ENCYCLOPEDIA OF
RELIGION
SECOND EDITION

ENCYCLOPEDIA OF RELIGION

SECOND EDITION

4

DACIAN RIDERS
•
ESTHER

LINDSAY JONES
EDITOR IN CHIEF

MACMILLAN REFERENCE USA
An imprint of Thomson Gale, a part of The Thomson Corporation

THOMSON
GALE

Detroit • New York • San Francisco • San Diego • New Haven, Conn. • Waterville, Maine • London • Munich

THOMSON
GALE

Encyclopedia of Religion, Second Edition

Lindsay Jones, Editor in Chief

For more information, contact
Macmillan Reference USA
An imprint of Thomson Gale
27500 Drake Rd.
Farmington, Hills, MI 48331-3535
Or you can visit our Internet site at
http://www.gale.com

LIBRARY OF CONGRESS CATALOGING-IN-PUBLICATION DATA

Encyclopedia of religion / Lindsay Jones, editor in chief.— 2nd ed.
p. cm.
Includes bibliographical references and index.
ISBN 0-02-865733-0 (SET HARDCOVER : ALK. PAPER) — ISBN 0-02-865734-9 (V. 1) — ISBN 0-02-865735-7 (v. 2) — ISBN 0-02-865736-5 (v. 3) — ISBN 0-02-865737-3 (v. 4) — ISBN 0-02-865738-1 (v. 5) — ISBN 0-02-865739-X (v. 6) — ISBN 0-02-865740-3 (v. 7) — ISBN 0-02-865741-1 (v. 8) — ISBN 0-02-865742-X (v. 9) — ISBN 0-02-865743-8 (v. 10) — ISBN 0-02-865980-5 (v. 11) — ISBN 0-02-865981-3 (v. 12) — ISBN 0-02-865982-1 (v. 13) — ISBN 0-02-865983-X (v. 14) — ISBN 0-02-865984-8 (v. 15)
1. RELIGION—ENCYCLOPEDIAS. I. JONES, LINDSAY, 1954-

BL31.E46 2005
200'.3—dc22 2004017052

This title is also available as an e-book.
ISBN 0-02-865997-X
Contact your Thomson Gale representative for ordering information.

Printed in the United States of America
10 9 8 7 6 5 4 3 2 1

EDITORS AND CONSULTANTS

Harvard Forum on Religion and Ecology
Ecology and Religion

JOSEPH HARRIS
Francis Lee Higginson Professor of English Literature and Professor of Folklore, Harvard University
Germanic Religions

URSULA KING
Professor Emerita, Senior Research Fellow and Associate Member of the Institute for Advanced Studies, University of Bristol, England, and Professorial Research Associate, Centre for Gender and Religions Research, School of Oriental and African Studies, University of London
Gender and Religion

DAVID MORGAN
Duesenberg Professor of Christianity and the Arts, and Professor of Humanities and Art History, Valparaiso University
Color Inserts and Essays

JOSEPH F. NAGY
Professor, Department of English, University of California, Los Angeles
Celtic Religion

MATTHEW OJO
Obafemi Awolowo University
African Religions

JUHA PENTIKÄINEN
Professor of Comparative Religion, The University of Helsinki, Member of Academia Scientiarum Fennica, Finland
Arctic Religions and Uralic Religions

TED PETERS
Professor of Systematic Theology, Pacific Lutheran Theological Seminary and the Center for Theology and the Natural Sciences at the Graduate Theological Union, Berkeley, California
Science and Religion

FRANK E. REYNOLDS
Professor of the History of Religions and Buddhist Studies in the Divinity School and the Department of South Asian Languages and Civilizations, Emeritus, University of Chicago
History of Religions

GONZALO RUBIO
Assistant Professor, Department of Classics and Ancient Mediterranean Studies and Department of History and Religious Studies, Pennsylvania State University
Ancient Near Eastern Religions

SUSAN SERED
Director of Research, Religion, Health and Healing Initiative, Center for the Study of World Religions, Harvard University, and Senior Research Associate, Center for Women's Health and Human Rights, Suffolk University
Healing, Medicine, and Religion

LAWRENCE E. SULLIVAN
Professor, Department of Theology, University of Notre Dame
History of Religions

WINNIFRED FALLERS SULLIVAN
Dean of Students and Senior Lecturer in the Anthropology and Sociology of Religion, University of Chicago
Law and Religion

TOD SWANSON
Associate Professor of Religious Studies, and Director, Center for Latin American Studies, Arizona State University
South American Religions

MARY EVELYN TUCKER
Professor of Religion, Bucknell University, Founder and Coordinator, Harvard Forum on Religion and Ecology, Research Fellow, Harvard Yenching Institute, Research Associate, Harvard Reischauer Institute of Japanese Studies
Ecology and Religion

HUGH URBAN
Associate Professor, Department of Comparative Studies, Ohio State University
Politics and Religion

CATHERINE WESSINGER
Professor of the History of Religions and Women's Studies, Loyola University New Orleans
New Religious Movements

ROBERT A. YELLE
Mellon Postdoctoral Fellow, University of Toronto
Law and Religion

ERIC ZIOLKOWSKI
Charles A. Dana Professor of Religious Studies, Lafayette College
Literature and Religion

ABBREVIATIONS AND SYMBOLS USED IN THIS WORK

abbr. abbreviated; abbreviation
abr. abridged; abridgment
AD *anno Domini,* in the year of the (our) Lord
Afrik. Afrikaans
AH *anno Hegirae,* in the year of the Hijrah
Akk. Akkadian
Ala. Alabama
Alb. Albanian
Am. *Amos*
AM *ante meridiem,* before noon
amend. amended; amendment
annot. annotated; annotation
Ap. *Apocalypse*
Apn. *Apocryphon*
app. appendix
Arab. Arabic
'Arakh. *'Arakhin*
Aram. Aramaic
Ariz. Arizona
Ark. Arkansas
Arm. Armenian
art. article (pl., arts.)
AS Anglo-Saxon
Asm. Mos. *Assumption of Moses*
Assyr. Assyrian
A.S.S.R. Autonomous Soviet Socialist Republic
Av. Avestan
'A.Z. *'Avodah zarah*
b. born
Bab. Babylonian
Ban. Bantu
1 Bar. *1 Baruch*
2 Bar. *2 Baruch*
3 Bar. *3 Baruch*
4 Bar. *4 Baruch*
B.B. *Bava' batra'*
BBC British Broadcasting Corporation
BC before Christ
BCE before the common era
B.D. Bachelor of Divinity
Beits. *Beitsah*
Bekh. *Bekhorot*
Beng. Bengali
Ber. *Berakhot*
Berb. Berber
Bik. *Bikkurim*
bk. book (pl., bks.)
B.M. *Bava' metsi'a'*
BP before the present
B.Q. *Bava' qamma'*
Brāh. *Brāhmaṇa*
Bret. Breton
B.T. Babylonian Talmud
Bulg. Bulgarian
Burm. Burmese
c. *circa,* about, approximately
Calif. California
Can. Canaanite
Catal. Catalan
CE of the common era
Celt. Celtic
cf. *confer,* compare
Chald. Chaldean
chap. chapter (pl., chaps.)
Chin. Chinese
C.H.M. Community of the Holy Myrrhbearers
1 Chr. *1 Chronicles*
2 Chr. *2 Chronicles*
Ch. Slav. Church Slavic
cm centimeters
col. column (pl., cols.)
Col. *Colossians*
Colo. Colorado
comp. compiler (pl., comps.)
Conn. Connecticut
cont. continued
Copt. Coptic
1 Cor. *1 Corinthians*
2 Cor. *2 Corinthians*
corr. corrected
C.S.P. Congregatio Sancti Pauli, Congregation of Saint Paul (Paulists)
d. died
D Deuteronomic (source of the Pentateuch)
Dan. Danish
D.B. Divinitatis Baccalaureus, Bachelor of Divinity
D.C. District of Columbia
D.D. Divinitatis Doctor, Doctor of Divinity
Del. Delaware
Dem. *Dema'i*
dim. diminutive
diss. dissertation
Dn. *Daniel*
D.Phil. Doctor of Philosophy
Dt. *Deuteronomy*
Du. Dutch
E Elohist (source of the Pentateuch)
Eccl. *Ecclesiastes*
ed. editor (pl., eds.); edition; edited by

ʿEduy. *ʿEduyyot*
e.g. *exempli gratia,* for example
Egyp. Egyptian
1 En. *1 Enoch*
2 En. *2 Enoch*
3 En. *3 Enoch*
Eng. English
enl. enlarged
Eph. *Ephesians*
ʿEruv. *ʿEruvin*
1 Esd. *1 Esdras*
2 Esd. *2 Esdras*
3 Esd. *3 Esdras*
4 Esd. *4 Esdras*
esp. especially
Est. Estonian
Est. *Esther*
et al. *et alii,* and others
etc. *et cetera,* and so forth
Eth. Ethiopic
EV English version
Ex. *Exodus*
exp. expanded
Ez. *Ezekiel*
Ezr. *Ezra*
2 Ezr. *2 Ezra*
4 Ezr. *4 Ezra*
f. feminine; and following (pl., ff.)
fasc. fascicle (pl., fascs.)
fig. figure (pl., figs.)
Finn. Finnish
fl. *floruit,* flourished
Fla. Florida
Fr. French
frag. fragment
ft. feet
Ga. Georgia
Gal. *Galatians*
Gaul. Gaulish
Ger. German
Giṭ. *Giṭṭin*
Gn. *Genesis*
Gr. Greek
Ḥag. *Ḥagigah*
Ḥal. *Ḥallah*
Hau. Hausa
Hb. *Habakkuk*
Heb. Hebrew
Heb. *Hebrews*
Hg. *Haggai*
Hitt. Hittite
Hor. *Horayot*
Hos. *Hosea*
Ḥul. *Ḥullin*
Hung. Hungarian
ibid. *ibidem,* in the same place (as the one immediately preceding)
Icel. Icelandic
i.e. *id est,* that is
IE Indo-European
Ill. Illinois
Ind. Indiana
intro. introduction
Ir. Gael. Irish Gaelic
Iran. Iranian
Is. *Isaiah*
Ital. Italian
J Yahvist (source of the Pentateuch)
Jas. *James*
Jav. Javanese
Jb. *Job*
Jdt. *Judith*
Jer. *Jeremiah*
Jgs. *Judges*
Jl. *Joel*
Jn. *John*
1 Jn. *1 John*
2 Jn. *2 John*
3 Jn. *3 John*
Jon. *Jonah*
Jos. *Joshua*
Jpn. Japanese
JPS Jewish Publication Society translation (1985) of the Hebrew Bible
J.T. Jerusalem Talmud
Jub. *Jubilees*
Kans. Kansas
Kel. *Kelim*
Ker. *Keritot*
Ket. *Ketubbot*
1 Kgs. *1 Kings*
2 Kgs. *2 Kings*
Khois. Khoisan
Kil. *Kilʾayim*
km kilometers
Kor. Korean
Ky. Kentucky
l. line (pl., ll.)
La. Louisiana
Lam. *Lamentations*
Lat. Latin
Latv. Latvian
L. en Th. Licencié en Théologie, Licentiate in Theology
L. ès L. Licencié ès Lettres, Licentiate in Literature
Let. Jer. *Letter of Jeremiah*
lit. literally
Lith. Lithuanian
Lk. *Luke*
LL Late Latin
LL.D. Legum Doctor, Doctor of Laws
Lv. *Leviticus*
m meters
m. masculine
M.A. Master of Arts
Ma ʿas. *Maʿaserot*
Ma ʿas. Sh. *Maʿ aser sheni*
Mak. *Makkot*
Makh. *Makhshirin*
Mal. *Malachi*
Mar. Marathi
Mass. Massachusetts
1 Mc. *1 Maccabees*
2 Mc. *2 Maccabees*
3 Mc. *3 Maccabees*
4 Mc. *4 Maccabees*
Md. Maryland
M.D. Medicinae Doctor, Doctor of Medicine
ME Middle English
Meg. *Megillah*
Me ʿil. *Meʿilah*
Men. *Menaḥot*
MHG Middle High German
mi. miles
Mi. *Micah*
Mich. Michigan
Mid. *Middot*
Minn. Minnesota
Miq. *Miqvaʾot*
MIran. Middle Iranian
Miss. Mississippi
Mk. *Mark*
Mo. Missouri
Moʿed Q. *Moʿed qaṭan*
Mont. Montana
MPers. Middle Persian
MS. *manuscriptum,* manuscript (pl., MSS)
Mt. *Matthew*
MT Masoretic text
n. note
Na. *Nahum*
Nah. Nahuatl
Naz. *Nazir*
N.B. *nota bene,* take careful note
N.C. North Carolina
n.d. no date
N.Dak. North Dakota
NEB New English Bible
Nebr. Nebraska

Ned. *Nedarim*
Neg. *Nega'im*
Neh. *Nehemiah*
Nev. Nevada
N.H. New Hampshire
Nid. *Niddah*
N.J. New Jersey
Nm. *Numbers*
N.Mex. New Mexico
no. number (pl., nos.)
Nor. Norwegian
n.p. no place
n.s. new series
N.Y. New York
Ob. *Obadiah*
O.Cist. Ordo Cisterciencium, Order of Cîteaux (Cistercians)
OCS Old Church Slavonic
OE Old English
O.F.M. Ordo Fratrum Minorum, Order of Friars Minor (Franciscans)
OFr. Old French
Ohal. *Ohalot*
OHG Old High German
OIr. Old Irish
OIran. Old Iranian
Okla. Oklahoma
ON Old Norse
O.P. Ordo Praedicatorum, Order of Preachers (Dominicans)
OPers. Old Persian
op. cit. *opere citato,* in the work cited
OPrus. Old Prussian
Oreg. Oregon
'Orl. *'Orlah*
O.S.B. Ordo Sancti Benedicti, Order of Saint Benedict (Benedictines)
p. page (pl., pp.)
P Priestly (source of the Pentateuch)
Pa. Pennsylvania
Pahl. Pahlavi
Par. *Parah*
para. paragraph (pl., paras.)
Pers. Persian
Pes. *Pesahim*
Ph.D. Philosophiae Doctor, Doctor of Philosophy
Phil. *Philippians*
Phlm. *Philemon*
Phoen. Phoenician
pl. plural; plate (pl., pls.)
PM *post meridiem,* after noon
Pol. Polish
pop. population
Port. Portuguese
Prv. *Proverbs*
Ps. *Psalms*
Ps. 151 *Psalm 151*
Ps. Sol. *Psalms of Solomon*
pt. part (pl., pts.)
1Pt. *1 Peter*
2 Pt. *2 Peter*
Pth. Parthian
Q hypothetical source of the synoptic Gospels
Qid. *Qiddushin*
Qin. *Qinnim*
r. reigned; ruled
Rab. *Rabbah*
rev. revised
R. ha-Sh. *Ro'sh ha-shanah*
R.I. Rhode Island
Rom. Romanian
Rom. *Romans*
R.S.C.J. Societas Sacratissimi Cordis Jesu, Religious of the Sacred Heart
RSV Revised Standard Version of the Bible
Ru. *Ruth*
Rus. Russian
Rv. *Revelation*
Rv. Ezr. *Revelation of Ezra*
San. *Sanhedrin*
S.C. South Carolina
Scot. Gael. Scottish Gaelic
S.Dak. South Dakota
sec. section (pl., secs.)
Sem. Semitic
ser. series
sg. singular
Sg. *Song of Songs*
Sg. of 3 *Prayer of Azariah and the Song of the Three Young Men*
Shab. *Shabbat*
Shav. *Shavu'ot*
Sheq. *Sheqalim*
Sib. Or. *Sibylline Oracles*
Sind. Sindhi
Sinh. Sinhala
Sir. *Ben Sira*
S.J. Societas Jesu, Society of Jesus (Jesuits)
Skt. Sanskrit
1 Sm. *1 Samuel*
2 Sm. *2 Samuel*
Sogd. Sogdian
Soṭ. *Soṭah*
sp. species (pl., spp.)
Span. Spanish
sq. square
S.S.R. Soviet Socialist Republic
st. stanza (pl., ss.)
S.T.M. Sacrae Theologiae Magister, Master of Sacred Theology
Suk. *Sukkah*
Sum. Sumerian
supp. supplement; supplementary
Sus. *Susanna*
s.v. *sub verbo,* under the word (pl., s.v.v.)
Swed. Swedish
Syr. Syriac
Syr. Men. *Syriac Menander*
Ta' an. *Ta'anit*
Tam. Tamil
Tam. *Tamid*
Tb. *Tobit*
T.D. *Taishō shinshū daizōkyō,* edited by Takakusu Junjirō et al. (Tokyo,1922–1934)
Tem. *Temurah*
Tenn. Tennessee
Ter. Terumot
Ṭev. Y. *Ṭevul yom*
Tex. Texas
Th.D. Theologicae Doctor, Doctor of Theology
1 Thes. *1 Thessalonians*
2 Thes. *2 Thessalonians*
Thrac. Thracian
Ti. *Titus*
Tib. Tibetan
1 Tm. *1 Timothy*
2 Tm. *2 Timothy*
T. of 12 *Testaments of the Twelve Patriarchs*
Ṭoh. *ṭohorot*
Tong. Tongan
trans. translator, translators; translated by; translation
Turk. Turkish
Ukr. Ukrainian
Upan. *Upaniṣad*
U.S. United States
U.S.S.R. Union of Soviet Socialist Republics
Uqts. *Uqtsin*
v. verse (pl., vv.)
Va. Virginia
var. variant; variation
Viet. Vietnamese

viz. *videlicet,* namely
vol. volume (pl., vols.)
Vt. Vermont
Wash. Washington
Wel. Welsh
Wis. Wisconsin
Wis. *Wisdom of Solomon*
W.Va. West Virginia
Wyo. Wyoming
Yad. *Yadayim*
Yev. *Yevamot*
Yi. Yiddish
Yor. Yoruba
Zav. *Zavim*
Zec. *Zechariah*
Zep. *Zephaniah*
Zev. *Zevaḥim*

* hypothetical
? uncertain; possibly; perhaps
° degrees
+ plus
– minus
= equals; is equivalent to
× by; multiplied by
→ yields

D

DACIAN RIDERS. The so-called Dacian Riders were associated with a mystery religion of the Getae and the Dacians, peoples of Thracian stock who lived in ancient Dacia (roughly equivalent to modern-day Romania). The cult of the Dacian, or Danubian, Riders began to spread among Roman soldiers soon after 106 CE, when Dacia was conquered by Trajan and made a province of the Roman Empire. Traces of the cult have been found as far away as the Roman provinces of Gaul and Britain.

Numerous reliefs and gems depicting the Dacian Riders are extant. Of the 232 items catalogued by Dumitru Tudor (1969–1976), 60 were found in Dacia, 24 in Moesia Superior, 34 in Moesia Inferior, 47 in Pannonia Inferior, and 25 in Pannonia Superior. Most of the Dacian reliefs are made of marble. They were copied on a large scale in lead, a very expensive material whose use can be explained only by the magical purposes for which the images of the Dacian Riders were intended. Of the 90 lead copies extant, 44 were found in Pannonia Inferior.

The most ancient reliefs show only one horseman, whose iconography was influenced by that of the Thracian Rider. Later monuments show two riders at either side of a goddess whose principal symbolic attribute is a fish. Of the 31 pieces belonging to the one-horseman type, 18 were found in Dacia. The two-horseman type belongs to the later period of this cult, which flourished in the third century CE and declined in the fourth.

Besides the two horsemen and the goddess with a fish, the iconography of the monuments includes prostrated characters, attendants, and various symbols, such as the sun, the moon, stars, and numerous animals (including the ram, dog, lion, eagle, peacock, raven, cock, snake, and sometimes even the bull). Scholarly identifications of the goddess are widely divergent. The two horsemen have been identified with the Dioscuri by some scholars and with the Cabiri brothers by others. The Greek iconography of the Dioscuri has had a particular impact on that of the Dacian Riders, but all these scholarly hypotheses are more or less fanciful.

It is likely that certain beliefs and practices, borrowed especially from Mithraism, were added to a local Dacian cult and that these borrowings changed the cult into a mys-

CLOCKWISE FROM TOP LEFT CORNER. Women dance with skeletons in a fifteenth-century woodcut of the Dance of Death. *[©Bettmann/Corbis]*; Seventeenth-century Chinese nobleman's badge depicting a dragon-like beast. *[©Art Resource, N.Y.]*; Demeter hands Triptolemos a sheaf of corn in a fifth-century BCE Greek relief depicting the creation of agriculture. National Archaeological Museum, Athens. *[©Erich Lessing/Art Resource, N.Y.]*; Laozi riding a water buffalo, circa 960–1280. *[©Burstein Collection/Corbis]*; Ruins of Tholos Temple at Delphi, Greece. *[©Wolfgang Kaehler/Corbis]* .

tery religion. Although the myth of the Danubian Riders remains unknown, it is safe to state that it was based on some Dacian beliefs not shared by the Thracians south of the Danube. The two horsemen and the goddess were probably supposed to establish a link between three cosmic layers (heaven, earth, and underworld), as the partition of the reliefs into three registers seems to suggest.

Only three degrees of initiation were present in the mysteries of the Dacian Riders: Aries ("ram"), Miles ("soldier"), and Leo ("lion"). The first two were placed under the influence of the planet Mars, the last one under the influence of the sun. If we interpret the numerous animals depicted in the reliefs of the Danubian Riders as astrological entities, then we may surmise that the symbolism of this mystery religion was fairly complicated. Inscriptions are unusually scarce in number, short (especially those on gems), and indecipherable. Initiates in the mysteries identified their grade by badges and seals; for example, a gem of unknown provenance bears as its inscription the single word *leon.* In all probability, sacrifice of a ram played an important part in these mysteries.

See Also Thracian Rider.

Bibliography

On the Dacian Riders, see the excellent work of Dumitru Tudor, *Corpus monumentorum religionis equitum Danuvinorum,* 2 vols. (Leiden, 1969–1976). Volume 1, *The Monuments,* translated by Eve Harris and John R. Harris, is a detailed catalog; volume 2, *The Analysis and Interpretation of the Monuments,* translated by Christopher Holme, is a thorough survey of scholarly theories concerning the mysteries.

New Sources

Alexandrescu, Petre. "L'oiseau unicorne, Introduction à l'iconologie thrace." *Comptes rendues de l'Académie d'Inscriptions et Belles Lettres* (1993): 725–745. As well as the Dacian Rider, the god with the unicorn bird was an important presence in the Getan pantheon.

"Heros Equitans." In *Lexicon Iconographicum Mythologiae Classicae (LIMC),* vol. 6, 1–2. Zürich and Munich, 1992, pp. 1019–1081. Various specialists examine the iconography of the heroic horseman, including full lists of the monuments and the related illustrations. See especially the chapter on "Les Cavaliers Danubiens," pp. 1078–1081, providing a reappraisal of the relevant religious-historical issues.

Sanie, Silvin. "Kulte und Glauben im römischen Süden der Moldau (Ostrumänien)." In *Aufstieg und Niedergang der römischen Welt I,* vol. II, 18, 2. Berlin and New York, 1989, pp. 1272–1316. See especially pp. 1294–1296, dealing with the Dacian Rider and its mystery cult guaranteeing immortality.

Ioan Petru Culianu and Cicerone Poghirc (1987)
Revised Bibliography

DACO-GETIC RELIGION

See GETO-DACIAN RELIGION

DADDY GRACE.

Charles M. "Daddy" (1881–1960) Grace was the founder of the United House of Prayer for All People of the Church on the Rock of the Apostolic Faith. A combination of Daddy Grace's grandiosity, his followers' intense devotion, and popular confusion between Grace and the controversial Father Divine caused outsiders to be skeptical of the church for decades. After Grace's death, new leadership made superficial changes that allowed the United House of Prayer to move away from its marginal status and closer to the American religious mainstream. Early in the twenty-first century, its long-term stability invites an appreciation of the strength of the institutional foundations designed and laid by Grace.

Daddy Grace was born Marceline Manuel DaGraca on the island of Brava, Cape Verde (at that time a Portuguese territory), off the northwest coast of Africa. With his parents and four siblings, Grace immigrated to Massachusetts at the turn of the twentieth century. In his first years in the New Bedford area, Grace held odd jobs such as picking cranberries, dishwashing, and selling patent medicines. During this time he also Americanized his surname and began using the first name Charles. Grace had two brief marriages, from which one daughter and two sons were produced. He died from heart ailments at the age of seventy-eight.

Grace was baptized Roman Catholic in Brava, but his religious calling in the United States led him to Protestant forms of worship, particularly the holiness movement. His early attempts to start a church were unsuccessful. He found himself rejected from the pulpit of a Massachusetts Nazarene church and was unable to gain a following in southern states despite extensive travels in his "Gospel Car." Grace finally met with success when he returned to Wareham, Massachusetts, opening his first House of Prayer in 1919, with himself as bishop.

Grace's church grew quickly in its first two decades, spreading both south and west to over a dozen states. Regardless of its growth, the church was commonly perceived as an invalid organization in which the leader exploited the working-class membership for profit. Journalists attempted to make a mockery of the bishop because his flamboyant personal style made for good press. Not only did he have long hair, painted fingernails, suits of bright colors, and jewels on his wrists and fingers, but he also traveled with an entourage that included a chauffeur, bodyguards, and occasionally lawyers and other assistants. Grace's visibility as a man of means and power was certainly one element of the House of Prayer's early growth, but it also contributed to outsiders' skepticism.

The United House of Prayer, though remaining nondenominational during Grace's lifetime, is squarely in the Pentecostal tradition. It is charismatic by nature, and Grace's theological teachings were based on the ideas of one God, one faith, one baptism, and one leader. Although popular lore holds that Grace claimed to be God, evidence demonstrates that this is a misconstruction. Instead, the church's theology focuses on the coming of the end-time and the importance of church leadership in helping to prepare. Worship services include demonstrations of the gifts of the holy spirit, as well as music led by their popular brass shout bands. The House of Prayer's traditions, including annual festive convocations and group baptisms (first on beaches, later by fire hose in the streets) added to its visibility during Grace's reign. There has long been an emphasis on member participation in church auxiliaries, which once included such clubs as the Grace Flower Girls, the Grace Willing Workers Club, the Grace Gospel Choir, the Grace Soul Hunters, and the Grace Soldiers. Beyond the church, members are expected to conduct themselves with conservative behavior, and are encouraged to read and understand the Bible.

Grace was the figurehead of the church, supported by a vast number of individual ministers and a set of General Council Laws prescribing overall operations. Grace was not accountable to anyone, and likewise the many ministers operating under him had a large degree of independence in their practices and teachings. After opening each new church or mission, Grace's involvement with individual Houses of Prayer was primarily based on financial management. Originally, Grace performed healings, but in time he encouraged people to believe they would heal because of their faith rather than because of his direct touch. As he aged, Grace took decreasing roles in religious services, though he frequently traveled to make church appearances. His sermons and other speaking roles were not as important as his mere presence at church events, and as a result very few records of his sermons have been preserved.

Grace's innovative investments and business ventures allowed the church to flourish, and this is where his genius was put to best use. Though often perceived by outsiders as using his working-class followers' donations for his own ends, Grace quietly used the money to build a wealthy corporate empire for the church. The church offered a pension fund for ministers and elderly members, as well as a small insurance plan. It owned several manufacturing businesses that generated revenue for the church corporation. Grace increasingly invested in real estate. For example, when he first opened a House of Prayer in Harlem in 1938, Grace purchased the headquarters of Father Divine's Peace Mission Movement and evicted them. This building was one of the first pieces of a trophy real estate collection that grew to include the El Dorado on Central Park West, two apartment buildings in the Sugar Hill neighborhood, a large swath of property on 125th Street in Harlem, and other mansions, apartment buildings, and businesses in places as varied as Los Angeles, Philadelphia, Detroit, Newport News, Washington D.C., and Havana, Cuba.

Following Grace's death in January 1960, the church experienced confusion over questions of succession to the bishopric and the extent of church assets. Several issues had to be resolved by the courts, and at least one splinter group formed. When the dust cleared, "Sweet Daddy" Walter McCollough (1915–1991) of Washington, D.C., was elected bishop of the multimillion dollar organization that included approximately one hundred Houses of Prayer nationwide. Under McCollough, congregants' attention was turned to issues of social justice, and church investments expanded to include projects that were of direct benefit to members, such as affordable housing and scholarship programs. McCollough's less ostentatious style of leadership helped move the House of Prayer closer to the mainstream of African American religion. Just as it was under Daddy Grace, the church today continues as a thriving, forward-thinking organization that provides an example of the harmonious mix of otherworldly theology with present-world practicality.

BIBLIOGRAPHY

Brune, Danielle E. "Sweet Daddy Grace: The Life and Times of a Modern Day Prophet." Ph.D. diss., University of Texas, Austin, 2002. A cultural biography of Grace that offers particularly good treatment of the early years of his church and a critical analysis of popular misconceptions about his leadership.

Damon, Sherri Marcia. "The Trombone in the Shout Band of the United House of Prayer for All People." Ph.D. diss., University of North Carolina, Greensboro, 1999. A history of the use of the trombone in the shout bands of the United House of Prayer for All People.

Davis, Lenwood G. *Daddy Grace: An Annotated Bibliography.* New York, 1992. This bibliography provides a sketch of many noteworthy incidents and other highlights of the church's history during the time of Grace's bishopric.

Fauset, Arthur Huff. *Black Gods of the Metropolis: Negro Religious Cults of the Urban North.* Philadelphia, 1944. This early source includes a chapter on the House of Prayer based on the author's doctoral fieldwork, and compares it to other marginalized African American churches of that time period.

Hodges, John O. "Charles Manuel 'Sweet Daddy' Grace." In *Twentieth-Century Shapers of American Popular Religion,* edited by Charles Lippy, pp. 170–179. New York, 1989. A short and pithy essay on the history of the church and Grace himself.

Robinson, John W. "A Song, a Shout, and a Prayer." In *The Black Experience in Religion,* edited by C. Eric Lincoln, pp. 212–235. Garden City, N.Y., 1974. A detailed essay on the House of Prayer including information about its changes after Grace's death; intended as an update to Fauset's work.

MARIE W. DALLAM (2005)

DAGAN (Dagān) was a West Semitic god, well known in ancient Syria and ancient Palestine. He is mentioned in texts from Ebla (Tell Mardīḫ, in Northern Syria) dating to the mid-third millennium BCE, in which his name occurs as part of theophoric anthroponyms with the element *Da-gan* or *Da-ga-an.* The logographic abbreviation BE (for *bēlum*/*ba'alum;* lord) also occurs in texts from Ebla—both as part of personal names and independently as a deity present in diverse Syrian and Northern Mesopotamian towns. This BE has frequently been identified with Dagan. However, BE is most likely a divine epithet, which refers to Dagan only in some specific cases, primarily the BE of Tuttul (i.e., "the Lord of Tuttul" refers to Dagan), modern Tell Bīʿa, on the Balīḫ River. Outside Ebla, and also during the second half of the third millennium, Dagan is attested in texts from Mari (Tell Ḥarīri, Southern Syria), which had a temple devoted to this god, probably built toward the end of the third millennium, and Tell Beydar in the region of the upper Ḫābūr River. The mentions of the "King" of Terqa in early Mari documents also refer to Dagan (^{d}lugal *Terqa*, with the divine determinative ^{d} refers to DINGIR preceding the Sumerian word for king, *lugal*). In all these pre-Sargonic Syro-Mesopotamian texts (i.e., prior to c. 2340 BCE), the only clear attestations of Dagan are in personal names.

SARGONIC AND UR III PERIODS. During the Sargonic (c. 2340–2113 BCE) and Ur III periods (c. 2113–2004 BCE), Dagan appears in royal inscriptions of Mesopotamian kings, but always in a Syrian context and especially in personal names, as in previous periods. The only autochthonous Syrian mention of Dagan during these periods comes from a Mari inscription, in which he appears along with two properly Mesopotamian deities, Ishtar and Enki. In the Old Babylonian period (first half of the second millennium BCE), the figure of Dagan emerges as the most important deity in the pantheon of the Middle Euphrates region, and his name is abundantly attested in letters from Old Babylonian Mari, as well as documents from Terqa and Tuttul. Both at Mari and at Aleppo, Dagan appears as the recipient of funerary offerings. Moreover, he plays a role in prophecies and divination, especially extispicy (observation of the entrails of sacrificial animals). As in previous periods, Dagan is widely attested in theophoric personal names from the Middle and Upper Euphrates regions, as well as the Ḫābūr area.

MIDDLE BABYLONIAN PERIOD. In the Middle Babylonian period (second half of the second millennium BCE), Dagan is particularly well represented in texts from two Late Bronze sites: Emar (modern Tell Meskene), on the Middle Euphrates, and Ugarit (Ras Shamra) on the Syrian Mediterranean coast. In texts from Emar and smaller neighboring towns including Ekalte and Azu, along with the customary syllabic spelling of the name (*Da-gan*), one finds the logogram ^{d}KUR, the determinative for divine names followed by the logogram KUR (mountain; land). This spelling may be an abbreviation of the epithet ^{d}kur-gal (The Great Mountain), but it may also point to a chthonic nature of Dagan. The latter might be associated with a possible Indo-European etymology and with Dagan's funerary offerings. The most important religious festival in Late Bronze Emar, the *zukru* festival (related to the Semitic root **zkr*; to call, recall) was devoted to Dagan. Dagan also played an important role in most Emar rituals, as his temple seems to have been the epicenter of religious life in that city. An important corpus of mythological and epic narratives exists from Ugarit, in which Dagan is attested only in epithets of other gods (e.g, Ba⊏lu is "the son of Dagan") and in oblique references with no active role. On the other hand, in the ritual texts from Ugarit, Dagan is frequently mentioned and plays an important role.

ETYMOLOGY. In all these third and second millennium texts, Dagan appears as father of the gods and, along with his consort, Shalash, he belongs to the earliest generation of gods in the Syrian pantheon. In the first millennium, Dagan's name occurs as Dagon (Dāgôn) in the biblical historical narratives (with an expected *ā* to *ō* shift), in which he is designated a Philistine deity, with temples dedicated to him in Ashdod, Gaza, and probably Beth-Shan (*1 Sm.* 5:1–7; *Jgs.* 16:23; *1 Chr.* 10:10; *1 Mac.* 10: 83–84, 11:4).

Traditionally, three different Semitic etymologies of this theonym have been proposed: (1) the root **dg* (fish), which appeared already in Saint Jerome, the Talmud, and elsewhere, but which is now regarded as a folk etymology by most scholars; (2) the root **dgn* (grain; *dāgān*), with the expected fertility implications, but which works only in West Semitic and is likely to also be a folk etymology; and (3) the root **dgn* (cloudy, rainy), also bearing somehow a fertility connotation.

The latter possibility is not immediately evident, because the Semitic root in question (**dgn*) would seem to mean "cloudy, rainy" only in Arabic. Nonetheless, there is a related root in Syriac (a Christian Aramaic dialect) that occurs in a verb meaning "to be blind, to have blurry eyes" (*dgen*, with intransitive vocalization) and in nouns referring to ophthalmic maladies and blindness. The Arabic verb *dajana* means primarily "to be dusky, gloomy," as in *dujna/dujunna* (darkness) and *adjan* (dark). Nonetheless, Arabic exhibits occurrences of this root referring to rain or rainy conditions (*dajn*; heavy rain) and the Syriac cognate (*degnā, degānā*) has a distinctive secondary but frequent meaning concerning snow (packed snow).

Based on the problems posed by the aforementioned Semitic etymologies and the association of Dagan to the earth, an Indo-European etymology has been proposed for this theonym: $*d^{h}e^{h}om$ (earth), as in Sanskrit *kam*, Greek *khthōn* (with metathesis), Latin *humus* (and probably also *homo*; terrestrial, human being), Tocharian *tkaṃ*, Hittite *tegan* (genitive *taknaš*), and perhaps even part of the name of the goddess Demeter (*Dēmētēr *Gdan-mátēr*, with *gd $*g^{h}d^{h}$ $*d^{h}e^{h}$). As in most etymologies of proper names, tentative and speculative by nature, it is difficult to rule out this Indo-European hypothesis. Such an etymology would also match the possible linguistic identity of the Philistines.

BIBLIOGRAPHY

On Dagan in general, see Lluís Feliu, *The God Dagan in Bronze Age Syria* (Leiden, 2003) and Bradley L. Crowell, "The Development of Dagan: A Sketch," *Journal of Ancient Near Eastern Religions* 1 (2001): 32–83. On Dagan at Ebla, see Francesco Pomponio and Paolo Xella, *Les dieux d'Ebla* (Münster, 1997). For Dagan at Tuttul, see Manfred Krebernik, *Ausgrabungen in Tall Biʿa/Tuttul, II: Die altorientalischen Schriftfunde* (Saarbrücken, Germany, 2001). On Dagan at Late Bronze Emar, see Daniel E. Fleming, *Time at Emar*

(Winona Lake, Ind., 2000). On Dagan in Ugaritic rituals, see G. del Olmo Lete, *Canaanite Religion* (Bethesda, Md., 1999) and Dennis Pardee, *Les textes rituels, I–II (Ras Shamra-Ougarit XII)* (Paris, 2000). On the etymology of Dagan, see Fred Renfroe, *Arabic-Ugaritic Lexical Studies,* pp. 91–94 (Münster, Germany, 1992) and Itamar Singer, "Semitic *dagān* and Indo-European **dheǵhom*: Related Words?" in *The Asia Minor Connexion,* edited by Yoël L. Arbeitman, pp. 221–232 (Louvain, 2000).

GONZALO RUBIO (2005)

DAHOMEAN RELIGION SEE FON AND EWE RELIGION

DAINAS.

In Baltic cultures, the songs known in Latvian as *dainas* and in Lithuanian as *dainos* deal with two fundamental cycles, the life cycle of humans and the festival cycle of the agricultural seasons. Although they are often referred to by the common designation *folk song,* this modern term is misleading, for the *dainas,* with their trochaic and dactylic meters, differ from the folk songs known to European scholars. The original Lithuanian *dainos* have to a great extent disappeared because of the influence of the European folk song, but Latvian *dainas* have survived in great numbers. About sixty thousand (not including variants) have been collected and published by scholars. Their content reveals that they were an integral part of daily agrarian life among Baltic peoples; as such, they bear directly on Baltic religion.

Regarding the etymology of the term, Suniti Kumar Chatterji has pointed out that

> the Baltic word *daina* had unquestionably its Aryan [Indo-Iranian] equivalent, etymologically and semantically, which is perfectly permissible. . . . An Indo-European root **dhi-, *dhy-ei, *dhei-*, meaning "to think, to ponder over, to give thought to," appears to be the source of the Vedic *dhēnā* and the Avestian *daēnā*. An Indo-European form **dhainā* as the sourceword can very easily and quite correctly be postulated. (Chatterji, 1968, pp. 69–70)

From the age of Vedic literature words derived from this source word deal with the following notions: speech, voice, praise, prayer, panegyric, and song. The Pahlavi *dēn* ("religion") developed into the Avestan *daēnā*, which, in turn, appears in modern Arabic as *dīn,* meaning "religion," specifically, orthodox Islam. These etymological derivations and semantic relationships suggest that *dhainā* is an ancient Baltic word that has retained the meaning of "song" through the years.

LIFE CYCLE. *Dainas* figure prominently in an individual's life cycle at three major points: birth, marriage, and death. Each of these events determines not only the content but also the form of the *dainas.*

1. In songs dealing with childbirth, the mother figure appears not only as the one who bears the child but also as the one who rears it and determines its fate. These *dainas* are characterized by their deep emotionality. This is particularly true of *dainas* dealing with the fate of foster children. *Dainas* sung directly after the birth of a child during the cultic feast (*pirtīžas*) in the sauna, the traditional place of birthing, have a special significance because of their cultic character. These *dainas* are devoted to the goddess of fate, Laima.

2. *Dainas* dealing with love, the selection of a partner, and marriage are rather different from those associated with birth. They are imbued with joy and contain erotic and sexual elements intended to chafe and mock others. Some of the songs are so caustic that the seventeenth-century bishop Paul Einhorn, having heard the wedding songs of Latvian peasants, failed to comprehend their deep religious and cultic character. He wrote in dismay in his *Historie lettice* in 1649: "Afterwards such improper, brazen, and flippant songs were sung without interruption, day and night, that even the devil himself could not have devised and put forth anything more improper and lewd." Yet such fertility *dainas* belong to the very old family cult.

3. The third group of life-cycle *dainas,* those dealing with death, are rich in content, representing the individual's preparation for death. Their cultic character becomes evident in songs that describe the bearing of the casket from the home to the cemetery, which was the site of the cultic feast. There a particular type of *daina* was sung to guarantee that the dead person would have a favorable relationship with the ruler of the grave and the realm of death, occasionally referred to as Kapu Māte ("grave mother").

FESTIVAL CYCLE. The second cycle includes *dainas* that describe the agricultural work routine and festivals. In their sequence they mirror the yearly cycle, including its holidays. The most important holidays are the summer and winter solstices. The commencement and conclusion of particular work phases also have an important place in the cycle. In the spring, when planting began, bread and meat were plowed into the first furrow. Similarly, the leading of the first cattle to pasture and the first horses to night watch were also observed as special events. All of these occasions were associated with sacral feasts under the leadership of the paterfamilias. Appropriate *dainas* were an integral part of these rituals. The commencement as well as the conclusion of certain jobs was observed, especially during the fall harvest. This was a time of relative abundance, and therefore the feasts were especially lavish.

RELIGIOUS DIMENSIONS. Both of these cycles mirror the framework of the Baltic peasant's life, which consisted of both hard work and joyous festivity, represented by work *dainas* and festival *dainas.* The peasants, in close harmony with nature, performed their tasks with songs that helped them to adhere to the rhythm of work. Festival *dainas,* whether of the first or second cycle, introduce another ancient element inherent in the name *dainas* itself: that of dance. The verb *dainot* really means "to sing and move rhythmically in a group," that is, "to dance" in the broadest sense of the word.

The great majority of *dainas* are songs describing various chores that have no specific religious content. Many describe nature, using explicit personifications of and metaphors for natural phenomena. A significant number of songs, however, do have a religious dimension, which can be explained by the significance of religion in Baltic daily life. Man's place in nature and his dependence on it forced him to ponder the basis of his existence and to determine his relationship with the forces of nature. The *dainas* are the clearest proof of this close relationship. Furthermore, because the source material relating to the religious life of the Baltic peoples is limited, the *dainas* represent an irreplaceable source for the reconstruction of this religious framework.

Bibliography

Barons, Krišjānis. *Latwju dainas.* 2d ed. 6 vols. in 8. Riga, 1922. An academic complete-text edition with variants of Latvian *dainas.*

Chatterji, Suniti Kumar. *Balts and Aryans.* Simla, India, 1968.

Greble, Vilma. "Tautas dziesmas." In *Latviešu literatūras vēsture,* vol. 1, pp. 22–158. Riga, 1959. Historical survey of the different editions of *dainas* and a short introduction to the main problems.

Jonval, Michel. *Les chansons mythologiques lettonnes.* Paris, 1929. A selection of religious *dainas* concerning the pre-Christian Latvian deities.

Katzenelenbogen, Uriah. *The Daina.* Chicago, 1935. The only edition of *dainas* in English, with a brief introductory survey of their ethnological value.

Lietuviuh tautosaka, vol. 1, *Dainos.* Vilnius, 1962. A complete-text edition of Lithuanian *dainos* with a Marxist ideological introduction.

New Sources

Latviešu tautas dziesmas. Riga, 1979. Latvian folk songs.

Raudupe, Rudīte. *Dievatziņa vēdās un dainās.* Riga, 2002. Perception of God in vedas and *dainas.*

Sex Songs of the Ancient Letts. New York, 1969.

Švābe, Arvēds, Karlīs Straubergs, and Edīte Hauzenberga-Šturma, eds. *Latviešu tautas dziesmas. Chansons Populaires Lettonnes.* 12 vols. Copenhagen, 1952–56.

Vīķe-Freiberga, Vaira, ed. *Linguistics and Poetics of Latvian Folk Songs.* Kingston and Montreal, 1989.

Vīķe-Freiberga, Vaira, and Imants Freibergs. *Saules dainas.* Latvian Sun songs. Montreal, 1988.

HARALDS BIEZAIS (1987)
Revised Bibliography

DAIVAS. The Iranian term *daiva* originally signified "god," as is shown in several occurrences of the word in the Avesta (Av., *daēva;* OPers., *daiva;* MPers., Pahl., *dēw*). Like the Vedic *deva* or the Latin *deus, daiva* may be related to the Indo-European root meaning "shine, be bright." In Zoroastrian Iran, however, *daiva* had a negative sense. Other terms were used to refer to divine beings, such as *baga* ("one who distributes"), *ahura* ("lord"), and *yazata* ("one worthy of worship"), while *daiva* was used to designate malefic or demonic powers. For that reason one speaks of a "demonization" of the *daiva* as a phenomenon characteristic of Zoroastrianism.

In all probability *daiva* acquired a negative value in the Iranian world because of the condemnation by Zarathushtra (Zoroaster) of traditional religion. The prophet of Ahura Mazdā propounded a faith and a doctrine of monotheistic inspiration, and the gods of ancient polytheism were repudiated as illusions or chimeras.

Later, after Zoroastrianism had reached a compromise with the older religious sensibility and with the various forms of polytheism that had spread throughout the Iranian world in the first millennium BCE, the *daivas* were condemned not because they were considered, as Zarathushtra had seen them, the fruit of ignorance and superstition but because they were thought to be real demonic beings. The significance of *daiva* thus changed from "god" to "demon." In this later form of the religion, Indra, Saurva, and Nānhaithya—who had prominent positions in the Indian pantheon as Indra, Śarva, and Nāsatya—became archdemons. They were opposed, respectively, by the Amesha Spentas Asha, Khshathra Vairya, and Ārmaiti.

The Zoroastrian pandemonium is particularly rich. Among the most important *daivas* are Aēshma ("wrath, fury"), known throughout the Zoroastrian tradition; Apaosha ("dearth"), fought by Tishtrya, the *yazata* of the star Sirius; Astōvīdhātu ("dismembering of skeleton"); Būshyąstā ("sloth"); and Nasu ("corpse"), the demon of decay.

Zarathushtra's condemnation of the *daivas*, intended as the rejection of the gods of polytheism, always remained, if only with the modification explained above, a characteristic feature of Zoroastrianism. In all its subsequent historical manifestations—as, for example, in an inscription of Xerxes at Persepolis—there are traces, even if partly distorted, of Zarathushtra's original teaching.

Bibliography

Benveniste, Émile. "Hommes et dieux dans l'Avesta." In *Festschrift für Wilhelm Eilers,* pp. 144–147. Wiesbaden, 1967.

Bianchi, Ugo. "L'inscription 'des daivas' et le zoroastrisme des Achéménides." *Revue de l'historie des religions* 192 (1977): 3–30.

Boyce, Mary. *A History of Zoroastrianism,* vol. 1. Leiden, 1975.

Burrow, T. "The Proto-Indoaryans." *Journal of the Royal Asiatic Society* (1973): 123–140.

Duchesne-Guillemin, Jacques. *Ormazd et Ahriman.* Paris, 1953.

Gershevitch, Ilya. "Die Sonne das Beste." In *Mithraic Studies,* edited by John R. Hinnells, vol. 1, pp. 68–81. Manchester, U.K., 1975.

Gnoli, Gherardo. *Zoroaster's Time and Homeland.* Naples, 1980.

Gray, Louis H. *The Foundations of the Iranian Religions.* Bombay, 1930.

Henning, W. B. "A Sogdian God." *Bulletin of the School of Oriental and African Studies* 28 (1965): 242–254.

Kellens, Jean. *Le panthéon de l'Avesta ancien.* Wiesbaden, 1994.

Lommel, Herman. *Die Religionn Zarathustras nach dem Awesta dargestellt.* Tübingen, 1930.

Molé, Marijan. *Culte, mythe et cosmologie dans l'Iran ancien.* Paris, 1963.

Nöldeke, Theodor. "Der Weisse Dēv von Māzandarān." *Archiv für Religionswissenschaft* 18 (1915): 597–600.

Widengren, Geo. *Stand und Aufgaben der iranischen Religionsgeschichte.* Leiden, 1955.

GHERARDO GNOLI (1987)
Translated from Italian by Roger DeGaris

DAI ZHEN (*zi*, Shenxiu; *hao*, Dongyuan; 1724–1777), the most illustrious representative of the *kaozheng* school of evidential research and one of the leading philosophers of the Qing dynasty (1644–1911).

Dai Zhen was born into a modest mercantile family of Xiuning, Anhwei Province. He pursued his earliest education by borrowing books from neighbors. He learned very quickly and astonished his teachers by questioning the authority of everything he read. For a brief period he was apprenticed to a cloth merchant, but in 1742 he was sent to the home of a wealthy scholar and there studied with Jiangyong (1681–1762).

The scholar Jiangyong provided the formative influence during the first period of Dai Zhen's adult life. He was a specialist in the *Li ji* (Record of Rites) and in mathematics and phonology; the training he gave Dai Zhen in these areas became the foundation for much of Dai Zhen's later scholarship in the *kaozheng* tradition. This side of his education fitted him for the mainstream of Qing intellectual life. Jiangyong, however, also steeped his pupil in the philosophical systems of Song neo-Confucianism, inculcating the notion that practical scholarship and moral philosophy were the two legs of Confucian learning.

In 1754, Dai Zhen moved to Beijing, where he mingled with representatives of the *kaozheng* school of evidential research, notably Huidong (1697–1758). *Kaozheng* scholars accused the Song neo-Confucians of pointless speculation influenced by the Buddhists; such learning, they claimed, was disdainful of the practical problems of the real world and neglected solid scholarship in favor of subjectivism. Although during his early years in Beijing Dai Zhen defended the need to ask larger questions about morality and meaning, his writings published between 1758 and 1766 show the influence of *kaozheng* on his thinking. Some scholars interpret this period as a repudiation of his past philosophical training. It is certain that Dai Zhen brought to Beijing ideas that ran counter to the consensus of his peers, but whether his colleagues in Beijing convinced him to change his orientation, or whether he simply emphasized the nonphilosophical side of his work to gain acceptance at the capital, is a question that remains unanswered.

However superficial or profound his conversion to evidential research, Dai Zhen succeeded in gaining entry to the most illustrious intellectual circles. His publications in mathematics and waterway engineering earned him high renown. In 1773 the emperor appointed him to the elite board of compilers of the Imperial Manuscript Library (Siku Quanshu). He had risen to the very pinnacle of scholarship, yet even during his tenure at the library he continued to write books on philosophy.

His colleagues and peers tended to view his philosophical writings as incidental digressions from his scholarly work. Although one or two of his closest disciples recognized the importance of philosophy to Dai Zhen's intellectual life, none of them was able to carry on his philosophical work. Hu Shi revived Dai Zhen's philosophy at a memorial conference in 1923–1924, claiming that Dai Zhen, fully steeped in the empirical scholarship of his day, had attacked and transcended the errors and excesses of Song neo-Confucianism, laying the groundwork of a new Confucian vision. Others, notably Yu Yingshi, have argued that Dai Zhen's thought is in fact profoundly indebted to neo-Confucianism and is a continuous development of that heritage. Yu maintains that Dai was never fully converted to the antiphilosophical prejudices of his peers. He saw scholarship as a handmaiden to the larger task of philosophy. Arguing from Dai Zhen's letters and conversations, Yu contends that the real target of his philosophy was not the Song school, but his narrow and pedantic contemporaries in evidential research.

Dai Zhen's philosophy was based on a monism of *qi* ("ether"). He argued against the Song neo-Confucian distinctions between metaphysical and physical, between heaven-endowed nature and material nature. Such dualism, he claimed, led Confucians to neglect the empirical world and to believe that there was in human beings a dichotomy between nature and feelings. On the grand scale, Dai argued that the Dao was nothing other than the orderly patterns of the movements of ether; it was not a metaphysical principle. Analogously, he held that the realization of human nature was nothing other than the orderly patterns of one's feelings. As the sages had channeled the floodwaters to restore the order of Dao in the world, so feelings, properly channeled, are the manifestations of human nature. Human life in the material world is made up of feelings or response. When feelings are healthfully expressed and fundamental needs satisfied, both the body and *xin*, or mind and heart, of the person can be healthy and whole. To channel feelings and understand the order and movements of ether, the mind must weigh (*quan*) its perceptions and responses carefully. Weighing requires accurate and informed perceptions that take account of all the evidence and, carefully comparing the evidence, come to a balanced response.

An organic connection ran between Dai Zhen's scholarship and his philosophy. Only the former aspect of his work was appreciated during his lifetime, whereas the latter area is the subject of continued debate among Confucian scholars.

SEE ALSO Mengzi.

BIBLIOGRAPHY

Although during his lifetime Dai Zhen was best known for his essays on mathematics, waterworks, and phonology (Liang, pp. 58–59), he is today highly regarded for his philosophical writings. His *Yuan shan*, composed in 1763 and revised in 1776, has been translated by Cheng Chung-ying as *Dai Chên's Inquiry into Goodness* (Honolulu, 1971). In it Dai developed his monism of ether and his views of human nature and feelings. *Meng-zi zi i su cheng* (Elucidation on the meaning of words in Mencius) in 3 *chüan* (Beijing, 1956) was composed in 1769, but revised during his final years at the Imperial Manuscript Library. The *Elucidation* is his most systematic philosophical work and grounds his monism and his view of human nature in the writings of Mencius.

Fang Chao-ying has written a very useful biography of Dai Zhen in *Eminent Chinese of the Qing Period, 1644–1912*, vol. 1, edited by Arthur W. Hummel (Washington, D.C., 1943), pp. 695–700. Regarding the thought of Dai Zhen, Hu Shi's *Dai Dongyuan di zhexue* (Shanghai, 1927) makes the case that the originality of Dai's philosophy lays the groundwork for a new Confucian school. Yu Yingshi's *Lun Dai Zhen Yu Chang Xuecheng* (On Dai Zhen and Chang Xuecheng; Hong Kong, 1976) argues that Dai's thought develops organically out of his deep knowledge of the neo-Confucian tradition and in dialogue with the concerns of the greatest minds of the *kaozheng* school. Hou Wai-lu, in volume 5 of his *Zhongguo sixiang tongshi* (Beijing, 1963), pp. 430–464, provides a lucid analysis of Dai Zhen's thought and a succinct account of the twentieth-century revival of his philosophy.

Three English-language works provide a brief introduction to Dai Zhen's philosophy. Cheng Chung-ying discusses the philosophical system in the introduction to his translation (above). Liang Qichao provides an appreciative introduction to Dai's thought and scholarship in *Intellectual Trends of the Qing Period*, translated by Immanuel C. Y. Xu (Cambridge, Mass., 1959), pp. 54–62. Fung Yulan provides a critique of his philosophical position in *A History of Chinese Philosophy*, vol. 2, 2d ed., translated by Derk Bodde (Princeton, 1953), pp. 651–672. Finally Yu Yingshi's article "Some Preliminary Observations on the Rise of Qing Confucian Intellectualism," *Tsing-hua Journal of Chinese Studies*, n.s. 11 (1975): 105–146, provides a larger picture of the rise of evidential research that shows that Dai Zhen's moral philosophy motivates his evidential research.

JUDITH A. BERLING (1987)

DAKHMA. The Iranian term *dakhma*, which probably originally signified "tomb," seems to be derived from the Indo-European root **dhm̥bh*, "bury" (Hoffmann, 1965), and not from *dag*, "burn," as some scholars have proposed. It is occasionally used in the Avesta with a negative meaning, insofar as the burial of bodies was condemned: the funeral rites adopted by the Zoroastrian community (and which were already practiced in priestly circles in the Achaemenid period, as we know from Herodotus) were designed to avoid scrupulously any contamination of the earth, fire, and water and can be traced to earlier practices widespread among the nomads of Central Asia. These—as we learn from the *Vendidad*—prescribed that corpses, considered impure, be exposed to vultures so that the bones could be cleansed of flesh. Once they were purified of humors and putrefying flesh, the bones were placed in special ossuaries. According to Strabo, the exposure of corpses was also practiced in eastern Iran during the Parthian period.

Later, *dakhma* became the technical term for the "towers of silence," the buildings used for the rites of exposure of the corpses, whether in Zoroastrian communities in Iran or in Parsi communities of India. The modern translation "towers of silence" seems to have been used for the first time by R. Z. Murphy, Oriental translator for the British government at Bombay (Modi, 1937).

The *dakhma*, which continues to be used today, although in more limited forms, is a circular tower, constructed of stone and often located on a hill. An iron door opens onto a large platform consisting of three concentric circles. The first and largest is for the bodies of men; the second, in the middle, is for those of women; and the third is for those of children. After the corpse has been exposed and reduced to a skeleton, the bones are put in a large, deep hole at the center of the *dakhma*.

Zoroastrian ritual attaches great importance to funerals, which are consequently very detailed and complex, as well as meticulous in their purificatory practices. Equally complex are the rites for the consecration of the *dakhma*, which consist of ceremonies for the excavation of the site, for the foundation, and for the consecration itself.

BIBLIOGRAPHY

Boyce, Mary. "An Old Village *Dakhma* of Iran." In *Mémorial Jean de Menasce*, edited by Philippe Gignoux and A. Tafazzoli, pp. 3–9. Louvain, 1974.

Boyce, Mary. *A History of Zoroastrianism*, vol. 1. Leiden, 1975.

Boyce, Mary. *A Persian Stronghold of Zoroastrianism*. Oxford, 1977.

Boyce, Mary. *Zoroastrians: Their Religious Beliefs and Practices*. London, 1979.

de Jong, Albert. *Traditions of the Magi. Zoroastrianism in Greek and Latin Literature*. Leiden, 1997.

Duchesne-Guillemin, Jacques. *La religion de l'Iran ancien*. Paris, 1962.

Hoffmann, Karl. "Av. daxma-." *Zeitschrift für vergleichende Sprachforschung aus dem Gebiete der indogermanischen Sprache* 89 (1965): 238.

Modi, Jivanji Jamshedji. *The Religious Ceremonies and Customs of the Parsees*. 2d ed. Bombay, 1937.

GHERARDO GNOLI (1987 AND 2005)
Translated from Italian by Roger DeGaris

DALAI LAMA, title of the spiritual and formerly political leader of the Tibetan people, is a combination of the Mongolian *dalai* ("ocean"), signifying profound knowledge, and the Tibetan *blama* ("religious teacher"). The title dates from 1578 CE, when it was conferred by Altan Khan of the Mongols upon Bsod nams rgya mtsho (1543–1588), third hierarch of the Dge lugs pa school of Tibetan Buddhism, commonly called the Yellow Hat sect. The title was applied posthumously to the two preceding hierarchs, Dge 'dungrub pa (1391–1475), founder of Bkra śis lhun po (Tashilhunpo) monastery near Shigatse in Gtsaṅ province, and Dge 'dun rgya mtsho (1475–1542), founder of the Dalai Lama's residence in 'Bras spung monastery near Lhasa in Dbus province. After 1578 the title was given to each of the successive reincarnations of the Dalai Lama. The present Dalai Lama is fourteenth in the lineage.

Incarnation (Tib., *sprul sku*), the manifestation of some aspect of the absolute Buddhahood in human form, is an ancient doctrine and one common to various schools of Mahayana Buddhism, but the concept of the reincarnation *(yaṅ srid)* of a lama is unique to Tibetan Buddhism. The concept emerged in the fourteenth century in the hierarchic lineage of the Black Hat Karma pa and was soon adopted by the other Tibetan schools.

From the inception of the institution, traditional procedures for discovering the rebirth of a Dalai Lama, similar to those used for other reincarnate lamas, were followed. Indicative statements made by the previous Dalai Lama during his lifetime, significant auguries surrounding his death and afterward, and meditative visions by special lamas were recorded and interpreted as guides to finding his rebirth. In time, but no sooner than nine months after the death of the previous Dalai Lama, the people began to expect reports of an exceptional male child born in accordance with various omens. Such a child, usually two or three years old when discovered, was subjected to tests to determine physical fitness, intelligence, and the ability to remember events and objects from his previous existence. If more than one likely candidate was found, the final selection was made by drawing a name from a golden urn. Once the true reincarnation was determined, he was enthroned in the Potala palace as the Dalai Lama. The monastic education of a Dalai Lama, directed by learned tutors of the Dge lugs pa school, occupied his time for years. When he attained his majority, at about eighteen years of age, he assumed the religio-political power of the office of Dalai Lama.

In the beginning, the religious power of the Dalai Lama was limited to the monastic members and lay patrons of the reformed Yellow Hat school. By the middle of the sixteenth century, religio-political power in Tibet was unevenly divided between the Red Hat Karma pa, supported by the lay king of Gtsaṅ, and the Yellow Hat Dge lugs pa, patronized by lay princes of Dbus. The third hierarch of the Yellow Hat school was subsequently invited to Mongolia by Altan Khan, who gave him the title Dalai Lama. When the Dalai Lama died in Mongolia, his reincarnation was discovered to be none other than the great-grandson of Altan Khan himself. The fourth Dalai Lama, Yon tan rgya mtsho (1589–1617), is the only one in the lineage ethnically not a Tibetan. Escorted from Mongolia to Lhasa, he was enthroned in the Dalai Lama's residence in 'Bras spung monastery. Recognition of this Mongol prince as the reincarnation of the Dalai Lama thereafter bound the Mongols by faith to the Yellow Hat school, and in time they were to protect it militarily from its enemies.

The power struggle in Tibet between the Red Hat Karma pa and the Yellow Hat Dge lugs pa continued to escalate in favor of the Red Hats and the lay king of Gtsaṅ. Finally in 1642, at the invitation of the fifth Dalai Lama, Nag dban rgya mtsho (1617–1682), Gu śrī Khan of the Mongols led troops into Tibet, defeated the Red Hat opposition, and executed the lay king of Gtsaṅ. In effect Gu śrī Khan had conquered Tibet, but true to his faith, he presented the country to the fifth Dalai Lama as a religious gift. Thus the Dalai Lama became the religious and political head of Tibet. Because he was a monk, a civil administrator was appointed to handle the day-to-day affairs of state.

After the enthronement of this Dalai Lama, a prophetic scripture was discovered. It revealed that the reincarnate Dalai Lama was also an incarnation of the Bodhisattva of Compassion, Avalokiteśvara (Tib., Spyan ras gzigs), traditionally regarded as the patron bodhisattva of Tibet. The relationship between the noumenal Avalokiteśvara and the phenomenal Dalai Lama was attested by symbolism. According to Buddhist doctrine, the mystical abode of Avalokiteśvara is a mountain called the Potala; so the fifth Dalai Lama ordered a massive fortress, also called the Potala, to be built on a mountain in the Lhasa area. Begun in 1645, the Potala at Lhasa served as the palace of the Dalai Lama for more than three hundred years.

The most common Tibetan prayer is the six-syllable "Oṃ maṇi padme hūṃ." Printed on prayer flags, contained in prayer wheels, carved repeatedly in wood and stone, and chanted daily by Tibetan Buddhists, this is the vocative mantra in Sanskrit of Avalokiteśvara. In view of his relationship to the Dalai Lama, the six-syllable mantra symbolically serves at once as an invocation to both the noumenal and phenomenal manifestations of the Bodhisattva of Compassion. Because of the belief that the Dalai Lama is an incarnation of Avalokiteśvara as well as a reincarnation of his predecessor, he is frequently, but incorrectly, called the "God-King" of Tibet in Western writings.

The fifth Dalai Lama was a learned scholar and the author of many texts, including a history of Tibet. During the forty years he was head of state, the Mongols helped to protect his newly established government and to expand its territorial control. In recognition of the important role he played in religio-political history, he is referred to in Tibetan literature as the Great Fifth.

The death of the fifth Dalai Lama was kept secret for fifteen years by the civil administrator for political reasons. His reincarnation, Tshaṅs dbyaṅs rgya mtsho (1683–1706), was discovered in due course but was not officially acknowledged as the next Dalai Lama until 1697. Unlike the monastic training of his predecessors, who had been publicly enthroned and tutored as children, that of the sixth Dalai Lama was not only kept secret but was apparently less than strict. Already in his teens when enthroned in the Potala, he soon gained notoriety for his addiction to wine, women, and song. Censure caused him to renounce his vows as a monk in 1702, but he remained in the Potala as the Dalai Lama. Finally in 1706, he was deposed by Lha bzaṅ Khan, a great-grandson of Gu śrī Khan, and deported to China; he died enroute. The sixth Dalai Lama is perhaps best remembered for sixty-two four-line verses, commonly referred to as his "love songs." A recurring theme in his poetry is the psychophysiological conflict between his monastic obligations as the Dalai Lama and his passion for mundane pleasures.

After the deposition and death of the sixth Dalai Lama, Lha-bzaṅ Khan became undisputed ruler of Tibet. He enthroned a puppet in the Potala, but the Tibetan people refused to accept him as the Dalai Lama. Instead, a boy born in eastern Tibet was recognized as the true reincarnation. Owing to the unstable situation in Lhasa, the seventh Dalai Lama, Bskal bzaṅ rgya mtsho (1708–1757), was taken to Kumbum monastery in the Kokonor region for safekeeping. In 1717 Mongols from Dzungaria, in support of the seventh Dalai Lama, invaded Tibet and killed Lha bzaṅ Khan. The puppet Dalai Lama was deposed and later deported to China. The seventh Dalai Lama was escorted to Lhasa by a Manchu imperial army and enthroned in the Potala in 1720.

A significant change was made in 1721 in the structure of the Tibetan government. The office of the civil administrator, which had concentrated political power in one pair of hands, was abolished and replaced with a council of four ministers collectively responsible for the secular branch of the dyadic hierocracy.

The death of the seventh Dalai Lama in 1757 led to the creation of a new government position. The office of the Dalai Lama had become institutionalized by then, and there was no question but that his reincarnation would succeed to his position of ruling power. Thus, the death of a Dalai Lama meant an interregnum of some twenty years, during which his reincarnation had to be discovered and educated, and his majority attained before he would resume power. During that period, another reincarnate lama of the Dge lugs pa school was appointed regent to rule Tibet on behalf of the minor Dalai Lama. Reluctance of successive regents and their supporters to hand over power each time a Dalai Lama reached his majority is blamed, perhaps unjustly, for the fact that the eighth Dalai Lama ruled only for a few years, the ninth and tenth died young without assuming power, and the eleventh and twelth Dalai Lamas ruled only for short periods before their death.

The thirteenth Dalai Lama, Thubbstan rgya mtsho (1876–1933), assumed full power in 1895. He survived an attempt on his life by his former regent, who purportedly resorted to witchcraft in hopes of furthering his political ambitions. During his long reign as head of state, the thirteenth Dalai Lama was forced to flee to Mongolia in 1904 to escape British troops invading from India. He spent years traveling in Mongolia and China. Not long after his return to Lhasa, he was again forced to flee early in 1910, this time to India to avoid the invading Chinese forces. The Chinese revolution of 1911 that overthrew the Manchu dynasty and established the Republic of China also marked the end of Manchu domination of Tibetan affairs. The Manchu imperial garrison at Lhasa, which had been set up early in the eighteenth century, was deported to a man by the Tibetan government. From 1913 until his death in 1933, the thirteenth Dalai Lama was the head of an independent government. Living in exile in British India motivated the thirteenth Dalai Lama to implement various reforms in Tibet to improve the welfare of his people. His importance in Tibetan history can be compared with that of the Great Fifth Dalai Lama in the seventeenth century.

The fourteenth Dalai Lama, Bstan 'dzin rgya mtsho, was born in 1935 of Tibetan parentage in the Chinghai province of China. Two other likely candidates were also found; but the one from Chinghai successfully passed all the tests, the omens were in mystical agreement, and he was confirmed as the true reincarnation by the State Oracle of Tibet himself. The Chinghai candidate was duly enthroned in the Potala at Lhasa in 1940. During the next decade, half of which was taken up by World War II in Asia, the young Dalai Lama was educated and prepared for the time he would assume his role as religio-political ruler of Tibet.

The invasion of eastern Tibet late in 1950 by forces of the People's Republic of China precipitated the empowerment of the fourteenth Dalai Lama when he was just fifteen years old. He was escorted to a village near the Indian border to avoid capture by the Chinese. In 1951, an agreement was reached between the Tibetan government and the Peking regime, and the Dalai Lama subsequently returned to Lhasa.

In 1956, the Dalai Lama and the Panchen Lama, the high-ranking reincarnate lama of the Yellow Hat monastery of Bkra śis lhun po, were invited to India to attend the Buddha Jayanti, a great celebration marking the twenty-five-hundredth anniversary of the birth of the Buddha. After the Dalai Lama returned to Tibet, however, the constrained political situation there continued to deteriorate, and in March 1959 the Tibetan populace revolted against the Chinese regime in Lhasa. The Dalai Lama fled to India. That month the Chinese abolished the traditional Tibetan government, ending over three hundred years of hierocratic rule by the Dalai Lama, incarnation of Avalokiteśvara, Bodhisattva of Compassion.

The present Dalai Lama continues to live in exile in India. He has traveled internationally, visiting various Asian countries as well as continental Europe, the United Kingdom, and the United States. The leaders of two great religious traditions met when the fourteenth Dalai Lama of Tibetan Buddhism was welcomed in the Vatican by Paul VI in 1973 and by John Paul II in 1979.

SEE ALSO Dge lugs pa.

BIBLIOGRAPHY

The only book dealing with the first thirteen Dalai Lamas in some detail remains Günther Schulemann's *Die Geschichte der Dalailamas,* 2d ed. (Leipzig, 1959). Charles A. Bell's *Portrait of the Dalai Lama* (London, 1946) is a biographical sketch based on the author's personal friendship with the thirteenth Dalai Lama, but part 2 of the book explains what a Dalai Lama is and how he is discovered and educated. A scholarly listing, but with basic dates and data only, of all fourteen Dalai Lamas, as well as the regents who successively served them, can be found in Luciano Petech's "The Dalai-Lamas and Regents of Tibet: A Chronological Study," *Tuoung bao* (Leiden) 47 (1959): 368–394.

English translations of three books by the fourteenth Dalai Lama, Tenzin Gyatso, are recommended. His autobiography, *My Land and My People* (New York, 1962), is an interesting narrative of his selection, education, and experiences. The *Opening of the Wisdom-Eye and the History of the Advancement of Buddhadharma in Tibet* (Bangkok, 1968) and *The Buddhism of Tibet and the Key to the Middle Way* (New York, 1975) provide lucid expositions of the fundamental philosophical teachings of Tibetan Buddhism that must be mastered by a Dalai Lama.

Also recommended are David L. Snellgrove and Hugh E. Richardson's *A Cultural History of Tibet* (New York, 1968), Rolf A. Stein's *Tibetan Civilization* (Stanford, Calif., 1972), and Tsepon W. D. Shakabpa's *Tibet: A Political History* (New Haven, Conn., 1967). Each of these works contains an excellent bibliography.

TURRELL V. WYLIE (1987)

DAMASCENE, JOHN SEE JOHN OF DAMASCUS

DAMIAN, PETER

DAMIAN, PETER (1007–1072), also known as Pier Damiani; Italian author, monk, cardinal, doctor of the church, and Christian saint. Born in Ravenna, Damian acquired his training in the liberal arts, his superior command of Latin, and his knowledge of Roman law at Ravenna, Faenza, and Parma, where an urban culture survived. Ravenna, capital of Romagna and the old Byzantine exarchate, regained importance through the Ottonian revival. Throughout his lifetime, Damian retained ties with Ravenna's civil and clerical circles.

In 1035, when already a priest and teacher, he changed careers to join the disciples of the extreme ascetic Romuald (d. 1027) in the wilderness at Fonte Avellana, a hermitage near Monte Catria in the Marches. Damian is reticent about his conversion, but it is known that it was not sudden. *Vita Romualdi,* Damian's first datable work (1042), is as valuable for its view of eremitical life as the apex of Benedictine observance as it is as a source for the life of Damian's revered mentor. Chosen prior in 1043, Damian turned the colony into a stable community with a written rule, a library, and a temporal base, and saw it grow into a widespread congregation.

Damian's conviction that his pursuit of evangelical perfection did not exempt him from public service helped him cope with an important challenge of his day, namely the reform of the church, appeals for which mounted from outside monasteries, from Emperor Henry III, from Archdeacon Hildebrand (later Pope Gregory VII), and from others. A rare insight into the mystery of the church as the union of every member in Christ complemented his strong support of its hierarchical structure in the Roman tradition. His collaboration with the popes began under Leo IX (1049–1054) and was closest with the moderate Alexander II (1061–1073). Damian became cardinal bishop of Ostia in 1057, carrying out delicate missions in Italy, France, and Germany. After reconciling the archbishop of Ravenna with the Roman see, he died at Faenza, where his cult began.

The flow of writings from Damian's pen, matching his tireless activity in the church, includes 175 letters, small tracts, some 50 sermons, saints' lives, prayers, hymns, and poems. His efforts at reform, based on the norms of church law, reflect the issues of his times: clerical immorality (*Liber Gomorrhianus*), theological problems raised by traffic in church offices (*Liber gratissimus*), and political-ecclesiastical strife (*Disceptatio synodalis*). Of lasting interest are the fruits of his beloved solitude: his ideal of Christian virtue and fidelity to duty in all walks of society, and his spiritual counsel, scriptural comments, and meditations. He was steeped in the Bible and drew on the church fathers, especially Augustine, whose works he procured for Fonte Avellana. Still prized in the twelfth century, his writings were eclipsed by the intellectualism of the Scholastic age, but Dante's praise assured Damian recognition outside the church as well (*Paradiso* 21.106–111). Thanks to excellent transmission of the manuscripts, Damian's corpus was secured for the modern age in the *Editio princeps* of Costantino Gaetani (four volumes, Rome, 1606–1640). Scholarship has shifted from its earlier selectivity to a consideration of Damian's whole legacy and of the man himself, as evidenced in the studies published in 1972 for the ninth centennial of his death. Perhaps the major significance of Peter Damian for Western religion lies in the fact that he, like the Camaldolese and Carthusians, gave new life and form to the strain of contemplative life and asceticism stemming from the Desert Fathers of Egypt.

BIBLIOGRAPHY

The collected works are available in *Patrologia Latina,* edited by J.-P. Migne, vols. 144 and 145, (Paris, 1853). Single items have modern editions, and an edition of the letters is in preparation for the "Monumenta Germaniae Historica" series.

The only anthology in English is *Saint Peter Damian: Selected Writings on the Spiritual Life*, translated with an introduction by Patricia McNulty (London, 1959). Both Owen J. Blum's *Saint Peter Damian: His Teachings on the Spiritual Life* (Washington, D.C., 1947) and my own *Saint Peter Damiani and His Canonical Sources: A Preliminary Study in the Antecedents of the Gregorian Reform* (Toronto, 1956) have ample bibliographies. An expert portrayal is Jean Leclercq's *Saint Pierre Damien: Ermite et homme d'église* (Rome, 1960). Two important collections of new studies are *San Pier Damiano: Nel IX centenario della morte, 1072–1972*, 4 vols. (Cesena, 1972–1978); and *San Pier Damiani: Atti del convegno di studi nel IX centenario della morte* (Faenza, 1973).

J. Joseph Ryan (1987)

DANCE

This entry consists of the following articles:

DANCE AND RELIGION
POPULAR AND FOLK DANCE [FIRST EDITION]
POPULAR AND FOLK DANCE [FURTHER CONSIDERATIONS]
THEATRICAL AND LITURGICAL DANCE [FIRST EDITION]
THEATRICAL AND LITURGICAL DANCE [FURTHER CONSIDERATIONS]

DANCE: DANCE AND RELIGION

Dance is part of many systems of belief about the universe that deal with the nature and mystery of human existence and involve feelings, thoughts, and actions. From a comparative worldwide perspective, dance may be seen as human behavior composed (from the dancer's point of view) of purposeful, intentionally rhythmical, and culturally patterned sequences of nonverbal body movements in time, in space, and with effort. Different from ordinary motor activities, these movements have inherent and "aesthetic" values; that is, they have both appropriateness and competency. According to historical and anthropological research, people dance to express an awareness that is often difficult to express in words, and to fulfill a range of intentions and functions that change over time. Perceptions of orthodoxy and authenticity vary. People dance to explain religion, to create and re-create social roles, to worship or honor, to conduct supernatural beneficence, to effect change, to embody or merge with the supernatural through inner or external transformations, to reveal divinity through dance creation, to help themselves, and to entertain. Specific knowledge of dance practices associated with the supernatural is acquired through initiation, divination, oracle, observation, and copying.

The power of dance in religious practice lies in its multisensory, emotional, and symbolic capacity to create moods and a sense of situation in attention-riveting patterns by framing, prolonging, or discontinuing communication. Dance is a vehicle that incorporates inchoate ideas in visible human form and modifies inner experience as well as social action. The efficacy of dance in contributing to the construction of a worldview and affecting human behavior depends upon the beliefs of the participants (performers and spectators), particularly their faith in their ability to affect the world around them.

Dance has potency through sensory sensitivity and perception: the sight of performers moving in time and space, the sounds of physical movements, the odors of physical exertion, the feeling of kinesthetic activity or empathy, and the sensations of contact with other bodies or the dancer's environment. Meaning in dance relies on who does what, and on when, where, why, how, and with and to whom it is done. Such variables can convey gender roles, class status hierarchies, race, and other group identities. Skilled dancing may show spiritual excellence.

More like poetry than prose, dance may have cognitive, language-like references beyond the dance form itself. Meaning may be conveyed through various devices, such as metaphor (a dance in place of another expression that it resembles to suggest a likeness between the two), metonym (a dance connected with a larger whole), concretization (mimetic presentation), stylization (somewhat arbitrary religious gestures or movements that are the result of convention), icon (a dancer enacting some of a god's characteristics and being regarded or treated as that god), and actualization (a portrayal of one or several aspects of a dancer's real life).

Meaning may also exist in the spheres of the dance event, including nondance activity, the human body in special action, the whole dance performance, performance segments as they unfold as in a narrative, specific movements or style reflecting religious values, the intermeshing of dance with other communication media such as music, and the presence of a dancer conveying a supernatural aura or energy.

It is not possible to know the origins of religious dance. Rock art verifies its antiquity, however, and many peoples have explanatory myths. The Dogon of Mali, for example, say that god's son the jackal danced and traced out the world and its future; the first attested dance was one of divination that told secrets in dust. A spirit later taught people to dance. Hindus of India believe that Śiva danced the world into being and later conveyed the art of dancing to humans.

A popularly held psychological and theological theory found in numerous histories of dance suggests that dance evolved instrumentally to cope with unknown happenings in the human environment. Spontaneous movement—an outlet for the emotional tension endemic in the perpetual struggle for existence in a baffling environment—developed into patterned, symbolic movements for the individual and group. When a desired situation occurred following an instrumentally intended dance (for example, rain followed a danced request), the dance was assumed to have causative power and sacred association. Over time, style, structure, and meaning in dance changed through the perception of supernatural revelation, individual or group initiative, and contacts with other people. When different religious groups come together, one may dominate the other, sometimes leading to complete acceptance or syncretism. In many parts of the world, a group may practice both the old and new religions, as when African deities share their altars with Christian saints.

Acceptance of Dance as Religious Practice. Views of mind and body, especially concerning emotion and sexuality, affect dance in religion (as well as in other aspects of life). Whereas various arts use the body as an accessory to create sounds or visual objects, dance is manifest directly through the body and evokes bodily associations. Christian, Muslim, and Hindu beliefs and practices illustrate significantly different perspectives about dance and religion.

Christianity's love-hate relationship with the body and acceptance of a mind-body dichotomy—which the rationalism of sixteenth-century Europe intensified—has led to both positive and negative attitudes toward dance. Recognizing Christ's humanity, Christianity views the human body as a temple housing the Holy Spirit, and it calls its church the "body of Christ." Paul said, "Glorify Christ in your bodies" (*1 Cor.* 6:15–20). From the second century, Christians (e.g., Theodoret of Cyrrhus and Clement of Alexandria) described dance as an imitation of the perpetual dance of angels, the blessed and righteous expressing physically their desire to enter heaven. Christianity built upon the Hebrew tradition of demonstrating through pious dance that no part of the individual was unaffected by the love of God. Yet Christianity also scorned flesh as a root of evil to be transcended, even mortified. Misunderstandings of Paul's view of flesh, by which he meant to refer to the individual acting selfishly, led to negative attitudes toward the body in general that he did not share. Christianity's rejection of the body reflects an inability to come to terms with the passing of time and with death. Moreover that the body is the instrument of sex and of dance creates fear of unbridled arousal of the passions and sexuality. Consequently, religious and secular totalitarian governments try to exert control over dance.

Although the Greeks, Hebrews, and Christians took part in ancient fertility and sustenance dances, some of these dances took the form of unrestrained, sensual rites. This perceived debasement of religion led to the periodic proscription of dance and to penalties against dancers. Legends of Salome's sensuous dance, for which she received John the Baptist's head in reward (she either obeyed her revengeful mother in requesting this or expressed her anger about John's not reciprocating her sexual interest in him), have kept alive negative associations with dance. Some Christians hold any glorification of the body, including dancing, an anathema: outspoken enemies of physicality with an ascetic dislike of eroticism, which could undermine faith and unsettle the hierarchic status quo, they preach the ideal of the Virgin. Western philosophy and Victorian prudishness have not, however, affected the Eastern Orthodox Church to the extent of eliminating dance in worship.

Because the nineteenth- and twentieth-century European industrializing nations that imperialistically dominated the world economy were largely Christian, this religion has had a stifling impact on dance worldwide. Europeans recognized that non-European dance was intertwined with indigenous religions and moralities. Even though these dances often had themes and origins comparable to those of European folk dances, colonialists considered indigenous dances to be the manifestation of savage heathenism, and thus antagonistic to the "true faith." They therefore frequently sought to eliminate them. The British influence, for example, contributed to the demise of Hindu temple dancing without succeeding in spreading Christianity. However, even when proscribed or out of fashion, dance rises phoenixlike and transformed. The Hindu temple-dancing became an Indian nationalist symbol appropriated by middle-class women. Black slaves in the United States, members of Nigerian Yoruba Assemblies of God, and a number of white Christian groups have all included in their worship what appears to be dance—though under a different name, such as "play," "the shout," or "feeling the Lord."

As former European colonies in Africa, Latin America, and Asia regained independence, they frequently reevaluated and renewed their devalued dances. Moreover, counterreactions in the twentieth-century West to claims of the separation of mind from body have led to a renaissance of dance as religious practice in churches and temples. When Westerners developed more accepting attitudes about the body, and as biblical scholarship on dance increased after the 1960s, a sacred dance movement gave impetus to the resurgence of Christian congregational, choir, and solo dancing. Nevertheless, some Christian groups still ban dancing.

Islam generally disapproves of dancing as a frivolous distraction from contemplating the wisdom of the Prophet. Its religious leaders look upon dancing with contempt.

The sacred and secular, the ritualistic and playful, and the spiritual and sexual do not everywhere have the dichotomous character so common in Muslim societies and in industrial societies, where specialization and separation are hallmarks. For example, Hinduism generally merges the sacred and the sexual in a felicitous union. As religion is about mystery, potential danger, hope of heaven, and ecstasy, so too are sexual love and its ramifications. Rather than considering carnal love a phenomenon to be "overcome," as in some Christian denominations, a strand of Hinduism accepts sexual congress as a phase of the soul's migration. Through the path of devotion *(bhakti),* a surrender to the erotic self-oblivion of becoming one, a man and a woman momentarily glimpse spiritually and symbolically the desired absolute union with divinity. This is a microcosm of divine creation that reveals the hidden truth of the universe. The dance conveys this vision of life in telling the stories of the anthropomorphic gods. Hinduism has a pantheon of deities and is really a medley of hundreds of belief systems that share commonalities, as do Christian denominations. The supreme, all-powerful God is manifest in a trio of divinities: Brahma, Viṣṇu (who appears in the incarnation of Kṛṣṇa, of amorous nature and exploits), and Śiva (Lord of the Dance, who created the universe, which he destroys and regenerates through dance). Śiva's rhythms determine those of the world. The classic Indian sacred treatise on dance, the *Nāṭya Śāstra,* describes dance as an offering and demonstration of love to God, a cleansing of sin, a path of salvation, a partaking of the cosmic control of the world, and an expression of God within oneself.

Typology of Sacred Dance Practice. Dance is frequently an element of the process by which symbolic meanings related to the supernatural world of ancestors, spirits, and gods are exchanged among performers and spectators. From the perspectives of various religions and the functionalist, structuralist, feminist, and identity theories that view religion as part of the larger social system, there appear to be eleven categories of dance, which are neither exhaustive nor mutually exclusive. The specific dances referred to in the discussion below are from different times and cultures, removed from their rich historical and social contexts; they are chosen to illustrate kinds of beliefs and acts.

Explaining religion. Dance is part of ritual constructions of reality communicated to people so they may understand the world and operate in it. The lore of sacred and profane belief, often intertwined, is told and retold in dance.

In early Christendom, dancing began as metaphor and metonym for the mysteries of faith. During the first part of the Middle Ages, dancing accompanied Christian church festivals and processionals in which relics of saints or martyrs were carried to call attention to their life histories. Later, in the twelfth, thirteenth, and fourteenth centuries, dance was an accepted liturgical art form in mystery and miracle plays. Elaborate dramatic presentations flourished in the Renaissance, but then printed tracts, pamphlets, and books and other promotions of the ascendance of the mind began to erode the importance of dance as a medium of religious expression. The Jesuits sponsored ballet as honorable relaxation in the seventeenth and eighteenth centuries until its suppression for being veiled political commentary.

The Spanish Franciscans used dance dramas, especially those depicting the struggle of the church against its foes, to explain the Christian faith to the illiterate New World Indians they hoped to convert. Pageants of Moors and Christians were common. Appropriating indigenous Indian dances, the Franciscans suffused them with Christian meaning. Similarly, Muslims in East Africa at the end of the nineteenth century used indigenous attachment to the old Yao initiation dances to gradually introduce another dance that was regarded as an initiation into Islam.

Contemporary Western dance performances in places of worship, referred to as sacred, liturgical, or midrash dance (search for biblical meaning in the Torah through improvisational movement); public theaters; film; television; and on the internet perpetuate the tradition of dance explaining religion. Choreographers present biblical scenes, incidents, and concepts in addition to religious philosophy, characters, events, and processes. Of course, all religious dance may have an entertaining element.

Creating and re-creating social roles. Often used as a means to legitimize social organization, religion may employ dance as its agent to convey attitudes about proper social behavior at the same time that it fulfills other purposes and functions. An example comes from Hinduism, which has a rich ancient history in the arts and religion. Although both male and female royalty in early India may have been well versed in dancing, the *Nāṭya Śāstra* is the scripture of a male sage, Bhārata Muni, who upon receiving instruction from the gods later handed it down through his sons. Recognizing that dance is symbolic, he thought danced enactments of myths and legends would give people guidance in their lives.

Male Brahmans (members of the priestly class) taught dance to males who performed only as young boys *(gotipuas),* to males who performed in all-male companies *(kathakali),* and to women dedicated to serving in the temples *(devadāsīs).* A dancer usually performs both male and female roles and movement styles for the deities in private devotions and at religious festivals involving the larger community.

Some common religious dance themes are about male-female relations. In the allegories of Rādhā (loveliest of the milkmaids) and Kṛṣṇa (the eternal lover dancing in the heart of every man), for example, their illicit love becomes a spiritual freedom, a type of salvation, and a surrender of all that the strict Indian social conventional world values.

Human analogies explain Hindu divinity; conversely, the tales of the gods—more powerful versions of men and women with the same virtues and vices—provide sanctified models for human actions as well as fantasies with vicarious thrills related to cultural sexual taboos. Danced enactments of legends send messages of patriarchal dominance—that it is acceptable for men to lustfully wander outside of marriage, whereas, in contrast, women are supposed to be faithful to their husbands, forgive them, and bear their children in spite of the pain, risk of death, and agony from high infant mortality.

In the West Sepik District of Papua New Guinea, the Umeda people convey gender status through the annual Idā dance, a ritual for sago palm fertility and a celebration of survival in the face of physical and mystical dangers. Although the sexual division of labor is supposedly complementary, in this dance the cultural creativity of men is pitted against the biological creativity of women, and female culture is opposed and ultimately conquered by male culture.

The myths and metaphors of religious codes present basic propositions concerning expected behavior between leaders and followers, other than relations between the sexes. Such codes are danced for all to see. The Indian *kathakali* (in which feminine-looking boys learn to dance female roles) draws upon the physical training techniques from Kerala's military tradition. This powerful and spectacular drama, staged as a public ritual for the entire community, has been claimed to be a reaction to foreign aggression and a reaffirmation of the priestly and warrior social status, as well as an affirmation of masculine pride in matrilineal and matrilocal society.

Dance in preconquest Mexico was devoted to deities and agricultural success; its performance, as well as its representation in artifacts, appears to have served contemporary sociopolitical designs: to create, reflect, and reinforce social stratification and a centralized integrated political organization encompassing diverse, geographically dispersed ethnic groups. Nobles, priests, and commoners, old and young, male and female, each had distinct dances and spatial levels for performing at the pyramid temple.

Worship or honor. At regularly scheduled seasonal times, at critical junctures, or just spontaneously, dances are part of rituals that revere; greet as a token of fellowship, hospitality, and respect; and thank, entreat, placate, or offer penitence to deities, ancestors, and other supernatural entities. Not only may dance be a remedial vehicle to propitiate or beseech, it may also be prophylactic—gods may be honored to preclude disaster.

Dance is a means of religious concentration as well as of corporeal merging with the infinite God. The Jews dance to praise their God in sublime adoration and to express joy for his beneficence. Hasidic Jews communicate with God through ecstatic dancing designed to create a mystical state. Hebrew Scriptures refer to "rejoicing with the whole being," as well as to specific dances performed for traditional festivals. The God-given mind and body are returned to God through dance. As a result of the destruction of the Temple in 70 CE Jews generally eliminated dance and song from regular worship until such a time as they could return from the Diaspora and rebuild the Temple. The Talmud, ancient rabbinic writings that constitute religious authority for traditional Judaism, describes dancing as the principal function of the angels and commands dancing at weddings for brides, grooms, and their wedding guests. Procreation is God's will, weddings a step toward its fulfillment, and dancing a thanksgiving symbolizing fruitfulness. Even in exile there could be dancing, because out of the wedding might be born the Messiah who would restore the people to the Land of Israel.

In Christianity the Catholic Church allowed dances created for special occasions, such as the canonization of cardinals or commemoration of their birthdays. Throughout Latin America, devotional dances are part of a pilgrimage and processional fiesta system that fuses Indian and Catholic tenets. Dance training and production preparation are often undertaken as part of a religious vow to a powerful saint, the Virgin, or a Christ figure. The Mormons believe that, when engaged in by the pure of heart, dance (excluding the embracing-couple position of Western social dance) prepares the individual and community for prayer meetings or other religious activity; devotion and recreation unite the individual with God. Brigham Young, who led the Mormon migration from Illinois to Utah, discovered that dance was a means to strengthen group morale and solidarity through providing emotional and physical release from hardship.

In Orissa, India, the custom of small boys dancing dressed as girls has coexisted with a female dance tradition since the fifteenth century. The *sakhībhāva* cult believes that, because Kṛṣṇa is male, the most effective way of showing devotion is as a female, like the milkmaids *(gopīs)* who dance their love for Kṛṣṇa.

The Gogo of Tanzania dance the Cidwanga as a sign of reverence in the annual ritual for good rains and fertility. Groups in Nigeria provide many illustrations of worshipful dance. The Kalabari believe that human beings make the gods great. Fervent worship adds to a deity's capacity to aid the worshipers, and just as surely the cutting off of worship will render them impotent, or at least cause them to break off contact with erstwhile worshipers. Among the Efik, the worshipers of the sea deity Ndem briskly dance in a circle at the deity's shrine to express metaphorically the affective intensity of a wish, whether it be for a child or a safe journey. The brisker the dance, the more likely Ndem is to grant requests. Because the Ubakala Igbo dance to honor and propitiate the respected living, it is not surprising that the spirits of the departed and other supernatural entities are also honored in this way. Some deities, such as the Yoruba Ṣango, love to be entertained and can best be placated with good dancing.

Like the human creatures they basically are, the ancestors of the Fon of Dahomey (or the other spiritual entities who are given anthroposocial attributes) are believed to love display and ceremony. Thus both living and spiritual entities are believed to watch a dance performance, and both categories of spectators may even join the dancers, the latter often doing so through possession. Supernatural beings are sometimes honored to ensure that they do not mar festivals.

Conducting supernatural beneficence. Dance may be the vehicle through which an individual, as self or other (masked or possessed), becomes a conduit of extraordinary power. Among the Ganda of Uganda, parents of twins, having demonstrated their extraordinary fertility and the direct intervention of the god Mukasa, danced in the gardens of their friends to transmit human fertility supernaturally to the vegetation. Yoruba mothers of twins dance with their offspring and promise to bless all those who are generous with alms. Here the motional, dynamic rhythm and spatial patterns of dance transfer desired qualities to objects or individuals.

The men and women of Tanzania's Sandawe people dance by moonlight in the erotic Phek'umo rites to promote fertility. Identifying with the moon, a supreme being believed to be both beneficial and destructive, they adopt stylized signs or moon stances; they also embrace tightly and mimic the act of sexual intercourse. The dance, metaphorically at least, conducts supernatural beneficence.

Because dance movement is metonymical with life movement, dance parody of sorcerer-caused disease and death affects the ascendance of life spirits and health forces. The Tiv of Nigeria parody dropsy and elephantiasis through dance.

The Sun Dance of the hunting peoples of the Great Plains of North America was an elaborate annual pageant performed during full summer, when scattered tribal bands could unite in a season of plenty. Representatives danced to renew the earth, pray for fertility or revenge for a murdered relative, and transfer medicine. The typical Sun Dance involved a week of intense activity culminating in dramatic climactic rites. Male dancers participated in accord with personal vows made previously for success in warfare or healing of a loved one. Each dancer strove to attain personal power. Dancers were pierced through the breast or shoulder muscles and tethered with thongs to the central pole of a ceremonial lodge altar. Staring at the sun, they danced without pause, pulling back until the flesh gave way.

Effecting change. Dance may be used as a medium to reverse a debilitating condition caused by the supernatural or to prepare an individual or group to reach a religiously defined ideal state. This includes status transformation in rites of passage, death, healing, and prevention, as well as rites to reverse political domination.

The United Society of Believers in Christ's Second Appearing, commonly called Shakers because of their dramatic practice of vigorous dancing, believed that the day of judgment was imminent. Numbering about six thousand members in nineteen communities at its peak in the 1840s, the group held that salvation would come through confessing and forsaking fleshy practices. Notwithstanding their professed attitudes toward the body, the first adherents were seized by an involuntary ecstasy that led them to run about a meeting room, jump, shake, whirl, and reel in a spontaneous manner to shake off doubts, loosen sins and faults, and mortify lust in order to purify the spirit. In repentance they turned away from preoccupation with self to shake off their bondage to a troubled past. This permitted concentration on new feelings and intent.

Dancing for the Shakers, who believed in the dualism of spirit versus body, appears to be a canalization of feeling in the context of men and women living together in celibacy, austerity, humility, and hard manual labor. Shaker dance involved a sequence of movements, designed to shake off sin, that paralleled the sexual experience of energy buildup to climax and then relaxation. Individualistic impulsive movements evolved into ordered, well-rehearsed patterns. Shaking the hand palm downward discarded the carnal; turning palms upward petitioned eternal life.

For Buddhist Sherpa lamas, laymen, and young boys in Nepal, dancing is a means by which they resolve the necessity of simultaneously affirming and denying the value of worldly existence. The spring Dumje ceremony purges the forces of repression and guilt that oppose the erotic impulses so that life may continue. The young boys' highly lascivious *tek-tek* masked dances represent sexuality as well as the children who are its desired fruits.

Dance mediates between childhood and adult status in the Chisungu, the girls' initiation ceremony of the Bemba of Zambia. The women conducting the ceremony believe they are causing supernatural changes to take place as each initiate is "danced" from one group with its status and roles to another. Among the Wan of the Ivory Coast, a man must dance a female initiate on his shoulders. During the initiation to an ancestral cult, the Fang of Gabon carry religious statues from their usual places and make them dance like puppets to vitalize them.

Another form of status change occurs at death. The Ubakala perform the dance dramas Nkwa Uko and Nkwa Ese to escort a deceased aged and respected woman and man, respectively, to become ancestors residing among the spirits, later to return in a new incarnations. These forms are similar to the dances in the Christian tradition that enable one to enter heaven.

Among the Dogon, death creates disorder. But through the symbolism and orderliness of dance, humans metaphorically restore order to the disordered world. Symbolically spatializing things never seen, the Dogon represent heaven on earth. So too at the time of death the mask dance helps to mitigate the psychic distress and spiritual fear of the dead.

The funeral dance of the Nyakyusa in Tanzania begins with a passionate expression of anger and grief and gradually becomes a fertility dance. In this way dancing mediates the passionate and quarrelsome emotions felt over a death and the acceptance of it.

Dances related to death were common in medieval Europe, a largely preliterate society dominated by the Christian church. It interpreted an economically harsh and morally complex world as a fight between God and the devil. Part of a convivial attempt to deny the finality of death, dances also had other manifestations and functions. In the so-called Dance of Death, a performer beckoned people to the world beyond in a reaction to the epidemic Black Death (1347–1373), a bubonic plague outbreak in Italy, Spain, France, Germany, and England. Evolving with the image of the skeletal figure seen as one's future self, the dance was a mockery of the pretenses of the rich and a vision of social equality. The dance emphasized the terrors of death to frighten sinners into repentance. Hallucinogenic and clonic cramp symptoms of bread and grain ergot poisoning, called Saint Anthony's Fire, led some of its sickly victims to move involuntarily in dancelike movements. Such people were believed to be possessed. Other victims sought relief from pain through ecstatic dancing, considered to be of curative value and efficacious in warding off death. Dances were also connected with wakes for the dead and the rebirth of the soul to everlasting life. Dancing at the graves of family, friends, and martyrs was believed to comfort the dead and encourage resurrection as well as protect against the dead as demons.

Gregory of Nazianzus, bishop of Constantinople, Turkey, thought of dancing at the graves of martyrs as a means to cast out devils and prevent sickness. Dance could also trample vices and that which enslaves people and holds them down.

Among the Gogo, dance metaphorically effects a supernatural change through role reversal in a curative and preventative rite. When men fail in their ritual responsibility for controlling human and animal fertility, disorder reigns. Women then become the only active agents in rituals addressed to righting the wrong. Dressed as men, they dance violently with spears to drive away contamination.

The Hamadsha, a Moroccan Ṣufi brotherhood, performs the *hadrah,* an ecstatic dance, in order to cure an individual who has been struck or possessed by a devil. They seek a good relationship with a *jinni* (spirit), usually ʿĀʾishah. In the course of the dance, people become entranced and slash at their heads in imitation of Sidi, ʿAli's servant, who did so when he learned of his master's death. A flow of blood is believed to calm the spirit. The Hamadsha women fall into trance more readily and dance with more abandon than the men.

Dance was an integral part of many American Indian religious revivals and reaffirmations in response to historical, economic, and political situations they wanted to change. The northern Paiute and peoples of the Northwest Plateau believed that ceremonies involving group dancing, a visible index of ethnic and political alliances and action, would bring about periodic world renewal. The Indians thought certain group dances had the power to end the deprivation that resulted from defeat at the hands of whites and bring about the return of Indian prosperity. The Ghost Dance religion incorporated Christian teachings of the millennium and the second coming of Christ in order to attract acculturated Indians.

Mexican dance groups, known as *concheros, danza Chicimeca, danza Azteca,* and *danza de la conquista,* originated in the states of Querétaro and Guanajuato as a response to the Spanish conquest in the sixteenth century. The groups may also be seen as "crisis cults," syncretistic attempts to create prideful cultural identity and new forms of social integration. Participants, at the low end of the socioeconomic scale and heavily represented in the laborer and shoe-shine occupations, adopt the nomenclature of the Spanish military hierarchy and perform dances reenacting the conquest that were derived from Spanish representations of the Moors and Christians. The warlike dances involve women, the aged, and children as well as men.

Embodying the supernatural in inner transformation: personal possession. Dance may serve as an activating agent for a specific kind of change: giving oneself temporarily to a supernatural being or essence. This metamorphic process is usually accompanied by a devout state and altered consciousness aided by autosuggestion or autointoxication through learned frenzied movement that releases oxygen, adrenalin, and endorphins and sometimes promotes vertigo. Audience encouragement abets crossing the threshold into another state of being. The dance itself is often characterized by a particular type of musical accompaniment. A possessed devotee may achieve a consciousness of identity or a ritual connection with the supernatural iconically, metonymically, metaphorically, or experientially. Some practitioners retain their own identities; others become the spirit—and self-identity depends on the spirit that animates the body.

A supernatural possessor may manifest itself through the dancer's performance of identifiable and specific patterns and conventional signs. In this way it communicates to the entire group that it is present and enacting its particular supernatural role in the lives of humans. Thus fear of the supernatural entity's indifference is allayed. Possession may alter somatic states and cause a dancer's collapse. The specific characteristics of possession are culturally determined, and even children may play at possession.

There are four types of personal possession. Diviners, cult members, medicine men, and shamans are among those who participate in the first type "invited" spirit mediumship possession dances. Numerous African religions and their offshoots in Haitian vodou and Brazilian macumba, as well as other faiths, involve the belief that humans can contact supernatural entities and influence them to act on a person's behalf. The worshiper takes the initiative and lends his or her body to the tutelary spirit when there is an indication that the spirit wishes to communicate with the living or when the devotee desires a meeting. As a sensorimotor sign, the dance may indicate the deity's presence or a leader's legitimacy; as a signal, it may be a marker for specific activities. As a metonym, it may be part of the universe; and as a metaphor, it may refer to human self-extension or social conflict.

The Kalabari believe a possessed dancer invites a god as a guest into the village. "Dancing the gods" is considered an admirable achievement. Masquerade dancers may become possessed, and in some cases the performer is expected to await possession before dancing. In possession dances the ability of Water People gods to materialize as pythons is accented as they metamorphose from acting like people to writhing on the ground and slithering about the house rafters as the great snakes do. The *oru seki* (spirit) dancing occurs in the ritual to solicit a special benefit or to appease a spirit whose rules for human behavior have been infringed. Possession of the invoker, an iconic sign in the midst of the congregation, assures the spirit's presence, power, and acceptance of the invocation and offerings.

Among the Ga of Ghana it is through a medium, whose state of possession is induced by dance, that the god signifies its presence and delivers messages prophesying the coming year's events and suggesting how to cope with them. Possession legitimizes leadership among the Fanti of Ghana. Because the deities love to dance, the priests assemble drummers, become possessed, and then speak with the power and authority of the deity. The Korean shaman attains knowledge and power in the role of religious leader through trance possession induced by dancing.

Invited possession may be a mechanism for individuals to transact social relationships more favorably. Healing practices often mediate the natural, social, and supernatural. In Sri Lanka's Sinhala healing rites, an exorcist attempts to sever the relationship between a patient and malign demons and ghosts. The exorcist's performance of various dance sequences progressively builds up emotional tension and generates power that can entrance both the healer and the patient. Their bodies become the demonic spirit's vehicle, constitute evidence of its control, and convince spectators of the need, as the healer prescribes, for a change in social relations that will exorcise the demonic spirit and transform the patient from illness to a state of health.

A second kind of possession dance, known as "invasion" (also often a metaphor and signal of social pathology or personal maladjustment) indicates that a supernatural being has overwhelmed an individual, causing some form of malaise, illness, or personal or group misfortune. A deity or spirit who manifests itself in specific dances identified with the supernatural speaks or acts using the possessed's body. Some cultures—for example, in Africa, the Caribbean, the Middle East, Brazil, and Korea—recognize that a person's poor physical condition and related fear and helplessness may also be associated with difficult social relationships that the person feels helpless to remedy by himself or herself. Dance becomes a medium to exorcise and appease the being, thus freeing the possessed individual and ameliorating his or her irksome ascribed status or difficult situation. Meeting the wishes of a spirit as part of exorcism frequently imposes obligations on those related to the possessed.

The *vimbuza* healing dance of the Chewa and Tumbuka societies in Malawi is a socially sanctioned means of expressing those feelings and tensions that if otherwise broadcast would disrupt family or community relationships. The dance is medicine for the *vimbuza* disease, which causes terrifying dreams or visions, the eating of unusual meat, or the uttering of a specific groan.

A third kind of possession, called "consecration," involves initiation and the impersonation of a deity, during which time the dancer becomes deified. In India the audience worships the young performers in the Rāma-līlās who play Kṛṣṇa, Rādhā, Rāma, and other mythic heroes in the same way they would revere icons. Performers of the Tibetan sacred masked dance, or *'cham,* are viewed as sacred beings.

Not only may individuals be possessed by supernatural entities, they may also experience "essence possession," the fourth type, by an impersonal religious or supernatural potency. Among the Lango of Uganda, *jok* is liberated or generated in dancing. Similarly among the !Kung San of Namibia, dance activates *n/um,* that potency from which medicine men derive their power to protect the people from sickness and death. The medicine dancer may go into trance and communicate with spirits without being possessed by them. The ceremonial curing dance may be called for in crisis situations, or the dance may occur spontaneously; it is redressive and prophylactic.

Merging with the supernatural toward enlightenment or self-detachment. Illustrations of another form of inner transformation through dance come from Turkey and Tibet. In Turkey the followers of the thirteenth-century poet-philosopher Mawlana Jalāl al-Dīn Rūmī, founder of one of Islam's principal mystic orders, perform whirling dances. Men with immobile faces revolve in long white shirts with covered arms outstretched, slowly at first and then faster until they reach a spiritual trance. These men, the dervishes (the word refers to a person on the threshold of enlightenment), strive to detach themselves from earth and divest themselves of ties to self in order to unite with a nonpersonified God. This process occurs through revolving movement and repeated chanting that vibrates energy centers of the body in order to raise the individual to higher spheres.

The Tibetan Buddhist dance ritual called Ling Dro Dechen Rolmo permits imaging the divine. The dancer's circular path and turning movement aid the participants toward enlightenment by providing a means to realize that the deity is a reflection of one's own mind.

Embodying the supernatural in external transformation: masquerade. Sacred masquerade dances, part of a people's intercourse with the spirit world, make social and personal contributions through symbolic actions that are similar to those made through dances that explain religion, create and re-create social roles, worship and honor, conduct supernatural beneficence, effect change, and involve possession. The Midimu masked dancing of the Yao, Makua, and Makonde of Tanzania and Mozambique helps to explain religion by marking the presence of the supernatural (ancestors) in the affairs of the living. In effect, ancestors return from the dead to rejoice on the occasion of an initiate's return from the training camp. The Dogon's masked-society dancing patterns depict their conception of the world, its progress and order, and its continuity and oneness with the total universe. Dance is thus a model of the belief system. Participants in the Nyau society of Chewa-speaking peoples dance a reenactment of the primal coexistence of people, animals, and spirits in friendship and their subsequent division by fire. The people believe that underneath their masks the dancers have undergone transformation into spirits.

Social roles are emphasized when the Yoruba's Gẹlẹdẹ society masquerade figures appear annually at the start of the new agricultural year to dance in the marketplace and through the streets. They honor and propitiate the female *orișa* (spirits) and their representatives, living and ancestral, for the mothers are the gods of society and their children are its members—all animal life comes from a mother's body.

Although both men and women belong to the Gẹlẹdẹ cult (to seek protection and blessings and assuage their fear of death), only men dance, with masks portraying the appropriate sex roles of each character. Mothers have both positive (calm, creative, protective) and negative or witch (unmitigated evil affecting fertility, childbirth, and the functioning of men's sexual organs) dimensions. The mothers possess powerful *ase* (vital, mystical power). A man can have *ase* most fully when he is spiritually united with an *orișa.* When men symbolically externalize the vital life forces in dance, they may be asserting their virility and freedom in the presence of the powerful mothers and, in addition, recognizing and honoring their powers in order to appease them to ensure that they utilize their *ase* for male benefit.

Among the Nafana of the Ivory Coast, masked dancing occurs almost nightly during the lunar month of the year. The dancing is intended to worship and effect change. Living in the masks, the Bedu spirits bless and purify the village dwellings and their occupants and metaphorically absorb evil and misfortune, which they remove from the community so that the new year begins afresh.

The masked (antelope headdress) dance of the Bamana of Mali represents Chi Wara, the god of agriculture—a supernatural being who is half animal and half man—who first taught people how to cultivate the soil. Chi Wara's public presence is an invocation of his blessings. In a concretized form that makes appeals more understandable to the young, animal masked dances remind humans that they have some animal characteristics, and participants respond to the dancers both positively and negatively. In this way the masked dancing presents human foibles at a distance for examination without threat to individuals, thus helping to effect change.

Masked dancing can be a metaphor for both normative and innovative behavior. Under religious auspices the dancer is freed from the everyday restrictions on etiquette and thus is able to present secular messages and critiques. Presented by the unmasked, these messages might produce social frictions or hostilities rather than positive change.

Among the Nsukka Igbo of Nigeria, the council of elders employed masked dancers representing an *omabe* spirit cult whenever there was difficulty in enforcing law and order. In Zambia, Wiko Makishi masqueraders, believed to be resurrected ancestors and other supernatural beings, patrol the vicinities of the boys' initiation lodges to ward off intruders, women, and non-Wiko.

A Chewa man residing with his wife and mother-in-law often resorts to the male masked Nyau dancer to mediate between himself and a mother-in-law whose constant demands on him he resents. When the dancer dons the mask of the Chirombo (beast), he directs obscene language against her. No action may be taken against him, for in his mask he enjoys the immunity of the Chirombo. Afterward, the mother-in-law often reduces her demands.

Socially sanctioned ritual abuse with ribald and lewd movements and gestures in a highly charged atmosphere is permitted in the Bedu masked dance mentioned above. There appear to be humor and an underlying feeling that these acts are socially acceptable and that through them participants will be purged of whatever negative emotions they may harbor.

The masked dancer may be an iconic sign, revered and experienced as a veritable apparition of the being he represents, even when people know that a man made the mask and is wearing it. Because the Angolan Chokwe mask and its wearer are a spiritual whole, both in life and death, when a dancer dies, his mask is buried with him.

Revelation of divinity through dance creation. Within a Protestant Christian view, artistic self-expression is analogized to the creative self-expression of God as creator. Dancing a set piece is considered a reflection of the unknowable God's immanence, irrespective of the performer's intention. The dancer is to dance as God is to creation. The language of movement is God given, and both the progression of a dancer's training and the perfection of performance reveal God's achievement. Within the Franciscan view, God is present in good works and in the creative force of the arts. Through dance rituals in Latin America, performers become one with creation. When an individual dances with expertise—individuality, agility, and dexterity—the Gola of Liberia consider this to be a sign of a *jina*'s gift of love given in a dream.

Self-help. Many people wanting to stay well or to cope with stress seek out nontraditional spiritual pathways. They draw upon teachings from different religions and borrow movements for their own spiritual dances. Some people seek a "high" through vigorous dance and the release of endorphins.

Nonsacred theatrical and recreational dance. In many parts of the world that have become somewhat modernized and secularized, participants in nonsacred theatrical dance often choose to explain religion, to convey or to challenge its models for social organization and gender roles, to effect change, and to honor the divine by infusing their dances with elements drawn from religions worldwide. Many folk dances associated with religious holidays or events have been transformed into commercial theatrical, nightclub, tourist, and museum productions—and into performances (by dancers other than the "folk") for recreational purposes.

Choreographers interpretatively embody religious events in sensory storytelling or reflect theologically rooted affirmations and values without reference to specific stories in opera and dance concerts and on television and the Internet. Isadora Duncan, a pioneer of American modern (a form of dance that originally reflected a rebellion against formality) viewed her dance as a prayer through which one could become one with nature, itself sacred. Dance was an invocation for which Duncan desired audience participation. Yet women have mostly performed dances taught by male choreograpahers and interpreters, and thus helped to perpetuate both male dominance over females and stereotypes of women as virgin or whore. Good women in the Bible are tainted by using seduction (e.g., Judith). Martha Graham, another pioneer of modern dance, was a leader in choreographing a woman's viewpoint and dominance without guilt. Dancers in India are modifying the movement and story line of the epics to assert feminist perspectives.

Technology and religious practice. Access to new technology is sometimes manifest in ritual, such as the appearance of a telephone mask. Movements of contemporary disco have been incorporated into possession dance. Television broadcasts some rituals as they occur. There are replays and documentaries. Among the Edo in Benin City, Nigeria, videorecording capturing the span of real time became a mandatory assertion of the importance of individual participants. Visibility may effect efficaciousness. Choreography with the camera loses immediacy of the place of worship or theater but gains excitement through access.

IN SHORT. Dance is a barometer of theology, ideology, worldview, and social change within often overlapping categories of religious practice. Dance appears to be part of a cultural code or logical model enabling humans to order experience, account for its chaos, express isomorphic properties between opposing entities, and explain realities. Dance and religion merge in a configuration that encompasses sensory experience, cognition, diffused and focused emotions, personal and social conflicts, and technology. People dance to explain religion, convey sanctified models for social organization, revere the divine, conduct supernatural beneficence, effect change, embody the supernatural through internal or external transformation, merge with the divine toward enlightenment, reveal divinity through creating dance, engage in self-help, and convey religious themes in secular theater and recreation. Permeated with religious tradition, dance continually changes.

SEE ALSO Darwīsh; Drama; Ghost Dance; Human Body; Ritual; Spirit Possession; Sun Dance.

BIBLIOGRAPHY

Adams, Doug. *Congregational Dancing in Christian Worship.* Rev. ed. Austin, Tex., 1980. Biblical, historical, and theological perspectives provide the context for a discussion of dance principles and practices.

Adams, Doug, and Diane Apostolos-Cappadona, eds. *Dance as Religious Studies.* New York, 1990. Resources and explanation of dance and Scripture and women in dance and Scripture.

Amoss, Pamela. *Coast Salish Spirit Dancing: The Survival of an Ancestral Religion.* Seattle, 1978. A probing of the reasons for this revival within its new context.

Andrews, Edward Deming. *The Gift to Be Simple.* New York, 1940. A description of the history, songs, music, and dances of the Shakers.

Backman, E. Louis. *Religious Dances in the Christian Church and in Popular Medicine.* Translated by E. Classen. London, 1952. A rich source of historical material.

Bharata Muni. *The Nāṭyaśāstra: A Treatise on Ancient Indian Dramaturgy and Histrionics, Ascribed to Bharata Muni.* Translated by Manomohan Ghosh. Calcutta, India, 1950. Important source of many forms of dancing in India.

Bloch, Maurice. "Symbols, Song, Dance, and Features of Articulation: Is Religion an Extreme Form of Traditional Authority?" *Archives Européenes de Sociologie* 15 (1974): 51–81. A claim that formalizing dance is a kind of power or coercion by restricting options for expression.

Clive, H. P. "The Calvinists and the Question of Dancing in the Sixteenth Century." *Bibliothèque d'humanisme et Renaissance* 23 (1961): 296–323.

Coomaraswamy, Ananda K. *The Dance of Shiva: Fourteen Indian Essays.* New Delhi, 1971. Reprint ed. of *The Dance of Shiva* (New York, 1957). A discussion of dancing milkmaids as a metaphor of human souls.

Crapanzo, Vincent. "The Hamadsh." In *Scholars, Saints, and Sufis,* edited by Nikki R. Keddie, pp. 327–348. Berkeley, Calif., 1972. A description of the ecstatic dance of a Moroccan cult.

Cuisinier, Jeanne. *La danse sacrée en Indochine et Indonésie.* Paris, 1951.

Deren, Maya. *Divine Horsemen: Voodoo Gods of Haiti.* Foreword by Joseph Campbell. New York, 1970. An account of the principles and many of the rites of an African-based religion.

De Zoete, Beryl. *Dance and Magic Drama in Ceylon.* London, 1957. A description predating Kapferer's *A Celebration of Demons* (1983).

Drewal, Henry John, and Margaret Thompson Drewal. *Gẹlẹdẹ: Art and Female Power among the Yoruba.* Bloomington, Ind., 1983. A description of masked dancing and gender relations.

Fallon, Dennis J., and Mary Jane Wolbers, eds. *Religion and Dance.* Focus on Dance, vol. 10. Reston, Va., 1982. Twenty-two articles primarily in the area of Western culture.

Félice, Phillipe de. *L'enchantement des danses, et la magie du verbe.* Paris, 1957.

Fergusson, Erna. *Dancing Gods: Indian Ceremonials of New Mexico and Arizona.* New York, 1931. A descriptive presentation.

Friedlander, Ira. *The Whirling Dervishes, Being an Account of the Sufi Order Known as the Mevlevis and Its Founder the Poet and Mystic Mevlana Jalalu'ddin Rumi.* New York, 1975. Includes numerous photographs and bibliography.

Friedson, Steven. *Dancing Prophets: Musical Experience in Tumbuka Healing.* Chicago, 1996. An analysis of religious practice in Malawi.

Gell, Alfred. *Metamorphosis of the Cassowaries: Umeda Society, Language, and Ritual.* London, 1975. An insightful analysis of ritual dances.

Gore, Charles. "Ritual, Performance, and Media in Urban Contemporary Shrine Configurations in Benin City, Nigeria." In *Ritual, Performance, Media,* edited by Felicia Hughes-Freeland, pp. 66–84. Association of Social Anthropologists Monographs 35. London, 1998.

Granet, Marcel. *Danses et légendes de la Chine ancienne.* 2 vols. Paris, 1926.

Griaule, Marcel. *Conversations with Ogotemmêli: An Introduction to Dogon Religious Ideas.* London, 1965. A Dogon elder's account of his people's cosmology.

Hanna, Judith Lynne. *The Performer-Audience Connection: Emotion to Metaphor in Dance and Society.* Austin, Tex., 1983. Discussion of religious attitudes that shape performance expectations, focusing on two forms of Hindu dance and a black spiritual.

Hanna, Judith Lynne. *To Dance Is Human: A Theory of Nonverbal Communication.* Chicago, 1987. A theory based on contemporary knowledge that explains how dance works and how it can be studied. Extensive bibliography.

Hanna, Judith Lynne. *Dance and Stress: Resistance, Reduction, and Euphoria.* New York, 1988. Illustrations through history and across geography of how danced religion helps people cope.

Hanna, Judith Lynne. "The Representation and Reality of Divinity in Dance." *Journal of the American Academy of Religion* 56, no. 2 (1988): 501–526. A discussion of different ways of manifesting divinity.

Kapferer, Bruce. *A Celebration of Demons.* Bloomington, Ind., 1983. A descriptive analysis of the role of dance gesture and style in ritual healing among the Sinhalese.

Leeuw, Gerardus van der. *Sacred and Profane Beauty.* Translated by David E. Green. New York, 1963. Commentary on the secularization of dance, believed by author to be the original art form.

Lum, Kenneth Anthony. *Praising His Name in the Dance: Spirit Possession in the Spiritual Baptist Faith and Orisha Work in Trinidad, West Indies.* Studies in Latin America and the Caribbean. Amsterdam, 2000. Based on traditional Yoruba religion in West Africa, the Spiritual Baptist Faith persons possessed by the Holy Spirit retain their own identity, whereas in Orisha Work, those possessed by oriṣas (spirits) become the spirits.

McKean, Philip F. "From Purity to Pollution? The Balinese Ketjak (Monkey Dance) as Symbolic Form in Transition." In *The Imagination of Reality: Essays in Southeast Asian Coherence Systems,* edited by A. L. Becker and Aram A. Yengoyan, pp. 293–302. Norwood, N.J., 1979. A descriptive analysis predating Kapferer's study.

Oesterly, W. O. E. *The Sacred Dance.* Cambridge, U.K., 1923. An estimate of the role of sacred dance among the peoples of antiquity and non-Western cultures.

Paul, Robert A. "Dumje: Paradox and Resolution in Sherpa Ritual Symbolism." *American Ethnologist* 6 (1979): 274–304. A description of boys' dances that represent sexuality as well as the children who are the desired result of it.

Porter, Stanley E., Michael A. Hayes, and David Tombs, eds. *Faith in the Millennium.* Sheffield, U.K., 2001. Catholic missionaries allow syncretism among northern Australian aboriginal Tiwi that respects both native and Christian ideologies.

Rostas, Susanna. "From Ritualization to Performativity: The Concheros of Mexico." In *Ritual, Performance, Media,* edited by Felicia Hughes-Freeland, pp. 85–103. Association of Social Anthropologists Monographs 35. London, 1998. Rural tradition is politicized by urban dancers who reject colonialist taint to favor indigenous identity.

Sendrey, Alfred. *Music in Ancient Israel.* New York, 1969. Chap. 8 is about dance, verbs that express the act of dancing, and the functions of dance.

Taylor, Margaret F. *A Time to Dance: Symbolic Movement in Worship.* Philadelphia, 1967. An overview of dance in the history of the Christian church and its reawakened use in the twentieth century.

Tucker, JoAnne, and Susan Freeman. *Torah in Motion: Creating Dance Midrash.* Preface by Rabbi Norman Cohen. Denver, Colo., 1990. By asking pertinent questions about biblical passages and then answering them through movement activities that illustrate and explicate their nuances, midrash enlivens the Bible.

Wagner, Ann. *Adversaries of Dance: From the Puritans to the Present.* Urbana, Ill., 1997. A history of hostility toward dance in the United States.

Waterhouse, David, ed. *Dance of India.* Toronto, 1998. Includes feminist perspectives.

Wood, W. Raymond, and Margot P. Liberty, eds. *Anthropology on the Great Plains.* Lincoln, Nebr., 1980. Articles with bibliographies on the sun dance and the Ghost Dance religion.

JUDITH LYNNE HANNA (1987 AND 2005)

DANCE: POPULAR AND FOLK DANCE [FIRST EDITION]

Dance and religion have been intertwined in various ways through the centuries. The attitudes toward dance expressed in ancient Greek writings and the Bible are part of a philosophical legacy that has been influential throughout the intellectual and cultural history of the Western world. The ancient Greeks believed that dance was supreme among the arts, indeed that it was fundamentally inseparable from music and poetry. In the *Laws,* Plato writes that all creatures are prompted to express emotions through body movements, and he notes that such instinctive response is transformed into dance by virtue of a gift from the gods: rhythmic and harmonic order. Other Greeks held the general belief that dance was originally transmitted directly from the gods to humans, and consequently that all dancing is a spiritual endeavor. Whatever the origin of dance, classical historians maintain that religious rituals were indeed the source of many Greek dances, though dancing was not confined to rituals or occasions of formal worship. Dance was also an integral part of Greek social life, as recreation and as a means of solemnizing events or experiences. The spiritual nature of dance was apparently considered so all-encompassing that the Greeks made no rigid distinction between religious dancing and secular dancing.

The Hebrew scriptures contain numerous references to the dance activities of the Israelites in biblical times. Dancing was an expression of joy in all realms of life, a celebration of mental and corporeal fulfillment as well as a personal declaration of spiritual devotion. Modern scholars have debated whether dance was a part of actual religious rituals or formal worship in the Jewish faith. Some believe that there was no role for dancing in the Temple or in performances of the religious officiants during services and ceremonies. Even so, dance clearly played a significant part in the public festivals that accompanied the holy days. For example, the pilgrimages associated with seasonal festivals were sanctified by dancing, singing, and the playing of musical instruments such as the harp. Also, the triumphs of the Jewish people over their oppressors were celebrated in victory parades with dancing and special songs.

By the dawn of the Christian era, two major factors affected the status of dance in the philosophy of the church establishment. The first was the tangible and immediate heritage of attitudes toward dancing found among the Jewish people; the second was the active dance traditions of the various pagan cults that were now converting to Christianity. The Christian community shared with the Jews the fundamental belief that dance was a means of expressing reverence to God. The angels danced in heavenly joy, and mortals danced to celebrate their faith. Many ancient pre-Christian customs found in European cultures were preserved (e.g., the practice of dancing at burial grounds) and coexisted alongside the new rites of the church. Other dance customs were actually integrated into Christian religious ceremonies. Religious dances performed by the clergy included the ring dance and the processionals that formed part of the various saints' festivals. Other dances were performed only by members of the congregation, including ribbon dances, ring dances accompanied by songs and hand-clapping, and processionals. Over the centuries as Christianity spread, local enthusiasm for dancing remained strong, and church officials were compelled to limit the types of religious events in which dancing was acceptable. Regional church authorities forbade dancing in the house of the Lord: dancing would be permissible (to varying degrees) only in the religious observances that took place in public festivals outside the church structure itself. The fact that such restrictions were issued repeatedly indicates that they were not always obeyed, nor were they always enforceable in local communities.

The continued strength and tenacity of dance customs in the face of the declining approval of church authorities suggest the depth of the fundamental Western belief in the spiritual nature of dance. In *Religious Dances* (1952), Louis Backman provides a chronicle of historical references that illustrates individual dance forms and activities and their relationship to the Christian church in various regions. The interconnection of dance and religion, however, must be considered in a context that extends beyond the confines of official, formalized religion. The very definitions of folk dance and popular dance have developed from a spectrum of cultural beliefs that ranges from the organized religious establishment to the vernacular spirituality that animates everyday life.

FOLK DANCE AND POPULAR DANCE. Although the terms *folk dance* and *popular dance* did not enter common use until the early twentieth century, the dance phenomena they describe have existed for centuries. Rather than referring to particular dance choreography, *folk dance* and *popular dance* refer to the dancing found in certain social strata of European society in a certain period of history.

As Peter Burke notes in *Popular Culture in Early Modern Europe* (1978), by the sixteenth century European society was sufficiently stratified to be able to distinguish between the culture of the common people and the culture of the elite. The elite were a minority who had access to formal scholastic training; they were the innovators and primary beneficiaries of such intellectual movements as the Renaissance and the Enlightenment. The rest of society went about everyday life, molding and adapting time-worn traditions and values to accommodate the inevitable shifts demanded by social and economic change. It cannot be assumed, however, that the common people were a homogeneous group, or that the elite educated minority did not participate in popular culture. Burke illuminates the complexity of these issues, noting the diversity of the common people: there were poorer peasants and richer peasants, freemen and serfs, uneducated laborers and literate merchants, rural dwellers and urban dwellers, religious sects and regional subcultures. The elite took part in a broad range of popular culture outside the boundaries of their intellectual pursuits, if simply because they were surrounded by that culture.

By the late eighteenth century factors such as dramatic population shifts, the radical expansion of commercial capitalism, and the advent of industrialization contributed to the disruption of traditional community life in many parts of Western Europe and the subsequent demise of many popular traditions. In the same period, a new intellectual movement took root in which the folk or rural peasants became increasingly idealized in the eyes of the elite, and "folk culture" became a national treasure embodying the survivals of the uncorrupted national past. In the nineteenth century the anthropologist E. B. Tylor pointed to folklore, especially old customs and beliefs, as providing evidence of the historical development of primitive culture into civilized society. Folklore materials were seen as the vestiges of primitive culture, somehow preserved by the folk memory in the midst of an otherwise relatively civilized society.

This argument was supported further by comparing folklore to parallel cultural elements found in existing primitive societies. Seemingly irrational folk beliefs or antiquated folk customs were explained on the basis of their full-fledged primitive counterparts; the original function and meaning of the folklore survivals were considered equivalent to those of the related primitive practices, even when the forms or contexts of performance differed greatly. Many scholars believed that primitive religion was the ultimate source of folklore because religion played such a prominent role in primitive life.

If folklore was what remained of ancient pagan religion, then it might follow that folk dance was what remained of ancient religious ritual. Yet it is curious that the genre of folk dance was neglected in the heyday of naming and documenting folk cultural genres in the nineteenth century. There is no doubt that the folk were dancing, but most scholars mention dancing only in passing, generally in reference to seasonal or religious festivals or the celebration of rites of passage.

This puzzle still remains to be explored fully, but two factors can be suggested as important elements in this regard.

The first factor is that as a cultural commodity vying for scholarly attention, dance was of comparatively low status. The young fields of folklore and anthropology were intent on establishing themselves as scientific pursuits, and toward that end researchers were concerned with the task of generating texts. Dance was not a literary genre that could be recorded in words, and unlike music it did not have associated with it a common form of notation. To be sure, scholars did not hesitate to describe folk customs and celebrations in written accounts that were often illustrated with drawings and, later, photographs. The first studies of the late nineteenth century that discussed dance in any detail used that type of descriptive narrative: they presented dance customs, complete with notes on costumes, other related material paraphernalia such as swords, ribbons, sticks, or bells, unusual dramatic characters such as a man or woman impersonator or a hobbyhorse, and the social event of which the dance activity was a part. Yet very little explicit or technical description was included of the actual dance forms or styles themselves. It seems that, while writing about dance customs was certainly possible, the difficulty of rendering dance into documentary evidence hardly encouraged early scholars to invest their intellectual enthusiasm in such an elusive genre.

The second factor in the scholarly neglect of folk dance is that it was indeed believed to manifest the remnants of ancient religious ritual. This is ironic because that type of connection with primitive culture would generally have been considered a favorable quality in the evolutionary school of thought that considered folklore to be descended from ancient religion. In the case of dance, however, it may have contributed to some intellectual discomfort. By the nineteenth century, dance style was socially stratified, although the choreographic forms danced in the elite ballrooms were not dissimilar to those danced in peasant villages. The elite were responsible for infusing these dance forms with an educated and refined style of performance appropriate to their social class, for the physical abandon and overt emotionalism displayed in much peasant dancing would have been judged quite improper, even uncivilized, by the upper classes. The contemporary observations of European missionaries and travelers of wild, impassioned dancing in primitive societies served as a graphic comparison to dancing in folk communities in Europe and may have intensified the elite's sense of a debasing impropriety of folk dance. More so than any other folk performance genre, dance may have seemed a bit threatening—too primitive and too close to home; for it could be argued that the only thing separating the dancing of the elite themselves from the blatantly uncivilized dancing of the folk was a fine line of decorum. In addition, scholars were well aware of the fact that the Christian clergy had long believed that dance and dance customs (which nineteenth-century scholars would have equated with folk dance) were the survivals of pagan religious rituals. For centuries, throughout Europe, the church had been waging campaigns to cleanse Christian ritual of any taints of paganism, of which dance was one of the most insidious elements. Whatever their intellectual creeds, nineteenth-century scholars in Europe and America were good Christian gentlemen and ladies, and there can be little doubt that the official religious prejudice against dancing influenced scholarly perceptions. It is possible that this Christian heritage contributed to a sense of discomfort with folk dance material, which in turn further discouraged researchers from working in that field.

In the last decade of the nineteenth century, dance began to be considered with some seriousness. James G. Frazer included dance as one of the myriad customs examined in his comparative treatise on magic and religion, *The Golden Bough* (1890). The development of the open-air folklife museum in Scandinavia with its focus on traditional folkways gave impetus to the founding of the Friends of Swedish Folk Dance in 1893. This was one of the first organizations of its kind, dedicated to the preservation and perpetuation of regional folk dances. Lilly Grove, in her history of dancing (London, 1895), included whole chapters on national dances and dance customs. English folklore journals published essays on seasonal festivities that discussed rustic examples such as maypole dancing and morris dancing. The year 1903, in saw E. K. Chamber's *The Mediaeval Stage* (London), one of the earliest uses of the terms *folk dance* and *Volkstanz* in a scholarly study, signalling a subtle shift in intellectual attitudes: dance was finally included in the rank of folk-compound genres, and a whole group of dance forms and customs associated with the romantic notion of the folk became "folk dance."

Throughout the early twentieth century, the concept of the folk dance was codified through the collecting and publishing of dance materials and through work in the now growing fields of folklore studies and dance education. To differentiate certain important features of dance culture, particularly the origin and transmission of dance forms and styles and the contexts of dance performance, the term *popular dance* began to be used. *Folk dance* referred to dances whose origins were obscured in ancient customs and ceremonies that derived from primitive religious ritual. Folk dances were passed on from one generation to the next and were performed as part of traditional folk community festivals. Though popular dances might be adopted into the folk repertoire and performed in traditional contexts, they were not native to the folk community. Popular dances originated from an external source, such as a foreign culture or a professional dance instructor. Popular dances were transmitted through a broader variety of social relationships than would generally have been included in the traditional folk learning process; that is, people learned from non-community members, from strangers, or from dance teachers. Popular dances were most often performed during recreational events organized for the purpose of social dancing, often in a public setting such as a dance hall. Folk dance was believed to be a pure expression of national identity, whereas popular dance was a commodity in the aesthetic marketplace of a heterogeneous, multicultural society.

The development of the concepts of folk dance and popular dance is critical to a larger understanding of dance and religion. The very definition of folk dance is inextricably tied to Western ideas about the history of religion and human culture. In the end, however, the definitions of folk dance and popular dance have to do not so much with types of dance activity as with the progression of intellectual judgments about social and economic class. According to the nineteenth-century models on which they are based, folk dance is the dance performed by the folk, and popular dance is the dance performed by the working class, or bourgeoisie. These intellectual constructions are so romantically idealized and oversimplified, however, that they do not reflect the cultural reality of the time. Even if nineteenth-century peasants had been the pristine, homogeneous group the folk were supposed to be, there was constant interaction between folk and popular culture. Popular dances did circulate among rural peasant communities and in some cases were regarded as having more prestige than older traditional forms because they were new, different, innovative, or exotic. Likewise, the dancing of the new working class was full of deeply embedded traditional elements: a foreign or popular dance form would be performed in the traditional, regional body movement style of the performer, reflecting traditional concepts of the body; a laborer who paid an admission fee to enter a public dance hall would pursue social interaction with members of the opposite sex and different age groups according to traditional—and commonly shared—rules. Perhaps most importantly, the new popular dances were evaluated and accepted on the basis of how well they satisfied current fashions, but those fashions were at least partially rooted in a folk aesthetic. The complexity of the historical interrelations between folk dance and popular dance and the disparity between intellectual ideals and cultural reality must be considered seriously.

Fundamental beliefs about dance as a form of expresion run deep in Western culture and have influenced the intellectual fashions of every age. Whatever the criteria used to delimit folk dance and popular dance, it is in the meaning of dance in vernacular culture that the relationship between dance and religion can be explored most profitably. Vernacular dance, then, refers to dancing that is integral to the everyday life and beliefs of a given group of people, irrespective of whether that dancing might also be classified as folk or popular. Religion must also be contemplated in terms of everyday culture, ranging from the dogma of the official religious establishment to the traditional beliefs and practices that embody spirituality.

VERNACULAR DANCE, SPIRITUALITY, AND RELIGION. There are three general categories of dance as it relates to religion and spiritual values: religious dance, ceremonial dance, and social dance. Each of those categories can be distinguished on the basis of context, belief, and—to a lesser extent—form. *Religious dance* is dance performed as part of religious worship, often taking place in the church or sanctuary. It is believed to be devotion incarnate, more than just a symbol or gesture of piety. Common forms of religious dance include the processional, circle, and solo individual dance. In performance the dancer seeks to express reverence and to interact directly with the divine.

Ceremonial dance is a much broader category and includes dancing that is part of a whole spectrum of celebratory events, from the religious to the secular. Religious events such as saints' festivals and secular events such as civic parades frame a continuum of events that manifest many types and degrees of spiritual belief. Celebrations such as Carnival, certain rites of passage, and seasonal festivities embody an ambiguous spirituality that lies somewhere between the sacred and the secular, or perhaps encompasses elements of both. Ceremonial dance is believed to transcend the realm of everyday life, reaching toward a higher spiritual power, be it a deity, luck, or art. Of any category, ceremonial dance embraces the largest variety of dance forms including processionals, circle and line dances, various set formations, couple dances, and solo dancing.

Social dance, finally, refers to dancing that is performed for recreation, generally as part of events that are oriented around leisure activity and social interaction. Social dance is believed to be the expression of the individual or a social relationship and does not refer directly to any religious or spiritual concept, except in one sense. In that dancing is considered artistic performance, it attends to the immanent spirituality of art as a vehicle of power and meaning. The forms of social dance include various group and couple formations and solo individual dancing.

These three categories of dance—religious, ceremonial, and social—are somewhat fluid. Changes in one factor or another can result in a shift in category for a given dance. For example, with a change in context, social dance can become ceremonial dance; with a change in belief, ceremonial dance can become religious dance (this is what occurs in many cases when a dancer becomes "possessed" by a spirit or deity.) Thus it is clear that dance cannot be considered an inanimate cultural object. Its significance must be assessed in performance as it is actively employed in a social process. Following is a sampling of dance customs found in different cultures in Europe, the Middle East, and the New World, illustrating primarily examples of religious and ceremonial dance.

Europe. The religious revival movement of Hasidism developed in Europe in the eighteenth century. In reaction to the Jewish orthodoxy of the time, Hasidism emphasized the individual expression of devotion that was within the means of every man and woman and not limited to those educated few who were privileged to study the Torah. Dance became a primary mode of religious expression, and as Hasidism spread through eastern European Jewish communities, ecstatic dancing became an identifying marker of Hasidic worship. In fact, critics of the revival sometimes mocked or ridiculed the exaggerated dance style when voicing disapproval of religious extremism. Hasidic dance is religious dance in the fullest sense; it is a means of inspired communication with God. Not only is dance and ritual movement a revered element of religious services but dancing infuses the spirit of religious devotion into numerous other festivities and celebrations. A prominent form of Hasidic dance is solo improvisation, which sometimes consists of little more than simple shuffling steps or weight shifts, various distinctive body postures, and gestures of the arms and hands, which are often raised above the head. Specific dance steps are not required, and any decorous movement performed with a spiritual intent can be acceptable. Group and couple formations are also common, though men and women are strictly segregated in all aspects of religious worship, including dance. Couple forms include simple variations of linking elbows and turning, and of forward and back patterns; group forms include complex set dances in square and circle formations. The Ḥasidim have apparently never hesitated to adopt dance forms from surrounding gentile cultures, and this process continues in Hasidic communities today.

One end of the spectrum of ceremonial dance, that which is associated with the religious or sacred, is found in the Romanian ritual Căluş. For approximately one week beginning on Whitsunday, the villagers of southern Romania observe Rusalii, a period when the spirits of the dead are believed to return to be among the living. Also during this period, evil forces are believed to be unusually threatening, and various types of behavior are restricted or forbidden in efforts to ward off the illness caused by being "possessed by Rusalii." Such an illness can only be cured through the ritual Căluş. In addition to the general healing and protective properties of Căluş, the ritual is also seen as a source of good luck and fertility. Handerkerchiefs or small articles of clothing are sometimes attached to the dancers' costumes in hopes that they will be imbued with this luck, which is then brought back to the owner of the object. Likewise, threads from the dancers' costumes are throught to be charmed, and spectators often pluck them in hopes of deriving some magical benefit. Căluş involves a complex of performance genres, material culture, and beliefs, and it is believed they work together to effect some modicum of human control over nature and the supernatural.

In Căluş, women of the community sing long, emotional laments in the traditional manner to maintain contact between the dead and the living. All the dancing, however, is performed only by a select group of men, the Căluşari. These men are all highly skilled dancers and must take an oath not to reveal the secrets of Căluş and to obey certain behavioral interdictions. Dancing is a primary vehicle of ritual magic and healing and is performed with great seriousness and sense of responsibility. The Căluşari visit each house in the village, dancing in the courtyard to a group of eager spectators. The performance includes exhibition dances that are done only by the Căluşari and a final group dance in which the villagers dance with the Căluşari. The exhibition dances are of two types, one consisting of simple walking figures done in circle formation, the second being a combination of complicated steps, jumps, and acrobatic leaps that demand virtuosic skill from each dancer. In Căluş, dancing is an act of magic, an inexorable part of the healing ritual and beliefs about supernatural forces.

The Tuscan *veglia* offers an example of dancing that straddles the boundary between social and ceremonial dance. The *veglia* is the traditional evening social gathering that is held regularly through the winter season. This custom lingers on to this day in some areas but was common throughout Tuscany until a general decline that began in the 1970s. At the *veglia*, family and friends gather around the kitchen hearth in rural homes, and amid general socializing and merriment, the performance of traditional narratives unfolds. Through storytelling, children are instructed in the moral values of the community, young unmarried couples court each other with the singing of love songs, and the elders reflect on their experiences by exchanging tales of insight, happiness, and woe. Though the *veglia* is primarily a social occasion, it also has ceremonial qualities: it is a seasonal event; it is only open to people who have a certain relationship to the host family; there are prescribed rules for social intercourse between age groups; and there is a particular sequence that is appropriate for the performance of certain artistic genres. The *veglia* is a time of heightened social interaction defined by a community reverence for traditional values and a group negotiation of the boundaries of artistic performance.

Though dancing takes place throughout the year except during Lent, Carnival season is especially devoted to dance events. The "Carnival *veglia*" is often organized by the young unmarried men, who arrange for a suitable location, hire a musician, and provide refreshments. They then invite young women to the dance, who always come accompanied by a chaperon. At other times, the dance *veglia* is hosted by a given household, in which case one's attendance is dependent on being acquainted with the family and garnering an invitation. In either case, the dance *veglia* is specifically an event for the young to socialize. Every year during Carnival, the landlords hold a dance party to which people of all social classes are invited. Peasants and landowners dance together as equals, temporarily nullifying class differences.

There are also two instances when the dance *veglia* is held in a public hall. In one case, the young men arrange for a dance party to be held on a Sunday afternoon following the religious service. This dance is semi-secretive in that it is not announced formally in the community, thereby allowing the young women to attend without the knowledge of their mothers and chaperons. A public hall is also the setting for the special dance parties that are held on the three most important days of the Carnival period. These are organized by private social clubs whose members are confined to representatives of the families from a given village. The young people dress in elaborate finery, the men in dark suits with white gloves, the women in special outfits that are supposed to have never been seen before. The proceedings of the dance event are directed by the *caposala,* who is a well-known and respected man from the community. The *caposala* formally presides over the various and sundry forms of social interaction. He coordinates the sequence of dances, dance and courting games, and dancing competitions, and he serves as a matchmaker, employing both overt and covert methods to bring certain young couples together to dance and enforcing the etiquette that demands that no favoritism be shown in choosing dancing partners so that all the young women have at least one dance with each young man. He also maintains peaceful social equilibrium, settling any dispute and expelling troublesome participants. These dance *veglie* often last until dawn, although the party held on the final night of Carnival ends promptly at midnight, which marks the beginning of Lent. The last part of the Carnival season was, in years past, distinguished by the appearance of two costumed characters. The first of these masked men, dressed in fancy black formal attire, was the incarnation of Carnival itself, and he arrived just in time to dance the last dance of the evening. The second man entered at midnight, cloaked in a long gray coat decorated with smoked herrings; he was the embodiment of Lent, and he brought the festivities to a ceremonious end.

The dance forms performed at a *veglia* are always the same and are always danced in a particular sequence. The first dance is a polka, followed by a mazurka, a waltz, and a quadrille. The quadrille was considered the climax to the dance sequence, as it involved a variety of complicated steps and patterns and allowed the greatest opportunity for flirting during the changing of partners. Recently, other couple dances have been inserted after the waltz, such as the tango and the one-step. All of these forms are popular dances, and though they are all based on folk dance forms to varying degrees, none is specifically native to Tuscany. Despite the fact that these dances have been, at some point in history, imported into the Tuscan countryside from some foreign source, they have been unabashedly adopted into the community repertoire and through generations of performance have become thoroughly naturalized. The dancing that takes place at a *veglia* is social dancing in the most straightforward sense: young men and women dance together to be with each other, confirming and expanding an everyday relationship. It can also be considered ceremonial dancing by virtue of its central role in the *veglia,* transforming everyday life and social interaction into festivity and artistic performance.

MIDDLE EAST. The Middle East is the birthplace of three of the world's major religions—Judaism, Christianity, and Islam—and home to a variety of regional cultures and linguistic groups. Though all three religions and their subdenominations are found in the Middle East today, Islam predominates. In *The Middle East* (1976), anthropologist John Gulick distinguishes between the "great tradition" and "little tradition" in Islamic religion. The "great tradition" refers to the tenets of official religion based on the sacred written texts. The "little traditon" refers to the belief systems surrounding the veneration of saints, the control of evil spirits, and other spiritual endeavors. The beliefs and customs of the little tradition are not specified in the official religious texts and are, in fact, frowned upon by some religious functionaries. They are, nonetheless, an integral part of everyday religious prescriptions of devotion. It is in this little tradition of vernacular spirituality that we find dance customs related to religious life. There are few studies that discuss dancing in Muslim and Jewish communities, and virtually none that examine Christian settlements. Even these limited materials, however, suggest some cultural consistency or interrelationship between customs, and possibly dance forms, found among different religious groups in the Middle East. It remains for future research to explore fully the implications of ethnicity, religion, and regionality on artistic performance.

The "little tradition" of many Muslim communities includes a type of ceremonial dancing that plays a key role in a ritual process of exorcism known as the *zār.* Though found in several Middle Eastern countries, the *zār* appears to be most well known and vital in the Nile region, particularly in Egypt. The spirit that must be exorcised in the *zār* ceremony is also known as *zār.* The *zār* ceremony is performed to cure an individual of spirit possession. Though anyone is potentially vulnerable to possession, women are the most commonly afflicted. It is believed that pure spirits are ever present, wandering around the earth. These spirits demand respect, and humans are required to observe rules of spiritual etiquette, such as giving thanks or asking permission for certain actions. Pure spirits can impose good or evil upon human beings, but it is believed that committing some infraction or allowing a breach in deferential protocol will provoke a spirit to possess an individual and wreak punishment. Such possession can manifest itself in a variety of physical and mental symptoms, such as chronic aches and pains in certain body parts, general indolence, allergies, rheumatism, epileptic fits, and different feminine complaints, including barrenness.

The *zār* ceremony requires the services of two important ceremonial functionaries, as well as an ensemble of musicians. One role is that of the *shaykhah,* who is a spiritual intermediary. Through consultations, divination, and the prescription of different types of ritual behavior, the *shaykhah* ascertains what is needed to appease and expel the spirit. The second role is that of the *munshidah,* who is a singer versed in the specialized traditional repertoire of *zār* songs. The *munshidah* sings different songs throughout the ceremony, entreating the spirit to make itself known and interact with the *shaykhah.* Both the *shaykhah* and *munshidah* are generally hereditary roles passed on from mother to daughter.

The *zār* ceremony itself can last anywhere from one to several days, depending on the wealth of the possessed woman who has come for help. The "patient" must follow the advice of the *shaykhah* to wear special garments and ornaments or to consume certain foods and drinks. The patient provides whatever offerings the *shaykhah* determines are necessary, generally a combination of a few fowl and pieces of gold or silver jewelry. At sunset, a large circular table is covered with an elaborate meal, accompanied by chants and special songs. At two o'clock the following morning, the animals are ritually slaughtered according to Islamic custom, and the possessed woman is smeared with the warm blood. The next day the *zār* ceremony continues as the *shaykhah* guides the patient through various rituals while the *munshidah* sings the appropriate songs.

The emotional climax of the ceremony is reached when the possessed woman starts to dance. Individual spirits are associated with distinctive rhythmic patterns, and as the musicians play a particular beat the possesed woman will be drawn to dance. The dancing is frenzied and ecstatic, and the dancer speaks in the voice of her possessing spirit. The spirit makes demands that the *shaykhah* must then interpret and satisfy. The dancing continues and the excitement builds as the musicians, *munshidah*, and *shaykhah* encourage the dancer, who will dance until she is thoroughly exhausted. The dance is always a solo improvisational form, consisting of torso bending and swaying, head and arm gestures, and some simple stepping and floor patterns. The dancing performed in the *zār* ceremony is considered a vehicle for the spirit to express itself and a critical cathartic element in the process of exorcism.

Yemenite Jewish culture provides a vibrant example of the range of dance activity in the religious and spiritual life of a community. Jewish communities in Yemen were among the most isolated in the Middle East, and many ancient customs were preserved as an ongoing part of daily life. For example, religious dancing was an integral part of the observation of certain holidays, such as Simḥat Torah. In celebration of the yearly cycle of reading the Torah, the congregation sang special verses of the *pizmon*, which are religious texts sung only in the synagogue. Along with their joyous, exuberant singing, the congregation danced around with the Torah scrolls, carrying them from the central desk of the synagogue, where they were placed for reading, back to the ark, where they were stored. The dancing consisted of simple walking steps without much elaboration or stylization, but the dancing was considered an expression of devotion to Jewish religious law as written in the Torah.

There was also ceremonial dancing in Yemenite Jewish communities. Celebrations and rites of passage such as circumcisions or the two weeks of preparations and festivities that accompanied a wedding were commemorated with dancing and singing. Traditionally, men and women danced separately, each to the singing of special dance songs and the playing of a drum. The dance songs sung by the men had fixed religious texts in Hebrew, Aramaic, or literary Arabic and were performed by two singers who sat apart from the dancers. The women sang songs about everyday life, including the importance of the event being celebrated at the time. Their song texts were sung in local Yemenite Arabic dialect and were performed by the women as they danced. Though the women's songs were less overtly religious, the dancing of both men and women was considered a means of rejoicing and of honoring the celebrants.

New World. Among the European cultures in the New World, the religious sect known as Shakers offers a unique example of religious dancing in community worship. The Shakers originated in England in the mid-eighteenth century and settled in America shortly before the Revolution. They held that the second appearance of Christ was imminent and that true believers must follow certain tenets in order to transcend wordly existence and achieve everlasting life. The foundations of Shaker faith were observed through keeping apart from the world at large, the two sexes living separately and remaining celibate, sharing all property in common, diligently pursuing craftwork with their hands, and worshiping with joyful abandon. The early Shakers were overcome with ecstasy in their worship and were given to fervent and eclectic displays of divine inspiration including speaking in tongues, whirling or shaking, singing song fragments, shouting, and jumping.

As the sect grew and developed, their deranged array of spiritual responses was institutionalized into orderly forms of song and dance. Though the expression of their religious zeal was largely disposed to tidy devotional exercises, the Shaker's faith was no less impassioned. Dancing was considered a spiritual gift, or the "work of God," which they were most happy to receive. Devotional dancing was also believed to function as a means of expelling and pacifying carnal desires, thereby allowing a pure bodily manifestation of faith. There were instances of individuals dancing by themselves while receiving the spirit, but most Shaker dancing was performed in large groups consisting of all the able-bodied Believers. Men and women formed separate lines or circles and danced a variety of floor patterns and simple figures. There were dances in square and circle formations as well as processionals and sacred marches. Many of the dance patterns were said to have originated in spiritual visions and dreams received by the Shakers and were imputed with specific symbolic meanings illustrating Shaker beliefs.

The population of the New World is a panoply of different cultural groups, with a broad spectrum of religious beliefs and customs. Over the centuries different cultures have come into contact, influencing each other to varying degrees. Rather than dissolving into a homogeneous mass, however, distinct aspects from different cultural traditions were reblended into new creole forms. These creole cultures, languages, or performance traditions often contain elements that can be easily identified and traced to specific Old World origins, but the new incarnation is not an exact replica of the original. In all cases, there has been change, development, and adaption to suit new conditions and social contexts.

One of the most dramatic examples of this reblending process is found in Afro-American culture. The historical circumstances of the slave trade threw together Africans from several different national territories in west Africa, including at least five major cultural groups. The intermingling of different African traditions and beliefs has yielded an array of new Afro-American forms, which have also intermingled with other non-African traditions according to regional and historical conditions.

The *vodou* religion practiced in Haiti is one instance of this intermingling of African and non-African traditions. It incorporates a synthesis of different African beliefs and rituals that further interface with Roman Catholic practice and symbolism. Vodou is based on a complex mythology that relates major gods to lesser divinities. These spirits are called *lwa*, a Kréyol term, and they include ancestor spirits, gods and goddesses of nature, a trickster, a god of creativity, and a supreme god who presides over all the others. Every spirit has an individual personality and is associated with certain domains of everyday life or spiritual well-being. To ensure the goodwill of the *lwa* and be taken under their protection, a person must be initiated into the spiritual society. A priest or priestess, known as *hungan*, coordinates the ceremonies and rites that take place in their sanctuary and tends to community needs requiring divination, exorcism, and healing.

Vodou ceremonies and dances are generally performed in a covered shed that has a post standing in the center of the floor space. This center post is considered the means by which the spirits descend into the peristyle. Though the spirits communicate with initiates through symbolic dreams and visions, they commonly possess people and make their will known. Each spirit expresses itself through a distincitve repertoire of speech mannerisms, body movements, special dances, and a predilection for certain objects, such as a hat, bottle, or stick. It is said that a spirit "mounts" its "horse" when a person becomes possessed; the person is a vehicle for the spirit, an expressive body through which the spirit interacts with the crowd and other spirits. Possession behavior is regarded as tangible evidence of a spirit's personality and temperament, and watching the possessed during vodou ceremonies is believed to be an important way for potential initiates to learn about the spirits.

Dancing and possession are closely interrelated. Three dances are performed to honor each spirit, accompanied by songs and the playing of a drum ensemble. Rhythm acts as a kind of supernatural intermediary and entices the spirits themselves to dance. Each spirit has its own particular dances through which it reveals its power and aesthetic agility. Dancing is considered a ritual act on several levels. In one sense, dancing is held to be a gift, performed by initiates as an offering to please the spirits. In another sense, dancing is believed to be a means of divine communication by which a spirit imparts its essence or intentions to a devotee. On yet another level, dancing is transcendental, in that aesthetic fulfillment has spiritual significance. Both humans and spirits dance, seeking to achieve greater spiritual power through artistic performance. The dancing in vodou worship that is associated with possession is undeniably religious dancing, as it is the actual practice of religious belief and devotions.

SEE ALSO Carnival; Folklore; Folk Religion; Shakers; Vodou.

BIBLIOGRAPHY

A well-rounded and detailed study discussing the nature of dance in Greek civilization is Lillian B. Lawler's *The Dance in Ancient Greece* (London, 1964). This book also outlines the important Greek philosophical tenets that have influenced Western ideas about dance. A good historical study of literary references to dancing and Christianity, especially focusing on the dance epidemics, is Eugène Louis Backman's *Religious Dances in the Christian Church and in Popular Medicine*, translated by E. Classen (London, 1952). An excellent introduction to the history of popular culture and folk culture is Peter Burke's *Popular Culture in Early Modern Europe* (New York, 1978). This book also has a very useful bibliography.

The classic work that epitomizes the nineteenth-century study of comparative religion and ideas of cultural evolution is James G. Frazer's *The Golden Bough*, 3d ed., rev. & enl., 12 vols. (London, 1911–1915). Though his source materials are quite uneven, Frazer includes a multitude of references to dance-related customs. A further elaboration of evolutionary ideas is found in Curt Sachs's *World History of the Dance*, translated by Bessie Schönberg (New York, 1937). While this book has been used as a standard text for many years and offers interesting examples of dance customs, it ignores twentieth-century developments in the study of human culture and restates outdated nineteenth-century philosophy. One of the few examinations of dance by a historian of religions can be found in Gerardus van der Leeuw's *Sacred and Profane Beauty* (New York, 1963).

Additional source material on the history of folk dance, popular dance, and vernacular dance is discussed in my article "Folkdance," in the *International Encyclopedia of Dance* (New York, forthcoming). One of the first works to develop the concept of vernacular dance is Marshall Stearns and Jean Stearns's *Jazz Dance: The Story of American Vernacular Dance* (New York, 1964). A varied collection of short essays is *The Chasidic Dance*, edited by Fred Berk (New York, 1975). Of particular interest in that collection is the article by Jill Gellerman, "With Body and Soul: The Dance of the Chasidim" (pp. 16–21), which recounts the contemporary practices of Hasidic communities in Brooklyn, New York. A recent monograph that offers detailed description and analysis based on first-hand observations is Gail Kligman's *Căluş: Symbolic Transformation in Romanian Ritual* (Chicago, 1981). A delightful account of traditional social life, which includes a collection of song and narrative texts, is Alessandro Falassi's *Folklore by the Fireside: Text and Context of the Tuscan Veglia* (Austin, 1980). A good introduction to the culture of the Middle East written from an anthropological perspective is John Gulick's *The Middle East* (Pacific Palisades, Calif., 1976). This book contains useful annotated bibliographies after each chapter.

There are very few sources on dance in the Middle East, but a good overview is found in Lois Ibsen al-Faruqi's "Dance as an Expression of Islamic Culture," *Dance Research Journal* 10 (Spring-Summer 1978): 6–13. Two short studies that contain interesting history and illustrations are Metin And's "Dances of Anatolian Turkey," *Dance Perspectives* 3 (1959): 5–76, and Morroe Berger's "The Arab Danse du Ventre," *Dance Perspectives* 10 (1961): 4–67. Two longer studies that offer detailed descriptions and contextual information based on contemporary observations are Magda Ahmed Abdfel Ghaffar Saleh's *A Documentation of the Ethnic Dance Traditions of the Arab Republic of Egypt*, 2 vols., Ph.D. diss., New York University (Ann Arbor, 1979), and Shalom Staub's *The Yemenite Jewish Dance*, M.A. thesis, Wesleyan University (Ann Arbor, 1978).

The classic work on the Shaker sect remains Edward Deming Andrew's *The Gift to Be Simple: Songs, Dances, and Rituals of the American Shakers* (New York, 1940). A revealing examination of Afro-American art and the process of creolization, much of which is in relation to religion, can be found in Robert Farris Thompson's *Flash of the Spirit: African and Afro-American Art and Philosophy* (New York, 1981). A classic study in the field of Afro-American religion remains Alfred Métraux's *Voodoo in Haiti* (New York, 1959).

LEEELLEN FRIEDLAND (1987)

DANCE: POPULAR AND FOLK DANCE [FURTHER CONSIDERATIONS]

Traditionally, dance scholarship has privileged classical and theatrical dance over popular and social dance. Folk dance has been viewed since the nineteenth century as a special case study in expressions of group identity and of interest for specialists in folklore, mythology, and ritual. Popular dance has been a study in class distinctions and in modes of transmission, especially with regard to the ever-widening forms of late twentieth-century mass media. The dearth of scholarly publications related to popular and folk dance continues even among dance ethnologists and anthropologists.

Dance anthropologists Joanne W. Kealiinohomoku and Adrienne Kaeppler and dance sociologists like Helen Thomas, have found that dance—like language, art, and religion—is found in all human societies. Popular and folk dances are powerful forces in the shaping and experiencing of culture and values, but these terpsichorean modes are culturally distinct idioms, such as in Mircea Eliade's discussion of the *căluşuri* (1985).

However, the fundamental difficulty for any form of academic research is that the vehicle for dance is the human body, so that the ephemeral nature of dance presents a difficulty for "objective" analysis, as do the varied cultural attitudes toward the body. Further, all forms of popular dance, whether as a formal social dance such as the waltz or as informal and fleeting as teenage dance crazes, are perceived more as an "entertainment" than as a historically significant subject for scholarly attention.

Into the 1980s, dance scholarship had been divided into two groups: dance historians and critics who operated chronologically and based their evaluations upon traditional aesthetic criteria; and dance ethnologists and anthropologists who focused on the cultural role(s) and effects of dance. Ironically, the historians and critics traditionally concentrated their research efforts on the West while the ethnologists and anthropologists considered the non-western countries. The now classic hierarchy of dance forms from ballet through ballroom continues to function. However, since 1987 attention has been paid to the expanding universe inspired by gender studies, cultural attitudes toward the body, and the inclusion of the marginalized—that is, those who for reasons of race, ethnicity, gender, or class were omitted from earlier academic research and thereby the history of civilization. This transformation can be partially credited to the almost simultaneous airing of the eight-part television series *Dancing!* with its companion volume (1992) and the publication of the multi-volume *International Encyclopedia of Dance* (1998).

Throughout the 1990s, the oral history project of the Dance Collection of the New York Library for the Performing Arts has expanded its efforts into the collecting, supporting, and curatoring of the interviews, papers, ephemera, and film related to both popular and folk dance. In particular, the Dance Collection received funding support to coordinate with the Smithsonian Institution the videotaping of the American Folklife Festivals.

As an artistic, religious, and social practice, popular and folk dances generate a cultural and political identity for both dancer(s) and audience. These forms of dance have garnered the attention of folklorists, anthropologists, and historians of religion who typically study the interrelations among the arts, mythology, and dance of indigenous peoples as a way of learning and communicating cultural values and religious identity. Some expansions of the traditional boundaries of the interdisciplinary nature of the study of the religious connections with folk and popular dance have expanded into the realms of American Studies, Performance and Display, Popular Culture, and Religious Studies.

NEW PERSPECTIVES. Both from the perspective of religious studies and dance theory, the primary objective is to remove the "stigma of entertainment" from any intellectual analysis of either social or folk dance. The varied interpretations of the body and performance in contemporary scholarship may proffer a methodology for dance as kinesthetic modes for the politics of identity and difference. The category of "vernacular dance" (Spalding, 1995) has opened the borders within which dance had functioned and promises to re-shape the meaning and values of popular and folk dance for a new generation of scholars.

SEE ALSO Carnival; Folklore; Folk Religion, overview article; Performance and Ritual; Shakers; Vodou.

BIBLIOGRAPHY

Carty, Hilary S. *Folk Dances of Jamaica: An Insight. A Study of Five Folk Dances of Jamaica with Regard to the Origins, History,*

Development, Contemporary Setting, and Dance Technique of Each. London, 1988.

Desmond, Jane C. *Meaning in Motion: New Cultural Studies of Dance.* Durham, N.C., 1997.

Eliade, Mircea. *A History of Religious Ideas,* vol. 2. Translated by Willard R. Trask. Chicago, 1986.

Erenberg, Lewis A. *Swingin' the Dream: Big Band Jazz and the Rebirth of American Culture.* Chicago, 1998.

Harris, Janice A., Anne Pittman, and Maryls S. Waller. *Dance Awhile: Handbook of Folk, Square, Contra, and Social Dance.* 6th edition. New York, 1988.

Herbst, Edward. *Voices in Bali: Energies and Perceptions in Vocal Music and Dance Theater.* Hanover, N.H., 1997.

International Encyclopedia of Dance. 6 vols. New York, 1998.

Kaeppler, Adrienne Lois, Joanne W. Kealiinohomoku, and Cynthia Novack. *Sharing the Dance: Contact Improvisation and American Culture.* Madison, Wis., 1990.

Kaeppler, Adrienne Lois, Judy Van Zile, and Elizabeth Tatar. *Hula Pahu: Hawaiian Drum Dances.* Honolulu, 1993.

Mendoza, Zoila S. *Shaping Society through Dance: Mestizo Ritual Performance in the Peruvian Andes.* Chicago, 2000.

Mohd, Anis Md. Nor. *Zapin: Folk Dance of the Malay World.* New York, 1993.

Ness, Sally Ann. *Body, Movement, and Culture: Kinesthetic and Visual Symbolism in a Philippine Community.* Philadelphia, 1992.

Pearlman, Ellen. *Tibetan Sacred Dance: A Journey into the Religious and Folk Traditions.* Rochester, Vt., 2002.

Pegg, Carole. *Mongolian Music, Dance, and Oral Narrative: Performing Diverse Identities.* Seattle, Wash., 2001.

Peterson, Betsy. *The Changing Faces of Tradition: A Report on the Folk and Traditional Arts in the United States.* Washington, D.C., 1996.

Phim, Toni Samantha, and Ashley Thompson. *Dance in Cambodia.* New York, 1999.

Shay, Anthony. *Choreographic Politics: State Folk Dance Companies, Representation, and Power.* Middletown, Conn., 2002.

Spalding, Susan Eike, and Jane Harris Woodside. *Communities in Motion: Dance, Community, and Tradition in America's Southeast and Beyond.* Westport, Conn., 1995.

Thomas, Helen. *The Body, Dance, and Cultural Theory.* New York, 2003.

Van Zile, Judy. *Perspectives on Korean Dance.* Middletown, Conn., 2001.

Williams, Drid. *Anthropology and the Dance: Ten Lectures.* Urbana, Ill., 2004.

Zuhur, Sherifa, ed. *Images of Enchantment: Visual and Performing Arts of the Middle East.* Cairo, Egypt, 1998.

DIANE APOSTOLOS-CAPPADONA (2005)

DANCE: THEATRICAL AND LITURGICAL DANCE [FIRST EDITION]

A distinction often drawn between dance in the West (the Euramerican tradition) and dance in the rest of the world is that the latter is closely tied to religion, while dance in the West, especially theatrical dance, has developed outside religious institutions and often in opposition to them. Most of the major Asian dance–drama forms originated in religious contexts, involve religious themes, and, especially in the past, were often performed by religious practitioners. Outside Europe and Asia, dancing intended for presentation to an audience has been rare until recently and has usually taken place in a religious context. Divine possession has often been a vehicle for quasi-theatrical performance.

A dichotomy can also be discovered between the history of Western dance on the one hand and that of Western music, visual arts, and architecture on the other. While religion provided a legitimate context and a source of patronage for the growth of other European arts, this was not the case for dance. For the most part, the church not only did not support dance, it vehemently opposed it.

Yet, such broad generalizations about the divorce of dance from religion tend to obscure recognition of how influential religion has in fact been. While direct religious intent has been relatively rare, it has been strong in some periods and for some choreographers. A few have been motivated to express their religious conviction in dance, and others have sought in dance the wellsprings of spirituality. These choreographers have often found inspiration in non-Western religions where the connection between the spirit and the body is often a key principle. Whereas in earlier centuries myth and ritual were used as plot devices or as political metaphors, often in recent decades the choreography has explored the deeper dimensions of their symbolism.

Religious content has entered Western theatrical dance in a variety of ways, including (1) the use of biblical or folkloric religious themes; (2) the depiction of characters, rituals, and myths of non-Judeo-Christian religions or of unorthodox sects; (3) the influence of religious philosophies; (4) explorations of the concept of ritual or the stylizations of specific rituals; (5) the enactment of myths or the probing of mythic symbolism; (6) the use of general religious concepts or central characters, events, or processes, such as Death, Creation, and the Devil; (7) plots involving supernatural characters and stories; (8) the theme of religiously motivated sexual repression; (9) the use of religion as a device for exploring cultural identity; (10) explorations of altered states of consciousness as often occurs in sacred dance; and (11) settings of the Mass as theatrical works. In addition, many dance plots presuppose a knowledge of Judeo-Christian ethics, symbolism, ritual, and history in order to be understood fully. Religion has also indirectly affected theatrical dance history by its varying attitudes toward dance, which have included suppressing, supporting, and ignoring it.

Conflicting attitudes toward the human body and, by extension, toward dancing have characterized all three of the major monotheistic religions in the West—Judaism, Christianity, and Islam. Although the negative view has generally won out, alternative models and solutions constantly challenge any overwhelming orthodoxy. Biblical literature, for instance, provides both favorable and unfavorable pictures. On the one hand, there is the model of King David's joyous dance before the Ark of the Covenant (2 *Sm.* 6:14–16); on the other hand, there are the Israelites' idolatrous dance around the Golden Calf (*Ex.* 32:19) and Salome's allegedly lascivious dance before King Herod (*Mt.* 14:6, *Mk.* 6:22). Contradictory, too, are possible interpretations of the words of the apostle Paul. For instance, his statement that the "body is a temple of the Holy Spirit" (1 *Cor.* 6:19) has been interpreted as indicating the appropriateness of using the body in dance as a vehicle of worship and also as justification for condemning dance as a defilement of the "temple." Ambiguity about the relation of body and soul has plagued Jews, Christians, and Muslims alike, and has militated against the acceptance of dancing.

Interestingly, some heterodoxies in monotheistic religions have incorporated dance as a major focus of expression—the gnostic sects of early Christianity, the Sufis in Islam, the Hasidim of Judaism, and the Shakers of American Christianity. The Mormons are unusual in their embrace of dancing as both a social and theatrical experience.

There has been more interrelationship between religion and theatrical dance in the twentieth century, in quantity as well as in diversity of expression, than at any other time. With organized religions in general neither condemning nor supporting dance, perhaps dance has been freer to adopt religious themes without political ties or negative consequences. Perhaps the apparent secularization of society has rendered religious themes more neutral raw material. On the other hand, the growing popularity of dance has made this medium of expression more acceptable in religious contexts. In addition, while primarily growing up outside of religious institutions, theatrical dance in the twentieth century has returned to the church and synagogue in the burgeoning liturgical or sacred dance movement.

EARLY CHRISTIANITY THROUGH THE MIDDLE AGES. The strongest evidence that there was dancing connected with religion in the early Christian church is the persistent condemnation of dance chronicled in the writings of over six hundred years of church councils. At this time, dancing was particularly associated with ceremonies at the shrines of martyrs.

The disdain of the church for dancing stemmed in part from the state of dancing at the time. Much of the refinement of Greek and Roman dance and theater had degenerated into generally bawdy mime and acrobatic shows, or else the dancing had become associated with pagan rituals. The church even refused baptism to performers. A growing asceticism further divorced Christianity from dance. In addition, certain heretical movements incorporated dance into their liturgy, further fueling orthodoxy's condemnation of it. For instance, the gnostic sects enacted the "Round Dance of the Cross" from the *Acts of John* as an actual sacred ritual dance that enabled the participants to identify with Christ and to transcend human suffering. Such lines as the following have become a rallying point for other religious sects that wish to recognize sacred dance: "To the universe belongs the dancer. Whoever does not dance does not know what happens" (Acts of John 95:16–17).

Condemnation of dancing continued into the later Middle Ages. However, the inherent theatricality of the Christian liturgy, as well as of the biblical literature, could not be ignored. Dramatic performances were often elaborate, sometimes involving processionals and dancing. Dance roles tended to be comic or grotesque character parts. Starting around the twelfth century through about the fifteenth century, plays were associated with Easter and Christmas. Corpus Christi festivals involved dancing, often by guild members or under government sponsorship. Los Seises, a ritual dance performed by boy choristers, was initiated in Seville and is still performed today. The Pelota of Auxerre is thought to have been a complex dance in which the clergy passed a ball among themselves along the stations of a labyrinth. Dances moving along the paths of labyrinths on the floors of cathedrals, such as the one at Chartres, were also integrated into the liturgy.

Dancing in both a recreational and performance context took place mostly outside the church, often in conjunction with local saint days and religious festivals. Christmas was particularly enlivened by popular dancing often involving mumming, a practice that still accompanies this holiday in parts of the United Kingdom and in North and South America. The Feast of Fools provided the opportunity for burlesques of the established church. Many of the celebrations on these holidays had pagan roots, providing further reason for official condemnation.

The miracle, mystery, and morality plays of the Middle Ages were performed in the churchyards and contained some of the beginnings of professional dance. The dancing parts tended to be fools, shepherds, and demons. The Devil was often blamed for inventing dancing, and it is the Devil who was one of the most danced characters. Minstrels, jongleurs, and other traveling performers of this period often included acrobatics, mime, and dancing in their performances. Pageants included *tableaux vivants* depicting biblical scenes. While generally not dance per se, they involved the communication of meaning through postures and movement rather than through words. The Dance of Death was a pervasive visual and literary symbol.

Social dancing was practiced in the feudal manors of the Middle Ages, and performances including dancing began to enter the courts toward the end of the period. However, it was in the courts of Renaissance Europe that the roots of theatrical dancing emerged, roots not directly linked to religion, but affected by religious ideas in indirect ways.

RENAISSANCE. With the rediscovery of classical antiquity during the Renaissance came a desire to discover the relationship between Greek philosophy and dance. Renaissance courtiers viewed dance as a medium that could express cosmological, moral, and political principles. Aristotelian ethical theory, Plato's mystical geometry, and Neoplatonist ideas of love were exemplified in dance. While dance in the Renaissance was for the most part composed of simple patterns of stepping, there was also an emphasis on elaborate spatial formations. Much like the members of a contemporary marching band at a football game, the performers constantly created floor patterns that they skillfully transmuted to other patterns. To the Renaissance dancer and spectator, the geometrical figures that were formed had symbolic significance: the dissolution of the patterns revealed the mutability of nature, but underlying these shapes and changes was a grand unifying order emanating from God. The patterns of the dancing were interpreted in different ways. For example, in cosmological terms, they might reveal the harmony of nature as in the cycles of the heavenly bodies; in moral terms, they might exemplify order and virtue and the resolution of extremes; and in political terms they might demonstrate the court's control over these cosmic patterns. It was felt that dancing helped create order within the individual's soul and thereby could promote order and peace in political affairs as well. Dance linked the political, moral, and cosmological orders in an inseparable cycle. Dance did not just portray ritual, it was felt to affect the cosmic and mundane realms of existence.

The dance-plays had primarily mythological themes. The best-documented ballet of this period, *Le ballet comique de la reine* (1581), related the triumph of Minerva (Wisdom) and Jupiter (Virtue) over the evil Circe. The king is seen as her ultimate conqueror, restoring the cosmos to peace. Another important later work has a historical theme relating to Christianity. In *Le deliverance de Renaud* (1617), the Christian crusader Renaud is seduced away from battle by the enchantress Armide. Subsequently, the Christians lose, but Armide's powers fail and Renaud is able to escape and liberate Jerusalem. The plot was interpreted as an allegory for the king freeing France from chaos.

Thus although in European history dance has often been associated with immorality, the Renaissance also offered an alternative interpretation: the conception of dance as virtue. There are examples of this attitude in antiquity, in the writings of Plato and Cicero, for instance, but a fuller development of this theme blossomed in the sixteenth century with the developing concept of the gentleman. Sir Thomas Elyot's *Boke Named the Governour* (1531) and Sir John Davies's poem *Orchestra* (1594), among other works, reveal this perspective. Adapting the concept of correspondences, they discovered the symbolic relationship between dance and particular virtues or states of being. Elyot associated dance with prudence, reason, and order. Particular dance movements were analyzed for their moral symbolism. Davies saw the correspondence between dance and chastity and marriage in contradistinction to the usual correlation between dance and lust. Both authors describe couple dancing in terms of a model of cosmic harmony. Dance was elevated to the status of an ethical ideal. Political concepts were couched in mythological themes that were revealed in dance.

During the Renaissance, *Tanzhausen* were important institutions in the Jewish ghettos of northern Europe. They fostered many choreographers, then called "dance masters," who traveled throughout Europe, often arranging dances at various courts. The best-documented Jewish dance master was, however, a product of the court tradition of southern Europe: Guglielmo Ebreo (William the Jew of Pisaro) is the author of one of the earliest extant dance manuals, dating from the mid-fifteenth century.

In the later Renaissance and early Baroque period in Italy, ballet developed in conjunction with the growth of opera. Monteverdi's *Il combattimento di Tancredi e Clorinda* (1624) featured a duel between the Christian crusader Tancredi and the disguised Muslim maiden Clorinda whom he loved. He kills her, and as she lies dying she asks for baptism. The same theme has been treated by others, most notably by the American choreographer William Dollar in his 1949 ballet *The Duel.*

With the rise of Protestantism, the opposition to dancing grew and was taken to extremes in Calvinist contexts. Although the Puritan condemnation of dance was not so vehement or all-encompassing as often painted, it was strong enough to squelch much social dancing and to thwart theatrical dancing in America and in some strongly Calvinist countries in Europe.

The objection was especially strong to "mixed" or couple dancing and to women appearing on the stage. Such ambivalance toward dance persists to the present and was dramatically represented until well into the twentieth century in the United States in the so-called blue laws, which prohibited dancing and similar activities on Sunday. From the eighteenth century into the twentieth, dance performances often had to be billed as lectures or sacred concerts. Puritanical repression of the body and dancing has been a theme in several twentieth-century choreographies, especially in the works of Martha Graham.

BAROQUE AND PRE-ROMANTIC PERIODS. It is in the French court of Louis XIV (r. 1643–1714), called the Sun King, that theatrical dance germinated. In numerous court pageants the king himself was the star dancer, and his favorite role was Apollo, the personification of the sun. The subject matter of court ballets continued to be mythological or pastoral, and the message was still a political one. Professional dancers began to appear, and with the establishment of the Paris Opéra, ballet finally left the confines of the court. With the evolution of the proscenium stage, the figure-based style of the Renaissance with its attendant symbolism was no longer viable; the frontal view of the body was the focus. The ballet vocabulary rapidly expanded in this context. The aesthetic still had a moral overtone; *complaisance*, an air of refined constraint, was the ideal.

Religious institutions were also directly involved in the ballet of the Baroque period in the form of the performances regularly produced by the Jesuit colleges. These colleges were not seminaries, but rather institutions of higher secular education. Unlike most other orders, the Jesuits embraced dance as *divertissements honnêtes.* They performed plays at different times throughout the year, but the principal event was during graduation. They generally staged a five-act tragedy with a biblical, classical, or national theme. A four-act ballet was performed between the acts of the play. The ballets were sometimes loosely connected to the play, but they did not deal overtly with religious themes, favoring the Greek mythological or allegorical plots prevalent also in the court and opera ballets. They were performed in the colleges throughout Europe by the students and were immensely popular. They served as a welcome relief from the heaviness of the often obscure Latin rhetoric of the plays. In Paris the students were joined by the most famous dancers of the Paris Opéra, and the ballets were choreographed by the same preeminent dance masters, such as Pierre Beauchamps and Louis Pécour, who created the masterpieces of the secular theater.

The ballets were often veiled social and political commentaries couched in mythological terms. Themes ranged from "Crowns," a depiction of methods of royal succession, to "The History of Dance," an apologia for dance, to "The Empire of Fate," a critique of the doctrine of predestination promoted by the Jansenists, a group that was ultimately to cause the downfall of the Jesuits in the mid-eighteenth century. Dancing was compatible with the Christian humanist, this-worldly orientation of the Jesuit order. Their ballets differed from their secularly sponsored counterparts in having no female performers or romantic plots and in always having a moral point.

Dance also developed in England, where choreographer-scholars like John Weaver (1673–1760) debated the significance of the dance. The French choreographer Jean-Georges Noverre (1727–1810) shared similar concerns with Weaver, and both were instrumental in the development of *ballet d'action,* which led into another phase of dance history, the pre-Romantic. The characters were still mythological or pastoral, but rather than being merely allegorical symbols, they often displayed emotions and showed some sense of characterization. Important ballets of this period were the mythologically based *The Loves of Mars and Venus* (1717) of Weaver and Noverre's *Medea and Jason* (1763). It was the Age of Reason, and theatrical dance also emulated these ideals.

The French Revolution affected the development of ballet in several ways. For one, it dispersed many of its aristocratic dancers to other countries, including the United States, where theatrical dancing ran up against Puritan disdain. At this time, too, a different energy was at work outside the Opéra in the boulevard theaters of Paris. Catering to the middle class, they featured comic, acrobatic movements, themes from exotic lands and medieval times, grand visual spectacles, and sometimes characters drawn from life rather than from mythology or antiquity. The boulevard theater also discovered the potential for spectacle in biblical themes, producing such ballets and pantomimes as *Samson, Suzanne et les vieillards, Daniel,* and *David et Goliath* during the period from 1816 to 1838. Many of the production techniques and themes of this Theater of Marvels were adopted and refined at the Opéra.

One curiosity of this period was the highly popular, somewhat sacrilegious, political satire *The Ballet of the Pope* (1797) by Dominique Le Fevre, performed at La Scala in Milan. The choreographer danced the role of Pope Pius VI, who engaged in most unpopelike behavior. An important work of this period was Salvatore Viganó's *La vestale* (1818), which told the story of the forbidden love of a Roman Vestal Virgin, ending in the dual murder of the two would-be lovers. Pierre Gardel's *L'enfant prodigue* (1812) was perhaps the first of a long succession of interpretations of this story.

The Romantic Ballet. With the rise of romanticism in the arts, another type of religious theme entered ballet. The beginnings of the Romantic ballet are commonly traced to the 1831 opera *Robert le diable* in which Marie Taglioni, the dancer who was to become the quintessential ethereal ballerina, led a group of the spirits of nuns in a supernatural scene. The development of ballet technique, especially the beginning of *pointe* work, created a mechanism to promote the otherworldly ideals of romanticism. *La sylphide* (1832) and *Giselle* (1841), versions of which are still widely performed, are considered the epitomes of romanticism in ballet. Both exist in a context of the depiction of otherworldly spirits and the desire to escape from this-worldly reality. Because of the Romantic emphasis on emotionalism, subjectivity, malaise, and the attraction to ungovernable forces, this aesthetic trend has often been labeled as un-Christian. Yet a pervasive theme is the contrasting of these uncontrolled states with the tranquility and harmony of nature and Christian values.

Overtly religious themes were rare, but Christian ethics were pervasive. The conflict between Christian values and the supernatural or wild unknown was displayed in many guises. The Romantic litterateur Théophile Gautier characterized the two leading ballerinas of his day, Marie Taglioni and Fanny Elssler, respectively, as a Christian and a pagan dancer, referring to the virginal ethereality of the former and the voluptuous passion of the latter. The roles available to the Romantic ballerina in this era also reflected this kind of dichotomy: supernatural wood and water nymphs alternated with female bandits, gypsies, and exotic temptresses. Plots often contrasted the two.

In *Giselle,* the peasant girl is betrayed by an aristocratic suitor, goes mad, and dies, joining the ranks of avenging *wilis,* spirits who dance men to death. At one point, Giselle protects her lover by shielding him against the cross on her tomb. Thus, religious symbolism often entered the ballet in incidental or subtle ways. The Devil also showed up in many

Romantic ballets—for example, *Le Diable boiteux* (1836) and *Le violin du Diable* (1849).

Another variation of the Romantic ballet thrived in Denmark under the choreographer Auguste Bournonville (1805–1879). His ballets also reveal the fascination with the supernatural and the exotic, but Bournonville emphasized the optimistic and harmonic aspects of the Romantic spirit, for the most part eschewing the darker emotionalism of the Romantic ballets in France, England, and Russia. Contemporary Danish dance critic Erik Aschengreen noted: "Bournonville's ballets rest on the idea of spiritual aspiration, with poetry and beauty as important qualities and with Christianity as the conqueror of all dissonances" (Aschengreen, 1979, p. 111).

While rarely dealing with religious subject matter per se, Bournonville's ballets are suffused with Christian values and symbolism. His ballets contrast social harmony with uncontrolled forces outside society. Christian symbols often are the devices that effect the triumph of human values over the danger of the irrational. He often uses two women (or one woman in two transformations) as a device for contrasting the rational and irrational, Christian and pagan. A striking example of this is in his extant ballet *A Folk Tale* (1854). This is the story of the human baby Hilda who was snatched from her cradle and replaced by the troll baby Birthe. Each grows up unaware of the truth. Birthe struggles to conform to the human world, but bursts of temper and uncontrolled and vulgar movements reveal her troll nature. Hilda, on the other hand, instinctively bows to church bells in the distance and fashions herself a cross from sticks. Her calm nature soothes the chaos around her. The ballet ends happily with each character acknowledging the rightness of remaining true to one's nature. A wedding, the sanctioning of love by the church, ends this ballet, as in many other Romantic works. In *Napoli* (1842) and *The Flower Festival in Genzano* (1858), the heroine invokes the aid of the Madonna. In *Napoli*, for instance, the heroine is saved from her transformation into a sea nymph by an amulet of the Virgin Mary.

The theme of another ballet, Arcona (1875), is overtly Christian—a chronicle of the christianization of the Slavs in Denmark. The heroine is about to be initiated into the pagan religion when she sees the cross worn by a Danish prisoner. Bournonville's libretto states: "No sooner has Hella hung the cross around her neck . . . than her whole being is suffused with a religious feeling hitherto unknown to her" (McAndrews, 1982–1983, p. 330). She proceeds to free the Christian prisoner. In Bournonville's *La sylphide* (1836), which is still his most widely performed work, the hero's rejection of home to quest after the sylphide results in his losing everything, an example of how the choreographer contrasted the virtues of the Christian home with the disruptive forces of the nonsocial.

Classical Ballet. The Romantic ballet began to decline in Europe and the United States, and the values changed to promote spectacles that were often merely vehicles for flaunting women's legs. Ballet became more the province of the music hall. However, the evolution of ballet continued in Russia, where the great classical ballets *Swan Lake* (1895), *The Nutcracker* (1892), and *Sleeping Beauty* (1890) were choreographed. The themes were primarily fairy tales or exotic spectacles, but the choreographic quality of the works of Marius Petipa (1818–1910) and Lev Ivanov (1834–1901) elevated the genre. Few ballets from this period are extant, but it seems that very few had more than a gloss of religious significance. Thus, Petipa's *La bayadère* (1877) continues a tradition of depicting Hindu priests and temple dancers, and his *La fille du pharon* (1862) depicts his notion of Egyptian religion. Ironically, Ivanov's *The Nutcracker*, and the many versions of this work rechoreographed by others, has become almost synonymous with Christmas. It takes place at a Christmas party, but it has no Christian significance per se although it involves religious phenomena such as magical transformation. It is probably performed by more companies in more performances all over the world than any other work and might be said to be a symbol of the secular Christmas.

Delsarte. During the nineteenth century, another trend with religious overtones was developing that was to have profound impact on the growth of twentieth-century dance. François Delsarte (1811–1871) developed a system for analyzing and explaining the source of expression in movement, especially as it relates to singing, acting, and oratory. In the United States, a primary application was to dance. Underlying his quasi-scientific categorization of movement possibilities and their meanings are two basic laws. The Law of Correspondence states, "To each spiritual function responds a function of the body; to each grand function of the body corresponds a spiritual act." The Law of Trinity led him to divide all nature, and therefore movement too, into a series of triads. For instance, he presented the following series:

Life	Soul	Mind
Physical	Emotional	Mental
Ease	Coordination	Precision
Motion	Space	Time
Energy	Love	Wisdom

There were three corresponding zones of the body: limbs (or lower torso), torso (or upper torso), and head. Each body part could be further subdivided into three areas, each of which replicated the physical, emotional, and mental layering. Thus, which body part one used, in conjunction with which other parts, in what section of space determined the expressive message of the movement. Outgrowths of Delsarte's work were the art of statue-posing, in which the performers created *tableaux vivants* according to Delsartean principles; aesthetic gymnastics, a form of physical fitness for Victorian women; and pantomiming of poetry. These forms of performance were precursors of modern dance.

To some followers of Delsarte, the system was "the basis of a new religious education, destined to perfect the children of men . . . and redeem the earth" (quoted in Ruyter, 1979, p. 20). An underlying idea was that since man was made in the likeness of God, then his movements must inherently reveal God. The three great precursors of twentieth-century dance—Isadora Duncan, Ruth St. Denis, and Ted Shawn—were explicitly influenced by Delsartean philosophy, and through their teachings Delsarte indirectly affected the first generation of modern dancers.

EARLY TWENTIETH-CENTURY MODERN DANCE. Isadora Duncan (1878–1927) is usually credited with pioneering the break with the past and ushering in a twentieth-century dance form. She discarded what she felt was the artifice and vulgarity of the theatrical dance that surrounded her and looked to an idealized conception of Greek spirit embodied in dance. She found her models also in nature, as in the curves and flow of waves and shells. She drew on Delsartean principles and philosophy, but she also developed her own ideas, which were impregnated with religion and politics. Through dance she believed that one could liberate not only the body but also the soul. One could become united with nature, and nature was sacred. She wrote: "This is the highest expression of religion in the dance: that a human body should no longer seem human but become transmuted into the movements of the stars" (quoted in Pruett, 1982, p. 57).

She found inspiration in the writings of the philosopher Friedrich Nietzsche, often quoting his statement: "Let that day be called lost on which I have not danced" (Duncan, 1928, p. 77). She was fascinated by his distinction between the Apollonian and the Dionysian. She wanted the audience to experience her work as more than entertainment, as participation in her "invocation."

She searched for inspiration in Greek antiquity. She contemplated the Parthenon and sought a dance form that would be worthy of this temple. When she found it, she exclaimed, "And then I knew I had found my dance, and it was a Prayer" (Duncan, 1928, p. 65). Her dancing was composed of simple runs, skips, and walks, often accompanied by gestures pregnant with meaning. Although one of her best-known pieces was *Ave Maria* (1914), her dances rarely had overtly religious themes.

The next major figures of twentieth-century dance were Ruth St. Denis (1879–1968) and Ted Shawn (1891–1972), her husband. Out of Denishawn, their school and company, came the three most influential pioneers of modern dance: Martha Graham, Doris Humphrey, and Charles Weidman. Not only were St. Denis and Shawn seminal in the development of modern dance but they were also the most directly involved in exploring the relationship between religion and dance in their choreography and in their teachings—and both pioneered the return of dance to the church.

St. Denis (born Ruth Dennis) ransacked the world's dances searching not only for visually exciting forms but insight into the use of dance in religion that was so prevalent outside the West. While the religious intent of her choreography was so often buried in the spectacle of her performances in the vaudeville circuit, her writings and teachings emphasized spiritual intent. In her later years, she was able to fulfill some of her dreams to create religious theatrical dancing, becoming the first major choreographer to develop liturgical dance.

In St. Denis's biography, appropriately titled *Divine Dancer*, a distinction between her own and Duncan's views on dance in relation to religion is succinctly phrased as follows: "[Duncan and St. Denis] followed the polar paths of mysticism: one, seeking the Self in the Universe; the other, seeking the Universe in the Self. St. Denis . . . probed toward an unseen center, cultivating an interior space. Duncan . . . created an expanding consciousness that seemed to consume the cosmos" (Shelton, 1981, p. 97).

From childhood St. Denis had been exposed to various forms of spiritual philosophy, from "American Transcendentalism to Swedenborgian mysticism of her parents' Eagleswood colony, to her explorations of Christian Science and, ultimately, the Vedanta" (Shelton, 1981, p. 93). Her dance was deeply influenced by Delsartean principles both in the techniques of movement and in her belief in the correspondence between the physical and the metaphysical. She believed that "the Creative Dancer is always striving to give expression to Divine Intelligence" (quoted in Cohen, 1974, p. 134) and that "dancing is a living mantra" (quoted in Shelton, 1981, p. 244).

As early as St. Denis's first concert, she choreographed works based on Eastern religions. In *Radha* (1906) she was a goddess surrounded by worshiping priests. She danced a solo built on each of the five senses, culminating in a final dance in which she renounced all sensuality, ending in the yogic Lotus Position, lost in *samādhi* (meditative trance). Her costume featured a bare midriff, and even more daring, she danced in bare feet. Other of her signature works were *Incense* (1906), in which she performed a *pūjā* ritual, and *The Yogi* (1908), based on a passage from the *Bhagavadgītā*, which was a very austere unfolding of a few simple gestures revealing a yogin's spiritual state. She also danced *White Jade*, in which she portrayed Guanyin, the Chinese goddess of mercy, and in other dances she took the roles of various goddesses (Isis, Ishtar, et al.) and biblical heroines. In her later years, she danced Madonnas. She presented pageants in churches and theaters dancing the role of the Virgin in *Masque of Mary* (1934), *Ballet of Christmas Hymns*, and *Healing*. In the *Blue Madonna of St. Mark's* she portrayed Mary's life from the birth of Christ to the crucifixion. She was eighty years old at its premiere. In the "He Is Risen" section of *Resurrection*, she danced Mary Magdelen. She formed the Society of Spiritual Acts, a Christian Science discussion group for which she choreographed dances based on religious themes. Out of this grew her Rhythmic Choir, which performed in churches.

Edward (Ted) Shawn had studied to be a Methodist minister but found dance instead. He described the basis for the Shawn-St. Denis relationship as follows: "She, pursuing the dance upstream to its source, found there religion, and

I, pursuing religion upstream, found the dance was the first and finest means of religious expression, and so we have wedded artistically and humanly ever since" (Shawn, 1926, p. 12). In a taped interview he explained his calling as follows: "I feel my whole life as a dancer has been a ministry . . . because it includes in it every attribute of God; it has lightness and rhythm and proportion and expressiveness . . . the only way you can describe God is to describe him in the terms of a great dancer." He often quoted Nietzsche's comment, "I could not believe in a God who did not know how to dance." He was more directly Christian in his intent and choice of themes, while St. Denis was immersed in Eastern religions and mystical philosophy.

Among his many works were *Brothers Bernard, Lawrence, and Masseo: Three Varieties of Religious Experience*; *O Brother Sun and Sister Moon, a Study of Francis of Assisi*; *Dance of the Redeemed*, inspired by religious visual arts such as William Blake's illustrations for the Book of Job; and Mevlevi Dervish. He often incorporated the dancing of the Doxology into his concerts.

The religious import of St. Denis's dances was usually lost to the audience, which saw only exotic spectacle. Realizing this, Shawn and later St. Denis turned to explicit Christian themes and contexts. As early as 1917, Shawn choreographed an entire church service held in the Scottish Rite Temple of San Francisco. (In 1921 the same work was censured by the local clergy and the commissioner of public safety of Shreveport, Louisiana.)

An accompanist and composer for Denishawn was to become a major force in shaping American modern dance choreography. Louis Horst (1884–1964) became mentor to at least two generations of modern dancers. He developed a systematic method for composing dances, using musical composition as a guide to teach dancers about form and style. One of his choreographic devices was based on "modern dance forms," that is, stylistic models garnered from the arts of an era and translated into dance. What he called Primitivism embraced two styles, Earth Primitive and Air Primitive. Both were characterized by awkward asymmetrical movements, the former revealing a sense of vitality, the latter of awe. The Archaic style was conceived of as ritualistic, and the movement style was based on Egyptian and Greek bas-reliefs. Medievalism had two aspects, religious and secular. It included the symbolism of denial of the flesh as revealed in off-balance, distorted postures. The ecstasy of saints and the exuberance of courtly love and minstrelsy were the essence of secular life. In Horst's outline, the nineteenth and twentieth centuries were characterized by Introspection/Expression, Cerebralism, Jazz, Americana, and Impressionism. Primitivism, the Archaic, and Medievalism took clues from visual arts and music, and all had religious connotations. Those themes have been repeated throughout twentieth-century modern dance and ballet, whether or not directly as a result of Horst's teaching. Stylized gestures have often been used to evoke an archaic context, as in Nijinksy's *L'après-midi d'un faune* (1912), which predates Horst, and in Paul Taylor's *Profiles* (1979). The stylization of religious ecstasy has characterized the many versions of *The Rite of Spring*. Horst worked with almost all the early modern dancers, but he had an especially close collaboration with Martha Graham.

Doris Humphrey and Martha Graham. Nurtured by "Miss Ruth's" spiritual lectures and later influence by Horst's methodology and theories of movement style, the two great pioneers of American modern dance, Martha Graham (1894–1991) and Doris Humphrey (1895–1958), brought to their independent careers Delsartean principles and religious themes. During the early period of modern dance, in the late 1920s and the 1930s, ritual was a common theme. Two classics are Graham's *Primitive Mysteries* (1931) and Humphrey's *The Shakers* (1931). The former was inspired by the rituals of the Native American Christians of the southwestern United States. It is an abstraction of the passion play as seen through the experience of the Virgin Mary. The three sections—"Hymn to the Virgin" (adoration), "Crucifixus" (Virgin's grief), and "Hosannah" (exaltation)—are punctuated at the beginnings and ends by processions of the Virgin and her attendants, composed of weighted, solemn steppings. Processions are a frequent device in Graham's works, and they lend to virtually any theme a ritualistic quality. In the same year, *The Shakers* depicted the essence of the dance ritual of the American religious sect, the Shakers, who used dance and song as their primary modes of worship. Both works created fictitious rituals based on actual sources.

Religious themes per se were not common in Humphrey's choreography or that of her colleague Charles Weidman (1901–1975). Their choreography was, however, religious in the wider sense of showing a concern for the fundamental issues of human life. For instance, Humphrey described her *New Dance* (1935) trilogy as having the theme of the relationship of man to man. To her, *New Dance* represented "the world as it should be, where each person has a clear and harmonious relationship to his fellow beings" (quoted in Cohen, 1972, p. 137). It conveys its message without overt narrative; it is through the organization and disorganization of group relationships that the theme is developed.

Humphrey's *Passacaglia and Fugue in C Minor* (1938) is a plotless work to Bach's music. However, she found in the music religious import that colored the dance. For instance, in a program note she points out that the "minor melody . . . seems to say 'How can a man be saved and be content in a world of infinite despair?'" (quoted in Cohen, 1972, p. 149). Dancing to Bach was highly controversial. Even his secular music has been interpreted as being suffused with spirituality. One of Humphrey's earliest pieces was to Bach's so-called *Air for the G String* (1929), which consists of a group of women with a leader who basically walk, pose, dip, and sway in sumptuous draperies inspired by the paintings of Fra Angelico. Although there is no plot or context, the costumery, music, and the rapturous poses (often in Gothic sway as in sculptures of the Madonna), suggest a pious ritual. Humphrey later defended her use of Bach, especially in the context of World War II, by stating: "Now is the time for me to tell of the nobility that the human spirit is capable of" (quoted in Cohen, 1972, p. 243). Choreographers continue to use Bach as a means of lending a spiritual aura to their works. In later years Weidman choreographed *Christmas Oratorio* (1961), *Easter Oratorio* (1967), and *Bach's St. Matthew's Passion* (1973).

It is impossible to look at Martha Graham's towering sixty-year career without considering the role of religion. Her work can be seen as falling into several periods. Her earliest works were stark, ascetic, often ritualistic pieces. She later turned to more narrative works, exploring facets of female psychology and aspects of Americana. In the 1940s she began her epic treatment of mythological and biblical themes, which has continued for forty more years. Almost all her early works are lost, but some of their titles are suggestive: *Figure of a Saint, Resurrection, Vision of the Apocalypse, Heretic,* all choreographed in 1929, stand out among other titles.

El penitente (1940), inspired by the Spanish-Indian flagellant sects of the American Southwest, is the depiction of Christ's journey to Calvary as performed by a troup of touring players. *Appalachian Spring* (1944) is the story of a wedding in the nineteenth-century frontier. The figure of the Revivalist who weds the couple is a crystallization of one aspect of American religion. The ambivalence about physical enjoyment (whether in the sexual connotations of marriage or in the abandonment of dance and play) is expressed in the Revivalist's movements. He dances a tormented solo of self-condemnation characterized by crawling on his knees, breast beating, and fervent praying. The moralistic dilemma of ambivalence toward sexuality is explored in many of Graham's works, especially in her treatment of women, such as in her *American Provincials: Act of Piety, Act of Judgment* and the *Scarlet Letter.* In Graham's *Letter to the World* (1940), the poet Emily Dickinson battles repression as personified in an ancestress figure. Graham's family was staunchly Presbyterian, and her father had objected to dancing for moral reasons.

Graham's *Dark Meadow* (1946) is a ritual of rebirth and procreation with strong erotic overtones and pervasive Jungian and Freudian symbolism. Archetypal characters, such as She of the Ground (representing the female principle), dance a myth of rebirth. There are allusions to the worship of phallic monuments and to sacrifice in the name of fertility. Her monumental works based on Greek mythology include *Cave of the Heart* (1946), retelling the Medea legend; *Night Journey* (1947), the Oedipus story through the experience of Jocasta; the full length *Clytemnestra* (1958); and *Cortege of Eagles* (1967), the story of Hecuba; and lesser-known works, such as *Phaedra* (1962), *Circe* (1963), and *Andromache's Lament* (1982). Other biblical works include *Herodiade*, the Salome story as seen through the psyche of her mother; *Judith* (1950) and *Legend of Judith* (1962); *Gospel of Eve* (1950); *Embattled Garden* (1958), a major retelling of the Adam-Eve-Lilith myth; and *Lucifer* (1975). A major historical work, *Seraphic Dialogue* (1955), is based on the story of Joan of Arc. The characters are Saint Michael, Saint Catherine, Saint Margaret, and Joan at the moment of canonization. Joan recalls the three facets of her life as the Maid, the Warrior, and the Martyr.

Graham uses religious themes as a device for probing psychological dimensions. She treats mythology as the psychology of another age and seeks to reveal the "inner landscapes" of the human psyche in her dance. Even in her less frequent plotless works there are religious reverberations. *Diversion of Angels* (1948) is a rare lyrical and joyful work for four couples and three solo women, yet at the end the soloist in white is crowned with the splayed fingers of a symbol of benediction. The title of *Acrobats of God* (1960), derived from the name of a group of early church fathers who lived in the desert, alludes to a comparison of the ascetic spiritual life of the Desert Fathers to the arduous training of dancers. Both works celebrate the dancer, and their titles may reveal Graham's conception of their superhuman quality. In the last section of the abstract *Acts of Light* (1981), the "Ritual of the Sun" is evoked by the stylization of a technique class.

Other first-generation American modern dance choreographers. Two other pioneers were Lester Horton (1906–1953) and Helen Tamiris (1905–1966). Very few of their works survive. Horton often used themes from other cultures that were inherently religious: *Siva-Siva* (1929), *Voodoo Ceremonial* (1932), *Sun Ritual* (1935), and *Pentecost* (1935) are examples of works utilizing such themes. His three best-known works all have religious themes: *Salomé* (several versions from 1934 to 1950), *Le sacre du printemps* (1937), and *The Beloved* (1948). *The Beloved* is still in active repertory. Although it is not expressly religious, it is an example of the theme of sexual repression implicitly derived from religious beliefs. It is a duet for a husband and wife. The man, outwardly a symbol of rectitude, proceeds to manipulate and then to strangle his wife, who presumably is guilty of a sexual transgression.

Tamiris (born Becker) choreographed many works of social protest. She is best known for her *Negro Spirituals.* This is a suite of dances (solos and group pieces) to which she added over a period of fifteen years beginning in 1928. She is credited as the first to use black spirituals. *Negro Spirituals* is set to music representing a gamut of moods. Partially pantomimic in degrees of abstraction, each piece is a distillation of a theme. The crucifixion section, for instance, was inspired by the visual imagery of medieval religious paintings. Her goal was to reveal the human side of suffering, oppression, and joy. Ted Shawn also choreographed *Negro Spirituals* in 1933, and the theme became very popular among black choreographers beginning with Alvin Ailey's *Revelations* (1960).

Central European modern dance. In Europe, another approach to modern dance developed. The foremost figure there was Rudolf Laban (1879–1958), better remembered today for his theoretical work (now called Laban Movement Analysis) and the development of a dance notation system (Labanotation or Kinetography Laban), than for his choreography, which has been lost. Laban believed in the spiritual source of movement and felt that dance was a means of attuning to the harmony of the universe. He had been impressed in his youth by the dancing of Muslim dervishes and sought to find and understand the link between movement and spirituality. He developed the idea of "movement choirs," communal dancing of lay dancers, as an expression of the festive spirit of humanity. His stage choreography often dealt with cosmic themes. For example, *The Swinging Temple* was a choreodrama of all types of dancing from primordial rhythms through priestly processions, to ecstatic, comic, and combative dances. His writings and the scenarios for many of his dance works have a strain of mysticism, a search for the divine power of movement, whereas the system for the analysis of movement that developed from his theories is known for its objectivity.

Laban's two most famous students were Mary Wigman (1886–1973) and Kurt Jooss (1901–1979). Wigman is considered the principal dancer-choreographer of central European modern dance. While not concerned with themes from any specific religion, her work in general grapples with spirituality and the larger issues of life. Many of her works deal with death or the cycle of nature. Her signature work was the solo *Witch Dance* (1914, rechoreographed in 1926), which probes the demonic side of human nature. Many of her works revolved around the darker, grotesque aspects of life, themes that seem to have been appropriate to Germany between the two world wars, her most productive period.

Jooss is best known for *The Green Table* (1932), an antiwar ballet still widely performed. In this work, he draws on the medieval image of death as the Grim Reaper, placing the work in a religious historical context.

The European tradition of modern dance was established in America by Wigman's student Hanya Holm (1898–1992). Her works of the 1930s often made social and political statements but can also be seen as having an underlying moral message. Her masterwork, *Trend* (1937), was nonliterary, but its theme was the discovery of the meaning of life.

At the same time that Laban was beginning his experimentation, there were several others in Europe exploring the relationship between movement and spirituality in the context of new religions. Among these were Rudolf Steiner (1861–1925) and G. I. Gurdjieff (1877?–1949). Steiner developed a comprehensive religious and philosophical system called Anthroposophy, which encompassed a movement and dance system called Eurythmy. In this practice, specific gestures and floor patterns are correlated with specific sounds and spiritual functions. Performing the movements thereby promotes physical and spiritual health. Structured choreography to works of classical music is one form of expressing this philosophy. Gurdjieff, influenced by Sufism, developed dancelike movement exercises designed to effect certain mystical states. The work of Steiner and Gurdjieff was part of a tradition that centered on the belief that mystical knowledge could be manifested in physical behavior and that the altered states of consciousness generated by movement could put one in touch with the underlying patterns of the universe.

SECOND GENERATION OF AMERICAN MODERN DANCE. Humphrey's closest protégé was José Limón. Several of his major works were based on religious themes. He often drew on his Mexican and Native American heritage. *La Malinche* (1949) is a form of the passion play as performed by a troupe of traveling Mexican peasants. *The Visitation* (1952) is based on the Annunication; *The Apostate* (1959) captures a battle between Christianity and paganism; and *There Is a Time* (1956) is a danced version of *Ecclesiastes* 2. Limón's *Psalm* (1967) includes the theme of the Jews under Hitler, and *The Unsung* (1970) deals with the spirituality of Native Americans. In *The Traitor* (1954) he retells the story of Jesus and Judas, casting Judas as a symbol of modern man. *Missa brevis* (1958), first performed in a bombed-out church in Budapest, is a dance of pain and an affirmation of faith. At certain points, women dancers are carried like the statues of the Madonna in Mexican religious processions.

The choreography of Alwin Nikolais, a student of Holm, rebels against the emotionalism of the first generation of modern dance. He turns instead to portraying the moving body as just one element of a multimedia theater. He has often been criticized for dehumanizing the dancer, but he interprets his work in a religio-philosophical manner; he sees man as a "fellow traveller . . . rather than the god from which all things flowed. . . . He lost his domination but instead became kinsman to the universe" (quoted in Siegel, 1971, p. 11). His pieces often are glimpses into the ritualistic lives of what seem to be alien tribes of people whose activities make profound comments on human existence. His *Tower* (1965), for example, details the building of a metaphorical Tower of Babel to which each dancer contributes a piece only to have the whole monument topple at the end.

Erick Hawkins is among those choreographers who worked with Graham. His choreography is notable as a rejection of her aesthetic and technique. He has been inspired by Zen philosophy and feels that an audience should be brought to enlightenment. His goal has been to develop a technique that would be harmonious with nature, gentle and free of tension. His choreography is often ritualistic and deals with the human relation to nature and the oneness of body and soul. The mood of his works is often meditative with poetic resonances. In *Plains Daybreak* (1983), for example, masked dancers represent the essences of animals during a mythical time near the beginning of creation. *Lords of Persia* (1965) is a portrayal of an ancient game of polo stylized as sacred ritual.

Paul Taylor has produced a wide range of works that frequently make comments on the human condition and social relationships. Sometimes his works involve religious themes. One of his most enduring works is *Three Epitaphs* (1960), in which dancers covered in black appear as figures whose postures and gestures convey both humor and pathos. The title of this work and the accompaniment of early New Orleans jazz funeral music provide an ironic commentary to the antic interactions of these creatures. His *Churchyard* (1969) is a dance of piety transformed into wild eroticism; *Runes* (1975) creates a prehistoric ritual of sacrifice and regeneration.

Merce Cunningham made a radical break with the past. He creates plotless works in which movements, music, and decor are conceived of as separate elements. Pure movement is the primary content of his works, and therefore religious themes are irrelevant. However, underlying Cunningham's choreography is a philosophy based on Zen Buddhism. Like his principal musical collaborator, John Cage, Cunningham often composes according to chance principles; for instance, throwing the *I ching* (casting lots) determines the order in which movement phrases will be combined. Such an indeterminate method of choreography helps him to feel liberated from becoming attached to his possessions, which are his choreographic creations.

POSTMODERN DANCE. Cunningham signaled the beginning of a reconception of dance. The idea that theatrical dance was marked by storytelling, emotional expression, and a fixed relationship to music and decor was shattered by his work. Many choreographers in the next generation of modern dance have been called "post-Cunningham" or postmodern. One of the more prominent characteristics of this trend in dance has been the focus on movement for movement's sake. Dances were often composed of everyday movements danced by untrained performers. They wished to return dance to the people, rather than reserving it for the virtuosic performer. Religious themes would not seem relevant to plotless works that aimed to expose the nature of movement rather than the nature of human and spiritual existence. Yet, a major stream of postmodern dance has been the exploration of the concept of ritual. Many choreographers shared the aims of the experimental theater of the 1960s and 1970s, especially the idea that dance and theatrical performances could be rituals for both performers and audience. A goal was to provide a transformative experience, a function of many religious rituals. The means of effecting these changes in physical and mental states were also modeled on a conception of ritual that often emphasized symbolism, manipulations of time and space, repetititons, nonlinear development of actions, and a highly formal structure. Some aimed at the creation of a feeling of community; others reached for a spiritual experience, a feeling of holism or integration with the universe. They were concerned with experiencing dance as a metaphor for life.

Anna Halprin has been a pioneer in this area. She explored the use of trance, the expression of communal feeling through dance, and the healing nature of movement. Deborah Hay created a series of Circle Dances based on simple movements to be performed in a group with no spectators. She was influenced by *taiji quan* and Daoist philosophy. The goal of these dance experiences was to understand the inner self, the power of the group, and the individual's connection to the cosmos. Meditation as well as ecstatic movements have characterized these ritualistic dances.

Meredith Monk, on the other hand, creates multimedia theatrical works that are often ritualistic in character. She creates layers of evocative imagery and archetypal characters and transforms ordinary speech into chants and spectacular sounds. Her *Vessel* (1971) dealt with Joan of Arc. Many of her other works, such as *Quarry* (1976) and *Education of the Girlchild* (1972), have presented themes of human life and history in a ritual structure.

TWENTIETH-CENTURY BALLET. While modern dance grew out of a desire for self-expression, ballet traditionally has been concerned with telling stories. The twentieth century saw the development of plotless (or abstract) works that inherently give limited scope for interior states or religious themes. Yet, ballet also expanded its expressive powers in such a way as to become a vehicle for religious ideas as well.

The first major break with nineteenth-century ballet in both form and content was Sergei Diaghilev's Ballets Russes. This company produced a few biblical works: *Salomé* (1913), *The Legend of Joseph* (1914), and *Prodigal Son* (1929). *Le dieu bleu* (1912) was based on the Hindu god Kṛṣṇa. The most remarkable religious work was also perhaps the most revolutionary ballet in dance history—*Le sacre du printemps* (1913), choreographed by the great dancer Vaslav Nijinsky. The dance and its music by Igor Stravinsky caused a riot at the premiere, and the ballet was performed only a few times. It drew on a mythic history of Old Russia, but its pounding rhythms, ecstatic dancing, circular floor patterns, and sacrificial dance of death became a model for many other rituals in twentieth-century dance. There have been many other rechoreographings of the Stravinsky music, including Léonide Massine's 1930 reworking for Diaghilev (in which the Chosen Maiden was danced by Martha Graham, who fifty-four years later was to choreograph her own *Rite of Spring*). Other notable examples were by Horton, Wigman, ballet choreographer Maurice Béjart, German Expressionist modern-dance choreographer Pina Bausch, and Paul Taylor, who transformed the ritual into a gangster play within a play.

Two of the last works that Diaghilev produced were *Apollon musagète* (1928) and *Prodigal Son* (1929), both choreographed by George Balanchine, who was to become the most influential ballet choreographer in the United States, if not the world. Though Balanchine is known primarily for his plotless works, these two early ballets with religious themes are counted among his greatest, and both are performed in many companies around the world. *Apollon musagète*, now titled *Apollo*, retells the birth of the god and his coming of age under the tutelage of three of the Muses. In

Prodigal Son, Balanchine drew on motifs from his native Russia, including visual imagery from religious icons, especially the two-dimensional quality, and certain gestures and liturgical movements from the Russian Orthodox church, such as beating the chest and back.

Other Balanchine works of some religious significance include his *Nutcracker* (1954), *Noah and the Flood* (1962), and his Greek mythological masterpiece, *Orpheus* (1948). His *Don Quixote* (1965) also has much religious imagery. Despite the relative lack of religious themes in his choreography, religion was very important in Balanchine's personal life. One of the last works he created incorporated much religious symbolism and has been interpreted as his comment on death. In 1981, he choreographed the last movement of Tchaikovsky's *Pathétique* Symphony as a ballet of the same name. A dance of grief is followed by a procession composed of angels with enormous wings, hooded figures, and monks who prostrate themselves in the form of a cross. A child extinguishes a candle to the final notes of the symphony.

Another choreographer for the Ballets Russes was Léonide Massine. Although he is best known for his character ballets, he also choreographed several ambitious but short-lived works based on religious themes. Seventh Symphony (1938), set to Beethoven's *Seventh Symphony*, was a chronicle of the world from its creation to its destruction; *Noblissima visione* (1938) was the story of Saint Francis of Assisi; and *Laudes evangelii* (1952) was the translation into dance of a fourteenth-century text depicting eight episodes from the life of Christ.

Frederick Ashton has been the principal choreographer in Great Britain. Like British ballet in general, his works tend to be literary, although he occasionally has used religious themes. An early Ashton work was the choreography for the Virgil Thomson-Gertrude Stein opera *Four Saints in Three Acts* (1934). His *Dante Sonata* (1940), based on the *Inferno* of Dante's *Commedia*, was a reaction to World War II. It was conceived as a battle between the Children of Light and the Children of Darkness. *The Wise Virgins* (1940) was also an antiwar ballet. Performed to Bach cantatas and chorale preludes, it created visual images reminiscent of Baroque art. The work had a devout atmosphere. He also occasionally used mythical themes, as in *Cupid and Psyche*, *Leda*, *Mercury*, *Mars and Venus*, and *Daphnis and Chloe*. His *The Quest* (1943) was the story of Saint George; his *Tiresias* (1951) depicted a Cretan athletic ritual.

Other choreographers in England include Ninette de Valois, founder of the Royal Ballet. One of her most successful works was *Job, a Masque for Dancing* (1931) based on William Blake's drawings. As an example of Western ambivalence toward the relationship between religion and dance, censors prohibited the depiction of God in this work, leading de Valois to create a character called Job's Spiritual Self. *Miracle in the Gorbals* (1944) by Robert Helpmann was a morality play in dance in which Christ comes to the slums of Glasgow, revives a suicide, and in turn is murdered by the crowd.

Antony Tudor is known for his psychologically motivated ballets, and few of his works are religious in content. His *Shadowplay* (1967), which depicts a wild boy as lord of the jungle, however, was influenced by Zen Buddhism. Underlying his masterwork *Pillar of Fire* (1942) is the theme of religiously induced sexual repression. His *Dark Elegies* (1937) is a ritualization of grief.

In modern ballet, mythic characters are often used to create a psychological dimension. Tudor's *Undertow* (1945), for example, is a contemporary murder story, but the characters have mythological names, and his *Judgment of Paris* (1938) is set in a Paris bar where Juno, Minerva, and Venus are tawdry showgirls.

The American John Butler, who choreographs in both the ballet and modern dance idioms, has produced a large opus of religious works. He was the principal choreographer for the American religious television series *Lamp unto My Feet* in the 1960s. One of his major works is *Carmina burana* (1959), which is set to thirteenth-century poems discovered at a Benedictine monastery. The monks and nuns of the dance temporarily discard the discipline of their order to engage in the passions of secular life and to experience the wheel of fate.

Robert Joffrey and Gerald Arpino, choreographing for the Joffrey Ballet, have created several works based on religious themes. Joffrey's *Astarte* (1967), which has been called the first psychedelic ballet, is a contemporary depiction of the Akkadian Ishtar, moon goddess of love and fertility who was called Astarte by the Greeks, though audiences are often unaware of this theme. Set to loud electronic rock music, flashing lights, and projected film, the dance evokes the atmosphere of an après-discotheque seduction. The man strips to his briefs, the goddess lets down her hair, and an erotic *pas de deux* of power and submission takes place in a hallucinatory sequence. It was the first multimedia rock ballet to receive widespread attention, and it ushered in a new trend in ballet, enticing new audiences into the theater. Arpino's *Sacred Grove on Mount Tamalpais* (1972) is a paean to the "flower children" of the 1960s, an innocent romp of renewal depicting a wedding ceremony and the birth of a son who promises to be a kind of prophet to the celebrants. His *Trinity* (1969) is a three-part contemporary ritual of young people employing some popular dance movements set to a rock orchestration of Gregorian chant and other sacred music styles. In the third section, "Saturday," the dancers carry lighted candles. A male soloist dances to a rock version of the hymn "Ite, missa est" that concludes the Latin Mass. The final image is of the stage, empty except for the pattern of votive candles on the floor.

Contemporary European choreographers have been more attracted to religious themes than their American counterparts. John Neumeier, mainly choreographing for the Hamburg Ballet, created the four-hour *Saint Matthew's Passion* (1981) set to Bach's work. The story is conveyed through *tableaux vivants* interspersed with dancing commenting on the deeper aspects of the drama. Neumeier's *Mahler's Third Symphony* has a theme of redemption and incorporates Mahler's idea of the quest for divine love.

The Czech Jiri Kylian, working primarily for the Nederlands Dans Theater, has offered *Psalm Symphony* (1978), based on Psalms 39, 40, and 150, among other works. Further examples include John Cranko's *Kyrie eleison* (1968) and Kenneth Macmillan's *Requiem* (1976). Maurice Béjart, choreographer for his Belgian company, Ballet of the Twentieth Century, is known for tackling grand epic themes. Several of his works have themes with religious connotations. In his *Nijinsky—Clown of God* (1971), the Ballets Russes is cast as Nijinsky's Paradise with Diaghilev as its overseeing God. His *Bhakti* (1968) draws on Hindu mythology, and his *Notre Faust* (1975) is one of several dance treatments of this work over the centuries.

Contemporary ballet has incorporated many movements and much of the sensibility of modern dance. It often does not use *pointe* work but may reserve this kind of movement to portray particular ideas. A ballerina on *pointe* sometimes is cast in a higher spiritual mode. For instance, in Ashton's *Illuminations* (1950), Sacred Love dances on *pointe*, while Profane Love has one bare foot; in Neumeier's *Mahler's Third Symphony*, the figure of idealized love dances on *pointe* while most of the other dancers do not.

Biblical Themes. The flexibility of interpretation inherent in biblical literature has been an inspiration for many different treatments that range from literal interpretations to the probing of universal psychological truths to political and social commentary. Several characters and episodes have been particularly appealing. These include: the theme of creation, the garden of Eden, the story of Cain and Abel, Noah and the Flood, Job, David and Goliath, Joseph, Samson and Delilah, Salome, the Prodigal Son, the Wise and Foolish Virgins; and the many biblical heroines, including Miriam, Jephthah's Daughter, Esther, Deborah, Judith, Ruth, the Virgin Mary, and Mary Magdalene. The life of Christ and interpretations of various psalms have also been frequently choreographed themes. One of the more popular subjects has been the story of Adam and Eve. Treatments of this theme indicate some of the range of interpretations of biblical stories. Graham's *Embattled Garden* (1958) introduces Lilith into the domestic routine of the Garden of Eden, whereas Butler's *After Eden* (1966) and Limón's *The Exiles* (1950) both deal with the fate of Adam and Eve after the expulsion, while Roland Petit's *Paradise Lost* (1967) featured a pop interpretation with Adam plunging into a backdrop of a huge lipsticked mouth at the end of the dance. The story has been treated with awe and wonder and irony, and as tragedy and comedy.

The *Book of Genesis* has provided a source of comedic ballets. *Billy Sunday* (1946), choreographed by Ruth Page, is the retelling of these familiar stories as they might have been explained by the baseball-player-turned-preacher Billy Sunday, who used the vernacular and often employed baseball analogies in his exuberant evangelical addresses. In this work Bathsheba does a striptease behind a screen fashioned from a scarf, and Joseph's seducer is the contemporary Mrs. Potiphar. Page emphasizes those stories that portray women betraying men. Taylor's *American Genesis* (1973) recasts the stories as episodes in American history, using bits of Americana—such as minstrel-show techniques—as ironic commentary on both United States history and the biblical stories themselves.

Other ways in which biblical stories have served as a means of social commentary include interpreting the story of Joseph as a message about overcoming political oppression and the story of Esther as a metaphor for Nazism's "final solution." Jooss's *Prodigal Son* found his downfall not in the pursuit of decadent living but in the quest for power, a poignant theme for Germany in 1931.

Religious Themes and Cultural Identity. Modern dance, built on a philosophy of the expression of emotions and personal identity, has provided a vehicle for the exploration of ethnic and religious identity through dance. This has been true, in particular, for Jewish, Afro-American, and Asian choreographers.

Jewish history, ritual, and music have inspired several twentieth-century works in both modern dance and ballet. Several topics have been particularly popular: Jewish village life of tsarist Russia and eastern Europe, the Holocaust, Hasidism, Sefardic Judaism, and Jewish folk tales. Some works employ movement qualities and steps associated with dances from Jewish communities or with prayer movements, while others use Jewish themes or music without any particular ethnic movement style.

The second generation of modern dancers were particularly drawn to social and political themes. This period of growth also coincided with World War II and the attendant Holocaust, providing thematic material for powerful dances. Many of the works of Pearl Lang have Jewish themes. Perhaps her best-known work is *The Possessed* (1975), based on the dybbuk legend. She also choreographed dances using Hasidic themes, biblical stories, and poems composed by Holocaust victims. Her *Tailor's Megillah* is the retelling of Esther's story in a tailor's shop.

Anna Sokolow created the solo *Kaddish* (1946); *Dreams* (1961), an abstract enactment of the horrors of the Nazi concentration camps; and *The Holy Place* (1977), based on Psalm 137 and dealing with the theme of the Jews in exile. The first part of *The Exile* (1939) is set in ancient times, the second deals with persecution, culminating in Nazism. She created both *The Bride*, in which a shy Jewess faces a wedding to an unknown groom, and *Mexican Retablo*, in which she danced a Madonna.

Tamiris choreographed *Memoir* (1957), depicting themes of Jewish life. Holm offered *Tragic Exodus* (1939) and *They Too Are Exiles* (1940), which dealt with the dispossession and persecution of all peoples, but at that time, reference to the Jews in Hitler's Germany was all too apparent. Sophie Maslow choreographed *The Village I Knew* (1950) as an evocation of Jewish life in tsarist Russia.

In ballet, Eliot Feld has contributed *Tzaddik* (1974), a representation of a scholar's intensely emotional introduction of two students into the world of religious study. His *Sephardic Song* (1974) was influenced by traditional Sefardic music. Jerome Robbins choreographed *The Dybbuk Variations* (1974), an abstract version of this story. Robbins is also well known for his staging and choreography of the musical-theater work *Fiddler on the Roof* (1964), which drew on many dance forms and images of turn-of-the-century Jewish life in Russia.

Israel has a very active theatrical dance culture. Many choreographers there naturally turn to Jewish and biblical themes. One of the more prominent companies, the Inbal Dance Theatre, whose principal choreographer is Sara Levi-Tanai, draws on the dances and rituals of the Jewish minorities of the Middle East, especially the Yemenites. Some examples of works by Israeli choreographers include Levi-Tanai's *Psalm of David* (1964), which features the story of Avishag, the girl brought to the aging David; Margalit Oved's *The Mothers of Israel*, choreographed for Ze'eva Cohen, draws on the image of the biblical Sarah, Rebecca, Rachel, and Leah; the Bat-Dor Company performs Domy Reiter-Soffer's *I Shall Sing to Thee in the Valley of the Dead My Beloved* (1971), which tells the history of Israel through the story of King David's loves; Rina Schoenfeld choreographed *Jephthah's Daugher* for the Batsheva Company; and the Russian dancer Rina Nikova founded the Biblical Ballet of Israel.

African Americans have also drawn on dance as a vehicle for the expression of cultural identity. Religious practices and music are a major component of this identity and have formed the basis for many ballet and modern dance works. *Revelations*, a work by Alvin Ailey, was one of the first of these works, and it has also proved to be the most popular and enduring. It is a suite of dances to black hymns and gospel music, each section revealing the theme or spirit of the song—from the solemn abstraction of "I've Been 'Buked'" to the rousing church service of the finale. The audience is often whipped into an enthusiastic hand-clapping and foot-stomping participation that is akin to the atmosphere of many black churches. In this way, *Revelations* has introduced to the Western theater a different model for the role of the spectator at a ballet performance. Some of the other religiously inspired Ailey works include *Three Black Kings* (1976) and the often humorous *Mary Lou's Mass* (1971), in which biblical stories are reenacted.

Many African and African American choreographers also draw on African religious practices. Katherine Dunham, Pearl Primus, and Asadata Dafora were among the first to do this. Dunham's *Rites of Passage* (1941) depicted a fertility ritual, and *Shango*, a vodou rite. Primus's Fanga (1949) created a ritual in an African context.

Asian religious themes have often been popular in Western dance history. In the past, Eastern themes tended to be used as a device for creating exotic spectacle. St. Denis promoted a form of Orientalism that adopted the color and sensuality of Asian dance but also attempted to expose its spiritual import. Cunningham, Hawkins, and Tudor have been influenced by Zen Buddhism. Starting in the 1960s, but especially in the 1970s and 1980s, there has been an explicit attempt to create a dance form that assimilates Eastern and Western dance and that especially captures the spiritual quality of Asian dance. Asian and Asian-American choreographers have been particularly active in adopting Eastern techniques and themes to the modern dance context, often emphasizing the creation of ritual. Kei Takei and the duo Eiko and Koma are particularly noteworthy for their use of Japanese rituals and movement qualities, and Mel Wong is known for his synthesis of Chinese culture and American modern dance.

The discovery of Asian religions in the context of the drug-influenced counterculture of the 1960s led to works such as Béjart's *Bhakti*, a ballet about love as manifested in the relationships between Rāma and Sitā, Kṛṣṇa and Rādhā, and Śiva and Śakti. In the 1970s and 1980s, there has been a growing interest in Ṣūfī dancing, and choreographers have adopted spinning techniques, as in the work of Laura Dean, and have explored the mystical symbolism of Muslim faith.

Modern dance also took root in Japan, where a unique synthesis of American and central European Expressionist modern dance, Japanese *nō*, and *kabuki* combines with a post-World War II sensibility. An avant-garde trend called *butoh*, a word referring to an ancient dance, exists in the shadow of Hiroshima and Nagasaki and lends itself to the creation of ritualistic theatrical probings of primordial and postapocalyptic images.

SACRED OR LITURGICAL DANCE. Dance has returned to the church and synagogue in the twentieth century. With St. Denis and Shawn as its foremost pioneers, the sacred dance or liturgical dance movement has grown rapidly. Another early experiment with ritual dancing in the church took place at Saint Mark's-in-the-Bowerie Church in New York, beginning in the 1920s. Choreographed by the rector of the church, William Norman Guthrie, the dance, depicting the Annunication, was performed by six barefooted women robed in flowing white material probably dancing in the Duncanesque style of the avant-garde of the time. For this scandalous act, Saint Mark's was suspended from the Episcopal church. The ritual dance was performed annually for many years and continued to cause controversy.

Contemporary sacred dance covers a range of ways in which movement can be incorporated into the liturgy. These include (1) rhythmic or dance choirs, analogous to singing choirs, (2) performances based on religious themes or stories by lay or professional dancers, which the congregation watches, (3) congregational dancing in which everyone participates, (4) dancing based on ritual dances of other cultures,

(5) charismatic dancing, (6) danced individual prayers, and (7) dance with therapeutic intent (spiritual healing through dance). Aims of sacred dance include promoting the affirmation of the body, offering dance to God, creating a sense of community, finding the festive nature of life and religion, and integrating body and soul. Leaders in the sacred dance movement have been, among others, Margaret Fiske Taylor, Douglas Adams, Mary Jane Wolbers, Judith Rock, and Carla de Sola. Exponents of liturgical dance have also been unusually prolific writers. In the United States, the Sacred Dance Guild was formed in the late 1950s, and the movement grew rapidly in the 1960s and 1970s in many countries, fed by other related trends: the reemergence of exuberant social dancing, the growth of alternative religions and religious practices, and the rise of dance therapy. While the sacred dance movement is mainly a Christian movement, there is also a growing following in Judaism. A central controversy within the movement is whether to emphasize the liturgical aspect or the aesthetic aspect, whether sacred dance should be performed by the laity with a communal, participatory focus or whether it should be performed by professionals with an aesthetic goal. Ironically, the success of theatrical dance in America, despite the opposition of religious orthodoxies, has led to the addition of a new (or rediscovered) dimension of religious practice—the expressive power of dance.

SEE ALSO Anthroposophy; Circumambulation; Drama; Gurdjieff, G. I.; Labyrinth; Procession; Steiner, Rudolf.

BIBLIOGRAPHY

There has been very little written about religion and theatrical dance. Aside from a few isolated articles or books on particular topics, most information must be gleaned from general books on dance. There are, however, a few anthologies that cover aspects of this topic. In 1979, an International Seminar on the Bible in Dance was held in Israel. The papers from the conference were not published as a group, but the manuscripts are available at the Dance Collection, New York Public Library at Lincoln Center, and elsewhere. Papers of special interest to this topic are those on Limón, Graham, The *Prodigal Son*, *Billy Sunday*, labyrinths, and biblical dance on television. In conjunction with this event, Giora Manor published an extensive study of the use of biblical themes in ballet and modern dance, *The Gospel according to Dance* (New York, 1980). *Worship and Dance*, edited by J. G. Davies (Birmingham, 1975), is particularly useful for information on dance in the church, both historically and as part of the contemporary liturgical dance movement. *Focus on Dance X: Religion and Dance*, edited by Dennis J. Fallon and Mary Jane Wolbers (Reston, Va., 1982), includes Lynn Matluck Brooks's "The Catholic Church and Dance in the Middle Ages," Diane Milhan Pruett's "Duncan's Perception of Dance in Religion," and Georganna Balif Arrington's "Dance in Mormonism: The Dancingest Denomination." A thought-provoking article by Douglas Adams and Judith Rock, "Biblical Criteria in Modern Dance: Modern Dance as Prophetic Form," also delivered at the seminar in Israel, is an application to dance of Paul Tillich's four categories of the relation between religion and visual arts. About half the articles in this volume are devoted to the liturgical dance movement. The journal *Parabola*'s issue on "Sacred Dance," vol. 4, no. 2 (May 1979), contains articles on the dance of Jesus by Elaine H. Pagels and on labyrinths by Rosemary Jeanes. Jamake Highwater's *Dance: Rituals of Experience* (New York, 1978) is a personal view on the importance of reaffirming the ritual nature of dance; his book includes a discussion of which contemporary theatrical choreographers create works that fulfill his conception of ritual.

Most information about religion and theatrical dance must be pieced together from a general history of Western dance. A basic introduction to this topic is Jack Anderson's *Dance* (New York, 1979). A more detailed, although somewhat out-of-date book is Lincoln Kirstein's *Dance: A Short History of Classical Theatrical Dancing* (New York, 1935). Marcia B. Siegel's *The Shapes of Change* (Boston, 1979) analyzes some of the important works of American dance including *Negro Spirituals, Shakers, Revelations*, and several of Graham's works. A brief description and listing of dances by major modern dance choreographers can be found in Don McDonagh's *The Complete Guide to Modern Dance* (Garden City, N.Y., 1976). Anthologies of primary sources include *Dance as a Theatre Art*, edited by Selma Jeanne Cohen (New York, 1974), and, for theoretical essays, *What Is Dance?*, edited by Roger Copeland and Marshall Cohen (New York, 1983). One of several books of synopses of ballet librettos is *101 Stories of the Great Ballets* by George Balanchine and Francis Mason (Garden City, N.Y., 1975).

For dance in the early Christian church and in the medieval European tradition, see Eugène Louis Backman's *Religious Dances in the Christian Church and in Popular Medicine* (London, 1952). For later attitudes held about dance by the Christian church, see *The Mathers on Dancing*, edited by Joseph E. Marks III (Brooklyn, N.Y., 1975), which contains an extensive bibliography of antidance literature from 1685 to 1963. On the Renaissance, see James Miller's "The Philosophical Background of Renaissance Dance," *York Dance Review* 5 (Spring 1976), and Roy Strong's *Splendour at Court* (London, 1973).

For the Baroque, see Shirley Wynne's "Complaisance, an Eighteenth-Century Cool," *Dance Scope* 5 (Fall 1970): 22–35, and Wendy Hilton's *Dance of Court and Theater: The French Noble Style*, 1690–1725 (Princeton, 1971). On the Jesuit theater, see Régine Astier's "Pierre Beauchamps and the Ballets de Collège," *Dance Chronicle* 6, no. 2 (1983): 138–151. for pre-Romantic ballet, the principal history is Marian Hannah Winter's *The Pre-Romantic Ballet* (Brooklyn, N.Y., 1975). Ivor Guest has written extensively on the Romantic ballet; his books include *The Romantic Ballet in Paris*, 2d rev. ed. (London, 1980), and *The Romantic Ballet in England* (Middletown, Conn., 1972). On Bournonville, see his autobiography, *My Theater Life*, translated by Patricia N. McAndrew (Middletown, Conn., 1979), and Erik Ashengreen's "Bournonville: Yesterday, Today and Tomorrow," *Dance Chronicle* 3, no. 2 (1979): 102–151. His librettos have been translated by McAndrews in various issues of *Dance Chronicle* (1980–1983).

On Delsarte and his impact, see Nancy Lee Ruyter's *Reformers and Visionaries: The Americanization of the Art of Dance* (New

York, 1979), which also contains an extensive bibliography of primary sources, and Ted Shawn's *Every Little Movement* (Pittsfield, Mass., 1984). Duncan's own writings in *The Art of the Dance* (New York, 1928) reveal her thoughts on religion and dance. Suzanne Shelton's *Divine Dancer* (Garden City, N.Y., 1981) gives an excellent analysis of St. Denis's beliefs and choreography. Some of Shawn's ideas are in *The American Ballet* (New York, 1926). On Humphrey, see Selma Jeanne Cohen's *Doris Humphrey: An Artist First* (Middletown, Conn., 1972) and my "The Translation of a Culture into Choreography: A Study of Doris Humphrey's *The Shakers*, Based on Labananalysis," *Dance Research Annual* 9 (1978): 93–110. *The Notebooks of Martha Graham* (New York, 1973) provides unique perspective on the development of her choreographic ideas. For information on Laban, see his autobiography, *A Life for Dance*, translated by Lisa Ullmann (New York, 1975). On Wigman, see her *The Language of Dance*, translated by Walter Sorell (Middletown, Conn., 1966). For information on Steiner and Gurdjieff, see the "Occult and Bizarre" issue of *Drama Review* 22 (June 1978).

For the second generation of modern dance, Margaret Lloyd's *The Borzoi Book of Modern Dance* (New York, 1949) is the most detailed. Hawkin's ideas are explained in *Erick Hawkins: Theory and Training*, edited by Richard Lorber (New York, 1979). Nikolais discusses his work in "nik: a documentary," edited by Marcia B. Siegel, *Dance Perspectives* 48 (Winter 1971). For an overview of the Ballets Russes, see John Percival's *The World of Diaghilev* (New York, 1971). For Balanchine, see among others, *Choreography by George Balanchine: A Catalogue of Works*, edited by Harvey Simmonds (New York, 1983), and Marilyn Hunt's "*The Prodigal Son*'s Russian Roots: Avant-Garde and Icons," *Dance Chronicle* 5, no. 1 (1982): 24–49. Postmodern dance is introduced in Sally Banes's *Terpsichore in Sneakers* (Boston, 1980). Anna Halprin's *Movement Ritual* (San Francisco, 1979) is an example of one of the outgrowths of this movement.

On the sacred dance movement, see Carlynn Reed's *And We Have Danced: A History of the Sacred Dance Guild and Sacred Dance, 1958–1978* (Austin, 1978), which contains a useful bibliography.

SUZANNE YOUNGERMAN (1987)

DANCE: THEATRICAL AND LITURGICAL DANCE [FURTHER CONSIDERATIONS]

Academic studies related to the topic of theatrical and liturgical dance have remained predominantly within the circles of dance scholarship. Traditionally, such studies have been divided into two categories of analysis: dance history and criticism, which have premised their evaluations according to chronological and classic aesthetic criteria; or ethnography and anthropology, which have inquired into the cultural formations and functions of dance. The former has emphasized typically the West and the latter non-Western cultures. The publication of the *International Encyclopedia of Dance* (1998) and the televised presentation of the eight-part series *Dancing!* (1992), with its companion volume, generated both scholarly and public interest in the global and multi-cultural correspondences among dance traditions. Since 1987, the central investigations by dance scholars have moved beyond the "how, what, where, and why" of dance to those related to dance as a communicator of meaning and values throughout world cultures and religions.

Interest in the investigation of liturgical and theatrical dance has extended into the realm of religious studies—especially world religions—beyond the traditional categories of "dance and liturgy," ritual studies, and the umbrella of art and religion. These are evidenced in the work of Ann Cooper Albright, Diane Apostolos-Cappadona, and Ann Dils. While J.G. Davies' texts remain as classics for the study of liturgical dance in Christianity, Doug Adams, Helga Barbara Gundlach, Thomas A. Kane (in *Introducing Dance in Christian Worship*), Judith Rock, and Carla De Sola continue to expand the discussions about the nature, styles, and meaning of Christian liturgical dance into the contemporary scene. Other religion scholars have incorporated analyses of ritual and ceremonial dance into their studies of individual religious traditions, i.e., Hinduism and Native America, which might otherwise not culturally identify these dances as "liturgical." Issues of gender studies, investigations of the body, and the study of the economic, ethnic, engendered and/or racial minorities have affected the modes and methods for studying liturgical and theatrical dance. This appears in the work of Jane C. Desmond, Brenda Dixon Gottschild, Judith Lynn Hanna, and Cynthia Novack.

Both the performance and the study of liturgical and theatrical dance have incorporated the technologies of video, mass media, and the internet as well as a place within the academic spectrum in the newer categories of "performance and display," and "visual culture" (Mitoma, 2003). Scholarship in the fields of liturgical and theatrical dance has entered geographic areas previously investigated to a lesser extent, such as Southeast Asia, Pre-Columbian Latin America, Oceania, and Africa. These are shown in the work of Judy Mitoma, Richard Anderson Sutton, Robert Farris Thompson, and Elizabeth Zimmer. The influence—historically and from post-1960s global cultures—of non-Western religious dance traditions on Western dance, whether religious or secular, is emerging as an investigative focus for both dance history and religious studies scholars. However, more often than not the study of the influences of non-western dance and religion is in terms of a particular dancer in historical studies, such as Isadora Duncan, Ruth St. Denis, José Limon, and Martha Graham. Exciting possibilities for new scholarship include analyses of the "east-west" connectives in such contemporary choreography as that of Eiko and Komo, Meredith Monk, Peter Sparling, and Yin Mei.

NEW PERSPECTIVES. The new directions for the study of theatrical and liturgical dance will emerge in coordination with a growing recognition of global and multi-cultural discourses, especially in terms of cross-cultural analyses of the creative process and the human body as evidenced for example in the work of Mitoma and Zimmer. New questions about the definition of dance—liturgical and/or theatrical—are raised with the advent of technology and the merging of dance with other media to create "performance pieces," such as the collaboration between architect Zaha Hadid and the Charleroi Dance Company (2001). Analyses of dance as a communicator of cultural values and ideas will re-frame the mode and methods of studying theatrical and liturgical dance from the perspective of dance studies in the work of Ruth Solomon and John Solomon, and in religious studies as evidenced in the work of a new generation of scholars, most notably Kimerer Lewis LaMothe.

SEE ALSO Anthroposophy; Circumambulation; Gurdjieff, G. I.; Labyrinth; Performance and Ritual; Procession; Steiner, Rudolf.

BIBLIOGRAPHY

Adams, Doug. *Changing Biblical Imagery and Artistic Identity in 20th Century Liturgical Dance.* Austin, Tex., 1984.

Adams, Doug, and Diane Apostolos-Cappadona, eds. *Dance as Religious Studies.* Eugene, Ore., 2001.

Albright, Ann Cooper. *Choreographing Difference: The Body and Identity in Contemporary Dance.* Middleton, Conn., 1997.

Desmond, Jane C. *Dancing Desire: Choreographing Sexualities On and Off Stage.* Madison, Wis., 2001.

De Sola, Carla. *The Spirit Moves: A Handbook of Dance and Prayer.* Austin, Tex., 1986.

Dils, Ann, and Ann Cooper Albright, eds. *Moving History/ Dancing Cultures: A Dance History Reader.* Middleton, Conn., 2001.

Fernández Olmos, Margarite, and Lizabeth Paravisini-Gebert, eds. *Sacred Possessions: Vodou, Santería, Obeah, and the Caribbean.* New Brunswick, N.J., 1997.

Gagne, Ronald. *Introducing Dance in Christian Worship.* Portland, Ore., 1984.

Gottschild, Brenda Dixon. *The Black Dancing Body: A Geography from Coon to Cool.* New York, 2003.

Gundlach, Helga Barbara. *Religiösen Tanz: Formen-Funktionen-Beispiele.* Marburg, Germany, 2000.

Hanna, Judith Lynne. *Dance, Sex, and Gender: Signs of Identity, Dominance, Defiance, and Desire.* Chicago, 1988.

Heth, Charlotte, ed. *Native American Dance: Ceremonies and Social Traditions.* Washington, D.C., 1992.

International Encyclopedia of Dance, 6 vols. New York, 1998.

Kehoe, Alice Beck. *The Ghost Dance: Ethnohistory and Revitalization.* New York, 1989.

Kirstein, Lincoln. *Dance: A Short History.* Princeton, N.J., 1987. Anniversary edition.

Lonsdale, Steven. *Dance and Ritual Play in Greek Religion.* Baltimore, Md., 1993.

Mazo, Joseph H. *Prime Movers: The Makers of Modern Dance in America.* Hightstown, N.J., 2000. 2d edition.

Mitoma, Judy, and Elizabeth Zimmer. *Envisioning Dance on Film and Video.* New York, 2003.

Needham, Maureen, ed. *I See America Dancing: Selected Readings, 1685–2000.* Urbana, Ill., 2002.

Novack, Cynthia. *Sharing the Dance: Contact Improvisation and American Culture.* Madison, Wis., 1990.

Richmond, Farley P., Darius L. Swann, and Phillip B. Zarilli, eds. *Indian Theatre: Traditions of Performance.* Honolulu, 1990.

Rock, Judith, and Norman Mealy. *Performer as Priest and Prophet: Restoring the Intuitive in Worship through Music and Dance.* San Francisco, 1988.

Roseman, Janet Lynn. *Dance Was Her Religion: The Sacred Choreography of Isadora Duncan, Ruth St, Denis, and Martha Graham.* Prescott, Ariz., 2004.

Rust, Ezra Gardner. *The Music and Dance of the World's Religions: A Comprehensive, Annotated Bibliography of Materials in the English Language.* Westport, Conn., 1996.

Shelton, Suzanne. *Ruth St. Denis: A Biography of the Divine Dancer.* Garden City, N.Y., 1990.

Solomon, Ruth, and John Solomon, eds. *East Meets West in Dance Voices in the Cross-Cultural Dialogue.* Chur, Switzerland; New York, 1995.

Sutton, Richard Anderson. *Calling Back the Spirit: Music, Dance, and Cultural Politics in Lowland South Sulawesi.* New York, 2002.

Thompson, Robert Farris. *Flash of the Spirit: African and Afro-American Art and Philosophy.* New York, 1983.

Zuhur, Sherifa, ed. *Colors of Enchantment: Theater, Dance, Music, and the Visual Arts of the Middle East.* Cairo, 2001.

DIANE APOSTOLOS-CAPPADONA (2005)

DAN FODIO, USUMAN (AH 1168–1232, 1754/5–1817 CE), renowned Fulbe Islamic teacher and shaykh. Shehu (Hausa for *shaykh*) Usuman dan Fodio was born in the Hausa kingdom of Gobir, in the north of the present-day state of Sokoto, Nigeria. He came of a line of Muslim scholars of the Fulbe clan Torodbe that had been established in the area since about 854/1450. They worked as scribes, teachers, and in other literate roles and contributed over several generations to the dissemination of Sunnī Islam among the inhabitants of Gobir. As a result, the Gobir royals were superficially won over to Islam. Nonetheless, authority in Gobir still rested on customary norms, not the Islamic *sharīʿah*, at the end of the eighteenth century CE. This caused mounting frustration among these Muslim literates and resulted in the emergence of an Islamic reform movement that reached its peak at that time. The Shehu Usuman became widely accepted in Gobir and neighboring kingdoms as its leader.

The Shehu Usuman spent his early manhood as a teacher and preacher of Islam in Gobir and the nearby kingdoms of Zamfara, Katsina, and Kebbi. He appears to have had no initial intention of pursuing reform by force, but the prolonged resistance of the Gobir chiefs and courtiers to demands for stricter adherence to Islam built up tension. After several violent incidents, organized warfare broke out between the Gobir forces and the Shehu's followers in 1219/1804. For the Muslim reformers this was *jihād*, war against unbelievers.

The campaigns in Gobir ended in 1223/1808, when the Gobir dynasty collapsed and was replaced by a polity organized along Islamic lines that the reformers described as a "caliphate" (Arab., *khalīfah*). The Shehu remained its titular head until his death in 1232/1817, when he was succeeded by his son, Muhammadu Bello. Elsewhere in the Hausa kingdoms and even as far south as Yorubaland and the Nupe kingdom other *jihāds*, led by the Shehu's "flag bearers," or military commanders, continued until brought to a halt by the colonial occupations of the late nineteenth and early twentieth centuries.

The Shehu was not only a war leader but also a scholar and poet in the classical Arabic tradition. Best known among his verse works is his panegyric to the prophet Muḥammad, *Al-dālīyah (The Ode Rhyming in Dāl)*, that helped to spread the prophet's Ṣūfī cult and was seminal to a genre of Hausa prophetic panegyric (Hau., *madahu*) among the generations that followed him.

His Arabic prose works are numerous (see Last, 1967). Their main thrust is against all manifestations of indigenous, non-Islamic Hausa culture—song, music, ornate dress, architecture, social mores, and so on—and an insistence that these be replaced by Islamic alternatives. His works also influenced his society, and posterity, by disseminating the ideas of the Qādirī order of Ṣūfīs, to which he was deeply committed, especially as regards the cult of the *awliyā'* (Arab.; sg., *walī*, "one near" to Allāh). Indeed, the Shehu's own charisma stems largely from his reputation as a *walī*.

The immediate political consequences of the *jihād* were to overthrow the discrete Hausa principalities based on traditional, unwritten customary codes and to substitute the unified Islamic system of the caliphate governed by the revealed and written *sharī'ah*. More long-term cultural and religious consequences were to displace, to some extent, indigenous African notions about cosmology and replace them with the Islamic celestial architecture, to challenge African cyclical explanations of life and death with the finality of the Islamic doctrine of divine punishment and reward, and to enhance the status of Arabic literacy in Hausa society.

The Shehu is still a much revered personality among Hausa Muslims, having become something of a symbol of Hausa Muslim nationalism. However, the Ṣūfī aspects of his teaching are now less emphasized than in the past, perhaps because the Wahhābī doctrine has become more influential in West Africa.

BIBLIOGRAPHY

The bibliography on the Fulbe *jihād* is extensive, and the student is advised to consult lists in Murray Last's *The Sokoto Caliphate* (London, 1967). The following will also be found useful in the first instance: my edition and translation of *Tazyīn al-waraqāt* (Ibadan, 1963), an account of the Shehu's life and the *jihād* from the Muslim reformers' own viewpoint; my *The Sword of Truth* (New York, 1973), a study of the life and times of the Shehu based on the Arabic and Hausa sources; my *The Development of Islam in West Africa*, (New York, 1984), which places the Fulbe reform movement in the wider West African context; and *Bayān wujūb al-hijrah 'alā al-'ibād*, edited and translated by F. H. el-Masri (Khartoum and Oxford, 1978), the edited Arabic text and English translation of one of the Shehu's major works with an excellent critical introduction. There are also many articles in learned journals that deal with aspects of the Shehu's life and writings. These are conveniently listed in Hiskett (1973 and 1984) and Last (1967).

MERVYN HISKETT (1987)

DANIEL, or, in Hebrew, Daniyye'l; hero of the biblical book that bears his name. Daniel is presented as a Jew in the Babylonian exile who achieved notoriety in the royal court for his dream interpretations and cryptography and for his salvation from death in a lion's pit. He also appears in the last chapters of the book as the revealer of divine mysteries and of the timetables of Israel's restoration to national-religious autonomy. As a practitioner of oneiromancy in the court, described in *Daniel* 1–6 (written in the third person), Daniel performs his interpretations alone, while as a visionary-apocalyptist, in *Daniel* 7–12 (written in the first person), he is in need of an angel to help him decode his visions and mysteries of the future. It is likely that the name Daniel is pseudonymous, a deliberate allusion to a wise and righteous man known from Ugaritic legend and earlier biblical tradition (*Ez.* 14:4, 28:3).

The authorship of the book is complicated not only by the diverse narrative voices and content but by its language: *Daniel* 1:1–2:4a and 8–12 are written in Hebrew, whereas *Daniel* 2:4b–7:28 is in Aramaic. The language division parallels the subject division (*Daniel* 1–6 concerns legends and dream interpretations; 7–12 concerns apocalyptic visions and interpretations of older prophecies). The overall chronological scheme as well as internal thematic balances (*Daniel* 2–7 is chiliastically related) suggest an attempt at redactional unity. After the prefatory tale emphasizing the life in court and the loyalty of Daniel and some youths to their ancestral religion, a chronological ordering is discernible: a sequence from King Nebuchadrezzar to Darius is reported (*Dn.* 2–6), followed by a second royal sequence beginning with Belshazzar and concluding with Cyrus II (*Dn.* 7–12). Much of this royal dating and even some of the tales are problematic: for example, *Daniel* 4 speaks of Nebuchadrezzar's transformation into a beast, a story that is reported in the Qumran scrolls of Nabonidus; Belshazzar is portrayed as the last king of Babylon, although he was never king; and Darius is called a Mede who conquered Babylon and is placed before Cyrus II of Persia, although no such Darius is known (the Medes followed the Persians, and *Darius* is the name of several Persian kings). Presumably the episodes of *Daniel* 2–6, depicting a series of monarchical reversals, episodes of ritual observances, and reports of miraculous deliverances were collected in the Seleucid period (late fourth to mid-second century

BCE) in order to reinvigorate waning Jewish hopes in divine providence and encourage steadfast faith.

The visions of *Daniel* 7–12, reporting events from the reign of Belshazzar to that of Cyrus II (but actually predicting the overthrow of Seleucid rule in Palestine), were collected and published during the reign of Antiochus IV prior to the Maccabean Revolt, for it was then (beginning in 168 BCE) that the Jews were put to the test concerning their allegiance to Judaism and their ancestral traditions, and many refused to desecrate the statutes of Moses and endured a martyr's death for their resolute trust in divine dominion. All of the visions of Daniel dramatize this dominion in different ways: for example, via images of the enthronement of a God of judgment, with a "son of man" invested with rule (this figure was interpreted by Jews as Michael the archangel and by Christians as Christ), in chapter 7; via zodiacal images of cosmic beasts with bizarre manifestations, as in chapter 8; or via complex reinterpretations of ancient prophecies, especially those of *Jeremiah* 25:9–11, as found in *Daniel* 9–12.

The imagery of the four beasts in chapter 7 (paralleled by the image of four metals in chapter 2), representing four kingdoms to be overthrown by a fifth monarchy of divine origin, is one of the enduring images of the book: it survived as a prototype of Jewish and Christian historical and apocalyptic schemes to the end of the Middle Ages. The role and power of this imagery in the fifteenth- and sixteenth-century work of the exegete Isaac Abravanel, the scientist Isaac Newton, and the philosopher Jean Bodin and among the Fifth Monarchy Men of seventeenth-century England, for example, is abiding testimony to the use of this ancient topos in organizing the chiliastic imagination of diverse thinkers and groups. The schema is still used to this day by various groups predicting the apocalyptic advent.

The encouragement in the face of religious persecution that is found and propagandized in *Daniel* 11–12 contains a remarkable reinterpretation of *Isaiah* 52:13–53:12, regarding the suffering servant of God not as all Israel but as the select faithful. Neither the opening stories about Daniel and the youths nor the final martyrological allusions advocate violence or revolt; they rather advocate a stance of piety, civil disobedience, and trustful resignation. Victory for the faithful is in the hands of the archangel Michael, and the martyrs will be resurrected and granted astral immortality. Presumably the circles behind the book were not the same as the Maccabean fighters and may reflect some proto-Pharisaic group of *ḥasidim*, or Pietists. The themes of resistance to oppression, freedom of worship, preservation of monotheistic integrity, the overthrow of historical dominions, and the acknowledgment of the God of heaven recur throughout the book and have served as a token of trust for the faithful in their darkest hour.

BIBLIOGRAPHY

Bickerman, Elias J. *Four Strange Books of the Bible: Jonah, Daniel, Koheleth, Esther.* New York, 1967. See pages 53–138.

Braverman, Jay. *Jerome's Commentary on Daniel.* Washington, D.C., 1978.

Hartman, Louis F., and Alexander A. Di Lella. *Book of Daniel.* Anchor Bible, vol. 23. Garden City, N.Y., 1978.

New Sources

Collins, John J., and Peter W. Flint, eds. *The Book of Daniel: Composition and Reception.* Boston; Leiden, 2002.

Van der Woude, A. S., ed. *The Book of Daniel in the Light of New Findings.* Leuven, 1993.

Wills, Lawrence Mitchell. *The Jew in the Court of the Foreign King: Ancient Jewish Court Legends.* Minneapolis, 1990.

MICHAEL FISHBANE (1987)
Revised Bibliography

DANTE ALIGHIERI (1265–1321), Italian poet, theologian, and philosopher. Dante offered in his *Commedia* a "sacred poem" of enormous erudition and aesthetic power, which more than any other work of Christian literature merits the appellation conferred on it by a mid-sixteenth-century edition: "divine." After producing the *Vita nuova* in 1295, Dante entered the volatile world of Florentine politics, which, however unjustly, subsequently led to his banishment from the city in 1302. In exile for the remainder of his life, he wrote the *Convivio*, the *De vulgari eloquentia*, and the *De monarchia* in the following decade, works that together reveal a commonality of themes: an admiration for the Latin classics, a dedication to the study of philosophy, and a commitment to the revival of the Roman imperial ideal. These concerns are all transfigured in the long and elaborate course of the *Commedia* (*Inferno, Purgatorio, Paradiso*), which represents an encyclopedic synthesis of late medieval thought subsumed within an overarching theological vision. The poem is at once profoundly traditional in its religious ordering of human experience and an innovation of substance and form that suggests an utterly new mentality at work. It can be seen both as an attempt to exorcise what would shortly become the spirit of the Renaissance and yet also as a brilliant precursor of it.

Dante came of age in Florence at a time when the papacy was embroiled with the Holy Roman Empire over temporal jurisdiction in Italy. Widespread corruption in the church, as well as within the powerful mendicant orders of the Franciscans and the Dominicans, seemed to give rise to many individualistic and charismatic expressions of piety that, while passionately Catholic, nonetheless found themselves alienated from the established religious institutions and hierarchies. It is in this context that a devout layman like Dante, discovering himself a mere "party of one," could dare to arrogate to himself the quasi-biblical role of prophet. He became a voice crying in the wilderness, instructing the powers of church and state in their true responsibilities at the same time that he was attempting to woo the ordinary reader (in a daring use of the vernacular for so ambitious a poetic work) into a full conversion of the heart.

Whatever the poet's personal upbringing may have given him, it is known that he studied for an extended period "in the schools of the religious orders and at the disputations of the philosophers" (*Convivio* 2.12). At Santa Croce he would have been exposed to the wealth of Franciscan piety, while at Santa Maria Novella the Dominican Remigio de' Girolami expounded the theology of Thomas Aquinas with special regard for the Aristotelian philosophy that subtends it. In such an intellectual atmosphere Dante found validated what was to be one of the most impressive characteristics of his own work: the massive appropriation of pagan and classical writers for Christian reflection and use.

In assessing Dante's relation to medieval theology and religious thought it is commonplace to emphasize the formative influence of "the Philosopher" (Aristotle) and the "Angelic Doctor" (Thomas); that is, to stress his strong debt to Scholasticism. It must be remembered, however, that the poet everywhere shows himself to be an independent and eclectic thinker, whose imaginative meditation on the Christian faith leads him far and wide: to the systematics of Peter Lombard, the Platonism of Bonaventure, the mysticism of Bernard of Clairvaux and the Victorines, the biblical exegesis (as well as the retrospective confessional mode) of Augustine. Thus, while we may well speak of Dante as standing at the crossroads of medieval religious thought, the intersection is one that he personally constructed rather than discovered ready-made. The synthesis of the *Commedia* is idiosyncratically his own.

As a propagator of the Christian religion Dante must, of course, be assessed by the achievement of his great poem, with its account of the state of the soul after death portrayed in the course of a journey undertaken by the poet himself (lasting from Good Friday 1300 to the Wednesday of Easter Week) through the realms of damnation, purgation, and beatitude. Granted this extraordinary experience through the intercession of his deceased love, Beatrice, the pilgrim-poet is led step by step through a process of conversion by a series of guides and mediators: the pagan poet Vergil, Beatrice herself, and the churchman-mystic-crusader Bernard. But in its larger aspect, the poem is itself an invitation to conversion: to the individual reader, to rediscover the Gospels' "true way"; to the church, to recover its spiritual mission; and to the state, to exercise its divinely ordained mandate to foster temporal well-being.

There are other transformations as well. Hell is portrayed not as a place of arbitrary horror, but as the eternal living out of the soul's self-choice, whereby punishments not only fit but express the crimes of sin. Dante also brings Purgatory aboveground and into the sun, turning the traditional place of torturous penance into more of a hospital or school than a prison house. No less striking is the presentation of Beatrice, at once the earthly lover praised in the youthful pages of the *Vita nuova* and the Christ-event for Dante: a woman in whom we see human eros accorded an unprecedented place in the scheme of human salvation. But perhaps most significant of all—and most singularly responsible for the *Commedia*'s immense and enduring popularity—is Dante's superb representation of the self: ineradicable even in death; more vivid than the theological context in which it is eternally envisioned; more subtly and realistically portrayed than in any other work of medieval literature. The poem's itinerary leads us along the paths of theology to a vision of God, but its hundred cantos offer an investigation of human nature and culture that grounds the reader's attention in the complex realities of earth.

Bibliography

The quantity of secondary material on Dante written in English alone is staggering. Carole Slade's extensive and somewhat annotated bibliography in *Approaches to Teaching Dante's Divine Comedy* (New York, 1982) gives a fine sense of the whole range. Among those works that deal sensitively with Dante's relation to Christian belief and tradition, one needs to accord special tribute to the critical oeuvre of Charles S. Singleton, who has exerted a powerful influence on American studies of Dante by underscoring the importance of the poem's theological assumptions. In addition to Singleton's translation and commentary (Princeton, 1970–1975), there are his earlier works: *An Essay on the Vita Nuova* (Cambridge, U.K. 1949), *Dante Studies 1: Commedia, Elements of Structure*, 2d ed. (Baltimore, 1977), and *Dante Studies 2: Journey to Beatrice*, 2d ed. (Baltimore, 1977). Charles Williams's *The Figure of Beatrice* (London, 1958) gives a coherent theological reading of all of Dante's works, whose point of view informs not only Dorothy Sayers's commentary and notes (Harmondsworth, 1951–1967) but her *Introductory Papers on Dante* (New York, 1954) and *Further Papers on Dante* (New York, 1957). There are also brilliant insights into the religious ethos of the *Commedia* in Erich Auerbach's *Dante: Poet of the Secular World* (Chicago, 1961) as well as in an important chapter of his *Mimesis* (Princeton, 1953). Robert Hollander's *Allegory in Dante's Commedia* (Princeton, 1969) and *Studies in Dante* (Ravenna, 1980) deal masterfully with the poet's claim to write an "allegory of the theologians" (and therefore in the manner of scripture itself). John Freccero's many brilliant essays on the *Commedia*, collected under the title *The Poetry of Conversion* (Cambridge, Mass., 1986), stress the poet's debt to Augustine's *Confessions* and the Christian Neoplatonic tradition. The latter connection is explored in Joseph Anthony Mazzeo's *Structure and Thought in the Paradiso* (Ithaca, N.Y., 1958). Finally, William Anderson's *Dante the Maker* (Boston, 1980) takes seriously the visionary origin of the *Commedia* and therefore forces us to examine again the literal level of the poem and its bid to be believed as a genuine vision of God.

Peter S. Hawkins (1987)

DAO'AN (312–385), also known as Shi Dao'an, Chinese Buddhist monk, scholar, and gifted exegete whose organizational abilities and doctrinal acumen helped shape the direction of early Chinese Buddhism. Dao'an was born to a family of literati in what is now Hebei Province in North China. He became a novice at the age of twelve. In 335 he journeyed to Ye (Hebei Province), the new capital of the Later Zhao kingdom, where he studied with Fotudeng (d. 348), the thaumaturge-monk whose magical prowess and success at predicting the outcome of battle had served to recommend Buddhism to the non-Chinese rulers of the kingdom. With the death of Shi Hu, then ruler of the Later Zhao, in 349, Dao'an left Ye and began a peripatetic career in North China that was to last until 365, when he was forced by war to flee south to Xiangyang (Hubei Province). During this period he gathered around himself an ever-growing band of disciples and developed the scholarly and organizational skills for which he is esteemed.

Dao'an's interests during the period 349–365 were conditioned by the pronounced orientation of the Buddhism of North China around primarily Hinayanistic techniques of meditation designed to advance the practitioner through successively rarefied transic states (Skt., *dhyāna;* Chin., *chan*). The enumeration of these states constituted the topic of several sūtras introduced to China in the second century CE by the Parthian translator An Shigao. During his time in the North, Dao'an wrote commentaries to no fewer than six of An Shigao's translations, remarking at one point that the study of *dhyāna* categories constituted "the very pivot of the religious life." That the practice of the techniques described in An Shigao's translations occupied a central role in the community of monks gathered around Dao'an can scarcely be doubted.

This interest in some of the earliest products of the interaction between India and China may reflect something of the growing historiographical and text-critical concerns that would become the hallmark of Dao'an's later years. His biographies emphasize his concern lest the meaning of the scriptures be obscured by the translation process or by the efforts of well-meaning exegetes to couch Buddhist ideas in equivalent Chinese terms bearing only a nominal relationship to the original Sanskrit. Like no one before him in the history of Chinese Buddhism, Dao'an recognized that profound differences separated the original teachings of the scriptures from the hermeneutical framework devised for them in China. In light of this, he undertook his own program of textual exegesis, including careful notation of the history of various texts in China, and formally repudiated a prevailing method of textual interpretation known as *geyi* (matching meanings), under which numerical categories from the scriptures were paired with terms from secular literature.

The year 365 found Dao'an in Xiangyang with an entourage of over four hundred disciples. Once there he moved quickly to establish a monastic center and to forge links with the local government and aristocracy that would ensure its institutional stability. Aware of the difficulties in regulating monastic life in the absence of a complete translation of the Vinaya, or monastic rules, he promulgated a series of ordinances of his own devising. These appear to have treated the daily regimen of the monks and their observance of the Upoṣadha (Pali, Uposatha), or fortnightly confessional ceremony.

But the distinguishing feature of Dao'an's fifteen-year stay in Xiangyang was his shift in attention from *dhyāna* texts and practices to the Mahāyāna Prajñāpāramitā (perfection of wisdom) literature. Although there is evidence that he had become acquainted with these sūtras prior to 365, the years in Xiangyang were characterized by a radical reorganization of his religious interests: six of Dao'an's commentaries from this period are devoted to the Prajñāpāramitā literature. He is also said to have lectured twice yearly on the *Fangguang jing*, Mokṣala's translation (291 CE) of the *Prajñāpāramitā Sūtra* in twenty-five thousand *ślokas*. It is as an outgrowth of this interest in speculations on *prajñāpāramitā* that he is credited with establishing the teaching of original nonbeing (*benwu zong*), one of seven so-called *prajñā* traditions that flourished in China during the fourth and fifth centuries. From the scant evidence remaining to us, Dao'an's teaching appears to have emphasized the existence of an underlying substrate (*benwu*) that stands to phenomena (*moyou*) as both fundamental substance and source. By focusing the mind in meditation upon this radically other, empty absolute, Dao'an taught, release from phenomenal existence can be won.

Two other hallmarks of Dao'an's stay at Xiangyang bear mentioning. The first is his compilation, in 374, of the first critical catalog of Chinese Buddhist texts. As a culmination of his lifelong interest in the fidelity of the sources available to the Chinese, the *Zongli zhongjing mulu* (Comprehensive catalog of the collected scriptures) became a model for all future works of this sort. Dao'an personally inspected each of the more than six hundred works in the catalog, laboriously copied the colophons, where available, and scrupulously passed judgment on the authenticity of the information given there. The other noteworthy feature of Dao'an's career in Xiangyang is his inauguration of a cult to the *bodhisattva* Maitreya. In this cult, clearly the model for his disciple Huiyuan's own Amitabha confraternity (402 CE), Dao'an and seven other devotees gathered before an image of Maitreya and collectively vowed to be reborn in Tusita Heaven, the abode of the *bodhisattva* prior to his rebirth in this world. His biography relates how, in a miraculous visitation to Dao'an shortly before his death, Maitreya vouchsafed to him a vision of Tusita.

The final era of Dao'an's career began in 379 when Fu Jian, ruler of the Former Qin kingdom, laid siege to Xiangyang. In the aftermath of the capitulation of the city Dao'an was brought to Chang'an to preside over a monastic community several times larger than that at Xiangyang. With Fu Jian's restoration of Chinese hegemony over Central Asia, Chang'an was once again the eastern terminus of a trade and information network that stretched through Chinese Turkistan, beyond the Hindu Kush, and into India itself. In the final years of Dao'an's life a number of important missionaries and translators arrived in Chang'an from the western regions, especially from Kashmir, where the Sarvastivada community was exceptionally strong. They brought with them texts that gradually began to fill the lacunae in the canon so lamented by Dao'an. The *Ekottara* and *Madhyama Āgamas*, the *Jñānaprasthāna* (the central work in the Sarvastivada Abhidharma Pitaka), and important sections of the Sarvastivada Vinaya were all introduced at this time. As head of an officially sponsored translation bureau, Dao'an advised the translation team in matters of style (Dao'an, of course, knew no Sanskrit), and composed prefaces to some of the texts. His classic guidelines for translators, consisting, formulaically, of five parameters for changing the text (*wu shiben*) and three conditions under which deviation from the original was not encouraged (*san buyi*), date from this period.

Dao'an's influence over the exegetical and bibliographical traditions of Chinese Buddhism during its formative years can scarcely be overestimated. As the first Buddhist on Chinese soil to confront the problem of understanding Buddhist texts on their own terms, free from the conceptual distortions imposed on them by their association with indigenous thought, Dao'an brought to the young church a new measure of maturity. He is also significant for having combined in a single career the emphasis on Pietism and *dhyāna* practices characteristic of the Buddhism of North China with the Gnostic speculations of Prajñāpāramitā and *xuanxue* thought that engaged the Buddhist thinkers of the South. That Buddhism emerged with the doctrinal and institutional autonomy that it did during the fifth century is attributable in no small measure to Dao'an's efforts.

SEE ALSO Huiyuan; Kumārajīva; Maitreya.

BIBLIOGRAPHY

Extensive discussions of Dao'an's role in the development of Chinese Buddhism can be found in Tang Yongtong's *Han Wei liang-Jin Nan-bei chao fojiao shi* (Shanghai, 1938), vol. 1, pp. 187–277; Itō Giken's *Shina bukkyō seishi* (Yamaguchi-ken, 1923), pp. 111–206; and Erik Zürcher's *The Buddhist Conquest of China* (1959; reprint, Leiden, 1972), vol. 1, pp. 181–204. Kenneth Ch'en's *Buddhism in China: A Historical Survey* (Princeton, 1964) offers a summary of Dao'an's career on pages 94–103.

For a good introduction to the Buddhism of North China in Dao'an's time, see Arthur Wright's essay on Dao'an's teacher, "Fo-t'u-têng: A Biography," *Harvard Journal of Asiatic Studies* 11 (1948): 321–371. Dao'an's biography in the *Gaoseng zhuan* has been translated by Arthur Link in "The Biography of Shih Tao-an," *T'oung pao* 46 (1958): 1–48. Useful for their treatments of Dao'an and the *prajñā* traditions of the fourth and fifth centuries are Arthur Link's "The Taoist Antecedents of Tao-an's Prajñā Ontology," *History of Religions* 9 (1969–1970): 181–215; Kenneth Ch'en's "Neo-Taoism and the Prajñā School during the Wei and Chin Dynasties," *Chinese Culture* 1 (October 1957): 33–46; and Fung Yu-lan's *A History of Chinese Philosophy*, vol. 2, *The Period of Classical Learning*, translated by Derk Bodde (Princeton, 1953), pp. 243–258. Ui Hakuju's *Shaku Dōan kenkyū* (Tokyo, 1956) reviews Dao'an's career and includes annotated editions of his major prefaces. For a discussion of Dao'an's translation guidelines, see Ōchō Enichi's "Shaku Dōan no hon'yakuron," *Indogaku bukkyōgaku kenkyū* 5 (1957): 120–130.

MARK D. CUMMINGS (1987)

DAO AND DE, the "way" and "virtue," respectively, are basic Chinese philosophical concepts with particular relevance in the Daoist tradition. They are important separately as politico-philosophical and religious terms. Joined as a binomial, *dao-de* appears first in the third century BCE and plays a key role in religious Daoist speculation. In modern Chinese, *dao-de* means "morality."

Dao is the word for "road" or "pathway." It has no other sense in the earliest texts—that is, in the oracle bones of the Shang dynasty (c. 1200 BCE). By the time of the Eastern Zhou (770–256 BCE), *dao* comes to mean the correct or natural way something is done, especially in the actions of rulers and kings (Vandermeersch, 1980). Used as a verb, *dao* also means to "show the way," "tell," or "guide," and hence gains the meaning "teaching" or "doctrine." In both these senses, the term is central to the various philosophical schools of ancient China and the formulation of political doctrines; it often designates a meta-way of talking about specific ideas or political measures (Hansen, 1992). A. C. Graham accordingly entitled his volume on ancient Chinese thought *Disputers of the Tao* (1989).

In the philosophical texts, *dao* means both "the way the universe operates" and "the teachings people follow." Thus, the *Lunyu* (the *Analects* or "Sayings of Confucius," dated to about 400 BCE) speaks of the "*dao* of the ancient kings" and says a state "has *dao*" if it is well governed. A Confucian gentleman "devotes himself to *dao*" and people do not all "have the same *dao*" if they adhere to different principles. The classic of all texts on *dao*, the *Dao de jing*, states, "*dao* that can be *dao*'ed is not the eternal *dao*" (chap. 1), emphasizing the ineffable nature of the way that underlies existence.

Despite this, it is possible to create a working definition, such as that by Benjamin Schwartz in his *The World of Thought in Ancient China* (1985). He describes *dao* as "organic order"—organic in the sense that it is not willful. It is not a conscious, active creator, not a personal entity, but rather an organic process that just moves along. It is mysterious in its depth and unfathomable in its essence.

Beyond this, *dao* is also order, clearly manifest in the rhythmic changes and patterned processes of the natural world. As such, it is predictable in its developments and can be analyzed and described in ordered patterns. These ordered patterns are what the Chinese call *ziran*, or "self-so," which is the spontaneous and observable way things are naturally. Yet while *dao* is very much nature, it is also more than nature. It is also the essence of nature, the inner quality that makes things what they are. It is governed by laws of nature, yet it is also these laws itself.

In other words, it is possible to explain the nature of *dao* in terms of a twofold structure. The "*dao* that can be *dao*'ed" and the "eternal *dao*." The latter is the mysterious, ineffable *dao* at the center of the cosmos; the former is the *dao* at the periphery, visible and tangible in the natural cycles. About the eternal *dao*, the *Dao de jing* says:

> Look at it and do not see it: we call it invisible. Listen to it and do not hear it: we call it inaudible. Touch it and do not feel it: we call it subtle. . . . Infinite and boundless, it cannot be named;. . . Call it vague and obscure. (chap. 14; see LaFargue, 1992)

This *dao* is entirely beyond the perception of ordinary humans. It is so vague and obscure, so subtle and so potent, that it is utterly beyond all knowing and analysis, and cannot be grasped however much one may try. The human body, the human senses, and the human intellect are not equipped to deal with *dao* on this level, and the only way a person can ever get in touch with it is by forgetting and transcending his or her ordinary human faculties, by becoming subtler and finer and more potent, more like *dao* itself.

Dao at the periphery, on the other hand, is characterized as the give and take of various pairs of complementary opposites, as the natural ebb and flow of things as they rise and fall, come and go, grow and decline, are born and die. The *Dao de jing* says:

> To contract, there must first be expansion. To weaken, there must first be strengthening. To destroy, there must first be promotion. To grasp, there must first be giving. This is called the subtle pattern. (chap. 36)

Things, as long as they live, develop in alternating movements, commonly described with the terms *yin* and *yang*. It is the nature of life to be in constant change, and of things to always be moving in one or the other direction, up or down, towards lightness or heaviness, brightness or darkness, and so on. Nature is in a continuous flow of becoming, latent and transparent, described as the alternation of yin and yang, complementary characteristics and directions, that cannot exist without each other. This is the nature of *dao* as it can be observed and followed in politics and self-cultivation. If practiced properly, following this aspect of *dao* will ultimately lead to a state of spontaneous alignment with the ineffable *dao*, the creative force at the center (see Roth, 1999). Attaining this state of perfect alignment is described as sagehood and being in complete nonaction *(wuwei)*.

De as a term goes back further than *dao*. It has been identified in the oracle bones, where it seems to indicate a psychic quality of the king that is approved by the spirits and that gives him influence and prestige (Nivison, 1978–1979). Thus, in the Shang dynasty, heaven or the ancestors would recognize and "approve" the *de* of a sacrificer, preferring the "fragrance" of his offerings to those of others (*Shangshu* 30). The good king observes the religious duty to care for *de* in himself, seen as a psychic entity implanted in the person by heaven. Not unlike the concept of *mana* in Polynesian religions, *de* is thus the personal power inherent in a person that allows him or her to be vibrant and strong and rule in harmony with the wishes of the gods and ancestors. By extension, the word also came to mean a basic "goodness" or "generosity," as well as "to admire someone for his generosity," indicating the moral quality (virtue) and psychic force of a person (Munro, 1969).

Used frequently in the politico-philosophical texts of ancient China, *de* denotes an energy in the ruler that enables him to found or continue a dynasty. The theory was that heaven, surveying the world and finding the people suffering from disorder, conferred its mandate (*ming*) on the person with the greatest *de*. His subsequent success attested to and supported heaven's choice. Usually, the first ruler of a dynasty is heavy with *de* and thus able to govern without effort (*Lunyu* 2.1). He does not need to use punishment to gain obedience; the wisest of the land are eager to serve him, knowing that he will heed their advice. Accordingly, the dialogue of Mengzi with the king of Qi is centrally concerned with the question: "What innate *de* does one need to be king?"

Following the establishment of a dynasty, the usual pattern was that the ruler's *de* diminished over time, until a new dynasty needed to be established and received the mandate of heaven. This diminishing, however, was not inevitable, but involved the active forfeiture and loss of *de* by subsequent rulers. It could be prevented through personal restraint and ritual correctness, and many political texts serve to advise rulers on just how to maintain these. If not prevented, a bad last ruler, who was entirely without *de*, would appear on the scene. He would neglect the proper rituals, engage in sensual indulgence, follow the advice of greedy counselors, exploit the people to build grandiose palaces, and govern by punishment and harsh measures.

The result of this vision of *de* is a paradox: the ruler who needs to be straightened out most lacks good counsel and would not listen if he had it, while the one who has good counselors and is wise enough to recognize their wisdom and listen to them is "virtuous" already. As the concept of *de* becomes more recognizably "virtue," which all people may have, it leads to a persistent difficulty in moral philosophy: the question of how *de* is to be imparted to the person who lacks it. The problem exasperated Confucius (e.g., *Lunyu* 5.9, 6.10). Later philosophers had various solutions, such as Mengzi and his famous principle of the inherent goodness of human nature.

Another paradox arises not from the aspect of *de* as moral virtue but from its aspect as psychic force. The person with *de* has prestige, effectiveness, and status—things people desire. However, in order to acquire and strengthen *de*, one must be self-denying, sincerely generous, and generally good. Therefore, efforts to gain more *de* must be self-defeating, unless one seems to be trying to avoid it. The *Dao de jing* solves this issue by saying:

> The person of superior *de* is not conscious of his *de*; therefore he has *de*. The person of inferior *de* never loses sight of his *de*; therefore he loses *de*. The person of superior *de* takes no action and has no ulterior motive

> for doing anything. The person of inferior *de* takes many actions and follows ulterior motives in doing so. (chap. 38)

Thus, the person with the greatest *de* is unassuming and unimpressive, follows the patterns of *dao* in nonaction, and comes to serve all. Again, the text says: "Strong *de* appears as if unsteady; / true substance seems to be changeable" (chap. 41).

The person in the *Dao de jing* who has perfect *de* is also most in line with *dao*: the sage, who can be, but does not have to be, the ruler. The sage is described as unobtrusive, inactive, and independent, free from all possessions or attachments and without a formal teaching or program of action. Because he is all these things, which match him to the natural forces of heaven and earth, "the sage is whole" (chap. 22) and his accomplishments are thorough and long-lasting. Part of his permeating effect is that he subtly and imperceptibly—like the *dao*—spreads *de* by just being, imposing some of his psychic force and inherent goodness on others. Thereby he "causes people to be unknowing and free from desires, so that the smart ones will not dare to impose" (chap. 3). He is "always there to help the people, rejecting no one and no creature" (chap. 27), never puts himself forward in any way yet finds himself a nucleus of social and cosmic activity.

> Not presenting himself, he is radiant. Not thinking himself right, he is famous. Not pushing himself forward, he is meritorious. Not pitying himself, he is eminent. (chap. 22)

The *Dao de jing* is a good example of a text where the political quality of *de* as virtue is conflated with the more psychological aspect of *de* as inherent life force. In this latter sense, *de* indicates the essential character of anyone or anything, effective in interaction with people and things. The same is also apparent in other philosophical texts. Thus, Confucius says that "the *de* of the ruler is wind; that of the people is grass" (*Lunyu* 12.19); and the correspondence system of the five phases, which fully developed in the Han dynasty, describes its different aspects as the *wu de* or the "five powers" (see Yates, 1997).

In the *Zhuangzi* (the *Book of Master Zhuang*, the second major text of ancient Daoism, compiled in the third century BCE), this more physical yet intangible aspect of *de* is made clear in a chapter called "The Sign of Virtue Complete" (chap. 5), and particularly in the story of the suckling pigs. Told in the voice of Confucius, it tells of a group of little pigs nursing at the body of their dead mother. "After a while they gave a start and ran away, leaving the body behind, because they could no longer see their likeness in her. . . . They loved not her body but the thing that moved her body"(i.e., her *de*). By the same token, several other stories in the same chapter tell of people who have lost a part of their body (maimed in war or as punishment) but are in no way impaired in their *de*, their inherent life force—the thing that moves the body—still being complete.

To sum up, *de* means the inherent force and power that moves the world and makes people and animals come to life. It can be held to a greater or lesser degree, be purer or cruder, superior or inferior. When strong and radiant, it imparts itself to others and creates harmony and good government, thus resulting in a "virtuous" situation and imbuing its carrier with virtue—in the original sense of *virtus*, the power that makes a man strong and valiant. When lost, it results in death or the loss of inherent integrity—both cosmic and moral—which in turn causes political corruption and the downfall of dynasties.

Dao and *de* in combination occur mainly in Daoist texts. The *Dao de jing* is the classic example. Divided into eighty-one chapters, the text also has two major parts, a *Dao jing*, and a *De jing*. The former discusses the more cosmic dimensions of life and the larger perspective of Daoist thought; the latter focuses on the concrete activities and patterns of daily life. *De* here describes the activation of *dao* in the visible cycles of existence; that is, *dao* at the periphery. Both parts are of equal importance in the text, but while the standard version of the *Dao de jing* places the *dao* part first, the manuscripts found at Mawangdui (168 BCE) reverse the order (see Henricks, 1989).

A fifth-century religious Daoist text that takes up the *Dao de jing* in its mystical dimension and links it to practices of ritual and self-cultivation also discusses the relationship between *dao* and *de*. Section 10 of the *Xisheng jing* (Scripture of western ascension) relates *dao* and *de* and connects both to the social virtues of Confucianism:

> In *dao*, make nonbeing the highest; in *de* make kindness your master. In ceremony, make righteousness your feeling; in acting, make grace your friend. In benevolence, make advantage your ideal; in faith, make efficaciousness your goal. . . .When kindness, social responsibility, ceremony, and faith are lost, *dao* and *de* are also discarded, they perish and decay. When social *de* is not substantiated by *dao*, it will be supported only by material wealth. (Kohn, 1991, p. 242)

In the same way, the texts suggests that "the way the good person acts in the world can be compared to the bellows: he never contends with others, his *de* always depends on *dao*. This is because he is empty and void and utterly free from desires" (sect. 18). *Dao* and *de* in this text are thus seen as closely related, and one cannot be cultivated without the other. More importantly, the concept of *de* is expanded to include the various specific virtues of Confucian society.

The most detailed Daoist discussion of the relation of *dao* and *de* is found in the *Daoti lun* (On the embodiment of *dao*), a short scholastic treatise associated with Sima Chengzhen (647–735), the twelfth patriarch of Highest Clarity (Shangqing) Daoism. According to the text, "*dao* is all-pervasive; it transforms all from the beginning. *De* arises in its following; it completes all beings to their end. They appear in birth and the completion of life. In the world, they have two different names, yet fulfilling their activities, they return to the same ancestral ground. *Dao* and *de* are two and yet always one. Therefore, there is no *dao* outside of the omnipresence of *de*. There is no *de* different from the completion of life through *dao*. They are one and still appear as two. *Dao* is found in endless transformation and pervasive omnipresence. *De* shines forth in the completion of life and in following along. They are always one; they are always two. Two in one, they are all-pervasive. All-pervasive, they can yet be distinguished. Thus their names are *dao* and *de*" (*Daoti lun* 1a; see Kohn, 1998, p. 130).

According to this, *dao* and *de* are two aspects of the underlying creative power of life; they need each other and depend on each other. They are different yet the same, separate yet one, nameless yet named, at rest yet in constant movement. Pervading all, penetrating all, they are indistinct, yet can also be distinguished and named, creating a particular vision of reality. Names and reality, then, raise the problem of epistemology and knowledge of *dao*. Both names and reality ultimately belong to the same underlying structure that essentially can never be grasped. But they are also an active part of the world.

The practical application of this concept of *dao* and *de* as two aspects of the same underlying power is realized in Daoist cultivation. Through mystical practice, adepts strip off all names and classifications in their minds, and allow the "chaos perfected" nature of *dao* to emerge. *Chaos*, as the text explains, means "without distinctions," something, not a thing, that cannot be called by any name. *Perfected* means "total and centered in itself," some not-thing that has no referent outside of itself. Speaking of self or beings as "chaos perfected" thus creates a dichotomy that is not there originally. Any name, even that attached to the human body, arises from a conscious self and is mere projection. The concept is a formal expression of a perceived difference—it is unrelated to the being as being, as chaos perfected (*Daoti lun* 5a).

Knowledge of *dao* is thus a contradiction in terms, yet that is precisely what Daoism is about, what adepts strive to realize. It can only be attained in utter so-being, a state that is both empty and serene and not empty and not serene at the same time. It thereby comes close to *dao*, which embodies emptiness and rests originally in serenity, yet is also actualized in the living world and moves along with beings and things (*Daoti lun* 5b).

The close connection of *de* to *dao* in this vision is applied to guide practitioners to an integrated mystical vision of the universe and lead them toward the attainment of sagehood and oneness with *dao*. *De* helps to explain why, "if there is no difference between all beings and *dao*, should one cultivate it at all?" The answer is that "cultivation makes up for the discrepancy, however minor, between the root and its embodiment, and leads back to original nonbeing" (*Daoti lun* 8b). *De*, the visible, tangible, and active part of *dao* in the world is the bridge that allows the first step in this direction—a major stepping stone in the recovery of the original flow of life in *dao*.

SEE ALSO Chinese Religion, overview article; Daoism, overview article.

BIBLIOGRAPHY

Graham, A. C. *Disputers of the Tao: Philosophical Argument in Ancient China.* La Salle, Ill., 1989. Overview of ancient Chinese thought, discussing different dimensions of the concept of *dao*.

Hansen, Chad. *A Daoist Theory of Chinese Thought: A Philosophical Interpretation.* New York, 1992. Presentation of *dao* as meta-language in relation to various philosophical discourses.

Henricks, Robert, ed. and trans. *Lao-Tzu: Te-Tao ching.* New York, 1989. Translation of the *Dao de jing* as found in several manuscript versions at Mawangdui.

Kohn, Livia. *Taoist Mystical Philosophy: The Scripture of Western Ascension.* Albany, N.Y., 1991. Translation and discussion of the fifth-century scripture *Xisheng jing*.

Kohn, Livia. "Taoist Scholasticism: A Preliminary Inquiry." In *Scholasticism: Cross-Cultural and Comparative Perspectives,* edited by José Ignacio Cabezón, pp. 115–140. Albany, N.Y., 1998. Discussion of the speculative dimension of religious Daoism, including a presentation and partial translation of the *Daoti lun*.

LaFargue, Michael, trans. and ed. *The Tao of the Tao-te-ching.* Albany, N.Y., 1992. Translation and interpretation of the *Dao de jing* with particular attention to the vision of *dao*.

Munro, Donald J. "The Origin of the Concept of *Te*." In *The Concept of Man in Early China,* edited by D. J. Munro, pp. 185–197. Stanford, Calif., 1969; reprint, Ann Arbor, Mich., 2001. On the earliest understanding of the concept of *de*.

Nivison, David S. "Royal 'Virtue' in Shang Oracle Inscriptions." *Early China* 4 (1978–1979): 52–55. On the most ancient forms and meanings of *de*.

Roth, Harold D., trans. and ed. *Original Tao: Inward Training* (Nei-yeh) *and the Foundations of Taoist Mysticism.* New York, 1999. Translation and discussion of mystical chapters of the *Guanzi*, an ancient Daoist text.

Schwartz, Benjamin. *The World of Thought in Ancient China.* Cambridge, Mass., 1985. Overview of ancient Chinese philosophy.

Vandermeersch, Leon. *Wangdao ou La voie royale: Recherches sur l'esprit des institutions de la Chine archaique.* 2 vols. Paris, 1980. Extensive discussion of the "*dao*" of the king in ancient China, examining historical and philosophical sources.

Yates, Robin D. S., trans. and ed. *Five Lost Classics: Tao, Huang-Lao, and Yin-Yang in Han China.* New York, 1997. Translation and discussion of proto-Daoist materials found at Mawangdui.

LIVIA KOHN (2005)

DAOCHUO (562–645), known in Japan as Dōshaku; Chinese pioneer of Pure Land Buddhism in East Asia. Daochuo advocated devotion to Amitābha Buddha and rebirth in his Pure Land as the only practice in our age that would guarantee salvation. Although Pure Land devotion was popular among most Mahāyāna Buddhists as a supplementary practice, Daochuo followed Tanluan (c. 488–c. 554) in regarding it as necessary for salvation. Other forms of Buddhism he branded as the "path of the sages" *(shengdao),* too difficult to practice during these times.

A religious crisis caused in part by the bewildering demands of Indian Buddhist texts in the eyes of Chinese practitioners was exacerbated by famine and war in the Bingzhou area of Shansi Province where Daochuo lived, and he became the first Pure Land thinker to proclaim that the ten-thousand-year historical period predicted by the scriptures for the final decline of Buddhism (i.e., the *mofa;* Jpn., *mappō*) was at hand. Accordingly, he deemed traditional practices inadequate since no one could attain enlightenment based on self-effort. For Daochuo, the only hope was through outside help. He preached that the *Wuliangshou jing* (the *Larger Sukhāvatīvyūha Sūtra*) was designed for this period and that reliance on the compassionate vows of the Buddha Amitābha—which guarantee people of ordinary religious capacities rebirth in his Pure Land followed by speedy and painless enlightenment there—was the only soteriologically effective action remaining.

After his conversion to Pure Land in 609, Daochuo took up residence in the Xuanzhong Monastery. There, he lectured over two hundred times on the *Kuan wu-liang-shou ching (*Amitāyurdhyāna Sūtra)* and advocated its practices, especially the vocal recitation of Amitābha's name *(nianfo;* Jpn., *nembutsu).* Departing from the view of Tanluan, for whom *nianfo* involved a transcendent quality of mystical union with Amitābha's name, Daochuo was the first Chinese Buddhist to teach reliance on verbal recitation, which was to be aided by bushels of beans or rosaries to record the number of recitations. (Daochuo himself is alleged to have recited the name of Amitābha as much as seventy thousand times a day.) As a consequence, Pure Land devotion spread rapidly among the laity under the slogan "chant the Buddha's name and be reborn in the Pure Land" *(nianfo wangsheng)* and rosaries became ubiquitous in Chinese Buddhism.

Because the prajñāpāramitā literature affirmed that reality is characterized by both form and emptiness, Daochuo argued for the legitimacy of using verbal recitations and attention to the physical aspect of Amitābha and his Pure Land. These practices, he believed, were temporary expedients to lead people to formlessness, nonattachment, and nonduality after rebirth in the Pure Land. In his only surviving writing, the *Anloji,* Daochuo acknowledges that understanding the Pure Land as formless is superior to seeing it as form, and that one's original motivation should be a desire for enlightenment *(bodhicitta)* in order to save others, not just desire for the bliss of Pure Land. However, according to the Mahāyāna doctrine of "two truths," those who understand the ultimate truth of emptiness are able to use the conventional truth of form to save beings, thus legitimizing temporary attachment to concrete forms in Pure Land devotionalism.

The most important disciple of Daochuo was Shandao (613–681), who wrote systematic works that firmly established Pure Land as a major religious tradition in East Asia and influenced Honen in Japan. It was the sense of crisis and urgency that permeates the *Anloji* that dramatized the necessity of Pure Land devotion, while the concrete methods of practice that Daochuo promoted made Pure Land attractive and accessible to common people. Pure Land devotion thus became a popular social movement in China for the first time, and the sound of Amitābha's name has been chanted unceasingly in Chinese Buddhist worship ever since.

See Also Honen; Jingtu; Mappō Shandao; Tanluan.

Bibliography

The *Anloji* (Jpn., Anrakushū) of Daochuo is available in George Eishin Shibata's "A Study and Translation of the *Anraku Shū*" (M.A. thesis, Ryūkoku University, 1969).

Readers of Japanese will want to consult Nogami Shunjō's *Chugoku jōdo sansoden* (Kyoto, 1970) and Yamamoto Bukkotu's *Dōshaku kyōgaku no kenkyū* (Kyoto, 1957).

David W. Chappell (1987 and 2005)

DAOISM

This entry consists of the following articles:

AN OVERVIEW
THE DAOIST RELIGIOUS COMMUNITY
DAOIST LITERATURE
HISTORY OF STUDY

DAOISM: AN OVERVIEW

The English word *Daoism,* with its nominalizing suffix, has no counterpart in the Chinese language. The term has been used in Western writings on China to refer to a wide range of phenomena. First, scholars employ the term *Daoism* to designate early philosophical texts classified as representing *daojia* (schools of the Dao) in early Chinese bibliographic works. Some of these, such as the *Dao de jing* (The classic of the way and its power), also known as the *Laozi* after its supposed author, propounded methods of governance based on mystical gnosis, inaction on the part of the ruler, and a metaphysics centered on the concept of the Dao. Others, such as the eponymous *Zhuangzi,* emphasized mystical union with the Dao and equanimity in the face of death and other natural processes.

Second, given the staunch antipathy toward Confucian methods of social organization common to texts classified *daojia,* the term *Daoism* has been employed in modern scholarship to mark a wide range of anti-Confucian, utopian, and escapist strains of thought. For instance, eremitic withdrawal from government service, a practice with deep roots in the Confucian tradition, was until recently routinely portrayed as "Daoism."

Third, and even more loosely, *Daoism* has been used in works on China to express a sort of free-flowing effortlessness informing individual endeavors, especially the arts of calligraphy, painting, music, and the like. Fourth, *Daoism* has been used to refer to any Chinese religious practice that is not identifiably Confucian or Buddhist. Fifth, and more strictly, the term *Daoism* is used by scholars to translate the Chinese term *daojiao* (literally, "teachings of the Dao"), the closest analogue for our term *Daoism.* The Chinese, like the Japanese, had no formal name for their native religion until the arrival of Buddhism. The term *daojiao* was thus fairly widely adopted to distinguish Daoist religious practice from *fojiao,* "the teachings of the Buddha," or Buddhism.

The present entry deals solely with these religious movements. Even with our narrower focus, problems of definition remain. Most Daoist organizations lacked or failed to emphasize elements deemed essential in other religions. With some exceptions, most Daoists throughout history would agree that their religion did not have a single founder, a closed canon of scriptures, a unified creed, exclusive criteria of lay membership, or a stable pantheon. Historically speaking, the most important structuring force was not internal, but external to the religion. In its efforts to impose order on the realm, the state from time to time sought to control Daoism through overseeing the initiation of clerics, the number of temples, the approved canon, and the like. While none of these attempts were ultimately successful, they did provide impetus for stricter organizational cohesion than would otherwise have been the case.

The high degree of doctrinal flexibility deployed by Daoist organizations often leads modern scholars to debate which specific ideas and practices might or might not be called *Daoist.* A more productive approach, one that emphasizes not what Daoism is, but how various traditions functioned within society, will notice how Daoism has remained an open system, accepting elements drawn from diverse sources and organizing them according to a constellation of key principles and practices. None of these constituents are exclusive to or original with the Daoist traditions. Yet the distinctiveness of the religion lies in the combination of such elements into a structure of beliefs and practices with distinct priorities. These priorities are explored in the following section.

KEY ASPECTS OF DAOISM. The defining concept of the Daoist religion is the Dao itself, understood in a particular way. The term *dao,* originally denoting a "way" or "path," came to be used in pre-Han philosophical discourse to refer to the proper course of human conduct and, by extension, to the teachings of any philosophical school, especially insofar as these were based on the venerated ways of the sages of antiquity. In the *Laozi,* the *Zhuangzi,* and other early writings, the Dao came to be seen not as human order, but as the metaphysical basis of natural order itself, inchoate yet capable of being comprehended by the sage, primordial yet eternally present. This *Dao* of the early thinkers informs religious Daoist texts as well, but with an added dimension of great significance. For Daoists, the Dao underwent further transformations, analogous to those it underwent at the beginnings of time, to incarnate itself in human history. The Dao itself is seen as anthropomorphic, possessed of likes and dislikes, desires, sentiments, and motivations—the full range of human emotions. At the same time, the Dao might act in history through avatars, such as Laozi, who were fully human in appearance. Finally, a number of deities, including those resident in the human body, are regarded as divine hypostases of the Dao.

Qi has been variously translated as "breath," "pneuma," "vapor," or "energy." Seen as the basic building block of all things in the universe, *qi* is both energy and matter. In its primordial form, before division, the Dao is described as "nothingness," void and null. The first sign that it was about to divide, a process that would eventuate in the creation of the sensible world, was the appearance within this nothingness of *qi,* a term that originally seems to have meant "breath" or "steam." All physical objects in the universe are thus composed of relatively stable *qi,* while rarified *qi* is responsible for motion and energy and is the vital substance of life. In that the Dao is characterized by regular and cyclical change, the transformations of *qi* could be described in terms of recurring cycles, marked off in terms of *yin, yang,* the five phases, or the eight trigrams of the *Yi jing.* In such interlocking systems, *qi* was the intervening matrix by which things sharing the same coordinates in the cycle might resonate and influence one another.

Daoists, building both on such cosmological speculation and on various practices for extending life that featured the induction into the body of pure, cosmic *qi,* came to regard *qi* as the primary medium by which one might apprehend and eventually join with the Dao. Most meditation practices, in one way or another, involve swallowing *qi* and circulating it within the body. The primary difference between Daoist meditations and similar hygiene practices is that Daoists visualize the substance either in deified form or as the astral sustenance for *qi*-formed deities resident in the body. In fact, all of the gods are held to be concretions of *qi* from the earliest moments of the Dao's division. *Qi,* particularly that mysterious substance known as *yuan qi* (primal *qi*) thus bridges the gulf between the sensible and the supramundane worlds.

Macrocosm-microcosm. While all existence is seen to be part of the Dao, movements away from its primordial condition of unity are held to be destructive, evil, and transgressive. The perfect human is thus imagined to be a flawless microcosm of the cosmic whole, with the bodily spirits perfectly attuned to their counterparts in the macrocosm. The most common depiction of the body in Daoist writings holds that it is divided into three realms, corresponding to the tripartite cosmic division into heaven, humanity, and earth. A spot in the brain, between and behind the eyebrows, controls the palaces of the head; the heart, organ of sentience and emotion, controls the center; and a spot above the pubis, center of reproduction, controls the life force. These are sometimes called the "three primes" or the "three cinnabar fields." From an initial unity before birth, the human body moves towards increased diversity and closer to death.

Daoist ritual is much concerned with identifying and combating the forces of aging, degeneration, and illness. The goal, at once temporal and spatial, is to bring the various aspects of the body back into unified harmony. Beings who existed in this state are called *xian* (Transcendents) or *zhenren* (Perfected). Generally, *xian* had once been human, while *zhenren* are pure manifestations of aspects of the Dao, though this distinction is not always strictly maintained.

In the correlative cosmology of Chinese science developed during the early Han dynasty, the earth was held to mirror the heavens, so that each portion of the realm corresponded precisely with a sector of the heavens. This correspondence was the basis for the determination of the celestial omens that were regularly reported to the throne. The pole star and surrounding constellations corresponded to the emperor and his court, so that "invasions" of meteors or comets in that portion of the sky were held to be particularly dire portents. In addition, four (and later five) mountains, or "marchmounts," were designated the corners and center of the square earth, symbolically encompassing the realm and corresponding to the five phases. These mountains, which support the sky dome, were thus points where communication with heaven was easiest. Most important in this regard was the eastern marchmount, Taishan, associated with the east, the rising of the sun, and new beginnings. Here a number of Chinese emperors ascended to perform a rite called the *fengshan* to seal with heaven their mandate to rule.

These concepts were further developed in Daoism. Daoist ritual often focuses on the northern dipper, whose movements mark the passage of time, and on the palaces of the apex of heaven, the higher gods of which are described in great detail. The other asterisms, the sun, and the moon also house gods responsible for the orderly revolutions of these celestial bodies who could be accessed through ritual. Eventually, all of the marchmounts boasted Daoist temples.

Bureaucratic pantheons. Imperial symbolism extends into almost every aspect of the Daoist religion. Aspects of the Dao are visualized as the lord of heaven with a dizzying number of spirit-officials. Just as the well-run kingdom depended on the labors of its bureaucracy, so the workings of the cosmos depend on this pantheon of spirits. The human body is held to house a corresponding pantheon of spirits. Daoist methods for communicating with the spirits of the body and the heavens involve both visualization meditations and the actual delivery of documents, swallowed for the internal spirits and buried, submerged, or burned for delivery to the cosmic pantheon. Illness, like disorders in the human realm, can be cured through such petitioning rites, the goal of which is to bring disharmony to the attention of the highest gods. When the priest presents such documents, he or she is acting as an official in this celestial pantheon. Because of this, Daoist priests are sometimes called "officials of the Dao."

The gods who fill various ranks in the pantheon, including the highest, are not fixed. Daoists hold that gods, as part of a changeable cosmos, are themselves subject to change and can be promoted or demoted. A number of rituals end with a procedure to "establish merit," whereby the gods invoked in the rite are recommended for promotion in gratitude for their prompt aid. Divinities from Buddhism and the gods worshiped by local cults could also be absorbed into the pantheon. New revelations almost always include information on new gods or rearrangements of the existing pantheon.

Ritual. Meditations and ritual practices are designed to bring individuals and communities back to a state of integration with the Dao. Modeled on the dawn assemblies held by the human monarch to review his officials, the basic ritual program brings the Daoist priest in vision before the assembled bureaucracy of heaven where, through his merit, he can formally request the rectification of disease or other disorder. Ritual robes, headgear, and paraphernalia, all carefully described in Daoist manuals, are fashioned after the styles of the imperial court. Communication with the spirits of heaven takes place sometimes through recitation of petitions, sometimes through their presentation by burning. In addition, some documents—talismans and longer texts—are written in "celestial script," an imaginative form of writing loosely resembling ancient forms of Chinese graphs, but illegible to ordinary mortals.

One striking feature of Daoist ritual is the way it collapses space and time. The ritual space is constructed to symbolize the cosmos, overlaid with the vertical dimension of the center, which represents the highest courts of the heavens. Temporally, Daoist ritual seeks to bring its performers back to the moment of cosmogenesis, when the Dao was integrated and whole. In its fully developed form, Daoist ritual became a colorful pageant that had a marked influence on Chinese drama. The ascent of the priests to the courts of heaven is outwardly symbolized with banners, retinues of acolytes bearing incense and flowers, and ritual pacing accompanied by austere music.

Eschatology. In its concern with time, Daoism adopted the notion of cyclical return common to ancient Chinese metaphysics. One component of the "Mandate of Heaven" concept was that empires rose and fell in a regular cycle, a cycle that was eventually associated with the cyclical progress of the five phases. Daoist contributions to this system of thought came to the fore particularly when the religion was employed by one or another aspirant to the throne to support his program. But, given that Daoism came into being as a religious entity during the final days of the Han empire, dire pronouncements concerning an imminent sweeping away of the unjust and the establishment of a new kingdom of Great Peace were always part of the religion, helping to support its program of moral reform. One early version promised that the righteous would be the "seed people" of the coming age, chosen to repopulate the new divinely sanctioned kingdom. Equally important were the contributions of Buddhist scripture, whose vast cosmological visions and descriptions of "kalpa cycles" came to inform eschatological writings.

Morality. The idea that humans, through indulging their desires and hoarding what should be shared, block the correct circulation of energies that should exist in the ideal Daoist kingdom has been present from the beginning. As noted above, illness was seen by early Daoists as a sign of such transgression. Followers were urged to repent of transgressions and to petition the deities to repair the imbalances caused thereby. The primary transgression mentioned in Daoist writings seems to be covetousness or desire. Even when providing explanations for the *Laozi*, however, early Daoists did not follow that text in its rejection of Confucian virtues such as humaneness and responsibility. Instead, they argued that such virtues were too often merely outward and advocated the practice of "secret virtue," good acts performed secretly so that only the gods would know and reward the agent. Eventually, Daoist texts and morality tracts regularly came to include lists of precepts to be followed by priests and by the laity.

Relations with other religions. The doctrinal flexibility of Daoist practice meant that the system was quite accommodating to Buddhism, and later to such foreign imports as Manichaeism. This ability to absorb the beliefs and practices of other religions could elicit a negative response from proponents of the targeted religion. One idea that resurfaced several times in Chinese history was that Buddhism was but a foreign version of Daoism, created by Laozi himself when he disappeared through the western gates of the Chinese kingdom. Insofar as this story was related to show that Daoism was fit for the Han peoples, while Buddhism had been specifically crafted for "foreign barbarians," it was rightly seen by Buddhists as an attempt to co-opt their religion. Books propounding this theory were imperially banned several times.

Most Daoist adaptations of Buddhist doctrine and practice were innocent of such motives. Since Buddhist sūtras were translated into Chinese, it was natural that Buddhist doctrine had to be explained in native terms. Daoism often informed or, through adapting Buddhist doctrine and practice to its own uses, reconfigured those native understandings. While appropriations went both ways, it is undeniable that many features of the Daoist religion are adaptations of ideas brought in with Buddhism. The distinctive Daoist ideas of rebirth, of the underworld purgatories, of monastic life—to name but a few—all grew from productive interactions with Buddhism. Generations of Chinese scholar-officials and Buddhist scholiasts sought to clarify the boundaries between the two religions, but the attempt proved less than successful. Indeed, as Erik Zürcher (1983) has remarked, China's three great religions—Buddhism, Daoism, and Confucianism—might be envisioned as a floating iceberg with three peaks. Above the waterline, the peaks are distinct, but below, where the religion of the common masses is situated, they merge into undifferentiation.

Such is not the case for Daoist interactions with the popular, or common, religion of the Chinese people, which is centered on cults to the powerful dead who are often consulted through mediums and propitiated with meat sacrifice. Originally, Daoist organizations forthrightly banned all such worship of "blood eaters," arguing that these unholy gods only drained the sustenance of those who worshipped them. Eventually, a few such figures were admitted to the Daoist pantheon and other associated practices, such as fortune-telling, were allowed. Nonetheless, most Daoist lineages strove first and foremost to distinguish their practice from that of common cult religion.

DAOISM AT THE BEGINNING OF THE IMPERIAL ERA: FIRST AND SECOND CENTURIES CE. As mentioned above, the Daoist religion began with the founding of the Way of the Celestial Masters (*Tianshi dao*) in the second century CE. Recent archeological finds and increased scholarly attention have begun to clarify the lively religious scene of the Han dynasty (206 BCE–220 CE) that provided the backdrop to this event and contributed elements that were shaped into the Daoist synthesis.

From later Warring States times, shadowy *fangshi* or "masters of prescriptions" sought patronage with various rulers, promulgating esoteric techniques passed from master to disciple. These included knowledge of paradises beyond the seas, alchemical, magical, and medical techniques, and the ability to contact spirits. From such sources there grew a widespread popular belief in the existence of *xian*, "Transcendents" or "Immortals," winged beings who could bypass death, travel vast distances to inhabit remote paradises, or confer blessings on deserving mortals. One of the most powerful of these was the Queen Mother of the West, who was held to reside on the mythical cosmic mountain Kunlun. In the opening years of the common era, a panic spread through the Shandong peninsula when farmers left their fields and traveled west to greet what they said was the imminent arrival of this deity. The Queen Mother would eventually find a place in the Daoist pantheon. From around the same time we have records of others sacrificing to the deified Laozi, regarding him as a salvific, cosmic deity in the fashion of the archaic deity Taiyi.

Another aspect of Han belief that was adapted into Daoism was the idea that documents addressed to the bureaucracy of the otherworld should be interred with the dead to facilitate the transfer from one realm to the other and to ensure that the dead did not return to injure the living. Archeologically recovered documents, addressed to the Yellow, or Heavenly, Thearch and his officers attest to this belief.

Perhaps the most important ingredient, however, was the constellation of ideas surrounding Han imperial religion. These include the belief that heaven responds directly to human actions, rewarding good and evil, and that heaven forecasts its will through signs and portents. The Han court invested a good deal of administrative energy in collecting and analyzing such portents. This led to the composition of apocryphal addenda (*chenwei*) to the imperially-sanctioned Confucian classics that detailed the systems underlying celestial omens and explained how to interpret them. According to these texts, heaven regularly intervened in human history by sending its envoys in human form. Normally, these divinely engendered beings were seen to be the founders of new dynasties. But cultural heroes, such as Confucius, were also born in this fashion.

In the chaotic years leading up to the fall of the Han dynasty, a number of aspirants to the throne, holding that celestial approbation had departed from the Liu house, employed religious persuasions of the sort that had supported the divine mandate of the dynasty to mobilize followers. Among the rebel groups mentioned by court historians was the organization to which later Daoists traced the beginnings of their dispensation, the Celestial Masters. Sometimes mentioned by historians in the same tone was a more infamous group, the Yellow Turbans.

Centered in the eastern reaches of the Han empire, the Yellow Turban rebellion, led by a man named Zhang Jue, was a well-planned insurrection organized around a millennial religious ideology. Zhang called his movement the "Way of Great Peace" and, under the slogan that the "Yellow Heaven is about to rise," sought to position himself and his followers as the vanguard of a new and perfect society. It is likely that this ideology was drawn from a revealed book, the *Scripture of Great Peace*, perhaps a version of a work that had been promulgated earlier in the Han dynasty by a court faction. The *Scripture of Great Peace*, which survives only in fifth- or sixth-century recensions, promotes an ideal social structure based on cosmic principles, particularly the idea that the moral action of each person determines not only individual wellbeing, but also the health of the body politic and the smooth functioning of the cosmos.

The Yellow Turbans converted people to their cause through healing practices, including incantation, doses of water infused with the ashes of talismans, and confession of sins. The *Scripture of Great Peace* relates confession to the idea that political and cosmic disease is caused by humans and must be cured on the individual level. Sin, in this text, is the failure to act in accord with one's social role, thereby blocking the circulation of the Dao's energies. Those who should labor with their bodies fail to do so, but live in idleness; those who possess wealth keep it for their own enjoyment rather than allowing it to circulate; and those who should teach virtue only "accumulate" it for their personal benefit. These and other blockages to the circulation of goods and life forces lead, by this account, to illness and death. This strict correspondence between microcosm and macrocosm was to be a prominent feature of later Daoist practice.

Zhang Jue organized his followers into thirty-six administrative regions. The new age of the Yellow Heaven was to dawn in the year 184, the beginning of a new sexagesimal cycle by the Chinese calendar. Despite well-laid plans, news of Zhang Jue's uprising reached the court and the Yellow Turbans were defeated within the year.

The ideologies and practices of the early Celestial Masters were superficially similar to those of the Yellow Turbans. Historians note that the early Celestial Masters knew of the *Scripture of Great Peace*, but there is no conclusive evidence of any direct connection between the two movements. The Celestial Masters revered as founder Zhang Ling (Zhang Daoling in Daoist texts), a man of Pei (in modern Jiangsu province) who traveled to the kingdom of Shu (the western part of modern Sichuan) to study the Dao on Mount Cranecall. Daoist texts record that there, in the year 142 CE, he was visited by the "Newly appeared Lord Lao," the deified Laozi. Laozi granted him the title "Heavenly [-appointed] Teacher" or Celestial Master. On Ling's death, the title of Celestial Master was passed on to his son Heng, and eventually to his grandson, Lu. The line of transmission, it is claimed, remains unbroken this day, but the first three Celestial Masters, and their wives, are the most important. Later Daoist ritual regularly includes the invocation of their names.

Some scholars have suggested, however, that the legends of the first two Celestial Masters were fabrications, since only Zhang Lu is mentioned in non-Daoist historical records. Nonetheless, a stele inscription found in the modern province of Sichuan, recording the initiation of a group of libationers, or priests, in 173 CE, attests to the fact that Celestial Master practice existed at that time and already had produced a corpus of scriptures.

The Celestial Masters divided their followers into twenty-four parishes or dioceses, each headed by a libationer. But this hierarchy was not organized along traditional lines. Women and non-Han peoples—two groups so devalued in traditional Chinese society that accounts of them, if they appeared at all, were placed at the end of standard histories—were welcomed as full members of the Celestial Masters' community. Both could serve as libationers, and men were encouraged to emulate virtues specifically associated with women.

Libationers instructed the people by means of the *Dao de jing*, which was to be recited chorally so that even the illiterate could be instructed. The *Xiang'er* commentary to the *Dao de jing*, attributed to Zhang Lu and surviving in part in a Tang dynasty manuscript recovered from Dunhuang, attests to the novel ways in which they interpreted the text.

As Terry Kleeman (1994) has shown, the central teaching of the Celestial Masters, called "the Correct and Orthodox Covenant with the Powers," held that "the gods do not eat or drink, the master does not accept money." This stricture, as clarified in the *Xiang'er* commentary, mandates the rejection of blood sacrifice, central to popular and imperial cult. In place of gods, and their priests, who could be swayed by offerings, the Celestial Masters revered deities who were pure emanations of the Dao and ate only *qi*. Agents of this unseen bureaucracy resided even in the human body and so could not be deceived. They would be moved only by good deeds or ritually presented petitions of contrition. In any event, they kept detailed records of each person's merits and demerits.

The Celestial Masters cured illness with confession and the ingestion of talisman water. The ill were to confess their transgressions in specially constructed "chambers of quietude" and to present the necessary written petitions to the offices of heaven, earth, and water. Three times a year—the seventh of the first month, the seventh of the seventh month, and the fifth of the tenth month by the lunar calendar—people were to assemble at their assigned parish. There, libationers would verify records of death and birth, and communal meals would be held. On this occasion, members of the community were to present a good-faith offering of five pecks of rice. This gave rise to an alternate name for the community, the "Way of the Five Pecks of Rice" or, in less favorable sources, "the rice bandits." Beyond these faith-offerings, the community was enjoined to perform acts of merit, such as the building of roads or the provision of free food for travelers.

As Kristofer Schipper (1982) shows in detail, libationers were also responsible for bestowing on the faithful registers recording the number of transcendent "generals," residents of their own bodies, that they were empowered to summon and control. Children of six years of age received a register with one general. By marriageable age, initiates could receive registers listing seventy-five generals, a number that they could double by performing the Celestial Master marriage ritual. This ritual, known as "merging *qi*" included instruction in a precise method of intercourse that could replenish the bodily forces of male and female participants, normally deficient in *yin* and *yang qi* respectively, without the exchange of bodily fluids that led to reproduction. As the *Xiang'er* commentary explains, the Dao wishes people to reproduce, but not to squander their vital energies. Later reformers were to criticize and rectify this practice, which was considered "lascivious" by outsiders.

By the end of the second century, Zhang's grandson, Zhang Lu, then head of the community, took sanctuary in the Hanzhong Valley, just north of the Sichuan basin and over 200 kilometers southwest of the Han capital of Chang'an (modern Xian). In 215 CE, Zhang Lu surrendered to Cao Cao, the Han general whose son was to inaugurate the Wei dynasty (220–265) of the Three Kingdoms period. As a result of this act of fealty, a large portion of the Celestial Master community was relocated from Hanzhong to areas farther north, while many of its leaders were enfeoffed or otherwise ennobled. While some followers doubtless remained from the early period in Sichuan, the spread of Daoism throughout China as a whole begins with this diaspora of the original Celestial Master community.

A fascinating document found in the Daoist canon, the "Commands and Admonitions for the Families of the Great Dao," dated to the first of the three yearly assemblies in 255, gives us some idea of how the community fared under the Wei kingdom. Delivered in the voice of Zhang Lu, who had doubtless died by that time, the document warns the community of the impending fall of the dynasty and excoriates them for lapses in practice. From this document, we learn that the system of parishes had fallen into disarray and that a number of new texts, including the important *Scripture of the Yellow Court* were in circulation. The "Admonitions" further states that Zhang Lu himself, or at least the medium who now spoke in the voice of Zhang, authored the *Scripture of the Yellow Court*, which presents detailed meditations on the gods of the body.

DAOISM OF THE SIX DYNASTIES: FOURTH THROUGH SIXTH CENTURIES. We hear no more of the Celestial Masters until the Jin dynasty's (265–420) hold on northern China began to weaken early in the fourth century. A group of ethnic Ba families, some two hundred thousand strong, returned to the region of Chengdu where Li Te inaugurated the short-lived theocracy known as the Cheng-Han (302–347). Other Celestial Master adherents came into the region around present-day Nanjing when the Jin dynasty relocated there in 317. The writings of Ge Hong (283–343), a member of an influential southern gentry family, provide detailed information on the vibrant religious scene that the Celestial Masters encountered.

At a young age, Ge Hong formally received from his tutor—a man who claimed that his lineage extended through Ge's great-uncle—"Grand Purity" alchemical scriptures and the *Esoteric Writings of the Three Sovereigns*. Throughout the remainder of his life, Ge collected as many such texts as he could. Though his poverty prevented him from ever concocting an elixir himself, Ge Hong became an ardent proponent of practices of transcendence that extended back to the *fangshi* of the Han. Two works bearing his name have survived. The inner chapters of the eponymous *Baopu zi* (Master who embraces simplicity), known by Ge Hong's style name, represent a spirited defense of the arts of transcendence and include transcriptions of some of the methods Ge studied. Ge ranks such practices, listing herbal recipes meant to prolong life as a distant second to the ingestion of the mineral and metallic products of the alchemist's furnace. The *Traditions of Divine Transcendents*, which survives only in later redactions, provides vivid hagiographies of important transcendent figures, including Laozi and Zhang Daoling, who is here portrayed as a practitioner of alchemy.

While Ge Hong shows only a limited awareness of Celestial Master religion, as Robert Campany (2002) has shown, his writings provide invaluable testimony to the ways religious practitioners operated in the society of the time, gaining reputations for their esoteric arts, seeking patronage, and initiating disciples. Further, Ge's written works attest to several scriptural traditions that were eventually to find their way into the Daoist canon. The most important of these are the two traditions into which Ge was initiated as a youth and the *Five Talismans of Lingbao,* a book of visualization practice and herbal recipes. Indeed, it was through Ge's own family, as well as families related to his by marriage, that Celestial Master Daoism was to be reshaped through an infusion of these southern traditions.

Between the years 363 and 370, the Daoist Yang Xi (330–c. 386) was employed as a spiritual advisor by a gentry family related to Ge's through marriage. Yang's patrons, who had employed before him a Celestial Master libationer, were Xu Mi (303–373), a minor official at the imperial court, and his son Hui (341–c. 370). From his meditation chamber, Yang brought to them enticing revelations from the unseen world. These concerned both the whereabouts in the underworld or heavens of the relatives and acquaintances of the Xus and their circle, as well as complete scriptures outlining new practices. Transmitted from person to person among this privileged group, Yang's *Shangqing* (Upper clarity or supreme purity) scriptures and revealed fragments of divine instruction eventually came to be collected in the first of the tripartite divisions of the Daoist canon. Thereafter, the Shangqing scriptures, augmented by later revelations and additions, became the center of one school of Daoist practice, with its own patriarchs, priests, temples, and liturgies.

Several features distinguished the Shangqing scriptures from the mass of scriptural material produced during this period. First of all, the texts emanated from the highest reaches of the heavens. The Transcendents (*xian*) of earlier scripture occupy only lower positions in the celestial hierarchy. Above them are ranks of even more exalted and subtle beings, the Perfected (or "Authentic Ones," *zhenren*), a term originating in the *Zhuangzi* but here made part of a bureaucratic pantheon of celestial deities. The Perfected, male and female, are clothed in resplendent garb, described in terms of mists and auroras. They are decked out with tinkling gems, symbols of their high office. Their bodies are formed of the purest *qi* and glow with a celestial radiance as they move about the heavens in chariots of light. The texts such beings brought were likewise exalted in that they described the practices the Perfected themselves employed to subtilize their bodies. In fact, one form the Shangqing scriptures take is that of a biography of one or another of the Perfected, replete with descriptions of the practices associated with that deity.

Secondly, the Shangqing scriptures clearly earned their eventual popularity in large part through the compelling way in which they are written. Yang Xi must be counted among the major innovators in the history of Chinese letters. The language of his texts—both poetry and prose—is abstruse, dense, and obscurely allusive. It seems to exemplify as much as express the mysterious qualities of the spirit world to which he had been granted privileged access as the result of his strivings. The macrocosm-microcosm identity familiar from other Daoist texts becomes for Yang license for a multivalence of signification whereby literally whole passages refer simultaneously to, for instance, the placement of palaces in the heavens and the arrangement of spirit-residences in the viscera. Yang frequently uses such devices as synesthetic metaphor to portray how apparent contradictions collapse in the Dao. In addition, because Yang's revelations described spirit marriages with young female Perfected awaiting both him and the Xus, one cannot discount the erotic component of Yang's productions. Yang's unique style was immediately and widely imitated, both by writers of Daoist scripture and by later secular writers.

Finally, the Shangqing texts were prized for their message. The Shangqing texts do not represent a radical break with the past. All of the meditations and rituals found in them have analogues in earlier religious literature. A number of scriptures contain improvements on earlier Celestial Master techniques, while one fragment proves to be a rewritten version of the Buddhist *Sūtra in Forty-two Sections.* What is really new is the way in which the constituent parts are modified to give preeminence to the guided meditations and visualizations of the practitioner. The meditation practice of the Shangqing scripture includes both visionary journeys into the heavens and more direct ways of working with the body.

Visionary journeys have an ancient pedigree in Chinese religion. In the Shangqing scriptures, the adept is instructed to perform purifications and then to visualize his or her body ascending to the sun, moon, stars, or up into the celestial timekeeper, the northern dipper. There, the adept imbibes astral sustenance, the food of the gods, pays homage to the gods, or exchanges documents with them. Practices aimed at perfecting the body also typically involve visualization. While there are quite a few references to drugs and elixirs in the Shangqing texts, the tradition tended to transform more physical practices into meditative experience. Generally, the spirits that inhabit the body are energized through the ingestion of pure *qi,* enjoined not to leave, and merged with their celestial counterparts. In some practices, the joining of bodily gods with those of the macrocosm functions as an interiorization of the Celestial Master sexual practice known as "merging *qi.*" Other techniques teach ways of reenacting the process of gestation using the *qi* of the nine heavens to create an immortal body.

After the death of Yang and the Xus, the fragments of personal revelation and the scriptures Yang had received from the Perfected were scattered. The preservation of such a significant portion of Yang's writings is due to the efforts of Tao Hongjing (456–536), perhaps the foremost scholar of early Daoism. Tao collected the more personal revelations that Yang Xi wrote for the Xus in his *Zheng'ao* (Declarations of the Perfected), an extremely diverse work that includes records of the Perfected mates promised to Yang Xi and Xu Mi, injunctions to Xu Mi and Xu Hui concerning the details of their practice, letters between them, accounts of the underworld topography of Mount Mao, and even records of dreams. As this work cites a number of scriptures, it has proven invaluable to scholars' attempts to reconstruct Daoist history. In addition, Tao Hongjing edited a number of the scriptures that he was able to acquire and preserved annotated passages from them in his *Dengzhen yinjue* (Secret instructions on the ascent to perfection), which survives only in part.

At the very beginning of the fifth century, another southern corpus of scriptures began to emerge, attesting to yet another attempt to reform Daoist practice. These scriptures, collectively known as *Lingbao* (Numinous gem), represent at once a return to the communal practices of the Celestial Masters and a renewed attempt to make Daoism the common religion. The Lingbao scriptures drew upon the religious traditions of the day (*fangshi* practice, Han-period apocrypha, southern practices known to Ge Hong such as those found in the *Lingbao wufu jing* itself, Celestial Master Daoism, Shangqing Daoism, and Buddhism), sometimes copying entire sections of text and presenting them so as to accord with its central doctrines in order to fashion a new, universal religion for a unified China. While Lingbao proponents failed in this attempt—the emperor upon whom they based their hopes, Song Wudi (r. 420–422) failed to reunify the kingdom, and monks expert in the texts they plagiarized, Buddhist and Daoist alike, denounced their productions as forgeries—the Lingbao texts they produced did lead to a new Daoist unity.

While Lingbao descriptions of the spiritual cosmography of the human body differ little from those of the Shangqing scriptures, their soteriology are very different. The Lingbao texts describe an elaborate cosmic bureaucracy that has survived the destruction of the cosmos through countless kalpas, or "world-ages," a concept adapted from Buddhism. At the apex of the pantheon is the Celestial Worthy of Primordial Commencement, a deity who plays somewhat the same role in the Lingbao scriptures as the cosmic Buddha in Buddhist scriptures. By joining with the enduring Dao through keeping its precepts and conducting rituals for the salvation of others, adherents hope to ensure for themselves either a favorable rebirth "as a prince or marquis" or immediate promotion into the celestial bureaucracy. The hymns and liturgies of the scriptures reenact and prepare practitioners for this latter, final destination. This was the first instance in which a version of the Buddhist concept of rebirth was fully integrated into Daoist doctrine. Significantly, Daoists, holding that their religion valued life while Buddhism valued death, did not forward *nirvāṇa* (cessation) as a religious goal. Because later Daoist ritual practice was based on these early Lingbao texts, this explanation of rebirth was to become an enduring feature of the religion.

The moral component of the Lingbao scriptures—a mixture of traditional Chinese morality and Buddhist salvational ethics—is much more prominent than that found in earlier texts. There is also a pronounced proselytizing emphasis. The texts argue that contemporary Daoist and Buddhist practices are but variant paths that lead to the same goal and that the rewritten versions of some practices found in their pages are the original, authentic pronouncements of the Celestial Worthy from prior kalpas. As a result, the Lingbao scriptures give what amounts to the earliest attempt to grade religious practices, an emphasis that led Lu Xiujing (406–477), the Daoist who first catalogued the Lingbao scriptures, to also make a listing of all Daoist texts, entitled the Catalog of the Three Caverns. Lu's catalog originally comprised 1,228 *juan* (scrolls) of texts, of which 138 had not yet been revealed on earth. The texts were divided into three "caverns" or "comprehensive collections": *Dongzhen* (comprehending perfection, containing Shangqing texts), *Dongxuan* (comprehending the mysterious, containing Lingbao texts), and *Dongshen* (comprehending the spirits, containing early southern scriptures). All subsequent Daoist canons were organized into these "three caverns." Three deities, each regarded as a transformation of the former, were designated the ultimate sources of these three collections of texts. These were: (1) for Dongzhen, the Lord of Celestial Treasure, residing in the Heaven of Jade Clarity; (2) for Dongxuan, the Lord of Numinous Treasure, residing in the Heaven of Upper Clarity; and (3) for Dongshen, the Lord of Spiritual Treasure, residing in the Heaven of Grand Clarity. With some modifications, this trinity, also known as the "three pure ones," continued to be central to later Daoist ritual traditions.

In the north of China, reform of the Celestial Masters' practice took a different turn. In 415 and again in 423, Kou Qianzhi (365–448), a Celestial Masters' priest, received from the deified Laozi revelations containing codes explicitly meant to reform aberrant practice and lead to a more tightly organized ecclesia. With the help of a high official, he presented these to the throne of the Toba (a Turkish people) Wei dynasty (386–534). Because the foreign rulers in the north of China were interested in controlling religions that might disguise rebellion, the Toba emperor agreed to make Kou's new dispensation the official religion of the kingdom. The demand for orthodoxy increased to the extent that the emperor was eventually urged to proscribe Buddhism. The Daoist theocracy barely outlived Kou.

Subsequent northern emperors continued to harbor suspicions of unregulated religious practice, however, leading to a series of court debates between Buddhists and Daoists and concomitant attempts to abolish one religion or the other. The best documented of these occurred during the reign of Yuwen Yong, Emperor Wu of the Zhou dynasty (r. 560–578). Harboring the ambition to reunify China, Emperor Wu, who had himself received initiation into Daoist scriptures, held several debates between Buddhists and Daoists to determine which of their doctrines would best complement the Confucian state orthodoxy. Daoist apologists argued, apparently with some success, that their practice extended back into the prehistorical golden age of the Central Kingdom, while the Buddhist religion was a recent foreign import. But the debates were still inconclusive and the emperor charged one of his officials, Zhen Luan, to compose a treatise comparing the two religions. When Zhen produced the "Treatise Deriding the Dao," which debunked the claim of antiquity of Daoist scriptures and undermined the hope for a unifying ideology, the emperor ordered it burned and commissioned the scholarly monk Dao'an to write a new treatise, "Treatise on the Two Teachings." Both works survive in the Buddhist canon, providing scholars with opposition views regarding the Daoist practice of the day. Daoist apologists, on the other hand, preserved no similarly detailed documentation of the debates.

As would happen again and again throughout Chinese history, Emperor Wu's attempts at central control of religion were neither effective nor long lasting. In 574, he ordered that Buddhist and Daoist monks return to lay life and confiscated temple holdings. Later in the same year, he established a central Daoist temple, the Tongdao guan (Observatory for Comprehending the Dao) and commissioned the composition of an encyclopedic collection of Daoist writings, the *Wushang biyao* (Secret essentials of the most high). While the proscriptions did not endure beyond Emperor Wu's death in 578, the controversies continued as subsequent emperors attempted to co-opt the prestige of Buddhism and Daoism to bolster their dynastic designs. Within Daoism, the *Wushang biyao* did have the effect of providing its contents with the stamp of orthodoxy, though at some point the more egregious passages claiming that Buddhist doctrine and practice originated with Daoism were expunged from the collection.

DAOISM UNDER THE TANG (618–907). The rulers of the short-lived Sui dynasty (581–618), which did manage to unify China, favored Buddhism to lend cosmological authority to their state orthodoxy. But millennial expectations, drawn from both Buddhism and Daoism, arose in force again to contribute to the downfall of the dynasty. Foremost among these expectations was the idea, derived from early Daoism and given prominence in the Shangqing scriptures, that the "Perfect Lord" Li Hong would soon descend to sweep away the unjust and establish a rule of great peace. Among those who took on the mantle of the Perfect Lord was Li Yuan, founder of the Tang dynasty. Further, he claimed descent from Laozi, whose given name was said to have been Li Er. Given this, Tang emperors tended thereafter to favor the Daoist religion.

As a result, the Tang period marked a time of consolidation and expansion for the Daoist tradition. Even Wu Zhao (r. 684–705), who proclaimed herself "emperor" and renamed the dynasty Zhou, while giving secondary status to the religion that had lent support to those she sought to replace, took recourse to Daoist symbolism, ritual, and prestige to establish her rule. The most fervent imperial supporter of Daoism was Li Longji (the Xuanzong Emperor, r. 712–756). The emperor's personal involvement with the cult of the dynastic ancestor built up slowly over the course of his long reign. At first he sponsored rituals for the welfare of the state, employing prominent priests such as Sima Chengzhen (647–735) to help revise state ritual and music. He also introduced Laozi's text, the *Dao de jing*, into the state exam system, even composing an imperial commentary to the text. The favor he bestowed on the religion was matched by imperial oversight. He instituted the office of commissioner for Daoist ritual to control at the national level the ordination and registration of the priesthood. Similar oversight was accorded Buddhist institutions.

It was during the second half of Xuanzong's reign that his enthusiasm for the religion came most fully to the fore. The watershed events were the appearance of the divine ancestor to the emperor in dreams and the discovery of a talisman, the whereabouts of which was also revealed by Laozi. As a result of this latter discovery, the emperor changed the reign-name to "Celestial Treasure." He distributed images of Laozi, fashioned after his dream vision, throughout the empire, granted grand titles to the sage, and established official institutes for Daoist study in each prefecture of the realm. As Timothy Barrett (1996) shows, graduates of these institutes could take part in the newly inaugurated Daoist examination in the capital and enter the civil service, the first time religious examinations had ever been used for this purpose. Meanwhile officials reported apparitions of Laozi and other signs of divine approbation with great frequency. Even Xuanzong's flight from the capital as a result of the An Lushan rebellion and his removal from power are not without legends of Laozi's continued support of the emperor.

Due in part to this imperial favor, the Tang dynasty marked a rapid expansion of Daoist belief and practice into the gentry class, with a concomitant growth in Daoist scholarship. A number of encyclopedias, annotations, and local histories survive from the period. In response to the subtleties of Buddhist philosophy, Daoist scholars evolved a number of philosophical approaches to Daoism, from meditations on the self and nurturing life to analyses of the processes by which one might join with the Dao. Distinctive styles of music, art, and dance were also developed. With the regularization of Daoist monasticism, we learn more about women who entered Daoist orders, some clearly attracted by the prospect of gaining more control over their lives. A few gained kingdom-wide reputations for their piety. Once such was Huang Lingwei (c. 640–721), who after a long period of training restored and occupied the shrine of the Shangqing goddess Wei Huacun. Her reconstruction of the site was aided at each step by divine visions and dreams. The number of poems presented to her by famous figures and the laudatory biography written after her death by the official and calligrapher Yan Zhenqing (709–784) attest to her fame.

The practice of alchemy also came into prominence during the Tang. As in other areas of Daoist scholasticism, ancient texts were collected and compared. One representative work is the *Essential Instructions from the Scriptures on the Elixirs of Great Clarity* (Sivin, 1968) by the physician and pharmacologist Sun Simiao (581–682). While the exact extent of elixir ingestion is unknown, a number of literati mention the practice in their writings. In addition, Tang emperors patronized masters of alchemy and several of the later emperors may have died as a result of such experimentation. Meanwhile, the use of alchemical experimentation as a means to observe the workings of the cosmos led to the gradual creation of "inner alchemy," a term that refers to various methods for merging "cinnabar" and "lead" within the body to create the immortal embryo without actual ingestion of mineral or metallic substances. As Fabrizio Pregadio (2000) has shown, this trend began during the late Six Dynasties period (220–589 CE) with the *Zhouyi cantong qi* (Token of the concordance of the three, based on the *Book of Changes*), a work that shows operative alchemy to be a replication of cosmic processes as defined by the symbol systems of the ancient fortune-telling manual, the *Book of Changes.* Widely studied during the Tang, this work, together with the dangers of elixir ingestion, led to the eclipse of operative alchemy.

Later Daoists were to look back on the Tang as a golden age, and often traced their own lineages to real or mythological Tang figures. A more balanced picture of the religion appears in the works of Du Guangting (850–933), the foremost Daoist priest of the Shu kingdom (in present-day Sichuan). Writing as the Tang dynasty lay in ruins, Du's collections of hagiographies, miracle tales, inscriptions, and ritual summaries attest to aspects of the religion that are given short shrift or lacking in earlier sources (Verellen, 1989). Here we learn of the importance of Daoist practice at the local level, the veneration of holy women, and the importance of lay benefactors for the maintenance of temples and images.

DAOISM UNDER THE SONG (960–1279) AND YUAN (1206–1368). In gauging the development of Daoism during the Song and Yuan dynasties, we must avoid the "documentary fallacy." More than half of the texts found in our primary source for the study of the religion, the Ming canon printed in 1445, were compiled after the mid-twelfth century. This dramatic increase in documentation, in part the result of the invention of printing and consequent spread of literacy, provides evidence, unavailable from earlier times, on how the religion operated at all strata of society. This has sometimes led scholars to underestimate the penetration of Daoism into lower levels of society in earlier periods and to overstate the spread of the religion during the Song and Yuan. Even accounting for this distorting factor, however, it does appear that social changes—especially the rise in mercantilism, increased literacy, and the relaxation of governmental control—led to new forms of organization, an increase in the number of literate priests, heightened religious competition, and a consequent burgeoning of pantheons and practices. Increasingly, localities, regional associations of various kinds, and minority communities came to adopt Daoist deities and practices. At the same time, scholarly Daoists composed vast ritual compendia, consolidating and formalizing practice. And, again under foreign rule in the north of China, another counter-trend emerged. This was Quanzhen Daoism, a well-organized and highly centralized monastic movement.

These disparate features of the religion endure to the present day. In many ways, then, scholars tend to see the Song period as the beginning of modern Daoism. The most thoroughly studied example of a local therapeutic and exorcistic tradition that rose to national prominence, and eventually received court recognition, is the Rectifying Rites of Tianxin (the center of heaven, that is, the northern dipper). While serving the fourth ruler of the state of Min (present-day Fuzhou) during the years 935 to 939, a Daoist priest by the name of Tan Zixiao was asked to interpret a set of talismans that had come to light. These, he pronounced, were part of a secret patrimony, the Rectifying Rites of Tianxin, passed down from Zhang Daoling. The talismans, as they developed in the tradition, were held to embody the power of the celestial emperor of the north, of the Department of Exorcisms, and his agents, the fearsome generals Tianpeng, Heisha, and Zhenwu, among others. Daoist priests visualized Tianpeng in Tantric form and the latter two with disheveled hair, bulging eyes, brandished weapons, and martial dress. And thus they are depicted in Daoist statuary and painting. The rites of Tianxin were passed from master to master, finally coming to the Daoist Deng Yougong, who between 1075 and 1100 wrote ritual manuals that were eventually included in the imperially sponsored Song Daoist canon of 1120, the first ever to be printed.

Another ritual tradition was founded by Lu Shizhong (fl. 1100–1158), a native of Chenzhou (modern Henan) who received visits from the deified Zhao Sheng, who had been a disciple of the first Celestial Master. Lu's manuals, known as the Rites of the Jade Hall, blend the Rites of Tianxin with Lingbao funeral rites and show an increased emphasis on meditation practice. Characteristic of these and other therapeutic rituals of the early Song was the practice of *kaozhao,* "summoning for investigation." In *kaozhao* ritual, the master transforms himself into a martial deity, identifies the demon causing problems, seizes it, and causes it to descend into the troubled person or a surrogate where it might be interrogated and the problem resolved (Davis, 2001). Such practices could only arise once illness was no longer linked to morality, as it had been in earlier Daoist traditions.

Early Song rulers, who like the Tang rulers before them traced their ancestry to a Daoist deity, here the Yellow Emperor, had recourse to the protection offered by demon-quelling ritual. Threatened by peoples to their north, they found special protection from the celestial general Heisha, whom they ennobled with the title "the Perfected Lord who Supports the Sage [ruler] and Protects [his] Virtue." They also ordered the construction in the capital Kaifeng of a massive temple complex dedicated to Zhenwu, the Perfected Warrior. In addition, rulers patronized ritual specialists, built temples throughout the realm and sponsored the collection and printing of Daoist texts. The *Yunji qiqian* (Seven slips from the book bags of the clouds), a 120-chapter collection of Daoist texts extracted from the canon of 1120, survives from this period.

The imperial support of Daoism culminated in the brief theocratic reign of Huizong (r. 1101–1125), who called to court Daoists from the major ordination centers. In addition to confirming the prestige of old Daoist lineages—Shangqing was represented by its putative twenty-fifth patriarch and the Celestial Masters, now centered at Mount Longhu (in modern Jiangxi), by their thirtieth—several new lineages were also created in response. Lin Lingsu (1076–1120) arrived in the capital with revelations he had received from *Shenxiao* (Divine empyrean), the highest reaches of heaven. Lin revealed the divine identity of Huizong as the deity "Great Thearch of Long Life" and promulgated a set of rituals based on earlier Shangqing and Lingbao texts. Yang Xizhen (1101–1124) claimed to have emerged from the caverns hidden in Mount Mao, the ancient center of Shangqing practice, with a set of therapeutic rituals that had been bestowed upon him in this underworld study center. These were called the "Rites of Youthful Incipience." Huizong's enthusiasm for these Daoist traditions went to such extremes that he commanded that all Buddhists of the realm be demoted to Daoists of the second rank. This and other excesses incited further disputes between Buddhists and Daoists. But Huizong's reign was short and in 1127 the court moved south to evade the Jurchen Jin dynasty (1115–1234).

During the southern Song, the most noteworthy developments involved the codification of innovations begun in the north. Lin Lingsu had presented his Shenxiao tradition as an extension of the ancient Lingbao canon and the culmination of Shangqing revelation. In line with these claims, he had presented to the throne a sixty-one-chapter version of the originally one-chapter Lingbao *Scripture of Salvation.* This important text formed the basis for another ritual tradition, the Lingbao *dafa* (Great Rites of Lingbao). While there were regional variations, the centerpiece of this tradition was the rite of *liandu* (roughly, "salvation by fiery smelting"). Through an extremely elaborate external ritual—involving chants, pacing, and the use of talismans—and an equally complex internal ritual through which the bodily spirits of the master descended into the hells, the rite aimed to purify and rescue the dead.

Under the Jin in northern China, several new traditions appeared. The most important and enduring of these was the Quanzhen ("Perfect Realization" or "Completion of Authenticity"). The movement was inaugurated by the ascetic and visionary Wang Zhe (1113–1170), also known as Wang Chongyang. After achieving enlightenment in 1167, Wang wandered the Shandong peninsula, converting followers and founding associations for the promulgation of his doctrine. Wang gathered around him a coterie of favored disciples, all highly literate men among whom Ma Danyang (1123–1184) was his designated heir. The later tradition settled on a list of *qi zhen* (Seven Perfected or "Authentic Ones") as the foremost disciples. This list included Sun Bu'er (1119–1183), Ma's wife, thus signaling the vital role female clerics had come to play in the movement.

Wang's most famous disciple, Qiu Changchun (1148–1227), was summoned to the Jin court in the 1180s and, in 1220, to the itinerant court of Chinggis Khan (r. 1206–1227), who hoped to obtain the drug of immortality from him. Although Qiu allowed that he knew only hygienic techniques for prolonging life, he made a favorable impression on the khan, who bestowed special privileges on the Quanzhen order, including authority over the religious in his realm. Quanzhen Daoism grew explosively during the Yuan dynasty, despite prescriptions of the order ordered by Kublai Khan (r. 1260–1294) in retribution when his armada sent against Japan was destroyed by a typhoon in 1281. According to the estimates of Vincent Goossaert (2001), by 1300 there were some four thousand Quanzhen temples in northern China, housing an estimated twenty thousand clerics, around one-third of whom were women.

As an order, Quanzhen was devoted to both communal discipline and self-cultivation. Priests and nuns took vows of celibacy and left the home to live communally in one of the many temples. There, submitting to monastic discipline, they would work to cultivate lack of attachment, purity of mind, and immortality through the practice of inner alchemy. As they often took up residence in the temples of local cults or other orders, the rituals conducted by Quanzhen clerics derived from all the major traditions of Daoism. Sometimes their eclecticism led them into difficulties, as when Quanzhen clerics championed a later version of the *Huahu jing*, the scripture that held that Laozi was the Buddha, before the Yuan emperors in a series of debates with Buddhists. In a final debate before Kublai Khan in 1281, the enraged emperor ruled against them and, as we have seen, eventually suppressed the order. In mature form, Quanzhen doctrine was less doctrinaire, drawing from the quietist aspects of Confucianism and Ch'an (Jpn., Zen) Buddhism and revering both the Buddhist *Heart Sūtra* and the Confucian *Classic of Filial Piety.*

The remarkable spread of Quanzhen during the Yuan period can be attributed to several factors. First, clerics tended to travel widely, spreading the doctrine. Second, Quanzhen adepts, more than those of other contemporary religious groups, tended to use literary works—dialogic treatises, poetic accounts of practice, public inscriptions, organizational histories, and the like—as proselytizing tools. Third, Quanzhen adepts easily assimilated themselves to existing religious establishments, reinterpreting the texts of their rivals and even occupying their temples.

DAOISM IN THE MING (1368–1644) AND QING (1644–1911). Scholars have only recently begun to turn their attention to post-Yuan developments in the Daoist traditions traced above. One difficulty derives from the often-strained relationship between Daoist practitioners and the throne. Increasingly stringent controls placed on Daoist institutions and practitioners during the Ming and Qing attest to the continued vitality of the religion. At the same time, tight imperial oversight tended to erase from the public record much that we would like to know.

The first Ming ruler, Taizu (r. 1368–1399), attempted to manage Daoism by establishing various agencies governing the religion, regulating the number of monks and nuns who could be ordained, and mandating the maximum age at which they could do so. Taizu favored the Zhengyi order, but tolerated the Quanzhen movement. Clerics of many ritual traditions thus began to take refuge in these two orders, a situation that continues. It is clear, however, that Taizu's restrictions, though continued by subsequent emperors, only superficially limited the numbers or activities of Daoists.

Chengzu (r. 1402–1425), also known by his reign-title as the Yongle Emperor, provided more protection for Daoism. He ordered the compilation of a new canon (completed after his death) and designated Zhenwu, the Perfect Warrior, the dynastic protector. Claiming that Zhenwu had aided him in unifying the realm, the emperor set up a sanctuary for this deity in Beijing's forbidden city when he took residence there in 1421. He also provided support for the god's cult center on Mount Wudang in Hubei. For similar reasons, Chengzu supported other deities, including the popular "god of war," Guandi, one of a list of popular deities who were adopted into the Daoist pantheon.

Subsequent Ming emperors continued the dual policy of support and control begun by the first rulers of the dynasty. Despite official patronage for some, there seem to have been few doctrinal developments during this period. The main trend seems to have been one of amalgamation of diverse practices into a single way, something that pleased rulers as evidence of unity. One important tradition that provided a foundation for this search for unity was the tradition of inner alchemy. Zhao Yizhen (d. 1382), a master trained in Quanzhen and Qingwei ritual, proposed a strict course of self-examination through the use of "ledgers of merit and demerit," a widespread practice at the time. Such self-criticism, he held, could bring human emotions into harmony with reason, dispel illusion—whether that of demons, spirits, or *bodhisattvas*—and prepare the way for proper absorption of cosmic essences through meditation. Zhang Yuchu (1361–1410), the forty-third Celestial Master of the Zhengyi tradition, carried on Zhao's understandings of inner alchemical practice, explicitly incorporating into his system the insights of Chan Buddhism on inner nature.

An even more syncretic teaching was propounded by Lin Zhao'en (1517–1598), scion of an official family from Fujian who studied with various Daoist masters and eventually styled himself "Master of the Three Teachings." His group became the "Three in One Teaching," merging insights from Confucianism as the principle doctrine, with Daoism and Buddhism. Lin taught a method of inner cultivation in nine stages, culminating in "breaking through the void," a final step of inner alchemical practice for forming the internal embryo. To this stage of ultimate attainment, Lin assimilated the "perfect sincerity" of neo-Confucian understanding of the *Doctrine of the Mean* and the Buddhist concept of moving beyond illusion into the ground between being and nonbeing. The group spread throughout southeastern China and endured for about 150 years after Lin's death.

Another result of Ming attempts at religious control was the strengthening of lay associations, both trade guilds and those local groups organized for the purpose of sponsoring a temple or religious site. One prominent example is the famous Yongle Gong (Palace of Eternal Joy), a temple dedicated to Lü Dongbin first occupied by Quanzhen adepts in the 1240s that had, by the mid-Ming, fallen into disrepair. Beginning in 1614, local leaders organized subscription campaigns for the repair and ritual use of the temple. To the efforts of such associations we owe the remarkable preservation of fourteenth-century murals depicting scenes from the life of Lü Dongbin, perhaps drawn from popular Yuan plans, and depictions of Daoist divinities used in ritual (Katz, 1999). The support of temple associations is also responsible for the incorporation into Daoism of popular deities such as Ma Zu, goddess of merchants and fishermen.

Another sign of popularization was the printing and distribution of Daoist tales. Among these, one of the most completely studied concerns the mysterious figure Zhang Sanfeng. Pierre-Henry de Bruyn (2000) relates the origins of this figure: When Chengzu (r. 1402–1424) usurped the throne by having his nephew murdered, he still entertained doubts that the burnt corpse presented to him was in fact his nephew. He consequently sent secret police throughout the realm on the pretext of seeking the immortal "Zhang Sanfeng," but actually to seek for his nephew. As a result of this apparent imperial interest, all sorts of legends began to circulate concerning this figure. These were duly published and circulated by the faithful, and a cult arose.

The same trends—strict imperial control, standardization of Daoist traditions under the aegis of Zhengyi and Quanzhen, and growing lay involvement—intensified during the Qing dynasty. The Manchu rulers of the Qing venerated Tibetan Buddhism and promoted neo-Confucian doctrine as state orthodoxy, even to the extent of promulgating its tenets among the populace through imperial "sacred edicts." The Confucian elite, feeling that excessive emphasis on personal cultivation had led to the collapse of the Ming, tended to support the state orthodoxy. As a result, officially sanctioned "three teachings" movements during the Qing tended to exist for the purpose of spreading Confucian morality. An unintended consequence of this imperial initiative was an upsurge in lay associations and sectarian movements organized under the pretext of spreading morality. *Shanshu* (Morality books) promoting Confucian ethics based on Buddhist notions of *karma* and Daoist concepts of longevity and of the bureaucratic organization of the unseen worlds had circulated since the Song dynasty but now were produced in even greater numbers.

Beginning in the Ming, sectarian movements published similar works, known as *baojuan* (precious volumes) of a more striking religious character. A number of these were produced by "spirit writing," a type of revelation whereby spirits of gods, Transcendents, or even cultural heroes were believed to compose texts by taking control of a writing implement. The most common means, still in use today, involved two mediums wielding a double-handled planchette that would inscribe the deity's words, graph by graph, in a shallow box filled with sand. This message would then be "transcribed" by several observers. Texts produced in this way began to appear as early as the Song dynasty (Kleeman 1994), but the popularity of such works seems to have increased radically during the Ming.

One of the most widespread of the sectarian movements, named by Susan Naquin (1985) "White Lotus Sectarianism," centered on the Maitreya-like goddess, the Eternal Venerable Mother, who, it was believed, would reappear to eradicate evil and create a new heaven and earth. These movements, only loosely organized, were a threat both to the Buddhist and Daoist establishments and to the government. Imperial attempts at suppression only succeeded in spurring millenarian movements.

While Qing rulers gave precedence to the Zhengyi order in state ritual, they also appreciated the organizational strengths of Quanzhen, with its strict rules for clerics. Over the course of the dynasty, the Longmen branch of Quanzhen rose to domination. The Longmen branch traces its founding back to Qiu Chuji of the Song, but, as Monica Esposito (2000) has shown, it actually originated during the Ming among southern Daoist movements. The importance of the Longmen branch can with assurance be traced to Wang Changyue (d. 1680), who from 1656 until his death served as abbot of the Baiyun guan (White Cloud Abbey) in Beijing. Wang reorganized Quanzhen precepts to include neo-Confucian rules for living that were favored by Qing rulers. He divided the precepts into three ascending stages: (1) initial precepts of perfection; (2) intermediate precepts; and (3) precepts of celestial transcendence. He also held that anyone could gain immortality through their careful cultivation. Under Wang's direction, Baiyun guan became a central training center for all Daoist traditions, formally granting the precepts to male and female clerics from all over the kingdom as part of their official investiture. This, in itself, was crucial to the spread of Longmen branch teachings.

As Wang Changyue's example shows, while Quanzhen and other Daoist organizations continued to discourse on and practice the inner alchemy of earlier days, there was an increased emphasis on universalism. Simplified descriptions of the discipline were promulgated not only by Daoists, but by sectarian groups and lay organizations, and even in popular plays and novels. Schools of martial arts and physical cultivation adopted some inner alchemical learning to their own purposes, leading to the widespread practice of *qigong* (roughly, "breath achievement") in modern times. While many *qigong* schools have their own origin myths, a more scholarly account of their origins is that, while some of their practices are quite ancient, they in fact grew from the intellectual and social conditions of Ming and Qing times.

DAOISM IN JAPAN. There is no clear evidence of the transmission of organized Daoism to Japan. No records of Daoist investiture or even the presence of Daoist priests have yet been detected. A number of scholars have cited references to immortality seeking, alchemy, and other practices and words associated with Daoism in texts from the seventh century CE forward. For example, the *Nihonshoki* (Chronicle of Japan), under entries for the years 456 to 479, mentions several mountaintop establishments it styles *dōkan* (Daoist temples), but it is uncertain what sort of establishment might have been meant. Most Japanese scholars, then, agree with the 1933 findings of Tsukami Jikiryō that "Daoist ideas transmitted to Japan in ancient and Heian (794–1185) times came first under the umbrella of esoteric Buddhism and yin-yang divination, and then spread to the wider populace" (cited in Masuo, 2000, p. 824). A number of the practices scholars point to in support of this assertion, however, are best considered part of Chinese common religion, rather than specifically Daoist.

One example is the practices associated with the *gengshen* (Jpn., *kōshin)* day, the fifty-seventh day of the sexagesimal cycle of days according to the Chinese calendar. According to texts as early as the *Baopuzi*, the human body played host to three worms or "corpses" that sought the death of their host and would, on the night of this day, ascend to heaven to report on his or her transgressions. Since these evil-minded residents might depart the body only during sleep, one method to frustrate them included an all-night vigil. While Daoist texts taught that abstention from meat, sexual abstention, and purification procedures were also necessary, the vigil in Japan (as sometimes in China) became the occasion for an all-night party.

Introduced in the mid-ninth century, *kōshin* practice was modified in the eleventh century by Tendai monks, who added further Daoist and Buddhist elements from a variety of scriptural sources. During the Edo period (1603–1687), esoteric monks and *yamabushi* began delivering morality lectures on the practice throughout the country and a number of *kōshin* halls were established to accommodate those holding vigils. Thriving *kōshin* halls still exist in Osaka and Nara. Although specific practices for ridding the body of the three worms found a place in Daoism, the belief in the three worms was not confined to Daoism, as its presence in Buddhist texts composed in China attests.

Other practices associated with Daoism—methods of appeasing the celestial bureaucracy, the use of apotropaic talismans and spells, even the ritual "pace of Yu" (a magical gait held to avert evil originating in ancient Chinese occult traditions and adapted into Daoism)—can be found in similar form, mixed with Chinese common religion and Buddhism. One group that seems to have been particularly receptive to Daoist practice was the *yamabushi* practitioners of Shugendō (roughly "way of practice for inciting auspicious response"). According to legend, Shugendō began in the seventh century, but was certainly widespread by the end of the Heian period. The practice of *yamabushi,* who undergo austerities in the mountains to gain spiritual powers, includes healing, the dispelling of misfortune, a version of the pace of Yu, and the use of spells and talismans. While some of these can be traced to Daoist works, the precise vectors of transmission are unknown. In addition, the twelfth-century Shintō schools of Ise and Yoshida developed a view of spirits (Jpn., *kami*) divided according to function and sometimes associated with the northern dipper and other asterisms that made specific use of Daoist works.

In the seventeenth and eighteenth centuries, a number of Daoist practices, including those associated with Quanzhen Daoism, arrived in Japan as a result of the popularity of neo-Confucianism. Morality books were another source of knowledge of Daoist deities, such as the martial god Guandi, and of practices meant to satisfy the moral oversight of the celestial bureaucracy. In line with the flexible nature of Daoist belief, such foreign elements were easily modified to conform with Japanese society.

DAOISM IN KOREA. Unlike the case of Japan, there are records of the formal transmission of Daoism into the Korean peninsula. In the early seventh century, Tang emperors, who traced their lineage to Laozi, sent priests on at least two occasions to teach Daoist ritual in the court of the king of Koguryŏ (37 BCE–668 CE). During the late Tang, monks of the unified Silla (668–935) are recorded as having visited the Chinese capital to study Daoism. Not much is known, though, about how well established the religion became as a result of such exchanges.

During the Koryŏ dynasty (918–1392), however, Daoist ritual became part of imperial practice. King Taejo (r. 918–943) set up some fifteen Daoist sites, ordered rites for the welfare of the state, and gave Daoism a ranking equal to that of Buddhism. Subsequent emperors followed suit. Under King Sŏnjong (r. 1083–1094), Daoist rituals were no longer confined to the capital and, in 1115, Song Huizong provided clerics to assist in imperial Daoist rites. Jung Jae-seo (2000) has found that there were a total of 191 recorded *jiao* rituals performed during the Koryŏ. During this period, Korean intellectuals also became interested in Daoist practice, sometimes modeling their associations on the hagiographies of Chinese Transcendents.

The Chosŏn dynasty (1392–1910) promoted neo-Confucianism as the state doctrine and closed many of the temples built during the Koryŏ, but still allowed some Daoist rituals for the welfare of the royal family. A version of Chinese methods of control was instituted early in the dynasty whereby candidates for the priesthood were examined in the Lingbao scriptures, a *Zhenwu* scripture, and other important texts. Eventually only one temple, the Sogyŏk sŏ, with one hall dedicated to Grand Unity and another to the Three Pure Ones and patronized by officials, was allowed to conduct formal Daoist rituals. These were entirely Chinese-style Daoist rites. The temple was finally abolished as a consequence of the Japanese invasion. Nonetheless, private study of inner alchemy continued in the form of private *danhak pai* (schools of alchemical studies), which developed in distinctive ways and began to claim transmissions from shadowy ancient figures of Korean history.

The "new religions" that developed in Korea in the nineteenth century drew extensively on Daoist scriptures and practices. The Donghak (Eastern Doctrine), established in 1860 by Choi Jaewu (1824–1864) and others, includes sacrifices to Daoist gods, the use of talismans, and the practice of visionary journeys to the celestial realms.

DAOISM TODAY. The official body governing Daoist practice in modern China is the Chinese Daoist Association, formed in 1956 and officially approved by the Ministry of Internal Affairs on May 20, 1957. Operating from the White Cloud Temple in Beijing, the organization coordinates Daoist practice and controls the initiation of priests and nuns. At first, the association, following Qing precedent, recognized only Zhengyi (Celestial Master) and Quanzhen traditions. During the government-sponsored mass movements of the 1960s and 1970s, all Daoist holdings were returned to state control. Following the Cultural Revolution, and particularly from 1979 forward, governmental control of religious practice has relaxed considerably and researchers report a resurgence of Daoist practice throughout the country. This has been matched by an exuberant growth of scholarship on all aspects of the religion.

In Taiwan, free exercise of religion existed since the founding of the Nationalist government in 1949. All forms of religious practice flourished and the crafts necessary to ritual—the painting of religious images, construction of ritual garb and implements, and so on—thrived. Many early Western researchers into the Daoism, beginning with Kristofer Schipper, began their studies with fieldwork on the island. In 1951, Zhang Enpu, the putative sixty-third generation Celestial Master founded the Taiwan Daoist Society to provide coordination for Daoist activities. This quasi-governmental organization represents only one facet of the vibrant Daoist practice seen in Taiwan; Daoist practitioners and scholars have also entered into fruitful communication with their counterparts in mainland China.

Outside of China, Daoist practice exists wherever there is a substantial Chinese community. In premodern times, one of the vectors of transmission seems to have been non-Han peoples who had been converted to Daoism as part of strategies of Sinification. For instance, the Yao people, resident in northwest Thailand, practice a form of the Rectifying Rites of the Center of Heaven, dating to the Song. Michel Strickmann (1982) has provided evidence that the Yao acquired their traditions from officially sponsored missionaries, perhaps as early as the Song. Comparable evidence for the Daoism of other parts of Southeast Asia has not so far been discovered.

More common was the spread of Daoism with Chinese mercantile communities, something that we know to have occurred from early times. Today Singapore and Malaysia host the most widespread practice of the religion. Active associations for the coordination of Daoist practice were founded there in 1979 and 1995, respectively. These umbrella organizations frequently coordinate with the Daoist Associations of China, Hong Kong, and Taiwan.

SEE ALSO Dao and De; Fangshi; Huangdi; Shugendō; Taiji; Xi Wang Mu; Yinyang Wuxing; Yuhuang.

BIBLIOGRAPHY

General Works

Bokenkamp, Stephen R. *Early Daoist Scriptures.* Berkeley, Calif., 1997. A translation and study of the *Xiang'er* commentary to the *Laozi* and other Celestial Master, Shangqing, and Lingbao Daoist scriptural works from the third to the fifth centuries CE.

Boltz, Judith M. *A Survey of Taoist Literature: Tenth to Seventeenth Centuries.* Berkeley, Calif., 1987. A comprehensive survey of genres of writing found in the Daoist canon and the traditions that produced them.

Campany, Robert Ford. "On the Very Idea of Religions (In the Modern West and Early Medieval China)." *History of Religions* 42, no. 4 (2003): 287–319. This article contains important insights on the ways "religion" was referred to in medieval China.

Ch'en Kuo-fu. *Daozang yuanliu kao.* 2d ed. Beijing, 1963. An important early Chinese study of Daoist history.

Dean, Kenneth. *Taoist Ritual and Popular Cults of Southeast China.* Princeton, N.J., 1993. A study based on fieldwork that attests to the vivacity of modern Daoist practice.

Granet, Marcel. *La pensée chinoise* (1934). Reprint, Paris, 1968. A classic on the systems of Chinese thought with their symbols and categories. A brilliant pioneering study, it contains interesting chapters on the Daoist schools and the techniques of longevity.

Maspero, Henri. *Mélanges posthumes sur les religions et l'histoire de la Chine,* edited by Paul Demiéville; Vol. 2: *Le taoïsme.* Paris, 1950. Reprinted in *Le taoïsme et les religions chinoises* (Paris, 1971) and translated by Frank A. Kierman Jr. as *Taoism and Chinese Religion* (Amherst, Mass., 1981). Written by one of the founders of modern French Sinology, this posthumous work contains important essays on religious Daoism.

Needham, Joseph. *Science and Civilisation in China.* 5 vols. Cambridge, U.K., 1954–1983. This work is an ambitious and successful undertaking on Chinese scientific thought, with chapters on Daoism (vol. 2) and a presentation of alchemy and the techniques of longevity (vol. 5).

Ren Jiyu, ed. *Zhongguo daojiao shi.* Shanghai, 1990. The best general account of Daoist history produced in China to date.

Robinet, Isabelle. *Les commentaries du Tao Tu King jusqu'au septième siècle.* 2d ed. Paris, 1981. A study of the main commentaries of the *Laozi.*

Robinet, Isabelle. *Histoire du taoïsme des origines au XIV siècle.* Paris, 1992. Translated by Phyllis Brooks as *Taoism: Growth of a Religion.* Stanford, Calif., 1997. One of the foremost scholars of Daoist texts here traces the early development of the religion.

Schafer, Edward H. *The Divine Woman: Dragon Ladies and Rain Maidens in T'ang Literature.* Berkeley, Calif., 1973. A survey of Chinese mythology on water goddesses, some of whom were adapted into Daoism.

Schipper, Kristofer. *Le corps taoïste.* Paris, 1982. Translated by Karen C. Duval as *The Taoist Body.* Berkeley, Calif., 1993. Schipper offers an overall analysis of the Daoist religion with an excellent chapter on ritual.

Sivin, Nathan. "On the Word 'Taoist' as a Source of Perplexity." *History of Religions* 17 (1978): 303–330.

Historical Studies

Barrett, Timothy H. *Taoism Under the T'ang.* London, 1996. A survey of relations between the state and the Daoist religion drawn largely from the official histories.

Davis, Edward L. *Society and the Supernatural in Song China.* Honolulu, Hawaii, 2001. A study of spirit-possession and its relationship to Daoist and Buddhist practice.

de Bruyn, Pierre-Henry. "Daoism in the Ming (1368–1644)." In *Daoism Handbook,* edited by Livia Kohn, pp. 594–622. Leiden, Netherlands, 2000.

Esposito, Monica. "Daoism in the Qing (1644–1911)." In *Daoism Handbook,* edited by Livia Kohn, pp. 623–658. Leiden, Netherlands, 2000.

Goossaert, Vincent. "The Invention of an Order: Collective Identity in Thirteenth-Century Quanzhen Taoism." *Journal of Chinese Religions* 29 (2001): 111–138. The centerpiece of a special section devoted to studies of *Quanzhen.*

Jao Tsung-i. *Laozi xiang-er zhu jiaojian.* Hong Kong, 1956. A study of the *Xiang'er* commentary to the *Laozi.*

Jung Jae-seo. "Daoism in Korea." In *Daoism Handbook,* edited by Livia Kohn, pp. 792–820. Leiden, 2000.

Katz, Paul R. *Images of the Immortal: The Cult of Lü Dongbin at the Palace of Eternal Joy.* Honolulu, 1999. A detailed study of an important temple and its artwork.

Kleeman, Terry F. *Great Perfection: Religion and Ethnicity in a Chinese Millennial Kingdom.* Honolulu, 1998. A study of the Ba converts to Daoism and the kingdom they founded in Sichuan in the fourth century CE.

Kohn, Livia, trans. and ed. *Laughing at the Tao: Debates Among Taoists and Buddhists in Medieval China.* Princeton, N.J., 1995. A translation and study of the *Xiaodao lun* of Zhen Luan.

Masuo Shin'ichirō. "Daoism in Japan." In *Daoism Handbook,* edited by Livia Kohn, pp. 821–842. Leiden, 2000.

Naquin, Susan. "The Transmission of White Lotus Sectarianism in Late Imperial China." In *Popular Culture in Late Imperial China,* edited by David Johnson, Andrew J. Nathan, and Evelyn S. Rawski, pp. 255–291. Berkeley, Calif., 1985.

Seidel, Anna K. *La divinisation de Lao tseu dans les taoïsme des Han.* Paris, 1969. An excellent study of the divinization of Laozi.

Seidel, Anna K. "Imperial Treasures and Taoist Sacraments: Taoist Roots in the Apocrypha." In *Tantric and Taoist Studies* II, edited by Michel Strickmann, pp. 291–371. Brussels, 1983. The seminal article on the relations between early Daoism and Han imperial religion.

Stein, Rolf A. "Remarques sur les mouvements du taoïsme politico-religieux au IIe siècle ap. J.-C." *T'oung pao* 50 (1963):

1–78. A study of sectarian revolts that brought about the downfall of the Han dynasty.

Strickmann, Michel. *Le taoïsme du Mao-Chan: Chronique d'une révélation.* Paris, 1981. A historical survey of an important sect of the Chinese middle ages.

Strickmann, Michel. "The Tao Among the Yao: Taoism and the Sinification of South China." In *Rekishi ni okeru minshū to bunka,* edited by Sakai Tadao, pp. 23–30. Tokyo, 1982.

Verellen, Franciscus. *Du Guangting (850-933): Taoïste de cour à la fin de la Chine médiévale.* Paris, 1989. One of the few book-length studies of the life and works of an important Daoist figure, this works provides valuable information on the development of Daoist practice during the Tang dynasty.

Daoist Hagiography

Campany, Robert Ford. *To Live as Long as Heaven and Earth: Ge Hong's Traditions of Divine Transcendents.* Berkeley, Calif., 2002. A translation and study of the *Shenxian zhuan,* this work contains important insights into transcendent cults of the fourth century CE and their relations with Daoism.

Kaltenmark, Max. *Le Lie sien tchouan: Biographies légendaires de immortels taoïstes de l'antiquité.* Beijing, 1953. A fully annotated translation of the earliest collection of transcendent biographies.

Kleeman, Terry F. *A God's Own Tale: The Book of Transformations of Wenchang, the Divine Lord of Zitong.* Albany, N.Y., 1994. A translation and study of a work produced by planchette in 1181.

Ngo Van Xuyet. *Divination, magie, et politique dans la Chine ancienne.* Paris, 1976. A thorough study of the occult sciences and *fangshi* in China during the Han dynasty and the Three Kingdoms period.

Schipper, Kristofer. *L'Empereur Wou des Han dans la légende taoïste.* Paris, 1965. A translation of an ancient Daoist novel, important for the study of the legends and practices of the Mao-shan school.

Daoism and Fine Arts

Chang Chung-yüan. *Creativity and Taoism: A Study of Chinese Philosophy, Art, and Poetry.* New York, 1963. Examines the influence of Daoist thought on the arts and poetry.

Little, Stephen, ed. *Taoism and the Arts of China.* Chicago, 2000. The illustrated catalog of the first Western exhibit of Daoist-related art, this book includes essays by scholars on a variety of subjects.

Daoist Ritual

Hou Ching-Lang. *Monnaies d'offrande et la Notion de Trésorerie dans la religion chinoise.* Paris, 1975. An interesting work that helps to understand some aspects of Daoist ritual.

Kaltenmark, Max. "Quelques remarques sur le *T'ai-chang Ling-pao wou-fou siu.*" *Zinbun* 18 (1982): 1–10. Includes a description of an ancient ritual.

Kleeman, Terry F., "Licentious Cults and Bloody Victuals: Sacrifice, Reciprocity, and Violence in Traditional China." *Asia Major* (3d series) 7, no. 1 (1994): 185–211. The primary study of the sacrificial religion against which Daoism developed its "Pure Covenant" with the gods.

Lagerwey, John. *Wu-shang pi-yao: Somme taoïste du sixieme siècle.* Paris, 1981. A study of the first Daoist anthology.

Lagerwey, John. *Taoist Ritual in Chinese Society and History.* New York, 1987. An account of the cosmology of Daoist ritual.

Schipper, Kristofer. "The Written Memorial in Taoist Ceremonies." In *Religion and Ritual in Chinese Society,* edited by Arthur P. Wolf, pp. 309–324. Stanford, Calif., 1974.

Schipper, Kristofer. *Le Fen-Teng: Rituel taoïste.* Paris, 1975.

Schipper, Kristofer. "Taoist Ritual and the Local Cults of the T'ang Dynasty." Taipei, 1979. This work, as well as the preceding two, written by one of the best specialists of Daoism, examines various aspects of ritual.

Longevity Techniques and Meditation

Anderson, Poul, trans. *The Method of Holding the Three Ones: A Taoist Manual of Meditation of the Fourth Century A.D.* Copenhagen and Atlantic Highlands, N.J., 1980. A good translation of a meditation text of the Mao-shan school.

Baldrian-Hussein, Farzeen. *Procédés secrets du Joyau magique: Traité d'alchimie taoïste de l'onzième siècle.* Paris, 1984. An introduction to a Song dynasty system of internal alchemy, with translation.

Despeux, Catherine, trans. *Traité d'alchimie et de physiologie taoïste.* Paris, 1979. A translation of Zhao Bichen's important work of modern internal alchemy.

Despeux, Catherine. *Taiji Quan: Technique de longue vie et de combat.* Paris, 1981. An interesting study of Chinese boxing, with good translations.

Gulik, Robert H. van. *Sexual Life in Ancient China: A Preliminary Survey of Chinese Sex and Society from ca. 1500 B.C. till 1644 A.D.* (1961). Reprint, New York, 2003. A pioneering work on an important subject, with an interesting chapter on the various interpretations of alchemical language.

Maspero, Henri. "Les procédés de 'nourrir le principe vital' dans la religion taoïste ancienne." *Journal asiatique* 229 (1937): 177–252, 353–430. Reprinted in *Le taoïsme et les religions chinoises* (Paris, 1971). Fundamental work on physiological practices.

Robinet, Isabelle. *Méditation taoïste.* Paris, 1979. Translated by Norman Girardot and Julian Pas as *Taoist Meditation* (Albany, N.Y., 1993). A study of Shangqing visualization techniques by the foremost scholar of Shangqing literature.

Schafer, Edward H. *Pacing the Void: T'ang Approaches to the Stars.* Berkeley, Calif., 1977. Tang dynasty astronomical lore, including the foundations of Daoist dipper practice.

Alchemy and Medicine

Pregadio, Fabrizio. "Elixirs and Alchemy." In *Daoism Handbook,* edited by Livia Kohn, pp. 165–195. Leiden, Netherlands, 2000.

Sivin, Nathan. *Chinese Alchemy: Preliminary Studies.* Cambridge, Mass., 1968. A first-rate study of an alchemical treatise written by Sun Simiao of the Tang dynasty.

Ware, James R., trans. *Alchemy, Medicine, Religion in the China of A.D. 320: The Nei-P'ien of Ko Hung* (1967). Reprint, New York, 1981. Complete translation of the Daoist section of the *Baopuzi.* Unfortunately it is not always reliable.

Diverse Collections and Articles

History of Religions 9 (November 1969 and February 1970). Proceedings of the First International Conference of Taoist Studies.

Welch, Holmes, and Anna K. Seidel, eds. *Facets of Taoism: Essays in Chinese Religion.* New Haven, Conn., 1979. Proceedings of the Second International Conference of Daoist Studies.

Zürcher, Erik. "Buddhist Influence on Early Taoism." *T'oung pao* 66 (1980): 84–147.

Bibliographies

Loon, Piet van der. *Taoist Books in the Libraries of the Sung Period: A Critical Study and Index.* Ithaca, N.Y., 1984. A work intended for specialists; however, the introduction on Daoist literature in Song times is of general interest.

Seidel, Anna. "Chronicle of Taoist Studies in the West, 1950–1990." *Cahiers d'Extrême-Asie* 5 (1989–1990): 223–348. This journal continues to publish important articles on Daoism.

Soymié, Michel. "Bibliographie du taoïsme: Études dans les langues occidentales." *Études taoïstes* 3–4 (1968–1971): 247–313 and 225–287.

Tōhō shūkyō (Journal of eastern religions). Sponsored by the Japan Society of Daoistic Research, this journal publishes important articles and each year a bibliography of scholarship on Daoism in Japanese and Western languages from the preceding year.

STEPHEN R. BOKENKAMP (2005)

DAOISM: THE DAOIST RELIGIOUS COMMUNITY

There is no trace in the historical records of any organized Daoist community before the Latter Han dynasty (25–220 CE). Among the various politico-religious movements that sprang up during the second century as the dynasty went into decline, the most famous are the Way of the Heavenly Masters (Tianshi Dao) and the Way of Great Peace (Tai ping Dao). Although the historical evidence linking these two groups is slim, both clearly aimed at the total transformation of society and the establishment of a Daoist utopia; both were founded by people surnamed Zhang, probably because the Zhang clan was thought to be descended from the Yellow Emperor, who, together with Laozi, was revered in Han Daoism as the divine source of Daoist teachings; both organized the faithful into cosmologically determined units; and both considered sickness a sign of sin and therefore prescribed confession as a prerequisite for healing.

HAN PERIOD. At least partly inspired by a *Tai ping jing* (Scripture of great peace), presented to the throne during the reign of the emperor Shun (r. 126–145 CE), the Way of Great Peace was founded by three brothers who called themselves the generals of the lords, respectively, of Heaven, Earth, and Man. In addition to healing by means of confession and "symbol-water" (*fu-shui*), they and their subordinates spread the message that a new era, the era of Yellow Heaven, was about to begin. Having organized their adherents, known as the Yellow Turbans, into thirty-six military regions (*fang*) covering eight of the twelve provinces of the empire (all of eastern China), they rose in revolt in the first year of a new sixty-year cycle, a *jiazi* year (184 CE). It took government forces a full ten months to crush the revolt.

The Way of the Heavenly Masters was founded, according to the mid-third century *Zhengi fawen Tianshi jiao-jie k'o-jing* (Scripture of the rules and Teachings of the Heavenly Masters, a Text of the Method of Orthodox Unity), by Zhang Daoling. He is there said to have received, in the year 142, from the Newly Manifested Lord Lao (Xinzhu Laojun), the "Way of the Covenant of Orthodox Unity with the Powers" (zhengyi mengwei dao). He set up twenty-four "governances" (*zhi*) and "divided and spread the energies of the mysterious (celestial), the original (terrestrial), and the beginning (the Way) in order to govern the people." The earliest list of these governances appears in the late sixth-century *Wushang biyao* (Essentials of the supreme secrets): it places all but one of the governances in what is now Sichuan province and clearly confirms that the movement started in the western part of that province.

According to the dynastic histories, Zhang Daoling was succeeded by his son Heng, and Heng by his son Lu. Zhang Lu controlled northeastern Szezhuan for over thirty years, until he surrendered in 215 to Cao Cao, future founder of the Wei dynasty (220–264). Cao Cao gave him the title "General Who Controls the South" (*zhennan jiangjun*), enfeoffed him, and married his son Pengzu to Lu's daughter. It was probably at this time that the last of the twenty-four governances was located in the capital city of Luoyang and that the Way of Orthodox Unity (Zhengyi Mengwei Dao) became the dominant religion in the state of Wei. It remains to this day the most important form of religious Daoism.

SIX DYNASTIES PERIOD. The dynastic histories note that the adherents of Zhang Daoling were called "rice rebels" because a tax of five bushels of rice was levied on initiates. Throughout the Period of Disunion (220–589), the nickname Way of the Five Bushels of Rice (Wudoumi Dao) continued to be applied to the "church" of the Heavenly Masters. Its original organization consisted of a hierarchy of laypeople called "demon soldiers" (*guizu*), low-level priests called "demon clerks" (*guili*), higher-level priests called "libationers" (*jijiu*), and chief priests called "head libationers." Each of the libationers was in charge of an "inn of equity" (*yishe*). Said to be like the postal relay stations of the Han government, these inns were open to travelers, and free "meat and rice of equity" were supplied them.

That the "church" had in fact virtually supplanted the state may be seen from the fact that justice was administered by the libationers. Minor infractions were punished by the obligation to repair the routes between the inns: the word *dao* means "way, route," and free circulation of goods, persons, and ideas was considered essential to a society built on Daoist principles.

The basic institutions and attitudes of the movement all reveal its utopian character. Perhaps most striking in this regard is the equal treatment accorded to men and women—both could become libationers—and to Chinese and tribal populations. There were, as a result, a large number of these tribal people among the adepts of the Heavenly Masters. The various titles given the leaders of the movement, and in particular that of libationer, were taken from the Han system of local administration, where they referred to individuals selected locally for their moral qualities and their wisdom. The hierarchy envisaged was one that was communally oriented and merit based. Although the position of Heavenly Master was in later times a hereditary one, it is not certain that this was true at first; until as late as the Five Dynasties period (907–960) there are many references to heavenly masters of surnames other than Zhang.

In addition to running the inns of equity, the libationers were charged with the task of explaining the *Laozi* (*Dao de jing*) to the faithful. Part of a commentary on the *Laozi,* the *Xiang'er zhu,* found in the Dunhuang caves at the beginning of this century, is generally attributed to Zhang Lu. The commentary insists above all on the moral conduct of the faithful: "Who practices the Dao and does not infringe the commandments will be profound as the Dao itself; Heaven and Earth are like the Dao, kind to the good, unkind to the wicked; therefore people must accumulate good works so that their spirit can communicate with Heaven."

The "demon clerks"—so called, no doubt, because they had direct charge of the "demon soldiers"—had as their chief task the recitation of prayers for the sick. After the sick person had first meditated on his sins in a "quiet room" (*jingshi*), the demon clerk would write down the person's name and the purpose of his confession. He drew up this "handwritten document for the Three Officers" in three copies, one to be sent to each of these governors of Heaven, Earth, and the Waters. It was for this service that the faithful contributed five bushels of rice, as well as the paper and brush for preparing the documents.

An early Daoist text, the *Tai-zhen ke* (Regulations of the most perfect) states that every household should set up a meditation room and place the list of the names of its members in five bushels filled with "faith-rice" (*xinmi*). Every year, at the beginning of the tenth month, all the faithful were to gather at the governance of the Heavenly Master himself and contribute their faith-rice to the Heavenly Granary. They would then go in to pay their respects to the Heavenly Master and listen to an explanation of the rituals, ordinances, and commandments. The family registers of all the faithful were to be brought up to date at this time, that is, births, deaths, and marriages were to be recorded, so that the centrally held registers agreed with the family registers.

Similar gatherings were held in the first and seventh months, the former to determine, according to their respective merits, the advancement of the officers of the movement, the latter that of the laypeople. On each of these three "days of meeting" (*huiri*), linked respectively to the Three Officers (San Guan) of Heaven, Earth, and the Waters, a "memorial stating the merit [of each and all] was sent up." These days of meeting, especially the grand assembly of the tenth month, are clearly the origin of the community Offerings (*jiao*), which continue to constitute, to this day, the most elevated service performed by Daoist priests at the request of temple communities.

Progress in this vast meritocracy was marked by the graded transmission of a whole series of commandments and registers. According to the *Regulations of the Most Perfect,* the first series of commandments was transmitted to seven-year-old children. Starting at the age of eight, they could receive a register with the name and description of one general on it, then the register of ten generals at age twenty. Next came the registers of seventy-five generals, of which there were two, a feminine (*yin*) one giving control over seventy-five immortals (*xian*), and a masculine (*yang*) one, to which were attached the same number of potentates (*ling*). The *Regulations* state simply that these two registers are to be transmitted successively to the same person. It is probable, however, that the second transmission occurred only after successful accomplishment of the rites of sexual union called "mingling the energies" (*heqi*), for the reform-minded Heavenly Master Kou Qianzhi (d. 448), in forbidding the practice of these rites by other than married couples in his *New Regulations,* refers explicitly to the "registers of male and female officers."

These registers gave the names and physical descriptions of these generals and the armies of immortal and spiritual officers under their command. The role of these armies was to guard and protect the adept, just as the gods of the popular pantheon, who are also often called generals, were supposed to do. The adept who received further registers was called a "Daoist who distributes his energies" (*sanqi Taoshi*), that is, one who had moved beyond self-protection to saving others: a priest.

In general, each additional register increased the adept's power over the invisible world of the spirits and added thereby to his understanding of the Covenant of Orthodox Unity with the Powers. To enter the Way of the Heavenly Masters meant to worship only those powers enrolled, like the adepts themselves, on official registers and to cease to worship the "gods of ordinary people" (*sushen*). According to the *Xiang'er* commentary, "the Way is most venerable, it is subtle and hidden, it has no face nor form; one can only follow its commandments, not know or see it." The ultimate goal was to know this invisible way, to "hold on" to its mysterious—"orthodox"—Unity. This required forswearing all contact with the multiple "heterodox cults" (*yinsi*) current among the people. Throughout the Period of Disunion and, in somewhat diluted form, down to the present day, Orthodox Unity Daoists have been, like the Confucians, implacable opponents of these cults.

This well-formed, cosmologically comprehensive ecclesiastical organization survived, more or less intact and with appropriate modifications, through the Tang dynasty (618–907). One of the reasons for its survival was its readiness to come to terms, in the manner of Zhang Lu, with the state. The Scripture of the Teachings of the Heavenly Master cited above explicitly criticizes the Yellow Turbans as a "perverse way" (*Xiedao*) responsible for the death of millions. The same text states that the Dao, that is, Lord Lao, had often in the past appeared as the "teacher of kings and emperors." But after his "new manifestation" in the year 142, he would appear no more, for "Lord Lao had then bestowed on Zhang Daoling the position of Heavenly Master." Now, in the year 255, the Heavenly Master urges the faithful to obey the "pure government of the Wei."

The power and the appropriateness of this conception in the context of the Confucian state may be seen from the fact that in 442 the emperor Taiwu (r. 424–452) of the Northern Wei (386–535) became the first of a long line of emperors to "receive registers" (*shoulu*), that is, to receive a Daoist initiation that was tantamount to ecclesiastical (divine) investiture. Emperors—especially, but not exclusively, those favorable to Daoism—perpetuated this practice until the end of the Northern Song dynasty (960–1126).

The man who thus invested the emperor Taiwu was Kou Qianzhi. In 425, Kou was named Heavenly Master and his *New Regulations,* partly of Buddhist inspiration, was promulgated throughout the realm. In 431, in what may be considered a forerunner of the system of officially sponsored abbeys (*guan*) begun under the Tang and continued through the Qing (1644–1911), altars (*tan*) were set up and priests assigned to officiate on them in every province.

It is also noteworthy that the first great persecution of Buddhism occurred under the reign of the emperor Taiwu: inspired by Kou's Confucian friend, Cui Hao (381–450), and with Kou's reluctant cooperation, a decree promulgated in the year 444 attacked, in the same breath, the "heterodox cults," with their mediums and sorcerers, and Buddhism. Although the proscription of Buddhism that followed in the year 446 was rescinded by a new emperor in 454, these events proved to be the opening round of a long competition for imperial favor. In southern China, in 517, the emperor Wu (r. 502–549) of the Liang dynasty (502–557) abolished all Daoist temples and ordered the return of Daoist priests to the laity. In the year 574, after a series of debates between representatives of the "three teachings" (*sanjiao*)—Buddhism, Daoism, and Confucianism—the emperor Wu (r. 560–578) of the Northern Zhou dynasty (557–581) proscribed Buddhism and made Daoism the state religion. Daoists were later instrumental in bringing about the suppression of Buddhism by the Tang emperor Wuzong (r. 841–847) in the year 845 and its reduction to subordinate status by the emperors Huizung (r. 1101–1126) of the Northern Song dynasty, in 1119, and Taizu (r. 1206–1229) of the Yuan dynasty, starting in 1224.

The most telling arguments used in these various conflicts were, on the Buddhist side, that the only authentic Daoist works were those of its philosophers, the *Laozi* and the *Zhuangzi* and, on the Daoist side, that Buddhism was a foreign religion suitable only for barbarians. The court debates themselves often focused on a Daoist text called the *Huahu jing* (Scripture of the conversion of the barbarians). The idea that Laozi, at the end of his life, had gone into the western regions beyond China and there transformed himself into the Buddha in order to convert the barbarians is first attested in a memorial presented to the throne in the year 166 by one Xiang Kai. At that time, Buddhism was still perceived in China as a form of Daoism, and so the legend was useful, even complimentary to the Buddhists. But by the time the libationer Wang Fou wrote the first known (now lost) version of the *Huahu jing* around the year 300, Buddhism had become an entirely autonomous force in Chinese life, and the compliment had turned into a polemic slur.

The Daoists rarely won the court debates, and the *Huahu jing* was regularly proscribed over the centuries, starting in 668 with its suppression by Tang Gaozong (r. 650–684). But before the work disappeared definitively from circulation, after Yuan Shizu (r. 1260–1295) ordered all copies burned in 1281, it had served for nearly a millennium as a means of conveying a central Daoist conviction, based on many a passage in the *Laozi,* that the Dao embraced all things, large and small, high and low, Chinese and barbarian. To the Daoists it followed logically that "Daoism"—the "teaching of the Way" (*daojiao*)—included within itself all other teachings.

Outrageous from the Buddhist point of view, Daoist universalism was most attractive to Chinese emperors. The emperor Wu of the Northern Zhou dynasty, for example, began the decree in which he ordered the foundation of the Abbey for Communicating with the Way (Tongdao Guan) a mere eleven days after proscribing Buddhism as follows: "The supreme Way is vast and profound: it envelops both being and nonbeing; it informs highest heaven and darkest hell." According to Buddhist sources, the people appointed to staff this state abbey were all "enthusiasts of the *Laozi* and the *Zhuangzi* and proponents of the unity of the Three Teachings."

Another expression of Daoist universalism constantly attacked by the Buddhists was its regular "fabrication" of new texts by plagiarizing Buddhist sūtras. This criticism applied especially to the Lingbao ("numinous treasure") scriptures that began to appear in southeastern China in the 390s. The most important of these texts, the *Wuliang duren jing* (Scripture of universal salvation), may be described as pure "Mahāyāna Daoism." From start to finish, it has the flavor of a Buddhist scripture, but the revealed words come from the mouth, not of the Buddha, the "World-honored One" (*Shizun*), but from that of the "Heaven-honored One of the Primordial Beginning" (Yuanshi Tianzun), that is, the Dao. These texts also take over Buddhist notions of karmic retribution and introduce Buddhist-inspired rituals for the dead.

Some twenty years prior to the appearance of the first Lingbao texts, another group of texts had been revealed in the same part of China that was to play an extremely important role in the court Daoism of the Tang dynasty. Owing little to Buddhism, this new Shangqing ("high purity") literature completely transformed the methods of the traditional, eremetic Daoism of the South—alchemy, gymnastics, diet, visualization, and sexual practices—by incorporating them into a complex system revealed in ecstatic prose and poetry by a kind of automatic writing during séances. Recitation of these sacred texts and visualization of the spirits described in them became the high roads to spiritual realization in this movement.

The milieu in which these revelations occurred was that of the southern aristocracy, a group that recently had been supplanted by émigrés fleeing North China after the barbarian capture of the capital city of Luoyang in 311. These émigrés, who founded the Eastern Jin dynasty (317–420), with its capital in Jiankang (modern Nanking), brought with them the Way of the Heavenly Masters, and many Southerners—among them the father and uncle of Xu Mi (303–373), one of the main recipients of the new revelations—had adopted the Northerners' religion. Wei Huazun (d. 334) herself, the "teacher in the beyond" of the inspired calligrapher of the revealed texts, one Yang Xi (330–?), had been, during her life on earth, a libationer. Xu Mi continued to employ his father's libationer, Li Tung. One of the "real persons" (*zhenren*) who was revealing to Xu the new methods for spiritual (as opposed to physical) rites of union criticized Xu for his excessive use of the old methods of the Heavenly Masters: "The method for mingling the energies is not practiced by the Real Persons; it is an inferior Way that destroys the orthodox energies of the real vapors." Also, illness was attributed not to sin and consequent attacks by demons, but to physiological causes, and massages and drugs were therefore prescribed instead of the confession of sins. The demons of the Shangqing texts are those forces that try to keep the adept from achieving the level of concentration necessary for the spiritual union with a divine spouse, which alone can lead to "realization" (immortality).

It was probably a second- or third-generation practitioner of the new techniques of realization who first classified Daoist literature into the "three caverns" (*sandong*). Traditionally, it is Lu Xiujing (406–477) who is credited with this hierarchical classification, which places Shangqing texts first, Lingbao second, and Sanhuang (Three Sovereigns) last. The Sanhuang scriptures, of which only small portions survive, represent the talismanic, exorcistic literature of popular Daoism. It may be that they represent the tradition of the Yellow Turbans, for the Three Sovereigns are those of Heaven, Earth, and Man, whose lords the brothers Zhang served as generals.

Heavenly Master texts are conspicuously absent from this classification, but it may well be that they were felt by Lu, who is one of the most important liturgists in Daoist history, to be unnecessary: not only would he have shared, as a practitioner of Shangqing methods, the dim views of the sexual rites of the Heavenly Masters, but also, and more importantly, he had incorporated the basic Heavenly Master liturgy into the Lingbao texts, which he himself had edited. The Three Caverns thus constituted a complete and self-contained canon of exorcistic, liturgical, and meditational texts: together, they met every religious need, from that of a sick peasant requiring an exorcism to that of the refined aristocrat seeking sublime spiritual union.

The idea of this tripartite division was no doubt inspired by the Buddhist Tripiṭaka, but whereas the division of the latter was generic, that of the Daoist was practical. Correspondingly graded registers, moreover, were created to accompany initiation into each successive level of texts. Five separate rituals of transmission were included in the original *Wushang biyao* (compiled c. 580 at imperial behest): progressive initiation into the texts of the Three Caverns was preceded by the transmission of ten commandments (against murder, robbery, adultery, etc.) and of the *Laozi.*

The addition of these two rituals of initiation was a clear sign that the idea of the Three Caverns, however coherent ideologically, was too far removed from the reality of Daoist practice to survive without major modifications. The other ritual chapters in the *Wushang biyao* provided further evidence of this: nine of ten chapters were taken directly from the texts of the Three Caverns, but one, the "mud and soot fast" (*tutan zhai*), a ritual of confession, required an officiant who was at once a "libationer belonging to a diocese of the Heavenly Masters" and a "ritual master of the Three Caverns." This situation was remedied, probably in the early Tang period, by adding the Four Supplements (*gsifu*) to the Three Caverns. In the resulting initiation hierarchy, Orthodox Unity texts occupied, appropriately, the bottom of the seven rungs: emperors interested in Daoism invited Shangqing masters to court and received their registers, but the typical country priest required no more than the registers of Orthodox Unity—and the skills they implied. The remaining three of the Four Supplements also incorporated older Daoist traditions: alchemy, the Scripture of Great Peace, and the *Laozi.*

TANG PERIOD. The Tang dynasty saw the development of the more or less definitive forms not only of the Daoist canon, but also of Daoist messianism and monasticism. Closely related to its utopianism, Daoist messianism always had an intensely political character. In the second-century *Laozi bianhua jing* (Scripture of the transformations of Laozi), Laozi puts himself forward as the messianic leader. But during the Period of Disunion, it was usually a "descendant" of Laozi, the Perfect Lord (*zhenjun*) Li Hung, who excited the messianic hopes of the people. Thus Kou Qianzhi, in his *Laojun yinsong jiejing* (Scripture of the recitation of the prescriptions of Lord Lao), complains that many false prophets "attack the orthodox Dao and deceive the common people. All they have to say is, 'Lord Lao should reign, Li Hung ought to manifest himself.'" Li Hung messianism even appears in the Shangqing scriptures: according to the *Shangqing housheng daojun liji* (Shangqing biography of the Latter-day Saint and Lord of the Way), Li Hung will appear in a *jen-renchen* year (the twenty-ninth year of the sixty-year cycle, possibly 392) to establish a new world populated by the chosen and governed directly by the Latter-day Saint.

The centuries-old conflict between this popular Daoist messianism and the Heavenly Master tendency—seen in the careers of both Zhang Lu and Kou Qianzhi—to opt for the role of spiritual advisor to the emperor, found its perfect resolution in the Tang dynasty when, at last, not Li Hung himself, but another family of the same surname as Laozi, Li, came to power. This advent, moreover, is said to have been predicted toward the end of the Sui dynasty (589–618) by one Ji Hui, a Daoist who had entered the Abbey for Communication with the Way at the beginning of the Sui dynasty: "A descendant of the Lord Lao is about to rule the world, and our teaching will prosper." No sooner had Tang Gaozu (r. 618–627) come to power than he asked Ji Hui to celebrate an Offering to pray for divine benediction on the dynasty. He then ordered the complete rebuilding of the Lou Guan (Tower Abbey) and, in 620, changed its name to Zungsheng Guan (Abbey of the Holy Ancestor). In 625, after holding a debate between representatives of the "three teachings," Gaozu ranked them in the order Daoism, Confucianism, and Buddhism.

Tower Abbey occupied the site where Laozi was said to have revealed the *Laozi* to the keeper of the pass, Yin Xie, before disappearing into the western regions. Daoist sources make it out to have been a center for the cult of Laozi already in the time of Qing Shihuang (r. 221–209 BCE) and describe it as an important northern Daoist center throughout the Period of Disunion. In the Tang dynasty it became a dynastic cult center. In 679 its abbot, Yin Wencao (d. 688) compiled, on the order of the emperor, the *Sheng Ji* (Annals of the saint) in ten volumes. Judging on the basis of its Song-dynasty successor, the *Hunyuan sheng ji* (Annals of the saint of the womb), this was a "salvation history" of Daoism, presented as the successive divine interventions of Lord Lao in human history. In 741, after the emperor Xuanzong (r. 713–756) had encountered his divine ancestor in a dream, a statue corresponding to the face he had seen in his dream was found near the Abbey of the Holy Ancestor. The emperor had the statue set up in the inner palace for his own worship. He then ordered that similar statues be cast and sent to all the state-sponsored abbeys in the country, declared a general amnesty, and had an inscribed tablet set up at the Zongsheng Guan to commemorate these events.

The first network of Daoist buildings was that associated with the twenty-four governances of Heavenly Master Daoism in the second century. The first state-sponsored Daoist abbey in history is generally thought to be the Chongxu Guan (House for the Veneration of the Void) founded in 467 by the emperor Ming of the Liu Song (420–479) for Lu Xiujing. But it was not until 666, after performing the *feng-shan* ritual of celestial investiture on Taishan, that the Tang emperor Gaozong (r. 649–683) decreed the creation of a system of state-sponsored Daoist (and Buddhist) monasteries in each of the prefectures—there were over three hundred—in the empire. This dual system was perpetuated under all successive dynasties, until the fall of the empire in 1911.

It is generally assumed, with good reason, that these and other non-state abbeys were populated by monks and nuns. First, people who entered these institutions were said, like their Buddhist counterparts, to have "left the family" (*chujia*). Second, from the mid-sixth to the mid-eighth century, a new type of Lingbao scripture, clearly designed for monastic living was very much in vogue: the vocabulary and long-winded style of these texts is that of Buddhist scholastics; repeatedly, they recommend such Buddhist virtues as charity and compassion and such Buddhist practices as scripture-copying, recitation, and preaching; above all, they explicitly recommend celibacy. The *Taishang icheng Haikong zhizang jing* (The reservoir of wisdom of sea-void, a scripture of the unique vehicle of the Most High), after speaking in derogatory manner of Orthodox Unity Daoists, affirms that only those who "leave the family" can liberate themselves from all attachments and achieve enlightenment. Preaching is important in this *ekayāna* ("unique vehicle") Daoism because it frees people from doubt and ignorance.

Other texts in this group, however, such as the *Yuanyang jing* (Scripture of the primordial Yang) suggest that these Buddhist practices are but a preparation for more traditional Daoist ones, among which it names the rites of sexual union. Indeed, Daoist monks and nuns often lived in the same community and are known to have practiced these rites: they had "left their families," but Daoist commandments forbade only concupiscence, not intercourse. On the contrary, carefully regulated sexual intercourse was one of the oldest of Daoist roads to immortality, said to have been practiced by Laozi himself.

State support entailed state control. The emperor Xuanzong introduced registration of Buddhist and Daoist monks and nuns and restriction of their movement. He set limits on the size of monastic communities and on their land holdings. He ordered all monks who had not received official ordination certificates to pass an exam. A commissioner was appointed for each religion to ensure that these various ordinances were respected. Specific ritual services were also required of these state clergy: both Buddhists and Daoists were to perform services for the deceased of the imperial family on the anniversaries of their deaths; Daoists also celebrated rituals for the prosperity of the state on the three "days of origin" (the fifteenth day of the first, seventh, and tenth months) and on the emperor's birthday. This latter was made a three-day national holiday, to be celebrated with feasting throughout the empire.

Xuanzong favored Daoism in still other ways: he inaugurated imperial use of a ritual known as "throwing the dragon and the prayer slips" (*tou longjian*), its aim was to report dynastic merit to the Three Officers and to pray for personal immortality. In 731, upon the suggestion of the Shangqing patriarch Sima Chengzhen (647–735), sanctuaries dedicated to the Daoist Perfect Lords of the Five Sacred Peaks were set up on these mountains and Daoist priests selected to staff them. In early 742 the emperor ordered all Daoist temples in the empire to copy the *Benji jing* (Scripture of the original term) throughout the coming year. At the end of the year he issued a second decree attributing the good harvest to the merit thus obtained. In 748 he added to the Daoist monastic network a system of shrines on all forty-six mountains that had "cave-heavens" (*tongtian*). He also ordered the establishment of abbeys on the various sites where famous Daoists of the past had "obtained the Way." Between two and five Daoists were appointed for each of these new shrines and abbeys.

Xuanzong also went to considerable lengths in giving institutional form to the special relationship between the ruling house and its divine ancestor: in 737 he placed the Daoist clergy under the jurisdiction of the Office of the Imperial Clan; in 741 he ordered the creation of temples for the worship of Laozi in the two capitals (Chang'an and Luoyang) and in each prefecture, as well as a parallel network of Daoist academies and examinations. The imperial ancestral tablets were henceforth to be kept in the temple dedicated to Laozi in Chang'an, and statues of the imperial ancestors were set up in the Taiqing Gong (Palace of Grand Purity), which had been built in Pozhou, Laozi's birthplace. In the mid-740s Xuanzong had his own image set up next to that of Laozi in the Taiqing Gong in Chang'an, and later added those of his chief ministers as well. A first imperial commentary on the *Laozi* was published in 732, a second in 735, and in 745 the *Laozi* was declared superior to the Confucian classics. Among Xuanzong's successors—at least five of whom died of elixir poisoning in their Daoist-inspired quest for immortality—only Wuzong (r. 840–846) found anything to add to Xuanzong's ideological edifice: he made Laozi's birthday a three-day national holiday.

FIVE DYNASTIES, SONG, AND YUAN PERIODS. Later dynasties naturally could not make use of this link with Laozi; the Song replaced it with a similar genealogical tie to the equally Daoist Yellow Emperor, but the Tang system of state control and support survived. Registration statistics preserved over the centuries provide interesting insight into the shape and functioning of the system. (See table 1.)

Monastic Populations

Year	Registrations	Buddhism	Daoism
739	Monasteries	3,245	1,137
	Convents	2,113	550
1077	Monks	202,872	18,513
	Nuns	29,692	708
1677	Monks	110,292	21,286
	Nuns	8,615	——

TABLE 1.

The figures for the year 739 show that even the extravagant patronage of Xuanzong did not suffice to bring the number of Daoist monastic centers on a par with those of the Buddhists. This is not a reflection of the relative popularity of the two religions, but of the fact that lay clergy continued to be the norm among Daoists. A text compiled at imperial behest around 712, the *Miaomen youqi* (Origins of the school of mystery) distinguishes between hermits and those who "leave the family," on the one hand, and libationers and those who "live at home," on the other. These latter categories, whose chief function is healing, are said to be particularly numerous in Sichuan and the South.

The figures from the eleventh and seventeenth centuries show a marked decline for the Buddhists and remarkable stability for the Daoists. Although Buddhism is generally said to have lost much influence under the last two dynasties, what these figures really demonstrate is the success of the policy restricting the number of ordinations. Ordination implied exemption from taxation, conscription, and corvée. A Southern Song-dynasty (1127–1260) compilation of the Qing-Yuan period (1195–1201) restricts the number of Daoist novices to one per fifty and of Buddhist to one per hundred of the population as a whole. Qing-dynasty (1644–1911) law allowed monks and nuns of both religions to adopt a single pupil to whom they could transmit their ordination certificate. No religious institution could be founded without imperial permission.

All nineteenth-century observers note that the result of these restrictive policies was a glaring gap between the law and reality. At the beginning of the Qing dynasty, a state census revealed 12,482 monasteries and temples founded with imperial permission and 67,140 without. Already in the eighth century, Zhang Wanfu (fl. 711), in his *Shou sandong jingjie falu zheri li* (Calendar for the selection of days for the transmission of the registers, prescriptions, and scriptures of the Three Caverns), complains that the Daoists of these areas paid attention neither to the fasts of the official liturgy nor to the proper transmission of ritual knowledge: "Their only interest is in Offerings and sacrifices." Moreover, their "vulgar ways" had become popular of late in the capital cities of Chang'an and Luoyang as well.

These comments of Zhang suggest that, by his time, the aristocratic, meditative Shangqing tradition already was losing ground to more popular forms of Daoism. Other indications of this are the gradual rise of a "Confucian" Daoist movement called the Way of Filial Piety (Xiaodao). First heard of in the seventh century, claiming to have been founded by one Xu Sun (239–292?), it was in fact a local cult whose growth from its base in Hongzhou (Jiangxi) had led to its adoption and absorption by Daoism. This process was to be repeated many times in the future, most notably in the case of a local Fujian cult of two brothers, which was converted by imperial decree in 1417 into a state Daoist cult. The emperor Chengzu (r. 1403–1425) decided on the elevation of these two "perfect lords of boundless grace" (*hong'en zhenjun*) after a nagging illness had been cured by a drug prescribed, apparently, by the Fujian temple's medium. The brothers' official titles in the imperial "canon of sacrifices" were lengthened, a second temple built for them in the capital, a special Daoist liturgy created, and, in 1420, a Lingbao scripture produced. It taught the virtues of loyalty to one's superiors, filial piety, charity, and justice, and the emperor had it printed for dissemination on a wide scale in order to repay his debt to the divine brothers.

Another example of the increasing imbrication of popular cults, imperial ideology, and Daoist liturgy occurred at the beginning of the Song dynasty. Between 960 and 994, a commoner by the name of Zhang Shouzhen received a series of revelations on Mount Zhongnan, the site of Tower Abbey. The god, who was an assistant of the Jade Emperor, revealed himself to be the divine protector of the new ruling house and instructed Zhang to find a Daoist master. Having been initiated by a Daoist of Tower Abbey, Zhang received further revelations leading to the establishment of an imperially funded temple in 976, an official title in 981, and, above all, a system of Daoist Offerings that has survived, at least in part, until the present day.

The basic feature of the new system is the grading of Offerings according to the number of "stellar seats" (*xingwei*)—from 24 to 3,600—used to construct the altar. Divided into nine grades (3 x 3), the upper three altars were reserved for the emperor, the middle three for his ministers, and the lower three for gentry and commoners. The upper three altars had, respectively, 3,600, 2,400, and 1,200 stellar seats, corresponding to the Grand Offerings of All Heaven (*Putian*), the Entire Heaven (*Zhoutian*), and Net Heaven (*luotian*). Perfect expression of the hierarchical universalism common to both Daoist and imperial ideology, this system was adopted as the universal norm in the year 1009 by the emperor Zhenzong (r. 998–1023). It was to remain in official use throughout the Yuan (1279–1368) and perhaps beyond.

A 1,200-seat version, based in part on an official edition of Daoist ritual promulgated under Huizong (r. 1101–1126), has been preserved by Lü Taigu in his *Daomen dingzhi* (The Daoist system normalized) of 1201: starting from the highest celestial and stellar divinities, the list descends—by way of the celestial officials linked to the texts of the Three Caverns, the perfect lords and immortals of Daoist history and geography, the vast bureaucracy of the Three Officers, and all the governors of hell—to the humblest gods of the soil and agents of the time cycle. Among the Daoist sites for whose lords a seat is reserved are the Five Sacred Peaks, the various "cave-heaven" paradises, and the twenty-four governances; famous Daoists mentioned include Zhang Daoling, Xu Sun, Lu Xiujing, Du Guangting, various patriarchs of the Shangqing lineage, Tan Zuxiao, Jao Tongtian, Zhongli Quan, and Lü Dongpin.

The last two named are semi-legendary Daoist immortals who came to be revered together as the patrons of an important school of *neidan* (internal elixir alchemy) first heard of in the eleventh century. Dan zixiao (fl. 930) and Jao Tongtian (fl. 994) were the co-founders of the Tianhsin Zhengfa ("orthodox rites of the heart of heaven"), a new form of exorcistic healing based on texts discovered on Mount Hua-kai (Jiangxi province) and attributed to Zhang Daoling himself. The movement spread throughout southern China—the Yao tribes that have since migrated to Thailand still practice these rites today—and by the start of the twelfth century was deemed important enough to merit imperial attention (the oldest extant collection of these rites was presented to the throne by one Yuan Miaozong in 1116).

Du Guangting (850–933) was at once an important Daoist liturgist and one of Daoism's greatest hagiographers. His liturgical compilations draw on both the Lingbao and the Zhengi traditions; his collections of anecdotal literature are a gold mine of information on local cults and popular Daoism. The liturgies may be described as a synthesis of past practice, the stories as a harbinger of future developments: Du's career marks a watershed in the history of Daoism.

Suddenly, the veil is lifted on the world of popular piety—a world of miracles, exorcisms, pilgrimages, and portents—and on the place of Daoism in that world. In his *Daojiao lingyan ji* (Records of Daoist miracles), for example, Du tells a story about Xu Sun's magic bell: when a military governor tried to remove it from the Daoist abbey where it had been ever since the time of Xu Sun, Xu appeared to the governor in a dream and told him his life was in danger. The governor returned the bell and went to burn incense and confess his fault in the abbey, but his sin was too grave to be pardoned and he died in battle soon afterward.

Another tale recounts how a mysterious visitor, later rumored to have been Zhang Daoling himself, visited the Heavenly Master of the eighteenth generation and repaired the sword used by the first Heavenly Master to "punish and control gods and demons." The sword had been in the family, adds Du, for twenty-one generations. Elsewhere in the same book, in introducing the story of a man who was released from hell because he was wearing a register transmitted to him in the year 868 by the nineteenth-generation Heavenly Master, Du notes that, until the thirteenth-generation descendant of Zhang Daoling, the registers transmitted to the faithful had been made of wood, but "because they were being transmitted on such a vast scale, the thirteenth Heavenly Master could not make them in sufficient numbers and so started using paper and silk instead."

Du no doubt owed his knowledge of such events to his own master, Ying Yijie (810–894), who, at the age of eighteen, had gone to Longhu Shan (Dragon-tiger Mountain) in Jiangxi to be initiated by the eighteenth Heavenly Master. Much later accounts claim that Zhang Sheng, the fourth-generation descendant of Zhang Daoling, had been the first to take up residence on Mount Longhu. The first contemporary trace of a Zhang family in southern China dates to 504, when according to a stele, the twelfth-generation descendant lived in an abbey in what is now Jiangsu. In the mid-eighth century Sima Chengzhen mentions a Zhang living on Mount Longhu. The next reliable witness is Du Guangting.

It is therefore impossible to ascertain whether the Zhang family, which apparently lived on this mountain in unbroken succession from at least the mid-eighth century until 1949, was indeed descended from the first Heavenly Master.

What is certain is that, from Du Guangting's time on, the lineage grew steadily more important in Chinese religious life. Already in 1015, the emperor Zhenzong (r. 997–1023) recognized its hereditary rights. By 1097 Mount Longhu had won official recognition as an authorized center for initiation into Daoist practice, along with Mount Mao (Jiangsu) for the Shangqing tradition and Mount Gezao (Jiangxi) for the Lingbao. The thirtieth Heavenly Master (1092–1126) played a prominent role at the court under Huizong, and his reputation for magical powers was already celebrated in a contemporary novel. Full consecration came in the thirty-sixth generation, to Zhang Zongyan (d. 1291): invited to the capital by the emperor Shizu (r. 1260–1295) in 1277, he was commissioned to perform a Grand Offering of the Entire Heaven (2,400 divinities) in the Changchun Gong (Palace of Eternal Spring). Shortly thereafter, he was appointed head of all Daoists in southern China. The emperor Chengzong (r. 1295–1308) decreed in 1295 that Heavenly Master texts for the Offering be used throughout the empire. Finally, under the first Ming emperor, Taizu (r. 1368–1399), the Heavenly Masters were put in charge of all Daoist affairs.

During the Yuan dynasty the control of Daoism in the North was entrusted to the successive leaders of the Quanzhen ("integral perfection") order. One of three major Daoist movements to emerge in the North during the twelfth century, when that part of China was ruled by the foreign Jurchen Jin dynasty (1115–1234), it alone was destined to survive beyond the Yuan. Its founder, Wang Zhe (1112–1170), a native of the same village in Shaanxi as Zhongli Quan, had witnessed, at the age of eighteen, the takeover of his native province by the invading Jurchen. He nonetheless served for a time in the military before deciding to abandon both his career and his family. In 1160, after a period of living in reclusion in Liujiang village, not far from Tower Abbey, two mysterious encounters with Daoist immortals led him to dig a grave, to which he gave the name "tomb of the living dead," and to live in it for three years; having built a thatched hut, he lived next to it for another four. In 1167 he suddenly burned down his hut and left for Shandong to begin proselytizing. According to Wang's hagiographers, the three immortals who appeared to him were Zhongli Quan, Lü Dongpin, and Liu Haichan, all of whom Wang refers to in his writings as his teachers.

Wishing to shock people into enlightenment, which necessarily entailed a complete break of the sort he had made from his own family and career, Wang's methods were apparently uncompromising and even violent. In this manner he selected seven disciples, including one separated couple, to carry on his work. He also established five *sanjiao hui* ("assemblies of the three teachings") before dying while on his way back to his home in the west. His disciples are portrayed by their hagiographers as ascetics and, in some cases, eccentrics. Qiu Changchun (1148–1227) lived for seven years in a cave. Hao Datong (1140–1212) spent six years under a stone bridge neither moving nor speaking and eating only when people offered him something. For nine years Wang Chui (1142–1217) spent his nights in a cave standing on one foot so as not to fall asleep. Wang is also depicted as a wandering exorcist and healer (herbal medicine was one of the arts that Wang Zhe insisted "those who study the Way must master").

The reputations of the Seven Real Persons (*qizhen*), as Wang's disciples came to be known, soon made the movement of Integral Perfection a force to deal with. It attracted lay followers from all levels of society, including the gentry class, to which most of the seven and Wang Zhe had belonged. Their following seems to have been particularly large among women. The emperor Shizong (r. 1161–1190) summoned Wang Chui in 1187, questioned him about the methods for "preserving life and ruling the country," and constructed for him the Xiuzhen Guan (Abbey for the Cultivation of Perfection). In 1197 Wang was involved, together with the Zhengi Daoist Sun Mingdao, in the celebration of a Grand Offering of the Entire Heaven in the Tianchang Guan (Abbey of Celestial Longevity) in the capital. In 1202 the emperor Zhangzong (r. 1190–1208) ordered Wang to perform an Offering in the Palace of Grand Purity in Laozi's birthplace.

But it was Qiu Changchun's three-year westward trek to meet Chinggis Khan in Central Asia that assured the order's future, for when Qiu returned to China in 1223, he did so armed with decrees granting tax and labor exemption to himself and his disciples and control over "all those in the world who leave their families" to him. The result was the rapid growth of the Integral Perfection order and the start of another round of confrontrations with the Buddhists. When Qiu died, the Tianchang Abbey was renamed the Abbey of Eternal Spring (Changchun Guan), in Qiu's honor, and his disciples inherited his position. One of them, Li Zhichang (1193–1273), abbot between 1238 and 1256, precipitated the crisis with the Buddhists by printing and distributing the *Laozi bashii huatu* (Pictures of the eighty-one transformations of Laozi). One of these transformations, of course, was that into the Buddha. The Buddhists protested and also accused the Daoists of appropriating their temples. Debates were held in 1255, 1258 (the burning of the offending books was ordered, but not carried out), and 1281 (Zhang Zongyan also participated in this debate). After the last confrontation, the Daoist canon was ordered destroyed—an order carried out, at least in part, and the Quanzhen order went into a partial eclipse until the end of Shizu's reign. It was replaced at the court by the Heavenly Masters and their ambassadors.

Strictly speaking, Integral Perfection Daoism taught nothing new. It was a reform movement that sought, in the tradition of Daoist universalism, to synthesize the best in the

Three Teachings. Like Chan Buddhism, which Wang Zhe apparently knew fairly well, it preached celibacy and "sitting in meditation" in order to control the "apelike mind and the horselike will"; as in neo-Confucianism, perfect authenticity was prized as the ultimate goal of self-cultivation. But it was eminently Daoist in insisting that both one's "nature" (*xing*) and one's "life force" (*ming*) had to be nurtured, and in having recourse for the latter to the usual panoply of physiological practices. Quanzhen masters were also frequently renowned adepts of the martial arts, and Wang Zhe himself must have practiced internal alchemy inasmuch as his divine teachers were its patrons.

Zhongli Quan and Lü Dongpin, especially the latter, appear frequently to convert and save people in a number of Yuan operas (*zaju*) of clearly Quanzhen inspiration. A temple on the presumed site of Lü Dongpin's house was converted into a Quanzhen abbey toward the end of the Jin dynasty and then, after the abbey had burned down in 1244, rebuilt on a vast scale between 1247 and 1358. The three surviving halls of the resulting Yonglo Gong (Palace of Eternal Joy) are dedicated, respectively, to the Three Pure Ones, Lü Dongpin, and Wang Zhe. The magnificent murals of the latter two halls tell the stories of Lü and Wang and of Wang's conversion by Lü. The murals of the first hall portray many of the same divinities as were listed in Lü Taigo's list of 1201: they are all "going in audience before the Origin" (*chaoyuan*), that is, before the Three Pure Ones. The other great surviving monument of Daoist history, the fabulous complex of abbeys and palaces on Mount Wu-tang (Hubei), built by the Ming emperor Chengzu in honor of Pei-ti (Emperor of the North), divine patron of the exorcistic and martial arts, was also a Quanzhen center. Reopened in 1982, it has since been recognized by the UNESCO World Heritage Fund. The Tower Abbey was first taken over by the Quanzhen order in 1236, when disciples of Qiu Changchun rebuilt it.

Later Developments. Both the site of Lü Dongpin's house and Mount Wu-tang were important pilgrimage centers from the twelfth and thirteenth centuries on. As such, they reveal an important aspect of Daoism's role in Chinese society in those centuries: Daoists occupied and ran important cult centers and their temples. In particular, the Daoists, together with the Buddhists, inhabited the many sacred mountains of China and took care of the pilgrims who came to them. Several of the more important pilgrimage centers also developed networks of "branch offices"—local centers where the lay-person who lacked the means or the motivation to make a long pilgrimage could nonetheless worship the divinity of his choice. On the Daoist side, the most numerous temples of this kind were those dedicated to Lü Dongpin, the Emperor of the North, and the Emperor of the Eastern Peak. The first two were centers for the practice of divination by selection of slips, which were then interpreted by an attendant. The halls dedicated to Lü Dongpin in most Quanzhen abbeys served simultaneously as temples for the local populace.

The temples of the Eastern Peak (Dongyue Miao), on the contrary, were without exception run by Orthodox Unity Daoists. According to an inscription written by one Zhao Shiyan in 1328 and set up on the grounds of the Temple of the Eastern Peak in Beijing, such temples "first become widespread in the middle of the Song dynasty." By the Yuan dynasty they were to be found in every town of any size, and mediums and their Daoist masters worked in them side by side, the former to contact the souls of the dead and the latter to save them, for the Eastern Peak, the abode of the dead already in Han times, was associated at once with the tribunals of hell and the hope of immortality. Veritable nerve centers of the traditional Chinese religious system, the temples of the Eastern Peak seem to have been singled out for destruction by the Red Guards during the Cultural Revolution (1966–1976).

It is not known when the original Daoist community organized by the Heavenly Masters disappeared. As early as the third century, leaders of the community were complaining that libationers were increasingly self-appointed or at least not appointed by the hierarchy. The office of libationer, moreover, seems very early on to have become a hereditary one. It is nonetheless fairly certain that laypersons continued to practice the initiatory rites of sexual union as late as the mid-Tang, and Heavenly Master "congregations" must therefore have continued to exist. But by the mid-Song, when the Heavenly Masters themselves began once again to play a political role, it was as hierarchs not, as in the time of Zhang Lu, of an organized lay community, but of all Orthodox Unity priests. Over the centuries, laypersons of means continued to make the pilgrimage to Dragon-Tiger Mountain in order to be invested before death with a "register of immortality," but the main function of the Daoist "pope" was the transmission of registers to priests. By the 1920s and 1930s even the number of such registers had dropped off to from one to three hundred a year, and it was estimated that only one percent of Zhengi priests actually applied for such a register.

This situation was in part due to the fact that the foreign Qing dynasty had terminated the special relationship between the ruling house and the Heavenly Masters. During the Ming dynasty, by contrast, emperors were constantly inviting the Heavenly Master to the capital to perform Offerings, the compilation of the *Daozang* (Daoist canon) was entrusted to the Heavenly Masters, and several emperors even arranged high marriages for what had in effect become their spiritual counterpart: the emperor controlled the (Confucian) administration; the Heavenly Master had final authority over all gods and demons. He was, in other words, not only the nominal head of all Daoist priests, but also the overseer of all local cults. Throughout the Ming period, the Heavenly Master continued to be associated with imperial campaigns against heterodox cults. At the same time, local Orthodox Unity priests were "infiltrating" local temples—of the Eastern Peak, of the City God (Chenghuang Miao), of the third-century patriot and general Guan Yü (Guanti Miao)—and performing Offerings for the consecration of temples dedicated to gods who, although not "Daoist," had been officially invested by imperially promulgated titles inscribed in the "canon of sacrifices." The collective ceremonies of initiation of original Daoism seem to have survived only among tribal peoples such as the Yao: there, ordination remains a prerequisite for salvation and is therefore extended to the entire community.

The number of Daoist monks—mostly of the Quanzhen order since the Yuan dynasty—never approached that of lay Daoist priests (or Buddhist monks). The monks nonetheless played an important part in shaping Daoist history from the fifth century on. Not only did their leaders have privileged relations with emperors, at least until 1281, they also regularly exchanged visits and poems with the members of the gentry class from which many of them came. Wang Zhe's first convert and eventual successor, for example, Ma Yü (1123–1183), was known locally as Ma *panzhou,* Ma "half-the-prefecture," because of his extensive land holdings. Also, it was these Daoists who controlled the network of official abbeys first created in the Tang dynasty.

At the beginning of the Qing dynasty, the White Cloud Abbey of Beijing, originally built around the grave of Qiu Changchun became the center of a reinvigorated, imperially recognized Quanzhen lineage. In the 1940s it still had at least nominal control of twenty-three such abbeys throughout the country. Qiu's birthday on the nineteenth day of the first lunar month was one of Beijing's biggest festivals. The only complete copy of the Ming-dynasty Daoist canon to survive to the present is that of the same White Cloud Abbey. It was only natural, therefore, that it was selected by the government in the 1950s as the seat of the National Daoist Association. Among the major abbeys that have been restored since the government began, in the early 1980s, to allow and even encourage the restoration of religious buildings, many are on the 1940s list of twenty-three, and all reopened abbeys send their best novices to Beijing for a six-month training period. Gradually, however Zhengi Daoists have joined the hitherto Quanzhen-dominated national association, and they now perform rituals in their temples as in the past.

SEE ALSO Du Guangting; Jiao; Kou Qianzhi; Laozi; Liang Wudi; Lu Xiujing; Millenarianism, article on Chinese Millenarian Movements; Priesthood, article on Daoist Priesthood; Sima Chengzhen; Taiping; Wang Zhe; Worship and Devotional Life, article on Daoist Devotional Life; Zhang Daoling; Zhang Jue; Zhang Lu; Zhenren.

BIBLIOGRAPHY

For good general surveys of early Daoism see *Daoism Handbook,* ed. Livia Kohn (Leiden, 2000): Barbara Hendrischke, "Early Daoist Movements" (chap. 6); Peter Nickerson, "The Southern Celestial Masters" (chap. 10); Livia Kohn, "The Northern Celestial Masters" (chap. 11); Charles Benn, "Daoist Ordination and *Zhai* Rituals" (chap. 12). Excellent introductions to the ideological content of pre-Tang Heavenly Master Daoism may be found in Anna Seidel's "Das neue Testament des Dao: Lao Tzu und die Entstehung der daoistiszhen Religion am Ende der Han-Zeit," *Saeculum* 27 (1978): 147–172, and Rolf A. Stein's "Remarques sur les mouvements du daoïsme politico-religieux au deuxième siècle ap. J.-C.," *T'oung pao* 50 (1963): 1–78. On Daoist rejection of "heterodox cults," see Rolf A. Stein's "Religious Daoism and Popular Religion from the Second to the Seventh Centuries," in *Facets of Daoism,* edited by Holmes Welch and Anna Seidel (New Haven, 1979), pp. 53–81. On Daoist messianism, see Anna Seidel's "The Image of the Perfect Ruler in Early Daoist Messianism: Laozi and Li Hung," *History of Religions* 9 (November 1969 and February 1970): 216–247, and Christine Mollier's *Une apocalypse taoïste du Ve siècle: Le livre des Incantations divines des grottes abyssales* (Paris, 1990). On the early history of zhurch-state relations and the development of Daoist sanction of imperial power, see Anna Seidel's "Imperial Treasures and Daoist Sacraments: Daoist Roots in the Apocrypha," in *Tantric and Daoist Studies in Honour of R. A. Stein,* edited by Michel Strickmann (Brussels, 1983), vol. 2, pp. 291–371, and Richard B. Mather's "Kou Qianzhi and the Daoist Theocracy at the Northern Wei Court, 425–451," in *Facets of Daoism,* pp. 103–122. My *Wushang biyao: Somme daoïste du sixième siècle* (Paris, 1981) describes the ideological content of Daoist universalism under the Northern Zhou dynasty. For the sociological background and early history of Shangqing Daoism, see Michel Strickmann's "The Mao-shan Revelations: Daoism and the Aristocracy," *T'oung pao* 63 (1977): 1–64. Isabelle Robinet's *Méditation daoïste* (Paris, 1979) and *La révélation du Shangqing dans l'histoire du daoïsme,* 2 vols (Paris, 1984), gives thorough surveys of Shangqing practices and their prehistory.

For the Tang dynasty, the best introduction is Timothy Barrett's *Daoism under the T'ang: Religion and Empire During the Golden Age of Chinese History* (London, 1996). Charles David Benn's "Daoism as Ideology in the Reign of Emperor Xuanzung (712–755)" (Ph.D. diss., University of Michigan, 1977) gives a detailed study of the period up to the mid-Tang. On the pivotal figure Du Guangting, Franciscus Verellen's *Du Guangting (850–933): taoïste de cour à la fin de la Chine médiévale* (Paris, 1989) gives an exemplary study of the intertwining of religious and political history. On Huizong, the "emperor as Daoist god," see Michel Strickmann's "The Longest Daoist Scripture," *History of Religions* 17 (February-May 1978): 331–354. *Procédés secrets du Joyau magique. Traité d'alchimie daoïste du onzième siècle,* edited and translated by Farzeen Baldrian-Hussein (Paris, 1984) is a translation and study of the main text on internal alchemy in the Zhongli Quan/Lü Dongpin tradition.

A special issue of *The Journal of Chinese Religions* (no. 29, 2001), edited by Vincent Goossaert and Paul Katz, is entirely devoted to "New Perspectives on Quanzhen Taoism." *The Yongle Palace Murals* (Beijing, 1985) gives beautiful reproductions of the Yonglo murals. An excellent study is provided by Paul R. Katz in *Images of the Immortal: The Cult of Lü Dongbin at the Palace of Eternal Joy* (Honolulu, 1999). David Hawkes's "Quanzhen Plays and Quanzhen Masters," *Bulletin de l'École Francaise d'Extrême-Orient* 69 (1981): 153–170, is a delightful introduction to the subjects named.

On the legislation governing official abbeys, see Werner Eichhorn's *Beitrag zur rechtlizhen Stellung des Buddhismus und Daoismus im Song-Staat: Übersetzung der Sektion "Daoismus und Buddhismus" aus dem Qing-Yuan T'iao-Fa Shih-Lei* (Leiden, 1968) and J. J. M. de Groot's *Sectarianism and Religious Persecution in China,* vol. 7 (Amsterdam, 1903), chap. 3.

Excellent introductions to Daoism from the Song through the Qing may be found in Livia Kohn, ed., *Daoism Handbook* (Leiden, 2000): Lowell Skar, "Ritual Movements, Deity Cults, and the Transformation of Daoism in Song and Yuan Times" (chap. 15); Lowell Skar and Fabrizio Pregadio, "Inner Alchemy (*Neidan*)" (chap. 16); Pierre-Henry de Bruyn "Daoism in the Ming (1368–1644)" (chap. 20); Monica Esposito, "Daoism in the Qing (1644–1911)" (chap. 21). New light on the role of Tantrism in transforming Daoism's relationship with popular religion may be found in Edward L. Davis, *Society and the Supernatural in Song China* (Honolulu, 2001).

On Daoism among the Yao, see Jacques Lemoine's richly illustrated *Yao Ceremonial Paintings* (Atlantic Highlands, N.J., 1982). On Daoism as it functions in modern Chinese society, see my *Daoist Ritual in Chinese Society and History* (New York, 1987) and Kenneth Dean, *Taoist Ritual and Popular Cults of Southeast China* (Princeton, 1993).

John Lagerwey (1987)
Revised Bibliography

DAOISM: DAOIST LITERATURE

Compared to Buddhism, the literature of Daoist traditions remains largely unexplored. Large-scale study in this area was greatly enhanced in 1926 with the appearance of the first widely accessible reprint of the *Daozang*, or Daoist canon, which, at 1120 fascicles, is the largest repository of Daoist literature ever compiled. Research on Daoism prior to that time was, with few exceptions, generally confined to studies of texts such as the *Laozi* and *Zhuangzi* that are widely available in editions outside the canon. For the most part, the West has also had its understanding of the Daoist legacy shaped by what has been summarized from the writings on the subject by Buddhist polemicists and unsympathetic Chinese literati. The one-sided view of Daoist traditions that such limitations promote is easily amended when the resources of the *Daozang* are taken into account, together with subsidiary compilations and pertinent collections of epigraphy and manuscripts. The social and historical context of much of this material has only recently come under intensive scrutiny. Continued research on the Daoist literary heritage is likely to challenge many long-held perceptions about the nature of religious traditions in Chinese society.

The Daozang. Before 1926, very few copies of the Daoist canon were available outside of those kept in the temple archives of China. The state traditionally sponsored both the compilation and distribution of the *Daozang*. While it cannot be said that the newly founded Republic of China was a patron of Daoism, the reprinting of the canon between 1923 and 1926 came about only through government subvention. The former minister of education and renowned bibliophile Fu Zengxiang (1872–1950) was instrumental in convincing President Xu Shichang (1855–1939) of the scholarly value of the *Daozang* and to underwrite its publication by the Commercial Press of Shanghai. The copy that was selected for photographic reproduction in the 1920s and that has since been reprinted in at least three modern editions was the wood-block concertina canon housed in the Baiyun Guan (White Cloud Abbey) of Beijing, the central Daoist seminary of the People's Republic of China. It is thought that this copy of the canon was largely derived from the 1445 printing, apart from the lacunae reconstituted in 1845.

History of compilation. Among the earliest inventories of Daoist writings are those recorded in the bibliographic monograph of Ban Gu's (32–92) *Han shu* (History of the Han) and Ge Hong's (283–343) *Baopuzi.* It was not until the late fifth century, well after the establishment of the Shangqing and Lingbao scriptural traditions, that a single, comprehensive catalogue of Daoist texts was attempted. Lu Xiujing (406–477), principal codifier of the Lingbao corpus, undertook the task on the order of Song Mingdi (r. 465–472). The *Sandong jingshu mulu* (An index to the scriptural writings of the three caverns), which Lu presented to the emperor in 471, was said to list over twelve hundred *juan* (scrolls or chapters), ranging from scriptures and pharmaceutical works to talismanic diagrams. Nearly three centuries later, Tang Xuanzong (r. 712–756), confident that he was the descendant of Laozi, issued a decree dispatching his envoys throughout the empire in search of all existing Daoist writings. The collection that followed was given the title *Sandong qionggang* (Exquisite compendium of the three caverns) and reportedly included around thirty-seven hundred or fifty-seven hundred *juan.* It was the first canon from which multiple copies were to be transcribed for distribution to Daoist temples. But not long after Xuanzong officially authorized this undertaking in 748, the imperial libraries of the capitals of Chang'an and Luoyang were destroyed during the An Lushan and Shi Siming rebellions, and much of the *Sandong qionggang* was apparently lost.

Subsequent compilations were attempted upon the command of various Song emperors, who similarly viewed their mandate as part of a larger Daoist dispensation. Song Zhenzong (r. 998–1022) assigned his trusted adviser Wang Qinruo (962–1025) the task of preparing a new catalogue of Daoist texts in the imperial archives. By 1016 an assistant draftsman named Zhang Junfang (fl. 1008–1029) was put in charge of a staff of Daoist priests to make copies of a new canon for distribution to major temples. The *Da Song tiangong baozang* (Precious canon of the celestial palace of the great sung; 4,565 *juan*) that resulted was the first definitive edition of what has come simply to be called the *Daozang.*

A century later Song Huizong (r. 1101–1125) initiated an even more ambitious program for the compilation and dissemination of a new Daoist canon. In 1114 he issued an edict ordering all local officials, clergy, and laity to submit whatever Daoist texts they had to the capital of Kaifeng. A number of Daoist priests answered his call to help with the collation of the incoming literature. Their work culminated in the *Zhenghe wanshou Daozang* (Daoist canon of the longevity of the Zhenghe reign), the first canon to be printed. The blocks for nearly fifty-four hundred *juan* were cut sometime around 1118 to 1120. It is not known how many copies of the *Daozang* were subsequently made and there is also some question as to how much was lost upon the Jurchen takeover in 1127. But it appears that at least some blocks survived, for in 1188 it is reported that Jin Shizong (r. 1161–1189) commanded their removal from Kaifeng to the Tianchang Guan (Abbey of Celestial Perpetuity) in the central capital of the Jurchen empire, the predecessor to the Baiyun Guan in Beijing. His grandson and successor, Jin Zhangzong (r. 1190–1208), had the temple enlarged in 1190 and then appointed two imperial academicians to assist the abbot in reediting the canon. With the carving of additional blocks two years later, the *Da Jin xuandu baozang* (Precious canon of the arcane metropolis of the great Chin) totaled over sixty-four hundred *juan.*

In 1215 the capital of the Jurchen fell into the hands of the Mongols and it is not known how much of the enlarged canon of the Jin escaped destruction. But by 1237 work on a new edition was undertaken, sponsored this time by the local administration of Shanxi province. Two Quanzhen masters, Song Defang (1183–1247) and his disciple Qin Zhi'an (1188–1244), oversaw a staff in the hundreds. The *Xuandu baozang* (Precious canon of the arcane metropolis), completed in 1244, was apparently the largest ever, comprising altogether seven thousand *juan.* Over a hundred copies were said to have been made, but in 1281 Khubilai Khan decreed that all texts and printing blocks of the *Daozang* be burnt, save the *Dao de jing.* Fragments of the 1244 canon were nonetheless spared and, together with what remained of the Jurchen and Song canons, came to serve as the foundation of the Ming *Daozang.*

The canon currently in print is based on the compilation completed between 1444 and 1445 and a supplement dating to 1607. Ming Chengzu (r. 1402–1424) initiated the project in 1406 by appointing the forty-third Celestial Master, Zhang Yuchu (1361–1410), as compiler-in-chief. But the final version of the *Da Ming Daozang jing* (Scriptures of the Daoist canon of the great Ming) was actually completed under the guidance of Shao Yizheng, a prominent Daoist master at the court of Ming Yingzong (r. 1436–1449). The fiftieth Celestial Master, Zhang Guoxiang (d. 1611), supervised the preparation of a 240-*juan* supplement to the 5,318 *juan* of this edition. It is known as the *Xu Daozang* (Supplementary Daoist canon) of the Wanli reign (1573–1619), whereas the fifteenth-century core is sometimes referred to as the *Zhengtong Daozang* or Daoist canon of the Zhengtong reign (1436–1449).

Organizational divisions. As the title of Lu Xiujing's catalogue of 471 suggests, Daoist writings were traditionally classified according to the "Three Caverns" (*sandong*). This tripart division became a fundamental organizational feature of the *Daozang.* Although there has been a tendency in the past to equate these three compartments of texts with the "Three Receptacles" (*sanzang*) of the Buddhist canon, the closer parallel is actually the Buddhist *triyāna* or *sansheng* ("three vehicles"). Rather than being representative of three genres of literature such as the Sūtra, Vinaya, and Abhidharma of the Three Receptacles, the Three Caverns reflect three distinct revelatory traditions. And like the Three Vehicles, the Three Caverns are viewed as a ranking of textual legacies. The Dongzhen section evolved around the Shangqing (Supreme Clarity) scriptures, the Dongxuan around the Lingbao (Numinous Treasure), and the Dongshen around the San huang (Three Sovereigns). Since this categorization gives primacy to the Shangqing traditions, it is assumed that it was devised well before Lu Xiujing compiled his catalogue, perhaps by the end of the fourth or beginning of the fifth century. There is less certainty about the origins of the Four Supplements that follow the Three Caverns, what are known as the Taixuan, Taiping, Taiqing, and Zhengyi components of the canon. The term *ssu-fu* ("four supplements") does not seem to date before the turn of the sixth century. The first three have commonly been regarded as individual appendices to the Three Caverns, but in fact they appear to have been organized around very specific literary collections. Central to the Tai-xuan division is the *Dao de jing.* Likewise, the *Taiping jing* (Scripture on the grand pacification), the Taiqing (Grand Purity) legacy of alchemical writings, and the Zhengyi (Authentic unity), or Celestial Master heritage lie at the heart of the Taiping, Taiqing, and Zhengyi subdivisions. It may be that these four supplements were inspired by demands to establish a more cohesive body of Daoist literature vis-à-vis the rapidly developing corpus of Chinese Buddhist writings. Although the preeminence of the Shangqing revelations was apparently never in question, it seems that by the sixth century there was more awareness of the diversity of inspiration from which they arose. Liturgical texts of the Tang dynasty, moreover, seem to suggest that the arrangement of the canon corresponds to descending ranks of ordination, from the top level of Dongzhen down to the first step of the Zhengyi initiation.

Whatever the underlying significance of the organization of the *Daozang,* accretions over the centuries have resulted in a less than systematic presentation of texts. Each of the Three Caverns is subdivided into twelve sections: (1) original revelations, (2) divine talismans, (3) exegeses, (4) sacred diagrams, (5) histories and genealogies, (6) codes of conduct, (7) ceremonial protocols, (8) prescriptive rituals, (9) special techniques (i.e., alchemical, geomantic, numerological), (10) hagiography, (11) hymnody, and (12) memorial communications. The distribution of texts is not always in keeping with either the major headings or these subheadings. No categorical distinctions are applied to the Four Supplements and the *Xu Daozang,* the contents of which are as diverse as the Three Caverns.

Facets of research. Nearly half of the volumes in the canon either bear dates after 1126 or can be directly linked to new scriptural traditions developing after the Northern Song dynasty. Moreover, the prefaces of at least sixty titles in the *Daozang* indicate that they circulated in printed editions prior to their incorporation into the canon. Prefaces and colophons, however, are not always reliable guides to the history of a text. Fictive lineages are often invoked in order to establish the historical antiquity of newly codified writings. It is not unusual to find, for example, the provenance of a text traced directly to the founder of the Tianshi Dao (Way of the Celestial Masters), Zhang Daoling (fl. 142 CE). An even larger number of texts are simply presented as the word of divine authority. The names of the deities cited often prove critical to the identification of a text vis-à-vis established scriptural traditions. Other internal dating features that help clarify the historical and social origins of a compilation include reign titles, datable place names and official titles, as well as the titles of canonization granted by imperial decree to various patriarchs and apotheosized cultic figures. The language itself, particularly the use of specialized terminology, also helps determine the setting in which a text arose. The *terminus a quo* or *terminus ad quem* of a work can likewise be determined with the help of a number of inventories of Daoist texts.

Contents. The range of literature in the canon is as diverse as the beliefs and practices associated with Daoism since the Han dynasty. Much research to date has concentrated on the scientific significance of Daoist alchemical and pharmaceutical works. Aside from the early Shangqing and Lingbao scriptural traditions, little has been reported on the textual legacy of Daoist revelatory and cultic inspiration. The *Daozang*, furthermore, has yet to be fully appreciated as a valuable repository of belles-lettres in its own right. The following survey highlights a few of the texts in the canon with enduring literary and religious interest.

Revelation and ritual. As a work ostensibly transmitted from master to disciple, the *Dao de jing* or *Laozi* has long been regarded as a revelation in itself. The writings that Laozi reportedly delivered to the gatekeeper Yin Xi on his journey west have served as the inspiration for centuries of instruction on the attainment of the Dao. To the Celestial Masters, the *Dao de jing* seems to have functioned foremost as a code of behavior for young initiates. It is thought that the Xiang'er commentary on the *Laozi* (*Xiang'er zhu*) discovered at Dunhuang was compiled by one of the first, if not the first, patriarch of the Celestial Masters. The commentary extrapolates not only rules of conduct but also techniques of meditative practice from the text and is the only substantial writing associated with the early Celestial Masters to survive. The apotheosis of Laozi, that is, Taishang Laojun, or Lord Lao the Most High, who appeared before the founder Zhang Daoling was said to have revealed not scriptures but the sacred registers and talismans of divine guardians. Both were essential to the demonifuge mission of the Tianshi Dao. Divine commanders on high could be summoned only by those privy to their names and capable of infusing talismanic communications with their vitality. Countless texts, including even Ge Hong's *Baopuzi*, purport to preserve the apotropaic talismans of the Celestial Masters. The manipulation of such talismans was and still is thought to keep spectral forces at bay. Throughout the centuries the codifiers of later revelatory and ritual writings have never forgotten the ultimate heritage of the Tianshi Dao as a healing cult. Many anthologies of ritual are based precisely on the understanding that the ultimate mission of their founders was to convey hope in the salvation of humankind from all forms of suffering.

Salvation was also the message behind one of the earliest scriptures recorded in the canon, the *Taiping jing* (Scripture on the grand pacification). An early version of a text by this title was apparently promoted during the Western Han in support of a faction that sought to influence the direction of the ruling house through its expertise in the interpretation of cosmological omens. What circulates as the *Taiping jing* can be traced in part to another faction that arose during the Eastern Han on the Shandong Peninsula. Because of the text's link with Zhang Jue, leader of the Yellow Turban peasant rebellion, and the fall of the Han empire, the *Taiping jing* fell out of favor for several generations. It was not until the sixth century that a new, and much larger, edition of 170 *juan* appeared, portions of which are preserved in the canon as well as in Dunhuang manuscripts. This edition, the provenance of which can be traced to the Shangqing *axis mundi* of Maoshan (in present-day Jiangsu), seems to retain many of the major themes promoted in the Han dynasty works. The text was generally regarded as the omen of a more prosperous era. While there is difficulty in distinguishing the second-century text from later accretions, it appears that one consistent feature was the hint of an apocalypse should the divine teachings recorded within not be put into effect. The sixth-century editors enlarged upon this theme by interpolating references to the promise of deliverance by a messianic figure sacred to Shangqing, Housheng Jun, or the Sage-lord to Come. Overall, however, the *Taiping jing* stresses the importance of creating a utopian society in the present, one in which the political, social, and economic welfare of all could be assured upon the recitation of the scripture and the keeping of behavioral precepts in accordance with the will of the heavens above. This ideal of equity is tempered in part by instructions on techniques for prolonging life, a pastime in which only a select few could indulge.

The common denominator between the practices prescribed for attaining longevity in the *Taiping jing* and in the Shangqing scriptures is a large body of macrobiotic literature that is traditionally associated with the *fangshi* or technocrats of Chinese society. The titles of many of these works are recorded in early hagiographies. Central to these guides on the pursuit of a life everlasting is the ability to gain communion with the gods residing within one's own body as well as with those on high. One of the earliest and more provocative instruction manuals on gaining communication with the corporeal hierarchy is the *Huangting jing (Scripture of the Yellow Court).* The innate ambiguities of this lengthy verse composed in heptasyllabic meter were apparently thought to be at least partially resolved upon repeated recitation. A revised and less arcane version of the *Huangting jing* was reportedly among those texts conveyed to Yang Xi (b. 330), the prime recipient of the Shangqing revelations during the years 364 to 370. The most comprehensive record of Shangqing beliefs and practices was made over a century later by the eminent Daoist master Tao Hongjing (456–536). The *Zhengao* (Declarations of the perfected) that he edited is largely intended to be a verbatim account of the instructions given Yang during the visits of divine transcendents. Central to the expectations of those promoting the new dispensation of Shangqing was the imminent descent of a messiah who could replace the disorder of their age with order. The eschatological scenario for the advent of a savior by the name of Li Hong is set forth in the *Shangqing housheng daojun lieji* (Annals of the Lord of the Tao, the sage-to-come of Shangqing). The vision of Li Hong's epiphany continued to inspire a number of messianic movements as reflected, for example, in the *Dongyuan shenzhou jing* (A scripture of spirit spells from the caverned abyss), a composite work dating from the fifth and sixth centuries that has its analogues in the newly compiled *dhāraṇī* sūtras of that era.

The Shangqing visionaries worked not only toward the restoration of terrestrial order but also toward their own promotion into the ranks of the divine. The methods by which their eschatological hopes could be realized ranged from the rigid control of diet to stringent respiratory exercises and experimentation with pharmaceutical compounds. But the main sustenance for adepts pursuing such a regimen were the vital forces of the sun, moon, and stars. It was thought that the regular and concentrated absorption of these powerful sources of radiance would lead ultimately to one's cosmic transmigration. Feeding on the illumination of astral bodies is among the most fundamental techniques of the Daoist master (central to his private meditative sessions as well as his liturgical performances) and is by and large a technique of visualization, the skill of which is the concern of many manuals predating the Shangqing revelations. Those texts in which the ultimate goal specified is ascent to the celestial realm of Taiqing are commonly regarded as part of a Taiqing scriptural tradition, the origins of which remain unclear. The teachings of these Taiqing manuals were incorporated into both the Shangqing revelations and the slightly later scriptural tradition known as Lingbao. The prolongation of life through the ingestion of astral essences is, for example, a lesson in the *Taishang Lingbao wufu xu* (Prolegomena on the five talismans of the numinous treasure of the most high), a text originally dating to the late third century and recycled by spokesmen for the Lingbao tradition in the late fourth century.

The major recipient of the Lingbao revelations was Ge Chaofu, a nephew of Ge Hong. In the 390s, Ge Chaofu began ascribing the origin of some twenty-seven Lingbao scriptures to his grand-uncle Ge Xuan (164–244). This set of sacred writings actually owes its inspiration to not only the centuries-old arcana of southern Chinese religious practice and the more recent Shangqing innovations, but also to the Mahāyāna Buddhist traditions of the Nanjing area. The message of Lingbao, as epitomized in the *Duren jing* (Scripture on the salvation of mankind), was that all could ultimately be released from the cycle of suffering and ascend to the celestial realm by adhering to the teachings of the Yuanshi Tianzun, or Celestial Worthy of Primordial Commencement. The foremost contribution of the Lingbao tradition was in fact a whole program of liturgical services to be performed on behalf of the living and dead. Equally significant was the articulation of a code of behavior to be followed by the faithful in their struggle to escape the bonds of the mundane realm. As with the Shangqing tradition, a systematic presentation of the Lingbao corpus came some time after the original revelations. What is preserved in the canon from this syncretic development is due to the efforts of Lu Xiujing, the compiler of the first known catalogue of Daoist writings.

Expansion on the Lingbao rituals continued for centuries, as is reflected, for example, in the *Wushang huanglu dazhai licheng yi* (Protocols on the establishment of the great *Zhai* retreats of the Yellow Register), a compilation based on the writings of Lu, as well as two major Tang liturgists, Zhang Wanfu (fl. 711) and Du Guangting (850–933), and the Song Daoist masters Liu Yongguang (1134–1206) and Jiang Shuyu (1156–1217). Du Guangting was by far the most prolific Tang liturgist, for in addition to editing a number of Lingbao codes, he also compiled the protocols for various ordination rituals, including those marking the bestowal of the *Dao de jing* and the divine registers of Shangqing and Zhengyi. He issued, moreover, a series of ritual texts associated with the *Scripture of Spirit Spells*, as well as with the archaic practice of casting propitiatory prayers inscribed on metal or wood into caves and streams. The diversity of Du's contributions reflects in general the trend of his age toward a consolidation and systematization of diverse ritual practices in which the Daoist priesthood was engaged.

The editorial enterprises of the Tang dynasty soon yielded to a new wave of scriptural innovation during the Song dynasty. The creation of more innovative ritual traditions was apparently stimulated in large part by Song Huizong's patronage of Daoist masters. Among the most influential at his court was Lin Lingsu (1076–1120) of Wenzhou (in present-day Zhejiang). Lin convinced the emperor that he was the incarnation of Changsheng Dadi (Great Sovereign of Long Life) and, as such, was responsible for the salvation of all under his domain. To this end, Lin drew on the soteriological features of the Lingbao legacy and the messianic expectations of the Shangqing tradition to devise what he called the Shenxiao (Divine Empyrean) dispensation. The *Gaoshang shenxiao zongshi shoujing shi* (Formulary for the transmission of scriptures according to the patriarchs of the exalted divine empyrean) is a record of the evolution of the Shenxiao scriptures from their origins as cosmic script to their bestowal upon the Grand Sovereign himself. Large ritual compendia were eventually compiled based on this new scriptural heritage, with the *Duren jing* uniformly established as the central focus. Among the largest of such corpora are those associated with the teachings of Ning Benli (1101–1181), also of Wenzhou, namely the *Shangqing Lingbao dafa* (Great rites of the Shangqing Lingbao legacy), compiled by a disciple named Wang Qizhen, and the *Lingbao lingjiao jidu jinshu* (Golden writings on salvation, based on the instructions conveyed by the Lingbao legacy), edited originally by Lin Weifu (1239–1302) of Wenzhou.

Another scriptural tradition codified during Song Huizong's reign was the Tianxin Zhengfa (Authentic Rites of the Celestial Heart), the origins of which were traced to the discovery in 994 of sacred texts at Huagai Shan (in present-day Jiangxi). One of the Daoist masters working on the compilation of a new canon at Kaifeng, Yuan Miaozong (fl. 1086–1116) sought to make amends for a lack of talismanic healing rituals by compiling the *Taishang zhuguo jiumin zongzhen biyao* (Secret essentials of the most high on assembling the perfected for the relief of the state and delivery of the people). At the heart of this corpus are the instructions on the application of the three talismans central to the Tianxin legacy: San'guang (Three Sources of Radiance; i.e., sun, moon, and stars); Zhenwu (Perfected Martial Lord); and Tiangang (Celestial Mainstay; i.e., Ursa Major).

The best testimony to the diversity of healing ritual from the twelfth to the fourteenth centuries is the *Daofa huiyuan* (A corpus of Daoist rites), compiled after 1356. The most voluminous work in the canon, this corpus is devoted largely to what are known as *leifa* ("thunder rites"), based on the practice of quelling demonic forces through the absorption and projection of thunder pneumas. The opening chapters of the work are derived from one of the later Thunder Ritual traditions called Qingwei (Purified Tenuity), codified in part by Zhao Yizhen (d. 1382). Many rituals that evoke the authority of the Zhengyi tradition appear to reflect the influence of the thirty-ninth Celestial Master Zhang Sicheng (d. 1343). Most outstanding of all are the ritual instructions to be enacted on behalf of various astral deities and cultic figures such as the martial lord Guan Yu (d. 219). These therapeutic rites were prescribed for a wide range of ailments, from conjunctivitis to manifestations of possessing spirits. Many attest, moreover, to a long tradition of collaboration between Daoist masters and spirit-mediums.

Hagiography. Not unlike Confucian and Buddhist biographical accounts, Daoist hagiographies were compiled primarily as commemorative works, usually with a didactic message in mind. The lives of transcendents were generally intended to instruct on the paths by which one's divine destiny might be realized, as well as on the rewards inherent in venerating those who gained entry into the celestial ranks. The visionary Yang Xi was reportedly conveyed the full biographies of a number of divine transcendents with whom he was in communication, but only a few survive. Some of his contacts are memorialized in the *Liexian zhuan* (Lives of the immortals), traditionally attributed to Liu Xiang (77–6 BCE) but apparently based on several centuries of oral tradition surrounding various local cults.

More extensive hagiographic accounts were compiled during the Tang dynasty, most notably by Du Guangting. One work of his, the *Yongcheng jixian lu* (A record of the transcendents assembled at Yongcheng), is entirely devoted to the lives of divine women, starting with an account of the cosmic evolution of the primordial goddess who gave birth to the historical Laozi. Du Guangting was above all a good storyteller and, as his *Daojiao lingyan ji* (An account of the divine efficacy of the teachings of the Dao) and *Shenxian ganyu zhuan* (A record of inspirational encounters with divine transcendents) further attest, he was most interested in recording accounts of sacred phenomena. Such works, together with Buddhist miracle tales, contributed significantly to the development of the narrative in Chinese literary history.

By far the most comprehensive hagiographic work in the canon is one compiled by a specialist in Thunder Ritual named Zhao Daoyi (fl. 1297–1307), the *Lishi zhenxian tidao tongjian* (A Comprehensive mirror on successive generations of perfected transcendents and those who embody the Dao). Largely derivative of earlier works, this text preserves much material that has otherwise been lost. Among more specialized works is the *Xuanpin lu* (A record of the ranks of the sublime) edited by a prominent literatus named Zhang Yu (1283–c. 1356). The author, who was himself temporarily in residence at Maoshan, dedicates a large portion of his text to the Shangqing heritage, from Yang Xi to the twenty-fifth patriarch Liu Hunkang (1035–1108). A separate account of the Zhengyi patriarchs, the *Han Tianshi shijia* (A genealogy of the Celestial Masters since the Han), is a composite work, based on editions dating from the fourteenth to the sixteenth century. The imprimatur of the fiftieth Celestial Master, Zhang Guoxiang (d. 1611), is found not only in this text but in the latest hagiography of the canon, the *Soushen ji* (In search of the sacred), edited by Luo Maodeng (fl. 1593–1598). Also a composite work, this text opens with the biographies of Confucius, Śākyamuni, and Taishang Laojun. Most predominate thereafter are the accounts of apotheosized cultic figures from south of the Yangtze. The dates of birth and ascension recorded in many of these entries give some indication as to the annual cycle of festival days authorized by church and state.

Several hagiographic works honor the Quanzhen heritage founded by Wang Zhe (1113–1170). One of the earliest is the *Jinlian zhengzong ji* (An account of the true lineage of the golden lotus), completed in 1241 by Qin Zhi'an, editor of the 1244 canon. This work was apparently lost in the book burning of 1281 and only recovered in the Ming. It was unknown to the compilers of a similar hagiography, the *Jinlian zhengzong xianyuan xiangzhuan* (An illustrated biographical account of the transcendent origins of the true lineage of the golden lotus). Liu Zhixuan and Xie Xichan completed this text in 1326, according to what written documents and stone inscriptions remained. They differ with Qin in attributing the origins of Quanzhen teachings to Laozi, but there is unanimity on the following four patriarchs: Donghua Dijun (Sovereign Lord of Eastern Florescence), Zhongli Quan, Lü Yan (b. 798?), and Liu Cao (fl. 1050). Central to both works are the hagiographies of the founder Wang and his seven disciples, known to the tradition as the Seven Perfected Ones (*qi zhen*) of Quanzhen: Ma Yu (1123–1183), Tan Chuduan (1123–1185), Liu Chuxuan (1147–1203), Qiu Chuji (1148–1227), Wang Chuyi (1142–1217), Hao Datong (1140–1212), and the single matriarch, Sun Bu'er (1119–1183).

Among hagiographies for individual Quanzhen patriarchs is an anonymous compilation in tribute to Wang Chuyi, the *Tixuan zhenren xianyi lu* (A record of the marvels manifested by the perfected who embodies sublimity). The nineteen episodes in this text offer a rare view of the therapeutic mission of Quanzhen masters, in the roles of healer, rain-maker, and demon queller. Even more well-known is the patriarch Qiu Chuji, whose journey into Central Asia for an audience with Chinggis Khan is commemorated in the *Changchun zhenren xiyou ji* (The journey to the west of the perfected Changchun). Qiu's disciple Li Zhichang (1193–1256) completed this work in 1228, following Qiu's death at the Tianchang Abbey in Beijing. The transcendent Lü Yan, conventionally credited with Wang Zhe's enlightenment, is the subject of a lengthy chronicle by Miao Shanshi (fl. 1324), the *Chunyang dijun shenhua miaotong ji* (Annals of the wondrous communications and divine transformations of the sovereign lord Chunyang). As with similar narrative sequences, this text appears to have evolved from centuries of storytelling traditions that also found their expression in temple wall paintings.

Most numerous of the hagiographies focused on local cults are those dedicated to Xu Sun (239–292?), whose career as a healer and subduer of malevolent dragons was established from Sichuan east to the central Jiangxi River valleys. The earliest text to survive intact is the *Xiaodao Wu Xu er zhenjun zhuan* (A Hagiography of Wu and Xu, the two perfected lords of the filial way). Xu's association in this account with Wu Meng, the legendary exemplar of filiality, attests to an early ritual tradition that evolved around his cult in Jiangxi, apparently a Tang variation on Lingbao liturgy. The *Yulong ji* (An anthology of jade beneficence), a later work compiled by the well-known specialist in Thunder Rites, Bai Yuchan (fl. 1209–1224), reveals the extent to which Song Huizong patronized this cult as a symbol of unity in the face of the Jurchen invasions. Veneration of Xu Sun eventually led to the development of a nationalistic cult known as the Jingming Dao (Way of Purity and Perspicacity), generally thought to have been founded by Liu Yu (1257–1308), an abbot of the Yulong Guan, an abbey established in Jiangxi at the putative site of Xu's ascension. Liu's disciple Huang Yuanji (1270–1324) edited the *Jingming zhong xiao quanshu* (A comprehensive compilation on the Jingming tradition of loyalty and filiality), the biographies of which exemplify the role of Xu's disciples as guarantors of political stability. The traditional attributes of *zhong* (loyalty) and *xiao* (filiality) are reinterpreted in this context as metaphors for submission to authority and the suppression of rebellion. Shrines to Xu are still maintained in Taiwan today and, even more remarkably, the Yulong Abbey is officially designated as a historical monument worthy of preservation.

A number of other hagiographic accounts testify to the popularity of local cults at various sacred mountain sites, including Lu Shan on the northern border of Jiangxi, once a popular missionary resort, and Huagai Shan, the source of the Tianxin revelations. Most well-known perhaps is the guardian of Wudang Shan (in present-day Hubei), referred to as Xuanwu (Dark Martial Lord) or Zhenwu (Perfected Martial Lord). How early this deity associated with the north was enshrined in China is not known, but well over three hundred shrines are established in his name on Taiwan today. Xuanwu's role as defender of the Song empire against the Western Xia invasions and other threats is commemorated in the *Xuantian shangdi qisheng lu* (An account of the revelations conveyed to the sages by the supreme sovereign of the dark celestial realm). A composite work, it is derived largely from the textual counterpart to the wall paintings of a shrine dedicated to the Martial Lord by Song Renzong in 1057. A later anthology reveals in turn that many literati of the thirteenth and fourteenth centuries promoted Xuanwu as the special guardian of the Mongol empire. Similarly, the *Da Ming Xuantian shangdi ruiying tulu* (An illustrated account of the auspicious responses of the supreme sovereign of the dark celestial realm during the great Ming) is a collection of encomia dating from 1405 to 1418 that honor the deity's role in establishing the mandate of the Ming.

Topography, epigraphy, and historiography. The chorography of sacred space, in the heavens above, on the earth below, and in the subterranean caverns beyond, is the subject of many works in the Daoist canon. Certainly among the most renowned of such texts from antiquity is the *Wuyue zhenxing tu* (Mappings of the true form of the Five Sacred Peaks), talismanic variations of which were introduced into the Lingbao textual corpus. The apotropaic value of these diagrams was recognized by Ge Hong and inspired Daoist liturgists for many generations later. The Five Sacred Peaks also serve as a crucial point of reference in Du Guangting's *Dongtian fudi yuedu mingshan ji* (A record of the celebrated mountains, conduits, sacred peaks, munificent terrains, and caverned heavens). In addition to mapping out the *wuyue* ("five [sacred] peaks," e.g., Tai Shan in the east, Heng Shan in the south, Song Shan in the center, Hua Shan in the west, and Heng Shan in the north) and the interlocking network of ranges, Du identifies ten major and thirty-six supplementary *dongtian* or subterranean chambers, as well as seventy-two sites traversed by various transcendents and the twenty-four original parishes established by Zhang Daoling in western Sichuan.

Larger descriptive topographies date from the Song to Ming. The canon preserves individual records for three of the Five Sacred Peaks. That compiled in commemoration of the Sacred Peak of the East, *Dai shi* (A history of Dai), was presented to Ming Shenzong (r. 1573–1619) on New Year's Day of 1587. In compiling this work the editor, Zha Zhilong (fl. 1554–1586), sought to reinforce the ritual obligations of the court toward Tai Shan, devoting large portions of the text to the history of imperial sacrifices and various temple compounds, as well as the supernatural phenomena witnessed at the site from 78 BCE to 1586.

Earlier and less ambitious accounts are available for the sacred peaks of the west and south. The *Xiyue Huashan zhi* (A treatise on Hua Shan, sacred peak of the West) is attributed to a Wang Chuyi, not to be confused with the Quanzhen patriarch of the same name. This text, derived in part from the *Huashan ji* (A record of Hua Shan) dating to the Tang, may in fact be the work of the author of an 1183 preface, Liu Dayong. Unlike the treatise on Tai Shan, there is little discussion of ritual traditions in propitiation of the spirits embodied in the mountain. Instead, the compiler was far more interested in recounting stories about supramundane forces and in identifying indigenous plants and minerals with magical properties.

The *Nanyue zongsheng ji* (An anthology on the collective highlights of the sacred peak of the south) is wholly devoted to the history of Daoist sanctuaries on Heng Shan. The edition of this text in the *Daozang* is an extract from a fuller account of sacred shrines, including Daoist, Buddhist, and folk, that is printed in the Buddhist canon. Chen Tianfu (fl. 1131–1163), who completed this text in 1163, relies in part on the *Nanyue xiaolu* (A short account of the sacred peak of the south) compiled by Li Chongzhao in 902. Of considerable interest are Chen's own contributions on the history of rituals on behalf of the emperor's longevity and national prosperity. As the inventory of canonizations reveals, Song Huizong was a particularly avid patron of the shrines at Heng Shan.

Five topographies in the canon celebrate mountain ranges in Zhejiang, the most famous of which is Tiantai Shan. Central to the *Tiantaishan zhi* (A treatise on the Tiantai Mountains) is the history of the Tongbo Abbey, located on a peak of that name. It was for centuries the most prominent temple compound in the Tiantai range. Built originally for the Daoist master Sima Chengzhen (647–735), the Tongbo Guan reportedly once housed one of the largest collections of Daoist texts in the country. With the fall of Kaifeng and the reestablishment of the Song mandate at Hangzhou, the temple became an even more important talisman of the state and was evidently at the height of its glory in 1168, following thirty-seven years of construction activity. It later served as a haven for refugees during the fall of the Mongol regime and by 1367 went up in flames.

To the sacred font of the Shangqing revelations is dedicated the largest topography in the canon, the *Maoshan zhi* (A treatise on Maoshan). The forty-fifth Shangqing patriarch, Liu Dabin (fl. 1317–1328), completed this text in 1328, at a time when the site enjoyed a renewal of royal patronage. His account opens with a comprehensive collection of imperial communications concerning Maoshan, dating from 1 BCE to 1319 CE. Other outstanding features include the hagiographies of the three eponymous transcendents surnamed Mao as well as the ranks of Shangqing patriarchs and matriarchs, the history of various shrines and hermitages, an anthology of stone inscriptions dating from 520 to 1314, and a large selection of prose and prosody sustaining the sanctity of the region.

The *Daozang* also preserves a few works solely comprised of texts carved on stone. Most notable are the anthologies of epigraphy prepared on behalf of the Quanzhen heritage. The largest is the *Ganshui xianyuan lu* (An account of the origins of transcendents at Ganshui) compiled by the Quanzhen archivist Li Daoqian. The title refers to the Ganhe Garrison (in present-day Shaanxi), where the founder Wang Zhe reportedly achieved enlightenment in 1159. Most numerous are the tomb inscriptions commemorating worthies ranging from Wang Zhe to a contemporary of the editor. Another anthology, the *Gongguan beizhi* (Epigraphic memorials of palaces and abbeys), is devoted largely to the early history of the Baiyun Guan in Beijing. One inscription marks the conclusion of a massive renovation of the Tianchang Guan, as the earlier abbey was known, in 1179. Also included is the proclamation issued upon the completion of the Jin canon at the Tianchang Guan in 1191.

Zhu Xiangxian (fl. 1279–1308) of Maoshan is the editor of two works commemorating the site where Laozi reputedly left behind the *Dao de jing* in answer to the gatekeeper Yin Xi's pleas for instruction. One is a set of hagiographic inscriptions entitled *Zhongnanshan shuojing tai lidai zhenxian beiji* (An epigraphic record of the successive generations of perfected transcendents at the pavilion for the recitation of scripture on Zhongnan Shan). Zhu composed these accounts and had them inscribed on stone following a pilgrimage in 1279 to the Lou Guan (Tiered Abbey) established in honor of Yin Xi's discipleship. He derived much of his data from an earlier work compiled by Yin Wencao (d. 688), a Daoist master who apparently regarded himself as a descendant of Yin Xi. The second work compiled by Zhu, the *Gu Louguan ziyun yanqing ji* (An anthology from the abundant felicity of purple clouds at the tiered abbey of antiquity), includes inscriptions on the history of the shrine dating from 625 to 1303.

The historical works in the *Daozang* do not match the size and scope of those in the Buddhist canon. There are a large number of brief historical surveys embedded in various texts, composed generally to establish the ultimate antiquity and thus authority of a scriptural tradition. The earliest separately compiled history in the Daoist canon is the *Lidai diwang chongdao ji* (A record of reverence for the Dao on the part of sovereign rulers over successive generations) of Du Guangting. The opening summary of the pre-Tang era is little more than a statistical analysis of the number of temples established and Daoist masters ordained from one period of state patronage to the next. The discussions thereafter focus on the role of Taishang Laojun as the ancestral guardian of the Tang, especially his defense of the empire during the uprising of Huang Chao (d. 884).

The unifying feature of all later histories in the canon continues to be the providential manifestations of Lord Lao. Prototypes of this historiographic approach include the early writings on *huahu* ("converting the barbarians") that were essentially chronicles of Laozi's incarnations as the supreme preceptor of all peoples. To write a history of the faith was, in other words, to write a hagiography of Lord Lao as the messiah. This approach is exemplified in Jia Shanxiang's (fl. 1086) *Youlong zhuan* (Like unto a dragon), the title of which is drawn from Confucius's putative characterization of Laozi as recorded in the *Shi ji* (Records of the historian) of Sima Qian (145–86 BCE). Jia concentrates on Lord Lao's role as instructor to the ruling house and the history of the Taiqing Gong (Palace of Grand Clarity, in present-day Luyi, Henan province), the reputed birthplace of the "historical" Laozi.

Nearly a century later, Xie Shouhao (1134–1212), a prominent Daoist master at the site of the Xu Sun cult in Jiangxi, presented an even more comprehensive chronicle to Song Guangzong (r. 1190–1194). In compiling the *Hunyuan shengji* (A chronicle of the sage from the primordiality of chaos), Xie sought to correct the inconsistencies in Jia's account by drawing on a wider range of readings from the *sanjiao*, or "three teachings" (i.e., Confucianism, Daoism, and Buddhism). Xie's work is an invaluable source of citations from works no longer extant, such as the early chronicle on Lord Lao compiled by Yin Wencao. He is also particularly attentive to the history of the compilation of the canon. Among those who found Xie's work indispensable was the hagiographer Zhao Daoyi.

LITERARY COLLECTIONS AND DIALOGIC TREATISES. Among the most informative sources on the beliefs and practices of Daoist masters are their collected writings, editions of which were commonly prepared by devotees. The prime example is of course Tao Hongjing's assiduous collation of Yang Xi's revelatory verse. The writings of Wu Yun (d. 778), an ordained Zhengyi master often summoned by Tang Xuanzong, were brought together more expeditiously. According to a preface by Quan Deyu (759–818), a scribe named Wang Yan rescued what remained of the master's writings and presented them to the imperial archives. The edition in the canon, the *Zongxuan xiansheng wenji* (A literary anthology of Master Zongxuan) is that which a disciple Shao Yixuan conveyed to Quan. Among Wu's most well-known compositions is a sequence of verse entitled *Buxu ci* (Lyrics on pacing the Void) and a lengthy essay arguing that divine transcendence can indeed be learned. The history of a second Tang anthology in the canon, the collected works of the renowned Du Guangting entitled *Guangcheng ji* (An anthology of Guangcheng), is more obscure. It, too, is a valuable resource on the ritual activities of Daoist masters whose reputations made them favorites at court.

By far the most numerous of literary collections in the canon are those compiled after the Tang. A vast corpus, for example, has evolved around the semi-legendary Lü Yan, claimed as the patriarch of both the Quanzhen and Nanzong (Southern Heritage) traditions. A substantial collection of verse conventionally ascribed to him in truth probably dates no earlier than the thirteenth century. One anthology, the *Chunyang zhenren hunchengji* (An anthology of the perfected on arising from turbulence), was prepared by He Zhiyuan, a disciple of Song Defang. He was among those assigned to work on the Canon of 1244, the opportunity of which no doubt led to this edition. What he claimed to be the product of Lü's divine inspiration appears instead to reflect the literary legacy of Wang Zhe and his disciples.

Over a half-dozen works alone purport to be the teachings and writings of founder Wang. A number of the texts were compiled in direct tribute to Ma Yu's discipleship under Wang. The master's basic pedagogy was apparently to recite a verse that would provoke a response from his devotees. Two works, the *Chongyang jiaohua ji* (An anthology on the proselytism of Chongyang) and the *Chongyang fenli shihua ji* (An anthology of Chongyang on the ten transformations according to the sectioning of a pear), preserve hundreds of these missives between Wang and Ma. The exchange began, according to legend, when Wang locked himself up for one hundred days on the grounds of his hosts Ma and wife Sun Bu'er and communicated with them merely by submitting a gift of food, often a section of pear, accompanied by instruction in verse. There is unfortunately no comparable record of Sun's responses, although late editions of her writings available outside the canon suggest that at least a few considered her to have been equally literate.

Other texts in the canon reveal that Wang was also willing to entertain the questions of his disciples. Records of such question-and-answer sessions, known as *yulu* or dialogic treatises, were as popular with the Quanzhen masters as with their Chan Buddhist counterparts. A somewhat redundant example of this genre, the *Chongyang shou Danyang erhshisi jue* (Twenty-four lessons conveyed by Chongyang to Danyang), is composed of a series of questions and answers attributed to Ma and his master Wang. Among the lessons taught is that the devotee should speak very little, control all emotions, and minimize anxiety and cravings. Further details on Wang's instruction are found in the *Chongyang lijiao shiwu lun* (Fifteen discourses on the teachings set forth by Chongyang). Moderation in all things appears to be the central message of this dialogue. According to the concluding statement ascribed to Wang, departure from the mundane realm was to be accomplished mentally, not physically. The closing simile, obviously borrowed from the Buddhist translator and exegete Kumarajiva, is that one's body is like the root-stock of a lotus mired in mud, whereas one's heart-mind is suspended in space as the lotus blossom itself.

The writings associated with Ma Yu are even more numerous than those of his master. Aside from three works based on exchanges with Wang, there are altogether six separate collections of prose and prosody printed under his name in the canon. One compilation, the *Dongxuan jinyu ji* (An anthology of the gold and jade of Dongxuan), includes a particularly revealing verse that exhorts Buddhist monks and Daoist masters to come together in accord and do away with slander. Another work, the *Jianwu ji* (An anthology on gradual enlightenment), features onomatopoeic verses that were apparently designed to illustrate, as the title implies, that enlightenment is a gradual process. A significant number of Ma's verses are expressly dedicated to female adepts, including his wife Sun. All men and women of the Dao, he urges, would best bring under control their *yima xinyuan,* or "horse of the will and monkey of the mind."

Qiu Chuji, the youngest disciple of Wang and eventually the most renowned, has comparably fewer writings to his name in the canon. The *Changchunzi Panxi ji* (An anthology of Changchunzi from the Pan tributary) preserves compositions dating both from Qiu's seclusion in the upper reaches of the Yellow River valley as well as from his later ritual activities at Qixia (in present-day Shandong). Among his verses are commemorations of various *jiao* fetes over which he had presided, personal communications to Jin Shizong (r. 1161–1189), and instructions on meditative practices. In addition to Li Zhichang's account of Qiu's later years, the *Xuanfeng qinghui lu* (A record of a felicitous convocation on the sublime spirit of the Dao), ascribed to Yelü Chucai (1189–1243), provides a record of the sermons delivered before his patron, Chinggis Khan.

All but a fraction of the collected writings associated with the other select members in Wang's circle are lost. The single anthology of Tan Chuduan's teachings in the canon arose directly from the initiative of the junior patriarch Liu Chuxuan. Of the five anthologies attributed to Liu, only one survives, although a dialogic treatise compiled by his disciples reveals somewhat more about his career. Liu's sayings, many of which were inspired by lines in the *Dao de jing,* were reportedly so popular as to have become part of the local culture of his circuit. The two paragons of filial piety, Wang Chuyi and Hao Datong, are remembered with one anthology each. The *Yunguang ji* (An anthology from Yunguang), named for the cavern in which Wang secluded himself for nine years, is a valuable supplement to the hagiographic *Xianyi lu.* The one edition of Hao's teachings to be preserved attests to his training as a diviner and abiding interest in the *Yijing.*

The influence of the early Quanzhen patriarchs is easily measured by the volume of writings that emerged from later generations. Among those whose teachings expanded upon this legacy are Qiu's successor Yin Zhiping (1169–1251), Liu's disciple Yu Daoxian (1168–1232), and Hao's disciple Wang Zhijin (1178–1263). Later syncretists for whom there is ample record in the canon include Li Daochun (fl. 1290), Miao Shanshi (fl. 1324), Wang Jie (fl. 1310), Chen Zhixu (fl. 1329–1336), Wang Weiyi (fl. 1294–1304), and Zhao Yizhen (d. 1382). Many of these figures drew equally from the Quanzhen and Nanzong traditions. The fullest documentation on the latter is to be found in late encyclopedic anthologies of the *Daozang.*

Encyclopedic anthologies. The earliest comprehensive encyclopedic work in the canon is the *Wushang biyao* (The essentials of unsurpassed arcana). Only two-thirds of the original one hundred *juan* survives of this anonymous compilation. Citations from a wide selection of texts are organized under 288 headings, ranging from cosmology and sacred topography to the protocols for transmitting divine scriptures and instructions on meditative practices. The origins of this text are revealed in a Buddhist, not Daoist, compilation, namely the *Xu gaoseng zhuan* (Supplementary biographies of exalted monks) of Daoxuan (596–667), which states that Zhou Wudi (r. 561–578) ordered its compilation following his pacification of the state of Northern Qi in 577. It is thought that work began on this vast anthology as early as 574, when Wudi issued a decree establishing the Tongdao Guan (Abbey of Communication with the Dao) as a symbol of the anticipated political and ideological reunification of the empire. The text is not only an invaluable resource for citations from the original Shangqing and Lingbao revelations, but also for the later codifications they inspired.

Two smaller compendia were compiled a century later by a relatively unknown recluse named Wang Xuanhe (fl. 683). The larger of the works, the *Sandong zhunang* (Pearl bag of the three caverns) is organized under thirty-four categories dealing with various aspects of conduct befitting an adept and includes extracts from a number of texts on contemplative pursuits that are otherwise lost. The second corpus attributed to Wang is the *Shangqing daolei shixiang* (A categorical survey of the Dao of Shangqing), which specializes in citations dealing with six types of sacred quarters, from private retreats to the cosmic chambers of revealed literature.

A much larger encyclopedic anthology, the *Yunji qiqian* (Seven lots from the book-pack of the clouds), was compiled by Zhang Junfang, inspired apparently by his assignment to oversee the copying of a new canon on the order of Song Zhenzong. Zhang states in his preface that his intention was to prepare a reference work for the emperor's personal use. But since the *Yunji qiqian* was not completed until 1028 or 1029, it was obviously presented to his successor Renzong (r. 1023–1053). The writings Zhang selected for this work date from the earliest revelations to the first decades of the eleventh century. Recorded, for example, in the opening essays on cosmogony and scriptural transmission are unique copies of the prefaces composed for the first catalogues of Shangqing and Lingbao literature. Additional subheadings include sacred topography, behavioral precepts, ritual purification, visualization techniques, and hagiography. Notably absent are any instructions on liturgical procedure, a subject that Zhang clearly considered to be beyond the scope of this corpus.

Two remarkable collections of writings treating "inner alchemy" (*neidan*) appeared during the Southern Song period. The first in print was the *Dao shu* (Pivot of the Dao) compiled by the bibliophile Zeng Cao (fl. 1131–1155). Among the rare texts Zeng records is the *Baiwen pian* (A folio of one-hundred questions), based on a putative exchange between Lü Yan and his mentor, the late Han transcendent Zhongli Quan. The entire last chapter is devoted to the *Lingbao pian* (A folio on Lingbao), a variant edition of the *Lingbao bifa* (Conclusive rites of Lingbao), which was also compiled as a tribute to this legendary discipleship. A related theoretical work on the cultivation of the *jindan* (metallous enchymoma), the *Zhong Lü chuandao ji* (An Anthology on Zhong [li]'s transmission of the Dao to Lü), is found in both the *Dao shu* and a later Song collectaneum of *neidan* literature, the *Xiuzhen shishu* (Ten writings on the cultivation of perfection). This anonymously compiled anthology also includes many texts associated with the Nanzong, or Southern Heritage, the "five patriarchs" (*wuzu*) of which are: Liu Cao (d. ca. 1050), Zhang Boduan (d. 1082), Shi Tai (d. 1158), Xue Zixian (d. 1191), and Chen Nan (d. 1213). The establishment of this patriarchy appears to be a rather late innovation inspired by the legacy of the Seven Perfected of Quanzhen. By the early fourteenth century a number of texts began to assert that Liu conveyed the teachings of the venerable Zhongli Quan and Lü Yan to both Wang Zhe in the north and Zhang Boduan in the south.

Zhang Boduan is popularly regarded as the "founder" of Nanzong. His writings were initially viewed as treatises on *waidan*, "exterior," or laboratory, alchemy. More recent research suggests that they fall, rather, into the mainstream of *neidan* literature. An edition of the major corpus attributed to him, the *Wuzhen pian* (Folios on the apprehension of perfection), is recorded in the *Xiuzhen shishu*, with a preface by Zhang dating to 1075. The same anthology also includes variant editions of similar lyrical sequences ascribed to Shi Tai, Xue Zixian, and Chen Nan. But by far the most dominant in the *Xiuzhen shishu* are the writings of Chen's putative disciple, the renowned Thunder Ritual specialist Bai Yuchan. Nearly half of the text is devoted to a record of his instructions on *jindan* and Thunder Ritual traditions, as well as his liturgical activities in Fujian and his accounts of the Xu Sun cult in central Jiangxi. It may be that the *Xiuzhen shishu* was compiled by devotees of Bai, for the latest work included is a set of texts on *jindan* by Xiao Tingzhi (fl. 1260), a second-generation disciple.

OTHER SOURCES. While the *Daozang* is the most comprehensive collection of Daoist literature, it is by no means the only source available. Among the number of publications issued during the Qing dynasty, the next largest corpus is the *Daozang jiyao* (An edition of essentials from Daoist canon). The reedition of this work in 1906 includes 287 titles, compared to nearly fifteen hundred in the canon. Over half of the titles are found in the *Daozang* as well, but this anthology also contains works otherwise unknown, including tracts attributed to Sun Bu'er and Liu Cao, as well as the writings of later syncretists such as Wu Shouyang (d. 1644).

Perhaps one of the most neglected resources for Daoist literature is epigraphy. Aside from the few, mainly Quanzhen, collections in the canon, there is a wide range of stone and bronze inscriptions pertinent to the history of the faith. An anthology of epigraphy compiled by Wang Chang (1725–1806), for example, includes a transcription of the *Taishang Laojun riyong miaojing* (A wondrous scripture of Lord Lao and most high for daily use) carved on stone in 1352 at the Pavilion for the Recitation of Scriptures in Shaanxi. A variant redaction of this text is found in the *Daozang* and, at 141 words, is among the shortest works in the canon. It is essentially a code of conduct based on many traditional Chinese attributes such as filiality. Study of epigraphic documents will soon be greatly facilitated by the imminent publication of a comprehensive anthology of inscriptions bearing on the history of Daoism, a project begun by Chen Yuan and now being completed by Chen Zhichao at the Chinese Academy of Social Sciences in Beijing.

Scriptures and related sacred writings found in various archives constitute another essential source of Daoist literature. The Dunhuang manuscripts preserved in a number of libraries worldwide, for example, include texts that clarify the early history of several scriptural codifications. One such work, of which only a portion survives in the canon, is the *Benji jing* (Scripture on the original juncture). Over seventy fragments of this text are in the British and French archives of Dunhuang manuscripts. One of the compilers is known to have taken part in debates before the court of Tang Gaozu (r. 618–626) on the issue of whether the Buddha was a disciple of the Dao. The text itself, designed apparently in part to support this theory, seems to have taken its inspiration from discussions on the cosmogonic concept of *pūrvakoṭi* (Chin., *benji*) in the *Madhyamāgama* and *Saṃyuktāgama*, Chinese translations of which appeared in the fourth and fifth centuries. Parables in one section of the *Benji jing*, moreover, were evidently drawn from the *Dharmapada*. The text reached the height of its popularity during the reign of Tang Xuanzong, who ordered all Daoist priests not only to copy it out but also to recite and lecture on it during official religious festivals. In short, the lessons within were thought to lead to the salvation of the state as well as of the individual.

Later collections of manuscripts and rare blockprints also have much to reveal about the continuity and change in Daoist traditions. Among published works is the *Zhuang Lin xu Daozang* (Supplementary Daoist canon of the Zhuang and Lin clans) edited by Michael Saso, a collection of Daoist works largely gathered from a Zhengyi fraternity in Xinzhu of north Taiwan. These texts, as well as those recovered by Kristofer Schipper in the Tainan area of south Taiwan, suggest a remarkable continuum of Daoist liturgical practice. A scripture dedicated to Tianfei (i.e., Mazu) in the Schipper Archives of Paris, for example, proves to be a variant of a text in the canon dating to 1409–1412. The manuscript version conveys an image of this well-known Fujianese patroness of seafarers that accommodates a folk vision of her as an *avatāra* of Guanyin. Tianfei's assimilation to this all-compassionate *bodhisattva* is promoted in popular narratives on the life of the goddess compiled during the late Ming dynasty. Just as she continues to inspire poets, novelists, and even scriptwriters in this age, so, too, has much of the Daoist literature both in and outside the canon left its mark on centuries of Chinese belles-lettres. Further study of this literature can only disclose how deeply the Daoist heritage pervades all aspects of Chinese society.

SEE ALSO Alchemy, article on Chinese Alchemy; Du Guangting; Fangshi; Ge Hong; Laozi; Lu Xiujing; Millenarianism, article on Chinese Millenarian Movements; Sima Chengzhen; Tao Hongjing; Wang Zhe; Xian; Zhang Daoling; Zhang Jue.

BIBLIOGRAPHY

Baldrian-Hussein, Farzeen. *Procédés secrets au joyau magique: Traité d'alchimie taoïste du onzième siècle.* Paris, 1984. An investigation into the textual history of the *Lingbao bifa*, with a full translation.

Boltz, Judith Magee. "In Homage to T'ien-fei." *Journal of the American Oriental Society* 106 (1986). A study of the Tianfei scripture in the canon, collated with manuscripts in the Schipper Archives.

Boltz, Judith Magee. *A Survey of Taoist Literature, Tenth to Seventeenth Centuries.* Berkeley, 1987. An introduction to over two hundred titles in the Daoist canon from revelation and ritual to encyclopedic anthologies.

Chavannes, Édouard. *Le jet des dragons.* Paris, 1916. A remarkable study of the tradition of casting prayers inscribed on stone or metal into caves and waterways, including an annotated translation of a ritual manual compiled by Du Guangting (850–933).

Ch'en Kuo-fu. *Tao-tsang yüan-liu k'ao* (1949). 2d ed. Beijing, 1963. A pioneering work in the history of the Daoist canon.

Kandel, Barbara. *Taiping jing: The Origin and Transmission of the "Scripture on General Welfare"; The History of an Unofficial Text.* Hamburg, 1979. A brief study on the history of texts circulating under the title *Taiping jing.*

Lagerwey, John. *Wu-shang pi-yao: somme taoïste du sixième siècle.* Paris, 1981. A detailed analysis of the organization and contents of the sixth-century anthology of Daoist literature entitled *Wushang biyao.*

Loon, Piet van der. *Taoist Books in the Libraries of the Sung Period.* London, 1984. An analytic index to Daoist writings cited in private and official Song bibliographies dating from 945 to 1345, with introductory essays on the history of these compilations and the Daoist canon.

Maspero, Henri. *Le taoïsme et les religions chinoises.* Paris, 1971. Translated by Frank A. Kierman, Jr., as *Taoism and Chinese Religion* (Amherst, 1981). A collection of essays on the origins of Daoist practices, drawn largely from the early literature on various macrobiotic techniques.

Naundorf, Gert, et al., eds. *Religion und Philosophie in Ostasien.* Würzburg, 1985. Contributions include studies on *neidan* and the *Taiping jing.*

Needham, Joseph, and Lu Gwei-Djen. *Science and Civilisation in China*, vol. 5, pt. 5. Cambridge, U.K., 1983. A broad survey of instructions on *neidan* (physiological alchemy) and other macrobiotic techniques in the Daoist canon and subsidiary collections.

Robinet, Isabelle. *Méditation taoïste.* Paris, 1979. An introduction to early manuals on techniques of visualization such as the *Huangting jing.*

Robinet, Isabelle. *La révélation du Shangging dans l'histoire du taoïsme.* 2 vols. Paris, 1984. A comprehensive study of the origins and development of the Shangqing scriptural legacy.

Schipper, Kristofer. *Le Fen-teng: Rituel taoïste.* Paris, 1975. An annotated translation of eighteenth- and nineteenth-century Daoist ritual texts in illustration of a continuum of Lingbao liturgy since at least the Song dynasty.

Schipper, Kristofer. *Le corps taoïste.* Paris, 1982. An introduction to Daoist beliefs and practices with a special emphasis on teachings concerning the hierarchies of gods within and without.

Strickmann, Michel. *Le taoïsme du Mao Chan: Chronique d'une révélation.* Paris, 1981. On the social history of the Shangqing scriptural tradition, with special attention to its messianic eschatology.

Strickmann, Michel, ed. *Tantric and Taoist Studies in Honour of R. A. Stein*, vol. 2. Mélanges chinoise et bouddhique, vol. 21. Brussels, 1983. Includes studies on ritual investiture, the early Shangqing and Lingbao textual legacies, and a Shenxiao soteriological meditation technique.

Waley, Arthur, trans. *The Travels of an Alchemist.* London, 1931. A study and translation of *Changchun xiyou ji* by Li Zhichang (1193–1256), on the journey west of the Quanzhen patriarch Qiu Chuji (1148–1227).

Welch, Holmes, and Anna Seidel, eds. *Facets of Taoism.* New Haven, 1979. Includes studies on the origins of the *Daozang*, the *Taiping jing*, and the Shangqing revelations.

Wu Chi-yu, ed. *Pen-chi ching: Livre du terme originel.* Paris, 1960. Textual history of the early seventh-century Daoist scripture *Benji jing*, inspired in part by Chinese translations of Mahāyāna texts.

Yoshioka Yoshitoyo. *Dōkyō kyōten shiron.* Tokyo, 1952.

JUDITH MAGEE BOLTZ (1987 AND 2005)

DAOISM: HISTORY OF STUDY

Although Daoism represents a tradition as ancient and as rich as any other major religion, the serious study of this tradition has been almost entirely a twentieth-century phenomenon and largely a phenomenon of the second half of the twentieth century at that. The reasons for this are not far to seek. From its fourth and last printing in 1445 until its reproduction by photomechanical means in 1926, the Daoist canon (*Daozang*), a compendium of over one thousand different works representing the full scope of the tradition, was a decidedly rare work, the jealously guarded possession of a handful of monasteries. Until the twentieth century, moreover, few outsiders would have been inclined to persist in seeking them out. To the traditional Chinese scholar, raised in the neo-Confucian belief that Buddhism and Daoism alike were little more than gross superstition, there was little reason to take an interest in such literature.

Although certain eighteenth- and nineteenth-century scholars made use of the Daoist canon to obtain good editions of ancient philosophical or historical texts (which, as in the case of the *Mozi*, were often not Daoist works but were included in the canon for reasons unrelated to their contents), it was not until 1911 that a Chinese scholar lingered over the rest of the canon. This scholar was Liu Shipei, a fervent nationalist whose attitude toward tradition had been enlarged by the modern world to embrace a less orthodox range of study.

By the time Liu published the results of his readings, non-Chinese scholars who had inherited the best of the traditional Chinese polymath's zeal for knowledge (without the polymath's blind spot with regard to religion) had begun to show a lively interest in Daoism also. French Sinologists, such as Édouard Chavannes and Paul Pelliot, and Japanese, such as Tsumaki Naoyoshi, came to Daoism out of a general interest in Chinese civilization, but also from societies where the study of religion was an accepted branch of learning. Japan, in particular, had at an early stage accepted much of China's medieval culture, including the Buddhist faith, but had not undergone a neo-Confucian rejection of this legacy to the same degree. Thus, learned Buddhists, such as Tokiwa Daijō, were already confronting the complex issue of the relationship between Chinese Buddhism and Daoism in the 1920s. One of them, Ōfuchi Eshin, had even traveled abroad to investigate the millennium-old manuscripts of Daoist scriptures that had been discovered among other ancient materials at Dunhuang in Northwest China at the turn of the century.

The increased political role of Japan in China during the 1930s also brought many Buddhist scholars to China. Some, such as Fukui Kojun, returned to Japan to pursue research in the Daoist canon, now available in its modern printing in academic libraries, while others, such as Yoshioka Yoshitoyo, stayed longer to gain firsthand experience of Daoist monastic life. Yoshioka's 1941 *Dōkyō no jittai* (The actual state of Daoism), published in Beijing, remains an invaluable source on a mode of religious life now largely vanished. The expulsion of the Japanese from China after 1945 effectively halted all such opportunities for fieldwork and even led to the loss of much material already painstakingly collected. However, as *Dōkyō to Chūgoku shakai* (Daoism and Chinese society), a slim volume published in Tokyo in 1948 by Kubo Noritada, demonstrates, even after their return to Japan these scholars were concerned to relate their historical and bibliographical research to the fuller picture of Chinese society they had witnessed. Their numbers were also sufficient to found in 1950 the Japan Society of Taoistic Research (Nippon Dōkyō Gakkai) and to start, the following year, the publication of a journal, *Tōhō shūkyō*, a serial still published with an annual update on Daoist bibliography.

In contrast, 1950 saw the publication in Paris of the posthumous writings on Daoism of the sole French scholar to have followed up the pioneering work of Chavannes and Pelliot by carrying out research into materials in the Daoist canon. Henri Maspero (1883–1945), like others of his generation, came to the study of Daoism not as a specialist but as a broad-ranging scholar. He had published in the fields of Egyptology and Vietnamese studies and had produced a Sinological masterpiece, a one-volume survey of preimperial China, before his research into the China of the latter Han period and thereafter brought him face to face with the Daoist religion. During the 1930s he applied himself to unraveling the formative stages of the religion, working independently of, but using similar methods to, his Japanese contemporaries (for example, comparing materials in the Daoist canon with the Dunhuang manuscripts and with Buddhist sources). Maspero perished at Buchenwald in 1945 before he had published more than a portion of his findings. In his three-volume collected writings, compiled by Paul Demiéville, his equally erudite literary executor, an entire volume is devoted to Daoism. Maspero's description of Daoism remains a highly rewarding record of the first encounter between a modern European mind and the full complexity of this ancient religion.

Sadly, Maspero had no students. Maspero's great contemporary in the study of Chinese religion, Marcel Granet, more immediately influenced the experts on Chinese religion who rose to prominence in postwar Paris. Yet Granet was not unaware of the importance of Daoism, and the work of such men as Max Kaltenmark, Rolf Alfred Stein, and Michel Soymié helped maintain the primacy of Paris as the center of Daoist studies in the Western world. Nor were these men, for their part, unaware of the achievements of their Japanese colleagues: Soymié established with Yoshioka in 1965 a second Japanese journal devoted to Daoism, the *Dōkyō kenkyū*. By this time a number of studies of Daoism had been published in Japan, and many points of controversy were hotly debated. A new generation of European researchers specifically interested in Daoism emerged, and the new publication soon introduced the findings of Anna Seidel and K. M. Schipper to a Japanese audience.

While the two major streams of Daoist studies were beginning to flow together, research in China remained almost as it had been in France in the 1930s, the domain of one lone scholar. Since the reprinting of the Daoist canon, established specialists in the history of Chinese religion, such as Chen

Yinke and Chen Yuan, had devoted articles to aspects of Daoist history, and one small volume attempting an account of the whole development of Daoism had been published, partly on the basis of early Japanese research. But from 1949 onward the only aspects of Daoist studies to see publication were those connected with the history of peasant uprisings or the history of science. In the former area the textual scholar Wang Ming produced in 1960 an excellent edition of the *Taiping jing*, a major Daoist scripture associated with the Yellow Turban insurgents of the Han dynasty, but subsequent discussion of the text by a number of academics tended not to focus on religious issues.

In 1963 Chen Guofu, a historian of science and the "lone scholar" referred to above, managed to republish an expanded version of an outstanding monograph, originally published in 1949, on the formation of the Daoist canon. Chen had initially undertaken his lengthy and painstaking research during the 1940s, when his interest in the history of Chinese alchemy led him to the question of the dating of Daoist texts on this subject. But especially in the 1963 edition of his *Daozang yuanliu kao*, he also included gleanings on many other topics that had caught his eye in the course of his readings. Other scholars, unable to claim to be furthering the study of science rather than religion, were less fortunate. Man Wentong, who had published some worthwhile research on Daoist texts in the 1940s, saw his work confiscated during the late 1950s; only a few further notes were published posthumously in 1980. The Chinese Cultural Revolution of the 1960s ended for a while the activities of the Zhongguo Daojiao Xiehui (the Chinese Daoist Association), a group formed in 1957 but unable even then to achieve much in either religious or academic terms.

Chen Guofu had begun his alchemical researches while studying in the United States under Tenney L. Davis at the Massachusetts Institute of Technology, and it was almost exclusively this scientific aspect of Daoism that had continued to attract the attention of the English-speaking world—apart, that is, from the perennial fascination with the *Dao de jing*, reinvigorated for academics in the 1970s and 1990s by discoveries of early versions of its text. Thus, when the first international conference on Daoism met in Italy in 1968, two historians of science, Joseph Needham from Great Britain and Nathan Sivin from the United States, joined with experts on religion such as Schipper and Seidel. No Chinese scholar attended, nor did any senior scholar from Japan. This situation was rectified in 1972 at the next conference, which was held in Japan so a number of Japanese scholars could attend, as did Hou Ching-lang, originally from Taiwan but trained in Paris. Hou was by no means the first Chinese to have conducted research into Daoism there. In 1960 Wu Chi-yu had used the Dunhuang manuscripts to compile an edition of an important Daoist scripture, the *Benji jing*. A few other Chinese scholars had by now published on Daoism in Hong Kong, Taiwan, or farther afield—Liu Ts'un-yan in Australia, for instance. But it was not until 1979, at a third conference held in Switzerland, that the situation in Beijing had changed sufficiently for Chen Guofu to participate. Daoist studies were thus finally able to achieve true international status and to win a degree of recognition in Daoism's native land.

The change of climate in the People's Republic of China manifested itself in a number of other ways. The year 1979 also saw the first publication of a new academic periodical, *Shijie zongjiao* (World religion), marking the start of the officially recognized study of religion in post-1949 China. Although it was initially much concerned with the history of atheism, in the following year articles on Daoism were included. The first volume of an outline history of Chinese Daoist thought, *Zhongguo Daojiao sixiang shigang*, and a new textual study by Wang Ming also appeared at this time. By 1980 the Chinese Daoist Association was active once more. In 1981 a dictionary of religion (*Zongjiao cedian*) containing a large number of entries on Daoism, was published. The first dictionary of Daoism as such, the *Daojiao dacidian* by Li Shuhuan, appeared in 1979 in Taiwan, but while Li's status as a Daoist priest contrasts markedly with that of the Marxist compilers of the later volume, inasmuch as neither dictionary incorporated the findings of non-Chinese scholars, both fell well below the standard that could have been achieved through international cooperation.

Although Chinese scholarship on Daoism lagged behind that of France and Japan, the potential for development was great. In the early 1980s Daoist priests appeared once again in China's streets and marketplaces, showing that the living tradition of the religion had not been cut off entirely by the Cultural Revolution and that scholars might still learn from it firsthand. Furthermore, China's bibliographic resources remained (and still remain) the envy of the outside world. One might mention, for example, the epigraphical sources on Song Daoism used by the historian Chen Yuan, besides those related to canonical literature. At this point international work was already under way on a complete bibliographic guide to the canon in its modern reprinted form. Based in Paris under the direction of Schipper, it was sponsored by the European Association for Chinese Studies and involved scholars from European countries and beyond. Even before publication of the guide, the project led to the publication of concordances to important Daoist texts and to an analysis by John Lagerwey of a sixth-century Daoist encyclopedia, published by Lagerwey as the *Wushang piyao* (1981). It also indirectly stimulated a monograph by Piet van der Loon titled *Taoist Works in the Libraries of the Sung Period* (1984).

In Japan, major collaborative ventures were preceded by publications reflecting the work of individual careers. First Yoshioka and then Kubo produced histories of Daoism aimed at general audiences. Ōfuchi Ninji completed a catalog of all the Daoist manuscripts from Dunhuang with a companion volume of photographs of every text. These two works were published as *Tonkō Dōkyō*, respectively subtitled

Mokuroku-hen and *Zuroku-hen,* in Tokyo in 1978 and 1979. Collaborative ventures began when a volume on Daoism was required for a series on the rich material of Dunhuang, and no fewer than ten writers (including Schipper) joined under the editorship of Yoshioka. Yoshioka died in 1979, but the volume, *Tonkō to Chūgoku Dōkyō,* eventually appeared in 1983. It includes a sixty-two-page general bibliography of Daoism based on material he had earlier collected. Yoshioka had in a sense initiated cooperative scholarship in Japanese Daoist studies somewhat earlier. A Festschrift in his honor, *Dōkyō kenkyū ronshū* (Collected essays in Daoist studies), drawing on the work of fifty-four Japanese and foreign contributors, was published in Tokyo in 1977.

In 1983 a comprehensive survey of Daoism involving the work of twenty-three scholars was published in Japan under the general title *Dōkyō.* This was the first collaborative attempt at a full description of the religion in any language. The three volumes of this survey, *Dōkyō to wa nani ka?, Dōkyō no tenkai,* and *Dōkyō no dempō,* are devoted respectively to a description of Daoism itself, an assessment of its importance in relation to other aspects of Chinese life and thought, and a survey of its spread beyond its Chinese origins. The last volume also contains surveys of research in Japan and elsewhere. The study of Daoism outside mainland China became increasingly prominent, especially as it moved from historical to anthropological research. Historical research has not, however, decreased in importance. Pioneering works such as the *Han'guk Togyosa* of Yi Nŭng-hwa, a study of the history of Daoism published in Seoul, South Korea, in 1959, have successors in the publications of Japanese scholars concerned to reassess the impact of Daoist beliefs on the history of their own culture. Of these, the symposium *Dōkyō to kodai tennōsei,* which appeared in Tokyo in 1978 under the editorship of Fukunaga Mitsuji, deals with an issue of no slight importance to the modern Japanese, namely the possibility of Daoist influence on such a quintessentially Japanese institution as the emperorship.

However, it is in the investigation of Daoism as practiced nowadays outside mainland China that the greatest diversity of scholarly activity became apparent. Kubo, in his research into Daoist beliefs associated with the hour *gengshen,* has covered not only Japan but also Okinawa. Of the many ethnographers and others concerned with recording Daoist practices in Taiwan, one scholar based on that island, Liu Zhiwan, published the first part of his study *Chūgoku Dōkyō no matsuri to shinkō* in Tokyo in 1983. In 1975 the American Michael Saso published in Taipei twenty-five volumes of Daoist texts used under the title *Zhuanglin xu Daozang.* The Daoist practices of the Yao people of northern Thailand were recorded by Japanese scholars and have attracted the attention of French, American, and Dutch scholars. Daoism in Hong Kong, Singapore, and other overseas Chinese communities was investigated to some extent as well.

By the mid-1980s, Daoist studies were thus no longer confined to one or two pioneers working in isolation, and in the late twentieth century and early twenty-first century the trend toward the internationalization of Daoist studies has continued, even though the initial series of international conferences has not been maintained. The steady revival and progress of academic life in the People's Republic of China saw the emergence of strong centers of research outside the Institute for the Study of World Religions in the China Academy of Social Sciences, Beijing, which launched *Shijie zongjiao.* Sichuan University in Chengdu, for example, has since 1986 published a journal, *Zongjiaoxue yanjiu* (Religious studies), which consistently carries articles on Daoism, and also completed publication between 1988 and 1995, under the editorship of Qing Xitai, of the first comprehensive history of Daoism up to the twentieth century, spread over four volumes, a work now available in English translation. The Chinese Daoist Association, meanwhile, published not only its own journal but also a major encyclopedic dictionary in 1994, a year before an even larger work of the same type from the Chinese Academy of Social Sciences, which had already produced a comprehensive guide to the literature in the canon in 1991. In some respects, publication on Daoism in China (notably the series *Zangwai daoshu* and its continuation, supplementing existing canonical collections, and especially the republication of traditional works on self-cultivation) was assisted by the rapid rise of interest in *qigong* in the late 1980s, though government worries about the implications of the craze eventually led to its increasing regulation in the following decade, especially after 1999.

The stream of monographs and research aids produced in Japan has increased to a flood, and more concise encyclopedic dictionaries drawing on a wider range of international scholarship have been published in Japan. The French language has remained important for scholarship in the field, even though scholars who had initially published in French often choose to publish in English or see their work translated. The same holds true for the less conspicuous but not unimportant tradition of Daoist studies in Germany. During the last decade of the twentieth century the study of Daoism in English at last came into its own. The only journal exclusively dedicated to it, *Taoist Resources,* lasted less than a decade (1988–1997) before being absorbed into the *Journal of Chinese Religions,* but this and other established periodicals find much more room for contributions on Daoism. Stephen Bokenkamp's pioneering *Early Daoist Scriptures* initiated the first monographic series in English dedicated to Daoism (in 1997), whereas established social historians like Robert Hymes and Edward L. Davis publish volumes exploring the role of Daoism in local society from the eleventh century onwards.

In part, this willingness of North American university presses to venture into what had been before the 1980s a virtually unknown area was the result of the emergence of a wider reading public in the English-speaking world, a public still primarily interested in the *Dao de jing, feng-shui,* or the martial arts, but also prepared to explore further. To cater to such interests a number of websites emerged, including some of real academic value, such as that maintained by the Italian expert on alchemy, Fabrizio Pregadio, who is also editor of a substantial and groundbreaking encyclopedia of Daoism in English. Livia Kohn, who had from early in her career attempted to provide materials in English to meet the needs of higher education in North America, edited the first major work of reference on Daoism in English, the *Daoism Handbook*, though her student James Miller has achieved an even more remarkable feat by condensing knowledge into a readable introductory volume. Miller's work has earned the approbation of at least one ordained Daoist priest engaged in doctoral research in English. The combination of religious and academic qualifications goes back to Schipper's contacts with Daoist circles in Taiwan, but the increasingly obvious strength of the religion throughout the Chinese world suggests it is a combination that may become more common in the future. Certainly the revival of Daoist practice on a large scale in China itself has enabled scholars such as Kenneth Dean and Lagerwey, partly inspired by the pioneering work of der Loon, to combine textual scholarship and fieldwork to bring new insights into many aspects of Daoist ritual and its relationship to Chinese social life.

Meanwhile, the very vibrancy of the religion in the contemporary world has started to stimulate reflection on the way it was originally represented in Western scholarship as a moribund tradition perpetuated only by ignorant charlatans. In this, the lead has been taken by the Australian scholar Benjamin Penny, who has briefly examined some of the influences working on nineteenth-century accounts of Daoism. In 2003 Elena Valussi challenged the rhetoric of decline in later Daoism through a London doctorate devoted to the emergence in the Qing period of texts promoting the self-cultivation of women. These show an ongoing pattern of adaptation and innovation into the twentieth century not easy to reconcile with the negative assessments of Western missionary observers. The early twenty-first century is at last seeing the recognition of Daoism as a religious tradition of remarkable richness and historic depth that has by no means been extinguished by modernity and that may yet have much to teach. Several of those responsible for demonstrating this, like Anna Seidel (1938–1991), Michel Strickmann (1942–1994), and Isabelle Robinet (1932–2000), did not live to see the full fruits of their efforts.

BIBLIOGRAPHY

Retrospective surveys with a narrow focus are K. M. Schipper, "The History of Taoist Studies in Europe," in *Europe Studies China*, edited by Ming Wilson and John Cayley (London, 1995), pp. 467–491; and Fukui Fumimasa, "The History of Taoist Studies in Japan and Some Related Issues," *Acta Asiatica* 68 (1995), pp. 1–18. J. J. Clarke, *The Tao of the West: Western Transformations of Taoist Thought* (London, 2000), is an outsider's account useful for its information on the broader context of the acceptance of Daoism as a topic of study. Lai Chi-Tim, "Daoism in China Today, 1980–2002," *China Quarterly* 174 (June 2003), pp. 413–427, is an account of the religion in its homeland. James Miller, *Daoism: A Short Introduction* (Oxford, 2003), is an up-to-date summary. Livia Kohn, ed., *Daoism Handbook* (Leiden, 2000), is a compendious source of information in English. Fabrizio Pregadio's website, available at http://venus.unive.it/pregadio/taoism.html, is a gateway to the mysteries of Daoism.

T. H. BARRETT (1987 AND 2005)

DAOSHENG

DAOSHENG (360?–434), also Zhu Daosheng; Chinese Buddhist monk, student of the *Nirvāṇa Sūtra*, and early proponent of a doctrine of sudden enlightenment. The precise age at which Daosheng entered the religious life is unknown. Accounts of his early career state only that he studied under Zhu Fatai (a disciple, with Dao'an, of Fotudeng) in Jiankang, the southern capital. In 397 he journeyed to Mount Lu and became the disciple of Dao'an's most famous student, Huiyuan. During his first year on Lushan, Daosheng took advantage of the presence of the Kashmiri monk Saṃghadeva to study the Sarvāstivāda Abhidharma literature. Around 406 he left Lushan for the northern capital of Chang'an, where he presumably attended Kumārajīva's translation seminars of the *Vimalakīrti* and *Saddharmapuṇḍarīka Sūtras*. Later, he wrote commentaries to both of these scriptures.

In 407 Daosheng abruptly left Chang'an and returned to Lushan, bearing with him a copy of Sengzhao's *Boruo wu zhi lun* (*Prajñā* is not knowledge). Liu Yimin's correspondence with Sengzhao regarding this text, included in the *Zhaolun*, resulted from this fortuitous transmission. Shortly after arriving on Mount Lu, Daosheng was off again, this time to Jiankang, where in 418 Faxian translated a recension of the Mahāyāna *Mahāparinirvāṇa Sūtra*. This text, like its Hīnayāna namesake, purported to record the last discourse of the Buddha, a fact that very naturally conferred on it a prestige and authority all its own. Quite unlike the Hīnayāna version, however, the Mahāyāna text preached that *nirvāṇa* was "permanent, joyous, personal, and pure" (Chin., *chang, le, wo*[!], *jing*), assertions that are substantially at odds with the normative Mahāyāna teaching that the nature of *nirvāṇa*, like that of all *dharmas*, is itself empty (*śūnya*) of all attributes. More curious to Daosheng's ears, however, was the statement in Faxian's translation that the *icchantikas* (Chin., *yichanti*, beings who have cut off their roots of virtue and seek only to gratify their desires) could never attain buddhahood. To Daosheng, such a statement vitiated the central claim of Mahāyāna Buddhism to be a vehicle of salvation for all beings. Disdaining to accept the letter of the text, he insisted on the ultimate buddhahood of the *icchantikas*, and in so doing brought down upon himself the wrath of the monastic community in Jiankang. Daosheng was forced to leave the capital in 428 or 429 when accusations of heresy were formally brought to the attention of the emperor.

Back on Lushan, Daosheng did not have to wait long for vindication. In 430 a new recension of the

Mahāparinirvāṇa Sūtra, translated by Dharmakṣema in Liangzhou in 421, reached the southern capital. Eight chapters longer than Faxian's recension, this text contained passages in the sections hitherto unavailable to the Chinese that explicitly guaranteed salvation to the *icchantika*s. When the contents of this text became known in Jiankang, Daosheng was invited to return to the capital. He died on Mount Lu in the year 434.

Daosheng's works, nearly all lost, reflect the broadened textual horizons of the Chinese Buddhist world of the early fifth century. They include essays on the Buddha nature and the *dharmakāya* (the transcendental, absolute body of the Buddha); a treatise on the two truths, presumably a Mādhyamika-oriented work deriving from the influence of Kumārajīva; and commentaries on several sūtras, including the *Vimalakīrti,* the *Saddharmapuṇḍarīka* (Lotus), the *Nirvāṇa* (the principal scriptural warrant for many of his notions), and the *Aṣṭasāhasrikā-prajñāpāramitā.* But what we know of his thought is based principally on secondary sources, the testimony of Sengzhao, for instance, who liberally cites Daosheng's views in his own commentary on the *Vimalakīrti Sūtra.* Of Daosheng's scriptural commentaries only that on the *Lotus* survives.

For Daosheng, the phenomenal world is supported by an absolute, a principle of cosmic and moral order (*li*) that is unitary, indivisible, and immanent in all things. This cosmic order is *dharma.* As the source of things, it is also their *ti,* or substance, and yet it is ultimately without any qualifying attributes whatsoever: it is *kong,* empty, *wu,* without existence, or *ziran,* self-same, what is naturally so. The personification of this principle is, of course, the Buddha, but as the Buddha is in a sense no more than a reification of the *dharma,* the body of the *dharma* (*dharmakāya*), buddhas and ordinary beings share a common substance. The *Nirvāṇa Sūtra* asserts, in its most well-known passage, that all beings possess this buddha nature (*foxing*). If so, argues Daosheng, the religious life does not culminate in the acquisition of some new quality but in an awareness within each of us of an already present enlightenment. Once this awareness dawns, there then arises what the *Nirvāṇa Sūtra* refers to as the true self (*zhen wo*), an unqualified, blissful, and unchanging consciousness. It was in terms of this True Self that Daosheng understood the *Nirvāṇa Sūtra*'s teaching that *nirvāṇa* is permanent, joyous, personal, and pure.

Classical Mahāyāna thought conceives of the religious path as commencing with a mind set on enlightenment (*bodhicitta*) and progressing through a series of ten *bodhisattva* stages (*bhūmis*) in which deluded thought is suppressed and nondual insight (*prajñā*) into reality cultivated. The seventh of these *bhūmis* is usually considered a decisive point in the spiritual life. From that point on, the practitioner is considered no longer subject to spiritual retrogression; his consciousness is wholly oriented toward enlightenment, even if that path involves, as it must, the decision to delay final *nirvāṇa* for the sake of others. But is the experience of enlightenment itself a sudden, radical break in consciousness, or is it of a piece, more rarefied perhaps, with the gradual steps of spiritual progress along the *bodhisattva* path?

A document contemporary with Daosheng, Xie Lingyun's *Bianzong lun* (Discussion of essentials; included in the *Guang hongming ji,* T.D. no. 2103) apprises us that for many Chinese the *bodhisattva* path was seen as a course of gradual progression and graded stages of enlightenment. Against this view, the *Bianzong lun* sets forth what it calls the new doctrine of Daosheng. According to this doctrine, as the Absolute is unitary, indivisible, and without any qualifiers whatsoever, so too must the wisdom that comprehends it be a sudden, intuitive insight (*dunwu*) into the whole of reality. Such an insight can admit to no gradation. Daosheng likens the process of enlightenment to that of a fruit ripening on a tree. Religious practice may inculcate confidence and faith in the *dharma,* but at the moment when one reaches enlightenment there is a qualitative leap or disjunction, just as the fruit suddenly falls away from the tree when it reaches maturity.

Daosheng's teaching of sudden enlightenment was not the first such doctrine in China. Previous thinkers such as Zhi Dun and, allegedly, Dao'an, had spoken of the seventh *bhūmi* as the critical stage at which insight dawns. For them, however, this insight was deepened in later stages. Daosheng rejected this lesser doctrine of sudden enlightenment (*xiao dunwu*), as he did the gradualist notions of his former companion in Chang'an, Huiguan (354–424), who argued that practitioners of different levels of spiritual maturity perceive the truth in different ways and to differing degrees: the truth may be whole, but some are capable of seeing only a portion of it. This subitist versus gradualist controversy was one of the issues subsumed within the discourse of fifth- and sixth-century debates on the *jiaopan,* the divisions of scriptures that attempted to account for the diversity, even incongruity, the Chinese found among the teachings of the Indian sūtra literature. These organizing schemes classified texts both genetically, according to the type of teaching embodied therein, and historically, according to the period in the career of the Buddha in which they were said to have been preached.

In one of the most prominent of these early systems, Huiguan proposed that the Buddha preached at least two types of doctrine, *dunjiao,* or sudden teachings, and *jianjiao,* gradual teachings (a third type, indeterminate, is often attributed to Huiguan and was widely found in *jiaopan* contemporary with his). But Huiguan's emphasis here does not bear directly on the nature of the enlightenment experience itself; as the term *jiao* (teaching) implies, what is at issue is the *method* employed in various texts to bring beings to enlightenment, suggesting that in their quest for a systematization of the Buddhist scriptures, the scholar-monks of Daosheng's time admitted, in best Mahāyāna fashion, a plurality of religious paths without necessarily denying the suddenness of enlightenment itself.

For his part, Daosheng too proposed a classification of the Buddha's teachings according to the capacities of the audience. In the *Miaofa lianhua jing su,* his commentary to the *Lotus Sūtra,* Daosheng acknowledges the need for various devices to provoke faith in *dharma* and posits a fourfold division of the Buddha's teachings: (1) Good and Pure Wheel of the Law; (2) Expedient Teachings; (3) True Teachings; and (4) Teachings without Residue. Whether these refer, as commonly interpreted, to specific texts or, as also maintained (Ōchō, 1952, pp. 232–238), merely to teaching methods, they are indicative of Daosheng's recognition that although the Truth may be indivisible, the means to attract people to it must take heed of their capacity to comprehend what is taught. Clearly, Daosheng never intended to preclude the necessity for religious cultivation by promulgating his doctrine of sudden enlightenment.

Crucial as these issues may have been for the Indian Buddhist tradition, where both subitist and gradualist tendencies are attested, it is important to recognize the extent to which the debate over the topic in China was carried out against a backdrop of indigenous values and perceptions. Despite the provocative fact that Xie Lingyun classed as sudden the doctrines of Confucius, Confucian teachings were perennially associated with a gradual path of moral and intellectual cultivation epitomized in their concept of the ideal person, the *junzi.* By contrast, the very notions most typically associated with the subitist doctrine, the unity and indivisibility of the Truth and the ineffability and spontaneity of the experience of it, are characteristically Daoist. As Demiéville points out (1973, pp. 256–257), Daosheng's most well-known assertions—that works are in vain, that acts engender no retribution, that *karman* is a mere nominal designation, and that buddahood is innate in all beings—handsomely recapitulate the notions of sagehood championed in the immediately preceding centuries by the *xuanxue* thinkers.

In later centuries, subitist and gradualist patterns would manifest themselves again in the controversies of the Southern and Northern Chan teachings (upon which Daosheng's thought has no real bearing whatsoever) and, in another form altogether, in the division of the neo-Confucian teachings into the so-called Cheng-Zhu and Lu-Wang traditions, testifying to the power of these motifs over Chinese intellectual and religious history. It is thus important to see in Daosheng's thought the extent to which Buddhist and indigenous patterns of religious thinking fertilize each other and to recognize in the concerns of the still young Chinese Buddhist church of Daosheng's day the resumption of perennial Chinese themes and conflicts.

SEE ALSO Bodhisattva Path; Guo Xiang; Huiyuan; Kumārajīva; Sengzhao; Wang Bi.

BIBLIOGRAPHY

Ch'en, Kenneth. *Buddhism in China: A Historical Survey.* Princeton, 1964. Daosheng's thought is introduced on pages 112–120.

Demiéville, Paul. "Busshō." In *Hōbōgirin,* edited by Paul Demiéville, fasc. 2, pp. 185–187. Tokyo, 1930.

Demiéville, Paul. "La pénétration du bouddhisme dans la tradition philosophique chinoise." In his *Choix d'études bouddhiques,* pp. 241–260. Leiden, 1973. Includes a discussion of subitist versus gradualist tendencies in Chinese Buddhism.

Fung Yu-lan. *A History of Chinese Philosophy,* vol. 2, *The Period of Classical Learning.* 2d ed. Translated by Derk Bodde. Princeton, 1953. See pages 270–284.

Fuse Kōgaku. *Nehanshū no kenkyū.* 2 vols. Tokyo, 1942. See especially volume 2 for an extensive treatment of the development of the notions of sudden and gradual enlightenment (pp. 139–171) and the thought of Daosheng and Huiguan (pp. 172–196).

Hurvitz, Leon N. *Chih-i (538–597): An Introduction to the Life and Ideas of a Chinese Buddhist Monk.* Brussels, 1962. Daosheng is discussed on pages 193–201.

Itano Chōhachi. "Dōshō no tongosetsu seiritsu no jijō." *Tōhō gakuhō* 7 (December 1936): 125–186.

Itano Chōhachi. "Dōshō no busshōron." *Shina bukkyō shigaku* 2 (May 1938): 1–26.

Liebenthal, Walter. "A Biography of Chu Tao-sheng." *Monumenta Nipponica* 11 (1955): 284–316.

Liebenthal, Walter. "The World Conception of Chu Tao–sheng." *Monumenta Nipponica* 12 (1956): 65–103.

Liebenthal, Walter. "The World Conception of Chu Tao-sheng (Texts)." *Monumenta Nipponica* 12 (1956–1957): 241–268.

Liebenthal, Walter, ed. and trans. *The Book of Chao.* Beijing, 1948. Appendix 3 contains a useful discussion of sudden and gradual enlightenment.

Ōchō Enichi. "Jiku Dōshō sen *Hokekyōsho* no kenkyū." *Ōtani daigaku kenkyū nenpō* 5 (1952): 169–272.

Tang Yongtong. *Han Wei liang-Jin Nan-bei chao fojiao shi.* 2 vols. Shanghai, 1938. See volume 2, pages 601–676, for a full treatment of Daosheng.

New Sources

Kim, Young-ho. *Daosheng's Commentary on the Lotus Sūtra Sūtra: A Study and Translation.* Albany, 1990.

Lai, Whalen. "Some Notes on Perceptions of Pratitya-Samutpada in China from Kumarajiva to Fa-yao." *Journal of Chinese Philosophy* 8 (1981): 427–435.

Lai, Whalen. "The Mahaparinirvana-Sutra and Its Earliest Interpreters in China: Two Prefaces by Tao-lang and Daosheng." *Journal of the American Oriental Society* 102, no. 2 (1982): 99–105.

Lai, Whalen. "Daosheng's Theory of Sudden Enlightenment Re-Examined." In *Sudden and Gradual: Approaches to Enlightenment in Chinese Thought,* edited by Peter Gregory, pp. 169–200. Honolulu, 1987.

Yu, David C. "Skill-in-Means and the Buddhism of Daosheng: A Study of a Chinese Reaction to Mahāyāana of the Fifth Century." *Philosophy East and West* 24, no. 4 (1974): 413–427.

MARK D. CUMMINGS (1987)
Revised Bibliography

DĀRĀ SHIKŌH, MUḤAMMAD.

DĀRĀ SHIKŌH, MUḤAMMAD. (According to some sources, Dara Shukōh.) Sultan Muḥammad Dārā

Shikōh (AH 1024–1069/1615–1659 CE), the eldest son of the Mughal emperor Shāhjahān and Mumtāz Maḥal, was born in the city of Ajmer. Dārā's political career began in 1634, when he was given the first *manṣab* (rank) in command of 1,200 *dhāt* (soldiers) and 6,000 *sawār* (horsemen). By 1657 the number of troops under Dārā's command had reached 100,000. Moreover, later in the same year, due to the illness of his father, Dārā was appointed as regent to look after the affairs of the empire.

Dārā was not a successful warrior, however. His three expeditions against the Persian army, in 1639, 1642, and 1653, ended in humiliation and cost him the chance of capturing Kandahar. His later career, moreover, saw two detrimental defeats in the war of succession at the hands of his brothers, who refused to accept Dārā as the new regent. First he lost against Murād and Aurangzēb in Samūgarh, and then a few months later he suffered his final defeat in 1659 at the hands of Aurangzēb in Deorai. Although Dārā was a brave warrior, his lack of diplomatic and leadership skills lost him his crown, and he was forced to flee to Dadar for refuge. There he was betrayed by his host, Malik Jīwan, and handed over to the new emperor, Aurangzēb. Finally, Dārā was paraded in disgrace through the streets of Delhi and beheaded in Dhū al Ḥijja AH 1069 (August 1659).

Dārā was a patron of arts, architecture, and literature and was himself a skilled calligrapher, artist, poet, writer, and translator. He wrote several works on Sufism and translated a few remarkable Sanskrit works into Persian. Dārā appears to have been interested in the Qādiriyya Ṣūfī *silsila* (literally, "order") from his childhood. He was formally initiated by Mullā Shāh into the Qādiriyya *silsila* sometime in 1639 or 1640. He remained committed to his *silsila* throughout his life, and as a poet he adopted "Qādirī" as his pen name.

It was his interest in Sufism that led Dārā to start writing in 1639 or 1640. His first four works were on Sufism. The first, *Safīnat al-Awliyā'* (Ship of the saints), contains more than four hundred short biographies of Ṣūfī saints of various orders. The second, *Sakīnat al–Awliyā'* (Tranquility of the saints), encompasses the lives of twenty-eight Qādirī Ṣūfīs, mostly Dārā's contemporaries. The third work, *Risāla-i Ḥaqq numā'* (The compass of the truth), is a manual aimed at explaining the theory and practice of Ṣūfī meditation. The fourth work, *Ḥasanāt al-ʿĀrifīn* (Merits of the Gnostics), is a collection of the *shaṭḥiyyāt* (ecstatic utterances) of the Ṣūfī saints from the eleventh century down to Dārā's own time. His Ṣūfī writings show that he was an enthusiastic follower of the doctrine of *waḥdat al-wujūd* (oneness of being) and advocated an inclusive approach towards other religions.

It was Dārā's broad-minded Ṣūfī attitude that brought him to the study of Hinduism. He held a series of dialogues with a Hindu yogi, Bābā Lāl Dās, and discussed with him various concepts of Hinduism, at times comparing them with Islam. This conversation was later compiled as *Sū'āl-o-jawāb Dārā Shukōh-o-Bābā Lāl Dās* (The dialogue between Dārā Shukōh and Bābā Lāl Dās). As a result of his discussion with Bābā Lāl and other Ṣūfīs he wrote *Majmaʿ al-Baḥrayn* (*The Mingling of the Two Oceans*). This work represents one of the most important attempts to reconcile Islam and Hinduism in the history of Indian thought, and specifically in the field of comparative religion. Yet despite its ecumenical nature, *Majmaʿ* became the most controversial work written by Dārā.

Dārā also translated fifty Upaniṣads—under the title *Sirr-i Akbar* (The greatest veil)—from the original Sanskrit into Persian. Later, Anquetil Duperron, a French scholar, translated the Persian rendering of Dārā into French and Latin and introduced his work to Europe. In his preface to the *Sirr-i Akbar,* Dārā assigned the Upaniṣads the status of *kitāb-i maknūn* (a well-guarded book)—a status previously assigned by Muslim scholars only to the Qur'ān. For Dārā, the Upaniṣads and the Qur'ān represented two facets of the same truth. Dārā's other scholarly efforts in the field of Hinduism include a translation of the *Bhagavadgītā* and his commission of a translation of the *Jōg Bāshist,* also known as *Minhāj al-Sālikīn* (The path of the wayfarers). In the preface to *Jōg,* he praises the prophet Muḥammad and admires the Hindu avatar Ramchand. This also demonstrates that, for him, both personalities were guides of the same stature. Dārā Shikōh's efforts to forge a new relationship between Hinduism and Islam was the most remarkable ecumenical achievement in the history of Mughal India.

BIBLIOGRAPHY

Chand, Tārā. "Dara Shikoh and the Upanishads." *Islamic Culture* (1943): 397–413.

Dārā Shukōh. *Ḥasanāt al-ʿĀrifīn.* Edited by Sayyid Makhdoom Rahīn. Tehran, Iran, 1973.

Dārā Shukōh. *Majmaʿ-ul-Bahrain, or, The Mingling of the Two Oceans.* Edited and translated by M. Mahfuz-ul-Haq. Calcutta, 1929.

Dārā Shukōh. *Risāla-i Ḥaqq-numā', Majmaʿ al-Baḥrayn, Upanikhat Mundak.* Edited by Sayyid Muḥammad Rizā Jalālī Nā'īnī as *Muntakhabāt-i Āthār.* Tehran, Iran, 1956.

Dārā Shukōh. *Safīnat al-Awliyā'.* Kanpur, India, 1900.

Dārā Shukōh. *Sirr-i Akbar: The Oldest Translation of Upanishads from Sanskrit into Persian.* Edited by Tārā Chand and Muḥammad Rizā Jalālī Nā'īnī. Tehran, Iran, 1957.

Dārā Shukōh. *Sakīnat al-Awliyā'.* Edited by Sayyid Muḥammad Rizā Jalālī Nā'īnī and Tārā Chand. Tehran, Iran, 1965.

Ernst, C. W. *Words of Ecstasy in Sufism.* Albany, N.Y., 1985.

Göbel Gross, Erhard. *Sirr-i Akbar: Die persische Upaniṣadenübersetzung des Moġulprinzen Dārā Šukoh.* Marburg, Germany, 1962.

Hasrat, Bikrama Jit. *Dārā Shikūh: Life and Works.* Allahabad, India, 1953; 2d ed., New Delhi, 1979.

Huart, Clement, and Louis Massignon. "Les entretiens de Lahore (entre le prince impérial Dārā Shikūh et l'ascète hindou Baba La'l Das)." *Journal Asiatique* 208 (1926): 285–334.

Karim, Arshad Syed. "Muslim Nationalism: Conflicting Ideologies of Dara Shikoh and Aurangzeb." *Journal of the Pakistan Historical Society* 33, pt. 4 (1985): 288–296.

Narain, Sheo. "Dārā Shikoh as an Author." *Journal of the Punjab Historical Society* 2 (1913–1914): 21–38.

Qanungo, Kalika-Ranjan. *Dara Shukoh.* 2d ed. Calcutta, 1952.

Shayegan, Darius. *Les relations de l'Hindouisme et du Soufisme d'après le Majma' al-Bahrayn de Dārā Shokūh.* Paris, 1979.

PERWAIZ HAYAT (2005)

DARKNESS SEE LIGHT AND DARKNESS

DARŚANAS SEE MĪMĀṂSĀ; NYĀYA; SĀṂKHYA; VAIŚEṢIKA; VEDĀNTA; YOGA

DARWIN, CHARLES SEE EVOLUTION; SCIENCE AND RELIGION

DARWĪSH. The Persian word *darwīsh,* from the Pahlavi *driyosh,* is most likely derived from the term *darvīza,* meaning "poverty," "neediness," "begging," and so forth. The word *darwīsh* has entered the other Islamic languages, such as Turkish and Urdu, and is even found in classical Arabic sources. It has become an English word in the form of *dervish.* In all these cases, including the original Persian, it is related primarily to spiritual poverty, equivalent to the possession of "Muhammadan poverty" *(al-faqr al-muḥammadi).* Hence the term *darwīsh* referring to a person who possesses this "poverty" is the same as the Arabic term *faqīr* used in Sufism in many Islamic languages besides Arabic (including Persian itself) for Muhammadan poverty. Within Ṣūfī circles, these words are used interchangeably, along with *mutaṣawwif,* "practitioner" of Sufism.

The term *darwīsh* appears in Persian literature as early as the tenth century and in such early Persian Ṣūfī texts as the works of Khwājah ʿAbd Allāh Anṣārī of Herat, where it carries the basic meaning referred to above but encompasses such variations as "ascetic," "hermit," and "wandering Ṣūfī" *(qalandar).* Later it also became an honorific title bestowed upon certain Ṣūfīs such as Darwīsh Khusraw, the leader of the Nuqṭawiyah school at the time of Shah ʿAbbās I. Throughout the history of Sufism, the state of being a *darwīsh,* or *darwīshī,* has been held in great honor and respect, as seen from the famous *ghazal* of Ḥāfiẓ that begins with the verse

> Rawḍiy-i khuld-i barīn khalwat-i darwīshānast
> Māyiy-i muḥtashimī khidmat-i darwīshanast
>
> The sublime eternal Paradise is the spiritual
> retreat of the dervishes;
>
> The essence of grandeur is the service of the dervishes.

There is, however, a secondary meaning associated with *darwīsh* that carries negative connotations, interpreting simplicity of life, limitation of material needs, reliance upon God for sustenance, and other aspects of Muhammadan poverty or Sufism as laziness, lackadaisicalness, indifference to cleanliness, neglect of duties toward oneself and society, and other injunctions emphasized by the *sharīʿah,* or Islamic law. This negative aspect of the term increased with the decay of certain Ṣūfī orders during the past two or three centuries and also with the attempt by some people to pass themselves off as *darwīsh* without any involvement with Sufism at all. Nonetheless, the association with spiritual poverty, self-discipline, and the basic virtues of humility, charity, and veracity remains the primary meaning of the word.

BIBLIOGRAPHY

Arberry, A. J. *Sufism: An Account of the Mystics of Islam* (1950). Reprint, London, 1979.

Birge, John K. *The Bektashi Order of Dervishes* (1937). Reprint, New York, 1982.

Ernst, Carl W. *The Shambala Guide to Sufism.* Boston, 1997.

Keddie, Nikki R., ed. *Scholars, Saints, and Sufis: Muslim Religious Institutions in the Middle East since 1500.* Berkeley, Calif., 1972.

Nicholson, Reynold A. *The Mystics of Islam* (1914). Reprint, London, 1963.

Schimmel, Annemarie. *Mystical Dimensions of Islam.* Chapel Hill, N. C., 1975.

SEYYED HOSSEIN NASR (1987 AND 2005)

DASAM GRANTH. The *Dasam Granth* (Tenth book) is a collection of writings attributed to Gurū Gobind Singh, the tenth Sikh gurū (1666–1708). It was compiled sometime after his death by Bhāī Manī Singh, one of his devoted followers. The *Dasam Granth* is 1,428 pages long, so it is almost the same size as the *Gurū Granth* (1,430 pages). The *Gurū Granth,* also known as the *Ādi Granth* (First book), is the sacred scripture of the Sikhs, but some parts of the *Dasam Granth* are also used in Sikh prayers. The authorship and authenticity of a large proportion of this work is questioned. Most of the *Dasam Granth* is in the Braj language, but the entire work is printed in the Gurmukhi script.

Gurū Gobind Singh was a superb poet who introduced vigorous meters and rhythms to revitalize his people and created novel images and paradoxes to stretch their imagination. He was also a great patron of the arts and employed numerous poets from different religious backgrounds. Much of the poetry written by Gurū Gobind Singh himself as well as that by his court poets was lost during his evacuation from Anandpur in 1705. Bhāī Manī Singh spent years collecting whatever materials he could salvage, and from these he produced the first recension of the *Dasam Granth.*

The *Dasam Granth* remains controversial among scholars, and it elicits a range of responses from devotees. Such compositions as the *Jaapu, Akāl Ustat, Bicitra Nātak, Caṇḍī*

Caritra, Caṇḍī di Vār, Śabad Hazāre, and *Gyān Prabodh* are generally accepted as Gurū Gobind Singh's compositions, and these are revered by the Sikhs. A large proportion of the *Dasam Granth* (about 1,185 pages) is devoted to stories, many of them based on Indian myth, others dealing with amorous intrigues. Most people believe that these sections were written by the poets of the gurū's entourage. They are therefore neglected, but the *Benati Chaupai* from this section is one of the daily Sikh prayers.

The *Dasam Granth* opens with the *Jaapu.* Analogous to Gurū Nānak's *Japu* (the first hymn in the *Gurū Granth*), Gurū Gobind Singh's *Jaapu* carries forward in breathtaking speed Nānak's message of the One reality. Many Sikhs recite the *Jaapu* daily in the morning. It is also one of the hymns recited as part of the Sikh initiation ceremony. Through dynamic metaphors and rhythm, the *Jaapu* exalts the animating and life-generating One that flows through and interconnects the myriad creatures: "salutations to You in every country, in every garb" (*Jaapu* 66). Like Nānak's *Japu,* Gobind Singh's *Jaapu* celebrates the presence of the transcendent within the glorious diversity of the cosmos: "You are in water, You are on land" (*Jaapu* 62); "You are the sustainer of the earth" (*Jaapu* 173).

The *Jaapu* is followed by *Akāl Ustat* (Praise of the timeless one), which occupies twenty-eight pages of the *Dasam Granth.* It proclaims the unity of humanity:

> Hindus and Muslims are one . . . . The Hindu temple and the Muslim mosque are the same. . . . All humanity is one. (*Akal Ustat* 86)

Mahatma Gandhi (1869–1948) popularized these verses in his famous prayer, "Īśvara and Allah are your names, temple and mosque are your homes." Verses from the *Akāl Ustat* are central to the Sikh initiation ceremony. They rhythmically repeat that without love all religious practices are ineffective: "They alone who love, find the Beloved."

The thirty-eight-page *Bicitra Nātak* (Wondrous drama) follows the *Akāl Ustat.* This poetic autobiography is a magical mixture of biographical facts and literary imagination. It is the only autobiographical work by any of the Sikh gurūs.

The three Durgā-Caṇḍī poems come next and retell the story of Durgā's titanic battles against the demons from the *Devīmāhātmya.* With all his artistic zeal, the gurū amplifies the warrior role of the ancient Hindu heroine.

Khālsā Mahima (Praise of the Khālsā), which comes later in the *Dasam Granth,* is a favorite hymn amongst the Sikhs. It celebrates the democratic Khālsā community created by Gurū Gobind Singh: "The Khālsā is my special form . . . the Khālsā is my body and breath." Another popular text from the *Dasam Granth* is the defiant *Zafar Nāmā* (Letter of victory), written in Persian, and addressed to the emperor Aurangzeb.

Like his predecessor gurūs, Gobind Singh appropriates love as the highest form of action. His devotional compositions reiterate Sikh ideals and ethics. Their tone is forceful, and their imperatives are clear:

> Recognize the single caste of humanity
> Know that we are all of the same body, the same light.
> (*Akāl Ustat* 85)

The tenth gurū's verse continues to have great resonance for the global society. Difference should not stand in the way of people getting to know one another:

> Different vestures from different countries may make us different. But we have the same eyes, the same ears, the same body, the same voice. (*Akāl Ustat* 86)

SEE ALSO Ādi Granth; Sikhism; Singh, Gobind.

BIBLIOGRAPHY

For the text in the original Punjabi, see Bhai Randhir Singh's *Sabdharath Dasam Granth,* 3 vols. (Patiala, India, 1988). This text has been reproduced with a translation by Jodh Singh and Dharam Singh, *Sri Dasam Granth Sahib: Text and Translation* (Patiala, India, 1999). Excellent scholarly works in Punjabi include Rattan Singh Jaggi, *Dasam Granth da Kartritav* (New Delhi, 1966); and Piara Singh Padam, *Dasam Granth Darsan* (Patiala, India, 1990). Studies written in English include D. P. Ashta, *The Poetry of the Dasam Granth* (New Delhi, 1959); C. H. Loehlin, *The Granth of Guru Gobind Singh and the Khalsa Brotherhood* (Lucknow, India, 1958); J. S. Grewal, *Contesting Interpretations of the Sikh Tradition* (New Delhi, 1998); Hew McLeod, *Sikhs of the Khalsa: A History of the Khalsa Rahit* (New Delhi, 2003); and Robin Rinehart, "Strategies for Interpreting the *Dasam Granth,*" in *Sikhism and History,* edited by Pashaura Singh and N. Gerald Barrier (New Delhi, 2004).

NIKKY-GUNINDER KAUR SINGH (2005)

DAVID [FIRST EDITION], second king of Israel and Judah (c. 1000–960 BCE), and founder of a dynasty that continued until the end of the Judean monarchy. David was the youngest son of Jesse from Bethlehem in Judah.

DAVID'S PLACE IN THE HISTORY OF ISRAEL. David is regarded by both tradition and modern scholarship as the greatest ruler of the combined states of Israel and Judah. He was able to free them from the control of the Philistines and to gain a measure of domination over some of the neighboring states (Edom, Moab, Ammon) and some of the Aramean states of Syria. At the same time he established treaty relations with Tyre and Hamath. He also extended the territories of Judah and Israel to include a number of major Canaanite cities and took Jerusalem by conquest. It became his capital and remained the ruling center of Judah until the end of the monarchy.

There are no references to David in any historical source outside the Bible. One contemporary ruler, Hiram of Tyre, mentioned in *2 Samuel* 5:11, is known from other historical sources, but the correlation of the chronologies of the two kings remains problematic.

The assessment of David's career is based upon sources in *1 Samuel* 16 through *1 Kings* 2. Some of these that mention his military activities reflect annalistic or formal documents. These are now embedded within two literary works often regarded as nearly contemporary with David and an important witness to the events: the story of David's rise to power (*1 Sm.* 16 through *2 Sm.* 2:7, *2 Sm.* 5), and the court history, or succession story (*2 Sm.* 2:8–4:12, 6:16, 6:20–23; *2 Sm.* 9–20; *1 Kgs.* 1–2). It remains less clear how *2 Samuel* 6–8 relates to either of these works or how they all fit into the larger history of the monarchy. The materials in *2 Samuel* 21–24 are supplemental additions that do not belong to the other sources.

There are, however, two serious questions about this literary analysis. First, the identification of a distinct literary work, the story of David's rise to power, may be doubted, since it may be viewed as a continuation of earlier materials in *Samuel* and as having strong ties to the rest of the so-called Deuteronomist's history of the monarchy—in which case it would be a work of the exilic period. Second, the court history was not originally part of this history but constitutes a later addition with quite a different perspective. If these two views can be sustained, then both works are comparatively late, and great caution must be exercised in using them as historical sources for the time of David.

DAVID IN THE TRADITION OF ISRAEL. Whatever their historical value might be, the literary works within *1 Samuel* 16 through *1 Kings* 2 establish David's place within the Israelite-Jewish tradition. Two quite different views of David's character and his significance for later Israel are given in these works.

Rise to power. David's introduction is directly linked to God's rejection of Saul, so that he immediately appears as the "one after God's own heart" to replace Saul. Shortly after David enters Saul's service as personal armor bearer, musician, and successful military leader, Saul becomes jealous and turns against David. While Saul's son Jonathan, his daughter Michal, his servants, and all the people grow to love David, Saul grows to hate him and makes various attempts on his life so that David flees. David establishes a band of followers in Judah and becomes a vassal of the Philistines. Saul, demented, cruel, and forsaken by God, ultimately dies on the battlefield with his sons. David, after offering a lament for Saul and Jonathan, is made king at Hebron, first by Judah and subsequently by Israel. David then captures Jerusalem and wages successful warfare against the Philistines. All of this comes to David because "God is with him." Throughout the entire account, David is viewed as one who can do no wrong. Heroic and magnanimous, he is the obvious replacement for Saul.

The dynastic promise. Once the land is at peace, David is able to bring the Ark to Jerusalem (*2 Sm.* 6) and build himself a palace (*2 Sm.* 5:11). He then proposes a plan to Nathan the prophet to build a temple for the Ark, and this leads to a dynastic promise by God through the prophet (*2 Sm.* 7). Although some have argued that this promise is based upon a special document of the early monarchy, it seems preferable to regard it as the thematic center of the larger Deuteronomic history of the monarchy and its ideology of kingship.

The dynastic promise is the real climax to the account of David's rise to kingship. With David a new era begins in two respects. God promises David an eternal dynasty but assigns the task of building the Temple—a permanent abode—to his son Solomon. God will be "a father" to the king, and he will be God's "son." He may be disciplined for disobedience to God's laws, but the dynasty will remain in perpetuity.

David as the "servant of Yahveh" who is completely obedient to God becomes the model for all future kings, especially those of Judah. Not only is his obedience rewarded with an immediate heir, but it is said to merit the perpetuation of his dynasty even if some future kings are disobedient to God's laws.

This dynastic promise also becomes the basis for the hope of a restoration of the monarchy after the destruction of the state in 587/6 BCE and ultimately leads to messianism—the belief that a son of David will arise and restore the fortunes of Israel and usher in the final reign of God.

Court history. The so-called court history, or succession story, variously regarded as a unique piece of early history writing, a historical novel, and a work of royal propaganda, is a literary masterpiece of realistic narrative. Some view it as written in support of Solomon, while others understand it as anti-Solomonic. If this work is an early source used by the historian of *Samuel* and *Kings*, then it is not clear how he could have been reconciled to such a pejorative view of David, since the rest of the history so completely idealizes him.

The court history, in fact, was a later addition to the history that seeks to counter the idealized view of David by suggesting that he gained the throne from a son of Saul under doubtful circumstances and that the divine promise to David was constantly used by David, Solomon, and others to legitimize very questionable behavior. The "sure house" of David is characterized by endless turmoil, and Solomon finally succeeds David after a palace intrigue. David himself commits adultery and murder. One of his sons, Amnon, rapes his sister Tamar and is avenged by his brother Absalom. After an exile Absalom returns to lead a revolt against his father that finally ends in Absalom's death. This is followed by yet another revolt between north and south.

This pejorative view of David's monarchy and the dynastic promise did not suppress the royal ideology or its evolution into messianism. At most it "humanized" David and gave added appeal to the tradition as a whole.

DAVID IN THE *BOOKS OF CHRONICLES*. The historian of *1* and *2 Chronicles* sees in David the real founder of the Jewish state, a state dominated by the Temple and an elaborate priestly hierarchy (*1 Chr.* 10–29). The Chronicler's source for David was the history in *Samuel* and *Kings* modified by his perception of the state, which was based upon his own times in the Hellenistic period. He presents David as immediately coming to the throne over all Israel after the death of Saul. There is no account of his struggle with Saul or of his warfare with Saul's son, Ishbosheth. The whole of the court history has been excised as too derogatory. In its place David becomes the real founder of the Temple, laying all the plans, providing for all the workmanship and the materials, and even establishing the whole hierarchy of priestly and Temple officials. Of particular importance for later tradition is the association of David with the Temple music, which did much to identify him as the "sweet singer of Israel." In this history David is completely idealized, and the time of David is an anachronistic legitimation for the ecclesiastical state that developed in the time of the Second Temple.

David and the Psalms. David is directly mentioned in only a few psalms (78, 89, and 132), those that make reference to the dynastic promise, all of which are dependent upon *Samuel* and *Kings*. In the Hebrew scriptures the superscriptions, which are all late, and which modern scholarship considers secondary additions, attribute seventy-three psalms to David. This continues the tradition of David's association with the sacred music of the Temple. But in a number of instances the individual laments (e.g., *Ps.* 51) are associated with particular events in David's life. Thus the psalms that were originally anonymous become increasingly associated with the figure of David.

David in Prophecy. While the royal ideology had at most a minor place in preexilic prophecy, it was only in late prophecy and in exilic and postexilic editing of prophetic books that the dynastic promise to David plays a major role in visions of the future (*Is.* 9:5–6 [Eng. version 6–7], 11:1–10, 61:1–7; *Jer.* 33:14–26; *Ez.* 34:23–24; *Am.* 9:11ff.; *Mi.* 5:1–3 [EV 2–4]; *Zec.* 12:7–9). Hope is expressed for the restoration of the Davidic dynasty and times of prosperity. In their most elaborate form these prophecies predict an "anointed one" (the Messiah) who would manifest all the idealized attributes of royalty, liberate Israel from its enemies, and bring in the reign of Yahveh.

David in Rabbinic Judaism, Christianity, and Islam. The most important development in the Davidic tradition in postbiblical Judaism was the regarding of David as the author of the Psalter, or at least as author of most of the psalms within it. This meant that David, as the composer of Israel's sacred hymns and prayers, was a model of Jewish piety. In the psalms David speaks not only for himself but for all Israel. His praise represents the spiritual life of the worshiping community, and in his prayers he supplicates God for Israel in all time to come. Furthermore, a number of the psalms have as their theme the glorification of the Law (Torah) and the ardent devotion of the psalmist to the study of the Law day and night (*Ps.* 1, 19, 119). Consequently, David was viewed as a great authority on the Law, and his words and example could often be invoked to settle a point at issue in the discussions of legal matters (*halakhah*) (B. T., *Ber.* 4a; B. T., *Yev.* 78b–79a). Since the Psalter came to be regarded as holy writ, David was also considered a prophet through whom God spoke and gave his revelation to Israel.

Some elements in the Davidic tradition gave the rabbis difficulty, most notably David's sin of adultery with Bathsheba. Some attempted to exonerate him, but those who found him guilty of wrongdoing saw a divine purpose in the events, namely that David was to be an example of contrition and repentance to give hope and encouragement to Israel when it sinned (*Midrash Tehillim* 40.2, 51.1, 51.3). Another problem was the tradition that David was descended from Ruth the Moabite (*Ru.* 4:17), since this would make him ineligible for participation in the congregation of Israel. As a compensation, every attempt was made to enhance David's genealogical line and give him the strongest possible pedigree. The dynastic promise to David represented the future hope of Israel, but many rabbis were concerned that it not be used for political or ideological manipulation by messianic adventurers. At the same time the liturgical tradition continued to embody the hope in a restoration of the kingdom of David in the age to come.

Christianity, as reflected in the New Testament, also recognized David as author of the psalms, as an example of piety, and as a prophet of divine revelation; but the emphasis was clearly on the messianic aspects of the tradition. Since Jesus was identified as the Messiah, he received the title "son of David," although he repudiated the political connotation of such a designation. Matthew and Luke, in their birth stories, connect Jesus with Bethlehem, the city of David, and supply genealogies that trace his lineage back to David. David as prophet also bears witness in the psalms to Jesus as the Messiah (*Acts* 2:25–37).

Islam's tradition about David is slight. The Qurʾān knows of a few episodes in David's life, such as the victory over Goliath, but this and other stories are confused with those of other biblical figures (2:252). The Qurʾān also recognizes that God gave *Psalms* to David as a divine book in much the same way as Moses and Muḥammad received their revelations (17:56).

Bibliography

Treatments of the historical periods of David's reign may be found in John Bright's *A History of Israel*, 3d ed. (Philadelphia, 1981); the contribution by J. Alberto Soggin, "The Davidic-Solomonic Kingdom," in *Israelite and Judaean History*, edited by John H. Hayes and J. Maxwell Miller (Philadelphia, 1977); and those by Benjamin Mazar and David N. Freedman in *The World History of the Jewish People*, vol. 4, pt. 1, edited by Abraham Malamat (Jerusalem, 1979), pp. 76–125.

The standard treatment on the story of David's rise to power is Jakob H. Grønbaek's *Die Geschichte vom Aufstieg Davids, 1 SAM. 15–2 SAM. 5: Tradition und Komposition*, "Acta Theologica Danica," vol. 10 (Copenhagen, 1971). The classic work on the so-called succession story is Leonhard Rost's *Die Überlieferung von der Thronnachfolge Davids*, "Beiträge zur Wissenschaft vom Alten und Neuen Testament," vol. 3, no. 6 (Stuttgart, 1926), translated by Michael D. Rutter and David M. Gunn as *The Succession to the Throne of David* (Sheffield, 1982). Building upon this study was the important essay by Gerhard von Rad, "Der Anfang der Geschichtsschreibung im Alten Israel," *Archiv für Kulturgeschichte* 32 (Weimar, 1944): 1–42, translated by E. W. Trueman Dicken as "The Beginning of Historical Writing in Ancient Israel," in Gerhard von Rad's *The Problem of the Hexateuch and Other Essays* (Edinburgh, 1966), pp. 166–204. See also the studies by Roger N. Whybray, *The Succession Narrative* (London, 1968), and David M. Gunn, *The Story of King David: Genre and Interpretation* (Sheffield, 1982). A more detailed treatment of my own views may be found in chapter 8 of my *In Search of History: Historiography in the Ancient World and the Origins of Biblical History* (New Haven, Conn., 1983).

For a more detailed treatment of the Jewish and Christian traditions with bibliography, see the article "David" in *Theologische Realenzyklopädie*, vol. 8 (New York, 1981).

JOHN VAN SETERS (1987)

DAVID [FURTHER CONSIDERATIONS].

The most important recent developments in the study of the biblical king David have to do both with the degree of historicity of the Bible's account and with new textual material. Fueled by a more skeptical approach to biblical historiography and by new interpretations of the archaeological evidence, in recent years some scholars have come to question the historicity of the entire united monarchy of Israel (the biblical reigns of Saul, David, and Solomon). Nonetheless, the fragments of the Tel Dan inscription discovered in 1993 and 1995 seem to contain the first and only early mention so far of David outside the Bible.

The Bible's account of the united monarchy of Israel in *1-2 Samuel* and *1 Kings* (part of the so-called Deuteronomistic history) is no longer accepted by many scholars as accurate documentation about the tenth century BCE, but instead as an idealized portrayal of a past golden age. Some scholars (especially Thomas L. Thompson, Niels Peter Lemche, and Philip Davies) have gone so far as to argue that the united monarchy never really existed but was merely the propagandistic invention of post-exilic or even Hellenistic Jewish writers. According to this, the twin kingdoms of first Israel in the ninth century and later its sister Judah in the seventh century would have arisen independently and would not have been the result of a split of Israel under Solomon's son, Rehoboam, in the last quarter of the tenth century. Other scholars, however, maintain a pre-exilic or exilic date for the main portions of the Deuteronomistic history, but suggest that the Bible has exaggerated the extent and might of the historical David and Solomon's tenth-century kingdom (e.g., Israel Finkelstein, Neil Silberman, Amihai Mazar).

With regard to the archaeology of tenth-century Israel, certain sites with monumental gates and palaces that had been previously connected to the reign of David's son Solomon, are now dated by Finkelstein and others to the following ninth century. For example, Hazor, Megiddo, and Gezer, which are said to be rebuilt by Solomon in *1 Kings* 9:15, have been reinterpreted on the basis of pottery analysis, carbon-14 dating, and other means, as early ninth-century cities. Even if one might disagree with the new dating of these large cities, however, one is still left with the numerous small settlements elsewhere, especially in the south around Jerusalem. These small sites do not at all bear evidence of the significant political reorganization or population and settlement growth that would have taken place with the united monarchy.

As for excavations in Jerusalem itself, the great capital of David and Solomon in the Bible, they have produced an almost total lack of evidence for significant tenth-century occupation. Either subsequent occupation of Jerusalem throughout the centuries destroyed or obscured its monumental buildings, or else Jerusalem was merely a highland village in the tenth century, without the great temple and palace of the Bible's united monarchy. Population estimates for the environs of Jerusalem and points south suggest that only around five thousand people lived in that area, whereas up to forty-five thousand lived in settlements north of Jerusalem. Thus, it is unlikely that Jerusalem in the tenth century was the capital of a large kingdom, or a city of any particular importance whatsoever, let alone the center of an empire stretching from Egypt to the Euphrates, as is described in *1 Kings* 4:21 for Solomon's reign.

Interpretations of the Tel Dan inscription, found at Tel Dan in northern Israel in three fragments in 1993 and 1995, add to the discussion. Perhaps dating to just before 800 BCE, the inscription is written in Aramaic, probably by a king of Aram who celebrates his defeat of a king of Israel and perhaps also of a king of *byt dwd*, "the house (i.e., dynasty) of David." The fragments preserve at most only four words in each of twenty-one lines, and thus it remains difficult to piece together the historical situation that is commemorated. The simplest interpretation is that the inscription reflects the existence at that time in some form of both Israel an early form of Judah, with the latter signified by the name of the dynastic hero, David, from days long past.

However, while the Tel Dan inscription shows that there was a *byt dwd*, "house of David," recognized by Arameans around 800 BCE, it does not prove the historicity of the biblical narratives concerning king David. (Note that it has also been suggested that the phrase *byt dwd* should be restored to line thirty-one of the Moabite inscription from the late ninth-century BCE, but that proposal is problematic and unlikely.)

In sum, the biblical narratives about David are particularly important for what they tell historians about political theology, apologetic writing, and literary devices in biblical historiographic discourse. However, for the purpose of historical reconstruction, the search for the historical kernel of the Davidic traditions may well belong to the realm of modern apologetics and contemporary political theology.

BIBLIOGRAPHY

On David, see especially S. L. McKenzie, *King David: A Biography* (Oxford, 2000); Baruch Halpern, *David's Secret Demons: Messiah, Murderer, Traitor, King* (Grand Rapids, Mich., 2001); and Amihai Mazar, et al., *David, King of Israel: Alive and Enduring?* (in Hebrew; Jerusalem, 1997).

Essential essays on biblical historiography and the historical reconstruction of the tenth century BCE include Thomas L. Thompson, *Early History of the Israelite People from the Written and Archaeological Sources* (Leiden, 1992) and *The Bible in History: How Writers Create a Past* (London, 1999); Philip Davies' *In Search of Ancient Israel* (Sheffield, U.K., 1992); Niels Peter Lemche, *The Israelites in History and Tradition* (London, 1998); V. Philips Long, *Israel's Past in Present Research: Essays on Ancient Israelite Historiography* (Winona Lake, Ind., 1999); and Mario Liverani, "Nuovi sviluppi nella studio della storia dell'Israele biblico," *Biblica* 80 (1999): 488–505.

Archaeological studies of the tenth century BCE may be found in Israel Finkelstein, *The Archaeology of the Israelite Settlement* (Jerusalem, 1988), and a more popular presentation in Israel Finkelstein and Neil Silberman, *The Bible Unearthed: Archaeology's New Vision of Ancient Israel and the Origin of Its Sacred Texts* (New York, 2001). In opposition to Finkelstein's dating of the "Solomonic" cities, but supporting the idea that the extent of the united monarchy has been exaggerated in the Bible, see Amihai Mazar, "Iron Age Chronology: A Reply to I. Finkelstein," *Levant* 29 (1997): 157–167.

On the Tel Dan inscription see George Athas's *The Tel Dan Inscription: A Reappraisal and a New Interpretation* (Sheffield, U.K., 2003).

TAWNY L. HOLM (2005)

DAʿWAH. The Arabic term *daʿwah* (lit., "call, invitation, summoning") is used especially in the sense of the religious outreach or mission to exhort people to embrace Islam as the true religion. The Arabic root *dʿw* occurs frequently in the Qurʾān, where it can also mean calling upon God in prayer (as in *duʿāʾ*). The Qurʾān contains many imperatives to spread Islam, as in *sūrah* 16:125–126:

> Call [*udʿu*] thou to the way of thy Lord with wisdom and good admonition, and dispute with them in the better way. Surely thy Lord knows very well those who have gone astray from his way, and he knows very well those who are guided. And if you chastise, chastise even as you have been chastised; and yet assuredly if you are patient, better it is for those patient. And be patient; yet it is thy patience only with the help of God.

Daʿwah can also mean simply an invitation to a mundane affair, such as a meal, or propaganda for a political or sectarian cause. A specialized meaning of *daʿwah* has been the quasi-magical practice of spell and incantation through invocation of the names of God and his good angels and jinn, in pursuit of personal goals such as healing, success in love or war, avoidance of evil, and other things. This occult practice became highly elaborated and included astrology, a magical alphabet, numerology, and alchemy.

During the early centuries of Islamic history, *daʿwah* often had strong political orientations when used to mean a summons to support a claimant to Islamic rule. New movements would spread their ideologies of Islamic statehood through highly organized and disciplined networks of information and indoctrination. The most forceful and long-lived *daʿwah* enterprise was the Shīʿī sect known as the Ismāʿīlīyah, which insisted that the true Muslim community should be ruled by a politico-religious leader descended from the family of Muḥammad through the line of Ismāʿīl Jaʿfar al-Ṣādiq (d. 756 CE), one of the great Shīʿī imams. The Ismāʿīlīyah developed *daʿwah* into a comprehensive political theology aimed at their ultimate dominance of the Muslims. The movement inducted converts into a fanatically devoted community that observed a hierarchy of degrees of membership, marked by initiation into ascending levels of esoteric knowledge. The leaders at each level were called *dāʿīs*, "summoners," who exercised authority by regions in which they preached and taught the doctrines of the movement. The *dāʿīs* were considered by the Ismāʿīlīyah to be the representatives of the imam. In some cases, the head *dāʿī* was the highest religious leader of a country, a sort of Shīʿī "bishop." More often, the *dāʿīs* functioned in an underground manner, spreading their doctrines in territories not under Ismāʿīlī rule. As well as preaching and propaganda, advanced theology and philosophy were major activities of the *dāʿīs.*

In the modern period, *daʿwah* most often refers to Islamic missionary activities, which are increasingly characterized by long-range planning, skillful exploitation of the media, establishment of study centers and mosques, and earnest, urgent preaching and efforts at persuasion.

Daʿwah as mission should never be spread by force (*sūrah* 2:256). If the hearers refuse to embrace Islam, then they should be left alone, at least for a time. But a committed Muslim should not give up the task of *daʿwah.* If nothing else succeeds, the silent example of a devout Muslim may be used by God as a means to someone's voluntary conversion.

In the strong Islamic revival the post-colonial period, *daʿwah* has a less specifically political and a more marked spiritual and moral emphasis than in earlier times. The *ummah*, the Muslim community, is believed to transcend national political entities, and the *sharīʿah*, the sacred law, is said to make claims on Muslims even when it is not embodied as the actual legal code (except in certain countries). *Daʿwah*, then, is the cutting edge of Islam and as such is directed at fellow believers as well as at the multitudes outside the *ummah* who nevertheless possess the God-given *fiṭrah* (*sūrah* 30:30), or "inherent character," also to be intentional Muslims and thus vicegerents (*khulafāʾ*; s. g., *kha-līfah*, "caliph") of God on earth (2:30). From North Africa to Indonesia, and beyond, Muslim individuals and organizations are strenuously dedicated to missionary activities, utilizing the media and other advanced means of communication and "market research." *Daʿwah* faculties are prominent in Muslim training schools and universities, and the hope is that the strong obligation to spread Islam will be felt by Muslims at all levels of society. *Daʿwah*, as well as migration, is responsible for the significant recent growth of Muslim populations in Western countries.

SEE ALSO Shiism, article on Ismāʿīlīyah.

BIBLIOGRAPHY

Maurice Canard's article "Daʿwa," in *The Encyclopaedia of Islam*, new ed. (Leiden, 1960–), offers a detailed analysis with extensive source citations, although it does not treat modern Islamic mission. A provocative collection of exploratory essays and discussions is *Christian Mission and Islamic Daʿwah: Proceedings of the Chambésy Dialogue Consultation*, edited by Khurshid Ahmad and David Kerr (London and Ann Arbor, Mich., 1982), first published as a special issue of the *International Review of Mission* 65 (October 1976). For an introduction to *daʿwah* as occult spell and incantation, see the article "Daʿwah" in Thomas Patrick Hughes's *A Dictionary of Islam*, 2d ed. (London, 1896). A standard survey of Shīʿī sectarian concepts and practices of *daʿwah* as propaganda is Bernard Lewis's *The Origins of Ismāʿīlism* (1940; reprint, New York, 1975).

FREDERICK MATHEWSON DENNY (1987)

DAY, DOROTHY (1897–1980), personalist revolutionary, journalist, and lecturer. Between 1933, when she brought out the first penny-a-copy issue of the *Catholic Worker*, and 1980, when she died, Dorothy Day became, in the opinion of many, America's foremost Roman Catholic voice calling for peace and a profound change in the major institutional forms of the contemporary world. She opposed what she regarded as the enslaving colossus of the modern state and the technological giantism to which it was a partner. Fundamental to her ideas of social reordering was her insistence on the personal transformation of value based on the primary reality of spirit rather than the spirit of acquisitiveness. For her, this meant taking her directions from church tradition, the papal encyclicals, and her literal reading of the Gospels. She used these sources to justify her absolute pacifism and her communitarian ideas on social reconstruction.

For Day, the ultimate and transfiguring value was love, a subject that was the theme of her best writing. The exercise of a sacrificial love was at the heart of her personalist revolt against the enlarging domain over life of institutional forms. The world would be renewed by persons who loved and not by state management. In her own case she chose to wage her revolution by establishing "houses of hospitality" in the destitute areas of lower Manhattan in New York City, by promoting communitarian farms, and by an immense writing and speaking regimen that left few Catholic parishes or schools untouched by her ideas by the time of her death.

She was born the third in a family of five children in Brooklyn on November 8, 1897, the daughter of Grace Satterlee and John Day. An opening in journalism for John Day took the family to San Francisco in 1903, but the earthquake there, three years later, forced a removal to Chicago. In 1915 the family moved to New York where Dorothy, having finished two years at the University of Illinois, began her own life in journalism as a reporter for the Socialist *Call*.

For the next five years she dabbled in radical causes, moving from one cheap flat to another, mostly in the lower New York area. In 1919 she left a hospital nurse's training program to live with a flamboyant journalist, Lionel Moise. The affair ended with her having an abortion, a circumstance that filled her with such grief that she was brought to the brink of suicide. Later, living in a fisherman's shack on Staten Island as the common-law wife of Forster Batterham, she bore a daughter, Tamar Therese. Out of gratitude for her daughter and a mystical rapture she felt in living on such close terms with nature, she turned to God and was subsequently baptized a Catholic. In 1932 she met the French itinerant philosopher, Peter Maurin, and after some months of tutelage she acquired from him the idea of "the correlation of the spiritual with the material." This was the beginning point of her vision of social re-creation.

Her personality was remarkably forceful and engaging, but she could be given to moments of authoritarian harshness. After a series of retreats during World War II, the unremitting struggle of her life was to grow in sanctity. In her later years the impression she gave was of one who had achieved a rare level of holiness. She died on November 29, 1980, and was buried at Jamestown, Long Island, not far from the site of her conversion.

BIBLIOGRAPHY

Dorothy Day wrote five books, all of which, from various perspectives, are autobiographical. The best and most comprehensive is *The Long Loneliness* (New York, 1952). A full-length biography is my *Dorothy Day* (New York, 1982), based on personal acquaintance with Day and for which I had access to all of her personal manuscript materials. An excellent edition of Day's writings is Robert Ellsberg's *By Little and Little: The Selected Writings of Dorothy Day* (New York, 1983).

WILLIAM D. MILLER (1987)

DAYANANDA SARASVATI (1824–1883), leading Hindu reformer and founder of the Ārya Samāj, known by the westernized form of his religious name, Dayānanda Sarasvatī. What is known of Dayananda's early years comes from two autobiographical statements made after he founded the Ārya Samāj in 1875. Although he refused to reveal his family and personal names or place of birth in order to preserve his freedom as a *saṃnyāsin* ("renunciant"), these statements allow a reconstruction of his life before he became a public figure.

Dayananda claimed to have spent his childhood in a small town—from his description, most likely Tankara—in the princely state of Morvi in northern Kathiawar, now in Gujarat's Rajkot district. His father was a high-caste *brahman* landowner and revenue collector and a devout worshiper of Śiva. Dayananda received Vedic initiation at eight and began to study Sanskrit and the Vedas. Although his father preferred that he become a devotee of Śiva, an experience in the local Śiva temple undermined Dayananda's faith that the temple icon was God, and turned him away from Śaiva ritual practice involving images. The deaths of a sister and a beloved uncle a few years later made him realize the instability of worldly life, and when, around 1845, he learned that his family had secretly arranged his marriage, he fled to become a homeless wanderer.

The young mendicant studied the monistic philosophy of the Upaniṣads with several teachers before being initiated into an order of *saṃnyāsins* as Dayananda Sarasvati in 1847. He lived as an itinerant yogin for the next thirteen years, but in 1860 he settled in Mathura to study with the Sanskrit grammarian Vrijānanda (1779–1868). Vrijānanda, whom Dayananda accepted as his *guru,* aided Dayananda in perfecting his Sanskrit and also convinced him that the only truthful texts were those composed by the *ṛṣis* ("seers") before the *Mahābhārata,* since, he taught, all later works contained false sectarian doctrines. Dayananda committed himself to spreading this message when he left his *guru* in 1863, though it took him most of his life to decide which individual texts were true and which were false.

Between 1863 and 1873, Dayananda spent most of his time in small towns along the Ganges River in what is now western Uttar Pradesh meeting representatives of various Hindu communities and debating sectarian *paṇḍits.* These experiences confirmed his early doubts about image worship and led him to reject all of the Hindu sectarian traditions—not only Vaiṣṇavism, to which he had an early aversion, but eventually even worship of the formless Śiva. In place of sectarianism and the related religious and caste restrictions, he argued with growing conviction for a united Hinduism based on the monotheism and morality of the Vedas.

Throughout this period Dayananda continued to dress as a yogin in loincloth and ashes and debated only in Sanskrit; thus his message was restricted mainly to those orthodox upper-caste Hindus who were most solidly opposed to his views. Early in 1873, however, he spent four months in Calcutta as the guest of the Brāhmo Samāj leader Debendranath Tagore, met the great Brāhmo spokesman Keshab Chandra Sen, and discussed religious issues with these and other westernized Hindu intellectuals. Dayananda saw firsthand the influence of the Brāhmo organization, learned the value of educational programs, public lectures, and publications in effecting change, and accepted from Sen some valuable advice to improve his own reception: abandon the loincloth and the elitist Sanskrit in favor of street clothes and Hindi.

Dayananda left Calcutta with an unchanged message but a broader perspective and a new style, lecturing and writing in Hindi and seeking a receptive audience for his message. He found the first such audience in Bombay, where he founded the Ārya Samāj ("society of honorable ones") on April 10, 1875. His major breakthrough, however, came two years later in the Punjab, where a rising class of merchants and professionals was seeking a defense of Hinduism against Christian missionary activity. A chapter of the Ārya Samāj was founded in Lahore in 1877, and this soon became the headquarters for a rapidly expanding movement in the Punjab and western Uttar Pradesh.

Dayananda left control of the Ārya Samāj in the hands of local chapters and spent his last years perfecting his message. He completed the revision of his major doctrinal statement, *Satyārth prakāś,* shortly before his death on October 30, 1883. With final conviction, he declared that the Vedic hymns revealed to the *ṛṣis* were the sole authority for truth, and he reaffirmed his faith in the one eternal God whose revelation thus made salvation possible for all the world.

SEE ALSO Ārya Samāj.

BIBLIOGRAPHY

Dayananda's longest autobiographical statement appeared in *The Theosophist* in three installments in 1879–1880. This statement has been supplemented by an excerpt from one of his lectures in Poona in 1875 and published with explanatory notes, a doctrinal statement, and a chronology of his life in *Autobiography of Swami Dayanand Saraswati,* edited by K. C. Yadav (New Delhi, 1976). The best scholarly study of Dayananda's life and thought is J. T. F. Jordens's *Dayānanda Sarasvatī, His Life and Ideas* (Delhi, 1978). A more focused analysis of the central element in Dayananda's belief system is provided by Arvind Sharma's "Svami Dayananda Sarasvati and Vedic Authority," in *Religion in Modern India,* edited by Robert D. Baird (New Delhi, 1981), pp. 179–196. The standard account of Dayananda's life by one of his followers is Har Bilas Sarda's *Life of Dayanand Saraswati, World Leader,* 2d ed. (Ajmer, 1968).

THOMAS J. HOPKINS (1987)

DAY OF ATONEMENT SEE RO'SH HA-SHANAH AND YOM KIPPUR

DAY OF THE DEAD.

The feast of All Saints Day and the liturgical celebration of All Souls Day have long histories in Western Christendom. The origins of these occasions in the Christian yearly cycle are uncertain, but by the fourteenth century they ranked immediately after Christmas and Holy Week in importance, and their celebration had been fixed on November 1 for All Saints Day and November 2 (or November 3 if November 2 fell on a Sunday) for All Souls Day. Since then these two festivities, most commonly known as the Days of the Dead, have been inextricably interrelated in the liturgy of the Western Church. At the onset of, perhaps even as the result of, the Reformation and the rise of modern science during the Renaissance, there was a significant decline in the ritual and ceremonial underpinnings of Christendom, but in the New World (more precisely in the Catholic New World) the rites, ceremonies, and symbolic meaning of All Saints Day and All Souls Day have been reinvigorated and in many ways have achieved their maximum elaboration.

DEVELOPMENT OF THE OBSERVANCES. All Saints Day commemorates those individuals who in the service of the church have achieved that ambivalent status of "sainthood." Although the transcendentally different natures of the omnipotent-omnipresent almighty God of Christian monotheism and its underlings, the saints, may be clearly understood and explained by theologians, this has not been the case for significant segments of practicing Christians since probably the formative period of Christianity between the first and fourth centuries CE. Indeed there is plenty of historical evidence that for sizable segments of Christendom the proliferation of saints and their relationship to God have come to look suspiciously like polytheism and have led to practices incompatible with monotheism. Moreover there are anthropologists (Ralph Linton, John M. Roberts, L. Keith Brown, Hugo G. Nutini) who maintain that the bulk of Christianity for centuries has been practicing monolatry (or polylatry) and not monotheism—that is, that in behavior (psychologically) and practice (ritually and ceremonially) no transcendental difference emerges between God and the saints, including the many manifestations of the Virgin Mary. This is certainly the case with Mesoamerican Indians in the early twenty-first century. Most contemporary Mexican Indians have not internalized the theological distinction between God and the saints, even if they somewhat vaguely understand it, and in their actual religious behavior and practice God is little more than a primus inter pares, a more powerful deity than the many saints and the various forms of the Virgin Mary. Mexican Indians, and often rural mestizos, often rank the village patron saint higher than God the Father, God the Son, and God the Holy Ghost or they center their Catholicism on the cult of the Virgin of Guadalupe, thus in effect abandoning the central tenet of monotheism.

Lest the reader think that the syncretic nature of Catholicism in this region of the New World is a special case, two examples from other parts of the world may be cited. In their ranking and expressive analysis of the saints as conceived and practiced by Chinese Catholics in Hong Kong, John M. Roberts and John T. Myers found that the array of Catholic supernaturals (God the Father, God the Son, God the Holy Ghost, several dozen saints, and half a dozen manifestations of the Virgin Mary) was similar to the Chinese pantheon of gods. The respondents conceived of these Catholic supernaturals as gods who have definite rankings and spheres of action. In many peasant communities in the West as well—such as southern Italy, Sicily, and southern Spain—the saints are conceived as deities of sorts, with powers in their own right and not infrequently arranged in arrays similar to classical polytheistic pantheons. Whether or not the distinction between God and saints is understood or explicitly made by these subsocieties, the fact remains that in behavior and practice these segments of Christendom are practicing monolātry, not monotheism. Indeed at least in Catholicism it may be difficult to be a theologically pure monotheist.

The feast of All Saints Day is in a sense democratic in that it commemorates all the saints of God, canonized and uncanonized, known and unknown. It is a rite of propitiation and intensification, in which the church celebrates the external glory of God in the company of those who are closest to his perfection. The origins of the feast are lost, but there are indications that as early as the middle of the fourth century a day was set aside to commemorate the martyrs who had died before Christianity became the official religion of the Roman Empire. Specifically May 13 commemorated all the martyrs of Edessa (an important early center of Christianity, now the city of Urfa in southern Turkey), and it appears that this date soon spread to the western empire. By the early seventh century most bishoprics in the West celebrated on this day their own and other martyrs of Christendom. Some scholars doubt that there is a connection between May 13 and November 1, and no one has determined how and under what circumstances a feast of all saints came to be celebrated on the latter date. Scholars also are not agreed as to when the category of "saint" or the status of "sainthood" appears in Christian theology and practice. It is safe to assume, however, that there were no saints as ritual and ceremonial objects of worship until the beginning of the seventh century. It is reasonable to surmise an evolution from martyr to saint, but the social and religious condition of this transformation and amalgamation are not clear. In any case, by the beginning of the ninth century November 1 was widely celebrated as the day of all martyrs and saints in Western Christendom, and in the latter part of the eleventh century, during the papacy of Gregory VII, that date officially became All Saints Day in the modern sense of the feast. Since then All Saints Day has steadily increased in importance as a ritual occasion in the yearly cycle, and in southern Europe, especially Spain, it developed elaborate proportions beginning in the early fourteenth century.

All Souls Day, November 2, is a liturgical celebration of the Western Church commemorating the "faithfully departed"—that is, those who have died within the fold of the church. It is observed as a day for honoring and rejoicing with those who are in heaven, offering prayers for those who are in purgatory so that they may soon enter the kingdom of heaven, and in general supplicating with the dead to watch over the living and thanking them for past intercessions. All Souls Day is a yearly rite of propitiation and thanksgiving and, in the popular conscience, a veritable cult of the dead. Indeed it is a form of ancestor worship somewhat reminiscent of the Roman gods of the household, the *lares* and *penates* (the feast of Parentalia), from which it probably developed. Among the many organizational, ritual, ceremonial, and symbolic examples of syncretism as Christianity developed out of the confluence of Hebrew monotheism and Roman polytheism, All Souls Day is one of the clearest.

Until well into the Middle Ages the church was reluctant to establish a specific liturgical day for propitiating and thanking the dead. The reason for this reluctance was the desire to dissociate the church from the persistent and tenacious pre-Christian rites and ceremonies of the cult of the dead and ancestor worship, widespread among all branches of Indo-European polytheism, which from the beginning the church regarded as "superstitious" and theologically impure. The efforts of the early church fathers (Augustine, Jerome, Athanasius, Boniface, and Chrysostom) to render what they regarded as superstitious and heretic remains of the polytheistic past (many aspects of witchcraft and sorcery, rites and ceremonies associated with particular festivities and the cult of the gods, the cult of the dead itself, and so on) indicate that a significant amalgam of beliefs and practices of the old and new religions already existed. By the beginning of the eighth century, at least in the circum-Mediterranean area, many aspects of Christianity had been significantly syncretized. Despite these efforts and the efforts of subsequent theologians, as Christianity spread to more marginal areas of Europe, syncretism placed a permanent mark on several practices of the Christian faith. More than the other two great branches of monotheism (Judaism and Islam), Christianity has been unable to divest itself completely of polytheistic beliefs and practices out of which it arose. Christian theologians have always insisted on an ideologically pure monotheism, and ever since the church became an imperial force in the middle of the fourth century, it has successfully obliterated deviations that smacked of polytheism, pantheism, monolatry, and other deviant supernatural conceptions. Nevertheless the syncretic aspects of Christianity have manifested themselves in many contexts and segments of Christian worship, and theologians, sometimes to their embarrassment, have had to accommodate rituals, beliefs, and behaviors with a distinct polytheistic, pantheistic, or monolatrous character within a strict monotheistic ideology. The often marked dichotomy between theology and practice appears to be a constant from Christianity's folk beginnings to its imperial maturity during the first half of the sixteenth century.

Although prayers to the dead were encouraged from earliest times, the church, for the reasons given above, was slow in giving liturgical recognition to the rites and ceremonies concerning the dead that probably had been going on for centuries in many parts of Christendom. However, Pentecost Monday was dedicated to the worship of the dead in Spain by the middle of the seventh century. For reasons unknown, November 2 was set aside for commemoration of All Souls Day, a practice that was well established in the Cluniac monasteries in northern France by the middle of the twelfth century—that is, not long after November 1 had officially become All Saints Day. Unlike All Saints Day, however, All Souls Day never acquired official liturgical status—further evidence that the church was unwilling to formally sanction a celebration so pregnant with pagan elements and unchristian evocations. All Souls Day came to have liturgical status only by custom. Nonetheless by the second half of the fifteenth century All Saints Day and All Souls Day were liturgical feasts celebrated as a unit and ranked among the four most important occasions in the yearly ritual cycle of Western Christendom.

What the church was up against throughout the Dark and Middle Ages is well known; the situation has been replicated several times during the past five hundred years in the context of the expansion of western European peoples throughout the world. With specific reference to All Souls Day, many beliefs and practices of pagan origins or corruptions of Orthodox Christian beliefs concerning the dead were associated with this celebration and ancillary concerns. Throughout Western Christendom, these beliefs and practices survived until well into the sixteenth century. With the onset of secularization in Western society, they were displaced to marginal areas and to the lower levels of the social order, but they are still found in circum-Mediterranean areas and in other parts of Europe.

Beliefs and Practices. Among the best-known beliefs and practices that were associated with the All Souls Day complex and relevant to the cult of the dead, the following may be mentioned. During the vigil of November 2 the souls of the dead came back in spirit to bless the household where they had died. On November 2 the souls in purgatory came back in the form of phantoms, witches, and toads, lizards, and other repellent animals in order to scare or harm persons who wronged or injured them during their lives. Food offerings were made to the dead in the cemeteries, ritually disposed of by those concerned after the souls had symbolically tasted the food. Special food offerings, consisting of a dish or drink that he or she had particularly liked, were made to prominent departed members of the household. Garments that had been worn by particularly good or pious members of the household were displayed on the family altar so that the souls would rejoice upon contemplating such a display of affection and become effective protectors of their living kin. The way to the house was marked by recognized signposts of flowers and other decorations so that the returning souls could more easily find their earthly homes. This veritable cult of the dead during the Dark and Middle Ages had probably changed little since Roman times.

All Saints Day, on the other hand, was rather heavily influenced by northern Indo-European polytheism and by the liturgical feasts of the Byzantine (Orthodox, Armenian) and Coptic churches, which in turn were doubly influenced by other Near Eastern polytheistic systems. Both the Germanic and Celtic traditions, particularly the latter, celebrated in the late autumn a complex of rites and activities associated with the end of harvest and the impending arrival of winter and intended to honor the gods of agriculture and natural elements. During the process of conversion to Christianity, the church condemned this complex as dealing with the devil and dabbling in witchcraft and sorcery. In the British Isles this was the celebration of Samhain, which has survived among English- and Gaelic-speaking peoples and is variously known as Hallow E'en, Allhallows, Hallowmas, and most commonly Halloween. Probably by the middle of the fifteenth century Halloween had coalesced as a syncretic component of English, Irish, Scottish, and Welsh Catholicism. By that time the high point of the celebration was the vigil of All Saints Day, and since then Halloween has been intimately associated with this liturgical feast as well as All Souls Day. The Protestant Reformation kept the celebration of All Saints Day, but for several reasons (most significantly the denial of the belief in purgatory) it abolished the feast of All Souls Day. With the increasing secularization of northern European societies, the Halloween–All Saints Day complex was transformed into what it is in the early twenty-first century, a secular feast. In many parts of northern Europe, however, the church was never able to stamp out completely many beliefs and practices associated with regional complexes that were instrumental in shaping the combined liturgical celebration of All Saints Day and All Souls Day. Thus even in the early twenty-first century, from Ireland to Russia, the ethnographer or folklorist finds survivals of these beliefs and practices (related mainly to food, drink, and special rites performed in the household or cemetery) among peasant and rural folk.

The syncretic background of All Saints Day in the Byzantine Church is not well known and still less that of the Coptic Church. However, the contemporary celebration of All Saints Day and All Souls Day in the East indicates that syncretism there was perhaps more influenced by pagan elements than in the West. The celebrations of the Greek and Armenian Churches appear to be more diversified and exhibit more traits of early Christian origin that is the case in the Western Churches. The Eastern Churches celebrate All Souls Day on several different dates: the Greek Church on the Saturday before Sexagesima Sunday (the second Sunday before Lent); the Armenian Church on Easter Sunday (as in Spain in the seventh century). The most interesting celebration of All Souls Day is in the Syrian-Antiochene Church. On the Friday before Septuagesima (the third Sunday before Lent), dead priests are honored; on Friday before Sexagesima, all the blessed souls in heaven and purgatory are worshipped; and on Friday before Quinquagesima (the first Sunday before Lent), all those who have died away from home and parents and friends are remembered. An even more elaborate division of labor in the celebration of All Souls Day is present in rural Tlaxcala, Mexico. Perhaps there is a connection with the Syrian-Antiochene rites, or it may be simply a continuation of pre-Hispanic practices.

It is probably in southern Italy and Spain that the celebration of the combined feasts of All Saints Day and All Souls Day acquired its most complex and elaborate form. In Spain this may be attributable to the Christian reconquest of Spain from the Moors in particular and Muslims inputs in general, but the evidence is not conclusive. It is certain, however, that the Dominican order was instrumental in enhancing the importance of All Saints Day–All Souls Day during the fifteenth century. For example, the Dominicans initiated the custom of having a priest celebrate three masses for the eternal glory and rest of the faithfully departed on All Souls Day. This action gained quick acceptance throughout Spain, and All Souls Day became ritually more important than All Saints Day. (This apparently never happened in any other country of western Europe.) By the middle of the fifteenth century the combined celebration of All Saints Day and All Souls Day in Spain was commonly referred to as Todos Santos. This combined liturgical celebration had become increasingly important and ranked just below Christmas and Holy Week in the yearly ritual cycle of Spanish Catholicism, popularly if not theologically. It was in this form that Todos Santos was introduced into the New World by the mendicant friars in the first half of the sixteenth century, and All Souls Day has remained the most ritually significant of the two days.

In Mexico the Day of the Dead is also known as Todos Santos and, after Christmas and Holy Week (Easter), is the most important celebration in the annual religious cycle. In several respects it is more elaborate than in Spain due to its syncretic component, which reinforced the Spanish Day of the Dead with similar beliefs and practices of Pre-Hispanic polytheism. The celebration of Todos Santos has three main components: the offerings to the dead on the household altar, the decoration of the graves in the cemetery, and the celebration of the different kinds of dead from Palm Sunday to Easter Sunday. All three of these components, but particularly the last, are heavily laden with pre-Hispanic elements. Moreover the sociological significance of the Todos Santos greatly departs from its Spanish antecedents. November 1 and 2, the central core of the celebration, are homecoming for Mexican folk people (rural Indian and mestizo communities); those who have migrated to the city return to visit their kin and together remember the dead, and if they do not return for three consecutive years, they are no longer regarded as members of the community. Throughout the Todos Santos cycle (from a week before to a week after November 1) people are on their best behavior, exchange offerings, and make special efforts to intensify kinship, ritual kinship (*compadrazgo*), and friendship relationships. This, in other words, is a "sacralized" period or a kind of *treuga Dei* (truth of God) in the community's annual cycle.

See Also Afterlife, article on Mesoamerican Concepts; Funeral Rites, article on Mesoamerican Funeral Rites.

Bibliography

Duchesne, Louis. *Le Liber Pontificalis.* Paris, 1955–1957. An indispensable source for reconstructing the evolution of All Saints Day and All Souls Day throughout the Dark and Middle Ages.

Gaillard, Jacques. *Catholicisme.* Paris, 1950. From the Catholic standpoint, this book offers many insights into the chronology, evolution, and interrelationship of All Saints Day and All Souls Day.

Hatch, Jane M. *The American Book of Days.* New York, 1978. A good source on the origins of All Saints Day in late antiquity and on the celebration of All Saints Day and All Souls Day in the United States.

Hennig, John. "The Meaning of All the Saints." *Medieval Studies* 10 (1948): 132–167. Provides a good account of the evolution of the cult of the dead in Western Christendom.

Kellner, Karl Adam Heinrich. *Heortology.* London, 1908. A good source in English on Catholic festivals with detailed information on the celebration of All Saints Day and All Souls Day.

Lane, Sarah, Marilyn Turkovich, and Peggy Mueller. *Los Días de los Muertos, The Days of the Dead.* Chicago, 1987. A useful source that includes some interesting ideas on the belief system and realization of Todos Santos in Spanish-speaking countries.

Leies, John A. *Sanctity and Religion according to St. Thomas.* Fribourg, Switzerland, 1963. An excellent source for understanding the concept of sainthood in Catholicism and how it is related to dead souls in general and the role saints play as mediators between humans and the deity.

Linton, Ralph, and Adelin Linton. *Halloween through Twenty Centuries.* New York, 1950. An excellent account of Halloween, its evolution throughout the centuries, and how it is related to the Christian cult of the dead.

Nutini, Hugo G. *Todos Santos in Rural Tlaxcala: A Syncretic, Expressive, and Symbolic Analysis of the Cult of the Dead.* Princeton, N.J., 1988. This book provides an exhaustive account of the Days of the Dead in Tlaxcala in the early twenty-first century, including the syncretic origins of the cult of the dead in the interaction of sixteenth-century Spanish Catholicism and Mesoamerican Indian polytheism.

Radó, Polikarp. *Enchiridion Liturgicum.* 2 vols. Rome, 1961. A good handbook on Catholic liturgical practices that includes many entries on the cult of the saints and the cult of the dead.

Las Tradiciones de Días de Muertos en México. Mexico City, 1987. Good regional descriptions of beliefs and practices of All Saints Day and All Souls Day for an area of Christendom where the Day of the Dead is probably most pronounced.

HUGO G. NUTINI (2005)

DAZHBOG was the pre-Christian sun god of the East and South Slavs. The name *Dazhbog* (Old Russian, *Dazh'bog*) is first mentioned in the Kievan pantheon, listed in the Russian *Primary Chronicle* (c. 1111 CE). His connection with the sun is clearly stated in the *Malalas Chronicle* of 1114: "Tsar Sun is the son of Svarog, and his name is Dazhbog." (Svarog, the creator of the sun, is identified in Greek translation with the smith Hephaistos. Like his Lithuanian counterpart, the heavenly smith Kalvelis, whose achievement is described in the *Volynian Chronicle* of 1252, Svarog probably hammered the sun into shape and placed it in the sky. For the chroniclers, he was identical with Helios.) The importance of this god is attested in the thirteenth-century Old Russian epic *Slovo o polku Igoreve,* where the phrase "grandchildren of Dazhbog" is used to refer to the Russian people.

Dazhbog seems to have been one of the various manifestations of the Indo-European god of the "shining sky" or "heavenly light." In the Kievan pantheon his name appears next to that of Khors, another sun deity (cf. Persian *khursīd,* "sun"), and he was identified with the Greek god Apollo by early Russian translators. Dazhbog is possibly an analogue of the northwestern Slavic deity Svarozhich (Svarožiči, Zuariscici; "son of Svarog"), who was worshiped in the temple at Radigast (Rethra), near Feldberg, in present-day northern Germany. There, as noted in 1014 by Thietmar, bishop of Merseburg, were a number of carved idols dressed in armor and helmets, each dedicated to some aspect of the god. The most important one was that of Svarozhich.

In Roman Jakobson's view, Dazhbog, like the Vedic Bhaga, is "the giver of wealth," and the name of Dazhbog's immediate neighbor in the Kievan pantheon, Stribog, means literally—like that of Bhaga's partner Amsa—"the apportioner of wealth" (see Jakobson, 1972). The name *Dazhbog* is a compound of *dazh'* (the imperative form of *dati,* "to give") and *bog* ("god"). Both Slavs and Iranians eliminated the Proto-Indo-European name for the "god of heavenly light," **dieus,* and assigned the general meaning of "god" to a term that originally signified both wealth and its giver, *bog.* The origin of the name *Dazhbog* may go back to the period of close Slavic-Iranian contacts, not later than the Scythian-Sarmatian period.

In Serbian folk beliefs, Dabog (i.e., Dazhbog) is an adversary of the Christian God: "Dabog is tsar on earth, and the Lord God is in heaven." Dabog is also known as "the silver tsar"; in mining areas as Dajboi, a demon; and as Daba or Dabo, the devil.

BIBLIOGRAPHY

Čajkanović, Veselin. *O srpskom vrhovnom bogu.* Posebna izdanja, Srpska Kraljevska Akademija, vol. 132. Belgrade, 1941.

Dickenmann, E. "Serbokroatisch *Dabog.*" *Zeitschrift für slavische Philologie* (Leipzig) 20 (1950): 323–346.

Jagić, V. "Mythologische Skizzen: 2, Daždbog, Dažbog-Dabog." *Archiv für slavische Philologie* (Leipzig) 5 (1881): 1–14.

Jakobson, Roman. "Slavic Mythology." In *Funk and Wagnalls Standard Dictionary of Folklore, Mythology, and Legend* (1949–1950), edited by Maria Leach, vol. 2, pp. 1025–1028. Reprint, 2 vols. in 1, New York, 1972.

New Sources

Kapica, F. S. *Slavyanskije tradicionnije verovanija, prazdniki i rituali* [Slavic traditional beliefs, festivities and rituals]. Moscow, 2001.

Shaparova, N. S. *Kratkaya enciklopedija slavyanskoj mifologii* [A short dictionary of Slavic mythology]. Moskva, Astrelj, 2001.

MARIJA GIMBUTAS (1987)
Revised Bibliography

DE SEE DAO AND DE

DEA DIA.

DEA DIA. The worship of the Roman goddess Dea Dia was in the hands of a priesthood of twelve, the *fratres arvales* (Arval brethren), and she possessed a shrine in a grove outside Rome at the fifth (or sixth, depending on the period) milestone on the Via Campana, in the modern suburb of La Magliana. The deity, her cult, and her priesthood supposedly date back to very early in Roman history, but they underwent a major renovation by Augustus (r. 27 BCE–14 CE). From the previous period, we only know of the existence of the *arvales* and of a public sacrifice, mentioned by Varro (*De lingua latina* 5, 74). The site itself bears testimony of cultic occupation since at least the third century BCE. But it is impossible to be sure whether these items belonged to Dea Dia or to Fors Fortuna, who possessed a temple on the same spot.

After Augustus's reform the priesthood consisted of twelve members chosen by cooptation from the most distinguished families. The reigning emperor was always a member. The reorganization was one element in Augustus's policy of directing enthusiasm for his person and policies into traditional religious channels. Under the empire the Arval brethren offered sacrifices not only to Dea Dia but to a wide variety of divinities to secure the health and prosperity of the emperor and his family. Along with sometimes lengthy descriptions of the rituals celebrated in the grove of Dea Dia, and of other sacrifices of the brotherhood in Rome, the records of the Arval brethren were inscribed on marble, and numerous fragments have been preserved. These records, extending from 21 BCE to 241 CE, are a major source for traditional Roman religion in the imperial age. The cult and its priesthood are documented as late as 304 CE.

Dea Dia, who was the owner of the *lucus fratrum arvalium* and the main addressee of the cult celebrated by the Arval brethren, is only known by the proceedings of this brotherhood. Thus, there has been much speculation about her identity. During the nineteenth century, when scholars tended to assimilate gods, Wilhelm Henzen (1874, p. ix) saw her as a goddess similar to Ceres, if not Ceres herself. In the *Römische Mythologie* (1831) of Ludwig Preller and Heinrich Jordan, Dea Dia was supposed to embody certain aspects of the numen otherwise venerated under the names of Ceres, Tellus, and perhaps Ops or Acca Larentia (see also Fowler, 1911, p. 435; Wissowa, 1912, p. 195). One also finds assimilations to Diana, Hebe, and the Mother of the Gods. In short, Dea Dia was supposed to be an indigitation (the assimilation of minor deities to one major god or goddess) of Ceres or another goddess linked to agriculture.

In a similar vein, Ida Paladino has tried to present Dea Dia as a minor *paredros* of Fors Fortuna. Paladino thinks that, with the Lares, also present in the *lucus* of the Arvals, and Diana (whose name relies on the same etymon), Fors Fortuna shared a marginal position, as well as a link to Servius Tullius and the plebs. When Augustus reformed this cult, he preferred, according to Paladino, the less plebeian goddess Dea Dia. According to an isolated inscription from Amiternum (CIL I, 2d ed., 1846), Dea Dia herself could be of Sabine origin.

As Henri Le Bonniec (1958, p. 202) has shown, Dea Dia cannot possibly be taken as another form of Ceres because the ritual of the Arval brethren, which is the best known in ancient Rome, forbids this assimilation. Moreover, the Arval proceedings never mention Ceres (the hypothesis of Kurt Latte that her "real" name was secret and taboo is not convincing). And generally speaking, the trend of indigitation, as surmised by Greek and Roman antiquarians and grammarians, has been denied pertinence in religious history (Le Bonniec, 1958, p. 203). Accordingly Ileana Chirassi-Colombo and Robert Schilling have reconsidered the problem. Both start with the name of the goddess, from *dius* (luminous) and *diuum* (sky), and consider her as the goddess of the sky (Chirassi, 1968) or of the beneficial light necessary to agriculture (Schilling, 1969; Franz Altheim [1931] links her, unconvincingly, to the moon). Chirassi considers this Dia as an archaic paredros of Jupiter, or Dius, with whom she is supposed to have formed a couple representing the sky and the earth.

Referring to the cultic evidence, Schilling shows that the name Dea Dia is an emphatic doublet, meaning literally, "the celestial goddess." According to the Arval proceedings, Dea Dia performed her divine function between the periods of sowing and harvesting and was thus the good light of heaven that brought the crops from germination to maturation. This is evident in both the date and the ritual of her festival. Her feast was always held in May, about a month before the beginning of the harvest in central Italy. Its exact date was announced in January, on the 7th or the 11th. The ritual at her festival employed, among other offerings (a lamb, meatballs, sweet wine, and pastries), green ears from the current crop, together with dried ears of grain from the previous year's crop. The other gods and goddesses mentioned in her *lucus* are to be considered her assistants or her guests; the precise link to her neighbor Fors Fortuna is not known. The temple and the grove of Dea Dia could have been built at La Magliana only after Augustus's reform, which could have so monumentalized an aristocratic ritual.

SEE ALSO Arval Brothers; Roman Religion, article on the Early Period.

BIBLIOGRAPHY

The records of the Arval Brothers are available in *Acta Fratrum Arvalium,* edited by Wilhelm Henzen (Berlin, 1874, also CIL VI, 2023–2119; 32338–32398), and in *Commentarii fratrum arvalium qui supersunt: Les copies épigraphiques des protocoles annuels de la confrérie arvale (21 av.-304 ap. J.-C.),* edited with a French translation by John Scheid (Rome, 1998). Some of the records can be found in translation in Frederick C. Grant's *Ancient Roman Religion* (New York, 1957), pp. 233–238, and in *Roman Civilization,* vol. 2, edited by Naphtali Lewis and Meyer Reinhold (New York, 1955), pp. 254–257.

A survey and study of the problems posed by the character and cult of Dea Dia is offered by John Scheid in *Romulus et ses frères: Le collège des frères arvales, modèle du culte public dans la Rome des empereurs* (Rome, 1990). For details see Wilhelm Henzen, *Acta fratrum Arvalium quae supersunt* (Berlin, 1874); Ludwig Preller and Heinrich Jordan, *Römische Mythologie,* 3d ed. (Berlin, 1881), vol. 2, p. 26; William W. Fowler, *The Religious Experience of the Roman People* (London, 1911); Georg Wissowa, *Religion und Kultus der Römer,* 2d ed. (Munich, 1912); Franz Altheim, *Terra mater: Untersuchungen zur altitalischen Religionsgeschichte* (Berlin, 1931); Henri Le Bonniec, *Le culte de Cérès à Rome: Des origines à la fin de la République* (Paris, 1958); Ileana Chirassi, "Dea Dia e Fratres Arvales," *Studi e materiali di storia delle religioni* 39 (1968): 191–291; Robert Schilling, "Dea Dia dans la liturgie des frères Arv ales," in *Hommages à Marcel Renard,* edited by Jacqueline Bibauw (Brussels, 1969), vol. 2, pp. 675–679; and Ida Paladino, *Fratres Arvales: Storia di un collegio sacerdotale romano* (Rome, 1988).

J. Rufus Fears (1987)
John Scheid (2005)

DEAD SEA SCROLLS. The manuscripts unearthed between 1947 and 1956 in the Judean desert, in caves along the coast of the Dead Sea, have come to be known collectively as the Dead Sea Scrolls. The main body of materials comes from Qumran, near the northern end of the Dead Sea, 8.5 miles (13.7 km) south of Jericho. Other texts, including the Masada scrolls and the Bar Kokhba texts, are occasionally also referred to as Dead Sea Scrolls, but this article will pertain only to the Qumran scrolls themselves. These scrolls constituted the library of a sect of Jews in the Greco-Roman period that has been identified by most scholars as the Essenes.

Discovery. In the second half of the nineteenth century, Hebrew manuscripts discovered in the *genizah* ("storehouse") of the Ben Ezra synagogue in Cairo began circulating in Europe. Much of this collection, known as the Cairo Genizah, was acquired for the University of Cambridge by Solomon Schechter in 1896. Among these texts was a strange composition, known as the *Zadokite Fragments* or the *Damascus Document,* that outlined the life and teachings of a Jewish sect. Eventually, this same text was found at Qumran.

There, in 1947, a young bedouin entered what is now designated Cave I and found a group of pottery jars containing leather scrolls wrapped in linen cloths. These scrolls, the first finds, were sold to Athanasius Samuel, the Syrian metropolitan of Jerusalem, and to Eliezer Sukenik, a professor representing the Hebrew University of Jerusalem. The scrolls in the possession of the Syrian metropolitan were purchased in 1954 by Yigael Yadin, Sukenik's son, on behalf of the Hebrew University.

Scientific exploration of the cave in 1949 by G. Lankester Harding and Roland de Vaux uncovered additional fragments and many broken jars. From 1951 on, a steady stream of manuscripts has been provided by bedouin and archaeologists. Some of these manuscripts are held in the Archaeological (Rockefeller) Museum in East Jerusalem. Many are displayed in the beautiful Shrine of the Book, a part of the Israel Museum built especially for the display and preservation of the scrolls.

Dating. From the beginning, the dating of the scrolls was a matter of controversy. Some saw the new texts as documents of the medieval Jewish sect of the Karaites. Others believed they dated from the Roman period, and some even thought they were of Christian origin.

Of primary importance for dating the scrolls was the excavation of the building complex immediately below the caves on the plateau. In the view of most scholars, those who lived in the complex copied many of the scrolls and were part of the sect described in some of the texts. Numismatic evidence has shown that the complex flourished from circa 135 BCE to 68 CE, interrupted only by the earthquake of 31 BCE.

Similar conclusions resulted from carbon dating of the cloth wrappings in which the scrolls were found. Study of the paleography (the form of the Hebrew letters) in which the texts are written has also supported a similar dating. It is certain, then, that the scrolls once constituted the library of a sect that occupied the Qumran area from after the Maccabean Revolt of 166–164 BCE until the great revolt against Rome of 66–74 CE.

The Scrolls. The many scrolls that were found in the Qumran caves can be divided into three main categories: biblical manuscripts, apocryphal compositions, and sectarian documents.

Fragments of every book of the Hebrew scriptures have been unearthed at Qumran, with the sole exception of the *Book of Esther.* Among the more important biblical scrolls are the two *Isaiah* scrolls (one is complete) and the fragments of *Leviticus* and *Samuel* (dated to the third century BCE). William Albright and Frank Moore Cross have detected three recensional traditions among the scrolls at Qumran: (1) a Palestinian, from which the Samaritan Pentateuch is ultimately descended, (2) an Alexandrian, upon which the Septuagint (the Greek translation of the Bible) is based, and (3) a Babylonian, which serves as the basis of the Masoretic (received and authoritative) text fixed by rabbis in the late first century BCE.

The apocryphal and pseudepigraphical writings were known until recently only in Greek and Latin translation. The Cairo Genizah yielded Hebrew and Aramaic fragments of medieval recensions. Among the important fragments found at Qumran are *Ben Sira*, *Jubilees*, Aramaic fragments of the *Enoch* books, the *Testament of Levi*, and additions to *Daniel*.

By far the most interesting materials are the writings of the sect that inhabited Qumran. The *pesharim* are the sect's biblical commentaries, which seek to show how the present premessianic age is the fulfillment of the words of the prophets. Prominent among these texts are the *pesharim* to *Habakkuk*, *Nahum*, and *Psalms*, and the *florilegia*, which are chains of verses and comments. The commentaries allow us a glimpse of the sect's self-image and allude to actual historical figures who lived at the time during which Qumran was occupied.

The *Damascus Document* describes the history of the sect and its attitudes toward its enemies. It also contains a series of legal tracts dealing with various topics of Jewish law, including the Sabbath, courts and testimony, relations with non-Jews, oaths and vows, and so forth.

Admission into the sect, the conduct of daily affairs, and the penalties for violating the sect's laws are the subjects of the *Manual of Discipline*. This text makes clear the role of ritual purity and impurity in defining membership in the sect as well as detailing the annual mustering ceremony of covenant renewal. Appended to it are the *Rule of the Community*, which describes the community in the End of Days, and the *Rule of Benedictions*, which contains praises of the sect's leaders.

The *Thanksgiving Scroll* contains a series of poems describing the "anthropology" and theology of the sect. Many scholars see its author as the "teacher of righteousness" (or "correct teacher") who led the sect in its early years.

The *Scroll of the War of the Sons of Light against the Sons of Darkness* describes the eschatological war. The sect and the angels fight against the nations and the evildoers of Israel for forty years, thereby ushering in the End of Days. This scroll is notable for its information on the art of warfare in the Greco-Roman period.

Unique is the *Temple Scroll*, which is an idealized description of the Jerusalem Temple, its cult, and other aspects of Jewish law. This text is the subject of debate as to whether it is actually a sectarian scroll or simply part of the sect's library.

THE SECT AND ITS BELIEFS. The Qumran sect saw itself as the sole possessor of the correct interpretation of the Bible, the exegesis of which was the key to the discovery of God's word in the present premessianic age. Like other apocalyptic movements of the day, the sect believed that the messianic era was about to dawn. Only those who had lived according to sectarian ways and had been predestined to share in the End of Days would fight the final battle against the forces of evil. In order to prepare for the coming age, the sect lived a life of purity and holiness at its center on the shore of the Dead Sea.

According to the sect's own description of its history, it had come into existence when its earliest members, apparently Zadokite priests, decided to separate themselves from the corrupt Judaism of Jerusalem and left to set up a refuge at Qumran. The sect was organized along rigid lines. There was an elaborate initiation procedure, lasting several years, during which members were progressively received at the ritually pure banquets of the sect. All legal decisions of the sect were made by the sectarian assembly, and its own system of courts dealt with violations and punishments of the sectarian interpretation of Jewish law. New laws were derived by ongoing inspired biblical exegesis.

Annual covenant renewal ceremonies took place in which the members of the sect were called to assemble in order of their status. Similar mustering was part of the sect's preparations for the eschatological battle. The Qumran sect believed that in the End of Days, two messiahs would appear, a Davidic messiah who was to be the temporal authority, and a priestly messiah of Aaron, who was to take charge of the restored sacrificial cult. They were both to preside over a great messianic banquet. Meals of the sect were periodically eaten in ritual purity in imitation of this final banquet.

The sect maintained a strictly solar calendar rather than the solar-lunar calendar utilized by the rest of the Jewish community. The sect was further distinguished by its principle of communal use of property. Although private ownership was maintained, members of the sect could freely use each other's possessions. The scrolls themselves refute the widespread view that the sectarians of Qumran were celibate.

IDENTIFICATION OF THE SECT. Dominant scholarly opinion has identified the Dead Sea sect as the Essenes described in the writings of Philo Judaeus and Josephus Flavius of the first century CE. Indeed, there are many similarities between this group and the sect described by the scrolls.

In many details, however, the Dead Sea Scrolls do not agree with these accounts of the Essenes. Josephus himself calls the Essenes a "philosophy" and makes clear that it was composed of various groups. If, indeed, the Dead Sea community was an Essene sect, perhaps it represented an offshoot of the Essenes who themselves differ in many ways from those described by Philo and Josephus. A further difficulty stems from the fact that the word *essene* never appears in the scrolls and that it is of unknown meaning and etymology.

Scholars have noted as well the points of similarity between the Qumran writings and aspects of the Pharisaic tradition. Louis Ginzberg has called the authors of these texts "an unknown Jewish sect." Indeed, many groups and sects dotted the spiritual and political landscape of Judaea in the Greco-Roman period, and the Dead Sea sect, previously unknown from any other sources, may have been one of these groups.

QUMRAN AND THE HISTORY OF RELIGIONS. The Dead Sea Scrolls have illuminated the background of the emergence of rabbinic Judaism and of Christianity. In the years leading up to the great revolt of 66–74, Judaism was moving toward a consensus that would carry it through the Middle Ages. As Talmudic Judaism emerged from the ashes of the destruction, other groups, like the Dead Sea sect, fell by the wayside. Nonetheless, the scrolls allow us an important glimpse into the nature of Jewish law, theology, and eschatology as understood by one of these sects.

The scrolls show us that Jews in the Second Temple period were engaged in a vibrant religious life based on study of the scriptures, interpretation of Jewish law, practice of ritual purity, and messianic aspirations. Some Jewish practices known from later texts, such as phylacteries, thrice-daily prayer, and blessings before and after meals, were regularly practiced. Rituals were seen as a preparation for the soon-to-dawn End of Days that would usher in a life of purity and perfection.

The scrolls, therefore, have shown us that Jewish life and law were already considerably developed in this period. Although we cannot see a linear development between the Judaism of the scrolls and that of the later rabbis, since the rabbis were heirs to the tradition of the Pharisees, we can still derive great advantage from the scrolls in our understanding of the early history of Jewish law. Here, for the first time, we have a fully developed system of postbiblical law and ritual.

The Dead Sea sect, and, for that matter, all the known Jewish sects from the Second Temple period, were strict adherents to Jewish law as they interpreted it. At the same time, with their emphasis on the apocalyptic visions of the prophets, the sects provide us an understanding of the emerging Christian claims of messiahship for Jesus. Only against the background of the Dead Sea Scrolls can the worldview of early Christianity be understood.

The contribution of the biblical scrolls to our understanding of the history of the biblical text and versions is profound. We now know of the fluid state of the Hebrew scriptures in the last years of the Second Temple. With the help of the biblical scrolls from Masada and the Bar Kokhba caves, we can now understand the role of local texts, the sources of the different ancient translations of the Bible, and the process of standardization of the scriptures that resulted in the Masoretic text.

In the years spanned by the Dead Sea Scrolls, the text of the Hebrew scriptures was coming into its final form, the background of the New Testament was in evidence, and the great traditions that would constitute rabbinic Judaism were taking shape. The scrolls have opened a small window on these developments the analysis of which will reshape our knowledge of this crucial, formative period in the history of Western religion.

See Also Essenes.

Bibliography

An excellent introduction is Yigael Yadin's *The Message of the Scrolls* (New York, 1957). The archaeological aspect is discussed thoroughly in Roland de Vaux's Schweich Lectures of 1959, *Archaeology and the Dead Sea Scrolls* (London, 1973). Important scholarly studies are Frank Moore Cross's *The Ancient Library of Qumran and Modern Biblical Studies*, rev. ed. (Garden City, N.Y., 1961), and Géza Vermès's *The Dead Sea Scrolls: Qumran in Perspective* (Philadelphia, 1981). The theology of the Qumran sect is studied in Helmer Ringgren's *The Faith of Qumran*, translated by Emilie T. Sander (Philadelphia, 1963). On the relationship to Christianity, see Matthew Black's *The Scrolls and Christian Origins* (London, 1961) and William S. LaSor's *The Dead Sea Scrolls and the New Testament* (Grand Rapids, Mich., 1972). Two studies of the importance of the scrolls for the history of Jewish law are my books *The Halakhah at Qumran* (Leiden, 1975) and *Sectarian Law in the Dead Sea Scrolls* (Chico, Calif., 1983).

New Sources

Charlesworth, James H. *The Pesharim and Qumran History: Chaos or Consensus?* Grand Rapids, Mich., 2002.

Davies, Philip R., George J. Brooke, and Philip R. Callaway. *The Complete World of the Dead Sea Scrolls.* London, 2002.

Orion Center for the Study of the Dead Sea Scrolls and Associated Literature. 5th International Symposium, 2000. *Liturgical Perspectives: Prayer and Poetry in Light of the Dead Sea Scrolls: Proceedings of the Fifth International Symposium of the Orion Center for the Study of the Dead Sea Scrolls and Associated Literature, 19–23, January, 2000.* Edited by Esther G. Chazon with the collaboration of Ruth Clements and Avital Pinnick. Leiden and Boston, 2003.

VanderKam, James C. *The Meaning of the Dead Sea Scrolls: Their Significance for Understanding the Bible, Judaism, Jesus, and Christianity.* [San Francisco], 2002.

Vermès, Géza. *An Introduction to the Complete Dead Sea Scrolls.* Minneapolis, MN, 2000.

Lawrence H. Schiffman (1987)
Revised Bibliography

DEATH

DEATH is a fact of life. This statement is at once banal and profound. It is banal insofar as it is common knowledge that all human life is limited in duration; it is profound, however, insofar as serious reflection on the end of life challenges the limits of human language, conceptual thought, symbols, and imagination. In an important sense, the meaning of life is dependent in part on one's understanding of death. That death is a fact of life is also paradoxical, for it suggests a coincidence of opposites—death-in-life and life-in-death. How people have imagined death-in-life and life-in-death has shaped their experience of biological death both individually and collectively. Death is paradoxical, as well, in that although every death is an individual experience—only individuals die, even when they die together in large numbers—death is also a profoundly social experience.

Death as a biological fact or as a physiological state is uniform across time and space. However, this universal sameness in biological terms should not lull one into the error of assuming that the human sense or experience of death has been—or is also—uniform across space and time. When contemplating death today, people must avoid the anachronism of projecting their contemporary understanding and experience of death back onto others in the past. Similarly, they must also avoid the cultural imperialism of assuming that their understanding and experiences are normative and that those of other cultures should be measured in their terms. This entry on death is concerned with the diverse ways in which death has been imagined and the many different ways it has been experienced in different cultures and different ages. To say this is to recognize that although death is "a given" in one sense, it is culturally and historically constructed in various ways.

The study of beliefs and ritual practices surrounding death has been pursued using a number of different methodological approaches, including ethnographic, sociological, psychological, historical, morphological, and structural to name a few. The best comparative studies of death in the history of religions build upon the large number of available detailed ethnographic descriptions of specific communal beliefs and ritual practices, but move beyond these in a number of ways. Comparative studies in the history of religions are interdisciplinary in nature, integrating the findings of different disciplines in an effort to understand the complex existential meanings of religious beliefs and practices. The classic ethnographic monograph tended to present a historically "flat" and socially undifferentiated picture of the conception of death and the performance of mourning and funerary rites in a given culture. Unfortunately, such "snapshot" studies of different cultures implied that religious beliefs were static over time and uniformly held by all members of a given culture or religious tradition. More recently, the subfield of historical anthropology has reintroduced history into the mix and produced numerous sensitive studies of change in beliefs and practices. Scholars have also paid more attention to the effects of cultural contact, colonialism, and issues of gender, resulting in more complex representations.

In this essay, no attempt will be made to present an exhaustive survey of beliefs and ritual practices related to death. Rather than providing ethnographic detail and careful historical analysis, the entry focuses on selected themes and issues that emerge from a broad survey of cultures and religions, and in so doing offers some general reflections concerning the human imagining and experience of death. In passing, it also touches upon methodological issues involved in the comparative, cross-cultural, and historical study of beliefs and ritual practices surrounding death.

The Concern with Death. Death has been a central concern of religious persons across space and time. The brute fact of death raises pressing questions: Why do people and other living things have to die? What happens to a person after death? Do the dead have a continued existence of some sort? Are they happy? Where do the dead go? Can the dead return to the world of the living? Can the dead communicate with the living? Is death permanent, or is it a temporary or transitional state? These and many other questions have long spurred speculation concerning death and the possibility of an afterlife.

Recognizing that death raised questions for people, numerous nineteenth- and early twentieth-century scholars were led to speculate on the relationship of human ponderings on death to the origins of religion. These theories of the origins of religion were often written in the Enlightenment genre, represented by Rousseau's essay *Discourse on the Origin of Social Inequality.* Such works of imaginative reconstruction are based on pure speculation, not historical evidence. These reconstructions also are based on the ill-advised belief that modern psychological assumptions are universally applicable. Finally, such accounts are based on logical inferences (often faulty) that are presumed to have been drawn by the earliest human beings. The British anthropologist E. E. Evans-Pritchard dismissively labeled this sort of "*a priori* speculation, sprinkled with illustrations" the "if I were a horse" fallacy and unworthy of the name historical reconstruction (1965, p. 24). While there is little or no historical evidence to support these imaginative flights, it is salutary to note the broad influence they once had.

Today scholars strive to understand how different conceptualizations of death, the afterlife, and the body, as well as different ritual practices, affect the individual and collective experience of death. The cultural historical constructions of death, the body, the afterlife, and so on also directly affect one's religious valuations of life in this world. In thanatology (the study of death), among other things, it is important to consider the religious anthropology (i.e., the specific understanding of human nature and divine nature and the relationship between them), the understanding of the body, and the operative cosmology of a given culture or religious community. Moreover, one must take into account a given culture's epistemology of death and the afterlife (i.e., how people claim to know things about death and the afterlife). After all, most people would deny that their concepts about death are based on mere speculation. Cultures have established means of obtaining evidence on matters related to death and the afterlife. This evidence is commonly found in the content of dreams, reports from shamans concerning their ecstatic flights through the multiple realms of the universe, or individual accounts of visionary experiences or events witnessed in trance states. Alternatively, the "proof" may be found in the authoritative proclamations of myths or sacred texts.

Death may be accepted as a fact of life by many persons today, but historians of religions have clearly demonstrated that humans have rarely imagined death to have been a natural and inevitable condition from the beginning of time. Throughout the world, a myriad number of myths tell how death came into the world and how humans came to be mortal beings. Death is often claimed to be the result of an accident of some sort or an unfortunate mistake or choice made by a god or an ancestor. It may be the result of an act of forgetfulness, trickery, or theft, or it may have resulted from the breaking of a taboo or perhaps the commission of some major or minor transgression. The *Genesis* account of the fall, with the consequential changes in the human ontological condition and in the world itself, is only one such myth. It is important to recognize that this myth, like other such stories, continues to exercise power over the collective imagination and lives of millions of people. In yet other religions, the length of human life is imagined to be different in different cosmic ages, with the length usually decreasing as the devolutionary process continues.

OVERCOMING DEATH. If death was not always a fact of life, then the possibility suggests itself that death might be overcome in some way. The study of death in the history of religions is, in part, the history of how different cultures and religious communities have sought to deny the finality of the seemingly "given" nature of death. Many religious beliefs and practices aim to overcome death in some way or to restore humans and the world to conditions prior to the introduction of death. Eschatologies, for example, imagine the end of the world as it now exists, including the end of death. Similarly, the so-called cargo cults that emerged in the face of radical cultural disruption and rampant disease in situations of cultural contact are expressions of a desperate anticipation of the destruction of this world and the inauguration of a renewed world.

More generally, scholars have long noted that initiatory rites involve symbols and scenarios of death and rebirth. The performance of an initiatory rite rehearses death followed by a scenario of rebirth of some kind. This death may be imagined in biological terms, or it may be the death (end) of a specific status or ontological condition. In many religions, religious healers gain their powers precisely by having overcome death through an initiatory trial of some sort. Such initiatory trials are often unsought, but they need not be. Many examples of what one might call "dying onto the world" are found in the history of religions, including the elaboration of religious vocations defined over against mundane life in the world. These include, to name only two of the most common types, the renunciation of the world by monks and nuns and individuals going into the mountains, desert, or the bush in order to practice some form of asceticism and to seek visions. In many religions, lay persons or ordinary men and women can also ritually gain a foretaste of death and the afterlife. Altered states of consciousness of various sorts provide access to knowledge of the afterlife in many religions. For Pentacostal Christians, for instance, the psychosomatic experience of the descent of the Holy Ghost—the loss of consciousness, speaking in tongues, the radiant sense of divine infusion—is a form of dying onto life as, while at the same time a foretaste of what the Second Coming will bring.

Religious seekers have also proactively pursued various means of achieving immortality, sometimes in human-embodied form and other times by seeking to overcome the human body. The ancient Egyptians exemplify those who imagined the afterlife to be similar to life in this world, with the body surviving death. Thus, the corpse was carefully embalmed in order to preserve its form, while items the deceased would need in the afterlife were also buried with the body.

Practitioners in alchemical traditions around the world have searched for the elixir of immortality. Alchemists provided recipes and proffered various techniques to transform the mortal body into an immortal one. Some religions speak of a spiritual body existing after death. In such traditions, the decomposition or immolation of the physical body is often seen as a form of release into a spiritual existence. Such a belief informs the Ainu bear festival in Northern Japan in which a deity *(kamui)* visits the world of the living in the form of a bear cub. The cub is nursed and raised by the Ainu; it is also entertained before it is ritually killed, thereby releasing the deity from its temporary physical form and sending it back to the spirit world (Kimura, 1999).

Other traditions, such as yoga in its many forms, have sought to overcome the embodied nature of human existence (i.e., to overcome the body itself, which is identified as the locus of mortality) in order to achieve an immaterial and timeless state of pure consciousness. In Indian religious traditions, biological death is believed to lead to rebirth in another physical form, whereas *moksa,* release from the karmic cycle of birth-death-rebirth, puts an end to death. Death, then, has been imagined in many different ways, some positing another form of embodied existence and others a disembodied state. Only a few religions, such as the ancient religion represented in the *Enuma Elish,* viewed death as a real end, with no form of existence following it.

THEORIES OF DEATH AND THE ORIGINS OF RELIGION. As noted above, the recognition of the central importance of death in the conceptual worlds of human beings throughout time has occasionally led Western scholars to make some overblown claims concerning death and the origins of culture or civilization. Before returning to a brief consideration of some of the issues related to death that remain central to the study of the history of religions today, it is necessary to review in a cursory manner a few of the most famous—and wrongheaded—grand theories of the origins of religion that were based in part on the scholars' imagined human response to death in the misty past.

Edward B. Tylor. The famous nineteenth-century armchair anthropologist Edward B. Tylor no doubt went too far in claiming that death was the reason religion existed. In his highly influential two-volume work *Primitive Culture* (1871), Tylor argued that the concept of the soul or an animating spirit arose when primitive peoples reflected on death, trance states, visions, and dreams. He asserted that the belief in the existence of the soul was the logical deduction that primitives drew from putting together two separate experiences. First, according to Tylor, the primitives' awareness of the sudden transformation of a vibrant human body into a corpse at the moment of death must have suggested to them that the animating source of life was not to be found in the physical body. At the moment of death, the material body remained, but it was cold, immobile, and lifeless. In dreams and visions, however, people often saw and conversed with dead persons, who thus seemed to continue to "exist" in some form even after their bodily demise. Putting two and two together, this led to the logical deduction that an animating spirit or soul must exist that was invisible, immaterial, and detachable from the physical body.

Tylor believed that this type of primitive reasoning was the basis of the most primitive cultural stage of development, which he labeled "animism." Animism is the belief that both animate and inanimate things, natural phenomena, and the universe itself possess a vital animating power or soul. Like many nineteenth-century theorists, Tylor assumed that all cultures passed through evolutionary stages. The precise enumeration of these stages varied from scholar to scholar, but in general they follow the pattern of evolution from a belief in magic to religion and, ultimately, to the triumph of reason and science. At each stage, it was believed that belief in the earlier form of magic or religion would decline. Moreover, contemporary peoples living in technologically primitive cultures were held to be living fossils, as it were. As such, the study of "primitives" seemed to hold the promise of providing scholars in various disciplines the opportunity to view what the life of their own ancestors must have been like millennia earlier.

Ghosts and ancestral spirits. Herbert Spencer, one of the founders of modern sociology, offered a similar theory in *The Principles of Sociology* (1885). However, he maintained that the origins of religion were to be found in the belief in ghosts rather than the soul. Significantly, visions of the dead—as well as encounters with them in dreams—again played a central role in Spencer's theory. Because the dead were believed to still be present somehow in the world, Spencer claimed that they came to be propitiated and offered food, drink, and so on by their living relatives and friends. Moreover, the most important and powerful members of society were believed to retain their position and power even after death. Thus, they were treated with special respect and decorum, as they had been while alive. Over time, these ancestors evolved into deities. Thus, according to Spencer, primitive ancestor worship was the basis of all religions. Unfortunately, there is no hard historical evidence for this assertion or for the other universal claims he proffered.

Sigmund Freud. For his part, Sigmund Freud made a stunning series of claims about death, sex, and religion in both his psychological writings and in his works of cultural historical interpretation. The latter include *Totem and Taboo* (1918), *Civilization and Its Discontents* (1930), *The Future of an Illusion* (1928), and *Moses and Monotheism* (1939). Freud offered a psychological explanation of the paradoxical coincidence of opposites of death-in-life and life-in-death. He argued that *eros* and *thanatos*, the drives to reproduce oneself and to annihilate oneself, were both primordial in human nature and deeply intertwined at the unconscious level. Indeed, he claimed that a universal psychological connection existed between sexual activity and death. He found evidence for this assertion not only in the lives of his neurotic patients and ethnographic descriptions of primitive rites, but in such things as a colloquial phrase for male ejaculation, which translates as "the little death." Freud was not an anthropologist, though he used the work of anthropologists, sociologists, and ethnographers in his works of cultural interpretation. Nor was he really interested in cultural diversity. Rather, his interest, like so many others of his age, was only in different psychological-*cum*-cultural stages of development.

Few anthropologists or historians of religions today would accept Freud's universal claims or offer competing universal claims of their own for that matter. For instance, rather than make a universal assertion about the significance of "the little death," they would note that the male anxiety implicit in this phrase flows from the widely-held (but not universal) archaic belief that the vital fluids and life energy in one's body are finite in quantity and that they are not replenished. For those holding this understanding of the male body, any expenditure of seminal fluids is assumed to deplete the man's life force. Ironically then, the act that leads to the creation of new life ultimately contributes to the male's own physical decline and death.

Menstruation and lactation, to name two prominent female physiological functions, are also highly-charged symbols in many cultures and religions, but Freud paid considerably less attention to them. Had he, he would have found that they, too, are often associated with death-in-life and life-in-death. Freud was equally unaware of the significant impact the differences in the religious anthropologies of diverse people or their different understandings of the human body could have on their experience of sexual activity and death, among other things. Indeed, Freud dismissed native explanations of such things outright, claiming that conscious explanations never got to the real unconscious causal sources of human psychology and behavior.

In *Totem and Taboo*, Freud again associated death with the origin of religion, society, and civilization. Building upon the now long-discredited hypothesis that the earliest human beings lived in hordes each ruled by a dominant male and the mistaken concept of totemism, Freud produced a gothic tale (or, perhaps, a modern psychological myth) of primordial patricide. In Freud's telling, a single dominant male claimed exclusive sexual rights to all of the women in the horde. The sons produced by this supreme male must have looked up to their father and aspired to be like him, even as they hated and envied him. They no doubt became increasingly frustrated, Freud suggested, as they reached sexual maturity, but were still denied a sexual outlet within the horde. Then, one day the sons collectively hatched a plan to kill their father in order to gain sexual access to the women. After the dastardly deed had been done, "cannibal savages as they were," the sons instinctually devoured their victim in order to incorporate his power. Then, according to Freud, something momentous happened.

The sons' love and admiration of the father, which had been repressed in order to commit the murder, resurfaced as pangs of guilt and psychological ambivalence. These quickly overwhelmed them. On the one hand, they were grieved by their father's death and horrified by their role in it, but on the other they experienced a sense of satisfaction in having replaced the father. Yet Freud claims that in death the father became even stronger than he had been in life through the workings of psychological repression and substitution. In the wake of the murder, the sons forbid themselves sexual access to the local women (this is the origin of the incest taboo and exogenous marriage rules) and forbid the slaying of the father. The latter taboo was expressed through the deflected form of the totem animal or plant, the surrogate for the father, which was normally taboo but which was eaten in a collective ritual meal. In this way, Freud connected the origins of the totemic festival with the primitives' ambivalent psychological response to the death or murder of the father.

The psychological ambivalence felt towards the dead father was, Freud claims, the origin not only of the universal incest taboo and various taboos surrounding death, but also of the totemic meal, social organization, moral restrictions, and even religion itself. Significantly, Freud's narrative and analysis was concerned not only with instincts, but with the ways instincts and primitive desires are affected and controlled by the psychodynamics of family and social organization. For the primitive, the totemic object or animal is a surrogate for the murdered father, while in a more developed stage of culture the figure of God clearly serves this purpose.

Applying the biological theory of Ernst Haeckel that ontogeny recapitulates phylogeny to psychology (i.e., the stages of biological development of an individual from conception through maturity replicate in abbreviated form the evolution of the species), Freud argued that the study of the mental life of children, as well as dreams and neuroses, could shed light on the primitive stage of human development. He believed that the earliest object of sexual desire for every infant boy is incestuous and forbidden—his mother. Like the grown-up sons in the primal horde, an infant son is jealous of the father's sexual possession of the mother and desires to eliminate him as a rival. Freud posited that the Oedipal complex, as he labeled it, was a universal psychological complex, but one which healthy children in civilized societies could now overcome through submitting to social controls and, thereby, learning to control their instincts and deferring the immediate gratification of their desires.

For Freud, religion was the crucial link between the individual and society. Religious myths and rituals were the collective expressions of the same unconscious desires and psychological processes that produce dreams and neuroses in individuals. Freud famously claimed that religion was a collective neurosis that would eventually be outgrown, although not in the near future. Unlike Spencer and Tylor, though, Freud did not consider primitives to be rational beings; rather, he compared them to neurotics and children. Yet, just as most healthy boys work their way through the psychological conflicts of the Oedipal stage, he believed that cultures, too, evolved psychologically, with reason gradually replacing fantasy.

Modern studies of death. Today few people ascribe to the psychological assumptions underlying these and other theories that connect death to the origin of religion. The search for origins of this sort has been abandoned. Still, scholars have been struck by the patterned ways in which death has been associated with life in many cultures. For instance, scholars have long noted the striking association of death with fertility and/or the regeneration of life in religions around the world. In *Versuch über Grabersymbolik der Alten* (1859), J. J. Bachofen noted the prominence of symbols of fertility (e.g., eggs) and women on the tombs of ancient Greece and Rome, which he interpreted as indicating a belief in life coming out of death. For his part, Sir George Frazer made the image of the dying-and-rising god a central theme of his influential comparative study, *The Golden Bough,* which went through multiple editions during the early twentieth century. Other scholars, such as the classicist Jane Harrison, carried the study of the ancient mystery cults further, demonstrating in *Themis* (1911) how the social order was related to the natural order through these religious rites.

In 1906, Robert Hertz, a student of Emile Durkheim, published a seminal essay on the collective representation of death in *Année Sociologique* in which he analyzed double or secondary burial practices in Southeast Asia (Hertz, 1960). In the cultures he studied, the first burial period was temporary and dedicated to mourning. After the flesh of the corpse had rotted away, the dry skeletal remains were disinterred and then reburied elsewhere. With this secondary burial, the deceased was integrated into the society of the dead, while the mourners were reintegrated into the society of the living. Hertz also pointed to structural and symbolic parallels between funerary rites and initiation rites and marriages, an insight that numerous other scholars subsequently followed up and detailed in many other societies. More recently, Maurice Bloch and Jonathon Parry have revived interest in the symbolic association of death and fertility in a culturally wide-ranging collection of essays entitled *Death and the Regeneration of Life* (1982).

One final scholar deserves special mention. In a series of important publications, Philippe Ariès presented an unprecedented survey of the changing attitudes toward and representations of death in Europe over a thousand years from the eleventh through the twentieth centuries. Ariès used an interdisciplinary approach in his quest to trace these changes, working with literary, liturgical, testamentary, epigraphic, and iconographic sources of evidence. Specialists may quibble over specific details and dispute some of Ariès' interpretations, but his work has demonstrated beyond a doubt that the experience of death is subject to change over time within the same culture. On the other hand, scholars have also disclosed the remarkable continuity of some funerary practices over several millennia. Margaret Alexiou's study, *The Ritual Lament in Greek Tradition* (1974), and more recent anthropological field work (e.g., Danforth, 1982), has demonstrated that the performance of funerary laments and the practice of secondary or double burial continues down to the present in some rural areas, in spite of the dominant presence of Greek Orthodox Christianity.

To his credit, Ariès did not attempt to offer a grand overarching psychological or sociological theory about death. Rather, he sought to organize in a significant way the huge amount of historical evidence he had surveyed and then to trace the changes that occurred over broad sweeps of time. In his magnum opus, *Homme devant la mort* (1977; English translation, *The Hour of Our Death*, 1981), Ariès suggested that the history of the Western representations and experiences of death could be organized around variations on four psychological themes: the growing awareness of the individual; the defense of society against untamed nature; belief in an afterlife; and belief in the existence of evil.

Death in Comparative Perspective. Death has rarely been taken as an end as such, a real terminal point. Rather, for most humans throughout time, physiological death has signaled a transitional moment and state, not an absolute end. At death, life as previously lived in this world ends for the deceased, but the memory and imagination of the living open up paths to the past and the future and to other worlds and other modes of existence. A survey of the history of religions clearly shows a widespread affirmation that death creates the potential for new beginnings, for a new stage of the cycle of birth-death-rebirth, or for transitioning to different ends. The transformative possibilities signaled by death are numerous and extremely variable. However these possibilities are imagined, though, humans have rarely been content to "let nature take its course," as it were. Upon closer inspection, even those religious groups that apparently let nature take its course following a death (e.g., when the Parsi Zoroastrians of India exposed the corpse on top of a tower to be consumed by carrion birds, or the Lakota Sioux exposed the corpse on a bier to the elements), will be found to have performed ritualized acts intended to symbolically integrate the deceased into a cosmological world of meaning.

Death almost inevitably moves the living to perform ritual work of some sort in an effort to control what happens posthumously both in the world of the living and in that of the dead. The transformations made possible by death are not automatic, nor are they necessarily without danger. By and large, people have assumed that the desired transitions and transformations after death can be accomplished safely only through proper ritual acts. The performance of such rituals may require specific changes in dress, bodily decoration, voice (e.g., in ritual mourning), diet, daily activities, and so on among the living.

Liminality. Death creates a liminal time and space for the living and for the deceased. For a given period of time, those closely related to the deceased often have specific ritual obligations placed upon them, as well as a number of prohibitions (e.g., they cannot comb or wash their hair, wear colorful clothing, participate in certain activities, eat certain foods, go to certain places). The deceased is often imagined as being in a liminal condition as well, betwixt-and-between the world of the living and the world of the dead. In these cases, the funerary and mourning rites are designed to assist the deceased in his or her journey to the otherworld or to effect the transformation into an ancestor, spirit being, and so on. These rites are often viewed as aiding the dead, but at other times they are also clearly designed to keep the dead from returning to the world of the living or otherwise causing havoc. The liminal status of the newly dead or the dead for whom funerary rites were not performed is often imagined to be potentially dangerous. Such liminal beings haunt the world of the living and may cause illness, death, or other calamities; they may also possess individuals or cause them to go mad. Thus, many posthumous rituals are prophylactic in nature and designed to protect the living from the dead.

The liminal status of the corpse almost always requires that it be prepared or handled in specific ritualized ways. In some societies, the deceased is buried or cremated with objects he or she will need in the other world; in other societies, the dead may be buried in a fetal position, perhaps indicating a belief in rebirth. The care taken with the remains of the dead throughout human history has provided archaeologists with some of their most important evidence about the religious beliefs and practices of diverse peoples.

In many societies, death does not terminate all relationships between the deceased and living relatives. Throughout East Asia, for instance, ancestral cults involve regular ritual interactions often for up to thirty or more years, including prayers, offerings of food, drink, and incense, memorial services, and even dances to entertain the dead during the festival of the dead. In Japan, the corpse is cremated and the ashes buried in a cemetery. The deceased is given a posthumous name, which is inscribed by a Buddhist priest on a wooden tablet that is installed in a domestic Buddhist or Shinto ancestral shrine. After the requisite period of memorial rites has passed, the ancestral tablet is itself burned in a symbolic second cremation. Thereafter, the individual identity of the deceased ends and he or she is incorporated into the anonymous class of ancestors.

Communicating with the dead. Many religions also have ritual techniques for communicating with the dead. In traditional societies, a shaman or medium often serves as a conduit of communication with the dead. The deceased may possess a ritual functionary in order to communicate his or her needs or desires, or the ritual specialist may travel through ecstatic flight to the land of the dead to speak with the dead. In other religions, dreams or visions induced by hallucinogens may provide a means of interacting with the ordinary dead. Many societies have regular festivals to which the dead are invited, such as Obon in Japan or the Days of the Dead in Mexico.

In many mourning rites, mourners converse with the deceased by speaking, singing, or otherwise performing both voices in the dialogue. The desire to maintain some contact with deceased loved ones is widespread, although such contact is carefully controlled and of limited duration. In some societies one finds that—more than death itself—it is the fear of being forgotten after death that is paramount. One thinks of the ancient Greeks and the cult of heroes in which posthumous fame was more valued than life itself.

Many religions encourage visits to the gravesites of the deceased, where tears are shed, prayers are said, offerings of flowers, food, and incense are made, and communion with the deceased occurs. In many societies, songs associated with the dead are sung to recall the deceased, including an enumeration of the places he or she used to visit or the lands the deceased may have hunted or tilled. The deceased is often ritually mourned or keened at the gravesite, although in societies that practice double or secondary burial, these songs or mourning rites are sometimes offered at the now-empty initial burial site. In some societies, physical objects, songs, or specific places associated with the dead function as souvenirs or memento mori, recalling the deceased to mind. In ancient Japan, people employed objects (e.g., a comb, an item of clothing) called *katami* (to see the form/shape [of the deceased]) to conjure up an image of the dead (Ebersole, 1989). In the Victorian period, people often carried lockets containing a snippet of hair from a deceased or absent loved one. Victorian women also made elaborate hair weavings or flowers, birds, and other decorative forms—by using the hair of dead family members—for similar purposes. With the emergence of photography, photos of the deceased, including those of dead infants and children carefully posed to appear to be sleeping, became extremely popular. Today many persons find these objects macabre and disturbing, witnessing to a major shift in cultural sensibility surrounding death.

Many religions provide rituals to be performed for the benefit of the dead, as noted earlier. The practice of endowing Christian masses to be performed or the reading of Buddhist sutras for a deceased individual are examples. Sometimes individuals made arrangements for such rites to be performed on their behalf after their death, a clear indication of the belief in the continued existence of the self and personal identity. In other cases, it is the surviving family members who are expected to perform memorial or ancestral rites or to have them performed by religious functionaries. The Hindu *pinda* rite of offerings of food and drink to one's deceased parents is a prime example of a daily domestic practice.

Preparation for facing death, pacification, and the grieving process. Many religions also developed rites designed to help those facing imminent death to accept this fate. The Catholic rite of last unction is but one example. Such rites are based on the widespread belief that one's state of mind and mental focus at the time of death are critical in determining one's posthumous condition. Those who die in an emotionally agitated state, whether it be of fear, anger, jealousy, or lust, will not find peace in the afterlife and, thus, become potentially dangerous. Many different ritual practices seek to overcome the arbitrary nature of death precisely by controlling the timing and/or manner of death, but also one's mental response to it. By overcoming the survival instinct, one overcomes the fear of death and even death itself. The so-called self-mummified buddhas of Japan are the desiccated remains of Shugendō priests, now enshrined as objects of worship, who took a vow to have themselves buried alive in the mountains. Thousands of people gathered to witness the event, while the priest, breathing through a hollow bamboo tube, continually beat a drum and recited the *nembutsu,* or the ritual invocation of the Bodhisattva Amida (Amitābha), until death, or release, came (Hori, 1962).

Many religions feature rituals of pacification of the dead, designed to assist the deceased to accept his or her new status and surroundings. A certain ambivalence is evident in many of these rites. On the one hand, surviving loved ones wish for a continued relationship with the deceased; on the other hand, there is some fear or anxiety expressed over the possible return of the dead. The living seek to tightly control their interactions with the dead through ritual means. Although the dead are invoked to be present, the rites also usually include formal send-offs to return the deceased to the land of the dead.

Some scholars have long argued that mourning, funerary, and memorial rites are really for the living and answer to their psychological or social needs. Durkheim, for example, claimed they responded to the need for renewed social solidarity; more recently, psychologists and others insist on the need for individuals to work through the grieving process. (The findings of the history of religions, though, might well lead one to question whether there is a single universal grieving process.) Obviously, religious rituals serve multiple purposes, and need not be mutually exclusive. A brief consideration of the different scholarly interpretations of Japanese Buddhist rites of pacification for aborted fetuses (*mizuko kuyō*) will demonstrate this. These rites were newly created in late twentieth-century Japan, where abortion was a common form of birth control. Some have argued that *mizuko kuyō* rites answer the psychological needs of the parent(s), who experience pangs of guilt after the decision to abort (cf. La Fleur, 1992). Others, such as Helen Hardacre (1997), have argued that entrepreneurial Buddhist priests created the need for such rites through skillful marketing techniques. Significantly, advertisements represented aborted fetuses as haunting spirits in need of pacification rites.

The corpse. Whenever death occurs, a corpse is created—an object at once like a living body and radically different from it. Yet, one finds numerous reports of anomalous cases that deny this truism a universal status—the Taoist immortal who leaves the physical world, leaving behind only sandals, mysteriously empty tombs or graves, and so on. No matter what the details are, such reports imply that the "death" involved was not an ordinary biological death. In some cases, death is denied by claims that an individual has gone away or into hiding (e.g., the Shīʿah Hidden Imam in Iran), perhaps to return triumphantly at a later time. In ancient Japan, the emperor or empress did not die; rather, as a "living deity," he or she had returned to the High Heavens and there become secluded behind the bank of clouds. In many cases, death restores a person to true form, as in the case of a deity who had temporarily taken on material or human form. In yet other cases, at death the individual is reportedly changed instantly into another now permanent or eternal form—a star in the heavens, a rock formation, a spring—leaving no corpse

When a corpse is present, however, it is usually considered to be polluted, leading to numerous avoidance procedures. In many societies, only designated individuals may touch and prepare the corpse. In India, these ritual functionaries are outcastes; in other societies, they may be close relatives, who take on a polluted state for the duration of the funerary and mourning rites. In modern technologically developed societies, these roles have been assumed by medical professionals and professional morticians.

In a striking number of cultures, though, it is predominately women who perform these ritual duties. Bloch and Parry have provocatively argued that the prominence of women in funerary rites is not, as Frazer and many others believed, so much a part of the symbolic regeneration of life as it is a symbolic elaboration of female sexuality and fertility precisely in order to oppose it to "real" vitality. That is, female sexuality and biological reproduction are equated with death-in-life, which must be overcome. Among other religions Bloch and Parry cite, they suggest that Christianity epitomizes this pattern. They contrast the role the woman Eve played in the Fall in the Garden of Eden—which led to human sexuality, biological procreation, and death—to that of the Virgin Mary. The asexual conception of Jesus and his subsequent death and resurrection restore the possibility of access to the life eternal of Paradise. The meaning and valuation of physiological death, fertility, and regeneration can be totally transformed by shifts in symbolic and ritual representations, which recontexualize these (Bloch and Parry, 1982).

Whatever the merit of Bloch and Parry's overall thesis, it is clear that the meanings of concepts such as death, fertility, sexuality, and rebirth are not singular, nor are they culturally determined for all time or for all persons within a culture. The meanings for such fundamental categories can be renegotiated over time within the same religious tradition, as Ariès and others have shown. At an individual or subgroup level, they may also be affected by one's class, gender, or occupation among other things. A few admittedly extreme examples allow a more general point about these factors to be made. Take, for instance, Egyptian pharaohs. They no doubt anticipated death and rebirth differently than did their slaves, especially insofar as the afterworld was believed to replicate the social, political, and economic structures found in this world. Similarly, the ruling Mayan and Aztec elites must have understood and experienced the ritual sacrifice of the many human captives offered as tribute differently than did many of the conquered people, who were regularly forced to provide the persons for these bloody sacrifices. Unfortunately, most of the records and representations of these sacrificial deaths come from the elite sectors of the societies. Such evidence must be used carefully, always bearing in mind that the voices of the powerless and the disenfranchised were rarely recorded.

Sacrificial rites. Modern scholars have with little difficulty reconstructed the symbolic logic informing the ritual taking of human life in Mesoamerican empires. There once again myths and rituals proffer the paradoxical claim that life comes out of death. In order to renew the cosmos and to guarantee fertility and regeneration, blood must be shed at a specific time, at a specific place, and in a specific choreographed manner. This might be in the form of ritual bleedings from the penis of the Mayan king or through human sacrifice at the Aztec New Year and other appropriate moments of transformative potential (cf., Carrasco, 1999).

Such rituals clearly represented the religio-political ideology of the power elites. It should not be uncritically assumed, however, that such ritual performances accurately represented the shared cultural understanding of all people in the empire. At the same time, neither should it be uncritically assumed that the rites were nothing more than a vehicle for ideological obfuscation on the part of the ruling elites. To be sure, in significant ways, human sacrifice was a forced performance, but cases exist in which persons voluntarily went to their own deaths, and as such require an understanding the power such symbolic activities—designed to effect the magic of transforming death into life or even immortality—can have over individuals and groups. At a minimum, the question here is one of what constitutes a meaningful voluntary death for specific groups.

The history and complex multiple and competing meanings of the Hindu ritual practice of sati—the self-immolation of a widow on her husband's funerary pyre—may serve as an exemplar of voluntary ritual death. Sati has long captured people's imagination, but only recently have scholars begun to explore its history and the complex, ongoing, and contested representations of its meaning. For instance, Catherine Weinberger-Thomas (Chicago, 1999) sensitively explored how British merchants and later colonial authorities used the ritual as a rationale for taking control of India; how Western scholars have depicted it and why; how fundamentalist Hindu religious and political groups have embraced it; the complex issues of gender; and the at times intense social and familial pressures a widow faces. She also seeks to understand why some young women chose to follow their husbands in death. She discloses the power of the belief that the widow's self-immolation makes two human bodies into one indivisible body, which is ritually transformed into a sacrificial oblation and rice ball—a *pinda.* The funeral pyre becomes the mirror image of the marriage bed in which male and female powers were first conjoined, although now this union of opposites is forever. This ritual suicide is also the inverse of the primordial self sacrifice of Purusha, as detailed in *Ṛgveda* X: 40. In the latter, the primordial divine sacrifice leads to the creation of the material world, the caste system, and so on; with the ritual sacrifice of sati, all of these are overcome and the couple escapes the cycle of birth-death-rebirth.

Continued presence of death in life. It is a commonplace to say that religions create worlds of meaning. But they also create meaningful deaths. Death is never far from human experience, no matter how people may try to banish it from sight and mind. It permeates daily life just as it structures the rhythms of collective life. Graveyards, ossuaries, tombs, memorials, and museums bring the presence of death and the dead into human consciousness and landscape. Monumental architectural buildings and structures seek to guarantee and to control the memory of the dead by future generations. The mall of Washington, D.C., for instance, is a public space filled with memorials to the dead designed to evoke a sacred sense of the past and a collective American identity. Today in secular scientific cultures, human genes and DNA have become yet another way of re-imagining the continued presence of the dead in the living.

Religious calendars are punctuated with festivals and observances related to the dead, but so are secular calendars. The citizens of modern nation-states celebrate memorial days of various sorts for their war dead, the victims of genocide, presidents, and kings, but they also celebrate birthdays and beginnings. Even when the dead are feared or are considered polluting and, thus, are segregated and separated spatially from the living, they hover nearby. Ritual avoidances of specific places, foods, words, names, and so on also bring the dead—even in their physical absence—into the consciousness of the living. The dead live in memory, in dreams, and in physical tokens. In other cases, the dead are physically near to hand—buried under the cathedral floor, enshrined in part or in whole as holy relics in temples and sanctuaries, or interred under the entranceway to a house. The dead may even be literally incorporated into the living through some form of endocannibalism (e.g., Amazonian natives drinking the cremation ashes of a villager). Scholars have noted the striking similarity to the symbolism (or the reality of the miracle of transubstantiation) of the Christian Eucharist—"This is my body; this is my blood."

Death is everpresent, as well, in the privileged myths and stories told again and again in song and poetry, in the arts (painting, sculpture, weaving, mosaics, pottery, etc.), in dance and dramatic performances, in children's play ("Ring around a rosey/ pocketful of posies/ ashes, ashes, all fall down."), and today on television, in the movies, and in video games. Bringing the ubiquity and the absolute redundancy of death before the mind's eye of the living has often served didactic purposes, moving persons to act in spiritually and morally proper and ascribed ways. The Buddhist ritual contemplation of putrefying corpses, the ritual visualization of the inevitable future of all human bodies, visiting collective ossuaries, and so on have been used to move people to renounce the material body and the world. Graphic pictures of hells and the land of the dead in many religions have similarly served to keep death in the minds of people, just as images of heaven and the afterlife have proffered hope to many.

The ubiquitous presence of death, however, can also make it banal and rob it of any sense of sacrality or meaning. People can become inured to death by the numbing effect of the sheer numbers of the dead in times of plague, war, and, to use a modern term, natural disaster. Death's seemingly relentless redundancy can lead persons to perform horribly immoral acts as death's banality threatens the foundations of society. Akira Kurosawa's film *Rashomon,* set in Kyoto in an age of terrible civil war and a time of rampaging plague, is an unforgettable portrait of death's power to destroy law and order and to create utter chaos. Sheer desperation, coupled with the drive to survive, can lead humans to depravity as the moral order of the universe collapses. In the European Holocaust, the carrying out of the Nazi policy of extermination of the Jews, gypsies, and others was possible in part because in the camps killing became so banal.

There is also the "death without weeping"—the resignation at times of the poorest of the poor to the necessity of death for some if others are to live. The myriad images of a happier life in the future that many religions have proffered must not blind one to the desperate, horrible, and yet rational decision that innumerable mothers have made throughout history to stop feeding one child so that others might live (cf., Scheper-Hughes, 1992). Similarly, in much of the world today and in all countries before the advances of modern medicine, giving birth was an extremely dangerous act. All too often, bringing life into the world meant the death of the mother.

Yet, in the history of religions, few societies have collectively embraced an existential fatalism, which assumes that death is meaningless. Rather, plagues, wars, and natural disasters have often been taken to be cosmological signs of some sort. They have generated eschatological visions on a cosmic scale of the end of the world as we know it and the beginning of a new world. Or they have stimulated calendrical speculation on a cosmic scale, with the positing of ages through which the universe must pass. Examples are legion, ranging from ancient Indian speculation on devolutionary cosmic ages (*yugas*) and Buddhist writings on the present time as the Age of Declining Dharma to the elaborate intermeshing calendars of the Aztecs and the Mayans, which inexorably move through their cycles of change and ends and beginnings. In almost all cases, as has been seen in the case with the death of an individual, the end is imagined as a beginning. The end of a cosmic age is a moment of transition and transformation, one marked by death, destruction, and danger. Yet the religious imagination of humans turns this dark time—this descent into chaos—into a prelude to a renewed time and a return to order. Often this denouement is rehearsed in ritual performance and mythic narration.

The need to explain death. Death is both uniform and arbitrary. It is uniform in so far as all persons, regardless of social status, position, and wealth are subject to dying. Death is arbitrary, though, in terms of when it strikes, how it strikes, and often who it strikes. In this sense, death is enigmatic, mysterious, and unnerving. Although death is inevitable, specific deaths need to be explained. In many societies, the corpse or skeletal remains were examined for evidentiary purposes, or other ritual means, such as divination, were employed to determine who or what had caused a death. Today in scientifically developed countries, a special medical practitioner will perform an autopsy for these purposes.

In the past and in many traditional cultures today, ritual autopsies of a different sort were and are performed. In rural Greece, for instance, as in centuries past, old women and female relatives will fondle and closely examine exhumed skeletal bones for signs of the moral condition of the deceased and, thus, his or her posthumous fate (cf. Danforth, 1982). In other societies, the condition of a corpse after death is taken to be a sign of his or her spiritual status. In Buddhist and Christian lore, for example, the corpses of saints do not decay, nor do they emit disgusting odors. Rather, they release aromatic smells. Such extraordinary corpses are, of course, the source of relics in the cults of religions around the world. Such body relics are the repository of healing and saving powers; they are also yet another expression of the belief in life-from-death.

If the timing of death often seems arbitrary, societies and religious communities seek to regularize it temporally by punctuating religious and political calendars with days memorializing the dead. Whether it be the Shīʿah Muslims' annual memorialization and re-enactment of the martyrdom of al Husain, Christians' annual ritual remembrances of the crucifixion of Jesus and his resurrection, the celebration throughout East Asia of the festival of the dead, a ritual time when the spirits of the dead are invited to return to the world of the living and are entertained there, or modern national memorial days for the war dead, calendars are filled with days dedicated to the collective recollection of the dead. Through such collective reflections on death, communal values are reaffirmed. In an important sense, life cannot have meaning until death does.

While death is universal, it is imagined, encountered, and responded to in a myriad number of different ways across space and time. Death in the history of religions is the history of the ever-changing imagination and revaluation of death, as well as of the stylized responses to it. Philippe Aries' magisterial thousand-year history of death in Europe is one notable attempt to interpret and understand the existential meaning of the shifting representations of death over time. Aries' work reminds one that the manner in which death and the afterlife (or, the different possible consequences of death) are imagined and represented informs the lived experience of death both by the dying person and the survivors. Aries describes "the tame death" in medieval Europe when a dying individual accepted his or her coming death and met it at home. Surrounded by loved ones, the dying person said her or his last goodbyes and prepared to face death calmly, for one's state of mind at the time of death helped to determine one's fate.

Many religions have taught ways of preparing for death and facing this inevitability calmly. Holy men of the Agora sect in India meditate on death in the cremation grounds, spread the ashes of the dead over their own bodies, use human skulls as begging bowls, and pursue other practices in order to live with death continually (cf. Parry, 1994). Some Japanese samurai also practiced daily meditation in which they envisioned their deaths in battle. By practicing dying in this way, they sought to prepare themselves to face death unflinchingly (Reynolds and Waugh, 1977). In a myriad number of different ways, humans have sought to control death, even if it could not be conquered. The query "Death where is thy sting?" is an expression of the achievement of this control over death (*1 Corinthians* 15:55).

One way to gain control over death is to control the timing of one's death or to overcome the arbitrary timing of death by foretelling it. The ability to predict one's own death or to will it to happen at a certain time and place are widely recognized as a sign or a power of a holy person. The Japanese Buddhist poet-monk Saigyō (1118–1190) wrote a well-known poem (no. 77) included in his collection, *Sankashū* (*Nihon koten bungaku taikei,* Vol. 29, p. 32), that reads:

> negawaku wa Let me die, I pray, hana no shita nite under the cherry blossoms haru shinan of spring. sono kisaragi no around the full moon mochizuki no koro of the month of Kisaragi.

Kisaragi is the classical Japanese name for the second lunar month. Gotama the Buddha passed away on the fifteenth of this month, so Saigyō's wish was to emulate the Buddha even in death. When Saigyō died on the sixteenth of Kisaragi, many people took this as an auspicious sign. Saigyō's posthumous fame rested in part on this "proof" of his extraordinary spiritual nature. Similar miraculous powers of forecasting one's own death are found in religions around the world.

CONCLUSION. These general comments on death in the history of religions have done little more than present a brief introduction to the subject. In many ways, conceptions of death are subject to change over time, just as they vary dramatically in different religions. The imagining of death is not an empty exercise; it shapes the individual and communal experience of death and life. That death is a fact of life remains one of the most intractable mysteries that human beings must confront. Human beings past and present have always sought to find meaning in death and, thereby, in life.

The history of this search for meaning in the history of religions is both poignant and ennobling.

See Also Afterlife; Ages of the World; Alchemy; Ancestors; Ashes; Banaras; Birth; Bones; Bushido; Cannibalism; Cargo Cults; Day of the Dead; Descent into the Underworld; Dying and Rising Gods; Easter; Eschatology, overview article; Fall, The; Funeral Rites, overview article; Ghost Dance; Heaven and Hell; Human Sacrifice; Initiation; Life; Otherworld; Pure and Impure Lands; Relics; Rites of Passage; Sacrifice; Sati; Suicide; Tombs; Underworld.

Bibliography

Alexiou, Margaret. *The Ritual Lament in Greek Tradition.* London, 1974.

Ariès, Philippe. *The Hour of Our Death.* New York, 1981.

Bachofen, Johann Jakob. *Versuch uber Grabersymbolik der Alten,* Basel, Germany, 1859.

Bloch, Maurice, and Jonathon Parry, eds. *Death and the Regeneration of Life.* Cambridge, U.K., 1982.

Carrasco, Davíd. *City of Sacrifice: The Aztec Empire and the Role of Violence in Civilization.* Boston, 1999.

Danforth, Loring M. *The Death Rituals of Rural Greece.* Princeton, 1982.

Durkheim Emile. *The Elementary Forms of the Religious Life.* London, 1915.

Desjarlais, Robert. *Sensory Biographies: Lives and Deaths Among Nepal's Yolmo Buddhists.* Berkeley, Calif., 2003.

Ebersole, Gary L. *Ritual Poetry and the Politics of Death in Early Japan.* Princeton, 1989.

Evans-Pritchard, E. E. *Theories of Primitive Religion.* Oxford, 1965.

Frazer, James. *The Golden Bough: A Study in Magic and Religion.* London, 1912.

Freud, Sigmund. *Totem and Taboo: Resemblances Between the Psychic Lives of Savages and Neurotics.* New York, 1918.

Freud, Sigmund. *The Future of an Illusion.* New York, 1928.

Freud, Sigmund. *Civilization and Its Discontents.* London, 1930.

Freud, Sigmund. *Moses and Monotheism.* New York, 1939.

Hardacre, Helen. *Marketing the Menacing Fetus in Japan.* Berkeley, Calif., 1997.

Harrison, Jane. *Themis: A Study of the Social Origins of Greek Religion.* Cambridge, U.K., 1911.

Hertz, Robert. "A Contribution to the Study of the Collective Representation of Death." In *Death and the Right Hand,* trans. Rodney C. Needham. London, 1960.

Hori, Ichiro. "Self-Mummified Buddhas in Japan: An Aspect of the Shugen-dō ('Mountain Asceticism') Sect." *History of Religions* 1, 2 (1962): 222–242.

Kimura, Takeshi. "Bearing the 'Bare Facts' of Ritual: A Critique of Jonathan Z. Smith's Study of the Bear Ceremony Based on a Study of the Ainu Iyomante." *Numen* 46, no. 1 (1999): 88–114.

LaFleur, William R. *Liquid Life: Abortion and Buddhism in Japan.* Princeton, 1992.

Metcalf, Peter, and Richard Huntington. *Celebrations of Death: The Anthropology of Mortuary Ritual.* Cambridge, U.K., 1979; 2d ed., 1991.

Nihon koten bungaku taikei, vol. 29. Tokyo, 1958.

Parry, Jonathon. *Death in Benares.* New York, 1994.

Reynolds, Frank E., and Earle H. Waugh, eds. *Religious Encounters with Death: Insights from the History and Anthropology of Religions.* University Park, Pa., 1977.

Scheper-Hughes, Nancy. *Death Without Weeping: The Violence of Everyday Life in Brazil.* Berkeley, Calif., 1992.

Spencer, Herbert. *Principles of Sociology.* London, 1885.

Stannard, David E. *The Puritan Way of Death: A Study of Religion, Culture, and Social Change.* Oxford, 1977.

Tylor, Edward B. *Primitive Culture.* London, 1871.

Weinberger-Thomas, Catherine. *Ashes of Immortality: Widow Burning in India.* Chicago, 1999.

Gary L. Ebersole (2005)

DECALOGUE See TEN COMMANDMENTS

DE CHARDIN, PIERRE TEILHARD See TEILHARD DE CHARDIN, PIERRE

DECONSTRUCTION. The word *deconstruction* was coined by French philosopher Jacques Derrida (1930–2004), with whom the movement of that same name is identified. Derrida rejects the classical anthropological model of language, according to which the speaking subject gives verbal expression to inner thoughts that are subsequently written down. In such a model, writing is a sign of speaking; speaking is a sign of thinking; and thinking is a sign of being. Instead, Derrida follows the *structuralist* thesis of Swiss linguist Ferdinand de Saussure (1857–1913), which posits that language is to be understood scientifically as a purely formal system of signs *(langue)* internally related to one another (like a dictionary in which one word is defined by other words) and underlying the utterances of speaking subjects *(parole),* thus eliminating both the subjective-psychological and objective-metaphysical factors. In Saussure's model, *signifiers* are arbitrary (the word *king* has no natural likeness to a real king) and differential (they differ by the "space" between, say, *king* and *ring*). The *signified* is the effect produced by the rule-governed use of signifiers. Derrida's thought is *post-structuralist;* it criticizes Saussure for privileging speech over writing, in violation of the arbitrariness of the linguistic sign, and for treating linguistic strings as closed systems of fixed structures. Metaphors and wordplay illustrate the uncontainable capacity of linguistic chains to network out indefinitely in new directions, pushing endlessly against the limits imposed by the rules. Derrida encapsulated his adaptation of Saussure in the neologism *différance,* French philosophy's most famous misspelling. The idea is to keep networks open-ended, to resist their tendencies to closure, in order to allow new and unforeseen effects.

Deconstruction is not a settled body of substantive theses or positions but a style of thinking that applies in any field of inquiry, theoretical or practical, by virtue of which any present set of beliefs or practices is held to be indefinitely revisable (deconstructible) in the light of something unrevisable (undeconstructible). Inasmuch as the undeconstructible is never actually present or realized, the undeconstructible is also said to be "the impossible." According to Derrida, the least bad definition of deconstruction is the "experience of the impossible." "Least bad" because, in deconstruction, which is resolutely anti-essentialist (nominalistic), words have only a relatively stable unity of meaning, shifting histories of use, and no fixed or defined borders. Derrida uses the word *experience* in the sense not of empirical data gathering but of running up against something unexpected, even traumatic. "The impossible" does not mean a simple logical contradiction, such as (*p & ~p*), but something that shatters the horizon of expectation, that is not accountable (or possible) under prevailing presuppositions.

The same sense is conveyed when Derrida describes deconstruction as the "invention of the other." *Invention* has the more literal sense of "coming upon" and even of "in-coming" (Latin, *in-veniens*), running up against something that comes in upon or comes over us, overwhelming our powers of anticipation. By the "other," Derrida means not the relatively other—that is, new evidence confirming an existing horizon—but the "wholly other" *(tout autre),* a phrase he borrows from the Jewish ethicist Emmanuel Levinas, meaning something unforeseeable, unrepresentable, for which we have no concept. A deconstructive analysis thus prepares the way for or explores "the possibility of the impossible." Jean-François Lyotard makes a comparable distinction between making a new move in an old game (the possible or relatively other) and inventing a new game altogether (the impossible or wholly other). That, in turn, invites comparison with Thomas Kuhn's distinction between *normal science,* which makes new discoveries within an existing paradigm, and *revolutionary science,* when an anomaly forces a fundamental reconfiguration of the current schema, resulting in a "paradigm shift."

Derrida has recourse to a family of *venir* ("to come") words picked up in English in both Latinate *(invention)* and Anglo-Saxon forms *(coming).* Deconstruction is turned to the "in-coming," the invention, or the advent, of the "event," which is a unique and "singular" happening, not an instance or example of a universal (Derrida's idea of "singularity" is derived from Søren Kierkegaard, Martin Heidegger, and Levinas). The event defies convention, where everything is regularized and routinized. Deconstructive thinking is guided by the invocation "come" *(viens),* which Derrida has not hesitated to call a certain "prayer," by which he means a deep desire or love of the event to come, which is not without anxiety since the future is also an absolute risk. The motif of the "come" clearly has messianic overtones that Derrida acknowledged in later, more autobiographical, essays like "Circumfession," where he reflects on his birth as a Jew and on his early life in a Jewish family in French Algeria. The motifs of love and desire have overtones of Augustine's *cor inquietum,* of what Derrida calls the "prayers and tears of Augustine," which also surface in these same essays about his life in the Franco-Christian colony that is the historic land of Augustine.

The word *deconstruction,* which has the predominantly negative sense of disassembling something, is clearly not the best word for this deeply affirmative mode of thinking. Coined by Derrida as a translation of Heidegger's *Destruktion,* and used by him to characterize his own work, it owes its currency just as much to commentators who seized upon it. Heidegger himself was likely referring to Martin Luther's use of *destructio,* which itself goes back to *1 Corinthians* 1:19. Just as for Luther, destroying the wisdom of the wise meant nothing destructive, but rather the recovery of the original sense of scripture by breaking through the crust of Scholastic theology. And just as Heidegger did not mean anything negative but rather the recovery of the unthought sense of "being" that was hidden in the history of metaphysics, so Derrida does not mean anything negative, but rather the releasing of the possibility of the impossible, or the coming of the event, that threatens to be closed off by conventional interpretation and practices. While the word has entered the general vocabulary (e.g., "deconstructing Woody Allen") with the negative sense of knocking down and exposing faults, to deconstruct something in Derrida's sense is not to ruin it but to give it a history, to open it up to a future. Something that is insulated from deconstruction is not protected but petrified, having hardened over into a dogma, like a law that could never be reformed or repealed. The word enjoyed, or suffered from, a *succès de scandale,* particularly in American literary theory circles in the 1970s, where it seemed to invite a kind of interpretive anarchy that licensed any interpretation, however bizarre. When Derrida protested against such interpretations, critics thought him involved in the self-contradiction of insisting that his own texts should be interpreted carefully, thus refuting his own theory that anything goes.

In fact, careful reading is what deconstruction is all about. A philosophical theory with wider implications, deconstruction first gained ascendancy in the 1960s and 1970s as a literary theory. A deconstructive reading settles deeply into the grain of a text, sensitizing itself to its tropes and metaphors, its choice of words, the chains in which those words are caught up, and the complex and even anonymous operations of the linguistic system in which the author is working, in order to show that the text contains an unmasterable complexity—*dissemination*—that cannot be contained by the author's own intentions or conscious logic. Thus, Derrida's well-known critique of "logo-centrism." Derrida's frequent use of puns and wordplay is not a substitute for an argument but an exemplification of a theory about wordplay, which illustrates the unmasterable, unintended dimension of language, the semantic, graphic, and phonic chains that no intentional agent can contain. James Joyce, an early hero of Derrida's, embodies this point about language almost perfectly. This disseminative effect is not something that a clever writer or reader is doing to the text, exerting a kind of violence or mastery over it, but an auto-deconstructive operation going on within the linguistic network itself.

That this is not interpretive anarchy but responsible work, Derrida thinks, is clear to anyone who reads carefully. Anyone who reads Greek philosophy carefully knows that there is all the difference between "Plato," a shorthand for a cluster of condensed philosophical theses, summarized and passed along in prepackaged histories of philosophy, and a close, careful reading of or immersion into Plato's writings, which reveals multiple voices, dramatic devices, conflicting and suggestive counter-motifs, and loose threads—in short, a "text," a highly woven and interwoven complex, not a neatly argued "book" under the absolute conscious control of an "author." We might add that anyone who has studied the Jewish or Christian scriptures carefully will understand that these are "texts" in just this sense; that is, a complex weave (or "palimpsest") of many voices, competing theological and political agendas, redactive layerings, anonymous interventions, lost stories, liturgies, and multiple extra-textual references or reinscriptions of earlier texts, texts without fixed "margins." In the same way, conservative critics charge deconstruction with being out to destroy "tradition," but Derrida would respond that he only wants to show its immense complexity and competing voices; there is no such thing as "tradition" in the singular but rather an interweaving of many traditions and counter-traditions, of dominant and recessive voices, and even of chance mutations in manuscripts. Close readings of the past—the uncovering of forgotten women, for example—opens up hitherto closed possibilities for the future. Deconstruction is very conservative, Derrida once quipped, because the only way to love and be loyal to the past is to deconstruct it.

Although Derrida's avant-garde style of writing, especially early on, lent superficial credibility to the misinterpretation of deconstruction as a form of relativism or even nihilism, no one today can mistake the sustained seriousness of the later writings, whose ethical, political, and even religious character is beyond doubt. Reading his account of the "gift without return" or "forgiving the unforgivable," more informed critics today will accuse him of a Kantian rigorism or unrealistic ethical purism, an accusation that he also rejects. From the early 1980s on, Derrida has written not only about the gift and forgiveness, but about justice and the law, hospitality, friendship, democracy, capital punishment, and international human rights. In 2003 he published *Voyous,* a book about the denunciation of "rogue states" by the Western democracies.

Religious thinkers are fascinated by a distinction Derrida introduced in the 1990s between the concrete "messianisms"—the three great monotheistic religions of the book, as well as the philosophical eschatologies of G. W. F. Hegel, Karl Marx, and Heidegger—and the pure "messianic" or "messianicity." The *pure messianic* means the formal structure of desire, expectancy, or openness, the pure structure of the "to come" *(à venir)*—like the hospitality to come, the justice to come, and, most famously, the "democracy to come"—that is concretized in the historical messianisms. In virtue of the pure messianic, one can speak of a "religion without religion," a religious desire without confessional dogma or institutional ties. The "democracy to come" is not a Kantian regulative ideal, which brings a concept to ideal completion beyond its empirical limits, because, for Derrida, *democracy* is not a concept or an essence on which we are making asymptotic progress, but a moment in the open-endedness of history that makes possible an event, whose coming cannot be foreseen and whose name is not known, and where nothing guarantees that it will not bring forth a monster instead of a messiah. "Secular" political theory, and philosophy generally, is always transcribing an "unavowed theologeme," like the messianic promise, thus skewing any rigorous distinction between the religious and secular, faith and reason, religion and the nonreligious, prayer and social hope, theism and atheism.

This is not to say that religious thinkers were not interested in deconstruction from the start. The early essay "Differance" (1967) started a discussion with negative theology that dominated the dialogue between deconstruction and theology until the late 1990s. As Derrida says, he loves the syntax, semantics, and the tropes of negative theology, which is a self-effacing discourse, a discourse that attempts to erase its own traces. Beyond matters of style, the critique of the metaphysics of presence in deconstruction (what is present is deconstructible; the undeconstructible is never present) bears a substantive analogy to the critique of idols in apophatic theology (if you comprehend it, it is not God; if it is God, you cannot comprehend it). Nonetheless, while negative theology clearly uses deconstructive techniques, deconstruction is not negative theology, because it has no commitment to a *hyperousios,* to a Godhead beyond God or a God beyond being. The exchange between Derrida and Jean-Luc Marion is the most important in this regard.

In the 1980s, deconstruction was appropriated by the theology of the "death of God," most notably in Mark C. Taylor's *Erring: A Postmodern A/theology* (1984). Taylor argued that the first wave of death-of-God thinking in the nineteenth century left the old God standing under the new name of *Humanity.* Deconstruction is the true hermeneutics of the death of God because it has displaced any absolute center, human or divine, with the free play of signifiers. God has descended into the world without remainder, even as scripture has descended into *écriture* without remainder, a reading that reflected the Nietzschean understanding of Derrida then dominant in American departments of literature. Since then a different appreciation of the religious dimension of deconstruction has emerged in thinkers such as John Caputo, Kevin Hart, and Hent de Vries, for whom deconstruction is the hermeneutics not of the death but of the desire for God.

SEE ALSO Heidegger, Martin; Literature, article on Critical Theory and Religious Studies; Structuralism.

BIBLIOGRAPHY

Altizer, Thomas J. J., ed. *Deconstruction and Theology.* New York, 1982.

Caputo, John D. *The Prayers and Tears of Jacques Derrida: Religion without Religion.* Bloomington, Ind., 1997.

Carlson, Thomas A. *Indiscretion: Finitude and the Naming of God.* Chicago, 1999.

Derrida, Jacques. *Writing and Difference.* Translated by Alan Bass. Chicago, 1978.

Derrida, Jacques. "Circumfession: Fifty-nine Periods and Periphrases." In *Jacques Derrida,* by Geoffrey Bennington and Jacques Derrida, translated by Geoffrey Bennington. Chicago, 1993.

Derrida, Jacques. *On the Name.* Edited by Thomas Dutoit. Stanford, Calif., 1995.

Derrida, Jacques. *The Gift of Death.* Translated by David Wills. Chicago, 1995.

Derrida, Jacques. *Monolingualism of the Other, or, The Prosthesis of Origin.* Translated by Patrick Mensah. Stanford, Calif., 1998.

Derrida, Jacques. "On Forgiveness: A Roundtable Discussion with Jacques Derrida." In *Questioning God,* edited by Mark Dooley, Michael Scanlon, and John D. Caputo. Bloomington, Ind., 2001.

Derrida, Jacques. *Acts of Religion.* Edited by Gil Anidjar. London and New York, 2002.

Derrida, Jacques. *Voyous.* Paris, 2003.

Derrida, Jacques, and John D. Caputo. *Deconstruction in a Nutshell: A Conversation with Jacques Derrida.* Edited with a commentary. New York, 1997.

Derrida, Jacques, and Jean-Luc Marion. "On the Gift: A Discussion between Jacques Derrida and Jean-Luc Marion." In *God, the Gift, and Postmodernism,* edited by John D. Caputo and Michael J. Scanlon. Bloomington, Ind., 1999.

de Vries, Hent. *Philosophy and the Turn to Religion.* Baltimore, 1999.

Hart, Kevin. *The Trespass of the Sign: Deconstruction, Theology, and Philosophy.* New York, 2000.

Horner, Robyn. *Rethinking God as Gift: Marion, Derrida, and the Limits of Phenomenology.* New York, 2001.

Taylor, Mark C. *Erring: A Postmodern A/theology.* Chicago, 1984.

JOHN D. CAPUTO (2005)

DEFILEMENT SEE PURIFICATION; TABOO

DE GROOD, J. J. M. SEE GROOT, J. J. M. DE

DEIFICATION.

The Latin term *deificatio* does not appear until late in the Roman era, and then first in Christian literature, particularly in the controversies involving the Nestorians, who blamed the orthodox for "deifying" the body of Christ. In current usage, the English term *deification* is equivalent to *apotheosis.* In light of history, however, *apotheosis* might be reserved to refer to the consecration of heroes, of political personages, of Hellenistic sovereigns and, notably, of Roman emperors. In this article the subject will be the deification of individuals or of things generally through means that correspond to certain general tendencies of Greco-Roman paganism.

PYTHAGOREANISM AND CATHARTIC DEIFICATION. Since death makes the radical difference between men and gods, the problem of deification is indeed that of immortalization. In the Classical epoch, the Greeks attributed the power of immortalizing (*athanatizein*) to the Getae and to the Thracians through a kind of shamanism that may have involved Zalmoxis. No evidence exists of the ritual patterns of these practices, but they must have been based on a doctrine of the soul and on the existence of spiritual elites. Zalmoxis was regarded as a *daimōn* and as a disciple of Pythagoras. The connection is significant, since belief in metempsychosis is sometimes attributed to the Thracians.

The belief in metempsychosis is tied to the first explicit formulation of a deification of persons through asceticism and the satisfaction of penalties consequent upon the pleasures of previous lives. It is found in the writings of the Pythagorean philosopher Empedocles (frag. 145–146): a soul is a kind of "demon" that is bound to the cycle of reincarnation in expiation for its faults. At the end of purifying reincarnations, after having been "prophets, cantors, physicians . . . ," these fallen and ransomed "demons" are "reborn as gods": they become the "table companions of the immortals." The last two verses of the Pythagorean *Golden Verses* (70f.) offer hope of a state like that of an immortal god for the sage "who, having left his body behind, goes forward into the free ether." Hierocles would explain this deifying liberation of the soul as the "highest aim of the hieratic and sacred craft," that is, of philosophy. Deification, then, consists of restoring the personal *daimōn* to its authentic status as an immortal god. It is the goal of a spiritual asceticism confirmed by various means of testing.

The same teaching is implicit in Plato, notably in the *Phaedo* (69c, 114c), where the philosopher is talking not expressly about a deification, but rather about a sojourn among the gods. It is also seemingly implicit in the inscriptions engraved upon the noted golden tablets of Thurii (fourth to third century BCE) and of Rome (second century CE). These assure the deceased that he will be a god by virtue of his heavenly ancestry, his divine race, and the sentence that he has served. Caecilia Secundina "became divine according to the law," that is, by the law that governs reincarnations (*Orphicorum fragmenta* 32g.4). The deceased in one of these tablets states expressly that he has escaped at last the "circle of sorrows," an image that elsewhere is applied to the cycle of rebirths. Whether these tablets bear inscribed fragments of an Orphic "book of the dead," of a *missa pro defunctis*, or of a Pythagorean *hieros logos* ("sacred teaching"), their formulary promises a posthumous deification.

The same point of view is declared on the new tablet of Hipponium: the soul of the deceased woman will take "the sacred path along which the other initiates and Bacchants walk unto glory." The reference is to Orphic Bacchants. It is significant that Orphic vegetarianism expresses the desire to live not as men but as gods. This asceticism had the aim of purifying man from his Titanic components by liberating the Bacchus within him. A liberation of this sort coincides, as it does in Empedocles and Plato, with the escape from the "circle of genesis." The Orphic-Pythagorean deification thus presupposes a persevering action directed toward oneself, a cathartic and mystic tension. When Hippolytus (*Philosophumena* 6.9.25) attributes to Pythagoras the statement that souls "become immortal, once they are detached from their bodies," this does not mean that physical death liberates them automatically, but that immortality is the reward for continual effort at personal purification. This conviction is based upon a dualist anthropology.

The Mysteries and Initiatory Deification. Orphic-Pythagorean ideas were disseminated with variations (especially involving metempsychosis) by advocates of Platonism and Neoplatonism. Ever since the Classical epoch, the Orphic mystics, as well as various wandering charlatans, had promised, through the use of specialized formulas, not a religious purification, but only an ethical purification in the spirit of the philosophers. Later, during the Hellenistic age, the multiplication and success of mystery religions popularized a new form of deification.

These cults—centered on deities who were regarded as having lived and suffered among men—put into question the radical distinction between cursed mortals and blessed immortals. Insofar as they made their initiates relive in a liturgical way the trials of the gods who had died and revived (Osiris) or were reborn (Attis), the mystery religions connected their devotees with an adventure that ended with victory over death. Indeed, the initiation that, at first, was regarded as giving the candidates some assurance of a kind of privileged status in the beyond (Eleusis) tended also to safeguard them against bad luck, and even to deify them by a form of ritual identification with Dionysos, Attis, or Osiris. The Dionysian mysteries made a Bacchus of the initiate; the consecration of the initiate by means of the winnowing basket and the phallus regenerated him by immunizing him against death and infernal demons. Dionysos was held to have returned from the nether regions along with his mother Semele, and to have been "reborn." His myth provided a model for the rebirth of any initiate, to whom the same immortality was promised (Turcan, 1966, pp. 396ff., 436ff., 466ff.). This regeneration required the (figurative) death of the initiate, who was subjected to a rite of katabasis. The initiate was seen as undergoing the same trials of initiation that had turned Dionysos into a true Bacchus (ibid., pp. 406ff.). The Neoplatonists compared the restoration of the soul (purified and reintegrated in God) to the awakening of Dionysos Liknites (ibid., p. 401). The initiation of the cult of Isis offers many comparisons. The neophyte had to die to his previous life, and the ritual involved a descent into hell, with some kind of mystical or hallucinatory journey through the cosmos. Yet as recompense the initiate was defied, adorned *"ad instar Solis"* ("as a likeness of the Sun," that is, Osiris-Helios), and held up to the faithful as an idol. The benevolence of Isis, who judged someone to be worthy, made the neophyte into a new Osiris. The funeral rites of mummification in ancient Egypt had the same purpose. Yet in figuratively anticipating the initiate's death, the mysteries of Isis during the Roman epoch in some way democratized apotheosis, in that in its beginnings only pharaohs were the beneficiaries.

The mysteries of Cybele likewise promised a regeneration to their adherents and an elevation (*epanodos*) toward the gods. Just as in the initiation of the cult of Isis, the initiate is thought of as dying like Attis, in order to share in the love of Cybele in a blessed *hieros gamos*. The Galli, by castrating themselves, identified with Attis. To avoid this personal bodily sacrifice, use was made of the *taurobolium*, the ritual sacrifice of a bull. The function and meaning of the *taurobolium* are debated (R. Duthoy, *The Taurobolium: Its Evolution and Terminology*, Leiden, 1969). Yet the fact remains that the beneficiary of the *taurobolium* was factitiously identified with the victim by drenching himself in the victim's blood, thereby becoming an Attis that those present could worship. Just like the initiate of Isis, the initiate of Attis was "reborn" through the *taurobolium: in aeternum renatus*. Whatever the rites or mysteries, the resting with a divine nature was thought of as a regeneration (Nilsson, 1974, p. 653). This feature is also seen in Hermetic deification.

Hermetism and Gnostic Deification. Comparing astrology with an initiation, Vettius Valens (second century CE) identifies contemplation of the stars with a kind of mystical union with God: the knowledge of the heavens "divinizes" the man who possesses it, as if the subject came to merge with the object. This is even more true of the knowledge of God when, in the imperial epoch, philosophy becomes theosophy. In the *Corpus Hermeticum*, this idea recurs frequently, "for this is the blessed end of those who have the knowledge: they become God" (*Corpus Hermeticum* 1.26). The good choice—that of divine things—"deifies man" (ibid., 4.7). We are "divinized" by the birth into spiritual life that constitutes gnosis. *Asclepius* 41 gives thanks to the supreme God, that he has deigned to "consecrate for eternity," that is, to deify men in the flesh. This affirmation seems to conflict with that in *Corpus Hermeticum* 10.6, where it is denied that the soul can be divinized while in a body.

Indeed, Hermetic gnosis supposes a complete regeneration. It is the new man enlightened and reborn in God who becomes a god by dying to physical life and by becoming alien to the world even in this life. Regeneration consists of the substitution of ten good "powers" (including "the knowledge of God") for twelve evil "powers" attributable to the zodiac. The disciple then identifies himself with the cosmic eternity, Aion, and he is then divinized. This is the very recommendation that Nous makes to Hermes: "Become Aion, and you will understand God" (ibid., 11.20). Here again it is a matter of restoring the soul to its original state: "You are born a god and a child of the One," declares Hermes to Tat (ibid., 13.14).

Similarly, the Gnostic systems derived from Christian inspiration, whatever the variations in their myths and their soteriology, envision only the final restoration of the spirit to its original divine state. Finally, the idea that by knowing oneself one learns to know God and to be known by him so as to be "deified," or "generated into immortality," is expressed by orthodox Christians (Hippolytus, *Philosophumena* 10.34). In contrast with Hermes Trismegistos, Hippolytus promises the Christian a body that will be as immortal and incorruptible as the soul itself. But, like the Hermetist, the Christian must also die to the old man and to the profane life.

MAGICAL AND THEURGIC DEIFICATION. Certain procedures of deification are comparable to Hermetic gnosis, at least insofar as they are presented as "formulas for immortality" that feature magical concepts. This is true in the case of the so-called Mithraic liturgy (end of the third century CE), where the name of Mithra appears as only one of those associated at that time with the sun. The ritual involves prayers and a journey of the spirit that in some way anticipates the posthumous ascension of the soul unto Helios and the heavenly Aion, both invoked for the occasion. As in Hermetism, the *apathanatismos* asserts that a subject is regenerated by the very object of his theosophical quest, but this is conditional to the exact application of a formula. Other magical texts insist upon the importance of knowledge revealed by the god or gods: "We thank you for . . . having divinized us through the knowledge of your being," states one papyrus. Following the death of the magus, Aion carries away his breath (*pneuma*) by way of rescuing it from Hades, "as befits a god." The neophyte is "reborn" and freed from fate, as was the initiate of Isis. Neoplatonic theurgy would give its approval to pagan magic, and Psellus could believe that it was capable of making gods of men.

The magus could also deify animals by ritually mummifying them in accordance with traditional Egyptian practices. Further, he could deify idols through telestic action and theurgy. In this sense, *Asclepius* 23 affirms that man is the creator of gods. It was precisely for this reason that Christians reproached pagans: the very idea that men could make gods! The most frequently denounced example of idolatrous fiction is that of Serapis who, according to Origen (*Against Celsus* 5.38), owed his existence "to the profane mysteries and to the practices of sorcerers invoking demons." Indeed, telestic action consists of causing divine influence to enter into idols, to "animate" them or to illuminate them through the magical process known as *phōtagōgia.* This consecration of statues employing magical formulas played a great role in late paganism.

FUNERARY AND ICONOGRAPHIC DEIFICATION. The adornment of tombs displays the concern for deifying individuals by analogy or through iconography. This tendency was first evident in Rome among the class of freedmen who sought thus to insure themselves some kind of moral promotion. Their cippi or stelae represent, from the first century CE, Herakles, Hermes, Dionysos, and Artemis portrayed after the image of the deceased man or woman. The epitaphs, the architecture of the tombs, and the literary tradition confirm the intention to identify the dead with gods, goddesses, and heroes. When the use of sarcophagi began to prevail at the time of the Antonines, sepulchral imagery manifested even more clearly the same concerns that are evident among higher social circles; emperors and empresses provided the example. This style of funerary deification consisted either of featuring the deceased's medallion portrait (*imago elipeata*) as being carried by the gods (Tritons, Centaurs, Victories, Erotes) or of giving the sculpted god, goddess, or hero the same features as the dead man or woman, who could then be seen as Dionysos, Ariadne, Mars, Hercules, Endymion, or Selene. Imagery of predatory animals (eagles, griffins) or gods (Dioscuri, Pluto) also implies a deification by analogy. Finally, sarcophagi with figures of the Muses, or with scenes of teaching, of battle, or of hunting, heroize the deceased through association with the depicted qualities of gallantry or erudition.

Thus, in the Hellenistic and Roman world, philosophy, theosophy, magic, mystery religions, and the cult of the dead all aspired to the same goal (one that on principle was excluded in Classical Greek religion): for the individual person to become or become again a god.

SEE ALSO Apotheosis; Soul, article on Greek and Hellenistic Concepts; Theurgy; Thracian Religion.

BIBLIOGRAPHY

Bianchi, Ugo. *The Greek Mysteries.* Leiden, 1976.

Bianchi, Ugo, and Maarten J. Vermaseren, eds. *La soteriologia dei culti orientali nell 'Impero Romano.* Leiden, 1982.

Dieterich, Albrecht. *Eine Mithrasliturgie.* 3d ed. Leipzig, 1923.

Dodds, E. R. *The Greeks and the Irrational.* Berkeley, 1951.

Festugière, A.-J. *La révélation d'Hermès Trismégiste,* vols. 3 and 4. Paris, 1953–1954.

Festugière, A.-J. *Hermétisme et mystique païenne.* Paris, 1967.

Festugière, A.-J. *Études de religion grecque et hellénistique.* Paris, 1972.

Festugière, A.-J. *L'idéal religieux des Grecs et l'evangile.* 2d ed. Paris, 1981.

Jonas, Hans. *The Gnostic Religion.* 2d ed., rev. Boston, 1963.

Nilsson, Martin P. *Geschichte des griechischen Religion,* vol. 2, *Die hellenistische und römische Zeit.* 3d rev. ed. Munich, 1974.

Reitzenstein, Richard. *The Hellenistic Mystery Religions.* Translated by John E. Steely. Pittsburgh, 1978.

Rohde, Erwin. *Psyche: The Cult of Souls and Belief in Immortality among the Greeks* (1925). Translated by W. B. Hillis. London, 1950.

Schilling, Robert. "La déification à Rome: Tradition latine et interférence grecque." *Revue des études latines* 58 (1980): 137ff.

Turcan, Robert. *Les sarcophages romains à représentations dionysiaques.* Paris, 1966.

Wrede, Henning. *Consecratio in formam deorum: Vergöttlichte Privatpersonen in der römischen Kaiserzeit.* Mainz am Rhein, 1981.

Zuntz, Günther. *Persephone: Three Essays on Religion and Thought in Magna Graecia.* Oxford, 1971.

Robert Turcan (1987)
Translated from French by Paul C. Duggan

DEISM. The term *deism* was originally equivalent to *theism,* differing only in etymology: *theism* based on the Greek word for god (*theos*), and *deism* on the Latin (*deus*). In the seventeenth and eighteenth centuries, however, *deism* came to signify one or another form of rationalistic theological unorthodoxy. Often used pejoratively, it was also sometimes worn as a badge of honor. The first known use of the term occurs in the *Instruction chrétienne* (1564) of the Calvinist theologian Pierre Viret: "I have heard he is of that band who call themselves 'Deists,' a wholly new word which they would oppose to 'Atheist.'"

In its principal meaning, *deism* signifies the belief in a single God and in a religious practice founded solely on natural reason rather than on supernatural revelation. Thus Viret characterizes deists as "those who profess belief in God as creator of heaven and earth, but reject Jesus Christ and his doctrines." John Dryden's preface to his poem *Religio Laici* (1682) defines deism as "the opinion of those that acknowledge one God, without the reception of any revealed religion." The currency of the term in the eighteenth century was undoubtedly enhanced by the article on Viret in Pierre Bayle's *Dictionnaire historique et critique* (1697).

Like most epithets of controversy, *deism* was used in a number of senses other than its principal one. It was often used as a vague term of abuse with no determinate meaning at all. Among the chief subordinate or deviant senses of the term are (1) belief in a supreme being lacking in all attributes of personality (such as intellect and will); (2) belief in a God, but denial of any divine providential care for the world; (3) belief in a God, but denial of any future life; (4) belief in a God, but rejection of all other articles of religious faith (so defined by Samuel Johnson in his *Dictionary,* 1755).

Some Deists completely rejected all revealed and ecclesiastical religion, adopted anticlerical attitudes, challenged the scriptural canon, questioned the credibility of miracle narratives, or even rejected the New Testament as fabrication and imposture. Thus Edward Stillingfleet, bishop of Worcester, described the addressee of his polemical *Letter to a Deist* (1677) as "a particular person who owned the Being and Providence of God, but expressed mean esteem of the Scriptures and the Christian Religion." Yet a number of influential seventeenth- and eighteenth-century British thinkers described themselves as "Christian Deists" on the grounds that they accepted both the Christian religion based on supernatural revelation and a Deistic religion based solely on natural reason, consistent with Christianity but independent of any revealed authority.

Thus, even the principal sense of *deism,* which refers to belief in God without belief in supernatural revelation, is inherently imprecise. No sharp dividing line can be drawn between Christian or revelationist Deists and Deists who recognized no revelation. The former often accepted Christian revelation precisely because it accords with natural or rational religion and sometimes advocated allegorical readings of scripture in order to secure this agreement, while the latter often disavowed any "mean esteem" of Christian scriptures and expressed admiration for the inspiring way in which the truths of natural religion were presented in them. Further, there is no sharp line separating Christian Deists and orthodox Christian theologians (such as Thomas Aquinas or Duns Scotus) who maintain that some parts of Christian doctrine can be known by natural reason.

Deism was most prominent in England, the only place where it approached the status of a movement. Among its best-known representatives were Lord Herbert of Cherbury (1583–1648), author of *De veritate* (1624); his disciple Charles Blount (1654–1693); John Toland (1670–1722), author of *Christianity not Mysterious* (1696); Anthony Collins (1676–1729); and Matthew Tindal (1657–1733), author of *Christianity as Old as the Creation* (1730), often described as "the Deist's Bible." The powerful influence of English Deism is attested by the sizable number of attacks on it by the orthodox, including not only Stillingfleet, but also Richard Bentley, Charles Leslie, Samuel Clarke, and (most famously) Joseph Butler in his *Analogy of Religion* (1736). Deism also met with vicious persecution in England, where blasphemy was punishable by forfeiture of civil rights, fines, and even imprisonment. At least two prominent Deists were imprisoned for expressing their blasphemous opinions: Thomas Woolston (1670–1733) was sent to prison in 1729 and died there; Peter Annet was fined, pilloried, and imprisoned to hard labor in 1764 at age seventy.

Deism is generally associated with British religious thought. However, a number of major continental religious thinkers of the late sixteenth, seventeenth, and eighteenth centuries clearly qualify as Deists under the principal meaning of the term. They include Giordano Bruno (1548–1600) and Lucilio Vanini (1584–1619), both burned as heretics for rejecting ecclesiastical authority and scriptural revelation; Barukh Spinoza (1632–1677); François-Marie Arouet (Voltaire; 1694–1778); Jean-Jacques Rousseau (1712–1778); Hermann Samuel Reimarus (1694–1768); Gotthold Ephraim Lessing (1729–1781); Moses Mendelssohn (1729–1786); and Immanuel Kant (1724–1804). (Both Voltaire and Kant, however, repudiated the label "Deist" and always described themselves as "Theists.") There were outspoken Deists among the founding fathers of the United States of America, notably Benjamin Franklin (1706–1790), Thomas Paine (1737–1809), and Thomas Jefferson (1743–1826).

Deism appears to be exclusively a seventeenth- and eighteenth-century phenomenon, but this is partly an illusion. There are special reasons why the term *deism* attained currency then but did not survive longer. The rise of modern science did not immediately initiate warfare of science with religion, but it did initiate warfare within religion, between the orthodox who held fast to tradition, authority, and the supernatural, and the freethinkers, who sought a religion that harmonized with nature and reason. A term was needed by the orthodox to distinguish the freethinkers from themselves, and by the religious freethinkers to distinguish themselves from mere atheists. *Deism* served both needs. The term has fallen into disuse in the past two centuries, however, perhaps chiefly because in nineteenth- and twentieth-century philosophical and religious thought the distinctions between reason and tradition, nature and supernature, have lost the sharpness they had for thinkers of the seventeenth and eighteenth centuries. Greater tolerance of diversity of opinion within Christian society has also lessened the need for an epithet whose principal function was to scourge independent thinkers. Deism itself has also become a less popular position, owing to the increasing tendency of rationalists to become simple unbelievers rather than to settle for compromises and half-measures. Yet deism—in fact, if not in name—still survives in all religious communities and individuals whose convictions arise from autonomous thinking rather than from the submission of reason to ecclesiastical or scriptural authorities.

SEE ALSO Bruno, Giordano; Doubt and Belief; Enlightenment, The; Kant, Immanuel; Lessing, G.E.; Mendelssohn, Moses; Reimarus, Hermann Samuel; Rousseau, Jean-Jacques; Spinoza, Barukh; Theism.

BIBLIOGRAPHY

An excellent nineteenth-century account of British Deism is to be found in Leslie Stephen's *History of English Thought in the Eighteenth Century*, vol. 1 (1876; reprint, New York, 1963). A detailed account of Deistic thinkers is presented by J. M. Robertson in *A History of Freethought, Ancient and Modern*, vol. 2, *To the Period of the French Revolution*, 4th ed. (London, 1936). For the social background of Deism, see W. K. Jordan's *Development of Religious Toleration in England*, 4 vols. (1932–1940; reprint, Gloucester, Mass., 1965). Two very good studies of aspects of Deism are Norman L. Torrey's *Voltaire and the English Deists* (1930; reprint, Hamden, Conn., 1967) and Ernest C. Mossner's *Bishop Butler and the Age of Reason* (New York, 1936). Perhaps the two most classic works on religion by thinkers identified above as Deists are Barukh Spinoza's *Tractatus theologico-politicus* (1670), translated by R. H. M. Elwes in *Chief Works*, vol. 1 (1883; reprint, New York, 1955), and Immanuel Kant's *Religion within the Limits of Reason Alone* (1793), translated by Theodore M. Greene and Hoyt H. Hudson (LaSalle, Ill., 1960).

ALLEN W. WOOD (1987)

DEITY.

DEITY. As a symbol, deity represents the human struggle at its highest; it represents humanity's effort to discover its identity in confrontation with the limits of its universe. Deity is the symbol of what transcends the human being and the symbol of what lies hidden most deeply within. While other creatures merely accept their environments as a given, human beings exist as such only when they realize both their solidarity with the universe and their distinction from it. In the journey toward self-identity humanity encounters deity. In a cross-cultural context, deity symbolizes the transcendence of all the limitations of human consciousness and the movement of the human spirit toward self-identity through its encounter with the ultimate. Deity symbolizes humanity's knowledge that it is not alone nor the ultimate master of its fate. And yet this knowledge, dim though it may be, associates humanity with this same deity. Deity both transcends and envelops humanity; it is inseparable from humanity's awareness of its own identity and yet is always elusive, hidden, and for some, seemingly nonexistent.

THE POLYSEMY OF THE WORD. *Deity* is a word with a diversity of meanings. It is an ambiguous and often polemical word. The different interpretations that it has been given show that it is also a relative word.

Ambiguity. The word *deity* is ambiguous. It is not a proper name. It is not even a common name, since its possible referents are hardly homogeneous. It is the product of many and heterogeneous abstractions. Most names referring to divine beings or the divine were originally common names singled out in a peculiar way. What was general became specific, concrete, and, like a single being, evocative of emotion. Thus *Allāh* probably comes from *al-illah*, that is, "the God." *Ńinyi* or *Nnui*, the name for God among the Bamum of Cameroon, means "he who is everywhere"—and thus is at once concrete and elusive. *Yahveh* means "he who is" (or "he who shall be"), which becomes being par excellence for Christian Scholasticism. *Śiva* means "auspicious, benign, kind"—what for the Śaivas represents the highest symbol of the deity stripped of any attribute.

In short, there are gods called Allāh, Nnui, Yahveh, Śiva; but there is no god called Deity. One worships Viṣṇu, or even the Buddha, but one does not worship deity as such. One may worship only a particular deity. We often speak of "major" and "minor" deities in religious traditions. The word *deity,* in short, has a higher degree of abstractness than does the word *God.*

In Western antiquity, in the Middle Ages, and up to the present, *deity* in its adjectival or pronominal form is a word applied to creatures and used without theological misgivings. Works and persons are called "divine" and "deities" because they share in deity in a way in which they would not be said to share in God. Spiritual writers or popular heroes are called "divines" in many languages. The word simply denotes a character of (divine) excellence, which can be shared by many creatures.

The word *god* was also originally a common name, but soon became the proper name of the one God of the theists (and also of the atheists, for many atheists are merely antitheists; both live within the mythic horizon of the one personal God, accepting or rejecting it). By extension scholars speak of the African gods, discuss the nature of a supreme god, and the like.

At any rate, *deity* is not identical with *god.* One does not believe in deity in the individualized sense in which one may believe in God. Yet one may accept that there is something referred to by the word *deity.* The referent will always retain a certain mystery and show certain features of freedom, infinity, immanence, transcendence, or the like. For others, this mysterious entity becomes the highest example of superstition, primitivism, unevolved consciousness, and a pretense for exploiting others under the menace of an awesome and imaginary power. The ambiguity of the word is great.

Polemical usage. At the same time *deity* is also a polemical word. It has sometimes stood against some conceptions of God without rejecting the divine altogether. The philosophical Deism of the last centuries in Europe, which developed a concept of the divine more congenial to the natural sciences emerging at the time than to the idea of a personal god, could serve as an example. The deity of the Deists was to substitute for and correct the *theos* of the theists without discarding the belief in the existence of some supreme being or first cause. Yet this polemic was not new to the eighteenth century. The prolific Greek writer-priest at Delphi, Plutarch of Chaeronea (c. 46–c. 119 CE), our first source for the word *theotēs,* uses it in his polemic against the mythological interpretations of historical heroes as they appeared in the work of Euhemerus of Messina (fl. 300 BCE). In the New Testament this word, in the only passage in which it appears (*Col.* 2:9), is translated by the old Latin *deitas,* whereas the Vulgate uses the more current *divinitas*—a word unknown before Cicero (106–43 BCE). In the *Letter to the Romans* 1:20 we find the word *theiotes* derived from the adjective *theios* and also translated as *divinitas* in the Vulgate.

Deity is not only polemical in regard to a personal conception of God. It is polemical also as a symbol of the political use of the divine. We should not forget the wars of religion, the attempted legitimation of power and use of violence in the name of God, gods, and divinity, nor the justification of so many ideologies by slogans such as "In God we trust" or "*Gott mit uns.*" Deity has been all too often the cause of strife and war, sometimes under the guise of peace.

Relativity. From the perspective of a sociology of knowledge, the modern use of the word *deity* could be interpreted as the Western effort to open up a broader horizon than that of a monotheistic God but without breaking continuity with tradition. *God* was a common name. It became a proper name: the Abrahamic God. And it was then that this *God* came to designate the one God, which Muslims or Christians wanted to propagate around the world. All others were "mere" gods or, at most, inappropriate names for the true God. It is interesting to see how Western scholarship today tries to disentangle itself from its monolithic and colonial mentality. Is the word *deity* the last bulwark of this attitude?

We may draw two opposing conclusions from the paradoxical fact that this word denotes both the most communicable and the most exclusive aspects of the "divine" reality: everything that is shares a divine character, and nothing—no thing—that is can be said to embody or exhaust the divine, not even the totality of those things that are. In sum: the word says everything, every thing, and nothing, no thing. One legitimate conclusion from this ambiguity may be that one should avoid the word altogether or speak of deities in the plural as special superhuman (divine) entities.

There is another possible conclusion, however. Precisely because of its polysemic nature, this word may become a fundamental category for the study and understanding of religion. The subject matter of religion would then be related to deity, and not just to God or to gods. Polysemy does not need to mean confusion. It means a richness of meanings, a variety of senses. *Deity* could then become a true word, that is, a symbol not yet eroded by habit, rather than a univocal concept.

I should now try to describe the field of the symbol "deity" and study its structure. Regarding its field I shall analyze the means of approach to this symbol in its broadest aspect. Then, I shall examine the structure of deity by analyzing the different avenues, contexts, and perspectives under which deity has been studied. I shall then mention the structure of human consciousness when referring to deity. I shall further briefly compare deity with other equally broad categories in order to get a more accurate picture, and finally I shall try to summarize my findings.

AN APPROACH TO DEITY. This article does not deal primarily with the concept of God as it is generally understood in the Western world, and therefore it is not necessary to discuss, for instance, atheism or the nature of God. Further, this essay's cross-cultural perspective requires that the viewpoints of other cultures be integrated with our own instead of simply reported. Still we are engaged in what is predominantly a Western activity: taking a perspective from one tradition (as betrayed by the very use of the word *deity*) and expanding it in order to achieve a more universal viewpoint.

Linguistic background. Johann Gottlieb Fichte (1762–1814) provides us with a caution: "Deity appears only in the highest performance of thinking." We must keep in mind at the very outset that discourse about deity is unique, because the locus of deity is beyond both the things of the senses and the things of the intellect. Yet the way to deity belongs to the dynamism of our intellect. This is expressed in the first sentence of the *Brahma Sūtra:* "Athāto brahmajijñāsā" ("Now therefore the desire to know *brahman*"). The text refers to the "desiderative knowledge" or the "knowing desire" (*jijñāsā*), which arises out of an existential situation (*atha*). It liberates us from the weight of selfishness (*ahaṃkāra*), permitting us to soar in the search for deity. The process follows both an existential and an intellectual path, with no separation between pure and practical reason. Deity is as much at the beginning as at the end of the human quest—and also in between. The search requires purity of mind, strength of will, and a change of life.

While speaking of deity we have already had occasion to refer to God, and we now introduce *brahman.* Do all these words designate the same "thing"? Or have they at least the same meaning?

Brahman is certainly not the one true and living God of the Abrahamic traditions. Nor can it be said that Shang-ti or *kami* are the same as *brahman.* And yet they are not totally unrelated. Can we affirm that all those names refer to deity as a broad category? Is *deity* perhaps the common name for God, the godhead, the divine, *brahman, mana,* and so forth?

To begin with, it must be stressed that *brahman* and God, for instance, are not the same. The one is passive and does not need to care, it is at the bottom of everything and is the very condition of possibility for all that there is. The other is active and provident; it is above everything, personal, the creator of all that is. But they are not so different as to make the translation of the one by the other totally inaccurate. The Christian Scholastics, while affirming the ineffability of divine names, did not deny that some names are more applicable than others. We shall call *brahman* and God homeomorphic equivalents, because they perform corresponding yet different functions in their respective systems.

It is tempting to use the word *deity* as an abstract noun for all such homeomorphic equivalents. *Deity* would then refer to God, *kami, brahman,* Zeus, Rudra, Tien, the Dao, El, Baal, Urðr, Re, Kālī, and so on. This enterprise is relatively simple as long as we remain within more or less homologous cultures, making it easier to find common properties like infinity, omniscience, goodness, immutability, omnipotence, simplicity, unity, and so on. But when we attempt to include such properties as futurity, nothingness, or illusion, we find that these attributes are not at all common and are incompatible with the previous ones. In point of fact there is no common structure other than the purely formal one of being a vague something different from and perhaps superior to human beings, and sometimes only apparently so. Deity would then be a purely formal concept with no significant content whatsoever.

We may note the tendency, especially common to the West, to universalize what is familiar, as in the following sentences: "The Christian God is an absolute value for all; modern technology is fit for the entire world; the natural sciences are universally valid; truth is universal." We shall have to avoid such pretension if we are to take other cultures as seriously as we take Western cultures. The word *deity* cannot encompass all that other traditions have said about what in one group of cultures can be rendered by *deity.* Were we to use the term *brahman* or *kami* instead of *deity,* our meaning would change. The context being different, the results would also be different. Thus we must be careful in making extrapolations and avoid generalizations that are not warranted by the self-understanding of the different cultures of the world.

With these preliminary warnings in mind, we may now examine the distinction between God and deity. This distinction was known to medieval Christianity and was given clear expression by Meister Eckhart in his distinction between the godhead and God. The godhead, or deity, is as far from God as heaven is from earth. Deity is here the inner and passive aspect of the divine mystery and is related to the *deus absconditus* that was much commented upon during the patristic period. God, on the other hand, would be the outer and active aspect of the same mystery. Be this as it may, however, we will use the word *deity,* in distinction to *godhead,* to mean not just God's essence (as in Thomas Aquinas) or the "God beyond God" or the ground of God (as in Eckhart), but simply that divine dimension elusively present everywhere, which only our highest thinking performance can glimpse and which is the goal of our existential human quest.

Deity, then, not only may denote God or gods as substantial beings but also may be used as a generic name connoting all those forces, energies, entities, ideas, powers, and the like that come from "above" or "beyond" the human realm. In this sense *deity* represents the element of reality that belongs neither to the material world nor to the merely human realm but is above or beyond the sensible and intellectual order. *Deity* may thus stand for one of the three dimensions of reality that practically all human traditions reveal. First, there is the realm of heaven: the gods, the superhuman powers, the supraintelligible. Then there is the realm of the human: consciousness, ethics, life, mind, the intelligible, and so forth. And finally, the realm of the earth: the cosmic, the material, the spatiotemporal reality, the sensible, and so on.

We cannot proceed further in the study of the human approach to deity until we examine the nature of the "thing" we are trying to investigate. It is irrelevant now whether the world of deity is the paradigm of the human world, in which case the latter would be only a shadow of the real, or whether on the other hand the divine universe is only a projection of the unfulfilled desires of humans. The fact remains that the human experience crystallized in language witnesses to the existence of such a divine world, be it populated by *daimones* or by *theoi*, by *devas*, *elohim*, spirits of all types, the one God, or by nobody. Have we a common name to designate that universe? Can we say that this is the world of deity? For this we need a historical interlude.

Historical background. How have human beings come to the notion of deity? For some scholars this notion has been the result of an inference of some type of causal thinking. Deity is then a supreme being or beings, of a celestial or other type. The human question about the origin of life, the world, and the like triggers the search for a cause that then will be "located" in whatever place appears to be more appropriate for the dwelling of a supreme being or beings, whether in the heavens or in the earth. Others would see the origin of deity not so much in the intellectual quest as in the existential anxiety of the human being facing the elemental mysteries of life and nature. Still others have seen the search for deity as based neither on causal thinking, nor on anxious feeling, but on simple awareness.

For others deity is the disclosure of a supreme being through its own initiative, which explains why man has come to the idea of deity. If such a supreme being exists, even if its "revelation" is progressive and related to the intellectual development of the peoples concerned, it is always from that power that the first step comes.

Contemporary discussions are the aftermath of that great controversy of past decades about the origin of the idea of God, a controversy that resulted from the conflict of the emerging theory of evolution with traditional beliefs in God. Wilhelm Schmidt (1868–1954), rejecting the evolutionary scheme, searched for traces of a primitive revelation of a "primordial monotheism" among primitive peoples. Schmidt was elaborating the insights of Andrew Lang (1844–1912), who had argued for the existence of a belief in supreme beings among archaic peoples, in opposition to the then pervasive theory of primitive animism, represented by E. B. Tylor (1832–1917). Finally, atheistic movements—scientific, dialectical, or historical—will make of deity a superfluous hypothesis, an artificial tool for the subjection of humans, an undue extrapolation of our present ignorance, a mere illusion to console us in the midst of our impotencies.

It seems fair to say that the most universal, primordial human experience is neither monotheistic, nonatheistic, nor polytheistic but rather a deep-rooted belief in a divine world, a world populated by different kinds of superhuman beings or forces. Whether those beings are one or many, whether they represent a polytheistic hierarchy or an *Urmonotheismus*, is not the most important point. What is most important is that these beliefs express a human experience that says that man is not alone in the universe and that the sensible world is not all there is to reality. This is made clear not only by innumerable oral traditions and written texts in nearly every culture but also by the existence of a veritable jungle of names for the divine. All human languages have an enormous treasure of words denoting the super- or extrahuman realm.

It belongs to a second moment of human reflection to try to put order into that world, to assign to it its degree of reality, to decide what kind of hierarchy reigns there, and to elucidate the relationship of that world with the human world and the rest of the universe. One does not prove the existence of deity in a primordial civilization. The gods are simply there.

The Structure of Deity. Historical investigation is only a part of the question about deity. How people have come to this idea is less important than the structure of the idea itself. This structure is not an "objective" datum, however. It is in part a function of human interest. We have here an example of how any human enterprise is motivated and conditioned by human interests and prevailing myth. Because deity has no detectable referent outside human consciousness, its structure depends in part on one's opinions about it and on those of any human consciousness for which the notion makes sense. In other words, what deity *is* is inseparable from what people have believed it to be.

We must try then to make sense of the ideas and experiences humankind has had on the subject. For this we must attempt to understand the context in which the problem has been put. This leads us to distinguish between the methods that can be employed to elucidate the question and the horizons within which the problem of deity is set. The main methods are theological, anthropological, and philosophical. These methods are all interrelated, and distinguishing them is really a question of emphasis. The possible horizons of the problem consist of the presuppositions that we make about what we are looking for when we set about asking about deity and its origins. Horizons are a function of our universe and of the myths we live by. I shall distinguish three such horizons. Combining these with the methods just mentioned would give nine different sets of notions about deity. Brevity requires, however, that I do not develop these nine representations of the divine. I will describe only the three fundamental horizons that predetermine the question of deity.

Horizons. In order to understand what kind of deity we are talking about, it is essential to reflect on the horizon of the question. Is the deity to be conceived as absolute consciousness? As a supreme being? As the perfect, ideal individual? Or as the creator of the world? In short, where do we situate the divine? Where is the locus of deity? The horizons are, of course, dependent on the culture of any given time or place. Viewed structurally, however, the function of deity always seems to provide an ultimate point of reference. We may situate this point outside the universe or at its center, in the depths of man (in his mind or heart), or simply nowhere. Cosmology, anthropology, and ontology offer us the three main horizons.

Metacosmological. The human being in ancient times lived facing the world. The main concern was the universe as a human habitat. Humanity's vision is directed toward things in heaven and on earth. The horizon of deity is precisely this universe, but not just as one thing among others.

The locus is metacosmological. Deity is here related to the world. Certainly, it may be identified as immanent to the world, or more probably transcendent to it, but deity is the deity of the world, and the world is the deity's world. What type of function or functions deity is supposed to perform and what kind of relation it has with the world are left to the different cosmologies and traditions. In any case, deity is a kind of pole to the world, a prime mover that sets the world into motion, sustains it, directs it, and even creates it. A temporal metaphor can be used to say the same thing. In this case, the deity is represented as the beginning, present before the big bang, or at the end of the evolution of the physical universe, as the omega point. Or the deity may be both alpha and omega, at the beginning and at the end of the universe. The most common name for this deity is "God," whether this be Varuṇa, "supreme lord, ruling the spheres" (*Ṛgveda* 1.25.20), or Yahveh who "made heaven and earth" (*Gn.* 1:1). This God is "that from which truly all beings are born, by which when born they live, and into which they all return" (*Taittirīya Upaniṣad* 3.1). This God is the *pantokratōr* of many traditions, Eastern and Western. Even the *deus otiosus* belongs to this group. Deity is here a metacosmological category. Its most salient feature is its infinity. The world we experience is contingent, and all things are transient, finite. Only the deity is infinite.

Meta-anthropological. At a certain moment in history the main interest of humanity was no longer nature or the world outside, above and mysterious, but humanity itself. Humanity's visions were directed toward the inner recesses of the human spirit: the feelings, the mind. The locus of deity is here the human realm, but not just a human field made wider. It has to be deeper as well. The locus is meta-anthropological.

Here deity is seen as the symbol for the perfection of the human being. The notion of deity does not come so much as the fruit of reflection on the cosmos or as an experience of its numinous character as it does from anthropological self-awareness. Deity is the fullness of the human heart, the real destiny of man, the leader of the people, the beloved of the mystics, the lord of history, the full realization of what we really are. This deity does not need to be anthropomorphic, although it may present some such traits. Deity is here *ātman-brahman*, the fully divinized man, the Christ, the *puruṣa*, or even the symbol of justice, peace, and a happy society. Here deity may be considered immanent or transcendent, identified with or distinguishable from man, but its functions are related to the human being. It is a living, loving, or menacing deity, inspiring, caring, punishing, rewarding, and forgiving. In this deity all pilgrimage ends, all longing disappears, all thoughts recoil, and all sin is blotted out. The deity is a meta-anthropological category.

The vexed problem of divine personality belongs here, as do psychological analyses of human belief in deity. The most salient feature of this horizon, however, is the attribute of freedom. The deity is here freedom itself, liberating man from his often painful limitations. Modern theologies of liberation belong here, as does the notion of a god acting in history.

Meta-ontological. We are told that the culmination of man's development is self-awareness. The power of reflection makes *Homo sapiens* the superior being that he believes himself to be. The locus of the deity here cannot be just a superman or a ground of the world. It has to be a superbeing. The locus is meta-ontological.

Humanity is proud of the human power of abstraction. Deity is here not only beyond the physical world but also outside any natural realm, including that of the human world, the intellect, the desires, and the will. Deity is totally above and beyond nature, including human nature. The transcendence or otherness of deity is here so absolute that it transcends itself, and thus it can no longer be called transcendence. Deity does not exist; it is meta-ontological, beyond being. It is not even nonbeing. The apophatism is absolute. The deity neither is nor exists, nor is it thinkable or speakable. Silence is the only proper attitude toward it, not because we are incapable of speaking about it, but because silence is what befits it. This silence neither hides nor reveals. It is silence because it says nothing, there being nothing to say. Possible names for this deity are *śūnyatā*, Neither Being nor Nonbeing, Huperon, and so on. Deity is here a meta-ontological reality. Seen from below, as it were, it belongs to the unthinkable. Seen from within, it belongs to the unthought. To think about it would be idolatry.

Here we encounter the problem of the nothingness of deity, the radical apophatism developed in many traditions. The most salient feature here is immanence and transcendence, the two belonging together. Deity is the immanence and transcendence inserted in the heart of every being.

We should hasten to add that these three horizons are not mutually exclusive. Many a thinker in many a tradition has tried to elaborate a conception of deity embracing all three. Within Hinduism, for instance, *nirguṇa brahman* would correspond to the third type, *saguṇa brahman* to the first, and *īśvara* might be the personal deity of the devotee. Similarly, the Christian Scholastic tradition would like to combine God, the prime mover (the first type), with the personal God of the believers (the second type), and that of the mystics (the third type). How far all three can be reduced to an intelligible unity is a philosophical and theological problem that different traditions try to solve in different ways.

The morphological traits of deity may be summarized according to these three horizons, suggesting a threefold structure for deity. The ultimate experience of the meta-ontological deity is the character of the "I." Deity is the ultimate "I," the final subject of activity. "Who am I?" The "I" who can respond to this question without further questioning is the ultimate "I," the deity.

The meta-anthropological deity represents the experience of the "thou." In the human urge toward the deity this latter appears as the ultimate "thou" with whom dialogue and human relations can be established.

The deity as the ultimate cause and prime mover of the world is the "he, she, or it" that only an inference discloses. One speaks of this deity always in the third person.

Methods. We may now turn to the different methods used in the attempt to understand deity. Whatever deity may be, it is neither a sensible nor an intelligible thing. The deity is neither a visible thing nor a mere thought. Modern hermeneutics speaks of "pre-understanding" as a necessary condition of understanding, of a "hermeneutical circle" that is needed in all interpretation. Within the realm of sensible or intelligible objects we may be able to ascertain what pre-understanding is. We acquire an idea of the whole, which we may modify while investigating the parts. It is on the basis of this pre-understanding that a given method is applied to understanding an object. But how can this be done in the case of deity? If every method implies a proleptic jump into the alleged object, a coming back to our starting point, and a methodical process afterward, it is difficult to see how such a method can be applied in our attempt to understand deity. We do not know in which direction we should make the first jump nor with what instruments to approach it—unless we start from the received tradition or with an authentic mystical experience. This amounts to saying that we renounce finding a method of searching for deity and replace it by methods of research, interpreting the opinions of people about it. We know, further, that if we start with some "instruments," the results will greatly depend on the nature of those instruments. We can then neither jump (if we do not know the direction) nor come back (if the subject matter is beyond the senses and the intellect). In a word, the method for seeking the deity is sui generis—if indeed there is a method at all.

How do we come to a pre-understanding of deity? We may receive it from tradition. In the case of a direct mystical experience there is not a pre-understanding but an immediate insight that the mystic afterward explicates in terms of the culture in which he or she lives, and so ultimately it comes to the same thing. The mystic needs a post-understanding, as it were, in terms of his or her time and culture, which amounts to an initial pre-understanding for all the others. The pre-understanding of deity is, therefore, a traditional datum. Now, there are three main attitudes toward this datum. If one accepts it as a starting point and proceeds to a critical effort at understanding it, this is the *theological method.* The theologian tries to clarify something from within. If one tries to bracket one's personal beliefs and attempts to decipher the immense variety of opinions throughout the ages regarding the idea of deity, this is the *phenomenological method.* The datum is then the sediment of the history of human consciousness. Finally, if one reflects on one's own experience, enriched as much as possible by the thoughts of others, this is the *philosophical method.*

These methods are not mutually exclusive, and all three play a role in the human quest for deity. All are required and they imply each other. We distinguish between them for heuristic reasons only. Each one presents divisions and subdivisions. Sociology, psychology, anthropology, and so forth are among the important disciplines within these three approaches, each with its own particular methods.

We refer to methods in the plural, for there is not one single theological, phenomenological, or philosophical method. Each of these approaches presents a variety of methods. What we describe here is only a general pattern of methods, which acquire a proper physiognomy when applied to particular cases.

Theological. The theological method begins with an accepted datum: there exists a world of the gods, the world of deity. We will therefore have to clarify and eventually justify the raison d'être of such a world, but we do not necessarily have to prove its existence. In short, the origin of the idea of deity is the deity itself—whatever this deity may be. This forms the core of the so-called ontological argument and of any religious enterprise that wants to clarify the nature of deity. Deity could not be known if it did not exist. The theological problem here consists of determining what kind of existence this is. When Thomas Aquinas, for instance, ends each one of his five proofs for the existence of God by saying "and that is what all call God," he shows his theological method of clarifying the existence of something that we already call God. The deity was already there, certainly, as an idea, but also as a reality that hardly anyone doubted, although its rationality had to be demonstrated and its existence verified as real and not merely apparent. Theological proofs thus presuppose faith and only prove that such faith is rational. They are a form of *fides quaerens intellectum* ("faith seeking understanding").

We have already indicated that each combination of method and horizon yields a distinct picture of deity. In fact, theological methods have been mainly combined with the cosmological and the ontological horizons. They have been less conversant with the anthropological one, and this explains the uneasiness in theological circles when dealing with the emerging sciences of man, like psychology and sociology. The theological dialogues with Freud, Jung, and Weber are typical examples. There are serious studies on the psychology and sociology of religion, but little attention has been given to the psychology and sociology of deity from a theological perspective. Hans Urs von Balthasar's work on a theology of aesthetics is a notable exception.

Phenomenological. The phenomenological method could also be described as morphological, or even historical, since it is used in the new science of religions, often called the history of religions. On the whole there is a consensus regarding the phenomenological method, as the study of people's beliefs drawn from their own self-understanding, as reflected in the critical consciousness of the scholar. Here is the place for a typology of the conceptions of deity. This method is important today, in a world in which people of different religions mingle in the concerns of daily life, that is, in the stresses of technological civilization.

Use of the phenomenological method uncovers an immense variety of types of deity. We find the so-called animistic conception of deity as an all-pervading and living force animating everything that there is. We find so-called polytheism, the presence of many "gods" as supernatural entities with different powers and functions. We find so-called deism as the belief in a supreme being, probably a creator, who is afterward passive in relation to his creation, a notion that excludes any kind of specially revealed god. We find monotheism of the type of the Abrahamic religions, religions of a living, provident, and creator god. We find the various theisms that modify the exclusiveness of the monotheistic model, and pantheism, the identification of the deity with the universe. We also find all sorts of atheisms, as reactions to theism and especially to monotheism. And of course we find a number of distinctions and qualifications of these broad notions that are intended to respond to the demands of reason or answer difficulties raised by particular or collective experiences.

These types, and the changes that they have undergone through the ages, have been the subject of many useful and comprehensive studies by well-known scholars like Mircea Eliade, Gerardus van der Leeuw, Geo Widengren, Kurt Goldammer, W. Bede Kristensen, and Friedrich Heiler. With the possible exception of Widengren, none of these authors uses the notion of God as a major religious category. Even Widengren, who emphatically wants to distinguish religion from magic, while affirming that "faith in God constitutes the intimate essence of religion," has a very large idea of what God means. All the others recognize that there is a particular sphere that is at the center of religious life.

Philosophical. The philosophical method proceeds differently, although, in ways, not totally disconnected from those of the previous ones. Pascal's famous *mémorial*, which was found stitched in his coat after his death, "The God of Abraham, the God of Isaac, the God of Jacob, not of philosophers and scholars," has since served in the West to emphasize this difference. Without entering into the discussion of whether the "living God" is the *actus purus* or whether one can fall in love with the prime mover, the quintessence of the philosophical method consists in the willingness to question everything. The philosophical method is that of the radical question, be it the question of salvation, *mokṣa*, happiness, or whatever form in which it may be conceived. It is within this framework that the question of deity appears. Here in a cloud either of knowledge or of unknowing, in a science of good and evil, lies the philosophical locus of deity. This locus is the ultimate question, even if there is no final answer.

When this ultimate locus is considered to be being, the question of deity turns out to be what Heidegger calls an "onto-theology," a reflection on the being of beings. Here, the philosophical method meets the historical controversy. Is deity the highest being or is it being as such? In the latter case it cannot be a supreme being. The ontological difference is not the theological one. The history of religions puts the same question by simply asking how the supreme being is related to the entire reality. This polarity between being and supreme being permeates most of the conceptions about deity. We could phrase it as the polarity between the deity of the intellectuals (being) and the deity of the people (supreme being). A more academic way of saying it is this: deity may appear as a result of a thinking reflection (discovering being) or an existential attitude (requiring a supreme being). For the former, deity is the subsisting being, source of being, the foundation, the being "being" in all beings. For the latter, deity is the supreme being, the lord, the divine person, the ultimate in the pyramid of reality. The former conception will have to clarify the relation between deity as a ground of being and an undetermined and general *ens commune*. The latter will have to define the relation between deity as *esse subsistens* and the rest of beings that the deity creates, rules, and directs.

Is deity being (*Sein, sat, esse*) or the supreme being (*höchstes Seiendes, paramatman, ens realissimum*)? One can think about the first, but one cannot worship it. One can adore the second and trust in it, but this God cannot be reasoned about; it is corroded by thinking.

If the philosophical locus of the deity is the ultimate question, we may find as many conceptions of deity as there are ultimate questions. Thus the many and varied answers. The diversity of religions can also be explained from this perspective. Religions give different answers to ultimate questions, and the questions themselves are different. But philosophical reflection may ask still further: what is it that prompts man to ask the ultimate question, whatever this question may be? Why is man an asking being, ever thirsty for questions?

In a word, the issue of the deity has to do with the peculiarity of man as a questioning animal. "God acts without a why and does not know any why," says Meister Eckhart. What prompts man to question is ultimately the consciousness of not being realized, of not knowing, of being finite. This consciousness can be expressed as the anthropological discovery that man is imperfect, still in the making; the cosmological observation that the universe is moving, that is, also still becoming; or the ontological thought of nothingness lurking over being. In sum, the problem of becoming emerges here as the theological problem par excellence. If becoming is possible, it is because being is still "being." What covers this gap between being and becoming (encompassing or not encompassing the two) is the locus of the deity: it keeps open the flow of being.

THE TEXTURE OF HUMAN CONSCIOUSNESS OF DEITY. The different perspectives on the human approach to deity that we have found end in a healthy pluralism: reality is itself pluralistic. We cannot, of course, encompass this plurality in a unified scheme of intelligibility on a universal scale. Yet if we keep in mind our particular situation in time and place and its various viewpoints and prejudices, we may venture some further valid considerations.

Our point of departure is the lost innocence of our present situation. Whatever deity may be, whatever peoples of other epochs have felt, thought, or believed about deity, even if they have told us that it was the deity itself who spoke to them, it remains always the conviction of contemporary man that all relation to deity takes place in and through human consciousness. This in no way weakens the reality or the objectivity of deity. It only affirms that human consciousness is always a fellow traveler in this journey. If we want to reach a consensus regarding the many opinions on the nature of deity, we shall have to fall back upon the texture of our consciousness, even while accepting that deity may be much more than an act or content of consciousness and that this consciousness may vary with time and place and even be shaped by the power of deity.

In view of the many opinions about deity we have to rely upon the one factor that is common to them all, namely the human consciousness that uses the word *deity* or its homeomorphic equivalents. Deity has this one constitutive feature: it is disclosed to us in an act of consciousness, an act of consciousness that, in spite of having a transcendent intentionality, has no verifiable referent outside of consciousness. The reference of the word *deity*, in fact, is neither visible nor intelligible, and yet every culture in the world witnesses to the fact that men constantly speak about a "something" that transcends all other parameters. We have then to rely on the cultural documents of the past and the present that witness to this *tertium* we call *deity*.

We rely on the fact that people have meant something when using this word or its equivalents. The analysis of deity is based therefore not on the empirical presence of the object nor on the immediate evidence of thought but on tradition in its precise and etymological meaning, that is, on some cultural good that is being transmitted to us. One exception seems to be the case of mystics, who say that they have directly experienced this extra-empirical and supra-intellectual reality. Yet the moment that the mystics speak they have to fall back upon their consciousness. The thought and speech of the divine belong to that unique field of human consciousness whose contents are disclosed in the very experience that has them and nowhere else. This explains the elusive character of the divine and also accounts for the fact that the question is more important than the answer.

Deity is visible only in its alleged manifestations—and there is no way to make visible the manifesting power beyond what is manifested. Nicholas of Cusa says pointedly that God is the invisibility of the visible world, just as the world is the appearance of the invisible God.

Nor is deity intelligible. It would cease to be divine if we could grasp its meaning as something belonging to the human or worldly sphere. The divine is not subject to observation, nor can there be a science of the divine. Thus Meister Eckhart says that we must transcend not only the things of the imagination but even those of the understanding.

Long before Śaṅkara, the Indian world made crucial the distinction between appearance and reality and recognized that the latter transcends both the senses and the mind. The short *Kena Upsaniṣad* is perhaps one of the best scriptural texts to underline the transcendence and immanence of the deity:

> That which cannot be expressed by words but by which the word is expressed . . . That which cannot be thought by the mind, but that by which, they say, the mind is thought . . . That which cannot be seen by the eye, but that by which the eyes have sight. . . . It is not understood by those who understand; it is understood by those who do not understand. (1.5ff, 2.3)

In sum, of the divine there is only *logos* ("word"): *theologia.* But it is a *logos* irreducible to *nous;* that is, it is a word only revealed in the experience itself. This does not allow us to conclude that the divine is just a subjective state of experience. All things are related to states of experience, but of all others we have a communicable referent; we can get at the *res nominis*, that is, at the thing named. This is not the case with the divine. The *res nominis* is in the *ratio nominis*, that is, in the meaning of the name itself. And this is what has made theological and religious disputes so uncompromisingly serious. The names of God are all we have. Considering names as mere labels of things (as in nominalism) is the proper procedure of modern science, but this method is not adequate if applied to deity. Without the names we have no way of reaching the referent.

The names of deity are also different from abstract names like justice and beauty. We may infer the meaning of justice by observing a certain pattern of behavior among people and acquire some sense of beauty by contrasting some of our experiences with similar ones of other people. Both human behavior and sensible objects fall in the category of commonly shared experiences. In other words, the referent in all these cases is verifiable outside of consciousness although not independent of it. This is not the case with deity. We cannot verify it as an object outside the field of our own consciousness, nor can we compare our states of consciousness as we can in the case of other abstract concepts. In this latter case we can point to the things or acts reflecting, revealing, or somehow defining the meaning we give to such words. In the case of deity we can certainly infer the idea people have of it from what they say and do, but there is one difference: a dimension of transcendence, of ineffability, inadequacy, ultimacy, or uniqueness, which necessarily leaves a gap between the manifested and its source. This is the reason why some traditions have postulated a special "seventh" sense related to the divine, which is neither reducible to the five senses nor to the "sixth" sense of the intellect.

Now, to affirm that all the names of deity mean ultimately the same thing assumes at the start that "our" name is the real one. We make of our conception of it, expressed in the name we give it, the pattern for all other conceptions. The name we give it would then name the "thing" that is supposed to have other names as well. This is not the case. Not everybody is looking for the same thing, either the ultimate cause, the ground of being, or absolute nothingness, if any of these is what we mean by deity. Much less are the worshipers of Kālī ready to give up their practice and worship Allāh, or true Christians ready to deny Christ and adore Caesar. Deity is not a Kantian "thing in itself." Words matter. The conception we have of deity is certainly not identical with its reality. But it is our way of access to it, which we cannot deny without betraying ourselves. Martyrdom for the sake of a name is a human fact not reducible to sheer fanaticism.

The name we give it, or the name anyone else gives it, does not exhaust the nature of deity. Strictly speaking we do not name it. We only refer to him, her, or it. Or we simply believe, call, pray, shout, dance, or whatever. Deity is not an object of naming but of invocation. Deity is what we appeal to, implore, and worship precisely because it is beyond our apprehending faculties.

In the Greek tradition *theos* is a predicative name. Things are divine, and a particular entity is godly. *Theos* is an attribute. God is not a concept but a name. But when the name loses its power no amount of conceptualization can give it back.

There has been a shift in the idea of deity from the predicate to the subject. This is a great revolution. In the West this could be said to represent the genius of the Abrahamic traditions. While many traditions say that light, love, or goodness is God, that is, divine ("Truth is God" was a slogan of Mohandas Gandhi), the New Testament reverses the sentence and affirms that God is light, love, or goodness. Something similar could be said of the great Upanisadic revolution: in the Upaniṣads we witness the passage of the god of the third person (the Vedic gods) to the god of the first person (*aham brahman*, "I am *brahman*") by means of the second person (*tat tvam asi*, "that thou art"). The revelation of the "I" dawns in the very realization of the aspirant to liberation; the "I" is not a third person (he, she, it, or even they). The language of the deity cannot be the third person. The deity has to be the first person. It is only the real "I" when it says "I," or rather when "I" says "I," and more exactly when I say "I." This is what is called realization—the realization of the I (by the I). Only the I can say "I."

At any rate the divine is so linked to our state of consciousness that there is no way of deciding what ontic status it has outside the ontological statement. Or, rather, the deity has no ontic status. An ontological statement has an accepted currency only with people who share in the same myth, one in which a particular form of the divine is taken for granted.

The claim to universality is the temptation of any complex and sophisticated culture. This aspiration to universality is built into human nature. But we often fail to recognize that we cannot make a claim for universality in our own terms, which are far from being universal.

Meaningful talk about the divine is thus restricted to those belonging to the same mythical sphere. Others will hear but not really understand. Each culture or subculture has a myth in which their particular form of the divine is possible and talked about. In this sense it cannot be generalized. It is restricted to those of the same faith, to the initiated. Properly speaking, we do not know what we are talking about when we refer to the divine. We are already taking it for granted, which is the function of any myth, that is, to offer the unquestioned horizon of intelligibility where our words are meaningful.

And yet the world of deity is an ever-recurrent world in the history of mankind. What do all these traditions refer to? If asked, believers might answer that the divine is not just a purely subjective state of consciousness; most will assert that they refer to the highest realm of reality, a realm so high that it is beyond the reach of human powers. And yet they continue to speak of it. It belongs to their myth. The myth is the locus of belief. It is only when pressed by those outside their group that they concede that there is no possibility of showing any referent in the world of common human experience. At most they may point to an homeomorphic experience if they have found a language of communication.

What is, then, the content of such an experience of deity? We have said that the content of the experience is inseparable from the experience itself, so that it cannot be "shown" outside the experience: the divine is neither sensible nor intelligible. Is there something else? Common sense and historical evidence say that of course there is something else, since everybody seems to speak about the divine in one form or another. The critical mind will say that it makes no sense to speak about something that we cannot think. That is why many a philosopher feels more comfortable calling the content of that experience nothingness. All theology ends by being apophatic.

From these considerations we may infer that there is something in human consciousness that points to something beyond, and yet we are unable to "locate" it outside that consciousness. God has been described as a "transcending center of intention" (John E. Smith). No wonder that many thinkers in both the East and West then identify deity with consciousness in its highest form. Others defend a sort of transcendental dynamism of human consciousness toward a superior and perfect form of consciousness, which they then call divine. Still others affirm that it is only a pathological growth of our own consciousness, triggered perhaps by fear of the unknown or fostered by religious priestcraft for the sake of power. Finally, while recognizing both the divine immanence of human consciousness and the human intentionality toward a divine transcendent consciousness, some do not dare to consider deity as the all-encompassing reality but only as a dimension of it. Reality is primary to consciousness.

Consciousness is always consciousness *of*, of reality, of being, even of itself. This last is the *noēsis noēseōs* of Aristotle, the absolute reflection of Hegel, and the *svayamprakāśa* ("self-illumination") of Vedānta. Now pure consciousness cannot be of anything, not even of itself. This is what lets Vedānta say that *brahman* is not even conscious of being *brahman*. It is Īśvara, the Lord, who is the full consciousness of *brahman*. Something similar could be said of the Father, the *plenitudo fontalis* of the Christian Trinity.

The Deity between God and the Sacred. Having tried to present the problematic of deity in its broadest aspect, we may ask whether speaking of "the divine" is not preferable to speaking of "deity." It may better describe what we are looking for, namely a super- or metacategory that can serve to express the religious phenomenon in its universality. In fact, *deity*, because its grammatical form is substantive, suggests a certain kind of substantialization that is inappropriate for many religious traditions, which we could call the *nāstikās* or *anātmavādins* (such as the Buddhists who say that there is no God because there is no substance). Thus, in spite of some modern efforts at adaptation, the Buddhist world, for one, feels uncomfortable with the word *deity*—although not, of course, with deities.

There is another category of similar generality that has often been presented as the center of the religious traditions of humankind. Every religion, we are told, deals with the sacred. It was Nathan Söderblom who, in 1913, described the notion of holiness as even more essential than the notion of God. For Söderblom, there is no real religion without a distinction between the holy and the profane. Mircea Eliade is today the most important spokesman for the centrality of the sacred as the religious phenomenon par excellence. But, we may ask, if the sacred is the central category of religion, what is the place and role of deity?

There is a danger in wanting to reduce the immense jungle of man's religious experience, as crystallized in the different religions of the world, to a single category or even to a single set of categories. Even if this were possible, its only purpose would be to give a panoramic and coherent picture of the whole. But what cannot be universalized is precisely the perspective of the observer. Let us assume that the sacred is a convincing category for understanding and describing religious phenomena. It would still be true that it is only a suitable category for us—that is, a very special class of readers in time and space. If our parameters of understanding change, then the perspective must also vary. In short, we cannot universalize our perspective, and a "global perspective" is obviously a contradiction in terms. There is thus room for more than one attempt to focus the religious experience of man. Let me try then to point out the locus of deity in the panorama of human religious experience and distinguish it from the sacred.

One feature seems to permeate all the varied meanings of deity: personality. Deity does not need to be a substance nor a person in the modern sense of the word. But on the other hand, *deity* does not denote merely a character of things, as does the word *sacred*. Deity is a source of action, an active element, a spontaneous factor: it is free. Its actions cannot be anticipated; it has initiative. We cannot deal with deity as with an object that we can imprison in the web of our thoughts. Deity has a mysterious quality of being able to act and not just react, to take the lead, even if in a purely passive way.

We should distinguish between personality and person on the one hand and person and substance on the other. We may recall that the concept of person in the West was developed not as a meditation on man but as a theological problem. To speak of the personality of deity is no more an anthropomorphism than is speaking of God as a supreme being, which some would call an anthropomorphism simply because man is also a being. Here the polemical aspect of the notion of deity comes to the fore. Almost everyone will admit that there is a third dimension in reality, since man and the world, as they are experienced by us, do not exhaust that other pole that is neither man nor the world as we experience them now. But not everyone is prepared to admit that this third pole has personality, that is, that it is endowed with freedom, is a source of action, has an identity, and is relationship.

In this sense, the concept of deity is not just the idea that there is a third pole in reality. Nor is it identical with the concept of God. It stands between the sacred and God. It shares with the former its immanence and with the latter its personality (in the sense we have indicated). But while the concept of God seems to imply a certain substance, the idea of deity does not need to present this characteristic. It says only that this third dimension is not a mere mental hypothesis, a piece of mental equipment necessary for making sense of reality or merely something to fill in the gaps in our understanding. The notion of deity affirms boldly that this other dimension is real, that is, active, free, efficacious, and powerful on its own account. But it does not make it independent of the two other poles and thus not even independent of our conceptions of it. In a word, deity connotes the highest form of life.

Conclusion. This cross-cultural approach to the mystery of deity has one liberating consequence. It liberates us from the many aporias that, for centuries, have tortured the human mind as it attempts to consider God as the supreme being. Among these are the questions: is it personal or impersonal? If almighty, how can it condone evil? If infinite, what is the place of finite beings? If absolutely free, why can it not make two and two equal five? If omniscient, what about human freedom? Subtle theological and philosophical answers have been put forward. But the answers could be made simpler by cutting the Gordian knot of a universal theory about God and rediscovering the divine as a true dimension of reality.

Whether the word *deity* means a plurality of divine beings, absolute consciousness, perfect happiness, the supreme being, a divine character of beings, or being as such, thought about deity has no referent. At the same time it seems to be one of the most unvarying and powerful factors in human life throughout ages and across cultures. Words referring to deity or its homeomorphic equivalents are unique. Philosophy avers that the intentionality of human consciousness, while pointing outside itself, cannot show in the realm of the sensible or the intelligible the referent of this intentional act. In a word, there is no object that is deity. Either human consciousness transcends itself, or thought about deity is an illusion, albeit a transcendental illusion of historical reality.

We should return now to one of our earlier queries. Is the word *deity* broad enough to include all the types of the mystery we have tried to describe? We know that its original field is the cosmological, but we have also noted that we distinguish it from the name *God* precisely to allow it other horizons.

The word *deity* may partially fulfill this role on one essential condition: that it strip itself of all connotations coming from a single group of civilizations. This amounts to saying that it cannot have any specific content, because any attribute, be it being, nonbeing, goodness, creatorship, fatherhood, or whatever, is meaningful only within a given cultural universe (or a group of them). Deity becomes then an empty symbol to which different cultures attribute different concrete qualifications, positive or negative. *Deity* would then say something only when translated into a particular language.

I am still critical of such an option, however, and would like to propose a compromise that may appear obvious once explained. Were this article to be translated into Chinese, Arabic, or Swahili, what word would we use to convey this idea of deity? Either we would coin a new name or use an old one with the connotations of the particular language. So we can say that for the English language *deity* may be a convenient name to use to transcend the provincial limits of certain groups of cultures such as the one that thinks, for instance, that Buddhism was not a religion and Confucianism only a philosophy because they do not accept the Abrahamic idea of God. But we should not elevate the word *deity* as the name for that metacategory. It is only a pointer toward the last horizon of human consciousness and the utmost limit of human powers of thinking, imagining, and being. Now, an abstract name like *the Ultimate* or a metaphor like *horizon* are equally dependent on particular cultural systems or ways of thinking. Perhaps the word *mystery* is more adequate, in spite of its Hellenic flavor. Or should we say *brahman, kami, numen...?*

At any rate we should insist that this does not mean that all those quests search for the same thing but in different places. The quest is different in each case, and so are the ways or methods involved. We leave open the question (ultimately as a pseudo-question) whether we use different methods because we look for different things or whether we find different answers because we use different methods. Both possibilities are intrinsically related, and their relation does not lie on the level of the *logos* but on the level of the *mythos*, as we have suggested. All our ways and means, all our quests and perspectives already belong not only to the searching but also to what is sought. Deity is not independent of our own search for it. If we radically destroy all the ways to the peak, the entire mountain will collapse. The slopes of the mountain also make the mountain.

Scholars may debate whether humankind is or is not monotheistic, whether a personal god is a universal truth or there actually is a creator, whether the so-called atheists are right in denouncing anthropomorphisms and dogmatisms of all sorts, whether there is a divine origin of this universe or a glorious or catastrophical Parousia. One thing seems to emerge as a cultural universal and a historical invariant: besides the world and man there is a third pole, a hidden dimension, another element that has received and is still receiving the most varied names, each name being a witness of its power and of the impotence of human beings to reduce everything to a common denominator.

The human being both individually and as a species is not alone. Man is not alone not only because he has an earth under his feet but also because he has a heaven above his head. There is something else, something more than what meets the eye or comes into the range of the mental. There is something more, a plus that humans cannot adequately name but that haunts them nevertheless. This plus is freedom and infinity. Deity stands for all that is unfinished (infinite) and thus allows for fulfillment in one sense or another. Man needs—and discovers—an opening, a way out of the strictures of the exclusively empirical or ideological affairs of daily life. The idea of deity can provide such an opening, provided that it can be kept free of any particular content. It would then become a symbol for the emerging myth of a human race that can no longer afford to transform cultural discrepancies into a cosmic tragedy.

SEE ALSO Anthropomorphism; Evolution, article on Evolutionism; God; Gods and Goddesses; Otherworld; Sacred and the Profane, The; Study of Religion; Śūnyam and Śūnyatā; Theism; Theology; Transcendence and Immanence; Truth.

BIBLIOGRAPHY

Balthasar, Hans Urs von. *Herrlichkeit.* Einsiedeln, 1961. A treatment of the topic from the perspective of a theology of aesthetics.

Balthasar, Hans Urs von. *Theodramatik.* Einsiedeln, 1978.

Castelli, Enrico, ed. *L'analyse du langage théologique: Le nom de Dieu.* Paris, 1969. Offers a philosophical perspective.

Eliade, Mircea. *A History of Religious Ideas*, vol. 1, *From the Stone Age to the Eleusinian Mysteries.* Chicago, 1978.

Gilson, Étienne. *God and Philosophy.* New Haven, 1941.

Heidegger, Martin. *Holzwege.* Frankfurt, 1950. Offers distinctions between concepts of God, deity, the sacred, and salvation.

James, E. O. *The Concept of Deity.* London, 1950. A historical treatment.

Kumarappa, Bharatan. *The Hindu Conception of the Deity as Culminating in Rāmānuja.* London, 1934.

Owen, H. P. *Concepts of Deity.* New York, 1971.

Panikkar, Raimundo. *The Unknown Christ of Hinduism.* Rev. & enl. ed. New York, 1981. See pages 97–155.

Panikkar, Raimundo. *Il silenzio di Dio: La risposta del Buddha.* Rome, 1985. An analysis of the Buddhist idea of the emptiness of deity.

Pettazzoni, Raffaele. "The Supreme Being: Phenomenological Structure and Historical Development." In *The History of Religions: Essays in Methodology,* edited by Mircea Eliade and Joseph M. Kitagawa. Chicago, 1959.

Pöll, Wilhelm. *Das religiöse Erlebnis und seine Strukturen.* Munich, 1974. See the chapter titled "Der göttlich-heilige Pol." A positive analysis of the divine/sacred from a psychological perspective.

Schmidt, Wilhelm. *Der Ursprung der Gottesidee: Eine historisch-kritische und positive Studie.* 12 vols. Munster, 1912–1955. A response to the evolutionary hypothesis concerning the concept of deity.

New Sources

Benard, Elisabeth, and Beverly Moon, eds. *Goddesses Who Rule.* New York, 2000.

Lang, Bernhard. *The Hebrew God: Portrait of an Ancient Deity.* New Haven, 2002.

Leeming, David, and Jake Page. *God: Myths of the Male Divine.* New York, 1996.

Maxwell, T. S. *The Gods of Asia: Image, Text, and Meaning.* Oxford, 1997.

Miles, Jack. *God: A Biography.* New York, 1995.

Smith, Mark S. *The Early History of God: Yahweh and the Other Deities in Ancient Israel.* San Francisco, 1990.

Stark, Rodney. *One True God: Historical Consequences of Monotheism.* Princeton, N.J., 2003.

Stroud, Joanne, ed. *The Olympians: Ancient Deities as Archetypes.* New York, 1996.

Wilkinson, Richard. *The Complete Gods and Goddesses of Ancient Egypt.* London, 2003.

RAIMUNDO PANIKKAR (1987)
Revised Bibliography

DE LAS CASAS, BARTOLOMÉ SEE LAS CASAS, BARTOLOMÉ DE

DE LA VALLÉE POUSSIN, LOUIS SEE LA VALLÉE POUSSIN, LOUIS DE

DELAWARE PROPHET SEE NEOLIN

DELITZSCH, FRIEDRICH (1850–1922), German Assyriologist.

Friedrich Conrad Gerhard Delitzsch was the son of the Old Testament scholar Franz Delitzsch (1813–1890). Both were men of extremely high linguistic ability, but in other respects they formed a striking contrast. The father was pious and conservative in theology, and although he was interested in Christian missions to the Jews, he was warmly appreciative of Judaism; the son became iconoclastic and contemptuous toward traditional doctrine and hostile to the entire dependence of Christianity upon Judaism.

The leading figure in the Assyriology of his time, Friedrich Delitzsch placed grammar and lexicography of the languages of ancient Mesopotamia on a sound and exact basis. In the area of biblical scholarship, his *Die Lese- und Schreibfehler im Alten Testament* (1920) provided an exhaustive classification of ways in which copying errors, such as writing one consonant in place of another, may have affected the text of the Hebrew Bible. His main influence on religious studies came with the "Babel-Bible" controversy. Advances in Assyriology had already made a difference to scholarship but had hardly affected the general public. Delitzsch's two lectures "Babel und Bibel" were delivered, in 1902, before the German Oriental Society and were attended by Kaiser Wilhelm II, who took an active interest in these matters. In the past, the Bible had been considered the oldest book: it was believed to reach back to the beginnings of the world. Now Assyriology presented new knowledge, knowledge that went back to an epoch much earlier than that of which the Bible had known. The similarity between the Babylonian and the biblical worlds was enormous. But this meant that the Old Testament material was not unique and could not count as pure revelation. The Babylonian material confirmed the antiquity of the biblical material but put in question its finality. In fact the Old Testament rose little above the religious and ethical level of Mesopotamian civilization.

By relativizing the authority of many elements within the Bible, the new discoveries made room for a conception of religion that was more in accord with "reason." Delitzsch insisted on the spiritual and universal nature of God as discerned, he thought, by the German Reformation. In this light, what Delitzsch considered the limited, parochial, and sometimes immoral world of the Old Testament could not continue to have authority. These ideas met with a storm of opposition. In his later work *Die grosse Täuschung* (The great deception; 1921), Delitzsch continued in the same vein but became more extreme. The Old Testament was a collection of fragments which had some literary and cultural value but had no relevance for Christianity. Christianity had as close a relation to paganism, Delitzsch claimed, as it had to Judaism, and he emphasized to an almost hysterical degree the "defects," "inaccuracies," and "immoralities" of the Old Testament.

Delitzsch was facing real problems in the existence of common ground between the Bible and its antecedent religious environment and of religious differences between some strata of the Bible and others. But the controversial stand he took was rooted more in modern ideological conflicts than in a dispassionate study of the ancient religions. His use of ancient evidence was often exaggerated and distorted, as when he argued that Jesus, being a Galilean, was not of Jewish blood and when he asserted that Jesus' teaching was "anti-Jewish." Similarly, Delitzsch's conception of Christianity draws from only a very narrow strand in the Christian tradition. As history of religion, his assessment of the data was intemperate, and his outbursts had the effect of retarding rather than advancing the cool assessment of the problems that Assyriological discovery had created for the relationship between Bible and religion.

BIBLIOGRAPHY

Delitzsch's controversial lectures were published in German as two books under the same title, *Babel und Bibel* (Leipzig, 1902–1903); the English edition, *Babel and Bible* (Chicago, 1903), contains not only the lectures but a selection from the comments they engendered, including those of Kaiser Wilhelm II and of Adolf von Harnack, along with replies by Delitzsch. *Die grosse Täuschung* (Stuttgart, 1921) appears never to have been published in English.

New Sources

Arnold, Bill T., and David B. Weisberg. "A Centennial Review of Friedrich Delitzsch's 'Babel und Bibel' lectures." *Journal of Biblical Literature* 121, no. 3 (Fall 2002): 441–457.

Larsen, Mogens Trolle. "The 'Babel/Bible' Controversy and its Aftermath." In *Civilizations of the Ancient Near East,* vol 1. New York, 1995.

JAMES BARR (1987)
Revised Bibliography

DELORIA, ELLA CARA (1889–1971). Ella Cara Deloria was born January 31, 1889, on the Yankton Sioux Indian Reservation in southeastern South Dakota. She was the daughter of the Reverend Philip Deloria, an Episcopal priest, and Mary Sully Bordeaux. Her parents were enrolled members of the Yankton Sioux tribe, and both were descended from Dakota (Sioux) and Euro-American ancestors. The year after Ella's birth, her father was given charge of St. Elizabeth's Mission in north-central South Dakota, on the Standing Rock Reservation. Because his parishioners and the children attending the mission school were primarily Hunkpapa and Blackfoot Tetons (Lakotas), the Deloria family adopted the *l* dialect of the Tetons in place of the *d* dialect of the Yanktons. Therefore, Deloria, although a Yankton, grew up speaking the Lakota dialect of the Sioux language.

Deloria's primary schooling was at St. Elizabeth's until 1902, when she attended All Saints, an Episcopal boarding school in Sioux Falls, South Dakota. In 1910 she entered Oberlin College, then transferred to Columbia Teachers College in 1913, where, two years later, she earned her bachelor of science degree. During her senior year at Columbia Teachers she met Franz Boas, professor of anthropology at Columbia University, who introduced her to the formal study of American Indian languages and cultures, thereby setting in motion the course of much of the rest of her life.

For the next thirteen years Deloria was involved in Indian education. She taught at All Saints from 1915 to 1919, worked for the YMCA supervising health education in Indian schools from 1919 to 1923, then taught dance and physical education at Haskell Indian school in Lawrence, Kansas. In 1927 Boas, finally learning Deloria's whereabouts, visited her to propose that she resume the Lakota language studies that she had begun with him in New York. She readily agreed. He proposed that she record "all the details of everyday life as well as of religious attitudes and habits of thought of the people" (Boas quoted in Deloria, 1988, pp. 235–236). From 1928 until 1938, with support from Columbia University, Deloria studied the language, recorded stories and ethnographic material from Lakota elders throughout South Dakota, and translated historical texts written by tribal members. From 1939 until 1948 she continued to work as time allowed on the materials she had collected.

Deloria's collaboration with Boas himself culminated in a grammar of Lakota (Boas and Deloria, 1941). However, most of her studies were carried out under the supervision of Ruth Benedict, a cultural anthropologist who was Boas's assistant and colleague. After Boas's death in 1942, Deloria continued to collaborate with Benedict until the latter's death in 1948.

One of the first projects Deloria undertook for Boas was the translation of a native language text on the Sun Dance, the most important traditional Lakota religious ceremony. A long and detailed account, it had been written in the early 1900s by George Sword, a religious leader among the Oglala Lakotas on the Pine Ridge Reservation in southwestern South Dakota. Deloria read the text aloud to an Oglala elder and with his guidance edited and retranscribed it. The text, printed in both Lakota and English, was her first professional publication (Deloria, 1929).

As a member of a prominent Episcopal family, Deloria had little familiarity with traditional Lakota religion, but she became very interested in it. She recorded a large number of myths and sacred stories, many of which have been published in Lakota and English (Deloria, 1932; Rice, 1992, 1993, 1994). While recording autobiographical texts from elders she learned a good deal about the individual's role in religious ceremonies, visions and other supernatural experiences, and conflicts between traditional religion and Christianity. Benedict pressed her to interview medicine men and record their visions, but this forced Deloria into a personal dilemma. Her father was a prominent missionary, and her younger brother, Vine V. Deloria, had followed in his footsteps and begun his career as a missionary at Pine Ridge. Showing undue interest in traditional religion jeopardized the family's reputation, and, in any case, traditional religious leaders were not comfortable sharing their sacred knowledge with a devout Christian, who might ridicule them. Deloria focused instead on the forms of ceremonies, starting with the Sun Dance. She hypothesized that all the Sioux groups shared common ceremonies but that each performed them in different ways. She worked for years on a study that would document the variations from group to group, but failed to complete it.

Deloria's *Speaking of Indians* (1944) was intended to introduce American Indians to a broad popular audience. In it, with great insight and empathy, she succinctly summarized her understanding of traditional religion. She considered the Lakotas before they had learned of Christian teachings to be naturally religious, "always subconsciously aware of the Supernatural Power. Before it they felt helpless and humble" (Deloria, 1944, p. 51). She exemplified this with an account of the Sun Dance, making the esoteric ritual comprehensible to the general public.

The concern with communicating to the public motivated Deloria to write an ethnographic novel, *Waterlily,* that told the story of three generations of women before the reservation period. It masterfully summarizes the important themes of her study of Lakota culture and is the only written source that explores the religious life of Lakota women. When she completed the book in 1948 she could not find a publisher; it was published posthumously (Deloria, 1988) and rapidly became the most widely read of her works.

After Benedict's death in 1948 Deloria struggled to continue her work and received a number of grants for studies of religion and social life. From 1955 to 1958 she returned to St. Elizabeth's Mission to run the school she had attended as a girl. A grant for work on a Lakota dictionary provided her a position at the University of South Dakota from 1962 to 1966. After retiring, she continued to live in Vermillion, South Dakota, until her death on February 12, 1971.

Deloria was the most prolific native scholar of the Lakotas, and the results of her work (much of which is still unpublished, archived in the American Philosophical Society Library, Philadelphia, and the Dakota Indian Foundation, Chamberlain, South Dakota) are an essential source for the study of Lakota religion.

See Also Lakota Religious Traditions; North American Indians, article on Indians of the Plains.

Bibliography

Boas, Franz, and Ella C. Deloria. "Dakota Grammar." *Memoirs of the National Academy of Sciences* 23, no. 2. Washington, D.C., 1941. The standard reference grammar of Lakota.

Deloria, Ella C. "Dakota Texts." *Publications of the American Ethnological Society,* vol. 14. New York, 1932. Comprises sixty-three Lakota stories (and one in Dakota) printed in the original as recorded by Deloria with word-by-word and free English translations.

Deloria, Ella C. *Speaking of Indians.* New York, 1944. Deloria's popular introduction to American Indians, including a succinct and insightful summary of Lakota culture.

Deloria, Ella C. *Waterlily.* Lincoln, Neb., 1988. An ethnographic novel focusing on three generations of Lakota women. Contains a biographical sketch of the author by Agnes Picotte

Murray, Janette K. "Ella Deloria: A Biographical Sketch and Literary Analysis." Ph.D. diss., University of North Dakota, 1974.

Rice, Julian. *Deer Women and Elk Men: The Lakota Narratives of Ella Deloria.* Albuquerque, 1992. A literary analysis of Deloria's Lakota stories and other writings.

Rice, Julian. *Ella Deloria's Iron Hawk.* Albuquerque, 1993. A bilingual presentation and literary analysis of a long, previously unpublished sacred story recorded by Deloria.

Rice, Julian. *Ella Deloria's The Buffalo People.* Albuquerque, 1994. A bilingual presentation and literary analysis of five previously unpublished stories recorded by Deloria.

Raymond J. DeMallie (2005)

DELPHI. The Delphic oracle was the most important oracle of ancient Greece. Archaeological excavations at Delphi have shown that the temple of Apollo, which was the center of the oracular activities, was not built before 750 BCE. It was a time of extensive Greek colonization, and one in which the oracle, for obscure reasons, managed to play an important role. This activity may well have been the decisive factor in establishing Delphi almost immediately as an authoritative oracle, and Homer's *Iliad,* most commonly dated to the eighth century BCE, already mentions the wealth of its votive offerings. Its geographical location, far from powerful Greek city-states, undoubtedly helped its rise to fame; for none of the consulting states had to fear that its rich presents would foster the development of a rival state. On the other hand, Delphi was not so remotely situated as the oracle of Dodona (in northwestern Greece), its older rival. The Delphic oracle's fame was highest in the Archaic period, when even kings from Lydia and Cyrene came for consultation.

Earlier studies went so far as to stress the role of Delphi in supporting new moral and religious values such as requiring purification following a murder, but the evidence for such Delphic initiatives is actually very slight. It is indeed hard to see why Delphi, unlike all other oracles, should try to influence its clients beyond their immediate needs. The famous sayings "Nothing in excess" and "Know thyself," which in the sixth century were fitted into the wall of the Delphic temple, reflect existing ideas rather than new ones. Both sayings exhort man to remain within his human limits—a common idea in Archaic Greek literature. It seems therefore more likely that the oracle, through its central position in Greek society, functioned as a sounding board that could amplify current religious conceptions and preoccupations.

The ritual of consulting the oracle was relatively simple. After making various sacrifices, consultants of the oracle had to enter the temple of Apollo where they presented their questions, orally or written on a tablet, to the priestess of Apollo, the Pythia. She was an older woman, whose age made it socially acceptable for her to mix in the company of men such as priests and ambassadors. At the same time, she was dressed as a girl; the conception of the Pythia as the bride of Apollo was at least hinted at in Delphic mythology. The priestess made her utterances seated on a tripod and holding a spray of laurel, but unfortunately we are not informed about the exact process whereby she arrived at her oracles. Later reports, both ancient and modern, mention prophetic vapors emerging from a chasm below the priestess, but this has been disproved by modern archaeological findings. Such reports were evidently rationalizing explanations of the Pythia's skill in giving oracles. Her voice was supposed to change when she responded to the inquiries, which seems to indicate an altered state of consciousness. At the "séance," special "prophets" were present who translated the Pythia's utterances into acceptable prose or hexameters. It is not known to what extent the consultants could influence the outcome of the oracle, but it seems clear that the opinion of powerful clients was regularly taken into consideration. The grateful consultants dedicated votive offerings to the god, and in the highly competitive Greek society the exhibition of these offerings encouraged a kind of potlatch in dedications: at the end of the fifth century, there were nearly thirty special buildings in which Greek cities displayed their dedications.

Many of the inquiries and the oracle's corresponding answers have been preserved, although a number of these answers are demonstrably forgeries—products of hindsight. Greek cities as well as individuals sought the oracle's advice on a wide range of religious, political, and private matters. The evidence shows that in general the oracle helped to decide between various alternatives rather than to predict the future; recourse to the oracle must often have been a convenient way of avoiding the risk of being blamed for the wrong decision.

Delphi's prestige remained high until the fourth century BCE, when it was looted and, perhaps more fatal, when Alexander the Great moved the center of the Greek world to the East. The rulers of the warring factions after Alexander's death (c. 323 BCE) had no time for embassies to Delphi. Although on a much lower level, the oracle continued functioning in Roman times when the prolific author Plutarch (c. 45–120 CE) was one of its priests; his two treatises *The Oracles at Delphi No Longer Given in Verse* and *The Obsolescence of Oracles* are a mine of information on Delphi's rich mythology and ritual. In the fourth century CE, Delphi still attracted the attention of Roman emperors, but the prohibition of all pagan cults in 392 by the Christian emperor Theodosius I also meant the end of this age-old institution.

SEE ALSO Oracles.

BIBLIOGRAPHY

The best survey of the history of the oracle, together with a collection of all the extant oracles, is H. W. Parke and D. E. W. Wormell's *The Delphic Oracle*, 2 vols. (Oxford, 1956). The oracles are translated and discussed, if in a sometimes too skeptical way, by Joseph Fontenrose in *The Delphic Oracle* (Berkeley, 1978). For recent, revisionary studies of the oracle see L. Maurizio, "Anthropology and Spirit Possession: A Reconsideration of the Pythia's Role at Delphi," *Journal of Hellenic Studies* 115 (1995): 69–86 and "Delphic Oracles as Oral Performances: Authenticity and Historical Evidence", *Classical Antiquity* 16 (1997): 308–34. R. C. T. Parker's "Greek States and Greek Oracles," in R. Buxton, (ed.), *Oxford Readings in Greek Religion* (Oxford, 2000), pp. 76–108 analyses the questions Greek states posed and the answers they received.

JAN N. BREMMER (1987 AND 2005)

DELUGE, THE SEE FLOOD, THE

DE MARTINO, ERNESTO.

An ethnologist and historian of religions, Ernesto de Martino (1908–1965) was born on December 1, 1908, in Naples, Italy, where he studied under Adolfo Omodeo, graduating with a degree in philosophy in 1932. His degree thesis, subsequently published, dealt with the historical and philological problem of the Eleusinian *Gephyrismi* (ritual injuries addressed to the goddess) and provides an important methodological introduction to the concept of religion. Clearly influenced by reading *Das Heilige* by Rudolf Otto, de Martino preferred to emphasize the choleric nature of the believer, overturning the German scholar's thesis and making it capable of being applied to relations with gods in polytheistic religions and spirits in animist religions. Attracted by the ideological stance of the regime, for several years de Martino worked on an essay interpreting Fascism as a historically convenient form of civil religion. However, the attempt was insubstantial and the work, still unpublished, was gradually rejected by the author. At this time, which we now call the "Neapolitan" period, lasting until 1935, de Martino fell under the spell of the personality and work of an archaeologist who was particularly open-minded concerning the ancient history of religions and who was disliked by both the regime and its intellectual opponents: Vittorio Macchioro, known for his Orphic interpretation of the frescoes in the Villa of Mysteries in Pompeii and advocate of a theory of religion understood essentially as experience.

De Martino moved to Bari, where he became a history and philosophy teacher at a *regio liceo.* He almost immediately had the opportunity to become part of the philosopher Benedetto Croce's circle and to move in an anti-regime environment. He slowly distanced himself from Fascism completely, so that in 1941 he was one of the founders of the Liberal Socialist Party. Meanwhile, he had singled out religious ethnology as his main subject of study and edited the essays that made up his first book (*Naturalismo e storicismo nell'etnologia,* printed in the 1940s by Laterza) and formed the basis of the research that would in time develop into his most famous work, *Il mondo magico.* In the first book, which is primarily methodological, de Martino set out an idealistic theory of ethnology, perhaps in a negative rather than positive sense, refuting those theories that appeared least appropriate to the understanding of magical religious phenomena, such as the prelogical thought of Lucien Lévy-Bruhl and the *Urreligion* of Father Wilhelm Schmidt. If the criticism of the Viennese school (highly regarded in Italy) seems somewhat expected today and in line with that already put forward by Raffaele Pettazzoni, the dispute with Lévy-Bruhl would develop fruitfully, in that de Martino ended up making use of his insight regarding "magic participation," not just in sociological but in ontological terms.

After September 8, 1943, he was at Cotignola (near Ravenna) with the partisan adherents of the Partito d'Azione (Party of Action), and it was during the course of that year, the low point of European civilization, that the central theory upon which *Il mondo magico* was based took shape. Extensive study of parapsychology and psychopathology led him to reconsider radically the problem of magic in primitive societies, hitherto neglected or avoided by ethnologists; in particular, paragnomic powers were interpreted by de Martino as useful and vital tools in a culture in which the individual is unable to separate himself from the world around him and continually risks vanishing. In this dramatic scene, which is centered upon the crisis of "presence" (perhaps a translation of Heidegger's *Dasein*), the sorcerer or shaman is someone who knows how to lose the presence voluntarily and regain it by ritual action, playing the part of actor and director in a collective drama, which allows the group to recover the energy that has been lost. Edited after the end of the war, the book was published in 1948, provoking discussion rather than agreement, but nonetheless marking the author as one of the leading postwar Italian intellectuals.

In 1947, meanwhile, de Martino moved to Rome. He did not manage to find a permanent university post (he only became a qualified university teacher in 1952), and he had to make do with high school teaching, something he found rather unsatisfying. To supplement the paltry salary and especially to maintain a leading position in the political and cultural life of the capital, he worked directly with the Rome office of the Einaudi publishing house, where liberal socialist and communist intellectuals were brought together and where he would establish—along with Cesare Pavese (1908–1950)—a collection of ethnological and religious studies that were to go down in history as "La Collana Viola": this series would also contain irrational religious and ethnological classics (by Kerényi, Eliade, Jensen, Frobenius, and others), giving great offense to the supporters of Croce and the communists and rightly gaining de Martino a formidable intellectual reputation. All this took place at the very moment when, like many other politically committed scholars of his generation, he was beginning an intense, fervent period of militancy: for a time he joined the Socialist Party and traveled to Bari and Lecce, first in his role as commissar of the provincial federation and then as an inspector, experiencing at first hand the great land struggle of those years in the countryside of the South, or as he said in a much discussed essay of 1949, "the explosion of the lower-class people's world into history." Two literary works, along with his direct political experience, impelled him to see the south of Italy as an area in need of urgent study, to be wrested from the domain of folklore: *Quaderni del carcere* by Antonio Gramsci (1891–1937) and *Cristo si è fermato a Eboli* by Carlo Levi (1902–1975). In the former he found a conceptual framework that allowed him to set Marxism in a historical context, placing it within the structure of Italian cultural life, and of seeing religious belief and practice in southern Italy as the historical result of the interaction, not entirely contradictory, between the ruling and lower classes, between the Catholic Church and a core of pre-Christian traditions. In the work of Levi, on the other hand, he found a map of the spread of magic in the former Kingdom of Naples, an invaluable guide, enabling him to select places and subjects to study, according to a different perspective to meridionalist writing, which was more interested in aspects of material poverty than in forms of cultural poverty. This was a gap that would be closed to some extent with the work de Martino would carry out during the 1950s, specifically looking to set out a "religious history of the South."

Driven by the urgency of this project, which was also political, de Martino undertook a lengthy and substantial series of ethnological excursions into the world of magic described by Levi, seemingly not limited by time but restricted in terms of location, centered around the *sassi* (*terminus technicus*) of Matera and delimited by the Naples of Croce. These expeditions were groundbreaking for several reasons: first, he was in charge of a team of trained professionals and experts in related disciplines (such as social work, psychiatry, parapsychology, ethnomusicology, sociology, and photography), but most of all because he was concerned about setting out the problem of the relationship between the subject and object of research. The most extensive of these field studies gave rise to and produced the greatest contributions to the religious history of the South that de Martino himself had begun to carry out: the 1952 expedition, organized to acquire information concerning Lucanian ceremonial magic, gave rise to the first part of *Sud e magia* (1959); the expeditions of 1953 to 1956, recording the funeral laments of Lucania, formed the basis of the ethnographic chapters of *Morte e pianto rituale nel mondo antico* (the largest and most detailed of de Martino's books, published in 1958 and winning the prestigious Premio Viareggio literary prize); while the 1959 expedition to Galatina, in Puglia, which was interested in gathering such information as still existed on the ancient "tarantula" rituals, formed the harsh starting point of *Terra del rimorso* (1961), the third and unfortunately final stage of this lay pilgrimage to places where mere existence itself is something of an endeavor. From these three works, the cultural institutions surveyed and studied, corroborated by historiographical case study, were given a sense of worth that previous folkloric research had neglected or even sometimes crushed.

The rapid transformation of the south of Italy as a result of the so-called economic miracle and the gradual withdrawal of de Martino from active politics (partly as a result of disillusion with the unself-critical position adopted by the Italian Communist Party after the events of 1956) are the most obvious reasons that led to the end of the meridionalist period begun in 1949. In 1958 the writer finally gained a university chair in Cagliari, and the following year he began to hold a course on the history of religions. At first he seemed to be concerned with collecting and revising the more theoretical essays that he had been writing in the meantime (in 1962 *Furore simbolo valore* was published), but contrary to what some thought he had not in fact ceased his research and was in fact already working on a magnum opus concerning cultural apocalypses, which was to represent a compendium of his philosophy. This work would remain largely unfinished, but from the preliminary notes (published posthumously in 1977 by Clara Gallini as *La fine del mondo*), he was already embarked upon an intensive program to reestablish human sciences on the basis of an extremely detailed and careful indisciplinary study: the madness of the end of the world, the drama of the Christian apocalypse, the eschatological elements of Third World religions, the collapse of the bourgeoisie prophesied by Marxism, the "loss of the center" in the artistic expression of the twentieth century, are all themes that are analyzed throughout the respective texts (psychiatric, religious and historical, ethnological, philosophical, and literary) and return once again to that distinct contemporary sense of "ending," which the author interprets, at times ecumenically, as the "ontic" risk of losing forever the world as a cultural homeland. One of the means of salvation is ethnographic humanism, and it was this message, albeit not yet in complete detail, that the author found the time to convey. He was taken ill with a lung tumor and died in a Roman hospital on May 6, 1965.

BIBLIOGRAPHY

To date (2003) there is still no systematic and comprehensive biography of de Martino. Scholars should refer to: Giuseppe Galasso, "Ernesto de Martino," in *Croce, Gramsci e altri storici* (Milan, 1969); and Mario Gandini, "Ernesto de Martino. Nota bio-bibliografica," in *Uomo e Cultura* 10 (1972). There are useful items also in: Andrea Binazzi, "Ernesto de Martino," in *Belfagor* 196 (1969); Clara Gallini, in his introduction to *La fine del mondo* (Turin, 1977); and Ricardo Di Donato, ed., *La contraddizione felice? Ernesto de Martino e gli altri* (Pisa, 1990). Further information can be found in his correspondence with Cesare Pavese in *La collana viola*, edited by Pietro Angelini (Turin, 1991) with Pietro Secchia in *Compagni e amici*, edited by Ricardo Di Donato (Florence,1993) and Renato Boccassino in *Una vicinanza discreta*, edited by Francesco Pompeo, (Rome, 1996). See also the profile by Vittorio Lanternari in the *Dizionario biografico degli italiani*, vol. 38 (Rome, 1990) and by the same author, *La mia alleanza con E. de Martino* (Naples, 1997).

A catalog of the works of de Martino, which is almost complete, has been edited by Mario Gandini and Silvio Previtera for l'Associazione Internazionale E. de Martino (Rome, 1995). In addition to the works referred to in the article, the following should be noted: "Angoscia territoriale e riscatto culturale nel mito Achilpa delle origini," in *Studie Materiali di Storia delle Religioni* 23 (1951–1952); "Fenomenologia religiosa e storicismo assoluto," in *Studi e Materiali di Storia delle Religioni* 24–25 (1954); "Storicismo e irrazionalismo nella storia delle religioni," in *Studi e Materiali di Storia delle Religioni* 28 (1957); and *Magia e civiltà* (Milan, 1962). In 1995 the publisher Argo (Lecce) began a collection of the unpublished works of de Martino, and a large number of unpublished works can also be found in the author's personal archive, maintained by Vittoria De Palma and deposited with the aforementioned Associazione Internazionale E. de Martino.

The vast majority of critical work on de Martino is posthumous. Here we will only mention those works that form an essential starting point: Benedetto Croce, "Intorno al 'magismo' come età storica," in *Filosofia e storiografia* (Bari, 1949); Enzo Paci, *Il nulla e il problema dell'uomo* (Turin, 1950); Renato Solmi, "E. De Martino e il problema delle categorie," *Il Mulino* 7 (1952); Cesare Cases, in his introduction to the edition of *Mondo magico* (Turin, 1973); Pietro Clemente, "Morte e pianto rituale. Riflessioni su un lavoro di E. De Martino," *Annali della Facoltà di lettere e filosofia dell'Università di Siena* 4 (1983); Pier Giorgio Solinas, "Idealismo, marxismo, strutturalismo," in *L'antropologia italiana. Un secolo di storia,* edited by A. R. Leone (Bari, 1985); Placido and Maria Cherchi, *Ernesto de Martino. Dalla crisi della presenza alla comunità* (Naples, 1987); Carlo Ginzburg, "Momigliano e De Martino," in *Rivista storica italiana* 100 (1988); Ricardo Di Donato, "Preistoria di Ernesto De Martino," *Studi storici* 1 (1989); Giuseppe Giarrizzo, "Note su Ernesto de Martino," *Archivio storico di cultura* 8 (1995); *Ernesto de Martino nella cultura europea,* edited by Clara Gallini and Marcello Massenzio (Naples, 1997); Silvia Mancini, Postscript to the French edition of *Mondo magico* (Paris, 1999); and Gennaro Sasso, *Ernesto de Martino fra religione e filosofia* (Naples, 2001). Numerous journals, such as *Studi e Materiali di Storia delle Religioni* 51 (1985) and *La ricerca folklorica* 13 (1986), have devoted whole issues to de Martino.

PIETRO ANGELINI (2005)

DEMETER AND PERSEPHONE. In the Homeric epics, no link is established between the two goddesses Demeter and Persephone, to whom later sources attribute a close mythical and ritual relationship, insofar as they are mother and daughter. In the *Iliad* (14.326), Demeter is presented as the bride of Zeus; elsewhere in the same poem (2.696) and in the *Odyssey* (5.125–129), her specific function as goddess of the harvest is also mentioned. Although Demeter appears to play a marginal role in the Homeric religious panorama, she is a figure of extreme antiquity, perhaps related to the Sitopotinja (mistress of the wheat) mentioned in the Linear B texts of Mycenae (twelfth century BCE), and she performs a fundamental role in the polytheistic Greek system. In Hesiod's *Theogony,* Demeter is one of the many brides of Zeus, and in the *Erga* (vv. 465ff.), the poet presents Demeter Chthonia, partnered with Zeus Chthonios, as the sovereign dispenser of the fruits of the land.

In both of Homer's epics, Persephone, daughter of Zeus (*Odyssey* 11.217), is referred to as queen of the underworld and bride of Hades. The fact that no link between the two goddesses is mentioned does not imply that such a link was unknown at the time of composition. Nor does it follow that one may identify in Persephone the figure of a pre-Hellenic underworld goddess, different from the Kore (maiden) of the wheat and daughter of Demeter, as proposed by some scholars and comprehensively argued by Gunther Zuntz (1971). The first reference to their relationship and to the dramatic circumstances that led to Persephone becoming the bride of Hades is found in Hesiod (*Theogony,* 912–914). The narration of the event meanwhile, which represents one of the longest-lived and most geographically widespread mythical traditions in Greek history, is the subject of the *Hymn to Demeter* in the pseudo-Homeric collection, datable to around 600 BCE. This text, although literary and nonliturgical in nature, represents a sort of manifesto of the mythical-ritual context of Eleusis, because it links Persephone's abduction to Demeter's founding of the mysteries. Demeter's refusal to accept the loss of her daughter leads Zeus to allow them to periodically meet on Olympus, despite the fact that Persephone has since become queen of the underworld. The successful resolution of the problem involves the human world, to which Demeter grants not only agrarian fertility, which had ceased as a consequence of her mourning, but also a new ritual dimension within which initiates may experience direct and intimate contact with the two goddesses and obtain, with their goodwill, the guarantee of happiness after death. The mythical and cultic role of Demeter and Persephone in Greek religion is not limited to the Eleusinian mysteries, even though these are essential to defining their identity and prerogatives. Their role is actually extremely wide-ranging and diversified, and they are found both in the typical formula of the mother and daughter pair and as distinct figures with respective cults.

DEMETER CULTS. A wealth of sources testifies to the cult of Demeter throughout the area to which Hellenism spread, from the islands of the Aegean and Asia Minor to Magna Graecia. Sicily was particularly devoted to the worship of Demeter. A characteristic aspect of Demeter cults was the central importance of the abduction and search for Kore; in many parts of Greece and the colonies, and in particular in Sicily, the foundation of the cult and the structure of its places of worship are often linked to the mythical theme of the goddess visiting human hosts. Therefore the divine experience has an etiological function toward the numerous local cults, influencing both the arrangement of the sacred area (temple, enclosure, grove, or even vast sanctuary) and the ritual practice, which assumed a great variety of forms, at times connected to the Eleusinian model, at others Thesmophorion. There is thus created a sort of map of the Demeter cult that reflects the movements of the divine figures in the cosmos, with the earth as their meeting point. The sacred site and the ritual praxis celebrated there are in turn configured as a tangible sign of the divine passage along two vectors: vertical, through the underworld, the surface of the earth, and Olympus; and horizontal, representing Demeter's wandering in search of her daughter. This mythical theme in fact provides a wealth of material for the various cults, constituting the common thread that links the many pieces of the vast mosaic of Demetrian sites.

Among the sources that testify to the functional relationship between myth and sacred place, the *Periegesis* by Pausanias in particular offers extensive material for the reconstruction of a basic Demetrian cartography, whereas the remaining documentation—literary, epigraphic, and archaeological—helps fill in the details. Among the numerous cults connected with the theme of Demeter's wanderings, the most significant are those of Megara and Pheneos. In the first location, Pausanias mentions the rock called "Anaclethris because Demeter (if the story be credible) here too called her daughter back when she was wandering in search of her. Even in our day the Megarian women hold a performance that is a mimic representation of the legend" (*Periegesis,* 1, 43, 2). Every year at Pheneos a festival with evident aspects of the mysteries was celebrated in a construction known as the Petroma, formed by two large stones with a circular opening, "with a mask inside of Demetra Cidaria. This mask is put on by the priest at the Greater Rites who for some reason or other beats with rods the Folk Underground. The Pheneatians have a story that even before Naon arrived the wanderings of Demeter brought her to their city also. To those Pheneatians who received her with hospitality into their homes the goddess gave all sorts of pulse save the bean only" (*Periegesis* 8, 15, 1–4). Insofar as the divine mask—many examples of which have been found in the Demeter sanctuaries—is worn by the celebrant, this leads one to suppose that the latter aims to impersonate Demeter herself. The beating of the rods on the ground would thus seem to be aimed at "recall" and may be considered similar to the ritual performed at the Anaclethris rock in Megara in memory of the despairing wail of the mother looking for her abducted daughter.

Reports of Diodorus Siculus illustrate a different but parallel mythical tradition by placing the divine event in a Sicilian setting. It is difficult to establish the antiquity of this version, whereby the island is the place of the abduction, of Demeter's search, and also of the maiden's return, although this version was already formed by the high Hellenistic period. Nevertheless the spread of the Demetrian cult, starting from the most ancient colonial foundations (eighth to seventh centuries BCE) in Sicily, leads one to believe that the process of "transferring" the cult and its adaptations to local conditions induced the corresponding mythical narration to become rooted in the territory, along with the cultic structures. Diodorus situates the Sicilian version of the abduction in the Heroic Age and attributes the foundation of the magnificent festival of Syracuse to Herakles (*Bibliotheke,* 4.23). He goes on to provide an extended narration of the myth that, while reflecting the existing pan-Hellenic pattern, is characterized by its entirely Sicilian setting, which unfolds on the road linking Enna, where the abduction of the divine maiden took place, and Syracuse. Here the king of the underworld "ripped open the earth, plunged with the abducted maiden into Hades and made a spring flow forth, where the Syracusans every year celebrate a famous festival" (*Bibliotheke*, 5.3–4).

Having completed the union between mythical event and ritual practice, the historian offers a detailed description of two festive cycles, with sacrifices and grandiose ceremonies dedicated respectively to Persephone at the time of the ripening of the wheat (May–June) and to Demeter at the time of sowing of the seed. The first festival is called the *katagoge* of Kore, a name intended as the "recall" of the divine maiden rather than as her "descent" (into the underworld). The result is that in the Sicilian context the positive outcome of the story, with Persephone's periodic return to her mother, was the premise and foundation for a special cultic practice.

The second festival, dedicated to Demeter, concerns the theme of the goddess's laughter, which marks the end of her grief, and which is usually provoked—according to the various traditions—by *aischrologia* or by more or less explicitly obscene behavior. These attitudes are transferred from the mythical level, on which a female figure with various names (Iambe, Baubo, or a nameless old woman) intervenes, to a ritual level representing one of the most typical and recurrent elements of the Demeter cults, from the Eleusinian mysteries to the Thesmophoria. The seasonal collocation of the Syracusan festival at the time of the sowing or of the first germination of the wheat (October–November) confirms its connection with agriculture and the analogy with Thesmophorion practice, despite the duration of the rite (ten days) and its public aspects. Many archaeological finds from the city and surrounding territory confirm, in the wealth of votive materials portraying the two goddesses and their worshipers, just how pervasive and deep-rooted Demetrian and Persephonean religiosity was.

Whereas Demeter cults distinguished all of Sicily, some of the main centers were in Agrigento, which Pindar celebrates as the "dwelling place of Persephone" (*Pythics*, 12, 1–5); Gela, the site of a characteristic Thesmophorion (Bitalemi); and Enna, where Cicero—who witnessed the tradition whereby "the island of Sicily is entirely consecrated to Ceres and to Libera"—recognized the presence of the "more ancient Ceres," venerated in a famous sanctuary (*In Verrem Actio* 2, 2, 4, 48, 106–108). Archaeological research has brought to light in these and many other Sicilian locations sacred areas and votive hoards of such richness as to completely confirm the opinion, again reported by Cicero, of the ancient inhabitants of the island, who claimed that "these two goddesses were born in those places and the cultivation of cereals was introduced for the first time in that land."

The service of Demeter, without being an exclusive prerogative of women, was nevertheless usually performed by priestesses. In the priestly hierarchy of Eleusis, an essential role was played by the *hiereiai* ("priestesses") and by the *hierophantis* ("she who reveals the sacred things"), who acted as the female counterpart of the highest-level priest, the hierophant who revealed the sacred symbols of the mysteries. The other esoteric Demeter cults, particularly the Thesmophoria, are entirely characterized by female aspects, with only a few exceptions, in which men's involvement was limited to certain phases of the rite. This exclusive female Demetrian rituality is not configured as being in opposition to the male sphere but rather in a dialectic relationship and complementary to it. In almost all cases the cults in question have an evident political dimension in the sense that, inserted in the official calendar of the city, they are connected to the promotion of the well-being and prosperity of the entire community. Whereas generally excluded from the judicial-administrative activities of the Greek city, women nevertheless played a crucial role on the sacred level, which represented an essential and irreplaceable element of city life, for it was on this level that the city depended for its legitimacy and for the strength that ensured its survival and continuity.

The Thesmophoria are the oldest and most pan-Hellenic in diffusion of the female esoteric Demeter cults. The name *Thesmophora* was given to the goddess as an expression of her role as giver of civilizing laws (*thesmoi*), in particular of the rules of marriage. Agriculture and marriage, as well as chthonic and human fertility, are Demeter's functional prerogatives and the cornerstones of human identity. Humans, in the Greek ideological panorama, are defined as different from the gods due to their double roles as eaters of bread and generators of children, insofar as they are mortal but producers of culture. The Thesmophoria, which was reserved for married women with full rights of citizenship, took place once a year, although on different dates in the festive calendars of the various Greek cities. The festival is also connected to the abduction of Persephone; sources relate that on the days of the festival the *thesmophoriazousai* (the women who celebrated the Thesmophoria) ritually evoked Demeter's grief, the search for Persephone, and Persephone's retrieval. The festival involved both of the goddesses; in many cases a male figure, Eubuleus or Zeus Eubuleus; and a triad that included a married couple, probably identifiable as Persephone and an underworld Zeus, who corresponded to Hades/Pluto. Extensive archaeological evidence confirms the pervasive nature of this cult, with numerous finds dating from the archaic age up to late Hellenism spread throughout the Hellenized Mediterranean world, with particular concentrations in the Aegean Islands, in Magna Graecia, and in Sicily. The recurrent image of the female figure in votive deposits (the worshiper or goddess herself) with various attributes (a piglet, a cist, a dish of fruit, a torch) vividly express its central element, with its double reference to agrarian and female fertility. The presence of various figures of *kourotrophos*, a divine or human nursing mother, in the Thesmophorion places of worship strengthens the female connotations of the mythical-ritual scenario gravitating around the two goddesses.

Numerous other exclusively female rituals gravitate around Demeter, often together with her daughter and in relationship with the mythical theme of the abduction. In Athens there was the Stenia, a nocturnal festival in which women kept a vigil, perhaps awaiting the return of the two goddesses, and the Scire, connected also with Athena, Poseidon, and Erecteus. Sources of the imperial age attest the presence of mysteries of one or the other goddess in numerous centers, above all in the Peloponnese and in Asia Minor, and in cities in which the cult of Demeter had a long and consolidated tradition, such as Smyrna, Ephesus, and Pergamus.

PERSEPHONE CULTS. Some cults were dedicated solely to Persephone without Demeter, albeit often coupled with her underworld husband Hades, whereas others included her mother but merely in a sporadic or marginal role. Among these, particularly significant is the Magna Graecian cult in Locri, whose flourishing is shown by a few literary sources and by extensive archaeological evidence. Whereas its period of greatest splendor was between the end of the sixth century and the mid-fifth century BCE, this cult also spread outside the Locri Persephoneion to Medma and other towns of Magna Graecia and to Francavilla in Sicily. It was characterized by the enthusiastic participation of the local people and by a rich mythical background with a corresponding ritual praxis, whose reconstruction depends entirely on the exegesis of the complex iconography. The votive *pinakes* (tablets) that have been found in large numbers in the *favissae* (underground chambers for sacred deposits) of the sanctuary present numerous scenes in which the divine and mythical levels intertwine deeply with human life and ritual. The scenes are dominated by the majestic figures of Persephone and Hades on their thrones, often accompanied by other divine figures (Dionysos, Hermes, Ares) and above all human images, such as maidens with various attributes (ball, cockerel) and women engaged in picking fruit, in ritual procession, and in scenes of sacrifice or nuptial significance. A particularly interesting depiction is that of a female figure (goddess or woman?) sitting at a table upon which is placed a basket that she holds open to reveal a boy inside. Another scene that stands out for the frequency and variety of figurative motifs is that of a chariot drawn by winged horses carrying a maiden, who is led, often by force, by an abductor, who is sometimes a youth and sometimes an older man. The two levels of the divine and human are inextricably intertwined, because the scenario of the mythical marriage is superimposed by the reference to the common female experience of marriage perceived as a maiden's separation from her family and her assumption of the new role of adult woman, wife, and mother.

Lastly, the varied ancient religious literature attributed to the mythical Thracian poet Orpheus displayed a great interest in the myths and rituals gravitating around the mother and daughter pair. Although the thesis of an influence of Orphic doctrines in Eleusis has been convincingly confuted by Fritz Graf (1974), numerous testimonies reveal the existence of particular mythical versions of the abduction, which the Orphic *Argonautika* link explicitly to the Thesmophoria. In some formulas relative to the otherworldly journey of the soul contained in the well-known gold leaves from Thurii (fourth–third centuries BCE) that seem to reflect an eschatology of Orphic inspiration, Persephone is invoked as "pure Queen of them below" (in Kern, 1922, fr. 32 c-f), and Demeter is also mentioned.

SEE ALSO Baubo; Eleusinian Mysteries; Goddess Worship, overview article, article on Goddess Worship in the Hellenistic World; Greek Religion; Hades; Hekate; Orpheus; Thesmophoria.

BIBLIOGRAPHY

Publication of the complete edition of the Locri *pinakes*, after extensive analyses of the iconography and underlying religious concepts, was successfully started with publication of the first four volumes, various authors, in *Atti e Memorie della Società della Magna Grecia*, ser. 4, 1, 1–4 (Rome, 1999). For a picture of the historico-cultural situation in Locri, a useful source is *Atti del sedicesimo Convegno di studi sulla Magna Grecia Taranto, 3–8 ottobre 1976*, vols. 1–2 (Naples, 1977). The problem of Persephone's identity as been analyzed by Gunther Zuntz, *Persephone: Three Essays on Religion and Thought in Magna Graecia* (Oxford, U.K., 1971).

Claude Bérard's *Anodoi: Essai sur l'imagerie des passages chthoniens* (Rome, 1974) analyzes extensive iconographic material relative to myths of crossing cosmic levels in which various divine figures are involved, including Persephone. The agricultural connections of the various forms of the Demeter cult in Attica are highlighted by Allaire Chandor Brumfield, *The Attic Festivals of Demeter and Their Relation to the Agricultural Year* (New York, 1981). Walter Burkert's excellent manual on Greek religion, *Die Griechische Religion der archaischen und Klassischen Epoche* (Stuttgart, Germany, 1977), translated by John Raffan as *Greek Religion: Archaic and Classical* (Cambridge, Mass., 1985), provides indispensable data for collocating the cult in the wider context of Greek religious history. The typology of the nursing deities is examined by Theodora Hadzisteliou Price in *Kourotrophos: Cults and Representations of the Greek Nursing Deities* (Leiden, Netherlands, 1978). An exhaustive overview of the Sicilian and Italian centers of the cult, with comprehensive archaeological documentation, is provided by Valentina Hinz, *Der Kult von Demeter und Kore auf Sizilien und in der Magna Graecia* (Wiesbaden, Germany, 1998). See also Otto Kern, *Orphicorum Fragmenta* (Berlin, 1922), and Alberto Bernabé and Ana Isabel Jiménez San Cristóbal, *Instrucciones para el más allá: Las laminillas órficas de oro* (Madrid, 2001). The relation between Eleusis and Orphism has been discussed in detail by Fritz Graf, *Eleusis und die orphische Dichtung Athens in Vorhellenistischer Zeit* (Berlin and New York, 1974).

A useful commentary with a wide range of parallel documentation accompanies the translation by N. J. Richardson of *The Homeric Hymn to Demeter* (Oxford, 1974). Giulia Sfameni Gasparro's *Misteri e culti mistici di Demetra* (Rome, 1986) offers a picture of the Demeter cults as intended to set up an intense relationship between the faithful and the goddess through the ritual reevocation of the mythical event, often in an esoteric context.

On the methods of access to the priesthood by Greek women, see Judy Ann Turner, "*Hiereiai*: Acquisition of Feminine Priesthoods in Ancient Greece," Ph.D. diss. (University of California, Santa Barbara, 1983). For the complex religious and social dimension of feminine priesthood in the ancient world, see Sfameni Gasparro, "Ruolo cultuale della donna in Grecia e a Roma: Per una tipologia storico-religiosa," in *Donna e culture: Studi e documenti nel III anniversario della "Mulieris Dignitatem,"* edited by Umberto Mattioli (Bologna, Italy, 1991), pp. 57–121.

GIULIA SFAMENI GASPARRO (2005)

DEMIÉVILLE, PAUL (1894–1979), French Sinologist and Buddhologist. Demiéville was born in Lausanne, Switzerland, and completed undergraduate studies at Bern in 1911. He subsequently studied in Munich, London, Edinburgh, and Paris, finishing work for a doctorate in music at the University of Paris in 1914. He began his study of Chinese the following year at King's College in London, but he returned to Paris to study first at the École Nationale des Langues Orientales and then at the Collège de France, where he worked with Édouard Chavannes. Demiéville graduated from the École des Langues Orientales in 1918, having mastered not only Chinese but Japanese and Sanskrit as well. In 1920 he moved to Hanoi, and from 1924 to 1926 he taught Sanskrit and Western philosophy at the University of Amoy. From 1926 to 1930 he lived in Japan, where he edited the first four volumes (1929–1931) of the encyclopedic dictionary of Buddhism *Hôbôgirin*, compiled under the direction of Sylvain Lévi and Takakusu Junjiro. (The dictionary resumed publication in the 1960s.)

In 1931, Demiéville returned to France to become professor of Chinese at the École Nationale des Langues Orientales, a post he held until 1945, at which time he became director of studies at the École Pratique des Hautes Études, teaching courses in Buddhist philology. In 1946 he succeeded Henri Maspero to the chair of Chinese language and civilization at the Collège de France, the position he held until his retirement in 1964.

Demiéville was a corresponding member of the British Academy, the Association for Asian Studies, and the School of Oriental and African Studies in London and was an honorary member of Tōyō Bunko and of the Académie du Japon. He was awarded honorary doctorates by the universities of Louvain and Rome, and he was elected a member of the Académie des Inscriptions et Belles-Lettres in 1951. He served as codirector of the journal *T'oung pao* (Leiden) from 1945 to 1976.

Demiéville was a prolific writer, publishing 179 studies (books and articles) and 104 book reviews. His works are characterized by philological precision and a thorough examination of the sources. They are models of scholarship. He wrote on Chinese language, art, literature, archaeology, history, philosophy, and religion. But he is best known for his work on Buddhism in China, the school of Chan (Zen) in the Tang dynasty in particular, and for his work on the Buddhist materials found at Tun-huang.

BIBLIOGRAPHY

Book-length studies by Demiéville include the following: *Les versions chinoises du Milindapañha* (Hanoi, 1924); *Le Concile de Lhasa: Une controverse sur le Quiétisme entre bouddhistes de l'Inde et de la Chine au huitième siècle de l'ère chrétienne* (Paris, 1952); and *Entretiens de Lin-tsi*, translated and edited by Demiéville (Paris, 1972). Demiéville was the author of numerous articles, the most important of which are reprinted in two volumes: *Choix d'études sinologiques* (Leiden, 1973) and *Choix d'études bouddhiques* (Leiden, 1973). Both of these volumes contain extensive bibliographies, which are updated in Yves Hervouet's obituary for Demiéville, published in *T'oung pao* 65 (1979): 1–12.

New Sources

Gregory, P. N., and Kuroda Institute. *Sudden and Gradual: Approaches to Enlightenment in Chinese Thought.* Honolulu, 1987.

ROBERT G. HENRICKS (1987)
Revised Bibliography

DEMIURGE. The Greek term *dēmiourgos* (together with its variants) is derived from the words *dēmos* ("people") and *ergon* ("work") and thus has the basic meaning of "one who works for the people," an artisan or a professional. This etymological base subsequently developed in two directions. On the one hand, *dēmiourgos* came to refer to a magistrate; on the other, it became a name for the original creator of the world, in the specific sense of an ordainer or arranger, someone who as an artist fashions the world out of preexisting matter in accord with a preexisting model. It is this second meaning that is of primary concern here.

The term *dēmiourgos* occurs only twice in Homer, each time in the *Odyssey*. At 17.383 it refers to a professional man such as a soothsayer, physician, carpenter, or inspired poet. At 19.135 it refers to a herald, "one who performs a public function" (*kērukon hoi dēmioergoi easin*). Here the development of the later meaning, that of "magistrate," is already perceptible. Sophocles uses the term in its original sense when he calls Hades "the savage artisan of Hector's girdle" (*Ajax* 1035). Similarly, Aristophanes links the *dēmiourgoi* ("artisans") with other categories of workers (*Peace* 297) and uses the term *dēmiourgikos* ("in the style of an artisan, a specialized worker") to refer to Hermes, the versatile god of inventions (*Peace* 429). At one place *dēmiourgos* possibly takes on the specialized sense of "potter" (*Knights* 650), which suggests the future evolution of the word in the sense of "(cosmic) molder." The same term is used in its original meaning by Herodotos (7.31), whereas Thucydides uses it in the sense of "magistrate" (5.47.9; cf. 1.56). The pre-Socratic philosophers use the term *dēmiourgiai* in its original meaning (see, for instance, Philolaos, frag. 11t), whereas in the doxography of these philosophers, the term may refer to a molder or a former, in the sense of a cosmogonic agent (as in Empedocles).

Plato uses the term *dēmiourgos* to refer both to an artisan and to an original arranger of the world. Meaning "artisan" or "craftsman," the term occurs in *Laches* 185e and 195b and in *Charmides* 162e, 164a–b, 171c, 173c, 174e, and 175a. The last two cases include the sense of something that affects or causes; compare *Sophist* 219c, *Philebus* 55d, and *Laws* 829d, where the suggestion is of performers of noble deeds. See also *Gorgias* 452a, 453a–e, and 454a, where rhetoric and arithmetic "produce" persuasion, as do the arts in general. Compare, however, the term used as "creator of phantoms," that is, the opposite of a real creator, in *Republic* 599a–d and 601b, and see also *Republic* 340e, 346c, 597d; *Apology* 22d and 23e; *Alcibiades 1* 131a and 140b–c; *Gorgias* 447d and 455b; and *Euthydemus* 280c. Note particularly *Republic* 389d, which quotes Homer's *Odyssey* 17.383. In the context of the theory of the three categories of citizens in the *polis*, see *Republic* 415a; *Phaedrus* 248e; and *Sophist* 219c (cf. *Statesman* 280c). See also *Critias* 110c and 112b and *Laws* 746c and 921b.

Closely associated with the meaning "artisan" is the meaning "professional man" or "specialist," which appears in Homer. In this sense the term occurs in *Laches* 195d and *Charmides* 164b (cf. *Philebus* 55d and *Sophist* 229d); *Protagoras* 312b and 322b (*dēmiourgikē technē*, "the professional art" or "skill in handiwork," the gift of Prometheus to mankind, as opposed to the more spiritual or ethical *politikē technē*, the "political art," which is the gift of Zeus); *Cratylus* 389a, where the legislator is the most rare among the "specialists" or "experts" (cf. 428e and *Laws* 921d, respectively, referring to specialists in the arts of instruction and of war); *Euthydemus* 301c and *Phaedo* 86c, where it is a question of artists (cf. also the *Symposium* 186d, among others; *Republic* 401c; and *Sophist* 236a, where it refers to the sculptors of statues); and *Hippias Maior* 290b, where Phidias is mentioned as "a good craftsman knowing the beautiful" (here we are close to the meaning of a molder of the universe inspired by an invisible model). Finally, see *Republic* 596b, where a craftsman "fixes his eyes on the idea or form."

Dēmiourgos in the sense of a divine artisan or creator of the world is found in the *Timaeus, Statesman, Philebus, Republic, Sophist,* and *Laws.* It is the *Timaeus*, however, that provides us with the most complete description of the Demiurge. In fact, in the *Timaeus* nearly every occurrence of the noun *dēmiourgos* and the verb *dēmiourgeō* refers to the divine molder of the universe. The only exception to this is 24a, where the reference is to an ordinary artisan. The *Timaeus* presents the role of the Demiurge as essential to both the world and man, since it is responsible for their correspondence as microcosm and macrocosm. Although this theme of the microcosm and macrocosm has led some scholars to posit the survival of (reconstructed) ancient Indo-Iranian speculations on an alleged myth of a primordial man (*makranthrōpos*) in the *Timaeus*, a myth that would express a kind of pantheistic unity of God and world, such a survival is unlikely. In fact, in Plato's *Timaeus* the role of the Demiurge is incompatible with an essentially monistic conception of the world as a gigantic organism. Rather, this text is informed by Plato's fundamental dualism, a dualism that describes an ontological reality while at the same time providing a principle of philosophical hermeneutics.

Plato distinguishes two realms. On the one hand there is the ideal world, the world of the Ideas, the models of all reality. Opposite this stands the sensible world, which comes into being through the activity of the Demiurge, who projects the efficacy of the ideal models that he contemplates into the receptive *chōra* ("receptacle"). Clearly the Demiurge is here to be distinguished both from the Ideas, including the supreme idea, the idea of the Good, and from the soul of the world, the soul that the Demiurge introduces into the "body" of the world in order to animate it.

Plato refers to the Demiurge as a cause or principle (*aitia*) of the world, a term that he also applies to the world of Ideas in its relation to the sensible world. Even the *chōra* itself, the receptacle that preexists the molding activity of the Demiurge, is called an *aitia*, although due to its inferior ontological status it is sometimes referred to inaccurately in translation as "prime matter," in relation to the Demiurge and the world of Ideas.

The molding and animating activity of the Demiurge is an ordering activity that opposes the primordial chaotic disorder of the elements, progressively reducing their disorderly movement. The world is said to be generated by the Demiurge, who is also termed its "maker and father" (*poiētēs kai patēr*, *Timaeus* 28; cf. 41 and "maker and father," *dēmiourgos kai patēr*, at *Statesman* 273; at *Republic* 597d the painter is not *dēmiourgos kai poiētēs*). The Demiurge is also described as "the most perfect of causes," while the world is described as "the most beautiful of generated beings" (*Timaeus* 29). The model that inspires the maker is eternal, always the same, uniform and ungenerated. The Demiurge itself is said to be difficult to know; knowledge of it is impossible to divulge (*Timaeus* 28). Nevertheless, despite these difficulties, the role of the Demiurge does not seem to be in doubt. The beauty of the world sustains the belief that the activity of the Demiurge is beneficent, inspired by an eternal model. As we shall see, this belief stands in marked contrast to the ignorance and the *modus operandi* attributed to the demiurge in Gnostic systems. Plato's Demiurge, being good and without envy (*phthonos*), excludes as much as possible every imperfection from the world.

The role of the Demiurge in fashioning the world is primarily one of providing order. He takes the visible, preexistent mass that moves without measure and order (*kinoumenon plēmmelōs kai ataktōs*) and orders it, placing intellect within the soul of the world and the soul within the world's body, so that the world as a whole might be truly a living being, having a soul and an intellect, and born through the providence of God (29–30). The fashioning of man is somewhat more complex. The Demiurge provides man only with the higher, immortal part of his soul. The soul's inferior, mortal part, as well as the human body, are the creation of the inferior gods. Once brought into being, the Demiurge locates the souls among the stars and notifies them of the "laws of fate" (*nomous tous heimarmenous*). All souls begin as equals, each enjoying the same original conditions. Their individual destinies are to be determined by either their observance or neglect of piety and righteousness. The just soul is destined to return to its star, while the others are subjected to the law of metensomatosis, according to which a first reincarnation would be in the form of a woman, to be followed by rebirth in the form of an animal, if the soul should persist in its evil (here Plato is heir to the Orphics). Only submission to reason can insure the soul's return to its star. Plato adds that the Demiurge "dictated to them all these laws in order to be in the subsequent times innocent of the evil (*kakia*) of each of them," which can mean either that the Demiurge is innocent of moral evil or, more probably, that it is not responsible for evil souls. It is only after the establishment of this original justice by the Demiurge that the lower gods create for every individual the remaining part of the soul and the body.

Plato discusses the Demiurge in other dialogues as well, although these discussions are not always consistent with the doctrine presented in the *Timaeus* concerning the creation of man. Further discussions may be found at *Statesman* 270, 273 and 308; *Philebus* 27 (cf. 26 and 39); *Republic* 507, 530 (cf. 596 and *Sophist* 234a–b); and *Laws* 902.

The development that leads from the Demiurge of Plato to the demiurge of the Gnostics is a long one. As a transitional figure we may mention the Middle Platonist Numenius, who to an extent foreshadowed the pessimistic outlook of the later gnostics. The demiurge of Numenius, which he called the Second God, was an ambivalent figure torn between the possibilities of contemplating the ideal world or, alternatively, directing his attention downward toward the sensible world. A quite different development of the Platonic Demiurge is found in Philo of Alexandria. Philo employs the narrative of the *Timaeus* when he introduces the notion that in creating man God had not worked alone but had been assisted by other heavenly agents. This introduction of demiurgic intermediaries was intended to keep God separate from human evil.

Coming to the Gnostics, we encounter the notion of an inferior demiurge, a notion more or less common to the various gnostic schools, sects, and religions, with their anticosmic attitudes, and in clear-cut opposition to the far more positive Platonic notion. This opposition was noticed by the founder of Neoplatonism, Plotinus (third century CE), who wrote a treatise "against those who say that the Demiurge of the world is bad and that the world is bad," namely the Gnostics (*Enneads* 2.9). It is true that the Gnostic demiurge continues to function as the fashioner of the world and as an intermediary presence. But there is an immense difference: the Gnostic demiurge itself belongs to this inferior world, the world of ignorance that holds the spiritual soul in bondage. It is accordingly inferior to the human soul, which, when enlightened by *gnōsis*, realizes its consubstantiality with the divine *pneuma*, or spirit. The inferiority of the demiurge is sometimes reflected in its name, as when it is called Saklas ("foolish one").

More precise characterization of the demiurge varies considerably according to the different Gnostic schools and sects. On the one hand, there is the monstrous, almost demonic figure of the lion-headed demiurge Ialdabaoth found in the Gnostic *Apocryphon of John* and the ignorant, "psychic" (i.e., nonspiritual) Ialdabaoth of the Valentinians. The latter was assigned a role in the preliminary education of man and was destined to be taken up at the end of time into the heavenly realm known as Ogdoad. Significantly, this latter realm was not included in the higher, divine realm of the *plērōma*. On the other hand, among some followers of Basilides one finds the demiurge Sabaoth, who was conceived of as just and who cooperated with the pneumatic or spiritual beings, though he always remained unassimilable to them and was presented as the son of the evil, dethroned Ialdabaoth.

Common to all these Gnostic demiurges, however, whether in the Valentinian or Sethian currents, is a complete lack of spiritual or pneumatic nature: they are essentially inferior. In addition, they are often described in terms originally applied to the creator god of the Hebrew scriptures, a god debased in the Gnostic ideology. This explains the popularity of Hebrew or pseudo-Hebrew names for the demiurge, such as Ialdabaoth.

The demiurge is also found in other Gnostic groups and religions. We may mention the ambivalent demiurge of the Mandaeans, Ptahil, and the demiurge of the Manichaeans, the Spiritus Vivens ("living spirit"), who was an evocation of the Father of Light and was believed to have fashioned the world from the dark, demonic substance of slaughtered demons.

See Also Archetypes; Gnosticism.

Bibliography

Boyancé, Pierre. "Dieu cosmique et dualisme: Les archontes et Platon." In *The Origins of Gnosticism*, 2d ed., edited by Ugo Bianchi, pp. 340–356. Leiden, 1970.

Bréhier, Émile. *The Philosophy of Plotinus.* Translated by Joseph Thomas. Chicago, 1958.

Dodd, C. H. *The Bible and the Greeks* (1935). London, 1964.

Dodds, E. R., et al. *Les sources de Plotin.* Geneva, 1960.

Elsas, Christoph. *Neuplatonische und gnostische Weltablehnung in der Schule Plotins.* Berlin, 1975.

Festugière, A.-J. *La révélation d'Hermès Trismégiste.* 4 vols. Paris, 1950–1954.

Guthrie, W. K. C., et al. *Recherches sur la tradition platonicienne.* Vérone, 1957.

Horst, P. W. van der, and Jaap Mansfeld, eds. and trans. *An Alexandrian Platonist against Dualism: Alexander of Lycopolis' Treatise "Critique of the Doctrines of Manichaeus."* Leiden, 1974.

Jonas, Hans. *The Gnostic Religion.* 2d ed., rev. Boston, 1963.

Merlan, Philip. *From Platonism to Neoplatonism.* 2d ed., rev. The Hague, 1960.

Pétrement, Simone. *Le dualisme chez Platon, les gnostiques et les manichéens.* Paris, 1946.

Places, Édouard des. *Pindare et Platon.* Paris, 1949.

Robinson, T. M. *Plato's Psychology.* Toronto, 1970.

Rose, H. J., et al. *La notion du divin depuis Homère jusqu'à Platon.* Geneva, 1954.

Simon, Marcel. "Eléments gnostiques chez Philon." In *The Origins of Gnosticism,* 2d ed., edited by Ugo Bianchi, pp. 359–376. Leiden, 1970.

New Sources

Benitez, Eugenio E. "The Good or the Demiurge." *Apeiron* 28 (1995): 113–140.

Brisson, Luc. "Le démiurge du Timée et le créateur de la Genèse." In *Le style de la pensée. Recueil de textes en hommage à Jacques Brunschwig,* edited by Monique Canto-Sperber and Pierre Pellegrin, pp. 25–39. Paris, 2002.

Burkert, Walter. "Sacrificio-sacrilegio: il trickster fondatore." *Studi Storici* 4 (1984): 835–845.

Carpenter, Amber Danielle. "Phileban Gods." *Ancient Philosophy* 23 (2003): 99–111.

Classen, Carl Joachim. "Schöpfergott oder Weltordner. Zu den Gottesvorstellung der Griechen von Homer bis zu Platon." In *Ansätze. Beiträge zum Verständnis der frühgriechischen Philosophie,* pp. 3–27. Würzburg, 1986.

Deuse, Werner. "Der Demiurg bei Porphyrios und Jamblich." In *Die Philosophie des Neuplatonismus,* edited by Clemens Zintzen, pp. 238–278. Darmstadt, 1977.

Fossum, Jarl. "The Origin of the Gnostic Concept of the Demiurge." *Ephemerides Theologicae Lovanienses* 61 (1985): 142–152.

Hadot, Ilsetraut. "À propos de la place ontologique du démiurge dans le système philosophique d'Hiéroclès le Néoplatonicien." *Revue des Etudes Grecques* 106 (1993): 430–459.

Jackson, Howard M. *The Lion Becomes a Man: The Gnostic Leontomorphic Creator and the Platonic Tradition.* Atlanta, 1985.

Mansfeld, Jaap. "Bad World and Demiurge. A 'Gnostic' Motif from Parmenides and Empedocles to Lucretius and Philo." In *Studies in Gnosticism and Hellenistic Religions presented to G. Quispel on the Occasion of His 65th Birthday,* edited by Roelof van den Broek and Maarten J. Vermaseren, pp. 261–314. Leiden, 1981.

Perl, Eric D. "The Demiurge and the Forms." *Ancient Philosophy* 18 (1998): 81–92.

Quispel, Gilles. "The Origins of the Gnostic Demiurge." In *Kyriakon. Festschrift Johannes Quasten,* ed. by Patrick Grenfell and Josef A. Jungmann, pp. 271–276. Münster, 1970.

Quispel, Gilles. "The Demiurge in the Ap Jn." In *Nag Hammadi and Gnosis. Papers Read at the First International Congress of Coptology, Cairo December 1976,* pp. 1–33. Leiden, 1978.

Reydams-Schils, Gretchen. *Demiurge and Providence, Stoic and Platonist Readings of Plato's 'Timaeus'.* Turnhout, 1999.

UGO BIANCHI (1987)
Revised Bibliography

DEMONS

This entry consists of the following articles:

AN OVERVIEW
PSYCHOLOGICAL PERSPECTIVES

DEMONS: AN OVERVIEW

Except in some monotheistic religions, all demons are not assumed to be evil. Many kinds of spiritual beings who are not obviously gods may be described as demons. Demons are far more powerful than humans, though their powers are limited and they are longer-lived, though not necessarily immortal. Demons often seem to be the anthropomorphic conceptualization of discrete, invisible natural forces that are perceptible mainly through their effects, such as wind or specific diseases. In prescientific cosmologies, air, wind, and the "breath" *(spiritus)* of life are usually conceived as invisible or even immaterial. As spirits, demons are normally invisible, becoming perceptible either through their effects on humans, or through language or signs. When becoming visible, demons may exhibit their own inherent shapes or assume familiar or monstrous forms.

Demonic spirits may protect or inhabit places, bodies of water, or vegetation. Demons may also inhabit or be guardians of an underworld, and may torment human souls there. At times ghosts have demonic characteristics. They may be the ancestors of the culture that describes them, or recently deceased family members who, it is feared, could return to claim surviving relatives or neighbors.

In some religions (particularly Judaism, Christianity and Islam), demons may be identified with or compared to angels or devils. However, in English and other modern languages, the three terms, all derived from ancient Greek, have differing implications. *Daimon,* and its derivatives *daimonios, daimonion* (*daemon, daemonium* in Latin), denote a suprahuman spiritual being that interacts directly with humans. The *daimon*'s character may be good, evil, or changeable, but late Judaism and Christianity eventually define demons as profoundly, irredeemably evil.

Angel (aggelos or *angelos;* Latin *angelus)* denotes a messenger, and was originally applicable to human as well as suprahuman envoys. In Judaism and Christianity, the *angel* is a spirit messenger sent to humans by the god, but the term could include other functions, such as rewarding or punishing humans.

The noun *devil (diabolos;* Latin *diabolus)* derives from a verb meaning "to throw across" and by extension to attack, accuse, or slander. The devil is the sworn enemy of the god, and attempts to harm, subvert, or seduce the god's worshippers. The devil is inferior in power and wisdom to the god; in the three principal monotheistic religions, he is a renegade creature of the god. Devil and demon can thus be synonymous common nouns, particularly in Christianity, which defines *the* Devil as leading an army of subordinate demons. (In fully dualistic religions deriving from the ancient Iranian prophet Zarathushtra [c. 600 BCE], the evil opponent of the god is not his inferior but his inverted twin, fully as divine and powerful.)

Aside from ruling certain phenomena for all or many members of a society, demons may dedicate continuous attention to a single individual. A spiritual guardian protects the interests of his devotee. Conversely, a demon can afflict or even "possess" humans, entering their bodies and creating disease or an alien, transgressive personality.

Demons' invisibility implies that they either have bodies of finer matter than that composing the visible world, or else lack bodies altogether. Yet demons are in many cultures thought to behave like ordinary embodied humans: they may have sexual relations among themselves or with humans, and procreate demonic or semi-demonic children who are superhumanly powerful, charismatic, or evil.

TRIBAL CULTURES. The belief in invisible beings who control or strongly affect the conditions of human life is universal. It appears to be an essential trait of humanity to think of its own interactions with the physical world in anthropomorphic terms, considering forces and even objects as if they had personalities and desires. From the point of view of cultures possessing writing, demonic modes of thinking resemble the literary and ethical device of allegory, wherein psychological and physical phenomena are described as well-defined "people." According to the critic Angus Fletcher, demons "share [a] major characteristic of allegorical agents, the fact that they compartmentalize function," explaining limited aspects of the world: "Constriction of meaning, when it is the limit put upon a personified force or power, causes that personification to act somewhat mechanistically" (Fletcher, 1964, 40, 55). This relative predictability expresses a desire to tame or domesticate the world: "Coming from the term that means 'to divide,'; *daemon* implies an endless series of divisions of all important aspects of the world into separate elements for study and control" (Fletcher, 1964, 59). The need to understand the conditions of life leads to a belief that good—and especially, bad—fortunes are due to the agency of spirits. Demons give shape to inchoate fears of sudden vulnerability, dependence or victimization, triggered by solitary wastelands, darkness, or sexual anxieties. Attempts to control or placate these invisible forces take the form of exorcism, trickery (e.g., substituting effigies for potential human victims), or worship.

HINDUISM. In Hinduism the question of gods and demons reflects a complex, multimillennial history of religious and cultural beliefs. In the Vedas and epics, suprahuman beings are mentioned whose exact nature, and their differences from everyday humans, are often unclear. *Rakshasas*, *pisacas*, and *vetalas* are demon-like beings that haunt graveyards, threaten the living, and feed on human flesh; some are ghosts, others are suprahuman. *Pitrs* are ancestral spirits. In Hinduism reincarnation eliminates the absolute ontological barrier between humans and suprahumans that modern western cultures take for granted. The term *deva* refers to godlike beings, but even they are subject to reincarnation; moreover, humans may be reincarnated as *devas*. *Devas* are in conflict with *asuras* or "not-gods" (cf. Greek Titans). Yet *asuras* are neither radically evil nor the dedicated opponents of a single supreme deity, unlike demons of Judaism and, especially, Christianity. Nor is the enmity of the *devas* and *asuras* a historic constant; it appears that *asura* corresponds to "god" in some Vedic texts. When its meaning evolved to approximate "demon," the word *sura* was coined as its antonym. Though occasionally opposed to divinities and humans, Hindu "demons" are not inimical to them inherently or by definition.

In Iranian religion, which apparently descended from the same "parent" religion as Hinduism, a similar conflict existed between beings called *daevas* and *ahuras*. "In Iran, the ahuras defeated the daevas, the leader of the ahuras became the high God, Ahura Mazda, the god of light, and the Iranian daevas, consigned to the ranks of evil spirits, became minions of Ahriman, the lord of darkness. In India, the devas defeated the asuras" (Russell, 1977, p. 58). In both cases, "One group of deities was vanquished by another and relegated to the status of generally evil spirits" (Russell, 1977, p. 58). In Iranian religions, however (Zoroastrianism, Zervanism, Mazdaism), the "demonization" of the defeated gods created a dualistic system, a dichotomy between the forces of good and evil more absolute than in Christianity, Islam, or Judaism (Russell, 1977, 104ff.).

BUDDHISM. Many of the suprahuman beings important to Buddhist ontology were inherited from Hinduism. The *asura* is a jealous or hostile god/demon, while the *preta* is a ghost condemned to constant hunger; they are two of the unhappy destinies to which persons who have lived badly can be reborn in the world of sense experience. The *asuras* have been ejected from a divine realm of contentment ruled by its King, Indra. Māra, whose name means "death," promotes illusory thinking and vice, and behaves as a sort of Devil-figure in Buddhism. He tempted the Buddha with doubt as the latter was approaching enlightenment, even sending his own daughters and other minions to frighten and seduce him. Evil, however, is not personified by Māraas it is by Iranian evil gods or by the Judeo-Christian Devil, since evil, defined as suffering, is inevitable and necessary in the Buddhist world view. Mārais not responsible for cosmic evil as Satan is.

GREECE AND ROME. *Theos* (god) and *daimon* are near-synonyms in Homer (c. 800 BCE); *daimon* denotes more the power or agency of a god, rather than personality (cf. Latin *numen*). From Hesiod (c. 700 BCE) on, demons were considered inferior to the gods. Socrates' (d. 399 BCE) *daimon* was a kind of tutelary instinct, not necessarily external to him.

In the *Symposium,* Plato (d. 347 BCE) held that the gods, who have no direct contact with humans, use *daimons* as their messengers (*aggeloi*). Greek gods had no fixed good or evil character; nor did demons until the late Hellenistic period, when they were generally considered evil. Other spirits, not always explicitly called *daimons*, might have either fixed or changeable character. *Keres* were fate-like powers of evil and death for individuals; *heroes* were spirits of the dead; *Lamia, Empusa, Gello, and Mormo* were names for a female spirit that killed infants and (in some cases) coupled with sleeping men. The *Erinyes* and the *alastor* were spiritual avengers of the dead. Other figures, more important to mythology than to ordinary experience, were probably demons at their origin: the *Harpies* may have been wind-demons, and the *Gorgons* underworld- or sea-demons.

Roman spirits (*lares, manes, penates* and *genii*) were not unambiguously godlike or demonic or ghostly. The *Lamia,* however, had the same characteristics as her Greek namesake, while the *stryx,* a nocturnal demon who appeared as a screech-owl or a human shapeshifting witch, also assaulted sleeping babies (or according to some authors, suckled them with her own milk). Roman religion adopted the Etruscan death-demon *Charun,* making him the ferrier of souls to the underworld.

In Hellenistic demonology the Jew Philo of Alexandria (d. 40 CE) distinguished between angels and demons as good and evil spirits, although he classified some Gentile gods as angelic, against traditional Jewish "demonization" of them (see below). The Septuagint, a Greek translation of the Hebrew Bible begun in the third century, also made the angel/demon distinction. The Middle Platonist Plutarch (d. c. 120 CE) distinguished demons from gods and agreed that demons were entirely evil. In his *Platonic Theology,* Proclus (d. 485 CE) rationalized the system of gods, goddesses, heroes, and demons in Hellenistic religion, building on the Neoplatonism of Plotinus (d. 270 CE). But Proclus's concept of the Good as the highest principle, transcending all being, minimizes the distinctions between gods and demons, making Neoplatonic theology seem a de facto demonology. Accordingly, when Marsilio Ficino (d. 1499), Giovanni Pico della Mirandola (d. 1494), and other European philosophers of the fifteenth through seventeenth centuries revived Neoplatonic and Hermetic theology, guardians of Christian orthodoxy often suspected them of demon-worship.

JUDAISM. There are few recognizable demons in pre-exilic texts of the Hebrew Bible. Several beings mentioned there resemble spirits, and seem traceable to evil spirits of the Mesopotamians, Canaanites, and other neighbors, who believed that demons frequented remote and dangerous places. Desert demons were assimilated to or described as wild animals (*Isa.* 13:21; 34:14). Hebrew words for these spirits were rendered as *daimon* and *daimonion* by the translators of the Septuagint.

Lilith appears in the Hebrew Bible only once, as a nocturnal demon (*Isa.* 34:14); her name probably derives from Akkadian demonology. In middle Babylonian times, words related to Hebrew *līlīt* designate sterile, sexually frustrated, or uninitiated female demons, or a succubus demon (*Lilitu*). Later, Rabbinic commentators describe Lilith as the rebellious first wife of Adam, who, vainly claiming parity with him, left him and bore endless broods of demons. Lilith threatens newborn Jewish children with crib death, and must be warded off by an inscription invoking three angels God originally sent to subdue her. Saint Jerome (d. 420 CE) translated *līlīt* in Isaiah 34 as *Lamia;* his commentary identified the two infanticidal demons, maintaining that other Hebrew sources identify Lilith as an Erinys, or Fury.

Yahweh himself sometimes sent entities defined as or resembling evil spirits to punish erring Israelites or destroy their enemies (*1 Sam.* 16:14; *Judg.* 9:22–23; *1 Kings* 22:19ff.; *Exod.* 12:23; *Sirach* 39:28f.). But these agents had no more specificity or character than is implied by the tasks they performed for Yahweh; they were his "projections," and he could even accompany them (as in *Exod.* 12).

The role of Satan as chief of the demons evolved gradually. In pre-exilic texts, Hebrew *satan* was a common noun, designating any opponent or adversary. During the exile, the Israelites became acquainted with dualistic theologies deriving from the teachings of Zarathushtra, wherein divine rivals of equal power compete for human allegiance. Post-exilic texts (*1 Chron.* 21:1; *Job* 1:11; 2:5) describe a unique demonic adversary or *satan* of Israel or individual humans. This personage has an ambivalent relation to Yahweh, relieving him of responsibility for evil, but furthering, rather than opposing, his designs. The Septuagint translated this usage of *satan* as *diabolos.*

Post-exilic texts dismissed the gods and tutelary spirits worshipped by rival civilizations as empty idols. The Septuagint rendered the Hebrew terms for such foreign deities (especially *shedim*) as *daimon* even when translating pre-exilic texts (*Deut.* 32:17; *Ps.* 95:5, 105:37; *Isa.* 65:11).

The Jewish apocrypha and pseudepigrapha accelerated the dualistic process that turned all demons into the enemies of God. Notable is the demon Asmodeus of *Tobit* 3:8 and 17, who killed the first seven husbands of Sarah, and whose name may reflect a Persian phrase, *aeshma daeva,* or "demon of wrath." He was defeated by Raphael, an angel of the Lord.

Ancient tradition related that, on the Day of Atonement, the scapegoat, laden with the sins of the Israelites, was sent into the desert wastes "for Azazel" (*Lev.* 16:8–28). In *1 Enoch* and other pseudepigrapha, Azazel became a recognizable Devil-figure: ringleader of demons, enemy of God, and tempter of humans. According to these texts demons were originally holy angels, or "Watchers" (*egregori*) who rebelled because of their lust for human women (see below). Aside from Azazel, other texts named the demons' leader as Belial, Mastema, Satanael, Sammael, Semyaza, and *Satan.*

Pseudepigraphic and Talmudic sources identify some demons as the souls of deceased evil giants, who were born when the Watchers, also called *bene ha-elohim* or "sons of God," mated with the "daughters of men" (*1 Enoch* 6:2, etc.; cf. *Gen.* 6:1–4; *Deut.* 1:28; *Num.* 13:22, 33). The title "sons of God" reflects an older, semipolytheistic view of Yahweh as the sovereign of a heavenly court (cf. *Job* 1; *Ps.* 82). The dead-giant demons were numerous; one text counts 409,000 giants drowned by Noah's Flood (*3 Maccabees* 2:4; *Wisdom* 14:5–6; *1 Enoch* 15:8–16:1; *Jubilees* 10:1–3; *Testament of Solomon* 17:1; *3 Apocalypse of Baruch* 4:10). Demons are more frequently discussed in the Babylonian Talmud and the Midrashim than in the Jerusalem Talmud. Demons are important to Qabbalah, which drew on Christian and Muslim demonologies, including folklore, pursuing a systematic understanding of the subject. Although long-lived, demons are mortal, and may have been saved from extinction by Noah's Ark. The *Zohar* and later works of Qabbalah describe demons having natural bodies of fire and air and an inherent (rather than fictive or virtual) gender. Mating between male demons and women, and between female demons and men, is common, and produces demonic or hybrid children. Demons may depend on human semen even to reproduce their own species. Demons are organized into hosts, and control or meddle in most areas of human life; they must be carefully avoided or approached through incantations or by learning and using their individual seals.

CHRISTIANITY. As with Judaism, the Christian scriptural canon was formed gradually, creating an eclectic and evolving body of doctrine about spiritual beings. Like the contemporary Jewish apocrypha, new Testament demonology elaborated on canonical Hebrew texts. It also shows resemblances to various strains of Hellenistic religion and philosophy. Christian innovations took place mainly on two fronts, exorcism and the role of Satan. The Gospels describe demons or evil spirits (*daimon, daimonion, pneuma akatharton, pneuma poneron*) who possess or afflict humans, but fear and obey Jesus. Demons proclaim Jesus's power before witnesses by obeying his adjurations (*Matt.* 8:32; *Mark* 5:13; *Luke* 8:33), and through explicit verbal declarations (*Luke* 4:41; *Mark* 1:23–25, 34; *Matt.* 8:29; cf. *Mark* 5:7). By affirming his power, both miraculous healing and demonic utterances prove Jesus's divinity (cf. *Matt.* 8:16–17). Saint Paul (d. 65/67 CE) refers infrequently to demons (*1 Cor.* 10:20–21 [cf. *Deut.* 32:17]; 1 Timothy 4:1); other New Testament books concentrate on Satan and (in *Revelation*) the host of fallen angels.

Jesus and the Gospel writers present Satan as Jesus's declared personal adversary (*Mark* 3:23; *Luke* 11:18–21), paralleling the representation of Satan as Yahweh's adversary in Jewish apocrypha and further confirming Jesus's divinity. The rivalry between Jesus and Satan is developed in Saint Paul's *Epistles* and the *Book of Revelation*; the latter provides dramatically explicit visualizations of the divine Christ and the demonic hordes arrayed against him. *Luke, John, Paul,* and *Revelation* (e.g. chapter 12) consolidate the portrait of Satan as the leader of numerous evil angels who fell from Heaven because of their rebellion—not against Yahweh but against Christ (*Luke* 10:18; *Eph.* 2:1–2; 6:11–13; *2 Cor.* 6:14–16; *Col.* 2:15). "By the end of the New Testament period, Christian tradition made no distinction between fallen angels and demons" (Russell, 1977, p. 236).

Subsequent Christian literature internalized and spiritualized the danger of demonic persecution. Christian writers continued to see demons as responsible for human physical and psychological suffering, but also developed the notion of *temptation:* Satan tempts every Christian to oppose God through sin, just as he tempted Jesus in the desert (*Mark* 1:12–13; *Matt.* 4:1–11; *Luke* 4:1–13). All temptation, from Adam and Eve onward, was eventually credited to Satan. For most of the Middle Ages, demons were assumed to be ubiquitous and constantly tempting Christians and others. Such temptation usually happened privately and invisibly, though demons could act visibly and even publicly. The early monastic desert fathers regularly encountered demons who tempted them extravagantly, an experience detailed in Athanasius's (d. 373 CE) *Life of Saint Anthony* and elsewhere. The *incubus* demon was a sexual predator who polluted or violated sleeping women. The magician Merlin was supposedly born to a nun thus impregnated, while Saint Bernard of Clairvaux (d. 1153) allegedly defeated another incubus who tormented a pious laywoman. The popular legend of Theophilus (ninth to thirteenth centuries) described a priest who, disappointed in his career, contracted his soul to the Devil but was eventually rescued by the Virgin Mary.

After 1100, Western Christian interest in demons increased dramatically. The Fourth Lateran Council of 1215 declared that "the Devil and the other demons" (*diabolus et alii daemones)* were created good but became evil through free choice. The Book of Job, whose sophisticated theodicy explicitly portrayed "the satan's" responsibility for human suffering, became highly influential for both writers and visual artists. The apocryphal Book of Tobit, novelistically recounting the archangel Raphael's defeat of Sarah and Tobias's demonic persecutor Asmodeus, also evoked interest. Peter Lombard (d. 1160), Saint Thomas Aquinas (d. 1274), Saint Bonaventure (d. 1274), and many other theologians devoted systematic attention to good and—especially—evil angels, inventing *angelology* and *demonology* as a scientific subdiscipline of Christian theology. Treatises discussed the moral qualities of angels but also their history, social organization, psychology, physiology, and sexuality. Demonic corporeality became a major concern: since demons were thought sometimes to interact visibly and tangibly with humans, the question arose whether they had bodies, and if so, of what sort. Aquinas's solution prevailed: demons are pure spirit without matter, but can fabricate virtual bodies; thus they can afflict humans both internally (by possession and other invisible means) and in external reality (through apparition "in person"). Visual representations of demons became progressively more horrific after 1200, emphasizing a grotesque hybrid corporeality that seemed increasingly "real" rather than a visual allegory of spiritual perversity. This process was particularly notable in depictions of the Last Judgment and Hell, which were practically ubiquitous by the late Middle Ages. In these pictures, the interaction of spirits—human souls and demons—was portrayed as physical, corporeal violence.

Detailed literary and visual representations of the biblical demonic world relate to a growing interest in narratives about more recent human encounters and interactions with demons. About 1225, Caesarius of Heisterbach collected several dozen such tales in his *Dialogue on Miracles;* other collections of miracles and saints' biographies did likewise. In this period, exorcism, which had become formalized over the centuries, inspired intense interest in necromancy. This form of "black magic" arose in what Richard Kieckhefer (1989) has called the "clerical underworld" (pp. 153ff) of relatively learned professional exorcists. Originally defined as persons who commanded the souls of the dead (as in *Odyssey,* book 11 and the biblical story of Saul and the "Witch" of Endor [*1 Sam.* 28]) necromancers were redefined by Christian authorities as necessarily—and often willingly—contacting demons. While proponents defined necromancy as effected in the name of God, ecclesiastical consensus countered that it necessarily involved unholy alliances with demons.

"Demonization" of individuals and social groups, based on the notion of the demon as *satan* or *diabolos*—adversary—became a major vehicle of political and religious persecution during the Christian Middle Ages. Jews, heretics, "infidels," political enemies and vulnerable targets of opportunity (e.g., the Templars) were defined as unremittingly evil, and as literally in league with the Devil; their destruction was incumbent on the pious or orthodox. Between the twelfth and the fifteenth centuries, Catholic enforcers of orthodoxy, becoming sensitized to the spread of necromancy, also encountered widespread and alarming heresies among the laity (e.g., Catharism, Waldensianism, Hussitism). They thus began attempting to verify rumors, dating to the eleventh century, that even unlettered heretics had regular demonic encounters. Stereotypical "confessions" of such experiences, extracted under torture from real or suspected heretics, were cited to explain the origin and appeal of heretical doctrines. Confessions further stimulated officials' curiosity by portraying demons with vivid and shocking immediacy, creating a vicious cycle of inquiry and confirmation.

By the 1430s both ecclesiastical and secular judges were pursuing a new variety of super-heretic, the Witch, created by this process. Unlike previous heretics, witches were not considered merely deluded about doctrine. The Witch voluntarily sought to encounter Satan and his demons "in person," attending vast but secret mass meetings (the Sabbat or "Witches' Dance") where humans worshiped Satan as their god and had orgiastic sex with demons. Official theories about witches grew exponentially more sensational and complicated, making witchcraft responsible for society's most intractable problems—crop failure, disease, infertility, infant, adult, and animal mortality, religious and political turmoil.

In fact, the Witch was a phantom of the inquisitorial imagination, evoked by a coercive dialogue between tortured defendants and demon-obsessed prosecutors and judges, but the witch stereotype resisted facts, proof, and compassion until after 1700, killing some 50,000 to 60,000 defendants in western Christendom. Thanks to this "witch craze," narratives of human-demon interaction are an important preoccupation of western culture and a major subgenre of its literature. From Christopher Marlowe's *Dr. Faustus* (1590s), John Milton's *Paradise Lost* (1674), and Johann Wolfang von Goethe's *Faust* (1790), to Aldous Huxley's *Devils of Loudun* (1952), Arthur Miller's *Crucible* (1953) and Ira Levin's *Rosemary's Baby* (1967), the Devil and the demonization of his accused allies have retained their fascination.

Nor is the phenomenon of demonization limited to Christianity—or to religion. The perception of an imperfect natural or social order leads in extreme cases to a kind of collective paranoia: disasters are blamed on powerful saboteurs, who mask their immense malignant power beneath a pretense of marginality or benignity. Like demons, they are imagined as powerful, omnipresent, and immune to conventional methods of discovery or ordinary human justice. Extraordinary, extralegal measures are required to unmask and neutralize the threat, or legality itself must be redefined. The *Protocols of the Elders of Zion,* the Holocaust, and aspects of more recent genocides (e.g., Rwanda, Kosovo) bear witness to the powerful appeal of this myth. Evidence of its appeal also appears in the "show trials" and gulags of Stalinism (1930s), Mao Zedong's Cultural Revolution (1960s), Pol Pot's Cambodia (1970s), and the House Un-American Activities Committee under Joseph McCarthy (1950s). When "things go wrong," and no external enemy is clearly to blame, the evil will be sought inside the afflicted social body. Manifest powerlessness or a clear record of benignity offer no protection from persecution: as was often proclaimed in early modern Europe, the devil's subtlest trick is to convince us that he doesn't exist. Demonization occurs interculturally as well: a society's internal cohesion is enhanced by a dualistic world-view that identifies foreign antagonists as completely evil. It is more important that the antagonist be completely wrong and evil than for "us" to be completely right and good.

ISLAM. The most widespread figures in Islamic demonology are the *djinn* or jinns. They are ontologically intermediate, somewhat like the Greek *daimonia* and the Judeo-Christian angels and devils. According to the Qurʾān (LV, 14), their bodies were created of smokeless flame, while human bodies came from clay and angelic bodies from light. Jinns are of both sexes. Given their ethereal composition, jinns are normally imperceptible to humans, but may become perceptible in a variety of guises, including giants, dwarves, or animals. In pre-Islamic Arabia, jinns were desert beings like nymphs and satyrs, and hostile to humans; they were gradually "spiritualized." By Muḥammad's time, Arabs of Mecca were sacrificing to them and seeking their favor (Qurʾān VI, 128; LXXII, 6).

Jinns have a social organization and family life, and interact variously with humans, including through romantic love and intermarriage. They can be contacted through various forms of magic, and may respond favorably, but can also be easily offended and will react accordingly. At times they behave playfully, teasing and tricking humans. Jinns are prominent in folklore, popular magic, and literature, from the *Thousand and One Nights* onward. The notion of the jinn has been transmitted from Arabia to non-Arabic centers of Islamic culture, where it blends variously with local traditions about spirits.

Subclasses of the jinn are the *Ghūl,* the *si'lat,* and the *'ifrīt.* For ancient Arabs, the *Ghūl* (etymon of English *ghoul*) was a shape-shifting being who lived in desert wastes and led travelers astray. The *Ghūl* may be male or female; according to differing traditions, the *si'lat* may be either a female *Ghūl* or a kind of witch among the ghouls; some writers maintain that men can sire children on a *si'lat* but not on a *Ghūl.* In popular usage *Ghūl* may designate a human or demonic cannibal; this usage has inspired English and French concepts of ogres and vampires (*ghoul, goule*). The *'ifrīt* is a powerful, cunning, frightening jinn, and may also be thought identical to a *marid;* alternatively, one may be more powerful than the other.

The *shaytān* for pre-Islamic Arabs was a jinn, a kind of "genie" or "genius" or guardian spirit who was sometimes good, sometimes evil; as tutelary spirit it was also called the *karin.* It was responsible for inspiration of all sorts, and human progress in general, but particularly for poetic inspiration. The *shaytān* could also be a rebellious jinn, thus an "evil spirit" or "demon."

In Islamic usage, the singular *al-Shaytān* is a personal name paralleling Jewish and Christian references to Satan. This figure is also named Iblīs (possibly a contraction of *diabolos).* His epithets include *'Aduww Allāh* (Enemy of God) and *al-'Aduww* (The Enemy). The Islamic Satan resembles the Christian and late Jewish figure, as portrayed in the two Testaments and in apocrypha such as the *Life of Adam and Eve.* Areas of uncertainty or disagreement about Iblīs/*al-Shaytān* remain in Muslim commentary, especially regarding whether he is an angel (*mal'ak*) or a jinn. Angels are considered ontologically sinless by some, and have other characteristics incompatible with Iblīs's fundamental rebelliousness and even his physical makeup as presented in the Qur'ān. Also unclear is the exact nature of his sin, particularly the relation between his pride and his disobedience.

DOUBT, SKEPTICISM, UNBELIEF. Since demonic beings are by definition invisible most or all of the time, belief in their responsibility for human welfare or suffering—and belief in their very existence—varies considerably over time.

Until recently, the narrative of progress by which western societies define themselves inspired confident assertions that these societies were "outgrowing" or had already abandoned the belief in demonic reality. However, developments since the 1980s belie such a facile scenario. In the United States, polls register a majority of persons claiming to believe in spirit phenomena. The literal, personal existence of the Devil has been strongly affirmed by charismatic and fundamentalist Protestants and by Catholics alike. Meanwhile, exorcism, which the Second Vatican Council of the 1960s had de-emphasized, has become a divisive issue, even in the Pope's own diocese of Rome. In the United States and elsewhere, the same period has witnessed panics over alleged Satanic cults and "satanic ritual child abuse," along with enthusiastic New Age variants of angelolatry, benign or "white" witchcraft and magic, and the space-age demonology of "alien abduction syndrome" and "multiple personality syndrome." These movements variously express a lost sense of religious connection or "spirituality"—a term that defies precise definition and often seems not to require belief in actual spirits.

On the other hand, the assumption that, before the advent of scientific thinking in the seventeenth century, all Christians and Jews, or the overwhelming majority of them, believed in the literal existence of demons and angels, is equally erroneous. Skepticism about spirit did not arise suddenly in the 1600s; Aquinas himself had recognized the need to rebut it. Skepticism provoked the earliest treatises by militant witch-hunting demonologists (1460s), and remained a constant anxiety of Christian demonology even after 1700, when widespread witch-hunting had ceased.

The Sadducees, a Jewish sect in the time of Jesus, refused to believe in spirit (*Mark* 12:18; *Acts* 23:8). As detailed above, the oldest books of the Hebrew Bible make no mention of angels and demons as beings distinct from and subordinate to Yahweh, or to an individual named "Satan." The Jewish philosopher Moses Maimonides (d. 1204) opposed the belief in demons. Among Muslims, the question of the real existence of *jinn* was problematic. Ibn Sina (Avicenna, d. 1037) denied their existence, and Ibn Khaldūn (d. 1406) opined that only God knew the truth, while other philosophers variously evaded the question. Scholars also debated the nature or the real existence of the *ghūl,* which does not appear in the Qur'ān. It is uncertain to what extent the Buddha believed in the empirical reality of demons.

Epicurean and other ancient materialistic philosophies, which asserted the perishability of the human soul, remained familiar—mostly through hostile paraphrases—throughout the "Age of Faith," or Christian Middle Ages. Thomas Aquinas observed that some contemporary Aristotelian philosophers denied the reality of angels and devils; on one occasion he attributed the attitude to Aristotle himself. Accusations of philosophical skepticism were periodically leveled at innovative thinkers during the thirteenth and following centuries, at times with apparent justification. The philosopher Pietro Pomponazzi argued exhaustively between 1516 and 1520 that Aristotle's philosophy lent no support to the reality of angels, demons, magic, or human immortality, while the Fifth Lateran Council of 1513 dogmatically reaffirmed human immortality as an article of faith. From Aquinas until nearly 1800, Christian apologists regularly invoked the phenomena of witchcraft and exorcism as proof that angels, demons, and the immortal soul were not imaginary.

Between about 1550 and 1700, epidemics of demonic possession among Western Christians, often linked to accusations of witchcraft, provided compellingly theatrical arguments for demons' reality, but also provoked widespread skepticism. As demonic witchcraft was progressively discredited, interest shifted to ghosts (in the eighteenth century) and spiritualism (in the nineteenth) among those interested in defending the reality of spirit and human immortality. Yet purported demonstrations continued to produce skepticism and ridicule.

The enduring controversies over the reality of demons and spirits provide ample evidence that the drive to understand cosmic forces in human terms is not restricted to "primitive," "medieval," or "unscientific" societies.

SEE ALSO Angels; Devils; Monsters.

BIBLIOGRAPHY

Still useful is the entry "Demons and Spirits" in *The Encyclopedia of Religion and Ethics,* edited by James Hastings, vol. 4 (Edinburgh, 1911), a series of twenty articles concerning as many cultures. Although they concentrate on the figure of the Devil in Christian religion, the books by Jeffrey Burton Russell (below) contain frequent and useful discussions of demonology in several cultures from the ancient Near East to modern times. Karel van der Toorn, Bob Becking, and Pieter W. van der Horst, *Dictionary of Deities and Demons in the Bible: (DDD),* 2d ed. (Leiden, 1999) has in-depth articles regarding not only the Hebrew and Christian Bible but also its ancient sources and analogous demonological lore elsewhere.

Tribal Cultures

Collins, John J. *Primitive Religion.* Totowa, N.J., 1978. Chap. 8, "Supernatural Beings and Myths," pp. 190–227, includes cross-cultural examples and bibliography.

Fletcher, Angus. *Allegory: The Theory of a Symbolic Mode.* Ithaca, N.Y., 1964.

Tylor, E. B. *Primitive Culture,* vol. 1, *Religion in Primitive Culture* (1871; reprint [of chaps. 11–19], Gloucester, Mass., 1970). One of the founding texts for the topic.

Hinduism

Lochtefeld, James G. *The Illustrated Encyclopedia of Hinduism.* 2 vols. New York, 2002. See articles "Ancestral Spirits," "Deities," "Demons," "Deva," "Rakshasa," "Vetala."

Witzel, Michael. "Veda and Upaniṣads," in *The Blackwell Companion to Hinduism.* Edited by Gavin Flood, pp. 68–98, esp. 71–73, "Ṛgvedic Mythology." Oxford, 2003

Buddhism

Bunce, Fredrick W. *An Encyclopaedia of Buddhist Deities, Demigods, Godlings, Saints and Demons: With Special Focus on Iconographic Attributes.* Illustrations by G.X. Capdi. 2 vols. New Delhi, 1994.

Buswell, Robert E., gen. ed. *Encyclopedia of Buddhism.* 2 vols. New York, 2004. See articles "Ancestors" (Mariko Namba Walter); "Divinities" (Jacob N. Kinnard); "Evil" (Maria Heim); "Ghosts and Spirits" (Peter Masefield); "Hells" (Stephen F. Teiser); "Hells, Images of" (Karil J. Kucera); "Local Divinities and Buddhism" (Fabio Rambelli); "Māra" (Jacob N. Kinnard); "Realms of Existence" (Rupert Gethin); "Saṃsāra" (Bryan J. Cuevas); "Yakṣa" (Jacob N. Kinnard).

Greece and Rome

Luck, Georg. *Arcana Mundi. Magic and the Occult in the Greek and Roman Worlds.* Baltimore, 1985. A now-classic collection of texts; see pp. 163–175 for a succinct analysis of kinds of spirits.

Ogden, Daniel. *Greek and Roman Necromancy.* Princeton, N.J., 2001. See esp. pp. 219–230.

Ogden, Daniel. *Magic, Witchcraft, and Ghosts in the Greek and Roman Worlds.* Oxford, 2002. Another excellent anthology of texts.

Price, Simon, and Emily Kearns, eds. *The Oxford Dictionary of Classical Myth and Religion.* Oxford, 2003.

Judaism

Jung, Leo. *Fallen Angels in Jewish, Christian and Mohammedan Literature.* New York, 1974.

Langton, Edward. *Essentials of Demonology: A Study of Jewish and Christian Demonology, Its Origin and Development.* London, 1949.

Rappoport, Angelo S. *Ancient Israel: Myths and Legends.* 1928. Reprint, New York, 1987.

Roth, Cecil, and Geoffrey Wigoder, gen. eds. *Encyclopaedia Judaica.* 16 vols. Jerusalem, 1971. See articles "Asmodeus" (Editorial Staff, 3.754–755); "Azazel" (Shmuel Aḥituv, 3.999–1002); "Demons, Demonology" (Delbert Roy Hillers, Louis Isaac Rabinowitz, Gershom Scholem, 5.1521–1533); Lilith (Gershom Scholem, 11.245–249); "Samael" (Gershom Scholem, 14.719–722); "Satan" (Louis Isaac Rabinowitz and Editorial Staff, 14.902–905).

Christianity

Clark, Stuart. *Thinking with Demons: The Idea of Witchcraft in Early Modern Europe.* Oxford, 1997.

Cohn, Norman. *Europe's Inner Demons: An Enquiry Inspired by the Great Witch-Hunt.* New York, 1975.

Flint, Valerie. "The Demonisation of Magic and Sorcery in Late Antiquity: Christian Redefinitions of Pagan Religions." In *Witchcraft and Magic in Europe. Ancient Greece and Rome.* Philadelphia, 1999, pp. 277–348.

Keck, David. *Angels and Angelology in the Middle Ages.* Oxford, UK, 1998.

Kieckhefer, Richard. *European Witch Trials: Their Foundations in Popular and Learned Culture.* Berkeley, Calif., 1976.

Kieckhefer, Richard. *Magic in the Middle Ages.* Cambridge, U.K., 1989.

Russell, Jeffrey Burton. *The Devil: Perceptions of Evil from Antiquity to Primitive Christianity.* Ithaca, N.Y., 1977.

Russell, Jeffrey Burton. *Satan: The Early Christian Tradition.* Ithaca, N.Y., 1981.

Russell, Jeffrey Burton. *Lucifer: The Devil in the Middle Ages.* Ithaca, N.Y., 1984.

Russell, Jeffrey Burton. *Mephistopheles: The Devil in the Modern World.* Ithaca, N.Y., 1986.

Strickland, Deborah Higgs. *Saracens, Demons, and Jews: Making Monsters in Medieval Art.* Princeton, N.J., 2003. Comparison of negative stereotypes and demonizations.

Islam

Gibb, H. A. R., B. Lewis, E. van Donzel, C. E. Bosworth, P. J. Bearman, et al., eds. *The Encyclopedia of Islam, New Edition.* Leiden, 1960–2002. 11 vols. plus supplements. See articles "Ḍjinn" (P. Voorhoeve 2.546–550); "Ghūl" (D. B. Macdonald, Ch. Pellat, 2.1078–1079); "Iblīs" (A. J. Wensinck, L. Gardet, 3.668–669); "ʿIfrīt" (J. Chelhod, 3.1050–1051); "Malāʾika" (D. B. Macdonald, W. Madelung, 6.216–219); "al-Shaytān " (T. Fahd, A. Rippin, 9.406–409).

McAuliffe, Jane Dammen, ed. *The Encyclopaedia of the Qurʾān.* 3 vols. issued. Leiden, 2001—. "Angel" (Gisela Webb, 1.84–92); "Devil" (Andrew Rippin, 1. 524–527); "ʿIfrīt" (Thomas Bauer, 2.486–487); "Jinn" (Jacqueline Chabbi, 3.43–50); "Spiritual Beings" (as yet unreleased).

Doubt, Skepticism, Unbelief

Popkin, Richard H. *The History of Skepticism: From Savonarola to Bayle.* New York, 2003. The standard text in this field; the third rev. ed. of a book first published in 1960.

Stein, Gordon, ed. *The Encyclopedia of Unbelief.* 2 vols. Buffalo, N.Y., 1985. See especially "Devil, Unbelief in the Concept of" (George V. Tomashevich); "Evil, Problem of" (Peter H. Hare); "Immortality, Unbelief in" (Leon J. Putnam); "Skepticism" (Richard H. Popkin). Though it purports to describe phenomena of unbelief, this work often dedicates most of its attention to belief. There are no entries for unbelief in spirits, demons, or angels.

Stephens, Walter. *Demon Lovers: Witchcraft, Sex, and the Crisis of Belief.* Chicago, 2002. Argues that early modern European demonic witchcraft was an invention of literate Christian elites, and that it constituted "resistance to skepticism," reinforcing their own faltering belief in the reality of spirits, sacraments and divine benevolence by providing supposed evidence of human-demon encounters.

WALTER STEPHENS (2005)

DEMONS: PSYCHOLOGICAL PERSPECTIVES

The experience of the demon as a supernatural being that can affect human life for good or for bad is found all over the world. Modern depth psychology provides us with a fuller understanding of the nature of this phenomenon. Even in modern civilization where there is no longer the belief in demons, demons continue to play an important role. The existence of demons is a fact. The question of central importance is "How does consciousness interpret this fact?"

The interpretation depends upon the development of consciousness and the awareness of the multiple forces that determine human personality and experience. A more advanced stage of consciousness can look back at the preceding stage and describe it. For the present stage of consciousness, however, there exists no outside objective and critical standpoint from which to observe it. C. G. Jung has distinguished five different stages in the development of consciousness (also referred to as stages of the relation between object and subject). I would like to discuss the attitude toward the existence of demons at each of these five stages with reference first to cultures in which the stage of consciousness dominates and then to cultures of modern Western civilization.

Examples of each of these five stages can be found in human psychology side by side with the more advanced stages. There is no civilization in which consciousness belongs only and exclusively to one stage alone, because different psychological faculties will be developed to a different degree at any one time. Even though the main function may become advanced and rational, the inferior function remains archaic and closely aligned with the unconscious psyche.

THE MYTH OF THE COSMIC MAN: ARCHAIC MENTALITY. The unconscious psyche is the original mind of man, his primeval mentality, with which he still functions through his instincts. All persons function in this archaic way when unconscious; that is, to be unconscious in psychological terms is to be governed simply by the unconscious forces of instinct. Humankind has survived for hundreds of thousands of years supported by this primordial mentality, living in a state of identify with the environment called by Lucien Lévy-Bruhl "the participation mystique." The fact that humankind survived the Stone Age points to the value of this instinctive behavior.

The consciousness of these early stages of humankind and of today's hunters and gatherers resembles that of early childhood. At this stage man lives undifferentiated from his surroundings. This does not mean that he cannot differentiate between himself and the objects around him, but rather that for him these objects are alive: they have soul and behave like animated beings. In the words of Jung, the individual lives as though he were immersed "in a stream of events in which outer and inner worlds are not differentiated, or are differentiated very indistinctly."

For archaic man, the whole world reflects his psyche, or his psyche is just as much outside as inside, because as long as a psychic content is unconscious, it will appear in both realms. This stage of consciousness is mirrored in the myth of the cosmic man, a giant who pervades the entire universe; examples are the Indian Puruṣa or the Scandinavian Ymir. The psyche of archaic man is everywhere. All of the objects in the universe of archaic man lead their own purposeful lives, influencing or even dominating him. He feels inferior to these powers of nature and worships or propitiates them. Religion and magic are at his disposal in order to deal with these powers. Because his own ego is ill defined, it is easily transformed into an animal or possessed by one of the surrounding powers, by a spirit or a demon, or transformed into an animal. Possession belongs to this mentality, and one can be exorcised as easily as possessed.

By worshiping these powers, human beings acknowledge their reality and importance, and they are kept in the awareness of the entire community. Only when something escapes our attention and is thus neglected are we in danger of being possessed by it.

Possession—when our actions are determined by some psychic (or spiritual) force that overwhelms the ego—is by no means a phenomenon restricted to primitive societies, nor is it limited to those in our present civilization whom we call possessed. On the contrary, it is a universal experience. Whenever an unconscious power takes over the ego, possession occurs. Archaic man is threatened by all the demons and spirits around him, but at the same time he is wrapped also in the protection of the symbolic mother; that is, he is protected by powers that look out for him and provide him with sustenance so that he does not have to worry about himself. For example, when the Kusase people hear a certain tree in the village ask for a new dress and for new offerings, they are not surprised since this happens from time to time. In the context of their world, this is a common event and demands no explanation.

The idea of an all-pervading power in nature (*mana, manitou, orenda, wakanda*) forms part of this animistic view of existence. And magic is the primitive technology that seeks to manage this power. But the religious attitude is already prominent at this stage in the person of the shaman, rainmaker, or weathermaker, who is a specialist in dealing with spiritual powers. Furthermore, the power becomes embodied in certain sacred persons such as the chief, warrior, or blacksmith, as well as in sacred objects such as swords, stones, and medicine.

In modern Western civilization this archaic attitude still survives. Not only fairy tales and legends but also the words of poets reflect this attitude. And whenever an emotion lays hold of us, we fall back into such archaic behavior; for example, we kick the corner that "hit us," or we swear at the car that refuses to budge. We treat things as if they had a will of their own. This indicates that we believe that things share our human nature: the lime tree in the famous folk song bears all the feelings of love and the sorrow of farewell that men and women experience beneath its branches. We find ourselves feeling attached to objects as well as to persons, and when either fails to act according to our expectations, we experience strong emotion, because we identify with them to a certain extent.

If we look closely at our fears, we may detect the old demons and spirits in modern disguise: irrational fear of cancer or of atomic energy, idiosyncrasy, fear of war and power. We do not trust our modern consciousness to be able to handle these mighty things; there might be a demon in them that would make a fool of us. And we still worship the body of Christ in the host or the represented person in icons. In Switzerland, mountain climbing was avoided for a long time because of the belief in a divine numen living on top of the mountain. Old names point to this fact, such as the Vrenelisgärtli of Glärnisch, or "garden of Venus." Many names of parcels of land or of rivers also refer to the ancient spirits of nature that formerly lived in these places. Most vegetation rites in May and on midsummer's night recall the spirits of grain. Many Europeans still put a fir tree with colored ribbons on a newly built house in order to appease the spirits who will enter and dwell there. In Greek religion, the spirits of nature are personified as nymphs, dryads, and satyrs as well as in the form of the god Pan and numerous other local deities. Many of the sanctuaries of the Virgin Mary found in the woods, in a grotto, or by a well have inherited the site from pagan spirits. In the beginning of the common era, Christian churches were built on the site of earlier temples, sometimes with the stones of the earlier temples, because the power of the numen was already present there. Modern exorcists continue to banish ghosts in places that have been haunted for ages.

THE SACRIFICE OF THE COSMIC MAN: PROJECTION. In the myth of the cosmic man, the giant is sacrificed by the gods or by the wise men of old. This sacrifice symbolizes the cultural moment when the archaic mentality is sacrificed in favor of a different level of consciousness. This moment seems to correspond to the great Neolithic revolution of humankind, the transition from a life of hunting and gathering foods (living off the gifts of nature, the symbolic mother) to the life in which both plants and animals were domesticated. In agriculture and the herding of animals, humankind assumed some responsibility for husbanding natural resources and providing a steady food supply the human being. At this point he becomes separate from its environment; for the first time there occurs a split between human as subject and nature as object. Differentiation from the environment is one of the most difficult tasks for humankind. Psychic development (individuation) depends upon the ongoing continuation of this process. However, the individual is constantly threatened by demons, threatened, that is, by forces that are unconscious. The mythical combat between the hero and the dragon mirrors this dangerous situation.

Therefore it is consciousness that, in effect, creates the cosmos, for in the differentiation of consciousness the world comes into being as a realm separate from man. From this stage onward we can properly speak of a projection whenever there is any doubt as to whether or not a phenomenon does, in fact, belong to the outer world in which we seem to experience it. For example, when a schizophrenic of our civilization hears the voice of the devil, it is correct to interpret the voice as a projection of something that exists within him rather than something existing in the world.

Usually a demon is understood to be a supernatural being of a nature intermediate between that of gods and men. In the writings of Homer, the word for "demon," *daimōn*, can still refer to a god or, in a rather vague sense, to a divine efficacy. In a famous passage of Plato's *Symposium*, Diotima describes Eros as a "great spirit [*daimōn*], and like all spirits a being intermediate between the divine and the mortal" (202e). Psychologically speaking, this corresponds to the complex of the collective unconscious as defined by Jung. The complex, which is a necessary and normal component of the psyche, is intermediate between the ego and the archetype, having both a personal and an impersonal aspect. Whereas the archetypes are inborn dispositions, the complex comes into being through experiences in the individual life.

At this stage of consciousness, for example, the warrior is no longer believed to be generally demonic, but rather he becomes the berserker who fights with a mad frenzy only when he is possessed by the god Odin. Mediumship and possession attributed to specific gods or spirits are regular phenomena at this stage of consciousness. At this level, every disease is explained as the result of a spirit or demon. They are primitive forms of what we call mental disorders or *Geisteskrankheit* ("spirit-illness"). In psychological terms, a complex, also called a partial personality, takes over the ego.

The shaman is the master of spirits, the one who has overcome his own states of possession. Demons are far from being only noxious. In spirit-mediumship the spirits mediate the power of divination, providing information about the future and about matters removed from ordinary perception. They mediate between the spirit world and men and convey to their society the beneficial power of the gods. Everyone may have his own guiding spirit that controls to some effect his behavior. Mediumship may be experienced as a vocation whereby a spirit chooses a specific person as its vehicle. Our word *inspiration* means that a spirit is whispering wisdom into the ear of the inspired. When the world as a whole is no longer believed to be alive, it remains, nevertheless, filled with spirits and demons. One must be careful lest one be tripped up by a demon unnoticed. Spirit possession can even be contagious, especially during adolescence.

Spirits, particularly those of dead ancestors, may have control over the fertility of the earth, because they are believed to live in the earth under the ground or above the rain clouds. Passing by a cemetery one must take care not to be bewitched by a lurking ghost, the spirit of an ancestor that might cause illness or even death. (Psychologically, this appears to be the same fear that one experiences today when passing by a graveyard late at night.) Furthermore, a young girl has to be careful when she walks by a pond lest one of the unborn souls lurking there might jump into her womb and make her pregnant. The ghosts of the dead are especially hungry and desirous of blood or meat, food that must be provided through sacrifices. The great power of a mighty man continues to hold sway even after his death. In the vicinity of the grave of a *shaykh* there is a palm tree and a conical stone; barren women may silently step over the stone seven times and eat dates from the tree in order to become pregnant.

A regressive appearance of demons and spirits occurs when the high gods become remote. This often happens when a new civilization overlays an older one, whether by historical change or by conquest. The conquerors impose their social and administrative systems upon the conquered people, but they are themselves unconsciously infected by the spiritual culture of the latter. Some conquering tribes believe that the vanquished tribe survives in spirit form. In the new religious system the high gods become demons and spirits. As high gods they had received a cult and were represented in the collective consciousness, but in the new system they sink into relative unconsciousness. The Greek magical papyri are full of ancient high gods and goddesses, among them both Hekate and Hermes. Hellenistic syncretism absorbed many gods of the Mediterranean culture. In early Christianity the pagan gods became demons or spirits. The medieval iconography of the Devil, for example, depicts the Greek god Pan, who in ancient times was first a spirit of nature and the god of shepherds and finally became god of the universe. (In Greek *pan* means "all.") Plutarch relates the story of the death of the great Pan, according to which some sailors learn of the event and bring the tale to an island, whereupon a great lamentation ensues. This story marks the end of the archaic worship of nature, an end that resulted from the rise of Christianity. Our modern dilemma deriving from the pollution of nature demonstrates the practical value in the worship of ancient nature spirits, which served to render the superhuman quality of nature conscious to humankind, forming a consciousness that has been lost up to our present time. Today, natural science is searching again for the mysteries of nature, albeit with a rationalistic attitude.

MORAL DIFFERENTIATION: BELIEF IN A WORLD OF GOOD AND EVIL DEMONS. In the ancient story of Jacob's fight with the angel at the Jabbok River (*Gn.* 32:24) Yahveh is a deadly but not evil power. In the tale of Job from a later period, Satan ("the adversary") is one of the sons of God and represents the partial separation of an inner opposition generated by God himself. Similar is the history of the *deva/daēva* common to both prehistoric India and Iran. Originally the term was a neutral one referring to the celestial, daytime sky. After further development in India the term *deva* came to signify the high gods. In Iran, however, *daēva* acquired the meaning of "demon" in the evil sense.

Moral differentiation splits the world further into the opposites of night and day, earth and sky, left and right, good and evil. The collective consciousness is always in danger of identifying with one of a pair of opposites, abandoning the second to the demonic powers of the unconscious. Such an attitude gave rise, for example, to the Black Mass. Neglected aspects of the psyche are not simply repressed and forgotten, they become more and more powerful in the unconscious psyche and more disturbing to the conscious personality. A worldview that fails to acknowledge and experience the original unity of the opposites is in danger of an invasion from the neglected or rejected side. Psychologically, every optimistic or exclusively good attitude calls forth a reaction from its opposite. The more one-sided the conscious attitude, the larger grows the demonic counterworld.

THE ENLIGHTENMENT: DENIAL OF THE EXISTENCE OF DEMONS. Modern literature on demons is written for the most part from the standpoint of rationalism and attempts to explain demons as superstitious phenomena of a primitive mentality. The psychoanalytic approach developed by Sigmund Freud toward religious phenomena in general shares this attitude. It is a necessary transitional stage in the development of consciousness for man to ask "Who creates the demons?" and to answer "It is I!" In fact, man cannot help assuming responsibility for the products of his own imagination. They have arisen in him, and therefore he is their creator. Thus man identifies with his consciousness and explains all unconscious phenomena as derivative of that consciousness.

But in our time we can observe a certain counterreaction to this one-sided view in the form of irrational reactions: the new religions; the parapsychology enthusiasts; drug-based religion and fascination with science fiction among the youth; the "worship" of the natural wisdom of animals by some modern scientists; and the popularity of modern myths such as J. R. R. Tolkien's *Lord of the Rings.*

OBJECTIVITY OF THE PSYCHE: *UNUS MUNDUS.* Modern analytical psychology attributes to demons a reality of their own, recognizing the important role they play in the psychology of man. Because the *Auseinandersetzung* (Ger., "coming to terms") with the world of demons and spirits in the individuation process is so important, Jung specified a method called active imagination in which the figures of the unconscious are regarded as autonomous living entities of the psyche. Using this method it is possible to approach the archaic mentality from a position of conscious responsibility, acknowledging the unconscious and its personifications (demons, spirits, ghosts, fairies, angels, and so on) and seeking to find the appropriate way to respond to them. For these personifications may become conscious to the ego, but they are not created by it. The ego is obligated to take the unconscious realities into consideration. (This process recalls the Latin *relegere,* "*to gather up again.*") Spirits and demons must be allowed to arise as inner figures so that the ego can come to terms with them.

Sometimes one central spirit becomes the leading principle. This figure is called the archetype of the Anthropos, or the Self in human form (the unconscious principle of personality). Often the Anthropos is experienced as an inner guide, as, for example, Poimandres ("shepherd of men"), Agathos Daimōn ("good spirit"), and Hermes-Thoth in antiquity; Mercurius in alchemy; and Khidr in Islam. The *daimōn* of Socrates was a figure or a voice of a similar kind who forbade him certain things. A later variation is the guardian spirit who mediated between the spirit world and man, bringing dreams and foretelling the future.

The contemporary notion of spirits affects our understanding of mental illness as well as the psychic side of physical illness. Lauri Honko has studied the belief in so-called sickness projectiles, and he demonstrates the appearance of this belief in numerous cultures. For example, the German expression for lumbago is *Hexenschuss,* which means literally "the witch's shot."

The projection plays an important role in the transference of complexes from one person to another. Unconscious complexes are always projected onto other persons whom they may harm. Emotions are energy-laden phenomena that also affect other people. Typically, the gods of love (Eros, Cupid, Amor, Kāma) are armed with a bow and arrow, indicating that projections are sent by the divine principle or demon. But Job's plague, too, was caused by the arrows of Yahveh (*Job* 6:4), and the Vedic god Rudra sends death and illness with his arrows (*Rgveda* 7.46). A demon can be either a pathological complex or a new, creative impulse; both issue forth in connection with an archetype and embody a value that can destroy or save the individual person.

Further, the reality that analytical psychology attributes to demons provides insight into the parapsychological meaning of ghosts. The autonomy of the complex, together with the concept of synchronicity (the meaningful coincidence of events), provides tools with which we can understand, though not explain, the psychology of apparitions. French and English literature on this topic is extensive and points to a common belief in locally bound spirits, the *genius loci,* often depicted as a snake. In Roman families the genius was also a spirit of fertility. Modern parapsychology takes into account the psychological conditions that give rise to the appearance of apparitions. Beyond any doubt there are some people who are simply more aware of or sensitive to such phenomena; they are often said to possess second sight. Nevertheless, such occurrences are not uncommon for the less sensitive.

There is little doubt of the existence of the phenomena that have been called demons, angels, spirits, ghosts, and so on. But since these are experiences of a psychic nature, they can never be known except by means of such inner images.

SEE ALSO Spirit Possession.

BIBLIOGRAPHY

The most important work for this topic from the standpoint of analytical psychology is Marie-Louise von Franz's *Projection and Re-Collection in Jungian Psychology* (La Salle, Ill., 1980). Recent encyclopedic works mostly treat the topic historically and geographically. I mention here only the more recent and extensive ones. Lutz Röhrich gives a concise survey of demons in legends and fairy tales, including a psychological section, under "Dämon," in *Enzyklopädie des Märchens,* vol. 3 (Berlin, 1979). Material from the standpoint of the history of Christianity is collected in Otto Böcher's article "Dämonen," in *Theologische Realenzyklopädie,* vol. 8 (Berlin, 1981); articles include extensive bibliographies, with mention of Judaism. Even more comprehensive is the article "Geister (Dämonen)," with extensive bibliography, by Carsten Colpe and others in *Reallexikon für Antike und Christentum,* vol. 9 (Stuttgart, 1976). The standard reference for the Bible and Judaism is Werner Foerster's article "Demon," in the *Theological Dictionary of the New Testament* (1935), translated by Geoffrey W. Bromiley (Grand Rapids, Mich., 1964), which also gives the meaning of the term in folklore. Andres's article "Daimōn," in *Pauly's Real-encyclopädie der classischen Altertumwissenschaft*, supp. 3 (Stuttgart, 1918), is still useful for Greek material. The Church Fathers' standpoint is found in G. W. H. Lampe's *A Patristic Greek Lexicon* (Oxford, 1978), pp. 327–331. The *New Catholic Encyclopedia* (New York, 1967) gives a very short survey, as does Bernhard Kötting's article "Dämon," in *Lexikon für Theologie und Kirche*, vol. 3 (Freiburg, 1959). The articles under "Démon," in the *Dictionnaire de spiritualité, ascétique et mystique: Doctrine et histoire*, vol. 3 (Paris, 1957), give very interesting material not found elsewhere.

The classical survey of ancient authors is Julius Tambornino's *De antiquorum daemonismo*, "Religionsgeschichtliche Versuche und Vorarbeiten," vol. 7 (Giessen, 1909). Another classical work is *The Devils and Evil Spirits of Babylonia*, 2 vols., translated by Reginald C. Thompson, which consists of Babylonian and Assyrian incantations against the demons, ghouls, vampires, hobgoblins, ghosts, and kindred evil spirits that attack humankind (London, 1903–1904). The entry in the *Encyclopaedia of Religion and Ethics*, edited by James Hastings, vol. 4 (Edinburgh, 1911), summarizes the material in an extensive and comprehensive way; the introductory article by Louis H. Gray is the most useful.

No important recent works dealing with the subject in a scientific way exist. An outdated, although still useful, book is *Demonology and Devil-Lore*, 3d ed., rev. & enl., 2 vols. (London, 1889), by Moncure D. Conway. Ilmari Manninen's *Die daemonistischen Krankheiten im finnischen Volksaberglauben* (Helsinki, 1922) and Lauri Honko's *Krankheitsprojektile: Untersuchung über eine urtümliche Krankheitserklärung* (Helsinki, 1959) are high-quality standard collections of material related to this topic.

The iconography of demons and spirits is very enlightening, but unfortunately Herbert Schade's article "Dämonen," in *Lexikon der Christlichen Ikonographie*, vol. 1 (Freiburg, 1968), is too short. One needs to refer to Enrico Castelli's *Il demoniaco nell' arte: Il significato filosofico del demoniaco nell' arte* (Milan, 1952), Heinz Mode's *Fabulous Beasts and Demons* (London, 1975), or Jurgis Baltrusaitis's *Réveils et prodiges: Le gothique fantastique* (Paris, 1960). A classical work with pictures is Edward Langton's *Essentials of Demonology: A Study of Jewish and Christian Doctrine, Its Origin and Development* (London, 1949).

Important for our topic is the profound work of Dieter Harmening, *Superstitio: Ueberlieferungs- und theoriegeschichtliche Untersuchungen zur Kirchlich- theologischen Aberglaubensliteratur des Mittelalters* (Berlin, 1979), as well as Wilhelm Dupré's *Religion in Primitive Cultures: A Study in Ethnophilosophy*, "*Religion and Reason*," vol. 9 (Paris, 1975). An exhaustive collection of material and history of ideas can be found in Karl R. H. Frick's *Die Erleuchteten* (Graz, 1973), *Licht und Finsternis* (Graz, 1975), and *Das Reich Satans* (Graz, 1982).

New Sources

Bhattacharyya, Narenda Nath. *Indian Demonology: The Inverted Pantheon.* New Delhi, 2000.

Cuneo, Michael. *American Exorcism: Expelling Demons in the Land of Plenty.* New York, 2001.

Licence, Tom. "The Gift of Seeing Demons in Early Cistercian Spirituality." *Cistercian Studies Quarterly* 39 (2004): 49–65.

Ribi, Alfred. *Die Dämones des Hieronymus Bosch.* Küsnacht, 1990.

Stephens, Walter. *Demon Lovers: Witchcraft, Sex, and the Crisis of Belief.* Chicago, 2002.

Velasco, Sherry M. *Demons, Nausea, and Resistance in the Autobiography of Isabel de Jesús.* Albuquerque, 1996.

Worobec, Christine. *Possessed: Women, Witches, and Demons in Imperial Russia.* DeKalb, Ill., 2001.

Alfred Ribi (1987)
Revised Bibliography

DENOMINATIONALISM.

DENOMINATIONALISM. Denominationalism is one of the least understood aspects of Protestantism. In both popular usage and dictionary definition, *denominationalism* is commonly equated with *sectarianism.* This is a strange reversal in meaning, for in origin and intention the concept of denominationalism was the opposite of sectarianism.

The fact that few Protestants take offense when their church is called a denomination is evidence of a lingering awareness that the term has a positive connotation quite different from the negative implication of *sectarianism.* A sect by definition is exclusive. It claims the authority of Christ for itself alone, whereas the word *denomination* was adopted as a neutral and nonjudgmental term that implied that the group referred to was but one member, denominated by a particular name, of a larger group to which other Protestant denominations belonged. It was an inclusive term conveying the notion of mutual respect and recognition. Albert Barnes, minister of the First Presbyterian Church of Philadelphia (1830–1867), summarized the meaning of denominationalism when he said that the spirit it fostered

> is opposed to all bigotry and uncharitableness; to all attempts to "unchurch" others; to teaching that they worship in conventicles, that they are dissenters, or that they are left to the uncovenanted mercies of God. . . . The Church of Christ is not under the Episcopal form, or the Baptist, the Methodist, the Presbyterian, or the Congregational form exclusively; all are, to all intents and purposes, to be recognized as parts of the one holy catholic Church.

Denominationalism, in origin, was related to religious toleration and religious freedom. The latter were political and constitutional responses to religious diversity and were designed to enable a religiously diverse people to live together in peace. Denominationalism, on the other hand, was a response to problems created by the division of adherents of a single religious tradition into separate and competing ecclesiastical bodies. They shared a common faith but were divided by issues of church government and worship. Denominationalism took toleration and, later, religious freedom for granted, accepted arguments put forward in their defense, and then moved beyond the goal of peace among competing groups to a quest for unity in the midst of the acknowledged differences of those who shared a common faith. To this end, both an ideology and a system of relationships were devised that would permit members of the several Protestant denominations to acknowledge the unity that transcended their divisions and thus encourage them to maintain friendly coexistence and to engage in concerted action to promote shared concerns and forward common ends. It is interesting that a similar ideology and rationale for mutual respect and cooperative activity, utilizing the equally neutral term *sector* for *denomination*, was adopted by Jacob Neusner, noted professor of Judaic studies at Brown University, to explicate the unity that exists within a divided Judaism. (See his *Sectors of American Judaism*, 1975, pp. 259–277.)

Denomination as a nonjudgmental term in Protestantism was brought into vogue in the eighteenth century by leaders of the Evangelical Revival in Great Britain and of the parallel Great Awakening in North America. John Wesley was representative of British leadership when he declared: "I . . . refuse to be distinguished from other men by any but the common principles of Christianity. . . . I renounce and detest all other marks of distinction. But from real Christians, of whatever *denomination*, I earnestly desire not to be distinguished at all. . . . Dost thou love and fear God? It is enough! I give thee the right hand of fellowship." Gilbert Tennant, based in New Jersey but itinerating throughout the colonies, was even more precise in defining what the word implied: "All societies who profess Christianity and retain the fundamental principles thereof, notwithstanding their different denominations and diversity of sentiments in smaller things, are in reality but one Church of Christ, but several branches (more or less pure in minuter points) of one visible kingdom of the Messiah."

Although the revivalists made current coin of the term, it had been used as early as 1688 by Samuel Willard, minister of Old South Church in Boston, in a lecture later published as part of his *Compleat Body of Divinity*, in which he commented: "Through our knowing *but in part*, it is come to pass that professors of Christianity have been of diverse opinions in many things and their difference hath occasioned several *denominations*, but while they agree in the *foundation* they may be saved." Moreover, the denominational concept was implicit in the participation of Increase and Cotton Mather in 1717 in the ordination of a Baptist minister. And it was equally implicit at about the same time in the acceptance by Harvard College of funds from Thomas Hollis, a Baptist, for the endowment of a professorship of divinity and for a scholarship fund that would be available to Baptist as well as to other ministerial students. Such incipient manifestations of a irenic denominational temper were precipitated by policies of James II and then by the perceived consequences of the Glorious Revolution of 1688 and the Act of Toleration of 1689. Still, the creative moment in forging the concept of denominationalism antedated the crisis of the years following 1688–1689 by almost half a century.

SEVENTEENTH-CENTURY ORIGIN. Usually a movement or a theology is born before it is named. This was true of denominationalism. The denominational understanding of the church had been hammered out by non-Separatist Puritan preachers prior to and during the sessions of the Westminster Assembly of Divines, a body of clergymen summoned in 1643 during the English Civil War to advise the "Long Parliament" in the shaping of a religious settlement. The problem that stymied the Parliament and the Westminster Assembly was the splintering and fragmenting of a triumphant Puritanism. Puritans of several hues had united to bring down rule by "lordly prelates" in the church, but, having done this, they were unable to agree on an alternate policy. A solution to this problem was proposed by non-Separatist Independents (Anglicans of a congregational persuasion) both within and outside the assembly. Those who were members of the Westminster Assembly were called the Dissenting Brethren.

The non-Separatist Independents were indebted to the Protestant reformers of the sixteenth century for their basic insights. They recalled repeated cautions against sanctifying churchly forms. The true church, the reformers had insisted, is not an institution, although it finds institutional expression in the world. Calvin was more confident than Luther that external ecclesiastical arrangements could be deduced from the Bible; still, he had a word of caution for those "who are not satisfied unless the church can always be pointed out with the finger." This, he said in the preface to the *Institutes*, cannot be done in any final sense. The whole question of the boundaries of the church must be left to God, "since he alone 'knoweth them that are his.'" The reformers acted upon this insight only to a limited degree, but they did recognize as true churches, more or less adequate in external form, those possessing an essentially common faith, whether they were Lutheran churches as in various political units of Germany and Scandinavia, Reformed churches as in other political divisions of Europe, or an Anglican church as in England. The new element introduced in mid-seventeenth-century England was the application of this understanding to a situation where divisions were within a geographical area rather than between geographical areas.

As the fragmentation of Puritanism increased after 1640, the moderates associated with the Dissenting Brethren became increasingly aware of "the danger of rending and dividing the godly Protestant party" at its moment of triumph when there was "an absolute necessity of their nearest union." Not only did divisions threaten the achievement of reforms desired by all the godly, they constituted a denial of the spirit of Christianity itself. "We are wrangling, devising, plotting, working against one another," said Jeremiah Burroughes, their most eloquent spokesman in the Assembly, whereas "love and unity are Christ's badge." It was an unhappy fact that "we are divided notwithstanding we are all convinced of the evil of our divisions." The problem was to find a way to peace and unity when Christians did not all agree. "If we stay for peace and love till we come to the unity of faith in all things," Burroughes confessed, "we must stay for ought I know till we come to another world."

With this dilemma in mind, seventeenth-century Independents elaborated a series of principles as a basis on which Christians could be united notwithstanding their differences.

First, so long as people live "in this muddy world" and "deceitfulness" lurks within the human heart, it is inevitable that there shall be differences of opinion even among the godly.

Second, even when differing convictions do not involve fundamentals, they cannot be lightly regarded. Those who fear God must first be persuaded themselves before they can accept the judgment of others.

Third, differences must be approached with humility and a degree of tentativeness. No one put this more vividly than Thomas Hooker of Connecticut, as his contribution to the ongoing discussion in England. "The sum is, we doubt not what we practice, but it's beyond all doubt that all men are liars and we are in the number of those poor feeble men; either we do or may err, though we do not know it; what we have learned we do profess and yet profess still to live that we may learn."

Fourth, as a corollary to human fallibility, Burroughes contended that "God hath a hand in these divisions to bring forth further light. Sparks are beaten out by the flints striking together." How can people know that they are right, asked another, until they "by discussing, praying, reading, meditating, find that out?"

Fifth, "though our differences are sad enough," they do not make us of "different religions." While "godly people are divided in their opinions and ways . . . they are united in Christ." Nor does the mere fact of separation constitute schism. It is schismatic only when it is not "loving and peaceable," only when it is "uncharitable, unjust, rash, violent."

Burroughes gave several illustrations of what he had in mind. Both Scots and refugees from abroad, he noted, had been permitted to have their own churches in England without being regarded as schismatics. This also had been true of Independents when they were in exile on the continent. Furthermore, persons of sufficient means in England had the liberty of "choosing pastors" by "choosing houses," moving from a parish where in good conscience they could not enjoy the means of grace to another parish where they could. When they did so, no cry of schism was raised. Should the same liberty be denied the less affluent who could not afford to move their dwelling from one side of the street to the other? Were they to be condemned as schismatics when their richer brethren were not?

What Burroughes and others were pleading for was a recognition that, although Christians may walk in different "ways" of outward obedience, they are still united in Christ and may work together for common ends of "godliness." They did, in fact, unite in defense of "the good old cause" of religious toleration. Many (those of Episcopal persuasion as well as Presbyterians, Congregationalists, and Baptists) did participate in Oliver Cromwell's "voluntary national establishment" during the 1650s. Later there were the "Heads of Agreement" of 1690, the joint petition to Queen Anne in 1702 from those who came to be called the "three old denominations," and the establishment in 1732 of a formal representative committee, known as "the Dissenting Deputies," to protect and expand the rights of the dissenting churches and their members.

DENOMINATIONALISM IN THE UNITED STATES. The denominational concept of the church was accepted in New England from the beginning. "We do not go to New England as Separatists from the Church of England," said Francis Higginson, "though we cannot but separate from the corruptions of it." As did their brethren at home, they adopted the neutral term *way* when explaining points of distinction from other orthodox Protestants (e.g., John Cotton, *The Way of the New England Churches Cleared*, 1648). Moreover, the elders of the Massachusetts Bay Colony expressed the same willingness to learn from others when responding to an inquiry concerning their practice. "We see as much cause to suspect the integrity of our own hearts as yours; and so much the more as being more privy to the deceitfulness of our own hearts than to yours . . . which causeth us with great reverence to accept and receive what further light God may be pleased to impart unto us by you. But as we have believed, so have we hitherto practiced." They were upset, however, when dissidents challenged their attempt to fashion a new Zion in the American wilderness, since there was ample room for dissidents to establish their own communities. Banishment was the response, but as John Cotton explained, perhaps somewhat blandly, "Banishment in this country is not counted as much a confinement as an enlargement," pointing out that "the jurisdiction (whence a man is banished) is but small, and the country round about it large and fruitful; where a man may make his choice of variety of more pleasant and profitable seats than he leaveth behind him."

Although New Englanders did not always match profession with practice, their understanding of the church was well adapted to the situation in other colonies where religious diversity prevailed and no single group occupied a dominant position. Even North Carolina could be regarded as a southern Pennsylvania in its ethnic composition and religious complexion, and the valley of Virginia and late-blooming Georgia were not greatly different.

Not only was the denominational theory of the church popularized by leaders of the Great Awakening, since 1690 it had been reinforced by the growing influence of John Locke, who had adopted and set forth, in his *Letter Concerning Toleration*, a view of the churches that he derived from his non-Separatist Puritan antecedents. (See George L. Hunt, *Calvinism and the Political Order*, 1965, pp. 111–113.)

By their acceptance of religious freedom following the American Revolution, most Protestant churches (with their general assemblies, general conventions, general conferences, general councils, or general associations) were committed to voluntarism and became, from a legal point of view, voluntary societies. They were under no legal restraint in dealing with their own internal affairs. Nor were most of them the least inhibited in following the practice developed during the years of the Great Awakening in joining together in efforts to promote concerts of prayer and religious revivals. In addition, in the early decades of the nineteenth century, out of their concern for the whole of society, a host of additional voluntary societies, both denominational and interdenominational, were founded to promote missionary, educational, benevolent, and reform activities. These societies became so ubiquitous that Orestes Brownson complained that "matters have come to such a pass that a peaceable man can hardly venture to eat or drink, to go to bed or get up, to correct his children or kiss his wife" without the guidance and sanction of some society.

This pattern of institutional activity persisted into the twentieth century, with new societies being formed as new needs were perceived to supplement the work of the older societies. Such newer societies were as varied as the Student Volunteer Movement, the League for Industrial Democracy, the Fellowship of Reconciliation, and the Southern Christian Leadership Conference. In addition, Protestant churches became linked by such official agencies as the Foreign Mission Conference of North America.

Countervailing Attitudes in the United States. Not everyone was enamored with denominationalism as an expression of Christian unity. There were manifestations of "high church" sentiment by some groups (e.g., Landmark Baptists) who insisted that they alone represented the true church and refused to recognize or cooperate with those outside their ranks. Others (e.g., Old School Presbyterians) established official boards firmly under church control to carry on work hitherto delegated to voluntary societies. Still others, such as Thomas and Alexander Campbell, sought to fashion a unified movement in which denominational distinctions would disappear. They preempted the name Christian for themselves and called upon others to reject party names and nonbiblical creeds and practices that were a source of division and to unite instead on the basis of biblical names and practices alone. Typical of their point of view was the slogan "Where the Scriptures speak, we speak; and where the Scriptures are silent, we are silent." Although the adherents they gathered were regarded as a denomination by others, they repudiated the name and spoke of themselves as a brotherhood.

A major shift in attitude toward denominationalism began in the late nineteenth century. It grew out of a growing conviction among a few key leaders that unity should find expression in a comprehensive church sufficiently broad in outlook and tolerant in spirit to minimize differences of opinion. Phillips Brooks, pastor of Trinity Church in Boston (1869–1891) and briefly Episcopal bishop of Massachusetts, was one who helped cultivate the temper that led in this direction when he declared that humanity itself, not any organized body of believers, is the instrument through which God effects his purposes. This is the true church where "the great human impulses" lead people to do "Christian work in the spirit of Christ" even when they "studiously" disown him. Broad churchmanship, it was sometimes called, or catholic Christianity.

The roots of this catholic Christianity can also be traced back to seventeenth-century England, to the "latitudinarians" of the decades following 1660. Two streams converged to inform the views of the "men of latitude." One was derived from the Cambridge Platonists, non-Separatist Independents at the university, who, unlike fellow Independents serving as pastors, faced the problem of finding a basis for unity within an institution (the university) rather than between institutions (the churches). After 1660 they joined forces with those influenced by the rationalism of the Enlightenment to fashion a defense of diversity (latitude) within a comprehensive state-established church. Thus they stood in opposition to those who insisted upon a narrowly defined Caroline Christianity (i.e., during the reign of Charles II) as the only true faith of the Church of England. The latitudinarian apologetic initially had little relevance to a situation where religious diversity was widespread and there was no dominant state church. Additional changes in the climate of opinion were necessary before it could become pertinent.

Another impulse leading to unhappiness with the denominational concept was the belief that, from an organizational and administrative point of view, the denominational system was inefficient and financially improvident. John D. Rockefeller Jr., a Baptist who was deeply devout and devoted to the mission enterprise and whose social concerns had been awakened by men who surrounded his father, is a prime illustration of this second impulse. A careful steward, Rockefeller sought efficiency and economy through consolidation of missionary endeavor and other aspects of Christian activity. He used his influence and his money to make Christian outreach cost-effective by initiating such breathtaking schemes to redeem a global society as the Interchurch World Movement of 1919–1920 and the Laymen's Foreign Mission Inquiry of 1930–1932. In the end he ceased contributing to denominational projects, restricting his stewardship to consolidated efforts.

A third factor bringing denominationalism into disrepute was a by-product of German sociological studies, notably those of Ernst Troeltsch (1865–1923). The key concept was a typology that drew a distinction between "church" and "sect" applicable to countries with a predominant state church. A "denomination," however, was difficult to fit into this scheme, for it was neither "church" nor "sect" in terms of Troeltsch's analysis. Still, his views were intriguing. The most influential attempt to adapt Troeltsch's typology to the American scene was H. Richard Niebuhr's *The Social Sources of Denominationalism* (1929), which in a curious way idealized European state churches because they were institutions into which everyone was born, rich and poor alike.

A scathing indictment of denominationalism preceded Niebuhr's analysis of "the ethical failure of a divided church" and his descriptions of the churches of the disinherited, the middle class, and those produced by nationalism, sectionalism, and the color line. "Denominationalism in the Christian church," he declared,

> is an unacknowledged hypocrisy. It represents the accommodation of Christianity to the caste-system of human society. . . . The division of the churches closely follows the division of men into the castes of national, racial, and economic groups. It draws the color line in the church of God; it fosters the misunderstandings, the self-exaltations, the hatreds of jingoistic nationalism by continuing in the body of Christ the spurious differences of provincial loyalties; it sets the rich and poor apart at the table of the Lord, where the fortunate may enjoy the bounty they have provided while the others feed upon the crusts their poverty affords.

Niebuhr acknowledged the insights he had derived from Troeltsch's typology. "Churches" are natural social groups "akin to the family or the nation" into which people of all classes are born, whereas "sects" are "voluntary associations." Sects compromise the universality of the Christian faith by their surrender to various caste systems. As generations pass, sects become denominations that are inclusive in the sense that people are born into them, with membership being determined by custom and family tradition. But as denominations, these former sects perpetuate in the body of Christ the caste systems of society. The volume closed with a summons to organic unity. Denominations were challenged to transcend their social conditioning and coalesce into a comprehensive church that would express the brotherhood of the Christian gospel.

By 1937 Niebuhr had second thoughts and published *The Kingdom of God in America* as a partial corrective to his earlier volume. He was still aware of the ways in which ethnicity, race, sectionalism, and economic circumstance had led to the formation of separate Christian groups. But this was not the whole story. He had not taken into account that denominationalism in its initial manifestation was the product of a new religious vitality with a dynamic sense of mission that placed primary emphasis on inner Christian experience. While differences of outward form and structure were not deemed unimportant and although there were competing claims as to their relative adequacy to express and advance the claims of Christ, stress was upon changed lives and a shared mission that encouraged cooperative activities and a not unfriendly coexistence. Slowly, however, the differing patterns took on greater importance as they became institutionalized. Here the problem was not compromise with caste systems but the process by which institutions over a long period of time begin to regard their own perpetuation as an end in itself. The earlier Puritan and the later evangelical sense of mission that provided the denominations with their reason for existence and bound them together in common causes began to fade. Becoming self-satisfied and self-congratulatory, they made peace with the world. This acculturation won from Niebuhr a stinging rebuke: "A God without wrath brought men without sin into a kingdom without judgment through the ministrations of a Christ without a cross." Niebuhr's summons was a call for renewal, for the recovery of a sense of mission that must precede and accompany any movement toward unity. Only a renewal that translated the love of God into love of brother would be powerful enough to overcome the walls of partition—institutional, ethnic, racial, sectional, economic—that fragmented the body of Christ.

The strictures of *The Kingdom of God in America* did little to mitigate the negative connotation evoked by the term *denominationalism* as a result of its being equated with sectarianism. Niebuhr's earlier *Social Sources of Denominationalism* continued for more than half a century to be his most influential book. Many Protestants seemed oblivious to his second thoughts. Instead of responding to the summons for renewal as a prerequisite for unity, many had become converts to a twentieth-century version of "latitudinarianism" or "catholic Christianity" that sought a united church that would be ample enough to accommodate the views and opinions of everyone. Instead of seeking renewal as a first step, such leaders opted for the more direct approach of tinkering with institutional arrangements to increase the scope of comprehension, a procedure that did not differ in kind from the preoccupation with institutional concerns that Niebuhr regarded as the nub of the problem.

Since the common core of Protestantism had become so badly eroded, it is possible that *Protestant denominationalism* may no longer be a viable term to indicate anything more than Protestant diversity. Perhaps Sidney Mead, author of numerous perceptive and incisive essays dealing with the shape of Protestantism in America, is right in using the words *church, denomination,* and *sect* as synonyms. There is an overabundance of Protestant denominations in this sense, but only minority segments are linked by a common faith and few of these segments possess a theological concept of denominationalism to express their unity and undergird their cooperative activities.

Recognizing this situation, and conceding that the use of the word *denomination* is likely to persist, Martin E. Marty of the University of Chicago in 1982 made a sensible suggestion. As the Bible justifies the use of the word *church* only for a local congregation or the entire church, the word *denomination* can serve as a useful "in-between" term to designate existing ecclesiastical groupings that have provided "family tone" and clusters of memories and symbols that still can be invoked to sustain Christians in their daily lives. "Denominations," Marty noted, "are an offense only when they undercut the local church or the whole church," but when Christians are faithful to their "particular heritage," without condemning others, they enrich the whole church. Such an observation is not far removed from the spirit of those who initially fashioned the denominational concept of the church.

SEE ALSO Anabaptism; Anglicanism; Baptist Churches; Christian Science; Church, article on Church Polity; Congregationalism; Disciples of Christ; Jehovah's Witnesses; Lutheranism; Mennonites; Methodist Churches; Moravians; Mormonism; Pietism; Presbyterianism, Reformed; Puritanism; Quakers; Salvation Army; Seventh-day Adventism; Shakers; Unitarian Universalist Association.

BIBLIOGRAPHY

While there are many histories of individual denominations, numerous handbooks or guides with accounts of the different religious bodies (e.g., Arthur C. Piepkorn's *Profiles in Belief*, 7 vols., New York, 1977–), and much discussion of the churches as voluntary associations, bureaucratic structures, and ethnic groupings, surprisingly little attention has been given to the theory and concept of denominationalism itself.

The most important discussions of denominationalism, from a variety of perspectives, have been assembled by Russell E. Richey in *Denominationalism* (Nashville, 1977). Richey includes a chapter from H. Richard Niebuhr's *The Kingdom of God in America* (Chicago and New York, 1937) and calls attention to the importance of Niebuhr's *Social Sources of Denominationalism* (Hamden, Conn., 1929). He includes Sidney E. Mead's essay "Denominationalism: The Shape of Protestantism in America," reprinted from Mead's *The Lively Experiment* (New York, 1963), which contains other pertinent material. Other essays included are by E. Franklin Frazier, Fred J. Hood, Winthrop S. Hudson, Martin E. Marty, Elwyn A. Smith, and Timothy L. Smith. Richey notes that the understanding of Protestant denominationalism presented in this entry represents a fairly general consensus, having been adopted by Sydney E. Ahlstrom in *A Religious History of the American People* (New Haven, Conn., 1972), pp. 96, 381–382; Robert T. Handy in *A History of the Churches in the United States and Canada* (New York, 1976), p. 112; Winthrop S. Hudson in *Religion in America*, 3d ed. (New York, 1981), pp. 81–82; Martin E. Marty in *Righteous Empire: The Protestant Experience in America* (New York, 1970), p. 69; and *The Westminster Dictionary of Church History* (Philadelphia, 1971), "Denominationalism." For the most theologically informed explication of denominationalism, see Jacob Neusner's "Conservative Judaism in a Divided Community," in *Sectors of American Judaism* (New York, 1975), vol. 2 of his *Understanding American Judaism.*

New Sources

Brauer, Jerald C., ed. *The Lively Experiment Continued.* Macon, Ga., 1987.

Muller, Robert Bruce, and Russell E. Richey, eds. *Reimagining Denominationalism.* New York, 1994.

Newman, William M., and Peter L. Halvorson. *Atlas of American Religion: The Denominational Era.* Walnut Creek, Calif., 2000.

WINTHROP S. HUDSON (1987)
Revised Bibliography

DEPROGRAMMING.

The term *deprogramming* has been used since the 1970s to refer to a range of behaviors, all of which are aimed at convincing members of so-called new religious movements (NRMs) to leave such groups and return to more mainstream social and religious lifestyles. Such groups might be "cultic," that is, communal and with high-demand authoritarian leadership, or they may simply hold unconventional beliefs and rituals. Definitions of *cult* have been extremely variable and inclusive, and the term has been used to refer to groups ranging from Old Catholics, Mormons, and Jehovah's Witnesses to members of the Unification Church, the Hare Krishnas, the Seventh-day Adventist–derived Branch Davidians, and even Pentecostals.

Deprogramming is regarded by its advocates as a "liberating" process that frees NRM members from a presumed hypnotic state of involuntary servitude or "mind control" that has been previously "programmed" into them. Deprogramming (as a term and practice) began in 1971 as the ad hoc vigilante response of one man, Theodore (Ted) Roosevelt Patrick Jr., to the intense missionizing activities of the Children of God, a fundamentalist Christian sect that was later renamed The Family. Patrick was a civil rights activist and Special Representative for Community Relations under California governor Ronald Reagan. According to Patrick's autobiographical *Let Our Children Go!* (1976), his teenage son and nephew met several missionaries of the Children of God and returned home noticeably and "mysteriously" disoriented. Patrick attended a meeting of the group and, by his account, found himself powerfully drawn to surrender his rationality and free will. Patrick claimed that he was contacted within a single week by fifty-two families who complained that their children had been similarly affected by the Children of God. Patrick developed a rough explanation of the "programming" (or conditioning) performed by that group. At the time, he had no knowledge of the post–Korean War coercive influence/brainwashing literature developed by U.S. Central Intelligence Agency (CIA) propagandists and psychologists.

DEPROGRAMMING INTERVENTION. The style of intervention that Patrick developed to "rescue" young persons from NRMs included sudden forcible abduction of a NRM member, detainment for days or longer in secured locations, the demeaning of the NRM, constant argumentation, and a barrage of verbal assaults on the integrity, sincerity, values, and activities of the religion and its leaders, all frequently interspersed with biblically based references. Patrick and other deprogrammers never claimed to be proselytizing their own personal credos—a claim that is contradicted by the sworn depositions and testimonies of some deprogrammees—but rather to simply "free minds" so that NRM members could once again think for themselves.

Noncoercive deprogramming attempts also occurred, as when a parent or clergyperson—by telephone, mail, or face-to-face—tried to create doubts or second thoughts in the mind of a young "cult" member who, in the absence of more than moral or emotional persuasion (i.e., without forcible restraint or violence), decided to leave the new faith. However, the coercive form of deprogramming caught public attention and became the object of opposition by such groups as the American Civil Liberties Union.

By the fall of 1971, Patrick had resigned his state position to devote himself full-time to mostly coercive deprogrammings. By early 1972 he was actively pursuing such interventions nationwide against a variety of NRMs, and he inspired a cottage industry of imitators, some of whom had been his apprentices. These deprogrammers represented a variety of backgrounds, from private investigators, insurance salesmen, and used-car salesmen to attorneys, degreed psychologists, and convicted felons.

The heyday of deprogramming occurred at the same time that some highly visible new religions were in apparent expansion. One source of deprogrammers' clientele was a subculture of relatives of previous NRM members who referred subjects to Patrick and other deprogrammers. Other sources included several anticult or counter-NRM organizations, such as the Citizens Freedom Foundation and its successor, the Cult Awareness Network (CAN).

There are few reliable estimates of how many deprogrammings took place. In the late 1980s sociologist David G. Bromley used a triangulation of media reports and internal organizational documents to track down almost four hundred attempted deprogrammings of members of the Unification Church. Bromley found that most of the successful deprogrammings were performed on persons either newly affiliating with the church or just beginning the process of disaffiliating, which suggests that the deprogrammers' faith in the efficacy of their techniques was overblown. Nevertheless, Bromley concluded that "the practice of forcibly separating individuals from religious groups for the purpose of inducing them to renounce their memberships is unprecedented in American religious history" (1988, p. 203).

Deprogrammings in Decline. By the late 1980s deprogrammers were seeking to shed Patrick's legacy of kidnapping and forcible confinement of deprogrammees, and they tried to upgrade their image to that of mental health therapists, or "exit counselors." Meeting at annual CAN conferences over a period of several years, they struggled to craft a code of ethics and to work out details, including a sliding scale of counseling fees that differentiated between academically trained and nondegreed practitioners. However, the resulting code of ethics focused mainly on the abuses of some deprogrammers who took drugs during deprogrammings and had sex with their captive clients, indicative of the unregulated "profession" that deprogramming had become.

Deprogrammings became all but extinct by the late 1990s for several reasons. First, there were some spectacularly bungled attempts, as when deprogrammers abducted the wrong person or allowed targeted persons to escape. In addition, the deprogrammings frequently did not work; it was relatively easy for deprogrammees to pretend to be deconverted ex-members ready to rejoin mainstream society, and then, when the counseling was supposedly finished, to bolt back to the NRM group. Few families could afford repeated deprogramming attempts since the practitioners began to charge upwards of $30,000.

Second, there were mounting legal costs for unsuccessful deprogrammers in criminal and civil proceedings. Several high-profile deprogrammers, including Patrick and private investigator Galen Kelly, served time in prison as judges became more aware of the religious liberties implications of deprogramming, as well as its status as an unrecognized, ersatz therapy. Coercive deprogramming and its questionable brainwashing assumptions were also aggressively criticized by civil liberties advocates, behavioral science scholars, and NRM spokespersons. Such criticism eventually tainted anticult "rescue" heroics with an odious reputation.

With the collapse of the CAN in 1996 due to bankruptcy as a result of civil suits brought against it (mostly by members of the Church of Scientology), deprogrammers, who now called themselves "thought reform" counselors or consultants, lacked a national referral conduit and either had to establish internet websites or gain footholds in local church community networks. However, the single legal case that finally brought an end to the CAN was *Scott v. Ross* (1995), a civil suit brought by Jason Scott, a United Pentecostal adult whose mother hired an "exit counselor" named Rick Ross to deprogram her three sons from a church of which she disapproved. After Scott's two brothers were successfully deprogrammed, Scott was violently abducted, physically abused, and forcibly detained at a remote Washington State location for almost a week.

The jury was clear in its decision to award damages to Scott ($875,000 in compensatory damages, as well as punitive damages in the amount of $1,000,000; against CAN; $2,500,000 against Rick Ross; and $25,000 each against Ross's two accomplices). The CAN's primary activity in this and other operations was to provide the public and the media with false or inflammatory opinion in the guise of "information" about unconventional religions. The jury's decision, under the definitions provided in Washington law, was that CAN was an organized hate campaign. In a curt note to the defendants, who appealed the verdict, U.S. district court judge John C. Coughenour concluded:

> Finally, the court notes each of the defendants' seeming incapability of appreciating the maliciousness of their conduct towards Mr. Scott. Rather, throughout the entire course of this litigation, they have attempted to portray themselves as victims of Mr. Scott's counsel's alleged agenda. Thus, the large award given by the jury against both CAN and Mr. Ross seems reasonably necessary to enforce the jury's determination on the oppressiveness of the defendants' actions and deter similar conduct in the future (*Scott v. Ross*, 1995).

The final death knell for deprogramming was shrinking public and official concern over many NRMs, some of which (such as the Unification Church) accommodated to the larger society and became, therefore, less visible, while others simply disappeared. In a time of war and fear of foreign terrorism, which characterized most of the 1990s and the early twenty-first century, NRMs in North America were not a major source of disquiet, and the market for interventions dramatically declined.

See Also Anticult Movements; Brainwashing (Debate); Cults and Sects; Law and Religion, article on Law and New Religious Movements.

Bibliography

Bromley, David G. "Deprogrammings as a Mode of Exit from New Religious Movements: The Case of the Unification Church." In *Falling from the Faith: Causes and Consequences of Religious Apostasy,* edited by David G. Bromley, pp. 185–204. Beverly Hills, Calif., 1988.

Bromley, David G., and Anson D. Shupe Jr. *Strange Gods: The Great American Cult Scare.* Boston, 1981.

Jason Scott, Plaintiff, v. Rick Ross et al., Defendants. Case no. C94–00796, November 29, 1995. Remarks of U.S. district court judge John C. Coughenour, pp. 8, 14. Seattle, Wash.

Patrick, Ted, with Tom Dulack. *Let Our Children Go!* New York, 1976.

Richardson, James T. "A Social Psychological Critique of 'Brainwashing' Claims about Recruitment to New Religions." In *The Handbook on Cults and Sects in America,* edited by David G. Bromley and Jeffrey K. Hadden, pp. 75–97, vol. 2, part B. Greenwich, Conn., 1993.

Shupe, Anson D., Jr., and David G. Bromley. *The New Vigilantes: Deprogrammers, Anti-Cultists, and the New Religions.* Beverly Hills, Calif., 1980.

Shupe, Anson, Susan E. Darnell, and Kendrick Moxon. "The Cult Awareness Network and the Anticult Movement: Implications for NRMs in America." In *New Religious Movements and Religious Liberty in America,* edited by Derek H. Davis and Barry Hankins, pp. 21–43. Waco, Tex., 2002.

Wright, Stuart A., and Helen Rose Ebaugh. "Leaving New Religions." In *The Handbook on Cults and Sects in America,* edited by David G. Bromley and Jeffrey K. Hadden, pp. 117–158, vol. 2, part B. Greenwich, Conn., 1993.

Anson Shupe (2005)

DERVISH See DARWĪSH

DESCARTES, RENÉ

DESCARTES, RENÉ (1596–1650), French philosopher. Descartes is held to be the father of modern philosophy and chief architect of the modern approach to the relationship between science and religion. The scholastic tradition, already ably criticized by Descartes's time, was in effect obviated by a new, universal metaphysical construction based on the conceptual apparatus of Descartes. The entire development of European philosophy, in all its diverse tendencies, has been dependent, directly or indirectly, on the Cartesian legacy. If it is true, as Whitehead said, that European philosophy consists of footnotes to Plato, modern European philosophy, in the same sense, consists of footnotes to Descartes.

Born to a noble Roman Catholic family, Descartes was educated in the physics and metaphysics of an Aristotelian and Thomist tradition, and in medicine and law. He joined the Dutch army, and, while in the Netherlands, became interested in mathematics and the new physics. Having traveled in various countries, he returned to France, where he outlined the first version of a new method of thinking based on mathematics *(Rules for the Direction of the Mind),* but he did not complete or publish it. After settling in the Netherlands, he maintained contact with scholars by letter; Marin Mersenne was his main correspondent. He passed the last year of his life in Sweden at the court of Queen Christina.

Descartes's aim was to use mathematics as a model for developing a fully unified form of human knowledge. He applied this method in his *Treatise on the World.* The trial of Galileo and condemnation of Galileo's *Dialogues* convinced Descartes not to print his own work, which clearly confirmed the heliocentric theory. In 1637 he published several parts of it with a methodological introduction, called *The Discourse on Method,* which was to become one of the greatest texts of modern thought. In 1641 he published his other major work, *Meditations on First Philosophy,* which had previously been sent to a number of scholars, among them Gassendi, Hobbes, and Arnauld; their objections and Descartes's replies were subsequently published with the main text. *The Principles of Philosophy* appeared in 1644 and *The Passions of the Soul* in 1649. Some other works and his voluminous correspondence were published posthumously.

The *Discourse* indicates that for Descartes philosophy was a methodological and conceptual basis for the sciences, to make them useful in the domination of nature. Although the metaphysical problems he discussed in his *Meditations* are not subordinated to this goal, it is clear that Descartes was interested only in matters that could be solved by rational means and that his mental attitude was essentially antihistorical.

Cartesian method demands that we accept as true only what is presented "clearly and distinctly" to our mind, leaving no room for doubt. We should suspend our judgment in all matters where the slightest doubt is possible, including all the truths of common sense, in order to find something that resists all doubts. Sense-perception does not provide us with any indubitable knowledge, since we cannot be a priori certain that we are not dreaming or that we are not being deceived by a malicious demon. But my very act of doubting, however far extended, and therefore the fact that I am thinking, cannot itself be doubted. And thus I find at least this one certainty in which I cannot be deceived: I think, and I, the thinker, must exist; no demon could induce me to err on this point. This reasoning, summarized in the famous formula "Cogito ergo sum," can be admitted as the basis of knowledge.

The cogito, accepted as a kind of epistemological absolute, is in Descartes's work an implicit challenge to the authority of tradition and an appeal to look for truth only in the reason of a thinking individual. And it implies that the only object that is directly and indubitably accessible to one's mind is its own activity; wherever else we start, our beliefs will be exposed to doubt.

While I grasp my existence as identical with the awareness of existence, I observe, according to Descartes, that nothing belongs necessarily to my nature except the fact that I think; therefore I may describe myself as a thinking thing, or thinking substance, or immaterial soul. This transition from "I think" to "I am a thinking substance" was strongly criticized by Descartes's contemporaries and later. It gave rise to the question, much debated in the twentieth century, whether or not the "self" or "I" can be described at all in "objective" categories.

Our mind, according to Descartes, has a natural light whereby it is capable of acquiring knowledge on most important issues without relying on sense-perception. We have in our mind a natural idea of God, or a perfect being. Since our mind clearly perceives that it is not perfect itself (of which the fact of doubting is evidence, if indeed evidence is needed), it could not have fabricated this idea, as a more perfect thing cannot be produced by a less perfect; consequently the very presence of this idea is a proof of the actual existence of the perfect being. This psychological argument for God's existence, like the ontological argument in traditional version, which Descartes accepts as well, implies nothing about God's presence and signs in the world. God's first function, in Descartes's construction, is to assure the reliability of human knowledge: being perfect, God cannot deceive us, therefore we can rely both on our commonsense belief in the reality of the material world and on our intellectual intuition. (Many critics pointed out the circularity in this reasoning: acts of intuition are necessary to acquire the certainty of the existence of God, who subsequently appears as a guarantor of the infallibility of those very acts.) We can thus affirm the reality of the material world.

Descartes conceived the material world, or "extension," in strictly mechanistic terms. All processes are explained by the laws of mechanics; living organisms behave according to the same principles that govern artificial automata; there is no specific realm of life. To be sure, human beings are endowed with an immaterial soul, which is the seat of all sensations; animals, having no soul, are no more than mechanisms, and their reactions are just mechanical movements. In human beings, organic (that is, mechanical) processes, should be distinguished from psychological events in the soul. The human organism does not differ from other mechanisms; its death is a physical phenomenon, whereas the separation of the soul is not the cause but the effect of death. The two substances—soul and body—that make up the human being cannot affect each other; therefore the question of how we can realize, in perception, the mechanical impacts of other things on our bodies and cause movements of our body by the sheer act of will becomes difficult to solve; and Descartes's followers, when trying to explain the unity of soul and body and their mutual influence, naturally tended to materialist or occasionalist explanations, none of which conformed to the master's doctrine, which implied both that the soul is absolutely free and capable of dominating the affects, and that the affects are passive states caused by the movement of blood.

Descartes's philosophy almost instantaneously produced new lines of division in European intellectual life. Though attacked, mainly for its rationalist rigor, by both Protestants (the school of Voetius) and Catholics (all Descartes's works were put on the Index of Prohibited Books in 1663), its impact was soon to be felt not only among philosophers, scientists, and physicians, but among theologians as well. In the Netherlands, Coccejus's school tried to apply Descartes's methods in theological investigations; in France, Malebranche and other occasionalists attempted a Catholic assimilation of a somewhat modified Cartesianism. In the Jansenist milieu the influence of Descartes was very strong. By the end of the seventeenth century few orthodox Cartesians remained, but the impact of the doctrine was felt throughout the early French Enlightenment; its general rationalist and determinist approach laid the foundation of eighteenth-century materialism, while its skeptical side and the cogito were crucially important in the rise of modern idealism, starting with Berkeley.

Although there are no reasons to doubt that Descartes himself believed in God and in the immortality of the soul, his philosophy made God absent in the world and thus useless in interpreting it. Descartes was not, strictly speaking, a deist, insofar as, according to him, the force needed to sustain the universe in existence is the same as that needed to create it; yet he contributed decisively to the deist and atheist movements of the subsequent centuries. He was the modern founder of totally secularized thinking. Outstanding twentieth-century Thomists (Gilson, Maritain) saw in Descartes the main author of what they believed to be the aberration of modern intellectual life, of its individualist, idealist, and rationalist tendencies. And the problem of the transition from the cogito to the world and vice versa has remained, thanks to Descartes, one of the crucial issues in modern phenomenology and existential philosophy.

BIBLIOGRAPHY

Works by Descartes

Correspondance. 8 vols. Edited by Charles Adam and Gérard Milhaud. Paris, 1936–1963.

Descartes: Philosophical Writings. Selected, translated, and edited by Elizabeth Anscombe and P. T. Geach. Edinburgh, 1964. Contains a good bibliography.

Œuvres de Descartes. 2d ed. 12 vols. Edited by Charles Adam and Paul Tannery. Paris, 1956–1957.

Philosophical Letters. Translated and edited by Anthony Kenny. Oxford, 1970.

Works about Descartes

Adam, Charles. *Descartes: Sa vie et son œuvre.* Paris, 1937.

Alquié, Ferdinand. *La découverte métaphysique de l'homme chez Descartes.* 2d ed. Paris, 1966.

Doney, Willis, ed. *Descartes: A Collection of Critical Essays.* Garden City, N.Y., 1967.

Gilson, Étienne. *La doctrine cartésienne de la liberté et la théologie.* Paris, 1915.

Gilson, Étienne. *Études sur le rôle de la pensée médiévale dans la formation du système cartésien.* Paris, 1930.

Gouhier, Henri. *La pensée religieuse de Descartes.* Paris, 1924.

Laporte, Jean. *Le rationalisme de Descartes.* 2d ed. Paris, 1950.

Leroy, Maxime. *Descartes, le philosophe au masque.* Paris, 1929.

Mouy, Paul. *Le développement de la physique cartésienne.* Paris, 1934.

Sebba, Gregor. *Bibliographia Cartesiana.* The Hague, 1964.

LESZEK KOLAKOWSKI (1987)

DESCENT INTO THE UNDERWORLD. Narratives the world over tell of descents into the underworld. Many traditions include myths connected with journeys to the "otherworld" undertaken by both human and suprahuman beings. Experiences of such journeys are especially common in the shamanistic traditions, but they are also found in association with various ecstatic religious phenomena and various heroic and visionary contexts within a great number of cultures.

An important differentiation can be made between the descent with no return (accomplishing the due of human mortality) and the descent with return made by heroes, shamans, and other extraordinary humans. The imaginary experiences with return could fulfill different objectives: to explain the cosmic subterranean topography, to rescue someone from the realm of the dead, and to expose the punishments and sufferings in the otherworld with a moral purpose. The descent into the underworld, particularly to the kingdom of the dead, is one of the central themes in myths explaining the cosmic order, the limits and possibilities of the human being, the relationships between gods, and human relationships with god or the gods.

But the descent into the underworld is also a powerful imaginal and, on occasion, stereotyped literary motif. In the European traditions, due to the influence of the Homeric *Nekyia* (ninth book of the *Odyssey*), the descent (Greek, *katabasis*), an imaginary motif is present in major literary and artistic works despite the cultural, chronological, and religious differences between contexts and authors (between, for instance, Vergil's sixth book of the *Aeneid* and the *Inferno* in Dante's *Commedia*). Such a literary motif is also found in the Middle Eastern traditions from the *Epic of Gilgamesh* to the *Book of Enoch* or the *isra* of Muḥammad. There are cross-relationships among all of these literary traditions. Christ's descent into hell and medieval Christian literature developing the topic of the descent and the description of hell have, therefore, a long literary tradition.

The beliefs concerning descent into an underworld inhabited by spirits and supernatural beings could be based in part on experiences in which the soul is believed to leave the body during a state of altered consciousness—such as trance, sleep, or near-death experiences—or during the visions and hallucinations associated with these states. The content of such experiences, however, is determined to a large extent by the cultures and traditional beliefs of the persons undergoing them, but these phenomena also have remarkable similarities in different cultures and ages, a fact that encourages intercultural comparisons.

THE ROADS TO DEATH: TOPOGRAPHIES OF THE DESCENT. Beliefs concerning the descent into the underworld are often connected with the concept of a three-layer cosmos, according to which the human world is located midway between the realm of spirits above and the realm of the dead below—the "underworld." The underworld itself may also be thought of as divided into layers. In certain Asian, European, Mesoamerican, and Oceanic cultures, for instance, the underworld is believed to be divided into as many as nine layers. Mayan cultures recognized nine levels of the underworld, and some funerary temples reproduce a descent in nine phases. Scandinavians called the ninth and lowest level Niflhel.

These cosmic levels are often believed to be connected to one another by a cosmic tree or mountain, which is frequently believed to be located in the north. In inner and northern Asia, India, and northern Europe, the "center of the world" is found in the north. The cosmic tree that connects the levels of the cosmos also acts as a path of communication among them. The Vasyugan Khanty, the Maya, and the Scandinavians, for instance, believe that it has its roots in the underworld. In the shamanistic tales of Siberia, the opening leading to the underworld is represented as lying at the foot of the cosmic tree or at the foot of its counterpart, the shaman's tree. The Altaic Turks, on the other hand, locate this opening at the "center of the cosmos" and describe it as a "smoke hole." Many northerly peoples locate the opening to the different cosmic levels in the North Star that shines at the center of the world and symbolizes supernatural stability and eternity.

In all cultural traditions the most important part of the underworld is the realm of the dead. Most of the traditions describing the descent into the underworld are in fact concerned with visiting the dead, though this realm may be described differently in various cultures. In some cultures of the East, in central Asia, and in ancient Greek religion, for instance, it is described as the palace of the sovereign of death or as a mighty dwelling place. In ancient Scandinavian folklore it is a great hall, whereas in the Finnish epic it is a large living room. Among the hunting peoples of Siberia, it is conceived of as a yurt village, in the Celtic culture it is in an insular location, and in ancient Greek tradition Hades (the realm of Hades, the god of the underworld) seems to be described as a palace. Despite the variety in representations, however, many of the concepts surrounding the realm of the dead and the roads to entrances are similar in all parts of the world.

Belief in a local opening and a road leading to the underworld are common in the cultures of Europe, Asia, America, West Africa, Melanesia, and Polynesia. On the west side of Rarotonga, in the Cook Islands, for instance, one finds the Black Rock, from which the souls of the dead are thought to set off on their journey to the otherworld. Volcanoes, such as Etna, or caves, such as that of Lough Derg in Ireland, mark the beginning of the road to hell or purgatory, as in medieval Christian literature. In the ancient Greek imaginary topography, subterranean entrances to the realm of Hades are not uncommon (more than fifty are testified in the ancient sources), and sanctuaries could be located in caves or entrances to the underworld: the best-known example is the Nekyomanteion (oracle of the dead) at Ephyra.

One of the universal features of such a road to the underworld is darkness. This is why the Yakut shaman has disks representing the sun and moon sewn onto clothing—to provide light on the route to the otherworld. The road is also dangerous, fraught with difficulties and preternatural obstacles that only an initiate or a spirit being can overcome. In Finnish folklore such obstacles include a great eagle, a snake, a fiery pond or waterfall, and a river bristling with swords. Similar obstacles are also found in the mythologies of the Middle and Far East, of classical antiquity, and of the Germanic peoples, and they were also cultivated in the Christian vision literature and art of the Middle Ages. According to the ancient Germans and the Yakuts of Siberia, the dead had to be equipped either with shoes or a horse to protect them on their difficult journey.

Traditions familiar in both Asia and Europe tell of a stream surrounding the realm of the dead that must be crossed on a ferry or by a narrow bridge made dangerous by swords, or they speak of a wall surrounding the underworld over which the soul must leap. In ancient Greek mythology the ferryman Charon helps the dead cross the labyrinthine underworld waters and enter the realm of Hades. But Charon, as a literary and iconographic motif, is found even in Western Christian literature and arts (e.g., in the Sistine Chapel), despite the religious changes produced in the idea of the underworld by Christianization. It could be used as an example of the plurality of beliefs about the underworld that coexist in a culture or a religion and that encourage the microanalysis of cases, contexts, and points of view.

Another widespread concept connected with the underworld is that of the beast or dog that guards its gates. Examples include the Greek Kerberos, with its three heads; the Scandinavian Garmr, a huge and bloody monster; the Babylonian Nedu, with its lion's head, human hands, and bird's feet; and the Egyptian Ammut, the watchdog of the underworld god Osiris that has the body of a lion, the front limbs of a crocodile, and the rear limbs of a hippopotamus.

The Shamanic Initiation and the Descent into the Underworld. A journey to the underworld under the helpful guidance of the spirits is the cornerstone of the classical shamanism of Siberia and inner Asia, and corresponding practices connected with the activities of a seer or an ecstatic healer are found in other parts of the world as well: in North America, in Oceania, in the folk religion of Indochina, among the early religions of Europe, and especially in the various religions of South America. One typical feature of this type of otherworldly journey is the use the shaman makes of ritual techniques intended to induce ecstasy.

Where there is a belief in an underworld, it is not uncommon for people to have chance experiences of descending into it during sleep or trance. In shamanistic cultures such spontaneous experiences were interpreted as proof that the spirits had selected a candidate as a future shaman. According to a Nentsy myth, a woodcutter suddenly found himself on the back of a *minryy* bird, from which he fell through a hole into the underworld. There he wandered from the dwelling of one spirit to that of another and had to recognize each in turn. He was then cut into pieces and put together again, after which one of the spirits guided him back to the earth's surface. This experience was taken to be the initiation as a shaman, particularly in view of the dissection and reassembling of the body by the spirits.

Chance visions, pains, and torments were interpreted as the shaman's sickness and were taken as signs of a person's candidacy as a shaman. While learning to use the drum and sing the shaman's songs, the candidate withdrew from the normal life of the community, fasted, and sought contact with the spirits. A journey to the underworld, experienced through visions and auditions, was a prerequisite for initiation. The central element of this journey was the experience of rebirth. The reports of such initiation visions prove that the initiate's experiences were shaped by the shamanistic tradition of the community in question. The older shamans interpreted the candidate's experiences in such a way as to channel them toward accepted, traditional patterns. During this initiation period the new shamans became familiar with that part of the spirit world to which they would later journey during shamanic séances.

A number of the peoples of inner Asia and southern Siberia referred to the shaman's journeying to the underworld as "black." This seems to be a reference to the fact that the underworld contained not only the abodes of the dead but also the dwelling places of various disease-causing or otherwise dangerous spirits. In order to be an accomplished shaman, one had to know the roads leading to these places and be able to recognize their inhabitants. This made it all the more important for a candidate to study the topography of the underworld during the initiation period. In the more northerly regions, this study was conducted under the guidance of special spirits, usually zoomorphic spirits of nature.

The Descent as Shamanic Ritual. The ritual descent into the underworld takes place during a shamanistic séance, in the course of which the shaman describes in song the stages of the journey. In northern Siberia and the Arctic regions in particular, the actual transfer to the otherworld was thought to coincide with the highest point in the shaman's altered state of consciousness and was indicated by loss of external consciousness. The shaman's soul was then thought to have left the body and to be traveling in the otherworld in the form of an animal or accompanied by benevolent spirits.

The visit to the underworld was sometimes portrayed through performable means. The journey of the "black" shamans of the Altaic Tatars to Erlik Khan, the lord of the underworld, was expressed not only in song but also in mime and movement. The shamans gave detailed descriptions of the stages of the journey and the meeting with Erlik Khan. First they rode southward, climbed the Mountain of Iron, on whose slopes lay the fading bones of unsuccessful shamans, and then descended through a hole into the underworld. They next crossed the sea of the underworld by an extremely narrow and dangerous bridge and arrived at the dwelling of Erlik Khan. At first the lord of the underworld was angry, but as the shamans offered him drink and sacrifices, he became benevolent and promised to fulfill the shamans' wishes. The shamans then returned to earth riding on a goose.

When descending into the underworld, the shaman tried to solve problems that were thought to be caused by the spirits. The reasons for the journey to the underworld thus depended on the sorts of spirits living there and on the way they were thought to influence human life. If an illness was believed to be caused by a loss of soul, it was the shaman's task to fetch the patient's soul from the malevolent spirits who had stolen it. Other typical reasons for descending into the underworld were to acquire knowledge concerning the future, the weather, lost objects, or persons; to meet the spirits who assisted at a birth; to meet the keepers of the game during a period of famine; to escort the soul of a sacrificial animal to its destination; or to accompany the souls of the dead to the underworld. For example, the initiatory vision of the Nganasani shaman Sereptie Djaruoskin reveals that he knew the roads leading from the foot of the shaman's tree to the spirits responsible for every kind of sickness, to the main guardians of the game, and to the spirits who provide protection at births.

If the soul of a dead person should fail to go to the underworld but instead keep disturbing the peace of the living, the shaman was called upon to play the role of psychopomp (guide of souls). Indeed among the Nanay (Goldi), the Altaic Turks, and the Nentsy, escorting the soul of the dead to its new abode was one of the shaman's most important tasks. After a death, the Nanay arranged a festival, during which the shaman caught the wandering spirit and placed it on a cushion specially made for the occasion. A big clan memorial festival was then held, and the shaman escorted the soul of the dead to Buni, the clan's own kingdom of the dead. On the way the shaman and the soul in keeping were assisted by the spirit Buchu, who knew the way, and the bird Koori, who carried the travelers to the underworld on its back. At the séance during which all this took place, the shaman expressed the stages of the journey with dramatic effects, giving instructions to the assisting spirits and expressing in song the horror and relief over the difficulties along the way. As described at such séances, the road to Buni included eighteen stages that had special names and generally known features. The most difficult task along the journey was crossing the river separating the living from the dead. The shamans could tell when they had reached their destination from strange footmarks, the sound of dogs barking, and other traditional signs.

In modern shamanism (and in neoshamanism), because of undergoing the process of adaptation to the modern world and global society, some of the classical themes of the descent into the underworld are objects of redefinition and psychological interpretation (using, for example, the Jungian and New Age concept of shadow as explanation). The descent into the underworld has become an inner experience of combat against a personal alter ego. The cosmic topographical implication and the social interest of the shamanic exploit are transformed in a private experience without social or cosmic relevance.

The Heroic Descent and the Orpheus Theme. The journeys to the underworld undertaken by shamans and mystics typically involve visions experienced during trance. There are, however, myths and tales in parts of the world that tell of journeys to the underworld undertaken by humans or gods without the aid of ecstatic techniques or powers. Visiting the underworld was thought to be one of the standard deeds of mythical heroes. The heroes descending into the underworld need not necessarily be human, for Ishtar makes the journey in the Akkadian myth, Lemminkäinen's mother does so in the Finnish tradition, and the Mayan twins Hunahpu and Ixbalanque descend into Xibalba (the realm of the deities of the death) in the *Popol Vuh.*

The reasons for the descent were many. One of the most popular was the rescue of a relative or loved one who had died young. But the journey also could be undertaken to search for immortality, knowledge, or some special favor, to escort the dead to their final resting place, or to receive initiation in the mysteries of the underworld. Here exists a close parallel to the reasons given for the shaman's journey.

A test of strength between love and death is the basis of the legends and myths in which one left behind in this world follows the beloved or relative "to the land of no return." And when the result of the journey is positive, the inexorable law of mortality—the power of Thanatos—is overcome by the power of Eros. The best-known representative of this type of narrative is the Orpheus theme, various forms of which are found not only in Eurasia but also in North America, Oceania, and Melanesia.

In Vergil's version, in the fourth book of the *Georgics,* perhaps the best literary expression of the classical myth (because the Orphic versions, included in *Katabasis of Orpheus,* have unfortunately disappeared), Orpheus sets off for Hades in search of his wife Eurydice, who has died young. With his songs and his music, Orpheus relieves the suffering in the underworld and wins the favor of the gods. Eurydice is promised to him on condition that he not turn to look at her on the road up. The impatient Orpheus breaks his vow and loses his wife. Despite the negative result of the *katabasis,* for the followers of the Greek mystery cults who use the name of Orpheus as a sign of identity this underworld exploit is a demonstration of the possibility of acquiring knowledge that can defeat death. The Orphic initiation offers the wisdom to find the appropriate path in the underworld journey and the knowledge of the correct descent that is inscribed in the Orphic-Dionysiac gold lamellae (sheets) found in a number of burial sites in Greece and southern Italy.

A negative result is also obtained by the god Izanagi in his underworld search for his twin sister and wife Izanami in the realm of Yomi as reported in the Japanese *Kojiki.* The episode explains a cosmic division into two layers, upper and lower, ruled by the twin gods, a provisional arrangement changed by the following generation of gods.

Greater happiness befalls the heroes of the Polynesians, including the Maori of New Zealand, who rescue their loved ones by deceiving the spirits trying to prevent their escape. In one Maori narrative, Hutu follows Pane, who has died of love for him, to the underworld. There Hutu entertains the spirits, having them sit on the top of a tree that has been bent over and fastened to the ground by a rope. When Hutu lets go of the rope, the spirits are hurled into the air, and he escapes with his beloved.

In addition to spouses or lovers, the main characters in these tales may also be people who are attached to one another by some other tie. For example, there are stories among the Indians of North America that stress sibling attachment. The Tatars of the Sayan steppes tell the story of Kubaiko, who goes to look for her brother in the kingdom of death ruled by Erlik Khan. After carrying out the superhuman tasks imposed upon her by the princes of death, Kubaiko receives the body of her brother and brings him back to life with the water of life. The story gives a long description of the state after death and the punishment of sinners. The torments inflicted in Hades to the enemies of the gods (Sisyphos, Tantalos, Tityos) are described in the story of Odysseus's journey to the land of the dead. But because the goal of the hero is not to rescue someone but to obtain information, the episode seems more an invocation followed by a vision than a descent.

The related idea of the death and resurrection of a god lies behind certain invigoration rites. There is a myth connected with the Akkadian Ishtar and her Sumerian counterpart Inanna that describes the descent of the goddess into the underworld, probably to try to subjugate that realm. On her way, Ishtar takes off her clothes and her ornaments as she passes through the gates that lead to Arallu. On reaching her destination, she dies, and the earthly vegetation wilts. When the gods sprinkle her with the water of life, she recovers and returns to earth.

The Heroic and Initiation Descent: Immortality and Apotheosis. In some cases a hero penetrates the kingdom of death to gain immortality. One of the oldest known examples is the Sumerian myth of Gilgamesh, in which Gilgamesh crosses the waters of death and reaches the land of eternal life. There he finds a plant that guarantees immortality. But a snake snatches it from him on his return trip, and he is forced to accept mortality for humankind. The account of Gilgamesh's journey has been compared to the account of Herakles's visit to Hades and Odysseus's *Nekyia.* But Odysseus refuses the immortality promised to him by Calypso in order to to maintain his own identity. Herakles reaches apotheosis (the transformation into a god) after a number of exploits (crucially the visit to the garden of the Hesperides), not simply after his victorious return from the underworld, when he brings with him the watchdog Kerberos and delivers Alcestis and Theseus.

The pursuit of immortality is also part of the tradition woven around the Polynesian trickster and culture hero Maui. Maui believed he could make himself immortal by crawling through the body of his giant grandmother Hine-nui-te-po. Hine-nui-te-po wakes as Maui enters her mouth and, closing her mouth, kills the intruder. This swallowing motif, also found in the story of Jonah and the great fish, is quite common in traditions concerned with initiation and takes both mythical and ritual forms. It is found in the Finnish folk epic, in which Väinämöinen enters the belly of a giant sage who had long been dead. Väinämöinen descends to the underworld in the role of a sage to seek knowledge and incantations. In this respect he is reminiscent of a shaman. A similar seeking journey is made by the Scandinavian god Odin, who is described as having ecstatic powers.

Further reasons for traveling to the underworld include the search for some special object, as in the descent of Psyche, or the mere satisfaction of curiosity. In each case the journey is described as extremely dangerous and difficult, with its success depending on special conditions: the travelers should not eat any food offered in the underworld, nor should they look back on the return journey, lest they fall under the power of the spirits giving chase from below (which happens to Izanami in the Japanese myth and Persephone in the Greek myth).

In some cultures, a main reason to endure the descent is to demonstrate the supernatural condition of the traveler, a recognition of his or her extraordinary or divine nature. The *katabasis* of Dionysos, with the rescue of his mother Semele, shows without a doubt to his followers the power of the god over death. And then Dionysos, like a sort of mystic Hades, could offer to those who had endured the initiation into his mysteries the liberation from death: the Dionysian path (difficult to distinguish from the Orphic path) to overshadow the mirage of common underworld destiny as it appears in the words inscribed in the golden intiatory lamellae.

In a similar way, some Christian theologians explain Christ's descent into the underworld as a complete victory over hell, overcoming the power of evil and rescuing the "saints of the Old Testament," highlighting the new alliance that changes the foundations of the cosmic topography with the descent. The complex theological implications of the episode have been understood in different ways in the various Christian denominations (a number of which discarded the cosmic implications of the descent, simply understood as a paraphrastic reference to the act of dying). But the iconographical possibilities of the episode have been widely exploited in art and literature, especially in the Middle Ages and in Oriental Christianity, due to the values of glory and sovereignty that underlie the episode and the classical and oriental imaginal implications of the descent into hell.

The Visionary Descent with Moral Purposes. Visions of descending into the underworld are a part of the traditions of the religions of the Middle East and the ancient Mediterranean world, Hinduism, Buddhism, Islam, and Christianity. The visit in question is usually to the kingdom of the dead, and one of its main themes is the observation of the torment awaiting sinners in the other world, along with the judgment of souls. The moral purposes of the journey are evident and serve as arguments to reinforce the belief in the ethical mainstream proposed by these religions.

One of the earliest records in the Greek tradition of the transformation of the literary heroic descent into a descent with moral purposes is the Platonic myth of Er, related at the end of Plato's *Republic* (c. 380 BCE), in which the visions of the postmortem destiny had a propaedeutic purpose in the philosophical way of life proposed by Plato. Earlier accounts about the punishment in Hades for amoral or criminal attitudes certainly existed—for instance, in the *Nekyia* painted in the fifth century BCE by Polygnotos in the Cnidian Lesche at Delphi (and described by Pausanias)—but in Plato the description had a moral purpose.

Multiple examples of the imaginal and moral effectiveness of these sorts of visionary descents exist in the ancient world. The *Book of Enoch* relates a descent into the She'ol that shows the diversity of the ideas about the underworld in Hellenistic Judaism. The judgment of the dead in an Egyptian papyrus of the first century CE describes how Setne Khamuas, a high priest of Memphis, descended into the halls of Amenti under the guidance of his son Si-Osiris. In the Christian *Apocalypse of Peter* (c. 135 CE), the visions detail, in an explicit and meticulous way, the terrible punishments of the sinners. These themes were particularly popular in the Christian literature and art of the Middle Ages, and the descriptive and imaginal possibilities of the journey were exploited in Christian countries. The popular medieval English mystery play *The Harrowing of Hell* is an example of this, although the most accurate and famous artistic expression of such beliefs is Dante's *Commedia* (1321).

But these descriptions of journeys into hell (and eventually paradise and other locations) repeat beliefs that are familiar from the Mediterranean and Middle Eastern traditions, and the relationships between authors and religious traditions are difficult to trace. The influence of a literary tradition that overcomes religious backgrounds using identical imaginal resources is undeniable, but the final purposes of the descriptions are also significant. For example, Aeneas's descent in Vergil's sixth book of the *Aeneid,* Christ's descent into hell in the *Gospel of Nicodemus,* the visions exposed in the Iranian *Ardā Wirāz Nāmag,* the journey described in the *Book of the Scale,* or other descriptions of the *isra* of Muḥammad had specific religious significance within each religious tradition.

The visionary descent appears also in Far Asian traditions. The ascetic practices known as *gyo,* practiced by Buddhist priests in Japan, sometimes led to trances that included visions of journeys to the underworld. Some of the visions were of an initiatory nature and had structural and thematic similarities to the shamans' visions. In the *Nihon ryōiki* a priest called Chikō, while feigning death, found himself accompanied by two messengers on the road to the underworld. The road led westward and finally to a golden palace, the door of which was guarded by two terrible beings. Three times the messengers ordered Chikō to clasp a burning hot pillar so that his flesh was burned and only his bones remained, and three times the spirits put him together again. They finally sent him back to earth, ordering him to renounce the sin of envy. In addition to such reports of initiatory trials, the Japanese narratives also contain revelations of the sentences passed by the king of the underworld and the horrors awaiting sinners. One type of narrative, which has parallels in the Chinese tradition, tells of persons descending into the underworld to save one of their relatives from the torments of hell. Such descriptions of the judgment and punishment of sinners could serve as a moral warning to lead a virtuous life, but they could also be used as a meditation resource (e.g., the visonary visit to the realm of the punished during the meditative practice with *bhava chakra* in Mahāyāna Buddhism).

The theme of visionary descent experienced a renewal in European tradition with Emanuel Swedenborg's (1688–1772) description of a supposed visit to the underworld in his *De coelo et ejus mirabilibus, et de inferno, ex auditis et visis* (Heaven and its wonders and hell from things heard and seen, 1758). He proposed a Christian esoterical topography of hell and an angelology, in which the torments of the sinners are transformed in an inner postmortem experience of the evil committed in life. Swedenborg is useful as an early example of the modern prevailing tendency to the interiorization brought about by the loss of imaginal fascination of the heroic motif of the descent. (The powerful 1998 iconographical adaptation of the classical *descensus* in Vincent Ward's film *What Dreams May Come* is perhaps an exception.) In fact, the descent into the underworld seems to be of little interest in the theological speculations and ritual practices developed in Christianity in particular and in the world religions in general, excluding perhaps some shamanic contexts.

SEE ALSO Judgment of the Dead; Shamanism; Underworld; Visions.

BIBLIOGRAPHY

Bishop, J. G. "The Hero's Descent to the Underworld." In *The Journey to the Other World,* edited by Hilda R. Ellis Davidson, pp. 109–129. Totowa, N.J., 1975.

Blacker, Carmen. "Other World Journeys in Japan." In *The Journey to the Other World,* edited by Hilda R. Ellis Davidson, pp. 42–47. Totowa, N.J., 1975.

Böcher, Otto, Walter Sparn, and Karl Christian Felmy. "Höllenfahrt Jesu Christi." In *Die Religion in Geschichte und Gegenwart,* edited by Hans Dieter Betz et al., 4th ed., vol. 2. Tübingen, Germany, 1998–2000.

Casadio, Giovanni. "Dioniso e Semele: Morte di un dio e resurrezione di una dona." In *Dionysos, mito e misterio,* edited by Fede Berti, pp. 361–377. Ferrara, Italy, 1991. The article was reprinted in Giovanni Casadio, *Il vino dell'anima,* pp. 145–167 (Rome, 1999).

Colpe, Carsten. "Höllenfahrt." In *Reallexikon für Antike und Christentum,* edited by Ernst Dassmann et al., vol. 15, cols. 1015–1023. Stuttgart, Germany, 1991.

Colpe, Carsten. "Jenseitsfahrt II (Unterwelts- oder Höllenfahrt)." In *Reallexikon für Antike und Christentum,* edited by Ernst Dassmann et al., vol. 17, cols. 466–489. Stuttgart, Germany, 1995.

Colpe, Carsten, and Peter Habermehl. "Jenseitsreise." In *Reallexikon für Antike und Christentum,* edited by Ernst Dassmann et al., vol. 17, cols. 490–543. Stuttgart, Germany, 1995.

Davidson, Hilda Roderick Ellis. *The Road to Hel: A Study of the Conception of the Dead in Old Norse Literature* (1943). Westport, Conn., 1977.

Dieterich, Albrecht. *Nekyia. Beiträge zur Erklärung der neuentdeckten Petrusapokalipse.* Leipzig, Germany, 1893.

Diez de Velasco, Francisco. *Los caminos de la muerte: Religión, rito e iconografía del paso al más allá en la Grecia antigua.* Madrid, 1995.

Eliade, Mircea. *Shamanism: Archaic Techniques of Ecstasy.* Translated by Willard R. Trask. Rev. and enl. ed. New York, 1964.

Eliade, Mircea. *Birth and Rebirth* (1958). New York, 1975.

Ganschinietz (Ganszyniec), Ryszard. "Katabasis." In *Pauly's Real-Encyclopädie der classischen Altertumswissenschaft,* edited by August Friedrich von Pauly et al., vol. 20, cols. 2359–2449. Stuttgart, Germany, 1919.

Gounelle, Rémi. *La descente du Christ aux enfers: Institutionalisation d'une croyance.* Paris, 2000.

Harris, W. Hall, III. *The Descent of Christ: Ephesians 4:7–11 and Traditional Hebrew Imagery.* Leiden, Netherlands, 1996.

Himmelfarb, Martha. *Tours of Hell.* Philadelphia, 1983.

Hultkrantz, Åke. *The North American Indian Orpheus Tradition: A Contribution to Comparative Religion.* Stockholm, 1957.

Kuusi, Matti, Keith Bosley, and Michael Branch, eds. and trans. *Finnish Folk Poetry: Epic; An Anthology in Finnish and English.* Helsinki, 1977.

Loofs, Friedrich. "Descent to Hades (Christ's)." In *Encyclopaedia of Religion and Ethics,* edited by James Hastings, vol. 4. Edinburgh, 1911.

Lopatin, Ivan Alexis. *The Cult of the Dead among the Natives of the Amur Basin.* The Hague, 1960.

MacCulloch, J. A. "Descent to Hades (Ethnic)." In *Encyclopaedia of Religion and Ethics,* edited by James Hastings, vol. 4. Edinburgh, 1911.

MacCulloch, J. A. *The Harrowing of Hell: A Comparative Study of an Early Christian Doctrine* (1930). New York, 1982.

Patch, Howard Rollin. *The Other World according to Descriptions in Medieval Literature* (1950). New York, 1970.

Popov, A. A. "How Sereptie Djaruoskin of the Nganasani (Tavgi Samoyeds) Became a Shaman." In *Popular Beliefs and Folklore Tradition in Siberia,* edited by Vilmos Diószegi, pp. 137–145. Bloomington, Ind., 1968.

Quinn, J. D., and J. H. Rohlings. "Descent of Christ into Hell." In *New Catholic Encyclopedia,* 2d ed., vol. 4, pp. 683–686. Detroit, Mich., 2003.

Sullivan, Lawrence E. *Icanchu's Drum: An Orientation to Meaning in South American Religions.* New York, 1988.

Swedenborg, Emanuel. *De coelo et ejus mirabilibus, et de inferno, ex auditis et visis.* London, 1758. Translated by George F. Dole as *Heaven and Its Wonders and Hell: Drawn from Things Heard and Seen* (West Chester, Pa., 2000).

ANNA-LEENA SIIKALA (1987)
FRANCISCO DIEZ DE VELASCO (2005)

DESERTS. In areas of continuous occupation, the presence of the sacred transcends and resolves the stresses produced by the environment. In the desert, humankind, deprived of the support of social solidarity and helplessly confronted by supernatural forces, is beset by anguish and fear.

THE DESERT AND PERSONAL RELIGIOUS EXPERIENCE. The first visions of the desert, therefore, are pessimistic. It is the region of the savage beasts and malevolent spirits, of demons of all kinds. In primitive societies it is the place of trials, of initiations. It is the place to which the rejected and the exiled are banished: Cain (*Gn.* 4:11–16), Hagar and Ishmael (*Gn.* 21:9–15), and the scapegoat that was burdened with the sins of Israel (*Lv.* 16:8–10). Particularly characteristic of the most ancient sedentary societies of the Middle East (Haldar, 1950), this conception was long lived. For the prophets of Israel (e.g., *Ez.* 20) and in the accounts of the Exodus, the time in the desert is that of infidelity (*Ex.* 17:7), of the golden calf (*Ex.* 32), and of punishment before the entrance into the Promised Land.

But another, parallel attitude also developed: the desert as apprenticeship and self-knowledge. As a terrain of struggle, the desert leads to the discovery of one's own being and, thereby, to the affirmation of the individual. At a more evolved stage of religious thought, it is the privileged place of divine revelation, of the betrothal of Israel with Yahveh

(Gillet, 1949), of the offer of alliance, and of law that brings liberation. After the infidelities in the land of Canaan, it was by means of a return to the desert, the place of love and intimacy with the divine, that reconciliation with Yahveh was achieved (*Hos.* 2:14–16; *Jer.* 2:2–3). The desert thus becomes a refuge from corruption and depravity. Philo Judaeus (d. 45–50 CE) adds to this specifically Jewish conception a theme of Hellenistic mysticism—the romantic yearning of the world-weary city dweller for solitude, for retreat to the desert, where he can find peace. The desert, where the air is pure and light (*On the Contemplative Life* 22–23), assumes for Philo an absolute value. It was for this reason that God gave his laws to his people "in the depths of the desert" (*On the Decalogue* 2). This idea leaves its trace, then, through a whole series of Christian authors, for example, Origen: "John the Baptist, fleeing the tumult of the cities, went into the desert, where the air is purer, the sky more open, and God more intimate" (*Homilies on Luke* 11). It is the point of departure of the entire Christian monastic movement toward settlement in the desert after the fourth century—a movement that to a large extent regains the primitive pessimistic vision in its land of choice, Egypt.

The desert is where the devil is encountered and where Christ contended with him (Mauser, 1963). Monastic asceticism developed as a struggle in a fearsome place that was the land of demons par excellence. But this struggle was victorious. The presence of the pious anchorites integrated the desert into the realm of faith either by transforming it into a city, *desertum civitas* (Athanasius, *Life of Anthony* 14; cf. Chitty, 1966), or by fertilizing it and making it bloom according to the prophecy of *Isaiah* 35:1: *desertum floribus vernans* (Jerome, *Letters* 14). Finally, it was in the desert that the monks would find *hēsuchia,* the serenity of solitude. Christian tradition would thus, in the course of centuries, base the movement toward the solitary life that was to become as essential component of it on the image of the desert as a place of solitude (*ēremia*).

This approbation of solitude, brought to its apogee in Christianity, was to be more or less present in all higher religions in which the ascetic imperative is based on meditation, which is facilitated by life in the desert: Buddhism, particularly in the Tantric forms, Daoism, and Islam. However, in the case of Islam, the acceptance was relatively cautious. For the Muslims, the desert was above all a *thème d'illustration* (Arnaldez, 1975). It is necessary to "realize" the desert of spiritual solitude before the sole existent being, God. But it is dangerous to actually take abode in the desert. It is true that there man can avoid hypocritical ostentation (*riʾāʾ*) and the artificial social role that destroys authentic sincerity (*ikhlās*). But he thereby runs the risk of arrogance, of developing the cult of his inner self. This more reserved attitude of Islam in regard to the reality of the desert does not affect the value attributed to the desert as a synonym for solitude and retreat, ending in the solitariness (*infirād*) that culminates in mystical ascension. Both by its nature and its symbols, the desert brings man closer to God.

The Desert in the History of Religions. Does this proximity to the divine lead to the development of a particular religious structure? Ernest Renan thought so. In his *Histoire générale des langues sémitiques* (1885), inspired by the long Christian tradition, he wrote: "The desert is monotheistic. Sublime in its immense uniformity, it first revealed to man the idea of infinity, but not the perception of an unceasingly creative life that a more fertile nature inspired in other races" (p. 6). He later returned to this idea and defined it more precisely in his *Histoire du peuple d'Israël* (vol. 1, 1887, pp. 45, 59). He found the basis for the development of primitive monotheism, which he attributed to the Semitic peoples, to be "the customs of nomadic life," where there is little room for cultic practice and where "philosophical reflection, exercised intensely within a small circle of observation, leads to extremely simple ideas." More than a century after Renan, his idea of the desert as source and origin of Jewish monotheistic thought would again inspire the works of a master of biblical archaeology, William Albright (1964, pp. 154–156).

Actually, this idea is now largely outdated and has been vigorously disputed. All the studies on pre-Islamic Arab religion in particular (Wellhausen, 1897; Ryckmans, 1951; Henninger, 1959) have drawn a picture of it that has little to do with monotheism and that associates with the supreme deity, Allah, a numerous and varied cortege of deities. The desert is the domain of polymorphous and diffuse ritual. It is, to repeat the expression of the Qurʾān, "associationistic," and the desert bedouin are "the most obdurate in their impiety and hypocrisy" (sura 9:97).

However, the situation remains ambiguous. Beside and above the other gods was Allāh. He was incontestably a god of the nomads, a provider of rain (Brockelmann, 1922), and one can easily imagine the extreme importance that he assumed for a nomad whose survival depends entirely on the condition of the grazing land. Not only among the Arabs was the god of rain the unique god. It has been possible to reconstruct the special characteristics of the religion of pastoral peoples in general in conjunction with the peculiarities of their social structure and their way of life; such a reconstruction has been made for the first time in an environment very different from the desert, namely, that of the high grassy savannas of East Africa (Meinhof, 1926). The creation of powerful personages, of heroic saviors who are then frequently enrobed in historic myths connected with the origins of the tribe, is an expression of the instability of the pastoral tribe, which assembles or disperses in accordance with the importance of the individuals that direct and guide it within a context of aggressive relationships between groups. This orientation often accompanies that which consists of making the god of rain the unique god, dispenser of all benefices. The herdsman soon breaks free of polytheism. Ancestor worship is unknown to him, and the dead are forgotten. The herdsman is knowledgeable and intrepid, little inclined toward fear and superstition.

One is here indeed on the way to the monotheistic god, but under the impetus of a somewhat different logic. It is not that the desert is monotheistic but rather that the pastoral nomad has the tendency, at least, to become monotheistic. In contrast with the profusion of rituals in the Australian desert traversed by primitive hunters or gatherers is the evolution toward the monotheistic god of the warlike pastoral tribe, herders of large beasts of the African savannas or the bedouin of the deserts of the Old World. This trend toward monotheism is a late development in the cultural history of humanity. Contrary to Wilhelm Schmidt's opinion, this "great god of the herdsmen" is not the legacy of a primitive monotheism. Today we know that the pastoral nomads were, in the main, descendants of the first agrarian civilizations of the Old World, or were at least posterior to them. They constitute, in the world of the deserts and the steppes, a relatively recent cultural development, first in the form of the prebedouin herders of bovines, and then, after the domestication of the horse and the dromedary, in the form of the widespread, aggressive, warlike nomadism of the bedouin type, which in the Middle East does not go back further than the second millennium BCE.

But the appearance of monotheistic tendencies in the tribes of pastoral nomads can be rapid, as is shown by the analysis of neopastoral civilizations of the New World (Planhol, 1975). The Navajo of the Colorado plateaus of North America, whose pastoral mode of life did not emerge until the second half of the eighteenth century, still do not recognize a supreme deity (Reichard, 1950). But among the Goajira of Colombia and Venezuela, whose aggressive, cavalieristic, pastoral life goes back at least two or three centuries, there is a process of elaboration that seems much more advanced. Involved here is the predominance of a demiurgic creator (Maleiwa) and a rain giver (Juya), who are, however, not yet confused with each other, although the first signs of such a confusion are evident (Perrin, 1976). Among the herdsmen of East Africa, such as the Maasai, whose formation of a pastoral system goes back at least a thousand years, pastoral monotheism is well defined.

But, rather than being a true monotheism, it is in fact a monolatry in that it is willing to recognize the existence of other gods, who fulfil the same functions for the benefit of neighboring tribes or peoples; it is a protomonotheism in Baly's sense of the term (1970, pp. 258–259). The moral monotheism (Baly's "absolute" or "transcendent" monotheism) is a much more complex and revolutionary structure (Pettazzoni, 1950), the birth of which implies a break, not a simple evolution. Its occurrence exclusively in the Middle Eastern and Old World cultural environment reflects conditions of conflict. Here the presence of groups of pastoral nomads with still rather primitive monotheistic tendencies certainly played an essential role within the orbit of sedentary, sacerdotal civilizations that were polytheistic but much more highly developed (as Weindl, 1935, demonstrated). These conflicts could not be resolved except by a universalistic aspiration such as that of which the birth of Islam, following that of Judeo-Christian monotheism and Zoroastrian dualism, constitutes the final manifestation (Watt, 1953, 1956; Rodinson, 1961). Although Yahvism, as Nyström (1946) has shown, surpasses and in many particulars contradicts and transcends the bedouin ideal, this ideal is nonetheless necessary to it.

There is, therefore, no "religion of the desert." But, in the historical evolution of humanity in the Old World, the deserts have indeed been the privileged place for the development of the pastoral nomadic cultures that evolved precociously toward monotheism and that constituted an essential component in the genesis of the great monotheistic religions.

SEE ALSO Arabian Religions; Eremitism; Monotheism; Retreat.

BIBLIOGRAPHY

Albright, William F. *History, Archaeology, and Christian Humanism.* New York, 1964.

Arnaldez, Roger. "Le thème du désert dans la mystique musulmane, thème d'inspiration ou thème d'illustration." In *Les mystiques du désert,* pp. 89–96. Gap, France, 1975.

Baly, Denis. "The Geography of Monotheism." In *Translating and Understanding the Old Testament,* edited by Harry Thomas Frank and William L. Reed, pp. 258–278. New York, 1970.

Bartelink, G. J. M. "Les oxymores *desertum civitas* et *desertum floribus vernans.*" *Studia Monastica* 15 (1973): 7–15.

Brockelmann, Carl. "Allah und die Götzen, der Ursprung des islamischen Monotheismus." *Archiv für Religionswissenschaft* 21 (1922): 99–121.

Chitty, Derwas J. *The Desert a City.* Oxford, 1966.

Gillet, Jacques. "Thème de la marche au Désert dans l'Ancien et le Nouveau Testament." *Recherches de science religieuse* 36 (April–June 1949): 161–181.

Guillaumont, Antoine. "La conception du désert chez les moines d'Égypte." In *Les mystiques du désert,* pp. 25–38. Gap, France, 1975.

Haldar, Alfred O. *The Notion of the Desert in Sumero-Accadian and West-Semitic Religions.* Uppsala, 1950.

Henninger, Joseph. "La religion bédouine pré-islamique." In *L'antica societa beduina,* edited by Francesco Gabrieli, pp. 115–140. Rome, 1959.

Mauser, Ulrich W. *Christ in the Wilderness: The Wilderness Theme in the Second Gospel and Its Basis in the Biblical Tradition.* London, 1963.

Meinhof, Carl. "Religionen der Hirtenvölker." In his *Die Religionen der Afrikaner in ihrem Zusammenhang mit dem Wirtschaftsleben,* pp. 71–84. Oslo and Cambridge, Mass., 1926.

Les mystiques du désert dans l'Islam, le judaïsme, et le christianisme. Gap, France, 1975. Papers delivered at a conference of the Association des Amis de Sénanque, 28 July–3 August 1974.

Nyström, Samuel. *Beduinentum und Jahwismus: Eine soziologisch-religionsgeschichtliche Untersuchung zum Alten Testament.* Lund, 1946.

Perrin, Michel. *Le chemin des Indiens morts: Mythes et symboles goajiro.* Paris, 1976.

Pettazzoni, Raffaele. "La formation du monothéisme." *Revue de l'Université de Bruxelles* 2 (1950): 209–219.

Planhol, Xavier de. "Le désert, cadre géographique de l'expérience religieuse." In *Les mystiques du désert,* pp. 5–16. Gap, France, 1975.

Reichard, Gladys A. *Navajo Religion.* 2 vols. New York, 1950.

Rodinson, Maxime. *Mahomet.* Paris, 1961. Translated by Anne Carter as *Mohammed* (New York, 1971).

Ryckmans, Gonzague. *Les religions arabes préislamiques.* 2d ed. Louvain, 1951.

Schmidt, Wilhelm. *Der Ursprung der Gottesidee,* vols. 7–12, *Die Religionen der Hirtenvölker.* Münster, 1940–1955.

Watt, W. Montgomery. *Muḥammad at Mecca.* London, 1953.

Watt, W. Montgomery. *Muḥammad at Medina.* London, 1956.

Weindl, Theodor. *Monotheismus und Dualismus in Indien, Iran und Palästina als Religion junger, kriegerisch nomadistischer Völker im Gravitations bereich von Völkern alter Kultur.* Vienna, 1935.

Wellhausen, Julius. *Reste arabischen Heidentums.* 2d ed. Berlin, 1897.

XAVIER DE PLANHOL (1987)
Translated from French by Roger Norton

DESIRE is one of those important subjects that are seldom discussed under their own names, so that one hardly knows where to go for answers to questions about the nature of desire and its significance for the religious or spiritual life. The term *desire* is only rarely found in the index or tables of contents of books on religion, even when the term figures prominently in the author's description or interpretation of religion. In addition, there is no widely shared consensus about the meaning of the term, so it is put to a variety of uses. There is no standard inventory of experiences, realities, or relations to which the term refers.

In order to clarify the subject of desire and indicate some representative ways in which desire has been religiously and spiritually interpreted, its scope and boundaries will be discussed through a cross-cultural overview. In this context, the varieties of desire and of the experiences, realities, and terms closely associated with desire—and of other terms antithetical to it, terms of contrast through which some of the particular meanings of desire become fixed—will be examined. The dimensions of desire will thus be reflected upon by charting the regions of human experience to which the term *desire* refers.

In a discussion of the term *desire,* three kinds of questions need be considered. First, what is it that is being named? How is desire thought of, imagined, represented to oneself, and located in relation to other phenomena? Second, how does desire enter into human experience? In what circumstances does it become an issue for the religious or spiritual life? Third, how do people deal with desire in their religious or spiritual lives? What are the negative and positive strategies with which religious and spiritual individuals, communities, and traditions have dealt with desire? Where desire has been taken as a threat to the religious life or to spiritual integrity, what strategies have been developed to discipline, train, overcome, transcend, detach from, or eradicate desire? Where desire has been viewed more positively, what strategies have been developed to channel, direct, release, render articulate, or otherwise enlist and incorporate the energies and vitality of desire into the spiritual or religious life? In other words, how have individuals and communities sought to share and pass on what they have learned about desire and how to deal with it?

What is named when speaking of desire? How is it thought about, imagined, represented to oneself, and located in relation to other phenomena—particularly to matters of religious or spiritual importance?

Desire is commonly understood in volitional terms, in which case it is identified with such things as willing, wanting, and wishing, choice and appetite, inspiration and motivation, and even with intention. Desire is also understood in more emotional or affectional rather than volitional terms, in which case it is associated or identified with such things as emotion, feeling, passion, love, eros, (and eroticism), attachment, craving, yearning, greed, and lust. These volitional and affectional vocabularies for interpreting desire are, of course, not incompatible—especially if, as is often the case, the affections are understood as central to or constitutive of the self as willing and loving. Where reason is set over against and valued above either will or emotion, desire will usually be viewed as spiritually problematic.

In discussions of religious ethics, desire will figure more positively in teleological than in deontological ethics. Teleological ethics is likely to involve some consideration of the *telos* (goal or object) of desire—its satisfaction or fulfillment in happiness, well-being, pleasure, ecstacy, and/or union or communion or some other form of participation in the divine or sacred reality. In deontological ethics, on the other hand, desire will be seen in tension or conflict with the governing moral principles of obligation and duty. Yet here, too, reality goes beyond the terms of analysis, as when through the agency of religious rituals duty is sometimes converted into desire. According to anthropologist Victor Turner, sacred symbols have two semantic poles, one abstract and normative, the other physiological and "orectic"—that is, relating to desire or appetite, willing and feeling. The drama of ritual action, he suggests, may cause an exchange of properties between these semantic poles, condensing their many referents into a single cognitive and affective field, the biological referents ennobled and the normative referents charged with emotional significance. By such an exchange of qualities between semantic poles, what is socially necessary is rendered desirable, and duty becomes desire.

There is at least one striking contrast in the cultural and religious treatment of desire between Oriental and Occidental cultures. In Western cultures desire is generally given a more positive place in the vision of human being and well-being. But that affirmation tends to remain at a fairly abstract level, formulated by theologians. At the more pedestrian level of spiritual guidance and of daily life among ordinary people, desire is hedged about with all sorts of constraints. In both East and West, desire is treated in a highly differentiated fashion, but the pattern of differentiation varies significantly. In Asia desires are viewed in the context of the stages of life and are judged and constrained or released and licensed differently, according to the stage of life in question. In the West, desires are viewed more consistently in relation to their objects rather than to the stages of life, and desires are evaluated and graded according to higher and lower, finer and coarser objects of desire.

Desire figures in human experience in many ways and becomes religiously valid or problematic under a variety of circumstances. To illustrate the spiritual importance and power of desire and the complexity of the issues raised by desire, consider two of the greatest religious texts: the *Dao de jing,* the principal classic of Daoism, a collection of about the fourth century BCE attributed to Laozi, and Augustine's *Confessions,* a Christian classic written near the end of the fourth century CE. The *Dao de jing* is divided into two books. Book 1 begins and ends on the subject of desire:

> The way that can be spoken of
> Is not the constant way;
> The name that can be named
> Is not the constant name.
> The nameless was the beginning of heaven and earth;
> The named was the mother of the myriad creatures.
> Hence always rid yourself of desires in order to observe its [the way's] secrets;
> But always allow yourself to have desires in order to observe its [the way's] manifestations.
>
> The way never acts yet nothing is left undone.
> Should lords and princes be able to hold fast to it,
> The myriad creatures will be transformed of their own accord.
> After they are transformed, should desire raise its head,
> I shall press it down with the weight of the nameless uncarved block.
> The nameless uncarved block
> Is but freedom from desire,
> And if I cease to desire and remain still,
> The empire will be at peace of its own accord.
>
> (*Dao de jing,* trans. D. C. Lau, Baltimore, 1963, pp. 57, 96)

The ambiguity of desire is recognized, as well as the need to be acquainted with it. But real power and serenity lies in freedom from desire and in the active inactivity that is here identified with the "nameless uncarved block." Desire is presented as a problem rather than a resource for true spirituality.

In contrast, Augustine takes a very different view of desire. Addressing himself to God, he begins the *Confessions* by proclaiming the greatness of God and the desire to praise Him. "Thou movest us to delight in praising Thee; for Thou hast formed us for Thyself, and our hearts are restless till they find rest in Thee." But Augustine goes on to write of other desires that distract him from desire for God—desires for success and adulation, sexual desires, that great complex of desires that he came to identify as belonging to the City of Man in contrast with those of the City of God.

How do people deal with desire in their religious or spiritual lives? For some, desire itself, of whatever sort, is spiritually destructive. The primary—or at any rate initial—aim of their spiritual practice and discipline is to wean themselves from all desire, even the desire for enlightenment, self-transcendence, liberation, salvation, *nirvāṇa,* or mystical union with God. For others, desire is not itself intrinsically problematic but is seen as an essential and even a central mark of their humanity and of their spirituality. The issue for them is the right direction of desire, the right ordering of the various desires toward their appropriate objects, and a true perception of appropriate rank among possible objects of desire.

The experience of desire is often powerful and demanding. One may experience a single powerful desire as all-consuming and overriding all others. Or one may experience conflicting desires and find ourselves wrestling with their competing claims. Even if one has resolved the issues raised by a particular desire or set of desires, one may well find that resolution challenged and upset by the appearance of yet new desires, and at some point in this process one's response may well be to seek a path away from all desire—a way of apathy, disinterestedness.

Desire invokes, if it does not actually generate, tension and contrast—between the present and the future, the actual and the possible, the real and the ideal—and tends to nourish or express restless dissatisfaction with the former in each of these pairs and to assign higher value to the latter. And yet the disquieting role of desire can be seen as undermining complacency, mobilizing creative energies, and generating new achievements.

EASTERN CONCEPTS. A representative range of religious movements and texts will be selectively analyzed to illuminate the issues raised by the religious significance of desire. This examination will be a topical study rather than a chronological survey of historical records. For this reason some of the early religious movements are passed over entirely, and modern movements, texts, and developments have generally not been considered.

In India various sentiments have been recorded to define desire. At both the intellectual-scholarly and the popular levels, the element of desire has been discussed and analyzed.

Hinduism. Among the ancient sacred texts that deal with desire, the *Bhagavadgītā* (the most revered of Hindu texts, composed between the fifth and second centuries BCE) has been generally considered the most important one. In this tradition *kāma* (Skt., "desire") is one of the four basic aims or drives (*puruṣārthas*) that need to be either satisfied, redirected, or transcended in life. The four basic aims are *dharma* (in its narrower meaning of social duty), *artha* (enjoyment of material things), *kāma* (pleasurable experiences generally, but often, as in the context of the *Gītā,* the satisfaction of sensual desire), and *mokṣa* (release, liberation). They are to be realized, transformed, or transcended in such a way as to realize one's personal obligation (*svadharma*) in accordance with one's social station and stage of life. Thus the exact nature of one's response to desire depends upon one's place in the class system (*varna*) and one's advancement along the path marked by the four basic stages (*āśramas*) of life—student, householder, forest dweller, and renunciant.

The appropriate measure for the enjoyment or the control of desire and its objects and related passions is also seen in Hinduism in terms of the three *guṇas* (energy fields, or strands), which differently combine to form all things in nature (*prakṛti*). In ascending order of spiritual health, these three *guṇas* are *tamas, rajas,* and *sattva.* A life in which ignorance, insensibility, and lethargy predominate is *tamas* (dullness), one in which emotion and subjectivity predominate is *rajas* (turbulence), and one in which intelligence and objectivity predominate is *sattva* (dynamic equilibrium).

Fulfillment of one's own *dharma* (*svadharma*), again, involves some combination of three types of discipline (*yoga*), each of them requiring the sublimation and transcendence of desires, passions, and emotions together with an intensification of (1) action without attachment in *karmayoga,* the *yoga* of work and action, (2) loving devotion to a personal deity in *bhaktiyoga,* and (3) knowledge and wisdom in the most demanding path of *jñānayoga.* The aim is to rise above both *tamas* and *rajas* toward the equilibrium and detachment of *sattva,* knowing neither attraction nor repulsion, neither pleasure nor pain, having passed from both the absence and the turbulence of desire to the renunciation of all desires and aversions into a condition of equilibrium or serenity beyond desire.

In the *Gītā,* desire, anger, and greed are described as "the threefold gate of Hell that leads to the ruin of the soul" (16.21). Arjuna, the protagonist, learns that he must move among the objects of sense "with the senses under control and . . . free from desire and aversion" (2.62) if he would attain "serenity of mind" and that the same is required if he would attain intelligence, concentration, peace, or happiness. "He attains peace into whom all desires flow as waters into the sea, which, though even being filled, is ever motionless" (2.70). Yet it is only particular desires that are to be abandoned, for action without attachment involves "desiring [only] to maintain the order of the world" through one's action (2.71), and Kṛṣṇa, the god, declares: "I am the strength of the strong, which is free from desire and passion," but also "I am the desire in all beings, which is not incompatible with dharma" (7.11).

The *Gītā* is the most important sacred text in a tradition in which desires are ultimately to be overcome in detachment. In the Vedas and the Upaniṣads, desire is given a prominent place in the description of human nature, but then precisely for that reason it is ultimately desire that must be uprooted in order to achieve liberation from bondage to the wheel of existence. Nonetheless, in that same tradition, desires appropriate to the stages of life on the way to liberation are affirmed and even celebrated with imaginative exuberance. *Kāma* (desire, most especially erotic and sensual desire, delight, and pleasure) is often assigned a very positive role in the spiritual life and in the religious vision of reality. At one level of this tradition is the *Kāma Sūtra,* a manual for the enrichment of erotic and sexual pleasure appropriate to the householder stage of life.

At a deeper and broader level of this tradition there is the rich and complex Hindu mythology in which the place of desire in the life of the gods is portrayed. Wendy O'Flaherty, in *Asceticism and Eroticism in the Mythology of Śiva* (London, 1973), has shown, for example, how in the mythology of Śiva, desire and asceticism, chastity and sexuality, quiescence and energy, are variously related and yet in a fashion that affirms even where it does not clarify a profound inner connection between asceticism and eroticism and the power inherent in the transformation of one into the other. The tension is exhibited in part through the conflict between Śiva and Kāma—Śiva, the eternal *brahmacārin* (student), the god whose essence is chastity, and Kāma, the god of desire. But the conflict is also evident within Śiva himself, for he sometimes appears in the ambiguous figure of an erotic ascetic, both yogin and lover, (even a yogin because he is a lover) and is sometimes represented in images with an erect phallus, the ithyphallic yogin. While in Hindu mythology asceticism and eroticism revolve about each other in cycles of alternating ascendancy, chastity building into desire and the fulfillment of desire leading to chastity, the balance of these energies is found ideally through the control and transformation of desire.

Tantrism, a complex of teachings and practices that takes both Hindu and Buddhist forms, develops some of these last themes in a radical direction. Tantric teaching envisages the world as a field of energy generated through the sexual union of masculine and feminine aspects of sacred energy, *śakti.* The mobilization of *kāma,* desire, plays an important part in Tantric practice designed to participate in the restoration of the universe to its original unity with its sacred source. That practice involves the sublimation rather than the conquest or destruction of desire. It includes the ritually controlled performance of sexual union, but without consummation, redirecting the energy spiritually upward rather than physically outward. In emulation of the sacred activity of world-generation, erotic desire and play is thus ritually elevated into a vehicle of meditative discipline and devotion (*bhakti*)—and a means of sharing in the plenitude of sacred power by which the world is sustained.

Buddhism. The *Dhammapada,* an early Theravāda Buddhist collection of teachings about the moral life and the path to spiritual perfection, includes much on the subject of desire. Desire is a principal manifestation of the selfish craving, grasping, or blind demandingness (Pali, *taṇhā*) that, according to the four noble truths of Buddhism, is the cause of unhappiness, pain, and sorrow (*duḥkha*), and that can only be destroyed by following the eightfold path toward the freedom and joy of *nirvāṇa.* The 423 aphorisms of the *Dhammapada* offer guidance for those who would follow that eightfold path. Humanity is portrayed as besieged by dangerous and destructive desires on every side. "When the thirty-six streams of desire that run towards pleasures are strong, their powerful waves carry away that man without vision whose imaginings are lustful desires" (339). "The creeper of craving grows everywhere," and one must "cut off its roots by the power of wisdom" (340). Only if you "cut down the forest of desires" and its undergrowth, and not only a particular tree of desire, will you "be free on the path of freedom" (283). Beyond that, if the very "roots of craving are not wholly uprooted" (338) the tree and forest of desires will flourish again. Desire is specifically associated with pleasure, passion, lust, sensuousness, and craving (212–216), and all of these are portrayed as generating sorrow, fear, hatred, bondage, and disharmony. On the other hand, the surrender of all desires leads to the joy, wisdom, and freedom of *nirvāṇa.* "The loss of desires conquers all sorrows" (354). "When desires go, joy comes: The follower of Buddha finds this truth" (187). The true *brahman,* "leaving behind the desires of the world" (415), "has nothing and desires nothing" (421). "He who has no craving desires, either for this world or for another world, who free from desires is in infinite freedom—him I call a brahman" (410).

In Zen Buddhism, a Japanese religious movement of Chinese origin that emphasizes the direct experience of enlightenment, desire is treated in a somewhat different fashion. A Mahāyāna Buddhist text, popular in the Zen school, the *Laṅkāvatāra Sūtra,* extresses compactly the aim of *dhyāna* (Jpn., *zen,* "meditation, trance"): "The goal of tranquilization is to be reached not by suppressing all mind activity but by getting rid of discriminations and attachments." As discrimination dissolves and distinctions—between self and other, between this and that, even between *saṃsāra* and *nirvana*—are experienced as illusory, desire and attachment fall away as well, and delusion is displaced by enlightenment (Jpn., *satori*).

Zen Buddhism in Japan is most powerfully represented by the Rinzai and Sōtō sects, whose principal discipline is *zazen,* sitting meditation. The Rinzai practice is to concentrate meditation on a *kōan,* a riddle designed to break the grip of the discriminating rational mind, opening the way for *kenshō,* the experience of seeing into one's essential Buddha nature and realizing one's unity with all that is. In Sōtō practice the adherent moves through the unity of body and mind in sitting, to concentrate on the sitting itself, *shikantaza,* "just sitting"—not sitting in order to accomplish some objective but just sitting, letting the activity of the "monkey mind" come and go as it will, letting come what may and letting it go, accepting what comes but not desiring and not holding on, simply letting the mind be emptied of all discriminations and attachments, and in that simplicity of presence actualizing one's undefiled Buddha nature and opening the way to *satori,* enlightenment. In all of this there is no place for desire—except of course, paradoxically, for the desire to break through one's own illusory view of reality and experience the true reality of Buddha nature. That desire, too, is dissolved rather than conquered in the sustained discipline of Zen—a way of just being in accord with the Way, letting go of any desire that the "thatness" (*tathatā,* "suchness") of things be otherwise. The practice of meditation then becomes a model for activity in everyday life, with everything to be done just for what it is, just doing, just being, and not aiming at some desired end.

Daoism. Daoism is an important Chinese movement whose influence extended beyond the sectarian confines of the Daoist church to the arts, literature, and Chinese philosophy in general. Its influence can also be discerned in the formation of the Chinese Chan school (known in Japan as Zen) of Mahāyāna Buddhism. As is evident from the passages from the *Dao de jing* already cited, Daoism recommends freedom from desire as essential to the Way (the Dao) and its power or virtue (*de*). But it proposes to achieve that freedom, not by disciplined control of desire or even of the mind, nor quite by rising above desire, but rather by going beneath it, by following the wisdom of the valley, of water, in which is to be found the power of the Way. "The highest virtue is like the valley" (41). "Highest good is like water. Because water excels in benefiting the myriad creatures without contending with them and settles where none would like to be, it comes close to the Way" (8). Nature rather than empire provides the models. "The river and the sea" are powerful, and their power endures, because "they excel in taking the lower position" (66). Even the empire will be at peace if the ruler will but say with the sage, "I am free from desire, and the people of themselves become simple like the uncarved block" (57). Abandon desires, simply let them drop. Seek not to control them or the world, but find spiritual health—and, not incidentally, survival—in a life of simplicity, humility, and harmony with nature, the flow of which is only disturbed by desires. In *wuwei,* the action that is no action, lies the power of the Way. "The Way never acts yet nothing is left undone" (37). Do not try to establish harmony, as though it depended upon you, but let go and let harmony reign, as it will do of its own accord. Such is the perspective of Daoism on desire.

WESTERN CONCEPTIONS. Turning now from religions of Eastern origin to religions of Middle Eastern and Western origin, it is necessary to again be very selective, because there is no hope of even surveying the relevant literature on desire or of describing the many strategies for addressing desires. The principal sources that provide the themes upon which variations have been played are to be found in ancient Israel and in ancient Greece, in the Bible and in Hellenistic cultures. The variations are themselves substantial, although for the most part they share a generally more positive assessment of desire as an ingredient in human nature and as contributing to spiritual fulfillment than is characteristics of the religious movements already examined.

Stoicism. Among the traditions in the West, Stoicism provides a unique perspective. The *Enchiridion* of Epictetus, a Hellenistic philosopher who taught in Rome in the late first century and early second century CE, is the most influential formulation of basic Stoic teachings. Epictetus begins by distinguishing things within one's power from things beyond one's power. Desire is among the former things, and in a world where there is much that is beyond one's power, one can achieve spiritual serenity and freedom only to the extent that one disregards things beyond one's control and focuses on those things one can control. The basis of such a life is the perception that there is a universal *logos* (reason) and *nomos* (law) at work in all that happens and that if one keeps one's mind in harmony with that universal nature, responding to events according to reason and not emotion, then one's external circumstances will be of little consequence. One can live in simplicity, with moderate desires and expectations, not demanding that events happen as one wishes, but wishing them to happen as they do happen. Stoicism is a religious philosophy of lowered expectations and reflective responsibility in the station to which one is assigned by God.

Old Testament. The Old Testament contains many observations about various desires, ranging from the use of erotic love and desire and pleasure as metaphors for God's relationship to Israel to expressions of God's frustrated desire and longing for a covenant faithfulness on the part of the people of Israel and expressions of comparable desire on their part for intimacy with God, as well as injunctions to detach from or to discipline various desires in accordance with God's commandments and laws. What the Bible has to say directly about desire may fairly be summed up in three passages: the Lord's declaration through the prophet Hosea, "For I desire steadfast love and not sacrifice, the knowledge of God, rather than burnt offerings" (*Hos.* 6:60); the exclamation, "My soul thirsts for God, for the living God" (*Ps.* 42:2); and the saying of Jesus, "For where your treasure is, there will your heart be also" (*Mt.* 6:21).

Early Christianity. Augustine (354–430 CE) gives the most powerful classical formulation of the convergence of Hellenistic and biblical traditions. It is from Augustine that has come the most influential expression of Western religious thought about desire and also the most important expression of what has proved for many to be most problematic about the orientation toward desire. There is in Augustine something of the whole range of Christian attitudes toward desire.

Augustine affirms the basic biblical conviction that everything that is has its origin in God and is essentially good and that by the grace of God the world is being restored from a fallen condition to its proper destiny in God. The appropriate human role in that process is to conform the will to God in a covenant of faith and obedience to God's laws, or, to put the same matter differently, to conform the heart to God in love to God and neighbor. In either case the critical human response is a matter of will or of love more than it is of reason or of knowledge, and desire is central to Augustine's understanding of both will and love—or, more precisely, of willing and loving as different terms for the same activity. So, in the *City of God,* Augustine says: "The right will is . . . well-directed love, and the wrong will is ill-directed love. Love, then, yearning to have what is loved, is desire; and having and enjoying it, is joy; feeling what is opposed to it, is fear; and feeling what is opposed to it, when it has befallen it, is sadness" (14.7). In the *Confessions,* Augustine had said that "the mind can experience four kinds of emotion—desire, joy, fear, and sorrow" (10.14). It is these same four emotions that he here presents as forms of love, with the critical and spiritually constructive role assigned to the affirmative affections of desire and joy.

The way in which Augustine appropriates Hellenistic and especially Platonic ideas into his formulation of Christian thought is illustrated by his also presenting the four classical Greek virtues as forms of love:

> Temperance is love giving itself entirely to that which is loved; fortitude is love readily bearing all things for the sake of the loved object; justice is love serving only the loved object, and therefore ruling rightly; prudence is love distinguishing with sagacity between what hinders it and what helps it. The object of this love is not anything, but only God, the chief good, the highest wisdom, the perfect harmony. So we may express the definition thus: that temperance is love keeping itself entire and incorrupt for God; fortitude is love bearing everything readily for the sake of God; justice is love serving God only, and therefore ruling well all else, as subject to man; prudence is love making a right distinction between what helps it towards God and what might hinder it. (*Morals of the Catholic Church,* chap. 15)

The passage is worth quoting at length in this context, for the second formulation shows clearly that the first formulation is also about four forms of that true virtue that for Augustine is not just any love or all love but specifically the love of God. It is also clear that these forms of love are all manifestations of desire, that is, of that phase in the life of the virtuous lover marked more by yearning for what is loved than by the joy of actually or fully having and enjoying it.

Indeed, for Augustine all of human life is moved by desires. He takes it for granted that "we all certainly desire to live happily" and that without desire people do nothing. The problem is not to uproot or transcend desire, which is an essential mark of humanity and of belonging to God. It is right rather to direct desires toward their appropriate objects and to order all objects of desire in accordance with their true relation to God, the *summum bonum,* the source and center of all value and beauty, in whom alone restless human hearts will find the satisfaction of all their deepest desires. It is for Augustine the dynamic of desires that draws the heart toward God, though only an infusion of divine grace is sufficient to turn desire from all lesser goods toward God. Augustine makes a major distinction between desires directed upward, which he calls *caritas,* or love, and those directed downward, which he calls *cupiditas,* or lust. The one tends toward God, the other toward worldly goods. An even sharper contrast is invoked as he distinguishes between the City of God and the City of Man, the heavenly and earthly cities into which all humanity is divided, the one formed by the desire or "love of God, even to the contempt of self," the other by the "love of self, to the contempt of God" (*City of God,* 14.28). An otherwise Platonic contrast between lower and higher desires and their corresponding hierarchy of objects cumulating in God is thus transformed into a more historical contrast culminating in heaven and hell—a contrast and contest between those moved to seek God and respond to God's grace and those moved to seek self and the world.

Three kinds of objections have been raised against Augustine's views related to desire. Mention of them can serve as a shorthand way of indicating some alternatives to Augustine among Christians that cannot be surveyed here. One objection is that even if Augustine is right that all of human life is moved by desires, he is wrong in identifying the love of God with desire, and that he is led into that error by adopting the Platonic idea of love as *eros,* an aspiring love moved by the beauty of its object and the desire to possess and enjoy that object. Anders Nygren, a Lutheran theologian, has been most forceful in claiming that "*agape,* Christian love . . . has nothing to do with desire and longing" (*Agape and Eros,* London, 1932–1939), because it is a love which bestows value rather than being attracted by it. M. C. D'Arcy in *The Mind and Heart of Love* (New York, 1947) and Daniel D. Williams in *The Spirit and the Forms of Love* (New York, 1968) are among those who have challenged Nygren's diametrical opposition between *eros* and *agape.*

A second objection has been that Augustine, and with him Thomas Aquinas and much of Christian orthodoxy, has been led by Greek ideas about the impassibility of God—the idea, for example, that God's perfection includes his being unchanging and self-sufficient—into either denying or distorting the biblical view that God, too, is moved by desire, because desire is the mark of some need, some lack, which would be remedied or satisfied by what is desired. The issue is whether a God who is understood to love and act with a purpose in the world can without contradiction be construed as unchanging, impassible, unmoved by desires such as those that are often attributed to God in the Bible and in the piety of both Jews and Christians.

A third objection has been against Augustine's repudiation of sexual desire and his influence on the long history of the Roman Catholic Church's requirement of celibacy for the priesthood and its teaching that sexual pleasure and even the expression of love are at best only secondary ends of sexual intercourse, the primary end of which is said to be conception.

Medieval and Renaissance Christianity. The pivotal role of Augustine is illustrated by the fact that the other three most important theologians of Roman Catholic and Protestant Christianity, Thomas Aquinas (1225–1274), Martin Luther (1483–1546), and John Calvin (1509–1564), are all essentially Augustinian and in most respects do not depart from Augustine's views on desire. Thomas Aquinas, following Aristotle, assigns more importance to the intellect and reason in directing the will than does Augustine and gives a more Aristotelian turn to the ranking and the formation of intellectual and moral virtues in the governance of appetites, passions, and desires by reason. The classical Greek virtues are not presented by him as forms of love but are rather supplemented by the three theological virtues of faith, hope, and charity, through which God's grace makes possible and completes the natural desire of all intelligent creatures for the "vision of God."

On the subject of desire, Luther departs from Augustine principally in connection with his insistence upon the universal priesthood of all believers, the dignity of all callings and not only of the priesthood, and hence the abandonment of celibacy as essential to the priesthood. He also exhibits a certain lustiness of character and a more affirmative attitude toward the expression of sexual desire within the context of married love.

John Calvin departs from Augustine primarily by developing a distinctively political strategy in both church and state for the encouragement and the enforcement of sober, righteous, and godly lives turned from ungodliness and worldly lust. He was at war against what he called "irregular desires" or "inordinate desires of the flesh" (*The Institutes of the Christian Religion* 3.3.2). Such desires are considered sinful "not as they are natural, but because they are inordinate" and are contrasted with "those desires which God implanted so deeply" in human nature "that they cannot be eradicated from it without destroying humanity itself." Desires are to be drawn away from the world and toward God. "Whatever is abstracted from the corrupt love of this life should be added to the desire for a better" one in full communion with God (3.2.4). But Calvin rejected too great an austerity as well as a stoic divestment of all affections, arguing that God's gifts are given for human pleasure and delight as well as for human necessity—though people are to use them as though they used them not, according to the requirements of their calling.

European Enlightenment. Barukh Spinoza (1632–1677), a freethinking but "God-intoxicated" philosopher (as some have called him), developed a religious philosophy akin to Stoicism in its determination to see things from a universal and rational perspective. But he assigns to desire a much more crucial and positive role in human experience than does Epictetus. In his *Ethics* he examines the conditions under which desire can spring from reason, from the knowledge and love of God. In his view, there are but three primary emotions—joy, sorrow, and desire. Of these three, to which all other emotions are related, it is the two affirmative affections of desire and joy that are most important, and of these "desire is the very nature or essence of a person" (3.57). It is the intellectual love of God that gives the mind power over its emotions, and the *Ethics* is an elaborate analysis of how this process culminates in and flows from a condition of blessedness.

MONASTICISM. Monasticism has been an important strategy for spiritual discipline and the control of desires in most religious traditions. For Buddhism it is the *saṃgha,* the community of monks. For Christians there have been a variety of monastic orders, many of them following variations on the rule drawn up by Benedict of Nursia (480–543), with many desires renounced by the three vows of chastity, poverty, and obedience. The Benedictine rule requires manual labor in part to control desires by diverting energy and employs the image of the "ladder of humility" for the disciplinary steps by which "desires of the flesh" are cut away and displaced by the love of God and a "second nature" that delights in virtue. The *Little Flowers* of Francis of Assisi (thirteenth century), a collection of legends and traditions about the saint, reflects a different pattern of monastic discipline, more severe in its insistence upon poverty and freedom from all compromise with the world, but it also offers a more joyful asceticism, sending monks out of the cloister to delight in the created world and its beauty and to celebrate the realized desire for ecstatic union with Christ.

MYSTICISM. For the mystics, desire is generally equated with search for the transcendent. The testimony of Francis of Assisi has much in common with religious mysticism around the world, in which the experience as well as the language of desire and joy, of ecstasy and delight, play an important role. For the mystic, the spiritual desires cultivated and realized are of far greater significance than all the abandoned worldly desires. In his *Sayings of Light and Love,* John of the Cross (1542–1591) advises: "If you desire that devotion be born in your spirit and that the love of God and the desire for divine things increase, cleanse your soul of every desire and attachment and ambition in suchwise that you have no concern about anything." In *The Spiritual Canticle* he notes that "the soul lives where she loves more than in the body she animates," and that "God does not place His grace and love in the soul except according to its desire and love." And in *The Living Flame of Love* he declares to God:

> What you desire me to ask for, I ask for; and what you do not desire, I do not desire, nor can I, nor does it even enter my mind to desire it. . . . Tear then the thin veil of this life and do not let old age cut it naturally, that from now on I may love you with the plenitude and fullness my soul desires forever and ever.

Similiarly, the Ṣūfīs considered spiritual union with the transcendent beloved as the pivotal aspect of all their desires and endeavors. All else in existence was generally regarded as superfluous. The urgent quest for the almightly is thus reflected in the prayers of Rābiʿah al-ʿAdawīyah (d. 801):

> O God, my whole occupation and all my desire in this world, of all worldly things, is to remember Thee, and in the world to come, is to meet Thee. This is on my side, as I have stated; now do Thou whatsoever Thou wilt. O God, if I worship Thee for fear of Hell, burn me in Hell, and if I worship Thee in hope of Paradise, exclude me from Paradise; but if I worship Thee for thy own sake, grudge me not Thy everlasting beauty. (quoted in Arberry, p. 51)

As the prayer indicates, for Rābiʿah all aspects in life were subservient to her intense desire for spiritual elevation and union with God.

SEE ALSO Four Noble Truths; Logos; Mystical Union; Tantrism.

BIBLIOGRAPHY

Arberry, A. J. *Muslim Saints and Mystics.* London, 1964.

Nygren, Anders. *Agape and Eros.* 2 vols. London, 1932–1939.

O'Flaherty, Wendy Doniger. *Ascetism and Eroticism in the Mythology of Śiva.* London, 1973.

Turner, Victor. *The Forest of Symbols.* Ithaca, N.Y., 1967.

ROLAND A. DELATTRE (1987)

DESTINY SEE FATE

DETERMINISM SEE FREE WILL AND DETERMINISM

DEUS OTIOSUS.

The Latin term *deus otiosus* (pl., *dei otiosi),* meaning literally "god at leisure" or "god without work," denotes a god who has withdrawn or retired from active life. The paucity of detailed descriptions of these deities, when coupled with their widespread appearance in cultures around the globe, presents a puzzle for the study of religions. Athough the outline of these divine personalities is usually sketchy, they maintain a firm hold on the religious imagination. The study of gods who have retired from their arena of activity has provoked deep reflection on the meaning and function of symbols, especially of divine forms, in religious life.

CELESTIAL ASSOCIATIONS. Many African creation myths involving *dei otiosi* recount how the divine sky lay flat on the earth at the beginning of time. Nuba and Dogon myths, for example, describe how the chafing of the sky against the earth stunted human growth and disrupted normal routines of work. (R. C. Stevenson, "The Doctrine of God in the Nuba Mountains," in *African Ideas of God,* ed. E. W. Smith, London, 1950, p. 216; Marcel Griaule, *Masques Dogons,*

Paris, 1938, p. 48). "In particular, women could not pound their grain without knocking against the sky, and so close relations finally ended when the sky's anger at the annoying blows of the women's pestles caused it to withdraw from the earth" (Dominique Zahan, *The Religion, Spirituality, and Thought of Traditional Africa*, Chicago, 1979, p. 16). In other African societies, such as the Nyarwanda and Rundi of central Africa, the creator god lived with the first people at the beginning of time (or the first people lived in the sky with the god). For one reason or another, the god moved away from the company of his creatures—upstream, downstream, to a mountaintop, or to the sky (R. Bourgeois, *Banyarwanda et Barundi*, Brussels, 1957, vol. 3, pp. 19–25).

Most forms of the *deus otiosus* cluster around the symbolism of the sky. The manifestation of the sacred in the sky and the belief in supreme beings of the sky is most often overwhelmed and replaced by other sacred forms. We do not mean to say that devotion to the beings of the sky was the first and only religious practice of archaic humankind. In the first place, we do not have the data we need to reconstitute the first forms of religious practice and belief in human history. More important, the study of histories that we know more fully indicate the unlikelihood that a belief in a supreme being of the sky would exclude all other religious forms. The point to begin with is that the experience of the sky as a religious reality, in fact as the divine sphere, places emphasis on the religious value of withdrawal and transcendence. The sky itself, as a symbol of sacred being, embraces or constitutes these elemental structures of a *deus otiosus*, withdrawal and transcendence. For this reason, countless other hierophanies can coexist with this sacred manifestation of the remote sky.

For example, Puluga is an omniscient sky-dwelling divinity revered in the Andaman Islands. After a stormy relationship with the first people, Puluga reminded them of his commands and withdrew. Men have never seen him since that time of estrangement at the beginning (Paul Schebesta, *Les Pygmées*, Paris, 1940, pp. 161–163). In a similar way, Témaukel, the eternal and omniscient creator of the Selk'nam of Tierra del Fuego, is called *so'onh-haskan* ("dweller in the sky") and *so'onh kas pémer* ("he who is in the sky"). Témaukel created mythical ancestors who took over the process of creating the world. Once creation was accomplished, he withdrew beyond the stars. For his part he remains indifferent to human affairs. Correspondingly, human beings possess no images of Témaukel or regular cult dedicated to him, and they direct their prayers to him only in cases of dire illness or bad weather (Martin Gusinde, "Das höchste Wesen bei den Selk'nam auf Feuerland," in *Wilhelm Schmidt Festschrift*, Vienna, 1928, pp. 269–274). The Muring people of the east coast of Australia recount in their myths the story of Daramulun, their "father" (*papang*) and "lord" (*biamban*). Daramulun, the true name of this divine being of the sky, is known only to initiates. For a brief time he lived on earth and instituted the rites of initiation. Since his return to the heavens his presence is made known mostly in the sounds of thunder, the eerie groans from the nocturnal jungle, and through the sound of sacred bull-roarer used in initiation rites (Alfred W. Howitt, *The Native Tribes of South-East Australia*, New York, 1904, pp. 362ff., 466ff.). Similarly, Bunjil, the heavenly supreme being of the Kulin tribes of Australia, created earth, trees, animals, and human beings and then left the world to live in the heaven beyond the "dark heaven" visited by holy men (ibid., p. 490).

ABSENCE OF MYTH AND CULT. The most striking feature of the *deus otiosus* is the absence of an active cult dedicated to the god. Even where there is sporadic and spontaneous devotion, it is remarkable how often there is no regular calendar of seasonal rituals celebrated in honor of the god. Mythic accounts of the *deus otiosus* are scanty. Even those myths that exist are short compared to the dramatic epics of heroes, storm gods, or the divine forms associated with the agricultural cycle. A large number of celestial supreme beings receive no regular worship. Among them we may mention Muladjadi of the Batak of central Sumatra, Petara remembered by the Sea Dyaks of Kalimantan (Borneo), Ndengei of Fijian mythology, and Yelefaz from the island of Yap.

The absence of scheduled cult and the brevity of mythic reference to the *deus otiosus* led scholars to a misconception. At the end of the nineteenth century and beginning of the twentieth (and even today, in some circles), scholars of religion and culture overlooked the importance of this religious form. The *deus otiosus* was seen as an anomalous piece of speculation, as a recent addition to the divine pantheon in response to contact with Christian missionaries, or as an archaic idea that had lost the clarity of its expression and meaning. It did not fit into the schemata that evaluated mythic thinking as infantile, unsubtle, or undeveloped. Rather than regard the absence of the *deus otiosus* from myth and cult as an inherent feature of its structure, scholars frequently ignored the issue or slighted its value in favor of theories that portrayed tribal peoples as theologically naive or intellectually underdeveloped.

WITHDRAWAL OF GOD. Myths that mention the *deus otiosus* usually face head-on the question of the god's absence from the preoccupations of culture. The narratives themselves describe the withdrawal or substitution of the supreme being. For example, Ọlọrun, the Yoruba divinity whose name means "lord or owner of the sky," turned over the project of creating the world to Ọbatala, one of his sons. When Ọbatala became drunk and mismanaged the creation of humans from clay, Oduduwa, his younger brother, usurped the task of creation. Ọlọrun then permanently absented himself from human history. He does not intervene directly in human affairs, for he delegated the care of human creation to his sons and to the *orisa*, a collection of deities each with its own precinct, priesthood, temple, and devotees. Although absent from the unfolding course of human affairs, Ọlọrun remains an essential presence, for he inspires the breath of life into all individuals and allots them their destiny. Furthermore, the Yoruba call upon Ọlọrun in times of desperate calamity (E. Bọlaji Idowu, *Olódùmarè: God in Yoruba Belief,* London, 1962; Peter Morton-Williams, "An Outline of the Cosmology and Cult Organization of the Oyo," *Africa* 34, 1964; Benjamin C. Ray, *African Religions: Symbol, Ritual, and Community,* Englewood Cliffs, N. J., 1976, pp. 49–76, esp. pp. 52ff.).

Myths describe the origins of the status of the *deus otiosus* in cultural life as well as in the religious imagination. On the one hand, the god withdraws on his own initiative after finishing his work of creation or of overseeing its accomplishment. On the other hand, another frequent scenario is the usurpation of the supreme being's sovereignty by a younger and more active god. In the Hittite translations of Hurrian texts made around 1300 BCE, there is an initial episode that describes the struggle for the "kingship of heaven." At first, the god Alalu was king, then the divinity named Anu overpowered him. At the beginning of Anu's reign, Kumarbi, the main protagonist of Hittite myth and the father of the gods, was Anu's servant. After nine years, Kumarbi chased Anu into the sky, tossed him to the ground, and bit off his loins (Hans G. Güterbock, "The Hittite Version of the Hurrian Kumarbi Myths: Oriental Forerunners of Hesiod," *American Journal of Archaeology* 52, 1948, pp. 123–124; and C. Scott Littleton, "The 'Kingship in Heaven' Theme," in *Myth and Law among the Indo-Europeans,* edited by Jaan Puhvel, Berkeley, 1970, pp. 93–100). A parallel in Greek mythology describes the castration of the sky god Ouranos and the forced separation of Heaven (Ouranos) from Earth (Gaia). In Mesopotamian mythology as well, the young gods led by Marduk guarantee that the great gods such as An, Enlil, and Ea lose their supremacy in the cult.

The existence in mythology of this most streamlined and ethereal of divine forms, the *deus otiosus,* teaches a lesson about the dynamics of the religious imagination. The *dei otiosi,* especially those supreme beings of the sky who retire after the creative episode, withdraw from the world in several senses. They withdraw on high and leave their creation behind. They also withdraw to the outer margins of the religious imagination and define the outermost reach of creativity, for they assume the most wispy of images. No doubt, contact with outsiders, especially Christians or Muslims, has often played a role in shaping the contemporary forms of *dei otiosi.* However, such contact does not preclude the existence of an indigenous structure of the *deus otiosus.* In fact, the existence of a myth of an otiose god enabled many cultures to recognize aspects of the foreign supreme being and reconcile them with their own. Far from remaining insignificant, the features of the *deus otiosus* exhibit definite signs, especially of vagueness and sublimity, that demarcate the outer reach of imaginable being.

SYMBOLIC CHARACTERISTICS. The *deus otiosus* is a limit-image, for before and beyond the *deus otiosus* nothing exists. The Winnebago Indians of Wisconsin admitted, "What there was before our Father Earthmaker came to consciousness, we do not know."

Sublimity. The descriptions of supreme beings who withdraw on high introduce students of religion to the most sublime end of the spectrum of divine forms, for the *deus otiosus* is often the most sublimated of sublime forms. By narrating descriptions of the most remote, transcendent, invisible, or intangible reality, cultures offer themselves and scholars expressions of an experience of being that, by definition, most transcends the senses. The myths of the *deus otiosus* are statements about the nature of creativity itself and about the subtle powers and rarefied capacities of the religious imagination. The Witóto of Colombia offer the following example: in the beginning nothing existed except "mere appearance," which was "something mysterious." Moma, the supreme being, touched this phantasm. Moma calls himself Nainuema, "he who is or possesses what is not present." He is an illusive appearance linked to sacred sounds associated with ritual words and chants. By means of dream, Nainuema held the phantasm against his breast and fell into deep thought, his breath helping him hold onto the illusion with the thread of his dream. Moma plumbed the dream-contained, breath-held phantasm to its bottom and found that it was empty. He fastened the illusion to his dream-thread with a gluey substance and then stamped on the bottom of the illusion until he came to rest on the earth. He made the forests rise by spitting and covered the earth with heaven (Konrad T. Preuss, *Religion und Mythologie der Uitoto,* vol. 1, Göttingen, 1921, pp. 27, 166–168). Such sublime features of the *deus otiosus* have great value for the student of religious forms, for they describe the outer boundaries of imaginable being.

Passivity. The passive character of the *dei otiosi* leaves the gods' personalities vague and ill-defined. The deities often avoid dramatic action and remain inert or aloof. In fact, the creativity of the *dei otiosi* is often described in negative terms. Their omnipresence comes across as a lack of presence in any single or definable place over another. Their omnipotence implies an uninvolvement with any single or specific cosmic operation, such as the growth of crops or the transitions of the human life cycle. Their omniscience implies a certain indifference to, or lack of interest in, any one fact over another. Their immortality implies a certain stasis, immobility, and inability to change. These negative valences are a function of the gods' association with creation at the very beginning. Once creation is accomplished and being has appeared for the first time, the function of a creator is completely exhausted and the god becomes otiose. The divinities and their unique creative powers retire from the active world they have initiated. They remain the ground of all created being and of all creative possibilities and, for that very reason, retire into infinity, beyond the bounded spaces of creation. Once the universe comes into existence, the supreme being's active mode is no longer in need of full manifestation, nor is it desired.

Primordiality. The withdrawal of the *deus otiosus* from the creative scene marks the end of the primordium. Therefore, it may be said that the presence of the *deus otiosus* defines primordiality, a potent condition full of possibilities. *Dei otiosi* have always existed; they bespeak the meaning of eternity and antiquity. The sky, or whatever paradisal place the gods dwelled in, has always been inhabited by supernatural beings. For example, for the Aranda of Australia, the "great father" (*knaritja*) is an eternal youth (*altjira nditja*) who lives in an eternally green countryside covered with flowers and fruits. The Milky Way transects this immortal dwelling place. The great father and his heavenly companions, all equally young, take no interest in the affairs of earth; the great father leaves the management of such affairs to the ancestors. The Aranda great father represents the primordium, the state of being that has no immediate significance, although it has unprecedented ontological bearing. Beatific existence, immortality, anteriority, or static antiquity are unmatched conditions of being. That primordial state was interrupted, and direct contact with it became difficult or impossible. Only a few privileged people, such as mythic heroes or specialists in ecstasy, can revisit a situation that has become irretrievably lost. Primordiality reveals something about the very nature of time and space. It is a quality that cannot be recaptured in terms of the present conditions of the cosmos. The withdrawal of the *deus otiosus* is part of the definition of a primordial world that stands over and against history. Primordiality is the milieu in which reality and eternity can truly manifest themselves. Knowledge of the existence of a *deus otiosus* affirms that even unique modes of being can be apprehended as a species of time.

Transcendence. The fate of the *deus otiosus* in mythic history guarantees that the first state of being becomes something less immediate and pressing. The god withdraws and becomes distant, and, for its part, human history becomes enveloped by the wrappings of symbolic life. For example, in the very beginning of the Makiritare creation cycle, all that existed was sky and eternal light. Shi, the invisible sun, had already created Wanadi, the heavenly creator, by blowing on quartz crystal. During that first period, there was no separation between the sky and the earth; the sky had no door in it as it does now, and Wanadi was bright and shining everywhere. He wished to make houses and place good people in them, and for this reason sent aspects of himself to earth. Attawanadi ("house-Wanadi"), the third aspect of Wanadi, specialized in constructing enclosures. He created the enclosed stratum called earth. Attawanadi made a new, visible sky for the earth so that the real sky could no longer be seen. The *atta*, the house or village of the Makiritare, is an exact replica of the first universe created by Attawanadi. Attawanadi's creation of the house-world achieved symbolic closure. He withdrew from his creation.

Myths of creation involving a *deus otiosus* frequently recount the lifting up of the sky and the installation of that heavenly body, the primordial image of transcendence. The sky becomes the paradigm of distance and difference. As the object of first real separation, the *deus otiosus* and its celestial manifestations betoken the possibility of distance between one kind of being and another; their continued transcendence and absence guarantee the symbolic life they signify. Many myths portray the danger that the sky will fall; that is, they portray the fear of the collapse of symbolic possibilities. If the symbolism of withdrawal of the *deus otiosus*, the reality transcendent above all others, will not stand up to scrutiny and cannot stay removed, then no symbolic distance of any kind can be guaranteed, and representational life fails. In fact, it is only at the end of time that many *dei otiosi* make their return. Attawanadi, for example, will return to the Makiritare when the earth ceases to exist (Marc de Civrieux, *Watunna: An Orinoco Creation Cycle*, ed. and trans. David M. Guss [San Francisco, 1980, pp. 28ff.]. The relationship between gods and humans comes into being when the separation of creator from created is acknowledged. "The period of man's 'religiousness' is not at all the 'paradisiac' era when God lived in the 'village' of men but the period following when God had lost his earthly and human qualities in order to live separately from mankind" (Zahan, *The Religion, Spirituality, and Thought of Traditional Africa*, p. 16). The withdrawal of the *deus otiosus* becomes the foundation-stone of religious life: "the African feels deeply that the more inaccessible God seems to be, the greater is his need of him" (Zahan, p. 16).

Symbolic life, made possible by the withdrawal of primordial being, offers humankind the freedom of the symbolic condition, a dynamic existence that could never have flourished if the creator had continued to crush or overwhelm his creation with his ponderous presence and immediacy. Mediation, intermediaries, and symbolic distance become indispensable and possible when the god retires from the scene.

Implications for the Study of Religious Symbols. The knowledge of the mythic history of the *dei otiosi*, the story of their creative acts and the transformations they undergo while disappearing into the starry vault or into the forest or downstream, are an indispensable part of culture. Equipped with this knowledge, members of a culture live in awareness of the sacred nature of their environment and of their sociocultural order because they know the mythic history of each one of its forms. The withdrawal of the primordial being, the *deus otiosus*, leaves indelible marks on the physical universe and its organic contents.

For example, the Campas of Peru describe the migration of the sun (Pava) into the sky. He enlisted the aid of the hummingbird Neoronke, who carried one end of the sky-rope to the highest level of the universe. As Pava ascended, transformations occurred that gave nature its present condition. Many primordial beings, which at that time existed in protohuman form, became animals such as the tapir or the mouse. Certain trees and flowers used to demarcate the calendrical year were daughters of Pava. The trees are the clothes that these young women shed when they migrated to heaven with him. When the sky-rope dropped to the earth after the ascent, a number of beings fell from heaven to earth, including the wasp, the porcupine, and the sloth (Gerald Weiss, *Campa Cosmology: The World of a Forest Tribe in South America*, New York, 1975, pp. 219–588; esp. pp. 389–390).

There is no guarantee that the divine form of the *deus otiosus* will remain balanced on the periphery of the religious imagination. In some cases it seems that the god lapses into total oblivion. In other instances, prophets re-form and revitalize the concept of the supreme being and reinstate his cult. Where mythic knowledge of the retired god disappears entirely, the deity becomes completely otiose and no longer has religious value. Such was probably the fate of Dyaus, the Indo-European sky god, who eventually was no longer worshiped. No hymns or myths present this oldest Vedic religious form. The name simply designates the "sky" or "day." However, there lingers the memory that the "Sky knows all" (*Atharvaveda* 1.32.4) and that there is the "sky father" (*Atharvaveda* 6.4.3), who is one element of the primordial pair, Dyāvāpṛthivī, "sky and earth" (*Ṛgveda* 1.160). This draws Dyaus into the circle of similarly named Indo-European sky gods for whom we possess mythologies: Greek Zeus Pater, Roman Jupiter, Illyrian Daipatures, Scythian Zeus-Papaios, and Thraco-Phrygian Zeus-Pappos.

The god Mwari of the Shona people of Zimbabwe appears to be an instance of the recovery of the *deus otiosus.* Since the fifteenth century, circumstances have contributed to the revitalization of this remote sky god's cult. The Rozvi royal dynasty patronized the cult in the center of the city of Zimbabwe and the priests of Mwari have become important political figures (Daneel, 1970, pp. 30–35).

The form of the *deus otiosus*, even if it is recalled only in wispy outline, is an essential stimulus to the life of the religious imagination. To one degree or another such a form is implied in every complete corpus of myths. Since every reality appearing in the mythic beginnings of the world is a total and absolute statement of its kind of being, the change and dynamism that undergird human history provoke a total eclipse or disintegration of primordial form. The death, transformation, or withdrawal of supernatural beings into the heights or into the extremes of the cosmos exemplifies the fate of primordial existence as a whole.

SEE ALSO Sky; Supreme Beings.

BIBLIOGRAPHY

Daneel, M. L. *The God of the Matopo Hills: An Essay on the Mwari Cult in Rhodesia.* The Hague, 1970.

Danquah, J. B. *The Akan Doctrine of God.* 2d ed. London, 1969.

Eliade, Mircea. "The Sky and Sky Gods." In his *Patterns in Comparative Religion*, pp. 38–123. New York, 1958.

Eliade, Mircea. "South American High Gods." *History of Religions* 8 (1968): 338–354 and 10 (1970–1971): 234–266.

Ikenga-Metuh, Emefie. "The Paradox of Transcendence and Immanence of God in African Religions: A Socio-historical Explanation." *Religion* 15 (1985): 373–385.

Lienhardt, Godfrey. *Divinity and Experience.* Oxford, 1961.

Long, Charles H. "The West African High God: History and Religious Experience." *History of Religions* 3 (1964): 328–342.

Pettazzoni, Raffaele. "The Formation of Monotheism." In his *Essays on the History of Religions*, translated by H. J. Rose. Leiden, 1954.

Pettazzoni, Raffaele. "The Supreme Being: Phenomenological Structure and Historical Development." In *The History of Religions: Essays in Methodology*, edited by Joseph M. Kitagawa and Mircea Eliade, pp. 59–66. Chicago, 1959.

Verger, Pierre. "The Yoruba High God." *Odu* 2 (January 1966): 19–40.

New Sources

Casadio, Giovanni. "El and Cosmic Order: is the Ugaritic Supreme God a *deus otiosus?*" In *Studia Fennica* 32 (1987): 45–58. For a bibliography on the *deus otiosus* in the religious-historical literature see p. 57.

Casadio, Giovanni. "A ciascuno il suo: *otium* e *negotium* del dio supremo dalla Siria alla Mesopotamia." *Studi e materiali di storia delle religioni* 58 (1992): 59–79. After a discussion of the bibliography on the *deus otiosus* as a cross-cultural type, the controversial case of the Mesopotamian celestial god is examined.

Flamand Jean-Marie. "Deus otiosus: recherches lexicales pour servir à l'histoire de la critique religieuse d'Épicure. " In *Sophies Maietores. Chercheurs de sagesse: hommage à Jean Pépin*, edited by Marie-Odile Goulet-Cazé, Goulven Madec, and Denis O'Brien, pp. 147–166. Paris, 1992.

MIRCEA ELIADE AND LAWRENCE E. SULLIVAN (1987)
Revised Bibliography

DEVĀNAṂPIYATISSA (247–207 BCE), king of Sri Lanka. According to the *Mahāvaṃsa*, Devānaṃpiyatissa was an ally of Aśoka and through Aśoka's influence introduced Buddhism to Sri Lanka. At the outset of his reign, Devānaṃpiyatissa sent envoys to India with gifts for Aśoka. In return, Aśoka sent gifts and implicit support for Devānaṃpiyatissa's kingship. The Sinhala chronicles also relate that the Buddhist elder, Mahinda, who was either the son or the brother of Aśoka, visited Devānaṃpiyatissa to establish the Buddhist tradition in Sri Lanka.

Mahinda is said to have arrived in the island on the full-moon day of Poson (May–June), a day still celebrated in Sri Lanka as the date of the founding of Buddhism there. Devānaṃpiyatissa greeted Mahinda on Missaka Hill, now called Mihintale, and proceeded from there to the site of Anurādhapura. Near the royal pavilion in Mahāmegha Park at Anurādhapura, Mahinda and Devānaṃpiyatissa laid out and subsequently built the monasteries and shrines that came to be the international center for the Theravāda Buddhist tradition. The heart of their complex was the Mahāvihāra, the Great Monastery, which was established 236 years after the Buddha. The king also built the first stupa or *cetiya* in Sri Lanka, the Thūpārāma, to enshrine the collarbone relic of the Buddha.

At the request of the women in Sri Lanka, Devānaṃpiyatissa arranged for Mahinda's sister Saṃghamittā to come from India to ordain women into the Buddhist order of nuns. Saṃghamittā brought with her a branch from the bodhi tree under which the Buddha attained enlightenment. The king planted this branch at Anurādhapura, where it remains today as a sacred shrine for Buddhists.

See Also Aśoka.

Bibliography

The primary source for this subject is *The Mahāvaṃsa, or, The Great Chronicle of Ceylon,* translated and edited by Wilhelm Geiger (1912; reprint, Colombo, 1950). A reliable secondary source is C. W. Nicholas and Senarat Paranavitana's *A Concise History of Ceylon* (Colombo, 1961).

New Sources

Dissanayake, Wimal. "The Poetics and the Politics of the Mahavamsa [The Great Chronicle of Sri Lanka]." In *Handcuffed to History: Narratives, Pathologies, and Violence in South Asia,* edited by S. P. Udayakumar, pp. 147–164. London, 2001.

George D. Bond (1987)
Revised Bibliography

DEVĪ See GODDESS WORSHIP, *ARTICLE ON* THE HINDU GODDESS

DEVILS.

DEVILS. The definition and derivation of the term *devil* need to be carefully delineated. This need for care in defining *devil* arises from the fact that the very class of creatures being designated as malign may have been originally benign or may be capable of acting in either a benign or malign way. One species of devils in classical Hinduism consists of the *asuras*, also called *pūrvadevas*, or "those who were formerly gods or benign beings." In Zoroastrianism, the same *asuras*, by contrast, are called *ahuras*, or "lords." In Christianity, Satan, the Prince of Darkness, is regarded as a fallen angel. According to Origen (whose view is considered heresy by orthodox Christians), he will, in time, be reinstated in his "pristine splendor and original rank." There are, however, also classes of intermediate beings whose association with evil is equivocal. In Islam, genies or, more properly, *jinn* provide a useful illustration: "They were vaguely feared, but were not always malevolent" (Watt, 1970, p. 153).

Biblical Terminology. The problem is also, in part, etymological. The English word *devil* derives from the Greek *diabolos*, which has the original sense of "accuser" or "traducer" (from *diaballein*, "to slander, traduce," lit., "to throw across"). The Hebrew Bible (Old Testament) uses the word *satan* in the sense of "adversary," and it was translated in the third century BCE by Egyptian Jews as *diabolos*. When the Greek Septuagint (Old Testament) was translated into Latin, *diabolos* was rendered as *diabolus* (in the early translations) or as *saṭan*, in the standard Vulgate text (Robbins, 1959, p. 130). In the New Testament, on the other hand, the name *Satanas* is used to mean not just any adversary, as is often the case in the Old Testament, but *the* adversary of God. Throughout the New Testament, *Satanas* refers to the Devil, and *Revelation* 12:9 describes "the great dragon . . . that ancient serpent, who is called the Devil and Satan." As Robbins points out (p. 130), English translations generally render both the *saṭan* of the Hebrew scriptures and *Satanas* of the New Testament as "Satan."

Thus two different conceptions were fused, and this idea of an evil demigod became the common heritage of Judaic and Christian traditions. The word *devil* as used in the New Testament fuses two elements—the Greek and the Judaic. The Greek element is provided by the inclusion of the sense of *daimōn* ("demon"), which referred to a guardian spirit or a source of inspiration. The description of the Devil as the "prince of the demons" (*Mt.* 9:35) is particularly significant in this respect, for, according to Russell (1977, p. 229), the association of the Devil with the demons is paralleled by his association with the fallen angels (see *Rv.* 12:4, 12:7ff.; *Eph.* 2:1–2). However, the Greek Septuagint "used *demon* for the Hebrew words meaning 'vengeful idols' (*schedim*) and 'hairy satyrs' (*seîrim*). The Vulgate Latinized accordingly and the English authorized version (1613) translated both by 'Devil,' while the revised version (1881) substituted 'demon' in Deuteronomy and the Psalms [and] retained 'Devil' in the New Testament." The overall result of these philological developments was that "originally distinct species of spirits were unified by interchangeable translations of Devil, demon, fiend. All these terms devolved on Satan" (Robbins, 1959, p. 131). This explanation should clarify the use of the terms *demon* and *devil* as they are employed here. The word *demon* denotes spirits in general while the word *devil* denotes evil spirits, malign beings viewed as embodiments of evil.

Typology. Several typologies of devils are possible, and consideration may be limited to those that proceed by habitation and function. Psellus (eleventh century CE) distinguishes devils by habitat as fiery, aerial, terrestrial, aqueous, subterranean, and heliophobic. A simpler scheme may be applied in the case of Africa and Oceania, where devils could be associated with animals, waters, forest, and mountains. The former scheme has the merit of being comparable with those of otherworld religions, wherein, however, the site of habitation may not be described in terms of elements but may be located in space. Islam provides a link between the two types. The *jinn* are created out of a single element, fire, but are "associated with deserts, ruins and other eerie places, and might assume such forms as those of animals, serpents, and other creeping things" (Watt, 1970, p. 153). But the *jinn* are not necessarily evil like the devils, or *shayṭāns*, who prompt human beings to evil.

According to one tradition the species (for which we may use "genies" as a convenient westernized rubric) is made up of five orders, namely, *jānn, jinn, shayṭāns, ʿifrīts*, and *mārids*. The last are said to be the most powerful and the first the least; *shayṭān* is generally used to signify any evil genius; an *ʿifrīt* is a powerfully evil genius, while a *mārid*, as indicated, is an evil genius of the most powerful class. At this point it should be noted that sources admit to some confusion between *jānn* and *jinn;* while it is held that *jānn* are transformed *jinn*, just as certain apes and swine were transformed men, it is also admitted that the two are often used indiscriminately as names for the whole species, whether good or bad (*jinn* is the more common term, however). As for the characteristics of *jinn*, they are of different shapes, appearing as serpents, scorpions, lions, wolves, jackals, and so on; they are of land, sea, and air; and either have wings that allow them to fly, move like snakes or dogs, or move about like men. Other embodiments of evil in Islam may also be mentioned: *quṭrub*, *gharrār*, *siʿlah*, *shiqq*, and *nasnās*. Of these, the *gharrār* is comparable to the ogre inasmuch as the latter is also a figure of folklore who feeds on human beings.

In the Indic worldview the devils have been provided with a habitation and a name. Jainism provides an example of the many typologies of devils in Indic religions. The seven netherworlds contain the hells, one of which, the Vyantaras, includes demons, goblins, ghosts, and spirits, which are divided into eight ranks—*kinnaras*, *kimpuruṣas*, *mahoragas*, *gandharvas*, *yakṣas*, *rākṣasas*, *bhūtas*, and *piśācas*, all of which are found in Hindu mythology in nearly the same forms (Jacobi, in Hastings, 1911, p. 608).

Anthropological studies of Buddhism, particularly as practiced in Burma (Spiro, 1978) and Thailand (Tambiah, 1970), have led to the identification of devilish beings in Buddhism. Thus it has been noted in the case of Burmese Buddhism that *nats*, witches, ghosts, and demons, though substantively different, share the functional attribute of causing pain (Spiro, p. 40). It is noteworthy that although Hinduism does not acknowledge a specific devil, which Buddhism does in the form of Mara, it acknowledges the existence of devilish beings, who are also functionally differentiated. Hindu lore distinguishes between *asuras*, a class of supernatural beings continually opposed to the gods; *rākṣasas*, demonic beings who roam about at night, disturb the penances of ascetics, and harass and kill people; *piśācas*, who frequent cremation grounds; *vetālas*, or vampires; and *pretas* and *bhūtas*, phantoms of the dead who bother human beings on occasion. Sometimes the word *bhūta* is inclusive of *preta* and *piśāca* (Crooke, in Hastings, 1911, p. 608). The Hindu god Śiva, incidentally, presides over his own *gaṇas*, or malevolent troopers, who include some of the abovementioned creatures and can act in extremely unpleasant ways when incensed.

By contrast, in Islam, the various functions of the one and same class of demons—the *shayṭāns*—may be distinguished: they teach humans magic, lead them to unbelief, try to eavesdrop on heaven, and accompany obstinate unbelievers. An intermediate form of functional differentiation, between the Hindu one, organized by class as well as function, and the Islamic one, where different functions are performed by members of the same class, is provided by Zoroastrianism, where the devil, Angra Mainyu, rallies around his standard Aka Manah ("evil thought"), Indra, Saurva, Nanhaithya, (parallel with three Indian deities who are opposed), Taurvi ("hunger") Zairich ("thirst") and Aēshma ("fury"), so that one finds closely allied devil figures performing several diabolical functions, only some of which have been listed. One of the clearest formulations of devilish functions in Christianity is found in the *Admirable History* (1612) of Sebastien Michaëlis, which is set forth in three sets of hierarchies, each specifying the name of the devil, his function, and his adversary (Robbins, 1959, p. 129).

Another way in which devils could be typologized is by gender differentiation, for female devils are not unknown. In popular Hinduism the Churalin, a demoness regarded as the composite spirit of women who have died in childbirth (Babb, 1975, p. 248), is referred to as identifiable by an inverse foot formation. Islam speaks of beings called *ghūl* in general, though properly speaking it is said to apply only to the female, whose male counterpart is the *gharrār*. She is supposed to lead a solitary existence in the deserts, to waylay travelers and practice cannibalism. The case of the lamia, a vampire or (night-)mare, may also be discussed here. The word serves a dual sense, which may cut across gender differentiation: it could mean a succubus demon or a witch. It was suggested in the fifteenth century in Germany and Czechoslovakia that lamiae were demons in the shape of old women who stole children and roasted them.

POSSESSION. As universal as belief in evil spirits is belief in the phenomenon of possession of the body by these evil spirits. The history of Christianity records epidemics of possession, and a distinction is drawn between possession and obsession, the former being more grave inasmuch as it involves actual residence by the evil spirit in the body of the possessed.

Exorcism has been associated with Christian evangelization since its inception. This is also true of other religions. Tambiah (1970) clearly distinguishes between possession by benevolent and malevolent spirits (*phī*) in the context of Thailand, and notes how the distinction figures in Buddhist mortuary rites. Although the Thai beliefs about such evil spirits are so free-floating as to resist typologizing, certain kinds of devilish spirits most often cited as attacking people may be mentioned. Spirits of the rice field (*phī rai phī naa*) can attack villagers; so can the spirit that lives on a mountain (*phī pu loob*) but the attack of the *phī paub*, a malevolent disembodied spirit, is to be feared most as it may be hosted by some living being. Its origin is attributed to the transformation of spells into an evil force inside a magical expert, either a man or a woman. The force then acquires an existence of its own and can possess others.

DEBATE ON ORIGINS. Speculation regarding the origin of belief in devils has proceeded along several routes. According to one view, belief in devilish beings may have its roots in the experience of prehistoric man. At this time wild animals of strange shapes and sizes roamed the earth, and it would have been easy for early human beings to assume that nonhuman evil spirits abounded and assumed animal forms. Alongside this explanation may be placed the anthropological view, according to which beliefs in all classes of spiritual beings—benign or malign—are derived from belief in the disembodied spirits of the dead. Considerable controversy surrounds this view, but it may be safe to affirm that among many peoples the hostile spirits of the dead would be identified as devils. Psychological explanations for the origin of devils include the ideas of hallucinations and projection with various degrees of sophistication. As early as 1218, Gervase of Tilbury suggested that belief in lamia or nightmare was simply nocturnal hallucination, and some modern scholars would argue that man manufactures his devils out of his fears. It is often considered self-evident that the "conception of such beings doubtless stems from man's instinctive fear of the unknown, the strange and horrific. It is significant that belief in evil spirits or Devils can exist without the idea of the Devil, i.e. the personification of the principle of evil in a single being" (Brandon, 1970, p. 229).

In addition to the historical (i.e., prehistorical); anthropological (i.e., animistic); and psychological (i.e., psychoanalytical) explanations, one must consider also the theological aspect, for what is really involved is an explanation of the problem of evil. How is its existence to be reconciled with belief in a benevolent God? Evil creatures that defy God, despite his potential supremacy, may offer the scaffolding for some kind of a theological explanation. Given the existence of evil, one can offer a certain range of justifications: (1) what is perceived as evil is necessary for greater good; (2) evil exists as a necessary part of a good creation; (3) the universe is not perfect but is being perfected, hence the existence of evil; and (4) evil is necessary to retain free will. The existence of devils, as of the Devil, can be reconciled in various ways, as representing the principle of evil either singly or collectively and emerging out of an attempt to come to existential grips with the fact that evil exists. Since most events are caused by an agent, one might assume that evil is also caused by an agent, which may itself be either intrinsically or instrumentally evil.

SEE ALSO Ahuras; ʿĀshūrāʾ; Demons, article on Psychological Perspectives; Evil; Satan; Spirit Possession; Theodicy.

BIBLIOGRAPHY

Still useful are the articles grouped under "Demons and Spirits" in the *Encyclopaedia of Religion and Ethics*, edited by James Hastings, vol. 4 (Edinburgh, 1911); see particularly the pieces by Edward Anwyl (Celtic), William Crooke (Indian), Hermann Jacobi (Jain), Arthur Lloyd (Japanese), P. J. Maclagan (Chinese), V. J. Mansikka (Slavic), Eugen Mogk (Teutonic), L. A. Waddell (Tibetan), and A. V. Williams Jackson (Persian). *A Dictionary of Comparative Religion*, edited by S. G. F. Brandon (London, 1970), also contains a useful entry under "Demons," and *The Encyclopedia of Witchcraft and Demonology* (New York, 1959), by Rossell Hope Robbins, offers much information. In addition to these reference works, the following books provide information on devils in particular cultures and religious systems.

Awn, Peter J. *Satan's Tragedy and Redemption: Iblis in Sufi Psychology.* Leiden, 1983.

Babb, Lawrence A. *The Divine Hierarchy: Popular Hinduism in Central India.* New York, 1975.

O'Flaherty, Wendy Doniger. *Women, Androgynes, and Other Mythical Beasts.* Chicago, 1980.

Russell, Jeffrey Burton. *The Devil: Perceptions of Evil from Antiquity to Primitive Christianity.* Ithaca, N.Y., 1977.

Spiro, Melford E. *Burmese Supernaturalism.* Exp. ed. Philadelphia, 1978.

Tambiah, Stanley J. *Buddhism and the Spirit Cults in North-East Thailand.* Cambridge, 1970.

Watt, W. Montgomery. *Bell's Introduction to the Qur'ān.* Edinburgh, 1970.

ARVIND SHARMA (1987)

DEVOTION.

DEVOTION. Religious *devotion* is ardent affection, zealous attachment, piety, dedication, reverence, faithfulness, respect, awe, attentiveness, loyalty, fidelity, or love for, or to, some object, person, spirit, or deity deemed sacred, holy, or venerable. Devotion may also be thought of as action, such as worshiping, praying, and making religious vows.

Devotion is a very common phenomenon in all areas of the world and in most religious traditions. In some traditions, sects, or cults, devotion is the central religious concern or is almost synonymous with religion itself. This is the case, for example, in some versions of Chinese and Japanese Pure Land Buddhism, several Hindu devotional movements, and some Christian movements, such as Pietism. The centrality of devotion seems to be more common in religious traditions in which theistic tendencies are central, although its importance in Pure Land Buddhism is sufficient evidence to caution against equating devotion with theism. Religious devotion frequently exists in a theological context of hierarchy where there is at least functional if not ontological theism and divine being(s) are considered to be superior to and have power over a human devotee.

OBJECTS OF DEVOTION. The extensiveness of devotion in religion becomes evident when the variety of objects of devotion is considered. While deities are usually considered the principal objects of devotion, a great many other things are also given devotion in the world's religions. In many African religions, as well as in such historical traditions as Hinduism and Confucianism, ancestors are important objects of reverence, awe, and devotion. Various people, living and dead, are also objects of devotion or the focus of devotional cults. *Gurūs* in Hinduism, saints in Christianity, the *xian* (immortals) in Daoism, the sage kings in Confucianism, *imāms* in Islam, *tīrthaṃkaras* in Jainism, and the buddhas and *bodhisattvas* in Buddhism are only a few examples of divine personages who receive devotion in the world's religions.

In most religions, devotion is primarily addressed to a deity. This could be male, female, or androgynous (as in the half-male, half-female deity Ardhanārīśvara in Hinduism,). The deity or divinity could be in the form of an animal or tree; sometimes, the deity may temporarily possess a human being and during the period of possession that person is the object of veneration. Devotion can also be shown to saints, *gurūs,* and charismatic teachers.

Relics associated with sacred personages are the objects of devotion in many religions. The physical remains of the Buddha were incorporated into stupas, the shrines around which devotional Buddhism began. To this day, parts of the Buddha's physical body are enshrined in temples such as the Temple of the Tooth in Kandy, Sri Lanka. In Christianity, particularly in the late medieval period in Europe, there was a lively traffic in relics, which became extremely important in popular piety. Relics were incorporated into church altars and often represented the concrete, objective aspect of the divine around which the church was built. Pieces of the true cross, bones of martyrs, vials of the Virgin Mary's milk, even the foreskin of Jesus, were among the holy relics that were the objects of popular devotion. In contemporary Christianity the Shroud of Turin is probably the best-known example of a holy relic. In other traditions as well, the physical remains of saints are commonly revered, and the burial places of saints, where purported miracles attributed to devotion are not uncommon, often become centers of healing cults.

In many societies, charismatic leaders, relics, and shrines of saints also become the devotional focus of adherents from communities different from the one to which they were originally associated. Thus, Hindu devotees throng the *dargāhs* (shrines where Ṣūfī saints are entombed) in India. In many cases, the land where these shrines were built was donated by Hindu rulers to the Muslim saints they venerated. Sites where miraculous cures and healing are said to take place also draw devotees from a variety of religious affiliations. Thus, Lourdes, Fátima, Velankanni, and other places where it is held that Marian apparitions took place are pilgrimage centers for devotees from a variety of religious traditions. Devotion in these cases is focused on a person, site, or object not ordinarily considered to be part of the religious tradition to which one officially belongs. These "fuzzy boundaries" between religions abound in South, Southeast, and East Asia, where rigid affiliation to a religious tradition has historically not been part of a community's ethos.

Rivers in Hinduism and mountains in Shintō are often especially revered; indeed, most religious traditions associate sacredness with specific places. Certain cities, such as Vārāṇasī in Hinduism, Jerusalem in Judaism and Christianity, Mecca in Islam, and Ise in Shintō, play an important role in the tradition of many religions and are often themselves the centers of pilgrimage and devotion. Sometimes whole geographical areas or countries are the objects of devotion, such as the Indian subcontinent as a whole for Hindus and Israel for many Jews.

Where it is not possible to visit an original pilgrimage site, devotion often focuses on ritual objects such as the Ark of the Covenant in ancient Judaism and the Host in Christianity. Sacred texts are also objects of devotion in some religions, insofar as they are seen to be the locus of divine revelation. Although the place and function of these texts in the various religious traditions are quite different, the Torah in Judaism, the *Lotus Sūtra* in Nichiren Buddhism, the *Adī Granth* in Sikhism, and the Qur'ān in Islam are books held in great reverence. Indeed, the sacred, holy, or divine has revealed itself to, or been apprehended by, humankind in so many different ways and in such a variety of forms that at some point in the religious history of the world almost every conceivable object has received religious devotion.

And finally, in a circular fashion, people perceived to be paradigmatic devotees themselves become the objects of devotion. Many saints, teachers, and devotees are honored, venerated, and prayed to as bestowers of earthly favors, as mediators between human beings and gods, and as exalted divinities in themselves.

Types of Devotion. Devotion is of different types and takes place in different physical settings, with different attendant moods, and within different kinds of communities. It is often meditative, emotionally disciplined, and subdued, and consists primarily of the willful directing of one's attention to the object of devotion. This is the nature of devotion, for example, as described in the *Bhagavadgītā.* There, Kṛṣṇa teaches Arjuna to center himself mentally on God in all his actions in order to make his entire life an act of devotion. There is a similar emphasis in most theistic traditions in which the devotee is taught to be attentive to God in all things.

Devotion may also express itself in emotional frenzy and passion. Ṣūfī devotion is usually accompanied by music and dance, and much Ṣūfī devotional poetry is intensely passionate. The *Bhāgavata Purāṇa,* a medieval Hindu devotional text, says that true devotion is always accompanied by shivering, the hair standing on end, tears, and sighs of passion. The Hindu saint Caitanya (1486–1533) exemplified this kind of devotion. He was so often overcome by fits of emotional devotion to Kṛṣṇa, in which he would swoon or become ecstatic, that he could barely manage the normal routines of daily life.

The setting of devotion may be quite formal. Churches, synagogues, temples, and mosques are all places in which people devote their minds and hearts to the divine. In such settings devotion may be highly formalized, even routinized, and under the direction of professional clergy. In its formal expression devotion is often communal or congregational and arises from, or is even dependent upon, the coming together of a group of people for a common devotional purpose. On the other hand, devotion in such formal physical settings may also take the form of a lone individual performing an act of devotion to a special saint.

Devotion may also be highly informal and unstructured. The best examples of this are the lives of famous saints who were great devotees. Francis of Assisi (1182–1226) in Christianity and Caitanya in Hinduism were both characterized by spontaneous outbursts of passionate devotion in nearly any setting.

Devotional communities (groups formed primarily as a result of, or in order to cultivate, devotion) also vary from the highly structured to the very unstructured. Monastic orders in Christianity and the Ṣūfī orders in Islam, in which devotion serves a central role, are examples of highly structured devotional communities. The South Indian devotee-saints of Śiva (the Nāyaṉārs) and Viṣṇu (the Āḻvārs), in comparison, were part of unstructured traditions in which individual poet-devotee-saints wandered the countryside or resided at temples and sang devotional hymns to their lord. The devotional community may extend no further than an individual saint and his or her admirers, students, followers, or devotees. Such was the case in the early days of Saint Francis's religious life and for such Hindu saints as Lalleśvarī or Kashmir (fourteenth century) and Mīrā Bāī of Rajasthan (1498–1546).

The practice of devotional rituals may also have several goals. While most religions portray the ideal goal as submission to the deity's love without any expectation of reward or fear of punishment, millions of devotees pray or perform votive rituals for the fulfillment of specific desires. Thus prayers may be offered or devotional exercises performed for the cure of a family member, achievement of a particular career goal, the birth of a child, the marriage of a son, or even the selling of a house. These prayers and votive rituals form the bulk of most devotional petitions in many religions.

CHARACTERISTICS OF DEVOTION. Although the contexts, objects, and moods of devotion vary, there are several characteristics that typify most religious devotion. These involve the emotions, the will, and the mind.

1. The object, person, or deity to whom devotion is directed is regarded with awe and reverence. There is a recognition, often more emotional than mental, that the object is imbued with sacred power. This awe or reverence may assume a passionate intensity, exclusivity, or ardor that overwhelms the devotee.
2. There is faith—conviction, trust, or confidence—on the part of the devotee that the object of devotion is real, that it underlies, overarches, or in some way epitomizes reality. This aspect of devotion is usually associated with the will; it involves commitment, loyalty, and often submission to the object of devotion.
3. Single-mindedness, at least for the time that a particular person, object, or deity is venerated, often involves mental concentration on its object. Spiritual techniques that aim at focusing and concentrating the mind are often part of religious devotion.

Characteristics of theistic devotion. When religious devotion is theistic in nature it is further typified by the following characteristics.

1. Theistic devotion involves a personal relationship in which the deity is imagined and approached as a person and is expected to respond to his devotees accordingly. In Islam, for example, the term *manājāt,* meaning "intimate converse," is supposed to characterize a person's devotion to God. The attitude the devotee adopts in this personal relationship varies and is often dependent upon how the deity is perceived.
2. One of the most common metaphors used in theistic devotion is that of a love relationship. The love of the devotee may be like that of a servant for the master, child for a parent, parent for a child, friend for a friend, or lover for the beloved. In theistic devotion the mood of love, especially when the relationship is familial, erotic, or romantic, introduces great intimacy, passion, and tenderness into the devotional experience. When devotion is expressed in terms of a love relationship, the deity is usually cast in a very approachable role and is described as reciprocating the devotee's love with a passionate love of his or her own. Many goddesses, for example, are portrayed as mothers who are attentive to and fiercely protective of their devotees/children, while the Lord's Prayer in Christianity describes God as the devotees' father. Throughout theistic devotion, deities assume the roles of loving parent, intimate friend, playful child, or impassioned lover in response to the devotee's own devotional role. In some roles of intimacy, the devotee may even tease or scold the deity; such is the case with Andal (c. eighth century) and Nammāḻvār (c. ninth century), who composed Tamil devotional hymns, hailing Kṛṣṇa as harsh and cruel and as the person who knows no righteousness.
3. Theistic devotion is also characterized by expressions or feelings of praise and submission. Both attitudes presuppose that the deity is morally superior to, wiser, and more powerful than the devotee, and usually that the devotee has been created by the deity or is wholly dependent on the deity for his or her continued existence and well-being. In praise, the deity's qualities of goodness, greatness, and generosity are often mentioned. The deity is praised for bestowing various blessings, particularly the blessing of life, on the devotee, the country or nation, or the world as a whole. Theistic devotion typically expresses itself by praising the deity as the source of all good things and as the embodiment of all good qualities. In Islam, for example, the term *ḥamd,* meaning "thankful praise," often characterizes devotion. The relationship that is frequently spoken of when praise and submission dominate is that of a master and servant.

The devotee of a deity often expresses total dependence upon the god by feelings, attitudes, gestures, or acts of submission. In Arabic the word *muslim* means "one who surrenders (to God)," suggesting the centrality of this attitude in Islamic tradition. The Muslim term *ʿibādah* (worship) is often used to characterize devotional observances to God, clearly indicating that the divine-human relationship is like that of a master to a slave *(ʿabd)*. In Śrī Vaiṣṇavism, a Hindu devotional movement, the theme of complete self-surrender *(prapatti)* is central; such submission is held to epitomize *bhakti*, or devotion to God.

The style of submission may depend upon the type of relationship envisioned by the devotee. The submission of a child to its mother, for example, might be quite different from the submission of a slave to his owner. In many traditions the devotee is affirmed to be greatly inferior to the deity; men and women are often described as morally weak, sinful, corrupt, and insignificant, and the deity as overwhelmingly superior. In this relationship the proper attitude of the devotee is abasement and submission.

Devotion in the context of nontheistic traditions. Devotion, most prominent in theistic traditions, is sometimes considered a form of justification for letting loose the flow of divine grace. One may ask if it has any place in philosophical schools such as Zen Buddhism and Advaita Vedānta, where individual meditation in a nontheistic context is seen as the way to reach the final goal. Zen, Advaita Vedānta, and some yogic traditions have ontologies which consider the distinction between the deity and devotee meaningless or challenge concepts of reality as we know them. In many of these schools there is no ultimate gracious deity whose grace will give salvation or liberation. Thus, in the nontheistic traditions, philosophically speaking, devotion has no ultimate value as a path to liberation, *nirvāṇa*, or the final goal. Yet, many adherents of these traditions have, in fact, composed devotional hymns addressed to teachers and deities.

Devotion and Religious Practices. Devotion is often associated with or expressed in the context of several common types of religious practices.

Prayer. Devotion often takes the form of prayer. In prayer a deity is entreated, supplicated, adored, or praised in a mood of devotional service or attentiveness. In some cases, the devotee cultivates a mood of devotion before praying, in order to ensure sincerity and concentration. In medieval Judaism, for example, some authorities recommended the practice of *kavvanah*, the directing of attention to God, before prayer so that prayer might be undertaken with the proper mental inclination.

Moving and dramatic expressions of devotion are found in poems and hymns that articulate the prayers of devotees to the divine in many indigenous religions and in every theistic religious tradition among the world's historical religions. Hymns, such as those central to Protestant Christianity, are devotional prayers set to music. Collective prayer, common in many religions, is another example of formalized devotion.

Worship. As a formal expression of homage, service, reverence, praise, or petition to a deity, worship is closely related to, or expressive of, devotion. Much worship represents a formal, periodic, structured expression of devotion. The prescribed daily and Friday prayers in Islam, called *ṣalāt*, for example, are essentially devotional in nature. In Hindu *pūjā* (worship), which occurs in both temple and domestic settings and which may be performed by an individual or by large groups, the basic pattern of ritual actions denotes personal attendance upon and service of the deity by the worshipers. The deity is symbolically bathed, fanned, fed, and entertained by the priest or directly by the devotee. It is common in worship to make an offering to the deity, which again is often done in the spirit of devotion. Some forms of worship are primarily occasions for devotees to express together their devotion to their god. This is the case, for example, with Hindu *kīrtana* and *bhajan*, gatherings of devotees at which songs are sung in praise of a deity. The setting is usually informal and the mood warm and emotional. It is not uncommon for devotees to dance and leap for joy while they sing their hymns of praise. In Protestant revival meetings, too, open expression of emotional devotion to God is encouraged and expected of those present.

Performing and fine arts. Devotion in many religions is expressed through music and dance. Many church and synagogue services deploy music, chants, and ritual action to express devotional intensity in an aesthetic framework. Making joyful noise or using the body to depict one's longing for the divine have been hallmarks of almost all religious traditions. Deities and devotees in many traditions dance the cosmos, dance their relationship to each other, and dance to the powers of the universe. Devotees in the Hindu tradition emulate the dance of the deities Śiva, Pārvatī, or Kṛṣṇa. Many dances portray a soul's longing for the supreme being; the devotional songs of Hindu schools are standard accompaniment for dancers. Devotion to the deity is expressed through a number of *bhavas* or attitudes, including the attitudes connected with service, maternal love, and romantic love. Singing emotional lyrics with devotion is said to be a path through which one can reach salvation. In the Hebrew scriptures, Miriam took a tambourine in her hand and danced with all the other women; *Psalm* 149 exhorts one to praise the Lord's name in dance. There is a palpable expression of devotion in the dances of some Ṣūfī traditions and in the circular dances seen among the Ismāʿīlīs.

Divine beings are often painted, carved, or fashioned out of various materials to be used as objects of devotion. These objects are frequently invested with life and the divine is said to reside in them after ritual consecrations. Many of these icons are carved with devotion for worship by other devotees.

Pilgrimage is a popular undertaking in many religions, and for many pilgrims the journey is an act of devotion. Setting off on a long trip to a sacred place is a sort of physical prayer. Through the pilgrimage the pilgrim may be making a special appeal to a deity or expressing gratitude for a blessing received from the deity. In Islam a pilgrimage to Mecca is enjoined as one of the fundamental acts of submission incumbent upon all Muslims.

The pilgrim may be making the pilgrimage simply to steep himself or herself in an atmosphere of piety and devotion that is far more intense than in ordinary circumstances. The feeling of community that arises among pilgrims is often strong, and the entire journey, which can last for weeks or even years, may turn into a devotional extravaganza with hymns being sung all day long, devotees swooning in fits of ecstasy or possession, and miraculous cures or incidents being reported. The annual pilgrimage to Pandharpur in Maharashtra is an act of mass devotion sustained for weeks, not unusual in Hinduism.

Devotion is also closely connected with patronage. The large cathedrals of medieval Europe, the Hindu temple complexes of South and Southeast Asia, Buddhist stupas and temples, and Shintō shrines were frequently built by royalty, nobility, or wealthy patrons as a testimony to their devotion and piety.

Meditation. Although many kinds of meditation may not involve devotion, devotion often uses meditative techniques. Meditation usually involves disciplining the mind so that it can focus on something without being distracted by frivolous thoughts or bodily needs and discomforts. For many practitioners the goal is to achieve or maintain attentiveness to a deity. Meditation is used to perfect, deepen, sharpen, or enhance devotion. In such cases meditation and devotion may become synonymous. In Japanese Pure Land Buddhism the term *anjin* (which is sometimes translated as "faith") refers to a meditative calm in which the heart and mind are quieted through concentration on Amida Buddha and his paradise. A particularly common meditative technique used to engender, express, or enhance devotion is the constant repetition of the deity's name or a short prayer to the deity. Ṣūfīs invoke the names of God over and over as part of their *dhikr* (a term meaning recollection that refers to devotional techniques); Eastern Orthodox Christian monks chant the Jesus Prayer ("Lord Jesus have mercy on me a sinner") as often as possible; devotees of Kṛṣṇa chant his names repeatedly. In Pure Land Buddhism, devotees chant a short prayer ("Hail to Amida Buddha") over and over to sharpen and concentrate their faith in Amida.

Asceticism and monasticism. Asceticism and monasticism are often undertaken in the context of devotion, especially in the theistic and Pure Land Buddhist traditions. The Desert Fathers sought solitude in the desert in order to develop their attentiveness to God without distractions or hindrances from society or other people. Their asceticism was clearly associated with, and intended to cultivate, devotion. An ascetic strain is also strong in Sufism, a highly devotional expression of Islam, and many of the most important Hindu devotional leaders and saints have been world renouncers. In many cases, it is clear that asceticism, or renunciation of the world, has been found not only compatible with devotion but a positive encouragement of it.

The case is similar with monasticism. An isolated, cloistered, highly regimented religious community was for centuries esteemed in Christianity as the best place to devote oneself to God. Life in the monastic community was dominated by regular worship and prayer several times a day and imposed a devotional discipline on the individual. To a great extent, monasticism in Christianity was a systematic attempt to perfect a human being's devotional predilections. As in Christian asceticism, the goal was to become attentive to God at all times, except that in the monastic context this goal was sought with the help of a like-minded community and under the guidelines of a carefully regulated spiritual discipline or rule. In many respects, several Ṣūfī brotherhoods and Pure Land Buddhist monastic communities were also organized attempts to create the ideal environment for cultivating the devotional sentiment.

Apart from acts of renunciation in which a devotee may make a clean break with the world he or she lives in, there are many acts of asceticism that are woven into the daily life of the faithful. Thus, Muslims may fast during the month of Ramaḍān, from sunrise to sundown. Hindu women fast on particular days of the week, lunar month, or year for the welfare of their families. In many situations, acts of devotional asceticism addressed to specific deities may be performed for immediate worldly benefits, rather than for salvation or liberation.

Mysticism. For many devotees, particularly in theistic traditions, there is a deep longing to be close to, in the presence of, or absorbed into the deity. This is also the goal of mysticism in theistic traditions, and devotion and mysticism are often closely associated. In medieval Jewish mysticism, *devequt*, which is usually translated as "cleaving to God," is considered the highest religious state that can be attained. This state of cleaving to God is synonymous with an intense devotion in which the devotee is completely preoccupied with and absorbed into the divine. In Sufism the term *fanā'* describes a point in the devotee's or mystic's spiritual quest in which all feeling of individuality and ego fall away and the Ṣūfī is overwhelmed by God. In Christianity, Paul expresses the idea of union with the divine as follows: "It is no longer I who live, but Christ who lives in me" (*Gal.* 2:20). In trying to describe the intimacy of his unmediated experiences of God, John of the Cross (1542–1591), a Spanish mystic, spoke of a river merging with the ocean and of iron heated until it becomes one with the fire. Mystical union, then, represents the ultimate goal of many devotees in several different traditions, and the mystical path is often understood as being the highest path a devotee can embark upon. In many of these cases, devotion is gendered and a submitting devotee is portrayed as a woman in the ecstatic embrace of her lover.

Social action and charity. In some religious traditions, charitable service to one's fellow human beings is considered the most perfect form of devotion to the divine. Several Christian movements with a strong devotional bias have emphasized works of charity as central to devotional life. With the inauguration of active religious orders for men by Francis of Assisi in the thirteenth century, and for women by Mary

Ward and Vincent de Paul in the seventeenth century, the focus of religious life, which had earlier been cloistered, shifted from the cultivation of one's spiritual predilections in isolation from society to serving the poor and needy in the world. Several religious brotherhoods and sisterhoods in Protestant Christianity aim at serving the poor, while the Social Gospel movement of the nineteenth century in the United States represents an attempt to provide theological justification for social involvement as central to Christian life.

A dramatic modern example of devotion as inextricably associated with social service is the life of Mother Theresa of Calcutta and her Sisters of Charity, who minister to the "poorest of the poor" as a way of life. Mother Theresa said that she taught the women who joined her order to see Jesus in each person they served; in serving men and women, they serve Jesus.

Other traditions, too, equated service to human beings with service to God. Mahatma Gandhi, for example, who had a strong devotional bent, was once asked why he did not withdraw from the world in his search for God. He replied that if he thought for one moment that God might be found in a Himalayan cave, he would go there at once, but he was convinced that God could only be found among human beings and in their service.

DEVOTION AND ETHICS. Some narratives depict devotees as flouting the accepted norms of ethics of the tradition. Thus, a devotee may resort to highway robbery or may sell her body so that the money may be used for charity or a pious cause. In some such narratives, the devotee is depicted as undergoing a test. In some there is a miraculous intervention and the devotee is vindicated, but in others, the story may aim to show that within the world of devotion, the normal code of behavior may be nuanced or even reversed, with a logic of its own that is not seen in everyday life. In some traditions, this philosophy is taken one step further to make the point, in an exaggerated manner, that the devotion of a so-called sinner is more "pure" or acceptable to a devotee than the half-hearted or mindless devotional ritual of one who is considered to be virtuous or morally upright.

The philosophy of devotion. The Hindu and Buddhist traditions, in which there are very strong competing paths alongside the devotional path, put forth two kinds of arguments in defending the excellence of the devotional way. Both traditions assume that the world has entered a final period of moral, religious, and ethical decline (the *kaliyuga* in Hinduism, and *mappō* in Japanese Buddhism), in which human beings are no longer spiritually capable of undertaking certain religious paths that were popular among people in earlier ages. Asceticism, meditation, monasticism, and religious ceremonialism, in particular, are held to be too demanding for people of the present age, whose spiritual capacities are weak. In this age, devotion is the best way to reach the spiritual goal, the best because it is the easiest. It can be practiced by anyone, by monk and peasant, rich and poor, priest and layman, man and woman, young and old.

The second argument follows from the first. Why is devotion the easiest path? Because it is the most natural to human beings. In some Hindu devotional movements, *bhakti* (devotion) is said to represent one's inherent *dharma* (proper way of acting) as opposed to one's inherited *dharma*, which is equated with one's caste, occupation, and social roles. All human beings, according to this logic, have an inner longing to love God, and until they do they remain frustrated, incomplete, lonely, and lost. Devotion is understood as a person's cultivation of this natural urge to serve and love the creator, who has instilled in human beings at the deepest level a longing to be reunited with their source.

The idea of devotion representing a person's natural inclination is also expressed in many Ṣūfī images that speak of one who is not devoted to God as being like a fish out of water, a camel far from a watering hole, a bird separated from its mate. To seek God by means of the mystic way is to return home, to seek the familiar and comfortable, to indulge one's natural longings. A similar idea is expressed in Augustine of Hippo's (354–430) famous saying to the effect that human beings are restless until they find their rest in God.

In the vision of Francis of Assisi, all creation was brought into being in order to praise the creator; every species in existence praises God in its own special way. Even inorganic nature celebrates the creator in some way. For Francis, devotion to God represents the inherent and underlying law of the creation and is apparent everywhere. Some Ṣūfīs write that the entire creation is said to be pervaded by the presence of God, that his divine presence intoxicates all creatures and sets them singing and dancing in ecstatic praise.

In the *Bhagavadgītā*, when Kṛṣṇa teaches Arjuna how to discipline his actions so that he will not reap the fruits of *karman*, he tells him to dedicate all of his actions to God, to become God's instrument in all that he does (9.27). One who is truly devoted to a deity makes every action, no matter how apparently insignificant, routine, or frivolous, an act of devotion to the divine. Similarly, Hasidic Judaism teaches that the state of *devequt*, or cleaving to God, should be a person's constant state of mind. In everyday life, even while performing the most mundane acts, a person should cleave to the Lord.

SEE ALSO Worship and Devotional Life.

BIBLIOGRAPHY

There is a lack of books on devotion as a religious phenomenon. Friedrich Heiler's *Prayer: A Study in the History and Psychology of Religion*, translated by Samuel McComb (London, 1938), seeks to describe a widespread devotional phenomenon in religion, but it focuses primarily on Western religious traditions. There are more and better sources for individual traditions. Abraham Zebi Idelsohn's *Jewish Liturgy and Its Development* (New York, 1967) has sections on devotion in the Jewish tradition. Owen Chadwick's *Western Asceticism* (London, 1958) contains translations of important ascetic texts in the Christian tradition and deals with the exemplary role of the ascetic in Christian piety. David Knowles's *Christian Monasticism* (New York, 1969) is a standard work on the monastic ideal in Christian life. Annemarie Schimmel's *Mystical Dimensions of Islam* (Chapel Hill, N.C., 1975) treats the Ṣūfī traditions in Islam, which are highly devotional in nature. Constance Padwick's *Muslim Devotions: A Study of Prayer-Manuals in Common Use* (London, 1961) surveys popular devotional manuals in Islam. A. K. Ramanujan has translated several devotional hymns of a South Indian Hindu devotee and presented an overview of Hindu devotion in a volume entitled *Hymns for Drowning: Poems for Visnu by Nammalyar* (Princeton, 1981). Edward C. Dimock and Denise Levertov have translated several Bengali Hindu devotional hymns in a book entitled *In Praise of Krishna: Songs from the Bengali* (New York, 1967). Alfred Bloom's *Shinran's Gospel of Pure Grace* (Tucson, Ariz., 1965) and Gendo Nakai's *Shinran and His Religion of Pure Faith* (Kyoto, 1946) deal with devotional Buddhism in Japan.

DAVID KINSLEY (1987)
VASUDHA NARAYANAN (2005)

DE VRIES, JAN SEE VRIES, JAN DE

DGE LUGS PA.

The Dge lugs pa (Geluk pa) order of Tibetan Buddhism was founded in the early fifteenth century by Tsong kha pa (1357–1419) in the area of Lhasa, the capital of Tibet. He established a monastic university on a mountain called Dga' ldan ("the joyous") in 1409, and his sect was thus originally called Joyous Way (Dga' ldan pa'i lugs); later it came to be called Virtuous Way, Dge lugs pa. Students built two other large monastic universities in the Lhasa area, 'Bras spung (Drepung) (1416) and Se ra (1419), and the system gradually spread throughout the country. Within two hundred years the sect had become an important political force, such that around 1640, with the help of the Mongolian potentate Gushri Khan, the fifth Dalai Lama (1617-1682) assumed power as head of the government. The lineage of Dalai Lamas maintained this position until the Chinese takeover in 1959.

The Dge lugs pa educational system so captured the imagination of Tibetans that its universities attracted great numbers of men. Dge lugs pa gradually became the dominant mode of religious education and the dominant cultural force in an area ranging from the Kalmyk Mongolian lands in Russia near the Caspian Sea through Outer Mongolia, Inner Mongolia, Mongolian Siberia, parts of China, and Tibet. Lhasa, with its large Dge lugs pa universities, became the cultural, religious, educational, medical, and astrological capital of Buddhist Inner Asia. Great influence was exercised by a complex system of education, devotion, meditation, and cultism, the pattern for which was set by brilliant Dge lugs pa leaders in Lhasa over several centuries.

In Lhasa each monastery had at least two competing faculties and student bodies, which periodically met to debate in intense competition. Factionalism between groups of differing philosophic opinion was highly encouraged; thus there was more intellectual activity within the Dge lugs pa order on this level than between Dge lugs pa and the other orders of Tibetan Buddhism.

Although the Western study of Dge lugs pa education is scarcely more than a half century old, it is possible to piece together a picture of this highly developed program for stimulating the metaphysical imagination. In general, Dge lugs pa doctrinal training is classified into two types, sūtra and Tantra, based on a division of the texts regarded as the Buddha's word. Training in the sūtra system is further divided into a more "practical" and a more "theoretical" system of study. Both practical and theoretical systems are based on great Indian books and Tibetan texts that consist of either explicit commentaries on those texts or expositions of main themes in them.

The practical system centers on Tsong kha pa's *Lam rim chen mo* (Great exposition of the stages of the path) and Indian texts such as Śāntideva's *Bodhicāryāvatāra* (Engaging in the Bodhisattva deeds). The theoretical system centers either on comparative systems of tenets, both Buddhist and non-Buddhist, or on the "Five Great Books." The large Dge lugs pa universities take the latter approach for a curriculum of sūtra study that begins when the student is around eighteen and continues for twenty to twenty-five years.

To prepare students for study of these texts, the curriculum begins with a class on introductory debate that serves to establish the procedure of combative and probing analysis used throughout the entire course of study. The approach is at once individualistic (as used in the preparation and execution of specific debates) and group-stimulated (in that information and philosophic positions are acquired from fellow debaters in an ongoing network of communication). The preliminary classes further study basic psychology and basic theory of reasoning. Then begins a reading of the first of the Five Great Books: the future Buddha Maitreya's *Abhisamayālamkāṃra* (Ornament for clear realization), a rendering of the hidden teaching on the path structure in the *Perfection of Wisdom Sūtras;* this work is usually studied for six or seven years.

The class then passes on to the second Great Book, Candrakīrti's *Madhyamakāvatāra* (Supplement to [Nāgārjuna's] treatise on the middle), to explore for two years the explicit teaching on the emptiness of inherent existence expounded in the *Perfection of Wisdom Sūtras.* Next is Vasubandhu's *Abhidharmakośa* (Treasury of manifest knowledge), a compendium of the types and nature of afflicted phenomena (*kliṣṭadharma*) as well as the pure phenomena (*vaiyavadānikadharma*) that act as antidotes to them; this takes two years. The fourth Great Book is Gunaprabhā's *Vinaya Sūtra* (Aphorisms on discipline), also studied for two years.

Each year throughout the entire twenty-year program, time is taken out for pursuit of the last of the Great Books,

Dharmakīrti's *Prāmaṇavarttika* (Commentary on [Dignāga's] compilation of prime cognition), largely epistemological and logical studies. At the end there are several years for review and preliminary rounds of debate in preparation for the national yearly debate competition in Lhasa; the winner becomes a national hero.

Throughout the long course of study reasoned analysis is stressed, but at the same time the student maintains daily practice of Tantric rites revolving around visualization of himself as a deity. He also participates in cultic rites at the university, college, and subdivision levels to appease and satisfy various protector deities associated with those units, and participates in devotional assemblies on a daily basis centered on deities like the savioress Tārā. Because of the long training period in sūtra studies, this less obvious, yet very strong and even dominant Tantric side of Dge lugs pa often goes unnoticed by foreign observers.

After taking a *dge bśhes* degree, a monk can proceed to a Tantric college, the two prime ones being the Tantric College of Upper Lhasa and the Tantric College of Lower Lhasa. Both have as their main purpose the study, transmission, and practice of the *Guhyasamāja Tantra,* again through the extensive commentaries of Tsong kha pa. The distinguishing feature of Tantrism is deity yoga; its practitioners meditate on themselves as having the physical form not of an ordinary person, but of a deity embodying the highest levels of wisdom and compassion.

Underlying this entire program of religious immersal through doctrinal, devotional, ritualistic, and meditational means is a commitment to reason. The harmony of reason with the most profound religious experiences of compassion, wisdom, deity yoga, and manifestation of the fundamental innate mind of clear light is stressed. Meditation is viewed as being of two varieties, stabilizing (or fixating) meditation and analytical meditation, with the latter receiving great stress in Dge lugs pa. To develop compassion, reflective reasoning is used to enhance basic feelings that are recognized as part of common experience. To develop wisdom, reflective reasoning is used in an intricately devised process so that the student may penetratively understand the incorrectness of assent to the false appearance of phenomena as if they existed in their own right. The aim is not merely to defeat rival systems but to overcome an innate, unlearned misconception of the nature of phenomena.

Such analytically derived realization of emptiness constitutes the first step in practicing deity yoga in Tantrism. The wisdom consciousness—the realization of emptiness impelled by compassion—is then used as the basis for manifesting as a divine being. The wisdom consciousness itself appears as a deity in an indivisible fusion of wisdom and compassion that is symbolized by a *vajra,* a diamond. Utilizing these continuous divine appearances, stabilizing meditation can then be performed on essential points within the body to induce subtler levels of consciousness that are used to realize the same emptiness of inherent existence. When the most subtle consciousness, the fundamental innate mind of clear light, is actualized, the wind (Skt., *prāna;* Tib., *rlung*), or energy, associated with this most subtle consciousness is said to be used as the substantial cause for appearing in an *actual* divine body such that one no longer needs the old coarse body. Transformation is literally both mental and physical.

This most subtle mind is the same as the clear light of death that terrifies ordinary beings, who fear they are being annihilated when it manifests. The Dge lugs pa system of education is aimed at overcoming this fear of one's own most basic nature; thus it suggests that the sense of otherness that many of the world's cultures associate with profound religious experience of the awesome is based on a misconception about the basic nature of one's own being. Further, it suggests that this fear and sense of otherness can be caused to disappear through an understanding of the actual status of phenomena, which is gained through reasoned investigation brought to the level of a profoundly moving experience. This highly developed view of the compatibility of reason and deep mystic insight, expressed in a system of education and ritual exercise, is a distinctive feature of Dge lugs pa.

Since the Dalai Lama's flight from Tibet in 1959, just prior to the takeover of the government by Chinese Communists, a refugee community of Dge lugs pas under his leadership (which is not confined to members of the Dge lugs pa order) has, in scattered places throughout India, reestablished smaller versions of Lhasa's three main monastic universities (each having two competing colleges as subdivisions) as well as two of the Tantric colleges and the monasteries of the Dalai Lama and Panchen Lama. Thus the Dge lugs pa educational system has been reestablished in India and, as of 2003, involved approximately ten thousand monks. There are also approximately eight hundred Dge lugs pa nuns in India and Nepal, with scholastic education being introduced in the early 1990s in some nunneries, a remarkable development in the empowerment of women. Clearly this re-establishment of monastic training in exile is a feat of considerable achievement by an overall Tibetan refugee population in India and Nepal of 120,000.

See Also Buddhism, Schools of; Dalai Lama; Tsong kha pa.

Bibliography

The study of Dge lugs pa is in its infancy, but several helpful expositions have emerged. For a historical and political study, see David L. Snellgrove and Hugh E. Richardson's *A Cultural History of Tibet* (1968; reprint, Boulder, Colo., 1980), pp. 177–267. An anthropological treatment of Dge lugs pa power structures is found in Martin A. Mills' *Identity, Ritual and State in Tibetan Buddhism: The Foundations of Authority in Gelukpa Monasticism* (London and New York, 2003). A short biography of Tsong kha pa, the founder of Dge lugs pa, and scattered samples of his teachings are given in *The Life and Teachings of Tsong Khapa* (Dharamsala, 1982), edited by Robert A. F. Thurman. Tsong kha pa's *Lam rim chen mo* is being translated as *The Great Treatise on the Stages of the Path to Enlightenment* by the Lamrim Chenmo Translation Committee, Joshua W.C. Cutler, editor-in-chief (volume one: Ithaca, N.Y., 2000; volume three: Ithaca, N.Y., 2003). Tsong kha pa's analytic style in which reason dominates over and interprets tradition is evidenced in his *Tantra in Tibet,* translated and edited by me (London, 1977, Ithaca, N.Y., 1987). Glenn H. Mullin's *The Fourteen Dalai Lamas: A Sacred Legacy of Reincarnation* (Santa Fe, 2001) includes biographies of all fourteen Dalai Lamas. Janice D. Willis's *Enlightened Beings: Life Stories from the Ganden Oral Tradition* (Boston, 1995) presents hagiographies of a number of saints from the Dge lugs pa order. For a stirring autobiography of a Dge lugs pa scholar and lama as well as a description of the course of training and basic teachings of the school, see *The Life and Teaching of Geshé Rabten,* translated and edited by B. Alan Wallace (London, 1980). Georges B.J. Dreyfus's *The Sound of Two Hands Clapping: The Education of a Tibetan Buddhist Monk* (Berkeley, Calif, 2003) compares the educational systems of Dge lugs pa monasteries with that of Rnying ma pa. A sense of how a Dge lugs pa scholar's mind probes issues can be gained from Lati Rinbochay's *Mind in Tibetan Buddhism,* edited, translated, and introduced by Elizabeth Napper (London, 1980); in this work the topic of basic psychology is examined in depth. The themes of death, the subtler levels of consciousness, and the mind of clear light, as presented by an eighteenth-century Dge lugs pa scholar, Yang jen ga way lo drö, is given in Lati Rinbochay and my *Death, Intermediate State, and Rebirth in Tibetan Buddhism* (London, 1979, Ithaca, N.Y., 1985), and these topics are also treated in intimate and practical detail in His Holiness the Dalai Lama's *Advice of Dying and Living a Better Life* (New York, 2002). The doctrine of emptiness and its place in the Dge lugs pa worldview is presented in considerable detail, drawing from several works of their scholastic tradition, in my works *Meditation on Emptiness* (London, 1983,1996), *Emptiness in the Mind-Only School of Buddhism* (Berkeley, Calif., 1999), and *Reflections on Reality* (Berkeley, Calif., 2002). How the doctrine of emptiness and expression of compassion is practiced in Anuttarayoga Tantra is presented in detail in Daniel Cozort's *Highest Yoga Tantra* (Ithaca, N.Y., 1986).

PAUL JEFFREY HOPKINS (1987 AND 2005)

DHAMMAKĀYA MOVEMENT.

DHAMMAKĀYA MOVEMENT. At the turn of the twenty-first century, the Dhammakāya (Thai, *Thammakāi*) movement was one of the most dynamic and controversial aspects of Thai Theravāda Buddhism. The Pali word *dhammakāya* corresponds to the Sanskrit term *dharmakāya,* which in Mahāyāna Buddhism has come to refer to one of the three aspects of the buddha-nature, specifically its unmanifest yet all-pervading essence. By the late twentieth century the term had also been applied to a specific meditation method and to the movements that taught it. By the early twenty-first century, the most prominent of these movements, based at Wat Phra Dhammakāya on the north edge of Bangkok, had attracted tens of thousands of followers in Thailand and established several branch centers abroad. Highly skilled at organization and proselytization, this movement was also plagued by public controversies and periodically threatened with suppression.

ORIGINS AND GROWTH. Dhammakāya meditation was developed in the early twentieth century by the Thai monk Luang Phọ̄ Sot Jandasarō (Thai: Čhanthasarō). Supporting his teaching with references to the Pali texts of Theravāda Buddhism, Sot claimed his new method of meditation was taught by the Buddha and resulted in an actual vision of the Buddha's essence. Though these teachings eventually proved controversial, they drew little note in Sot's day. He was eventually appointed abbot of Wat Paknam in what is now western Bangkok, which he made a center of dhammakāya teaching and practice, a role continued into the late twentieth century.

Following Sot's death in 1959, several disciples continued teaching his method. By the late 1960s one of them, a white-robed nun named Chandra Khonnokyoong (Thai, Čhan Khonnokyūng), had attracted a group of university students into her circle. In 1969 one of them, a recent graduate of Kasetsart University, took ordination as Phra Dhammachaiyo (Pali, Dhammajayō; Thai, Thammachaiyō) and served from then on as titular head of this new branch of the movement. By 1970 Chandra's core of devotees had attracted the funds to establish a new meditation center just north of Bangkok, and the movement's activities rapidly expanded. By the early 1980s the movement had attracted thousands of devotees, and its meditation center was now registered as a monastery under the name Wat Phra Dhammakāya.

The founders of Wat Phra Dhammakāya had a talent for organization. The movement's core of university and technical-school students quickly took control of the student Buddhist clubs at several of the most prestigious campuses in Bangkok. In the 1980s on-campus activities expanded rapidly, and by the late 1980s the movement controlled clubs on more than fifty campuses around the country. The group also organized annual meditation and indoctrination retreats that gradually increased in length and numbers. In Thai Buddhism, young men have long been expected to undertake temporary ordination before assuming adult responsibilities, but for many urban men this tradition had become increasingly abbreviated, and the movement was seeking to reverse this trend. By the late 1980s the Dhammakāya movement's program of meditation retreats, which it dubbed *dhammadāyāda* (Thai, *thammathāyāt,* meaning "heir of the *dhamma"*), was enrolling more than a thousand participants a year in a program that entailed a two-month commitment and culminated in a highly publicized mass ordination.

In the 1980s a competing center opened in Ratchaburi province, a little west of Bangkok. This center, led by Phra Sermchai Chaiyamanggalo, became registered as the monastery Wat Luang Pho Sodh Dhammakāyaram, which takes great pains to distance itself from Wat Phra Dhammakāya. A third center, Wat Paknam, reportedly also functions as a center of dhammakāya teachings. However, as of late 2003, the largest, best known, and most controversial of the movements continued to be the one based at Wat Phra Dhammakāya.

By the late 1980s Wat Phra Dhammakāya was drawing a congregation of more than 1,000 on Sundays (more than 5,000 at the beginning of the month), and claimed to draw more than 50,000 on major Buddhist observances. Its followers also organized branch meditation groups and centers throughout the country, and by the 1990s several overseas branches had also been organized. By the late 1990s the crowds had gotten even larger, and the organization had acquired a full square mile of land and was nearing completion of a massive stupa faced by a pavilion said to accommodate 100,000 people. Meditation retreats continued to multiply (including *dhammadāyada* retreats for young women), and the movement had required additional land for temples and meditation sites throughout the country.

CONTROVERSIES. The Wat Phra Dhammakāya movement has been plagued by controversy throughout its existence. Criticisms have focused variously on its style of meditation, its interpretation of the terms *dhammakāya* and *nirvāṇa,* the alleged self-aggrandizement of its leaders, and the potential threat to competing streams of Thai Theravāda Buddhism entailed by its size, its financial power, and its political connections.

The exact nature of the controversies changed over time. In the 1970s, the movement was thought to be communist because of its successes among university students, who at the time tended to be leftist. By the late 1980s the movement was more likely to be considered right-wing due to its connections with the government and military officials; criticism shifted to the movement's size, ambitions, and organizational methods, though few in this period raised questions about doctrinal issues. In addition, visible and sometimes violent rifts arose between the movement's educated urban followers and the farmers, who tended to be less well-connected and outside the movement and who sometimes lost their livelihoods as the movement expanded its land holdings. These conflicts came to a head in the late 1980s as the movement was expanding its main center near Bangkok.

By the late 1990s, leading critics had amplified their attacks to include allegations of doctrinal heresy. During this period several of the movement's leading monks were also charged with financial improprieties. In the midst of this, the most serious crisis in the movement's history, leading governmental officials seriously proposed replacing the monastery's entire leadership with non-dhammakāya monks. In 1999 Wat Phra Dhammakāya's abbot was briefly suspended, but the monastery and movement remained in the hands of his deputies, and in late 2003 neither abbot nor movement seemed to have suffered lasting damage.

TEACHINGS. Wat Phra Dhammakāya is known for its emphasis on meditation and on a strict lay morality. It is dhammakāya meditation that has drawn the greatest attention.

The meditation. Participants in dhammakāya meditation are urged to relax, focus on a meditative object such as a clear crystal ball, and recite the *mantra sammā āraham̐* (Thai, *sammā ārahang,* literally, "fullness of spiritual attainment"). When devotees meditate in groups, as they often do, the voice of the session leader becomes an additional (unacknowledged) meditative object.

Leaders teach that when meditators have become sufficiently skilled, or their store of merit sufficiently full, they will see a glowing sphere called the *paṭhommamagga* (Thai, *pathommamak,* or "beginning of the path"). As they continue to gaze upon the sphere, it should pass through a series of self-representations (or "sheaths") of increasing clarity, resulting in a vision of the dhammakāya. Visual representations of these successive sheaths show a glowing circle containing a man sitting in meditation; in the later spheres he is wearing a yellow robe, and in the final, "dhammakāya," sheath he looks like a glowing saint, or Buddha.

The dhammakāya seen in meditation is a self-representation both of the Buddha's eternal essence and of the buddhahood within. Thus the meditator does not attain something he or she does not have, but rather sees what was already there. This clarity is founded on the merit accumulated in past lives, but is enhanced by the practice of meditation, especially dhammakāya meditation. Not only can meditation on the dhammakāya speed attainment of *nirvāṇa,* owing to the tremendous amount of merit it generates, but advanced practitioners can also use meditation to explore past lives and to visit the heavens and hells of traditional Thai Buddhist cosmology.

Points of orthodoxy. In many ways the Dhammakāya movement operates entirely within the norms of Thai Theravāda Buddhism. Its emphasis on meditation is paired with an emphasis on lay morality and the promotion of Buddhist identity and Buddhist missions. The movement justifies its teachings with references to the Pali texts of the Theravāda traditions, and the majority of its practices (other than the meditation itself) are grounded in Thai Buddhist convention. The cosmology is also fairly conventional, asserting the reality of past and future lives, as well as the existence of multiple heavens and hells, all of which can be visited (and experientially verified) through meditation.

Heterodox teachings. The movement also promotes several heterodox teachings, two of which deserve special note. The first has to do with the notion of the dhammakāya. The Dhammakāya movement says that this notion, which is found in the Pali texts, refers to the Buddha's eternal essence, or to the buddhahood within, which can be viewed directly through meditation. Opponents say that the Pali references to dhammakāya refer solely to the inwardly comprehended truth of the Buddha's teachings.

The second of these teachings has to do with the nature of *nirvāṇa.* Although most Theravāda teachers hold that *nirvāṇa* refers to a "snuffing out," or the end of the cycle of existence and suffering, the Dhammakāya movement asserts, again with references to the Pali scriptures, that *nirvāṇa* is a place where past buddhas can be visited through meditation.

It appears that these teachings were developed by Luang Pho Sot, and versions of them are propagated by all of the movement's competing branches. As noted above, until the 1990s these teachings drew little public comment, but late in the decade they were the subject of much controversy, as opponents branded them heretical.

SIGNIFICANCE. In terms of the educated, relatively urban Thai culture from whom the movement draws most of its followers, Wat Phra Dhammakāya takes a middle of the road position, appealing to the mind while avoiding intellectualism, and appealing to popular fascination with the miraculous while rejecting traditional magical rituals. The movement's leaders lecture in classroom style, its followers read religious literature voraciously, and the organization sponsors Pali quiz contests, yet its commitment to building its own organization, and the relatively simple nature of its teachings, separate it from more intellectual Thai Buddhist leaders such as Buddhadāsa and Prayut Payutto. On the practice side, the movement believes strongly in the action of karma and the beneficial power of merit (especially merit accumulated through meditation); many devotees expect that the practice of dhammakāya meditation will not only help to calm the mind, but can also have miraculous effects on external circumstances. Yet the movement also discourages allegedly "non-Buddhist" or "magical" practices such as traditional divination, possession, and healing rituals.

Wat Phra Dhammakāya is an extension of the nineteenth-century reforms of Prince Mongkut (later King Rama IV) and Prince-Patriarch Vajirañāṇa (Thai, Wachirayan), who fully accepted Western science for investigating and mastering the material world, while asserting traditional Thai Buddhist cosmology as the means of understanding one's place in the world and strict textualism as a means of understanding Buddhism. To this reformist stance the Wat Phra Dhammakāya movement added late-twentieth-century organizational and public-relations techniques, along with a pragmatism, emphasis on lay practice, and advertisement of success that appeals to many educated city dwellers. Unlike most earlier Buddhist movements, Wat Phra Dhammakāya organizes lay practice much like a school would organize its students or a corporation its workers, while continuing to proclaim the superiority of the monastic path. The organization views its role as calling people, especially secularly educated people, back to a whole-hearted devotion to Buddhism, while hoping to make Wat Phra Dhammakāya the primary center through which meditation's meritorious power will be channeled for the benefit of the world.

SEE ALSO Buddhism, article on Buddhism in Southeast Asia; Buddhist Meditation, article on Theravāda Buddhist Meditation.

BIBLIOGRAPHY

Despite the movement's size and notoriety, there are few examples of English-language scholarship based on fieldwork with the movement's devotees. The best examples of fieldwork-based writings include Apinya Fuengfusakul, "Empire of Crystal and Utopian Commune: Two Types of Contemporary Theravāda Reform in Thailand," *Sojourn: Social Issues in Southeast Asia* 8, no. 1 (February 1993): 153–183, which includes a description of the movement's organizational structure; Edwin Zehner, "Reform Symbolism of a Thai Middle-Class Sect: The Growth and Appeal of the Thammakai Movement," *Journal of Southeast Asian Studies* 21, no. 2 (September 1990): 402–426, which includes discussion of the controversies of the 1980s and a description of a major religious observance at Wat Phra Dhammakāya; and Jeffrey Bowers, *Dhammakaya Meditation in Thai Society* (Bangkok, 1996), a published master's thesis that includes an extended description of dhammakāya meditation from the perspective of the rival center at Wat Luang Phor Sodh Dhammakāyaram. Of these, Apinya has conducted the most sustained fieldwork with the Wat Phra Dhammakāya movement. Unfortunately, most of her fieldwork results are available only in the Thai-language research report titled *Sātsanathat khǭng chumchon mư̄ang samai mai: sưksā karanī wat phra thammakāi* [Religious perspectives of contemporary urban society: A case study of Wat Phra Dhammakāya] (Bangkok, [undated, but appearing sometime between 1996 and 1998]).

For information on the controversies of the 1980s, see Zehner (1990, cited above) and Peter A. Jackson, *Buddhism, Legitimation, and Conflict: The Political Functions of Urban Thai Buddhism* (Singapore, 1989). The best set of English-language materials on the controversies of the late 1990s is the archive of articles maintained by the Bangkok Post at http://www.bangkokpost.com. Wat Phra Dhammakāya (under the guise of its Dhammakāya Foundation) maintains its own website at http://www.dhammakaya.or.th/, and the rival Wat Luang Phor Sodh Dhammakāyaram maintains a website at http://www.concentration.org/. Both websites include information about teachings and recent events.

For scholarly interpretations of the Wat Phra Dhammakāya movement, see Donald K. Swearer, "Fundamentalistic Movements in Theravāda Buddhism," in *Fundamentalisms Observed*, edited by Martin E. Marty and R. Scott Appleby, pp. 628–690 (Chicago, 1991), which analyzes the movement as a kind of Buddhist fundamentalism; also Charles F. Keyes, "Buddhist Politics and Their Revolutionary Origins in Thailand," *International Political Science Review* 10, no. 2 (1989): 121–142, which cites the movement as an example of the recently increased emphasis in Thai Buddhism on seeking a better future through ethically impelled practical action. Several authors, including Zehner, Jackson, and Keyes (all cited above), have explored aspects of the movement's appeal to its primarily urban, middle-class following. Additional information on the social and economic contexts of the movement is provided in Pasuk Phongpaichit and Chris Baker's respected survey *Thailand: Economy and Politics* (Kuala Lumpur, 1995).

EDWIN ZEHNER (2005)

DHARMA

This entry consists of the following articles:

HINDU DHARMA
BUDDHIST DHARMA AND DHARMAS

DHARMA: HINDU DHARMA

The term *dharma,* central to Hindu conceptions of morality, tradition, and national identity, is a notoriously difficult one to define. Standard definitions relate the word variously to the individual's duty to observe custom or law, to the individual's conformity to duty and nature, or to divine law itself. An examination of the word in context, however, quickly reveals that all of these simple definitions gloss over numerous complexities and contradictions. This is primarily due to the fact that *dharma* both embraces and tries to bridge a foundational ambiguity in Hindu thought.

Hindu cosmologies, histories, and normative traditions describe a wide gap that separates that which is essentially true and eternal from its historic and contingent manifestations. The broadest and most compelling way of putting the matter is in the distinction between Veda (transcendent knowledge) and *itihāsa* (history), or between *śruti* (revelation) and *smṛti* (tradition based on memory). *Śruti* represents the source of absolute authority—revealed knowledge—while *smṛti* is the tradition that humans obey in order to live the sanctioned life. At the heart of Hinduism, then, is this paradox: the tradition that tells Hindus how to live in the world is a tradition of recollection, and memory must bridge a daunting gap between the present and the timeless absolute.

The concept of *dharma* encompasses this paradox and reflects Hindu cosmology's understanding of the ambiguous relationship between absolute truth and history and time, between revelation and remembrance. This can be seen, for example, in the story that holds that Prajāpati composed a book on *dharma* that, at one thousand chapters, was so vast it had to be reduced to a mere four thousand *ślokas* in order to accommodate human frailty (*Nāradasmṛti,* Introduction). It can also be seen in the belief that at the end of each cosmic age (*yuga*) the Veda will disappear, requiring recurring *dharma* legislation at the beginning of each successive new age (*Viṣṇu Purāṇa* 3.2). Something eternal and absolute remains forever, but what we as humans see of it changes, gets lost to forgetfulness, and must be gleaned from limited memory in order to serve as a binding moral tradition. These profoundly important ideas must be taken into account in any attempt to understand the concept of *dharma* and the nature of ethical discourse within Hinduism.

THE LEXICAL DIVERSITY OF *DHARMA*. *Dharma* is generally understood as a concept that encompasses several meanings, including morality, law, religion, and tradition, as well as the nature of reality or the nature of individual members of society. For contemporary and western scholarship this is far too ambiguous: the conceptual distinction between the nature of reality and morality, or between religious and legal rules is too important to gloss over by means of one term. Nonetheless, the lexical meanings of *dharma* remain extremely diverse and the decision to translate the word into one term or another remains difficult and context-sensitive.

In fact, the wealth and subtlety of meanings denoted by *dharma* belies any brief definition. Even a cursory glance at the numerous textual examples reveals a number of broad meanings. Like the term *ṛta,* which refers to the Vedic conception of cosmic and social order, *dharma* is depicted as a cosmological principle that encompasses both the structure of reality and the essential rightness of this structure. It is Varuṇa's *dharma* that separates Heaven and Earth, and Mitra-Varuṇa are the two guardians of this order, whose laws are truth itself (*Ṛgveda* 6.70.1; 5.63.1). Both of these gods are wise with *dharma* (*Ṛgveda* 5.63.7). This conception extends to the much later *dharma* texts. *Manusmṛti* (Manu), for example, argues that the practice of appointing a childless widow to another man is unacceptable because it destroys the eternal *dharma* or the natural order of things (9.64).

Dharma often recurs in the plural nominal form in Vedic literature, referring either to religious laws or ritual practices. Agni is said to cherish the laws (*dharmani*) (*Ṛgveda* 5.26.6; 8.43.24). Soma, like a steer, which is both powerful and fecund, ordains laws (*Ṛgveda* 9.64.1), while Varuṇa enforces them (*Ṛgveda* 7.89.5), but the sacrifices are the first laws (*Atharvaveda* 7.51). In fact, several Vedic gods are given the name Dharma or some variation of it, most notably Agni, who is called Svadharma—"whose very self is the law" (*Ṛgveda* 3.21.2). Other gods who bear the name Dharma are Savitṛ, Viśvadeva, Mitra, and Varuṇa. And, of course, Dharma himself is a Vedic god (*Ṛgveda* 8.35.13) and the post-Vedic divine father of Yudhiṣṭhira in the *Mahābhārata* (1.1.69).

The strong religious and ritual meanings of *dharma* extend to post-Vedic literature, including Dharmasūtras and Dharmaśāstras, but more specialized meanings are added as well. *Dharma* can mean "Law" as a sacred normative order of reality, as in the *Āpastamba Dharmasūtra,* in which a student is encouraged to take delight in *dharma* (5.11). A similar meaning attaches to *dharma* in Manu, in which the birth of a *brāhmaṇa* is described as the eternal physical form of *dharma* (1.98).

The renowned cosmological doctrine of the four *yugas* (aeons) entails the successive deterioration of *dharma.* In Manu, *dharma* is compared to a bull that loses one leg in each age following the initial *Kṛtayuga.* This conception, along with the implication that the loss of *dharma* leads to a deterioration of health and longevity in each age, resembles the Vedic doctrine of *ṛta* in which moral and natural factors are inseparable. A sense prevails here that *dharma* implies some substance that increases or diminishes with the rise or fall of order—or, for that matter, with the observance of rituals or good and bad actions. This "substance" has often been translated as "merit" in texts that use *dharma* in the following sense: "Four things increase and thrive for a man who habitually greets other people . . . long life, *dharma,* fame and strength" (Manu 2.121; 3.131). This sense of *dharma* overlaps with the ethical and eschatological domain of karma in its psychological implications as *puṇya* (merit) or *pāpa* (demerit or sin)—the attendant consequences of doing right or wrong. Perhaps "virtue" would be a fair translation for *dharma* in the sense of a quality that attaches to individuals who follow the law—though the distinction between the law that is followed and the virtue that increases may be arbitrary here.

The meanings of *dharma* extend far beyond the topics mentioned above to areas that circumscribe the social domain, particularly law and morality. A paradigmatic expression of this usage is the famous statement in the Śanti Parvan of the *Mahābhārata* that *dharma* restrains the evil acts of men and helps the acquisition and preservation of wealth (12.91.5). In other words, *dharma* can be broadly understood as the law that underlies social order—a juridical equivalent of law as cosmic order, or a principle of absolute justice: "Because of *dharma* alone people are sustained in their separate stations" (*Mahābhārata* 12.110.11). The broad principle that upholds social order and economic activity becomes instantiated in the work of the king as the dispenser of justice: "No one should violate the justice (*dharma*) that the king dispenses" (Manu 7.13). The king is the guardian of *dharma* in this sense, and the paradigmatically righteous king, Yudhiṣṭhira in the *Mahābhārata,* is the *dharma rāja.*

But *dharma* also refers to the specific laws that the king enforces, such as the law (*dharma*) for the division of inheritance (Manu 1.115), the duties of husband and wife (Manu 8.7), the duties of the priest (Manu 12.71), and others. The distinction made between rules of conduct that are enforced by the court ("positive law") and those that are sanctioned by religious principles (God's revenge, hell, *karman*), does not apply here. The legal concept of *vyavahāra* (legal transaction), often contrasted with *dharma,* simply refers to the manner by which a legal dispute is brought to the attention of the court, not to the source of authority or sanction. In other words, whatever particular problem the king addresses (settling inheritance disputes; defining the boundary between the rights of two castes), the issue is always regarded as a matter of *dharma,* in this case, *rāja dharma.*

***DHARMA* AND AUTHORITY.** The complexity and richness of *dharma* reflects not so much the failure to make conceptual distinctions as the multiplicity and durability of the traditions in which the term figures. A great number of texts over millennia simply cannot speak with one voice. Nonetheless, Hindu theorists began to synthesize and unify the conception of *dharma* from an early age. Their theories seek to ground *dharma* as rule of conduct in some type of metaphysical foundation such as the Vedic conception of *ṛta.* Possibly the oldest such theory is found in the *Gautama Dharmasūtra,* which lists three sources (*mūla*) of *dharma* (1.1–2). These are Veda, tradition, and good custom. Later *dharma* texts (such as Manu and Yājñavalkya) added a fourth, namely "self-contentment" (*ātma-tuṣṭi*) or conscience. The doctrine of the four sources (or "feet"—*pada*) of *dharma* achieves two primary goals: one is technical, the second ideological. Technically, the four sources reflect a hierarchy of prestige and therefore the ranking of applicability among rules. One may look to tradition only where the Vedas are silent and to good custom only where the first two say nothing. In a conflict between rules—for instance, the widow's right to inherit as opposed to her obligation to perform *satī* (self-immolation) on the funeral pyre—the rule that originates in a higher source of *dharma* prevails.

The ideological goal of this doctrine is to ground *dharma* (as contingent law and morality) in a transcendent and fixed source of authority. The law on the books, the customary practice in the region, even moral common sense, ultimately point to the Veda and to the sacred order of reality.

Despite the efforts of some scholars, such as P. V. Kāne, to show that the Vedas do cover a wide array of *dharma* topics, and even specific rules, most contemporary scholars agree that the Vedic texts (*saṃhitā*) contain little in the way of explicit rules of conduct. Consequently, the Veda should be regarded as a source of authority, a metaphysical constitution, so to speak, rather then a positive source for rules of conduct or ethical reasoning. This recognition underlies the later synthesizing theories of Mīmāṃsā philosophers. When the foundational Mīmāṃsā text, Jaimini's *Mīmāṃsāsūtras* (c. 100 BCE), states that *dharma* is a beneficial act indicated by Vedic injunction, it is attempting to ground the authority of contingent rules of conduct on the eternal validity of Vedic language and its meanings (1.1.2). In other words, the Mīmāṃsā philosopher, like his colleagues within the Nyāya and Vaiśeṣika schools, is aware of the gap that separates present circumstances and the justifying norm, which is said to be eternal and immutable. The commentaries on the *Mīmāṃsāsūtras,* such as that of Kumārila, argue that what makes *dharma* binding even as it changes over time, is precisely this grounding of the language of *dharma* in the language of Vedic injunctions. What makes *dharma* known are the rules of interpretation based on Mīmāṃsā hermeneutics of Vedic language, primarily the distinction between injunction (*vidhi*) and statement of fact or embellishment (*arthavāda*). In short, the doctrine of the four sources of *dharma* in its basic form, and the philosophical-grammatical speculations on the link between *dharma* and Veda, reflect a sharp awareness of the problematic nature of law and morality in relation to ultimate authority.

THE LITERARY SOURCES OF *DHARMA*. Among its many lexical meanings *dharma* can indicate "tradition" in a very broad sense, or, as *sanātana dharma* (eternal *dharma*), it can refer to the normative tradition loosely identified with Hinduism. However, in the narrower technical sense of rule of conduct (religious, moral, legal), *dharma* is found mainly in a large but clearly circumscribed literary corpus.

The Vedic Saṃhitās do contain some references to matters of *dharma,* and the newer Gṛhyasūtras are systematic expositions of procedures for domestic and life-cycle rituals. However, the explicit and comprehensive enumeration of *dharma* rules begins with the Dharmasūtras, which originally belonged to Kalpasūtras associated with specific Vedic schools. The four major Dharmasūtras are attributed to Gautama, Baudhāyana, Vasiṣṭha, and Āpastamba. The texts, written in the post-Brāhmaṇa period but notoriously difficult to date, were probably composed between 600 and 200 BCE. The sūtra texts were composed in a brief aphoristic prose style, and they are regarded as parts of the *smṛti* (rather than Veda) tradition within the broad classification of the four sources of *dharma.* Far grander in scale and elaboration are the Dharmaśāstras, written in *śloka* (a four-part meter) verse using the classical Sanskrit that was the hallmark of the *Rāmāyaṇa* and *Mahābhārata* as well. The Śāstras cover the same topics as the Dharmasūtras but they expand and add detail, and they reflect many of the social changes that took place in the intervening centuries. The major, and oldest, works are *Mānava Dharmaśāstra* (or *Manusmṛti*), *Yājñavalkyasmṛti,* and *Nāradasmṛti.* Like the preceding sūtra texts, these works are impossible to date with precision. The most renowned and often-discussed of all *dharma* texts, *Manusmṛti,* reveals the hand of several compilers and contains both internal and external evidence of a contradictory nature (see Doniger and Smith, 1991). Its dating is very broadly placed between the third century BCE and the second or third century CE. Yājñavalkya and Nārada are slightly more recent, as are additional *dharma* texts such as *Parāśarasmṛti, Bṛhaspatismṛti,* and *Kātyāyanasmṛti.*

Roughly contemporary texts with the early Dharmasūtras, and serving as respected sources of *dharma,* are the two great epics, the *Rāmāyaṇa* and *Mahābhārata.* The latter is a consciously framed model of good conduct, and the twelfth book (Śanti Parvan) is a virtual encyclopedia of *dharma.* Georg Bühler believed that a full 10 percent of the *ślokas* in Manu were shared with the *Mahābhārata,* and P. V. Kāne gives the nod of precedence to the Dharmaśāstra. The *Arthaśāstra* of Kauṭilya, though specializing in matters of statecraft and polity over law and morality, was nonetheless a valuable source of *rāja dharma,* or the rules that apply to the king. It dates to the first two centuries BCE, perhaps to the court of Candragupta Maurya.

Far more specialized as sources of *dharma* are the commentaries (*bhāṣya*) that have been attached to the Dharmaśāstras, especially Manu and Yājñavalkya. The oldest is Bhāruci's commentary on Manu—an incomplete work, possibly of South Indian origins. The most prestigious commentary on Manu from the perspective of adjudication, is *Medhātithi,* dating to the ninth or tenth century. However, the *Manvartha Muktāvali* of Kullūka, a fifteenth century work composed in Banaras, is far more comprehensive and clear. The Dharmaśāstra of Yājñavalkya also inspired several commentaries. By far the most important was the *Mitākṣarā,* authored by Vijñāneśvara in the eleventh century. This large work had a vast influence on family law, especially matters of succession and inheritance, throughout India, with the exception of Bengal, where the *Dāyabhāga* digest of Jīmūtavāhana (twelfth century) prevailed. The Anglo-Indian courts turned the *Mitākṣarā* into the virtual law code for personal law under British dominion.

While commentaries were being composed in medieval and early modern India for the sake of clarifying and promoting legal schools, large compendia or digests (*nibandhas*) also began to appear. These were collections of quotes from the older *dharma* texts, logically arranged under various headings, with occasional brief commentaries. The most prominent among the many digests were the *Kṛtyakalpataru* of Lakṣmīdhara (twelfth century), which was a vast collection of nearly 30,000 *ślokas.* The *Smṛti Candrikā* of Devanna Bhaṭṭa is a South Indian digest from roughly the same period and contains a very important commentary on the Dharmaśāstra. Additional works of note include the *Vivāda Ratnākara* of Caṇḍeśvara, the *Smṛti Sindhu* of Nanda Paṇḍita, and the *Vyavahāra Mayūkha* of Nīlakaṇṭha Bhaṭṭa.

It is important to note that along with the specialized sources of *dharma* there have always been the informal or popular sources of moral and religious norms. Among many others, these include mythical and folk narratives contained in the *Mahābhārata* and *Rāmāyaṇa* (along with explicit *dharma* sections), oral and theatrical performances in temples or during festivals, the *Pañcatantra* and *Hitopadeśa* (collections of stories about moral and pragmatic conduct), the *Kathāsaritsāgara,* the plays of Kālidāsa and other dramatists, the Purāṇas, and devotional songs.

THE TOPICS OF *DHARMA*. Because the concept of *dharma* is so fluid and encompasses so many domains, it is difficult to limit the range of *dharma* to a fixed set of "topics." In a sense, everything is *dharma.* Still, the most prestigious and systematic literary source of *dharma,* Manu, does consciously enumerate a number of clearly defined areas. Manu 1.111–118 serves as a general table of contents for the work as a whole and includes the following major topics, among others: rituals of change (*saṃskāras*—"rites of passage"), the duties of a student, rules for marriage, sacrifices and last rites, rules that describe and restrict means of livelihood, food, purification, the duties of women, rules for the ascetic, matters relating to the king and court procedure, rules for husband and wife, inheritance, protection of the state, rules for time of emergency, expiation, and rules that apply to foreigners and heretical social groups.

***VARṆĀŚRAMADHARMA*.** The central domain of *dharma,* which gradually came to be equated by several texts with *dharma* itself, is *varṇāśramadharma:* the duties of the four social classes (*varṇas*) and the four stages of life (*āśramas*) (*Viṣṇusmṛti* 1.48; *Yājñavalkyasmṛti* 1.1). The social classes include the *brāhmaṇa* (priest), *kṣatriya* (warrior), *vaiśya* (merchant), and *śūdra* (laborer). The Dharmaśāstras explicitly regard these as social categories rather than specific or definitive occupations. All *kṣatriyas* are not warriors and many *brāhmaṇas* perform tasks different than officiating in rituals.

Still, the rules that indicate the appropriate duties (*svadharma*) befitting each social class are firm, enforced by the rule of law and fortified by the threat of ritual pollution and the retributive psychology of *karman.* Some *svadharma* rules may be suspended during times of emergency (*āpaddharma*). The rules or duties that apply to all members of society are designated *sādhāraṇa* (or *sāmānya*) *dharma.* These are not very numerous and, though prestigious, they have never gained the sanctity one sees invested within Judaism in the Ten Commandments. There are several lists of *sādhāraṇadharma* but Manu specifies nonviolence (*ahiṃsā*), truthfulness, not taking other people's property (*asteya*), purity, and restraint of the senses as the *dharma* of all the *varṇas.* The *Vāmana Purāṇa* describes a tenfold *dharma* common to all, adding generosity, forbearance, quiescence, not demeaning oneself, and ascetic discipline to Manu's list (Kāne, 1968–1975, vol. 2, p. 11).

The doctrine of the four stages of life, so central to the Dharmaśāstras, follows the older Dharmasūtra version (*Gautama Dharmasūtra, Baudhāyana Dharmasūtra*), which included only three stages: the student (*brahmacārin*), the householder (*gṛhasthin*), and the forest-dweller (*vānaprasthin*) who is not a complete renouncer. Only from the sūtra texts of Āpastamba and Vasiṣṭha onwards does a fourth *āśrama* emerge—that of the *saṃnyāsin* who renounces all social relations and identity in full pursuit of *mokṣa* (liberation). The addition of the fourth stage of life represents, according to Patrick Olivelle, the attempt to resolve a perceived tension between the competing values of *dharma* and *mokṣa* in the enumeration of life's four supreme values: *kāma* (love), *artha* (wealth), *dharma* (morality), and *mokṣa* (liberation). In broader terms yet, the addition of the fourth stage of life is another effort to encompass, by means of *dharma,* both contingent reality and transcendent or ultimate value. The synthesis corresponds to the contemporaneous drive to ground *dharma* in Veda as transcendent authority (*prāmaṇa*). Both types of synthesis may have been historic reactions to the challenges of heterodoxy (Buddhism, Jainism), or more specifically, the threat that the quietist or monastic life (*nivṛtti*) posed to the pursuit of active engagement (*pravṛtti*) in social life. Hence, in Manu both *nivṛtti* and *pravṛtti* are regarded as domains of *dharma,* and the fourth stage of life (*saṃnyāsa*) is fully integrated into the *āśramadharma.* In a different vein, the roughly contemporary *Bhagavadgītā* resolves the tension between meditative inactivity and *varṇa* duty (*svadharma*) by postulating yet other integrative concepts—devotion (*bhakti*) to God (Kṛṣṇa) and selfless action.

DHARMA, TIME, AND SOCIAL REFORM. The *dharma* texts, which tipped their hats to the eternal Veda as their eternal source of authority (in theory), contained several rules of conduct that later communities were bound to find unworthy of their values. A small number of hermeneutic and ideological devices were constructed either by the compilers of *dharma* texts or by subsequent theorists to admit changes into an ostensibly immutable tradition. Chief among these were the doctrines of *Kālī-varjyas* (rules unfit for the Kālī age) and *āpaddharma* (rules for time of emergency). But additional techniques included the Mīmāṃṣā distinction between injunctive text (*vidhi*) and mere explanatory passages (*arthavāda*), as well as the concept of *loka-vidviṣṭa*—norms that are odious to the public despite their origin in *dharma* texts.

The *dharma* literature does not provide more than a few dozen explicit examples of exceptions to the immutability of *dharma.* But the principle is familiar and prestigious, and so it may be invoked to substantiate legal and social reforms when the time is right. The most notorious examples among the fifty or so *Kālī-varjya* rules are the prohibitions against *nīyoga*—the pairing of a childless widow with her deceased husband's brother, the remarriage of widowed virgins, eating meat, or killing a *brāhmaṇa* aggressor (in self-defense) (Kāne, 1968–1975, vol. 3, pp. 930–968). The rules of *āpaddharma* tend to loosen prohibitions against upper-caste freedom: A *brāhmaṇa* may study under a *kṣatriya,* upper-caste members may engage in low-caste professions (which are usually polluting), a *vaiśya* may lend money at interest, and, most notoriously, a high-caste Hindu may steal and eat polluting meat. This latter case is illustrated in the famous story of Viśvāmitra who stole dog meat from a *caṇḍāla* (untouchable) during time of drought and famine (Manu 10.108; *Mahābhārata* 12.141.90), as well as in the lesser-known stories of Uṣati Cakrāyaṇa and, earliest of all, Vāmadeva (*Ṛgveda* 4.18.13).

Like the ranking of the four sources of *dharma,* these concepts were intended to situate law and ethics in the historic and contingent world while preserving *dharma*'s authority as grounded in Veda. However, when pressure for reform began to build up under Anglo-Indian courts in the nineteenth century, these devices were seldom explicitly invoked by either reformers or conservatives, although they occasionally figured in substance. The abolition of *satī* (widow burning), known as the Bengal Satī Regulation of 1829, was the first major case to test the Dharmaśāstra and the judicial autonomy given by the British to Hindu law in modern times. Reformers claimed that *satī* did not originate in *smṛti* (authoritative tradition—Dharmasūtras and Dharmaśāstras) but in custom, and that it was "revolting to the feelings of human nature." The opponents of reform appealed both to *smṛti* (although the texts were sharply divided on the matter) and to the sanctity of "immemorial" practice in matters of religious belief. In other words, both sides appealed to the prestige invested in the hierarchy of the four sources of *dharma,* but the reformers also introduced the matter of *loka-vidviṣṭa.* Similar legal battles followed (for instance, the Caste Removal of Disabilities Act of 1850; the Hindu Widow Remarriage Act XV of 1856). In the case of widow remarriage, the opponents of reform appealed to the *Kālī-varjya* principle as showing that precisely because the Kālī age was morally depraved: widows, even the very young and virgins, should not be allowed to remarry. These conservatives showed that the principle of overriding positive legal rules could be used as a tool for protecting the status quo and not only for reform. The reformers, as usual, argued that the rule they wished to reform was not Sastric but rooted in custom, and that the change promoted social morality by enshrining what the British called "equity." Backed by British courts and power, reformers consistently won the legal battles, but social practice was far slower to change.

Due to the fact that Hindu *dharma* has always encompassed religious, social, and juridical matters, twentieth-century legislation has been strongly shaped by the culture of *dharma.* The social and legislative battles of the nineteenth century continue to influence various aspects of Hindu law today in topics such as marriage, succession, adoption, guardianship, caste law, and minority rights. In other words, conflicting interpretations of *dharma* still effect social policy in India today. Moreover, the question of *dharma* has spilled out of the courtroom and legislature to become part of a far more impassioned ideological contest over what constitutes Hindu consciousness (*Hindutva*) in the face of competing values such as feminism, social equality, and religious pluralism.

The concept of *sanātanadharma,* which both conservatives and liberals now often equate with normative Hindu identity, emerged in the early years of the nineteenth century in response to Anglo-Indian social legislation. The orthodox opponents of Ram Mohan Roy (members of the Dharma Sabha) used it as an ideological response to the reformers' claim on the Veda as a source of equity and a blueprint for reform. *Sanātanadharma* thus became conflated with Hindu identity and national pride. This is how even such figures as Aurobindo Ghose and India's president-scholar Sarvepalli Radhakrishnan used the term. For social and religious conservatives, "*satīdharma*" could then be defended—as it is still defended in some nationalist circles today—as a voluntary affirmation of national and religious ideology by Hindu women of courage. And, although no one justifies dowry murders (the killing of brides whose dowry was deemed unsatisfactory), or the violence toward Dalits (scheduled castes, tribes) over matters of land or labor, the remedy for such tragedies has been complicated by the ideological contest over the meaning of *dharma* and the seemingly ageless conflation of religious and ethical discourse within matters of *dharma.*

SEE ALSO Karman, article on Hindu and Jain Concepts; Śāstra Literature; Sūtra Literature; Varṇa and Jāti; Vedas.

BIBLIOGRAPHY

Primary Sources

Bhattacharya, Bhabatosh, trans. *Daṇḍaviveka of Vardhamāna Upādhyāya.* Calcutta, 1973.

Derrett, J. Duncan M., trans. *Bhāruci's Commentary on the Manusmṛti.* 2 vols. Wiesbaden, Germany, 1975.

Doniger, Wendy, and Brian Smith, trans. *The Laws of Manu.* Harmondsworth, U.K., 1991.

Gharpure, J. R., trans. *Hindu Law Texts: Yājñavalkya Smṛti with Commentaries by Vijñāneśvara, Mitra-miśra, and Śūlapāṇi.* 7 vols. Bombay, 1936–1942.

Mandlik, Vishwanath Narayan, ed. and trans. *Vyavahāra Mayūkha.* New Delhi, 1982.

Olivelle, Patrick, ed. and trans. *Rules and Regulations of Brahmanical Asceticism: Yatidharmasamuccaya of Yādava Prakāśa.* Albany, N.Y., 1995.

Olivelle, Patrick, trans. *The Dharmasūtras: The Law Codes of Āpastamba, Gautama, Baudhāyana, and Vasiṣṭha.* New York, 1999.

Critical Studies

Creel, Austin. *Dharma in Hindu Ethics.* Calcutta, 1977. A detailed and systematic ethical analysis of *dharma.*

Derrett, J. Duncan M. *Religion, Law, and the State in India.* New York, 1968.

Gupta, Ram Chandra. *The Wonder That Is Hindu Dharma.* Delhi, 1987. A close and textually detailed study of *dharma* in a variety of legal, religious, and social contexts.

Kāne, Pānduranga Vāmana. *History of Dharmaśāstra.* 2d ed. 5 vols. Poona, India, 1968–1975. A monumental historical and textual study of *dharma,* both in its narrower senses and more broadly as the ritual and scriptural traditions of ancient India.

Lingat, Robert. *The Classical Law of India.* Translated by J. Duncan M. Derrett. Berkeley, Calif., 1973. A clear and concise introduction to *dharma* as legal tradition and as religious ideology in history.

Narang, Sudesh, Urmi B. Gupta, and Urmila Rustagi, eds. *Dharmaśāstra in Contemporary Times.* Delhi, 1988. Collection of essays linking Dharmaśāstra to social and legal issues in recent decades.

O'Flaherty, Wendy, and J. Duncan M. Derrett. *The Concept of Duty in South Asia.* New Delhi, 1978. Studies by several scholars on the religious and philosophical aspects of *dharma.*

Olivelle, Patrick. *The Āśrama System: The History and Hermeneutics of a Religious Institution.* New York, 1993.

Saraswati, Baidyanath. *Thinking about Tradition: The Indian Vision.* Varanasi (Banaras), India, 1988. Analytical and normative essay on the meaning of *dharma* as tradition.

Sternbach, Ludwik. *Juridical Studies in Ancient Indian Law.* 2 vols. Delhi, 1965–1967.

Weinberger-Thomas, Catherine. *Ashes of Immortality: Widow-Burning in India.* Translated by Jeffrey Mehlman and David Gordon White. Chicago, 1999. Phenomenological and historical study of *satī* ideology.

ARIEL GLUCKLICH (2005)

DHARMA: BUDDHIST DHARMA AND DHARMAS

The pan-Indian term *dharma* (from the Sanskrit root *dhṛ,* "to sustain, to hold"; Pali, *dhamma;* Tib., *chos*) has acquired a variety of meanings and interpretations in the course of many centuries of Indian religious thought. Buddhism shares this term and some of its meanings with other Indian religions, but at the same time it has provided a set of unique and exclusive interpretations of its own. *Dharma* can imply many different meanings in various contexts and with reference to different things. Here we shall consider it under two general headings: the first as *dharma* in a general sense, comprising a variety of meanings, and the second as *dharma*(s) in a technical sense, denoting the ultimate constituents or elements of the whole of the existing reality.

GENERAL USAGES. *Dharma* was and still is employed by all the religious denominations that have originated in India to indicate their religious beliefs and practices. In this sense, *dharma* refers broadly to what we would term "religion." *Dharma* also designates the universal order, the natural law or the uniform norm according to which the whole world (*saṃsāra*) runs its course. Within the Buddhist context this universal order is coordinated in the doctrine of dependent origination (*pratītya-samutpāda*). This rigorous natural law, which controls the sequence of events and the behavior and acts of beings, has no cause or originator. It is beginningless and functions of its own nature. It is said in the *Aṅguttara Nikāya* and the *Saṃyutta Nikāya,* and later rephrased in the *Laṅkāvatāra Sūtra,* that the nature of things is such that the causal law as the inevitable determination of *karman* continues to evolve spontaneously whether or not the *tathāgata*s appear in this world. It is an inherent and all-pervading law that does not depend for its existence on the appearance of the Buddhas, whose mission in this world is merely to reveal it. Śākyamuni Buddha first perceived and understood this fundamental law and then proclaimed and explained it to his followers. The discovery of the nature of *dharma* is compared in some sūtras to the discovery of an old and forgotten city. In the Mahāyāna, especially within the context of the doctrine of the three Buddha bodies (*trikāya*) and the reinterpretation of the relationship between *saṃsāra* and *nirvāṇa* as two aspects of the same reality, *dharma* as the universal norm received a wider and deeper interpretation. As a part of the compound *dharmakāya,* it signifies both the immanent and transcendental reality of all beings and appearances. Thus, it clearly denotes the essence of sentient beings as well as the nature of the Buddhas. In the sense of denoting phenomenal existence, it is also referred to as reality (*dharmatā*), the essence of reality (*dharmadhātu*), suchness (*tathatā*), emptiness (*śūnyatā*), or store-consciousness (*ālaya-vijñāna*). In the sense of referring to the nature of the buddhas, it is known as buddhahood (*buddhatā*), as the self-nature of the buddhas (*buddhasvabhāva*), or as the womb of the buddhas (*tathāgata-garbha*).

Dharma as the Buddha's teaching or doctrine as a whole comprises his exposition of the universal order of nature as described above and his proclamation of the path toward deliverance. Thus, when his teaching is meant as a whole system it is the term *dharma* (or *śāsana*) that is employed. When his teachings are referred to or explained from two different angles, that is, when theoretical and practical aspects are differentiated, two terms are employed: *dharma,* as a body of religio-philosophical discourses as contained in the Sūtras, and Vinaya, or monastic discipline, the rules and regulations for the application and practice of *dharma.* The Prātimokṣa (monastic code) contains rules of conduct, each of which is also called *dharma.*

The shortest and yet the clearest exposition of *dharma* as the Buddha's word (*buddhavacana*) is epitomized in Śākyamuni's first sermon, when he "set in motion" (i.e., proclaimed) the wheel (lore) of *dharma:* the four noble truths and eightfold noble path. There is suffering and it has a cause that can be eliminated through the knowledge and practice of the path of *dharma* as summarized by the Eightfold Noble Path: right views, right conduct, and so forth. Another presentation of the same path is articulated within the basic trilogy of monastic practice of cultivating wisdom (*prajñā*), morality (*śīla*), and meditation (*dhyāna*). Through wisdom one acquires a full vision of *dharma,* through morality one purifies all that obscures the vision of *dharma,* and through meditation one matures *dharma* within oneself and indeed transforms oneself into an epitome of *dharma.*

Dharma denotes truth, knowledge, morality, and duty. It is the truth about the state and function of the world, the truth about how to eliminate its evil tendencies, and the truth about its immutable spiritual potentiality. It is knowledge in the sense that once one becomes aware of *dharma* one acquires the knowledge to become free from the bonds of phenomenal existence. It is morality, for it contains a code of moral conduct that conduces to spiritual purification and maturation. It is duty, for whoever professes *dharma* has a duty to comply with its norms and to achieve the goal that it sets forth. In this sense there is only one duty in Buddhism: the ceaseless and constant effort to strive for *nirvāṇa.*

Dharma, together with the Buddha and the *saṃgha,* constitute a "threefold jewel" (*triratna*) before which one makes prostrations and in which one takes refuge. Here *dharma* does not so much represent a body of teachings as it assumes a character of awesomeness, protection, and deliverance wholly appropriate to the Truth. One stands in awe of *dharma* as a self-sustained righteousness whose universal legacy is to protect through its righteousness those who profess it. Soon after his enlightenment, realizing that there is no one more perfect than himself in virtue, wisdom, and meditation under whom he could live in obedience and reverence, Śākyamuni decided that he would live honoring and revering *dharma,* the universal truth he had just realized. As one of the Three Jewels, the Buddha is *dharma*'s embodied personification, revealer, and teacher. The *saṃgha* constitutes a body of *dharma*'s followers among whom *dharma* thrives as the norm of daily life, becoming an inspiration and a path to deliverance. The Three Jewels as conceived in the early period can be paralleled, as a somewhat general compar-ison, with the later concept of the three buddha bodies. *Dharma* as *dharmakāya* represents its own sublime and absolute aspect, the Buddha as a *saṃbhogakāya* represents the pure and glorified state of *dharma*, and the *saṃgha* as *nirmāṇakāya* represents *dharma* as discovered and operating within the world.

TECHNICAL USAGES. The strictly technical meaning of *dharmas* as ultimate elements or principles of existence as systematized in the Abhidharma literature, especially in the Abhidharma works of the Sarvāstivāda school, is not so distinct or rigidly formulated in the four Nikāyas (Āgamas). In the sūtras of the four Nikāyas we find many descriptions of *dharmas* and their various classifications, but their systematization into what we could call "*dharma* theory" took place within the Abhidharma literature. Thus, in the Nikāyas *dharmas* are usually characterized as good or bad with reference to ethical conduct, but receive little attention as coherent metaphysical or epistemological systems. The *Dasuttara Sutta* enumerates some 550 *dharmas* to be cultivated or abandoned. The *Saṅgīti Sutta* gives an even larger number of them, and the *Mahāparinibbāna Suttanta* lists some 1,011 *dharmas*. In this latter work we also find a set of *dharmas* that Śākyamuni ascertained to be for the benefit of living beings. These include the thirty-seven *bodhipakṣya dharmas* that constitute the thirty-seven practices and principles conducive to the attainment of enlightenment.

Rather than providing further examples from the sūtras I propose now to concentrate on describing the *dharma* theory of the Sarvāstivāda school. Within its systematized presentation one finds practically all the important aspects of *dharmas* and their role; the variant interpretations of other schools will be mentioned wherever appropriate.

Buddhism makes an emphatic and "dogmatic" statement that a "soul" (*ātman*) as interpreted by non-Buddhist schools in India does not exist. By denying the existence of a soul as a permanent and unifying factor of a human entity it has removed all grounds for asserting the permanency of the human entity or the existence of any indestructible element therein. With reference to the substantiality of physical things it has removed the concept of substance and replaced it by modalities: there is no substance but only the appearances of what we call substances or things. Having removed the notion of substance Buddhism has construed an explanation as to how this world functions. According to this explanation, the universe is seen as a flux of *dharmas*, the smallest elements or principles of which it consists, but this flux is not merely a flux of incoherent motion or change. On the contrary, the world evolves according to the strict law of dependent origination (*pratītya-samutpāda*).

This universal flux can be conveniently viewed, for the moment, at three simultaneous and interrelated levels. If we take the inanimate world (matter) alone, it flows in accordance with a uniformly homogeneous and natural law of change. Similarly, the organic world (vegetation) flows according to its own uniform evolution of natural life (germination, growth, etc.). The third level is constituted by sentient life. This last one, apart from comprehending the other levels (matter and organic functions), includes a sentient element (consciousness or mind) as well. In general, we can say that it includes material as well as immaterial elements. Such sentient life, in which the material and immaterial elements are tied together, evolves or flows according to the strict law of causality as decreed in the causal nexus of dependent origination. Furthermore, this constant flux of sentient life coordinated by the law of dependent origination has a moral law superimposed upon it: the "law" of *karman*. It is with regard to such a flux that the *dharma* theory attempts to provide an explanation. There is no substance or person but there are *dharmas* (psychophysical elements) that flow according to the law of dependent origination that is set in motion by the law of *karman*. Basically, the *dharma* theory provides an explanation of how the universe functions within the context of a sentient life, in particular a human flux, for it is human life that Buddhism is concerned with. *Dharma* theory constitutes then not so much an explanation of what the universe is as it does an attempt to describe of what it consists and how it functions. Thus, in the detailed enumeration of *dharmas* as basic and infinitesimal elements that constitute the conglomeration of the universe we find an analysis of human life and its destiny. But this analysis is not "Buddhist psychology," as many call it; it is an exposition of both the constant and inevitably coordinated flux of phenomena and the inherent potentiality of bringing this flux to a halt.

I shall now describe some general classifications of *dharmas* (again, after the Sarvāstivāda Abhidharma). *Dharmas* are divided into conditioned (*saṃskṛta*) and unconditioned (*asaṃskṛta*). The conditioned *dharmas* (seventy-two in all) comprise all the elements of phenomenal existence (*saṃsāra*). They are called conditioned because by their nature and in their flow they cooperate in and are subject to the law of causality; they conglomerate or cooperate in the production of life (*pṛhagjana*). The unconditioned elements (three in all) are those that are not subject to the law that governs phenomenal existence. *Dharmas* are also divided into those that are influenced or permeated by negative tendencies or depravities (*āsrava;* in a moral sense, bad *karmas*) and those that are not under the influence of depravities (*anāsrava;* morally, good *karmas*). These are the same *dharmas* as in the previous classification but here they are viewed from two aspects: when they are influenced chiefly by ignorance (*avidyā*) their flux has the tendency to perpetuate itself; when they are under the influence of intuitive wisdom (*prajñā*) they acquire the tendency toward appeasement or tranquillity. By their nature the unconditioned *dharmas* must be classed among the *dharmas* that are not under the influence of depravities. We should recall here that the chief characteristic of *saṃsāra* is motion or unrest, *duḥkha*, and that of *nirvāṇa* is tranquillity, *nirodha*. The *dharmas* can be also divided in relationship to the four truths. Here again we have a twofold division. The first two truths (unrest, *duḥkha*, and its cause, *samudaya*) refer to the seventy-two *dharmas* that are permeated by depravities or that are conditioned. The two other truths (rest, *nirodha*, and the means to it, *mārga*) refer to the three unconditioned *dharmas* that are always at rest (*nirodha*) and to the *dharmas* that are on the way (*mārga*) to become extinguished (*nirodha*).

Having described the general divisions I shall now proceed to list a set of three standard classifications within which individual *dharmas* are distributed. The first classification, which includes the conditioned *dharmas* alone, refers to their grouping as perceived in a sentient life. This classification divides *dharmas* into five aggregates or *skandhas*. Here we have (1) matter or body (*rūpaskandha*): eleven *dharmas*; (2) feelings, sensations, or emotions (*vedanāskandha*): one *dharma*; (3) perceptions (*saṃjñāskandha*): one *dharma;* (4) impulses or will-forces (*saṃskāraskandha*): fifty-eight *dharmas*; (5) consciousness or mind (*vijñānaskandha*): one *dharma.* This division into five *skandhas* not only constitutes an analysis of all phenomena but also serves to prove that there is no soul (*ātman*) in a human entity, for none of the five *skandhas* can be identified with or regarded as a soul.

The second classification divides *dharmas* with reference to the process of cognition. Here we have the six sense organs (*indriya*) and the six sense objects (*viṣaya*) jointy called the "bases" or "foundations" (*āyatana*) of cognition. The six sense organs or internal bases are (1) sense of vision (*cakṣur-indriyāyatana*); (2) sense of hearing (*śrotra-*); (3) sense of smell (*ghrāna-*); (4) sense of taste (*jihvā-*); (5) sense of touch (*kāya-*); and (6) consciousness or intellectual faculty (*mana-*). The six sense objects or external bases are (7) color and form (*rūpa-āyatana*); (8) sound (*śabda-*); (9) smell (*gandha-*); (10) taste (*rasa-*); (11) contact (*spraṣṭavya-*); and (12) nonsensuous or immaterial objects (*dharma-*). The first eleven *āyatanas* have one *dharma* each; the immaterial objects comprise sixty-four *dharmas*.

The third classification groups *dharmas* in relationship to the flow (*santāna*) of life that evolves within the threefold world (*kāma-*, *rūpa-*, and *ārūpya-dhātu*) as described by Buddhist cosmology. This group is divided into eighteen *dhātus*, or elements. It incorporates the previous division into the twelve bases, to which is added a corresponding set of six kinds of consciousness to the intellectual faculty. Thus we have (13) visual consciousness (*cakṣur-vijñānadhātu*); (14) auditory consciousness (*śrotra-*); (15) olfactory consciousness (*ghrāṇa-*); (16) gustatory consciousness (*jihvā-*); (17) tactile consciousness (*kāya-*); and (18) nonsensuous consciousness (*mano-*). Within this group the five sense organs and their five objects contain one *dharma* each (ten *dharmas* in all). Consciousness (no. 6) is divided here into seven *dhātus* (no. 6 plus 13–18). The *dhātu* that represents immaterial objects (no. 12) contains sixty-four *dharmas*. All the eighteen *dhātus* exist in the sensuous world (*kāmadhātu*) or the world in which the mind operates through the sense data. In the world of refined matter (*rūpadhātu*), the objects of smell and taste (nos. 9–10) and the olfactory and gustatory consciousnesses cease to exist. In the world without matter (but frequently interpreted as very subtle matter for we are still within *saṃsāra*) all the *dhātus* cease to exist except for consciousness (no. 6), its immaterial objects (no. 12), and its nonsensuous aspect of cognition (no. 18).

Now at last we come to enumerate the individual *dharmas*. Within the classification into the five *skandhas*, matter (*rūpa*) contains eleven *dharmas*: five sense organs (*āyatanas* 1–5) and their five corresponding sense objects (*āyatanas* 7–11), plus an additional element to be discussed below. *Āyatana* (*dhātu*) number 12 (nonsensuous objects) is in this system classified as an immaterial *dharma*, as we shall see, and hence is not considered here.

Matter or body is conceived as consisting of the four primary elements (*mahābhūtas*)—earth, water, fire, and air. Secondary or refined matter (*bhautika*, derived from or related to matter) is represented by the senses and their objects (i.e., sense data). As already mentioned above, there is no substance as such. The four primary elements are talked about in Buddhism, but rightly understood these are taken to refer to properties: hardness (earth), cohesion (water), heat (fire), and motion (wind). The primary matter (four elements) present in a body sustains the secondary matter (the senses and their objects). Since the Buddhists analyze matter within the context of a sentient life, their description of matter is mainly concerned with discerning how it functions and how it appears, not with what it is, for properly speaking it does not exist. The world is in constant flux, the living life changes from one moment to the next. Consequently, because Buddhists are constrained from speaking in terms of soul or substance, matter is styled as sense data alone. Such a definition of the physical *dharmas* that constitute the sense data (ten *dharmas*) accounts for the component of matter that sustains consciousness, the other component of sentient life. What then is the eleventh *dharma*?

The Sarvāstivāda, viewing the human personality as a threefold aspect of body, speech, and mind, divided *karman* (as it operates within a sentient life) into mental action (*manas*, identified with volition, or *cetanā*) and physical and vocal actions. Mental action was classed as immaterial but physical and vocal actions that proceed from mental action were classed as belonging to matter (*rūpaskandha*). Furthermore, physical and vocal action was seen as being an (external) "expression" (*vijñapti*), but when mental action was committed but not externalized its "material" concomitant was seen as "nonexpression" (*avijñapti*). It is the latter "unexpressed matter" (*avijñaptirūpa*) that constitutes the eleventh *dharma* among the *skandha* division. Although immaterial, it was classed as matter because physical and vocal action with which it was associated was classed as such.

Three *skandhas* (feelings, perceptions, and impulses) contain jointly sixty *dharmas*, which are included as immaterial objects within the two other (*āyatana*, *dhātu*) classifications (no. 12 in both). The three immutable elements (*asaṃskṛta*) and *avijñapti* are also included among the immaterial *dharmas* of these two latter divisions, thus making a total of sixty-four *dharmas*.

Now I shall describe the sixty *dharmas* that are included in all three classifications (*skandha*, *āyatana*, and *dhātu*). They are divided into two main groups: one group comprises forty-six associated *dharmas* or mental *dharmas* (*caittadharma*), that arise from or in association with pure consciousness or mind (*citta-saṃprayuk-tasaṃskāra*); the second group comprises fourteen unassociated *dharmas*, that is to say, *dharmas* that can be associated neither with matter nor with mind (*rūpa-citta-viprayukta-saṃskāra*).

The forty-six associated *dharmas* include ten mental *dharmas* that are present in a sentient life (*citta-mahābhūmika*): (1) feeling, (2) perception, (3) will, (4) contact, (5) desire, (6) comprehension, (7) memory, (8) attention, (9) aspiration, and (10) concentration; ten morally good (*kuśala-mahābhūmika*) *dharmas* that are present in favorable conditions: (11) faith, (12) courage, (13) equanimity, (14) modesty, (15) aversion to evil, (16) detachment from love, (17) detachment from hatred, (18) nonviolence, (19) dexterity, and (20) perseverence in good; six obscuring (*kleśa-mahābhūmika*) *dharmas* that enter the stream of a sentient life in unfavorable moments: (21) confusion (ignorance), (22) remissness, (23) mental dullness, (24) lack of faith, (25) indolence, and (26) addiction to pleasure; ten additional obscuring (*upakleśa-bhūmika*) *dharmas* that may occur at different times: (27) anger, (28) hypocrisy, (29) maliciousness, (30) envy, (31) ill-motivated rivalry, (32) violence, (33) malice, (34) deceit, (35) treachery, and (36) self-gratification; two universally inauspicious (*akuśala-mahabhūmika*) *dharmas*: (37) irreverence, and (38) willful tolerance of offences; and eight *dharmas* that are called undetermined (*aniyata-bhūmika*) or undifferentiated in the sense that they can have different moral implications: (39) remorse, (40) deliberation, (41) investigation, (42) determination, (43) passion, (44) hatred, (45) pride, and (46) doubt. All forty-six *dharmas* listed above cannot be associated with (or cofunction with) consciousness at the same time on the general principle that their inner inclinations are variously geared toward either good or evil.

The fourteen unassociated *dharmas* are (47) acquisition (*prāpti*), or the controlling force of an individual flux of life, (48) force (*aprāpti*) that suspends some elements, (49) force of homogeneity of existence, (50) force that leads to trance, (51) force produced by effort to enter trance, (52) force that stops consciousness, thus effecting the highest trance, (53) force that projects life's duration, (54) origination, (55) duration, (56) decay, (57) extinction, (58) force that imparts meaning to words, (59) force that imparts meaning to sentences, and (60) force that imparts meaning to sounds.

Pure consciousness or mind constitutes one *dharma* (fifth *skandha*, sixth *āyatana*). In the division into *dhātus vijñāna* is, as it were, subdivided among seven *dhātus* (no. 6 plus 13–18) where the same consciousness is viewed in relation to the sense organs and immaterial objects.

Adding all the conditioned *dharmas* together yields eleven material *dharmas*, one *dharma* representing consciousness, forty-six associated *dharmas*, and fourteen unassociated *dharmas*—seventy-two in all. These are the *dharmas* into which the whole of phenomenal existence is analyzed and which account for all events that take place within it.

The Sarvāstivāda also enumerate three unconditioned *dharmas*: space (*ākāśa*), emancipation through discerning knowledge (*pratisaṃkhyānirodha*), and emancipation through nondiscerning knowledge (*apratisaṃkhyā-nirodha*). Thus, the total of *dharmas* both conditioned and unconditioned amounts to seventy-five in the Sarvāstivāda school.

The Theravāda tradition enumerates only one unconditioned *dharma* (*nirvāṇa*) and eighty-one conditioned *dharmas*: four primary elements; four secondary elements; five sense organs; five sense objects; two aspects of sex (male and female); heart as the sustaining element of psychic life; two kinds (bodily and vocal) of *avijñaptirūpa;* a psychic vitality of matter; space; three properties (agility, elasticity, and pliability) of body; three characteristics (origination, duration, and decay) of conditioned *dharmas*; material food; fifty-two mental elements, including twenty-five wholesome, fourteen unwholesome, and thirteen morally neutral elements; and consciousness.

The Sarvāstivāda asserted that all the conditioned *dharmas* are real (they exist for they happen) and that they have the characteristic of coming into existence, lasting for a short period, and disappearing again in order to reappear in a new karmically determined formation. They also maintained that *dharmas* exist in all three times: past, present, and future.

The Lokottaravāda school, a Mahāsāṃghika subsect, treated all the conditioned *dharmas* as unreal and held that only the unconditioned *dharmas* are real. The Prajñaptivāda school, another Mahāsāṃghika group, argued that the twelve *āyatanas* are not real because they are the products of the *skandhas*, which are the only real entities. The Sautrāntikas admitted the existence of thought but rejected the reality of the majority of the associated and all the unassociated *dharmas*, denied the reality of the past and future, and maintained that only the present exists. They also rejected the existence of the unconditioned *dharmas*, considering them mere denominations of absence. The Mādhyamika school rejected the ultimate reality of *dharmas* altogether. The Vijñānavāda school recognized mind as the only reality (*cittamātra*) and treated the whole of phenomenal existence as its illusive projection. Finally, a well-known Buddhist formula (*ye dharmā hetuprabhavā*, etc.) expresses the soteriological aspect associated with the analysis of sentient beings in terms of *dharmas*: "Whatever events arise from a cause, the Tathāgata has foretold their cause, and the Great Hermit has also explained their cessation."

SEE ALSO Buddhist Philosophy; Four Noble Truths; Karman, article on Buddhist Concepts; Mādhyamika; Nirvāṇa; Pratītya-samutpāda; Sarvāstivāda; Sautrāntika; Soteriology; Soul, article on Buddhist Concepts; Yogācāra.

BIBLIOGRAPHY

The *dharma* theory of the Sarvāstivādins is systematically set forth in Vasubandhu's *Abhidharmakośa*, translated by Louis de La

Vallée Poussin as *L'Abhidharmakośa de Vasubandhu*, 6 vols. (1923–1931; reprint, Brussels, 1971). Theodore Stcherbatsky's *The Central Conception of Buddhism and the Meaning of the Word "Dharma"* (1923; reprint, Delhi, 1970) is a lucid introduction to the topic. For the Theravāda view, see especially *A Buddhist Manual of Psychological Ethics: Dhammasangani*, translated by C. A. F. Rhys Davids (London, 1923), a rendering of the first book of the Theravāda Abhidharma. Ñyāṇatiloka's *Guide through the Abhidhamma Pitaka*, 3d ed., revised and enlarged by Ñyāṇatiloka Thera (Colombo, 1957), is the single most useful guide to the study of the Theravāda Abhidhamma. The reader will also find useful A. K. Warder's "Dharmas and Data," *Journal of Indian Philosophy* 1 (1971): 272–295.

New Sources

Bhuti, Tsewang. "Klong rdol bla ma's List of 108 Dharmas of Prajnaparamita and the Commentary." *Tibet Journal* 25, no. 3 (2000): 48–68.

Cox, C. *Disputed Dharmas, Early Buddhist Theories on Existence: An Annotated Translation of the Section of Factors Dissociated from Thought from Sanghabhadra's Nyayanusara.* Tokyo, 1995.

Dessein, Bart. "Dharmas Associated with Awarenesses and the Dating of the Sarvastivada Abhidharma Works." *Asiatische Studien* 50, no. 3 (1996): 623–651.

Frauwallner, E., S. F. Kidd, and E. Steinkellner. *Studies in Abhidharma Literature and the Origins of Buddhist Philosophical Systems.* Albany, 1995.

Ganguly, S. *Treatise on Groups of Elements: The Abhidharmadhatukaya-padasastra: English Translation of Hsüan-tsang's Chinese Version.* Delhi, 1994.

Mejor, M. *Vasubandhu's Abhidharmakosa and the Commentaries Preserved in the Tanjur.* Stuttgart, 1991.

TADEUSZ SKORUPSKI (1987)
Revised Bibliography

DHARMAKĪRTI (c. 600–660), Buddhist philosopher of South Indian origin, pupil of Īśvarasena, and teacher at Nālānda. Dharmakīrti's thought brings the tradition of Buddhist epistemology and logic as founded by Dignāga (c. 480–540) to its culmination and final accomplishment.

Dharmakīrti's philosophical work consists of seven treatises still extant either in the original Sanskrit or in Tibetan translation. Dharmakīrti's stated intention was to give an explanation of Dignāga's ideas, and tradition accepted his explanation as such. His works, however, surpassed those of the earlier philosopher to become the basis for the study of this tradition by later Indian and Tibetan Buddhists. His first major work, *Pramāṇavārttika* (Commentary on the means of valid cognition), is a verse text in four chapters. The first chapter, "On Inference," was written with a prose commentary, thus constituting his earliest work, and was only later joined with the other chapters, "Establishment of the Means of Valid Cognition," "On Perception," and "On Proof." The *Pramāṇaviniścaya* (Analytical determination of the means of valid cognition), contains chapters on perception, on inference, and on proof, and is the final formulation of Dharmakīrti's epistemological and logical thought in mixed verse and prose. For its clarity in structure, presentation, argument, and verbal expression, it is a masterpiece of Indian scholarly literature. In what is largely an excerpt of the latter work, the *Nyāyabindu* (A drop of logical argumentation), Dharmakīrti gives a succinct *sūtra*-like formulation of his epistemology.

The *Hetubindu* (A drop of logical reason) examines logical reason, negative cognition, and causality. The *Vādanyāya* (The rule for disputations), his last work, attempts to apply the new logical theory to the dialectical practice. Dharmakīrti refuted solipsism in his *Santānāntarasiddhi* (A proof of other mental continuities) and rejected the reality of relations in *Sambandhaparīkṣā* (Examination of Relation).

Most of Dharmakīrti's thought is devoted to epistemological and logical themes. In its context, this must be understood as an attempt to establish a philosophical foundation of meaningful everyday and Buddhist practice. For Dharmakīrti, valid cognitions can be established only with regard to the Buddha, who—himself a means of valid cognition—can provide the motifs and goals of all human actions that are the frame of judgment necessary to differentiate the validity or invalidity of cognitions. At the same time, perception and inference, the two kinds of valid cognition, can be used to demonstrate that the Buddha is the only conceivable source from which we can derive such advice.

In the field of logic, Dharmakīrti overcomes the formal character of Dignāga's theory, in which only three forms or characteristics of logical reason are formulated as the necessary conditions of logical certainty, by giving an ontological explanation for such certainty. According to this explanation, concepts are related to each other only when they refer to the same real entity or to an entity caused by that referred to by the other concept. The necessary logical relation is thus based on a relation of real identity or of causality. Consequently, only such concepts may be used as logical reasons (*hetu*) that are either "essential properties" (*svabhāva*), "effect" (*kārya*), that is, concepts referring to something as the effect of something else, or "non-perception of something perceivable" (*dṛśyānupalabdhi*).

Dharmakīrti's theory of concepts (*apoha*) explains a concept as the difference from other things that is common to individual entities. Lacking any principle of unity, absolutely different individual entities nonetheless cause the same judgments precisely on account of such experience of them that differs from experience of others. The resultant concept is nothing real, but by recourse to experience and practice there is nevertheless a relation between reality and the false realm of linguistic constructs of varying degrees of reliability. While perception is a direct valid cognition of what is real, inference is an indirect valid cognition, since it is conceptual by nature and must be gained under strict control by means of logical reason (*hetu*). Concepts that may be used as logical reasons serve to infer other concepts as necessarily true or to remove or correct wrong concepts. One of the most influential results of this new logical theory is a new form of the inference of universal momentary destruction (*kṣaṇikatva*) in which Dharmakīrti derives it from the concept of being (*sattvānumāna*), thereby offering a new method for establishing the first of the four noble truths, "All is suffering."

SEE ALSO Buddhist Philosophy.

BIBLIOGRAPHY

Stcherbatsky, Theodore. *Buddhist Logic* (1930–1932). Reprint, New York, 1962. An introduction to Buddhist logic, including many references to Dharmakīrti.

Steinkellner, Ernst, trans. *Dharmakīrti's Hetubinduḥ*, vol. 2. Vienna, 1967. German translation of the first Indian text on logic as such, including the important proof of momentariness as the essential character of being; also contains an elaborate discussion of causality and a theory of negative cognition.

Steinkellner, Ernst, trans. *Dharmakīrti's Pramāṇaviniścayaḥ*, vol. 2. *Kapitel: Svārthānumānam.* Vienna, 1979. A German translation of the chapter on inference that constitutes the essence of Dharmakīrti's logical thought.

Vetter, Tilmann. *Erkenntnisprobleme bei Dharmakīrti.* Vienna, 1964. A study of Dharmakīrti's theories of cognition, concepts, perception, and being.

Vetter, Tilmann, trans. *Dharmakīrti's Pramāṇaviniścayaḥ*, vol. l, *Kapitel: Pratyakṣam.* Vienna, 1966. Text and German translation of the chapter on perception, with an investigation of congition in general and the problem of extra-cognitional reality.

Vetter, Tilmann, trans. *Die Lehre des Buddha in Dharmakīrti's Pramāṇavārttika.* Vienna, 1984. German translation of a major part of the second chapter of the *Pramāṇavārttika.* Includes an introductory study of Dharmakīrti's presentation of the essence of Buddhist interpretation of reality and religiouspractice, providing the motifs, conditions, and purpose of epistemological theory.

New Sources

Jackson, Roger R. "Atheology and Buddhalogy in Dharmakirti's Pramanavarttika." *Faith and Philosophy* 16, no. 4 (1999): 472–505.

Namai, Chisho Mamoru. "Dharmakirti on Compassion and Rebirth." *Indo-Iranian Journal* 44, no. 1 (2001): 84–90.

Steinkellner, Ernst. "Kumarila, Isvarasena and Dharmakirti in Dialogue: A New Interpretation of Pramanavarttika I 33." *Bauddhavidyasudhakarah* (1997): 625–646.

ERNST STEINKELLNER (1987)
Revised Bibliography

DHARMAPĀLA (530–561), Indian Buddhist thinker associated with the Yogācāra school and founder of a Vijñānavāda ("consciousness only") tradition that was to become highly influential in the scholastic traditions of East Asian Buddhism. His numerous followers include Śīlabhadra, his successor as abbot of Nālandā and teacher of the famous Chinese monk Xuanzang (569–664). It was Xuanzang who introduced Dharmapāla's thought to China, where, under the name of Faxiang ("dharma characteristics"), it supplanted the traditions transmitted by Paramārtha (499–569) and Bodhiruci (d. 527) to become the dominant form of Yogācāra there. The Faxiang "school" was introduced to Japan beginning in the late seventh century by the monk Dōshō (629–710), enjoyed three subsequent transmissions, and, as the Hossō school (the Japanese pronunciation of the Chinese Faxiang), became perhaps the most eminent of the six scholastic traditions that flouished during the Nara period (710–784).

The eldest son of a minister in Kāñcīpuram, Dharmapāla became a Buddhist monk in his youth. He studied Buddhism at the Nālandā monastic university and later became its head. In several doctrinal debates Dharmapāla defeated philosophers representing both non-Buddhist and Buddhist (especially Hīnayāna) opinion. At twenty-nine, however, realizing that he was not destined to live long, he retired from his post at Nālandā to concentrate on writing. He died two years later. Despite the relative brevity of his career, Dharmapāla wrote a number of works, some of which are preserved in the Chinese canon. These include the *Guansuo yuan lun shi* (T.D. No. 1625), the *Cheng wei shi lun* (T.D. no. 1585), and the *Dasheng guang bolun shi lun* (T.D. no. 1571). The second of these, Xuanzang's translation of the *Vijñāptimātratāsiddhi*, a compilation of ten commentaries on Vasubandhu's *Triṃśika* (Thirty verses), includes a commentary by Dharmapāla's own hand. More than a mere gloss of the original text of Vasubandhu, however, Dharmapāla's commentary constitutes an original doctrinal treatise in its own right.

Unlike the Mādhyamika thinkers, who concentrated on the refutation of fallacies without explaining how the magic (i.e., the illusion, in Buddhist terms) of "self" should arise in every living being, Dharmapāla offered an intricate analysis of this process from the Yogācāra point of view. This analysis begins with an interpretation of causality, or "dependent co-origination" (*pratītya-samutpāda*): every action creates a pattern or potential for future action, just as in legal cases a single decision becomes a precedent for the future. The precedents, karmic residues in this case, are technically referred to as "seeds" (*bīja*), which are "deposited," as it were, in a "receptacle" or "store" consciousness, from which, under the proper conditions, they manifest themselves at some future time. The process by which actions "deposit" seeds in the subconscious is known as "impression" (*vāsāna*); the actualization of these seeds in the mental life of the being involved is known as "manifestation."

The accumulation of these numerous potentials suggests a division of labor between the storage function, the coordinating function, and the discriminating function. In Yogācāra thought, these functions represent concrete activities of different levels and types of consciousness, usually numbered eight in the system championed by Dharmapāla. The storage function is referred to as *ālaya-vijñāna* ("storehouse consciousness"). It is the *ālaya* that receives the *bījas* deposited by actions and as such functions as a karmic repository in which the continuity of past actions in the stream of an individual's lives is preserved. The coordinating function is called the "cognitive" center (*manas*); it serves to synchronize all the activities of mind so that they function as an integrated whole. It is the *manas* that, turning inward, fails to perceive that the *ālaya* essentially has no existence other than the seeds that it stores, and thus falsely imputes to the *ālaya* the permanence and unity of a self or *ātman*. Such a (false) belief in the existence of a self is traditionally regarded by Buddhists as the very source of suffering. Ordinary sentient beings (as opposed to Buddhas and very highly advanced *bodhisattvas*) are unaware of the actions of these two functions. *Ālaya* and *manas* thus constitute unconscious functions of mind.

The discriminating function is represented by the six types of consciousnesses of which we are all aware: the five senses and the thinking process itself (*mano-vijñāna*). These, like the *manas*, are ultimately the very creations, "evolutes," of the seeds stored in the *ālaya*, which manifest themselves under the proper causal conditions as our psychophysical "selves." What appears in consciousness, under this interpretation, is thus not an external reality but simply the products of previous actions and cognitions thrown into consciousness by the functioning of the *ālaya*. Thus the mind, which should be indivisible, is, in Dharmapāla's view, fundamentally fractured into subjective and objective components: that which is conscious and that which we are conscious of.

The interaction of the three functions, further complicated by the subject-object split, transforms the reality of the illusional existence of living beings. These functions are therefore referred to as the "three sources of transformation." What is usually called "self" is merely the "subject portion" of the *ālaya* as interpreted by the *manas*. Similarly, what is usually called the "external world" is the "object portion," a mere sense of externality. Whether or not there exists a world outside of consciousness is not at issue here: it is the sense of externality that obtains *within* consciousness that is the subject of Dharmapāla's analysis, for deliverance or enlightenment consists in realizing that the "self" and the "real" world are mere reifications, enforced in language, of consciousness.

Yogācāra analysis of reality, a term as ambiguous in Sanskrit as it is in English, thus must take into account the varying ways in which a thing may be construed as real. According to Yogācāra doctrine, a "triple nature" (*trisvabhāva*) is inherent in all things. First, there is the sense in which all things are mere constructs of mind, mental fabrications devoid of reality outside of the consciousness that creates them. This character of things is referred to as *parikalpita-lakṣaṇa* ("imaginary character"). Second, there is the sense in which things are dependently originated, devoid of any independent reality but "real" in the sense that they exist as part of a nexus of events that mutually condition and reinforce each other. This character of things is referred to as *paratantra-lakṣaṇa* ("dependent character"). Finally, things are characterized as "ultimately real" when viewed without the distortions of conceptualization. But what constitutes this "perfected character" (*pariniṣpanna-lakṣaṇa*) is precisely the "emptiness" (*śūnyatā*) of the thing, its *lack* of self-nature (*svabhāva*) or the "ultimate absence of a reality-in-its-own-right." Such a reality is also referred to as "suchness" (*tathatā*).

Dharmapāla's *Vijñāptimātratāsiddhi* was the subject of at least three major commentaries (T.D. nos. 1830, 1831, 1832) and a host of subcommentaries. Although Faxiang thought failed to survive the challenges posed by the creation of the new, more fully sinicized, Buddhist traditions of the Tang period (618–907), its doctrines were kept alive in the wide dissemination of the commentaries to the *Cheng wei shi lun*. In Japan, Hossō thought continues to this day to serve as part of the basic Buddhist training of scholars and clerics alike.

SEE ALSO Ālaya-vijñāna; Kuiji; Paramārtha; Tathatā; Vasubandhu; Xuanzang; Yogācāra.

BIBLIOGRAPHY

Fukaura Seibun. *Yuishikigaki kenkyū*. 2 vols. Kyoto, 1954.

Fukihara Akinobu. *Gohōshū yuishikikō*. Kyoto, 1954.

La Vallée Poussin, Louis de, ed. and trans. *Vijñāptimātratāsiddhi: La Siddhi de Hiuan-tsang*. 2 vols. Paris, 1928–1929.

Nakamura Hajime. "A Brief Survey of Japanese Studies on the Philosophical Schools of the Mahāyāna." *Acta Asiatica* 1 (1960): 67–88.

Radhakrishnan, Sarvepalli. *Indian Philosophy*, vol. 1. 2d ed. London, 1927. Dharmapāla's contributions to Buddhist thought are discussed in the chapter entitled "The Yogācāras."

Sharma, Chandradhar. *A Critical Survey of Indian Philosophy*. Livingston, N. J., 1971. For treatment of Dharmapāla, see chapters entitled "Vijñānavāda" and "Svatantra-Vijñānavāda."

Ueda, Yoshifumi. "Two Main Streams of Thought in Yogācāra Philosophy." *Philosophy East and West* 17 (1967): 155–165.

New Sources

Keenan, J. P., ed. *Dharmapalas's Yogacara Critique of Bhavaviveka's Madhyamika: Explanation of Emptiness: The Tenth Chapter of Ta-ch'eng Kuang pai-lun shih lun, Commenting on Aryadeva's Catuhsataka Chapter Sixteen*. Lewiston, N.Y., 1997.

Tillemans, T. J. F. *Materials for the Study of Aryadeva, Dharmapala and Candrakirti: The Catuhsataka of Aryadeva, Chapters XII and XIII, with the Commentaries of Dharmapala and Candrakirti*. Vienna, 1990.

Vasubandhu, et al. *Treatise in Thirty Verses on Mere-Consciousness: A Critical English Translation of Hsüan-tsang's Chinese Version of the Vijñaptimatratatrimsika with Notes from Dharmapala's Commentary in Chinese*. Delhi, 1992.

RICHARD S. Y. CHI (1987)
Revised Bibliography

DHIKR (Arab., "remembrance, mention") is an important Islamic concept and practice best known in the West as a form of Ṣūfī ritual. Because it signifies a kind of prayer, the term *dhikr* is usually translated as *invocation*, since it involves the repetition of a name or names of God, often within a set phrase such as "Praise belongs to God." The sources frequently discuss it in conjunction with supplication (*duʿaʾ*, "calling [upon God]"), which normally adds a request to the mention of a name or names; supplication may take the form of a personal prayer in any language, while *dhikr* employs Arabic names drawn from the Qurʾān. Both are fundamentally voluntary and in any case need to be distinguished from the daily prayer (*salāt*), which is incumbent upon all the faithful.

Studies of *dhikr* in Western languages usually emphasize the bodily movements and the techniques for bringing about concentration that are employed by various Ṣūfī groups and thus neglect the centrality of the concept in the Qurʾān, where the term is employed, along with various closely related derivatives, about 270 times. Although techniques have certainly fascinated a number of Islamicists and travelers to the East, they have always been of secondary interest within the Ṣūfī tradition itself. Nor is it necessary to search for outside influence to explain their genesis: perseverance in remembering God—and sincere Islam is nothing if not this—will eventually entail a certain concern with the technical aspects of controlling one's thoughts and attention.

The basic meaning of the term *dhikr* can be brought out by answering three questions:

1. What is the object of remembrance? God, whose nature is defined succinctly by the first *shahādah*, or creedal statement, "Lā ilāha illā Allāh" ("There is no god but God"), and in detail by the whole range of names and attributes (*al-asmāʾ wa-al-ṣifāt*) mentioned in the Qurʾān.
2. Why should God be remembered? Because human beings are commanded to remember him by his revelations to the prophets and because ultimate human felicity depends upon this remembrance.
3. How can God be remembered? By imitation of the Prophet, who provides the model through his *sunnah* (practice or custom) for all religious and spiritual activity.

In short, to understand the full implications of the term *dhikr* as it is employed in the Qurʾān and the tradition one needs to have a clear grasp of the three "principles of religion" (*uṣūl al-dīn*), namely divine unity, prophecy, and the return to God (in its widest sense, embracing both the "compulsory return" through death and the "voluntary return" through spiritual practice).

QURʾANIC SOURCES. The Qurʾān refers to itself as a remembrance (*dhikr*) or reminder (*dhikrā, tadhkirah*) more than forty times and also alludes to other revelations by the same terms (*sūrahs* 10:71, 21:48, 21:105, 40:54). God had to send a long series of prophets—124,000 according to a *ḥadīth*—because Adam's children keep on falling into forgetfulness, the shortcoming of their father (20:110). If the Qurʾān is a remembrance, so also is the human response to it (here the root's fifth verbal form, *tadhakkur*, is often employed). To be human is to remember: to acknowledge and confirm the obvious. "Not equal are the blind and the seeing man, those who have faith and do deeds of righteousness and the wrongdoer. Little do you remember!" (40:58).

The ultimate object of remembrance is God, since nothing else is truly worthy of human devotion, which is to say that "there is no god but God." The Qurʾān employs the term *dhikr Allāh*, "the remembrance of God," twenty-six times in nominal or verbal form. In a number of other instances where the word *ism* ("name") is inserted into this phrase, the emphasis is placed upon the verbal mentioning of the name *Allāh*, for example, when people are commanded to remember/mention God's name before sacrificing animals (5:4, 6:118, and elsewhere), but the command to remember/mention God's name is also a general one: "And remember the name of thy Lord, and devote thyself to him" (73:8; also 2:114, 22:40, 24:36, 76:25, 87:115). In any case the remembrance of God is almost invariably interpreted to coincide with the mentioning of his name, whether vocally or mentally.

Fifteen verses actually command the remembering of God. But beyond obedience to such commands, human beings must remember God because true life—life with God in the next world—depends on it. In Qurʾanic terms, "to be forgotten by God" is to burn in the Fire; to be remembered by him is to dwell in Paradise. If we want God to remember us, we must follow the divine command to remember him: "Remember me, and I will remember you" (2:152), since God will forget those who disobey this command. Speaking of the resurrection, God says, "Today we do forget you, even as you forgot the encounter of this your day; and your refuge is the Fire" (45:34; also 20:126, 32:14, 38:26, 59:19). Such verses help explain why the Ṣūfī Ibn ʿAṭāʾ Allāh al-Iskandarī (d. 1309) can say in his well-known treatise on *dhikr*, "All acts of worship will disappear from the servant on the Day of Resurrection, except the remembrance of God" (*Miftāḥ al-falāḥ*, Cairo, 1961, p. 31).

Just as *dhikr* brings about felicity in the next world, so too it provides the way to achieve proximity to God in this world. In contrast to the hearts of the godfearing, the hearts of the unbelievers are "hardened against the remembrance of God" (39:22–23). Note the emphasis through repetition in "Those who have faith, their hearts being at peace in God's remembrance—in God's remembrance are at peace the hearts of those who have faith and do righteous deeds; theirs is blessedness and a fair resort" (13:28). The way to achieve this peace of heart (cf. the "soul at peace with God," 89:27) is to follow the Prophet, one of whose names is Dhikr Allāh: "You have a good example in God's Messenger, for whosoever hopes for God and the Last Day and remembers God frequently" (33:21). The Prophet is the perfect embodiment of

God's remembrance; hence, his *sunnah* provides all the details of how to remember God in every act of life. Ibn ʿAṭāʾ Allāh quotes a short *ḥadīth* that epitomizes the pervasive rationale for the love of the Prophet: "He who remembers me has remembered God, and he who loves me has loved God" (*Miftāḥ*, p. 46).

Ḥadīth. The *ḥadīth* literature provides a wealth of material on *dhikr* corroborating the Qurʾān picture while emphasizing the practice of mentioning or invoking God's names and the benefits it provides beyond the grave. The Prophet calls *dhikr* the best act of worship. Every word a person utters in this life will be counted against him or her in the next life, except "bidding to honor and forbidding dishonor" (sura 3:11, 7:157, and elsewhere) and remembering God. When a companion of Muḥammad complained about Islam's many ordinances and asked for a single practice to which he could cling, the Prophet replied, "Let your tongue remain moist in the remembrance of God." The Prophet reported that God says, "I am with my servant when he remembers me. If he remembers me in himself I remember him in myself, and if he remembers me in an assembly, I remember him in an assembly better than his." Such "assemblies" of God's remembrance are well attested in the Prophet's time and became the model for Ṣūfī gatherings.

The *ḥadīths* make clear that the important formulas of remembrance or invocation are those still heard throughout the Islamic world on every sort of occasion: "There is no god but God," "Praise belongs to God," "Glory be to God," "God is greater," and "There is no power and no strength save in God." Only the last is non-Qurʾanic, while the first, the Shahādah, is said to be the most excellent. The *ḥadīths* also make clear that all of God's names, traditionally said to number ninety-nine, may be employed in invocation and supplication, though certain names, such as *All-Merciful* or *All-Forgiving*, have always been employed far more than others, such as *Avenger* or *Terrible in Retribution*.

The idea that each name of God has a specific characteristic is already well reflected in the *ḥadīth* literature. Thus, for example, many *ḥadīths* allude to "the greatest name of God" (*alism al-aʿẓam*), the name "when called by which he answers and when asked by which he gives." Litanies (*awrād*, *aḥzāb*) composed of divine names, formulas of remembrance, and Qurʾanic verses have been common among Muslims from earliest times. Some of them mention the ninety-nine "most beautiful names"; others, such as *al-jawshan al-kabīr* (quoted from the Prophet in Shīʿī sources, e.g., ʿAbbās Qummī, *Mafātīḥ al-jinān*, Tehran, 1961/2, pp. 179–207), list one thousand names of God.

Ṣūfī Tradition. The Shīʿī *ḥadīth* literature, which includes sayings from all twelve imams as well as from the Prophet, helps to demonstrate that the remembrance of God remained central to Islamic piety in the two centuries following Muḥammad. But while the Qurʾān commands the faithful to remember God, the jurists could not impose remembrance upon the community except in the form of the ritual prayer and other outward acts of worship, since by its nature remembrance is a personal affair related more to the domain of intention than to outward activity. In general, therefore, the Ṣūfīs more than any other group emphasized the importance of the devotional practices. In the words of Khwājah Muḥammad Pārsā (d. 1420), "The root of being a Muslim *[aṣl-i musalmānī]* is 'No god but God,' words that are identical with remembrance.'" Hence, he says, the soul of the daily prayer and the other ritual practices, such as fasting and pilgrimage, is "the renewal of God's remembrance in the heart" (*Qudsīyah*, ed. Aḥmad Ṭāhirī ʿIrāqī, Tehran, 1975, p. 30). In the same way, the Ṣūfīs considered all Islamic doctrine and theory to be aimed at awakening remembrance in the soul. If on the one hand the Qurʾān commands human beings to remember God, on the other it provides a full justification for the necessity of this remembrance in its teachings about human nature and ultimate felicity, as, for example, in its description of the "trust" given to human beings in preference to all other creatures (33:72).

In commenting on the Qurʾanic teachings, the Ṣūfīs in particular demonstrate that remembrance of God implies far more than just the ritual activities that go by this name. Full remembrance means actualizing all the ontological perfections latent within the primordial human nature (*fiṭrah*) by virtue of its being a divine image. These perfections belong ultimately to God, the one true being, and in his case they are referred to as the divine names. Al-Ghazālī and many others speak of human perfection as "assuming the traits of the divine names" (*al-takhalluq bi-al-asmāʾ al-ilāhīyah*); Ibn al-ʿArabī (d. 1240) even offers this phrase as the definition of Ṣūfīsm (*Al-futūḥāt al-makkīyah* 2.267.11). Since *Allāh* is the all-comprehensive name (*alism al-jāmiʿ*), the referent of all other divine names, the stage of full human perfection is also known as "being like unto Allāh " (*taʾalluh*), or "theomorphism." For Ibn al-ʿArabī and others, the remembrance of the name *Allāh* is the sign of the fully realized human individual to whom reference is made in the prophetic saying, "The Last Hour will not come as long as there remains someone in this world saying, 'Allāh, Allāh!'" (*Futūḥāt* 3.248.17, 3.438.21).

The hallmark of this potential theomorphism is the particular nature of human intelligence, which sets men and women apart from all other creatures. Turning to God—remembrance—actualizes the divine image latent within humans; ultimate felicity is nothing but the remembrance of our own true nature, or the realization of genuine human character traits, the names of God.

Ṣūfī teachings and practice can be summarized by the "best of invocations," the Shahādah: "La ilāha illā Allāh " ("There is no god but God"). The aim is to "annihilate" (*fanāʾ*) all "others" (*aghyār*) and to "subsist" (*baqāʾ*) in the divine. In the words of Ibn ʿAṭāʾ Allāh, "No one says correctly 'No god but God' unless he negates everything other than God from his soul and heart" (*Miftāḥ*, p. 28). Likewise Najm al-Dīn Rāzī (d. 1256): "When one pursues the *dhikr* and persists in it, the attachment of the spirit to other than God will be gradually severed by the scissors of *la ilaha*, and the beauty of the monarch of *illa Allāh* will become manifest and emerge from the veil of might" (*The Path of God's Bondsmen*, p. 270). For Rūmī as for many other Ṣūfīs, the fire of love drives the seeker to remember God constantly; only this can effect the final transformation: "Love is that flame which, when it blazes up, burns away everything except the beloved. It drives home the sword of *lā ilāha* in order to slay other than God" (*Mathnavī* 5, vv. 588–590).

Though many authorities agree that "Lā ilāha illā Allāh" is the most excellent invocation, others hold that the "single invocation" (*al-dhikr al-mufrad*)—the mention of only the name *Allāh*—is superior. Ibn al-ʿArabī often quotes approvingly the words of one of his masters, Abū al-ʿAbbās al-ʿUraybī, who held that this invocation is best, since in invoking "no god but God" one could die in the terror of negation, but in invoking Allāh one can only die in the intimacy of affirmation (*Futūḥāt* 1.329.2, 2.110.21, 2.224.34).

Ṣūfī masters employed various names methodically to bring out the spiritual potentialities and shape the character traits of their disciples. Many Ṣūfī works provide information on names that can be appropriately invoked—though never without the permission and inculcation (*talqīn*) of a master—by disciples at different stages of spiritual growth. Works on the "most beautiful names," such as al-Ghazālī's *Al-maqṣad al-asnā* (partially translated by R. Stade, *Ninety-nine Names of God*, Ibadan, 1970), often discuss the moral traits and spiritual attitudes that reflect each of the individual names on the human level. Ibn ʿAṭāʾ Allāh devotes several pages to the properties of various names and their influence on disciples at different stages of the path. He points out, for example, that the name *Independent* (*al-Ghanī*) is useful for a disciple who seeks disengagement (*tajrīd*) from phenomena but is unable to achieve it (*Miftāḥ*, p. 35). Nonetheless, those who invoke the name *Allāh* should not be interested in specific benefits but should exemplify the attitude expressed in the famous prayer of the woman saint Rābiʿah al-ʿAdawīyah (eighth century): "O God, if I worship thee for fear of Hell, burn me in Hell, and if I worship thee in hope of Paradise, exclude me from Paradise; but if I worship thee for thy own sake, grudge me not thy everlasting beauty" (A. J. Arberry, *Muslim Saints and Mystics*, London, 1966, p. 51).

Some Ṣūfīs wrote of transcending *dhikr*, since in the last analysis it is an attribute of the seeker and is therefore "other than God," a veil concealing God from sight (al-Kalābādhī, *The Doctrine of the Sufis*, p. 107). Ibn al-ʿArabī explains that there can be no invocation after the veil has been lifted and contemplation (*mushāhadah*) takes place, for "invocation disappears in the theophany of the invoked" (*Futūḥāt* 2.245.21). According to al-Nūrī (d. 907), true invocation is "the annihilation of the invoker in the invoked" (Rūzbihān, *Mashrab al-arwāḥ*, ed. Nazif H. Hoca, Istanbul, 1974, p. 139). Ibn al-ʿArabī's foremost disciple, Ṣadr al-Dīn al-Qūnawī (d. 1274) writes that the Ṣūfī must gradually abandon all invocation, both outward and inward, until total emptiness is achieved (*Al-risālah al-hādiyah al-murshidīyah*, MS; cf. M. Valsan, "L'épître sur l'orientation parfaite," *Études traditionnelles* 67, 1966, pp. 241–268). But the final word for most seekers remains with Ibn al-ʿArabī: "Invocation is more excellent than abandoning it, for one can only abandon it during contemplation, and that cannot be achieved in an absolute sense" (*Futūḥāt* 2.229.24).

Many classifications of types of *dhikr* can be found in Ṣūfī works. Some of these refer to the depth of concentration achieved by the disciple, such as invocation of the tongue, of the heart, of the innermost mystery. Another common classification distinguishes between loud or public and silent or private *dhikr*. The former was usually performed in groups according to various ritual forms that took shape within the different Ṣūfī orders. Sessions of public invocation range from the reserved to the ecstatic; some groups, such as the Mawlawīyah, or "whirling dervishes," considered music and dance aids to concentration, while others banned anything but sober recitation. Most Ṣūfīs would probably agree that public sessions are really a secondary form of Ṣūfī practice, since the individual's progress on the path, to the extent it does not derive totally from God's grace, depends upon his or her own efforts. Thus Saʿdī (d. 1292) is not speaking metaphorically when he says at the beginning of his famous *Gulistān*: "Every breath taken in replenishes life, and once let out gives joy to the soul. So each breath contains two blessings, and each blessing requires thanksgiving." It is the silent and persevering remembrance of God with each breath or each heartbeat, always within the context of the prophetic *sunnah*, that takes the seeker to the ultimate goal.

SEE ALSO Attributes of God, article on Islamic Concepts; Shahādah; Sufism.

BIBLIOGRAPHY

For a representative sampling of the *ḥadīth* literature, see al-Khaṭīb al-Tabrīzī's *Mishkāt al-maṣābīḥ*, 4 vols., translated by John Robson (Lahore, 1963–1965), pp. 476–492. Shīʿī sources provide more of the same in far more detail, for example, Majlisī's *Biḥār al-anwār* (1956–1972; reprint, Beirut, 1983), vol. 90, pp. 148–285. Al-Ghazālī brings together Qurʾān, *ḥadīth*s, the sayings of the pious, and the views of contemporary theologians and Ṣūfīs in the chapter on *dhikr* and supplication in his *Iḥyāʾ ʿulūm al-dīn*, 5 vols. (Cairo, 1932), translated by K. Nakamura as *Ghazali on Prayer* (Tokyo, 1973).

For *dhikr* in the Ṣūfī tradition, see Louis Gardet's entry in *The Encyclopaedia of Islam*, new ed. (Leiden, 1960–), and J. Spencer Trimingham's *The Sufi Orders in Islam* (New York, 1971), pp. 194–217, both of which deal mainly with techniques. A far more insightful treatment is provided by Annemarie Schimmel's *Mystical Dimensions of Islam* (Chapel Hill, 1975), pp. 167–178. Among translated texts a brief overview of the views of the early Ṣūfīs is provided by al-Kalābādhī's *The Doctrine of the Sufis*, translated by A. J. Arberry (Lahore, 1966), pp. 105–108, while a comprehensive explanation of its significance is given by Najm al-Dīn Rāzī's *The Path of*

God's Bondsmen from Origin to Return, translated by Hamid Algar (Delmar, N.Y., 1982), pp. 268–285. For a description of various forms of *dhikr* within the context of contemporary Egyptian Sufism, see Michael Gilsenan's *Saint and Sufi in Modern Egypt* (Oxford, 1973), pp. 156–187.

William C. Chittick (1987)

DIALOGUE OF RELIGIONS. Etymologically, the word *dialogue* (Gr., *dialogos*) means simply "conversation," although in Western intellectual history its dominant meaning has been "a piece of written work cast in the form of a conversation." In the history of religions, "conversations" about the meaning of beliefs, rituals, and ethics have no doubt been taking place, though informally and unrecorded, from the very beginning, or at least from the first encounter of divergent belief systems. However, the phrase *dialogue of religions* has become common in various religious traditions only since the second half of the twentieth century.

Written dialogues on religion and on philosophical subjects have a long history. The most celebrated Western examples are no doubt the dialogues of Plato, and particularly those in which the teaching methods of Socrates are presented on a question-and-answer basis. Within many religious traditions, dialogues between teachers and their pupils were recorded as a means of communicating and deepening insights. But in virtually all such cases the neophyte occupied a position of submission to the teacher, whose authority derived from what he had learned orally from his mentor and proved in practice. This type of dialogue is especially marked in the Indian traditions, Hindu and Buddhist alike. A relationship of faith and trust is set up between master and disciple, whereupon the disciple receives instruction, often in response to respectful questioning. Many of the Upaniṣads are cast in dialogue form, as is the *Bhagavadgītā* and a portion of the Buddhist Pali canon. The Judeo-Christian tradition likewise contains much instruction in dialogue form: the Law (Torah) is interpreted orally by rabbis to the circle of their disciples, whereas the teachings of Jesus are often placed in the context of conversations and instruction sessions within the company of followers. It is hardly possible in any of these instances to speak of a dialogue between equals, since the disciple or pupil comes seeking the insights that only that particular teacher can provide. In the Socratic dialogue the pupil is made to play a more active role, certainly, but the presence of the master is what guarantees that insights will emerge.

Artificial or imaginative dialogues on religious and metaphysical subjects also occur frequently in Western literature, following the pattern established in classical antiquity. An early medieval example of the genre was the Icelander Snorri Sturluson's *Prose Edda* (early thirteenth century), in which Gangleri asks three informants about the contents of Norse mythology. Later examples are very numerous, and include works as diverse as David Hume's *Dialogues Concerning Natural Religion* (1779), R. A. Vaughan's *Hours with the Mystics* (1856), and Ninian Smart's *A Dialogue of Religions* (1960). This type of dialogue relates closely to the conventions of the theater and the novel, which may serve a similar purpose and of which this type of dialogue is a didactic offshoot. Less artificial were attempts to record the conversations and informal statements of literati and religious leaders—Martin Luther's *Tischreden* (*Table Talk*, 1566), Boswell's *Life of Johnson* (1791), *Dialogues of Alfred North Whitehead* (1954), and, from India, *The Gospel of Sri Ramakrishna* (1897).

Imaginative dialogue has also served the cause of interreligious controversy—for example, by convincing an imaginary opponent of the error of his ways. An early missionary example was K. M. Banerjea's *Dialogues on Hindu Philosophy* (1861), which set Indian traditions against one another in the interests of Christianity. This apologetic method was, however, short-lived.

Common to the older forms of didactic or controversial dialogue was the assumption that religious truth is to be arrived at rationally, by reasonable discourse and the weighing of evidence and proofs. Doubtless there were cases in which this actually happened. In the eighteenth and nineteenth centuries, contacts between religious traditions increased rapidly, and along with them actual (as opposed to imaginary) conversational encounters between believers. How often these followed an ideally rational course must remain a moot point: one suspects they seldom did so. But since during this same period the Western countries were politically and economically dominant, and the Christian missionary enterprise was experiencing its greatest successes, conversations usually involved Christians, and were seldom between equal partners. Where other traditions were concerned, for instance in confrontations between Hindus and Muslims in India, there could be a level of mutual suspicion that prevented constructive conversations from taking place at all. The West was, however, becoming steadily better informed on matters concerning other religious traditions, while the rapid onset of theological liberalism was modifying the terms in which Western religion was expressed. Before World War I, the dominant concepts were "sympathy" and "fulfillment," and although innumerable conversations took place, no one applied to them the word *dialogue*.

Apologetics and controversy aside, in the late nineteenth century began a serious attempt to bring the religious leaders of the world together in a spirit of reconciliation, concentrating on what united them rather than what kept them apart. The pioneer assembly was the World's Parliament of Religions, held in Chicago in 1893; its original impulse came from Swedenborgians, yet it gathered under the banner of a common theism. The parliament at least attracted delegates from every major tradition, and although it dismayed the orthodox of many creeds (especially within evangelical Christianity), it established many important contacts. It also marked the beginning of the modern Hindu "mission" to the

West in the person of Swami Vivekananda, who taught, following Ramakrishna, the equal value of all religions as pathways to the Real. This view was strongly supported in theory by organizations like the Theosophical Society (founded in 1875) and Bāhā'i. A Chicago "continuation committee" was formed, though no further full-scale parliaments were ever held. The Chicago spirit survived, however, in an International Council of Unitarian and Other Liberal Religious Thinkers and Workers, which worked between 1901 and 1913. Its aims were to introduce believers to one another, to emphasize the "universal elements" in all religions, and to work for the "moral uplift of the world." World War I brought these efforts to a temporary halt, but after the war, when internationalism was held to be one safeguard against further conflict, various interfaith movements emerged, culminating in the World Fellowship of Faiths (1929).

Eight years earlier, Rudolf Otto had instituted his Religiöser Menschheitsbund (Interreligious League) with the same end in view—the lessening of international tensions through the banding together of believers. These moral objectives were accepted on the liberal wing of Christianity, coming to expression at the Jerusalem conference of the International Missionary Council in 1928, and classically in the liberal manifesto edited by W. E. Hocking, *Re-Thinking Missions* (1932). In general, however, Christians were uneasy about interfaith cooperation. Hindus adjusted to it more easily, and in the person of Sarvepalli Radhakrishnan gained an international spokesman of great force and clarity. Radhakrishnan held that the comparative study of religion made exclusive claims on the part of any individual tradition impossible, and that behind all empirical forms of religion there is "the same intention, the same striving, the same faith" (Radhakrishnan, *East and West in Religion*, London, 1933, p. 19).

Between the wars, world congresses and fellowships of faiths continued to meet regularly, even under the lengthening shadow of various forms of totalitarianism. Mention might also be made of the Oxford Group Movement (subsequently retitled Moral Re-Armament), which was basically Christian but which was more concerned with moral than with theological issues: it enjoyed its heyday in the late 1930s, and attracted many non-Christians. On another level, the *philosophia perennis* proclaimed by Coomaraswamy, Schuon, and Guénon gained followers from various traditions, Eastern as well as Western. This, however, was less a meeting place of religious traditions than a means by which they might be transcended. In the area of scholarship, although the study of religion on a multicultural basis undoubtedly did increase mutual respect among the traditions and further dialogue between them, few individual scholars were prepared to pronounce on the issue. One exception was Friedrich Heiler of Marburg, who stated at an international conference in Tokyo in 1958 that "a new era will dawn upon mankind when the religions will rise to true tolerance and co-operation on behalf of mankind. To assist in preparing the way for this era is one of the finest hopes of the scientific study of religion" (quoted in Sharpe, 1975, p. 272). Other scholars, however, regarded this ideal as less than "scientific."

Parliaments, congresses, and conferences continued to bring together religious leaders in a spirit of irenic idealism, on the pattern of the League of Nations. Yet there was an increasing sense of the threat to religion being posed by the European totalitarian regimes, as well as by materialism, and frequent calls were made for the world's religious leaders to band their people together to meet these pressures. What the leaders could not guarantee to do, however, was change the religious configurations of the world. Local situations were still, during the interwar years, dominated by local concerns. Within the Christian churches, there were several notable moves in the direction of increasing visible unity—among Methodists in Britain, Presbyterians in Scotland, Protestant churches in Canada and South India—but relatively little could be done on the interfaith level.

The notion of dialogue in its modern sense entered the world of religion during the confused and confusing years after World War I, and was closely connected with the philosophy of existentialism. Its first and most widely read manifesto was Martin Buber's *I and Thou* (1923), which urged that human beings should cease to look upon one another merely as objects ("I-It") and approach one another directly and with mutual acceptance as fellow humans ("I-Thou"). Buber was Jewish and therefore well acquainted with racial, religious, and economic oppression. But such forms of oppression might emerge whenever and wherever negative value judgments were applied by a dominant group to their (supposed) inferiors. The only cure was the recognition of common humanity, and the personal discourse—or dialogue—of individuals, whatever their beliefs, on that level.

Although Buber and the other existentialists were widely read, and although, as we have seen, many interfaith initiatives were begun between the wars, the application of the term *dialogue* to the relation between religious traditions did not become common until the years after World War II. By that time the political and religious patterns of the world had begun to change more and more rapidly. Western political imperialism was being rapidly dismantled; former colonies were becoming independent almost daily, with a consequent questioning of the values of the colonial period, religious values not excepted; but at the same time Christianity was an important factor in the lives of the new nations, and needed to find a new role, independent of the former governing powers. The newly independent nations were seldom other than partly Christian. India became officially "secular," while having a massive Hindu majority, and Pakistan was created as a Muslim state, for Hindu-Muslim dialogue on the subcontinent had been a marked failure. Elsewhere in the world, whether official ideology was Muslim, Buddhist, Jewish (in the sole case of Israel), or "secular," Christianity was in almost all cases thrust on to the defensive. In the Western countries themselves the Christian pattern underwent a progressive polarization between conservative and liberal views, with liberals in particular suffering greatly from postcolonial guilt on the one hand and an uncertainty as to ultimate religious values on the other.

It was in this atmosphere that the word *dialogue* began to emerge as the only workable term with which to describe the proper attitude of one group of believers over against another. It should be remembered, however, that during the time of its greatest popularity, between the mid-1960s and the mid-1970s, the word was used almost exclusively by the liberal wing of Christianity (both Catholic and Protestant) in the West, and by similarly liberal Christians in the developing nations. Conservatives found the term unacceptable, since it implicitly placed religious traditions on a par with one another, or at least was less than explicit when it came to affirming the claims of Christianity. In the non-Western world, too, there were those who suspected that the new emphasis on dialogue was no more than a subtler and more insidious form of missionary apologetics.

An important symbolical breakthrough was achieved by the Second Vatican Council (1962–1965) of the Roman Catholic church, which spoke in several documents about dialogue, the church for instance urging "her sons . . . prudently and lovingly, through dialogue and collaboration with the followers of other religions," to "acknowledge, preserve, and promote the spiritual and moral goods found among these men, as well as the values in their society and culture" (*Nostra aetate* 2). Similarly, the disciples of Christ "can learn by sincere and patient dialogue what treasures a bountiful God has distributed among the nations of the earth" (*Ad gentes* 2.11). Statements of this kind had the effect of liberating Catholics from previous restrictions on fellowship with non-Catholics, and of releasing a flood of "dialogue literature," in the production of which Protestants were soon to share.

But not all this literature saw the nature and purpose of dialogue in the same light. In addition, much of it suffered in that it was not actually emerging from discussions between believers belonging to different traditions, but remained on the level of theorizing *about* dialogue. Various types of activity seemed to be capable of being contained beneath the "dialogue" canopy.

1. *Discursive dialogue* (previously "debate" or "discussion") involves meeting, listening, and discussion on the level of mutual competent intellectual inquiry. As such it was neither very new nor very remarkable, though it had always been fairly uncommon. As an intellectual activity, it could only ever be profitable among equally equipped partners, since it presupposes the willingness of both to listen, as well as speak.
2. *Human ("Buberian") dialogue* rests on the existential foundations previously described, and assumes that it is possible for human beings to meet purely and simply as human beings, irrespective of the beliefs that separate them. The great drawback to this approach is its individualism. Although suitable enough among intellectuals in the semisecular West, it leaves out of consideration the extent to which the individual is shaped by the community of which he or she, depending on its support and adhering to its values, is part. To bypass the community is often simply impossible, and although this approach rests on high ideals, it may prove to be little more than a theoretical stance.
3. *Secular dialogue* stresses that where there are tasks to be performed in the world, believers in different creeds may share in a program of joint action, without regard to their respective convictions. In the theological climate of the 1960s and 1970s, dialogue very frequently appeared to be pointed in this direction. It simply bypassed the belief question in the interests of practicalities. "Desacralization turns the eyes of men to the world, to time and history, and the realities of history are often more manageable for purposes of dialogue than the supramundane things of an ethereal world" (Jai Singh, 1967, pp. 43–44).
4. *Spiritual dialogue* has been advocated chiefly by those who have been trained in the contemplative and monastic traditions, and who have learned to set high value upon Eastern (or other) spirituality, while not wishing to lessen their hold upon their own. Its locus is not debate and discussion, but prayer and meditation, and in recent years it has given rise to a considerable number of ashrams and meditation centers in East and West alike. In theoretical terms, it rests on a monistic theology similar in many ways to Vedānta; in practical terms, it often concedes to the East a level of attainment in matters of spirituality superior to that of the West, and is prepared to use non-Christian scriptures, liturgies, and techniques alongside those that are specifically Christian. Often it will stress the importance of *theologia negativa,* negate the primacy of logic and conceptual knowledge, and rely on experience, intuition, and contemplation. In this respect it was a typical product of the 1960s.

Since about the mid-1970s, the term *dialogue* has been somewhat less used than during the previous decade, partly on account of changing fashions, partly in response to socioeconomic pressures. There is little real evidence that the stated goals of dialogue (at least as formulated by Christians) were ever reached, and in any case, each new generation has had to take up the task of meeting other believers afresh. But at least the "dialogue period" helped to banish some of the impatience and the inaccuracies of the past, although doubtless creating fresh problems of its own. While it taught many Christians the importance of sympathy and seriousness in interreligious discourse, it failed to engage the attention of most other traditions on anything but a superficial level. As such, what has often been called a "dialogue of religions" and set forth as a practical activity, has remained on the level of theory and ideals. Actual encounters of believers there will always be. They will undoubtedly remain haphazard, unpredictable, sometimes violent, and always determined by local conditions.

See Also Religious Diversity; Truth.

Bibliography

Jai Singh, Herbert, ed. *Inter-religious Dialogue.* Bangalore, 1967.

Klostermaier, Klaus Konrad. *Hindu and Christian in Vrindaban.* Translated by Antonia Fonseca. London, 1969.

Klostermaier, Klaus Konrad. "Hindu-Christian Dialogue: Its Religious and Cultural Implications." *Studies in Religion* 1 (1971): 83–97.

Sharpe, Eric J. "The Goals of Inter-religious Dialogue." In *Truth and Dialogue in World Religions: Conflicting Truth-Claims,* edited by John Hick, pp. 77–95. Philadelphia, 1974.

Sharpe, Eric J. *Comparative Religion: A History.* London, 1975. See the discussion on pages 251–266.

Sharpe, Eric J. *Faith Meets Faith: Some Christian Attitudes to Hinduism in the Nineteenth and Twentieth Centuries.* London, 1977.

Eric J. Sharpe (1987)

DIAMOND. The diamond, first of all, participates in the hierophany of stones signifying in religious consciousness that which is hard, rugged, and unchanging. Above all, stone *is.* Like all precious stones, the diamond also partakes of the general symbolism of treasures and riches, which in religious terms represent moral and intellectual knowledge.

As a symbol the diamond, as the hardest of all stones, has a wide range of meanings, among them indestructibility, constancy, the unyielding, and dominance. Because of its brilliance it also signifies unconquerable light, excellence, frankness, joy, life, and purity.

In Greek the word for "diamond" is derived from *adamas,* meaning "invincible, unconquerable." In some places, and especially on Greek emblems, it indicated the irradiant mystic center, a meaning discovered in the most obscure examples as well as in the most prominent. Jean Chevalier and Alain Gheerbrant (1982) point out that the German word *Eckstein* ("cornerstone") also refers to the diamond in a deck of cards. The cornerstone is one of many symbols for the center. In a more obvious example, Plato likens the axis of the world to a diamond.

Until the nineteenth century, diamonds were found almost entirely in India. On the subcontinent the word *vajra* meant both "lightning" and "diamond." Thus, the *vajra* of the god Śiva has a double aspect as thunderbolt and diamond scepter. *Vajra* also belongs to the god Agni as a spiritual power and to Indra as a temporal power. As a diamond *vajra* is adamantine and depicts spiritual power, but as thunderbolt and lightning it also represents both destruction and fertilization, death-dealing and life-giving powers, the alternating and complementary forces of the universe.

The symbol of the *vajra* is important in Buddhism as well, where it symbolizes the power of the Buddha's teaching (the *dharma*) to overcome the deluding passions of sentient beings. The Diamond Throne or Seat is the place of enlightenment. Situated at the foot of the bodhi tree, it is the unchangeable axis or center of the world.

In Tantric Buddhism *vajra* represents immutable, unalterable spiritual power. Symbolizing clarity and light, it also refers to the indeterminate character and ultimate emptiness of the Buddha nature. Mircea Eliade cites a Tantric text that makes a clear identification between *śūnyatā* ("voidness") and *vajra.* The Chan patriarch Huineng is said to have declared that neither that which is waxing nor that which is waning is the diamond.

In the traditional mineralogy of the Indian subcontinent, the diamond represents perfection. Stones and metals were thought to grow within the earth's womb, each with its own lethargic pace and rhythm. The crystal was unripe (Hindi, *kacchā)* and constituted a state of intermediate maturation. The diamond was the epitome of maturity and ripeness (Hindi, *pakkā).* The crystal is not hard; the diamond is. The Indian alchemist, associating the diamond with immortality, identified it with the philosophers' stone.

Similarly, in Tibetan iconography the diamond scepter signifies the adamantine or immutable world, which is also potential or nonmanifest. The bell or *tilpa* refers to the phenomenal world, which is manifest and changing. The diamond scepter is the active principle; the bell is the passive. The former is wisdom and the latter, human reason.

The diamond has also been linked with the supreme female divinity, who is usually associated with the earth. In Tibet the earth goddess Tārā has a human incarnation, the Diamond Sow. She is also traditionally regarded as the consort of or feminine counterpart to the *bodhisattva* Avalokiteśvara. In the transition from tarot cards to modern playing cards, diamonds replaced the ancient suit of pentacles, which had been symbols of Mother Earth (Tārā) and of the earth as feminine.

The characteristics of hardness and durability have lent themselves to other meanings. In the Old Testament the diamond could symbolize hardness of the heart and forehead (*Jer.* 17:1). In Rome it was believed that the stone promoted harmony, and that it guarded health and vitality if worn on the left hand, close to the heart. This belief probably informed its character as an emblem of reconciliation in the Middle Ages and as a sign of betrothal in the modern world.

In some places the diamond's brilliance and lucidity made it a symbol for Christ. In Hebrew culture the sixth stone of the high priest's breastplate, a diamond, was said to become dark or light according to the guilt or innocence of an accused person.

Mircea Eliade (1958) has related diamonds to "snake stones," which in many cultures are thought to have fallen from the heads of snakes or dragons. In ancient India, and later in the Hellenistic and Arab worlds, it was believed that the stones were poisonous if anyone touched them with their lips, because they had once been in a snake's throat. The notion that precious stones came from snake spittle has been found in areas ranging from China to Great Britain.

Pliny the Elder (23–79 CE) described the *dracontia*, or dracontites, that were to be found in the brains of dragons. Philostratus the Lemnian (b. c. 190 CE) reported that the eyes of some dragons were stones of blinding brilliance imbued with magical powers. Sorcerers, he relates, after they have worshiped reptiles, cut off their heads and take out the precious stones.

Given such beliefs, it is not surprising that the diamond has a reputation as a remedy for snakebite. Indeed, Pliny describes it as a universal talisman, rendering poisons and every malady harmless and causing evil spirits and bad dreams to depart. In occidental Europe, the diamond has been thought to chase away savage beasts, phantoms, sorcerers, and the terrors of the night. In Russia, its purity and lucidity have made it a charm to impede lust and to strengthen the resolve of the chaste.

BIBLIOGRAPHY

Jean Chevalier and Alain Gheerbrant, in *Dictionnaire des symboles* (Paris, 1982), have written an interesting and often provocative essay on the diamond. Mircea Eliade, in *Patterns in Comparative Religion* (New York, 1958), primarily discussed the diamond as a magical object. His description of the significance of the stones in the same book is also helpful. Berthold Laufer's book *The Diamond: A Study in Chinese and Hellenistic Folklore* (Chicago, 1915), is one of the few sources that include substantial material on the diamond as a symbol rather than a physical object.

New Sources

Harlow, George, ed. *The Nature of Diamonds*. New York, 1997.

Hart, Matthew. *Diamond: A Journey to the Heart of an Obsession*. New York, 2001.

Kendall, Leo P. *Diamonds Famous and Fatal: The History, Mystery and Lore of the World's Most Famous Gem*. Fort Lee, N.J., 2001.

ELAINE MAGALIS (1987)
Revised Bibliography

DIANA. Latin grammarians offer the oldest and most commonly accepted etymology of the name of Diana. She is the female counterpart of Zeus/Deus, following the etymological chain: *Deus, dius, Divus, Diovis, dies, duius, Diviana, Diana.* Therefore, Diana is "the goddess," and she is often defined as such in inscriptions of the imperial era, which honor her as *Dea Diana, Deana,* or simply, *Diana.*

Varro (*De lingua Latina* 5.68), following the ancient texts of Epicharmus and Ennius, states that "the Moon (*luna*) takes her name from *lucere* (to illuminate) because it shines alone at night." For this reason it is called *Noctiluca* over the Palatinus, where her temple shines at night. Varro adds that *lucere* derives from *luere* (to undo, to dissolve), because light (*lux*) dissolves darkness; from *lux* derives *Noctiluca* (*De lingua Latina* 6.79). In her temple a lamp remained lit, illuminating the night. That rite is not Greek, but Italian. For his part, Cicero commands that "just as the Sun receives the name of Apollo, so the Moon receives that of Diana" (*De natura deorum* 3.20.51); the same duality of day versus night appears in Horace's *Ode* 4.6, when the poet, in this hymn honoring Augustus, praises Apollo *Phoibos* (= Sun) and, later, the rites celebrated in honor of Diana-*Phoibe*, whose flame grows, ripening the wheat fields: *rite crescentem face Noctilucam, prosperam frugum celeremque pronos volvere mensis* (As with a torch that rekindles the moonlight, to bring back favorable prosperity and swift fruitfulness).

Catullus dedicates his *Carmen* XXXIV to Diana. Here, the rhythmic repetitions transform the poem into a true hymn or a prayer where she is invoked as Mistress (*domina*) of wild life in verses 9 through 12: *montium domina ut fores / silvarumque virentium / saltuumque reconditorum amniumque sonantum* (Thus you are mistress of the hills, and the flourishing woods and the secluded pasture land and the resounding river). The verses show the duality of Diana as a midwife and protector of children, and as regent of the gloomy night. Thus, Diana is the light that rules the night. This is why she is also invoked as *Lucina* (and by the Greeks as *Lucifera*), stealing the role from Juno herself, who aids women in labor (Cicero, *De natura deorum* 2.68).

The Italic cult to Diana is very ancient. Legend attributes to King Tatius the establishment of her cult in Latium, brought from the land of the Sabines. According to Livy (27.4.12), a temple and a forest (*templum et lucus*) were consecrated to her in Anagnia, the land of the Hernici, as was a hill near the *Tusculum.* These natural landscapes defined from early on the sacred surroundings of Diana: dark forests, luxuriant woods, and caves.

The paradigm of such a cult can be found in the oldest and most renowned of Diana's sanctuaries in Latin worship, that of *Diana Aricina,* located in the forest of Nemus, on a lakeshore at the foot of the Alban hills (Pliny, *Naturalis historia* 16.91). From the name of the lake and the forest, the goddess takes the epithet *Nemorensis.* In Aricia, the worshipers of Diana were mostly female, and her night rituals were impressive. Once the women had performed the rites, they returned to Rome in a procession, carrying torches and illuminating the night with the fire of their goddess. The procession was repeated, more theatrically, on the ides of August, when the women, carrying the torches, would stand around Lake Nemi until they could feel the presence of the goddess: "Diana herself, who crowns with flowers her chosen hounds, sets her darts and lets the wild beasts lose, while in their chaste homes, the people, throughout the land of Italy, celebrate the day of Hecate" (Statius, *Silvae* 3.1.55–60).

This archaic temple held extraordinary importance in the organization of the later cult of the goddess, for, when it was moved to Rome, the priest of the temple of Diana in the Aventine was addressed by the "archaeological" title *rex nemorensis* (Ovid, *Fasti* 3.265; 6.735). The title conferred sacred respect, and was evidence of the ancient barbarism. The priest of Diana "always had to defend himself sword in hand against his foes" (Ovid, *Ars amandi* 1.260). The notion of barbarism and a constant state of "defense and vigilance" are probably at the heart of Diana's success among slaves and gladiators. In the time of Augustus, the bronze tables with the founding decree of the confederate temple, the *lex arae Dianae in Aventino*, were still preserved. As in Aricia, in Rome the anniversary of her cult was August 13. On that date, slaves received symbolic freedom and women purified themselves by washing their hair and combing it delicately (Plutarch, *Quaestiones Romanae* 100).

The early commingling with Artemis can explain those aspects of Diana that contrast with her virginal nature. At Aricia, votive objects have been discovered that take the form of vulvas and phalluses. Syncretism progressively altered the Latin goddess to the point of conferring various features of the Greek goddess upon her beyond her lunar function; thus she became a midwife like Artemis *Locheia*, a huntress-goddess, and, as Diana *Trivia*, a goddess of crossroads, after the example of Hekate *Trioditis*. By the time of Augustus, the absorption of Diana by Artemis was virtually complete, as can be seen in the *Carmen saeculare* of Horace. On the other hand, Strabo (4.1.5) relates that the cultic statue on the Aventine displayed the same traits as the Artemis of Marseilles, which in turn was identical with the Artemis of Ephesus.

In Campania, north of Capua, there was another great archaic sanctuary to Diana, called the Diana Tifatina because of the abundance of evergreen oaks on its surrounding hills. It was created around the third century BCE. The numerous inscriptions found there suggest the popularity of her cult, especially between the first century BCE and the first century CE, which depict Diana Tifatina as "huntress." The temple received generous tributes from Sulla in gratitude for his victory over C. Norbanus not far from the temple of Tifatina (Velleius, *Paterculus* 2.25.4; Plutarch, *Sulla* 6). Economic activity, based on the ownership and farming of the land, extends to the imperial era. The policies of protection of the temple by the emperors is exemplified by the actions of Vespasian in 77 or 78 against private individuals who improperly occupied lands surrounding the temple of Diana Tifatina—by illegally expanding the size of adjacent plots during the first century CE. The emperor demanded that the land be returned to the temple *(quibus secundum instrumentum fines restituuntur)*. Sulla granted the land to the temple of Diana in 82 CE, and its boundaries were legally recorded in the land registry under Augustus. The imperial judgment is preserved in an inscription in Capua, stating that Emperor Vespasian "restored the limits of the lands under litigation to the temple of Diana Tifatina, donated by Cornelius Sulla" (*CIL* X 3828).

After the burning of Rome in 65 CE, Nero ordered the construction of a temple to Diana in the Aventine, which is also mentioned by Vitruvius (5.5.8) and Ovid (*Fasti* 3. 883–884). The temple took the place of another one, in a different location, that "Servius Tullius had consecrated to the moon," according to Tacitus (*Annales* 15.41.1). Livy also refers to the temple (40.2.2) when he tells the prodigious story of how, in the year 182, the door to the sanctuary was blown down by a hurricane.

During the first and second centuries CE Diana was highly honored by the military, especially equestrian officers throughout the Roman Empire. Dedications allude to Diana's ancient names, as well as her earlier functions as goddess of the forests and ruler of wild animals. Thus, in Altava (Mauretania Caesariensis) she is invoked as "Diana Dea nemorum comes, victrix ferarum" (*CIL* VIII, 9831); Diana Nemorensis is worshiped in Narona (Dalmatia) (*CIL* III, 1773); while in Intercisa (Lower Pannonia), honors go to Numen Dianae Tifatinae (*Année Epigraphique*, 1968, 429). In an important inscription in León (Hispania), dating to the second century CE, a senator who was also *legatus* in legion VII *Gemina*, writes a long votive invocation of the goddess, building a temple in her honor and offering her his hunting trophies: boar tusks, deer antlers, and a bear skin, all of them hunted by Tullius Maximus, who calls himself "general of the descendants of Aeneas" (Del Hoyo, 2002).

In late antiquity, the name of Diana and her nocturnal names (such as Hekate, *Triva*, Selene, Luna) had great acceptance in the religion of the people and in magic.

SEE ALSO Artemis; Dea Dia; Moon; Roman Religion, article on the Early Period.

BIBLIOGRAPHY

Blagg, T. F. C. "The Cult and Sanctuary of *Diana Nemorensis*." In *Pagan Gods and Shrines of the Roman Empire*, edited by Martin Henig and Anthony King, pp. 211–219. Oxford, 1986.

Cels-Saint Hilaire, Janine. "*Numen Augusti* et Diane de l'Aventin: Le témoignage de l'ara narbonensis." In *Les grandes figures religieuses: Fonctionnement pratique et symbolique dans l'antiquité*, pp. 455–502. Paris, 1986.

Del Hoyo, Javier. "*Cvrsv certari*: Acerca de la afición cinegética de *Q. Tvllivs Maximvs* (*CIL* II 2660)." *Faventia* 24, no. 1 (2002): 69–98.

Gras, Michel. "Le temple de Diane sur l'Aventine." *Revue des études anciennes* 89 (1987): 47–61.

Guldager, Pia. "The Sanctuary of *Diana Nemorensis*: The Late Republican Acrolithic Cult Statues." *Acta archaeologica* 66 (1995): 191–217.

Montero, Santiago, and Sabino Perea. *Romana religio/religio romanorum: Diccionario bibliográfico de religión romana*. Madrid, 1999. See the entry on "Diana" (p. 150), with the relevant bibliography.

Ruiz Sánchez, Marcos. *Confectum Carmine: En torno a la poesía de Catulo.* Murcia, Spain, 1996. See volume 2, pages 65–70, for a commentary on poem XXXIV.

ROBERT SCHILLING (1987)
SABINO PEREA YÉBENES (2005)
Translated from Spanish by Fernando Feliu-Moggi

DIETARY LAWS SEE KASHRUT

DIETERICH, ALBRECHT (1866–1908), German philologist and historian of Greco-Roman religions. Born in Bad Hersfeld (in the Hesse region of Germany), Albrecht Dieterich completed his secondary studies in the school where his father (who wanted Dieterich to become a theologian) was a member of the faculty. At the University of Leipzig in 1885–1886, Dieterich studied the New Testament and church history; he also took an interest in the philosophy of religion in general and enrolled in courses in classical philology (taught by Georg Curtius, Otto Crusius, and Otto Ribbeck). He pursued higher studies at the University of Bonn from 1886 to 1888, where the teaching of Hermann Usener (whose daughter he later married) had decisive influence upon his scientific orientation. He also studied under Franz Bücheler, who introduced him to funerary epigraphy, and under Reinhard Kekulé, who taught him to appreciate iconography.

Dieterich consolidated the bases of his philological training at Usener's urging, who had him write a dissertation on Aeschylus. He then worked on an edition (with comments) of the magical papyrus J 384 of Leiden; it was submitted to a competition sponsered by Bücheler and won the prize (the text was published in the *Jahrbücher für klassische Philologie,* supp. vol. 16, 1888). In this work Dieterich showed his concern for historical and linguistic comprehension of the papyrus's strange elements (that at first glance appear irrational) by paying attention to how these elements manifest the marginal strains of Greco-Roman religion (e.g., Orphism, Hermetism, and Gnosticism). Having obtained his doctoral degree in 1888, he passed his state examination in 1889 with his dissertation addressing the question, "What do we know about the theism or pantheism of Plato?" In 1891 he qualified as a doctor of philosophy at the University of Marburg with his work *De hymnis Orphicis capitula quinque,* in which the problems of literary and religious history are treated together. (The hypothesis that he advanced in this book—that of an Alexandrian elaboration of some "Orphic hymns"—is no longer supported, but nevertheless it is still generally agreed that certain aspects of Orphism in Ptolemaic Egypt deserve attention.)

He had at first planned to edit another magical papyrus of Leiden (J 395) as part of his doctoral work; it was instead published as an appendix to his *Abraxas* (1891). This book, written in homage to Usener, displayed Dieterich's remarkable mastery over hermetic and Gnostic literature. He applied himself in *Abraxas* to uncovering in this literature elements of Stoic, Orphic, astrological, Egyptian, and Judaic origin. Yet for all that he did not neglect Classical Greek literature (especially Aeschylus and Aristophanes). He wrote the article "Aischylos" for the *Real-Encyclopädie* (1893); in this article the religious sense of tragic grandeur surpasses the level of purely verbal and bibliographical erudition. The origins of Christianity were part of his concern as well. His study of the *Apocalypse of Peter,* a text discovered in a tomb in Akhmim, Egypt, led to the publication of *Nekyia* (1893), an in-depth study of the Greek tradition of descent (*katabasis*) into the underworld and of Judeo-Christian apocalyptic tradition. It stressed the importance of popular beliefs and of beliefs of popular origin at the periphery of official cults or of Classical paganism.

During 1894 and 1895, a long Mediterranean voyage took him to Greece, Asia Minor, Naples and Pompeii, Sicily, and finally Rome. He thus made direct contact with the objects of his studies: the countrysides, the representational monuments, the common people's way of life, and the ever-living folklore in rustic festivals. The paintings of Campania (commented upon by August Mau) and Italian theater inspired Dieterich's book *Pulcinella* (1897), a perspicacious study of the history of comic characters from classical antiquity extending into the present. His visit to the Lateran Museum resulted in his publication in 1896 of a commentary on the epitaph of Aberkios (a bishop of Hierapolis, Phrygia) in which he proposed a pagan interpretation, which generated both enthusiastic support (e.g., from Salomon Reinach) and sharp criticism (e.g., from Franz Cumont).

In 1895 he became an auxiliary professor of philology at the University of Giessen, and then became in 1897 a full professor there, succeeding Edvard Schwartz. His teaching on Greek and Latin literature made reference to iconography as well as to popular mythology. Greatly impressed by Erwin Rohde's *Psyché* (1890–1894) and Wilhelm Mannhardt's *Wald- und Feldkulte* (1875–1877), he became fascinated with ethnography and collaborated in the projects of the Hessische Vereinigung für Volkskunde. In this activity he always insisted upon the necessity of providing a philological basis for comparisons. He held conferences at Frankfurt on the rites of birth and death that served as a prelude for his book *Mutter Erde* (1905).

Dieterich was interested in the magical aspect of literature manifested in the mysticism of signs, in demonology, and in all the aberrant and disturbing fringes of Greco-Roman paganism, which until then were somewhat neglected by classical philologists. In a similar way, Oriental religions also concerned him. In a letter written in 1897, he argued that the Egyptian deity Sarapis was a syncretic god foreshadowing a kind of henotheism that would pave the way for Christian monotheism. Hugo Hepding, with his book *Attis* (1903), inaugurated the series "Religionsgeschichtliche Versuche und Vorarbeiten," which Dieterich, along with Richard Wünsch, edited until Dieterich's death. The same year saw the publication of Dieterich's *Eine Mithrasliturgie,* an expansion of an article he had published in 1902 ("Die Religion des Mithras" in the journal *Bon ner Jahrbücher*); the topic was the famous papyrus in the National Papyrus Library in Paris (Supplementum Graecum 574) that contains the "formula for immortality." Although Dieterich's description of this text as a Mithraic liturgy is no longer generally accepted, his commentary does display prodigious erudition.

Dieterich moved to the University of Heidelberg in 1903, succeeding Crusius as professor of classical philology. There he dedicated himself mainly to the history of religions. Beginning in 1904, his editing (at first with Thomas Achelis but from 1905 to 1908 alone) of the journal *Archiv für Religionswissenschaft* occupied the greater part of his time. This, however, did not prevent him from writing a *magnum opus* that he had been nurturing for some time: *Mutter Erde: Ein Versuch über Volksreligion* (1905). In it he defends the thesis that rites of birth and death can be explained as functions of a fundamental belief, a primitive and universal given in the history of religions. His idea enjoyed considerable success. It was answered with justified criticisms (for example, by Olof Pettersson in his book *Mother Earth,* Lund, 1967); yet the work still has merit, and any criticisms of it ought to be nuanced (see my review of Pettersson's book in *Revue de l'histoire des religions* 175, 1969, pp. 69–71). Significantly, *Mutter Erde* was dedicated to Usener on the occasion of his seventieth birthday. In the same year (1905), a supplement to *Archiv für Religionswissenschaft* was also dedicated to Usener; in it, a piece entitled "Sonnentag" by Dieterich drew a relationship between a Heidelberg custom and the ancient and modern feasts of Palm Sunday. He was planning one work on popular religion and another on the origins of Christianity.

Dieterich died of a cerebral apoplexy shortly after beginning a course of lectures at Heidelberg; he was fully active and in the prime of his career. His students (notably Friedrich Pfister, Eugen Fehrle, and Otto Weinreich) bear the clear stamp of his teaching. He contributed to a greater understanding of Greco-Roman paganism by opening classical philology to the exegesis of obscure texts from late antiquity; he also contributed to the comparative study of religions and to the study of popular traditions without ever losing sight of the great Hellenic literary tradition.

Bibliography

Dietrich's published works include the following:

De hymnis orphicis capitula quinque. Marburg, 1891.

Abraxas: Studien zur Religionsgeschichte des spätern Altertums. Leipzig, 1891.

Nekyia: Beiträge zur Erklärung der neuentdeckten Petrusapokalypse. Leipzig, 1893.

Die Grabinschrift des Aberkios. Leipzig, 1896.

Pulcinella pompjanische Wandbilder und römische Satyrspiele. Leipzig, 1897.

Eine Mithrasliturgie (1903). 3d ed. Edited by Otto Weinreich. Leipzig, 1923.

Mutter Erde: Ein Versuch über Volksreligion (1905). 3d ed. Leipzig, 1925.

Kleine Schriften. Edited by Richard Wünsch. Leipzig, 1911. Includes detailed biographical information on Dieterich.

New Sources

Betz, Hans Dieter. *The "Mithras Liturgy," Text, Translation, and Commentary.* Tübingen, 2003. See pages 14–26.

Marchand, Suzanne. "From Liberalism to Neoromanticism: Albrecht Dieterich, Richard Reitzenstein, and the Religious Turn in fin-de-siècle German Classical Studies." In *Out of Arcadia: Classics and Politics in Germany in the Age of Burckhardt, Nietzsche and Wilamowitz,* edited by Ingo Gildenhard and Martin Ruehl, pp. 129–160. London, 2003.

Pettersson, Olof. *Mother Earth: An Analysis of the Mother Earth Concepts according to Albrecht Dieterich.* Lund, 1967.

Wessels, Antje *Ursprungszauber. Zur Rezeption von Hermann Useners Lehre von der religiösen Begriffsbildung* (RGVV 51). Berlin and New York, 2003. See pages 96–128.

ROBERT TURCAN (1987)
Translated from French by Paul C. Duggan
Revised Bibliography

DIETERLEN, GERMAINE (1903–1999), a towering figure in French ethnography, is especially known for her exhaustive documentation of the Dogon of Mali. In 1931 she joined the famous ethnographic expedition, the Dakar-Djibouti mission, led by Marcel Griaule (1898–1956). She became an integral part of Griaule's interdisciplinary research team and his closest associate. Dieterlen's interests and investigations were wide-ranging. She made more than forty expeditions, mostly to Mali but also to Burkina Faso, Ivory Coast, Niger, and Ghana. She researched Bozo, Peul, and Bambara (Bamana) as well as Dogon cultures, including music and instruments, statuary and art, jewelry, oral literature, language, and religion.

Dieterlen was already married and thirty years old when she decided to earn her baccalaureate in order to pursue a vocation in the nascent science of ethnography. That she defied the constricting social conventions of her day shows the extraordinary will and determination that she extended into the field, where she was reputed to be both exacting and tireless.

Dieterlen's first work, "Calebasses dahoméennes" ("Documents de la mission Dakar-Djibouti"), published in 1935 in collaboration with Griaule, was a descriptive study of the more than thirty-six hundred objects brought back by the Dakar-Djibouti mission for the Trocadero Museum. Dieterlen's careful attention to material culture reflects the influence of her teacher Marcel Mauss (1872–1950). Her first great work, *Les âmes des Dogons* (1941), inaugurated her innovative research on religious ethnology. During three subsequent expeditions she deepened her focus on belief systems, producing the classic *Essai sur la religion des Bambara* (1951). These three works, though disparate in content and style, reflect the two orientations in Dieterlen's scientific life: concrete objects and symbolic representations. Dieterlen's fascination with the relationship of concrete manifestations to systems of belief is evident in another work coauthored with Griaule, *Signes graphiques soudanais* (1951).

Dieterlen carefully attended to the very words of those she studied as a means of understanding their beliefs and systems of representation. Her method was to note their language and then later develop reflections and deepened insights by examining their words. This was the method used in *Le renard pâle* (1965), which she published after Griaule's death under both their names. An extraordinary work, it is the extended study and amplification of the cosmogonic system first expounded by a Dogon elder seventeen years before and related by Griaule in his landmark book, *Dieu d'eau* (Conversations with Ogotemmêli) in 1948. Her comprehensive synthesis of Dogon cosmogony is complemented by a thorough analysis of its concrete manifestation in their social arrangements. Dieterlen's respect for the authority of her native informants' own self-representation is epitomized in *Le titre d'honneur des Arou* (1982), almost entirely comprised of direct transcription.

Dieterlen's assumption that key informants were articulate exponents of local knowledge provided the guiding impulse for her novel use of ethnographic film as a research tool. She viewed filmed ceremonial events with informants to elicit a dialogue and insights that led to fuller comprehension. A unique achievement in the history of ethnography was the series of eight films she made with Jean Rouch (1917–2004) between 1967 and 1973 consecrated to the Sigui, a Dogon masking ritual held every sixty years that extends over a seven-year period. A pioneer of the medium, Dieterlen eventually served as the president of the Committee on Ethnographic Film.

Another critical contribution Dieterlen made to the field was her promotion of dialogue between the French and British schools of anthropology, which employed characteristically opposing means of interrogating West African culture. The French approach, personified by Griaule and Dieterlen, gave primacy to the symbolic and mythical features of culture, while the British method, more analytical than metaphysical, documented social organization, particularly kinship and politics. Collaborating extensively with British colleagues, Dieterlen played an ambassadorial role that fostered constructive discussion about method even as it promoted work that cut across the boundaries of Francophone and Anglophone countries. Dieterlen served on the Council of the International African Institute (CIAI) along with Daryll Forde (1902–1973), who edited the important collection *African Worlds: Studies in the Cosmological Ideas and Social Values of African Peoples* (1954) that also bridged French and British preoccupations.

During the mid-1960s the CIAI organized two seminars on the Voltaic region. The result was an important collection, *African Systems of Thought* (1965), coedited by Dieterlen and the British anthropologist Meyer Fortes (1906–1983). The volume initiated a wide and enduring debate on the meaning of non-Western thought. It also explored the degree to which the contrasting theoretical orientations and methods of the two schools determined strikingly different appraisals of similar cultures.

A founding member and director of research for the Centre National de la Recherche Scientifique (CNRS), Dieterlen created a research group on African religions. She organized the CNRS's influential 1971 international colloquium on what later became a fashionable theme in anthropology, the "notion of personhood." Dieterlen's contribution recovered the feminine as important aspects of the Dogon mythology and social system, including a consideration of pregnancy, childbirth, and the placenta as the bearer of the sacred signs of creation. In an astounding homage to Dieterlen, the Dogon gave her the status *yasiguine* (sister of Sigui), which entitled her to be a member of the male masking society.

See Also Griaule, Marcel.

Bibliography

Dieterlen, Germaine, in collaboration with Marcel Griaule. "Calebasses dahoméennes" ("Documents de la mission Dakar-Djibouti"). *Journal de la Société des Africanistes* V, no. 2 (1935): 203–246.

Dieterlen, Germaine. *Les âmes des Dogons.* Paris, 1941.

Dieterlen, Germaine. *Essai sur la religion Bambara.* Paris, 1951. Translated as *An Essay on the Religion of the Bambara* (New Haven, Conn., 1960).

Dieterlen, Germaine. "Mythe et organization sociale au Soudan français." *Journal de la Société des Africanistes* 25 (1955): 39–76.

Dieterlen, Germaine. "Mythe et organization sociale en Afrique occidentale." *Journal de la Société des Africanistes* 29 (1959): 119–138.

Dieterlen, Germaine. "Colloque sur les cultures voltaïques (Sochamp, 6–8 décembre 1965)." *Recherches voltaïques* 8 (1967): 33–44.

Dieterlen, Germaine. "L'image du corps et les composantes de la personne chez les Dogon." In *La notion de personne en Afrique noire, Paris, 11–17 octobre 1971.* Colloques internationaux du C.N.R.S., pp. 205–229. Paris, 1973.

Dieterlen, Germaine. *Systèmes de signes: Textes réunis en hommage à Germaine Dieterlen.* Centre National de la Recherche Scientifique. Paris, 1978.

Dieterlen, Germaine. *Le titre d'honneur des Arou (Dogon, Mali).* Paris, 1982.

Dieterlen, Germaine, and Marcel Griaule. *Signes graphiques soudanais.* Paris, 1951.

Dieterlen, Germaine, and Marcel Griaule. "The Dogon of the French Sudan." In *African Worlds: Studies in the Cosmological Ideas and Social Values of African Peoples,* edited by Daryll Forde, pp. 83–110. London, 1954.

Dieterlen, Germaine, and Marcel Griaule. *Le renard pâle.* Paris, 1965. Translated by Stephen C. Infantino as *The Pale Fox,* Chino Valley, Az., 1986.

Ferry, Marie-Paule. "Hommage à . . . Germaine Dieterlen." *L'humanité* (November 29, 1999).

Griaule, Marcel. *Dieu d'eau.* Paris, 1948. Translated as *Conversations with Ogotemmêli* (London and New York, 1970).

International African Seminar (3d, 1960, Salisbury, Southern Rhodesia). *African Systems of Thought: Studies Presented and Discussed at the Third International African Seminar in Salisbury, December 1960.* Prefaces by M. Fortes and G. Dieterlen. London, New York, 1965.

Lewis, I. M. "Obituary." *Anthropology Today* 16, no. 2 (April 2000): 25–56.

Piault, Marc-Henri, and Joelle Hauzeur, eds. "Les empreintes du renard pâle: Pour Germaine Dieterlen." *Journal des Africanistes* 71, no. 1 (2001): special issue.

LAURA S. GRILLO (2005)

DIFFUSIONISM SEE EVOLUTION, *ARTICLE ON* EVOLUTIONISM; KULTURKREISELEHRE

DIGNĀGA (c. 480–540 CE), founder of the Buddhist school of epistemology and logic in India. Born near Kāñcī in South India, Dignāga first belonged to the Vātsīputrīya school of Hīnayāna Buddhism, but unconvinced of the adequacy of its doctrine, he left the school. Some source materials record that he became a pupil of Vasubandhu, a renowned scholar of Buddhist philosophy, but his direct relationship to Vasubandhu may be questioned: a passage in one of Dignāga's works indicates an uncertainty concerning the authorship of a book traditionally attributed to Vasubandhu. Dignāga stayed for some time in Nālandā, then the center of Buddhist learning, and obtained mastery of the Vijñānavāda philosophy and of logic. His later years were spent in Orissa.

Dignāga composed many philosophical treatises. Most are no longer extant in Sanskrit, but a certain number of them are available in Tibetan or Chinese translation. The important ones are (1) *Prajñāpāramitā-piṇḍārtha-saṃgraha,* a summary of the *Prajñāpāramitā Sūtra* from the Yogācāra standpoint; (2) *Traikālya-pa-rīkṣā,* a treatise on the concept of time consisting of verses taken from Bhartṛhari's *Vākyapadīya* with a slight but significant modification: it is intended to set forth the Yogācāra view that phenomenal existences are produced by the consciousness (*vijñāna*); (3) *Abhidharmakośa-marma-dīpa,* an abridgment of Vasubandhu's book treating the dogmatics of the Hīnāyana schools; (4) *Hastavāla-prakaraṇa,* an examination of the Sautrāntika concepts of ultimate reality (*paramārtha-sat*) and empirical reality (*saṃvṛti-sat*); (5) **Upādāya-prajñapti-prakaraṇa,* a clear explanation of the Sautrāntika concept of empirical reality, arguing at the conclusion from the Yogācāra viewpoint that empirical reality is a product of the consciousness; (6) *Ālambana-parīkṣā,* an examination of the object of cognition; (7) *Hetucakraḍamaru;* (8) *Nyāyamukha;* (9) *Hetumukha* (not extant except for a few fragments); and (10) *Pramāṇa-samuccaya.* These last four works treat logic and epistemology.

Dignāga was a proponent of the Yogācāra doctrine insofar as he maintained that phenomenal existence was fabricated by the consciousness. However, the notion of the *ālaya-vijñāna* ("receptacle consciousness"), a central Yogācāra doctrine, is not mentioned in any of his works. He belonged to that school of the Yogācāras that did not recognize the *ālaya-vijñāna* and the "I-consciousness" (*manas*) separately from the six kinds of ordinary sense consciousness: visual, auditory, olfactory, gustatory, tactile, and discriminative. In some of his works he evinces an interest in Sautrāntika doctrine, and in fact, Dignāga's epistemological theories as expounded in the *Pramāṇasamuccaya* were made acceptable for both the Sautrāntikas and the Yogācāras.

Among the treatises concerning the Yogācāra philosophy, the *Ālambana-parīkṣā* is most important. In this work Dignāga repudiates the realists by arguing that a cognition cannot take for its object a thing in the external world, whether it is an individual atom or an aggregate of atoms. His discussions are similar to those presented by Vasubandhu in his *Viṃśatikā-vijñaptimā-tratāsiddhi.* However, the originality of Dignāga lies in his insistence that an object of cognition (*ālambana*) must fulfill two necessary conditions: first, the object must be the cause (*kāraṇa*) of a cognition, and second, it must possess the same form (*ākāra*) as that which appears in the cognition. To satisfy these two conditions the object must be a real entity (*dravya-sat*) and possess a gross form (*sthūlākāra*). With these two conditions in view Dignāga examined and rejected the realist theories and drew the conclusion that the object of cognition is nothing other than the form of an object that appears in the cognition.

Dignāga's major contribution in the field of logic is the invention of the "wheel of reasons" (*hetucakra*), which shows nine possible relations between a logical reason (*hetu*) and what is to be proven (*sādhya*), and enables one to distinguish a valid reason from invalid ones. The *hetucakra* was first presented in the *Hetucakraḍamaru,* and later incorporated in the *Nyāyamukha,* a work treating the dialectic on the model of Vasubandhu's *Vādavidhi,* and in the *Pramāṇasamuccaya,* a systematic exposition of the theory of knowledge.

The *Pramāṇasamuccaya* is the most important of Dignāga's works, for it is the synthesis of the doctrines expounded by him in different treatises. It comprises six chapters focusing on, respectively, (1) perception (*pratyakṣa*), (2) inference *svārthānumāna*), (3) syllogism (*parārthānumāna*), (4) proper and improper examples in syllogism (*dṛṣṭānta-dṛṣṭāntābhāsa*), (5) "differentiation from others" (*anyāpoha*) as the meaning of a word, and (6) futile rejoinder (*jāti*). In the first chapter, Dignāga makes a radical distinction between the two means of cognition, namely, perception, which apprehends the particular (*svalakṣaṇa*) with no conceptual construction (*kalpanā*), and inference, which apprehends the universal (*sāmānyalakṣaṇa*) produced through conceptual construction. The doctrines that invited attack from opponents, such as that of the identity between the means (*pramāṇa*) and the result (*pramāṇaphala*) of cognition and that of "self-awareness" (*svasaṃvitti*) of cognition, are advocated in this chapter. Chapters 2, 3, 4, and 6 deal with logical problems. In these chapters Dignāga discusses in full detail such topics as the distinction between inference for oneself (*svārthānumāna*) and inference for others (*parārthānumāna*), the three character-istics (*trirūpa*) of an inferential mark (*liṅga*), the object of inference (*anumeya*), the "wheel of reasons" (*hetucakra*), and the concomitance in agreement (*anavaya*) and in difference (*vyatireka*) between inferential mark and example, and establishes the system of three-membered syllogism. The fifth chapter is devoted to the elucidation of the *apoha* doctrine, that is, the doctrine that the function of a word consists in the "differentiation (of an object) from other things" (*anyāpoha*) and not in the direct reference to a real entity. This doctrine also aroused controversy among the scholars of the different philosophical schools.

Dignāga had a great influence on the scholars of both Brahmanic and Buddhist schools. Uddyotakara (c. sixth century) of the Nyāya school, Kumārila Bhaṭṭa (c. seventh century) of the Mīmāṃsā school, and Mallavādin (c. sixth century) of the Jain school made vehement attacks on his doctrines as presented in the *Pramāṇasamuccaya.* Praśastapāda (c. sixth century), a Vaiśeṣika philosopher, was much indebted to Dignāga for the formulation of his theory of inference. Among Buddhist scholars, Dharmakīrti (c. 600–660) wrote an elaborate commentary on the *Pramāṇasamuccaya*, the *Pramāṇavārttika*, in which he fully developed the ideas formulated by Dignāga. Soon this work took the place of the *Pramāṇasamuccaya* in academic circles, and was studied both by Buddhists and by members of rival schools.

See Also Dharmakīrti; Indian Philosophies; Vasubandhu; Yogācāra.

Bibliography

Frauwallner, Erich. "Dignāga, sein Werk und seine Entwicklung." *Wiener Zeitschrift für die Kunde Süd- und Ostasiens* 3 (1959): 83–164. On the basis of the careful examination of Dignāga's works, the author proposes a chronological order for them and sketches the development of Dignāga's thought. The Sanskrit or Tibetan texts of some short treatises are appended.

Hattori Masaaki, trans. *Dignāga, On Perception, Being the Pratyakṣapariccheda of Dignāga's Pramāṇasamuccaya.* Cambridge, Mass., 1968. An annotated English translation of chapter 1 of the *Pramāṇasamuccaya*, based on the Sanskrit fragments and the Tibetan versions. In the annotation references are made to the philosophical arguments of the rival schools and Dignāga's followers. Transliterated texts of two Tibetan versions are printed on facing pages.

Kitagawa Hidenori. *Indo koten ronrigaku no kenkyū: Jinna no taikei.* Tokyo, 1965. A lucid exposition of Dignāga's system of logic (part 1) and a Japanese translation of the main portions of the *Pramāṇasamuccaya*, chapters 2, 3, 4, and 6, with explanations based on Jinendrabuddhi's commentary (part 2). Appendix A consists of an annotated English translation of Dharmakīrti's *Saṃtānāntarasiddhi*, and an abridged English translation of Dignāga's *Ch'ü yin chia she lun* (**Upādā-yaprajñapti-prakaraṇa*). Appendix B presents two Tibetan texts of the *Pramāṇasamuccaya.*

New Sources

Franco, Eli. "Did Dignaga Accept Four Types of Perception?" *Journal of Indian Philosophy* 21 (1993): 295–299.

Ho, Chien-Hsing. "How Not to Avoid Speaking: A Free Exposition of Dignaga's Apoha Doctrine." *Journal of Indian Philosophy* 24 (1996): 541–562.

Robbins, Robert. "A Reexamination of Dignaga's Concept of Self Awareness." In *Contacts Between Cultures,* edited by A. Harrak, pp. 242–248. Lewiston, N.Y., 1992.

Tillemans, Tom J. F. "Pre-Dharmakirti Commentators on Dignaga's Definition of a Thesis (paksalaksana)." *Buddhist Forum* (1994): 295–305.

Tuske, Joerg. "Dinnaga and the Raven Paradox." *Journal of Indian Philosophy* 26 (1998): 387–403.

Hattori Masaaki (1987)
Revised Bibliography

DIHLAWĪ, SHĀH WALĪ, ALLĀH

See Walī Allāh, Shāh

DILTHEY, WILHELM

DILTHEY, WILHELM (1833–1911), German philosopher of history and intellectual historian. Dilthey was born in Biebrich am Rhein, where his father, a liberal Calvinist theologian, was court chaplain to the duke of Nassau. Following graduation at the head of his *Gymnasium* class in nearby Wiesbaden, he enrolled at Heidelberg in 1852 to study theology. After only a year, however, he left for Berlin and there began to concentrate on history and philosophy, studying with some of the greatest representatives of German historical scholarship: Leopold von Ranke, Theodor Mommsen, Jakob Grimm, August Boeckh, Franz Bopp, and Karl Ritter. In philosophy, his principal mentor was the Aristotelian F. A. Trendelenburg. Dilthey's interest in the German theologian and philosopher Friedrich Schleiermacher also stems from this Berlin period. In 1860, his essay on Schleiermacher's hermeneutics was awarded two prizes by the Schleiermacher Society and was followed by a commission to complete an edition of Schleiermacher's correspondence and write his biography. Dilthey defended his doctoral dissertation on Schleiermacher's moral principles in 1864. In the same year he presented a monograph on the analysis of moral consciousness that served as his *Habilitationsschrift*, the thesis that qualified him for university teaching. After a brief period of teaching at Berlin, he was called to Basel in 1867, and then to Kiel in 1868.

In 1870, Dilthey published the initial volume of his *Leben Schleiermachers* (Life of Schleiermacher), the first of several ambitious projects that would remain unfinished. In 1871, he accepted a chair at Breslau, where his main efforts were devoted to the problem of the nature and methods of the human sciences. In 1883, he published the first part of his major philosophical work, *Einleitung in die Geisteswissenschaften* (Introduction to the Human Sciences). In 1883, Dilthey also returned to Berlin to succeed Hermann Lotze in the chair that had once been occupied by Hegel. Election to the Prussian Academy of the Sciences followed in 1897. In 1900, he gave up his seminars, and in 1907 he retired from teaching altogether in order to develop more systematically the philosophical ideas put forward in the *Einleitung*. Dilthey died while on a working holiday in the Austrian Tyrol in 1911.

Dilthey's research on Schleiermacher and his account of the process of understanding the activity of a religious thinker constituted an important component of his work on the theory and practice of intellectual history. Yet his major contribution to religious studies lies in his theory of the human studies and its implications for the scientific investigation of religion.

Dilthey's theory of the human studies may be understood as an attempt to establish the idea that these disciplines have a distinctive subject matter and method that differentiate them from the natural sciences. The difference in subject matter is not grounded in two different modes of being but is, rather, based on two different ways of experiencing the world. Each is empirical, and each has its own definitive scientific objectivity and validity. The distinctive subject matter of the natural sciences is the world as given in the abstractions of sense perception and structured by reference to causal laws. The distinctive subject matter of the human sciences is the world as the person actually experiences it: the historically constituted ensemble of meanings and values that are the objects of his practical projects and interests. Because the artifacts of this historical world are all expressions of the human spirit, or *Geist*, the human sciences are the *Geisteswissenschaften*, the disciplines that investigate expressions of the human spirit.

Verstehen, or understanding, the distinctive method of these disciplines, is a consequence of the attitude that defines their subject matter. Because the actions and artifacts that express the human spirit are meaningful entities, a kind of knowledge is possible in the human sciences that cannot be reduced to explanation, or knowledge of the nomological structure of natural phenomena. *Verstehen* identifies the meaningful content of expressions of the spirit and the structures in which they are implicated. Much of Dilthey's work in the philosophy of the human sciences was concerned with the elucidation of this process of understanding and its distinctive epistemological quality, which he called the hermeneutic circle. An interpretation of the Romantic movement, for example, presupposes prior knowledge of which persons, actions, and artifacts fall within it. However, the latter are identifiable only on the basis of a general criterion that defines the features of romanticism. Thus knowledge of the whole rests on knowledge of the parts, which in turn presupposes knowledge of the whole.

The main aim of Dilthey's philosophical work was to develop a critique of historical reason that would resolve the question of how knowledge in the human sciences is possible. Dilthey struggled with this enterprise for more than forty years in the attempt to identify a basic or foundational science for the human sciences. In his writings of the 1880s and the early 1890s, he seems to have envisaged a descriptive, analytical, and phenomenological psychology as this foundation. Beginning in 1895, however, he stressed hermeneutics, or the theory of interpretation, as the basis for a valid theory of knowledge on which the human sciences can be grounded. Nevertheless, in his last works Dilthey retained intact many of the psychological theses of his earlier writings; moreover, the hermeneutic doctrines of his later work are also present in his earlier writings. As a result, the relationship between psychology and hermeneutics in the development of Dilthey's thought remains one of the most controverted issues among scholars who have attempted to understand his project of a critique of historical reason.

BIBLIOGRAPHY

The standard edition of Dilthey's works is the *Gesammelte Schriften*, 2d ed. (Stuttgart, 1957–), of which twenty-three volumes, prepared by various editors, have appeared. Also being published is a six-volume English edition of selected works by Dilthey. Under the general editorship of Rudolf A. Makkreel and Frithjof Rodi, five volumes have so far been issued. Major works on Dilthey in English include Makkreel's *Dilthey: Philosopher of the Human Studies* (Princeton, 1975), Michael Ermarth's *Wilhelm Dilthey: The Critique of Historical Reason* (Chicago, 1978), H. P. Rickman's *Wilhelm Dilthey: Pioneer of the Human Studies* (Berkeley, 1979), and Theodore Plantinga's *Historical Understanding in the Thought of Wilhelm Dilthey* (Toronto, 1980). For extant English translations of Dilthey's works, see Plantinga's bibliography. Since 1983 there has also been a scholarly journal devoted to Dilthey's work, with some articles in English and current bibliography: *Dilthey-Jahrbuch für Philosophie und Geschichte der Geisteswissenschaften* (Göttingen).

New Sources

Bambach, Charles R. *Heidegger, Dilthey, and the Crisis of Historicism.* Ithaca, 1995.

Makkreel, Rudolf A., and John Scanlon. *Dilthey and Phenomenology.* Washington, D.C., 1987.

Owensby, Jacob. *Dilthey and the Narrative of History.* Ithaca, 1994.

Rickman, H. P. *Dilthey Today: A Critical Appraisal of the Contemporary Relevance of his Work.* New York, 1988.

Tuttle, Howard N. *The Dawn of Historical Reason: The Historicality of Human Existence in the Thought of Dilthey, Heidegger, and Ortega y Gasset.* New York, 1994.

GUY OAKES (1987)
Revised Bibliography

DINÉ RELIGIOUS TRADITIONS SEE NAVAJO RELIGIOUS TRADITIONS

DINKA RELIGION SEE NUER AND DINKA RELIGION

DIOLA RELIGION. Numbering some four hundred thousand people, the Diola inhabit the well-watered coastal plain between the Gambia and São Domingo rivers of Senegambia and Guinea-Bissau. They are sedentary wet-rice farmers and usually described as a stateless people, governed by village councils. Despite a common ethnic label the various Diola subgroups speak distinct dialects and have somewhat divergent religious beliefs and political organizations.

The past two centuries of Diola religious history have been characterized by the increasing interaction of Diola religion with Islam and Christianity. While Muslims and Christians have been in contact with the Diola at least since the sixteenth century, few conversions occurred before the late nineteenth century. On the north shore of the Casamance River, where contact with Islam was both earliest and most violent, many Diola have embraced Islam and, to a lesser extent, Christianity. However, the growth of these new religions had to await the firm establishment of colonial rule and the growth of commerce in peanuts before gaining dominance over the traditional religion. On the south shore the vast majority of the population resisted the advance of Islam and Christianity until after World War II. While Christianity has made substantial inroads since that time, Diola religion remains dominant. This may partly result from the south's escape from the devastation of the Mandinka invasions and its slower integration into the colonial economy. A major factor, however, was the ability of south shore religion to adapt to rapidly changing conditions in the nineteenth and twentieth centuries. Innovations in ritual structures, the creation of new cults, and the emergence of Diola prophets have all contributed to the vitality of Diola traditional religion. This study will focus on south shore Diola religion.

Adherents of Diola religion believe in a creator god and in a number of lesser spirits whose powers originate with the supreme being but who are more accessible to the religious community. A study of Diola ritual might suggest that the supreme being, variously known as Ata-Emit or Emitai, was a remote high god whose name was rarely invoked in prayer, who had no shrines, and who was not a moral force in community life. The lesser spirits, variously known as *ukine* or *sinaati*, dominate ritual life. By examining the history of various cults and other religious beliefs, it becomes clear that Emitai is an active force in Diola life as a provider of life itself, as a source of spiritual aid in a time of crisis, and as the creator of the various cults. His name is derived from *emit*, meaning both "sky" and "year," thus indicating a strong relationship with the heavens and the order of an agricultural year. Furthermore, *Emitai ehlahl*, which means "it is raining," indicates Emitai's crucial role in the disbursement of that life-giving resource.

Emitai is seen as the creator of the world and all its inhabitants and as the source of human knowledge of farming, ironworking, and healing. He established a set of duties and interdictions to which he holds people accountable. At the time of death, Emitai decides whether a person has lived morally enough to become an ancestor or whether, if the individual concerned disregarded Emitai's interdictions, he will become a phantom wanderer or, ambivalently, a village dweller in a land to the south. All fates are temporary; the dead are eventually reincarnated.

Emitai communicates with people through dreams and visions and endows some of them with powers to communicate with him and with lesser spirits. While lesser spirits receive the bulk of ritual attention, prayers are ultimately received by Emitai. In times of crisis or when people feel they have exhausted other means, Emitai is prayed to directly. This is especially true during droughts when a ritual known as Nyakul Emit is performed. Rituals are conducted at all the village shrines, and prayers are offered directly to the supreme being: "Ata-Emit, is it true that this year's rice is destined to wither in the rice paddies? . . . The misfortune will be so large that we will not have the strength to speak. Give us water, give us life."

In Diola religion, the lesser spirits provide specific ways for individuals, families, and communities to resolve recurrent problems and to sustain a religious community. Thus there are shrines associated with rain, women's fertility, farming, hunting, fishing, war, ironworking, healing, family welfare, and village councils. These cults were introduced in a variety of ways. Some are said to have existed since the time of the first ancestors, that is, beyond the memory of Diola historians. Others were borrowed from the Bainounk, a people who were conquered by the Diola but who still retain a spiritual authority as the first inhabitants of the region. Still others were introduced by people who had spiritual powers, who were said to be able to travel up to Emitai or make contact with spirits through dreams or visions. Others were learned about from neighboring Diola or from other neighboring peoples. Such shrines were installed by elders from the outside community who also initiated a local group of shrine elders. The large number of shrines helps to ensure that one path can resolve any particular problem, and it allows a broad access to religious authority. Most people eventually become shrine elders. The shrines themselves contain ritual objects associated with spirits but not the spirits themselves. These objects help to summon the spirits and focus the attention of the worshipers.

While the preceding description represents broad continuities in Diola religion since 1700, environmental disruption, political and economic changes, and prophetic leaders have all influenced Diola religion. Droughts and epidemics have created spiritual challenges that have led to the formation of new cults and changes in ritual structure. Diola participation in the slave trade generated new sources of community vulnerability as well as new sources of social stratification, each of which had religious consequences. Men who gained wealth from the ransom or sale of captives often invested their wealth in the acquisition of priestly offices, thereby changing the role of priests and the ability of the less fortunate to gain religious authority. A new series of cults stressing lavish sacrifices to gain ritual authority became increasingly important to the Diola in the eighteenth century.

During World War II a Diola woman named Alinesitoué had a series of visions of Emitai. It was a time of severe drought and increasing French military conscription and confiscation of rice and cattle. Alinesitoué revealed that Emitai had given her a series of shrines that would help procure rain but whose ritual offices would be open to all, regardless of wealth, age, or sex. She advocated a renewed commitment to community, a stripping away of social and religious hierarchies, and a reaffirmation of many customs that had fallen into disuse. She taught that Emitai was deeply involved in the lives of the Diola and that they could expect his assistance if they followed his ways. Alinesitoué's teachings enabled the Diola to meet the crisis generated by the French occupation and a renewed Christian mission challenge. They allowed the Diola to adapt to their increasing integration into the rapidly changing order of a colonial and independent Senegal with the support of a vital Diola religion.

Bibliography

The major ethnographic study of the Diola, with extensive discussion of religious issues, is Louis-Vincent Thomas's *Les Diola*, 2 vols. (Dakar, 1958). Thomas has also written a vast number of articles on Diola ritual, concepts of death, initiation, and so on. J. David Sapir has written a number of articles on Diola symbolic thought, of which "Kujamama: Symbolic Separation among the Diola-Fogny," *American Anthropologist* 72 (December 1970): 1330–1348, is the most important. On the relationship between religious beliefs and legal and economic change, see Francis G. Snyder's *Capitalism and Legal Change: An African Transformation* (New York, 1981). Historical approaches to Diola religion include Jean Girard's *Genèse du pouvoir charismatique en Basse Casamance (Sénégal)* (Dakar, 1969) and my "Belief and Value Change among the Diola-Esulalu in Eighteenth and Nineteenth Century Senegambia" (Ph.D. diss., Yale University, 1986). There are also two important studies of the influence of Islam among the Diola: Frances Anne Leary's "Islam, Politics and Colonialism: A Political History of Islam in the Casamance Region of Senegal, 1850–1914" (Ph.D. diss., Northwestern University, 1970) and Peter Allen Mark's "Economic and Religious Change among the Diola of Boulouf (Casamance), 1890–1940" (Ph.D. diss., Yale University, 1976).

Robert M. Baum (1987)

DIONYSIUS THE AREOPAGITE (c. 500 CE),

Christian mystical theologian, also known as Pseudo-Dionysius. In the early sixth century, a set of treatises and letters appeared under the name of Dionysius the Areopagite, whom Paul had converted in Athens (*Acts* 17:34). At a synod in Constantinople in 533, the writings were used to support the monophysite position, but their authenticity was challenged. Nevertheless, the works soon came to be accepted as both apostolic and orthodox, and assumed nearly canonical status and authority in Eastern and Western Christendom.

Hilduin first translated the works into Latin (c. 832), and mistakenly identified Dionysius the Areopagite with Denis, the first bishop of Paris and patron saint of France. Though Abelard challenged this last identification, not until the Renaissance did Lorenzo Valla and Erasmus again question the authenticity of the writings' apostolic claims. These claims were decisively overturned in 1895, when two scholars, Joseph Stiglmayr and Hugo Koch, documented the dependence of the Dionysian corpus on Proclus, the fifth-century Neoplatonic philosopher. The works were thus composed in the late fifth or early sixth century. Despite many scholarly attempts to identify their author, he remains hidden behind his influential pseudonym. Dionysius's treatises are *Divine Names, Celestial Hierarchy, Ecclesiastical Hierarchy*, and *Mystical Theology*. The titles indicate Dionysius's principal concerns: religious language, hierarchy, and spirituality.

Divine Names poses the problems of religious knowledge and language by contrasting divine transcendence and theophany. In itself the divine nature is beyond being (*huperousios*), yet God becomes manifest in all being as its cause. God is both utterly transcendent and present in all things. This paradox underlies Dionysius's affirmative and negative theology. Affirmative theology focuses on divine causality and knows God through God's self-manifestations. It traces the causal procession from God's unity, through the divine ideas, or forms, to celestial hierarchy and thence to the sensible world; as it follows this descent, affirmative theology discovers an increasing variety of divine names, from "good" and "one" to "ancient of days," "sun," and "rock." Conversely, negative theology retraces the procession of beings in a return that moves from the sensible world, through the intelligences and forms, and to divine unity. Thus Dionysius emphasizes the dissimilarities in sensible symbols and the limits of all intelligible divine names. His work *Mystical Theology* negates all language about God because divinity cannot be known in its transcendence. For Dionysius, therefore, God is both nameless and praised in all names.

In *Celestial Hierarchy* Dionysius defines hierarchy as "a sacred order, activity and knowledge" that seeks "as far as possible [an] assimilation and union with God" (3.1–2). Its order is defined by each rank's capacity for assimilation to God, and its activity is purification, illumination, and perfection as it receives and communicates divine knowledge.

The celestial hierarchy consists of nine ranks of angelic intelligences, arranged in groups of three: (1) seraphim, cherubim, thrones; (2) dominations, virtues, powers; and (3) principalities, archangels, angels. The first triad is immediately united to God, whose light and knowledge it communicates to the lower ranks. In its turn the third triad presides over the human hierarchies. The ecclesiastical hierarchy stands between the celestial hierarchy and the hierarchy of the Mosaic law, which it supersedes (*Ecclesiastical Hierarchy* 5.2). Within the church there are six ranks in two triads: (1) bishops, priests, and ministers or deacons; and (2) monks, the "holy people of God," and those being purified (e.g., penitents and those awaiting baptism). Dionysius again stresses the activities of perfecting, illuminating, and purifying, but his focus here is symbolic and sacramental. Baptism is the sacrament of initiation and illumination, and the eucharistic liturgy exemplifies both the christological mystery and the perfecting "communion and union with the One" (*Ecclesiastical Hierarchy* 3.1). Contemplation (*theoria*) of the sacraments' hidden meanings purifies and illumines the understanding, and produces an intellectual insight akin to that of the celestial hierarchy.

The brief treatise *Mystical Theology* both completes and transcends the schemes of the divine names and of the hierarchies. It emphasizes the divine nature's radical transcendence, and it envisions mystical union in terms of unknowing (*agnōsia*). The concluding chapters present negative theology's ascending motion by stripping away the sensible and intelligible names of God. Dionysius then denies that God can be named adequately even in negative terms, because God is prior to all affirmation and negation. In itself the divine nature remains beyond all the contrasts that arise in its causal self-disclosure—and thus beyond all knowledge and speech. For Dionysius, mystical theology is an austere, intellectual ascent to union with God, and because divinity is essentially unknowable, this union occurs in the cloud and darkness of unknowing. This assimilation to God also completes the task of hierarchy. It is the perfection that the intellect seeks in symbols, sacraments, and intelligible divine names. Yet mystical theology accomplishes this ecstatically, by going out from intellect and hierarchy to their hidden source in the divine nature itself. In this way mystical theology completes the return to the God "beyond being."

The Dionysian writings are the product of a thoroughly hellenized Christian mind. Their reliance on Proclus and Damascius continues and even exaggerates the Greek patristic use of Platonic and Neoplatonic thought to interpret Christian faith. Dionysius was drawn into the mainstream of Byzantine theology by Maximos the Confessor, John of Scythopolis, and John of Damascus. Dionysius's major impact, however, came in the medieval West, where he was an immensely authoritative but alien figure. As the only Greek father to be fully and widely welcomed in the West, Dionysius influenced the whole range of Latin theology and spirituality. His account of the angelic hierarchy became standard, and his treatment of liturgy and the sacraments enriched the symbolic thinking of the Middle Ages. The Dionysian corpus became a major source for speculative thinkers, including John Scottus Eriugena, Albertus Magnus, Thomas Aquinas, and Nicholas of Cusa. Perhaps most important was the influence of Dionysius on mystical theology, evident in the Victorines, the Rhineland and English mystics, and in John of the Cross. Even while these Western thinkers were transforming his doctrine in their schools and monasteries, they consistently revered him as the "divine Dionysius." Although Dionysius's influence waned with the increasing suspicion concerning his identity, he still speaks powerfully on the issues of religious knowledge, language, and symbolism and their inherent limits.

BIBLIOGRAPHY

The standard edition of the extant works of Dionysius remains that of Balthasar Cordier (Antwerp, 1634), published in volume 3 of J.-P. Migne's *Patrologia Graeca* (1857; reprint, Turnhout, 1977). Gunther Heil has prepared a new edition of *La hiérarchie céleste* with a French translation by Maurice de Gandillac and an introduction by René Roques (Paris, 1970). The Dionysian corpus is available in English translations: John D. Jones's *Pseudo-Dionysius Areopagite: The Divine Names and Mystical Theology* (Milwaukee, 1980); *Mystical Theology and the Celestial Hierarchies*, 2d ed. (Fintry, U.K., 1965); Thomas L. Campbell's *The Ecclesiastical Hierarchy* (Lanham, Md., 1981; from a Ph.D. diss., 1955); and Ronald F. Hathaway's translation of Dionysius's letters in his study *Hierarchy and Order in the Letters of Pseudo-Dionysius* (The Hague, 1969). An excellent survey of Dionysius and his influence is the series of articles by René Roques and others under "Denys l'Aréopagite," in the *Dictionnaire de spiritualité*, vol. 3 (Paris, 1957), edited by Charles Baumgartner. Other studies include Denys Rutledge's *Cosmic Theology: The Ecclesiastical Hierarchy of Pseudo-Denys* (Staten Island, N.Y., 1965); Bernhard Brons's *Gott und die Seienden* (Göttingen, 1976); and Jan Vanneste's "Is the Mysticism of Pseudo-Dionysius Genuine?," *International Philosophical Quarterly* 3 (1963): 286–306.

DONALD F. DUCLOW (1987)

DIONYSOS is included in the pantheons of the majority of Greek cities and is present at such very early festivals as the Apaturia, the festival of the phratries, and the Anthesteria, that of new wine and the assembly of the dead. The youngest of the Olympian gods, he is somewhat insecure about his divine identity because he was conceived in the womb of a mortal woman, Semele. His semidivine status may account for his consistent interest in mortals and wine drinkers. As the god of masks, Dionysos appears in many forms, but he most loves to disguise himself as a god of the city, posing as a political deity and expressing absolute power. He appears in this form at Teos, where the city and the territory are consecrated to him and where he has a magnificent temple. In the town of Heraia in Arcadia, one of the two Dionysian temples is reserved for Dionysos the Citizen (Dionysos Polites). In Patras, where he is promoted to the rank of tyrant and given the title of Aisymnetes, he is the magistrate in charge of giving every person his rightful share. His political career begins in the seventh century on the island of Lesbos. Here he appears alongside Zeus and Hera in the common sanctuary as the god who is an "eater of raw flesh" (Alcaeus, *Fragment* 129). Thus the keystone of this political and religious edifice is Dionysos's subversive character, expressed in his rejection of the sacrificial system of eating food that is cooked according to the proper order (roasted then boiled) in favor of *omophagia*, the desire to eat raw flesh. The most extreme form of *omophagia* is *allelophagia*, in which men devour one another, becoming like wild beasts and ferocious animals. Such behavior allows them to escape from the human condition: it is a way of getting outside oneself by imitating those animals least subject to domestication.

It is at Delphi, in the great pan-Hellenic sanctuary of the eighth century, that Dionysos presents the full extent of his influence. In partnership with Apollo, the most ambitious god in the pantheon, Semele's son dominates not only the assemblies of local gods but also the whole course of Greek religion. Although he is originally from Thebes, Dionysos can be found in two parts of Delphi: in the heights of Mount Parnassus, where the members of the Thyiads, "the agitated ones," gather every other year in the Corycian cavern to honor him in the secret liturgy of the *trietēris* ("triennial festival"); and in the sanctuary of the Pythia, in a tomb-cradle beside the golden statue of Apollo, where he waits in mortal slumber until his servants come to wake him and where the Pure Ones, the priests of Apollo, privately offer sacrifice to him. At Delphi, Dionysos holds himself aloof from the giving of oracles, whereas in other sanctuaries oracles are closely connected with him. But this is because at Delphi he forms, together with Apollo, one of a pair of forces who are alternative poles in a system open to all of the altars or sanctuaries they share. Apollo has his Dionysian side, just as Dionysos presents more than one Apollonian aspect. The close connection between them at Delphi is the culmination of all the alliances that link them together at other places and in other ways.

Dionysos and Apollo are particularly joined in Orphic thought and its theogonic discourse, which was wholly at variance with the official dogma of Hesiod's theology. The religious system of the city and of the world, Hesiod's theology categorically rejected the way of life advocated by followers of Orpheus, who renounced the world and sought to be saved by returning to the primordial unity that preceded diversity. In the succession of divine ages described in the Orphic theogony, Dionysos is at once the last ruler and the first. In the last age he appears in the guise of the child who is lured by the Titans with toys—a spinning top, a devilish rhombus, and a mirror—and then slaughtered and devoured after being first boiled and then roasted (in breach of the normal order of the sacrificial ceremony). In being torn apart, scattered abroad, and broken into seven pieces, Dionysos experiences for himself the effects of the utmost differentiation, in accord with the process that began after the first age under the aegis of Phanes-Metis, another name for Dionysos. The primordial god of the perfect Unity, Phanes-Metis comes back at the end in order to return things once again to the beginning. In this scenario Apollo, even at Delphi, plays a role in the odyssey of Dionysos. Apollo buries the remains of Dionysos's murdered body at the foot of Mount Parnassus; shares the sovereignty of the oracle with Night, the primordial power; and, finally, becomes the Sun, the greatest of the gods even to Orpheus himself, rising to the summit of Mount Pangaeus in Dionysos's Thracian kingdom.

The success of Dionysos in Orphic theology reveals more than his ability to appear as the youngest of the Olympians and the oldest of the ancient gods. It demonstrates too his mystical calling, his natural tendency to rule over mysteries. In Ephesus, in the late sixth century, the philosopher Heraclitus denounced those who prowl in the night, in particular "magi, Bacchants, and mystics." It is sacrilegious, according to Heraclitus, for people to be initiated into what they dare to call mysteries. From the discoveries at Olbia on the shores of the Black Sea, we now believe that Dionysos first appears as the initiator in the sixth century, long before a Scythian king had enrolled in the band of Bacchus (Gr., Bakchos) in this same city, where he was fond of going for the aesthetic pleasure of living *à la grecque*—even to the extent of becoming a follower of Dionysos. This initiation was already known to King Scylas (Herodotos, 4.79), who had already begun preparations for it when a prodigy occurred: his palace of white marble, struck by lightning, was reduced to ashes. Nonetheless Scylas went ahead with the initiation ceremony, during which he publicly played the Bacchant, staggering through the town with a band of revelers.

What Herodotos implies in his account of Scylas going through with the initiation (*teletē*) is stated clearly in Euripides' *The Bacchae* in the voice of Dionysos. To Pentheus, who has failed to recognize his divinity and who will remain firmly entrenched in a ridiculous error, Dionysos, appearing as a stranger, recounts how the god introduced him to his rites, during which Dionysos watched him while he himself looked upon the god. In this mirror image, the initiation seems to denote an experience in which the Bacchant comes face to face with his god: he becomes as much a Bacchus as is Dionysos. The lord of the Bacchanalia refuses to reveal this experience to Pentheus; these are unspeakable things (*arrēta*) that non-Bacchants may not know (1.472). At Cumae, in the fifth century, a similar formula prohibited entry to a Greek cemetery "save to those who have been initiated to Dionysos."

At Olbia and at Cumae, Dionysos obviously does not receive the official, public worship that so many cities practice during the winter months, when solemn processions are attended by the entire population. Sacred laws from Asia Minor clearly distinguish between regular sacrifices, in which a goat or even a large ox is offered to Dionysos in full view of the city, and more private ceremonies in which the priestess of Dionysos celebrates an initiation into the cult of the god who drives people mad, inciting men and women to raving lunacy. There is a difference between *thuein* and *telein.* The same holy law of the Miletians, in 276 BCE, specifies that the rites of consecration (*telestēria*) should be invested in the priestess, who can initiate people into Dionysos Bakcheios "in the city, in the country, or in the islands." These are the so-called trieteric mysteries, which take place every two years. At Miletus they were celebrated at the same time as the Feast of the Return, when the god, escorted by the priests and priestesses, came back and entered the town.

In more than 150 cities of Asia Minor and the islands, Dionysos appears in the guise of Bakcheios, the god of the bacchanals—those who, like him, have become *bakchoi.* "Many are those who carry thyrsi; few are the Bacchants," according to a saying of the initiation masters quoted by Plato in his *Phaedo* (69c). To the initiate is reserved the experience of frenzy and possession, seeing the god face-to-face and sharing his madness and delirium. In the last golden tablet, a book of the dead unearthed at Vibo Valentia in Calabria in 1974, the titles *mystic* and *bacchant* are given to the chosen ones who go to the right, under the sign of memory, and take the sacred path that leads to the gods. Dionysos follows the same direction, from the sixth century on, to enter, via Iacchos, into the system of Eleusinian gods—the mysteries founded by Demeter on the fringes of Athens.

In connection with Dionysos the Initiate—who, under the name of Mustes, has a temple between Tegea and Argos (Pausanias, 8.54.5)—we find esoteric practices and rules of secrecy. Near Mantinea, in a great ancient chamber known as the *megaron,* the honey companions (*meliastai*) worship Dionysos, a neighbor of Black Aphrodite (Pausanias, 8.6.4). At Brysai, on the slopes of Mount Taigetos in Laconia, only women are permitted to view the statue of Dionysos, ensconced in an open-air sanctuary, and the sacrifices they perform are carried out in the greatest secrecy (Pausanias, 3.20.3). Males are also excluded on Lesbos, at Aigai, and on the island on the shores of the Atlantic described by Posidonius. The privilege of experiencing a private, face-to-face encounter with Dionysos or of being truly possessed by him is restricted to women, notwithstanding the violent objections of some modern-day feminists, who condemn the Dionysian interest in women as another way of oppressing them. The most unfortunate effect of this misinterpretation is to obscure the Dionysian union and its fundamental aspect: it is an individual allegiance that rejects kinship or feudal ties and, in the fluid form of the private *thiasos,* creates associations and communities independent of authority and outside the control of the state. If the mystical and mysterious side of Dionysos appears less clearly in the Athenian city-state—no doubt because the mystical pole there is called Eleusis—still it is a major component of Dionysianism in very many cities from the earliest times. Whether he resides in the center of town or camps on its outskirts, Dionysos is always the lord of dementia and of the ability to get outside oneself.

The popular tales of his coming and his manifestations describe, often in explicit terms, the favored *modus operandi* of Dionysos. It has to do with what the Greeks call the god's *epidēmia:* the tendency of a power to take up residence in one sanctuary and then switch to another temple and another country. Thus Apollo likes to spend the winter in the company of the Hyperboreans, making it possible for Dionysos to be "woken" by his priestesses, who proclaim his return. This is *epidēmia* in the sense of appearance or presence (*parousia*) and not in the sense of contagion, which would suggest that Dionysos moves from one place to another like a contagious disease whose infectious source is located on foreign soil (in the country of the Thracians) and is responsible for the violent fevers that invade the healthy, vigorous body of the Hellenic nation. One need only peel the outer shell of legend from this picture, only recently revealed with the aid of a number of myths concerning Dionysian Thrace and the god's enemies, to uncover the reality of a very faithful history. The Dionysian *parousia,* as originally intended, presents two interlocking aspects. The god who comes is a foreigner and remains so, carrying within him the most unwavering strangeness.

Yet the opposite side of Dionysos, and his appearance vis-à-vis the other gods, is that he affirms through his disavowal that he is a god too strange, and too much a stranger, to be believable. In Greece, the stranger, as opposed to the "barbarian," belongs to the society of those who share the same blood, the same language, and the same gods, according to Herodotos's definition. Dionysos, indeed, is no barbarian god, even when his outrages smack of barbarism. Born in Thebes, in the town of Kadmos, he is a great god, the equal of Apollo, the oracular power known as Ismenios. Dionysos presents himself in his status as a foreigner in more than one of his Joyous Entrances. For example, at Patrae in Achaia (Pausanias, 7.19.7–9), Dionysos enters as an idol in a sealed chest, like a demon god classed as a foreigner, and is conveyed by an equally strange king, a prince stricken with madness for having looked at the face, the mask, of Dionysos. This strange team puts an end to an equally outlandish sacrifice in which the human blood of both sexes had to be shed, bringing forth a sickness (*nosos*) in the land; the earth is diseased with punishment imposed by a cruel Artemis.

But the stranger who comes with Dionysos, instead of making himself a host and returning the gracious generosity seen in a feast like the Xenia, appears ungrateful to those who find him. The strangeness of Dionysos seems to imply that he cannot be recognized as a god at first sight. Thus he is obliged to offer a public demonstation of his divine power so that all people can see what a great god they have failed to acknowledge.

The appearance of Dionysos requires the revelation of Otherness through its exacting violence. There are those who do not know him and still slight him, doubters and those who neglect, scorn, or refuse to believe in or accept him. And there are those who are called on to persecute him, whom he has chosen to be his tormenters and thus the most striking witnesses to his *parousia*, once they have become his rightful victims. In Boeotia, in the city of Orchomenus, the daughters of King Minyas, absorbed in household tasks, pay no heed to Dionysos. But then the god, in the guise of a young girl, carefully encourages them to join in his mysteries. Suddenly, all three are entranced by Dionysos's metamorphoses—the girl disappears, and the god is a bull, a lion, a leopard. They watch in fascination as milk and nectar flow along the weaver's loom. Already they are caught in the web; wishing to honor the unknown god by offering sacrifice, they draw lots to see who will have the privilege of providing the chosen victim. The tragically elected Leucippe falls upon her own son and, with the help of her sisters, tears him to pieces in front of Dionysos (Antoninus Liberalis, *Metamorphoses* 10).

In Thrace, where Dionysos is also treated as a stranger, Lykurgos embodies the irreconcilable foe whose blindness compels the god, despite himself, to unleash the cruelest of deeds. Like a madman, Lykurgos brandishes his double ax, the *pelekus*, to kill Dionysos, not knowing that in Thessaly, at Pagasai, Dionysos is called the god of the ax, Pelekus. Lykurgos, hallucinating in his *mania*, turns the weapon back upon his own flesh and blood: he strikes down his children, whose living limbs, arms, and lopped-off legs appear to him as so many branches on a vine. This happens before the Edonians, incited by Dionysos, attempt to put an end to the fatal barrenness of their land by handing over their king to wild horses. The king is to be torn apart on Mount Pangaeus, where the oracle of Dionysos, like that at Delphi, will be erected. On its peak, Orpheus, the worshiper of the greatest of the gods, whom he names Apollo, is torn to pieces by Thracian women with a violence borrowed from Dionysos.

The stranger-god finds the full measure of his *parousia* in murderous frenzy, in the *mania* that leads to killing and to the spilled blood of a son torn apart by his mother, to children who are cut down alive by their father, and to father and daughter, such as Icarus and Erigone, losing their lives for lack of pure wine. Dionysos is truly himself only in *unyielding* madness, when the *mania* creates, through murder, a taint, a *miasma*, a sickness or pestilence. One must be cleansed of this stain; it is urgent to escape the plague, for in it appears the contagious power of those who fall into madness, which affects an entire town or even a whole country. In the *mania* of Dionysos is a taint that the god himself experiences in the course of his life (Apollodorus, *Library* 3.5.1). When he discovers the vine, Hera, his stepmother, breathes madness into Dionysos, dooming him to the wanderings of all madmen. Dionysos goes to Proteus, then to Cybele in Phrygia; at last he finds Rhea, who eases and puts an end to his nomadic delirium. Dionysos is purified, delivered from the taint of his madness. While with Rhea he learns the rites of his cult, and he receives from her his raiment, his Bacchus outfit, which he gives to Pentheus in *The Bacchae*.

The tales of his epiphany thus show how the worship of Dionysos, with its formalized mythology, establishes itself within the sphere of the purification called for by the insanity that the stranger carries. Dionysos the Purificator (Lysios) is the opposite side of the Bacchanal, the god who leads men and women astray in his frenzy. That he is a dual god is shown by his pairs of neighboring temples, at Thebes, at Corinth, and at Sicyon. The unclean madness that forms the basis of his cult is always part of him, however disciplined and civilized Dionysos may seem in the pantheons of cities unmindful of his fundamental wildness.

BIBLIOGRAPHY

Detienne, Marcel. *Dionysus Slain.* Translated by Mireille Muellner and Leonard Muellner. Baltimore, 1979.

Detienne, Marcel. *Dionysos à ciel ouvert.* Paris, 1986.

Farnell, Lewis R. *The Cults of the Greek States*, vol. 5 (1909). Reprint, New Rochelle, N.Y., 1977. See pages 85–344.

Jeanmaire, Henri. *Dionysos: Histoire du culte de Bacchus.* Paris, 1970.

Kerényi, Károly. *Dionysos: Archetypal Image of the Indestructible Life.* Princeton, 1976.

Nilsson, Martin P. *The Dionysiac Mysteries of the Hellenistic and Roman Age* (1957). New York, 1975.

Otto, Walter F. *Dionysos: Myth and Cult.* Bloomington, Ind., 1965.

Segal, Charles. *Dionysiac Poetics and Euripides' Bacchae.* Princeton, 1982.

West, M. L. *The Orphic Poems.* Oxford, 1983.

New Sources

Bierl, Anton F. Harald. *Dionysos und die griechiche Tragödie.* Tübingen, 1991. See the review by Giovanni Casadio, in *Quaderni di storia* 38 (1993): 185–198.

Carpenter, Thomas H. *Dionysian Imagery in Archaic Greek Art.* Oxford, 1986.

Carpenter, Thomas H. *Dionysian Imagery in Fifth Century Athens.* Oxford, 1997.

Carpenter, Thomas H., and Christopher A. Faraone, eds. *Masks of Dionysus.* Ithaca and London, 1993.

Casadio, Giovanni. *Storia del culto di Dioniso in Argolide.* Rome, 1994.

Casadio, Giovanni. *Il vino dell'anima. Storia del culto di Dioniso a Corinto, Sicione, Trezene.* Rome, 1999.

Cazanove, Oliver de, ed. *L' association dionysiaque dans les sociétés anciennes.* Rome, 1986. See the review by Giovanni Casadio, in *Dialogues d'histoire ancienne* 15 (1989): 285–308.

Frontisi-Ducroux, Françoise. *Le dieu-masque. Une figure de Dionysos d'Athènes.* Paris and Rome, 1991.

Henrichs, Albert. "Loss of Self, Suffering, Violence: the Modern View of Dionysus from Nietztsche to Girard." *Harvard Studies in Classical Philology* (1984): 205–240.

Henrichs, Albert. "Dionysus." In *The Oxford Classical Dictionary*, pp. 479–482. Oxford and New York, 1996.

McGinty, Park. *Interpretation and Dionysos. Method in the Study of a God.* The Hague, 1978.

Merkelbach, Reinhold. *Die Hirten des Dionysos.* Stuttgart, 1988.

Pailler, Jean-Marie. *Bacchus. Figures et pouvoirs.* Paris, 1995.

Privitera, Giuseppe Aurelio. *Dioniso in Omero e nella poesia greca arcaica.* Rome, 1970.

Seaford, Richard. *Reciprocity and Ritual.* Oxford, 1994.

Turcan, Robert. *Les sarcophages romaines à rpr̃ésentations dionysiaques.* Paris, 1966.

Turcan, Robert. *Liturgies de l'initiation bacchique à l'époque romaine (Liber).* Paris, 2003.

Versnel, Hendrik Simon. *Ter Unus. Isis, Dionysos, Hermes.* Leiden, 1990.

MARCEL DETIENNE (1987)
Translated from French by David M. Weeks
Revised Bibliography

DIOSCURI SEE TWINS

DISCIPLESHIP.

Scholars of the world's religions have contributed much to the study of discipleship in the settings of specific religious communities. But there remains much to be done in framing a general estimate of the social meaning and historical impact of discipleship as a communal pattern in the history of religions. The present entry, therefore, offers a model of discipleship that might be helpful in organizing comparative studies of this important type of religious society.

Religious discipleship, in the sense defined below, seems to be specifically rooted in the great civilizational religious and philosophical systems that arose in the Mediterranean world, Mesopotamia, South Asia, and East Asia from the middle of the first millennium BCE through the middle of the first millennium CE. Buddhism, Christianity, Confucianism, Greco-Roman philosophical tradition, Islam, Hinduism, Judaism, Daoism, and Zoroastrianism are the most influential traditions to have emerged or reached classical expression during this period. At the conceptual center of each stands a moral seriousness that challenges adherents to transform themselves in light of a comprehensive vision of the place of human life in the cosmic order. At the social center of these traditions stand strikingly similar types of authoritative figures—literate intellectuals (priests, scribes, teachers, or prophets) who claim, on the basis of learning in ancient tradition or personal insight, to mediate wisdom about the essential purposes of life. Communities established for the perpetuation and transmission of such wisdom were probably the earliest settings for the practice of religious discipleship.

A WORKING MODEL OF DISCIPLESHIP. Discipleship can be defined most generally as a particularly intense mentoring relationship in which a body of knowledge deemed essential to the wise conduct of life is transmitted from the mentor (or master) to the protégé (or disciple). This wisdom, about how to properly live, necessarily combines practical matters of daily life with more esoteric bodies of theory or doctrine. In the practice of discipleship, moreover, such wisdom is believed to be available only within the mentoring relationship. The disciple's belief that the master is uniquely capable of communicating wisdom is crucial to the master's continuing authority in the relationship. It is also crucial to the disciple's ongoing willingness to emulate those elements of the master's way of living that are taken to embody the latter's own possession of wisdom.

Indeed, emulation of the master is the essence of the master–disciple relationship. It is both a primary strategy in the disciple's quest for wisdom and proof that this knowledge has been properly mastered. So, for example, the disciples of Stoic philosophers in the Hellenistic world would seek to embody the attitude of *apatheia* (indifference to pleasure or pain) modeled in the lives of such masters as Epictetus (50–130 CE). Similarly, initiates into Islamic Ṣūfī circles would be expected to emulate the specific discipline or path (*ṭarīqah*) modeled by the guide (*shaykh*). Another common aspect of emulation involves, as in early rabbinic Judaism (from about the third century CE) and Tibetan Buddhist monastic settings even in contemporary times, memorizing the master's formal teaching in oral or written texts, and interpreting their meaning in oral instructional settings.

In many cases, orally recited stories that first circulated among disciples about the deeds of a master were written down to provide hagiographic material for circulation both within and beyond the immediate circle of disciples. The diverse oral collections of Jesus' sayings and deeds that underlie the canonical and extra-canonical Gospels may well have been collected by Jesus' disciples prior to the point at which they were combined into a broader evangelical literature. Later, more formal examples of hagiography in the Christian tradition include the *Life of Anthony* and the *Life of Pachomius,* both of which were fundamental to the development of fourth-century asceticism as a pattern of Christian discipleship. Comparable writings are transmitted in Sufism (e.g., *The Way of Aḥmad ibn ʿAlī ar-Rifāʿī* of the twelfth century), Jewish contemplative circles (*The Life of the Holy Lion Rabbi Isaac Luria* of the early seventeenth century), and Daoism (*Collected Accounts of the Perfected* of the tenth century), among many others.

Emulation of the master necessarily involves disciples in intense psychological identification with, and dependence upon, their mentors. Thus the virtue of humility or self-effacement before the master is a prized trait of the disciple. Symbolic postures of subordination can be as simple as carefully observed protocols governing, for example, which rabbinic disciples walked to the left or the right of the sage, and which the sage actually chose to lean upon when walking. In this context, it is not unusual for disciples to expect and receive corporal punishment as a form of discipline, as specified, for example, in the *Rule* of the Christian monastic order of Saint Benedict. In other systems of discipleship, as in some Tantric traditions of India or in ancient Greek philosophical discipleship, identification with or subordination to the master can also be expressed via sexual intimacy.

DISCIPLESHIP AND SOCIAL HIERARCHY. The basic social protocol of discipleship involves practices for ordering human relationships in view of hierarchy of power and authority. The fundamental purpose of that relationship is to authorize the transmission of knowledge and wisdom from the superior (the master) to the subordinate (the disciple). The nature of this knowledge will be discussed below. For now, it is important to focus upon the nesting of the discipleship relationship within a web of other types of hierarchical institutions in which the transmission of knowledge is also an essential goal.

Most historical examples of religious discipleship involve not simply a teacher and a student, but a group. This group is the discipleship community. Such communities, in many respects, are analogous in intention and structure to such common social institutions as kinship systems and schools. The social hierarchy created within the discipleship community is different from that of family and school, but dependent upon both. In discipleship, the community is a kind of school that recapitulates at a more refined level the cultural task of the family. Here the disciple returns to the psychological situation of childhood to be fundamentally reformed as a human being. Now the task of emulation involves absorbing the teaching of a master in such a way as to embody the master's own achievement.

What is that achievement? It is at this point that the question of special knowledge and wisdom arises. The master's achievement is greater than that of the biological parent or other elder, who has merely become a participant in the received cultural or religious tradition. The master, by contrast, has reached that form of human perfection held out by tradition as the highest attainable. The master, then, is a parent, but more so. Often called "Father" or "Mother," the master can displace the biological parents in the disciple's scale of loyalties and affections. Certain Greco-Roman philosophical paths, echoed by some rabbinic teachers of the early common era, as well as medieval Ṣūfī masters, held, for example, that a disciple owes more respect to a master than to a biological parent. The reason should not be hard to predict: parents only bring their child into physical life, whereas the master, by contrast, brings the disciple into eternal, life-transforming knowledge.

The master is also more than a teacher, for a system of discipleship is more than a school. Schools transmit the knowledge expected of functional participants in the religious tradition or culture. Whether at a relatively fundamental or at a more sophisticated level, they transmit "formative" knowledge, knowledge that shapes the cultural and autobiographical identity of the knower and enables one to both share in and contribute to creativity in the culture. In the setting of discipleship, however, students are trained to reconceive their own human perfection in emulation of the model presented by their master. In this sense, the knowledge offered in the discipleship relationship is not formative but "transformative." It holds out to the disciple the promise of becoming in some fundamental sense a new being. In possessing the master's transformative knowledge and embodying it, one passes from a state of ignorance to one of wisdom, illumination, or grace, depending upon the symbolic vocabulary native to the traditions that nourish specific discipleship communities.

CHARACTERISTICS OF TRANSFORMATIVE KNOWLEDGE. As mentioned above, transformative knowledge can be known only through a direct relationship of discipleship with the master. Familiarity with a master's teaching alone, either as oral tradition or written text, does not constitute a transformative appropriation of the master's knowledge. Rather, it is necessary to hear the master's own teaching accompanied by the master's explanation; it is necessary to observe the master's behavior in various settings, in order to emulate the ways in which the master's teachings are embodied in concrete models of execution.

The master, from this perspective, is a living medium through which a truth, otherwise hidden from natural sight, is disclosed and made tangible. The master is a disclosure of truth, and this disclosure is only in part mediated through specific verbal teachings. Its fullness must be found in the actual existence of the master. Thus the disciple commonly views the master as a kind of text to be decoded and interpreted. The full, transformative knowledge imparted by the master is available only to the disciple who knows how to read the master's text—and this text includes more than the master's verbal utterances. It includes the entire being of the master as it is disclosed to the disciple in the personal encounter.

In the history of religions, the nature and significance of the transformative knowledge made available to disciples by masters is always linked to broader cultural and religious traditions within which the discipleship communities themselves have emerged. In other words, masters control, focus, and refine symbol systems that penetrate widely throughout a given culture. They transform "culture" into a disciplinary path that creates a "subculture," a community living out the larger values of a cultural tradition in particularly intense and concentrated form. Monasticism in the diverse Christian and Buddhist traditions are examples of discipleship communities that are perceived, by both insiders and their lay or royal patrons, to represent the purest representation of the path of life defined by Christ or the Buddha. Depending upon circumstances, however, discipleship communities can define themselves, under a master's guidance, in an adversarial relationship to the larger cultural and religious tradition. A "subculture" of discipleship, in other words, can become a "counterculture."

Thus the so-called Dead Sea sect of second-century BCE Jewish Palestine, founded by a priest known as the Righteous Teacher (*moreh tzedek*), was certainly a discipleship community that framed itself in opposition to the existing culture of the Jerusalem Temple priesthood. It is highly probable as well that the original discipleship communities surrounding Siddhārtha Gautama, the founder of Buddhism, were defined in some sort of adversarial relationship to socially dominant forms of Hindu asceticism and Brahmanic traditionalism. Buddhism and Christianity, from this perspective, are examples of countercultural discipleship communities that ultimately became comprehensive religious civilizations in their own right, and that lived to spawn further subcultures of discipleship.

The precise social agendas of discipleship communities are distinct, at least theoretically, from the specific sorts of transformative knowledge that they offer to their members as the pinnacle of and reward for a life of self-discipline. For the present introductory purpose, it will be helpful to organize the patterns of transformative knowledge transmitted within discipleship communities into the following clusters: (1) knowledge concerning the cultivation and interpretation of visions; (2) knowledge concerning the cultivation of conditions of ego-lessness and loss of self-consciousness; and (3) knowledge concerning self-mastery in view of ultimately authoritative laws or norms. It is important to remember that, like all typological exercises in the history of religions, these types rarely appear in "pure" form. Rather, students should be prepared to find various degrees of admixture of one or more of these patterns in any given discipleship community.

The cultivation of visionary experience, especially associated with healing, is, according to some historians of religion, among the oldest forms of religious activity. Often referred to under the general rubric of shamanism, its roots lie in the preagricultural societies of hunters and gatherers, and it continues in a variety of forms into contemporary times. It is impossible to know how prehistoric shamanic experiences were transmitted or whether training in the cultivation of such experiences took the form of discipleship communities as defined here. It is clear, however, that guidance in the shamanic arts among contemporary practitioners often takes forms quite similar to discipleship, although the life-defining vision that inaugurates the life of the shamanic healer is commonly sought in isolation.

The point is that the formation of discipleship communities for the cultivation of extraordinary visions is not limited to classical shamanic rites of healing. The prophetic guilds of ancient Israel and other Mediterranean and Mesopotamian cultures also cultivated visionary experiences. Here, however, the healing of individuals was not a primary concern, but rather the disclosure of divine purposes in relation to communities or to society as a whole. Many scholars have suggested, moreover, that the tradition of pseudepigraphic apocalyptic literary prophecies of Second Temple period Judaism (c. 520 BCE–70 CE) and early Christianity (c. 30 CE–120 CE) had its roots in visionary discipleship communities formed among scribes in particular. The ability to receive visions of a heavenly world, to interpret their meaning for others, and to cultivate new visions, was read as a sign of the visionary's transformation into a new being, no longer entirely earthbound, but capable of tasting in this life the immortality of the divine world. This form of visionary pursuit proved to be of particular salience among the various Christian communities of Late Antiquity labeled by their Orthodox Christian theological opponents as Gnostics. It was richly apparent as well among neighboring Jewish communities associated with heavenly ascent to the *merkavah*, or divine Throne, who witnessed angels bathed in divine light and surrounded by rivers of fire singing hymns to the hidden God of Israel.

The cultivation of experiences of ego-lessness and loss of self-consciousness is commonly found among contemplative traditions frequently defined as mysticism. It is entirely fair to assert that mysticism is among the most frequent settings for the flourishing of discipleship communities. Contemplative exercises associated with yogic disciplines for focusing awareness beyond the self, necessarily mediated by a guide or *gurū*, have very ancient roots in the Indian subcontinent and continue to be widely practiced in traditional and westernized forms. Equally well known are the contemplative traditions of Japanese Zen Buddhism, Tibetan Buddhism, Islamic Sufism, some forms of Jewish Qabbalah, and a host of Christian meditative practices cultivated primarily in monastic settings. All of these require protracted periods of discipleship to a master in order to achieve and control the interpretation of various states of loss of self.

In one sense, the search for self-mastery in view of ultimately authoritative norms or laws is common to any form of discipleship, for the essence of discipleship is the incorporation of a discipline framed by rules. In certain types of discipleship circles, however, self-mastery is viewed not merely as a means toward the acquisition of transformative knowledge, but as the essence of wisdom itself. This is particularly so when heroic cultivation of memory is regarded as part of the discipline of self-transformation. Scrupulous Brahmanic performance of ancient Vedic rituals, associated with the memorization of vast corpora of orally transmitted Sanskrit texts, is one of the oldest continuous traditions of this sort of discipleship community. In Judaism, this type of discipleship became prominent in the rabbinic communities of late antiquity (c. 200 CE–700 CE). Disciples in this tradition studied under masters who had memorized the traditions of Oral and Written Torah that had been revealed on Sinai to Moses and incorporated them into their very being. Like their masters, disciples sought to be transformed into "living books" from which the revelation of God could be read.

Some Questions for Further Study. As stated above, the comparative study of discipleship as a pattern of religion remains relatively undeveloped, especially in light of the massive documentation of discipleship communities in specific religious traditions. It is useful, therefore, to pose some pointed questions for further research on the nature of discipleship and the relationship of discipleship communities to the larger patterns of the religious cultures in which they emerge.

The first is as follows: What structural and historical roles have discipleship communities played in forming and transmitting traditions central to religious traditions as a whole? To what degree, in other words, does the discipleship community constitute a formative, culturally influential context for the production and transmission of aesthetic, ideological, ritual, or other traditions? Are there religious civilizations that appear to have been largely generated by discipleship communities; are there others in which discipleship communities appear relatively late in the articulation of the tradition? What historical or ideological factors might explain such differences?

The second question concerns the wisdom cultivated within discipleship communities. How is transformative knowledge constructed in relationship to the sorts of ritual or theological knowledge mediated beyond the discipleship community? That is, in what settings do discipleship communities represent themselves as self-selecting elites who must protect their special knowledge from outsiders? What conditions account for moments in which discipleship communities seek to expand the circle to include and transform those originally outside the circle? How have discipleship communities been involved in the politics of knowledge within their several host cultures?

A third question focuses upon the media in which transformative knowledge is communicated in the situation of disciple mentoring. Discipleship as such seems to be largely associated with religions in which literacy and the interpretation of writings play important roles. Yet the importance of the mentoring relationship commonly places a premium on orally transmitted knowledge. Can the study of discipleship communities shed light on the relative importance of written and oral forms of communication within the broader religious traditions in which they participate? Many discipleship communities are profoundly hostile to, or at least ambivalent about, the use of written sources in the teaching of disciples. These include the following: Brahmanic priests, rabbinic sages, Hindu *sants*, Greco-Roman philosophers, and Christian monastic ascetics, among others. How do such attitudes mirror broader cultural attitudes regarding the authority of books and teachers as repositories of knowledge?

Finally, a fourth question: To the degree that the discipleship community is constructed hierarchically, how does its hierarchy replicate or undermine other social hierarchies beyond the community? At times, for example, initiation into discipleship communities offers relief from confining gender roles (as in female monasticism in Buddhism and Christianity). What principles explain this creation of a space in which normal gender practices are suspended? Why are such principles absent in other discipleship traditions, such as those created in Judaism, where—with the possible exception of the first-century Therapeutrides of Alexandria—female discipleship is largely unknown?

SEE ALSO Leadership.

BIBLIOGRAPHY

Asad, Talal. "Discipline and Humility in Medieval Christian Monasticism." In *Genealogies of Religion: Discipline and Reasons of Power in Christianity and Islam*, pp. 125–167. Baltimore, Md., & London, 1993.

Brown, Peter. "The Rise and Function of the Holy Man in Late Antiquity." *Journal of Roman Studies* 61 (1972): 80–101.

Brown, Peter. *The Body and Society: Men, Women, and Sexual Renunciation in Early Christianity.* New York, 1988.

Byrskog, Samuel. *Jesus the Only Teacher: Didactic Authority and Transmission in Ancient Israel, Ancient Judaism, and the Matthean Community.* Stockholm, 1993.

Cabezón, José Ignacio. *Buddhism and Language: A Study in Indo-Tibetan Scholasticism.* Albany, N.Y., 1994.

Cabezón, José Ignacio, ed. *Scholasticism: Cross-Cultural and Comparative Perspectives.* Albany, N.Y., 1998.

Cannon, Dale. *Six Ways of Being Religious: A Framework for Comparative Studies of Religion.* Belmont, Calif., 1996.

Carruthers, Mary. *The Book of Memory: A Study of Memory in Medieval Culture.* Cambridge, UK, 1990.

Chamberlain, Michael. *Knowledge and Social Practice in Medieval Damascus, 1190–1350.* Cambridge, UK, 1994.

Elm, Susanna. *"Virgins of God": The Making of Asceticism in Late Antiquity.* Oxford, 1994.

Ernst, Carl W. "The Textual Formation of Oral Teachings in Early Chishti Sufism." In *Texts in Context: Traditional Hermeneutics in South Asia*, edited by Jeffrey R. Timm, pp. 271–297. Albany, N.Y., 1992.

Fowden, Garth. "The Platonic Philosopher and His Circle in Late Antiquity." *Philosophia* 7 (1977): 359–383.

Fowden, Garth. "The Pagan Holy Man in Late Antique Society." *Journal of Hellenic Studies* 102 (1982): 33–59.

Gammie, John G., and Leo G. Perdue, eds. *The Sage in Israel and the Ancient Near East.* Winona Lake, Wis., 1990.

Gold, Daniel. *The Lord as Guru: Hindu Sants in North Indian Tradition.* New York, 1987.

Gold, Daniel. *Comprehending the Guru: Toward a Grammar of Religious Perception.* Atlanta, Ga., 1988-.

Hadot, Ilsetraut Hadot. "The Spiritual Guide." In *Classical Mediterranean Spirituality: Egyptian, Greek, Roman*, edited by A. Hilary Armstrong, pp. 436–458. New York, 1986.

Hadot, Pierre. "Forms of Life and Forms of Discourse in Ancient Philosophy." *Critical Inquiry* 16 (1990): 183–205.

Hengel, Martin. *The Charismatic Leader and His Followers.* Translated by James C. G. Greig. Edinburgh, UK, 1981.

Hevelone-Harper, Jennifer. "Spiritual Direction." In *Late Antiquity: A Guide to the Postclassical World*, edited by G. W. Bowersock, Peter Brown, and Oleg Grabar, pp. 704–705. Cambridge, Mass., 1999.

Hezser, Catherine. *The Social Structure of the Rabbinic Movement in Roman Palestine.* Tübingen, Germany, 1997.

Idel, Moshe. *Hasidism: Between Ecstasy and Magic.* Albany, N.Y., 1995.

Ivanhoe, Philip J. *Confucian Moral Self Cultivation.* 2d ed. Indianapolis, Ind., 2000.

Jaffee, Martin S. "A Rabbinic Ontology of the Written and Spoken Word: On Discipleship, Transformative Knowledge, and the Living Texts of Oral Torah." *Journal of the American Academy of Religion* 65 (1997): 525–549.

Jaffee, Martin S. "Transformative Knowledge." In *Early Judaism,* pp. 213–243. Upper Saddle River, N.J., 1997.

Jaffee, Martin S. "Torah in the Mouth in Galilean Discipleship Communities." In *Torah in the Mouth: Writing and Oral Tradition in Palestinian Judaism, 200 BCE–400 CE,* pp. 126–152. New York, 2001.

Katz, Steven T. "Models, Modeling, and Mystical Training." *Religion* 12 (1982): 247–275.

Klein, Anne C. *Knowledge and Liberation: Tibetan Buddhist Epistemology in Support of Transformative Religious Experience.* Ithaca, N.Y., 1986.

Klein, Anne C., ed. and trans. *Path to the Middle: Oral Mādhyamika Philosophy in Tibet.* Albany, N.Y., 1994.

Malamud, Margaret. "Gender and Spiritual Self-Fashioning: The Master-Disciple Relationship in Classical Sufism." *Journal of the American Academy of Religion* 64 (1996): 89–117.

McMahon, David. "Orality, Writing, and Authority in South Asian Buddhism: Visionary Literature and the Struggle for Legitimacy in Mahayana." *History of Religions* 37 (1998): 249–274.

Rousseau, Philip. *Ascetics, Authority, and the Church in the Age of Jerome and Cassian.* Oxford, 1978.

Schimmel, Annemarie. *Mystical Dimensions of Islam.* Chapel Hill, N.C., 1975.

Schofer, Jonathan. "Virtues in Xunzi's Thought." *Journal of Religious Ethics* 21 (1993): 117–136.

Snyder, H. Gregory. *Teachers and Texts in the Ancient World: Philosophers, Jews, and Christians.* New York, 2000.

Swartz, Michael D. *Scholastic Magic: Ritual and Revelation in Early Jewish Mysticism.* Princeton, N.J., 1996.

Tambiah, S. J. *The Buddhist Saints of the Forest and the Cult of Amulets: A Study in Charisma, Hagiography, Sectarianism, and Millennial Buddhism.* Cambridge, UK, 1984.

Trimingham, J. Spencer. *The Sufi Orders in Islam.* New York, 1971; reprint, 1998.

Valantasis, Richard. *Spiritual Guides of the Third Century: A Semiotic Study of the Guide-Disciple Relationship in Christianity, Neoplatonism, Hermetism, and Gnosticism.* Minneapolis, Minn., 1991.

Valantasis, Richard. "A Theory of the Social Function of Asceticism." In *Asceticism,* edited by Vincent L. Wimbush and Richard Valantasis, pp. 544–551. New York, 1995.

Wach, Joachim. "Master and Disciple: Two Religio-Sociological Studies." *Journal of Religion* 42 (1962): 1–21.

Weber, Max. *The Sociology of Religion.* Translated by Ephraim Fischoff. Boston, 1963.

Yearley, Lee. "Teachers and Saviors." *Journal of Religion* 65 (1985): 225–243.

MARTIN S. JAFFEE (2005)

DISCIPLES OF CHRIST. The Disciples of Christ is an American-born religious group formed in 1832 by the merger of the Christian movement led by Barton Stone with the "Reforming Baptists," headed by Thomas and Alexander Campbell. Most of the early leaders of the movement, including Stone and the Campbells, had been Presbyterians, but they imbibed deeply of the spirit of religious freedom in the wake of the American Revolution. Stone was one of the leaders of the Kentucky revival at the turn of the nineteenth century. Distressed by Presbyterian opposition to the revival, in 1804 he and five other ministers left the church, announcing their plan to be "Christians only" in "The Last Will and Testament of the Springfield Presbytery."

Thomas Campbell came to America in 1807, having been a Presbyterian minister in Northern Ireland. Disturbed by the sectarian spirit of the American church, Campbell clashed with the synod, and in 1809 he was suspended from the ministry. Campbell and a few of his supporters almost immediately formed the Christian Association of Washington (Pennsylvania), and Campbell wrote a fifty-six page explanation of his views, called the *Declaration and Address.* Thomas Campbell's son, Alexander, arrived in America shortly after the publication of the *Declaration and Address.* Twenty-one years old at the time, Alexander Campbell had been influenced by the reforming ideas of Scottish evangelist Robert Haldane while spending a year in Glasgow, and he immediately embraced his father's independent position. He quickly rose to the leadership of the movement. The Campbells joined with Baptist associations from 1815 until 1830 and were known by the name Reformers.

Preaching similar pleas for Christian union and in frequent contact with one another in Kentucky, the Stone and Campbell movements sealed a remarkably successful union in 1832. Alexander Campbell and his followers generally favored the name Disciples of Christ, while the Stone churches continued to use the name Christian Church. Many local congregations were called Churches of Christ. All three names have been used throughout the movement's history. The new church spread rapidly with the westward migration of population; at the time of the union in 1832 it was estimated to have 22,000 members, and by 1860 that figure had grown to nearly 200,000.

Two ideas undergird Disciples thought, both of them highly attractive amid the optimism on the American frontier in the 1830s. First was an emphasis on Christian union. Second was an appeal for the "restoration of the ancient order of things" as a means of attaining unity. The battle cry of the movement, stated in 1809 by Thomas Campbell, was "Where the Scriptures speak, we speak; and where the Scriptures are silent, we are silent."

The Disciples were Arminian, believing in freedom of the will, and they were revivalistic, although never given to extreme enthusiasm. They held traditional views on most questions and were most visibly set apart by their restorationist views on the local church. They organized autonomous congregations presided over by elders and deacons and emphasized weekly observance of the Lord's Supper. In the early years of the movement, Alexander Campbell was caustically anti-institutional, but by the 1840s antimission sentiment abated. Most early Disciples were also strong postmillennialists, believing that the second coming of Christ would be ushered in by the world reformation begun by Luther and capped by their own restoration movement.

In addition to the Campbells and Stone, the most prominent early leader of the Disciples was another Scottish Presbyterian minister, Walter Scott, who is credited with formulating the "five-finger" plan of salvation—faith, repentance, baptism, forgiveness of sins, and gift of the Holy Spirit—which was preached by a generation of pioneer Disciples evangelists. The Disciples were slow in developing denominational institutions; consequently, the most powerful leaders of the movement were editors of religious journals. Alexander Campbell edited the *Christian Baptist* from 1823 to 1830 and the *Millennial Harbinger* from 1830 until 1864, just two years before his death. Stone, Scott, and scores of other preachers also published papers that tied the loose-knit movement together.

While conceiving of themselves as a protest against sectarian division, the Disciples quickly became a part of the denominational competition in the American Midwest and South. Alexander Campbell's influence among the Baptists was particularly strong, and in some parts of the West, the Disciples devastated Baptist associations. The church spread rapidly westward from Ohio and Kentucky and as far south as Tennessee and Texas.

The years after the Civil War form a second era in Disciples history. By 1866, all of the first generation leaders of the church were dead, and dramatic shifts in power occurred within the church. The Disciples continued to grow rapidly; the religious census of 1906 listed around 1,150,000 members in the movement. But the census also revealed that a major schism had taken place within the church. Deep sectional and sociological tensions had begun to appear shortly after the Civil War.

In spite of the facts that the Disciples were strongest in the border areas and that most of the church's leaders had urged moderation during the slavery controversy, Disciples were seriously divided by the Civil War. In 1863, northern Disciples passed a resolution of loyalty to the Union at the meeting of the American Christian Missionary Society, which had been formed in 1849. Southern Disciples were deeply angered. Although most Disciples argued that the church could not divide because it had no denominational apparatus, in the years after the Civil War northern and southern newspapers and other institutions became increasingly antagonistic. In the census of 1906 the most conservative wing of the movement (which was almost entirely southern) was identified separately and designated the Churches of Christ.

Although the tensions of the nineteenth century had clear sectional and sociological underpinnings, the debate also had a doctrinal focus. As it became ever more apparent that the hoped-for millennium of peace and unity was not imminent, conservative Disciples lost interest in Christian union as a practical goal, and liberal Disciples increasingly discarded legalistic restorationism as a means of attaining union. The most visible issues that divided churches were support for the missionary society that had been founded in 1849 and the scripturality of the use of instrumental music in worship. The founding of the society (which had Alexander Campbell's tacit approval) seemed to some an abandonment of the anti-institutional principles of the early movement; the society further alienated many southerners because of the passage of political resolutions during the Civil War; finally, the organization was attacked as "unscriptural" by rigid restorationists. The introduction of organs into the churches also rankled conservatives, who considered them symbols of decadence and found no evidence of their presence in the New Testament churches. By 1900, hundreds of conservative local congregations had separated from the movement as independent Churches of Christ.

The most powerful Disciples journal during the late nineteenth century was the *Christian Standard*, published in Cincinnati, Ohio, by Isaac Errett until his death in 1888. The most influential journal among the conservatives of the South was the *Gospel Advocate*, edited for over half a century by David Lipscomb in Nashville, Tennessee. By the end of the century, however, leadership of the movement had drifted toward James H. Garrison, who in 1874 became editor of the Saint Louis-based *Christian-Evangelist*. Garrison was grounded in the nuances of Disciples theology, but he was irenic in spirit and encouraged a new generation of Disciples leaders to take the mainstream of the movement into the center of liberal American Protestantism.

In the early twentieth century the Disciples suffered a second major division and a slowing growth rate. As a new generation of Disciples liberals, particularly a group associated with the University of Chicago, pressed for a more ecumenical view of the Disciples mission and a more liberal understanding of the scriptures, conservative opposition solidified around the *Christian Standard*. Finally, in the 1920s, the conservatives began withdrawing their support from Disciples organizations and in 1927 established the rival North American Christian Convention. These dissentient conservative congregations remained loosely associated in the Undenominational Fellowship of Christian Churches and Churches of Christ. The more liberal wing of the movement adopted the name Christian Church (Disciples of Christ).

A full body of boards and commissions developed in the twentieth century, headquartered mostly in Indianapolis and Saint Louis. In 1968 the church restructured into a representative and more centrally controlled organization, losing perhaps one-third of its listed congregations in the move and completing the second schism, which had been in progress since the 1920s.

Disciples have been important leaders in modern ecumenical activities. The *Christian Century* began as a Disciples journal (founded as the *Christian Oracle* in 1884), and its editorial corps was long dominated by Disciples. The Disciples have also been prolific builders of universities and colleges, perhaps the most widely known being Texas Christian University, Butler University, Drake University, and Bethany College.

See Also Campbell, Alexander.

Bibliography

The best general summary of Disciples history is William E. Tucker and Lester G. McAllister's *Journey in Faith* (Saint Louis, 1975). A sociological interpretation of Disciples history in the nineteenth century can be found in my books *Quest for a Christian America* (Nashville, 1966) and *The Social Source of Division in the Disciples of Christ* (Atlanta, 1973). A survey of the movement written by a leader of the conservative Christian churches is James D. Murch's *Christians Only* (Cincinnati, 1962). A Churches of Christ perspective can be found in Earl I. West's *The Search for the Ancient Order,* 2 vols. (Indianapolis, 1950). Three older works that remain significant are William T. Moore's *A Comprehensive History of the Disciples of Christ* (New York, 1909), and two books by Winfred E. Garrison, *Religion Follows the Frontier* (New York, 1931) and *An American Religious Movement* (Saint Louis, 1945).

David Edwin Harrell Jr. (1987)

DISCIPLINE, SPIRITUAL See SPIRITUAL DISCIPLINE

DISMEMBERMENT.

Among the many procedures that are carried out in sacrificial ritual, dismemberment and distribution of the victim's body figure prominently. Moreover, beyond its physical dimension, dismemberment also possesses complex and highly significant social, symbolic, and intellectual dimensions, as has been shown, for instance, in Jean-Pierre Vernant's analysis of the primordial sacrifice performed by Prometheus, according to Hesiod's *Theogony.* For, as Vernant has argued, the division of the victim's body in effect establishes the difference between gods, who are immortal and have no need of food (since they receive only the victim's bones and fat) and humans, who receive portions of bloody meat wrapped in an ox's stomach and whose lives are thus characterized by hunger, death, and ultimate bodily decay.

Whereas the Promethean model of sacrificial division (evident also in the sacrifices of the Greek city-states) served to discuss and establish the distinction between human and divine, other sacrificial patterns are more attuned to gradations of social hierarchy. Such is the case in Dinka sacrifice, as described by Godfrey Lienhardt, who presents what appears to be a "butcher's chart" detailing the assignment of different cuts of meat to different social groups, the prestige of group and cut being directly correlated. That the butcher's chart is, in effect, a diagram of social hierarchy is not lost on the Dinka themselves, who observe: "The people are put together, as a bull is put together." Lienhardt (1961) goes on to elaborate: "Since every bull or ox is destined ultimately for sacrifice, each one demonstrates, potentially, the ordered social relationships of the sacrificing group, the members of which are indeed 'put together' in each beast and represented in their precise relations to each other in the meat which it provides."

A similar pattern is also evident in one of the most ancient Italic sacrifices, the *Feriae Latinae,* a ritual that dates to the period prior to Roman domination of central Italy but subsequently was taken over by the Romans and adapted to their purposes. Thus, according to Dionys of Halikarnassos (4.49), all forty-seven cities that were members of the Rome-dominated Latin League were called upon to send representatives each year to the Alban Mount "to congregate, feast together, and take part in common rituals." Within the *Feriae Latinae,* however, were celebrated both the cohesion of the Latin League and the unequal status of its members, themes that found expression in the sacrificial banquet at the center of the rite. Thus, each city was assigned to contribute a different, carefully graded portion of food to the celebration ("some lambs, some cheeses, some a portion of milk"), while hierarchically ranked portions of meat taken from the sacrificial bull were distributed to all the participants. Given its sociopolitical importance, the distribution of meat was carefully scrutinized, and any mistake in the assignment of portions could force the repetition of the entire ritual, as could the failure of any participant to pray for the welfare of the whole Roman people. The latter offense would mark a failure of social solidarity; the former, of proper hierarchy.

A similar case is found in one of the best-documented sacrifices performed by the ancient Germanic peoples, that of the Semnones, as reported in chapter 39 of Tacitus's *Germania*:

> They say that the Semnones are the oldest and most renowned of the Suebi. This belief is confirmed in a religious ceremony of ancient times. At a fixed time, all the people of the same blood come together by legations in a wood that is consecrated by the signs of their ancestors and by an ancient dread. Barbaric rites celebrate the horrific origins, through the dismemberment of a man for the public good. . . . There the belief of all looks back [to the primordial past], as if from that spot there were the origins of the race. The god who is ruler of all things is there. Others are inferior and subservient. The good fortune of the Semnones adds to their authority. One hundred cantons are inhabited for them, and this great body causes them to believe themselves to be the head of the Suebi.

Several points must be made regarding the logic and intent of this grisly rite in which the public dismemberment of a human victim was the central feature. First, this was done in repetition or representation of creation, insofar as the sacrifice celebrating the "horrific origins" (*horrenda primordia*) was performed at the very place where the "origins of the race" (*initia gentis*) were believed to be. This comes as little surprise, however, given the well-known Germanic myths that describe creation as resulting from the bodily dismemberment of a primordial giant by the gods themselves. (For the fullest account, see Snorri Sturluson's *Gylfaginning* 6–8.) Second, the sacrifice was performed to confirm the Semnones' claim to primacy within the Suebian confederation, of which they considered themselves the "oldest and most renowned" (*vetustissimos se nobilissimosque*) members. This claim was also expressed in bodily terms: the Semnones regarded themselves as the "head of the Suebi" (*Sueborum caput*), something that was perhaps no idle metaphor, but one reflected—and justified—in the formal distribution of the dismembered remains of sacrificial victims.

The theme of creation as the result of a primordial act of sacrificial dismemberment is also common in ancient India. As one celebrated text relates:

> When they divided Man [Skt., Puruṣa], how many pieces did they prepare? What are his mouth, arms, thighs, and feet called? The priest was his mouth, the warrior was made from his arms; His thighs were the commoner, and the servant was born from his feet. The moon was born of his mind; of his eye, the sun was born; From his mouth, Indra and fire; from his breath, wind was born. From his navel there was the atmosphere; from his head, heaven was rolled together; From his feet, the earth; from his ear, the cardinal points. Thus the gods caused the worlds to be created. (*Ṛgveda 10.90.11–14*)

The text is remarkable for the way in which it describes society and the cosmos alike as having both been formed from the bodily members of the first sacrificial victim. Thus, we are first presented with a set of social homologues to the human body, wherein four differentially ranked classes—priests (Skt., *brāhmaṅa*), warriors (*kṣatriya*), commoners (*vaiśya*), and servants (*śūdra*)—derive their respective hierarchic positions and characteristic modes of action (speech, force of arms, production and reproduction, and running of errands) from that bodily part with which they are associated (mouth, arms, thighs, and feet). Similarly, a second set homologizes parts of the cosmos to bodily members or faculties: moon to mind, sun to eyes, wind to breath, and so on. Moreover, the social and the cosmic sets themselves are implicitly correlated through the mediation of the body, for the cosmos—like the body and society—is organized into hierarchically ranked vertical strata: heaven (including the celestial bodies), atmosphere (including the wind), and earth.

The logic of dismemberment thus establishes the priestly class as concerned with heavenly matters, such as sacred speech and the ritual fire, by their very nature, for priests and fire alike have their origin from the mouth (fire being thus the "eater" of whatever is placed into it, the sacrificial fire being called the "mouth of the gods"). The lower classes, in contrast, are relegated to more lowly, mundane pursuits; warriors occupy an intermediate status.

The model that is established within this myth (as also within the practice of Vedic sacrifice) is, quite literally, that of an "organic" cosmos and a "corporate" society, the parts of which are ordinarily unified but are also analytically detachable, whereupon their hierarchic interrelations become fully evident. Moreover, the corporate nature of society also finds expression within the very rhythms of sacrificial ritual. Lienhardt's observations regarding Dinka sacrifice are, once again, most instructive:

> It is at the moment immediately preceding the physical death of the beast, as the last invocation reaches its climax with more vigorous thrusts of the spear, that those attending the ceremony are most palpably members of a single undifferentiated body, looking towards a single common end. After the victim has been killed, their individual characters, their private and family differences, and various claims and rights according to their status, become apparent once more. In the account of the role of cattle, I mentioned the Dinkas' way of figuring the unity and diversity of kin-groups in the unity of the bull or ox and in the customary division of its flesh. Similarly in a sacrifice, whilst the victim is still a living whole, all members of a gathering are least differentiated from each other in their common interest in that whole victim. With its death, interest turns towards the customary rights of different participating groups in the division of its flesh. . . . Sacrifice thus includes a recreation of the basis of local corporate life, in the full sense of those words. The whole victim corresponds to the unitary solidarity of human beings in their common relationship to the divine, while the division of the flesh corresponds to the social differentiation of the groups taking part. (Lienhardt, 1961, pp. 233–234)

Although he does not use these terms, Lienhardt here masterfully describes the phases of aggregation and segmentation that mark most rituals. As is clear in the accounts of the *Feriae Latinae* and the Semnones' sacrifice, individuals and groups gather for the performance of a ritual in which they gradually surrender their sense of separate identity as they come to feel part of a broader social totality, united by bonds of kinship, polity, commensality, and/or common purpose. Then, toward the end of the proceedings, this social totality breaks into its constituent parts once again, only to be reunited at the next sacrifice. Further, as Lienhardt recognized, the moment at which the phase of aggregation ends and that of segmentation begins is that moment in which the victim is killed and its flesh divided.

Social segmentation thus coincides with sacrificial dismemberment, while aggregation corresponds to a victim that is whole. That victim, like society, contains within its body the potential to be cut into hierarchically differentiated pieces, but its life depends upon the preserved unity and cooperation of those pieces within an organic whole. These same processes also find abstract, philosophical expression at times, as in the thought of Empedocles (fifth century BCE), who describes the entire cosmos as being ruled by two competing processes: Strife, which tears things apart and finds its representation par excellence in sacrificial dismemberment (see, for example, his fragments numbered B128, B137, and B20 in the Diels-Kranz collection), and Love, the force that reunites those things rent asunder by Strife. For that matter, things are not so dissimilar when it comes to the celebrated Aristotelian tools of analysis (i.e., separating a whole into its constituent parts) and synthesis (i.e., reassembling the parts into an organic whole), whereby thought is dismembered and put back together, after the fashion of a sacrificial ox.

SEE ALSO Cosmogony; Greek Religion; Puruṣa; Sacrifice.

BIBLIOGRAPHY

An important collection of essays on the general theme of dismemberment within sacrificial ritual has appeared under the editorship of Christiano Grottanelli, Nicola F. Parise, and Pier Giorgio Solinas: "Sacrificio, Organizzazione del cosmo, dinamica sociale," *Studi storici* 25 (October–December 1984): 829–956. Further studies on the same theme, organized by the same editors, will be forthcoming in *L'Uomo.* Also of great interest are the essays that appear in *La cuisine du sacrifice en pays grec,* edited by Marcel Detienne and Jean-Pierre Vernant (Paris, 1980). Discussion of the Dinka materials is found in Godfrey Lienhardt's *Divinity and Experience: The Religion of the Dinka* (Oxford, 1961). On the *Feriae Latinae* (and its possible connection to myths of creation by sacrificial dismemberment), see Walter Burkert's "Caesar und Romulus-Quirinus," *Historia* 11 (1962): 356–376; on the Semnones, see L. L. Hammerich's "Horrenda Primordia: Zur 'Germania' c. 39," *Germanisch-Romanische Monatsschrift* 33 (May 1952): 228–233, and Alfred Ebenbauer's "Ursprungsglaube, Herrschergott und Menschenopfer: Beobachtungen zum Semnonenkult (Germania c. 39)," in *Antiquitates Indogermanicae: Gedenkschrift für Hermann Güntert,* edited by Manfred Mayrhofer et al. (Innsbruck, 1974), pp. 233–249. I have also discussed many of these materials at greater length in *Myth, Cosmos, and Society: Indo-European Themes of Creation and Destruction* (Cambridge, Mass., 1986).

New Sources

Ulrich, Katherine Eirene. "Divided Bodies: Corporeal and Metaphorical Dismemberment and Fragmentation in South Asian Religions." Ph.D. diss., University of Chicago, 2002.

BRUCE LINCOLN (1987)
Revised Bibliography

DĪVĀLĪ, also known as Dīpāvalī, is an important renewal festival celebrated all over India in October–November at the time of the autumn equinox. Dīvālī marks the end of the rainy season and the harvest of the summer crops. The name *Dīvālī* can be translated as "row of lights," in reference to lights lit on the nights of the transition from the waning to the waxing moon. These lights stand for the hope kindled by the new season that comes at the end of the dangerous monsoon. In many ways the festival is a celebration of a new year. Accordingly, debts are paid off, and merchants close their accounts in anticipation of new wealth.

Dīvālī is a three-night festival, the last night of which is the first night of the waxing moon. The celebrations incorporate a number of mythic elements, many of which find colorful regional variations. As in any renewal rite, care is taken to cleanse and purify homes and shops, and people make certain to perform special ablutions in a ritual bath. The festival is most obviously characterized by the seemingly infinite number of oil lamps that are lit everywhere, as well as by the noise of exploding firecrackers that are said to frighten away evil spirits and to welcome the arrival of Lakṣmī, goddess of prosperity. In some regional practices the lamps are said to light the darkness for departed ancestors or to welcome the demon king Bali.

It is to Lakṣmī, however, that the people offer jewels and money, delicate foods, and special new clothes made for the occasion. Much importance is placed on the giving of gifts to all members of the family and to the neighborhood servants who help people throughout the year. Men gamble at various games in a ritual reenactment of the dice tournaments played by the gods to determine the fate of human beings.

The festival is associated with several Puranic myths. Their underlying idea calls forth what was at issue during the rainy season and centers on the notion, which holds true for ancestors as well, that underworld creatures play a crucial role in the acquisition of wealth. A well-known myth relates how the dwarf Vāmana (an incarnation of Viṣṇu) asked Bali to grant him as much land as he could cover in three steps. The generous demon king agreed. To his amazement, two of the dwarf's steps covered the earth and the sky; the third, planted on Bali's head, sent the demon to the underworld, a region that became his domain. For his generosity, Bali was then allowed to come to the surface of the earth during Dīvālī in order to bestow wealth on human beings.

Another myth, one in which the god Kṛṣṇa is said to slay Naraka (or Narakāsura, the "demon of hell"), similarly marks the momentary halt of evil underworld powers. Naraka is the son of Bhūdevī, the earth goddess, and Varāha, the incarnation of Viṣṇu as a boar, who had rescued the goddess when she lay buried under the waters of the sea. Although he was ultimately killed by Kṛṣṇa—as all demons must eventually be killed by a god—Naraka, like Bali, is nevertheless paid homage when the question of wealth is at stake.

In North India the second day of Dīvālī is reserved for the worship of the hill Govardhana, near the town of Mathura, a site of deep religious significance for devotees of Kṛṣṇa. Once Indra had captured all of the world's cattle. Kṛṣṇa freed the cows, but the enraged Indra flooded the earth with a downpour of rain to drown the valuable animals. Kṛṣṇa then raised Govardhana so that the cows would be saved. The importance of the myth is clear in the context of Dīvālī, for in Hindu thought the cow is a powerful and evocative symbol of prosperity. The ritual here primarily involves worship of cattle, but—in a play on the word *govardhana* (lit., "cow-increasing")—offerings are made to mounds of cow dung (*govar*) to ensure continued prosperity and wealth (*dhana*).

One final ritual marks the celebration of Dīvālī. Girls and women, who at the onset of the rainy season had tied protective threads around their brothers' wrists, now invite the boys and men for delicacies in exchange for gifts. This rite is accompanied by the worship of Yama, lord of the dead, and his twin sister, Yami. Yama is also known as Dharmarāja ("king of the social and cosmic order"), for that very order is then restored with the return of prosperity, which is dependent upon women and on controlled underworld powers.

See Also Gambling; Hindu Religious Year; Yama.

BIBLIOGRAPHY

For textual details on the festival, see P. V. Kane's *History of Dharmaśastra,* 2d ed. (Poona, 1958), vol. 5, pt. 1, pp. 194–210. Some interesting regional variations are given in Lawrence A. Babb's *The Divine Hierarchy: Popular Hinduism in Central India* (New York, 1975) and in Oscar Lewis's *Village Life in Northern India* (Urbana, Ill., 1958).

MARIE-LOUISE REINICHE (1987)

DIVINATION

This entry consists of the following articles:

AN OVERVIEW
GREEK AND ROMAN DIVINATION

DIVINATION: AN OVERVIEW

is the art or practice of discovering the personal, human significance of future or, more commonly, present or past events. A preoccupation with the import of events and specific methods to discover it are found in almost all cultures. The culture possibly least interested in divination is that of the traditional Australian Aborigines, yet even they hold divinatory "inquests" at funerals to discover the identity of the sorcerers responsible for the deaths.

Much of science itself has evolved from forms of divination and may be said to continue certain aspects of it. Astronomy, for example, is deeply indebted to ancient Near Eastern and Hellenistic astrological researches; mathematics and physics were advanced by Indian, Pythagorean, and Arabic divinatory cosmological speculations; and several leading Renaissance scientists were inspired by the divinatory schemes of Qabbalah and hermitism in their search for the moral harmonies and direction of the universe. Yet it would be incorrect to label divination a mere infantile science or pseudoscientific magic, for modern science and traditional divination are concerned with essentially distinct goals. This helps to explain the continuing fascination with divination even today on the part of well-educated people, notably in regard to astrology, the *Yi Jing,* and spiritualism or necromancy (séances with the dead). Divination involves communication with personally binding realities and seeks to discover the "ought" addressed specifically to the personal self or to a group. Science, however, if faithful to its own axioms, cannot enunciate any "oughts" because of its methodological, cognitive, and moral neutrality: it only offers hypotheses about reality and is concerned with general statistical regularities, not with unique persons or events. The existential situation and binding transcendental realities are beyond its concern. It may be argued that, precisely to the degree that such modern disciplines as psychotherapy and Marxist theory leave science behind, they take on divinatory (and therefore religious) functions, and represent modern contributions to the history of divination.

BASIC FORMS. Anything can be used to divine the meaning of events. It is very common to assign spontaneous and arbitrary meaning to signs or omens when one is deeply anxious about the outcome of a personal situation. But the cultural form of divinatory methods and signs is seldom entirely random: each one expresses a specific logic.

A full list of divinatory agents, therefore, would amount to a catalog of both nature and culture. H. J. Rose, in his article "Divination, Introductory and Primitive," in volume 4 of the *Encyclopaedia of Religion and Ethics* (Edinburgh, 1911), classifies the most common means used to obtain insight as follows: dreams (oneiromancy); hunches and presentiments; involuntary body actions (twinges, sneezes, etc.); ordeals; mediumistic possession; consulting the dead (necromancy); observing animal behavior (e.g., ornithomancy, interpreting the flight of birds); noting the form of entrails of sacrificial victims (extaspicy or haruspicy), or the victims' last movements before death; making mechanical manipulations with small objects such as dice, drawing long or short stalks from a bundle, and so on (sortilege); reading tea leaves (tasseography), or using playing cards (cartography), etc.; decoding natural phenomena (as in geomancy, palmistry, phrenology, or astrology); and—of course—"miscellaneous." Plato—in an analysis that still forms the basis of most modern treatments (as in the world survey of divination edited by Caquot and Leibovici, 1968)—distinguished "ecstatic" and "nonecstatic" types, with the latter including all inductive and empirical systems of noting portents, studying entrails, and so forth. But ecstatic states and inductive methods can be mingled confusingly; indigenous interpretations of so-called objective omens often assume spirit possession of the omens and/or ecstatic insight in the diviner, while some mediums appear quite normal when "possessed."

It would be more useful to establish what the indigenous theory of divination is, rather than to attempt to assay the states of mind actually experienced by diviners in different cultures and periods. The same conscious experience of heightened awareness can be interpreted in one culture as deep wisdom and in another as spirit possession. Under the influence of such interpretations, in fact, an individual diviner might permit himself to drift into a deeper mediumistic trance, or on the contrary strive toward a more intense lucidity. How a condition is interpreted influences the way it unfolds and realizes itself.

Stressing the indigenous theory of divination also directs us to the cosmological assumptions and the attitudes toward the self that unit various seemingly unrelated methods. For example, cultures that stress mediumistic interpretations of trance usually also explain the casting of lots or the conformations of entrails in terms of spirit possession: divination, according to this overarching viewpoint, consists of the forms of communication developed by invisible beings to instruct humanity on the meaning of events. But cultures that have developed a concept of a decodable impersonal and elemental divine order would see the entrails or the sortilege in terms of microcosmic echoes of vaster harmonies. In general, then, we may distinguish three general types of divination, based on indigenous meanings: those based on the immediate context when interpreted by the spiritual insight of the diviner (intuitive divination); those based on spirit manipulation (possession divination); and those reflecting the operation of impersonal laws within a coherent divine order (wisdom divination).

Intuitive divination. The Shona of Zimbabwe esteem their *hombahomba* diviners above all other kinds because these remarkable men, consulted by strangers who travel from far off to seek their help, can spontaneously tell their visitors' names, family connections, urgent problems, and even minor experiences encountered on the journey. People speak in awe of the piercing eyes and aura of penetrating awareness of these diviners, whose fame can spread over great distances. And yet—an example of how types of divination can run into one another—the *hombahomba* may attune himself to the consultation by casting *hakata* dice (a form of wisdom divination), after which, in one reported case, the diviner became possessed before returning to a state of mind in which he could begin the inquiry.

Intuitive divination is perhaps the elementary form out of which, through various interpretations, the other two developed. It is seldom much stressed, although its distribution as hunches and presentiments is universal. The reliability of amateur intuitions is not usually considered very great, yet in many cultures extraordinary spiritual masters are often credited with this type of divinatory insight, which then has more prestige and credence than any other. For example, disciples of a *tsaddiq* or saintly master in Hasidic Judaism frequently claim that their master can look into a person's soul at first meeting and determine not only the past lives but also the future course of that person. Precisely the same claims are made for many Hindu *gurūs.* These insights by the *gurū* are regarded as far more reliable and authoritative than the various forms of wisdom divination common to India, and these in turn are more esteemed than folk mediumistic and possession divination methods.

Possession divination. There are many varieties of possession divination. The most common is augury: divining the message sent by spiritual beings through nonhuman creatures or things. The classic form of augury, much used in ancient Greece and Rome, consisted of attending to the flight of birds, which were thought to be seized by the gods or spirits and directed according to a code known to the diviner. But all other forms of interpreting supposedly objective spirit messages were also included in the Latin term *augurium.*

Even when human agents are seized by the spiritual beings, this does not always imply trance: a popular form of divination in ancient Near Eastern, medieval European, and even modern societies such as Mexico, is to pose a question and then attend to the first chance words one overhears from passing strangers on the street. Another almost universal method whereby spirits or divinities communicate with a person is to induce twitches or sudden pains in the body. Quite explicit meanings can be derived from this, depending on the part of the body affected and other indications, and of course varying according to the specific cultural context. The theory behind the contemporary use of the Ouija board is explicitly spiritualistic, yet all that one must do to use it is put oneself in a receptive mood: ordinary awareness remains. A very similar state is apparently involved in some cases of glossolalia, according to American Pentecostals I have interviewed, but full mediumistic trance is reported in many studies (see, for example, Felicitas Goodman, *Speaking in Tongues,* Chicago, 1979). The divinatory interpretation of dreams is another very widely used method; here manipulation by spiritual beings begins to require outright alteration of consciousness, although only when the ego has already dimmed its awareness.

Full divinatory possession of human beings may be of several theoretical forms: prophetic inspiration, shamanistic ecstasy, mystical illuminations and visions, and mediumistic or oracular trance. They differ according to the degree of ego awareness and lucidity, awareness of the ordinary world, and the theoretical recipient of the divinatory message. The prophets of the Bible seem to retain a lucid sense of themselves and the world as they exhort their audience, although they are gripped by an overmastering sense of the integral meaning of events as illuminated by God's presence. The recipient of this revelation of temporal meaning is both the prophet and the human community. In shamanistic trance the struggle between ego awareness and the spirits is often portrayed as being so intense that it forces a displacement of the shaman from this world: the shaman may fly far away to interrogate the spirits or God, and may have to struggle with bad spirits and force them to confess their role in human events. As recipient of the divinatory communications, the shaman may later report on his conversations to an assembled audience, or may permit the audience to eavesdrop on the actual interviews or even to be directly addressed by the spirits through his mouth, but in any case he remains self-possessed and afterward can recall everything that occurred. For the mystical visionary, on the other hand, the entire ordinary world is eclipsed by the ecstatic revelations, and the mystic is the sole direct recipient of the communications. The oracular medium, however, loses all awareness, it is said, and therefore often remains ignorant of the message that is communicated directly from the spiritual being to the audience.

The dependency in particular cultures or subgroups of a culture on "objective" augury methods, or on methods that progressively encroach on or even obliterate ego awareness, suggest differing views of the self, society, and the world. Satisfactory cross-cultural studies of divinatory theories from this point of view have not yet been made, but some points may be tentatively suggested. All kinds of possession divination assume a mysterious, arbitrary world governed by personal powers who are involved with a vulnerable humanity. The human self must learn how to submit to or cajole these capricious and often dangerous spirits. However, in loosely organized, relatively egalitarian societies with an emphasis on personal initiative, we can expect more confidence in the ability of the human ego to sustain its integrity when faced with the spiritual powers. This is what we find, for example, in circumpolar and related cultures in Europe, Siberia, and North America. A study by H. Barry, I. L. Child, and M. K. Bacon (cited by Erika Bourguignon, *Possession*, San Francisco, 1976) shows that hunting-fishing cultures generally depend on short-term risks and personal initiative, so that individuals are trained from childhood to be self-reliant and self-sufficient: each adult can master all the cultural skills necessary to survive, and ego alertness is highly valued. In such societies mediumistic divination is not found; instead, individuals possess an encyclopedic knowledge of portents, and of methods for obtaining auguries of the capricious spirits' intentions. The autonomous ego can negotiate its way through a mysterious cosmos, while the shaman, able to retain ego awareness and control even in the most intimate relationship with the spirits, is the group guide.

The same cross-cultural study indicates that children in agricultural societies are trained to be obedient, reliable, cooperative, and patient—qualities needed for ceaseless cultivation of crops and for interaction with fixed communities. The social group, not the individual, is the survival unit; personal success is obtained through accommodation to others. Even the powerful must submit to the more powerful and the spirits, while the weak survive only through self-effacement. Here, mediumistic trance expresses the natural state of things. A survey of African cultures by Lenora Greenbaum (in *Religion, Altered States of Consciousness, and Social Change*, edited by Erika Bourguignon, Columbus, Ohio, 1973) has shown that mediumistic divinatory trance is most common in societies having slaves and two or more hereditary (i.e., fixed) classes, such as commoners and nobility, and possessing populations over 100,000. I might add that in such societies a sense of relative deprivation and ego diminution must be common, since individuals meet people every day who enjoy other roles in life. Less advantaged groups (the poor, women, and so on) might well seek transcendental release from the resultant frustrations through mediumistic trance more often than more privileged sectors of society (see I. M. Lewis, *Ecstatic Religion*, Baltimore, 1971). In any case, here one obtains power only through radical self-effacement; even kings become divine only through being possessed. This is the opposite view from that underlying shamanism.

It is perhaps inevitable that, at the center of social power, attempts are made in such cultures to master all that can be known of the arbitrary will of the gods. The court diviners frequently compile mountainous records of precedents of monster births or other omens, the results of centuries of haruspicy, and so forth, as in Babylonia, where we see the fruit of intense efforts to maintain clarity as far as is possible. The Babylonian priests noted every heavenly sign over many centuries, identifying each celestial body with a god. But no system emerged from this, for the classical Babylonian worldview was polytheistic and predicated on power, passion, and personal whims of the divinities. Yet the result was a hierarchy of divination methods: present at the courts were alert, learned priests who interpreted the will of the gods in elaborate augury ceremonials, while among the lower classes mediumism and a much more random and confused use of omens indicated the insecurity of ego control.

When the entire social structure and even the cosmos is felt to be inauthentic, as in late antiquity, mediumistic ecstasy may tend to apocalyptic predictions of the end of the age: the muted protest becomes radical and explicit. Or mystical visions may teach the negation of the entire world. In such cases, divination merges with salvation cults.

Wisdom divination. The elaboration of divination systems based on a unified field of impersonal and universal processes that can be studied, harmonized with, and above all internalized by nonecstatic sages, is an important but rare development in the history of religion. It is most often found in complex civilizations that have been defeated by equally powerful cultures and therefore must integrate their own indigenous views with other perspectives. Wisdom divination is a syncretistic movement beyond specific cults, approaching the elemental ground from which all personal spirits and cultic gods as well as cultural groups arise. But the speculative effort must usually begin in court and priestly circles, for it depends on a cumulative effort of generations and a specialized learning of which, in most early civilizations, only centralized priesthoods are capable. Only after literacy and education become general can the sagelike diviner detach himself from court circles and apply himself to individual and nonpolitical concerns.

Thus it was only after Babylonia fell to Persian conquest in the sixth century BCE that its priestly thinkers were challenged by a view that placed "Truth" (the Zoroastrian *artha*) and a cosmic order founded in a supreme being above the capricious gods. The new empire embraced many cultures, making possible as a real option personal conversion to such missionizing, universal monotheisms as those espoused by the Jews and the Persians. The old social boundaries—and their gods—now became part of a vaster order, and an attempt was begun to link individual lives directly to a single cosmic pattern rather than to any intermediate hierarchies. Inevitably, the effort was eventually to lead to a kind of pagan monotheism, but it began as an attempt to confirm the polytheistic view. With the new radical improvements in mathematics and astronomy, the first personal horoscope known to us was made of a ruler in 410 BCE. The new cities and academies of the Hellenistic world spurred the fusion of Zoroastrian, Babylonian, Jewish, Syrian, and Greek currents; as Franz Cumont (1912) has made clear, astrology came to function as nothing less than a universal and syncretistic religious perspective that underlay or influenced all the religions of late antiquity. Even synagogues, as we know from recent excavations, commonly traced the zodiac on their sanctuary floors or walls.

The growing separation of divination and wisdom from the central institutions of power was resented by many kings and emperors. One of Augustus's first acts as emperor was the burning of about two thousand collections of pseudo-Sibylline oracles circulating among the people, since some of the oracles favored rival figures or criticized Roman policies, while others, by Jewish proselytizers, predicted the impending messianic era. Several Roman emperors outlawed all non-official divination; Constantine the Great and his successors used Christianity as an excuse to roast to death any astrologer and client caught in private consultation (see Cramer, 1954, and D. Grodzynski's article in Vernant et al., 1974). Even in modern times astrology can have political aspects: the Nazis directed certain agents to gain reputations in the United States and England as astrologers, and then to predict the success of Nazi endeavors or otherwise demoralize Western efforts. Within Nazi Germany itself, astrology was strictly an instrument of state.

Today, however, astrology serves usually as a muted protest against everyday social identity or generally accepted scientific values and cosmology. While interest in astrology is widespread, it has been especially favored by the so-called counterculture, and by many in the lower and lower-middle classes, particularly women, since it desubstantializes oppressive personal relationships, offering instead an exotic alternative identity in which faults are erased or elevated into association with a "star family" embracing strangers. In an increasingly fluid, anonymous, and heterogeneous society, pattern and typological identities are discovered within a larger cosmic harmony, and a sense of control is restored to personal life through the aesthetic and probabilistic terms in which predictions are couched. The power of such a vision is seen in the fact that it persists, even though the zodiac houses and their stellar correlates, fixed as they were during the hellenistic period, are now literally two thousand years out of congruence, making the system obsolete even in its own terms.

A quite similar history of a wisdom divinatory system is that of the *Yi Jing* in China. It was the practice in court circles of the Shang dynasty to consult the nature spirits and royal ancestors—and especially the celestial supreme being—concerning all significant state decisions. Scapulimancy was the favored technique—in the late Shang period tortoise shells were generally substituted, supplemented by sortilege with long and short yarrow stalks. These methods had their roots, respectively, in hunting-fishing cultures to the north and in agricultural tribes to the south. Although these methods already involved a conception of heavenly and earthly polarities, it was apparently only after the Shang were overthrown by the Zhou, and after the Zhou had expanded rapidly in succeeding centuries to embrace cultures throughout northern, central, and even southern China, that an elemental metaphysics arose that transcended all gods and spirits and was encapsulated in the *Yi Jing* as such. There is no reference to personal spirits or gods anywhere in the text of the *Yi Jing* in its present form, which stems from the late Zhou and former Han dynasties. Instead, all of reality is regarded as woven out of a dialectic of yin and yang forces (contracting and expanding, respectively): all things and persons are composites in the process of transformation. Using the elaborate binary code of this method, one can discover what the transformations imply, but only if one has attained true nobility and tranquility of character. Confucian mandarins and philosophers through the ages ruled their lives by this text, but only in the Ming dynasty did its use become widespread among the general populace, reflecting the growth of literacy and the escalating complexity of Chinese civilization. The *Yi Jing* had come to serve as a quiet intellectual aid to personal transcendence and mastery of immediate social pressures. This function—the same one it serves today in the West—differed from its earlier Confucian use as a guide in official life and in social activity often associated with the court.

The Chinese had a number of other forms of wisdom divination, in particular a distinctive form of astrology and an elaborate geomancy. The latter offered detailed instructions on the cosmic forces affecting any specific site, and professional geomancers were consulted whenever a house was to be built, a road laid, or a grave site chosen. Astrology too governed all aspects of village life by the later medieval period, despite the general folk use of many possession divination methods, ranging from countless omens and portents to outright mediumistic séances.

Hindu astrology combined some elements of the Chinese system and more of the Middle Eastern system into its own configuration. Other significant forms of wisdom divination include the Islamic *hati* system *(al-khaṭṭ bi-raml)* and the several derivations of it in West Africa (especially the Yoruba and Fon Ifa systems), Zimbabwe, and Madagascar.

DIVINATION IN WESTERN RELIGIONS. The Jewish and Christian traditions are markedly ambivalent about divination. For example, the rabbis criticized the use of folk methods found in surrounding cultures, just as the Torah itself forbids all appeals to local nature spirits or to the dead. While the efficacy of such appeals is not necessarily denied (*1 Sm.* 28), such acts were thought to suggest that God is not the one source of all events and of all truly reliable knowledge. (See *Dt.* 18:10–22; *Lv.* 19:26, 19:31, 20:6–7, 20:27; *Jer.* 10:2; and the tractates *Pes.* 113a and *Ned.* 32a from the Talmud. For a full discussion, see Cohen, 1949.) Thus prophetic inspiration directly from God, the use of Urim and Tummim in the Temple, certain kinds of omens, and even dream divination by Joseph in Egypt and at local shrines in ancient Israel were certainly acceptable. So most Talmudic rabbis permitted dream divination, water gazing, and the use of omens; contradictory views were expressed concerning astrology, but by the Middle Ages most rabbis accepted what was in effect the science of the day. Moses Maimonides, however, made a scathing attack upon it: freedom of will, he said, is fundamental to Torah spirituality; those who follow God cannot in any case by subject to the stars (see, e.g., *Dt.* 4:19–20), while a close analysis of astrology shows it to be based on poor reasoning and worse science. Necromancy was explicitly condemned in the Torah (*Dt.* 18:11), and there is very little reference to any kind of spirit possession in the Talmud; the late medieval dybbuk possession chiefly involved tormented but not malicious spirits who sought expiation for sins. Yet qabbalistic meditations resulted in a wide variety of wisdom divinatory methods based on the divine image sustaining the whole of creation, and prophetic ecstatic visions were sought by mystics from the Talmudic age on.

In Christianity some of the same themes and ambiguities reappear, but now the antithesis between good and bad divination is understood as part of a war between Christ and Satan. For example spirit possession, mediumistic and otherwise, is a frequent phenomenon and is generally viewed as demonic and requiring exorcism. However, astrological signs can be good, for they marked Jesus' birth. Dream divination by Joseph or Pilate's wife, casting lots, and mediumistic glossolalia are all approved (*Mt.* 1:20, 2:2, 2:12, 27:19; *Acts* 1:26, 10:10), unless performed by non-Christians like Simon Magus or by sorcerers (*Acts* 8:9, 13:6, 16:16). Folk methods used in the Roman Empire and afterward were readily incorporated into Christian and official usage, although the fourth-century Synod of Laodicia and the contemporaneous Theodosian Code outlawed divination (drawing on earlier precedents in Roman legislation). Thus divinatory invocation of pagan deities or spirits, schismatic prophetic movements within Christianity, and even oracular attempts to criticize or delegitimize the ruling regime were all stamped as "Satanism."

Similar attitudes continued into later European cultures, but a rich and highly varied regional folk practice of divination persisted. From Islamic civilization—itself the inheritor of Middle Eastern, Persian, and even Indian methods of divination—came scholarly catalogs of divinatory significances of dreams, omens, and studies of specialized systems such as palmistry, astrology, and crystal gazing. Astrology—despite the rejection of it in the late Roman Empire by church leaders who often cited critical analyses by earlier pagan philosophers—came to be regarded as a universal science in the Middle Ages. The Renaissance renewed acquaintance with classical criticisms (permitting astronomy to develop as an independent science), but the increasing literacy of later generations spread knowledge of these systems and encouraged devotees to elaborate their own methods further and publish studies of them. Cartomancy (including the use of tarot cards), phrenology (divination by head conformations), graphology (handwriting analysis), and many other novel systems or elaborations of earlier systems developed at this time. Pietists of the Reformation heartily condemned these alternative systems of wisdom, but continued to use dreams, omens, and even scriptures opened at random to comprehend events.

In the modern period, devotees of such systems as astrology or water witching often feel constrained to offer "scientific" explanations for the claimed success of their methods—explanations often extrinsic to the methods themselves. Extrasensory perceptions (precognition, etc.), for example, have been cited, or the "synchronicity" invoked by C. G. Jung for the power of the *Yi Jing:* with the mind tuned in by the divinatory apparatus and method, the diviner may notice the minute evidences of interconnections and processes in the environment that are usually ignored, or the diviner may in this heightened state even comprehend vaster elemental wholes leading inevitably to certain outcomes. It is even suggested that divinatory consciousness may be able to pick up unobservable rhythms in events, in somewhat the same way that a radio picks up invisible transmission. These hypotheses may describe real processes; unfortunately, they are at present untestable.

SACRIFICIAL MOTIFS. In any case, divination is fundamentally directed by religious, not scientific, concerns. Its basic curiosity is not about how the world is constructed apart from the pulsing heart of the observer, but about the existential meaning of particular human lives. Above all, divination illuminates suffering and alleviates doubt. It restores value and significance to lives in crisis. But to achieve this, all systems of divination demand the submission of the inquirer to transcendental realities, whether these be divine persons (possession divination) or the underlying divine order (wisdom divination). The inquirer is made to achieve spiritual distance from the self and the immediate crisis.

This recentering of the self is usually directed by sacrificial motifs and rituals. Almost all African divination, for example, ends in sacrifice to the spirits named in the consultations as responsible for the crisis, and many rites also begin with sacrifice. Very often the act of divination is simply a sacrificial rite: in Nilotic and Bantu cultures, the answer is "read" from the entrails of victims. Often the actions of the sacrificed victim give the spirit's answer. In the Democratic Republic of the Congo and nearby culture areas, chickens may be fed a partially toxic substance: if the bird dies, God has accepted it and signified "yes" to the question; if not, the answer is "no." A similar logic directs witch ordeals. As in Africa, so also in Europe is the observation of the last convulsive movements of a sacrificial victim a divination practice. Strabo tells us that the ancient Gauls often killed a slave or captive by a sword stroke in the back: the future was then told from the way he fell, his movements, and the way the blood flowed. Even wisdom divination is frequently given a mythical source in a primal sacrifice (as in the case of the African Dogon and Bambara rites, and also the Yoruba and Fon systems of divination, called Ifa and Fa, respectively. The oracle bone divination of Shang dynasty China had a sacrificial context, and the actual procedure by which one consults the *Yi Jing* is basically structured by sacrificial ideas. Mediums perhaps most dramatically embody a sacrificial logic: those initiated in the spiritualistic religions of Nigeria and Dahomey, for example, and in their perpetuations in recent centuries in the Caribbean, must undergo a symbolic and psychic death and resurrection—one so experiential that occasionally the offering to the spirits, the medium-candidate, does not rise again from the ground.

All this expresses a deeper truth, that divination requires the radical submission of the diviner and indeed the client to the transcendental sources of truth, before their lives can be transformed and set straight, before they can be reincorporated harmoniously into the world. In short, divinatory rites follow the pattern of all rites of passage. The client, having learned in the course of the rite to offer up to the divine all egocentric resistance, ends the session reoriented to the world and able to take positive and confident action in it.

G. K. Park (in Lessa and Vogt, 1965) has suggested that divination assists in political and personal decision making precisely by removing the decision from contesting parties and giving it an objective legitimacy, both through its spiritual source and its convincing ritual drama. O. K. Moore (ibid.) has added that even the "randomizing" of decision outcomes in divination is actually adaptive in situations where egoistically obvious or socially customary decisions might end up limiting personal or group survival chances. By hunting in accord with the cracks that appear on heated deer shoulder blades, the Naskapi Indians of Labrador are prevented from overhunting favorite areas and are therefore more likely to find game year-round.

Wisdom divination also often works in this way: by freeing the inquirer from customary ways of thought, it frequently reveals fresh insight into problems. Thus the cryptic proverbs or aphorisms (as in the Ifa system or the *Yi Jing*), or the nonbinding details and universalizable generalities (as in astrology), open up a cosmic perspective that in itself bestows tranquility and a renewed ability to cope effectively with crises. One learns to see behind appearances and to cultivate a continual attitude of tranquil self-offering. The momentum of wisdom divination, in short, is to internalize the basic attitude operating in all divination; it does this by rendering the structures of the transcendent into a form in which they can be grasped consciously and autonomously. The very vagueness of the answers in most forms of wisdom divination aid in this personal appropriation, making the client participate in shaping meaning out of the session.

See Also Dreams; Geomancy; Necromancy; Oracles; Yinyang Wuxing.

Bibliography

Useful historical surveys of divination and related topics in world cultures include Lynn Thorndike's monumental *A History of Magic and Experimental Science,* 3 vols. (New York, 1923–1958), and Auguste Bouché-Leclerq's still very useful *Histoire de la divination dans l'antiquité,* 4 vols. in 2 (1879–1889; reprint, New York, 1975). Thorndike's history is chiefly oriented to Western culture, but the first two volumes deal with antiquity. Bouché-Leclerq focuses on classical Greco-Roman cultures. A total of seventeen learned articles on divination in particular cultures, and an additional twelve articles on astrology and other religious aspects of heavenly phenomena in world cultures, can be found in the *Encyclopaedia of Religion and Ethics,* 13 vols., edited by James Hastings (Edinburgh, 1908–1926), under "Divination" (vol. 4, 1911) and "Sun, Moon, and Stars" (vol. 12, 1921). More up to date is the excellent survey edited by André Caquot and Marcel Leibovici, *La divination: Études recueillies,* 2 vols., (Paris, 1968), which, in addition to the expected essays on the major ancient Near Eastern, classical, and Asian cultures, contains numerous essays on pre-Christian European cultures; the ancient civilizations of the Americas; native or tribal cultures in Siberia, Africa, and elsewhere; and modern folk and urban Western societies—all with helpful bibliographies. The most recent English symposium is Michael Loewe and Carmen Blacker's *Divination and Oracles* (London, 1981), with nine authoritative essays ranging from Tibetan culture to Islam.

An anthropological symposium on divination that refers to political aspects as well is *Divination et rationalité,* by Jean-Pierre Vernant and others (Paris, 1974). A useful selection of important theoretical anthropological essays on divination is included in *Reader in Comparative Religion: An Anthropological Approach,* 2d ed., edited by William A. Lessa and Evon Z. Vogt (New York, 1965); later editions include some more recent studies but omit much from the second edition. Mediumship has evoked the greatest attention from anthropologists; see, for example, *Spirit Mediumship and Society in Africa,* edited by John Beattie and John Middleton (New York, 1969), in addition to the studies mentioned in the text of the foregoing article.

For an authorative summary of what we know about ancient Mesopotamian divination, see A. Leo Oppenheim's *Ancient Mesopotamia* (Chicago, 1964), pp. 198–227, or W. H. P. Römer's "Religion of Ancient Mesopotamia," in *Historia Religionum,* edited by C. Jouco Bleeker and Geo Widengren, vol. 1 (Leiden, 1969), especially pp. 172–178. H. W. Parke has summarized his many authoritative studies on Greek mediumship in his brief *Greek Oracles* (London, 1967); he does not ignore social and political implications. Still outstanding is Franz Cumont's *Astrology and Religion among the Greeks and Romans* (1912; reprint, New York, 1960). More recent are Hans Lewy's *Chaldaean Oracles and Theurgy: Mysticism, Magic and Platonism in the Later Roman Empire*, new edition by Michel Tardieu (Paris, 1978), and Frederick Henry Cramer's *Astrology in Roman Law and Politics* (Philadelphia, 1954).

Talmudic views of divination are well discussed by Abraham Cohen in his *Everyman's Talmud*, new ed. (New York, 1949), pp. 274–297; further information is available in the article "Divination" by Shmuel Ahituv and others in the *Encyclopaedia Judaica*, 16 vols. (Jerusalem, 1971). A general survey of Muslim divination is available in Toufic Fahd's *La divination arabe* (Leiden, 1966), and in the various symposia mentioned above. On *hati* geomancy, see the article by Robert Jaulin in the collection by André Caquot and Marcel Leibovici, cited above, and Robert Jaulin's *La géomancie: Analyse formelle* (Paris, 1966). For a penetrating study of the Yoruba Ifa system, see Wande Abimbola's *Ifa: An Exposition of Ifa Literary Corpus* (London, 1976).

Any study of Chinese divination should begin with Joseph Needham's brilliant study *Science and Civilisation in China*, vol. 2 (Cambridge, 1956), pp. 216–395; an excellent bibliography is appended. Among the many perceptive studies of the *Yi Jing* is Hellmut Wilhelm's *Heaven, Earth and Man in the Book of Changes: Seven Eranos Lectures* (Seattle, 1977). A useful survey of other forms of Chinese wisdom divination as well as of allied forms of the *I ching* is Wallace A. Sherrill and Wen Kuan Chu's *An Anthology of I Ching* (London, 1977). Also see Stephan D. R. Feuchtwang's *An Anthropological Analysis of Chinese Geomancy* (Vientiane, Laos, 1974).

New Sources

Aguilar, Mario I. "Divination, Theology and Healing in an African Context." *Feminist Theology* no. 7S (1994): 34–38.

Ciraolo, Leda, and Jonathan Seidel, eds. *Magic and Divination in the Ancient World.* Leiden, 2002.

Cryer, Frederick H. *Divination in Ancient Israel and Its Near Eastern Environment: A Socio-historical Investigation.* Sheffield, England, 1994.

Davis, David. "Divination in the Bible." *Jewish Bible Quarterly* 30, no. 2 (April–June 2002): 121.

EVAN M. ZUESSE (1987)
Revised Bibliography

DIVINATION: GREEK AND ROMAN DIVINATION

People tend to think of divination as a process concerned with the future and with such questions as "Will I marry?" and "Will I be rich?" But in ancient Greece and Rome, as in many other cultures, divination was predominantly concerned with discerning the will of the gods and other superhuman entities (e.g., demons, ghosts) and then learning how to bring oneself into harmony with them. Thus, the enquirer might try to find out why famine was harming his city: Had the dead not received the cult that was due them? Was a god being ignored? Alternatively, an enquirer might ask a god's advice: shall we institute a new political system in Athens? In the latter sort of cases, the enquirer typically presented a detailed plan to the god and then asked for his or her approval, rather than giving the god completely free rein to decide what should be done. The knowledge that one sought from divination usually was not all that different in its nature from what one could learn from another person. It differed mainly insofar as the gods, demons, and ghosts might know more because they had a greater range of sources of knowledge; they knew what was going on among the dead, among the gods, and in distant parts of the world that the average enquirer could not reach.

Almost any object, person, statement, or event could convey information; the challenge was to learn how to choose, interpret, and act upon it correctly. Sometimes divinatory information aroused debate among its recipients as to how to interpret it. For example, during the Persian Wars of the early fifth century BCE, the Athenians received an oracle from Apollo at Delphi advising them to protect themselves "by wooden walls," but prominent citizens argued for different interpretations. Themistocles (c. 524–c. 460 BCE) finally convinced the others that this meant they should increase the size of their navy (ships being built of wood) rather than seek refuge on the Acropolis, which had in former times been protected by a "wall" of thorn bushes. Themistocles was proven correct when the fortified navy saved not only Athens but all of Greece (Herodotos, *Histories* 7.140–143).

This story also demonstrates that anyone, not only a specialist, was free to interpret divinatory information; indeed, the Greek *chrêsmologoi*, or professional interpreters of oracles, had urged the Athenians to abandon their city after they heard the oracle, but their advice was ignored. Professional seers (*manteis*) traveled with armies to provide advice, but the general Xenophon (c. 431–c. 352 BCE) stated that he himself was knowledgeable enough in the arts of divination so that his seer could not deceive him with false information (*Anabasis* 5.6.29). This statement also reflects the common presumption that, far from being unimpeachable, professional diviners were motivated by the same things as other people and might put their own interests before those of their clients. Moreover, even when the source and interpretation were considered trustworthy, divinatory information might be challenged. The "wooden walls" oracle was the second oracle the Athenians had received from Delphi; they had rejected an earlier one because it offered the city no hope at all, and they asked the god for a more optimistic response. Similarly, in Rome the results of sortition (a method whereby an answer was obtained by shaking or drawing lots out of a jar) might be overturned in the civic and military arena when participants judged them to be "ill-omened." For example, if the results commanded that a man serving in the office of *flamen Dialis* (a prominent priesthood) should accept a foreign posting, the results were overturned because the *flamen* was forbidden from sleeping outside his own bed for more than two nights running. Divination, in short, was always as much a process of negotiation as it was of obtaining knowledge.

GREECE. Although Greek and Roman divinatory methods and the contexts in which they were used were very similar in many regards, there were also distinctions, and it is therefore best to treat the two cultures separately. We begin with Greece.

Institutional oracles. Both of the oracles that Athens received during the Persian Wars came from the Delphic Oracle, one of the oldest (perhaps dating to the late ninth century BCE) and most prestigious of Greek institutional oracles, which were situated in a fixed spot and administered by a priesthood. At Delphi, in an inner chamber of Apollo's temple, the Pythia (a woman who had pledged to remain a virgin) sat on a sacred tripod, wore a crown of sacred laurel, and was inspired by the god himself. Through her mouth, Apollo issued statements that were transmitted to enquirers by priests called "prophets"—literally, "those who speak for" someone else. The statements might be worded so as to require interpretation, as we have seen, but the truly enigmatic Delphi response, whose meaning proves to be quite different from what it seems (as in the story of Oedipus), is probably only a literary motif.

Although Delphi was the most famous oracle in the ancient world, there were others. Most were sponsored by Apollo (including those at Didyma and Claros), but Zeus had one at Dodona, and other gods had oracles, too. Dead heroes might also convey information through oracles: Amphiaraus had one in Oropus and Trophonius had one in Lebadeia. The means by which the information was conveyed varied from place to place; at the oracle of Trophonius, enquirers descended into an underground shrine and apparently encountered the hero himself.

Independent practitioners. Independent experts who went by a variety of titles provided divination as well; *ornithomanteis* (interpreters of birds' behavior), *oneiromanteis* (dream interpreters), and *teratoskopoi* (interpreters of portents) were among them. The word *mantis,* the most general term of all, might be applied to any of these and many other types. Neither the titles nor the methods of divination that they represented were mutually exclusive, and many practitioners used more than one technique as the situation demanded. *Manteis* might provide other services as well, such as purification and initiation into private mystery cults. Although myths that made *manteis* such as Melampus and Amphiaraus members of prominent royal families may reflect the status of *manteis* during some early period of Greek history, by the classical age *manteis* were marginalized members of society. For important matters it was preferable, when possible, to consult one of the institutional oracles. *Chrêsmologoi* (interpreters of oracles) not only interpreted information delivered by institutional oracles, as mentioned in the story of Themistocles, but also oracles that had been collected together and were believed to be very old, such as those of Bacis and the Sibyls. "Belly-talkers" (*engastrimuthoi*) had gods or demons in their stomachs that prophesied (see Plato, *Sophist* 252c, and Plutarch, *On the Obsolescence of Oracles* 9, 414e).

In later antiquity there were other divinatory techniques that private practitioners might employ. It is likely that many of these were available earlier but simply do not show up in the more meager sources of that time; examples are scrying (gazing at water or some other reflective surface), lychnomancy (gazing at a flame), and "direct vision"—that is, a personal encounter with a god. The later sources make it clear that the practitioners often combined and adapted divinatory procedures that we would consider separate from one another. Thus, a practitioner might call a spirit into a child to prophesy at the same time as he asked the child to scry. In short, divination was a collection of practices open to improvisation, even if modern scholars (and already some ancient intellectuals such as Cicero) have attempted to categorize its varieties.

Everyday divination. Divinatory methods were available to ordinary people as well. Typically, these involved a person interpreting some spontaneous occurrence that seemed significant. In the *Odyssey* (17.541), Telemachus sneezes unexpectedly, and his mother, Penelope, interprets this to mean that she will soon be rid of her troublesome suitors. Dreams were viewed as having hidden meanings (but see *Odyssey* 19.562–567, where Penelope dismisses attempts to find hidden meanings in her dreams). Although one could call in professional help for especially strange ones, the average person usually could manage without such help.

Intellectuals became fascinated with dreams: Aristotle (384–322 BCE) wrote a short treatise, *On Divination in Sleep,* in which he denied that dreams were predictive, but the Stoics went on to explore in depth the "scientific" reasons that dreams might be so. In the second century CE, Aelius Aristides kept a "dream diary" that described his nightly visions and proposed interpretations for them. Artemidorus's dream book, also from the second century, includes the dreams of people whom he interviewed, with notations as to what subsequently happened—an early effort at systematizing and testing dream interpretation. He also attempted to catalogue and categorize symbols that might appear in dreams, somewhat in the way that Sigmund Freud later would (and indeed, Freud, in his study of dreams, sometimes quotes Artemidorus). At the shrine of the hero Amphiaraus, people "incubated" (slept) in a special building and waited for the hero to advise them in dreams. Priests might help the dreamers interpret the dreams.

There are many more divinatory methods about which only a little is mentioned in the sources, making it impossible to say how common or respected they were. Aristophanes (c. 450–c. 388 BCE) shows us a woman asking a statue of Hekate outside her house whether she should go out that day (*Lysistrata* 63). At dice oracles, which were set up in marketplaces of Greek Asia Minor during the Roman Imperial period, merchants apparently took the initiative, when they pleased, of rolling the dice and then looking up the significance of the roll on a chart engraved on the base of a statue of Hermes (the god of merchants). There were also a few people who were what today would be called "clairvoyant"—that is, they could "see" what was happening in distant places (Philostratus, *Life of Apollonius* 8.26; Eunapius, *Lives of the Sophists* 468).

Sometimes the conversation of other people (especially children), when overheard by someone who needed advice, was interpreted as a divine message. The story of the conversion of Saint Augustine (354–430 CE) to Christianity plays on this practice: while sitting in his garden he heard a child on the other side of the wall sing out "pick it up and read it," which Augustine took to refer to the Bible that lay on a table next to him; later, after he had converted, Augustine decided that it must have been an angel rather than a child (*Confessions* 8.12.29).

ROME. Much of what was said about Greek methods of divination is also true for Rome; in fact, in many cases, Greek sources explicitly discuss Roman participation as well. The Romans, for example, frequently visited the institutionalized oracles that the Greeks had established, such as Delphi, as well as a few of their own, such as the lot oracle of the Roman goddess Fortuna at Praeneste. But Roman divination differed from that of the Greeks in two important ways. First, the state exerted far greater control over the methods that were used for public matters—and eventually tried to exert control over private divination as well. Second, although Greek intellectuals already had mocked and challenged divinatory procedures, Roman writers provide a much richer picture of debates that swirled around the topic. It must also be noted that the Romans at least believed (and were probably to some extent correct in believing) that their methods of divination had been inherited from the Etruscans, who were viewed as especially sagacious in such matters.

Civic divination. Roman civic divination can be divided into three main types, organized according to whether the information conveyed was sought or unsought, and to the circumstances that surrounded each individual divinatory incident.

Taking the *auspices* was an act initiated by people seeking a sign from the gods to ensure that an undertaking would be successful—that is, that the gods approved of it or were at least open-minded about it. A famous form of this type of divination was feeding sacred chickens and watching whether they consumed the food. Obviously, this was open to manipulation—a starving chicken will eventually eat. Another form required defining a *templum,* that is, designating a rectangular section of the sky that was then divided into left, right, front, and back subsections. One then watched for signs to appear within the *templum*'s subsections (e.g., lightning, particular birds such as [Jupiter's] eagle) and drew meaning from these signs. Such *auspices* were interpreted by experts known as *augures;* until they gave the go-ahead, no public business (such as elections, Senate meetings, or initiation of new priests) could be conducted. Their role was strictly interpretative, however; the actual taking of the *auspices* was carried out by a magistrate. The *augures* also determined whether ritual faults had been committed during the taking of *auspices*—if so, the act had to be repeated correctly.

Prodigies or *portents* were unbidden omens sent by the gods to warn humans of imminent disaster. These might take any of myriad forms: the birth of a two-headed calf or a hermaphrodite, sudden strokes of lightning, and eclipses are examples. Before a prodigy was studied, the Senate had to decide that it really was a prodigy; if so, either of two types of experts were called in: *haruspices* or *pontifices.* (*Haruspices* were from Etruria, reflecting the Roman belief that the Etruscans were masters of many religious practices, especially divinatory ones.) The *haruspices* and *pontifices* gave advice about how to avert the disaster that the prodigy had portended. Although this implicitly included interpreting the prodigy, emphasis was always on aversion rather than explanation; in this sense, Roman divination was an eminently practical rather than a theoretical art. We also hear of portents in Greece, and of experts (*manteis,* for example) sometimes being called in to interpret them, but Greek cities had no similarly complex, official system in place for dealing with them.

Entrail reading (also called extispicy or *haruspinica*) is a form of divination found throughout the Mediterranean. (Typically, the liver and other internal organs of every sacrificial animal were "read" to determine whether the gods were pleased with the sacrifice, and if the sacrifice occurred at the outset of an important endeavor, the gods' pleasure or displeasure was construed as sending a message about the endeavor itself.) In Rome, extispicy was especially associated with military matters. Before battle, the *haruspices* looked at the entrails of the sacrificial animal and determined, from the pattern of bumps and other characteristics upon them, whether the gods were pleased. If they were not, that did not necessarily mean that the endeavor had to be abandoned; the sacrifice might be repeated numerous times until the entrails signified that it was all right to go ahead.

None of the three methods just described foretells the future, strictly speaking; at most they indicate what might happen if proper actions are not taken to avert crisis, or what might happen if the gods' advice (e.g., not to go into battle) were ignored. Roman divination, even more than Greek, was an ongoing consultation with the gods in which humans attempted to discover how they must modify their behavior to maintain the *pax deorum* (peace with the gods) that lay at the center of Roman religion.

A final form of official Roman divination that should be mentioned involved the Sibylline Books, collections of oracular verses in Greek dactylic hexameter, supposedly purchased from the Cumaean Sibyl (one of several sibyls or prophetesses inspired by Apollo) during an early period of

Roman history; the collection was occasionally supplemented as time went on and was completely rebuilt after the original books were lost in a fire in 83 BCE. The collection was under the care of a priestly group called the *quindecemviri sacris faciundis* (fifteen men concerned with sacred actions), but only the Senate could decide when the collection would be consulted for advice. In later antiquity, Christians and Jews read their own meanings into these oracles, finding within them, for instance, predictions of Christ's coming.

State control of divination. Of course, Romans needed advice concerning private as well as public matters, and by and large the same methods were available to them as to the Greeks: everything in the world potentially carried meaning, if properly observed and interpreted. Knowledge is power, however, and periodically, particularly during the Imperial period, certain forms of divination were either condemned or kept under strict governmental control. The most important of these was astrology. In the second century BCE, catarchic astrology (the reading of star signs at the outset of an endeavor) was introduced into Rome (Pliny, *Natural History* 35.199), and by 139 BCE the Senate had already passed a law expelling all astrologers (Valerius Maximus 1.3.3). The purge was constantly repeated; the first century CE alone saw eleven new attempts to expel astrologers. Other forms of divination came under fire, as well; the emperor Augustus had more than two thousand oracular books burned to prevent unauthorized access to them. In general, these purges fell into line with other attempts by Roman rulers to control religion and thereby access to the divine—purges of Jews, of magicians, of members of mystery cults in honor of Dionysos, and, of course, of Christians.

Response to divination. As mentioned above, Aristotle already had formally critiqued dream divination in the fourth century BCE, and many other Greeks had challenged particular operators as being dishonest or inept. But there is more evidence for intellectual engagement with the question of how (or whether) divination worked in sources from the Roman period, perhaps because people of this time were more interested in the topic or perhaps because the sheer luck of survival has left more.

Cicero's treatise, *Concerning Divination,* is an articulate investigation of arguments for and against divination that takes the form of a dialogue between Cicero and his brother, Quintus. The latter represents those who believe divination works, particularly the Stoics; Cicero himself presents philosophical arguments against it, particularly those of the Platonists and Cynics. No resolution is reached, but in the course of the discussion Cicero not only offers a lengthy résumé of divinatory methods, but also elaborates on a division of divinatory methods that had first been proposed by the Stoics and that still holds considerable sway: that between natural divination (e.g., dreams, inspired prophecy such as that of the Delphi Pythia or the Sibyls) and artificial divination, which required special training or tools (e.g., reading bird flights, astrology, sortition). Another important topic that Cicero takes up from the Stoics is cosmic *sympatheia,* the idea that everything in the cosmos is connected to other things; thus, movements or changes in the heavenly world should be signaled by changes in the world below. Once one knew how to read and interpret the system, these changes could provide information that was not otherwise available. *Sympatheia* continued to be debated by philosophers throughout antiquity and into the Middle Ages.

BIBLIOGRAPHY

Beard, Mary. "Cicero and Divination." *Journal of Roman Studies* 76 (1986): 33–46.

Bouché-Leclercq, Auguste. *Histoire de la divination dans l'Antiquité.* 4 vols. Paris, 1879–1882.

Dodds, E. R. "Supernormal Phenomena in Classical Antiquity." In *The Ancient Concept of Progress.* Oxford, 1973.

Graf, Fritz. "Magic and Divination." In *The World of Ancient Magic,* edited by David Jordan, Hugh Montgomery, and Einar Thomasson. Bergen, Norway, 1999.

Johnston, S. I. "Charming Children: The Use of the Child in Ancient Divination." *Arethusa* 34, no. 1 (2001): 97–117.

MacBain, Bruce. *Prodigy and Expiation: A Study of Religion and Politics in Republican Rome.* Brussels, 1982.

North, John. "Diviners and Divination at Rome." In *Pagan Priests: Religion and Power in the Ancient World,* edited by Mary Beard and John North. London, 1990.

Parker, Robert. "Greek States and Greek Oracles." In *Crux: Essays Presented to G. E. M. de Ste. Croix on His 75th Birthday,* edited by P. A. Cartledge and F. D. Harvey. London, 1985.

SARAH ILES JOHNSTON (2005)

DIVINE, THE

SEE HOLY, IDEA OF THE; SACRED AND THE PROFANE, THE; TRANSCENDENCE AND IMMANENCE

DIVINE CHILD

SEE CHILD

DIVING PRESENCE

SEE SHEKHINAH

DIVINITY

SEE DEITY; GODS AND GODDESSES; SUPREME BEINGS

DIVINIZATION

SEE APOTHEOSIS; DEIFICATION; HEROES

DJAN'KAWU. The name Djan'kawu (also spelled as Djang'kawu or Djanggawul) refers to ancestral beings described in the mythology of the Dhuwa moiety, or descent group, of the Yolngu people, who live in northeast Arnhem Land in the Northern Territory of Australia. The Yolngu people divide themselves into two moieties called Dhuwa and Yirritja. People inherit their moiety identity from their father and paternal grandfather, and are required to marry someone from the other moiety. Land and water areas, totemic ancestors and ceremonies, natural species, and other phenomena are all assigned to one or the other moiety. Djan'kawu traditions are found in many patrilineal groups of the Dhuwa moiety, especially coastal groups.

The ancestral beings called Djan'kawu comprise an elder and younger sister in some groups' stories while others add a brother. Their names also vary from group to group. Dhuwa moiety myths describe the journey of the Djan'kawu "following the sun" from Burralku, an island across the sea to the east, to the eastern coast of northeast Arnhem Land, then along the coast and islands to the west towards the sunset. The Djan'kawu are said to have traveled on foot and by canoe or bark raft, each carrying two long sticks called Garninyirdi, one in each hand. The Garninyirdi were used as walking sticks on land and as paddles for the canoe.

The Djan'kawu also carried twined pandanus baskets, or dilly bags, decorated with the orange feathers of the red-collared lorikeet, and containing many strings of lorikeet feathers as well as *rangga,* which are sacred objects made of wood and other materials. The sisters had with them conical *ngarnmarra* mats of the kind that Dhuwa women use as aprons, bassinets, and mosquito nets, and which served as fishing nets in the myths and songs.

The Dhuwa stories relate how the Djan'kawu saw and named many fish, birds, reptiles, and animals on their journey. They gave birth to many children in the country of each Dhuwa moiety group, and left the powers of continuing reproduction in the water holes and springs they made with their sticks. The springs bubbled up on the beaches or in the saline mud of the mangroves, the fresh water mixing with salt water at high tide. The Djan'kawu placed sacred objects in the waters of each group and reserved some water holes for older men.

As in the doctrines of Aboriginal people from other regions of Australia, the Djan'kawu left traces of their journey, activities, and physical presence in the land and waters. In Yolngu terminology, the traces of the ancestors and the songs and other gifts that they left behind are their footprints, or *luku,* the foundation (*rom*) of ancestral law (*mardayin*). A group may identify a specific locale in their country as the place where the ancestors pulled their canoe up to the mangroves. They planted one of their sticks and it became a tree. They heard men chanting from a ceremony ground in the forest. A certain causeway of shell was their path. The Djan'kawu endowed each group with the myths, songs, dances, designs (painted or made in the sand), and sacred objects that describe and "follow" their journey, actions, and presence.

DJAN'KAWU SONGS. The songs of the Djan'kawu constitute a distinctive genre in the repertoire of Dhuwa moiety groups, and are called *birlma,* or clap stick songs. Male singers use heavy ironwood clap sticks to create a slow steady rhythm unaccompanied by a didgeridoo, or Aboriginal drone pipe. The songs have a chant-like sound with a low pitch and shallow melodic profile. They "follow" songs sung by the Djan'kawu themselves, and so are often sung in the first person as if the Djan'kawu themselves were singing. The songs do not have a direct narrative structure but rather evoke images related to the Djan'kawu and places associated with them.

The songs tell of the catfish the Djan'kawu caught with their *ngarnmarra* mats, of shellfish in the mangrove swamps, of flying foxes and black cockatoos (fruit bats) in the trees, of water monitor lizards in the creeks and water holes, and of monsoon rains and floods. A particularly interesting feature of the Djan'kawu songs is the way they manipulate time and space. On one level they represent the long journey of many days, during which the Djan'kawu gave birth to people from all the Dhuwa moiety groups and gave them their ancestral law. On another level the songs trace the passage of the sun through a single day, for singers often begin the song series early in the morning (for a purification ceremony, for example) and sing through the day until sunset, when the ceremony ends. On one level the songs represent the ancestral beings' journey from Burralku in the east through the lands and waters of many groups, to those belonging to people far to the west towards the sunset. On another level the songs follow the Djan'kawu around a particular group's country, through the sea to the mangroves, up to the saline mud flats and across to the swamps and lagoons, into the forest and patches of jungle. The song cycles may be construed as following the seasons of the year, ending with the monsoon rains. They also seem to recapitulate the human life cycle, beginning with conception (represented by the sisters catching fish with their conical mats and putting them in their dilly bags), and ending with the Djan'kawu, exhausted from their labors, walking or paddling toward the setting sun.

DJAN'KAWU DESIGNS. Designs associated with the Djan'kawu belong to the Dhuwa groups who possess the myths. They are painted on the body for ceremonies and on sacred objects; drawn with ridges of sand or soil on the earth to mark ceremony grounds; or reproduced on bark paintings or prints for sale. The Djan'kawu designs have some features in common. One is the use of a circular form that radiates vertical and horizontal bands with diagonal divisions between the bands. This design may represent the sun, a waterhole made by the Djan'kawu, or other aspects of the Djan'kawu stories. It may be drawn as two circles joined by a band, representing springs and channels in the mangroves, or repeated several times to form a grid of circles, bands, and diagonal lines. These multivalent images have many meanings, including symbolic references to a group's country that function as a kind of map, as well as references to the group's sacred objects.

A second design associated with the Djan'kawu consists of horizontal stripes of white, red, and yellow ochre painted on the body for ceremonies or on a ritual digging stick or hollow-log coffin. This polysemous design has a rich array of meanings ranging from the red-collared lorikeet to the bands on a mangrove tree left by the tides. The adult males of the moiety keep the design's other meanings secret.

DJAN'KAWU DANCES AND CEREMONIES. Adults and children follow the ancestors' journey in a sacred dance accompanied by male singers. The dancers move in a line or as a pair through the camp, each dancer provided with a pair of long sticks, and painted in horizontal stripes of red and yellow ochre and white clay. From time to time the dancers form a circle and spear the ground with their sticks, working them back and forth, representing the Djan'kawu making waterholes and giving birth to each group along their journey. Finally they surround the deceased (in a funeral) or the initiate (in a circumcision), or the sacred Riyawarra tree (in a Nga:rra ceremony), where the leader calls out the ancestral names of the Dhuwa moiety groups whose countries lie along the ancestral track.

The Nga:rra revelatory ceremony is an important ritual in which young men are gradually admitted to participate in secret dances and see the sacred objects. The young women learn the dances at the public ground. Each day during the ceremony, the men dance out from the men's ground to the public dance ground where the women represent the Djan'kawu sisters at the Riyawarra tree. The men then chase the women away and perform the dances of Salmon, Catfish, and other fish. The leader calls out the ancestral names of a Dhuwa moiety group, which changes on each day of the ceremony, and all the men and women participate in the Kingfisher dance.

These daily dances represent central episodes in the mythology of each Dhuwa group. According to one group's myths, the ancestral sisters leave their dilly bags full of sacred objects hanging in a tree by the swamp while they go to the mangroves to collect crabs and shellfish. The men then sneak out from a secret ceremony ground, steal the dilly bags, and take them back to the ceremony ground, where the sisters are not admitted because they are women. From that moment on, the teller of the myth remarks, the men possessed the ancestral sacred objects and the women became the "workers" at the hearth. Each group's story, however, varies in its details: in one version a fire destroyed the dilly bags, in another the men attempted to have intercourse with the women but failed, in still another the sisters were joined by a brother. But the dances are sufficiently abstract to accommodate each group's version of the story—a necessary characteristic because many Dhuwa moiety groups participate jointly with their Yirritja moiety relatives.

On the final day of the Nga:rra ceremony, the men dance out from the secret ground through the camp to the Riyawarra tree. The participants are all painted with stripes and carry the long sticks required to reenact the creative journey of the Djan'kawu. At the tree the women are lying under conical *ngarnmarra* mats. As the men surround the women, working the long sticks back and forth, the women burst out of the mats to represent the birth of children to the moiety groups. Then all participants bathe in the sea, or a lagoon or river nearby, their body paints mixing together in the water.

The Djan'kawu songs, dances, and designs may be used in other ceremonies. The men may paint a Djan'kawu design on the initiate's chest during a circumcision ceremony or on the deceased during a funeral ceremony. The Djan'kawu rituals and designs are also incorporated in purification ceremonies following a death, in which the mourners wash themselves while standing in a sand sculpture representing the springs made by the Djan'kawu.

The Djan'kawu were credited with setting down precedents for such matters as kin relations and customary rights in the countries associated with them. A body of designs and ceremonies are the ancestral inheritance of each group and form part of its ancestral law (*mardayin*). Each patrilineal group is differentiated from others by the particular constellation of sacra associated with its country (or countries), the specific details of its mythology, its particular sacred objects, and the form of its designs. The groups are linked by the common features described above.

The Djan'kawu mythology and associated sacra are but one of a vast array of Yolngu mythological traditions. A second major Dhuwa moiety tradition is that of the Wagilak sisters, whose long journey began in the south. Their story is associated with a cycle of ceremonies in a "desert" style, in which wild cotton is stuck to the body in patterns and ritual songs are accompanied by boomerangs used as clap sticks. Yirritja moiety mythology includes several long journeys as well, such as those of Lany'tjung. Yirritja patrilineal groups, however, recognize many beings, creators, and ancestors, including Shark, Honeybee, Saltwater Crocodile, Long-Necked Turtle, Whale, and Dingo. What distinguishes the Djan'kawu mythology is its association with the Nga:rra ceremony of the Dhuwa moiety.

SEE ALSO Australian Indigenous Religions, articles on Mythic Themes; Gadjeri; Gender and Religion, article on Gender and Indigenous Australian Religions; Iconography, article on Australian Aboriginal Iconography.

BIBLIOGRAPHY

Berndt, Ronald M. *Djanggawul.* Melbourne, 1952.

Keen, Ian. *Knowledge and Secrecy in an Aboriginal Religion.* Oxford, 1994.

RONALD M. BERNDT (1987)
IAN KEEN (2005)

DOCETISM. The term *docetism* is primarily used with reference to ancient Christologies where the reality of Jesus Christ's physical body was denied, or at least various of the normal carnal properties and functions were refused in favor of those more spiritual or ethereal. Christ had only the appearance (Greek, *dokesis*) of a human, and only seemed *(dokein)* to be a man. Such docetists were accused by their opponents of putting forward a phantasm, and obviating the fundamental Christian hope in the resurrection with a birth and death that were not entirely real.

Beliefs in the divine origin and nature of the Christ inevitably put pressure on the full humanity of Jesus from the earliest times. Many found it hard to accept that he would eat and drink in the normal way, let alone perform more gross human functions, suffer the debilitations of old age and disease, or emit bodily fluids. Thus, some texts ascribe special characteristics to his body, such as that he could alter his appearance at will, or, in the *Acts of John,* that his eyes never closed and he left no footprints. A particular issue was his conception and birth, and here one can argue that docetic tendencies have affected mainstream Christian beliefs, where the virgin birth and associated doctrines have had enormous devotional power. Another problem was the reality of his death, and again one can track a variety of strategies that have attempted to circumvent that most human of fates, such as substitution of another on the cross or survival somehow of the experience to awaken in the tomb.

Certainly, the resurrection narratives, with their curious portrayals of Jesus unrecognized by his closest associates—or suddenly disappearing or appearing in their midst, implicate docetism in the basic Christian story, while the notion of "the resurrection body" enables it to coexist with imperatives requiring his full humanity. The disciples fear that they have seen a ghost, and thus he must eat a piece of grilled fish before their eyes (*Lk.* 24:37–43), just as he puts Thomas's hand into his side (*Jn.* 20:27).

Apart from these contentious issues about the canonical gospel narrative itself, it is clear that docetic beliefs received support (whatever the original intention) from phrasing in the early hymn embedded in *Philippians* 2:5–11, which states that Christ Jesus took "the form of a slave, being born in human likeness," as this echoes as a proof-text through the writings of adherents to such views. Conversely, *1 John* 1:1–3 and 4:1–3, and *2 John* 7 evidence anti-docetic emphasis on the flesh that has been touched. Already, by the early second century, Ignatius of Antioch and Polycarp were combating those who denied the fleshly reality of Jesus' birth, life, and death, as well as those who claimed that his suffering was only apparent. Marcion can be taken as indicative of the trajectory of an indigenous Christianity in Asia Minor that now sought divorce from its Jewish and historical origins, and for whom Jesus descended suddenly from the third heaven to Capernaum in the fifteenth year of Tiberius Caesar, fully formed but in appearance only.

Although docetism is frequently associated with Gnosticism—and many variations of such ideas can be found in the Nag Hammadi and similar writings—it is best understood as a collection of widespread tendencies that evidence the imperatives of popular piety, the impress of pagan notions of divinity or archetypal polarities between heaven and earth, and the influence of the glorified Christ already envisioned in the transfiguration and resurrection appearances. The term *docetist* first appears in a letter of Serapion of Antioch as quoted in Eusebius of Caesarea's *History of the Church* (6.12.6) with reference to those who circulated the *Gospel of Peter,* dating from around the mid-second century; but indications of pressure in this direction are evident from virtually the earliest strata of Christian belief that can be tracked historically. There is no evidence for any single sect of "docetists," and (even though Clement of Alexandria ascribes it to Julius Cassianus) no founder or point of origin can be supposed other than in theologically driven histories of heresy. However, docetic Christologies are useful in tracking the heritage of later systems, such as the understanding about the advent of Jesus (that he came "without body") assumed in Manichaeism; the duplication of the docetic Jesus in the Mandaean savior figure Anosh-Uthra; and possibly the Qur'anic teaching at 4:157 about the crucifixion (that Jesus was not killed, but rather a resemblance of him on another). It has even been suggested as a source for the development of the triple-body of the Buddha doctrine in Mahāyāna texts.

Essentially, *docetism* is a term of opprobrium utilized by opponents to highlight the supposed correctness of their own views. Its usage reflects a refusal to accept the worth or impetus driving divergent Christologies, and thus the development of varied Christianities, some of which (such as Marcionism or Manichaeism) placed a premium on a noncorporeal savior free from limitations of time or matter. The term is still found in contemporary discussions of Christology to indicate particular emphases, but it remains rooted in theological or value-laden assumptions.

BIBLIOGRAPHY

Standard accounts of early Christian doctrine provide references to primary sources. See, for example, Alois Grillmeier, *Christ in Christian Tradition,* 2d rev. ed., vol. 1, *From the Apostolic Age to Chalcedon (451),* translated by John Bowden (London, 1975); J. N. D. Kelly, *Early Christian Doctrines,* 5th rev. ed. (London, 1977); and Jaroslav Pelikan, *The Christian Tradition: A History of the Development of Doctrine,* vol. 1, *The Emergence of the Catholic Tradition, 100–600 A.D.* (Chicago, 1971).

IAIN GARDNER (2005)

DOCTRINE. Most dictionaries record two related senses of the term *doctrine:* according to the first, it is the affirmation of a truth; according to the second, it is a teaching. The two are not mutually exclusive: to affirm something as true is a way of teaching it, and that which is taught is usually held to be true.

The denotation of the term is thus reasonably clear. However, the connotations (i.e., the feelings and attitudes associated with it), differ according to where the emphasis is placed in a given instance. As the statement of a truth, doctrine has a philosophical cast; as a teaching, it suggests something more practical. The first connotation prevails among the secular sciences. The doctrine of evolution, for example, comprises a body of knowledge that is appropriately characterized as a theory, but not a teaching. Philosophical discourse reveals more variation: according to the context, "the doctrine of the equality of man" may be taken either as a precise axiom belonging to a political theory, or as a practical maxim designed to guide political action.

Religious doctrines tend to be characterized by their practical intent. Even when a doctrine appears in the shape of an abstruse theoretical disquisition, it is usually the case that any speculative interest is strictly subordinated to the spiritual, which is the dominant concern. For example, the orientation of Judaism is toward practical obedience to the law of God, not speculative knowledge of his being. The doctrinal element in Judaism thus reveals an intimate connection with the notion of teaching. The most important figure is the rabbi ("teacher"); the most important word is *torah* ("instruction"), which refers to God's revelation in the Hebrew scriptures and, more specifically, to his law as presented in the five books of the Pentateuch. In a broader sense, *torah* encompasses the oral as well as the written law, together with the continuing tradition of rabbinical interpretations. The Talmud ("study") is an authoritative compilation of expositions of the law and applications of it to particular circumstances. It has been observed that the phrase "to read the Talmud," while grammatically correct, is a violation of the text's religious character, since the only appropriate response to the Talmud is to study it.

In Islam, the *sharīʿah*, or study of God's law, is of paramount importance. Here the doctrinal element is subordinated, of course, to judgments about moral and ritual behavior. The term *kalām*, however, indicates a kind of thought very close to that indicated by the English terms *doctrine* and *theology*. *Kalām* literally means "word" or "speech," and the Qurʾān is deemed *kalām Allāh*, the word of God. In the course of time, *kalām* has come to mean both a single truth and a system of truth (as is the case with the English term *doctrine*), and has played an important role in the history of the Islamic tradition.

Christianity uses the terms *doctrine* and *dogma* to designate the teachings through which salvation is offered to all those who hear and respond. An early example of such a doctrinal affirmation is Paul's claim that Christians have been "reconciled to God by the death of his Son" and that "much more, being reconciled, [they are] saved by his life" (*Rom.* 5:10).

The development of Christian doctrine is closely allied with the task of instructing catechumens who are being prepared to receive the sacrament or rite of baptism. As late as the third century, Augustine, in *De magistro* (Concerning the teacher), reveals a major concern with doctrine in this sense. His specific tractate on Christian doctrine, *De doctrina christiana*, is not an exposition of the content of Christian doctrine but a discussion of the most effective way to teach it. Indeed, the immense Augustinian corpus contains no speculative overview of Christian knowledge; his most memorable works in the field of doctrine are devoted to specific themes that troubled the faith of Christians in his time: free will (*De libero arbitrio*); divine providence *(City of God);* the Trinity (*De Trinitate*). Even the great disquisitions on doctrine by Thomas Aquinas (the *Summa theologiae* and *Summa contra gentiles*) are in the form of questions and answers that reveal an obvious affinity for the method of catechetical instruction. Luther's most important contribution to the area of doctrine is his *Longer Catechism* and *Short Catechism;* Calvin's *Institutes of the Christian Religion* is an expanded version of a small handbook he originally produced to assist Christians in understanding the teachings presented in Luther's catechisms.

The examples of such major Catholic and Protestant figures are evidence of the dominant focus of Christian doctrine on spiritual instruction. The teaching focus of doctrine has both a constructive and defensive thrust. It is, in part, an attempt to refute heresies within the church and false teachings without, as many historians of doctrine have pointed out. This polemical aspect offers a partial explanation for the greater emphasis on certain themes and the neglect of others at a particular time and place. Still, the refutation of error is not an end in itself, but a means through which to enhance the efficacy of the soteriological aspect of the teaching, which remains the paramount concern.

A CATEGORY OF COMPARATIVE RELIGION. Doctrine is not restricted to Christianity. There are examples in each of the world's major religious traditions of affirmations that possess the same kind of authority and intent: in Judaism, the Shemaʿ ("Hear!") with its admonition "Hear, O Israel! The Lord is our God, the Lord is one"; in Islam, the testimony of the Shahādah that "there is no god but God, and Muḥammad is his prophet." Examples of doctrine central to other religions include the doctrine of the permanent self, or *ātman*, in Hinduism; the doctrine of nonself, or *anātman* (Pali, *anatta*), in Buddhism; the Confucian doctrine of "humanity" or *jen;* the Daoist doctrine of the efficacy of nonaction, or *wuwei;* and the Shinto belief in *kami*, the presence of sacred power in things.

It is even more significant that each religion makes use of words that, though not exact synonyms for the terms *doctrine* or *teaching*, are very close to them in meaning: *torah* ("instruction") in Judaism and *kalām* ("doctrine, theology") in Islam; *darśana* ("school, viewpoint") in Hinduism; dharma ("teaching") in Buddhism; *chiao* ("teaching") in Confucianism and Daoism; *Butsudo* ("way of the Buddha") in Japanese Buddhism; *kami no michi* ("way of the Japanese divinities") in Shintō.

The prevalence of a doctrinal factor in all of the world's major religions suggests that it ought to be treated as a general category in the academic study of religion. This has, at times, not been recognized with sufficient clarity because of a romantic bias that exalts feeling over thought and deems "doctrine" an alien intrusion into a religious form of existence that is essentially nonrational in character.

However, the notion of a dichotomy between thought and feeling in the religious life is not tenable. Feelings, perceptions, and emotions require form and structure to become the content of human experience. By the same token, mysticism and rationalism reveal an intimate affinity, since most mystics become known to us through the discursive accounts of their ineffable experiences that they produce. Even the symbol systems of nonliterate societies have a doctrinal or rational aspect that gives religious shape to communal life.

Doctrine, then, is a category in the comparative study of religion that belongs with ritual, sacrament, mystical experience, and other factors whose importance has been recognized for some time. Like them, doctrine is designed to focus the mind, emotions, and will on the religious goal that the community has accepted as its ultimate concern.

Buddhism. Buddhism provides a striking example of the role played by doctrine in the realization of a religious goal. According to the Buddhist dharma, or teaching, the existence of man is determined by limitless craving (*tṛṣṇā*) that produces anguish (*duḥkha*) and a fundamental distortion of one's thoughts and feelings about the world. The teaching offers release from the tyranny of those disordered perceptions and a path of deliverance from the endless cycle of birth and rebirth (*saṃsāra*) to which man's obsessive desires have bound him. The teaching consists of training in the control of thoughts and feelings, conscientious ethical behavior, and an intensive discipline of inner concentration and meditation. The doctrinal component supports the posture of mind and heart that is to be assumed throughout the various stages of the training.

However, in his present state of illusion, the seeker is never able to discern the true difference between the theoretical and the practical. He does not know what is a mere palliative and what truly heals. In this state he perceives Buddhist teachings as paradoxical: metaphysical reticence is advised in meditations that seem endlessly speculative; simplicity is advocated in arcane terms. These paradoxes are themselves symptoms of the ignorance of the seeker, who does not even know what constitutes the simplicity and healing that he seeks. The doctrine or teaching leads him along a path that, by both wakening and frustrating his speculative curiosity, brings about a transformation of thought and feeling that is the prerequisite for the authentic liberation that is his goal.

The doctrine of *nirvāṇa* (Pali, *nibbāna*) is a striking case in point. The term literally means "blowing out," as when a candle is extinguished. It is used to indicate the final end of man. But what is it? Four possibilities have been suggested: (1) it is absolute nonexistence; (2) it is a positive state of bliss and tranquillity; (3) it is a state that can only be indicated in terms of what it is not; and (4) it is something ineffable, incapable of being rendered in either positive or negative terms. Depending upon the Buddhist text or school that is consulted, each of these options receives some sort of support. On what basis is one to choose among them?

The scholar-observer who, as a speculative venture, examines the doctrine from without, will probably make a choice based on historical grounds (which option is closest to the original teachings of the historical Buddha?) or on systematic considerations (which is most consistent with Buddhist thought as a totality?). On the other hand, a Buddhist will judge them according to their efficacy as religious vehicles. From this perspective, it may appear that each option makes a contribution according to changes in circumstance as the Buddhist seeker proceeds along his religious path.

The notion of *nirvāṇa* as extinction is as austere and forbidding to the average member of a Buddhist society as it is to a nonbeliever. Still, it may be effective as a means to separate the seeker from some of the distorted perceptions of "existence" that are one cause of his anguish. In different circumstances, the prospect of an end that includes bliss and tranquillity may be more therapeutic; at other times, the way of negations, or an even more intricate path of "spiritual agnosticism," eschewing both negations and affirmations, may be efficacious. While man remains in a state of bondage to his anguish and illusions, a definitive description of his final end is of little value. The authority of the doctrine of *nirvāṇa* lies rather in the therapeutic role it plays in the attainment of a goal that will only be truly known in the process of its concrete realization. When this takes place, it will become apparent that the "goal" was in the seeker's possession all the time. The doctrine has led him on an arduous journey to a destination that, once reached, coincides with the place of departure that he never left.

Theology and Doctrinal Form. At the present time, doctrine is frequently associated with systematic theology. For over a thousand years of church history, theology had diverse meanings, some of which were remote from those of Christian doctrine. Plato used the word *theology* to describe the stories about the gods told by poets; Aristotle used it to describe his doctrine of immutable substance. Augustine distinguished three senses: the theology of the poets, a civic theology based on public ceremonies, and a theology of nature. Sometimes the term was used in a narrow sense by Christian thinkers, who restricted it to the doctrine of God.

Muslim theologians such as al-Ghazālī (1058–1111 CE) participated in a golden age of theology devoted to the task of reconciling Greek philosophy with the faith of Islam. During the same period, Maimonides (Mosheh ben Maimon, 1135/8–1204) worked on the reconciliation of Greek thought with Judaism; Thomas Aquinas (1225–1274) undertook a similar task in respect to the Roman Catholic faith. Even more important is the fact that during the twelfth and thirteenth centuries revisions in medieval education were made that, among other things, introduced the notion of doctrinal theology as an academic discipline with a status similar to that of the secular subjects taught in the university curriculum.

Hugh of Saint-Victor (c. 1096–1141) developed an approach to theology that subsumed the two senses of the term *theory* (i.e., both intellectual endeavor and contemplation of God) under the complex notion of "speculation," which had previously been applied, for the most part, to religious meditation. Hugh characterized the method of theology as a kind of thought that is theoretical, both in the rational sense of submission to the norms of logic and in the contemplative sense of religious aspiration and vision. However, the delicate balance that he proposed is the prescription of an ideal and not what most works of systematic theology are, in fact, like. Theologians readily acknowledge that the norms of rational adequacy as a rule take precedence over a devotional focus. They deem it sufficient that theology provides rational support for the spiritual life without functioning as a direct expression of it.

The institutionalization of systematic and doctrinal theology in universities and seminaries has guaranteed for it a place of continuing importance in the history of the church from the time of the Renaissance to the present. However, it is evident that in the course of its long history the church has also made use of other forms (e.g., epistles, catechisms, creeds, tractates, and biblical commentaries) to express the concerns of doctrine. At the present time, there is some evidence that the essay is replacing the systematic tome as the preferred means for doctrinal discussions among both Catholic and Protestant thinkers.

The fourth book of Augustine's *Christian Doctrine* offers comments about doctrine that are still relevant to the contemporary scene. Augustine suggests that rhetoric is as important as logic in the communication of doctrine, though, like Plato in his attack on the Sophists, he is aware that the eloquence of rhetoric may deceive rather than enlighten. Augustine accepts, however, Aristotle's defense of the notion of a viable rhetoric that deals with the distinction between probative arguments and those based on a misuse of eloquence analogous to a formal logic that distinguishes between valid and invalid syllogisms. Augustine makes use of the rhetorical tradition derived from Aristotle to explore the capacity of Christian doctrine to teach, delight, and persuade. He recommends a subdued style for the task of careful instruction, a moderate style for condemnation and praise, and a grand style, forceful with the emotions and the spirit, for those moments when the need emerges to move the reader to action.

Contemporary experiments in the communication of doctrine through literature and other media are thus not unprecedented; they are, in fact, the continuation of a classical tradition of rhetoric toward which many thinkers, in both religious and secular disciplines, are at present showing a renewed respect.

See Also Creeds; Dharma; Dogma; Jiao; Kalām; Theology; Torah; Truth.

Bibliography

The most up-to-date extended history of doctrine from a Protestant perspective is Jaroslav Pelikan's *The Christian Tradition: A History of the Development of Doctrine*, 4 vols. (Chicago, 1971–1984). The work provides many revaluations of conventional historical judgments and includes an extensive bibliographical apparatus of primary and secondary sources. Nineteenth-century studies like Adolf von Harnack's *History of Dogma*, 7 vols. translated by Neil Buchanan (London, 1895–1900), and Reinhold Seeberg's *Text-Book of the History of Doctrines*, 2 vols. translated by Charles E. Hay (Grand Rapids, Mich., 1952), among others, remain indispensable in spite of inadequacies of interpretation corrected by later historians. Bernhard Lohse's *A Short History of Christian Doctrine: From the First Century to the Present*, translated by F. Ernest Stoeffer (Philadelphia, 1978) is a brief summary that is also a helpful essay of interpretation; George A. Lindbeck's *The Nature of Doctrine: Religion and Theology in a Postliberal Age* (Philadelphia, 1984) offers an approach to doctrine that makes use of the categories developed by philosophers of language. The *Dictionnaire de theologie catholique*, 15 vols., edited by Jean-Michel-Alfred Vacant et al. (Paris, 1903–1950), is important for an understanding of doctrine from a Catholic perspective. Also useful is the *Encyclopedia of Theology: The Concise Sacramentum Mundi*, edited by Karl Rahner (New York, 1975). "Dogma," an essay by Rahner in this encyclopedia, together with his "Considerations on the Development of Dogma," in his *Theological Investigations*, translated by Kevin Smyth, vol. 4 (Baltimore, 1966), pp. 3–35, offer a sophisticated statement of the standard approach to Catholic doctrine and dogma. An informative account of the emergence of doctrinal theology as an academic discipline is G. R. Evans's *Old Arts and New Technology: The Beginnings of Theology as an Academic Discipline* (Oxford, 1980).

The following works offer useful discussions of rhetorical and literary genres other than systematic theology appropriate for contemporary statements of doctrine: Giles B. Gunn, *The Interpretation of Otherness: Literature, Religion, and the American Imagination* (Oxford, 1979); David Tracy, *The Analogical Imagination: Christian Theology and the Culture of Pluralism* (New York, 1981); Nathan A. Scott, Jr., ed., *The New Orpheus: Essays toward a Christian Poetic* (New York, 1964).

The following are useful studies of the role of doctrine in religions other than Christianity. For Judaism: Judah Goldin, ed. *The Living Talmud* (New York, 1957); Jacob Neusner, *The Way of Torah: An Introduction to Judaism* (Belmont, Calif., 1970); Leo Trepp, *Judaism: Development and Life* (Belmont, Calif., 1982). For Islam: Charles J. Adams, "The Islamic Religious Tradition," in *Religion and Man*, edited by W. Richard Comstock (New York, 1971), pp. 553–617; Fazlur Rahman, *Islam*, 2d ed. (Chicago, 1979). For the religions of India: Robert Baird, "Indian Religious Traditions," in *Religion and Man* (cited above), pp. 115–250; Ninian Smart, *Doctrine and Argument in Indian Philosophy* (London, 1964). For Buddhism: Edward Conze, *Buddhism: Its Essence and Devel-*

opment (Oxford, 1951); Melford E. Spiro, *Buddhism and Society: A Great Tradition and Its Burmese Vicissitudes*, 2d ed., exp. (Berkeley, 1982). For the religions of China: Tu Weiming, *Humanity and Self-Cultivation: Essays in Confucian Thought* (Berkeley, 1978); C. K. Yang, *Religion in Chinese Society* (Berkeley, 1961). For the religions of Japan: Alfred Bloom, "Far Eastern Religious Traditions," in *Religion and Man* (cited above), pp. 254–396; H. Byron Earhart, *Japanese Religion: Unity and Diversity*, 3d rev. ed. (Belmont, Calif., 1982). For the religions of preliterate societies: W. Richard Comstock, *The Study of Religion and Primitive Religions* (New York, 1972); Mary Douglas, *Natural Symbols: Explorations in Cosmology* (New York, 1970); Clifford Geertz, "Religion as a Cultural System," in *Anthropological Approaches to the Study of Religion*, edited by Michael Banton (New York, 1966), pp. 1–46.

W. RICHARD COMSTOCK (1987)

DŌGEN (1200–1253), more fully, Eihei Dōgen (or Buppō Dōgen, but never Dōgen Kigen or Kigen Dōgen as has been mistakenly suggested), was the founding abbot of the Eiheiji Zen monastery. Since the late nineteenth century, he has been officially designated, along with Keizan Jōkin (1264–1325), as one of the two founding patriarchs of the Japanese Sōtō Zen school, and, most recently, he has been widely celebrated as one of Japan's most creative and original religious thinkers, whose writings and novel use of language seem to anticipate many modern philosophical concerns.

Dōgen lived at a time of political and religious unrest. Shortly before his birth, the Buddhist monastic centers in the ancient capital of Nara had been destroyed by warfare in 1185, Japan's first military government (shogunate) had been established in Kamakura in 1180, and the royal court in Kyoto in 1194 had banned the establishment of independent Zen temples, which were just beginning to appear. During the year of Dōgen's birth (1200), however, the fortunes of the new Zen movement changed when the shogunate began to support the pioneer Japanese Zen teacher Eisai (1141–1215).

Dōgen entered monastic life as a youth. From 1212 to 1217 he studied the mixed exoteric-esoteric (*kenmitsu*) Buddhism of the Japanese Tendai tradition on Mount Hiei. From 1217 to 1225 he studied Zen Buddhism under Myōzen (1184–1225), who was Eisai's successor as abbot of Kenninji temple in Kyoto. In 1223 Dōgen accompanied his teacher Myōzen on a pilgrimage to China. In 1225, after Myōzen died, Dōgen became the disciple of the Chinese monk Rujing (1163–1227), who was then abbot of the major state monastery on Mount Tiantong (i.e., Mount Taibei in Zhejiang province). Two years later, in 1227, Dōgen inherited Rujing's Caodong Chan (Japanese, Sōtō Zen) lineage and returned to Japan.

Once back in Japan, Dōgen initially resided at Kenninji. In 1230 he established a new Zen community (officially designated the Kōshōji monastery in 1236) in Fukakusa outside of Kyoto, where in 1241 he was joined by a group of Zen practitioners known as the Darumashū (the lineage of Bodhidharma). In 1243 Dōgen secured the patronage of a powerful warrior family, the Hatano, and relocated his Zen community to the Hatano estates in Echizen province where the following year he founded the Daibutsuji Monastery (renamed Eiheiji in 1246). In 1253 Dōgen became deathly ill and returned to Kyoto for medical treatment, which proved ineffective. Today, Eiheiji is one of the two headquarter temples, along with Sōjiji, of the Sōtō Zen school, one of Japan's largest religious denominations. In 1878 the Meiji emperor (Mutsuhito, 1852–1912) awarded Dōgen with the posthumous name Jōyō Daishi.

Dōgen was an extremely prolific author who wrote essays, sermons, and poetry, both in literary Chinese and in Japanese. His early short compositions—such as *Bendōwa* (A talk on practicing Buddhism, 1231), *Fukan zazen gi* (Universal exhortation to practice sitting Zen, 1233), and the Chinese-language *Shōbōgenzō* (True dharma eye collection, 1235, a compilation of 301 *kōan*, or topics for Zen study)—comprise a concise introduction to key Zen doctrines and methods of practicing Zen meditation.

In midcareer, and especially after being joined by members of the Darumashū, Dōgen wrote a series of books in Japanese also collectively titled *Shōbōgenzō*. While this Japanese-language *Shōbōgenzō* apparently never reached the final form intended by Dōgen, he nonetheless completed at least three compilations: an initial draft in sixty books, a revised draft in seventy-five books, and a new draft in twelve books. After Dōgen's death, books from these three compilations were mixed together (sometimes with unrelated compositions) to produce many other separate editions, each independent from the others. In 1796, monks at Eiheiji began work on publishing an officially sanctioned "Head Monastery" (*honzan*) edition of the *Shōbōgenzō*. It was revised in 1906 to include ninety-five books, arranged in a rough chronological order that bares no relationship to the order of books in any of the three compilations by Dōgen. Each individual book in the *Shōbōgenzō* typically is organized around a series of quotations from Chinese *kōan* or Chinese translations of the Buddhist scriptures. Dōgen then comments in Japanese on each of these passages to show how they should be read and understood as expressions of religious truth. Together the books in the *Shōbōgenzō* comment on approximately 512 *kōan*, thereby providing an encyclopedic overview of Zen (and general Buddhist) teachings.

In later life, Dōgen seems to have concentrated his literary efforts on composing works in Chinese. After his death, his disciples compiled these Chinese-language compositions into the *Eihei kōroku* (Extensive recorded sayings of Eihei Dōgen, ten fascicles), which contains sermons, lectures, and verse organized into sections from Kōshōji, Daibutsuji, and Eiheiji. It contains the only writings by Dōgen that can be positively dated to his mature years between 1247 and 1252. In all, it includes Dōgen's comments on approximately 298 *kōan.* Finally, in 1667, monks at Eiheiji compiled a collection of Dōgen's independent essays on monastic procedures, which they published as *Eihei shingi* (Eihei Dōgen's monastic regulations). The proper practice of Buddhist monasticism was of major concern to Dōgen, and many of the books in the *Shōbōgenzō* also address this topic.

Dōgen died in almost complete obscurity, known only to his immediate disciples. The Sōtō Zen community he founded, however, prospered. At first it expanded slowly but steadily, and then it grew rapidly under the leadership of monks affiliated with the Sōjiji monastery, which had been founded by a fourth-generation dharma heir of Dōgen named Keizan Jōkin. During this period of expansion, manuscript copies of Dōgen's prodigious oeuvre were stored in the head monasteries of each major temple network, where they served more as symbols of religious authority and legitimacy than as sources for studying Zen Buddhism.

This situation changed during the Tokugawa period (1600–1868) as a result of government policies that simultaneously promoted Buddhist scholasticism and reorganized many Sōtō temple networks. At that time, reform-minded Sōtō monks, such as Manzan Dōhaku (1636–1714), who sought to challenge temple policies, cited Dōgen's writings to support their positions and began publishing excerpts from his Japanese-language *Shōbōgenzō.* Sōtō authorities reacted by asking the government to ban its publication, which was done from 1722 to 1796. With the subsequent publication of the Head Monastery edition of the *Shōbōgenzō,* however, Dōgen eventually came to be identified with doctrinal orthodoxy for the Sōtō Zen school. Influential Sōtō monks, especially Menzan Zuihō (1683–1769) and Nishiari Bokusan (1822–1910), interpreted Dōgen as advocating a religion of "just sitting" (*shikan taza*), in which the practice of sitting Zen (*zazen*) is itself the complete authentication of awakening (*shushō ichinyo*). Meditation on *kōan* and striving to see nature (*kenshō*; i.e., attain *satori*) are to be rejected. In this way, Dōgen's Zen came to be contrasted to other forms of Zen Buddhism, now usually associated only with Japanese Rinzai or Ōbaku Zen lineages. More recently, some Sōtō scholars have advocated a "Critical Buddhism" (*hihan Bukkyō*), which portrays Dōgen's teachings as standing in opposition to many Buddhist doctrinal norms, such as original awakening (*hongaku*), that are widely accepted in East Asia.

In 1868 the Tokugawa regime was overthrown, and Japan entered a period of rapid transformation into a modern political state, with an industrialized economy fully engaged in the world. In 1906 the Head Monastery edition of the *Shōbōgenzō* was published for the first time in a modern typeset edition readily accessible to a mass audience. It soon came to the attention of Japanese intellectuals who had not been educated in Buddhist doctrines but trained in Western philosophy. Leading scholars and educators, such as Watsuji Tetsurō (1889–1960), Tanabe Hajime (1885–1962), and Akiyama Hanji (1893–1980), discovered in Dōgen an original Japanese philosopher whose ideas and methods of analysis presented innovative responses to ontological, phenomenological, and linguistic issues posed by Western thinkers such as Martin Heidegger (1889–1976), Jean-Paul Sartre (1905–1980), and others. Dōgen's notion of time as discontinuous moments (*uji*), in particular, has attracted much attention. Just as important, but less discussed in Western-language scholarship, is Dōgen's innovative methods of reading Chinese-language texts. In a manner with many parallels to postmodern literary deconstructionism, Dōgen's Japanese-language comments frequently dissect and rearrange individual words or phrases from Chinese-language passages in ways that defy the ordinary rules of grammar to reveal hidden layers of significance. Today Dōgen's importance to philosophy is widely recognized, not just in Japan, but throughout the world.

There have been sporadic attempts to translate Dōgen's writings, especially his Japanese-language *Shōbōgenzō,* into Western languages. None of the results has been wholly satisfactory, however, with paraphrased interpretation frequently substituting for the complex linguistic gymnastics of Dōgen's original prose. Moreover, any translation must confront the thorny problem of how to reconcile the existence of at least three separate versions of Dōgen: the thirteenth-century Zen teacher, the eighteenth- and nineteenth-century Sōtō sectarian patriarch, and the twentieth-century Western (or world) philosopher. Dōgen has become too big to be defined by any one audience.

See Also Eisai; Keizan; Zen.

Bibliography

Abe, Masao. *A Study of Dōgen: His Philosophy and Religion.* Edited by Steven Heine. Albany, N.Y., 1992.

Bielefeldt, Carl. *Dōgen's Manuals of Zen Meditation.* Berkeley, 1988.

Bodiford, William M. *Sōtō Zen in Medieval Japan.* Honolulu, 1994.

Faure, Bernard. "The Daruma-shū, Dōgen, and Sōtō Zen." *Monumenta Nipponica* 42, no. 1 (1987): 25–55.

Gunn, Robert J. *Journeys into Emptiness: Dōgen, Merton, Jung, and the Quest for Transformation.* New York, 2000.

He, Yansheng. *Dōgen to Chūgoku Zen shisō* (Dōgen and Chinese Zen doctrines). Kyoto, 2000.

Heine, Steven. *Existential and Ontological Dimensions of Time in Heidegger and Dōgen.* Albany, N.Y., 1985.

Hubbard, Jamie, and Paul L. Swanson, eds. *Pruning the Bodhi Tree: The Storm over Critical Buddhism.* Honolulu, 1997.

Ishii Shūdō. *Dōgen Zen no seiritsu shiteki kenkyū* (Historical researches in the development of Dōgen's Zen). Tokyo, 1991.

Kagamishima Genryū. *Dōgen Zenji to sono shūhen* (Zen teacher Dōgen and his surroundings). Tokyo, 1985.

LaFleur, William R., ed. *Dōgen Studies.* Honolulu, 1985.

Nakaseko Shōdō. *Dōgen Zenji den kenkyū* (Research in the biography of Zen teacher Dōgen). 2 vols. Tokyo, 1979–1997.

Shaner, David E. *The Bodymind Experience in Japanese Buddhism: A Phenomenological Perspective of Kūkai and Dōgen.* Albany, N.Y., 1985.

Stambaugh, Joan. *Impermanence Is Buddha-nature: Dōgen's Understanding of Temporality.* Honolulu, 1990.

WILLIAM M. BODIFORD (2005)

DOGMA. Dogma, in the strictest sense, whether embodied in the sacred scripture of the Old and New Testaments or in tradition, is understood by the Roman Catholic Church to be a truth revealed by God (directly and formally), which is presented by the church for belief, as revealed by God, either through a solemn decision of the extraordinary magisterium (pope or council) or through the ordinary and general magisterium of the church (episcopacy). It is to be accepted by the same faith that is due to the divine word itself (*fides divina*) or to the church's tradition (*fides catholica*).

This magisterial definition, as it was given by the First Vatican Council, has the following historical antecedents: (1) the ancient philosophical (Platonic-Stoic) use of the word *dogma* to designate that which seems right to all, as opinion or teaching, as foundation or decision, as decree or edict, as a rational judgment that is identical to a moral decision, or as a decree of a legitimate authority; (2) the New Testament use, in which Old Testament law is said to be the dogma of God and the decisions of the apostolic council are designated as dogmas in *Acts* 16:4; and (3) the patristic and medieval transmission of both these strains, the dogma of God in distinction to the teachings of human beings or of the philosophers. The close connection between the "dogmas of the Lord" and the "fidelity to the church" is already asserted in the *regula fidei*, the canon of truth. Finally, synodal decrees are also considered dogmas in opposition to the dogmas of the heretics. The content referred to by *dogma* also occurs in the patristic and scholastic tradition under equivalent designations, for instance, *professio* and *confessio*, or (Catholic) truth in general; *fides*, the correct doctrine handed down by the church; and, in Thomas Aquinas, over against the concept of dogma, the narrowed concept of *articulus fidei*. What led to an emphasis on the formal authority of dogma was, finally, the emphasis on the claim to the limitless autonomy of human reason in the eighteenth and nineteenth centuries.

The definition of the concept and function of dogma in the Eastern Orthodox churches, in spite of the multiplicity and differing historical development of these churches, can begin with their formal unity in terms of doctrine, law, and liturgy. Faith is based upon the dogmas that have been transmitted in part through scripture and in part through the oral *paradosis* ("handing down" of tradition) of the apostles and have then been interpreted by the councils and church fathers. Because and to the extent that the church speaks with the authority of the Holy Spirit, it is infallible in the same way as scripture. The believing acceptance of the revealed truth of faith is necessary for salvation. The dogma of the church is present and closed in the doctrinal decisions of the first seven ecumenical councils (325–787), whose formulations are considered the embodiment of dogma and the summary of the teachings of scripture. The further dogmatic development of the Latin church is rejected. Dogma in the Orthodox churches has not so much a doctrinaire-intellectual function as it does a doxological and life-defining one.

The relationship to dogma of the churches and communities produced by the Reformation is defined by the theology of the reformers, which, on the one hand, does not dispute that the church may have to make obligatory statements and that the truth of scripture may only be able to be revealed through a painstaking process. It therefore accepts at least the Trinitarian-Christological dogma of the old church as an appropriate expression of the matter of the gospel. But, on the other hand, through the principle of *sola scriptura* (over against an association of scripture and tradition), the theology of the reformers takes up a different position, scripture being for them no longer merely the source and norm of all Christian speech, teaching, and preaching, but, rather, the single final authority. All confessions and dogmas are to be measured against it. In this sense, dogmatic statements (even the Trinitarian-Christological) are only secondarily binding for Protestant theology, and then only when it has been demonstrated whether and to what extent dogmas open up an access to direct biblical instruction, where it is presupposed that scripture, on the basis of its transparency, is its own interpreter. In spite of all confessional-theological discussions among the churches and communities growing out of the Reformation, and in spite of the changing theological positions and the change in the functional definition of dogma connected with them (from orthodoxy through rationalism and Pietism and from the purely ethical and practical interpretation to dialectical and existential theology), they agree both negatively and positively. Negatively, they agree in their rejection of the Roman Catholic understanding of dogma and its function for faith and church as "doctrinal law." Positively, they agree in the conviction that God's word must not only be existentially recognized but also known as objective truth and reproduced in statements and doctrinal teachings, however these may then be interpreted and qualified with regard to their binding character.

In the question of the development of dogma, Roman Catholic theology must proceed from the fact that the church defines statements as revealed by God if they satisfy one of the following conditions: (1) Even if previously stated, they were not always expressly defined or bindingly taught as revealed. (2) They articulate the express contents of statements of the earlier tradition in very different or newly developed conceptual terms (by defending the always known meaning of the revealed statement more expressly against heretical misinterpretations, by setting off more clearly individual aspects of these statements, or by placing these aspects in a dialectical interplay of faith and reason or in a more explicit relationship to other truths of faith and of reason). (3) They refer to statements in the tradition that may not be immediately equivalent to them or explicitly capable of being traced back to the apostles or that cannot even be supposed with historical probability to have been once previously available. Thus not only theology but also revelation (to the extent that it is only present in proclamation, acceptance of faith, and practice) has a history, a "development," and a "progress" after Christ, even if this history is essentially different from the development of revelation before Christ.

The problem of the development of dogma and its solution consists in the task of demonstrating the fundamental possibility and the actuality, in individual cases, of the identity of the later, "developed" matter of faith with the apostolic matter given in Christ. The difficulty of the problem lies in the fact that, according to church doctrine, the entire "public" revelation, entrusted to the church and its teaching office and involving an obligation of belief, was closed with the death of the apostles, that is, that the church can only continue to bear witness to what it has heard about Christ in the apostolic generation and has recognized as belonging to the deposit of faith. Therefore an additional, later, ecclesial revelation is not possible, does not expand the old Christian revelation, and cannot undergo an epigenetic transformation in the sense that might be implied by modernism. Because the solution to the problem (formally speaking and in general) must be sought in the fact that a new dogma is contained "implicitly" in an old dogma or in the whole of what was previously believed, the problem and its solution may be formulated in the following way.

1. What is the status of implicitness and what is the process of explication such that these can be recognized as factually given in the development of dogma? That is, how can the identity of faith, as expressed in an actual history of faith, and revelation after Christ be explained?
2. What implications are sufficient so that the explicated can be considered as revealed by God (and not simply taught by the church with infallible authority)? Such an implication is obviously to be applied, however, in such a way that it can be said not only that the new dogma, as derivative in its truth and certainty upon the original revelation, could thus legitimately appeal to the witness of God (purely objective implication) but also that it, of itself (even if in a different form), has always been witnessed to by God's self and has always been believed by the church (subjective implication).

The problem, precisely posed, has only been clearly present since the nineteenth century, that is, since there has existed a history of dogma that not only (as still in the post-Tridentine period) doxographically collects the proofs from an earlier time for the doctrine of the present and thereby considers these proofs to be only different from the contemporary doctrine in their external form but also sees that the recognition of revelational truth has a real history after Christ.

The problem is stated differently in Protestant theology, because there is in evangelical theology no faith statement of the church that could be an absolutely binding norm for the private understanding of scripture, and thus there can actually be, from the start, only a history of theology, not really a history of dogma and faith after scripture. Behind this problem is, as its natural presupposition, the problem of the historicity of the (ever the same) recognition of truth in general and that of reconciling a present continuing immediacy of the divine revelation in the church (which is necessarily historically new) with the relegation of the present proclamation back to an earlier historical past, that is to say, back to the apostolic period.

The first three centuries of Christianity and perhaps the following one and a half centuries, which saw the development and culmination of the first three, present a history of Christian belief and dogma in a confrontational struggle with the simultaneous assimilation of a non-Christian spiritual and cultural (Hellenistic-Roman) environment. However, the second long period after the waning of antiquity, that is, from the early Middle Ages to the Enlightenment, was a time of unfolding and differentiation of the substance of faith from within its own center outward into even more systematized distinctions that, because of their one point of departure from within, could be considered without really major confrontation with external contradictions and as a more or less homogeneous abstraction presupposed by all to be self-evident. (This was so in spite of the continuing influence of Platonism and the medieval reception of Aristotelianism, and in spite of the crises that occurred with the split between the Eastern and Western churches and with the Reformation of the sixteenth century.) This was, therefore, a time for summae and simultaneously and for the same reasons a time (because the whole was taken for granted) when one threw oneself into theological questions with enormous passion and almost became lost in them. It was a time the effects of which are reflected in the great catechisms of the modern period. It was a time in which one could take for granted long papal encyclicals over relatively small questions of detail of the Christian faith; in which the magisterium reacted carefully and quickly to real or imagined attacks against individual doctrines of this detailed system; and in which one had the impression that the entire system was clear and could hardly be further developed, except in the case of individual questions, so that the major work of theology had to be turned backward upon its own history.

Today (after a long preparation since the Enlightenment, from which time also dates the defensive dialogue with liberalism and modernism) we have doubtless entered upon a new, third phase in the history of faith and thus also in the history of dogma and of theology. Today it is no longer a question of an ever more detailed unfolding of the basic substance of faith within a homogeneous environment that has a common horizon of understanding with the church. It is much more a question of winning a new understanding (naturally preserving the substance of faith which has been handed down) of the one totality of faith in a non-Christian environment, in a new epoch of a global world civilization in which world cultures that were never Christian have appeared. It is also a question of a history of faith and dogma in a new diaspora, with confrontation and assimilation to be simultaneously carried out in a radically new way that includes even the most divergent belief, that of atheism and the doubt as to whether religion in general will survive. To that extent, there is a formal similarity between the period of the history of dogma now beginning and the first period, even if the matter and the tasks of the first and the third periods are radically different.

The history of faith and dogma will probably develop in the future not in the style of the second period, as an evolutionary unfolding and systematizing differentiation of the basic substance of faith, but rather as the transposition of this lasting faith into new and pluralistic horizons of understanding. Because of the incommensurable and not synthesizable pluralism of contemporary and future horizons of understanding, transpositions of faith will have to occur by means of a plurality of theologies that, despite the necessary readiness for dialogue of these theologies among themselves, will not be able to be synthesized adequately for the preservation and rediscovery of the one faith.

The task of the magisterium in this incipient period will, therefore, hardly consist any more in the definition of "new" individual dogmas, no longer so much in the anxious monitoring of supposed or real deviations from individual traditional doctrines, but rather in the preservation of the one entirety of the faith in its basic substance and, in fact, not so much through a "censuring," but rather through the positive, constructive, collaborative work on this new interpretation of the old faith that is demanded today in a new and not necessarily Christian environment.

The history of faith and dogma will continue, but it will have a different character, not so much the history of individual, newly articulated statements of faith and of the theology that reflects upon them, but rather the history of the restatement of the old basic substance of faith in the confrontation with and assimilation of the future horizon of understanding. It is self-evident that this history will be then no longer merely the history of the formulation of early Christian and Western dogmas and their theology (including their export to other countries) but rather the history of the faith and dogma of a universal church, however little we can concretely imagine today what is materially and formally meant by that. This naturally does not exclude but rather includes the fact that the changing new conception of the one entirety of the Christian substance of faith will also have consequences for the interpretation of many or all individual doctrines.

See Also Creeds; Doctrine; Theology.

BIBLIOGRAPHY

A summary introduction to the history of the concept of dogma and the history of the problem of the development of dogma from a Catholic point of view can be found in Georg Söll's "Dogma und Dogmenentwicklung," in *Handbuch der Dogmengeschichte*, vol. 1, fasc. 5 (Freiburg, 1971), which includes an extensive bibliography. From the Protestant perspective the following articles in *Theologische Realenzyklopädie*, vol. 9 (Berlin and New York, 1982), pp. 26–125, should be consulted: "Dogma" by Ulrich Wickert and Carl H. Ratschow, "Dogmatik" by Gerhard Sauter, Anders Jeffner, Alasdair Heron, and Frederick Herzog, and "Dogmengeschichtsschreibung" by Wolf-Dieter Hauschild. See also Karlmann Beyschlag's *Grundriss der Dogmengeschichte*, vol. 1 (Darmstadt, 1982), pp. 1–54.

The relationship between kerygma and dogma (also in conversation with Protestant positions) is analyzed in Karl Rahner and Karl Lehmann's *Kerygma and Dogma* (New York, 1969), Walter Kasper's *Dogma unter dem Wort Gottes* (Mainz, 1965), and Karl Rahner and Joseph Ratzinger's *Offenbarung und Überlieferung* (Freiburg, 1965).

The problem of the development of dogma from a theological-systematic perspective is treated by Karl Rahner and Karl Lehmann in *Das Problem der Vermittlung*, "Mysterium Salutis," vol. 1 (Einsiedeln, 1965), pp. 727–787; by Karl Rahner in "The Development of Dogma," in *Theological Investigations*, vol. 1 (New York, 1961), pp. 39–77; by Karl Rahner in "Considerations on the Development of Dogma," in *Theological Investigations*, vol. 4 (New York, 1966), pp. 3–35; by Joseph Ratzinger in *Das Problem der Dogmengeschichte in der Sicht der katholischen Theologie* (Cologne, 1966); and from an evangelical point of view by Gerhard Ebeling in *Die Geschichtlichkeit der Kirche und ihrer Verkündigung als theologisches Problem* (Tübingen, 1954). An instructive analysis of the more recent Catholic models of the development of dogma can be found in Herbert Hammans's *Die neueren katholischen Erklärungen der Dogmenentwicklung* (Essen, 1965). For the modernist theological-critical approach, the broadly based source study by Émile Poulat, *Histoire, dogme et critique dans la crise moderniste*, 2d ed., rev. (Paris, 1979), should be consulted. It is written, however, from a somewhat sociological perspective.

With regard to the theory and the history of the development of dogma (as well as of the historiography of dogma), the prolegomena of the classic handbooks and manuals of dogmatic history are to be consulted: for example, those by Harnack, Seeberg, Ritschl, Köhler, Schwane, Tixeront, et al. In addition, see, for Catholic theology, *Handbuch der Dogmengeschichte*, edited by Michael Schmaus et al. (Freiburg, 1971–), which is arranged according to treatises; for the Protestant perspective, see Alfred Adam's *Lehrbuch der Dogmengeschichte*, 2 vols. (Gütersloh, 1965–1968), and *Handbuch der Dogmen- und Theologiegeschichte*, 3 vols., edited by Carl Andresen (Göttingen, 1980–1984). Recent positions can also be found in Avery Dulles's *The Survival of Dogma* (New York, 1971) and Gerald O'Collins's *The Case against Dogma* (New York, 1975).

New Sources

Crowley, Paul G. *In Ten Thousand Places: Dogma in a Pluralistic Church*. New York, 1997.

Hines, Mary E. *The Transformation of Dogma: An Introduction to Karl Rahner on Dogma*. New York, 1989.

McGrath, Alister E. *The Genesis of Doctrine: A Study in the Foundations of Doctrinal Criticism.* Oxford and Cambridge, Mass., 1990.

Pannenberg, Wolfhart. *Systematische Theologie.* 3 vols. Göttingen, 1988.

Segundo, Juan Luis. *The Liberation of Dogma: Faith, Revelation, and Dogmatic Teaching Authority.* Translated by Phillip Berryman. Maryknoll, N.Y., 1992.

Theissen, Gerd. *Biblical Faith: An Evolutionary Approach.* Philadelphia, 1985.

ADOLF DARLAP (1987)
KARL RAHNER (1987)
Translated from German by Charlotte Prather
Revised Bibliography

DOGON RELIGION. The Dogon inhabit the cliffs of Bandiagara, an area located in the southwestern region of the bend of the Niger River in Mali. This area consists of a vast, rocky plateau that ends in its southern part in a 124-mile-long (200-kilometer-long) cliff overlooking a vast plain. Numbering approximately 225,000, the Dogon are cultivators of millet and other cereals and breeders of small livestock; owing to the scarcity of permanent water sources on the plateau and on the cliffs, they have had to exploit all resources available to them. Onion and pepper gardens and plantations of large trees (ficus, baobab) surround the villages whose clay houses picturesquely conform to the jagged contours of the rock.

The Dogon are well known in ethnographical literature. Since 1931 they have been the subject of numerous publications by the French ethnologist Marcel Griaule (1898–1956) and by other researchers schooled in his methods. The Dogon are perhaps best known for their art, whose consummate form is sculpture in wood (masks, statuettes, locks).

The traditional religion of the Dogon is complex and involves, among other things, a rich myth of origin, belief in a unique god, and an intricate cult of the ancestors. Christianity has had little impact on their culture, but Islam, during the late twentieth century, made significant inroads, without, however, destroying the vitality of long-standing religious beliefs and practices.

THE CREATION MYTH. The Dogon myth of origin provides both an explanation of the world and a justification of Dogon social organization. The creation of the world was the deed of the god Amma, the one god and image of the father who existed before all things. He traced the plan of the universe using 266 signs (a number corresponding to the gestation period for human beings). The design (the preliminary act of creation) corresponds to thought, which "conceives" before action or speech. Following an unsuccessful initial attempt, from which he salvaged only the four elements (water, earth, fire, and air), Amma placed in the "egg of the world," or the original placenta, two pairs of androgynous twins in the form of fish (to Sudanese peoples the catfish *Clarias senegalensis* represents the human fetus). Their gestation inside the egg was interrupted by an act of rebellion: one of the male beings prematurely left the "mother" (the placenta), deserting both "her" and his female counterpart, thus prefiguring the birth of single beings even though Amma had envisaged twin births. The solitary being descended into space and primordial darkness, taking with him a piece of the placenta that became Earth. Aware of his solitude, he traveled through space, attempted to reascend to heaven to join his female twin again, and even sought her out in the bowels of Earth, an incestuous act that brought to a climax the disorder he had already introduced into the world by leaving the placenta. The piece of placenta rotted and thus death appeared on earth.

Amma put an end to the male being's disorderly acts by transforming him into a fox, an animal that occupies a very important position in Dogon ideology. This small, wild creature, which is known more properly as *Vulpes pallida,* goes about only at night and never drinks water from ponds near the village—which, for the Dogon, explains why the fox was chosen to symbolize this enemy of light, water, fertility, and civilization.

The mythical fox Yurugu (also known as Ogo) was condemned to an eternal search for his lost twin. Moreover, he lost the ability to speak when Amma, from whom he had stolen speech, punished him by cutting off his tongue (indeed, actual foxes emit only a brief, almost clipped cry); but he still retained the power to foretell the future by "speaking" with his paws.

Unable to restore total order to his universe, Amma sought to mitigate the disorder let loose by the fox; he sacrificed Nommo, the other male twin who had stayed in the egg. Nommo's dismembered body purified the four cardinal points of the universe, and the blood that flowed forth gave birth to various heavenly bodies, edible plants, and animals.

Amma then burst the *Digitaria exilis,* a minuscule grain into which he had "rolled" all the elements of creation; these elements emptied into an ark of pure earth (the remains of the placenta). In that ark Amma also placed Nommo, whom he had already resuscitated, and his other "sons," the four pairs of heterosexual twins who are the ancestors of the human race. He lowered the ark from the heavens by means of a copper chain; the ark crashed onto Yurugu's earth at the time of the first rainfall, which formed the first pool of water. The sun also rose for the first time. Nommo went to live in the pool while the eight ancestors settled on the spot where they had landed. Using the pure earth from their ark, these ancestors created the first cultivated field, and cultivation then spread throughout Yurugu's impure earth (the bush).

The ancestors initially communicated by means of cries and grunts until one of the Nommo twins, the master of water, life, speech, and fertility, taught them language at the same time that he instructed them in the art of weaving. He then revealed to the ancestors such other fundamental techniques as agriculture, blacksmithing, dance, and music. The first human society was thus founded; marriage was introduced when the ancestors exchanged sisters.

The descent of the ark is analogous to birth. The ancestors of humanity who began their life on earth can be seen as newborns emerging from the maternal womb; the ark is the placenta, and its chain is the umbilical cord; the rains are the fetal waters.

Cults and Social Organization. The four male ancestors founded the four major religious cults, which are also the pillars of social organization; among the Dogon, social order cannot be dissociated from religion. The eldest of the ancestors, Amma Seru ("witness of Amma"), is associated with the creator god and with air (sky). The patriarch of the extended family is Amma Seru's representative in the human community. His residence, known as the "big house," is the focal point of the paternal lineage, and this is where the altar to the ancestors is situated. The altar is composed of pottery bowls (deposited there whenever a family member dies) into which the patriarch pours libations in honor of the ancestors.

Paternal lineages combine to form a totemic clan; all members of a particular clan must respect the same taboo, be it animal or vegetable. The clan is headed by a priest whose vocation is revealed through trances that incite him to seek an object hidden by dignitaries of the clan at the death of the priest he will succeed. He remains subject to these trances, which force him to wander through the countryside prophesying; he is said to be possessed by Nommo. As the representative of the ancestor Binu Seru ("witness of the *binu*"), the priest is responsible for the cult of the *binu*, the ancestors associated with the various animal and vegetable species. According to the custodians of profound knowledge, the *binu* are also symbols of the different parts of Nommo's dismembered body; the ensemble of these *binu* represents the body resuscitated in its entirety. The cult itself is associated with water, and its ritual is celebrated in sanctuaries whose façades are periodically redecorated with paintings done in thin millet paste; each transformation favors a specific event—the coming of the rains, the harvesting of various crops.

The cult of Lébé is dedicated to the ancestor Lébé Seru ("witness of Lébé") who, having died, was subsequently brought back to life in the form of a large snake; this ancestor is associated with Earth (the planet and soil, as well as the mythic archetype Earth), and with vegetation that periodically dies and comes back to life. His priest is the *hogon*, the most senior of the region, whose authority once had political impact, since it was he who administered justice and controlled the marketplaces. The *hogon* and the totemic priest together celebrate the feast of sowing (*bulu*) before the coming of the rains; they distribute to the villagers the millet seeds that have been stored in the preceding year. These seeds are thought to contain the spiritual essence of this cereal. The mythical snake Lébé is said to visit the *hogon* every night to lick his body and thus revitalize him.

The fourth ancestor, Dyongu Seru ("witness of healing"), has a different status. He was in effect the first human to die, following the breach of an interdiction. His cult is celebrated by the mask society (which exists only on the cliff and on the plateau). It is an exclusively male association, which all boys enter after their circumcision; each one must carve his own mask and must learn the society's secret language. The dance of the masks takes place as part of funeral ceremonies for men. Objects of death, the masks are strictly forbidden to women, who are associated with fertility and the forces of life. Women can only observe the dances from far away.

The death and resurrection of Dyongu Seru are commemorated through the Sigi, a spectacular ceremony that takes place every sixty years; the last one was held between 1967 and 1974. This feast also marks, on the human plane, the renewing of the generations (sixty years is thought to be the average human life span) and, on the celestial plane, the revolution of the "star of *Digitaria exilis*" around the "star of Sigi," or Sirius. The Dogon's longstanding knowledge of this Sirius satellite, which was only recently discovered by astronomers, is a mystery that science has not yet uncovered. The ceremony, celebrated from village to village over a period of eight years, includes dances executed by men in single file (each generation is ranked according to age-group). Their costumes and paraphernalia refer to both maleness and femaleness: for example, the cowrie shells that decorate the dancers' costumes and the fish-head design of their embroidered bonnets are symbols of fertility; when they drink the ritual beer, they sit on a ceremonial seat, which is a masculine symbol. Another important component of the Sigi ceremony is the erection of the "great mask," a single tree trunk or log carved in the shape of a snake to represent the resurrected ancestor.

Dyongu Seru is associated with fire, death, the wilderness (in his role as hunter and healer), and, consequently, disorder—connections that, in turn, link his cult with the mythical fox Yurugu who, on a more mundane level, is commemorated in divination rites. Diviners trace framed grids in the sand, and during the night small foxes come to eat the food offerings placed on these "tables"; the configuration of spoors left by the animals are then interpreted as responses to questions about the future. Yurugu, however much decried for being the source of disorder, is respected for his ability to foretell the future, a gift that even Amma could not take away from him. In effect, by liberating himself from all rules through his act of rebellion, Yurugu placed himself beyond time. Ultimately he incarnates individual liberty, in opposition to the group solidarity essential for the survival of traditional societies, and therein lies his ambiguity.

The Dogon religious universe is also peopled by various categories of spirits who haunt the wilderness, the trees, and inhabited sites; these spirits are the outcome of Yurugu's incestuous coupling with Earth. They represent natural forces and the original proprietors of the soil, with whom men had to ally themselves in order to gain possession of cultivable land. Offerings presented to these spirits on different occasions propitiate them and renew the original alliance.

SPEECH AND BEING. A human being is viewed as a whole composed of a body and the eight spiritual principles of both sexes. A vital life force (*nyama*) animates the entire being. The ambivalence of the human condition (that is, its simultaneous maleness and femaleness), which recalls the law of twin births ordained by Amma but later destroyed by Yurugu, is mediated by circumcision and clitoridectomy; these procedures free the child from the influence of the opposite sex (located in the prepuce and the clitoris) and thus have an equilibrating function. Death destroys the tie that holds together the various components of a person's being; funeral ceremonies assure that each component is restored to its place and facilitate the transference of the vital force from the deceased to an unborn child, who will establish a cult for that ancestor.

Speech is fundamental in Dogon thought. It forms itself in the body, all of whose organs contribute to its "birth," and like human beings, it possesses vital energy and spiritual principles. The four basic elements enter into its composition, but water is the most essential component. In symbolic rapport with all technological processes, especially the art of weaving (the organs of the mouth are said to "weave" sounds), speech is both creative (on the divine plane) and fertilizing (on the human plane); in fact, intercourse between spouses is successful only if "good words" make the woman fertile. Speech is also the cement that holds together all social relationships and facilitates the advance of society, its progress and survival.

If ancestor worship and the belief in Amma dominate the religious beliefs of the Dogon, the mythical figures who command their worldview are Nommo and Yurugu: the two incarnate opposed and complementary principles (order/disorder, life/death, humidity/dryness, fertility/sterility) that wrangle over possession of the universe. That struggle, which is constantly rekindled, assures both the equilibrium and progress of the world.

BIBLIOGRAPHY

The most complete and most detailed version of the Dogon origin myth is given in Marcel Griaule and Germaine Dieterlen's *Le renard pâle* (Paris, 1965). The first published version of the myth can be found in *Dieu d'eau: Entretiens avec Ogotemmêli* (Paris, 1948), Griaule's very popular book translated into English by Robert Redfield as *Conversations with Ogotemmêli* (London, 1965). Griaule's *Masques dogon* (Paris, 1938) still remains the definitive reference work on the mask society and on funerary ceremonies, as does that by Michel Leiris, *La langue secrète des Dogons de Sanga* (Paris, 1948), on the society's secret language. For information on perceptions of the person in Dogon society, one can consult Dieterlen's *Les âmes des Dogons* (Paris, 1941), even though our understanding of this question has been considerably enriched since that book's publication. Speech and its utilization at different levels of social life is analyzed in my own study *Ethnologie et langage: La parole chez les Dogon* (Paris, 1965), which has been translated into English by Dierdre La Pin as *Words and the Dogon World* (Philadelphia, 1986).

New Sources

Additional sources are Dirk Verboven's *A Paxiological Approach to Ritual Analysis: The Sigi of the Dogon* (Gent, 1986) and Germaine Dieterlen's *Les Dogon: Notion de Personne et Mythe de la Creation* (Paris, 1999).

GENEVIÈVE CALAME-GRIAULE (1987)
Translated from French by Brunhilde Biebuyck
Revised Bibliography

DOGS.

Recent archaeological discoveries place the domestication of the dog thousands if not tens of thousands of years prior to that of any of the other animals with which humanity has shared its cultural evolution. This shared heritage is reflected in the ritual, mythology, and religious doctrine of nearly every human society. The ancient Phoenicians, Chinese, Meso-Americans, and Egyptians buried, entombed, or mummified dogs, separately or together with their human masters; archaic astronomical systems from Europe, Asia, Africa, and North America identify star clusters or planets with supernatural dogs; and dogs figure prominently in a wide variety of myths and rituals, particularly those concerned with death and afterlife.

The place of *Canis familiaris* in religious traditions closely corresponds to the social roles, behaviors, and spatial orientations of dogs in relationship to humans, as protectors of the home, in hunting, and in herding. In every case, the dog is located at a problematic boundary between "us"—the living members of a human community—and "them": the dead, wild animals, interlopers, and human enemies of that community. As a watchdog, it prowls the zone of demarcation between within and without, inhabited space and outside world. As a herding animal, it constitutes a moving periphery, enclosing the herd that it guards from savage predators and human rustlers, but also culling animals that have been designated for slaughter. In the hunt, the hound leads—seeing, hearing, and scenting the prey before its master, who follows its bark, is able to do so—and fetches back small game in its mouth. Man's best friend has a dark side as well: the domesticated dog can turn rabid, predatory, or feral, in which cases it may endanger the very humans and livestock it normally protects. Furthermore, the dog's gluttony may be a stronger impulse than its faithfulness to its master, and its indiscriminate eating habits allow it to consume carrion, excrements, and other impure substances, including the bodies of humans slain in battle.

All of these canine qualities and behaviors have made for an intimate association between dogs and death in the world's religions. Gods of death, such as the Greek Hekate, the Indian Yama and Bhairava, and the Teutonic Garmr, are often identified with or accompanied by dogs that guard the gates to their realms. Very often, the dog is cast as a hellhound that tracks down and even devours the errant dead, for which reason the dead may be buried together with a sop to distract it, as in the case of the Sārameya—the twin dogs of the Indian death god Yama—the Greek Cerberus, and the Nicaraguan Tausun Tara. Alternatively, the dog serves as a psychopomp, a guide who leads or herds the recently deceased over the dangerous paths leading to the world of the dead—hence the sacrifice of dogs or the burial of dog effigies with the dead in Nahuatl, Chamba (northern Nigeria), and ancient Chinese traditions. In several northern European traditions, a spectral pack of dogs accompanies the storm god Woden, or the Christian Devil, on his wild hunt after the souls of the damned. At different periods, the Tibetans, Kalmuks, Parsis, Bactrians, Hyrcanians, Mongols, Javanese, and Kamchatkans have exposed their dead in "sky burials," relying on necrophagous dogs and birds of prey to consume the bodily remains and thereby carry off the pollution of death.

Numerous myths of the origin of death involve a dog. In several western African traditions, the dog is a messenger whose failure to deliver a message to a high god results in human mortality. A central Asian mytheme, found from the Balkans to Siberia and northern Japan, features a primal dog who is charged by a *deus otiosis*-type figure with protecting the bodies of a primal human pair; the dog succumbs to the temptations of the Devil, who befouls humans and dog with his spittle, thereby rendering them mortal.

Judaism, Christianity, and Islam generally cast the dog in a negative light, especially by emphasizing its impurity, and often identify dogs as demons or minions of the Devil. A striking exception is the role of the dog in the early Christian and later Islamic myth of the "Cave of the Seven Sleepers," which draws on a widespread Indo-European mytheme that has a faithful watchdog guard the mouth of a cave where six saints sleep for hundreds of years. From the high Middle Ages down to the twentieth century, a greyhound was venerated in the Dombes region of southeastern France as Saint Guignefort, the healer of sick children, in spite of repeated attempts by the Roman Church to suppress the cult of this decidedly noncanonical saint.

In Zoroastrianism, the dog plays a particularly positive role in postmortem ritual. A dog is fed three times daily for three days following a death, as a conduit for nurturing the soul of the dead. In the celebrated rite of *sag did*, the powerful gaze of a "four-eyed dog" drives away the demonic Nasus spirits that swarm around the corpse of the deceased. In Zoroastrian otherworldly geography, one or two four-eyed dogs are present at the Cinvat bridge in order to aid the souls of the just to cross over to the "Best Existence," which lies beyond. The same four-eyed dog is found, this time with a negative valence, in ancient India, where this creature was put to death beneath the feet of a horse representing the king, as a part of the famous *aśvamedha* sacrifice. This apotropaic (evil-averting) sacrifice identified the dog with the king's rival in what was essentially a ritual of royal conquest, which concluded with the sacrifice of the horse itself.

This doubling of dogs' eyes is not limited to Indian or Indo-Iranian religions, and is of a piece with a broader phenomenon of doubling in the symbolism of death. Four-eyed dogs are found in the mythology and ritual of numerous cultures, including the Ibo of Nigeria who behead a four-eyed dog (that is, a dog with pronounced markings over its eyes) when burying their chiefs. This they do in order that the dog may transfer its powers of clairvoyance to the deceased. Similar practices involving dogs of this sort are found in hunting rituals in many parts of Africa, while Finnish and Slavic traditions employ four-eyed dogs to root out and protect against evil spirits. Hellhounds are often found in pairs, or with two heads (as in the case of the Greek Orthos, Cerberos's less famous elder brother); and the name of the Indian Yama may itself be read as "Twin," the brother of Manu, "Man," who sacrifices him. As the first being to die, Yama becomes the lord of the world of the dead. A parallel mytheme is found in ancient Rome, in which Romulus kills his twin brother Remus (whose name is an Indo-European cognate of Yama) as a foundation sacrifice. In Mesoamerica, the Nahuatl dog god Xolotl is considered to be the twin brother of Quetzalcoatl, and together the two represent the planet Venus, as the morning and evening stars respectively. The eastern and western entrances to East Asian Buddhist temples are guarded by Foo (or Foh) dogs, which are said to symbolize the yin and yang principles. In ancient Egypt, the jackal- or dog-headed Anubis of Cynopolis was considered to be the "opener" of the northern paths of the dead, while the wolf-god Up-uaut or Ap-heru of Lycopolis opened the southern paths. Likewise, the "entrance" to the Milky Way, the starry path of the gods and the dead in several Indo-European traditions, is guarded by two dogs, Canis Major and Canis Minor, with the dog star Sirius being located in the former constellation of the Greco-Roman system. Located at the threshold of two worlds, these beings that symbolize the transition between death need two bodies, two heads, or four eyes to look both backward and forward, toward both the living and the dead who live in a symbiotic relationship not unlike that obtaining between man and dog.

In Roman mythology, the aforementioned twins Romulus and Remus, who had been forsaken at birth, are suckled and protected by a she-wolf in a cave at the base of the Palatine hill. They enjoy the same mythic fate as Cyrus, the founder of the Achaemenid dynasty and the Persian Empire: according to Herodotos, the infant Cyrus, who had been left to die at the order of the Median king Astyages, was saved by a Median woman named "Bitch." Other versions of the story, such as that of Trogus Pompeius, simply state that Cyrus was raised by a she-dog, as were also the Greek Aesculapius, the Persian Afrasiyab, and Lugaid Mac Con of Irish legend. A variation on this Indo-European mytheme of a dynastic founder or culture hero being fostered by an animal nurse, is a central and east Asian ethnogenic myth, which likely spread into the circumpolar regions. This is the myth of the origin of a people or race through the union of a human woman and a male dog, a most illustrious example being that of Chinggis (Genghis) Khan, as is related in the opening lines of the *Secret History of the Mongols* (c. 1240 CE). The Inuit of the central Arctic trace the origin of the "five human races" back to the union of the daughter of the primordial human pair, a maiden named Uinigumasuittuq ("She Who Did Not Wish to Marry"), with the family dog, Siarnaq. A similar myth is found among several of China's "southern barbarian" peoples, including the Man, Yao, and Liao. In both Chinese and European medieval literatures, this mytheme, which was transmitted along the Silk Road from its original Central Asian source, underwent a transformation that made it a stock fixture of world mythology. As it traveled east and west, it became an account of a remote "Kingdom of Women" that shared its borders with a "Kingdom of Dogs." During the mating season of the former, these dogs, or Dog-Men would cohabit with the women, with female offspring being kept by the women, and males by the dogs or Dog-Men. This was the source of the rich European mythology of races of Dog-Men (Cynanthropoi) or Dog-Headed Men (Cynocephali), who figure in the Alexander Legend and the writings of Marco Polo, as well as in the legends of several medieval Christian saints, who sought to convert these monsters to the true faith.

Numerous mythical traditions cast supernatural dogs in various types of foundation myths. According to the mythology of two Mesoamerican peoples, the Huichol and the Tlapanec, the repopulation of the earth is effected, following a great flood, through the union of a man and a she-dog. The Nahuatl Xolotl reanimates humanity at the beginning of a new creation cycle by fetching the bones of dead humans from a prior cycle back to his dwelling and bleeding on them from his penis. The North American Shoshone and Achowami, as well as several African peoples, identify the dog as the bringer of fire to humanity. Maya manuscripts depict the dog as the bringer of maize to the world, while several southern Chinese and Southeast Asian myths portray the dog as swimming over the waters of a primal flood while carrying grains of rice on its tail, to feed a starving humanity.

Poised on the uncertain boundary between humanity and animality, wildness and domestication, inside and outside, the living and the dead, purity and impurity, even the divine and the demonic, dogs have, throughout the long history of their relationship to humans, been especially "good to think with," whence the abundance of mythology, ritual, and religious precept that we humans have generated around canine modes of being in the world.

SEE ALSO Animals.

BIBLIOGRAPHY

The most comprehensive surveys of dogs in world religions concentrate on mythology. These include Freda Kretschmar's *Hundestammvater und Kerberos,* 2 vols. (Stuttgart, 1938; reprint, New York, 1968), Maria Leach's *God Had a Dog: Folklore of the Dog* (New Brunswick, N.J., 1961), and Patricia Dale-Green's *The Lore of the Dog* (Boston, 1967). Studies with a wide cultural area focus include David Gordon White's *Myths of the Dog-Man* (Chicago, 1991), which limits itself to Europe and Asian mythology, Barbara Frank's *Die Rolle des Hundes in afrikanischen Kulturen* (Wiesbaden, 1965), and Wilhelm Köppers's "Der Hund in der Mythologie der zirkumpazifischen Völker," *Wiener Beiträge zur Kulturgeschichte und Linguistik* 1 (1930): 359–399. Several studies extensively treat the dog in death-related mythology and ritual. These include Manabu Waida's "Central Asian Mythology of the Origin of Death: A Comparative Analysis of Its Structure and History," *Anthropos* 77 (1982): 663–701, Bruce Lincoln's "The Hellhound," *Journal of Indo-European Studies* 7, nos. 3–4 (Fall/Winter 1979): 273–285, Manfred Lurker's "Der Hund als Symboltier für den Übergang vom Diesseits in das Jenseits," *Zeitschrift für Religions- und Geistesgeschichte* 35 (1983): 132–144, and Franke J. Neumann's "The Dragon and the Dog: Two Symbols of Time in Nahuatl Religion," *Numen* 22, no. 1 (1975): 1–23.

Works focusing on a single cultural area include Mahasti Ziai Afshar's *The Immortal Hound: The Genesis and Transformation of a Symbol in Indo-Iranian Traditions* (New York, 1990), Eduard Erkes's "Der Hund im alten China," *T'oung Pao* 38 (1944): 186–225, Frank Jenkins's "The Role of the Dog in Romano-Gaulish Religion," *Latomus* 16, no. 1 (January–March 1957): 60–76, Carla Mainoldi's *L'image du loup et du chien dans la Grèce ancien d'Homère à Platon* (Paris, 1984), and Jean-Claude Schmitt's *Le saint lévrier: Guignefort guérisseur d'enfants depuis le XIIIe siècle* (Paris, 1979), which focuses on the remarkable cult of a greyhound, which persisted well into the twentieth century in the Dombes region of southeastern France.

DAVID GORDON WHITE (2005)

DOLGAN RELIGION. The Dolgans are a small, Turkic-speaking nationality living on the Taimyr Peninsula in northern Siberia. Their primary occupations are hunting and fishing; they also breed a small number of domesticated reindeer, which are utilized as means of transport during nomadic migration. During the winter season the Dolgans live in the forest-tundra zone, and toward summer they migrate northward into the tundra in pursuit of wild reindeer herds. In 1989 there were seven thousand Dolgans, 80 percent of whom spoke their native tongue, which is derived from the Yakut language. The Dolgans appeared as a distinct nationality during the last three hundred years and are largely descended from the Tunguz and the Yakuts; their religion had its origin in the culture area of their formation.

The Dolgans are converts to Christianity, and they bear Russian names. Their calendar—a six-sided small stick carved from mammoth bone—is known as the *paskaal* (from Russian *paskhal'nyi,* "relating to Easter"); the basic Russian Orthodox holidays are marked on the sides of the *paskaal.* The old men who can calculate time by this calendar are called *paskaalcit* and are deemed to be sages. Icons are found in each Dolgan dwelling, but the Russian Orthodox saints represented on them are no more revered than are the other spirits of the Dolgan pantheon.

In their mobile dwellings (*urasa*), special sanctity is attached to the four foundation poles (*suona*) in which the spirits who protect the people living in the *urasa* dwell. After a successful hunt, these poles are smeared with the blood of a wild reindeer and purified by the smoke of burning fat. When a dwelling's owner dies, the weeping of the *suona* is heard. The cover of the *urasa* is sewn out of reindeer chamois, on which are drawn the sun, moon, reindeer, or *urasa*, according to a shaman's instructions. The *urasa* functions as a barrier impenetrable to evil spirits. In building a permanent dwelling, the Dolgans leave two tall trees by the side of the entrance, so that the souls of the dwellers may live in their branches. The trees are termed *serge* ("post") in Yakut.

The Dolgans call all supernatural beings *saĭtaan*, a word of Arabic origin brought to the Dolgans by the Russians, who borrowed it from Turkic-speaking Muslims. In practice, small stones and anthropomorphic and zoomorphic images carved from wood or reindeer antler, as well as certain household objects, figure as *saĭtaans*.

All these objects are revered because they are bearers of spirits, either independently or by means of the shaman. A *saĭtaan* may be a personal helper of its owner or the protector of an entire family or nomadic group; it may, for example, be the hook used to hang the caldron in the *urasa*. Facing the hook, the Dolgans smear it with the blood or fat of a slaughtered animal and address it, saying, "May the caldron hung on thee be full lifelong!" One type of *saĭtaan*, with human form, is called the *baĭanaĭ*. The idea of the *baĭanaĭ* and the term itself are borrowed from the Yakuts, among whom Bai-baianai is master of the forest. But among the Dolgans a *baĭanaĭ* becomes the personal helper of the hunter who made its image. However, the *baĭanaĭ* acquires power only after the shaman animates the figurine by placing his breath within it. Before going on a hunt, the hunter smears his *baĭanaĭ* with the fat of a wild reindeer and tosses it into the air in order to divine his chances of catching game. If the figurine falls on its back, there will be success; if it falls on its belly, there will be failure. Wooden images of birds and animals, called *singken*, also belong to the category of *saĭtaans* that assist hunters. Hunters carry them along on the hunt, together with the *baĭanaĭ*.

At the beginning of each winter month, the hunter purifies his *baĭanaĭ* with the smoke of burning fat. Upon killing a wild reindeer, he cuts the fat from the animal's knee and suspends it from the figurine. After a particularly successful hunt, the Dolgans feed not only the *baĭanaĭ* but all their *saĭtaans*. They hang them on poles over the hearth, into which they throw small pieces of fatty food. Then they arrange a low table near the hearth and place on it pieces of the heart and lungs of slain animals. Afterward, the *saĭtaans* are smeared with blood and placed in a box, where they remain.

During nomadic treks, white or piebald reindeer carry the boxes containing *saĭtaans* and icons in cases. Such a reindeer is decorated with a beaded, embroidered headband and a bell is hung on its neck. This reindeer is always placed just before the end of the animal train; the reindeer transporting the dwelling poles is tied to it. When they arrive at a new place, the Dolgans avoid setting up their *urasa* where another stood earlier, since strange *saĭtaans* might prove powerful and feel wrathful toward the newcomers.

The activities of the Dolgans are accompanied by many religious rites. After killing a reindeer, the hunter smears his rifle with its blood. The bones of a reindeer that has been eaten are buried in the ground, and a tripod of poles is placed above them so that other reindeer will not go near that place. Upon killing an arctic fox, the hunter cuts off its nose so as not to give away his luck with its skin. The Dolgans rarely hunt bears, which they fear and which they regard as women transformed into beasts. The hunter who has killed a bear lies on its back imitating sexual intercourse. Then the participants in the hunt take out the bear's heart, eat it, and caw like ravens. While fishing, the Dolgans present to the Master of the River or Lake beads or scraps of red wool tied to nets. Near the body of water they hang a fox skin from a rope attached to the ends of two sticks thrust into the ground. Some Dolgans throw small, flat pieces of dough into the water; impressions of crosses worn on the body are made on these.

Shamans play such a large role among the Dolgans that the emergence of each new shaman is met by his kinsmen with great joy. According to Dolgan tradition, a shaman owns one to three Tuuruu trees, the term designating the "world tree" among the Tunguz, and he sets the souls of the persons under his protection on their branches. Signs of a shaman's power are the number, height, and extent of branching of his trees. A weak shaman's tree will be sickly, and the people in his charge may die. On the second day after death, the shaman must accompany the dead person's soul into the netherworld.

Among the Dolgans, as among the Yakuts, shamans are called *oĭun*; a female shaman is called *udaghan*, as among the Yakuts, Buriats, and Mongols. The Dolgans divide shamans into several categories according to their ability. The strongest shamans, *ulakan oĭun*, can cure diseases, divine events, and generally know all that happens on earth. In the past, the frequent wars between groups of Dolgans were decided by shamanic duels, with each shaman trying to increase the *ilbis* or power of the war spirit of his group. He sheltered the *kut*, or soul, of his leader on a cloud and killed the soul of the opposing leader. The shamanic séance, which in some cases continued for several days and nights, is called *kyyryy* by the Dolgans, from the Yakut word *kyyr*, "to hop."

In the spring, when the first grass appeared, the shaman performed the annual shamanic ritual Djilga Kyyryy, by which he would divine what awaited his nomadic group. This ritual, the greatest religious festival of the year, is also called D'yly Oduuluur. To conduct this rite a new *urasa* was made, and seven or nine images of birds with heads turned toward the sun were fastened on top of the poles making up the *urasa*'s frame. The shaman departed on these birds to meet the chief of the upper world in order to secure his support for the forthcoming year. During this festival, the Dolgans and their shaman performed the ritual dance Kisi Kaamy Gynan ("people's step-by-step procession"). They circled the hearth three times clockwise, then exited from the tent and continued the same movement around it. This festival probably came to the Dolgans from their neighbors the Nganasani, who called it Any'o Dialy ("big day") and conducted it on the summer solstice. However, the dance is Yakut in origin.

BIBLIOGRAPHY

Dolgikh, B. O. "Proiskhozhdenie dolgan." *Sibirskii etnograficheskii sbornik* (1963), fasc. 5, pp. 92–141.

Popov, A. A. "Materialy po rodovomu stroiu dolgan." *Sovetskaia etnografiia* (1934), fasc. 6, pp. 116–139.

Popov, A. A. "Okhota i rybolovstvo u dolgan." In *Sbornik statei "Pamiati B. G. Bogoraza,"* pp. 146–206. Moscow, 1937.

Popov, A. A. "Kochevaia zhizn' i tipy zhilishch u dolgan." *Sibirskii etnograficheskii sbornik* (1952), fasc. 1, pp. 143–172.

Popov, A. A. "Perezhitki doreligioznykh vozzrenii dolganov na prirody." *Sovetskaia etnografiia* (1958), fasc. 2, pp. 77–99.

Popov, A. A. "The Dolgan Sajtans." In *Shamanism in Siberia,* edited by Vilmos Diószegi and Mihály Hoppál, pp. 449–456. Budapest, 1979.

Popov, A. A. "Shamanstvo u dolgan." In *Problemy istorii obshchestvennogo soznaniia aborigenov Sibiri,* pp. 258–264. Moscow, 1981.

BORIS CHICHLO (1987 AND 2005)
Translated from Russian by Demitri B. Shimkim

DÖLLINGER, JOHANN

DÖLLINGER, JOHANN (1799–1890), more fully Johann Joseph Ignaz von Döllinger; Roman Catholic professor of dogmatics and church history at the University of Munich (1826–1872), who became the controversial center of scholarly liberal Catholicism in Europe. Son of a pious Catholic mother and an educated, anticlerical father, he was ordained at age twenty-three and served briefly as a curate before finishing his doctoral dissertation and being appointed to Munich. There he was somewhat novel among Roman Catholics, though not unprecedented, in his emphasis upon the scholarly study of church history.

The key principle in Döllinger's thought, "organic growth," or "consistent development," gave not only approval but also limits to changes in the Catholic church. Early in his career, defending established developments in Catholicism, he denounced mixed marriages, affirmed the authority of the pope (1836), and favored the policy that Protestant soldiers be required to kneel at the consecration when they were present at a Catholic mass (1843). Likewise, in his works on Luther (1851) and the Reformation (1846–1848), he denounced the break in historical continuity effected by the Protestant schism. Later in his career, however, he came to oppose as "inconsistent with tradition" new prerogatives of the papacy, such as the opposition to modern scholarship and the assertion of infallibility. In 1863, Döllinger organized, without ecclesiastical permission, a meeting of one hundred Catholic theologians in Munich, to evaluate the scientific study of history. In his opening address he denounced scholasticism and called boldly for a thorough use of critical tools in examining church history, independent of Roman authority. Although hailed by liberal Catholics throughout Europe, such principles were soon condemned by Pope Pius IX, in his 1864 *Syllabus of Errors* and in his encyclical *Quanta cura.* Such disagreements intensified as rumors grew that unrestricted papal infallibility was to be affirmed at the First Vatican Council (1869–1870). For his opposition to infallibility, Döllinger was excommunicated, with both haste and publicity, in March 1871, by Archbishop Scherr of Munich. Some have seen the excommunication as gratuitous. Döllinger's opposition resulted partially from conciliar secrecy, which kept him from learning until too late the restrictions placed on infallibility. Because of the enforced ignorance, some of his arguments (1869–1871) sound more rhetorical than relevant.

Döllinger provided a rallying cry for the development in Germany of the "Old Catholic" church (which denied papal infallibility). He admitted he belonged to this church "by conviction," but he never formally joined. His refusal of an offer to become the first German Old Catholic bishop hampered that church's growth. Even after excommunication, he continued to attend Roman Catholic services, even though he was denied the sacraments by his excommunication. Despite political ability sufficient to hold national office under Ludwig I of Bavaria, neither his scholarship nor his statecraft was adequate to reconcile Catholicism with modernity. As important to Germany as Cardinal Newman was to England, Döllinger influenced Lord Acton and widened the ambit of historical consciousness in the Roman Catholic church. He has not yet found his definitive place in that church's history. Extolled in a book by his close friend the Old Catholic priest Johannes Friedrich (*Ignaz von Döllinger,* 3 vols., 1899–1901), he also was castigated by the Jesuit Émile Michael (*Ignaz von Döllinger,* 1892), whose criticism was so severe that Döllinger was repudiated even by the usually nonjudgmental modernist Friedrich von Hügel. The definitive Döllinger biography has not yet been written.

BIBLIOGRAPHY

For an interesting survey of Döllinger's development, from apologist for Rome to staunchly pre-Vatican I Roman Catholic, see Peter Neuner's *Döllinger als Theologe der Ökumene* (Paderborn, 1979). Showing similarities and differences between Newman and Döllinger, though with surprisingly superficial analysis of some materials, is Wolfgang Klausnitzer's *Päpst-liche Unfehlbarkeit bei Newman und Döllinger* (Innsbruck, 1980). Lacking in details, but with an evenhanded treatment of the Vatican I infallibility controversy, is Walter

Brandmüller's *Ignaz v. Döllinger am Vorabend des I. Vatikanums* (Saint Ottilien, 1977). Important correspondence is included in the work edited by Victor Conzemius, *Ignaz von Döllinger: Briefwechsel 1820–90,* 3 vols. (Munich, 1963–1971). An unsurpassed bibliography of Döllinger's writings, including translations, is in Stephan Lösch's *Döllinger und Frankreich* (Munich, 1955).

RONALD BURKE (1987)

DOMESTIC OBSERVANCES

This entry consists of the following articles:

JEWISH PRACTICES
CHRISTIAN PRACTICES
MUSLIM PRACTICES
HINDU PRACTICES
CHINESE PRACTICES
JAPANESE PRACTICES

DOMESTIC OBSERVANCES: JEWISH PRACTICES

Besides the synagogue, the home has traditionally been a main focus of religiosity both for the Jewish family as a unit and especially for women. Women were traditionally excluded from the duty of Torah study, which for men was, and to some extent remains, a major focus of spirituality. Moreover, women were not obligated to observe many of the religious practices that bound men. In particular, their place in public synagogue ritual was minimal. Consequently, domestic rituals, and especially those governed by women, are important focuses of their spirituality. For all Jews, certain ritual customs (*minhagim*) and rabbinic laws (*halakhot*) actually require a domestic setting. These rituals may be divided into those that are held on specific occasions of the Jewish calendar and those that are a constant presence in daily life.

PERIODIC DOMESTIC OBSERVANCES. The annual festival cycle begins in the spring with Passover, which focuses on two major domestic activities: the thorough cleaning of the home to remove leavened food, and then the Seder, the Passover eve feast, which has traditionally been led by the father and requires the participation of the children. Shavu'ot, in early summer, is accompanied by only minor domestic customs, such as decorating the home with greenery and partaking of dairy foods. The period of mourning for the destroyed Temple, which follows in midsummer, affects the home in a fashion opposite to that of the festivals: enjoyment of music, food, new clothing, and vacations, and joyfulness in general, are restricted. The fall holy days start with Ro'sh ha-Shanah and Yom Kippur, which are primarily synagogue-centered occasions but which include secondary domestic activities. On Ro'sh ha-Shanah, foods symbolizing good fortune are served at the family meal, and on Yom Kippur, family elders bless the young. During the weeklong Sukkot festival the domestic focus is again pronounced. Temporary booths or huts (*sukkot*) are erected near or adjacent to each family home. Meals are eaten there, and some males follow the rabbinic tradition of sleeping in the booths at night. People entertain guests and generally pass time in the family *sukkah.* Ḥanukkah, in early winter, is focused domestically as well. Lights are ritually kindled in the home, and special holiday foods are prepared. Ḥanukkah also has indoor child-centered activities (gift-giving and living-room games). In late winter, Purim requires a formal feast at home, and women and children become particularly involved in the traditional sending of gifts of food to friends.

PERENNIAL DOMESTIC OBSERVANCES. Besides seasonal events, the Jewish home also has perennial ritual activities, primarily on the Sabbath, when the routine of the home is transformed. Domestic rituals are observed on the Sabbath: candles are lit by the housewife on Sabbath eve; the Qiddush ("sanctification of the day") is chanted at the first of the three mandatory festive meals; families sing Sabbath songs (*zemirot*) and sometimes study Torah together. Of these customs, candle-lighting is a major rite for women, a virtual symbol of female religious identity. In recent times, with the attenuation of many more-burdensome Jewish customs, candle-lighting has remained vital and thus has become more prominent. According to some traditions, parents formally bless their children on Sabbath eve, and Sabbath night is a preferred time for conjugal relations. In the home the Sabbath ends with the ceremony of *havdalah* ("separation" of the Sabbath from the week), which involves the use of wine, spices, and a special braided candle, and at which a new fire is lit. Another perennial domestic ritual element is the display of religious artifacts. Foremost of these is the mandatory *mezuzah* inscription of biblical verses, encased on all doorposts. Brass or silver candelabra, wine goblets, and collections of Judaica books are common in the more prosperous homes. It is a custom to leave a section of wall in the home (about one square foot) unpainted, as a symbol of pain over the destruction of ancient Jerusalem (*zekher le-ḥurban*).

The celebration of rites of passage spills over into the home through the holding of festive meals. Domestically, the most marked rites of passage are mourning rites, which restrict the bereaved to their homes and require them to receive condolence visits. Memorial candles for the dead are lit at home. In the past, marriages in Mediterranean countries were patrilocal and some marriage observances paralleled mourning rites. The bridal couple were restricted to their new home for seven days of festivity, and daily rites were held in the presence of visitors. In our time, owing to the attenuation of patrilocality, the practice among many young Orthodox bridal couples, both in Israel and elsewhere, is to travel distances to visit their kin, and to be hosted in different homes where rites are held for the duration of seven days.

In Orthodox and traditionally observant families, the home is the scene of innumerable daily acts of individual piety: the ritual washing of hands upon arising, before meals and after voiding; the uttering of grace after meals, and of shorter benedictions before and after the partaking of any food. Prayers are recited upon waking and upon retiring at night, and three daily prayer services (*shaḥarit,* in the morning, *minḥah,* in the afternoon, *ma'ariv,* in the evening) are required of all adult males. In recent times, because of the weaker hold of the community, weekday prayers are frequently said at home rather than at the synagogue; hence, the role of the home in daily prayer has increased.

The most pervasive home observances are those that concern food and conjugal relations. Observance of the rules of *kashrut* (maintaining a ritually pure, kosher kitchen), is dependent upon the foods introduced into the home, and on the separation of various categories of foods in the kitchen and dining area. *Kashrut* also requires the services of extra-domestic agents, such as a *shoḥet* (ritual slaughterer), and of manufacturers of kosher foods. The maintenance of "family purity" (*ṭaharat ha-mishpaḥah*) depends to a greater extent on the privacy of domestic practice. Family purity consists of the maintenance of a monthly schedule of conjugal separation and reunion based on the menstrual cycle, and on the woman's periodic immersion in a *miqveh* (ritual bath). While the availability of an external agent, the *miqveh,* is required here as well, the element of domestic autonomy in this area of intimacy is nonetheless very strong. The autonomy of the home in this area was curtailed in traditional times (in Northern Europe roughly until the mid-nineteenth century, in Mediterranean lands until close to the mid-twentieth century). Decisions concerning the proper timing of immersion were not handled exclusively by the woman then, but rather in conjunction with a circle of elder females, family and neighbors. If there was any physiological irregularity, male rabbis were consulted. In contemporary Orthodoxy, middle-class sensitivities concerning the privacy of sexual matters have eliminated the role of the outside female circle; rabbis are consulted only in the most unusual cases. But it is in the maintenance of *kashrut* that the role of the home has increased most in contemporary times, and has assumed a novel symbolic weight. The affective term *kosher home* is now commonly used in reference to *kashrut* observance, which has gained much greater prominence in relation to its historical place in Jewish practice and thought. Over time, additional domestic practices have become more prominent (contemporary domestic Sabbath practices are innovations of the late sixteenth century). Most recently in the West, the pressure of Christmastime commercialism has encouraged Jewish families to elaborate the observance of Ḥanukkah, especially with parties, gift giving, and the decoration of the home, as an ethnic counterpoint to Christian symbols such as the tree and Santa Claus.

There are two major exceptions to this development (i.e., the increasing emphasis on Jewish domestic ritual). One is the virtual disappearance of the *ḥallah*-separation rite. Married women baking their bread used to separate and burn a small portion of the dough, as a symbol of the tithe that was due the priests in Temple times. *Ḥallah*-separation used to be a major female responsibility, similar to Sabbath candle-lighting and to the maintenance of family purity (*niddah*). But as bread production has shifted from a domestic to a commercial setting, the rite has become uncommon. Another exception is in practices of the Hasidic movement, which encourages male groups to congregate by themselves, or at the court of the *rebbe,* the sect leader. In these congregations, adult males eat the third of the three required meals together, away from their families, on the Sabbath afternoon. Hasidism also encourages men to spend some of the holy days and Sabbaths at the distant court of the *rebe,* again separating them from their families.

See Also Kashrut.

Bibliography

For a masterly, though brief, overview of the position of formal *halakhah,* see Aaron Lichtenstein's "Ha-mishpahah be-halakhah" in *Mishpeḥot Yisra'el: Divrei ha-kinus ha-shemonah-'asar le-maḥshavah Yehudit* (Jerusalem, 1976), pp. 13–30. On Ashkenazic Jewry, Jacob Katz's *Tradition and Crisis: Jewish Society at the End of the Middle Ages* (New York, 1961) provides a fine sociological overview; much pertinent information is scattered in the chapters on the family, religion, and Hasidism. In a shorter monograph, *Tsibbur ve-yiḥidim be-Maroqo: Sidrei ḥevra ba-kehillot ha-Yehudiyot ba-me'ot ha-18–19* (Tel Aviv, 1983), I describe eighteenth- and nineteenth-century Moroccan Jewry and thereby provide documentation for a section of Sephardic Jewry; some of this material appears in English in "Women in the Jewish Family in Pre-Colonial Morocco," *Anthropological Quarterly* 56 (July 1983): 134–144. A comprehensive ethnographic survey of religious and other home feasts in a village of Moroccan immigrants in Israel is given in Moshe Shokeid's "Conviviality versus Strife: Peacemaking at Parties among Atlas Mountains Immigrants in Israel," in *Freedom and Constraint: A Memorial Tribute to Max Gluckman,* edited by Myron J. Aronoff (Assen, Netherlands, 1976). One such feast is described in detail in my *Immigrant Voters in Israel: Parties and Congregations in a Local Election Campaign* (Manchester, 1970), pp. 140–147. The qabbalistic sources for some of the comparatively recent domestic Sabbath customs are cited in Gershom Scholem's *On the Kabbalah and Its Symbolism,* translated by Ralph Manheim (New York, 1965), pp. 142–146. In an overview of U.S. suburban Jewry, *Jewish Identity on the Suburban Frontier* (Chicago, 1979), Marshall Sklare and Joseph Greenblum analyze the novel weight of Ḥanukkah child-centered activities.

New Sources

Broner, Esther M. *Bringing Home the Light: A Jewish Woman's Handbook of Rituals.* San Francisco, 1999.

Dahbany-Miraglia, Dina. "Negotiating Passover: Women, Food and Power." *Women in Judaism: Contemporary Writings* (June 11, 2003). Available from http://www.utoronto.ca/wjudaism/contemporary/contemp_index1.html.

Goldberg, Harvey E. *Jewish Passages: Cycles of Jewish Life.* Berkeley, 2003.

Plumb, Marcia. "Filling the Bookcase: Women's Rituals in Rabbinic Texts." *Journal of Progressive Judaism* 2 (1994): 49–70.

Sered, Susan Starr. "Husbands, Wives, and Childbirth Rituals." *Ethos* 22 (1994): 187–208.

Shlomo Deshen (1987)
Revised Bibliography

DOMESTIC OBSERVANCES: CHRISTIAN PRACTICES

Contemporary forms and practices of Christian religious life in the home vary widely among the various denominations and branches of Christianity, as well as among ethnic and socioeconomic groups within those broader divisions. The usual division of Western Christians into Roman Catholic and Protestant is, for the purpose of the present discussion, more suitably replaced by a distinction between those denominations, such as Roman Catholic, Episcopalian, and Lutheran, with strong liturgical traditions, and those, such as Baptists and Pentecostals, that have a less fully developed ritual heritage.

Western Christians often adorn their homes with religious images such as crucifixes and holy pictures, and Eastern Christian homes traditionally contain an icon corner where images of Christ and the saints are honored and where family prayers are said. A lighted candle or oil lamp usually burns before these icons. In the homes of families of the Eastern churches and the Western churches with more developed liturgies, palm or other branches blessed in church on Palm Sunday may be placed behind these images.

Traditional Roman Catholics sometimes provide small fonts for holy water at the doors of bedrooms, and during the month of May a Marian shrine may be set up in a corner of the home. The blessing of a new home, usually conducted by a priest, is practiced by some liturgically oriented Christian families of both East and West, with Eastern Christians observing an annual renewal of the house blessing during the period following the Feast of Theophany (Epiphany) on January 6.

Some form of grace, said daily at the main meal or at each meal, is common among Christians, at least on special occasions. Also common among most denominations is the practice of an adult or older member of the family hearing a child's bedtime prayers. Christian families observe the Lord's Day (Sunday) in various ways. A festive meal is often part of the day, which may be honored as a day of rest. Among some families of the nonliturgical traditions, family gatherings for prayer, often held early in the morning and consisting of Bible readings, hymn singing, and prayers by a leader, are customary.

Devout Christian families often say prayers for sick family members. These prayer services can include the laying on of hands and anointing with oil by a priest (in the liturgical traditions) or by a layperson (in the nonliturgical traditions). These rites of anointing are usually reserved for the seriously ill and dying in more conservative religious families. In the Eastern tradition, a priest, or, among Western Christians, a layperson or priest sometimes brings the Eucharist from the church to the sick person; in the less liturgically oriented churches the Lord's Supper may be celebrated by an ordained person in the sickroom.

Families of different denominations observe anniversaries of the deaths of family members and friends in various ways. Not uncommon among Eastern Christians, especially those of Slavic extraction, is the custom of burning a lighted candle before a picture of the deceased person during the day of the anniversary. A festive dinner, with gifts for the honored person, is commonly given on the saints' name days of family members, and various national groups enjoy festive meals featuring traditional ethnic foods on the feast days of their important saints.

The cycle of feasts and seasons of the Christian calendar provides many occasions for religious observances in the home, especially among Christians with strong liturgical traditions. During the pre-Lenten Carnival season, doughnut making and pancake suppers are common, such customs originating from earlier times when lard and other meat products had to be consumed before the beginning of Lent. While Lenten fasting and abstinence have become merely token or even nonexistent among many Western Christians, Eastern Christians commonly abstain from meat, butter, eggs, milk, and other animal products throughout this period, as well as during other penitential times. Some families in the nonliturgical churches are returning to the ancient practice of fasting twice weekly, usually on Tuesday and Friday. In the West during Lent, families often give money saved by having simple meals to charitable organizations. Also, soft pretzels continue to be served in some homes, a practice that originated in the Middle Ages when the shape of the pretzel was thought to resemble the crossed arms of a person at prayer. Hot cross buns, another customary food of medieval origin, are served in some Christian homes on the Fridays of Lent and during the last days of Holy Week.

Eastern Christian families continue their tradition of creating intricately decorated Easter eggs to be included in a basket of foods (with sausage, butter, cakes, and other foods proscribed during Lent), which is taken to the church and blessed at the all-night Easter service and eaten at a holy breakfast following that service on Easter morning. A similar breakfast has become popular among some Western Christian families in recent years following the restoration of the Easter Vigil service to its original time in the middle of the night. Two unique Eastern Christian family customs practiced during this season should be noted: (1) the bringing home of a lighted flame from the matins service of Holy Saturday (held on Holy Friday evening) and the marking of the form of a cross on the underside of every door lintel with smoke from this flame; and (2) the blessing of and picnicking at the graves of departed relatives and friends on the Sunday following Easter Day.

Many Western Christian families observe a similar memorial custom, but in the autumn season rather than at Easter. Picnicking at the graves of the departed on November 2 (All Souls Day) is common especially among Hispanic Christians; visits to cemeteries on that day, or the following Sunday, are also made by members of various denominations.

Eastern Christians continue the ancient practice of preparing fruit on the Feast of the Transfiguration of Christ (August 6) and flowers on the Feast of the Dormition of Mary (August 15) to be taken to the church for a special blessing. Some Western Christians have renewed a similar practice of bringing freshly baked bread to the church to be blessed at Lammastide (the first two weeks of August).

The Advent season encompasses immensely rich and varied family observances. The custom of the Advent wreath enjoys widespread popularity in the West. On the Advent wreath, constructed from a circle of evergreens surmounted by four candles (usually three purple and one rose colored), Christians light one additional candle each week during the four weeks of Advent. In some families the wreath is lighted before the evening meal to the accompaniment of brief prayers and often the singing of the Advent carol *O Come, O Come, Emmanuel.* Among Western Christians three traditional feasts during Advent are regaining the popularity they had in earlier centuries: Saint Barbara's Day (December 4), when a dormant branch of flowering cherry, known as the Barbara branch, is brought indoors and blooms on or near Christmas Day; the Feast of Saint Nicholas (December 6), which is often celebrated with small gifts placed in the children's shoes left outside bedroom doors on the eve of the feast; and the Feast of Santa Lucia (December 13, usually the date of the earliest sunset of the year), which is observed with customs dating from pre-Christian times and features saffron-yellow yeast buns, known as Lucia cakes, baked in the form of a spiral sun.

Among Hispanic people the last nine days of Advent are known as Posadas ("lodgings"). Children, portraying Mary and Joseph seeking shelter on their way to Bethlehem, go from door to door and are turned away repeatedly. Finally, the last home welcomes them, which then becomes the site of a joyful service and feast.

Some families honor the religious significance of the traditional Christmas tree by a ritual blessing of the tree. Often they place a crêche or nativity scene under or near the tree and adorn it with other traditional decorations, such as candles and glittering tinsel.

A festive family dinner on Christmas Eve is common among many ethnic groups, often with a prescribed number of courses (usually seven, nine, eleven, or twelve) limited to fish or vegetable dishes. The fact that the day before Christmas was one of strict fast and abstinence in previous centuries accounts for the tradition of a meatless festive meal. Ethnic variations abound at this Christmas Eve meal; among the better known is the Polish custom of the distribution by the head of the family of portions of a waferlike rectangle of unleavened bread, known as *oplatek,* with prayers and good wishes for the holy season and the coming year.

The Feast of the Epiphany (traditionally celebrated on January 6 but observed by some denominations on a Sunday near that date) is little observed in most Western Christian homes, although Twelfth Night parties on the eve of the feast, a custom dating from the Middle Ages, continue to be held or are being revived. In Hispanic cultures, January 6, known as the Day of the Three Kings, is a major feast, and families of Slavic extraction continue the centuries-old custom of using blessed chalk to mark the doorways of their homes with the numerals of the current year and the initials of the Three Kings. Known as the Feast of Theophany among Eastern Christians, January 6 celebrates the manifestation of God's presence in the world that was given at the baptism of Jesus. Water, as the primal element representing all creation, is blessed in the churches and preserved by families at home; the custom of the reverent drinking of some of this blessed water by members of the family persists, and the priest uses the same water to bless the home on the traditional annual visit during this season.

Recent developments in Christian domestic religious observance include the adoption by some Christian families of Jewish feasts. These include Ḥanukkah near the winter solstice, with its custom of lighting the menorah (an eight-branched candelabrum), and the feast of Purim in the spring, when the story of Queen Esther is read aloud to the accompaniment of joyous noisemaking by children. Christian families celebrating these festivals serve traditional foods, such as potato pancakes for Ḥanukkah and prune-filled three-cornered pastries for Purim. Of particular interest is the celebration of the Seder (the Jewish Passover meal) in some Christian homes during Holy Week. As Christians rediscover the centrality of Jewish Passover imagery to their own beliefs and practices, especially its relevance to the Eucharist, they have begun to extend invitations to family and friends to celebrate a Seder with them annually; some families follow the Jewish ritual strictly, while others adapt it in various ways.

See Also Carnival; Christmas; Easter; Epiphany; Halloween.

Bibliography

Much information on the domestic practice of European Catholics up until recent times can be found in Pius Parsch's *The Church's Year of Grace,* 5 vols. (Collegeville, Minn., 1953–1959). Francis X. Weiser's *Handbook of Christian Feasts and Customs: The Year of the Lord in Liturgy and Folklore* (New York, 1958) deals more directly with domestic practices among Catholics of European heritage prior to the Second Vatican Council. No comparable texts exist on domestic practices among families of the nonliturgical traditions or of those of the Eastern Christian tradition, although Constance J. Tarasar's *The Season of Christmas* (Syosset, N.Y., 1980) provides much information on family practices among Eastern Christians for the period between November 15 and February 2.

The more recent contemporary trend toward self- or family-generated ritual is discussed by Virginia H. Hine in "Self-Generated Ritual: Trend or Fad?" in *Worship* 55 (September 1981): 404–419. My book *Passover Seder for Christian Fami-*

lies (San Jose, Calif., 1984) provides an example of the adaptation of Jewish traditions among contemporary Christians. The bimonthly periodical *Family Festivals* (San Jose, Calif., 1981–) offers numerous examples of contemporary adaptations by Christian families of observances from diverse non-Christian religious traditions.

New Sources

Cox, Harvey Gallagher. *Common Prayers: Faith, Family, and a Christian's Journey through the Jewish Year.* Boston, 2001.

Gutiérrez, Ramón, Salvatore Scalora, and William Beezley. *Home Altars of Mexico.* Albuquerque, 1997.

Nissenbaum, Stephen. *The Battle for Christmas.* New York, 1996.

Restad, Penne L. *Christmas in America.* New York, 1995.

Schmidt, Leigh Eric. *Consumer Rites.* Princeton, N.J., 1995.

SAM MACKINTOSH (1987)
Revised Bibliography

DOMESTIC OBSERVANCES: MUSLIM PRACTICES

Owing to the segregation of the sexes and the belief that a woman's primary roles are as wife, mother, and manager of domestic affairs, the traditional Muslim home is largely the domain of women. Accordingly, many religious practices that occur within the home are performed exclusively by or facilitiated by women; these tend to be less formal and are often placed in the realm of folk practice. None of the five obligatory Muslim religious observances—the profession of faith, daily prayers, fasting, the pilgrimage, and almsgiving—is fundamentally bound up with the home. Indeed, public religious institutions and performances are generally the provinces of men. Women may attend the mosque and public religious gatherings, but their presence is seldom essential and frequently discouraged. They often remain onlookers or are relegated to separate areas where it is difficult to follow the central activity, such as a sermon, in any detail. Thus women's religious activities tend to take place in the home, where they can exercise some control and express their religiosity with a degree of freedom.

THE HOME ENVIRONMENT. Even within the home, a woman's behavior reflects on her family's reputation in the Muslim community. It is expected that she will be modest and circumspect in her dress and behavior, keep a good home, and be careful in performing her religious duties. Women are responsible for the protection of family health and well-being, which is achieved in part through vows and procedures to ward off the evil eye; both practices are popularly regarded as Islamic. Women are also charged with the care of young children and must see to their religious upbringing.

As managers of the home, women are responsible for creating and maintaining an environment conducive to proper Muslim behavior for all family members. Consequently, conventional domestic tasks take on religious significance. Ritual purity (*ṭahārah*) is an essential precondition for acts of worship. Things such as blood, certain bodily fluids, wine, pigs, and dogs are regarded as ritually unclean (*najis*). A person, place, or object that comes into contact with any of these must be properly cleansed in order to be ritually pure (*ṭāhir*). The state of ritual purity may be achieved by ritual washing *(wuḍū'*, *ghasl)* for personal cleanliness and by washing in running water or a sufficiently large body of water for objects. Women are themselves often considered ritually unclean because of menstruation, childbirth, and child care and must work hard at keeping themselves and their families, as well as their homes, appropriately clean. Clothes to be worn for prayer and other religious observances must be ritually pure. The vessels in which food and drink are cooked and served should be scrupulously clean as well. Some women devote a great deal of time and energy to these tasks: cleanliness is indeed next to godliness and often a prerequisite for it. In two *ḥadīth*s (traditional accounts), the Prophet is reported to have drawn attention to the importance of ritual purity, saying "Purification is half of faith," and "The key to Paradise is worship [*ṣalāt*]: the key to worship is purification" (M. M. Ali, *A Manual of Ḥadīth*, Lahore, 1944, pp. 41–42).

The preparation and consumption of food also have religious overtones. Bread, the archetypical food, is regarded as a symbol of God's generosity and must be treated with respect. Housewives take care not to dispose of uneaten bread with other scraps; rather, it is fed to beggars or animals or transformed into breadcrumbs for later cooking. Because certain foods are said to have been preferred or recommended by the prophet Muḥammad, their preparation has religious merit. In Iran dates are said to have been recommended by the Prophet as the first food to eat upon breaking the Ramaḍān fast. Other dishes are prepared as the result of vows to particular saints or, for Shīʿī Muslims, to the *imāms;* their distribution is regarded as a praiseworthy religious act. In addition, entire meals are prepared for religious reasons and served at home. These include evening meals during the fasting month of Ramaḍān, to which the poor may be invited, or ritual meals served in consequence of vows, such as the *sufrah*s in Iran. Women are expected to know when and how to prepare dishes that have religious significance: some Iranian women, for example, recognize a different dish as appropriate for each night of the month of Ramaḍān. The exact round of meals is a matter of local tradition, known to the women of a particular town or region. The careful avoidance of prohibited foods in cooking is equally important. As the primary guardians of their families' Muslim identity, Chinese Muslim women go to great lengths to avoid cooking with pork and pork products in the midst of the non-Muslim, pork-eating Chinese majority.

Hospitality is considered one of the hallmarks of a good Muslim, and the burden of caring for guests falls chiefly on the shoulders of the host family's women. Here too, this responsibility takes on particular importance in areas where

Muslims are a minority and proper accommodations and food are hard to find.

RITUALS AND CEREMONIES. Specifically religious domestic observances for which time is set aside and special preparations are made include Qur'anic readings during Ramaḍān and special sermons at which women may officiate. In Iran and Iraq, Shīʿī Muslim women attend sermons combined with mourning for the martyred *imāms,* particularly on ʿĀshūrā' (10 Muḥarram), which commemorates the seventh-century CE martyrdom of Imam Ḥusayn and other men in his family along with the imprisonment and mistreatment of the women. The rituals may be sponsored by and for women; if sponsored by families and attended by men as well, separate areas are set off for the women.

Observances to mark regained health and answered vows may take place at any time of the ritual year. Auspicious days, such as the Prophet's birthday, are preferred. In Iran, ritual dinners (*sufrahs*) are often held on such occasions. A sermon commemorating the martyrdom of the *imām* or saint who answered the vow is followed by a dinner at which foods associated with the holy figure are served. Friends and family join in preparation of the dinner, then celebrate the answered vow and take home some of the remaining blessed food for their menfolk and children.

Many ceremonies marking rites of passage are held at home, and women play a major role in preparing for them. Among the ceremonies marking important stages in Muslim life are the formal naming of a child, circumcision, wedding contract ceremonies, and the reading of the Qur'ān over a body before it is taken away for washing and burial.

In Ethiopia, Egypt, the Sudan, and the Arabian Peninsula women participate in *zār* ceremonies. *Zār* refers to both the belief in possession by spirits (*jinn;* sg., *jinni*) and ceremonies designed to alleviate illness caused by spirits. The ceremonies, which involve dancing and trance, often take place at the homes of afflicted women. Women who attend do not feel that belief in the *zār* and its effectiveness conflicts with Islam. *Jinn* are mentioned in the Qur'ān and are popularly identified with the spirits that can possess and trouble people.

The extent to which a woman is willing and able to participate in group religious activities depends on her socioeconomic status, her education, the attitudes of senior men and women in her family, and her stage of life. For more observant and less traditional women, legitimate religious activity is determined by formal interpretations of religious law and includes formal religious education. Highly educated or strictly observant Muslim women may regard certain rituals, such as the *sufrah* or *zār,* as non-Islamic and avoid them. Denigrated practices are often viewed as vestiges of pre-Islamic rituals. Iranian Shīʿī *sufrahs,* for example, somewhat resemble *sufrahs* displayed in Zoroastrian ritual contexts. Women bearing heavy responsibility for the care of young children, food preparation, and housework have little time to attend religious gatherings.

Women perform essential services to their families and define themselves as good women in discharging their duties as Muslims, but the opportunity to socialize with other women in preparing for and celebrating religious occasions doubtless constitutes part of the rituals' attraction as well. By participating in individual and group religious observances at home, women are able to express their religious sentiments in ways that suit them personally and are socially acceptable. As women move into the public world of education, paid employment, and politics, circumspect behavior at school and in the workplace is added to their responsibilities as representatives of their families and their faith.

SEE ALSO ʿĀshūrā'; Folk Religion, article on Folk Islam; Islamic Religious Year; Rites of Passage, article on Muslim Rites; Worship and Devotional Life, article on Muslim Worship.

BIBLIOGRAPHY

An excellent introduction to the religious practices of Muslim women, with particular attention paid to women in Iraq, can be found in Robert A. Fernea and Elizabeth W. Fernea's "Variation in Religious Observance among Islamic Women," in *Scholars, Saints, and Sufis,* edited by Nikki R. Keddie (Berkeley, 1972), pp. 385–401. *Women in the Muslim World,* edited by Lois Beck and Nikki R. Keddie (Cambridge, Mass., 1978), is a useful collection of articles; part 4, "Ideology, Religion, and Ritual," includes information on women in Algeria, Morocco, Egypt, Iran, and China. Further material on the status, responsibilities, and views of women in contemporary Muslim societies is presented in *Women and the Family in the Middle East: New Voices of Change,* edited by Elizabeth W. Fernea (Austin, Tex., 1985).

A detailed explanation of ritual purity is provided under "Taharah" in the *Shorter Encyclopaedia of Islam,* edited by H. A. R. Gibb and J. J. Kramers (Leiden, 1953). For information on food preparation and hospitality, see Aida Sami Kanafani's *Aesthetics and Ritual in the United Arab Emirates: The Anthropology of Food and Personal Adornment among Arabian Women* (Beirut, 1983), esp. chap. 2, "Food Rituals," and chap. 10, "Islam, Rites of Hospitality and Aesthetics." See also Bess Ann Donaldson's *The Wild Rue: A Study of Muhammadan Magic and Folklore in Iran* (1938; reprint, New York, 1973). Women's religious practices in Iran are discussed in two articles in *Unspoken Worlds: Women's Religious Lives in Non-Western Cultures,* edited by Nancy Auer Falk and Rita M. Gross (San Francisco, 1980). Erika Friedl's "Islam and Tribal Women in a Village in Iran" (pp. 159–173) provides an interesting contrast to the material on urban women in my article on *sufrahs,* "The Controversial Vows of Urban Muslim Women in Iran" (pp. 141–155).

Lucie Wood Saunders describes the involvement of two Egyptian village women in *zār* ceremonies and includes references to other articles on the *zār* in "Variants in Zar Experience in an Egyptian Village," in *Case Studies in Spirit Possession,* edited by Vincent Crapanzano and Vivian Garrison (New York, 1977), pp. 177–191. Fatimah Mernissi's "Women, Saints and Sanctuaries," *Signs* 3 (1977): 101–112, offers a compelling discussion of women's visits to local shrines in Morocco.

Patricia Jeffery's *Frogs in a Well: Indian Women in Purdah* (London, 1979), one of the few works on Muslim women outside the Middle East, studies the domestic life and religious responsibilities of the women of *sayyid* families who administer a shrine south of Old Delhi.

Elizabeth Fernea has also worked on a number of films that vividly present the role of religion in Muslim women's lives. In particular, *A Veiled Revolution*, by Fernea and Marilyn Gaunt (1982, distributed by Icarus Films, New York), addresses the issue of veiling in contemporary Egypt, and *Saints and Spirits*, by Fernea and Melissa Llewelyn-Davies (1979, distributed by Icarus Films, New York), portrays personal dimensions of religious experience among Moroccan women. *Some Women of Marrakesh*, by Llewelyn-Davies and Fernea (1977, Granada Films, London) provides a finely detailed look at the lives of traditional women in Morocco.

ANNE H. BETTERIDGE (1987)

DOMESTIC OBSERVANCES: HINDU PRACTICES

The Hindu home provides a necessary center for all social and religious life. A man has not fulfilled his duties and obligations to his ancestors unless he has been a householder. A woman is considered to be auspicious and blessed while she is married, and incomplete if she is not. Indeed, neither men nor women in Hindu society normally perform calendrical or life-cycle rituals unless they are wedded and their spouses are still alive. The home is where the major turning points in the life cycle (birth, marriage, and death) occur. Although practical considerations now make the hospital and the temple possible alternative locales, Hindus still associate such major occasions with the family living quarters. Traditional domestic architecture, wherever possible, anticipates the celebration of these periodic and grand events at home.

HOUSEHOLD OBSERVANCES. At a symbolic level, the household of a couple serves as a miniature of cosmic principles. Ideally, a home should be laid out as a series of rooms surrounding a single, larger courtyard. This is the same plan that astrologers use to depict the organization and movement of planetary deities and that priests use in laying out a sacred space for ritual purposes. Because of physical constraints, a shortage of proper building materials, and other economic and social concerns, contemporary Hindu homes in South Asia frequently deviate from the traditional ideal. Nonetheless, life in a modern house can still be linked, in several symbolic ways, to this basic design.

Where Viṣṇu is the prime deity it is common to have a tulasi plant growing in the family courtyard. This plant, treated as sacred, will always be tenderly cared for. Even when the tulasi itself is missing, a distinctively shaped pedestal intended for it often forms part of the basic household layout. No exact parallel exists for homes where Śiva is the foremost god. Nonetheless, there are other ways to mark off the symbolic center of family living space for special occasions. One common practice is to erect a square canopy made of bamboo stakes, mats, cloths, and vegetable greenery. This structure will generally be tied to one or more green branches, which serve symbolically as ritual center posts. Often these are further festooned with small pouches of grain, suggestive either of household fertility or simply of abundance. Like the tulasi plant, the ritual post functions as the *axis mundi.* Alternative expressions of the same idea take form through elaborate floor designs, complete with a pleasing vertical centerpiece. During the month of October–November, Hindus in Bengal traditionally put an oil lamp on a pole tied to the roof. Now often replaced by an electric bulb, this light helps the ancestors see their way in an annual journey made across the sky. In South India similar lights are placed on the central pillar of the temple for the same period. These folk concepts utilize a pillar-of-heaven concept. In this way, Hindu homes symbolically link family and temple life to ordered energy in the cosmos at large.

The Hindu home also shares its form with cosmic space by its customary orientation to the four cardinal points. Walls, doors, and even sleeping or eating locations inside are often identified in this manner. In Tamil-speaking areas people say that, ideally, the main door of the house should face the rising sun. The building's interior lines will then presumably allow the passage of morning air and light through the house in straight lines. Some orthodox homes in the South actually have a large mirror that faces the eastern entry, where a hall leading through the whole is not possible. This way the same effect is achieved in an illusory but still highly visual manner. Similar cosmic overtones govern other aspects of house layout. The family hearth, for example, recalls the sacred fire used in many Hindu rituals, just as a domestic well (if there is one) symbolically leads to the underworld. A typical Hindu residence also reserves space for the gods. The household shrine can be as grand as a separate room or as simple as a small picture or wall niche. Often a family's favorite gods are pictured in poster form, but they can also be represented in other, more traditional ways, such as by lamps, pots of water, or measures of grain.

No verbal terminology explicitly associates the parts of the house with parts of the body, yet the two are intimately linked. Indeed, the human body is considered by many Hindus to be a temple of the Lord, just as the household living space is a shrine. Hence daily bathing is a key part of the Hindu toilet, and the body should be internally cleansed by fasting in preparation for important events. Similarly, daily sweeping is essential to the maintenance of the house, as is the regular whitewashing or repainting of interior walls. The use of a medicinal cow-dung wash on the floors is also part of traditional preparations for many ceremonial events. After such preliminaries, homes in many parts of India are further decorated with powdered floor designs, ritual wall paintings, bunches of specially tied leaves, or strings of flowers. These adornments help protect a dwelling against evil spirits and serve, as well, to beautify personal space. Similarly, a Hindu's own body is frequently beautified with scented powders after bathing. Protective strings or amulets, and black eye paste, can be added to ward off various unwelcome forces.

In a striking way, images of fire and cooking further link these two forms—the human body and the "body" of the home—within Hindu religious life. On the domestic hearth each day, foodstuffs are transformed through water and heat into consumable meals. Human digestion also provides a fire that refines and transforms food internally. Fire, for a Hindu, is itself a god (Agni), yet it is also the vehicle through which offerings at domestic rituals are carried to other gods via an open flame and rising smoke. Food consumption is often seen as a parallel process that makes offerings to an internal god. Thus all eating, but especially the partaking of full meals, is a semisacred activity. Orthodox Hindus bathe and change into clean clothes before meals, and prefer not to talk while seated for any significant feeding purpose. Many Hindus are also sensitive about having maximum privacy at this time. No one but an approved cook should tend the domestic hearth, and no one but the eater should look at the meal set before him. Because of the presence of an internal fire, the period reserved for food consumption is also a time of transformation. The threat of mismanaging this process, and hence of subsequent spiritual and physical disorder, is always present at such moments. Careful controls surround the eating process for this reason.

Firm rules also govern body movements in the home. Because personal or household space should be respected and kept clean, shoes or sandals must always be left at the door. Furthermore, Hindus are very aware of the symbolism of vertical placement. The lowest floor of a house is reserved for unclean visitors. Washermen or itinerant merchants sit or stand there. Higher levels are reserved for honored guests and for family members, while the very highest spots are used for sacred shrines and for valued photos of deceased relatives. One always sits and lies at a level lower than that allocated to these revered symbols. Similarly, much family etiquette revolves around bowing to senior members, often touching their feet. Women generally cover their shoulders (and in the North, their heads) in the presence of certain relatives. Such gestures indicate an attitude of special respect. Correct male behavior is similar. Men partially uncover themselves (legs, head, chest) when performing services for pay, thus acknowledging inferior status, but cover up (at least their legs) to express deference to senior relatives and to gods.

It is difficult to delineate male roles from female roles in discussing domestic observances. In wealthy homes male servants often cook, but among close relatives it is usually women who tend the family hearth. An exception arises when women in the house are menstruating, at which time they are not supposed to touch anything in the kitchen, or indeed to even enter that room. If no other female relatives are available, men may temporarily assume the task of food preparation at this time. Hindus can also be quite particular about taking cooked food from strangers, since in such a case they know little about the caste and pollution restrictions that were observed during its preparation. Many Hindu men who travel, or who live alone for other reasons, learn to cook for themselves.

A somewhat similar division of labor by gender governs worship at domestic shrines. Many Hindu women regularly tend a family altar, laying or hanging fresh flowers around the gods and saying prayers. In homes where elaborate daily rituals are performed, however, these are usually left to a senior male. Such intensive worship is by personal preference and is generally associated with individual orthodoxy. It is also common for families to conduct day-to-day rituals themselves but to hire a priest-specialist for the more elaborate work associated with honoring family gods during special festivals or at key domestic events.

Relation to Nondomestic Observances. It would be incorrect to draw any sharp division between Hindu household rites and nondomestic observances. The human body, the domestic living space, and the public temple, as pointed out earlier, are ritually similar. Worship relating to one, for a Hindu, is often equivalent to worship at another.

Hospitality, another key theme, also runs through both temple and domestic events. The reception accorded special household visitors has its own rituals of greeting, seating, and feeding. Gods are treated as household guests, while human visitors may be treated like gods. Foods appropriately offered a guest, as well as the sequence in which they are presented, have been codified in detail. In traditional circles even the serving dishes used to welcome guests are made of special metals and molded into special shapes. Details of gesture and posture are also important when one is receiving visitors. Such gestures are sometimes carefully described in folktales. Details of such hospitality rules, but not the principles, vary by region and by a family's social or community status.

For any Hindu, the house guest *par excellence* is the religious mendicant. Many devout, well-to-do people make a point of feeding ascetic wanderers daily. Family honor and personal merit both increase with the generous giving of food to one who has renounced the world. Popular religious legends tell of gods who become beggars in order to test a devout householder. These holy persons challenge the donor, testing to see if he or she is willing to sacrifice personal abundance for religious devotion. In all such encounters divine grace enters the household with the guest's presence, just as a deity is thought to enter the household shrine during worship. It is not uncommon, furthermore, to give foods that were first offered at the family shrine to strangers who later appear at the door.

Public and domestic elements also come together in other Hindu observances. One tradition, becoming more and more popular at present, is the hymn-singing evening among friends. This event can be held in a public temple, but it is also commonly organized in private. The participants either seat themselves facing a household shrine or use an image taken from that altar as a centerpiece. Such gatherings redefine space in a personal home, so that it becomes more like the space of the public temple.

Hindu domestic rituals spill into the wider world in other ways. A good illustration is provided by the popular southern rite called Poṅkal. This is the special boiling of raw rice *(poṅkal)* on a festive occasion, and its subsequent offering to one or more divinities. The symbolism of Poṅkal carries with it many of the associations between body, home, shrine, and cosmos already mentioned. At an overt level, Poṅkal transforms raw rice into a milky, mushy gruel that is then offered to a god or goddess with a short ceremonial *pūjā*. In a third step, the same food is later distributed among the key participants and eaten. At a deeper level Poṅkal is symbolically associated with the harvest of rice or the birth of a child. In each of these three transformations there is both careful control and the application of heat. In Poṅkal the cooking is confined by a pot; in a field rice is ripened or cooked by the sun, there held to the earth in which it was planted; in gestation a child matures or "cooks" inside the mother's belly while still confined to her womb. The Poṅkal ceremony is also linked to key calendrical festivals such as the Tamil New Year, where yet a further temporal transition is celebrated.

The *poṅkal* is generally cooked in new pots, often on a new stove. Normally it is prepared in the open, on a house threshold, or at the border of a temple compound. In this sense cooking *poṅkal* is a little like cooking at a picnic. The place is unusual and the method of preparation slightly different from normal. There is also a special ritual involved in the cooking, whereby each pot must boil up and spill out in an auspicious direction, but not substantially overflow. This rice-cooking ritual may be performed at home and the product directly offered to deities there, or it may be prepared in an open temple yard by women from separate households. It will then be offered to a publicly enshrined god or goddess. The rite of Poṅkal thus moves a key domestic activity out of the inner sanctum of the kitchen and into more marginal and more open spaces. The preparation of this most vulnerable of food substances, boiled rice, is also opened up on such occasions to an unusual degree of public view. Both these changes suggest the temporary merger of domestic with wider human domains.

If the cooking of *poṅkal* involves a relaxation of the distinction between household and temple, it is also a key ritual in events that mark the overlap of a household social grouping with other key dimensions of community structure. A share of Poṅkal rice, for example, is often offered to immediate family ancestors. Furthermore, cooking *poṅkal* is a common ritual ingredient of festivals celebrated by much larger groupings of kinfolk, such as whole lineages, clans, or subcastes. The preparation of *poṅkal* is also a big event at calendrical celebrations for the village goddess. Here members of many different castes participate overtly. By joining in such an event, they define their common membership in a unit larger than the hamlet or single community.

POLLUTION. Hindu men and women both contract ritual pollution upon the death of close relatives. Complex rules govern how long one is disqualified from participating in festival events after a family funeral has taken place. Both sexes also suffer from temporary pollution after sexual intercourse (requiring a bath) and after eating foods cooked by persons of low caste (traditionally requiring additional acts of expiation). Hindu women acquire pollution during childbirth and menstruation as well. The rules vary by caste, region, and the general orthodoxy of the household as to the action and precautions necessary in such circumstances. Most urban or educated Hindus now consider some or all of these pollution ideas outdated. The enforcement of such restrictions persists, however, in many rural areas.

The Hindu concept of pollution is still imprecisely and incompletely understood by theorists, but it is known that this idea interweaves, in complex ways, such elements as domestic precautions, detailed rules for social intercourse, and several concepts of danger. Pollution, for the Hindu householder, involves a social misalignment, the loss of bodily substances, or a lapse in key biological functions. Either matter is out of place or primal energies have been misaligned. Pollution-linked restrictions serve to prevent such disorders from spreading. As in the Poṅkal ceremony, unusual admixtures and the heat that they generate are a necessary force in transformation. Such processes, though necessary, must be properly contained and monitored in order to confine the chaos produced as their by-product. Hindu domestic ceremonies symbolize the need for regulation and control. They thus ensure a fruitful channeling of vitalizing and heating forces of many kinds.

SEE ALSO Rites of Passage, article on Hindu Rites.

BIBLIOGRAPHY

Two classical sources of great importance on domestic matters are *The Dharmaśāstras*, best summarized by P. V. Kane in *History of Dharmaśāstra*, 5 vols., 2d ed., rev. & enl. (Poona, 1968–1975); and *The Laws of Manu*, translated by Georg Bühler, Sacred Books of the East, vol. 25 (1886; reprint, Delhi, 1964). No recent sourcebook provides a reader with the same colorful detail on a full range of Hindu domestic practices and at the same time charts an overview of first principles. Current works, however, do give a better idea of day-to-day household observances. An in-depth discussion of cooking, gastronomy, and food exchange, for example, can be found in Ravindra S. Khare's *The Hindu Hearth and Home* (Durham, N. C., 1976). A more technical treatment of a broad range of domestic and temple ritual is provided by Carl Gustav Diehl in *Instrument and Purpose: Studies on Rites and Rituals in South India* (Lund, 1956). Another excellent description of household ceremonies, especially those celebrating the life cycle of individuals, is to be found in Margaret S. Stevenson's *Rites of the Twice Born* (London, 1920). A still earlier work by Abbé Jean Antoine Dubois, *Hindu Manners, Customs and Ceremonies*, translated by Henry K. Beauchamp (Oxford, 1906), describes the whole range of Hindu ceremonials he encountered between 1792 and 1823, during his sojourn in southern India as a Catholic missionary. Though highly judgmental in places, the ethnographic detail he includes retains its value to this day. Much contemporary information about rural domestic practices in the North is contained in Ruth S. Freed and Stanley A. Freed's *Rites of Passage in Shanti Nagar* (New York, 1980). Information on central India can be found in Lawrence A. Babb's *The Divine Hierarchy: Popular Hinduism in Central India* (New York, 1975), and traditions in the Tamil-speaking area of South India (especially those surrounding the Poṅkal ceremony) are discussed by Louis Dumont in *Une sous-caste de l'Inde du Sud; Organization sociale et religion des Pramalai Kallar* (Paris, 1957).

New Sources

Bühnemann, Gudrun. *Puja: A Study in Smarta Ritual.* Vienna, 1988.

Rodrigues, Hillary. *Ritual Worship of the Great Goddess: The Liturgy of the Durga Puja with Interpretations.* Albany, 2003.

Tachikawa, Musashi. *Puja and Samskara.* Delhi, 2001.

BRENDA E. F. BECK (1987)
Revised Bibliography

DOMESTIC OBSERVANCES: CHINESE PRACTICES

Chinese domestic rituals are rich and varied, differing from place to place and over time. We know most about the observances of the southeastern provinces (Kwangtung, Fukien, and Taiwan) in the nineteenth and twentieth centuries; what follows reflects this imbalance in our knowledge. Widespread hints and a few fuller accounts of other provinces and other periods, however, give us confidence that, despite considerable variation in specific rituals, the same basic themes have shaped domestic ritual throughout China for several hundred years.

The Chinese word *jia* means both "house" and "family," and everywhere in China there exists a close ritual connection between the building and its inhabitants. It is convenient to divide Chinese domestic rituals into three types: those concerning the house itself, those dealing with the life cycle of the family and its members, and those calendrical rites that are ordinarily performed by the household corporately, or by one or more household members for the benefit of the family as a whole.

RITES OF THE HOUSE. The placement and spatial proportions of a house are believed to affect greatly the fortunes and well-being of its inhabitants. Before building, then, care is taken to site and orient a house in a way favorable to those who will live in it. This is done by selecting a site, if possible, with the advice of a geomancer, a specialist in the technique of *feng-shui* ("wind and water"). A geomancer can tell from the topography of a potential site and its surroundings how well the "cosmic breaths" or "natural forces" *(qi)* set up by building the house will harmonize with those of the natural environment and the potential inhabitants. Geomantic siting and orientation are particularly important in a farmhouse, which can be built without regard to streets or nearby structures.

An urban house, of course, must be built on an empty lot and must face a street, so the opportunities for geomantic siting and orientation are correspondingly restricted. But in both urban and farm houses, the internal proportions of construction are another important consideration in assuring a harmonious dwelling. Such measurements as the size and placement of gates and doors, the arrangement of rooms, and, in particular, the placement of the ritual altar are deemed to affect the relations between a house and its inhabitants. Accordingly, not only geomancers but also carpenters must be familiar with correct proportions; carpenters' manuals contain both explicit instructions for the proper proportioning of a house and an occasional hint at how to cause discord in an enemy's family by purposefully building the house incorrectly.

Disharmony in family relations is sometimes attributed to bad geomantic siting or improper proportioning or layout of a house. To correct such spatial dissonance, it is not uncommon for people to erect a screen to prevent the direct entry of certain undesirable forces or spirits, reorient a door so it will face the domestic altar at a different angle, or perhaps build or take down a wall in order to restore harmonious relations between a house and neighboring structures. In extreme cases, houses geomantically diagnosed as incurable may be abandoned in favor of more salubrious sites.

Not only must a house harmonize with its spatial surroundings, it must also be occupied at a harmonious, and thus auspicious, time. A family moves into a new house during a two-hour period selected by a horoscope reader (who may double as a geomancer) to harmonize with the hours, days, months, and years of birth of as many of the family members as possible. The actual act of moving is marked by lighting incense to the household gods and ancestors on the new altar. The full celebration of moving into a new house is an elaborate one, often complete with major ritual sacrifices, officiated by Daoist or other priests, and including a large feast for relatives, friends, and neighbors.

Even after taking all prudent geomantic and horoscopic precautions, a family may still find its house a source of domestic disharmony. Certain rituals are designed to protect against this or to remedy it should it occur. Families who have moved into a previously occupied house will protect themselves against the spirit of the original owner, who is thought to reside in the house: on certain calendrical holidays this spirit, Ti-chi-chu ("lord of the foundation"), is worshiped with a small offering. In many areas, exorcisms, performed by Daoist or other priests, are employed either as precautions against possible haunting or in order to banish a ghost or spirit thought to be causing trouble.

In addition to such malevolent spirits, more benevolent or protective spirits also reside in the Chinese house. The local gods and family ancestors are enshrined on an altar, usually a prominent feature of a central parlor or another auspiciously located room in the house. They are the object of many of the calendrical and life-cycle rituals described below. Besides these, the house also plays host to some lesser spirits, the most important of which is Zaojun, the so-called kitchen god or, more accurately, "lord of the stove." The stove god is a low-ranking divinity, but many people consider him important because he is a sort of spy, sent by the Jade Emperor in Heaven to report on the activities of household members. As there is one stove for each household, even if there is more than one household in a dwelling, each household also has its own stove god, represented either by a picture or by his title written on red paper and pasted on the wall near the stove. This provides the stove itself with a certain sanctity. Thus, polluting substances (such as laundry, which is presumed to contain menstrual blood) cannot be placed on or hung in front of the stove, any more than these substances can come in contact with the altar. In addition, in some areas people ritually send the stove god back to Heaven to make his report on one of the last days of each lunar year; sometimes they place a bit of sticky candy on his lips so that his report will be brief and inarticulate, or alternatively, a bit of opium to soften his mood. Some families occasionally offer incense to a minor divinity associated with the household pigs or other livestock; rituals and stories surrounding this spirit are not as important or as elaborated as those concerning the stove god.

LIFE-CYCLE RITUALS. Domestic rites and celebrations accompany almost every stage in the life cycle of family members, including pregnancy, birth, early childhood, marriage, family division, death, and the passage to ancestral status. At each stage, both the family as a social unit and the house as a ritually charged space play an important part.

When a woman becomes pregnant, a spirit known as the "fetus spirit" (*taishen*) comes into being. This spirit, thought by some to be the soul of the unborn child, is not yet firmly attached to the fetus, but migrates around the house, changing its position from day to day. By reading a ritual calendar, people can discern, for example, that the fetus spirit will be in the bedroom today, on the roof tomorrow, in the front door the day after, and so on. No one worships or propitiates the fetus spirit, but all must be careful not to offend it for fear of harming the unborn child. Thoughtlessly driving a nail into a wall where the fetus spirit is staying, for example, may cause the child to be born with a harelip; sawing or cutting cloth in the fetus spirit's current room can cause missing limbs or digits; moving things that have long lain still at a time when the fetus spirit is in that room can cause spontaneous abortion.

Aside from such considerations, the pregnant woman has but few ritual restrictions placed on her. Birth ordinarily occurs in the woman's bedroom. The blood of birth, like the blood of menstruation, is polluting, and thus offensive to the gods. For one month following the birth, a new mother is treated as being in a state of ritual pollution, and is confined to the house. During that month, the room where the birth took place is also considered polluted, as is anyone who enters it. For a first son, a first-month feast often marks both the lifting of the state of pollution and the introduction of the child to the community; for subsequent sons and for daughters the ritual is often omitted.

A mother with young children has special ritual duties incumbent on no one else; she makes daily prayers and offerings to Chuangmu ("bed mother"), a low-ranking spirit whose special concern is the health and growth of young children. Closely associated with the bed, the bedroom, and motherhood, the Bed Mother is ignored by other members of the household; she is also, unlike such domestic spirits as the Lord of the Stove, unaffected by pollution. After a woman's children are all of school age or older, she will no longer need the special protection of the Bed Mother, and will cease the prayers and offerings to her.

Since no rituals have marked puberty or other coming of age for Chinese boys or girls in late traditional or modern times, the next ritually important event in the life cycle of the family is marriage. Marriage, like the other life-cycle rituals mentioned above, is closely connected with both the family group and the house itself. After the initial negotiations and matching of horoscopes of the prospective spouses, the first major ritual is the engagement, in which members of the groom's family (but in most areas, excluding the groom himself) deliver the betrothal payment (*pinjin*) and other gifts to the bride's family, and the groom's mother places a ring on the bride's hand. A few weeks or months later, at a horoscopically determined day and time, the marriage itself takes place. The day before the wedding, members of the groom's family go to the bride's house to exchange some ritual presents for the bride's dowry, which they then proceed to take home with them. Part of the dowry—the clothing, jewelry, cosmetics, and bedroom furniture—is installed in the "new room" (*xinfang*), ideally a newly built room, but minimally a newly outfitted one, in which the new couple will sleep. The next visit of the groom's relatives fetches the bride herself, who comes in splendor in a red sedan chair, and at a ritually auspicious moment is carried into the bedroom, the act marking the actual wedding. Later, she and her new husband worship the ancestors of his house, symbolizing the incorporation of the bride into her marital family. A feast follows, introducing the family's bride to relatives and neighbors.

With all sons bringing their brides to live as part of a joint family, the household will, inevitably, grow too large and its conflicts too intense to remain together as a joint corporation. The eventual establishment of separate household groups involves not only the equal division of property and residential space among the brothers but also the division of ritual responsibilities. After the households are divided, brothers may continue to share an altar for household gods and ancestors, but they can no longer share a stove or a stove god. A simple ritual of division involves a final common meal, followed by division of the ashes from the original stove and the consecration of a new stove, with a new stove god, for each of the newly independent households.

Death, like other phases in the life cycle, is an affair both of the family and of the house. A person's death places all family members, as well as the house (whether or not the person died at home), in a state of ritual pollution for a month, and initiates the most elaborate and sustained series of life-cycle rituals. At a ritually auspicious time, a priest or monk, depending on local tradition, places the body in its elaborately painted wooden coffin, which remains in the family's parlor until the burial. A paper soul-tablet with its own incense burner is set up on a special table adjacent to the family's altar. Copious offerings of food and incense are made night and day until the funeral, which must occur at a ritually opportune time, and thus may be delayed several weeks. The funeral involves the participation of many people besides the family members, and as such, is not a purely domestic observance. But the connection to the house remains strong; the two ritually crucial acts of the funeral, those that must be performed at proper times on pain of severe illness for family members, are carrying the coffin out of the house and lowering it into the grave. The family pays all funeral expenses, including a modest feast for a large gathering of relatives, neighbors, and friends. Those who come to pay their respects help offset the cost by bringing the family gifts of money.

After the funeral the temporary, paper spirit-tablet remains on its table for a few weeks, after which it is moved to the family altar, where it is still worshiped separately from the wooden tablets of previously deceased ancestors. After one or two years, a carved wooden tablet replaces the paper one, and the deceased takes a place among the ancestors of the household, to be worshiped as part of the domestic ritual calendar.

Calendrical Rituals of the Family. Calendrical rituals center around the altar, which is usually divided into two halves. The left-hand part (which stands at the observer's right when facing the altar) is the ritually superior half, and enshrines the household gods. These may include deities of Buddhist origin such as Guanyin or one of the Buddhas; historical heroes, such as the Three-Kingdomsera fighter Guangong or one of the more local heroes; or purely traditional gods of the folk religion, such as Tudigong ("earth spirit"). There is usually a scroll hanging on the wall behind the gods' half of the altar, depicting whatever gods are popular locally. Families who feel particular devotion to an individual god may in addition place that god's carved wooden image on the altar in front of the scroll. A single incense pot serves for offerings to all the gods or, if need be, to a particular god on his or her birthday or other special occasions, such as the anniversary of the day when the god saved a family member's life or aided in some other extraordinary way.

The subordinate side of the altar, the right side (which stands at the observer's left), is the seat of the family's ancestral tablets. Depending on region and on individual preference, there may be a separate tablet for each ancestor or married pair of ancestors, there may be a single tablet-cabinet, containing rectangular wooden strips, one for each ancestor or pair, or the names of all the ancestors may be written on a broad, rectangular wooden board. In any case, the names of individual ancestors are always written on the tablets, together with their birth and death dates, and often the number of sons erecting the tablet. Exactly which deceased forebears are worshiped as ancestors varies from household to household, but the general rule is that a family should worship the household head's father and mother, father's father and father's mother, and so on back three to five generations from the current head. In fact, however, other ancestors are often included. For example, if a woman with no brothers marries into the family, she will bring her ancestors' tablets with her, and if a man marries into his wife's family, he may also bring his parents' tablets, or more if he has no brothers to take care of the tablets at home. Ancestors with surnames other than that of the primary ancestral line of the household cannot be worshiped together with the primary ancestors; they must have their own incense burner, and may be relegated to a separate, subordinate altar.

Daily devotions at the altar include incense offered morning and evening, first to the gods and then to the ancestors. Often, a third stick of incense is placed in a burner just outside the front door of the house and offered to dangerous ghosts. Any family member may perform these simple rites; in practice the duty most often falls to the senior woman.

More complex offerings to various spirits may come on the first and fifteenth days of each lunar month, corresponding roughly to the dates of the new and full moon, respectively. These offerings may include presentation of food and burning of ritual money as well as the customary lighting of incense. But the truly elaborate domestic offerings are reserved for special occasions of three kinds. First are the holidays, which are dispersed differently through the Chinese lunar and solar years from one region to the next; only the New Year and the Mid-Autumn festival, celebrated the fifteenth day of the eighth lunar month, approach universality. Second are the birthdays of individual gods, on which occasions households may worship individually or as part of a larger, community celebration. Finally, there are the death-day anniversaries of the family's individual ancestors; these are of course different for each family.

For any of these three sorts of calendrical occasions, each family will prepare and present its own offerings, which always include incense, food, and paper money, and may also include other paper offerings, such as clothing for the ancestors, and on some occasions firecrackers. Offerings always differ according to the particular occasion and according to which spirits are being worshiped. As a general rule, gods receive large, symbolic offerings, such as whole fowl or meat cuts and "gold" paper money. Ancestors receive smaller and more intimate presentations, including food cooked, chopped, and ready to eat, along with silver spirit money and in some places clothes or other practical goods, burnt in paper form. Ghosts, worshiped in many places in the seventh lunar month, receive massive and impersonal offerings, such as uncooked foods, and always the lowest denomination of paper money.

A calendrical ritual of any sort represents the discharge of a family's ritual obligations, either alone or along with other households in the community. At the same time, ritual occasions of this sort provide families with the opportunity to socialize and to strengthen ties with other families. All food offerings are eventually eaten, and all but the simplest are elaborate and expensive enough to be suitable for entertaining guests. Even on the private occasion of an ancestor's death-day, a family will invite a few relatives or neighbors to a ritual meal, and on a major community holiday or god's birthday every house in a village or a city street will be full of guests from outside the local community. On these holidays, as on so many other private and public occasions, the Chinese family affirms its good standing and its unity through ritual.

SEE ALSO Chinese Religion, article on Popular Religion; Chinese Religious Year.

BIBLIOGRAPHY

The best single source of modern analyses of Chinese domestic observances is Arthur P. Wolf's edited collection *Religion and Ritual in Chinese Society* (Stanford, Calif., 1974). Particularly informative for domestic rites are Wolf's "Gods, Ghosts, and Ancestors," pp. 131–182; Stephan Feuchtwang's "Domestic and Communal Worship in Taiwan," pp. 105–129; and Wang Songxing's "Taiwanese Architecture and the Supernatural," pp. 183–192. A good general account, including interesting descriptions of exorcistic rituals, is David K. Jordan's *Gods, Ghosts, and Ancestors* (Berkeley, 1972). Maurice Freedman's writings are notable for their comprehensiveness and wealth of ideas, particularly those concerning ancestor worship and geomancy. See particularly his *Lineage Organization in Southeastern China* (London, 1958), *Chinese Lineage and Society: Fukien and Kwangtung* (London, 1966), and many of the articles collected and reprinted in *The Study of Chinese Society: Essays by Maurice Freedman*, edited by G. William Skinner (Stanford, Calif., 1979). These latter include not only treatments of ancestor worship and geomancy but rich accounts of marriage rituals as well. The most detailed and satisfying study of ancestral rites, including those in the home, is Emily M. Ahern's *The Cult of the Dead in a Chinese Village* (Stanford, Calif., 1973).

All the above sources concern the three southeastern provinces of Taiwan, Kwangtung, and Fukien; accounts of domestic rites in other areas of China consist primarily of descriptions of festivals and of life-crisis rituals, with little analysis. Good descriptions for Shantung can be found in Martin C. Yang's *A Chinese Village: Taitou, Shantung Province* (New York, 1945) and Reginald F. Johnston's *Lion and Dragon in Northern China* (New York, 1910); for Hopei, there is much useful material in Sidney Gamble's *Ting Hsien; A North China Rural Community* (New York, 1954; reprint ed., Stanford, Calif., 1968).

New Sources

Benn, Charles D. *Daily Life in Traditional China: The Tang Dynasty.* Westport, Conn., 2002.

Ebery, Patricia Buckley. *Confucian and Family Rituals in Imperial China: A Social History of Writing about Rites.* Princeton, N.J., 1991.

Goodrich, Anne Swann. *Peking Paper Gods: A Look at Home Worship.* Nettetal, 1991.

Gunde, Richard. *Culture and Customs of China.* Westport, Conn., 2002.

Hayes, James. *South China Village Culture.* New York, 2001.

Holzman, Donald. *Immortals, Festivals, and Poetry in Medieval China: Studies in Social and Intellectual History.* Brookfield, Vt., 1998.

Knapp, Ronald G. *China's Living Houses: Beliefs, Symbols, and Household Ornamentation.* Honolulu, 1999.

STEVAN HARRELL (1987)
Revised Bibliography

DOMESTIC OBSERVANCES: JAPANESE PRACTICES

The Japanese dwelling once was a sacred place in which images and symbols of numerous deities and spirits were the object of purely domestic ritual. Over the past century, and with increasing acceleration since the end of World War II in 1945, both the number of objects of veneration and the frequency of the rituals directed toward them have declined precipitously. Despite the decline, there nevertheless remain ceremonies and practices that speak directly to the notion that the dwelling and its occupants will enjoy the protection of an array of tutelary deities and spirits so long as they are fittingly propitiated.

In analyses of Japanese religious behavior it is common to distinguish three general domains: Buddhism, Shintō, and folk beliefs and practices. Although the categories are by no means exclusive, this tripartite division affords a useful way of organizing a discussion of change. The postwar period has seen the near eclipse of domestic practices belonging to the realms of folk religion and Shintō. Both were closely bound up in the annual cycle of agricultural and fishing communities, whose way of life has been irreversibly altered by the massive social and economic transformation of the twentieth century. Shintō, furthermore, has long been deprived of its privileged position as the vehicle for the government's efforts to construct a national cult centered on emperor worship. Rites in the Buddhist idiom alone survive as the chief focus of domestic religious observances.

Before turning to these Buddhist rites, however, it is appropriate to survey briefly the rapidly vanishing world of household deities and spirits, for only a generation or two ago their benign presence was thought essential to the well-being of the domestic unit. Few dwellings would have contained all of them, given the very great regional variation in these matters, but it is safe to say that most would have had at least one.

Known by many names, the *yashikigami* (house deity) was found in one form or another throughout the country. Customarily enshrined in the corner of the house yard or on other land owned by the family, it served as the tutelary deity of the household or the community and in some places was thought to represent the spirits of the ancestors of the contemporary population. The rites associated with the house deity were essentially Shintō in character, but lacked any connection with the state cult. Equally common, perhaps, was the *toshi no kami* or *toshigami* (year deity), enshrined in the Shintō style on a shelf set high on the wall of the main room of the house. As the name implies, it was venerated chiefly at the New Year, at which time its vaguely tutelary powers were invoked to see the family safely through the coming year.

Once almost universal but quite rare since the disestablishment of state Shintō was the practice at the New Year and on some other festival occasions of hanging a scroll in the *tokonama* (alcove) of the main room of the house bearing the characters *Tenshō kōtaijin* (i.e., the name Amaterasu Ōmikami, the sun goddess, founder of the imperial line). Offerings to this premier deity of the Shintō pantheon consisted of rice or glutinous rice cake and branches of the *sakaki* tree. Less ordinarily enshrined in homes than in places of business, Inari, usually referred to as the fox god but in reality the goddess of rice, was found in some house yards. In other areas, an image of the *bodhisattva* Jizō (Skt., Kṣitigarbha), the protector of children, was installed somewhere outside the house and, like Inari, was made the object of occasional offerings.

Many houses contained a pair of images of two other deities thought to bring good fortune. Ebisu, usually depicted with a large fish under his arm, and Daikoku, shown standing or sitting astride bales of rice and holding a hammer from which money and other valuables flow, were placed together on a separate shelf, and offerings of food were made to them periodically. Daikoku appeared in another form as well, as the largest of the four main pillars supporting the roof of the house. Called *daikoku bashira,* this post was the central point of the geomantic diagram from which all auspicious and inauspicious directions were calculated. Although no offerings were made to it, care was taken that the pillar was not defaced and that no one leaned disrespectfully on it.

Ritual of a combined folk and Shintō character is also a feature of the construction of the house itself. The site itself is protected by the placing of emblems of purity and sanctity called *shimenawa* (twisted straw rope) and *gohei* (folded white paper streamers). When the ridgepole is raised, a priest or the head carpenter, accompanied by the head of the house and his sons, performs rites designed to secure the good fortune of the family and from atop the structure throws down rice cakes to family members, helpers, and neighbors. The ceremony is followed by a feast featuring numerous dishes symbolizing prosperity, longevity, and felicity. Less widely practiced in cities than in the countryside, both the sanctification of the house site and the ridgepole ceremony are still widely observed.

There remain three other major domestic deities associated directly with the dwelling itself, *kama no kami* (deity of the stove), *suijin* (deity of the well), and *benjō-gami* (deity of the toilet), all of whom received offerings primarily at the New Year. The first was enshrined on a shelf, where offerings of rice, tea, *sakaki* branches, candles, and incense were made. The well god, represented by a stone image or a small clay shrine set near the well or pump, received offerings of flowers. The toilet god has been of little importance in most areas for a long time, but was given a little rice at the New Year. Of the minor household deities, many were worshiped in limited areas or by certain kinds of households. It would be impossible to enumerate them here.

Until the end of World War II, which ended in a defeat so catastrophic that the carefully crafted structure of national Shintō was totally discredited, most houses had a shelf for Shintō deities called the *kamidana.* Made of plain wood and bearing unglazed pottery vessels for offerings, it held a miscellany of amulets (*fuda* or *omamori*), souvenirs from Shintō shrines, and most particularly a talisman from the imperial shrine at Ise, seat of the imperial ancestors. At the end of the war many people took down the *kamidana* or failed to incorporate one into new dwellings built in the postwar period. Nonetheless, the practice of collecting amulets from both Shintō shrines and Buddhist temples remains a vigorous one, and almost anyone on a visit or pilgrimage will purchase them to bring back to keep in the house, on his or her person, or, more recently, in the family automobile. These amulets are for easy childbirth, traffic safety, curing alcoholism, success in school examinations, and a host of other mundane concerns. Never the object of veneration or offerings, they are thought to serve a generally protective function.

Most of the rites associated with the household deities so far discussed are performed rather casually. An offering may be made by anyone who thinks of it, although the wife of the family head or the grandmother of the house is most likely to discharge this function as part of her domestic duties. Very different are the rites associated with veneration of the spirits of the deceased members of the household, for in this context the family coalesces as a worshiping unit. These rites center on the *butsudan* (Buddhist domestic altar), a cabinet with doors that normally stands in the main room of the dwelling. The altar doors are opened only when a ceremony is held or someone wishes to speak to the ancestral spirits. Although the altar may contain certain Buddhist paraphernalia, perhaps an image of a *bodhisattva* or scroll bearing a picture or sacred text, it is first and foremost the repository for the memorial tablets of deceased family members. For this reason it is called the ancestor shelf (*senzodana*) in many parts of the country.

On major occasions of worship, priests may be called to the home to conduct the services, but all the other ceremonies for the ancestral spirits are performed by members of the family. They may assemble as a collectivity or approach the altar individually, but on such occasions the presence of a ritual specialist is not required. Because the matter is rather complicated, it will be well at this juncture to lay out the variety and kinds of circumstances that lead the living members of the household to interact ritually with the spirits of their dead kin.

Particular attention is given the ancestral spirits on four occasions in the annual ritual cycle: New Year, the vernal and autumnal equinoxes, and Obon (Festival of the Dead) in the middle of July or August by the Western calendar. By far the most important of these is Obon, when the spirits are welcomed back to the house and given a feast by the members of the family. They remain for three days and are sent off again with gifts of food and flowers. On all four of these calendrically determined occasions, the collectivity of the ancestors is worshiped by the collectivity of the family. Other occasions for domestic worship center on the deceased individual. Special offerings and sūtra reading mark every seventh day of the first forty-nine days after death. Memorial services are held at the altar in a sequence of anniversaries of the person's death (*nenki* or *shūki*), generally the first, third, seventh, thirteenth, seventeenth, twenty-third, twenty-seventh, thirty-third, fiftieth, and one-hundredth. Depending on the family's sectarian affiliation and preferences, one of the last three anniversaries may terminate the series of observances for the deceased as an individual. In addition to these prescribed rites, rice, tea, and other foods are placed in the altar daily, usually at the time of the morning meal. For the more elaborate and formal rites, most people deem it appropriate that the family head officiate, but at all others any member may make the offerings. Inasmuch as responsibility for care of the ancestors is conceived as an extension of a woman's domestic role, it is not surprising to find that adult female members of the family are heavily involved in the daily offering of food and drink to the ancestral spirits, who are clearly thought to remain in need of care and sustenance.

More casual, less routinized contact between the living and the domestically enshrined ancestors is also common. Individuals may petition the ancestors for assistance in some endeavor, report successes to them and apologize for failures, seek their advice rhetorically by raising problems and expressing doubts about the best course of action in some matter, and offering them a portion of gifts of food brought to the family by visitors. At such times no formal offerings are made, but such interaction, in which conventional rather than ritual speech is used, clearly supports the contention that, as David W. Plath (1964) has put it, the Family of God is the family and the dwelling the site of the most intense religious activity in which most Japanese ever engage.

Until recent times the house was also the site of births, weddings, and funerals, as well as a number of other events marking stages in the life cycles of its members. Each was marked by the preparation of ceremonial foods and the display of ritual objects. Auspicious and festive occasions, as well as somber and inauspicious ones, were observed in the context of a concern for the continuity of the domestic unit, celebrating the addition of new members through birth or marriage, changes in their social position, and transition to the realm of ancestorhood. Today, however, women give birth in hospitals and weddings are held in commercial establishments. Only the funeral service remains a household event.

The annual round is punctuated by the observance of a combination of secular and religious occasions on which, as in the life-cycle events, special foods are prepared by the women of the house and ritual objects specific to the event are displayed. There is still considerable variation in the scheduling of these rites and practices, but the establishment of a series of national holidays and adoption of the Western calendar in rural and urban areas alike have served to encourage standardization of the annual cycle. Many official holidays and not a few informal practices retain some vestiges of religious elements, although for the most part these have become much attenuated in recent years.

The annual ceremonial calendar begins with the great three-day celebration of Oshōgatsu, the New Year, which is essentially a family-centered holiday. Decorations are placed in and around the dwelling and offerings made to the ancestors and the deities. In many rural areas January 15 is marked as Koshōgatsu, Little New Year, by the preparation of special foods and other observances. On March 3 families with daughters celebrate Momo no Sekku or Hina Matsuri, Girls' Day, by setting up displays of dolls and making or purchasing special cakes and preparing a meal of auspicious dishes. The vernal equinox, Shūbun no Hi, today observed on March 21, is a religious occasion for cleaning the family graves and venerating the ancestors. On May 5 families with sons mark Boys' Day, Tango no Sekku or Shōbu no Sekku, by flying cloth banners and carp streamers over the house, displaying objects such as miniature helmets, spears, swords, and masculine dolls, and as on Girls' Day, preparing or purchasing special cakes. Since the end of World War II, both these days have been combined into Children's Day, May 5, but the old distinction is still widely observed.

Tanabata, the Star Festival, now held on July 7 for the most part, is the occasion for practicing calligraphy and setting up branches of living bamboo festooned with decorations in the yard of the house. The Festival of the Dead, Obon, is the paramount religious holiday. Formerly held on the thirteenth to the fifteenth days of the seventh lunar month, it is now observed in July in some areas and in August in others. The autumnal equinox, Shūbun no Hi, like the vernal, is an occasion for veneration of the ancestral spirits. The annual cycle formerly concluded with Setsubun, the eve of Risshun, first day of the old solar year. Today it falls out of sequence about February 3. Each family member eats a number of boiled beans equal to his or her age in years and tosses roasted beans outside the house with the cry "Oni wa soto, fuku wa uchi" ("Devils out, good fortune in"). Like many of the formerly religious occasions, Setsubun increasingly is regarded as an observance children will particularly enjoy.

With the passage of time, many of these festive occasions, which formerly played such a significant role in the life of the household, will continue to fade in importance, and their meaning will be lost. Already most young Japanese have seen them performed in the traditional manner only in costume dramas on television or read about them in accounts of life before World War II. Nonetheless, the core of domestic ritual concerned with the care of the ancestors of the house remains the bedrock on which rests what is left of the sacred character of the domestic unit in Japanese society.

Bibliography

In the interest of encouraging further reading, only sources in English are cited here. For treatments of the annual ceremonial cycle, household deities and spirits, and other religious practices centering on the family dwelling and its residents, see Richard K. Beardsley, John W. Hall, and Robert E. Ward's *Village Japan* (Chicago, 1959); Ronald P. Dore's *City Life in Japan: A Study of a Tokyo Ward* (Berkeley, 1958); John F. Embree's *Suye Mura: A Japanese Village* (Chicago, 1939); Edward Norbeck's *Takashima: A Japanese Fishing Community* (Salt Lake City, 1954); and Robert J. Smith's *Kurusu: The Price of Progress in a Japanese Village, 1951–1975* (Stanford, Calif., 1978). These topics are also dealt with in two important articles: Hiroji Naoe's "A Study of *Yashiki-gami,* the Deity of House and Grounds," in *Studies in Japanese Folklore,* edited by Richard M. Dorson (Bloomington, Ind., 1963) and Michio Sue-nari's "Yearly Rituals within the Household: A Case Study from a Hamlet in Northeastern Japan," *East Asian Cultural Studies* 11 (1972): 77–82. Domestic veneration of the ancestors is discussed in detail in my study *Ancestor Worship in Contemporary Japan* (Stanford, Calif., 1974), which includes an exhaustive bibliography on the subject. An excellent succinct statement concerning the meaning of the ancestral rites is David W. Plath's "Where the Family of God Is the Family: The Role of the Dead in Japanese Households," *American Anthropologist* 66 (April 1964); 300–317.

New Sources

Hanley, Susan B. *Everyday Things in Premodern Japan: The Hidden Legacy of Material Culture.* Berkeley, 1997.

Kato, Etsuka. *The Tea Ceremony and Women's Empowerment in Modern Japan: Bodies Re-Presenting the Past.* New York, 1994.

Mizuta, Kazuo. *The Structures of Everyday Life in Japan in the Last Decade of the Twentieth Century.* Lewiston, N.Y., 1993.

Perez, Louis G. *Daily Life in Early Modern Japan.* Westport, Conn., 2002.

Pitelka, Morgan, ed. *Japanese Tea Culture: Art, History, and Practice.* New York, 1994.

Sand, Jordan. *House and Home in Modern Japan: Architecture, Domestic Space, and Bourgeois Culture, 1880–1930.* Cambridge, Mass., 2003.

Robert J. Smith (1987)
Revised Bibliography

DOMINIC (1170–1221), Christian saint and founder of the Order of Friars Preachers, popularly known as the Dominicans. Born at Caleruega in Old Castile, Spain, of parents of the lesser nobility, Domingo de Guzmán received his early education for the clerical state from his archpriest uncle before going to Palencia to study arts and theology from 1186 until 1196. In the latter year he became a canon regular of the reformed cathedral chapter of his home diocese of Osma, where he was ordained to the priesthood and spent the next seven years. A diplomatic mission to Denmark in 1203 brought Dominic, as the traveling companion of his bishop, Diego d'Acebes, into contact with the Albigensian, or Catharist, movement in Languedoc.

This dualist heresy, which had its origin in the teachings of the Persian religious thinker Mani (216–276), had come to western Europe from the Bogomils of Bulgaria, spreading along medieval trade routes in the eleventh and twelfth centuries. The Albigensians (the name derives from the city of Albi, near Toulouse) offered a viable religious alternative for many men and women in southern France who were disenchanted with the institutional church, and the austere lives of the Albigensian teachers, known as the perfect, often stood in marked contrast to the wealth and immoral behavior of the Roman Catholic clergy.

Confronted with a profound challenge to Catholic teaching and authority, Innocent III (1198–1216) had enlisted the services of the Cistercians as preachers among the Albigensians. When Dominic and Diego arrived at the papal court in 1205 on their way home to Spain, after the unsuccessful completion of their Danish mission, Innocent sent them to join the Cistercian preaching mission. The nine years of Dominic's preaching among the Albigensians (1206–1215) constituted the germinating period for his understanding that the ecclesial crisis represented by the Albigensian movement could be met only by a group of doctrinal preachers who would proclaim the gospel and live in apostolic poverty. While in Languedoc, Dominic established a form of religious life for a group of converted Albigensian women at Prouille. This first community of Dominican nuns marked the beginning of countless ways in which women over the centuries would come to share in and help create the Dominican vision.

In 1215 Dominic gathered his first companions in Toulouse, and with the approval of Bishop Fulk they began to preach and live a communal religious life within the diocese. Dominic's vision, however, extended far beyond the confines of Languedoc. Hence he accompanied Fulk to the Fourth Lateran Council in 1215 to obtain papal approval for his dream of a band of doctrinal preachers available to serve the universal church wherever there was need. Innocent III approved of Dominic's idea in principle, but since the council had just forbidden the establishment of any new religious orders, the pope told him to return when he and his companions had selected an already approved rule under which they would live.

Dominic and the first friars chose the rule of Augustine, the rule under which Dominic had already lived as a canon regular, supplemented with legislation borrowed from the Premonstratensians and modified in ways appropriate to their new circumstances. In a series of three bulls between December 1216 and February 1217, Honorius III (1216–1227) officially approved Dominic's plan for a universal preaching brotherhood and addressed its members as "the Order of Preachers."

In 1217 only four years remained of Dominic's life, but they were to be years of intense activity in which he set forth the basic design for the Order of Preachers with bold strokes. Since Dominic believed that doctrinal preaching was required to meet the spiritual needs of men and women in an increasingly urban and academic culture, he saw study as essential to a universal preaching mission. Upon his return from Rome in 1217, Dominic dispersed the first sixteen friars gathered in Toulouse throughout Europe, sending seven of them to establish a religious house at the University of Paris. From the dispersal in 1217 until the spring of 1220, Dominic was on the road, preaching, visiting the friars he had sent out, gathering new members for the order, founding new houses, and seeking continued papal support for the work of the preachers.

Dominic's thought has survived not in his writings, for only a few of his letters are extant, but rather in the formative guidance that he gave to the first two general chapters of the order in 1220 and 1221. The idea of a general chapter was not unique to Dominic; begun by the Cistercians in the previous century, it had become the common form of unifying and promoting the life of a religious order. Dominic, however, saw the general chapter not as a gathering of abbots but as an assembly of brothers elected by their peers who would legislate for the common good. In Dominic's vision the master of the order was to be the center of unity on the universal level, the provincial on the regional level, and the prior on the local level. But the friars themselves, functioning through the general, provincial, and local chapters, were to assume responsibility for carrying on the life and mission of the order.

Under Dominic's dynamic leadership, the chapters of 1220 and 1221 established the basic constitutional framework that would ensure constant flexibility in adapting the order's preaching mission to diverse situations. They gave a primary place to study as essential to doctrinal preaching, embraced mendicant poverty, provided for dispensations from the constitutions when necessary so as not to impede preaching or study, and universalized the mission of the order by establishing eight provinces in western Europe. The chapters of 1220 and 1221 brought Dominic's vision to life: an order of preachers whose preaching would flow from a life of study and common prayer, lived in a community of brothers professing the vows and being jointly responsible, through a chapter system of representative government, for a universal preaching mission in cooperation with the bishops and with the papacy's protection and support.

Dominic fell ill during a preaching tour in Lombardy after the meeting of the general chapter of 1221, and he died in Bologna (where he is buried) on August 6, 1221. In 1234 he was canonized by Gregory IX (1227–1241), and he is commemorated in the Roman calendar on August 8. The influence of Dominic perdures in the shared vision of a religious family of men and women dedicated to preaching the gospel to all people while living in a community that is committed to common prayer and simplicity and whose members are jointly responsible for their life and mission.

See Also Dominicans.

Bibliography

The most scholarly and reliable biography of Dominic is the work by M.-H. Vicaire, O.P., *Saint Dominic and His Times,* translated by Kathleen Pond (London, 1964). The documents that constitute the primary sources for Dominic's life have been collected by Francis C. Lehner, O.P., in *Saint Dominic: Biographical Documents* (Washington, D.C., 1964).

Thomas McGonigle (1987)

DOMINICANS. The popular name of the Order of Friars Preachers (Ordo Praedicatorum, abbreviated O.P.) was derived from the name of the order's founder, Domingo de Guzmán (1170–1221), generally called Dominic. In France the Dominicans were once known as Jacobins, from their priory of Saint Jacques at the University of Paris, and in England they were known as Black Friars, from the black mantles that they wore over their white habits.

Along with the Franciscans, the Dominicans constitute the heart of the mendicant friar movement of the thirteenth century. After the renaissance of the twelfth century, the presence within medieval society of a growing number of urban-dwelling and literate laypeople, critical of and often alienated from the institutional church, posed a great pastoral problem. The secular and religious clergy at the beginning of the thirteenth century seemed ill equipped to meet the spiritual needs of an urbanized laity and unable to cope with the rapid spread of the Albigensian and Waldensian heresies in the cities of southern France and northern Italy.

Between 1215 and 1221, Dominic with papal approval founded a religious order whose members would not be bound by monastic stability but would be itinerant doctrinal preachers, living a life of poverty in community and educated to minister to the spiritual needs of a literate urban laity. The presence of the Dominicans at the burgeoning universities of Europe established a mutual relationship that would have profound consequences for the history of European thought. From the local priory, which was seen as an ongoing theological school for preachers, to the great centers of study at Paris, Oxford, Bologna, and Cologne, the houses of the order constituted a vast educational network. Albertus Magnus (1193–1280) and Thomas Aquinas (1225–1274), with their monumental achievements of utilizing the insights of Aristotelian thought in the formulation of a new Christian philosophical and theological synthesis, represent the best of the Dominican tradition of study at the service of preaching the gospel in ever new and challenging milieus.

The same creative élan that marked the Dominican presence at the great university centers of Europe was also manifest in missionary activity. Within the first hundred years of their existence, the Dominicans had established missions in Scandinavia, the Baltic area, eastern Europe, Greece, Persia, the Holy Land, and North Africa.

Dominican emphasis on doctrinal preaching led popes and bishops to use the order in the work of the Inquisition. This darker aspect of Dominican history is somewhat counterbalanced by the positive impact that the order's model of government by elected representatives had upon the emerging parliamentary system of Europe.

From its earliest days the Order of Preachers embraced not only priests, student brothers, novices, and lay brothers, all of whom constituted what came to be called the first order, but also contemplative nuns (the second order) and women religious and laypeople living in the world (the third order). The first order grew rapidly in the first hundred years of the order's existence. In 1277 there were 12 provinces and 404 priories with about thirteen thousand friars whereas in 1303 there were 18 provinces and 590 priories with about twenty thousand friars. Because the Black Death took a great toll in the middle of the fourteenth century, the number of Dominican friars probably never exceeded thirty thousand at any one time during the Middle Ages.

The monasteries of Dominican second-order nuns, which numbered 4 during the last years of Dominic's life, increased to 58 in 1277, 141 in 1303, and 157 in 1358. Munio of Zamora, seventh master of the order (1285–1291), drew up a rule in 1285 for lay men and women who wished to be Dominicans while continuing to live in the world. It is impossible to estimate how many men and women shared the Dominican life and mission as members of the third order, but Catherine of Siena (1347–1380), mystic and doctor of the church, stands as an eloquent witness to the third order's profound influence upon medieval society.

The German Dominicans Meister Eckhart (1260–1327), Johannes Tauler (1300–1361), and Heinrich Suso (c. 1295–1366) were leaders in the fourteenth-century mystical movement, but like all other religious orders the Dominicans experienced a considerable loss of members and a marked decline in observance and morale as a result of the Black Death. Raymond of Capua, twenty-third master of the order (1380–1400), inaugurated a reform movement in the last decades of the fourteenth century that resulted in the renewed life of the order in the fifteenth century, exemplified by Antoninus of Florence (1389–1459), Fra Angelico (1387–1455), and Girolamo Savonarola (1452–1498).

The Dominicans Johann Tetzel (1465–1519) and Thomas de Vio Cajetan (1469–1534) played key roles in the events that inaugurated the Reformation, and Dominicans were to be found both joining the ranks of the Reformation preachers and defending the old faith before and after the Council of Trent (1545–1563). Although religious changes in Europe caused the disappearance or decline of the Dominican provinces in northern Europe, seven new provinces were founded in Central and South America. Dominican missionary activity in the New World was rendered illustrious by the preaching of Louis Bertrand (1526–1581), by the charitable work of Martín de Porres (1579–1639) and Juan Macias (1585–1645), and by the struggles of Bartolomé de Las Casas (1474–1566) to protect the Indians from the exploitation of Spanish colonial officials.

Although the order numbered between thirty and forty thousand friars and nuns in forty-five provinces in the seventeenth century, and Thomism flourished under such distinguished commentators as John of Saint Thomas (1589–1644), much of the outward structure of the order was swept away during the difficult period from 1789 to 1848. Under the impulse of the French Dominican preacher Jean-Baptiste-Henri Lacordaire (1802–1861) and the outstanding leadership of Vincent Jandel, seventy-third master of the order (1855–1872), the Dominicans entered upon a new spring in the mid-nineteenth century that ultimately produced in the early decades of the twentieth century the biblical scholar Marie-Joseph Lagrange (1855–1938) and the Thomistic theologians Reginald Garrigou-Lagrange (1877–1964) and Juan Arintero (1860–1928).

Dominican theologians Yves Congar, Dominic Chenu, and Edward Schillebeeckx were leaders in the new theological movement that flourished after World War II in Europe and culminated in Vatican II. The renewal of the order in accordance with the norms of the council began with the publication of the new constitutions written at the general chapter held at River Forest, Illinois, in 1968. The four subsequent general chapters have continued the renewal process and given special emphasis to new forms of preaching and to the modern media of communication, the ministry of social justice, and the development of the order in South America, Africa, and Asia. In 1974 the concept of the first, second, and third orders was replaced by that of the Dominican family. New emphasis was given to the common mission of the men and women of the order to preach the gospel, while recognizing the diverse ways in which the ministry of preaching is carried out by the clerical, religious, and lay members of the order.

Over the past seven centuries 18 Dominican men and women have been canonized, and 334 members of the Dominican family have been beatified. Furthermore, 4 popes, 69 cardinals, and several thousand bishops have been drawn from the Dominican order to the service of the universal church. In 2000, the Dominican family throughout the world included 5,171 brothers in solemn vows, 4,672 priests, and 477 lay brothers. In 1983 there were 4,775 nuns in 225 cloistered monasteries, 40,816 women religious in 140 congregations, and 70,431 laity or secular Dominicans.

SEE ALSO Albertus Magnus; Catherine of Siena; Dominic; Eckhart, Johannes; Las Casas, Bartolomé de; Savonarola, Girolamo; Tauler, Johannes; Thomas Aquinas.

BIBLIOGRAPHY

The most scholarly history of the Dominican order from its beginnings to the Reformation is *The History of the Dominican Order,* 2 vols., by William A. Hinnebusch, O.P. Volume 1 is titled *Origins and Growth to 1500* (New York, 1966); volume 2, *Intellectual and Cultural Life to 1500* (New York, 1973). Hinnebusch's untimely death in 1981 prevented his completing two further volumes that would have taken the history of the order from the Reformation to the present. However, a concise summary of the material planned for the two final volumes can be found in his work *The Dominicans: A Short History* (New York, 1975).

The publication of two works edited and translated by Simon Tugwell, O.P.—*Early Dominicans* (New York, 1982) and *On the Beginnings of the Order of Preachers by Jordan of Saxony* (Oak Park, Ill., 1982)—have provided excellent selections of primary documents necessary for an understanding of the early history of the Dominican family. Both works also contain superb introductions to the sources of Dominican spirituality.

New Sources

Borgman, Eric. *Dominican Spirituality.* New York, 2001.

Conrad, Richard. *The Catholic Faith: A Dominican's Vision.* New York, 1994.

THOMAS MCGONIGLE (1987)
Revised Bibliography

DÖMÖTÖR, TEKLA (1914–1987) was a Hungarian folklorist and pioneering scholar of folk religion in the Hungarian context. Born in Budapest, Hungary, she studied English and German philology at the Pázmány Péter University in Budapest from 1932 to 1936. Her Ph.D. dissertation (1937) was about German medieval ritual drama. She became a university teacher in 1953, then was professor and chair of the folklore department in Budapest—the university's first woman chairperson and professor—from 1973 to 1984. Her primary field of research was the history of Hungarian theater and Hungarian folk customs and folk beliefs. Beginning in the 1960s she participated in international conferences and societies of European folklore. In 1985 she won the Herder Prize for fostering comparative folklore research in central Europe.

Dömötor's major works are devoted to Hungarian folk calendar customs and Hungarian ritual poetry, including references to folk beliefs and folk legends. Extending her earlier popular books, she wrote the first new summary on Hungarian folk beliefs (1981 in Hungarian, English translation 1982). Dömötör wrote a biographical sketch about János Honti (1910–1945), the closest friend of her husband, Aladár Dobrovits, professor of Egyptology at the Budapest University. In this biographical sketch of Honti, who was one of the first modern Hungarian folklorists and who was killed by the Nazis, she gave a detailed picture of the work before World War I of the Hungarian Section of the Folklore Fellows in organizing the rich Hungarian folklore collections.

Dömötör's monograph on Hungarian folk beliefs is a careful work. She avoids the use of such basic religio-scientific concepts as the term *mythology* as regards the Hungarians. Contrary to many Finno-Ugric scholars, she prefers historical interpretations of folklife and belief and is reluctant to say anything about "Hungarian shamanism." In the introduction she lists the previous attempts to describe the "ancient Hungarian religion," but in general she finds unconvincing their reconstructions and historic stratifications concerning the ancient Hungarian "mythology" or "religion," because in such works "the scope of speculation remains very wide indeed" (1982, p. 42). When Hungarians adopted the Christian faith (during the reign of King Stephen I, 997–1038), the old pattern of social organization disintegrated, to be replaced by the emergence of a feudal social structure. According to Dömötör, Hungarian medievalist historians have interpreted the true historic data related to beliefs and customs according to their own expectations. Regarding the time of the Reformation, she discusses "diabolic beings," evil-eye cases, and witches. The witch trials existed in Hungary until 1768, and their pattern does not significantly modify the general European picture. At the time of the Enlightenment a tendency toward teaching the people not to trust superstitions appeared.

Dömötör did not address the later sociohistorical stratification of Hungarian folk beliefs. She wanted to draw an overall picture of the nineteenth and twentieth centuries. The major chapters of her description are: animistic beliefs (mythical beings, metamorphosis, *ignis fatuus,* "fair lady," "fair maid" and fairies, revenants and ghosts, demons of nature, giants and dwarfs, the devil and his accomplices, Lucy, malevolent spirits, bogeymen, demons of disease, changeling, werewolf, dragon, snake, and other mythical animals and plants); the "cunning folk" (people with special skills); healers and their cures; magic (and divination); the magical power of words (incantations and prayers); man and nature (creation of the earth and weather lore); laicized traditions of the church (popular religion), pilgrimages, and sects; and the living and the dead (grave posts).

As is evident from these contents, Dömötör's book does not give a deep historical analysis and does not follow any system of phenomenology of religion. The order of the several subchapters in the book remains unexplained. In fact the differences between old traces of "mythology," folk beliefs, superstitions, and forms of everyday popular religion are not distinguished or systematized. Dömötör was afraid of making any terminological or theoretical suggestions or conclusions. The fear of giving concess to mystical or nationalistic interpretation (of the primordial Hungarian religion) paralyzed the systematization of Hungarian worldview studies. On the other hand, most of the data Dömötör refers to are historically correct, put into European context, and without boasting speculations. In particular she refers to the results of Géza Róheim, Vilmos Diószegi, Éva Pócs, and Mihály Hoppál but with idiosyncratic restrictions. Superfluously she stresses the importance of the social context, whereas in fact she was never a follower of any social or historical interpretation of the beliefs. (Except for some slogans, she was never a Marxist either.) Empiricism and eclecticism prevail in her studies on Hungarian folk legends and folk customs. Dömötör wrote the short entry "Hungarian Religion" in the first edition of *The Encyclopedia of Religion,* however, without any reference to gender problems.

SEE ALSO Hungarian Religion

BIBLIOGRAPHY

Balázs, Géza, and József Hála, eds. *Folklór, életrend, tudománytörténet: Tanulmányok Dömötör Tekla 70. születésnapjára.* Budapest, 1984. A Festschrift in honor of Dömötör's seventieth birthday, in Hungarian, without a detailed biography, and without any bibliography.

Dömötör, Tekla. *Hungarian Folk Beliefs.* Budapest, 1977. Translation of *A magyar nép hiedelemvilága.* Good illustrations and references.

Dömötör, Tekla. *János Honti, Leben und Werk.* Folklore Fellows Communications no. 221. Helsinki, 1978.

Dömötör, Tekla. *Táltosok Pest-Budán és környékén.* Budapest, 1987. Novelistic stories about her life.

Dömötör, Tekla. *Hungarian Folk Customs* (1983). Budapest, 1988. Updated edition of a popular book.

Dömötör, Tekla, ed. *Népszokás, néphit, népi vallásosság.* Budapest, 1990. For this volume on folk customs, folk beliefs, and popular religion in the new Hungarian "academic" handbook of folk traditions, she wrote a chapter on the research history of Hungarian folk beliefs (pp. 501–526), the same text as in the first chapter of *Hungarian Folk Customs* (1988), in English, pp. 21–75.

Magda, S. Gémes. "Dömötör Tekla önálló művei." *Néprajzi Hírek* 16 (1987): 105–106. Includes an incomplete bibliography.

VILMOS VOIGT (2005)

DONATISM is the name given to the schism that divided the North African church from around at least 311 until the end of the sixth century. The immediate cause was the refusal of part of the clergy and congregations of Carthage, supported by bishops from Numidia, to accept the election of the archdeacon Caecilian as bishop of Carthage in succession to Mensurius. It was claimed that one of Caecilian's consecrators, Felix of Apthungi, had been a *traditor* (i.e., one who had handed the scriptures to the authorities during the Great Persecution of 303–305) and was therefore unworthy. It was also claimed that Caecilian had maltreated confessors in prison at Carthage by preventing food supplied by well-wishers from reaching them.

In the background of the schism, however, were important theological and nontheological issues. Since its emergence into history in 180, the North African church had been a church of martyrs. Its members believed themselves to be under the continuous guidance of the Holy Spirit. For many, the ideals of purity, integrity, and zeal for martyrdom took precedence over that of universality. Under Cyprian's guidance, the church had decided that a valid sacrament could not be administered by a cleric in a state of sin or to one who was outside the church. Congregations should separate themselves from a priest who was a sinner. In addition, in the latter part of the third century, the less romanized province of Numidia had become a separate province of the church, and its primate had acquired the right of consecrating each new bishop of Carthage. Now the bishops of Numidia were eager to assert the claim of their province in the government of the North African church.

These factors helped to consolidate opposition to Caecilian, and in 312 he was condemned to deposition by a council presided over by the primate of Numidia. The emperor Constantine, however, supported Caecilian, put a considerable sum of money at his disposal, and exempted from municipal levies clergy loyal to him. In April 313, the opposition appealed to Constantine, outlining their complaints against Caecilian and requesting arbitration from bishops in Gaul, as Gaul, they claimed, had not suffered in the persecution.

Long-drawn-out legal processes ensued. Constantine first delegated the opposition's complaint to Pope Miltiades, himself an African, but on the rejection of the pope's decision in favor of Caecilian (October 5, 313) by the opposition, summoned a full council of Western bishops at Arles on August 1, 314, to decide the issue. The opposition, now led by Donatus of Casae Nigrae in southern Numidia, rejected this decision also. Only after the acquittal of Felix of Apthungi in February 315, another appeal, and the dispatch of a commission of bishops to Carthage did Constantine conclude that Caecilian was innocent; he pronounced judgment in that sense on November 10, 316.

Persecution (317–321) failed to destroy the Donatists, as they were now known. Under Donatus's leadership they became the majority party among North African Christians, and this predominance was only threatened temporarily by the exiling of Donatus by the emperor Constans in 347/8. Under the emperor Julian the Donatist leaders returned in strength. Their leader was now a cleric named Parmenian who was not a North African but described as a "Gaul or Spaniard." As bishop of Carthage, until his death in 391/2, he witnessed Donatism at the height of its power in North Africa. His death, however, was followed by schism between his followers. The new bishop of Carthage, Primian, was supported by the Numidians but opposed by Maximian, a descendant of Donatus who represented more moderate tendencies within the church.

The Maximianist schism was contained and unity within the Donatist church restored at the Council of Bagai on April 24, 394. Four years later, however, one of the principal Donatist leaders was implicated in the revolt against Emperor Honorius by the native chieftain, Count Gildo. On its failure, the Donatist church faced attack by the North African catholics, now ably led by Aurelius, bishop of Carthage, and Augustine of Hippo. Augustine took advantage of the fact that nearly all Christendom had remained loyal to Caecilian and hence regarded his Catholic successors as the true bishops of Carthage. In addition, by their practice of rebaptizing converts the Donatists rendered themselves liable to the antiheretical laws of the emperor Theodosius. Moreover, the extremist Donatists and social revolutionaries known as Circumcellions, who since 340 had been terrorizing the landowners of the day and the Catholic population in general, were considered a menace to civil authority. Augustine persuaded the government of the emperor Honorius to promulgate edicts banning the Donatists in February and March 405 and finally in May 411 maneuvered them into a conference with the Catholics under an imperial commissioner, Marcellinus, to decide what party was the "catholic church" in North Africa.

In the previous twelve years Augustine had written a series of tracts designed to show that there was no historical justification for the schism and that rejection of universality as the standard of catholicism as well as erroneous teaching on the church and sacraments made the Donatists heretics. In addition, Bishop Aurelius's yearly conferences of Catholic bishops of Carthage had revitalized the organization and sense of purpose of the catholics. When the conference met, all the advantages lay with them, although the Donatists still managed to match the Catholics in number of bishops, namely 284. After three session of debate Marcellinus gave his decision against the Donatists. This was followed on January 30, 412, by an edict that effectively banned Donatism, confiscated Donatist property, and ordered the exile of Donatist leaders.

This time the repressive measures succeeded. Augustine provides evidence for the conversion of Donatist congregations and surrender of Donatist church property. The Circumcellions, however, remained active and eventually contributed to the downfall of Roman Africa when the Vandals invaded from Spain in 429. In the Vandal occupation (429–534) little is heard of the Donatists, but at the end of the sixth century, after the Byzantine reconquest, Donatism emerged again in southern Numidia. Descriptions of the progressive advance of the movement are found in a series of letters from Pope Gregory to his representatives in North Africa, to imperial officials, and to the emperor Maurice. After 601 nothing more is heard of the movement. Only further archaeological investigation of Numidian rural sites is likely to add to our information about the final phase of the sect.

Donatism demonstrates the continuance in the West of the biblical rigorist and individualist pattern of early Christianity that placed individual holiness under the guidance of the spirit as its highest ideal. The Donatists were the true successors of Tertullian and Cyprian in the African church, and they were protesters. Church and state must always be separate. Martyrdom must be accepted as a Christian duty. As far as the Donatist was concerned, the conversion of Constantine might never have taken place. In addition, Donatism, unlike any other Christian movement in the Roman Empire, gave scope for revolutionary stirrings among the peasantry, for it expressed the peasants' hopes for the great reversal of material fortunes that would presage the millennium. Its forceful repression by church and secular authorities also provided precedents for the persecution of heresy in the Middle Ages and in the Reformation and Counter-Reformation periods.

Material remains of Donatism are still to be seen in North Africa, especially in Numidia, where the great church of Bishop Optatus of Timgad (388–398) is an outstanding monument to Donatism at the height of its power. Many Donatist chapels have been found in rural sites of Roman and Byzantine date in Numidia. Some Donatist literature has survived, notably the circular letter written by Bishop Petilian of Constantine to his clergy about 400; it is preserved in Augustine's *Contra litteras Petiliani.* Tyconius was a Donatist biblical exegete of first caliber whose work was used extensively in the early Middle Ages by orthodox writers such as Bede. Finally, Donatism found expression in peasant art forms, especially in woodcarving. These art forms often incorporated a biblical text or the watchword used by the Circumcellions, "Deo laudes."

See Also Augustine of Hippo; Christianity, article on Christianity in North Africa; Constantine; Cyprian.

Bibliography

Bonner, Gerald. *St. Augustine of Hippo: Life and Controversies.* London, 1963.

Brisson, Jean-Paul. *Autonomisme et christianisme dans l'Afrique romaine.* Paris, 1958.

Brown, Peter. *Religion and Society in the Age of Saint Augustine.* London, 1972.

Diesner, Hans-Joachim. "Die Circumcellionen von Hippo Regius." *Theologische Literaturzeitung* 85 (1960): 497–508.

Frend, W. H. C. *The Donatist Church: A Movement of Protest in Roman North Africa* (1952). Reprint, Oxford, 1971. Includes bibliography and a list of Donatist writers.

Frend, W. H. C. *Town and Countryside in the Early Christian Centuries.* London, 1980.

Lancel, Serge, trans. and ed. *Actes de la conférence de Carthage en 411.* Sources chrétiennes, vols. 194, 195, and 224. Paris, 1972–1975.

Mandouze, André. "Encore le Donatisme." *L'antiquité classique* 29 (1960): 61–107.

Monceaux, Paul. *Histoire littéraire de l'Afrique chrétienne,* vols. 4–6 (1901–1923). Reprint, Brussels, 1966.

Saumagne, Charles. "Ouvriers agricoles ou rôdeurs de celliers? Les Circoncellions d'Afrique." *Annales d'histoire économique et sociale* 6 (1934): 351–364.

Simpson, W. J. Sparrow. *St. Augustine and African Church Divisions.* London, 1910.

Tengström, Emin. *Donatisten und Katholiken.* Göteborg, 1964. Includes a bibliography.

W. H. C. Frend (1987)

DONG ZHONGSHU (also Tung Chung-shu, c. 195–c. 115 BCE) is one of the most important thinkers of Han dynasty (206 BCE–220 CE) Confucianism. His concept of the relationship between Heaven and humans has been influential for the development of Confucianism. Yet Dong's contribution to the history of religion is a matter of dispute due to diverging evaluations of the sources connected to him. Today, four sorts of sources with possible information about Dong Zhongshu exist.

Sources. The *Records of the Grand Historian (Shiji)* written by Sima Qian around 100 BCE contains a biography of Dong Zhongshu, the earliest and most reliable source about his life and thought. According to *Shiji,* Dong in his early years was interested in the principles operating within the forces of yin and yang. On the basis of these principles he created a ritual that should seek and stop the rain, and he attempted to interpret historical and contemporary anomalies and catastrophes as omens.

In the biography of Dong Zhongshu in the *Dynastic History of the Han* (*Hanshu*) written by Ban Gu at the end of the first century CE, Dong is depicted rather as patriarch of Han Confucianism and as a political teacher. Appended to the biography are three memorials, which contain a question-and-answer exchange between Dong and Emperor Wu. In these memorials Dong refers to two ultimate authorities that should serve as guidelines for the Han government: Heaven and antiquity. Dong claims that Heaven responds to human action according to the same principles that Confucius's judgments of praise and blame respond to the action of the historical actors in the *Spring and Autumn Annals* (*Chunqiu*). According to Dong, Confucius inserted his judgments in the *Chunqiu* in correspondence with the laws and the will of Heaven, and has thus proven how Heaven responds to human action. Heaven's response is not a conscious choice—it is mechanical and automatic, but it does not always respond in a one-to-one analogy to the actions. Instead, Heaven appears as a rather lenient and gracious force that starts signaling with small tokens of anomalies as warnings before sending harsh punishments in the form of catastrophes.

The *Chunqiu fanlu* (*CQFL*) is a post-Han collection that was probably edited six centuries after Dong's death. It is a compilation of extremely heterogeneous and contradictory materials, including chapters on *Chunqiu* exegesis, Huang-Lao philosophy (the philosophy of the Yellow Emperor Huangdi and Laozi which focuses on questions of inner spiritual self cultivation, the void, the dao, the emptying of the mind, non-action and non-being), Confucian virtues, state institutions, cosmological speculations on *yin-yang, wuxing,* Heaven and Earth, and sacrificial and rain rituals. Which of these materials was written by Dong Zhongshu is highly controversial.

Other Han sources contain many quotations from Dong Zhongshu, but larger fragments of his writing are also transmitted. The "Wuxing zhi" chapter in *Hanshu* includes Dong's commentaries and explanations to historical and contemporary anomalies and catastrophes. Furthermore, the fragments of the *Chunqiu jueyu,* a handbook on law cases ascribed to Dong, give an impression of the pragmatic and formal usage of the *Chunqiu* as a book of legal precedents.

Critical Interpretation of the Sources. The evaluation and interpretation of these sources determines the different reconstructions of Dong Zhongshu's life, religion, and philosophy.

In the sources that most probably stem from Dong's hand—in *Shiji* and *Hanshu,* in the first 17 *Chunqiu* exegetical chapters and the ritual chapters of the *CQFL,* as well as any of the above mentioned fragments—Dong Zhongshu is never connected to *wuxing* or to Huang-Lao thought. He appears as a specialist on prognostication and religious rites employing the theory of yin and yang. Moreover, he is depicted as an important political thinker and instructor who professes Heaven and antiquity as the most important models upon which a state should be molded. In the *Chunqiu jueyu* he is quoted as an important exegetical voice in legal court cases. These sources present him as a serious traditional scholar whose thought was rooted in the classical Confucian writings and in his belief in a Heavenly way and its signs.

There is little theoretical innovation in his work. It is rather mainly important in the history of thought because of decisive selections and new evaluations of traditional concepts like the will of Heaven, the law of stimulus and response, correspondence between human action and Heaven, love for the people, cyclical change of institutions, and human nature. Dong is not developing these concepts further but rather applies and combines old traditions in new contexts like text exegesis, modification of cosmological cycles, devaluation of yin (punishment) against yang (education), or the introduction of a lenient aspect in Heaven's clockwork of mechanical resonance. Innovative is Dong's connective approach through which he interrelates different areas such as prognostication, human nature, politics, cosmology, and text exegesis on the basis of a singular Heavenly scheme that reaches into all of these realms. However, he therewith does not intertwine these realms into one unified system that could function as a universal organism, but rather establishes structural parallels and analogies in order to defend his moral, political, and philosophical position against Legalists, Mohists, and Huang-Laoists.

Critique on Traditional Interpretations of the Sources. Dong Zhongshu appears rather differently under the premise that he is the author of the whole *CQFL,* a premise which has been upheld by the mainstream of traditional scholarship. As the material of the *CQFL* is so abundant, complex, and comprehensive, Dong, as the assumed author, has subsequently been depicted as the architect of Han Confucianism, the founder and theorist of Han cosmology and Han political philosophy who ingeniously created the great synthesis of *yin-yang, wuxing,* and exegetical scholarship on the Confucian classics in a great unified theological and teleological system.

Further research shows that this picture can not be upheld. Han Confucianism is a collective term covering highly complex and contradictory philosophies of very different synthetic teachings, which vary strongly from thinker to thinker. Dong's philosophy is neither theological nor teleological, but rather a traditional philosophy of a balance of extremes. Heaven as a willful institution plays a crucial role in Dong's philosophy; however, this institution is strictly subdued to the working rules of yin and yang and should not be compared to a deity. Dong's *Chunqiu* scholarship is nowhere connected to or mixed with cosmological theories. It rather develops from concrete text exegesis to a theory of abstract political and moral principles. Although historical *Chunqiu* precedent cases are sometimes taken to illustrate cosmological principles, theories of cosmology and of *Chunqiu* scholarship remain strictly disconnected.

The central position of Heaven as a model and argumentative foundation of the design of the imperial position within the political philosophy of the *CQFL,* and, moreover, the interpretation of the *CQFL* material as a systematic whole, has led Chinese reformers at the end of the nineteenth century to declare Dong Zhongshu's Confucianism to be the correct and pure form of Chinese Confucianism. Accordingly, this ostensible systematic and religious Confucianism, constructed as an indigenous form of unified Chinese national state religion, was used to oppose Western religion and culture. In a counterreaction, Chinese Marxist histories of Chinese thought evaluate Dong's philosophy as feudal idealist theology because of this alleged fixation on Heaven as the systematic center of his thought. It is correct that Heaven in Dong's writings is revived as a central philosophical authority. However, the way in which Heaven is brought into the argumentation is far from "theology" in the sense of a unified religious system founded in something like *theos.* Dong's theories, and even the theories concerning Heaven in the later chapters of the *CQFL,* merely reflect a cosmo-political discourse and nowhere show an attempt to unify or systematize different models of Heaven's operations. Therefore, they should not be regarded as an innovative outline of a Chinese theology, but rather be read in the context of other cosmopolitical writings of Dong's time contained in the *Lüshi Chunqiu,* the *Huainanzi,* and the *Xinyu.* Religious theory in Han times developed rather in the realm of the search for immortality in the *fangshi,* Huang-Lao, and Mohist spheres. Dong Zhongshu used the concepts of Heaven and yin and yang for political, prognostication, and ritual purposes. He did not formulate a religious theory of his own.

BIBLIOGRAPHY

Arbuckle, Gary. "Restoring Dong Zhongshu (BCE 195–115): An Experiment in Historical and Philosophical Reconstruction." Ph.D. diss., University of British Columbia, Dept. of Asian Studies, Vancouver, 1991.

Bujard, Marianne. "La vie de Dong Zhongshu: enigmes et hypothèses." *Journal Asiatique* 280 (1992): 145–217.

Queen, Sarah A. *From Chronicle to Canon: The Hermeneutics of the Spring and Autumn, according to Tung Chung-shu.* New York, 1996.

JOACHIM GENTZ (2005)

DÖNMEH. The followers of the Ottoman Jewish messiah Shabbetai Tsevi (or Shabtai Zvi; 1626–1676), subsequent to his conversion to Islam, are known as the Dönmeh. Despite hostility originating from the belief that they had converted to Islam deceitfully, though perhaps with a salvific intent, the Dönmeh adhered to Tsevi and his successors. They maintained a certain degree of unity even after their removal in 1924 from Salonika, which had become their capital early on, to Turkey (where they are still present). Tsevi's conversion is understood to have been the model for their own, undertaken in imitation of his and intended to assist him in his attempt to defeat demonic forces associated with Islam by descending among them. There were, however, several different theologies and theologians of the Shabbatean sects, including some that did not convert to Islam or counsel conversion until long after the seventeenth century, and several that converted sincerely, whether to Christianity, to Islam, or to Turkish secular, progressive nationalism. All the sects retained a certain unity based in their history, their belief (or the memory of one) in Tsevi's divine role and destiny, and their practice of a number of rituals and customs from the late seventeenth century recalling Tsevi's passion and his liberationist, even antinomian, praxis. In general it may be more useful to consider the Dönmeh as a movement of revitalization, looking back to the *conversos* of Iberia, and as counterparts of their contemporaries, the Portuguese-Dutch Jews.

Among themselves the Dönmeh (Turkish: turners, converts) are known collectively as the *ma'aminim* (Hebrew, believers); few of the earlier sectarian groups—Izmirli (from Izmir), also known as *kabayeros* (knights); Yakubiler (followers of Tsevi's brother-in-law); Konyousos (followers of Tsevi's chief successor, Barukhya Russo Counio)—remained distinct after the rise of secular Turkey and the population transfer of 1924. The members of the groups occupied themselves as merchants, bureaucrats, and artisans and developed a great interest in progressive schooling, religion serving as moral instruction, and scientific training served by modern pedagogy. Basic beliefs (in the messiahship of Shabbetai Tsevi and in his "spiritual [antinomian] Torah" and its trinity), practices (spousal exchanges, consumption of ritually impure foods), and festivals (invented by Tsevi or commemorating deeds of his passion) have held the Dönmeh together to a certain degree. This cohesion has been assisted by bonds of secrecy and privacy and by the marginalization of the group from both Jewish and Islamic communities. Dönmeh attachment to progressive social politics has been of great importance and can be seen as arising from this marginalization.

The most important literature of the Dönmeh that remains from the early periods includes their prayer book, collections of praise-songs, and some homiletic material. The late nineteenth century witnessed the rise to prominence of Dönmeh in Ottoman Salonika. Dönmeh bankers and textile and tobacco merchants played a large role in global trade and finance; headed the city's Chamber of Commerce; founded influential progressive schools, literary journals, and architectural styles; and engaged in local and then imperial politics—serving as mayors, members of parliament, and ministers, and generally espousing modernization and, in time, secularization. Some Dönmeh became so committed to radical new philosophies and political ideas that they played an important role in the revolutionary movement that deposed the sultan in 1908 and laid the groundwork for the creation of the Republic of Turkey in 1923. At the same time, many remained faithful to ancestral Shabbatean traditions.

Because they were considered Muslims by the Greek government, the Dönmeh of Salonika were subject to deportation to Turkey as part of the population exchange of 1923–1924. Relying on their Jewish origins, some Dönmeh asked the Greek government to excuse them from the expulsion, as other Dönmeh approached Turkish officials with the same aim. Despite their protests, the estimated ten to fifteen thousand Dönmeh were compelled to abandon their native Salonika. Immediately following their arrival in Turkey in 1924, the Dönmeh faced a wave of controversy as Muslims sought to determine whether they were Jews or Muslims, foreigners or Turks. For over two decades, newspapers published sensationalized accounts of Dönmeh beliefs and practices. Throughout the 1930s many kept Shabbetai Tsevi's memory, traditions, and customs fully alive. Actively practiced customs included the recitation of passages from traditional Dönmeh literature—such as "*Shabtai Zvi, esperamos a ti*" (from the *kaddish*, as in the Dönmeh prayer book)—at the Festival of the Lamb held on the seashore, and at other Dönmeh feasts, fasts, burials, and festivals.

After World War II the Dönmeh managed to integrate into the mainstream of Turkish society, marrying into secularized Muslim families and almost entirely losing their distinctive religious beliefs and customs, other than rituals attending burial at predominantly Dönmeh cemeteries in Istanbul. At the same time, Dönmeh retained social ties among themselves by sending their children to the originally Salonikan Dönmeh schools relocated to Istanbul and serving on their boards, residing in the same neighborhoods in Istanbul, maintaining the textile and tobacco businesses and business relationships established in Salonika, and retaining membership in the same Masonic lodges.

Anti-Dönmeh journalism in Turkey has increased in intensity since the 1990s. Typically driven by anti-Semitic, populist, and religious motives, this writing has defined the Dönmeh community in ways that stress its alienation from Turkish social, political, and religious norms.

See Also Messianism; Shabbetai Tsevi.

Bibliography

Baer, Marc David. "Revealing a Hidden Community: Ilgaz Zorlu and the Debate in Turkey over the Dönme/Sabbatians." *Turkish Studies Association Bulletin* 23, no. 1 (Spring 1999): 68–75. An important review of the book by Zorlu listed below, and an updating of research on the Dönmeh.

Scholem, Gershom. "Doenmeh." In *Encyclopaedia Judaica,* edited by Cecil Roth and Geoffrey Wigoder, vol. 6. Jerusalem, 1971. Summarizes much of this scholar's work on the topic (with bibliography to that date) including his own essays and publications of Dönmeh literature and religion.

Zorlu, Ilgaz. *Evet, Ben Salanikliyim: Türkiye Sabetaycilik üstüne Makalaer.* Istanbul, 1998. A modern "confession."

Harris Lenowitz (2005)
Marc David Baer (2005)

DONNER, KAI. Finnish scholar Karl Reinhold (Kai) Donner (1888–1935) united British anthropology and Northern ethnography. Born into a Swedish-speaking family, Donner was educated in the religious liberalism and bilingualism that prevailed in Finnish universities at the beginning of the twentieth century. His father, Otto Donner, was a professor of Sanskrit and comparative linguistics at the University of Helsinki; in 1883 he founded the Finno-Ugric Society, a nationalistic organization that studied the languages, ethnology, and history of Finno-Ugric peoples.

In 1908 Donner's studies in Budapest introduced him to Hungarian research in Finno-Ugristics (Hungarian is an Ugric language). Three years later he went to Cambridge University, where he became familiar with British anthropological models. This is significant because until the turn of the twentieth century Finnish scholars wrote mainly in German and rarely ventured outside the spheres of German and Russian science.

The ranking scholars of British anthropology at that time were A. C. Haddon and W. H. R. Rivers in Cambridge, who established the first British anthropological field laboratory on the western Pacific islands of the Torres Strait. Other leading lights were Charles G. Seligman, Edward Westermarck, and Bronislaw Malinowski in London, as well as Robert R. Marrett and Alfred R. Radcliffe-Brown at Oxford. The Torres Strait study launched functionalism (a theory that emphasized the interdependence and importance of institutions and behavioral patterns—particularly cultural practices—for a society's survival) as a method for conducting field work; this became Donner's model for his studies in Siberia.

Donner's association with these British anthropologists was formative and through them he learned the basics of ethnological field work. Haddon introduced him to Malinowski; Sir James Frazer, another Cambridge fellow and author of the seminal *Golden Bough,* donated his portable grammophone for Donner's linguistic studies. Donner was also deeply influenced by Rivers's article "The Genealogical Method as Anthropological Inquiry," published in a 1910 issue of *Sociological Review*: "I have had only positive results from its use among the Samoyeds and later on in Finland," he remarked. "It will be the key to the gate to the world already gone. It makes [it] possible to remember in a touchable manner the old beliefs and customs, ancestral worship."

Donner made two expeditions to Siberia, the first a two-year venture, begun in August of 1911, in which he travelled from Tomsk to Narym, Tymskoye and in the settlements by Ob and Tym rivers—the main areas of the Samoyedic peoples, who numbered about 18,000 at that time. Donner's second tour took place in 1914, during World War I and the Russification of the Samoyeds he had met during his first tour.

Donner categorized his Siberian field data according to the typological and genealogical models he learned in Britain. He was particularly influenced by Haddon's 1908 publication *The Study of Man,* which defines ethnology as "description of a man, a tribe, people in a smaller or larger area" demanding special characteristics from the scholar. Donner used these methods in Siberia even though he believed that the Samoyeds had little collective knowledge about their ancestors. Haddon's genealogical methods, for example, helped explain the inheritance of shamanic prestige symbols in a Ket River clan that Donner described in 1915. He also used anthropometry (the collection, correlation, and comparison of human body measurements) as a research tool.

Between his two Siberian treks he took part in a research seminar led by Westermarck at the University of Helsinki, where he was encouraged to write his doctoral thesis on the Samoyed. Although there was no department of religious history at the university, Heikki Paasonen (1865–1919), a Finno-Ugrist, suggested that Donner write his dissertation on comparative religion instead of philology (the study of languages and literature) as he had intended.

Donner's fieldwork followed Castrén's footsteps as faithfully as possible, although he sought to disprove some of the less-likely hypotheses proposed by Castrén—whose nationalistic fervor had sought too many relatives on the Finnish family tree. Donner believed, for example, that Castrén's inclusion of Uralic and Mongolian-Turkic peoples in the Finno-Ugric family was wrong. While they shared some common vocabulary, this was due to their long-lasting contacts in Siberia.

Donner's field notes are also interesting from a historical perspecitve. On his journeys he met Russian officials, Orthodox missionaries, European emigrants, as well as other Finns who were merchants, ministers, and even prisoners in Siberia. His memoir *Siperian samojedien keskuudessa vuosina 1911–1913 ja 1914* (Among the Siberian Samoyed), first published in 1915, was republished in 1979 with a preface written by his son Jörn Donner (b. 1932), a filmmaker and author.

See Also Finno-Ugric Religions.

Bibliography

Donner, Kai. *A Samoyede Epic.* Helsingfors, 1913.

Donner, Kai. *Bei den Samojeden in Sibirien.* Stuttgart, 1926.

Donner, Kai. *Ethnological Notes about the Yenisey-Ostyak (in the Turukhansk Region).* Suomalais-ugrilaisen seuran toimituksia, vol. 66. Helsinki, 1933.

Donner, Kai. *La Sibérie: La vie en Sibérie—Les temps anciens.* L'espèce humaine, vol. 6. Paris, 1946.

Donner, Kai. *Among the Samoyed in Siberia.* Translated by Rinehart Kyler and edited by Genevieve A. Highland. New Haven, 1954.

Donner, Kai. *Ketica: Materialen aus dem Ketischen oder Jenisseiostjakischen.* Suomalais-ugrilaisen seuran toimituksia, vol. 108. Helsinki, 1955.

Pentikäinen, Juha. "Northern Ethnography: On the Foundations of a New Paradigm." *Styles and Positions: Ethnographical Perspectives in Comparative Religion.* Comparative Religion 8. Helsinki, 2002.

Juha Pentikäinen (2005)

DOORWAYS See PORTALS

DOSTOEVSKY, FYODOR

DOSTOEVSKY, FYODOR (1821–1881), Russian novelist. Fyodor Mikhailovich Dostoevsky's childhood was spent in the constrained atmosphere of a Muscovite charity hospital, where his father served as a doctor. It was the murder of his father (1838) that was alleged by Freud to have determined the course of Dostoevsky's epilepsy. This theory is usually discounted, but there is no doubt about the epilepsy itself, nor about its capacity to inspire in its victim something of a "higher awareness." Early symptoms of the condition were experienced in 1849 during his first period of imprisonment. By this time the young Dostoevsky, a graduate of the Academy of Military Engineering in Saint Petersburg, had already established a reputation with some works of fiction, the earliest and most acclaimed of which was *Poor Folk* (1846).

But it was not for his writings that Dostoevsky had been arrested. His crime was having participated in a utopian-socialist discussion group. At a time of repression in the aftermath of the European revolutions of 1848, Dostoevsky and his fellow "conspirators" found themselves arbitrarily sentenced to death. Only minutes before the execution was the sentence commuted. The years of penal exile in Siberia that followed (four years of hard labor and four of military service in the ranks) could not efface the memory of the cynically contrived mock execution, and Dostoevsky was to return to this near experience of death more than once in his later fiction.

The penal exile itself provided ample material for a semidocumentary study of it, *Notes from the House of the Dead* (1860–1861), which was to be published on Dostoevsky's return to European Russia. Part of the book was to be serialized in the short-lived journal *Vremia,* which Dostoevsky founded with his brother (1861). Despite the suppression of this journal, Dostoevsky was to revert to journalism throughout the years to come in order to ensure a modest income. But the greater part of his rarely adequate income was derived from the serial publication of his novels and novellas in the well-established literary periodicals of the day.

It was in the second of Dostoevsky's own periodicals, *Epokha,* that the first of his major works appeared, *Notes from the Underground* (1864). This anguished work ushered in the period (and introduced some of the thematics) of the great novels. The majority of these novels were composed in western Europe, to which Dostoevsky withdrew to escape his creditors. He found it necessary to mortgage his writings for some time, much to his disadvantage. Only after completing abroad much of *Crime and Punishment* (1866), all of *The Idiot* (1868), and *The Possessed* (1871–1872) was Dostoevsky in a position to return to his homeland. *A Raw Youth* (1875) and the unfinished *The Brothers Karamazov* (1879–1880) were thus exceptional in being composed on Russian soil by this most Europhobic of Russian patriots. Even so, with rare exceptions (such as *The Gambler,* 1867) all the novels have a Russian setting.

This is not to say that the novels are restricted by their time and place, deeply rooted though they are in each. In the dismal byways of Dostoevsky's Saint Petersburg or his provincial towns, problems and myths with universal implications are encountered. The significance of suffering, the limitations of reason, and the importance of free will are debated as early as *Notes from the Underground.* Each of the major novels has moral and religious problems at its center. Yet answers to these problems are not necessarily to be expected. Rather (as one of Dostoevsky's characters urges in *The Idiot*), "it is the continuous and perpetual process of discovery [which is important], not the discovery itself." Dostoevsky does not set himself up as an arbitrator between the characters engaged in this process. Indeed, in *The Possessed* and *The Brothers Karamazov* he even abandons his role as narrator to "independent" surrogates.

It is one of these surrogates who notes that "reality strives toward fragmentation." The world of the novels is replete with disorientation and disorder. Yet in the privacy of his notebooks Dostoevsky still insists that there is or ought to be some "moral center" or "central idea." However eroded such a central idea may be, however obscured in the contemporary mind, merely to depict its erosion should not be sufficient for someone like himself who has progressed to his "hosanna" through what he describes as "a great crucible of doubt."

After his second marriage (1867), and especially in the last decade of his life, Dostoevsky gradually reverted to the Orthodox Christianity of his youth. Indeed, even in the darkest days of his exile, he had never abjured his residual loyalty to "the image of Christ," regardless (as he wrote in 1854) of whether it corresponded to the truth or not. Nor had he abandoned a certain faith in some kind of golden age, yet to be recaptured. But none of this was enough to overcome a deep-seated reluctance, an organic inability, to proceed with a didactic novel. The creative process inevitably involved him in the production of works that are multicentered and polyphonic in both their philosophical and psychological concerns.

Nevertheless, he continued to nurture the hope that he might one day "compel people to admit that a pure and ideal Christianity is not an abstraction, but a vivid reality, possibly near at hand; and that Christianity is the sole refuge of the Russian land from all its evils." Toward the end of his life it seemed that *The Brothers Karamazov* might prove the appropriate vehicle for such a demonstration. The saintly figure of the elder Zosima would be called upon to act as the principal spokesman of faith in the work. Thus, the spokesman was required to perform a task to which his author was ill-suited. Equally important, the faith that Dostoevsky invokes was curiously diluted, even secularized. Not that it fails to reflect a "process of discovery"—but necessarily a part of that process are the incisive arguments presented by Ivan Karamazov and his Grand Inquisitor, critics of the divine dispensation.

The Dostoevsky whom one emperor had seemingly sought to execute was to be offered a state funeral by another. The didacticism that had little opportunity to flourish in the novels had found an outlet in the brash and chauvinistic journalism of the writer's later years—hence at least some of the acclaim which accompanied him to his grave. But it was the reputation of a novelist who had given his readers an insight into his crucible of doubt which was to live on. Had he not taken pride in the fact that he "alone had brought out the tragedy of the underground"? It was a tragedy, he had noted in 1875, "which consists of suffering and immolation; of the awareness of that which is better, and of the inability to attain it."

BIBLIOGRAPHY

Generally recognized as an outstanding survey of Dostoevsky, and one written with considerable insight into his development as a religious thinker, is Konstantin Mochul'skii's *Dostoevsky: His Life and Work* (Princeton, 1967). Another wide-ranging survey is provided by Richard Peace, *Dostoyevsky: An Examination of the Major Novels* (Cambridge, U.K., 1971). This contains interesting material on the novelist's treatment of religious sectarians. Robert L. Jackson's *Dostoevsky's Quest for Form* (New Haven, 1966) is concerned with the subject's idealism and his reluctance to confine himself merely to the phenomena of everyday life. Malcolm V. Jones, in his *Dostoyevsky: The Novel of Discord* (London, 1976), discusses the centrifugal forces in the fiction with erudition and tact. The classic treatment of the novelist's polyphonic technique is Mikhail Bakhtin's *Problems of Dostoevsky's Poetics* (Ann Arbor, Mich., 1973). By contrast, L. A. Zander in *Dostoevsky* (London, 1948) argues that his subject is essentially a proponent of Orthodox Christianity. Less partisan is the useful study of *The Religion of Dostoevsky* by A. Boyce Gibson (London, 1973). The symposium *New Essays on Dostoyevsky*, edited by Malcolm V. Jones and Garth M. Terry (Cambridge, U.K., 1983), contains my analysis of the teachings attributed to the elder Zosima, "The Religious Dimension: Vision or Evasion? Zosima's Discourse in *The Brothers Karamazov*," pp. 139–168.

SERGEI HACKEL (1987)

DOUBLENESS. The prehistoric cultures of Europe used images of doubles to indicate potency or abundance. This can be seen in the frequent use of double images of caterpillars, crescents, eggs, seeds, spirals, snakes, phalli, and even goddesses. Dualism is also expressed by two lines on a figurine, or in the center of an egg, vulva, or seed, and by a double-fruit symbol resembling two acorns.

The exaggerated buttocks of Upper Paleolithic and Neolithic figurines (called "steatopygous" in the archaeological literature) are probably a metaphor of the double egg or breasts, that is, of intensified fertility or pregnancy. Such figurines usually have no indication of other anatomical details; the upper part of the body is totally neglected. An intensification of the meaning can be seen in whirls, snake coils, spirals, and lozenges engraved on the buttocks of figurines created during the Copper Age of east-central Europe (5500–3500 BCE). Obviously, the fat female posteriors that appear on prehistoric figurines had other than erotic significance or simple aesthetic purpose. They were, in fact, the actualization of a cosmogonic concept. Egg symbolism made manifest certain basic beliefs, hopes, and understandings concerning creation, life origins, and the birth process as well as reverence for supernatural potency, expressed by the doubling device, the "power of two."

A glyph formed by two ellipses connected at one end—a double grain or double fruit—appears on ceramics, seals, and megaliths throughout the duration of Old Europe (6500–3500 BCE). The sign may have been retained from the Upper Paleolithic period: a sign of two connected ovals that look much like buttocks can be seen in Magdalenian parietal art. Similar signs are engraved on Irish megaliths. The double-fruit glyph continued to be significant in Minoan ceramic art. By the middle Minoan period, it can be seen in association with a tree and a sprouting bud, incorporated in the hieroglyphic inscription on seals.

The mystique of the power of two lingers in European folk tradition, especially in the East Baltic countries, which have remained a repository of ancient beliefs and traditions. Latvians have preserved to this day the word *jumis* and the deity of the same name. The meaning of the word is "two things grown together into one unit," such as apples, potatoes, and so on. *Jumis* and *jumm*, Finnish and Estonian words considered to be ancient borrowings from the Baltic, mean "two things or beings joined together," "bundle of flax," and "divinity who gives wedding luck."

Twin ears of rye, barley, or wheat—a relatively rare phenomenon in nature—are a manifestation of *jumis*. When a double ear is found at harvest time, it is brought home by the reaper and put in a place of honor on the wall beside the table. In the following planting season, the *jumis* is mixed with the seed grain and sown in the field. *Jumis* is a force that increases wealth and prosperity, signified by double ears, double fruit, and double vegetables.

Neolithic images of the great goddess are frequently marked with two dashes over the hips, arm stumps, between the breasts, or on the pubic triangle. Often two horizontal or vertical lines are painted or incised across the face or a mask of the goddess. The double line also typically appears on mother and child figurines, which suggests that these lines may have connotations of resurgence and new life.

Double-headed goddesses convey the idea of twin birth on a cosmic plane. Figurines of "Siamese twins" are known throughout the Neolithic period and the Copper Age. The heads of these figurines are beaked and masked; the bodies are marked by chevrons, meanders, and crossbands. These attributes identify the image as a bird goddess. In Anatolia and the Agean area, two-headed figurines continue into the Archaic period of Greece. The twin aspect of the great goddess is also expressed by double-bodied or double-necked vessels from the early Bronze Age in the Aegean, Crete, and Malta.

SEE ALSO Baltic Religion; Dualism; Numbers; Prehistoric Religions; Twins.

BIBLIOGRAPHY

Butler, Michael. *Number Symbolism.* London, 1970.

Crawley, A. E. "Doubles." In *Encyclopaedia of Religion and Ethics*, edited by James Hastings, vol. 4. Edinburgh, 1911.

Schimmel, Annemarie. *Das Mysterium der Zahl: Zahlensymbolik im Kultur-Vergleich.* Cologne, 1984.

New Sources

Doniger, Wendy. *Splitting the Difference: Gender and Myth in Ancient Greece and India.* Chicago, 1999.

MARIJA GIMBUTAS (1987)
Revised Bibliography

DOUBT AND BELIEF. [*This entry is a philosophical discussion of the interrelation of doubt and belief in the Western tradition.*]

Doubt and skepticism, although popularly accounted antithetical to religious belief and alien to the religious attitude, are in fact inseparable from every deeply religious disposition. The fact that twentieth-century philosophical critique of religion focused on questions of meaning rather than on questions of truth (the usual preoccupation in the nineteenth century, when T. H. Huxley coined the term *agnostic*) does not at all diminish the importance of doubt as part of the intellectual process of religious belief. All authentic religious faith, indeed, may be viewed as a descant on doubt.

THE MEANING OF DOUBT. The word *doubt*, although often regarded as the opposite of *belief*, signifies primarily vacillation, perplexity, irresolution. These primary meanings are discoverable in the Latin word from which *doubt* is derived: *dubito*, which is grammatically the frequentative of the Old Latin *dubo*, from *duo* ("two"). To doubt means, therefore, to be of two minds, to stand at the crossroads of the mind. The regular German word for doubt (*Zweifel*, from *zwei*, "two") brings out the vacillating connotation more obviously than does the English word. In German, *Zweifelgeist* means "skepticism, the spirit of doubt," and *Er zweifelte was er tun sollte* means "He was in doubt what he should do"—that is, he was of two minds about it. The Greek *doiazō* ("I doubt") also exhibits this two-mindedness.

Doubt, therefore, is not to be equated with unbelief or disbelief but rather with a vacillation between the two opposites: unbelief and belief. In doubt there are always two propositions or theses between which the mind oscillates without resting completely in either. To the extent that religious people deprecate doubt, what they are deprecating must be indecision rather than unbelief, and what skeptics find praiseworthy in it must be not unbelief but a willingness to recognize two sides to a question. Doubt is the attitude of mind proper to the skeptic, who is by no means necessarily an unbeliever any more than a believer. The only serious reproach that either believer or unbeliever may justly direct to the skeptic is that of declining to make up his mind in one direction or the other—that is, a moral rather than an intellectual reproach.

MODES OF DOUBT. Doubt may be considered in three modes: an attitude of mind, a philosophical method, and a necessary ingredient in or component of belief.

1. The characteristic attitude both of the ancient Greek thinkers and of the Renaissance men who admired and followed them has doubt as one of its fundamental inspirations. (By *attitude* is meant here an inclination of the will.) That is, rather than conceiving philosophy as a way of showing this or that proposition or thesis to be such as to lead logically to a settled conviction, thinkers in this tradition insist upon an openness of mind sustained by an ongoing attitude of questioning. Even when inclining to one view or another, such thinkers will always not only pay homage to doubt as a methodological principle but will endeavor in practice to keep their minds constantly alert to the claims of both sides of every question: they will show a judicial rather than a prosecuting or defensive attitude. Such an attitude, to the extent that it is successful in terms of its own aims, is creative, engendering openness of the will as well as of the mind. Like all attitudes it is, of course, susceptible to deformity. It may be feigned, for instance, to disguise a moral unwillingness to reach a decision because of the implications of making such a commitment. That the attitude of doubt can lead to such a moral deformity or perversity is of itself, however, no argument against its salutariness or its integrity. It is an attitude that has sustained the greatest minds of all ages in human history; a notable exemplar is Socrates.
2. Doubt as a philosophical method is exhibited in the thought of many important thinkers. Celebrated instances include Augustine and Descartes. In Augustine's dictum "*Si fallor, sum*" ("If I doubt, I exist") and in the well-known Cartesian formula "*Cogito, ergo sum*" ("I think, therefore I am") are to be found intellectual assurances that in the act of doubting one's own existence is an awareness of that existence, since if one can catch oneself doubting, one cannot be doubting that one exists and so at least one can be certain of the proposition "I exist," whatever that proposition be taken to mean. Doubt, then, is a methodological point of departure as well as an implicate of all thought. Thinking, in the sense in which it is understood in this intellectual tradition, which goes far beyond any computerlike function of the human brain, entails doubting.
3. While both of the foregoing modes of doubt are relevant to questions of religious belief, that which most sharply illuminates an understanding of the nature of religious belief is the notion that doubt is an implicate of religious faith and therefore of the religious belief that formulates that faith. By taking the view that authentic religious faith does not entail blind, thoughtless belief but must always be accompanied by an element of doubt, we recognize that such faith and the belief that formulates it are in some way sustained by doubt, making doubt and belief as inseparable from each other as are, in the human body, the arteries and the veins. If one hopes to preserve the vigor and vivacity of one's thought, one must conserve in it the element of doubt that sustains it. Authentic religious faith, whatever it is, can never be as the schoolboy is said to have defined it: believing steadfastly what you know isn't true; instead, it must always entail doubt. Some religious philosophers in the modern existentialist tradition, such as Kierkegaard, Unamuno, and Marcel, have emphasized that a faith unshaken by doubt cannot be authentic faith at all but is a mere blind nodding without either intellectual content or moral decision. I have called faith a descant on doubt, by which I mean, of course, that it rises beyond the doubt that is at the same time its necessary presupposition: one cannot have a descant with nothing to descant upon, nor can a descant ever leave the rest of the music permanently behind it.

Contemporary religious thinkers in the tradition of Kierkegaard talk of the "leap of faith," a phrase that sometimes exasperates their hearers. How does one jump from doubt to belief without injuring, not to say destroying, the integrity of the belief? Before dealing with this vital question, we must first clarify the relation between faith and belief, more particularly as these terms arise in religious contexts.

FAITH AND BELIEF. In religious literature faith and belief often have been identified with each other. In medieval usage the Latin *fides* ("faith") generally means both. Even in the New Testament the distinction between the two is not entirely clear, for the Greek word *pistis* ("faith") often has the older connotation of intellectual conviction alongside the notion of trust, the bending of one's whole being to God in complete confidence in his infinite goodness and in his ability to guard and to guide one's entire life in the best possible way. The thirteenth-century Thomas Aquinas, who became a quasi-official spokesman of the Roman Catholic church, and even Martin Luther, leader of the sixteenth-century Reformation, when they wrote of *fides*, often meant intellectual assent as much as an act of the will. The classic Lutheran dogmatic treatises usually distinguished three elements in *fides: notitia* ("knowledge"), *assensus* ("assent"), and *fiducia* ("trust"). By this they implied that both intellect and will are involved in *fides;* nevertheless, following Luther himself, they recognized *fiducia* as the principal element and the others as subordinate to it.

In much Christian literature, however, not least among heirs of the Reformation, the term *faith* is invested with a volitional connotation and *belief* with an intellectual one. The distinction is useful, for faith has an ethical content, with implicates of courage and perseverance that are irrelevant to intellectual assent to any proposition or thesis, religious or otherwise. Nevertheless, faith also entails a metaphysical stance. The object of faith is an "is," not merely an "ought to be." It is the postulated real, so that no matter to what extent authentic faith may be called volitional rather than cognitive, an act of the will rather than an intellectual affirmation, it must be somehow connected with the intellectual activity by which it comes to be formulated. Since, as we have seen, thought itself implies doubt, every assertion of belief that is not to be dubbed mere credulity presupposes an intellectual choice between two alternative possibilities. And since, as we have seen, doubt is an implicate of belief and all authentic faith has in it an intellectual element of belief, then doubt must be called an implicate of faith, no matter how much the volitional element in faith be emphasized.

Beliefs, moreover, cannot be held in isolation: they are part of a creedal system that may be called authentic only to the extent that they are not mere uninformed opinions or thoughtless presuppositions. As soon, therefore, as we start developing either faith or reason, the question of accepting this belief and rejecting that one inevitably arises. Without the coherence that is thereby achieved, one would seen be in a position like that parodied in apothegms such as "I believe there is no God and Our Lady is his mother." So although faith is an act of the will, it must be expressed not only in a particular belief but by a whole system of beliefs, each of which is believed to illumine the others. Hence there is in the mainstream of Western theological tradition the tendency to set forth creedal statements that call for believers' assent, as does, for example, the Nicene Creed. In Indian thought and practice, by contrast, one may hold one's own view (*darśana*) without repudiating that of another that seems logically incompatible with it. That attitude, however, arises from an emphasis on the inadequacy of all formulations of truth *(dharma)*. The West, except in the more philosophical types of religious literature and in the more mystical varieties of religious experience, has been less skeptical about the capacity of religious symbols to portray the realities of the spiritual dimension of being.

Faith, although it entails an intellectual element of belief, plays a special and often misunderstood role in the Bible and therefore in all biblically oriented Jewish and Christian thought. A classic series of illustrations of the fundamental religious significance of faith is provided by the author of the *Letter to the Hebrews* (*Heb.* 11), who points to the actions of Abraham, Noah, and other biblical figures, upholding them as exemplars of the courage of those who have lived by faith. Such faith is typified in Abraham's going out "not knowing whither he went" (*Heb.* 11:8). It is closely akin to trust. We should note carefully, however, that although Abraham's courage may have been boundless, his ignorance was by no means absolute. He was not totally uninformed. He did not wander forth haphazardly as in a game of blindman's buff. Yet, considerable as his knowledge presumably was, his act entailed both great personal courage and a firm personal conviction that he could rely on the guidance and guardianship of God, in whom he reposed his trust and to whom he dedicated both his courage and his intelligence, using all the willpower and the knowledge at his disposal.

The "knight of faith," whom Kierkegaard depicts in *Fear and Trembling*, engages in a paradoxical movement that presupposes and transcends the "purely human" courage that mere renunciation of the world demands. His is a uniquely humble courage that makes him perfectly obedient to God. Faith is "the greatest and hardest" enterprise in which one can engage, entailing as it does a leap beyond even the highest ethical decisions of which anyone is capable. From all rational standpoints the leap is absurd, running counter to everything to which human wisdom directs our attention as reliable guideposts to right decision and noble action: common sense, logic, and experience. In his journals, Kierkegaard expressly asserts that "faith's conflict with the world is a battle of character. . . . The man of faith is a person of character who, unconditionally obedient to God, grasps it as a character-task that one is not to insist upon comprehending" (*Journals and Papers*, vol. 2, pp. 13–14). Kierkegaard was by no means an enemy of either the aesthetic or the intellectual or of the ethical life of man; his concern was to show the uniqueness of faith as a category transcending all other modes of human consciousness.

This distinctiveness that Kierkegaard saw in faith has warranty in the New Testament, from which he drew his principal inspiration. Through such faith the Christian is saved (*Eph.* 2:8) and made righteous in the sight of God (*Rom.* 5:1). Inseparable though faith is from belief, it is not to be equated with it. It has a quality that distinguishes it from every other activity of mind and will. Nevertheless, having recognized that distinctiveness, we must now explore further the relation of faith to whatever cognitive status can be assigned to belief.

Prevalent but erroneous is the notion that faith, especially in the tradition of the Protestant reformers, excludes claim to knowledge of God. Hence faith is often contrasted with sight. In the teaching of the Christian school at Alexandria, faith tended to be treated as a vestibule to knowledge, a prolegomenon to a Christian gnosis. By contrast, the reformers glorified living by faith. Yet the French reformer Calvin expressly states: "Faith consists in the knowledge of God [*cognitio Dei*] and of Christ" (*Institutes* 3.2.5). He is not claiming knowledge of God as God is in himself (*apud se*); he does mean that we know him as he is in his dealings with us (*erga nos*). Faith, then, ever for so doughty a champion of its volitional character, has a cognitive element in it. Indeed, as good theologians no less than great mystics have always seen, faith yields a kind of knowledge, a gradual unfolding of awareness of God in human experience, apart from which awareness faith could not be indefinitely sustained. This awareness of that to which the name God is given is formulated in a set of beliefs that express in one way or another the stance to which faith leads the person who exercises it. Faith, practical and volitional as it is, is the means by which the knight of faith actually arrives at what he comes to call communion with (that is, entailing knowledge of) God. Just as we learn to drive or skate or play the piano less from books than by doing the thing, so through faith we arrive at the cognitive element to which it leads and is expressed in a set of beliefs.

Human knowledge is always limited and subject to revision, except in the case of mathematics, which is a closed system, a vast tautology that is indispensable as an instrument in scientific inquiry yet incapable by itself of yielding new information. Knowledge of the empirical world, based on observation and experiment, can never yield certainty. As Kant showed, we cannot know the "thing-in-itself." Doubt is therefore inseparable from all inquiry into and discoveries about the empirical world. Yet through advancement in the sciences we do have a better grasp of the world around us than did our primitive ancestors. We would not propose to go back to our forebears' view that the earth is flat with a blue dome of sky above it, but we must be prepared to doubt that our present knowledge of astronomy is irreformable and to recognize that a thousand years hence it, too, may seem primitivistic. When the knight of faith, whose adventures take him to a dimension beyond the empirical world as commonly understood, expresses his faith in a creedal statement, he can claim only a kind of knowledge. Many philosophical objections attend his claim. For instance, has he merely experienced a psychological state within himself, or has he in any sense encountered the ground of existence, the ultimate reality? Or, again, might he have encountered God through the superego of his own psyche? He can never be consistently and constantly sure; yet his faith, ever challenged by such questions, survives the challenges. When the authentic believer goes on to proclaim his belief "in" God, he is speaking from experience, as is the swimmer who says he believes "in" swimming and knows that he knows what he is talking about.

Since the knight of faith is engaged in a practical, not a theoretical, inquiry, his method, like the method of the sciences, is inductive. The inductive method used so habitually and extensively in modern science entails making hypotheses and subjecting them to tests that result in their verification or falsification. While the knight of faith cannot verify or falsify the beliefs that express his faith in the same way that the scientist tests his hypotheses, his procedure is in some important respects analogous. As the creative scientist invests his time and may stake his reputation on the eventual verification of his hypothesis, so the knight of faith stakes his life and his final destiny on his. Although he cannot hope to provide a definitive, assent-compelling verification of his faith here and now, the claim implicit in his faith is verifiable or falsifiable in the long run. Such faith entails risk. It is, as Pascal saw, a gamble; yet it is by no means a mere idle gamble, for it is informed by one's whole interpretation of life, as the scientist's hypothesis is no mere guess, but is founded on the whole range of his scientific experience and inquiry.

We have seen that in the thought of the Middle Ages faith (*fides*) was generally equated with belief. The great thinkers of the thirteenth century were much more familiar with deductive methods of reasoning than with inductive ones. Despite the foundations for inductive methods that were laid by original medieval minds such as Robert Grosseteste, Roger Bacon, and Johannes Duns Scotus, medieval science did not advance as physics, chemistry, and biology have advanced in recent times. The medieval men certainly did not lack powers of observation. They made astonishingly perceptive discoveries and invented many ingenious technological tools. They were hampered, however, by not taking seriously enough those inductive methods by which modern science has made its advances. For the same reason they tended to underestimate the meaning and power of faith as the volitional, practical, risk-taking catalyst of authentic awareness of God, apart from which both the beliefs and the doubts that spring from it must lack authenticity. This peculiar role of faith was expressed in the nineteenth century by John Henry Newman. In his *Apologia pro vita sua* he reports that it was not logic that carried him on any more than it is the mercury in the barometer that changes the weather: "The whole man moves; paper logic is but the record of it."

The difference between the medieval and the post-Renaissance understanding of the nature of faith may be due also, at least in part, to a general change of outlook that the Renaissance brought about in respect to the nature of man. In medieval thought the will was treated as but one of several "faculties," or powers of the soul. Such was the change wrought by the Renaissance that a tendency developed to see the will as virtually synonymous with the whole person. In this view the whole person is the agent; hence the act of faith comes to be seen more and more as an act of the will.

BELIEF AND KNOWLEDGE. The twentieth-century philosopher Bertrand Russell, in one of his best books, *Human Knowledge* (London, 1948), reminds us that "all knowledge is in some degree doubtful, and we cannot say what degree of doubtfulness makes it cease to be knowledge, any more than we can say how much loss of hair makes a man bald" (p. 516). He goes on to say that all words outside mathematics and logic are vague. After pointing out that empiricism as a theory of knowledge is inadequate, though less so than any previous one, he concludes that "all human knowledge is uncertain, inexact, and partial" (p. 527).

Russell's thought on this subject represents a development of the empiricist view championed in the eighteenth century by David Hume. According to Hume all human knowledge is reducible to more or less strong beliefs. Although some modern philosophers have argued for a clear distinction between knowledge and belief, they show only that it may be convenient to dub certain very strong beliefs knowledge in order to distinguish them from other beliefs that are weak. While I may feel so certain about some beliefs that I wish to assign to them a special place among my beliefs and so call them knowledge, I can never claim to be entirely certain that I have examined all possible alternatives, if only because I cannot know all the possible alternatives. When belief in a geocentric universe was fashionable, many must have felt confident that such a universe was demonstrable beyond a shadow of a doubt. If anyone doubted it, he could be asked to follow the movement of the sun from its rising to its setting and so be shown conclusively that the sun moved; yet that conclusion would be wrong according to today's reckoning.

For practical purposes one may choose to call one's strongest beliefs knowledge, but it can never be knowledge in the sense of an infallible grasp of truth or an acquaintance with reality. Even to say "I know I am in pain" is not an exception since it adds nothing to saying "I am in pain." If I did not know myself to be in pain, I could not be in pain; and if I were in pain, I could not have neglected to notice it. Of course I feel pain; but to say "I know" is to claim knowledge of what pain is, and this I cannot properly claim. Nor could such a claim to know result in any objective knowledge at all. As my friend you would presumably trust my word; nevertheless, you would be entitled to disbelieve me. John Austin in his essay "Other Minds" (*Proceedings of the Aristotelian Society*, supp. vol. 20, 1946) recognized this by pointing out that saying "I know" registers the highest possible cognitive claim in a form that authorizes someone to rely on the statement, so that it functions in a way similar to "I promise." Thus the claim to know is no more than a strident way of asserting a particular belief.

It is one thing to contend that everyone has the right to be sure of his beliefs; it is another thing to affirm that the beliefs are justified as claims to knowledge. By claiming to know, I would claim—judiciously or rashly—to have no doubt. If I affirm that something is a known fact, I am contending that no one has any need or any right to doubt it. No alleged facts, however, can be said to be so indubitable, and none, therefore, is so indisputable. When in creedal statements such as the Nicene Creed or the so-called Apostles' Creed we use the traditional "I believe" or "We believe," we exhibit the characteristically religious disposition of openness and its implication of the possibility of doubt. This doubt may be transcended by faith, yet the faith is meaningless apart from it. Perceptive, then, was the poet Alfred Tennyson's observation that more faith lives in honest doubt than "in half the creeds"; for unless the believer's affirmation recognizes the possibility of doubt, his faith has no vitality. The absence of doubt is the height of irreligion. Both the will to believe, which the psychologist and philosopher William James popularized in the late nineteenth century, and the will to doubt, which Bertrand Russell said he would prefer to preach, are necessary for a lively faith. When the authentic believer says "I believe," he omits a hidden qualifier—"*Nevertheless*, I believe." For if there can be nothing (outside the tautologies of logic and mathematics) that justifies a claim to certainty, then doubt is proper to every belief. Authentic belief does not sidestep doubt. On the contrary, when one seriously intends to live by faith, one does not at all claim that the formulation of that faith is adequate or irreformable.

NIHILISM AND CERTAINTY. The role of doubt in belief can be clarified by a glance at two extremes: nihilism and certainty. Nihilism (from the Latin *nihil*, "nothing") consists in the dogmatic tendency to deny not only the existence of God but the permanence of any entity. According to such a view one can therefore say nothing that is absolutely true of anything since no claims to truth have any objective grounds. A classical exponent of nihilism in its intellectual aspect is Gorgias in Plato's dialogue of that name. In contrast to the earlier philosopher Protagoras, who held that "man is the measure of all things" (i.e., truth is relative to persons and circumstances), Plato's Gorgias taught that there can be no truth at all. On the practical or ethical side the nihilist denies all "higher" and "objective" values. In the nineteenth century the German philosopher Friedrich Nietzsche held that the interpretation of existence that Christianity bequeathed to Europe was fundamentally a life-negating pessimism. A particular form of nihilism emerged in Russia. Mikhail Bakunin (1814–1876) taught that society's only hope lies in its destruction, while, even more radically, Dmitrii Pisarev (1840–1868) taught that society is so evil that its destruction is a good in itself. Existentialism, by contrast, is not necessarily nihilistic, although some forms of it (e.g., those of Jean-Paul Sartre and Albert Camus) have nihilistic elements in them.

Certainty is a peculiarly difficult concept. After the Renaissance, John Locke, George Berkeley, and David Hume all paved the way for Kant's demonstration that we can have no certain knowledge of the "thing-in-itself." Noteworthy is the fact that down to the present century the papal index of prohibited books included these writers only in respect to those of their works that cast doubt on the possibility of certain knowledge. Although from Augustine to Thomas the medieval thinkers had discussed the conditions of certain knowledge, all of them held that at least some kind of knowledge is possible. Otherwise, how else could one know, for instance, that God exists? Modern thinkers, however, have generally been reluctant to recognize the possibility of absolute certainty except in the realm of logical and mathematical relationships that are (as we have seen) tautologies. Russell distinguished three kinds of claims to certainty: (1) logical, or mathematical, certainty—for example, if we grant that man is a rational animal, we may be certain that by implication man is an animal; (2) epistemological certainty, according to which a proposition is credible in the highest degree as a result of the abundance of evidence adduced for it—for example, we can be certain that the earth moves around the sun; and (3) psychological certainty, which occurs when a person merely feels no doubt about the truth of a proposition—for example, if after having known you for two minutes I were to say, "I am an excellent judge of people, and I know for certain that you are not to be trusted."

THE ROLE OF DOUBT IN AUTHENTIC FAITH AND BELIEF. Superficial critics of religion tend to ask, "How genuine is the believer's belief?" Such a question never yields—nor could it ever yield—any satisfactory answer. The questioner, having taken care to steer between the Scylla of nihilism and the Charybdis of a claim to certainty, would more fruitfully formulate the question by asking, "How genuine is the doubt behind the belief?" For when a believer says, "In spite of *x*, I believe *y*," that which is most likely to determine the significance of *y* is knowledge of the content to be assigned to *x*.

Doubt is a profound expression of humility. Without the humility that is and always has been at the root of all creative philosophical and scientific inquiry from Socrates onward, pretensions to religious faith are shown for what they are: at best a caricature, at worst a mockery, of religion. For humility is not only the virtue that corresponds to the vice of pride—which according to the teachings of all the great religions of the world is the fundamental obstacle to spiritual perceptivity; it is also closely connected with love, which is in Christian teaching the spring of all virtues. So faith and love respectively have as their implicates doubt and humility. If humility be radical enough it can become the best means of access to God, who "resisteth the proud, but giveth grace unto the humble" (*Jas.* 4:6). We may also say with E.-Alexis Preyre that "the man whom doubt, pushed to its extreme consequences, has led to total indetermination may 'find' God or not. But if he find God, the faith of that man is immovable" (*À l'extrême du scepticisme*, Paris, 1947, p. 168).

Laughter is likewise relevant to the spirit of humility and doubt. To be able to laugh at oneself is surely the hallmark of humility. Neither the religious fanatic nor the antireligious propagandist is likely to be able to do so, and so neither can ever laugh lovingly about religion. The mirth that springs from self-forgetfulness is a potent instrument in the attainment of religious insight, for it springs from deep humility and a childlike love that have matured into intellectual openness and awe before the mystery of being. That is impossible apart from doubt.

Faith, to have any value at all, emerges in personal encounter with divine being: "*Scio cui credidi*" ("I know whom I have believed"; *2 Tm.* 1:12). In childhood we learn to trust those who surround us with love. In due course we discover that, like all human beings, they, too, have their limitations. The deeply religious person, however, claims to have encountered the being in whom alone such trust may be placed without reserve, and so such a person sets no limits on the faith that issues from the encounter. What such a person may and should question is what precisely the encounter signifies and how it is to be interpreted. If the faith does not entail any doubt at all, surely it is a straw in the wind.

Moreover, without a willingness to doubt, religious tolerance is impossible. True, religious tolerance is not in itself the mark of authentic faith, for it may spring from mere indifference to or ignorance of the cardinal issues of the religious consciousness; but a faith that is fundamentally intolerant of any expressions of religion other than its own merely reveals its lack of confidence and the trivial nature of its thrust. Genuinely religious persons, whatever their beliefs, are always thoroughly impressed by the mystery of faith. The tendency to explain rather than to contemplate mystery is the vice of much popular, institutional religion and has immensely contributed to the disunity of Christendom as well as to the maintenance of barriers between one religion and another. The apocalyptic literature of religion unfolds the presence of mystery; it does not purport to explain it. Genuine religion is always full of wonder and therefore full of doubt, while irreligion is wonderless. With wonderless belief the devotee can offer only wonderless love, which is tantamount to blasphemy since it entails a casualness such as one might properly express in saying, for instance, "Of course I love candy, doesn't everyone?" Such religion, shorn of doubt, lacking humility, and therefore loveless, surely reveals its own ignorance and depravity, for it expresses a mere narcissistic looking at oneself in a mirror rather than an outpouring of love to the source and ground of being, apart from which religion is indeed vain.

SEE ALSO Enlightenment, The; Epistemology; Existentialism; Faith; Intuition; Knowledge and Ignorance; Logical Positivism; Philosophy, articles on Philosophy and Religion, Philosophy of Religion; Skeptics and Skepticism; Truth.

BIBLIOGRAPHY

The classic source on doubt as a philosophical method is René Descartes's *Discourse on Method* (especially part 3). For a discussion of a "doubtful faith" that can partake of rational checks and balances yet allow beliefs that go beyond theoretical knowledge, see Immanuel Kant's *Critique of Judgment* (especially section 91). Another classical treatment of the nature of belief is Blaise Pascal's *Pensées.* Søren Kierkegaard's singularly important perceptions on doubt and belief are scattered throughout his works, but especially important are his *Journals and Papers,* 7 vols., edited and translated by Howard V. Hong and Edna H. Hong, assisted by Gregor Malantschuk (Bloomington, Ind., 1967–1978) and his *Either/Or,* 2 vols., translated by David F. Swenson, Lillian M. Swenson, and Walter Lowrie, with revisions and foreword by Howard A. Johnson (Princeton, 1959). John Henry Newman discusses belief in terms of an "illative" sense in *An Essay in Aid of a Grammar of Assent* (1870; reprint, with an introduction by Étienne Gilson, New York, 1955) and in his *Apologia pro vita sua,* 2d ed. (1865; reprint, New York, 1964). On the meaninglessness of "radical" doubt, see G. E. Moore's "The Refutation of Idealism," reprinted in *Philosophical Studies* (London, 1922); "A Defence of Common Sense," in *Philosophical Papers* (New York, 1959); and *Some Main Problems of Philosophy* (New York, 1953), especially chapter 1. Frederick R. Tennant's theory of belief and faith is expounded in his *Philosophical Theology,* 2 vols. (Cambridge, U.K., 1928), especially volume 1, chapter 11, and in his *The Nature of Belief* (London, 1943), especially chapter 6. Martin C. D'Arcy, S.J., in *The Nature of Belief* (London, 1931), gives an account consonant with the Thomist tradition. Also important are Dorothy Emmet's *The Nature of Metaphysical Thinking* (London, 1945) and John Hick's *Faith and Knowledge,* 2d ed. (Ithaca, N.Y., 1966). In several of my books, notably *Christian Doubt* (London, 1951) and *God beyond Doubt* (Philadelphia, 1966), I have discussed faith as a descant on doubt.

New Sources

Bookchin, Murray. *Re-Enchanting Humanity: A Defense of the Human Spirit against Anti-humanism, Misanthropy, Mysticism and Primitivism.* London, 1995.

Gellner, Ernest. *Reason and Culture: The Historic Role of Rationality and Rationalism.* Malden, Mass., 1992.

Gratzer, Walter. *The Undergrowth of Science: Delusion, Self-Deception, and Human Frailty.* New York, 2000.

Howard-Snyder, Daniel, and Paul Moser, eds. *Divine Hiddenness: New Essays.* New York, 2002.

Kitcher, Philip. *The Advancement of Science without Legend; Objectivity without Illusions.* New York, 1993.

Shermer, Michael. *How We Believe: The Search for God in an Age of Science.* New York, 1999.

Wilson, A. N. *God's Funeral: The Decline of Faith in Western Civilization.* New York, 1999.

Wilson, David Sloan. *Darwin's Cathedral: Evolution, Religion, and the Nature of Society.* Chicago, 2002.

GEDDES MACGREGOR (1987)
Revised Bibliography

DOV BER OF MEZHIRICH (c. 1704–1772), Hasidic teacher and leader of the movement from 1760. A scholar and an ascetic qabbalist from his youth, Dov Ber sensed a lack in the rigorous routine of study, fasting, and self-mortification that provided the standards for intense Jewish spirituality in his day. Tradition has it that he was a physically frail man, rendered so in part by the voluntary self-denial of his early years.

Toward the middle of the eighteenth century, Dov Ber came under the influence of Yisraʾel ben Eliʿezer (1700–1760), the Besht, a wandering healer and folk teacher and the central figure of a spiritual revival movement that had met with some modest success among Jews in Podolia. The Besht, though a person of significantly less rabbinic learning than Dov Ber, was a natural mystic and a charismatic personality who probably had mastered the supranormal powers of perception. Their meeting transformed Dov Ber's life. The Besht taught a religion of divine immanence, of the palpable presence of God in each place, each moment, and every human soul. In this teaching Dov Ber felt his own religious life come alive, and he was liberated by it from the excessive demands of his earlier asceticism.

While the death of the Besht occasioned a struggle for leadership in the nascent movement, most of the master's disciples followed Dov Ber as he moved the center of Hasidic teaching westward to Volhynian Mezhirich, where he served as preacher *(maggid).* In the twelve years of his leadership, he attracted to Hasidism a dazzling group of young seekers, many of whom were to become important teachers, leaders, and authors in their own right. These include such well-known Hasidic figures as Menaḥem Mendel of Vitebsk, Shneʾur Zalman of Lyady, Levi Yitsḥaq of Berdichev, Elimelekh of Lizhensk, and Aharon of Karlin. It was Dov Ber who sent them forth to spread the Hasidic message throughout the Jewish communities of eastern Europe, and it is largely due to his impact that Hasidism became a far-flung and important force in Jewish history. His death in 1772 occurred just as the controversy and bans against the Ḥasidim were first being issued by the rabbinical authorities.

Dov Ber was a mystic intoxicated by the single idea of *devequt* ("attachment to God") as a return to the state of primal nothingness. He taught a panentheistic doctrine that bordered on acosmism: the transcendent God also fills all the worlds; his life force is the only true vitality in all of being. The outer human self as well as the exterior appearance of all reality are the infinitely varied garb of God. As the devotee learns to transcend such externals, he will find only the One, that nothing that is in fact the only Being. Paradoxically, this highly abstract immanentism was combined frequently with entirely personalistic religious metaphors. God is often described by Dov Ber as a father who reduces the intensity of his presence in the world, a process called *tsimtsum,* the way a patient parent lessens the complexity of a concept while trying to impart it to a beloved child.

Much of Dov Ber's work focuses on issues of devotion. He taught that proper prayer must be for the sake of the Shekhinah (the exiled divine presence) and that supplication for one's own sake was selfish. Prayer as practiced in the Mezhirich circle was an ecstatic ascent to *devequt,* with the externals of worship successively cast aside as the worshiper, even while continuing to recite the prescribed liturgy, basked in the glow of God's presence. The heights of such prayer bordered on the prophetic; moments passed in which the worshiper's own voice was silenced as "the Shekhinah spoke from his mouth."

Unlike earlier Jewish mystics, who seemed to shy away from unitive formulations in discussing their experiences, Dov Ber freely advocated union with the divine. The human soul, wholly identified with *shekhinah,* the lowest of the ten divine emanations, had to return to *ḥokhmah,* or primordial wisdom, the highest of the ten and often called by the name *Ein,* representing the divine *nihil.* In this act of mystical self-annihilation, man served as a channel by which all the divine energy released in creation was reunited with its source, effecting a foretaste of ultimate redemption.

In Dov Ber's teaching, the messianic urgency that characterizes much of the earlier Qabbalah is set aside or "neutralized"; the immediate and highly individual act of *devequt* seems to mitigate the need for the long-range and collective striving for *tiqqun,* or cosmic redemption. This neutralization was also made possible by a vision that denied the ultimate reality of evil, considered an illusion that stood as a temporary barrier to our sight of the good.

Dov Ber's teachings were edited by his students and published after his death in *Maggid devarav le-Ya'aqov* (1784), *Or Torah* (1804), and *Or ha-emet* (1899). He is also frequently quoted throughout the many writings of his disciples, and his dominant influence is felt throughout the later Hasidic literature.

Bibliography

Dov Ber's *Maggid devarav le-Ya'aqov* has been published in a critical edition by Rivka Schatz Uffenheimer (Jerusalem, 1976). His other works are available in reprinted traditional editions. While no work of Dov Ber's as such has been translated into English, the reader can obtain an idea of his teachings from the works of his disciple Menaḥem Naḥum of Chernobyl, *Upright Practices* and *The Light of the Eyes,* translated by me (both, New York, 1982). Dov Ber's thought is the chief subject of Rivka Schatz Uffenheimer's important study *Ha-Ḥasidut ke-misṭiqah* (Jerusalem, 1968). For biography, see volume 1 of Samuel A. Horodetzky's *Ha-Ḥasidut ve-ha-ḥasidim* (Tel Aviv, 1951), pp. 75ff.

New Sources

Goldstein, Niles Elliot. *Forests of the Night: The Fear of God in Early Hasidic Thought.* Northvale, N.J., 1996.

Kushner, Lawrence Square. "Bratslav and Mezritch: The Two Poles of Jewish Spirituality." In *What Kind of God? Essays in Honor of Richard L. Rubenstein,* edited by Betty Rogers Rubenstein and Michael Berenbaum, pp. 357–366. Lanham, Md., 1995.

Schatz Uffenheimer, Rivka. *Hasidism as Mysticism: Quietistic Elements in Eighteenth Century Hasidic Thought.* Translated by Jonathan Chipman. Princeton, N.J. and Jerusalem, 1993.

Arthur Green (1987)
Revised Bibliography

DOVES

See BIRDS

DRAGONS.

The etymology of the term *dragon* (from the ancient Greek *drakōn* and the Latin *draco, -onis*) points to serpents, for the Greek term means "serpent," and it refers to real snakes as well as to mythical snakes or snakelike figures; the Latin term may also refer to actual serpents. By dragons we mean mythical creatures shaped like serpents or with serpent features, and often endowed with features or parts belonging to various animals (a body like a lizard's or a crocodile's, with a feline's or a reptile's head, a bat's wings, an eagle's or a lion's paws and claws, and a mouth endowed with many tongues and pointed fangs). Dragons are often presented as fierce, devouring monsters; according to many traditions, they spit fire; they may be chthonic, aquatic, or aerial beings.

Even though the specific shape of the dragon's monstrous body becomes increasingly standardized in time and assumes a heraldic fixity in the art of many cultures, as in the European or in the Chinese and Japanese, the dragon is better defined by its meaning and function in mythical thought than by that shape. Dragons are the symbols of elements, forces, or principles present, or active, in the cosmic (or precosmic) world. They thus express, in mythical language, aspects of the natural setting of the various societies, and the dangerous or positive qualities of those aspects, such as drought or rain, flood, and so on. Beyond this "natural" meaning they possess a more complex value on the cosmic level, being forces of stability or of disorder, of staticity or of dynamism, of death or of life. Again, they may have a similar meaning on a "social" or "political" level, symbolizing the enemies, or, in some cases, the champions, of a given culture, society, group, or class. In this case also, however, the symbolism of this first level expresses a second-level, "cosmic" symbolism of evil, disorder, and injustice, or of protection and strength.

The main Old World traditions about dragons can be classified in two different groups. A tradition belonging to cultures located in the western part of Eurasia and in some parts of East Africa presents dragons as chaotic beings, responsible for death and disorder, and vanquished by gods or heroes. This tradition has its roots in the ancient mythologies of the Near East, and of the Indian, Iranian, and European world, and it continues into the Christian culture of the European Middle Ages as well as into the Christian mythology of Egypt and Ethiopia. A second tradition is typical of East Asia (notably China, Japan, and Indonesia) and presents dragons as powerful and helpful beings. The distinction, however, is not a totally simple and straightforward one, for "positive" aspects are present in the dragon lore of the western area, notably in India (where myths present dragonlike beings that are similar to the dragons of East Asia), and dragon-slaying myths are not unknown to the East Asian cultures. In order to respect the complexity of the material, a more detailed treatment is required, based upon specific aspects and motifs of the dragon lore of the Old World, rather than upon the usual twofold classification.

Dragons in Cosmogonies and Eschatologies. The most ancient traditions about dragons go back to the Sumerian, Akkadian, and Egyptian mythologies of the first three millennia BCE. In these contexts dragons (often clearly serpentine; in some cases, as in that of Tiamat, of different, though unclear, shapes) represent forces or elements that interfere with the correct order or functioning of the world, and they are vanquished by gods who shape and organize the cosmos and, through their victory, acquire authority and power over the newly ordered world. The god Enlil defeats a monstrous being, the Labbu, in a Sumerian text. The god Marduk vanquishes the monsters Tiamat and Kingu in the Akkadian text *Enuma elish* of Babylon. In the mythology of the Syrian city of Ugarit (end of the second millennium BCE) the god Baal defeats the monsters Yamm ("sea") and Mot ("death"). The dragon Apopis is slain by the god Seth in Egyptian mythology. In similar mythical traditions the serpentine Vṛtra is killed by the warrior god Indra (or by the hero Trita) in Indic mythical narratives that go back to the *Ṛgveda.* In the Hittite texts of Bogazköy, the serpent Illuyanka is killed by the storm god. In Greek mythology, Zeus slays the monster Typhon, who had a hundred snake heads, and Apollo kills the female serpent (*drakaina*) at Delphi, and then builds his own sanctuary on the spot where the monstrous being has been slain.

In some cases, these myths have been interpreted as myths of fertility and of the seasonal pattern, because the victorious deity is often a storm god, and drought, rain, and the life of vegetation are often at stake. But the cosmogonic quality of these myths is clear in all cases: in order to construct, or to defend, the world order, the god has to destroy the primeval, chaotic dragon. In some cases (as in that of Apsu and the female Tiamat, who represent two parts of the original watery chaos, and of the younger monster Kingu) the dragonlike monster represents the preexisting, static, chaotic matter that must be broken, divided, and restructured to build the cosmos. In other cases (as in the myths about Apopis, the serpent who tries to stop the sun from rising and setting, or of Vṛtra, the "withholder" who blocks the cows symbolizing water and dawn) the serpentine monsters are beings that cause staticity and death by stopping the correct functioning of the world, and they must be eliminated.

The Hebrew Bible contains many traces of an ancient mythology, wherein Yahveh, in primeval times, defeats monsters that are extremely similar to the dragonlike beings dispatched by the various Near Eastern gods: to names already present in the more ancient Ugaritic texts (*Yamm, Mavet,* or *Mot*) one can add names such as *Peten, Nahash, Rahab, Leviathan, Tannin, Behemoth.* Indeed, this seems to have been an ancient Israelite myth connecting creation to the fight against one or more primeval monsters, and thus a cosmogonical motif alternative to the one(s) contained in the first chapter of the *Book of Genesis.*

Given the structural correspondence between cosmogonies and eschatologies, it is not surprising to find that eschatological myths of various societies show a dragon as the being (or as one of the beings) responsible for the lapse into chaos and death that is to take place at the end of time. Thus in late biblical texts (e.g., *Dn.* 7, *Jb.* 7:12), as well as in Judaic and Christian texts of "apocalyptic" content (e.g., *Rv.* 12–13, 20), the primeval dragon is said to have been defeated but not totally destroyed, and to return at the end to wreak havoc, only to be finally annihilated. Other religious traditions also present dragonlike beings as eschatological enemies: thus the Germanic mythology (the Midgarðr serpent of the *Prose Edda*) and the Iranian (the serpentine Azhi Dahaka, later called Zohak, who is chained to Mount Demavend by the hero Thraetaona/Feridun and who returns at the end of time).

Dragons as Abductors and Devourers. To the above themes one should connect the similar mythical complex that presents dragons as robbers who steal wealth or abduct women, and the theme of the devouring dragon. In some of the "cosmogonical" myths listed above (e.g., in the Ugaritic myth of Baal, Mot, and Yamm) the"chaotic" enemy is also presented as a devourer, or as a tyrant levying tribute; in other cases, such as the ancient Egyptian myth about Astarte and the sea (nineteenth dynasty), a goddess is sent (as "tribute"?) to the monster by the gods it terrorizes. But a more precise motif of this type has recently been reconstructed and called the Indo-European cattle-raiding myth. In the mythologies of many Indo-European-speaking societies (Indic, Iranian, Hittite, Greek, Roman, Germanic, and Armenian) versions or traces of a type of myth have been found, wherein a monstrous, serpentine, three-headed being steals cattle from a hero or a community; a god or hero retrieves the cattle and dispatches the monster. The Indic example is the very myth of Indra (and/or Trita) mentioned above, that is clearly cosmogonic; the Hittite example is the myth, also cited above, of Illuyanka and the storm god. This overlapping, and the eschatological developments of the Germanic and Iranian myths of this group (see above), point to a typological and historical connection between the theme in question and the cosmogonical myths mentioned in the preceding section, though there is no consensus among scholars on the original cosmogonic value of the cattle-raiding myths.

In the Iranian myth belonging to this group, the monster Azhi Dahaka/Zohak steals not cattle (though an interpretation of the stolen female as cattle has been proposed for the most ancient versions) but royal women, and his opponent Thraetaona/Feridun regains the young women (and, in the later versions, the usurped throne) by defeating the dragon. This theme of a dragon who steals women and is defeated by a hero who thus regains them is no less widespread than the theme of the devouring or greedy dragon. It is attested in ancient Greek mythology (e.g., the hero Perseus saves Andromeda from the dragon), and it is a central theme in medieval and modern dragon lore in Europe and Asia, appearing in folk tales collected from the oral tradition of European peasants down to the nineteenth and twentieth centuries, in which a "princess" is stolen by a dragon (or by some other monstrous enemy) and recovered by a young man of the lower social strata, who kills the monster and is promoted, often by gaining the hand of the "princess." In other folk tales of the same traditions, the dragon steals or devours vital elements such as light or water, or pollutes the soil or the air of whole regions.

Dragons as Withholders and Custodians. The tradition of the dragon as a greedy usurper, robber, devourer, or withholder may be combined with two other widespread motifs: the theme of the serpent who in primeval times deprived humankind of immortality—a theme attested, for example, in the biblical *Book of Genesis* (3:1–15) and in the Mesopotamian *Epic of Gilgamesh*—and the widespread theme, which is especially important in many Asian mythologies, of the snake that resides at the foot of the tree of life or the cosmic tree. Such combinations probably gave rise to the theme of the dragon as a custodian of the tree of life or of other sources of immortality or longevity: one should quote the ancient Greek myth of the dragon that guarded the golden apples of the Hesperides, killed by Herakles when the hero conquered the apples, or the *nāgas* of Indic tradition, that guarded the White Mountain and its wonder-tree Mahāsankha, "tall as Mount Meru," that produced a special fruit. In other cases the dragon is shown not guarding but attacking the holy tree: thus, in Iranian mythology (*Bundahishn* 18.2) the reptile created by Ahriman that damages the miraculous plant Gayo-kerena, or, in Germanic traditions, the serpent Níðhǫggr that attacks the roots of the cosmic tree Yggdrasill.

The theme of the dragon as guardian of the tree of life or cosmic tree is connected typologically to the theme of the dragon who guards treasures, widely attested in China, India, and Europe. See, for instance, the ancient Greek tradition about the dragon that guarded the Golden Fleece and was killed by the hero Jason, who thus obtained the precious token of kingship; the serpents guarding the gold of Apollo among the Scythians (Herodotus, 3.116); and the Germanic myth of the snake Fafnir who guards the gold coveted by Regin and is killed by the hero Sigurd. The theme of the dragon guarding the tree of life became an important iconographical motif in ancient and medieval art of Asia and Europe: it is found, in a rigid heraldic scheme, even in the reliefs of the Baptistery of Parma and of other medieval churches.

Dragons as Enemies and Devils. In other traditions, dragons are ever-active, menacing symbols of evil. In some cases, their symbolic value is drastically "historicized," and they are identified by various societies or groups with real, external enemies such as foreign nations or oppressive powers and rulers. It has been shown that in many traditions of the cattle-raiding myth type the serpentine cattle raider (or abductor of women) is seen as the representative of an enemy (often non-Indo-European) group, against which the society that created the myths was engaged in a continuous warfare; in the Hebrew Bible and in the most ancient Christian texts the various monsters listed above are quoted to indicate neighboring nations (Egypt, Assyria, Babylon, etc.) or tyrannical rulers that oppressed Israel or persecuted the believers.

In later Judaic and in other religious and magical texts of the eastern Mediterranean of Hellenistic and Roman times, dragons and serpents are increasingly presented as symbols and instruments of the evil forces, and from this background, as well as from the eschatological value of dragons in biblical and other traditions (see above), the identification of the dragon with the enemy of God, Satan, arose. This interpretation was already explicit in the "canonical" Christian apocalypse (*Rv.* 20:2; see above), and it became the most generally accepted in the Christian world. In the new Christian context, numerous hagiographic and other traditions contained a restructured version of the ancient mythical theme of the battle against the dragon or monster, in which the dragon was an embodiment or an emissary of Satan. The best-known type of battle between a holy being and the devilish dragon in Christian traditions opposes the satanic enemy to a warrior figure. One might mention Saint George, a saintly knight of Anatolian origin, who often replaced the "pagan" dragon slayers of local, pre-Christian traditions; or Michael, the Archangel, an important figure of Christian angelology that is presented as a dragon slayer already in the earliest texts (*Rv.* 12:7–9). These two figures are extremely popular in Christian iconography from the earliest times; they are usually shown dispatching the satanic dragon with a lance or sword, clad in full armor, and Saint George is often depicted on horseback.

Saints George and Michael are not, however, the only Christian dragon-slayers. The Virgin Mary, mother of Jesus, for example, is often depicted as trampling a serpent, as the Second Eve who defeats the forces of evil, in fulfillment of the verse of the *Book of Genesis* (3:15) that announced an eternal enmity between the seed of Eve and the serpent; the iconographical type continues, today still, in Catholic sacred art. Finally, other dragon-fighters of Christian tradition, such as Saint Marcellus of Paris (fifth century) or Saint Hilary of Poitiers, appear not as warriors, but as bishops, their weapon against the dragon being not the sword or lance but the bishop's pastoral staff. The connection established by the hagiographic sources between their victory over the dragon and their role as culture heroes and as peaceful leaders of their communities shows that their treatment of dragons (often not slain, but tamed or chased away) has specific meanings, different from those of the other Christian narratives about dragons, and probably less concerned with a theological symbolism: we are told of Hilary that "he gave more land to humankind, for colonists migrated to the place that had been held by the beast" ("addidit terra hominibus, quia in loco beluae incola transmigravit").

DRAGONS AS GIVERS OF FECUNDITY AND LIFE. In spite of the systematic "demonization" of dragon figures in the Christian Middle Ages, specialists of European folklore and medieval culture have shown that many aspects of the dragon lore of Europe point to a more complex symbolic and mythical value of dragons. It will suffice here to quote the heraldic use of dragons in crests, banners, and insignia, from late antiquity to modern times; the identification (that has been compared to "totemic" practices of tribal societies) of nations and lineages with dragons; the presence of dragons (often as symbols of fecundity and prosperity) in liturgical processions (such as the Rogations of western Europe) or in folkloric festivals (such as Carnival).

The "positive" traits of dragons in European traditions show the dragon lore of Europe to be polysemous. They may be usefully compared to the "positive" traits of dragons in East Asia, and especially in China, where dragon figures are no less polysemous than in the Western tradition. In China, the theme of dragons as forces or beings that have to be controlled and confirmed in order to "create" the cosmic order is well attested by, for example, the Confucian *Shujing* (Book of stories). That text recounts how the mythical emperor Yu, the founder of the Hsia dynasty, who gave the world its correct order, built the first canals, freed the land from the chaotic waters, and chased away the serpents and dragons, forcing them to reside in the marshes.

To this tradition one could add many others, such as the deeds of the dragon-slaying emperor Chuan-hin. However, one should note that Nü-kua (the goddess who ordered the world in primeval times according to another ancient text, the *Lizi*, and killed the black dragon) and her spouse, the mythical emperor Fuxi, are represented as dragonlike beings in sculptures of the first centuries CE. This paradox of the dragonlike dragon-slayer is emblematic of the complexity of Chinese dragon lore. Chinese dragons embodied the fertilizing qualities of water, and the importance of rain in the agricultural life of that region explains the increasingly ouranic traits of dragons, their wings, their connections with lightning.

Far from being a mere symbolic expression of the natural elements, however, Chinese dragons represent the rhythmic forces that rule the life of the cosmos. This is explicitly stated by the Daoist Zhuangzi, who writes that the dragon is a symbol of rhythmic life because it embodies the waters that guarantee the living order of the cosmos by their harmonious movement. The cosmic value of dragons as symbols of rhythm and flux is not distinguished, in this text, from their value on the level of the material elements of nature.

The connection of Chinese dragons with rain is well exemplified by the ritual practices of ancient China; during droughts, images of the Ying dragon, a water figure, were made, to propitiate rainfall. Yet dragons are also important in rituals of cosmic renewal, as is shown by the presence of dragon masks during the lamplit, nightly festivities that close the Chinese New Year feast; and many traditions and practices point to the other value of dragons as symbols of cosmic rhythm. In particular, this is clear in the symbolic correspondences and ties between dragons and the Chinese emperors or Sons of Heaven who were also representative of cosmic rhythms and givers of fecundity. Thus we are told that an emperor of the Hsia dynasty ate dragons in order to ensure magically the welfare of his kingdom, and that when that same dynasty underwent a crisis and lost its vital force, dragons appeared to reestablish the correct rhythmic flux in various ways. Finally, mythical dragons were responsible for the ascension of monarchs to the heavenly regions, as happened, we are told, when Huangdi, the Yellow Emperor, was abducted with several members of his court by a bearded dragon and carried to the sky.

Throughout Southeast Asia, in South India, Indochina, and Indonesia, dragons are water figures and symbols of fertility. This is attested not only by narrative traditions but also by ritual practices. Thus, in modern Cambodian weddings the bride is identified with the moon, her teeth are treated as if to deprive them of serpent venom, and the rituals are explicitly connected with myths about a dragonlike royal ancestress; in Tenasserim (Burma), to stop the rainy season and to bring in the dry weather, a statue of Upagutta, a mythical serpent king, is plunged in water and offered sacrificial gifts, in a ritual that is a symmetrical reversal of the Chinese dragon rite mentioned above.

DRAGONS AS PARENTS AND ANCESTORS. Many traditions of Asia and Europe present dragons as the parents of heroes and holy men and as the mythical ancestors of kingly dynasties. The ancient Greek myth of the origin of the Boeotian city Thebes combines this theme with the theme of the serpent as guardian and withholder: the hero Kadmos kills the dragon that barred the way to the site of the future city and then sows the dragon's teeth in the earth, thus giving rise to the Spartoi ("sown men"), who become the first Thebans. Alexander the Great (r. 336–323 BCE) was believed by some to be born from his mother's encounter with a god in the shape of a serpent, and a similar legend was told of the Roman emperor Augustus. According to a Chinese tradition, the princess Liu was resting by a pond with her husband, when she was raped by a dragon and conceived thus the future emperor Gaozu; and the culture hero Fuxi was said to have been born from a pond that was famous for its dragons. Similar traditions are attested in Annam and Indonesia; and the Indian kings of Chota Nagpur were believed to have descended from a *nāga*, or serpentlike spirit, named Puṇḍarīka.

A series of Asian traditions recount the birth of a famous kingly ancestor or holy man from a prince or priest and a *nāgī* (female counterpart to the male *nāga*). Thus, according to a Palaung myth, the *nāgī* Thusandi and the son of the solar deity, Prince Thuryia, gave birth to three sons who became the kings of three lands (China, the land of the Palaung, and Pagan). Similar traditions about the origins of royal dynasties from female dragon figures exist in South India, Indochina, and Indonesia. In India the birth of the sage Agastya from the *apsara* Urvasi is recounted in a comparable fashion.

In the legends, the dragon-woman is often recognized as such suddenly, because she smells strongly of fish, or because she is spied upon while she takes a bath and plays in the water with a *nāga.* In modern traditions of this kind from Cambodia, the female dragon is a moon figure, and her mythical marriage with a solar prince is the prototype of today's marriage rituals, as well as a symbol of cosmic union between opposites. Similarly, the traditions about the birth of a dynasty from the union of a watery, dragonlike female and a fiery solar male are symbolic of a primeval unity of opposites that prepares the new cosmos represented by the new dynastic order.

A comparable symbolic interpretation has not been offered by scholars for the European traditions of the same type, that also derive princely dynasties from dragonlike females, and are known both from medieval chronicles and other texts, and from modern folklore. In the best-known of these European narrative traditions (the story of the extrahuman female Mélusine or Mélusigne, often classified as a fairy by its medieval redactors) the female protagonist is spied upon by her husband, who discovers that she turns into a snake when taking a bath. The Mélusine stories have been compared to the myth told by Herodotus (4.8–10) about the birth of the ancestors of the three Scythian "tribes" from the hero Herakles and a powerful female being, who was half woman, half serpent, but decidedly chthonic rather than watery.

See Also Chaos; Monsters; Snakes.

Bibliography

G. Elliot Smith's *The Evolution of the Dragon* (New York, 1919), although outdated, is still useful as a general study. The best discussion of dragons and their symbolic meaning is in Mircea Eliade's *Patterns in Comparative Religion* (New York, 1958), chaps. 5 and 8. This book has an excellent bibliographical appendix. On dragons as chaotic beings of primeval times and on the theme of the cosmogonic battle against such monsters in the ancient Near East, Indic, and Greek worlds, see Mary K. Wakeman's *God's Battle with the Monster: A Study in Biblical Imagery* (Leiden, 1973). For still wider comparative material, see Joseph Fontenrose's *Python: A Study of the Delphic Myth and Its Origins* (Berkeley, Calif., 1959).

On the "cattle-raiding myth," see Bruce Lincoln's *Priests, Warriors, and Cattle: A Study in the Ecology of Religions* (Berkeley, 1981), esp. pp. 103–122. On the Indo-European myths about the fight against the dragon, consult Viacheslav Ivanov and V. N. Toporov's "Le mythe indo-européen du dieu de l'orage poursuivant le serpent: Réconstitution du schéma," in *Échanges et communications: Mélanges offerts à Claude Lévi-Strauss,* edited by Jean Pouillon and Pierre Maranda, vol. 2 (The Hague, 1968), pp. 1180–1206.

A good source for medieval European dragon lore, especially the theme of the bishop as a dragon tamer, and an important critical study is Jacques Le Goff's "Culture ecclésiastique et culture folklorique au Moyen-Âge: Saint Marcel de Paris et le dragon," in *Richerche storiche ed economiche in memoria di Corrado Barbagallo,* edited by Luigi De Rosa, vol. 2 (Naples, 1970), pp. 53–90. This essay has been translated as "Ecclesiastical Culture and Folklore in the Middle Ages: Saint Marcellus of Paris and the Dragon," in Le Goff's *Time, Work and Culture in the Middle Ages* (Chicago, 1980), pp. 159–188. Le Goff and Emmanuel Le Roy Ladurie's "Mélusine maternelle et défricheuse," *Annales: Économies, sociétés, civilisations* 26 (1971): 587–622, offers a source on Mélusine.

Bibliography for East Asian dragons can be found in Eliade's *Patterns in Comparative Religion* (cited above), Barbara Renz's *Der orientalische Schlangendrache* (Augsburg, 1930), and Hampden C. Du Bose's *The Dragon, Image, and Demon, or The Three Religions of China* (London, 1886). On the mythical serpentine ancestress in Southeast Asia, see the bibliography provided by Eliade (cited above), adding Éveline Porée-Maspéro's "Nouvelle étude sur la nagi Soma," *Journal asiatique* 236 (1950): 237–267.

New Sources

Avil, François. *Interprétation symbolique du combat de saint Michel et du dragon.* Paris, 1971.

Jones, David E. *An Instinct for Dragons.* New York and London, 2000. A cross-cultural study on the origins and spread of dragon lore, following a socio-biological approach and including an excellent bibliography.

Lurker, Manfred. "Drache." In *Wörterbuch der Symbolik.* Stuttgart, Germany, 1983, pp. 138–139.

Morris, Henry M. *Dragons in Paradise.* El Cajon, Calif., 1993.

Nigg, Joe. *Wonder Beasts: Tales and Lore of the Phoenix, the Griffin, the Unicorn, and the Dragon.* Englewood, Colo., 1995.

Passes, David. *Dragons. Truth, Myth and Legend.* New York, 1993.

Shuker, Karl. *Dragons. A Natural History.* New York, 1995.

Visser, Willem de. *The Dragon in China and Japan.* Wiesbaden, Germany, 1969. Original edition Amsterdam, 1913.

Watkins, Calvert. *How to Kill a Dragon. Aspects of Indo-European Poetics.* Oxford, 1995. After an introduction to the field of comparative Indo-European poetics the author examines the structure of the dragon/serpent-slaying myths throughout the Indo-European tradition. A copious bibliography is provided.

Cristiano Grottanelli (1987)
Revised Bibliography

DRAMA

This entry consists of the following articles:

INDIAN DANCE AND DANCE DRAMA
BALINESE DANCE AND DANCE DRAMA
JAVANESE WAYANG
EAST ASIAN DANCE AND THEATER
AFRICAN RELIGIOUS DRAMA
NORTH AMERICAN INDIAN DANCE AND DRAMA
MESOAMERICAN DANCE AND DRAMA
EUROPEAN RELIGIOUS DRAMA [FIRST EDITION]
EUROPEAN RELIGIOUS DRAMA [FURTHER CONSIDERATIONS]
MODERN WESTERN THEATER

DRAMA: DRAMA AND RELIGION

Although it can be said that the presentation of drama and religious ceremony are analogous, the two practices are not always directly related in world history. The notion popularized in the early twentieth century by the Cambridge School that drama springs directly from ritual has been largely discredited. However, religious practices and dramatic presentation often share many common elements: costume, storytelling, a playing space, and an audience. Also many of the world's dramatic forms are derived from religious rituals and are still, in some way, connected to religious celebration. With that in mind, drama has had a long, sometimes intimate, sometimes adversarial relationship with religion.

Scholars generally assign drama and religious ritual to a continuum with the following divisions: ritual with performative elements, ritual drama, drama presented as part of a religious festival, and secular drama. While this continuum cannot be used as a trajectory of theatrical development, it provides a useful tool with which to understand the many kinds of relationships theatrical performance has had with religious practice. Some societies developed rituals with advanced elements of performance but never developed anything approaching a secular drama. Conversely, some societies adopted a secular performance form independent of religious ritual. At the same time, many in Western society have assigned the secular theater a religious importance and power, particularly during the mid–twentieth century, when interest in so-called primitive cultures surged.

RITUAL COMPRISING PERFORMATIVE ELEMENTS. To understand the relationships between these various forms and concepts it is useful to examine the ritual practice of Egungun. Egungun ritual influenced later performance forms in Yorubaland and what came to be known as Nigeria. Yoruba religion centers on deities related to nature (the *orisha*) and ancestor worship. The followers of Yoruba believe human spirits travel back and forth to a spiritual plane between lives, and followers look to the spirits of their ancestors for guidance.

The ancestor may appear to someone in material form embodied by a dancer from the Egungun secret society. The ancestor can be summoned at particular times of need or may appear regularly during cyclical rituals, such as the Egungun Festival. The dancer wears elaborate costumes, which consist of a mask and long strips or panels of fabric. The dancer whirls around so that the long strips of fabric fan out and create a breeze. This breeze is said to be a blessing passed from the ancestors to the living. No one may touch the dancers, however, and men with whips or sticks keep the dancers and the spectators separated.

The Egungun ritual contains other performative elements, including songs of praise for the *orisha* and satirical sketches. The ritual does not possess the elements of a ritual drama in that it does not contain a set narrative, characters, or specific dialogue, but according to Joel Adedeji (1972), Egungun had a direct influence in the development of dramatic forms such as the Yoruba Alarinjo theater and on the postcolonial drama of such writers as Wole Soyinka (b. 1934) (Adedeji, 1972, p. 254).

RITUAL DRAMA. The earliest known record of ritual drama comes from an Egyptian stele erected around 1868 BCE. It is the account by Ikhernofret of his participation in the Mysteries of Osiris at Abydos. The stele reads like a list of heroic accomplishments: "I overthrew the enemies of Osiris. I celebrated the *Great-Going-Forth,* following the god at his going. I sailed the divine boat of Thoth." The drama he is recounting, often called the *Abydos Passion Play,* recounts the life, death, and resurrection of Osiris. It is difficult to get an accurate idea of how elaborate or developed the performance may have been or where one might place it on the continuum between ritual and drama.

Another example of ritual drama is the Mayan dance drama *Rabinal Achí* (also known as the Dance of El Tun). Scholars have long studied the accounts of ritual warfare among the Mayans, but in the 1990s Nikolai Grube deciphered the glyph for the word *dance.* Several precolonial dances have survived, including the Dance of Giants, a solstice ritual of the lunar gods in conflict with the solar gods, and a pole dance in which dancers attached to ropes wound tightly around a pole slowly descend (fly) to the ground from the top as the ropes unwind.

The text of *Rabinal Achí* is the only Mayan precolonial dramatic text to survive. In the nineteenth century a Queché actor named Bartolo Zis first transcribed the text into Queché using the Roman alphabet. The French priest-explorer Charles Brasseur de Bourbourg, after seeing a performance, convinced Zis to recite it to him. The drama retells the story of the ritual warfare between the Rabinal and Queché warriors during the Mayan Classic period (300–900 CE). In the story the Rabinal warrior has captured Cawek, a Queché warrior. Rabinal brings Cawek before the Rabinal chief, where Cawek's request to say good-bye to his homeland is met with silence. Cawek leaves the room and returns sometime later angry at the idea that anyone might have assumed that he had fled. He then bravely faces his sacrificial death.

The dancers of the drama, the Twelve Yellow Eagles and Twelve Yellow Jaguars, wore elaborate costumes and masks. The drama was accompanied by music, and Brasseur included musical notation in his description. His version includes two trumpets (probably European-style) and a drum, although scholars assume that other native instruments were used in the precolonial performances. The anthropologist Georges Reynaud made special note of the "parallelism" of the dialogue. The ritualistic dialogue consists of "parallel" responses in which the second speaker repeats what the first speaker says before adding more dialogue to the conversation. The dialogue also contains ritualistic salutations and closings.

Dancers continued to perform the ritual drama into the twenty-first century, although as Carlos Escobar (2001) points out, some question how much the text must have changed through the ages, especially after the Spanish priests outlawed such rituals in 1625. Zis inherited the oral text in secret, and subsequent translations present an even greater filter of the text. Richard Leinaweaver (1968) noted that in a twentieth-century production the masks, costumes, and musical instruments were placed on a sacred altar the night before the drama was staged, a syncretic practice that performers of the sacred *autos,* the Catholic liturgical dramas, also occasionally observe (Leinaweaver, 1968, p. 15).

THE DIFFERENCE BETWEEN RITUAL AND SECULAR DRAMA. Ritual drama developed in many societies in large part because drama and religious ritual share so many elements and structural qualities. As Richard Schechner notes in *Between Theater and Anthropology* (1985), both employ the use of "restored behavior," or behavior that is repeated. The repetition sets dramatic performance and ritual behavior apart from the behavior of everyday life. The distance of the performers from the behavior makes the behavior "symbolic and reflexive" in a way that regular behavior is not.

Religious ritual and dramatic performance both employ the use of a "frame" to set these behaviors apart from everyday life. These may be as complex as the concentric circles of ritual sacrifice that separate the world of the sacred from the world of the profane or as simple as the rectangle of the proscenium arch in the Western theater. But herein lies the key difference between ritual and the performance of secular drama.

Arnold van Gennep (1960) explained that in the ritual, such as the rite of passage, the ritual subject moves through three phases: separation, transition, and incorporation. The subjects pass through the ritual frame into a marginal, or liminal, state where their status is ambiguous. Then the subjects are restored to everyday life in a new state, with a new status. Henri Hubert and Marcel Mauss (1964) also defined ritual as "a religious act which, through the consecration of a victim, modifies the condition of the moral person who accomplishes it or that of certain objects with which he is concerned" (Gennep, 1960, p. 13). As Victor Turner (1982) noted, while ritual behavior can be defined as obligatory, collective, integrated, and transforming—or liminal—secular drama is optional, individual, removed, and although it may question the status quo or experiment with form, it is ultimately void of the transforming quality of ritual. It is, therefore, merely *liminoid.*

DRAMA OF RELIGIOUS FESTIVALS. Of the secular dramatic traditions, many coincide with religious festivals, and many of those can be traced back directly to a ritual drama or a ritual practice. Nigerian scholars have traced the Egungun ritual origin of Alarinjo theater, the court theater of the Oyo Yoruba kingdom that predated colonialism. While the drama may be tied to religious practice, dramatic traditions such as Alarinjo demonstrate an elaborate theatrical practice in which artisans train for specific tasks within the theatrical art, such as acting, dance, costuming, mask making, set design, or music. Often a system of guilds and schools control the selection and training of the artists and oversee the production of the theatrical event. In other words, artists are producing art for art's sake.

SANSKRIT DRAMA. Scholars know very little about the origin of Sanskrit drama, a performance form that remained popular from approximately the second century CE to the ninth century. While some say that Sanskrit drama has its origins in the popular traditions, others argue that it shares many elements with certain religious rituals. Regardless of its origins, the Sanskrit theater of India has a close relationship with Hindu temple festivals. According to Farley Richmond and his colleagues (1990), the *Nāṭya Śāstra,* the ancient Indian dramaturgical text, equates dramatic performance with holy sacrifice (Richmond et al., 1990, p. 47). The *Nāṭya Śāstra* also gives Sanskrit drama divine origins. In the story, Brahmā creates drama as an alternative to the less desirable behavior in which people were engaged. The gods gave the priests the charge of creating and maintaining the dramatic tradition (Richmond et al., 1990, pp. 25–26).

While Sanskrit drama, in its ancient form, did not last past the ninth century, other forms grew up in its place. Wealthy families offer *kathakali* performances at temple festivals and other important events. *Kathakali* evolved from a Sanskrit drama derivative and plays devoted to celebrating the life of Kṛṣṇa. Although it may have sprung from devotional worship, *kathakali* is an institution unto itself. The *kathakali* actor undergoes extensive training from a young age. *Kathakali* students learn elaborate makeup art specific to their character types. In addition to the dance steps, the actor must learn a series of hand gestures and complex facial expressions. It is through the face that the actor evokes the appropriate *rasa* and reflects the psychic state of the character.

THE ORIGINS OF GREEK DRAMA. Also associated with a religious festival, Greek tragedy supposedly evolved from dithyrambs, or choral dance drama, to honor the demigod Dionysos. To some extent, high school and college textbooks have oversimplified the relationship of tragedy to Dionysian worship, influenced perhaps by the century-old theory of Gilbert Murray that rituals of vegetation deities, specifically the Dionysian *sparagmos* (ritual rending), were evident in the tragedies of Euripides. However, as William Ridgeway suggests (and Herodotus before him), dithyrambic performance was not limited to religious worship as the people of Sicyon used the dithyramb as a tribute to ancestors and dead heroes. Also while the dithyramb may have influenced the development of tragedy, the dithyramb continued to develop as an independent form. Scholars have begun to look at Greek dramatic forms as having a multitude of influences instead of looking for one ritualistic ur-drama that must have predated Aeschylus.

In the sixth century BCE Peisistratus established the Greater Dionysia. The festival included many activities celebrating wine and fertility, such as the procession of the phallus. Like two of the other Dionysian festivals, the Greater Dionysia included dramatic contests. According to the *Marmor Parium,* the first tragic contest occurred in 534 BCE. Although the priest of Dionysos occupied the central seat at the dramatic performance, the dramas themselves do not reflect a particular religious belief. Rather, they reinforce Athenian class and political ideology. Athenian playwrights of the fifth century BCE seem particularly interested in analyzing the benefits of Athenian institutions, such as democracy or the courts. The plays were performed at a religious festival but other than that have very little connection with religious thought.

RELIGION AND DRAMA AT ODDS. While many religions included drama as an important part of religious observance, some religions (especially the Christian and Islamic) forbade theater. Even before Rome became a Christian empire in the late fourth century CE, the early Christian Church looked with disfavor on dramatic performance. Tertullian wrote *De Spectaculis* at the end of the second century CE, sometime after his own conversion to Christianity. He devoted his entire treatise to explaining why Christians should not attend any of the entertainments such as races, gladiatorial combat, Atellan farce, and tragedies.

Most of Tertullian's explanations are simple: Christians should not take pleasure in watching others being harmed, nor should they witness licentious behavior. His thinking also reflects some of the complexities of early Christian thought. He noted that watching such entertainment aroused passions that could lead to sinful feelings and actions. Tertullian condemns the practice of acting itself, stating: "[God] regards as adultery all that is unreal. . . . He never will approve any putting on of voice, or sex, or age; He never will approve pretended loves, and wraths, and groans, and tears" (chapter 23). Tertullian found the very idea of performing a role sinful.

In the first half of the treatise, Tertullian lays out what seem to be the most vehement of his reasons for avoiding the entertainments: their pagan origins. The fact that the theater of Rome was a temple of Venus and that the Greek theater came from the Dionysian festivals, Tertullian states, are reason enough to avoid theatrical entertainment. The theater became the site of conflict between Roman pantheism and emerging Christianity.

The Catholic Church, in its quest for a monopoly on spectacle during the medieval period, continued to campaign against the theater, decreeing excommunication for anyone who attended theater instead of church and declaring that no plays should be performed on Sundays. While very little evidence exists of secular drama's persistence and development during this time, scholars deduce that the continual stream of declarations by the church is evidence enough.

LITURGICAL DRAMA: MEDIEVAL RITUAL DRAMA. In the late medieval period the Catholic Church began to develop a theatrical practice of its own. Many scholars believe that the liturgical drama grew out of the Mass in the form of a trope, or a lengthened musical passage used to elaborate some moment in the liturgy. The most widely cited trope is the *Quem Queritis,* the trope that accompanies the Easter Mass in the form of a dialogue between the three Marys and the angel at the tomb. This simple passage was accompanied by stage directions written in the tenth century by Bishop Ethelwold in the *Regularis Concordia,* instructing the monks to position themselves around the tomb "in imitation of the angel seated in the tomb, and of the women coming with spices to anoint the body of Jesus" (Gassner, 1963, p. 37). The tropes were performed on the *platea* (a flat space in the front of the church) in front of a mansion (a small structure that signified a location such as the sepulcher, manger, or Hellmouth).

The theory of the development of liturgical drama holds that these miniature dramatic presentations in the form of tropes became more elaborate and developed into the later outdoor vernacular religious drama, following the ritual-to-drama trajectory. But some scholars, such as Dunbar Ogden (2002), dispute that, pointing to the fact that the tropes continued to develop as a separate form parallel to the outdoor drama (Ogden, 2002, p. 35).

CYCLE PLAYS, MIRACLE PLAYS, AND MORALITY PLAYS: MEDIEVAL RELIGIOUS DRAMA. With the establishment of the Feast of Corpus Christi as a churchwide celebration by Pope Urban IV in 1264, outdoor religious drama began to form. Whether it developed from the trope or not, the festival allowed for several developments: the presentations could be much more elaborate outdoors, and the stories could be performed in the vernacular because they were situated outside of the formal Mass. Furthermore, since the festival was an annual festival, all the events of the church calendar were covered at one time, allowing for the dramatization of the life of Jesus or even the entire Bible from the Creation to the Last Judgment. The outdoor cycles continued to use the mansion and *platea* staging from the indoor pieces.

In addition to the cycle plays, groups of performers began to perform miracle plays and morality plays. Miracle plays dealt with the lives of saints or participated in debating a church controversy. *The Croxton Play of the Sacrament* examined the issues of transubstantiation and whether Jews can convert to Christianity. Morality plays instructed the audience in how to be a good Christian. For instance, *Everyman* instructs Christians to attend confession regularly in order to assure that their accounts are in order when death unexpectedly arrives.

Christian Drama in the Americas. By the dawn of the Renaissance, Christian drama was popular all over Europe from the cycles of the British Isles to the *autos* of Spain. The *autos* quickly spread to the Americas with the colonization of much of the New World by the Spanish in the sixteenth century. The priests who accompanied the conquistadors attempted to supplant indigenous rituals with *autos* to indoctrinate the indigenous people in the ways of Christian practice.

The priests also encouraged the converted native people to stage their own Christian pageants, which became an opening for the performance of political subversion. Many scholars have noted the contradictory semiotics of *La conquista de Jerusalén* (The conquest of Jerusalem, 1543). The Franciscans charged the indigenous converts of Tlaxcala to perform the pageant during the Feast of Corpus Christi. The frame of the pageant is the liberation of Jerusalem from the Moors. In a layering of symbols, the Christians were dressed as the new captain general of New Spain. The Moors were dressed like the former captain general, the conqueror of the Aztecs, Hernando Cortés. This created a performance of the "reversal of the conquest," with the indigenous people defeating Cortés at Jerusalem.

Church Influence on Modern Secular Drama. With the Renaissance came a new secular drama, especially in places where the religious drama was outlawed to prevent religious conflict in a Europe increasingly divided along Catholic and Protestant lines. In England, Elizabeth I outlawed religious drama in 1559 and specifically suppressed cycle plays in 1570. University students continued to study the classic plays of Rome and used them as models along with a variety of other sources, including the Bible, for Renaissance drama. Christopher Marlowe's *Doctor Faustus* (c. 1588) reflects the conflicting cosmologies of the medieval world and the English Renaissance. The play resembles a morality play with the forces of good and evil fighting for Faustus's soul. Although Faustus condemns himself to hell for the knowledge he gains, he remains a Renaissance man, a humanist, and a seeker of scientific truth.

In Italy, with the power of the church on the wane, powerful Italian families, such as the Medici family, began to celebrate an Italian culture that preexisted the church. The Medici family poured money into creating spectacles that often used Roman mythology as the main theme. But Christian morality maintained an influence on the high arts, and morality occupied an important position as a central component of the concept of verisimilitude in drama. The neoclassicists, who advocated returning to the ideals of Horace and Aristotle in the sixteenth century, stressed that truthfulness meant a higher, moral truth rather than a specific, historical truth.

Christian clergy continued to be a powerful force in shaping the direction of the development of Western drama. A few years after Protestants in England had managed to successfully close the theaters during the Commonwealth, the Protestant minister Jeremy Collier helped to put an end to Restoration comedy when he wrote his "Short View of the Immorality and Profaneness of the English Stage" in 1698. Unlike some of his predecessors, Collier felt that drama should not be banned because drama could be used for didactic purposes. But Collier disliked how evil was rewarded in Restoration comedy. He objected to the licentious behavior of Restoration comedy characters, particularly the women. He also objected to characters taking the Lord's name in vain and mocking the clergy. These were sentiments that were shared by the increasingly powerful merchant class, initiating a sea change in the nature of English drama.

Modern Theater as Religion. While experimental movements in the nineteenth and twentieth centuries seemed to challenge the Christian moral imperative, many avant-garde artists became interested in the spiritual practices of non-European cultures. One of the most influential of these artists was Antonin Artaud (1895–1948). In 1931 Artaud witnessed a Balinese dance at the Colonial Exposition, a performance that had an immediate and profound effect on Artaud and launched his writings about his "Theater of Cruelty." For Artaud, the key to the truth lay hidden deep within the human psyche, a psyche that had been perverted and repressed by civilization. Artaud wanted a theater that would act on the senses with sounds and images visceral enough to force the members of the audience to see their true selves. For Artaud, the so-called primitive societies of Bali and Mexico had escaped the effects of European civilization and were able to convey something deeper in their performance by way of gesture and facial expression.

This primitivism of Artaud's Theatre of Cruelty influenced several avant-garde artists: Jerzy Grotowski of the Polish Laboratory Theatre, Richard Schechner's Performance Group, Julian Beck and Judith Malina of the Living Theatre, and Joseph Chaikin of the Open Theatre. Grotowski (1968) sought to use ritual to induce actors into "casting off his everyday mask" and to lose themselves as a kind of sacrifice (Grotowski, 1968, p. 34). He advocated a theater without lights, a stage, or elaborate costumes so that he could remove the separation of the actors from the audience; and he used long and arduous rehearsal workshops to create *communitas* among his actors.

In 1968 the Open Theatre embarked on the Bible Workshops, a series of improvisations designed to explore some of the concepts in the Bible. Through these workshops the Open Theatre explored the life of Jesus and the stories in *Genesis*. Chaikin encouraged the company members to read Carl Jung and Joseph Campbell to inform their exploration. The improvisations developed into the dramatic work *The Serpent: A Ceremony*, a play that drew connections from modern political assassinations to what the group believed were the roots of such violence in the Bible.

Feminist Spirituality and the Theater. In the 1970s and 1980s cultural feminist theater took up the use of ritual in performance. As Jill Dolan noted in *The Feminist Spectator* *as Critic* (1988), many women left avant-garde groups and formed their own when it became clear to them that women's issues were being ignored. As part of the feminist theater movement in France, Hélène Cixous reiterated Artaud's belief that gesture and movement could somehow subvert language, which to Cixous was phallocentric. But as Dolan pointed out, women's groups in the United States rarely followed her lead and looked instead to discover a feminist narrative, which was seen as cyclical and connected to the earth. The cultural feminist groups often used ritual in performance. For example, the group At the Foot of the Mountain used ritual as a companion to their performance of *Ashes, Ashes* in which they asked the audience to visualize saying good-bye to someone close to them as the apocalypse approached. Dolan recounted a ritual performed in conjunction with *Story of a Mother II* in which the group encouraged the audience to celebrate mother-daughter relationships and their matrilineal history. This development in cultural feminist theater fit within a larger trend by cultural feminists to return to Wiccan spirituality in what was perceived as a return to a matriarchal society that predated patriarchal religions such as Christianity.

POSTCOLONIAL DRAMA AND RELIGION. In the nations formerly colonized by the British, many scholars have documented the ways colonial administrators, uneasy with the idea of using Christianity to teach English morality, used Shakespeare in place of the Bible. Now, as part of the project to revive national traditions, many native dramatists have employed religious elements from their precolonial cultures.

Miguel Ángel Asturias used the Mayan dance of Los Gigantes in his play *Soluna* (1955), a title that literally means *Sun/Moon.* The central character envies the spiritual life of the indigenous peasants around him. He has been told that a mask he received from a sorcerer will make time run backward. He dreams that the peasants act out Los Gigantes, the Mayan ritual fight between the agents of the Sun and the agents of the Moon. When he awakens, the train carrying his wife, who had been in the process of leaving him, wrecks after an eclipse and an earthquake, and she returns to him. While Asturias appropriated Mayan spiritual elements in his work, it should be noted that Asturias was not a Mayan but rather a white Guatemalan anthropologist who studied with Georges Reynaud at the Sorbonne. Some scholars have been critical of his European-informed look at the Guatemalan native people.

Wole Soyinka has written about Yoruba spiritual practices in his plays, such as *Death and the King's Horseman* (1975), which involves Egungun and the ritual suicide of the king's horseman on the night of the king's burial. The foreign administrators, who lack understanding and sensitivity to the Yoruba religion, continually trivialize Yoruba practice, even to the point of wearing Egungun costumes to a Western masked ball. They attempt to stamp out the "barbaric" customs and interfere with the horseman's task to tragic effect.

THE FUTURE OF DRAMA AND RELIGION. The future of drama and religion is impossible to predict. In some cases, religion will continue to act as a censor, suppressing seemingly objectionable material, as in the case of funding being pulled from four performance artists who were National Endowment for the Arts recipients in 1990. Certainly the two will continue to share common elements, especially their creative potential. As Schechner says of ritual, dramatic performance "opens up a time/space of antistructural playfulness" where creative choices and solutions can be explored and rehearsed (Schechner, 1993, p. 233). The exploration of new religious ideas will continue to spur new material and create new dramatic practices, and drama will continue to be shaped by religious ideas.

SEE ALSO Performance and Ritual; Ritual.

BIBLIOGRAPHY

Adedeji, Joel A. "The Origin and Form of the Yoruba Masque Theatre." *Cahiers d'études Africaines* 12 (1972): 254–276.

Breasted, James Henry. "The Ikhernofret Stela." In *Ancient Records of Egypt,* vol. 1, pp. 663ff. Chicago, 1906. Available from http://www.nefertiti.iwebland.com/texts/ikhernofret.htm.

Brockett, Oscar G., and Franklin J. Hildy. *History of the Theatre,* 9th ed. Boston, 2003.

David, A. Rosalie. *A Guide to Religious Ritual at Abydos.* Warminster, U.K., 1981.

Dolan, Jill. *The Feminist Spectator as Critic.* Ann Arbor, Mich., 1988.

Drewal, Margaret Thompson. *Yoruba Ritual: Performers, Play, Agency.* Bloomington, Ind., 1992.

Emigh, John. *Masked Performance: The Play of Self and Other in Ritual and Theatre.* Philadelphia, 1996.

Escobar, Carlos René García. "Hacia un suceso prehispánico con los k'ichés." *La Hora,* November 9, 2001. Available from http://www.lahora.com.gt/06-11-01/paginas/cult_2.htm.

Gassner, John, ed. *Medieval and Tudor Drama.* New York, 1963.

Gennep, Arnold van. *The Rites of Passage.* Translated by Monika B. Vizedom and Gabrielle L. Caffee. Chicago, 1960.

Grotowski, Jerzy. *Towards a Poor Theatre.* New York, 1968.

Grube, Nikolai. "Classic Maya Dance: Evidence from Hieroglyphs and Iconography." *Ancient Mesoamerica* 3, no. 2 (1992): 201–218.

Hubert, Henri, and Marcel Mauss. *Sacrifice: Its Nature and Function.* Translated by W. D. Halls. London, 1964.

Kirby, E. T. *Ur-drama: The Origins of Theatre.* New York, 1975.

Leinaweaver, Richard E. "*Rabinal Achi:* Commentary" and "*Rabinal Achi.*" *Latin American Theatre Review* 1, no. 2 (1968): 3–53.

Monterde, Francisco. *Teatro indígena prehispánico.* México City, 1955.

Nagler, A. M. *The Medieval Religious Stage: Shapes and Phantoms.* New Haven, Conn., 1976.

Ogden, Dunbar H. *The Staging of Drama in the Medieval Church.* Newark, Del., London, and Cranbury, N.J., 2002.

Richmond, Farley P., Darius L. Swann, and Phillip B. Zarrilli. *Indian Theatre: Traditions of Performance.* Honolulu, Hawaii, 1990.

Rozik, Eli. "The Ritual Origin of Theatre—a Scientific Theory or Theatrical Ideology?" *Journal of Religion and Theatre* 2, no.1 (Fall 2003). Available from http://apollo.fa.mtu.edu/~dlbruch/rtjournal/vol_2/no_1/rozik2.html.

Schechner, Richard. *Between Theater and Anthropology.* Philadelphia, 1985.

Schechner, Richard. *The Future of Ritual: Writings on Culture and Performance.* London and New York, 1993.

Soyinka, Wole. *Myth, Literature, and the African World.* Cambridge, U.K., 1976.

Tedlock, Dennis. *Rabinal Achi: A Mayan Drama of War and Sacrifice.* Oxford and New York, 2003.

Tertullian. *De spectaculis.* Florence, 1961.

Turner, Victor. *From Ritual to Theatre: The Human Seriousness of Play.* New York, 1982.

Versényi, Adam. *Theatre in Latin America: Religion, Politics, and Culture from Cortés to the 1980s.* Cambridge, U.K., 1993.

Vince, Ronald W. *Ancient and Medieval Theatre: A Historiographical Handbook.* Westport, Conn., 1984.

E. J. WESTLAKE (2005)

DRAMA: ANCIENT NEAR EASTERN RITUAL DRAMA [FIRST EDITION]

It is now commonly recognized that drama in the ancient Near East originated as a program of ritual acts performed at seasonal festivals, especially at the New Year festival. The central theme of this program was "off with the old, on with the new"; it was designed to mark the end of one lease of communal life and to ensure the next. The program is attested in many parts of the world and survives—albeit in attenuated form—in folk plays still performed in northern Greece and in such popular diversions as the English mummers' play.

The principal components of this ritual program are as follows:

1. The deposition (or even execution) of the reigning king, regarded as the embodiment of communal life momentarily ended, followed by the installation of a successor, regarded as a new avatar (or incarnation) of the ideal, perpetual kingship ("Le roi est mort; vive le roi!"). Often a temporary king is appointed during the interval.
2. The ceremonial "marriage" of the new king to a chosen bride in order to ensure the continued fecundity of the people. This epitomizes a brief period of sexual license observed by the community as a whole to the same end.
3. A combat between principals or teams symbolizing, respectively, new year and old, summer and winter, rainfall and drought, or simply life and death. When waged by principals, the victor (necessarily the embodiment of regeneration) becomes the king. Often the defeated antagonist is identified as a dragon who has impounded the subterranean waters and caused drought, or who has embroiled the sea and rivers and brought floods. His discomfiture ensures the irrigation of the soil in proper measure, and the power to control it is then formally vested in the victorious new king.
4. A communal feast, whereby members of the community recement their bonds of kinship by commensality, thus becoming companions in the literal sense of the word. The community's gods are thought to be present either as guests or as hosts. The ancestral dead are likewise in attendance, since the ongoing existence of the community necessarily involves the past as well as the present and future ("Our founders are with us in spirit").

Often the ritual program takes the form of the burial and subsequent disinterment of a puppet representing the temporary death and subsequent revival (resurrection) of vegetation and fertility.

Six factors turn this ritual program into drama in the modern sense of the term:

1. It comes to be interpreted as the representation in present time of a situation or process that essentially transcends the particular moment when it is performed—that is, as the punctualization of something essentially transtemporal. This is accomplished by representing the successive functional acts as incidents (or episodes) in a myth or story, the actors then impersonating supernatural beings, such as deities, or demons.
2. There is shift of focus from the ritual plot to the interplay of characters. The actors are no longer cardboard figures representing such abstractions as old year and new, life and death; the combat becomes one of conflicting personalities.
3. The action comes to be performed by a professional class (e.g., priests) rather than by the community as a whole. The broad masses then constitute an audience. This converts drama in the original sense of the term, namely, something done (Gr., *draō,* "do"), into theater, something watched (Gr., *theaomai,* "watch"), that is, into a spectacle.
4. Subsidiary elements are introduced in order to enhance popular interest and attention. Familiar songs are inserted in which the audience may join; messages are repeated verbatim when delivered, so that latecomers to the performance may catch up with the preceding action; the several incidents are tricked out with details drawn from traditional folklore; things are done abortively twice and successfully only at the third try, thereby increasing momentum and excitement.
5. The ritual combat is sometimes rationalized as the commemorative reenactment of a historical event, the actors being identified with traditional heroes and their adver-

saries. In certain parts of Greece, for instance, the opposing teams were portrayed as the followers of Alexander and Darius respectively, and in the English mummers' play they become at times King George and Napoleon. Indeed, by this process the ritual purport may be obscured altogether, as when the folk play develops into the enactment of an incident from scripture (e.g., the Flood, the Annunciation, or the Crucifixion in the medieval mystery plays or the story of Esther in Jewish plays staged at Purim).

6. In the course of time, when the original function of the performance has been forgotten, the action may degenerate into burlesque, farce, or masquerade, as is often the ase in the modern survivals. This development eventually gives rise to comedy.

The earliest examples of ritual drama come from the ancient Near East. They are preserved in hieroglyphic and cuneiform texts emanating from the civilizations of the Egyptians, the Babylonians and Assyrians, the Hittites of Asia Minor, and the Canaanites of ancient Syria. These texts date in general from the second and third millennia BCE, although their contents in several cases represent traditions older than the documents themselves. Most of them are explicitly associated with seasonal ceremonies, either being accompanied by a formal "order of service," or else containing interspersed liturgical rubrics. It should be observed, however, that since the ritual drama was (and still is) often performed in pantomime, the dialogues being recited and the story narrated by a "lector," some of the texts appear to be scripts for these "presenters" rather than libretti for the actors.

EGYPT. The Egyptian texts are the oldest. The *Ramesseum Coronation Drama* is inscribed on a papyrus unearthed in 1896 in the precincts of the Ramesseum at Thebes. The manuscript dates from the reign of Sen-Wosret (Sesotris) I (c. 1970 BCE), but it is believed that the contents go back some thirteen centuries earlier to the time of the first dynasty. The text was designed for the ceremony of installing (or reinstalling) the pharaoh at a New Year festival. It includes such elements of the ritual pattern as the combat, the death of the old king and the lamentation over him, the investiture and enthronement of the new king, a communal feast attended by the governors of the several provinces (nomes) of Egypt, and various acts (for example, the threshing of grain and the milking of goats) designed to promote fertility.

The successive ritual acts are construed as an enactment of the mythic discomfiture of the god Osiris by his evil brother Seth. The combat is taken to represent the fight between them. The new king is identified with Horus, son of Osiris, who avenged his father and defeated Seth. The two sacred women who bewail the slain king are the goddesses Isis and Nephthys, who bewailed Osiris. The official who invests the new king is the god Thoth, who adjudicated the contest between the gods. The various regalia are explained symbolically: the maces handed to the new king are the testicles of Seth wrested from him by Horus and then grafted upon himself to increase his vigor. The threshing of the grain represents the belaboring of Osiris by his rival. Interspersed rubrics identify the actors with their mythic counterparts and list props for the various scenes.

The *Edfu Drama* is engraved, with illustrative reliefs, on one of the walls of the temple at Edfu (Idfu; ancient Bekhdet); this text was composed for a ritual performance at a spring festival. Its central theme is the reinvigoration of the king as the epitome of communal life. It consists of a prologue, three acts (subdivided into scenes), and an epilogue. At one point, there is mention of a "chief lector," and since there is no indication of separate speakers, it is probable that the action was performed in pantomime and that what we have before us is simply the script for that "reciter."

The contents include such ingredients of the ritual pattern as the combat, the installation of the victor as king, and a "sacred marriage" at which he is the bridegroom. The action is interpreted mythically: the king is the local god, Horus of Bekhdet; his adversary, termed "the Caitiff," or "Monster," is identified as a hippopotamus (analogous to the dragon elsewhere), and the bride is the goddess Hathor of Dendera.

The *Memphite Theology* (or *Memphis Drama*), inserted on a slab of black granite now in the British Museum, was written in the reign of Shabaka (c. 712–697 BCE), but a preamble states expressly that it was copied from an original, which has been dated by modern scholars some eighteen centuries earlier. It was designed to be performed at a festival.

The theme is, once again, the death or discomfiture of the old king, the ritual lament over him, the combat, and the installation of the victor as the new king in the city of Memphis. The king is again identified with Horus, his defunct predecessor with Osiris, the wailing women with Isis and Nephthys, and the combat as that between Horus and Seth. The action, however, is not only mythified, but also historicized; the upshot of the combat is that the god Geb awards Upper Egypt to Seth and lower Egypt to Horus, but both areas are eventually united in a single country whose capital is Memphis. The text concludes, in fact, with a hymn to Ptah, patron god of that city.

It has been suggested also that certain mythico-magical texts engraved on plaques and stelae depicting Horus treading triumphantly on snakes, crocodiles, and scorpions were copied from ritual drama. There is, however, no indication that these myths were associated with seasonal festivals, nor do they include several of the typical elements of the ritual pattern.

BABYLONIA AND ASSYRIA. The evidence for drama among the Babylonians and Assyrians is inferential and indirect but nonetheless persuasive. First, we have a long mythological poem, the *Enuma elish* (wrongly called an epic of creation), which was recited by a priest as part of the liturgy of the New Year festival. This relates how Marduk, the primary god of Babylon, vanquished a rebellious marine monster named

Tiamat and her cohorts, how he thereby acquired sovereignty over the gods, was installed in a newly built palace, and, at a banquet, determined the world order. Although this text is a literary composition and not a scenario, it clearly conforms to the ritual pattern of combat, enthronement, and renewal, and it is therefore reasonable to conclude that it is based on some more ancient seasonal drama.

Second, we have a series of texts—albeit fragmentary—in which what seem to be successive acts in a seasonal ritual are interpreted mythologically as representing incidents in a story concerning Marduk. This has suggested that these texts accompanied a dramatic performance. It has been proposed alternatively, however, that they refer rather to historical events that learned academicians explained as exemplifications of a traditional myth.

From the Hittites comes a text that describes how the weather god, with the aid of a mortal, defeated a marine dragon named Illuyanka, how this was followed by a desired precipitation of rain, and (apparently) how control of the subterranean waters was thereafter vested in the king. The story is tricked out with folkloric motifs and was designed for recitation at an annual festival. It is prefaced by a petition for rain and is accompanied by a description of the festival ceremonies. Hence, although it is once again a liturgical recitation rather than the actual text of a play, it clearly derives, like its Mesopotamian counterpart, from some earlier dramatic performance. Another Hittite text describes a ritual combat, in which the antagonists are historicized respectively as the Hittites themselves and a neighboring people called the Masa (possibly the Maeonians of Lydia).

That sacred drama was known also to the Canaanites in the second millennium BCE may be confidently deduced from a lengthy mythological poem discovered at Ras Shamra (ancient Ugarit) on the north coast of Syria. This relates how Baal, god of rainfall and fertility, successively vanquished Yamm, lord of seas and rivers, and Mot, genius of aridity and death. By virtue of defeating the former, he acquired sovereignty over the gods and was installed in a newly built palace. At an inaugural banquet tendered to the gods, he deliberately excluded Mot, whereupon his offended rival lured him down to the netherworld. During his sojourn there, all fertility failed on earth. An interrex was appointed in the person of a young god named Athtar—probably the genius of artificial irrigation—but he was too small to "make the grade," and the languishing earth was revived only when Baal's sister Anat, aided by the Lady Sun, descended into the lower regions, retrieved him and gave him burial, as a necessary prelude to his eventual resurrection. Thus revived, Baal finally discomfited Mot in combat and made known his return by an impressive display of sheet lightning.

Clearly a myth of the alternation of wet and dry seasons in the Syrian year, this poem reflects unmistakably in its contents and sequence the characteristic features of the standard seasonal ritual—the combat, interrex, enthronement, and banquet. A colophon states expressly that it was redacted (or recited?) by a disciple of the high priest. It was therefore a liturgical chant, probably recited at an autumnal festival that inaugurated the rainy season after that of the winter squalls and the dry summer months.

A burlesque version of the primitive seasonal drama may be seen to underlie another composition from Ras Shamra, conventionally known as the *Poem of Dawn and Sunset.* This consists of two sections: the first gives the rubrics for a ritual ceremony at the time when grapes ripen, and the second an accompanying mythological narrative. Two women encounter the aged supreme god El at the seashore while he is shooting down a bird and boiling it for his dinner. They make ribald remarks about his senility and seeming sexual impotence. Thereupon he gives forthright proof to the contrary. The ladies bear a pair of siblings. Someone—apparently the cuckolded husband of each—reports to the god that the children (of whose true parentage he is evidently unaware) glow like dawn and sunset—a common trait of divine offspring—whereupon El cynically suggests that their proper place would be up in the sky alongside the sun, moon, and fixed stars. Subsequently, further children, called "the gracious gods," are born. El is informed that these have insatiable appetites—another common folkloric trait of divinely begotten children. He thereupon consigns them to the desert, there to forage for their food. After a time, they fall in with the official custodian of grain and beg food and drink. Although he has only a meager supply to meet his own needs, he apparently feeds them, or they break into his silo. The rest of the story is missing, but a few fragmentary words at the end may be interpreted to mean that as a reward for his generosity, the gods annually bestow a due measure of crops and fruits. The text would thus be a more or less comic version of the ritual drama acted out at a festival of renewal in June, when vines are preliminarily trimmed. The seduction of the two women would then reflect the sacred marriage, and the children would be the gods subsequently astralized as the Heavenly Twins (Dioscuri), the regnant constellation of that month.

HEBREW SCRIPTURES. Literary echoes of the sacred drama have also been recognized by several modern scholars in certain of the biblical psalms. Those, for instance, that begin with the words, "The Lord reigneth" (or "hath become king"), Psalms 97 and 99, for example, would have been patterned after a traditional type of hymn composed for the annual enthronement of the god at the New Year festival (even though the ceremony itself may have been discarded); while Psalm 93, which acclaims the Lord as having acquired sovereignty by subduing "the mighty waters," as occupying a gorgeous temple, and as issuing eternal decrees for the government of the world, would reflect the same myth as the Mesopotamian and Hittite texts, based on the seasonal pattern.

Some scholars have also suggested that the *Song of Songs* is really a pastoral drama, in which a country maiden (the Shulammite) abducted by the king (Solomon) for his harem, is won back by her shepherd lover. There is, however, no evidence of such secular drama in the ancient Near East. Moreover, this view depends very largely on dubious interpretations of certain passages, and the assumed scenes of the drama sometimes consist of a single verse! It is therefore more probable that the biblical book is simply a repertoire of love songs.

RITUAL PATTERNS IN GREEK AND OTHER LITERATURE. Much of the same ritual pattern that underlies the ancient Near Eastern texts may be recognized also as one of the main sources of classical Greek drama, for Gilbert Murray (1912) has pointed out that in several of the classical Greek tragedies that have come down to us, notably in those of Euripides, it is possible to discern—albeit through a glass darkly—such standard elements of the primitive ritual pattern as the combat (usually attenuated to a mere verbal altercation), the discomfiture of the loser (e.g., Pentheus or Hippolytus), the ceremonial lament, and sometimes also the resurrection of the fertility spirit (modified, to be sure, into a mere final theophany, like that of Dionysos in *The Bacchae*). On this theory, the prologue, which came eventually to summarize the background of the play, would have developed out of a more primitive ritual formula that served originally not to introduce the characters but to inaugurate the religious ceremony at which the play was performed. (Such a prologue indeed occurs in the aforementioned Canaanite *Poem of Dawn and Sunset.*) So, too, the division of the chorus into two halves would be a survival of the two opposing teams in the ritual combat.

A striking example of how the primitive ritual drama survived in literary form has been detected by Murray in *The Bacchae* of Euripides. Here he finds a mythified version of the combat, the dismemberment (in this case, of Pentheus), the lament, the retrieval of the scattered members, and, as "by a sort of doubling," the resurrection, attenuated into the final epiphany of the true god Dionysos instead of the revivification of the slaughtered victim.

Some twenty years later, Francis Cornford (1934, 1961), an eminent British classicist, applied this theory to Greek comedy, arguing that traces of the combat, the death-and-resurrection, the sacred marriage, and the banquet could be recognized in each of the extant plays of Aristophanes. It must be noted, however, that other scholars have questioned this assumption.

Nor is it only in Greek drama that survivals of the ritual pattern may be recognized. Equally impressive is the evidence afforded by the so-called Homeric *Hymn to Demeter.* This describes the rape of Demeter's daughter Persephone and the search for her by her mother and the goddess Hekate. But the successive incidents in the narrative reproduce to a nicety certain features of the ritual associated with the festival of Thesmophoria and with the Eleusinian mysteries. Thus, the search by torchlight reproduces the torchlight procession by female worshipers; the fast observed by Demeter reproduces the period of abstinence and mortification characteristic of seasonal ceremonies; the emphasis on her glum abstention from mirth and laughter finds its explanation in the statement of Plutarch and other writers that the festival was observed in a grim, lugubrious mood and that all merriment was forbidden; while the obscene gestures and jokes of the crone Iambe correspond to the chanting of ribald songs couched in iambic meter as a means of stimulating fertility.

It is not, however, in the seasonal pattern alone that the origin of Greek drama may be recognized. Other scholars—notably William Ridgeway (1915) and even Murray himself—have suggested that an alternative source lay in some cases in the commemorative stories of ancient heroes recited on the anniversaries of their births or deaths or at annual festivals when their shades were believed temporarily to rejoin their kinsmen (this would be like the reenactment of historical incidents in modern pageants, for example, on President Washington's birthday).

Finally, survivals of the primitive ritual pattern have been recognized by several modern scholars not only in drama but also in other forms of literature. It has been claimed, for instance, that some of the hymns of the Hindu *Ṛgveda* were chanted in seasonal masquerades and that some of the odes in the Chinese *Shih ching* were the libretti of crude harvest pantomimes. The Scandinavian *Elder Edda* and the legend of the Holy Grail have likewise been derived from ritual archetypes. Doubtless in certain cases, enthusiasm has outrun sobriety, but this can scarcely detract from the fact that a set of usages so constant and recurrent in ancient communities may be expected to have left its impress on their literature and art.

SEE ALSO Egyptian Religion, article on The Literature; Enuma Elish; Epics; Literature, article on Literature and Religion; New Year Festivals; Poetry, article on Poetry and Religion; Psalms; Purim Plays.

BIBLIOGRAPHY

The most comprehensive account of standard seasonal rites, ancient and primitive, and of their survival in popular usages is still James G. Frazer's monumental *The Golden Bough,* 3d ed., rev. & enl., 12 vols. (London, 1911–1915). Of several condensed editions, my abridgement, with notes, is the most recent: *The New Golden Bough* (1959; New York, 1977). Highly stimulating also, though sometimes exaggerated, is Jane Ellen Harrison's general treatment of the subject in her *Ancient Art and Ritual* (London, 1913).

Translations and discussions of the ancient Near Eastern texts can be found in my *Thespis: Ritual, Myth, and Drama in the Ancient Near East,* 2d ed. (1961; New York, 1977); translations alone appear in *Ancient Near Eastern Texts relating to the Old Testament,* 3d ed., edited by James B. Pritchard (Princeton, 1969). For a translation and discussion of the Egyptian Edfu drama, see A. M. Blackman and H. W. Fairman's "The Myth of Horus at Edfu I–II," *Journal of Egyptian Archaeology* 21 (1935): 26–36, 28 (1942): 32–38, and 29 (1943): 2–36. On the relations of the seasonal patterns to classical Greek tragedy, see Gilbert Murray's "Excursus on the Ritual Forms

Preserved in Greek Tragedy," in Harrison's *Themis* (Cambridge, 1912), pp. 341–363, and on their assumed relation to Greek comedy, see Francis M. Cornford's *The Origin of Attic Comedy*, 2d ed. (1934; New York, 1961). On traces of the pattern in Euripides' The Bacchae, see E. R. Dodds's edition, *Bacchae* (Oxford, 1944), and on the ritual background of the Homeric *Hymn to Demeter*, see N. J. Richardson's *The Homeric Hymn to Demeter* (Oxford, 1974). Survivals in modern Greek folk plays are described by R. M. Dawkins in "The Modern Carnival in Thrace and the Cult of Dionysus," *Journal of Hellenic Studies* 26 (1906): 191–206, and by A. J. B. Wace in "North Greek Festivals," *Annual of the British School at Athens* 16 (1910): 232ff. The alternative view that Greek drama developed out of recitations at the annual or periodic commemoration of heroes is best presented in William Ridgeway's *The Origin of Tragedy* (London, 1910).

On the medieval mystery and miracle plays, the best source is E. K. Chambers's *The Mediaeval Stage*, 2 vols. (Oxford, 1903), but the older collection of texts in William Hone's *Ancient Mysteries Described, Especially in English Miracle Plays* (London, 1823) is still useful. The standard work on the English mummers' play is R. J. E. Tiddy's posthumous *The Mummers' Play*, edited by Rupert S. Thompson (Oxford, 1923), where some twenty-three specimens are collected.

Regarding literary forms of the ritual pattern, see, for the odes in the Chinese *Shih ching*, Bruno Schindler's essay in *Occident and Orient*, edited by Schindler (London, 1936), pp. 498–502; for the *Elder Edda*, Bertha S. Phillpotts's *The Elder Edda and Ancient Scandinavian Drama* (Cambridge, 1920); and for the legend of the Holy Grail, Jesse L. Weston's ingenious, but much controverted work *From Ritual to Romance* (Cambridge, 1920). For possible echoes of the pattern in the Psalter, see my *Thespis*, 2d ed. (1961; New York, 1977), pp. 442–452, and Aubrey R. Johnson's "The Role of the King in the Jerusalem Cultus," in *The Labyrinth*, edited by S. H. Hooke (London, 1934), pp. 73–111. For a skeptical critique of this view, however, see S. G. F. Brandon's essay "The Myth Ritual and Position Critically Considered," in *Myth, Ritual and Kingship*, edited by S. H. Hooks (Oxford, 1958), pp. 261–291.

THEODOR H. GASTER (1987)

DRAMA: ANCIENT NEAR EASTERN RITUAL DRAMA [FURTHER CONSIDERATIONS]

Beginning with his 1936 master's thesis, Theodor H. Gaster (1906–1992) focused most of his research on the analysis of Ancient Near Eastern mythological compositions (especially those from Ugarit, modern Ras Shamra in Syria) as religious dramas that were performed within a ritual setting. Gaster was deeply influenced by James G. Frazer's (1854–1941) understanding of the relation between myth and ritual, as well as by his preoccupation with seasonal patterns in mythological narratives and discourses. Although this approach, exemplified by Gaster's famous work *Thespis*, was predominant in North American and British scholarship during the 1950s and 1960s, now it can also be regarded as a modern intellectual construct rather than as a historical reconstruction.

ANCIENT EGYPT. Gaster was excessively optimistic about the possibilities of knowing the actual setting of many ancient compositions. In the case of the Ancient Egyptian, some compositions have been regarded as ritual dramas by some scholars, including the *Dramatic Ramesseum Papyrus*, the *Triumph of Horus* from the Ptolemaic temple at Edfu, and the Ptolemaic papyri concerning the mysteries of Osiris at Abydos. In fact, in some instances (e.g., the Mysteries of Osiris at Abydos and the Bremner-Rhind Papyrus), the papyri include annotations about the performance of songs and switch between first person singular and plural—the latter may indicate solos sung by Isis and duets by the two goddesses (Isis and Nephthys) in the Bremner-Rhind Papyrus. Nevertheless, the evidence is generally ambiguous, and even the indications of the expected performative nature of songs and hymns do not imply an actual dramatic performance with different roles enacted by actors. The compositions themselves and the rituals connected to them were literary dramatizations of divine deeds, which would have taken place in a mythical time. However, there is no clear indication that these compositions were ever staged as actual dramas.

MESOPOTAMIA. The Mesopotamian case is even more complicated. One can question whether the Sumerian and Akkadian religious narratives had any actual life outside the narrow walls of the scribal world. For many of the ritual texts and exorcisms, specific instructions do prescribe their recitation at various points in rituals. Moreover, there are some letters stating that certain rituals were performed or instructing them to be performed. Nonetheless, almost all the texts whose performance seems more or less well attested in different sources are nonnarrative and mostly performative utterances (i.e., incantations and rituals whose illocutionary linguistic nature qualify them as speech acts). However, for the Mesopotamian religious narratives—the kinds of compositions that articulate a theological or theologico-political discourse—very little evidence exists that they were ever performed. Ironically, the *Enuma elish* (the Babylonian story of creation) is the only religious narrative for whose performance there seems to be some explicit evidence. One fragmentary tablet refers to the recitation of the whole *Enuma elish* on the fourth of Nisan (i.e., on the fourth day of the Akitu festival). The Akitu was the Babylonian New Year festival, celebrated from the first to the twelfth of Nisan (the first of Nisan would be near the vernal equinox, about March 21). In Babylon, the Akitu was a sowing festival. In other Mesopotamian cities, however, especially in earlier periods, the Akitu took place twice a year—during harvest season and during sowing season.

That the *Enuma elish* was probably the only Mesopotamian religious narrative ever performed is ironic because this is an exceedingly atypical work: The style, dialect, grammar, and lexicon of the composition seem to point to an individual author, an erudite scholar trained in all the intricacies of the most arcane scribal traditions. Most Assyriologists date the composition to the reign of Nebuchadrezzar I (c. 1100 BCE), and the scribal and scholarly setting of the text can hardly be doubted. The poem abounds in puns and word play based on signs and compound signs, which can make sense only in writing. The famous list of the fifty names of Marduk in Tablet VII of the *Enuma elish* is understandable only in its written form: Every line of the text is an expansion based on homophonic and homographic Sumerograms evoked by each specific name of Marduk. The text is itself a scholarly commentary. Thus, the only religious narrative that may have ever been publicly performed in Mesopotamia constitutes the epitome of artificiality, the prototype of scholarly literature. Even if regarded as part of the official cult, the *Enuma elish* stands alone in the history of Mesopotamian religious texts and little can be inferred from its uniqueness.

SACRED MARRIAGE. Also with regard to Mesopotamia, many assume that the cycle of lyric compositions focused on the relation between Inanna and Dumuzi reflects a ritual usually called *hieròs gámos* (sacred marriage) and that these texts would have been connected to its performance. However, very little is known about such a ritual. As part of the celebration of the new year from the second half of the third millennium to the beginning of the second, the king, representing Dumuzi, would have had (or pretended to have) sexual intercourse with a woman (usually a high priestess) who was representing the goddess Inanna. Echoes of this ceremony survived in first millennium texts that describe royal rituals and the epithalamia of, for instance, Nabu and Tašmētu in Assyria, and Nabu and Nanaya in Babylonia. Most of the details of this sacred marriage are unknown. In documents from the Ur III period (c. 2100–2000 BCE), there are some mentions of priestesses spending the night in the god's bedchamber. Other possible sacred marriage rites have been proposed for earlier periods, especially those involving the moon god (Nanna/Suen), and his high priestess at Ur. In spite of all of this more or less oblique evidence, important doubts have been cast on the actual existence of such a rite. The arcane character of this ritual and the unclear and scanty evidence can be explained in the light of the inherent nature of the ritual, whatever its actual performative mechanisms were. Nonetheless, the Mesopotamian sacred marriage may well have been a mere intellectual construct, a religious narrative in which the mythical and historical discourses intersect as part of the Mesopotamian political theology.

HITTITE. Probably the only area in which Gaster's enthusiasm was partly justified is Anatolia. A number of Hittite rituals have been regarded as the forerunners of drama. Some of these rituals are labeled as *uttar* (utterance, word, spell) in their colophons and refrains and have sections clearly noted as direct speech (with the quotation particle *-wa*). Moreover, some Hittite compositions can be regarded as ritual dialogues, as in the case of the text describing the "great road" the soul takes at death. Nonetheless, most Anatolian texts in Hittite, Luwian, and Palaic are actually rituals, and rituals are performative by nature. Some of these rituals include dialogues that were perhaps dramatized, but this is still a far cry from staged drama. Likewise, in the realm of Mesopotamian secular literature, the Sumerian dialogues and disputations might seem pieces of a chamber theater of sorts, if it were not for the fact that these are strictly scribal compositions whose life was limited to the confines of the Mesopotamian schools.

The Ugaritic cycle of Baʿlu has been interpreted by Gaster and others as a ritual dramatization of a seasonal pattern. This approach makes several assumptions for which there is no textual evidence: (1) the Baʿlu narrative mentions very few terms or expressions that could be linked to a ritual or seasonal cycle; (2) the identification of Yammu (the sea) with a dragon or monster; (3) the banishment of Môtu (death) prior to his confrontation with Baʿlu; (4) the seasonal pattern reverses the order of the texts; (5) the cycle would correspond to an autumnal festival of which there are no traces in the Ugaritic corpus (e.g., rituals, administrative documents, letters); and (6) the palace of Baʿlu in the cycle cannot be the temple excavated at Ras Shamra, because the composition places it on Mount Sapanu (*ṣpn*, Ṣapānu, biblical *ṣāp̱ôn*, Saphon), presumably north of Ugarit. Therefore, there is no textual basis for an interpretation of this mythical cycle as a ritual drama. As in the case of the Egyptian compositions above, a composition may narrate a mythical event in a dramatized fashion, but this does not imply that the composition was performed as a drama, especially in the absence of any specific evidence (e.g., administrative texts concerning festivals or references to performance within the composition itself or in other texts). This would also apply to the biblical *Song of Songs,* which is simply a lyrical dialogue between the Shulammite and her lover, sometimes seemingly portrayed in the poems as King Solomon. The *Song of Songs* may have been performed as a series of recitatives, but can hardly be labeled as a drama and was probably never a hierogamic text.

In sum, it is a misguided effort to search for the historical or typological roots of Greek drama in the Ancient Near East. Some compositions include dialogues between characters and some concrete genres (rituals, incantations, exorcisms) were performative by nature. However, there is no internal or external evidence of any actual dramatic, staged performance of any of these mythological and ritual texts.

BIBLIOGRAPHY

On Theodor H. Gaster, see Richard H. Hiers and Harold M. Stahmer, "Theodor H. Gaster, 1906–1992," *Ugarit-Forschungen* 27 (1995): 59–114; 28 (1996): 277–285, and Mark S. Smith, *Untold Stories: The Bible and Ugaritic Studies in the Twentieth Century,* pp. 73–75, 88–90 (Peabody, Mass., 2001). On ritual drama in Hittite texts, see Calvert Watkins, *How to Kill a Dragon: Aspects of Indo-European Poetics,* pp. 135–44, 284–88 (Oxford, 1995). On the ritual interpretation of the Ugaritic cycle of Baʿlu, see Mark S. Smith, *The Ugaritic Baal Cycle, I,* pp. 60–75 (Leiden, 1994). On the Mesopotamian sacred marriage, see Johannes Renger and Jerrold S. Cooper, "Heilige Hochzeit," *Reallexikon der Assyriologie* 4 (1975): 251–269, J. S. Cooper, "Sacred Marriage and Popular Cult in Early Mesopotamia," in *Official Cult and Popular Religion in the Ancient Near East,* edited by E. Matshushima, pp. 81–96 (Heidelberg, 1993), R. F. G. Sweet, "A New Look at the 'Sacred Marriage' in Ancient Mesopotamia," in *Corolla Torontonensis: Studies in Honour of R. M. Smith,* edited by Emmet Robbins and Stella Sandahl, pp. 85–104 (Toronto, 1994), Gonzalo Rubio, "Inanna and Dumuzi: A Sumerian Love Story," *Journal of the American Oriental Society* 121 (2001): 268–274, Philip Jones, "Embracing Inana: Legitimation and Mediation in the Ancient Mesopotamian Sacred Marriage Hymn Iddin-Dagan A," *Journal of the American Oriental Society* 123 (2003): 291–302, and Pirjo Lapinkivi, *The Sumerian Sacred Marriage in the Light of Comparative Evidence* (Helsinki, 2004). Emmanuel Laroche's *Catalogue des textes hittites* (Paris, 1971) is available online at http://www.asor.org/HITTITE/CTHHP.html. Also see *Keilschrifturkunden aus Boghazköi* (Berlin, 1921–1990).

GONZALO RUBIO (2005)

DRAMA: MIDDLE EASTERN NARRATIVE TRADITIONS

Popular religious storytelling has been widespread in the Islamic Middle East since the earliest times, and its forms have varied considerably according to time, place, and branch or sect of Islam. For the period before 1500, sources for religious storytelling are few and widely scattered; nevertheless, some idea of the situation can be gained. With the establishment of Shiism as the state religion in Persia in about 1500, important new forms of religious oral narrative appeared, some of which are still practiced in the twentieth century.

Religious storytelling on the popular level has its roots in formal preaching in the mosque. In its broadest sense, it attempts to interpret the religion and meet the spiritual needs of the common people in a manner more accessible to them than that of a preacher representing the religious establishment. This kind of storytelling quickly came to reflect the values and beliefs of popular Islam and in doing so widened the gap between the Islam of the theologians and jurisprudents and that of the common people. The sources for the study of popular religious storytelling reflect, by and large, the views of the small educated class, including the religious class, and deplore the existence and influence of popular oral narrators.

In the first century of Islam it became the practice of governing authorities to appoint a preacher for the local mosque and pay him a stipend from the state treasury. At the same time, unofficial preachers (*qāṣṣ*, lit. "story-teller"; pl., *quṣṣāṣ*) began delivering sermons in mosques and elsewhere. While the official preachers represented the views of the religious establishment, the free preachers were not so restricted. Enlightenment mixed with entertainment in their sermons, and edifying tales slowly developed into entertaining ones, always within the framework of transmitting and interpreting the tradition of the Prophet. Some popular preachers were highly respected men of great learning, and al-Jāḥiẓ (d. 868/9) included Ḥasan al-Baṣrī (d. 728/9) in his list of learned popular preachers. Most, however, were bent on impressing their audiences, and since it is easy to pass from edifying tales to profane ones, they began to enjoy great success among the uneducated. By about 892, popular preaching was considered a problem in the Muslim community, and the government announced that storytellers, astrologers, and fortune-tellers were not to appear in the streets and mosques of Baghdad. In Spain in the twelfth century, religious storytellers were banned from performing in cemeteries and from telling tales in which the Prophet's name was mentioned, and municipal authorities were charged with preventing women from attending their sessions in tents.

Because of the bias of the sources in favor of the religious establishment, most accounts of popular preachers and storytellers after the ninth century describe them as charlatans and often associate them with beggars and confidence men. They were accused of mixing edifying narratives from the Qurʾān with fanciful biblical legends, stories from pre-Islamic Arabia and Persia, eschatological and cosmological tales based on invented chains of authorities, romances with religious associations, and popular etymologies, leaving no questions unanswered. Among the public, they became more highly regarded than the theologians, who condemned them for falsifying the religious tradition. They were also opposed by the Ṣūfīs, who maintained that they did not transmit true mystical experiences. More than one source describes their practices used to impress their audiences, which included painting their faces, artificially stimulating the flow of tears, making histrionic gestures, pounding on the pulpit, running up and down its stairs, and even throwing themselves off it. These storytellers flourished in Iraq, Persia, and Central Asia but were relatively scarce in the Hejaz and in Muslim North Africa. Whatever the accuracy of these accounts may be, it is clear that the popular religious storytellers, like the friars of medieval Christianity, bridged the gulf between an intellectual and distant religious establishment and an illiterate populace needing spiritual guidance and education in terms they could comprehend.

When the Safavids (1500–1732) were establishing Shiism as the official religion in Persia, one of the means they used to spread their message was the oral storyteller. This appears to have stimulated the development and specialization of oral narration, and to judge from the sources, religious storytelling flourished in Persia from the sixteenth to the early twentieth century. I shall describe here the three most important forms.

Rawẓah-khvānī began with public readings from *Ruwẓat al-shuhadā* (The garden of martyrs), a collection of stories by Ḥusayn Vāʿiẓ Kāshifī (d. 910 AH/1504–1505 CE) about the Shīʿī *imāms.* Soon moving out of the mosque and into public places and private houses, *rawẓah-khvānī* became an integral part of religious life. It is still practiced widely in Iran. Another form of oral religious narrative, rarer today, is a variety of picture storytelling called *pardah-dārī.* Working in pairs, narrators make use of a large canvas on which are painted pictures of the imams in their struggles with the opponents of Shiism. The canvas is slowly unrolled or unveiled as the story is related in a mixture of prose and verse. Finally, there is *sukhanvarī*, which began in Safavid times and is all but extinct in Iran today. Probably deriving from an older rivalry between Shīʿī and Sunnī religious storytellers, *sukhanvarī* was a contest in which two narrators attempted to outdo each other in improvising verses praising the imams and condemning the Sunnīs. The contests would usually take place in coffeehouses and were most popular during the nights of Ramaḍān.

Among the Sunnīs of Ottoman Turkey and the Turkic peoples of Central Asia, religious storytelling was practiced to a modest extent. It is believed that the *meddah*s (dramatic storytellers) of Turkey were originally religious storytellers, and nineteenth-century travelers report hearing popular religious narratives in Kabul and Bukhara. Today the practice has almost disappeared from Sunnī Islam, but it is still popular among the Shīʿī communities of Iraq and Anatolia, in addition to Iran. There a variant of *rawẓah-khvānī* is common: passages from *maqtal*s, books that relate the martyrdom of the *imām*s, are recited, most often during the first ten days of Muḥarram (the first month of the Muslim lunar year).

SEE ALSO Taʿziyah.

BIBLIOGRAPHY

Because references to religious storytelling are so widely scattered, the following sources have been chosen for their bibliographical references as well as their information on the subject. Charles Pellat's "Ḳāṣṣ," in *The Encyclopaedia of Islam*, new ed., vol. 4 (Leiden, 1978), gives a basic introduction to the subject but focuses on Arabic sources. Ignácz Goldziher in his *Muslim Studies*, edited by S. M. Stern, vol. 2 (New York, 1973), pp. 149–159, discusses the early preachers of Islam and the rise of popular preaching. This was originally published as *Muhammedanische Studien*, 2 vols. (Halle, 1889–1890). The scandalous side of popular religious storytelling is depicted vividly by C. E. Bosworth in his *The Mediaeval Islamic Underworld*, vol. 1 (Leiden, 1976), pp. 15, 24–29. The various forms of dramatic religious storytelling in Iran are described by Bahrām Bayẓāʾī in his *Namāyish dar Irān* (The Theater in Iran; Tehran, 1965), pp. 71–76. Metin And describes Shīʿī religious practices and storytelling in his "The Muharram Observances in Anatolian Turkey," in *Taʿziyeh: Ritual and Drama in Iran*, edited by Peter Chelkowski (New York, 1979), pp. 238–254.

WILLIAM L. HANAWAY, JR. (1987)

DRAMA: INDIAN DANCE AND DANCE DRAMA

In the cultures of the Indian subcontinent, drama and ritual have been integral parts of a single whole from earliest recorded history. The first evidences of ritual dance drama performances occur in the rock paintings of Mirzapur, Bhimbetka, and in other sites, which are variously dated 20,000–5000 BCE. The ancient remains of Mohenjo-Daro and Harappa (2500–2000 BCE) are more definitive. Here archaeological remains clearly point to the prevalence of ritual performance involving populace and patrons. The Mohenjo-Daro seals, bronze figurines, and images of priests and broken torsos are all clear indications of dance as ritual.

The aspect of Vedic ritual tradition closest to dance and drama was a rigorous system called *yajña*. Various types of sacrifices called *yajña*s were held at different astronomical confluences and lasted for five, seven, fifteen, or twenty-one days. These rituals were dramatic performances presented in a sacred enclosure. Usually three altars symbolized the celestial, terrestrial, and mundane worlds. The altars were in the shape of a square, a circle, and a semicircle. The performance included incantation, verses recited in different meters in specific intonation, movement in eight directions along a circumambulatory path in the sacred enclosure, and offerings of sixteen auspicious objects. Combined, these activities constituted a comprehensive ritual drama. Participating were the priests and the *yajamana*, the person desiring the performance of the sacrifice. Roles were clearly defined: the patron, his wife, the priest, his assistants, and members of the society representing the various vocations.

The ritual's movement pattern was dramatic from inception to conclusion. The cosmos was symbolically recreated for the duration of the performance, and the movement of the universe in its process of involution, evolution, and devolution was suggested. The ritual's ultimate conclusion was the ritual burning of the sacred enclosure.

The concern of the Vedic poet was also focused on images of dance and drama, as evidenced by the inumerable textual references to these arts. Some members of the Vedic pantheon were dancers: Ūṣa, the goddess of the dawn; Indra, the god of the thunderbolt; and the two sets of twin gods, the Māruts and the Aśvins.

Archaeological remains from the Mauryan period provide evidence of the prevalence of ritual dance and dance drama. The terra-cotta figures of the dancing girls, the drummer, and others of this period suggest preoccupation with ritual dance. The tradition continues in the Sunga, Stavahana, and Kushan periods (second century BCE to second century CE), culminating with the great Buddhist stupas, Jain monuments, and early Hindu temples of the Gupta period (fourth to sixth centuries CE). The frequency of ritual performance is evident from the architectural remains of sacrificial enclosures, sculptural reliefs, and literary evidence.

THE NĀṬYA ŚĀSTRA. Attributed to Bhārata, the *Nāṭya Śāstra* (second century BCE to second century CE) enunciates a theory of aesthetics and the techniques of dramaturgy in thirty-six chapters. These chapters discuss dramatic evolution, theatrical and stage construction, and the presentation of drama. Drama is viewed as a reenactment of the cosmos, which is composed of celestial, terrestrial, and mundane worlds. It is compared to a ritual performance (*yajña*) and aims at emancipation or release (*mokṣa*) gained through the purification of emotion (*rāsa*).

Like the stupa and temple, the theater is a sacred enclosure, and the stage is the sacred altar. A center is established, and all else radiates from it. The stage center is demarcated. The performance is a ritual that begins with offerings to the sacred center and the deities of the eight directions. The *Nāṭya Śāstra* devotes a full chapter to the preliminary rituals (*pūrvaraṅga*). These comprise various entries and exits of three principal dancer-actors who establish the ritual space through song and mime. Drama proper follows. The *Nāṭya Śāstra* clearly draws upon Vedic ritual drama to create the edifice for dramatic ritual. It extracts elements from the four Vedas: intonation, recitation, gesture, language, music, and the internalized states of emotion, to create a fifth whole that Bhārata called the fifth Veda of drama. With speech, movement, music, and costumery, the performance is early multimedia. The *Nāṭya Śāstra* recognizes regional variations and can be presented in either stylized or natural modes.

Enunciated in oral tradition two thousand years ago, the precepts of the *Nāṭya Śāstra* are still followed in India in many dance and drama forms in whole or in part. The preliminaries invariably invoke principal deities; the sacred enclosure is demarcated. Whether the performance is in open space or in a closed theater, a center is established. Offerings are made of eight auspicious things, such as coconut, water, turmeric, and so forth. Once the director and his companions have established the consecrated space, the audience is invited to participate in the mythical, consecrated time of the drama.

The architectural plans of many stupas and temples built between the second and thirteenth century provide evidence of adhering to a sacred geometry of the square and circle. In each instance, a center is fundamental. Many rituals were performed in different areas of the temple, from the inner sanctum to outer enclosure. By the eighth century and particularly between the tenth and thirteenth century, special structures called *naṭamaṇḍapa* were built for ritual dance and dance drama.

Music and dance were included as part of temple offerings (*sevas*) involving flowers and incense. A solo dancer performed before the deity. Hereditary dancers called *devadāsīs* also performed in the temple sanctum. This practice was prevalent in all parts of India. Many other ritual dance dramas were performed in the courtyard, a tradition that continued and developed in many parts of India.

RITUAL DANCE DRAMA. The ritual dance-drama form with the longest continuity, called *kuttiyattam,* is performed today in special theaters (*kuttambalamas*) in Kerala. The spectacle held in these special theaters within the temple precincts is performed by professional acting families called *chakyars*. Such families can trace their genealogies back to the tenth century of the common era.

The play starts with the sounding of a large, pitcher-shaped drum, the *mizhavu.* The director and his companions enter, almost exactly as described in the *Nāṭya Śāstra,* carrying a brimming vase and a pole. In the central area of the stage, eight auspicious gifts, *aṣṭa-maṅgala,* are offered; these offerings almost replicate the offerings within the temple sanctum. The actors then circumambulate the stage, establishing the eight directions and the three spaces of the universe—nether, terrestial, and celestial.

A single play takes from seven to nine nights to complete. Each act is elaborated upon in minutest detail. A repertoire of ten plays is extant, although today only excerpts are presented. Night after night audiences witness these performances in rapt attention. Participation in the performance is a ritual act comparable to the daily worship the devotee offers to the deity inside the temple.

In the Guruvayur Temple (c. fifteenth century CE), the dance drama called *Kṛṣṇattam* is presented in the temple courtyard rather than in a *kuttambalama.* The life of Kṛṣṇa is enacted by a totally male cast of actors over a period of eight nights. The performance is based on the *Kṛṣṇagiti,* a text composed by King Manavedan. The favorite episodes of Kṛṣṇa's life—his birth in a dark prison, his childhood pranks, his conquest of the snake demon Kaliya, his destruction of the demonness Pūtanā and the demons hidden in tree trunks, his playful sport with the cowherdesses (*gopīs*), and his final journey to heaven (*svargarśana*)—are all re-created in a charming spectacle full of lyricism and fluidity. The faces of some actors are painted in green or red, symbolizing good and evil characters, respectively; other characters wear large masks.

The *kathakali* dance drama form was inspired by *kuttiyattam.* By some accounts it developed as a reaction to *kṛṣṇattam.* Eclectic in character, it is a highly sophisticated art form utilizing the preliminary rituals of *kuttiyattam* and presenting dance dramas based on the Indian epics, the *Rāmāyaṇa* and *Mahābhārata.* While *kathakali*'s ritualistic origins are not immediately clear, it draws essentially upon the rituals held in the temple sanctum.

The countless ritual dance drama forms of several village communities in Kerala are fundamental to the evolution of all temple dance drama forms. The preserve of the socioeconomically deprived and backward classes, these forms are known as *teyyams*, a name derived from the word *daivam* ("to be god"). Many different forms of *teyyam* and *teriyattam* continue to be performed in Kerala. In these performances, the spirit of the deity enters the actor so that the ritual enactment invariably culminates in magic and trance. These forms characteristically feature elaborate makeup, high headgears, and oversize costumery, all designed to create an otherworldly vision. In the form called *mudiyettu,* an enclosure is made, and the image of the goddess Kālī is traced on the ground with the powders of different cereal grains. Another person, who many be considered devotee or priest, worships the image. Then this priest/devotee dances in a trance state and obliterates the image. A second enclosure is made, and the action of the dance drama shifts to this second space. A lamp, which had accompanied the first part of the performance, is moved to the second enclosure, symbolizing continuity. The story of Kālī vanquishing the demon Darika is enacted in the second enclosure. Until about the mid-twentieth century, the role of Kālī was performed by the same actor who worshiped and obliterated the image in the first enclosure; today they are different actors. At the end of the performance, the actors who take the roles of Kālī and Darika become possessed.

It is important to remember that for those forms drawing inspiration from the temple, the ritual precedes the dramatic spectacle, and the actors always are narrators and performers of the myth. In village dance drama rituals, however, the performer is not an actor but is transformed for the duration into the deity. The performance, therefore, invariably ends in trance with the actor possessed.

Similar dance-drama forms are known elsewhere in India. The patterns of chanting *mantras* in the temple sanctum; singing inside the temple; and performing dances in the dance hall (*manadappam*), dance drama in the temple courtyard, and dance drama in the village field or open spaces are pan-Indian.

One can identify three major systems of dance as ritual process and ritualistic dance drama from the thousands of distinctly regional or local forms. The first is an offering of music and dance, usually performed by a solo female dancer or a group of dancers. This genre owes its repertoire in varying degrees to the traditions followed by *devadāsīs*, *māharis*, and others, and includes the *bhāratanāṭyam* of South India, the *orissi* of Orissa, and the *ardhananṛtyam* of Andhra Pradesh.

The second system includes the dance dramas within and without the temple courtyard. Here the performers are largely male dancer-actors, not devotee-narrators as in the solo offering. The medieval cycle plays concerning the life of Kṛṣṇa or Rāma emerged within this broad category. While known throughout India, they are special to the North and East. The third system is characterized by the presentation of themes from the *Mahābhārata* and *Rāmāyaṇa.*

Performances of Rāma-līlā are pervasive throughout India. The life cycle of Rāma, hero and god, is also presented during early autumn in Java, Bali, Thailand, and Malaysia. Commencing with ritual preliminaries—invoking gods of the water, earth, and sky and the deities of the quarters, and seeking benediction—the life of Rāma is enacted nightly in episodes about his birth, his ultimate coronation, the banishing of Sītā, and, in some versions, his immersion in the waters of the river Saryu. The Rāmnagar Rāma-līlā and the Tulsīghāṭa Rāma-līlā are held in different parts of the city of Banaras. These ritual dance-drama performances take on a special quality because the locale itself is transformed into the situs of the story. Each episode is performed in a different place. The singer-director recites verses from the *Rāmacaritamānas*, a sixteenth-century work by Tulsīdās. Young boys, especially trained for the annual performance, act their roles in the changing locales; the audience identifies them with the mythical heroes. During the performance of the Rāma-līlā, a period of over twenty days, the actors who play the main role of Rāma and his brothers are considered deified. They are consecrated through ritual before the beginning of the dance drama; from that time on the human is icon come to life. Only after their final performance when they remove their headgear do the actors return to mundane life. Until that time, the audience worships them as they would an icon, the sacred and the profane are concurrent without tension, and actual time and place become mythical while also retaining their own ordinary identities.

Ritual and dance drama around the Kṛṣṇa theme constitute another performance system throughout India. Inspired by the early life of Kṛṣṇa, especially that narrated in the *Bhāgavata Purāṇa* (c. ninth century), the cycle of Kṛṣṇalīlā plays is performed two weeks before the Janmāṣṭamī, the day of Kṛṣṇa's birth on the eighth day of the waning moon of July–August. The most important of these is the *Vṛndāvana Kṛṣṇalīlā*. Again, as in the case of Rāma-līlā, young boys are trained for their roles, initiated, and consecrated. For the duration of the cycle plays, these young boys, as Kṛṣṇa, his consort Rādhā, and other cowherdesses (*gopīs*), are considered deified. Beginning with Kṛṣṇa's birth, a new episode in his life is presented each day. This is known as *līlā*. The enactment of the stories in the early life of Kṛṣṇa culminates in the *rāsa*, the circular dance of great antiquity in which Kṛṣṇa stands in the center with the *gopīs* surrounding him. During the dance, Kṛṣṇa creates the illusion in which each *gopī* believes her partner to be Kṛṣṇa. In the *Vṛndāvana Kṛṣṇalīlā* the one young Kṛṣṇa suddenly is multiplied, leading to complex circle dancing until Kṛṣṇa and his consort Rādhā finally stand in the center. All others pay obeisance to the icon (*mūrti*) of Kṛṣṇa and Rādhā as they would within the temple. Ecstatic cries fill the arena. Devotees prostrate themselves before the young dancers who are, for that time and space, deities.

In Manipur, the same Kṛṣṇalīlā becomes Rāsalīlā and is performed five times yearly to coincide with the full moon of spring, the monsoons, late autumn, and so forth. Instead of young boys, young girls before puberty take the principal roles. The *gopīs* can be women of any age, from ten to more than sixty. The enactment of Kṛṣṇa's early life is a moving spectacle, but the presentation of *rāsa* provides the most heightened ecstatic experience. The *rāsa* is held in the Govindjī Temple precincts in Manipur in springtime; the *mahārāsa*, or grand *rāsa*, in the November full moon. The *gopīs* arrive in two files of twenty to forty dancers each, dressed in glittering skirts and transparent veils. They sing verses from the tenth section of the *Bhāgavata Purāṇa*, each *gopī* vying with the others to communicate her yearning for the Dark Lord. Tears flow effortlessly. Singing in falsetto, with minimal restrained gestures, also occurs. Always played by a young girl, Kṛṣṇa appears, dances, and looks for the *gopīs*. Rādhā, dressed in a green skirt to distinguish her from the red-skirted *gopīs*, then appears. This provides an opportunity for a solo dance of great beauty. A dialogue through music and dance takes place between the two, followed by estrangement and then reunion. As in the *Vṛndāvana Kṛṣṇalīlā* the dance ends with a circular movement but without a number of Kṛṣṇas appearing.

The atmosphere is charged with devotion (*bhakti*). Members of the audience enter the arena and bow down or prostrate themselves before the dancer-deities, offer gifts, and then retreat. The dance can last all night until early in the morning, when the *gopīs* and the audience worship the child actors portraying Kṛṣṇa and Rādhā as they would the icons inside the temple sanctum.

See Also Līlā.

Bibliography

Bhattacharya, D. H. *Origin and Development of the Assamese Drama and Stage.* New Delhi, 1964.

Blank, Judith. *The History, Cultural Context and Religious Meaning of the Chau Dance.* Chicago, 1972.

Desai, Sudha. *Bhavai: A Medieval Form of Ancient Indian Dramatic Art.* Ahmadabad, 1972.

Ghosh, Manomohan, ed. and trans. *Natyasastra.* 2 vols. 2d rev. ed. Calcutta, 1967.

Guha, Thakurta P. *The Bengali Drama.* London, 1930.

Hawley, John Stratton. *At Play with Krishna: Pilgrimage Dramas from Brindavan.* Princeton, 1981.

Hein, Norvin. *The Miracle Plays of Mathura.* New Haven, 1972.

Jones, Clifford, and Betty True Jones. *Kathakali: An Introduction to the Dance-Drama of Kerala.* San Francisco, 1970.

Raju, P. T. *Telugu Literature: Andhra Literature.* Bombay, 1944.

Ranganath, H. K. *The Karnataka Theatre.* Dharwar, 1960.

Shekhar, Indu. *Sanskrit Drama: Its Origin and Decline.* Leiden, 1960.

Vatsyayan, Kapila. *Traditional Indian Theater: Multiple Streams.* New Delhi, 1980. Includes extensive bibliography.

New Sources

Sax, William S., ed. *The Gods at Pay: Lila in South Asia.* New York, 1995.

Kapila Vatsyayan (1987)
Revised Bibliography

DRAMA: BALINESE DANCE AND DANCE DRAMA

Balinese dance and dance drama are integral to the distinctive Hindu-Buddhist religious practices found in Bali, Lombok, and parts of East Java, Sumatra, and Celebes recently converted to Bali-Hindu religion or settled by Balinese under Indonesia's national program to relocate population. Many sourcebooks for Balinese drama derive from the pre-Muslim period of Javanese civilization. Beginning in the fourteenth century, Java's Hinduized courts confronted first Islamic, then Western forces of trade, political authority, and religious instruction; the ritual and drama apparently central to Javanese statecraft altered accordingly. Neighboring Bali, in part isolated from these developments and from the more intensive style of Dutch colonialism, provided a context for the continuing cultivation of both scribal and performing arts tied to rites of ancestor commemoration and a cult of kingship, to wet-rice agricultural cycles, and to intricate temple systems that organize productive lands, civic units, domestic space, and funerary areas into networks of shrines. Hindu deities and local ancestors make periodic visitations to these shrines to be entertained. Moreover, demonic agents both regularly and occasionally upset the social and cosmic equilibrium and must be appeased at places vulnerable to their influence, such as the ground, the sea, and all crossroads.

Balinese temple celebrations always include the playing of gongs and metallophones (*gamelan*, the instruments for which the percussion orchestra is named) and specific dances in ritual processions; they may also include shadow puppet theater (*wayang*), masked dance drama (*topeng*), or many unmasked dance dramas. Performances may be used to upgrade life-crisis rites, such as tooth filings, weddings, and cremations. A specific orchestral ensemble accompanies each variety of dance and drama. Important genres include *gambuh, topeng, parwa,* and *wayang.* In *gambuh,* unmasked courtly dramas dating back at least four hundred years, the orchestra adds haunting flutes to its percussions. *Gambuh* tales come from the indigenous cycle of love and political intrigue called Malat in Bali and Panji in Java. Masked *topeng,* performed either by a soloist or by multiple actor-dancers, stages narratives from dynastic chronicles. *Parwa,* probably originating around 1885, is similar to *wayang wong,* in which masked dancers replace the famous leather puppets of *wayang kulit;* but *parwa* contents are restricted to episodes from the *Mahābhārata.* Bali's versions of the *Rāmāyaṇa* remain the basic source for *wayang,* both the renowned nighttime varieties that project puppet shadows onto a screen and the daytime version without shadows, regarded as a more potent message to ancestral shades. Myriad additional genres represent one of the fullest flowerings of dramatic dance in the history of civilizations.

Complex rules delimit which episodes in what performance mode are suited to which rituals; variations reflect Bali's history of shifting sponsorships by courts, ancestor groups, localities, and now national and commercial agencies. Several types of dance involve divine or demonic possession (for example, the prepubescent trance dancers of *Sanghyang Dedari*). Trance occurs frequently in Balinese ritual, most spectacularly among the participants in the famous exorcist battles based on the Tantric tale of *Calonarang,* in which the witch Rangda (whose dread masks belong to village-area temples) engages the friendlier force of lionlike Barong (whose costumes are usually owned by hamlets). The end is inevitably a standoff. Most Balinese dance dramas, however, are thought to be given not by deities or demons, but for them. Bali's traditional concept of "audience" includes the ordinarily remote deities, lured to their "seats" for the show; partisan ancestors, to whom descendants may have "promised in their hearts" a particular performance; human spectators of all social ranks; and outsiders as well, including foreigners and tourists. Indeed commoners, called "outsiders" to noble courts (*puri*), are essential spectators. That ritual and drama are seldom designed for a closed public, despite the culture's exclusivistic hierarchies, helps explain the resilience of Bali's semiprofessionalized dance and drama organizations: talented peasants moonlighting in troups for hire.

Any Balinese ritual mobilizes an array of specialists, some restricted by caste or social position, others not. Brahmana priests (*pedanda*) specialize in Sanskrit and esoteric manuals that prescribe rituals for purifying water (*tirtha*) required by their clients for ceremonies. Puppeteers (*dhalang*), not restricted to a particular caste but sometimes concentrated in certain ancestral lines, are highly respected virtuosi: a *dhalang* is the actors, propmen, screenwriter, director, and conductor rolled into one. Young dancers are intensively exercised in choreographic codes that replicate in gestures what a *dhalang* depicts through puppets. A temple celebration, cremation, wedding, or other ritual may be elaborated into a bustling, muted circus, with multiple rings of performers and onlookers, perhaps including a priest intoning *mantras*, a reading group reciting select texts, a *wayang*, various phases of the ritual itself, extra attractions, and several *gamelan*. Historically transforming genres of dance and drama have combined and recombined select channels of refined versus agitated form: sound (in phased periodicities of percussion), voice (in chant and prayer, individual and choral song, and spoken dialogues), languages (Sanskrit; Old Javanese, or Kawi; High Balinese; vernacular Balinese; Indonesian), styles of movement, and levels of gesture. Certain performers—the puppeteer, the *topeng* soloist, the translating and paraphrasing servant-clowns of *wayang wong*—must master all codes.

Dance and drama in Bali portray stock types of conventional characters, ordered into cosmically opposed sets, right-hand ("mountainward") and left-hand ("seaward"). The familiar panoply from Hindu myth and epic includes gods; heroes; adventurous knights; ladies; prime ministers; ladies-in-waiting; servants; ogres; demons; animals (some anthropomorphic); and clowns, the most popular figures, marked by specifically Balinese characteristics. Stage layouts, the situation of performances in and around temples, and the punctuation of ritual by dance and drama help articulate such conceptually opposite attributes as refined and crude and divine and demonic implicit in all spatial arrangements, interactions, and temporal flow. Styles of offerings and priestly functions, too, activate complementary cycles of patterned sound, gesture, story, and ritual regalia: from the esoteric *mantras* and *mudrās* (hand postures) of *pedanda* (high priests of the right-hand powers) or *sengguhu* (high priests of the left-hand powers), to the charms, tokens, and homey icons of the many *balian* ("curers") dealing in sorcery and love magic. The realms of health and disease, activities of allure and cure, and the values of aesthetics and exorcism remain intertwined in Bali-Hinduism, where any analytic separation of the theatrical, the political, and the religious arts is difficult to sustain.

Recent studies of Balinese dance and drama adopt helpful, although conscientiously rationalized, schemes advanced by I G. Sugriwa, R. Moerdowo, and other Indonesian scholars. They distinguish four types of dances. There are dances indispensable to ritual sacrifice, performed in the inner temple by the deities' female attendants and male guardians, drawn from the community concerned. There are optional dance dramas of the middle courtyard that heighten a temple ceremony or a crisis rite; masks and costumes and the performers themselves, perhaps hired from outside, are ritually consecrated. A third type encompasses "secular" dances performed in conjunction with a temple ceremony, but outside the walls, along with cockfights and games of chance; one example is the flirtatious Joged, a dance that recalls precolonial royal involvement in prostitution and other service monopolies. Finally, commercial dances, casually performed with unconsecrated masks, have flourished in tourist shows; the consummate example is the picturesque monkey dance (the Cak), which has become the trademark of Balinese culture in Indonesia.

The rich interplay among dance, drama, and religious practice and belief in Bali pertains to many important issues. Balinese Hinduism's stress on dance in popular ritual sets it off vividly from Islamic values of neighboring islands and of the Indonesian nation. Although many dramatic texts in Bali originated in India, its dance is very different from South Asian varieties, as are its temples. The rituals garnished with Balinese dance drama have counterparts among non-Hindu Indonesians, particularly wet-rice growers and societies organized into rival centers of authority marked by competitive displays during rituals of death, reburial, marriage, circumcision (not practiced by Balinese), or other passage rites. A major problem in interpreting Balinese arts concerns their place in rivalries among rajas, among localities, and among other sponsors. The manufacture of sacred objects—gongs, masks, daggers, written texts, and the like—and expertise in rituals necessary to maintain and periodically cleanse and reconsecrate them remain important in Balinese notions of status and prestige. Moreover, dramas often contain stories of their own origins and credit different social segments, dynasties, and ancestors with instituting distinct arts and performances. Contrary claims in these matters still vitalize Balinese social and political processes and introduce complications into the historiography of Balinese religion, dance, and drama.

Explicit Bali-Hindu philosophies of religion correlate action, word, and thought, thus orchestrating ritual deed, spoken syllables, and mental images in a theory of the interrelation of visual, verbal, spatial, and sonic arts. Some Balinese experts make fine distinctions between trance and "inspiration" (*taksu*) as well as other conditions of dramatic and religious awareness. Although several modern institutes and schools for the preservation and advancement of Balinese arts have promoted new experiments in training and documentation (including musical notation systems), traditional court-based or village-centered training techniques persist for music, dance, drama, sculpture, painting, and so forth. Certain principles of Balinese religion seem manifest less in popular creed than in ideals of transmitting from masters to novices complex aesthetic skills, such as musically structured muscular coordination of postures plus pulsations of eyes, limbs, feet, and fingers. Performers achieve exemplary concentration, self-control, and personal effacement; their poise seems to exist in dynamic tension with the risk of demonic abandon. Judging from Balinese culture, a religion can be danced as much as believed.

Bibliography

A recent, insightful general description of Balinese dance is I. M. Bandem and Fredrik De Boer's *Kaja and Kelod: Balinese Dance in Transition* (2d ed. New York, 1995). The classic account, which accentuates dramatic narrative, remains the splendid volume by Beryl de Zoete and Walter Spies, *Dance and Drama in Bali* (1938; reprint, Oxford, 1973). There are fine illustrations with concise descriptions and case studies in Urs Ramseyer's *The Art and Culture of Bali* (Oxford, 1977). The abundant philological work on Balinese texts, many involved in dance drama, can be surveyed, beginning with Christiaan Hooykaas's *Religion in Bali* (Leiden, 1973) and *Drawings of Balinese Sorcery* (Leiden, 1980); Hooykaas alone produced a score of major books of translation and commentary. On performance contexts for right-hand and left-hand magic, see Marie-Thérèse Berthier and John-Thomas Sweeney's *Bali: L'art de la magie* (Paris, 1976). For a guide to the intriguing collection of work done by assorted artists, musicologists, anthropologists, and performers in the 1920–1930s, see *Traditional Balinese Culture*, compiled by Jane Belo (New York, 1970). Still vivid and relevant are many parts of Miguel Covarrubias's *Island of Bali* (New York, 1937). Background on social and historical processes at work in religion and dramatic arts is reviewed in my book *The Anthropological Romance of Bali, 1597–1972* (New York, 1977) and Clifford Geertz's *Negara: The Theater State in Nineteenth-Century Bali* (Princeton, 1980). All of the works listed include extensive bibliographies with copious relevant literature in Dutch, Indonesian, and Balinese.

New Sources

George, D.E.R. *Balinese Ritual Theatre.* Alexandria, Va., 1991.

Herbst, E. *Voices in Bali: Energies and Perceptions in Vocal Music and Dance Theater.* Hanover, N.H., 1997.

Lewiston, D. *Music from the Morning of the World: The Balinese Gamelan & Ketjak, the Ramayana Monkey Chant.* New York, 1988.

James A. Boon (1987)
Revised Bibliography

DRAMA: JAVANESE WAYANG

Wayang kulit, also known as *wayang purwa* ("shadow play"), is a type of puppet theater that is indigenous primarily to Java, the most populous island of Indonesia, but that flourishes also on the Indonesian islands of Bali and Lombok and in the state of Kelantan on the Malay Peninsula. *Wayang kulit* is performed by a sacral puppeteer (*dalang*), who, accompanied by the percussive yet flowing music of the *gamelan* orchestra, moves intricately crafted leather figures in front of an oil lamp to cast flickering shadows on a white screen as he chants mythological narrative in old sanskritized Javanese or other languages. Variants of *wayang kulit* include the wooden-rod puppet form *wayang golek* among the Sundanese of West Java and a human dance drama (*wayang wong*) patterned after the puppet plays.

Wayang kulit traditionally lasts all night—from 9 PM to 7 AM—and is a rite as well as a drama. It is performed at weddings and circumcisions, to exorcise evil spirits, and to cure. *Wayang kulit* also embodies an elaborate mythology and philosophy. The two great Hindu epics, the *Mahābhārata* and the *Rāmāyaṇa*, are the mythological sources for some of the *wayang kulit* narrations. The *Rāmāyaṇa* depicts the quest of Prince Rāma, aided by the white monkey god Hanuman, for Princess Sītā, who is abducted by the monster king Rāvaṇa. The *Mahābhārata* portrays the battle between the five knightly brothers, the Pandavas, and the hundred rival princes, the Kurawas. But these plots are only a skeleton for a vast cycle of interlocking episodes developed by the Indonesians. In addition to the Hindu epics, variants of *wayang kulit* draw on stories from Arab, Javanese, and other traditions, as well as contemporary plays, including some addressing such topical matters as family planning or national ideology.

Wayang kulit characters are categorized according to their status, temperament, and manner, and their interrelationships are plotted through intricate genealogies that trace them to the origins of the world. The refined characters tend to appear on the puppeteer's right, the crude ones on his left. The refined princes, epitomized by Arjuna of the Pandavas, have narrow, almond-shaped eyes, down-turned noses, slightly bowed heads, no chin whiskers, and delicate physiques. Crude monsters, typified by Buriswawa, are fat, with heavy, bristling eyebrows, round eyes, bulbous noses, and red faces. Battles between refined heroes and crude monsters carry psychological as well as political meanings, symbolizing the tension between fleshly desire and spiritual tranquillity. Related themes include the hero's search for his origin and destiny as he passes through temptations represented by forest nymphs, and his search for the self, symbolized by his climbing inside the ear of his own miniature replica to discover the universe inside the person. For Javanese, to experience the symbolism of a *wayang* play is vicariously to struggle through the life cycle and to undergo mystical exercises, and they have composed meditations and treatises on the plays that explicate their meanings in relation to Javanese philosophies and theologies, as well as world religions.

A central role is played by Semar, the short-legged, stout, hermaphroditic, and misshapen clown. Brother to Batara Guru (Śiva), Semar was of pre-Hindu, local Javanese origin (c. 600 CE), and he combines the earthly role of lowly servant with the powers and wisdom of the highest god. It is he who appears on the screen at midnight, when the elements rage, to restore order. Having a relation to the princes somewhat like that of Shakespeare's Falstaff to Prince Hal, Semar balances their extreme refinement, heroism, and nobility with his earthiness and buffoonery (a buffoonery that, when necessary, is transformed into awesome might).

If the clown-servant Semar represents, as some have suggested, the earthy Javanese substance beneath the courtly Hindu glaze, Prince Arjuna is the consummate Satriya, the cultured and noble knight. Before a great battle, Arjuna is troubled by the need to kill his cousins and boyhood playmates, the Kurava. In his distress he turns to his divine mentor, Kṛṣṇa, who is driving Arjuna's chariot. Kṛṣṇa explains that Arjuna must fulfill the code of his knightly caste and follow the predetermined path of his life: he must slay the enemy. He should perform that deed, however, while maintaining an inner detachment from it. Spiritual tranquillity in the midst of worldly conflict is a core ideal of Hinduized Javanese philosophy.

Wayang kulit has been part of Javanese experience for perhaps a thousand years, dating back at least to the time of King Airlangga in the eleventh century CE. Yet *wayang kulit* remains very much a living tradition, influencing the political and secular as well as the religious life of Indonesians. The late President Sukarno once wrote a newspaper column under the penname Bima, the blunt and strong Pandava brother, and he named a regiment after the female warrior Srikandi. Sukarno also referred to his relation to Indonesia as analogous to that of a *dalang* to his puppets, and in other ways he and others have drawn on the imagery of *wayang* in interpreting political life. Comic books on newsstands depict the adventures of Semar's sons Petruck and Gareng in contemporary costumes and situations. Pedicabs are painted with the image of Semar, and he is the guardian figure for a contemporary mystical cult. Classical performances of *wayang kulit* abound, not only in palaces and schools but also as part of community life—at weddings and village festivals, amid the laughter of children and the gossip and meditative conversation of their elders.

BIBLIOGRAPHY

A standard source on *wayang kulit* is J. Kats's *Het Javaansche tooneel*, pt. 1, *Wajang poerwa* (Weltevreden, 1923), which describes principal characters and some stories. *Sedjarah wajang purwa*, edited by Raden Hardjowirogo (Djakarta, 1955), provides descriptions of a larger number of characters. For Balinese dance and drama, the classic source is Beryl de Zoete and Walter Spies's *Dance and Drama in Bali* (New York, 1938). Regarding *wayang kulit* in Malaya, see Jeanne Cuisinier's *Le théâtre d'ombres à Kelantan*, 2d ed. (Paris, 1957). An excellent brief introduction is Mantle Hood's "The Enduring Tradition: Music and Theater in Java and Bali," in *Indonesia*, edited by Ruth T. McVey (New Haven, 1963).

Translated texts of the Javanese plays, together with helpful interpretations, appear in *On Thrones of Gold: Three Javanese Shadow Plays* (Cambridge, Mass., 1970), edited by James R. Brandon. A profound comment on the meaning and worldview of the *wayang* is provided in A. L. Becker's "Textbuilding, Epistemology, and Aesthetics in Javanese Shadow Theater," in *The Imagination of Reality: Essays in Southeast Asian Coherence Systems*, edited by A. L. Becker and Aram A. Yengoyan (Norwood, N.J., 1979). A fascinating interpretation of mystical meanings of the *wayang kulit* is provided by Mangkunegara VII of the court of Surakarta in his *On the Wajang Kulit and Its Symbolic and Mystical Elements*, translated by Claire Holt (Ithaca, N.Y., 1957). A provocative sociological interpretation is given in Benedict R. O'G. Anderson's *Mythology and the Tolerance of the Javanese* (Ithaca, N.Y., 1965), and a useful ethnographic view is Clifford Geertz's *Religion of Java* (Glencoe, Ill., 1960), chap. 18.

Concerning ritual aspects of Balinese shadow plays, see Christian Hooykaas's *Kama and Kala: Materials of the Study of Shadow Theatre in Bali* (Amsterdam, 1973). For recent studies of *wayang kulit*, consult Mimi Herbert's *Voices of the Puppet Masters* (Jakarta and Honolulu, 2002), Alit Veldhuisen-Djajasoebrata's *Shadow Theatre in Java* (Amsterdam, 1999) and the University of Michigan Centers for Southeast Asian Studies' *Puppet Theatre in Contemporary Indonesia* (Ann Arbor, 2002).

JAMES L. PEACOCK (1987 AND 2005)

DRAMA: EAST ASIAN DANCE AND THEATER

From ancient times, theater and religion have had a close, often symbiotic, relationship in East Asia. Theatrical performance is an integral part of certain animistic, Confucian, and Buddhist rites in China, Korea, and Japan. Priests have been performers, and even today temples and shrines provide places for performance. Play cycles based on religious myth and legend are numerous. Aesthetic systems reflect religious worldviews. Although drama is increasingly secularized in the contemporary world, religious values and beliefs continue to be projected to audiences through masked plays (*sandae* in Korea, *satokagura* and *nō* in Japan), popular dramas (*kabuki* in Japan and *jingxi* and other forms of Chinese opera), and puppet plays (*gogdu gagsi* in Korea and *bunraku* in Japan).

SHAMANISM AND ANIMISM. Since prehistoric times people in northeast Asia have communicated with animistic spirits for the benefit of the living through songs and dances. In the fourth millennium BCE, the inscription on a Chinese oracle bone mentions a dance of sympathetic magic performed to induce the spirits to bring rain. Before the time of Confucius (or Kongsi, c. 551–479 BCE), songs and dances dedicated to the Eight Deities and supervised by the royal steward constituted an important state ritual of the Chinese court. Performing a masked play is a folk ritual in northwest Korea, intended to repulse evil spirits at the beginning of summer. Dances of demon exorcism (*namahage* and *emburi* for example) are central features of lunar New Year festivals in scores of villages in Japan. The Lion Dance, familiar through East Asia, may have derived from totem worship in prehistoric times.

The three-part structure of the rituals of Shintō, containing many animistic elements, reveals one reason performing arts in Japan are naturally linked to the practice of animism: the god (or *kami*) is summoned into this world, entertained, and sent away. Because deities had to be entertained, a large number of religious dances developed. In Japan many dances enact, often in attenuated, symbolic form, myths of the islands' founding gods and goddesses. The god remains enshrined in his or her god-house during court or shrine dances (*mika-gura*), hence the dancer and the god are separate. At agricultural festivals, village actors wear the costumes and masks of ferocious demons (*oni*). In these folkloric dance dramas (*satokagura*), the spirit moves freely into the world of humans by possessing the performer.

From these primal traditions has come the concept of a sanctified stage area. A sacred playing space, often on the ground, is set apart from the mundane world by the placement of tree branches at the four corners. This idea, in developed form, can be seen in the Japanese *nō* stage. A plain square platform is marked off by four pillars and covered by a roof in the style indicating the dwelling of a god. The bridgeway *(hashigakari)*, on which the spirit-protagonist of a *nō* play enters, mirrors the sacred passageway marked out on a shrine ground along which a god would make his or her journey from the other world to a temporary home at festival time.

In shamanistic traditions, the shaman is a professional communicator with the spirits. Throughout East Asia and from earliest times, dance and song have been essential shamanic skills. The Chinese *Li ji* (Book of rites; fourth century BCE) tells of shamans wearing animal skins who drive out evil spirits, and *The Elegies of Chu* of the first century BCE describes elegantly dressed male and female shamans singing and dancing seductively to woo deities to make the passage down into this world. Contemporary shamans continue the tradition of being skilled singers and dancers. Dances of Japanese shamans are relatively simple, while seances (*kut*) of present-day Korean shamans contain complex dances designed to please the god being invoked. The purely theatrical skill of juggling can be part of the shaman's repertory in Korea. In Japan, juggling and acrobatics were associated with Shintō agricultural festivals in medieval times as "field music" (*dengaku*), and they are still performed today during Shintō festivals such as the New Year celebration.

The origin of theater in Japan is described in the *Kojiki* (Records of ancient matters; 712) and the *Nihongi* (Chronicles of Japan; 720) in a myth that has the shape of a shamanistic performance. The sun goddess, Amaterasu, has withdrawn in anger from the community of fellow deities into a rock cave, thus plunging Japan into darkness. Another goddess, Ame no Uzume, tries to lure her from the cave by showing her breasts, lowering her skirt, and dancing joyfully on an overturned tub. The assembled gods and goddesses cry out and clap with delight. Hearing their laughter, Amaterasu leaves the cave to see what is causing so much merriment—thus light is restored to the world. Like a shaman, Ama no Uzume entices a goddess to leave her private world and join the community on whose behalf she is performing. Like a shaman, she entices the goddess with joyful singing and dancing. And like a shaman, she uses a mirror and holds a sprig of a tree, two favorite shamanic implements.

Links between shaman and performing artist are not difficult to identify. The Chinese ideograph for shaman represents two people practicing a skill, by inference, the skill of performance. The same ideograph is used in Japan for a Shintō priestess (*miko*), who serves at a shrine as a *kagura* dancer. The old Korean term *kwangdae* meant shaman or popular performer interchangeably. In Korea the husbands of female shamans performed masked plays (*sandae*) and puppet plays (*gogdu gagsi*). One of the standard roles in plays of both genres is the female shaman, usually depicted as a young and alluring prostitute. It is also believed that *pan'sori* narrative singing was developed into a Korean national art by these same low-status performers in the eighteenth and nineteenth centuries. (Confucian and Buddhist teaching equally hold the shaman in contempt.) A Japanese myth says that the spreading pine tree painted on the back wall of a *nō* stage symbolizes the Yogo Pine, the tree through which the god descended to earth during performance. Stamping at the conclusion of a *nō* play and the earth-stamping dance sequences in village *kagura* are contemporary examples of Ama no Uzume's stamping steps described twelve hundred years ago. The four flags worn on the back of a Chinese opera general are averred to derive from the Chinese shaman's flags of exorcism.

It has been theorized that acting originated in East Asia in the shamanic act of possession. There are difficulties with such an argument. The village actor in Japan who wears the mask and costume of a demon may or may not be possessed by the mask's spirit; in neither case, however, is he functioning as a trained shaman. Conversely, the shaman, possessed by a deity and speaking the deity's words, rarely enacts past events in that deity's life as the actor would do. Rather, the shaman's function, at least as we know it today, is to bring the god's knowledge and power into the mundane world in the service of practical needs (curing sickness, assuring prosperity, et al.). The art of mimesis (acting) and especially the enactment of a story about a character (drama) are not essential to this function. Similarly, the action of a *nō* drama has been likened to a shamanistic seance because in the typical play an intermediary, usually a Shintō priest, summons a dead spirit or deity to enter this world. But the parallel is inexact: the enticed spirit does not possess the intermediary but becomes independently manifest on stage. Finally, and in a more general sense, the performing arts may have had their origin in shamanism. If so, we must imagine ancient man waiting for a shaman professional to create the first songs and dances. What is more likely is that after song and dance existed, shamans utilized these theatrical arts for religious purposes.

CONFUCIANISM. While less influential perhaps than primal traditions, Confucianism has affected the performing arts in three main ways. First, according to Confucian doctrine, the performance of appropriate music and dance helped assure the harmonious working of the universe. Confucian rulers supported court performance as a ritual function, often co-opting preexisting animistic rituals. During the Tang dynasty (618–907) in China, the Koryŏ dynasty in Korea (from c. the eleventh century), and at the Japanese imperial court during the Nara and Heian periods (710–1185), rulers patronized large contingents of palace performers, and they established official schools to preserve the ritually correct forms. The Pear Garden school, founded by the emperor Xuanzong (712–754), was the most famous of these in China. The Japanese form of court dance, *bugaku*, continues to be patronized by the emperor in modern Japan and thus represents an unbroken tradition of some thirteen hundred years. Second, Confucian ideals of proportion, moderation, and symmetry set the aesthetic tone of court performance. *Bugaku* is an excellent reflection of Confucian ideals in its sedateness, repeated patterns, and geometric symmetry of form.

Third, the ethical norms of Confucianism—social duties as expressed in the "five human relationships"—set the standards of morality for dramatic characters, especially in popular theater. Filial piety is celebrated in Chinese operas such as *The Lute Song* (c. 1358), and duty to one's lord in scores of Japanese *kabuki* and *bunraku* plays such as *The Forty-seven Loyal Retainers* (1749) and *The Subscription List* (1841). Korean *sandae* present a peasant's view of Confucian morality: unfilial sons and unfaithful wives are mockingly satirized. Domestic plays (*sewamono*) in eighteenth-century *kabuki* and *bunraku* use the conflict between human feelings (*ninjo*) and social duties (*giri*) as a major plot device. Chikamatsu Monzaemon (1653–1724) wrote a score of domestic plays in which young lovers, unable to meet the heavy demands of duty—to spouse, parents, children, employer—choose to die together rather than live under Confucian restrictions.

BUDDHISM. Between the seventh and the eleventh centuries, Buddhism was widely propagandized in East Asia by popular forms of masked drama. *Giak*, the Buddhist masked dance drama of Korea, was brought to Japan in 612 by the Korean immigrant, Mimaji (Jpn., Mimashi), who had learned the art in China. Called *gigaku* ("elegant entertainment") in Japan, it was supported by the imperial court as a means to spread the new state religion. *Gigaku* is described in a fourteenth-century book on music, *A Short Manual of Instruction*, as a procession that passed through the city streets in which masked performers enacted comic scenes ridiculing the evils of drunkenness, lechery, and lewdness. Court-supported performances died out, but village masked plays, such as the widespread *sandae* in Korea, and the Lion Dance (Jpn., *shishimai*) that is seen everywhere in East Asia, are believed to be their descendants. Remnants can also be seen in contemporary *gyōdō* processions in Japan, in which monks wearing masks of *bodhisattvas* circle a statue of the Buddha. Popular, anticlerical views of Buddhism can be seen in contemporary Korean *sandae*. Buddhist monks are ridiculed for being venal and lustful.

The origin of *nō* in Japan can be traced back to ninth-century performances of sorcerers (*jushi* or *noroji*) who would impersonate a guardian deity of Buddhism such as Bishamon at the New Year exorcism ceremony, and of temple sextons who would play his *oni* (demon) antagonists. In the twelfth and thirteenth centuries, Buddhist priests enacted teachings and legends of Buddha in *ennen nō* and *sarugaku nō*. Even after professional actors took over in the thirteenth and fourteenth centuries, troupes lived at Buddhist temples. The troupe organized by Kan'ami Kiyotsugu (1333–1384), the nominal founder of *nō*, was attached to the Kofukuji in Nara, and most of Kan'ami's life was spent performing at Buddhist temple festivals around the country. A dozen *nō* plays out of the repertory of 240 concern Shintō deities. *Ōkina*, a ceremonial piece commemorating felicitous longevity, is the most ancient and sacred. The majority, however, are deeply imbued with Buddhist teachings. By the time of the great actor Zeami Motokiyo (1363–1443), the protagonist (*shite*) of a typical *nō* play was the ghost of a famous man or woman who was suffering torment in Buddhist hell. At the conclusion of such a play, the spirit abandons the sinful human ties binding him or her to this world and, through the mercy of Amida Buddha, attains salvation in Western Paradise. While Zen philosophy is expressed by characters in some *nō* plays, the Pure Land salvation of Amida is far more pervasive (as it is in *kabuki* and *bunraku* plays).

Early puppet plays in Japan emphasized Buddhist miracles and legends. *The Chest-Splitting of Amida*, showing the Buddha saving a dying girl by placing his heart in her chest, was a sixteenth-century favorite. Buddhist ghosts of the dead and reincarnated spirits are standard characters in Chinese opera, *nō*, *bunraku*, and *kabuki*, becoming, in the latter, objects of parody in the nineteenth century. Buddhist concepts underlie several features of playwriting. Coincidence abounds, not because playwrights were careless, but because of the belief in reincarnation: people whose paths had crossed in previous lives were fated to meet again in later incarnations. The Buddhist idea that the world is transient and in constant flux finds its parallel in the episodic structure of Chinese operas, Korean *sandae*, and Japanese *kabuki* and *bunraku* dramas. The relative unimportance of climax, so noticeable to the Western theatergoer, is a reflection of the belief that each moment is equal to any other, that life is a stream constantly flowing. Zen concepts of intuitive apprehension—as opposed to explicit statement—underlie the *nō* aesthetics of restraint, suggestion, and abhorrence of realistic detail in staging. A practical man of theater, Zeami nonetheless formulated a particularly Buddhist vision of the ideal *nō* performance. It should express *yūgen*, a quiet beauty tinged with dark, melancholy emotion. The *nō* actor and theoretician Komparu Zenchiku (d. between 1468 and 1471) carried Zen aesthetics to its furthest when he spoke of the art of *nō* passing through "six wheels," an image relating to the Buddhist duality of illusion-reality, and leading to ultimate enlightenment, symbolized by the wheel of emptiness and the sword.

For the sake of convenience, the contribution of each religion to the performing arts has been discussed separately here. Yet such a division is necessarily arbitrary and perhaps misleading. One aspect of dance or theater may reflect several East Asian religions. To cite but one example, the annual cycle of full-moon festivals that is celebrated by performances in all parts of East Asia relates to local traditions, Confucianism, Buddhism, and, indeed, Daoism as well.

See Also Music, articles on Music and Religion in China, Korea, and Tibet, Music and Religion in Japan.

BIBLIOGRAPHY

No single book adequately addresses the topic of this article. Halla Pai Huhm describes the unique role of shamanism in the performing arts of one country in *Kut: Korean Shamanist Rituals* (Elizabeth, N.J., and Seoul, 1980), while the classic study of shamanism in East Asia remains Mircea Eliade's *Shamanism: Archaic Techniques of Ecstasy*, rev. & enl. ed. (Princeton, 1964). There are interesting chapters on Shintō ritual and myth in performance in Fred Mayer and Thomas Immoos's *Japanese Theatre* (New York, 1977). Buddhist contributions to *nō* are covered in detail in Inoura Yoshinobu's *A History of Japanese Theater*, vol. 1, *Noh and Kyogen* (Tokyo, 1971), and in Patrick Geoffrey O'Neill's *Early No Drama* (London, 1958). Oh Kon Cho's *Korean Puppet Theatre: Kkoktu Kaksi* (East Lansing, Mich., 1979) discusses Buddhism and shamanism as butts of satire. In *Major Plays of Chikamatsu* (New York, 1961), Donald Keene offers an analysis of Confucian and Buddhist values in Japanese popular drama. The most complete accounts of early religious influences on Chinese theater are still those of A. E. Zucker, *The Chinese Theatre* (Boston, 1925), and Cecilia S. L. Zung, *Secrets of Chinese Drama* (1937; New York, 1964).

James R. Brandon (1987)

DRAMA: AFRICAN RELIGIOUS DRAMA

In traditional Africa, everyday life, blending profane and sacred activities, is permeated with music, dance, rhythmic movement, symbolic gestures, song, and verbal artistry. Body adornment—costuming, painting, tattooing, decorating, and masking—is not only a mark of status, age, and sex differentiations but also serves as an element of beautification, play, imitation, impersonation, and visual communication of religious values.

Dramatic performances by soloists and groups of actors interacting with active spectators originate from the combination of these features in recurring formal settings. Simple routine activities as well as momentous events—the hoeing of a field, the telling of a tale, the recitation of an epic, the coming out ceremony of a newborn child, the celebration of a marriage, the initiation of young men and women, the enthronement of a chief, or the burial rites of a headman—are accompanied by dramatic performances, all with more or less explicit religious content. Groups of interacting participants (protagonists, preceptors, experts, attendants, musicians, singers, active audience), in specific settings and at prescribed moments, portray characters and enact events through the combined use of words, songs, gestures, rhythms, dances, mimicry, music, and artifacts. The narration of a tale, for example, becomes a performance event in which narrator and audience may enhance the presentation of a text through phonic, verbal, and mimetic features, including dialogue, choral singing, handclapping, gestures, and sometimes music and special costumes (Ben-Amos, 1977, pp. 13–16; Finnegan, 1970, pp. 500–502).

In the performance of an epic, Nyanga bards identify with the central hero by acting out select passages before an audience that responds with encouragements and sung refrains (Biebuyck and Mateene, 1969). Accompanied by song and music, Pygmy hunters among the Bembe perform spectacular solo and duo dances. Painted and dressed in animal hides and feather hats, the hunters imitate the behavior of certain animals and the techniques used to spear them in a display of skill and prowess that placates the deities presiding over the hunt. The Khomani of southern Africa stage plays in which men and boys act out, with appropriate sound effects, the hunting of a gemsbok or a fight between baboons and dogs, or plays in which women and girls imitate the movements and habits of turtles (Doke, 1936, pp. 465–469). After harvest time among the Malinke and Bamana of West Africa, disguised men, accompanied by a female chorus, present nocturnal comical and satirical sketches that portray characters such as a thief, a braggart, or an adulterous woman. Each performance is a structured entity that starts with a ballet with male and female participants. A prologue, which is both sung and acted, follows, introducing the individual actors. Last are the actual plays in which the actors also engage in dialogue with the musicians (Labouret and Travélé, 1928). Countless other examples could be given of such performances where dramatic action offers an opportunity for entertainment, display of artistic skill, social prestige, and reward. Broad religious conceptions are implicit in the overall purposes of such performances, which show the close bond between animals and humans or the disastrous consequences of not living in conformity with standards set by the ancestors.

The elements of religious drama emerge more directly in activities linked with hunting, planting, harvesting, and other seasonal events. These performances not only ensure a successful hunt or abundant crops but also placate the supernatural beings that are responsible for order in nature, appease the spirits of the animals, attract and neutralize evil beings, purify humans of their sinful interference with natural forces, and protect against witchcraft.

In dances preceding an actual expedition, elephant hunters among the Baasa are painted and specially dressed to present the village audience with a sequence of realistic skits in which elephants are praised and appeased before being symbolically killed (to increase the chances for a safe and successful hunt). The movements of the elephant are vividly re-created by a disguised hunter who carries two small elephant tusks. At the same time, actors painted to portray marauding leopards symbolically evoke the dangers of the deep forest, while others brandish spears and display medicines to depict the power, tribulations, and joys of the specialist hunters. The song texts are specifically addressed to famed ancestors, divinities, and elephant spirits to protect and purify the hunters.

Divination and therapeutic sessions may be simple events in which a diviner or healer submits the patient to private consultation and treatment. If masks, figurines, and other sculptures are used, the sessions develop into a sequence of dramas in which mystic powers are captured, controlled, and released for the benefit of the patient.

Among the Kongo, when a person is diagnosed by a diviner to be suffering from a sickness or misfortune caused by *nkosi*, the patient must be treated by a ritual expert who holds complete control over this mysterious power. *Nkosi* is contained in a secret mixture of mineral, vegetal, and animal ingredients placed in the cavity of a wooden figurine and consecrated by the sacred words and deeds of a healer initiated to this power.

The treatment consists of an ordered sequence of dramatic events. The invited healer, accompanied by attendants playing small slit-drums, carries the figurine to the outskirts of the village. Dialogue and action including the patient's relatives follows. After receiving gifts, healers and assistants proceed to the patient's house. The figurine is placed on a mat while the patient, surrounded by many relatives, is seated outside. There follows a series of dramatic actions, accompanied by songs, imprecations, gestures, music, and rhythmic movements. The figurine is manipulated like a puppet while the power contained in it is exhorted, conjured, and appeased with words, gestures, and sacrificial blood; the patient and relatives are aspersed with lustral liquid; the patient is rubbed successively with white clay, oil, and the medicines contained in the figurine; and the rules and prohibitions linked with *nkosi* are interpreted (Van Wing, 1941, pp. 89–90).

Funerary ceremonies are sometimes accompanied by a spectacular dramatic finale intended to honor the deceased and their families. An elaborate example is the Bobongo of the Ekonda of west-central Africa. Organized *équipes* of men or women rehearse for several weeks before presenting the theatrical spectacle three to fifteen months after the death of an important man. The performance includes a combination of special body ornamentation, dance, acrobatics, pantomime, song, panegyrics, tales, lessons in ethics, and invocations of nature spirits and dead quasi-divinized twins. It also involves the construction of special decors, platforms, fences, and litters in which solo dancers are brought to the village (Iyandza-Lopoloko, 1961; Vangroenweghe, 1977).

Dramatic forms of expression climax in those rituals and festivities in which masked, painted, and costumed actors, sometimes carrying artifacts (clubs, whips, scepters, staffs, swords, axes, rattles, phalli, figurines), engage in prescribed and staged performances. The intricate action involves a combination of sung and spoken texts, vocal signals, music, dance, gestures, and mimicry by specially disguised performers who interact with one another and with the participating audience. These maskers represent ancestors, divinities, nature spirits, monsters, and mythological or undefinable *sui generis* creatures. In many ethnic groups these total performances, incorporating elements of what is conventionally called drama, sacred opera, and ballet, form an intrinsic part of men's initiations (for example, puberty rites, induction into voluntary associations and cult groups, enthronement rites for chiefs and headmen, and initiation schools for ritual experts). The numerous activities of these initiations—which may extend over a considerable period of time and may be staged in several prescribed settings—are interspersed with performances in which the actors embody supernatural beings and human prototypes.

Outstanding examples of traditional African dramatic art are found in the young men's Mukanda rites, held periodically by a large number of related ethnic groups in southern parts of the Democratic Republic of the Congo, northeastern Angola, and northern Zambia. Novices are circumcised at an early stage of the rites as part of the transition from boyhood to manhood, but the overall aims of the Mukanda institution are social, didactic, moral, and aesthetic. Living in prolonged seclusion, the young men are not only trained in vital economic activities but are thoroughly educated in values and beliefs. They spend a large part of their secluded life learning how to perform dances, music, and songs and how to manufacture costumes, masks, and other paraphernalia. Throughout the Mukanda, the elders and ritual experts who organize and direct the rites, and even the women and noninitiated males who are excluded from their secret activities, are involved in a series of celebrations in which choreographic and musical performances are as essential as the material and social aspects. Masked and costumed male performers, singly and in groups, participate in the secret and public events.

Among the Chokwe, who have the most highly developed mask institution, maskers appear in all major stages of the Mukanda rites and in the public festivities that follow. The masks, hierarchically organized, fall into distinctive semantic, morphological, and functional groups. They also differ in the materials used (some are sculptured in wood; others are constructed of fibers, beaten bark, and resin), in size and volume, in the ornamental designs, and in the related accessories, costumes, and paraphernalia. Each fully outfitted masker impersonates a unique character and refers symbolically to a range of religious, cosmological, moral, philosophical, and social concepts.

Masks may represent an ancestor of a chief or a lineage founder, a nature spirit, a mythological being, or some *sui generis* creature that exists only through the mask, as well as social and psychological types. All maskers are thought to be *ikishi*, beings who rise from the dead for the Mukanda through the intercession of ritual experts and devotees. For both insiders and outsiders, masks and maskers are always surrounded with an aura of sacredness, mystical power, danger, and mystery. The maskers have distinctive roles as impersonators of "others." Those that directly embody specific ancestors or nature spirits perform in situations of social control: they lend authority, dignity, integrity, and conformity to the proceedings; they protect against witchcraft or interference by noninitiates; they supervise and sanction the fermentation of corn, the brewing of the sacred corn beer, and the preparation of medicines; they sanction the secrecy and accuracy of the rites; they discipline and test moral and physical strength. Others that depict prototypical characters in the guise of legendary figures assume the roles of entertainers, comedians, and social critics to underscore basic social and moral values. All maskers stir strong emotions among novices and initiates as well as among noninitiates: they spread terror and anxiety; they create an atmosphere of severity and restraint; they engage in the burlesque, the libidinous, the satirical.

The danced and masked dramas of the Mukanda rituals alternate between reality and fiction, tragedy and comedy, and combine the performing arts to convey deep religious, moral, philosophical, and sociopolitical messages. Moreover, in several ethnic groups, the closing of the Mukanda period is followed by dance tours. Organized by previous and recent novices and their tutors, these masked dances function as displays of individual artistic talent and skill and as sources of prestige and material reward. These dance tours have gradually become independent dramatic performances in which the secular element of entertainment and fun overshadows the lingering sacredness attributed to the masks (Bastin, 1982; Lima, 1967).

In numerous festivals imbued with religious meanings among West African peoples (e.g., the Yoruba, Igbo, Abua, Urhobo, and Ijo of Nigeria), the central actors are maskers, often recruited from the members of secret societies, cult groups, and certain age groups. The spectacles performed at designated times by Yoruba Gẹlẹdẹ maskers follow a precise plot pattern in danced sketches that include social comments, satires, caricatures of strangers, and scenes honoring important persons and depicting hunters and women at markets. Artistic competition and the search for prestige in such performances are keen (Drewal, 1975, pp. 142–146). Their overall purposes, however, are the propitiation of witches through prayers, offerings of food, and sacrifices. Typical Yoruba masquerades linked with the Egungun cult start with a sequence of songs and invocations to divinities, ancestors, and elders along with acrobatics and dances; next are plays in which mythical themes are enacted together with satirical and burlesque sketches of characters; the performance ends with a procession to collect gifts (Drewal, 1975, pp. 46–48). Among the northwestern Igbo of Nigeria, some of the maskers in plays produced by males of the same age group represent women. These plays are performed at feasts held soon after harvest or at celebrations for the earth spirit. The forms of the masks depict ideal feminine beauty and character; the male maskers imitate female dancing style and portray women at work or at leisure (Boston, 1960). In the Afikpo-Igbo Okumkpa play, which is part of a calendar of seasonal festivals, as many as one hundred maskers (always thought to be personifications of ancestral and nature spirits) present danced and sung satirical and topical scenes that are conceived as commentaries on the lives of real persons (Ottenberg, 1975, pp. 87–127).

Dramatic impersonations of supernatural beings and mythological, legendary, and prototypical characters are accomplished not only through masks but also by simpler methods of mimicry, dance, word, object, and gesture. A case in point is the initiation of men and women into the hierarchically graded Bwami association of the Lega. Most phases of these initiations consist of structured dramatic sequences. Stereotypical characters are depicted in pantomimes by expert dancers and preceptors or are represented by natural objects and artifacts (including masks and figurines) that are displayed and manipulated in song and dance contexts. The characters are ancestors, legendary persons, illustrious initiates of the past, personified animals and objects, or social, physical, and psychological types. All of them positively or negatively illustrate the association's code of values.

In one episode, for example, an initiate represents Kyamunyungu za Baitindi ("big arrogant one of the passionate dice players"). The sickly old man, stumbling, irascible, and loaded with bags containing valuables, arrives uninvited in a village to play the dice game. In highly dramatic action that involves a cast of other initiates, the old man provokes the villagers by quarreling with the headman, interfering with the dice throwing, and challenging his opponents to a fight; unwilling to listen to advice, he is chased away. This scene refers to the novice who must passively listen to the advice of his tutors and show respect and restraint in all his actions.

The countless episodes in which ancestors (generalized or specifically named), stereotypical characters (e.g., Great Old One or Beautiful One), personified animals (e.g., pangolin or turtle), objects (e.g., a bark pounder or a shell), and activities (e.g., poison ordeal or divination) are enacted are always performed with dance, music, and song and with appropriate objects and paraphernalia. In many instances the dramatic effects are enhanced by light and dark contrasts (some of the action takes place at night, at dawn, or in a closed initiation house lighted with burning resin torches), special vocal features (dialogues, orations, praises, name shouting) and musical features (imitation of nature sounds; use of mirlitons, bull roarers, and other unusual and sacred musical instruments; message drumming), and by alternating solo dances and ballets by initiated men or women (Biebuyck, 1973).

Theater in the modern Western sense may be a fairly recent development in Africa, but from immemorial times drama has been an intrinsic part of narrative sessions, rituals, and other celebrations (Schipper-de Leeuw, 1977, pp. 7–38). Moreover, the dramatic enactment of characters and events may become the most important feature in initiations and cult activities and as a result may be established as a partly independent form. The dramatic performances—short, self-contained sketches, longer, conceptually interrelated scenes, or elaborate plays—are multifunctional. They are total aesthetic expressions in which the participants, using a multimedia system of communication, display individual and collective skills in the arts of dance, song, music, sculpture, design, and costume to emphasize beauty, pageantry, inventiveness, harmony, and perfection. They are sources of entertainment for the actors and for the audience, which often actively participates as part of a chorus or an orchestra or by responding with its own dance, song, hand clapping, and dramatic action. They provide means of gaining prestige and reward and of reaffirming status, rank, and authority not only of the participants but also of the ancestors and supernatural beings. They incorporate multifaceted messsages on religious, moral, social, and political themes. Finally, those performances in particular that involve maskers are thought to be sacred occasions during which divinities, ancestors, nature spirits, and mythical beings return to the human world to be honored and placated, to bring communal well-being, and to sanction the rules and practices of initiations and rituals.

BIBLIOGRAPHY

Bastin, Marie-Louise. *La sculpture tshokwe.* Meudon, 1982.

Ben-Amos, Dan. "Introduction: Folklore in African Society." In *Forms of Folklore in Africa: Narrative, Poetic, Gnomic, Dramatic,* edited by Bernth Lindfors, pp. 1–34. Austin, Tex., 1977.

Biebuyck, Daniel P. *Lega Culture: Art, Initiation, and Moral Philosophy among a Central African People.* Berkeley, 1973.

Biebuyck, Daniel P., and Kohombo C. Mateene. *The Mwindo Epic from the Banyanga.* Berkeley, 1969.

Boston, J. S. "Some Northern Ibo Masquerades." *Journal of the Royal Anthropological Institute* 90 (1960): 54–65.

Doke, C. M. "Games, Plays and Dances of the Khomani Bushmen." *Bantu Studies* 10 (1936): 461–471.

Drewal, Henry John. "African Masked Theatre." *Mime Journal* 2 (1975): 36–53.

Finnegan, Ruth. *Oral Literature in Africa.* London, 1970.

Graham-White, Anthony. *The Drama of Black Africa.* New York, 1974.

Hanna, Judith Lynne. *To Dance Is Human: A Theory of Nonverbal Communication.* Austin, Tex., 1979.

Iyandza-Lopoloko, Joseph. *Bobongo, danse renommée des Ekonda.* Tervuren, 1961.

Labouret, Henri, and Moussa Travélé. "Le théâtre mandingue (Soudan français)." *Africa* 1 (1928): 73–97.

Lima, Mesquitela. *Os "akixi" (mascarados) do Nordeste de Angola.* Lisbon, 1967.

Ottenberg, Simon. *Masked Rituals of Afikpo: The Context of an African Art.* Seattle, 1975.

Schipper-de Leeuw, Mineke. *Toneel en Maatschappij in Afrika.* Assen, 1977.

Traoré, Bakary. *The Black African Theatre and Its Social Functions.* Ibadan, 1972.

Vangroenweghe, Daniel. "Oorsprong en verspreiding van Bobongo en Iyaya bij de Ekonda." *Africa-Tervuren* 23 (1977): 106–128.

Van Wing, J. "Bakongo Magic." *Journal of the Royal Anthropological Institute* 71 (1941): 85–97.

DANIEL P. BIEBUYCK (1987)

DRAMA: NORTH AMERICAN INDIAN DANCE AND DRAMA

In all regions of North America, indigenous peoples practiced various public rituals for the purpose of communicating with the supernatural spirits and powers that controlled their universe. The most ubiquitous and theatrical form of the dramatic performance was dance in which actors wore elaborate costumes and masks representing the supernatural beings they sought to appease. These dance dramas often involved a special performance area that included entrances and exits for the performers; a chorus of singers and dancers; principal dancers; scenic backdrops; special lighting effects; and, most importantly, plots revolving around myths of creation and supernatural beings and powers who were perceived to inhabit the everyday world. These dance dramas were characterized by masquerade, imitation, role reversal, burlesque, and reenactments of myths and personal visions.

American Indians relied greatly on their ability to mime the behaviors of those animals and birds that were important to their religious life. The environment played a great role in ritual performance, which was grounded empirically in knowledge of the seasons, flora, and fauna. As might be expected, hunters chose to emulate in their dances those animals that were important to their survival, while farmers performed rituals that focused on the agricultural cycle.

Dance drama was performed to the accompaniment of vocal music sung by an individual or chorus. The songs might contain meaningful text, sometimes short phrases that poetically captured the theme of the dance, or meaningless vocables that despite their lack of semantics were highly structured both melodically and rhythmically. The range of native musical instruments in North America was comparatively limited. Various sizes and shapes of drums served as the major accompaniment to song in all regions. Rhythmic patterns were characterized mainly by single unaccented beats, duple accented beats, and accented triplets. Only in the Pueblo Southwest do we find a highly structured sense of rhythm, particularly in some of the mimetic animal and bird dances, in which there is a perfect correspondence between song, drum, and dance steps without benefit of measured beats in the strict Western sense of time.

Costumes were both realistic and stylized. On the Plains, a Buffalo dancer would dress in the hides of a bull, complete with a headdress of horns, a robe over his shoulders, leggings made from the hairless part of the hide, and a buffalo tail hanging conspicuously from his waist. Similarly, Eagle dancers of the Pueblo Southwest soared gracefully in the dance plaza wearing costumes made from eagle feathers topped with a headdress representing the bald eagle's crown and golden beak. But in the Northwest Coast region, where wood sculpture reached its highest aesthetic form in all of North America, intricately carved masks, made to be manipulated by strings revealing masks within masks, and carved and painted dance houses and scenery frequently featured stylized representations of ravens, whales, bears, and other animals and birds significant to the coastal culture.

All ritual performances were for the benefit of the general public as well as the principal performers, and all performances required a specially constructed performance area. Frequently, the public part of the performance represented only a small part of a longer ritual that sometimes took several days or weeks. For example, among the Lakota on the Great Plains, the vision quest was regarded as a personal and private form of mediation and propitiation. However, it was necessary for a medicine man to interpret the candidates' visions. Frequently, in order to legitimate the experiences, the supplicants were directed to reenact their visions before the entire village. This reenactment took the form of imitation of various animals or birds that had informed them, and appropriate costumes representing the buffalo, wolf, elk, bear, or eagle were worn.

On a larger scale, Plains Indians performed the Sun Dance collectively, after individual dancers had participated in private vision quests. An integral part of the ceremony, the elements of which were widely diffused to nearly all Plains tribes, was the erection of the medicine lodge, or sacred arbor, in which the performance occurred. Dancers wore special costumes including long kilts, necklaces representing sunflowers, and wreaths of sage around their wrists, ankles, and forehead. The segments of the dance in which the Sun was propitiated were directed by the Sun Dance leader. The performance lasted for several days and was accompanied by other intrusive dances prior to going on the buffalo hunt.

The Kwakiutl of the Northwest Coast were unsurpassed as dramatists with a full sense of lighting, scenery, costumes, and plot. The dance dramas were presented in cycles and depicted the kidnapping of the hero by a spirit who bestowed supernatural power upon him before returning the hero to the village. The hero was most frequently possessed by a "cannibal spirit" and therefore craved human flesh. In the reenactment, a frenzied hero was led back into the dance house by villagers and fed flesh believed to have been taken from a human corpse, although more likely it was animal meat. The dance house was replete with trap doors and tunnels, and performers could quickly appear and disappear magically. The dancers wore huge masks with movable parts, some representing the large beak of a bird, through which the dancers cried out "Eat! Eat!" Hollow stems hidden beneath the floor were used as microphones through which the voices of the actors could emanate from any part of the house. Dolls strung on ropes partly obscured by the dim firelight flew through the air for dramatic effect. Finally, the principal dancer, believing he had consumed human flesh, calmed down to end the event gracefully.

In the Northeast, the best-known Iroquoian sodality was the False Faces. The society was formed when a supernatural being called False Face appeared to the Iroquois in the form of detached faces and taught them the art of curing. The elaborate masks were carved and painted in grotesque ways, and when worn by the society, members were believed to frighten away malevolent spirits that caused sickness. The mask was carved from a living tree and was painted red or black depending on whether the carver began work in the morning or afternoon. Noses, mouths, and eye holes were twisted and contorted, and long shocks of horsehair fell over the wearer's shoulders. The False Faces performed during the midwinter festivals on the New York and Canadian reservations. Additionally, they visited every Iroquois house in fall and spring in order to exorcise evil spirits. Wearing the masks and tattered clothing, the False Faces carried turtle-shell rattles and hickory sticks. When someone had contracted a disease over which the False Faces had power, the leader of the society was informed, and the troop of False Faces appeared at the patient's house, striking and rubbing their rattles against the house as they entered. Once inside they sang and danced, accompanied by the shaking of rattles. Some of the dancers would scoop up hot embers from the fire and blow them on the patient in order to cure him.

In the Great Lakes area the ritual of the Midewiwin was enacted by the Ojibwa and other central Algonquians. Translated as "Great Medicine Society," the Mide (the shortened form of the name) held its meetings once a year in a special lodge resembling a large wigwam varying in length from one hundred to two hundred feet and in width from thirteen to thirty feet. In height it was seven to ten feet with an open apex that was covered with cattail mats and birchbark during inclement weather.

The Midewiwin was a membership organization, and people were admitted on the basis of application, of having a suitable dream, or by replacing a deceased relative who had been a member. Both men and women could join, and the religious leaders of the Mide were elected by its membership.

The main annual functions were initiatory, and curing rites were conducted by carefully trained Mide shamans.

The Mide priests determined which candidates would be accepted into the society, and candidates were expected to pay for the rites of initiation, which included knowledge of the myths, rituals, songs, and remedies of the society. All ceremonies had originated in revelations and were carefully transcribed on birchbark scrolls with a bone stylus and handed down pictographically from generation to generation.

The initiation rite was the most dramatic. The candidates knelt on mats surrounded by four posts inside the medicine lodge. Two members held the candidates' shoulders, while four others thrust their medicine bags at them. As the four leaders approached, the candidates were overcome by the power of the leaders' spirits and fell lifeless to the ground. When revived, each candidate spat out a small cowrie shell called *migis*, which was the sacred emblem of the Mide. The initiator then offered the shell to the four directions and sky after which it magically disappeared again into the candidate's body, and the candidate was fully resuscitated. All members were required to attend meetings once a year for the renewal of their spiritual powers, but smaller gatherings could be held for the treatment of the sick, singing songs, and strengthening their belief in the power of the Mide. A feast was an inseparable part of all Mide functions.

One of the most important ceremonies of the Southeast was the Green Corn Dance, a celebration of the harvesting of one of the major food staples of North America. Known among the Creek as the Busk (from the Creek word *puskita*, "to fast"), the ceremony of first fruits took place in August. The Busk was actually an aggregation of different ceremonies, including the drinking of *Ilex cassine*, or "black drink," used as an emetic to purge the participants and purify themselves. A sacred fire was built, and young initiates had their flesh scratched to make them brave. Both men and women performed various dances including the Stomp dance, which was performed in a serpentine pattern by a line of alternating men and women. The women wore turtle-shell shakers around their knees that accompanied the antiphonal singing of the group. At the end of the Busk, the various clans participated in a stickball game that marked the conclusion of the ceremony. Variations of the Green Corn Dance were found also among the Seminole, Cherokee, Choctaw, Chickasaw, and Yuchi of the Southeast, as well as among other tribes where corn was cultivated.

The Southwest is where the highest concentration of dance drama is found not only with the elaborate agricultural rituals of the Pueblos, but with the various curing rituals, puberty ceremonies, and mimetic animal dances. Literally hundreds of these rituals were performed by the Navajo, Apache, and Pueblo peoples each year. In many cases native rituals are still held in conjunction with feasts of the Catholic Church. All provide colorful spectacles equal to any of the religious pageants of North America and Europe.

The Hopi of Arizona perform a number of masked dances on their mesas. The *kachina* dances, named after the spirits of the dead, are the most intriguing. The Hopi believe that in mythological times the *kachinas* came from their homes in the West to bring them rain and to ensure them long and happy lives. Later, the *kachinas* showed the people how to make masks and costumes and taught them their songs and dances with the understanding that if the people performed the ceremonies correctly, the supernaturals would continue to bring prosperity to the villages. There are over 250 named *kachina* spirits among the Hopi, each represented by a different mask and costume. It is believed that the men who impersonate the spirits at the *kachina* performances become the spirits they represent. Women and uninitiated youth are not supposed to know that the *kachina* dancers are really their clansmen. At each performance the *kachinas* bring gifts for the children and place them in the center of the village plaza. The *kachina* dances are performed during the first half of the year, when their appearance is supposed to ensure the successful planting of crops. The ceremonies represent intense periods of ritual performance in which all men and women in the village undergo instruction in their faith. It is also a time when the people entertain their spiritual benefactors.

At the time of the summer solstice, the Niman dance is performed in which all the *kachinas* appear en masse before the villagers who thank the supernaturals for the gift of a good harvest. It is believed that the *kachinas* then leave to return to their homes. When they return to their homes, they visit the dead, who are performing rituals of the winter solstice while similar ceremonies are being performed by the living during the summer.

In New Mexico among the Zuni the Shalako ceremony is held in November or December each year. Six dancers are dressed to represent giant birds, the messengers of the rain gods, with conical costumes attached to their waists measuring in height from ten to twelve feet. They have birdlike faces complete with beaks that are movable, protruding eyes, and upcurved tapered horns. At midnight, they enter special houses that have been built for their performance. They utter birdlike calls and clack their beaks in rapid succession. They dance and make speeches telling the people to pray for an abundant harvest and long lives for the villagers.

The Shalako dancers are joined in their ritual by the ten Koyemshi, or "Mudheads," the children of a legendary incestuous union. These impersonators are appointed by the Zuni priests to serve for one year and are then free from further duties for another four years. The Koyemshi entertain at all public rituals when the *kachinas* are away from the village by providing comic, and sometimes obscene, interludes between the more serious dances. Sometimes they play Euroamerican games such as beanbag. The jokes, puns, and riddles that they cry out to the villagers are filled with scatalogical references, and they play pranks and make obscene jokes about the most respected and sacred aspects of

Zuni religion. In this manner they make moral and ethical points by burlesquing those institutions and individuals with whom people come in contact every day. They also burlesque their most sacred beliefs through vulgar references that strongly constrast with appropriate Zuni behavior. For the duration of the ritual, the onlookers participate vicariously in what is temporarily socially approved behavior.

The Koyemshi appear as ludicrous figures. They wear formless baglike cotton masks that have bumps or knobs protruding from them. The knobs are filled with raw cotton seeds and earth or dust taken from the footprints made by the people in the streets around the village. Sometimes feathers are tied to the knobs, and the lower part of the mask is tied to the knobs with black cotton in scarflike fashion. Under the scarf they wear a small bag containing squash, corn, and gourd seeds. Their masks and bodies are painted with pink clay that comes from the sacred lake. These clowns also wear black homespun kilts, and the leader adds to his kilt a black tunic worn over his right shoulder. As is true with the Hopi, the Zuni dancers and clowns serve to underscore the religious values of the society by occasionally emphasizing the absurd.

Nearby in Arizona and parts of New Mexico and Oklahoma, numerous bands of Apache perform a ceremony used variously as a puberty ceremony, or to cure illness and avert catastrophe. The Mountain Spirits dance, or Gahan, as it is properly known, is an essential feature of the female puberty ceremony, in which the young initiate ritually represents White Painted Woman, the divine mother of the Apache culture hero, or in some cases, Mother Earth. The Apache believe that performance of the ritual brings good fortune to the initiate, her family, and to the entire tribe.

In this ceremony four male dancers represent the four directions, or Mountain Spirits, powerful supernatural beings who act as intermediaries between humans and the Great Spirit. The initiate is secluded in a special lodge. She is painted and dressed by a woman of impeccable reputation who also has received a vision from the White Painted Woman. Each day a male singer sings appropriate songs for her. Each night the masked dancers appear in spectacular and grotesque costumes. They are dressed and painted by a shaman in a special brush arbor before the evening ceremonies begin. The shaman paints their bodies with designs representing the sun, moon, lightning, planets, rain, and rainbow. After being painted and instructed, the dancers line up facing east. They then spin clockwise, spit four times into their headdresses, and put them on after feigning this action three times. A fire is made in the ceremonial lodge by rubbing sticks together, and each night the masked dancers enter the lodge and dance around the lodge in a prescribed manner. They wear wooden headdresses shaped like huge rainbows projecting from their black-hooded faces. Yellow buckskin kilts are tied from their waist, cuffed by long fringed boots. They carry wooden swords in each hand, and as they dance in rigid, angular patterns, bending and crouching in near-balletic movements, they slap their swords vigorously against their thighs and legs. On the fourth night, the candidate joins the dancers dressed in a yellow buckskin fringed dress with designs like those of the masked dancers. At the end of the four days, the young woman scatters pollen over the people who were brought to her to receive her blessings.

The Apache regard the dance as particularly powerful, and each of the aspects of the dance must be done properly lest harm befall the tribe. If the dance is not executed properly, it is believed that the dancers may have trouble with their eyes and noses, their faces will swell, or paralysis will set in.

Among one of the most vivid ritual performances of the Navajo of the Four Corners region of the Southwest is the Yeibichai, also known as Night Chant. The word *yeibichai* is partly a corruption of the Zuni word for "spirit" plus the Navajo term for "maternal grandfather," hence it literally means "grandfather of the gods." The ceremony was handed down by supernaturals and was thought to be particularly efficacious in curing both psychosomatic and somatic disorders, especially insanity, deafness, or paralysis.

The ritual is sponsored by one man and his clan relatives in winter and is performed outdoors on a barren plateau. A sacred hogan is built at the west and a brush arbor shelter for the dancers at the east. Between the two a row of bonfires is built.

The ceremony takes nine days, the first eight being composed of secret ceremonies, and the last day, a public performance. In the dance the Grandfather of the Gods is personified by the lead dancer, who wears buckskin hunting clothes. The other dancers wear masks and kilts and resemble Pueblo *kachinas*.

The ritual specialist in charge of the Yeibichai is the chanter, a person who has chosen to learn the sacred ritual. He pays to be taught and studies for many years learning by rote every detail. During this time he collects sacred objects such as prayer sticks, herbs, turquoise, white shell, abalone, and jet, which he will use in his ceremonies. The specialist also may learn a few lesser rites plus the Blessingway, a ritual that must follow every other ritual to atone for any possible mistakes in them.

During the first four days, the patient and his relatives purify themselves by sweating and taking emetics. The patient and the chanter pray to the supernaturals to aid them in the ceremony. Each supernatural must be named in the proper order lest misfortune befall them. The chanter sings sacred songs and administers potions and sacred pollen to help rid the patient of evil forces.

During the next four days, the chanter and helpers coax the supernaturals into the ritual area by constructing sand paintings of them. The final power will arrive when pollen has been sprinkled on the sand painting. In these paintings, male divinities are represented as having round heads, while females have square heads. The *yeis*, as these male and female divinities are called, are pictured as standing on clouds or lightning and guarded by rainbows. The completed painting forms an altar sometimes ranging in width from four to eighteen feet.

Next, the patients are bathed and dried with cornmeal and painted with the symbols of the supernaturals. They are then brought into the hogan to receive power from the supernaturals represented in the sand painting. Sand from various parts of the painted figures is pressed against their ailing parts, and they are made one with the supernaturals and share their power. Finally the sand is swept up so that it may not be contaminated. The Navajo word for the design means the "going away of the group" and the design itself is regarded as a temporary visit from the supernaturals. On the ninth night, both the chanter and the patient must stay awake until dawn while the power increases in them. The Yeibichai impersonators are dressed in grotesque masks and decorated kilts with as many turquoise and silver necklaces, bracelets, and bow guards as they can put on. They spend the night publicly dancing and singing. The patients must not sleep until sunset, when they enter the sacred hogan and stay there for four nights. The rite is ceremonially concluded with the Bluebird Song, sung in honor of the bird of the dawn that brings promise and happiness.

Although most dance dramas were performed by groups of singers and dancers, the Deer Dance of the Yaqui of the Southwest is a unique solo performance. The Yaqui believed that the deer had the power to cure or cause illness and also to bring thunder, lightning, and rain. Dancing to the deer deity also ensured food and fecundity for the people and animals.

A religious pageant announcing the Deer Dance, which took place just before Easter, was suddenly interrupted by the presence of four to six dancers and four singers striking gourds with sticks to create a rasping sound. All dancers were naked from the waist up and wore grotesque masks representing human faces. The lead dancer, however, wore small deer antlers attached to his head and a cocoon rattle, six to eight feet in length and filled with pebbles, wrapped around one leg.

The lead dancer performed most of the Deer Dance alone. His movements mimicked that of the deer with great realism, his head moving quickly and erratically from side to side as if he had picked up the scent of danger. His feet scratched the earth before he quickly bolted upward, leaping gracefully over some imaginary barrier. Then, as the dance came to a close, the dancer became hunter and hunted, imitating the actions of a man with bow and arrow carefully stalking his prey. Letting fly the arrow that mortally wounded him, he fell to the ground quivering as he breathed his last.

See Also Clowns; Iconography, article on Native North American Iconography; Music, article on Music and Religion; Sun Dance.

Bibliography

Densmore, Frances. *Chippewa Music.* Bulletin of the Bureau of American Ethnology, no. 45. Washington, D. C., 1910. A classic work on the Chippewa with detailed discussion of the Midewiwin.

Densmore, Frances. *Yuman and Yaqui Music.* Bulletin of the Bureau of American Ethnology, no. 110. Washington, D.C., 1932. A good description of the Yaqui Deer Dance.

Drucker, Philip. *Indians of the Northwest Coast.* Garden City, N.Y., 1955. A discussion of various tribes of the Pacific Northwest with some emphasis on material culture and ritual drama.

Kurath, Gertrude P. *Iroquois Music and Dance: Ceremonial Arts of Two Seneca Longhouses.* Bulletin of the Bureau of American Ethnology, no. 187. Washington, D.C., 1964. A description of music and choreographic patterns of numerous Iroquoian rituals including the False Face society.

Ortiz, Alfonso, ed. *New Perspectives on the Pueblos.* Albuquerque, 1972. The section entitled "Ritual Drama and Pueblo World View," by Ortiz, himself an anthropologist and Pueblo, is one of the best theoretical introductions to ritual drama.

Powers, William K. *Oglala Religion.* Lincoln, Neb., 1977. Includes a description and analysis of the vision quest, sweat lodge, and Sun Dance of the Lakota Indians of the Great Plains.

Powers, William K. *Sacred Language: The Nature of Supernatural Discourse in Lakota.* Norman, Okla., 1986. Contains descriptions and illustrations of various animal impersonators among the Lakota.

Reichard, Gladys A. *Navaho Religion.* New York, 1950. Perhaps the best work ever done on Navajo symbolism.

Roediger, Virginia More. *Ceremonial Costumes of the Pueblo Indians.* Berkeley, 1941. An excellent illustrated book of ceremonial costumes, including those described for the Hopi and Zuni.

Tyler, Hamilton A. *Pueblo Gods and Myths.* Norman, Okla., 1964. A good historical background to the Pueblo with an emphasis on cosmology and worldview.

Underhill, Ruth M. *Red Man's Religion.* Chicago, 1965. Although stylistically dated and somewhat patronizing, there are excellent descriptions of ritual drama from most parts of native North America.

William K. Powers (1987)

DRAMA: MESOAMERICAN DANCE AND DRAMA

Mesoamerican dance and other dramatic performances not only serve as public entertainment but also are inextricably linked to native society, religion, and worldview. In Mesoamerica, dance encompasses the interplay of physical, historical, and spiritual aspects of human existence. On a basic corporeal level, dance encompasses concepts of sensuality, sex, and fertility—not only of humans, but also of the world as a whole, such as the summer season of warmth, growth, and abundance. This is commonly expressed through flowers that symbolize sexual organs, pleasure, beauty, the soul spirit, as well as the numinous realm of ancestors. Through dance, historical events and political and social relationships are defined and expressed through bodily presentation and movement. Mesoamerican dance includes both song and nonverbal aspects of communication including distinct gesture, posture, position, and *pasitas,* or steps. In addition, dance forms a conduit linking the living to the gods, ancestors, and other supernatural beings. Drama encompasses basic concepts such as reenactments of creation mythology, and through ritual pageants, the definition of communities. Drama was also a fundamental part of ritual sacrifice and public humiliation of captives. In fact, because public dance and performance were so intensely interwoven in Mesoamerican cultures, during the colonial era, community dances, dramas, and theatrical events formed a locus for mass conversion throughout New Spain. Although it will never be known how any of these performances were viewed or received in the past, in general, Mesoamerican dances today do not eliminate the observer. Spectatorship and vicarious participation are integral components in community festivals and contribute greatly to the success of the event.

PHYSICALITY OF DANCE. Given the essentially physical nature of dance, it is not surprising that throughout Mesoamerica it relates to somatic sensations. For example, the Dominican friar Diego Duran disapprovingly describes the Aztec Tickling Dance as "so roughish as to be compared to our own Spanish dance called the *saraband,* with all its wriggling and grimacing and immodest mimicry." Duran also mentions that the term for this dance, *cuecuechcuicatl,* can also mean "dance of the itch," a connotation very similar to conceptions of dance among the ancient Mixtec of Oaxaca. Thus there is the Mixtec town called Zahuatlan, which means "place of itching" in Nahuatl. The original Mixtec term for this community is Yucu Cata, meaning "mountain of itching," but in Mixtec, *cata* also signifies "dancing," and in the pre-Hispanic *Codex Selden* (c. sixteenth century), this town is rendered as a mountain marked by an obviously dancing man holding rattles in his upraised arms. The Aztec and Mixtec relation of dance to itching suggests a restless and agitated physical need much like intense sexual desire.

In Mesoamerica, dance is a basic form of interaction between the sexes. Among the Aztec it provided a means to meet and interact with possible future paramours and spouses. Finely dressed warriors danced during the day at the *cuicacalli* ("house of flowers") to attract women for potential trysts. These dances promptly ended when children from the various wards arrived for their lessons, indicating the erotically charged nature of these adult events. However, during children's dances it often became evident that certain boys and girls had a special affinity and fondness for one another, and this was often the prelude to future marriage. Two Aztec deities closely identified with dance and music were the male Xochipilli and the female Xochiquetzal, youthful and beautiful beings of sensuality, pleasure, and fertility. Although there is little direct evidence indicating that they were a couple, they shared very similar symbolic domains. Aztec figurines frequently depict Xochiquetzal wearing her flower headband while in a position of dance, with bouquets of flowers in her extended hands. Duran mentions that the "most enjoyed" Aztec dance, the Dance of Flowers, was dedicated to Xochiquetzal. Both Aztec deities contain the term *xochitl,* of "flower" in their names, a basic symbol of sensuality and fertility in Mesoamerica.

Aside from condoned aspects of comportment, Mesoamerican dance frequently lampoons egregious conduct of both sexes. Masked performers reinforce accepted models of behavior through burlesque and clowning, which is the antithesis of socially accepted norms expressed by other dancers during the same occasion. However, for the Aztec, there was a being of dance decidedly different from Xochipilli and Xochiquetzal—the bestial Huehuecoyotl, the old and corrupt coyote god of dance identified with drunkenness, excess, and unseemly sexual demeanor. In the Aztec calendrical system he is the patron of the thirteen-day week called "one flower," and in the ancient manuscripts illustrating this period he appears with grotesque monkey-like dancers in the context of alcohol and wanton excess. At the time of early contact in Yucatan there was a rich variety of comical dances, theatrical lampoons, and social parodies. Officials were openly addressed and ridiculed by costumed dancers who used cleverly phrased metaphors and witty allusions to make reference to their improper activities. Either performed on stage or indoors, these humorous farces were closely associated with the god K'uk'ulkan, or Quetzalcoatl. Titles of the comedies provide clues to some of the favored targets of these direct displays, including "the parasite," "the cacao grower," and "the chile vendor." The last mentioned dance is suspiciously similar to the well-known and infamous Aztec account of the last king of Tula, Huemac, and his daughter. In this legend the daughter falls hopelessly and lustfully in love with a Huastec Maya chile vendor who, tellingly, wears no breechcloth.

Ritual clowns are commonly portrayed in figurines of the Late Classic Maya (600–900 CE), portable images that may well have been passed out at festival events as mementos. Quite frequently, such figures were aged beings displaying bestial attributes and wielding dance rattles or fans, clearly marking them as performers. At times these grotesque characters, the converse of Classic Maya conventions of comeliness, were paired with beautiful young women in erotic embraces, scenes surely meant to be humorous. One of the most common themes addressed in ritual humor in contemporary Maya communities was inappropriate sexual behavior of senior and typically aged public officials. On a fundamental level, ritual clowning defines and normalizes appropriate gender roles through a folk or "popular" medium. This is especially true for children, who learn during socially focused and framed events some of the most elemental aspects of individual public identity and responsibility.

One of the most common dance positions portrayed in ancient Mesoamerican art is with the arms upraised and the elbows bent at right angles to the sides of the body. This convention occurs with the wildly grinning performers of the ceramic art of Nopiloa and Remojadas, Veracruz (c. 500–800 CE). These figures often display attributes of spider monkeys in their headdresses. Frequently amusing creatures, spider monkeys of the verdant, humid jungles were widely identified with dance and sexuality in Mesoamerica. In addition, when they run they adopt the same basic upwardly raised arm position enjoyed by dancers. Dancers adopted this position in many areas of ancient Mesoamerica besides Remojadas, including the Classic Maya and highland Mexico.

SOCIAL POLITICS OF DANCE. What were the social politics of dance and performance, and what were the stakes? Aside from parodies, one essential reason for community dance was undoubtedly related to notions of self-display and social prestige. Aristocratic participants, including members of the royalty, presented themselves publicly to affirm their ancestry, identity, and current place within courtly society. Sixteenth-century chroniclers mention that the Aztec had professional singers who composed songs and public performances concerning the glorious deeds of ancestors and nobles; especially important were the "feats, victories, and conquests" of kings. Among the Classic Maya, including such ancient cities as Copan, Palenque, Yaxchilan, it is clear from numerous works of art that rulers frequently personified and incarnated gods, demonstrating their unique link to the supernatural world. Imagery of elaborately costumed dancing nobles appears in a wide variety of media, from large permanent monuments carved in stone to smaller painted or incised elite vessels and innumerable ceramic figurines, indicating that these motifs were available for commoners as well as for the upper echelons of society. These "mass market" objects, which were widely circulated throughout the urban centers as well as rural outliers, must have expanded the desire for these important ceremonial events.

For the Aztec, members of the royal court adhered to strict rules of conduct that established what the scholar Susan Evans described as a "theater for courtly behavior." Public speaking, song, and dance were all important aspects of palace life. Even the title of king, or *tlatoani,* signifies "speaker," denoting the importance of oratory and rhetoric. According to sixteenth-century chroniclers, the Nahuatl "lordly language" of the court, *tecpillatolli,* was quite distinct from the language of the commoners, known as *macehuallatolli.* Music, song, and poetry were closely identified with royalty and courtly behavior, and the god of music was Xochipilli, the "flower prince," the god of the palace folk. In Aztec thought flowers symbolize both music and rulership. The king of Tetzcoco, Nezahualcoyotl, was renowned as a gifted poet, and a number of Nahuatl texts ascribed to him survive to this day. The *Florentine Codex* (c. 1577) describes the public demeanor of Aztec kings:

> When the ruler went forth, in his hand rested his reed stalk which he went moving in rhythm with his words. His chamberlains and his elders went before him; on both sides, on either hand, they proceeded as they went clearing the way for him. . . . He sang; songs were learned; chants were intoned. They told him proverbs and pleasantries to pass the time.

The same source also mentions a palace courtyard with flowering trees where the king danced, as well as a detailed list of the sumptuous items worn by the king during his performances. Diego Duran records that during the coronation of King Tizoc, some 2,000 nobles danced in his honor within the palace. In this event, dance served as a social contract acknowledging Tizoc as king of Tenochtitlan.

At an early age Aztec children were taught songs, music, and dance at the aforementioned *cuicacalli,* the house of song, located near the central temple area of each community. According to Diego Duran, boys and girls between twelve and fourteen years of age were brought separately from the various wards of the city; each group of boys was accompanied by an old man, and each group of girls by an old woman. Serving essentially as chaperones, these old men and woman would walk behind the children as they marched to and from the *cuicacalli,* closely watching for any inappropriate or disrespectful behavior. The *cuicacalli* is described as a compound of many spacious chambers surrounding a large courtyard used for the dance. According to Duran this courtyard also featured a stone statue of the god of dance with his arms extended and hands hollowed to receive bouquets of flowers and feather fans.

REPRESENTATIONS IN ART AND LITERATURE. Classic Maya art is filled with portrayals of dance, which are identifiable by the accoutrements of the dancers, including masks, rattles, and fans. In addition, the dancers are frequently attended by musicians playing drums, trumpets, flutes, and rattles, as well as by male and female singers. However, perhaps the clearest indications of dance are the poses adopted by these performers. Aside from the symmetrically upraised arm position mentioned above, dancers gesticulate dramatically, with the arms extended and the hands bent sharply at right angles. Very rarely are dancers depicted in profile; instead, they tend to be represented in a frontal or three-quarter body position with the head almost invariably in profile. This position affords the spectator the most direct and probably preferred viewing perspective. Typically, the feet are turned out sharply at right angles with one foot raised. In an almost life-size in-the-round sculpture from Structure 10L–16 at Copan, the founding king of the Copan dynasty, K'inich Yax K'uk' Mo,' is explicitly portrayed with his feet turned sharply outward from the central axis of his body, indicating that this was a true pose of dancers, and not an artistic convention deriving from matters of perspective. This position is strikingly similar to second position *plié* of French ballet, developed during the reign of King Louis XIV, its first star. This stance derived from a particular presentation of the body intended to intensify viewership of the central performing figure, whose outturned legs heightened the impact of physical movement.

For the Classic Maya, not only are there detailed portrayals of particular forms of dance, but also the accompanying glyphic texts often provide specific terms for distinct dances. Thus, the epigrapher Nikolai Grube deciphered the glyph denoting dance, probably read as *ak'ta.* Another glyph following this term refers to the specific form of dance, and among these are dances with staffs, an axe-like scepter known as the god K'awil, and even live serpents. In addition, there are references to a ballplayer dance and military dances. Quite frequently, Maya kings impersonated particular deities, and in Maya texts such performances are phrased by a clause that could be glossed as "in the famous image of," followed by the name of the particular deity portrayed. It is likely that as with the contemporary *katsina* dancers of the Hopi, Zuni, and other Puebloan peoples of the American Southwest, such dancers were considered not simply as skilled performers but rather the spiritual embodiments of conjured beings. For the Great Plaza at Copan, many of the elaborately carved stelae of the thirteenth ruler Waxaklahun Ub'ah K'awil portray the king as various gods frozen in dance, suggesting that such plazas were important *loci* for public dances.

War Dances. Among the ancient Maya, dance also served to celebrate military victories. Not surprisingly, such dances involved the display of war trophies, including body parts, and the strength and virility of the male warriors. The Franciscan friar Diego de Landa mentions such war dances as the Holcan Ok'ot and the Batel Ok'ot, during which hundreds of warriors danced in long strides in perfect unison to the beat of the drum. Landa also notes that during the month of Pax, warriors danced with the jawbones of the vanquished. Similarly, many Classic Maya vessel scenes depict musicians and elaborately dressed striding warriors with captives, severed heads, and other body parts; quite probably these were scenes of celebratory war dances. One of the more elaborate portrayals of this type of celebratory dance is found in Room 3 of Structure 1 at the site of Bonampak', Chiapas, Mexico. In this chamber, warriors dance with severed heads and other body trophies to the accompaniment of trumpets and rattles. In the center of the south wall scene, men display massive fan-like elements extending laterally from the side of their groins. Although this has been interpreted as a supreme act of penis perforation and self-sacrifice, it is entirely possible that is it a mock bloodletting event celebrating male virility and bravery.

Aside from the dancing men with their phallic fans, the pivotal element in the Room 3 scene from Structure 1 is a beheaded figure swung above the heads of two celebrants. The murals of this chamber almost surely concern the sacrificial climax of a particular historical event. However, these events were not limited to one particular occasion, rather they were re-created in pageants celebrated by the entire community, quite possibly over generations. Each drama not only recalled the original event, but all subsequent performances as well, revivifying the accomplishments and pride of the population with each presentation. One remarkable Late Classic vessel seems to depict the original historical event, one episode removed. In this scene, published by Justin Kerr (K2025), a masked figure accompanied by musicians threatens an unarmed young man with his spear and shield. Rather than in the typical pose of the captive, this figure stands in a dramatic position of dance with one arm fully upraised and the other flexed behind his waist. Behind the youth are contortionists, who with their grotesque faces appear to personify trophy heads. Such a theme of historical reenactment is consistent with the sixteenth-century *Rabinal Achi,* which concerns the arraignment and eventual execution of Cawek of the Forest People from the Quiche nation by the court of Rabinal. Although this was an event cast in the fifteenth century, the dance continues to be celebrated in the community of Rabinal to this day.

Dance Accoutrements. In the most tragic moments of the *Rabinal Achi,* Cawek muses how his bones will be used by future generations in celebrations. In a similar manner, it is clear that war trophies worn by dancers in Mesoamerica were not simply for one occasion, but were esteemed regalia of past heroic events that were passed down through generations as valuable family possessions and inscribed memories. It is likely that such pieces were tied into the original performances when they first appeared before the public. It is also clear that many of the fine jewels and other accoutrements presented by royal courts of the ancient Maya, Mixtec, Aztec, and other peoples of Mesoamerica were esteemed as physical testimonies of special moments of royal favor. For the Aztec, there are descriptions of the emperor bestowing elaborately worked necklaces and other jewels during specific celebrations. When one handles these pieces, it is clear that they were meant for music and dance, for both the gold pendants and the jades make light tinkling noises. Although the Classic Maya lacked metals, they did possess a rich array of shell and jade jewelry and dance regalia. As Rosemary Joyce noted, the jewels worn for these events would accumulate an heirloom quality. Perhaps the most important objects of royal Maya dance were three jade plaques hanging from a belt mask. When worn in dance, these items emit a powerfully vibrant sound, quite possibly denoting the voice of the ancestral head from which the plaques depend. In a number of examples, including the famed Leiden Plaque, such jades have anachronistic texts that refer to historical episodes well before the style of the carving, suggesting that the pieces are indeed heirlooms of ancient peoples and events.

The frequent use in dance of shining jewels of jade, shell, and precious metals, as well as the elaborate plumage of tropical birds, is not simply related to sumptuary goods of the elite. Rather, such beautiful and precious items relate to the symbolism of brilliant colored flowers, a basic representation of the soul and paradise, not only in Mesoamerica but the American Southwest as well. In these regions, a common and ancient metaphor for the numinous state of contact between the world of the living and the supernatural realms of the gods and ancestors is the "rain of flowers." Thus in the remarkable early colonial Aztec songs known as the *Cantares Mexicanos,* there is frequent mention of raining flowers and jewels, along with the presence of incense. Diego Duran mentions that during his accession, emperor Tizoc carried a smoking censer to the pivotal drum to inaugurate the dance of nobles. Still today, *copal* incense and music are used to open the path for religious processions. Along with flowers, incense is one of the most basic offerings for the honored ancestral dead in both ancient and contemporary Mesoamerica. Even today, among the contemporary Jakaltek Maya of highland Guatemala, dance is a means of "untying," feeding, and communicating with the ancestral beings, for them the most compelling reason for traditional dance. Although scenes of the rain of flowers do appear in Aztec portrayals of dance and music, such scenes are much more widespread in Classic Maya art, where not only dancers but also kings are portrayed in this shining place of sweet music and incense, contacting their ancestors from the other realm.

Bibliography

Acuña, René. *Farzas y representaciones escénicas de los Mayas antiguos.* Mexico City, 1978.

Bierhorst, John. *Cantares Mexicanos: Songs of the Aztecs.* Stanford, Calif., 1985.

Bricker, Victoria. *Ritual Humor in Highland Chiapas.* Austin, Tex., 1975.

Duran, Diego. *Book of the Gods and Rites and the Ancient Calendar.* Translated and edited by Fernando Horcasitas and Doris Heyden. Norman, Okla., 1971.

Duran, Diego. *The History of the Indies of New Spain.* Translated by Doris Heyden. Norman, Okla., 1994.

Grube, Nikolai. "Classic Maya Dance: Evidence from Hieroglyphs and Iconography." *Ancient Mesoamerica* 3 (1992): 201–218.

Kerr, Justin. *The Maya Vase Book: A Corpus of Rollout Photographs of Maya Vases.* 5 vols. New York, 1989–1997.

Martí, Samuel, and Gertrude Prokosch Kurath. *Dances of Anáhuac: The Choreography and Music of Precortesian Dances.* Chicago, 1964.

McArthur, Harry S. "Releasing the Dead: Ritual and Motivation in Aguacatec Dances." *Cognitive Studies of Southern Mesoamerica* (1977): 6–35.

Sahagún, Fray Bernardino. *Florentine Codex: General History of the Things of New Spain,* edited and translated by A. J. O. Anderson and C. E. Dibble. 13 vols. Santa Fe, N. Mex., 1950–1982.

Taube, Karl A. "Ritual Humor in Classic Maya Religion." In *Word and Image in Maya Culture,* edited by William Hanks and Donald S. Rice, pp. 351–382. Salt Lake City, 1982.

Taube, Karl A. "Dance." In *The Oxford Encyclopedia of Mesoamerican Cultures: The Civilizations of Mexico and Central America,* edited by Davíd Carrasco, pp. 305–308. Oxford, 2001.

Tedlock, Dennis. *Rabinal Achi: A Mayan Drama of War and Sacrifice.* Oxford, 2003.

Karl Taube (2005)
Rhonda Taube (2005)

DRAMA: EUROPEAN RELIGIOUS DRAMA [FIRST EDITION]

Ancient drama ceased to be performed at the beginning of the Middle Ages. Christian authors like Tertullian (third century) complained that it was cruel, obscene, and idolatrous. Whatever the justification for such complaints, by the fifth century it was no longer relevant to the dominant Christian culture. Performances in the ancient manner may have been offered in Byzantium as late as the seventh century, but they were sporadic and culturally insignificant. A Christian imitation of classical Greek tragedy, *Christos paschon* (fifth century?), may or may not have been performed. Curiously, in spite of the memories of ancient drama that lingered in Byzantium, European religious drama was created in the Latin West rather than the East.

Ancient dramatic texts were copied and read in the West throughout the Middle Ages. The tenth-century nun Hrosvitha of Gandersheim wrote attractive Christian comedies imitating the comedies of Plautus, but it is unlikely that they were performed. In the later Middle Ages, the terms *tragedy* and *comedy* referred to narrative works like Dante's *Commedia.* The mimes, folk plays, and quasi-dramatic entertainments performed sporadically during the Middle Ages did not establish a significant dramatic tradition, and they have disappeared almost without a trace.

In the tenth century several brief plays appeared that were written for performance. These plays were not imitations of ancient drama but original compositions. They all depict the visit of the Marys to the sepulcher of Christ on the morning of the Resurrection. They are to be sung rather than spoken, and they begin with the Angel's question: "Quem quaeritis in sepulchro?" ("Whom do you seek in the sepulcher?"). Since they are attached to the Easter liturgy they are called liturgical dramas.

Liturgical dramas of the nativity of Christ appeared in the eleventh century. By the twelfth century there were dramas of the postresurrection appearances of Christ, the Ascension, Pentecost, the Slaughter of the Innocents, and the Prophets of Christ. There were also dramas on less explicitly liturgical subjects: Lazarus, the apostle Paul, Joseph and his brothers, Saint Nicholas, and the Antichrist. Two long vernacular plays survive from this period: *Le mystère d'Adam* and *La seinte Resurreccion.* Both require more sophisticated acting and staging than the liturgical plays. By the fifteenth century vernacular religious drama was flourishing throughout Europe. In addition to plays on biblical subjects there were saints' plays, miracle plays, and morality plays. Some of the plays were gigantic by modern Western standards, requiring a whole day or even several days for performance and using huge casts and elaborate stage machinery.

During the Renaissance, Protestant and Roman Catholic authorities discouraged the performance of medieval religious drama, and it was gradually supplanted by the secular theater. Only one medieval play has survived to the present in more or less continuous performance: *The Mystery of Elche*

(c. 1420), which is presented annually in the town of Elche in Spain on the Feast of the Assumption. The well-known *Oberammergau Passion* is of later origin (seventeenth century) and is performed only at ten-year intervals. A few medieval plays have occasionally been revived in the twentieth century. Of these, the fifteenth-century morality play *Everyman* is the most enduringly popular.

There has been much speculation about the origins of the tenth-century Resurrection play. Historical scholarship has sought a specific "source" and located this source in a ninth-century lyric composition (trope) that was used to ornament the regular liturgy. In *The Drama of the Medieval Church* (1933) Karl Young argues that the Resurrection play began as a trope of the Introit of the first mass of Easter day. This trope was eventually separated from the Introit and attached to Easter matins. In the new position its dramatic quality could be exploited, and it began to be acted.

The possibility of a deeper relationship between the Resurrection play and the liturgy of the church is suggested by the fact that in every culture in which drama is an indigenous form, the earliest examples are closely associated with religious rituals. The rituals are dramatic in quality and the dramas have obvious ritual elements and themes. The relationship between Greek religious ritual and Greek drama was apparent to Aristotle, and the lingering influence of this relationship can be seen in several of the extant Greek tragedies. Both the form and the theme of the Resurrection play point to a similar relationship with Christian ritual.

Baptism is the Christian rite of initiation. The sequence of events in a liturgical ceremony is described in what the Middle Ages called an *ordo*, an order of procedure. As performed in the early centuries, the *ordo* of baptism required the candidate to descend naked into the font, to be immersed three times, and, on emersion, to be signed in holy oil and blessed by a bishop. This sequence is itself a generalized drama in which immersion in water is the visible expression, or "imitation," of cleansing from sin.

In elaborating Paul's ideas of baptism and resurrection (*Rom.* 6:3–4) Cyril of Jerusalem (fourth century) uses the terminology of Greek dramatic criticism: "O Paradox! We did not really die, we were not really buried, we were not really crucified and raised again; but our imitation [*mimēsis*] was a likeness [*en eikoni*], and our salvation a reality" (*Catechesis mystagogica* 2.5).

Cyril understands baptism in two ways. The ritual occupies the foreground. It is a real action because it produces "a reality," namely, the rebirth and salvation of the candidate. This reality is absolute. It is caused by the intervention of the divine—the Holy Spirit—in the world of time. Baptism is also a stylized enactment by imitation (*mimēsis*) of the death and resurrection of Christ. This historical drama defines the ritual by giving it a specific meaning that is true, rather than conjectural, as far as Christianity is concerned.

Throughout the earlier Middle Ages the Easter Vigil was the preferred time for baptism. The candidates prepared for their initiation during Lent. They were baptized at around midnight on Holy Saturday. Dressed in white robes, they then proceeded to their first Communion, which occurred early on Easter morning, a time roughly coincident with the moment of Jesus' resurrection, which baptism enacts.

Like baptism, the Mass is a real action. By means of consecration, bread and wine are transformed into the body and blood of Christ. The change is a transubstantiation, a change of substance, not a symbolic change or a commemoration.

The Mass *ordo* is a sequence of discrete ritual moments arranged in the form of prologue, rising action, climax, and denouement. This structure took shape over centuries and with innumerable variants. It was regarded, however, as divinely ordained, which means that the arrangement of the ritual moments follows the will of God rather than natural causality. The structure cannot be explained, but it must be observed if the ritual is to produce its miracle.

The initial tone of the Mass is solemn and the concluding tone is joyful. The climax is the miracle of the real presence. It is both a recognition (*anagnōrisis*) of Christ and a reversal (*peripeteia*) of the tone of the ritual. Medieval liturgists described the reversal as a change from sorrows (*tristia*) to rejoicing (*gaudium*). The Mass, in the Classical Greek sense, is therefore comic rather than tragic in structure.

Bits of scriptural history are embedded in the structure of the Mass. When the celebrant repeats the words of Christ at the Last Supper during the consecration he is, for the moment, representing the historical Christ. Representation also occurs during the celebrant's "extension of hands" *(extensio manuum)* in imitation of the arms of Christ on the cross.

In the ninth century these and related historical elements led to a full-scale interpretation of the Mass in which each ritual moment was equated with an event in the life of Christ. The most elaborate description of the Mass from this point of view is the *Liber officialis* of Amalarius of Metz. According to Amalarius the climax of the Mass is the commingling. Because Christ's body and blood are united in the commingling, it corresponds to the Resurrection. The two subdeacons who assist represent the two Marys who visited the sepulcher on Easter morning. At the moment of the commingling, their solemnity is changed to joy, as though through the announcement of the angel to the historical Marys.

In this interpretation the Mass is both a ritual and an elaborate historical drama. The ritual provides the absolute reality on which the drama rests. It is, however, a generalized reality, a sacramental ground. The drama gives this sacramental reality a specific narrative meaning that allows it to be "understood." It seems probable that the Amalarian interpretation was popular in the ninth and later centuries precisely because the laity no longer understood the Mass on its own terms and welcomed the assistance that the interpretation provided. At any rate, for the reasons outlined above, ninth-century Easter liturgy was dominated by the theme of the Resurrection.

The Resurrection play of the tenth century was performed at Easter. Its structure reproduces in little the structure of the Mass: a movement from sorrow, through a climax which is a recognition and a reversal, to rejoicing. And the historical moment that is its subject, namely the Resurrection, is the moment Amalarius equated with the climax of the Mass. Liturgy also provides the stage on which the play is performed, the clerics who act its roles, and vestments that serve as its costumes.

In the Mass generalized ritual action is primary and narrative drama secondary. In the transition from ritual to drama this relationship is inverted. The Resurrection play makes the story primary and ritual action secondary, secondary in the sense of being a submerged sacramental ground, an *a priori* shaping principle that must be deduced *a posteriori* from the materials it has shaped. The sequence of ritual moments is not a plot. It is, rather, a form that can be the shaping principle of many different plots, both historical and fictional. It provides the absolute reality on which medieval religious drama builds it appearances.

When the ritual structure of the Mass becomes the ground for a play about the Resurrection, this structure seems to be replaced by a plot, a story with characters. The clerics who perform the actions of the ritual become actors. Their ceremonial gestures become mimetic gestures expressing human motives. Their prayers and chants become stylized dialogue, still sung, but dialogue in which questions produce replies and commands are visibly obeyed. Meanwhile, because the congregation no longer participates, as it does in the ritual, it becomes a group of spectators, an audience.

Underlying these visible changes there is a movement from ritual sequence to natural causality. The ritual moments in the Mass follow one another in a given order because they must be in that order. Natural causality is not so much absent from the *ordo* as irrelevant to it. On the other hand, because the events of a plot occur in natural time, they are subject to causality. If scriptural history says they occurred, they are necessary; if not, they are only probable. Scripture, for example, states that when the Marys came to the sepulcher they encountered an angel. The angel is thus a necessary element of the Resurrection play, even though outside of the sphere of natural causality. Scripture is vague, however, about the gestures of the Marys when they encountered the angel. The actors performing the roles of the Marys must decide what gestures the Marys probably used. In several extended versions of the Resurrection play the Marys report their experience to the apostles. The Bible says that such a report occurred but does not provide the dialogue. Several plays therefore use a well-known lyric composition (sequence) that begins "Dic mihi Maria" ("Tell me, Mary") for the dialogue. The popularity of this composition demonstrates that it was widely considered an acceptable—therefore probable—version of the dialogue. Hence its appropriateness for the play.

Unlike ritual reality, the reality of drama is contingent. Scriptural history is true in a special sense, and, therefore, necessary; but other kinds of history can err, and elaborations based on probability are contingent by definition. The reality of medieval religious drama is therefore a hypothetical reality, "reality in appearance," in which the reality of the appearance is sustained by the absolute reality of the sacramental ground on which it rests.

Ritual reality is an *ordo*, absolutely determined. "Reality in appearance," however, is plastic and can be manipulated. Three kinds of manipulation are common in medieval religious drama: extension, invention, and imitation.

Extension is the addition of historical episodes to an already existing drama. The visit of Mary Magdalene to the cross can be added, for example, at the beginning of the Resurrection play, and the appearance of Christ at Emmaus at the end, without changing the play's structure. The limit of extension for scriptural drama is shown by the English Corpus Christi plays; they begin with the Fall of Lucifer and end with the Last Judgment, but they retain the comic structure, including the visit to the sepulcher as the climax, of the Resurrection play. For religious drama based on historical sources other than scripture (the *Legenda Aurea*, for example) the limit of extension is the limit of the historical narrative.

Invention is the creation of episodes that are not found in history. As is evident from the problem of the gestures of the Marys confronting the angel, even the briefest historical drama uses extension because history never provides all of the details that drama requires. Whenever extension occurs it moves the drama from history toward fiction. The report of the Marys to the apostles is scripture, but the dialogue beginning "Dic mihi Maria" is fiction. Scripture states that the Marys brought ointment to the sepulcher. Where did the ointment come from? Probably from a spice merchant. How was the ointment obtained? Probably by bargaining. Bargaining has its humorous as well as its serious aspects, so an invented spice-merchant episode, freed of the restrictions of the biblical narrative, has the potential of becoming amusing or satirical. One of the earliest episodes invented for the Resurrection play is the "spice merchant" (*unguentarius*) scene. It is mildly satiric. It is also anachronistic. Historical research might have produced something like a Palestinian merchant of the first century, but the result would have baffled the audience. Therefore the dramatist produced a character who is "probable" in the sense of resembling the sort of merchant with whom his audience was familiar. This means also that the character has the quality of "realism."

A brilliant instance of realistic invention is provided by the *Second Shepherds' Play* of the Wakefield Cycle (fifteenth century). Scripture states that shepherds visited the infant Jesus. What were the shepherds like? The Wakefield dramatist creates a comic vignette of medieval English shepherds that is so effective that it all but eclipses the Nativity scene that is the play's subject. A similar impulse toward free invention is evident in the gigantic French *mystères* of the late Middle Ages, which are based on saints' lives rather than scripture. This playful impulse is made possible by the fact that, as long as the sacramental ground is respected, it will sustain—that is, make acceptable—almost any kind of invention. The playfulness is expressed in passages that are alternately humorous, grotesque, satirical, serious, and intensely devout, and in abrupt juxtapositions of the comic and the ploddingly didactic, the realistic and the miraculous.

The late medieval morality play is entirely fictional, being made up out of the probabilities of theories of religious psychology. Because it is fictional it is more cautious—more rationalistic—than the plays based on scriptural history and saints' lives. Its characters are more consistent, its dialogue more restrained, and its use of digressive, comic, and realistic materials and abrupt juxtapositions more conservative. Its reliance on the sacramental ground of ritual is evident in its comic plot, which regularly hinges on the miraculous conversion or salvation of its protagonist, and in its use of religious themes and characters from the invisible world: good and bad angels, departed souls, demons, and comic "vices" who reappear in Renaissance drama rationalized as villains, like Iago, or as comic embodiments of the principle of disorder, like Falstaff.

Imitation is simply the use of models. The Resurrection play embodies the concept of a "reality in appearance" resting on a sacramental ground. Once the original form of the play became widely known, it could be a model for other Resurrection plays and for plays using the same techniques but different subject matter. As the dramas became more complex through extension and invention, the possibilities for imitation multiplied. By the fifteenth century (and probably much earlier) medieval religious drama had institutionalized itself, and its authors drew their techniques primarily from other dramas. Because the "reality in appearance" of religious drama is explicit and the sacramental ground is *a priori* and invisible, the surface eventually came to seem real—that is, autonomous—while the sacramental ground came to seem a corollary of subject matter and hence either an accident of history or a liability, rather than the foundation on which the drama rests.

During the Renaissance, French and Italian drama rejected the medieval tradition. At first the alternative was direct imitation of the tragedies of Seneca and the comedies of Plautus and Terence. Since ancient drama rests on a ground entirely different from, and alien to, the ground of medieval drama, it is not surprising that most of the direct imitations were stillborn. In seventeenth-century France direct imitation gave way to a neoclassicism that paid homage to ancient models but was based on rationalist principles of verisimilitude, decorum, and the norm of nature. The dramas of Molière and Racine assume that appearance is autonomous and seek to create the illusion of reality by subjecting all of their materials to the rule of probability. Their plays resemble thought-experiments arising from the question, "Given this situation and these characters, what would be the probable result?" The comic plots are pure fiction. The myth and legend that provide the subject matter of the tragic plots are drained of their ancient religious import: myth and legend provide a means of distancing the thought-experiment, or drama, from immediate experience and thus of emphasizing its status as "autonomous appearance."

Spanish and English drama of the Renaissance took an opposite path. As neoclassic critics rightly observed, Shakespeare's plays ignore verisimilitude and decorum and are filled with extravagant language, improbable inventions and characters, and astonishing juxtapositions of the serious and the comic. They may be considered in this regard a final flowering in a secular context of the traditions of religious drama. Shakespeare's enormous history cycle, extending from the "fall" of England through the murder of Richard II to its miraculous "salvation" following the defeat of Richard III, is a secular equivalent of the Corpus Christi play. Several of his tragedies end on a note emphasizing the redemptive quality of suffering: *Romeo and Juliet*, *Hamlet*, and *Macbeth*. The motif of salvation by miracle is rationalized by the "unrealistic" devices of coincidence and disguise in comedies like *The Comedy of Errors*, *Twelfth Night*, and *Measure for Measure*; it becomes explicit in *The Winter's Tale* and *The Tempest*. The medieval tradition also appears in characters influenced by medieval conventions (Falstaff as comic vice), in ritualistic scenes (Othello kneeling to pledge allegiance to Iago), in magic and miracles (*Midsummer Night's Dream*, the rebirth of Hermione), and in the emphasis at the end of many of the plays on reestablishment of community (*As You Like It*, *Hamlet*, *Measure for Measure*, *The Tempest*). According to later, neoclassic (eighteenth-century) criticism, Shakespeare's plays should be failures. They are sprawling, loosely constructed, improbable, and indecorous. The fact that they succeed is evidence of their reliance on a reality deeper than the "autonomous appearance" of neoclassic drama and of the continuing importance of this deeper reality for the modern audiences who respond to them.

Liturgical drama is emphatically not an antiquarian subject, and its reemergence in extremely popular vernacular forms is significant. Paul Claudel and T. S. Eliot, among others, attempted to revive religious drama in the twentieth century; their efforts were not fully successful. Perhaps this is because their plays are concerned primarily with subject matter, that is, with appearance. A few twentieth-century plays began with ritual rather than subject matter, and these seem moderately effective: Timothy Rice and Andrew Lloyd Webber's *Jesus Christ Superstar* and Leonard Bernstein's *Mass*. Popular movie and television entertainments—Westerns, thrillers, science fantasies—retain the comic structure of ritual and its convention of "salvation by miracle," although the miracles are always rationalized as coincidence, luck, or "intervention from beyond." Popular entertainment, however, is limited by its dependence on stereotypes and formulas. Its "reality in appearance" is thin and predictable when compared to the "reality in appearance" observable in medieval religious drama and in English and Spanish drama of the Renaissance.

BIBLIOGRAPHY

The standard bibliography of medieval drama is Carl J. Stratman's *Bibliography of Medieval Drama*, 2d ed. (New York, 1972). Supplements are provided by C. Clifford Flanigan in *Research Opportunities in Renaissance Drama* 18 (1975): 81–102 and 19 (1976): 109–136. The best history of the Roman Mass is Josef A. Jungmann's *The Mass of the Roman Rite*, rev. ed., 2 vols. (New York, 1959). E. K. Chambers's *The Mediaeval Stage*, 2 vols. (1903; reprint, Oxford, 1925) is dated but has interesting material on medieval folk drama. Karl Young's *The Drama of the Medieval Church*, 2 vols. (1933; reprint, London, 1967), remains the standard treatment of the subject from the historical point of view and reprints most of the texts of the surviving liturgical plays. The most complete collection of texts of Latin liturgical dramas is Walther Lipphardt's *Lateinische Osterfeiern und Osterspiele*, 9 vols. (Berlin, 1975–1991). An analysis of medieval religious drama emphasizing its reliance on liturgy is offered in my *Christian Rite and Christian Drama in the Middle Ages* (Baltimore, 1965). See also J. D. A. Ogilvy's "*Mimi, Scurrae, Histriones*: Entertainers of the Middle Ages," *Speculum* 38 (1963): 603–619; George La Piana's "The Byzantine Theatre," *Speculum* 11 (1936): 171–211; and H. A. Kelly's *The Devil at Baptism: Ritual, Theology, and Drama* (Ithaca, 1985). European vernacular drama is surveyed in Richard Axton's *European Drama of the Early Middle Ages* (London, 1974), and the English cycle plays are reviewed in V. A. Kolve's *The Play Called Corpus Christi* (Stanford, Calif., 1966). Very suggestive general discussion of ritual and drama is found in Northrop Frye's *Anatomy of Criticism* (Princeton, 1957). C. L. Barber's *Shakespeare's Festive Comedies: A Study of Dramatic Form and Its Relation to Social Custom* (Princeton, 1959) and E. M. W. Tillyard's *Shakespeare's History Plays* (1944; reprint, New York, 1964) are representative of discussions of Shakespeare from a ritual and generally Christian point of view.

O. B. HARDISON, JR. (1987)

DRAMA: EUROPEAN RELIGIOUS DRAMA (FURTHER CONSIDERATIONS)

The origin of the Latin *Visit to the Sepulcher* and the related ceremonies of the Good Friday *Depositio* (usually involving the burial of a consecrated wafer and/or image) and Easter *Elevatio*, which first appeared in the *Regularis Concordia* (c. 980 CE) from Winchester, remains controversial, but the various forms taken by these dramatic rites have been most fruitfully studied from the standpoint of the geographical distribution of texts and music, rather than of theory (especially the discredited theory of evolutionary development). While centers of this music-drama activity were monasteries and cathedrals, widespread records of parish church presentation exist at least for the *Depositio* and *Elevatio*. The Easter sepulchers required for these are recorded in great numbers throughout much of Europe, and many still exist.

The distinction between rite and mimetic drama is necessarily blurred. The semidramatic Palm Sunday procession is a case in point. In German-speaking countries and Poland, the procession included a *Palmesel*, a carved life-size image of Jesus riding on a donkey. This ceremony, along with certain other semidramatic rites, would be maintained for some centuries in spite of the prohibitions of the Council of Trent. Brigittine nuns, using a carved corpus of Jesus for the *Burial*, continued traditional Good Friday ceremonies into the twentieth century.

The first of the medieval music-dramas to become something of a modern box-office success was the twelfth-century *Play of Daniel* when it was staged by the New York Pro Musica in the 1950s. This play, originally composed by young men of Beauvais Cathedral for the Christmas season, has eschatological overtones and is an impressive collation of biblical history and prophecy. Another very effective play is the slightly earlier *Sponsus* from Saint Martial of Limoges, which stages the Wise and Foolish Virgins (with the latter seeking to buy oil from oil merchants); the reward of the Wise is to be invited in to the marriage feast by the Bridegroom, while the Foolish are cast into darkness, as specified in *Matthew* 25.

The most remarkable example from this period, however, is the *Ordo Virtutum* (c. 1151) of Hildegard of Bingen, which was virtually unnoticed by scholars until the 1980s. It dramatizes the fall of Anima (the Soul) and her return to the circle of the Virtues, over whom Humility presides as queen. The music of this ambitious play, which has twenty singing roles (the number of nuns in Hildegard's abbey), is based on chant but is unique for its time. The single male character, the Devil, is unmusical and only shouts indecorously; his appearance may be surmised from the illustrations in the manuscript of Hildegard's *Scivias*, which also contained an earlier draft of the play.

These music-dramas were not intended to be entertainment. As Katherine of Sutton, Abbess of Barking in Essex, indicated circa 1370 when offering a *Harrowing* play in which the nuns of the convent were to take part, the purpose was to bring the participants out of their spiritual lethargy. Such a motive is particularly evident in the *Peregrinus*, which adapted the Emmaus story to the religious community's desire for the sight of the absent God. Ritually, singers and congregation were to be brought into sacred time as if present at the original events.

Little direct connection can be claimed between the liturgical drama and the vernacular plays of the late Middle Ages. The ambiguity of the Middle English term *play* has created some scholarly confusion, but for the most elaborate examples of the vernacular drama—for example, the great Creation-to-Doom cycles presented at York and possibly Coventry on the feast of Corpus Christi and at Chester during Whitsun week—the purpose of the producers seems principally to have been to involve the audience aesthetically and spiritually in the depiction of salvation history. These dramas attempt to make visible and to stage-manage the violence connected with the life of Jesus from the massacre of the innocents to the crucifixion in a way that focuses the audience's compassion toward the sufferer, the Lamb of God. Audience response is difficult to ascertain when we are dealing with productions from the fourteenth, fifteenth, and sixteenth centuries. Occasional evidence of inappropriateness appears, as in the play of the Funeral of the Virgin at York that dramatized the attack by a Jew on her bier—a case of anti-Semitism in which the audience apparently participated raucously, and of which the sponsoring guild disapproved. But, in general, the producers—the guilds and the city corporation of York—would never have been able to carry on the tradition of staging the plays in the cycle on pageant wagons through the streets at such enormous expense for nearly two hundred years unless a serious religious purpose had been involved. They clearly were setting out to make visible for audiences the same scenes that were depicted in religious art of the city churches and the minster, and they were doing this in a manner that brought the stories forth in a lively rather than a static way. Audiences were therefore being invited to imagine themselves as onlookers at the events of sacred history. The popular *Meditations on the Life of Christ,* translated by the Carthusian Nicholas Love of Mount Grace Priory in Yorkshire, indeed told people that it was necessary for their salvation to be able to *imagine* the passion of Christ visually in all the stages of his suffering. Both in England and on the continent people felt they received spiritual benefit from watching plays on the lives and suffering of saints.

Just as the vernacular plays of the late Middle Ages did not directly evolve out of liturgical drama, so too the plays of Shakespeare and his contemporaries cannot be viewed as having emerged through an evolutionary process that brought about the secularization of earlier biblical, morality, or saint plays. Secularization was largely forced on the public stage in England by the iconoclastic bias of the Reformation and the fear of the authorities that the medieval saint and biblical plays promoted Catholicism. Nevertheless, at their best, Renaissance dramas retain a religious dimension that extended to both stage picture and the invocation of religious iconography in their texts, and they have rightly been seen (in Heideggerian terms) to facilitate the "deconcealment of Being."

With the rise of modernity, the plays of Henrik Ibsen and of August Strindberg examine religious themes in an unorthodox but powerful way. Strindberg in his late plays presents a rich visual symbolism that reflects a world in which God is simultaneously absent and present. T. S. Eliot's *Murder in the Cathedral* (1935), as well as, to a lesser extent, Charles Williams's *Thomas Cranmer of Canterbury* (1936) retain their interest. After World War II, perhaps some of the most striking treatments of religion appeared in the films of Ingmar Bergman. *The Seventh Seal* (1957) explores human doubt and fragility against the background of death in the plague years of 1348 to 1350—a symbolic treatment of the possibility of nuclear annihilation during the Cold War—while some of his films from the early 1960s treat the tremendous power of religious experience over against the terror of the void in a world without God.

Some current challenges for scholarship will involve more thorough exploration of the following: the connections between traditional religion and early drama; the significance of positional symbolism (to use Mary Douglas's term) or its displacement, and the applicability of other anthropological insights in dramas, both medieval and more recent; the spread of early religious drama to the East (e.g., the adaptation of European forms such as the Magi play to Indian dance drama in South India) and to the New World; comparisons of European vernacular plays with dramas such as the Shīʿī passion plays of the death of Ḥusayn in Iran and Iraq; and the sponsorship and reception of religious drama since the Middle Ages, as well as, more specifically, the engagement of audiences with religious content.

Bibliography

Battenhouse, Roy, ed. *Shakespeare's Christian Dimension: An Anthology of Commentary.* Bloomington, Ind., 1994.

Davidson, Audrey Ekdahl, ed. *Holy Week and Easter Ceremonies from Medieval Sweden.* Kalamazoo, Mich., 1990. Includes Brigittine examples, with musical transcriptions.

Davidson, Audrey Ekdahl, ed. *The Ordo Virtutum of Hildegard of Bingen: Critical Studies* (and reduced facsimile of the manuscript). Kalamazoo, Mich., 1992. Supplemented by Gunilla Iversen, "*O Virginitas, in regali thalmo stas;* New Light on the *Ordo Virtutum:* Hildegard, Richardis, and the Order of the Virtues." *Early Drama, Art, and Music Review* 20, no. 1 (1992): 19–22.

Davidson, Clifford, ed. *The Saint Play in Medieval Europe.* Kalamazoo, Mich., 1986.

Fassler, Margot. "The Feast of Fools and *Danielis Ludus:* Popular Tradition in a Medieval Cathedral Play." In *Plainsong in the Age of Polyphony,* edited by Thomas Forrest Kelly, pp. 65–99. Cambridge, U.K., 1992.

Gardiner, F. C. *The Pilgrimage of Desire: A Study of Theme and Genre in Medieval Literature.* Leiden, 1971.

Gibson, Gail McMurray. *The Theater of Devotion: East Anglian Drama and Society in the Late Middle Ages.* Chicago, 1989.

Muir, Lynette R. *Biblical Drama of Medieval Europe.* Cambridge, U.K., 1995.

Ogden, Dunbar, ed. *The Play of Daniel: Critical Essays,* with a transcription of the music by A. Marcel J. Zijlstra (and facsimile of the manuscript). Kalamazoo, Mich., 1997.

Puthussery, Joly. "Chavitunātakam: A Music-Drama of Kerala Christians." *Early Drama, Art, and Music Review* 19, no. 2 (1997): 93–104; and 20, no. 1 (1997): 27–33.

Sheingorn, Pamela. *The Easter Sepulchre in England.* Kalamazoo, Mich., 1987.

Simon, Eckehard. *The Theatre of Medieval Europe: New Research in Early Drama.* Cambridge, Mass., 1991.

Stockenström, Göran. "Strindberg's Cosmos in *A Dream Play:* Medieval or Modern." *Comparative Drama* 30 (1996): 72–105.

Much new research on early religious drama, both English and continental, appears in the journals *Comparative Drama, Early Drama* (superseding *The REED Newsletter*); *The Early Drama, Art, and Music Review* (formerly *EDAM Newsletter*); *Medieval English Theatre;* and *Research Opportunities in Renaissance Drama;* while for documentation concerning original performance and sponsorship, see the volumes of *Records of Early English Drama.*

CLIFFORD DAVIDSON (2005)

DRAMA: MODERN WESTERN THEATER

Where religion has kept alive its affinity with dance, drum, and the dramatic appearance of the gods, it has remained vital. Where drama has kept alive its quality of magic disclosure, it has remained indispensable. These legacies have proved difficult to maintain in Western society, but they contain the heart of the expectations people bring to theater and to religious ceremony alike. The ancient and persistent link between religion and drama may be viewed as the result of factors that include the emergence of theater from religious ritual, the acting out of sacred myth and story, the quasi-priestly or shamanic characteristics of theatrical performers and, conversely, the theatrical qualities of religious liturgies.

It is often supposed that the theater in modern Europe and North America, like Western civilization in general, has steadily become more secular, which is to say, less and less concerned with religion. The truth of this assumption, with respect to theater and modern society alike, is debatable. To the extent that it may be true, it is balanced by the fact that Western religion itself has undergone a kind of secularization: it has, in many quarters, undergone demythologizing, the "death of God," and a radical turn toward political action in "this world," all without losing its identity as religion. More significant than the phenomenon of secularization is the fact that, in most European and American societies in modern times, the professional theater and institutional religion have both become culturally marginal—perhaps for similar reasons.

Before 1700, the principal places for public storytelling were theaters and churches. The advent of novelistic fiction in the eighteenth century meant that stories could be told to a wide audience without people having to gather in a public place. Even so, theater remained a popular institution throughout the nineteenth century while revivalistic religion, if not regular church attendance, was also vigorous, especially in the United States. The immense success of motion pictures and television in the twentieth century reduced the audience for live theater to a very small portion of the population. Although, compared to this, the number of churchgoers remains very large, perhaps twenty to twenty-five times as great in the United States, it too has shrunk as the audience for film and television has grown. New methods of communication, the proliferation of channels on television, the advent of virtual-reality meeting places on the World Wide Web, and multiplex movie palaces have all brought about a change in the way people gather in public—or do not so gather—to participate at the performance of stories, rituals, and myths.

The change in patterns of assemblage has not been quite the same for all social classes. The popularity of religious gatherings continues more vigorously among the marginalized than among the affluent. One might even argue that religion serves as a theater of the poor, although it would be more accurate to say that among them the bifurcation between religion and drama is not as deep as among those with higher incomes.

The rise of the charismatic movement within traditional and established churches, as well as the growth of Pentecostal denominations, may indicate a renewed quest for theatrical and ecstatic worship, paralleling the revivalism of an earlier age.

It would be a mistake, of course, to link forms of worship too closely to social strata. In the United States, for instance, congregations of evangelical churches now occupy middle- to upper-level income brackets and are flourishing. In some cases their messages, saturated with apocalyptic themes, are inherently dramatic and conjure up spectacular imagery. However, it must be said that insofar as religion and theater are middle-class institutions, both are, ironically, of less and less importance to the middle class. The social bracketing of the two institutions leads to a kind of aesthetic bracketing as well: theater becomes pictorial (and hence no significant competition for film and television), while religious rituals become archaic, not to say quaint. In this situation, theater and religion often look to each other for some lost component to help restore their immediacy. The fundamental link between them is their use of performance to make what is unseen seen and what is absent present, and this in the immediacy of a specific time and place.

CHRISTIANITY AND RENAISSANCE THEATER. Although European Christianity was much indebted to classical Greek and Roman civilization, it also inherited the Bible's view of history as fulfillment of divine promise and of Christ as a redeemer who did not fit either the tragic or the comic prototypes of antiquity. Hence, Christianity brought into European culture many sensibilities concerning human character, experience, and historical existence that were significantly different than those upon which the drama of Greece and Rome had been based. It is likely that these sensibilities became mixed with those of the religions that were already practiced in Europe when Christianity arrived. Several nonclassical ideas emerged that proved important to drama: for example, that human nature is not divided into a limited number of fixed character types; that some individuals are subject to marked changes in character as a result of experiences they undergo; and that human history is capable of genuine novelty and surprise. As they worked their way into dramatic expression on stage, these ideas led to a mode of drama concerned with processes of history, the dynamics of class interaction, and the confrontation of the human soul with temptation, with conscience, and with God.

An unprecedented outburst of dramatic genius occurred in the sixteenth century. The greatest talents were those of William Shakespeare in England and Lope de Vega in Spain. Their writing for the stage was based upon very different ideas of dramatic form from the Greek and Roman classics. These ideas led to a form more loose, more episodic, more open to variety in human characterization, more concerned with reflective consciousness, and more open to depictions of the grotesque and the ugly. The immediate sources of the new sensibility, with its profound effect upon dramatic form, theater design, and modes of acting, are thought to lie in medieval Christian dramas known as *mystery plays,* in popular religious festivals, whether Christian or not (some of which gave rise to mummers' plays, concerned with death and resurrection), in biblical literature, and in Christian homilies.

In England, the new dramatic sensibilities were expressed by Shakespeare and most of his contemporary dramatists, using themes much indebted to the humanists and to Protestant (mostly Puritan) reformers of that age and showing the strong influence of a rising middle class. In Spain, the new sensibilities were expressed by Lope de Vega and Pedro Calderón de la Barca, using ideas more congenial to feudalism and to Roman Catholicism. The Renaissance, with its ambivalent attitude toward Christianity, the church, and dogma, empowered dramatists not only to express their own religious ambivalence but also, in the process, to fashion a new dramatic form.

Puritan influence on drama, noticeable during the reign of Elizabeth I in England, soon changed to hostility toward theatergoing. By the early seventeenth century, most Puritans would have been startled to know that John Calvin had spent many Sunday afternoons watching the performance of plays, even if those were indeed plays on scriptural subjects by Theodore Beza. In 1642, English Puritans, who had achieved municipal power in London, closed all theaters, partly because the stage was thought conducive to loose morals, but also because it was associated with the royal court, the nobility, and Roman Catholicism. Although the theaters were allowed to reopen in 1660 with the accession of Charles II to the throne, this forced closing left its mark on all subsequent relations between church and theater throughout the Western world, relations that are sometimes intense but most often strained.

Drama in the Seventeenth and Eighteenth Centuries. With some exceptions, the seventeenth and eighteenth centuries were not periods of important interaction between religion and drama. In the Counter-Reformation, Jesuits throughout Europe made widespread use of dramas to propagate the faith, producing a legacy of postmedieval didactic theater that has had widespread influence, for example on the twentieth-century Marxist playwright Bertolt Brecht. The neoclassic dramas of France in the seventeenth century, especially those of Jean Racine and Thomas Corneille, and also the comic dramas of Molière, are not well understood without knowledge of Christian doctrine and ethics in that age, including, for example, Jansenist theology, which was important to the work of Racine. The anticlericalism that spread during the Enlightenment, especially in France and Germany, exacerbated ancient tensions between religion and theater, with the result that the rift between them was at its widest in the Age of Reason. Whether that has anything to do with the fact that this was not an especially creative period of playwriting, as compared to epochs before and after, is a matter for speculation. The theater of the eighteenth century went in for extraordinary scenic effects and allied itself with experiments being made by painters and architects. It tended more toward the pictorial than the performance aspect of theater and hence was distant from any deep religious sensibility.

The Romantic movement that began in the late eighteenth century was a different matter. It stimulated the use of religious themes in drama, often in unorthodox forms. Goethe's *Faust* (1808/1832) is perhaps the most famous example, but it is difficult to think of a Romantic playwright in whose dramas religious ideas or experiences do not make an appearance, whether in a positive manner (as in Faust), a negative manner (as in much of Henrik Ibsen), or a highly charged ambivalent manner (as in the works of Wilhelm von Kleist, Georg Büchner, and others).

Social Realism. During the nineteenth century, European drama began to display two major interests: the effect of social conditions upon human existence (leading to a style usually known as *realism*) and the quest for meaning in life amid the uncertainties occasioned by the French Revolution, the Industrial Revolution, and the emerging evolutionary view of nature. Depictions of the quest for meaning, more than the positivistic concern for social realism, led frequently to plays depicting a search for God or for the protagonist's soul. Ibsen's *Brand* (1866) and *Peer Gynt* (1867) fall into this category, as do many plays by August Strindberg, such as *Advent* (1898), *To Damascus* (1898–1904), *Easter* (1900), and *The Ghost Sonata* (1907). At the same time, there was also a tendency for the more realistic or "secular" plays to develop a symbolic mode that verges on myth and confronts an audience with quasi-religious mystery. Ibsen's *The Wild Duck* (1884) and *The Master Builder* (1892) are of this kind, as well as Strindberg's horrifying plays about marriage, *The Father* (1887) and *The Dance of Death* (1901). It is worth noting that Ibsen was interested in the religious existentialism and anticlericalism of Søren Kierkegaard, and that Strindberg was at one time a practitioner of alchemy and at another a disciple of Emanuel Swedenborg.

To this tendency among major nineteenth-century playwrights to evince an interest in religious themes, the most notable exception is Anton Chekhov. In him the heavens are closed. The symbolism of plays like *The Seagull* (1896) and *The Cherry Orchard* (1904), strong and beautiful as it is, does not hint at transcendent mystery. The closing speech of Sonya in *Uncle Vanya* (1897), with its vision of an eventual heavenly peace, is moving precisely because the audience recognizes that her words are only wistful.

George Bernard Shaw, a fourth luminary among playwrights at the turn of the century, was a severe critic of contemporary Christianity, mostly because of what he saw as its moral hypocrisy and its alliance with capitalism; yet he introduced religious motifs in almost all his plays, and it may be said of him, as of William Butler Yeats, that he invented a religion of his own. Made up of ideas taken from Christianity, from the philosophers Friedrich Nietzsche and Henri Bergson, and from Fabian socialism, Shaw's faith amounted to a divination of the creative force of life. While concern for life as both rational and holy is never absent from Shaw's work, the plays in which it is most prominent are *Man and Superman* (1903), *Major Barbara* (1905), *Back to Methuselah* (1922), and *Saint Joan* (1923). Meanwhile, Shaw's Irish compatriot, the poet Yeats, was making use of theater to communicate not only the legends of Irish patriotism but also poetic religious visions, especially in plays written late in his life, such as *Calvary* (1921), *The Resurrection* (1927), and *Purgatory* (1938).

TWENTIETH-CENTURY THEATER. World War I put an end, not to romanticism in the arts, as used to be said, but to its nineteenth-century phase. Following the war, the theatrical motifs and styles of the preceding century continued, but in a deeper, more tortured form. The quest for meaning became more desperate. One result in the theater was a form known as *expressionism,* which used theatrical resources—decor, costuming, lighting, music, scene construction, performance technique—to achieve effects more like painting, cartooning, clowning, and poetry than like the narrative art that most Western theater has been. Indeed, from Yeats onward the experimental Western theater has reached out to Eastern (mostly Japanese) stylistic conventions, which are themselves firmly rooted in religious tradition.

In the work of German expressionist playwrights such as Ernst Toller, Ernst Barlach, and Oskar Kokoschka (better known as a painter) is found an outrage against existence that is at once moral and religious, the latter with varying degrees of explicitness. Art of this kind, in the theater as well as in other forms, was employed by the theologian Paul Tillich to depict the religious situation in Germany in the late 1920s. He wrote of such art as engaged in a religious protest against "bourgeois self-sufficient finitude," as he termed the attitude that had infiltrated both the churches and other social institutions and against which much serious theater of the time protested.

Such a theater of antireligious religious protest (to use a very dialectical expression for it) was also brought forth by the first playwright of the American theater to achieve an international reputation—Eugene O'Neill, whose plays often depict "the creative pagan acceptance of life," as he put it, "fighting eternal war with the masochistic, life-denying spirit of Christianity" (quoted in Cole, 1961, p. 237ff.). The plays of O'Neill that treat this religious theme include *Desire under the Elms* (1924), *The Great God Brown* (1926), *Lazarus Laughed* (1928), *Dynamo* (1929), and *Mourning Becomes Electra* (1931).

In O'Neill's works there is also another, slightly different understanding of the modern religious situation, one closer to the views of Tillich. O'Neill articulated this in a letter to the critic George Jean Nathan. Here he wrote of his desire to dig at "the roots of the sickness today," which he described as "the death of an old God and the failure of science and materialism to give any satisfying new one for the surviving primitive religious instinct to find a meaning for life in, and to comfort its fears of death with" (quoted in Clark and Freedley, 1947, p. 690). Such a sense of the loss of God, of meaning, of satisfaction and comfort, may be called post-Nietzschean, after the German philosopher who was the first among modern intellectuals to write of the "death of God." This view of the modern human situation, when held with passion, gives rise to a conviction known as existentialist, of which O'Neill was the first and remains the foremost exponent in American theater. His deepest expressions of this attitude are to be found in his late plays, particularly *The Iceman Cometh* (1939) and *Long Day's Journey into Night* (1940), but it is anticipated much earlier in his expressionist plays, such as *The Emperor Jones* (1920) and *The Hairy Ape* (1922).

In Europe, too, one can discern a line of development from the pre-expressionist, anarchist outcry of Alfred Jarry's *Ubu roi* (1896) through the expressionist drama—including many examples from Russia, France, and Italy not mentioned here—continuing in specifically existentialist dramas such as *No Exit* (1944) by Jean-Paul Sartre and *Caligula* (1944) by Albert Camus, thence into the post-1945 "theater of the absurd" (including the work of Eugène Ionesco, Arthur Adamov, Jean Genet, Fernando Arrabal, Edward Albee, and others) and culminating in the plays of Samuel Beckett, most famously in his first published play, *Waiting for Godot* (1952).

Crucial to this development, as also to the experimental theater of the 1960s and 1970s, were the ideas put forward by Antonin Artaud in a book of essays entitled *Le théâtre et son double* (1938, translated as *The Theater and Its Double,* 1958). Artaud's "theater of cruelty," as he called it, is actually a theater of pure gesture in which words and ideas are "cruelly" subordinated to actions performed for their own sake (*l'acte gratuit*). This concentration upon the theatrical gesture per se would return theater to the domain of ritual. Theologically speaking, an *acte gratuit* is the action of a divinity that is answerable only to itself. Avant-garde theater in the twentieth century has been an attempt to return theater to its religious roots without necessarily adopting—indeed, often opposing—religious faith.

There was, however, a movement in midcentury to restore religious faith to the theater by way of a return to poetic drama. The movement's most prominent figure was the poet T. S. Eliot, who in 1934 was asked by E. Martin Browne, a theater director working for the Anglican diocese of London, to compose some verses (later known as "Choruses from the Rock") for a diocesan stage production. This was followed by a commission from Browne and Canterbury Cathedral that resulted in the play *Murder in the Cathedral* (1935), an explicitly religious play, which made Eliot famous as a playwright and which is arguably the best poetic drama written in modern times. Eliot later aspired to the writing of religious plays composed in verse about people in modern circumstances, partly because of the aesthetic challenge such a task presented, partly for the sake of propagating Christian faith in the modern world, and partly as an answer to existentialist playwrights. He wrote five of these, of which the most popular has been *The Cocktail Party* (1949). Others active in the revival of poetic religious drama have been Christopher Fry, Ronald Duncan, Henri Ghéon, and André Obey. However, the Belgian Michel de Ghelderode, who wrote perhaps the most forceful religious dramas of the century, chose not to use verse. Instead, he adopted a theatrical style somewhere between that of expressionism and absurdism, yielding works of strong religious and theatrical interest, including *Barabbas* (1929), *Chronicles of Hell* (1929), and *The Women at the Tomb* (1928)

During this period, Brecht was seeking a theater that synthesized both the aesthetic value of expressionism and the instructional value of naturalism. He sought a theater that was poetic, parable-like, didactic, and epic, portraying the large configurations of power while locating the dilemmas of the little person within these configurations. In his play, *Galileo* (1943), for example, he demonstrates how the authority of an institution supersedes the rationality of scientific truth. Garbed in papal vestments, the otherwise supportive prelate must force Galileo to renounce his discovery. To watch Brecht's Berliner Ensemble perform one of his plays was to watch a calm ritual unfold. The dramaturgy is antinaturalistic and yet captivating. Although there is controversy over the precise meaning of Brechtian concepts like "the alienation effect" (*Verfremdungs-effekt*) and "epic," the result was a certain spaciousness that allowed audiences to contemplate ideas that might form a basis for decisions in real life. Although Brecht, with his Marxist orientation, derided religious piety, his work seems to lie within a biblical tradition of prophecy in its analysis of an era and its denunciation of the destructive forces within society

PERFORMANCE THEATER. An important result of the competition given to theater by film and television has been the recognition by innovative theorists and practitioners that theater is not necessarily an art of representation. Instead, leading innovators began to view theater as an art of performance that focuses upon the actuality of the performer's existence and the interaction between the performer, the other performers, and the spectators. There have been attempts to work from an aesthetic of actuality rather than one of imitation. This awareness, and the techniques of performance associated with it, tend to move theater in the direction of ritualization and thus bring to the surface one of its more important yet hidden connections with religion.

For this reason, it may be argued that there has been no more significant development in the relation between theater and religion in the twentieth century than the experimental theater movement of the 1960s and 1970s. The most influential exponent of this movement was Jerzy Grotowski, founder of the Polish Laboratory Theater. The notion of theater as religious ritual has become more explicit for many of Grotowski's successors. Peter Brook has acknowledged the inspiration of G. I. Gurdjieff, also a major influence for Grotowski. Inspired by yogans and dervishes, Gurdjieff's concept of theater was that of a spiritual quest employing movement and music to achieve enlightenment. Brook turned increasingly to an exploration of religious themes, including performance adaptations of Ṣūfī poetry and a spectacular dramatization of the Hindu epic, *Mahābhārata.* Brook's 1998 production about a Russian mnemonist, *Je suis un Phénomène,* implied, according to the London *Times,* "that the brain remains unknowable and exists in relation to yet more imponderable issues to do with friendship, God and death" (quoted in Moffitt, 1999, p. 164). Indeed, the intensity of such work necessitates the formation of quasi- or actual religious communities of performers who often abandon the role of entertainer in favor of both improving technical skills and finding an absolute immediacy of the performing gesture in a quest for a transcendent awareness.

One such troupe, Dzieci (Polish for "children"), founded by Grotowski disciple Matt Mitler in 1999, is "dedicated to a search for the 'sacred' through the medium of theater." Carrying this idea to pastoral lengths, Dzieci regularly visits patients in hospitals, where moments of nonverbal interaction result in therapy for the patient, learning for the performer, and transcendent awareness for both. In the course of developing a theater project inspired by Aldous Huxley's *Devils of Loudun,* the Dzieci troupe stumbled upon the idea of creating a Fool's Mass, which has become its signature piece, performed repeatedly in various church settings. The performers wear vestments not of priests but of medieval bedlam idiots who are called upon by circumstance to celebrate a Mass even though they do not know how. Moving easily between the sublime and the ridiculous, drawing its audience through laughter toward participation and contemplation, the work resists being categorized as either theater or religion, becoming both at once in an event experienced by many as transformative. As they stand beside these grotesque characters in prayer, worshippers begin to participate in the liturgy with new understanding.

AFRICAN AMERICAN THEATER. African American religion in the United States, unlike the religion of most white Americans, has made a direct artistic contribution to the theater, largely because worship in African American churches has retained a vigorous performance tradition. Narrative recitation in African American preaching, for example, is theatrical in the deepest sense of the word. Music and rhythm provide the structure of the service, and dancing often occurs. The religious service aims at a visible experiential encounter between the suppliants and a God who provides security, dignity, and freedom.

There has also been a close connection between African American church music and music performed for entertainment in clubs and theaters. In the commercial theater, this connection has been manifest in many productions, among them Langston Hughes's *Tambourines to Glory* (1949), with gospel music by Jobe Huntley, and *Black Nativity* (1961), as well as Vinette Carroll's *Your Arms Too Short to Box with God* (1975). Lee Breuer's *The Gospel at Colonus* (1983) is a powerful musical with a book drawn from Sophocles' *Oedipus at Colonus, Oedipus Rex,* and *Antigone.* This text was sung, orated, and preached as if it were part of an African American church service. Here gospel music, African American preaching, an avant-garde approach to theater, and the ritual basis of Greek theater as echoed in the Sophoclean text all joined to provide a glimpse of the ecstasy that a living tradition of religious theater can provide.

CONTEMPORARY THEATER. It would be a mistake to assume that religious themes are not part of the work of the major playwrights of late twentieth and early twenty-first century. British playwright David Hare's *Racing Demon* (1990) critiques the Church of England in a wry Shavian manner. The play portrays how the kindly vicar of an inner city parish is sabotaged and ultimately ousted by the establishment and its ecclesiastical allies. In a scene reminiscent of Brecht's *Galileo,* a bishop dons his vestments as he grows ever more merciless in his condemnation of the saintly but naive vicar. At the heart of this play and Hare's *The Secret Rapture* (1988) is the question of the survival of goodness in a system of ruthless greed and exploitation.

For the inchoate characters of American writer David Rabe, religion seems a vague notion that has been mislaid in the recent past. Rabe's characters flail about in a violent, fragmented world at the mercy of moment and emotion. Although they reach out for a moral authority, they find none, and question one another helplessly and often comically. A character in Rabe's *Hurly Burly* (1985) asks, "What I'm wondering here is, you got any particularly useful, I mean, lead on this karma stuff?" Rabe's is a postmodern vision to which even existentialism can bring no comfort. The works of South African playwright Athol Fugard, including *The Island* (1973) and *Master Harold and the Boys* (1982), create a dialogue across racial and religious barriers. His plays are a combination of righteous anger and yearning for reconciliation.

The vibrancy and common elements of theater and worship in African American culture continue to produce rich results. The playwright August Wilson brings to his work a sense of spiritual continuity. Everything from African animism, slavery, and the history of the African American church appears in Wilson's symbols in plays where the ghosts are both destructive and constructive. Wilson's characters challenge one another over what has the greater power—the devil or God, oppression or loving-kindness.

African-Canadian playwright Djanet Sears deals with both feminist and racial issues in her work. In 2002 Sears wrote and directed a powerful spectacle about a young woman struggling to see God through a veil of personal tragedy. The staging incorporates dance, Caribbean and African choral elements, and perhaps classical Greek theater. Sears reached back to Shaw for the title to this work, and, in an act of cultural reappropriation, named her play *Adventures of a Black Girl in Search of God.*

CURRENT POSSIBILITIES. An expanding use of drama within liturgy itself can be expected in twenty-first-century theater. Playwrights and liturgists are turning for inspiration to the dynamics of early church drama, the mystery plays, and the work of Swedish theologian and playwright Olov Hartman. The nonecclesiastical work of Brazilian director Augusto Boal, who breaks down distinctions between audience and actor as a method of working out practical solutions to oppressive situations, may also provide a helpful resource in future liturgical and dramatic exploration. These approaches provide clues both to the enrichment of participative ritual and theater, and to the discovery of a dramatic vehicle for the proclamation of a theology of liberation.

BIBLIOGRAPHY

On the ancient connections between religious rituals and drama, see Theodor H. Gaster's *Thespis: Ritual, Myth, and Drama in the Ancient Near East* (New York, 1950); A. W. Pickard-Cambridge's *The Dramatic Festivals of Athens,* 2d ed., revised by John Gould and D. M. Lewis (Oxford, 1968); *Ritual, Play, and Performance,* a collection of readings edited by Richard Schechner and Mady Schuman (New York, 1976); and Schechner's *Essays on Performance Theory, 1970–1976* (New York, 1977). The rise of European drama from liturgy has been documented by Karl Young in *The Drama of the Medieval Church* (London, 1933), but the standard view of the growth of European drama solely from Christian origins has been challenged in *The Origin of the Theater: An Essay,* by Benjamin Hunningher (New York, 1961). Indispensable for understanding how Western drama has been structured to represent changing views of reality, some religious and some not, is *The Idea of a Theater,* by Francis Fergusson (Princeton, 1949). For the influence of biblical thought on Renaissance drama, see *The Sense of History in Greek and Shakespearean Drama* by Tom F. Driver (New York, 1960) and Juliet Dusinberre's *Shakespeare and the Nature of Women,* 2d ed. (New York, 1996). An analysis of developments in nineteenth- and twentieth-century drama as they pertain to modern consciousness and its search for meaning is to be found in *Romantic Quest and Modern Query: A History of the Modern Theater* by Tom F. Driver (New York, 1970). The views of Paul Tillich cited above are from his book *The Religious Situation,* translated by H. Richard Niebuhr (New York, 1932). *European Theories of the Drama,* rev. ed., edited by Barrett H. Clark (New York, 1947), is the standard sourcebook for theoretical writings about the whole of Western drama, both ancient and modern.

There is no book dealing comprehensively with religion and modern drama. A good book of limited scope is *The Great Pendulum of Becoming: Images in Modern Drama,* by Nelvin Vos (Grand Rapids, Mich., 1980). See also *The Making of T. S. Eliot's Plays,* by E. Martin Browne (London, 1969). Among reference works on modern drama, Myron Matlaw's *Modern World Drama: An Encyclopedia* (New York, 1972) is particularly useful.

For an overview of Peter Brook see, *Between Two Silences: Talking with Peter Brook,* edited by Dale Moffitt (Dallas, 1999), and Brook's *Threads of Time: Recollections* (Washington, D.C., 1998). For the theatrical theories of Boal, Brook, and others see, *In Contact with the Gods? Directors Talk Theatre,* edited by Maria M. Delgado and Paul Heritage (Manchester, UK, 1996). For commentary on Brecht see, Martin Esslin, *Brecht: The Man and his Work,* rev. ed. (New York, 1971), and John Fuegi, *The Essential Brecht* (Los Angeles, 1972), as well as Fuegi's *Brecht and Company: Sex, Politics, and the Making of Modern Drama* (New York, 1994). Some of the ideas contained in the above entry are explored more thoroughly in *Liberating Rites: Understanding the Transformative Power of Ritual* by Tom F. Driver (1997); see especially the preface and Part 2: "Modalities of Performance." For examples of liturgical drama, see *Three Church Dramas* by Olov Hartman, translated by Brita Stendahl (Philadelphia, 1966).

See also Toby Cole, ed., *Playwrights on Playwriting: The Meaning and Making of Modern Drama from Ibsen to Ionesco* (New York, 1961), and Barrett H. Clark and George Freedley, eds., *A History of Modern Drama* (New York, 1947).

TOM F. DRIVER (1987)
REX DEVERELL (2005)

DREAMING, THE. If one asks: Why do you call out before approaching a sacred site? Why do you sweep the paths clean the first time you visit the camping site of a deceased relative? Why do you click your fingers to move rain clouds? Why does the hunter not get the best part of the catch? Why do you never look directly at or speak to your mother-in-law? Why do you marry a classificatory matrilateral cross-cousin? Why do you kill an iguana by hitting it behind the ear? Why is the baby carrier rubbed with red ochre? Why do you always ask a particular relative if you can go to a certain place to hunt or gather? The first answer will most likely be, "because that's the Law," or "that's the Dreaming."

Although Aboriginal beliefs and practices are not consistent across the Australian continent, at the core is the concept of the Dreaming, a moral code that informs and unites all life. The dogma of Dreaming states that all the world is known and can be classified within the taxonomy created by the ancestral heroes whose pioneering travels gave form, shape, and meaning to the land, seas, and skies in a long-ago creative era that W. E. H. Stanner, in his classic 1962 article "Religion, Totemism, and Symbolisim," called the "founding drama" (Stanner, 1979, pp. 113–114). Here a rocky outcrop indicates the place where the ancestral dog had her puppies, there a low ridge the sleeping body of the emu; the red streaks on the cliff face recall the blood shed in a territorial dispute; ghost gums stand as mute witness to where the Lightning Brothers flashed angrily at their father Rain; the lush growth of the bush berries is the legacy of prudent care by two old grandmothers; the clear sweet water holes the home of the rainbow serpent. The water holes stay sweet and pure because the Law is followed. Sacred places, imbued with the power of the ancestral heroes, must be approached according to the Law laid down in the Dreamtime. The ritual work necessary to keep the Law alive is often called "business," and those schooled in the Law, "business men" and "business women."

DREAMINGS, RELIGION, AND TOTEMISM. Tracing the genealogy of the term *Dreaming* or *Dreamtime* has been the subject of a spirited exchange between Patrick Wolfe, in "On Being Woken Up: The Dreamtime in Anthropology and in Australian Settler Culture" (1996, pp. 197–224) and Howard Morphy in his response, "Empiricism to Metaphysics: In Defence of the Concept of the Dreamtime" (1996, pp. 163–189). While it is interesting to ascertain the first documented usage of the term, it is perhaps more important to consider the context within which terms such as Dreaming were being employed.

Ronald Berndt (1987) noted:

> The basic indicator of what is (or was traditionally) regarded as sacred, the Dreaming serves to articulate the main components of Aboriginal religion. Variously defined, this concept has its own identifying terms among differing Aboriginal groups: *alcheringa* (Aranda), *djugurba* (Western Desert), *bugari* (La Grange), *ungud* (Ungarinyin), *djumanggani* (eastern Kimberley), *wongar* (northeastern Arnhem Land), and so on. Such words are not necessarily translatable, but nearly all of them refer in one sense to a category of actions and things, mythic beings, natural species and elements, and human or human-type characters of the far distant past, the creative era, or the beginning. In addition, however, they imply a condition of timelessness. They do not refer only to the past as such but to the past in the present and into the future—a past that is believed to be eternally relevant to all living things, including human beings. (pp. 479–480)

For the most part, the observers and recorders in the nineteenth and early twentieth centuries were reluctant to call Aboriginal beliefs and practices "religion." They were more comfortable with concepts of "magic" and "superstition." In his 1962 article (reprinted in 1979) Stanner traced the resistance to the idea that Indigenous Australians had what might properly be called "religion." Skeptical and dogmatic pronouncements held sway. The blindness, he argued, was not that the men would not see but rather that the idea of religion without God, without creed or priests, "was organic with the European mind of the day" (1979, p. 108). In 1915, in *The Elementary Form of the Religious Life,* Émile Durkheim would write of the profoundly religious character of Aboriginal culture, and it is this notion in part that Stanner explores in his sketch of positive characteristics of Aboriginal religion. First, the world was full of signs of intent; second, at its best religion put a high worth on the human person; third, it magnified the value of life by making its conservation and renewal into a cult; fourth, it privileged the spiritual over that material domain; fifth, it was a discipline that subdued egotistical man to a sacred continuing purpose; sixth, the religious philosophy entailed assent to life's terms; and lastly, the use of symbolism in major cults inculcated a sense of mystery (1979, pp. 113–114).

Stanner's article also explored the notion of "totemism." He argued:

> What is meant by Totemism in Aboriginal Australia is always a mystical connection, expressed by symbolic devices and maintained by rules, between living persons, whether as individuals or as groups or as stocks, and other existents—their "totems"—within an ontology of life that in Aboriginal understanding depends for order and continuity on maintaining the identities ad associations which exemplify the connection. (1979, p. 128)

In 1933 A. P. Elkin proposed a threefold classification of individual totem, social totem, and cult totem. Stanner looked at four modes of acquiring a totem—dream, conceptual, augury, and descent-affiliative, but admitted that there was no satisfactory classification and much research was yet to be done.

The Ngarrindjeri of the lower Murray River translate their word *ngatji* as totem and explain its significance as "friend, countryman, and protector." *Ngatji* bring messages and reassurance that the land is indeed alive and "full of signs of intent." In central Australia ceremonial participants refer to ritual paraphernalia representing sacred places and Dreamings by kin terms. In this region Aborigines trace their relationship to the land through both mother's father and father's father. Other considerations are also important. Some are specific and individualistic, such as the place where one's forebears are buried and the place where one was born and conceived. The latter is usually reckoned by the first sensation of movement felt by the mother-to-be, the quickening around the sixteenth week of pregnancy. Both birth and conception sites are open to a degree of manipulation in that one can plan to be in a particular area when a birth is imminent, or one can choose not to acknowledge a pregnancy until near a site with which one would like to have one's child associated. Other considerations are more general and community based, centering on ties of kinship and ritual sharing or exchange. People also have sentimental ties to the places where they worked and lived. These are the places they know, and in Aboriginal society it is only with knowledge of the ways of the land that one may assert a right to use that land and tell the stories of the Dreaming.

BEARING WITNESS. It is only since the late 1970s, with the presentation of evidence from Aboriginal witnesses in land claims brought under the *Aboriginal Land Rights (Northern Territory) Act,* 1976, the *Aboriginal and Torres Straits Islander Heritage Protection Act,* 1984, and the *Native Title Act,* 1993, that Aboriginal voices have been given primacy in defining their relationships to land and their Dreamings. However, the constraints of the Australian law that seeks to "recognize" traditional ties to land specifies that to be granted title to the land of their ancestors, the claimants must meet the criteria of traditional ownership enshrined in legislation. What has happened is that a once-dynamic, negotiable, accommodating, and integrative set of beliefs and practices has been rendered static by statute. The assertion by indigenous Australians that their Law remains unchanged has been taken as a lived reality by Anglo law, and those who cannot measure up to early written records are deemed to have "lost" their culture or to have fabricated it. For a number of reason, accounts of the Dreaming were not recorded by nineteenth- and early twentieth-century observers and when recorded were presented as myths and "just so" stories rather than understood as religion.

In a central Australian land claim brought by the Kaytej, Warlpiri, and Warlmanpa in 1981, three women, Nampijinpa, Napurrula, and Nungarrayi, cooperated in explaining about their Dreamings, or Yawakayi (meaning bush berry), in the country of Waake and Wakulpu, southwest of Tennant Creek (Transcript of Evidence, pp. 175–191). The witnesses were careful to locate the Dreamings in place and in relationship to each other and to themselves. Their conversational style draws the audience into this account of the founding drama, and the repetition underscores the moral lessons being imparted. They were there to bear witness to the fact that none had ventured onto the territory or knowledge of another. Although the narrators mention secrets of the Dreamings, the story has been told in a public context and may be shared with persons not bound by the Law.

> *Yawakayi* comes from Waake and went to visit his brother as Wakulpu, the other one comes from Yanganpali [Wauchope]. He stopped at the soakages along the way . . . at Warnku, he was just sitting in the shade . . . There is a creek there . . . Then he got up and went straight to Wakulpu . . . The one from Waake, he stopped at Jajilpernange, Wulpuje. His brother at Wakulpu told him to go straight back. There was one *Yawakayi* who was sitting by himself at Wakulpu. He was sitting by himself. His name was Amberanger. He was the oldest brother. That is his secret name. That is the Dreaming's own name. The other *Yawakayi* came and was asking this one. "Nambinyindu?" which means, "What name are you?" "I am food, I am vegetable food. What about you?" He refused to answer. He made a sign which means, "I don't know. I don't want to let on." "I said mine. I'm hungry." What they were doing [Napurrula explained], is calling each other's secret names. Another name was Yarrirnti. "You can be Yarrirnti," he answered. "What about you?" He then said, "I am Wakuwarlpa" which is a fruit like *yawakayi.* These two Yawakayi were asking each's secret names and also for secret places that they held [Napurrula ex-

> plained]. That is all, and then he went back—the one who was visiting from Wakulpu . . . to Waake . . . back to Waake. The one who was at Wakulpu stayed living there permanently. He stayed there and that is it . . . and the one who came from Wauchope . . . he was staying there, where that house, that hotel at Wauchope is. He went from there, from Wauchope, he went to Warnku from Wauchope. He went from Warnku where there is a swamp and he slept there, at Wirlilunku. That is the name of the swamp where the Dreaming camped . . . then he went in at Wakuplu for ever. He entered the ground. The soakages of Wakulpu, Kirlartakurlangu. Wirlilunku, a swamp, Jarnapajinijini, Amarralungku, Martunkunya, Kungku, Alajiyte, Kunanyirre, all Yawakayi places.

The women continued to name the places the Dreaming visited, but as they neared the boundary of their country, one said, "Stop there. We're getting too close to someone else's country."

What were the responsibilities of these women as the descendents of these Dreamings? Nungarrayi explained:

> We do that *yawulyu* for Wakulpu all the time. We make the country good . . . for fruit. So it will grow up well, so we can make it green, so that we can hold the Law forever. My father told me to hold it always this way. So I go on holding *yawulyu* for the country. . . . Sometime we dance, man and women together . . . For Wakulpu. So we can "catch him up," "hold him up."

Knowledge of the Dreamings is passed down the generations through song, ceremony, and ritual designs and through being in the country of one's ancestors. When it is shared, the correct people must be present to make sure the Law is followed and to bear witness should any challenge as to the propriety of ceremonies arise.

Dreamings and Art. It is partly through the growing popularity of Aboriginal art and endeavors such as the exhibit entitled Dreamings at the Asia Society in New York in 1987 that the concept of the Dreamings has reached an international audience. There is a long tradition of illustrating Aboriginal Dreamtime stories for a popular audience such as *The Dreamtime: Australian Aboriginal Myths in Paintings* by Ainslie Roberts with text by Charles P. Mountford. This and similar collections of "myths and legends" pandered to Anglo sensibilities rather than reflecting Indigenous storytelling modes. But now Indigenous artists are speaking directly to their audiences. In *Kuruwarri: Yuendumu Doors* Dreaming stories referring to more than two hundred sites are presented in Warlpiri and English. The 1983 project involved five artists painting thirty doors at the Yuendumu settlement school with Dreaming designs. They negotiated the content with other Warlpiri men and women who also collectively owned the designs. Their goal was to teach their children, but the doors, now unhinged, are owned by the South Australian Museum and have traveled widely.

Change and Continuity. The Law is inscribed on the land and encoded in relationships that are testimony to the continuance of the Law. The Law binds people, flora, fauna, and natural phenomena into one enormous interfunctional world. It is the responsibility of the living to give form and substance to this heritage in their daily routines and their ceremonial practices; to keep the Law, to visit the sites, to use the country, and to enjoy its bounty. It is in the living out of the Dreamtime heritage, particularly in the ceremonial domain, that we see how the past is negotiated in the present, how men and women position themselves vis-à-vis each other and vis-à-vis the Law. The common core of knowledge of the Dreamtime concerns knowledge of ancestral activities (the major sites and their Dreaming affiliations), the rights of the living descendents, and the responsibilities of the ritual bosses of the particular business. It is a structural grid onto which people, place, and relatedness are mapped.

It is through ceremonial activity that men and women give form to their distinctive interpretation of the heritage. Thus, although the dogma of Dreaming states that the Law continues unchanged and immutable, the living shape and negotiate beliefs and practices. In most parts of Australia there is a taboo on calling the names of the dead. When an important ceremonial leader dies, songs, designs, place names, and ritual paraphernalia associated with him or her will also become taboo. This knowledge will eventually come back into circulation through the dream of a person who stands in the right relationship to the songs, dances, and places to be able to carry on the Law.

In an oral culture the Law can be given meaning only through the expressions of the living. As long as one has contact with the land and control over sacred sites, the Dreamtime, as an ever present, all-encompassing Law, can be asserted to be a reality. But land, as the central tablet, the sacred text, is no longer under Aboriginal control across the country. Accounts of the Dreaming reflect these altered circumstances, and in the accounts of contact with the colonizers and the changing use of land, Indigenous Australians have attempted to contain the changes, to assimilate the intruders, and thus make them amenable to their law. The narratives of travels through the country of the ancestors, of family, and of outsiders now meld details of the ruptures in relations to the Dreamings and to country with those of continuing connectedness asserted with the past.

Although each song, dance, and design bears the stamp of its finder, the dogma of Dreaming that entails this necessary and continuous process of reinvention ensures that only one person may claim to be an individually inspired creator: Living persons may only assert and reaffirm the law and act as the custodians of knowledge of the Dreaming. The process of reinvention is necessary because of the taboos on a person's property at death. It is continuous because the Dreamings must be shown to have continuity and people to have access to that power. Renewal depends on access to country. Over the generations a song that referred to a specific incident will become shrouded in oblique references, intelligible only to the contemporaries of the person depicted in the song or design. However, once the reference is no longer to a particular person but to a subsection, the song becomes part of a more general repertoire of ancestral activity in the area. Ultimately, it will concern the ancestors themselves. In *Daughters of the Dreaming* Diane Bell traces the way in which a song that began as a reference to a specific event becomes assimilated into the general body of Dreaming activity (2002, pp. 92–94).

Fred Myers (1986, pp. 64–68), writing of the Pintupi of central Australia, describes the process of deductive reasoning by which landscape is assimilated to narrative structure and the underlying impulse to find explanations within the framework of known stories for anomalous formations is satisfied. Ian Keen (1994, pp. 296–297), writing of the Yolngu of Arnhem Land, a people whose stories have become the standard references in the study of religion, points out, "Yolngu assimilated introduced ritual forms to their own mythology and interpreted old forms in terms of mythologised newcomers." Robert Tonkinson, writing of the religious life of the Mardudjara of the Western Desert, identifies "four related aspects of its internal dynamism" (1978, p. 113).

In the southeast, where ties to land have been disrupted and knowledge of ancestral activity has been challenged, people still validate Stanner's 1962 edict: "Aborgines thought the world full of signs to men: they transformed the signs into assurances of mystical providence; and they conceived life's design as fixed by the founding drama" (1979, pp. 113–114). For the Ngarrindjeri the land is still alive with signs of intent, foreboding, and significance. The *ngatji* (totems), such as Ritjuruki, the little willy wagtail bird, and Nori, the pelican, bring messages. The past is constantly being refound and reincorporated into the present, albeit a radically altered one.

As Keen (1994) argued, rather that trying to record changes to a "traditional" order, we should "trace trajectories of transformation in relations, powers, trends, events, and the forms into which people try to shape their worlds" (p. 297).

History and Dreamings. One debate concerning the relationship between history and myth has been pursued with some vigor by Steven Hemming in "River Murray Histories" (1995) and Philip Clarke in "Myth as History?" (1995) with reference to the Ngurunderi exhibit in the South Australia museum in the mid-1990s. To be sure, some narratives are grounded in history. For example one of the major creative heroes of the Lower Murray River, Ngurunderi, is said to have called out in the voice of thunder to his escaping wives. As they ran into the Southern Ocean, the seas rose and separated the land from the nearby islands. The bodies of the fleeing wives can be seen as the rocky islands known as The Pages. If this is to read as history, the story recalls events of 6,000 to 10,000 BCE when Kangaroo Island was cut off from the mainland and the sea rose to near present levels.

Several Dreamings are associated with the opening on the Murray River mouth to the sea. In one, Thukapi, a pregnant turtle, looking for a place to lay her eggs, drags her swollen body to the sea and pushes open a channel for the river waters to flow into the sea. In another complex of stories, the creative hero Ngurunderi creates the landscape. The actual location of the Murray mouth does shift, silt up, and change shape. The multiplicity of myths reflects the changing nature of the land itself.

At one level the Dreaming is an era shrouded in the mists of time from which people claim to be descended without actually tracing the links. Information concerning past generations is difficult to locate on a chronological scale because there is a taboo on calling the names of the dead. This is often given as a reason for the shallowness of genealogies, patrilines, matrilines, and so on. Such an explanation is tautological. It is more pertinent to recognize that the remembering of a unique name and exact dates adds little to Aboriginal understanding and perceptions of the past. What is stressed when identifying a person, alive or dead, is their relationship to others, their Dreaming affiliations, and their ritual associations. In this way it is possible to locate every person as a unique individual: no two persons share exactly the same social rituals and kin field. Siblings are perhaps the closest. To say "our grandparents were siblings" is sufficient to bind two people as sharing the same Dreaming, rights, and responsibilities.

The shallowness of genealogical memory is not a form of cultural amnesia but rather a way of focusing on the basis of all relationships—that is, the Dreaming and relationships to the land. By not naming deceased relatives, people are able to stress a relationship directly to the Dreaming. It is not necessary to trace back through many generations to a founding ancestor to make a claim. By stating that a person is of a certain country, usually by reference to a grandparent who was from the area, the identity of a person is known.

Relations to country that underpin relationships between people are evident also in the way people refer to ritual objects. During a ceremony it is not unusual to hear participants refer to a sacred object that represents a particular ancestor, Dreaming track, or sacred site as "mother," father," or "aunty."

At another level the Dreaming is only two generations behind the present generation, moving concurrently with the present, its heritage entrusted to the "old people," to the deceased grandparents. It is this aspect of the Dreaming that makes any attempt to establish an ethnographic baseline an uneasy enterprise. The Dreaming is not a long dead and fixed point of reference. It is a living and accessible force in the lives of people today, just as it was in the past. Here, then, is the structural potential for change, the Indigenous mode of incorporating change within their cosmos.

Those who give form and substance to the Dreaming live increasingly divergent lifestyles from those envisaged as correct in the Dreaming of a century or two ago. People no longer live in small mobile bands but on large settlements and outstations, in towns and fringe camps, on cattle stations (ranches), and in the cities. They no longer subsist by hunting and gathering but have become members of the cash economy. People are no longer independent producers but rely on wage labor and social security. New items have been accommodated in the ceremonies that bring forth the Dreamings. Wooden digging sticks are now metal crowbars, car springs are used as adzes. These incorporations are seamless. Other resources can be brought under the control of the Dreaming law by classifying them within the subsection system. Thus, one's car may be known as a particular relative and be painted for ceremony with Dreaming motifs. Even residence in a new territory can eventually be legitimated once evidence is found of Dreamtime activity in the locality. Being born on the country, even if it is not that of one's grandparents, confers some rights that will strengthen over several generations of residence, births, and burials in an area. The Law is not challenged by certain changes, but others such as alcohol present significant problems.

The twin notions of an ideologically fixed universe and a structural potential for change through actual behavior are not irreconcilable rather; they allow one to maintain a secure position known to be underpinned by the Law while leaving room to respond within particular constraints. Stanner (1966, p. 169) put it well when he wrote, "They attained stability but avoided inertia." It is possible to establish how life ought to be lived and to be relatively certain that in these values there is continuity with the past. It is somewhat more difficult to determine what is or was the actual behavioral content of the Law as applied or acted upon in any given situation, unless one has actual documented observations.

See Also Australian Indigenous Religions, overview article; Ecology and Religion, article on Ecology and Indigenous Traditions; Law and Religion, article on Law and Religion in Indigenous Cultures.

Bibliography

Bell, Diane. *Daughters of the Dreaming,* 3d ed. Melbourne, 2002 (originally published, 1983).

Berndt, Ronald M. "The Dreaming." In *Encyclopedia of Religion,* edited by Mircea Eliade, vol. 4, pp. 479–81. New York, 1987.

Clarke, Philip A. "Myth as History? The Ngurunderi Dreaming of the Lower Murray, South Australia." *Records of the South Australia Museum* 28, no. 2 (1995): 143–156.

Durkheim, Émile. *The Elementary Form of the Religious Life.* New York, 1915.

Elkin, A. P. *Studies in Australian Totemism.* New York, 1978 (originally published, 1933).

Hemming, Steven. "River Murray Histories: Oral History, Archaeology and Museum Collections." In *Work in Flux,* edited by E. Greenwood, K. Neumann, and A. Sartori, pp. 102–110. Melbourne, 1995.

Keen, Ian. *Knowledge and Secrecy in an Aboriginal Religion.* Oxford, 1994.

Morphy, Howard. "Empiricism to Metaphysics: In Defence of the Concept of the Dreamtime." In *Prehistory to Politics: John Mulvaney, the Humanities and the Public Intellectual,* edited by Tim Bonyhady and Tom Griffiths, pp. 163–189. Melbourne, 1996.

Myers, Fred R. *Pintipu Country, Pintupi Self: Sentiment. Place and Politics Among Western Desert Aborigines.* Washington, D.C., 1986.

Roberts, Ainslie (illustrator), and Charles P. Mountford (text). *The Dreamtime: Australian Aboriginal Myths in Paintings.* Adelaide. 1965.

Stanner, W. E. H. *On Aboriginal Religion.* Oceanic Monographs, No. 11, Sydney, 1966.

Stanner, W. E. H. "Religion, Totemism, and Symbolism." In *White Man Got No Dreaming,* pp. 106–143. Canberra, 1979.

Tonkinson, Robert. *The Mardudjara Aborigines.* New York, 1978.

Transcript of Evidence. "Kaytej, Warlpiri and Warlmanpa Land Claim." Aboriginal Land Rights (Northern Territory) Act, 1976, 1981.

Warlukurlangu Artists. *Kuruwarri: Yuendumu Doors.* Canberra, 1992.

Wolfe, Patrick. "On Being Woken Up: The Dreamtime in Anthropology and in Australian Settler Culture." In *Prehistory to Politics: John Mulvaney, the Humanities and the Public Intellectual,* edited by Tim Bonyhady and Tom Griffiths, pp. 197–224. Melbourne, 1996.

Diane Bell (2005)

DREAMS

DREAMS. The category of dreams designates both sleeping and imaginal states of consciousness together with waking descriptions and other representations of these states. Sleeping consciousness includes healing dreams, prophetic dreams, archetypal dreams, nightmares, and lucid dreams. Imaginal consciousness includes guided fantasies known as waking dreams, omens, and visions.

Dreaming is both a sleeping and a waking experience that is activated whenever energy flows inward toward the spiritual and intellectual senses rather than outward toward the worldly and perceptual senses. When one falls into a trance or falls asleep, the worldly senses vanish inside, the everyday mind stops functioning, and one is sleeping. After a period of nothingness, the mind begins to function again, and dreaming begins. As this happens one slowly moves from private sensations, personal memories, images, and symbols to transpersonal imagining as an interactive social process.

The Cross-Cultural Study of Dreams. From the earliest times sleeping dreams and waking visions have been of considerable interest to humankind. Dream narratives have also been examined to learn how members of different cultures categorize and use their dreams. Some researchers have shown both the tactical use of dreams in social interaction and the cultural influences on dream content. Others have chosen not to focus their attention on dream narratives or social context but rather to use dreams to investigate psychological issues, such as personality and values.

Before Sigmund Freud published *The Interpretation of Dreams* (1900), scholars described dreams as the ultimate source of religious beliefs concerning the supernatural and the nature of the human soul. After Freud's book, many people followed him in separating the nature of the dream experience, or the "manifest dream," from the so-called real meaning of the experience, which he labeled the "latent dream." The manifest dream content is investigated with the help of a dreamer's associations to the key elements in the dream that are traced to the dreamer's hidden or latent thoughts, consisting of a combination of wishes and conflicts. The manifest dream content—though often distorted, disguised, or presented in metaphorical form—and the latent dream content are in turn linked to a distinction between two modes of thought: primary and secondary process. Primary process consists of nonlogical symbolic imagery, whereas secondary process is predominantly verbal and logical.

A number of researchers who were interested in the cross-cultural study of dreams utilized Freudian concepts and methodologies. Some, however, remained skeptical and tested the key hypotheses. Others ignored the approach altogether. Those who followed Freud's psychoanalytic theories and methods argued that similar latent contents—including incestuous family attachments, sibling rivalry, anxiety about maternal separation, and fear of castration—are revealed in dream reports gathered in vastly different cultures. The ethnographer Anthony Wallace (1958) even described the Iroquois of North America as having independently invented their own psychoanalytic techniques of dream interpretation.

Other researchers employed one or more of the following Freudian methodologies in working with dreams:

1. eliciting associations to dream images as they are related,
2. focusing on an element containing a metaphorical key to the meaning of the dream,
3. asking for the previous day's events connected with the dream,
4. allowing the subject to freely associate to the dream.

The ethnographer Dorothy Eggan (1966), for example, did not press her Hopi consultants for the previous day's residue or free associations but allowed them to take the initiative in dream telling and free association. The psychoanalyst Géza Róheim (1952), on the other hand, obtained associations from Australian Aborigines for each dream episode and elicited personal anecdotes, myths, and songs. Because he was focused on the infantile wish rather than on current conflicts, he suggested that an analyst need only be familiar with the simple factual knowledge required to follow the manifest narrative content of a dream.

The psychoanalytically trained ethnographer Waud Kracke (1979) disagreed with Róheim, noting that in order to understand what a person's dreams reveal about his or her personality it is necessary to learn the language of dreaming within that individual's culture. Researchers who use a psychoanalytic approach to dreams often combine it with an ethnographic approach to the culture in order to probe both the psychological and the cultural significance of dreams. Visionary or prophetic dreams, for example, often transform the psyche of the dreamer, and they may be a source of inspiration for the founding of new religions and charismatic movements as well as for triggering anticolonialist revolts. Would-be prophets commonly experience revelatory dreams that underlie both their personal access to charismatic power and their spiritual message. Examples include the origins of the Dream and Ghost Dances of Native North America as well as Melanesian cargo cults and Japanese new religions (Michelson, 1923; Burridge, 1960; Fabian, 1966; Worsley, 1968; Franck, 1975; Lanternari, 1975; Stephen, 1979).

Freud's hypothesis concerning type dreams states that the same manifest content—for example, flying, climbing, or the loss of a tooth—reveals identical latent meanings across cultures. Charles Seligman (1923) tested this idea by publishing a request for British colonial officials and missionaries to send him records of native dreams. He believed that if type dreams of the Freudian sort were found frequently in this data base, then the human unconscious was qualitatively so alike worldwide that it constituted a common store on which fantasy might draw. His store metaphor points to the objectifying notion of dream symbolism as a simple trait that might be measured or weighed by colonial officials. It ignores the importance of communicative context both within these cultures and in the negotiation of reality between colonial administrators and indigenous peoples. This lack of sensitivity to the context and manner in which one conducts research is also true for the Navajo research of Jackson Steward Lincoln (1935). He ignored the influence of social setting on his own collection of dreams: transactions that took place at the Black Mountain Trading Post.

While Seligman and Lincoln found that similar sorts of dreams occurred worldwide, the Freudian premise that universal type dreams should mean the same thing everywhere they occurred was never tested empirically until Benjamin Kilborne (1978) asked a group of Moroccan dream interpreters to explain the meaning of a set of fifteen dreams he culled from Freud. Kilborne found that whereas Freud treated dream reports as analyzable structures requiring secondary associations before they could be adequately interpreted, Moroccans did not make an analyzable entity of either the dream or the context of interpretation. Thus in a woman's dream of a deep pit in a vineyard created when a tree was removed, which Freud used as a classic example of a female castration dream, Moroccan dream interpreters focused primarily on the pit, leaving out the tree, or else focused on the tree, leaving out the pit. In the first instance the pit was described as representing a trap for the dreamer, whereas in the second case the tree represented a good person who died. Whereas the Freudian explanation of dream symbols draws on the notion of universal latent content, the Moroccan explanation centers on the dreamer's social position.

Although most dream researchers chose the Freudian path of analysis, a few, including John Layard (1988), Vera Bührmann (1982), and Lawrence Petchkovsky (1984), followed Carl Jung. The sharpest disagreement between the Freudians and the Jungians centers on Freud's hypothesis that the manifest dream is simply a disguise of the latent dream that embodies an infantile erotic wish. Jung (1974) argued that images in dreams reflect the structure of psychological complexes in the personal unconscious that rest upon archetypal cores in the psyche and are subject to the individuating force of the self.

Dreaming encourages a variety of attitudes and responses: pragmatic, cognitive, and spiritual. The pragmatics of dreaming centers on the tactical use of dreams and visions in dream sharing, social interaction, and healing. A cognitive response focuses on expectations concerning the theoretical nature of dreaming and dream interpretation systems together with the languages of dream telling. Spiritual approaches to dreaming combine symbolic, mythic, and ritual elaborations of consciousness. Although these responses overlap, the following sections introduce them one after the other.

The Pragmatics of Dreaming. Deciding which dreams to share, how, and with whom are important issues. Informal dream telling upon awakening with members of one's immediate family is found in all societies. More formal public dream sharing, although it is far less common, also occurs in many places. However, the significance given to the act of dream sharing, whether formal or informal, varies markedly from one society to another. In some societies people place a high value on both the personal and the public use of the many forms of dreaming, including waking dreams, lucid dreams, visions, and nightmares. In other societies dreaming is regarded as insignificant and is given limited importance or even ignored. Epistemological differences between these attitudes toward dreaming are evident when people relate their life stories.

Many Amerindian societies, for example, honor dreaming and construct personal biographies around dreams and visions. The Lakota holy man Black Elk, when he first met his biographer John Neihardt (1932), immediately shared his power dreams with him. Likewise in Chile, when the Mapuche shaman Tomasa first met Lydia Degarrod (1990), she shared her power dreams and visions. In northern California and Oregon there were in the past, and in some cases there remain, organized schools of shamans in which novices shared their dreams with their teachers. After listening carefully to the novices' dreams, the teachers encouraged them to receive specific types of dreams or visions that allowed them to heal patients.

For Mayans in Mexico and Central America it is routine to awaken one's spouse or other sleeping partner in the middle of the night to narrate a dream (Tedlock, 1992, p. 120). Parents also ask their children each morning about their dreams. In most of these societies, even though there may be no recognized dream interpreters, dreams and dream interpretations of respected elders are taken seriously. Children's dreams, while they are always given the benefit of interpretation, have little effect on adult's actions. Other societies urge their children to experience and report certain types of culturally approved dreams and visions that help them to allay anxiety and bring them power and prestige. In yet other cultures parents carefully monitor their children's dream reports lest they begin receiving nightmares. If a youngster receives such dreams, the parents do what they can to alter them by taking the child into the mountains, where they ask that person's spirit to stay away.

The first issue in dream sharing is to categorize the dream as to its type: good or bad, lucky or unlucky. Once this has been decided, a dreamer chooses whether or not to tell the dream. This depends on a combination of personal preference and wider cultural patterns. At Zuni Pueblo in western New Mexico, for example, the dreams that are immediately told are only those that are considered to be "bad," in that dead people appear and attempt to lure the dreamer to visit the Land of the Dead (Tedlock, 1992, p. 118). The way Zunis prevent the completion of such nightmares is to tell them while inhaling the fumes of a burning piñon branch, then to plant feathered prayer sticks for the ancestors asking them not to appear. If the dream is frightening, the dreamer may even ask for a ceremonial whipping at the hands of a masked ancestral figure. Such whippings remove the bad thoughts and turn them around, reversing their meaning. Good dreams, on the other hand, are not reported until they have been "completed," in other words until they have come true.

Among Quechua speakers in the Peruvian Andes, dreams are premonitory of the day's events (Mannheim, 1992, p. 145). If you experience a bad dream, when you get out of bed in the morning you should step on the left instead of on the right foot. Then before telling anyone your dream, you must find a young sheep or llama and recount the dream to the animal then spit in its mouth three times saying, "Disappear, disappear, disappear."

In China from the earliest times the nature of dreams—whether lucky or unlucky—was considered to be determined by the spirits (Fang and Zhang, 2000). During the Zhou dynasty (c. 1150–256 BCE) the emperors practiced rituals to solicit lucky dreams and to avoid unlucky dreams. Texts containing charms to help one avoid bad dreams or turn them into good dreams were eventually written down. *The New Collection Zhou Gong's Dream Interpretations* (Tang dynasty, c. 618–907 CE), for example, explains that those who have evil dreams should not tell anyone. When they rise in the morning they should instead write on a piece of paper "Red sunshine, the sun rises in the east." If they read this charm three times and place it under their beds, the ghosts will immediately flee.

After a dream is categorized, it can be enacted or interpreted in various ways. Jungians and certain other dream workers regard one's dream images as aspects of the self.

Thus all of the symbols within a dream are "translated" into words upon waking and are shared later during an analytic session or dream-group meeting. During this period the dreamer, with the help of the analyst or facilitator, moves into the inner space of the dream and brings out or elaborates the dream events, often amplifying them through mythic or visual similarities, rhymes, or wordplays.

K'iche' Mayans handle their dreams in a similar but slightly different manner. Unlike Western dream enthusiasts, Mayans do not wait for the dream to end to integrate it. Instead they begin during the process of dreaming whenever an important mythic symbol appears. If they miss this opportunity, they wait for a later dream when the symbol recurs in a somewhat different form. At that time the dreamer awakens slightly, cognitively enters the dreamscape, and interrogates each and every symbol as it appears, one after the other, so that each reveals its true nature. This practice, called "completing the dreaming," is similar to both Dream Yoga and lucid dreaming.

Dreaming, Cognition, and Interpretation. The dichotomy between dreaming as an internal subjective reality and waking as an external objective reality, together with a devaluation of dreaming, is an inheritance from the ancient Greeks, most especially from Aristotle. He dismissed dreams as nothing but mental pictures that, like reflections in water, are not the real objects. This idea was elaborated at the end of the Middle Ages, when the notion of the person as having a soul or spirit that could temporarily leave the body during dreaming became heretical. Whereas dreaming was already devalued within the West by the time of the emergence of naturalistic or scientific thought, it was not until the development of Cartesian dualism in the seventeenth century that dreams were firmly placed within the realm of fantasy or irrational experience.

It must be remembered, however, that the irreducible dualism of "spirit" and "matter," which denies the common principle from which the terms of this duality proceed by a process of polarization, was a historical development within Western philosophy. A majority of the world's peoples have not focused their thinking around oppositionalism and thus have not isolated dreaming within the "unreal" realm of spirit. Rather, it is a rationalist proposition that dreaming is somehow a more subjective, false, private, illusory, or transient reality than the more objective, true, public, real, or permanent reality of waking life.

This difference in attitudes toward dreaming is demonstrated by a set of interchanges between Rarámuri Indians living in northern Mexico and the ethnographer William Merrill (1992). Merrill noted that he was frustrated when on numerous occasions people described to him incredible personal experiences but failed to mention that the events had taken place in dreams until he specifically asked. Another researcher living in a Tzeltal Mayan community in Chiapas, Mexico, noted that since dream events were deeply integrated into conscious behavior, it was often difficult for her to decide whether a person was referring to an actual occurrence or to a dream (Hermitte, 1964, p. 183). A third ethnographer who was editing a Tzotzil Mayan's life story reported that she found herself asking him over and over again whether a particular event he was describing occurred in conscious waking life or in a dream while he was sleeping (Guiteras Holmes, 1961, pp. 256–257).

During fieldwork at Zuni Pueblo in western New Mexico, Barbara Tedlock sometimes found it difficult to tell whether a person was narrating a nighttime dream or a waking experience. When she asked a middle-aged man whether he ever had dreams that foretold the future, he answered: "Yes, awhile back a sheep herder found a dead rabbit, badly torn up, and he cooked and ate it. Later on the man was thrown from a burro, his foot caught in the stirrup, and he was dragged around in some rocks. When his partner found him, he was all tore up, dead" (Tedlock, 1973 field notes).

Instead of narrating one of his own dream experiences, this man related a waking omen. Thus although there are separate terms in the Zuni language to distinguish dreaming from the perception of omens, the fact that the rabbit was eaten in life rather than in a dream seemed to be a matter of indifference to the narrator. Either way, the incident of the rabbit portended the incident with the burro. This blending of waking omens and sleeping dream signs into a single category of premonitions is found more generally among Amerindians.

This remarkable creative potentiality of dreaming occurs because dreams are a way of thinking and of organizing knowledge. At some level all people believe this, as is revealed by the common saying "I'll have to sleep on that decision." At the same time people often profess the belief that dreams are meaningless fantasies or confused mental imaginings with little truth value. This ambivalence arises from the educational system that teaches that only fully conscious rational thoughts can provide true knowledge. Nevertheless people also believe that irrational, or better yet nonrational, unconscious thoughts or intuitions are a sign of "genius."

The Language of Dreaming. It has been suggested that dreaming is the original native tongue, a common language shared by all human beings. However, when discussing dreams, people often neglect the important fact that in any given society the language or languages spoken deeply affect the perception and narration of dreams. Both the structure of the language and its available vocabulary help to channel the imagination of dreamers. Thus within a number of languages, including French, Italian, K'iche' Mayan, and Xavante, the verb stem for dreaming is transitive, indicating that a dreamer acts upon or "makes" something while dreaming. In other languages, such as English, German, Spanish, Zuni, Kalapalo, and Egyptian hieroglyphics, the verb stem used to describe the process of dreaming is intransitive, indicating that dreaming is a passive state of being, that one simply "has" or "sees" a dream. This difference underscores the variable attention paid to dreaming as a passive observation by a dreamer and dreaming as an active experience of the dreamer's soul, psyche, or self.

In dream telling a dreamer's source of knowledge or authority as a narrator is also marked grammatically. Wherever dreaming is conceived as involving the actions of the soul rather than of the dreamer's ego, third-person singular forms are used. Epistemological concern with a dreamer's source of knowledge or authority is often marked grammatically. On the Northwest Coast of Canada Kwakiutl speakers use a suffix that indicates that the action of the verb occurred in a dream. There is also another suffix meaning apparently, seemingly, and it seems like as well as in a dream. Since these two suffixes include adverbial and conjunctional ideas possessing a strong subjective element, they are categorized as word suffixes and are placed in a single classification expressing the sources of subjective knowledge. As a grammatical category these suffixes indicating events known only indirectly have been classified by linguists as *evidentials.* There are several kinds of evidentials—tense particles, adverbs, and quotatives—that require the speaker to adopt a particular stance toward the truth value of an utterance.

The use of evidentials demonstrates major epistemological differences among various traditions. In a number of cultures report forms consisting of verbs as well as particles indicate that the preceding or following utterance is an animation of the speech of a deity, ancestor, or other supernatural. In these examples there is no distinction, as there is in English, between direct discourse that is faithful to the wording and indirect discourse that is faithful to the meaning. Instead, for many peoples there appears to be an irreducible dialectic between linguistic structure, practice, and ideology. It also reveals the existence of separate dream interpretation codes for lay dreamers and professional dream interpreters within the same society. Only people who have been trained as dream interpreters use the quotative.

Psychologists of both psychoanalytic and cognitive bents have read anthropology to compare the dreams of preliterate, tribal, traditional, or peasant peoples with their own findings concerning the dreams of literate, urban, modern, or industrial peoples. This dichotomy, however, denies people living in other cultures contemporaneity with industrial peoples. Instead of using typological time to create and set off an object of study, such as "tribal dreaming," cultural anthropologists have become interested in intersubjective time in which all of the participants involved are coeval or share the same time. This focus on communicative processes among people living in the same time but in vastly different cultures demands that coevalness not only be created and maintained in the field but also that it is carried over during the write-up process. Robert Dentan (1986), while discussing the principle of contraries in which dreams indicate the opposite of what they seem, noted that practitioners of this type of dream interpretation include such widely separated peoples as Ashanti, Malays, Maori, Semai, Zulu, Polish American schoolgirls, and psychoanalysts. In other words Euro-Americans share this principle of dream interpretation with people living in faraway, exotic places.

This underlying sameness in human cognition is also stressed within structuralism. A structural approach to dreaming demonstrates that dreams, like myths, constitute a set of systematic transformations of a single structure consisting of a set of oppositions representing a dilemma or conflict facing a dreamer. Philippe Descola (1989), in research among Jivaroan people in South America, found that the individual unconscious and the collective unconscious are related less by contiguity or universal archetypes than by use of encoding devices for the diversity of reality within elementary systems of relationships. He noted that, like structualists, indigenous dream interpreters emphasize the logical operations through which symbols are connected and suggests that a comparative grammar of dreams is needed that might elucidate how various cultures choose and combine a set of rules or codes for dream interpretation.

The turn away from treating non-Western dreams as totally other, fully knowable objects to be gathered, analyzed, tabulated, and compared with Western dreams toward paying attention to the problematics of dream communication and interpretation worldwide has occurred within anthropology for several reasons. First, ethnographers came to distrust survey research in which "data" is gathered for the purpose of testing Western theories concerning universals in human psychology. Cross-cultural content analysis, in which statistical assertions about dream patterns within particular ethnic groups or genders were the goal, have been critiqued by anthropologists. There are several reasons for this, including the fact that sample surveys aggregate respondents who are deeply distrustful of the researcher with those who are not, as if suspicion made no difference whatsoever in the validity of their replies. Further, a comparativist focus on the extractable contents, underlying structure, or cognitive grammar of a dream report not only omits important phenomena, such as pacing, tones of voice, gestures, and audience responses, that accompany dream narrative performances but is also an expression of the culture of alphabetic literacy and thus is culture-bound.

Another reason for the abandonment of content analysis by most anthropologists is their formal training in linguistics, which encourages them to reject the basic assumption of aggregate statistical research, namely that meaning resides within single words rather than within their contexts. Furthermore dream symbols taken in isolation can be misleading if the researcher has not spent sufficient time observing and interacting within the culture in order to make sense of local knowledge and produce a "thick description" of that culture. Rather than interpreting the language of dream narratives in semantico-referential, context-independent terms, it is more appropriate to utilize context-dependent or pragmatic meaning.

Because of these considerations, researchers no longer set out to elicit dream reports as ethnographic objects to be used primarily as raw data for comparative hypotheses. Instead, since the attitudes toward and beliefs about dreams held by a people reveal important aspects of their worldviews, constructing a detailed ethnography of dreaming has become an important research goal. Ethnographers tape-record and transcribe verbatim dream narratives along with dreamers' interpretations. The method of ethnographic semantics, in which direct and formal questioning is used, may also be applied to ascertain how members of a particular linguistic group categorize their dreams. The goals of this methodology are to produce a taxonomic system of types of dreams, good, bad, true, false, and to reveal native dream theory and techniques of dream interpretation.

This combination of linguistic and ethnographic methodologies, applied within different domains, particularly suits contemporary cultural anthropology, which requires researchers to enter the field for extended periods of time with broad sets of research interests. By living in the community they learn the local language as well as how to interact appropriately, and they are present for various formal and informal social dramas. Sooner or later they are present when a dream is narrated within a family or to a practicing shaman or other dream interpreter. If this event attracts their attention, they make notes about it in their field journals, and they may later record other such occurrences on audio- or videotape. Once they have translated their texts, they may ask the narrator, who may or may not be the dreamer, questions about the meaning, significance, and use of the dream account.

This shift in research strategy from eliciting dozens of dreams as fixed objects to studying naturally occurring situations, such as dream sharing, representation, and interpretation, is part of a larger movement within the human sciences in which there has been a growing interest in analyses focused on practice, interaction, dialogue, experience, and performance together with the individual agents, actors, persons, selves, and subjects of all this activity. A number of new books in the human sciences display this shift from a focus on the dream as an object to the social context surrounding both the personal experience and cultural uses of dreaming (Dombeck, 1991; Parman, 1991; J'edrej and Shaw, 1992; Tedlock, 1992; Shulman and Stroumsa, 1999; Young, 1999; Lohmann, 2003).

Dream Sharing. Lydia Degarrod (1990) recorded the majority of her subjects' dreams within a natural setting rather than by arranging formal interviews. During her research in southern Chile with the Mapuche Indians, she gathered dreams and interpretations from members of two families who were coping with serious stress caused by witchcraft and illness. Through dream sharing and interpreting, the afflicted members of the families were able to express their anxieties and externalize their illness, and other family members were able to participate in the healing of their loved ones. Degarrod hypothesized that these types of family interventions were possible due to the general belief that dreams facilitate communication with supernatural beings and due to the nature of the communal dream sharing and interpreting system that allowed the combination of elements from different individual's dreams to be related through intertextual and contextual analysis.

During her research among Australian Aboriginal peoples, Sylvie Poirier (2003) found that dreaming was closely intertwined with religious beliefs. In Western Australia, for example, dreams represent the privileged space-time of increased receptivity among individuals, the environment, and the ancestral world. Through studying local epistemology, she found that not only was the interpretation of dreams open to multiple readings depending on context but that dream experience was also a primary step in the social construction of the person. This sensitivity to the crucial importance of the social and cultural context in understanding and interpreting dreams has been elaborated by historians of religion to include the integration of dream interpretation into the culture's ontological and semiotic maps and the further integration of dream theory into culturally specific notions of personality and economies of consciousness, so that dreaming can be seen in the context of metapsychology (Shulman and Stroumsa, 1999, p. 7).

By studying dream sharing and the transmission of dream theories in their full social contexts as communicative and integrative events, including the natural dialogical interactions that take place within these events, scholars have realized that both the researcher and those who are researched are engaged in the creation of a social reality that implicates both of them. Although ethnographers have long subscribed to the method of participant observation, it still comes as a shock when they discover how important their participation is in helping to create what they are studying. Gilbert Herdt (1992) reported his surprise at discovering the therapeutic dimension of his role in New Guinea as a sympathetic listener to his key consultant, who shared with him erotic dreams that the consultant could not communicate to anyone within his own society.

Likewise the importance of the psychodynamic process of transference, or the bringing of past experiences into a current situation with the result that the present is unconsciously experienced as though it were the past, has only recently been fully realized and described for anthropology. Waud Kracke (1979), during his fieldwork with the Kagwahiv Indians of Brazil, kept a diary containing his personal reactions, dreams, and associations. In an essay discussing these field responses, Kracke not only analyzed his personal transference of his own family relationships to certain key Kagwahiv individuals but also his cultural transference of American values to Kagwahiv behavior patterns.

The Spirituality of Dreaming. Throughout history humans have perceived the visible world of daily living as containing an invisible essence or world of the imagination that manifests in sacred places. This may be located above, below, behind, or alongside of the everyday waking world. Melanesians picture a magical underground mirror world, in Celtic myths the Otherworld lies somewhere in the west, entered through lakes or caves, and in Korean shamanism it lies just across a river from the everyday world. During dreaming, human spirits leave the body and wander in these mythic realms, meeting and engaging with other spirits.

Dreams are perceived as an experience of the shadow, spirit, or soul. As such they are fertile ground for reflection, spiritual growth, and prophecy. Insights derived from dreams have challenged people to deepen and refine their understandings of the sacred. The process of dreaming lies at the heart of shamanism and those religions such as Daoism and Buddhism that have long intermingled with shamanism.

In shamanic cultures dreams allow increased receptivity among persons, ancestors, animals, and indeed the entire natural world. The visible entities that surround one—rocks, persons, animals, trees, leaves—are crystallizations of conscious awareness. The invisible medium between such entities is a dreamlike realm from which all conscious forms emerge. In a number of traditions the rainbow is the outside edge of dreaming, a place where the invisible potentials become manifest, and flashes of lightning are discharges from the depth of dreaming. It is through the nightly experience of dreaming that shamans learn to connect themselves to the cosmos in order to gain knowledge and power.

This shamanic approach toward dreaming is highly developed in hunting-and-gathering societies. When a hunter falls asleep, the spirit detaches itself from the body, tracks and catches a prey animal. The following morning the awakened dreamer goes into the forest to the dream place and gets his or her prey. In far northern Canada hunters explain this ability to communicate with and influence animals as the spiritual practice of "deep hope." They envision this form of dreaming as learning how to untie or lay out a straight mental-spiritual path to the goal of getting meat. In yet another form of dream hunting a person develops an amorous dream alliance with a forest spirit who becomes his or her hunting guide. The spirit falls in love with the dreamer, visiting often in dreams, and enjoys intercourse with the dreamer. This intimate relationship eventually turns the dreamer into a successful hunter. A third type of dreaming involves spirit animals who visit hunters and "sing through them" while they are sleeping, granting them special songs that ensure their later success in hunting. These types of power dreams are sources of spiritual entities, such as divine partners or spouses, attending spirits, companion animals, co-essences, or spirit doubles.

Worldwide there is a close connection between dreaming and shamanic initiation. Essie Parrish, a famous Kashaya Pomo shaman from northern California, told Tedlock one of her earliest power dreams. She was eleven years old at the time she was selected to serve her people as a healing shaman.

> As I lay asleep, a dream came to me. I heard a man singing way up in the sky. It was as if the singing entered deep into my chest, as if the song itself were singing in my voice box. Then it seemed as if I could see the man. After I awoke the song was singing in my voice box. Then I myself tried, tried to sing, and amazingly the song turned out to be beautiful. I have remembered it ever since. (Tedlock, 1972 speech to the New School)

In Myanmar (formerly Burma) a young woman dreamed repeatedly of a spirit suitor in human form. After sharing her dreams with her friends, she was encouraged by them to symbolically wed him. As an orchestra played, she performed a special dance and then entered a screened-off area where a group of women shamans waited. One of them moved a mirror back and forth in front of her face, hypnotizing her, while pressing another mirror against her back. A second woman shaman attached cotton strings to her ankles and wrists, placed a longer cord diagonally across her shoulders, and pierced her hair knot with a needle to which a cotton string was attached. As the young woman drifted into sleep, she became both the wife of the spirit and an initiated shaman. From this point onward she was not only in love with and loved by her spiritual spouse, but she also was able to transform herself into his spirit double through appropriate dress and dance gestures (Spiro, 1967, p. 322).

Within Buddhist nations, such as Myanmar, Mongolia, and Tibet, there are both clerical (written) and shamanic (oral) spiritual traditions. Whereas each accepts dreams as spiritually meaningful, the clerical tradition, in which dreaming is primarily used as an aid to achieving enlightenment, holds that dreams are examples of the empty and illusory nature of this world. In the shamanic tradition dreaming leads directly to the esoteric practice of Yoga or lucid dreaming, both of which involve cultivating and controlling one's dreams. Tibetan dream practice combines indigenous shamanic beliefs about the spiritual power of dreams with the Buddhist goal of enlightenment (Young, 1999).

Lucid Dreaming. Within many spiritual traditions the key moment of lucidity is described as the result of an interior dialogue or imaginal conversation between different parts of the self, psyche, or soul. The dreamer is simultaneously cognizant of being asleep and removed from the external world and of being awake and receptive to the inner world. At this crossover point between sleeping and waking there are often complex synesthesias—visual, auditory, and tactile—as the lucid dream emerges from the dream landscape. This new element, which interrupts the imagery and narrative flow of an ongoing dream, fuses dreamer to dreamscape in such a way that it may be experienced as fearful or joyful.

Several methods for achieving lucidity while dreaming are described in the autobiography of the well-known Cahuilla shaman Ruby Modesto (Modesto and Mount, 1980). This remarkable woman spent her adult life as an herb doctor, spiritual healer, and midwife within her home community outside Palm Springs. She explained that directing the course of dreaming, or what is called in her tradition "setting up dreaming," was the most important spiritual practice within her culture. It had been actively sought, used, and taught for generations by shamanic healers.

Dreams and Prophecy. In monotheistic religions, such as Judaism and Christianity, dreaming is closely related to prophetic traditions. The prophet Muḥammad was chosen for his mission late in his life, when the angel Gabriel appeared to him in a dream. The Old Testament records the prophetic dreams of Joseph, the son of Jacob (*Gn.* 37:5–11), and in the New Testament both the Magi and Mary's husband Joseph are warned in dreams to beware of King Herod. The Magi are warned to return to their country by another route, whereas Joseph is told "take the child and his mother and escape to Egypt. Stay there until I tell you, for Herod is going to search for the child to kill him" (*Mt.* 2:13).

A widespread type of prophetic dream is the conception dream that parents experience shortly before the birth of extraordinary children. Stories about the birth of Christian and Muslim saints contain many such dreams, which are believed to be signs of divine involvement, sometimes even actual divine fathering. For example, Joseph, the stepfather of Jesus, received a dream in which an angel appeared to him saying, "Joseph, son of David, do not fear to take Mary your wife, for that which is conceived in her is of the Holy Spirit" (*Mt.* 1:20–21). This dream proclaims Jesus' divine origin and encourages Joseph to accept Mary's child as the son of God.

Women also have conception dreams. According to Korean Daoist beliefs, whenever heavenly spirits and those of a woman's body join together and crystallize to make a baby, a dream emerges. One night a Korean woman dreamed that she was bathing in a stream all alone in the moonlight. "I saw a red pepper floating around me. Without thinking, I picked it out of the water, and woke up. Ten months later I had a gentle, though obstinate, boy" (Seligson, 1989, p. 15). In the West during the Middle Ages a pregnant woman's dream was recorded in an eleventh-century text, *The Life of Saint Thierry*. The future mother of Thierry was disturbed by her dreams and consulted a woman renowned for her gift of interpreting dreams.

> She confided her vision, first begging [the woman] to pray for her, so that the vision would not forecast for her an unnatural event, and then begging her to tell her the meaning of the vision. After praying, invested with prophetic grace, [the dream interpreter] said: "Have faith, woman, since what you have seen is a vision coming from God." (Schmitt, 1999, p. 277)

Conception dreams can also be experienced by a fetus while still inside its mother's womb. Desert-dwelling Yuman speakers in the American Southwest remember their earliest dreams from the time they are within their mothers' wombs (Kroeber, 1957). These unborn souls are said to journey to a sacred mountain, where their deceased elders give them special spiritual powers. After the baby is born, he or she totally forgets this prenatal journey, but dreams of the mountain reappear during adolescence. In these traditions all songs, myths, good fortune, and in fact all knowledge itself is derived from dreams. Thus the Mohave and other Yumans are said to interpret their culture in terms of their dreams, rather than their dreams in terms of their culture.

Robert Desjarlais (1991), during his fieldwork in Nepal with the Yolmo Sherpa, noted a large degree of agreement among individuals concerning the meaning of dream imagery and found an implicit dictionary of dream symbolism that individuals relied upon most frequently in times of physical or spiritual distress. In this dream interpretation system the experience of dreaming is believed to have a close, even causal connection with the future life of the dreamer. This principle is also found in many other cultures. However, such interpretations are often provisional. Not all people in a given society place their faith in them, and in some societies only certain individuals are believed to be able to experience prophetic or precognitive dreams. Researchers who have undertaken substantial fieldwork within American society have found that middle-class dreamers also admit to having experienced dreams of the prophetic or precognitive sort in which they obtain information about future events. The Western conception of dreams as predictors of misfortune or success, together with the anecdotal literature on "psychic dreams," indicates that this form of dream interpretation is far from rare in Western societies.

Labeling certain dream experiences prophetic or precognitive, however, does not explain how these and other dream experiences are used within a society. In order to learn about the use of dreaming, researchers cannot simply gather examples of different types of dreams by administering a questionnaire but must interact intensively with local populations for long periods of time. Thus whereas Desjarlais discovered an implicit metaphorical dictionary of dream symbolism among the Sherpa early in his fieldwork, it took him some time as an apprentice shaman to learn the precise way these dream symbols served as symptoms and signifiers both shaping and reflecting distress.

Among the Navajo of the American Southwest and the Maya of Guatemala, as people age their dreams become more and more continuous with waking life, predicting, causing, or expressing events in the world. As a result they no longer clearly distinguish what they discover in dreams from what they learn through direct sensory experience or from other people. Elders sometimes even manipulate their dream narratives to blur the distinction between the present and the mythological past.

Myths and Dreams. Whereas dreams have been described as private, highly fluid experiences and myths as public, fixed linguistic forms, they are actually closely related. Both myths and dreams have a story line that is expressive of an inner emotional-aesthetic structure together with an imagistic, metaphor-rich tapestry of spiritual feeling. Links between dream portents and the events they predict are often made by way of myths. Examples include Daoist practices in ancient China as well as those of contemporary peoples living in the Amazon Basin in Brazil.

For Daoists the appearance of a peach in a dream was an extremely favorable omen, because the Queen Mother of the West loved peaches and invited her favorites to partake of them in order to acquire immortality (Fang and Zhang, 2000). In the Amazon Basin to dream of an armadillo smoked out of his burrow indicates that a kinsman will die, because in a myth a man lures his brother-in-law into an armadillo's home and tries to kill him there (Reid, 1978). On the other hand, to dream of either leaf-cutter ants or a white-lipped peccary entering the house indicates that the person will be killed. This is based on a set of myths in which twin heroes kill their grandmother by transforming leaf-cutter ants into poisonous spiders then create and destroy white-lipped peccaries with thunder sticks (Reid, 1978).

As processes dreams and myths are inversions of one another. Whereas dreams move from sensory imagery to verbal form, myths move from language to sensory imagery. Thus among the Sharanahua of eastern Peru, when shamans elicit dream reports from their patients, they typically consist of single images, such as "peccary" or the "sun," that simultaneously echo myths and overlap with the shamans' categories of songs and symptoms. These thoughts may be shared through "representation" by talking about, drawing, painting, or describing a dream or through "presentation" by reenacting the dream in poetry, song, and dance.

In representational symbolism intentional reference is paramount, the medium of expression is relatively automatic, and inductive reality is paramount. In presentational symbolism meaning emerges as a result of an experiential immersion in the emotional patterns of the dream that is grasped intuitively. Dream workers of various kinds—prophets, *gurus,* shamans, theologians, and psychoanalysts—use a combination of these techniques to help dreamers engage with the image-filled mythic world of dreaming. It has been noted by healers that in many cultures dramatizations of dreams are a highly effective treatment for disoriented and alienated persons. The psychiatrist Wolfgang Jilek (1982) observed that Northwest Coast shamans who encouraged their clients to perform their dreaming in public are 80 percent effective in healing, compared with the 30 percent effective rate for psychiatrists using the private representational techniques favored by depth psychology.

Some Western dream workers have independently come to a similar conclusion about the presentational power of dreaming. They have noted that because dreams involve an imagistic healing process, it is best if the cogitating mind stays out of the process. Consequently many of them no longer interpret dreams but instead focus on reenacting and reexperiencing the feelings and images of the dream as fully as possible. Others take the position that the healing power of dreaming requires both experiencing, for energy, and interpretation, for meaning.

SEE ALSO Asklepios; Consciousness, States of; Visions.

BIBLIOGRAPHY

Black Elk. *Black Elk Speaks.* As told to John G. Neihardt. New York, 1932.

Bührmann, M. Vera. "The Xhosa Healers of Southern Africa: A Family Therapy Session with a Dream as Central Content." *Journal of Analytical Psychology* 27 (1982): 41–57.

Bulkeley, Kelly. *The Wilderness of Dreams: Exploring the Religious Meanings of Dreams in Modern Western Culture.* Albany, N.Y., 1994. A thoughtful evaluation of the major modern approaches to the study of dreams.

Burridge, Kenelm. *Mambu: A Melanesian Millennium.* London, 1960.

Crapanzano, Vincent. "Text, Transference, and Indexicality." *Ethos* 9 (1981): 122–148.

Degarrod, Lydia N. "Coping with Stress: Dream Interpretation in the Mapuche Family." *Psychiatric Journal of the University of Ottawa* 15 (1990): 111–116.

Dentan, Robert K. "Ethnographic Considerations in the Cross-Cultural Study of Dreaming." In *Sleep and Dreams,* edited by Jayne Gackenbach, pp. 317–358. New York, 1986.

Descola, Philippe. "Head-Shrinkers versus Shrinks: Jivaroan Dream Analysis." *Man* 24 (1989): 39–45.

Desjarlais, Robert. "Dreams, Divination, and Yolmo Ways of Knowing." *Dreaming* 1 (1991): 211–224.

Dombeck, Mary-Therese. *Dreams and Professional Personhood.* Albany, N.Y., 1991.

Eggan, Dorothy. "Hopi Dreams in Cultural Perspective." In *The Dream and Human Societies,* edited by G. E. von Grunebaum and Roger Caillois, pp. 237–266. Berkeley, Calif., 1966.

Fabian, Johannes. "Dream and Charisma: 'Theories of Dreams' in the Jamaa-Movement (Congo)." *Anthropos* 61 (1966): 544–560.

Fang Jing Pei, and Zhang Juwen. *The Interpretation of Dreams in Chinese Culture.* New York, 2000.

Franck, Frederick. *An Encounter with Oomoto: "The Great Origin."* West Nyack, N.Y., 1975. The story of the founding of a new religion based on a woman shaman's dreams.

Freud, Sigmund. *The Interpretation of Dreams.* In *Standard Edition of the Complete Psychological Works of Sigmund Freud.* London, 1900.

Grunebaum, G. E. von, and Roger Caillois, eds. *The Dream and Human Societies.* Berkeley, Calif., 1966. A wide-ranging analysis of dreams within various cultures. The focus, however, is not the culture or religion-specific perception of dreams but rather the observation that the modern age seems to have less need of dreams.

Guiteras Holmes, Calixta. *Perils of the Soul: The World View of a Tzotzil Indian.* New York, 1961.

Herdt, Gilbert. "Selfhood and Discourse in Sambia Dream Sharing." In *Dreaming: Anthropological and Psychological Interpretations,* edited by Barbara Tedlock, pp. 55–85. Santa Fe, N.Mex., 1992.

Hermitte, M. Esther. *Supernatural Power and Social Control in a Modern Mayan Village.* Chicago, 1964.

Hunt, Harry T. *The Multiplicity of Dreams: Memory, Imagination, and Consciousness.* New Haven, Conn., 1989. Hunt challenges prior theories based on the characteristics of a single type of dream and develops a cognitive psychological understanding of the visual-spatial imagery that generates the various dream types.

J'edrej, M. C., and Rosalind Shaw, eds. *Dreaming, Religion, and Society in Africa.* Leiden, 1992.

Jilek, Wolfgang G. *Indian Healing: Shamanic Ceremonialism in the Pacific Northwest Today.* Surrey, British Columbia, 1982.

Jung, Carl. *Dreams.* Extracted from vols. 4, 8, 12, and 16 of *The Collected Works of C. G. Jung.* Princeton, N.J., 1974.

Kilborne, Benjamin. *Interprétations du rêve au Maroc.* Grenoble, France, 1978. An extended comparison of Freudian with Moroccan dream interpretation practices.

Kracke, Waud. "Dreaming in Kagwahiv: Dream Beliefs and Their Psychic Uses in an Amazonian Culture." *Psychoanalytic Study of Society* 8 (1979): 119–171.

Kroeber, Alfred. "Mohave Clairvoyance: Ethnographic Interpretations." *University of California Publications in American Archaeology and Ethnology* 47 (1957): 230–239.

Lanternari, Vittorio. "Dreams as Charismatic Significants: Their Bearing on the Rise of New Religious Movements." In *Psychological Anthropology,* edited by Thomas R. Williams, pp. 221–235. The Hague, 1975.

Layard, John. *The Lady of the Hare: A Study in the Healing Power of Dreams.* Boston, 1988.

Lincoln, Jackson Steward. *The Dream in Primitive Cultures.* London, 1935. A comparative study of the cultural uses and functions of dreams in various Native American societies.

Lohmann, Roger Ivar, ed. *Dream Travelers: Sleep Experiences and Culture in the Western Pacific.* New York, 2003.

Mannheim, Bruce. "A Semiotic of Andean Dreams." In *Dreaming: Anthropological and Psychological Interpretations,* edited by Barbara Tedlock, pp. 132–153. Santa Fe, N.Mex., 1992.

Merrill, William. "The Rarámuri Stereotype of Dreams." In *Dreaming: Anthropological and Psychological Interpretations,* edited by Barbara Tedlock, pp. 194–219. Santa Fe, N.Mex., 1992.

Michelson, Truman. "On the Origin of the So-Called Dream Dance of the Central Algonkians." *American Anthropologist* 25 (1923): 277–278.

Miller, Patricia Cox. *Dreams in Late Antiquity: Studies in the Imagination of a Culture.* Princeton, 1994.

Modesto, Ruby, and Guy Mount. *Not for Innocent Ears: Spiritual Traditions of a Desert Cahuilla Medicine Woman.* Angelus Oaks, Calif., 1980.

Parman, Susan. *Dream and Culture: An Anthropological Study of the Western Intellectual Tradition.* New York, 1991.

Petchkovsky, Lawrence. "A Jungian Commentary on the 'Ordinar' Dreams of the Yolngu." *Australian and New Zealand Journal of Psychiatry* 18 (1984): 245–249.

Poirier, Sylvie. "This Is Good Country: We Are Good Dreamers." In *Dream Travelers: Sleep Experiences and Culture in the Western Pacific,* edited by Roger Ivar Lohmann, pp. 196–229. New York, 2003.

Reid, Howard. "Dreams and Their Interpretation among the Hupdu Maku Indians of Brazil." *Cambridge Anthropology* 4 (1978): 1–28.

Róheim, Géza. *The Gates of the Dream.* New York, 1952. A compendium of central Australian dream reports together with Freudian analysis.

Schmitt, Jean-Claude. "The Liminality and Centrality of Dreams in the Medieval West." In *Dream Cultures: Explorations in the Comparative History of Dreaming,* edited by David Shulman and Guy G. Stroumsa, pp. 274–287. New York, 1999.

Seligman, Charles G. "Type Dreams: A Request." *Folklore* 34 (1923): 376–378.

Seligman, Charles G. "Anthropology and Psychology: A Study of Some Points of Contact." *Journal of the Royal Anthropological Institute* 54 (1924): 13–46.

Seligson, Fred Jeremy. *Oriental Birth Dreams.* Elizabeth, N.J., 1989.

Shulman, David, and Guy G. Stroumsa, eds. *Dream Cultures: Explorations in the Comparative History of Dreaming.* New York, 1999. An important source for readers interested in the intersection of dreams, religion, and culture. The essays center on dreams as witnessed, transmitted linguistically, and framed as texts.

Spiro, Melford E. *Burmese Supernaturalism.* Englewood Cliffs, N.J., 1967.

Stephen, Michele. "Dreams of Change: The Innovative Role of Altered States of Consciousness in Traditional Melanesian Religion." *Oceania* 50 (1979): 3–22.

Tedlock, Barbara, ed. *Dreaming: Anthropological and Psychological Interpretations.* Santa Fe, N.Mex., 1992. Essays centering on the communicative context of dream sharing and interpretation.

Tedlock, Barbara. *The Woman in the Shaman's Body: Reclaiming the Feminine in Religion and Medicine.* New York, forthcoming. A review and reevaluation of the important role of women as shamans, dream interpreters, and healers in many cultures worldwide.

Wallace, Anthony F. C. "Dreams and Wishes of the Soul: A Type of Psychoanalytic Theory among the Seventeenth Century Iroquois." *American Anthropologist* 60 (1958): 234–248.

Worsley, Peter. *The Trumpet Shall Sound: A Study of "Cargo" Cults in Melanesia.* London, 1968.

Young, Serinity. *Dreaming in the Lotus: Buddhist Dream Narrative, Imagery, and Practice.* Boston, 1999.

BARBARA TEDLOCK (1987 AND 2005)

DRUGS SEE PSYCHEDELIC DRUGS

DRUIDS. The term *druid* is used by Greek and Roman authors, medieval Irish writers, and modern scholars alike to designate a priest of the ancient Celts. The word is thought to mean something like "those knowledgeable about the (sacred) oak," being derived from two Celtic words meaning "oak" and "knowledge." (This etymology seems more plausible than the identification of the first element *dru- with an intensive prefix, which is not well attested in the Celtic languages; cf. also the Galatian term *drunemeton,* which presumably means "oak grove".) As there is no unequivocal archaeological evidence concerning the druids, our knowledge of them rests exclusively on a rather small number of written sources, which are fragmentary and difficult to interpret. This poses the fundamental question of to what extent the classical and early medieval statements about druids may be taken as an adequate reflection of historical reality.

The Druids of the Greek and Roman Authors. The oldest classical reference to druids may be contained in a passage written in the third century CE by the philosophical writer Diogenes Laertios. Discussing the supposition of some earlier writers that philosophy had its origins among the barbarians, he mentions Persian magi, Babylonian or Assyrian Chaldeans, Indian gymnosophists, and Celtic druids, referring to the philosophers Aristotle and Sotion of Alexandria as his sources. If Diogenes' identification of these sources is correct, the druids may have attracted the attention of classical authors as early as the fourth century BCE. However, the earliest detailed description of druids apart from this brief and somewhat doubtful reference is given in the first century BCE by the Stoic philosopher Posidonius of Apamea. His description of druids can be reconstructed in outline by comparing the statements to be found in Strabo, Diodorus Siculus, and Timagenes (as cited by Ammianus Marcellinus), which are demonstrably dependent on Posidonius. In addition to these authors, there is information about druids in Julius Caesar, Pliny the Elder, and other authors writing in the imperial period.

Diodorus mentions the druids in the context of his description of Celtic society. He groups them together with poets and soothsayers, saying that they were highly respected theologians and philosophers that were held responsible for all matters of sacrificial offerings. An allusion to his view of their teaching may be seen in his explanation of Celtic bravery, which he attributes to a belief in the transmigration of souls. Strabo gives a very similar account, stating that the druids were natural and moral philosophers. According to him, the druids were considered to be most just and therefore entrusted with settling both private and public disputes. The druids' preoccupation with natural philosophy is also mentioned by Cicero, who differs from the other sources by ascribing to them the pursuit of divination by means of the interpretation of signs. (Cicero, incidentally, also tells us that the Gaulish noble Diviciacus frequently referred to by Julius Caesar was a druid.) To this description Ammianus Marcellinus (referring to Timagenes) adds that the druids were organized in brotherhoods, in accordance with the teaching of Pythagoras.

A more elaborate description of the druids is given by Julius Caesar, whose account concurs to a large extent with the above-mentioned writers but offers much additional information not to be found elsewhere. Caesar describes the druids as the most important social group (making no mention of either poets or soothsayers). According to him, they did not pay any taxes, had immunity from military service, and were exempt from all lawsuits; organized on a national basis, they were presided over by a single druid with the highest authority. They were reported to commit to memory a great number of verses, some of them remaining in training for some twenty years. Yet another piece of information is provided by Pliny the Elder, according to whom the designation "druid" was derived from the Greek name of the oak, because the druids chose oak groves for their sacrificial rites and held nothing more sacred than the mistletoe and the oak on which it grew. Describing a druidic sacrifice, Pliny mentions a druid in white clothing climbing the tree and cutting the mistletoe with a golden sickle.

As Suetonius in his biography of the emperor Claudius reports, Roman citizens were forbidden to participate in the religion of the druids even in the time of Augustus, long before the entire priesthood was totally banned in the middle of the first century CE. However, druids continue to be mentioned sporadically, and there are even some references to female druids (who are not known from pre-Roman times) as kinds of female soothsayers in the late imperial period.

In evaluating this body of evidence, it should be noted that all Greek and Latin statements about druids refer to Gaul in the immediately pre-Roman and Roman period, and that there is virtually no information about druids in earlier times or in other Celtic-speaking regions, such as the Iberian Peninsula, Italy, the Balkans, and Asia Minor. Furthermore, most if not all information about pre-Roman druids is demonstrably contained in or derived from Caesar and Posidonius, whereas sources from the late imperial period referring to contemporary druids may use this term in a rather loose sense meaning no more than "Gaulish soothsayer." On stylistic grounds, Pliny the Elder's description of a druidic sacrifice may also be considered to be based on Posidonius, whose highly influential Celtic ethnography is known only in outline. Thus, any evaluation of the evidence rests on an estimate of the trustworthiness of two authors, Posidonius and Julius Caesar. As regards Posidonius, it should be noted that his comparison of druids and Greek philosophers may mirror both his own philosophical turn of mind and the influence of Greek culture on the Celts of southern Gaul, where he collected most of his information. As for Julius Caesar, it seems possible that he deliberately depicted the druids as a worthy counterpart to the Roman pontifices presided over by the *pontifex maximus,* just as he depicted the Gaulish gods along the lines of the Roman pantheon, in order to emphasize the Gauls' adaptability to Roman civilization and to stress their cultural superiority over the Germanic tribes east of the Rhine. It is probable that the elaborate and large-scale sacrificial rites at major Gaulish sanctuaries, such as those of Gournay-sur-Aronde or Ribemont-sur-Ancre, presuppose the existence of a specialized cult personnel, and it stands to reason that the performance of divinatory practices (which may leave no archaeological traces) would also have been one of their functions. However, both Posidonius's view of the philosophical quality of the druids' teaching and Julius Caesar's account of the hierarchical and national structure of their organization are somewhat open to doubt.

The Druids of Medieval Irish Literature. In looking for druids in medieval Insular Celtic literature, it will be noted that Welsh sources are completely silent on this point and that the oldest Irish references to druids tend to assimilate the druids to pagan priests as known or, rather, imagined from biblical and apocryphal writings. (The Welsh term *derwydd* [prophet], though superficially similar to Old Irish *druí*, is to be analyzed as *do-are-wid-, so that its usage does not tell us anything about druids in the technical sense of the term.) Thus the hagiographer Muirchú in his *Life of Patrick* modeled the saint's confrontation with King Loegaire's druids on the Old Testament account of Moses's confronting the magicians of Pharaoh. Conversely, an Old Irish gloss on the New Testament calls the pharaoh's magicians "two Egyptian druids." Among the most prominent features of the druids in Irish literature is their association with magic. However, this should not be taken to reflect any genuine tradition, being most likely based on the medieval Christian association of pagan religion with the workings of demons. In fact, it may be questioned whether there are any clear recollections of pagan priests to be found in medieval Irish writings, as in many cases the druid appears to be depicted as a negative counterpart of the Christian priest. A typical example of this tendency would seem to be Muirchú's description of a contest between Saint Patrick and a pagan druid, in the course of which both of them throw their books into a river. Clearly, sacred writings were for the early medieval author of this story of such paramount importance that he could not envisage a pagan priest doing without them. Similarly, some other medieval Irish narratives credit the druids with performing ceremonies of name-giving that seem to be modeled on the Christian baptism, presumably because medieval clerics found it hard to believe that there should have been no pagan equivalent of this fundamental Christian rite. In fact, the survival of the Continental Celtic word for "druid" in Old Irish cannot be taken to warrant a continuity of either social organization or religious teaching.

The Druids of Modern Scholarship. Much modern writing about the druids has been bedeviled by the fact that, from the seventeenth and eighteenth century onward, the fragmentary and often contradictory classical and medieval statements were invoked to buttress more or less ill-founded assumptions about Celtic culture and religion in general. A general tendency has been to interpret the pagan Celtic past in the light of the present and to "explain" the present with reference to alleged pagan antecedents. Ideas of continuity have been especially prominent in Great Britain and Ireland due to linguistic continuity, but also in France where the idea of "our ancestors, the Gauls" was used to establish and propagate a cultural identity different from and superior to that of the Germans. Major factors in the creation of these ideologies were an uncritical reliance on the credibility of the written sources and the absence of a firm chronology, so that Stone and Bronze Age artifacts and monuments came to be associated with the druids. Influential figures in this development were the British antiquaries John Aubrey (1626–1697), Henry Rowlands (1655–1723), and William Stukeley (1687–1765), who popularized the idea that Stonehenge and contemporary monuments were to be interpreted as temples of the druids. Mention should also be made of the Welsh antiquary Iolo Morgannwg (Edward Williams, 1747–1826), who from patriotic motives tried to demonstrate a continuity of tradition stretching from the pre-Christian druids to the modern Welsh poets. When, in the course of the nineteenth century, Indo-European linguistics and Celtic studies came to be established as academic disciplines, great store was set by correspondences between the writings of classical and medieval authors, and by real or alleged Indo-European parallels. Especially influential have been the ideas of Georges Dumézil (1898–1986) and his followers, who derived the druids from a prehistoric Indo-European priesthood that they believed was also at the base of the ancient Indian Brahmans. More recently, however, an increased awareness of methodological problems involved in this approach and substantial advances in Indo-European linguistics, Celtic studies, classical philology, and prehistoric archaeology have helped to show the fragility of many facile interpretations of that written evidence which, without exaggeration, may be said to have generated an amount of discussion inversely proportionate to the verifiable facts.

See Also Celtic Religion, overview article.

Bibliography

Jones, Leslie Ellen. *Druid, Shaman, Priest: Metaphors of Celtic Paganism.* Enfield Lock, UK, 1998. An account of the druids and modern druidic ideologies.

Kendrick, Thomas Downing. *The Druids.* London, 1927. A classic study which, though dated from an archaeological point of view, gives a convenient survey of the Greek and Roman evidence in the original languages and in English translations.

Maier, Bernhard. *The Celts: A History from Earliest Times to the Present.* Translated by Kevin Windle. Edinburgh, 2003. A discussion of the druids and their significance for Celtic religion and modern Celtic ideologies within a broader historical context.

Owen, A. L. *The Famous Druids: A Survey of Three Centuries of English Literature on the Druids.* Oxford, 1962. A study of the references to druids in English works of literature dating from the sixteenth to the nineteenth centuries.

Piggott, Stuart. *The Druids.* London, 1968. A general account, embracing archaeology, written evidence, and the history of scholarship.

Bernhard Maier (2005)

DRUMS are instruments that produce sound through the striking, rubbing, or plucking of stretched membranes. The religious use of drums is historically and geographically extensive, but by no means universal. They are conspicuously lacking in many Christian and Islamic liturgical traditions, as well as in various African religions. Their absence from the oldest forms of religious music of such well-known hunter-gatherers as the African Pygmies and San (Bushmen), the Australian Aborigines, the Väddas of Sri Lanka, and others suggests that drums are not particularly archaic or "primitive" but rather are associated with the later cultural systems of sedentary agriculture and urban civilization. They are important in both local traditions and in the "great" intercultural, literate religious traditions.

Drums have relatively low value in Middle Eastern and European religious traditions, somewhat more in East Asia, Oceania, and Native America, and high value and variety of uses in South Asian, African, and Inner Asian and circumpolar shamanistic traditions. Where drums are used, they may have considerable symbolic or ritual value: E. Manker (in Diószegi, 1968, p. 32) describes how, when Christian missionaries burned the drums of Sami (Lapp) shamans, the Sami protested that the drums were their compasses; how could they find their way in the world without them?

DESCRIPTION. Drums belong to the organological class membranophones, instruments that produce sound by means of a stretched flexible membrane (skin, plastic, etc.). Instruments shaped or played like drums, but lacking membranes—the "slit-drums" or "log drums" of many tropical areas, the "bronze drums" of Southeast Asia, the "steel drums" of Trinidad, and so forth, are idiophones or solid instruments. Other mislabels, such as "tambourine" (correct only for frame drums with jingles) or "tom-tom" (corruption of a Sinhala/Tamil name for paired kettledrums), often have been indiscriminately applied by Westerners to non-Western drums in much the same way as labels like "witchcraft" and "vodou" have been widely and derogatorily applied to non-Western religions.

Drums are described by number of membrane heads (one to five), by material composition (wood, earth/clay, metal, bone, etc.), by shape of body (shallow frame, round-bottomed kettle, straight-sided cylindrical, bulging barrel, narrow-waisted hourglass, etc.), and by playing technique (hands, sticks, suspended clappers), decorations, and other physical features. Although such features are the basis of scientifically accurate descriptions, religious traditions themselves often categorize and evaluate drums in terms of less tangible but religiously more significant factors.

SYMBOLISM. Drums may carry a wide range of symbolic values, both positive and negative. The negative symbolism best known in the West, that of sensuality and licentiousness, is based on culture-specific associations of drums, rhythmic dance, and sexual abandon. Because this particular symbolism is not universal (for example, dance and sexuality may be seen as normal, as religiously beneficial, or as unrelated to drums), the negative symbolism of sensuality may be rarer than other negative associations. Another important one is the association of drums with pollution. In South Asia, for example, drums have sometimes been considered religiously polluting because the hands of those who touch or play them must come in contact with the skins of slaughtered animals, or because of associations with powerful, dangerous beings and forces; hence, both making and playing drums have been restricted to low castes. The negative association of drums with noise and chaos may be less widespread than is sometimes assumed: for example, drums were included only in a few scattered, atypical cases in the European Christian "Instruments of Darkness" complex described by Claude Lévi-Strauss in *From Honey to Ashes* (New York, 1973). Christian and Buddhist images of hells with sinners imprisoned in drums gain at least some of their negative impact from the demons shown beating them.

In their positive roles, drums may be associated with almost any aspect of religious experience, and may even themselves be considered deities. One common symbolic complex links them with elements of nature, biology, and cosmology. A drum may embody an *axis mundi* of the cosmic tree or mountain in its wooden or earthen body, the life force of a helping spirit in the form of the animal that supplied its skin, the voice of thunder or of an animal/spirit in its sound, and elements of hunting or pastoral lifestyles in its manufacture, treatment, and use. Another widespread symbolic complex derives from social relationships: drums may form "family" relationships with one another or with humans; sets of them may constitute hierarchies that parallel or are included within human and divine hierarchies; and they may play functional roles within society and the pantheon, ranging from invoking the deities to functions as practical as telecommunication. The "royal drums" of Africa and ancient South India were part of the property, symbols, and tools of divine kingship, considered so powerful and important in some cases that it might be more appropriate to speak of the king as a symbol of the royal drums than the reverse. The model of royal and divine proclamation is often central to the religious symbolism of drums, whether or not they are actually sounded for communication or musical purposes. Where the symbolic connection of drums, dance, and sensuality exists, it may become a positive symbol of divine enjoyment and celestial pleasures, with court and village dances serving as models for, or sacramental participations in, their heavenly counterparts.

It should be emphasized that the symbolism of drums does not support any unitary hypothesis of universal sexual symbolism. Drums may be seen as feminine because of their hollow bodies and soft skins; as masculine because of their intrusive sounds and the rigid sticks or hand tensions required to play them; or as neuter, androgynous, or symbolic of sexual union because of any of these or other reasons. The paired high/low-pitch kettledrums of Asia are often considered male/female; but if low is "male" in one culture, it is just as likely to be "female" in a neighboring culture. The multioctave drum sets of West African and African American possession religions are often viewed as "families," with the largest and lowest drum acting as "mother," and with primary contrasts drawn across generational rather than gender

SACRED MATTER

Understandings of matter, of the physical, obdurate objects that make up the everyday world, vary considerably among religions. Matter is sometimes regarded as evil or void of real being, sometimes as infused with spiritual realities that animate it. In other traditions, matter and spirit are inextricably joined and the idea of a dualist split between the two is inconceivable. Likewise, the experience of matter as sacred varies from the idea of holy substance, to consecrated matter, to objects sacred to memory, to objects that are morally useful but in no manner sacred in the sense of being infused with an intrinsic power. But in every case the power or use ascribed to natural or artificial objects is inseparable from the cultural webs of meaning-making that invest them with the power to signify. It is in this sense that sacred matter of whatever kind helps construct the life-worlds of those who harness its power by using objects in their rites and ceremonies.

Perhaps the root of sacred matter in many if not all religions is the physical remains of saints, heroes, and founders. Bones, teeth, and hair endure far beyond the decay of flesh and viscera and are commonly prized as the material trace of the saint's existence. These items become relics when they are recognized as the locus of spiritual power and presence, and they therefore offer access to the holy figure for the sake of blessing. In many religions holy men and women are thought to acquire such an excess of merit that it forms a reservoir that may be accessed by prayer in the presence of the saint's relics. The relic becomes part of a metaphysical economy in which

(a) Svayambhūnāth Stupa, west of Kathmandu, Nepal, during a celebration of the birth, enlightenment, and death of the Buddha. *[©Macduff Everton/Corbis]*

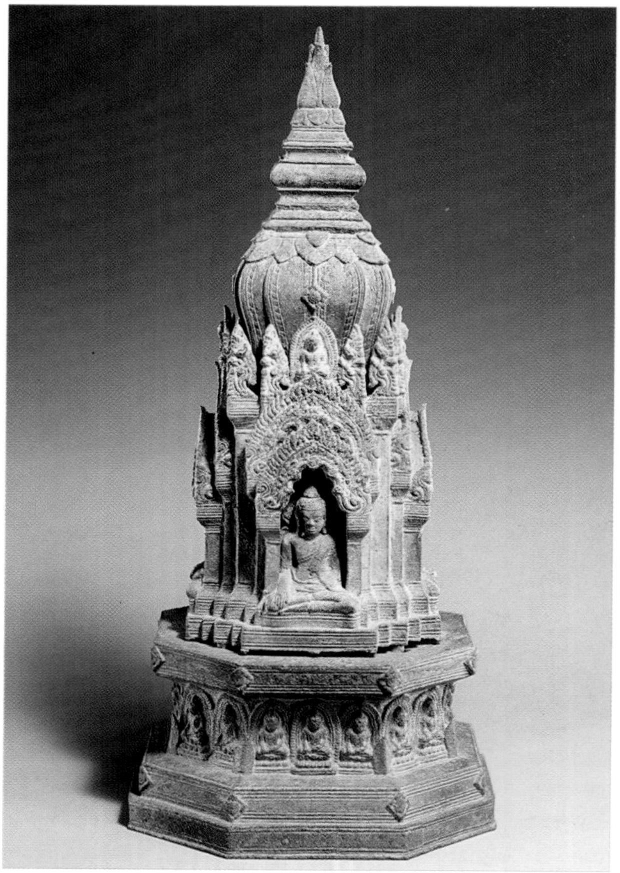

blessing is procured by pilgrimage, prayer, or penitential deed or offering. Within a few centuries of the Buddha's death a cult of relics of his body formed in India and Sri Lanka and moved with the faith as it spread north and south across Asia. The relics were placed in funerary mounds called stupas **(a)** and in portable shrines designed like stupas **(b)**. Stupas became major sites for local as well as international pilgrimage and were eventually surrounded by temple and monastery complexes and towns. Pilgrimage and relic veneration built their metaphysical economy over the commercial economies of local and far-flung populations, offering material well-being to craftsmen, townspeople, and religious communities.

The veneration of relics likely originates in devotion to the deceased at the graveside and in the dynamics of proselytism as religions spread to new regions, where the convert's need for shrines and access to the founder and other saints is fueled by competition with indigenous rival religions. In the case of Roman Catholicism, the practice

(b) LEFT. Portable Buddhist shrine, thirteenth century, bronze, Thailand or Cambodia. The Metropolitan Museum of Art, Gift of Enid Haupt, 1993. (1993.387.7a-d) *[Photograph ©2001 The Metropolitan Museum of Art]* **(c)** BOTTOM. Etruscan sarcophagus made of carved travertine, from a tomb in Cerveteri, Italy, late fifth century BCE. *[©Scala/Art Resource, N.Y.]*

of relic veneration was energized by the cult of martyrs during the first centuries of the church's existence. But there is reason to believe that the cult of relics built on the ancient practice of ancestral worship and prayer to the dead to secure blessing in the present. Long before Roman Catholicism existed, inhabitants of the central Italian peninsula, the Etruscans, practiced an elaborate form of funerary cult in which the dead were interred in figural sarcophagi **(c)** in underground tombs carved as domestic interiors that collectively formed part of an ever-expanding necropolis, or city of the dead. The catacombs beneath Rome are their descendents.

Gothic cathedrals, much of the art, and many of the liturgical items of the later medieval Catholic Mass functioned as reliquaries to house the sacred items that had become especially important to European Christians, including the relics pilfered during the Crusades in Palestine and the Byzantine world. The bodily suffering and vindication of Jesus became the focal point of many different devotions, both cloistered and lay. Religious leaders and monastic orders endorsed devotion to saints and their relics and to the Eucharist. Elaborate monstrances **(d)** displayed the host or relics of Mary or other saints in crystal chambers housed in structures that depicted the church. Portions of the "true cross" were avidly collected in the Holy Land and brought back to cathedrals and chapels in Europe for veneration.

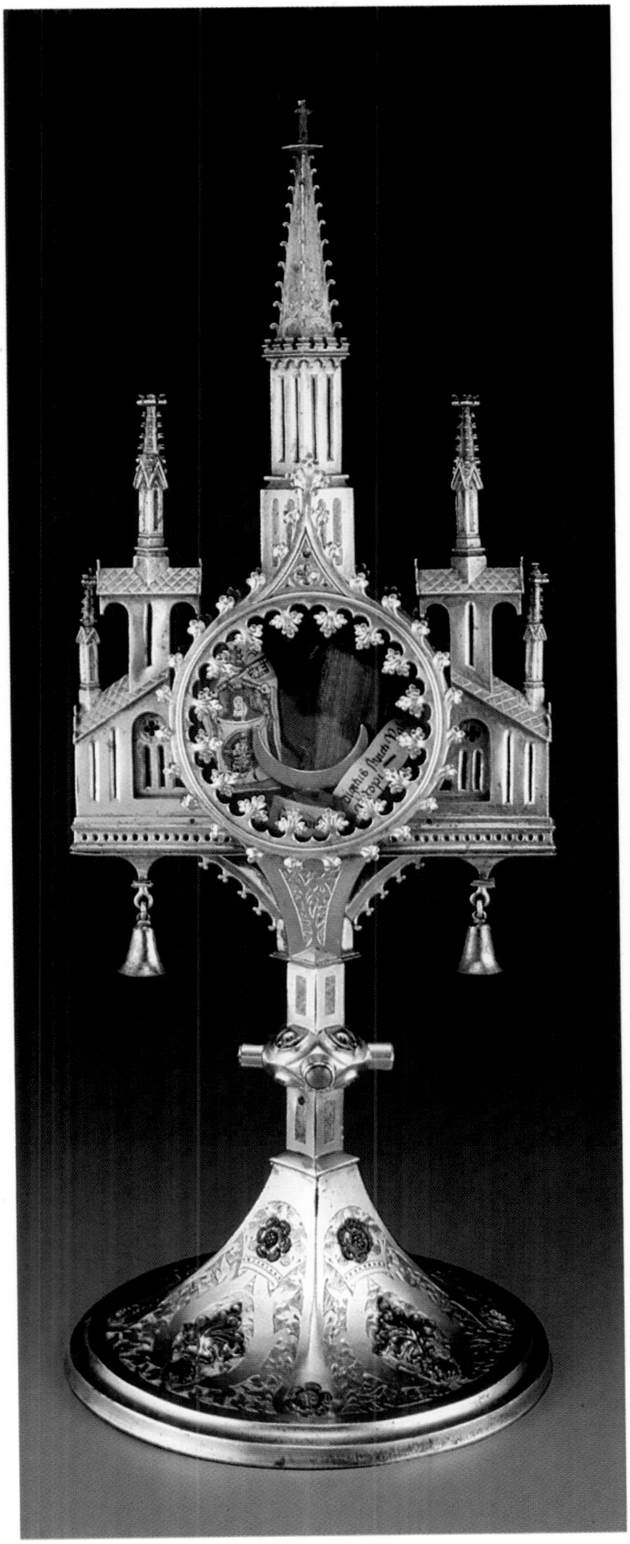

(d) Early-fifteenth-century German reliquary monstrance from the Guelph Treasure, engraved copper-gilt, silver, translucent enamel. *[The Museum of Fine Arts, Houston; museum purchase with funds provided by the Laurence H. Favrot bequest]*

Objects can also become sacred by ritual preparation, when spiritual power comes to reside in them. Such objects may be found or manufactured. Vodou and its West African precursor Vodun consist of ritual practices that are designed to solve problems of spiritual malevolence caused by one's misdeeds or the harmful intentions of another. Shamans or priests and priestesses are able to invest objects with a counteractive power **(e)**, or to enter trances or perform libations at altars **(f)**. Another Caribbean religion that originated in West Africa, Santería, fashions beautiful garments **(g)** for initiates and practitioners to wear when they are ritually transfigured into an *orisha*, one of the spirits of natural forces, such as thunder, fresh water, or the sea. The garments are worn only a few times, including during consecration as a priest and at one's burial.

Like the performative garment, masks are a familiar aspect of African and Oceanic as well as some Native

(e) TOP. A Fon *bocio* figure, a Vodou protective object, made of wood, hide, fiber, cowrie shell, and cord, southern Benin. *[©Werner Forman/Art Resource, N.Y.]* **(f)** RIGHT. A Vodou altar constructed by Silva Joseph in Port-au-Prince, Haiti, 1987. *[Photograph ©Maggie Steber]*

American religions. The mask and the costume it accompanies assume a sacred power and are kept by their owner, and even handed down among family members. The mask reproduced here **(h)** was worn by the Nootka people on Vancouver Island in dances in the spring and fall to invoke ancestral spirits. The founding myth of the group related that they descended from a family of eagles that flew from heaven and transformed themselves into human beings when they arrived. Accordingly, during the ceremonial dance the eagle mask transforms into a human face that is contained within. The annual performance of the rite connects the people with their primordial origins.

(g) RIGHT. Sequined taffeta garment for wear by a male Santería initiate. *[Photograph by Ysamur Flores-Peña]* **(h) BELOW.** A Nootka transformation mask, used in reenactments of the community's primordial origins, 1890s, feathers and wood, Vancouver Island, British Columbia. *[©The Field Museum; photograph by John Weinstein]*

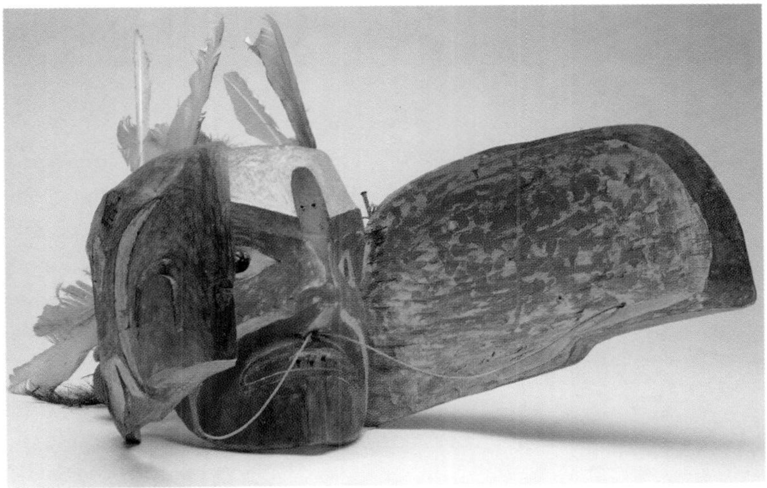

(i) Jewish worshipers parade Torah scrolls at the Western Wall in Jerusalem. *[©Peter Guttman/Corbis]*

But for some religions the idea of a spiritual energy inhering in material forms is repugnant because it confuses the divine with the merely phenomenal. Some Christians, Jews, and Muslims, as well as Sikhs and some Hindus and Buddhists, maintain that objects and rituals are merely convenient and time-honored forms of commemoration and the useful expression of devotion and communal solidarity. The very idea of sacred matter, substance endowed with power, conflicts with the stark distinction of spirit and matter of some religions, or the radical transcendence of the divine among others. For many Jews, for instance, liturgical objects **(i)** are prized for their association with orthopraxy, with strict adherence to the liturgical calendar and its prescription of ceremony. Some Christians, such as those of the Anabaptist and Puritan traditions, do not consecrate objects for use in worship spaces, and indeed, may not even set aside spaces to be exclusively used for worship. Any such privileging of objects threatens idolatry, the confusion of the divine with a created or material form.

Yet even within these traditions material forms can acquire a powerful quality that imbues their visual display with a meaning that is not merely symbolic, such as the

(j) Crystals, rocks, and statuary deposited at the center of a labyrinth in northwestern Indiana. *[Photograph by David Morgan]*

display of the Torah scroll in Jerusalem **(i)**. For other religious traditions, material forms are an integral part of evoking divine power and communicating with forces that transcend the human sphere. Often these forms are found objects, as in the case of the rocks left by visitors to labyrinths **(j)** or other sacred spaces important to earth-centered spiritualities. Crystals are believed by many to possess healing powers in their vibrational energy, which is transferred to humans in therapies of placing stones on the body at the chakras, the seven centers of energy derived from yogic teaching.

Other powers are attributed to stones by priests and users. Joseph Smith, founder of Mormonism, used a seer stone, a small, brightly colored, perforated stone, in his practice of divining, looking for hidden treasures buried in the New York landscape. Smith is said to have claimed that possession of one such stone gave him the divine power of the all-seeing eye. He used the seer stones that he possessed to search for buried money, but it was on one such quest that he found the golden plates that he claimed were the source of the *Book of Mormon*.

Managing the sacred power of objects occupies a good deal of attention and ritual practice. Since they are

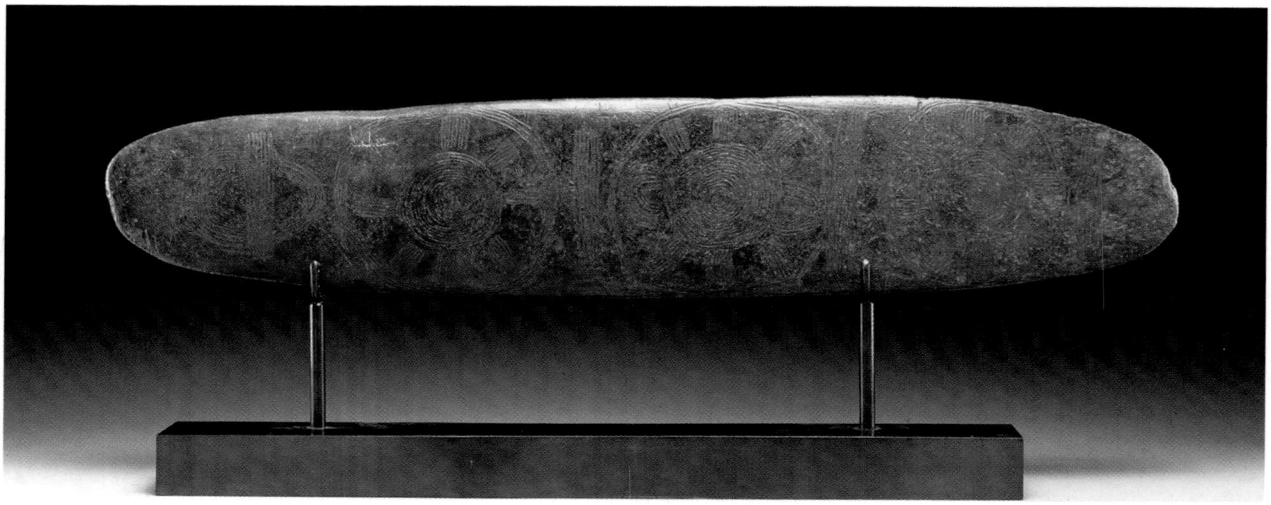

(k) TOP. A 34-inch stone *tjurunga* with linear incisions, found in Australia before 1935. *[Masco Collection; photograph by Dirk Baker]* **(l)** ABOVE. A *brāhmaṇa* priest bathes an ancient stone symbol of Śiva in Mamallapuram, Tamil Nadu, India. *[©Photograph by Stephen P. Huyler]*

the locus of power, the objects must be stored properly and carefully prepared for use and display. Often, as in the case of the Australian Aboriginal sacred stone called *tjurunga* **(k)**, the object is kept from sight except when in ritual use since it embodies the totemic spirits of its owner and serves as the dwelling of creator spirits. The sacred stones are displayed during initiations and are used by elders to relate traditions to those undergoing initiation. Hindu priests dedicate themselves to the daily preparation of the stone lingam of Śiva **(l)** at temples around the world, where they ritually bathe the ancient stone in honey, milk, or fragrant water before covering it with a dress and mask in order for its presentation to the devout.

BIBLIOGRAPHY

Brooke, John L. *The Refiner's Fire: The Making of Mormon Cosmology, 1644–1844.* New York, 1994.

Cosentino, Donald J., ed. *Sacred Arts of Haitian Vodou.* Los Angeles, 1995.

Fitzhugh, William W., and Valérie Chaussonnet, eds. *Anthropology of the North Pacific Rim.* Washington, D.C., 1994.

Flores-Peña, Ysamur, and Roberta J. Evanchuk. *Santería Garments and Altars: Speaking without a Voice.* Jackson, Miss., 1994.

Pike, Sarah M. *Earthly Bodies, Magical Selves: Contemporary Pagans and the Search for Community.* Berkeley, 2001.

Trainor, Kevin. *Relics, Ritual, and Representation in Buddhism: Rematerializing the Sri Lankan Theravada Tradition.* Cambridge, U.K., 1997.

DAVID MORGAN (2005)

lines. As with most instruments, drums are more widely played by men than by women; but for almost every case of a male-oriented drum tradition or practice, a corresponding female-oriented example can be found somewhere, occasionally even in the same culture or religious tradition.

Religious Use. Drums may be excluded from religious uses, used peripherally to demarcate the temporal, spatial, or structural boundaries of religious occasions, or integrated in positive, essential ways into religious thought and performances. If they are used religiously, their role is usually musical; but sometimes they function instead as signaling or communication devices, as silent cult objects or offerings, or in other capacities. Drums may or may not have special religious status compared with other musical instruments. For example, many Islamic traditions exclude all instruments equally from religious observances. Some Christian traditions have admitted other instruments while excluding drums. Many African and South Asian traditions assign special roles and status to a wide variety of drums. In most of Central and North Asia, drums were the prime focus of ritual, while other instruments were used for secular music. Generally, the great intercultural religious traditions of Near Eastern origin have shown more hostility or indifference to drums than have many others; but this ultimately may be due as much to the lack of early wide distribution and musical importance of drums in the area as to religious factors.

The vast range of religious valuations and uses of drums can be suggested by a few specific examples.

African and African American traditions. Although images of a "dark continent" filled with compulsively throbbing, obsessively omnipresent drums, witch doctors, and similar colonialist missionary-in-the-cannibal-pot stereotypes have partially faded away in the post-independence period (1950s onward), the ideal pan-African perspective of many writings continues to mask a range of cultural, religious, and musical diversity as great as is found in Europe or in Asia. The use of drums in African religions is a typical example of this diversity, with cases ranging from drums playing central, essential religious roles to their total absence from a religious tradition.

Colin Turnbull, in *The Forest People* (New York, 1961) and *Wayward Servants* (New York, 1965), found the drums used occasionally by the Mbuti Pgymies to be a late import from contacts with sedentary non-Pygmy villagers. Drums were not suitable by reason of their heavy wooden construction to the traditional Mbuti nomadic-forager lifestyle and their associated religious observances—a point equally worth noting in regard to other hunter-gatherers who lead a nomadic life without the assistance of draft animals. Even the pastoralist Fulbe, distributed through nearly the entire sub-Saharan borderland, adopted drums only in ceremonial contexts arising from culture contact with neighboring sedentary agricultural peoples such as the Hausa. Agriculturalists, in turn, need not accord drums a significant place in religion: Maraire (n.d.) reports that the Shona of Zimbabwe assign a very high religious value and function to the plucked idiophone *mbira* used in Bira possession rituals, while considering drums and their music appropriate to less sacred contexts oriented around socializing and entertainment. In the last analysis, neither race, place of residence, nor ecological adaptation is an accurate predictor of the importance or unimportance of drums in African music and religion.

Against this background of diversity, of contrasting occurrences interspersed with significant blank spaces where no uses are found, the pattern of use of drums in African religions stands out clearly as one of remarkable religious and artistic richness. In some cases, drums and ritual are so closely associated with each other that the same term can be used to refer to both (Turner, 1968, p. 15). If drums are not universally present, they nevertheless occur throughout the continent in nearly every possible physical shape (beside those mentioned above, goblet-shaped, conical, cylindroconical, and footed varieties are widespread), musical function, and religious value, and application. Drums may be found in every position and role from that of peripheral accessories that signal the start of ceremonies to that of spirit beings in their own right, called to life through invocations and rituals, tended by priests and acolytes, and housed, unseen by profane eyes, in sacred dwellings. They are so widespread and important that even religious traditions of Near Eastern origin—those of the Falāshā Jews and Coptic Christians of Ethiopia, as well as of the Islamic Ṣūfīs—overcome the reservations widespread among non-African branches of their respective religious traditions to the extent of allowing some liturgical drumming by cult members, leaders, or priests. Frequently, however, the drumming is less extensive and elaborate than that used by neighboring religious traditions of local African origin. The paired kettledrum apparently spread with Islamic conquests and conversions. Its most widespread ritual use, however, is in ceremonies of state, rather than in Islamic worship.

Although only extensive reading in the ethnographic, religious, and ethnomusicological literature would give an adequate sense of the religious uses of African drums, a few topics of broad interest are worth mention.

Talking drums. The widely mentioned "talking drums" that transmit verbal messages by playing tonal and rhythmic abridgments of stylized phrases are frequently slit-drums (i.e., wooden percussion tubes) or xylophones, rather than true drums with membranes; but drums may also be used for communication, as in the cases of the *atumpan* two-drum set of Ghana or the variable-tension hourglass drums widespread in West Africa. Most reported cases of religious use have involved announcements and communications among cult members (e.g., to invite guests to an initiation ceremony), a peripheral application sometimes combined or alternated with the widespread practice of using drums to accompany religious dance. However, there have also been reports (e.g., among the Ewe and Yoruba) of "talking drums" used for direct communication with gods or spirits, transmitting messages in the form of invocations or prayers—a function of greater apparent religious centrality and importance than announcing and signaling.

Royal drums. One especially characteristic function, best documented in East Africa but occurring in other regions as well, is the use of drums as royal emblems or regalia, a religious function insofar as it usually relates to concepts and cults of sacral kingship. Drums may be personalized spirits or ancestors, or conduits of power; in either case, they are the sacralizing and legitimizing emblems of royal rule, and as such receive honor, offerings, and ritual care that may be greater than that accorded the king himself. Royal drums are the prime example of drums that may be religious artifacts without necessarily being musical instruments as well: some royal drums are never played, and a few may exist entirely on a divine plane, invisible to all but the gods themselves (Lois A. M. Anderson, n.d.). Other royal drums may have a full range of musical uses while still enjoying a higher ritual status than their profane counterparts; such was the case with the *entenga* tuned-drum ensemble of the Buganda court. Often, as with the Buganda and Rwanda royal drums, several sets existed, each with its own kind and degree of religious, political, and musical function. Playing and/or priestly service of the royal drums might be restricted to male members of either hereditary noble or service classes. As was also the case with royal drums in ancient South India, some African royal drums were the recipients of ritual blood sacrifices.

Possession. Drums may not be used at all in possession cults (cf. the Shona Bira, mentioned above). But their importance in West African areas exploited by the slave trade led to their use in African American possession religions such as Haitian vodou, Brazilian Candomblé, the Lucumi of Cuba, the Shango religion of Trinidad, and others. In keeping with their West African sources, these religions use drums in cross-generational "families" of three or more to accompany spirit-possession rituals and dances. There has been some controversy as to whether the sounds of the drums actually "cause" or induce possession, that is, whether their effects are best understood in physiological or cultural and religious terms.

Rhythm and time. The musical variety of African religious drumming extends from the austere patterns of widely spaced single beats used by the Falāshā Jews, to elaborate polyrhythms (one rhythm played simultaneously with one or more contrasting rhythms) of the complex and compelling sort that most listeners associate with African styles. The question of possible conceptual relationships between musical rhythm and cosmological/calendrical time has been raised by Alan P. Merriam in his article "African Musical Rhythm and Concepts of Time-Reckoning" (in Thomas Noblitt, ed., *Music East and West*, New York, 1981, pp. 123–141) and by others. The unresolved issue is whether the perception by foreign observers of "time" and cyclicity in African music (or their being labeled as such in European languages) corresponds significantly to African conceptions, given the apparent lack in African languages of a "time" domain that extends to musical categories. J. H. Kwabena Nketia (n.d.) has suggested that music itself might constitute an extralinguistic, complementary system of conceptualization. We might hypothesize that musical rhythm is one fundamental human mode of perceiving and conceptualizing time, whether lexically labeled as such. If so, the apparent "polyrhythm" of simultaneous contrasting-length market weeks in West Africa may share an underlying conceptual unity with musical polyrhythms. On the other hand, we might equally hypothesize that musical polyrhythms result at least in part from the proliferation of conceptually multigenerational drum "families" that replicate socioreligious concepts of ancestor-descendant relationships. While research trends during most of the twentieth century moved gradually away from consideration of such broad issues, favoring a view of music as an autonomous "art" intelligible only in terms of acoustic-structural principles peculiar to itself, new approaches in the century's final decades suggested a growing interest in the conceptual bases of the close links between music and religion that are so evident in African behavior and performance.

Buddhism. Buddhist traditions share a common symbolic valuation of drums but differ widely in patterns of use. The act of proclaiming the Buddhist teaching is traditionally known as "sounding the drum of the Dharma," either because of a proclamation by Śākyamuni Buddha (c. 560–480 BCE) after his enlightenment that he would sound the "drum of immortality" (*amata-dundubhiḥ*), or because of an edict of the Indian emperor Aśoka (d. 232 BCE) that "the sound of the war drum [*bherighoṣa*] has now become the sound of *dharma* [*dharmaghoṣa*]." Both *dundubhiḥ* and *bherī* were royal/military drums. Perhaps because of the Buddha's *kṣatriya* (warrior/princely) caste origin, Buddhist drum symbolism relies heavily on the concepts of royal authority and invincibility. Drum sounds reach everywhere, filling earth and sky; they are clear and unmistakable; and they cannot be ignored or overwhelmed by lesser sounds. These are all characteristics both of the royal drums themselves and of the teaching proclaimed by the Buddha.

The use of drums in Buddhist ritual, derived from the stupa (reliquary mound) cult sanctioned in the *Mahāparinibbana Sutta*, is said to date back to the death of the Buddha (c. 480 BCE). They are pictured on the railings of the stupa in relief sculptures of the first century BCE–first century CE period. In Indian Buddhism up to the early second millennium CE, drums served the function of elaborating and ornamenting the *tāla* rhythmic cycle outlined by the cymbals, according to standard Indian musical practice of the time. Written drum notations were introduced before the mid-eighth century CE.

Sri Lanka. Modern practice varies with traditions and cultures. Generally, Theravāda Buddhism restricts the use of instruments to laymen, while Mahāyāna and Vajrayāna traditions allow monks to play them as well. In present-day Sri

Lanka, Theravāda Buddhism exists in conjunction with a variety of indigenous *yakkha* (local spirit) cults whose priests are hereditary low-caste drummer-dancers using their ritual and artistic skills to control a variety of powerful forces. Just as their gods are admitted to the Buddhist pantheon in a subordinate role, so also their instruments and performances find a subordinate, boundary-marking role in some Buddhist ceremonies.

Two kinds of drums, the *dawula* (cylindrical drum) and the *tammätamma* (paired kettledrums), play a more central role in the orthodox Buddhist cult of stupas and other types of *cetiya* (relics), in the *pañcavādya*, or fivefold instrumental music that can be traced back to the first centuries of Indian Buddhism. The drums play auspicious music based on beat patterns conventionally associated with the Buddha, with acts of offering or circumambulation, and so on. The players are of the same caste and are often the very same persons as those who serve as priests of the *yakkha* religions. The primary drum of the *yakkha* cult, the *gäta bere* barrel drum, also finds an important place in Buddhist rituals as the *mangulbere*, or "auspicious drum." In the chief Buddhist temple of Kandy, even high-caste specialists play the hourglass *udäkki* drum to accompany secret songs of praise in the inner shrine.

Nepal. In the Vajrayāna Buddhism of the Newars of Nepal, drums find both more diverse and more central ritual roles. Parallels with Theravāda include the use of paired kettledrums in the fivefold offering music and the adoption of drums from local cults, such as the barrel drums adorned with ram's horns (*yakkakhiṃ*) embodying the indigenous god of dance (Nasadyah) which accompany some dances with Buddhist contents. Specific drums are allocated to specific castes, from the small barrel drum (*naykhiṃ*) of the butchers to the deified barrel drums (*damaḥkhiṃ*), decorated with masks of the deities they embody and played by the highest castes of Buddhist Tantric priests. In processions farmers play the *dhimay*, which is made from an irregularly shaped cross section of tree trunk. They and the oil-presser caste play the *mākhiṃ* barrel drum to accompany songs of praise at Buddhist temples. Vajrācārya priests accompany some of their Tantric *cārya* songs and dances with the *kwotaḥ*, a three-headed drum set made by joining a large horizontal and small vertical barrel drum together. The drum becomes the embodiment of both the god of dance and the buddha Vajra-sattva during performance, and it plays musically structured, notated compositions of *mantra* syllables evoking the presence of buddhas and gods. Drumming, singing, and dancing, along with meditation, become the technical means for generating the *maṇḍala* of buddhas in the performers' own bodies, voices, and minds.

Central and East Asia. Outside the South Asian homeland of Buddhism, drums lose their caste associations and some of their practical musical importance, while retaining their symbolic value. In Tibetan Vajrayāna, the double-headed frame drum (*rnga*) is used in both vocal and instrumental performances, but in a role supporting the cymbals, which provide a primary musical structure based on elaborate mathematical sequences. The hourglass drum made from two human skulls (Skt., *kāpāla-ḍamaru*), adopted from the Indian *Kāpālika* yogic tradition, is also largely subordinate, often being replaced by a similar wooden drum. Nevertheless, such drums may symbolically embody the entire range of Buddhist concepts and teachings and enjoy greater practical importance in specialized ritual/meditational traditions. In East Asian Mahāyāna Buddhism, drums are often used, together with an assortment of metal and wooden idiophones, to mark off the subdivisions of musical structures. Japanese Buddhist practices range from the elaborate drumming in Zen temples to the greatly lessened use of drums in traditions such as Buzanha Shingi Shingon, in which idiophones such as the wooden fish-shaped *mokugyō* play beat patterns accompanying chants. Some traditions give drums a practical role to match their symbolic value, as with the Nichiren school Nihonzan Myohonji pacifist monks who walk about chanting and beating a small single-headed frame drum, literally "sounding the drum of the Dharma" to call attention to their Buddhist teachings and way of life.

Shamanism. In the "classical" shamanism of Inner and North Asia, drums play central roles in religious belief and practice. The drum is the shaman's primary religious tool for attracting helper gods or spirits, for taming or inciting them to action, and for carrying the shaman away on spiritual flights to heavenly realms or to the underworld. The drum itself is part of the shaman's pantheon, a living spirit helper or a theriomorphic steed such as a horse or a deer. It may serve as object as well as agent of religious acts, being treated to life-cycle rituals, like those performed for humans, from its "birth" to its "death," as well as to cyclic or occasional ceremonies encouraging or exhorting it to perform its helping function. It may also serve the shaman as a tool for specialized ritual purposes, as in drum-divination ceremonies in which the upturned skin of the drum is sprinkled with small grains that move about through sympathetic vibration when a second drum is played nearby (or, if the drum has two playing heads, when the second head is beaten) to form divinatory patterns on the drumhead. The type of drum used may indicate the shaman's status in a graded hierarchy of initiatory rankings. In contrast to many religious drum traditions, shamanic drumming is frequently performed by women, as female shamans are fairly widespread.

The shaman's drum is usually a shallow frame drum with a wooden circular or ellipsoidal body and one skin head, played with a stick. Small jingling pieces of metal or bells may be mounted either on or inside the drum, or worn separately on the shaman's costume. Making the drum recapitulates a primordial cosmological quest, as in this song of the Tibetan Bon tradition:

> seek a drum, where do I seek? I seek in the four directions, and the eight between; On the Chief of Mountains, in the center of the world, There, there is a tree growing; A mighty sandalwood tree has grown. Now,

> having cut a branch from it, Bending, bending, forced in a coiled circle, Knowing the method, hewn by an ax's blade, With the hide of a black antelope covered over, That amazing drum, that swastika-circle drum, Sewn together with effort, by the pressure of a tendon, Has a miraculous, melodious, sweet sound, full of meaning: Beaten, it is beaten in the highest heaven; Sounds, it sounds at the peak of the world-mountain; The realm of demons trembles: *Shig shig!* When I beat on that great drum, then Even all the ocean, churned, clouds up with mud; The massive Chief of Mountains, shaken, is thrown down; The water-serpent children are uneasy in their minds; *E ma!* How great this most superior of wonders!

The feeling of joyful mastery expressed here is the result of spirits, called and subjugated by the drum, entering the player's body and merging into a single identity under his control. Siberian ethnographic accounts are seldom detailed enough to show exactly what role the drumming plays in this course of events, but the process is quite clear for the related Himalayan shamanic traditions. The shaman begins by drumming at moderate speed in a dotted-rhythm beat pattern, singing an invocation of the "first shaman"; he then changes to a slightly slower, steady rhythm, as he sings an invitation song to the spirits who will come to help in the ritual. As he senses the approach of the spirits, his body begins to shake, sounding the metal bells on his costume or in the drum, and the beating grows louder. The drumming becomes irregular, suddenly breaking off into short periods when the drum is silent, and only the sound of the shaking bells carries on the emotional momentum of the performance. The singing is interspersed with special vocal effects: singing into the face of the drum, grunting, whistling, sneezing, and altered tones of voice. These events are signs of the entry of a spirit into the drummer's body, and of the struggle for control between him and the spirit. As the shaman asserts mastery over the spirit, the drum reenters with a strong, steady beat, the shaman begins a song of praise to the helping spirits, and the way is open for subsequent ritual stages of dancing, travel to spirit worlds, diagnosis, divination, curing, or whatever is required by the ritual.

The combination of heightened emotion and use of the drum to summon and control spirits, evident both in shamanic songs, as quoted above, and in the actual events of the ritual, is characteristic of the full geographic range of Asian shamanism. Use of the drum as a "steed" for a flight to the spirit world is a more limited phenomenon. Mircea Eliade (1964) argues that ecstatic flight is the historical and religious core of the shamanic complex, and that those traditions that lack it represent a degenerate stage; I suggest in "Musical Flight in Tibet" (in the journal *Asian Music* 5, 1974, pp. 3–44) that the practice of drumming to attract the tame theriomorphic spirits is a religious transformation of widespread use of music by Asian hunters and pastoralists to lure and control animals, and that the ideology of spiritual flight is a later and more localized superimposition on a conceptual basis of the shaman as a spiritual hunter-pastoralist. In some religious traditions outside the "classical" Asian/circumpolar area, broad similarities in ideology and practice seem to justify comparative extension of the term *shaman* (originally from the language of the Tunguz of Siberia); some of these traditions (e.g., the Mapuche of Chile) use drums in ways similar to Asian shamans, while many "shamanic" traditions of Latin America use hallucinogenic drugs and/or rattles whose symbolic and functional status so closely parallel that of the shaman drum as to suggest that they are local substitutes for it.

Other traditions. Drums have seen religious use on every inhabited continent, although in Aboriginal Australia they were characteristic only of coastal zones of contact with Melanesian cultures. They have been used throughout most of human history and found a place in the religions of ancient civilizations of both the Old and New Worlds.

Near East and Mediterranean. Drums appeared rather late in Mesopotamia. Clapper idiophones were shown in the artwork of the Mesilim and Ur I periods (c. twenty-eighth–twenty-fourth centuries BCE). Drums alone begin to appear in depictions of ritual dances in the neo-Sumerian period (twenty-second–nineteenth centuries BCE). Frame drums (*adapa?, balag?*) existed in sizes ranging from extremely large varieties played by two men down to small handheld types carried by dancers; the latter apparently spread to Egypt (sixteenth–eleventh centuries), Israel (*tof,* mentioned in *Exodus, Psalms,* etc.), Greece (*tumpanon,* sixth–fifth centuries?), Rome (*tympanum,* c. 200 BCE), and eventually throughout the Near East, where it is still widespread under the Arabic name *daff.*

In Sumeria, drums were ideographically linked with the god Enki and by ritual and symbolic attention to their skins with the bull, symbol of sacred strength. The small frame drum became associated (c. 2000 BCE) with women players and with revelry and has generally retained these associations throughout its geographical and historical range. Even today it is widely played by women at weddings. In Israel the small-frame drum was excluded from Temple ritual. Other drums may have been employed until the ban on instrumental music following the destruction of the Temple in 70 CE. The small-frame drum was associated in Egypt with the goddess Isis and in Greece with the imported Cybele and native Dionysos cults. Eventually it spread to Rome along with these three "orgiastic" religions.

Cultic associations with dance and sexual license helped to shape Judeo-Christian attitudes to drums up to the present day, but they may not be entirely responsible for the subsequent exclusion of drums from the Jewish, Christian, and Islamic liturgies. In fact, such associations applied only to one type of drum (the small-frame drum); but this was, perhaps significantly, in an area where few types were available as more "respectable" liturgical alternatives. Cylindrical drums, goblet-shaped or footed drums, and a few other types were known in Sumeria and Egypt. In Israel, Greece, and Rome frame drums may have been the only drums available. There is no evidence of musically important or elaborate rhythmic traditions that might have stimulated the importation or invention of other types. Even the drum perhaps most characteristic of the Near East, the paired kettledrum, did not appear until the beginning of the second millennium CE.

At any rate, we see the disappearance of drums and other instruments from the Jewish liturgy in the first century CE, after the destruction of the Temple and the rise of the less ritualistic synagogue tradition. Christianity, perhaps simply following the lead of its parent tradition and culture, seemed to mirror the synagogue in its apparently exclusively vocal musical practices. Islam, in its turn, excluded drums, instruments, and "music" from its worship, which nevertheless came to include melodically chanted "readings" from the Qur'ān and religious poetry; these in turn eventually came to embrace possible rhythmic accompaniment with drums, even the once-suspect frame drum. By the early second millennium CE the Ṣūfīs movement began to develop, leading to ritual traditions that use drums along with other instruments to accompany inspirational dancing. Drums would likewise gradually reenter Christian religious music through the influence of European folk, military, and art music traditions.

India and China. Textual evidence indicates the presence of drums in India and China by at least the late second millennium BCE; they are probably considerably older in both regions. There is some evidence for the use of drums in the Indus Valley civilization of the third millennium BCE. The earliest Indian sacred texts, the Vedas, seem to regard drums as primarily military instruments used by the Central Asian Aryan tribes who migrated into India some time after the middle of the third millennium. Later Tamil (South Indian) literature, which may reflect a much earlier culture, describes a cult of sacred royal drums reminiscent of African traditions, including sacrifice and ritual care by priests who were avoided because of their association with powerful, dangerous beings. Such cults may have provided the initial impetus that led to the eventual high religious value of drums in Hinduism. Another stimulus was provided by the decline of Vedic sacrificial ritual and its supplanting by the performance of *pūjā* offerings, a development particularly stressed in Buddhist traditions, where we find the first evidence of musical *pūjā*. Hindu traditions parallel their Buddhist counterparts in variety and richness, incorporating drum music at every level; and one of the three supreme post-Vedic gods, Śiva, is identified with the hourglass-shaped *ḍamaru* drum, which he plays to accompany his own cosmic dance. The elaborate rhythms of Indian drumming were, at least until the growth of Islamic dominance in the second millennium CE, part of a tradition that was inseparably both aesthetic performance and religious offering, whether Hindu, Buddhist, or Jain, and hence a reflection of the same ideals of complexly multifaceted individuality that appear in Indian pantheons and ritual practices.

In China, by contrast, drums and their music were a balanced component in both a carefully orchestrated musical structure and the elemental cosmic structure it embodies. Drums were part of an ideal system of *ba yin* or "eight sounds" represented by the names of eight characteristic materials from which instruments are constructed: metal, stone, silk, bamboo, wood, skin, gourd, and earth. Each of the instrument groups corresponding to these materials in turn corresponds to a cardinal point of the compass, a season of the year, a natural element or phenomenon, and other cosmological features. Drums are classified under their most characteristic constituent material, skin, and they correspond to the north, to winter, and to water. In Confucian ceremonial music, they play a musical part that is slow and simple in terms of technique and rhythmic density but that, together with the other instruments of the ensemble, forms part of a restrained, carefully regulated, and balanced whole. Barrel drums, some very large, are the most characteristic type used.

Americas and Oceania. New World civilizations, like their Old World counterparts, made use of drums. Ritual applications included sacrifices that sometimes involved human victims and, among the Incas at least, used their skins as drumheads. However, reports of at least one "drum" used in sacrificial rituals are the result of misidentification: the Aztec *teponaztli* was a slit-drum, or wooden percussion tube, rather than a membranophone.

The drum most widely used in American music and ritual is the frame drum, the form, ideology, and use of which in many regions show general parallels to that of the Asian shaman's drum. In addition to their shamanic use, frame drums were utilized in a wide variety of local religious contexts; among the best-known examples are the Plains Sun Dance and War Dance, as well as the late nineteenth-century Ghost Dance and other postcontact syncretistic and revitalization movements. Frame drums are played with sticks held in one hand only, a practice that links them with other unacculturated Native American drum traditions and distinguishes them from Euro-American and African American traditions and styles.

Two relatively recent traditions show some unusual features. Thomas Vennum, in his *The Ojibwa Dance Drum* (Washington, D.C., 1982) and subsequent work, has examined the history of the "dream drum" revealed in a vision by the Great Spirit to Tailfeather Woman of the Sioux in the nineteenth century and passed on to the Ojibwa (Chippewa) and other Northeast Woodlands peoples through manufacturing and song-learning rituals ultimately intended as a way of creating intertribal peace. While the "dream drum" is a larger and more elaborate version of the widespread frame drum, other physical types of drums may also attain religious importance. The best-known example is the water drum used to accompany songs in the sacramental peyote rituals of the Native American Church. The drum consists of a solid-bottomed body that forms a vessel into which water is poured and with the single playing head covering it at the top. Using more or less water creates a higher or lower sound; the dampness also changes the tension of the drumhead (which can be tuned by making it wetter or dryer), and the sound has a characteristic wavering reverberation caused by the movement of the water inside.

In Oceania, the area richest in variety of musical instruments was Melanesia, where log slit-drums (percussion idiophones) generally enjoyed more religious and musical prominence than true drums with membranes. Oceanian drums tend to have only one playing head, often made from fish or shark skin and to be set or held in vertical position and played with the hands. Hourglass shapes are common in Melanesia, and cylindrical types are widespread in Polynesia.

Drums were accorded sacred status in Polynesia, kept and tended by priests in temples, and considered receptacles of *mana* (sacred power). Some were associated with sacrifice, including, in Tahiti, human sacrifice. Many were "royal drums," used to honor chiefs as well as gods; one Hawaiian king traveled with such a drum in his canoe. Important drums of chiefs or gods were often large, with smaller versions used in lesser contexts; ensembles of varying sizes were found in some areas. The Hawaiian ceremonial Mele Hula dances utilize two drums: the larger *pahu hula* of wood, played with the hands, and the smaller *pūniu* made from a coconut shell, played with a braided fiber "stick." Although other instruments are also used, the drums are reserved for the most important dances.

Drums and Possession. African American religions, shamanism, and many other religious traditions employ drums in conjunction with, and apparently to induce, a kind of experience known in the research literature as "possession" or "altered states of consciousness." Behind such standard labels lie essential differences in both the experience itself and the process of achieving it: Haitian priestesses and Tibetan oracles, for example, are controlled by the beings who enter their bodies, while the Tamang shaman asserts control over the spirits who enter his. Both of the former rely on others to play drums for them during the ritual, but the shaman acts as his own drummer. What all these traditions have in common is a varied range of techniques for transformation of personal consciousness into a correspondingly varied range of experiences of identity with a god or spirit and, in many but not all cases, the use of drums with or without additional instruments.

A famous and controversial hypothesis by Andrew Neher (1961, 1962) posits an automatically causal, physiological link between drumming and ritual experiences of consciousness-transformation. Neher cites laboratory experiments with photic driving (pulsating lights) and covariation of alpha rhythms in the brain to support a suggestion that rhythmic drumming, with its wide frequency spectrum and high energy content, would automatically affect a normal brain in such a way as to affect alpha rhythms and produce reactions similar to those reported by laboratory subjects: visual, tactile, kinesthetic, and emotional sensations for experiments with light, but only "unusual perceptions" and muscle twitching reported for actual tests with drums. He predicts (1962) that a beat frequency of 8–13 cycles per second (the range of normal alpha variation) will be found to predominate in "possession" rituals with drums.

Neher's hypothesis has been accepted without further examination by a number of ethnologists and scholars of religion (e.g., Siikala, 1978) but has been questioned or rejected by ethnomusicologists investigating actual drum usage in transformation rituals. Gilbert Rouget (1977, 1985) argues, based on extensive studies of African and African American traditions, that the laboratory experiments differ greatly from the conditions and experiences of actual ceremonies; that automatic physiological causation is out of the question because most of those who hear the drumming (even the same individuals on different occasions) do not experience trance or possession; and that if Neher's quantitative predictions were correct, "then the whole of sub-Saharan Africa should be in trance from the beginning to the end of the year." But in fact, given the speeds that occur in drum music elsewhere, if Neher's (1961) dubious alternative of a lower limit of 4 beats per second were accepted, much of the world would be in perpetual trance.

While proponents and opponents of the hypothesis have tended to argue over its merits on the basis of logic and conviction, Neher's quantitative prediction has not been subjected to quantitative testing by comparison with measurements of drum rhythms in actual performances. Figure 1 shows a comparison of (A) Neher's (1962) predicted minimum tempo of 8 beats per second for "trance" rituals, with transcriptions of actual drumbeat tempos in (B) the "invitation" song to helping spirits sung by a Tamang shaman; (C) the instrumental "Invitation to the Protector of Religion" (*Chos skyoṅ Spyan 'dren*) played for the Tibetan state oracle (*Gnas-chuṅ chos skyoṅ*) before he sinks into a quiescent state to receive the god Pehar; and (D) the "Song of Invitation" (*Spyan 'dren gyi dbyaṅs*) sung to the oracle just before he begins to show evidence of having been transformed into a state of conscious identity with the god.

Clearly, the minimum quantitative requirements of the hypothesis are not satisfied by two of the best-known Asian traditions that ought to fall within its intended scope. Example B of figure 1 is 58 of the required minimum speed, while Example C would have to be 280 times as fast to reach the minimum 8 beats per second. Other well-known Asian traditions (e.g., Tibetan and Newar Tantric *sādhanas*) likewise fail to satisfy the hypothesis; and, while one might expect to find more cases of African and African American traditions that fall in the predicted quantitative range, there are also African cases that do not meet the requirements of the hypothesis (John Blacking, n.d.). In any case, the hypothesis in its given form must be rejected, as the occurrence of exceptions to its predictions show the operation of cross-cultural variables external to the species-universal mechanisms of human physiology. The possibility cannot be excluded that a more sophisticated reformulation of a physiological-causation theory will lead to verifiable, significant results. Current research on musical and religious practices show, however, such a wide range of variation as to render the search for causal universals progressively more difficult, and also greater apparent progress in the investigation of cultural and ideological factors that seem to underlie both religious and musical practices.

See Also Shamanism; Spirit Possession.

Bibliography

Although drums are both musical and religious instruments, it is difficult to find studies that do not ignore or misinterpret one of these two aspects. Information is scattered in journal articles and general religious and musical studies of particular areas; and many important findings of recent researchers are still unpublished, as indicated by the number of "n.d." (no date) citations for information used in this article.

The most extensive previous general study, A. E. Crawley's article "Drums and Cymbals," in the *Encyclopaedia of Religion and Ethics*, edited by James Hastings, vol. 5 (Edinburgh, 1912), is flawed by outdated and inaccurate ethnographic data and by discredited interpretive approaches. These faults are common to many nineteenth- and early twentieth-century ethnographies (and almost universal in travelers' and missionaries' accounts); while later studies have increasingly tended to treat music and religion as autonomous, mutually unintelligible domains. Thus, even such excellent ethnographic studies of drum-centered ritual traditions as Victor Turner's *The Drums of Affliction: A Study of Religious Processes among the Ndembu of Zambia* (Oxford, 1968) or Bruce Kapferer's *A Celebration of Demons: Exorcism and the Aesthetics of Healing in Sri Lanka* (Bloomington, Ind., 1983) exclude drums and their music from the depth of analytical attention paid to other components of ritual symbolism and performance.

The scientific, physical description of drums is given accurate and readable treatment in the "Terminology" section ("Membranophones," pp. 459–463) of Curt Sachs's *The History of Musical Instruments* (New York, 1940), an organological classic with a wealth of accurate information organized around partly outdated historical viewpoints. The most comprehensive and up-to-date organological information will be found in the *New Grove Dictionary of Musical Instruments*, 3 vols., edited by Stanley Sadie (New York, 1984).

The most ambitious recent effort to relate African drumming and ideology, criticized by some specialists for lack of methodological explicitness and generalization of localized West African experience to a pan-African scale, is John M. Chernoff's *African Rhythm and African Sensibility* (Chicago, 1979). A less exciting but perhaps more reliable ethnomusicological study, also from West Africa, is J. H. Kwabena Nketia's *Drumming in Akan Communities of Ghana* (Edinburgh, 1963). The classic work on "talking drums," with an old-fashioned perspective and pronounced missionary bias, is John Carrington's *Talking Drums of Africa* (London, 1949). Among the more technically oriented organological studies of specific regions, Olga Boone's *Les tambours du Congo Belge et du Ruanda-Urundi* (Tervuren, Belgium, 1951) is one of the more comprehensive. There are a number of good studies of religious and symbolic aspects of drumming-centered ritual traditions in Africa, among which Victor Turner's works (including the book already cited) are outstanding examples.

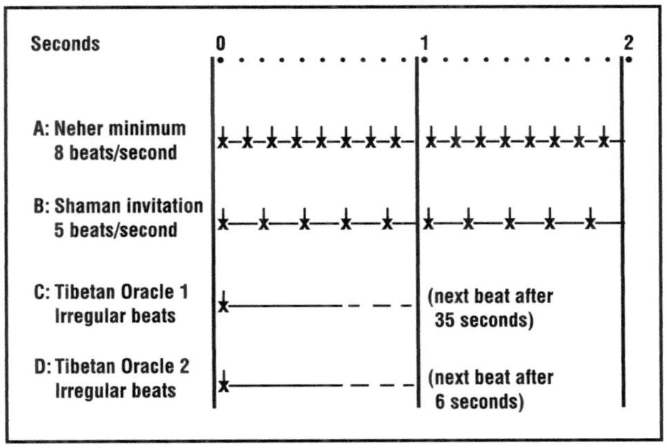

Figure 1. Neher's minimum projected tempo figures compared with drum tempos in two ritual traditions.

General works on Buddhist drums are unavailable; and on drum symbolism, only Rinjing Dorje and Ter Ellingson's article "Explanation of the Secret *Gcod Ḍa ma ru'*: An Exploration of Musical Instrument Symbolism," *Asian Music* (1979): 63–91, gives Buddhist primary source material, a text on the symbolism of a Tibetan drum. The standard work on shamanism, Mircea Eliade's *Shamanism: Archaic Techniques of Ecstasy*, rev. & enl. ed. (New York, 1964), contains valuable information on the ideology and use of drums, as do various articles in *Popular Beliefs and Folklore Tradition in Siberia*, edited by Vilmos Diószegi, (Bloomington, 1968); *Shamanism in Siberia*, edited by Vilmos Diószegi and Mihaly Hoppál (Budapest, 1978); and sections of Anna-Leena Siikala's *The Rite Technique of the Siberian Shaman* (Helsinki, 1978). The only detailed study of music and drumming in a "classic" Asian shaman tradition is Valerie Jill Poris's "Shamanistic Music in the Bhuji River Valley of Nepal" (M.A. thesis, University of Wisconsin, Madison, 1977). Andrew Neher describes his drum-possession hypothesis in two journal articles, "Auditory Driving Observed with Scalp Electrodes in Normal Subjects," *Electroencephalography and Clinical Neurophysiology* 13 (June 1961): 449–451, and "A Physiological Explanation of Unusual Behavior in Ceremonies Involving Drums," *Human Biology* 34 (February 1962): 151–160. The best counterarguments to Neher are given by Gilbert Rouget, in a short article, "Music and Possession Trance," in *The Anthropology of the Body*, edited by John Blacking (London, 1977), pp. 233–239, and in a book that is so far the most complete study of its subject, *Music and Trance: A Theory of the Relations between Music and Possession* (Chicago, 1985).

New Sources

Ahlbäck, Tore, and Jan Bergman. *The Saami Shaman Drum: Based on Papers Read at the Symposium on the Saami Shaman Drum Held at Åbo, Finland, on the 19th–20th of August 1988.* Åbo, Finland, and Stockholm, 1991.

Hart, Mickey, Jay Stevens, and Frederic Lieberman. *Drumming at the Edge of Magic: A Journey into the Spirit of Percussion.* San Francisco, 1990.

Hawkins, Holly Blue. *The Heart of the Circle: A Guide to Drumming.* Freedom, Calif., 1999.

Houk, James T. *Spirits, Blood, and Drums: The Orisha Religion in Trinidad.* Philadelphia, 1995.

Jacobs, Adrian. *Aboriginal Christianity: The Way It Was Meant to Be.* Rapid City, 1998.

Keshavarz, Fatemeh. *Reading Mystical Lyric: The Case of Jalal al-Din Rumi.* Columbia, S.C., 1998.

Powers, William K. *Beyond the Vision: Essays on American Indian Culture.* Norman, Okla., 1987.

Redmond, Layne. *When the Drummers Were Women: A Spiritual History of Rhythm.* New York, 1997.

Sindima, Harvey J. *Drums of Redemption: An Introduction to African Christianity.* Westport, Conn., 1994.

Vélez, Maria Teresa. *Drumming for the Gods: The Life and Times of Felipe García Villamil, Santero, Palero, and Abakuá.* Philadelphia, 2000.

Wardwell, Allen. *Tangible Visions: Northwest Coast Indian Shamanism and its Art.* New York, 1996.

TER ELLINGSON (1987)
Revised Bibliography

DRUZE. The title *Druze* (Arab. *Durzī;* pl. *Durūz)* was given to the community by outsiders who derived it from the name of Muḥammad ibn Ismāʿīl al-Darazī (d. 1019). Al-Darazī is considered by Druzes to be the "deviate" or "great heretic." Druzes refer to themselves as *Muwwaḥḥidūn* (Unitarians) or *Ahl al-Tawḥīd* (the People of Unitarianism). In addition to these titles, the community is often known in the Middle East as *Banū Maʿrūf* (Sons of Mercy, or Sons of Beneficence). The term *Maʿrūf* is derived from the Arabic words *ʿarafa* (to know), *maʿrifah* (knowledge), and *ʿirfān* (esoteric knowledge, gnosis). More importantly, the Druze manuscripts refer to the community as *madhhab ʿirfānī* (a gnostic school), and to its members as *Aʿrāf* (those who possess knowledge).

There are approximately one million Druzes in the world today, with the majority of them living in Syria (40–50%), Lebanon (30–40%), and Israel (6–7%). Syrian Druzes can be found mainly in the Ḥawrān and Ṣuwaydāʾ provinces, with the city of Ṣuwaydā having the largest Druze population. In Lebanon, Druzes live primarily in the ʿAlayh and the Shūf regions, with smaller populations in Bʿabdā, Marjʿuyūn, Rāshayyā, and al-Matn. Some Druze families also reside in Beirut, where the judiciary and administrative center of the community has its headquarters. In Israel, Druzes live in the Galilee and Carmel Mountain regions, with smaller numbers in other parts of the country. There are also a few thousand Druzes living in Jordan.

In addition to these larger concentrations of Druzes in the Middle East, smaller communities can be found in Australia, Canada, Europe, the Philippines, South America, West Africa, and the United States. These Druze diasporas have established communal associations, such as the American Druze Society, the British Druze Society, the Druze Association of Toronto, the Sidney Druze Society, and La Druzo Brazileiri.

INITIATED VERSUS UNINITIATED. Religious beliefs unite Druzes into socially cohesive communities and divide them into two main classes: the initiated or wise *(ʿuqqāl)* and the uninitiated or "ignorant" *(juhhāl).* The initiated members learn the precepts of their faith through readings and discussions of the sacred writings in the Druze house of prayer *(khalwah* or *majlis).* Only those believers who demonstrate piety and devotion and who have withstood the lengthy process of candidacy are introduced to the esoteric teachings and oral traditions of the faith. The Druze doctrine considers women more spiritually prepared than men, and women therefore undergo a less rigorous initiation process. The initiated men and women are easily identified by their modest dark clothes and white head covers.

Initiated persons are further subdivided into a number of categories, with the *Ajāwīd* (plural of *juwayyid,* the diminutive form of *jayyid,* which means "good") as the most devout among the initiated. The *Ajāwīd* serve as models for behavior, truthfulness, and wisdom, and whenever disputes arise their opinions are both revered and followed. Thus, they provide exclusive authority on the religious doctrine and dictate the proper conduct of members of the community, reinforcing its interactions within families, villages, and the rest of the world.

Uninitiated persons make up the majority of Druze society. They may seek initiation at any age, but their acceptance is based on their character. Although the uninitiated are indeed "ignorant" of the Druze doctrine, they are expected to behave according to certain prescriptions, both spiritual (e.g., devotion to God and his prophets) and moral (e.g., respect for elders, care for the young, and honor for women).

The division of Druzes into the initiated and uninitiated also has important ramifications for the political behavior of members of the community. This social structure may have facilitated Druze political cohesiveness, since religious leadership is provided by the *ʿuqqāl,* while political leadership is exercised by the *juhhāl.* However, despite the power held by the political leaders, families continue to consult, revere, and defer to the initiated members of their own families and of the community as a whole. Even though almost none of the initiated members hold political office, their perspectives carry political weight, influencing the decisions of the community's political leaders. Thus, while the initiated exercise strong yet indirect power in enforcing accepted standards for the community, the uninitiated draw strength from, as well as provide protection for, the initiated and the way of life, beliefs, and values they represent.

HISTORY VERSUS GENEALOGY. Druzes trace their genealogy to the beginning of time, believing that *tawḥīd* has existed in several phases or cycles *(adwār)* since the creation. They hold that before the biblical (or historical) Adam, there were 343 million years of human existence, and that during that period and up to the present certain communities have professed *tawḥīd* in one form or another. The Druze manuscripts include an elaborate cosmological doctrine that begins with the prebiblical Adam, referred to as "the pure Adam" (*Adam al-Ṣafā'*), and known as *Adam Kadmun* (Primordial Adam) in the Jewish Qabbalah and other religious traditions.

Druze historical origins, on the other hand, are traced to eleventh-century Fāṭimid Egypt. The Fāṭimis (r. 909–1171 CE) are Ismāʿīlī Shīʿah who originated in North Africa but conquered Egypt and built Cairo in 969 CE as their seat of power. According to almost all scholarly accounts, and based on Druze manuscripts, the Druze religious doctrine was founded, approved, supervised, or simply tolerated by the sixth Fāṭimid caliph, al-Manṣūr, known as al-Ḥākim bi-Amr Allāh (r. 996–1021 CE).

In the eyes of many historians, al-Ḥākim was the most controversial among Fāṭimid caliphs, due partly to rumors about a claim for divinity, which he apparently never made, and partly to his early resolutions against the ritualistic practices of several religious communities. Descriptions of al-Ḥākim as insane and eccentric became dominant in mainstream Islamic scholarship and later in the West as well. However, more recent historians have come to view him as an antagonist to ritualistic practices and as a reformer with his own style and approach.

A second important figure in the Druze religious reform movement is Ḥamzah ibn ʿAlī (b. 985), who is considered the main authority behind Druze teachings. Ḥamzah came to Cairo in December 1016 CE, and in May 1017 al-Ḥākim officially conferred the title of *imām* on him, announcing that he and his associates could begin disseminating their religious reforms. Druze manuscripts tell us that Ḥamzah ibn ʿAlī sent missionaries in every direction of the earth with a document or "proclamation of faith" known as *al-Mithāq* (the Covenant) by which the prospective converts could commit themselves and pledge their loyalty to the new movement and its religious doctrine. Then he sent twenty of his followers to the supreme Muslim judge, Aḥmad ibn al-ʿAwām, asking him not to adjudicate cases by members of the new movement because the movement's doctrine, among other things, prohibited polygamy and the remarriage of one's divorcee, practices that were authorized in the Islamic courts. Ḥamzah's emissaries were attacked and some were killed.

During this external resistance to the new movement, an internal power struggle arose between Ḥamzah and one of the activists mentioned earlier, al-Darazī. Although Ḥamzah was technically al-Darazī's superior, he decided to withdraw from public preaching in order to prevent any confusion in the ranks of new and prospective converts. Al-Darazī exploited the opportunity of Ḥamzah's withdrawal and not only claimed the title of *imām* for himself, but also began to falsify Ḥamzah's writings and teachings in order to present al-Ḥākim as divine. This was apparently in the hopes that al-Ḥākim would favor him over Ḥamzah. Instead, al-Ḥākim withdrew his support from al-Darazī and public opposition to al-Darazī's teachings increased. As his defeat neared, al-Darazī redirected the public's attack by declaring that he had acted on Ḥamzah's instructions.

Ḥamzah's previous withdrawal from preaching now worked against him by reinforcing al-Darazī's assertion that he was indeed following Ḥamzah's directives. Consequently, instead of attacking al-Darazī, the crowd turned against Ḥamzah's residence at the Ridan mosque. Although al-Darazī was eventually executed by al-Ḥākim and his teachings were repudiated, some writers thereafter attributed his teachings to the followers of Ḥamzah. In doing so, they referred to such followers as *Druzes* after Darazī's name, and erroneously portrayed al-Darazī as the founder of Druzism.

In 1021 CE, al-Ḥākim departed on one of his routine trips, but he never returned, leaving fertile ground for speculation. His contemporaries said that he could have been assassinated by his sister's agents, attacked by nomads who had not recognized him, or he could have simply died of natural causes. Whatever the case, his body was never found, and historians have been unable to resolve the mystery surrounding the caliph's life and disappearance. In the same year, Ḥamzah withdrew completely from the public eye and delegated the leadership of the community to Bahā' al-Dīn al-Sāmmūqī, who is considered the third important figure in the emergence of the Druze movement.

Bahā' al-Dīn took office in a period when the Fāṭimid caliph, al-Ẓāhir, successor of al-Ḥākim, began persecuting members of the new movement. This period of persecution is known in the Druze tradition as a "testing phase" or "hardship" that lasted over five years. After 1026 CE, Bahā' al-Dīn wrote letters both to prospective converts in new locations and to those members who had seceded from the movement as a result of the persecution. He also sent missionaries to strengthen and guide believers. Bahā' al-Dīn continued his activity until the closing of the Druze *tawḥīd* movement in 1043. In that year Ḥamzah ibn ʿAlī, Bahā' al-Dīn and the other luminaries left Egypt to an unknown destination. Druzes believe that they will all return on the Day of Judgment. Since 1043, Druzism has remained closed to new converts.

In the past nearly one thousand years, Druze communities have faced various challenges, most notably their religious and spiritual decline during the fourteenth and fifteenth centuries. That period led to the emergence of several important spiritual leaders, the most important being the prolific theologian al-Amīr al-Sayyid al-Tanūkhī (d. 1479), who is the author of a number of treatises and commentaries. On the social and political levels, Druzes have remained a close-knit community and have almost always stayed loyal to the governments under which they lived. Exceptions that are worth mentioning may include the Maʿnīs' uprisings against the Ottoman Empire in the sixteenth century and the Aṭrashs' rebellion against French rule in the 1920s. Both the Maʿnīs and Aṭrashs were also supported by non-Druze residents of the region.

Beliefs versus Practices. The Druze manuscripts advocate that the sources of *tawḥīd* are many and include the Hebrew Bible, the New Testament, and the Qurʾān. The Druze (holy) book, known as *The Epistles of Wisdom (Rasāʾil al-Ḥikmah),* is in actuality a hermeneutic of biblical and Qurʾanic doctrines rather than an independent book of revelations.

Several beliefs and practices may be highlighted. The first Druze belief is in God and his oneness, without an attempt to penetrate the nature of his being and attributes. With minor variations, the Druze belief in God is consistent with the Judeo-Christian-Islamic tradition.

Secondly, Druzes believe in the teachings of several intermediaries, including seven spokesmen (*nutaqāʾ*) who preached *tawḥīd* in their times: Adam, Noah, Abraham, Moses, Jesus, Muḥammad, and Muḥammad ibn Ismāʿīl. For each of these seven spokesmen, God provided a foundation *(asas)* to help in spreading *tawḥīd.* These helpers are, respectively, Seth, Shem, Ishmael, Aaron/Joshua, Simeon Peter, ʿAli ibn Abī Ṭālib, and al-Qaddah. Because these spokesmen and their helpers came from God, introduced his teachings, and obeyed and worshiped him, Druzes acknowledge and revere them. In addition to the spokesmen and foundations, Druzes believe that there was also a hierarchy of luminaries *(ḥudūd)* in each cycle. The five central luminaries are, in descending order, the Universal Intellect (*al-ʿAql al-Kullī*), the Universal Soul (*al-Nafs al-Kullīyah*), the Word (*al-Kalimah*), the Preceding (*al-Sābiq*), and the Following (*al-Tālī*). Each of these spiritual luminaries was also represented by a human in each respective period.

Third, Druzes believe in the phenomenon of the transmigration of souls, or more precisely perhaps, *metempsychosis.* They use the unique term *taqāmus,* derived from *qāmis,* meaning "shirt," and not the common Arabic term *tanāsukh* (reincarnation). Druzes rely on biblical and Qurʾanic passages, as well as on Platonic and Neoplatonic arguments, to support their belief in *taqāmus.* Generally, and in contrast to other traditions, Druzes believe that after the death of the body the soul is instantly reborn into a new human body. Thus, Druzes do not accept the doctrine that the soul "hovers" without the body, nor the belief that humans are reborn as animals, plants, or things. Moreover, they believe that the soul's punishment or reward is granted only on the Day of Judgment and after a large number of lives in which the soul would have experienced all possible roles, being poor and rich, healthy and ill, and having had long and short lives.

In addition to the above three beliefs in God, intermediaries, and metempsychosis, Druzes believe in the centrality of wisdom *(ḥikmah)* as a collective body of knowledge concerning theology, cosmology, and eschatology. The word *ḥikmah* is often associated with *The Epistles of Wisdom,* but here the use of *ḥikmah* is distinctive and more cumulative, going beyond the eleventh-century religious doctrine. Some Druze sages are aware of such distinction between the *book of ḥikmah* and the *body of ḥikmah,* and they confirm that the world's printed spiritual texts are only a few drops in a vast ocean of wisdom. These drops are partially recorded in a number of ancient and medieval texts, some of which represent versions of older manuscripts with some degree of error.

Related to the belief in *ḥikmah* and its place in the Druze community is the belief in accessing such *ḥikmah* through initiation. As stated earlier, initiation in Druzism is a lengthy and arduous process. Like other esoteric and mystical groups, such a process demands that the initiated member be not only of the right character and personality, but also in a ready mental and spiritual state in life.

Finally, Druze religious practices, as distinguished from beliefs, include the following:

1. Speaking the truth *(ṣidq al-lisān);*
2. Protecting coreligionists *(ḥifz al-ikhwān);*
3. Abandoning the worship of idols/sin *(tark ʿibādat al-awthān);*
4. Fleeing from devils and oppression *(baraʾah min al-abālisah wa-al-tughyān);*
5. Declaring the unity of the creator *(tawḥīd al-Bārīʾ);*
6. Being contented with God *(riḍāʾ);*
7. Submitting to God's will *(taslīm).*

Bibliography

Abu Izzeddin, Nejla M. *The Druzes: A New Study of Their History, Faith, and Society.* Leiden, 1984.

Ben-Dor, Gabriel. *The Druzes in Israel: A Political Study.* Jerusalem, 1979.

Betts, Robert Brenton. *The Druze.* New Haven, 1988.

Firro, Kais. *A History of the Druzes.* Leiden, 1992.

Firro, Kais. *The Druzes in the Jewish State: A Brief History.* Leiden, 1999.

Hitti, Philip K. *The Origins of the Druze People and Religion.* New York, 1928.

Makarem, Sami Nasib. *The Druze Faith.* Delmar, N.Y., 1974.

Silvestre de Sacy, Antoine Isaac. *Exposé de la religion des Druzes.* Paris, 1838. Reprint, Amsterdam, 1964.

Swayd, Samy S. *The Druzes: An Annotated Bibliography.* Los Angeles, 1998.

Samy Swayd (2005)

DUALISM. As a category within the history and phenomenology of religion, dualism may be defined as a doctrine that posits the existence of two fundamental causal principles underlying the existence (or, as in the case of the Indian notion of *maya* as opposed to *atman,* the painful appearance of the existence) of the world. In addition, dualistic doctrines, worldviews, or myths represent the basic components of the world, or of humans, as participating in the ontological opposition and disparity of value that characterize their dual principles. In this specific religio-historical sense, dualism is to be distinguished from the more general philosophical doctrines of transcendence and metaphysical irreducibility, which are opposed to monistic or pantheistic doctrines of immanence. This article will examine dualism only in the former sense, as a religio-historical phenomenon. It begins with a systematic overview of the nature and types of dualism, then proceeds to a closer examination of some specific historical instances.

As a religio-historical phenomenon, dualism is more specific than either simple duality or polarity. Not every duality or polarity is dualistic—only those that involve the duality or polarity of causal principles. Thus not every pair of opposites (such as male and female, right and left, light and darkness, good and bad, spirit and matter, and sacred and profane) can be labeled as dualistic, even when their opposition is emphasized. They are dualistic only when they are understood as principles or causes of the world and its constitutive elements. In addition, in order for pairs of opposites to be dualistic, it is not necessary that they be mutually irreducible or coeternal. Indeed, one may be the creation of the other, as in the dualistic doctrine of the Bogomils, where Satan, created by God, is in turn the creator of the human body. In short, there is no dualism where there is no question of cosmogony or anthropogony, where there is no account of the principles responsible for bringing the world and humans into existence. This means that a concept of mere ethical dualism, stressing the moral opposition between good and evil and their respective protagonists (as in the Christian concepts of God and the devil), is not properly dualistic in the religio-historical and phenomenological sense—unless, however, good and evil are also connected with opposite ontological principles, as in Zoroastrianism and in Manichaeism. The simple contrasting of good and evil, life and death, light and darkness, and so on is in fact coextensive with religion itself and cannot be equated with the much more specific phenomenon of dualism.

Dualism in Religio-Historical, Philosophical and Sociological Discourse. In 1700 the English Orientalist Thomas Hyde (1636–1703) used in his *Historia religionis veterum Persarum* (1700) the term "dualistae" in reference to the ancient religion of the Persians, whom he described as professing a belief in two principles—respectively the Light and Good one and the Dark and Evil one, a belief he traced to Zarathushtra. Subsequently, the terms "dualist" and "duality" were employed in reference to Zarathushtra by Pierre Bayle and Gottfried Leibnitz, and in 1734 Christian Wolff in his *Psychologia rationalis* introduced the term "dualism" to define philosophical systems like that of René Descartes (1596–1650), which posit that mind and matter are two distinct substances. Subsequently, the term came into use for philosophical descriptions of Cartesianism, the mind-body problem, and the doctrines of transcendence. More generally, the term dualism came to be applied also to philosophical systems that contained important and paradigmatic pairs of oppositions like that of Plato, with its dualities between the mortal body and the immortal soul, the "One" and the "Many," the finite and the infinite, as well as the world perceived by the senses and the world of eternal ideas comprehended by the mind or the Kantian ontological distinction between the phenomenal and the noumenal world.

Although the term "dualism" entered forcefully into philosophical terminology, theories, and arguments, in the field of religious history and theology throughout the nineteenth century, it would retain its original association with Zarathushtra and the ancient Persian religion. The development of Oriental scholarship, the history of religions, and ethnology in the second half of the nineteenth century, however, led to the application of the term beyond ancient Iran in the discussions of the religions of ancient Egypt and Mesopotamia, the Greek and the Hellenistic world—particularly with regard to some currents in Pre-Socratic philosophic traditions, Orphism and Pythagoreanism)—and the first studies trying to identify dualist strands in the preliterate cultures of North America and Eurasia. Consequently there appeared the first attempts to determine the place of religious dualism in the history of religions on the whole. Dualism came to be variously defined as a reaction against monotheism; as an intermediate phase of passage between polytheism and monotheism; as a protest against the presence of evil in the world; as a corrective to monism's tendency to effect a premature synthesis (Rudolf Eucken); and as a response to the experience of irrationality in the world (Max Weber).

Another approach to the problem in which dualism and monotheism are treated as intimately related phenomena was also to find its early expressions in literature, for example, in Ludwig Stein's *Dualismus oder Monismus* (1909). The widening of the scope of the study of religious dualism in the early twentieth century was also effected by the historical-critical methods of inquiry introduced by the *Religionsgeschitliche Schule.* At the same time, the prominent focus on the impact of ancient Iran and Mesopotamia on Judaism, Christianity, and Gnosticism in the most influential works of the *Religionsgeschitliche Schule*, as well as the postulation of Iranian redemption myths—like that of the "redeemed redeemer," believed by Richard Reitzenstein to have crucially influenced Gnosticism—helped to retain what should have been by then an anachronistic paradigm of Iran as the cradleland of religious dualism.

Meanwhile, the contemporary advance in research in the dual organization of a number of mainly preliterate societies generated increasing interest among anthropologists and sociologists in its origins, development, and ways of functioning. This had direct implications for the study of dualism, polarity, and contrariety in religious and cultural history. Coupled with the widening exploration and understanding of the phenomenon of dual symbolic classification in such preliterate (as well as some later) societies, this led to the conceptualization of some influential anthropological and sociological approaches to the problem of dualism and dual social organization. For Emile Durkheim and his followers, as well as related theorists—like the Russian scholar A. Zolotarev—the bipartite classification of society and the world (and the related religious and mythological/cosmological notions) had its origins in dual models developed in society itself. Other scholars favored "historical" explanations for the rise of social organization of a binary type—decoded largely as a consequence of the historical mixture of two different ethnic entities.

Although making some major contributions to the study of dual social organizations, particularly in relation to the use of dual symbolic classification and religious traditions such as the cult of the divine twins, these historicizing and sociologizing approaches were frequently marred by obvious reductionism. According to the influential alternative approach offered by the structural anthropology of Claude Lévi-Strauss and his followers, the principles of dual social organization derive from a "deep structure" operating unconsciously in the human mind, one of whose most important mechanisms is that of the binary opposition intrinsic to the mind's perception of the world.

Structural anthropology stimulated a number of studies and widespread debates across a range of fields, ranging from whether binary differentiation and oppositions form the primal and permanent basis of human consciousness and culture (including theories that it could be related to the bicamerality of the human mind) to their posited correlations with the general formal characteristics of language and the diffusion and history of binary systems of thought and action in various civilizations. The studies and debates also ranged from preliterate societies, to the use of a "polar mode of thought" in classical Greece and China, and the preoccupation of binary opposites and contrariety in medieval and early modern Europe.

The resultant expanding study of binary social organizations and symbolic classifications on the whole, and separate problems—such as the correlation between beliefs/cosmology based on the binary cosmos of certain cultures and the related social institutions (binary or not)—has not always distinguished sufficiently the term dualism from duality, polarity, contrariety, and oppositional thought. With the prevalent focus being on the sociological or psychological interpretation of religion, this has led to some ambiguity and uncritical use in the application of the term dualism in anthropological and sociological discourse, as well as a frequent lack of terminological specification, which has to be contrasted with the terminologically well-defined usage of the term in philosophical discourse gradually established throughout the nineteenth and twentieth centuries.

Indeed the term dualism may have originally been introduced in a religio-historical framework, but the parameters of its legitimate and specific usage were determined earlier in philosophical discourse—this process was somewhat delayed in religious studies of the phenomenon, at least prior to the appearance of the first more systematic works on religious dualism. The unearthing and publication of new sources for Manichaeism between the two World Wars, and the eventual discovery of the Nag Hammadi Gnostic corpus in 1945, revolutionized the study of Gnosticism and led to increasing numbers of studies, such as Hans Jonas's *The Gnostic Religion* (1958), that focused on various aspects of Gnostic dualism. Employing the newly redefined methods of form criticism, redaction history, and tradition history, these studies revisited and reassessed the theories and arguments of the *Religionsgeschitliche Schule* regarding the origins of Gnostic dualism, and often broke into completely new territories.

A new stage in the research on religious dualism and a movement towards the accomplishment of its *Weltgeschichte* was inaugurated in the studies of Ugo Bianchi between 1958 and 1995. Among the many contributions of these studies was the elaboration of a systematic typology of dualism with the simultaneous and balanced use of comparative-historical and phenomenological approaches to the various historical and theological problems posed by dualist traditions (pertaining to, among others, diffusion, cultural exchange, parallel development, and acculturation). Thus depth, meticulousness, and variety were finally given to the religio-historical senses in which dualism can be validly used. Bianchi's discussions, typology, and definitions of dualism—which integrated material both from literate and nonliterate religions—have recently been further elaborated, specified, and in some cases challenged by other scholars working in the various fields of religious studies.

ROLE IN MONOTHEISM, POLYTHEISM, AND MONISM. In the historical phenomenology of religion, dualism need not be opposed necessarily to either monotheism, polytheism, or monism.

Dualism in monotheism. Dualistic manifestations of monotheism can be found in the *Gathas* of the Zoroastrian Avesta and in Christian Gnosticism. Here one finds an ontologically inferior and often demonic figure, such as Ahriman (Angra Mainyu) in the Avesta or the Prince of Darkness in Manichaeism or the psychic demiurge in Gnosticism, all of which exist as a second principle along with the supreme God. Only in Marcionism does this dualism lead beyond monotheism to a properly ditheistic doctrine (the supreme god of perfect goodness, as opposed to the inferior god of "justice"). Additionally, some forms of non-Gnostic Christian speculation deeply influenced by Platonism can be regarded as dualistic. Rather than a Gnostic belief in two irreducible agencies that account for the existence of humans and the universe, there is in the speculation a belief in the fundamental opposition of the immaterial human soul and the material—that is, physical—body. Although present here is the same God who creates both the soul and the body, the occasion for the creation of the latter is the primordial sin of what were originally "incorporeal"—that is, not bound to a material body—rational souls. This primordial sin can accordingly be viewed as a second principle or cause that motivates God to create the human body in its present constitution and the visible world in which people must live until the final apocatastasis, or restoration of his primordial, "immaterial" condition.

Such is the picture presented by the platonizing anthropology of Origen (c. 185–c. 254 CE. In this case, one can speak of an anthropological dualism, which implies not only the dual constituents of soul and body, but more importantly a duality of causes: the omnipotent will of God and the sin of a created soul, the latter motivating the creation of the human physiological body and the material world. Clearly, sin is not to be understood here as the efficient cause of this "second creation"; it merely motivates the subsequent (second) creative act of God. Rather, sin is to be understood here as "previous sin," as distinct from the original sin of Adam. Whereas the latter was committed by Adam as a fully corporeal man, this "previous sin" was committed by the preexisting souls in a kind of "prologue in heaven." Elements of this Origenian tradition of anthropological dualism are also found in Gregory of Nyssa, who thought that God created the human (sexual) body because of his foreknowledge of the (not sexual) sin of Adam and his fall from paradise.

One finds a somewhat different form of non-Gnostic, dualistic monotheism in certain Jewish thinkers who admit the existence of angelic agents who cooperate with God the creator. In Philo Judaeus (c. 20 BCE– after 42 CE), for instance, these angels are particularly concerned with the creation of people or their lower constituents. Philo shows here the clear influence of Plato, who in his *Timaeus* had opposed the great Demiurge, creator of the immortal part of the soul, and the "generated gods," whom the Demiurge appoints to create the lower, mortal parts of the soul and the human body.

Needless to say, dualistic formulations of monotheism were criticized by Christian theologians, who sought to avoid any limitation of the absolute creativity of God. Nevertheless, it should be noted that some of the abovementioned conceptions (those of Philo and Plato) were originally intended to safeguard God's innocence in relation to evil. Thus the Platonists attributed human evil not to God, but to the freedom of the will and to the corporeal nature of humans.

Dualism in polytheism. Dualistic conceptions can also be found in polytheism. In some polytheistic cosmogonies there is an opposition between two distinct causal principles, represented on the one hand by the older, semipersonal *archai,* or principles of an elementary character, and on the other by a new race of youthful and energetic gods. Thus Ouranos, in the cosmogony of Hesiod, and Apsu, in the Mesopotamian *Enuma elish,* are each violently opposed in their egocentrism and ontological passivity by new gods, among whom figures a wise and energetic demiurge who creates or sets in order the world, apportions lots, and fixes destinies. It should be noted that in this type of cosmogony, the vanquished primordial entities do not completely lose their sacredness. Ouranos, for instance, retains a prophetic function, Apsu remains pure, and Vrtra (an analogous figure in Vedic cosmogony) remains a brahman. In other words, the character of these primordial entities, fated to a final defeat and transformed substantially into the elements of the universe, is far from demonic; they remain different from the aggressive beings that characterize the Zoroastrian and Gnostic worldviews.

Dualism in monism. Finally, even monism can be expressed in dualistic terms. This is the case, paradoxically enough, in the classical Advaita doctrine of Sankara (c. 788–820), and in other systems that reduce the multiplicity of the material world to illusion—that is, to metaphysical nonexistence. These systems in fact correspond to the definition of dualism put forth earlier, inasmuch as *maya* (illusion), though ontologically insubstantial, nevertheless gives rise to the phenomenal world and its suffering. Instances of dualistic monism can be found outside India as well. In Greece the monistic doctrine of Parmenides is not without dualistic overtones, with its opposition between truth and opinion (*doxa*)—a distinction that was also proper to Plato. More profoundly intermingled, and at the same time opposed, are the coeternal principles of Love and Discord in the ontology and cosmology of Empedocles. One also thinks of Heraclitus's essentially dualistic doctrine of "war" (*polemos*), where the "way downward" and the "way upward" oppose each other, all within the context of the axiological preeminence attributed to the principle of Logos, which has as its material aspect fire.

TYPES OF DUALISM. In order to provide a more systematic examination of dualism, it is necessary to review a typology of its basic forms. These forms, however, require verification through comparative historical research. From the systematic point of view, every form of dualism may be classified by type as either radical or moderate, either dialectical or eschatological, and as either cosmic (or procosmic) or anticosmic. Each of these pairs is examined in turn below.

Radical versus moderate. Radical dualism and moderate dualism may be distinguished from each other on the basis of their respective views of the two fundamental principles. Radical dualism admits two coequal and coeternal principles (in the sense that both of them exist and act from the very beginning, whatever may be their final destiny; see below). Late Avestan and medieval Zoroastrianism, as well as the early Gathic doctrine of the two primordial spirits, are examples of such radical dualism. In particular, the two Gathic spirits are to be understood as existing independently from the beginning of the world with their perfectly contrary natures. Notwithstanding the interpretation given by most Iranologists, the conflicting moral choices of the two Gathic spirits between *asha* (Truth) and *druj* (Untruth) means merely the declaration of their inborn natures, and the bad spirit has nothing in common with Ahura Mazda, the high god. That the Gathic spirits are mentioned in the Gathas as "twins" does not imply more than their being symmetrical and contrary in essence to each other. (Manichaeism and some varieties of medieval Catharism also belong within this form.) Among the Greeks there exists a radical dualism in Orphism, with its conception of the *kuklos tes geneseos* ("the cycle of birth") and the dualistic implications of its metaphysics; in Empedocles' theory of the two opposed principles of Love and Discord; in Heraclitus; and in Plato's doctrines of the two alternating revolutions of the world, mentioned in the *Statesman,* and of the coeternity of the Ideas and the "receptacle" *(chora).* There are also several forms of radical dualism in India, particularly in the Samkhya system, with its opposed principles of *purusa* and *prakrti.*

Unlike the radical dualism, moderate (or monarchian) dualism exhibits only one primordial principle, while a second principle somehow derives from the first, often through an incident that took place in a kind of prologue in heaven. This second principle then plays a central role in bringing the world into existence. Many of the Gnostic systems provide examples of moderate dualism, in particular the systems of Valentinus, where the structure of the divine, pneumatic world (the *pleroma*) allows for the possibility of a fall in heaven. The fall of Sophia, the last Aion, is a result of her location on the periphery of the divine *pleroma.* This dangerous position amounts to a kind of predestination. Although this does not destroy the moderate, or monarchian, character of Valentinianism, it does show that Gnostic metaphysics here includes a concept of crisis or instability in the divine that is fundamentally dualistic. It also provides evidence of Gnosticism's connections with other speculative trends during the Hellenistic period, such as the Orphic, Pythagorean, and Platonic traditions. Other examples of moderate dualism are the anthropogony of Plato's *Timaeus,* and medieval sects (some of the Cathari and the Bogomils).

Evidence of radical or moderate dualism among nonliterate cultures is ambiguous, and this fact may be significant for an understanding of the formation process of dualistic ideologies and creeds. Thus, whereas the Algonquin myth of the two brothers Ioskeha and Tawiskaron, born of Ataentsic (a primordial female being) can be traced to a type of radical dualism—because the brothers have, respectively, a positive and negative relation to creation from the beginning—other American myths of a dualistic character are different. They may present a supreme being who in the beginning is unopposed but is later joined by a second figure of unknown origin who begins to interfere in the creation process. The unknown origin of the rival, who is often characterized as a demiurgic trickster, may be intended to indicate that his earlier absence was really an unmanifested presence, and that he is in fact an integral part of a single, all-inclusive scenario.

The same seems to be true of the North American myth of Nih'asa (or Napiwa), the "hard man" who arrives late, his origin unknown. He succeeds in taking control of the earth with the creator god's permission, but then immediately acts against the latter's purposes. The less tragic Chukchi myth of the primordial times conveys the same impression. The supreme being creates everything, but forgets to create Raven (who in other Northeast Asian myths is a trickster and a secondary demiurge). The supreme being's forgetfulness points to the fact that Raven is implicitly, even before his birth, a constituent element of the universe. In fact, the myth tells us that he comes into being in darkness, during the night following creation, born of a creator god's abandoned garment. Thus the creator is, in one way or another, responsible for the totality of existence, and Raven owes his existence to a kind of inborn necessity.

It would seem, therefore, that the most ancient formulations (or at least the simplest) did not choose between the two possibilities of radical and moderate dualism. Perhaps such an alternative was not recognized. Such may also have been the case with what we have called the moderate dualism of the Valentinians and of other Gnostics and sectarians, whose mythologies are frequently reminiscent of the dualistic scenarios of archaic cultures.

In this connection one may also mention the mythologies of the Yazīdīs, the Ahl-i Haqq, and the dualistic myths and legends found in the folklore of eastern Europe. The latter have been influenced both by the doctrines of the Bogomils, who themselves drew upon certain Christian apocryphal writings; but they also have some features in common with the dualistic mythologies found among the Tatars of the Altai and among other Turkish and Mongolian populations of Central Asia.

Dialectical versus eschatological dualism. Dialectical dualism may be distinguished from eschatological dualism by the fact that the two irreducible principles recognized by the former function eternally, whereas in the latter case they do not. In dialectical dualism the two principles are often conceived of as good and evil, respectively, both in the ethical and metaphysical sense. Samples are to be found in Orphic speculation on the one and the many, in Empedocles and Heraclitus, and in Platonism. The Hindu opposition of *atman* and *maya* also represents this type of dualism, as does the Chinese ideology of *yin* and *yang,* and various theosophical speculations.

The distinctive feature of eschatological dualism is the belief that the evil principle will be overcome at the end of history. Examples of this type of belief can be found in Zoroastrianism, Manichaeism, Gnosticism, Bogomilism, and Catharism. As can be seen from this list, many forms of eschatological dualism are historically dependent on doctrines within Christianity, where soteriology is strongly eschatological (though nondualistic). Similarly, some forms of dialectical dualism are connected with monistic speculations. It should also be noted that whereas dialectical dualism is always radical dualism, eschatological dualism can be grounded on either radical dualism, as in the case of Zoroastrianism and the Manichaeism influenced by it, or on moderate dualism, such as one finds in most Gnostic traditions, in Bogomilism, and in Catharism.

Cosmic (Procosmic) versus anticosmic dualism. Cosmic and anticosmic forms of dualism are distinguished by their attitudes towards the world. Cosmic dualism contends that creation is fundamentally good, and evil comes to it from the outside. Zoroastrianism can be named as a typical example. Anticosmic dualism contends, to the contrary, that evil is intrinsic to the world and present in an essentially negative or delusive principle or substance such as matter, the body, or the inferior soul. Examples here include Orphism, Gnosticism, Manichaeism, Bogomilism, Catharism, and certain forms of Hinduism. In Manichaeism, for instance, we find the notion of the world as being made out of the dark, material substance of demons, molded by a divine demiurge, the Spiritus Vivens. The cosmos is created as a providential engine in order to permit the progressive liberation of the souls trapped within it, which are eventually guided to the heavenly paradise.

OTHER TYPOLOGIES OF RELIGIOUS DUALISM. With the expansion of research on religious dualism, other typologies have also been put forward that should be taken into account when considering separate disciplines like that of Dead Sea Scrolls studies, in which such alternative typologies of dualism have become more influential. Some modern scholars have added more dichotomies to the above scheme of Bianchi's three pairs, as in the case of Ioan Coulianu, who added to the scheme the dichotomy of antihylic (against matter) versus prohylic dualism (*The Tree of Gnosis*, 1992), while effectively not recognizing mitigated dualist teachings as belonging to religious dualism and, accordingly, the first pair in Bianchi's typology. In her *Le Dieu Separé* (Paris, 1984) Simone Pétrement puts the main focus on the dichotomy of horizontal dualism (where the division is between beings on the same level as in Zoroastrian and Qumran dualism) and vertical dualism (where the division is between realities of different levels as in Platonic, Christian, and Gnostic dualism as well as the Cartesian and Kantian systems). A. H. Armstrong ("Dualism: Platonic, Gnostic, and Christian," 1992) proposes as a main dichotomy a distinction between cosmic dualism, which perceives the whole existence as constituted by the interaction of two opposite principles, and two-world dualism, which posits the division between two levels of reality, the normal and the higher one. The cosmic dualism in this scheme is further divided into four varieties: conflict-dualism of the Iranian pattern, in which the two principles are intrinsically opposed and in a constant conflict; dualism in which the two principles are seen as independent but complementary or interacting in harmony—as frequently speculated in Chinese thought; and two types of dualism in which the second principle derives from the first, accordingly either in revolt or opposition against the first principle, or in harmony and collaboration with it.

Another kind of typology of religious dualism is widely used in the study of the Qumran texts and differing from Bianchi's scheme in several important respects. Advanced by James H. Charlesworth and elaborated by other Qumran scholars, it distinguishes ten types of dualistic thought: metaphysical dualism, denoting the opposition of two prominent causal powers of equal standing; cosmic dualism, expressing the division of the universe and humankind into opposed forces of good and evil—which are, however, not viewed as coeternal or causal; spatial dualism, which divides the world in two spatially differentiated parts, like heaven and earth; and eschatological dualism focused on the bisection of the world into two temporally separated parts like the present age and the future one (also referred to as spatial dualism); ethical dualism, indicating the splitting up of humanity into two mutually exclusive camps on the basis of their adherence to virtue or vice; soteriological dualism, signifying the bisection of humans into two groups on the basis of their acceptance or rejection of a messianic figure; theological dualism, denoting the contrast between God and humans or the creator and his creation (a contrast approaching genuine dualism only when the element of antagonism between the two is accentuated); physical dualism, referring to the radical separation between spirit and matter; anthropological dualism, designating the contrariety between body and soul as dissimilar principles of being (obviously related to the previous type of physical dualism) and finally, psychological dualism, denoting the opposition of two principles or impulses—good and evil—within people and struggling to prevail upon them. It is obvious that the types of cosmic and eschatological dualism refer to different kinds of dualist concepts in this typology and Bianchi's scheme, differences that should be reckoned with when dealing with studies in the relevant fields

RELATIVE IMPORTANCE OF TYPES. A general consideration of the typologies that have just been presented permits one to make several interesting observations. First of all, the first opposition—that between radical and moderate forms of dualism—seems to be the least significant. This calls into question the frequent assumption that dualism in its genuine form implies the coeternity of the two principles. That this particular alternative caused important clashes in the Cathar churches of the Western Middle Ages should not lead us to overestimate its importance. The fundamental ambiguity involved in the question of the origin of the rival of God, the demiurge-trickster, in the dualistic mythologies of a number of nonliterate cultures points rather to the relative unimportance of this opposition. From the metaphysical point of view, the second form of typological opposition, that between dialectical and eschatological dualism, which is the most important. Finally, in relation to the actual conception and practice of life, it is the third opposition, that between cosmic and anticosmic dualism, that is central.

This final point enables us to recognize the specific character of Zoroastrianism in relation to the other types. As an outstanding form of cosmic dualism, Zoroastrianism is to be distinguished sharply from anticosmic Manichaeism, in spite of their similarities as both radical and eschatological. Manichaeism, which is generally Gnostic and Western in character, nevertheless shares in the radical and eschatological form of Zoroastrian dualism and suggests the conceptual and iconographic influence of the Iranian religious milieu.

The opposition of cosmic and anticosmic is less helpful for arriving at a specific characterization of Platonic and Hermetic forms of dualism. Both Plato and Plotinus strongly affirmed the beauty and order of the cosmos (something that sets Plotinus apart from the Gnostics). Nevertheless, they occasionally expressed less optimistic views. In the *Laws,* for example, Plato formulated an opposition between two souls of the world, one good and the other evil. Furthermore, both he and Plotinus shared the Orphic doctrine of the body as the tomb or prison of the soul and the view of life as a kind of death. In the end, it is impossible to describe the thought of either as consistently cosmic or anticosmic.

DUALISM IN HISTORY. Up to this point in the entry, the approach to dualism has been systematic. But the history of religions entails more than a purely phenomenological or systematic outlook. Employing a comparative-historical method raises the question of possible historical connections between different forms of religious dualism, and engages one in analyzing the historical milieus in which these phenomena arise. A historical-comparative treatment of dualism as a specific category of religious thought and experience need not revert to diffusionist explanations that presuppose a single historical origin of dualism and explain its subsequent geographical extension as a consequence of cultural diffusion and adaptation. The diverse historical forms of dualism can be better explained on the basis of parallel development, provided this approach avoids the presuppositions of evolutionism and physiological development. Yet it is not less historical in character than the diffusionist approach.

What is intended, then, is a historical typology that would explain the independent development of analogous religious phenomena such as dualism on the basis of comparable religious and historical circumstances or presuppositions. In any case, with the modern scholarship available, it would be hard to support a diffusionist explanation of the widespread presence of dualism in different cultures, times, and religions. Given the presence of forms of dualism in the archaic cultures of North America, it is clearly impossible to view all forms of dualism as having a single geographical point of origin, such as Iran. Here it is best to focus only on those connections that can be historically documented.

As was pointed out above, such connections can be found between some forms of Manichaean and Zoroastrian dualism. Similar comparative-historical conclusions could be drawn concerning the relationship between the dualistic conceptions found in eastern European folklore and in such western Asian sects as the Yazīdīs. One could possibly speak of a certain dualistic propensity in the ethnological background of these areas without losing sight of the opposite possibility—namely, the direct influence of the great dualistic religions and the active dualistic sectarian movements such as the Bogomils. Similar possibilities exist in the case of the well-established dualistic mythologies of the Inner Asian Turks and Tatars (see, for example, the dark figure of Erlik, an antigod particularly connected with the realm of death). These may have been influenced not only by Iran but also by the dualistic folklore traditions of eastern Europe.

The earth-diver cosmogonies and dualism. Even in Iran, there have occasionally been peripheral formulations of dualism that cannot be explained on the basis of Zoroastrian ideology alone. The characterization of Ahriman as a kind of demiurge-trickster, for instance, is not unlike the characterization of similar figures in the nonliterate cultures of Asia. Ultimately one is led to question the origins of Zoroastrian dualism itself: to what extent was it influenced or predetermined by the figure of Zarathushtra? To what extent, and in which ways, was Iranian religion characterized by dualistic tendencies prior to Zarathushtra? And, what was more important for this: those elements that were paralleled in the Vedic literature of India (such as the parallel figures of Indra-Vrtrahan and Verethraghna), or those that recall Inner Asian folklore?

However these questions are to be answered, one possibility deserves special mention, namely that of what one might call a "dualistic imperialism." This may be illustrated by considering the historical fate of the so-called earth diver, the mythical theme of a bird or animal that dives into the primordial sea in order to bring up some mud for the creator, who then spreads it on the surface of the waters to create the earth. This motif is widespread, being found in Inner Asia, eastern Europe, and North America. What is interesting is that it has dualistic implications only in the Old World, which seems particularly significant because other dualistic myths are far from rare in the New World. It may mean that the originally nondualistic motif of the diver was first given a dualistic interpretation in Asia, some time after versions of it had spread to North America. The reasons for such an insistence on a dualistic interpretation of the motif in Asia can only be guessed at, but once it had taken hold, it could have modified the earlier situation and led to the appropriation of themes previously extraneous to dualism. Thus one would have a kind of "dualistic imperialism" whose more peculiar manifestations would have appeared in Iran or at its borders. Such a hypothesis need not have anything to do with the theory that dualism as such originated in these regions.

Whereas it is still early to conclude that the earth-diver cosmogonic scenario can be seen as the core of a widespread "Eurasian dualism," various East European, Siberian, and Central Asian earth-diver cosmogonies display dualist elements in different stages of development and combination. It would be safe to assume that both internal factors (like inherited binary cosmogonies and the divine twins mythology) and external influences (in the Eurasian cases: Christian diabology, with its inherent dualist tendencies; as well as possible Zoroastrian and Manichaean influences in the central Asian cosmogonies) conditioned the overall general movement towards dualism, as the mythic scenario came to be reinterpreted and modified, particularly in Eurasia.

Traces of the earth-diver cosmogonic lore may be found in the cosmogonies of Islamic heterodox groups such as the

Alevi, the Yazīdīs, and the Ahl-i Haqq, but its dualist elements have been variously tamed. In most of the mature east European versions of the cosmogonic scenario, the two primordial beings are identified as God and Satan, and it is God who dispatches Satan to dive in the primal sea (whether in ornithomorphic form or not) upon which there follows the antagonism between the two figures. These east European dualist cosmogonic legends vary in detail, yet all of them emphasize the role of Satan as an original companion of God and a crucial vehicle for the creation of the material world.

Diffusion of dualism. It is now time to focus attention on other territories and cultures in which dualism, in forms different from those found in Inner Asia and North America, was once widespread. These territories extend from the border of the Achaemenid empire in the East to Sicily and Magna Graecia in the West. Here, Orphism and Pythagoreanism—both typical forms of dualism—took forms different from those found in Iran, Inner Asia, and North America. Rather than a supreme being opposed by a devilish or trickster-like demiurge, we find a form of anthropological dualism that is at the same time ontological and cosmological. The doctrines of *soma-sema* (body-tomb), *metensomatosis,* and purification from "previous sin" characterize this mysteriosophical, anthropological dualism, which is rooted in a metaphysics that opposes oneness and multiplicity in the context of an eternally recurring cycle. The term "mysteriosophical" is intended to refer to the tendency of Orphism and Pythagoreanism, and later Plato and Platonism, to adapt elements from the theology of the mystery religions to their own philosophies. The mystery religions themselves seem to have been free from the antisomatic attitudes typical to Orphism and Pythagoreanism.

The anticosmic and antisomatic doctrines of Greek mysteriosophy are comparable in some respects to the monistic-dualistic speculation found in the Indian Upaniṣads, some of which were roughly contemporary with the mysteriosophic currents of the West. Greek mysteriosophy no doubt contributed to the development of similar trends in the West— for example, in the form of Gnostic, Hermetic, Neoplatonic, and Neo-Pythagorean dualism, and in Gnostic antisomatism, which connected death with *eros* and *genesis* (birth) with *phthora* (corruption, death). Although Gnosticism, and in particular Christian Gnosticism, was undoubtedly heir to the eschatological setting of non-Gnostic Christianity, these objective historical and phenomenological connections with pagan mysteriosophy should not be overlooked.

Also not to be overlooked is the question of the influence of North Asian, northeast European, and Balkan forms of animism and shamanism on the development of dualism in the Mediterranean area, as well as in Iran and Central Asia. The problem of the relation between such non-Greek forms of animism and shamanism and some of the "irrational" aspects of Archaic and Classical Greek culture is well known. Although the issue is certainly of primary importance, it should not be forgotten that important differences separate the *metensomatosis* and asceticism of Orphism and Pythagoreanism from the animistic creeds and practices of northeast European shamanistic cultures. In particular, the ethical and ontological motivations of the Greek mysteriosophic traditions are conspicuously absent in such cultures. The same is true of those Balkan personages, such as Zalmoxis, who are connected in Thrace with practices and beliefs of "immortalization" that are different from the Orphic conception of death and reincarnation in the context of ethical and ontological purification. Nevertheless, these so-called barbarian elements may form an essential part of the history of European dualism.

The "Pythagorean" abstention from meat was also attributed to Zalmoxis. Moreover, for the celibate sect of the Ktistai, and also the pagan sect of the Pious Ones (Eusebeis) of Balkan antiquity, abstaining from meat (Strabo, *Geographia* 7.3.3.5) may recall some corresponding aspects of the medieval Balkan sect of the Bogomils, founded by a priest named Bogomil ("he who prays to God," or perhaps "he who loves God"). The dualistic folklore of the Balkans and eastern Europe, as well as the more or less dualistic apocrypha popular there, are also a part of this history. These oral and literary instances are particularly interesting in that they may show the influence of Gnostic motifs drawn from literary texts and oral legends originating in the East. Generally speaking, one can say that "Oriental" dualism—derived from both literary and oral traditions and characterized by the opposition of a creator and an inferior demiurge (the lower god of Gnosticism, or the demiurge-trickster of ethnology and folklore)—was influential in those Balkan and eastern European regions where dualistic trends were already in evidence. The di-theism of those imported mythologies may have been prepared for by indigenous conceptions of a duality of gods, such as the white god and the black god mentioned by a medieval—and not authoritative—text: Helmold's *Chronica Slavorum* (twelfth century).

DUALIST DENOMINATIONS AND TENDENCIES IN JUDAISM, CHRISTIANITY, AND ISLAM. The ostensibly contradictory views of early Zoroastrianism as "dualist monotheism" or "monotheistic dualism" (and the related debates on whether Zurvanism should be considered a "heretical" monistic deviation from dualist Zoroastrianism or just its triadic version) have been continuously challenged and redefined against the background of the monotheistic worlds of Judaism, Christianity, and Islam. Concerning early Zoroastrianism, the main debates have been focused on whether Angra Mainyu can be regarded as proceeding from Ahura Mazda or as a likewise uncreated being who is directly opposed to him, as well as on whether Angra Mainyu should be considered evil by nature or by choice.

Dualism in Judaism. To a great extent these debates have been provoked by the various chronological problems posed by nature of the primary sources for Zoroastrianism and the difficulties in separating the early stages of Zoroastrian thought from later sources. These problems have also affected the study of the religious interchange between ancient Iran and Israel and the emergence of dualist tendencies in postexilic Judaism. Previously focused on the development of Jewish angelology and demonology and the emerging notion of Satan as the personification of cosmic evil opposed to God and humanity in the intertestamental period, the arguments for Zoroastrian influence on postexilic Jewish thought received a fresh impetus with the discovery and publication of the Dead Sea Scrolls, among which documents like the *Community Rule* and the *War Rule* offered explicit dualist proclivities and terminology. This was coupled with the related expansion of research into the intertestamental Enochic apocalyptic tradition with its generative, novel, and dualistically-oriented notion of the superhuman origin of evil caused by the sinful descent of the fallen angels—the Watchers—in the early section of the apocalyptic corpus of *1 Enoch, The Book of the Watchers.*

Although Qumran cosmic dualism ("cosmic" as in Charlesworth's scheme above) remains a dualism under one God who determines the dualistic structure, a number of studies have sought a Zoroastrian or Zurvanite pedigree for the Qumran teachings of the "Two Ways" and the "Two Spirits" and the temporal and eschatological dimension of the "war dualism" in the *War Rule.* As Qumran thought presents varied dualist traits with a complex evolution, such arguments for a certain outside dualist impact on them need to be balanced by a proper analysis of their links with late sapiential theology (with its "embryonic" ethical dualism and the related dual classification of the creation into pairs of opposites and antitheses) and the cosmic antagonism of opposed supernatural powers in intertestamental pseudepigrapha such as the *Aramaic Testament of Levi, The Book of Jubilees,* and the Enochic apocalyptic works.

Rabbinic Judaism. Following the destruction of the Second Temple in 70 CE, rabbinic Judaism tended to counterbalance the dualist trends developed in apocalyptic Judaism, although it retained elements of the impact of Platonic soul-body dualism on Jewish thought in the Hellenistic period (on figures such as Philo). Rabbinic texts from the second century CE warn against the heresy of the "Two Heavenly Powers" linked to speculations about the exalted status of an angel or vice-regent of the Lord that may have been related to nascent Gnostic thought.

In rabbinic Judaism the figure of Satan and the myth of the downfall of the angels lost much of the intensity and the dualist traits that had marked some earlier Jewish apocalyptic trends, although the aggadic tradition preserved and elaborated various stories about Satan (Samael) and the evil spirits. Otherwise, in rabbinic theory Satan was linked to the evil inclination within man (*yetser ha-ra*) which was opposed to the good inclination (*yetser ha-tov*). Dualistic tendencies were retained, however, in the Jewish Merkabah (Divine Chariot) and later Hekhalot traditions, especially in the speculations surrounding the status and functions of the highest of the archangels and God's vice-regent, Metatron, as the "Lesser Yahweh."

More explicit dualist tendencies reappear in Judaism from the twelfth century onwards in early Qabbalistic traditions (along with other parallels to Gnostic notions from late antiquity which have not been historically explained), particularly those concerned with the problem of evil and positing the existence of another, parallel world of a *sitra' ahra,* waging a constant war with the "side of holiness"(in contrast with the non- and often antidualist theodicy in contemporary Jewish philsosophy). These dualist tendencies were magnified in the later Lurianic Qabbalah of Isaac Luria (1534–1572), with the elaboration of its fundamental doctrines of the divine *tsimtsum* (contraction), the breakup of the spiritual vessels and the discharge of the demonic *kelippot* (shells) in creation.

Dualism in early early Christianity and gnosticism. In early Christianity some of the concepts of Satan and his opposition to God and man—developed in postexilic and particularly apocalyptic Judaism—were accepted with all their ambiguities and potential for radical new developments. Early Christianity retained a tension between its monotheistic theology and the dualist implications of its evolving diabology and the evident spirit-flesh opposition in the New Testament. The inherited heavenly antagonism between Michael and Satan was reflected in Revelation; there are definite dualist traits in John and Paul where the Devil is the "god of this world," with his imperium embracing not only the evil spirits and wicked men but also "this age" (*Aion*) and this world (*kosmos*)—he was the "Prince of this World" and "the whole world . . . lies in the power of the evil one" (*1 Jn* 5:19), although his prevalence in the world has been broken with Christ's advent. In early Christian thought, the Devil was the personification and source of evil and death—an angel—who has fallen, through his pride and free will, to lead the hosts of evil against the "Kingdom of God" and Christ. At this time the Enochic story of the downfall of the angels was still popular and known among the Church Fathers. As well, the Church Fathers also had to defend the orthodox Christian tenets of evil as privation of good and Godness against the more radical, dualist solutions of the origin of evil advanced in the contemporary Gnostic schools of the second and third centuries.

Despite the evident dualism of spirit and flesh in early Christianity, the world was viewed as a creation of the benevolent God-Creator and was not evil by nature. Conversely, the multifarious Gnostic schools did share, on the whole, an anti-cosmic dualism—the material world was negated as an imperfect and evil creation of an inferior demiurgic, or clearly "Satanic" power, and was opposed to the supernal spiritual world of the true but remote and unknown God. The Gnostic schools drew widely on the syncretistic heritage of antiquity to embellish their basic dualist myths and concepts related to the creation of the world by the demiurge, the fall of the soul, the missions of the redeemer and revealer of the *gno-*

sis, and finally the release and ascent of the soul to its spiritual abode. Gnosticism shared its preoccupation with the divine knowledge, *gnosis*, the soul's search for its divine origin, and its final salvation with another religio-spiritualist current whose teachings crystallized in the early Christian era, Hermeticism, which also presented some dualist traits—yet there were also important differences between the two movements in the spheres of theology, cosmology, and anthropology.

Gnostic groups, moreover, adopted and further elaborated esoteric traditions current in early Christianity and Jewish Christianity that were believed to have been transmitted both orally in apostolic times and through apocryphal (understood as "hidden") texts. Whereas the classification and provenance of the various Gnostic schools (Christian and non-Christian Gnosticism, for example) continues to provoke debates and conflicting theories, a general distinction between Gnostic radical dualism of the two primal principles (as in Manichaeism) and Gnostic moderate dualism (Valentinianism and Sethian Gnosticism) has found a wider acceptance. Gnostic groups—and particularly Manichaeism—retained the use of pseudepigraphy, and the Manichaeans continued to resort to the composition and compilation of new apocrypha in their later history.

After the collapse of the Manichaean westward mission, and amid the intense persecution during the early reign of Justinian the Great (527–65), Manichaeism remained mostly confined to Asia, where it survived as a separate religion until the end of the Middle Ages. Following the widespread dissemination of manifold Gnostic and dualist teachings during late antiquity, traces and actual transmitters of Gnostic and dualist traditions in the early Middle Ages become increasingly difficult to discern and identify. In the Near East, such teachings enjoyed an uninterrupted historical maintenance within the still-existing small religious group of the Mandaeans in southern Iraq and Khuzistan in Iran, rightly considered the last survivors of the great Gnostic movements of late antiquity.

Medieval forms of Christian dualism. In the early Middle Ages, traces and elements of Gnostic and dualist teachings in varying degrees of intensity were also preserved in various apocryphal works from late antiquity that, despite being banned, were preserved, maintaining their circulation mainly in the eastern Christian world in heterodox, sectarian, or simply learned circles. Under the right circumstances these Gnostic or dualist residues in apocryphal works could effect a revival of related attitudes through simple borrowing of their themes, or through creative interpretation spreading from these works to the canonical scriptures, complete with all of the possibilities for the formulation of new heterodoxies and heresies. A number of such apocryphal texts were preserved in Byzantium, where the process of the creation of new apocrypha, like apocalyptic revelations about the course of world history, continued throughout the early Middle Ages.

The first important early medieval version of Christian dualism was formulated by the Paulicians who emerged in the complicated world of early medieval Armenia. Whereas Paulician radical dualism has been often traced in the past to Manichaean, Gnostic, or Marcionite influences, it seems more plausible that Paulicianism developed its dualist version of Christianity through a spiritualist and allegorical reading of the New Testament, its dualist element being influenced directly or indirectly by the various dualist residues still active in the religious scene of late antique and early medieval Armenia, ranging from Zoroastrian to Gnostic survivals. The Paulicians entered Byzantium around the mid-seventh century, and in 759 entered the Balkans for the first time to establish a long-lasting presence in Thrace, continuing to play a frequently important role in the development of Balkan-Byzantine—and consequently medieval European Christian—dualism.

The history of medieval Christian dualism entered a new, crucial stage with the emergence of the Bogomil heresy in the first half of the tenth century in the newly Christianized Bulgarian kingdom. The origins of Bogomilism are surrounded by many riddles, but it is now apparent that whereas the antisomatic and anticosmic aspects of Bogomil dualism should be explored in the wider context of Byzantine heresy, heterodoxy, and alternative demonology, there are strong parallels between the main Bogomil theological formulas and diabology, on the one hand, and apocryphal traditions, preserved in a number of apocryphal works, and which were translated and disseminated in the Slavonic Orthodox world around the time of the formation and spread of Bogomilism, on the other.

Given this wide-ranging translation and diffusion of apocryphal texts in the initial phases of the development of Slavo-Byzantine culture, it seems not so surprising that the formulation of the Bogomil new version of Christian dualism was strongly stimulated by the influx of teachings, themes, and notions rediscovered in the newly translated apocryphal works from late antiquity. The expansion of the Bogomil mission, both eastwards in Byzantium, and westwards, stimulated the diffusion of the Christian dualist tradition in western Europe in the twelfth and thirteenth centuries and reached its culmination in the growth of an organized Cathar movement in northern Italy and southern France (contemporary Catholic accounts often refer to the crucial impact of Balkan-Byzantine dualism on its formation). Modern theories may differ in their estimation of the chronology and the scale of Bogomil influence on original Catharism, but invariably confirm its vital role in providing a new dualist framework for western heretical and heterodox currents. Bogomil and Cathar dualism had a strongly anticosmic, antisomatic, and eschatological character.

Original Bogomil dualism had a monarchian nature that clearly contrasted with the mature Paulician radical dualist dogma of the two principles: the evil creator of this world and the good Lord of the world to come. By the last three decades of the twelfth century, however, both Bogomil and Cathar dualism divided into two strands, a monarchian and a radical trend, which advanced different versions of Christian dualism. Generally, according to the first, monarchian strand, there was one sublime God, Father of All, yet the material universe was created and ruled by his rebellious firstborn, Satan or Lucifer, the Lord of the Old Testament. The one sublime God's younger son, Jesus Christ, was sent in a semblance of the human body to "save that was lost" during the satanic reign through his baptism in the Holy Spirit and with fire (*Lk.* 19:10). Generally, the radical branch of Bogomil and Cathar dualism taught that Satan-Lucifer was a son of an eternal evil god whose attack on the heaven of the good God caused the fall of the angels, and that the mission of Christ was to redeem angelic souls from their imprisonment in human bodies.

Both versions of Bogomil-Cathar dualism present a number of differences from the variants of theological dualism and related teachings professed by earlier antiecclesiastical and heretical movements such as Manichaeism and Paulicianism. To a considerable extent, this is due to the Bogomil-Cathar indebtedness to earlier apocryphal and apocalyptic traditions and their predilection for the elaboration of new vivid mythic stories in support of their dualist doctrines. This practice presents a telling parallel to Gnosticism, in which the creation of Gnostic secret dualist myths was, as pointed out by Guy Stroumsa in his *Hidden Wisdom* (1996), a crucial part of the process of a "self-conscious re-mythologization" by the Gnostic theorists. In both cases this re-mythologization and creation of a dualist mythology was accomplished through a determined inverse exegesis of the normative scriptures to produce alternative and striking accounts of cosmogony, fall, and salvation of the soul. Whereas the campaigns of the Inquisition, the rise of spiritual currents in Catholicism, and the work of the Mendicant orders all effected the eclipse of Catharism in the early thirteenth century, reports of Bogomil activities in the eastern Christendom discontinue only in the early fifteenth century, amid the spread of new syncretistic and sectarian movements in the early Ottoman era.

Dualism in Islam. Although the diabology and cosmology of the Qur'ān and early normative Islam was notably strictly monotheistic and antidualistic, veiled or explicit dualist tendencies eventually appeared in Islamic mystical and *ghulāt* (heterodox) traditions, as Islam expanded and encountered a multitude of other religious traditions. Still, one needs to distinguish the definite dualistic traits in such traditions from the heightened use of dualities and polarities, as in the system of ninth-century mystic al-Hakim al-Tirmidhi or the use of Zoroastrian themes and imagery in al-Sohrawardi's thought; one needs also to be extremely cautious regarding the antidualist polemical clichés of Sunnī heresiologists who could attack the Ismāʿīlīs as followers of dualist Manichaeism. In this context the appearance of gnostic-like and dualist traits in the syncretistic and revelatory *Umm al-kitāb* and in the pre-Fatimid early Ismāʿīlī cosmological tract of Abū ʿĪsā al-Murshid deserve greater attention and study which can indicate whether their revival of dualist and gnostic tendencies is the outcome of an assimilation of Neoplatonic and related traditions from late antiquity or novel religious syntheses in Islamic garb. Likewise, the dualist tendencies in the cosmology and diabology of Islamic heterodox communities such as the Alevi, the Yazīdīs and the Ahl-i Haq need to be considered in the context of their conglomerate-like belief systems in which the later and locally-adopted elements need to be differentiated from the more archaic components of their beliefs which include versions of the ancient and dualistically-oriented earth diver cosmogonic scenario.

In the case of the Yazīdīs and the Ahl-i Haqq the archaic layer of beliefs includes pre-Islamic Iranian traditions, both Zoroastrian and pre-Zoroastrian. In the case of the Alevi, any search or claims for influences of the Balkan and Anatolian Christian dualist sectarians on their teachings and practices of Alevism should consider first the arguments for traces of a Manichaean impact on Alevi traditions, again arguably traceable to the pre-Islamic exposure of some Central Asian Turkic groups, most famously the Uighurs, to Manichaeism. And when one considers the greater problem of dualism vis-à-vis Islam, one should take into account that when even these Islamic heterodox traditions have inherited a cosmogonic tradition with strong dualist leanings like the earth-diver one, they generally tended to minimise its dualist potential (without neutralising it altogether) in contrast to the hardening of the dualist elements in the Christian heterodox and popular cosmogonies based on the same cosmogonic scenario.

Plutarch's View. Some of the more important historical and systematic forms of dualism as found in different religious contexts have been considered in this entry. Consider briefly, now, a type of dualistic thought that, far from being limited to the expression of a particular creed, was a key to the interpretation of different religious systems and of religion in itself. This type of dualistic thought is exemplified in Plutarch's treatise *Isis and Osiris.* The aim of the philosopher and theologian of Chaeronea is to show, on the basis of Platonic or Middle Platonic hermeneutics, that dualism, as the idea of two opposing forces manifesting themselves in the universe, is a notion common to most of the religions of his time.

In the course of developing his thesis, Plutarch provides precious information concerning the Persian, Mesopotamian, and especially the Egyptian religions. The information he gives concerning the Osiris-Seth opposition in Egypt is the sole ancient literary document containing a complete form of that basic myth. His interpretation of the different characters of the myth and of the different forms of relationship that link them together is clearly Platonic and heavily speculative. He goes so far as to introduce different kinds of opposition: a hostile opposition between Osiris/Horus and

Seth, and an opposition of cooperation and transcendence between Osiris and Isis, a married couple. Osiris is interpreted as the ideal world, or the transcendent model that informs matter; that is, Isis, the female, is the nourishing agency of all beings in the visible world.

It is important to note that Plutarchian hermeneutics synthesizes these two different kinds of dualistic opposition into a unitary structure. As a result, in Plutarch's interpretation, Isis does not totally eliminate the evil figure of Seth from the world after the victory of Horus over him. Despite his inborn malignity, Seth is clearly conceived of as a presence necessary for the equilibrium of the world. Thus, despite his acceptance of the Platonic notion expressed in *Theaetetus* 176ab that evil is intrinsic to the lower world, Plutarch's speculative Platonism actually goes beyond Plato. Plato had never managed to unite the two different forms of dualism found in the *Laws* (the two opposing souls of the universe, one good and one bad) and in the *Timaeus* (the invisible and the visible as necessary constituents of being).

Would it be too much to suspect that Plutarch, though aided by the use of Platonic speculation, did not himself purely invent this complex, yet unitary, "Egyptian" structure? Egyptian documentation lends support to the idea that Seth, god of deficiency, sterility, and loneliness, god of the desert and of hostile countries, was explicitly acknowledged as a constituent element of the Egyptian pantheon and universe. He has, for instance, a positive role in the daily struggle against the serpent Apophis, the enemy of the sun. That is not all. Recent studies of the Egyptian Seth have demonstrated that he possesses traits characteristic of a trickster. Moreover, the comparative study of the Egyptian mythology of Seth and that of Yurugu (Ogo) among the Dogon of West Africa has shown considerable structural affinities between the two. In the Dogon myths, Yurugu is a sterile, lonely, adversarial character; yet at the same time he is an indispensable element in the universe. He is furthermore a trickster; he is "pale fox" (the name refers to *Vulpes pallida,* an African fox).

It is remarkable, having made peregrinations among the many forms of dualism, to come across something reminiscent of that pedantic, aggressive, unhappy, and inescapable dualistic figure, the demiurge-trickster (Raven, Coyote, and others) typical of a number of preliterate mythologies. Could this mean that, far from being a protest against monotheism, a protest intended as an option in favor of the innocence of God over his omnipotence, dualism may be interpreted (in at least some of its forms) as rather an insufficient actualization of God's omnipotence? And that the most extreme and irreconcilable form of dualism—namely dialectical dualism, both in its quietistic and combative forms—was fated to present monotheism with its most radical challenge? This can be seen also in the dialectics of Hegel, Nietzsche, Marx, and Freud, all of which are samples of "dualism" in the modern world.

See Also Demiurge; Gnosticism; Manichaeism; Orpheus; Plato; Tricksters; Twins; Zoroastrianism.

Bibliography

Armstrong, A. H., "Dualism: Platonic, Gnostic, and Christian." In *Neoplatonism and Gnosticism,* edited by Richard T. Wallis, pp. 33–55. New York, 1992.

Bayle, Pierre. *Dictionnaire historique et critique.* 2d ed. Paris, 1702.

Besch, Bernt. *Der Dualismus in der Kermsehriften von Pumren.* Rome, 1996.

Bianchi, Ugo. *Il dualismo religioso: Saggio storico ed etnologico.* Rome, 1958; 2d ed., 1983. A seminal, broad exposition of the problems concerning the forms and the diffusion of dualism in the nonliterate and literate religions.

Bianchi, Ugo *Selected Essays on Gnosticism, Dualism and Mysteriosophy.* Leiden, 1978. Contains some of Bianchi's most important studies of religious dualism.

Bianchi, Ugo. "Tipologie stoica delle religioni e comparazione: il easo del dualismo." *Annals of the Lergiu* Al-George Institute 6-8 (1997-1999): pp. 7-16.

Bianchi, Ugo, ed. *Le origini dello gnosticismo.* Leiden, 1967.

Boyce, Mary. *A History of Zoroastrianism.* 3 vols. (vol. 2 with F. Grenet). Leiden, Netherlands, 1975–1991. A thorough, vigorous and often polemical survey of the Zoroastrian history from its origins to Late Antiquity with important discussions of Zoroastrian encounters and interchange with other religious traditions.

Casadio, Giovanni and Guy G. Stroumsa. "Dualismus." In *Religion in Geschichte und Gegenwart,* edited by Hans Dieter Betz et al., vol. 2, pp. 1004–1006. Tübingen, Germany, 1999.

Charlesworth, James H. "A Critical Comparison of the Dualism in 1QS 3:13–4.26 and the Dualism' contained in the Gospel of John." *New Testament Studies* 15 (1968/69): 389–418.

Coulianu, Ioan Petru. *The Tree of Gnosis: Gnostic Mythology from Early Christianity to Modern Nihilism.* San Francisco, 1992. Coulianu's survey of the transmission and repeated resurrection of Gnostic religiosity and spirituality from antiquity through the Middle Ages to the modern period frequently challenges accepted notions about the nature and varieties of Gnostic (and Neo-Gnostic) dualism.

Dähnhardt, Oscar. *Natursagen, Eine Sammlung Naturdeutender Sagen, Märchen, Fabeln und Legende 1: Sagen zum Alten Testament.* Leipzig and Berlin, 1907. Contains valuable material related to popular East European and Asian cosmogonies with strong dualist elements, particularly the so-called earth-diver cosmogonic lore.

Duchesne-Guillemin, Jacques. *The Western Response to Zoroaster.* Oxford, 1958.

Duchesne-Guillemin, Jacques. *La religion de l'Iran ancien.* Paris, 1962. A comparative perspective on Iranian dualism.

Duhaime, J. "Dualist Reworking in the Scrolls from Qumran." *Catholic Biblical Quarterly* 49 (1987): 32–56.

Durkheim Emile and Marcel Mauss. "De quelques formes primitives de classification." *Année sociologique* 6 (1903):1–72.The paradigmatic study of the sociological approach to the phenomena of duality, dual social organization and dual symbolic classification.

Duvernoy, Jean *Le Catharisme I: La Religion des Cathares.* Toulouse, France, 1976.

Eliade, Mircea. "Prolegomenon to Religious Dualism." In *The Quest: History and Meaning in Religion.* Chicago, 1969. This essay challenges some of the prevalent sociological and anthropological approaches to dualism to propose a comparative analysis of the phenomenon in literate and nonliterate cultures using the hermeneutic approach of the history of religions.

Eliade, Mircea. *De Zalmoxis à Gengis-Khan.* Paris, 1970. Chapter 3 contains an important comparative study of the so-called "earth-diver" cosmogonies a number of which present marked dualist features.

Eucken, Rudolf. "Dualism." In *Encyclopedia of Religion and Ethics,* edited by James Hastings, vol. 5. pp. 99–101. Edinburgh, 1912.

Fontaine, P. F. M. *The Light and the Dark: A Cultural History of Dualism.* 18 vols. Amsterdam, 1986–2003. Fontaine bases his typology on Bianchi's scheme but uses a much broader definition of the term "dualism" (unsolvable or unbridgeable opposition between concepts, principles or groups of people) and applies it to a variety of religious, cultural, political, and social phenomena in antiquity and the Middle Ages such as dualism in ancient Greek social and political history, Roman "imperialistic dualism," interior politics and social life, Byzantine hooliganism, medieval imperialism, etc.—a commendable effort but with a neglible use of the available anthropological and sociological work and theory on dual symbolic classification and dual social organization.

Frey, Jörg. "Different Patterns of Dualistic Thought in the Qumran Library: Reflections on their Background and History." In *Legal Texts and Legal Issues: Proceedings of the Second Meeting of the International Organization for Qumran Studies, Cambridge, 1995, Published in Honour of J. M. Baumgarten,* edited by M. Berstein et al., pp. 275–337. Leiden, 1997.

Gamie, J. G. "Spatial and Ethical Dualism in Jewish Wisdom and Apocalyptic Literature." *Journal of Biblical Literature* 93 (1974): 356–85.

Granet, Marcel. *La Pensée chinoise.* Paris, 1950. Incorporates analysis of the dual classification by *ying* and *yang* in Chinese thought.

Griaule, Marcel, and Germaine Dieterlen. *Le renard pâle,* vol. 1. Paris, 1965.

Halm, H. *Die islamische Gnosis. Die extreme Schia und die Alawiten.* Zurich, 1982.

Hamilton, Janet, and Bernard Hamilton eds. *Christian Dualist Heresies in the Byzantine world c. 650–c.1450,* translations of Old Slavonic texts by Yuri Stoyanov. Manchester, U.K., 1998.

Hyde, Thomas. *Historia religionis veterum Persarum eorumque Magorum.* Oxford, 1700.

Insler, S., trans. *The Gathas of Zarathustra.* Leiden and Téhéran, 1975.

Ivanov, V. V., and V. N. Toporov. *Slavianskie iazykovye modeliruiushchie semioticheskie sistemy.* Moscow, 1965.

Ivanov, V. V. *Issledovaniia v oblasti slavianskikh drevnostei.* Moscow, 1974. One of the major and most representative works of the Russian scholarship investigating duality and dual symbolic classification, applying often an innovative methodology.

Ivanow, W. *The Truth-Worshippers of Kurdistan: Ahl-i Haqq texts.* Leiden, Netherlands, 1953.

Jonas, Hans. *The Gnostic Religion: The Message of the Alien God and Beginnings of Christianity.* Boston, 1958; 2d ed., rev.& enl. 1963. Jonas's seminal study of the nature and types of Gnostic dualism, defined as "anticosmic and eschatological in character; on the basis of the specific dualist features of the Gnostic schools Jonas distinguished between Syrian-Egyptian and Iranian types of Gnosticism."

Kehl-Bodrogi, K. *Die Kizilbaş/Aleviten: Untersuchungen über eine esoterische Glaubensgemeinschaft in Anatolien.* 1988.

Kehl-Bodrogi, K. (ed.) *Syncretistic Religious Communities in the Near East.* Leiden, Netherlands, 1997.

Kreyenbroek, P. *Yezidism: Its Background, Observances and Textual Tradition.* Lewiston, N.Y., 1995.

Lambert, Malcolm. *The Cathars.* Oxford and Malden, Mass., 1998.

Lévi-Strauss, Claude. *Le Structures élémentaires de la parenté.* Paris, 1949.

Lévi-Strauss, Claude. *Anthropologie structurale.* Paris, 1958.

Maybury-Lewis, David, and Uri Almagor, eds. *The Attraction of Opposites: Thought and Society in the Dualistic Mode.* Ann Arbor, Mich., 1989. The volume contains important contributions to the study of dual symbolic classification, offering some significant reassessments of earlier approaches to and interpretations of the phenomenon.

Mélikoff, I. *Sur le traces du soufisme turc. Recherches sur l'Islam populaire en Anatolie.* Istanbul, 1992.

Moosa, M. *Extremist Shiites: The Ghulat Sects.* Syracuse, N.Y., 1987.

Needham, Rodney. *Symbolic Classification.* Santa Monica, Calif., 1979. This book demonstrates Needham's influential approach to the phenomena of duality and dual symbolic classification.

Needham, Rodney, ed. *Right and Left: Essays on Dual Symbolic Classification.* London, 1973

Numazawa, Franz Kiichi. *Die Weltanfänge in der japanischen Mythologie.* Fribourg, 1946. A comparative analysis of the Chinese *yin-yang* ideology.

Pagels, Elaine. *The Origins of Satan.* New York, 1995. An exploration of the legacy of Jewish apocalyptic satanology and vision of the cosmic struggle, involving the split of society into two opposing forces, in the early Christian tradition, focusing mainly on the social implications of the figure of Satan.

Pétrement, Simone. *Le dualisme dans l'histoire de la philosophie et des religion.* Paris, 1946.

Pétrement, Simone. *Le dualisme chez Platon, les gnostiques et les manichéens.* Paris, 1947. Pétrement's approach to the history and phenomenology of religious dualism differs somewhat from that of Bianchi and Eliade and she furnishes further her own version of dualist typology

Pétrement, Simone. *Le Dieu separé.* Paris. 1984. Pétrement endeavours to redefine Gnostic theology as not dualistic in a strict sense but a rigorous accentuation of transcendence indebted to dualist tendencies in John and Paul.

Reitzenstein, Richard *Die Vorgeschichte der chtistlichen Taufe.* Leipzig and Berlin, 1929.

Rottenwöhrer, Gerhard, *Der Katharismus,* 4 vols., Bad Honnef, Germany, 1982–1993.

Schmidt, Wilhelm. *Der Ursprung der Gottesidee.* Vols. 9–12. Münster, Germany, 1948–1955. Comprises important East European and Asian popular cosmogonic traditions of the dualist-oriented earth-diver versions.

Shaked, Shaul. *Dualism in Transformation: Varieties of Religion in Sasanian Iran.* London, 1994. A lucid survey of the transformations of Zoroastrian dualism in Sasanian Iran, making a full and often pioneering use of the extant sources.

Stein, Ludwig. *Dualismus oder Monismus. Eine Untersuchung über die doppelte Wahrheit.* Berlin, 1909. Stein argues that monism and dualism are intimately related not in terms of opposition but as a contrasted pair of notions.

Stoyanov, Yuri. *The Other God. Dualist Religions from Antiquity to the Cathar Heresy.* New York and London, 2000. An up-to-date, broad survey of dualist religions and currents from the ancient Middle East to medieval Europe, with a particular focus on medieval Christian dualist heresies.

Strabo. *The Geography of Strabo,* edited by H. J. Jones. London, 8 vols., 1917–1932.

Stroumsa, Guy. G. *Hidden Wisdom: Esoteric Traditions and the Roots of Christian Mysticism.* Leiden, 1996.

Weber, Max. *Soziologie, weltgeschichtliche Analysen, Politik,* edited by Johannes Winckelmann. Stuttgart, Germany, 1956.

Widengren, Geo. "Der Iranische Hintergrund der Gnosis." *Zeitschrift für Religions und Geistesgeschichte* 4 (1952): 97–114.

Widengren, Geo, A. Hultgård, and M. Philonenko. *Apocalyptique iranienne et dualisme Qoumrânien.* Paris, 1995.

Wolffe, Christian. *Psychologia rationalis.* Frankfurt, Germany, 1734.

Zaehner, Robert C. *Zurvan: A Zoroastrian Dilemma.* Oxford, 1955.

Zolotarev, A. *Dual'naia organizatsiia pervobytnykh narodov i prozhozhdenie dualisticheskikh kosmogonii.* Moscow, 1964 (written 1941). One of the most thorough and well-researched works on the interrelations between dual social organization and the related religious and mythological/cosmological traditions in a number of cultures.

UGO BIANCHI (1987)
YURI STOYANOV (2005)

DU GUANGTING (850–933; adult style, Binsheng; epithet, Dongying zi; name in religion, Master Guangcheng) was born in the region of Chuzhou in Zhejiang. Around 870, after failing to obtain the civil service examination degree (*mingjing*) in the Confucian classics, Du underwent Daoist training and initiation at Mount Tiantai in Zhejiang. His master Ying Yijie (810–894) belonged to the Tiantai branch of the Shangqing lineage that descended via Xue Jichang (d. 759), a disciple of Sima Chengzhen (647–735). Soon after the accession of Emperor Xizong (r. 873–888), Du was summoned to court. He performed various functions as a Daoist prelate and official redactor at the capital Chang'an up to the outbreak of the Huang Chao rebellion (880–885). After the sack of the capital by the rebels in early 881, Du followed the court into exile in Chengdu (Sichuan). As a textual and liturgical scholar, Du deplored the loss of Daoist sacred books in the wake of the destruction of Chang'an and eventually reconstituted parts of the canon from temple libraries in Sichuan. Du announced the divine restoration of the Tang dynasty under the auspices of Lord Lao in his memorial *Lidai chongdao ji* (*Daozang* 593), which he presented to the emperor on the eve of the court's return to the capital in 885. When Xizong was once again obliged to flee Chang'an the following year, Du Guangting obtained permission to return to Sichuan.

Many of Du's works were written during the period of transition from the Tang (618–907) to the Five Dynasties (907–960), while he was a priest in the temple Yuju guan in Chengdu and a frequent visitor to nearby Mount Qingcheng. This phase in Du's career brought him into contact with the future emperor Wang Jian (847–918) and his local staff and allies, who were to proclaim the kingdom of Shu after the fall of the Tang in 907. Under the first two rulers of the independent Shu kingdom, Du resumed his earlier functions as court Daoist and official, reaching the rank of vice president of the board of finance (*hubu shilang*) in 916. Around the time of the fall of the Former Shu in 925, Du seems to have retired to Mount Qingcheng, where he died in 933.

Du Guangting was a prolific author. His lifelong mission to preserve and transmit works from the Daoist canon led Du to patronize the burgeoning printing industry in tenth-century Sichuan. Under the Song (960–1279), Du was recognized as the foremost patriarch of the Daoist liturgical tradition, handed down by Lu Xiujing (406–477) and Zhang Wanfu (fl. 711–713). His voluminous writings, compendia, and editions in this domain (see, for example, the "Liturgical Manual for the Yellow Register Retreat," *Taishang huanglu zhai yi* [*Daozang* 507]) are regarded as authoritative to this day. Du's contributions to philosophical and scriptural exegesis are epitomized in his massive annotation of the Tang imperial commentary on Laozi's "The Way and Its Power" (*Dao de zhenjing guangsheng yi* [*Daozang* 725]). Active in the religious and political arenas under three imperial governments, Du was a well-placed observer of a key period in Chinese history, which is now recognized as the transition from the medieval to the modern periods. Hundreds of his court and liturgical memorials document his activity at various social levels, from the emperor to the newly risen merchant class (see especially *Lidai chongdao ji* [*Daozang* 593] and the surviving seventeen-*juan* fragment of his collected works, the *Guangcheng ji* [*Daozang* 616]). His writings probe contemporary events from the perspective of an overarching, sacred history of Daoism that was intertwined with the destiny of imperial government. Du's narrative oeuvre, in particular, reveals a keen observation of the place of religion in a society undergoing the violent dislocations and upheavals of rebellion and civil war. Belonging ostensibly to the genre of Daoist hagiography—devoted to the lives of immortals and chronicles of sacred sites—his anecdotal histories are also akin to the imaginative literature known as "traditions of the supernatural" (*chuanqi*) that was popular in Tang times. Du Guangting authored or transmitted hundreds of tales of this genre, which he collected into separate books. With some overlap, these collections are organized around recognizable themes. For example, the "Evidential Miracles in Support of Daoism" (*Daojiao lingyan ji* [*Daozang* 590]) focuses on the interaction of the Buddhist and Daoist communities in late medieval society; the "Record of Marvels" (*Luyi ji* [*Daozang* 591]) on the cultural distinctiveness and sacred destiny of the Sichuan region; the "Encounters with Immortals" (*Shenxian ganyu zhuan* [*Daozang* 592]) on the Daoist theme of the supernatural encounter as revelation; and the "Record of the Assembled Immortals of Yongcheng" (*Yongcheng jixian lu* [*Daozang* 783]) on the legends of female immortals in the entourage of the Queen Mother of the West (Xi wang mu). Du's classification of these rich materials offers significant insights into the order of a medieval Daoist's mental universe. His works, despite many losses, constitute one of the richest testimonies to have come down from medieval China.

SEE ALSO Daoism, overview article.

BIBLIOGRAPHY

Cahill, Suzanne. *Transcendence and Divine Passion: The Queen Mother of the West in Medieval China.* Stanford, Calif., 1993. Based on the biography of the goddess in *Yongcheng jixian lu.*

Chavannes, Edouard. "Le jet des dragons." *Mémoires concernant l'Asie Orientale* 3 (1919): 53–220. See pages 172–213 for a translation of one of Du's ritual protocols.

Imaeda Jirō. "To Kōtei shōkō." In *Dōkyō kenkyū ronshū: Dōkyō no shisō to bunka,* edited by Yoshioka Hakushi kanreki kinen ronshū kankōkai, pp. 523–532. Tokyo, 1977.

Qing Xitai. "Du Guangting dui daojiao lilun di zongjie he fazhan." In *Zhongguo daojiao sixiang shigang,* vol. 2, pp. 653–678. Chengdu, People's Republic of China, 1985.

Verellen, Franciscus. *Du Guangting (850–933): Taoïste de cour à la fin de la Chine médiévale.* Paris, 1989. See also the following studies of Du's works: "'Evidential Miracles in Support of Taoism': The Inversion of a Buddhist Apologetic Tradition in Late T'ang China," *T'oung Pao* 78 (1992): 217–263 (*Daojiao lingyan ji*); "A Forgotten T'ang Restoration: The Taoist Dispensation after Huang Ch'ao," *Asia Major* 3d ser., 7, no. 1 (1994): 107–153 (*Lidai chongdao ji*); "Shu as a Hallowed Land: Du Guangting's *Record of Marvels,*" *Cahiers d'Extrême-Asie* 10 (1998): 213–254 (*Luyi ji*); and "Encounter as Revelation: A Taoist Hagiographic Theme in Medieval China," *Bulletin de l'École Française d'Extrême-Orient* 85 (1998): 363–384 (*Shenxian ganyu zhuan*).

Zheng Suchun. "Du Guangting." In *Zhongguo lidai sixiang jia,* vol. 8, edited by Wang Shounan and Hong Anquan, et al., pp. 330–370. Taipei, 1999.

FRANCISCUS VERELLEN (2005)

DUMÉZIL, GEORGES.

Georges Dumézil (1898–1986) was a French scholar who revolutionized the study of comparative mythology, especially comparative Indo-European mythology. In the early decades of the twentieth century, largely as a result of the eclipse of Max Müller's "solar mythology" (Dorson, 1955), the science of comparative mythology—especially comparative Indo-European mythology—reached a low ebb. However, the basic questions to which Müller and his adherents had addressed themselves—the curious thematic, if not in all cases etymological, parallels among a great many ancient Indo-European gods and heroes—remained unresolved. In the early 1920s a young French scholar named Georges Dumézil set out to find a viable framework in terms of which these questions might once again be approached.

Born in Paris on March 4, 1898, Dumézil attended the Lycée Louis-le-Grand and later the prestigious École Normale Supérieure. After serving as an artillery officer in 1917 and 1918, he returned to his studies at the University of Paris, where in 1924 he completed his doctoral thesis. Entitled *Le festin d'immortalité: Étude de mythologie comparée indo-européenne* (*The Feast of Immortality: A Study of Comparative Indo-European Mythology,* 1924), it marked the beginning of one of the twentieth century's most distinguished scholarly careers.

Dumézil's initial attempts (e.g., 1924, 1929) to develop a "new comparative mythology" were grounded in James G. Frazer's now largely discredited theory, first enunciated in the latter's masterwork, *The Golden Bough* (1890), that religion everywhere reflects an attempt to magically renew the world by periodically killing and replacing kings and other persons symbolic of divine beings. But the Frazerian model ultimately failed to provide the theoretical framework Dumézil was seeking. By 1938, however, he had made a major discovery and had begun to draw upon a wholly different theoretical base. The discovery was that the several ancient Indo-European-speaking communities, at least in their earliest periods, were characterized by a tripartite social class system that broadly resembled the three Aryan or "twice-born" castes of classical and later Indian society (i.e., Brāhmaṇa, Kṣatriyas, and Vaiśya). The new theoretical base was the sociology of Émile Durkheim and his followers, to which Dumézil was introduced by Marcel Granet. Although it is unfair to characterize Dumézil as a full-fledged Durkheimian (his fundamental training was in philology and the history of religions), he nevertheless came to adopt one of Durkheim's most famous maxims: that important social and cultural realities are inevitably "collectively represented" by supernatural beings and concepts (Durkheim, 1912).

In a remarkable series of books and articles written during the course of the next decade, Dumézil successfully combined his newly discovered evidence for tripartite social structures, Durkheimian sociology, and the traditional methods of comparative philology, and he arrived at a comprehensive model of the common Indo-European ideology—that is, the tripartite cognitive model in terms of which the ancient (and not so ancient) Indo-European speakers ordered their social and supernatural universes. The salient features, or functions, as Dumézil labeled them, of this ideology are as follows: (1) the maintenance of cosmic and juridical sovereignty; (2) the exercise of physical prowess; and (3) the promotion of physical well-being, fertility, wealth, and so on. At least some evidence of this cognitive model can be seen in every ancient Indo-European tradition, from Vedic India, whose three-fold caste system was collectively represented, respectively, by Varuṇa and Mitra (first function), Indra (second function), and the Aśvins, or Divine Horsemen (third function), to the Old Norse figures Týr and Odin, Thor, and Njord and Freyr, who reflect the same functional paradigm. Moreover, it soon became clear that the three functions are endlessly replicated in an extremely wide variety of cultural phenomena, including triads of epic heroes, threefold categories of diseases (and cures), and even tripartite conceptions of physical space.

At first glance, Dumézil's approach might appear similar to that of his longtime friend and colleague, Claude Lévi-Strauss. However, where Lévi-Strauss (e.g., 1963) is concerned with the universal structure of the human psyche, Dumézil's purview is limited to the Indo-European-speaking domain (Littleton, 1982, pp. 277–275), and he was the first to admit that non-Indo-European speakers, such as the Sino-Tibetans, the Hamito-Semites, the Uto-Aztecans, and the Bantu are constrained by wholly different cognitive models, predicated on other functional paradigms.

To be sure, Dumézil's theories and methods have not met with universal approval. Some critics suggest that on more than one occasion he imposed the tripartite model on data that are perhaps amenable to other interpretations (Littleton, 1982, pp. 186–202). Still others have claimed that he was a crypto-fascist (Momigliano, 1983 and Lincoln, 1991, pp. 231–267), an unfortunate accusation that has been laid to rest by Didier Eribon in *Faut-il brûler Dumézil?* (*Is it necessary to burn Dumézil?*, 1992). In addition, Nicholas Justin Allen (1987) has suggested that a "fourth function" exists outside of the tripartite paradigm and can be characterized as "other."

After spending several years teaching at the University of Istanbul (1925–1932) and a year as a lecturer at the University of Uppsala in Sweden (1932–1933), Dumézil returned to France and settled into a career at the University of Paris, punctuated by visiting professorships at other universities, including the University of Lima, Peru (1955), and the University of California at Los Angeles (1971). In 1948 he was appointed Professeur de Civilisation indo-européenne in the Collège de France, a position that was created for him, where he remained until his retirement in 1968. In 1979, in the autumn of his eightieth year, he was elected to the Académie française.

In 1925 Dumézil married the former Madeleine Legrand, a union that produced a son, Claude, and a daughter, Perrine (Curien). After suffering a massive heart attack, he passed away in Paris on October 11, 1986.

BIBLIOGRAPHY

Major Works by Georges Dumézil

Dumézil published over seventy-five books and several hundred articles, reviews, replies, etc. For more comprehensive bibliographies of Dumézil's publications, see Rivière (1979) and Littleton (1982).

Dumézil, Georges. *Le festin d'immortalité: Étude de mythologie comparée indo-européenne.* Paris, 1924. Dumézil's doctoral thesis.

Dumézil, Georges. *Mythes et dieux des Germains: Essai d'interprétation comparative.* Paris, 1939. This book contains Dumézil's first systematic articulation of the tripartite ideology.

Dumézil, Georges. *Jupiter-Maris-Quirinus I: Essai sur la conception indo-européenne de la société et sur les origins de Rome.* Paris, 1941.

Dumézil, Georges. *Les dieux des indo-européens.* Paris, 1952. This book contains a comprehensive overview of Dumézil's model at midcentury.

Dumézil, Georges. *Aspects de la fonction guerrière chez les indo-européens.* Paris, 1956. Translated by John Lindow, Alan Toth, Francis Charat, and Georges Gopen as *Gods of the Ancient Northmen* (Berkeley, Calif., 1973).

Dumézil, Georges. *L'idéologie tripartie des indo-européens.* Brussels, Belgium, 1958. This monograph remains the best single introduction to Dumézil's basic ideas.

Dumézil, Georges. *La religion romaine archaïque, avec un appendice sur la religion des Etrusques.* Paris, 1966. Translated by Philipp Krapp as *Archaic Roman Religion* (Chicago, 1970). Dumézil's "*bilan romain.*"

Dumézil, Georges. *Mythe et épopée I: L'idéologie des trois fonctions dans les épopées des peuples indo-européens.* Paris, 1968. The first volume of a magisterial series of books concerning how the tripartite ideology manifests itself in Indo-European epics.

Dumézil, Georges. *Heur et malheur du guerriére: Aspects mythiques de la fonction guerriére chez les indo-européens.* Paris, 1969. Translated by Alf Hiltebeitel as *The Destiny of the Warrior* (Chicago, 1970).

Dumézil, Georges. *Mythe et épopée II: Types épiques indo-européens: un héros, un sorcier, un roi.* Paris, 1971. Part 1 translated by Jaan Puhvel and David Weeks as *The Stakes of the Warrior* (Berkeley, Calif., 1983); Part 2 translated by Jaan Puhvel and David Weeks as *The Plight of a Sorcerer* (Berkeley, 1986); Part 3 translated by Alf Hiltebeitel as *The Destiny of a King* (Chicago, 1973).

Dumézil, Georges. *Mythe et épopée III: Histoires romaines.* Paris, 1973. Translated by Antoinette Aronowicz and Josette Bryson as *Camillus: A Study of Indo-European Religion as Roman History.* (Berkeley, Calif., 1980).

Other Works

Allen, Nicholas Justin. "The Ideology of the Indo-Europeans: Dumézil's Theory and the Idea of a Fourth Function." *International Journal of Moral and Social Studies* 2, no. 1 (1987): 23–39.

Dorson, Richard. "The Eclipse of Solar Mythology." In *Myth: A Symposium*, edited by Thomas A. Sebeok, pp. 15–38. Philadelphia, 1955.

Durkheim, Émile. *Les formes élémentaires de la vie religeuse.* Paris, 1912. Translated by Joseph Ward as Swain as *The Elementary Forms of the Religious Life* (New York, 1961).

Eribon, Didier. *Entretiens avec Georges Dumézil.* Paris, 1987. These "conversations," which the author recorded a few months before Dumézil died in 1986, are the closest the French mythologist ever came to writing a memoir.

Eribon, Didier. *Faut-il brûler Dumézil?* Paris, 1992. The definitive answer to Momigliano, Lincoln, and others who have accused Dumézil of being a "crypto-fascist."

Frazer, Sir James G. *The Golden Bough* (abridged edition). New York, 1922.

Granet, Marcel. *La civilization chinoise.* Paris, 1929. Translated by Kathleen E. Innes and Mabel R. Brailsford as *Chinese Civilization* (New York, 1930). It was Granet who introduced Dumézil to the Durkheimian approach to religion.

Lévi-Strauss, Claude. *Anthropologie structurale.* Paris, 1958. Translated by M. Layton as *Structural Anthropology* (New York, 1963).

Lincoln, Bruce. "Shaping the Past and the Future." *Times Literary Supplement* (London), October 3 (1986): 1107–1108. Review of Georges Dumézil's *L'oublie de l'homme et l'honneur des dieux.*

Littleton, C. Scott. *The New Comparative Mythology: An Anthropological Assessment of the Theories of Georges Dumézil.* 3d edition. Berkeley, Calif., 1982.

Littleton, C. Scott. "Gods, Myths and Structures: Dumézil." In *Encyclopedia of Continental Philosophy*, edited by Simon Glendinning, pp. 558–568. Edinburgh, UK, 1999.

Miller, Dean A. *The Epic Hero.* Baltimore, Md., 2000. An important assessment of the role of the hero in the several ancient Indo-European epics; reflects current thinking about the nature and symbolism of the "second function."

Momigliano, Arnaldo. "Permesse per una discussione su Georges Dumézil." *Opus* 2 (1983): 329–341. The first scholar to accuse Dumézil of harboring fascist beliefs.

Strutynski, Udo. "Introduction." In *Camillus: A Study of Indo-European Religion as History* by Georges Dumézil, edited by Udo Strutynski, pp. 1–39. Berkeley, Calif., 1980. A succinct overview of Dumézil's contributions to Roman religion.

Wikander, Stig. *Der arische Männerbund.* Lund, Sweden, 1938. The late Stig Wikander was Dumézil's earliest disciple. This book had a profound impact on the evolution of his ideas, especially as they relate to the "second function"; that is, the Indo-European warrior ideology.

C. SCOTT LITTLETON (2005)

DUMUZI. The god Dumuzi (Akkadian: Tammuz) appears very early in the cuneiform documentation, and an echo of him is still present today, since the month of July in Middle Eastern calendars bears his name. In the history of cuneiform Mesopotamian literatures, the tradition on the god is discontinuous. From the Old-Babylonian period (the twentieth through the sixteenth century BCE), nonhomogeneous songs about the god and the goddess Inanna have been found. Thorkild Jacobsen (1976, pp. 23–73) gathered them into a single plot, segmented in four sections:

1. courtship songs
2. wedding songs
3. death and lament songs
4. search and return songs

There is no evidence to ascribe the search and return songs to the god's return from the netherworld, so it must be removed from Jacobsen's otherwise valid reconstruction. The first two sections are clearly connected to that type of *hieros gamos* in which the king, playing the role of Dumuzi, married the goddess Inanna. It is not known how this rite was actually celebrated, but direct evidence of its historical performance is available, since kings of the Third Dynasty of Ur and of the Dynasties of Isin and Larsa (from the twenty-first through the eighteenth century BCE) explicitly declare in their texts that they married the goddess Inanna (in particular, two of them, Shulgi and Iddin-Dagan, left celebrative hymns on regard). The king's personification of Dumuzi and his marriage with the goddess was intended to attract the gods' blessing on the reign. After the wedding the reign would become prosperous in all aspects, including agriculture. Dumuzi is also a character in a "contrast" (belonging to the gender of the *debates*) where he, the shepherd, is competing with the farmer to obtain the hand of the goddess Inanna. Two kings named Dumuzi are recorded in the great Sumerian King List (composed during the Isin period); one whose reign lasted thousands of years is included among the antediluvian kings, and the other is included with the mythical kings of Uruk.

After the Old-Babylonian period there was a change in the documentation: only lamentation songs, which mourn the god's departure, were transmitted; Dumuzi as a lover and a bridegroom was almost completely forgotten. Only the authority he took *post mortem* as a great officer of the netherworld is still mentioned. The *gala/kalû* priests (related to Ishtar) sang these lamentation songs when conducting funerals, at the beginning of an activity as a prophylaxis against evil entities, and during rituals for appeasing a god when his temple had to be touched for reconstruction or restoration. The change in the tradition coincides with a change in the use of the *hieros gamos* rite to apply only to marriage between divinities, excluding the form in which the king, personifying Dumuzi, unites with Inanna (for a possible exception, see Nissinen, 2001, p. 103).

At last the myth of Adapa must be considered. The myth tells how Adapa, because of an impious act, had to submit to the verdict of the heaven god An. Dumuzi and Gizzida, a divinity often confused with Dumuzi, were at the gatepost of heaven, as intermediaries with lofty An. The contradiction between the netherworld, where Dumuzi plays a role of responsibility, and the heavenly one is seemingly real, since the anthropomorphic aspect of the divinity is the mere representation of a cosmic power that can be manifested in other forms: Dumuzi and (Nin)gizzida are actually mentioned as constellations in an astronomic text.

Observation on the Documentation. Scholars still debate whether the whole of the love literature is related to the couple Inanna and Dumuzi, or whether a part is formed by merely profane songs, or whether a part is connected with the *Hieros gamos*. The discussion parallels the debate over the biblical *Song of Songs*. Because divinities, even in anthropomorphic forms, are not belles lettres characters but representations of cosmic powers, in the love songs the two lovers, even when they are depicted as laymen, are two persons who act under the influence of that particular cosmic power that is love. Under this point of view, the lovers are a manifestation of that cosmic power, and so they play exactly the same role as the anthropomorphic characters of Inanna and Dumuzi (Lambert, 1987, p. 26; Alster, 1999, p. 832; Nissinen, 2001, pp. 126ff.). Consider the exorcist who declares, "I am Asalluhi [/Marduk]," or Gudea who intends to tell his dream to the goddess Nanshe, to have its meaning cleared, but who in reality is given the oracle by the seers and the diviners of the goddess' temple (Waetzoldt, 1998). All these priests participate in the nature of the cosmic power the respective divinities represent. All the love songs, as well as the songs of the king's wedding, must therefore be included in the category of the songs of Inanna and Dumuzi.

There are two distinct traditions regarding Dumuzi's death. One tells how he was caught by demons who carried him into the netherworld, where he played an important role after his arrival there. Another is included in the finale of the Sumerian poem "Inanna's Descent to the Netherworld." Two versions of the poem exist, one in Sumerian (with minor variations according to local versions) and one in Akkadian. Both versions contain a narrative in which Inanna requests—for no apparent reason—to penetrate the netherworld. The queen of that kingdom, her sister Ereshkigal, allows Inanna access, ordering the porter to deprive Inanna of a piece of jewelry at each of the seven netherworld gates. Inanna is therefore naked, denuded of her divine powers (her jewels) when she arrives before the queen of the netherworld, and Ereshkigal hangs her, in a condition of suspended life, from a nail. Inanna's faithful vizier, the goddess Ninshubur, obtains help from Enki, who creates two beings to rescue her. These creatures enter the netherworld and gain Ereshkigal's gratitude, and in return they ask for the piece of meat hanging from the nail—such is Inanna's appearance. But because of the netherworld law that there must be a substitue for anyone leaving its reign, a replacement must be found to in order to set Inanna free. Demons escort Inanna from the netherworld, and she begins looking for someone to replace her. In an outburst of anger she chooses her unlucky husband Dumuzi, who is not displaying signs of mourning for her death, and the demons take him into the netherworld. His sister Geshtinanna generously agrees to replace him for a portion of the year. This is the only known case of Dumuzi's going up, and it represents the god's short sorties—in his role of netherworld officer—to bring back haunting ghosts. This function of the god is related to the series of incantations of Ishtar and Dumuzi (Farber, 1977).

Dumuzi's Portrait. Dumuzi was a young shepherd. After his premature death at the hand of demons, he became an officer in the netherworld, where he stayed. There are clues that his ascent in the final part of "Inanna's Descent" is related to his official task (Scurlock, 1992). Dumuzi's character in mythology is rather vague, mixing qualities of Amaushum gal anna, Ningizzida, and, in specific cases, Damu (a genuine vegetation god). Songs in his honor praised him with all these and other names, including those of the divinized kings of the Ur III and Isin dynasties (who took part in the *Hieros gamos*). The god shows solar traits as well in, for example, his driving the ghosts haunting the living back into the netherworld. Like the sun, he is closely related to kingship, so that for some time sovereigns personified him in the *Hieros gamos*. It must be remarked that both Dumuzi and Utu are masculine characters very close to Inanna, the former being her husband and the latter her elder brother.

Dumuzi as Dying and Rising God. Tammuz is mentioned in the Bible in a prophecy of Ezekiel (dated between the seventh and sixth century BCE). Because the biblical prophet lived in Babylonia, where he was deported after the conquest of Jerusalem, this passage should be considered as belonging to the Mesopotamian cultural area. The evidence for this is that (1) the sun god Shamash is mentioned in the same context and (2) there are no further mentions of Tammuz in the Old Testament. Mentions of Tammuz from periods after the Mesopotamian cuneiform literary tradition are relevant. Lamentations of the Sabians of Harran for the passing away of Ta'uz (Tammuz, identified with St. George by the Christians), are doumented, written in Arabic and dated to the tenth century CE. But the crucial feature—extraneous to the Mesopotamian cultural area—is the translation of the biblical "Tammuz" of *Ezekiel* to "Adonis." This translation has influenced scholars' opinions up to recent times. In the Septuagint translation, the name Tammuz was left untranslated, but later Christian authors (Origen, Saint Jerome) rendered it as Adonis. When the first cuneiform texts mentioning Dumuzi/Tammuz were discovered, the ancient identification of Tammuz with Adonis played a decisive role in scholars identifying a pattern of death and resurrection that could not be deduced from the surviving parts of the texts themselves (which, at the time, were but roughly understood). The existence of Tammuz's resurrection, symbolizing the vegetation cycle from sowing (death) to blooming (resurrection), became authoritative. This composite portrait placed him together with other divinities in the Eastern Mediterranean area, including the Egyptian Osiris (whose resurrection is well-established in myth), some Syro-Palestinian divinities, and the mythic-ritual complex of Demeter and Persephone. Dying and resurrecting were common to all these divine figures, hence their current label as dying and rising gods.

Theories on the Dying God. The Tammuz that emerged from philological research was forced into a preconceived pattern of dying and rising fertility gods, based on what was known about the connection between Adonis and Tammuz (François Lenormant in 1874). This identification began with the Akkadian version of "Ishtar's Descent to the Netherworld"—the first myth to be found—even if its meaning was far from certain. References in the Akkadian myth to the vegetative seasonal cycle provided evidence for what scholars already assumed, namely Dumuzi's inclusion in the dying and rising god class. Two opinions developed about this cycle. One, first proposed by the Assyriologist Lenormant (in 1880), identified the sun as the main character of the cycle. The second, following Sir James George Frazer's path (*The Golden Bough* in 1890 and *Adonis, Attis, Osiris* in 1905), saw the life cycle—in particular the vegetal one—as the deep meaning of that myth. A third line of thought located the myth's meaning in both the solar cycle and the vegetative one (indications of this direction can be found in Lenormant himself and in Barton in 1902). At the beginning of the past century Marduk joined the rank of these divinities; he was explicitly compared with Christ by Heinrich Zimmern, who in 1906 published the first exhaustive research on the Babylonian festival of Akitu, *Zum babylonischen Neujahrsfest.* Zimmern misunderstood some passages (which are not fully clear even today!), and thought that after Marduk was imprisoned (which Zimmern took to mean "death"), he was resuscitated. The scholar drew comparisons with New Year celebrations from other cultures to reach a parallel with Christ's passion. His thesis was expanded by Stephen Herbert Langdon (1923), who interpreted Marduk's apotheosis, the *Enuma elish*, and the Akitu festival, within the same cultural context as "Ishtar's Descent to the Netherworld," Tammuz's fate (since he was thought to alternate with the goddess in sojourning on earth), and the *Hieros gamos* rite. As Assyriologists advanced in their studies, they toned down some of this excess but nonetheless inclined to follow the underworld-agrarian interpretation. They considered Dumuzi to be a vegetation god; therefore, in the holy marriage the king was performing a fertility rite to restore life after the death of wintertime. Thorkild Jacobsen (1962) presented the most exhaustive exposition of this theory, linking it to the village society of the fifth and fourth millennium, before the rise of the city-state, when survival depended on the actions of natural agents. He compared the "intransitivity" of the gods from that era to the "transitivity" of the great gods of the third millennium, in the age of the fighting city-states. Ugo Bianchi became interested in Dumuzi while researching the origin of the mystery cults and Gnosticism. In Bianchi's opinion, four phases followed in sequence. First cults developed similar to those of Tammuz, followed in the order by the mystery cults, the so-called mysteriosophic cults, and Gnosticism. Bianchi saw Dumuzi as the earliest manifestation of the dualism that reached its apex in Gnosticism, and which is opposed to Hebrew and Christian monotheism. To further his theory, Bianchi (1965) accepted the intransitivity of the Dumuzi myth, relating it to the character of Adonis, as in Jacobsen's fatalistic-vegetative interpretation.

The pattern of the dying and rising gods has been reconsidered and re-interpreted. Henri Frankfort (1948) has the distinction of being the first to differentiate Osiris from other divinities in the supposed class of dying and rising gods. Based on new studies, the western Semitic Baal and the Phoenician Eshmun and Melqart have been reconsidered and recognised as prototypes of divinised dead sovereigns (del Olmo Lete, 1996).

Advancing studies opened new perspectives on Dumuzi as well. After Oliver R. Gurney's article (1962), which critically examined Langdon's, Anton Moortagart's, and Adam Falkenstein's positions, Bent Alster (1972) confirmed the myth's connection with kingship and the absence of references to the vegetative cycle. A by-form of Dumuzi, worshiped in Lagash in the third millennium and older than any mention of Dumuzi in that town, the god Lugal-URU-KAR2, has been shown to be related to kingship and to be extraneousness to the vegetation cycle, so indirectly confirming the genuine features of Dumuzi (Pisi, 1995).

M. M. Fritz (2003, pp. 291–301, 370) has shown how Dumuzi (and Amaushumgalanna, who is identified with him) is a distinct divine character not to be confused with Damu and Ningizzida. Both the latter gods are vegetation divinities, and because Damu was also worshiped as a healing god, some scholars thought that there were two distinct gods with the same name. Now Fritz uncovers evidence that this is not the case and that Damu was a single divine character who contained both qualities of healing and vegetation god. It is evident from the documentation Fritz adduced that the peculiar features of Damu do not match those of Dumuzi, and therefore, the latter cannot be considered a vegetation god (Fritz, 2003, p. 370). Nonetheless, in particular circumstances (which Fritz describes) Damu and Ningizzida may be included in the same context with Dumuzi (Fritz, 2003, pp. 249–268).

Is the Mythical Complex of Inanna and Dumuzi a Religion Apart? As mentioned, in *The Treasures of Darkness* Thorkild Jacobsen identified Inanna's and Dumuzi's songs as manifestations of "intransitivity." In the previous edition of this *Encyclopedia* he outlined the character Dumuzi's "passivity":

> Dumuzi was generally visualized as a young man or boy. Under some of his aspects he is of marriageable age; in others he is younger, a mere child. He is dearly loved by the women who surround him—his mother, sister, and later, his young bride—but there is no evidence to assume that his cult was predominantly a women's cult [Fritz, 2003, pp. 353–359]. The love songs of his wooing and wedding are all love songs to him or are self-praise of the bride hoping her body will please him; there are no love songs of his to Inanna.

Correspondingly, the laments for him are by his mother, sister, and widowed bride, never by a father. One may also cite here *Ezekiel* 8:14: There sat women weeping for Tammuz.

The intransitivity and passivity of the Inanna and Dumuzi complex differentiate it from a religion centered on the pantheon of the divine characters who transitively and actively operate in the cosmos. This opinion of Jacobsen—for completely unrelated reasons—is shared by other great interpreters of Mesopotamian thought. Both Falkenstein (1954), on an evemeristic ground, and Jean van Dijk (1971), who compared the hunters' cult to that of the farmers and breeders, who worshiped respectively Enlil and An, considered independent the mythological complex of Inanna-Dumuzi from the remaining religious beliefs. The myth's connection with kingship could provide a clue to this peculiarity. An active principle (Dumuzi), by his union with the goddess (Inanna) of the Venus planet (the crepuscolar nature of which, between day and night, represents the passage between opposites, here from heaven to earth), borrows Venus star's power of manifestation, spreading it all over the earth (this radiation is similar to the biblical Glory or the Hindu *shakti*). When this role is over, this power is cast into the netherworld, where it exercises its strength, since everything earthly is bound for death. It is from this pattern that the king's role derives, not because he is his people's leader, but because he is the conduit for divine power from heaven and therefore becomes the distributor of it over the earth. The autonomy and peculiarity of this pattern enabled its wide scattering outside Mesopotamian religion. A shadow of it could still be found in the fourth century CE, when the emperor Julian expanded philosophically the cosmological aspects of a peculiar version of the myth of Attis and Cybele (Mander, 2001). The Inanna and Dumuzi complex serves as a bridge between the human and the divine, between life and death, and between unity and multiplicity. Kingship is an essential component because it connects heavenly will and human society.

SEE ALSO Adonis; Dying and Rising Gods; Inanna; Kingship, article on Kingship in the Ancient Mediterranean World; Mesopotamian Religions, overview article.

BIBLIOGRAPHY

Bianchi, Ugo. "*Initiation, mystères, gnose.*" In *Initiation*, edited by C. J. Bleker, pp. 154–171. Leiden, 1965.

Del Olmo Lete, Gregorio. *El continuum cultural cananeo.* Barcelona, 1996.

Falkenstein, Adam. "Tammuz" *Compte Rendu de la Rencontre Assyriologique Internationale* 3 (1954): 41–75.

Farber, W. *Beschwörungsrituale an Ishtar und Dumuzi.* Wiesbaden, 1977.

Frankfort, Henri. *Kingship and the Gods.* Chicago, 1948.

Langdon, Stephen Herbert. *The Epic of Creation.* Oxford, 1923.

Van Dijk, Jean. "Sumerische Religion." In *Handbuch der Religiongeschichte—Band 1*, edited by J. P Asmussen and J. Læssøe, pp. 435–436. 1971.

Waetzoldt, Hartmut. "Die Göttin Nanse und die Traumdeutung." *Nouvelles Assyriologiques Brèves et Utilitaires* 60 (1998).

For Sumerian love songs, see the full edition in Yitzhak Sefati, *Love Songs in Sumerian Literature* (Bar-Ilan, 1998) and the studies by Bent Alster, "Marriage and Love in the Sumerian Love Songs," in Mark Cohen et al., eds., *The Tablet and the Scroll: Near Eastern Studies in Honour of W. W. Hallo* (Potomac, Md., 1993), pp. 15–27. On the reconstructed myth of Dumuzi and Inanna, see Thorkild Jacobsen, "Toward the Image of Tammuz" in W. L. Moran, ed., *Toward the Image of Tammuz and Other Essays on Mesopotamian History and Culture* (Cambridge, Mass., 1970), pp. 73–101, and *The Treasures of Darkness* (New Haven, Conn., and London, 1976), chapter 2. On love in Mesopotamian literature, see W. G. Lambert, "Devotion: The Languages of Religion and Love" in M. Mindlin et al., eds., *Figurative Language in the Ancient Near East* (London, 1987), pp. 25–40; G. Leick, *Sex and Eroticism in Mesopotamian Literature* (London and New York, 1994); M. Nissinen, "Akkadian Rituals and Poetry of Divine Love" in R. M. Whiting, ed., *Mythology and Mythologies*, Melammu Symposia II (Helsinki, 2001), pp. 93–136. On Dumuzi's death see Bent Alster, *Dumuzi's Dream* (Copenhagen, 1972), and for lamentations on his departure see Mark E. Cohen, *The Canonical Lamentations of Ancient Mesopotamia* (Potomac, Md., 1998). On Dumuzi as an officer in the netherworld, see J. A. Scurlock's "K 164: New Light on the Mourning Rites for Dumuzi?," *Revue d'Assyriologie* 86 (1992): 53–67. For insight on Dumuzi in later times up to the tenth century, see J. Hämeen-Anttila, "Continuity of Pagan Religious Traditions in Tenth-Century Iraq" in A. Panaino and G. Pettinato, eds., *Ideologies as Intercultural Phenomena*, Melammu Symposia III (Bologna, Italy, 2002), pp. 89–108. For discussions of Dumuzi's nature, see Oliver R. Gurney, "Tammuz Reconsidered: Some Recent Developments," *Journal of Semitic Studies* 7 (1962): 147–160, and Bent Alster, "Tammuz," in K. van der Toorn, B. Becking, and P. W. van der Horst's *Dictionary of Deities and Demons in the Bible*, 2d ed. (Leiden, 1999), pp. 828–834; and P. Pisi, "Il dio LUGAL-URUxKAR$_2$ e il culto degli antenati regali nella Lagash pre-sargonica," *Oriens Antiquus Miscellanea* II (1995): 1–40. For information about Dumuzi's relationship with other cultures see Pietro Mander, "Antecedents in the Cuneiform Literature of the Attis Tradition in Late Antiquity," *Journal of Ancient Near Eastern Religions* 1 (2001): 100–149; Pietro Mander, "Il contributo di U. Bianchi allo studio del pensiero mesopotamico antico" in G. Casadio, ed., *Ugo Bianchi. Una vita per la storia delle religioni* (Rome, 2002), pp. 87–143; and M. M. Fritz, "*. . . und weinten um Tammuz"—Die Götter Dumuzi-Ama'ushumgal'anna und Damu*, Alter Orient und Altes Testament, Band 307 (Münster, Germany, 2003).

PIETRO MANDER (2005)

DUNS SCOTUS, JOHN (c. 1266–1308), Franciscan philosopher and theologian, and founder of the school of Scotism. Born in Scotland and trained by his paternal uncle at the Franciscan friary at Dumfries, Scotland, Duns Scotus entered the Franciscan order at an early age and was ordained a priest. As a bachelor of theology he studied and taught at Oxford, completing his lectures on Peter Lombard's *Sentences,* which he began revising as the *Ordinatio* in 1300. When in 1302 the turn came for the English province to provide a talented candidate for the prestigious University of Paris, Duns Scotus was sent. During the demonstrations against Boniface VIII initiated by Philip the Fair, Duns Scotus sided with the pope and, as a consequence, was exiled from France. Just where he spent his exile is unknown, but with the death of Boniface and the accession to the papacy of Benedict XI, the church's ban against the king and the university was lifted, and Duns Scotus returned to complete his Paris lectures on the *Sentences.* He became regent master probably in 1305.

During his regency Duns Scotus conducted quodlibetic disputations covering a wide variety of theological and philosophical questions about God and creatures proposed by his audience. His later version of these questions (*Quaestiones quodlibetales*), like his *Ordinatio* (begun at Oxford, and hence referred to as the *Opus oxoniense*), was not finished at the time of his untimely death, yet these two works were widely copied for distribution and are largely responsible for his fame as a philosopher and theologian. In addition he left a number of important philosophical works on logic, psychology, and metaphysics, presented in the form of questions suggested by the works of Porphyry and Aristotle. Like *Collationes oxoniense et parisienses* (shorter questions on specific philosophical and theological topics), these were probably the result of disputations Duns Scotus conducted for the Franciscan students at Oxford and Paris. The most extensive and influential of these philosophical works are the *Quaestiones subtilissime super libros Metaphysicorum Aristoteles* and the important *Tractatus de Primo Principio,* a compendium of what reason can prove about God. Duns Scotus left Paris in the fall of 1307 to teach at the Franciscan house of studies in Cologne, where he died the following year. His remains rest in the nave of the Franciscan church near the Cologne cathedral, where he is venerated as blessed.

In his writings, Duns Scotus views theology as a practical science rather than a theoretical science, inasmuch as it gives human beings the necessary knowledge to reach their supernatural end. This end consists in sharing in the inner life of the Trinity in heaven. Developing Richard of Saint-Victor's insight that perfect love wants the beloved to be loved by others, Duns Scotus envisions the motive for creation as follows. God first loved himself, then he freely decided to create co-lovers of his infinitely lovable nature. Being orderly in his love, he next predestined Christ's human nature to share this glory and gave this nature the highest possible grace that could be bestowed upon a creature. Christ, the God-man, purchased grace for both angels and humanity. But because God foresaw Adam's sin and humanity's consequent fall from grace, Christ came as a suffering, rather than a triumphant, mediator. The most perfect form of mediation, however, would have been to preredeem, and Scotus proposes this as the rationale for Mary's immaculate conception, an argument that became basic for defenders of that doctrine until its declaration in 1854 as a dogma by Pius IX. Finally, God willed the sensible world to serve humanity.

As a philosopher, Duns Scotus modified the Aristotelian influence current in his day with insights of Augustine of Hippo, Anselm of Canterbury, Richard of Saint-Victor, and Ibn Sīnā (Avicenna). Developing Ibn Sīnā's conception of metaphysics, Duns Scotus provided a powerful rational proof for an infinite being, who he believed had revealed himself to Moses as the "I am who am."

In his philosophical system, Duns Scotus stressed the metaphysical primacy of the individual, each with its own unique "haecceity," which exists only because God's creative love wanted just "this" and not "that." On the other hand, he logically analyzed what individualized created natures must have in common, if scientific knowledge of them is to become possible.

Duns Scotus adopted the peculiar "Augustinian" tradition of the earlier Franciscan school, which stressed the "supersufficient potentiality" of the will for self-determination, and showed how it could be reconciled with the Aristotelian notion of an active potency, if one rejected the controversial principle that "whatever is moved is moved by another." In this and other ways he brought the earlier anti-Aristotelianism of his Franciscan predecessors into the mainstream of what contemporaries considered essential to Aristotle's philosophical system. For instance, he indicated how Aristotle's criteria for rational and nonrational faculties could be used to prove that the will, not the intellect, is the primary rational potency. Nonrational faculties are determined to act in one way, said Aristotle, all other conditions being the same; rational faculties are free to act in more than one way and thus are the basis of all creativity in the arts. If that be so, Duns Scotus argued, the intellect is nonrational, since it has but one mode of acting determined by the objective evidence. In this it resembles all active potencies that are collectively called "nature." The will alone has the basic freedom, when it acts with reason, for alternate modes of acting. Thus for Duns Scotus the distinction between nature and will represents the primary division of active potencies, corresponding roughly to the Aristotelian division of nonrational and rational.

Original also is Duns Scotus's development of Anselm of Canterbury's distinction of the will's twofold inclination, or "affection," namely, love of the advantageous on the one hand and love of what is right and just for its own sake on the other. As the seat of the former, the will is only an intellectual appetite that seeks happiness and self above all else. Only by reason of its affection for justice is the will free to moderate this self-seeking and, according to right reason, love what is good objectively for its intrinsic worth. Unlike Anselm, however, Duns Scotus understood justice not merely as a supernatural, infused gift, called "gratuitous grace" or "charity," but as a congenital or innate freedom of the will, free precisely because it liberates the will from that necessity Aristotle claimed was characteristic of all natural agents, namely, to seek happiness and the perfection of their nature above all else.

These two affections of the will are not volitions as such; though they incline the will, they do not necessitate it or cause it to act. The will itself determines how it will act, but when it does it acts in accord with one or the other of these affections. While the affection for the advantageous corresponds with Aristotle's conception of choice, the affection or bias for justice is an essentially Christian notion. This inclination, according to Duns Scotus, has a twofold effect: (1) it enables the will to love God above all else for God's own sake, and (2) it allows the will to moderate its natural inclination for happiness and self-actualization, either as an individual or as a species, and to love according to right reason. Thus the affection for justice provides the natural basis for a rational ethical philosophy. Both affections are essential to human nature, but they can be perfected supernaturally and directed to God as their object. Charity perfects the will's affection for justice, inclining it to love God for his own sake; hope perfects the will's affection for the advantageous, inclining it to love God because he has shown his love for us in this life and because he will be our ultimate happiness in the life to come.

Another important psychological notion of Duns Scotus' that influenced subsequent scholastics is his conception of intuitive intellectual cognition, or the simple, nonjudgmental awareness of a here-and-now existential situation. First developed as a necessary theological condition for the face-to-face vision of God in the afterlife, intellectual intuition is needed to explain our certainty of primary contingent truths such as "I think," "I choose," "I live," and to account for our awareness of existence. Duns Scotus never makes intellectual intuition the basis for his epistemology. Neither does he see it as putting persons into direct contact with the external sensible world, with any substance material or spiritual, or with an individual's haecceity, for in this life, at least, human intellect works through the sensory imagination. Intellectual intuition seems rather to be identified with the indistinct peripheral aura associated with all our direct sensory-intellectual cognition. We know of it explicitly only in retrospect when we consider the necessary conditions for intellectual memory.

The notion of intellectual intuition continued to be a topic of discussion and dispute down to the time of Calvin, who, influenced by the Scotist John Major, used an auditory rather than a visual sense model of intellectual intuition to explain our experience of God. Whereas Duns Scotus restricted intuition of God to the beatific vision in the afterlife or to the special mystical visions given to the prophets or to Paul of Tarsus, John Major explained that we may also experience God intuitively whenever he "speaks to our soul" through some special inspiration.

BIBLIOGRAPHY

The Scotistic Commission (Rome) began publishing a critical edition of the collected works of Duns Scotus in 1950. The Luke Wadding edition (Lyons, 1639), reprinted as *John Duns Scotus: Opera omnia*, edited by L. Vivès (Paris, 1891–1895), contains the major portion of his writings. A critical edition of the *Tractatus de Primo Principio*, edited by Marianus Mueller (Freiburg im Breisgau, 1941), has been reprinted with translations in several languages. I have added to my earlier edition and translation an extensive commentary on this work in *A Treatise on God as First Principle* (Chicago, 1983). Selections from the *Ordinatio* are available in my *Duns Scotus: Philosophical Writings* (Edinburgh, 1962). The most recent edition of the *Quodlibetal Questions* (Latin text and Spanish translation) is by Felix Alluntis, *Obras del Doctor Sutil Juan Duns Escoto* (Madrid, 1968); an English translation by Felix Alluntis and myself is entitled *God and Creatures: The Quodlibetal Questions* (Princeton, 1975). An extensive bibliography by Odulfus Schaefer, *Bibliographia vita operibus et doctrina Iohannis Duns Scoti* (Rome, 1950), covers nineteenth- and twentieth-century secondary literature. This has been updated to 1965 by Odulfus Schaefer in the *Acta ordinis Fratrum Minorum* (Florence) 85 (1966) and by Servus Gieben in *Laurentianum* 6 (1965). Contemporary interest in Duns Scotus's thought is apparent from the international Scotistic Congresses held every five years, the proceedings of which are published under special titles in the general series "Studia Scholastico-Scotistica" (Rome, 1968–) by the Societas Internationalis Scotistica. *Duns Scotus on the Will and Morality* (Washington, D. C., 1986) contains a large selection of Latin texts that I have translated into English.

ALLAN B. WOLTER (1987)

DURGĀ HINDUISM. In classical Hindu mythology the goddess Durgā is one of the principal forms of the wife of the great god Śiva. She is particularly celebrated for her victory over the buffalo demon Mahiṣāsura. At a higher level of abstraction she is considered to be the energy (*śakti*) of Śiva. Ultimately she is Devī, the Goddess, whose myriad names and forms are merely transient and adventitious disguises that overlay a unitary spiritual reality.

Most modern scholars have sought to find the ultimate origin of the goddess worship of Hinduism in the prehistoric Indus Valley civilization centered in what is now Pakistan. This theory is plausible, but the evidence for an important goddess cult in the Indus civilization is inconclusive, and the historical links of such a cult with classical Hinduism are impossible to document. Preclassical Vedic literature mentions numerous goddesses, but they are clearly of secondary importance. The earliest Vedic text, the *Ṛgveda*, praises several river goddesses, most notably Sarasvatī; the goddess Uṣas, the Dawn; Aditi, a rather vague mother of several gods; and the goddess Vāc, Speech. An ancillary Vedic text, the *Bṛhaddevatā* (2.77), includes Durgā among the many names of Vāc, but this is considered to be a late interpolation. The *Taittirīya Saṃhitā* (1.8.6.1) of the *Yajurveda* mentions

Ambikā, later one of the common alternate names of Durgā, as the sister of Śiva. In the later *Taittirīya Āraṇyaka* (10.18), Śiva is said to be "the husband of Ambikā, the husband of Umā." Umā appears in the *Kena Upaniṣad* (3.12) as Haimavatī, the daughter of Himavat, the Himalaya.

It is not until the early centuries of the Christian era, however, that either Durgā in particular or the Goddess as a unitary concept become important figures in Hindu religious texts. Hymns in praise of Durgā as the Goddess appear in the *Virāṭaparvan* (6) and the *Bhīṣmaparvan* (23) of the epic *Mahābhārata*, the critical edition of which considers them to be late interpolations. In the *Harivaṃśa*, the "appendix" to the *Mahābhārata*, the Goddess consents to be born as Yaśodā's child, who is exchanged for Kṛṣṇa and killed by Kaṃsa. There follows another long hymn dedicated to her, but the critical edition considers this also to be an interpolation. The three hymns provide lists of her names and forms and praises of her greatness, but they do not narrate her mythological exploits. These appear in great detail in the classical texts known as the Purāṇas, dated between the third and fifteenth centuries CE.

Most important in this context is the section of the *Mārkaṇḍeya Purāṇa* known as the *Devīmāhātmya*, also called the *Caṇḍīmāhātmya* and *Durgāsaptaśatī*. This text celebrates the Goddess's victory over the buffalo demon Mahiṣāsura and over the demons Śumbha and Niśumbha. The great prevalence of Durgā's buffalo-killer form, known as Mahiṣamardinī, in iconography shows this to be her most important exploit. The *Devīmāhātmya* tells how the gods are oppressed for a century by the demons led by Mahiṣāsura. Finally they appeal to the great gods Viṣṇu and Śiva to rescue them. The anger of Viṣṇu and Śiva, joined with the anger of all the other gods, produces a mass of luminous energy. This then takes the form of a woman, the Goddess. Each god gives her his principal weapon. The god Himavat gives her the lion, which becomes her "vehicle." During a great battle she destroys the armies of Mahiṣāsura and finally beheads the demon himself.

In classical mythology many of the forms assumed by the wife of Śiva can be divided into those that are terrifying and those that are benevolent. Durgā Mahiṣamardinī belongs among the former, together with Caṇḍikā, Kālī, Vindhyavāsinī, Cāmuṇḍā, and many others. Her benevolent forms include Satī, Umā, Pārvatī, Śiva, and Gaurī. These benevolent forms have their own distinct cycle of myths, recorded in the Purāṇas and other works, such as Kālidāsa's *Kumāra-saṃbhava*. She also appears as Yoganidrā ("cosmic sleep"); as Viṣṇumāyā ("world illusion"); as Ambikā ("the mother"); as Śakti ("divine energy"); and as simply Devī ("the goddess"). Since she is Śakti, those who worship her above all other gods are frequently called Śāktas. Śākta worship tends to blend into the somewhat heterodox current of Hinduism known as Tantrism, after the religious texts called the Tantras. Durgā as the one Devī, on the other hand, is one of the five great gods of the nonsectarian, orthodox Brahmanic cult known as Pañcāyatana.

As Hindu thinkers tend to conflate all her forms into a single great goddess, many modern scholars similarly consider these forms to be manifestations of a single archetypal mother-goddess concept. However this may be, it is also clear that most of these forms have distinct historical origins. They derive from a variety of goddesses from specific regions and localities, each associated with specific social or ethnic groups and fulfilling specific cultural functions. Many of the major terrifying forms of the Goddess, such as Durgā, seem to have arisen among semi-hinduized tribes such as the Śabaras and Pulindas and retain these associations in classical texts. Local forms of goddesses of disease, such as the goddesses of smallpox, may also have contributed to the evolution of these terrifying forms.

Durgā Mahiṣamardinī is popular especially in Bengal and Bihar in the east and in Tamil Nadu in the south. Her great festival is the Durgotsava, or Durgā Pūjā, also called Navarātri, celebrated during the first ten days of the waxing fortnight of the autumn month Āśvina. Clay images of Durgā are made and presented with varied offerings. Formerly many buffalo and goats were sacrificed to her, but this practice has been gradually dying out. Recitations of the *Devīmāhātmya* also play an important part in the festival. On the "Victorious Tenth Day" (Vijayadaśami) the images are paraded to a river or tank. Now considered lifeless, they are deposited in the water.

SEE ALSO Goddess Worship, article on The Hindu Goddess.

BIBLIOGRAPHY

The best work on the historical evolution of the Goddess is J. N. Tiwari's *Studies in Goddess Cults in Northern India* (Canberra, 1971). Also useful is M. C. P. Srivastava's *Mother Goddess in Indian Art, Archaeology and Literature* (Delhi, 1979). Translations of the basic myths from Sanskrit sources are easily found in Wendy Doniger O'Flaherty's *Hindu Myths: A Sourcebook* (Baltimore, 1975). Tamil myths are discussed in David Shulman's "The Murderous Bride: Tamil Versions of the Myth of Devī and the Buffalo-Demon," *History of Religions* 16 (1976): 120–146. A detailed description of the Durgā Pūjā festival appears in P. V. Kane's *History of Dharmaśāstra*, 2d ed., rev. & enl., vol. 5 (Poona, 1975).

New Sources

Sharma, Bulbul. *The Book of Devi.* New Delhi; New York, 2001.

DAVID N. LORENZEN (1987)
Revised Bibliography

DURKHEIM, ÉMILE (1858–1917), known generally as France's first sociologist, was far more than that. David Émile Durkheim was also a historian and theorist of pedagogy, moral education, and morals; a student of traditional societies, ritual life, and the world's religions; an active agent of social reform and religious change in his own milieu; a writer of patriotic tracts during World War I; a prominent defender of Alfred Dreyfus; a champion of charitable relief efforts for Jews fleeing the Russian pogroms of the early twentieth century; and a lifelong, although thoroughly eclectic and radical, philosopher.

In terms of his own strategic intellectual goals and his reputation among his contemporaries, Durkheim sought to infuse a sociological apperception into all areas of human life, especially religion. As an academic, he raised this awareness of the social dimension first by systematically challenging the identities of the two leading humanistic disciplines of his day—history and philosophy. In doing so, he sought to radically reorient their practice. To Durkheim, the historians of his day were dull describers and documenters; Durkheim sought instead to *explain* events by revealing their underlying sociological causes. He likewise thought that philosophy had stagnated by remaining speculative and locked into psychological introspection. Durkheim argued that philosophy could solve its perennial problems only by seeking the empirical social causes to the conditions it considered. Exemplifying this attempt to surpass both history and philosophy by seeking the underlying, collective, empirical causes of human action was one of Durkheim's earliest books, *Suicide* (1897). In this book, he tried to show that while suicide seemed at first like a lonely, deeply internal, even metaphysical matter, it was to be explained by the conditions of membership in social groups, such as religious communities, to which individuals taking their own lives belonged. Durkheim's mature sociological approach to religion emerged a decade or so later, but it retained many of the same methodological priorities established in *Suicide.*

Durkheim's life followed a similarly innovative pattern. The teenage Durkheim abandoned Jewish religious practice. He thus passed up the professional calling prepared for him as the eldest son in a family with a long history of rabbinic service. He left his home in Épinal, Lorraine, for a new life in Paris, where he attended one of the classical *collèges* to prepare for entry into the exclusive École Normale Supérieure, the elite institution for educating the influential *instituteurs* who staffed the nationwide system of rigorously secular state-run *lycées.* After teaching philosophy for several years at provincial *lycées,* interrupted by a short study tour of German universities (1885–1886), in 1887 Durkheim joined the faculty of the University of Bordeaux in a position created for him in social science and pedagogy, where he remained for fifteen years. There, he produced his first trademark books—*The Division of Labor in Society* (1893), *The Rules of Sociological Method* (1895), and *Suicide*—and many germinal articles. In Bordeaux, Durkheim also began to develop an interest in ethnological topics, such as totemism, and also religion.

Durkheim lived the final fifteen years of his life in Paris, where he succeeded Ferdinand Buisson in the chair of the Science of Education at the Sorbonne. He likewise continued the work he had already begun in Bordeaux, organizing the annual review *L'année sociologique,* and pursuing his work on pedagogy, religion, and social science. In the capital, he produced the work for which he is justly most famous, *The Elementary Forms of the Religious Life* (1912). He died on the eve of the end of World War I, considerably wounded in spirit by the death of his son, André, on the field of battle, but writing what he considered would be his masterpiece, a book to have been entitled *La Morale.*

Durkheim's years at the École Normale Supérieure (1879–1882) gave the new life he had fashioned for himself a definite intellectual and personal formation. Among his classmates were such future luminaries as the philosopher Henri Bergson and the statesman and socialist Jean Jaurès. Among his instructors, Durkheim was greatly influenced by the "scientific" history of Gabriel Monod, and even more perhaps by the historian of Roman religion and domestic rituals, Numa Denis Fustel de Coulanges. Among philosophers, the neo-Kantian Émile Boutroux exerted direct influence upon Durkheim with his notions about the independence of different levels of being, such as the social over the psychological. Linked with Boutroux in terms of Durkheim's emerging social realism was Alfred Espinas, a major figure in the "eclectic" tradition of philosophy and social thought in France. Durkheim credited Espinas with being the source of his sense of autonomous reality of the social realm over the realms of biology and personal psychology.

Another vital philosophical influence upon Durkheim was the neo-Kantian republican rationalist and founder of the periodical *Critique philosophique,* Charles Renouvier. Renouvier seems to have played a role in shaping Durkheim's reading of Immanuel Kant, as well as his passion for a science of morality. Renouvier's political liberalism, especially its affirmation of the sacredness of the individual human person, ran parallel to Durkheim's inclinations towards a "religion of humanity." Guided in large part by the values of Renouvier, and enhanced by his close friendship with the neo-Hegelian Renouvierian, Octave Hamelin, Durkheim articulated a form of humanistic liberalism that remained with him throughout his life. Like other progressives of his time and place, Durkheim's interest in Hegelian revisions of neo-Kantianism recalled not only Hamelin, but also such notables as the legendary promoter of left-wing Hegelianism, Lucien Herr. Over the dual extremes of a utilitarian individualism and materialism, on the one side, and a collectivist socialism and mystagogic spiritualism on the other, Durkheim sought to integrate an unruly French egoism with a broad, but concrete, communalism. His defense of Captain Alfred Dreyfus, articulated in terms of the French republic's collective valuation of the *individual* as a sacred being, captures what has aptly been called the eclectic "social individualism" at the core of Durkheim's values.

Although his years in Bordeaux were happy and productive, Durkheim's move to Paris in 1902 proved indispensable to the success of his celebrated periodical, *L'année sociologique* (1898–1913). Its success was facilitated in large part by his nephew, Marcel Mauss, and Mauss's close collaborator, Henri Hubert. These two Durkheimians also recruited members for what arguably was Durkheim's most important "work"—that lively and extravagantly talented team of coworkers, the Durkheimian "*équipe.*" This remarkable community not only absorbed and deployed Durkheimian ideas for generations, but would also shape a good deal of what and how Durkheim himself would think and write. As historians of religion themselves, Hubert and Mauss, for example, made significant contributions to Durkheim's articulation of the central notion of sacrifice in *The Elementary Forms.* Others associated with the *équipe* were Maurice Halbwachs, Robert Hertz, Célestin Bouglé, Antoine Meillet, Marcel Granet, Louis Gernet, Marc Bloch, Lucien Febvre, and Lucien Lévy-Bruhl. His location in Paris also placed Durkheim in the thick of the struggles over the future of the Third Rebublic against its Catholic adversaries, and along with that, all the attendant academic and national political struggles that shaped the times and Durkheim's work as well.

In terms of his study of religion, one can perceive the same socializing efforts that Durkheim had employed in regards to the fields of history and philosophy. At the time, the study of religion was dominated by various combinations of philosophy, psychology and Christian theologies. Bringing a social dimension to the study of religion meant that more attention would be accorded the collective, group, or institutional functions and contexts of religion. Durkheim thus spurred the study of religious communities like monastic groups, charismatics, local cults, "world" religions, ritual associations, ethnic and national religions, and such institutions as the church, synagogue, and so on. Further, insofar as his work concerned philosophical, psychological, or theological matters in religion, Durkheim wished to cast a social light upon them in order to show how they were dependent upon their social location for much of their form and content. How, for example, might the early Christian belief in the visitations of the Holy Spirit be related to the effervescent vitality of the young community and its avid ritual life? How and why was the notion and experience of the "sacred" so widely deployed in the religions of the world, and why was it so often linked with the identities of religious communities?

In this respect, the fruitfulness of the research fostered by this articulation of the social dimension of religion for modern religious studies far overshadows that upon which far too much attention has been focused by students of religion—the so-called sociological reduction of religion. Commonly regarded as the most important feature of Durkheim's thought about religion—doubtless because of the apologetic anxieties it stirs—this "reduction" takes the form of claiming that all talk of God can be reduced to talk about society. As a formula, this is to assert that society and God are identical. There is indeed ample warrant for the view that the Durkheimians believed that all talk of God was really about and derived from social experience. The religious experience of "spirit" is explainable in terms of the dynamics of crowd-induced enthusiasms in rituals. As atheists, the Durkheimians did not believe an experience of God or spirit was possible because gods or spirits either did not exist or were beyond the cognitive abilities of humans to experience. Ritual, on the other hand, was religion in tangible form.

On the other hand, the Durkheimian identity of society and God was also intended to be read as arguing that all social forms contained a spiritual or normative aspect to them. Materialists therefore attacked the Durkheimians for insisting upon the place of norms, values, consensus, beliefs, and other intangibles—"spiritual" factors—in the makeup of human reality. So, on this reading of the God-society identity, the Durkheimians were asserting the "godly" quality of social reality. Societies, whether families, tribes, nations, and so on, were not therefore just agglomerations of particulars, but units of humanity linked together by the common values that at once constitute them and that they hold to be sacred. It is this side of the God-society identity that fits with the deeply held Durkheimian views of the importance of religion and of its primacy in time and agency among other social institutions.

The genesis of Durkheim's consuming interest in religion is a subject of some debate. William Robertson Smith's *Lectures on the Religion of the Semites* (1889) is frequently, and with good reason, cited for its influence upon Durkheim's turn to the study of both simple societies and religion. Durkheim's first two major books, *The Division of Labor in Society* and *Suicide* dealt with social problems of so-called advanced industrial societies, while his masterpiece in the study of religion, *The Elementary Forms of the Religious Life*, explored so-called primitive ritual and religion and dealt with such topics as the sacred, totem, taboo, sacrifice, ordeals, myth, and symbolism—all set among the aboriginal folk of Australia. These were not the interests one might have expected from an author concerned mostly with the problems of the industrial society. Yet, in a way, a continuity may be discerned, at least from *Suicide* to *The Elementary Forms,* despite general agreement among scholars that around 1895 Durkheim shifted his interest to religion and to the so-called primitive societies. One might, for instance, argue that a social problem afflicting the France of his day was that of how to establish a secure and viable social order. How, given the threat of war with Germany or the fissiparous individualism bred by modern urban life (the political anarchism of the day was also a concern), could modern societies hope to maintain sufficient cohesion to continue surviving? Durkheim reasoned that the secrets of social integration and coherence were there to be learned in the "elementary forms of social life" in the societies of so-called primitive peoples, where coherence and well-regulated order was the norm. If one could isolate and identify the "elementary" institutions, practices, and mechanisms that "primitive" societies employed to secure their own coherence, then perhaps modern folk could either create or retrieve these aspects of a social technology of order and coherence for their own use. *The Elementary*

Forms answered this question by proposing Aboriginal Australian society and its elaborate sacrificial ritual religious life as a model for the France of its day. As ritual sacrifice functioned among the Aborigines to weld the people into a coherent whole, so also would the civic sacrifice of duty and devotion to country insure France's integrity against their foe.

A revival of interest in Durkheimian work, spurred by the publication of Steven Lukes's *Émile Durkheim: His Life and Work* (1972), shows no sign of letting up. Some of this may have to do with the steadily declining political and intellectual fortunes of Marxism. Despite their shared conviction about the social nature of human beings, Durkheimian social thought has escaped the downdraft in which Marxism was caught due to its links to a discredited totalitarianism. Even in his own time, while Durkheim's theories were seen as fully social, they were also seen as alternatives to the economic materialism of Marxism. Thus, Durkheim actually provided an alternative both to Marxian economic materialism and to the abstract individualist interpretations of human life that Marx attacked as well. Like Marx, Durkheim challenged the conventional wisdom of entrenched abstract individualism, and pushed people to seek the underlying social constraints and causes that shape the way they act—whether this be their religious behavior or anything else. Social and cultural constraints are thus paramount in Durkheim's view, and as such seem more subtle, complex, and diverse than Marx's economism would allow. Thus, today, when the sociocultural dimensions conditioning economic life itself are gaining new appreciation, Durkheim's emphasis upon the role of religion and kindred sociocultural factors in social formation will likely become more compelling as well.

BIBLIOGRAPHY

Besnard, Philippe, ed. *The Sociological Domain: The Durkheimians and the Founding of French Sociology.* Cambridge, U.K., 1983.

Durkheim, Émile. *Suicide.* (1897). Translated by John A. Spaulding and George Simpson. New York, 1951.

Durkheim, Émile. "Individuals and the Intellectuals" (1898). In *Durkheim on Religion,* edited by W. S. F. Pickering, pp. 59–73. London, 1975.

Durkheim, Émile. "Concerning the Definition of Religious Phenomena" (1899). In *Durkheim on Religion,* edited by W. S. F. Pickering, pp. 74–99. London, 1975.

Durkheim, Émile. *The Elementary Forms of the Religious Life: A Study in Religious Sociology* (1912). Translated by J. W. Swain. New York, 1915.

Durkheim, Émile. *Professional Ethics and Civic Morals.* Translated by Cornelia Brookfield. Westport, Conn., 1957.

Durkheim, Émile. "The Dualism of Human Nature and Its Social Conditions" (1914). In *Essays on Sociology and Philosophy,* edited by Kurt Wolff, pp. 325–340. New York, 1960.

Durkheim, Émile. *Moral Education: A Study in the Theory and Application of the Sociology of Education* (1925). Translated by Everett K. Wilson and Herman Schnurer. New York, 1961.

Durkheim, Émile. "Individual and Collective Representations" (1898). In *Sociology and Philosophy,* translated by D. F. Pocock, pp. 1–34. New York, 1974.

Durkheim, Émile. "Contribution to Discussion 'Religious Sentiment at the Present Time.'" In *Durkheim on Religion,* edited by W. S. F. Pickering, pp. 181–189. London, 1975.

Durkheim, Émile. *The Evolution of Educational Thought: Lectures on the Formation and Secondary Education in France* (1906). Translated by Peter Collins. 2d ed. London, 1977.

Durkheim, Émile. *The Rules of Sociological Method and Selected Texts on Sociology and Its Method.* Translated by W. D. Halls, edited by Steven Lukes. London, 1982.

Durkheim, Émile. "The Problem of Religion and the Duality of Human Nature" (1913). In *Knowledge and Society: Studies in the Sociology of Culture, Past and Present,* edited by Henrika Kuklick, vol. 5, pp. 1–44. Greenwich, Conn., 1984.

Jones, Robert Alun. "Durkheim in Context: A Reply to Perrin." *Sociological Quarterly* 15 (1975): 552–559.

Jones, Robert Alun. "On Understanding a Sociological Classic." *American Journal of Sociology* 83, no. 2 (1977): 279–319.

Jones, Robert Alun. "Robertson Smith, Durkheim and Sacrifice: An Historical Context for *The Elementary Forms.*" *Journal of the History of the Behavioral Sciences* 17, no. 2 (1981): 184–205.

Jones, Robert Alun. "Demythologizing Durkheim." In *Knowledge and Society: Studies in the Sociology of Culture, Past and Present,* edited by Henrika Kuklick, vol. 5, pp. 63–83. Greenwich, Conn., 1984.

Jones, Robert Alun. *The Development of Durkheim's Social Realism.* Cambridge, U.K., 1999.

Jones, Robert Alun, and Paul W. Vogt. "Durkheim's Defence of *Les formes élementaires de la vie religieuse.*" In *Knowledge and Society: Studies in the Sociology of Culture, Past and Present,* edited by Henrika Kuklick, vol. 5, pp. 45–62. Greenwich, Conn., 1984.

Karady, Victor. "The Durkheimians in Academe: A Reconsideration." In *The Sociological Domain,* edited by Philippe Besnard, pp. 71–89. Cambridge, U.K., 1983.

Karady, Victor, ed. *Émile Durkheim: Textes,* vol. 1, *Éléments d'une théorie sociale.* Paris, 1975.

Karady, Victor, ed. *Émile Durkheim: Textes,* vol. 2, *Religion, morale, anomie.* Paris, 1975.

Karady, Victor, ed. *Émile Durkheim: Textes,* vol. 3, *Fonctions sociales et institutions.* Paris, 1975.

Loisy, Alfred. "Sociologie et religion." *Revue d'histoire et de litterature religieuses* 4 (1913): 45–76.

Lukes, Steven. *Émile Durkheim: His Life and Work, A Historical and Critical Study.* New York, 1972; reprint, Stanford, Calif., 1985.

Pickering, W. S. F. *Durkheim's Sociology of Religion: Themes and Theories.* London, 1984.

Pickering, W. S. F. "Human Rights and the Cult of Individual: An Unholy Alliance Created by Durkheim?" In *Individualism and Human Rights in the Durkheimian Tradition,* edited by W. S. F Pickering and W. Watts-Miller, chap. 3. Oxford, 1993.

Strenski, Ivan. "Durkheim, Hamelin, and the French Hegel." *Historical Reflections/Réflexions Historiques* 16 (1989): 146–149.

Strenski, Ivan. "The Rise of Ritual and the Hegemony of Myth: Sylvain Lévi, the Durkheimians, and Max Müller." In *Myth and Method*, edited by Wendy Doniger and Laurie Patton, pp. 52–81. Charlottesville, Va., 1996.

Strenski, Ivan. *Durkheim and the Jews of France.* Chicago, 1997.

Strenski, Ivan. "Durkheim's Bourgeois Theory of Sacrifice." In *On Durkheim's Elementary Forms of the Religious Life*, edited by N. J. Allen, W. S. F. Pickering, and Willie Watts Miller, pp. 116–126. London, 1998.

Strenski, Ivan. "The Ironies of Fin-de-Siècle Rebellions against Historicism and Empiricism in the École Pratique des Hautes Etudes, Fifth Section." In *Religion in the Making: The Emergence of the Sciences of Religion*, edited by Peter Pels and Arie L. Molendijk, pp. 159–180. Leiden, 1998.

Strenski, Ivan. *Contesting Sacrifice: Religion, Nationalism and Social Thought in France.* Chicago, 2002.

Strenski, Ivan. *Theology and the First Theory of Sacrifice.* Leiden, 2003.

Tiryakian, Edward. "L'École Durkheimiennes à la recherche de la Société Perdue." *Cahiers internationaux de sociologie* 66 (1979): 97–114.

Vogt, W. Paul. "Durkheimian Sociology versus Philosophical Rationalism: The Case of Celestin Bouglé." In *The Sociological Domain: The Durkheimians and the Founding of French Sociology*, edited by Philippe Besnard, pp. 231–247. Cambridge, U.K., 1983.

Vogt, W. Paul, ed. "Obligation and Right: The Durkheimians and the Sociology of Law." In *The Sociological Domain: The Durkheimians and the Founding of French Sociology*, edited by Philippe Besnard, pp. 177–198. Cambridge, U.K., 1983.

IVAN STRENSKI (2005)

DUSHUN (557–640), also known as Fashun; first patriarch of the Huayan school in China. Dushun was born in the town of Wannien in Yongzhou Province, the birthplace of many important Buddhists. At the age of eighteen he was ordained by Senzhen of the Yinsheng Si, and studied Buddhist meditation under him. Some years later he went to Qingzhou Province and there recommended that people hold a Buddhist vegetarian feast. According to legend, he is said to have satisfied the hunger of a thousand people with food adequate for only five hundred. According to this same legend, he acquired such great supernatural power through meditation that he was able to effect miraculous cures. Indeed, it is principally for such charismatic powers, and not for his doctrinal contributions, that he is known to later church historians.

As a result of his growing reputation, Dushun was asked to preach at the court of Tang Taizong (627–645). It is said that the emperor bestowed upon him the honorary name *Dixing* (Imperial heart) in the year 632. In the years after his death at the Yishan Si temple in Nanjiao, popular legend declared Dushun to have been an incarnation of the *bodhisattva* Mañjuśrī.

Little precise information is known about Dushun's religious practice. It is said that he urged Fan Xuanzhi, one of his disciples, to chant the *Huayan jing (Mahâvaipulya-buddhagaṇḍavyūha Sūtra)* and to learn from it the practice of the *bodhisattva* Samantabhadra. We can infer from this that his own religious exercises were intimately related to such practices. Dushun had at least four disciples: the above-mentioned Fan Xuanzhi, Zhiyan, who was to become the Huayen school's second patriarch, a monk known simply as Da, and a child of a Li family. The latter two persons are otherwise unknown.

Tradition has long ascribed to Dushun authorship of the seminal *Fajie guanmen* (On the meditation of the *Dharmadhātu*), a work that sets forth the basic doctrinal and practical stance of Huayan Buddhism. Some modern scholars, however, doubt that this book was either edited or written by him. The *Xu gaoseng zhuan* (Further biographies of eminent monks), which contains the most reliable account of Dushun's life, makes no reference whatsoever to the *Fajie guanmen.* Nor is there any positive relation between the thought expressed in this work and the thought of Dushun's disciple and patriarchal successor Zhiyan. Finally, the *Fapudixin zhang,* written by Fazang, the Huayan school's third patriarch, has the same content as this work. Given these arguments, and considering the long tradition of pseudepigraphy in the Buddhist tradition, the association of Dushun with the *Fajie guanmen* appears doubtful.

SEE ALSO Huayan.

BIBLIOGRAPHY

Dushun's role in the formation of Huayan Buddhism is the subject of three important articles: Tokiwa Daijō's "Shina kegonshū dentō ron," *Tōhōgakuhō* (Tokyo) 3 (1932): 1–96 and its sequel, "Zoku kegonshū dentō ron," *Tōhōgakuhō* (Tokyo) 5 (1934): 1–85; and Yūki Reimon's "Kegon hokkaikanmon ni tsuite," *Indogaku Bukkyōgaku kenkyū* 6 (1958): 587–593. In my own study of early Huayen thought, *Shoki chūgoku kegonshisō no kenkyū* (Tokyo, 1977), I question the reliability of the traditional attribution of the *Fajie guanmen* to Dushun; see especially pages 325–370.

In addition, it is clear that the *Wujiao zhiguan* (Cessation and contemplation practice in the five teachings) cannot be attributed to Dushun based on its contents. Ishii Kōsei tried to demonstrate a new point of view that it appeared several decades after the third patriarch Fazang's death (712) in the article named "Kegonshū no kangyōbunken ni mieru zenshūhihan," *Matsugaokabunko kenkyū nenpō* 17 (Kamakura, 2003):47–62.

KIMURA KIYOTAKA (1987 AND 2005)

DUṬṬHAGĀMAṆĪ ("Gāmaṇī the wicked"), prince of a minor Sinhala kingdom who unified Sri Lanka as a Buddhist polity and ruled the island as overlord for twenty-four years (c. 161–137 BCE). In a manner characteristic of the rulers of classical India, Duṭṭhagāmaṇī marked his position as overlord by constructing numerous religious monuments and with great donative ceremonies (*mahādānas*) for the Buddhist monastic order.

Duṭṭhagāmaṇī established his polity through a series of military campaigns against the Sinhala and Tamil rulers of other minor kingdoms. His polity was fragile, however, maintained more by an ability to coerce than by administrative institutions; it collapsed soon after his death. The image of Duṭṭhagāmaṇī was more enduring. It provided a model of the ideal Buddhist king and the ideal layman, who have the responsibility to protect and promote Buddhist institutions materially, for which spiritual benefits accrue.

The image of Duṭṭhagāmaṇī was embellished in a folk epic tradition that extolled his virtues as a pious king and his exploits as a warrior. This epic tradition was the source for the many versions of the Duṭṭhagāmaṇī story found in the Sri Lankan monastic chronicles and in later Sinhala literature. The classic version is found in the *Mahāvaṃsa,* the most important of the chronicles.

The qualities of piety and violence—antithetical in canonical Buddhist ethics—are woven together in the *Mahāvaṃsa's* account of Duṭṭhagāmaṇī's military campaign to become overlord. He declares that his battles are "for the sake of the *sāsana* [i.e., Buddhism]" and "not for the pleasures of sovereignty." He goes into battle with monks in his army and a relic of the Buddha on his spear. The dramatic climax comes with Duṭṭhagāmaṇī's single combat with the Tamil king Eḷāra, who, while described as a just and righteous ruler, is judged by the *Mahāvaṃsa* as unfit to be overlord because he was not a Buddhist.

All versions of the story give prominence to the pious deeds done by Duṭṭhagāmaṇī after he became overlord. The *Mahāvaṃsa* says that, in addition to his construction of monuments (including the Great Stupa at Anuradhapura) and his many donations to the monastic order, he gifted sovereignty over the island to the relics of the Buddha, a sign of Sri Lanka's identity as a Buddhist polity. As a result of these meritorious deeds, we are told, he has been reborn in the Tusita (Skt., Tuṣita) heaven, and in the future will be reborn as a chief disciple of the next buddha, Metteyya.

A crucial element in the story is Duṭṭhagāmaṇī's remorse over the killing done in battle, a motif that recalls Aśoka, the first Buddhist imperial ruler. A delegation of enlightened monks (*arahants*) counsels the king that he has no reason to feel remorse. In different versions of the story, various explanations for this counsel are suggested, an indication perhaps that the counsel itself troubled Buddhists: Duṭṭhagāmaṇī's victims were not Buddhist, and thus killing them was somehow not equivalent to taking human life; his intentions to protect the *sāsana* were good, and would outweigh the evil of his actions; there would be no opportunity for the fruits of these evil deeds to mature, since his rebirth in heaven was assured by his good deeds, and this counsel was given only to comfort his mind.

The folk epic tradition assumed a strong communalist character—specifically anti-Tamil—which became increasingly visible in the later literature. This communalist character has made the Duṭṭhagāmaṇī story a vitriolic element in the political and religious rhetoric of modern Sri Lanka.

The story was an important part of the *dhammadīpa* ("island of truth") tradition, which viewed Sri Lanka as the repository of the Buddha's teaching. It emphasized the necessity of political unity for the island to fulfill its religious destiny, as well as the special and exclusive relationship its rulers were to have with Buddhism.

The Duṭṭhagāmaṇī story has also had a continuing significance in Sinhala Buddhism as a background for interpretation. It has provided a context for resolving conflicts about ethical issues (e.g., whether violence is ever permissible), for elucidating points of Buddhist doctrine, and for legitimizing social and religious charters.

BIBLIOGRAPHY

The *Mahāvaṃsa* version of the Duṭṭhagāmaṇī story has been translated by Wilhelm Geiger in chapters 22–32 of *The Mahāvaṃsa, or the Great Chronicle of Ceylon* (London, 1912). This classic version should be compared with the later versions found in the *Thūpavamsa,* translated from Pali by N. A. Jayawickrama (London, 1971), and in the *Saddharmālaṇkaraya,* a medieval Sinhala prose work, a translation of which is found in *An Anthology of Sinhalese Literature up to 1815,* edited by Christopher Reynolds (London, 1970). A classic discussion of the epic tradition is provided by Wilhelm Geiger in *The Dīpavaṁsa and Mahāvaṃsa and Their Historical Development in Ceylon,* translated by Ethel M. Coomaraswamy (Colombo, 1908). Many of the articles in the collection *Religion and Legitimation of Power in Sri Lanka,* edited by Bardwell L. Smith (Chambersburg, Pa., 1978), consider the place of the Duṭṭhagāmaṇī story in Sinhala "religio-nationalism"; related folk traditions are discussed by Marguerite S. Robinson in "'The House of the Mighty Hero' or 'The House of Enough Paddy'? Some Implications of a Sinhalese Myth," in *Dialectic in Practical Religion,* edited by Edmund R. Leach (Cambridge, U.K., 1968), pp. 122–152. An idea of how widely the story has functioned as a background for interpretation in Sinhala Buddhism can be gathered from the many references to Dutugämunu (the Sinhala cognate of Duṭṭhagāmaṇī) in Richard F. Gombrich's *Precept and Practice: Traditional Buddhism in the Rural Highlands of Ceylon* (Oxford, 1971).

New Sources

Bartholomeusz, Tessa. "In Defense of Dharma: Just-War Ideology in Buddhist Sri Lanka." *Journal of Buddhist Ethics* 6 (1999). Available from http://jbe.gold.ac.uk/6/current6.html.

Bretfeld, Sven. *Das singhalesische Nationalepos von König Duttha-gamani Abhaya: Textkritische Bearbeitung und Übersetzung der Kapitel VII. 3-VIII. 3 der Rasavahini des Vedeha Thera und Vergleich mit den Paralleltexten Sahassavatthuppakarana und Saddharmalankaraya.* Berlin, 2001.

Obeyesekere, Gananath. "Dutthagamani and the Buddhist Conscience." In *Religion and Political Conflict in South Asia,* edited by Douglas Allen, pp. 135–160. Westport, Conn., 1992.

CHARLES HALLISEY (1987)
FRANK E. REYNOLDS (1987)
Revised Bibliography

DVERGAR (dwarfs) are an all-male race of supernatural beings in Germanic mythology. Only in later sagas are they described as stunted and deformed. Molded from earth or quickened in the blood of giants in earlier eddic sources (*Gylfaginning*, ch. 13; *Vǫluspá*, st. 9), the dwarfs were created by the gods. This was the most successful of the gods' experiments in producing life by nonbiological means, for the dwarfs were craftsmen like the gods and served their interests. Artisans in wood and metal and gifted with magical creativity, dwarfs produced precious objects such as Þórr's hammer, Óðinn's spear, Sif's golden hair, Freyr's boat, and Freyja's necklace and boar. A particularly useful item that they forged for the gods was the magical fetter that kept the monstrous wolf Fenrir bound until the gods' last battle at Ragnarǫk. Dwarfs also engaged in creative enterprises of their own, such as brewing the mead of wisdom and poetic inspiration (*Skáldskaparmál*, ch. 1).

Dwarfs occupied an intermediate position between gods and giants (*Hávamál*, st. 143). Active, inventive, and humanlike, as were the gods, they lived in earth or rocks and associated with death and cold, as did the giants. Also like giants, dwarfs were assigned a place in Germanic cosmogony. Four dwarfs (Austri [East], Vestri [West], Suðri [South], and Norðri [North]) were said to uphold the four corners of the sky, which was made from the skull of the primordial giant Ymir. But where the giants were generally hostile to the gods, dwarfs were generally friendly, becoming vindictive only when they were treated unfairly. For example, the gold guarded by the dragon Fáfnir had originally been taken from a dwarf by Loki. The dwarf put a curse on it, which led to the tragedies of the Vǫlsungs and the Nibelungs. Unmotivated hostility by the dwarfs is seen in their capture and killing of Kvasir, from whose blood they brewed the mead of poetic inspiration.

Dwarfs could not reproduce, but the eddic poem *Alvíssmál* describes how Alvíss (All-Wise) persuaded the gods to give him Þórr's daughter. Like the giants who sought Freyja and Iðunn for their brides, this dwarf tried to redress the social imbalance that forbade the goddesses to be married to anyone but gods. Þórr thwarted Alvíss's effort by starting a riddle contest with him, with questions continuing until dawn, when the rays of the sun turned the dwarf into stone.

Depicted principally as craftsmen and resembling priests in their possession of secret knowledge and magic chants (*Hávamál*, st. 160), dwarfs show affinity with the earth-dwelling forces of magical creativity of the Mediterranean regions, such as Ptah of Egypt, Hephaistos of Lemnos, and the Daktyls of Crete, but they are more likely to have originated as demons of death, as suggested by their underground home and names like Bláinn (Blue, black), Dáinn (Dead), and Nár (Corpse). Alvíss is described as having a pale nose and looking as if he had spent the night with a corpse. There is little to suggest that the dwarfs were venerated.

SEE ALSO Eddas; Germanic Religion; Jǫtnar.

BIBLIOGRAPHY

See John Lindow's *Scandinavian Mythology: An Annotated Bibliography* (New York, 1988), particularly for the studies by Lotte Motz. Mircea Eliade discusses the significance of the artisan in early societies in *The Forge and the Crucible*, 2d ed. (Chicago, 1978), and Margaret Clunies Ross takes a sociological approach in the first volume of *Prolonged Echoes: Old Norse Myths in Medieval Northern Society* (Odense, Denmark, 1994). The encyclopedia-style entries of Rudolf Simek's *Dictionary of Northern Mythology* (Cambridge, U.K., 1993) and John Lindow's *Handbook of Norse Mythology* (Santa Barbara, 2001) are very detailed.

LOTTE MOTZ (1987)
ELIZABETH ASHMAN ROWE (2005)

DWIGHT, TIMOTHY (1752–1817), president of Yale College and leader of Connecticut orthodoxy. A grandson of Jonathan Edwards, Dwight viewed himself as within the Edwardsean "New Divinity" tradition. But by Dwight's time the Edwardsean "consistent Calvinism" had become an arid scholasticism that denigrated all human activity, or "means," used in the process of attaining salvation. As Harriet Beecher Stowe later commented, the high Calvinistic system as expounded by Edwards's intellectual followers was like a "rungless ladder" with piety at the top and no human way to ascend. "Consistent Calvinist" ministers of early national America alienated their parishioners and dampened religious fervor. On the other hand, liberal moralists of the time were compromising the historic doctrines of the reformed faith and veering toward Unitarianism. Dwight, an important transitional figure in the development of a nineteenth-century American evangelical consensus, devised a practical theology with the avowed purpose of countering America's late-eighteenth-century slide into secularism.

As president of Yale College between 1795 and 1817, Dwight forged his system of theology, which he preached in sermon form, exerting profound influence on a multitude of students who later entered the ministry. With his pragmatic approach, Dwight did not abjure such Calvinist doctrines as depravity, election, or absolute divine sovereignty, but he avoided giving them the effect of rendering humanity powerless in the process of salvation. He laid emphasis on the means by which one can attain piety, accentuating the spiritual potency of an environment saturated in "true religion." In many an emotion-laden sermon Dwight exhorted his students to repent and receive the Savior. In his revivalistic preaching and his enhancement of Christian nurture, Dwight influenced such important divines as Nathaniel W. Taylor and Lyman Beecher, both of whom studied under him at Yale. These men devised the practical, evangelistic orthodoxy that spawned the interdenominational "benevolent societies" and played a major part in spreading the Second Great Awakening. Dwight's emphasis on nurture was later picked up and expanded by the influential Hartford theologian Horace Bushnell, a forerunner of the Social Gospel.

BIBLIOGRAPHY

Dwight's best-known work is his *Travels in New England and New York* (1823; reprint, Cambridge, Mass., 1969). In this four-volume compendium, he comments editorially on the religion, culture, and politics, as well as the geographical features of his region. Republished, the *Travels* has been edited and given an excellent introduction by Barbara Miller Solomon. Dwight's *Theology Explained and Defended in a Series of Sermons*, 4 vols. (New Haven, 1823), went through a number of nineteenth-century editions. It is the best and most comprehensive exposition of his theology. There are three modern biographical studies of Dwight, each of which views his life from a different perspective. Charles E. Cunningham's *Timothy Dwight 1752–1817* (New York, 1942) concentrates on his attainments as educator. It is the most complete biography of Dwight. Kenneth Silverman's work, *Timothy Dwight* (New York, 1969) focuses on the development of his social and political views as expounded in his narrative and epic poetry. Stephen E. Berk's *Calvinism versus Democracy: Timothy Dwight and the Origins of American Evangelical Orthodoxy* (Hamden, Conn., 1974) considers Dwight as theologian and ecclesiastical politician, relating his career to the broader social and religious currents of his time. It contains the only detailed appraisal of Dwight's theology.

STEPHEN E. BERK (1987)

DYBBUK is a term used in Jewish sources for a dead soul possessing the body of a living person. The term first appears in seventeenth-century Ashkenazi (European) Jewish sources. Earlier Jewish sources and Sephardic (Middle Eastern) Jewry even after the seventeenth century refer to a possessed person as "adhered to by an evil spirit" (*davuk mi-ruah ra'ah*). Ashkenazi usage borrowed the root of the verb "to adhere" and made it into a noun signifying "the adherer" (Scholem, 1934). While cases of spirit possession are found in Jewish sources dating back to antiquity, the scattered references in ancient rabbinic literature were followed by a millennium of silence, which was finally broken by a dozen or so sixteenth-century narrative accounts. These first tales served as models for subsequent cases and their narration. Approximately eighty similar accounts were recorded from the seventeenth to the early twentieth centuries (Nigal, 1994).

ETIOLOGY. Although the early modern etiology of spirit possession most commonly regarded the possessing agent as a dead soul, earlier Jewish sources refer to the possessing agents as *shedim* or *mazzikim*, these being malevolent demons. The increasing tendency to identify the intruder as a dead soul is an indication of the growing prominence of the doctrine of reincarnation in sixteenth-century Judaism (Scholem, 1991). The Jewish doctrine, as articulated by contemporary mystical theorists, allowed both for reincarnation into a body at birth (*gilgul*; literally, "rolling"), as well as for the temporary transmigration of a soul into an adult body in a supplementary capacity (*'ibbur*; literally, "impregnation"). While the term *dybbuk* would come to be exclusively associated with the evil "impregnation" of the dead into bodies of the living, contemporary Jewish mystics actively pursued benevolent "impregnations" of saints into their own bodies, often through prostration upon the graves of the righteous (Kallus, 2003; Giller, 1994).

Classical Jewish sources generally regarded the afterlife as entailing a stay of up to a year in Gehenna, a purgatory that was thought to refine and purify the soul in preparation for its entrance into the Edenic heavens. According to sixteenth-century conceptions, however, particularly evil individuals lacked sufficient merit to gain admission to Gehenna. They would thus linger in a tortuous limbo of unspecified duration. Respite for such a soul could only be obtained through its taking refuge in the body of a living person; possession also allowed a soul to negotiate the terms of its admission to Gehenna through the intervention of a rabbinic exorcist.

LOCUS. The Galilean town of Safed was the epicenter of the efflorescence of spirit possession among Jews in the sixteenth century. The Jews of Safed in this period were predominantly pietistic refugees and penitent *conversos* of Iberian origin who, along with other new immigrants from Jewish communities from around the world, chose the town for its religious advantages as soon as political and economic conditions facilitated their doing so. Despite its small size, Safed became the religious capital of world Jewry, producing masterworks of legal, homiletical, and mystical literature that have remained influential to this day. Leading the Jewish religious revival in Palestine that followed in the wake of the Ottoman conquest of 1516, these mystics cultivated benevolent forms of possession while also serving as exorcists for those whose experiences were of an unwelcome variety. Just as centers of religious devotion in sixteenth- and seventeenth-century Europe were the focal points of outbreaks of demonic possession, cases of "*dybbuk*" possession notably emerge in Jewish society in the context of this community of self-selected mystical pietists. The monastic intensity of this small community, which took upon itself the burden not only to lead, but to atone for the sins of the entire Jewish people, may have been the driving force behind the eruption of spirit possession in Safed (Chajes, 2003).

Isolated cases from this period were also reported in Jewish communities elsewhere in the Ottoman Empire, as well as in Italy. Over the subsequent centuries, *dybbuk* possession was reported in Jewish communities from North Africa to eastern Europe. Accounts of spirit possession from Hasidic circles tend to focus less on the victim or spirit, as did earlier accounts, and more on the exorcist—in this case, a Hasidic master. While always serving a didactic function, *dybbuk* accounts in the nineteenth century thus became part and parcel of Hasidic hagiography. The last well publicized case of *dybbuk* possession took place in Dimona, Israel, in April 1999 when a 38-year-old widow was diagnosed by a prominent Jerusalem rabbi as possessed by the soul of her late husband.

SIGNS OF POSSESSION. Jewish sources note symptoms of *dybbuk* possession that closely correlate to those found in many other cultures. Physical signs include epileptic collapse, called "the falling sickness" *(holi ha-nofel)* in medieval sources; unnatural strength; and egg-shaped swellings under the skin, often seen in motion and identified as the source of the *dybbuk*'s speech. Impostors and insanity were thought to be ruled out, especially when the spirit spoke in a language unknown to the victim (xenoglossia) and when the sins of those present were exposed through its clairvoyance (Patai, 1978). *Dybbukim* (plural) were often thought to have entered their female victims through the vagina, but other orifices could also be subject to penetration. Food in which a *dybbuk* was lodged might thus enter a victim who innocently ate of it. Finally, while *dybbuk* possession was involuntary and the victim not culpable for what she said or did under the influence, many victims were thought to have been possessed as a punishment for a previous sin of omission or commission. Sins of belief seem to have been particularly common, especially what might be called "folk-skepticism" or unlearned disbelief in traditional doctrines and authority.

TRADITIONAL TREATMENT: JEWISH EXORCISM. While narrative accounts of spirit possession among Jews are lacking between antiquity and the sixteenth century, the evidence of Hebrew and Aramaic magical literature indicates a striking continuity in the approach to treating the possessed over the centuries. A typical Jewish exorcism would begin with the diagnostic examination of the suffering victim. If possession was confirmed, efforts to obtain the name of the spirit would begin. Without obtaining this name, there could be no successful adjuration (Gk., *horkos* [exorcism]; Heb., *hashba'ah*) of the spirit to depart. Threats of excommunication might be used, along with adjured angels and demons, as well as fumigations of burning sulphur. Such ceremonies were often punctuated by the thunderous blasts of a ram's horn (*shofar*), which Jewish sources dating back to antiquity believed had the power to discombobulate demonic forces (*le'arbev et ha-satan*). Finally, an amulet might be written to be hung upon the victim, lest she be repossessed by the dislocated spirit in the aftermath of a successful exorcism (Knox, 1938).

In the wake of the etiological shift of the sixteenth century and the increasing tendency to identify the spirit as the soul of a Jewish sinner, penitential liturgy on behalf of the spirit is added to the exorcism formulae. Thus the exorcist comes to advocate on behalf of this tormented soul and to facilitate its admission to Gehenna in a negotiated quid pro quo, in exchange for leaving the victim quickly and unharmed.

According to the extant accounts, women were more likely to be victims of *dybbuk* possession by a margin of about two to one. While heterosexual penetration was most common, we also find cases of male souls possessing men; possessions by female souls rarely occur. This predominance of possessed women, not unique to the Jewish possession idiom, has often been viewed as resulting from their social or sexual deprivation in patriarchal cultures. Possession affords its primarily female victims with a licit opportunity for public expression and for the release of suppressed beliefs and feelings; exorcism, in this interpretation, reintegrates the victim into the community (Bilu, 1985). While such functionalist interpretations are compelling, critics charge that they are invoked too quickly in the analysis of women's religiosity, thus disallowing for the possibility of women acting religiously for religious (rather than social or psychological) reasons (Sered, 1994). Indeed, there is reason to believe that at least some of the women described as *dybbuk*-possessed may have been female visionaries and clairvoyants venerated by segments of the community unrepresented in the accounts composed by men (Chajes, 2003; Deutsch, 2004).

Dybbuk possession is known today primarily through the Yiddish play, *Between Two Worlds: The Dybbuk,* written in the early twentieth century by S. Ansky, and first performed shortly after his death in 1920 (Werses, 1986; Ansky, 2002). Ansky's ethnographic research in eastern Europe and his keen grasp of the dramatic potential of possession narratives resulted in a mythic tale of a righteous young scholar who gives up everything, including life itself, to be united with his true love. Denied her as his bride in life, he possesses her upon his death on the day she was to have married another. Adapted for film and shot in Poland in 1937, *Der Dibuk* is one of the finest Yiddish films of the period and, in retrospect, a poignant time-capsule of Jewish life in Poland in its final hour. The play, directed by Evgeny Vakhtangov, was also performed in 1922 in a Hebrew version by the Habima theater troupe in Russia; Habima would later stage popular revivals of the play in Tel Aviv, lending it a formative role in the history of Israeli theater. More recent works by Leonard Bernstein, Tony Kushner, and others testify to the enduring appeal of this material.

SEE ALSO Exorcism; Hasidism; Magic; Qabbalah; Spirit Possession.

BIBLIOGRAPHY

Ansky, S. *The Dybbuk and Other Writings.* Edited by David G. Roskies and translated by Golda Werman. New Haven and London, 2002.

Bilu, Yoram. "The Taming of the Deviants and Beyond: An Analysis of Dibbuk Possession and Exorcism in Judaism." In *The Psychoanalytic Study of Society: Essays in Honor of Paul Parin,* edited by L. Bryce Boyer and Simon A. Grolnick, pp. 1–32. Hillsdale, N.J., and London, 1985.

Chajes, J. H. *Between Worlds: Dybbuks, Exorcists, and Early Modern Judaism.* Philadelphia, 2003.

Deutsch, Nathaniel. *The Maiden of Ludmir: A Jewish Holy Woman and Her World.* Berkeley, Calif., 2004.

Giller, Pinchas. "Recovering the Sanctity of the Galilee: The Veneration of Sacred Relics in Classical Kabbalah." *Journal of Jewish Thought and Philosophy* 4 (1994): 147–169.

Kallus, Menachem. "Pneumatic Mystical Possession and the Eschatology of the Soul in the Lurianic Qabbalah." In *Spirit Possession in Judaism: Cases and Contexts from the Middle Ages to the Present,* edited by Matt Goldish. Detroit, 2003.

Knox, W. L. "Jewish Liturgical Exorcism." *Harvard Theological Review* 31, no. 3 (1938): 191–203.

Nigal, Gedalyah. *Sippurei Dybbuk be-Sifrut Yisrael.* Jerusalem, 1994.

Patai, R. "Exorcism and Xenoglossia among the Safed Kabbalists." *Journal of American Folklore* 91 (1978): 823–835.

Scholem, Gershom. "'*Golem*' and '*Dibbuk*' in the Hebrew Lexicon." *Leshonenu* 6 (1934): 40–41.

Scholem, Gershom. "Gilgul: The Transmigration of Souls." In *On the Mystical Shape of the Godhead: Basic Concepts in Kabbalah,* edited by Jonathan Chipman, pp. 197–250. New York, 1991.

Sered, Susan Starr. *Priestess, Mother, Sacred Sister: Religions Dominated by Women.* New York and Oxford, 1994.

Werses, Shmuel. "S. An-ski's '*tsvishn Tsvey Veltn* (*Der Dybbuk*)' '*beyn Shney Olamot* (*Hadybbuk*)' '*Between Two Worlds* (*The Dybbuk*)': A Textual History." In *Studies in Yiddish Literature and Folklore,* edited by Chava Turniansky, pp. 99–185. Jerusalem, 1986.

J. H. CHAJES (2005)

DYING AND RISING GODS.

The category of dying and rising gods, once a major topic of scholarly investigation, must now be understood to have been largely a misnomer based on imaginative reconstructions and exceedingly late or highly ambiguous texts.

DEFINITION. As applied in the scholarly literature, "dying and rising gods" is a generic appellation for a group of male deities found in agrarian Mediterranean societies who serve as the focus of myths and rituals that allegedly narrate and annually represent their death and resurrection.

Beyond this sufficient criterion, dying and rising deities were often held by scholars to have a number of cultic associations, sometimes thought to form a "pattern." They were young male figures of fertility; the drama of their lives was often associated with mother or virgin goddesses; in some areas, they were related to the institution of sacred kingship, often expressed through rituals of sacred marriage; there were dramatic reenactments of their life, death, and putative resurrection, often accompanied by a ritual identification of either the society or given individuals with their fate.

The category of dying and rising gods, as well as the pattern of its mythic and ritual associations, received its earliest full formulation in the influential work of James G. Frazer *The Golden Bough,* especially in its two central volumes, *The Dying God* and *Adonis, Attis, Osiris.* Frazer offered two interpretations, one euhemerist, the other naturist. In the former, which focused on the figure of the dying god, it was held that a (sacred) king would be slain when his fertility waned. This practice, it was suggested, would be later mythologized, giving rise to a dying god. The naturist explanation, which covered the full cycle of dying and rising, held the deities to be personifications of the seasonal cycle of vegetation. The two interpretations were linked by the notion that death followed upon a loss of fertility, with a period of sterility being followed by one of rejuvenation, either in the transfer of the kingship to a successor or by the rebirth or resurrection of the deity.

There are empirical problems with the euhemerist theory. The evidence for sacral regicide is limited and ambiguous; where it appears to occur, there are no instances of a dying god figure. The naturist explanation is flawed at the level of theory. Modern scholarship has largely rejected, for good reasons, an interpretation of deities as projections of natural phenomena.

Nevertheless, the figure of the dying and rising deity has continued to be employed, largely as a preoccupation of biblical scholarship, among those working on ancient Near Eastern sacred kingship in relation to the Hebrew Bible and among those concerned with the Hellenistic mystery cults in relation to the New Testament.

BROADER CATEGORIES. Despite the shock this fact may deal to modern Western religious sensibilities, it is a commonplace within the history of religions that immortality is not a prime characteristic of divinity: Gods die. Nor is the concomitant of omnipresence a widespread requisite: Gods disappear. The putative category of dying and rising deities thus takes its place within the larger category of dying gods and the even larger category of disappearing deities. Some of these divine figures simply disappear; some disappear only to return again in the near or distant future; some disappear and reappear with monotonous frequency. All the deities that have been identified as belonging to the class of dying and rising deities can be subsumed under the two larger classes of disappearing deities or dying deities. In the first case, the deities return but have not died; in the second case, the gods die but do not return. There is no unambiguous instance in the history of religions of a dying and rising deity.

THE DEITIES. The list of specific deities to whom the appellation "dying and rising" has been attached varies. In most cases, the decipherment and interpretation of texts in the language native to the deity's cult has led to questions as to the applicability of the category. The majority of evidence for Near Eastern dying and rising deities occurs in Greek and Latin texts of late antiquity, usually post-Christian in date.

Adonis. Despite the original Semitic provenance of Adonis, there is no native mythology. What is known depends on later Greek, Roman, and Christian interpretations.

There are two major forms of the Adonis myth, only brought together in late mythographical tradition (e.g., the second-century CE *Bibliotheca,* falsely attributed to Apollodorus of Athens). The first, which may be termed the Panyasisian form, knows only of a quarrel between two goddesses (Aphrodite and Persephone) for the affections of the infant Adonis. Zeus or Calliope decrees that Adonis should spend part of the year in the upperworld with the one, and part of the year in the lowerworld with the other. This tradition of bilocation (similar to that connected with Persephone and, perhaps, Dumuzi) has no suggestion of death and rebirth. The second, more familiar Ovidian form narrates Adonis's death by a boar and his commemoration by Aphrodite in a flower. There is no suggestion of Adonis rising. The first version lacks an account of Adonis's death; the second emphasizes the goddess's mourning and the fragility of the flower that perpetuates his memory. Even when the two versions are combined, Adonis' alternation between the upper and lower worlds precedes his death.

The rituals of Adonis, held during the summer months, are everywhere described as periods of intense mourning. Only late texts, largely influenced by or written by Christians, claim that there is a subsequent day of celebration for Adonis having been raised from the dead. The earliest of these is alleged to be the second-century account of Lucian (*Syrian Goddess* 6–7) that, on the third day of the ritual, a statue of Adonis is "brought out into the light" and "addressed as if alive"; but this is an ambiguous report. Lucian goes on to say that some think the ritual is not for Adonis but rather for some Egyptian deity. The practice of addressing a statue "as if alive" is no proof of belief in resurrection; rather it is the common presupposition of any cultic activity in the Mediterranean world that uses images. Besides, Lucian reports that after the "address" women cut their hair as a sign of mourning.

Considerably later, the Christian writers Origen and Jerome, commenting on *Ezekiel* 8:14, and Cyril of Alexandria and Procopius of Gaza, commenting on *Isaiah* 18:1, clearly report joyous festivities on the third day to celebrate Adonis (identified with Tammuz) having been "raised from the dead." Whether this represents an *interpretatio Christiana* or whether late third- and fourth-century forms of the Adonis cult themselves developed a dying and rising mythology (possibility in imitation of the Christian myth) cannot be determined. This pattern will recur for many of the figures considered: an indigenous mythology and ritual focusing on the deity's death and rituals of lamentation, followed by a later Christian report adding the element nowhere found in the earlier native sources, that the god was resurrected.

The frequently cited "gardens of Adonis" (the *kepoi)* were proverbial illustrations of the brief, transitory nature of life and contain no hint of rebirth. The point is that the young plant shoots rapidly wither and die, not that the seeds have been "reborn" when they sprout.

Finally, despite scholarly fantasies, there is no evidence for the existence of any mysteries of Adonis whereby the member was identified with Adonis or his fate.

Aliyan Baal. The Ras Shamra texts (late Bronze Age) narrate the descent into the underworld of the puissant deity Aliyan Baal ("the one who prevails; the lord") and his apparent return. Unfortunately, the order of the incidents in the several different texts that have been held to form a Baal cycle is uncertain. The texts that are of greatest relevance to the question of whether Aliyan Baal is correctly to be classified as a dying and rising deity have major lacunae at the most crucial points. Although these texts have been reconstructed by some scholars using the dying and rising pattern, whether these texts are an independent witness to that pattern remains an open question.

In the major narrative cycle, Baal, having won the rulership by vanquishing the dangerous waters, is challenged by Mot, ruler of the underworld, to descend into his realm. After some initial hesitation, and after copulating with a cow, Baal accepts the challenge and goes down to the lower realm, whence it will be said of him that he is as if dead. After a gap of some forty lines, Baal is reported to have died. Anat descends and recovers his corpse, which is properly buried; a successor to Baal is then appointed, and Anat seeks out and kills Mot. After the narrative is interrupted by another forty-line gap, El declares, on the basis of a symbolic dream, that Baal still lives. After another gap of similar length, Baal is described as being in combat with a group of deities. As is apparent from this brief summary, much depends on the order of incidents. As it stands, the text appears to be one of a descent to the underworld and return—a pattern not necessarily equivalent to dying and rising. Baal is "as if he is dead"; he then appears to be alive.

In another, even more fragmentary Hadad cycle (Hadad being identified with Baal), Hadad goes off to capture a group of monsters, but they, in turn, pursue him. In order to escape he hides in a bog, where he lies sick for seven years while the earth is parched and without growth. Hadad's brothers eventually find him and he is rescued. This is a disappearing-reappearing narrative. There is no suggestion of death and resurrection.

There is no evidence that any of the events narrated in these distressingly fragmentary texts were ritually reenacted. Nor is there any suggestion of an annual cycle of death and rebirth. The question whether Aliyan Baal is a dying and rising deity must remain *sub judice.*

Attis. The complex mythology of Attis is largely irrelevant to the question of dying and rising deities. In the old, Phrygian version, Attis is killed by being castrated, either by himself or by another; in the old Lydian version, he is killed by a boar. In neither case is there any question of his returning to life. There is a second series of later traditions that deny that Attis died of his wounds but do not narrate his subsequent death or, for that matter, his rebirth. Finally, two late, post-Christian theological reflections on the myth hint at rebirth: the complex allegory in the *Naassene Sermon* and the euhemerist account in Firmacus Maternus, in which a pretended resurrection is mentioned. Attis is not, in his mythology, a dying and rising deity; indeed, he is not a deity at all.

All of the attempts in the scholarly literature to identify Attis as a dying and rising deity depend not on the mythology but rather on the ritual, in particular a questionable interpretation of the five-day festival of Cybele on March 22–27. The question of the relationship between the Day of Blood (March 24) and the Day of Joy (March 25) caught the attention of some scholars, who, employing the analogy of the relationship of Good Friday to Easter Sunday, reasoned that if among other activities on the Day of Blood there was mourning for Attis, then the object of the "joy" on the following day must be Attis's resurrection. Unfortunately, there is no evidence that this was the case. The Day of Joy is a late addition to what was once a three-day ritual in which the Day of Blood was followed by a purificatory ritual and the return of the statue of the goddess to the temple. Within the cult, the new feast of the Day of Joy celebrates Cybele. The sole text that connects the Day of Joy with Attis is a fifth-century biography of Isidore the Dialectician by the Neoplatonic philosopher Damascius, who reports that Isidore once had a dream in which he was Attis and the Day of Joy was celebrated in his honor!

Scholars have frequently cited a text in Firmacus Maternus (22.3) as referring to Attis and his resurrection on the Day of Joy: "Be of good cheer, you of the mysteries, your god is saved!" However, the god is unidentified, and the notion of "cheer" is insufficient to link this utterance to Attis and the Day of Joy. The text most probably reflects a late antique Osirian ritual.

Neither myth nor ritual offers any warrant for classifying Attis as a dying and rising deity.

Marduk. The figure of the king-god of Babylon, Marduk, has been crucial to those scholars associated with the Myth and Ritual school as applied to the religions of the ancient Near East. For here, as in no other figure, the central elements of their proposed pattern appear to be brought together: the correlation of myth and ritual, the annual celebration of the dying and rising of a deity, paralleled by an annual ritual death and rebirth of the king. Marduk is the canonical instance of the Myth and Ritual pattern.

In 1921, F. Thureau-Dangin published the text, transcription, and translation of a Seleucid era text, preserved in two copies, presenting a part of the ritual for the New Year festival (the Akitu) in Babylon. Despite a large number of references to the performance of the ritual in Babylonian texts (although not always to the Akitu associated with Marduk or Babylon) and scattered mentions of individual items in the ritual, this exceedingly late cuneiform text is the only detailed description of the ritual program in Babylon to survive. It enjoins twenty-six ritual actions for the first five days of the twelve-day ceremony, including a double reading of a text entitled *Enuma elish.* Assuming that this reference is to some form of the text now known by that name, the "Babylonian creation epic" as reconstructed by contemporary scholarship, the ritual suggests a close link to the myth. However, not one of the twenty-six ritual actions bears the slightest resemblance to any narrative element in the myth. Whatever the significance of the recitation of the text during the Akitu festival, the myth is not reenacted in that portion of the ceremonies that has survived.

Realizing this, some proponents of the Myth and Ritual approach have argued that the first five days of the ritual were only purificatory in nature, and go on to speculate that the next three days of the festival featured a dramatic reenactment of a myth of the death and resurrection of Marduk. This sort of imaginative speculation gave rise to a new set of problems. There is no hint of Marduk's death in the triumphant account of his cosmic kingship in *Enuma elish.* If some such myth was enacted, it was not the one stipulated in the ritual program. Nevertheless, scholars turned to a cuneiform text that they entitled *The Death and Resurrection of Bel-Marduk.* The title is somewhat misleading. There are sixteen episodes in the text, which appears to narrate Marduk's imprisonment. The text is fragmentary and difficult to interpret, but it appears to be in the form of a ritual commentary in which a set of ritual gestures are correlated to events in a subtextual narrative of Marduk's capture.

For an older generation of scholars, Marduk's imprisonment was equivalent to his death, and his presumed ultimate release represented his resurrection. More recent interpretations have minimized the cosmic symbolism: Marduk has been arrested and is being held for trial. By either reading, such a narrative of the king-god's weakness or crime would appear odd in a Babylonian setting. This caution is strengthened by the fact that the text is of Assyrian provenance and is written in the Assyrian dialect. It is not a native Babylonian text and could have played no role in the central festival of Babylon.

The so-called *Death and Resurrection of Bel-Marduk* is most likely an Assyrian political parody of some now unrecoverable Babylonian ritual composed after the Assyrians conquered Babylon in 691/689 BCE. At that time, the statue of Marduk was carried off into Assyrian captivity. From one point of view, the text has a simple, propagandistic message: Compared to the gods of Ashur, Marduk is a weak deity. More subtly, for those Assyrians who held Marduk in some reverence, the notion of his crimes would provide religious justification for his capture.

The notion that the king undergoes an annual ritual of mimetic dying and rising is predicated on the fact that the deity, whose chief representative is the king, is believed to undergo a similar fate. If it is doubtful that Marduk was understood as a dying and rising deity, it is also doubtful that such a ritual was required of the king. Some scholars have held that the so-called ritual humiliation of the king on the fifth day of the New Year festival, with its startling portrayal of the king being dethroned, slapped, pulled by the ears, and reenthroned, is symbolic of his death and resurrection. But such an interpretation ignores both the manifest content of the ritual text and its date. During the humiliation ceremony, the king is required to recite a negative confession: that he did not overthrow his capital city of Babylon or tear down its walls, that he did not insult its protected citizens, that he did not neglect or destroy its central temple.

From one point of view, such a negative confession is ludicrous. What native Babylonian king ever contemplated, much less carried out, such actions? These were the actions of foreign kings (Assyrian, Persian, Seleucid) who gained the throne of Babylon by conquest and desecrated the native cult. However, as with Cyrus among the Israelites, so too for the Babylonians, foreign kings could be named who restored Babylon and its temple. Read in this light, the ritual humiliation of the king appears to be a piece of Babylonian nationalistic ritual rectification: Good fortune and continued kingship comes to the (foreign) king if he acts as a pious (native) king would act. If not, he will be stripped of his kingship.

This understanding is made more plausible by the date of the only surviving texts of the ritual. They are all from the Hellenistic Seleucid period, that is to say, from a period after the ending of native kingship and the installing of foreign kings on the throne. The pattern may be earlier, dating back, perhaps, to the time of Sargon II (r. 721–705 BCE), the earliest conqueror of Babylon to adopt consciously the Babylonian etiquette of kingship and during whose rule, for the first time, one finds legal texts guaranteeing Assyrian recognition of the rights and privileges of the "protected citizens" of Babylon. In the present text of the New Year ritual, a set of actions designed to deal with the more proximate Assyrian conquerors has been reapplied to the relatively more foreign Seleucid rulers.

There is no evidence that the Babylonian Marduk was ever understood to be a dying and rising deity, that such a myth was reenacted during the New Year festival, or that the king was believed to undergo a similar fate.

Osiris. In contrast to the other deities considered above, Osiris has a thick textual dossier stretching over millennia. Although the full, connected myth is only to be found in Greek, in Plutarch's *Isis and Osiris* from the early second century CE, the Osirian myth can be reconstructed from the Pyramid Texts of the fifth and sixth dynasties. While the names of the actors and details of the incidents vary, this record is remarkably consistent over twenty-five hundred years. Osiris was murdered and his body dismembered and scattered. The pieces of his body were recovered and rejoined, and the god was rejuvenated. However, he did not return to his former mode of existence but rather journeyed to the underworld, where he became the powerful lord of the dead. In no sense can Osiris be said to have "risen" in the sense required by the dying and rising pattern; most certainly it was never conceived as an annual event. The repeated formula "Rise up, you have not died," whether applied to Osiris or a citizen of Egypt, signaled a new, permanent life in the realm of the dead.

Osiris was considered to be the mythical prototype for the distinctive Egyptian process of mummification. Iconographically, Osiris is always depicted in mummified form. The descriptions of the recovery and rejoining of the pieces of his body are all elaborate parallels to funerary rituals: the vigil over his corpse, the hymns of lamentation, the embalmment (usually performed by Anubis), the washing and purification of the corpse, the undertaking of the elaborate ritual of the "opening of the mouth" with its 107 separate operations, as well as other procedures for reanimation, the dressing of the body, and the pouring out of libations. Through these parallels, the individual Egyptian dead became identified with, and addressed as, Osiris (perhaps earliest in Pyramid Texts 167a–168a). The myth and ritual of Osiris emphasizes the message that there is life for the dead, although it is of a different character than that of the living. What is to be feared is "dying a second time in the realm of the dead" (*Book of Going Forth by Day* 175–176).

Osiris is a powerful god of the potent dead. In no sense can the dramatic myth of his death and reanimation be harmonized to the pattern of dying and rising gods.

Tammuz/Dumuzi. The assessment of the figure of Tammuz (Sumerian, Dumuzi) as a dying and rising deity in the scholarly literature has varied more than any other deity placed in this class. For example, within a thirty-year period, one of the most significant scholars in the field, the Sumeriologist Samuel Noah Kramer, has revised his judgment regarding this question several times. Before 1950, Kramer thought it possible that Dumuzi was freed from death; between 1950 and 1965, he considered Dumuzi to be solely a dying god; since 1966, he has been willing to speak again of the "death and resurrection" of Dumuzi.

The ritual evidence is unambiguously negative. During the summer month of Tammuz, there was a period of wailing and lamentation for the dead deity. A substantial number of cultic hymns of mourning, going back to the second millennium BCE, have been recovered; by the sixth century BCE, the ritual was practiced in Jerusalem (*Ez.* 8:14); in Syria, it is witnessed to as late as the fifth century CE and, in variations, persisted through medieval times. If third-century Christian authors are to be trusted, the figure of Tammuz interacted with that of Adonis in Asia Minor. In all of these varied reports, the character of the ritual is the same. It is a relentlessly funereal cult. The young Tammuz is dead, and he is mourned. His life was like that of the shoot of a tender plant. It grows quickly and then withers away. It was a life that is "no more"—a persistent refrain in the lamentations. There is no evidence for any cultic celebration of a rebirth of Tammuz apart from late Christian texts where he is identified with Adonis.

Given the predilection of scholars concerned with Christian origins for a pre-Christian pattern of dying and rising deities, it comes as no surprise that, despite the lack of cultic evidence, it was widely supposed that the period of mourning for Tammuz must have been followed by a festival of rejoicing. This speculative conclusion seemed to gain support with the publication of the Akkadian *Descent of Ishtar* from the library of Ashurbanipal in Nineveh. The text narrates the descent of the goddess into the underworld and her return. However, the concluding nine lines of the text contain a series of enigmatic references to Tammuz, Ishtar's youthful lover, in the land of the dead. Although the text nowhere mentions it, scholars supposed that the purpose of Ishtar's descent was to bring Tammuz up. If so, this would place Tammuz securely within the dying and rising pattern.

Even on the basis of the Akkadian text alone, such an interpretation is unlikely. There is no connection stated in the text between Ishtar's descent and Tammuz. (Indeed, some scholars have suggested that the last lines referring to Tammuz were originally independent and added to the *Descent* as a scribal gloss.) Even more detrimental to the dying and rising hypothesis, the actions performed on Tammuz in these three strophes are elements from the funeral ritual. Ishtar is treating Tammuz as a corpse. Finally, the line rendered in the earlier translations as "on the day when Tammuz comes up" has been shown to be a mistranslation. It either refers to Tammuz greeting Ishtar (i. e., coming up to her) in the underworld, or it is a reference to the month Tammuz. In the Akkadian version, Tammuz is dead and remains so. Such an understanding is witnessed to in other Akkadian texts. For example, in the *Epic of Gilgamesh* (6.46–50), the hero insults and scorns Ishtar, reminding her that all her previous lovers—Tammuz heads the list—have died as a result of their relationship to her.

Such considerations seemed to become purely academic with the publication of the Sumerian prototype of the Akkadian text, *Inanna's Descent to the Netherworld* (Inanna is the Sumerian form of Ishtar) and the closely related *Death of Dumuzi.* These early texts made clear that the goddess did not descend to the realm of the dead to rescue her consort. Rather it was her descent that was responsible for his death.

Inanna, the queen of heaven, sought to extend her power over the underworld, ruled by her sister, Ereshkigal. As in the Akkadian text, Inanna descends through seven gates, at each removing an article of clothing or royal regalia until, after passing through the seventh gate, she is naked and powerless. She is killed and her corpse hung on a hook. Through a stratagem planned before her descent, she is revived, but she may not return above unless she can find a substitute to take her place. She reascends, accompanied by a force of demons who will return her to the land of the dead if she fails. After allowing two possible candidates to escape, she comes to Erech, where Dumuzi, the shepherd king who is her consort, appears to be rejoicing over her fate. She sets the demons on him, and after he escapes several times, he is captured, killed, and carried off to the underworld to replace Inanna. In this narrative, Dumuzi is a dying god.

In 1963 a new portion of the *Descent of Inanna* was announced. Here, it would appear, there is yet a further episode. Inanna, in response to Dumuzi's weeping, decrees an arrangement whereby Dumuzi will take her place for half the year in the underworld and then return to the realm of the living; his sister, Geshtinanna, will then take Dumuzi's place in the underworld for the other half of the year, and, likewise, return.

For some scholars, this new conclusion to *Inanna's Descent* was sufficient to restore Dumuzi/Tammuz to the class of dying and rising gods. Such an understanding is unlikely. The myth emphasizes the inalterable power of the realm of the dead, not triumph over it. No one ascends from the land of the dead unless someone takes his or her place. The pattern of alternation—half a year below, half a year above—is familiar from other myths of the underworld in which there is no question of the presence of a dying and rising deity (e.g., Persephone, as in Ovid, *Fasti* 4.613–4, or the youthful Adonis as described above), and is related, as well, to wider folkloristic themes of death delayed if a substitute can be found (e.g., Stith Thompson, *Motif-Index* A 316; D 1855.2; P 316). Such alternation is not what is usually meant in the literature when speaking of a deity's "rising."

As the above examples make plain, the category of dying and rising deities is exceedingly dubious. It has been based largely on Christian interest and tenuous evidence. As such, the category is of more interest to the history of scholarship than to the history of religions.

See Also Castration.

Bibliography

The classic formulation of the dying and rising pattern was made by James G. Frazer in *The Golden Bough,* 3d ed., 12 vols. (London, 1911–1915), esp. vol. 4, *The Dying God* (1912), p. 6. Frazer cites a representative sample of the older scholarly literature. A full bibliography, from the perspective of Old Testament scholarship, is supplied in Karl-Heinz Bernhardt's *Das Problem der altorientalischen Königsideologie im Alten Testament* (Leiden, 1961). Günter Wagner's *Pauline Baptism and the Pagan Mysteries,* translated by J. P. Smith (Edinburgh, 1967), offers not only a full bibliography from the perspective of New Testament research but also a brilliant critique of the notion of dying and rising deities.

For Adonis, the old collection of all the relevant texts and testimonia by W. W. Baudissin, *Adonis und Esmun* (Leipzig, 1911), has been partially superseded by Wahib Atallah's *Adonis dans la littérature et l'art grecs* (Paris, 1966). The most consistently critical position toward Adonis as a "rising god" is in Pierre Lambrechts's "La 'resurrection' d'Adonis," in *Mélanges I. Lévy* (Brussels, 1955), pp. 207–240; compare Lambrecht's *Over Griekse en Oosterse mysteriogodsdiensten: De zogenannte Adonismysteries* (Brussels, 1954).

The relevant texts on Aliyan Baal are collected and translated in Cyrus H. Gordon's *Ugaritic Literature* (Rome, 1949) and Godfrey R. Driver's *Canaanite Myths and Legends* (Edinburgh, 1956), both of which reject the dying and rising pattern. Theodor H. Gaster is thoroughly convinced of its applicability; see his *Thespis: Ritual, Myth, and Drama in the Ancient Near East,* 2d rev. ed. (1961; reprint, New York, 1977). Arvid S. Kapelrud is more cautious; see his *Baal in the Ras Shamra Texts* (Copenhagen, 1952).

Hugo Hepding's old collection and typology of sources for Attis, *Attis: Seine Mythen und sein Kulte* (1903; reprint, Berlin,

1967), remains standard. The fundamental work on Attis as a dying and rising god is a series of publications by Lambrechts: "Les fêtes phrygiennes de Cybèle et d'Attis," *Bulletin de l'Institut Historique Belge de Rome* 27 (1952): 141–170; *Attis: Van herdersknaap tot god* (Brussels, 1962); and *Attis en het feest der Hilariën* (Amsterdam, 1967).

For Marduk, the text of the New Year ritual is available in English translation by A. Sachs as "Temple Program for the New Year's Festival at Babylon," in *Ancient Near Eastern Texts relating to the Old Testament,* 2d ed., edited by J. B. Pritchard (Princeton, 1955), pp. 331–334. The *Death and Resurrection of Bel-Marduk* is available in a less adequate translation by Stephen H. Langdon: *The Babylonian Epic of Creation* (Oxford, 1923), pp. 34–49. A shorter recension, with an important essay that challenges the parodic interpretation, has been translated by Tikva Frymer-Kensky: "The Tribulations of Marduk: The So-Called 'Marduk Ordeal Text,'" *Journal of the American Oriental Society* 103 (January–March 1983): 131–141. The major critical treatment of Marduk as a dying and rising god is Wolfram von Soden's "Gibt es ein Zeugnis dafür das die Babylonier an die Wiederauferstehung Marduks geglaubt haben?" *Zeitschrift für Assyriologie* 51 (May 1955): 130–166.

The most useful treatment of Osiris, with full critical bibliography, is contained in the notes and commentary of J. Gwyn Griffiths's *Plutarch's De Iside et Osiride* (Cardiff, 1970). The newest material on Dumuzi and Inanna, with bibliography for the older, is found in Samuel Noah Kramer's *The Sacred Mar*riage Rite: Aspects of Faith, Myth, and Ritual in Ancient Sumer (Bloomington, Ind., 1969). Kramer and Diane Wolkstein's *Inanna* (New York, 1983) provides a highly literary translation.

JONATHAN Z. SMITH (1987)

DYNAMISM. In philosophy, dynamism is "the system, theory, or doctrine which seeks to explain the phenomena of the universe by some immanent force or energy" *(Oxford English Dictionary).* In the study of religion, dynamism is the theoretical viewpoint that finds a universal, immanent force or energy underlying—either logically or chronologically—all religious (and/or magical) beliefs, practices, and forms of association. This viewpoint has also been known as animatism, preanimism, dynamistic preanimism, and, very occasionally, predeism.

Religious dynamism received its most precise theoretical formulation at the beginning of the twentieth century, especially in the writings of R. R. Marett, Konrad T. Preuss, and Marcel Mauss. It contributed to the waning of the evolutionistic animism then prevalent and exerted a great deal of influence on both the study of religions generally and the study of certain cultural areas, but in the end it succumbed to criticism. In its classic form it finds no advocates today. Some of its elements, however, persist with varying degrees of vitality.

BEFORE PREANIMISM. Dynamism was formulated as a theoretical alternative to other proposed theories on the origin of religion. Its conceptual configurations took shape from contemporary general attitudes toward religion and other human cultural phenomena, from current theories against which it reacted, and from ethnographic data that had surfaced in the nineteenth century.

Nineteenth-century thought on religion was dominated, by and large, by the idea of evolution, its procedures by a historical, generally noncontextual comparison of surface features arranged in logical progression. Each of the several theories advanced along these lines took its name from the stage of religion it posited as earliest: fetishism, naturism, totemism, manism, animism, and so forth.

Dynamism reacted most directly to the view that at its earliest, religion comprised a belief in a multitude of supernatural, personal beings with whom human beings interacted. The most popular such theory, first formulated by the British ethnologist E. B. Tylor in *Primitive Culture* (1873), counted both human souls and independent spirits among those beings, and was called animism (from the Latin *anima;* hence "preanimism"). In developing his theory, Tylor deliberately neglected emotion in favor of intellect. In his view, animistic beliefs were originally explanatory: the belief in souls explained phenomena such as life and death, dreams, and apparitions; spirits formed elements in a full-blown theory of personal causation. A similar theory, manism, proposed by the British social thinker Herbert Spencer (*Principles of Sociology,* 1876), derived all higher religious forms from a belief in ghosts *(manes).* The work of James G. Frazer stood in a more ambiguous relation to dynamism. On the one hand, R. R. Marett called *The Golden Bough* the greatest compendium of preanimistic phenomena ever compiled. On the other, many of Frazer's interpretations were held suspect. Frazer conceived a stepwise development between religion and magic. In discussing magic, he emphasized external, immutable, and mechanical sequences of events, or laws, disregarding any possible efficient cause. Taboo he saw as a form of negative magic, while religion developed in the wake of magic's failure and posited the existence of potent superhuman beings whose wills one had to propitiate.

Principles of evolution and the common identification of modern nonliterate civilizations with prehistoric culture made the wealth of ethnographic material then becoming available to Western thinkers essential to all middle to late nineteenth-century theories of religion. Frazer's "magical stage" showed that not all ethnographic material fit an animistic or manistic model. For the dynamistic theories, the most important single ethnographic datum was the Melanesian word *mana,* bequeathed to the Western scholarly world by R. H. Codrington's *The Melanesians* (1891). Codrington spoke of *mana* as "a force altogether distinct from physical power, which acts in all kinds of ways for good or evil, and which it is of the greatest advantage to possess and control" (p. 118, n. 1). The American ethnologist Alice C. Fletcher had already spoken of "Sioux" religion in similar terms.

Some writers surpassed ethnography to anticipate features of the dynamistic theories. Apparently writing in ignorance of Marett's proposed animatism, J. N. B. Hewitt noted that a notion of magical potency was common among North American Indians. He suggested that the Iroquois word *orenda* was suited to denote this notion, and on it he based a definition of religion. Hewitt did not openly oppose other theories, nor did he set his definition in the context of further reflections on religion. Nonetheless, his article significantly influenced the development of dynamism on the European continent.

By contrast, John H. King's earlier work, *The Supernatural* (1892), lay in obscurity until Wilhelm Schmidt brought it to scholarly attention. King derived all religion from a sense of luck or chance. But he posited an intervening stage between this initial period and a later, more manistic one, an era of religion centered on nonpersonal, all-pervasive power, such as *mana*, *wakan* (Lakota), or *boylya* (Australia).

Classic Dynamistic Theories. Evolutionary thought can integrate evidence incompatible with previously formulated developmental schemes very economically by postulating further, formerly unrecognized developmental stages. These stages assume their preferred places at the beginning of developmental series. Insertion at the initial position allows the rest of the series to remain relatively undisturbed and at the same time claims the greatest possible significance for the newly posited stage or stages.

At the end of the nineteenth century, two new theories sought to redress the inadequacies of evolutionistic animism by assigning it a derivative position. One theory, first voiced by Andrew Lang in 1898, argued, mostly on historical-ethnographic grounds, that religion originally centered not on a multitude of spirits but on a supreme creator invoked to explain the existence of the cosmos. The other, dynamism, first enunciated by Marett, combined logic with certain ethnographic data to postulate not a preanimistic superpersonal deity but a preanimistic, nonpersonal power or, as it was commonly called, *mana.* Nevertheless, some dynamists, Marett among them, advanced only cautious evolutionary claims. They saw *mana* as logically primitive but not necessarily as temporally prior to the idea of deity.

In addition to the common emphasis on power as constitutive of religion, dynamistic theories shared several other characteristics. First, they denigrated the mental abilities of peoples at the dynamistic stage (the primitives). On the one hand, most abandoned the intellectualist orientation and considered religion a matter not so much of individual belief as of collective processes and actions prompted by collective emotion. Whether emotionalist or not, they generally denied that primitives were capable of, or interested in, the causal thought that Tylor and Frazer required of them. On the other hand, those who spoke of a universally pervasive power were forced to admit that primitives did not clearly conceive of power as such. These scholars often claimed to work out logically the notion of power implicit in primitive speech and action.

Second, dynamistic theories softened the sharp distinction between religion and magic that Frazer, among others, had postulated. The force underlying religious and magical practices was identical. In addition, dynamists usually balked when others based the separation of religion and magic on a distinction between coercion and propitiation. In their view, religious and magical acts alike could be coercive, propitiatory, or both simultaneously. When a distinction was made, dynamists tended instead to distinguish magic from religion—not altogether satisfactorily—on grounds of the agent's moral or social position (good versus bad intent, communal versus individual acts). Third, dynamistic theories envisioned taboos not as the result of cognitive imaginings about causal processes but as a reaction to immanent but fearful power.

By definition, dynamistic theories equate power with the beginning or most elementary form of religion. But the classic dynamistic theories did not all conceive of power in identical terms. For Marett, power was an aspect of the supernatural, manifested as the extraordinary and inexplicable. It evoked emotions, especially awe, that impelled those who encountered it to attempt to establish relations with it. Marett distinguished positive and negative modes of the supernatural: *mana* (the supernatural has power) and *taboo* (power may be harmful; be heedful of it). He imagined development proceeding from the undifferentiated and indistinct to the differentiated and distinct, and for him it made sense to distinguish magic and religion only on a more developed, moral level.

A second view was expressed by Preuss, in his highly influential article "Der Ursprung der Religion und Kunst." For Preuss, "supernatural" and "mystical" carried connotations of the spiritual, the animistic. As a result, unlike Marett, he posited at the initial stage of human development a distinctly nonmystical, efficacious power believed to reside in all objects, both animate and inanimate, and to operate in all activities, both those we consider magical and those we consider natural. Human actions with regard to this power were prompted by the intellect, or rather, by the so-called *Urdummheit* ("primal stupidity") of humanity transcending the bounds of instinct. In Preuss's view, this power was originally differentiated; the idea of a universal, indwelling power such as *orenda* developed late. The gods, Preuss thought, were in origin only natural objects of special magical efficacy. Thus, he derived religion (which he identified with a concern for gods) from the era of magic.

A third view was expressed by Mauss in his *General Theory of Magic.* Unlike Marett's and Preuss's notions, Mauss's power (he called it *mana*) was neither supernatural nor natural, but social and unconscious. Originating in collective emotions and impulses, *mana* consisted of society's relative values and differences in potential. It undergirded both religious and magical practices, which Mauss distinguished only with difficulty, and at the unconscious level it was universal and undifferentiated. But it was not opposed to differentiated representations. It called them into existence and provided a field for their operation. In the realm of magic (on which Mauss's work focused), differentiated representations occurred in three forms: the abstractly impersonal (laws of sympathy), the concretely impersonal (differentiated potentials), and the personal (demons).

Elaboration and Application. In the ensuing years, several writers expressed and expounded dynamistic views. Differences between various notions of power persisted, inherited in part along national lines, but no new major, theoretical positions developed. In England, for example, E. Sidney Hartland synthesized and refined a variety of positions but made no significant theoretical contributions of his own. Alfred Vierkandt sought to refine Preuss's views by prefacing his initial era of magic with a premagical stage and by supplementing the intellectual confusion of subjectivity and objectivity that Preuss saw underlying magic with a similar practical and affective confusion. But these were essentially modifications in detail.

In general, those with dynamistic leanings seemed bent on (rather superficially) conciliating rather than adjudicating differing views of power. For example, Émile Durkheim and Lucien Lévy-Bruhl maintained that Preuss's magical and intellectualist orientations, respectively, differed more in language than in substance from religious or magico-religious and emotionalist views. At heart, dynamism remained the simple assertion that in origin or in essence religion was a complex of acts and beliefs centering on a reified, autonomous, efficacious, quasi-substantive power residing in all objects, whether that power was differentiated or universal, and whether or not the practitioners themselves formed any clear ideas about it.

Dynamistic views influenced many areas of the study of religion outside theoretical ethnology. In these areas, too, different dynamistic heritages were displayed clearly. But in general writers did not appreciate and often did not discuss the different possible notions of power. In attempts to increase dynamism's scope and adequacy, some even took the movement toward conciliation one step further, combining dynamistic views with other theories.

In the human studies, for example, Durkheim linked dynamism above all with totemism. For him, *mana* was the imperative force of society manifested (more or less) as the totemic principle, while the soul was *mana* individualized. Thus, the soul was conceptually, though probably not temporally, posterior to *mana.* Not surprisingly, the philosopher Lévy-Bruhl developed his notion of "primitive mentality" in what came to be a clearly dynamistic context. Lévy-Bruhl thought that the primitive felt rather than represented (i.e., conceived) an all-pervasive, ever-dynamic "essential reality, both one and multiple, both material and spiritual" (Lévy-Bruhl, 1966, pp. 16–17). In the history of religions proper, Nathan Söderblom outlined three constituents of primitive religion: animism, *mana,* and a belief in a primitive "originator" *(Urheber).* Rather more exclusively dynamistic, Gerardus van der Leeuw made power the center of his phenomenology of religion.

Those who reflected more concretely on religion also applied dynamistic insights. Somewhat like Söderblom, Marett's student E. O. James discovered in his study of Australia that the impersonal power at the center of religion was manifested in animatistic, animistic, and anthropomorphic forms even at the primitive level. Summarizing a decade of intense dynamistic influence on North American ethnology, Franz Boas's article on religion in the *Handbook of American Indians* made the belief in magical power, with varying degrees of individualization and personification, "one of the fundamental [religious] concepts that occur among all Indian tribes" (Boas, 1910, p. 366).

Descriptions of literate cultures also found dynamistic formulations useful. John Abbott, a bachelor of Oxford in the British civil service, wrote a lengthy description of Indian practices that interpreted *śakti* as the Indian equivalent of *mana,* manifested in the positive and negative forms of *puṇya* ("merit") and *pāpa* ("evil"). In the second quarter of the twentieth century, H. J. Rose refused to assign priority to either dynamism or animism in discussing the earliest religion of the Greeks, but his treatment of early Roman religion was thoroughly dynamistic, equating the Latin *numen* with *mana* and Latin *sacer* with *tabu.*

On the Wane. The combination of the dynamist viewpoint with others could not forestall criticism. Because awareness of developments in anthropology and the history of religions has always varied, dynamism waned more slowly in some areas than in others. Eventually, however, several critiques devastated the classic dynamistic formulations.

The ethnographic and linguistic critique not only opposed dynamism's genetic or essential universality; it questioned whether the notion of an impersonal, fluid power was at all appropriate to the cultures to which it had been ascribed. For both major areas supplying dynamists with ethnographic material, this critique began in 1914. Paul Radin, reviewing the writings of the Americanists Hewitt, Fletcher, William Jones, John R. Swanton, and Boas, noted the common appearance of personal beings in their accounts and suggested that they had been misled by the North American Indians' lack of concern for a supernatural being's precise form. After surveying the cultures of several Polynesian islands—*mana* is as much a Polynesian as a Melanesian concept—Arthur M. Hocart contradicted not Codrington's accounts so much as the theorists' allegations that *mana* was nonpersonal and constantly evoked an emotional response. Radin characterized North American religions as "Tylorian animism"; Hocart declared *mana* to be "out and out spiritualistic." Later scholars would modify both characterizations.

A second critique, the historical, did not question dynamistic interpretations of *mana* but did doubt *mana's* place as the foundation of all religion. Nineteenth-century evolutionary thought had been content to establish developmental stages from a logic of forms. The early twentieth century witnessed efforts to establish the connections among nonliterate societies historically. When applied to Oceania, both Schmidt's culture-historical approach and A. Capell's historical linguistics led to the conclusion that, far from being primary, *mana* actually belonged to the youngest cultural stratum.

A third critique addressed the presupposed orientation of religious beliefs and practices that underlay dynamistic views. This took two forms, structural-functional and semantic-symbolic. With Preuss, many dynamists held that all behavior was actual and effective, directly aimed at fostering life. Symbolism arose only when acts that had been conservatively preserved were no longer believed to be actually efficacious. Structural functionalists rejected the dynamists' assimilation of religious acts to technical acts and looked not to purpose but to hidden function in explaining ritual's preservation. Bronislaw Malinowski conceived of religious observances as the "cement of the social fabric" (Malinowski, 1948, p. 50), magic as the result of a psychophysiological mechanism to allay anxieties in the face of dangerous human impotence. Because magical power resided in human beings, Malinowski felt that any theory seeking the essence of magic in a power of nature *(mana)* was totally misdirected. A. R. Radcliffe-Brown sought to avoid the distinction between magic and religion and saw rituals as expressions of common sentiments essential to an orderly social life, but he felt no compulsion to reduce common social values and sentiments to a reified, efficacious power.

The roots of the semantic-symbolic critique lay in the aftermath of World War I. Europe's search for meaning revitalized the symbol, first among theologians, philosophers, and litterateurs, later among historians of religions, anthropologists, and other students of humanity. In a critique of preanimism and certain animistic and theistic notions, the German anthropologist Adolf E. Jensen completely reversed Preuss's notion. In Jensen's view, practices arise as semantically full expressions. Over time, symbolic contexts change and a state of application sets in. Practices then become semantically depleted. They are conceived as some variety of purposive act. Thus, both structural-functional and semantic-symbolic critiques relegated to the interpretive sidelines the purposive orientation on which dynamistic notions were based.

Dynamism lingered longest, it seems, in discussions of Roman religion. In contrast to the situation at the turn of the century, classics and anthropology were not closely related after World War I. In a critique of H. J. Rose, Georges Dumézil employed each of the three arguments leveled at classic dynamism. Citing the practice of baptism, Dumézil warned scholars not to mistake symbolic acts for efficacious ones. He intensively examined rituals, sayings, and terms such as *numen* to show the extent to which dynamistic interpretations strain the evidence. Finally, he noted that personal gods were inherited from the time of the Indo-European migrations; hence it made no historical sense to posit a strictly Roman predeistic period.

Dispersed Remnants. Today, classic theories of dynamism exert virtually no influence in the study of religion or anthropology. Descriptive failures and the results and limits of historical work have contributed to the disregard not only of dynamism but of all evolutionary theories. Furthermore, the semantic-symbolic view of religion that dominates at present, again in combination with descriptive failings, has made dynamism's nonevolutionary side unappealing. Nonetheless, several dynamistic elements, now removed from their former theoretical context, float dispersed throughout the study of religion.

Of these, the least important is probably the name about which the theories congealed. *Dynamism* (often used in the plural, *dynamisms*) now refers blandly to the changes characteristic of religious phenomena. In this usage, change has lost its purposive, effective character and arouses no desire to identify an efficient cause. Some scholars, such as Ugo Bianchi, use the term in combating what they see as a falsely static view of religion, promoted particularly by phenomenological investigations (*The History of Religions*, Leiden, 1975). But in such a case, the term *dynamism(s)* refers to a characteristic of the metaphysical background against which all religious phenomena necessarily stand forth. It says little about religion itself.

More important are the continuing investigations of the original ethnographic materials upon which the dynamists built. Some phenomena still seem actually to permit a quasi-dynamistic interpretation. Of impersonal power, Åke Hultkrantz writes, "*Orenda* is one of the most convincing proofs of such a conception that can be found" (Hultkrantz, 1983, p. 39). But later dynamists, such as Hartland, had already recognized that *mana* could not be adequately described as impersonal. More recently, Julian Pitt-Rivers has built especially on fieldwork by Raymond Firth in interpreting *mana* in the light of political anthropology, as exemplifying the sacred dimension that must be included in any comparative study of political power.

Perhaps most important, however, is the notion of power in the study of religion. Even such a convinced symbolist as Mircea Eliade has stated that "every hierophany is a kratophany" (Eliade, 1960, p. 126). Eliade interprets power ontologically. For him it refers to what is real (sacred) and "therefore efficacious, fecund, fertile" (p. 129). Eliade also cautions students of religion to keep several points in mind: the particular conception of power denoted by *mana* is not universal; power is not the whole of religion; and kratophanies exhibit differences in degree and frequency.

The analysis of religious power requires a more subtle approach than the dynamists ever developed, an approach that abandons the evolutionistic and narrowly essentialistic concerns of classic dynamism and that does not treat power monolithically, as an impersonal, all-pervading, efficacious essence. For years the problem lay dormant, apart from rather isolated comments such as Eliade's. Today, there are signs of an inchoate resurgence of interest in questions of religious power as found in both literate cultures, such as India, and nonliterate cultures. The new interest derives in part from a general reaction to radically synchronic and semantic structuralist interpretations. In time it may gain strength, if a general concern with praxis and power replaces the current widespread concern with meaning, as it has to some extent done already. At present, discussions of religious power are limited to particularist accounts of varying scope, usually informed by some degree of theoretical reflection in anthropology or similar fields. It is impossible to predict whether these discussions will continue to flourish, to what extent they will contribute to a new, general vision of religion, and what insights, if any, such a general vision might share with classical dynamism.

SEE ALSO Animism and Animatism; Manism; Numen; Power.

BIBLIOGRAPHY

Surveys of dynamism or of the views of individual dynamist theorists, more or less extensive, are available in a large number of works written from a great variety of perspectives. The following are, perhaps, most useful or most readily available. Henri Pinard de la Boullaye's *L'étude compareé des religions*, vol. 1, *Son histoire dans le monde occidental*, 4th ed. (Paris, 1929), is an early work but a good bibliographical source that sets "dynamistic preanimism" in a detailed contest. Wilhelm Schmidt's *The Origin and Growth of Religion: Facts and Theories*, translated by H. J. Rose (1931; reprint, New York, 1972), is a detailed critique but is limited by subsuming dynamism under the category of "magism," by too facile a distinction between intellectual, emotional, and volitional theories, and by the author's thoroughly polemical concerns. Robert H. Lowie's *The History of Ethnological Theory* (New York, 1937) is sensitive to issues of historical ethnology and "primitive rationality," sympathetic to both Tylor and Marett, but scathing in its attacks upon Frazer. E. E. Evans-Pritchard's *Theories of Primitive Religion* (Oxford, 1965), a more recent account, discusses its subject in terms of psychological theories, both intellectualist and emotionalist, and sociological theories. Jan de Vrie's *Perspectives in the History of Religion*, tranlsated by Kees W. Bolle (Berkley, 1977), is readily available but annoying because it dismisses many theories simply on the grounds that they are "arbitrary." Eric J. Sharpe's *Comparitive Religion: A History* (London, 1975) is a useful survey that highlights personal biography as much as theoretical reflection.

Standard works by dynamistic theorists include R. R. Marett's *The Threshold of Religion* (London, 1909), a collection of his most important articles on dynamism; Konrad T. Preuss's "Der Ursprung der Religion und Kunst," *Globus 86* (1904): 321–327, 355–363, 375–379, 388–392 and 87 (1905): 333–337, 347–350, 380–384, 394–400, 413–419, which builds especially on the author's fieldwork in Mexico; Marcel Mauss's *A General Theory of Magic*, translated by Robert Brain (London, 1972); E. Sidney Hartland's *Ritual and Belief: Studies in the History of Religion* (London, 1914); Alfred Vierkandt's "Die Anfänge der Religion und Zauberei," *Globus 92* (1907): 21–25, 40–45, 61–65; and E. O. James's *Primitive Ritual and Belief: An Anthropological Essay* (London, 1917). John H. King's *The Supernatural: Its Origin, Nature and Evolution*, 2 vols. (London, 1892), is as interested in modern occultism as in the history of religions.

R. H. Codrington's definition of *mana* cited in the text was quoted already by F. Max Müller in the Hibbert Lectures of 1878 (from a letter by Codrington to Müller). Codrington's views on *mana* were most widely dispersed by his *The Melanesians* (1891; reprint, New Haven, 1957). Subsequently, mana has evoked a large critical literature, including Arthur M. Hocart's "Mana," *Man* 14 (June 1914): 46–47; Julius Röhr's "Das Wesen des Mana," *Anthropos* 14/15 (1919–1920): 97–124; F. R. Lehmann's *Mana, der Begriff des "ausserordentlich wirkungsvollen" bei Südseevölkern* (Leipzig, 1922); Ian Hogbin's "Mana," Oceania 6 (March 1936): 241–274; A. Capell's "The Word 'Mana' Linguistic Study," *Oceania* 9 (September 1938): 89–96; Raymond Firth's "An Analysis of *Mana:* An Empirical Approach," *Journal of the Polynesian Society* 49 (1940): 483–510, reprinted in his *Tikopia Ritual and Belief* (Boston, 1967), pp. 174–194 (*mana* as the ability to succeed, and, at the same time, successful results in areas of vital human interest beyond the capabilities of normal human effort and by divine gift); and, of more comparative than ethnographic interest, Julian Pitt-Rivers's *Mana: An Inaugural Lecture* (London, 1974), which discusses mana in connection with Mediterranean notions of honor and grace.

Early comments of a dynamistic flavor by Alice C. Fletcher are quoted in J. Owen Dorsey's "A Study of Siouan Cults," *Bureau of American Ethnology, Annual Report* 11 (1889–1890): 434–435; see also Fletcher's article "Wakonda" in the *Handbook of American Indians*, part 2, edited by Frederick W. Hodge (Washington, D. C., 1910). J. N. B. Hewitt's influential views on *orenda* were expounded in "Orenda and a Definition of Religion," *American Anthropologist*, n. s. 4 (1902): 33–46. Other works that interpreted North American religions in terms of impersonal power include William Jones's "The Algonkin Manitou," *Journal of American Folk-Lore* 18 (1905): 183–190; John R. Swanton's *Social Condition, Beliefs, and Linguistic Relationship of the Tlingit Indians*, "Bureau of American Ethnology, Annual Report," vol. 26 (Washington, D. C., 1907), see especially page 451, note c; and Franz Boas's "Religion," in the *Handbook of American Indians*, part 2, edited by Frederick W. Hodge (Washington, D. C., 1910), pp. 365–371. Paul Radin takes these theorists to task in his "Religion of the North American Indians," *Journal of American Folk-Lore* 27 (1914): 335–373. For an assessment of Radin's views, and for a survey of this interpretation of American Indian religions in a broader context, see Åke Hultkrantz's *The Study of American Indian Religions*, edited by Christopher Vecsey, (New York, 1983); see especially "Indian Religious Concepts," pp. 39–46.

Émile Durkheim discusses *mana* and the totemic principle in *The Elementary Forms of the Religious Life*, translated by Joseph Ward Swain (1915; reprint, New York, 1965). Lucien Lévy-Bruhl's notion of the primitive's prelogical participation in a homogeneous world is perhaps most easily accessible in his

Primitive Mentality, translated by Lilian A. Clare (New York, 1923); his introduction to *The 'Soul' of the Primitive*, translated by Lilian A. Clare (1928; reprint, New York, 1966) quite clearly endows his views on prelogical mentality with a dynamistic slant. For the other authors cited as applying dynamistic insights, see Nathan Söderblom's *Das Werden des Gottesglaubens: Untersuchungen über die Anfänge der Religion*, 2d rev. ed., edited by Heinrich Karl Stübe (Leipzig, 1926); Gerardus van der Leeuw's *Religion in Essence and Manifestation*, 2 vols., translated by J. E. Turner (1938; reprint, Gloucester, Mass., 1967); John Abbott's *The Keys of Power: A Study of Indian Ritual and Belief* (1932; reprint, Secaucus, N. J., 1974); and H. J. Rose's *Ancient Greek Religion* (London, 1946) and *Ancient Roman Religion* (London, 1948).

Critiques of dynamistic views may be found in the later studies of Oceania and North America cited above. In the well-known *Argonauts of the Western Pacific* (1922; reprint, New York, 1953), Bronislaw Malinowski speaks of *mana* as figuring largely in all magical practices and beliefs. Only a few years later, however, in the title essay (1925) of *Magic, Science, and Religion and Other Essays* (New York, 1948), he finds dynamistic theories to be "pointing altogether in the wrong direction." A. R. Radcliffe-Brown discusses clearly his rejection of the search for origins and of culture-history in favor of "meaning" and "function" in the preface to the 1933 edition of his *The Andaman Islanders* (1922; Glencoe, Ill., 1948); for his interpretation of religion and magic, see especially *Structure and Function in Primitive Society: Essays and Addresses* (London, 1952), chapter 7, "Taboo" (1939), and chapter 8, "Religion and Society" (1945). The other critiques of dynamism mentioned in the text may be found in Adolf E. Jensen's *Myth and Cult among Primitive Peoples*, translated by Marianna Tax Choldin and Wolfgang Weissleder (Chicago, 1963), and Georges Dumézil's *Archaic Roman Religion*, 2 vols., translated by Philip Krapp (Chicago, 1970), especially the preliminary remarks and chapter 3, "The Most Ancient Roman Religion: *Numen* or *Deus*?," pp. 18–31.

For Mircea Eliade's views on power, see especially *Myths, Dreams and Mysteries: The Encounter between Contemporary Faiths and Archaic Realities*, translated by Philip Mairet (New York, 1960), especially chapter 4, "Power and Holiness in the History of Religions," pp. 123–154. Scholars interested in Indian religions are today devoting a good deal of attention to religious power, usually conceived in terms of interaction. Among writings by Wendy Doniger O'Flaherty, see, for example, *Women, Androgynes, and Other Mythical Beasts* (Chicago, 1980). Recent anthropological writings that display an interest in power include Jay Miller's "Numic Religion: An Overview of Power in the Great Basin of Native North America," *Anthropos* 78 (1983): 337–354, and Adrian Campion Edwards's "Seeing, Believing, Doing: The Tiv Understanding of Power," *Anthropos* 78 (1983): 459–480.

GREGORY D. ALLES (1987)

DZOGCHEN, the Great Perfection (or Great Completion, *Rdzogs chen*), also known as Atiyoga (*a ti yo ga*), is considered the pinnacle of all systems of thought and practice in the Nyingma (Rnying ma) and Bon traditions of Tibetan religion. It is widely associated with a rhetoric stressing naturalness, spontaneity, and simplicity, as well as a deconstructive critique of Buddhist philosophical positions and normative practices. It has an ambiguous relationship with Tantra, since at times it stresses its transcendence and distinctness from Tantric forms, whereas in most forms it is clearly indebted in its concepts, diction, and practices to esoteric Buddhist traditions. The Great Perfection is thus often portrayed as a tradition that lacks any type of systematic philosophic inquiry or even actual praxis. From the outside it is often viewed on these terms as a fairly homogenous tradition.

The truth is that the rubric the Great Perfection embraces an astonishingly varied array of traditions that, for example, range from a systematic rejection of all praxis to complex systems of Tantric rituals, and from a rejection of all Tantra, including its sexual and horrific elements, to a full incorporation of esoteric funerary and sexual rituals. This diversity finds its expression in different doxographical schemes, which hierarchically rank diverse Great Perfection traditions in relationship to each other, each having its own distinct lineages, scriptures, and unitary rubric of self-identification. Despite this diversity, however, there is a common rhetorical and contemplative thread that runs through all these traditions, which can be summed up as a tendency toward naturalness, innateness, and simplicity/simplification and a strong suspicion of techniques and rule-governed processes of all types.

EARLY HISTORIES. The Great Perfection's lineage holders and historians claim transcendental origins tracing back to divine figures and other world systems, with different histories for the Nyingma and Bon lineages, respectively. Nyingma lineages trace the origins of their lineages on this planet and this era back to India and a variety of other countries, and they were then transmitted into Tibetan translations and lineages during the latter half of the eighth century CE onward from diverse languages and sources. The most important early sources are attributed above all to the Indians Padmasambhava, Vimalamitra, and Śrīsiṃha, as well as the Tibetan Vairocana, all of whom lived in the latter half of the eighth century. Many of these teachings are then claimed to have been concealed within Tibet shortly afterward during the ninth century as the Tibetan empire disintegrated. Innovations in the tradition were thus largely introduced historically in Tibet through the medium of revelations of these concealed scriptures via visionary and physical excavations known as "Treasures" (*gter ma*) that were revealed from at least the tenth century and right into the present.

Bon lineages and histories of the Great Perfection are similar in character, but quite different in details. Traditional histories describe lineages flowing into the Tibetan plateau from the western realm of Takzik and first appearing in the Zhang Zhung empire (fifth to seventh centuries) as translated into the Zhang Zhung language. These materials were then retranslated into Tibetan as the Tibetan empire's seventh-century rise eclipsed its western Zhang Zhung rivals and then gradually subsumed them. However, only minor fragments of Zhang Zhung language still exist in literary form, and all Bon literature currently exists only in Tibetan manuscripts, the earliest of which can only be attested in roughly the eleventh century. Remarkably, Bon lineages continue to this day to maintain a strong historical memory of their non-Tibetan Zhang Zhung origins and affiliations. Bon lineages of the Great Perfection, like their Nyingma counterparts, transformed over time largely through the medium of revelations of past concealments known as "Treasures" from at least the eleventh century onward.

Despite these traditional claims, there is no independent attestation of the existence of any separate traditions or lineages going under these rubrics outside of Tibet, though the nomenclature Atiyoga and the Great Perfection does appear in eighth- and ninth-century Indian Tantric Buddhist literature. Admittedly, there is no question that its characteristic discursive language, marked by an esoteric naturalism, a strong language of negation, and a celebration of divine creation, is pronounced in some Indian Tantras. However, we have no evidence of any independent tradition outside of Tibet known under Atiyoga, Great Perfection, or any of the other rubrics that gradually emerge over time in the Nyingma and Bon traditions for these movements. Nontraditional scholarship since the 1980s suggests that most of the early literature claiming to be "translations" are original compositions that date much later than the claimed eighth-century dates for their translation—much less their, at times, even far earlier claims for composition back in India or elsewhere before translation. Scholarship has thus begun to focus on how these traditions reflect the indigenization of Buddhism into Tibet during the ninth to the fourteenth centuries, in particular, rather than on its supposed ancient roots.

Thus, the doxographical diversity of the Great Perfection—despite all its variants claiming to be rooted in eighth-century (and earlier) translations—appears to be the hidden key to the still secret history of the Great Perfection on Tibetan soil. Within the Nyingma tradition we can trace the lineaments of this secret history with a certain degree of confidence. The tradition first appeared in the first half of the ninth century with a series of short texts attributed to Indian saints that at some point were codified into a canon of eighteen texts referred to as "mind oriented" (*sems phyogs*) or later as "mind series" (*sems sde*). These texts were then gradually transformed over the next two centuries into full-fledged Tantras attributed to the divine authorship of Buddhas, as well as into ever longer and more numerous texts. This culminated in the emergence of *The All-Creating King* (kun byed rgyal po) at an uncertain date in the last half of the tenth century to the first half of the eleventh century. This Tantra was historically perhaps the most important and widely quoted of all Great Perfection scriptures, and it clearly was in part formed by incorporating earlier shorter texts as chapters. These texts represent what appears to have been the dominant form of the tradition during the ninth to the tenth centuries.

This early literature is almost entirely without any references to practice of any kind and indeed is renowned for its rhetoric of transcendence and spontaneity, suggesting that all forms of practice are superfluous given the primordial purity of "awareness" (*rig pa*) possessed by all living beings. However, they are still inextricably bound up with normative Tantra, which in eighth- and ninth-century Tibet was represented by Tantric movements known as the "Great Yoga" (*mahāyoga*), with intricate forms of ritualism including visualization of self as deity, peaceful and wrathful maṇḍalas, and complex initiations. The Great Perfection thus originates on the periphery of the vast discursive terrain of the *mahāyoga* by creating a vacuum within its landscape through the systematic expulsion of an array of standard Tantric principles. This absence is defined by what it has excluded, since it is an absence of precise systems that are thus inexorably evoked under erasure. The entire spectrum of rejected Tantric ideologies and praxis thus haunts the Great Perfection's pristine space of rhetorical absence.

Historical transformations. This landscape was completely transformed in the eleventh century as a series of new Treasure revelations gradually articulated into an entirely different series of Great Perfection movements with distinctive rubrics of self-identification and radical new developments in doctrine and practice. This transformation was part and parcel of the renaissance of Tibetan culture occurring from the late tenth century to the early twelfth century as new Buddhist literature and practices were imported anew from India. This period, under the rubric the "later dissemination" (*phyi dar*) of Buddhism, is often misunderstood as primarily involving new movements called "modernists" (*gsar ma*), but the truth is that the older Bon and Nyingma lineages were just as deeply involved as creative agents of change. The point of delineation involved the former explicitly acknowledging their debt to new imports that they "translated," whereas the latter groups tended to glide over this indebtedness by assimilating new developments seamlessly into their older traditions through the process of Treasure revelation. The eleventh century in particular was dominated by the rise of *yoginī* Tantras deriving from the final efflorescence of Indian Buddhist culture. These striking documents involved horrific imagery and violent rituals, erotic imagery, and sexual practices and somatic practices involving a cult of the body's subtle interior. They were also marked by transgressive rhetoric and an evocative imagery of long-haired *siddhas* celebrating lay values in ritual assemblies called "circles of the group" (*tshogs gi 'khor lo*, Sanskrit *gaṇa-cakra*). While Nyingma or Bon lineages on the whole neither formally transmitted nor wrote about these traditions in this or the next few centuries, it is clear that in fact these new esoteric transmissions made a deep if unacknowledged impact on their own rapidly evolving traditions.

In the case of the Great Perfection, its new variations emerging in the eleventh century were clearly deeply indebted to the *yoginī* traditions. Its influences were clear in the rise of subtle body representations and practices, new pantheons of wrathful and erotic Buddhas, increasingly antinomian rhetoric, and a focus on motifs of death. At the same time these influences were transformatively assimilated with each strand modified and integrated on the basis of the Great Perfection's commitments to naturalism, Gnosticism, simplicity, and divine creation. This influence can be traced progressively through movements that come to be known as the Secret Cycle (*gsang skor*), Ultra Pith (*yang tig*), Brahmin's Tradition (*bram ze'i lugs*), and others and culminates in the late eleventh and twelfth centuries with the emergence of the Seminal Heart (*snying thig*). The Seminal Heart represents a stunningly creative and deeply Tibetan reinterpretation of many central Buddhist traditions around the central motif of the divine creativity of the Buddhas' creation of Pure Lands. The central literature is a body of revealed Tantras collected together as *The Seventeen Tantras* (rgyud bcu bdun) and a body of exegetical literature organized as *The Seminal Heart of Vimalamitra* (bi ma snying thig).

The Seminal Heart. The Seminal Heart is characterized by an intensely philosophical discourse, a distinctive doctrinal intersection of divine creation and naturalism, and a unique contemplative system integrating visionary practices of spontaneous image cultivation with earlier practices of technique-free cultivation of pure awareness. In each of these areas there is a deep grounding in exoteric and esoteric forms of Indian Buddhism, but there is also a startlingly creative assimilation. The first facet is its systematic philosophical character, which is unusual because of its esoteric nature. Tantric Buddhism in India tended on the whole to be far more focused on ritual practice than on philosophical speculation, even if there gradually developed a cottage industry in scholastic exegesis on these rituals and iconography. In Tibet, however, many esoteric traditions came to develop complex philosophical discourses, which some have termed *philosophic Vajrayāna.* The Seminal Heart represents perhaps the most interesting philosophical system to emerge out of this development.

Its doctrinal heart is a unique blend of the older strains of naturalism with a new doctrine of Gnostic creation intertwined with esoteric conceptions and practices of death. Its basis is what can be best termed a Gnostic orientation, which entails a Buddha's primordial *gnosis* (*ye shes*, Skt. *jñāna*) being portrayed consistently as the principal creative agent driving manifestation, even if its effects are often clouded by derivative processes fueled by emotionally fueled activity (*las*, Skt. *karman*). Thus, rather than *gnosis* being a product of contemplative practice, it is seen as a preexistent agent that precedes, not follows, *karma.* This divine creativity is modeled on juxtaposing two basic doctrines found in the Great Vehicle (*theg chen*, Skt. *Mahāyāna*): buddha-nature (*de bzhin gshegs pa'i snying po*, Skt. *tathāgatagarbha*) and a buddha's creation of Pure Lands and Enjoyment Bodies (*longs sku*, Skt. *sambhogakāya*). Buddha-nature is the idea that all life is characterized by an internal divinity, though just how inert or active this divinity is, and its relationship with a manifestly realized buddha, often remains unclear. Pure Lands are special cosmic locales believed to be created by buddhas as realms with optimal spiritual conditions into which Buddhists could be reborn after death. Enjoyment Bodies are resplendent forms that a buddha manifests out of the pure emptiness of his or her enlightenment experience and that typically reside at the center of these Pure Lands. The philosophical innovation of the Seminal Heart was to integrate buddha-nature with this buddha-creativity, and then articulate this internal Gnostic creativity as the central driving force of all being and manifestation.

This process of creativity marked by the unfolding of Pure Lands and divinely resplendent buddhas—itself depicted clearly in the esoteric form of the creation and articulation of a maṇḍala—is found, most importantly, in three intertwined processes: cosmogony, post-death experience, and contemplation, as well as more minor contexts such as embryology, dreaming, and cognitive activity. Each of these is described as centrally involving a buddha's Gnostic creativity engendering Pure Lands, or maṇḍalas of buddhas. This notion of buddhas creating worlds was a standard component of Great Vehicle literature, but the innovation of the Seminal Heart was to apply it so systematically to a wide variety of contexts in which creation, transition, and development take place. Thus, a buddha's *gnosis* is identified as the preeminent creative agent in the universe, rather than the more typical depiction of *karma* as what generates the world, embodiment, mental action, dreaming, post-death experience, and other such human experiences. The Seminal Heart presents an unusual divine cosmogony, in which a Buddha's *gnosis* is presenting as driving the emergence of being out of nonbeing, which unfolds as a primordial array of Pure Lands. The karmic process of conditioned existence only emerges as a secondary process following a lack of recognition of those divine arrays as "self" by an emergent cognitive capacity. Second, out of the experience of complete collapse into emptiness that marks death, the experience of the intermediate process (*bar do*) between death and rebirth is marked by the experience of rich maṇḍalas of serene and horrific buddhas. The karmic experiences of memories of one's past life, and visual premonitions of one's impending rebirth, only occur in a secondary post-death process should one fail to recognize the divine manifestations as "self-manifestations." Third, the core contemplative practice, termed *direct transcendence*, involves stimulating a flow of Pure Lands out of one's heart through one's eyes into the sky, so that one reflexively experiences, and recognizes, these divine maṇḍalas of buddhas as self. Thus, in the birth of worlds, in the emergence out of death, and in contemplation, we find *gnosis* as the primary agent and *karma* as a derivative and secondary process.

Finally, its contemplative system consists of a massive anthology of varied Tantric and non-Tantric contemplative techniques capped by two unique contemplative processes named "breakthrough" *(khregs chod)* and "direct transcendence" *(thod rgal).* Breakthrough signifies the older style of

Great Perfection contemplation, and its descriptions are typically poetic evocations of pure awareness that strictly avoid discussions of techniques that might be understood to generate such states of awareness. Direct transcendence, however, is an innovative practice that involves relying on yogic postures, breathing practices, and gazing directed at the complete darkness of a specially prepared retreat hut, or at sources of light such as the sun. The practice aims at generating a spontaneous flow of luminous, rainbow-colored images that gradually expand in extent and complexity, proceeding from fragments of buddha-bodies and sacred icons to gradually become vast maṇḍalas of buddhas pervading the sky. While innovative, these practices clearly represent a transmutation of Tantric practices typically classified as "perfection phase" techniques (*rdzogs rim*). These practices involve manipulation of a yogic or subtle body of winds, channels, and nuclei within the coarse physical body, which engender ever more subtle states of consciousness marked by experiences of flashes of light. These experiences of light are typically discussed in terms of eight, ten, or eleven signs described imagistically as like fireflies, a mirage, smoke, or lightening. These practices, as outlined in the early-eleventh-century Indian Tantric cycle *The Wheel of Time* (Kālacakra), culminate in the vision of a buddha, and the close association with staring into darkness and at the sky make it highly probably that it was a direct inspiration for the Seminal Heart.

Despite this influence, the practice was deeply assimilated into the Great Perfection with its focus on naturalness, release rather than control, spontaneity rather than fabrication, simplicity rather than complexity, and interpenetration of the external and internal rather than the deeply interior world of subtle body yogas. Likewise, when we turn to the vast anthologies of practices presented as preliminaries and auxiliary contemplative techniques, we find a wide range of ordinary and unique exoteric and esoteric practices that have been thoroughly assimilated into the world of the Great Perfection. Throughout, common Buddhist practices have been subtly and extensively altered, again, to be simple rather than complex, natural rather than artificial, spontaneous rather than contrived, governed by letting go rather than taking control, and focused on the intersection of the external and the internal rather than on deeply internal processes. Most notably absent is any focus on the mainstream Tantric practice of deity yoga, with its ritual transformation of self into deity by complex visualizations and mantric recitations of a Buddhist deity.

THE DOMINANCE OF THE SEMINAL HEART. The Seminal Heart's radical transformation of the Great Perfection was not without its internal critics from conservative Nyingma figures. It seems that the most important Nyingma of the twelfth century, Nyangrel Nyima Özer (Nyang ral nyi ma 'od zer, 1136–1204), in particular developed his Crown Pith (*spyi ti*) tradition to reassert the older traditions in new form as supreme. He appears to have felt that the Great Perfection should transcend prescriptions of specific practices as well as the rhetoric of violence, sexuality, and transgression. His revelations are marked by the relative absence of *yoginī* Tantra influence and appear to substitute instead a lovely rhetoric of metaphors and images.

Despite such reservations, however, the Seminal Heart was ultimately to triumph and become the dominant tradition of the Great Perfection for the Nyingma. This was due in no small measure to the towering achievements of Longchenpa (*klong chen pa*, 1308–1364) in the fourteenth century. Longchenpa, considered to be one of the greatest authors, intellects, and poets in the history of Tibetan Buddhism, both systematized the Seminal Heart and integrated it with broader Mahāyāna literature and motifs. His corpus is marked as much by poetic beauty as by intellectual mastery and includes *The Seven Treasuries (mdzod bdun), The Trilogy of Natural Freedom (rang grol skor gsum), The Trilogy of Relaxation* (*ngal gso skor gsum*), and three of the five parts of *The Seminal Heart in Four Parts (snying thig ya bzhi).* Most of the Seminal Heart content stems from the earlier literature, but Longchenpa's writings refine its terminology, systematize it into powerful intellectual architectures, and provide brilliant interpretations. In addition, most previous Nyingma authors bothered little with nonesoteric philosophy, at least in their exegetical compositions. In contrast, Longchenpa was deeply learned in exoteric Buddhist thought and wrote extensively on it, as well as explicitly integrating it with the Seminal Heart, thereby articulating its deep roots in mainstream Buddhist thought and practice.

Following Longchenpa, there were many other major Great Perfection corpuses of literature in terms of revelation, exegesis, and poetry. Throughout, we can see the dominant influence of the Seminal Heart, though the earlier traditions of a pristine transcendence continue to play a vibrant though lesser role. Important bodies of literature include *The Penetrating Wisdom* (dgongs pa zang thal), revealed by Rinzin Gödem (*rig 'dzin rgod ldem*, 1337–1409); *The Nucleus of Ati's Profound Meaning* (rDzogs pa chen po a ti zab don snying po), by Terdak Lingpa (*gter bdag gling pa*, 1646–1714); and others. Of particular note is the seventeenth-century revelations of Jikme Lingpa ('Jigs med gling pa, 1729/30–1798) in *The Seminal Heart of the Great Matrix* (*klong chen snying thig*). These revelations emerged as the most popular ritual system of the Great Perfection over the last two centuries. In addition, they represented the culmination of an increasing ritualization of the Seminal Heart with an ever greater focus on evocation rituals of deities (*grub thabs*, Sanskrit *sādhana*) that had to come to be the lynchpin of monastic esotericism.

EARLY BON TRADITIONS. The Great Perfection in nominally non-Buddhist Bon circles in Tibet is deeply intertwined with that of Nyingma lineages in all ways, though these complex interdependencies are unacknowledged. It is clear that identical terminology, structures, and even whole passages are shared by the Nyingma and Bon traditions, while many of the key elements of the Seminal Heart are found within pre-fifteenth-century Bon literature. The standard Bon doxography outlines three main traditions of the Great Perfection (*a rdzogs snyan gsum*): Guidance on the Syllable *A* (*a khrid*), Great Perfection (*Rdzogs chen*), and the Oral Transmission (*snyan rgyud*). In short, the Great Perfection is said to be more philosophical and the oral transmission more experiential, whereas the Guidance on the Syllable *A* falls in between. The key authoritative figure in these traditions' background, paralleling that of Śākyamuni and Padmasambhava for the Nyingmas, is Shenrab Miwoche (*gshen rab mi bo che*), a divine figure said to have historically founded the Bon Tantric traditions in the land of Takzik to the west of Tibet.

In the Tibetan imperial period—a difficult time for *Bonpos,* given their valorization of the suppressed Zhang Zhung Empire—key figures were Tapihritsa and Gyerpung Nangzher Löpo (eighth century). The former is said to have orally transmitted *The Oral Transmission of Zhang Zhung* to the latter in a vision, and his student Gyerpung then committed it to writing to become the core text of the Oral Transmission tradition. The cycle has strong connections to the Seminal Heart synthesis, as it is distinctive among the early Bon Great Perfection traditions for its view's emphasis on embodiment, along with its pervasive focus on visions of light. It seems to be the earliest Bon literature that evidences this movement beyond the more common early focus on the Great Perfection consisting of a pristine view similar to the austere perspective of the non-Tantric Mādhyamaka school. However, its redaction is presumably centuries later than the eighth century—much of its present one-volume redaction does not even claim to go back to Tapihritsa, though the two key, but short, texts (*The Twelve Little Child Tantras* and *Instructions on the Six Lamps*) both claim to have been orally transmitted to Gyerpung from a vision of Tapihritsa.

Instructions on the Six Lamps is historically intertwined with the early Seminal Heart canon with similar discussions of the six lamps: All Good as the primordial Buddha, the dying process, post-death intermediate state liberation, and, of course, the importance of visionary experiences of lights and Buddhas. However, it is not a mere adaptation of any known Nyingma Tantra, as it uses terminology and concepts in its own distinctive way. At least one other text of the *Zhang Zhung* cycle, however, appears to be directly derived from *The Seminal Heart of Vimalamitra.*

The other central figure for Bon during the imperial period was Drenpa Namkha, a shadowy *siddha*-style figure in the eighth century as well, but whose name is said to have been used by at least three different figures from Tibet, the Dakpo (dwags po), and the Zhang Zhung, respectively. His most important teachings on the Great Perfection are said to be contained in *The Magical Treasury of the Magical Sky (nam mkha' 'phrul mdzod),* but this was only transcribed as an oral transmission in the twelfth century by Tulku Lungbön Lhanyen (Sprul sku lung bon lha gnyan, b. 1112?) after receiving them from Tsewang Rindzin (Tshe dbang rig 'dzin, twelfth century).

LATER BON TRADITIONS. During the later renaissance period, Shenchen Luga (Gshen chen klu dga, 996–1035) was one of the earliest and most important of Bon treasure-finders, whose revealed Treasures in 1017 were part of *The General Heap (sPyi spungs)* canon, including the famous Great Perfection text *The Ninefold Cycle of the Hidden Enlightening Mind.* Shenchen Luga also excavated a commentarial cycle on the latter text, which itself appears to be centered on classic mind-series rhetoric as found in early Nyingma Tantras of that classification.

Zhötön Ngödrub (g/bzhod ston dngos grub grags, c. 1050) further mined Great Perfection literature from *The General Heap* cache when he excavated *The Trilogy of Proclamations (sgrags pa skor gsum),* a single volume with forty-six individual texts that claims to be a translation from the Zhang Zhung language. Its root Tantra is *The Golden Tortoise* (gser gyi rus sbal) and Samten Karmay (1988) shows that this text was subsequently copied with minor modifications to partially elide its Bon character by Nyingmas. This latter Tantra was then circulated as a mind-series text claiming to be translated from Sanskrit by Mañjuśrīmitra and Vairocana, and rediscovered by the obscure Khyungdrak (khyung grag of Lhodrak [lho brag], thirteenth century?). However, the Bon text itself in at least two cases reproduces lines from one of the earliest Nyingma Atiyoga texts, indicating that this Bon revelation was itself drawing on earlier Buddhist sources in its own composition. The cycle is also connected to *The Oral Transmission of Zhang Zhung* by the presence of the identically titled *The Twelve Little Child Tantras,* located in the collection right after *The Golden Tortoise.*

Zhötön also revealed *The Great Sphere of the Great Perfection's Ultra Summit* (yang rtse'i klong chen) from the same location in 1088, which became the basis for the Great Perfection tradition in Bon. It claims to have been originally composed by the eighth-century *siddha* Nyenchen Lishu Takring (snyen chen li bshu stag rings) from Takzik Long, who translated it from the Zhang Zhung language into Tibetan and then concealed it. Zhötön evidently considered himself to be the reincarnation of Nyenchen, just as Dangma himself was considered to be an incarnation of Vimalamitra when he initially excavated the latter's Treasure cache at Zha (zhwa) temple. One of the texts from the cycle, *The Lamp Illuminating the Signs of Dying,* is nearly identical to a text on the same subject attributed to Mañjuśrīmitra titled *Examining for Death,* which is redacted within *The Turquoise Letters* section of *The Seminal Heart of Vimalamitra.*

Only a few decades later Gongdzö (dgongs mdzod, 1038–1096) of the Meu (rme'u) clan founded the *A* Guidance tradition, which differs from the other two divisions of Bon Great Perfection by having a precise historical origin in Tibet rather than transcendental origins. It appears the tradition was more associated with the Nyingma mind-series movement with its central focus on inner calm (*zhi gnas*) techniques revolving around concentrating on a written letter *A.* Drugom Gyelwa Yungdrung's (bru sgom rgyal ba gyung drung, 1242–1290) later condensation of the tradition does involve a simple channel visualization practice and dream yoga, but it remains to be seen if these date back to the original synthesis of Gongdzö.

However, Drugom is arguably the most important Bon Great Perfection figure after the eleventh century. He partially corresponds to the role of Longchenpa in the Nyingma tradition and composed important works in both the Guidance on the Syllable *A* and Oral Transmission traditions. He wrote a series of nine interlinked texts on *The Oral Transmission of Zhang Zhung* that present the contemplation of spontaneous light images within darkness, in sky gazing, and in sun gazing—the similarities with the Seminal Heart are detailed. He also contributed a long exegesis to yet a third important Great Perfection cycle, namely *The Lamp Commentary Dispelling Darkness*, which was included within *The Commentarial Cycle on the Great Sphere of the Ultra Summit.* Special mention should also be made of Shardza Tashi Gyeltsen (shar rdza bkra shis rgyal mtshan, 1859–1933), the prolific Bon author who drew extensively on Longchenpa's own Great Perfection corpus to create compositions whose system is basically identical to the Seminal Heart.

BIBLIOGRAPHY

Achard, Jean-Luc. *L'Essence Perlée du Secret.* Turnhout, Belgium, 1999. A survey of early Great Perfection traditions with a focus on the Seminal Heart via an annotated translation of a key text from *The Seminal Heart of Vimalamitra,* including comments on Bon traditions and possible connections with Kashmiri Shaivism.

Dudjom Rinpoche, Jikdrel Yeshe Dorje. *The Nyingma School of Tibetan Buddhism: Its Fundamentals and History,* vol. 1. Translated and edited by Gyurme Dorje with the collaboration of Matthew Kapstein. Boston, 1991. An annotated translation of a twentieth-century survey of Nyingma religions and history, including extensive sections on the Great Perfection.

Germano, David F. "Dying, Death and Other Opportunities." In *Religions of Tibet in Practice,* edited by Donald S. Lopez Jr., pp. 458–493. Princeton, N.J., 1997. A translation with an introduction of Longchenpa's treatment of death-related meditations in the Great Perfection from *The Treasury of Words and Meanings.*

Germano, David F. "Architecture and Absence in the Secret Tantric History of rDzogs Chen." In *Journal of the International Association of Buddhist Studies* 17, no. 2: 203–335. A survey of the growth of Nyingma Great Perfection movements from the eighth to the fourteenth centuries that stresses the nature and diversity of contemplative praxis.

Germano, David F. "The History of Funerary *rDzogs chen.*" *Journal of the International Association of Tibetan Studies* 1 (2004). A study of early Nyingma Great Perfection movements depicting a fundamental divide between types stressing earlier "pristine" forms and later "funerary" forms that focus on late Tantric practice and iconography with a special focus on death motifs.

Karmay, Samten. *The Great Perfection (rDzogs chen): A Philosophical and Meditative Teaching of Tibetan Buddhism.* Leiden, 1988. A study of some of the earliest of the Great Perfection texts with a history of the movement's early evolution.

Kvaerne, Per. "Bonpo Studies: The A-khrid System of Meditation." *Kailash* 1, no. 1 (1973): 19–50; 1, no. 4 (1973): 247–332. A detailed study of the Bon Guidance on the Syllable *A* tradition of the Great Perfection.

Longchenpa. *Kindly Bent to Ease Us: From the Trilogy of Finding Comfort and Ease.* 3 vols. Translated by Herbert V. Guenther. Emeryville, Calif., 1975–1976. A translation of the root verses form Longchenpa's *The Trilogy of Resting at Ease,* including interpretative introductions to each chapter.

Neumaier-Dargyay, E. K., trans. *The Sovereign All-Creating Mind: The Motherly Buddha.* Albany, N.Y., 1992. A pioneering and important translation of *The All-Creating King,* though not always correct in the fine details of the text's meaning.

Rossi, Donatella. *The Philosophical View of the Great Perfection in the Tibetan Bon Religion.* Ithaca, N.Y., 1999. A study of the philosophical system of the Great Perfection in Bon traditions, including annotated translations of key texts from *The Oral Transmission of Zhang Zhung* and *The Trilogy of Proclamations.*

Thondup Rinpoche, Tulku. *Buddha Mind: An Anthology of Longchen Rabjam's Writings on Dzogpa Chenpo.* Ithaca, N.Y., 1989. An anthology of translations of classic Great Perfection of literature with a special focus on Longchenpa.

DAVID GERMANO (2005)

E

EA See ENKI

EAGLES AND HAWKS.

EAGLES AND HAWKS. The terms *eagle* and *hawk* can be taken to refer generally to birds of prey, although there is much confusion as to the particular species (eagle, hawk, falcon, vulture, osprey, etc.) in bird symbolism and its description. Eagles and hawks seem to gather their symbolic value from their swiftness, soaring ability, and fierceness; through these qualities they are equated and associated with various religious principles and with deities of all kinds.

The sacred roles of the eagle and hawk in many religions derive from their association with the life-giving and life-sustaining powers of various deities who represent the forces of nature. The Aztec god of sun and war, Huitzilopochtli, is symbolized by an eagle. The sun's efforts to regain the sky from its daily rising in the east symbolize the struggle between the principles of the celestial, or spiritual, spheres and those of the lower world. The sun gods Re and Horus of ancient Egypt, who share similar attributes, are depicted as hawks or hawk-headed men.

A myth of the Iroquois describes how Oshadage, the Big Eagle of the Dew, bears a lake of dew on his back, which brings water and life to the earth after forces of fire have parched all plant life. Assyro-Babylonian religion provides a similar example: the divine lion-headed eagle Imdugud spread his wings after a drought, shrouding the skies in rain-bearing clouds. An Olmec deity, the dragon monster, is a composite of caiman, eagle, jaguar, serpent, and human, a figure that fuses sun, water, earth, and fertility symbolism.

Eagle and hawk symbolism is also associated with death, for the birds often act as the bearers of souls "heavenward." This is true of the hawk in California Indian religions as well as in the religious system of ancient Egypt, where the hawk was itself the emblem of the soul. In ancient Rome an eagle was released from an emperor's funeral pyre to signify the soul departing for the afterlife.

Clockwise from top left corner. Colossus of Ramses II at the Temple of Amun in Karnak, Egypt. *[©Gian Berto Vanni/Corbis]*; Coptic ceremonial fan depicting Ethiopian saints. *[©Werner Forman/Art Resource, N.Y.]*; Reverse of an early-fourth-century BCE Etruscan bronze mirror showing the mythical seer Calchas dressed as an haruspex and examining an animal liver. Museo Gregoriano Profano, Vatican Museums. *[©Scala/Art Resource, N.Y.]*; Twelfth-century mosaic of Jesus as Pantocrator. Duomo di Cefalu, Sicily. *[©Adam Woolfitt/Corbis]*; Glazed pottery eagle from second- to third-century CE Italy. Museo Ostiense, Ostia. *[©Erich Lessing/Art Resource, N.Y.]* .

Because of their swiftness, eagles and hawks are the messengers and bearers of the gods. The *Iliad* and *Odyssey* of ancient Greek culture make reference to the gods' use of eagles as messengers. In Eddic mythology, both Freyja and Odin possessed a hawk's plumage that gave them the capacity for swift flight. The swiftness of the eagle Garuḍa is noted in the Hindu *Mahābhārata.* It was Garuḍa who stole the soma for Viṣṇu and so became Viṣṇu's mount. In Christianity the swiftness of the eagle's flight associates the bird with prayer rising to the Lord and with his grace descending to man.

As birds of prey, the eagle and hawk are often identified with gods of war and with supernatural malice in general. The eagle was the weapon bearer of the Roman gods and was often shown clutching a thunderbolt in its talons. According to the *Mahābhārata,* hawks are unlucky omens except when they precede a warrior into battle. As Jupiter's bird in Roman religion, the eagle was also a "storm bird," just as the hawk was among the ancient Greeks; both were identified with violent winds associated with the earth's malignant forces.

Eagles and hawks represent divine majesty, the superiority of the intellect over the physical and of the spiritual over the material. Thus the opposition of eagle (or hawk) and serpent represents the domination of baser forces by higher spiritual forces; so also, more generally, does the symbolic equation of eagle and thunderbolt. This principle is found also in such mythical creatures as the Christian griffin, the Olmec jaguar-monster deities, and the Assyro-Babylonian god Imdugud; in Greek imagery depicting a hawk ripping apart a hare; and, similarly, in Hindu imagery of the eagle Garuḍa and a serpent.

Bibliography

An early work comparing themes and symbols that are found repeatedly in the myths and practices of many religions worldwide is Ellen R. Emerson's *Indian Myths, or Legends, Traditions and Symbols of the Aborigines of America Compared with Those of Other Countries, Including Hindostan, Egypt, Persia, Assyria, and China* (1884; Minneapolis, 1965). A more detailed study of Semitic symbolism is to be found in Maurice H. Farbridge's *Studies in Biblical and Semitic Symbolism* (New York, 1970). This is a rich historical discussion of Semitic religious and cultural symbols, including a brief but interesting discussion of the use of animal imagery. A very useful collection (with index) of myths representing cultures and religious traditions worldwide can be found in *The Mythology of All Races,* 13 vols., edited by Louis H. Gray (Boston, 1916–1932). E. Washburn Hopkins's *Epic Mythology* (1915; New York, 1969) and William J. Wilkins's *Hindu Mythology: Vedic and Puranic,* 2d ed. (London, 1973), offer extensive discussions of the Hindu epics, with detailed accounts of the various roles played by eagles and hawks. An authoritative discussion of the use of animal imagery in religious and cultural contexts is Jocelyn Toynbee's *Animals in Roman Life and Art* (London, 1973). This work makes extensive use of historical accounts and of the described behavior of animals in explaining their symbolic roles.

New Sources

Baird, Merrily. "Birds and Insects." In *Symbols of Japan: Thematic Motifs in Art and Design.* New York, 2001.

Taylor, Pamela York. *Beasts, Birds, and Blossoms in Thai Art.* New York, 1996.

Vogel, Dan. "Ambiguities of the Eagle." *Jewish Bible Quarterly* 26 (June 1988): 85–92.

S. J. M. Gray (1987)
Revised Bibliography

EARTH. "May the rain-maker water the Earth-Mother that she may be made beautiful to look upon." Thus opens a prayer to Awitelin Tsita, the earth divinity of the Zuni of New Mexico. The chant continues, "May the rain-makers water the Earth-Mother that she may become fruitful and give to her children and to all the world the fruits of her being that they may have food in abundance. May the Sun-Father embrace our Earth-Mother that she may become fruitful, that food may be bountiful, and that our children may live the span of life, not die, but sleep to awake with their gods" (Matilda Coxe Stevenson, "Ethnobotany of the Zuñi Indians," in *Annual Report of the Bureau of Ethnology,* Washington, D. C. 1915, p. 37). Many North American peoples revered the earth and remained deeply impressed by its sacredness. In the first years of the twentieth century, a Cheyenne explained to a visitor, "It is by the earth that we live. Without it we could not exist. It nourishes and supports us. From it grow the fruits that we eat, and the grass that sustains the animals whose flesh we live on; from it come forth, and over its surface run, the waters which we drink. We walk on it and unless it is firm and steadfast we cannot live" (George Bird Grinnell, "Tenure of Land among the Indians," *American Anthropologist* 9, 1907, p. 3).

Native Americans are not the only people to speak of the earth with intimacy and emotion. Throughout history and across cultures, people have clung to their images of the sacred earth. It is worthwhile and necessary to come to grips with these images. In the first place, they reveal a reality that remains veiled in any other terms. Furthermore, the study of the images of the earth bears directly on our understanding of the human condition as it has been plumbed by so much of the human family. In this article we review several important aspects of the earth, seen as a religious condition: earth as the source of life, earth as it appears at the beginning of time, the image of earth as the primal mother, and earth as the locus of regenerative life.

Source of Life. The cosmos is a reservoir of sacred forces. From a religious perspective, the earth is the clearest epiphany of an ensemble of sacred apparitions: soil, stones, trees, water, shadows, vegetation, and the jumbled landscape of the world. These form a single, living, cosmic unity. The soil, the earth, signifies this tangle of concrete vitalities. The earth is the foundation, the generative source, of every expression of existence. From the earliest records we possess of religious history, the earth, united with everything else that is, supports and contains all the life forms that reveal themselves to human beings. Earth is a tireless fount of existence. The lesson that the Cheyenne man taught his visitor is that the religious meaning of the earth remains indistinguishable from all the life that takes manifest form through the powers of the earth: mountains, forests, water, vegetation, and so on.

The Creative Role of Earth in the Beginning. A great number of myths describe a distant time when the earth produced or helped create life in the world. Among the many mythic themes, we call attention to five: androgyny, parthenogenesis, hierogamy, sacrifice, and emergence.

Androgyny: fullness of being. Androgyny is an ancient and widespread image of wholeness. Myths make clear that the meaning of androgyny goes beyond its overtly sexual manifestation to symbolize the perfection of a primordial, nonconditioned state of being. In fact, every beginning must start in the wholeness of being. Gods who manifested powerful aspects of the earth, especially divinities of vegetation and fertility, reveal traces of androgyny (cf. Nyberg, 1931, pp. 230ff., for bisexual earth divinities). These sources of holiness and power, such as Attis, Adonis, and Cybele in the Mediterranean world, portray the overfullness from which life springs. In cosmogonic myths, chaos often represents the perfect totality, the undifferentiated unity, on which all subsequent existence bases itself. In such circumstances, the creative role of the earth is obscure but discernible. The earth exists "in germ."

Such is the case in the Japanese texts recorded in the *Kojiki* and *Nihongi*. In the beginning, heaven and earth were inseparably mingled together. These male and female principles formed a perfect and androgynous totality within an egglike chaos. Eventually a tiny, amorphous island was precipitated out of the chaos. In this island was a reed, a development of the germ that first existed in the center of the cosmic egg. The reed was the first articulate transformation undertaken by the earth; it generated a number of gods. Later, when heaven and earth separated definitively from one another, they took on the human forms of a man and a woman, Izanagi and Izanami. The union of the two separate principles generated the world. When the woman died giving birth to the fire god, the deities of local places, hearths, and vegetation arose from her body. For the moment we focus our attention on the first stage of creation and on the incipient, androgynous being that embraces the sacred powers of the earth. These are not yet clearly defined, but they include all possibilities of life. As such, the divine androgyny in which the earth shares at the most primordial stage of creation is the ultimate ground of the realities that follow.

Parthenogenesis. According to Hesiod, "Earth [Gaia] herself first of all gave birth to a being equal to herself who could overspread her completely, the starry heaven [Ouranos] who was to present the blessed gods a secure throne forever" (*Theogony* 5126f.). This divine couple procreated the gods, the cyclopes, and a slew of mythical monsters, arrogant children with a hundred arms and fifty heads. Although Gaia finds no prominent place in the Homeric Hymns, one of them is addressed to her: "It is the earth I sing, securely enthroned, the mother of all things, venerable ancestress feeding upon her soil all that exists. . . . To thee it belongs to give life to mortals and to take it from them" (*Hymn to Earth* 1ff.).

Ancient Greek traditions affirm that the earth existed before heaven, to whom the earth gave birth by parthenogenesis (i.e., without any male assistance or insemination; for treatment of parthenogenesis among Greek and other Mediterranean goddesses, see Uberto Pestalozza, *Pagine di religione mediterranea*, Milan, 1942, vol. 1, pp. 191ff.). Through such myths the power of the creative possibilities of the earth are portrayed as limitless. The motif of parthenogenesis by the primordial earth reappears in myths that account for all the species of animals and plants as having been born from the body of a primordial being, as well as in myths of virgin birth such as the Greek accounts of Hera who, alone and unaided by men, gave birth to Typhon, Hephaistos, and Ares. Izanami, the Japanese goddess of the earth, gave birth to a number of gods who issued from her own substance.

Hierogamy. Perhaps the most lavish and numerous myths depicting the role of the earth in creation are those that describe a marriage between heaven and earth, a hierogamy. Myths of this sort are reported from Oceania, Indonesia, Micronesia, Asia, Africa, Europe, and the Americas. When heaven encounters earth, life flows forth in innumerable forms. The union of heaven and earth is a fundamental act of creation; it generates life on a cosmic and biological scale. The Greek accounts about Gaia and the Japanese myths concerning Izanami show that the views of androgyny, parthenogenesis, and hierogamy are related and, on occasion, even overlap one another. All of these images, which are expressions of a coincidence of opposites, struggle to express the notion of creativity and of the cosmic fecundity of the earth. In the beginning of time, according to the Maori tradition, the sky, Rangi, and the earth, Papa, were locked together in a sexual union. Their children longed for the light of day. In the eternal darkness of their earthen womb, they plotted a way to separate their parents. Eventually, the children severed the bonds that tied heaven to earth and shoved their father into the air until light appeared.

According to Zuni accounts, the creator, Awonawilona, contained all being within himself. At first he existed alone in the universe, but then changed himself into the sun and produced two seeds from his own substance. With these he inseminated the waters. Under his warmth, the sea turned green and grew in size until it became the earth mother (Awatelin Tsita, the "fourfold-containing mother earth"), on the one hand, and the sky father (Apoyan Táchu, "all-covering father sky"), on the other. These cosmic twins embraced in union to produce the countless numbers of creatures. After many complications, the sun and the first ancestors he created managed to free the creatures germinating in the dark womb of the earth. Previously they had crawled over one another like reptiles, hissing and spitting out indecent words. Eventually, when the sky was lifted off the earth, these children escaped along a ladder to freedom and light (Frank Hamilton Cushing, "Outlines of Zuñi Creation Myths," in *Annual Report of the Bureau of American Ethnology*, Washington, D. C., 1896, pp. 379–384).

In myths of hierogamy, a sacred union with heaven, often symbolized by lightning, hail, or rain, is indispensable to the fruitfulness of the earth. It also serves as the model of fruitful human marriage. Hierogamy explains creation from some primordial whole that precedes it. The separation of heaven from earth is the first cosmogonic act, a fundamental shearing of primordial unity. In this widely known mythic drama, the fecundity of the earth with heaven is noticeably absent or sparsely distributed among the peoples of Australia, the Arctic, Tierra del Fuego, and the hunters and herders of North and Central Asia.

Sacrifice. In some myths of creation, the earth appears as a primordial victim of destruction (e.g., through conflagration, deluge, earthquake, petrification), especially through sacrifice, or even self-sacrifice. In such circumstances the fertility of the earth is never suppressed, for from the immolated or dismembered remains spring the species of plants, animals, linguistic groups, or races of humankind. The mystery of the creation of edible plants through the sacrifice of a goddess of the soil or earth was reenacted through agrarian rituals.

Most often, ritual sacrifices associated with the fertility of the soil were symbolic. In some cases, however, we possess reports of the actual sacrifice of living human victims. Such was the case, for example, among the Khonds of early nineteenth-century India. The Khond community, a Dravidian tribe inhabiting the hills of Orissa, a province of southern Bengal, bought a *meriah*, a voluntary victim who lived in the community for years, married, and fathered children. In the days preceding his sacrifice the *meriah* was ritually identified with the sacrificed divinity. The community danced in reverence around him. The victim was led in procession from the village to the virgin forest, the location of sacrifice. Participants anointed him and decorated him with flowers. They called upon the earth god, Tari Pennu (or Bera Pennu): "O God! We offer the sacrifice to you. Give us good crops, seasons, and health" (Frazer, 1926, p. 389). In front of representatives from every village in the vicinity, the *meriah* was slain, and a priest distributed fragments of the sacrificed body. These pieces were brought to the villages and ceremonially buried in the fields. The remains were burned so that the ashes could be spread over plowed fields to guarantee a good harvest.

In connection with the sacredness of the earth, the Aztec of central Mexico also performed acts of ritual sacrifice and dismemberment. When plants first sprouted, people sought the "god of the maize," a new shoot that was brought home, revered, and furnished with food offerings. That evening the new sprout was carried to a temple. The goddess of maize was honored by three different female age-groups. When the crop was ripe, the community celebrated a sacrifice in which a young girl represented Xilonen, the goddess of the new maize. After the young woman was sacrificed, the new crop could be consumed as food. Two months later, at the end of the harvest, another woman, representing the goddess Toci, was beheaded in sacrifice. A priest wore the flayed skin of the victim; another ritual specialist fashioned a mask from the victim's thigh. The masked participant played the role of a woman in childbirth in the harvest ritual.

These sacrifices ritually repeat the creation scenario in which the violent death of a primordial earth (e.g., through flood, fire, or violent self-sacrifice) gave rise to new forms, especially plants. Cut to pieces, the victim's body is identified with the mythic being whose death gave life to the cereal grain.

Emergence. We have seen how the earth figures largely in the creation of cosmic structures, as well as plant and animal life. A large number of myths emphasize the role of the earth in the origins of human life. As mentioned above in the opening scenes of the Zuni creation account reported by Cushing, the solitary creator became the sun and impregnated the great waters with two seeds from his own substance. These germs of men and of other creatures eventually hatched in the darkness. Pośhayank'ya, the great sage (who perhaps represents the nocturnal sun), then emerged from the foamy body of the earth mother, who possessed four wombs, one on top of another. It was in the deepest of these womb-caverns that all creatures dwelled in the beginning. For the first time, Pośhayank'ya pleaded with the sun father to liberate humanity from the dank and crowded bowels of the earth. In order to deliver the forms of life from the obscure and indistinct conditions of its fertile matrix, the sun father began another round of creation, but this time he aimed to produce intelligent beings who could find their way out of the dark, uterine hold of life-engendering earth. These beings would have the freedom that comes from the knowledge of magical power and ritual.

For a second time the sun father inseminated the foamy earth mother to produce twins. The twins sliced open the mountains and slipped into the subterranean darkness. With their warm breath they hastened the growth of a climbing plant, enabling it to break through to the light above. They then fashioned a ladder from its stalk, thus permitting the creatures to ascend from the lowest cavern into the second chamber. The beings who stayed behind or fell along the way became terrible monsters, creatures of the deep. Step by step, the twins provided the plant-ladder to grow and led the earthly pilgrims toward open space and heavenly light. At each stage, the people grew in wisdom, and humanity multiplied along the way, filling up whatever space was made available in the earth by the twins. Eventually, the twins led out, one after another, six distinct groups of people, the ancestors of the six human races. They emerged on the surface of the earth still bearing signs of their fetal existence in the ground: their toes were webbed and their ears, like those of bats and other creatures of the night, were attached to their heads by large membranes. They could not yet stand erect but crawled on their bellies like lizards or hopped like frogs.

The Caniengas Mohawk, an Iroquois group, also reported that humans once dwelled in the dark womb of the earth, without sunlight and in strange form. One day, during a hunt, one of the intraterrestrials accidentally discovered a hole that led to the surface of the earth. On the surface, this huntsman captured a deer. Drawn by the good-tasting game and the fine countryside, the subterranean creatures decided to emerge into the light of day. Only the groundhog remained in the earth.

Similarly, referring to the Lenni Lenape or Delaware Indians, the nineteenth-century scholar John Hockewelder remarked that "Indian mythologists are not agreed as to the form in which they existed while in the bowels of the earth. Some assert that they lived there in a human shape, while others, with greater consistency, maintain that their existence was in the form of certain terrestrial animals, such as the groundhog, the rabbit, and the tortoise" (cited in Frazer, 1926, p. 427).

These myths of emergence from the earth illustrate to what extent the earth is seen as a mother. In fact, the gestation of the fetus and the act of parturition are viewed as recapitulations of the cosmic birth of humankind and the creation of life in general, when humans emerged from the deepest chambers of the earth. Within the earth humanity lived an embryonic existence; for that matter, all the forms of creation existed as embryos within the earth. All living beings passed through the various stages of development in a "ripening" process that has not yet come to completion. For that reason the fruits of the earth reflect many different degrees of transmutation. Some Indian minerological tracts, for example, describe the diamond as "ripe" (*pakka*), whereas crystal is "unripe" (*kacca*), and the emerald, still wrapped in its stone womb, is only an embryo. In the same way, base metals and unrefined ores are not yet fully "ripe," but human smiths and alchemists may imitate, hasten, and complete the powerful functions of the earth mother.

This passage from the darkness of unconscious and preformal life to articulate form through emergence becomes a model for many human activities. When cultures wish to create something new, restore something worn, or regenerate a being, they reenact the pattern that was powerful enough to produce life in the first place. The act of procreation and birth of individual human beings in a culture is considered a reenactment of the primordial drama of emergence. The condition of the unborn child parallels the preexistence of humanity in the womb of the earth. Every fetal child relives the primal experience of humanity though its signs (darkness, water, enclosure, larval form, etc.). In other words, because the emergence myth is known, cultures recognize that every individual possesses a firsthand experience of the entire significant history of humanity. The human mother and her fertile powers are brought completely within the compass and sacredness of the great earth mother.

MOTHER EARTH. Across the face of the globe, people cling to the belief that human beings were born from the earth. In some cases, human maternity is believed to result from the direct insertion of a child, an earthling, into a human woman's womb (whether in the form of a seed, an ancestral soul, or a miniature fetus). Up until the moment of its translocation into the human womb, the child had lived an embryological existence in the earth—in a cave, well, fissure, or tree. In Lithuania, for example, children were said to come from springs, lakes, or hills intimately associated with Zemyna, the earth mother, for she alone was responsible for the creation of new beings (Haralds Biezais, *Die Hauptgöttinnen der alten Letten*, Uppsala, 1955, pp. 338–342).

In many societies, the presence of a child in a mother's womb is attribued to her contact with some animal, stone, or other object. Whatever role the father and his sexual union with the mother might play, the fertility of the earth as the primordial mother is directly responsible for human motherhood and offspring. In such a setting of beliefs, human beings are, in a profound sense, people of their native land. Like the first humans in the earth, each new generation of children first lives among the rocks or in chasms. Aquatic animals such as frogs, crocodiles, fish, swans, or storks then bring them and place them magically in their mothers' wombs. Here again, fecund earth, the fertility of cosmic being, is represented by specific fruits or forms that take life from her (e.g., mountains, fertility stones, the waters of grottoes or springs, animals). A human mother simply receives children in their embryonic state. She is a container that helps the larval life of the earth attain a specifically human form. The belief is that the subterranean womb is the true *fons et origo* of embryological life, and once that is understood, the religious beliefs and practices described below make sense.

Memories of life in the womb. The experiences of mystics and shamans may be compared with prenatal existence in the womb of the earth. The primordial dark night of the soul portrays the opacity of subterranean life before emergence onto the surface of the earth. The power of North American shamans, for example, sometimes depends on their extraordinary abilities to remember their prenatal life. The images they recall from life in the womb bear striking similarity to the chambers, fixtures, sounds, and sensations of the subterranean world. The Guayaki of Paraguay often consult pregnant women as diviners, since their unborn children reveal secrets and truths to them. Fetal children possess the power to know obscure facts because they relive the primordial experience of the divine twins. These, in the first utter darkness of chaos, knew the germinal possibilities of all subsequent life forms and experienced them at first hand, in the darkness, before they pursued their diverse historical destinies.

At times the cultural community longs to return to the womb of the earth mother. The Yaruro people of Venezuela revered their great mother, who lived in the remote area of Kuma in the east, where the dead go. In the late 1930s, the Yaruro expressed the desire to reenter the realm of their mother in order to be reborn into the paradisal existence that preceded life and the arrival of colonial invaders (Vicenco Petrullo, *The Yaruros of the Capanaparo River, Venezuela,* Bureau of American Ethnology Bulletin 123, Washington, D. C., 1939, pp. 226ff.).

Labyrinths. The image of the earth as mother (with openings to the world in the form of galleries, mines, grottoes, and caves) and the desire to return to the embryonic stage of existence in the womb explain why the labyrinth can be an image of the body of the earth mother. The labyrinth, or meandering underground cavern, was an initiatory arena as well as a place to bury the dead. Entering a labyrinth (among other religious motivations for doing so) amounted to a ritual return to the womb of the mother. Labyrinthine caves were the sites of initiation, funerals, and marriages. It is in the fruitful womb of the earth that new forms of life first quicken. The labyrinth dramatizes the difficulty of discovering the past back to the sources of limitless creativity.

Malekula funeral symbolism, for example, describes Tenes (or Le-he-he), a frightening female being who lies in wait for dead men's souls. She stands at the entrance to a cavern; in front of her, outlined on the ground, is the sketch of a labyrinth. As the dead soul approaches, she rubs out half of the design. If the deceased has been properly initiated, he will know the entire outline of the labyrinth and find his road easily to the afterlife; otherwise the woman will swallow him. The labyrinths that one finds drawn on the earth in Malekula teach the living the road to the land of the dead. That is, they provide the living with the initiatory key that enables them to return into the bowels of the earth mother (A. Bernard Deacon, "Geometrical Drawings from Malekula and the Other Islands of the New Hebrides," *Journal of the Royal Anthropological Institute* 64, 1934, pp. 132ff.; John Layard, "Totenfahrt auf Malekula," *Eranos-Jahrbuch* 5, 1937, pp. 242–292).

Agrarian rites. Rites that mark significant moments in the agricultural calendar repeat what happened to the earth in mythical times. The mysteries of how life emerged from a germ hidden in an undifferentiated chaos, or was engendered in the sacred union between heaven and earth, or resulted from the violent death of divinities associated with the soil are reenacted in the rituals of the earth. Agricultural operations in the Andes, for example, are scheduled around the menstrual periods of Pachamama, Mother Earth. Special restrictions are observed at the times when Pachamama is "open," for the life of the community and the cosmos depend on her fertility.

Women usually play crucial roles in the rites associated with earthly fecundity. Insofar as women are symbolically assimilated with the land and insofar as agricultural work is homologous with the sexual act (so that the plow or spade is an emblem of the phallus, for example), women become epiphanies of the sacred power of the earth. The acts of women have worldly significance, for they channel the effects of the earth's ability to bear fruit and modulate its intensity. The Qur'ān declares, "Your wives are to you as fields" (2:223). The *Śatapatha Brāhmaṇa* (7.2.2.5) identifies the furrows of a plowed field with a vulva and the seeds sown in the furrow with semen. These ideas are widespread; they account for the prominent ritual role of women in agriculture. Many communities consider it auspicious if a pregnant woman sows the new seed; it augurs a good harvest, for the crops will grow apace with the fetus. Often women put the seed in the ground cleared by men, or women choose and store reservoirs of the fertile powers of the earth. Agricultural labor keeps one cognizant of the sacred origins of gardening; labor is the vehicle of meaning as well as the vehicle of its transmission from one generation to another.

For example, after the Canelos Quechua women of Ecuador have set a new field, they remain in it with their children and recount episodes from ancient myths about Nungui, the goddess of garden soil, whose power underlies all fertility. The neighboring women of the Jivaroan community also sing to Nungui at the time of planting. Nungui is short, fat, and black (characteristic features of many "dark virgins" or black madonnas associated with the soil). She forces crops to break through the surface of the earth by making them grow. Nungui dances at night in gardens that are well maintained; the new shoots of manioc are her dancing partners. Since plants tend to shrink during the daylight hours, Jivaroan women harvest them in the morning.

In a related ritual Jivaroan women ask Nungui for "babies," three red jasper stones (*nantara*) whose hidden location in the earth is revealed to them by the goddess in dreams. The nantara contain the female souls of manioc plants. Women hide the stones in the earth and keep them dark with an overturned food bowl placed in the center of the garden. The stones carry out the role of Nungui's mystical child who, in the primordial past, helped women accomplish all the tasks of farming with a single magical word. The prescribed layout of the contemporary Jivaroan garden and the red "children-stones" hidden there remain as signs of the perfect garden that existed at the beginning of time. When the time arrives to plant manioc seedlings, Jivaroan women gather to sing to Nungui while squatting over the new slips. The woman gardener places the first manioc cutting against her vaginal opening and paints the plant red before placing it in the ground. The identification of the fertility of women with the fertility of the soil is thus complete and direct. When they finish planting the fields, women dance for five nights in a row in honor of Nungui and request that her presence spur on the growth of the plants (Michael J. Harner, *The Jívaro: People of the Sacred Waterfalls,* Garden City, N.Y., 1973, pp. 70–76; Julian H. Steward and Alfred Métraux, "Tribes of the Peruvian and Ecuadorian Montaña," in *Hand-*

book of South American Indians, vol. 3, New York, 1948, p. 620).

The religious role of women, who are identified with the land, appears dramatically in ritual sexual unions performed in fields or in orgies with which the entire community punctuates the agricultural calendar. With these sacred acts, women and their partners commemorate the union of heaven and earth in order to stimulate the fruitfulness of the virgin soil. Communal sexual frenzy evokes the image of the divine couple during the confusion of the long cosmic night in the period before creation, or in their primal state within the cosmogonic egg. During orgies, the whole community celebrates this return to the undifferentiated state of the earth at the beginning of time. The custom of streaking naked across the earth to provoke the virility of the sky or of the fertilizing rains shows how rites associated with the earth break down the barriers between individuals, society, cosmic nature, and divine forms. The experience of society during orgy is that of seeds and primordial embryos. The community as a whole loses its articulate shape during the period of subterranean merging and disintegration that is an integral part of the process of germination. Individuality dissolves in the orgy, for neither law nor social form is maintained in the total fusion of sexes and emotions. As in the ritual of immersion in water, orgy undoes the structures of the community and identifies human life with the formless, precosmic chaos in the bowels of the earth before creation. Even when orgies are not literally carried out but are only staged as performances (e.g., phallic dances or parades, dancing between series of unmarried partners), the fruitfulness of life derived from the earth depends on the symbolic dissolution of norms through carousing, obscenity, debauchery, insult, or choreographic and choral union of bodies and voices normally held separate from one another. For example, it is in connection with the fertility of the earth that many of the so-called *hadaka matsuri* (literally, "naked festivals") celebrated throughout Japan find their meaning.

Lying on the soil. We have already seen that the conception and birth of human individuals are scaled-down versions of the creative process performed by the earth since the beginning of time. Human mothers repeat that sucessful first act by which life first appeared in the womb of the earth mother. For that reason, at the moment of birth, women from many cultures put themselves directly in touch with the earth and mimic her actions. In this way they partake as fully as possible of her powers and remain under her protection. In numerous societies women give birth in such a way as to deposit the child onto the earth, or else place the child on the soil immediately after birth. In some cases women in childbirth lie prostrate on the ground or move into the forest or fields. "To sit on the ground" was a common expression in ancient Egypt meaning to give birth (Nyberg, 1931, p. 133). Every authentic birth of an Aché of Paraguay repeats the first act of standing upright upon the primordial earth. The Aché birth rites include two moments: *waa*, a "falling" from the womb onto the soil, and *upi*, a "lifting up." The act of touching the earth introduces the child to the biotic condition shared by all animals and plants. By lifting him up from the earth, the mother repeats his transition from amorphous biological form to fully human stature—just as it was obtained by the primordial ancestors when they first emerged from the earth and stood upright upon it (Pierre Clastres, *Chronique des Indiens Guayaki*, Paris, 1972, pp. 14–16). The earth must be the mother who gives birth to every true human being.

Placement on the soil was also an integral part of healing rites. Sick persons were restored to health when they were created anew, remade in the image of the ancestral beings in their primordial situation within the earth. The Huichol of Mexico, for example, when on pilgrimage to Wirikuta, their place of mythic origins, stop by pools of water that open into the creative depths of the earth. The healer asks his patients, especially barren women, to stretch out full-length on the ground, which is the powerful body of the primal mother. The rite of placing a newborn child on the earth existed in ancient China, where a dying person was also set on the soil. The earth represents the powers both of birth and of rebirth to a new existence. The powers of the earth determine whether the transitions of birth and death are valid and well accomplished (Granet, 1953, pp. 192–198).

DEATH AND REGENERATION. As a form of regenerative darkness, the earth, in its sacredness and fertility, includes the reality of death. This was clear already in the myths of the sacrifice of a primordial divinity associated with the soil. The death of the god gives rise to life in new forms, especially that of plants. Life and death are simply two phases in the career of Mother Earth. In fact, "life" in the light of day consists of a hiatus, a brief period of detachment from the earth's womb. It is death that returns one to the primordial or eternal condition that existed before the cycle of life began.

Many of the terrifying aspects of the earth mother, in the form of the goddess of death or the recipient of violent sacrifices, are rooted in her status as the universal womb, the source of all life. Death itself is not annihilation, but rather the state of the seed in the bosom of the earth. This helps explain why the bodies of the dead are buried in fetal positions in so many cultures. These "embryos" are expected to come back to life. In some cases, as stated above, the dead reenact the experience of the earth mother herself, who was the first person to die (e.g., Izanami of Japanese mythology, who died giving birth to fire). In such circumstances, the negative depictions of the earth mother as the goddess of death portray her role in the sacrificial mode of existence that makes passage from one form to another possible. The ubiquitous sacrificial dimension of symbolic existence guarantees the unending circulation of life. "Crawl to the earth, your mother," proclaims the *Ṛgveda* (10.18.10). "You, who are earth I place you in the earth," is a funerary formula from the *Atharvaveda* (12.1.11, 12.1.14). The Kraho of Brazil make every attempt to transport a dying man back to the soil of his maternal village. The inscriptions on ancient Roman tombs illustrate the same desire to rest in one's native earth. The vitality and fecundity of the earth, its sacred power to generate life without end, assures the reappearance of the dead in a new living form.

The rich symbolism of the earth is not exhausted by the cosmogonies, agricultural feasts, or burial practices of archaic peoples or tribal societies. The earth remains a powerful image of the possibility of new life and radically new social existence. In contemporary religious movements of rebellion or revolution prompted by desperate and oppressive circumstances, the earth becomes a focal image of renewal (Bruce Lincoln, "'The Earth Becomes Flat': A Study of Apocalyptic Imagery," *Comparative Studies in Society and History* 25, 1983, pp. 136–153; see also Werner Müller, *Geliebte Erde: Naturfrömmigkeit und Naturhass im indianischen und europäischen Nordamerika*, Bonn, 1972). In the eschatological or utopian visions of new regimes or revolutionary kingdoms the face of the earth will be renewed or the end of the world will intervene to impose a new and just order, symbolized by the leveling of mountains and the filling of valleys. All forms of life, without discrimination, will obtain easy and equal access to the plenteous vitality of the earth.

COSMIC SOLIDARITY OF LIFE. The religious imagery of the earth engenders a kinship among all forms of life, for they are all generated in the same matrix. The intimate relationship between earth and the human, animal, and vegetal life forms inheres in the religious realization that the life force is the same in all of them. They are united on the biological plane; their fates, consequently, are intertwined. Pollution or sterility on one level of existence affects all other modes of life. Because of their common origin, all life-forms constitute a whole. Unlike the sacredness of the sky, which appears vividly in the myths of the separation of the sky from the creaturely forms dependent on it, there is no rupture between the earth and the forms it engenders.

Furthermore, earth protects the existence of life in myriad forms, and safeguards against abuses (e.g., incest or murder) that threaten the good order of reproductive life. Ritual union between sexual partners and orgies celebrated in ceremony are restricted to decisive moments of the agricultural calendar. During the rest of the time, the earth mother is often a patroness of morality and a guardian of the norms conducive to fruitful existence. The earth punishes certain categories of criminals, especially adulterers, murderers, and sexual miscreants. In some cases, as in ancient Greece, the shedding of blood on the earth and incest could render the earth barren, with catastrophic consequences. Thus, in the opening of Sophocles' *Oedipus Rex*, a priest bewails the fate of Thebes because women suffer birth pangs without living issue and the fruits of the earth and the oxen in the fields are dying, as is the city itself.

CONCLUSION. The earth reveals the meaning and sacredness of life's ceaseless ability to bear fruit. This point comes home strongly in all the images we have examined. There is a tendency for agricultural divinities, active and dramatic, to draw attention from the primordial divinities of the soil. But in all the great goddesses who represent the capacities of agriculture and the fruitfulness of the tilled soil there exists the underlying presence of the earth as a whole, the sacredness of the physical place of life. It is true that the earth often appears in cosmogonic myths as a figure vaguer in outline than the more clearly delineated goddesses of specific crops or particular rites in the agricultural cycle. However, the role of the earth in the earliest stages of mythic history testifies to the abiding sacredness of life itself, regardless of the distinct forms that it may include. The myths of parthenogenesis, of the androgyny of the earth, of hierogamy, of the sacrifice of the primordial earth, and of emergence from the dark womb of the first times affirm the sacredness of the soil. That is, they disclose the meaning of its tireless creativity. That manifestation of the sacred in the form of the soil, whether as a general presence or divine figure, helps make sense of rituals and symbolic forms linked to the earth.

Descents into caves and grottoes, the imagery of subterranean embryos, scenarios of return to a prenatal existence, labyrinths, rites of swearing by the earth, deposition of the newborn on the earth or interment of the dead in earthen graves, the iconographic tradition of black madonnas, and the terrifying figures of great goddesses, as well as the stylized sexual orgies of agricultural feasts return the attention of the religious imagination to one of its most important sources: the inexhaustible powers of the universal procreator of life. Few images have generated such power within the religious imagination or held such a command over it throughout the course of human history. It is possible that the rise of the earth to primacy as a sacred form in the religious imagination was stunted by her sacred marriage with the sky and other male divinities (e.g., storm gods) who are important in agriculture. Nevertheless, the earth, especially in the image of the great mother, has never forfeited her role as the locus of life, the source of all forms, the guardian of children, and the womb where the dead await their rebirth.

SEE ALSO Alchemy; Androgynes; Caves; Dismemberment; Hieros Gamos; Labyrinth; Nature.

BIBLIOGRAPHY

Several fundamental works recommend themselves for their comprehensive coverage of the phenomenon, as well as for their insight. Although dated, these studies are still important and valuable: Albrecht Dieterich's *Mutter Erde* (Berlin, 1905); Theodor Nöldeke's "Mutter-Erde und Verwandtes bei den Semiten," *Archiv für Religionswissenschaft* 8 (1905): 161–166; Ernst Samter's *Geburt, Hochzeit und Tod* (Berlin, 1911), pp. 1–20; Wolf Wilhelm Baudissin's *Adonis und Esmun* (Leipzig, 1911), esp. pp. 443ff. and 505ff.; James G. Frazer's *The Worship of Nature* (London, 1926), pp. 316–440; Marcel Granet's "Le dépôt de l'enfant sur le sol," in his *Études sociologiques sur la Chine* (Paris, 1953), pp. 159–202; Henri Théodore Fischer's *Het heilig huwelik van hemel en aarde* (Utrecht, 1929); Bertel Nyberg's *Kind und Erde* (Helsinki, 1931); Willibald Staudacher's *Die Trennung von Himmel und Erde* (Tübingen, 1942); Vittore Pisani's "La donna e la terra," *Anthropos* 37–40 (1942–1945); 241–253; Uberto Pestalozza's *Religione mediterranea: Vecchi e nuovi studi* (Milan, 1951), esp. pp. 191ff.; and Gerardus van der Leeuw's "Das sogenannte Hockerbegräbnis und der ägyptische Tjknw," *Studi e materiali di storia delle religioni* 14 (1938): 151–167.

Mircea Eliade's *Myths, Dreams, and Mysteries: The Encounter between Contemporary Faiths and Archaic Realities* (New York, 1960), pp. 155–189, and *Patterns in Comparative Religion* (New York, 1958), chaps. 7 and 9, deal with earth and agriculture and offer ample bibliograpies. For a discussion of the images of the goddess in relation to the sacredness of the earth, see Andrew Fleming's article "The Myth of the Mother-Goddess," *World Archaeology* 1 (October 1969): 247–261, and *The Book of the Goddess: Past and Present*, edited by Carl Olson (New York, 1983), which deals with the role of the goddess in prehistory, Mesopotamia, Egypt, Greece, Rome, Canaanite-Hebrew culture, in Christianity, gnosticism, Hinduism, Buddhism, Japanese religion, Afro-American culture, Amerindian religions, and in contemporary thought and practice. Bibliographies for these topics are included on pages 251–259. *Mother Worship: Theme and Variations*, edited by James J. Preston (Chapel Hill, N. C., 1982), presents several cases from the New World, Europe, South Asia, and Africa.

Jürgen Zwernemann's *Die Erde in der Vorstellungswelt und Kultpraktiken der sudanischen Völker* (Berlin, 1968) is an example of a study of the full range of earth symbolism in a single culture. A most thorough and penetrating study of the earth is Ana Maria Mariscotti de Görlitz's *Pachamama Santa Tierra* (Berlin, 1978), which examines the history of belief and practice surrounding the earth mother in the South American Andes. Olof Pettersson's *Mother Earth: An Analysis of the Mother Earth Concepts according to Albert Dieterich* (Lund, 1967) redresses some of the hasty generalizations of Dieterich.

New Sources

Berthrong, John, and Mary Evelyn Tucker, eds. *Confucianism and Ecology: The Interrelation of Heaven, Earth, and Human.* Cambridge, Mass., 1998.

Chapple, Christopher Key, and Mary Evelyn Tucker, eds. *Hinduism and Ecology: The Intersection of Earth, Sky, and Water.* Cambridge, Mass., 2000.

Cloud, Preston. *Oasis in Space: Earth History from the Beginning.* New York, 1988.

Cooper, David E., and Joy A. Palmer, eds. *Spirit of the Environment: Religion, Value, and Environmental Concern.* New York, 1998.

Elvin, Mark and Liu Ts'ui-jung. *Sediments of Time: Environment and Society in Chinese History.* Cambridge, Mass. 1998.

Emiliani, Cesare. *Planet Earth: Cosmology, Geology, and the Evolution of Life and Environment.* New York, 1992.

Girardot, N.J., James Miller, and Liu Xiaogan, eds. *Daoism and Ecology: Ways within a Cosmic Landscape.* Cambridge, Mass., 2001.

Gottlieb, Roger S., ed. *This Sacred Earth: Religion, Nature, Environment.* New York, 1996.

Hessel, Dieter T., and Rosemary Radford Reuther, eds. *Christianity and Ecology: Seeking the Well-Being of Earth and Humans.* Cambridge, Mass., 2000.

Wright, M. R. *Cosmology in Antiquity.* New York, 1995.

MIRCEA ELIADE (1987)
LAWRENCE E. SULLIVAN (1987)
Revised Bibliography

EARTH FIRST! Earth First!, the best known among the so-called radical environmental groups, was founded in 1980 in the southwestern United States. With its slogan "no compromise in defense of mother earth," it underscored its anti-anthropocentric ideology. In contrast to the anthropocentric point of view it promoted a "biocentric" or "ecocentric" axiology that insisted that every life form, and indeed every ecosystem, has intrinsic value and a right to live and flourish regardless of whether human beings find it useful.

DEEP ECOLOGY. This axiology has a significant affinity with deep ecology, a philosophy and term derived from the work of the Norwegian philosopher Arne Naess (1912–). Naess developed deep ecology to critique what he considered the "shallow" anthropocentric ethics of most forms of environmentalism as well as to articulate a biocentric perspective in which nature is considered to have intrinsic value.

Naess's path to that perspective was grounded in his joyful and mystical experiences in wild nature, which led him to appreciate and draw from the pantheistic philosophy of Baruch Spinoza as well as from the Hindu Vedas, especially as interpreted by Mohandas Gandhi (1869–1948). Naess's version of deep ecology suggested that a path to one's personal self-realization can involve expanding one's sense of self to include nature. Consequently, biocentric ethics can be understood as a form of self-love rather than a duty or obligation. Naess was clear, however, that there are many experiential, religious, and philosophical bases for a deep ecology perspective and that his represents only one of them.

After hearing about it in the early 1980s, the earliest Earth First! activists adopted deep ecology as a descriptor for their own ethics even though few had read Naess's philosophy in detail. However, they identified with what they understood to be his critique of anthropocentrism and his biocentric ethics. The early affinity between Earth First! and deep ecology was animated by two shared perceptions: first that all life evolved in the same way and from the same single-celled organism and thus all life forms are related, and second that the biosphere and all its life forms are sacred.

Whereas Naess insisted that there are many tributaries to a biocentric perspective, radical environmentalists tended to believe that monotheism cannot be one of them. Such activists generally blame monotheistic religions and the agricultural practices that evolved simultaneously with them for environmental deterioration as well as the destruction of premonotheistic foraging cultures. They also believe that the societies that preceded monotheism and/or agriculture were more environmentally sustainable because they considered nature sacred. These activists often single out Christianity as the most powerful global form of Western monotheism in part because it is seen as devaluing the earthly realm and locates the sacred beyond this world and in part because it has been aligned with political power. The earliest Earth First!ers found such critiques in the work of historians such as Paul Shepard, Lynn White, Perry Miller, and Roderick Nash. Earth First! cofounder Dave Foreman, the most charismatic of the group's early leaders and the one most responsible for articulating its critical perspective, asserted:

> Our problem is a spiritual crisis. The Puritans brought with them a theology that saw the wilderness of North America as a haunt of Satan, with savages as his disciples and wild animals as his demons—all of which had to be cleared, defeated, tamed, or killed. (*Harpers Forum*, 1990, p. 44)

THE PHILOSOPHY OF EARTH FIRST! Foreman and his earliest Earth First! comrades found substantial evidence that such attitudes were alive and well in contemporary America. During the years leading up to the formation of Earth First!, when he was still working for the Wilderness Society, Foreman concluded that ordinary political advocacy had become ineffective because the government had been corrupted by corporations, which were assisted by a virulently antinature Christian ideology, including that of President Ronald Reagan and his secretary of the interior, James Watt, a devout evangelical Christian. That antinature religious ideology, which desacralizes nature and unleashes a voracious appetite for "natural resources," combined with modern science and advanced technology, had produced an environmental calamity in which most of the world's life forms were jeopardized, Foreman and his cohort believed. This belief that human beings are precipitating an environmental apocalypse that imperils a sacred natural world provides the urgency felt by Earth First!ers and undergirds their conviction that resistance to these trends is a moral imperative.

TACTICS AND GOALS. The general public knows less about the social, religious, and ethical perceptions of Earth First!ers than it does about the movement's controversial tactics. Earth First! activists have engaged in rowdy and well-publicized protests that often have involved civil disobedience, including innovative blockades of logging roads and industry or governmental offices as well as clandestine sabotage operations that increasingly have utilized arson.

These tactics sometimes are employed by individuals associated with offshoot groups such as the Earth Liberation Front (ELF), which believes that tactics more aggressive than those usually deployed by Earth First! are essential. The ELF first emerged in the United Kingdom in 1992. Its participants called themselves "elves" to evoke playfully a sense that they were spirits of nature or other representatives of the natural world who were defending themselves. The moniker was also a way for many of them to signal their pagan identity.

Soon radical activists in North America also were calling themselves elves as they took credit for a series of dramatic and costly sabotage and arson attacks. Their targets included forest service offices and equipment, ski resort lodges built in habitats considered critical for endangered species, genetic engineering laboratories, and gas-guzzling sport utility vehicles. Whatever the targets or the descriptors they choose when announcing their actions, radical environmentalists consider civil disobedience and sabotage to be forms of economic warfare against the destroyers of nature. They hope that those tactics will thwart destructive commercial enterprises by making them unprofitable.

Some Earth First!ers consider themselves anarchists and seek the overthrow of all industrial nation-states. The majority, however, have a less revolutionary goal of securing legal protection for habitats large enough to ensure the survival of biological diversity. Indeed, the movement helped bring that term, which often is abbreviated as *biodiversity*, into popular parlance and public debate. This broader objective depended on environmental legislation and law enforcement, which most Earth First!ers, despite their justification of extralegal tactics, hoped to strengthen. Indeed, the earliest Earth First! activists theorized that an uncompromising radical environmental movement could strengthen the resolve and lobbying power of mainstream environmentalists.

Although it is difficult to judge whether the presence of a radical environmental front makes mainstream groups more effective, after the formation of Earth First! some mainstream environmental groups did develop stronger positions, at least in part as a response to Earth First!. A number of them also adopted biodiversity protection as a central priority, something that had not been prevalent before Earth First!'s emphasis on it. Some of the leaders of mainstream groups who publicly criticized the movement's illegal tactics privately acknowledge that the radicals have played a positive role politically.

ROAD SHOWS, WILDERNESS GATHERINGS, AND OTHER RITUALS. Equally important, the critique of anthropocentric attitudes that the militants of Earth First! forcefully articulated contributed significantly to the spread of deep ecology spirituality within the wider environmental movement. One way that occurred was through the creative efforts of the movement's leaders, artists, and musicians.

Some of the first generation of Earth First! activists, for example, toured the United States conducting "road shows" that also could be labeled biocentric revival meetings. Those shows sometimes would juxtapose photographic slides of intact "sacred wilderness ecosystems" with wilderness habitats ruined by logging. The epistemological assumption behind the presentations was that a spiritually receptive heart would know that a great wrong had been committed. The American Earth First! singer Alice DiMicelle, for example, once explained during an interview that her role during performances in a 1992 Earth First! tour of the United Kingdom was, through her photographs and music, to awaken in the audience, many of whom had never experienced a sacred wilderness ecosystem, the mystical experience that is available in such places.

Perhaps the most common theme in the road shows was conversion stories, frequently that of Aldo Leopold, who is considered by many the greatest ecologist of the twentieth century. In the 1930s Leopold, who had contributed to the federal government's campaign to exterminate the wolf and other predators, encountered a female wolf and her pups and with his Forest Service mates shot the wolf, only to witness the "green fire" dying in her eyes as she expired. That experience precipitated Leopold's biocentric epiphany of the intrinsic value of predators, even those labeled varmints by the mainstream culture. This led to his repentance and subsequently to some of the most poignant biocentric nature writing of the twentieth century. In the 1980s and afterward Dave Foreman became well known for ending his road show performances by recalling Leopold's conversion, urging those assembled to repent, howling with him the cry of the wolf as a sign of their reconnection with and ethical commitment to wild nature.

Wilderness gatherings of Earth First! activists provided another important venue for earth-based religious rituals. Movement poets and musicians performed their own works, which reflected and reinforced perceptions of the sacredness of life while providing activists with powerful bonding experiences. Others took on the role of religious leaders, developing sometimes elaborate pageants that depicted a "fall" from an early nature-and-goddess-worshipping paradise of foragers (caused by the advent of sky-god-worshipping agricultural societies) that precipitated an ecological calamity. In those performances a cosmic redemption also was enacted as a remnant community of resistance, which understood the earth's sacred nature, arose and fought for the reharmonization of life on earth. Movement members who were also involved in Neopaganism, Wicca, or New Age rituals often played significant roles in shaping the ritual life of the emerging movement. Indeed, Earth First! has many of the sources and characteristics of a wide variety of contemporary nature religions and arguably has contributed to a number of them.

Even more influential than the rituals at wilderness gatherings was the invention of a ritual process that became known as the Council of All Beings. It was developed primarily by two Buddhists, the American Joanna Macy and the Australian John Seed, both of whom became pioneering figures in the deep ecology movement internationally. They achieved this in part by spreading this process and similar ones primarily though not exclusively in North America, Australia, and Europe. The heart of the ritual involves an imaginative, if not mystical or shamanic, process in which the human participants take on or represent the identity of other beings and entities of nature, expressing during the council's deliberations their anguish about environmental deterioration, their hopes for the future of life on earth, and their counsel and support in pursuing ecological justice.

Further illustrating the role that Buddhism has played in the movement, John Seed was introduced to Earth First! by the American Pulitzer Prize–winning poet Gary Snyder, a Buddhist who variously calls himself a deep ecologist or a "Buddhist animist." Snyder also has been one of the leading proponents of bioregionalism, a decentralist environmentalist ideology that has become the de facto social philosophy of radical environmentalism. It envisions local political self-rule within political units whose boundaries would be redrawn to cohere with the contours of differing types of ecosystems.

Snyder attempted to communicate with the Earth First! movement soon after he heard about it but criticized tactics he considered violent that were being advocated by some Earth First!ers, including Foreman. However, Snyder was strongly supportive of Earth First!ers' deep ecological intuitions and direct action resistance as long as it remained nonviolent and thus, in his view, effective political theater. After hearing about Earth First!, Seed quickly arranged to participate in one of the earliest North American road shows, which contributed to his own fusion of Buddhism, deep ecology ritualizing, and radical environmental activism.

Sabotage as Ritual. For some Earth First! activists, however, the most important ritual actions are sabotage and civil disobedience, which constitute acts of earth veneration and can lead to spiritual experiences that reconnect their participants with nature. For example, early in his Earth First! period Dave Foreman, who left Earth First! but not its overall ethical commitments around 1990 primarily because of political differences with a growing faction of anarchistic newcomers, spoke of sabotage as a form of ritual worship. A number of other Earth First! activists have described mystical experiences of "earth bonding" or reported communicating with the trees they inhabited during antilogging campaigns. Those experiences reflected or helped shape the pantheistic and animistic worldviews that Earth First! activists often share. Indeed, so many Earth First!ers consider themselves pagan that a possible description for the movement would be the pagan environmental movement.

Whatever terminology Earth First! activists identify with, during its initial decade at least, the movement probably received its greatest inspiration from the southwestern novelist Edward Abbey (1927–1989). His *Desert Solitaire* (1968) described mystical experiences in the desert that taught him humility and a proper spiritual perception; for him, that meant biocentrism and reverence for the land. Abbey's novel *The Monkeywrench Gang* (1975) portrayed ecological saboteurs fighting back against a totalitarian and relentlessly destructive industrial civilization that was in league with religions that seek salvation beyond this world. Though a work of fiction, the book was based on an actual group of ecological saboteurs (mentioned briefly in *Desert Solitaire*) who in the 1950s battled the strip mining of the Black Mesa plateau by the Peabody Coal Company. Through its characters *The Monkeywrench Gang* captured the various types of nature religion that animated those early green rebels, such as Doc Sarvis's hope that "Pan shall rise again!" (Abbey, 1975, p. 44) and George Washington Hayduke's pondering of "the oceanic unity of things" and his rationale for sabotage, which was grounded in his understanding that the desert is "holy country" (Abbey, 1975, pp. 227, 128).

EARTH FIRST! AS A RELIGIOUS MOVEMENT. The human perception of sacred places, along with battles over them, is common in the history of religion. Often there is an environmental dimension to such perceptions of sacredness; sometimes places are invested with an aura of holiness because they are remote, dangerous to access, or characterized by great biomass or geomorphological uniqueness (as is the case with caves, geothermal vents, and mountains). What is religiously innovative in the Earth First! movement and other radical environmental groups is the notion that the greater is the contribution of a place to the planet's genetic and biological diversity, the greater is its sacredness.

Although Earth First! activists affirm that the entire biosphere is sacred and worthy of defense, because they cannot be everywhere at once, they must make hard choices and decide which parts they will act to protect or heal. Consequently, the most important ethical priority is to prevent extinctions and the destruction of the world's most important biological reserves. Even decisions about where to camp are determined on the basis of such considerations: a site should be near enough to connect spiritually to the most fragile and thus sacred ecosystems but not so close that it damages or defiles them.

Apocalyptic expectations of the end of the world or a lesser disaster also have been common in the history of religions. Environmental degradation may have played a role in fostering the kind of suffering that gives rise to such expectations. What is novel in the apocalypticism characteristic of Earth First! is that for the first time such an expectation is grounded in environmental science or at least on one credible reading of currently available scientific data. Moreover, as Earth First!ers are drawing on the same countercultural religious elements as others involved in contemporary nature religion, many of them also are drawing on contemporary science as a religious resource, and this represents another innovation. Many Earth First!ers, for example, consider James Lovelock's Gaia hypothesis spiritually meaningful, inspiring or supporting their pantheistic religious sentiments. Others have been moved by those, such as Thomas Berry, who endeavor to consecrate scientific narratives of the evolution of the universe and biosphere, making them into new sacred stories that promote the veneration and defense of nature.

Not all radical environmentalists, however, are comfortable calling themselves religious, including a number of biologists who have supported radical environmental initiatives. This discomfort is usually the result of equating religion with the Western institutional forms of religion that they consider authoritarian and antinature. Nevertheless, those environmentalists rarely object to and almost always rely on metaphors of the sacred to express their conviction that nature has intrinsic value. They also often describe environmental destruction as desecration or defilement. Even though a few participants in these movements call themselves atheists, this generally means that they do not believe in otherworldly deities or divine rescue from this world, not that they deny a sacred dimension to the universe and earthly life. Indeed, they often characterize their connections to nature as spiritual.

The Earth First! movement can be considered religious in that it views the evolutionary process, the diversity of life, and the entire biosphere as precious, sacred, and worthy of defense. Another religious aspect is that its participants construct myths, rituals, and ethical practices that cohere with such beliefs. This kind of nature religion attempts to express a form of spirituality that coheres with evolutionary understandings of the origins and diversity of life. It claims to offer a solution to intractable and intensifying environmental problems, and if nothing is done to halt the unfolding environmental catastrophe, it offers hope that some may survive and eventually live on the earth respectfully and sustainably, especially those who develop spiritual humility.

As the radical environmental worldview is at odds with that of many of the earth's other peoples, viewing most religions as part of the problem, it enjoins resistance to them as well as efforts to persuade those who adhere to them to resacralize their perceptions of the earth. In light of these differences and because the environmental conditions that contributed to the rise of Earth First! and other radical environmental groups show no signs of abating, it is likely that such groups will continue to precipitate or become involved in environment-related social conflicts. It is also likely that for the indefinite future such religiosity and movements will continue to play a role in shaping religious attitudes and behaviors toward the earth's living systems.

SEE ALSO Ecology and Religion, articles on Ecology and Buddhism and Ecology and Nature Religions; Gandhi, Mohandas; Neopaganism; New Age Movement; Wicca.

BIBLIOGRAPHY

Abbey, Edward. *Desert Solitaire.* Tucson, Ariz., 1968. A memoir of Abbey's years as a National Park Ranger, with vivid accounts of the spiritual experiences that led to his biocentric outlook.

Abbey, Edward. *The Monkeywrench Gang.* New York, 1975. The novel (about a band of environmentalist saboteurs) that inspired the Earth First! movement.

Abbey, Edward. *Hayduke Lives!* Boston, 1990. Drawing on Abbey's experiences with the movement that *The Monkeywrench Gang* helped to precipitate, this humorous novel depicts, in exaggerated fashion, the diverse religious and political subcultures drawn to the movement.

Abram, David. *Spell of the Sensuous: Perception and Language in a More-Than-Human World.* New York, 1996. A sophisticated argument defending animistic religious perception, written by a scholar who identifies with them. It has been well received by many radical environmentalists.

Andruss, Van, Christopher Plant, Judith Plant, and Eleanor Wright. *Home!: A Bioregional Reader.* Philadelphia, 1990. An early collection of essays from the pioneers of the bioregional movement.

Bari, Judi. *Timber Wars.* Monroe, Maine, 1994. A compendium of writings by Northern California Earth First! activist Judi Bari, who was a lightning rod both within the movement and to her adversaries, and who was the victim of a unsolved car bombing in 1989.

Foreman, Dave. *Confessions of an Eco-Warrior.* New York, 1991. Foreman's perceptions of the first decade of Earth First!, including his reasons for leaving the movement he co-founded.

Harpers Forum. "Only Man's Presence Can Save Nature." *Harper's,* April 1990, 37–48.

Hill, Julia Butterfly. The Legacy of Luna: The Story of a Tree, a Woman, and the Struggle to Save the Redwoods. San Francisco, 2000. An account by an activist who initially affiliated with Earth First! of her long, illegal occupation of a redwood tree, and the spiritual and political experiences she had during and afterward.

LaChapelle, Dolores. *Earth Wisdom.* Silverton, Colo., 1978. LaChapelle's works exemplify the religious experiences and perceptions often associated with a radical environmental perspective.

LaChapelle, Dolores. *Sacred Land, Sacred Sex: Rapture of the Deep.* Silverton, Colo., 1988. This book includes interesting firsthand descriptions of the earliest connections between Earth First! activists and Deep Ecology proponents.

Lee, Martha F. *Earth First!: Environmental Apocalypse.* Syracuse, N.Y., 1995. A book claiming to identify a sharp distinction between apocalyptic and millenarian Earth First! factions, based largely on a reading of the early years of *Earth First!,* the movement's journal.

Loeffler, Jack. *Adventures with Ed: A Portrait of Abbey.* Albuquerque, 2002. A biography of Ed Abbey, who died in 1989, written by his best friend.

Manes, Christopher. *Green Rage: Radical Environmentalism and the Unmaking of Civilization.* Boston, Little, Brown, 1990. A book written by an early Earth First!er, synthesizing and drawing on the movement's early journal articles; it provides a good introduction to the thinking animating the majority of early Earth First! activists.

Mason, Jim. *An Unnatural Order: Uncovering the Roots of Our Domination of Nature and Each Other.* New York, 1993. This articulates the view—common among radical environmentalists—that agriculture led to social injustice and environmental deterioration.

McGinnis, Michael Vincent, ed. *Bioregionalism.* New York and London, 1999. A recent collection of essays describing and mostly promoting bioregionalism; it includes historical accounts of its genesis and evolution.

Naess, Arne. "The Shallow and the Deep, Long-Range Ecology Movement: A Summary." *Inquiry* 16 (1973): 95–100. This is the essay in which Naess coined the trope "deep ecology."

Scarce, Rik. *Ecowarriors: Understanding the Radical Environmental Movement.* Chicago, 1990. An early journalistic treatment with good descriptions of the views of the animal liberationists and anarchists drawn into the movement, and of the controversies that followed this development, it largely ignores the movement's religious dimensions.

Seed, John, Joanna Macy, Pat Fleming, and Arne Naess. *Thinking Like a Mountain: Towards a Council of All Beings.* Philadelphia, 1988. Explains this important ritual process.

Shepard, Paul. *Coming Home to the Pleistocene.* San Francisco, 1998. Published posthumously, this is the best introduction to Shepard's defense of foraging cultures, with their animistic spiritualities, over the monotheistic agricultures that have widely supplanted them.

Smith, Samantha. *Goddess Earth: Exposing the Pagan Agenda of the Environmental Movement.* Lafayette, La., 1994. An example of the common perception among conservative Christians that radical environmentalists are pagans who must be resisted.

Snyder, Gary. *Turtle Island.* New York, 1969. Snyder's Pulitzer Prize–winning book, which contributed significantly to both the radical environmental and bioregional movements.

Taylor, Bron. "Resacralizing Earth: Pagan Environmentalism and the Restoration of Turtle Island." In *American Sacred Space,* edited by David Chidester and Edward T. Linenthal, pp. 97–151. Bloomington, Ind., 1995. A historical analysis of the antecedents to radical environmentalism in the United States, with a contemporary case study depicting the ways that perceptions of sacred space are involved in radical environmental campaigns.

Taylor, Bron. "Earthen Spirituality or Cultural Genocide: Radical Environmentalism's Appropriation of Native American Spirituality." *Religion* 17, no. 2 (1997): 183–215.

Taylor, Bron. "Religion, Violence, and Radical Environmentalism: From Earth First! to the Unabomber to the Earth Liberation Front." *Terrorism and Political Violence* 10, no. 4 (1998): 10–42. An analysis of charges that radical environmentalism is a terrorist movement.

Taylor, Bron. "Green Apocalypticism: Understanding Disaster in the Radical Environmental Worldview." *Society and Natural Resources* 12, no. 4 (1999): 377–386. Focuses on the movement's apocalypticism and a critique of the book by Martha Lee cited above.

Taylor, Bron. "Deep Ecology as Social Philosophy: A Critique." In *Beneath the Surface: Critical Essays on Deep Ecology,* edited by Eric Katz, Andrew Light, and David Rothenberg, pp. 269–299. Cambridge, Mass., 2000. Assesses the contributions and limits of the bioregional social philosophy that inheres in most radical environmentalism.

Taylor, Bron. "Earth and Nature-Based Spirituality (Part I): From Deep Ecology to Radical Environmentalism." *Religion* 30, no. 2 (2001): 175–193;and "Earth and Nature-Based Spirituality (Part II): From Deep Ecology to Scientific Paganism." *Religion* 30, no. 3 (2001): 225–245. This two-part study explores the breadth of nature-related religion, which includes Earth First! and Deep Ecology.

Taylor, Bron. "Diggers, Wolfs, Ents, Elves and Expanding Universes: Bricolage, Religion, and Violence from Earth First! and the Earth Liberation Front to the Antiglobalization Resistance." In *The Cultic Milieu: Oppositional Subcultures in an Age of Globalization,* edited by Jeffrey Kaplan and Heléne Lööw, pp. 26–74. Lanham, Md., 2002. Explores the movement with greater ethnographic depth than the earlier ones.

Taylor, Bron, ed. *Ecological Resistance Movements: The Global Emergence of Radical and Popular Environmentalism.* Albany, N.Y., 1995. Examines the continuities and discontinuities among diverse forms of radical environmentalism around the world, providing comparisons between Earth First! in the United States and Europe.

Wall, Derek. *Earth First! and the Anti-Roads Movement: Radical Environmentalism and the Anti-Roads Movement.* London, 1999. A partisan book lauding Earth First!'s anti-roads movement in the United Kingdom; provides good descriptions of the campaigns but reflects a number of misperceptions about Earth First! in the United States.

Watson, Paul. *Ocean Warrior: My Battle to End the Illegal Slaughter on the High Seas.* Toronto, 1994. An account by a proponent of biocentric religion, whose group, the Sea Shepard Conservation Society, has been called the navy of Earth First!; their controversial tactics have included sinking whaling vessels believed to be operating in defiance of international laws.

Wolke, Howie. *Wilderness on the Rocks.* Tucson, Ariz., 1991. Written from jail by one of the cofounders of Earth First! after a conviction for removing survey stakes from a logging road, this book provides a good example of the ecological analysis motivating many of the movement's activists.

Zakin, Susan. *Coyotes and Town Dogs: Earth First! and the Environmental Movement.* New York, 1993. A journalistic treatment of the early years of Earth First!, highly favorable to Dave Foreman and his allies when examining internal movement disputes.

Zimmerman, Michael E. *Contesting Earth's Future: Radical Ecology and Postmodernity.* Berkeley and Los Angeles, 1994. A sympathetic scholarly analysis of the promise and perils of deep ecology and radical environmentalism.

BRON TAYLOR (2005)

EAST AFRICAN RELIGIONS

This entry consists of the following articles:

AN OVERVIEW
ETHIOPIAN RELIGIONS
NORTHEAST BANTU RELIGIONS

EAST AFRICAN RELIGIONS: AN OVERVIEW

East African religions do not form a single coherent body of beliefs and practices. They show great diversity in myths and cosmologies and in beliefs about the nature of spiritual powers; in kinds and authority of ritual experts; in the situations when ritual is performed; and in responses to the advent of Islam and Christianity. This diversity is consistent with the ethnic, geographical, and historical diversity of the region. Our knowledge of East African religions is very uneven, and this may also contribute to the seeming diversity.

The total population of the Eastern African region in 2003 was about 263 million people. The population comprises some two hundred more or less distinct societies, each defined by its own language and sense of identity, its own traditional territory and political structure, and its own system of family relations, marriage, and religious belief and practice. These groups are distributed very unevenly in areas of high and low population densities.

East Africa contains several clearly defined geographical and cultural areas, with an immense variety of societies, languages, and religions. It has been the meeting place of several main language groupings, and its peoples are remarkably diverse in their cultures and forms of economic, political, and familial organizations.

In the northern part of the region live peoples representing several main language families and groups: Semitic and Hamitic (Cushitic), mainly in Ethiopia and Somalia, and three subgroups of the Chari-Nile group of the Nilo-Saharan family—Sudanic, in the far northwest corner, Nilotic in the upper Nile Valley, and Para-Nilotic (Eastern Nilotic or Nilo-Hamitic) mainly in the Rift Valley region. To the south are many people speaking Bantu languages (of the Niger-Congo family). There are small pockets of speakers of other language families (such as Khoisan, or click, languages in northern Tanzania), and there are of course speakers of intrusive languages such as Arabic and English. In most parts of the region Swahili has long been used as a lingua franca, although in a debased form rather than in its proper form as spoken along the Indian Ocean coast. However, there appears to be no direct relationship between language and religious belief and practice.

The situation is different as regards economic, political, and familial types, and belief and practice are more obviously linked to them. Although there are a few hunting and gathering peoples, such as the Hadza of Tanzania and the Okiek of Kenya, the vast majority of the population consists of mixed farmers, growing grains and keeping some livestock, and pastoralist livestock herders.

A century of European colonial rule over the entire region and the long Arab colonial overrule along the coast have brought about degrees of unity and interaction. Trade and wars have also often linked peoples together in varying ways and degrees. Although East African peoples are traditionally farmers and livestock herders, large towns and urban centers exist throughout the region, from the ancient cities of Mombasa, Mogadishu, and Zanzibar on the coast to the modern cities of Nairobi, Addis Ababa, Kampala, and Dar es-Salaam. Scattered are many lesser towns that have attracted mixed immigrant populations from the countryside and from which modern Christian and syncretist movements have spread out into the rural areas. Today there are virtually no peoples in the region who are unaffected by Christianity or Islam (although the depth of influence of these faiths varies widely); but traditional local religions remain active in almost every part of the area.

DIVINITY AND MYTH. All East African religions have a belief in a high god, the creator. Perhaps the most accurate term to translate this concept here is *Deity.* As would be expected, even though there are variations, in all of them the Deity is attributed broadly similar characteristics: omnipotence, everlastingness, ubiquity, and being beyond the comprehension and control of ordinary living people. The variations lie in the idioms and symbols used to express these features and abilities. These general characteristics are found in the high gods representing all the cosmologies of the region: Kwoth (Nuer; the name also means breath or spirit), Juok (Shilluk), Nhialic (Dinka), Mbori (Azande), Adroa (Lugbara; the name also means power), Ngai (Kikuyu), Kyala (Nyakyusa), Mungu (Swahili), and so on. The names are different, but the divine nature is the same. Usually the Deity is considered to be spatially unlocalized, but in some religions it is thought to be associated with mountains and other terrestrial features, as among the Kikuyu, who state that Ngai dwells on Mount Kenya and on lesser mountains of the Rift Valley area.

The Deity is usually considered remote and otiose: after creating the world it retired, leaving men and women on earth ultimately dependent upon it but pursuing their own ways cut off from divine truth and perfection and with a memory of a primeval paradise that might one day be reached again with the help of prophetic leaders. Perhaps all peoples of the region have myths to explain the separation, often couched in terms of a Tower of Babel story in which a rope or a tree between heaven and earth was destroyed either by human foolishness or divine displeasure. (There is not the least reason to suppose that these separation myths are in any way due to diffusion from Christian sources.) There is considerable variation in the degree to which it is held that the Deity interferes in the everyday affairs of the living, beyond being responsible for death, and in beliefs held about the relationship between its creation of the world and the later formation of human societies. There is also much variation in its relationships with the many lesser deities that are found in all East African cosmologies.

These aspects and relations are stated in myth, each society having its own corpus of myth that tells of the creation of the world, the relationship between humankind and the Deity, and the formation of society. A typical example is that of the cosmogony of the Nilotic Shilluk of the upper Nile. Their myths tell of the creation of the world by Juok and of the later formation of the Shilluk kingdom by the culture hero or mediator, Nyikang. The mythical cooperation of creator and hero is a feature of many East African myths, their two activities being distinct in time and usually in place also. Nyikang, whose parentage is usually given as a father of heavenly provenance and a mother who was a creature of the River Nile with the attributes of the crocodile, is thus associated with sky, river, and earth; he separated the Shilluk from their neighbors and united his people as their first king. All later kings have been embodiments of Nyikang, and the installation of a new king is a dramatic representation of both the social diversity and the unity of the Shilluk as well as their mystical link with the Nile, on which they are ecologically dependent. The king, as Nyikang in immanent form, represents the ideal and true order of the world within himself. Godfrey Lienhardt has written about the Shilluk proverb that says "the Shilluk only believe what they see," pointing out that it is through their human king that they are also able to see what they believe.

Other than the distinction between the creation of the world and the formation of the particular society, the most widespread mythopoeic feature of the many and varied myths of the region would seem to be the attribution of reverse or inverted characteristics and behavior to the originally created inhabitants. They may be portrayed as incestuous or as being ignorant of kinship, the idiom used by most East African societies to express and validate everyday social relationships; they may be given close identification with animal species, the natural and the social thereby being brought into a single conceptual system; they may be said to have dwelt outside the present homeland in a state of primeval timelessness, their travels and adventures representing those of past migrations and final settlement into the present habitat; they construct a cosmic topography in which the particular society is set in both space and time as a moral community within an asocial and amoral wilderness.

With creation myths are found myths that tell of such matters as the relationships between people and wild and domesticated animals, between men and women, and between peoples of different societies and races; the origins of and reasons for death; the origins of fire and cooking, linked with the making of settlements and the exchange of primeval hunting for farming; and the nature and validation of the ties, rights, and obligations of descent, age, sex, and rank. It is frequently difficult to draw any meaningful distinction between what may be considered by outside observers to be myths and folk tales that tell of these and similar problems. As with myths, most folk tales are concerned with paradoxes and logical contradictions in the experience of the particular culture concerned. Perhaps the great majority of East African folk tales are told about agents who are animals or humans in the guise of animals; their adventures refer essentially and by implication to human behavior. Proverbs and riddles, many with similar implications, are found throughout the region.

In Ethiopia and the Swahili and Somali coasts, the areas with long-standing literacy and forms of writing, accounts of the formation of the world and society and their history may also be in written forms. They may profess to be historical chronicles of particular towns, peoples, or dynasties, but nonetheless they partake of the general nature of mythopoeic statements, using the same idioms as spoken myth.

LESSER DEITIES AND THEIR RELATIONS WITH THE LIVING. The Deity usually communicates with the living only indirectly, through refractions of its power in the forms of lesser deities, spirits, gods, powers, and ancestors, ghosts, or shades (almost every writer has his or her own terminology, which has led to a good deal of definitional confusion). These mystical entities may float freely or they may be attached to social groups (lineages, clans, neighborhoods, and others) by having localized shrines established for them. The relations of communication are complex, but essentially the deities may control or constrain the living by possessing them and making them sick, and the living may contact the deities by sacrifice, prayer, and self-induced trance. Both parties are seen as interdependent, even if the living may not understand the full nature and motivation of the deities; but if contact ceases, the deities cease to have power and to "exist" in the awareness of the living at all.

There are many kinds of these deities found in East African religions, but they may conveniently be divided into the categories of spirits and ancestors, each comprising many subtypes. Spirits are considered as different from the transcendent and otiose Deity (even though the same word may be used for both, as is *kwoth* among the Nuer). They are immanent, more dynamic, and more immediately demanding; they are usually regarded as so numerous as to be beyond counting. Whereas the Deity is only rarely localized in shrines (as among the Kikuyu, who recognize certain fig trees as shrines for Ngai), many kinds of shrines, temples, and images are built for the spirits where they may be contacted by the living. Since spirits are invisible and unknowable, being of a different order than human beings, they need some locus where the living may contact them.

A spirit may be considered as a representation of some aspect of human experience whose power is thought to be outside the immediate community and beyond the everyday knowledge or control of ordinary people, until it exercises some form of power over a living person by possession or sickness. This experience may be that of nature, as with the smallpox and other disease gods of the Ganda or the earthquake and lightning spirits of the Lugbara; it may be experience of outside historical events, as with the airplane and Polish (refugee) spirits of the Nyoro; or it may be the individual experience of inner psychological states such as guilt and fear, as with the sky divinities of the Dinka. The possession of a living person by a spirit places him or her into direct and palpable contact with the particular experience: divination identifies the spirit, and sacrifice removes it from the possessed victim and restores the proper status quo.

Another aspect of spirit possession is that the victim is thereby singled out and acquires a new or additional mystical and personal status. In East Africa women appear more usually to be possessed by spirits; it has been suggested that this is so because women suffer from a greater sense of cultural deprivation and ambiguity of role than do men. Women's roles are less clearly defined than those of men, with the exception of the role of mother. When a woman is barren, therefore, her role is wanting and ambiguous: she may acquire a more definite one, largely independent and less under the control of husband or brother, by becoming the adherent and communicant of a spirit and so linking herself to other women who have been possessed. In some societies, for example the Lugbara, these women acquire a degree of personal independence and clearly defined identity but no more. In others, such as the Swahili, they become members of spirit cults and so of socially recognized groupings that stress their joint identity as against that of the men, who are seen as affiliated to a particular mosque in which women are never full members. The Swahili spirits are localized in particular places, each of which is associated with a particular cult group under the control of a spirit priest who has the powers of mediumship and divination. The women thus form a kind of mirror organization to that of the men. Something very similar is found in the *zār* cult of much of Ethiopia, Somalia, and the Muslim Sudan. Women are possessed, healed by an exorcist-medium, and then considered as cult adherents. The high incidence of this possession would seem to be linked to the particular problems, both social and psychological, of women in these largely Muslim societies.

The other main category of deity in East African religions is that of the dead, who, unlike spirits, are of the same order of existence as the living and so more easily understood and approached. There are many kinds and levels of ancestral worship, corresponding to the various kinds of ancestors: those of the direct line of descent, those of submerged descent lines, and those of other kin. They may be considered as individual ancestors, remembered by their personal names, or as collectivities of unnamed ancestral kin who are of less importance in living memory. As they are like the living, they may easily be worshiped by sacrifice in which they are given food, which is shared between them and the living as it is among kin, each category of ancestors representing a particular group or constellation of living kin that comes into contact with the dead on particular occasions. Also, as might be expected, the ancestors may themselves act as senior kin and initiate communication by sending sickness or trouble to the living and so draw attention to themselves.

Sacrifice is made typically to remove sickness or as a response of gratitude for removal of sickness, to avoid sickness and other troubles, and at times on regular occasions of group or individual purification. Each kin or lineage group makes its own sacrifices (since ancestors of other groups are of no interest to it). In centralized societies the royal ancestors may be offered sacrifice on state occasions by the ruler and his priests on behalf of the entire kingdom.

An example of lineage sacrifice is that of the Lugbara of Uganda. Here the most important and frequent sacrifices are made to the ghosts, those dead of the patrilineal lineage who have left sons behind them. They are believed to send sickness to their living descendants to teach them if the latter have denied respect to the living elders, who may invoke the dead to do this as part of an elder's duty. When the sickness has gone, the lineage elder sacrifices an animal to thank the dead and so cleanse the home of sin. People may also sacrifice to their matrilateral ghosts for broadly similar reasons and to the collectivity of dead who left no children. Similar sacrifices are reported from the Nyakyusa of southern Tanzania, but besides their being made by lineages to their own ancestors they are also made on behalf of all the members of neighborhoods and chiefdoms.

The relationship between ancestor and spirit worship is essentially that ancestors are linked to, and typically localized in, a shrine established by their descendants, whereas spirits are freer and if localized are tied to neighborhoods and wider settlements instead of to descent groups. The identity of the group concerned is clearly of central importance.

Sacrifice is typically made by ritual representatives of living groups. They are of two kinds: priests who are regarded as having special spiritual characteristics and skills, and ordinary senior people (elders) who sacrifice by virtue of genealogical position rather than special skills as such (although by being nearer to the dead than juniors they do have greater spiritual authority). It is true that in most East African societies priests may also be appointed on genealogical grounds, but in those cases they come from priestly lines, as the office is not open to members of other groups. Priests are repositories of divine knowledge and power that are usually considered to be vested in a descent line, so that there are myths that explain how this line was originally selected by the Deity for this task. Examples are the Masters of the Fishing Spear among the Dinka, the Nuer Leopard-skin priests, the Mugwe of the Meru of Kenya, the rainmakers of the Lugbara, the *laibons* of the Maasai and their Para-Nilotic neighbors, the members of the most senior age-sets among the Kikuyu.

The priests who have these specialized duties are uniformly given aspects of sacredness and so set apart from ordinary people. For example, the Dinka Masters of the Fishing Spear carry life within themselves for their people and so may not die a natural death; when they feel their powers wane they ask to be buried alive so that the life remains for the community. At a politically higher level, the king of the Shilluk is smothered for the same reasons. The Lugbara rainmakers are considered almost as living ancestors, being symbolically buried at their initation as rainmakers, and they are buried at their real death later in ways that are the exact opposite of those of ordinary funerals.

Another universally found ritual expert is the diviner, a person, male or female, believed able to discover the mystical causes of sickness and other misfortunes in the everyday world of the living. Methods of divination used in East Africa are many, including the use of oracles (more or less mechanical devices believed to be beyond the physical control of the operators), trance and mediumship (often while possessed by a spirit associated with mediumship), the consultation of omens, and formerly, before colonial rule stopped the practices, the administration of ordeals and oaths. Diviners are usually also healers, treating both the material and the mystical aspects of sickness by the use of medicines and by divination.

In brief, sacrifice to spirits and ancestors removes sickness and guilt for the commission of sin (defined variously but essentially as an act against the will of the Deity and the proper order of authority within social groups) by the immolation of a victim identified with the sick person, thereby removing the experience that has disturbed or affected the local group and the moral role of the guilty person within it. Other rites are found throughout the region: those of tradition or transformation of status. The most widespread are rites of initiation at puberty and at death.

Initiation rites, more generally for boys than for girls, although these take place, are most elaborate in those societies in which age-sets and generation-sets provide the basis for political and military action and also regulate marriage. The best-known examples are the Para-Nilotic pastoralist societies such as the Maasai, Samburu, Nandi, Karamojong, and their related neighbors; some southern Ethiopian groups such as the Galla; and others such as the Nyakyusa of southern Tanzania, who also have age systems of political importance and complex initiation rites. These rites, as with all rites of transition, begin with a rite in which the initiates are separated symbolically (and often physically) from their families and is followed by a series of rites that takes place in seclusion or secret from the remainder of society. Finally there are the rites of reaggregation of the new person into society with his or her new role as an adult able to have sexual relations, marry, act as a warrior, and so on. In some cases, as traditionally among the Kikuyu, the period of seclusion might take many months and would finish with the elaborate symbolic rebirth of the new young man. But today initiation rites have lost much of their former importance and are performed somewhat perfunctorily in most of the region.

In those societies where ancestral cults are important, mortuary rites are likewise important; an example comes from the Lugbara of Uganda, where mortuary rites, especially for senior men, are long, drawn out affairs that involve the participation of kin over great distances. The disposal of the corpse is of little moment, but the symbolic destruction of the deceased's social identity, the restructuring of kin ties that were centered on him, and the rites of redomestication of the soul as a ghost in its new shrine are all of the greatest importance and elaboration. In societies where ancestral cults are lacking, such as the technologically simple hunting and gathering Hadza of Tanzania, these rites are of virtually no importance.

EXPLANATIONS OF AND RESPONSES TO EVIL AND MISFORTUNE. All East African religions have a concept of evil. Explanations of evil and responses to it are typically expressed in beliefs in witchcraft and sorcery, which are thus integral parts of any system of religion. The first fully adequate study of witchcraft—one which has not as yet been surpassed—concerns witchcraft beliefs among the Azande people of southwestern Sudan. The Azande distinguish between witchcraft (an innate mystical ability to harm others merely by wishing or thinking to do so) and sorcery (the use of material substances to do the same). Although this distinction is widespread in East Africa, it is not universal, and many societies refer merely to evildoers who use either or both means of harming others.

These beliefs are found throughout the region, although each culture has its own peculiarities of idiom in which to express the ideology of evil; in all of them, however, the ideology of a witch is that he or she is in some way a reverse of a full and properly behaving member of a community. The basic principles of the system of explaining coincidence, unexpected failure, disaster, or sickness are similar everywhere. It is consistent with the basic, small-scale, and personal relationships of everyday life in these societies that explanations of the unexpected and immediately inexplicable in technical terms should be sought in personal relations, as the activities of evil-intentioned persons. Their motivation is held to be hatred, envy, and jealousy against those who are more fortunate or successful. These emotions are felt toward others who are already known; it is extremely rare that such feelings are provoked by strangers. Their identity depends largely on the composition of the more important groups whose members should regard themselves as a community. Witchcraft is a kind of treachery, a perversion for ignoble ends of proper authority, obligation, and affection. Thus where the basic local group is a kinship one, witches are held to be kin of their victims and sorcerers thought to harm unrelated persons. Where such kin groups are unimportant, the distinction between witches and sorcerers may not be made.

These beliefs are linked to knowledge of technical causation. A belief in witchcraft regards the activities of witches as "the second spear," in the Zande phrase. It is clear that a man is gored by a buffalo: the belief in witchcraft is used to explain not that he was gored as such but why he was gored by a particular animal at that particular time and place. The identity of the witch is discovered by divination, and demands for reparation, vengeance, punishment, or other socially approved action can be taken by the community so as to restore proper relations between the concerned parties. The whole is an effective jural process once the premises are accepted.

Radical social change has occurred in almost all parts of East Africa during and since colonial times. Change leads to increases in disputes and tensions as traditional social roles break down and alter, and this is often expressed in terms of suspicions and fears of witchcraft and sorcery. These evildoers are traitors, coming symbolically from the outside of the community, and efforts are made to cleanse whole communities of them by mass purificatory religious movements led by prophets and healers, both Christian and non-Christian.

Religious Change and Prophetic Movements. East African societies have never been static, and at times in their history change has been rapid and radical. A usual response to the sense of confusion about the present, uncertainty about the future, and in some cases virtual breakdown of the social order has been and is the recourse to prophetic leaders. It is often held that East African prophets are a modern phenomena, but this is extremely unlikely; although historical records are few it may be safely assumed that they have always been a feature of the region.

If we omit here the famous Sudanese Mahdi Muḥammad Aḥmad who led his adherents to capture Khartoum in 1885 and established a theocracy there, the earliest cases for which reasonably reliable records are available include those from the southern Sudan and from what is now Tanzania (earlier prophets have been recorded from the Lake Nyasa region to the south).

Prophets have been a marked feature of the Nuer and Dinka of the Nilotic Sudan. At the end of the nineteenth century the Nuer prophet Ngundeng, claiming inspiration from a Dinka sky divinity and spending much time fasting and living in the wilderness, was able to bring together large, normally autonomous groupings to raid neighboring peoples and to stand together against Arab slavers and, later, British colonial rule. He built an earthen pyramid from which he would prophesy. After his death his son Gwek succeeded him, refusing cooperation with the government. A deformed man, Gwek would stand on top of the pyramid in a state of possession, uttering prophecies that foretold the end of colonial rule. He was killed and the pyramid destroyed some years later. Among the neighboring Dinka, Arianhdit was perhaps the greatest prophet, flourishing at the time of the First World War; he died in 1948. Dinka prophets were Masters of the Fishing Spear as well as Men of Divinity, thus being both priests and prophets with powers additional to those of ordinary priests. The main Dinka prophets may well have influenced the prophetic water cults that arose in Uganda at the time of the Uganda Mutiny, marked by the drinking of divine water that would remove the Europeans and their weapons.

Among the Lugbara, to the south, a water cult known as Yakan emerged about the turn of the century in response to human and cattle epidemics and to the intrusion of Arabs and Europeans, which seriously affected local life. The disturbance of a traditionally ordered society led the people to seek a famed prophet, Rembe, from the Kakwa people to the north. At first they obtained sacred water from him; later they invited him to enter their country to restore their damaged society. Rembe dispensed water that was imbued with divine power to his adherents, promising that drinking it would ensure the return of dead livestock and people (and so destroy the traditional ancestral cult), drive away disease and foreign newcomers, and make the drinkers immune to bullets. Adherents were regarded as equal, men and women, old and young, irrespective of clan differences, thereby symbolizing a primeval egalitarian society as portrayed in myth. The cult collapsed at his arrest in 1917, although the spirit Yakan who inspired him is to this day believed to be a wandering spirit. Like almost all prophets, Rembe tried to reconstruct society as it was thought to have been at the beginning of time, the utopia of the future being the same as the paradise of the mythical past.

The communal drinking of divine water was also found in southeastern and central Tanganyika during the Maji Maji rebellion (*maji* is Swahili for water) against the German colonial government in 1905–1907. It was begun by a diviner or prophet called Kinjikitile, who was possessed by a local spirit as well as by a panethnic deity called Hongo. Those who drank Kinjikitile's water would be immune to bullets and would drive the Germans into the sea. The movement turned beyond his control politically; he was hanged, but the revolt was put down only after as many as a quarter of a million Africans had died.

There were many other prophet-led movements of the time, such as the Giriama (a Mijikenda group of the Kenya coast) movement of 1914, led by prophetesses, and the Nyabingi movement in southwestern Uganda during the first quarter of the century and later, also led largely by women. Both of these began as religious responses to colonial rule and later became increasingly political in aim until they were put down by the colonial governments.

Many accounts of changes in East Africa have set conversion to Christianity apart from more traditional and pre-Christian prophetic movements (except in Ethiopia, the political center of which has been Christian since the fourth century—but Ethiopian Christianity has had no influence on other parts of the region, being physically so separate). This reflects the outsiders' distinction between true and false religions, but from the point of view of the local societies themselves the distinction is largely meaningless. Outside observers also distinguish between traditional and world religions, but here the differences are more significant. Christianity and Islam are parts of international networks of economic and political as well as religious relations, so that their adherents may become part of extrasocietal and extra-African groupings that are significant in the lives of educated and elite people. They are also literate religions and as such open up temporal and spatial visions and areas of knowledge of a wider world that are less accessible to traditional worldviews based upon particular local societies.

It may well and sensibly be argued that a person adopts a new faith both because he or she accepts, in an intellectual or emotional measure, its theological arguments and because he or she accepts it as a better way of dealing with the tribulations of everyday life than had been offered by the traditional faith. In all traditional East African religions the factor of healing is, and has probably always been, a central one. To this must be added a related factor: when fears and accusations of witchcraft and sorcery reach a critical stage, people turn to prophets who promise to cleanse the land of these evils. East Africa has had many new Christian and Islamic prophetic movements whose leaders promise a new society free of witchcraft, sickness, and poverty; in addition, the Christian message as expressed by missionaries refers, to a large extent, to the problems of physical and moral health and sickness. Another factor has been that of education. Until independence a high proportion of educational services were controlled by mission organizations; thus to acquire a Western education and enter the modern world one had to join a mission and become at least a nominal Christian. This kind of conversion has nothing to do with the individual sincerity of conversion and belief, which is a matter quite outside the competence of any outsider to evaluate.

African Independent Churches without any link to foreign bodies have long been a feature of East Africa. They began largely as responses to what were seen (justifiably or not is not the immediate question at issue) as overbearing colonialist attitudes on the part of the mission churches. These African Independent Churches (AICs) in East Africa seem to have developed rather later than those in other parts of the continent. They have been marked particularly in areas of very high population density, which have been those where, for obvious reasons, colonial efforts and influences were first directed and where the effects of external change and of land shortage and overcrowding have been the most severely felt. The Kikuyu, the Luhya, and the Luo of Kenya, the Chagga of Tanzania, and the Ganda of Uganda are among the most striking examples, and all of them have educated Christian elites and African Independent Churches. These areas also, as a not unrelated consequence, have produced most of the members of modern political and social elites.

Islam has been a feature of East Africa for many centuries. It has been a part of the religious situation in northern Ethiopia, the Sudan, and the Somali and Swahili coasts since the Middle Ages. The advent of Omani colonial rule based on Zanzibar in the eighteenth and nineteenth centuries revitalized it, and from the coast Islam penetrated into the interior along the trading and slave routes based on Zanzibar. In some cases whole groups near the coast became Muslim, as did the Yao, for example (often largely to prevent their being enslaved, often to enable them to participate in the slave trade as partners with Arabs and Swahili); in others, individual members of the trading settlements inland, such as Tabora and Ujiji in Tanganyika (now Tanzania), became Muslims. In addition, Muslims from the Indian subcontinent have been in the coastal towns for centuries and spread inland to the more modern colonial towns. In general, however, Islam has had relatively little religious impact on most of East Africa, and once the power of the Zanzibar sultanate was weakened it almost ceased to spread.

If traditional Christian and Muslim prophetic leaders are considered members of a single category of religious experts, it may be seen that there are certain clearly defined phases of these movements in East Africa since the latter part of the nineteenth century. The first phase was that of the earlier effects of colonial rule, with which a link was seen with epidemics and other disasters; here the prophets were ultimately unsuccessful as religious or political leaders (although their inspirational spirits have usually lingered on as free spirits of one kind or another). The second phase was during the second quarter of the twentieth century, when the political aspects were less in evidence and more importance was given to missionization, missionaries being seen as colonial agents and even as betrayers of the Christian message as it affected Africans. The third and fourth phases have been more contemporary but should be distinguished. One comprised the movements led by Christian prophets to reform mission churches and to found syncretist or reformed sects and churches; these continued the process mentioned in the second phase. The other has been the rise of more overtly political leaders during the period of gaining political independence from the colonial powers. The leaders' authority has usually had aspects of messianic and charismatic authority, but no more need be said about them here. The third phase, however, is distinctly relevant and provides a main link between the histories and followings of traditional and world religions, especially Christianity in this particular region of Africa. The acceptance of new faiths, with either the abandonment of the old or a syncretism of the two, does not happen in a historical or social vacuum and cannot be considered in isolation from the traditional religious past. The same people, as individuals, move from traditional to world religions (and often back again): they are not members of separate communities.

SEE ALSO African Religions, articles on Mythic Themes and New Religious Movements; Lugbara Religion; Muḥammad Aḥmad; Nuer and Dinka Religion; Nyakyusa Religion; Witchcraft, article on African Witchcraft.

BIBLIOGRAPHY

The basic accounts of East African religions are in the form of monographs on the religious systems of particular societies. Most, although by no means all, are by anthropologists, each of whom has lived among the people in question, has learned their language and ways of life, and can set the beliefs and rites firmly into their social, cultural, and historical contexts. They include two books by E. E. Evans-Pritchard. In *Nuer Religion* (Oxford, 1956), on the Nilotic Nuer of the southern Sudan, he discusses the complex Nuer beliefs of the soul, divinity, sin, sacrifice, and religious symbolism and relates them to the social structure. The other, *Witchcraft, Oracles and Magic among the Azande,* 2d ed. (Oxford, 1950), is essentially on notions of spiritual causation among a prescientific people of the southwestern Sudan. Both these books are classics in the study of African religions. The Dinka, neighbors of the Nuer and closely related to them, are the subject of Godfrey Lienhardt's *Divinity and Experience: The Religion of the Dinka* (Oxford, 1961, reprinted, 1987), in which the relationships of belief and sacrifice to Dinka efforts to understand and control their experience of the outside world are discussed with insight and subtlety. John Middleton's *Lugbara Religion* (London, 1960) deals in a more strictly sociological manner with the use made by the Lugbara of Uganda, who are related to the Azande, of ritual in everyday social and political affairs. The two books on the Nyakyusa, a Bantu-speaking people of southern Tanzania, by Monica Wilson, *Rituals of Kinship among the Nyakyusa* (London, 1957) and *Communal Rituals of the Nyakyusa* (London, 1959), deal in great detail with rituals of many kinds, set in their social context. Bernardo Bernardi's *The Mugwe: A Failing Prophet* (London, 1959) deals with a particular priestly office among the Meru, an offshoot of the Kikuyu of central Kenya. Abdul Hamid M. el-Zein's *The Sacred Meadows* (Evanston, Ill., 1974) is concerned with the elaborate beliefs and rites of the Swahili town of Lamu, on the Kenya coast, which has nominally been Muslim for many centuries. Frederick B. Welbourn's *East African Rebels* (London, 1961) and Frederick B. Welbourn and Bethwell A. Ogot's *A Place to Feel at Home* (London, 1966) deal in detail and with sympathy with African Independent Church movements in southern Uganda and western Kenya respectively.

The other main category of writings on East African religions are surveys of various kinds in which comparisons are made between several local religions. Benjamin C. Ray's *African Religions* (Englewood Cliffs, N.J., 1976) is an excellent introduction to African religions in which those of East Africa feature prominently, in particular the Nuer, Dinka, Shilluk, Ganda, Lugbara, and Kikuyu. *Witchcraft and Sorcery in East Africa,* edited by John Middleton and E. H. Winter (London, 1963), and *Spirit Mediumship and Society in Africa,* edited by John Beattie and John Middleton (New York, 1969), contain essays by various authors on these matters among several different peoples. J. Spencer Trimingham's *Islam in East Africa* (London, 1964) is a useful survey, and John V. Taylor's *The Primal Vision* (London, 1963) is a valuable short introduction to East African religion from a Christian viewpoint.

New Sources

Anderson, David M., and Douglas H. Johnson. *Revealing Prophets: Prophecy in Eastern African History.* London, 1995.

Ewel, Manfred. *From Ritual to Modern Art: Tradition and Modernity in Tanzanian Sculpture.* Dar es Salaam, Tanzania, 2001.

Hansen, Holger Bernt, and Michael Twaddle, eds. *Religion and Politics in East Africa: The Period Since Independence.* London, 1995.

Meeker, Michael E. *The Pastoral Son and the Spirit of Patriarchy: Religion, Society and Person Among East African Stock Keepers.* Madison, Wis., 1989.

Oded, Arye. *Religions and Politics in Uganda: A Study of Islam and Judaism.* Nairobi, Kenya, 1995.

Omari, Cuthbert Kashingo. *God and Worship in Traditional Asu Society.* Erlangen, Germany, 1990.

Ray, Benjamin. *Myth, Ritual and Kingship in Buganda.* New York, 1991.

Spear, Thomas, and Isaria N. Kimanbo. *East African Expressions of Christianity.* Athens, Ohio, 1999.

Wrigley, Christopher. *Kingship and State: The Buganda Dynasty.* New York, 1996.

JOHN MIDDLETON (1987)
Revised Bibliography

EAST AFRICAN RELIGIONS: ETHIOPIAN RELIGIONS

Situated in the northeasternmost part of the Horn of Africa, Ethiopia is populated by three major groupings of people.

These groups speak languages classified as being related to three branches of Afro-Asiatic: Cushitic (e.g., Agaw, Bilen, Sidama, Oromo), Semitic (e.g., Amhara, Tigriña, Tigre, Gurage), and Nilo-Saharan (e.g., Majangir, Berta, Gumuz, Koma). Linguistic affiliations roughly correspond with religious observances. Centuries ago Cushitic- and Semitic-speaking Ethiopians were converted to Christianity and Islam but they still retain some traditional beliefs and practices. The traditional religious observances of the Nilo-Saharan peoples have been among the least influenced by Christianity and Islam. Cushitic religious traditions, principally those of the Agaw, profoundly affected the beliefs and practices of Ethiopians on the central plateau.

AGAW. Inhabiting the northern and central plateaus in the region of Gonder province, the Agaw form the linguistic and cultural substrate population of the Semitic-speaking Amhara and Tigriña. Their most northerly relatives, the mainly Islamic Bilen, are sedentary and engage in agriculture, as nearly all Agaw do. Three Agaw groups—the Qemant, Kwara, and Falasha (the last sometimes called Ethiopian Jews, who practice a pre-Talmudic form of Judaism)—live west of the Takkaze River and north of Lake Tana. Other Agaw groups live south of Lake Tana in Agawmeder and Damot. At the beginning of the twenty-first century, the Agaw were estimated to number about 490,000.

The Qemant, who have a mixture of traditional and Hebraic religious beliefs, live in dispersed settlements that are defined by sacred groves, the abodes of culture heroes called *qedus*. Sacred groves, a feature widespread among other central Ethiopians, are the loci of all major religious ceremonies. Among the Qemant, these ceremonies are conducted by officiates (*wambar*) who hold the highest political and religious offices and belong to the Keber, or superior moiety. Keber moiety members trace their ancestry to the pure Qemant; all other Qemant belong to the Yetanti moiety. Both groups disdain manual labor other than agriculture. At the apex of the priesthood, the *wambar* are assisted on ceremonial occasions by higher and lower priests, who ritually sacrifice on behalf of the community a white bull or white sheep as an offering to the male high god, Mezgana, who is believed to reside in the sky. After performing purification rites, priests and laypeople fast from the eve of the ceremony until the sacrifice the following morning. Worship of *jinn* at their natural abodes is also held to regulate rain, restore fertility, and rid the community of pests and disease.

OROMO. The over twenty million Oromo, representative of the southern Cushitic, stretch from the southern tip of Tigre to Harar, then south to the Tana River in Kenya, and as far west as the tributaries of the Blue Nile. Their cultural life is varied, ranging from the seminomadic pastoralism practiced by the southern Boran, who have resisted conversion to Christianity or Islam, to the sedentary agricultural life of the Macha of western Shoa province. Shoan and Wollo Oromo long ago abandoned their traditional dependence upon cattle, a cultural transformation coinciding with their gradual acceptance of the religious beliefs and practices of the agricultural and Christian Amhara and Tigriña near whom they settled. By the close of the twentieth century, few traces of indigenous Cushitic rites existed among the Muslim Jimma Oromo, most of whom had become devout followers of the Tijānīyah order of Islam.

Macha, Boran, and Guji Oromo, with slight variation, all share in common the Kallu institution, which Karl Knutsson describes as a social bridge between humanity and divinity. Through the figure of the Kallu, a ritual expert, a person's wishes are carried to divinity; this dignitary also constitutes the channel through which divinity's will is passed down to humanity. Moral rules of conduct are made manifest in the Kallu's daily behavioral and ritual performances associated with divinity. Macha manifestations of divinity find expression in the belief in Waka (sky or god); Atete, a female deity; and *ayana*, or divine agents. Kallu rituals, performed in groves of tall trees, incorporate sacrifices for rainmaking or ceremonies in honor of Waka. Possession by *ayana* spirits at regular intervals gives the Kallu man or woman a wider sphere of influence and power as a ritual clan leader.

AMHARA-TIGRIÑA. Inheritors of the monophysite doctrine of Christianity (which became the official religion of the old Aksumite kingdom in about 350 CE), the Semitic-speaking Amhara and Tigriña, inhabit large areas of central Ethiopia. The provinces of Gonder, Shoa, and Gojam, and the district of Lasta in Wollo province are the traditional homelands of the Amhara, estimated at the beginning of the twenty-first century to number almost twenty million. Tigriña mainly inhabit the province of Tigre, their homeland, and more are dispersed throughout several districts in highland Eritrea. The Tigriña people numbered over four million at the beginning of the twenty-first century.

The Amhara-Tigriña have no cult associated with their supreme being and creator god, Egziabher (the god from across the sea). Predating the transplantation of Christianity, the Amhara-Tigriña worshiped good and evil spirits who were associated with trees, fountains, and animate and inanimate objects. Nowadays, extreme devotion is expressed to the Virgin Mary (Maryam), who is believed to dwell in such sacred natural areas as high mountains, springs, and groves of sycamore trees. Sacrifices and cult activities take place in sacred groves, though the church (*bet kristyan*) is the principal seat of religious worship. Dedicated in the name of a patron saint, the church is the focal point of the parish, the largest local, social, and political subdivision. At services, only the priest and deacons (and formerly the king) may enter the sanctuary, which is completely hidden from the view of the communicants. Priests and laypeople alike observe strict fasting laws throughout the year and always before major religious festivals. Before a modern system of taxation was introduced in this century, church and state administration was supported by an elaborate system of tithing in labor and kind, made possible by a surplus economy based on extensive agricultural production.

GURAGE. The southernmost speakers of Semitic Afro-Asiatic, the Gurage inhabit the region in Shoa province where Lake Zeway and the middle course of the Gibbie River form, respectively, the general east and west boundaries. The Shoan Oromo live to the north, and Sidama groups stretch across the southern flanks of Gurage territory. Language and dialectical differences sharply demarcate the largely Christian and Muslim eastern Gurage from the adherents of traditional religion, which is still observed among some western Gurage. These western Gurage numbered about 250,000 at the beginning of the twenty-first century. The cultural life of the western group is dominated by the cultivation of *Ensete ventricosum*, more commonly known as false banana, a food staple consumed in great quantities on all religious or ritual occasions.

The remote supreme god of the western Gurage figures less prominently in religious beliefs and practices than do lesser deities, on whom major cult activities center. Guardians of the shrines dedicated to the lesser deities—Wak, the male sky god; Dämwamwit, the female deity; and Božä, the thunder god (all of whom reside in sacred groves where the great annual festivals are held)—exercise quasi-political and judicial roles in their spiritual capacity and sanction the authority of secular leaders. The annual festival of the female deity gives women ritual license to shed their customary subservient role and abuse menfolk verbally.

MAJANGIR. Nilo-Saharan peoples, such as the Majangir, Anuak, and Nuer, occupy western Ethiopia, mainly along the Sudan border. In the early twenty-first century, the hunting and trapping Majangir were estimated to number about 28,000 people. They live on the southwestern edge of the Ethiopian plateau in dispersed homesteads adjacent to forest areas, which they exploit for game. The material culture of the Majangir is as simple as their political and religious organization; the ritual expert (*tapat*) possesses characteristics of both shaman and priest, exercising quasi-political, chiefly duties. He derives his power mainly by control over spiritual sanctions, the threat of which is sufficient to maintain peace and order.

SEE ALSO Aksumite Religion.

BIBLIOGRAPHY

Gamst, Fredrick C. *The Qemant: A Pagan-Hebraic Peasantry of Ethiopia.* New York, 1969. A brief, informative ethnographic account of social organization and religious ritual life of descendants of the proto-Ethiopians.

Knutsson, Karl Eric. *Authority and Change: A Study of the Kallu Institution among the Macha Galla of Ethiopia.* Göteborg, Sweden, 1967. An analysis of ritual and cosmology in the political organization of sedentary Oromo. A comparison is made of form and variation of the Kallu among other Oromo groups.

Legesse, Asmarom. *Gada: Three Approaches to the Study of African Society.* New York, 1973. A detailed analysis of the cyclical Gada age-grade system of the pastoral Boran Oromo of southern Ethiopia.

Levine, Donald N. *Greater Ethiopia: The Evolution of a Multiethnic Society.* Chicago, 1974. A bold, imaginative examination of the principal linguistic and sociocultural factors accounting for the shaping of modern Ethiopia.

Shack, William A. *The Gurage: A People of the Ensete Culture.* London, 1966. A comprehensive analysis of social and religious organization set against the cultural background of the food quest.

Stauder, Jack. *The Majangir: Ecology and Society of a Southwest Ethiopian People.* Cambridge, U.K., 1971. A model study of small-scale social organization of a hunting and gathering people.

Trimingham, J. Spencer. *Islam in Ethiopia.* London, 1952. Reprint, Totowa, N.J., 1965. The definitive study of the history and institutions of the Islamic peoples of the Horn of Africa.

New Sources

Aspen, Harald. *Amhara Traditions of Knowledge: Spirit Mediums and Their Clients.* Wiesbaden, Germany, 2001.

Eide, Øyvind M. *Revolution and Religion in Ethiopia.* Stavanger, Norway, 1996.

Ghebre-Ab, Habtu, ed. *Ethiopia and Eritrea: A Documentary Study.* Trenton, N.J., 1993.

Mengisteab, Kidane. *Ethiopia: Failure of Land Reform and Agricultural Crisis.* New York, 1990.

Shelemay, Kay Kaufman. *Music, Ritual and Falasha History.* East Lansing, Mich., 1986.

Yamauchi, Edwin M. *Africa and Africans in Antiquity.* East Lansing, Mich., 2001.

Zegeye, Abebe, and Siegfried Pausewang. *Ethiopia in Change: Peasantry, Nationalism, and Democracy.* London, 1994.

WILLIAM A. SHACK (1987)
Revised Bibliography

EAST AFRICAN RELIGIONS: NORTHEAST BANTU RELIGIONS

The northeastern Bantu-speaking peoples of East Africa include the Ganda, Nyoro, Nkore, Soga, and Gisu of Uganda; the Kikuyu and Kamba of Kenya; and the Gogo and Kaguru of Tanzania. Although these societies are united by their common usage of Bantu languages, they differ considerably in political, social, and economic organization and in religious ideas and practices.

In most of these societies the creator god is regarded as a remote and distant figure, except among the Kikuyu where he is thought to be involved in the major events of personal and community life and is the object of ritual activity. The Nyoro and Nkore say that the creator god, Ruhanga, made the world and everything needed for human life on earth. He also established the three classes of Nyoro and Nkore society: the agriculturalists, the rulers (or royal clan), and the cattle herders. Each class is descended from one of Ruhanga's sons, whom Ruhanga tested before assigning them their social role. The Nyoro say that Ruhanga disinherited his fourth son, Kantu, and that he became the source of evil in the world and eventually corrupted the people. For this reason, say the Nyoro, Ruhanga withdrew to the sky and later sent disease and death into the world to punish the people. Because of his remoteness, Ruhanga does not play any role in Nyoro and Nkore ritual.

Among the Ganda, the creator god, Katonda, had a small temple and a medium who gave oracles at night. Katonda was known as the Owner of Heaven and the Master of Life, and it is said that every morning the heads of families would pray to him for the protection of their households. Although Katonda was important to everyone's personal destiny, offerings were not often made to him, and he appears to have had less ritual significance than most of the other gods; today he has no shrine or medium. According to Ganda mythology, it was the culture hero, Kintu, who established the world, populated the country, and founded the kingdom of Buganda. Death also came into the world as a result of the misdeeds of Kintu and his wife, Nambi, and their children, who allowed Nambi's brother, Death (Walumbe), to come to earth with them. After Death started killing people and was chased into the underworld, Kintu solemnly declared that Death would never kill all the people.

The Gisu say that the creator, Were, is a distant deity who allots each person his life span. Were has no shrines, and no sacrifices are made directly to him, although there is a vague belief that he is the recipient of sacrifices made to the ancestors and nature spirits. Were is regarded as being invisible and present everywhere like the wind.

The Kikuyu say that the creator, Ngai, dwells on certain prominent mountains in western Kenya, including Mount Kenya. His presence is also said to be manifested in such natural phenomena as the sun, moon, stars, rain, rainbows, lightning, and thunder; he is also present in sacred fig trees, where sacrifices are made to him. According to Kikuyu tradition, Ngai gave the land to the ancestors, Kikuyu and Mumbi, and he told them to call upon him in times of need. Sacrifices are offered to Ngai in times of drought, famine, and epidemic and also during the agricultural cycle. The Kikuyu also pray to Ngai at the major stages of life: at birth, initiation, marriage, and death. On less important occasions, offerings and prayers are made to the ancestors.

The relationship between Ngai and the people is unilateral, while their relationship with the ancestors is reciprocal. People beseech Ngai for his blessings, which he may choose to give or to withhold, whereas they pour out beer and slaughter animals for the ancestors, who are expected to respond favorably. The shrines to Ngai are fig trees that are both publicly and privately owned. A diviner communicates with Ngai in his dreams and determines when it is appropriate to offer sacrifice. After a sheep is killed, its intestines are tied around a tree and a portion of meat is placed at the foot. Prayers are offered to Ngai while facing Mount Kenya and the other mountains at each of the cardinal points. Two days later a solemn beer-drinking ceremony may be held and prayers offered again to Ngai for rain, health, prosperity, and children.

The Kamba, who are neighbors of the Kikuyu, say that the creator god, Molungu, made all things, including men and animals; thus the Kamba call him Mombi, the molder of all creatures. First, Molungu created the ancestors, then he made man and woman and sent them down from heaven. Later, another couple came up through the ant holes in the earth, and their children married those of the sky couple. As time passed, the people multiplied and their livestock increased and their crops prospered. However, one year the people failed to offer sacrifice to Molungu and he became angry and refused to send the rains, and there was great famine. Many of the original clans migrated to distant places, and these people are now the neighbors of the Kamba: the Kikuyu, Maasai, Meru, and others.

Originally, Molungu intended to endow human beings with immortality. He sent a chameleon with a message of eternal life to the people. When the slow-moving chameleon finally arrived, he began to deliver his message, saying, "I was ordered to . . . I was ordered to. . . ." But before he could finish, he was interrupted by the swift-flying weaverbird that had been sent by Molungu with a new message that the people would die. The bird delivered his message quickly and concisely, and since that day mankind has been mortal. According to another version, the chameleon was interrupted by a clever and agile hare who had overheard the message that Molungu gave to the chameleon, only he heard incorrectly and delivered the message that people would die.

Molungu is said to dwell beyond the skies and to observe mankind from the tops of Mount Kilimanjaro and Mount Kenya. He is thought to be well disposed to human beings and to intervene in human affairs when people act against the moral principles of society, but no sacrifices are offered directly to him. His dealings with the Kamba are mediated entirely by the spirits of the ancestors. In times of drought, flood, or epidemic, women gather and a goat is sacrificed. The women ask the ancestors to intercede with Molungu on behalf of the people. The sacrifice is intended to remove the ills and sins committed by the people during the year. The sacrificial animal is burned and the women call out all the offenses done by people in the community in order to purify it and to ward off Molungu's punishment. Occasionally, the Kamba pray to Molungu at other times, for example, to give thanks for the birth of a child or to ask that initiated children turn out well. The prayers to Molungu are brief and general in nature, reflecting his distance and impersonal character.

Among the Ganda, Soga, Nyoro, and Nkore, the primary focus of the traditional religion is upon the hero gods, the *lubaale* (Ganda), *misimbwa* (Soga), and *cwezi* (Nyoro and Nkore). These deities are thought to have been human beings who died and became gods. Some of the *cwezi*, for example, are said to have been ancient kings while others are described as having once been their royal servants. Each god has several shrines and priests throughout the country. In Buganda the most important gods were also in the service of the kingship. In precolonial times the king consulted them about matters of state, while the common people consulted them about personal misfortunes. These gods are still active today, and they are consulted about a variety of personal troubles, such as illness, crop failure, loss of money, barrenness, and loss of employment. To discover the cause of the problem, a person goes to a medium and pays a token fee (often described as a kind of gift) and, under probing by the diviner, states the nature of the problem. The medium then goes into a trance and tells the client (in the voice of the god) the remedy for the difficulty and also the additional cost involved in order to make the remedy effective. The diviner may tell his client to use certain medicines, usually obtained at the marketplace, and/or to make a sacrifice. The diviner usually gives some practical advice about the client's behavior as well. Sometimes the remedy requires the client to become initiated into the cult of the god so that persistent troubles will cease. This entails some expense and a lifelong relationship with the deity and his shrine.

Ghosts of the dead may also be diagnosed as the cause of personal misfortune, though not as frequently as the gods. Like the gods, the ghosts are communicated with through spirit possession and mediumship. But unlike the gods, the ghosts may be destroyed or rendered harmless by being placed in a pot that is then burned or buried in the ground.

The Gisu place shrines for the spirits of the dead in the compounds of important men or in special groves. These groves, which contain a number of fig trees, are sacred to the ancestors. The shrines in the homesteads are shaped like small huts, with forked branches extending through the roof so that offerings of meat may be hung upon them. Sacrifices take place at these shrines on important family occasions, such as the naming of a child, the circumcision of a boy, or personal misfortune. The central act is the offering of beer and an animal (e.g., cow, goat, or fowl) with an invocation. During the invocation, all the names of the dead must be recited lest a spirit feel slighted and cause trouble. Beer is sprayed over the participants as a blessing; red clay, signifying the renewal of health, may also be rubbed on them.

The matrilineal Kaguru offer annual beer and animal sacrifices to the ghosts of the dead at clan ritual sites. These sites contain the graves of the founding female ancestor of the clan and those of her closest descendants. The graves are cleared of growth, and beer and flour are poured onto the gravestones. The blood of animal victims is also poured out. Often a miniature shelter for the ghosts is built on the site. The dead are said to gain nourishment from the offerings and to be made cool and quiet and therefore unlikely to bother the living. The fertility of the land depends upon such annual rites, for the spirits of the dead guarantee the productivity of the land. Cultivation and other work on the land is thought mystically to wear down the earth; and the misdeeds of the people, especially of the clan elders who live near the site, are also thought to disturb the ghost ancestors. The Kaguru believe that if such rituals were not performed, the land would be less fertile, the annual rains less favorable, and illness and misfortune more frequent.

Although the Kaguru do not believe in reincarnation, they say that newborn children come from the land of the dead, where, it is said, the ghosts have villages and live as do people on earth. The difference is that life and death in the land of the ghosts is the reverse of that on earth. The ghosts mourn when one of their number dies and is born on earth, and they rejoice when a person dies on earth and is born in their land. Hence, an infant's hold on life is precarious because the jealous ghosts wish to take it back, and many rites are performed for the ghosts in order to protect the child's life.

Gogo rituals are also concerned primarily with the ancestors, for they are believed to control the fertility of the land and the welfare of the clans who live on it. Cattle and beer are the chief offerings. These bridge the gap between human beings and the spirits because they belong both to the world of men and to the world of nature, as do the ancestor spirits themselves. The semipastoralist Gogo sacrifice cattle, their most valuable possession, to the ancestors for rain and good crops and to obtain their blessings at crucial stages in the life cycle. Beer is poured out around a post that is considered to be the architectural and ritual center of the household. Called the nose of the homestead, the post is the locus of contact between the world of the living and the world of the dead in the domestic rituals. Beer may also be poured onto the gravestones of the dead, which also link the living to the world of the spirits.

Among the northeastern Bantu-speaking peoples, certain rites, or aspects of rites, are not aimed at the gods or spirits but at impersonal mystical forces that affect the welfare of human society. By means of ritual action bad forces may be removed and society purified and thereby spiritually renewed. The Gogo distinguish between good and bad ritual states. For things to go well, a good or auspicious ritual state must be created. When things do not go well (for instance, if a woman miscarries or has a difficult childbirth or if cattle become diseased), a bad ritual state is said to prevail. In these circumstances it is assumed that the male ritual leaders have failed. Women must take over and act and dress like men and effect a ritual cure through dancing. The women's violent, masculine dancing is a reversal of normal female domesticity and a parody of the male's violent role in Gogo society. In this reversal of sex roles, the ritual state of society is turned around. The inauspicious ritual state is taken to the boundary of the ritual area and thrown down into a swamp or pool, and the area is thus purified and a good ritual state regained.

Divination is central to all East African religions. The Kikuyu say that a diviner, called a man of God (*mundu mugu*), is chosen by Ngai through dreams. "A father may teach, but it is God [Ngai] who chooses the [diviner]. He talks to him in the night: it comes into his head." Divination is performed by spilling out small counters (beans and stones) from a gourd that reveals the will of Ngai or, more frequently, the will of the ancestor spirits. The result of the inquiry is determined by the odd or even number of counters that are spilled out together with other small objects that have symbolic significance. Kamba diviners use the same technique. A few Kikuyu diviners are also inspired in dreams directed by the creator god, who gives long-range prophecies about future events. During the colonial period in Kenya, such prophecies about colonial intrusion helped to legitimate the Mau Mau cause against British rule. The Mau Mau, a pro-independence armed revolt led by the Kikuyu in the 1950s, was an attempt to establish traditional land rights and ways of governance.

The Gisu diviner diagnoses his clients' problems by using a small wooden dish with pebbles in it. After invoking his ancestors for assistance, he swings the dish in an arc over his head, calling out the names of spirits who might be responsible for the problem or of people who might be causing it through sorcery or witchcraft. If the pebbles shake and rattle, then the wrong cause has been identified. When the pebbles form a mass and do not move, the correct diagnosis has been reached. The questions that the diviner puts to the test in this fashion are based upon his local knowledge and upon information gained from his client.

In the lacustrine kingdoms of Bunyoro, Nkore, and Buganda, the death, burial, and installation of kings were major ritual events that affected the whole kingdom. The kings were symbolically identified with the country as a whole, and hence their well-being was essential to the well-being of the kingdom. Thus they were surrounded by ritual prohibitions that were intended to keep them in a state of health and ritual purity. In Bunyoro the king's life was also strengthened periodically by the killing of human beings, sometimes in his stead as a mock king. Although the kings were not regarded as divine beings, in Bunyoro and Nkore it was said that the kings were killed when they grew old or ill or were wounded in battle, although there is no evidence that this actually occurred. That the kingship was thought of in this way, however, indicates the symbolic significance of the king as the source of life, peace, and order in his kingdom. In Bunyoro and Buganda there were also shrines for the spirits of the royal ancestors, and in Buganda these shrines were major ritual centers of the kingship. The mediums at the royal shrines conveyed advice from the royal ancestors to the king regarding matters of state, and all of the king's officials went to the shrines to be confirmed in office.

Fundamental to the social systems of the Gisu, Kikuyu, Kamba, Kaguru, and Gogo are rites of puberty and of initiation into adulthood. Their purpose is to transform young boys and girls into adult men and women. In these societies circumcision and clitoridectomy (or labiadectomy) are practiced. These physical operations are regarded as the outward signs of a new social position and of an inner moral change. Among the Gisu and Kikuyu, circumcision is thought of as a form of ordeal that testifies to the strength of character necessary for the change from childhood to adulthood. During the seclusion period, the initiated boys and girls are taught the rules governing sexual relations and the moral principles of society. For the Gisu, such rites are transformational, not merely transitional, "for it is in your heart," and the newly initiated person is said to be "like another person." The emphasis upon self-determination is also important, for a boy chooses when he shall be circumcised. When he does, he presents himself as a fully responsible agent to bear the ordeal and to stick to his resolution. Of the Kikuyu initiation rites, Jomo Kenyatta has said that "the moral code of the tribe is bound up with this custom and . . . it symbolizes the unification of the whole tribal organization." The rites mark the beginning of participation in the various governing groups in Kikuyu society, because age-group membership begins at this time. The history and legends are explained, as are the moral rules of society. Ngai and the ancestors are invoked, the misdeeds of childhood are symbolically cast away, and the initiates take an oath of loyalty and service to the Kikuyu community. Elements of these rites were also used during the Mau Mau oathing ceremonies. The Kaguru say that initiation into adulthood is the most important and impressive experience of their lives, and they conduct themselves in a noticeably different manner after going through it. Afterward, the fully initiated boys and girls can marry and have children, and the boys can own livestock and become warriors and elders in their society.

In precolonial times belief in witchcraft and sorcery was fundamental to East African societies. Although witchcraft and sorcery accusations are illegal under present law, in the past belief in witchcraft and sorcery functioned as an explanation of misfortunes that were not attributed to the gods or ancestors, and the process of finding and punishing witches functioned as a means of controlling socially deviant behavior and of resolving tensions within the local community. Belief in witchcraft and sorcery is based upon the assumption that many of the ills of life, including death, are caused by the evil intentions of human beings: hence the portrayal of witches as human beings whose behavior is the reverse of what is normal for humans. Witches and sorcerers are supposed to walk and dance upside down, to commit incest, to work at night, to travel at fantastic speeds, to go about naked, and to practice cannibalism. In short, witches and sorcerers are thought to confound the rules of society because they are bent upon destroying it. For the most part, witches were thought to be relatives of the people they attacked. The powers of witchcraft were also thought to be inherited and to be operative without a person's being aware of it. Sorcery, by contrast, was regarded as a conscious and deliberate action in which specific magical techniques were used to destroy other people. Witchcraft accusations were generally directed against people who exhibited antisocial characteristics—jealousy, spite, deceitfulness; even physical ugliness and unaccounted wealth were grounds for suspicion. In the past, diviners were employed to identify witches and sorcerers, and the accused were forced to confess and were often executed. Despite the illegality of witchcraft and sorcery accusations in the late twentieth century, belief in witchcraft and sorcery still exists in most of these societies as a way of explaining misfortune, and accusations may still be covertly made and acted upon.

Throughout the region of the northeastern Bantu-speaking peoples, the modern era has been marked by the increasing interaction of the traditional religions with Islam and Christianity. Although Islam and Christianity had long been present in certain areas of East Africa, it was not until the implementation of colonial rule with its new economic, educational, social, and religious order (or, in the case of Islam, the establishment in 1832 of the Omani Sultanate on Zanzibar and the subsequent development of extensive trading networks) that the introduced religions gained widespread influence.

By the late thirteenth century Islam had spread to the trading ports along the East African coast, and in the fifteenth century Mombasa and Zanzibar had become important centers of Arabic influence; despite this, however, Islam did not penetrate beyond the coastal area until the early nineteenth century. In the nineteenth and early twentieth centuries Muslim teachers and religious leaders followed the Zanzibari traders along the inland routes that conveyed ivory and slaves from Buganda and northern Tanganyika. Through the agency of the kings of Buganda, notably Mutesa I, Islam took hold in Buganda, and Arabic literacy developed among the chiefly class. Despite the fact that Mutesa once martyred several dozen Muslim converts because of the zealousness of their faith and the threat it posed to the exercise of his authority, Buganda became the center of Muslim expansion and later the home of a community of Sudanese Muslims from the north.

Although the Portuguese established Christianity in Mombasa in the early sixteenth century, it vanished when the Portuguese were expelled in 1631. Christians were forced to convert to Islam. In 1844 missionary work began again in the Mombasa area, and in the 1860s missionary activity entered the inland, Bantu-speaking areas with the arrival of the Anglican Church Missionary Society and the French Catholic White Fathers at Mutesa's capital in Buganda. Several years later Mutesa's successor, Mwanga II, killed a number of royal pages for placing their Christian faith above their allegiance to the throne. After a prolonged struggle for power in the kingdom between adherents of Christianity and Islam, the Christian faction (with the support of British forces) was victorious, and Christianity became the established religion of Buganda. Thereafter, Buganda became the center of Christian expansion in the Bantu-speaking areas. One of the aims of missionary work was the suppression of the Arab slave trade, and this motive also contributed to the establishment of colonial governments in Uganda, Kenya, and Tanganyika. During the colonial period, Islam made little headway in the Bantu-speaking areas, especially in parts formerly affected by the slave raids. The original Protestant and Catholic missions in Uganda spread into neighboring Kenya and Tanganyika, and colonial authorities rapidly opened these areas to other missions, such as the African Inland Mission and the missions of the Salvation Army, Scottish Presbyterians, Baptists, German, and Swedish Lutherans, Seventh-day Adventists, American Mennonites, Moravians, and the Brethren.

While the European missionaries were primarily motivated by the teaching of the gospel, they also acted, consciously or unconsciously, as agents of colonialism, racism, and westernization. The establishment of mission schools and hospitals did much to break down African traditional culture, and the missionaries joined colonial officials in attempting to abolish many indigenous practices, such as circumcision rites (especially among girls), polygamy, bridewealth, mourning rites, twin ceremonies, and ancestor rituals. In this fashion the missionaries set about to educate and westernize the next generation of African leaders. The missionaries also taught about human equality and the importance of individuals and thereby helped to foster the seeds of anticolonialism among Africans who were later to take over the governments, schools, and churches of East Africa in the postcolonial period. From the beginning, African preachers and catechists assisted the European missionaries, and they played a major role in spreading Christianity outside the mission stations and in founding new churches. Sometimes the frustrations of European control and the upheavals of colonial and postcolonial life caused African religious leaders to found their own churches, especially in Kenya, where over 150 such churches were established before and after the independence period. These churches combined African and Christian beliefs and rites into indigenized Christian expressions; but many were short-lived, and a few had elements of political protest, such as the Dini ya Msambwa (Religion of the Ancestors) in western Kenya. After independence in the 1960s leadership in the mission churches gradually passed into African hands, and this was accompanied by a significant growth in church membership. At the same time there was a resurgence in traditional religion, especially in the practice of divination and healing, due largely to the absence of colonial repression and to the need for culturally suitable therapeutic techniques not found in Christianity, Islam, or Western hospitals. With the establishment of political parties and nationalist governments, the churches, which had originally shaped the leadership of the new nations, were effectively reduced to a marginal role in the politics of East Africa.

See Also Interlacustrine Bantu Religions.

Bibliography

Beattie, John. "Spirit Possession in Bunyoro." In *Spirit Mediumship and Society in Africa*, edited by John Beattie and John Middleton. New York, 1969. An excellent ethnographic survey.

Beidelman, T. O. *The Kaguru.* New York, 1971. Contains a brief but comprehensive account of Kaguru religion.

Heald, Suzette. "The Making of Men." *Africa* 52 (1982): 15–36. A perceptive psychological study of Gisu boys' initiation ceremonies.

Kenyatta, Jomo. *Facing Mount Kenya* (1938). New York, 1978. An important interpretation from a Kikuyu point of view.

Lindblom, Gerhard. *The Akamba in British East Africa.* 2d ed. New York, 1969. A classic ethnography.

Middleton, John, and Greet Kershaw. *The Central Tribes of the Northeastern Bantu.* Rev. ed. London, 1965. A comprehensive survey and bibliography that includes ethnic groups not covered in the present article.

Ndeti, Kivuto. *Elements of Ákámbá Life.* Ann Arbor, Mich., 1971. Contains an important interpretation of some Akamba religious ideas and practices.

Oded, Arye. *Islam in Uganda.* Jerusalem, 1974.

Ray, Benjamin C. "Sacred Space and Royal Shrines in Buganda." *History of Religions* 16 (May 1977): 363–373.

Rigby, Peter. "Some Gogo Rituals of 'Purification.'" In *Dialectic in Practical Religion,* edited by Edmund Leach, pp. 153–179. London, 1968.

Rigby, Peter. "The Symbolic Role of Cattle in Gogo Ritual." In *The Translation of Culture,* edited by T. O. Beidelman, pp. 257–292. New York, 1973. Both of Rigby's articles present substantive interpretations of Gogo rituals.

Roscoe, John. *The Baganda.* 2d ed. London, 1965. A classic ethnography.

Routledge, W. S., and Katherine Routledge. *With a Prehistoric People* (1910). London, 1968. A well-informed account of the Kikuyu in the early twentieth century.

Welbourn, F. B. "The Impact of Christianity on East Africa." In *History of East Africa,* edited by D. A. Low and Alison Smith, vol 3. London, 1976.

New Sources

Barrett, Anthony. *Sacrifice and Prophecy in Turkana Cosmology.* Nairobi, Kenya, 1998.

Hoehler-Fatton, Cynthia. *Women of Fire and Spirit: History, Faith, and Gender in the Roho Religion in Western Kenya.* New York, 1996.

Johnson, Douglas Hamilton. *Nuer Prophets: A History of Prophecy from the Upper Nile in the Nineteenth and Twentieth Centuries.* New York, 1994.

Maloba, Wunyabari O. *Mau Mau and Kenya: An Analysis of a Peasant Revolt.* Bloomington, Ind., 1998.

Ruel, Malcolm. *Belief, Ritual and the Securing of Life: Reflexive Essays on a Bantu Religion.* Leiden, Netherlands, 1997.

Voshaar, Jan. *Maasai: Between the Oreteti-Tree and the Tree of the Cross.* Kampen, Netherlands, 1998.

BENJAMIN C. RAY (1987)
Revised Bibliography

EASTER, the most important of all Christian feasts, celebrates the passion, the death, and especially the resurrection of Jesus Christ. The English name *Easter,* like the German *Ostern,* probably derives from *Eostur,* the Norse word for the spring season, and not from *Eostre,* the name of an Anglo-Saxon goddess. In Romance languages the name for Easter is taken from the Greek *Pascha,* which in turn is derived from the Hebrew *Pesaḥ* (Passover). Thus Easter is the Christian equivalent of the Jewish Passover, a spring feast of both harvest and deliverance from bondage. The Eastern Slavs call Easter "the great day" and greet one another, as do the Greeks, with the words "Christ is risen," receiving the response "He is risen indeed."

Easter is the earliest of all annual Christian feasts. It may originally have been observed in conjunction with the Jewish Passover on the fourteenth day of the month Nisan. Gradually, however, it was observed everywhere on Sunday, the day of Christ's resurrection. The Council of Nicaea (325) prescribed that Easter should always be celebrated on the first Sunday after the first full moon following the spring equinox.

Easter was fundamentally a nocturnal feast preceded by a fast of at least one day. The celebration took place from Saturday evening until the early morning hours of Sunday. In the fifth century Augustine of Hippo called this "the mother of all vigils." From at least the time of Tertullian (third century) the Easter Vigil (also called the Paschal Vigil) was the favored time for baptism, since the candidates for initiation mirrored the new life won by Christ from the darkness of death.

The symbolism of light became an important feature of this nocturnal festival. It was customary on the Saturday evening of the Easter Vigil to illuminate not only churches but entire towns and villages with lamps and torches; thus the night was called "the night of illumination." From at least the end of the fourth century in Jerusalem the lighting of lamps at vespers took on a special character at this feast. In Northern European countries the use of special lights at Easter coincided with the custom of lighting bonfires on hilltops to celebrate the coming of spring; this is the origin of the Easter fire later kindled in Western Christian Easter Vigils. Large Easter candles also became the rule, and poems were composed in honor of them and thus of Christ the light, whom they symbolized. Such poems stem from as early as the fourth century; the most famous, still employed in various versions, is the *Exultet,* which originated in the seventh or eighth century. In the East, among the Orthodox, Holy Saturday night is celebrated with a candlelight procession outside the church building. After a solemn entrance into the church, bells peal and the Great Matins or Morning Prayer of Easter begins. It is followed by a solemn celebration of the Eucharist according to the liturgy of Saint Basil.

The Easter Vigil also contains a number of biblical readings. In the East the baptisms took place during the long readings of the vigil, whereas in the West a procession to the baptistery took place after the readings had been completed. In both cases the celebration of the Eucharist followed the baptisms. With the decline in adult conversions and, hence, in Easter baptisms during the Middle Ages, the time for the vigil service (and thus the end to fasting) was moved up to Saturday morning; however, the Roman Catholic church restored the nocturnal character of the service in 1952 and other rites relating to Holy Week in 1956. In the current Roman Catholic, Lutheran, and Episcopalian rites the Paschal Vigil is the high point of a *triduum*, or three days of services, celebrating the death and resurrection of Christ.

From at least the end of the fourth century, Easter was provided in Jerusalem with an octave, eight days of celebration. With the medieval decline in the octave celebration, Monday and Tuesday of Easter week nevertheless retained the character of holidays. In a larger context the whole of the fifty days from Easter Sunday to Pentecost was properly called Easter, and so constituted a feast in its own right; the eight-day octave, however, was a time of special recognition of the newly baptized. The Sunday after Easter was called the "Sunday in white" because the newly baptized wore their baptismal garments for the last time on that day, and among the Orthodox the octave of Easter is still called "the week of new garments."

Devotions tied to the liturgy of Easter are the origins of liturgical drama. In the Middle Ages it was customary to bury the consecrated host and a cross, or simply a cross, in an Easter sepulcher on Holy Thursday or Good Friday. The host or cross was retrieved on Easter Sunday morning and brought to the altar in procession. From this practice developed a brief Easter play called the *Visitatio sepulchri* (Visit to the Tomb), which enacted the visit of the two women to Christ's empty tomb. The same dramatic dialogue can be seen in the eleventh-century poetic sequence *Victimae paschali laudes* (Praise to the Paschal Victim), which became part of the Western liturgy.

A number of popular customs mark Easter Sunday and the rest of Easter week. One such custom, allied to the coming of spring with its earlier sunrise, is an outdoor sunrise service celebrating the resurrection. Such celebrations are especially popular among American Protestants. Since Easter was a time in which the newly baptized wore shining white garments, it became customary to wear new clothes on Easter Sunday and to show them off by walking around town and countryside; thus originated the Easter promenade or Easter parade, popular in many places.

Among the most familiar Easter symbols are the egg and rabbit. The egg symbolizes new life breaking through the apparent death (hardness) of the eggshell. Probably a pre-Christian symbol, it was adapted by Christians to denote Christ's coming forth from the tomb. In many countries the exchange of colored or decorated eggs at Easter has become customary. The Easter Bunny or Rabbit is also most likely of pre-Christian origin. The rabbit was known as an extraordinarily fertile creature, and hence it symbolized the coming of spring. Although adopted in a number of Christian cultures, the Easter Bunny has never received any specific Christian interpretation.

Among Easter foods the most significant is the Easter lamb, which is in many places the main dish of the Easter Sunday meal. Corresponding to the Passover lamb and to Christ, the Lamb of God, this dish has become a central symbol of Easter. Also popular among Europeans and Americans on Easter is ham, because the pig was considered a symbol of luck in pre-Christian European culture.

SEE ALSO Baptism; Christian Liturgical Year; Drama, article on European Religious Drama; Egg; Passover; Pigs; Rabbits.

BIBLIOGRAPHY

For a comprehensive survey of the Western liturgical development of Easter, see Ildephonso Schuster's *The Sacramentary* (New York, 1925). Good treatments of Easter and associated popular customs can be found in Francis X. Weiser's *Handbook of Christian Feasts and Customs* (New York, 1958) and in the same author's *The Easter Book* (New York, 1954). For discussion from the point of view of the history of religions, see E. O. James's *Seasonal Feasts and Festivals* (New York, 1961).

JOHN F. BALDOVIN (1987)

EASTERN CHRISTIANITY. From the city of Jerusalem, the first Christian missionaries set out along the roads of the Roman Empire to the cities and villages of the Mediterranean world and beyond. Within only a few years after Christ, Christian communities existed in major cities of the southeastern Roman Empire. Some aspects of the church's rapid development from Jerusalem through Syria and Greece and on to the city of Rome are contained in the Acts of the Apostles. The areas where the Christian presence was the strongest were in the East: Syria, Asia Minor, Egypt, and North Africa. Beyond the eastern confines of the Roman world, there were also Christian communities developing in Persia, Armenia, Ethiopia, and India.

The dramatic growth of the early church was not without difficulties. Yet the influence and prominence of Christians within the Roman world gradually increased, especially in the more eastern areas of Syria, Asia Minor, and the Greek peninsula. Under the Roman emperor Constantine, the formal persecution of the church ceased in 311, and a new relationship between the church and government developed after 313. Before his death in 337, Constantine was baptized. Emperor Theodosius finally proclaimed Christianity the official faith of the Roman-Byzantine Empire in the year 380.

PARALLEL HISTORICAL DEVELOPMENTS: EAST AND WEST. Because of a variety of developments and characteristics in the church beginning in the first four centuries, it is common to speak generally of Eastern and Western Christianity. These broad descriptive designations have their limitations. Nevertheless, they do help us to sense the diversity in unity that was expressed in early Christianity. The designations also help us appreciate the fact that the theological and historical development of Eastern Christianity is distinctive from the forms of Christianity that are expressed today both by Roman Catholicism and by the many expressions of Protestantism. While centered upon Christ and his teachings, both Eastern and Western Christianity came to express different perspectives. At times, these perspectives were complementary, at other times opposed to one another.

Initially, the early distinctions between Eastern and Western Christianity reflected the structural developments of the early church, especially in the Roman Empire. From the beginning, the one church was a communion of local churches. They were bound together by a common faith, frequently referred to as the "faith of the apostles." Yet, each regional church had its own particular characteristics. As such, the church was not a monolithic body. The Christian faith was expressed in regional churches containing a wide variety of peoples in different cultural settings and using different languages, a diversity that also expressed itself in liturgical practices.

Moreover, the organizational association of local dioceses within the Roman Empire became more pronounced from the second century onward. Comprising local parishes, each diocese maintained its integrity under the leadership of its bishop. Yet a regional association of dioceses developed that served to strengthen the unity and mission of the churches in a particular area. These provinces, led by a metropolitan archbishop, were eventually structured along the lines of five regions within the Roman-Byzantine Empire. By the early fourth century, the centers were associated with the cities of Rome, Constantinople, Alexandria, Antioch, and Jerusalem. Politically, Emperor Diocletian already had divided the empire between East and West in the third century. Theodosius furthered this in the fourth century.

Subsequently known as patriarchs, the bishops of these five churches and cities exercised primatial leadership among the bishops of their ecclesiastical region, later termed patriarchates. In some cases, these ecclesiastical regions extended beyond the borders of the Roman Empire. The most significant of these bishops were the pope of Rome within the western part of the Roman-Byzantine Empire and the Ecumenical Patriarch of Constantinople in the East. The position of the patriarch of Constantinople was established in the late fourth century and increased in importance especially following the rise of Islam in regions of the other Eastern patriarchates in the seventh century. Likewise, the influence of the pope of Rome increased in Western Europe during late antiquity and the subsequent rise of the Carolingian Empire in the ninth century. The Eastern patriarchates, however, consistently repudiated efforts by the pope to exercise authority beyond his territory.

The early distinction between Eastern and Western Christianity reflects the differences in languages in the early church. The early church never supported a universal language. On the contrary, the faith was expressed in a variety of languages and through a variety of cultures. While Jesus and the earliest Christians spoke Aramaic, the books of the New Testament were composed in a simple form of Greek. During the first century, Greek was the "common language" of the Mediterranean world. In the eastern portion of the Roman Empire, Greek remained the preferred language of education and culture. In the western portion, Latin predominated at least from the fourth century. Beyond the borders of the empire, the early church communities were composed of believers of a wide variety of cultures who also used languages such as Syriac and Armenian. The differences of languages, most especially Latin and Greek, provided one significant basis for making a distinction between Western Christianity and Eastern Christianity, at least from the fourth century. Indeed, historians of early Christianity have often spoken of the "Latin West" and the "Greek East." This designation, however, neglects those other, early expressions of Eastern Christianity employing other languages in teaching and preaching. The Christian Scriptures, for example, were translated into at least five major languages of the East by the end of the fourth century.

The early distinction between Eastern and Western Christianity also reflects differences in theological perspectives and terminology in the early church. A number of theological perspectives and schools of Christian thought became more pronounced during the fourth and fifth centuries. Each of these sought to express the Christian faith within a distinctive cultural context with its own philosophical antecedents. Each provided important perspectives upon the meaning of the faith as expressed in Christian Scripture and tradition. The desire to maintain the unity of faith did not prevent the natural development of different theological emphases as well as the use of different theological terms in various regions.

By the early fourth century, important centers of Christian learning and thought could be found in the prominent eastern cities of Alexandria, Antioch, and Edessa as well as in the region of Cappadocia (modern central Turkey). The development of a distinctive Western Christian theology was initially linked with North Africa and only by the fifth century with Rome.

Patristic traditions that developed after the fourth century reflect the distinction between Eastern and Western Christianity. Important teachers of the early church were concerned with teaching the Christian faith within a particular setting and in relationship to particular theological challenges. The teachings of Tertullian (c.160–c. 225), Cyprian (d. 258), and Augustine (354–430) reflect the theological issues of the growing church in North Africa. Among the critical issues were Donatism and Pelagianism. The teaching of Ambrose (c. 339–397) reflects pastoral concerns dealing with Arianism and sacramental practices in the region of Milan. The teachings of Athanasius (c. 296–373), Ephraem (c. 306–393), and Cyril of Alexandria (d. 444) reflect their concerns with Christology. The teachings of Macrina (c. 327–379),

Basil (c. 330–379), Gregory the Theologian (329–389), and Gregory of Nyssa (c. 330–c. 395), referred to as the Cappadocians, clarified the theological terms used to describe the Trinity. The teachings of Leo of Rome (d. 461) reflect a concern with both Christology and with church organization.

Within the early Christian East, there were many outstanding teachers, but none predominated in anything like the role played by, say, Augustine in the West. Profound theological issues affected the eastern portion of the Roman-Byzantine Empire especially between the fourth and eighth centuries. These were addressed at local councils and at the ecumenical councils, convened in the cities of the eastern part of the Roman-Byzantine Empire.

Clearly, there were different trajectories in the patristic traditions of East and West. Especially from the seventh century onward, a number of serious theological debates, compounded by politics, deepened the historic differentiation between Eastern and Western Christianity. In the realm of theological reflection, Eastern and Western Christianity were engaged with different theological issues and were affected by the perspectives of different teachers. The East was preoccupied with Christological themes, iconoclasm, missions to the Slavs, hesychaism (a style of prayer and meditation leading to a personal experience of God), and the encounter with Islam. Among its influential teachers at this time were John of Damascus (c. 675–c. 749), Maximos the Confessor (c. 580–662), Photios of Constantinople (c. 810–c. 895), and Gregory Palamas (c. 1296–1359). The West was preoccupied with such theological issues as the atonement, the relationship of the church and the state, and the interplay between revelation and reason. Among its influential teachers were Anselm of Canterbury (c. 1033–1109), Pope Gregory VII (c. 1021–1085), and Thomas Aquinas (1225–1274).

The great theological themes in East and West were bound to be expressed in the worship, popular piety, art, and architecture of the churches. Here too one can sense simple differences that may reflect deeper theological concerns. The liturgy and art of the Christian East emphasized the intimate and natural relationship between the Triune God and humanity within the context of a good creation. The Eastern liturgy together with liturgical art and architecture were designed to provide a context through which this salutary relationship is celebrated, nurtured, and, when necessary, restored. With the coming of the Middle Ages, the developing liturgy and liturgical art of the Christian West was concerned more with overcoming the barrier between God and humanity caused by sin.

The early distinctions between Eastern and Western Christianity reflect the fact that there were also different cultural and intellectual contexts especially in the two major portions of the Roman Empire. The Byzantines, a term coined by Western historians, always described themselves as "Romans." They believed that their commonwealth continued the Roman Empire, albeit with a new basis in the Christian gospel. Following the transfer of the capital to the city of Byzantium in 324, it was termed "New Rome," or later "Constantine's City" (Constantinople). While they placed ultimate emphasis upon the Christian revelation, the Byzantines appreciated the cultural and intellectual inheritance of the ancient world. For the most part, elements of the intellectual tradition of the Classical world were viewed as imperfect forms of preparation for the coming of Christ. Unlike the Christian West, the Byzantines never experienced the "Dark Ages" and always maintained a high regard for learning. Founded in 425 by Emperor Theodosius II, the University of Constantinople existed for about seven hundred years before the medieval Western universities were established. The Byzantines never lost touch with Plato and Aristotle. Indeed, the West's contact with the Byzantine world during the Middle Ages frequently led to revivals of learning. Byzantine scholars coming to Western Europe after the fall of Constantinople nurtured the Renaissance of the fifteenth century.

Moreover, the Christian East had significant examples of charitable institutions, well developed by the late fourth century. The believer was expected to imitate God in acts of philanthropy. This personal responsibility was also expressed in a substantial way both by the church and by the government. Basil the Great, Gregory the Theologian, John Chrysostom (c. 347–407), Olympia the Deacon (c. 368–408), and John the Almsgiver (556–619) were notable teachers who called upon believers to care for the poor and needy. Moreover, the church took an active role in establishing charitable institutions. Basil is especially remembered for the creation, about the year 372, of a "city of healing," known as the *Basileias,* where the sick and poor were cared for regardless of their beliefs. His activity provided inspiration for other church leaders and governmental officials. Throughout its history, the Byzantine Empire was renowned for its hospitals, orphanages, homes for the elderly and the poor, and hospices for travelers.

Many of the early Eastern teachers and philanthropists were nurtured in monasteries. From the fourth century there was a strong monastic presence in the Byzantine world, rooted in a tradition established in Egypt by Anthony (c. 251–356) and by Pachomius (292–346). Basil and his sister Macrina also provided additional guidance for monastic communities. The Eastern insights were subsequently received in the West by Jerome (342–420), John Cassian (c. 415), and Benedict (480–540). The monasteries were communities of celibate believers whose lives revolved about services of prayer. In the East, many monasteries also were concerned with preservation of manuscripts and with schools and hospitals. The monasteries, frequently located in mountains, were also places of pilgrimages. Mount Athos, known as the Holy Mountain, contains a number of active monasteries dating from the late Byzantine period.

DIVISION AFTER THE COUNCIL OF EPHESUS, 431. The early church professed that Jesus Christ was not only divine but also human. Reflecting the witness of the New Testament and early Christian teachings, the Council of Nicaea in 325 and the Council of Constantinople in 381 opposed Arianism and Apollinarianism, teachings that denied either Christ's full divinity or full humanity. Essential aspects of the faith of the church were expressed in the Nicene-Constantinople Creed of 381. By this time, and after much discussion, the church had settled on terminology that described the Trinity as three persons (*hypostases*), one divine essence (*ousia*). However, further questions arose over the relationship of the divinity and the humanity of Christ as well as the theological terms to be employed. These issues led to serious and unresolved divisions primarily within Eastern Christianity following the Council of Ephesus in 431 and the Council of Chalcedon in 451. At their heart, these divisions of the fifth century reflect the differences between the theological schools of Alexandria and Antioch. Both acknowledged Christ to be divine and human. Yet both differed in their descriptions of the relationship of the divinity and humanity in Christ as well as the terms to be used in describing the relationship between them.

The controversy was initiated over the term to be used to describe Mary. Formerly a monk in Antioch, Patriarch Nestorius of Constantinople refused to speak of Mary as the *Theotokos* (Mother or Birthgiver of God) and preferred to use the term *Christotokos* (Birthgiver of Christ). The term *Theotokos* had long been part of the church's understanding of the Virgin Mary and her relationship to Christ. It was less preferable for Nestorius because it sounded as though the humanity of Christ was somehow lost. Following the noted exegete Theodore of Mopsuestia (c. 350–428), the Antiochian tradition in general and Nestorius in particular were concerned with safeguarding the integrity of the humanity and divinity of Christ. He was accused, however, of teaching not only that Christ was divine and human but also that Christ was two beings. In his teaching, there appeared to be no true connection between humanity and divinity in Christ.

Representing the Alexandrian school of thought, Patriarch Cyril of Alexandria (d. 444) was the chief opponent to Nestorius. Cyril emphasized the union of humanity and divinity in Christ. In so doing, he frequently used the phrase "One nature of the Incarnate Word." Not denying Christ's full humanity and divinity, Cyril emphasized their union in the one reality of Christ. He usually used the word "nature" *(physis)* to describe the concrete expression of the one Christ.

To resolve this dispute, a council of bishops convened in Ephesus in 431. When it began, however, not all the bishops from the region of Antioch had arrived. The council deposed Nestorius and affirmed Cyril's Christological perspectives. The Antiochian bishops subsequently refused to accept the decision of Ephesus and convened their own council. They held that the terminology of Cyril could be used to deny the integrity of the divinity and humanity in Christ. For some of them, the term "nature" (*physis*) was used to speak about the two realities of humanity and divinity.

In an effort to avoid division, Patriarch Cyril and Patriarch John of Antioch came to an agreement in 433 affirming a common Christological teaching and a common terminology. They spoke of Christ being one person (*hypostasis*) and being of two natures (*physis*). This agreement eventually led many in the Antiochian tradition to accept the decision of the Council of Ephesus. The moderate Alexandrians emphasized the union of the divinity and humanity in Christ. The moderate Antiochians emphasized the integrity of both the humanity and divinity in Christ. Either approach, though, could be pushed to an extreme.

The bishops of the church in the region of eastern Syria and Mesopotamia met in 484 and formally rejected the decision of Ephesus and its clarification of 433. They continued to be suspicious of the Alexandrian perspective and the attacks on Nestorius, whom they honored. The alienation became even more pronounced as time passed. It was compounded by proponents of an extreme Alexandrian Christology as evidenced by the monk Eutyches (fl. 450). Moreover, the subsequent decision of the Council of Constantinople in 553 to condemn posthumously the teachings of Diodore of Tarsus (died c. 390) and Theodore of Mopsuestia (c. 350–428) further deepened the alienation.

The church in the region of Mesopotamia dates from at least the second century. It was conquered in the third century by Persia, which never fully accepted Christianity. Zoroastrianism predominated, and Christians remained a minority. During the early fourth century, the bishops of the region were organized into an ecclesiastical structure under the leadership of a *catholicos,* the bishop of the Persian royal capital at Seleucia-Ctesiphon. He later received the additional title of patriarch. The city of Edessa became a noted center of Christian theology. The church in Persia had little formal connection with the church in the Roman-Byzantine Empire. Attempts to reconcile the divided churches, especially in the sixth century, were thwarted by the conflicts between the Roman-Byzantine Empire and the Persian Empire. Compounded by politics and distance, the schism deepened. In addition, the rapid rise of Islam in the early seventh century further aggravated the separation and prevented meaningful contacts.

The church in Persia eventually came to be called by some the Nestorian Church. More recently, it has been more properly known as the Assyrian Church or the Church of the East. From the seventh century, it was generally unaffected by the subsequent developments that touched the churches in the Mediterranean world through the Middle Ages and into the modern period. However, the Church of the East was engaged in remarkable missionary activity well into the fourteenth century. Missions were established for a period in Ceylon, India, Burma, Thailand, Indochina, and China. In recent centuries, membership in this church, however, has been considerably reduced. Some members accepted the authority of the Roman Catholic Church in the sixteenth century. Others were the objects of Protestant proselytism in the nineteenth century. A sizable number of its faithful were the victims of persecution in the early twentieth century. Today the majority of its 400,000 members live in present-day Iran, Iraq, and Syria. Because of recent immigration, there are new parishes in Western Europe and North America. It has had little formal contact with either the Orthodox Church or the Oriental Orthodox Churches.

DIVISION AFTER THE COUNCIL OF CHALCEDON, 451. The second notable church division in the Christian East followed the Council of Chalcedon in 451. In order to heal the growing division over Christology within the Roman-Byzantine Empire, a council of bishops met at Chalcedon, near Constantinople, in 451. This council was a response to an earlier meeting of bishops held in Ephesus in 449. Dubbed the "Robbers Synod" by Pope Leo of Rome, that council supported the extreme Alexandrian Christology expressed by the monk Eutyches. He maintained that in Christ there was a single nature, implying that Christ's humanity had been lost through its contact with his divinity. The bishops at Chalcedon forcefully repudiated the decisions of the council of 449 and its extreme Alexandrian Christology. They sought to express the apostolic faith in opposition both to extreme Alexandrian and extreme Antiochian perspectives. The council was also concerned with reconciling the growing division between the churches reflecting Alexandrian Christology and those reflecting the Antiochian version, especially the church in Mesopotamia.

The statement of the council reflected the theological debates reaching back to the council of Ephesus and the differing emphasis in Christology. The statement brought together the moderate elements of both Alexandrian and Antiochian Christology while opposing the extreme distortions of each. At the same time, the statement established a common terminology that could be received by both traditions. While recognizing the mystery of the incarnation, the statement affirmed that Christ is one person with two natures, both fully human and fully divine. Neither his divine nor his human nature is diminished or lost by the union in one person. Before this, the term "nature" had been used by some to describe the single reality of Christ (one nature). Others had spoken of two natures when referring to the divinity and humanity of Christ.

The churches related to the Patriarchate of Rome and the Patriarchate of Constantinople immediately received the statement. The Council of Chalcedon was eventually recognized in these churches as the Fourth Ecumenical Council. However, in the decades following Chalcedon, portions of the church in Egypt and in Syria as well as the church in Armenia rejected the statement of the council. For a time, the church in Georgia joined them. Following their lead, the churches in Ethiopia and in Malankara, India, subsequently also rejected the decision.

Upholding a very formal Alexandrian position, the opponents of Chalcedon believed that the use of the terminology of "two natures" had overtones of Nestorianism despite the fact that the council anathematized Nestorius. The opponents also claimed that the "two nature" terminology was a betrayal of Cyril's usual affirmation of "one nature of the incarnate Word." Generally overlooked was the fact that Cyril in the agreement of 433 recognized the use of the "two nature" terminology if understood properly. Those who rejected Chalcedon also repudiated the Monophysitism of Eutyches. They were subsequently accused of the heresy of Monophysitism because of they used the term "nature" as the Chalcedonians used the word "person" to describe the reality of Christ. While opposed to the doctrinal Monophysitism of Eutyches, they accepted a "linguistic Monophysitism" claiming to follow Cyril.

The division in the Christian East after Chalcedon not only reflected differences in Christology. It also reflected historical, political, and cultural differences between those Christians within the Roman-Byzantine world and those living on and beyond its boundaries. Following Chalcedon, those who rejected the council's teaching made up a significant portion of the Christians living on the periphery of the empire. The attempt by the Byzantines to impose the decision of Chalcedon through military force especially in Egypt only compounded the division.

Councils of bishops meeting in Constantinople in 553 and 661 attempted to heal the growing division. They also addressed ongoing questions related to describing the person of Christ. These councils were eventually recognized as the Fifth and Sixth Ecumenical Councils by the churches of the Byzantine-Roman world. By the seventh century, however, differences in Christology and theological perspectives were greatly complicated by cultural, political, and linguistic factors. In addition, the rise of Islam in the seventh century created a further wedge between those churches that accepted Chalcedon and the subsequent councils and those that did not. While there was some contact and dialogue during the Middle Ages, misunderstandings and language and cultural differences prevented an enduring reconciliation.

The portion of the Christian East that rejected the Council of Chalcedon developed parallel to those Orthodox churches of the Roman-Byzantine Empire. While some theological dialogues took place in the Middle Ages, no formal reconciliation was achieved. The fact that these churches, which did not accept Chalcedon, often existed in difficult political environments frequently limited their mission and theological development even into the twenty-first century. They have often been referred to as "Monophysite churches" and more recently as "Lesser Eastern Churches" or "Non-Chalcedonan Churches." Accepting the first three ecumenical councils, they claim to profess the Orthodox faith, express a different tradition in Christology, and possess distinctive liturgical traditions reaching back to the earliest days of Eastern Christianity.

Today, these churches use the title "Oriental Orthodox Churches." They are distinguished from the Orthodox Church, sometimes called Eastern Orthodox, which accepted Chalcedon and the related councils of 553, 680, and 787. The Oriental Orthodox Churches include: the Patriarchate of Alexandria (Coptic Orthodox) (3,900,000), the Patriarchate of Antioch (Syrian Orthodox) (250,000), the Church of Armenia (Armenian Apostolic; 6,000,000), the Church of Ethiopia (16,000,000), the Church of Malankara (India) (1,000,000), and the Church of Eritrea (1,700,000). While in full communion with one another, each church has its own distinctive history and liturgical traditions. Each also has a significant number of members living in Western Europe and North America.

Despite their formal division between the family of Oriental Orthodox churches and the family of Orthodox churches, theologians from both established an unofficial bilateral theological dialogue in 1964. This theological dialogue became formal in 1985. It is generally recognized today by theologians and church leaders in both families that the Christological differences between the Oriental Orthodox and the Orthodox were primarily a matter of terminological differences and that in fact both families of churches profess the same faith in Christ but use different theological terms.

Division Between the Orthodox Church and the Roman Catholic Churches. From the eighth century, signs of a growing estrangement between the Church of Rome and the Church of Constantinople together with portions of the churches of Alexandria, Antioch, and Jerusalem began to be evident in the wake of the iconoclastic controversy. Its first phase began following an imperial decree forbidding the veneration of icons by Emperor Leo III in 726. Initially, the veneration of icons was declared to be a form of idolatry, although the use of images, evidenced by the catacomb examples, dated from the earliest years of Christianity. With reference to the Old Testament, Leo III and his son Constantine V viewed "idolatry" as a cause of their political difficulties. Supported by Constantine V, a local council of bishops in 773 opposed the veneration of icons based upon Christological perspectives. Despite vicious persecution of the iconophiles, their theological perspectives eventually triumphed. The chief theological defenders of icons were John of Damascus, Theodore of Studios (759–826), and Nikephoros, patriarch of Constantinople (758–828). Empress Irene reversed the imperial policy and supported a new council held in 787 in Nicaea, which repudiated the iconoclastic positions. A second phase of iconoclasm arose in 714 but was formally ended in 843. A flowering of iconography followed. Throughout this period, the Church of Rome consistently opposed iconoclasm.

With the end of iconoclasm, the Church of Constantinople, supported by the government, entered into a vigorous period of missionary activity. Chief among the missionaries were Cyril (c. 826–869) and Methodios (c. 815–885). Sent by Patriarch Photios (c. 810–c. 895) first to evangelize the Khazars on the northeast side of the Black Sea in 860, the brothers eventually went to Greater Moravia. They created the Glagolithic alphabet and translated portions of the Scriptures and liturgical texts. Following their example, other missionaries worked especially among Slavic tribes of Central and Eastern Europe, inventing the Cyrillic alphabet as part of their activity. These missions provided the background for the formal conversion of the Kiev city-state under Prince Vladimir (956–1015) in 988. This established not only a bond with the Church of Constantinople but also a political and cultural relationship with the Byzantine world.

Photios was also involved in debates with the Church of Rome over issues that would subsequently be identified as the essential reasons for the "Great Schism." Pope Nicholas (d. 867) refused to recognize Photios's election in 863 following the deposition of the previous patriarch. Refusing to recognize the legitimacy of Nicholas's authority in the East, Photios in 867 authored a harsh letter denouncing Western missionaries in Bulgaria and the addition of the *filioque* (Latin for "and from the Son," professing the proceeding of the Holy Spirit from both the Father and the Son) to the Nicene-Constantinopolitan Creed in parts of the West. Ignatius, the previous patriarch, was restored in 867 and Photios was deposed. A council in Constantinople in 869 recognized the deposition. It was subsequently recognized as the Eighth Ecumenical Council by the Roman Catholic Church. Photios, however, was subsequently restored as patriarch. A new council in Constantinople in 879, with representatives of Pope John VIII, formally restored relations with Rome. Many Orthodox consider this the Eighth Ecumenical Council.

Since the ninth century, the *filioque* addition has remained a point of contention between the Orthodox East and the Catholic West. The Orthodox continue to recite the Nicene-Constantinopolitan Creed (381) in its original form, affirming that the Holy Spirit "proceeds from the Father," while the West expanded the wording to say that the Spirit "proceeds from the Father and the Son." The addition initially was introduced in Spain in the sixth century as a safeguard against Arianism. Behind the addition lies the Trinitarian theology of Augustine. The addition was adopted by the local bishop's council of Frankfurt (794). However, the addition was opposed by Pope Leo III. In the 860s Nicholas I supported the use of the *filioque* by Western missionaries in Bulgaria. The *filioque* was formally used in the Creed at the liturgy in Rome in 1014. From that time, Photios and the Byzantines held that the West had acted improperly to alter unilaterally the Creed that was the common heritage of the whole church. Photios also believed that the *filioque* expressed an incorrect understanding of the relationship among the persons of the Trinity.

Behind the *filioque* debate was also the question of the authority of the pope of Rome. Nicholas I had affirmed a universal supremacy of jurisdiction for the Roman see, over the East as well as the West. The Byzantines held that the pope, as senior among the five patriarchs, was accorded a "primacy of honor" but not a universal jurisdiction over and above other bishops. The bishop of Rome was regarded as the first bishop, but the first among equals. The Byzantines believed that while appeals could be made to the pope from the East, he did not have the right to intervene without request in the internal affairs of the other patriarchates. According to the Byzantine view, the pope cannot by himself decide questions of doctrine apart from the wider body of bishops. Thus, the East always looked to councils to resolve grave disputes.

There were also significant political developments in Western Europe. Determined to challenge the authority of the Roman Empire in Constantinople, Charlemagne was crowned Emperor of the Romans in 800 by Pope Leo III (d. 816). The papacy looked to the Carolingians for a political and military alliance. Likewise, Carolingian theologians were intent upon projecting Western theological perspectives and strengthening the position of the papacy, especially in relationship to the East. Misunderstanding the council of 787, the Carolingian theologians initially refused to accept its decision on the veneration of icons. Likewise, the Carolingians were firm proponents of the use of the *filioque* in the Creed. In a clear attempt to degrade the Byzantine Empire, the Carolingians refused to accord to it the title "Roman Empire," which the Byzantines consistently used. The Carolingians spoke disparagingly of it as the "Greek Empire," and they termed the Church of Constantinople as the "Greek Church."

The exact date of the Great Schism between East and West cannot easily be established because the separation was a gradual process extending from the ninth to at least the fifteenth century. The degree of alienation also varied in different places. The process focused chiefly upon the deterioration of the relationship between the Church of Rome and the Church of Constantinople. Differences in theological emphasis between the East and the West can be identified at least by the fourth century. Despite these, as well as the political estrangement, there was a fundamental sense of unity in faith and sacramental life that persisted well into the Middle Ages.

There were, however, serious differences developing in the understanding of authority in the church and especially the authority of the bishop of Rome. Different understandings of the role of the bishop of Rome in West and East were compounded by political developments in Western Europe. In the wake of the Germanic invasions and the growth of feudalism in Western Europe in the early Middle Ages, the church in Western Europe developed a highly centralized structure. This "feudal pyramid" placed the pope at the top. All other Western archbishops and bishops were placed in subservient positions to him.

The model of church governance in the West was compounded by political alliances between the papacy and the Franks in the late eighth and early ninth centuries. By the time of Pope Gregory VII (c. 1021–1085), however, the papacy sought to overcome political influence and other abuses that had developed during the feudal period. Influenced by the reform movements of Lorraine and Cluny, a number of influential popes advanced a strong doctrine of papal authority in relationship to Western political powers. As part of the reform movement, the papacy emphasized its independence from political rulers in Western Europe. It also reasserted the claim to universal jurisdiction over the churches of the East as well as the West. At the same time, the gradual Norman conquest of the Byzantine territories in Sicily and southern Italy, where Eastern Church traditions prevailed, also eliminated a significant bridge between East and West. The claims of the papacy were expressed with greater strength and emotion but with little appreciation for the perspectives of the East.

Sent by Pope Leo IX, Cardinal Humbert, bishop of Silva Candida, led a delegation to Constantinople in 1054. The mission of the delegation was to discuss growing tensions between Rome and Constantinople over theology and liturgical practices. Not received by Patriarch Michael Cerularios, Humbert placed a bull of excommunication against him on the altar of St. Sophia Cathedral on July 16, 1054, purportedly in the name of the pope. The anathema contained a number of charges against the East, including condemnation for failure to use the *filioque* in the Creed and neglect of papal authority. Also noted was the Eastern practice of using unleavened bread in the Eucharist and allowing a married priesthood. Believing that Humbert himself and not the pope initiated the action, Cerularios anathematized Humbert and his companions. While historians once used 1054 as the date of the schism, it is now recognized that the anathemas were very limited in scope. Humbert claimed to excommunicate Cerularios, not the emperor or the Eastern Church. Cerularios excommunicated Humbert, not the pope, who had died earlier. It appears that mutual acts were quickly forgotten, since sacramental communion between Rome and Constantinople and other parts of the East continued. The event of 1054 was a symptom of the deepening alienation.

While the Western Crusades sought to regain the Holy Land, they profoundly affected relations between Rome and the Eastern churches. In the captured cities, Eastern bishops were replaced by westerners, dividing the allegiance of the faithful and deepening the sense of alienation at the popular level. An expression of schism, rival patriarchs and bishops were commonplace in the Patriarchate of Antioch from 1100 and in Jerusalem from 1187. Diverted to Constantinople in 1204, the Fourth Crusade plundered the city and led to the temporary installation of a Latin patriarch there as well. The imposition of Western bishops loyal to Rome and to political powers in Western Europe became a tragic and visible expression of schism in Constantinople, Antioch, Jerusalem, and other cities. The clergy and faithful did not easily accept bishops imposed upon them. For them, this was a clear sign that Rome and Western rulers had little regard for the legitimacy of the ancient patriarchal churches of the East. While the Byzantines eventually recaptured the city in 1261 and the

Latin patriarch of Constantinople was removed to Rome, the destruction and sense of betrayal were not easily forgotten.

Between 1204 and 1453, when the Byzantine Empire fell, numerous attempts were made to address the theological and ecclesiological differences and to heal the schism between Rome and Constantinople. Two major attempts are noteworthy. At the Council of Lyons (1274), a small Byzantine delegation sent by Emperor Michael VIII Palaeologus (d. 1282) accepted the reunion terms of Pope Gregory X. Eventually repudiated in Constantinople, the meeting provided little opportunity for genuine dialogue. At the Council of Ferrara-Florence (1438–1439), there was a larger delegation from Constantinople, including Emperor John VIII and Patriarch Joseph II. With greater opportunity for discussion, the Byzantines recognized the Latin understanding of the procession of the Holy Spirit but were not required to add the *filioque* to the text of the Creed. The Byzantines also accepted an ambiguous view of the authority of the pope. Diverse practices were accepted in liturgical matters. A participant in the discussions, Mark Eugenikos (c. 1394–1445), archbishop of Ephesus, refused to accept the agreements, and the Council of Florence was formally rejected in Constantinople in 1484. At the same time, it was decided that individual Western Christians (Latins) would be anointed with holy oil upon entry into one of the other Eastern patriarchates. This was a liturgical expression of disunity with Rome, perceived to be in schism. The Roman Catholic Church, however, recognized the council and subsequently used it as a basis for the establishment of Eastern Catholic churches, known historically as the "unia" or "uniates," which accepted the full authority of the pope. The Patriarchate of Constantinople together with those of Alexandria, Antioch, Jerusalem, and the church of Cyprus, claiming to also be the apostolic and catholic church, eventually came to be known as the Orthodox Church.

During this period there was also a growing divergence in the theological traditions in the East and West and the issues with which their respective theologians dealt. Gregory Palamas (1296–1359) a monk from Mount Athos and later archbishop of Thessaloniki, represented the tradition of hesychaism. Especially significant was the recitation of the "Jesus Prayer." Confronted with the teachings of Barlam of Calabria (1290–c. 1350), Gregory affirmed the possibility of genuine personal encounter with God through prayer, experienced as divine light and involving the whole person, body and soul. In so doing, he followed Symeon the New Theologian (949–1022) and Gregory of Sinai (d. 1347). Gregory Palamas also spoke of the distinction between the divine essence, which is always hidden, and the divine energies or presence, which can be experienced in this life. His teachings were affirmed by three councils held at Constantinople (1341, 1347, 1351). A younger companion of Palamas, Nicholas Cabasilas (c. 1322–1395), a lay theologian, related hesychist theology especially to baptism and the Eucharist. The approach to God and the style of theological reflection exemplified by these teachers were quite different from that embodied in Western scholasticism expressed by Thomas Aquinas (c. 1225–1274). The Byzantines were not unconcerned with the relationship of reason and revelation. Yet in espousing an apophatic and more mystical approach to theology, they more readily affirmed the limitations of human speculation and the importance of prayer and worship for the transformation of the person.

The dramatic events of the fifteenth and sixteenth centuries hardened the alienation between the Roman Catholic Church centered on the pope of Rome and the Orthodox Church represented chiefly by the patriarchates of Constantinople, Alexandria, Antioch, and Jerusalem. The fall of Constantinople in 1453 marked the end of the Roman-Byzantine Empire. With the victory of the Ottoman Turks, the Church of Constantinople came under Muslim domination, thus joining the other patriarchates of the East.

While not directly involved in the Reformation debates, the Orthodox were not in a position to respond properly to the new issues raised in the West in the sixteenth century. After the fall of Constantinople in 1453, the Orthodox world, with the exception of Russia, was under the domination of the Ottomans. The Ottomans designated the Ecumenical Patriarchate of Constantinople as the head of the "Rum Millet," the Roman Orthodox people. Responsible to the sultan, the patriarch had ultimate religious and civil responsibility for all Orthodox regardless of language or culture in the Ottoman Empire. Treated as second-class citizens by the Ottomans, the life of the Orthodox and their church was gradually restricted. Orthodox had limited opportunities for advanced theological study in the East. Feeling oppressed, they adopted a defensive stance emphasizing survival. The Orthodox sought to maintain their patristic and liturgical inheritance, yet they failed to develop it in a creative manner. They were content with what has been called a "theology of repetition." During this period, a vast collection of spiritual texts known as the *Philokalia* was edited and published in 1782 by Makarios of Corinth (1731–1805) and Nikodimos of Mount Athos (c. 1749–1809). They were subsequently translated into Slavonic, Russian, Romanian, and more recently into English.

There was also a parallel tendency among some Orthodox theologians toward a form of westernization. Orthodox who could study in Western Europe were attracted to universities dominated by either Roman Catholicism or Protestantism. At the same time, some Roman Catholics and Protestants sought to enlist the Orthodox as their allies in the Western controversies. This meant that some Orthodox were challenged in difficult circumstances to reflect more deeply on new theological issues that had been raised during the Reformation and Counter-Reformation.

Between 1573 and 1581 Lutheran theologians at Tübingen engaged in correspondence with Patriarch Jeremias II of Constantinople (c. 1530–1595). In his responses the patriarch expressed traditional Orthodox teaching, generally avoiding both Catholic and Protestant perspectives and terminology. Later, however, Patriarch Cyril I (1572–1638) expressed clear Calvinist perspectives in his Confession of 1629 but gained few supporters among the Orthodox. Patriarch Dositheos of Jerusalem (1641–1707), in his Confession of Faith adopted at the Council of Jerusalem (1672), opposed Cyril but tended toward Roman Catholic perspectives and terminology. Metropolitan Petr Moghila of Kiev (1596–1646) expressed a strongly Latin style of theology within the Orthodox Church of the Ukraine. In the seventeenth century this "Latinizing" tendency later spread from Kiev to Moscow. Russian theology became increasingly influenced by Western perspectives, particularly through the influence of Feofan Prokopovich (1681–1736). Against this background, some discussions also took place between Anglicans and Orthodox between 1716 and 1725.

There were significant developments simultaneously in the Orthodox Church in Russia. Following the adoption of Christianity in Kiev in 988, the church flourished until the coming of Mongols in 1240. By the fourteenth century the center of civic and religious life had moved to Moscow. The Church of Russia, led by the metropolitan of Moscow, became autocephalous and independent from Constantinople in 1448. In 1589 Constantinople established the Patriarchate of Moscow and all Rus and ranked it after the ancient patriarchates. During the seventeenth century, a schism took place within the church following the reform of liturgical practices by Patriarch Nikon. Those who rejected the reforms were termed "Old Believers" or "Old Ritualists." Preferring closer governmental oversight, Czar Peter the Great abolished the patriarchal office in 1721 in favor of the synodical structure. Despite these limitations, there were significant missions in China, Japan, and Alaska in the eighteenth and nineteenth centuries. Likewise, a number of outstanding saintly teachers enriched church life. Among these were Paissy Velichkovsky (1722–1794), Seraphim of Sarov (1759–1833), Philaret of Moscow (1782–1867), and John of Kronstadt (1829–1908).

The Orthodox living in territories close to Catholic or Protestant countries eventually became the objects of proselytism. With political support from Poland and as a reaction to Protestantism, some Orthodox Christians living in the region of Ukraine entered into communion with Rome by decision of a council of bishops held in the city of Brest in 1595. Both clergy and laity were permitted to maintain many of their Eastern liturgical customs and much of their administrative organization. However, they professed ultimate loyalty to the pope of Rome and, in principle, Rome's view of the papacy. With Western political support, similar "unions" were established in Carpatho-Russia in 1646 and 1664, in Transylvania in 1700, and in Damascus in 1724. In other places, the Orthodox generally viewed these "unions" as tragic attempts to impose papal authority over their weakened church. By the year 1729, Rome formally forbade sacramental communion (*communio in sacris)* with the Orthodox, viewing them as schismatic. Being threatened both by Roman Catholic missionaries and Ottoman political influence, the Patriarchate of Constantinople in 1755 responded and advocated for a time the "rebaptism" of Roman Catholics who entered the Orthodox Church. This unprecedented recommendation did not reflect all of Orthodoxy and was subsequently overturned in 1888, yet such events indicate the level of estrangement and the formalization of the schism. Little formal contact between the Orthodoxy and Rome followed.

RECENT DEVELOPMENTS. The breakup of the Ottoman Empire led to the creation of new states in the Balkans. The Patriarchate of Constantinople granted autocephalous status to the churches of Greece (1833), Romania (1864), Bulgaria (1871), Serbia (1879), and later Albania (1937). Following the example of older Orthodox churches, these became fully responsible for their internal life while professing unity in the Orthodox faith.

The Church of Russia was profoundly affected by Bolshevik revolution in 1917 following the abdication of the czar and the civil war. On the eve of the revolution a historic church council reestablished the patriarchal office and elected Tikhon Belavin (1865–1925) of Moscow as patriarch. Other church reforms were prevented by the increase of persecution. Nearly all bishops and theologians were either executed or exiled in the 1920s and 1930s. About 85,000 priests were executed. Believers were systematically persecuted. Churches and monasteries were destroyed. With the Second World War, a *modus vivendi* between the church and the Soviet government was established, especially to defend against the Nazis threat. The internal life of the church, however, continued to be severely restricted. Only after 1989, with disintegration of the communistic system, did the plight of the church begin to improve. This has led to a dramatic growth of church members and the establishment of new churches, monasteries, and schools.

Following World War II the establishment of communist governments in Romania, Bulgaria, and Yugoslavia also led to restrictions on church life. Restrictions were lifted only after 1990 with the establishment of new governments. The church of Albania was especially impacted after the communist revolution of 1945. In the year 1967 the government began to close all churches and persecute Christians. Only in 1991, following the downfall of the communist government, was the church able to be restored. In many parts of Eastern Europe and the Middle East, Orthodox Christianity is only beginning to recover from the domination of repressive political and religious regimes.

The political and ecclesial developments of the late twentieth century led to new difficulties accompanied by the reemergence of ethnic and religious conflicts in the Balkans into which some Orthodox leaders were drawn, especially in Serbia. In Ukraine and Romania, tensions arose between Orthodox and Eastern Catholics over property rights. The Church of Russia repudiated the activities of evangelical

Protestant missionaries and the establishment of Roman Catholic dioceses. The churches of Bulgaria and Georgia experienced internal divisions reflective of political disputes. The undue emphasis on nationalism has tended to weaken a common witness and mission.

New and dramatic contacts between the churches of the Christian West and churches of the Christian East began in the late nineteenth century and intensified throughout the twentieth century. The ecumenical movement, with a goal of the visible unity of the churches, provided many opportunities for contact and theological dialogue. Each of the Orthodox Churches and the Oriental Orthodox Churches eventually became members of the World Council of Churches, founded in 1948. Their involvement provided opportunities for new contact and dialogues between the two Orthodox families, beginning informally in 1964, affirming agreement in a common Orthodox faith. In addition, the Orthodox, Oriental Orthodox, and the Assyrian Church of the East have established bilateral dialogues with the Roman Catholic Church. Participants in many of these dialogues have included leading contemporary Orthodox theologians.

The ecumenical dialogues have provided opportunities for a true engagement of Eastern and Western traditions of Christianity as well as for the examination and resolution of historic differences. At the same time, this encounter has enabled Western Christian theologians to move beyond a distorted perception of the Christian East. A false perception of the Christian East as essentially exotic, decadent, and moribund was reflected in the writings of Edward Gibbon (1737–1794) and Adolph von Harnack (1851–1930). Their influence can still be found in some studies that continue to marginalize the Christian East.

The migration of Eastern Christians to Western Europe, North and South America, and Australia in the late nineteenth and early twentieth centuries provided a basis for the growth of parishes and dioceses in cities where Western Christian churches were long established, sometimes improperly referred to as the "diaspora." Especially significant has been the steady growth of the Orthodox Church in the United States. While the Ecumenical Patriarchate claims ultimate canonical responsibility, most of the Orthodox jurisdictions remain directly connected to an autocephalous church. The largest, the Greek Orthodox Archdiocese, is a province of the Ecumenical Patriarchate. The Russian Orthodox Archdiocese (Metropolia), dating from the mission to Russian Alaska in 1794, received autocephaly (self-governing) status from the Church of Russia in 1970 and was renamed the Orthodox Church in America. This status, however, has not been recognized by most other Orthodox churches. While each jurisdiction began to serve a particular ethnic group, a remarkable process of indigenization has taken place as expressed in well-established parishes, dioceses, and theological schools serving about five million. This includes today persons from a wide variety of ethnic backgrounds, as well as persons raised in other religious traditions. Since 1960 the Standing Conference of Canonical Orthodox Churches (SCOBA), now representing nine jurisdictions, has been the major instrument of Orthodox unity and witness. It has also coordinated ecumenical dialogues, charitable endeavors worldwide, and missions especially in Africa and Asia. The presence of Orthodoxy in America has also provided many Western Christians with the opportunity to experience firsthand the spiritual and liturgical traditions of Eastern Christianity. This has been supported by a growing number of books and articles addressing various aspects of Eastern Christian theology, spirituality, liturgy, and history.

The Orthodox Church today is a communion of fourteen autocephalous churches and two autonomous churches. These are: the Ecumenical Patriarchate of Constantinople (3,500,000 approximate members), the Patriarchate of Alexandria (250,000), the Patriarchate of Antioch (750,000), the Patriarchate of Jerusalem (130,000), the Patriarchate of Russia (80,000,000), the Patriarchate of Serbia (8,000,000), the Patriarchate of Romania (19,800,000), the Patriarchate of Bulgaria (8,000,000), the Patriarchate of Georgia (3,500,000), the Church of Cyprus (442,000), the Church of Greece (9,025,000), the Church of Poland (570,000), the Church of Albania (160,000), and the Church of the Czech and Slovak Republics (55,000). The autonomous churches are: the Church of Finland (57,000) and the Church of Estonia (50,000).

Distinctive Theological Perspectives. Eastern Christianity, exemplified chiefly through the theology and life of the Orthodox Church, has had its own distinct historical development distinguishing it from both Roman Catholicism and Protestantism. At the same time, Orthodoxy has also preserved a distinctive expression of the Christian faith that its adherents believe is in continuity with the teachings of early Christianity and free from more recent Western Christian debates. Especially in the past five centuries, the Orthodox churches have not experienced the same theological discussions as those that took place within Roman Catholicism and Protestantism. These include, for example, Western debates over revelation and reason, faith and works, Scripture and tradition, or science and religion. The Christian East generally does not accept the dichotomies that have been part of the Western Christian traditions. One does not find a harsh distinction, for example, between the "City of God" and the "City of Man," between nature and super nature, body and spirit, Scripture and tradition, law and gospel, or sacred and secular.

The Triune God of revelation. Eastern Christianity teaches that the one God is a Triune God, known as Father, Son, and Holy Spirit. The one God has created all and is beyond all. Yet this God has acted to reveal himself and his love in history. While not diminishing the value of human reason and reflection, the Orthodox affirm that God is a mystery who is ultimately beyond human definition. The limited knowledge that we have of God results chiefly from the divine revelation and not from human speculation, important though it may be. Through this revelation, centered upon Christ, human persons have experienced a God who is a good God, *philanthropos,* a lover of humankind. This proclamation of the philanthropic God is at the heart of the worship and mission of the Orthodox Church. It is central to the life of each believer. Throughout the prayers of the Orthodox Church, one hears the affirmation: "You are a good God who loves humankind and to you we offer glory, Father, Son and Holy Spirit. . . ."

The reality of Christ and the event of his coming are the cornerstone of the Orthodox faith. The revelation of God to the ancient Israelites is fulfilled in the coming of Christ, the promised Messiah. Through his incarnation and in his person, a new relationship between divinity and humanity has been established that affects all. In the person of Jesus Christ, divinity is united with humanity in such a way that the distinctive character of each is maintained. The God who has created human persons and the entire world is not a distant and remote being. Rather, in order to express his love and restore persons to fellowship, God has united himself to humanity in the person of Christ.

The Orthodox have a high regard for the dignity and value of the human person, who is seen as naturally theocentric. From the moment of creation by God, the human person is fashioned with an orientation to God as the source of life. A natural and enduring relationship between each person and the Triune God is assumed, rooted in the very act of divine creation and deepened through the incarnation and the coming of the Spirit. This means that it is natural and healthy for the human person to live life in communion with the Triune God. It is unnatural for the human person not to be in a loving relationship with God. A source of much reflection in the Christian East, the biblical description of the human person as being created in the "image and likeness" of God (*Gen.* 1:26) is a profound affirmation that speaks both about the deep bond of love between God and each human person and the dignity of each person.

This bond was vividly expressed in the earthly ministry of Christ. Through his preaching and teachings, Christ revealed both the Triune God as *philanthropos* and the theocentric nature of the human person. In proclaiming the Kingdom of God, Christ announced a dramatic change in the course of history. Affirming the reign of God, Jesus spoke of the Father who loves each person and seeks a loving response from each person. He taught that the human person is most fully human when life is lived in communion with God and other persons through loving relationships. He promised that God the Holy Spirit would be a comforter and guide, nurturing those who know him as Lord. In his acts of forgiveness, Christ declared God's mercy for sinners and assistance to persevere. In his healings and exorcisms, Christ expressed the ability of God to overcome every evil power. Most importantly, the Resurrection of Christ is not only the heart of the gospel but also as the sign of God's ultimate victory over the power of death, evil, and Satan. The Resurrection of Christ is a bold proclamation that not even death is an obstacle to the Father's reconciling love. The Orthodox Easter hymn declares: "Christ is risen from the dead, conquering death by death, and upon those in the tombs he bestows life."

The Orthodox believe that Christ established the church with the call of his first disciples. It is a community of those who are called by God and who affirm Christ as Lord and Savior. The church is part of the divine plan of salvation centered upon Christ and enlivened by the Spirit from the first Pentecost. Through the life of the church, the Holy Spirit reveals the presence of the Risen Christ to persons of every age and every place and enables believers to share in his saving work. Because of the Spirit, Christ is not a distant person of history. The Holy Spirit leads persons from a life of self-centeredness to a life centered upon Christ and his gospel. The person of the Spirit is not subordinate to Christ, nor is the ministry of the Spirit inferior to that of Christ. The Spirit unites human persons to Christ, who leads them to the Father. Within this community of faith, believers have the opportunity to cultivate the bond of love not only with one another but also with the persons of the Holy Trinity. Both Christ and the Spirit work in harmony to accomplish the will of the Father, who desires that "everyone be saved and come to the knowledge of truth" (*I Tim.* 2:4). Under the guidance of the Spirit, the church has a mission to preach the gospel to all nations and to bear witness to the presence of the Risen Christ.

Salvation. These fundamental affirmations about God and the human person are the basis for the Eastern Christian view of salvation. From the very beginning the human person was fashioned in the "image and likeness" of God and given the vocation to live in communion with God (*Gen.* 1:26). A distortion in the natural relationship, however, was introduced into human history and is expressed in the story of the fall. The "ancestral sin," as the East speaks of "original sin," marked humanity's turning away from God. Yet the identity of the human person was never destroyed and the divine love was never diminished. While all sin and its consequences distorted the relationship between God and the human person, it could not destroy the fundamental bond between God the Father and his sons and daughters. Understood essentially as a new relationship with God the Father given in Christ, salvation is first an unmerited and free divine gift.

The term "deification" *(theosis)* is frequently used in the Christian East to describe the process of sanctification whereby the human person responds to the divine initiative and moves ever closer to the living God, through a life that reflects and imitates the divine love. The believer, following the example of Christ, must freely live in such a way that the relationship with God is deepened and strengthened. The gift of salvation must be freely received and actualized in the life of each believer. Through this relationship, the human person not only grows closer to God, the source of life and holiness, but also becomes more fully human. The process of deification begins at the very moment of personal creation and continues to the life that is to come. Love knows no limit and no boundary. For this reason, the great teachers of the church often declare: "God became human so that human persons may become divine."

Salvation is not simply personal but also communal. The Orthodox teach that believers grow in their relationship with God within the fellowship of the church. The rite of baptism establishes not only a personal relationship with Christ but also a relationship with all those others who are bound to Christ. Within this community of believers, the followers of Christ have the opportunity to deepen their love for as well as their understanding of God. They also have the support to live their lives in imitation of Christ within the responsibilities and obligation of daily life.

The theocentric person is also a person who is called to live in relationship with others. The inner orientation to the God of love is at the same time an orientation to other persons. The human person is not meant to be an autonomous or individualized self. Rather, the human person is meant to be a valuable member of a network of authentic relationships that contribute to well-being, wholeness, and holiness. Ultimately, these relationships of love contribute to the salvation of the whole world.

Authentic human relationships are those that nurture love, compassion, and mercy and make us more sensitive to the needs of the "other." Like God's relationship with us, our relationships with others are meant to be expressions of love, which heals and reconciles. In communion with God and others we grow in our human identity. The Orthodox take very seriously the old Christian adage "A solitary Christian is no Christian."

Relationships among believers are meant to be a constant reminder of the profound relationship that each of us has with every member of the human family. The Orthodox teach that each person, regardless of circumstance or belief, is created by the same God. Indeed, each of us has been united with God in a very intimate way through the humanity that Christ has shared.

Salvation also has its cosmic dimension. The Orthodox believe that human persons are not saved from the world but in and through the created world. The soul is not saved separately from the body but rather together with the body. The whole person, body and soul, is meant to share in the process of deification, beginning with the relationships and responsibilities of this life. Far from rejecting the body and the rest of the material creation, the Orthodox look upon the physical as the work of God and the medium through which the divine is manifest. The entire creation, good from the beginning, is related to the reality of the Incarnation of Christ.

The creation is the gift of a good and loving God, and although it is prone to distortion, both because of its createdness and because of human sin, it remains fundamentally valuable and "very good" because of its divine origin. By uniting himself with our humanity, Christ established a profound relationship not only with our human nature but also with the entire created order. The ultimate transfiguration of the entire cosmos is already prefigured not only in the lives of the faithful but also in the material of the Eucharist, the icons, and the relics of the saints.

The Orthodox Church makes constant use of the elements of the physical world in its worship. Bread and wine, water and oil, fruits and flowers are but a few of the many elements taken up by the church in its worship. In blessing these things of the earth, the church affirms that the physical world has its origins with God, that it possesses intrinsic value, and that it can be a vehicle of divine presence. This is the same principle that applies to the icon. It is composed of the "stuff of creation," wood and paint, or stone and glass. The icon is a valuable means of relating to God and one another.

Worship. Eastern Christianity has always emphasized the importance of worship. The gathering of believers, especially for the Eucharist, is an act of thanksgiving and praise offered in response to the presence and actions of the Triune God. Although Orthodox worship often can be very elaborate, solemn, and lengthy, it expresses a deep and pervasive sense of joy. This mood is an expression of belief in the Resurrection of Christ and the deification of humanity, dominant themes of Orthodox worship. In order to enhance this feeling and to encourage full participation, services are normally sung or chanted within a setting conducive to prayer.

Worship is not simply expressed in words. In addition to prayers, hymns, and Scripture readings, there are a number of ceremonies, gestures, and processions. The church makes rich use of nonverbal symbols to express God's presence and our relationship to him. Orthodox worship involves the whole person: intellect, feelings, and senses.

Services in the Orthodox Church follow a prescribed order, framework, and design, with a view to preserving its corporate dimension and strengthening a sense of unity and continuity. The content of the services is also prescribed. There are unchanging elements, and there are parts that change according to the feast, season, or particular circumstance. The regulating of the services indicates that worship is an expression of the entire church and not the composition on a particular priest and congregation.

Worship is also an important means of communicating the faith, especially through prayer. As the axiom says, the rule of prayer is the rule of faith (*lex orandi est lex credendi*). This means that the essential affirmations of the faith are expressed through worship. No universal or official language is prescribed, Orthodox worship having always been celebrated in the language of the people. Indeed, two or more languages may be used in the services to accommodate the needs of the congregation. Throughout the world Orthodox worship is celebrated in over fifty languages or dialects.

The Eucharist. Known as the Divine Liturgy, the Eucharist is the most important act of communal prayer for Orthodox Christians. In obedience to the command of the Lord given at the last supper (*Luke* 22:19), it has been celebrated regularly since the time of the apostles. At the Eucharist the community of believers gathers to hear Scripture, offer prayers, present the offering of bread and wine, recall the mighty acts of God, invoke the blessing of the Spirit, and receive Holy Communion as an expression of union with Christ and one another. It is an action, the Orthodox believe, that manifests the presence of Christ in the midst of his followers and is an expression of the kingdom to come.

The Eucharist is celebrated on Sunday morning, the day commemorating the Resurrection. It may also be offered on most weekdays, especially on feast days and saint days according to local custom. It is celebrated only once a day to emphasize and maintain the unity of the local congregation. While an ordained bishop or priest is necessary, the Divine Liturgy is never celebrated without a congregation. In many places the greater participation of the congregation and the frequent reception of Holy Communion are being strongly encouraged.

As it is celebrated today, the Divine Liturgy is a product of rich historical development. The fundamental core of the liturgy dates from the time of Christ and the apostles. To this, prayers, hymns, and gestures have been added. The liturgy achieved a basic framework by the ninth century. There are two principle forms of the Eucharist presently in use in the Orthodox Church. While their structure is the same, there are differences in prayers and hymns. The Liturgy of St. John Chrysostom is the version most frequently celebrated. The Liturgy of St. Basil the Great is celebrated especially during Lent. According to local custom, the Liturgy of St. James and the Liturgy of St. Mark are occasionally used. In addition, there is also the Liturgy of the Pre-Sanctified Gifts. Used on weekday evenings during Lent, this is a Vesper service followed by the distribution of Holy Communion reserved from the previous Sunday. The Orthodox affirm the presence of Christ in the eucharistic bread and wine but generally avoid using terms such as "transubstantiation" to express the reality. A portion of the eucharistic gifts is reserved for the communion of the sick, but it is not used for any other forms of devotions. Only baptized believers may receive Holy Communion. Except in emergencies, the Orthodox do not offer Holy Communion to members of other Christian churches because of the state of disunity over teachings.

Sacraments and prayers. The Orthodox Church has never formally determined a particular number of sacraments. In recent centuries, however, catechisms have frequently identified seven. With the Eucharist at the center, these rites are events of church life when the perception of God's actions in the lives of particular persons is heightened and celebrated. All the sacraments lead toward and flow from the Eucharist, which is at the center of the life of the Church. Traditionally, the sacraments are known as Mysteries in the Orthodox Church because they not only celebrate and reveal the presence of God but also make believers receptive to God. All the sacraments affect our personal relationship to God and to one another, although they are addressed to each person by name.

The sacraments are composed of prayers, hymns, Scripture lessons, and gestures. The Orthodox have avoided reducing the sacraments to a particular formula or action. Often, a whole series of rites make up a sacrament. Most use a portion of the material of creation as an outward and visible sign of God's presence and action. Water, oil, bread, and wine are but a few of the many elements employed. The frequent use of the material of creation affirms that matter is good and can become a medium of the Spirit. In addition, the use of creation affirms the central truth of the Orthodox Christian faith: that God became human in Jesus Christ and entered into the midst of creation, thereby redirecting the cosmos toward its Creator.

The sacrament of baptism with a threefold immersion in water in the name of the Holy Trinity publicly incorporates persons into the church. The act is a sign of new life and an identification with the death and Resurrection of Christ. Orthodoxy encourages the baptism of infants of believing parents. The sacrament bears witness to the action of God who calls a child to be a valued member of his people. From the day of their baptism, children are expected to mature in the life of the Spirit, through their family and the church. This practice reveals that Orthodoxy views children from their infancy as important members of the church. There is never time when the young are not part of God's people. Following a period of preparation, the baptism of adults is also practiced when there was no previous baptism in the name of the Holy Trinity.

Chrismation (confirmation) immediately follows baptism and is never delayed until a later age. It is a personal Pentecost, which signifies the coming of the Holy Spirit. The priest anoints the various parts of the body of the newly baptized with holy oil saying, "The seal of the gifts of the Holy Spirit." The sacrament emphasizes that the Spirit blesses each person with spiritual gifts and talents. The anointing also reminds us that our bodies are valuable and are involved in the process of salvation. Those who are received into the Orthodox Church and have been previously baptized in the name of the Holy Trinity are usually anointed with the same holy oil.

Confession is the sacrament through which sins are forgiven and the relationship to God and to others is restored and strengthened. According to Orthodox teaching, the penitent confesses to God and is forgiven by God. Viewed not as a judge but as a physician and guide, the priest bears witness to the presence and action of Christ and his people. Confession can take place on any number of occasions according to the needs of the believer. In the event of serious sin, however, confession is a necessary part of the preparation for Holy Communion. Orthodoxy encourages every believer to have a spiritual father or mother to whom the believer turns for spiritual advice and counsel.

The church blesses the relationship between a man and a woman and affirms the action of God in their lives through the sacrament of marriage. They enter into a new relationship with each other, God, and the church. Marriage is not viewed simply a social institution or legal contract. It is an eternal vocation of the Kingdom of God extending into the age to come. A husband and a wife are called by the Holy Spirit not only to live together but also to share their Christian life together so that each, with the aid of the other, may grow closer to God and become the persons they are meant to be. In the marriage service, after the couple have been betrothed and exchanged rings, crowns are placed on their heads as a sign of "glory and honor" of their vocation. Near the conclusion of the service, the husband and wife drink from a common cup of wine, reminiscent of the wedding of Cana and symbolizing the sharing of the burdens and joys of their new life together. It is expected that the marriage relationship is permanent and eternal. However, in cases where the marital relationship breaks down, the church may grant an ecclesiastical divorce and permit a second marriage.

Through the sacrament of ordination (holy orders), those who have been chosen from within the church are set apart by the church for special service to the church. God calls each through his people to serve the needs of the community. The process of ordination begins with the local congregation, but the bishop alone, who acts in the name of the wider church, can complete the action. Ordinations always take place within the context of the Eucharist. The rite involves the invocation of the Holy Spirit and the imposition of his hands on the person being ordained. There are three major orders—bishop, priest, and deacon—each of which requires a particular ordination. Often, other titles and offices are associated with these three orders. Each order is distinguished by its pastoral responsibilities within the community. Only a bishop may ordain. Persons may choose to marry before they are ordained. Since the sixth century, bishops have been chosen only from the celibate clergy. Since the early church, women have been ordained as deacons but less so in recent centuries. There have been formal calls for a revival of this practice.

The sacrament of the anointing of the sick (holy unction) is offered to believers who are ill or weak in body, mind, or spirit, not simply those in danger of death. As with chrismation, oil is also used as a sign of God's presence, strength, and forgiveness. After the reading of seven epistle lessons and seven gospel lessons and the offering of seven prayers, the priest anoints the body with the holy oil. In many places, this sacrament is also celebrated for all on Wednesday of Holy Week.

The Orthodox have many other blessings and special services of prayer that complement the major sacraments and that reflect the presence of God through the lives of the faithful. Among the more significant are the Great Blessing of Water on the Feast of the Theophany, January 6, the monastic profession, and the rites of burial.

There is also a fundamental connection between the prayers of the community and the prayer of the home, called the "domestic church." Prayer in the home also has a special importance for Orthodox believers. They are expected to have a personal "rule of prayer" to be followed during the course of the day, normally in the morning and evening. In most homes of Orthodox Christians, there is usually a corner or shelf where icons are prominently displayed with a vigil light. Here at the "home altar" family prayers are offered. The traditional Book of Prayers contains numerous prayers addressing the events and responsibilities of daily life. They serve to remind the believer of the presence of God through all aspects of life.

Holy Scripture. The Orthodox have a high regard for the Holy Scriptures. The book of the Gospels is prominently placed on the altar, and at least one selection from Scriptures is read at the every service of common worship. The Orthodox recognize twenty-seven books in the New Testament and forty-nine books in the Old Testament. The Orthodox recognize that the Bible, a collection of diverse texts written at different time periods and places, and in a variety of literary styles, is inspired by the Spirit through the hands of human persons. The books have been collected by the community of believers for the sake of nurture and teaching. This means that the Orthodox view the Scriptures as the "books of the church." They must be read by the faithful and interpreted within the broader context of the tradition of the church. The Scriptures are not always clear or self-explanatory. Here, tradition refers to the essential faith affirmations about the Holy Trinity, the human person, and all reality, which are professed by the church. These affirmations are rooted in the divine revelation centered on Christ, and they are transmitted in and through the believing community.

While Scriptures are given preeminence within tradition, reference can also be made to the faith expressed in other aspects of church life. These would include the Eucharist and other forms of liturgical prayer, hymns, iconography, the doctrinal decisions of the councils, the teachings of the Fathers and Mothers, as well as the witness of the saints. Through all of these, the Spirit can act to nurture the believer in the truth of the faith and deepen the relationship with the Triune God.

The Fathers and Mothers. Eastern Christianity has a special devotion to the Fathers and Mothers of the church. There is no absolute definition of such persons. Generally, the name is given to important teachers of the faith who are honored because of their sanctity and spiritual wisdom. Among the more prominent are those who were involved in the Trinitarian and Christological discussions of the early church. In every age, however, these teachers are concerned with relating the faith of the church to particular concerns and issues. They are very much people of their age and have to be understood as such. In facing the issues of their day, these teachers sought to affirm the intimate connection between theological reflection, the rule of prayer, and the life of virtue.

The icon. Eastern Christianity in general and the Orthodox Church in particular are especially known for its iconography. Forms of iconography have existed from the earliest days of the church, as evidenced by those primitive drawings in the catacombs of Rome. Icons may depict Christ, Mary, the Mother of God, and the other saints. At first glance, many icons appear simply educational because they can depict scenes from the Old and New Testaments or from the later history of the church. But more than this, icons are meant to assist the believer in being drawn closer to the person depicted. Icons are not worshiped, yet they may serve as vehicles through which veneration is offered to Christ and the saints and through which the presence of God is communicated to believers.

Most of the icons of the saints depict them in a historical setting. The saint is pictured in a manner that appears to express his or her transfiguration, sometimes accompanied by a symbolic expression of the saint's particular ministry or task in life. Sometimes the saint is depicted in the company of others, even pets or other animals. For the Orthodox, the saints dwell now in the glory of the kingdom. Yet the icon is a clear reminder that the saint grew in holiness within the context of the relationships and responsibilities of daily life. The icon is also a reminder that life is meant to be lived in harmony with God and others in the midst of the creation.

BIBLIOGRAPHY

Surveys

Valuable surveys covering history and doctrine of the Orthodox Church are John Meyendorff's *The Orthodox Church: Its Past and Its Role in the World Today,* rev. ed. (New York, 1981), and Timothy (Kallistos) Ware, *The Orthodox Church* (1964; reprint, New York, 1983). An older study by Nicholas Zernov, *Eastern Christendom: A Study of the Origins of the Eastern Orthodox Church* (London, 1961), provides a good overview. Other Eastern churches are covered extensively in A. S. Atiya's *A History of Eastern Christianity* (Notre Dame, Ind., 1965). For a comprehensive description of all the Eastern churches with contemporary information, see Ronald Robinson, *The Eastern Christian Churches: A Brief Survey,* 6th ed. (Rome, 1999).

Historical Development

An outstanding study of the church in Byzantium is J. M. Hussey, *The Orthodox Church in the Byzantine Empire* (Oxford, 1986). On the development of theology in the Byzantine period, the best summary is John Meyendorff's *Byzantine Theology: Historical Trends and Doctrinal Themes,* 2nd ed. (New York, 1979). See also his *Imperial Unity* (Crestwood, N.Y., 1989) and *Byzantium and the Rise of Russia* (Crestwood, N.Y., 1989). As part of his extensive history of doctrine, see Jaroslav Pelikan's *The Christian Tradition: A History of the Development of Doctrine,* vol. 2, *The Spirit of Eastern Christendom, 600–1700* (Chicago, 1974). Dimitri Obolensky's *The Byzantine Commonwealth: Eastern Europe, 500–1453* (London, 1971) provides a clear and authoritative picture. More specialized studies include, Anthony-Emil Tachiaos, *Cyril and Methodios of Thesalonika: The Acculturation of the Slavs* (Thessaloniki, 1989); Demetrios Constantelos, *Byzantine Philanthropy and Social Welfare* (New Brunswick, N.J., 1968); and Steven Runciman, *The Great Church in Captivity* (Cambridge, 1968). A small but very attractive introduction to the art of the Byzantine world is Rowena Loverance, *Byzantium* (Cambridge, Mass., 2004).

Issues of division in the fifth and sixth century are examined in John Meyendorff, *Christ in Eastern Christian Thought* (New York, 1975); Sabastian P. Brock, *Studies in Syriac Christianity* (Brookfield, Vt., 1992) and *From Ephrem to Romanos* (Brookfield, Vt., 1999; Paul Fries and Tiran Nersoyian, eds. *Christ in East and West* (Macon, Ga., 1987); H. Hill, ed., *Light from the East: A Symposium on the Oriental Orthodox and Assyrian Churches* (Toronto, 1988); and Wilhelm Baum and Dietmar Winkler, *The Church of the East* (London, 2003). Older but reliable studies are R. V. Sellers, *The Council of Chalcedon: A Historical and Doctrinal Survey* (London, 1953) and Karikin Sarksian, *The Council of Chalcedon and the Armenian Church* (London, 1965).

On the schism between Orthodoxy and Rome, Steven Runciman's *The Eastern Schism: A Study of the Papacy and the Eastern Churches during the Eleventh and Twelfth Centuries* (Oxford, 1955) is a classic, well-documented study. See also, Michael Fahey, *Trinitarian Theology East and West* (Brookine, Mass., 1977); Richard Haugh, *Photios and the Carolingians* (Belmont, Mass., 1975); Philip Sherrard's *The Greek East and the Latin West: A Study in the Christian Tradition* (London, 1959); Yves Congar's *After Nine Hundred Years: The Background of the Schism between the Eastern and Western Churches* (New York, 1959); Francis Dvornik, *Byzantium and the Roman Primacy* (New York, 1966); and George Every, *Misunderstanding Between East and West* (Richmond, Tenn., 1966). For a full treatment of the hesychastic controversy, see John Meyendorff's *A Study of Gregory Palamas* (London, 1964).

A classic account of the Turkish period, is Steven Runciman's *The Great Church in Captivity: A Study of the Patriarchate of Constantinople from the Eve of the Turkish Conquest to the Greek War of Independence* (Cambridge, 1968). On the Catholic communities, see Charles A. Frazee's *Catholics and Sultans: The Church and the Ottoman Empire, 1453–1923* (Cambridge, 1983). More recent developments in the Church of Russia and the Slavic world are found in James Cunningham, *A Vanquished Hope: Movements for Church Renewal in Russia* (Crestwood, N.Y., 1981); Dimitri Pospielovsky, *The Russian Church Under the Societ Regime, 1917–1982* (Crestwood, N.Y., 1984); and J. Ellis, *The Russian Orthodox Church: A Contemporary History* (London, 1986).

Essays on some developments in the Eastern churches can be found in Ion Bria, *Martyria and Mission: The Witness of the Orthodox Churches Today* (Geneva, 1980) and Petro Ramet, ed., *Eastern Christianity and Politics in the Twentieth Century* (Durham, N.C., 1988). For the development of the Orthodox Church in the United States, see Thomas FitzGerald, *The Orthodox Church* (Westport, Conn., 1995).

The story of the ecumenical movement, including Orthodox involvement, is found in Thomas FitzGerald, *The Ecumenical Movement: An Introductory History* (Westport, Conn., 2004). See also, Ion Bria, *The Sense of Ecumenical Tradition: The Ecumenical Witness and Vision of the Orthodox* (Geneva, 1991). For dialogue statements see: Christine Chaillot and Alexander Belopopsky, eds, *Towards Unity: The Theological Dialogue Between the Orthodox Church and the Oriental Orthodox Churches* (Geneva, 1998), and John Borelli and John Erickson, ed., *The Quest for Unity: Orthodox and Catholics in Dialogue* (Crestwood, N.Y., 1996).

Some contemporary issues are discussed in: Anastasios Yanoulatos, *Facing the World* (Crestwood, N.Y., 2003); Kyriaki Karidoyanes FitzGerald, *Women Deacons in the Orthodox Church* (Brookline, Mass., 1999); Emmanuel Clapsis, ed., *The Orthodox Churches in a Pluralistic World* (Brookline, Mass., 2004); and John Erickson, *The Challenge of the Past* (Crestwood, N.Y., 1991).

Doctrinal Themes

Among the contemporary treatments of Orthodox theology, see John D. Zizioulas, *Being as Communion: Studies in Personhood and the Church* (Crestwood, N.Y., 1985) and his *Eucharist, Bishop and Church* (Brookline, Mass., 2002); Dumitru Staniloae, *The Experience of God* (Brookline, Mass., 2000); Christos Yannaras, *The Freedom of Morality* (Crestwood, N.Y., 1984); Kallistos Ware, *The Orthodox Way* (Crestwood, N.Y., 1995); Maximos Aghiorgoussis, *In the Image of God* (Brookline, Mass., 1999); Boris Bobrinskoy, *The Mystery of the Trinity* (Crestwood, N.Y., 1999); and Stanley Harakas, *Wholeness of Faith and Life: Orthodox Christian Ethics*, Parts 1–3 (Brookline, Mass., 1999). An older valuable study is Vladimir Lossky, *The Mystical Theology of the Eastern Church* (London, 1957). The extensive writings of Georges Florovsky critically examine numerous theological themes. See his *Collected Works*, Volumes 1–5 (Belmont, Mass., 1974–1979). A comprehensive examination of Florovsky's contribution is Andrew Blane, *Georges Florovsky: Russian Intellectual, Orthodox Churchman* (Crestwood, N.Y., 1993). On approaches to the Scriptures, see Dimitrios Trakatellis, *Authority and Passion* (Brookline, Mass., 1987); Veselin Kesich's *The Gospel Image of Christ: The Church and Modern Criticism* (Crestwood, N.Y., 1987); and John Breck, *The Power of the Word in the Worshipping Church* (Crestwood, N.Y., 1986).

Worship and Spirituality

Rich insights into worship in the Christian East are found in the many books of Alexander Schmemann. See his *Introduction to Liturgical Theology* (Leighton Buzzards, U.K., 1996), *For the Life of the World* (Crestwood, N.Y., 1973), *Of Water and the Spirit* (Crestwood, N.Y., 1974), and *The Eucharist* (Crestwood, N.Y., 1988). See also Alkiviadis Calivas, *Aspects of Orthodox Worship* (Brookline, Mass., 2003) and *Great Week and Pascha in the Greek Orthodox Church* (Brookline, Mass., 1992).

Valuable perspectives into the Eastern Christian spirituality are found in: Kallistos Ware, *The Inner Kingdom* (Crestwood, N.Y., 2000); Andrew Louth, *The Origins of the Christian Mystical Tradition* (Oxford, 1981); Oliver Clement, *The Roots of Christian Mysticism* (London, 1993); K. M. George, *The Silent Root* (Geneva, 1994); Kyriaki Karidoyanes FitzGerald and Thomas FitzGerald, *Happy in the Lord: The Beatitudes for Everyday* Brookline, Mass., 2000); Tomas Spidlik, *The Spirituality of the Christian East* (Kalamazoo, Mich., 1986); and Paul Evdokimov, *The Sacrament of Love: The Nuptial Mystery in the Light of the Orthodox Tradition* (Crestwood, N.Y., 1985). Among the many collections of liturgical services, see Mother Mary and Kallistos Ware, eds., *The Festal Menaion* (London, 1969) and *The Lenten Triodion* (Boston, 1978). A collection of texts on the spiritual life see, Nikodimos of the Holy Mountain and Makarios of Corinth, eds., *The Philokalia*, translated and edited by G. E. H. Palmer, Philip Sherrard, and Kallistos Ware, vols. 1–4 (London and Boston, 1979–1984). An outstanding introduction to the theology of the icon is Leonid Ouspensky and Vladimir Lossky, *The Meaning of Icons* (New York, 1982).

THOMAS E. FITZGERALD (2005)

EAST SYRIAN CHURCH SEE NESTORIAN CHURCH

EBIONITES is the name given to a Jewish Christian sect that flourished during the early history of the Christian church. The origin of the term, a Hebrew word meaning *poor persons*, is obscure. It may have been an honorific title given to an original group of Christians who were Jews living in Jerusalem that needed assistance from Christians elsewhere in the Roman Empire (*Rom.* 15:25, *2 Cor.* 9:12). It was first used by the Christian bishop Irenaeus of Lyons (Gaul) in the late second century to designate a Jewish Christian sect. Some later writers used it ironically to refer to the poverty of understanding of the members of the sect, who did not believe that Jesus Christ was the divine Son of God. There is no evidence to support the claim of some Christian writers that it derived from a person named Ebion, the supposed founder of the sect.

The origin, history, and distinct character of the Ebionites have been subjects of intense debate. It is possible that the Ebionites go back to the earliest period of Christian history, when most Christians were Jews and some continued to observe the Jewish law. If so, they would be the earliest example of a Christian movement within Judaism that was eventually left behind as Christianity adapted to the influx of Gentile converts. These Christians eventually became a distinct group that, along with other groups (e.g., the Gnostics), was rejected as heretical by the emerging great church. They are sometimes identified with the minim (heretics), mentioned in the Talmud.

The Ebionites were Jews who accepted Jesus of Nazareth as the Messiah (Christ) while continuing to maintain their identity as Jews. They cultivated relations with Jews as well as Christians though they were welcomed by neither. They followed the Jewish law, insisting on circumcision, keeping the Sabbath and celebrating the Jewish festivals (Yom Kippur, Passover), and observing the dietary laws (e.g., abstention from pork) and other Jewish customs. They repudiated the apostle Paul because of his denigration of the Jewish law. They saw Jesus as a prophet, an exceptional man in the line of Jewish prophets (as described in *Deut.* 18:15), and denied the virgin birth. They justified their way of life by appealing to the example of Jesus' life: he was circumcised, observed the Sabbath and celebrated the Jewish festivals, and taught that all the precepts of the law should be observed. They celebrated Easter on the same day that the Jews celebrated the Passover, and they held the city of Jerusalem in high esteem.

Besides the Ebionites there were other Jewish Christian sects, such as the Nazarenes, the Symmachians, and the Elkesaites, but it is difficult to distinguish one from the other, and the names are not used with any consistency. Ebionite is the most common designation, and it may simply have been a term used to characterize any form of Jewish Christianity with a stress on the observance of Jewish law. Although early Christian writings directed against heresy sometimes linked the Ebionites with other heretical groups, such as the Gnostics, the distinctiveness of the Ebionites lies less in their doctrines than in their attitude toward the Jewish law.

The Ebionites had their own gospel, but it is not possible to reconstruct its content in any detail. Ancient writers mention three Jewish Christian gospels, but because of the fragmentary nature of our information, it is difficult to distinguish these works clearly. The *Gospel of the Ebionites* (a modern designation) may have been similar to the Gospel of Matthew, but it did not include the narrative of the virgin birth and Jesus' infancy.

Information on the Ebionites is scattered over three centuries, from the middle of the second to the middle of the fifth, suggesting that the sect had a continuous history as a distinct group from the earliest period. A continuous history cannot be documented, however, and it is more likely that the persistence of people called by the name Ebionites is evidence that within Christianity, in spite of the break with Judaism and the bitter polemic against Jewish practices, there continued to spring up groups of Christians who believed that one could be a Christian and still observe the Jewish law.

The greatest strength of the Ebionites was in Palestine and Syria, areas where Judaism flourished. One community of Ebionites lived in Pella, east of the Jordan River, and claimed to be descended from the original group of Christians, who were thought to have fled Jerusalem at the time of the war with the Romans in 70 CE. There was a resurgence of Jewish Christianity in the late fourth century, encouraged by Jewish messianism and the emperor Julian's attempt to rebuild the Temple in Jerusalem. Jews began to hope for their return to Jerusalem and Judaea, a rebuilding of the Temple, and restoration of sacrifices—the beginning of a messianic age. After this period little is known of the Ebionites.

BIBLIOGRAPHY

Klijn, Albertus Frederik Johannes, and G. J. Reinink. *Patristic Evidence for Jewish-Christian Sects.* Leiden, 1973.

Schoeps, Hans Joachim. *Theologie und Geschichte des Judenchristentums.* Tübingen, Germany, 1949.

Simon, Marcel. *Verus Israel: Étude sur les relations entre chrétiens et juifs dans l'Empire romain, 135–425.* Paris, 1964.

Strecker, Georg. "Ebioniten." In *Reallexikon für Antike und Christentum.* Stuttgart, 1959.

New Sources

Goulder, Michael. "A Poor Man's Christology." *New Testament Studies* 45 (1999): 332.

ROBERT L. WILKEN (1987)
Revised Bibliography

EBLAITE RELIGION.

EBLAITE RELIGION. The archaeological excavations carried out in the ancient city of Ebla have brought to light a library with thousands of clay tablets that inform us in detail about the politics, economy, and religion of third-millennium BCE Syria. These cuneiform texts have provoked great interest among scholars. Ebla's geographical position near the Syro-Palestinian region described in the Bible, as well as the presence in the Eblaite onomasticon of anthroponyms similar to those of the biblical patriarchs, have caused a heated debate among scholars of different tendencies.

THE EBLAITE PANTHEON. Although archaeologists have not been able to identify particular buildings from the third millennium as temples, it is clear from these texts that the city of Ebla must have contained a large number of religious buildings dedicated to the various divinities of their pantheon, since the Eblaites were in fact a polytheistic people. The pantheon, as seen in the epigraphic material, is clearly Western Semitic, and in this respect the Eblaite civilization differs from civilizations of the Mesopotamian world. Of course scholars at Ebla were aware of the Sumerian gods, and the Eblaite texts include a bilingual vocabulary with a section dedicated to listing the Sumerian gods who could be partly identified with Eblaite gods; for example, Inanna, the Sumerian goddess of love and war, is equated with Ishtar, the Western Semitic goddess with the same attributes, and Nergal, the Sumerian god of the underworld, is compared to Rasap, in later times Rasef, the god of plague.

Confirming what is already known from later literature, the texts from Ebla show that certain syncretic processes had not yet occurred. For example, Enlil, the supreme god of the Sumerian pantheon, was equated in the second millennium to the principal god of the Western Semitic pantheon; at Ebla, however, at least according to the bilingual vocabulary, the two divinities were not regarded as equivalent. At Ebla, as throughout the whole of Western Semitic civilization, Dagan is the principal god, and he is regarded as distinct from the Sumerian Enlil. This suggests deep intellectual reflection among the Eblaite writers, along with a spiritual maturity in their religious belief, indicating perfect knowledge of the divine world.

The Eblaite pantheon is indeed Semitic, and its chief god is Dagan, but together with familiar Semitic gods, such as Ishtar, Baal, Rasap, Kamish, Sipish, Adad, Sin, and Shamagan, we also find Hurrite gods, such as Ashtapi, Ishhara, and Hepat, and perhaps even Teshup. There are also gods that are otherwise completely unknown, such as the divine pair Kura and Barama, protective divinities of the Eblaite kingdom; Kakkab ("the star"), possibly Venus; and NI.DA.KUL (the spelling is uncertain), identified by some scholars as the moon god, who must have been part of the Eblaite pantheon, or more recently with Adad-Baal of later tradition. It is also striking that the guardian god of the city of Ebla is Dabir, who is known from the Bible.

Certain aspects of Eblaite religion are completely novel conceptually and anticipate much later developments. In particular, two pertinent and highly significant patterns of Eblaite thought reveal the remarkable flexibility and tolerance of this civilization. The first and most apparent novelty lies in the Eblaite practice of honoring not only their own divinities but also those of other cities and kingdoms both on lists of official offerings made by the royal household and in offerings made by private individuals. The recipients of the offerings are not only gods of the city and kingdom of Ebla, but also gods from various other kingdoms and cities of central-northern Syria. From sacrificial offerings to the god NI.DA.KUL of Arukatu, Æama, and Luban, as well as to Adad of Abati, Atanni, Æalam, Lub, and so on, we can clearly see that the Eblaites welcomed gods venerated in other cities into their pantheon. Frequent mention of gifts ("offerings to the gods") being dispatched by the Eblaite court to the most distant locations—Adab in southern Mesopotamia, Gasur in northern Mesopotamia, and Byblos on the Mediterranean coast in Lebanon—all lead to the same conclusion.

There would have been political reasons for this religious attitude towards foreign divinities, but it remains the case that the Eblaites, by behaving in this way, demonstrated open-mindedness, flexibility, and sensitivity to the needs of those with whom they came into contact. In contrast to the jealous reaction of the Sumerians, Assyrians, Babylonians, and Hebrews to the gods of other peoples and their rigid rejection of foreign religious traditions, one cannot help but be struck by the openness of the Eblaites in dealing with the varied religious observances of peoples with whom they had political and economic relationships.

The second novelty is the particular concept of divinity held by the Eblaites, which, notwithstanding their widespread polytheism, took the form of henotheism and a theoretical concept of god. Dagan in particular rises to a leading, nearly unique role. In votive texts and in onomastic writings Dagan is often referred to not by his own name but with the title *Lord*, which corresponds to the Semitic *belu.* In various religious references linked to particular cities, we find the expression "Lord of the gods" and "Lord of the country," confirming Dagan's leading role among the Eblaite gods and his undisputed position as the principal Semitic god in the third millennium. In an inscription of Sargon of Akkad, Dagan is said to have presented to the king the Upper Country, confirming what the Eblaite texts say about the status of this god.

The use of the term *Lord* instead of the name *Dagan* has profound implications in terms of religious history. It is clear that Dagan is present under a wide range of aspects and conceptual representations, as demonstrated by the numerous occasions where *^{d}Be Lord* is followed by a geographical reference. This perhaps provides an answer to an even more intriguing question, with all that this implies in terms of religious history: Dagan, although the principal god, or perhaps by virtue of being so, is not called by his own name, but rather by the term *Lord.* We thus find ourselves dealing with a religious concept very different from that in Mesopotamia, on the basis of which the name of the god could not be spoken, as is the case in other important ancient religions. This suggestive question, implicitly requiring an affirmative response, makes us realize the enormous contribution of Ebla to the understanding of later historico-religious phenomena.

This view of the role of Dagan finds unexpected onomastic support, permitting us to draw the conclusion that the Eblaites had already arrived at an abstract concept of divinity in the third millennium. It is indeed highly probable that the theophoric designations *-il* and *-ya* that are often mentioned in onomastic texts do not indicate the god Il or the god Ya as individual personal gods, but rather *god* as such or the concept of the divine. The use of the term *Be* for Dagan and of *-il* and *-ya* for divinity itself does not mean that we can talk of definite monotheism among the Western Semitic peoples; rather we can legitimately conclude that at the very least the Eblaites had an extremely advanced concept of the divine and were certainly very close to henotheism.

EBLAITE CULT. Turning from speculation to everyday life in Ebla, the deeply religious nature of the Eblaites is evident from the divine worship of both private citizens and the royal family. Eblaite texts concerning economic matters regularly catalogue offerings, bloody and unbloody, presented to the divine world in general and to individual gods to gain their favorable intercession in every aspect of life, and especially on important occasions, such as marriage or illness. The important influence of the cult on public life is also reflected in the six months of the New Calendar that refer to the festivals of various gods:

Festival of Dagan: 1st Month

Festival of Ashtapi: 2nd Month

Festival of Ada(d): 4th Month

Festival of Adamma: 9th Month

Festival of AMA-ra: 11th Month

Festival of Kamish: 12th Month

Two other festivals can be added to these official festivals: *itu er-me* and *itu hu-lu-mu*. Both are religious rituals, the first resembling the festival of tabernacles and the second that of the holocaust.

Such festivals presuppose the existence of sacred buildings or temples and the presence of cult worshippers or priests, but archaeologists have not managed to identify religious buildings of the third millennium, despite their presence as indicated by the written sources. It is recorded that one of the structures on the acropolis, specifically *é-mah* ("exalted house"), is the official temple area of the city of Ebla. Various temples mentioned in the documentary sources must have been located elsewhere in the Low City, especially the temples of Kura, Adad, and Ashtar, the three gods that were most worshipped at Ebla. Other texts tell us of the existence of a temple to all the gods called *e-mul*, where, inter alia, the marriage ceremony of the queen to the new sovereign was conducted. Located in the temples were statues of the various gods, made mostly of gold and silver and resplendent with jewels that the people had brought to them as gifts.

The ranks of the priesthood are not explicitly designated as such, but the priestly titles *dam-dingir*, reserved for female members of the ruling class, perhaps only royal princesses, and *pa*$_4$*-shesh* ND ("the god's anointed") stand out. One text indicates that the male head of the priestly class was called *a-bu-mul* ("father of the gods") and the female head *ama-mul* ("mother of the gods"); their respective relations to each other have not yet been investigated.

Religion also played a central role in Eblaite state events. The most weighty decisions were accompanied by oaths taken before the more important gods. Thus when Ebrium bequeaths his possessions to various children, he swears an oath before Kura, Siphish, Adad, and all the gods. Furthermore, in a curse mentioned in a treaty between Ebla and Assur, the sun god, Adad, and all the gods are invoked. Other ceremonies took place at the temple of Dagan at Tuttul.

The power structure at Ebla was essentially secular, in contrast to Mesopotamia and Egypt, where the sovereigns were either divine incarnations or simply their representatives. Nevertheless, Ebla was governed by firm religious principles: the marriage of the queen and sovereign was a religious rite that took place in the temple of the gods, and the queen herself was chosen by divination, which involved an inspection of entrails presided over by the "god of their fathers." The term *dingir* followed by a personal name did not indicate that this person had been made a god, but rather referred to the god of the individual concerned, and was actually the eponym of various Eblaite families, thus showing that the very structure of Eblaite society was based upon familial bonds. The choice of the queen of Ebla was made with the blessing of the god of the family to which she belonged.

Other important ceremonies include various divine processions in the area around Ebla, including one for the god NI.DA.KUL that occurred in the territories of over twenty other cities. Another even more splendid procession in celebration of the marriage of the queen lasted some six weeks, starting from Ebla and following a specific route to the town of Binash.

Eblaite royal power was the prerogative of the queen, that is, the female, and the sovereign became king not via dynastic descent but through marriage to the queen, who was the sole and real possessor of royal power, and who was chosen by the inspection of entrails. The marriage ceremony and subsequent enthronement took place in a time and manner described in the texts, from which it is clear that the ritual lasted some six weeks and featured cult acts not only in Ebla and Binash, but also in other cities where the marriage party would stop during the ceremonial procession. The Eblaite texts describe the enthronement of two well-known sovereigns, Arennum and Ebrium, the third and fourth rulers of Ebla, confirming theories advanced in previous studies regarding the nature of Eblaite sovereignty.

The rite of the scapegoat was one of the ceremonies in the complex ritual for the succession to the Eblaite throne. This rite was carried out when the procession arrived in Binash, and involved the purification of the sanctuary *é-mah* via the expulsion of a goat, a rite that Pelio Fronzaroli (1993) has rightly emphasized as "partly anticipating the well-known episode in *Leviticus* (16:21–22)." "Let us purify the exalted house (the sanctuary) before Kura and Barama go there, let us release a goat with a silver bracelet on its neck to the mountain of AliNI."

A passage from the Eblaite texts describing the purchase of a silver bracelet supports the idea that this rite must have occurred in the manner described above: "One Dilmunite *shiqlu* of silver for one bracelet for a goat for the purification of the exalted house of Binash (on the occasion of) the enthronement of the sovereign" (MEE 7, 34 v. VII 6–13). The text is only interested in the administrative dispatch of the silver and its intended destination and not in the fate of the goat, but the very mention of this transaction along with the purification of the sanctuary for the enthronement of the sovereign makes it clear that it was a part of this ceremony. This Eblaite practice marks the beginning of a rite that was to become very widespread, especially in the region of Syro-Palestine and Anatolia in the second and first millennium, as well as in the world of the Old Testament, as seen from the *Leviticus* passage cited above. Ebla is the oldest source for such a rite, which was to develop and extend until it included all the ceremonies described in the Bible: in Ebla there is no transference of the sins of the community to the head of the chosen goat, nor the sacrifice of another goat, the blood of which is sprinkled in the sanctuary. The Eblaite text emphasizes only that the temple was purified by sending a goat wearing a silver bracelet to the mountain. However, this ritual dating from the middle of the third millennium BCE is the nucleus of the highly detailed rite described in *Leviticus*. This fact demonstrates the attachment of the Syro-Palestinian peoples to religious tradition.

Among the most outstanding Eblaite prophetic figures, at least at Mari, a particular role is assigned to an individual called the *apilum* (var., *aplum*; fem., *apiltum*), which translators have rendered as "answering," basing their translation upon the literal meaning of the Akkadian. The translation is ill-suited to the role of the human being, however, and would be better rendered as "prophet." The surprise in the bilingual vocabulary of Ebla is not so much that the term contains the familiar Semitic root *ʾpl*, but that it includes the Sumerian syntagma *eme-bala*, which means "to translate" or "to interpret," and not the meaning expressed by the Semitic root, "to talk" or "to answer." The term corresponding to *eme-bala* in Akkadian and in other Semitic languages is *targumannu*, so that probably the Eblaite scribe intended a particular meaning of the Sumerian headword. The prophet therefore is no longer "the one who answers," as previously translated, but rather "the translator," that is, the person who interprets the divine message and renders it intelligible to humankind, just as the Greeks intended when they chose the word *prophet* to refer to someone who speaks for someone else—in this case God.

See Also Canaanite Religion; Hittite Religion; Israelite Religion; Mesopotamian Religions; Moabite Religion; Phoenician Religion.

Bibliography

Archi, Alfonso. "Die ersten zehn Könige von Ebla." *Zeitschrift für Assyriologie* 76 (1986): 213–217.

Archi, Alfonso. "Divinité sémitiques et divinités de substrat: Le cas d'Ishhara et d'Ishtar à Ebla." *MARI* 7 (1993): 71–78.

Dahood, Mitchell, and Giovanni Pettinato. "Ugaritic rshp.gn and Eblaite rasap gunu(m)ki." In *Orientalia* 46 (1977): 230–232.

Fronzaroli, Pelio. *Archivi reali di Ebla: Testi rituali della regalità (XI).* Rome, 1993.

Mander, Pietro. "Los dioses y el culto de Ebla." In *Mitología y Religión del Oriente Antiguo,* vol. 2.1: *Semitas Occidentales (Ebla, Mari),* edited by G. del Olmo Lete, pp. 5–123. Barcelona, 1995.

Müller; Hans-Peter. "Gab es in Ebla einen Gottesnamen Ja?" *Zeitschrift für Assyriologie* 70 (1981): 70–92.

Pettinato, Giovanni. *Culto Ufficiale ad Ebla durante il regno di Ibbi-Sipiš.* Rome, 1979.

Pettinato, Giovanni. "Pre-ugaritic Documentation of Ba'al." In *The Bible World: Essays in Honor of Cyrus H. Gordon,* edited by Gary Rendsburg, pp. 203–209. New York, 1980.

Pettinato, Giovanni. *Il rituale per la successione al trono ad Ebla.* Rome, 1992.

Pettinato, Giovanni, and Hartmut Waetzoldt. "Dagan in Ebla und Mesopotamien nach den Texten aus dem dritten Jahrtausend." *Orientalia* 54 (1985): 234–256.

Pomponio, Francesco, and Paolo Xella. *Les Dieux d'Ebla: Étude analytique des divinités Éblaïtes à l'époque des archives royales du IIIe millénaire.* Münster, Germany, 1997.

Xella, Paolo. "Tradition und Innovation: Bemerkungen zum Pantheon von Ebla." *Heidelberger Studien zum Alten Orient* 2 (1988): 349–358.

Giovanni Pettinato (2005)
Translated from Italian by Paul Ellis

ECCLESIASTES. The *Book of Ecclesiastes* belongs to the wisdom writings of the Hebrew Bible, along with *Proverbs* and *Job.* The Hebrew title of the book is Qohelet, a term related to the verb *qāhal,* "to gather, assemble." Most likely the noun *qōhelet* designates the function "gatherer," although it remains unclear whether the term refers to the author as a gatherer of wise sayings or as a gatherer of persons for instruction. Greek translators interpreted the word to mean *ekklēsiastēs,* "member of a citizen's assembly." Although the book identifies Qohelet as "king over Israel in Jerusalem, " that is, Solomon (1:12; cf. 1:1), scholars recognize this persona as a literary fiction, one that is maintained only for the section 1:12–2:26. In the epilogue Qohelet is referred to as a *ḥākām,* a "sage" who taught the people.

Date, Provenance, and Reception. The lack of specific historical references within the book makes it difficult to date *Ecclesiastes.* Consequently, its linguistic profile provides the best clue to the date of composition. The presence of Persian loan words and numerous Aramaisms, as well as Hebrew expressions and grammatical forms typical of other post-exilic texts, makes a date earlier than the mid-fifth century BCE all but impossible. Opinion is divided, however, as to whether the book is more likely to have been composed during the Persian period (540–332 BCE) or the Hellenistic period (332 BCE–165 CE). A date in the fourth or third century BCE is most likely.

Though the date remains somewhat uncertain, the social context of the book is reflected in the striking use of terms drawn from the commercial world. *Ecclesiastes* often uses these terms in a derived or metaphorical sense, but the commercial origin of words such as *yitrôn* (profit), *ḥesrôn* (deficit), *ḥeshbôn* (account), and *shallît* (proprietor) is readily recognized. Moreover, a number of the sayings concern money and economic relations. Beginning in the Persian period, the economy of Palestine was increasingly monetary and commercial. The competitive economic context of Persian and Hellenistic Palestine was also combined with an autocratic and often arbitrary system of political and economic hierarchy (royal grants, tax farming, etc.) that made it difficult for individuals to have a sense of control over their economic futures. This socioeconomic situation seems to inform the perspective of *Ecclesiastes,* in which the inability of persons to be able to grasp the order of the world becomes thematic. One of the ways in which this perspective is manifest in *Ecclesiastes* is the foregrounding of the contradictoriness of experience.

Not surprisingly, *Ecclesiastes* was one of the books about whose canonicity certain rabbis raised questions in the late first century CE, when such issues were being discussed. The shocking nature of a number of the observations of *Ecclesiastes* provoked some of the opposition. In addition, the book's odd, self-contradictory structure gave pause. As a remark in the Talmud observes, "the sages sought to withdraw the book of Qohelet because its words are mutually contradictory" (*b. Shabb.* 30b). Nevertheless, the book was received as canonical in Judaism and thus in the Christian canon. In fact, *Ecclesiastes* came to be recognized as one of the five Megillot, the scrolls read in connection with the calendar of Jewish festivals. *Ecclesiastes* is read during Sukkot, the Festival of Booths, presumably because of the connection between the repeated calls of *Ecclesiastes* to enjoy the present moment and the association of Sukkot with "the season of our rejoicing."

CONTENT AND THEMES. Although *Ecclesiastes* is often seen as a heterodox work, it fits quite well into the larger picture of wisdom writings in the ancient Near East. Ancient Near Eastern wisdom was fundamentally concerned with the quest for order in the natural world, especially as that order expresses itself in the sphere of human experience. While many wisdom texts, such as the *Book of Proverbs,* express confidence in human ability to discern and profit by perceiving such an order, there are also many that express a skeptical or pessimistic view. These include the Egyptian writings of the *Dialogue of a Man with His Ba, The Admonitions of Ipuwer,* and the conclusion to *The Instructions of Ani.* In Mesopotamian wisdom *The Babylonian Theodicy* and, in particular, *The Dialogue of a Master with His Slave* articulate skepticism toward the project of discerning the order of the universe. In Israelite wisdom the *Book of Job* is also reckoned among the skeptical works. It is probably incorrect to see these different opinions as representing a chronological movement from confidence to skepticism. It is rather more likely that both the confident and the skeptical perspectives were present within the dialogue of wisdom at most times.

The particular perspective of *Ecclesiastes* concerning the accessibility of order in the world is announced in the opening verse of the text (1:2). Following the translation of the King James Version, the line is often rendered "Vanity of vanities, says Qohelet; vanity of vanities; all is vanity." The word translated "vanity" is *hebel,* which literally means "a puff of air." It is, as C. L. Seow suggests in *Ecclesiates: A New Translation with Introduction and Commentary* (1997), "anything that is superficial, ephemeral, insubstantial, incomprehensible, enigmatic, inconsistent, or contradictory. . . . It cannot be grasped—either physically or intellectually" (p. 47). Thus, *Ecclesiastes* does not deny that there is an order to the world—indeed, he often suggests that there is—only it is one that cannot be grasped by human knowing. Consequently, translators sometimes render *hebel* by such terms as *futility* or even *absurdity.*

The conviction of *Ecclesiastes* that humans cannot grasp the order of the world helps make sense of a frequent literary strategy used in the book in which two sayings that contradict one another are placed side by side. Exposing contradictions as the way in which the world is in fact experienced demonstrates the elusiveness of any intellectual or moral order. Moreover, it also explains why his judgment concerning the utility of wisdom is so mixed. Wisdom may in some cases be an advantage, but in other cases it affords no advantage whatsoever. Hence, persons are unable to control their futures by discerning the right deed for the right time. For this reason *Ecclesiastes* often characterizes the work people do in their lives with a word that has negative connotations, *ʿamal,* meaning "burdensome toil." Similarly, *Ecclesiastes* notes that although God is just, injustice is often present in the world. Death becomes emblematic of the inability of humans to grasp any meaningful order, since "the same fate comes to all" (9:2), whether they are wise or foolish, good or evil, religious or not. Like the order of the world, God remains inscrutable for *Ecclesiastes.* Although much that *Ecclesiastes* says about God would be at home in *Proverbs,* he differs from that book in stressing the radical transcendence of God ("God is in heaven and you are on earth" [5:2]). Like an imperial monarch in the Persian or Hellenistic period, God is to be feared rather than loved (5:1–7).

Despite the conviction of *Ecclesiastes* that the order of things cannot be understood and used to human advantage, he addresses the concern of traditional wisdom for how to live appropriately in the world. Consistent with his analysis of the inability of persons to control their futures, *Ecclesiastes* endorses taking pleasure in the moment at hand. One should enjoy eating, drinking, being festive, loving one's spouse, working on the task at hand (9:7–10). Even this is not in one's own power, however, but rather is frequently described as God's "gift" or as a person's "portion" from God. Although this advice differs from what one finds in other Israelite wisdom texts, it is traditional wisdom, having a very close parallel in the Mesopotamian Gilgamesh epic. Thus, *Ecclesiastes* should not be seen as representing a crisis in Israelite wisdom, as is sometimes suggested, but rather as articulating the skeptical or pessimistic strand of traditional ancient Near Eastern wisdom.

BIBLIOGRAPHY

Crenshaw, James L. *Ecclesiastes: A Commentary.* Philadelphia, 1987.

Fox, Michael V. *A Time to Tear Down and a Time to Build Up: A Rereading of Ecclesiastes.* Grand Rapids, Mich., 1999.

Lohfink, Norbert. *Qoheleth: A Continental Commentary.* Translated by Sean McEvenue. Minneapolis, 2003.

Longman, Tremper, III. *The Book of Ecclesiastes.* Grand Rapids, Mich., 1998.

Murphy, Roland E. *Ecclesiastes.* Dallas, Tex., 1992.

Seow, C. L. *Ecclesiastes: A New Translation with Introduction and Commentary.* New York, 1997.

CAROL A. NEWSOM (2005)

ECCLESIOLOGY SEE CHURCH, *ARTICLE ON* ECCLESIOLOGY

ECK, JOHANN

ECK, JOHANN (1486–1543), German Roman Catholic theologian known for his opposition to the Protestant reformers. Born Johann Maier in the Swabian village of Eck, he entered the University of Heidelberg at age eleven. Thereafter he studied at Tübingen (master of arts, 1501), Cologne, and Freiburg (doctor of theology, 1510). In 1510 he began studies at Ingolstadt, where he received a second doctorate and assumed a position on the theological faculty. He quickly became the dominant theological force at Ingolstadt and retained his position and his dominance there until his death. Eck was ordained to the secular priesthood in 1508 and preached regularly during the years he spent in Ingolstadt.

Eck's early years revealed broad intellectual interests. He published on logic (*Bursa pavonis,* 1507; *In summulas Petri Hispani,* 1516; *Elementarius dialectice,* 1517) and on Aristotle (1517, 1519, 1520). He read geography and canon law, and his affinities for the humanists were reflected in his study of Greek and Hebrew and his fondness for classical sources. In theology, his most significant early work was the *Chrysopassus* (1514), a treatise on predestination. In it Eck declared his preference for the Franciscans Bonaventure and Duns Scotus but asserted that he would not be bound to any theological party—a notable declaration in view of his attachment to the nominalists during his years in Freiburg. The *Chrysopassus* expounded doctrines of merit and free will that would soon be under attack by Luther and other Protestants.

Luther's Ninety-five Theses (1517) changed Eck's life. At his bishop's request Eck responded to the theses, and ensuing exchanges led to the Leipzig Disputation (1519) between Eck and the Wittenbergers Luther and Karlstadt. Shortly thereafter Eck went to Rome and helped secure papal condemnation of Wittenberg theology. He was commissioned (1520) to publicize in Germany the papal bull *Exsurge Domine,* which condemned forty-one propositions attributed to Luther, and which Luther publicly burned.

The rest of Eck's life was devoted largely to combating Protestants in Germany and Switzerland. Although he had no confidence that disputation would convince his Protestant opponents, he engaged in debate when he thought public policy might be influenced—notably in Baden in 1524. He was the most important Catholic participant in discussions with Protestants at Augsburg (1530) and Ratisbon (1541). His anti-Protestant publications included the following: defenses of papal authority (*De primatu Petri,* 1520), the doctrine of purgatory (*De purgatorio,* 1523), the sacrament of penance (*De satisfactione* and *De initio poenitentiae,* both 1523), and the sacrifice of the Mass (*De sacrificio missae,* 1526); the *Enchiridion* (1525), a manual intended to refute common Protestant errors; cycles of sermons (German and Latin, 1530); and a German translation of the Bible (1537). Two memoirs (*Schutz red,* 1540, and *Replica,* 1543) are polemical tracts that also provide biographical details.

Eck's writings were the most widely distributed anti-Protestant theological works of his generation. He played a major role in convincing Roman Catholic authorities that Luther's teachings were novelties dangerous to the security of the faith. He helped shape the strategy widely used against the Protestants: to take positions representing a medieval consensus and, in defending them, to anticipate possible Protestant objections, avoid scholastic demonstration, and emphasize scriptural arguments.

BIBLIOGRAPHY

Despite its age and some serious flaws, the most satisfactory biography of Eck is still Theodor Wiedemann's *Dr. Johann Eck, Professor der Theologie an der Universität Ingolstadt* (Regensburg, 1865). For a thorough modern treatment of one aspect of Eck's theology, see Erwin Iserloh's *Die Eucharistie in der Darstellung des Johannes Eck* (Münster, 1950). Two exemplary critical editions of works by Eck are *Enchiridion locorum communium adversus Lutherum et alios hostes ecclesiae, 1525–1543,* edited by Pierre Fraenkel (Münster, 1979), and *De sacrificio missae libri tres, 1526,* edited by Erwin Iserloh, Vinzenz Pfnür, and Peter Fabisch (Münster, 1982).

WALTER L. MOORE (1987)

ECKANKAR

ECKANKAR was founded by Paul Twitchell (1909–1971) in California in the mid-1960s. Although the Hindi/Punjabi term *Ek Onkar* (literally "One God/Power") was most likely derived from Guru Nānak's *Japjī* (the first set of hymns in the Sikh holy book, *Gurū Granth Sāhib*), Twitchell altered its original phonetic spelling and definition, claiming that "Eckankar" was a Tibetan-Pali word meaning "coworker with God." According to Twitchell, Eckankar was an ancient spiritual path with a lineage of 970 "Eck" Masters who trace back to Gakko, who brought the true teachings of soul travel from the city of Retz on the planet Venus. Twitchell alleged that through this bilocation philosophy a neophtye can leave his or her body via an inner light and sound and soul-travel to higher regions of consciousness, which lead ultimately to the supreme lord, Sugmad.

The Living Eck Master (occasionally retaining the more exalted title of Mahanta, "the highest state of God consciousness on earth") is central to Eckankar theology because it is through his guidance that the student (known as a chela) receives various levels of initiation, usually involving instructions into new sacred tones and other higher-level practices of contemplation. In an early article entitled "The Cliff Hanger" published in *Psychic Observer* in 1964, Twitchell explained the basis behind his new group:

> Eckankar, which I formed out of my own experience, is the terms used for the philosophy I have developed for the Cliff Hanger. It is based on Shabd-Yoga, a way out form of yoga. The word is the Hindu locution for the cosmic sound current which is known in our vernacular as the cosmic river of God.

Twitchell attributed the evolution of his personal philosophy into a public spiritual path to his second wife, Gail Atkinson (whom he married in 1964 when he was fifty-four years old and she was twenty-one), saying, "The switchover from the Cliff Hanger to Eck began taking place after I met my present wife, Gail. She insisted that I do something with my knowledge and abilities" (quoted in Brad Steiger, *In My Soul I Am Free* [San Diego, 1974], p. 64).

Eckankar's organization and teachings have evolved since Twitchell died of heart disease on September 17, 1971, in Cincinnati, Ohio, shortly after giving a talk. Twitchell's widow, Gail Atkinson (his first wife, Camille Ballowe, whom he married in 1942, divorced him on the legal grounds of desertion in 1960), claimed to have had a dream in which her husband appointed Darwin Gross to be his spiritual successor and the leader of Eckankar. Gross, who eventually married and then divorced Atkinson, served as the Living Eck Master for ten years until 1981, when he appointed Harold Klemp to succeed him as the spiritual leader of the organization. Two years later, in 1983, there was an acrimonious split between Klemp and Gross, which resulted in the latter being excommunciated from Eckankar. A lawsuit was filed by the Eckankar organization against Gross for allegedly misappropriating funds and for trademark and copyright infringement. Gross subsequently cut off any formal ties with Eckankar and started his own group called ATOM (The Ancient Teachings of the Masters). Eckankar has more or less erased Gross's tenure (and books) from their official histories. After selling the copyrights of Twitchell's books to Eckankar, Gail Atkinson ended her association with Eckankar.

Under the present leadership of Klemp, Eckankar has expanded its core audience worldwide and has an estimated paid membership of anywhere between 40,000 and 100,000 members yearly (Eckankar does not provide exact numbers). Klemp has also produced a wide-ranging series of books and discourses and has moved Eckankar's former center of operations from Menlo Park, California, to Chanhassen, Minnesota, where he established the temple of Eck. According to its own accounting, Eckankar has members from over one hundred countries around the world.

During Klemp's tenure, Eckankar has also systematized its teaching and made it more accessible to the general reading public by lessening its emphasis on Twitchell's extensive use of Indian-influenced terminology (particularly Hindi/Punjabi). Eckankar's official website (http://www.eckankar.org) presents a codified version of its belief system:

> Soul is eternal and is the individual's true identity. Soul exists because God loves it. Soul is on a journey to Self- and God-Realization. Spiritual unfoldment can be accelerated through conscious contact with the ECK, Divine Spirit. This contact can be made via the Spiritual Exercises of ECK and the guidance of the Living ECK Master. The Mahanta, the Living ECK Master is the spiritual leader of Eckankar. Spiritual experience and liberation in this lifetime are available to all. You can actively explore the spiritual worlds through Soul Travel, dreams, and other spiritual techniques.

Eckankar has weathered a fair storm of controversy since its inception, primarily because of questions concerning Twitchell's alleged plagiarism, biographical redactions, and purported historical antecedents. First, Twitchell claimed that while traveling in Europe and India he was taught Eckankar by the two former Masters who preceded him, Sudar Singh of Allahabad and Rebazar Tarzs, a supposed five-hundred-year-old Tibetan monk. However, there is no documented evidence proving that Twitchell had visited these countries when he claimed he did or that either Sudar Singh or Rebazar Tarzs are genuine historical figures. Rather, there is ample evidence (even from Twitchell's own pen) that he was associated with Swami Premananda of the Self-Revelation Church of Absolute Monism in Washington, D.C., from 1950 to 1955, when he was asked to leave the church compounds for personal misconduct. Additionally, Twitchell received initiation into Shabd Yoga in 1955 from Kirpal Singh, the founder of Ruhani Satsang in Delhi, India, while the guru was on his first tour of the United States. He kept in close contact with Kirpal Singh via correspondence for at least a decade and took his wife Gail to see the Indian guru and have her receive initiation from him in San Francisco in 1963. Twitchell also joined L. Ron Hubbard's Church of Scientology in the 1950s and eventually served for a short time as his press agent and wrote a number of articles for the group.

With the founding of Eckankar, however, Twitchell altered his biography and redacted references to his former teachers and replaced them with a hierarchy of Eck Masters. He even changed his birth date, claiming on his second marriage certificate that he was born in 1922, subtracting some thirteen years off his age. He also eventually denied his initiation under Kirpal Singh and threatened to sue his former gurū over what he considered defamatory claims concerning his discipleship.

A number of Twitchell's books on Eckankar contain large chunks of material appropriated from sources he failed to reference. Twitchell seemed particularly fond of plagiarizing whole passages from Radhasoami Satsang Beas author Julian Johnson, whose two books, *With a Great Master in India* (1934) and *The Path of the Masters* (1939), contributed to much of Eckankar's specialized terminology that draws extensively from the Sant Mat tradition of North India, an eclectic spiritual movement that includes such poet-saints as Kabīr, Dādū, and Tulsi Sahib. While Gross denied such appropriations for over a decade, the current Eck leader, Harold Klemp, has acknowledged some of Twitchell's plagiarism by calling him a "master compiler." Regardless of these continuing controversies, Eckankar has become an exceptionally successful religion with centers spanning the globe. Interestingly, Eckankar has a strong presence in Africa (particularly Nigeria) and in Europe, and it continues to draw thousands to its yearly conferences.

While Eckankar has been directly influenced by the Self-Realization Fellowship, Theosophy, Scientology, and particularly Sant Mat (via its specialized version of sound-current yoga), it has, in turn, influenced a number of new religious offshoots, including the Movement of Spiritual Inner Awareness (MSIA), founded by John-Roger Hinkins; MasterPath, founded by Gary Olsen; The Ancient Teachings of the Masters (ATOM), founded by Darwin Gross; the Divine Science of Light and Sound, founded by Jerry Mulvin; the Sonic Spectrum, founded by Michael Turner; and the Higher Consciousness Society, founded by Ford Johnson. Each of the founders of these groups was at one time a member of Eckankar, and they have all incorporated many Eck terms and ideas into their respective organizations. Eckankar's future looks bright as it enters its fifth decade of existence.

See Also Hubbard, L. Ron; Scientology; Sikhism; Theosophical Society.

Bibliography

Johnson, Ford. *Confessions of a God Seeker: A Journey to Higher Consciousness.* Silver Spring, Md., 2003.

Klemp, Harold. *Autobiography of a Modern Prophet.* Minneapolis, 2000.

Lane, David Christopher. *The Making of a Spiritual Movement: The Untold Story of Paul Twitchell and Eckankar.* Del Mar, Calif., 1983.

Marman, Doug. *Dialogue in the Age of Criticism.* E-book available from http://www.littleknownpubs.com/DialogIntro.htm.

Twitchell, Paul. *Eckankar: The Key to Secret Worlds.* San Diego, 1969.

David Christopher Lane (2005)

ECKHART, JOHANNES

ECKHART, JOHANNES (c. 1260–1327?), called Meister Eckhart; German theologian and mystic. Eckhart was born at Hochheim in Thuringia (now Germany). After entering the Order of Preachers (Dominicans) at Erfurt, he began theological studies in Cologne about 1280, possibly being among the last students of Albertus Magnus. In 1293 Eckhart was in Paris as a young lecturer and in 1302 he held the chair once held by Thomas Aquinas. A versatile personality, Eckhart was chosen in 1303 and in 1307 to be the religious superior of a province of numerous Dominican houses and institutions. During his second teaching period in Paris, after 1311, Eckhart laid the foundations for what he intended to be his great work, the *Opus tripartitum,* a synthesis of commentaries on the Bible, philosophical-theological treatises, and sermons on the Christian life.

In 1314 Eckhart was active in Strassburg, a city rich in theological schools and centers of preaching and mystical prayer. Eckhart, without neglecting his theological teaching (among his students were the famous mystical writers Johannes Tauler and Heinrich Süse), traveled widely to Dominican and Cistercian houses as preacher and spiritual director. By 1322 this demanding apostolate had been transferred up the Rhine to Cologne.

By 1326 Eckhart was under attack for his theology by the archbishop of Cologne. Rivalry between Franciscans and Dominicans; the heated atmosphere of the excesses in piety, as well as the genius of Rhenish mysticism; Eckhart's preaching about God and human personality in a vivid, colloquial German—all contributed to Eckhart's difficulties. Mindful of the accusations leveled previously against Thomas Aquinas, and insulted by a local inquisition presuming to evaluate the Dominicans who stood under papal protection, Eckhart appealed to the papacy, then at Avignon. He spent the remaining months of his life traveling the roads to and from southern France, appealing his case before the papal Curia. In 1329 John XXII concluded formally that seventeen of the articles ascribed to Eckhart (only a sample of the longer list) were to be construed as heretical or supportive of heresy, but the papal document observed that Eckhart, prior to his death, had rejected error. Eckhart's place and time of death remain unknown.

Eckhart's professorial works in Latin together with his popular German sermons develop a single system that is a religious metaphysics of spirit-in-process. Spirit here has a twofold significance. In a daring appropriation of apophatic mysticism, Eckhart defends the otherness of the divine being, that "wilderness" that to us is nothing. For Eckhart, the Trinity exists only on the surface of the absolute, for the three persons display activity. The ultimate reality of the absolute is "the silent godhead" from which in love enormous processes come forth from transcendent peace. The second manifestation of spirit is human personality. Eckhart, whom some have called the greatest depth psychologist before Freud, describes human life both theoretically and practically as a birth. The true self that is being born in each person is a word of God, just as Jesus, the divine Logos, is a word of God. This birth happens in the midst of a metaphysics of psychological praxis: only by letting the world of finite being and desires be can the individual prepare for the birth at the center of his or her personality (in the "spark" of the psyche) of that new self that is the fulfillment of God's personalized love and of our individualized personality.

Eckhart exercised an extraordinary influence not only upon Tauler and Süse and other Rhenish mystics but also upon Nicholas of Cusa. Martin Luther too admired these and other mystics of the German school from the fourteenth century, but, because of the papal condemnation, he knew them only from anonymous collections. After 1800 the German thinker Franz von Baader rehabilitated a number of mystics, including Eckhart, who then influenced Hegel and, more extensively, Schelling. In the twentieth century, scholarship discovered more writings of Eckhart, employed critical methods to verify and comprehend them, and filled in the picture of a genius of extraordinary depth. Martin Heidegger, both Jungian and Freudian psychologists, and Asian scholars found Eckhart to be an inescapable voice in philosophy, theology, and personal life. Since 1965 a significant renaissance of interest in Eckhart's work has been taking place in Europe, North America, and Asia.

Bibliography

Texts of Eckhart's works, in Latin and medieval German, are available in *Die lateinischen Werke* (Stuttgart, 1956–1964) and *Die deutschen Werke* (Stuttgart, 1958–). On Eckhart's life, see Josef Koch's "Kritische Studien zum Leben Meister Eckharts," *Archivum Fratrum Praedicatorum* 29 (1959): 5–15. A bibliography of writings on Eckhart is available in my "An Eckhart Bibliography," *The Thomist* 42 (April 1978): 313–336. There are three new, worthwhile collections of Eckhart in English: Matthew Fox's *Breakthrough: Meister Eckhart's Creation Spirituality* (New York, 1980) offers numerous sermons with commentary and bibliography; Edmund Colledge and Bernard McGinn's *Meister Eckhart: The Essential Sermons, Commentaries, Treatises and Defense* (New York, 1981) offers selections from the Latin and German works, with bibliography; Maurice O. Walshe, in *Sermons and Treatises,* 3 vols. (London, 1980–), presents particularly fine translations. See also *Master Eckhart:* Parisian Questions and Prologues, translated by Alfred A. Maurer (Toronto, 1974).

Thomas F. O'Meara (1987)

ECOLOGY AND RELIGION

This entry consists of the following articles:

AN OVERVIEW
ECOLOGY AND INDIGENOUS TRADITIONS
ECOLOGY AND HINDUISM
ECOLOGY AND JAINISM
ECOLOGY AND BUDDHISM
ECOLOGY AND CONFUCIANISM
ECOLOGY AND DAOISM
ECOLOGY AND SHINTŌ
ECOLOGY AND JUDAISM
ECOLOGY AND CHRISTIANITY
ECOLOGY AND ISLAM
ENVIRONMENTAL ETHICS, WORLD RELIGIONS, AND ECOLOGY
SCIENCE, RELIGION, AND ECOLOGY
ECOLOGY AND NATURE RELIGIONS

ECOLOGY AND RELIGION: AN OVERVIEW

Religion and ecology is an emerging area of study, research, and engagement that embraces multiple disciplines, including environmental studies, geography, history, anthropology, sociology, and politics. This article will survey the field of study and some of the broader movements of religion and ecology. The field of study responds to both historical and contemporary quests for understanding the interrelationships of humans, Earth, cosmos, and the sacred. This field involves explorations of such topics as the creative and destructive dynamics of nature, divine presence and purpose in nature and the cosmos, the ways in which environments have shaped and been shaped by human culture, the symbolic expression of nature in myth and rituals, and the understanding of ecology as displayed in traditional practices of agriculture, commerce, fishing, or hunting. In short, it explores the complex and varied systems of human-Earth relations as expressed in religious traditions.

Religions are often thought to concentrate primarily on divine-human relations that aim at personal salvation or liberation from earthly travails. They also emphasize the importance of social and ethical relations between humans. The intersection of religion and ecology opens up for further investigation the broad interactions of humans as individuals and as communities with the natural world and the universe at large. It underscores the many ways that humans locate themselves by means of religious cosmologies within a universe of meaning and mystery. It explores the varieties of human flourishing in relation to nature, whether those interactions reflect reciprocity or respect, domination or manipulation, celebration or submission. It suggests as well that human interaction with the sacred often occurs in and through nature and the larger cosmos.

Religions have acknowledged that simultaneously with ongoing seasonal and geological changes there is a wholeness and a holiness in the earth. This evolving cycle of life and death is, in part, what has engaged religious systems seeking to integrate their intricate symbolic and ritual structures with life processes. Life, death, and rebirth in the natural world are frequently symbolized in religious traditions. This alignment of the passage of human life with natural systems constitutes a profound dynamic of religious energy expressed in cosmological myths, symbols, and rituals. Along with this alignment, religions have developed injunctions against overuse of land and species found in numerous scriptures. This interweaving of cosmological religious thought and environmental ethics is explored in the study of religion and ecology.

As an emerging field, religion and ecology is still defining its scope and limitations. The field embraces both descriptive and historical studies as well as prescriptive and constructive theologies. Most scholars in the field do not presume that environmentally friendly scriptural passages imply environmentally sensitive practices. Moreover, scholars acknowledge the vastly different historical contexts in which religious traditions evolve by comparison to current environmental problems. Nonetheless, some scholars of the world's religions have suggested that there are both concepts and practices from these traditions that can be integrated into discussions of environmental policy and ethics. For example, the Islamic concepts in the Qurʾān regarding *tawḥīd* (unity of creation), *mizan* (balance), and *amānah* (trust or stewardship) reflect values that have been interpreted in relation to the natural world. Furthermore, Islamic practices such as *hima* (protected sanctuaries) and *ḥaram* (sacred precincts) represent ancient customs whose contemporary environmental implications are currently being explored. It is the premise of many scholars of religion and ecology that the religions offer intellectual energy, symbolic power, moral persuasion, institutional structures, and a commitment to social and economic justice that may contribute to the transformation of attitudes, values and practices for a sustainable future. Yet scholars also recognize the challenges of historical complexities, the inevitable gaps between ideas and practices, and the extremes of idealizing or dismissing particular religions. Academics have written of the dangers of idealizing the "noble savage" or "noble oriental" in this regard. Correctives to such idealizations can be found in environmental history, which is itself a newly emerging field. These historical studies will help to shed light on actual environmental practices of various cultures, influenced in part by their religious traditions.

Diversity and Dialogue of Religions. The world's religions are inherently distinctive in their expressions, and these differences are especially significant in regard to the study of religion and ecology. Several types of religious diversity can be identified. First, there is historical and cultural diversity within and among religious traditions as expressed over time in varied social contexts. For example, Buddhism arose in India, spread to Southeast Asia and north across the Silk Road through Central Asia to China, and to Korea, Japan, and the West. This geographical expansion is paralleled by strikingly different cultural expressions of Buddhist thought and practice.

Second, there is dialogic and syncretic diversity within and among religious traditions. This does not override the historical and cultural diversity but instead adds another level of complexity. Dialogue and interaction between traditions engenders the sedimentation and synthesis of religious traditions into one another. This often results in new forms of religious expression that can be described as syncretic, the commingling of religions, or hybrid—the fusion of religions into new expressions. Such creative expressions occurred when indigenous peoples in the Americas adapted Christianity into local settings. In East Asia there is an ongoing dialogue between and among Confucianism, Daoism, and Buddhism that has resulted in various kinds of syncretism.

Third, there is cosmological and ecological diversity within and among religions. Religious traditions develop unique narratives, symbols, and rituals to express their relationships with the cosmos and with local landscapes. In Daoism the body is an energetic network of breathings-in and breathings-out that expresses a basic dialogical pattern of the cosmos. Through this process individuals open themselves to the inner meditative landscape that represents a path of organic unity with the cosmos.

Ecological diversity is evident in the varied environmental contexts and bioregions where religions have developed over time. For example, Jerusalem is the center of a larger sacred bioregion where three religious traditions, Judaism, Christianity, and Islam, have both shaped and been shaped by the environment. However, the formation and expression of symbols, rituals, laws and community life within these religions in relation to urban, piedmont, hill country, and desert settings that constitute "Jerusalem" are historically quite different. These complex interactions illustrate that religions throughout history have interacted in myriad ways with their natural settings.

Defining Terms. In the field of religion and ecology, religions may be broadly understood as a means whereby humans, recognizing the limitations of phenomenal reality, undertake specific practices to effect self-transformation and community cohesion within a cosmological context. Religions are vehicles for cosmological stories, symbol systems, ritual practices, ethical norms, historical processes, and institutional structures that transmit a view of the human as embedded in a world of meaning and responsibility, transformation and celebration. Religions connect humans with a divine or numinous presence, with the human community, and with the broader Earth community. They link humans to the larger matrix of mystery in which life arises, unfolds, and flourishes.

Nature is seen in this light as a revelatory context for orienting humans to abiding religious questions regarding the cosmological origins of the universe, the meaning of the emergence of life, and the responsible role of humans in these life processes. Religions thus situate humans in relation to both the natural and human worlds with regard to meaning and responsibility. This may be a limiting or liberating experience. For example, religious ideas regarding nature may have deep associations with social beliefs and practices that are seen as unchanging ideals authorizing hegemonic ideologies. At the same time, religions may become a means for experiencing a sustaining creative force in the natural and human worlds and beyond. For some traditions this is a creator deity, for others it is a numinous presence in nature, and for others it is the source of flourishing life.

This experience of a creative force gives rise to a human desire to enter into transformative processes that link self, society, and cosmos. The term *anthropocosmic* refers to the linkage in which the microcosm of the individual is connected to the larger human community and to the macrocosm of the universe itself. The anthropocosmic impulse is for relationality, intimacy, and communion with this numinous reality. Individual and communal transformations are expressed through rituals and ceremonies that celebrate natural seasonal cycles as well as various cultural rites of passage. Religions link humanity to the rhythms of nature through the use of symbols and rituals that help to establish moral relationships and patterns for social exchange.

The term *ecology,* as it is used here, locates the human within the horizon of emergent, interdependent life rather than seeing humanity as the vanguard of evolution, the exclusive fabricator of technology, or a species apart from nature. The term is also used here—rather than the term *environment,* which can suggest something apart from humans—to indicate the dynamic interaction of humans with nature. *Scientific ecology* is used to indicate the empirical and experimental study of the relations between living and nonliving organisms within their ecosystems. While drawing on the scientific understanding of interrelationships in nature, the term *religious ecology* is used here to point toward a cultural awareness of kinship with and dependence on nature for the continuity of all life. Religious ecology provides a basis for exploring diverse cultural responses to the varied Earth processes. In addition, the study of religious ecology gives insight into how particular environments have influenced the development of cultures. Therefore, one can distinguish religious ecology from scientific ecology, just as one can distinguish religious cosmology from scientific cosmology.

This awareness of the interdependence of life in religious ecology finds expression in the religious traditions as a sacred reality that is often recognized as a creative manifestation, a pervasive sustaining presence, a vital power in the natural world, or an emptiness (*śūnyatā*) leading to the realization of interbeing. For many religions, the natural world is understood as a source of teaching, guidance, visionary inspiration, revelation, or power. At the same time, nature is also a source of food, clothing, and shelter. Thus, religions have developed intricate systems of exchange and thanksgiving in relation to human dependence on animals and plants, on forests and fields, and on rivers and oceans. These encompass symbolic and ritual exchanges which frequently embody ecological knowledge of ecosystems, agricultural processes, or hunting practices.

The study of religion and ecology explores the many ways in which religious communities articulate relationships with their local landscapes and bioregions. Religious ecology gives insight into how people and cultures create complex symbolic systems from their perceived relationships with the world, as well as practical means of sustaining and implementing these relations. In other words, these symbolic systems are frequently embodied in hunting, agricultural, and ceremonial practices that reflect respect for the mystery of life, along with ritual exchanges for appropriate interactions with nature, especially as a source of nourishment for body and spirit.

HISTORICAL BACKGROUND IN THE WEST. While movements of religion and ecology can be found worldwide, the field of religion and ecology is largely situated in academic settings in the West. With the growing critique of the unintended ecological and social consequences of globalization, a period of intense self-reflection has emerged in the West. The causes of environmental destruction have sometimes been traced to particular views of nature in Western philosophy and religion. Some of the varied and intertwined conceptualizations of cosmology, nature, and religion that have arisen in Western thought are explored here. Significant conceptualizations have also emerged, for example, in South Asian thought regarding *rita* (cosmological order) and *deva* (natural forces); in East Asian explorations of *dao* (the Way) and *qi* (material force); in Buddhist reflections on *pratityasamutpada* (dependent origination); and in Indigenous lifeways regarding relationality to spirits in nature. However, other articles explore the multiple contributions of South Asian, East Asian, and Indigenous traditions, as well as the Abrahamic traditions.

The first formulation of an incipient environmental philosophy in the West is often attributed to the *Airs, Waters, and Places* of Hippocrates. This work describes the close formative influences of environment on peoples and their cultures. Concepts regarding the environment were actively explored in Hellenistic thought under the category of *oikumene*, or community of the inhabited world. These philosophical developments went beyond, but also complemented, ancient ideas of personification of natural forces in the classical religions of the Mediterranean region. Various Indo-European and Semitic myths of creation posited a universe of correspondences between material realities, cosmic bodies, and deities that mapped out personal identity, social stability, and cosmic hierarchies. Pagan worship in the Mediterranean world ritualized ancient ideas that brought self, society, and cosmos into meaningful relation, and the Hellenistic philosophers reformulated many of these ideas. Among Stoic thinkers the linkage between cosmology and ethics gave rise to a sense of cosmopolitan citizenship as a way for humans to participate in the divine order. One of the most significant and longest lasting concepts for describing the gradations of the natural and human worlds was that of a hierarchical view of life often imaged as a chain or ladder. Such a great chain of being effectively brought together Platonic and Aristotelian worldviews and provided the grounds for elevating humans above nature.

Cosmological concepts also commanded significant attention within the Abrahamic traditions derived from the attribution of creation to a monotheistic God. Both Rabbinic Judaism and early Christianity drew on the Hebrew Bible (e.g., *Gen.* 1:26–28; *Jb.* 26:8–13; and *Ps.* 65:5, 11–13) and Greek Platonic thought (e.g., *Timaeus* and Paul's epistles) to articulate ideas of design and order in nature as reflecting the power of the Divine Creator. The land ethic in the Hebrew tradition and the value of wilderness as places of encounter with the divine also passed into Christianity. Similarly, in Israel symbolic clusters were associated with shepherding in the hill country and agricultural productivity in the piedmont region. Such clusters were linked with the idea of a cosmic center in Jerusalem with which one could map the entire known world. Mapping the local and mapping the universe, or cosmography, often overlapped in cultures. These distinctive cosmological concepts coalesced around the Jewish and Christian notions of God's divine plan for creation. This is evident in the *hexaemeron* literature of the early Church Fathers describing the six days of creation, as well as in the writings of Philo, Origen, and Augustine.

Along with the sense of divine order in creation, another biblical and Qur'anic theme is God's loving care for creation. This is manifest in the imagery of the *Song of Songs* in the Hebrew scriptures, the parables of Jesus in the New Testament, and those passages in the Qur'ān evoking *ihsan*, love, care, and beauty. Individuals who embodied this quest for devotional love of the divine through the natural world include Qabbalistic and Hasidic teachers in Judaism like Baʿal Shem Tov, Christian figures like Bernard of Clairvaux and Francis of Assisi, and Jalāluddīn Rūmī among the many Ṣūfī masters of Islam. While this devotional exuberance inspired many in these traditions, the scholastic thinkers sought to circumscribe this experiential enthusiasm with more rational views of God, humans, and creation.

Scholastic thought in Judaism, Christianity, and Islam reflects the influence of the classical ideas of a divinely ordained beginning, an order to creation, the godlike form of creatures, and of nature as a work, like a product, resulting from an applied technique. God as manifest in His works became identified with views of the Divine as Artisan who contained within Himself the Divine Forms as articulated by Plato. Many Western thinkers depicted nature as similar to a scriptural book that revealed the mysteries and the mind of the Creator. However, like humans who suffered from the sin of the original fall, nature aged and experienced decay. It might be said that in all the Abrahamic traditions there is an ambivalence regarding nature. On the one hand, in Christianity nature is seen as good, as at the Nicene Council, and yet fallen, as in the writings of Augustine and Calvin. On the other hand, in different expressions in Judaism and Islam nature is at once God's handiwork as well as a potential place of chaos requiring transcendence.

Nature was worthy of admiration by humans only if that wonder and esteem was associated with the love of God. It is in this context that Ibn Sīnā, Ibn Rushd, Maimonides, Thomas Aquinas and other scholastic thinkers of the medieval period reinvigorated the direct investigation of nature based on Aristotle's notion that form is embedded in the world of matter. For example, in the *Summa contra gentiles,* Thomas Aquinas affirmed a diversity of created forms as coming closest to manifesting the divine. He wrote that, "The presence of multiplicity and variety among created things was therefore necessary that a perfect likeness to God be found in them according to their manner of being." (Bk. 1, chap. 45, para. 2) Despite this cosmological orientation within Christianity, as Roman Catholicism became dominant in Europe, it nonetheless suppressed indigenous nature-based religions and frequently leveled sacred groves and built churches on sacred sites. Thus, while such a devotional figure as Bernard of Clairvaux experienced a deep mystical union with the divine he also sought to tame the wild growth of the Clairvaux valley in France as an expression of that devotion.

The sixteenth-century Protestant Reformation did not significantly alter fundamental ambivalences within Christianity toward the natural world. Rather, with John Calvin and Martin Luther it deepened a sense of the fallen character of nature, emphasizing a need to control the wild and chaotic dimensions of the world. Thus, as Protestantism spread to the Americas it subtly engendered a fear of both new lands and new peoples as manifestations of the wild and chaotic. This resulted in a justification for the extraction of resources and the exploitation of peoples and animals as irrational, dark, chthonic entities. Such an objectifying worldview where the divine rested more fully in a transcendent realm accorded with emerging scientific perspectives evident in scientists such as Francis Bacon who advocated the torture of a feminine nature to make her reveal secrets.

By early modern times the discoveries of the Americas caused major revisions of Western cosmology and introduced a range of new ideas that refuted the presumed flatness, as well as the aging and senescence, of the Earth. Explorers noted the limits of the Earth's productivity, while increasingly observing a balance and harmony in nature evident both in the web of life and its potential loss in environmental destruction. By the seventeenth century in the West, philosophers such as Barukh Spinoza and natural theologians such as George Burnet, John Woodward, and John Ray, emphasized the order of the universe, nature's inherent design, its interrelationships, productivity, and capacity for positive manipulation and control. Enlightenment thought in the eighteenth century helped to shift conventional Western cosmology even further from a theological perspective focused on a personal Creator actively involved in creation to a predominantly scientific view of the universe as operating under machine-like principles.

As a result of the scientific revolution and Enlightenment thought, some theologians gradually muted their ideas about final cause and purpose in the universe itself. They broadly accepted the notion of Deism that God created nature with inherent mechanistic relationships that carried the whole cosmos forward. The presence of God's revelation in creation began to diminish for some Western religious thinkers. Thus, the revelatory character of nature was replaced by a linear unfolding of divine creation that connected God's care for creation and the ancient design arguments with the Deist notion of a clockwork universe. Deism and mechanism opened the way for the further objectification of nature.

The Romantic movement of nineteenth-century Europe, in reaction to the rational, objectifying emphases of the Enlightenment, brought a resurgence of the understanding of nature as vital, dynamic, and, for some, revelatory of the mind of God. Drawing on the writings of Jean Jacques Rousseau, such as *The Reveries of a Solitary Walker,* Romantic writers like Johann Fichte, Johann Herder, Friedrich Schelling, and Johann Goethe returned to the direct experience of nature as a way toward unity or harmony with the sacred in nature. This type of personal revelatory experience of nature was troubling to the orthodox teachers of the Abrahamic traditions because it fostered a religious path in nature apart from the authorized scriptures. The Romantic contemplation of nature later influenced the American transcendentalists, such as Ralph Waldo Emerson and Henry David Thoreau, as well as such early environmentalists as John Muir and John Burroughs.

By the twentieth century, religious traditions in the West had largely relegated cosmology and the understanding of Earth's geological development and biological diversity to the domain of Earth science and life science. Salvation history became identified with a Western anthropocentric view of salvation focused exclusively on the human existentialist condition apart from the world of nature. The focus on the individual that characterized both Protestant Reformation views of personal salvation and Enlightenment views of political liberties resulted in a highly anthropocentric view of the human as above nature. While Darwinism resituated Western anthropocentrism in an evolutionary worldview, an abiding tension surfaced in fundamentalist Christianity with its emphasis on the uniqueness of God's creation and the knowledge of reality and revelation localized in the Bible and not in nature.

Many critics have cited Western anthropocentrism in both its philosophical and religious expressions as an obstacle to a more comprehensive environmental ethics. They suggest that this anthropocentrism, in combination with the objectification of nature fostered by the scientific method of observation, has resulted in the economic exploitation of nature and consumption of its resources with little sense of restraint or limits.

Significant critiques of Western anthropocentrism and the objectification of nature are found in the work of Lynn White and Arne Naess, among others. The provocative essay of Lynn White titled "The Historical Roots of Our Ecologic Crisis" (1967) challenged many theologians and biblical scholars to explore the relationship of religion to the environmental crisis. White argued that the technological impact of humans on the planet's ecology has been largely deleterious. This is in part due to the influence of Christianity as a highly anthropocentric religion emphasizing a transcendent God removed from nature. These notions, White felt, contributed significantly to the desacralization of nature and, thus, to the ability to exploit nature without awareness of the consequences. White recommended alternative forms of Christianity, especially the comprehensive compassion for life of Francis of Assisi, whom White proposed as a patron saint for ecologists.

The Norwegian philosopher Arne Naess has also articulated an influential corrective to these positions of anthropocentrism and the objectification of nature. In *Deep Ecology: Living as if Nature Mattered* (1985), Bill Devall and George Sessions introduced Naess' concept of "deep ecology," which emphasizes the intrinsic ethical value of the natural world. They drew on Advaita Vedānta thought in Hinduism to emphasize human "self-realization" that recognized the larger dependence of humans on the entire community of life. This position also relied on the natural philosophy of Barukh Spinoza that highlights the unity of the divine in the natural world. Deep ecology has promoted a biocentric equality and the radical interdependence of species as values needed for protection of species diversity—both biological and cultural.

Such complex perspectives on nature in Western thought come into relief when considering anthropocentric responses to the first image of the Earth from the moon in 1969. One response can be characterized as a feeling of liberation similar to an ancient, classical Greek view of freedom from the constraints of the human condition that had been bound by the natural world. A second response follows from an appreciation of the beauty of the blue-green planet akin to a Romantic perspective that seeks to know this beauty more deeply through experience and contemplation. A third response reflects a thoroughly modern hubris derived from human technological accomplishments that sees the future of the Earth as a controlled, dominated, and managed sphere. The world's religious traditions themselves are influenced by these views. Yet, they continue to generate diverse responses by imaging the Earth from the standpoints of different cosmologies.

THE STUDY OF RELIGION AND ECOLOGY IN NORTH AMERICA. The field of religion and ecology arises from two disciplines that came more fully into the North American academy after the Second World War, namely, the study of religion and the science of ecology. Religious studies surfaced in the postwar era as an academic field focused on an analysis of religious experiences, myths, rituals, symbols, texts, and institutions. Distancing itself from creedal positions, religious studies developed as a distinctive area from theology that emphasizes particular denominational interpretations of religious life. The earlier emergence of the history of religions and comparative religions was an important spur to religious studies. This had taken place in nineteenth-century Europe under the leadership of such scholars as Max Mueller, who helped translate the *Sacred Books of the East,* and James Legge, who translated the *Chinese Classics.* Moreover, the appearance of the phenomenology of religion, the anthropology of religion, and the sociology of religion also prepared the grounds for a broader understanding of religion. A growing awareness of cultural diversity and the postwar affluence of the 1950s were accompanied by significant legal cases that made possible the establishment of departments of religion in higher education in North America. Previously, the study of religion had been largely confined to seminaries and schools of theology; now religion could be studied in the academy. Both undergraduate and graduate departments of religion thus emerged in the North American context.

The German biologist Ernst Haeckel coined the term *ecology* in 1866 as a combination of the Greek words *oikos* (house) and *logos* (science). The academic discipline in North America can be dated from the founding of the Ecological Society of America in 1915. As a field of study in higher education and as a movement for conservation it has come more fully into its own in the postwar period. The founding of the Nature Conservancy, which was established from the Ecological Society of America, occurred in 1951. This documents the concern and motivation of professional ecologists to preserve natural landscapes. A number of subdisciplines within ecology have emerged. For example, evolutionary ecology developed from a merger of ecology and evolution in the 1960s. The conservation biology subdiscipline developed with its own society in the late 1970s with the express goal of applying ecological principles to conservation issues. Other emerging subdisciplines include restoration ecology and landscape ecology.

Drawing on the natural sciences of biology and chemistry, and the social sciences of economics and politics, ecology has become the basis for interdisciplinary departments of environmental studies that have developed in higher education since the 1980s. In the 1990s the humanities began to participate in environmental studies with the emergence of environmental literature and history as well as environmental ethics, religion, and philosophy. Religious studies have contributed to environmental studies from such varied perspectives as the study of world religions and ecology, ecotheology and ecofeminism, social and environmental ethics, nature religions and alternative environmental movements, and cultural and ritual studies.

The fields of ecology and environmental studies have developed in relation to emerging environmental concerns that spanned the twentieth century. These included the challenging experiences of the Great Depression and Dust Bowl, dire predictions regarding growth in human population, glimpses of the limits of production and consumption, and awareness of the loss of species and ecosystems. This inspired an incipient conservation movement that gained attention with the publication of two key books. Fairfield Osborn's *Our Plundered Planet* (1948) described the devastation already facing many ecosystems. His major concerns focused on species loss and the cascading effects of human population growth. A year later, Aldo Leopold's classic text *A Sand County Almanac* (1949) called for a new land ethic. A forester with the U.S. Forest Service, Leopold described the land ethic as expanding the boundaries of the community to include soils, waters, plants, and animals, or, collectively, the land. The extension of ethics to the larger environment was, for Leopold, both an evolutionary possibility and an ecological necessity.

Walter Lowdermilk, a forester with the Soil Conservation Service, anticipated a similar conservation ethic after extensive travel and study of the effects of human civilization on soils. He wrote an essay in Jerusalem in 1940 in which he observed that each nation needed to appeal to national awareness for stewardship of soil and land for future generations. He called this the principle of an Eleventh Commandment. Scientists and others began to explore degradation of land due to industrial-technological processes and the dangers to biological life caused by new chemical compounds. With the publication in 1962 of Rachel Carson's *Silent Spring,* which documented the effects of DDT on bird life, the environmental movement was born.

APPROACHES WITHIN THE STUDY OF RELIGION AND ECOLOGY. While the field of religion and ecology arose in Western academic and philosophical contexts, it cannot be dissociated from the changing ideas and practices of the world's religious and cultural traditions, as well as from pressing environmental concerns, both global and local. Scholars in the field may draw on social-scientific studies of how a culture mediates between human populations and ecosystems while also relying on historical, textual, and interpretive studies from the humanities. Various creative approaches have emerged in the study of religion and ecology analyzing the ways in which cultures conceptualize, classify, and value their natural environments. Historical approaches have refuted older studies in this field that tended to fix a culture's ecological insights as synchronic patterns that never changed. Now, the mutual impacts of cultures and environments are more clearly understood as having changed and shaped one another through time. Moreover, postmodern approaches have affected many contemporary researchers in religion and ecology, attuning them to questions about the ways in which human individuals and groups construct systems of meaning and power concerning nature, society, and the environment. Studies of place-based conservation and biodiversity are being integrated with an understanding of religious ecology and sacred place. The mutual relevance of land, life, value, and sustainability are all included in the network of inquiry identified with the intersection of religion and ecology.

While a variety of methodologies are being used in the study of religion and ecology, three interpretive approaches challenge both scholars and the religious traditions themselves: retrieval, reevaluation, and reconstruction. Retrieval tends to be descriptive, while reevaluation and reconstruction tend to be prescriptive. Retrieval refers to the investigation of scriptural, commentarial, legal, and other literate and narrative sources in particular religions for evidence of traditional teachings regarding human-Earth relations. This requires that oral-narrative and historical and textual studies uncover the theoretical resources already present within the tradition. In addition, the method of retrieval examines ethics and rituals present in the tradition in order to discover how the tradition actualized these teachings in practices. Retrieval may be complemented by studies in the environmental history of cultures or geographical areas.

Interpretive reevaluation occurs when a tradition's teachings are evaluated with regard to their relevance to contemporary circumstances. In what ways can the ideas, teachings, or ethics present in these traditions be adopted by contemporary scholars, theologians, or practitioners who wish to help shape more ecologically sensitive attitudes and sustainable practices. Reevaluation also questions ideas that may lead to inappropriate environmental practices. For example, are certain religious tendencies reflective of other-worldly or world-denying orientations that are not helpful in relation to pressing ecological issues? It asks as well whether the material world of nature has been devalued by a particular religion, or whether exclusively human-centered ethics are adequate to address environmental problems.

Finally, reconstruction suggests ways that religious traditions might also adopt its teachings to current circumstances in new and creative ways. This may result in a new synthesis or in a creative adaptation of traditional ideas and practices into modern modes of expression. This is one of the most challenging aspects of the emerging field of religion and ecology and requires discrimination in the transformative adaptation of traditional ideas in relation to contemporary circumstances. Yet there are precedents for this in the ways religions have reshaped themselves over time, as is evident in theology and ethics.

RELIGIOUS THINKERS ADDRESS ENVIRONMENTAL PROBLEMS. Religious and moral reflections on environmental problems emerged from several Christian theologians in the second half of the twentieth century. One of the first to raise a voice of concern was Joseph Sittler, a Lutheran theologian at the University of Chicago. Writing in the 1950s, he decried the repudiation of Earth by Christians as a distorted reading of the biblical promise as exclusively oriented towards humans. Urging a larger cosmological vision, Sittler called for Christianity to recover a cosmic redemption of all creatures and of creation as a whole. Sittler's influence in the World Council of Churches led to the founding in 1963 of a Faith-Man-Nature group. For some ten years this group brought together leading theologians, such as Paul Albrecht, John Cobb, Philip Hefner, and Paul Santmire, to explore Christian understandings of appropriate human interactions with the environment.

Foremost among those thinkers who have urged Christianity to reconsider its relationship to the environment is the process theologian John Cobb. In the mid-1960s Cobb published *A Christian Natural Theology*, which reflected a traditional Christian understanding of "natural theology" as theology done within the bounds of reason apart from any reference to the natural world. Cobb's work later moved outside the framework of Kantian philosophy to find a basis in the process thought of Alfred North Whitehead for valuing the natural world and appropriate human interaction within it. Encouraged by the early work of the theologian Joseph Sittler and the biologist Charles Birch, and spurred by his son Clifford's concern for environmental degradation, in 1972 Cobb wrote *Is It Too Late? A Theology of Ecology*. Over the years Cobb has critiqued the harmful effects of growth-oriented economies on the community of life, especially in his work with the economist Herman Daly (*For the Common Good* [1989]). He and Daly challenged conventional economics, seeing it as engineered to promote development despite the environmental and social costs.

In 1972 Gordon Kaufman also published a seminal article, "A Problem for Theology: The Concept of Nature." Here, and in his later work, *In Face of Mystery: A Constructive Theology* (1993), he raised challenging questions about the anthropocentric model of God as developed in Christianity and the relationship of traditional models of God to creation. Kaufman critiqued the nature and names of the monotheistic, transcendent God that tends to distance humans from the sense of the sacred as residing in the natural world. He urged a new bio-historical understanding of humans as embedded in complex processes of "serendipitous creativity" in nature, and thus co-creators with the unfolding Earth processes.

The feminist theologian Sallie McFague has developed some of these ideas further, calling for new images of God as not simply a distant and transcendent father but also as friend and lover. Rosemary Radford Ruether draws on the Gaia hypothesis and ecofeminism for the development of a broader ecotheology. Both of these feminist theologians are indebted to the earlier historical work of Carolyn Merchant (*The Death of Nature* [1980]), which portrays the use and abuse of nature as comparable to patriarchal domination of women and the disintegration of older organic views of nature in which the sacred was experienced as immanent. Along with ecofeminism there has been an important alignment of social justice and environmental concerns among religious thinkers in both the developed and developing countries. The significance of this movement is that it creates new religious syntheses linking awareness of environmental degradation with insights from economic, political, and social analysis. The liberation theologian, Leonardo Boff, highlights this conjunction, as has the feminist theologian Ivone Gebara. Similarly, the emerging theologies and practices identified with eco-justice and environmental racism within Judaism and Christianity has been fostered by such writers as Roger Gottlieb and Dieter Hessel.

In response to the growing environmental and social crises facing the planet, and aware of the need for new modes of human-Earth relations, Thomas Berry drew on his studies of world religions and cultures to formulate a framework for rethinking cosmology. Beginning in the 1970s, Berry developed the cosmological thought of the Jesuit paleontologist Pierre Teilhard de Chardin (1881–1955) to present a radical revisioning of the scientific discoveries of universe emergence as the new cosmological story of our times. After many years of studying world religions and cultures, he published late in his career a sequence of books that elaborated this idea: *The Dream of the Earth* (1988), *The Universe Story* (with Brian Swimme, 1992), and *The Great Work* (1999). Berry understood the central roles of cosmologies in the world's religions as activating community identity, relationship with local bioregions, and communion with the Earth and universe itself. The challenge of contemporary societies, for Berry, is to realize and implement the transformative energies of the new cosmological story to effect a radical revisioning of human-Earth relations. From a cosmological perspective, this entails the transformation of individual and community in ways that foster the flourishing of the whole community of life.

The Islamic scholar Seyyed Hossein Nasr, while studying science at Harvard University in the 1960s, sensed the limited metaphysics of science and the loss of the transcendental unity he observed among the religions. He has been the leading spokesperson in the Islamic community for drawing attention to the seriousness of the environmental crisis as well as the need for a revival of the cosmological basis of religions where humans are seen as a microcosm of the macrocosm of the universe.

STUDIES IN ANTHROPOLOGY, CULTURAL STUDIES, AND GEOGRAPHY. Among the cultural theorists who investigated the connection of culture and the environment was the anthropologist Julian Steward, who proposed the study of cultural ecology. His studies of the Shoshone peoples of North America posited relations between the environment and the economic and technological aspects of society. While his work did not address religion directly, it marked a turning point in bringing together social, cultural, and environmental studies.

The Swedish historian of religions Åke Hultkrantz also studied the Shoshone and extended this research in cultural ecology to religion. Hultkrantz sought to understand the creative roles of environmental adaptation by evaluating its direct influences on technological, economic, and material culture, as well as the environment's indirect influences on social formations in specific cultures. Hultkrantz's article "Ecology" in the 1987 *Encyclopedia of Religion* was the only entry on this topic. He distinguished cultural ecology and geography of religions as the two major sources for modern studies of ecology of religion. Championing Steward's cultural-ecological approach, Hultkrantz stressed study of the impact of environment on religion, both directly through material culture and indirectly through social structures. Hultkrantz revealed how indigenous cultures have a "primary integration" in which religious complexes are ecologically adapted to basic traits of sustenance and technology. Cultures, such as those identified with Christianity and the so-called higher religions, adapted religion to their social structures. These Hultkrantz termed cultures of "secondary integration." Through research, he felt, religio-ecological types could be identified that would assess the interplay between environment and religion, especially among indigenous cultures.

Other anthropologists have contributed to the exploration of the relationships of ecosystems to symbol systems, rituals, and cultural life that have had significant implications for the study of religion and ecology. In *Pigs for the Ancestors* (1969), Roy Rapport's seminal study of liturgical cycles among the Maring of New Guinea, Rapport suggested that ritual among indigenous peoples functions as a conventional means for maintaining order between social groups and their environments. More than simply proximity to natural environments, then, indigenous peoples have coded into their ritual life a developed wisdom for sustaining their social life in specific environments.

The anthropologist Keith Basso drew attention to the significance of place-names among indigenous peoples, especially the Western Apache of North America. Basso reemphasized the importance of local knowledge about traditional places as connected to a broad array of ideas and values in indigenous communities, such as cosmology, identity, advocacy, and wisdom. In *Wisdom Sits in Places* (1996) Basso investigated disciplinary rituals and meditational practices in which the Apache "drink from places" so as to "work on the mind." In doing so, he developed an anthropological approach to the study of religion and ecology based on place.

Within medical anthropology, various approaches have developed that describe the interactions of ecological systems and religious beliefs. For example, George Foster and Barbara Anderson, in their work *Medical Anthropology* (1978), analyzed religions as functional sociocultural systems that adapt to different environments and thus bring new ethnomedical strategies into being. Arthur Kleinman, in *Patients and Healers in the Context of Culture* (1980), was among the first medical anthropologists to explore the complex relationships of environment, culture, and religious beliefs as impacting healing. Byron Good, in *Medicine, Rationality and Experience* (1994), challenged the instrumental rationality prevalent in biomedicine as well as functionalist approaches to religion, which he felt were insufficient interpretive tools for understanding the dynamic relationships of environment, religion, and healing. Like Kleinman, Good called for more attention to narratives about ecology, illness, and beliefs that reveal the voices of humane and socially committed individuals and communities.

Early social-science contributions to the study of religion and ecology emerged from the field of geography. In *The Geography of Religions* (1967), David Soper outlined a range of topics, modes of investigation, and examples of interactions between religious systems and landscapes. The geography of religion explores religions as material, social, and cultural expressions that evolved in relation to environments. Religions are thus viewed as molding environmental space in such diverse ways as ritualization of ecology, spatial and organizational structures, political processes and interactions with other religions. Investigation of these spatial and ecological characteristics of religions has steadily influenced the study of religion.

The geographer Yi-Fu Tuan has explored ways in which individuals' affective ties with the environment result from their being simultaneously biological organisms, social beings, and unique individuals with perceptions, attitudes, and values. For Tuan, the neologism *topophilia* describes this coupling of sentiment with multiple connections to place evident in human cultures. Thus, the images that emerge in religions, for example, are not directly shaped by the environment; rather, environments stimulate sensory commitments giving rise to emotions and ideals expressed in religion. In this context, the multiplicity of religious symbols are secondary manifestations of the deeper ecological connections described as *topophilia.*

This emphasis on symbols, imagination, and ecology was taken up by Richard Peet and Michael Watts in *Liberation Ecologies: Environment, Development, and Social Movements* (1996). Peet and Watts used Marxist dialectics to investigate the roles of religions in fostering "ecological imaginaries" within the overall contradictory character of the relations between humans and the Earth. Ecological imaginaries are the deep networks of affective association between bioregions and humans that surface in human imagination as symbols and concepts motivating individuals and communities to action. Ecological imaginaries bring political awareness to political ecology. Moreover, these affective and imaginative connections to ecology create the possibility for deeper liberation from the grip of seemingly intractable social and market forces.

Drawing on the social sciences and humanities, the two-volume *Encyclopedia of Religion and Nature* (2005), edited by Jeffrey Kaplan and Bron Taylor, continues the investigation of religion and ecology by exploring diverse nature-influenced religions as well as traditions that consider nature as sacred. These volumes are a major resource for study of the intersections of society, religion, and environment. Kaplan and Taylor not only attempt encyclopedic coverage of the historic roles of environments in the formation and development of religions, but they also address contemporary challenges to the religions raised by environmental crises.

MOVEMENTS OF RELIGION AND ECOLOGY: CALLS AND RESPONSES. Many organizations and individuals have called for the participation of religious communities in alleviating the environmental crisis and reorienting humans to show respect, restraint, and responsibility toward the Earth community. Several key documents contain this call. One is the statement of scientists titled "Preserving and Cherishing the Earth: An Appeal for Joint Commitment in Science and Religion," which was signed at the Global Forum meeting in Moscow in January 1990. It suggests that the human community is committing "crimes against creation" and notes that: "Problems of such magnitude, and solutions demanding so broad a perspective must be recognized from the outset as having a religious as well as a scientific dimension." It also acknowledges that:

> The environmental crisis requires radical changes not only in public policy, but in individual behavior. The historical record makes clear that religious teaching, example, and leadership are powerfully able to influence personal conduct and commitment. As scientists, many of us have had profound experiences of awe and reverence before the universe. We understand that what is regarded as sacred is more likely to be treated with care and respect. Our planetary home should be so regarded. Efforts to safeguard and cherish the environment need to be infused with a vision of the sacred. (http://www.environment.Harvard.edu)

A second key document, "World Scientists' Warning to Humanity," was produced by the Union of Concerned Scientists in 1992 and was signed by more than 2,000 scientists, including more than 200 Nobel laureates. This document also suggests that the planet is facing a severe environmental crisis:

> Human beings and the natural world are on a collision course. . . . Human activities inflict harsh and often irreversible damage on the environment and on critical resources. If not checked, many of our current practices put at risk the future that we wish for human society and the plant and animal kingdoms, and may so alter the living world that it will be unable to sustain life in the manner that we know. Fundamental changes are urgent if we are to avoid the collision our present course will bring about. (http://www.environment.Harvard.edu)

The document calls for the cooperation of natural and social scientists, business and industrial leaders, and religious leaders, as well as the world's citizens. It concludes with a call for environmentally sensitive attitudes and behaviors which religious communities can help to articulate:

> A new ethic is required—a new attitude towards discharging our responsibilities for caring for ourselves and for the Earth. We must recognize the Earth's limited capacity to provide for us. We must recognize its fragility. We must no longer allow it to be ravaged. This ethic must motivate a great movement, convincing reluctant leaders and reluctant governments and reluctant peoples themselves to effect the needed changes.

Although the responses of the religions to the global environmental crisis were slow at first, they have been steadily growing since the latter part of the twentieth century. Several years after the first United Nations Conference on Environment and Development, in Stockholm in 1972, some of the Christian churches began to address the growing environmental and social challenges. At the fifth Assembly of the World Council of Churches (WCC) in Nairobi in 1975, there was a call to establish the conditions for a "just, participatory, and sustainable [global] society." In 1979 a follow-up WCC conference was held at Massachusetts Institute of Technology on "Faith, Science, and the Future." This conference issued a call for a new biblical interpretation of nature and of human dominion. Moreover, there was recognition of the critical need to create the conditions for ecologically sustainable societies for a viable planetary future. The 1983 Vancouver Assembly of the WCC revised the theme of the Nairobi conference to include "Justice, Peace, and the Integrity of Creation." The 1991 WCC Canberra conference expanded on these ideas with the theme of the "Holy Spirit Renewing the Whole of Creation." After Canberra, the WCC theme for mission in society became "Theology of Life." This has brought theological reflection to bear on environmental destruction and social inequities resulting from economic globalization. In 1992, at the time of the UN Earth Summit in Rio de Janeiro, the WCC facilitated a gathering of Christian leaders that issued a "Letter to the Churches," calling for attention to pressing eco-justice concerns facing the planet. Principles of eco-justice that have had growing support in the last decade include: solidarity with other people and all creatures, ecological sustainability, sufficiency as a standard of distributive justice, and socially just participation in decisions for the common good.

In addition to major conferences held by the Christian churches, various interreligious meetings have occurred and movements have emerged that have shown significant levels of commitment toward alleviating the environmental crisis. Some of these include the interreligious gatherings on the environment in Assisi in 1984 under the sponsorship of the World Wildlife Fund (WWF), and under the auspices of the Vatican in 1986. Moreover, the United Nations Environment Programme (UNEP) established an Interfaith Partnership for the Environment (IPE) that has distributed thousands of packets of materials for use in local congregations and religious communities since 1985.

The Parliament of World Religions—held in Chicago in 1993, in Cape Town, South Africa in 1999, and in Barcelona in 2004—has issued statements on global ethics embracing human rights and environmental issues. The Global Forum of Spiritual and Parliamentary Leaders held international meetings in Oxford in 1988, Moscow in 1990, Rio in 1992, and Kyoto in 1993 that had the environment as a major focus. Since 1995 a critical Alliance of Religion and Conservation (ARC) has been active in England, and the National Religious Partnership for the Environment (NRPE) has organized Jewish and Christian groups on this issue in the United States. A member group of NRPE, the Coalition on Environment and Jewish Life (COEJL) has helped to mobilize the American Jewish communities regarding environmental issues, especially global warming. The Islamic Foundation for Ecology and Environmental Sciences (IFEES), based in England, has from its beginnings in 1984 established itself as a leader in environmental conservation and activism in Islamic settings. Religious groups have also contributed to the drafting of the Earth Charter. The World Bank has developed a World Faiths Development Dialogue on poverty and development issues with a select group of international religious leaders.

Religious leaders and laypersons have spoken out for protection of the environment. The Dalai Lama has made numerous statements on the importance of environmental protection and has proposed that Tibet should be designated a zone of special ecological integrity. Rabbi Ishmar Schorsch of the Jewish Theological Seminary in New York has frequently drawn attention to the critical state of the environment. Bob Edgar, president of the National Council of Churches, has led campaigns on environmental issues such as global warming and clean air. The Greek Orthodox Patriarch Bartholomew has sponsored several seminars to highlight environmental degradation in the Aegean, the Black, the Adriatic, and the Baltic Seas, as well as the Danube River. He has strongly critiqued human negligence and destruction of the environment by calling it "ecological sin." From the Islamic perspective, Seyyed Hossein Nasr has written and spoken widely on the sacred nature of the environment for more than two decades. In the Christian world, along with the efforts cited earlier of the Protestant community in the WCC, the Catholic Church, has issued several important pastoral letters since around 1990. Pope John Paul wrote a message for the World Day of Peace, January 1, 1990, titled "The Ecological Crisis: A Common Responsibility." He has also spoken of the need for ecological conversion, namely a deep turning to the needs of the larger community of life. In 1988 the Catholic Bishops of the Philippines issued an environmental letter titled "What Is Happening to Our Beautiful Land" and two years later the U. S. Catholic Bishops Conference published a statement called "Renewing the Earth." In 2000 the Boston Bishops wrote a pastoral letter titled, "And God Saw That It Was Good," and in February 2001 the Bishops of the Pacific Northwest published a document called, "The Columbia Watershed: Caring for Creation and the Common Good."

In October 2003 the Canadian bishops also published a letter on the environment. In August 2000 a gathering of more than one thousand religious leaders took place at the United Nations during the Millennium World Peace Summit of Religious and Spiritual Leaders, where discussion of the environment was a major theme. The UN secretary general, Kofi Anan, who addressed the summit, has called for a new ethic of global stewardship, recognizing the urgent situation posed by current unsustainable trends.

Religions of the World and Ecology Project. It was in light of these various initiatives and in response to the call of scientists that a three-year international conference series, titled, "Religions of the World and Ecology," took place at Harvard University. From 1996 to 1998 over eight hundred scholars gathered to examine the varied ways in which human-Earth relations have been conceived in the world's religious traditions. The intention of the series was to assist in establishing a new field of study within religious studies that would link to the interdisciplinary field of environmental studies and have implications for public policy on environmental issues. The series of ten conferences examined the traditions of Judaism, Christianity, Islam, Hinduism, Jainism, Buddhism, Daoism, Confucianism, Shintō, and Indigenous religions. Held at the Center for the Study of World Religions at Harvard Divinity School, the conferences were organized by Mary Evelyn Tucker and John Grim in collaboration with a team of area specialists. The series brought together international scholars of the world's religions, as well as scientists, environmentalists, and grassroots leaders. The papers from these conferences were published in ten volumes by the Center for the Study of World Religions and distributed by Harvard University Press. Recognizing that religions are key shapers of people's worldviews and formulators of their most cherished values, this broad research project uncovered a vast wealth of attitudes toward nature sanctioned by religious traditions. In addition, the project identified over one hundred examples of religiously inspired environmental practices and projects in various parts of the world ranging from reforestation in India and Africa to preservation of herbal knowledge in South America, from the protection of coral reefs in the Pacific regions to the conservation of wildlife in the Middle East.

Three culminating conferences were held at the American Academy of Arts and Sciences in Cambridge, Massachusetts, at the United Nations, and at the American Museum of Natural History in New York. These conferences brought representatives of the world's religions into conversation with one another as well as into dialogue with key scientists, economists, educators, and policymakers in the environmental field. It was at the United Nations press conference that an ongoing Harvard Forum on Religion and Ecology was announced to continue the research, education, and outreach begun at these earlier conferences. The forum has mounted an international website to assist the field of religion and ecology with introductory papers and annotated bibliographies on the major world religions as well as on science, economy, and policy issues (http://environment.harvard.edu/religion).

CONCLUSIONS. Several qualifications regarding the intersection of religion and ecology were identified by scholars in the Harvard research project. First, many suggest that no one religious tradition has a privileged ecological perspective. Rather, scholars frequently indicate that multiple perspectives are the most helpful in identifying the contributions of the world's religions to environmental problems. This field is thus conceived as an interreligious project. Second, it is assumed by many that while religions are necessary partners in this process, they are not sufficient without the indispensable contributions of science, economics, education, and policy to the varied challenges of current environmental problems. Therefore, this field can be regarded as an interdisciplinary effort in which religions have an important role. Third, it is acknowledged that there is frequently a disjunction between principles and practices, so that ecologically sensitive ideas in religions are not always evident in environmental practices in particular civilizations. Many civilizations have overused their environment, with or without religious sanction. Finally, there is an acknowledgment that religions have all too frequently contributed to tensions and conflict among ethnic groups, both historically and at present. Dogmatic rigidity, inflexible truth claims, and misuse of institutional and communal power by religions have often led to disruptive consequences in various parts of the globe.

Nonetheless, it is acknowledged that while religions have been preservers of traditional ways, they have also been provocateurs of social change. In other words, they can be both limiting and liberating in their outlooks and affects. In the twentieth century, for example, religious leaders and theologians helped to give birth to progressive movements such as civil rights for minorities, social justice for the poor, and liberation for women. In the 1990s, religious groups were instrumental in launching a movement called Jubilee 2000, advocating debt reduction for poor nations. In the early years of the twenty-first century, the National Council of Churches in the United States organized a campaign calling for attention to global warming and its deleterious consequences for human and biological communities.

As key repositories of enduring civilizational values, and as indispensable motivators in moral transformation, it can be said that religions have a role to play in shaping a sustainable future for the planet. This is especially true because attitudes toward nature have been consciously and unconsciously conditioned by religious and cultural worldviews. Lynn White observed this in the 1960s, when he noted, "What people do about their ecology depends on what they think about themselves in relation to things around them. Human ecology is deeply conditioned by beliefs about our nature and destiny—that is, by religion" (White, 1967). Recognition of the diverse roles of religions in shaping ecological worldviews, both historically and at present, has led to calls for their further involvement in addressing environmental issues.

A significant example of this occurred in autumn of 2003 in China. Pang Yue, director of the National Environmental Protection Bureau, gave an important speech in which he called for the creation of an environmental culture drawing on traditional values based in Confucianism, Daoism, and Buddhism. He said, "The inner spirit of traditional Chinese culture echoes environmental culture that the world is currently emphasizing. Traditional Chinese culture pursues harmony between human beings and nature. . .and as human beings we have the responsibility to maintain and protect our environment." These remarks are striking in their departure from the materialist Marxist ideology of the last fifty years in China, as well as China's current emphasis on development, seemingly at any environmental cost. This call for recovery of traditional values is being echoed in many parts of the world as environmental issues become ever more pressing.

BIBLIOGRAPHY

Abrecht, Paul, ed. *Faith, Science, and the Future.* Geneva, 1978.

Anderson, E. N. *Ecologies of the Heart: Emotion, Belief, and the Environment.* New York, 1996.

Barbour, Ian, ed. *Western Man and Environmental Ethic.* Reading, Mass., 1973.

Barnhill, David and Roger Gottlieb, eds. *Deep Ecology and World Religions: New Essays on Sacred Ground.* Albany, N.Y., 2001.

Basso, Keith H. *Wisdom Sits in Places: Landscape and Language among the Western Apache.* Albuquerque, 1996.

Berry, Thomas. *The Dream of the Earth.* San Francisco, 1988.

Berry, Thomas. *The Great Work.* New York, 1999.

Boff, Leonardo. *Ecology and Liberation: A New Paradigm.* Translated by J. Cumming. Marynoll, N.Y., 1995.

Brown, Lester. "Challenges of the New Century." In *State of the World 2000.* New York, 2000.

Callicot, J. Baird, and Roger Ames. *Nature in Asian Traditions of Thought: Essays in Environmental Philosophy.* Albany, N.Y., 1989.

Callicot, J. Baird, and Roger Ames. *Earth's Insights: A Survey of Ecological Insights from the Mediterranean Basin to the Australian Outback.* Berkeley, Calif., 1994.

Carson, Rachel. *Silent Spring.* Boston, 1962.

Chapple, Christopher Key, ed. *Jainism and Ecology: Nonviolence in the Web of Life.* Cambridge, Mass., 2003.

Chapple, Christopher Key, and Mary Evelyn Tucker, eds. *Hinduism and Ecology: The Intersection of Earth, Sky, and Water.* Cambridge, Mass., 2000.

Chryssavgis, John, ed. *Cosmic Grace, Humble Prayer: The Ecological Vision of the Green Patriarch Bartholomew I.* Grand Rapids, Mich., 2000.

Coates, Peter. *Nature: Western Attitudes since Ancient Times.* Berkeley, Calif., 1998.

Cobb, John. *A Christian Natural Theology.* Philadelphia, 1965.

Cobb, John. *Is it Too Late? A Theology of Ecology.* 1972; reprint, Denton, Tex., 1995.

Daneel, Marthinus. *African Earthkeepers: Holistic Interfaith Mission.* Maryknoll, N.Y., 2001.

Devall, Bill, and George Sessions. *Deep Ecology.* Salt Lake City, 1985.

DeWitt, C. B. *A Sustainable Earth: Religion and Ecology in the Western Hemisphere.* Mancelona, Mich., 1987.

Eldredge, Niles. *Life in the Balance: Humanity and the Biodiversity Crisis.* Princeton, N.J., 1998

Engel, J. Ronald, and Joan Gibb Engel, eds. *Ethics of Environment and Development: Global Challenge, International Response.* Tucson, Ariz., 1990.

Erhlich, Paul. *Human Natures.* Washington, D.C., 2001.

Foltz, Richard C., Frederick M. Denny, and Azizan Baharuddin, eds. *Islam and Ecology: A Bestowed Trust.* Cambridge, Mass., 2003.

Foster, George M., and Barbara Gallatin Anderson. *Medical Anthropology.* New York, 1978.

Fox, Matthew. *The Coming of the Cosmic Christ: The Healing of Mother Earth and the Birth of a Global Renaissance.* San Francisco, 1988.

Gardner, Gary. *Invoking the Spirit: Religion and Spirituality in the Quest for a Sustainable World.* Worldwatch Paper 164. Washington, D.C., 2002.

Gebara, Ivone. *Longing for Running Water: Ecofeminism and Liberation.* Minneapolis, 1999.

Giradot, N. J., James Miller, and Liu Xiaogan, eds. *Daoism and Ecology: Ways within a Cosmic Landscape.* Cambridge, Mass., 2001.

Glacken, Clarence. *Traces on the Rhodian Shore: Nature and Culture in Western Thought from Ancient Times to the End of the Eighteenth Century.* Berkeley, Calif., 1969.

Good, Byron. *Medicine, Rationality and Experience: An Anthropological Perspective.* New York, 1994.

Gottlieb, Roger, ed. *Liberating Faith: Religious Values for Justice, Peace, and Ecological Wisdom.* Burlington, Vt., 2003.

Granberg-Michaelson, Wesley. *Redeeming the Creation.* Geneva, 1992.

Grim, John A., ed. *The Shaman: Patterns of Religious Healing among the Ojibway Indians.* Norman, Okla., 1983.

Grim, John A., ed. *Indigenous Traditions and Ecology: The Interbeing of Cosmology and Community.* Cambridge, Mass., 2001.

Hallman, D. *Ecotheology: Voices from the South and North.* Maryknoll, N.Y., 1994.

Hargrove, Eugene, ed. *Religion and Environmental Crisis.* Athens, Ga., 1986.

Harvard Forum on Religion and Ecology. http://environment.harvard.edu/religion. This website includes a list of official statements on religion and ecology by scientists, churches, and other religious organizations.

Hessel, Dieter, and Rosemary Radford Ruether, eds. *Christianity and Ecology: Seeking the Well-Being of Earth and Humans.* Cambridge, Mass., 2000.

Hull, Fritz, ed. *Earth and Spirit: The Spiritual Dimension of the Environmental Crisis.* New York, 1993.

Hultkrantz, Åke. "Ecology." In *Encyclopedia of Religion.* New York, 1987.

Izzi Dien, Mawil. *The Environmental Dimensions of Islam.* Cambridge, U.K., 2000.

Kalland, Arne, ed. *Nature Across Cultures: Views of Nature and the Environment in Non-Western Cultures.* Boston, 2003.

Kaufman, Gordon D. "A Problem for Theology: The Concept of Nature." *Harvard Theological Review* 65 (1972).

Kaufman, Gordon D. *In Face of Mystery: A Constructive Theology.* Cambridge, Mass., 1993.

Kaza, Stephanie, and Kenneth Kraft, eds. *Dharma Rain: Sources of Buddhist Environmentalism.* Boston, 2000.

Kellert, Stephen, and Timothy Farnham, eds. *The Good in Nature and Humanity: Connecting Science and Spirituality with the Natural World.* Washington, D.C., 2002.

Kinsley, David. *Religion and Ecology: Ecological Spirituality in a Cross-Cultural Perspective.* Englewood Cliffs, N.J., 1995.

Kleinman, Arthur. *Patients and Healers in the Context of Culture: An Exploration of the Borderland between Anthropology, Medicine and Psychiatry.* Berkeley, Calif., 1980.

Knitter, Paul. *One Earth, Many Religions: Multifaith Dialogue and Global Responsibility.* Maryknoll, N.Y., 1995.

Leopold, Aldo. *A Sand County Almanac and Sketches Here and There.* New York, 1949.

Lincoln, Bruce. *Priests, Warriors and Cattle: A Study in the Ecology of Religions.* Berkeley, Calif., 1981.

Maguire, Daniel. *The Moral Core of Judaism and Christianity: Reclaiming the Revolution.* Philadelphia, 1993.

Matthews, Clifford, Mary Evelyn Tucker, and Philip Hefner, eds. *When Worlds Converge: What Science and Religions Tell Us about the Story of the Universe and Our Place in It.* Chicago, 2001.

McDaniel, Jay. *Of Gods and Pelicans: A Theology of Reverence for Life.* Louisville, Ky., 1989.

McFague, Sallie. *Models of God: Theology for an Ecological Nuclear Age.* Philadelphia, 1987.

McGrath, Alister. *The Reenchantment of Nature: The Denial of Religion and the Ecological Crisis.* New York, 2002.

McNeill, J. R. *Something New under the Sun: An Environmental History of the Twentieth-Century World.* New York, 2000.

Merchant, Carolyn. *The Death of Nature: Women, Ecology and the Scientific Revolution.* San Francisco, 1980.

Moltmann, Jurgen. *God and Creation: A New Theology of Creation and the Spirit of God.* Translated by M. Kohl. San Francisco, 1985.

Nasr, Seyyed Hossein. *Religion and the Order of Nature.* Oxford, 1996.

Nasr, Seyyed Hossein. *Man and Nature: The Spiritual Crisis in Modern Man.* Dunstable, U.K., 1997.

Nelson, Lance, ed. *Purifying the Earthly Body of God.* Albany, N.Y., 1998.

Osborn, Fairfield. *Our Plundered Planet.* Boston, 1948.

Peet, Richard, and Michael Watts. *Liberation Ecologies: Environment, Development and Social Movements.* New York, 1996.

Rapport, Roy A. *Pigs for the Ancestors: Ritual in the Ecology of a New Guinea People.* Oxford, 1969.

Rasmussen, Larry. *Earth Community, Earth Ethics.* Maryknoll, N.Y., 1997.

Reaka-Kudla, Marjorie, Don Wilson, and Edward O. Wilson. *Biodiversity II: Understanding and Protecting Our Biological Resources.* Washington, D.C., 1997.

Rockefeller, Steven, and John Elder, eds. *Spirit and Nature: Why the Environment Is a Religious Issue.* Boston, 1991.

Ruether, Rosemary. *Gaia and God: An Ecofeminist Theology of Earth Healing.* San Francisco, 1992.

Santmire, Paul. *The Travail of Nature: The Ambiguous Ecological Promise of Christian Theology.* Philadelphia, 1985.

Soper, David E. *The Geography of Religions.* Englewood Cliffs, N.J., 1967.

Steward, Julian. *Evolution and Ecology: Essays on Social Transformation.* Urbana, Ill., 1977.

Swimme, Brian, and Thomas Berry. *The Universe Story: from the Primordial Flaring Forth to the Ecozoic Era—A Celebration of the Unfolding of the Cosmos.* San Francisco, 1992.

Tirosh-Samuelson, Hava, ed. *Judaism and Ecology: Created World and Revealed Word.* Cambridge, Mass., 2003.

Tuan, Yi-Fu. *Topophilia: A Study of Environmental Perception, Attitudes and Values.* Englewood Cliffs, N.J., 1974.

Tucker, Mary Evelyn. *Worldly Wonder: Religions Enter Their Ecological Phase.* Chicago, 2003.

Tucker, Mary Evelyn, and Duncan Ryukan Williams, eds. *Buddhism and Ecology: The Interconnection of Dharma and Deeds.* Cambridge, Mass., 1997.

Tucker, Mary Evelyn, and John Berthrong, eds. *Confucianism and Ecology: The Interrelation of Heaven, Earth, and Humans.* Cambridge, Mass., 1998.

Tucker, Mary Evelyn, and John Grim, eds. "Religion and Ecology: Can the Climate Change?" *Daedalus* 130, no. 4 (2001).

Waskow, Arthur, ed. *Torah of the Earth.* Woodstock, Vt., 2000.

White, Lynn, Jr. "The Historical Roots of Our Ecologic Crisis," *Science* 155 (March 1967).

MARY EVELYN TUCKER (2005)
JOHN A. GRIM (2005)

ECOLOGY AND RELIGION: ECOLOGY AND INDIGENOUS TRADITIONS

In anthropology the term *indigenous* refers to small-scale societies with distinct languages, mythic narratives, sacred places, ceremonies, and kinship systems. Over 500 million people are considered indigenous; they live on every continent (except Antarctica) as well as in the Pacific Rim. They are known as First Nations (Canada), Adivasi (India), Orang Asli (Malaysia), Igorot (Philippines) and Indians or Native Americans (the Americas). Unfortunately these native societies are often marginalized within the larger culture; their existence is also threatened by the exploitation of corporations and extractive industries (such as fossil fuels and mining). Any discussion of indigenous traditions and ecology must necessarily involve political issues of cultural and biodiversity survival. Each indigenous society is unique, and a study of one regional community cannot be extrapolated to represent others. Each society has its own cosmological understanding of nature and its own regional, cultural, and historical issues with which to contend as it struggles to survive the challenges of a global economy.

The complete history of ecology and indigenous traditions is too complex and diverse to explore here, but three overview perspectives are useful. First, before and after contact with the civilizations of Asia, Europe, and Africa, indigenous cultures certainly interacted with one another, sharing forms of traditional environmental knowledge (TEK) as well as a mode of historical consciousness often embedded in myth. The transmission of knowledge of manioc cultivation in the Pacific region and yucca extraction from problematic tubers in South America are two examples of widespread sharing of technologies. Both of these food production techniques demonstrate widespread adaptation to local symbol systems and explanatory cosmologies. Quite often, historical notice of such a technological change was embedded in an ancient myth that would be narrated in a slightly different manner to mark the historical event. This first overview perspective can be identified with the ancient forms of traditional environmental knowledge found among specific indigenous peoples that also shows evidence of having become hybridized knowledge in other cultures. The spread of tobacco similarly illustrates the features of ancient sharing and adaptation. Tobacco became central to the socioreligious life of many indigenous peoples of the Americas holding its spiritual intentions intact to the present.

Second, with the advent of dominant and oppressive cultures that subverted indigenous ways of knowing, these small-scale cultures experienced massive deaths largely due to disease pathogens for which these native peoples had little or no immune resistance. These times of intense cultural fragmentation and despair have varied in world history, continuing to the present for some indigenous peoples. This has resulted in a tremendous loss of elders who would transmit traditional environmental knowledge as well as the cessation of the accompanying rituals that accompany that knowledge. Thus, indigenous peoples continue to experience the diminishment and loss of the actual ecological diversity itself that stimulates their deepest cultural religiosity. Certainly, not all traditional knowledge is lost, nor is the biodiversity of indigenous homelands extinguished, but in this overview perspective the religious sensibilities resulting from these profound losses among indigenous people often assumes prophetic forms that announce the end of a cosmological cycle before renewal reoccurs.

A final overview perspective has emerged more forcefully in the contemporary period that can be identified as resistance and regeneration. This is not exclusively a recent development as indigenous peoples have resisted the oppression and loss of the colonial period from its inception, but this historical perspective serves to emphasize the global activities of indigenous peoples who now often act in concert to make dominant cultures aware of their plight, to argue for their sovereignty in the larger arena of nation-states, and to articulate their contributions to human thought and their insights into contemporary challenges. A striking example occurred with the Zapatistas uprising in Chiapas, Mexico, in January 1994. This well-coordinated struggle linked labor issues with cultural survival, loss of homeland with growth of computer networks. Not only did this movement resist the age-old forms of oppression by the Mexican state, but it has also been a regenerative site for offering new thought on current issues. Increasingly, global forums of indigenous peoples and local communities critique international agreements on environmental or cultural issues that do not recognize the existence or contributions of indigenous peoples. These indigenous forums explore such issues as biopiracy, biocolonialism, and environmental racism, and propose traditional ideas and practices to counter the market-driven plans offered by developed nations. No one organization speaks for indigenous peoples, but some significant groups are the Columbia Coordinating Body of Indigenous Peoples Organizations of the Amazon Basin, International Alliance of Indigenous and Tribal Peoples of the Tropical Forests (Nepal), Amazon Alliance (Ecuador), Pacific Concerns Resource Centre (Fiji), International Research Institute for Maori and Indigenous Education, Ethnic Minority and Indigenous Rights Organizations of Africa (Nigeria), African Indigenous Women Organization, and the Inter-Mountain peoples Education and Culture in Thailand Association as well as the ongoing work of Cultural Survival and International Survival.

Traditional indigenous societies view all existence as interdependent, including interactions with nature and the technology of their subsistence practices. The term *lifeway* is used here to indicate this integration of thought, production, and distribution. This ecologically integrated knowledge has often been misconceived as animism or "failed epistemologies" too limited for consideration by modern societies. However, indigenous knowledge traditions—based on a relational knowing of their worlds—can contend as robust alternatives to modern worldviews that tend to objectify and distance the natural world from the human. Three significant political and social undercurrents must be considered in the study of indigenous religions and ecology.

First, despite mounting economic and political pressures indigenous communities have demonstrated remarkable resistance and regeneration. This has been evident through five centuries of contact with European culture and continues with the twenty-first-century struggle against complete absorption into dominant cultures. Cosmology (a society's view of the natural world and universe) and ecology play significant roles in this struggle, as well as in the adaptation of indigenous societies to contemporary culture and technology.

Second, what is known of indigenous lifeways, their integration of culture into local ecosystems, and their environmental knowledge has come from indigenous peoples themselves. Elders and teachers have been the source of knowledge about, and decision makers for, religious and environmental activities.

The third sociopolitical consideration is an ideology called *indigenism,* the promotion, defense, and/or politicization of native cultures. Romantic perspectives view indigenous lifeways as rigid, unchanging, and opposed to even appropriate development. At the other extreme, national governments sometimes devalue and demean the sustainable interactions that native peoples maintain with local bioregions to claim exclusive prerogatives over the use of indigenous lands. Both views are potentially misleading.

Indigenous Voices. Too frequently indigenous voices are not heard on ecological issues. Native American lawyer Vine Deloria, Jr., calls for the recognition of native peoples as national entities with sacred lands exempt from the arbitrary decisions of state and federal governments; this, he says would constitute a move from "greening" to "maturing." Deloria connects religion and ecology not simply with academic or conservationist concerns but with the struggle for legal and political rights to conserve traditional lifeways.

Indigenous logic is strikingly different from the linear, analytical, mechanistic, and concept-driven rhetoric of dominant modern societies. Traditional cultures often connect their regard for the protective power of spirits with concepts of cosmology and ecology. Spirits are differently understood, but these numinous beings are markedly place-based, relational, and felt presences. Affective, emotional ways of knowing are often cultivated in rituals by means of deprivation and body- or mind-altering substances, enabling indigenous leaders to address situations of community need through spirit-inspired messages.

Indigenous leaders know that environmental knowledge has long been operative in their communities and that, of late, nonnative peoples have been interested in this knowledge. They wonder, however, if this new interest is genuine or simply another type of exploitation.

Themes in the Study of Indigenous Religions and Ecology. Several prominent themes can be identified; this list is not exhaustive but represents efforts to understand the intricate and varied ways that indigenous peoples live in relation to their ecosystems.

Balance and conservation. Many indigenous lifeways recognize the balance that pervades both the ecosystem and the cosmos. Ruptures in this balance are addressed by ritual procedures intended to restore personal, social, ecological, and cosmological harmonies. Even hunting and fishing are believed to foster the balance of life. Thus, the Yup'ik Eskimo of Alaska view hunter and prey as part of a cycle of reciprocity in which animals visit the human world to be hunted, treated respectfully, and sent back to return the following season. Animals and plants are seen as spirit beings that willingly give themselves for human sustenance. Hunting and other activities are part of a cycle of reciprocity based on privilege and responsibility to a slain animal. These complex systems of limits on hunting, dietary prohibitions, and gender and kin rules regarding distribution of game and other foods constitute indigenous conservation ethics.

Religious ritual in the ecology of the Tsembaga horticultural peoples of highland New Guinea was described in 1968 by Roy Rappaport in *Pigs for the Ancestors.* This study provided important insight into indigenous concerns for cosmological and ecological balance. Previously, cultural ecology taught that indigenous religions had been formed passively by interactions with local environments. Rappaport suggested instead that ritual acted as a regulatory system whereby the Tsembaga maintained their environment, limited hostility, controlled population growth, promoted trade, and facilitated the distribution of protein. In short, Tsembaga religion had ecological implications as well as connections to political, social, and subsistence practices.

Richard Nelson's 1983 study of the Koyukon peoples of Alaska, *Make Prayers to the Raven* advanced this understanding of indigenous religions and ecology by showing how extensive Koyukon oral narratives of the Distant Time (*Kk'adonts'idnee*) contained detailed environmental knowledge of the boreal forest. Moreover, these narratives presented particular examples of Koyukon regard for plants and animals. Nelson explored ways in which these ecological insights linked a complex Koyukon ethical system (*hutlanee*) with cosmological narratives of the Distant Time and subsistence practices. Most importantly, Nelson's work described an indigenous conservation ethic flowing from the mutual interactions of lifeway and ecosystem.

Narrative and place. The Maori of New Zealand speak of themselves as *tangata whenua,* people of the land. By grounding their identity as a people in stories of their homeland, the Maori are not simply expressing a nationalistic patriotism. Rather, *whenua* means both land and placenta; this evokes the Earth-mother herself, Papatuanuku, and makes land the connection both to larger cosmic forces and the source of personal life. Myths describe how the Sky-father, Ranginui, was separated from the Earth-mother by the efforts of their children, who eventually differentiate all of creation. Thus, the mythic offspring bring about the primordial separation that introduces into creation disparate, yet interconnected, forces such as yearning, ambiguity, and fecundity.

For the Maori, interactions with the environment bring humans into contact with *mana* and *maori,* powers inherent in all of reality. A thing's existence carries within it *mana,* or the inherent right to be where it is. Maori myths explore predator and prey relations throughout existence in concepts of hard *mana*—competition and aggression—as well as soft *mana*—compassion and cooperation. All creatures also possess a personal life force, *maori,* suggesting that reality has intrinsic intention and value.

A Maori proverb presents a glimpse of this dynamic, interactive kinship with the Earth: "The blood (*toto*) of humans (*tangata*) comes from food *(kai);* our welfare (*oranga*) comes from land (*whenua*)." This links blood with the food that comes from the death of one's nonhuman kin, namely animals and plants. In addition to *mana* and *maori,* all beings-as-food carry individual *tapu,* or sacredness. Human subsistence practices may be harmful to the *mana* of those eaten, but recognition of *tapu* respects *maori.* Inner life, or blood, is thought to depend on correct spiritual relations with other creatures, including ritual treatment of their tapu. Welfare, or material prosperity, for the *maori* flows from ethical relations with the differentiated forces of life in creation.

According to the Maori, humans are people of the land when they maintain right relationships with the *mana, maori,* and *tapu* of creatures. These knowledge-based processes establish the *maori* of the human community, which can only be generated by acting responsibly. The Maori claim to be people of the land in Aoteroa New Zealand proceeds from a cosmology that establishes all creatures, not simply humans, in a web of kinship. Their ancestral prerogatives entail responsible, ethical interactions with both creatures and the land.

Person and power. In many indigenous cultures both male and female shamans cultivate intense, intimate, and transforming relationships with local lands and life forms. Shamans are persons of spiritual power whose symbolic practices mirror the understandings and interactions of their small-scale societies, with local environments as the source of efficacious power. Their exceptional ecological imagination makes shamans capable of interacting and identifying with local environments in innovative and creative ways.

A shaman's knowledge of plants, animals, terrain, and weather patterns is not merely empirical learning, but clearly has a religious perspective as well. Shamanistic views of the environment are relational and reflect personal and community identities and values. The shamans' healing and divining arts present a range of unique individual expressions of culturally specific religious ecologies.

Shamans transform the external environment of mountains, rivers, and biodiversity into inner experiential landscapes that resonate with the surrounding animate world, weaving together the outer environment of all beings with the shaman's inner psychic world, thus generating empathy and commitment from the people. As is evident in the following case study, this cosmology is presented as both the actual homeland and symbolic representations of it.

Arkadii Anisimov's study of the fishing and reindeer-herding Evenk peoples of the central Siberian plateau describes the shaman's tent and ritual as a "fencing" designed to protect the people from attacks by both harmful underworld spirits and neighboring shamans. Evenk cosmology envisions a tripartite world, and the ritual configures zones of symbolic activities that manifest this view. The shaman's tent is in the middle region, or human world, with an eastern gallery as the celestial realm and a western gallery as the underworld. The cosmological symbolism of the realms is evident to the Evenk. Thus, the eastern gallery has living green-leafed larch trees that are turned upside down with their roots on top as if anchored in the celestial world. Wooden plaques depicting spirit images of reindeer and pike symbolically swimming in the Milky Way are planted in the ground as guardians of this celestial region. Dead larch trees in the western gallery have their roots pointing down to the netherworld with wooden images of spirit birds and ancestral figures guarding the path to the departed. This western gallery, moreover, has multiple images of animals, fish, and larch trees with birds on top—all arranged in the form of a fish weir to capture any dangerous wolf spirits sent by neighboring shamans to attack during the ritual.

The shaman's tent, set on the human/earth level, has a central larch tree, a fire at its base, and a raft-seat for the shaman with wooden plaque images of salmon flanked by attending representations of knives, spears, and fish other than pike. In this symbolic setting the shaman becomes an animal and undertakes therapeutic journeys to heal members of the community who are ill. Along with healing symbolism, the shaman marshals considerable military might in the form of spirit-animal legions to oppose dangerous intruders. Should the shaman die, anxiety reigns until a new shaman can reestablish this protective spiritual fencing. The power-knowledge of the Evenk shaman, therefore, draws on a complex religious ecology that connects animal symbolism, military preparedness, and healing journeys to protect the people in their bioregion.

CONCLUSION. Indigenous lifeways do not foster individual, subjective beliefs, conceptualizations, or representations, nor do they divide a this-world reality from an other-world, transcendent reality. Rather, they live in a relational universe, striving to nurture and create a world that nurtures and creates them. Indigenous peoples undertake conversations with mountains, rivers, stars, animals, and plants that are not merely metaphorical or symbolic communication, but reciprocal conversations.

Ritual is but one example of this conversation in which the pragmatic and the religious, the material and the spiritual are interwoven. Body/mind connections between the human and the natural world are celebrated by indigenous peoples in ritual; human senses are activated as the highly crafted logic of ritual communication enables conversations with all living things. Life in the world is not without discord and disagreement—demands and limits are acknowledged. Rather than being symbolized as ecologists, indigenous peoples stand for commitment to place in the contemporary world.

BIBLIOGRAPHY

Anisimov, Arkadii F. "The Shaman's Tent of the Evenks and the Origin of the Shamanistic Rite." In *Siberian Shamanism*, edited by Henry Michael. Toronto, 1963.

Apffel-Marglin, Frederique, with the Andean Project on Peasant Technologies (PRATEC). *The Spirit of Regeneration: Andean Culture Confronting Western Notions of Development.* New York, 1998. A major study of the resistance and regeneration of traditional agricultural practices and knowledge among Aymara peoples of Peru and Bolivia.

Basso, Keith H. *Wisdom Sits in Places: Landscape and Language among the Western Apache.* Albuquerque, N.M., 1996. The classic study of place-based knowledge and wisdom among the Apache peoples in southwestern North America.

Callicott, J. Baird, and Michael P. Nelson. *American Indian Environmental Ethics: An Ojibwa Case Study.* Upper Saddle River, N.J., 2004. By examining the worldview of these Great Lakes Anishinabe peoples, these authors derive indigenous principles that they bring to a theoretical discussion of environmental ethics.

Crocker, Jon C. *Vital Souls: Bororo Cosmology, Natural Symbolism, and Shamanism.* Tucson, Ariz., 1985. A major ethnography on a South American Amazonian people exploring the relationships between cosmology and religious practice.

Grim, John, ed. *Indigenous Traditions and Ecology: The Interbeing of Cosmology and Community.* Cambridge, Mass., 2001. Perhaps the broadest collection of articles discussing different indigenous perspectives on environmental thought and issues.

Guss, David M. *To Weave and Sing: Art, Symbol, and Narrative in the South American Rainforest.* Berkeley, Calif., 1989. A beautiful and intricate discussion of cosmology and technical production among an Amazonian people.

Hughes, Donald. *North American Indian Ecology.* El Paso, Tex., 1996. One of the earliest texts on the environmental thought and practice of Native North American peoples.

Ingold, Tim. *Perception of the Environment: Essays in Livelihood, Dwelling and Skill.* London and New York, 2000. A major statement by an anthropologist investigating the contributions of indigenous traditions to the philosophical issues of environmental theory.

Karlsson, B.G. *Contested Belonging: An Indigenous People's Struggle for Forest and Identity in Sub-Himalayan Bengal.* 2d ed. Richmond, U.K., 2000. A major study of South Asian indigenous peoples and the environmental challenges unique to that area.

Kickingbird, Kirke, and Karen Ducheneaux. *One Hundred Million Acres.* New York, 1973. A study of the relationships between loss of land and cultural deprivation in North America.

Krech, Shepard, III. *The Ecological Indian: Myth and History.* New York, 1999. A response to the romantic imaging of indigenous peoples in North America as the "first ecologists."

Nelson, Richard K. *Make Prayers to the Raven: A Koyukon View of the Northern Forest.* Chicago, 1983. Continues to be a classic in the field of traditional environmental knowledge, traditional conservation practices, and insight into the deep affectivity for the natural world among indigenous peoples.

Ramos, Alcida Rita. *Indigenism: Ethnic Politics in Brazil.* Madison, Wis., 1998. A study of the romanticization of Brazil's indigenous peoples in terms of the politics of that country.

Rappaport, Roy A. *Pigs for the Ancestors: Ritual in the Ecology of a New Guinea People.* 2d ed. Prospect Heights, Ill., 2000. Classic study of the ways in which Maring peoples of New Guinea aspire to maintain socio-ecological balance by means of ritual.

Roseman, Marina. *Healing Sounds from the Malaysian Rainforest: Temiar Music and Medicine.* Berkeley, Calif., 1991. An ethnomusicologist investigates the close relationships between song, healing practices, and ecology among a Malaysian people.

Suzuki, David, and Peter Knudtson. *Wisdom of the Elders: Sacred Native Stories of Nature.* New York, 1992. Anthology of popular insights and concerns of indigenous peoples that is helpful in the classroom and useful for generating discussion.

Vecsey, Christopher, and Robert W. Venables. *American Indian Environments: Ecological Issues in Native American History.* Syracuse, N.Y., 1980. Early study of ecological consciousness among Native North American peoples.

Weaver, Jace, ed. *Defending Mother Earth: Native American Perspectives on Environmental Justice.* Maryknoll, N.Y., 1996. Examination of Native American attitudes toward environmental perceptions and problems largely written by native academics and activists.

Wilbert, Johannes. *Mystic Endowment: Religious Ethnography of the Warao Indians.* Cambridge, Mass., 1993. A major study of the ways in which myth is embedded in ritual and subsistence practices so as to affirm the traditional environmental knowledge of an indigenous people.

JOHN A. GRIM (2005)

ECOLOGY AND RELIGION: ECOLOGY AND HINDUISM

Hinduism, the major religious tradition in India and the faith of almost a billion people around the world, is extremely diverse. There are many philosophical, ritual, narrative, theistic, and nontheistic traditions within Hinduism and, therefore, Hinduism encompasses pluralistic views towards nature. Many Hindu communities value nature, think of the universe as the body of God, pray for peace between all the elements of the universe, urge nonviolence to all beings on earth, and personify nature and the earth as goddesses. However, others devalue nature by thinking of matter (homologized to women) as ensnaring the spirit and preventing it from achieving liberation. Yet other Hindus think of the universe as ultimately without reality, and some Hindus think of the final goal as transcending all dualities of good and evil, spirit and matter, culture and nature.

Several Indian words in Sanskrit and in vernacular languages have philosophical and colloquial meanings corresponding to the many meanings of *nature.* In general, the term *nature* will be used here to refer to those elements that are considered to be part of the lived or conceptualized environment in the many Hindu traditions. The most frequently used Indian term for "nature," *prakṛti,* may refer to matter as well as the inherent tendencies in material substances.

The many Sanskrit texts within Hindu traditions have had a limited role to play in the history of the religion. Hindu traditions consider custom and practice to be as important as the texts themselves. Nevertheless, with the intellectual colonization by the West and the advent of mass media, more Hindus today have started to focus on the sacred texts, and many search for answers to the environmental crises both in text and practice. This entry, therefore, will discuss textual sources, as well as eco-practices adopted by Hindus. This essay will consider the phenomena of nature in texts and then discuss the various forms of environmental activism in India that use religio-cultural concepts as sources of inspiration or guidance. Environmental activism has been largely guided by notions of *dharma* (duty, righteousness, "religion"). These concepts have been communicated through stories from the epics and Purāṇas (Sanskrit and vernacular texts glorifying deities and places composed primarily in the first millennium CE) and narrated by family or village elders.

NATURE IN SANSKRIT TEXTS. The earliest hymns of the Vedas are addressed to many gods, and many of them are connected with natural phenomena and the environment the people lived in. Agni, the god of fire, is seen as a messenger between human beings and the deities because offerings were placed in the fire to be carried to other worlds. Agni is the fire on earth, lightning in the atmosphere, and the sun in the sky. Usha, the goddess of dawn, Varuṇa, who presides over the waters, the oceans, and even aquatic animals, and Indra, who is associated with the thunderbolt and rain, are all worshiped. A goddess known as Sarasvatī is also spoken of, sometimes as a river, sometimes as representing learning. Some hymns speak of a connection between the rituals and the prevalence of cosmic and earthly order, *ṛta. Ṛta* is truth and justice, the rightness of things. It makes harmony and peace possible on the earth and in the heavens. Although *ṛta* is an impersonal cosmic principle, Vedic gods like Varuṇa were considered its upholders.

In retrieving and revisioning the Vedas, Hindus have emphasized those sections that speak of peace and harmony. Thus, the "Shanti path" (Song of peace) in the *Yajurveda* (36:17) has become popular in India and in the diaspora. Repeating a hymn composed more than three millennia ago, the Hindu devotee recites: "May there be peace in the skies, peace in the atmosphere, peace on earth, peace in the waters. May the healing plants and trees bring peace; may there be peace [on and from] the world, the deity. May there be peace in the world, peace on peace. May that peace come to me!"

The many texts that focus explicitly on *dharma* or righteous behavior were composed in the first few centuries of the Common Era. Many sections of the epics *Rāmāyaṇa* and *Mahābhārata* and the Purāṇas also focused on *dharma.* The epics and Purāṇas give detailed narratives of the periodic and cyclic destruction of the world. By the beginning of the third eon, things are perceived as going awry. The *Kūrma Purāṇa* says that because of greed and passion, the people of this age seize the rivers, fields, mountains, and clumps of trees and herbs, overcoming them by strength. That is just the beginning of the decline in virtue and behavior. The epic *Mahābhārata* (c. 500–200 BCE) is graphic in the portrayal of the events that will take place at the end of the fourth—and worst—eon and what will happen after a thousand such ages. At the end of the eon the population increases; there is a stench everywhere. The "natural" order of things becomes sluggish; the cows will yield little milk; and the trees, teeming with crows, will yield few flowers and fruits. The *brahmans*—the priestly class—it is said will plunder the land bare for alms. At the end of a thousand eons, the text continues, there will be a drought of many years, and all creatures will starve. The fire of destruction will rage, and large clouds will rise up in the sky. The epics say that at this time all humans will become omnivores and barbarians. They will destroy parks and trees, and the lives of the living will be ruined in the world. Thus, there seems to be an almost preordained structure in the destruction of the environment.

Other scriptural passages on *dharma*, however, focus on positive elements. They encourage the planting of trees, condemn the destruction of plants and forests, and assert that trees are like children. In this context, a passage from the *Matsya Purāṇa* is instructive. It is said that the goddess Pārvatī planted a sapling of the Aśoka tree and took good care of it. Her rationale was that there are many acts of *dharma* that one can perform—digging wells and reservoirs provide clean water to the public—but a tree is as good as ten sons in serving the community. Sentences such as these have been valorized by some temples to encourage the planting and care of trees. Other Purāṇas also celebrate the planting of trees; the *Varāha Purāṇa* says that one who plants five mango trees does not go to hell, and the *Viṣṇu Dharmottara* claims that one who plants a tree will never fall into hell. The *Matsya Purāṇa* also describes a celebration for planting trees.

ASPECTS OF NATURE. Most Hindus perceive divinity in many aspects of nature. Many animals, snakes, mountains, rivers, trees, and, indeed, the entire universe pulsate with something divine. Some Hindus personify natural phenomena as divine; others think of natural phenomena as having presiding deities. Although the divinity is considered invested in some natural phenomena and habitats, it does not follow that such habitats are not used or abused. As with many religious traditions, there is dissonance between perception and behavior.

Most of the rivers of India are considered to be female and the mountains male. Rivers are perceived to be nurturing (and sometimes judgmental) mothers, feeding, nourishing, quenching, and when angered, flooding the earth. Rivers are personified as deities. The River Gaṅgā (Ganges) is sometimes portrayed as a consort of Lord Śiva. In the south, Kāverī Amman (Mother Kāverī) is the name by which the river is fondly addressed. Hundreds of girls born in the area of Coorg, where the Kāverī has her source, are named after her. In the plains of Tamilnadu, Kāverī is seen as a devotee and sometimes the consort of Lord Viṣṇu, and several temples (such as Terazhundur, near Kumbakonam) include a striking image of this personified river in the innermost shrine.

Rivers such as the Gaṅgā, Kāverī, Godāvarī, and Narmadā are much venerated by devotees, both as rivers and as goddesses. By bathing in the great rivers of India, one is said to be both physically cleansed and morally purified of one's sins (*papa*), which are destroyed. Moreover, one acquires merit or auspiciousness in this way. Although there is strong belief in the religious purity of the rivers, from an environmental perspective, they have become severely polluted as a result of rapid industrialization and the release of toxic human and industrial waste. The rivers that are supposed to purify human beings, physically, morally, and ritually, are said to be at the receiving end of *adharma*, unrighteous behavior. The beliefs of devotees that the rivers are intrinsically pure, moreover, works against the cleansing of the rivers, for some people believe that they cannot really be polluted.

PHILOSOPHICAL TEXTS, *DHARMA*, AND *MOKṢA*. Hindu texts portray *dharma* and *mokṣa* (liberation from the cycle of life and death) as goals for all human beings. There are many meanings for *dharma.* In some of its manifestations, it is concerned with *loka sangraha* or the welfare of human beings. *Dharma* refers to many topics, including notions of righteousness and duty, as well as virtues such as gratitude and compassion, which are thought of ideally as common to all human beings. While in some philosophical traditions, doing one's *dharma* or duty led to *mokṣa,* in other cases the dictates and norms of *dharma* to sustain society (beget children, earn money) could be seen as binding one to the cycle of life and death and as tugging in a direction away from liberation. The pathways to liberation included meditative and reflective paths focusing on control of the human body and mind, as well as intellectual and emotional devotion to the deity of one's choice. Detachment from everyday life—even while living in the midst of the world—was an integral part of the enterprise.

It is important to keep this taxonomy in mind, because theological doctrines dealing with "reality" do not necessarily trickle down into dharmic or ethical injunctions. This disjunction between *dharma* and *mokṣa* is marked in some Hindu texts and practices. *Dharma* texts promote righteous behavior on earth, and *mokṣa* texts encourage one to be detached from such concerns. A few texts, such as the *Bhagavadgītā*, have tried to bridge the paradigms of *dharma* and *mokṣa.*

Thus, a theology that emphasizes the world as a body of God, a pervasive pan-Indian belief that goddess Earth (Bhūdevī/Vasundhara/Pṛithvī) is also a consort of Viṣṇu, or the notion that the mother goddess (Amba, Durgā) is synonymous with nature (*prakṛti*), does not necessarily translate to eco-friendly behavior. Likewise, renunciation, celibacy, and detachment are laudable virtues for one who seeks liberation from the cycle of life and death, but the texts on *dharma* say that begetting children is necessary for salvation. These biomorphic worldviews are significant if we are to assess the relevancy of philosophical viewpoints such as deep ecology for the Hindu traditions. On another front, the dissonance between *dharma* and philosophical texts explains why some Hindu traditions hold the Goddess to be supreme while women do not always have a high position in society. It is true that some theological/*tattva* texts speak of certain kinds of "oneness" of the universe and, in some cases, of the equality of all creation. Some philosophical texts speak of the oneness of creation and the creator, and the absolute identity between the supreme being (Brāhmaṇ) and the human soul (*ātman*)—a oneness that transcends the concept of "equality of many"; however, in the sphere of *dharma* and everyday life, the hierarchies of social classes pertaining to economics, gender, caste, and age are significant. Hindu institutions and eco-activists have therefore found more resources in the narratives in the *dharma* texts than in those of philosophy and theology in galvanizing people.

ENVIRONMENTAL ACTIVISM IN THE CONTEMPORARY PERIOD. In India there has been a fairly long, though sporadic, history of environmental activism. The faith of the Bishnoi and in the Chipko movement and the Narmadā Andolan have become well known. The Bishnoi tradition—or as some call it, the eco-religious revolution—was started around 1485 in Samrathal Dhora (north India) by Jambho-ji (b. 1451). Jambho-ji was said to have been influenced by the pastoral life led by the deity Kṛṣṇa and is believed to have preached his faith for about fifty-one years. Of the 120 sayings credited to him, twenty-nine *(bish-noi)* directives are said to be particularly significant. Many adherents today interpret these teachings as promoting biodiversity and the protection of trees.

The Chipko movement uses principles of nonviolent protest and resistance to protect trees from commercial developers. The movement was organized during the 1970s in the Himalayan region of the state of Uttar Pradesh and has since spread to many other parts of India. Local villagers embrace (*chipko* means "to hug") trees, and the movement promotes many slogans that help spread the message. These pithy sayings include such messages as "Ecology is permanent economy" and "What do forests bear? Soil, water, and pure air." The protests are based on Mohandas Gandhi's philosophy of nonviolence, pervasive Hindu notions of a harmonious relationship between human beings and nature, and respect for nature *(prakṛti),* which is seen as divine.

Some temples, such as the one at Tirumala Tirupati in South India, the largest and richest temple complex in the country, have also encouraged eco-activism. Billboards saying "Vriksho rakshati: rakshatah" ("Trees protect: Let us protect them" or "Trees, when protected, protect us") greet visitors to the sacred pilgrimage town of Tirumala-Tirupati in the state of Andhra Pradesh. The Tirumala-Tirupati temple is one of the oldest temples, and it carries a great deal of dharmic and financial clout both in India and in the diaspora. In response to the ecological crisis in India, the temple at Tirumala-Tirupati began what is called the Vriksha (tree) Prasāda scheme. Whenever a pilgrim visits a temple in India, he or she is given a piece of blessed fruit or food to take home. This is called a *prasāda* or "favor" of the deity; at Tirumala-Tirupati, a sapling, rather than food, is given as the symbol of the deity's grace. The nurseries of the Tirumala-Tirupati temple have many varieties of plants, both decorative plants and plants that are considered to be medically useful. The saplings cultivated are suitable for the soil in various parts of India, and by planting them at home, one can have an authentic piece of the sacred place of Tirumala wherever one lives.

The Tirumala-Tirupati temple, which is located on an elevation of 3,000 feet, was once surrounded by heavy forests. Apart from the giving of saplings, which is meant to raise the ecology-consciousness of the pilgrims, the forestry department of T. T. Devasthanam (the official bureaucracy of the temple) started the Shri Venkateswara Vanabhivriddhi scheme in 1981; it was initially called the "Bioaesthetic Plan." Following this plan, donations made by devotees are used for the purchase and planting of trees and plants. Over 2,500,000 indigenous trees are said to have been planted on the hills and the plains as a result of this program. In its support of this venture, the temple quotes relevant scriptural texts on the importance of trees and, most importantly, honors the devotee-participants in this thriving program. Both in texts and in practice, the Hindu traditions and some institutions have encouraged proactive approaches in the planting and protection of trees and plants.

Environmental activists have also deployed a number of religious strategies in the fight against the damming of rivers. Sunderlal Bahuguna, a well-known environmental activist, says that damming a river is like killing it. In opposing the building of the Tehri Dam in the Himalayas, a seismic zone, he has argued that several sacred pilgrimage sites will be destroyed if the dam were to break.

Several activists have drawn upon traditional Hindu narratives and rituals to save rivers like the Gaṅgā and the Yamunā from pollution, and more recently from corporate developers. Many of the movements and statements, such as the Haridwar Declaration, issued in 2002 to protect the river from privatization and commercial interests, draw upon the narratives and imagery of Gaṅgā as mother and goddess. The Haridwar Declaration correctly points out that rites of passages for Hindus, from birth to death, are conducted on the banks of these holy rivers and that the people will not let their Gaṅgā Mātā (Mother Gaṅgā) or its water be sold to multinational corporations. The declaration recalls the story of the descent of this river from the heavens, as narrated in the Purāṇas. It goes on to say that the sacred waters of this river cannot be the property of any one individual or company, and that Mother Gaṅgā is not for sale. In this, and many similar activist efforts, the Puranic narratives and notions of *dharma* are pressed into use.

Ramachandra Guha, a noted environmentalist, has urged a more practical environmentalism. He argues against an extremist, radical environmentalism, and advocates a balance between ecological concerns and social justice on the one hand, and economics and science and technology on the other.

In the hundreds of grassroots movements around India, leaders like Veer Bhadra Mishra and Sathya Sai Baba, institutions like the World Wide Fund for Nature, and pilgrimage sites such as Badrinath have all used religious narratives, ritual, and the values of *dharma* as ways of successfully motivating Hindus to take action and clean up the environment, plant new trees, and value biodiversity as an integral part of their activities. In many of these movements, women have played an active role.

Women and Contemporary Environmental Action. Beginning in the late twentieth century, environmental activists such has Vandana Shiva began to develop an ecofeminist critique of gender and the environment that was pertinent to India. They compared the denigration of the rivers to the denigration of women at various times in the history of Hindu civilization. Shiva has eloquently and forcefully explored as well the ways in which women suffer as "development" destroys forests near their homes. Shiva argues that many of the new corporations are involved in "maldevelopment" projects in which nature and women are turned into passive objects and exploited by and for the uncontrolled desires of men.

Shiva also works on issues of hazardous wastes, biodiversity conservation, globalization, and patenting and intellectual property rights (calling the profiteering of corporations from traditional ecological knowledge "biopiracy"). Shiva has highlighted colonialism as a major factor in the draining of resources from India and the dismantling of traditional ecological paradigms by which the earth is held in respect. She argues that the process of patenting will deprive India of its last resource—biodiversity. Inspired by such critiques, women from diverse social classes have become environmentally active in India.

Women in the Chipko movement, for example, have been involved in protecting trees, for women are generally the first to feel the impact of deforestation. In an important development, however, many women from the more powerful classes have become influential environmental activists in their own right, adding their strength to the cause. Women have been actively and creatively involved in communicating the tragedy of ecological disaster and facilitating environmental awareness and action, sometimes using traditional religious art forms, sometimes through mainstream media and technology.

Awareness of ecological concerns has also been raised through the medium of traditional Indian dance. The theory and practice of classical dance in India is seen as a religious activity. In the twentieth century, classical dance began to be used as a medium for a social commentary on women and the environment. Noted dancers choreographed many dances with environmental themes, portraying, through their art, the Chipko movement and the pollution of the landscape, and the importance of trees. Through this medium audiences around the country, urban and rural, literate and illiterate, soon came to understand the urgency of this message.

With the growing awareness of the ecological plight, Hindu communities are pressing into use many dharmic texts and injunctions. They are drawing on the epics and Purāṇas for inspiration as they plant gardens and revive traditional lore regarding the medicinal importance of trees and plants. Women, through song and dance, increasingly communicate the ways in which environmental deterioration injures both women and nature, and they call for environmental protection and restoration, sometimes engaging in direct action to resist environmentally destructive practices. The philosophical insights of Hinduism may not have been strong enough to prevent environmental disaster, but the dharmic resources have provided rich resources for the subcontinents' early initiatives to reverse these trends and make the subcontinent green and toxin free.

Bibliography

Alley, Kelly D. *On the Banks of the Gaṅgā: When Wastewater Meets a Sacred River.* Ann Arbor, Mich., 2002. An excellent discussion of the complex problems connected with the pollution of the Ganges River.

Chapple, Christopher Key. *Nonviolence to Animals, Earth, and Self in Asian Traditions.* Albany, N.Y., 1993.

Chapple, Christopher Key. "Hindu Environmentalism." In *Worldviews and Ecology*, edited by M. E. Tucker and J. A. Grim, pp. 113–123. Maryknoll, N.Y., 1994.

Chapple, Christopher Key, and Mary Evelyn Tucker, eds. *Hinduism and Ecology: The Intersection of Earth, Sky, and Water.* Cambridge, Mass., 2000. A wide variety of approaches and topics connected with Hindu environmentalism. Topics range from philosophical approaches to activism.

Feldhaus, Anne. *Water and Womanhood.* New York, 1995.

Gadgil, Madheva, and Ramachandra Guha. *This Fissured Land: An Ecological History of India.* Berkeley, Calif., 1992.

Gold, Ann Grodzins, and Bhoju Ram Gujar. *In the Time of Trees and Sorrows: Nature, Power, and Memory in Rajasthan.* Durham, N.C., 2001.

Gruzalski, Bart. "The Chipko Movement: A Gandhian Approach to Ecological Sustainability and Liberation from Economic Colonisation." In *Ethical and Political Dilemmas of Modern*

India, edited by Ninian Smart and Shivesh Thakur, pp. 100–125. New York, 1993. A concise and clear introduction to the Chipko movement

Narayanan, Vasudha. "'One Tree Is Equal to Ten Sons': Hindu Responses to the Problems of Ecology, Population, and Consumption." *Journal of the American Academy of Religion* 65, no. 2 (1997): 291–332.

Narayanan, Vasudha. "Water, Wood, and Wisdom: Ecological Perspectives from the Hindu Traditions." *Daedalus* 130, no. 4 (2001): 179–206.

Nelson, Lance E., ed. *Purifying the Earthly Body of God: Religion and Ecology in Hindu India.* Albany, N.Y., 1998. An excellent set of essays with detailed discussions on a wide variety of topics.

Prime, Ranchor, ed. *Hinduism and Ecology.* London and New York, 1992.

Shiva, Vandana. *Water Wars: Privatization, Pollution, and Profit.* Cambridge, Mass., 2002

VASUDHA NARAYANAN (2005)

ECOLOGY AND RELIGION: ECOLOGY AND JAINISM

The physical environment plays a key role in the Jaina worldview, which makes a direct connection between its cosmology and its ethical system. From the earliest extant text of the tradition, one learns that Jaina monks and nuns were keen observers of the elements and the living beings of the natural world. The *Ācārāṅga Sūtra,* which dates from the fourth or fifth century before the common era, indicates that Mahāvīra (c. 500 BCE), who established Jainism in its current institutional form, was a keen observer of nature. The text states: "Thoroughly knowing the earth-bodies and water-bodies and fire-bodies and wind-bodies, the lichens, seeds, and sprouts, he comprehended that they are, if narrowly inspected, imbued with life" (1.8.1.11–12; in Jacobi, 1884). These observations indicate the underpinning of the Jaina worldview: the belief that life *(jīva)* takes many interchanging forms. The life force exists in the four elements of earth, water, fire, and air as well as in microorganisms *(nigodha),* plants, and animals. At the point of death, this life force moves from one body to the next, depending on its karmic constitution. The life force attached to an earth body moves very slowly, whereas the life force found in an insect or microorganism might move on very quickly. The goal of Jainism entails an elevation of consciousness about one's *karma,* leading to rebirth in a human body and the adoption of a nonviolent lifestyle that will ultimately free a person from all karmic entanglements. At this final stage of blessedness, one ascends to the realm of perfection *(siddha-loka)* wherein one dwells eternally, observing the machinations of the world but never again succumbing to its allurement. The twenty-four great teachers or *tīrthaṃkaras* of Jainism all are said to have attained this state along with an undetermined number of saints.

The practice of nonviolence or *ahiṃsā* in Jainism sets an individual on the path of spiritual purification and ascent toward liberation. Jainas have been scrupulous in developing techniques for the avoidance of harm to living beings. The vows of Jainism provide the very foundation for Jaina identity. Nonviolence undergirds the human interpretation of and consequent relationship with the natural world. The commitment to not inflict harm extends far beyond anthropocentric concerns into the animal, plant, and even elemental realms.

The *Ācārāṅga Sūtra* lists five primary vows *(vrata)* for ethical practice: nonviolence, truthfulness, not stealing, sexual restraint, and nonpossession. These same vows inspired Mohandas Gandhi to lead a deeply abstemious life; he had learned of them during his childhood in Gujarat, an Indian state with a large Jaina presence, and from Raichandbhai, a prominent Jaina lay teacher. Nonviolence requires not only doing no harm to other human beings but also being informed about and respectful of all life forms. Truthfulness requires honesty in all one's dealings and vigilance about one's commitment to the nonviolent ideal. Stealing causes harm in innumerable ways, as does sexual promiscuity. In addition to the obvious emotional and medical hazards presented by wantonness, the very act of sexual intercourse kills innumerable microorganisms generated and obliterated by the heat and friction of sexual contact. Possessions weigh heavily on their owners. All material objects entail some sort of harm in their production and maintenance. Even to wear a heavy coat traps small insects and microorganisms. The Jaina philosophers and practitioners were mindful of such violations of the code of nonviolence and advocated minimal ownership of things. The ultimate ideal can be found in the story of Mahāvīra, who spent the last several years of his life totally naked, a practice emulated by the naked monks of the Digambara branch of Jainism.

In the early philosophical period of Jainism, Umāsvāti (c. 450 CE) composed the *Tattvārtha Sūtra,* a text that itemizes and describes the details of Jaina cosmology. The universe, shaped like a cosmic woman, consists of seven hells at its base, the surface of planet earth (Jambudvīpa) emanating from the navel region at its center, and nine heavens that rise through the torso of the cosmic person up to the crown of the cosmic head. Beyond the body of this person can be found the crescent realm of the liberated souls, the *siddhas* (adepts) and *tīrthaṃkaras* (great teachers), who have attained the fourteenth and ultimate state of unattached aloneness *(ayoga kevala).* These adepts have literally risen above and beyond all forms of *karma.* All other life forms can be found in lower stages of consciousness, with the overwhelming majority residing in the first stage, the deluded or ignorant view *(mithyādṛṣṭi).* Only human beings can begin the ascent along the spiritual path *(guṇasthāna)* that ultimately frees one from all karmic entanglement.

Umāsvāti categorized life forms according to the number of senses they possess. Earth, water, fire, and air bodies have only the sense of touch, as do plants. Worms add the sense of taste. Bugs possess touch, taste, and the capacity to smell. Winged insects add the ability to see. More complex beings, such as reptiles, mammals, and fish, can also hear and think. These higher life forms develop moral agency and make clear decisions about their behavior. These categories became embellished with great detail in the centuries following.

In the Middle Ages, some Jaina authors turned their attention to an exhaustive enumeration of biotic forms. Śāntisūri, a Śvetāmbara Jaina writer of the eleventh century, states in the *Jīva Vicāra Prakaranam* that hardened rock can survive as a distinct life form for twenty-two thousand years; "water-bodied souls" for seven thousand years; wind bodies for three thousand years; trees for ten thousand years; and fire for three days and three nights. He goes on to describe different forms of rock, such as quartz, gold, chalk, lava, and many others, and the variety of shapes assumed by water and fire and gives elegant descriptions of plant genres, worms, bugs, animals, hell beings, gods, and humans.

Jaina cosmology proclaims that all aspects of the surrounding world have feelings and consciousness. The earth feels and responds in kind to human presence. The earth one treads upon, the water one drinks, the air one inhales, the chair that supports one, the light that illumines one's day—all these entities feel one through the sense of touch, though one seldom acknowledges their presence. Humans, as living, sensate, sentient beings, have been given the special task and responsibility of growing in awareness and appreciation of these other life forms and of acting accordingly. Humans have the opportunity to cultivate ethical behavior that engenders respect toward the living, breathing, conscious beings that suffuse the universe.

The environmental message of this remarkable faith presents interesting challenges to the development of an ethical outlook. On the one hand, Jain precepts can support and correct the practice of an ecologically aware lifestyle. The practice of a Jaina monk or nun or carefully observant layperson challenges even the deep ecologist. Vegetarianism must be followed. One may not take up a profession that entails harm in any way. Only a few Jaina farmers can be found, as agriculture causes too much harm to the earth bodies and the two-sensed worms found in the soil. Jainas generally are careful about their professional choices, with few members of the community participating in warfare, directly or indirectly. Virtually none will involve themselves in the trafficking of animal products. Most Jainas take up careers that involve the production and sale of items manufactured from one-sensed beings and have found great success in the cotton industry and the diamond business as well as in accounting and banking. Many prosperous Jaina industrialists have used their wealth to support the extensive communities of Jaina monks and nuns in India and have contributed generously to the construction of Jaina temples.

However, other aspects of the faith present ambiguous challenges. Like the members of virtually all other religions, Jainas, despite their promotion of compassion toward all life forms and extensive construction of animal shelters *(pinjrapoles),* believe the highest form of life is human life. The inherent worth of other life forms is to be respected, but not for its own sake. Rather, a Jaina avoids harm for his or her own self-purification, not to advance the spiritual status of another. In traditional Jainism, to interfere with another's *karma* does harm to oneself. Despite Jainism's emphasis on the need for self-purification, the myriad practices resulting from the importance of nonviolence—the *Ācārāṅga Sūtra* even includes detailed instructions on how to empty one's bowels without harming living beings—have the unintended effect of guaranteeing that when in the presence of an observant Jaina even an ant has a much better chance for survival than it would if in the company of even well-intentioned members of other religious communities.

Perhaps one illustration of a positive attitude toward environmental protection stemming from the observance of *ahiṃsā* can be found in two Jaina stories that relate to trees. The first comes from a discourse in the *Ācārāṅga Sūtra* in which Mahāvīra tells a gathering of monks and nuns to "change their minds" about looking at big trees. He says that, rather than seeing trees as "fit for palaces, gates, houses, benches . . . , boats, buckets, stools, trays, ploughs . . . seats, beds, cars sheds," they should speak of trees as "noble, high and round, big," with "many branches . . . magnificent" (2.4.2, 11–12; in Jacobi, 1884). This advice indicates that Mahāvīra not only appreciated the beauty of trees but also encouraged his followers to set aside their utilitarian perspectives. Wood, the major material used at the time for nearly all aspects of human manufacturing, was to be viewed by Jainas not for its monetary value but for its inherent beauty.

Another tree story similarly warns against the wanton destruction of trees while simultaneously explaining the mechanics of *karma*:

> A hungry person with the most negative black *leśyā* karma uproots and kills an entire tree to obtain a few mangoes. The person of blue karma fells the tree by chopping the trunk, again merely to gain a handful of fruits. Fraught with gray karma, a third person spares the trunk but cuts off the major limbs of the tree. The one with orangish-red karma carelessly and needlessly lops off several branches to reach the mangoes. The fifth, exhibiting white or virtuous karma, "merely picks up ripe fruit that has dropped to the foot of the tree." (Jaini, 1916, p. 47)

Again, trees are not to be regarded covetously for their fruits but are to be given respect and treated in such a way as to avoid the inflicting of harm. This ethic of care may be extended to the entire biotic community, engendering an awareness of and sensitivity to the precious nature of life.

A ready example of Jaina involvement in the protection of life can be found in their long-standing practice of animal rescue. Quite often, the connection between treatment of animals and the environment is overlooked. The Jaina tradition has a long commitment to animal protection that can serve as a paradigm guiding interaction with the natural world. During the period of the Islamic incursion into India, the Jaina community was often in retreat and had some of its temples taken over and converted into mosques. However, some Jaina monks exerted influence within the Islamic world. Jinacandrasūri II (1531–1613), a leader of the Khartar Gacch order of the Śvetāmbaras, traveled in 1591 to Lahore, where he greatly influenced the Mogul emperor Akbar the Great. He gained protection for Jain pilgrimage places as well as legal protection ensuring that Jaina ceremonies would not be hindered. Akbar even lent support to Jaina advocacy for animals and forbade the slaughter of animals for one week each year.

A modern example of Jaina activism that extends into the realm of ecological ethics is in the work of two leaders of the Śvetāmbara Terāpanthī movement, Ācārya Tulsi (1914–1997) and his successor Ācārya Mahāprajña. Tulsi was appointed to the leadership of his order in 1936, when he was twenty-two years old. For fifty-eight years he served as leader and preceptor and worked tirelessly at promulgating the Jaina teachings on nonviolence. In June 1945, deeply disturbed by World War II, he issued a nine-point declaration of the basic principles of nonviolence. Starting with the proclamation that nonviolence should be widely propagated, he then stated that one must overcome anger, pride, deceitfulness, and discontent; that all persons should pursue education; that governments must become just; that science must not be used for purposes of war; that governmental pronouncements should promote "universal fraternity instead of national solidarity"; that people must not hoard; that the weak must not be oppressed; and that religious freedom should be granted to all (Kumar and Prakash, p. 42). Although some of these principles may certainly be seen though environmentalist spectacles, particularly the admonition against hoarding, not until 1949 did Ācārya Tulsi explicitly mention environmental pollution. He issued an eleven-point call for action, culminating in an eco-friendly message. Specifically, he asked his followers, laypeople and monastics, to observe the following admonitions: to not kill or attack; to not engage in destructive activities; to subscribe to the ideals of human unity and religious toleration; to follow good business ethics; to limit acquisitions; to not engage in falsification of elections; to abstain from bad habits and addictions; and finally, to be "alert to the problem of keeping the environment pollution-free" (Kumar and Prakash, p. 71).

Contemporary Jainas, particularly in North America, identify readily with values centered on environmental protection. Anne Vallely notes, "Rather than through the idiom of self-realization or the purification of the soul, ethics are being expressed through a discourse of environmentalism and animal rights" (Vallely, 2002, p. 193). One example of this trend is in *Resurgence,* the journal edited by the former Jaina monk Satish Kumar. This beautiful publication features works by prominent photographers, artists, and writers that highlight the beauties of nature and critique the many assaults on the environment caused by consumerism and the global economy. Whereas this journal enjoys worldwide distribution to diverse constituencies, a newer journal, *Jain Spirit: Sharing Jain Values Globally,* is distributed almost exclusively within the Jaina community. It includes articles on an array of topics, including essays on the integration of Jaina traditional values into contemporary life. One such piece, "Vote with Your Pocket," by Raju Shah, extols the virtues of hybrid automobiles, which "produce up to 90 percent less emission than a similar-sized normal vehicle" (Shah, 2003, p. 44). Numerous websites buttress the new global reach of the Jaina community, which continues to espouse vegetarianism and animal activism as key components of its ethical expression. As the twenty-first century progresses, the abstemious lifestyle of the Jainas may become increasingly instructive to those seeking to protect the environment.

BIBLIOGRAPHY

Babb, Lawrence. *Absent Lord: Ascetics and Kings in a Jain Ritual Culture.* Berkeley, Calif., 1996.

Chapple, Christopher Key. *Nonviolence to Animals, Earth, and Self in Asian Traditions.* Albany, N.Y., 1993. Includes an examination of how traditional Jaina texts and practices might contribute to debates over the global issue of environmental degradation.

Chapple, Christopher Key. *Jainism and Ecology: Nonviolence in the Web of Life.* Cambridge, Mass., 2002. Includes essays by Nathmal Tatia, John E. Cort, Paul Dundas, Padmanabh S. Jaini, and others on the contributions that Jainism can make to ecological discourse. It also examines the complex issue of whether a traditional system of ethical reflection based on self-purification can be adapted to adopt a more socially active role.

Dundas, Paul. "Jain Perceptions of Islam in the Early Modern Period." *Indo-Iranian Journal* 42, no. 1 (1999): 35–46.

Dundas, Paul. *The Jains.* 2d ed. London, 2002. Provides a comprehensive history of the Jaina faith.

Jacobi, Hermann, trans. *Jaina Sutras,* vol. 1: *The Akaranga Sutra. The Kalpa Sutra.* 1884; reprint, New York, 1968.

Jaini, Jagmanderlal. *The Outlines of Jainism.* Cambridge, U.K., 1916.

Jaini, Padmanabh S. *The Jaina Path of Purification.* Berkeley, Calif., 1979. Outstanding survey of Jaina history and doctrine.

Kumar, Muni Prashant, and Muni Lok Prakash. "Anuvrat Anushasta Saint Tulsi: A Glorious Life with a Purpose." *Anuvibha Reporter* 3, no. 1.

Lodrick, Deryck O. *Sacred Cows, Sacred Places: Origins and Survivals of Animal Homes in India.* Berkeley, Calif., 1981.

Śāntisūri. *Jīva Vicāra Prakaraṇam, along with Pāthaka Ratnākara's Commentary.* Edited by Muni Ratna-Prabha Vijaya, translated by Jayant P. Thaker. Madras, India, 1950.

Shah, Raju. "Vote with Your Pocket." *Jain Spirit* 14 (March–May 2003).

Tobias, Michael. *Ahimsa: Nonviolence.* PBS film, Los Angeles, Direct Cinema, 1989. A video that portrays leading Jaina teachers, shows Jaina pilgrimage sites, and explains fundamental teachings.

Tobias, Michael. *Life Force: The World of Jainism*. Berkeley, Calif., 1991. A gentle introduction to the life and business practices of contemporary Jainas in India.

Tobias, Michael. "Jainism and Ecology." In *Worldviews and Ecology: Religion, Philosophy, and the Environment,* edited by Mary Evelyn Tucker and John Grim. Maryknoll, N.Y., 1994. This important chapter delineates resources from the Jaina tradition that can be construed as eco-friendly.

Umāsvāti. *That Which Is: Tattvārtha Sūtra.* Translated by Nathmal Tatia. New York, 1994.

Vallely, Anne. "From Liberation to Ecology: Ethical Discourses among Orthodox and Diaspora Jains." In *Jainism and Ecology: Nonviolence in the Web of Life,* edited by Christopher Key Chapple. Cambridge, Mass., 2002.

CHRISTOPHER KEY CHAPPLE (2005)

ECOLOGY AND RELIGION: ECOLOGY AND BUDDHISM

In 1967 Lynn White, in an effort to address the roots of the growing global environmental crisis, put forward the thesis that the biblical worldview, which placed God outside of nature and authorized human beings to exploit nature for their proper ends, had been a major factor in the West's degradation of the natural environment (White, 1967). The ensuing controversy sparked by his thesis diverted attention from his underlying point at the core of the religion and ecology movement, namely, that human ecology is deeply conditioned by religious beliefs. Although White viewed Franciscan piety as having a more benign attitude toward nature than mainstream Christian theology, he found in Buddhism an even more holistic, egalitarian worldview and an environmentally friendly style of life. This entry seeks to explore White's sensibility regarding Buddhism by first analyzing four dimensions of the Buddhist worldview from the standpoint of their potential ecological significance, and then examining the normative values of a Buddhistically grounded lifestyle consonant with an ecology of human flourishing.

FOUR DIMENSIONS OF A BUDDHIST ECOLOGICAL WORLDVIEW. Although over the centuries Buddhism has developed diverse forms from the time the Buddha taught his *dharma* in India over 2,500 years ago, its holistic principle of causal interdependence (*paṭicca samuppāda, idappaccayatā*) has remained the normative core of its philosophical worldview. Buddhists view this interdependent world as conjoined in four ways: existentially, morally, cosmologically, and ontologically. Existentially, Buddhists affirm that all sentient beings share the fundamental conditions of birth, old age, suffering, and death. The existential realization of the universality of suffering lies at the core of the Buddha's teaching. Insight into the nature of suffering, its cause, cessation, and the path to the cessation of suffering constitutes the essence of the Buddha's enlightenment experience, formulated as the four noble truths and enunciated in the Buddha's first public teaching.

The tradition conveys this universal truth via the story of the founder's journey to *nirvāṇa*, the logical interrelationship among the four noble truths, as well as in many, often poignant, narratives. In one account a young mother approaches the Buddha after the death of her infant child. She pleads with the Blessed One to restore her child's life. In response the Buddha directs the grieving mother to bring him a mustard seed from a house in a village where death has never occurred, and if she finds such a household he will resuscitate her child. The mother returns to the Buddha not with the mustard seed but with the existential realization of the universality of suffering caused by death. The touching story of a mother's grief over the death of her baby speaks to the heart; the syllogistic logic of the four noble truths speaks to the mind.

Suffering and Compassion. Buddhism links the existential condition of the universality of suffering with the moral virtue of compassion. That the Buddha, after his enlightenment, decides to share his insight into the cause of and the path to the cessation of suffering rather than selfishly keeping this knowledge for himself, is regarded by the tradition as an act of universal compassion. Extrapolating from the example of the Buddha, Buddhist environmentalists assert that the mindful awareness of the universality of suffering produces compassionate empathy for all forms of life, particularly for all sentient species. They interpret the *Dhammapada's* ethical injunction not to do evil but to do good as a moral principle advocating the nonviolent elevation of suffering, an ideal embodied in the prayer of universal loving kindness that concludes many Buddhist rituals: "May all beings be free from enmity; may all beings be free from injury; may all beings be free from suffering; may all beings be happy." Out of a concern for the entire living environment, Buddhist environmentalists extend loving kindness, compassion, and respect beyond people and animals to include plants and the earth itself: "We humans think we are smart, but an orchid. . .knows how to produce noble, symmetrical flowers, and a snail knows how to make a beautiful, well-proportioned shell. We should bow deeply before the orchid and the snail and join our palms reverently before the monarch butterfly and the magnolia tree" ("The Sun My Heart," Nhat Hanh, p. 85).

***Karma*, rebirth, and Buddhist cosmology.** The concepts of *karma* and rebirth (*saṃsāra*) integrate the existential sense of a shared common condition among all sentient life forms with the moral nature of the Buddhist cosmology. Not unlike the biological sciences, rebirth links human and animal species. Evolution maps commonalties and differences among species on the basis of physical and genetic traits; rebirth maps them on moral grounds. Every form of sentient life participates in a karmic continuum traditionally divided into three world-levels and a hierarchical taxonomy of five or six life forms. Although this continuum constitutes a moral hierarchy, differences among life forms and individuals are relative, not absolute. While Buddhism traditionally privileges humans over animals, animals over hungry ghosts, male gender over the female, monk over laity, all forms of karmically conditioned life—human, animal, divine, demonic—are related within contingent, samsaric time: "In the long course of rebirth there is not one among living beings with form who has not been mother, father, brother, sister, son, or daughter, or some other relative. Being connected with the process of taking birth, one is kin to all wild and domestic animals, birds, and beings born from the womb" (*Laṅkāvatāra Sūtra*). *Nirvāṇa,* the Buddhist summum bonum, offers the promise of transforming karmic conditionedness into an unconditioned state of spiritual liberation, a realization potentially available to all forms of sentient life on the karmic continuum. The belief that plants and trees or the land itself have a similar potential for spiritual liberation became an explicit doctrine in Chinese and Japanese Buddhism and may also have been part of popular Buddhist belief from earliest times in the realization that all life forms share both a common problematic and promise: "*bodhisattvas* each of these, I call the large trees" (*Lotus Sūtra*).

Although the Buddhist doctrines of *karma* and rebirth connect all forms of sentient existence together in a moral continuum, Buddhist ethics focus on human agency and its consequences, and, in this sense, Buddhism is anthropocentric, not biocentric. The inclusion of plants and animals in Buddhist schemes of salvation may be important philosophically for the attribution of inherent value to nonhuman forms of life; however, it is humans who are the primary agents in creating the present ecological crisis and who will bear the major responsibility for its solution.

The myth of origins in the canon of Theravāda Buddhism (*Aggañña Sutta*) describes the deleterious impact of human activity on the primordial natural landscape. Unlike the Garden of Eden story in the Hebrew Bible, where human agency centers on the God-human relationship, the Buddhist story of first origins describes the negative impact of humans on the earth, which results from their selfishness and greed. In the Buddhist mythological Eden, the earth flourishes naturally but greed and desire lead to division and ownership of the land, which in turn promotes violent conflict, destruction, and chaos. It is human agency in the Buddhist myth of first origins that destroys the natural order of things. Although change is inherent in nature, Buddhists believe that natural processes are directly affected by human morality. From the Buddhist perspective our relationship to the natural environment implies an intrinsic moral equation. From a Buddhist perspective, therefore, an environmental policy based solely on a utilitarian cost-benefit analysis cannot solve the problem. At the heart of the matter remain the moral issues of greed, hatred, and violence.

The account of the Buddha's awakening (*nirvāṇa*) delineates the major elements of the Buddhist worldview in terms of the concrete particular, the general, and the universal. Tradition records that during the night of this defining experience the Blessed One first recalled his previous lives within the karmic continuum; then he perceived the fate of all sentient beings within the cosmic hierarchy; finally he fathomed the nature of suffering and the path to its cessation formulated as the four noble truths and the law of interdependent co-arising (*paṭicca samuppāda*). The Buddha's enlightenment experience is mapped in a specific sequence: an understanding of the *particular* (his personal karmic history), the *general* (the karmic history of humankind), and finally the *principle* underlying the cause and cessation of suffering. Subsequently, this principle is broadened into a *universal law of causality*: "on the arising of this, that arises; on the cessation of this, that ceases." Buddhist environmentalists find in this template a vision that integrates all aspects of the ecosphere—particular individuals as well as general species—in terms of the principle of mutual codependence.

These three stages, encompassed by the Buddha's enlightenment experience, suggest a model of moral reasoning applicable to environmental ethics that integrates general principles and collective action guides with particular contexts, or in the catchphrase of the popular bumper sticker, "Think globally; act locally." Effective schemes of environmental justice require both general principles, such as those embodied in the Earth Charter, and enforceable programs of action appropriate to particular regions and nation-states.

ONTOLOGICAL FOUNDATIONS OF BUDDHIST ECOLOGY. In the Buddhist cosmological model individual entities are by their very nature relational, which undermines the autonomous self vis-á-vis the "other," whether human, animal, or vegetable. Buddhist environmentalists see their worldview as one that rejects hierarchical dominance of one human over another or humans over nature, and as the basis of an ethic of empathetic compassion that respects biodiversity. In the view of the Thai monk Buddhadāsa Bhikkhu (1906–1993),

> The entire cosmos is a cooperative. The sun, the moon and the stars live together as a cooperative. The same is true for humans and animals, trees, and the earth. When we realize that the world is a mutual, interdependent, cooperative enterprise. . .then we can build a noble environment. If our lives are not based on this truth, then we shall perish (Swearer, 1998, p. 20).

In later schools of Buddhist thought the cosmological vision of interdependent causality evolved into a more substantive sense of ontological unity. The image of Indra's net found in the Huayan (Jap., Kegon) tradition's *Avataṃsaka Sūtra* has been a potent metaphor in Buddhist ecological discussions: "Just as the nature of earth is one, while beings each live separately, and the earth has no thought of oneness or difference, so is the truth of all the Buddhas." For the American writer Gary Snyder the Huayan image of the universe as a vast web of many-sided jewels, each constituted by the reflections of all the other jewels in the web and each jewel being the image of the entire universe, symbolizes the world as a universe of bio-regional ecological communities. Buddhist environmentalists argue, furthermore, that ontological notions, such as buddha-nature or *dharma*-nature (e.g., *buddhakāya, tathagata-garbha, dharmakāya, dharmadhātu*) provide a basis for unifying all existent entities in a common sacred universe, even though the tradition privileges human life in regard to spiritual realization.

For Tiantai monks in eighth-century China, the belief in a universal buddha-nature blurred the distinction between sentient and nonsentient life forms and logically led to the view that plants, trees, and the earth itself could achieve enlightenment. Kūkai (774–835), the founder of the Japanese Shingon school, and Dōgen (1200–1253), the founder of the Sōtō Zen sect, described universal buddha-nature in naturalistic terms: "If plants and trees were devoid of buddhahood, waves would then be without humidity" (Kūkai); "The sūtras [i.e., the *dharma*] are the entire universe, mountains and rivers and the great wide earth, plants, and trees" (Dōgen). Buddhist environmentalists often cite Dōgen's view as support for the preservation of species biodiversity, a view that ascribes intrinsic value to all species by affirming their shared dharmic nature.

For Buddhists the truth of the principle of causal interdependence as a universal, natural law was authenticated in the narrative of the Buddha's own *nirvāṇa* and his teaching (*dharma*). As has been noted, Buddhist scriptures and other texts employ the hermeneutical strategies of metaphor, story, and discursive logic to promote and explicate this truth. Throughout Buddhist history, poetry has also been an important literary tool for conveying the *dharma* and the truths of the interdependence of humans and nature. An early Pali *sutta* incorporates early Vedic traditions and extols nature's beauty by drawing on the metaphor of Indra and the landscape of abundance:

> Those rocky heights with hue of dark blue clouds
> Where lies embossed many a shining lake
> Of crystal-clear, cool waters, and whose slopes
> The herds of Indra cover and bedeck
> Those are the hills wherein my soul delights.
> (*Theragātā*)

East Asian traditions under Daoist influence best represent this poetic expression. The early ninth-century Chinese Buddhist poet and layman, Han-shan, writes:

> As for me, I delight in the everyday
> Way Among mist-wrapped vines and rocky caves
> Here in the wilderness I am completely free
> With my friends, the white clouds, idling forever
> There are roads, but they do not reach the world
> Since I am mindless, who can rouse my thoughts?
> On a bed of stone I sit, alone in the night
> While the round moon climbs up Cold Mountain
> (*Kaza and Kraft*, 2000, p. 54).

Although the various expressions of Buddhism's holistic, interdependent worldview that range from logical paradigms to poetry offer both guidance and inspiration to ecological thinking, the natural world looms largest for the achievement of an ecology of human flourishing.

An Ecology of Human Flourishing. Buddhism arose in north India in the fifth century BCE at a time when the region was undergoing a process of urbanization and political centralization accompanied by commercial development and the formation of artisan and merchant classes. The creation of towns and the expansion of an agrarian economy led to the clearing of forests and other tracts of uninhabited land. These changes influenced early Buddhism in several ways. For instance, the transformation of the natural environment that accompanied these changes was a factor in the Buddhist conception of human flourishing. Early monastic Buddhism was not biocentric, but naturalism seems to have played a role in popular piety, and naturalistic sentiments came to be infused in Buddhism in China, Korea, and Japan. As we shall see, while nature as an intrinsic value may be lacking in early Buddhist thought and practice, it nonetheless was always central to the Buddhist concept and articulation of the ecology of human flourishing.

The *Sangha* and Nature. Even though the picture of the Buddha seated under the tree of enlightenment traditionally has not been interpreted as a paradigm for ecological discourse, today's Buddhist environmental activists point out that the decisive events in the Buddha's life occurred in natural settings: the Buddha Gautama was born, attained enlightenment, and died under trees. The textual record, furthermore, testifies to the importance of forests, not only as the preferred environment for spiritual practices such as meditation, but also as a place where laity sought instruction. Historically, in Asia and increasingly in the West, Buddhists have situated centers of practice and teaching in forests and among mountains at some remove from the hustle and bustle of urban life. The Buddha's own example provides the original impetus for such locations: "Seeking the supreme state of sublime peace, I wandered. . .until. . .I saw a delightful stretch of land and a lovely woodland grove, and a clear flowing river with a delightful forest so I sat down thinking, 'Indeed, this is an appropriate place to strive for the ultimate realization of. . .*nirvāṇa*'" (*Ariyapariyesana Sutta*).

Lavish patronage and the traffic of pilgrims often complicated and compromised the solitude and simple life of forest monasteries, but forests, rivers, and mountains have remained important in the Buddhist ecology of human flourishing. Recall, for example, the Zen description of enlightenment wherein natural phenomena such as rivers and mountains are perceived as loci of the sacred, as in Dōgen's *Mountains and Water Sūtra.* Although some religious practitioners tested their spiritual mettle in wild nature, more often the norm appears to be a relatively benign state of nature conducive to quiet contemplation as suggested by the above quotation, or by the naturalistic gardens that one finds in many Japanese Zen monasteries originally located on the outskirts of towns. Buddhadāsa Bhikkhu called his forest monastery in south Thailand the Garden of Empowering Liberation (Suan Mokkhabalārāma), observing: "The deep sense of calm that nature provides through separation from the stress that plagues us in the day-to-day world protects our heart and mind. The lessons nature teaches us lead to a new birth beyond suffering caused by our acquisitive self-preoccupation" (Swearer, 1998, pp. 24–25). For Buddhist environmentalists, technology alone cannot solve the eco-crisis. A radical transformation of values and lifestyle will be required. Communities like Suan Mokkhabalārāma provide an example of a sustainable lifestyle grounded in the values of moderation, simplicity, and non-acquisitiveness.

Buddhadāsa's Garden of Empowering Liberation stands not as a retreat from the world but as a place where all forms of life—humans, animals, and plants—live as a cooperative microcosm of a larger ecosystem and as a community where humans are taught to practice an ecological ethic. Such an ethic is characterized by the virtues of restraint, simplicity, loving-kindness, compassion, equanimity, patience, wisdom, nonviolence, and generosity. These virtues represent moral ideals for all members of the Buddhist community—monk, lay person, political leader, ordinary citizen, male, female. Political leaders whose mandate it is to maintain the peace and security of the nation, are admonished to adhere to the ideal of nonviolence. King Aśoka (third century BCE), the model Buddhist ruler, is admired for his rejection of animal sacrifice and the protection of animals, as well as for building hospices and other public works. The Buddhist ethic of distributive justice extols the merchant who generously provides for the needy. Even ordinary Thai rice farmers traditionally left a portion of rice unharvested in their fields for the benefit of poor people and hungry animals.

The twin virtues of wisdom and compassion define the spiritual perfection of the *bodhisattva* praised by Śāntideva, the eighth-century Indian poet-monk, in these words:

> May I be the doctor and the medicine
> And may I be the nurse
> For all sick beings in the world
> Until all are healed.
> (*Bodhicaryāvatāra*)

For contemporary engaged Buddhists, most notably the Dalai Lama, a sense of responsibility rooted in compassion lies at the very heart of an ecological ethic: "The world grows smaller and smaller, more and more interdependent . . . today more than ever before life must be characterized by a sense of universal responsibility, not only . . . human to human but also human to other forms of life" (Sandell, 1987, p. 73).

A Critical Appraisal of Eco-Buddhism. For many Buddhist environmentalists, compassion naturally results from the intellectual understanding that all life forms are mutually interdependent. Others, however, argue that while a cognitive recognition of interdependence is necessary, it alone is not a sufficient condition for an ethic of mutual regard. These critics point to the centrality of practice in Buddhism, the threefold path to moral and spiritual excellence—virtue, mindful awareness, wisdom—as the key element in an ecological ethic. For the Vietnamese Zen monk, Thich Nhat Hanh (b. 1926), it is the practice of mindful awareness, in particular, that opens both heart and mind to the interbeingness of humans and nature:

> *Look deeply.* I arrive in every second to be a bud on a spring branch to be a tiny bird, with wings still fragile learning to sing in my new nest to be a caterpillar in the heart of a flower to be a jewel hiding itself in a stone. . . . ("Please Call Me By My True Names," Nhat Hanh, 1987)

Critics of the ethical saliency of the traditional Buddhist vision of human flourishing also argue that such nondualistic philosophical concepts as not-self (*anātman*) and emptiness (*śūnyatā*) undermine human autonomy and the distinction between self and other, essential to an other-regarding ethic. What are the grounds for an ethic or laws that protect the civil rights of minorities or animal species threatened with extinction when philosophically Buddhism seems to challenge their significance by deconstructing their independent reality as an epistemological fiction? Furthermore, they point out that the most basic concepts of Buddhism—*nirvāṇa*, suffering, rebirth, not-self, and even causality—were intended to further the goal of an individual's spiritual quest rather than engagement with the world. They affirm, therefore, that Buddhism serves primarily a salvific or soteriological purpose and that any attempt to ecologize the tradition distorts the historical and philosophical record. Buddhist environmentalists respond that their understanding of the tradition brings to the debates about human rights and the global environment an ethic of social and environmental responsibility more compatible with the language of compassion based on the mutual interdependence of all life forms than the language of rights. Furthermore, to apply Buddhist insights to a broad ecology of human flourishing represents the tradition at its best, namely, a creative, dynamic response to contemporary problems.

A related but more sympathetic criticism from within the Buddhist environmental movement suggests that for Buddhism to be an effective force for systemic institutional change, the traditional Buddhist emphasis on individual moral and spiritual transformation must be adjusted to address forcefully the structures of oppression, exploitation, and environmental degradation. While preserving the unique Buddhist emphasis on the practice of mindful awareness and a personal lifestyle of simplicity, under the inspiration of A. T. Ariyaratna, the founder of the Sarvodaya Shramadana movement in Sri Lanka, Sulak Sivaraksa, co-founder of the International Network of Engaged Buddhists, and other leaders, a new form of environmental and socially engaged Buddhism has emerged dedicated to the creation of a just, equitable, and sustainable world.

Bibliography

Badiner, Allan Hunt, ed. *Dharma Gaia: A Harvest of Essays in Buddhism and Ecology.* Berkeley, 1990.

Batchelor, Martina, and Kerry Brown, eds. *Buddhism and Ecology.* London, 1992.

Darlington, Susan M. "The Ordination of a Tree: The Buddhist Ecology Movement in Thailand." *Ethnology* 37 (1998): 1–15.

De Silva, Padmasiri. *Environmental Philosophy and Ethics in Buddhism.* Hampshire, U.K., 1998.

Harris, Ian. "How Environmental Is Buddhism?" *Religion* 21 (1991): 173–190.

Harris, Ian. "Buddhist Environmental Ethics and Detraditionalization: The Case of EcoBuddhism." *Religion* 25 (1995): 199–211.

Harris, Ian. "Getting to Grips with Buddhist Environmentalism: A Provisional Typology." *Journal of Buddhist Ethics* 2 (1995): 173–190.

Kaza, Stephanie, and Kenneth Kraft. *Dharma Rain: Sources of Buddhist Environmentalism.* Boston, 2000.

Nhat Hah, Thich, *Being Peace.* Berkeley, 1987.

Nyanasobhano, Bhikkhu. *Landscapes of Wonder: Discovering Buddhist Dharma in the World Around Us.* Boston, 1998.

Sandell, Klas. *Buddhist Perspectives on the Ecocrisis.* Kandy, Sri Lanka, 1987.

Schmithausen, Lambert. *Buddhism and Nature: The Lecture Delivered on the Occasion of the EXPO 1990, an Enlarged Version with Notes.* Tokyo, 1990.

Schmithausen, Lambert. "The Early Buddhist Tradition and Ecological Ethics." *Journal of Buddhist Ethics* 4 (1997): 1–42.

Swearer, Donald K. "The Hermeneutics of Buddhist Ecology in Contemporary Thailand: Buddhadāsa and Dhammapiṭaka." In *Buddhism and Ecology: The Interconnection of Dharma and Deeds,* edited by Mary Evelyn Tucker and Duncan Ryūken Williams, pp. 21–44. Cambridge, Mass., 1997.

Swearer, Donald K. "Buddhism and Ecology: Challenge and Promise." *Earth Ethics* 10 (1998): 19–22.

Swearer, Donald K. "Principles and Poetry, Places and Stories: The Resources of Buddhist Ecology." *Daedalus* 130 (2001): 225–239.

Tucker, Mary Evelyn, and Duncan Ryūken Williams, eds. *Buddhism and Ecology: The Interconnection of Dharma and Deeds.* Cambridge, Mass., 1997.

White, Lynn, Jr. "The Historical Roots of Our Ecological Crisis." *Science* 155 (1967): 1203–1207.

DONALD K. SWEARER (2005)

ECOLOGY AND RELIGION: ECOLOGY AND CONFUCIANISM

Within the Confucian tradition, there are rich resources for understanding how Chinese culture has viewed nature and the role of humans in nature. These are evident from the dynamic interactions of nature as expressed in the early classic *Yi jing* (Book of changes), to the Han period integration of the human into the triad with heaven and Earth, to the later neo-Confucian metaphysical discussions of the relationship of principle *(li)* and material force *(qi).* This does not imply, however, that there is not a gap between such theories of nature and practices toward nature in both premodern and contemporary East Asian societies. China, like many countries in Asia, has been faced with various environmental challenges, such as deforestation, for centuries. Thus, this is not to suggest an idealization of Confucian China as a model of environmental ideas or practices. This is an exploration of how Confucian thought contributed to the Chinese understanding of the relationship of humans to nature. China's complex environmental history would need to be examined for a fuller picture of the social and political reality of these relations. In addition, the spread of Confucianism would have to be traced across East Asia to Korea and Japan.

Confucianism, along with Daoism and Buddhism, has helped to shape attitudes toward nature in the Chinese context. These attitudes have changed over time as the three primary religious traditions have interacted with each other in a dynamic and mutually influencing manner. While distinctions have been made between various schools in these traditions, there has also been coexistence and syncretism among the traditions. Indeed, it is fair to say Confucianism and Daoism, in particular, share various terms and attitudes toward nature, although they differ on the role of humans in relation to nature. Confucians are more actively engaged in working with nature, especially in agricultural processes, while Daoists are more passive toward nature, wanting to experience its beauty and mystery without interfering in its rhythms.

Confucianism has conventionally been described as a humanistic tradition focusing on the roles and responsibilities of humans to family, society, and government. Thus, Confucianism is often identified primarily as an ethical or political system of thought with an anthropocentric focus. However, upon further examination and as more translations become available in Western languages, this narrow perspective needs to be reexamined. The work of many contemporary Confucian scholars in both Asia and the West has been crucial for expanding the understanding of Confucianism.

Some of the most important results of this reexamination are the insights that have emerged in seeing Confucianism as not simply an ethical, political, or ideological system. Rather, Confucianism is now being appreciated as a complex religious tradition in ways that are different from Western traditions. This is because Confucianism is being recognized for its affirmation of relationality, not only between and among humans but also between humans and the natural world. Confucians regard humans as not simply individualistic entities but as communitarian beings. It is this emerging understanding of the religious, relational, and communitarian dynamics of Confucianism that has particular relevance to the examination of Confucian attitudes toward nature. Some of these attitudes may be characterized as:

1. Embracing an anthropocosmic worldview.
2. Affirming nature as having inherent moral value.
3. Protecting nature as the basis of a stable agricultural society.

4. Encouraging human self-realization to be achieved in harmony with nature.

Anthropocosmic Worldview. The contemporary Confucian scholar Tu Weiming has spoken of the Confucian tradition as one based on an anthropocosmic vision of the dynamic interaction of heaven, Earth, and human. He describes this as a continuity of being with no radical split between a transcendent divine person or principle and the world of humans. Tu emphasizes that the continuity and wholeness of Chinese cosmological thinking is also accompanied by a vitality and dynamism.

This view is centered on the cosmos, not on the human. The implications are that the human is seen as embedded in nature, not dominant over nature. The Confucian worldview might be described as a series of concentric circles where the human resides in the center, not as an isolated individual, but as embedded in ever-expanding rings of family, society, government, and nature. The moral cultivation of the individual influences the larger circles of society and politics, as is evident in the text of the *Great Learning,* and that influence extends to nature, as is clear in the *Doctrine of the Mean.* All of these interacting circles are contained within the vast cosmos itself. Thus, the ultimate context for human flourishing is the 10,000 things, nature in all its remarkable variety and abundance.

Indeed, in Confucianism there is recognition that the rhythms of nature sustain life in both its biological needs and socio-cultural expressions. For Confucians, the biological dimensions of life are dependent on nature as a holistic, organic continuum. Everything in nature is interdependent and interrelated. Most importantly, for Confucians nature is seen as dynamic and transformational. These ideas are present as early as the classical texts of the *Book of Changes* and the *Book of Poetry* and are expressed in the *Four Books,* especially in *Mencius,* the *Doctrine of the Mean,* and the *Great Learning.* They come to full flowering in the neo-Confucian tradition of the Song (960–1279) and Ming (1368–1644) periods, especially in the thought of Zhu Xi, Zhangzai, Zhou Dunyi, and Wang Yangming. Nature in this context has an inherent unity, resulting from a primary ontological source (*Taiji*). It has patterned processes of transformation (*yin/yang*) and is interrelated in the interaction of the five elements (*wuxing*) and the 10,000 things. Nature's dynamic vitalism is seen through the movements of material force (*q qi*).

Within this Confucian worldview, human culture is created and expressed in harmony with the transformations of nature. Thus, the leading Confucian of the Han period (202 BCE–220 CE), Dong Zhongshu, developed a comprehensive synthesis of all the elements, directions, colors, seasons, and virtues. This codified an ancient Chinese tendency to connect the patterns of nature with the rhythms of humans and society. This theory of correspondences is foundational to the anthropocosmic worldview where humans are seen as working together with heaven and Earth in correlative relationships to create harmonious societies. The mutually related resonances between self, society, and nature are constantly being described in the Confucian texts. This early Han correlative synthesis, along with the institution of the civil service examination system, provided the basis for enduring political rule in subsequent Chinese dynasties. This is not to suggest that there were not abuses of political power or manipulations of the examination system, but simply to describe the anthropocosmic foundations of Confucian political and social thought. These Confucian ideas spread across East Asia to Korea and Japan and today are present in Taiwan, Hong Kong, and Singapore as well.

Nature Has Inherent Moral Value. For Confucians, nature is not only inherently valuable, it is morally good. Nature thus embodies the normative standard for all things. There is not a fact/value division in the Confucian worldview, for nature is seen as the source of all value. In particular, value lies in the ongoing transformation and productivity of nature. A term repeated frequently in neo-Confucian sources is "life-life" or "production and reproduction" (*sheng sheng*), reflecting the ever-renewing fecundity of life itself. In this sense, the dynamic transformations of life are seen as emerging in recurring cycles of growth, fruition, harvesting, and abundance. This reflects the natural processes of growth and decay in nature, human life, and human society. Change is thus seen as a dynamic force with which humans should harmonize and interact rather than from which to withdraw.

In this context, where nature has inherent moral value, there is nonetheless a sense of distinctions. Value rests in each thing in nature, but not in each thing equally. Differentiation is recognized as critical; everything has its appropriate role and place and should be treated accordingly. The use of nature for human ends must recognize the intrinsic value of each element of nature, but also its particular value in relation to the larger context of the environment. Each entity is considered not simply equal to every other; rather, each interrelated part of nature has a unique value according to its nature and function. Thus, there is a differentiated sense of appropriate roles for humans and for all other species. For Confucians, hierarchy is seen as a necessary way for each being to fulfill its function. In this context, then, no individual being has exclusive privileged status. The processes of nature and its ongoing logic of transformation (*yin/yang*) are the norms that take priority. Within this context, however, humans have particular responsibilities to care for nature.

Protecting Nature as the Basis of a Stable Agricultural Society. With regard to protecting nature, the Confucians taught that what fosters nature is valuable; what destroys nature is problematic, especially for a flourishing agricultural society. Confucians would ascribe to this in principle if not consistently in practice. Confucians were mindful that nature was the basis of a stable society and that without careful tending imbalances could result. There are numerous passages in *Mencius* advocating humane government based on appropriate management and distribution of natural resources. Moreover, there are various passages in Confucian texts urging humans not to wantonly cut down trees or kill animals needlessly. Thus, Confucians would wish (at least in principle) to nurture and protect the great variety and abundance of life forms. Again, it may be noted that this did not always occur in practice, especially with periods of population growth, military expansion, economic development, and political aggrandizement.

However, the goal of Confucian theory to establish humane society, government, and culture inevitably resulted in the use of nature for creating housing, growing food, and establishing the means of production. In this sense, Confucianism can be seen as a more pragmatic social ecology that recognized the necessity of forming human institutions and the means of governance to work with nature. Nonetheless, it is clear for Confucians that, in principle, human cultural values and practices are grounded in nature, are part of its structure and dependent on its beneficence. In addition, the agricultural base of Confucian societies across East Asia has always been recognized as essential to the political and social well-being of the country. Confucians realized that humans prosper by living within nature's boundaries—they are refreshed by its beauty, restored by its seasons, and fulfilled by its rhythms. Human flourishing is thus dependent on fostering nature in its variety and abundance; going against nature's processes is destructive of self and society.

SELF-REALIZATION IN HARMONY WITH NATURE. For Confucians, harmony with nature is essential; societal well-being and human self-realization are both achieved in relation to and in harmony with nature. The great intersecting triad of Confucianism—namely, heaven, Earth, and humans—signifies this understanding that humans can only attain their full humanity in relationship to both heaven and Earth. This became a foundation for a cosmological ethical system of relationality applicable to spheres of family, society, politics, and nature. The individual was always seen in relationship to others. In particular, the person was grounded in a reciprocal relationship with nature.

Nature functions in the Confucian worldview as great parents to humans providing sustenance, nurturing, intelligibility, and guidance. In return, nature requires respect and care from humans. Human self-realization is achieved by fulfilling this role of filiality toward heaven and Earth (nature) as beneficent parents who have sustained life for humans. This idea of heaven and Earth as parents is first depicted in the early classic of the *Book of History* and is later developed by thinkers such as Kaibara Ekken in seventeenth-century Japan. Humans participate in the vast processes of nature by cultivating themselves in relation to nature, by caring for the land appropriately, by creating benevolent government, and by developing human culture and society in relation to nature's seasons and transformations.

Human self-realization implies understanding the continuities of nature in its daily rhythms and seasonal cycles. Yet humans also recognize that these orderly patterns contain within them the dynamic transformations engendering creativity, spontaneity, and openness. This is the challenge for humans within a Confucian context: How to live within nature's continuities and yet be open to its spontaneities. Thus while nature has intelligible structures and patterns, it also operates in ways to produce and encourage novelty.

With regard to establishing human culture and maintaining institutions, the same dynamic tensions are evident within the Confucian tradition. How to be faithful to the past—the continuity of the tradition—and yet be open to the change and innovation necessary for the ongoing life of the tradition. Achieving self-realization for the Confucians required a creative balancing of these two elements of tradition and innovation against the background of nature's continuities and changes.

In the Confucian tradition there exists underlying patterns of cosmological orientation and connectedness of self to the universe and self to society. Indeed, one might say that Confucianism as a religious tradition is distinguished by a concern for both personal groundedness and cosmological relatedness amidst the myriad changes in the universe. The desire for appropriate orientation toward nature and connection to other humans is an enduring impetus in Confucianism. Indeed, this need to recognize and cultivate such relatedness is the primary task of the Confucian practitioner in attaining authentic personhood.

This relatedness takes many forms, and variations of it constitute one of the means of identifying different periods and thinkers in the tradition. In China, from the classical period of the *Book of Changes* to the Han system of correspondences and the Neo-Confucian metaphysics of the *Diagram of the Great Ultimate*, concerns for cosmology and cultivation have been dominant in Confucian thought. In Korea one of the most enduring expressions of this was the four-seven debates that linked the metaphysics of principle *(li)* and material force *(qi)* to issues of cultivating virtue and controlling the emotions. These debates continued in Japan, although without the same intensity and political consequences. Instead, in Japan the effort to link particular virtues to the cosmos became important, as did the expression of cultivation in the arts, in literature, and in practical learning. In this manner, one's cultivation was shared for the benefit of the society in both aesthetic and practical matters. Thus, in varied forms throughout East Asian Confucianism, the human is viewed as a microcosm in relation to the macrocosm of the universe,

NATURALISTIC IMAGERY OF CONFUCIAN RELIGIOSITY. Self-cultivation in this context is seen as essential to develop or to recover one's innate authenticity and one's connection to the cosmos. It is a process filled with naturalistic imagery of planting, nurturing, growth, and harvesting. It is in this sense that one might describe the religious ethos of Confucianism as a dynamic naturalism aimed at personal and societal transformation. This means that the imagery used to described Confucian religious practice is frequently drawn from nature, especially in its botanical, agricultural, and seasonal modes. Thus to become fully human one must nurture (*yang*) and preserve (*cun*)—that is, cultivate—the heavenly principle of one's mind and heart. These key terms may refer to such activities as nurturing the seeds of goodness that Mencius identifies and preserving emotional harmony mentioned in the *Doctrine of the Mean* (*Zhongyong*).

In *Mencius* there is a recognition of the fundamental sensitivity of humans to the suffering of others (IIA:6). This is demonstrated through the example of an observer's response on seeing a child who is about to fall into a well. Mencius suggests that the child would be rescued through activating the instinctive compassion of the observer, not by promising the rescuer any extraneous rewards. Indeed, to be human for Mencius means to have a heart with the seeds (or germs) of compassion, shame, courtesy and modesty, right and wrong. When cultivated, these will become the virtues of humaneness, righteousness, propriety, and wisdom. When they are developed in a person they will flourish, "like a fire starting up or a spring coming through" (IIA:6). Thus the incipient tendencies in the human are like sprouts or seeds that, as they grow, lean toward becoming fully cultivated virtues. The goal of Mencian cultivation, then, is to encourage these natural spontaneities before calculating or self-serving motives arise. This begins the art of discerning between the Way mind (*daoxin*) and the human mind (*renxin*).

In a similar manner, the *Doctrine of the Mean* speaks of differentiating between the state of centrality or equilibrium before the emotions (pleasure, anger, sorrow, joy) are aroused and the state of harmony after the emotions are aroused. This balancing between the ground of existence (centrality) and its unfolding process of self-expression (harmony) is part of achieving an authentic mode of human existence. To attain this authenticity (*cheng*) means not only that one has come into harmony with oneself but also that one has achieved a unity with heaven and Earth. Thus the identification of the moral order and the cosmic order is realized in the process of human cultivation. Self-authenticity is realized against the backdrop of the sincerity of the universe. This results in participation in the transforming and nourishing processes of heaven and Earth.

In *Mencius,* that self-cultivation is seen as analogous to the natural task of tending seeds and is thus enriched by agricultural and botanical imagery. Moreover, in the *Doctrine of the Mean* this cultivation is understood within the context of a cosmological order that is pervasive, structured, and meaningful. The human is charged to cultivate oneself and, in this process, to bring the transformations of the cosmos to their fulfillment. It is thus possible to speak of early Confucianism as having religious dimensions characterized by naturalistic analogies of cultivation within a context of cosmological processes of transformation. All of this, then, involves a religiosity of analogies between the human and the natural world.

The *Book of Changes* was also a major source of inspiration for spiritual practice and cosmological orientation for the neo-Confucians. This was seen amidst the transformations of the universe celebrated as production and reproduction (*sheng, sheng*). For the neo-Confucians it was clear that many of the virtues that a person cultivated had a cosmological component. For example, humaneness (*ren*) in humans was seen as analogous to origination (*yuan*) in nature. The growth of this virtue in humans thus had its counterpart in the fecundity of nature itself. To cultivate (*hanyang*), one needs to practice both inner awareness and outer attention, abiding in reverence within and investigating principle without. This requires quiet sitting (*jingzuo*) and extending knowledge through investigating things *(gewu zhizhi).* To be reverent has been compared to the notion of recollection (*shoulian*), which means literally to collect together or to gather a harvest.

Thus, from the early classical Confucian texts to the later neo-Confucian writings there is a strong sense of nature as a relational whole in which human life and society flourishes. This had implications for politics and society that were evident throughout Chinese history, even if the ideals of the tradition were not always realized in practice.

SEE ALSO Confucianism, overview article and article on the Classical Canon.

BIBLIOGRAPHY

Black, Alison Harley. *Man and Nature in the Philosophical Thought of Wang Fu-chih.* Seattle, 1989.

Forke, Alfred. *The World Conception of the Chinese.* London, 1925.

Henderson, John B. *The Development and Decline of Chinese Cosmology.* New York, 1984.

Huddle, Norie. *Island of Dreams: Environmental Crisis in Japan.* New York, 1975.

Hou, Wenhui. "Reflections on Chinese Traditional Ideas of Nature." *Environmental History* 2 (1997): 482–493.

Needham, Joseph. *Science and Civilisation in China.* 8 vols. Cambridge, U.K., 1954.

Smil, Vaclav. *The Bad Earth: Environmental Degradation in China.* Armonk, N.Y., 1984.

Smil, Vaclav. *China's Environmental Crisis.* Armonk, N.Y., 1993.

Taylor, Rodney L. *The Confucian Way of Contemplation: Okada Takehiko and the Tradition of Quiet-Sitting.* Columbia, S.C., 1988.

Totman, Conrad. *The Green Archipelago: Forestry in Preindustrial Japan.* Berkeley, Calif., 1989.

Tu Weiming. *Confucian Thought: Self-hood as Creative Transformation.* Albany, N.Y., 1985.

Tu Weiming. *Centrality and Commonality: An Essay on Confucian Religiousness.* Albany, N.Y., 1989.

Tu Weiming. *Way, Learning, and Politics: Essays on the Confucian Intellectual.* Albany, N.Y., 1993.

Tu Weiming, and Mary Evelyn Tucker, eds. *Confucian Spirituality.* 2 volumes. New York, 2003–2004.

Tucker, Mary Evelyn, and John Berthrong, eds. *Confucianism and Ecology: The Interrelation of Heaven, Earth, and Humans.* Cambridge, Mass., 1998.

Tucker, Mary Evelyn. "The Relevance of Chinese Neo-Confucianism for the Reverence of Nature." *Environmental History Review* 15, no. 2 (Summer 1991).

Tucker, Mary Evelyn. "Ecological Themes in Taoism and Confucianism." In *Worldviews and Ecology*. Lewisburg, Pa., 1993.

Tucker, Mary Evelyn. "An Ecological Cosmology: The Confucian Philosophy of Material Force." In *Ecological Prospects: Scientific, Religious and Aesthetic Perspectives*. Albany, N.Y., 1994.

Tucker, Mary Evelyn, with John Berthrong "Introduction." In *Confucianism and Ecology: The Interrelation of Heaven, Earth, and Humans*, edited by Mary Evelyn Tucker, with John Berthrong. Cambridge, Mass., 1998.

Tucker, Mary Evelyn."The Philosophy of *Ch'i* as an Ecological Cosmology." In *Confucianism and Ecology: The Interrelation of Heaven, Earth, and Humans*, edited by Mary Evelyn Tucker, with John Berthrong. Cambridge, Mass., 1998.

Tucker, Mary Evelyn. "A View of Philanthropy in Japan: Confucian Ethics and Education." In *Philanthropy and Culture in Comparative Perspective*, edited by Warren Illchman, Stanley Katz, and Edward Queen. Bloomington, Ind, 1998.

Tucker, Mary Evelyn. "Religious Dimensions of Confucianism: Cosmology and Cultivation." *Philosophy East and West* 48, no. 1 (January 1998).

Tucker, Mary Evelyn. "Cosmology, Science, and Ethics in Japanese Neo-Confucianism." In *Science and Religion in Search of Cosmic Purpose*, edited by John F. Haught. Washington, D.C., 2000.

Tucker, Mary Evelyn. "Confucian Cosmology and Ecological Ethics: Qi, Li and the Role of the Human." In *Ethics in the World Religions*,.edited by Joseph Runzo and Nancy Martin. Oxford, 2001.

Tucker, Mary Evelyn. "Working Toward a Shared Global Ethic: Confucian Perspectives." In *Toward a Global Civilization? The Contribution of Religions*, edited by Melissa Merkling and Pat Mische. New York, 2001.

Tucker, Mary Evelyn. "Confucian Ethics and Cosmology for a Sustainable Future." In *When Worlds Converge: What Science and Religion Tell Us about the Story of the Universe and Our Place in It*, edited by Mary Evelyn Tucker, with Cliff Matthews and Philip Hefner. Chicago, 2002.

Tucker, Mary Evelyn. "Kaibara Ekken's *Precepts on the Family*" in *An Anthology of Asian Religions in Practice*, edited by Donald S. Lopez, Jr. Princeton, N.J., 2002.

MARY EVELYN TUCKER (2005)

ECOLOGY AND RELIGION: ECOLOGY AND DAOISM

The study of Daoism and ecology has undergone rapid revision and expansion in the past ten years but is still in its infancy. The most important reason for the transformation of this field is the dramatic advance in Daoist studies since 1980. Whereas the focus of Daoist studies had previously been fixed on proto-Daoist wisdom literature such as the *Zhuangzi* (c. third century BCE) and the *Dao de jing* (c. fourth century BCE), scholars now understand Daoism to include a wide range of priestly, communal, and monastic traditions that began in 142 CE with the Way of the Celestial Masters under Zhang Daoling and continue to the present day in China, East Asia, and across the world. As knowledge of these traditions has broadened and deepened, so has the ability to make connections between Daoism and ecology, but despite the many possible areas of engagement that have opened up, the field of Daoism and ecology remains relatively unexplored, at least in comparison to such traditions as Christianity and Buddhism.

COSMOLOGY AND ENVIRONMENT. The starting point for any discussion on Daoism and ecology is the Dao itself. Daoist cosmology regards the Dao as the principle of vital creativity inherent within the diversity of phenomena within the universe. The Dao is transcendent in that it is regarded as the supreme wellspring of creativity for heaven, earth, and humanity. The Dao is also immanent within all life as the vital power (*de*) that informs the nature (*xing*) of each of the myriad beings (*wanwu*). Daoist religion can be regarded as ecological in its theoretical structure because it is based on the continuous negotiation between individuals and their cosmological environment or creative matrix (*dao*). Life is thus neither absolutely fated nor a matter of individual will but inscribed in a complex ecology of engagement with family, ancestors, deities, the seasons, the sun and moon, and even the Dao itself.

This ecological understanding of religion does not mean, however, that Daoists have always exhibited romantic views of nature or modern environmentalist sensibilities. More frequently, Daoists are concerned with the flow of vital fluid *(qi)* in their bodies and the cultivation of a divine (*shen*) or immortal (*xian*) body that transcends the conventional limits of time and space. Although this focus on self-cultivation has frequently taken the form of detachment from ordinary life and meditative internal visualization, the focus on the inner body is itself predicated on an understanding of the body as the world and the world as the body. This microcosm-macrocosm correspondence indicates an ecological resonance between the vitality of Daoist practitioners and the vitality of the cosmological matrix in which they exist.

Daoists thus came to imagine the body as a cosmic landscape incorporating stars, mountains, streams, vegetation, and other natural phenomena. The nineteenth-century *Neijing tu* (Chart of the inner passageways), for example, depicts organs of the body as groves of trees, and *qi* meridians as streams. Altogether it depicts the body, like the world, as an ecology of living beings that function together to create an integral life form. Other charts depict the body as a single solid mountain with an abundance of fountains, springs, and waterfalls. The implication is that the environment provides a natural analogy for understanding the functioning of the body.

Other more abstract schemes for mapping the connections between the body and the environment are also prevalent. The most widespread is the common Chinese system of the five phases (earth, metal, water, wood, and fire), which is correlated with the seasons of the year, directions, colors, the organs of the body, the emotions, tastes, and so on. The accompanying theory of impulse and resonance (*ganying*) provides a holistic scheme of synchronic correlation in which a change in one domain entails a corresponding change in another domain. This theory, which forms an integral part of the diagnostic scheme of Chinese medicine, is also central to the Daoist worldview, and it functions, for instance, to coordinate the directions, times, and colors of Daoist liturgies.

VIEWS OF NATURE. The resonance between human bodies and the Dao may be traced back as far as the *Dao de jing* and its seminal statement that "Dao follows [its] nature" (*dao fa ziran*; *Dao de jing*, chap. 25). Interpretations of this phrase vary but two themes predominate. The first interpretation is that this phrase indicates the Dao's transcendence: the Dao follows no principle other than its own so-being. The second interpretation points to the Dao's immanence: the Dao is inscribed in the patterns of nature, and thus the path to be followed is the natural path. This implies a core value of "naturalness" at the heart of Daoist ethics and leads to the formulation of the Daoist principle of nonaction (*wuwei*), that is, action that is so harmonious with the flow of the Dao that it seems as though it is no action (see Liu, 2001).

Daoist thinking regards the transcendent and immanent aspects of the Dao as complementary, not opposed. On the one hand, Dao transcends nature, and humans who follow the Dao aim for a transcendent state of unity with the Dao; on the other hand, Dao is implicated within nature, and humans must follow a natural path. A failure to understand the complementarity of these principles has led to the tendency to separate Daoism into a natural philosophy on the one hand, and a mystical-religious tradition on the other. If, however, we understand nature in the Daoist sense as pregnant with the capacity for self-transcendence it becomes easier to understand how Daoism can be both "natural" and "religious." This recursive, self-transcending view of nature is evident in two places in the *Dao de jing*. It is most clearly expressed in the cosmogony of *Dao de jing* chapter 42, in which "Dao gives birth to One; One gives birth to Two; Two gives birth to Three; Three gives birth to the ten thousand things." At each stage of this cosmogonic process, nature becomes, as it were, pregnant with itself, in a process of creative emergence and evolution. Secondly, we can look to the Daoist view of transformation (*bianhua*) according to which natural phenomena are in a process of constant change and creativity. This is not only a descriptive statement about the nature of nature but implies, prescriptively, an ethic of nonattachment to things. Although this Daoist view of nonattachment is not implicated, as in Buddhism, with a theory of unsatisfactoriness (*dukkha*) or impermanence, it does entail a similar set of negative ethical prescriptions rooted in the value of nonaction (*wuwei*), that is, noninterference in the creative process of the Way.

In the proto-Daoist *Zhuangzi*, the theory of transformation implies a skepticism with regard to the traditions of Confucian behavior and the conventions of logical philosophy. Since the natural world is constantly changing, human patterns of thinking and habits of action can never be adequate to orient humans towards nature. This attitude further implies an ethic of deference or respect for the spontaneity of nature's transformations. Some scholars infer from this an attitude of stoic, even mystical, passivity in regards to natural transformation that does not sit well with modern notions of environmental activism. According to this interpretation, even though Daoists may deplore the extinction of a species, they must not let themselves be moved to action by such a natural phenomenon. Other scholars infer from this concept of natural transformation not an ethic of passivity, but a more sophisticated Daoist form of "noninterventionist" action. Such nonaction is neither crassly heroic nor wildly precipitate, but functions mystically to create a harmonious balance within the natural order.

HISTORICAL SURVEY. The earliest two Daoist religious traditions were the Way of the Celestial Masters and the Way of Great Peace. Of the two, only the former is in some form extant, but scholars have investigated both in terms of their environmental and ecological orientation. Chi-tim Lai in *Taiping jing* (The Daoist concept of central harmony, the scripture of great peace) advocates a view of central harmony (*zhonghe*) between heaven, earth, and humankind: the role of humans is thus to achieve an optimal organic harmony between the three fundamental cosmological processes of heaven, earth, and humanity. This implies that although these early Daoists may not have been environmentalists in the modern sense, their religious worldview was founded on a cosmic ecology whose ideal state was a dynamic homeostatic equilibrium. This organismic, physiological worldview may be compared to James Lovelock's Gaia hypothesis, according to which the earth is understood as a unitary self-regulating organism. Unlike Lovelock, Daoists have generally regarded humans as the apex of creation with an active role to play in maintaining the creative harmony of heaven and earth.

The Way of the Celestial Masters codified specific measures for promoting this cosmic harmony, as evidenced in the *One Hundred and Eighty Precepts of Lord Lao*, its chief ethical code before the Tang dynasty (618–907). Central to this movement was the network of twenty-four "places of order" (*zhi*), all situated in the mountains or other natural spaces of the kingdom of Shu (present-day Sichuan province), which functioned as the religion's spiritual centers where assemblies were held and scriptures were kept. In "Daoist Ecology: The Inner Transformation," Kristofer Schipper writes that nature functioned as a sanctuary in the dual sense of a sacred space and as a refuge for the community.

This view of nature as sacred space continued in the Daoist alchemical movements that flourished in pre-Tang China. Here nature functioned as the alchemist's storehouse, an immense repository of numinous substances, particularly rare minerals and fungi, that were used for the decoction of elixirs of immortality. In these alchemical traditions the final goal was not the extension or nourishing of life as seen in China's ancient longevity (*yangsheng*) traditions, but rather the transcendence of ordinary human nature and the attainment of a celestial life. As Robert Campany writes in "Ingesting the Marvelous," nature is both the realm to be transcended and at the same time the means of transcendence.

As the Daoist alchemical vision became thoroughly interiorized in the *Shangqing dao* (Way of highest clarity) and subsequent meditative traditions, this led to an increasing emphasis on the inner landscape of the body. In the inner alchemy tradition, which continues to the present day, the marvelous substances previously sought in nature's bosom are instead found within the energetic systems of the body. Similarly, the alchemical reactions are carried out by an internal process of energy manipulation. Both the inner and outer forms of alchemy are predicated on a cosmology of transformation delineated in terms of the sixty-four hexagrams of the *Yi jing* (Book of changes).

Caverns and Mountains. Of particular importance in the cosmic landscape is the concept of caverns or grottoes (*dong*). In keeping with the polyvalent character of Daoist symbology, caverns have multiple meanings. Firstly, Daoist hermits often withdraw to mountain caves to engage in cultivation practices. Caverns are thus natural sacred environments in which Daoists have lived and cultivated the Dao and are the dwelling places of immortal beings. Secondly, caverns are understood as nodes in a network of sacred spaces that extend throughout the earth and are mirrored in a network of ten major and thirty-six minor grotto-heavens (*dongtian*). Daoist traditions grew up in and around these natural spaces, and became associated with the sacred mountains in which these grottoes are located. For this reason Daoist traditions may be classified not only by the lineage of their founders but by various sacred mountains around which they formed, for example, Maoshan (Mount Mao) Daoism. The term *cavern*, moreover, was used by Lu Xiujing (406–477) to denote the three major subdivisions of the Daoist canon. According to this bibliographical cosmology, caverns are understood to be celestial repositories of sacred texts, cosmic libraries formed of the fabric of the Dao. A further religious function of the earthly caves is thus to be a place where the revelation of sacred texts can take place. Texts are said to inscribe themselves on the walls of caves or at least become visible to adepts after years of meditation in caves.

The cave where Zhang Daoling, the first celestial master, is said to have meditated in the second century CE is now part of the monastery known as the *Tianshi dong* (Grotto of the Celestial Master), on Mount Qingcheng near Chengdu, the capital of Sichuan province. In the precincts of the monastery there is also a double gingko tree with two trunks joined together that Zhang Daoling is alleged to have planted nearly two thousand years ago. It is feted with a red sash. Since areas of outstanding natural beauty form the environments in which important Daoist figures have received religious revelations, it is not surprising that monasteries were established around these sites and continue today to mark out the sacred character of specific natural environments.

Daoist Precepts. Daoist communities formulated environmental ethical precepts that aimed to codify the relationship between humans and nature. The most important set of precepts for the early Celestial Masters community in Sichuan was known as the *Yibaibashi jie* (One hundred and eighty precepts). Community elders known as *libationers* were required to live by the code and thus set an example for the rest of the community. Approximately twenty of these precepts are injunctions against the wanton destruction of the natural environment. Members of the community were not to dry wet marshes, poison lakes, disturb birds, pick flowers, make lakes, or chop down trees without good reason. These precepts do not indicate a modern environmentalist concern with preserving nature but rather are there for the benefit of the libationers themselves. The admonition that "you should not light fires in the plains" contains the implication that this act will result in harm not only to the environment but to the community. These precepts can thus be regarded as a type of ecological ethics based on the notion that human fate is inextricably implicated in the natural environment. Although we can be sure that it was the fate of humans and not the environment that concerned the Celestial Masters, there was no concept of a human morality that somehow stood apart from the natural environment.

This ancient sentiment has been echoed in a recent statement on global ecology issued by the Chinese Daoist Association. This declaration points to an inflated image of the human self and subjective will as causes of the split between humans and nature in modern industrial and technological society. The text, written by Zhang Jiyu, argues that humans must nurture spontaneity and nonassertive action (*wuwei*) in order to restore the ecological balance between humans and nature. The practical effect of this declaration has been the attention to the local environments surrounding Daoist monasteries, where Daoists have been involved in planting trees and conserving rare plant species.

Contemporary Issues. The situation of Daoist monastic environments in China is precarious. On the one hand Daoist monasteries located in scenic locales are lauded for their environmental aesthetic and for actively promoting an environmental consciousness among China's people. The message that "Dao follows nature" receives a high profile in many temple inscriptions, and the Daoist complex on Mount Qingcheng contains many signs written in Chinese and English that make the connection between Daoism and environmental protection. The message is that China's cultural and religious traditions contain the wisdom that will help China succeed in creating economic development with ecological sustainability. But on the other hand these same Daoist mountains, precisely because of their natural beauty, are becoming local economic engines attracting significant numbers of tourists and infrastructure investment from local governments. The monasteries' economic success brings the danger of too many tourists and the possibility of environmental degradation. In this way the development of Daoist sites in China precisely mirrors the economic success and environmental problems of China's overall development.

SEE ALSO Daoism, overview article; Qi.

BIBLIOGRAPHY

The most comprehensive single-volume European-language work on Daoism and ecology is *Daoism and Ecology: Ways within a Cosmic Landscape,* edited by N. J. Girardot, James Miller, and Liu Xiaogan (Cambridge, Mass., 2001). This book, which contains the essays mentioned above, includes the "Declaration of the Chinese Daoist Association on Global Ecology" by Zhang Jiyu, pp. 361–372; Chi-tim Lai's "The Daoist Concept of Central Harmony (*zhonghe*) in the Scripture of Great Peace (*Taiping jing*): Human Responsibility for the Maladies of Nature," pp. 95–111; Liu Xiaogan's "Non-action and the Environment Today," pp. 315–339; Robert Ford Campany's "Investigating the Marvelous" pp. 125–147, and Kristofer Schipper's essay on the *One Hundred and Eighty Precepts* entitled "Daoist Ecology: The Inner Transformation, A Study of the Precepts of the Early Daoist Ecclesia," pp. 79–94. Robert Ford Campany's work on the idea of nature in the alchemy of Ge Hong can be found in his *To Live as Long as Heaven and Earth: A Translation and Study of Ge Hong's Traditions of Divine Transcendents* (Berkeley, 2002), and for theoretical treatments of alchemy see Fabrizio Pregadio's "Elixirs and Alchemy," in *Daoism Handbook,* edited by Livia Kohn, pp. 165–195 (Leiden, 2000). Sarah Allen's *The Way of Water and Sprouts of Virtue* (Albany, N.Y., 1997) contains an excellent discussion of how early Chinese philosophical concepts are rooted in images from nature; this philosophical inquiry is also treated in the set of essays in *Nature in Asian Traditions of Thought: Essays in Environmental Philosophy,* edited by J. Baird Callicott and Roger T. Ames (Albany, N.Y., 1989). E. N. Anderson's *Ecologies of the Heart: Emotion, Belief, and the Environment* (New York, 1996) discusses a wide range of Chinese folk traditions, such as *feng-shui* and diet, in terms of their ecology and culture. For an up-to-date annotated bibliography of works related to Daoism and ecology, consult the website of the Forum on Religion and Ecology at http://environment.harvard.edu/religion.

JAMES MILLER (2005)

ECOLOGY AND RELIGION: ECOLOGY AND SHINTŌ

Shintō and ecology cannot be called an established academic subject, either in Japan or in the West. However, in reply to the growing concerns for environmental politics, Shintō and many other religions have become a focus in the debate on inherent ecological thinking patterns in the established religious worldviews. In Japan, a discourse on the environmental aspects of Shintō that spans strictly academic research and Shintō theology has developed since the 1990s. One chief representative is Minoru Sonoda, who is both a Shintō priest and a Shintō historian and has published articles in English. His contributions to the subject will be discussed later. In the West probably the most remarkable effort so far has been an international conference called Shintō and Ecology that was organized by the Center for the Study of World Religions (CSWR) of Harvard University in 1997. This conference was part of a series of conferences on Religions of the World and Ecology. Still, there is no comprehensive study on the subject in a Western language, although the papers from this conference were published in Japanese.

This article will first discuss the ecological conditions and values of modern Japan before proceeding to a discussion of Shintō. As will become clear, the evaluation of Shintō's contribution to Japanese environmentalism depends on the respective interpretation of Shintō, which is in itself a controversial topic. Examples of religious symbolism applied to objects of nature and a discussion of Shintō's pragmatic ethics conclude the article.

ECOLOGY AND MODERN JAPANESE SOCIETY. Japan's environmental record is highly ambivalent. On the one hand, the country is known for its environmental catastrophes, such as the Minamata disease, a case of mercury poisoning that culminated in the 1960s, or its insensitive politics in connection with whale hunting and the exploitation of exotic timber wood. On the other hand, Japanese countermeasures against environmental pollution have proved surprisingly effective. Japan's laws and regulations concerning exhaust gases and the emission of sulfur dioxide and nitrogen have long been among the strictest in the world. These policies, which were started in the 1970s, have earned Japan something of a reputation as a model of environmentalism. According to Conrad Totman, a leading authority in the field of environmental history, in the long run, Japan's achievements in ecological preservation outweigh the harms Japanese society did to its environmental conditions. In his famous analysis of forestry in preindustrial Japan (1989), Totman argues that given the population density and the geographical conditions of the Japanese archipelago, one would expect Japan to be a "impoverished, slum-ridden, peasant society subsisting on barren, eroded moonscape characterized by bald mountains and debris-strewn lowlands" (p. 1). Instead, outside the urban centers Japan enjoys a wealth of verdant forests that has earned it the denomination "green archipelago." Totman argues that this is not the result of nature's benevolence but of "generations of human toil that have converted the archipelago into one green forest preserve" (p. 1).

To sustain his argument, Totman provides the following figures: Japan is not only one of the world's most heavily populated societies. Since 80 percent of the country consists of hard-rock mountains, it is by far the most populous society in terms of density by arable land (p. 172). In fact, Japan was on the verge of deforestation already in the seventeenth century. Totman's study concentrates on the policies that prevented forestry overexploitation, which elsewhere produced ecological calamities not only in the industrial age but, for instance, along the Mediterranean coast during the Roman Empire. The relative success of Japanese society in preserving and creating natural conditions that form the basis of the country's wealth naturally leads to the question of the extent to which Shintō, Japan's indigenous religion, has contributed to the ecological standards of Japan.

SHINTŌ AND THE PROVERBIAL JAPANESE LOVE OF NATURE. Shintō (literally, "Way of the Gods") comprises in its broadest sense a variety of beliefs in Japanese indigenous deities (*kami*). *Kami* range from powerful nature and ancestor deities to spirits of insignificant objects and are virtually infinite in number. Beliefs and forms of worship are equally heterogeneous but are often directed at objects of nature such as trees, rocks, or mountains, which are either interpreted as abodes of the *kami* or as *kami* themselves. Many Shintō shrines, even in urban areas, are further surrounded by small groves generally protected by religious taboos. One famous shrine, Kasuga Taisha in Nara, has even allowed a tree to protrude from the roof of one of its buildings, thus showing special respect for the sacredness of trees. Particularly in the eyes of Western observers, Shintō has been regarded therefore as a very ancient, "animistic" religion, maintaining features of times when people did not yet possess the capabilities to change their natural environment and instead strove for living in harmony with given environmental conditions. The French scholar Augustin Berque, for instance, contrasts the Christian "physicophobiac" tradition with the Japanese love for nature ("physicophily") and its strong affinity toward the forest (Berque, 1997). Other observers, such as Spanish author Luis Diez del Corral, directly associated Shintō architecture with this "physiophilic" attitude, regarding the Japanese shrine as the most compressed architectural expression of the forest as the home of the sacred (Diez del Corral, 1967).

Such harmonious, often romantic depictions stand in stark contrast to the historical role of Shintō in modern Japanese society, particularly in the area of ultranationalism from the 1930s to World War II. At that time Shintō was quintessentially equated with emperor worship. Every Japanese was obliged to perform religious service at the local shrine not as a reverence to the local *kami* or to surrounding nature but as a reverence to the state embodied by the figure of the emperor. This so-called State Shintō (*kokka shintō*) is nowadays often explained as an ideological misuse of the old indigenous religion, contrary to its original values and intentions. Emperor worship, however, had been an indispensable part of Shintō theology long before the existence of a modern nation-state. Until after World War II, the emperor was traditionally seen as descended from the Sun Goddess (Amaterasu), and thus divine himself. Even today, hardly any Shintō apologetic in Japan would go as far as to remove the emperor completely from the realm of Shintō.

Recent scholarship has attempted to overcome these inherently contradictory images by reducing the interpretation of Shintō to the facts gathered from historical sources. This implies a rejection of the still common notion that Shintō reflects a transhistorical Japanese mentality (including Japanese nature worship). Instead, special attention is given to the changing conceptions of indigenous deities and the interactions of Buddhism and Shintō. Since these interpretations are not yet familiar outside specialist circles, a short historical overview in light of recent studies seems necessary before discussing the ecological aspects of Shintō. More specific essays on this topic can be found, for instance, in *Shintō in History: Ways of the Kami* (Breen and Teeuwen, 2000) or *Tracing Shintō in the History of Kami Worship* (Teeuwen and Scheid, 2002).

HISTORICAL DEVELOPMENT. In ancient Japanese myth, the world (i.e., the Japanese islands) is a creation of a primordial, divine couple who are equally the ancestors of all divine beings populating the mundane world. Yet apart from a few mythical narrations, Shintō does not possess a theoretical concept of nature, the universe, or the divine, as developed for instance by Buddhism or Daoism. While there have always been individual attempts to establish something like a canonical Shintō view on these issues, such efforts drew mostly from existing explanations of other religions and did not reach canonical authority. This lack of religious doctrine is closely related to the fact that there is neither a founding figure nor a body of canonical texts, apart from ancient chronicles (most notably the *Kojiki*, or "Records of Ancient Matters" from 712, and the *Nihonshoki*, or "Records of Japan," from 720), which were never intended as religious writings by their authors. Shintō is defined by its belief in the local deities (*kami*), which existed through all phases of Japanese religious history. Yet the notion that belief in the *kami* is in itself an independent, self-sufficient religion is a comparatively new phenomenon. During most of Japanese religious history since the advent of Buddhism (sixth century CE), *kami* were seen either as minor spiritual beings such as demons or goblins or as manifestations of Buddhist entities.

In early historical times, probably inspired by the example of Buddhist temples, emperors as well as other local leaders began to erect permanent sites of worship to their ancestor deities, generally referred to as "shrines" (*jinja*). The most prestigious of these sites of ancestor worship is the well-known Ise Shrine dedicated to Amaterasu, the sun goddess, which is at the same time regarded as the ancestor deity of the imperial lineage. Only in the case of such big shrines, which became part of an elaborate system of state rituals, did a professional priesthood take over the affairs of religious service to the *kami*. On the local level, however, *kami* worship was mostly conducted by community leaders or was put into the hands of Buddhist monks. Buddhism was also instrumental in erecting sites of *kami* worship. Already in the Nara period (eighth century), every large Buddhist temple had its local protector *kami*, situated side by side with the local Buddha. Thus, from the beginning of Japanese Buddhism, efforts were taken to integrate *kami* worship into the Buddhist worldview and liturgy. *Kami* worship and Japanese Buddhism developed during most parts of their common history in mutual interaction and were not regarded as different or competing religious systems.

From the medieval period onward, however, individual thinkers engaged in a theology of *kami* worship independent from Buddhism. It is in this context that the word *shintō* was used for the first time to designate something comparable to Buddhism (in Japanese, *bustudō*, the Way of the Buddha) (Teeuwen, 2002). Only in these theologies, the way of the *kami* was regarded as a religion comprising, among other features, a cosmology based on Japanese myth, an ethical system different from Buddhism, and rituals for the dead, which had been entirely in the hands of Buddhist monks. While such efforts to establish Shintō as an independent religion were only partly successful, they induced a series of independence movements in many shrines from the beginning of the Edo period (1603–1867) onward. In the eighteenth century, a new intellectual movement, the so-called Nativist School (*kokugaku*), focused on the idea of Japanese culture from the times before the impact of Chinese and Indian civilizations and led to a new evaluation of ancient history, mythology, and the pure Way of the Kami. Later generations of this school were instrumental in the reestablishment of the political role of the *tennō* and the proclamation of Shintō as a kind of state religion in the political upheaval of 1868, generally known as the Meiji Restoration. Most notably, the early Meiji government commanded the separation of *kami* and Buddha worship (*shinbutsu bunri*), thereby destroying many existing syncretistic institutions and providing for the first time the necessary conditions for Shintō as an independent religion on a nationwide scale. The ideas of the Nativist School not only paved the way for the above-mentioned nationalistic ideologies of State Shintō, they also shaped the general depiction of Shintō as a repository of timeless, transhistorical Japanese values up to the present day.

As should be clear from this short sketch of recent approaches to Shintō history, it is not at all easy to determine a precise value system of Shintō, let alone Shintō attitudes toward nature. Yet there is an ample range of religious symbolism related to natural objects, which is nowadays attributed to the realm of Shintō. The following passages provide a few representative examples.

Mountains and rocks. Mountains were always seen as the realm of the divine in premodern times. Pilgrimages to Mount Fuji and other famous peaks trace their origins back to mountain cults that arose from a characteristic blend of ancient shamanistic and Buddhist religious features (*cf.* Miyake, 2001). But while modern pilgrimages are mass phenomena, undertaken mostly by bus, in olden times only very few people entered the higher mountainous regions. Those who did were almost by definition religious ascetics, called *yamabushi,* "those who sleep in the mountains." It is therefore no surprise that the mountains appear in folk legends either as the realm of the dead or as entrances to the Buddhist hell. All in all, the religious awe in relation to mountains is tightly connected with fear of their wild, menacing natural conditions. On the other hand, hills or smaller mountains close to human dwellings were sometimes regarded as a whole as a "divine body" (*shintai*), as the case of Mount Miwa near Nara demonstrates. Finally, there are certain scenic spots that owe their religious flair to their peculiar shapes. The "wedded rocks" at the Bay of Ise, two natural stone pillars formed by the sea and now united by a sacred rope (*shimenawa*), are a particularly famous example.

Trees. Sacred trees (*shinboku*) furnished with a simple cord of raw hemp to indicate their divine aura are a remarkable indication of the Japanese capability to endow nature with religious symbolism by using "almost natural" materials. Trees hold indeed a peculiar religious significance. In a recent article (2000), Shintō scholar Sonoda Minoru pointed out that in some of the earliest Japanese texts the word *mori,* which translates as "forest" in modern Japanese, could be used as a synonym of *yashiro,* the ancient word for *kami* shrine. According to Sonoda, this is an indication that in prehistorical times *kami* were venerated in simple groves. The groves around modern Shintō shrines are thus remnants of what shrines originally used to be—trees as abodes of the *kami.* To him, these "expressions of Japan's ancient animistic view of life" are part of an ancient forest culture, which has helped to limit ecological disasters in Japan so far (p. 45).

In fact, it remains open to debate to what extent Sonoda's relation between shrines and trees actually accounts for a special ecological consciousness. After all, Shintō does not protect forests in general but only a few select examples of trees. In the study of Japanese forestry mentioned earlier, Totman (1989) demonstrates that in the ancient period, religious institutions not only supported indiscriminate wood consumption but were actually among the chief consumers. Already in the eighth century the erection of shrines and temples, together with aristocratic mansions, led to the deforestation of vast regions in the Kinai region around present-day Nara, then the center of Japanese civilization. The practice of rebuilding shrines anew every twenty years, which is nowadays still performed in the case of the Ise shrines, was formerly a common technique related to prehistoric construction methods, which ceased when wood became sparse (p. 12). Totman raises these examples of "ancient predation" in his discussion of religious impacts on Japanese environmentalism, which he ultimately denies (p. 181). According to him, pragmatic considerations and a long period of trial and error with Japan's most important construction material, wood, were more important for early modern ecological successes than religious values.

SOCIAL ROLES OF *KAMI* WORSHIP. In spite of limitations of the received image of Shintō, it is quite obvious that *kami* worship played an important role in the religious life of communities during all times of Japanese history. *Kami* rites filled those gaps, where conventional Buddhist worship fell short in offering satisfactory solutions. In particular, rites related to agricultural production are primarily addressing local *kami.* Regular festivals (*matsuri*) in honor of the *kami* play an important role in sacralizing the annual cycle of production and in strengthening vertical and horizontal social bonds within local communities. In premodern times shrines seem to have also functioned as keepers of a kind of village constitution, which took the form of a pledge of the village to the local *kami*. In a recent study of shrines from the eighteenth century, Maeda Hiromi found many examples in which villagers were bound to raise only special crops or special animals by the will of their *kami*. As the economy changed and other forms of agriculture seemed more profitable, villages took great pains to change the provisions of their *kami*, which could only be done with the assistance of the highest Shintō authorities (Maeda, 2002). These examples testify to the severity of *kami* worship as well as to the flexibility and pragmatics of Shintō precepts.

CONCLUSION. All in all it becomes clear that the natural environment of Japan was and still is heavily endowed with religious symbolism. This symbolism is often, but not always, related to the native deities, the *kami*. Yet while the outer form of these symbols seems to have been transmitted with a remarkable degree of consistency and uniformity, the contents of *kami* worship is difficult to determine and subject to historical change.

From the earliest historical times indigenous Japanese religion, whether we call it Shintō or not, was related to the cultivation of nature, that is, agriculture. Natural conditions were perceived of as *kami*, and religion served to turn the powers of these *kami* into conditions favorable for agricultural production. Indigenous deities thus represented both nature's benevolent and nature's threatening aspects. They were neither morally good nor bad, but simply powerful. Also in later times, *kami* were worshiped not so much in the quest for moral guidance but in order to gain a *kami*'s favors. This is also one of the reasons for the well-known "this-worldliness" (*genze riyaku*) of Japanese religion in general and of Shintō in particular.

In the long run, Shintō seems to have always adapted to the conditions of human production, not the other way round. In particular, Shintō has been used to endow case-specific, pragmatic regulations with some religious dignity. It is certainly possible to sieve environmental ideas from the traditions of Shintō, but in historical retrospect there is no clear indication that Shintō served better to preserve environmental stability than any other religion.

BIBLIOGRAPHY

Berque, Augustin. *Nature, Artifice, and Japanese Culture.* Northamptonshire, U.K., 1997. (Translation of *Le sauvage et l'artifice: Les japonais devant la nature.* Paris, 1986.)

Breen, John, and Mark Teeuwen, eds. *Shintō in History: Ways of the Kami.* London, 2000.

Broadbent, Jeffrey. *Environmental Politics in Japan: Networks of Power and Protest.* Cambridge, U.K., 1998.

Diez del Corral, Luis. *Del Nuevo al Viejo Mundo, Revista de Occidente.* Madrid, 1967.

Kalland Arne. "Culture in Japanese Nature." In *Asian Perceptions of Nature: A Critical Approach,* edited by Ole Bruun and Arne Kalland, pp. 218–233. London, 1992.

Maeda Hiromi. "Court Rank for Village Shrines: The Yoshida House's Interaction with Local Shrines during the Mid-Tokugawa Period." In *Tracing Shintō in the History of Kami Worship,* edited by Mark Teeuwen and Bernhard Scheid, pp. 325–358. Special issue of *Japanese Journal of Religious Studies* 29, nos. 3–4 (fall 2002).

Miyake, Hitoshi. *Shugendō: Essays on the Structure of Japanese Folk Religion.* Ann Arbor, Mich., 2001.

Sonoda Minoru. "Shintō and the Natural Environment." In *Shintō in History: Ways of the Kami,* edited by John Breen and Mark Teeuwen, pp. 32–46. London, 2000.

Takeuchi Keiichi. "Traditional View of Nature and Natural Resource Management in Japan: Sustainable Development and Geographical Thought." *Hitotsubashi Journal of Social Studies* 30, no. 2 (December 1998): 85–93.

Teeuwen, Mark. "From *Jindō* to Shintō: A Concept Takes Shape." In *Tracing Shintō in the History of Kami Worship,* edited by Mark Teeuwen and Bernhard Scheid, pp. 233–263. Special issue of *Japanese Journal of Religious Studies* 29, nos. 3–4 (fall 2002).

Teeuwen, Mark, and Bernhard Scheid, eds. *Tracing Shintō in the History of Kami Worship.* Special issue of *Japanese Journal of Religious Studies* 29, nos. 3–4 (fall 2002).

Totman, Conrad. *The Green Archipelago: Forestry in Preindustrial Japan.* Berkeley, Calif., 1989.

BERNHARD SCHEID (2005)

ECOLOGY AND RELIGION: ECOLOGY AND JUDAISM

Judaism is rooted in two core beliefs: that God is the sole Creator of the universe and that God's will was revealed to Israel in the form of law, the Torah, as part of an eternal covenant. The dialectical relationship between the doctrine of creation and the doctrine of revelation, between nature and Torah, between what is and what ought to be, frames Jewish attitudes toward the natural world, reflecting changes over time.

Biblical cosmology envisioned an earth encompassed by a sphere of water, over which God's wind (*ruah*) hovers. Although the details of the creative act remain open to interpretation and debate, the act itself was broadly understood as one of establishing boundaries, separating heavens from earth, dry land from water, animate from inanimate things, human beings from other animals. Boundary formation at creation would serve as the rationale for the distinction between the sacred and the profane, the permitted and the forbidden in the legal parts of the Bible and in post-biblical Judaism.

In rabbinic Judaism (first to sixth centuries), cosmological speculations (*ma'aseh bereshit*) were regarded as esoteric lore to be divulged only to the initiated few (Mishnah *Hag.*

2:1). Although the rabbis debated the details of the biblical creation narrative, the dominant view was that the earth and the heavens are like "a pot with a cover." The "cover" was identified with the firmament (*raqi'a*), itself composed of water and stars of fire that coexist harmoniously (J. T. *R. H.* 2:5 58a), although it was believed that there were more than one firmament (*Hag.* 12b). The sun and the moon were believed to be situated in the second firmament, and beneath the earth there was the abyss.

In the Middle Ages, Jews reinterpreted the biblical creation narratives and rabbinic cosmological speculations in light of Greek and Hellenistic science and philosophy. Whether the world was created ex nihilo or out of a preexisting matter was hotly debated. Moses Maimonides (Mosheh ben Maimon, 1135/8–1204) held that the origin of the universe was beyond the ken of human reason and remained ambiguous whether God created the world ex nihilo or out of pre-existing matter. Unlike Maimonides, Levi ben Gershom (Gersonides, 1288–1344) argued that creation out of pre-existing matter is scientifically demonstrable and is in full accord with Aristotelian science.

Like its Muslim counterpart, medieval Jewish Aristotelianism was interlaced with Neoplatonic themes. The separate intelligences were said to emanate from God and the corporeal world emanated from the celestial spheres. Many Jewish thinkers understood creation to mean emanation and depicted the universe as a hierarchical great chain of being in which each thing occupies its natural place and acts in accord with its inherent telos. Whereas the doctrine of creation emphasizes the transcendence of God and the total dependence of all created beings on God, the doctrine of emanation highlights the immanence of God, viewing the natural world as an extension (albeit most remote) of divine reality. Both transcendentalist and immanentist outlooks informed medieval Jewish thought, but one view is not necessarily more "green" or "environmentally friendly" than the other.

During the early modern period, Jewish philosophers became increasingly more interested in the flora and fauna of their natural environment, and Jewish philosophical-scientific texts abound with information about minerals, plants, and animals. Yet such information was still framed by the theological assumptions of medieval rationalism: The natural world could be understood in light of the revealed Torah since it was the blueprint of creation. Jewish thinkers were also rather slow to respond to the scientific revolution of the seventeenth century, and most rejected Copernicus's heliocentric theory on religious grounds. While a small cadre of Jews earned doctorate degrees at European universities, especially in medicine, interest in natural sciences remained marginal among Jews. Instead, the study of halakhah (Jewish Law) and Qabbalah (Jewish mysticism) preoccupied Jewish intellectual interests, and both endeavors were textual, self-referential, and abstract.

With the onslaught of modernity and the secularization of culture, Jews began to re-examine their tradition, and many found it wanting precisely because Jewish life was divorced from nature. When Jews were granted civil rights, they flocked to the universities, excelling in the natural sciences such as physics, chemistry, and biology. Embracing science as a substitute to traditional Torah study, Jews no longer regarded the Bible as the source of truth about the physical world; cosmology now belonged to "science" rather than to "religion." As a result, Jewish philosophers no longer reflected about the origin of the universe, but instead focused on explicating the religious and existential meaning of the doctrine in relation to the doctrines of revelation and redemption.

DESCRIPTIONS OF NATURE IN JEWISH SACRED TEXTS. The doctrine of creation facilitates an interest in the natural world that God created. The more one observes the natural world, the more one comes to revere the creator because the world manifests the presence of order and wise design in which nothing is superfluous. *Psalms* 19:1 expresses the point poetically: "The heavens are telling the glory of God / and the firmament proclaims his handiwork." *Psalms* 148 depicts all of creation as engaged in praising God and recognizing God's commanding power over nature. Nature also fears God (*Ps.* 68:9); it observes the relationship between God and Israel and expresses either sorrow or joy at the fortunes of the Israelites (*Jl.* 1:12; *Am.* 1:2; *Jon.* 3:7–9; *Is.* 14:7–8). In the *Psalms*, however, awareness of nature's orderliness, regularity, and beauty never leads to revel in nature for its own sake. Nature is never an end but always points to the divine Creator who governs and sustains nature. The emphasis on orderliness of creation explains why in Judaism one does not find glorification of wilderness and why the cultivated field is the primary model for the created universe in the Bible.

The Bible abounds with references to the natural world and figurative usage of natural elements to teach about the relationship between God and Israel. In one famous parable, fruit trees and vines willingly serve the human in ritual observance by providing oil, fruit, and wine (*Jgs.* 9:8–13). Conversely, nature does God's bidding when it serves to punish and destroy the people of Israel when they sin; indeed, ungodly behavior leads to ecological punishment. Since God is the sole Creator, it is God's prerogative to sustain or to destroy nature (*Ps.* 29:5–6; *Zec.* 11:1–3; *Hb.* 3:5–8). Nature itself becomes a witness to the covenantal relationship between Israel and God, and the ongoing drama of righteousness, chastisement, and rebuke. Mostly the Bible emphasizes divine care of all creatures: God provides food to all (*Ps.* 147:9), God is concerned about humans and beasts (*Ps.* 104:14; 145:16), and God's care is extended to animals that can be used by humans such as goats and rabbits (*Ps.* 104:18) as well as to lion cubs and ravens that do not serve human interest. Because God takes care of animals, they turn to God in time of need (*Ps.* 104: 21; 27; 147:9; *Jb.* 38:41).

The rabbis were concerned about the relationship between revealed morality (prescriptive law) and the laws of nature (descriptive laws), but the rabbinic corpus harbors diverse, and even conflicting, views. One theme highlights the regularity of nature and its indifference to human concerns: "nature pursues its own course" (*olam ke-minhago noheg*; B.T. *A. Zar.* 54b). Accordingly nature is independent of the revealed Torah and the laws of nature are different from the laws of the Torah. A contrary viewpoint, however, holds that the natural world is contingent upon the acceptance of the Torah by the Jewish people; had they rejected the Torah, the world would have reverted to primeval chaos. The link between nature and the moral conduct of humans is expressed in yet a third view, that original natural order was perfect but suffered a radical change as a result of human original sin (B. T. *Kid.* 82b). A fourth view posits "the animals of the righteous" as models for human conduct. Since these animals live in perfect harmony with their Creator, humanity has much to learn from them, in terms of not only the principle of observing God's will but also specific lessons (B. T. *Pes.* 53b). Finally, there is a rabbinic teaching that not only do animals observe the moral laws, but all of nature is perceived as fulfilling the will of God in the performance of its normal functions (J. T. *Peah* 1:1).

The relationship between Torah and nature was the core of medieval philosophical speculations. Thus for Maimonides and Gersonides, God is the supreme telos of the universe, the intelligible apex of the entire cosmos accessible through philosophy and culminating in prophecy. Viewing nature itself as "wise," the goal of the medieval philosopher-scientist was to fathom the wisdom of nature in order to attain the ultimate end of human life: the knowledge of God to the extent this is possible for humans.

The notion that the Torah is the paradigmatic blueprint of nature was elaborated and radicalized in Qabbalah. Focusing on the linguistic aspect of the creative act, the qabbalists regarded the letters of the Hebrew alphabet as the building blocks of the created world, whose permutations account for the diversity of nature. This approach to nature assumed magical and theurgic dimensions: The one who knows how to decode the Torah can manipulate the physical environment (hence Qabbalah was closely associated with magic, astrology, and alchemy) and even affect and impact God's inner life (namely, reunify the feminine and masculine aspects of the Godhead). While qabbalistic texts abound with symbols derived from the natural world, corporeal nature was regarded as evil to be transcended or spiritualized.

Qabbalah gave rise to Eastern-European Hasidism in the eighteenth century. Hasidic theology treated all natural phenomena as ensouled: Divine sparks enlivened all corporeal entities and not just human beings. The divine sparks sought release from their material entrapment. Through ritual activity, the Hasidic master attempted to draw closer to the divine energy, the liberation of which would result not only in the sanctification of nature but also in the redemption of reality and its return to its original, non-corporeal state. The worship of God through the spiritualization of corporeal reality (*avodah ba-gashmiyut*) became a major Hasidic value.

Qabbalah and Hasidism contributed to the bookishness of Jewish culture and the alienation of traditional Jews from the natural world. With the rise of modernity, the very lack of Jewish interest in nature was cited by the Jewish Enlightenment (Haskalah) as the reason for Jewish backwardness. Only the return to nature could modernize the Jews, enabling them to recover their lost vitality and integrate as equals into modern society. The literature of the Haskalah movement in the nineteenth century is full of descriptions of nature, emphasizing its beauty, wisdom, and moral power.

The return to nature was one of the major goals of Zionism, the Jewish secular nationalist movement that emerged at the end of the nineteenth century in response to virulent anti-Semitism. The Zionist movement succeeded in reversing the traditional Jewish lifestyle and creating a new type of Jew, one who was rooted in nature rather than in sacred texts, but Zionism also illustrates the complex relationship between Judaism and ecology. In the State of Israel, intimate familiarity with the landscape of the land of Israel, its flora and fauna, and concern for the preservation of the physical environment are popular among secular Israelis. Yet environmentalism is generally not legitimated by appeal to the religious sources of Judaism.

The creative interweaving of Judaism and ecology belongs primarily to North America. Since 1970, considered the beginning of Jewish environmentalism, Jewish scholars (first Orthodox and later Reform and Conservative) have responded to the charge that the Judeo-Christian tradition is the cause of the environmental crisis. Jewish environmentalism has raised awareness about ecological problems such as pollution of natural resources, deforestation, erosion of topsoil, the disappearance of species, climatic changes, and other ecological disasters brought about by the industrial revolution, human greed, and unbridled consumerism. The nascent literature of Jewish environmentalism has shown that Jewish sacred texts and practices express concern for the earth and its inhabitants, and that the rhythm of Jewish religious life is rooted in the cycles of nature. Since 1993, the Coalition on the Environment and Jewish Life (COEJL) has coordinated a broad range of educational activities and brought a distinct Jewish voice to policy making on municipal, state, and federal levels.

Legal and Ethical Positions Regarding the Environment. In Judaism, Scripture frames legal and ethical positions regarding the environment. While clearly privileging the human perspective, the Bible places on humans special responsibilities toward the environment. Only the human species is said to be created "in the image of God" (*Gn.* 1:26), although humans, like other animals, were fashioned from the dust of the earth to which they return at death. Creation in the image of God did not entail a license to subdue and exploit the earth, as many environmentalists erroneously charge, but the task to protect God's created world. By following divine commandments, humans can sanctify nature and endow it with religious meaning. Nature itself is not sacred or holy, but it becomes sacred when humans interact with it in the framework of observing God's commandments. Jewish environmental responsibility is exemplified in the relationship between the people of Israel and the land of Israel, the land that belongs to God but which God gave to Israel, the chosen people, as collateral of the eternal covenant.

Land-based commandments. Various land-based commandments in the Bible express the belief that God is the rightful owner of the land of Israel and the source of its fertility. The Israelites working the land are but God's tenant-farmers who are obligated to return the first portion of the land's yield to its rightful owner in order to insure the land's continued fertility and the farmer's sustenance and prosperity. Accordingly, the first sheaf of the barley harvest, the first fruit of produce, and two loaves of bread made from the new grain are to be consecrated to God.

Scripture pays special attention to trees. *Leviticus* 19:23 commands that, during the first three years of growth, the fruits of newly planted trees or vineyards are not to be eaten (*orlah*) because they are considered to be God's property. When Israel conducts itself according to the laws of the Torah, the land is abundant and fertile, benefiting its inhabitants with the basic necessities of human life—grain, oil, and wine—but when Israel sins, the blessedness of the land declines, and it becomes desolate and inhospitable. When the alienation from God becomes egregious and injustice overtakes God's people, God removes them from the Holy Land. Thus the well-being of God's land and the moral quality of the people who live on the land are causally linked and both depend on obeying God's will.

***Bal tashchit* ("do not destroy").** The main legal principle of Jewish environmental ethics concerns the protection of vegetation, especially fruit-bearing trees. In war times, fruit-bearing trees must not be chopped down while a city is under siege (*Dt.* 20:19). This commandment is undoubtedly anthropocentric, but it indicates that the Torah recognizes the interdependence between humans and trees, on the one hand, and the capacity of humans to destroy natural things on the other. The Jewish legal tradition thus requires that one carefully weigh the ramifications of all actions and behavior for every interaction with the natural world; it also sets priorities and weighs conflicting interests and permanent modification of the environment.

***Tzaʿar baʿalei hayyim* ("distress of living creatures").** Although the Jewish tradition places the responsibility for management of God's creation in human hands, the tradition also recognizes the well-being of non-human species: Humans should take care of other species and be sensitive to the needs of animals. Cruelty toward animals is prohibited because it leads to other forms of cruelty. The ideal is to create a sensibility of love and kindness toward animals in order to emulate God's attribute of mercy and fill the commandment "to be Holy as I the Lord am Holy" (*Lv.* 19:2). Thus *Deuteronomy* 22:6 forbids the killing of a bird with her young because it is exceptionally cruel and because it can affect the perpetuation of the species. This commandment is one of seven commandments given to the sons of Noah and is therefore binding on all human beings, not just Jews.

The tradition prescribes particular modes of slaughter that are swift because they are performed with a sharp, clean blade. In Hasidism this principle was combined with the belief in the transmigration of souls into non-human bodies and the development of elaborate slaughtering practices designed to protect the human soul that may have transmigrated into the body of the animal about to be slaughtered. The concern for unnecessary suffering of animals is applied today to the industrial farming of animals for human consumption and with the use of animals in scientific experimentation.

Social justice and ecological well-being. The most distinctive feature of Jewish environmental legislation is the causal connection between the moral quality of human life and the vitality of God's creation. The corruption of society is closely linked to the corruption of nature. In both cases, the injustice arises from human greed and the failure of human beings to protect the original order of creation. From a Jewish perspective, the just allocation of nature's resources is indeed a religious issue of the highest order. The treatment of the marginal in society—the poor, the hungry, the widow, the orphan—must follow the principle of scriptural legislation. Thus, parts of the land's produce are to be given to those who do not own land. By observing the particular commandments, the soil itself becomes holy, and the person who obeys these commandments ensures the religio-moral purity necessary for residence in God's land.

The connection between land management, ritual, and social justice is most evident in the laws regulating the sabbatical year (*shemittah*). During the sabbatical year, it is forbidden to plant, cultivate, or harvest grain, fruit, or vegetables, or even to plant in the sixth year in order to harvest during the seventh year. Crops that grow untended are not to be harvested by the landlord but are to be left ownerless (*hefqer*) for all to share, including poor people and animals. The rest imposed during the sabbatical year facilitates the restoration of nutrients and the improvement of the soil, promotes diversity in plant life, and helps maintain vigorous cultivars.

Environmental virtues. In Judaism the ethics of duty are complemented by the ethics of virtue. The very virtues that rabbinic Judaism found necessary for standing in a covenantal relationship with God are the virtues that enable Jews to be the stewards of God's creation. The rabbinic tradition highlights the merits of humility (*anavah*), modesty (*tzniʿut*), moderation (*metinut*), and mercifulness (*rahmanut*), all of which are ecologically beneficial.

IMPORTANT RITUALS AND SYMBOLS. Ancient Israel was an agrarian society that lived in accord with seasonal rhythms and celebrated the completion of each harvest cycle by dedicating the earth's produce to God. Therefore, the Jewish tradition is rich with rituals that use natural objects and with symbolic language that is linked to natural phenomena. The rituals sanctify nature, making holy corporeal, physical reality.

Sukkot. Originally celebrating the end of the summer harvest and the preparation for the rainy season in the land of Israel, the pilgrimage festival of Sukkot was associated with the redemption of Israel from Egypt. In *Leviticus* 23:42, Israel was commanded to dwell in booths (*sukkah*) for seven days so "that your generations may know that I made the people of Israel dwell in booths when I brought them out of the land of Egypt." Removed from the protection of their regular dwellings, the Israelites were compelled by the temporary booths to experience the power of God in nature more directly and become even more grateful to God's power of deliverance. The rabbis elaborated the symbolic meaning of the *sukkah*, viewing it as a sacred home and the locus for the divine presence. They homiletically linked the four species (citron, palm, myrtle, and willow) used to celebrate Sukkot to parts of the human body, types of people, the four patriarchs, the four matriarchs, and even God. The festival of Sukkot was concluded by yet another festival, known as *Shemini Atzert* (Eighth Day of Assembly), which included prayers to God to deliver rain.

***Tu B'Shevat* (New Year for Trees).** A post-biblical festival that illustrates how humans sanctify nature is celebrated on the fifteenth day of the month of Shevat, which coincides with the time almond trees bloom after the period of winter dormancy. The day was celebrated as "the new year for trees" (*rosh ha-shanah la-ilanot*) paralleling the birthday of the world in the month of Tishrei. During the Middle Ages, when Jews no longer dwelled in the land of Israel, the festival assumed a new symbolic meaning, with new prayers and new customs. Fruits grown in the land of Israel were eaten by Diaspora Jews, and a special set of Psalms was added to the daily liturgy. The most elaborate ritual for the festival was constructed in the sixteenth century by qabbalists, for whom the land of Israel was no longer merely a physical place but rather a spiritual reality. Modeled after the Passover service, the qabbalistic ritual for the "new year for trees" endowed it with the capacity to restore the flow of divine energy to the broken world.

Shabbat. The most original environmental ritual in Judaism is the Sabbath, the introduction of imposed rest on nature. On the Sabbath, humans create nothing, destroy nothing, and enjoy the bounty of the earth. Since God rested on the seventh day, the Sabbath is viewed as completion of the act of creation, a celebration of human tenancy and stewardship. Sabbath teaches that humans stand not only in relation to nature but in relation to the Creator of nature. Most instructively, animals are included in the Sabbath rest (*Dt.* 5:13–14). There are specific cases in which it is permissible to violate the laws of the Sabbath in order to help an animal in distress. The observance of the Sabbath is a constant reminder of the deepest ethical and religious values that enable Jews to stand in a proper relationship with God.

Modern Jewish Ecological Thinking. The traditional Jewish ethics of stewardship or responsibility toward nature find an interesting advocate in the founder of modern Orthodoxy, Samson Raphael Hirsch (1808–1888). For him nature has a theological significance because not only is nature a model for the observance of its laws, but also it places on humans its own demands or commandments. Hirsch suggested that responsibility toward non-human creatures is commanded because empathy toward them is almost impossible. Because it is impossible for humans to understand these creatures, these laws appear irrational, binding humans to the world that is alien to them. Nature is a source of religious and moral commitment.

Human religious responsibility toward nature is also emphasized by Yosef Dov Soloveitchik (1903–1993), the spiritual leader of modern Jewish Orthodoxy in the twentieth century. Soloveitchik interpreted the two creation narratives in the Bible as two paradigmatic human postures toward nature. The first narrative presents "the majestic man" (Adam I) who celebrates the unique position of the human in creation. Creative, functionally oriented, and enamored of technology, Adam I aims to achieve a "dignified" existence by gaining mastery over nature. By contrast, the second creation narrative presents the "covenantal man" (Adam II), the human who was commanded "to till and tend" the earth. Adam II eschews power and control; he is a non-functional, receptive, submissive human type who yearns for a redeemed existence, which he achieves by bringing all of his actions under God's authority. The two postures exist simultaneously and remain permanently at war with each other within every religious Jew. Soloveitchik thus warned against the modern glorification of humanity (Adam I) that brought about the destruction of nature and pointed to religious commitment (Adam II) as the only response to our ecological and existential crisis.

Long before Soloveitchik, Aharon David Gordon (1856–1922), the spiritual leader of Labor Zionism, was keenly aware of the crisis of modernity and the causal connection between technology and human alienation from nature. Settling in Palestine in 1904, Gordon joined the agricultural settlements in order to create a new kind of Jewish life and Jewish person. He viewed humans as creatures of nature but warned that humans are in constant danger of losing contact with nature. For Gordon, the regeneration of humanity and of the Jewish people could come only through the return to nature and the development of a new understanding of labor as the source of genuine joy and creativity. Through physical, productive labor, humanity would become a partner of God in the process of creation. Rejecting the traditional Jewish focus on Torah study, Gordon viewed labor as a redemptive act, provided that the means humans employ are in accord with the divine order of things, that is, with nature. Gordon's "religion of labor" was a transvaluation of traditional Judaism.

Another Zionist leader, Martin Buber (1878–1965), reinterpreted traditional Jewish values in order to address the dilemmas of modern Jewish life. If the tradition understood the covenant to be law-centered, Buber insisted that the covenantal relationship culminating in revelation means a direct, non-propositional encounter with the divine presence. According to Buber, humans relate to the world either directly and unconditionally ("I-Thou") or indirectly, conditionally, and functionally ("I-It"). The "I-Thou" modality means a direct encounter that encompasses all of one's personality and treats the other as an end rather than as a means. The "I-It" relationship has a purpose outside the encounter itself and involves only a fragment of the other, not the entire person. Buber's ideas became ecologically relevant and influential because he extended the "I-Thou" relationship to an encounter with nature. In treating nature as a "Thou" rather than an "It," Buber personified natural phenomenon and recognized not only the need of humans to communicate with natural objects but also the inherent rights of nature as a "Thou" that waits to be addressed by the wholeness of one's own being.

Buber's colleague and successor as the leader of adult education in Germany, Abraham Joshua Heschel (1907–1972), is considered the most influential Jewish ecological thinker. A scion of a Hasidic family who received modern university training, Heschel escaped the Nazis in Germany, eventually settling in the United States in 1944. Intent on reversing the negative impact of modernity, which some suggest led to the atrocities of the Holocaust, Heschel's ecologically-sensitive depth theology spoke of God's glory as pervading nature, leading humans to radical amazement and wonder. Heschel viewed humans as members of the cosmic community and emphasized humility as the desired posture toward the natural world. Recognizing human kinship with the visible world, Heschel celebrated God's presence within the world, but he also insisted that the divine essence is not one with nature. God is simultaneously transcendent and immanent. Heschel's ecological teachings have been translated into concrete educational programs at the Abraham Joshua Heschel Center for Environmental Learning and Leadership in Tel Aviv.

The attempt to anchor Jewish environmentalism in the religious sources of Judaism was one characteristic of the Jewish renewal movement from the 1970s and 1980s. Environmental activists who were born Jews found their way back to the sources of Judaism by recognizing their ecological wisdom. Founded by Ellen Bernstein, the organization Shomrei Adamah (Keepers of the Earth) popularized the idea of Jewish environmentalism, revived nature-based Jewish rituals—such as the ritual meal for the minor holiday *Tu B'Shevat,* and organized wilderness trips with a strong Jewish component. The most significant ecological thinker in the Jewish renewal movement is Arthur Waskow, who coined the term "eco-kosher" to highlight the connection between human mistreatment of the natural world and social mistreatment of the marginal and the weak in the society. His concern for ecology is part of a deep passion for justice, and his recommendations include the cultivation of self-control, moderation in material consumption, sustainable economic development, and communitarianism.

While Waskow's environmentalism is linked to Heschel's social activism and indebted to social ecology, another disciple of Heschel, Arthur Green, has attempted to anchor Jewish ecological thinking in Qabbalah and Hasidism, the other dimension of Heschel's legacy. Adopting the ontological schema of Qabbalah, Green maintains that all existents are in some way an expression of God and are to some extent intrinsically related to each other. From the privileged position of the human, Green derives an ethics of responsibility toward all creatures that acknowledges the differences between diverse creatures while insisting on the need to defend the legitimate place in the world of even the weakest and most threatened of creatures. For Green, a Jewish ecological ethics must be a *torat hayim,* namely, a set of laws and instruction that truly enhances life.

While the Jewish tradition is rich with ecological wisdom, serious challenges are still posed to the future of the nascent Jewish environmental movement. First, the well-being of the natural world is still regarded as a marginal issue on the agenda of Jewish leadership, perhaps because Jews are generally preoccupied with the protracted Israeli-Arab conflict, relations between the State of Israel and Diaspora communities, Jewish-Christian dialogue, pluralism within Judaism, and gender equality. On a grassroots level, Jewish individuals are raising environmental issues and organizing educational activities to bring the ecological insights of Judaism to the attention of Jews, but it remains to be seen whether they will succeed in capturing the imagination of most Jews. Second, there is a conceptual gap between the religious nature of the Jewish tradition and the secularist outlook of the environmental movement. Thus, while in the State of Israel there is a vibrant environmental movement, its activities are secular and not legitimated by Jewish religious sources. In America, the Jewish environmental movement that speaks in the name of the religious tradition must translate its values and sensibilities to the language of the secular environmental discourse, and in some cases, as with nature-based feminist spirituality, Jewish environmentalism stands in direct conflict with self-conscious Neopagan sensibilities. Third, Jews all over the world share the habits of a consumerist society that puts a major stress on the limited natural resources of the planet. There is no indication that Jews, as a whole, will be interested in scaling down their lifestyles and markers of social mobility that they fought so hard to obtain. Ironically, it is the return to the oldest values in Judaism that might curb human behavior harmful to the environment.

Bibliography

Aubrey, Rose, ed. *Judaism and Ecology.* London, 1992.

Bernstein, Ellen, ed. *Ecology and the Jewish Spirit: Where Nature and the Sacred Meet.* Woodstock, Vt., 1998.

Cohen, Jeremy. *"Be Fertile and Increase, Fill the Earth and Master It": The Ancient and Medieval Carrier of a Biblical Text.* Ithaca, N.Y., 1989.

Eisenberg, Evan. *The Ecology of Eden.* New York, 1998.

Elon, Ari, Naomi Mara Hyman, and Arthur Waskow, eds. *Trees, Earth, and Torah: A Tu B'Shevat Anthology.* Philadelphia, 1999.

Felix, Yehuda. *Nature and Man in the Bible: Chapters in Biblical Ecology.* New York, 1981.

Gerstenfeld, Manferd. *Judaism, Environmentalism, and the Environment: Mapping and Analysis.* Jerusalem, 1998.

Heschel, Abraham Joshua. *Man Is Not Alone.* New York, 1951.

Heschel, Abraham Joshua. *The Sabbath: The Meaning for Modern Man.* New York, 1951, 1995.

Heschel, Abraham Joshua. *God in Search of Man: A Philosophy of Judaism.* Philadelphia, 1956.

Hirsch, Samson Raphael. *The Nineteen Letters on Judaism.* Edited by Jacob Breuer. New York, 1969.

Levy, Ze'ev, and Nadav Levy. *Ethics, Emotions, and Animals: On the Moral Status of Animals* (in Hebrew). Tel Aviv, 2002.

Samuelson, Norbert M. *Judaism and the Doctrine of Creation.* Cambridge, U.K., 1994.

Schwartz, Richard H. *Judaism and Global Survival.* New York, 1987.

Soloveitchik, Josef Dov. *The Lonely Man of Faith.* New York, 1992. Originally published in *Tradition* 7 (2) (1965).

Tirosh-Samuelson, Hava, ed. *Judaism and Ecology: Created World and Revealed Word.* Cambridge, Mass., 2003.

Waskow, Arthur. *Down-to-Earth Judaism: Food, Money, Sex, and the Rest of Life.* New York, 1995.

Waskow, Arthur, ed. *Torah of the Earth: Exploring 4000 Years of Ecology in Jewish Thought.* 2 vols. Burlington, Vt., 2000.

Yaffe, Martin D., ed. *Judaism and Environmental Ethics: A Reader.* Lanham, Md., 2001.

HAVA TIROSH-SAMUELSON (2005)

ECOLOGY AND RELIGION: ECOLOGY AND CHRISTIANITY

The problem of human distortion of ecological processes, to which much attention has been given since the 1960s, was not directly considered in most of Christian history. Whereas the teaching of Jesus reflects a rural context, the early church developed largely in urban centers of the Mediterranean world, where even the issues associated with agriculture were little considered. Christian theology dealt with human relations and especially the relation of human beings to God. Christian teaching in the early church had little bearing on how the natural world was treated at the time.

Nevertheless, retrospectively, the relevance of its teaching in this regard can be seen in the habits of mind and common practices that developed in Western Christendom after the fall of the Roman Empire in the West. Concepts of nature that primarily dealt with the human body and its sexuality colored attitudes toward the wider natural world. Doctrines of gender designed to support patriarchy also had their influence on the treatment of the natural world. The important doctrine of creation could be read either as a strong affirmation of the value of the natural world or as dethroning its claims to sacrality and opening it to exploitation.

Biblical scholars at the dawn of the twenty-first century can show that there are rich resources for the development of an ecological theology in the Christian canon. Historians of doctrine can show that traditional formulations have positive contributions to make. But the fact is that, at least in the West, these opportunities for the development of an ecological theology were neglected. Christian teaching generally led to the study of the natural world as testimony to God's greatness and to the use and manipulation of the world to satisfy human desires. It directed people away from a sense of kinship with other creatures and from treating the earth as worthy of respect in its own right.

Throughout most of Western history, Christian teaching focused on the process of personal redemption. The understanding of this process was heavily influenced by Paul's distinction between spirit and flesh. From a modern perspective, one can rightly emphasize that the flesh is to be identified not with the body but with an orientation of the whole person away from God. But through most of the history of Western Christianity, this theological duality was closely associated with the metaphysical dualism of mind, or spirit, and matter. The material world was understood to be inferior; to cultivate the spirit was to break away from that world. This required disciplining the body and repressing its desires.

Sexuality, in particular, was viewed as a threat to spirituality. Saint Augustine taught that original sin is transmitted from generation to generation by the sexual act. From the male perspective, sexuality was associated especially with women, so that the denigration of sexuality was used to denigrate women as well. Thus, the affirmation of domination of the body by the spirit justified the domination of women by men. Because the body and its sexuality were the main place where nature appeared in this treatment of redemption, nature as a whole was perceived as an object to be controlled by human efforts.

The tendency to disparage the physical, particularly its expression in sexuality, had immense practical effects in the church. It led to the ideal of celibacy and, in the West, to the rejection of marriage for secular priests as well as for members of religious orders. The only moral justification the Western church allowed for sexual acts was their necessity for procreation. It taught that the pleasure connected with these acts was sinful. The association of the natural world with fertility and sexuality meant that nature shared in the negativity of the human body.

However, the tendency to denigrate the physical world in general was checked by two central Christian doctrines:

incarnation and creation. Both of these doctrines required a defense against those who shared the Gnostic tendency to carry the hostility to the physical world through to its consistent conclusion.

The classic text for the doctrine of the incarnation of God in Jesus is in the prologue to John's gospel: "The Word *(Logos)* became flesh." Those who thought dualistically of the realm of spirit and the realm of flesh resisted this idea. They thought the purely spiritual God could not actually become a part of the physical reality. They argued that Jesus was not a real being of flesh and blood, but only an appearance in the physical world. This idea was called *docetism.* The church insisted that, on the contrary, the Word truly became "flesh."

There were repeated efforts to interpret incarnation as the replacement of some normally human function in Jesus by the divine. Against this, the creeds insisted that Jesus had all the dimensions of humanity, so that God assumed every aspect of the human. This cut against the sharp dualism of spirit and flesh and indicated that all aspects of human existence are subject to redemption. Although there were strong pressures toward the adoption of the doctrine of the immortality of the soul, the church insisted on the resurrection of the body. This can connect with occasional suggestions in the New Testament (especially *Romans* 8:19–23) that the redemption of our bodies is part of the redemption of the whole of creation.

The *locus classicus* for the discussion of creation is the first chapter of *Genesis,* which deals far more directly and extensively with the natural world than any passage in the New Testament. It has played the largest role in Christian history in shaping explicit teaching about the natural world, and while it has been read in many ways, it stands against any effort to treat the natural world as inherently unreal or evil.

Those who most strongly opposed the affirmation of the physical world argued that the God who created this world is an inferior god. It cannot, they thought, have been the Father of Jesus Christ. The most important advocate of this view was Marcion, who wanted to cut Christianity off from its Jewish roots. The church stood firm against him, insisting that the Father of Jesus Christ was the creator of the physical world, and that the Jewish scriptures are part of the Christian canon.

Nevertheless, in much of Western Christian history the chief lesson drawn from the *Genesis* creation story has been that human beings are the crown of creation. They differ from all other creatures in that they alone are in the image of God, and God has given all the other creatures to human beings to control and use. People are commanded both to subdue the earth and to increase in number. Hence, although the goodness of the world is recognized in this view, that goodness is understood to be a matter of its usefulness to human beings. A nature that resists subjugation to human control may still be viewed in a very negative light. Anthropocentrism and dualism both gain support from this reading.

This reading of *Genesis* provides the background for the dominant Western understanding of the story of the fall, in which the image of God in human beings is radically corrupted. From this it might be concluded that the difference between humans and other creatures is greatly diminished and the authorization to subdue them no longer valid. But the typical reading has been quite different. The emphasis has been, instead, that the good nature created by God for human enjoyment, depicted in the Garden of Eden, was also drastically corrupted by human disobedience to God. The earth is, therefore, no longer a friendly context for human life. This accents the need for human beings to dominate and manage the natural world.

A far less anthropocentric and dualistic reading of the creation story is possible. One may emphasize that God sees that creation is good before and apart from human beings. This suggests that the value of other creatures cannot be simply their usefulness to human beings. In most respects, God treats human beings like other animals. The dominion they are given in relation to other animals does not extend to eating them, and like other animals, humans are given only vegetation to eat. The sovereignty of human beings within the created order consists in representing God's rule. God's rule is for the sake of the ruled, not their exploitation. Today, lessons of this sort are drawn frequently from the story. But this was rare in the tradition.

One of the most famous and beloved Christians did draw conclusions from the Scriptures that have led to thinking of him as the patron saint of ecologists. Actually, he might better be thought of as the patron saint of animal lovers. The deep sensitivity of Saint Francis to the natural world was focused on animals. In this relationship he emphasized kinship instead of the dualism that justified exploitation.

Saint Francis was not alone in the medieval period in opposing dualism, however. Many people thought in terms of a great chain of being with many links and stages, rather than in terms of the dualistic either/or. There were many stories, especially from Irish Christianity, of saints who related positively to animals.

At the practical level, there was also some moderation of dualism. In contrast to the Desert Fathers in the East, Western monasticism balanced spiritual disciplines with physical labor in the fields. In contrast with much classical thought, it affirmed the dignity of such work and its worthiness as a form of service to God. Of course, this work was also a matter of manipulation and use.

Sacramental practice could give nature a deeper meaning. It tied spirit to nature in ways that are in tension with dualism. Bread and wine were held to be transmuted into the body and blood of Jesus so as to work salvifically for the believer. Participation in Jesus was attained by the physical act of eating and drinking. Sacramental thinking could extend this to the idea that spirit is found everywhere in nature. Nature is not thereby deified, but it testifies to the divine and communicates it to us.

Instead of advancing from medieval Christianity in an ecological direction, modernity hardened the dualism already well established in Christian teaching and practice. The Christian dualism of the premodern era was more practical than theoretical. God's concern was generally understood to be the redemption of human beings, not of all creatures; and humans were authorized to use other creatures as they saw fit. The church had resisted an ontological dualism that would have declared human beings to be of a different substance from other creatures or spirit to be a different substance from the physical world.

At the dawn of the modern era that resistance was ended in secular philosophy. Descartes affirmed the ontologically different character of mind and matter and set the task of modern philosophy. Many Christians, especially Protestants, followed his lead, only a little checked by their commitment to biblical interpretation. The influence of Saint Thomas on Catholic thought moderated its tendencies to dualism during the modern period.

The secularism that modernity encouraged also rigidified inherited anthropocentrism. This was checked in Christianity by belief in God. Christianity was, in principle, theocentric rather than anthropocentric. The door was open to thinking of the relation of God to the natural world as separate from that of humans to this world. The tendency to anthropocentrism resulted from the belief that God cares primarily for human beings and that the rest of creation was provided to serve and be used by humans. Thus it was derived from theocentrism. But modern secular thought eroded this check on human pretensions. God came to function only as needed by the human thinker, and finally disappeared from consideration altogether. The human world became self-contained.

Most Protestant thinkers have held back from this total atheism. But in many instances in the past two centuries, they have placed anthropology in the center of their work. For many modern Protestants, God seems to be an embarrassment. The anthropocentrism of these theologies goes far beyond that of the tradition.

After Descartes, the most important philosophical influence on Protestant theology has been Immanuel Kant. His dualism is even more extreme than that of Descartes, and his anthropocentrism is thoroughgoing. Whereas Descartes assigned a metaphysical status to nature different from that assigned to mind, Kant argued that nature is a construct of the human mind. It has no separate existence.

Most progressive Protestant theology on the continent of Europe followed Kant's lead in the nineteenth and twentieth centuries. In this way it was free to ignore the challenge of the natural sciences to traditional Christian teaching. The natural world simply disappeared from this theology. Gerhard von Rad, perhaps the greatest Old Testament scholar of the twentieth century, emphasized that Judaism focused on history, not nature. Its basic faith centered on the Exodus story of liberation from bondage in Egypt. The idea of creation was an extension of God's lordship over history. The clear implication is that this extension is dispensable.

Rudolf Bultmann (1884–1976), the greatest New Testament scholar of the twentieth century, taught that the true message of the Bible was to be found in existential interpretation of the texts. People are to ask of each text what it means in their personal existence. The idea of creation, from this point of view, speaks of a radical personal dependence on God. It says nothing about the natural world. This outcome of the long trajectory of Christian anthropocentrism and dualism highlights, by contrast, that these tendencies were by no means controlling in earlier periods.

Western Christianity was awakened from its dogmatic slumbers primarily by the famous 1967 essay of Lynn White Jr., "The Historical Roots of Our Ecologic Crisis." White wrote as a historian of science and technology. He showed that Western Christianity had, from an early point, a peculiarly strong tendency to dominate its environment. He traced this to the influence of the Western reading of the Bible, and especially the creation story. This attitude provided the context for the development of technology in the West even at a time when it was somewhat backward culturally. Later it provided the context for the rise of modern science. When science and technology came together in the chemical revolution, and later in the nuclear one, the mastery over nature that was called for in the Western reading of *Genesis* was dramatically realized. The result, however, is to endanger the future of life on the planet. Unless the goal of mastery is checked by other attitudes toward the natural world, the human venture, now led by the West, is likely to end in catastrophe.

Since the 1970s, Christians have scrambled, somewhat successfully, to contribute to the ecological worldview that is now so urgently needed. This has been done chiefly by highlighting aspects of the scriptures and tradition that had been progressively obscured. Official church teaching had already freed itself from the general denigration of sexuality and the human body that played so large a role in shaping its negativity toward nature. In the twentieth century it recognized that this view of sexuality is not biblical and has been profoundly harmful. This repentance for deeply entrenched teachings paved the way for the recovery of the positive affirmations of the natural world in the doctrines of creation and incarnation and the Pauline understanding of salvation (see *Rom.* 8:19–23).

Meanwhile, Eastern Orthodox thought has found new vitality in addressing ecological issues. It had never gone as far as the West in viewing human beings or nature as fallen, it rejected Augustine's understanding of original sin as transmitted through the sexual act, and it was not influenced by Cartesian dualism and Kantian idealism. Accordingly, it has never been as anthropocentric or dualistic as the West. Patriarch Bartholomew of Constantinople has given strong leadership in the Christian world in bringing the church's thought to bear on ecological issues in a positive way.

The Roman Catholic Church has also spoken powerfully through letters from the pope and from the bishops. Among Protestants, the World Council of Churches has done especially creative work since 1972 when it introduced sustainability into its vision of healthy societies. Later it called for respect for the "integrity of nature." Many member churches have developed their own statements. There is also a movement among evangelicals to develop an ecological theory influenced by the Bible.

In the West, most of the progress in formulating a more ecological theology has come from distinguishing Christian teaching from the Greek and modern philosophies that have so greatly influenced it. In the East, on the other hand, the philosophical theology of Gregory of Nyssa has been reemphasized for its positive value. In the West, process theology has called for a new connection with philosophy, this time with one that has systematically developed some of the biblical themes that are most useful for ecological purposes.

For example, the philosophy of Alfred North Whitehead (1861–1947) was developed to counteract the dualism and anthropocentrism of modern thought. By identifying process as basic, instead of substance, it connects more closely with the biblical emphasis on event and story. By affirming the intrinsic reality and value of all things, it picks up the teaching of *Genesis* 1. By showing how creaturely diversity contributes not only to the creatures but also to God, the biblical account of God's creation and the preservation of such diversity are underscored.

Perhaps most important, Whitehead stresses Paul's insight that Christ is in us and we are in Christ and that we are "members of one another" (*Eph.* 4:25). Nothing is more important to the ecological vision than the deep interconnectedness of all things. Whitehead shows that the entities that make up the world participate in the constitution of other entities as well as in the life of God, and that God participates in the constitution of all creatures. What humans do to other creatures, especially, in New Testament language, "to the least of these" (*Matt.* 25:40), they do to themselves and to God.

There is, of course, opposition to this view. Some conservative Christians suppose that any strong affirmation of the earth revives paganism and amounts to idolatry. The connection between feminism and much of the best work on ecological theology has added to this opposition, which is directed as much, or more, against feminist theology as against any supposed tendency to deify the natural world.

But by far the larger problem is the difficulty of changing basic attitudes even when the need for change is recognized. Earth Day is widely observed every year, but emphasis on the integrity of creation is still rare during the rest of the year. Christian habits direct attention to war and injustice, but not easily to ecological decline. This remains an afterthought. Even those who oppose anthropocentrism and dualism in theory find it difficult to incorporate a truly different way of viewing the world. When viewed in relation to the depth of change that is needed, what has been accomplished is disappointing. When viewed in relation to where the church was in the 1960s, the change appears remarkable and profoundly hopeful.

BIBLIOGRAPHY

Cobb, John B. Jr. *Is It Too Late? A Theology of Ecology.* Rev. ed., Denton, Tex., 1995. An early theological response to the recognition of Christian responsibility for the ecological crisis. Originally published in 1972.

Daly, Herman E., and John B. Cobb Jr. *For the Common Good: Redirecting the Economy toward Community, the Environment, and a Sustainable Future.* 2d ed. Boston, 1994.

DeWitt, Calvin B. *Caring for Creation: Responsible Stewardship of God's Handiwork.* Grand Rapids, Mich., 1998. An evangelical perspective on human responsibility toward nature.

Hessel, Dieter T., ed. *After Nature's Revolt: Eco-Justice and Theology.* Minneapolis, 1992. A carefully integrated collection of papers from American Protestants assessing the Christian legacy and dealing with such special concerns as global warming and economics.

Hessel, Dieter T., and Rosemary Radford Ruether, eds. *Christianity and Ecology: Seeking the Well-Being of Earth and Humans.* Cambridge, Mass., 2000. The largest and most varied collection of papers on the topic, derived from a major international conference. The book also contains an extended bibliography. This is the best place to start to get a sense of where Christians concerned about this topic now are.

McDaniel, Jay B. *Earth, Sky, Gods, and Mortals: Developing an Ecological Spirituality.* Mystic, Conn., 1990.

McFague, Sallie. *Super, Natural Christians: How We Should Love Nature.* Minneapolis, 1997. An ecofeminist perspective that emphasizes the need for changing economic understanding and practice.

Nash, James A. *Loving Nature: Ecological Integrity and Christian Responsibility.* Nashville, 1991. A careful study from the broadly neo-orthodox perspective.

Rasmussen, Larry L. *Earth Community, Earth Ethics.* Maryknoll, N.Y., 1996. A richly theological Lutheran perspective.

Ruether, Rosemary Radford. *Gaia and God: An Ecofeminist Theology of Earth Healing.* San Francisco, 1992. A Catholic feminist perspective that emphasizes the sacramental vision as supporting a healthy relation to the natural world.

Santmire, H. Paul. *The Travail of Nature: The Ambiguous Ecological Promise of Christian Theology.* Philadelphia, 1985. Santmire has done the most thorough study of major figures in the Christian tradition to examine their treatment of nature. He identifies promising themes as well as noting the obstacles their teachings pose to the development of an ecological theology.

White, Lynn, Jr., "The Historical Roots of Our Ecologic Crisis." *Science* 155 (March 1967): 1203–1207. White's essay was a challenge to the scientific community to recognize the influence of theology on its work and to the Christian community to revise its theology.

JOHN B. COBB, JR. (2005)

ECOLOGY AND RELIGION: ECOLOGY AND ISLAM

As with most religious traditions, in the Islamic world the attempt to retrieve environmental values in response to the present ecological crisis is a recent phenomenon. Moreover, the overwhelming majority of Muslim intellectuals remain preoccupied with other issues (such as Western hegemony, local and regional politics, gender issues, the role of religion in society), and accord environmental degradation a marginal status if they pay attention to it at all. Indeed, it might not be an exaggeration to state that environmental discourse is less developed within the contemporary Islamic tradition than among the followers of most other major religious traditions. Nevertheless, the few Islamic thinkers who have addressed environmental values specifically have found much in the tradition that could potentially lead Muslims to value nature and to adopt a more effective and responsible stewardship ethic than one typically sees throughout the Muslim world today.

HUMANS AND NATURE IN THE QUR'ĀN. The Qur'ān presents natural phenomena as signs (*ayat*) pointing to the existence of God (16:66, 41:53, 51:20–21, 88:17–20). The value of nature is therefore primarily symbolic. Scientific inquiry, which aims to understand the workings of the universe, thus constitutes for Muslims a sacred quest. Nature is perfectly proportioned and without any flaws (67:3), a reflection of the qualities of its Creator. It has a divinely ordained purpose (3:191, 21:16, 38:27) and is neither random nor meaningless. The "environment" is nothing less than God himself, since, according to the Qur'ān, "whithersoever you turn there is the presence of God" (2:115).

Within the hierarchy of creation, the Qur'ān accords humans a special status, that of God's *Khalīfa* (2:30, 6:165), which has been generally understood by Muslims to mean "vice-regent," thus one of stewardship or trust (*amanat*). Jafar Sheikh Idris (1990) has criticized this as a later interpretation, however, arguing that the original meaning of *Khalīfa* was "successor"; according to this view, humans are not the "deputies of God" but simply the "successors to Adam."

Nevertheless, the Qur'ān states that "all that is in the earth" has been subjected (*sakhkhara*) to humans (22:65) and that "It is He who has created for you all things that are on earth" (2:29). Yet ultimately, it is God "in whose hands is the dominion of all things" (36:83; *cf.* 2:107, 24:42). And though humans are said to have been created "in the best of forms" (*fi aḥsani taqwim*), the Qur'ān goes on to caution that "Assuredly the creation of the heavens and the earth is [a matter] greater than the creation of human beings: Yet most people understand not!" (40:57).

Humans are described in the Qur'ān as being more like other beings than unlike them. All creation is said to worship God (22:18), even if its praise is not expressed in human language (17:44, 24:41–42). Nonhuman communities are said to be like human communities (6:38), and nonhuman animals are explicitly said to possess speech (27:16). Nonhuman animals are said to have received divine revelation, as when God instructs bees on how to make honeycombs and honey (16:68). The earth was created for the benefit of all living beings (*anām*), not for humans alone (55:10). In fact, the only significant difference between humans and other beings is that humans alone possess volition (*taqwa*), and are thus accountable for their actions.

Humans will accordingly be held accountable for any acts of wanton destruction committed against the earth (2:205, 7:85). Wastefulness and overconsumption are also prohibited (7:31), as is hoarding. Water, arguably the most vital natural resource, is to be kept as common property (54:28). Balance (*mīizān*) is to be maintained in all things, including, presumably, natural systems (13:8, 15:21, 25:2); failure to do so, consequently, may be argued to be un-Islamic.

IN *ḤADĪTH*. The Arabs to whom the Qur'ān was revealed in the early seventh century CE had a long familiarity with the ecological constraints posed by their native desert environment. Reports about the words and deeds of Muḥammad (*ḥadīth*) indicate that the Prophet of Islam possessed both an awareness of these constraints and a sensitivity to the duties of humans toward the rest of creation.

Muḥammad received the first of his revelations while meditating in a cave on a mountain outside of Mecca. Thus, as in the case of numerous other seminal religious figures, his insights came within the context of immersion in the natural world. Perhaps the most illuminating of the *ḥadīth* in this regard is the one that states, "The earth has been created for me as a mosque [i.e., as a place of worship], and as a means of purification" (*Sahīh Bukhārī* 1:331).

A well-known *ḥadīth* has Muḥammad prohibiting his followers from wasting water, even when it is found in abundance and when it is used for a holy purpose such as ritual ablutions (*Musnad* ii, 22). Muḥammad also decreed that no more than an ankle depth of water (that is, sufficient for one season) could be taken for irrigation. Essential resources are to be common, not private property: "Muslims share alike in three things—water, pasture and fire" (*Mishkāt al-maṣābīḥ*).

Numerous *ḥadīth* speak to Muḥammad's concern for the interests of nonhuman animals. In regard to the killing of domestic animals for food he called for swift and conscientious slaughter with a sharp knife (*Sahīh Muslim* 2:11, "Slaying," 10:739) and not to slaughter an animal within view of its kin. He forbade hunting for sport and frequently reprimanded his followers for abusing or neglecting their camels and donkeys. He urged his followers to plant trees and cultivate land to provide food not only for humans but for birds and other animals as well (*Sahih Bukhari* 3:513). In a *ḥadīth* that is strikingly similar to a well-known rabbinical saying, Muḥammad is reported as saying, "When doomsday comes if someone has a palm shoot in his hand he should [still] plant it" (*Sunān al-Baīhaqī al-Kubrā*).

IN ISLAMIC LAW. The legal corpus known as the *sharīʿah,* codified by Islamic jurists during the eighth through the tenth centuries CE, was meant to address the breadth of human activity and thus includes aspects that could be said to deal with environmental protection and management of natural resources. Sunnī jurists based their prescriptions on interpretation of Qurʾanic injunctions, the example of Muḥammad as attested in the *ḥadīth,* analogical reasoning, and their own consensus of opinion, as well as preexisting customary practices of the Arabs and the Persians in particular, and to some extent of other Muslim peoples. Other schools of Islam also developed their own approaches to defining the *sharīʿah.*

Common aspects of *sharīʿah* law with the most explicit environmental applications may be the institution of the protected zone (*ḥarim*), which prohibited the development of certain areas, mainly riverbanks, for purposes of protecting watersheds. A related institution is that of the preserve (*ḥima*), which usually entailed the protection of trees and wildlife. Some traditional *ḥarim*s and *ḥima*s still exist today, but they are much diminished from former times and continue to disappear. The legal texts go into some detail about the distribution of water resources and also devote sections to the "bringing to life" (*iḥya*) of "dead" lands (*mawāt*), including the conditions and rights pertaining to one who engages in such "development."

Islamic law also extends many legal protections to nonhuman animals, including the "right of thirst" (*ḥaqq al-shurb*), which states that they cannot be denied drinking water (Qurʾān 91:13). A thirteenth-century work by ʿIzz al-dīn Ibn ʿAbd al-salam, *Qawaʾid al-ahkam fī masāliḥ al-anām* (*Rules for Judgment in the Cases of Living Beings*), includes what some contemporary commentators have called "an animals' bill of rights." Among the provisions are that animals should be properly cared for, not overburdened, kept safe from harm, given clean shelter, and allowed to mate.

Although there is little in the classical legal corpus that could be explicitly categorized as environmental law, there exist within it several basic principles that could, if so interpreted, serve to mitigate some of the main causes of global environmental degradation today. In particular, one may cite the principles of minimizing damage, the primacy of collective over individual interests, and the giving of priority to the interests of the poor over those of the rich. While some contemporary Muslims—notably Mawil Izzi Dien and Uthman Llewellyn—have attempted to provide such interpretations, these have not yet found their way into the legal codes of any existing Muslim societies.

IN ISLAMIC PHILOSOPHY. From around the tenth century CE Muslim philosophers, familiar with Classical works, appear to have been the ones to coin the Arabic term *tabiʿa* to represent the Latin and Greek equivalents *natura* and *physis.* (The word *tabiʿa* does not appear in the Qurʾān.) The derivatives *tabʿ* and *matbuʿ* may, on the other hand, have been the source of the Latin pairing *natura naturans* (the creating) and *natura naturata* (the created) (Nasr, 1993, p. 9). In Islamic philosophy the distinction between the Creator and creation is represented by the terms *haqq* (literally, "Divine Truth") and *khalq* (that which is created). The laws of the universe exist not in and of themselves but rather as expressions of the divine will, understood in Aristotelian terms as the First Cause. There are no "secondary" causes; thus, what appear to be the laws of nature are merely the "habits" of created things, which God could alter if he chose. Miracles, accordingly, are seen simply as instances in which God chooses to cause things to happen in other than their familiar, habitual manner.

Yet the relationship of the infinite (the Creator) to the finite (creation) is neither entirely one of immanence (*tasbīḥ*) nor one of transcendence (*tanziḥ*), since both extremes are incompatible with the ultimate oneness *(tawḥīd)* of God. Neither can creation be divine alongside the Creator, nor can there exist separate realities for each; either case would represent a kind of polytheism (*shirk*) unacceptable in Islam.

The Muslim philosophers developed further the Hellenistic model of the cosmos, which they understood to be spherical in shape and bounded by the stellar field. The planets, the sun, and the moon occupy the middle layers, with the earth constituting the center. The heavenly world (*al-ʿālam al-āʿla*), though made up of ether in contrast to the lower world *(al-ʿālam al-asfāl),* which is comprised of the four elements, shares with it the qualities of heat, cold, moistness, and dryness and acts upon it accordingly. The earth's geography was most often understood in terms of the pre-Islamic Iranian divisions of seven concentric climes (*keshvars*), although the fourfold division of the Greeks and the ninefold version of the Indians were also known.

Muslim philosophers affirm the position of humans near the top within the hierarchy of created beings, below angels but above other animals, plants, and minerals. Humans are the mediators between the heavenly and earthly realms and a major channel for divine grace. The human body, furthermore, is perceived as a microcosm of the universe, with specific parts of the body being identified with parts of the zodiac and thus subject to their influences.

The Ikhwān al-Ṣafa, in their tenth-century treatises collectively known as the *Rasāʾil,* write that the study of nature offers proof of God: "Know that the perfect manufacturing of an object indicates the existence of a wise and perfect artisan even when he is veiled and inaccessible to sense perception. He who meditates upon botanical objects will of necessity know that the beings of this reign issue from a perfect artisan" (quoted in Nasr, 1993, p. 45). For the Ikhwān, who admired Pythagoras, emphasized numbers, regarding them as an important means of insight into the ordering of nature. In one section of their treatise the Ikhwān present a fictitious court case in which nonhuman animals complain of their treatment by humans. Goodman has drawn attention to the similarity of ecological vision evoked in this tenth-century tract with that of contemporary ecologists (Goodman, 1978, pp. 5–6). The Ikhawān were a marginal group, however, and their views should not be taken to represent the mainstream Islamic thought of the time.

IN SUFISM. Muslim mystics, known as Ṣūfīs, have tended to interpret Qurʾanic references to the oneness of God (*tawḥīd*) as indicating an underlying unity to all reality. The Andalusian mystic Muḥyī al-Dīn ibn al-ʿArabī (1165–1240) described creation in terms of "unity of being" *(waḥdat al-wujūd)*, an idea that won wide popularity among Ṣūfīs especially in South Asia, where his work remains highly influential. Some Muslims have found this belief to verge dangerously close to pantheism, however; the seventeenth-century Indian Ṣūfī teacher Shah Waliullah preferred the term "unity of witness" *(waḥdat al-shuhud)* as more clearly maintaining the distinction between Creator and creation.

The Ṣūfī notion of the "Complete Man" (*insan al-kamil*), also elaborated by Ibn al-ʿArabī, expands the conception of the human being as microcosm of the universe. For Ṣūfīs, cultivation of the individual is analogous to cultivation of the cosmos as a whole; thus, one's personal spiritual development can affect the entire world.

To Ṣūfīs such as Jalāluddīn Rūmī (1207–1273), not just animals and plants but the entire universe of creation is alive. "Earth and water and fire are His slaves," he writes in the *Masnavī-yi maʿnavī*; "With you and me they are dead, but with God they are alive" (1.838). Nature also speaks, though only the mystics realize this: "The speech of water, the speech of the earth, and the speech of mud are apprehended by the sense of them that have hearts" (1.3279). The conversations of nature are indicative of affective relationships: "You yourself know what words the sun, in the sign of Aries, speaks to the plants and the date palms/You yourself, too, know what the limpid water is saying to the sweet herbs and the sapling" (6.1068–1069). Moreover, the Ṣūfīs often employ the symbolism of love (*ʿishq*) to describe the relationship of mutual attraction between the Creator and his creation. Yunus Emre, a thirteenth-century Turkish poet, composed the famous line, "We love all creation for the sake of its Creator."

Many Ṣūfī tales, such as those found in the works of Rūmī, Attar, and others, include animal characters, though these are almost always stand-ins for human characteristics associated with particular species. Nonhuman animals are seen as occupying a level below humans, and the "animal soul" of the philosophers is equated by the Ṣūfīs with the "lower self" (*nafs*), or one's own baser instincts, which along the path of spiritual development one strives to overcome.

CONTEMPORARY MUSLIM DISCOURSE ON THE ENVIRONMENT. The terms used by contemporary Muslims to denote "the environment"—for example, *al-biʿat* in Arabic, *mohit-e zist* in Persian, and *çevre* in Turkish—are all of recent derivation. In Muslim societies around the world discussions on environmental ethics and the protection of natural resources remain marginal and the level of discourse in most cases very low. When Muslim intellectuals address these topics at all—which is not often—their responses tend to be backward looking and self-exonerating: premodern Muslim societies are argued to have been perfectly ecological or nearly so, and current environmental problems to be the fault of hegemonic Western ideologies and lifestyles.

Given that among the world's billion-plus Muslims a disproportionately high number live in poverty, and that the poor suffer more immediately and dramatically from the effects of environmental degradation than do the rich, the lack of serious critical attention to environmental issues by Muslim intellectuals is striking. For all the attention given in current Islamic discourse to issues of social justice, the environment figures very little or not at all.

The number of Islamic voices calling attention to environmental issues is growing, though such voices remain so far outside of the mainstream of Islamic thought. It is perhaps significant that among the very few Muslim intellectuals to write on environmental values in Islamic terms, almost all have written their works in English. The first was Seyyed Hossein Nasr beginning in the 1960s. Since that time attempts to describe an Islamic environmental ethic have been undertaken by Mawil Izzi Dien, Bashir Ahmad al-Masri, Fazlun Khalid, and others.

For the most part the criticisms of several Muslim intellectuals have been directed at modernity as imposed on Muslim societies by the West, in particular such practices as interest taking (*riba*, which is forbidden in Islam) and the global economic system that is founded upon it, as well as the erosion of traditional Muslim social networks and the encouragement of materialistic lifestyles. Overconsumption by the West is held to be the major cause of global environmental degradation, while overpopulation in the developing world is not, a view believed justified by the Qurʾānic verse, "There is not a creature that walks on the earth but that Allāh provides for its needs" (11:6). One example of a trend against continuing fervent pro-natalism characteristic of traditional Muslim societies can be detected in the official policies of the Islamic Republic of Iran, which since the late 1980s have called for a reduction in birthrates.

The ecological remedies proposed by contemporary Islamic environmentalists generally involve some kind of "revival" of premodern models that are often highly idealized visions of traditional Islamic society. There has been little serious attempt to gauge critically the extent to which the life ways of premodern Muslim societies were in fact "more ecological" than present-day ones, or to which they resembled the guidelines provided in classical Islamic law, although there is much evidence that in areas such as land and water protection, hunting for sport, and so on, abuses were rampant, as indeed one may find in any human society.

In summary, it may be concluded that the discussion on Islam and ecology is in its very early stages but that it is likely to gain in relevance and sophistication as growing numbers of Muslims come to engage it as a vital contemporary issue.

BIBLIOGRAPHY

Ba Kader, Abu Bakr Ahmed, Abdel Latif Tawfik al-Shirazi al-Sabagh, Mohamed al-Sayed al-Glenid, and Mawil Y. Izzi Dien. *Islamic Principles for the Conservation of the Environment.* Gland, Switzerland, 1983. The first formal attempt by Islamic scholars to formulate an Islamic statement on environmental protection.

Foltz, Richard C., Frederick M. Denny, and Azizan Baharuddin, eds. *Islam and Ecology: A Bestowed Trust.* Cambridge, Mass., 2003. The most expansive collection of essays to date, most of them by scholars writing from within the tradition.

Goodman, Lenn Evan, trans. *The Case of the Animals versus Man before the King of the Jinn: A Tenth-Century Ecological Fable of the Pure Brethren of Basra.* Boston, 1978. An excellent translation of a fascinating, but highly unrepresentative medieval tract.

Idris, Jafar Sheikh. "Is Man the Viceregent of God?" *Journal of Islamic Studies* 1, no. 1 (1990): 99–110. A revisionist essay which seeks to correct long-held misperceptions about a key Islamic term.

Izzi Dien, Mawil Y. *The Environmental Dimensions of Islam.* Cambridge, U.K., 2000. The first book-length single-authored treatise on Islam and the environment by a practitioner. Limited to the Sunnī legalistic perspective.

Khalid, Fazlun, and Joanne O'Brien, eds. *Islam and Ecology.* London, 1992.

al-Masri, Hafez B. A. *Animals in Islam.* Petersfield, U.K., 1989. A short, early collection of essays.

Nanji, Azimed. *Building for Tomorrow.* London, 1994.

Nasr, Seyyed Hossein. *An Introduction to Islamic Cosmological Doctrines* (1964). Rev. ed. Albany, N.Y., 1993. A discussion of the cosmological thought of three early Islamic philosophers.

Nasr, Seyyed Hossein. *Man and Nature: The Spiritual Crisis in Modern Man.* London, 1967. One of the first books to address the spiritual dimension of the environmental crisis, written by a Westernized Muslim scholar for a Western audience.

Nasr, Seyyed Hossein. *Science and Civilization in Islam.* Cambridge, Mass., 1968. Argues that the scientific tradition in Islam, unlike in the West, never lost its sacred dimension.

RICHARD C. FOLTZ (2005)

ECOLOGY AND RELIGION: ENVIRONMENTAL ETHICS, WORLD RELIGIONS, AND ECOLOGY

Environmental ethics emerged as a new subdiscipline of philosophy in the early 1970s. It arose as a response to the widespread perception of an "environmental crisis" in the 1960s. The inspiration for a systematic exploration of environmental ethics was Lynn White Jr.'s (in)famous article, "The Historical Roots of Our Ecologic Crisis," published in *Science* in 1967. In this article White laid the blame for the "ecologic crisis" at the doorstep of the Judeo-Christian worldview—in which "man" is exclusively created in the image of God, given "dominion" over the earth (and all its creatures), and commanded to subdue it. In retrospect, of course, White's central and narrowly focused thesis seems jejune and cavalier. He claims that the Judeo-Christian worldview is anthropocentric, while the fragments of text from *Genesis* on which he bases his interpretation seem to be clearly theocentric.

THE JUDEO-CHRISTIAN STEWARDSHIP ENVIRONMENTAL ETHIC. Indeed, apologists eventually succeeded in developing a very powerful Judeo-Christian stewardship environmental ethic based on a fuller and subtler reading of the same texts. In several preceding verses God declares the creation to be "good." In the emerging technical terminology of academic environmental ethics, God thereby confers "intrinsic value" on the creation. And in subsequent verses the first man, Adam, is charged to "dress and keep" the Garden of Eden. If the Garden may be understood to represent nature as a whole, then the appropriate human relationship to nature seems to be that of caretaker, not conqueror. In light of this passage, the aforementioned (and somewhat ambiguous) "dominion" must then, the apologists go on to argue, surely connote not only special privileges but also special responsibilities—paramount among them the duty to steward and conserve creation.

THE RELATIONSHIP BETWEEN THOUGHT AND ACTION. The daring and lurid charge that the Judeo-Christian worldview—as its implications historically unfolded through two millennia—is to blame for the environmental crisis eclipsed a more general lemma, or fundamental assumption, that White reiterates throughout his essay: that what we do depends on what we think, and, corollary to that, that we cannot change what we do—to the environment in this case—until we change what we think about it and about ourselves in relationship to it. As long as we believe that we are rightfully lords and masters of creation, we shall never care for and conserve it. If this is true—and philosophers above all others are inclined to believe that it is—then to meet the challenge of the environmental crisis requires more than the development of scientific knowledge to better understand its proximate causes and the development of new "appropriate" technologies. It requires a revolution in our most basic beliefs and values—beliefs about the nature of nature, human nature, and the proper relationship between the two. That is a job not for scientists and engineers but for philosophers, theologians, and historians of religion.

AN AGENDA FOR ENVIRONMENTAL PHILOSOPHY AND COMPARATIVE ENVIRONMENTAL THEOLOGY. White thus sets the two-step agenda for a new domain of philosophical inquiry. There are other traditions of thought—most notably the Greco-Roman tradition—that have powerfully informed the modern Western worldview, in which context, White believed, the environmental crisis had been spawned. As a first step, these ideas about the nature of nature (such as the atomic theory of matter) and human nature (as, for example, defined by reason) and the relationship between the two (dualism) must also be identified and debunked. As a second step, new ideas—perhaps abstracted from such revolutionary twentieth-century sciences as quantum physics, evolutionary biology, and ecology—must be woven into a new, environmentally responsible worldview.

In suggesting that other religions—such as ancient European paganism and Zen Buddhism—espoused environmentally responsible worldviews, White also set an agenda for comparative religion and environmental thought. How do other religious worldviews picture the nature of nature, human nature, and the proper relationship between the two? White's interpretations of European paganism and Zen Buddhism were as jejune and cavalier as his interpretation of the Judeo-Christian worldview. But a more patient, thorough, and expert evaluation of the potential of all the world's religions to ground and foster environmental ethics was implicitly called for. In direct reaction to White's suggestion, Christian theologians led the way in formulating the stewardship environmental ethic. Scholars and representatives of various and diverse religious traditions of thought—Hinduism, Jainism, Daoism, Confucianism—soon followed by articulating very different environmental ethics. That enterprise—sometimes called the greening of religion—is now well advanced, spurred in large part by the Harvard conference series and subsequent books on "World Religions and Ecology."

Animal Liberation and Animal Rights. Creating a nonanthropocentric environmental ethic has been the central preoccupation of secular environmental philosophy. The first generation of environmental philosophers, steeped in modern Western ethical theory, tried to develop nonanthropocentric environmental ethics out of one or the other dominant strands of thought in (militantly anthropocentric) Western ethics—utilitarianism and Kantianism.

The most orthodox—and for that reason among the most compelling—of such efforts was mounted by Peter Singer and called "animal liberation." At the foundation of the utilitarian strain of modern ethical theory is the axiom that pleasure is good and pain is evil; and, further, that every moral agent should strive to maximize the good (pleasure) and minimize evil (pain), no matter where or by whom experienced—the agent him- or herself or anyone else. Singer simply pointed out that many nonhuman beings were also "sentient" (capable of experiencing pleasure and pain); therefore, for utilitarianism to be entirely consistent, the pleasure and pain of all sentient beings should be given equal consideration with human pleasure and pain. Singer thought animal liberation required vegetarianism—and billions of animals do indeed suffer grievously in the contemporary meat industry. But in an ideally reformed meat industry, animals might be comfortably raised and painlessly slaughtered. Thus, the pleasure human beings take in eating meat might be vouchsafed with no pain suffered by animals on the debit side of the utilitarian benefit-cost ledger.

To remedy the failure of animal liberation morally to condemn the killing and eating of some of our fellow animals, Tom Regan developed a case for animal rights. Rights, according to Regan, are based on the "inherent worth" (or intrinsic value) of the beings who have them. And, argues Regan, beings who are "subjects of a life," who have a sense of self, a remembered past, an anticipated future, desires, aversions—a life, in short, that can go better or worse from their own point of view—have intrinsic value. Kant thought that only rational beings have intrinsic value, but that doctrine, Regan believes, falls to the Argument from Marginal Cases. The "marginal cases" are prerational human infants, abjectly mentally challenged human beings, and postrational human seniors suffering from dementia. Because all such human beings are not rational, they have no intrinsic value, by Kant's reckoning, and thus no rights. Therefore, they can—if the Kantian criterion is consistently applied—be subjected to all the horrors and indignities to which we subject rightless animals: use them for biomedical experimentation, hunt them sport, or make dog food out of them. To bring the marginal cases into the class of beings protected by rights, we must relax the criterion for intrinsic value. Though not rational, the marginal cases are subjects of a life, but so are many other kinds of animals.

Biocentrism. Animals, however, represent only a tiny fraction of the environment that is alleged to be in a state of crisis. What about plants and other organisms that are certainly alive but that cannot be regarded as *subjects* of a life? A major school of thought in environmental ethics attempts to take Regan's reasoning a step further. All organisms, plants included, arguably have interests and goods of their own, even if they are not interested in their interests or care about what is good or bad for them. If they are not subjects of a life, they are, according to Paul Taylor, "teleological centers of life": they have unconscious ends (goals or purposes)—to grow, to thrive, to reproduce—which may be fostered or frustrated by moral agents. Being a teleological center of life should therefore, according to Taylor, be the criterion for intrinsic value (or inherent worth). However, no influential environmental philosophers are willing to go so far as to base universal organic *rights* on universal organic intrinsic value. Instead, according to Kenneth Goodpaster, all organisms deserve at least to have "moral considerability"—that is, a moral agent should at least take their interests into consideration when his or her actions would affect such beings. Holmes Rolston III has most fully developed this school of thought in environmental ethics. He insists that we have duties to species as well as specimens because the *telos* they are striving to realize is precisely their kind or species. And, Rolston also insists, we have duties to ecosystems and to biotic communities because they are the necessary contexts in which organisms thrive.

Despite Rolston's ingenuity, the main problem with this neo-Kantian strain of environmental ethics is that it does not directly address the actual environmental concerns that mandated the development of environmental ethics in the first place. In healthy ecosystems and stable biotic communities, individual organisms routinely and necessarily get their ends frustrated. What is of actual environmental concern is not the ups and downs in the careers of individual organisms.

Rather, concern focuses on abrupt, mass species extinction and the erosion of biodiversity; ecological degradation; global climate change; soil erosion; desertification; air and water pollution; and the hole in the earth's stratospheric ozone membrane. Other environmental philosophers—who seek to tailor a theory of environmental ethics to actual environmental concerns, rather than the other way around—have thus found it necessary to work outside the modern classical utilitarian and Kantian paradigms. The former terminates in animal liberation, the latter basically in plant liberation, not in the more comprehensive and holistic environmental ethic that the environmental crisis demands.

THE LAND ETHIC. Often called a prophet, Aldo Leopold anticipated the emergence of the environmental crisis by more than a decade and, in response, sketched a "land ethic." Leopold was not a philosopher by training. He was trained in forestry at Yale University and began his career with the U.S. Forest Service, eventually to become a professor of game management and wildlife ecology at the University of Wisconsin. Thus, he was less constrained by the modern Western ethical paradigms than latterly were academic environmental philosophers. He was apparently influenced instead by Darwin's theory of the origin and development of ethics in the *The Descent of Man.* J. Baird Callicott has filled in Leopold's outline of an environmental ethic and provided it with a full philosophical pedigree and expression.

According to Darwin, ethics evolved from "parental and filial affections," which were more widely directed to more distant kin (uncles, aunts, cousins, and so on) by natural selection—because they bonded individuals into united societies or communities. As members of united societies or communities, pursuing the struggle for existence collectively, individuals had a better chance to survive and reproduce than they would as loners. Certain kinds of individual behavior—murder, theft, adultery, treachery—threaten group solidarity. Ethics emerged when our earliest human ancestors evolved sufficient intelligence to trace the consequences of generalized forms of behavior on society, sufficient powers of imagination to envision those consequences, and, finally, language in which prohibitions against antisocial behavior could be encoded. Then, according to Darwin, as these small original human societies—which were scarcely anything more than extended families—flourished and began to compete with one another for limited resources, those that merged together to form larger, better organized communities won out. As Darwin envisioned it, over time this process of social evolution through merger was repeated several times. Clans, also known as gens, merged to form tribes; tribes merged to form nationalities; closely related nationalities merged to form sovereign states. Each of these moments in the evolution of human societies was accompanied by a correlative development of ethics. Darwin foresaw a time in the future—which is now upon us—in which a single human society, global in scope, would emerge. Facilitated by sophisticated transportation and communication technologies, loosely organized by such governing bodies as the United Nations (UN) and the World Trade Organization, and funded by financial institutions such as the World Bank and International Monetary Fund, we sanguinely call it the Global Village or, more ominously, the New World Order. The United Nations Universal Declaration of Human Rights, adopted in 1948, is its ethical correlative.

A year later after the UN human rights declaration, Leopold was, as Darwin before him, looking beyond his own time to the next step in this process. For, as Leopold was keenly aware, ecology had discovered that we are members not only of multiple human communities—our extended families, our ethnic groups, our municipalities and states, our nations or countries, and now the Global Village—we are also members of similarly nested biotic communities. If there is indeed an intimate—perhaps even an innate—correlation between our perception of community membership and an ethical response, as Darwin argued, then when, through universal ecological literacy, people become aware of their membership in biotic communities, they will respond with environmental (or land) ethics.

ECOCENTRIC HOLISM AND THE PROBLEM OF ECOFASCISM. Because Darwin thought of ethics as more focused on and concerned with society as a whole, not its members severally, the environmental ethic that Leopold erected on these Darwinian foundations makes for a better fit with actual environmental concerns. According to Leopold, "a thing is right when it tends to preserve the integrity, stability, and beauty of the biotic community; it is wrong when it tends otherwise." Leopold understood the biotic community to include not only plants and animals but also soils and waters. This broad, holistic precept thus addresses species extinction and loss of biodiversity—for nothing so violates the integrity of biotic communities than the loss of their component species—water pollution, soil erosion, and most of the other things that are of actual environmental concern. Further, it allows for the subordination of the interests of individual organisms to the good of the whole, to the integrity, stability, and beauty of the biotic *community.*

One should immediately worry, however, that it might also allow for the subordination of individual *human* interests to the good of the whole. Not surprisingly then, a charge of "ecofascism" has been leveled at Leopold's land ethic, first by Tom Regan. Fortunately, the charge will not stick because Leopold understood the land ethic to be an "accretion"—that is, an addition—to our older and more venerable traditions of human ethics, not a substitution or replacement for them. In the Darwinian foundations of the Leopold land ethic, when smaller societies merge to form larger societies, the older more venerable social strata do not dissolve. Even as we are now members of the Global Village, we are still very much also members of extended families and nation-states. And the ethics correlative to those social strata remain operative and in many circumstances preemptive. Unfortunately, the duties and obligations generated by our multiple community memberships are not always mutually consistent.

Family obligations and patriotic duties may conflict. One or another of the duties generated by our memberships in various human communities may conflict with the obligations generated by our membership in various biotic communities. Nor, also unfortunately, is there any algorithm that one may mechanically apply to them to resolve such moral conundrums. A person of goodwill must simply weigh and balance conflicting duties and obligations as best he or she can and try to choose wisely among them those that, under the circumstances, are the most compelling.

THE EARTH CHARTER. Just as the Universal Declaration of Human Rights crystallized the then-new ethic of the emerging Global Village, so the Earth Charter, also developed under the auspices of the United Nations, crystallizes the currently new ethic of the biospheric ecological community. The Earth Charter was anticipated in the early 1990s by Hans Kung's "Declaration of the Religions for a Global Ethic," commissioned by the Parliament of the World's Religions. It acknowledges, among other crises, a crisis of "global ecology" and, albeit largely focused on humanitarian concerns, declares that "the new global order" should be, among other things, "nature friendly." Kung's declaration was reviewed at an interdisciplinary colloquium with participants from various religions and continents and sent to various colleagues and friends who responded with dozens of suggestions for its improvement. The Earth Charter was drafted and repeatedly redrafted by an international committee based on systematic "consultations," spanning a decade, with thousands of individuals from different cultural backgrounds and sectors of society, representing hundreds of organizations, from all regions of the world. The first two of the four principles of the Earth Charter are, like the Leopold land ethic, holistic in scope and focus, respectively, on "respect and care for the community of life," and "ecological integrity." Two principles of the Earth Charter—concerning "social and economic justice" and "democracy, nonviolence, and peace"—spell out what Leopold only assumed, that environmental ethics must be harmonized with more traditional and familiar ethics concerned with individual human liberty, welfare, and rights.

THE PRAGMATIC APPROACH. Not all environmental philosophers have been happy with the search for a nonanthropocentric environmental ethic that has dominated the environmental-philosophy literature. Environmental pragmatists—Bryan Norton, most notably and persistently—have criticized the preoccupation of their colleagues with theory building, especially the construction of some comprehensive theory designed to embrace all environmental concerns. Instead they call for a bottom-up approach: beginning with actual issues, such as a proposal to dam a river, and then sorting out the attitudes and values at play in such cases, with the purpose of finding a course of action on which most interested parties can agree, irrespective of their attitudinal and moral differences. These two approaches to environmental philosophy—comprehensive theory building and an action-oriented search for pragmatic consensus—appear to be complementary, not competitive. The mainstream approach aims at the long term—what Hans Kung called a "transformation of consciousness"—something that will not occur in a human lifetime. The pragmatic approach aims at the (relatively) short term—environmental issues and public policies that are current for spans of time ranging from a few years to a decade or two (some of which of course may entrain long-term irreversible effects). The environmental crisis requires both approaches if ever it is to be adequately addressed.

BIBLIOGRAPHY

Barkey, Michael B. *Environmental Stewardship in the Judeo-Christian Tradition: Jewish, Catholic, and Protestant Wisdom on the Environment.* Grand Rapids, Mich., 2000.

Callicott, J. Baird. *In Defense of the Land Ethic: Essays in Environmental Philosophy.* Albany, N.Y., 1989.

Callicott, J. Baird. *Earth's Insights: A Multicultural Survey of Ecological Ethics from the Mediterranean Basin to the Australian Outback.* Berkeley, Calif., 1994.

Callicott, J. Baird. *Beyond the Land Ethic: More Essays in Environmental Philosophy.* Albany, N.Y., 1999.

Goodpaster, Kenneth E. "On Being Morally Considerable." *Journal of Philosophy* 75 (1978): 308–325.

Kung, Hans. "The Parliament of the World's Religions Declaration toward a Global Ethic," 1993. Available from http://astro.temple.edu.

Leopold, Aldo. *A Sand County Almanac and Sketches Here and There.* New York, 1949.

Norton, Bryan. *Toward Unity among Environmentalists.* New York, 1991.

Regan, Tom. *The Case for Animal Rights.* Berkeley, 1983.

Rockefeller, Steven. "The Earth Charter at the Johannesburg Summit: A Report Prepared by the Earth Charter Steering Committee and International Secretariat," 2002. Available from http://www.earthcharter.usa.org.

Rolston, Holmes. *Environmental Ethics: Duties to and Values in the Natural World.* Philadelphia, 1988.

Rolston, Holmes. *Conserving Natural Value.* New York, 1994.

Singer, Peter. *Animal Liberation: A New Ethics for Our Treatment of Animals.* New York, 1977.

Taylor, Paul W. *Respect for Nature: A Theory of Environmental Ethics.* Princeton, N.J., 1986.

White, Lynn, Jr. "The Historical Roots of Our Ecologic Crisis." *Science* 155 (1967): 1203–1207.

J. BAIRD CALLICOTT (2005)

ECOLOGY AND RELIGION: SCIENCE, RELIGION, AND ECOLOGY

The contemporary dialogue between religion and science is part of the foundation of the religion and ecology dialogue. Many of the contemporary luminaries in this dialogue—Ian Barbour, Holmes Rolston III, John Haught, John Cobb, Jr., and many others—also have published on ecological issues. Both fields try to understand the relationship of humans and nature.

Religion is an extremely diverse phenomenon, always plural, and difficult to philosophically define. The same can be said for science. For many today, there is a deep cultural ambivalence about one or the other. Science for many people brings to mind negative images of toxic industries, genetically modified foods, or nuclear holocaust. Similarly, religion also brings to mind negative images for many of religious wars, inquisitional torture, fanatical intolerance, genocidal persecutions, and deadly cults. Often juxtaposed to these negative images of one domain, either religion or science, is generally a positive and sometimes utopian orientation towards the other domain.

TYPOLOGY OF SCIENCE AND RELIGION. Ian Barbour has suggested a four-part typology for how different people relate science and religion—conflict, separation, dialogue, and synthesis. The conflict model sees religion and science as necessarily in opposition. Within the conflict model, one needs to choose sides, so there are two versions. Scienticism promotes science as an alternative belief system to religion against superstition and supernaturalism. It favors a commitment to materialistic and reductionistic understandings of reality often along with a commitment to human progress or betterment. Contemporary advocates of this position include Richard Dawkins, Daniel Dennett, and Stephen Weinberg.

The religious version of the conflict model promotes an absolute ontological and epistemic dependency on God as revealed in a scriptural tradition in which cosmological references are interpreted literally. The conflict generally revolves around accounts of natural history—evolution and cosmology—but also questions about the human person and ethics. These religious fundamentalists promote alternative "sciences" because they understand contemporary science to being necessarily atheistic and immoral. Both versions of the conflict model generate competing mythologies about the history of science and religion.

The separation model sees religion and science as different categories of endeavors. Stephen Jay Gould popularized the term "Non-Overlapping Magisteria" or NOMA to describe this view of science and religion (Gould, 2002). Science seeks to answer questions of "what" and "how," whereas religion seeks to answer questions of "why." Science deals with facts, religion deals with values. It is only when the two step out of their proper domains that conflict arises.

The problem with the separation model is that separate is never really equal. Religions necessarily make ontological claims about reality; the insights of science necessarily impinge upon questions of values and purpose. While religion and science are certainly distinct endeavors, they need to be in some kind of conversation. This then leads to the dialogue model, where religion and science need to engage each other on boundary questions of metaphysics and ethical dilemmas such as the ecological crisis or the challenges of new technologies. Science is sometimes understood to be mute on these questions, though it gives rise to new insights and technologies that present further challenges for humanity.

Others promote the synthesis model, wherein they seek to join science and religion in metaphysical, meaning, and moral systems. In this view, philosophers, theologians, and practitioners should be willing to reinterpret their fundamental beliefs in light of contemporary science; even as they mine their religious traditions to recover profound insights about the nature of the Divine, the nature of humanity, and the nature of nature. Advocates of this model note that there is not a metaphysical-free way of understanding the world and ourselves. Humanity would be better served if we develop a consistent, probable, and holistic understanding of science and religion. The contemporary conversation is profoundly influenced by the process philosophy of Alfred North Whitehead, the evolutionary mysticism of Pierre Teilhard de Chardin, and the hierarchical epistemology of Michael Polanyi. This synthesis model is particularly helpful for the religion and ecology field in that it affirms the importance of science in both its philosophical implications and practical understanding of the world of nature.

This four-part typology of the relationship between science and religion was turned into an alliteration by John Haught, who speaks of "conflict, contrast, contact," and "convergence" (Haught, 1995).

GENERAL PHILOSOPHICAL ISSUES. All science assumes some kind of *reductionism,* whereby a complex problem is broken down and analyzed in terms of its parts. Reductionism has led to increasing specialization in the familiar list of disciplines and departments of the modern university, as well as the growing lists of sub-disciplines and interdisciplinary communities of research. One can distinguish between philosophical reductionism and methodological reductionism. The latter is simply a tool for exploration and problem-solving, while philosophical reductionism becomes an all-encompassing worldview. There is a kind of reductionism that assumes everything can be broken down to constitutive parts, namely, consciousness is merely biology, biology is nothing but chemistry, and chemistry is just particle physics. Many scientists and philosophers, enamored with the incredible progress made in the last century, make intemperate claims about the power and prospects of reductionism to answer all questions, but this can lead to absurd category mistakes. A biologist need know nothing about particle physics to effectively practice biology. Cosmology is not likely to shed new light on economics. The concept of emergence is now being explored with scientific and philosophic rigor. The whole is often more than the sum of its parts. Novel entities come to be in an evolving universe that builds on existing structures and processes to create new levels of complexity. Many religious philosophers see the concept of emergence in science as a way of recovering religious understandings of the universe and the human person. Moreover, for some this is an important philosophical basis for understanding the large-scale evolutionary context for present day environmental questions.

Another philosophical debate within science and religion deals with the issue of materialism. The universe is nothing more than matter-energy and space-time. In this view, science cannot allow for any phenomena that are not material. All real phenomena, as opposed to imagined phenomena, can be analyzed as material or physical processes. In this extreme form, materialism precludes the truth claims of religion. Materialism also can leave no grounds for protecting the natural world.

However, religious and scientific philosophers today note that many scientific disciplines need the immaterial concept of information in order to understand material reality. Contemporary physics, for instance, assumes a transcendent understanding of mathematics, even as it deconstructs material reality into ephemeral subatomic particles, extend wave functions, and immaterial field equations. These new ontological categories open up a possibility for understanding aesthetic, moral, and spiritual realities as more than just imagined fantasies. Information science is also an important part of understanding the complex interactions of ecosystems and species.

Another philosophical debate within science and religion deals with the question of causation. The reductionist and materialist view understands causation to always be from the "bottom-up," while religious thinkers postulate modes of "top-down" causation. In contemporary physics, we also confront the conundrum of non-local causation in entangled quantum states. All of this opens up the possibility of a robust understanding of free will in human action, as well as divine action in the universe that need not violate the laws of science. Rather than simply a bottom-up or top-down approach to causation the complex interaction of chance and necessity is now part of the discussion.

Contemporary science challenges many of the traditional ontological hierarchies of religious worldviews. Science offers two kinds of hierarchies—chronology and size. On the one hand there is the chronological unfolding of the universe: from the infinitely dense and infinitely hot originating singularity some thirteen billion years ago; through the rise of stable particles to galaxy and star formation; the stellar fusion of heavier elements; the growth of solar systems out of second and third generation stars with complex chemistry; the rise of life on at least one planet; the stunning evolution of life into myriad forms over hundreds of million years; and the recent rise of our own species with its capacities of mind and language. Science also offers a new hierarchy of size, from orders of magnitude smaller and larger, unimaginable to our ancestors even one hundred years ago. This new epic of evolution and the new topography of the universe challenge some of our religious notions of human dignity and divine purpose. Many traditional religious cosmogonies seem quaint and parochial in light of this new scientific worldview. The science and religion dialogue seeks to offer new interpretations of the epic of evolution that integrates this new natural history with the enduring wisdom, spiritual quest, and cultural insights of our religious traditions. This context of the epic of evolution is also critical to the dialogue of religion and ecology. More people are realizing that the future of the evolutionary process is severely challenged by the presence of more than six billion people on the planet, along with the environmental destruction humans have wrought with their sophisticated technologies.

Another general philosophical issue explored at the intersection of science and religion is the question of dualism versus holism. Humans have often understood the metaphysics of the universe in terms of philosophical dualism—animate and inanimate, human and non-human, mind and brain, spiritual and material. Modern science undermines many of these dualisms. Religions have promoted both dualistic and holistic metaphysics. Humanity is lost in this new understanding of the universe without a compass or a map to the great moral, aesthetic, and ecological questions. The ecological sciences are offering a more holistic vision of life—human and non-human—which has implications for more comprehensive environmental ethics.

Specific Philosophical Issues. There are also a number of specific philosophical issues that science raises for religious thought and practice which are explored in the contemporary encounter between science and religion.

Physics and cosmology. Physics and cosmology raise a number of profound metaphysical questions. A number of the fundamental characteristics of the universe appear to be "fine-tuned" for the later development of complexity. This can be seen in the specific values of the four fundamental forces—gravity, electromagnetism, and strong and weak nuclear forces. Other characteristics, like the ratio of matter to anti-matter, the rate of expansion of the universe, or the particular properties of carbon, could all be hypothetically slightly different, in which case it would have been impossible for the universe as we know it to evolve. Sometimes referred to as the anthropic principle, physicists are often attracted to the idea that the universe, including our own consciousness, was some how intended and is sometimes interpreted as evidence for the existence of God, though the impersonal, mathematical God of Physics bares little resemblance to the God of Scriptures.

Contemporary physics understands the nature of space-time and matter-energy to be radically different than our common sense experiences would suggest. Time is relative to the location and speed of the observer; space bends and folds under the influence of intense gravitational fields. Little bits of matter can be converted into an enormous amount of energy, as seen in nuclear bombs or the stellar furnaces. Energy can be converted into matter, as seen in the bubble chambers of particle accelerators. Moreover, what we understand to be the concrete stuff of our everyday world turns out to be mostly empty space at the atomic level and ephemeral chimera at the subatomic level. These subatomic particles exhibit the strange properties of quantum mechanics. With both particle and wave, subatomic stuff is entangled, implicating both other subatomic particles and the observer, able to influence other quantum events at a distance or backwards into the past. The strangeness of quantum phenomena has led many a physicist to take a religious or philosophical turn, in spite of their prior materialist and mechanistic commitments.

Contemporary astronomy and cosmology also confront humanity with a scale and grandeur of an evolving universe difficult to imagine. Measured now in billions of light-years and hundreds of billions of galaxies, our lives on this planet might seem rather small and insignificant. On the other hand, our ability to even comprehend this new cosmic topography can also ennoble and enlarge our appreciation of these unique human abilities. In either case, this new view of the cosmos is an occasion for religious and philosophical reflection and an opportunity to expand our understanding of the divine. Moreover, it can enhance the reasons for protecting this remarkable planet.

Evolution and biology. Evolution and biology raise a series of different questions for religious thought. Where cosmologists see issues of elegant improbability in the design of the universe, evolutionary theory points towards a chaotic and brutal developmental process in which famine, predation, disease, and death are the ultimate editor of a story written through random drift. Darwinian evolution has been a flash point of conflict between science and religion, because it appears to undermine traditional religious understandings of nature as a product of a benevolent and powerful God. As applied to humans, social Darwinism also seems to undermine traditional religious morality, indeed in some cases to have contributed to ruthless political ideologies in the twentieth century.

Many religious and scientific thinkers have interpreted evolution through teleological or teleonomical lenses, arguing that natural history presents us with a progressive unfolding of greater levels of complexity and beauty in nature. Some scientists also point to mathematical patterns in nature, as well as the convergent evolution of similar life structures among unrelated species. It is important to remember that the problems of suffering, death, and evil have confounded humanity long before the theory of evolution, so the challenge of Darwinism is not a new issue for religious and theological thought. Some think it useful to extend the notion of free will beyond the human, that all of nature has elements of self-creative possibility not governed by causal processes or Divine fiat.

The lacuna of applying evolutionary theory to human behavior revolves around the question of altruism. If survival and reproduction are the key motive forces in evolution and human behavior, then why would anyone sacrifice his or her self for the benefit of someone unrelated? When science explores human nature, it necessarily confronts religious moral teachings, which universally teach some version of the Golden Rule. Many argue that humans evolve in a Lamarckian pattern by which acquired cultural adaptations are passed on directly to the next generation and that as such humanity transcends mere biological processes. Moreover, humans are a profoundly social and symbolic species; and we use narratives—for instance, sacred stories—to navigate existential moral and value choices. In that sense, everyone employs metanarratives, consciously or unconsciously, to navigate the uncertainties of life. *Homo sapien* is a moral and believing animal in which religion, broadly understood, is involved, even if that "religion" be atheism, pragmatism, or materialism.

Finally, evolution gives us a new perspective on the recent past and future prospects for humanity and the planet. Science, technology, economics, education, and government have given humans enormous power to engage in large-scale environmental engineering, even as we are about to embark upon wide-ranging genetic engineering of other species and ourselves. In the fields of bioethics and environmental ethics, religion and science discuss what it means to be human and the prospects of humanity's self-transcendence or self-destruction in a brave new world of twenty-first century technology. Science itself does not give much guidance as to whether such a future is desirable or whether it should be resisted.

Chaos and complexity theories. Applied in numerous scientific disciplines, chaos and complexity theories suggest that some of the most creative phenomena are distributed systems and iterative processes. In some cases, simple mathematical models can describe natural phenomena. In other cases, the multiplication of feedback loops and complexity confound us with known limitations of science and computation. Computer models are used to simulate climate change, which inform environmental policy debates. Computer models are now also used to simulate religious and cultural systems. Philosophers and theologians ponder the significance of this new paradigm for understanding the nature of God and creativity.

Aesthetics and ethics. In these domains the interaction of science and religion also plays itself out. Many philosophers realize that we cannot maintain a simple Is/Ought distinction. The nature of nature must inform our understanding about how humans desire to transform their lives, which values are possible and desirable to maximize. Traditional religious philosophy makes the distinction between natural moral law, knowable to any reasoning human being, and revealed moral law, knowable only those initiated in a particular tradition. The old natural law tradition needs to be conversant with the best of contemporary science, rather than fall back on antiquated Aristotelian notions of fixed natural kinds. All moral discourse presupposes sets of obligations and the necessity of sacrifice. There is a growing appreciation of the role of religious beliefs and practices in existentially grounding ethical deliberation, even as we debate issues like abortion, euthanasia, human and animal rights, and eco-justice.

Intra- and interreligious dialogue. Finally, science provides a powerful common denominator for this exciting and productive dialogue. In many conferences and workshops today around the world, organized by groups like the Center for Theology and the Natural Sciences (www.ctns.org), the Zygon Center for Science and Religion (www.zygoncenter.org), Metanexus Institute (www.metanexus.net), the John Templeton Foundation (www.templeton.org), and others, religious thinkers and practioners from diverse religious and philosophical traditions—as well as diverse scientific disciplines—find common ground and profound challenges in confronting some of the greatest questions of our time.

Ecology. Once dubbed "the subversive science," ecology also challenges the adequacy of reductionism and materialism, as it poses both new and enduring questions about the appropriate relationships between humans and the more-than-human world. By all accounts, we live at a unique moment in the natural history of our planet and the cultural evolution of our species, filled with challenge and promise. Whatever the future holds in store, the endeavors of science and religion, separately and together, will play an important part in the unfolding story.

BIBLIOGRAPHY

Barbour, Ian. *Ethics in an Age of Technology: The Gifford Lectures 1989–1991.* Vol. 2. San Francisco, 1990.

Barbour, Ian. *Religion and Science: Historical and Contemporary Issues.* New York, 1997.

Berry, Thomas, and Brian Swimme. *The Universe Story: From the Primordial Flaring Forth to the Ecozoic Era.* San Francisco, 1992.

Brooke, J. H. *Science and Religion: Some Historical Perspectives.* Cambridge, U.K., 1999.

Daly, Herman, and John Cobb, Jr. *For the Common Good: Redirecting the Economy toward Community, the Environment, and a Sustainable Future.* Boston, 1989.

Dawkins, Richard. *The Blind Watchmaker: Why the Evidence of Evolution Reveals a Universe Without Design.* New York, 1996.

Dennett, Daniel. *Darwin's Dangerous Idea.* New York, 1995.

Ellis, George F. R., and Nancey Murphy. *On the Moral Nature of the Universe: Theology, Cosmology, and Ethics.* Minneapolis, 1996.

Gould, Stephen Jay. *Rocks of Ages: Science and Religion in the Fullness of Life.* New York, 2002.

Grassie, William. "Biocultural Evolution in the 21st Century: The Evolutionary Role of Religion." *Metanexus Online.* 2004.

Harel, David. *Computers Ltd.: What They Really Can't Do.* New York, 2000.

Haught, John F. *Science and Religion: From Conflict to Conversation.* Mahwah, N.J., 1995.

Haught, John F. *God after Darwin: A Theology of Evolution.* Boulder, Colo., 2000.

Haught, John F. *Evolution and Divine Providence.* Philadelphia, 2001.

Huchingson, James Edward. *Pandemonium Tremendum: Chaos and Mystery in the Life of God.* Boston, 2001.

John, Arthur Fabel, and Donald St. John. *Teilhard in the 21st Century: The Emerging Spirit of Earth.* Maryknoll, N.Y., 2003.

McKinley, Paul Shepard, and Daniel McKinley. *The Subversive Science: Essays toward an Ecology of Man.* Boston, 1969.

Post, Stephen G. *Unlimited Love: Altruism, Compassion, and Service.* Radnor, Pa., 2003.

Rolston, Holmes, III. *Environmental Ethics: Duties and Values in the Natural World.* Philadelphia, 1988.

Rolston, Holmes, III. *Genes, Genesis and God: Values and Their Origins in Natural and Human History.* New York, 1999.

Smith, Christian. *Moral, Believing Animals: Human Personhood and Culture.* New York, 2003.

Weinberg, Steven. *First Three Minutes.* New York, 1977.

WILLIAM GRASSIE (2005)

ECOLOGY AND RELIGION: ECOLOGY AND NATURE RELIGIONS

The term *nature religion* or the plural *nature religions* most commonly is used as an umbrella term for religious perceptions and practices that despite substantial diversity are characterized by a reverence for nature and consider nature sacred. Over the last few centuries a number of phrases have been used to capture the family resemblance, including *natural religion, nature worship, nature mysticism,* and *earth religion,* and words have been invented to reflect what is taken to be the universal essence of such religiosity, such as *paganism, animism,* and *pantheism.* The term *nature religion,* which began to be employed regularly within religious subcultures at about the time of the first Earth Day celebration in 1970, is used increasingly to represent and debate such "nature-as-sacred" religion in both popular and scholarly venues.

HISTORY OF THE IDEA OF NATURE RELIGION. Regardless of the terminology, the idea has a long history that in significant ways parallels the evolution of the academic study of religion. Indeed, the most common contemporary understanding of nature religion resembles the nature-venerating religiosity described in E. B. Tylor's *Primitive Culture* (1871), F. Max Müller's *Natural Religion* (1888), James G. Frazer's *The Worship of Nature* (1926), and Mircea Eliade's *Patterns in Comparative Religion* (1958). As Lawrence Sullivan concluded in a broad comparative review of nature-related religiosity in "Worship of Nature" in this encyclopedia, there are diverse examples of the worship of nature in the history of religion.

This background helps explain why the study of religion has often involved an interpretive effort to understand nature religion (understood broadly as nature-venerating or nature-as-sacred religion) as well as "the natural dimension of religion," a term from Catherine Albanese's *Nature Religion in America* (1990), which urged scholars to examine not only religions in which nature is explicitly considered divine or worshiped but also those in which it serves as an important symbolic resource. This and other changes in the field of religious studies—where scholars focus less on notions such as worship and more on the way religion is integrated into everyday life and the way it promotes identity formation and serves power and material interests—have recast discussions and understandings of nature religion among religionists and scholars alike.

Despite some changes as scholarly perspectives come into and fall out of fashion, there have been important continuities in both popular and scholarly contestations over nature religion. In those contestations the line between the observer and the practitioner often has been blurred; scholars frequently become as involved in nature-related religious production as do their overtly religious subjects.

The most common debate has been between those who consider nature religions to be religiously or politically primitive, regressive, or dangerous and those who laud them as spiritually perceptive or authentic and ecologically beneficent.

NATURE RELIGIONS AS PRIMITIVE, REGRESSIVE, OR DANGEROUS. Perspectives that view nature religions as primitive, regressive, or dangerous may have originated with and throughout recorded history have been influenced by the ancient antipathy between Abrahamic religions and the pagan and polytheistic religions of the ancient Middle East. Frazer noted, for example, that the Hebrew King Josiah initiated a death penalty for those who worshipped the sun in the seventh century BCE and that subsequent Hebrew figures, including the prophet Ezekiel, continued to battle the solar cult and other forms of what they considered nature-related idolatry. The orthodox streams of Abrahamic religion, especially Christianity and Islam, maintained their hostility and helped push nature religions and the peoples who embodied them to extinction or marginalization through conversion, assimilation, and sometimes violence. Those actions were legitimated in religious terms as promoting the spiritual well-being of both believers and prospective believers.

However, criticisms of nature-related religiosity have not been restricted to the religiously orthodox. The tendency to view nature religions as primitive (though not necessarily dangerous) intensified as Occidental (Western) culture placed increasing value on reason and as many thinkers became less religiously orthodox. The German philosopher Georg Wilhelm Friedrich Hegel (1770–1831), for example, advanced an idealistic philosophy that viewed nature religions as primitive for failing to perceive the divine spirit moving through the dialectical process of history.

More important for the historical study of religion in general and scholarly reflection on nature religion in particular was the influence of Charles Darwin's theory of evolution published in *On the Origin of Species* (1859). Generations of scholars came to view nature religions as primitive misperceptions that natural forces are animated or alive. A friend of Darwin, John Lubbock, initiated that characterization in *The Origin of Civilization and the Primitive Condition of Man* (1889), citing Darwin's observation of the way dogs mistake inanimate objects for living beings. Lubbock asserted that religion had its origin in a similar misapprehension by primitive humans. Soon E. B. Tylor, who some consider the father of anthropology, would coin the term *animism* for that type of attribution of consciousness to inanimate objects and forces, asserting that that misapprehension was grounded in the dream states and sneezing of "primitive" or "savage" peoples. Not long afterward Max Müller, considered by some the father of the academic study of religion, traced the origin of Indo-European religion to religious metaphors and symbolism grounded in the natural environment, especially the sky and sun.

Both classical paganism and polytheistic religions, of course, involved the supplication to or veneration of celestial bodies and other natural entities and forces. According to Frazer, who was influenced by Tylor and Müller, belief and cultus related to the sun, the earth, and the dead were especially common in the worldwide emergence and ancient history of religion. Frazer approvingly quoted Müller's *Introduction to the Science of Religion* (1873): "The worship of the spirits of the departed is perhaps the most widely spread form of natural superstition all over the world" (Frazer, 1926, p. 18).

The idea of religion as involving nature-related beliefs and practices became widely influential, as did Frazer's "worship of nature" rubric to describe such religions:

> [By] the worship of nature, I mean . . . the worship of natural phenomena conceived as animated, conscious, and endowed with both the power and the will to benefit or injure mankind. Conceived as such they are naturally objects of human awe and fear . . . to the mind of primitive man these natural phenomena assume the character of formidable and dangerous spirits whose anger it is his wish to avoid, and whose favour it is his interest to conciliate. To attain these desirable ends he resorts to the same means of conciliation which he employs towards human beings on whose goodwill he happens to be dependent; he proffers requests to them, and he makes them presents; in other words, he prays and sacrifices to them; in short, he worships them. Thus what we may call the worship of nature is based on the personification of natural phenomena. (Frazer, 1926, p. 17)

This early nature religiosity, Frazer thought, was replaced first by polytheism and then by monotheism as part of a "slow and gradual" process that was leading inexorably among civilized peoples to the "despiritualization of the universe" (Frazer, 1926, p. 9). Most scholarly observers during the nineteenth and early twentieth centuries seemed to agree that the nature spirituality characteristic of early peoples and the world's remaining "primitives" eventually would be supplanted by higher, monotheistic forms or no religion at all.

They assumed that although such religion might be regressive, it could not be considered dangerous or threatening, at least to cultural and material progress.

More recently, however, a chorus of voices has suggested that some forms of nature religions have been or can be pernicious or at least not as ecologically beneficent as they may seem upon cursory observation.

Drawing on analyses of dominance and power in the work of the philosopher Michel Foucault and the sociologist Pierre Bourdieu, in *Nature Religion in America* (1990) Catherine Albanese argued that nature religion, although it is commonly thought to promote social and ecological well-being, often masked an impulse to dominate nature as well as other people. Specifically, she analyzed how some religions of nature that were prominent during the period of the nation's invention justified the subjugation of both the natural world and the continent's aboriginal peoples. She also broadened the field of view in regard to religion by including in it her own definition of religious phenomena in which nature was "a compelling religious center . . . [and] culture broker" even if it was not considered sacred. The study of nature religion, including, broadly "the natural dimension of religion," Albanese concluded, can illuminate "persistent patterns in past and present American life" (Albanese, 1990, pp. 200, 13).

Albanese's analyses of nature religion caused consternation among many scholars and religionists who had a positive attitude toward nature religion. By broadening the subject and complicating the understanding of its consequences, Albanese's study precipitated significant shifts and a more complicated discussion of the nature variable in religion among practitioners of nature religions and scholars. A number of scholars concluded that there have been worldview affinities and historical connections among some nature religions (especially northern European paganism and various pagan revival movements) and racist worldviews as well as between nature religions and radical environmental movements, which some view as prone to violence.

Perhaps the most influential among those critics was Anna Bramwell, whose *Blood and Soil: Walter Darré and Hitler's Green Party* (1985) was followed by *Ecology in the 20th Century* (1989). Bramwell's main argument has been that the environmental movement, which can be traced roughly to the middle of the nineteenth century, represents an entirely new "nature worshipping" ideology in which "a pantheistic religious feeling is the norm" (Bramwell, 1989, p. 17, cf. p. 13). This religious ideology, which she called "Ecologism," can be fused to many ideologies, she acknowledged. However, she argued that it has had its strongest affinities and historical connections to racist programs (such as eugenics) and political movements (such as Nazism) that rejected Enlightenment rationality, often in favor of an agrarian ideal.

Bramwell's discussion of Earnest Haeckel (1834–1919), who coined the word *ecology* in *Generelle Morphologie* in 1866, is noteworthy. She was careful to point out that Haeckel did not promote Nazi ideology. He did, however, promote an ecologistic spirituality that would be grafted to racist worldviews, according to Bramwell. Although Haeckel was atheistic and hostile to traditional monotheism, Bramwell believes he strongly advocated monistic pantheism, the belief that there is no supernatural realm and no spiritual substance distinct from matter but that nature in all its forms is divine. According to Bramwell, "Haeckel's most important legacy was his worship of Nature, the belief that man and nature were one, and that to damage one was to damage the other" (Bramwell, 1989, p. 53). To the extent that she was correct, the analysis of environmentalism as a new religious form would become important to religious studies.

Other books followed that explored connections between what some have called right-wing ecology and nature religion, including several by Nicholas Goodrick-Clarke that found occult and pagan roots in Nazism (Goodrick-Clarke, 1994, 1998, 2002). Richard Steigmann-Gall's *The Holy Reich: Nazi Conceptions of Christianity 1919–1945* (2003), however, argues largely to the contrary that Christianity, or a least an unorthodox strain of it, was far more important to Nazi ideology than were the few Nazis who were thinking romantically about the revival of a pre-Christian, Aryan nature religion that probably never existed.

Those studies of the Nazi period should be compared to fieldwork-based studies of contemporary movements. For example, the Swedish anthropologist Mattias Gardell, in *Gods of the Blood: The Pagan Revival and White Separatism* (2003), found significant affinities between contemporary nature religion, environmental ideals, and racist ideologies in Europe and North America. Another important work that took a fieldwork-based approach was edited by Jeffrey Kaplan and Heléne Lööw and titled *The Cultic Milieu* (2002), after an influential article by the sociologist Colin Campbell (1972). Several of its articles analyzed whether oppositional nature religions and environmental movements had developed or were likely to develop racist and violent characteristics. Although the conclusions varied with the specific subject matter, the book represented a turn toward field research in the effort to discern how nature religions are fused to political ideologies.

NATURE RELIGIONS AS SPIRITUALLY PERCEPTIVE, AUTHENTIC, AND ECOLOGICALLY BENEFICENT. Two historical works that bring the reader from ancient times nearly up to the present age of historical ideas, Clarence Glacken's *Traces on the Rhodian Shore: Nature and Culture in Western Thought from Ancient Times to the End of the Eighteenth Century* (1967) and Donald Worster's *Nature's Economy: A History of Ecological Ideas* (1977), demonstrate both the marginalization of nature religion and its persistence as a religious force.

Early in *Traces on the Rhodian Shore,* for example, Glacken urges his readers not to "forget the echoes of the primordial Mediterranean world: its age-old veneration of Mother Earth" or its "astrological paganism" (Glacken,

1967, pp. 13, 15). This is an appropriate injunction for the study of nature religion. In Glacken's and other studies, including Worster's *Nature's Economy,* it becomes clear that whereas belief in specific earthly and celestial nature gods may have declined or disappeared, the perception that nature's places and forces are sacred, which gave rise to classical paganism, has not withered way. That perception has been resilient, at least episodically, threatening the hegemony of the monotheistic consensus and later challenging secular, science-based worldviews.

Writing at the dawn of the "age of reason," the Jewish philosopher and theologian Baruch (or Benedictus) Spinoza (1632–1677) and the French social theorist Jean-Jacques Rousseau (1712–1778), provide two influential examples of such a challenge.

Spinoza articulated a sophisticated monistic pantheism that has directly or indirectly influenced generations of subsequent pantheistic nature religionists. Those embracing or being influenced by such philosophy include some of the greatest theologians and philosophers of the modern period, including Friedrich Schleiermacher, Alfred North Whitehead, and later generations of "process" philosophers and theologians, who have been either pantheistic or panentheistic in worldview. Spinoza was also very influential on the early philosopher-architects of the deep ecology movement, such as the Norwegian Arne Naess and the American George Sessions, as well as on a number of recent thinkers who have explicitly promoted pantheistic religion, including Michael Levine (1994), Robert Corrington (1997), and Donald Crosby (2002).

At least as important was Rousseau's inspirational role in the so-called Romantic movement. Rousseau rejected revealed Abrahamic religions in favor of a deistic "natural religion" that, he believed, helps people discern God's existence in the order and harmony of nature. For Rousseau, natural religion and an epistemological turn to nature could provide a way to live free of the alienation, inequality, prejudice, and competitiveness of "civilization." His *Reveries of a Solitary Walker* (1782), which fused botanical observation with reminiscences of his ecstatic experiences in nature, presaged an explosion of religious nature and natural history writing. His greatest legacy, however, may not have been his role in promoting reverence for nature but his respect if not veneration for indigenous peoples who lived closer to nature and were thus socially and ecologically superior to "civilized" peoples. Rousseau's belief that such peoples were worthy of emulation makes his nature religion not only a worldview; his belief also enjoined a practice that demands direct experience in nature as well as (at least eventually) ethical obligations to nature itself. For Rousseau and his progeny these obligations oppose the dominant social forces in the West: hierarchal religions, centralized nation-states, and the quest to harness nature for human purposes.

Spinoza, and Rousseau more directly, offered a direct rejoinder to those who viewed nature religion as dangerous or primitive. This viewpoint offered instead an antidote to the West's spiritual malaise, social violence, and economic inequality and the possibility of a harmonious future among the entire community of life.

ANTHROPOLOGY, THE STUDY OF RELIGION, AND NATURE RELIGION. Throughout the twentieth century and into the twenty-first anthropologists and scholars of religion often have continued to play the tunes common to nature religion. This is ironic since such scholars frequently have been directly or indirectly critical of such forms of religion. Even these critics, however, have, sometimes unwittingly, offered analyses that would be used to invent (or revitalize) nature religions.

Frazer provides a relevant example. Although he thought nature worship would disappear as scientific rationality spread, his wide-ranging descriptions of nature religiosity and his theory in *The Golden Bough* (1994) that much folk culture constitutes cultural survivals of a pagan past helped revitalize paganism or inspire new pagan religious production. Other scholars and religionists would offer historical interpretations of goddess or pagan societies that would be integrated into Neopaganism. Mircea Eliade's work, especially *Patterns in Comparative Religion* (1958) and *The Sacred and the Profane* (1959), functioned similarly as a resource. Unlike Frazer, however, Eliade apparently believed that the human experience of a sacred dimension of life represents not false consciousness but an authentic religious perception. A generation of religion scholars and popular writers followed his lead.

Equally important has been the work of the anthropologists who have developed several subfield specializations that have become known as ethnobotany, traditional ecological knowledge, and ecological anthropology or historical ecology. In various ways these disciplines have examined indigenous societies and sometimes peasant cultures as well in order to understand the relationships between ecosystems, livelihoods, and religions. The pioneers of these approaches, including the anthropologists Richard Schultes (1989), William Balée (1994), Roy Rappaport (1979, 1999), Gerardo Reichel-Dolmatoff (1976, 1996), Steven Lansing (1991), and Fikret Berkes (1999), concluded that indigenous societies and their spiritualities and religious practices and ethics, if not disrupted by outsiders, are usually environmentally sustainable and do not reduce biodiversity.

Many of these theorists have grounded their understanding of nature religion (and religion and nature) in evolutionary theory, wrestling with whether religious life can be seen as an evolutionary adaptation that promotes human survival. Roy Rappaport, one of the most influential theorists arguing along these lines, wrote, "Religious rituals [are] neither more or less than part of the behavioral repertoire employed by an aggregate of organisms in adjusting to its environment" (Rappaport, 1979, p. 28). Although this may sound like a scientifically reductionistic theory stating that religion can be explained as a mere epiphenomenon of evolution, Rappaport and many other anthropologists came to appreciate, if not have a personal affinity with, the nature religions of the indigenous people with whom they were well acquainted. The Harvard anthropologist Richard Schultes, who is widely considered the founder of ethnobotany and who studied indigenous cultures for decades in South America, concluded that the religion-related ecological knowledge of indigenous people was a precious treasury for humankind and that it was critically important to the conservation of biodiversity.

In addition to anthropologists, many scholars of religion have been involved in efforts to kindle a sense of reverence toward nature. In 1990 a group of scholars formed a Religion and Ecology Group within the American Academy of Religion. Its purpose was not only to understand the relationships between religions, cultures, and environments; many of its members sought to encourage religious environmental action. Some of its most active members became involved in the most comprehensive scholarly project to date in the emerging field of religion and ecology: a series of conferences titled "Religions of the World and Ecology" that were held between 1996 and 1998 and hosted by the Harvard Divinity School Center for the Study of World Religions (which at the time was directed by one of Eliade's most distinguished students, Lawrence Sullivan). Organized by two Bucknell University historians of religion, Mary Evelyn Tucker and John Grim, the conferences were followed by a ten-volume Harvard University Press book series, published between 1997 and 2004, which they edited. In the series introduction, Tucker and Grim indirectly confessed their belief in the earth's sacredness by lamenting "we no longer see the earth as sacred" and tracing environmental decline to this defective religious perception (Tucker and Grim, in Tucker and Williams, p. xvii). This statement seemed to also assume that earlier humans had a superior religious sensibility toward nature. The architects of the conference and the series held out the hope that a common religious ground for valuing nature could be found among all religions. They articulated their conviction that scholars could contribute to this effort by identifying and evaluating the "*distinctive ecological* attitudes, values, and practices of diverse religious traditions . . . that comprise . . . fertile ecological ground" (Tucker and Grim in Tucker and Williams, p. xxiii).

In the 1990s there were several conferences that focused explicitly on religions that consider nature to be sacred. Several important conferences were held in the United Kingdom. Graham Harvey and Charlotte Hardman organized the first one, "Paganism Today," which was held at the University of Newcastle upon Tyne in 1995. It and a number of edited books that followed represented, at least in part, an effort to blend rigorous scholarship with pagan identity, thereby legitimating that hybrid genre. Those books included a volume that took its title from the conference, Harvey and Hardman's *Paganism Today: Wiccans, Druids, the Goddess and Ancient Earth Traditions for the Twenty-First Century* (1996). Another volume, *Researching Paganisms* (2004), which Harvey later coedited with Jenny Blain and Douglas Ezzy, argued in favor of the use of diverse methods in the study of paganism and emphasized the value of committed pagan scholarship. The second conference was held at Lancaster University in 1996 and was organized by members of that university's religious studies department. It was titled "Nature Religion Today," and as in the "Paganism Today" conference the year before, many of the organizers and presenters were self-consciously pagan in their religious identity. This conference included a discussion of the revival or invention of Wicca, druidic religion, and Celtic nature spirituality. Also like the first conference, this one led to a scholarly publication, *Nature Religion Today: Paganism in the Modern World* (Pearson, Roberts, Samuel, and Roberts, 1998). At both conferences as well as afterward the participants engaged in their own forms of ritualized nature veneration. A third conference, a year later in 1997 at University College Winchester, was titled "Re-Enchantment."

The preceding examples illustrate that like some anthropologists, some scholars of religion not only study the various manifestations of nature religion but are directly involved in such religious production, both in scholarly ways and by participating in ritual and ethical action. The ethical action is most often deployed in defense of ecosystems and the indigenous peoples who are considered wise stewards of them.

SCIENCE AND NATURE RELIGION. In addition to anthropologists and religion scholars, a growing number of scientists are becoming engaged in nature religion. Nature religionists, scholarly and not, have embraced them and find reinforcement in the statements of scientists who confess their feeling that life is miraculous or that the natural world is sacred. Such shared sentiment has also led to interesting collaborations that appear to represent new forms of nature religion, including cases of scientific narratives being considered sacred and either grafted onto already existing religions in creative ways or offered as stand-alone sacred stories for modern, scientifically informed people. An example of science-based nature reverence can be found in a statement issued in the early 1990s by a group of prominent scientists that included Stephen Jay Gould, Hans Bethe, Stephen Schneider, and Carl Sagan:

> As scientists, many of us have had profound personal experiences of awe and reverence before the universe. We understand that what is regarded as sacred is more likely to be treated with care and respect. Our planetary home should be so regarded. Efforts to safeguard and cherish the environment should be infused with a vision of the sacred. (Suzuki and Knudtson, p. 227, cf. p. 167)

Some of these scientists had been influenced significantly by the former passionate priest and world religions scholar Thomas Berry (1914–), whose thinking was, in turn, influenced by Teilhard de Chardin, Alfred North Whitehead, and Mircea Eliade. Beginning in the late 1980s, Berry, sometimes collaborating with the physicist Brian Swimme, argued that the universe story—science-based cosmological and evolutionary narratives—should be considered sacred stories and inspire reverence for nature and environmental action. For scientifically inclined individuals who find implausible the supernaturalism that accompanies most forms of religion, Berry also articulated a spirituality that coheres with the feelings of awe and reverence that sometimes emerge from science itself. Published examples include Ursula Goodenough's *The Sacred Depths of Nature* (1998), the science writer Connie Barlow's *Green Space, Green Time: The Way of Science* (1997), and Loyal Rue's *Everybody's Story: Wising up to the Epic of Evolution* (2000).

In addition, some scientific theories were appropriated by nature religionists as evidence for their own perception of nature's sacredness. The atmospheric scientist James Lovelock articulated a scientific theory in *Gaia: A New Look at Life on Earth* (1979), in which he argued that the biosphere operates like a self-regulating organism, maintaining the necessary conditions of life. Although Lovelock borrowed the Gaia theory's name from the ancient Greek god of the earth, he regarded it as a scientific theory, not a religious treatise. He was, therefore, shocked at how nature religionists seized on it as evidence for their pantheistic, nature-venerating worldviews. But he eventually embraced the spiritual interpretation of his theory, concluding in 2001 that we must protect Gaia because "We are a part of it . . . and should revere it again."

Nature, Religion, and the Future. This discussion of nature religion illustrates some of the diverse ways in which the phenomenon has been understood. It has said little, however, about the invention or revitalization of paganism in the twentieth century and paid little attention to environmental and New Age groups, which often fit well into the nature religion construct.

Although nature religions usually consider nature to be sacred, they do not always agree about its location or where it manifests itself most powerfully. There are differing perceptions in nature religions of whether the sacred is primarily earthly (manifested in specific places such as caves, mountains, and water bodies), biotic (perceived in the earth's flora and fauna), or cosmic (reflected in a platonic way in earthly life but located beyond the biosphere).

Despite substantial differences, some convergence may be under way. Participants in contemporary nature religion often speak of their sense of "connection" and "belonging" to the earth, its living systems, or the universe as a whole. Such rhetoric is so widespread that it has become possible to define nature religions as *spiritualities of connection.* This would echo the etymological root of the word *religion,* which has to do with belonging or being bound to forces greater than the self. Such spiritualities usually are accompanied by kinship feelings and ethical obligations toward nonhuman life. They appear to be likely to play an important role in the human religious future, perhaps in part because such religion can be apprehended through the senses (sometimes magnified through scientific methods and technologies).

It is all but certain that nature religion will continue to evolve and encounter hostility. Nature religionists undoubtedly will continue to frame such opposition as the repressive tendency of religious zealots who seek to desacralize and desecrate the living natural world.

Scholarly theories regarding the evolutionary or "natural" roots of religion and analyses of the ubiquity of nature as a religious resource for veneration, worship, and symbolic thought suggest that religion will remain deeply intertwined with nature. The intersection of religion and nature therefore will continue to provide fertile ground for both nature religion and the scholarly analysis of it.

See Also Animals; Animism and Animatism; Earth; Earth First!; Nature; Neopaganism; Paganism, Anglo-Saxon; Pantheism and Panentheism; Sacred and the Profane, The; Vegetation.

Bibliography

Many of the sources provided below are introduced in the entry and require no additional annotation. Other cited works include those of Stephen Fox and Michael P. Cohen, who illustrate the prevalence of nature spirituality in the American environmental movement. Examples of deep ecology, an environmental philosophy that often is associated with radical environmentalism and can be understood as a nature religion, can be found in the cited works of Arne Naess, Paul Shepard, Gary Snyder, George Sessions, Bill Devall, John Seed, and Joanna Macy. Naess, Shepard, and Snyder are the most important intellectual architects of the movement, and Macy and Seed are its most influential evangelists and ritualizers. Michael Zimmerman is a philosopher sympathetic to deep ecology, radical environmentalism, and other forms of nature religion who has been troubled by the charges of right-wing connections to it, and his book is a reflection on that issue. The works of Bron Taylor, Sarah Pike, Michael York, and Catherine Albanese explore nature religion and its intersections with environmental movements, New Age spirituality, paganism, and other forms of countercultural spirituality. The novels by James Redfield about a "Celestine prophecy" provide a good example of the way in which environmental themes can be fused to New Age religion. Colin Campbell's theory of the Cultic Milieu, recently illustrated in the volume by Kaplan and Lööw, is helpful for understanding the processes by which such cross-fertilization occurs. The *Encyclopedia of Religion and Nature,* edited by Taylor, provides diverse examples of nature religion from around the world, and some of its entries that are especially relevant to nature religion are included below.

Albanese, Catherine L. *Nature Religion in America: From the Algonkian Indians to the New Age.* Chicago, 1990.

Balée, William. *Footprints of the Forest: Ka'Apor Ethnobotany—The Historical Ecology of Plant Utilization by an Amazonian People.* New York, 1994.

Berkes, Fikret. *Sacred Ecology: Traditional Ecological Knowledge and Resource Management.* Philadelphia, 1999.

Blain, Jenny, Douglas Ezzy, and Graham Harvey. *Researching Paganisms.* Lanham, Md., 2004.

Bramwell, Anna. *Blood and Soil: Walter Darré and Hitler's Green Party.* Buckinghamshire, U.K., 1985.

Bramwell, Anna. *Ecology in the 20th Century: A History.* New Haven, Conn., 1989.

Campbell, Colin. "The Cult, the Cultic Milieu and Secularization." *A Sociological Yearbook of Religion in Britain* 5 (1972): 119–136.

Capra, Fritjof, and David Steindl-Rast. *Belonging to the Universe: Explorations on the Frontiers of Science and Spirituality.* San Francisco, 1991.

Cauvin, Jacques. *The Birth of the Gods and the Origins of Agriculture.* Translated by Trevor Watkins. Cambridge, U.K., 2000.

Cohen, Michael P. *The Pathless Way: John Muir and American Wilderness.* Madison, Wisc., 1984.

Campolo, Anthony. *How to Rescue the Earth Without Worshipping Nature.* Nashville, Tenn., 1992.

Corrington, Robert S. *Nature's Religion.* Lanham, Md., 1997.

Crosby, Donald A. *A Religion of Nature.* Albany, N.Y., 2002.

Devall, Bill, and George Sessions. *Deep Ecology: Living as If Nature Mattered.* Salt Lake City, Utah, 1985.

Eliade, Mircea. *Patterns in Comparative Religion.* New York, 1958.

Eliade, Mircea. *The Sacred and the Profane: The Nature of Religion.* New York, 1959.

Fox, Stephen. *The American Conservation Movement: John Muir and His Legacy.* Madison, Wisc., 1981.

Frazer, Sir James George. *The Golden Bough: A History of Myth and Religion.* London, 1994.

Frazer, Sir James George. *The Worship of Nature.* London, 1926.

Gardell, Mattias. *Gods of the Blood: The Pagan Revival and White Separatism.* Durham, N.C., 2003.

Glacken, Clarence. *Traces on the Rhodian Shore: Nature and Culture in Western Thought from Ancient Times to the End of the Eighteenth Century.* Berkeley, Calif., 1967.

Goodenough, Ursula. *The Sacred Depths of Nature.* New York, 1998.

Goodrick-Clarke, Nicholas. *The Occult Roots of Nazism: Secret Aryan Cults and Their Influence on Nazi Ideology.* New York, 1994.

Goodrick-Clarke, Nicholas. *Hitler's Priestess: Savitri Devi, the Hindu-Aryan Myth and Neo-Nazism.* New York, 1998.

Goodrick-Clarke, Nicholas. *Black Sun: Aryan Cults, Esoteric Nazism and the Politics of Identity.* New York and London, 2002.

Guthrie, Stewart. *Faces in the Clouds: A New Theory of Religion.* New York and Oxford, 1993.

Haeckel, Ernest. *God-Nature.* London, 1906.

Haeckel, Ernest. *The Riddle of the Universe.* London, 1900.

Haeckel, Ernest. *The Wonders of Life.* London, 1905.

Haeckel, Ernest. *Monism as Connnecting Religion and Science: The Confession of Faith of a Man of Science.* London and Edinburgh, 1984.

Harvey, Graham. *Contemporary Paganism: Listening People, Speaking Earth.* New York, 1997.

Harvey, Graham, and Charlotte Hardman, eds. *Paganism Today: Wiccans, Druids, the Goddess and Ancient Earth Traditions for the Twenty-First Century.* New York, 1996.

Hutton, Ronald. *The Triumph of the Moon: A History of Modern Pagan Witchcraft.* Cambridge, Mass., 2000.

Kaplan, Jeffrey, and Heléne Lööw, eds. *The Cultic Milieu: Oppositional Subcultures in an Age of Globalization.* Lanham, Md. 2002. See especially Bron Taylor, "Diggers, Wolfs, Ents, Elves and Expanding Universes: Bricolage, Religion, and Violence from Earth First! and the Earth Liberation Front to the Antiglobalization Resistance" (pp. 26–74); Jeff Kaplan, "The Postwar Paths of Occult National Socialism" (pp. 225–264); and Heléne Lööw, "The Idea of Purity: The Swedish Racist Counterculture, Animal Rights, and Environmental Protection" (pp. 193–210).

Kellert, Stephen R. *Kinship to Mastery: Biophilia in Human Evolution and Development.* Washington, D.C., 1997.

Lansing, J. Stephen. *Priests and Programmers: Technologies of Power in the Engineered Landscape of Bali.* Princeton, N.J., 1991.

Levine, Michael. *Pantheism: A Non-Theistic Concept of Divinity.* New York and London, 1994.

Lubbock, John. *The Origin of Civilization and the Primitive Condition of Man.* London, 1889 (originally published in 1870).

Macy, Joanna. *Coming Back to Life: Practices to Reconnect Our Lives, Our World.* Blain, Wash., 1998.

Messer, Ellen, and Michael Lambek. *Ecology and the Sacred: Engaging the Anthropology of Roy A. Rappaport.* Ann Arbor, Mich., 2001.

Müller, F. Max. *Introduction to the Science of Religion.* London, 1873.

Müller, F. Max. *Natural Religion.* London, 1888.

Naess, Arne. *Ecology, Community and Lifestyle.* Edited and translated by David Rothenberg. Cambridge, U.K., 1989.

Noll, Richard. *The Aryan Christ: The Secret Life of Carl Jung.* New York, 1997. A work that buttresses allegations that nature religion, in this case that of Carl Jung, can contribute to fascist ideologies.

Pearson, Joanne, Richard H. Roberts, Geoffrey Samuel, and Richard Roberts, eds. *Nature Religion Today: Paganism in the Modern World.* Edinburgh, 1998.

Pike, Sarah. *New Age and Neopagan Religions in America.* New York, 2004.

Plotkin, Mark. *Tales of a Shaman's Apprentice.* New York, 1993.

Rappaport, Roy A. *Ecology, Meaning and Religion.* Richmond, Calif., 1979.

Rappaport, Roy A. *Ritual and Religion in the Making of Humanity.* Cambridge, Mass., 1999.

Redfield, James. *The Celestine Prophecy.* New York, 1993.

Reichel-Dolmatoff, Gerardo. "Cosmology As Ecological Analysis: A View from the Rainforest." *Man* 2, no. 3 (1976): 307–318.

Reichel-Dolmatoff, Gerardo. *The Forest Within: The Worldview of the Tukano Amazonian Indians.* Totnes, U.K., 1996.

Schultes, Richard Evans. "Reasons for Ethnobotanical Conservation." In *Traditional Ecological Knowledge: A Collection of Essays,* edited by R. E. Johannes. Geneva, 1989.

Schultes, Richard Evans, and Siri Reis. *Ethnobotany: Evolution of a Discipline.* Portland, Ore., 1995.

Seed, John, Joanna Macy, Pat Fleming, and Arne Naess. *Thinking Like a Mountain: Towards a Council of All Beings.* Philadelphia, 1988.

Sessions, George, ed. *Deep Ecology for the 21st Century.* Boston, 1995.

Shepard, Paul. *The Tender Carnivore and the Sacred Game.* New York, 1973.

Shepard, Paul. *Coming Home to the Pleistocene.* San Francisco, 1998.

Snyder, Gary. *Turtle Island.* New York, 1969.

Snyder, Gary. *The Practice of the Wild.* San Francisco, 1990.

Spinoza, Benedictus. *Tractatus Theologico-Politicus.* Leiden, 1991.

Steigmann-Gall, Richard. *The Holy Reich: Nazi Conceptions of Christianity 1919–1945.* Cambridge, Mass., 2003.

Suzuki, David, and Peter Knudtson. *Wisdom of the Elders: Honoring Sacred Native Visions of Nature.* New York, 1992.

Swimme, Brian, and Thomas Berry. *The Universe Story: From the Primordial Flaring Forth to the Ecozoic Era: A Celebration of the Unfolding of the Cosmos.* San Francisco, 1992.

Taylor, Bron. "Resacralizing Earth: Pagan Environmentalism and the Restoration of Turtle Island" In *American Sacred Space,* edited by David Chidester and Edward T. Linenthal, pp. 97–151. Bloomington, Ind., 1995.

Taylor, Bron. "Earth and Nature-Based Spirituality (Part I): From Deep Ecology to Radical Environmentalism." *Religion* 31, no. 2 (2001): 175–193.

Taylor, Bron. "Earth and Nature-Based Spirituality (Part II): From Deep Ecology to Scientific Paganism." *Religion* 31, no. 3 (2001): 225–245.

Taylor, Bron. "A Green Future for Religion?" *Futures Journal* 36, no. 9 (2004).

Taylor, Bron, ed. *The Encyclopedia of Religion and Nature,* London and New York, 2005. See especially Animism; Anthropology as a Source of Nature Religion; Berry, Thomas; Biodiversity and Religion; Biophilia; Conservation Biology; Council of All Beings; Deep Ecology; Earth Charter; Earth First! and the Earth Liberation Front; Ecology and Religion; Environmental Ethics; Epic of Evolution; Fascism; Gaia; Gaian Pilgrimage; Leopold, Aldo; Naess, Arne; Natural History as Natural Religion; Nature Religion; Paganism; Pantheism; Radical Environmentalism; Religious Naturalism; Religious Environmentalist Paradigm; Religious Studies and Environmental Concern; Spinoza, Baruch; Thoreau, Henry David; Traditional Ecological Knowledge; Wilson, Edward O.

Taylor, Sarah McFarland. *Green Sisters: Catholic Nuns Answering the Call of the Earth.* Cambridge, Mass., 2004.

Tylor, Sir Edward Burnett. *Primitive Culture: Researches into the Development of Mythology, Philosophy, Religion, Art and Custom.* London, 1871.

Wilson, Edward Osborne. *Biophilia.* Cambridge, Mass., 1984.

Wilson, Edward Osborne. *Consilience: The Unity of Knowledge.* New York, 1998. These are among Wilson's many works that have had the most influence on contemporary nature-religion discussions.

Worster, Donald. *Nature's Economy: A History of Ecological Ideas.* Cambridge, Mass., 1977; revised, 1994.

York, Michael. *The Emerging Network: A Sociology of the New Age and Neo-Pagan Movements.* Lanham, Md., 1995.

York, Michael. *Pagan Theology.* New York, 2004.

Zimmerman, Michael E. *Contesting Earth's Future: Radical Ecology and Postmodernity.* Berkeley, Calif., 1994.

BRON TAYLOR (2005)

ECONOMICS AND RELIGION.

[*To explore the relations between religion and economics, this article takes as its starting place the beginnings of modern economic theory and examines the perspectives on those relations that have developed within the sociology of religion since the late nineteenth century.*]

A sustained scholarly interest in the relationship between religion and economics crystallized in a number of Western societies in the early years of the twentieth century. Since that time it has been a topic of considerable research and debate.

DEVELOPMENT OF ECONOMIC ANALYSIS. The discussion of the relationship between economics and religion is plagued by a general problem having to do with how appropriate it is to speak of separate domains—such as the economic or the religious—in premodern, especially primal, societies, where such distinctions were or are not part of everyday life. Indeed, only during the last two hundred years or so have people become accustomed to speak of the *economy,* even though the term was used as long ago as the fourth century BCE by Aristotle to designate the relationships among members of the domestic household. Aristotle was particularly concerned to show, in the face of the commercial expansion of his time, that human wants and needs are not unlimited and that useful things are not, by their nature, scarce. In spite of the great expansion of trade, profit making, and eventually, price setting by market forces and the appearance of large-scale manufacture during the centuries following Aristotle, it was not until as recently as the end of the eighteenth century that "the economy" became fully thematized (and then only in the Western world) as a relatively autonomous realm of human life. That period saw the beginnings in Great Britain of the discipline that came to be called political economy and the first use of the term *économiste* by French intellectuals. The perception of the economy as a relatively autonomous realm (and, in the view of many of those who specialized in analyzing it, the most fundamental human realm) went hand-in-hand with the view that religion was of rapidly diminishing significance.

PRIMACY OF ECONOMIC ASPECT. The prevailing view among social scientists and historians has been that the economy, during the long period from ancient Greek civilization to the nineteenth century, became disembedded from the societal fabric, especially in the Western world. By the late nineteenth century, therefore, the economy was seen as standing apart from the rest of society. This move has been called the "naturalization" of the economy (in the sense that it came to be regarded as operating according to its own natural laws, particularly those issuing from the relationship between supply and demand, as expressed in monetary prices), and it constituted a crucial aspect of the nineteenth-century diagnosis of secularization (the decline in the significance of religion in modern society). The perception of the rapidly increasing autonomy of the economy inspired in Karl Marx and Friedrich Engels the idea that human history in its entirety had been motored by economic forces or, more specifically, by class conflicts centered upon economic concerns. In response to the view of the classical British political economists that the best form of society is one in which there is free competition among many private producers in line with universal economic laws, Marx argued that different modes of production have prevailed during different periods of history, and therefore the embryonic capitalist mode cannot be regarded as the paradigm of all other modes, let alone as a permanent and universal system.

Both the classical political economists, on the one hand, and Marx and Engels, on the other, thus saw the economy as fundamental to the operation of human societies and correspondingly regarded religion, particularly in modernizing societies, as of peripheral significance (for Marx and Engels, it was primarily an epiphenomenon), but they differed greatly with respect to the implications of the fundamentality of the economy. Religion was, according to Marx, being driven from human life by capitalist materialism and in any case impeded the realization of proletarian class consciousness, which would make possible the release of the class from the exploitative bondage of capitalism. Nevertheless, despite Marx's mainly negative assessment of the historical role of religion, he initiated an intellectual concern with the historical origins of capitalism and, more generally, with the relationship between economic matters and religion.

PRIMACY OF SOCIAL AND MORAL ASPECTS. Classical political economy as such did not encompass the sociological and historical themes that were developed by Marx and others during the nineteenth century. For the most part, the more sociologically inclined social scientists of the period shared Marx's belief in the increasing salience of the economy but tended to view it as a threat to the social and moral integration of industrial societies. In France, for example, Saint-Simon, after having written at length about the new industrial order, came to the conclusion that a new and in a sense secular version of Christianity was necessary in order to give the new form meaningful direction.

While Marx spoke of the new industrial order as providing the opportunity for deprived, exploited classes to seize control of the mainspring of human life (that is, its productive forces) and thus bring about the religionless humanization of the species, Saint-Simon had come to the conclusion that religion in a modernized form was essential in sustaining the meaningful sociality of human life in the face of the eruption of the economic factor. For Marx, religion is the definitive form of alienation, but for those who wrote from the perspective of Saint-Simon, religion cements society and in a sense expresses the sociality of humanity. The latter view was brought to its consummation by Émile Durkheim in the early years of the twentieth century. For Durkheim religion is the serious life, as he put it, and serves, inter alia, so as to elevate men and women above purely material interests.

RELIGION AND ECONOMIC LEGITIMATION. Although the developing nineteenth-century discipline of political economy (eventually known simply as economics) did not share the concern of Marxism and non-Marxist social science with religion, religious ideas and practices emerged in the major areas of capitalism—notably Britain and the United States—that legitimated the capitalist economy and sanctioned the existing social order. Indeed, capitalists themselves quite often expressed the view that certain forms of Protestantism encouraged a dedication to industrial work. More specifically, one may point to Wesleyan Methodism in England as an important example of the way in which religion played a significant part not merely in the development of the entrepreneurial attitude but also in the acquiescence of workers to their role in the system of social stratification. (That religion could, in spite of its allegedly imminent demise, perform this service for capitalism was conceded by Marx under the rubric of "false consciousness.") The greatest degree of religious legitimation of capitalism occurred in the United States, where the predominance of a basically Calvinist form of Protestantism encouraged the view that men proved themselves before God and their fellow men and women by successful, disciplined economic striving.

GERMAN CRITIQUES OF CAPITALISM. By the end of the nineteenth century, intellectuals in Europe and North America had become almost obsessed by the idea that a major transformation of the West had occurred, for by that time not only had capitalistic production greatly expanded but so had bureaucracy, science and technology, and urban forms of life. Thus in the declining years of the nineteenth century theories and diagnoses proliferated concerning the causes, magnitude, and implications of what was considered a more material and less religious mode of existence. It was in Germany, however, that the particular problem of the relationship between religious and economic factors was given the most sustained initial attention, particularly as far as its history was concerned.

The fact that an interest in the connection between economic matters and religion developed so strongly among German scholars can be attributed in part to their felt need to comprehend the character and the place in the modern world of Germany, which had only recently been politically united. Although it possessed a rich culture, the area that became the German empire in the 1870s had been relatively backward in economic terms and had not developed what came to be called by Max Weber "the spirit of capitalism" to the same degree as other parts of western Europe, notably

Britain and Holland, and the United States. A number of German intellectuals were thus greatly concerned (as well as ambivalent) about the origins and ramifications of the capitalist mode of production, which had in those other countries seemingly been responsible for rapid economic growth, urbanization, the increasing significance of money, and so on. They were also concerned with the problem of developing in Germany an integrated national society despite class conflicts largely produced, as they saw it, by changing economic circumstances, as well as by religious and other cleavages.

It should not be thought, however, that concern about the connection between religion and economic matters was confined to Germany, for in less self-consciously intellectual ways the link was addressed in many contexts and societies. During the rapid expansion of capitalistic forms of production, distribution, and exchange in the nineteenth century, religious leaders had responded in a variety of ways. By the 1890s the problems posed by materialism, rapid urbanization, inequality and poverty, the rise of labor unions and working-class political parties, and related conflicts between the lower and middle classes had attracted the attention of many religious leaders, organizations, and movements. Indeed the declining years of the nineteenth and early years of the twentieth centuries witnessed a spawning of movements concerned with the relationship between religion and capitalism. The most conspicuous of these movements deplored the social consequences that they attributed to the capitalist system.

SOCIAL GOSPEL, CHRISTIAN SOCIALISM, AND ROMAN CATHOLICISM. The social condition that aroused the most concern, as expressed in the Social Gospel movement in the United States and in Christian socialist movements in Britain and other predominantly Protestant societies (where capitalism had progressed the furthest), was the poverty and exploitation allegedly inherent in capitalism. In response, these movements ranged from the theological or moral denunciation of capitalism in toto to the more typical advocacy of methods for ameliorating the distress caused by urbanization and industrialization. Their opponents within religious organizations tended to argue either that the primary concern of religion should be with strictly spiritual matters or, as noted in the case of Calvinist Protestants, that capitalism was a God-sanctioned form of economy in the context of which individuals should strive to do their disciplined best. There were also those in American churches who were strongly opposed to anything resembling socialism, in which they saw the prospect of a world without religion, not least because of the open hostility to religion often found among secular socialists (especially those of a Marxist persuasion). Within Catholic circles and specifically in the pronouncements of the Roman Catholic church itself one did not find such conspicuous extremes. Generally speaking, what prevailed in official Catholicism was the view that capitalism contained the seeds of materialism and exploitation but that outright opposition to it in the form of socialism or labor unionism carried the potential for antireligious developments. Socialism and secular unionism were regarded as forms of attachment that rivaled commitment to the Catholic church itself. Consequently, the official Catholicism of the period expressed antagonism not only to most of the trappings of modernity but to what it saw as an ideology of modernism.

The intense religious concern with economic matters that characterized the early years of the twentieth century soon faded. While it would be an exaggeration to say that only slight concern was expressed between World War I and the 1970s, that period constituted something of a hiatus in the modern religious conciousness of the economic domain. This may be attributed in large part to the fact that during and in the aftermath of the phase of religious interest in economic matters that spanned the late nineteenth and early twentieth centuries, the modern welfare state came into being. Indeed, the concern expressed by religious leaders about poverty, health, and other issues had more than a little to do with the steps that many governments took in Europe and elsewhere to establish social welfare programs for their citizens. (Moreover, many religious organizations established their own welfare programs, partly following the lead of the Salvation Army.) During the 1970s and 1980s, however, the economic costs of maintaining the welfare state increased enormously, while serious problems of unemployment and poverty again became evident, partly due to the decline of traditional manufacturing industries in many of the more affluent societies. Meanwhile, the failure of most societies in the Third World to develop strong economies led to increasing concern about global poverty, material deprivation, and intersocietal inequalities. Against that background, there was a considerable renewal of religious interest in economic matters during the 1970s and 1980s, but this time on a much more global scale than at the beginning of the century.

CONTEMPORARY CONTEXT. One of the major sources of the revived concern with the religion-economics theme is the changed relationship between the economic and the governmental spheres. In the early decades of the nineteenth century the view developed that the economy, at least under classical capitalism, was naturelike and operated on its own terms. To that extent the government was thought to have only a small role to play in the production and distribution of wealth and material resources and that what is now called governmental intervention in the economy was inappropriate. However, thanks largely to the growth and monopolistic tendencies of industrial enterprise, governments were gradually conceded a definite role in the management of the economy. As the welfare state and strong central governments emerged, the economy was increasingly regarded as subject to state control or at least calibration rather than as an autonomous system following its own laws. The English economist John Maynard Keynes, by advocating a relatively high degree of governmental intervention in capitalist economies, did much to advance this view, which was further reinforced by the spreading influence of socialist, communist, and other conceptions of economic planning.

There has, however, been a reaction against the interventionist view, particularly in the United States, leading to a revival of the conservative idea that economic growth is best encouraged by the ethic that Weber considered crucial to the rapid economic growth achieved by the mainly Protestant societies of the West during the nineteenth century. On the other hand, the more recent rapid economic growth of some Asian societies, notably Japan, has further raised the possibility that it is not individualistic Protestantism as such that encourages industrial enterprise, but rather a generalized sense of sacrifice and collective involvement in work, at least in the modern corporative economy.

MAX WEBER'S CONTRIBUTION. In addressing the crystallization of scholarly interest in the relationship between religion and economics at the end of the nineteenth century it should be stressed that in the German context there was a general philosophical and sociological issue at the center of debate. In the later years of the nineteenth century Germany experienced a rapidly growing interest in the writings of Marx, due both to academic engagement with them and to the growth of the German Social Democratic Party, whose debates about ideology and strategy largely centered upon issues raised by Marx and Engels. For Marx and Engels and for those influenced by them, notably the historian and prominent ideologue of the Social Democratic Party, Karl Kautsky, the view that the economic realm was autonomous had led to analyses that rendered religion an effect of economic factors. This view became a major ingredient in the materialist, as opposed to the idealist, perspective on human life and history. It was against this general background that Weber began to make his highly influential contributions to the religion-economics theme.

Economics and religion. The novelty of the argument developed by Weber is best indicated at the outset by the fact that his colleague Ernst Troeltsch could emphatically remark that linking the scholarly discussion of economic matters to the analysis of religion and religious change, as he himself advocated, must have seemed strange to his readers, not least in the German context. The major reason for this was that for the majority of German intellectuals (not simply those of a Marxist persuasion), the modern world was characterized by the complete triumph of material, worldly concerns over spiritual ones, and religion was therefore retreating rapidly into the background. This was widely and often pejoratively perceived to have occurred most conspicuously in Britain and North America. At the end of his most important contribution to the discussion of the relationship between economic and religious matters, Weber indeed expressed the view that men and women were destined to live in an "iron cage" of concern with materiality, calculation, and routine, condemned to involvement in highly structured "intramundane" matters. However, writers such as Weber, Troeltsch, and Georg Simmel took the view that this self-interested concern with worldly matters, notably those of an economic kind, had not arisen autonomously but had developed out of changes in cultural presuppositions and psychological dispositions concerning such matters as the relationship between the individual and society. More specifically, in the writings of Weber there developed a particular interest in the relationship between what he came to call material interests and ideal interests in contrast to the prevailing distinction between material, economic forces and ideas.

Weber began his work *The Protestant Ethic and the Spirit of Capitalism* (1904–1905) by referring to the observations and complaints in the German-Catholic press and at German-Catholic congresses about the fact that business leaders and owners of financial capital, as well as skilled laborers and commercially trained business employees, were overwhelmingly Protestant. He set out to show that this circumstance, which was duplicated on a larger scale in contrasts between whole societies (such as Britain and Italy), could be largely explained in terms of what he called the "permanent intrinsic character" of religious beliefs. Weber did not deny that such "temporary external historico-political situations" as the migration of ethnic groups to societies in which they became commercially successful had been important in effecting economic change. But he insisted that such events had occurred over a very long period of human history and in many different places, whereas his exclusive interest was in the differential development of the distinctively modern spirit of entrepreneurial capitalism.

Origins of capitalism. After the publication of *The Protestant Ethic and the Spirit of Capitalism,* Weber began to situate his inquiries into the origins of modern capitalism within a more general inquiry into the origins of the calculative, rational-instrumental, and secular spirit of the Western world. In other words, his study of the ethos of modern capitalism, with its emphasis upon disciplined work, careful calculation, a willingness to forgo short-term for longterm gains, and so on, was subsumed by a wider interest in the making of the ethos of the modern Western world.

Weber argued that the tension between religious belief and what he sometimes called the economic impulse is central to the understanding of the human condition. The economic impulse is universal. But he asked, how and in what ways has it come to be tempered by rationality? In primitive society, he argued, religion is subordinated to the economic impulse and for that reason is best described as magic. Put another way, economic and religious matters are, from the modern point of view, conflated. Rituals and myths tend to be directed toward mainly economic functions. They are relatively instrumental in the provision of economic necessities and thus more magical than religious, not least because in primitive society there is virtually no development of economic ethics. In essence, economically based magic is the embryonic form of religion.

Dualist world images. From that primitive matrix there developed, argued Weber, dualistic world images, that is, images of a cosmos divided into two relatively independent realms, such as the opposed forces of good and evil in Zoroastrianism. Dualistic images of the cosmos gave rise to the problem of the relationship between an individual's action in the mundane world and the fate of the individual in relation to the supramundane world. Given the fundamentality of the economic impulse—or, put another way, the necessity of minimum levels of material satisfaction to support human life—it was inevitable that there should have been tension between the mundane world in its economic aspect and the supramundane world as a focus of meaning. As ideas about the two domains of the cosmos crystallized, a need developed, in turn, for what Weber called an ethical interpretation of the variations and vicissitudes in human fortunes.

Theodicy. Central to Weber's analysis of the economic ethics of the major religious traditions was the concept of theodicy. First systematically used by the philosopher G. W. Leibniz, the term *theodicy* in its most circumscribed sense has to do with the existence in this world of suffering, evil, and injustice in the face of belief in an omniscient, omnipotent, and just God. Weber expanded its range of application, particularly with reference to matters concerning economic circumstances, so as to embrace not merely monotheistic religions (notably Judaism, Christianity, and Islam) but also the major religions of India, China, and Japan (notably Hinduism, Buddhism, and Confucianism). It is crucial to recognize that in loosening the concept of theodicy (illegitimately, according to some) to encompass nontheistic religions Weber had a particular, guiding purpose: his quest for the origins of the modern ethos (a central part of which was, in his view, the instrumental, calculative rationality of entrepreneurial capitalism). In other words, although Weber in one sense followed Hegel and other Germans before him, and Troeltsch in his own time, in trying to establish a framework for the comparison of the major religious traditions, his work was unique in that he was not interested (as, for example, Hegel had been) in demonstrating that Christianity carried the greatest potential for the realization of the "idea of religion." Nor was Weber concerned, as others had been, with examining the degree to which Indian religion constituted a viable metaphysical alternative to Christianity. Closer to his project was Troeltsch's attempt to demonstrate the superiority of Christianity on the grounds that it promulgated both a particularly transcendent view of the supernatural and a definite set of social teachings. Nonetheless, Weber regarded Troeltsch's work as guided too much by theological purposes and a normative commitment to maximizing the relevance of religion to the modern world, as well as by too great an emphasis upon the social teachings that were explicitly developed by the Christian churches on the basis of official doctrine. Weber was interested in what he called the "practical-ethical" applications of religious teachings, the methodical, quotidian working out of theology and religious teaching in concrete circumstances.

Spirit of capitalism. Claiming that he was attempting only to show that it was just as possible to produce an idealistic interpretation of the rise of modern capitalism centered on religious matters as a materialistic one, Weber set out to provide an account of the "spirit" of modern capitalism. In emphasizing spirit (in the sense of the ethos that animates a certain kind of economic action and sustains certain kinds of economic institutions), Weber was in effect insisting that even though much of the behavior that informs the modern world is indeed sustained by what Marx had called the dull compulsion of economics, one could not plausibly account for its emergence solely in reference to economic change as such, not least because the monetary economy had initially become much more significant in the West than in the East, and then only in certain parts of the West. Weber thus set himself the task of stipulating what aspects of Christianity in general and of Protestantism in particular encouraged the growth of a positive orientation to the economic realm.

Weber began by emphasizing Martin Luther's injunction that the world should be made into a monastery. Whereas in traditional Christian teaching a clear distinction had been made between those who were called to live a monastic life of self-sacrifice (particularly in reference to the vows of poverty and chastity) and those who lived in the world, Luther argued that all Christians should be capable of following a God-inspired way of worldly life. Thus from Weber's point of view Lutheranism constituted a crucial unfolding and further rationalization of the inherently inner-worldly attitude of Christianity. The religious calling was, in other words, considered pursuable in this world. There was no need for a separate group of exemplary religious who turned emphatically away from the everyday world. Weber argued, however, that Luther's ideas in this and other respects were not so radical as those of John Calvin. The Lutheran conception of the calling was, in spite of its greater inner-worldliness in comparison with traditional, Catholic Christianity, essentially passive. It required the typical believer to live as religious a life as possible while remaining indifferent to the wider social context. In other words, the Lutheran was to take the world as he or she found it and respect the secular authorities and institutional characteristics of the wider society. The point of the religious life was to concentrate upon one's personal and familial circumstances in intimate relationship with God.

From Weber's point of view this Lutheran ideal was not sufficient to explain the development in the Western world of an ethos that positively encouraged active involvement in worldly and particularly economic affairs, even though it opened the door to such involvement. It was thus to the rather different Protestant attitude of Calvin that he turned in his search for the most significant source of the spirit of capitalism. Before considering what Weber saw in Calvinism in this respect it is necessary to emphasize again that Weber was concerned with the capitalism of the late nineteenth and early twentieth centuries. Capitalism in the sense of profit-seeking had existed in many parts of the world for many centuries, but modern capitalism of the kind that had developed in the West since the late eighteenth century had distinctive characteristics. It was a form of economic life that involved the careful calculation of costs and profits, the borrowing and lending of money, the accumulation of capital in the form of money and material assets, investment, private property, and the employment of laborers and employees in a more or less unrestricted labor market. Given Weber's interest in the spirit, or ethos, of modern capitalism it was what one may loosely call the attitudinal aspect of capitalism and even more particularly the attitudes of businessmen that concerned him. What he was thus looking for was an image of the economic realm that emphasized the virtue of disciplined enterprise and a positive concern with economic activity as such (more or less regardless of the material riches that the successful accumulated).

The central feature of Calvinism in terms of Weber's interest in the growth of the modern monetary economy was its special emphasis upon the doctrine of predestination, the idea that the conception of God as all-powerful, all-knowing, and inscrutable led inexorably to the conclusion that the fate of the world and of human individuals was predetermined. For Weber the crucial question hinged upon the practical problem posed to those who subscribed to this doctrine. Specifically, how did Calvinistic individuals decide to act in the world when they believed that God had already determined the fate of each individual and that only a relatively small proportion of human beings could be saved? Weber argued that individuals were constrained to look for signs of having been accorded an elite salvational status. Those who were most successful would tend to regard their worldly success as an indication that they were among God's chosen. While the conviction that one had been saved was the most general indicator of being of the elect, Calvinism's emphasis upon each person having a calling in life, a calling to strive in as disciplined a manner as possible, without self-indulgence, strongly encouraged the view that worldly success was a confirmation of acting as an instrument of God's will and a sign of elect status.

Thus, in Weber's interpretation, Calvinism constituted a further evolution of the Lutheran idea that life itself could be subjected to the monastic conception of the religious calling. Whereas Luther had adumbrated the relatively passive notion of being called to be as devout as possible in the world, Calvin had articulated a more dynamic and active conception of the calling. Calvin called upon individuals to be religious by engaging with the world. And even though Calvinism as a religious doctrine did not specify how one could be supremely confident that one was acting as an instrument of God, it certainly encouraged the faithful to become actively involved in the major institutional spheres of society and, in so doing, to take individual responsibility as agents of God. Weber maintained that it was psychologically inevitable that those who were most tangibly successful as a result of disciplined, ascetic striving in the world would tend to think of themselves as chosen by God. Because worldly indulgence and luxuriating in the fruits of one's endeavors were precluded by the Calvinist ethos, the result of disciplined economic action was the accumulation of financial capital. For Weber, the process of economic investment followed by accumulation of profit and more investment was intimately related to the process of gaining confirmation of salvation, even though such a calculating attitude toward salvation was not prescribed by Calvinist theology.

Weber regarded the Calvinist doctrine of predestination (which has appeared with much less explicitness in many branches of monotheistic religions) as the extreme theological extension of the Christianity that had developed after the founding of the Christian church. It was the logical consummation of the idea of an omniscient God and the commitment to religious involvement in the world. Calvinism thus constituted a logically perfected theodicy.

In *The Protestant Ethic and the Spirit of Capitalism* Weber concentrated on showing, as he put it, that a one-sided, idealistic account of the rise of capitalism (in the sense of stressing the role of ideas) was just as plausible as the equally one-sided materialist accounts produced by Marxists. In any case, he added, a historical account of the rise of capitalism ought to acknowledge the fact that capitalism (or any other mode of production) is not merely an objective structural phenomenon but is also, at least in part, sustained by a set of presuppositions that encourage specific interests in work and industry and discourage others. Thus, contrary to some interpretations of his work, he did not seek to provide a monocausal account of the rise of modern capitalism but rather to stress the ideational factors that had encouraged the capitalist work ethic and had been neglected by the Marxists. Even though he was intent on emphasizing the critical significance of religion in the rise of modern capitalism, Weber did not simply posit Protestantism as the cause and capitalism as the effect. Rather he insisted that a vital aspect of capitalism is the "spirit," or ethos, that legitimates it, and he sought the principal origins of that spirit. In this regard it should be emphasized that Weber undoubtedly exaggerated the degree to which the affinity between certain branches of Protestantism and capitalist economic success had been overlooked prior to his writings. Nevertheless, his own attempt to provide a detailed explanation of that affinity was unique and pathbreaking. It should also be stressed that according to Weber the spirit of capitalism had gradually become self-sustaining, so that by his own time it was no longer grounded upon the "Protestant ethic." Weber's major thesis about the link between Protestantism (particularly in its Calvinist and some other non-Lutheran forms) and capitalism was presented in the context of an expanding debate on that topic, notably, as has been emphasized, in Germany. His own ideas exacerbated the debate and have since been subjected to extensive criticism and appraisal. Indeed, the significance of his argument probably became greater in the course of the twentieth century. This is so not merely because of the purely scholarly interest in the making of the modern world and the crucial role of the West in that regard but also because the great economic disparities between contemporary societies became a matter of widespread concern, controversy, and conflict. Weber's major thesis about the promotion of the spirit of capitalism (and, more generally, of economic success) is thus of considerable relevance to the discussion of the making of the modern world as a whole and, more specifically, the distribution of resources and wealth within it. Before turning to such matters, however, it is necessary to indicate the ways in which Weber fleshed out his thesis about the origins of the modern Western consciousness.

Economic ethics. In the last decade of his life (1910–1920) Weber engaged in a series of studies of non-Christian civilizations with the express intent of explicating the economic ethics of their major religions. (He completed studies of India and China, as well as of the religion of ancient Israel, but not full-scale studies of medieval Christianity and Islam.) These efforts were largely guided by a general analytical contrast between Occidental and Oriental world-images, at the center of which were religious-metaphysical conceptions of the relationship between the cosmos and the world. His aim was to find out why there had arisen in the West (and more in some parts of the West than in others) the instrumental rationality that seemed to lie at the heart of not merely modern economic life but also modern science, modern forms of organization (what he called rational-legal bureaucracy), and modern life generally—or in other words, why modern capitalism and other aspects of modern life and consciousness had not arisen in Eastern civilizations.

The set of contrasts that Weber employed in his inquiries into economic ethics may be summarized as follows. The Eastern conception of the supramundane world centered upon a notion of eternal being, whereas the Western conception involved belief in a personal God. The first tended to encourage and to be consolidated by a mystical, otherworldly orientation, while the second was closely related to an ascetic, innerworldly orientation. The Eastern image was to be seen in its most acute and logically consistent form in classical Buddhism, which emphasized the basically illusory character of worldly life and regarded release from the contingencies of the everyday world as the highest religious aspiration. In contrast to Calvinism, its Western parallel and and opposite, Buddhism directed the attention of its adherents, particularly Buddhist monks, away from the conditions of everyday life and thus did not encourage the continuous application of religious ideals to the concrete circumstances of the world. More generally speaking, Weber maintained that in India, China, and Japan the dominant worldviews lacked the dynamic created in monotheistic religions, particularly in Christianity, by the conception of a demanding God who had enjoined believers to transform the world in his image. Thus in Eastern societies there was much more concern with the maintenance of an organically ordered society and the promotion of organic social ethics.

It is important to note that in his studies of Eastern societies, Weber took great pains to discuss the ways in which religious ideas and social structures were mutually reinforcing. In other words, even though he ascribed great significance to religion, he wished to demonstrate the specific links between religion and other aspects of human societies. But precisely because he did attend so closly to religion, his work has frequently been interpreted as an expression of religious determinism.

Weber's work on religion and economic life has been subject to an immense amount of exegesis and criticism, most of it centered on his thesis about the Western origins of capitalism. While much of the criticism has been well-grounded with respect to the historical record, a good deal of it has derived from tacit acceptance of the view that the modern economy is an autonomous realm lacking any kind of religious-symbolic grounding or relevance. During the 1970s and 1980s, however, renewed interest was generated in the religious foundations of economic life. The idea of the autonomy of economic life and action, as characteristically expressed in the work of professional economists, was strongly challenged, and religious organizations and movements became increasingly concerned about economic issues. Weber's work hovers explicitly or implicitly in the background of much of the contemporary interest in the relationship between religion and economics.

THE MODERN WORLD. While Weber was clearly conscious of the extent to which nineteenth-century entrepreneurial capitalism was itself being transformed, not least through the expansion of the modern bureaucratic state, his work on religion and economic life has primary relevance to the growth or lack of growth of classical, as opposed to what is now often called late, or advanced, capitalism. Moreover, Weber's work touched little, if at all, upon one of the most significant ingredients of modern economic life, particularly in capitalist societies—consumerism. Weber, as has been emphasized, was interested in the development of entrepreneurial asceticism (an asceticism that, for him, had become freed of its original religious mooring). In contemporary language he was concerned with the origins of the work ethic. However, a more hedonistic dimension of economic culture is to be found in the odyssey of capitalism. Certainly the value placed upon the accumulation of consumer goods is central to the modern form of capitalism. An interest in consumerism has led some social scientists—notably anthropologists—to attempt to lay bare the symbolic basis of patterns of consumption. That is, some analysts have become increasingly concerned with the underlying meanings that are produced and distributed by the advertising, purchase, and display of consumer goods. While not specifically involving the study of religion, this relatively new focus is part of a growing tendency to situate the study of economic behavior and institutions in a broader sociocultural context.

Among the more important specific developments that suggest a return to the thorough investigation of the relationship between religion and economic matters are these: the rapid economic growth in the second half of the twentieth century in societies, such as Japan, Taiwan, South Korea, and

Singapore, with religious traditions—sometimes called Neo-Confucian—that do not clearly conform to the Weberian image of Calvinist Protestantism; the emergence in the same period of religious movements, many of them inspired by forms of liberation theology, which stress the importance of linking economic ideas with theological ideas and religious practices; and the general problem of the global economy.

The capitalist world system. In fact these three phenomena discussed above are closely related, with the third probably being the most important. In the tradition largely initiated by Weber, the primary concern has been to connect the comparative economic success of societies (and of groups and regions within societies) with forms of religio-cultural tradition and religious commitment. But a contrasting approach, called world-system theory, has arisen out of the increasing awareness that the world constitutes a single sociocultural system, and that the affairs of particular societies, groups, and regions are inextricably bound up with it. In one of its most influential forms, the theory maintains that the modern world system is largely the result of the growth of capitalism and that the system should be understood as a primarily economic phenomenon. According to this view, the capitalist world system, which had its earliest beginnings in Europe some five hundred years ago, has spread to the point that it now embraces the entire world.

In the version developed by Immanuel Wallerstein, who has placed himself in the Marxist tradition, world-system theory reverses the priority that Weber's work gives to religion, for Wallerstein regards the religious cleavages that occurred in sixteenth-century Europe as consequences of the placement of societies in the nascent world economy. Specifically, he argues that those societies that became predominantly Protestant were the core societies of the embryonic world capitalist system, while those that remained or became Catholic were "peripheral" societies whose major economic function was the supply of raw materials to the dominant manufacturing centers. (Subsequently, as the world system expanded so as to become literally a worldwide system, those early peripheral units of the system became semiperipheral, insofar as they were economically situated between the core capitalist centers of economic domination and the peripheral societies of the world.)

Influence of religion. Thus, in the perspective of the school of thought largely led by Wallerstein, religion has played a significant, but nonetheless epiphenomenal, part in the making of the modern global system. It has, in other words, played an important ideological role, in the Marxist sense of ideology as the form in which inequality and exploitation are presented as justified. To a considerable extent this argument constitutes the highwater mark of the economistic view that everything in human life can be reduced to and explained by economic factors. Yet, in its very extremeness, it has stimulated what promises to be a constructive reaction in the form of a reassessment of the relationship between religion and economic life. In other words, just as the view, promoted by Marx and Engels, that individual societies are driven by conflicts attendant upon economic motivations stimulated the rich, if controversial, attempts by Weber to show that under certain circumstances religion could be a critical factor in sociocultural change, so the view of the entire world as governed by the dynamics of economic motivations and relationships is stimulating new ways of thinking about the economic significance of religion.

Talcott Parsons. A major example of such thinking, although not a direct reaction to the materialist form of world-system theory, is to be found in the work of Talcott Parsons. Greatly influenced by Weber, whose *The Protestant Ethic and the Spirit of Capitalism* he translated (1930), Parsons devoted much of his academic career to the question of what others have called the degree of embeddedness of economic life. At the center of his thinking in this regard is the general proposition that while economic activity is essential to human life, it is neither fully determining nor fully determined. Nonetheless, Parsons acknowledged that at certain points in history the economic realm has appeared to be particularly significant. Thus he attended to the various ways in which this apparent significance has been interpreted. Indeed, one of his main interests was the way in which the modern discipline of economics arose as one reaction among others to the cultural thematization of the idea that the economic realm is the central and most problematic realm of human existence. Specifically, Parsons examined the relationship between the responses to this idea and the industrial revolution that began in certain Western societies in the second half of the eighteenth century.

In this regard Parsons circumvented the perennial question of whether the economic or "material" aspects of life are more or less important than the "ideal" aspects. While conceding the great importance of the economic aspects, he tried to show that the ways in which they are interpreted and symbolized are of no less importance. The perception of economic autonomy yielded a number of different religious or quasi-religious interpretations, two of which carried it to the point of economic determinism. These were classical economics as it developed in the wake of the writings of Adam Smith and the particular socialist tradition initiated by Marx. Parsons regarded these economistic responses to the industrial revolution as being themselves quasi-religious in nature, for they carried with them sets of ideas concerning the nature and meaning of human existence. He proposed the important idea that nothing in social life is or can be purely economic.

Economic change. Wallerstein's world-system theory, it should be emphasized, originated as a direct response to the modernization theories of the 1950s and 1960s, which owed much to the writing of Weber on the relationship between religious and economic change. New life was given to Weber's work by the widespread concern with the economic gap between established societies, particularly those of the industrial West, and those that had won their independence during the wave of decolonization of the late 1950s and the 1960s. Many social scientists tried to account for disparities in economic circumstances and growth rates by assessing the degree to which religion encouraged or discouraged involvement in economic enterprise and the development of a work ethic.

A strong tendency among modernization theorists in the 1950s and 1960s was to maintain that cultural change, sometimes expressed more specifically as religious change, was a prerequisite of economic change, and that the mainly non-Christian societies of the world (as well as most of the Catholic Christian ones) needed either a Protestant ethic or its functional equivalent as a motivational base for engaging in economic activites that would produce economic growth. This was not at all an original idea, because, as has been seen, during the nineteenth century the claim that Protestantism in its Calvinist version encouraged commitment to enterprise and work had been quite widespread. Indeed in Latin America during that period it was not uncommon for the political leaders of newly independent states to encourage the spread of Protestantism in the hope that it would yield economic growth in the face of the dominant, largely anticapitalist Catholic ethos.

World-system theory achieved prominence largely because of its opposition to the view that poor societies can achieve prosperity by their own internal efforts (even if this means the importation of new cultural and religious forms). In place of this internalist conception of societal change, the theory afforded a basically externalist conception, one that regarded the position of individual societies in the world economic system as almost entirely the consequence of the character of the system as a whole. Rather than attributing economic growth or lack of growth to indigenous, including religious, characteristics, world-system theory maintained that the economic fates of individual societies are determined by the functioning and expansion of a capitalist world system (in which even internally socialistic societies are constrained to act capitalistically in their relations with other societies).

World as a whole. Even though a number of critical weaknesses have been exposed in this argument, there can be little doubt that it is to the world as a whole that one must now look in considering many of the most important questions about the relationship between economic and religious factors in modern life. One major example of this is the development of liberation theology, most conspicuously in Latin America. Latin American liberation theology, which has counterparts on all other continents, grew in part from a perspective on the world as a whole that is closely related to Marxist world-system theory. Dependency theory developed in Latin America in the 1960s in opposition to the view that the relatively backward economic state of Latin America should be attributed, inter alia, to its fatalistic Catholicism. Rather, it was argued, Latin America's condition was to be largely explained by its dependent status in relation to affluent countries, in particular the United States, whose very advantages were made possible by the economic underdevelopment of Third World societies. In combination with that perspective on the world system some leaders of the liberationist movement effected what during the late 1960s seemed an unlikely fusion of Christian theology and Marxist ideology, thus to a significant degree violating the traditional Marxist view that religion is, at least in the modern world, an enemy of socialist revolution. There is much debate as to the degree to which this fusion of Christian ideas concerning the achievement of the kingdom of God upon earth and the liberation of religious consciousness with Marxist ideas concerning the fundamentality of economic forces and relationships is simply a marriage of strategic convenience rather than a genuine synthesis. Nonetheless, the degree to which religion and politics, more specifically theology and ideology, have been recently combined among Marxist-tinged liberationist movements, as well as in movements often labeled as fundamentalist (ranging from Christian fundamentalism in the United States to Islamic fundamentalism in the Middle East), is very striking. Many such developments can best be understood in reference to the fact that the conspicuousness and evident fatefulness of the global economy (whether one calls it capitalistic or something else) elicits specific responses from movements, societies, regions, and so on, involving attempts to imbue the world order and its parts with some kind of symbolic meaning, such as the legitimation of privileged economic circumstances (what Weber called the theodicy of good fortune) or the attempt to overcome underprivileged conditions. In any case it is evident that the very different projections by Marx and Weber of a modern world without religion, which would allegedly yield to the force of economic interests and processes, have not yet been realized.

What thus has changed most of all since the period in which Weber wrote extensively about the economic ethics of the major religions is the highly conspicuous emergence of the global economy. This process has increasingly forced religions—more specifically, leaders of religious movements and organizations—to confront the economy and its appurtenances (such as materialism and consumerism) much more comprehensively than heretofore. Thus the original Weberian interest in the way in which religions differentially encourage or inhibit economic progress has been enlarged and refocused.

This is to be seen particularly in the case of Islam. Assisted in no small part by the economic circumstance of the world coming to depend so much, directly or indirectly, on the rich deposits of oil in a number of Islamic countries, Islam has reasserted itself in defiance of the West. In the process, many questions have been raised, both within Islamic contexts and by observers of it, as to whether the relative economic backwardness of Islamic societies in recent centuries has issued from inherent characteristics of Islam as a religious tradition, at one extreme, or from the subordinate position of Islamic societies in relation to those of West, at the other.

Weber's writings on Islam suggest strongly that it inhibited the growth of the instrumental rationality necessary for the emergence of a modern economic orientation, but that view is resisted by those who maintain that much of what appears, in Weber's terms, to be inimical to modern economic rationality is actually the consequence of Islamic culture's adaption to a subordinate politico-economic situation. Some scholars have argued that capitalism would have developed in Islamic societies but for this situation. Others have maintained that Islam is inherently more conducive to a socialist economic system, and that that is precisely what is developing in the modern period. In any case, unlike such societies as Britain and the United States, which led the way into, and in a sense created, the modern global economy, Islam, which not so many centuries ago was itself a dominant civilization, is currently engaged in a self-conscious, traumatic attempt to formulate very explicitly its economic ethics or, more generally, its economic culture. The self-conscious formulation of economic ethics or culture is also occurring to varying degrees in a number of other major religious contexts. Whether this will lead to a reunion of economics and religion of the kind that has prevailed in different patterns throughout most of human history remains to be seen.

See Also Marx, Karl; Modernity; Money; Political Theology; Revolution; Secularization; Troeltsch, Ernst; Wealth; Weber, Max.

Bibliography

Max Weber's major writings on religion and economic issues are available in the following English translations: *The Protestant Ethic and the Spirit of Capitalism* (1930; New York, 1977), *Economy and Society,* vol. 1 (Berkeley, Calif., 1978), *Ancient Judaism* (1952; New York, 1967), *The Religion of China* (1951; New York, 1968), *The Religion of India* (Glencoe, Ill., 1958); and *General Economic History* (1927; New Brunswick, N.J., 1981). A valuable exegesis of Weber's thesis about the economic consequences of Protestantism is Gordon Marshall's *In Search of the Spirit of Capitalism* (New York, 1982). Weber's sociology of religion in a more general sense is adumbrated, in comparison with the views of Marx and others, in my "Max Weber and German Sociology of Religion," in *Nineteenth Century Religious Thought in the West,* edited by Ninian Smart et al., vol. 3 (Cambridge, U.K., 1985), pp. 263–304. Weber's scattered writings on Islam are brought critically together in Bryan S. Turner's *Weber and Islam* (London, 1974). A very useful set of essays on Weber's ideas about economics in relation to religious change is to be found in *The Protestant Ethic and Modernization,* edited by Shmuel N. Eisenstadt (New York, 1968).

The French tradition of positive evaluation of religion in relation to economic factors is exemplified in Émile Durkheim's *Socialism,* translated by Charlotte Sattler and edited by Alvin Gouldner (New York, 1962), and in Durkheim's *The Elementary Forms of the Religious Life,* translated by Joseph Ward Swain (1915; New York, 1965). See also my essay "The Development and Modern Implications of the Classical Sociological Perspective on Religion and Revolution," in *Religion, Rebellion, Revolution,* edited by Bruce Lincoln (New York, 1985), pp. 236–265. A useful survey of Marxist theories of religions is contained in Delos B. McKown's *The Classical Marxist Critiques of Religion* (The Hague, 1975). Also relevant to understanding the late nineteenth- and early twentieth-century posing of issues regarding religion and economics is Ernst Troeltsch's *The Social Teaching of the Christian Churches,* 2 vols., translated by Olive Wyon (1931; Chicago, 1981).

Talcott Parsons's important writings on economic and religious factors are exemplified by his "Christianity and Modern Industrial Society," in *Sociological Theory, Values, and Socio-Cultural Change: Essays in Honor of Pitrim A. Sorokin,* edited by Edward A. Tiryakian (New York, 1963), pp. 33–70, and "Religious and Economic Symbolism in the Western World," *Sociological Inquiry* 49 (1979): 1–48. Immanuel Wallerstein's basic ideas are to be encountered in his *The Modern World-System* (New York, 1974). For the relation between religion and the world system, see my chapter, "The Sacred and the World System," in *The Sacred in a Secular Age,* edited by Phillip E. Hammond (Berkeley, 1985), pp. 347–457. For liberation theology, see my essay "Liberation Theology in Latin America," in *Prophetic Religion and Politics,* edited by Jeffrey Hadden and Anton Shupe (New York, 1987), pp. 107–139.

Finally, on more general questions of the varying significance of the economic factor, see Karl Polanyi's *The Great Transformation* (New York, 1944), Marshall D. Sahlins's *Culture and Practical Reason* (Chicago, 1976), Chandra Mukerji's *From Graven Images: Patterns of Modern Materialism* (New York, 1983), and Jürgen Habermas's *Legitimation Crisis,* translated by Thomas McCarthy (Boston, 1975).

New Sources

Dean, James, and A. M. C. Waterman. *Religion and Economics: Normative Social Theory.* Boston, 1999.

Graeber, David. *Toward an Anthropology of Value: The False Coin of Our Own Dreams.* New York, 2001.

Howell, Martha C. *The Marriage Exchange: Property, Social Place, and Gender in Cities of the Low Countries, 1300–1550.* Chicago, 1998.

Knitter, Paul, and Chandra Muzaffar. *Subverting Greed: Religious Perspectives on the Global Economy.* Maryknoll, N.Y., 2002.

Long, D. Stephen. *Theology and the Market.* Routledge Radical Orthodoxy series. London, 2000.

Mazu, Eric, and Kate McCarthy, eds. *God in the Details: American Religion in Popular Culture.* New York, 2001.

Neusner, Jacob. *Religious Belief and Economic Behavior in Ancient Israel, Classical Christianity, Islam, and Judaism, and Contemporary Ireland and Africa.* Atlanta, 1999.

Silver, Morris, ed. *Ancient Economy in Mythology: East and West.* Savage, Md., 1991.

Roland Robertson (1987)
Revised Bibliography

ECSTASY. The term *ecstasy* (Gr., *ekstasis*) literally means "to be placed outside," as well as, secondarily, "to be displaced." Both senses are relevant to the study of religion, the first more than the second perhaps, inasmuch as it denotes a state of exaltation in which one stands outside or transcends oneself. Transcendence has often been associated or even equated with religion. If such an understanding of ecstasy carries the historian of religion into the hinterland of mysticism, the second sense, involving as it does spirit possession and shamanism, carries one to the borderland of anthropology and even psychiatry. The vast range of phenomena covered by the term supports the adoption of an approach toward its understanding that uses a variety of methods, one of which, the philological, has already been engaged. *Ecstasy* can thus mean both the seizure of one's body by a spirit and the seizure of a human by a divinity. Although seemingly in opposition, the two senses are not mutually exclusive, and between them lies the vast and diverse range of phenomena covered by the umbrella term *ecstasy*, with the magician standing at one end of the spectrum and the psychiatrist at the other. The historian of religion tries to grasp the significance of the intervening terrain with the help of historical, anthropological, phenomenological, sociological, psychological, and philosophical approaches to the study of religion.

HISTORICAL APPROACH. Ecstatic techniques reach back to prehistoric times; utilizing the principle of survivals, the historian can reconstruct these techniques by extrapolating from the role of shamans in modern primal societies. In the realm of history proper, the mystery religions that flourished in the Greco-Roman world, such as those celebrated at Eleusis and those centering on Orpheus, Adonis, Attis, Isis and Osiris, Mithra, and others, provide examples of the role of ecstasy in religion. The emphasis on secrecy in these cults makes it difficult to delineate the exact role played by ecstasy in their rituals, but those rituals are generally believed to have led to ecstatic states that signified salvific union with their deities. Elements of ecstasy are not absent in Israelite religion, where groups or individuals were seized by the spirit of Yahveh; the case of Saul is often cited in this respect (*1 Sm.* 10:1–16).

It is significant that even the phenomenological approach to ecstasy, though it does not divorce the ecstasy of the shaman from communion with spirits, does point out that the "specific element of shamanism is not the incorporation of spirits in the shaman, but the ecstasy provoked by the ascension to the sky or by the descent to Hell" (Eliade, cited in Lewis, 1971, p. 49); the descent of Jesus into hell and his ascent to heaven, according to the Athanasian Creed, provide a rudimentary parallel to shamanistic ecstasy. Even when spirits are associated with the work of the shaman, the parallel persists. In *Revelation*, for instance, it is ecstasy that rules from the first moment: "I was in the Spirit on the Lord's Day, and I heard behind me a loud voice like a trumpet saying, 'Write what you see in a book'" (1:10–11). John turns to "see the voice," whereupon he sees seven lampstands and, in the middle of them, "one like a son of man": "When I saw him, I fell at his feet as though dead" (1:17). Later we are told how John saw an open door in heaven, and he heard a voice saying, "Come up hither, and I will show you what must take place after this" (4:1). John responds, or something within him responds: "At once I was in the Spirit" (4:2). Again he looked, saw, and heard. Another example may be provided from a later chapter of *Revelation*: "And he carried me away in the Spirit into a wilderness, and I saw a woman sitting on a scarlet beast" (17:3). Finally there is the vision of the New Jerusalem: "And in the Spirit he carried me away to a great, high mountain, and showed me the holy city Jerusalem coming down out of heaven from God" (21:10). Many religious traditions chart the path to ecstasy with precision and sophistication. Hinduism speaks of the various steps of Yoga leading to *samādhi*; Buddhism speaks of *jhānas* and *nirvāṇa*; Christianity speaks of the mystical way; and Islam speaks of the hal and maqam, or states and stations en route to divine knowledge (an imagery that may be compared to the "mansions" of Teresa of Ávila), as well as of wajd ("ecstasy").

ANTHROPOLOGICAL APPROACH. The anthropological approach emphasizes the role of the shaman and the phenomenon of possession in both prehistoric and contemporary preliterate societies. *Shaman* is a widely used term, the "lowest common denominator of which is that of the inspired priest" (Eliade, cited in Lewis, 1971, p. 49). In the anthropological approach, it is the shaman's role as a psychopomp that is preeminent. Through an ability to achieve a state of ecstatic exaltation, acquired after much rigorous training and careful, often painful initiation, the shaman is able to establish contact with the spirit world. In the course of this exaltation, the shaman may affect the postmortem fate of the deceased, aid or hurt the diseased in this life, as well as encounter the occupants of the spirit world, communicate with them, and then narrate the experiences of ecstatic flight on his or her return from there.

PHENOMENOLOGICAL APPROACH. It must be remembered, however, that while all shamans are ecstatics, all ecstatics are not shamans. Taking a broader phenomenological approach, one discovers that a variety of means, such as dancing, drugs, self-mortification, and so on, have been used across cultures and at various times to induce ecstasy and that these have generated ecstatic states ranging from the shamanistic to the mystical. If the first step of the phenomenological method is to classify, then one may employ Plato's distinction between "two types of mantic or 'prophecy', the first the *mantikē entheos*, the 'inspired madness' of the ecstatic, e.g. that of the Pythia; the second the systematic interpretation of signs, such as the augury of the flight of birds" (van der Leeuw, vol. 1, 1938, p. 225). This last category may be excluded from consideration here as a form of soothsaying. A further distinction has to be made between shamanistic and mystical ecstasy, with the experience of someone like Saul providing a bridge between the two. As Gerardus van der Leeuw writes: "With the *Shamans*, still further, we find ourselves on the road to the prophets, but of course only in the sense in which Saul too was 'among the prophets', that is as regards the ecstatic frenzy that renders possible a superhuman development of power" (ibid., p. 218). We must therefore consider three categories of ecstasies (and accordingly, ecstatics); they may not always be separable, but they are distinct: the shamanistic ecstasy, the prophetic ecstasy, and the mystical ecstasy. The differences among the three emerge clearly when we consider the nature of ecstatic utterances.

The ecstatic utterances of the shaman relate to the world of the spirits and to the shaman's movements in that realm. Eliade clearly distinguishes between non-shamanic, para-shamanic, and shamanic ecstasy, the characteristic feature of the last being the shaman's ability to communicate with dead or natural spirits. The ecstatic utterances of the prophet relate to God: the prophet literally speaks for God, though there are borderline cases, such as the priestess at the oracle at Delphi whose cryptic utterances had to be interpreted. These may be contrasted with the ecstatic utterances known as *shaṭḥīyāt* in Islamic mysticism; a typical example is provided by al-Ḥallāj's proclamation, "I am the Creative Truth" ("Anā al-ḥaqq"). This highly mystical utterance, which cost him his life, has been explained in later Sufism as resulting from a mistaken sense of identity with God due to God's overwhelming presence in mystical experience (as if a piece of red-hot coal in a furnace would call itself fire or a candle in the sunlight would mistake the light of the sun for its own).

Sociological Approach. The sociology of ecstasy or ecstatic religion, as explored by I. M. Lewis, provides another useful dimension to the topic. This approach relies heavily on the indirect application of the work of Émile Durkheim and Max Weber. Following Durkheim, Lewis draws attention to the socially integrative function of the shaman who, at ritual services, instills in the people a sense of solidarity by emphasizing the shunning of adultery, homicide, and other socially disruptive practices, and who often plays an active role in settling disputes. At the same time, however, the study of ecstasy also exposes the limitations of Durkheim's approach in certain contexts: the cultivation of ecstasy, especially in mysticism, may lead to a breach within a religious tradition instead of playing an integrating role in it. Thus, Sufism was viewed with suspicion by Islamic orthodoxy until the two were reconciled by al-Ghazālī. A more Weberian approach views the shaman as discovering through his ecstatic flights the reasons for whatever may have befallen his client, providing the client with "meaning," which according to Weber is one role of religion. Moreover, a subtler application of the Weberian approach makes further generalizations possible. Thus, according to the relative-deprivation theory, secret ecstatic cults may flourish particularly among women or dispossessed groups in patriarchal or authoritarian societies. This may be as true of women dancing ecstatically in Dionysian rituals in Greece in the fifth century BCE as it is in the *zār* cult in Sudan in modern times.

Another issue raised by the sociological approach to the study of religion is the role of ecstasy in societies that are in the process of secularization. Two views seem to prevail. One is to look upon the cultivation of cultic ecstasy as possessing cathartic value in a society undergoing rapid social change. A broader view suggests that the process of secularization does not so much do away with the need for transcendence as it provides surrogates for it. A convergence exists between the sociology of religion, which maintains that there are religious phenomena that belong to no determined religion, and the Tillichian theological viewpoint, which maintains that, though modern people think they have overcome their need for ultimate concern or transcendence, what has really happened is that they continue to seek it in secular contexts (as, for instance, in ecstatic participation in football matches). It may be further added that ecstasy is by definition an extraordinary experience that transcends routine, so that the increasing bureaucratization of modern life may impel the sort of person that Eliade called *homo religiosus* to seek such ecstasy all the more. It has been speculatively suggested, for instance, that the evidence in Indus Valley culture of yogic practices possibly possessing an ecstatic dimension may reflect that culture's highly organized, homogeneous, even monotonous appearance.

Psychological Approach. Various approaches to ecstasy have been discussed so far but, inasmuch as ecstasy is essentially concerned with the mind (or what lies beyond the mind), one might expect the psychology of religion to prove the most illuminating. The psychology of religion, however, is a discipline with boundaries that are difficult to define strictly; this is even more true when it is applied to a subject like ecstasy, which the psychology of religion itself approaches with methods that can vary from the transpersonal to the psychiatric. Thus, one must distinguish clearly among certain approaches within the psychology of religion: the psychoanalytical approach, the pharmacological approach, and the mystical approach.

The psychoanalytical approach has been applied to ecstasy at two levels, the shamanistic and the mystical. Claude Lévi-Strauss has argued that the cure administered by the shaman—who, unlike the modern analyst listening to the patient's words, speaks out on behalf of the patient—involves "the inversion of all the elements" of psychoanalysis yet retains its analogy with it. J. M. Masson sees in the ecstatic, oceanic feelings of the mystic a reversion to the experience of the fetus in the womb.

Modern developments in pharmacology have brought what might be called chemical ecstasy into the limelight. Drug-induced ecstasy was not unknown in ancient times. The *soma* of the Vedas, which R. Gordon Wasson identified with the mushroom called the *Amanita muscaria*, was supposed to be one such drug; it has even been suggested that techniques of yogic ecstatic trances were developed in post-Vedic Hinduism as a substitute for the *soma*-induced trances once the Aryans moved deeper into India and lost contact with the geographical source of the mushroom. Mexico provides another example of the religious use of drug-induced ecstasy in the peyote cult, which Aldous Huxley popularized in a modern version through his experiments with mescaline. But it was the discovery of LSD (lysergic acid diethylamide) that threw the door wide open to this avenue to ecstasy, with its open advocacy by modern experimenters such as Timothy Leary and Alan Watts.

Modern psychology tends to dismiss these experiences as chemically and artifically induced and therefore not genuine. Such a dismissive approach is difficult for a historian of religion to countenance; drugs can be the means to, rather than the cause of, these ecstasies. But the fact that such chemical experiences are not always ecstatic should not be overlooked; neither should the widespread assertion that drug-induced ecstasy may be distinguished from mystical experience primarily because the drug does not usually transform the personality and the subsequent life of the user, and that mystical experience usually does. Psychedelic drugs can be used not merely to induce ecstasy but also to gain power, a fact mentioned by Patañjali in his *Yoga Sūtra* and illustrated in the contemporary writings of anthropologist Carlos Castaneda.

For many, the classical focus of the discussion of ecstasy is still provided by mysticism, notwithstanding the elaboration of the role of archaic and chemical techniques in this context. Mysticism, for our purposes, may be conveniently defined as the doctrine or belief that a direct knowledge or immediate perception of the ultimate reality, or God, is possible in a way different from normal sense experience and ratiocination. The two channels in which the mystical tradition of mankind has flowed are thus naturally identified by emotion and intuition. The ecstatic experience resulting from them has been distinguished accordingly as "communion" in the first case, in which the devotee, though psychologically merged in God, remains a distinct entity, and as "union" in the second case, in which the aspirant achieves an ontological identity with God. The distinction is crucial to an understanding of mystical ecstasy: in the first case, access to the ultimate reality is "gained"; that is, it is something that originally did not exist; in the second case, access to the reality is "regained"; that is, it is something that always existed but was not recognized until the moment of ecstasy. Martin Buber's distinction between I-Thou and I-It relationships is relevant here. Some traditions recognize the existence of both these types of mysticism. The Hindu mystic Ramakrishna (1836–1886) contrasts the two ecstasies as offering a choice between "tasting sugar" and "becoming sugar," without insisting that the two be viewed as mutually exclusive.

Ecstasy in the Hindu tradition is basically experienced in three modes: nontheistic, theistic, and trans-theistic. In the nontheistic mode, it results from the suppression of all mental modifications; because of its restriction to the person of the practitioner and the absence of any outside referent, R. C. Zaehner refers to this mode as *enstasy*: "By 'enstasy' I understand that introverted mystical experience in which there is experience of nothing except an unchanging, purely static oneness. It is the exact reverse of ecstasy which means to get outside oneself and which is often characterized by a breaking down of the barriers between the individual subject and the universe around him" (*The Bhagavad-Gītā*, London, 1973, p. 143). Although the *Yoga Sūtra*, to which Zaehner's statement applies, also recognizes the existence of God, the theistic mode of ecstasy that flows from the love of God is best described in the *Bhakti Sūtra*: "It is as if a dumb man who has tasted a delicious food could not speak about it." The ecstasy experienced through the transtheistic or absolutistic mode in Hinduism is similarly considered ineffable because, in it, the distinction between the one who experiences and the experienced is annulled. Thus one is left with the Upanisadic paradox of the experience of the Absolute: "But where everything has become just one's own self, then whereby and whom would one see?" (*Bṛhadāraṇyaka Up.* 4.5.15). Does Meister Eckhart provide an answer to the question when he says "The eye with which I see God is the same with which God sees me"?

The Islamic mystical tradition emphasizes the passing away of individuality in God (*fanā'*), who alone represents divine unity *(tawḥīd);* this loss of self into God provides the experience of inward ecstasy. In Islamic mystical poetry wine symbolizes the "ecstatic experience due to the revelation of the True Beloved, destroying the foundations of reason" (Arberry, 1950, p. 114). Such ecstatic experience of God constitutes the ecstatic's knowledge of God (*ma'rifah*).

In Buddhism ecstasy plays an important role in the trances; the typical text of the first trance runs as follows: "Detached from sensual objects, O monks, detached from unwholesome states of mind, the monk enters into the first absorption, which is accompanied by Thought-Conception [*vitakka*] and Discursive Thinking [*vicāra*], is born of Detachment [Concentration: *samādhi*] and filled with Rapture [*pīti*] and Joy " (*Dīgha Nikāya* 1.182). It should be added, however, that in the fifth stage, ecstasy gives way to equanimity, and the final attainment of *nirvāṇa* is characterized not by ecstasy but by knowledge and bliss.

In Christian mysticism too, ecstasy plays a key role. We see it in the statement of John Cassian (360–435) that "by constant meditation on things divine and spiritual contemplation . . . the soul is caught up into . . . an ecstasy." It is at the heart of the fourteenth-century text *The Cloud of Unknowing*:

> God wishes to be served with both the body and the spirit together, as is proper, and He will give man his reward in bliss both in body and in soul. In giving that reward, He sometimes inflames the body of His devout servants with wonderful pleasures here in this life, not only once or twice, but very often in some cases as He may wish. Of these pleasures not all come into the body from outside through the windows of our senses, but come from within, rising and springing up out of an abundance of spiritual gladness and out of true devotion of spirit. (cited in Progoff, 1957, pp. 172–173)

It may be noted that, here as in other instances, ecstasy is not divorced from knowledge of God, and the text spells out stages for its attainment. In Christian mysticism, as in other forms of mysticism (especially theistic), different stages are delineated, perhaps the best known being the passage of the soul to God, first through the illuminative, second the purgative, and finally the unitive ways.

The Cross-Cultural Approach. Following Gershom Scholem's study of Jewish mysticism, we can ask why ecstatic experiences take particular forms constrained by each individual culture. Why, for instance, did Teresa of Ávila not have ecstatic visions of Kālī? The Hindu mystic Ramakrishna is said to have had visions of figures outside Hinduism, but he is known to have been somewhat familiar with the traditions in question. Yet C. G. Jung argued that some of his clients gave evidence of certain archetypal ecstatic visions that transcend the bounds of time and space. The role of depth psychology in uncovering the roots of ecstasy, it seems, has yet to be fully explored; the same is true of the other extreme, the physical symptoms accompanying the states of ecstasy. In ecstasies of the shamanistic and prophetic type the hypothalamus has been shown to become inactive so that people in trance become impervious to physical maltreatment or deprivation, though they still respond to speech and social communication. In ecstasies of the mystical type, signs of life have been known to fade, sometimes to the point of apparent disappearance.

Humanistic psychologists such as Abraham H. Maslow have taken some interest in ecstasy in its relation to the concept of peak experience. This interest is even more evident in Ernst Arbman's monumental work, *Ecstasy or Religious Trance* (1963–1970). In this psychological study of ecstasy, Arbman emphasizes the close relation between ecstasy and mystical experience and, within mysticism, between ecstasy and visionary experience. He classifies the latter as assuming three forms, which represents a trichotomy of medieval Christian mysticism traceable to Augustine: corporeal, imaginative, and intellectual. These three forms may be instantiated, respectively, by the experiences of the prophet Muḥammad in receiving the Qurʾān through an angel, some of the experiences of Teresa of Ávila, and the recorded experiences of Ignatius Loyola and Jakob Boehme. The distinction between these three forms of ecstatic visionary experience—the corporeal, the imaginative, and the intellectual—is said to lie in the fact that, while the first experience is felt as something actually or objectively perceived, in the second case it is something experienced only inwardly, in a psychic or spiritual sense. The third type of vision, in which the sense of the word *intellectual* seems to correspond more to Platonic than to modern usage, apprehends its object without any image or form.

How might we establish the genuineness of the experiences represented by this classification, even if the existence of a mystical realm is granted, and even if it is further accepted that the pathological state of mind might be the most receptive for such experiences? Or, to broaden the scale of skepticism, how do we know that the shaman's journeys do in fact occur? The phenomenologist of religion is disinclined to ask such questions, as are the followers of some other disciplines, but the historian of religion cannot choose to ignore them since almost every tradition concerned with ecstatic experience has provided evaluative criteria for distinguishing between genuine and spurious experience. More generally, what is the role of the philosophy of religion in ecstatic experiences? This is a thorny issue, complicated by a fundamental epistemological problem: philosophers use reason in order to know, but ecstatics reason because they know. And yet a philosophical approach to ecstasy still seems possible if two factors are taken into account: an ecstasy, however prolonged, is usually a temporary state, and it can be experienced by religious mystics and nonreligious mystics alike.

Duration and Efficacy. The duration of the ecstatic trance is variable. William James regarded transience as one of the four marks of the mystic state, but allowed only for "half an hour, or at most an hour or two." On the other hand, according to the Hindu mystical tradition, an ecstatic trance can be so profound that one does not recover from it at all. One reads of mystics who remained in a state of trance for six hours (Teresa of Ávila), three days (Ramakrishna), five days (Ellina von Crevelsheim), and even six months (again, Ramakrishna). Moreover, not merely mystics per se but also otherwise intellectually or aesthetically gifted persons have experienced ecstasy. Rabindranath Tagore describes one such experience:

> I suddenly felt as if some ancient mist had in a moment lifted from my sight and the ultimate significance of all things was laid bare. . . . I found that facts that had been detached and dim had a great unity of meaning, as if a man groping through a fog suddenly discovers that he stands before his own house. . . . An unexpected train of thought ran across my mind like a strange caravan carrying the wealth of an unknown kingdom. . . . Immediately I found the world bathed in a wonderful radiance with waves of beauty and joy swelling on every side, and no person or thing in the world seemed to me trivial or unpleasing. (cited in Walker, 1968, p. 475)

This passage raises a vital issue: if ordinary mortals can experience ecstasy along with the great mystics, and if ecstasies are terminable, then what do the great religious traditions of the world ultimately have to offer by way of salvation? If the answer is ecstatic union and ecstasy is a temporary phenomenon, then how lasting are the results of the spiritual path? Must one follow it to experience ecstasy?

The answer is not entirely clear, but both the theistic and nontheistic mystical traditions have approached an answer by asking whether ecstasy and union (in a mystical context) are identical. For Plotinus the two are one:

> For then nothing stirred within him, neither anger, nor desire, nor even reason, nor a certain intellectual perception, nor, in short, was he himself moved, if we may assert this; but, being in an ecstasy, tranquil and alone with God, he enjoyed an unbreakable calm. (Plotinus, *Enneads* 6.9)

For Teresa of Ávila, ecstasy and union are not identical:

> I wish I could explain with the help of God wherein union differs from rapture, or from transport, or from flight of the spirit, as they call it, or from trance, which are all one. I mean that all these are only different names for that *one and the same thing, which is also called ecstasy.* It is more excellent than union, the fruits of it are much greater, and its other operations more manifold, for union is uniform in the beginning, the middle and the end, and is so also interiorly; but as raptures have ends of a much higher kind, they produce effects both within and without (i. e., both physical and psychical). . . . A rapture is absolutely irresistible; whilst union, inasmuch as we are then on our own ground, may be hindered, though that resistance be painful and violent. (Teresa of Ávila, *Life* 20.1–3)

Apart from the question of whether, in either the theistic or nontheistic context, ecstasy represents union, and if so, to what extent and degree, there is a further question: does such ecstatic union constitute the summation of religious experience? There seems to be some difference of opinion on this point. Thus, according to W. R. Inge,

> Ecstasy was for Plotinus the culminating point of religious experience, whereby the union with God and perfect knowledge of Divine truth, which are the conclusion and achievement of the dialectical process and the ultimate goal of the moral will, are realized also in direct, though ineffable, experience. Plotinus enjoyed this supreme initiation four times during the period when Porphyry was with him; Porphyry himself only once, he tells us, when he was in his 68th year. It was a vision of the Absolute, 'the One', which being above even intuitive thought, can only be apprehended passively by a sort of Divine illapse into the expectant soul. It is not properly a vision, for the seer no longer distinguishes himself from that which he sees; indeed, it is impossible to speak of them as two, for the spirit, during the ecstasy, has been completely one with the One. This 'flight of the alone to the Alone' is a rare and transient privilege, even for the greatest saint. He who enjoys it 'can only say that he has all his desire, and that he would not exchange his bliss for all the heaven of heavens'. (Inge, 1912, p. 158)

Yet when we turn to other religious traditions, the culmination of the religious life seems to be distinguished not so much by a transient, if repeatable, ecstatic union as by a blissful state of being. The final goal of a Christian existence, for example, is the "eternal life" of the beatific vision or the kingdom of God, and not transient ecstasies; and the final goal of Buddhism is the attainment of the lasting happiness of *nirvāṇa*, which is attained for good, unlike the temporary ecstasies of the trances.

> Even the word 'happiness' (*sukha*) which is used to describe Nirvāṇa has an entirely different sense here. Sāriputta once said: 'O friend, Nirvāṇa is happiness! Nirvāṇa is happiness!' Then Udāyi asked: 'But, friend Sāriputta, what happiness can it be if there is no sensation?' Sāriputta's reply was highly philosophical and beyond ordinary comprehension: 'That there is no sensation itself is happiness.' (Rahula, 1967, p. 43)

Given the scope and variety of the phenomenon of ecstasy, our approach has been to use a variety of methods. It might then be proper to conclude by raising a methodological point: can or should one's approach to the study of ecstasy be translated into the terms of some other human phenomenon (a method often pejoratively described as "reductionist")? Eliade argues this point:

> Since ecstasy (trance, losing one's soul, losing consciousness) seems to form an integral part of the human condition, just like anxiety, dreams, imagination, etc., we do not deem it necessary to look for its origin in a particular culture or a particular historical moment. As *an experience* ecstasy is a non-historical phenomenon in the sense that it is coextensive with human nature. Only the religious *interpretation* given to ecstasy and the *techniques* designed to prepare it or facilitate it are historically conditioned. That is to say, they are dependent on various cultural contexts, and they change in the course of history. (Eliade, cited in Wavell et al., 1966, p. 243).

Thus, fasting, drugs, meditation, prayer, dancing, and sex have all been used to induce ecstasy in the course of human history.

A dominant trend in the study of religion on this point is reflected in what Charles Davis says of reductionistic explanations in general, which also applies to the explanations of ecstasy. His discussion is entitled "Wherein There Is No Ecstasy," a line from T. S. Eliot that refers not to the absence of ecstasy per se but to its absence in "the mystical dark night of the soul." Davis has this to say:

> There is no difficulty in accepting reductionistic explanations of particular religious beliefs and practices, if such explanations are sufficiently grounded. Every expression of the transcendent is a particular experience. The particularity of the experience is due to non-transcendent factors. Hence, in that particularity, it is open to non-religious explanations. As for a reductionistic explanation of religious faith as such, in my judgment a reductionistic explanation is so little grounded and so patently the result of an inadequate development of the subject who offers it that I do not grant it any degree of probability. But I am not infallible. Despite the certitude of my judgment, the possibility of error and illusion remains. (Davis, 1984, p. 398)

Scholars will no doubt continue to debate the issue of ecstasy, and shamans, prophets, and mystics continue to experience it—if a secularized world will let them do so.

See Also Enthusiasm; Mystical Union in Judaism, Christianity, and Islam; Mysticism; Psychedelic Drugs; Shamanism.

Bibliography

Arberry, A. J. *Sufism: An Account of the Mystics of Islam* (1950). London, 1979.

Arbman, Ernst. *Ecstasy or Religious Trance.* 3 vols. Edited by Åke Hultkrantz. Stockholm, 1963–1970.

Davis, Charles. "Wherein There Is No Ecstasy." *Studies in Religion / Sciences religieuses* 13 (1984): 393–400.

Eliade, Mircea. *Yoga: Immortality and Freedom.* 2d ed. Princeton, 1969.

Eliade, Mircea. *Shamanism: Archaic Techniques of Ecstasy.* Rev. & enl. ed. New York, 1964.

Inge, W. R. "Ecstasy." In *Encyclopaedia of Religion and Ethics,* edited by James Hastings, vol. 5. Edinburgh, 1912.

Leeuw, Gerardus van der. *Religion in Essence and Manifestation,* vol. 1. Translated by J. E. Turner. London, 1938.

Lewis, I. M. *Ecstatic Religion: An Anthropological Study of Spirit Possession and Shamanism.* Harmondsworth, 1971.

Mahadevan, T. M. P. *Outlines of Hinduism.* Bombay, 1956.

Maslow, Abraham. *Religions, Values, and Peak-Experiences.* Columbus, Ohio, 1964.

Nyanatiloka. *Buddhist Dictionary.* Colombo, 1950.

Progoff, Ira, ed. and trans. *The Cloud of Unknowing.* New York, 1957.

Rahula, Walpola. *What the Buddha Taught.* Rev. ed. Bedford, U.K., 1967.

Tart, Charles T., ed. *Altered States of Consciousness: A Book of Readings.* New York, 1969.

Underhill, Evelyn. *Mysticism* (1911). 12th ed. New York, 1961.

Walker, Benjamin. *The Hindu World,* vol. 2. New York, 1968.

Wavell, Stewart, Audrey Butt, and Nina Epton. *Trances.* London, 1966.

Zaehner, R. C. *Zen, Drugs, and Mysticism.* New York, 1972.

ARVIND SHARMA (1987)

ECUMENICAL MOVEMENT.

The long and varied history of Christian ecumenism is reflected in the many definitions attached to the word itself. The Greek *oikoumenē* comes from the noun *oikos* ("house, dwelling") and the verb *oikeō* ("to live, to dwell"). *Oikoumenē,* which is derived from the present passive participle of the verb, suggests the land in which people live or dwell and is usually translated "the inhabited world." The word initially had no theological implications; it was a descriptive term used by the Greeks to describe the world they knew, and later by the Romans to describe the Roman Empire.

Biblical usage of the word *oikoumenē* is sparse. Eight of the fifteen references are found in *Luke* and *Acts,* and with the exception of two references that suggest the Roman empire (*Lk.* 2:1, *Acts* 17:6) and one that may have cosmic import (*Heb.* 2:5), the remaining uses are no more than descriptive references to "the inhabited world" (*Mt.* 24:14; *Lk.* 4:5, 21:26; *Acts* 11:28, 17:31, 19:27, 24:5; *Rom.* 10:18; *Heb.* 1:6; *Rv.* 3:10, 12:9, 16:14).

As the early church extended its geographical boundaries, writers begin to refer to the church throughout the *oikoumenē* as a way of distinguishing it from local assemblies. And when Christians from different locations began to meet together to discuss aspects of belief and discipline, such gatherings began to be referred to as "ecumenical councils," that is, councils having representation from all parts of the *oikoumenē.* Eastern Orthodox churches acknowledge seven ecumenical councils before the Great Schism of 1054, while the Roman Catholic Church also claims as ecumenical subsequent councils in the West, such as the Council of Trent and the two Vatican councils. The Lutheran Formula of Concord (1577) described the early creeds (Apostles', Nicene, and Athanasian) as "ecumenical creeds" because they had been accepted by all branches of the Christian church. The meaning of the word *ecumenical* was thus extended beyond the theologically neutral notion of "the inhabited world" to include both an understanding of the church in its worldwide sense and expressions of belief that have universal ecclesiastical acceptance.

After a period of relative neglect, the word *ecumenical* reappeared in the twentieth century, with new meanings appropriate to a new situation. Many church bodies, disturbed by their divisions from one another, which were made particularly apparent by the competitive nature of nineteenth-century missionary activities, began to look for ways to overcome their diverse histories. Following a world conference of missionary societies in Edinburgh in 1910, the word *ecumenism* began to be used to signify a concern to reunite the divided Christian family. Alongside this concern for unity was a corresponding concern for mission (from *missio,* "a sending forth") to the *oikoumenē.* These twin poles of unity and mission have characterized what has come to be referred to as "the ecumenical movement." However, a broader use of the word *ecumenism* has also emerged to designate an attitude of active goodwill and concern for all peoples. Concerns about world hunger, racism, or political oppression are thus frequently described as "ecumenical concerns" and are often focal points of common action not only among Christians but in conjunction with all people of goodwill.

THE BIRTH OF MODERN ECUMENISM: EDINBURGH, 1910.

The fellowship of those who have been made "one in Christ" has almost always been marred by institutional division. In the earliest Christian literature, the letters of Paul, there are accounts of Paul's attempts to adjudicate between factions bitterly disputing with one another. The church at Corinth was particularly notorious in this regard. The creedal controversies in the early councils were attempts to set boundaries to the faith, and they provided canons for exclusion of heretics as well as inclusion of believers. In 1054 a radical division, the Great Schism, culminated the separation between Eastern and Western Christianity, and in the sixteenth century the Western church was further divided into the many separate denominations that resulted from the Reformation.

It is to the credit of the groups thus divided that they continued to believe that their divisions were "sinful," but not until the nineteenth century, with its missionary advance from Europe and North America to the rest of the world, was the situation recognized as intolerable. The efforts to "make disciples of all nations" (*Mt.* 28:19) was in fact imposing divisions of European origin on newly converted Christians in Asia, Africa, and Latin America in ways that distorted the unity in Christ that the message was supposed to bestow.

It is therefore significant that the first major attempt to begin a healing of the divisions within Christianity originated in the missionary societies. In 1910, a number of missionary societies held a conference in Edinburgh, Scotland, that by common consent is described as the birth of the modern ecumenical movement. The purpose of the conference was to develop a common missionary strategy that would not only avoid the scandal of the past but provide for a more creative and collaborative use of resources in the future.

The Three Streams Flowing from Edinburgh. As delegates to the Edinburgh conference looked ahead, they saw that some kind of structure would be necessary if the goals of the conference were to be accomplished. A continuation committee was established, and by 1921 it was clear that three concerns would need attention, continuing reflection, and structural implementation: (1) the missionary task of the church, (2) the kinds of common service the churches could render to the world even in their divided state, and (3) the doctrinal issues that were responsible for the ongoing divisions.

In response to the first concern, the International Missionary Council was established in 1921 to help various mission boards coordinate their previously separate and competing activities and to hold conferences that would enable members to think in new ways about the church's mission. During its forty-year life, the council held five conferences that dealt with the impact of secularism on the life of the church (Jerusalem, 1928); the relationship of the Christian religion to other world religions (Madras, 1938); the need to see missions as a two-way street on which the so-called younger churches would now be giving as well as receiving (Whitby, 1947); the imperative need for Christian unity, if mission was to retain its credibility (Willingen, 1952); and recognition that the time had come for missionary concern to be related structurally to those Christians already grappling with questions of unity and service (Ghana, 1957). The last conference translated into a decision to merge with the already established World Council of Churches, a decision that was implemented in 1961.

The Edinburgh-inspired concern for the church's common service to the world was embodied in a second structure, called the Commission on Life and Work. Recognizing that organic reunion was years if not light-years away, members of this commission sought to develop a consensus on matters to which divided churches could relate. "Doctrine divides, service unites" became the slogan. The first Conference on Life and Work, held in Stockholm in 1925, was widely representative—over 600 delegates from 37 countries attended and discussed the church's responsibility in such areas as international relations, education, economics, and industry.

A second Conference on Life and Work, held in Oxford in 1937, drew delegates from 40 countries and 120 denominations who discussed church and state, church and community, and the church and its function in society, while small groups dealt with education, the economic order, and the world of nations. Two realities loomed behind the Oxford discussions. One was the rapid consolidation of Adolf Hitler's power in Nazi Germany and the almost "emergency" situation it created for understanding the task of the church in such a world. The other was a realization that service could not adequately be discussed apart from considerations of doctrine. Consequently, the delegates voted that the Life and Work Commission should seek to merge with the Faith and Order Commission, the third outgrowth of Edinburgh.

This third structure provided a place for the doctrinal issues that divided the churches to be explored. The members, adopting the name Faith and Order, held an initial conference in Lausanne in 1927, with over 400 delegates from 108 churches, including not only Protestants but Eastern Orthodox representatives as well. The report of the conference exemplified a descriptive process called "comparative ecclesiology," which sought to pinpoint and describe doctrinal differences as well as similarities, without as yet attempting to resolve them. However, the commonly shared conviction at Lausanne that "God wills unity" led the delegates to project a second conference, which was held at Edinburgh in 1937, with delegates from 122 participating bodies. Unanimous agreement was reached on a statement about "the grace of our Lord Jesus Christ," although in other areas, such as church, ministry, and sacraments, awesome divergences remained. The delegates did acknowledge, however, that their task was not so much to create unity, which is God's gift, as to exhibit more clearly the unity that their empirical divisions obscured.

Members of the Faith and Order Commission realized that doctrine involves action and service, and they voted at Edinburgh (in complementarity with a similar action taken by the Commission on Life and Work) that the two groups should merge. Delegates from both groups therefore met in 1938 at Utrecht to work out proposals for "a world council of churches." World War II intervened, and until 1948 the world council was "in process of formation."

Other Ecumenical Advances. From 1910 to 1948, ecumenical activity was not limited to high-level consultations. Many denominations established international bodies, such as the Lutheran World Federation and the World Alliance of Reformed and Presbyterian Churches, so that global concerns could receive greater attention. National ecumenical agencies were created, such as the British Council of Churches and the Federal Council of Churches in the United States, which later became the National Council of Churches of Christ, providing vehicles through which Protestant groups could work cooperatively on many issues.

Another ecumenical impetus reminding Christians that "the world is too strong for a divided church" was the rise to power of Hitler, whose policies were bent on the extermination of the Jews, the suppression of any Christian groups opposing Nazi claims, and the extension of racially based totalitarian rule. The Barmen Declaration (1934) of the Confessing Church in Germany was a theological "no" to Hitler that brought Reformed and Lutheran groups together for the first time since the Reformation. Christians living under persecution from 1933 to 1945 discovered that in concentration camps or occupied territories their unity far outweighed their differences.

The World Council of Churches. In 1948 at Amsterdam, the World Council of Churches (WCC) became a reality, fusing the concerns of the Faith and Order and Life and Work commissions. In 1961 the International Missionary Council joined the WCC, thus completing the structural reunification of the three areas of concern originating at Edinburgh. Some 146 churches—Protestant, Anglican, and Orthodox—were the original members of the World Council. During World War II, a skeleton staff in Geneva engaged in refugee relief and found various ways for Christians to communicate across the national barriers created by the war. The person most responsible during these interim years, W. A. Visser 't Hooft, a Dutch lay theologian, was elected the first general secretary of the WCC, and permanent headquarters were established in Geneva.

At the time of its creation, the WCC defined itself as "composed of churches which acknowledge Jesus Christ as God and Savior." From the beginning the WCC has made clear (despite misunderstanding by outsiders) that its task is "to serve the churches," not to become a superchurch itself or to be a Protestant/Orthodox counterpart to the Vatican.

The issue of membership in the WCC has been a delicate one. All churches accepting the basic affirmation of "Jesus Christ as God and Savior" have been welcome to apply for membership, and at each world assembly (held every five or six years) new churches have joined, so that after the Vancouver world assembly (1983) there were three hundred member churches representing around four hundred million Christians and including almost all the major Protestant and Orthodox bodies in the world. Membership in the WCC, however, does not imply that member churches believe that their own doctrine of the church is inadequate, nor does it mean acknowledging that other members are "fully" churches. At the New Delhi assembly in 1961, a more fully developed basis for membership was approved. It reads: "The World Council of Churches is a fellowship of Churches which confess the Lord Jesus Christ as God and Savior according to the Scriptures and therefore seek to fulfill together their common calling to the glory of one God, Father, Son and Holy Spirit."

Although the WCC has gone through several structural reorganizations since its inception and will continue to respond structurally to new situations, the emphases of all three Edinburgh streams have remained central throughout its history. A brief description of the structure as it existed after the Vancouver assembly will indicate the wide variety and scope of WCC commitments.

There are three major foci of concern in the WCC, identified as "program units." Program Unit I, devoted to Faith and Witness, is where the earlier Faith and Order Commission is housed. In its new guise, Faith and Order has continued to have an active history since the formation of the WCC, dealing with issues related to the visible unity of the church and preparing reports on such topics as accounts of Christian hope; the theology of baptism, Eucharist, and ministry; the relationship between church and state; and the unity of the church in relation to the unity of humankind. The subunit on World Mission and Evangelism is clearly the repository of many of the concerns of the earlier International Missionary Council and deals with problems raised in proclaiming the faith today, discerning the true missionary congregation, and developing ways for churches throughout the world to share their resources, both material and spiritual.

The subunit on Church and Society is one of the continuing vehicles for the concerns of the earlier Commission on Life and Work; the WCC has held important conferences in this area, most notably a conference on "The Church in the Social and Technical Revolutions of Our Time" (Geneva, 1966), which included worldwide representation and set a new direction for Church and Society concerns. There have also been subsequent conferences on the uses of nuclear energy and issues in medical ethics. The subunit on Dialogue with People of Living Faiths and Ideologies has been a vehicle for widening contacts far beyond the Christian arena. The subunit on Theological Education seeks to make resources available for training for ministry in as ecumenical a context as possible.

Program Unit II is concerned with Justice and Service, another place where certain Life and Work emphases continue to be manifest in concrete ways. The subunit on Inter-Church Aid, Refugee and World Service has been a conduit for specific, practical, and immediate help to people in need. The subunit on Churches' Participation in Development enables churches to be involved in economic development in their own lands through grants and other acts of solidarity such as long-term low-interest loans, along with extensive educational programs and the sharing of technical services. The subunit on International Affairs calls the churches' attention to situations of injustice and conflict, particularly in such areas as the violation of human rights. The Program to Combat Racism, through separately solicited funds, gives financial support to groups of racially oppressed peoples so that they can work for their own liberation. The Christian Medical Commission engages in programs of community health care and education, particularly in areas that are without adequate hospitals or professional medical assistance.

Program Unit III is concerned with Education and Renewal and is oriented to new thinking about Christian education and its impact on parish life. The subunit on Education sponsors programs to develop leadership, educational curricula for churches, and Bible study. The subunit on Renewal and Congregational Life provides resources for local congregations and other Christian groups. The subunit on Women is helping the entire Christian family to rethink the roles of women in both church and society. A similar subunit on Youth gives special attention to the needs of young people.

Even this cursory listing indicates the council's breadth of concern. It directs ongoing attention to theological reflection in the context of the contemporary world (Program Unit I), specific actions in various projects of service (Program Unit II), and ongoing attempts at renewing the mind for the life of the people of God (Program Unit III). In addition to a staff of about 275 persons to administer these various activities, the WCC has a Central Committee, composed of about 135 members, chosen proportionately from among the member churches, which meets annually to determine the ongoing tasks of the WCC between assemblies.

At the world assemblies, member churches meet to discuss their common task and to work on problems that have emerged since the previous assembly. The topics of the assemblies give an indication of the central themes of the WCC's ongoing life. From 1948 to 1983, six assemblies were held: "Man's Disorder and God's Design" (Amsterdam, 1948), "Jesus Christ the Hope of the World" (Evanston, 1954), "Jesus Christ the Light of the World" (New Delhi, 1961), "Behold I Make All Things New" (Uppsala, 1968), "Jesus Christ Frees and Unites" (Nairobi, 1975), and "Jesus Christ the Life of the World" (Vancouver, 1983).

The most volatile storm center of controversy in the life of the WCC has been the Program to Combat Racism. Provided for at Uppsala (1975) shortly after the murder of Martin Luther King Jr., who was to have been the keynote speaker, the Program to Combat Racism assigns considerable sums of money each year to groups throughout the world who are victims of racism and are trying to find ways of escaping such repression. Small grants have occasionally been given to "freedom" groups, particularly in Africa, occasioning protest from others who feel that such gifts will foster violence. Although there have been no instances in which the charges have proven accurate, the issue has remained an emotionally charged one and has the effect of deflecting the public's attention from many of the other activities of the WCC.

The Development of Roman Catholic Ecumenism. During most of the developments described above, the Roman Catholic Church remained uninvolved. Its posture was clear: church unity could be achieved only by the return to the Roman Catholic Church of all the Christian bodies who had separated from it. Since full ecclesial reality was possible only for churches in communion with Rome, Roman Catholics were initially forbidden by Rome to participate in ecumenical activities. For example, Roman Catholic observers were not permitted to attend either the Amsterdam (1948) or Evanston (1954) assemblies of the WCC.

However, a few Roman Catholic ecumenical pioneers very cautiously began to initiate contact with non-Catholics. After World War I, Max Metzger, a German priest, founded the Una Sancta movement to foster dialogue between Protestants and Catholics. French priest Paul Couturier worked for revision of the prayers of the Christian Unity Octave of the Roman liturgy, so that Catholics and Protestants could begin to pray together. The Foyer Unitas in Rome was established for the study of non-Catholic traditions. Dominican priest Yves Congar in France, Jesuit Gustave Weigel in the United States, and other individuals trod a lonely path of seeking to put Protestants and Catholics on speaking terms with one another. After the Amsterdam assembly (1948), an "Instruction" was issued by the Holy Office in Rome in 1949, providing some cautious initial guidelines for Catholic and non-Catholic encounters; even so, an invitation to the Vatican to send Catholic observers to the Evanston assembly (1954) was declined. In 1961, however, during the pontificate of John XXIII, a similar invitation to send observers to the third assembly at New Delhi (1961) was accepted, and five priests attended.

A major ecumenical turning point occurred when John XXIII invited the major Protestant, Anglican, and Orthodox bodies to send observers to the Second Vatican Council, convened in the fall of 1962. Lasting warm and personal relationships that dissolved the frosty barriers of the centuries were established during the four sessions of the council (1962–1965).

Vatican II enhanced Catholic engagement in ecumenism in a number of ways. For one, the very calling of a council was seen as an instance of *ecclesia semper reformanda* ("the church always being reformed"), a concept Protestants had previously thought was anathema to Rome. Second, the inclusion of the observers demonstrated that Rome did not wish to continue to live in ecclesiastical isolation. Third, the influence of the "missionary bishops" who had often worked with Protestant missionaries brought fresh perspectives to other bishops trained in exclusivist patterns. Fourth, many of the council documents opened new doors of ecumenical understanding.

Of the sixteen promulgated conciliar documents, at least seven had significant ecumenical import. The document on ecumenism opened new doors for dialogue and understanding; the document on the liturgy restored the use of the vernacular and made Catholic worship less foreign to non-Catholics; the document on the church affirmed the "collegiality of the bishops," correcting certain one-sided emphases from Vatican I concerning the primacy of Peter that had been ecumenically counterproductive; the document on revelation gave scripture a greater prominence and authority in relation to tradition; the document on religious liberty dispelled fears about Catholic ecclesiastical imperialism; the document on the church and non-Christian religions created the possibility of dialogue between Roman Catholics and adherents of other world religions; and the document on the church and the world today indicated areas of concern, such as economics, labor unions, nuclear weapons, and culture, on which Catholics and non-Catholics could work together despite lack of full doctrinal consensus.

Assessments of the long-range impact of Vatican II are diverse. For many Catholics, the council brought the church into the modern world and made new levels of activity and dialogue possible. For other Catholics, the council created so many lines of rapport with modern thought and movements that the distinctiveness of the Catholic faith seemed to be placed in jeopardy. For most Protestants, the council unexpectedly legitimated Catholic attitudes that continue to enrich ecumenical life.

In the new atmosphere created by Vatican II, the relationship of Roman Catholicism to the WCC was raised anew. There is no theological reason why the Roman Catholic Church could not become a member of the WCC, since the basis of membership poses no challenge to Catholic faith. At the Uppsala assembly (1968), three years after the conclusion of Vatican II, the relations with Roman Catholic observers were so cordial that it seemed as though an application for membership might soon be possible, but by the Nairobi assembly (1975) such momentum had diminished. One important consideration, acknowledged by both sides, has been that, because of its size, the voting power of the Roman Catholic Church in the WCC would be disproportionate and cause alarm to member churches that have numerically small constituencies. Nevertheless, a close working relationship has been established between Geneva and Rome, not only in areas of social service projects, such as the Commission on Society, Development, and Peace, but in the theological arena as well, and Roman Catholic theologians have for some time been full voting members on the Commission on Faith and Order, contributing to discussions and reports about ministry, baptism, and Eucharist.

A further ecumenical contribution has come from Roman Catholicism. Building on the Vatican II document "The Church and the World Today," Catholics in Third World countries, particularly Latin America, have created a "theology of liberation," affirmed by the Latin American bishops in a meeting in Puebla, Mexico, in 1979, which involves committing the church to making "a preferential option for the poor." This has led to significant numbers of Catholics, frequently joined by Protestants, siding with the destitute at great personal risk in oppressive situations; Catholic-Protestant differences have paled before the awesome responsibility of ecumenical challenges to the oppressive status quo. This "practical ecumenism" provides a significant model for ecumenical involvement elsewhere.

Extending Intramural Christian Activity. Within the Christian family the impetus of ecumenical concern has not only led Christian bodies to seek closer contacts with one another and to work together whenever possible, but also led many denominations to seek organic union with one another. The motivations usually include at least a desire to respond organically and structurally to Jesus' high-priestly prayer "that they all may be one" (*Jn.* 17:21); a recognition that division is a "scandal" in the sight of both Christians and non-Christians, who cannot fail to perceive the hypocrisy of those who preach unity but do not practice it; and a desire to use institutional resources with more efficient stewardship by avoiding both overlapping and competition. Although not widely heralded by the secular press, there continue to be significant numbers of mergers between denominations that are members of the WCC. While the latter body does not act as the agent or broker for such reunions, its very existence has brought diverse groups of Christians into contact with one another and thereby helped to enhance the movement toward denominational reunion.

Many of the reunions have taken place among the so-called younger churches as they have sought to overcome the legacy of divisive denominationalism that the nineteenth-century missionary enterprise bequeathed to them. Although the period is exceptional, the reunifications that took place between the years 1965 and 1972 give some indication of the intensity of the concern to heal the Christian divisions of centuries. During that period, united churches were created out of two or more confessions in Zambia, Jamaica and Grand Cayman, Madagascar, Ecuador, Papua New Guinea and the Solomon Islands, Belgium, North India, Pakistan, Zaire, and Great Britain.

Other specific steps toward organic unity will be completed only after years of further discussion and exploration. A proposal for reunification of ten denominations in the United States, the Consultation on Church Union, is now, after years of high-level ecumenical discussion, moving into a time of local denominational reacquaintance at the grassroots level before any final decisions are made.

The tender spots in negotiating denominational mergers center less on theology than on polity. Theological agreement on most, if not all, issues is increasingly reachable, but the form and structure of new denominations is rendered difficult when any of the three major polities—congregational, presbyterian, or episcopal—are being combined. The Church of South India (1947) was the first such reunification to draw all three types of church government within a single new structure.

Within all denominations, and within the World Council of Churches, a new intramural issue has emerged with a vitality not anticipated even a short time ago: the role of women within the life of the church. Not only have such issues as the ordination of women and the holding of church office by women been treated very differently by the historic Christian confessions, but cultural influences, often unconsciously appropriated by various church groups and imposed on the intramural discussions, have made this a "radicalizing" issue for many women, who have been active in ecumenical affairs and have discovered that they have been the victims of conscious, or even unconscious, discrimination within the churches. The World Council of Churches has included a division within its structure to deal with the problem in an ongoing way, and a major consultation was held at Sheffield, England, in 1981; however, equality of status is far from a reality, either ecumenically or denominationally, and ongoing discussion and action on this matter will be high on the ecumenical agenda for the foreseeable future.

EXTRAMURAL ECUMENICAL DEVELOPMENTS. In addition to all the ecumenical concerns that center on mission and unity, there is the further meaning of *oikoumenē* that calls attention to the whole of "the inhabited world" and comprises not only service to every member of the human family but also a certain way of thinking about and relating to those who are part of the human family but not the Christian family. There are at least four areas in which the inner life of the ecumenical movement has been turning outward toward appraisal of and dialogue with groups that Christians cannot avoid confronting in an ever-shrinking world, and with whom they must seek terms of mutual understanding.

One of the most important of these areas has been the new attention accorded the relationship between Christians and Jews. Christians, born of the family of Abraham and Sarah, are beginning to acknowledge that they have been at best ungrateful heirs, and at worst despicable destroyers, of a faith apart from which they cannot truly define themselves. The ongoing history of destructive relations between Christians and Jews, frequently the result of a Christian theological imperialism, has been exacerbated in recent times by the Holocaust and the murdering by the Nazis of six million Jews, with the passive complicity and at times the active involvement of the Christian world. In the emerging ecumenical discussion, a new emphasis on the eternal nature of God's covenant with the Jews (based in large part on fresh study of *Romans* 9–11) is beginning to challenge the more traditional "supercessionist" view—that the coming of Christ superseded the divine covenant with Abraham—which has reduced the Jews living in the common era to objects for conversion. The WCC has sponsored several consultations on the relationship between Jews and Christians. Vatican II opened some doors for the new discussion by its clear declaration that anti-Semitism can in no way be grounded in the Christian scriptures, and many Protestant denominations, including a number in Germany, the location of Hitler's rise to power, have been exploring in fresh ways the implications of a view that Christians and Jews, who have lived in such destructive tension in the past, can create a more positive future together.

A concern to understand the relationship of Christianity to other world religions is a second area that has been the object of increasing ecumenical attention. A Vatican II declaration, "The Relationship of the Church to Non-Christian Religions" (1965), began to open doors on the Roman Catholic side, and the WCC has held a series of consultations, such as one at Chiang Mai, Thailand, in April 1977, on "Faith in the Midst of Faiths," which sought to explore new ways of dealing with the many communities of faith that exist in a world where Christians have often claimed to be the unique community of faith. The discussion goes back to a meeting of the International Missionary Council in Madras in 1938 on the Christian message to a non-Christian world. The issue is to discover a modus vivendi for all, between an attitude of theological imperialism, which implies that if one faith is the truth no other faiths really have a right to exist, and a syncretism, which implies that there are not enough differences between the faiths to pose an issue and that some amalgamating of them all can create a new faith for the future. The unattractiveness of both options means that the discussion will continue.

A third area of extramural ecumenical dialogue has had varying degrees of success and failure: the relationship between Christianity and Marxism. In the years immediately after World War II, an extended dialogue between Christians and Marxists flourished in Europe, since many Christians had been united with Russians and other communists in opposing the fascism of Hitler and Mussolini. However, the European dialogue was severely set back by Soviet takeovers in such places as Czechoslovakia. The issue of how Christians are to approach Marxism and communism is vitally important, as a matter of daily life as well as intellectual dialogue, because in many areas of the world Christians live under socialist or communist regimes. The entrance of the Russian Orthodox Church into the WCC at the New Delhi world assembly (1961) assured that the issue of Christian presence within a Marxist state would be under continual scrutiny.

The matter is rendered even more urgent in parts of the world where socialism or communism are seen as possible alternatives to oppressive governments that are perceived to be linked to imperialistic forms of capitalism. In Latin America, for example, the issue of Christian involvement in movements seeking to overthrow oppressive dictators cannot be separated from the question of the degree to which Christians are willing to work with Marxists in such situations or to accept certain elements of Marxist analysis in seeking to create a society more in keeping with their understanding of the Christian gospel. Although in the United States concern about Marxism is frequently interpreted as the camel's nose of subversion entering the tent of ecclesiology, the dialogue will remain crucial on an ecumenical level as long as Marxism represents an option for millions of people living in a world Christians are called upon to serve.

A further area of dialogical involvement centers on the appropriate relationship between Christians and those who are defined by a term such as *secularism.* A significant part of every world assembly of the WCC has addressed matters like international relations, racism, poverty, violence, and social embodiments of evil. Vatican II called attention to this new dialogue in its document "The Church and the World Today" (1965), which dealt with problems of culture, the spread of atheism (for which the church acknowledged some responsibility), the role of secular agencies in bringing about social change, and so forth.

But there is an even more fundamental issue, to which the Faith and Order division of the WCC has been directing attention and which is summarized in the title of one Faith and Order study: "Unity of the Church—Unity of Humankind." Recognizing that there is a unity that binds all people together as part of the human family, quite apart from the unity some of them have consciously chosen by their allegiance to Christ, how are those two kinds of unity to be related to one another? Does the former negate the significance of the latter, or vice versa? Can the two unities coexist? Is one too narrow, the other too broad?

The above are only a few examples of ways in which contemporary ecumenical concern is becoming broader and deeper. The original commitment to Christian cooperation has grown beyond issues of exclusive interest to Christians.

Some Unresolved Ecumenical Issues. The ecumenical movement is not so close to being successful that it will shortly render itself unnecessary. The three areas of mission, doctrine, and service still contain formidable obstacles to be overcome, though their formulation has shifted in some interesting ways since 1910.

In the area of mission the matter of "sending ambassadors of Christ" to faraway places must be viewed from a new perspective, since it now depends on who is deciding what is "far away." "Foreign missions" used to mean activities beyond the boundaries of North America and Europe. These continents constituted the "center," the rest of the world the "periphery." Mission was conceived of as a one-way street, emanating from the center toward the periphery. By the time of the Whitby conference of the International Missionary Council in 1947, it was clearly and even sternly affirmed that mission had become a two-way street and must remain that way. The new Christian vitality in the last half of the twentieth century seems to be coming from what used to be called the periphery, that is, the younger churches.

The real issue in the 1980s and 1990s and beyond may be the degree to which the "older churches" at the "center" can have the grace to be recipients of new understandings of the gospel that will come from the "younger churches" at the "periphery." For the time being, at least, it may be more ecumenically blessed for the older churches to receive than to give. (The WCC, which at its inception was made up almost entirely of "leaders" from North America and Europe, has responded creatively to the new situation. Increasing numbers of its staff and leadership are drawn from other parts of the world.)

In the area of doctrine there have been a surprising number of theological convergences, even though certain unresolved issues remain central to the question of church reunions. There are increasing degrees of consensus on the meaning of baptism and even on Eucharist, though the matter of ministry (i.e., who is properly validated to administer the sacraments) is far from resolved.

But Catholics and Protestants, for example, are much closer than before on such issues as the authority of scripture, the relationship of scripture to tradition, the meaning of "the priesthood of all believers," the nature of liturgy, the meaning of faith, and the necessity of social involvement on the part of Christians for the good of all. The office of the papacy naturally continues to divide Roman Catholics from the Orthodox, Anglicans, and Protestants, and the claim to infallibility of church teaching, while interpreted in different ways by the Orthodox and the Catholics, is an area where they are discernibly closer to each other than either of them is to the Protestants. The role of Mary in the economy of salvation is another unresolved area, although the Mary of the Magnificat (*Lk.* 1:46–55) is increasingly important to Protestants as well as Catholics.

The difference of atmosphere from earlier times, however, is marked. Rather than closing off unassailable areas from discussion, there is a willingness to reexamine and even restate deeply held truths in the light of what is learned in ecumenical dialogue. Many non-Catholics, for example, could now acknowledge the possibility of some form of papacy, if defined as *primus inter pares*, the pope as a "first among equals." While this is not a definition acceptable to Roman Catholics, many Catholics are nevertheless attempting to define more precisely the meaning of papal authority, especially in the light of Vatican II's conclusion that the bishop of Rome shares teaching authority with the other bishops in the "episcopal college."

Another doctrinal issue, however, will be increasingly important in the life of the ecumenical movement. It has little to do with formulations of a doctrine of the papacy or Eucharist or baptism, but a great deal to do with how doctrines are actually formulated. Protestant ecumenical theology has had a strong classical European stamp upon it, solidly rooted in the biblical heritage of Luther and Calvin. Roman Catholic ecumenical thought has likewise been nurtured by a European frame of reference, though, thanks to thinkers like Karl Rahner, it has been moving in new directions. Orthodox theologians have seen themselves as guarantors of past tradition, and their modes of describing that tradition have the stamp of centuries upon them.

But this is not the background from which Asians, Africans, and Latin Americans have come into the ecumenical movement. There is no reason, this new generation argues, why ways of doing theology in Europe should be normative everywhere. They are insisting that their own theology must now be done indigenously, arising out of their own cultures and using imagery appropriate to those cultures. Thus African Christians are drawing on images and experiences that maintain some continuity with their tribal pasts, to provide new metaphors to speak of the love of God in Jesus Christ. Asians are doing the same with a heritage more venerable than that of Europe, and "water-buffalo theology" (Kosuke Koyama) is more resonant for them than forensic images drawn from medieval courts of law. Latin Americans are insisting that theology must grow out of the experience of the poor, rather than being imposed on the poor by intellectuals in universities. A theological system arises out of human struggle, they are asserting, rather than being provided ahead of time by experts and then "applied" to specific situations. To the degree that the former "periphery" does begin to speak to the former "center"—and is heard—the issue of theological methodology will become an increasingly critical area of discussion.

In the third area, that of service, many difficult ecumenical issues have been posed for discussion, and the drawing of lines of difference bears little resemblance to the situation at the beginning of the modern ecumenical era. If, in the earlier period, it was true to say that "doctrine divides, service unites," the reverse has almost become the descriptive reality: service divides, doctrine unites.

A basic difference between two types of Christian approach to service seems to be part of a legacy that each era leaves to its successor. This legacy is a distinction between (1) those who see the Christian life as fundamentally an individual matter, in which, by giving sufficient attention to the personal and inner dimensions of life, a spirit is created that will transform the outer structures of society, and (2) those who believe that Christian faith is so incurably social that it is never enough just to change individuals and assume they will change society. This second view necessitates a simultaneous frontal attack on the unjust structures of society because they are causes of and manifestations of, as well as the results of, human sin. Almost all Christians, when pressed, would agree that both concerns must be present and that a theology containing one and not the other would be truncated and incorrect. But in practice, the matter of priority, or, even more, proportion, between the two is a significant cause of division.

What becomes ecumenically confusing is that divisions over such matters bear no resemblance to past denominational or confessional allegiances. For example, the lines between Roman Catholics and Protestants are not usually drawn on an issue such as the appropriateness from a Christian perspective of possessing nuclear weapons. Some Catholics will be closer to some Protestants than they will be to most other Catholics; some Presbyterians may be more at home in the company of Methodists on this matter than with their fellow Presbyterians. Within a Catholic religious order, the most diversified opinions may be found on the ethical responsibility of multinationals, and within member churches of the WCC similar divisions occur.

Issues of practice, then, are more often volatile sources of disagreement than issues of belief. For example, when "conservatives" attack the WCC, the issue is less likely to be a Faith and Order commission report on baptism than the allocation of funds for the Program to Combat Racism. Some Catholics appear to be more upset with the social analysis of Catholic liberation theologians than with Protestant views of the meaning of papal infallibility. Church members in the twenty-first century are better able to tolerate doctrinal differences on the meaning of the real presence in the Eucharist than to allow for two points of view on whether or not "class struggle" is a legitimate descriptive term in Christian social analysis. So it is tensions within the realm of service—how the church is to relate to the world, what it is to do in relation to revolutionary situations, how it is to make a critique of the economic order (or whether it is even appropriate to do so)—that have become the causes of the deepest ecumenical ruptures.

Beyond the focal points of mission, doctrine, and service, other unresolved, structural issues remain. For example, what should be the relationship of world confessional bodies, which are global expressions of denominationalism, to the WCC? Is the continuation of such groups as the Lutheran World Federation or the World Alliance of Reformed Churches a contribution or a detriment to ecumenism? Do they impede the cause of Christian unity, or are they provisionally necessary for the maintenance of certain doctrinal emphases and portions of a tradition that might otherwise be lost?

Coupled with such matters is the problem of size. Is there a "critical mass" beyond which concern for the Christian message will be dissipated simply because of the need to keep the wheels of a large organization running smoothly? To the degree that ecumenical dialogue brings about new understandings that render unnecessary the ongoing life of separate denominations, will the resultant mergers necessarily be vehicles for a refining of the prophetic nature of the gospel, or will bigness breed slowness and timidity? Whatever the answers to these and yet unanticipated questions, ecumenical concerns will persist in the life of the church as long as there is a discrepancy between the actual state of the church and the will of the head of the church "that all may be one."

SEE ALSO African Religions, article on New Religious Movements; Anti-Semitism; Australian Indigenous Religions, articles on Aboriginal Christianity, New Religious Movements; Christian Ethics; Christianity; Church, article on Church Polity; Councils, article on Christian Councils; Creeds, article on Christian Creeds; Denominationalism; Dialogue of Religions; Eucharist; Faith; Holocaust, The; Marxism; Mary; Ministry; Missions, article on Christian Missions; North American Indian Religions, article on New Religious Movements; Oceanic Religions, article on Missionary Movements; Papacy; Political Theology; Reformation; Sacrament, article on Christian Sacraments; Schism, article on Christian Schism; Theology, article on Christian Theology; Vatican Councils, articles on Vatican II.

BIBLIOGRAPHY

For a history of the mission and expansion of Christianity, the movement out of which modern ecumenism grew, the best overall resource is still K. S. Latourette's *Christianity in a Revolutionary Age: A History of Christianity in the Nineteenth and Twentieth Centuries*, 5 vols. (New York, 1958–1962). Documents pertinent to the development of the modern ecumenical movement are conveniently collected in *Documents on Christian Unity*, 4 vols., edited by G. K. A. Bell (London, 1924–1958), which includes Protestant, Catholic, and Orthodox materials. For a full history of the ecumenical movement, with special attention to the formation of the World Council of Churches, consult *A History of the Ecumenical Movement, 1517–1948*, 2d ed., edited by Ruth Rouse and Stephen C. Neill (London, 1957), and its sequel, *The Ecumenical Advance: A History of the Ecumenical Movement*, vol. 2, *1948–1968*, edited by Harold E. Fey (Philadelphia, 1970). An interpretive account of the Faith and Order movement can be found in *A Documentary History of the Faith and Order Movement, 1927–1963*, edited by Lukas Vischer (Saint Louis, 1963), which contains excerpts from all the Faith and Order conferences through the New Delhi assembly (1961). The closest comparable volume tracing the Life and Work movement is Paul Bock's *In Search of a Responsible World Society: The Social Teachings of the World Council of Churches* (Philadelphia, 1974). The reports of all the WCC assemblies contain speeches, reports of the various commissions, and other pertinent information. These are *The First Assembly of the World Council of Churches: The Official Report* (New York, 1949), *The Second Assembly of the World Council of Churches: The Evanston Report* (New York, 1955), *The Third Assembly of the World Council of Churches: The New Delhi Report* (New York, 1962), all edited by W. A. Visser 't Hooft; *The Fourth Assembly of the World Council of Churches: The Uppsala Report*, edited by Norman Goodall (Geneva, 1968); *Breaking Barriers: Nairobi 1975*, edited by David M. Paton (London, 1975); and *Gathered for Life: Official Report, Sixth Assembly of the World Council of Churches*, edited by David Gill (Geneva, 1983). My *The Ecumenical Revolution*, rev. ed. (Garden City, N.Y., 1969), is a history of both Protestant and Catholic ecumenism through the Uppsala assembly in 1968.

For an account of the "ecumenical pioneers" who were active before Roman Catholic ecumenism was widely sanctioned, see Leonard J. Swidler's *The Ecumenical Vanguard* (Pittsburgh, 1966), which gives special attention to the Una Sancta movement. Hans Küng's *Justification: The Doctrine of Karl Barth and a Catholic Reflection* (London, 1964) is a good example of one of the earliest serious attempts to bridge the Protestant-Catholic chasm.

Two accounts of the Second Vatican Council are of special interest: the reports from *Le monde* by the French journalist Henri Fesquet available as *The Drama of Vatican II* (New York, 1967), and Xavier Rynne's *Letters from Vatican City: Vatican Council II* (New York, 1963). The latter is an expansion of a famous series of *New Yorker* accounts, published pseudonymously throughout the council. The most easily available collection of the results of Vatican II is *Documents of Vatican II*, edited by Walter M. Abbott and Joseph Gallagher (New York, 1966). Since Vatican II, a series of volumes known as "Concilium," with more than a hundred titles, has been published by various publishers at regular intervals.

As an example of new theological and ecumenical understanding, Gustavo Gutiérrez's *A Theology of Liberation* (Maryknoll, N.Y., 1973) is the best introduction to post-Vatican II liberation theology, and Paul M. Van Buren's *Discerning the Way* (New York, 1980) and *A Christian Theology of the People Israel* (New York, 1983) represent fresh attempts to reconstitute Christian theology by taking its relationship to Judaism with new seriousness.

The most useful ecumenical periodical is *Journal of Ecumenical Studies* (Pittsburgh, 1974–), published triannually, with articles, extensive reportage on ecumenical activities throughout the world, and book reviews of new ecumenical literature. *The Ecumenical Review* (Geneva, 1948–), a quarterly publication of the WCC, contains articles, extensive journals of WCC activities, and book reviews covering ecumenical contributions from all over the world. *The Information Service of the Secretariat for Promoting Christian Unity*, published in Rome, gives papers, digests, and summaries of ecumenical activities in which the Secretariat is involved.

ROBERT MCAFEE BROWN (1987)

EDDAS. The Icelandic works known as the Eddas form our most important sources for Scandinavian mythology. The *Poetic Edda* is a collection of alliterative poems. First in the Danish Royal Library (hence the collection's name, *Codex Regius*), this manuscript was transferred to Iceland in 1971. Sixteen pages were lost from the middle between 1641 and 1643; the remaining ninety pages contain eleven poems about the gods and eighteen about Germanic heroes. A few poems in a similar style are found in other medieval manuscripts. The work known as the *Prose Edda* or Snorri's *Edda* is a handbook of poetry written by Snorri Sturluson between around 1225 and 1230. To explain circumlocutions such as "Freyja's tears" for "gold," Snorri relates myths about the gods. In one manuscript the work is given the title *Edda*. The derivation of this word is obscure, although several explanations have been proposed.

The authorship, date, and place of origin of the eddic poems are unknown. The *Codex Regius* was written about 1270, but its poems were copied from several manuscripts that are now lost. The poems quoted in Snorri's *Edda* must be from before 1230, and close echoes of them are found in court verse from the tenth and eleventh centuries. Their mythological lore must be older still, for it underlies the metaphors used by Norwegian court poets from the ninth century on. Eddic poetry was probably being composed in Scandinavia by the ninth century, although the content and form of these poems is unknown. Their mythological and heroic lore existed for two hundred years in Christian oral tradition, most likely for its entertainment value.

ORGANIZATION OF THE *CODEX REGIUS*. The *Codex Regius* has a clear hierarchical organization. It starts with cosmology; continues with Óðinn, Freyr, Þórr, and other supernatural beings; and concludes with human heroes. The poems on their own are not easy to understand, as they assume familiarity with the myths; therefore, the compiler supplies some commentary. But even so, knowledge of Scandinavian mythology would be sparse were it not for Snorri, who also organizes and explains the mythological lore he sets down. A prologue asserts that the heathen religion arose from nature worship and that the gods known as the Æsir are actually men, the descendants of King Priam of Troy. They emigrated from Asia, from which their name derives, and their king, Óðinn, gave his sons the rule of Sweden, Denmark, and Norway. This section, reflecting patristic approaches to paganism, may be intended to deflect any criticism of the retelling of pagan mythology.

The next part, the *Gylfaginning* (Deluding of Gylfi), uses a frame narrative—the quest of the Swedish king Gylfi to learn about the Æsir—to retell myths about the creation, cosmology, some two dozen gods and goddesses, and the end of the mythological world at Ragnarǫk. The triad of gods who answer Gylfi's questions appears to be modeled on the Christian Trinity. The third section, *Skáldskaparmál* (Language of poetry), uses a different dialogue to present additional myths, but it primarily discusses the diction of court poetry. The last section, *Háttatal* (Enumeration of meters), contains three of Snorri's poems illustrating many Norse verse forms, together with a prose commentary. Snorri most likely included mythology in his *Edda* because so many poetic circumlocutions required a knowledge of it. Viewing the heathen religion with detachment, he writes about the gods with irony and humor. He has little interest in allegorical or symbolic explanations of myths, and where he does offer an interpretation, it is an etiological one.

Given the inescapably mediated nature of the Eddas, can anything about authentic Scandinavian paganism be learned from them? The thirteenth-century forms were recorded by people who cannot have held them sacred, making them an unreliable source for religious history. Nonetheless, the myths do seem to be a reflex of paganism, as seen by the parallels between Snorri's myths and those of Saxo Grammaticus (c. 1150–after 1216), whose work predates Snorri's and was not known in Iceland. In addition, the eddic depictions of the gods correspond to what is known of the earlier Germanic pantheon.

THE FIRST FIVE POEMS. The *Poetic Edda* opens with *Vǫluspá* (Prophecy of the seeress), composed perhaps in late-tenth- or early-eleventh-century Iceland. It relates the creation of the worlds, the war between the two groups of gods (Æsir and Vanir), the death of Baldr, the fall of the gods, the destruction of the earth by fire and water, and its reemergence from the sea, beginning a new age. The poet was probably not a Christian, but the moral framework, the idea of punishment or reward for human beings after death, the coming of an unnamed new god referred to only as *inn ríki* (the mighty one), and the obsession with the end of the world do suggest syncretic use of Christian material. If the poet was a Christian, he was well versed in pagan mythology and does not display the hostility towards it common among early Norse Christians.

The second poem, *Hávamál* (Speech of the High One), begins the sequence about Óðinn. A composite work drawn from at least six sources, it lists the spells known to Óðinn and describes his winning the secret of runes by hanging from the World Tree for nine nights, wounded with a spear, a sacrifice of himself to himself. The elements of this myth all have parallels in Norse tradition, and it is probably not influenced by the Christian crucifixion. Next are two short narratives about Óðinn's unsuccessful wooing of a resolute maiden and his seduction of a giant's daughter in order to steal the mead of poetic inspiration. Finally, a long series of proverbs offers advice. References to cremation and memorial stones indicate the poem's origin in pagan Norway. In the third poem, *Vafþrúðnismál* (The lay of Vafþrúðnir), Óðinn holds a riddle contest with the giant Vafþrúðnir to see who knows the most mythological lore; defeat means death for the vanquished. They cover creation, the halls of the gods, the World Tree and the creatures that live on it, the life of warriors after death in the hall of Óðinn, and the events leading to Ragnarǫk. A variant of this myth is found in the fourth poem, *Grímnismál* (The lay of Grímnir).

The fifth poem, *Skírnismál* (The lay of Skírnir), tells of the wooing of the fair giantess Gerðr by Freyr, the fertility god. This myth seems quite archaic, and even if one sets aside the interpretations associating the story with any particular fertility ritual, there can be no doubt that sex and fertility lie at its core. The myth has also been interpreted as reaffirming the patriarchal structure of Old Norse society, depicting a male-female struggle for power and providing a matrix for resolving conflict between different families through a system of exchange and intermarriage.

ÞÓRR: FOUR POEMS. Þórr is the subject of the next four poems. In *Hárbarðsljóð* (The song of Hárbarðr) he tries to compel Óðinn, who is disguised as a ferryman, to take him across a fjord. When they recognize one another, they exchange insults referring to shameful incidents in the past. *Hymiskviða* (The lay of Hymir) describes how Þórr went fishing with the giant Hymir and nearly caught the sea serpent that encircles the earth. The tale is humorously told, but this does not diminish its underlying seriousness, for the emergence of the monster from the depths is the signal for the beginning of Ragnarǫk and the end of the world. The importance of this myth is seen from its depiction on Viking Age carved stones in Sweden, Denmark, and England. *Lokasenna* (Loki's exchange of insults) tells how the mischievous Loki is evicted from the gods' banquet for killing a servant. He immediately returns, and a heated exchange of abuse ensues in which he reminds each god of some humiliating incident. *Lokasenna* was grouped with the poems about Þórr because Loki leaves only when faced with Þórr's fury. The poet's purpose was probably to recite a catalogue of the important stories about the gods, perhaps as an *aide-mémoire.*

Þrymskviða (The lay of Þrymr), thought to be one of the youngest mythological poems (from the beginning of the thirteenth century), borrows phrases from older poems to describe the theft of Þórr's hammer by the giant Þrymr, who wants to exchange it for the hand of Freyja, goddess of love. Þórr goes to Þrymr disguised as Freyja, his face covered by the bridal veil, and Loki accompanies him disguised as a maid. Thanks to this ruse, Þórr is able to recover his hammer when it is brought in as part of the wedding ceremony. Like *Hymiskviða*, *Þrymskviða* treats a serious threat in a comic vein. Without Þórr's hammer to protect them, the gods would be at the mercy of the giants, but Þórr's unfeminine behavior and Loki's inspired excuses for him are truly amusing. However, this myth is otherwise unknown, and it may simply be a skillful imitation of "authentic" mythological poems.

THE FINAL POEMS ON THE GODS. The last two mythological poems nominally deal with lesser supernatural beings. *Völundarvkiða* (The lay of Völundr) tells the tragic story of the smith Völundr (in English: Weland, Wayland), who exacts a grisly vengeance on the king who captures him. Völundr is probably not a native figure of Scandinavian mythology, but his Norse appellation *álfa dróttinn* (Lord of Elves) seems to have led the compiler of the *Codex Regius* to place the poem here, rather than with the heroic poems with which modern scholars classify it. *Alvíssmál* (The lay of Alvíss) is a wisdom contest like *Vafþrúðnismál.* Here Þórr uses questions to keep the dwarf Alvíss (All-Wise)—who has persuaded the other gods to give him Þórr's daughter as a bride—up all night until the rays of the sun turn him into stone.

OUTSIDE THE *CODEX REGIUS.* Eddic poems not in the *Codex Regius* include *Baldrs draumar* (Dreams of Baldr), which describes how Óðinn seeks information from a seeress about the fate of his son Baldr. The incomplete *Rígsþula* (Rígr's list of names) treats the origin and structure of human society. Rígr (whom the medieval scribe says is the god Heimdallr) visits three farms, where each housewife gives birth to a boy nine months later. The child at the first farm is named Þræll (Slave), the child at the second is Karl (Freeman), and the child at the third is Jarl (Earl). Each has the stereotypical appearance of his social class. The poem thus employs an aristocratic, secular perspective in its survey of the social hierarchy and reflects archaic insular influences—such as the name Rígr, which corresponds to the Old Irish *rí* (king)—and the implicit sanction of the custom of allowing distinguished visitors to have sexual relations with the wife of the host. Scholars are split between regarding it as a mirror of Viking Age society (tenth century to c. 1100) and as a product of the learned milieu of late-twelfth-century and thirteenth-century Norway and Iceland.

Grottasöngr tells how King Fróði of Denmark had a mill that would grind out whatever its owner wished for. At first the king ordered it to grind gold and happiness for himself and peace for his kingdom, but his greed drove the two slaves who worked the mill to rebel and grind out vengeance and destruction. *Hyndluljóð*'s recounts how Freyja forces the giantess Hyndla to tell the genealogy of her protégé Óttarr. In addition to this information, Hyndla recites a version of *Vǫluspá.* Most scholars believe that this was originally a separate poem older than the verses about Freyja and Óttarr but younger than *Vǫluspá. Hyndluljóð*'s emphasis on genealogy and the interrelationship of noble families and legendary heroic figures suggests that it is a mythologization created for sociolegal purposes.

SNORRI'S SOURCES. When Snorri assembled the myths in his *Edda,* he made extensive use of the eddic poems and also drew on tales of the gods from other, unknown sources. He gives several traditional views about the creation of the world; describes the gods and goddesses and other supernatural beings, listing lesser ones about whom little or nothing is known; and explains how Óðinn and two companions created the first man and woman from logs of wood. Snorri also recounts a number of myths and legends concerning the gods and the giants. One is the tale of how a giant built the stronghold of Ásgarðr, whereupon the gods cheated him out of his wages and took his life; Óðinn's eight-legged horse Sleipnir was an unintended result of the gods' trickery. Another relates how the god Týr lost his hand in the process of binding the wolf Fenrir. Other tales relate how Óðinn brought the mead of poetry to Ásgarðr, which treasures the dwarfs fashioned for the gods, what befell Þórr in the land of the giants and at the court of Útgarða-Loki, and how he dueled with the giant Hrungnir. The defeat of the giant Þjazi results in the marriage of his daughter Skaði to one of the Vanir hostages, the sea god Njörðr. Loki's escapades culminate in the tale of how he caused the death of Baldr and was bound by the gods under the earth as a punishment. Finally, Snorri gives an account of Ragnarǫk that is based on *Vǫluspá* but which incorporates popular beliefs about the world's ending.

SEE ALSO Freyr; Óðinn; Saxo Grammaticus; Snorri Sturluson; Týr.

BIBLIOGRAPHY

Carolyne Larrington's *The Poetic Edda* (Oxford, 1996) is a good translation of the entire *Poetic Edda.* B. S. Benedikz and John McKinnell offer a translation with commentary in *Vǫluspá* (Durham, N.C., 1978). Ursula Dronke's *The Poetic Edda,* vol. 2, *Mythological Poems* (Oxford, 1997), does the same for *Vǫluspá, Baldrs draumar, Rígsþula, Völundarkvíða, Lokasenna,* and *Skírnismál.* The Everyman edition of *Snorri Sturluson: Edda* (London, 1987), translated and edited by Anthony Faulkes, is the best and most complete translation of Snorri's *Edda,* omitting only an appendix. For a translation of the prologue, *Gylfaginning,* and selections from *Skáldskaparmál,* see Jean I. Young, *The Prose Edda of Snorri Sturluson: Tales from Norse Mythology* (Cambridge, U.K., 1954).

Studies of the eddic myths include Gabriel Turville-Petre's *Myth and Religion of the North: The Religion of Ancient Scandinavia* (London, 1964) and Hilda Ellis Davidson's *Gods and Myths of Northern Europe* (Harmondsworth, U.K., 1965). In *Gods of the Ancient Northmen* (Berkeley, Calif., 1973), Georges Dumézil deals with the eddic myths in the light of other Indo-European mythologies. Papers on the *Poetic Edda* are gathered in *Edda: A Collection of Essays* (Manitoba, Canada, 1983), edited by Robert J. Glendinning and Haraldur Bessason. Jónas Kristjánsson's *Eddas and Sagas: Iceland's Medieval Literature* (Reykjavík, 1988), translated by Peter Foote, is a popular, illustrated treatment, while Margaret Clunies Ross takes an academic, sociological approach in the first volume of *Prolonged Echoes: Old Norse Myths in Medieval Northern Society* (Odense, Denmark, 1994). For bibliography and a valuable survey of scholarship up to 1985, consult Joseph Harris, "Eddic Poetry," in *Old Norse-Icelandic Literature: A Critical Guide*, edited by Carol J. Clover and John Lindow (Ithaca, N.Y., 1985). Further references can be found in John Lindow's *Scandinavian Mythology: An Annotated Bibliography* (New York, 1988). Phillip Pulsiano's *Medieval Scandinavia: An Encyclopedia* (New York, 1993), Rudolf Simek's *Dictionary of Northern Mythology* (Cambridge, U.K., 1993), and John Lindow's *Handbook of Norse Mythology* (Santa Barbara, Calif., 2001) supply useful encyclopedia-style entries.

ELIZABETH ASHMAN ROWE (2005)

EDDY, MARY BAKER (1821–1910), the American discoverer of Christian Science, founded the Church of Christ, Scientist, "to commemorate the word and works" of Christ Jesus and "to reinstate primitive Christianity and its lost element of healing" (Eddy, 1895, p. 17). The subject of vehement attack by the popular press and male theologians of her day, and of staunch defense by proponents of her teaching, Eddy remains a controversial figure.

Prayer, biblical readings, and religious discussion were prominent features of her rural New England upbringing, and Baptist, Methodist, and Congregational clergy frequented the family home. As a child, Eddy rebelled against the stern Calvinism of her father's religion, preferring the more loving deity of her mother's teaching. Despite her reservations about the doctrine of predestination, Eddy joined the Congregational Church and remained a member until she founded her own religious organization.

In the late twentieth century, feminist scholars turned to Eddy's life and leadership, hoping to find in her a model of empowerment for women. Eddy was not, however, primarily interested in political freedom but in a liberation theology that freed people from the "bondage of sickness and sin" (Eddy, 1875, p. 368).

Critics sought to dismiss Eddy by accusing her of being a hysterical female in the stereotypical nineteenth-century mode. This accusation failed to take into account an ancient precedent that may be more relevant in Eddy's case. In the second and third centuries CE Christian women were accused of hysteria by an emerging male religious hierarchy as a means of marginalizing women's religious authority. The accusation is particularly notable in patriarchal dismissal of female theologians who, like Eddy, functioned without deference to male authority. This precedent provides a historical antecedent, and not just a cultural one, for the opposition Eddy's teachings attracted.

EARLY LIFE. Eddy was born in Bow, New Hampshire, the youngest of the six children of Mark Baker and Abigail Ambrose Baker. Her formal education was sporadic, and she was often kept home from school due to illness. In her autobiography, *Retrospection and Introspection*, she wrote that her father was "taught to believe" her brain was too large for her body (Eddy, 1891, p. 10). Even though her schooling was uneven, she spent several terms at academies for young women.

Eddy was a keen learner and an avid reader, and throughout her life she kept scrapbooks of writings that had attracted her. In *Science and Health* she praised observation, invention, study, and original thought as "academics of the right sort" (Eddy, 1875, p. 195). Typically, what interested her were the ways thought was expanded through learning, rather than learning as mere acquisition of facts.

MARRIAGE AND MOTHERHOOD. Eddy's first marriage, in 1843, was to George Washington Glover. He died of yellow fever the following year, however. The pregnant widow returned to New England from her home in South Carolina, and eventually her young son was put in the care of a family retainer. Eddy was not reunited with him until he was grown and a parent himself.

In 1853, in the hope of providing a home for her son, Eddy married Daniel Patterson. He, however, was unwilling to have the boy. An itinerant dentist, Patterson was frequently absent from home, and in 1866 he abandoned his wife permanently. It was not until 1873 that Eddy applied for and was granted a divorce.

During these years Eddy suffered various illnesses that often kept her bedridden. She sought relief through a variety of alternative medical methods, including allopathy, homeopathy, and hydropathy. In 1862 she traveled to the Portland, Maine, clinic of Dr. Phineas P. Quimby, a magnetic healer. The extent of Quimby's influence on Eddy's thought is one of the more controversial aspects of her life.

After Eddy had become well known, Quimby's son and several of the doctor's associates claimed she had misrepresented Quimby's teaching as her own. Eddy acknowledged she had edited Quimby's notes but denied that he was her source for Christian Science. In fact, Quimby's techniques were based on mesmerism, while Eddy's practice was firmly rooted in the Christianity that had always been her strength.

Eddy's faith was tested after Quimby's death when in 1866 she suffered internal injuries following a fall on an icy path. Eddy later recalled that she turned to her Bible and read an account of one of Jesus' healings recorded in the Gospels. Subsequently she spoke of her instant recovery as a transformative experience in which she glimpsed "Life in and of Spirit" (Eddy, 1896, p. 24). The fall on the ice has assumed mythic importance in the history of Christian Science. Although the homeopathic physician who was called to Eddy's bedside later claimed it was his treatment that healed her, Eddy insisted it was her glimpse of a spiritual reality that effected the physical healing. The discovery of Christian Science is dated from this event.

Eddy's third marriage was to Asa Gilbert Eddy in 1877. Their brief union ended with his death in 1882. Gilbert

Eddy was one of his wife's early followers and the first to publicly advertise as a Christian Science healer.

Christian Science. Prior to her fall, Eddy's life had been fairly conventional. In nineteenth-century America, men held legal, financial, and decision-making power over women's lives. Women, especially genteel women, were daughters, sisters, wives, mothers, widows—and Eddy was all of these. Even in religion women were denied a public voice in worship and were expected to assent to the beliefs of their male relatives. In preaching a theology that promoted biblical authority over clerical teaching, and in founding a church, Eddy threatened established patriarchal positions and subsequently suffered legal, verbal, and even physical consequences.

Following her recovery, Eddy committed herself to a deep study of the Bible, spending the next several years seeking the spiritual significance of biblical accounts of healing. She searched for the "primitive Christianity" of Jesus and the early Christians in the period before the institutional church darkened its hue (Eddy, 1875, p. 139). This was her concept of evangelical religion. She wrote extensive exegetical notes, particularly reflecting on the books of *Genesis* and *Revelation.* Revisions of these books, and the addition of a glossary containing her interpretation of the spiritual meaning of selected terms mainly drawn from these two books, later formed the basis of her class teaching and the "Key to the Scriptures" section of the Christian Science textbook. As her radical ideas developed and she began to broadcast them, she found herself at odds with family and friends.

Over the next few years Eddy moved from boardinghouse to boardinghouse. She had little in the way of financial resources and made her living through modest literary contributions and eventually by taking students, to whom she began to teach her theology of healing. Her teaching was reinforced by her own healing practice. During this period she began writing her major work, *Science and Health with Key to the Scriptures,* the first edition of which was published in 1875. The book went through eight major revisions and over two hundred lesser versions before Eddy's death.

Initially Eddy hoped her ideas would be adopted by existing churches. When this did not happen, she organized her own church in 1879, only to abandon its charter in 1889. In 1892 she reorganized the church and named it the First Church of Christ, Scientist, in Boston, Massachusetts. Although Eddy herself preached both from the pulpit and in public halls, she decreed in 1895 that there would be no ordained clergy in her church. Instead she "ordained" the Bible and *Science and Health* as its pastor. Worship services consisted of readings from the Bible and "correlative passages" from her book. The readers, one man and one woman, were elected for a stipulated term from the lay membership.

In addition to Sunday and midweek worship, Eddy provided for lecturers who visited communities by invitation. Both women and men could be called to this position. She developed a highly centralized government for her church, delegating daily oversight to a board of directors. Both men and women were eligible to serve in this capacity, although female directors remained in the minority. Eddy also set up a structure for theological education, the teachers of which could be either men or women. Most notable, however, was the prominence of females in the public practice of what Eddy called Christian healing.

During the remainder of her life Eddy faced repeated internal dissension from followers wishing to supplement or supplant her teaching with their own. Most of these left Christian Science, and several of the women eventually became religious leaders in their own right, particularly in the New Thought movement. Eddy was convinced that the glimpse of spiritual reality she had experienced in 1866 and its subsequent refinement was divinely inspired and, as such, could not be modified by anyone else. Neither the church government she formed nor the denominational textbook she wrote can be revised. Her final achievement was the founding of an international newspaper, the *Christian Science Monitor,* in 1908.

At a time when many women lived domestically centered lives, Eddy's talent for organization and for conducting business, skills nineteenth-century society usually associated with men, attracted hostility and opposition. Followers defected and opponents criticized the control she maintained. At the same time, others found healing through the teachings of Christian Science.

Theological Teachings. As a child Eddy was immersed in the thought and language of the Bible. Her mature writings are replete with biblical allusions and citations. Her reading of the Bible, though, was often unconventional, and both nineteenth- and twentieth-century commentators criticized her theology as abstruse, uninformed, even heterodox.

In her spiritual interpretation of the Lord's Prayer, first published in 1891, Eddy defined God as Father and Mother. In 1900 she changed the designation to Father-Mother. Eddy was not the first female theologian to identify God in this way. Julian of Norwich (1342–after 1416) and the Shaker Mother Ann Lee (1736–1784) had described God as Mother, and there are biblical precedents as well. Hannah Whitall Smith, a contemporary of Eddy and a member of the Holiness movement in Philadelphia, also likened God to a Mother. However, there is no evidence that Eddy drew on any of these for her own interpretation.

From the third through the fifteenth editions of *Science and Health,* Eddy used the feminine pronoun for God in her chapter "Creation," reverting to the masculine pronoun in 1886. She also consistently employed nongendered terminology for God, referring to the deity as Life, Truth, Love, Spirit, Soul, Mind, and Principle.

Eddy's theological reflections in her chapter "Science, Theology, and Medicine" primarily relate to the nature of Christ and the character of Jesus. She wrote that Jesus was the highest human concept, inseparable from Christ, which she defined "as the divine idea of God outside the flesh" (Eddy, 1875, p. 482).

To a twenty-first-century reader, Eddy's use of *man* as a generic term sounds dated. However, she declared that masculine, feminine, and neuter genders are "human concepts," weakened by anthropomorphism (Eddy, 1875, p. 516). For Eddy, generic man was a nongendered spiritual idea, neither an "Eve or an Adam" (Eddy, 1887, p. 51). Feminist commentators operating out of a body-affirming late-twentieth-century and early-twenty-first-century imagination have been disappointed that Eddy's teaching does not relate to female bodies any more or less than to male bodies. Her rejection of corporeality as the real embodiment of woman and man is based on her teaching that the physical condition is a misapprehension. Eddy posits, on a biblical basis, that creation was originally and is ultimately spiritual. This spiritual image of body held in thought affects physical conditions in a redemptive manner that heals the human body.

A theologian, healer, teacher, author, and publisher, Eddy continued to function as leader of her church into her ninetieth year. In the twenty-first century Eddy has been recognized for her pioneering work in the field of spiritual healing.

SEE ALSO Christian Science; Lee, Ann; New Thought Movement.

BIBLIOGRAPHY

Eddy published *Science and Health with Key to the Scriptures* (Boston, 1875; reprint, Boston, 2000), the textbook of Christian Science. *Retrospection and Introspection* (Boston, 1891), Eddy's autobiography, is more of a theological statement than an account of her life. It is included in a collection, *Prose Works* (Boston, 1925), as is *Unity of Good* (Boston, 1887). *Miscellaneous Writings* (Boston, 1896) reprints addresses, letters, sermons, poems and articles written between 1883 and 1896. *Manual of the Mother Church* (Boston, 1895) specifies the governing structure of the First Church of Christ, Scientist.

Mary Farrell Bednarowski, *The Religious Imagination of American Women* (Bloomington, Ind., 1999), includes a short section on Eddy that considers her and the religious movement she founded as the outcome of her emphasis on a practical reciprocity between theology and healing. Bednarowski identifies several areas where, she argues, contemporary women healers owe an often unacknowledged debt to Eddy's efforts. Yvonne Caché von Fettweis and Robert Townsend Warneck, *Mary Baker Eddy: Christian Healer* (Boston, 1998), is a collection of testimonials from individuals who benefited from Eddy's healing gifts. The accounts are interspersed with biographical details and comments about events in the history of the church, and the book includes brief notes about persons cited in the text.

Martin Gardner, *The Healing Revelations of Mary Baker Eddy: The Rise and Fall of Christian Science* (Buffalo, N.Y., 1993), written by a person who is not an admirer of Eddy, relies heavily on material that has been published previously by other critics. Gillian Gill, *Mary Baker Eddy* (Radcliffe Biography Series, Reading, Mass., 1998), is a massive, heavily notated biography. Gill offers detailed analysis of Eddy's childhood and family relationships and chronicles her public life. Gill had unprecedented access to church archives, and much original material was published for the first time in this volume. She also provides a useful annotated bibliography of both the favorable and the critical literature on Eddy. Stephen Gottschalk, *The Emergence of Christian Science in American Religious Life* (Berkeley, Calif., 1973), includes biographical data on Eddy but is primarily a social-intellectual history of Christian Science as a cultural phenomenon. Bliss Knapp, *The Destiny of the Mother Church* (Boston, 1991), originally copyrighted in 1947 but not published until over forty years later, is a biography that caused profound internal church controversy. Richard A. Nenneman, *Persistent Pilgrim: The Life of Mary Baker Eddy* (Etna, N.H., 1997), offers an overview of key events in Eddy's life with particular emphasis on critical moments during the establishment of the Christian Science movement. Nenneman cites previously unpublished material from church archives.

Robert Peel, *Mary Baker Eddy*, vol. 1, *The Years of Discovery*; vol. 2, *The Years of Trial*; vol. 3, *The Years of Authority* (New York, 1966–1977), a biography written by a Christian Scientist, is a contextualized and well-documented treatment of Eddy with particular emphasis on her evolving leadership. Ann Braude, "The Perils of Passivity: Women's Leadership in Spiritualism and Christian Science," in *Women's Leadership in Marginal Religions*, edited by Catherine Wessinger, pp. 55–67 (Urbana, Ill., 1993), asks whether women are empowered in movements founded by women. Braude prioritizes organizational factors over theological ones when considering Eddy's relationships with potential rivals, either male or female.

DIANE TREACY-COLE (2005)

EDO RELIGION. The Edo-speaking peoples live in a tropical forest region of southern Nigeria. Their language formerly belonged to the Kwa family of Niger-Congo languages and is now classified with the South Central Niger-Congo group (Ruhlen, 1991). The Edo proper, centered in and around Benin City, are of long standing in this region. Oral traditions suggest that by the thirteenth or fourteenth century, the Edo were united into a powerful kingdom that by the fifteenth century had embarked on a course of aggressive military expansion in southern Nigeria. At the end of the fifteenth century, Portuguese explorers made contact with them, recording for the first time the name *Benin*, which has been used since to refer to the kingdom (the people are sometimes referred to as the *Bini*). In the ensuing 500 years following contact with Portugal, the Benin traded with many European nations until, in 1897, Benin fell to British colonial expansion and was incorporated into the wider political framework of Nigeria. Benin City, the capital of the kingdom from medieval times, is today the administrative center and capital of modern Edo State, one of thirty-three states created in late-twentieth-century, postcolonial Nigeria.

Traditional Edo religion divides the world into two realms: a visible world of ordinary human experience, and an invisible world of gods, ancestors, and other supernatural beings. The spirit world is a realm located under the ground or where the sky and earth meet. It has a parallel existence that constantly affects the everyday world. Rituals central to Edo religion, including prayers, offerings, and sacrifices, take place at meeting points between both realms, at shrines inside homes and villages, or at the foot of trees, crossroads, or the banks of rivers.

The two realms were created by the supreme being, Osanobua. He also established the framework of space and time and made the first humans by breathing lifeforce into molded clay images. Osanobua is envisioned as a king living in a palace from which he presides over the spirit world, having delegated responsibility for the everyday world to his children, the other gods of the Edo pantheon. The most important among them is Olokun, his son and ruler of the great waters, who resides in his own palace under the Ethiope River, which the Edo believe is the source of all the world's waters. From there Olokun sends the blessings of wealth and children to his faithful devotees, especially women who desire children. Olokun's wives and chiefs are the gods of the main rivers of the kingdom and are worshiped locally by villagers.

Ogun, another son of Osanobua, is the patron deity of all who work and use metal: the blacksmiths and brass and bronze casters; and the warriors, hunters, farmers, and modern vehicle drivers, for example. Ogun is seen as the god "who opens the way"—that is, he makes it possible for other deities and ancestors to be effective. Olokun and Ogun are vital forces in contemporary Edo religious life, but some deities, such as Ogiuwu, god of death, and Obiemwen, the great mother goddess, are no longer worshiped in Benin. Other deities, including Esu, Sango, and Oronmila, have been borrowed from the Yoruba to the west of Benin, especially in border areas where the two ethnic groups have been in close contact. Mammy Water is a cult borrowed from the Igbo area to the east.

Edo men and women alike may keep a shrine or shrines to Olokun, Ogun, or other gods. In addition, families and subdivisions (quarters) of towns and villages also keep communal shrines for the worship of various local deities. A family or ancestral shrine is kept in the house of the eldest son, who inherits all his father's property. Requests for assistance and appeals are addressed to these ancestors as well as to the gods.

Individuals both male and female become religious specialists through apprenticeship, attainment of seniority, or a by a religious "calling" signaled in trance states. There are two main religious roles: priest or priestess and Osun adept, Osun being the god of medicines. Priests and priestesses officiate at ceremonies, perform sacrifices, lead songs and prayers, and convey messages from a deity who "speaks" through them while they are dancing and/or in a trance. Throughout the year priests hold annual festivals to honor their own deity (usually Olokun or Ogun) and others. They also hold an annual festival to honor the deity who "speaks" through them. Although some priests have the knowledge to cure illness, the Osun specialists are the primary medical experts in traditional Edo religion and culture. The adept of Osun, seeking to gain knowledge of the power inherent in leaves and herbs, undergoes an apprenticeship, after which he is able to divine the causes of sickness, prescribe herbal treatments; in the old days, he also administered poison and other ordeals. Witchcraft is widely believed to be the ultimate cause of illness. Witches are identified as persons of evil intent who use their knowledge of herbalism to cause barrenness, disease, and premature death. At night witches are able to transform themselves into predatory birds and fly about. They meet in trees and plot to harm their innocent victims.

Adult men and women who have lived a full lifespan and have children receive a proper burial. The male heads of families join the group's ancestors who reside in the spirit world, but maintain their interest and involvement in the daily lives of their descendants. The ancestral altar located in the home of the senior male of a lineage, or the shrine in a special section of a ward or a village, is the focus of sacrifices and prayers at periodic rituals and in times of crisis, when appeals for help are made.

The ancestors of the king of Benin (who is known as the *oba*) are considered the protectors of the nation at large. Their altars are national shrines housed in the royal palace. As the descendant of these divine kings and the possessor of vast supernatural powers, the *oba* is a central figure in Edo religion. In Edo cosmology, the *oba* is called "king of dry land," and he is the earthly counterpart of the great deity Olokun, "king of the waters," giver of wealth and children. The king and his court are occupied throughout the year with public and private rituals aimed at preserving the well-being and prosperity of the Edo nation.

In the early sixteenth century the *oba* permitted Portuguese Catholic missionaries to establish their church in Benin City; it lasted until the late seventeenth century. The church was reestablished in the twentieth century and is known as the *oba*'s church, with worshipers at three locations in the city. Twentieth-century missionary activity by Protestant denominations and many evangelical groups converted some Edo to Christianity, and some Edo have converted to Islam, but traditional religion, with the *oba* at its core, continues to flourish.

BIBLIOGRAPHY

R. E. Bradbury's *The Benin Kingdom and the Edo-Speaking Peoples of South-Western Nigeria* (London, 1957) provides a brief overview of Edo religion, and his collected essays, *Benin Studies,* edited by Peter Morton-Williams (London, 1973), explore specific issues in depth. Paula Ben-Amos has discussed religious iconography in *The Art of Benin* (London, 1980) and in several articles: "Ekpo Ritual in Avbiama Village," *African Arts* 2, no. 4 (1969): 8–13, 79, written jointly with Osarenren Omoregie; "Symbolism in Olokun Mud Art," *African Arts* 6, no. 4 (1973): 28–31, 95; and "Men and Animals in Benin Art," *Man* n.s. 2, no. 2 (1976): 243–252. Flora Edouwaye S. Kaplan provides holistic views and context into Benin religion in: "Some Thoughts on Ideology, Beliefs, and Sacred Kingship among the Edo (Benin) People of Nigeria," in *African Spirituality: Forms, Meanings, and Expressions,* edited by Jacob K. Olupona (New York, 2002); and the roles of the Oba and of sacrifices in Benin religion in greater detail in "Understanding Sacrifice and Sanctity in Benin Indigenous Religion: A Case Study," in *Beyond Primitivism: Indigenous Religious Traditions and Modernity,* edited by Jacob K. Olupona (London and New York, 2003). African language classification is updated in Merritt Ruhlen's *A Guide to the World's Languages,* vol. 1: *Classification.* Stanford, Calif., 1991(1987). Additional important sources include Ekhaguosa, Aisen, *Iwu, the Body Markings of the Edo People* (Benin City, Nigeria, 1986); Imoagene, Oshomha, *The Edo and their Neighbours* (Ibadan, Nigeria, 1990); Momoh, Tony, *Edo Culture Group in the Nigerian Polity in Search of Sanity* (Lagos, Nigeria, 1996); and Oyakhire, George B. L., *An Edo Civilization: Owan Chieftancy Institution* (Benin City, Nigeria, 1997).

PAULA BEN-AMOS (1987)
FLORA EDOUWAYE S. KAPLAN (2005)

EDUCATION, RELIGIOUS SEE RELIGIOUS EDUCATION

EDWARDS, JONATHAN (1703–1758), was an American theologian and philosopher. Born in East Windsor, Connecticut, Edwards was the only son in a family of eleven children. His father, Timothy Edwards, a graduate of Harvard College, was the minister of the Congregational church in that town. His mother was the daughter of Solomon Stoddard, the minister at Northampton, Massachusetts.

LIFE AND WORK. As a youth Edwards was nurtured and instructed in the tenets of Reformed theology and the practices of Puritan piety. He entered the Collegiate School (later Yale College) in 1716; the course of study included classical and biblical languages, logic, natural philosophy, and the "new philosophy." He received the B.A. degree in 1720 and subsequently spent two additional years in New Haven studying theology. These early years, during which Edwards's inclination toward intellectual pursuits quickly became evident, were difficult but significant; the same period proved decisive religiously, too.

In August 1722 Edwards accepted his first pastorate at a Presbyterian congregation in New York City, a position he held until May of the following year. In the fall of 1723 he became the pastor at Bolton, Connecticut, but after a short time gave up the position. In May 1724 he assumed responsibilities as a tutor at Yale College. Two years later he resigned to become the ministerial colleague of his maternal grandfather in Northampton. He was ordained in February 1727 and in the same year married Sarah Pierrepont, the daughter of the Congregational minister in New Haven. Upon the death of Stoddard in 1729, Edwards became the full minister in Northampton.

The following years were times of expanding responsibilities. Edwards paid a great deal of attention to the preparation of sermons. A lecture he gave at Boston in 1731 became the first of his sermons to be published. He began to gain a reputation as a defender of Reformed doctrines. Edwards became a leading member of the Hampshire Association, an organization of clergymen in the county. His family also expanded with regularity, eventually reaching a total of eleven children.

The congregation at Northampton experienced an extraordinary manifestation of religious zeal during the winter of 1734–1735. The ferment spread to other communities in the Connecticut River valley. Accounts of these events sent by Edwards to Boston eventually circulated in expanded form throughout the American colonies and Great Britain, making him something of a celebrity. To his dismay, however, the religious fervor in Northampton proved short-lived.

In the fall of 1740 the languishing religious situation in New England changed dramatically with the arrival from England of George Whitefield, who in mid-October visited Northampton, where his preaching affected many, including Edwards. Scores of ministers adopted Whitefield's pattern of itinerancy and began to preach outside their own pulpits. In July 1741, for example, Edwards preached his now-famous sermon titled "Sinners in the Hands of an Angry God" at Enfield, Connecticut, having delivered earlier versions at several locations. The emotional outbursts accompanying the Great Awakening became increasingly controversial, causing critics to question the legitimacy of the revivalists and of the "New Lights." By 1742 the opponents of the revivals, led by Charles Chauncy of Boston's First Church, stepped up their attacks. Edwards answered these "Old Lights" by publishing a major defense of the revivals, declaring them the work of God's spirit and a harbinger of the millennial age. During the same period he preached a series of sermons that became the nucleus for his fullest statement on the evangelical nature of true religion, *A Treatise Concerning Religious Affections.* After the revivals waned again, he sought new ways to foster religious concern: For example, he supported a plan for a worldwide concert of prayer.

Late in the 1740s Edwards was forced to turn his attention to problems in Northampton. Conflict developed with members of his congregation over questions of ministerial authority. An open rupture was provoked by Edwards's announcement that he intended to discontinue his grandfather's practice of admitting to communion those in good standing, unless they could provide evidence of a work of grace in their lives. The conflict spread into town politics and into relations with neighboring ministers; bitter factionalism prevailed. After months of controversy, a council of ministers and laity recommended a separation, and Edwards's formal dismissal followed in mid-1750.

Edwards faced uncertain prospects following his removal. After receiving several offers to settle, including one tentative proposal from Scotland, in May 1751 he accepted a pastoral call to Stockbridge in western Massachusetts, a mission outpost populated by a few whites and more than 250 Indian families. Life at Stockbridge was difficult, especially after the outbreak of warfare in the mid-1750s. Despite the circumstances, these years were perhaps Edwards's most productive. Not only did he continue his pattern of study, but he wrote several major treatises. His writings gave voice to a lifetime of reflection.

In the fall of 1757 Edwards received an invitation from the College of New Jersey (later Princeton) to become president of that young Presbyterian institution. After some reluctance, he consented and in February 1758 journeyed to New Jersey. One week after his arrival he was inoculated against smallpox; less than one month later he became a victim of that disease. Edwards was buried in the cemetery at Princeton.

WRITINGS. The writings of Edwards fall into five categories: personal writings, sermons, occasional pieces, philosophical and theological works less directly occasional, and private notebooks. A substantial body of materials exists in each of these categories.

Edwards's most significant personal writings from the early period of his life, the "Diary" and "Resolutions," provide a contemporary record of his spiritual struggles and of his determination to pursue the religious life. The "Personal Narrative," a later recollection, records for spiritual edification his youthful experiences. Moreover, Edwards's correspondence was voluminous. He wrote to family members, students and colleagues, business associates, and evangelical leaders in America and Great Britain. His letters reveal a personal side not evident in the standard depictions of him as an intellectual, a preacher, and a polemicist.

Edwards's most pressing responsibility was preaching to his congregation. He invested heavily in the preparation of sermons, which often gave the first public expression to ideas developed in his notebooks. During his lifetime Edwards published eighteen sermons. The most famous of all, his Enfield sermon, continues to attract widespread attention today. Of greater significance, perhaps, is the "Farewell Sermon" in which he revealed his personal perspective upon the Northampton controversy. Two of Edwards's sermon series, *A History of the Work of Redemption* and *Charity and Its Fruits,* were published as treatises after his death. Today there is extant a collection of approximately thirteen hundred manuscript sermons.

A substantial number of Edwards's publications were written in response to particular circumstances. The most notable of his occasional writings describe and defend the revivals. *A Faithful Narrative* is clinically descriptive by contrast with the partisan, celebratory tone of *Some Thoughts. A Treatise Concerning Religious Affections* is theologically reflective, the *Life of Brainerd* didactic, and *An Humble Attempt* guardedly optimistic. All form part of an extended apology for evangelical religion. His publications relating to the communion controversy, although polemical, reinforce the same concerns.

Nearly all of Edwards's writings are in a sense occasional. Several of his publications, however, are more programmatic, defining fundamental theological and philosophical positions. For example, in the treatises *Free Will* and *Original Sin,* Edwards addressed himself to questions regarding human nature and human capacity. But they too were written in response to Enlightenment assaults upon traditional views and are part of his defense of classic Reformed doctrines. Shorter writings, titled *End of Creation* and *True Virtue,* have an even more abstract quality. At his death Edwards was at work on a rational defense of Christianity, a harmony of scripture, and a history of the work of redemption.

Edwards's study habits yielded an immense amount of material in his private notebooks. The notebooks "Natural Philosophy" and "The Mind" have received widespread attention, but the "Miscellanies," which contains theological, biblical, and philosophical reflections, is the most important source for tracing the development of his ideas. He also devoted separate notebooks to general biblical commentary, apocalyptic writing, typology, prophecy, history, sermon ideas, and symbolism in nature. Edwards's method of study included writing and rewriting his ideas, developing certain themes, and citing or paraphrasing works he read. The "Catalogue," a notebook referring to his reading, contains a working bibliography that documents the wide range of his interests.

THOUGHT. Edwards's religious and philosophical ideas form a coherent body of thought, but no complete system was stated by him. Among his unfinished projects were plans for such a statement. He must be viewed as a transitional thinker, looking back to the Reformed heritage and also drawing heavily upon the Enlightenment. Edwards employed biblical concepts as well as insights from the new science. He set for himself the task of defending orthodox views against liberal assaults from the Arminian party, but he also borrowed the ideas of his contemporaries to revise and restate the tradition.

One central theme in Edwards's thought is the universal depravity of humankind. According to him, all humanity shared in the original sin of Adam whereby a supernatural gift of grace was lost. The identity of humankind with Adam was constituted by divine decree, and by virtue of that identity, the fall condemned all to a life of certain and actual sin. Sin, in turn, merits condemnation and punishment; the greater the sin, the greater the deserved punishment. Transgressions against God are deserving of eternal retribution. Since the fall, humans are not truly free to choose the good.

Free will is a matter of semantics, for the will is free only to choose sin.

A second major theme in Edwards's thought is the sufficiency of God in the work of redemption. Humanity is totally dependent upon a gracious God who from eternity elected some for salvation. Edwards described God's nature variously. During his youth he spoke in idealistic categories, positing the necessary existence of an eternal Mind. Later he described God as the sun and the light from which everything derives its existence. He also employed the traditional language of the Trinity: The Father generates the Son from himself and is himself the source and object of his loving Spirit. In the redemptive act the Father appoints the Son as the Redeemer and accepts him as a sufficient price, and through his Spirit he communicates the good that has been purchased to those who have been chosen. The excellency of Christ is sufficient for the work of redemption. The presence of the Spirit defines a saint; only those with the indwelling divine principle are saved. The new birth signals the restoration of the supernatural gift lost with the fall into sin. Conversion is the moment when grace is infused into the life of the individual.

A third major theme is the legitimacy of the affections in true religion. Edwards believed that faith necessarily involves both the intellect or understanding and the volition or will. It is an act of affective knowledge, a sense of the heart. Belief inclines the heart toward what the understanding chooses. This holistic approach to religious experience was the linchpin for Edwards's case against both the rationalists and the enthusiasts. Against the former he held that, contrary to their belief, the emotions are legitimate in the religious life. Although he shared with John Locke a fear of the passions, he was unwilling to rule out the affections because he had investigated with great care specific cases of emotional religion and found them to be genuine. At the same time, he charged the enthusiasts with ignoring the role of the intellect in religious experience.

Edwards inherited his interest in practical religion from the Puritans, but the revivals raised the question of how to distinguish genuine religion from false. He sought to answer this question by establishing clear signs for the former. In true religion, he said, the witness of the Spirit is manifest both in the exercises of grace within the heart and in outward practice. True conversion is evident from the presence of both faith and love within the person. Self-examination is one way to test the state of grace, but the expression of holy affections in love of God and human beings is the chief means of assurance. Moreover, for Edwards conversion was never an end in itself but merely the beginning of the Christian life; the responsibility of the elect to pursue this godly life was another major theme in his thought. Sanctification, he held, follows justification as the product of the indwelling Spirit. Edwards insisted that true virtue consists in consent to or union with being in general, and that love of God for its own sake is the foundation for all other morality.

Finally, Edwards's system also embraced a vision of future glory. In his belief, the church comprises the community of the elect on earth, that is, those who have experienced grace in their lives. In covenant with others, the saints engage in the business of religion: good works, attendance at ordinances, worship, prayer, reading the Bible, and pursuit of their vocations. These activities reflect the kingdom of God in the world. Under the leadership of the ministry, the church seeks to expand and increase. Edwards's interest in missions reflected his larger understanding of history. The work of redemption, according to him, has progressed by God's direction from the time of biblical history to the contemporary moment and is moving toward a millennial climax on earth. The culmination of the Kingdom will bring the greater glory of God—the ultimate goal of creation and the purpose of the created order. Edwards looked eagerly for the fulfillment of this biblical vision.

Influence. During his lifetime Edwards achieved prominence and widespread reputation as a preacher, a leader of the revivalistic faction, and an evangelical theologian. Less than a decade after his death, Samuel Hopkins, disciple and close friend, declared that Edwards was one of the greatest theologians of the age. A school of New England theologians that emerged during the second half of the eighteenth century and that included Hopkins, Joseph Bellamy, and Jonathan Edwards, Jr., among its members held Edwards in high esteem even while beginning to depart from his specific views; that departure reflected the growing influence of the Enlightenment on American theology. Evangelicals in the first half of the nineteenth century continued this pattern of response. The publication and republication during this period of Edwards's works in collected editions is striking evidence of his stature, as is the circulation by tract societies of his works in abridged editions. On the other hand, the contrasting views of Charles Grandison Finney are a useful measure of the evangelical movement away from Edwards in antebellum America.

The second half of the nineteenth century witnessed an erosion of interest in Edwards and an increasing hostility toward his theological positions, particularly his commitment to the notion of human depravity, the doctrine of necessity, and the idea of eternal retribution. Although considerable praise was given to Edwards's skills as a metaphysician and logician, theological and cultural liberals condemned his ideas; even those who admired him and accepted his evangelical premises often viewed him as a tragic figure. The bicentennial of his birth produced only a small surge of interest in Edwards the man.

By the middle of the twentieth century, the prevailing attitude toward Edwards's work changed dramatically as a confluence of circumstances brought about a renaissance of interest in his ideas and a reassessment of his significance. This new interest, which had begun as a trickle of scholarship in the late 1930s, has in the present time risen to a flood tide. Edwards has become a major figure, a creative force, one of the most original thinkers in the American experience. Among the reasons for the change have been the new cultural climate in America following the Great Depression, the accompanying theological reappraisal that gave rise in American Protestantism to neoorthodoxy, and the growing concern about national origins, including the role of the Puritans in American life. An increasing number of conservative Protestants in America have also identified their thought with his evangelical views. This renewed engagement with the full range of Edwards's ideas has manifested itself among scholars in their support for a new critical edition of his writings. Today Edwards remains the object of sustained investigation by many in a variety of fields. For the moment, his place is secure within the pantheon of American thinkers.

BIBLIOGRAPHY

The works of Jonathan Edwards were collected several times in the nineteenth century. A new edition, *Works,* edited by Perry Miller and subsequently by John E. Smith, is in preparation (New Haven, 1957–). The monographic essays that constitute introductions to the volumes of this edition focus upon a range of particular religious issues relating to the life, thought, and influence of Edwards. The earliest biography of Edwards, which contains the text of the "Personal Narrative," is Samuel Hopkins's *The Life and Character of the Late Reverend Mr. Jonathan Edwards, President of the College at New-Jersey* (Boston, 1765). It has been reprinted in *Jonathan Edwards: A Profile,* edited by David Levin (New York, 1969). Numerous personal documents and items of correspondence from Edwards appear in Sereno E. Dwight's *The Life of President Edwards* (New York, 1829), the first volume of an edition of *The Works of President Edwards,* 10 vols. (New York, 1829–1830). The story of Edwards's life is told without undue concern for its intellectual dimensions in Ola E. Winslow's *Jonathan Edwards, 1703–1758* (New York, 1940), a prizewinning biography. The pastoral career of Edwards is the focus of Patricia J. Tracy's *Jonathan Edwards, Pastor: Religion and Society in Eighteenth Century Northampton* (New York, 1980). Perhaps the volume most responsible for the renaissance of scholarly interest in Edwards since the 1940s is Perry Miller's *Jonathan Edwards* (New York, 1949), a problematical interpretation focusing upon the influence of John Locke and Isaac Newton. The relationship between Edwards's thought and the tradition of Reformed theology is treated with care and precision in Conrad Cherry's *The Theology of Jonathan Edwards: A Reappraisal* (Garden City, N.Y., 1966). The influence of the English moral philosophers on Edwards is discussed in Norman Fiering's *Jonathan Edwards's Moral Thought and Its British Context* (Chapel Hill, N.C., 1981). The most comprehensive bibliography of writings about Edwards is M. X. Lesser's *Jonathan Edwards: A Reference Guide* (Boston, 1981). Lesser's volume consists of an excellent essay focusing upon the changing interpretation of Edwards and an annotated, descriptive bibliography. Three volumes that place Edwards centrally in the development of American thought and culture are Alan E. Heimert's *Religion and the American Mind* (Cambridge, Mass., 1966), Sacvan Bercovitch's *The American Jeremiad* (Madison, Wis., 1978), and Bruce Kuklick's *Churchmen and Philosophers: From Jonathan Edwards to John Dewey* (New Haven, 1985).

STEPHEN J. STEIN (1987)

EGG.

The egg has aroused feelings of wonder in cultures all over the world. Its smooth, elliptical shell conceals the mystery of new life in formation. The sight of an egg hatching and a young creature bursting out from an apparently lifeless object stimulated ancient peoples to think about the creative process. It would have been difficult for early humans to understand an abstraction such as the creation of the world, but they could watch a similar process in the hatching of an egg. Thus the egg became an important symbol in creation stories.

The concept of a world egg that hatched the first creator appears in many early myths. The Harris Magical Papyrus, an Egyptian manuscript of the New Kingdom period (1569–1085 BCE), contains the earliest known reference to a world egg emerging from the primeval waters. Several Egyptian deities are associated with the egg: Thoth, god of the moon; the sun god, Re; the celestial goose, Seb, god of the earth; Ptah of Memphis; and Khnum, god of creation, who shaped the world egg on his potter's wheel.

The Hindu Upaniṣads (c. 600–300 BCE) describe the first act of creation as an egg breaking in two. The *Ṛgveda,* a body of Hindu hymns, sacrificial formulas, and incantations collected in the first millennium BCE, speaks of Prajāpati, Lord of Creation, who fertilizes the waters of creation, which change into a golden egg. Inside sits the golden figure of Brahma, floating in the primeval waters for a thousand years, his golden light shining through seven shells. Land, sea, mountains, planets, gods, and humankind are all inside the egg with him.

In Chinese legend Pangu, the first man, emerged from the cosmic egg, as did Sun Wukong, the popular monkey king of Daoist and Buddhist legend.

Oceania has many stories of the origin of humankind from eggs. The divine bird laid one on the water, according to the Sandwich Islanders, and their islands hatched from its shell. Fijians attribute the origin of humans to Ngendei, who nurtured the world egg, and tribes in southeastern Australia believe the sun emerged from an emu egg thrown into the air.

In the Jewish tradition, eggs are used on many ceremonial occasions. Lag ba-ʿOmer, a joyful festival honoring the memory of Rabbi Shimʿon bar Yoḥai, falls on the thirty-third day between Passover and Pentecost. Children and their parents picnic with colored eggs. While the pious rabbi lived, God's symbolic rainbow, a sign that he would not destroy the world, was unnecessary. When he died, people needed the rainbow and hastened its coming by dyeing eggs in many colors.

The Seder, or Passover meal, always includes among its ritual foods a roasted egg. This is variously explained as a symbol of the additional sacrifice offered in the Temple at Passover, the sacrifice of travelers, or the departure from Egypt. More likely it signified rebirth, since Jewish mourners are traditionally fed baked eggs.

In the third and fourth centuries of the common era, the Christian church gradually adopted a Lenten fast of forty days commemorating the time Christ spent without food in the wilderness. Pope Gregory the Great (r. 590–604 CE) decreed that all Christians must renounce meat, cheese, butter, milk, and eggs at this time. The Orthodox church was very strict and permitted only the consumption of fruit, vegetables, bread, honey, and nuts. Hence it is not surprising that eggs form an important part of the festival food at Easter.

Easter is a major feast for Orthodox Christians in Russia and other countries of the former Soviet Union, and churches are filled for the midnight Mass. On Easter Sunday the dead are remembered. Hundreds visit the cemeteries to sit by the graves of their loved ones. They consume red eggs and scatter the shells on the soil.

It is not clear when the custom of exchanging eggs at Easter was first established. In his book *Easter: Its Story and Meaning* (1950), Alan Watts suggests that there are no western European records of Easter eggs prior to the fifteenth century. But the household accounts of the English king Edward I for 1290 record that eighteen pence was spent on decorating Easter eggs with gold leaf for presentation to members of his court. Poles were preparing Easter eggs before the eleventh century, and two goose eggs adorned with stripes and dots were found in a grave at Worms, Germany, dated 320 CE. Scholars are not sure whether this grave was the site of a Christian burial.

For Christians the Easter egg is a symbol of the resurrection of Christ. As a bird breaks out from its shell, so Christ arose from his tomb at the resurrection. In the Middle Ages it was a usual practice to place colored eggs in the replica of the tomb during the Easter service. Sometimes the clergy laid them on the altar as they greeted each other with the words "Christ is risen." This custom was observed in parts of France until the eighteenth century.

In traditional folk religion the egg is a powerful symbol of fertility, purity, and rebirth. It is used in magical rituals to promote fertility and restore virility; to look into the future; to bring good weather; to encourage the growth of the crops and protect both cattle and children against misfortune, especially the dreaded evil eye. All over the world it represents life and creation, fertility and resurrection. It appears at all the major events in the life cycle: birth, courtship, marriage, sickness, and death, as well as during Holy Week and the Easter period. It is the bearer of strength because it contains the seeds of life. In early times eggs were interred with the dead. Later they were linked with Easter. The church did not oppose this, though many egg customs were pre-Christian in origin, because the egg provided a fresh and powerful symbol of the resurrection and the transformation of death into life.

BIBLIOGRAPHY

Newall, Venetia. *An Egg at Easter: A Folklore Study.* Bloomington, Ind., 1971. A comparative treatment of the egg myth from the earliest recorded references until contemporary usage, and a study of the egg's symbolic role in tradition and belief.

Shoemaker, Alfred L. *Eastertide in Pennsylvania.* Kutztown, Pa., 1960. Provides information about Easter egg customs of the Pennsylvania Dutch community.

Václavík, Antonín. *Vyrocni obyceje a lidové umeni.* Prague, 1959. A handsomely illustrated volume that shows examples of the ornate Easter eggs prepared in Czechoslovakia. English and Russian summaries of the text are provided.

Weinhold, Gertrud. *Das schöne Osterei in Europa.* Kassel, 1967. A well-illustrated little book that provides a brief and popularly presented overview of the Easter egg customs in Europe.

Wildhaber, Robert. *Wir färben Ostereier.* Bern, 1957. An attractive booklet by the late director of the Swiss Folklore Museum, Basel, which contains a large and famous collection of decorated Easter eggs.

VENETIA NEWALL (1987)

EGYPTIAN RELIGION

This entry consists of the following articles:

AN OVERVIEW
THE LITERATURE
HISTORY OF STUDY

EGYPTIAN RELIGION: AN OVERVIEW

Before beginning to survey ancient Egyptian religion, a number of limiting factors must be considered. The data upon which this survey rests come from all periods and many different sites, but these times and places are very unevenly represented. Clearly, more data survive from the later periods, from the south of the country (Upper Egypt), and from the very highest social strata. Some cult centers were totally lost long ago. Others required periodic renovation, while the increased devotion and/or increased wealth of later generations also led to large-scale rebuilding efforts. Because of this it is often impossible to survey what went on for thousands of years at the major temples of Memphis and Heliopolis, difficult to assess the cultic changes at major sites such as the Karnak and Luxor temples, and almost impossible to reconstruct the pre-Greek beliefs and cultic practices from the largely Ptolemaic remains at the sites of Edfu, Dendera, and Philae. Material from numerous cemeteries in the deserts near town sites, sometimes on the opposite side of the Nile, provides more eschatological data than anything else, but it also occasionally provides doctrinal, devotional, ethical, or cosmological information about one or another of the creeds of ancient Egypt. Monumental architecture is often not synchronous with monumental pieces of religious literature, and some of the most commonly repeated texts are often much less insightful than some unique, fragmentary pieces.

RELIGIOUS TEXTS AND HISTORICAL SETTING. Of the texts that survive from ancient Egypt, the religious literature as a whole remains the most difficult to comprehend. There are a variety of explanations for this, including the carelessness of scribes, the composite nature of the collections, efforts to keep the material esoteric or arcane, and also factors having to do with the modern editing of the texts. In examples from both temple walls and papyri, the original scribe's efforts have been mishandled by copyists and artists. Texts chosen from different sources for a new purpose were not always fully understood by the scribes, who tried to incorporate old or unfamiliar bits. For much of the religious literature researchers are simply not familiar enough with all the mythological allusions, the magic, the rites, and the puns, and in the case of the Ptolemaic material, efforts were made originally to encode the texts with widespread and multifold sign substitution. These Ptolemaic hieroglyphs, which contain much of the accumulated myths and rituals at several major sites, also were not completely consistent from one site to another. One problem with modern editions of the religious literature is that the major concern has been to establish the best text by assembling parallels, with the result that the individual complete manuscripts are not understood or easily compared. The order of the texts in these editions is generally not that of any individual manuscript, and the variations that occur are completely lost in them, and in the translations made directly from them.

On the positive side, it should be noted that a large quantity of texts have been published now, and these include almost all the texts on several large temples. The temple texts furnish descriptions of the deities, their mythic significance, daily rites, and festivals, and to some extent the interaction between the human and divine worlds. Not all of the texts have been translated yet, but some important ones on rites and feasts have been, and attempts based on the texts found on the temple walls to explain the function of various parts of temples are not far off the mark. The major collections of mortuary or funerary texts from tombs are also available now, and preliminary published translations at least present the different Egyptian views concerning the afterlife and provide additional information concerning almost all aspects of Egyptian religion. There have also been numerous studies dealing with individual deities or concepts based on the phenomena encountered in all sources, and while these may not accurately reflect what the religion was for any one time or place, they do provide useful references for future synchronic studies, and again are probably not terribly far from the mark. Surveys of all of ancient Egyptian religion, also for the most part phenomenological, almost always have important observations to offer, though they do tend to be much less accurate in their generalizations and their subjectivity is often too significant an ingredient. Any details from which such generalizations are made may have applied to only an individual or a small group, when many different levels of belief and devotion were possibly current at the same time. To some extent, the survey that follows indicates trends, tendencies, and what apparently was appealing or approved at the highest levels, with the political motive often as weighty as the religious.

Already in prehistoric times, burial customs indicated a belief in life after death, which would have required that the body be preserved along with some household furnishings and food offerings. The expectation or hope was for a life after death that was not unlike human existence in this world. The locations of tombs and position of the bodies in their graves became traditional, and the traditions may have been more or less religious. Bodies were usually in a crouched position on their left sides with the head to the south and facing west, a custom that could be associated with the cult of Osiris or other gods of the dead in a western necropolis, or even with the location of the setting sun and perhaps the cult of the sun god. The exceptional site with a head to the north could also be understood in terms of an astral cult (reflected in later Pyramid Texts), with the goal of the deceased being to join the imperishable stars in the northern sky. There has been a great deal of speculation concerning the association of various cults with different localities in Egyptian prehistory, some of this based on finds but most on later evidence and claims. With the wealth of material available from historical context, it is surely best to omit speculation on undocumented origins and on the supposed interactions of the various prehistoric cult centers.

At the very beginnings of Egyptian history the slate palette of Narmer (c. 3110–3056 BCE) shows this king of Upper Egypt, who is wearing the white crown of the south, smiting a northerner, while on the reverse side of the palette Narmer is shown wearing the red crown of Lower Egypt. Whether Narmer or his son, Aha, was actually the first king (later known as Menes) of the first dynasty is still debatable, but some of the emblematic representations on the palette may have mythological significance. Both the bull and the falcon can represent aspects of the king's power, but the latter seems very likely to be associated with the identification of the king as the god Horus, a principal element in the myth of divine kingship. Since all but one king of Egypt is known to have been identified with the title "Horus," this myth is both very early and also, perhaps, one of the cornerstones of Egypt's success. There are several aspects of Horus, however, and even several Horuses, so that the full and precise meaning of this early representation could easily be overstated if it were said that all that is known of the association of the king and Horus from later texts had already been formulated at this stage. Many accretions must have occurred with later explication. The divinity of the pharaoh and the notion of divine or sacred kingship have recently been challenged because of specific later references indicating that there were clear distinctions between the respect accorded the kings and the worship accorded the greatest gods. It will be seen, however, that the myth persisted, undoubtedly supported by the kings, some without doubt more vigorously than others.

Menes, besides identifying with Horus and unifying or reunifying the Two Lands, traditionally founded the capital,

Memphis, and erected a temple there, presumably to the god Ptah. His civic contributions were equaled by his religious devotion, and he was thus an exemplary model for all succeeding kings. The kings of the first two dynasties probably had both tombs and cenotaphs that supported the new role of dual kingship, but their monuments at Abydos may also have had some bearing on the relationship of the living Horus to the deceased Osiris, whose cult was later at least maintained there. The fact that kings at the end of the second dynasty could take a "Seth" or a "Horus and Seth" title would indicate that the myth of the contending of Horus and Seth for the patrimony of Osiris was certainly known. But it is doubtful that this reflected a shift in religious belief; more likely a it was political move that was given a mythological framework.

For the first half of the Old Kingdom—the third and fourth dynasties—the great pyramids themselves remain, unfortunately, the principal monuments to the current beliefs. The attention given to these elaborate tombs clearly surpassed any other contemporaneous projects and would seem to show that the power of the king was reflected in the cult of his divine kingship. If the pyramids are not exclusively symbolic of royal power, they could also be symbols of divine power, either of the Horus-king or of his new father, the sun god, Re. The famous statue of Khafre with his headdress incorporating the Horus Falcon can be used to argue for the former, but the title "Son of Re," the use of *Re* in the theophoric royal names, and the true pyramid shape associated with the sun's rays and/or the Benben stone of Re point to the likelihood of either a developed or developing solar cult. In the second half of the Old Kingdom—the fifth and sixth dynasties—the central importance of the cult of Re is very well documented. The kings generally have *Re* in their name, and in addition to their smaller pyramids, they constructed substantial temples to the sun god. The story of the *Miracles That Happened in the Reign of King Khufu* (Westcar Papyrus) was probably written in the Middle Kingdom, but it reflects what was viewed as having happened earlier. The text purports to prophesy that a new dynasty will succeed Khufu's successors and that its first three new kings will be born to the wife of a priest of Re.

Much more significant for an understanding of the religion of this period and of much that had been developing and evolving before it are the Pyramid Texts, first recorded in the interior burial rooms of the pyramid of Unas, the last king of the fifth dynasty. These texts in vertical columns, lacking the illustrations and rubrics of later such mortuary or funerary literature, provided a combination of rituals, hymns, prayers, incantations, and offering lists, all designed to ensure that the king would reach his goal in the afterlife and have the information and provisions that he would need there. The texts were evidently compiled by priests connected with the temple of Re at Heliopolis. They indicate acceptance of the fact that the king is a god who ascends to the sky, joins Re on the solar bark for his voyage back and forth across the heavens, and guards Re and guides his bark past the perils, usually snakes, that threaten them. The rites, some of which may have taken place in these rooms or in the mortuary temple or valley temple to the east of the pyramid, included provision for opening the tomb, sacrificing an ox, and breaking jars for magical protection. The descriptions of the ascension in the tomb's antechamber provide alternative explanations that may have come originally from separate sources. They have the king ascending on the wings or backs of birds, on the incense wafting upward, on reed rafts, or on the outstretched arms of gods forming a ladder for him. On entering the tomb the king is still addressed as Horus; on ascension to the sky he is called Osiris. In the so-called cannibal hymn, he devours gods to acquire their attributes. He protests his guiltlessness and claims his divine perquisites. Within the burial chamber the king is presented to the great gods, and the offering-lists and spells are provided for him, while on the west gable are inscribed the serpent spells, incantations possibly intended to protect the tomb or to be used in guiding Re's bark.

Apart from the central theme of this collection, one learns much more about the religion of Egypt from these texts through the king's relationship to various deities and also through citations or mythological allusions from the texts of the other religions of the Egyptians. Here the king's genealogy is presented clearly by making him the product of the Heliopolitan Ennead. This family of nine gods represents a cosmological or cosmogonical explanation of creation by Atum (the complete one), who by himself created Shu (air) and Tefnut (moisture). From this pair, Geb (earth) and Nut (watery sky) came forth, and in the next generation they produced the two brothers Osiris and Seth and their sisters, Isis and Nephthys. Osiris, the eldest, ruled on earth in place of his father, but he was slain by his stronger brother, Seth. It fell to Osiris' son, Horus, born after his death, to avenge the slaying and assume the rule of this world.

In the form in which this genealogy survives, the significance of the Ennead is really subordinated to the son, Horus, on the one hand, and on the other to Re, who is alternately assimilated to Atum or placed before him as his creator. In the Pyramid Texts the Ennead is personified as the goddess Hathor (House of Horus), and so Re and Hathor are the parents of Horus just as surely as Osiris and Isis. Horus is also said here to be a son of Sekhmet, a statement of interest because Sekhmet was the consort of Ptah, the creator god of Memphis. According to later texts (the Shabaka Stone), Ptah sprang forth from primeval chaos conceiving the creator, Atum, in his heart and bringing him forth on his tongue by speaking his name. The chaos from which Ptah came is also known as the Hermopolitan Ogdoad: The four pairs of deities represent the different aspects of chaos from which an egg appeared as the inundation receded at Hermopolis, thus producing the creator. The names of the four pairs are not consistent in different texts, but they generally include Amun and Amaunet (hiddenness), Kuk and Kauket (darkness),

Huh and Hauhet (formlessness), and Nun and Naunet (the watery abyss). The creator god of Hermopolis might well have been Thoth, the moon god of that city, but in these Heliopolitan texts the creator remains Atum, while Thoth is included as a member of the Ennead and as a companion of Re in the sky. Because the son of Ptah and Sekhmet is Nefertem, the child appearing from the lotus, the king was associated with the scions and creator gods of all three of these important and early cult centers of Egypt.

It should be noted that the roles of both Thoth and Ptah in this connection are not spelled out, but they seem to be clearly alluded to. There were thus probably some limits on how far the Heliopolitan priests would go in assimilating the doctrines and deities of their counterparts or rivals. To some extent the priests of the other temples must have approved of some such accommodation to guarantee the continuing favor and actual support of the crown, but because the formulation had been Heliopolitan, the cult of Re became preeminent, and for the most part it remained so for most of Egyptian history.

In the fifth dynasty society in general became more open, and many of the highest offices in the land could be attained by people not related to the royal family. At least a few utterances from the Pyramid Texts indicate that they were not written originally for a king, so that the goal of a blessed hereafter was not exclusively a royal prerogative. Further decentralization of power occurs in the sixth dynasty, and local nomarchs are provided with quite respectable tombs. These tombs may have been equipped with religious texts on coffins or papyri that have not survived, but certainly in the First Intermediate Period, with the breakdown of central authority, several claimants to kingship, and actual civil war, the claimants to earthly power also made claim to divinity.

The texts on the interior of the single or nested wooden coffins of nobles from many sites in Egypt are in some cases identical to the earlier royal Pyramid Texts, and in other cases are considerably expanded. The texts from different sites vary more than the texts found at each site. The local differences are not all explained as yet, but some reasonably significant collections of spells labeled "books" on the coffins from El Bersha (the necropolis of Hermopolis) have been studied. These coffins have on their fronts (the side faced by the mummy lying on its left side) a false door to facilitate the deceased's mobility; a painted table of offerings to provide sustenance; a plan and description of the Field of Hetep, which is at least one version of the paradise these Egyptians hoped for; and a list of ship's parts, information useful for the deceased, who joins the sun god in his bark and guides it through the skies.

On the inside surface of the bottom of most of the El Bersha coffins was painted an elaborate illustrated plan or map with descriptive texts known today as the *Book of Two Ways.* (*The Book of Two Ways* is a collection within the Coffin Texts.) The plans are all roughly comparable, with a blue waterway surrounded by mounds to represent the day sky, and a black land route, surrounded by water, representing the night sky. This cosmological plan provided the earliest illustrated guidebook to the beyond and attempted to locate various uncommon demons as well as some commonly known terms for places in the afterlife. Apart from the central plan, however, the book is really two different books. The earliest version was apparently written as a guide for followers of the Osirian religion, and the goal of several of its sections was to aid these followers to pass the various gates and demon keepers leading to the mansion of Osiris. The later version has the plan and one section as a guide to the route leading to the mansion of Osiris, but it also has one whole section dealing with Thoth, another dealing with Re, and a conclusion that ties together the whole in terms of knowledge of spells about the beyond. If the deceased knows the spells to the first stage, he will become a star in the sky with the moon god, Thoth. If he knows them to the next stage he will join Osiris in his mansion, and if he knows all the spells he will join Re on his bark in the sky. These goals also appear to be put in terms of social standing, commoners being associated with Thoth, great ones with Osiris, and, obviously, royalty with Re. What this does is to democratize the hereafter by making the highest goals available to anyone who has the book. It was clearly based on an original Osirian text, and in the hands of the priests of Re it would have become a good prosyletizing text for the solar religion.

The *Book of Two Ways* concludes with the famous statement by the All-Lord, Re, that he "made the four winds that every man might breathe," "made the great flood that the poor as well as the great might have power," "made every man like his fellow (I did not command that they do evil. It is their hearts that disobey what I have said)," and "made their hearts to cease forgetting the West, in order to make divine offerings to the gods of the nomes." The All-Lord says, "it is with my sweat that I created the gods. Mankind is from the weeping of my eye," and a little later he adds that after the deceased has spent millions of years between Re and Osiris, "we will sit together in one place. Ruins will be cities and vice versa; house will desolate house." These remarks provide rather interesting insights into the metaphysics and ethics of the Re religion as well as a noteworthy example of early ecumenism. These particular Coffin Texts came from a necropolis of Hermopolis, in middle Egypt. Whether Re priests from Hermopolis or Heliopolis were responsible is still debatable. But another text of this same chaotic period, from Heracleopolis in middle Egypt, although it is a literary text in the "instruction" genre, is actually one of the most religious documents surviving from ancient Egypt. A compact section at the end provides in capsulized form the complete philosophy and theology of the Re religion:

> One generation of men passes to another, and God, who knows characters, has hidden Himself, . . . so worship God upon his way. . . . The soul goes to the place it knows. . . . Beautify your mansion in the West, embellish your place in the necropolis with

> straightforwardness and just dealing; . . . more acceptable is the character of the straightforward man than the ox of the wrongdoer. Serve God, that He may do the like for you, with offerings for replenishing the altars and with carving; it is that which will show forth your name, and God is aware of whoever serves Him. Provide for men, the cattle of God, for He made heaven and earth at their desire. He suppressed the greed of the waters, he gave the breath of life to their noses, for they are likenesses of Him which issued from His flesh. He shines in the sky for the benefit of their hearts; He has made herbs, cattle, and fish to nourish them. He has killed His enemies and destroyed His own children, because they had planned to make rebellion; He makes daylight for the benefit of their hearts, and He sails around in order to see them, . . . and when they weep, He hears. . . . He has made for them magic to be weapons to ward off what may happen.

From this it is seen that Re is hidden, omniscient, provident, responsive and just. Humans, who are created in the likeness of God, and for whom heaven and earth were created, must worship God, and provide for their fellow people. Hypocrisy is of no avail, but God gave humans magic to ward off "what may happen."

This text of the instruction of a Heracleopolitan king to his son, Merikare, anticipates the fall of the tenth dynasty (2040 BCE) to the Theban family of dynasty eleven. Coffin Texts continue to be used in the Middle Kingdom, and this indicates that for the most part the religion or religions of the people did not change drastically with this change in government. The official doctrine of the state, however, had to be supported by a great deal of political propaganda literature to account for the reunification under the new Theban king, Mentuhotep II, then the apparent usurpation by his vizier, and finally the assassination of this vizier become king, Amenemhet I. Amenemhet had already returned the capital to the north and constructed defenses on Egypt's borders, but he was apparently not prepared for the threat from within his own palace. The change from dynasty eleven to dynasty twelve was also marked by a shift in the Theban's titular god and the formulation of a new national god. Previously Montu, a war god, was worshiped at perhaps four separate temples in the Theban nome, but with Amenemhet ("Amun is in front") Amun and his new cult begin a long and steady growth in the south in spite of the fact that the kings of this and succeeding dynasties ruled from the north. The new god is perhaps a conflation of Montu with Min, the ithyphallic fertility god of Coptos, which had been allied with Thebes in the war against Heracleopolis, and also, of course, with Amun, the first of the primordial gods of Hermopolis. This latter element may have provided the priority of the new god in the minds of the formulators, but the association with Re as Amun-Re was probably the significant factor in guaranteeing some continuity with the earlier dynastic gods.

The king of the twelfth dynasty was still Horus, but beginning with Senusret I (1971–1928 BCE) important new claims to kingly divinity surface. In the *Story of Sinuhe* Senusret I is called a god without peer, "no other came to be before him." In order to consolidate his power, Senusret III deposed a number of powerful nomarchs and divided the country into departments that were to be administered from the capital by his appointees. At the same time, in a cycle of songs in his honor and in a loyalist instruction he is called the "unique divine being" and is identified as Re himself. Remarkably, the propaganda literature of this dynasty remained popular for at least 900 years, and the tradition of Senusret's special position among the kings of Egypt also survived through Greek sources to the present.

The Second Intermediate period was marked both by internal weakness eventually giving way to division and by foreign occupation of at least the major part of the delta. These Hyksos rulers were eventually driven out of their capital at Avaris by a new Theban family, which reunited the land and began the period of greatest imperialistic expansion, the New Kingdom. The new family was devoted to the cult of Amun-Re at Karnak, and also had a special interest in the moon god in several earlier forms, including Iah (the moon itself), Thoth, and Khonsu, who was now the son of Amun-Re and Mut (the mother). Thutmose I (c. 1509–1497 BCE), perhaps the first king of the eighteenth dynasty to have a palace in the north, was also responsible for leading expeditions far into Syria, perhaps to the Euphrates. His credentials as a god-king were evidently well established, but not those of his successors. His daughter by his chief wife had to become consort to his son by a lesser wife to secure that son's succession as Thutmose II. But when the latter died, handing over the throne to a son by another wife, his half sister and chief wife, Hatshepsut, took the throne for herself. There were probably very practical explanations for her success in this maneuver, but the justification she chose to propagate was her own "divine birth." She had this recorded on the walls of her mortuary temple at Deir al-Bahri, which depicted Amun-Re in the form of her father, Thutmose I, coming to her mother Ahmose, who conceived the goddess-king, the female Horus.

Hatshepsut's mythologizing goes beyond this with the commemoration of her restoration efforts since the expulsion of the Hyksos. They had "ruled without Re," and she was indeed favored by the gods of Egypt. She had extensive work done at the temple of Karnak, adding a new sanctuary, pylon gates, and very tall obelisks, monuments as much to herself as to Amun-Re, her father. Her small cult temple at Medinet Habu (ancient Djeme) probably has particular significance mythologically for the later association of the Hermopolitan Ogdoad with this sacred site. According to a Ptolemaic text in the Khonsu temple at Karnak, Amun was the father of the fathers of the Ogdoad who (as Ptah) created the egg at Hermopolis and later traveled *(khenesh)* to Thebes in his new name of Khonsu. Together with the Ogdoad, he is in the tomb chamber in the necropolis at Medinet Habu. Indeed, it seems likely that Hatshepsut and her supporters were concerned not only with her genealogy but with the genealogy of the Theban gods. Her husband's son, Thutmose III, who succeeded her and eventually tried to blot out her memory, was primarily involved with military expeditions to Syria and Palestine, and he used his additions to the Karnak temple to publicize his victories. The temple became wealthy and influential because of his generosity and devotion. His successors continued to benefit from and build upon his achievements in the international sphere; foreign alliances, foreign wives, and foreign deities were all introduced in this period, which peaked in the reign of Amenhotep III (1403–1366 BCE).

The son of Amenhotep III, who may have been his coregent for as long as ten years, changed his name from Amenhotep IV to Akhenaton by his fifth year and moved his residence to a new site, Akhetaton (modern Tell al-ʿAmarna). He devoted himself to one aspect of the solar cult, the sun disk (Aton) itself. He saw himself and perhaps his wife, Nefertiti, as the only representatives or intermediaries between the Aton and the rest of creation. Akhenaton's monolatry or henotheism, while apparently accepted by his chief officials, eventually did bring him into direct conflict with the powerful temple staff of Karnak. His supporters attacked the name "Amun" and the word *gods* throughout the Theban area. They were probably sent to eradicate the full name "Amun-Re, King of the Gods," but this attempt to erase (primarily from monuments) the term *gods* has been viewed by many as a monotheistic revolution. Later reaction to Akhenaton as a heretic is known, but what he intended or how far he went to not as clear. The Aton was not his creation either as an icon or as a deity. It had increased in significance in the early eighteenth dynasty. The emblems of almost all the gods of Egypt survive from Tell al-ʿAmarna, indicating that Akhenaton's followers either had no fear of keeping them or had greater fear of abandoning them. The fact that Akhenaton's own prenomen is Waen-Re ("the unique one of Re") is indicative of his continued acceptance of the old solar cult, or perhaps even of the Heliopolitan priests' support of the new cult. Something of Akhenaton's attitude toward the Aton in this international period can be seen in the following excerpt from his famous hymn to the Aton.

> How plentiful it is, what you have made, although they [the creatures made by Aton] are hidden from view, sole god, without another beside you; you created the earth as you wished, when you were by yourself, before mankind, all cattle and kine, all beings on land, who fare upon their feet, and all beings in the air, who fly with their wings. The lands of Khor and Kush and the land of Egypt: you have set every man in his place, you have allotted their needs, every one of them according to his diet, and his lifetime is counted out. Tongues are separate in speech, and their characters as well; their skins are different, for you have differentiated the foreigners. In the underworld you have made a Nile that you may bring it forth as you wish to feed the populace, since you made them for yourself, their utter master, growing weary on their account, lord of every land. For them the Aton of the daytime arises, great in awesomeness. All distant lands, you have made them live, for you have set a Nile in the sky that it may descend for them and make waves upon the mountains like the sea to irrigate the fields in their towns. How efficient are your designs, Lord of eternity: a Nile in the sky for foreigners and all creatures that go upon their feet, a Nile coming back from the underworld for Egypt.

Most aspects of this hymn can be found stated in almost identical terms in the universalist hymn to Amun-Re, so it cannot be regarded as totally original or epoch-making in itself. A claim in the hymn that there is no other who knows the Aton except his son, Akhenaton, is noteworthy, and the statement that the whole land was founded and its crops were raised by the Aton for Akhenaton and Nefertiti is egocentric, to say the least.

Akhenaton's coregent and short-lived successor, Semenkhkare, who some now believe may have been none other than Nefertiti herself, seems to have attempted reconciliation with the priesthood of Amun-Re. But Tutankhaton (c. 1348–1339 BCE), who next assumed the throne, changed his name to Tutankhamen, had statues of himself made both as Amun and as Osiris, and decorated the Luxor temple with scenes of the restored Opet feast. (The main feature of this feast was the procession of Amun's cult image from the Karnak temple to the Luxor temple and back.) He even had a restoration stela set up at Karnak. After his death and that of his successor, Ay, the temple reliefs and stela were usurped by his former general, Horemheb, who on becoming king began attacks on his four predecessors who were involved with the movement, now regarded as heretical.

Horemheb's successor was his vizier, who came from Tanis. As Ramses I he began the nineteenth dynasty, which for various reasons is seen as most significant in the history of Egyptian religion. On the one hand, the pharaohs of this dynasty had to indicate their continuity with the past and assure their support in all the cult centers of Egypt. They built extensively at all the old temple sites and went overboard to demonstrate their polytheism. Temples now had multiple chapels and sanctuaries dedicated to various deities, but the monuments also were used as propaganda to show the power of the kings, to depict their victories, to record their legitimate succession, and to indicate their great devotion to the gods and their munificence to both the gods and their own subjects. On the other hand, the pharaohs succeeded in reinstating their own god, Seth, whom they commemorated as having been in their new capital since the time of the Hyksos. Seth was included in the royal names now and also had one of the Egyptian armies named for him.

In the early Ramessid period the tombs of nobles had much less of the biographical material and scenes of everyday life that were common earlier. Now the emphasis was on the funerary rites and any religious offices the deceased had held. There appears to be a very conservative religious reaction to what had taken place in the eighteenth dynasty. Even the literary texts have primarily mythological settings and content for stories, but interestingly, these often make the gods look foolish and cannot be considered very pietistic. Women, even goddesses, in these texts are cast in an unflattering light, again perhaps in reaction to the powerful queens of the preceding dynasty. The long reign of Ramses II produced numerous temple constructions with colossal statues and representations of himself, but these seem to indicate that he was glorifying himself as much as any of the other gods. The group of four deities at the back of his temple at Abu Simbel shows that he was placing himself on the same level as the three earlier dynastic gods of Egypt—Ptah, Re-Harakhty, and Amun-Re.

The religious texts with which people were buried in the New Kingdom and later are now known as the *Book of Going Forth by Day* but they actually constituted at least two different collections, again emphasizing in introductions or conclusions either an Osirian or a solar afterlife, often with some elements of both in between. These papyri, illustrated with vignettes, vary greatly in length and include many interesting chapters, such as that with the servant statue or Shawabti spell (chap. 6), the heart spell (chap. 30), a spell to enable the deceased to have all requisite knowledge in one chapter (chap. 162), and the famous negative confession and judgment scene (chap. 125). The negative confession is not confession at all but rather a protestation of innocence between forty-two judges of the underworld. Following the psychostasia, or weighing of the deceased's heart, in relation to the feather of Maat, or Truth, the deceased inevitably escapes the devourer and is presented to Osiris, but most often goes forth past the gatekeepers and joins Re as well. The New Kingdom copies of the *Book of Going Forth by Day* are commonly called the Theban recension because so many copies come from Theban tombs. But the texts generally, even in the negative confession, indicate a northern origin, most likely Heliopolitan. Many texts outside of the negative confession are modifications or corruptions of the earlier Coffin Texts versions.

The negative confession, though less than ideal as a code of ethics, cannot be ignored, because it survived in thousands of copies spanning fifteen hundred years. A portion of the fuller list follows:

> O Wide-of-Stride, who comes forth from Heliopolis,
> I have not committed evil.
>
> O Embracer-of-Fire, who comes forth from Babylon,
> I have not stolen.
>
> O Nosey, who comes forth from Hermopolis,
> I have not been covetous. . . .
>
> O Dangerous-of-Face, who comes forth from Rosetau,
> I have not killed men.
>
> O Ruti, who comes forth from heaven,
> I have not damaged the grain-measure. . . .
>
> O Breaker-of-Bones, who comes forth from Heracleopolis,
> I have not told lies. . . .
>
> O White-of-Teeth, who comes forth from the Fayum,
> I have not trespassed. . . .
>
> O-Eater-of-Entrails, who comes forth from the Thirty,
> I have not practised usury. . . .
>
> O Wanderer, who comes forth from Bubastis,
> I have not gossiped. . . .
>
> O Wamemti-Serpent, who comes forth from the place of judgment,
> I have not committed adultery.
>
> O Maa-Intef, who comes forth from the Temple of Min,
> I have not defiled myself. . . .
>
> O Ser-Kheru, who comes forth from Wensi,
> I have not been quarrelsome.
>
> O Bastet, who comes forth from the sanctum,
> I have not winked.
>
> O His-Face-behind-Him, who comes forth from Tep-het-djat,
> I have not been perverted; I have not had sexual relations with a boy. . . .
>
> O Tem-sep, who comes forth from Busiris,
> I have not been abusive against a king.
>
> O Acting-with-His-Heart, who comes forth from Tjebu,
> I have not waded in water.
>
> O Flowing-One, who comes forth from Nun,
> My voice has not been loud. . . .

The judges and the places from which they come are not consistently prominent or frightening and cannot logically be connected with the forty-two nomes of Egypt, but while a few of the statements have uncertain meaning, the vast majority are perfectly clear and not particularly surprising.

From the beginning of the eighteenth dynasty the principal religious text selected to decorate the walls of the royal burial chambers was the so-called book of Amduat, or *That Which Is in the Netherworld.* This book, which resembles a large-scale papyrus unrolled on the walls, treats of the voyage of the solar bark through the hours of the night sky, but it involves Sokar, the god of the Memphite necropolis (Rosetau), as chief god of the underworld. The nineteenth-dynasty kings, different as they may have been from their eighteenth-dynasty counterparts, were also buried in tombs in the Theban Valley of the Kings, but their tombs were more elaborately decorated, with relief carving and paintings of the *Book of Gates* and the journey of the sun through the body of the goddess Nut.

When Ramses II made peace with the Hittites some time after the nearly disastrous battle of Kadesh, a thousand deities on either side were called to witness, and foreign deities such as Anat, Astarte, and Reshef became even more popular in Egypt. His successor, Merneptah, was beset with attacks from Libyans and the Sea Peoples. It is from his reign that the earliest surviving reference to Israel is found, but without other corroborating documentation for the story of the Exodus aside from its reasonably accurate setting.

Ramses III of the twentieth dynasty was the last great pharaonic ruler of Egypt. His building efforts included a separate small temple at Karnak, as well as a very large mortuary temple for himself at medinet Habu. This latter, which survives in very good condition, contains descriptions of the complete festivals of Min and Sokar in addition to the usual battle scenes, and it also has an elaborate calendar of feasts and offerings. The whole was surrounded by a wall with two fortifiable gateways, which probably reflect the worsening political situation of the whole country. There were strikes by the royal tomb workers, who had to be provisioned by the temple storehouses; there were attacks by a coalition of foreigners, principally Libyan; and finally, the king was slain in a harem conspiracy. In addition to punishing those responsible, his son Ramses IV recorded in a very interesting document, the great Papyrus Harris I (c. 1150 BCE), all the benefactions that his father had made to the temples of Egypt. The Wilbour Papyrus, of slightly later date (1140 BCE), confirms that the temple of Amun-Re alone controlled an exorbitant amount of land and the population of a large area in middle Egypt hundreds of miles away.

By the end of the twentieth dynasty the High Priest of Amun, Herihor, was for all practical purposes the ruler of Upper Egypt, and the twenty-first dynasty began with one of his sons assuming the kingship at Tanis in the north while another succeeded him as high priest in the south. Several of the priestly successors also claimed royal titles in the Theban area, and eventually the two offices were combined in one. Unlike the earlier usurpations of viziers or generals, who undoubtedly had a military power base, the base for the priests seems to have been primarily economic. The process can be traced back to the nineteenth dynasty, to a priestly family that gained control not only of the temple treasury but also of the royal treasury. Throughout the Ramessid period there are indications that all was not what it was supposed to be in this period of religious fervor. Banquet songs stress a *carpe diem* attitude; a workman in the royal necropolis shows no respect for his deceased king, and eventually almost all of the Theban tombs were systematically looted. Some of the robbers were accused and tried, but evidently those chiefly responsible got away with their crimes. The priests reburied the royal mummies, but with none of their original trappings or treasure. The priests apparently did not approve of the reinstatement of Seth by the Ramessid kings, and the god's name was attacked at their capital in the north.

When a Libyan family, the twenty-second dynasty, took over in the Third Intermediate Period they ruled from the north also, but controlled the south by appointing a daughter to serve as Divine Adoratress of Amun, a new position above that of high priest. The Nubian Piye (Piankhy), a very devout follower of Amun, conquered all of Egypt to set things right there but did not remain to rule himself, although he did appoint his sister (Amenirdis I) to be the successor of the current Divine Adoratress (Shepenwepet I) when she eventually died. His good intentions were not sufficient, however, and the Nubians (twenty-fifth dynasty) did return to rule the country, losing to the Assyrians, who installed the Saite (twenty-sixth) dynasty. This period marked one of the last Egyptian revivals, with a great deal of temple and tomb construction. In many respects the Saite period harked back to the Old Kingdom; several huge Theban tombs of this time had extensive collections of the Pyramid Texts.

With the Persian conquest of Egypt by Cambyses in 525 BCE, there are indications that the conquering kings had good intentions with regard to maintaining the cultural, legal, and religious traditions of the Egyptians. Although Herodotos, who was not unbiased, accused Cyrus of sacrilege in Egypt, it is known that this king dutifully performed burial rites for an Apis bull and also had small temples erected to the Egyptian gods. The Persian satraps who actually administered the country were doubtless less highly esteemed, probably deservedly so. With several native rebellions and one last gasp of independence in the thirtieth dynasty, Egypt fell again to the Persians, and in turn welcomed Alexander the Great in 332 BCE as a savior from the Persian oppressors.

Alexander was probably convinced of his own divinity on visiting the oracle of Amun at the Siwa oasis, but this was not enough to guarantee a long life. Under his successor, Philip Arrhidaeus, the sanctuary of the Karnak temple was rebuilt. When Alexander's general, Ptolemy, became king of Egypt, much new construction was begun. Alexandria, with its library, museum, and new government offices, was founded, while other Greek cities in Egypt were enlarged or planned. Under the Ptolemys truly great temples were erected at some ancient cult sites, and countless smaller temples, gates, appendages, and inscriptions were added to other places. All the main structures at the temple of Horus at Edfu are Ptolemaic. The vast main temple and its surrounding walls are covered from top to bottom with scenes and texts dealing with Horus, his myths and rituals. The texts have undergone a complicated encoding with a sixfold increase in the number of hieroglyphic signs used, and a wide range of possible substitutions for many standard signs is also encountered. The language is classical Middle Egyptian, and presumably the texts were from earlier material chosen by Egyptian priests from their own libraries, or perhaps from several sites in Egypt. The inscriptions are quite distinctive but often difficult to translate. They seem intentionally obscure despite their accessibility, and the encoding must have been used to make these texts more esoteric or arcane to their own followers and perhaps to the Greeks as well.

The temple of Hathor at Dendera has similar encoding of texts, as well as *mamisi* (birth houses) for the goddess, secret crypts, and a combined Egyptian-Greek zodiac on the ceiling of a small room on the temple's roof. The dual temple of Haroeris and Sobek (the crocodile god) at Kom Ombo may have had a crypt for oracular pronouncements. At Esna the creator god, Khnum, who fashions on the potter's wheel, is commemorated. The temple of Isis on the island of Philae had many separate buildings with inscriptions dating well into the Roman period. The cult of Isis, incorporating much of the cult of Hathor as well, is probably better known now from the Isiac temples in the rest of the Mediterranean than it is from this, the greatest center of the worship of the Egyptian goddess of love. Now that the entire temple complex has been moved to higher ground on a neighboring island, much more work will be possible here. Following construction of the old high dam at Aswan, the temple was under water for most of the year. Another major Oriental cult in the Greco-Roman world that had at least some roots in Egypt was that of Serapis, whose name comes from Osiris and the Apis bull of Ptah of Memphis. These particular sacred bulls, chosen for their markings, had been mummified and buried in large sarcophagi at the Serapium in Saqqara throughout much of the late period in Egyptian history.

Alexandria early became one of the principal centers in the world for the study of philosophy and theology, and when Egypt converted to Christianity many of the Alexandrian Church Fathers became deeply embroiled in controversies. Philo, Origen, Arrius, and Clement represent a few of the different positions originating in Alexandria. Traditional Greek philosophers and pagan, Jewish, Christian, orthodox, and heterodox interpretations—all had their adherents here, living virtually side by side for some time. The Septuagint and Hexapla were produced here, and the Coptic Gnostic library found in Upper Egypt at Nag Hammadi probably originated here as well. The hermetic tractates may provide some link to earlier Egyptian notions, but the apocrypha and *Gospel of Thomas* preserved in this archive most likely originated elsewhere.

Monasticism in both its eremetic and cenobitic forms originated and became very popular in Egypt, partially spread by conditions in the country under the Romans, who overtaxed the people and provided them little protection from the Blemmyes' invasions. The monasteries provided food, protection, and solace. The monastic rule of Pachomius became the standard in many Egyptian monasteries, and it was introduced to the west by John Cassian, becoming the basis of Western Benedictine monasticism.

The early Christians in Egypt suffered persecution under the Romans, but after Rome converted to Christianity, the pagans suffered as well. The Neoplatonic philosopher Hypatia was stoned to death in Alexandria in 415 CE, and the last outpost of paganism in the Roman Empire, at the temple of Isis at Philae, was finally overcome in the late fifth century. When the Arab general ʿAmr ibn al-ʿAṣ took Egypt in 641 conversion to Islam was rapid, due as much to economic advantages as to the attractions of the Qurʾān.

CONCEPTIONS OF THE UNIVERSE. The ancient Egyptians conceived of their universe in a number of different ways. One view was that the firmament (*bia*) was a huge inverted metal colander, from which pieces fell; these wonders or marvels (*biau*) included meteoric iron (*biat*), which was used in making ceremonial implements such as the adzes for the ritual of the Opening of the Mouth. This ritual was performed to give life to statues or other representations and also to revivify the mummies of the deceased. According to another view, the sky was a giant cow whose four legs were supported by four deities, while other deities (stars) on small crescent-shaped boats sailed on her belly. This heavenly cow may be associated with Hathor, who according to the Heliopolitan cosmogony was variously seen as consort of Re and mother of Horus, but also as consort of Horus and mother of Ihy, a form of the sun god to whom she gives birth. The sun god, Re, is also frequently shown being born to the goddess Nut, whose body spans the sky from east to west. According to the Heliopolitan cosmogony she should, of course, be descended from him. Nevertheless, as regularly depicted on the ceilings of royal bed chambers, the sun appears and crosses the goddess's body during the day, but is swallowed by her at night, passing through her body from west to east to be born again.

All of these concepts view the earth as quite solid, generally flat, and practically limitless in extent. The sky (Nut) receives her support from the earth (Geb), and sometimes is shown held apart from him by the air god, Shu. All that the sun encounters in its day and its night voyage is above the earth. The locations generally translated as "netherworld" or "underworld" (*imht* and *duat*) both actually appear to have been in the sky originally. Some descriptions indicate that the Egyptians also conceived of an undersky (*nenet*) and a topsy-turvy afterlife, so that one of the terms (*duat*) seems to have been relocated later. As if this were not confusing enough, another mythological cosmology would have one form of the falcon god, Horus, represent the entire sky, with his two eyes as the sun and the moon. The moon was the eye injured in the battle with his uncle, Seth, to avenge the death of his father, Osiris, in order to assume his inheritance. This great Horus would seem to be as much greater than Re, the sun, as the Heliopolitan Re of the Pyramid Texts is above his son, the Horus-king. Such seemingly incompatible cosmologies may represent either earlier separate traditions or later attempted rationalizations.

CONCEPTIONS OF HUMAN NATURE AND DESTINY. The Egyptians' view of their own nature certainly varied in some respects from time to time, place to place, and person to person, but a few terms persisted expressing notions about their ontology that are reasonably consistent. People were created in God's image, from the weeping of his (Re's) eye, were conceived in God's heart (mind) and spoken by his tongue (Ptah), or were fashioned on the potter's wheel (Khnum). One's body had to be preserved in order to enable it to properly live again in the afterlife. To ensure this a replica of the body was thought to have been fashioned by the gods at birth; more were made later by sculptors and painters as stand-ins for bodies that might be lost. These *ka* figures, enlivened by the Opening of the Mouth ritual, served as second effective personalities, but they could also be protecting genii. At least by the Late period even the great gods such as Re and Thoth have a number of these *ka*s or "attributes," including Hu (authoritative utterance), Sia (perception), Maa (sight), and Sedem (hearing).

The term most closely approximating "soul" for the Egyptians was *ba,* which was represented in hieroglyphic as a small bird and was also depicted in burial scenes departing from the body as a bird flying up to the sky. In at least one literary text, the *Dispute of a Man with His Ba,* this conscience or other self is present in life to be argued with and to help the person make up his mind after considering both sides of a question, in this case the serious question of whether to go on living. Another literary text, the *Lamentations of Khakheperreseneb,* has the scribe address his heart (*ib*), which cannot respond, rather than his *ba.* It was generally the heart that was considered the seat of both intellect and will.

Another significant aspect of an individual's person or personality is the *akh,* or "spirit," which is what remains apart from the body or at least is not limited by the body after death. A person wants to become an *akh aper,* an "equipped spirit" or "perfect spirit," in the afterlife, and to this end he prepares himself with the required religious spells from one or the other collections available, often including as many books and variations as possible and both full and shortened versions. The spirits in the hereafter were sometimes thought to be not content to rest in peace in a blessed state, nor were they always allowed to. Another literary text, the *Ghost Story,* tells of a long-dead spirit who appears to a priest and requests that his cracked and drafty tomb be repaired. Many letters to the dead are also found; they were left with food offerings by living relatives to urge some specific action on their behalf in the spirit world. These usually mention past favors and show confidence in the deceased's ability to effect change for righting the injustice.

GODS, CULTS, AND MAGIC. While the deceased in the necropolis were regularly called *akh*s, they were also occasionally termed *netjeru* ("gods"). A curse left on a square block at the door of a tomb threatened dire consequences to anyone who disturbed even a pebble in the tomb, and it advised finding a place that would not impinge upon the tombs of any of the gods in the necropolis. For the Egyptians the word *netjer* ("god") was used broadly to cover all levels of divinity, from the greatest gods to the justified dead (that is, those declared "true of voice" in the judgment before Osiris). Monotheism, if it ever existed in ancient Egypt, was never clearly formulated and apparently was never established as doctrine in any of the native religions. From almost all periods come texts that indicate the uniqueness of one or the other gods, usually some form of the sun god, but this monolatry or henotheism cannot be demonstrated to have the exclusivity necessary to fit the modern definition of monotheism.

There are numerous references to "god" and "the god" in Egyptian literary texts, particularly in the instructions. In some cases these may refer to a local god or to the king, but most frequently they refer to Re or Pre (the sun). He is often called the *neb-er-djer* ("lord to the limit, universal lord"), and can indeed appear practically transcendent, as in the *Instruction for Merikare,* quoted above. The only important point lacking here is a statement that no other god exists, but of course this can also be said of the Hebrew Bible and the New Testament. Tradition is the principal source for both the Jewish and the Christian monotheistic doctrine, but it is lacking for Egyptian religion. Without this tradition the multiplicity of denominations and sects, the veneration of saints, and the loose use of "divine" and "godlike" for popular heroes would all conspire to challenge the generally accepted monotheistic aspect of modern Western religions and of Western civilization. For the Atenist heresy of Akhenaton the situation is somewhat different, because the *Hymn to the Aton* states that there is no god beside (or like) Aton, there was an attack on other gods and the plural "gods," and Akhenaton was later clearly regarded as having attempted to disrupt the established religious system. Most likely the notion of monotheism was present in this period, in some minds at least, though it was harshly dispelled. By syncretizing the names and aspects of various deities into powerful new gods, the Egyptians widened the gap between the greatest god and all the rest. Re-Atum, Amun-Re, and Pre-Harakhty were unchallenged national gods each in his own time.

Probably second in importance to the great national gods was the cult of the god of the dead. This evolved very early, evidently from several separate cults. The cult of Osiris, originally from Busiris, superseded the cults of Khentyimentiu ("foremost of the westerners") and Wepwawet ("opener of the ways") from Abydos and Siut, respectively. The cults of Osiris and Re intermingle in most of the mortuary literature, and in at least one instance come close to merging. When the cult of Sokar becomes a major element in royal funerary literature and later in all the funerary literature of the New Kingdom, it leads to perhaps the ultimate syncretism in the late New Kingdom of Ptah-Sokar-Osiris-Tatenen.

The Osiris cult certainly permeated almost all aspects of Egyptian culture. Osirid statues decorated the courts of temples, and the Osiris suites are a major feature of the mortuary temples. Every owner of a book of mortuary literature is given the title "Osiris," and every deceased person named in tomb or stele has the epithet "true of voice" or "vindicated" with respect to his last judgment before this great god. The association of Osiris with death, resurrection, fertility, and the Nile touched everyone, and his cult center at Abydos, where he was supposed to have been buried, became the most important pilgrimage site in the country.

The living king is generally called the "good god," while the deceased king is the "great god." Whether death actually enhanced the king's status is debatable. As the embodiment or incarnation of the god Horus, he is already a major god on earth, and much of the doctrine of his divinity and his perquisites was widely published and accepted. Certainly the king who instructed Merikare was more aware personally of his limitations than Senusret III or Ramses II would have been. The whole concept could have been viewed in different ways at different times by different people. Based on the number of persons who had as their goal in the afterlife something approaching or equaling the goals of their kings, perhaps more would have believed in their sovereign's divinity and their own potential divinity than some modern scholars are now prepared to accept. Of course there are exceptions—the *Song of the Harper* and the story of the *Man Who Was Tired of Life* both reflect despair about the afterlife. Some kings were assassinated, and all the royal tombs were robbed. Aware of the difficulty of securing their burials, the Egyptians tried incredible masses of stone, secret hidden passages, tricks, provision of security guards, and also magic and curses. In a sense all of these would have been attempts by believers to thwart the unbelievers.

Some individuals, even nonroyal personages, attained a state of divinity far above the ordinary. The cult of deceased kings would generally not have outlived the endowment of their funerary establishment, but Amenhotep I, together with his mother, Ahmose Nefertari, continued for centuries to be venerated by the workmen of Deir al-Medineh as the great patrons or patron saints of the place. The architect of the step pyramid of Djoser at Saqqara, Imhotep, was deified, and his cult became ever more popular more than two millennia after his death. He was revered as a sage and was also identified with the Greek god Asklepios. Another architect and sage, Amenhotep Son of hapu (the epithet is traditionally part of his name), was also exceptionally revered. In sum, the Egyptians seem to have had a number of different levels of divinity, several equivalent to different levels of sainthood, with only one word, *netjer,* to cover them all.

Worship of animals does not seem to have been a significant element in any of the religions of Egypt. The use of animals to represent some attributes of gods, or the gods themselves, is frequent, and in most religious artwork their primary importance is clearly in differentiating the principals. The conventional linking of the falcon with Horus, the falcon and disk with Re, the cow with Hathor, the baboon or ibis with Thoth, the jackal with Anubis, the crocodile with Sobek, and the ram with Amun-Re was generally recognized throughout the country and in all periods following its formulation, whereas strictly anthropomorphic representations would have been confusing. It is possible that for some ritual reenactments priests would have worn the animal masks of the gods and recited the words attributed to the gods in numerous temple reliefs. The cobra Edjo of Buto and the vulture Nekhbet of Al-Kab are usually represented in their totally animal forms, but they are protective deities for the king of Upper and Lower Egypt, and were more intimidating in this form. The often malevolent but sometimes protective deity Seth is represented as either partially or totally animal, though there was in antiquity, and there is now, little agreement as to what the animal was. Pig, hippopotamus, donkey, hound, and giraffe are all plausible in different documents or reliefs. Evil beings or demons are often composite, fanciful creations that must be armed with knives to be really threatening. The evil serpent Apophis, perhaps the greatest demon, is repulsed from attacking the sun god by means of numerous serpent spells, but it is also driven back by the spears, and bows and arrows of protecting deities such as the four sons of Horus—Imesty, Hapi, Duamutef, and Khebeksenuef—who are also the protective gods represented on the Canopic jars containing the internal organs of the mummified dead.

Although oxen and smaller cattle were among the offerings made to the gods in their temples, the Apis bull, which was emblematic of and sacred to Ptah in the New Kingdom and later, had a very special position and would have been considered by many as the embodiment of a god on earth. Burials of each successive Apis bull and its cow mother were performed with great solemnity. Later, in the Greek period, the proliferation of cemeteries for mummified cats sacred to both Bast and Paket, crocodiles sacred to Sobek, ibises sacred to Thoth and Imhotep, baboons sacred to Thoth, and falcons sacred to Horus reached all parts of Egypt, to the point that demand for some of these creatures as votive offerings began to exceed the supplies available; sometimes people who thought they had purchased jars with mummified animals actually left sealed jars of sand to be buried in the huge catacombs at sacred sites.

Magic was clearly a significant aspect of Egyptian life. Again, as noted in the *Instruction for Merikare,* magic was considered a gift of the great god, Re. There was a goddess called Weret-Hekau (Great of Magic), and several texts refer to the books containing the secret knowledge of Thoth, whom the Greeks later identified with Hermes and whose legendary knowledge is still being touted by certain groups today (e.g., the Rosicrucians). The Egyptians had magical spells believed to prolong life, to alter fate, to help in romance, and to combat any number of physical and mental afflictions. A combination of entreaty and threat is found in one type of love charm:

> Hail to you, Re-Harakhty, father of the gods!
> Hail to you, Seven Hathors, who are adorned with strings of red thread!
> Hail to you, all the gods of heaven and earth!
> Come make so-and-so [f.] born of so-and-so come after me,
> Like an ox after grass, like a nursemaid after her children, like a herdsman after his herd!
> If you do not make her come after me, then I will set fire to Busiris and burn Osiris.

Some magic spells survive in the funerary literature, some references occur in the literature, and much is found in the medical texts. The rubrics of chapters in the New Kingdom *Book of Going Forth by Day* frequently provide information about the very ancient origins of these spells for transformation and glorification, and they also provide instructions concerning the rites accompanying recitation of the spells. In some cases complete secrecy is required, and one frequently encounters the claim that a particular spell was tried and proved a million times. Chapter 64 of the *Book of Going Forth by Day* is "The Chapter for Knowing the Chapters of Coming Forth by Day in a Single Chapter." Its rubric adds:

> If this chapter is known by the deceased, he will be mighty both on earth and in the otherworld, and he will perform every act of a living person. It is a great protection that has been given by God. This chapter was found in the city of Hermopolis on a block of iron of the south, which has been inlaid with real lapis lazuli, under the feet of the god during the reign of his majesty, the king of Upper and Lower Egypt, Menkaure, justified [i.e., deceased], by Prince Hordedef, justified. He found it when he was journeying to make an inspection of the temples. One Nakht was with him who was diligent in making him understand it, and he brought it to the king as a wonderful object when he saw that it was a thing of great mystery, which had never before been seen or looked upon. This chapter shall be recited by a man who is ritually clean and pure, who has not eaten the flesh of animals or fish, and who has not had intercourse with women. And you shall make a scarab of green stone, with a rim plated with gold, which shall be placed in the heart of a man, and it shall perform for him the opening of the mouth. And you shall anoint it with *anti*-unguent, and you shall recite over it these spells. . . .

The words that follow are the heart spell of chapter 30. The discovery of the text by such a famous sage in so significant a place clearly enhanced its value.

Those Egyptian medical texts that deal with surgical procedures tend to be reasonably scientific, but for the vast majority of human ailments treated in most medical texts the Egyptians relied on magic—potions, poultices, or salves applied with written or recited spells. Headaches and stomach disorders are obvious targets, and there are lengthy series of spells for hastening birth that recall the travail of Isis in giving birth to Horus.

Magic was also used in the Execration Texts, which the Egyptians devised to overcome enemies perhaps too difficult to overcome by any other means. These bowls or figurines, inscribed with a fairly standard selection of the names of Egypt's foreign and domestic enemies plus all evil thoughts, words, and deeds, were deliberately smashed to try to destroy any and all persons and things listed thereon.

The Opening of the Mouth ritual, already referred to above, was obviously a magical rite to bring to life mummies and other representations of individuals. Sculpted portraits (called reserve heads) in Old Kingdom mastaba tombs were magical stand-ins. The eradication from statues, stelae, and tomb and temple walls of names and representations of individuals was thought to be a way of eliminating those persons magically. The texts in some tombs had the animal hieroglyphs either halved or with knives in them, to prevent them from being a danger to the deceased. The names of individuals involved in the harem conspiracy against Ramses III were often changed in the records to evil-sounding names, primarily so that the evil person's memory would not live on. In this same conspiracy, magic was also apparently involved in the making of waxen images by the conspirators. Exactly how these were to be used is unclear.

In addition to reserve heads and *ka*-statues, the deceased in his tomb frequently had a supply of servant statues. In the earlier periods they were shown doing exactly what they would have done in life, but in the New Kingdom they were represented merely as mummified figures, with chapter 6 of the *Book of Going Forth by Day* written on them. This is the magic spell that says that if the deceased is called upon to do any work in the afterlife, such as moving sand from one bank to another, the "answerer" (the figurine) will respond that he is present to do it. A different type of magic is found in the *Cannibal Hymn,* in Pyramid Text utterances 273–274. Here the deceased king goes about devouring the gods, both to demonstrate that he has gained power over them in death and in order to acquire their strength and attributes.

Popular Religion and Personal Piety. Among the numerous amulets used by the Egyptians a few stand out and deserve attention. Probably the best-known amulet and symbol is the *ankh* sign, the hieroglyph for "life," which is most frequently shown being presented by the gods to humans. Considerably more important for the Egyptians was the *udjat,* the eye of Horus, which symbolized the sacrifice endured by Horus in his struggle to avenge his father's murder. This eye was used to designate any offering or sacrifice and also to represent the sun and the moon gods and their barks. Similar falcon eyes are found on the fronts of Middle Kingdom coffins, presumably to enable the deceased to see; on the prows of boats and in mummy wrappings these might also have been chosen to ward off evil.

The scarab beetle was a symbol that had religious significance, but it was frequently used for the very practical purpose of identification, as a seal bearing the owner's name on its flat underside. Some scarabs have ornamental decoration and the vast majority have royal names, usually of Thutmose III or Ramses II. The scarab itself was a symbol of the sun god, apparently derived from the image of this beetle slowly pushing along a nutritious ball of dung. The Egyptian word for this beetle was *kheper,* a homonym for their word meaning "to come to be" or "to happen," and the word also became the name of the early morning sun deity. Re, then, is the powerful and bright noonday sun, and Atum the old and worn-out evening sun.

Two symbolic figures often found on amulets seem to have been primarily associated with household deities and were particularly important for their connection with fertility and the successful conclusion of pregnancy. These are of the gods Bes, the grotesque human-faced baboon or monkey, and Taweret, the not very attractive female hippopotamus/crocodile who stands on her hind legs and holds another amulet, the "knot of Isis," in her hands. Amulets of the frog goddess, Heket, and the knot of Isis were probably used similarly by women. The feather of Maat (Truth or Justice) also symbolized order, and in those countless temple scenes showing the king presenting to various deities the small figure of the goddess wearing the feather and seated on a basket, the king is both claiming and promising to preserve order on earth on behalf of all the other gods. The plump hermaphrodite figures of Hapy are symbolic of the fertility of the Nile in flood and are frequently shown tying together the sedge plant of Upper Egypt and the papyrus of Lower Egypt.

The numerous stelae and votive offerings left at cult centers provide adequate testimony of the personal piety of the Egyptians. Many of the stelae were inscribed with a plea to the god of the place, and some had a human ear or ears carved on them as if to entreat the god to be especially attentive. Because the common people would not have had access to the god in the interior of his temple, they had their own preferred shrines, statues, or reliefs of the god (often Amun) "who hears prayers" outside the temple proper but within the sacred precincts. If they were patient they could wait to approach the god on his processions in connection with major feasts. These occasions were regularly used to make requests of the gods, and the nod of the god, perhaps aided by the shoulders of the men carrying the god, was considered a significant oracular response. The "power" or "manifestation" of a god is mentioned in several texts as punishment for an offense (e.g., being blinded for lying) or as a force compelling a person to recant earlier testimony. Some women called "knowledgeable" could use their powers for conjuring or healing. Omens were important to the Egyptians, many different dreams were interpreted as good or bad, and at least by the Late Period they had calendars of lucky and unlucky days.

One final indication of the religiosity of the Egyptians and also of their trust in magic is the very frequent occurrence, both on stelae and in graffiti, of a list of good works the writer had done, followed by his request that any passerby reading the text pronounce his name and the formula "A thousand bread, beer, oxen, and fowl," so that some day he would magically receive these stereotypical offerings. The Egyptians had a great deal of confidence in both the written and the spoken word and a proper respect for things sacred. A woman from Deir al-Medineh accused of stealing a workman's tool compounded her guilt enormously when she swore a false oath and it was discovered that she stole not only the tool but also a vessel from a temple.

Temples. The priests and priestesses of ancient Egypt included a very high percentage of the population. The king himself seems to have been the principal intermediary between gods and humans. He is shown making offerings, pouring libations, and burning incense before almost all the gods in all the temples. How much of the king's time was actually spent in religious ritual is not known and probably varied from dynasty to dynasty and from one king to another. The large amount of civil authority delegated to viziers would have released time for more religious activities if that were desired. Some kings, however, seem to have preferred leading military expeditions, perhaps finding these more essential or more interesting.

The actual high priests of each temple had different titles. The word used most frequently was *hem-netjer* ("servant of the god"), which the Greeks rendered as "prophet." The great temple of Amun-Re at Karnak had four ranked prophets, and the first prophet had one of the highest positions in the land. In addition to his religious duties involving the daily temple ritual and rites connected with many special feasts, he exercised temporal power over a vast amount of landholdings and over the people who worked those lands. He also served as a judge in the tribunal headed by the vizier. Some did rise to the higher priestly offices by coming up through the ranks and being recognized for their abilities, but it was also the case that they could start at the top, apparently with the king's patronage. Royal princes frequently held the post of high priest of the temple of Ptah at Memphis. At Thebes the office of high priest often was hereditary, and it became a power base from which individuals could claim and acquire the kingship of the entire land (twenty-first dynasty).

Little is known about the lesser prophets, though the office of second prophet seems in one case to have been given over to a queen, Akhmose Nefertari of the eighteenth dynasty, either to exercise the office or to award it to another. Later a famous fourth prophet of Amun, Montuemhet (twenty-sixth dynasty), was simultaneously mayor of Thebes, and his great wealth and prestige probably accrued from that position. It is not known whether any of these figureheads and administrators were also knowledgeable theologians.

Those temple scribes who were familiar with the sacred writings were called *chery-heb* ("lector priest"). It was their responsibility to interpret omens and dreams, to know the magical spells required for any eventuality, and to read the required texts for the rituals of embalmment and burial. The scribes most likely also provided the copies of funerary texts that people wanted to be buried with, and would either have served as physicians themselves or would have provided the magical medical spells that the physicians used.

In all the temples most of the lesser tasks were in the hands of the faithful. All would be called upon to do their monthly service, and because they were regularly divided into four phylae, this meant that they alternated but served three months out of the year. These common priests (*wabu*, "pure ones") shaved their hair, washed frequently in the sacred lakes near the temples, and maintained ritual purity to enable them to serve the god in his mansion. They served as porters, watchmen, and attendants, assisted with offerings and rites, and probably did their share of cleaning, polishing, painting, and moving things around.

There was of course a major distinction between the city cult temples and the mortuary temple establishments. The great mortuary temples grew out of the smaller chapels erected above shaft tombs, and these in turn developed from the small offering niches in Old Kingdom mastaba tombs. The offerings to be left at the chapels of nobles or temples of kings were provided by endowments, and the priests who administered the endowments were called *hemu-ka* ("servants of the *ka*"). If the endowment included lands, the produce would have provided offerings as well as an income for the individual "priests." They would also benefit from the unconsumed offerings that they provided each day. These endowments became an important part of the individual's property and tended to be collected and handed on to heirs.

Women in all periods shared at least some priestly responsibilities and enjoyed priestly titles. In the Old Kingdom many women were priestesses of Hathor, Neith, or Nut. In the early New Kingdom the great royal wives were also the "god's wives of Amun" and as such bore the next divine son, but they did as well participate with male priests in temple rites. Of course Hatshepsut as king (she took the masculine title, and even wore a false beard) was also priest, but remarkably, Nefertiti appeared alone or with her daughter, making offerings to her god, Aton. The wives of nobles and even the working women of Deir al-Medineh were very frequently called songstresses of Amun and were depicted in tombs bearing two symbols of this office, the sistrum and the *menit*-necklace, with which they provided musical accompaniment for rituals at both the great and the lesser temples. Women in general also served as *ka*-priests and professional mourners. In the late New Kingdom the wives of the high priests of Amun held the title of chief concubine of Amun-Re, but while it is known that they had a great deal of influence, it is not known precisely what religious responsibilities they had. Daughters of the first prophets of Amun were given the title of "God's Wife" in the twenty-first dynasty, and then, to assume greater control of the south, the Tanite kings gave this position to their own daughters. The next step in the process is the evolution of a new position, that of Divine Adoratress, from the office of God's Wife; the new position is clearly ranked above that of the high priest. Since the Divine Adoratress remains a virgin, she adopts her successor from among the daughters of the king.

The Egyptian temple was the mansion of the god, his abode on earth or, at least, the abode of his principal cult statue. The daily ritual for a god in his temple was limited to a few priests present, and consisted of their approaching the sanctuary, opening the shrine, removing the statue, undressing it, washing it, censing it, making offerings to it, clothing it in fresh garments, replacing it, sealing the shrine, and retreating, with care taken to sweep away their footprints. Although the faithful did not have the opportunity to participate in the daily ritual, they were able to see the god during special feasts, when the statue of the god would leave the temple. For the feast of Opet the statue and shrine of the god Amun-Re was taken from its sanctuary at the Karnak temple, placed on a bark held aloft by priests with carrying poles on their shoulders, and carried to its river transport for the two-mile voyage to the Luxor temple, the southern harem, for a sojourn there before the return voyage. The Beautiful Feast of the Valley involved Amun-Re's voyage across the river to western Thebes to visit the major temples there, but numerous stops were made at small temples and way stations along the route. In addition to these great feasts of Amun-Re recorded at the Luxor and Karnak temples, the mortuary temple of Ramses III at Medinet Habu contains records of the festival processions of Min and Sokar illustrated in great detail.

MYTHOLOGY. Mythology is encountered in almost everything that survives from ancient Egypt. Texts, whether religious, historical, literary, medical, or legal, or merely personal correspondence, all contain mythological allusions. Art of all kinds and on all scales, and artifacts of all types, made use of easily recognizable mythological symbols. This does not mean that everything had a ritual purpose or that the Egyptians had narrow one-track minds, but it does show how mythology and religion had permeated the culture, and also how artisans and craftsmen could capitalize on this.

It is not surprising to find that the Egyptians' mythology was not detailed and collected in any one place, but surely the various traditions were handed down by word of mouth and were generally well known. Temple libraries, known in the Late period as "houses of life," certainly contained medico-magical texts, and also would have had many ritual, historical, and theological texts and treatises. Many of these contained mythological material, but none was entitled *Egyptian Mythology*. There may have been individual texts relating to the individual cults or sites, such as Papyrus Jumilac. The cosmogonical myths that were excerpted for use in the mortuary literature and that have been briefly summarized above were included in the Pyramid Texts to indicate the power of the king, his genealogy, or his goal, rather than to explain or justify the other gods. The temple texts of individual gods are remarkable for the little mythological information they contain and the vast amount of knowledge they presume.

Some texts, such as the *Story of the Two Brothers* and the *Blinding of Truth by Falsehood*, are in large part mythological without being mythic in purpose. The *Contendings of Horus and Seth* has a totally mythological setting, but it is a burlesque of the real myth, and perhaps a sophisticated attack on the entire pantheon as well. The *Myth of the Destruction of Mankind* is slightly more serious in intent, showing humans to be totally at the mercy of the gods if they cross them. In this myth Hathor was sent to slay men because they had plotted in the presence of Re, but Re decided to save them by making bloodlike red beer to deceive and distract her. The goddess became so drunk that she could not perceive humankind, and what had begun as a story about punishment for sin becomes an etiological explanation for drinking to the point of drunkenness at the feast of Hathor. Another remarkable document from the late Ptolemaic period is Papyrus Jumilac, which provides the entire religious history, largely mythological, of the otherwise little-known eighteenth nome of Upper Egypt.

SURVIVALS. Egyptian religion does not seem to have been greatly changed by any outside influences. In the New Kingdom several Asiatic deities were introduced into the Egyptian pantheon, including Reshef, Kadesh, Anat, and Astarte. The story of *Astarte and the Insatiable Sea* has been proposed as one example of Egyptian borrowing from the Ugaritic *Poem of Baal,* but the counterargument for the indigenous nature of most of the contents of this text posits that only the names of the principals were changed to those of well-known Semitic deities. The Canaanite god Baal was regularly identified with Seth, and later many Greek gods became identified with the older Egyptian gods (e.g., Hermes-Thoth, Hephaistos-Ptah, and Min-Pan). The Isis-aretalogies that survive in Greek have a few descriptions of the goddess that may be traced back to Egyptian antecedents, but for the most part the composition appears to have been primarily Greek. Many scholars have seen similarities between the Egyptian *Hymn to the Aton* and the biblical *Psalms,* the *Instruction of Amenemope* and *Proverbs,* or the collections of Egyptian love songs and the *Song of Songs.* If there were instances of borrowing (and this is not universally accepted), they would in each case have been from the slightly earlier Egyptian texts.

Among the religious survivals from ancient Egypt, the language used in the Coptic Christian liturgy down to the present time represents the latest stage of ancient Egyptian, but it is written in the Greek alphabet. The decoration of early Coptic textiles used as vestments had incorporated *ankh* signs as well as *udjat.* As noted above, the institution of monasticism in both its eremetic and cenobitic forms, and the earliest monastic rule, can be clearly traced to Egypt. Whether the late cult of Isis had any influence on the story of the Blessed Virgin, or whether the story of the death and resurrection of Osiris influenced the gospel narrative of Christ, would be hotly contested by many Christians. In doctrinal matters it has been proposed that the Egyptian triads (such as that of Amun, Mut, and Khonsu of Thebes) influenced the concepts of the Trinity and the Holy Family, and that descriptions of the Field of Hetep (paradise) and of places of torment in the afterlife were predecessors for the concepts of heaven and hell. Slightly less controversial would be the question of Egyptian influence on the doctrines of the resurrection of the body and the communion of saints. The traditional sites for the finding of the infant Moses at the river's edge, and the places visited by the Holy Family on their sojourn in Egypt, are indeed very old, but how accurate they are historically is questionable. Surviving traditions in modern Egypt include the use of mourners at funerals, visits to tombs, the leaving of food offerings, and the burning of incense at services. Modern beliefs in afreets or ghosts certainly have ancient roots, and the modern Luxor processions carrying boats on the feast of the Muslim saint Abul Hagag are clearly reminiscent of ancient festivals.

CONCLUSIONS. In general the Egyptians seem to have been very religious, believed in an afterlife, and devoted much of their energy to preparing for this. Their preparations included both the physical burial equipment and the spiritual: rites, temple services, offerings, good works, and avoidance of evil deeds. They believed that they were destined from birth to a particular fate, but they were also optimistic that they could, perhaps with the help of a god, change an unfortunate fate. They desired a long life and eventually a proper Egyptian burial. To a great extent they wanted to continue living after death a life very like their life on earth. They were clearly optimistic about vindication in a last judgment and their ability to attain the highest goals in the afterlife.

Two characteristic features of Egyptian religious literature are syncretism and a multiplicity of approaches, and these perhaps show steps in the process of developing doctrine. In the case of the descriptions of the afterlife, the Egyptians could on the one hand place separate, mutually exclusive descriptions side by side without indicating that one is better or more accurate than another; on the other hand, they could combine in the same document aspects from different traditions in a new, apparently superior, composite, and theoretically logical entity. Perhaps this was one way of dealing with the problem of conservatively maintaining the old while also accepting the new.

The Egyptians did not believe in the transmigration of souls, but among the hymns, guidebooks, offering texts, and rituals with which the deceased were buried are many spells for transformations—often into the form of birds, perhaps because of a desire to achieve their apparent freedom. Presumably, an Egyptian purchased the texts he wanted well in advance of his death. Some manuscripts could have been read in advance by their owners, but many texts are quite flawed in extant copies and might not have been intelligible even if the person had bothered to read them. Scribes also had serious problems understanding some texts, and in at least one case (*Book of Going Forth by Day,* chap. 17) a tradition of various interpretations is handed down in the form of glosses incorporated into the text.

Hymns are probably a good gauge of the religiosity and sophistication of the priest-scribes and theologians, as well as of the believers, of ancient Egypt. The short hymns, perhaps excerpts, found in the earlier mortuary literature eventually developed into carefully constructed, easily read, edifying, and glowing tributes to the gods that spell out the gods' links with nature and their special concern for humankind. The *Hymn to the Nile,* the *Hymn to Amun-Re,* the *Hymn to the Aton,* hymns found in nobles' tombs to the rising and setting sun, and the hymns to Osiris and to Re in the *Book of Going Forth by Day* might not be as exciting and different as the so-called *Cannibal Hymn.* But these were very proper and popular works, indicating a considerable refinement in ancient Egypt that is not often recognized and appreciated by historians of religion.

BIBLIOGRAPHY

Allen, Thomas George. *The Book of the Dead or Going Forth by Day.* Chicago, 1974.

Anthes, Rudolf. "Egyptian Theology in the Third Millennium B.C." *Journal of Near Eastern Studies* 18 (1959): 170–212.

Assmann, Jan. *Ägyptische Hymnen und Gebete.* Zurich, 1975.

Bell, H. Idris. *Cults and Creeds of Graeco-Roman Egypt.* Liverpool, 1953.

Bonnet, Hans. *Reallexikon der ägyptischen Religionsgeschichte.* Berlin, 1952.

Breasted, James H. *The Development of Religion and Thought in Ancient Egypt.* New York, 1912.

Cerny, Jaroslav. *Ancient Egyptian Religion.* London, 1952.

Englund, Gertie. *Akh: Une notion religieuse dans l'Égypte pharaonique.* Uppsala, 1978.

Erman, Adolf. *Die Religion der Ägypter: Ihr Werden und ihr Vergehen in vier Jahrtausenden.* Berlin, 1934.

Faulkner, Raymond. *The Ancient Egyptian Pyramid Texts.* Oxford, 1969.

Faulkner, Raymond. *The Ancient Egyptian Coffin Texts.* 3 vols. Oxford, 1973–1978.

Frankfort, Henri. *Kingship and the Gods.* Chicago, 1948.

Frankfort, Henri. *Before Philosophy.* Baltimore, 1954.

Frankfort, Henri. *Ancient Egyptian Religion.* New York, 1961.

Greven, Liselotte. *Der Ka in Theologie und Königskult der Ägypter des Alten Reiches.* Glückstadt, 1952.

Griffiths, J. Gwyn. *The Origins of Osiris and His Cult.* Leiden, 1980.

Hornung, Erik. *Altägyptische Höllenvorstellungen.* Leipzig, 1968.

Hornung, Erik. *Ägyptische Unterweltsbücher.* Zurich, 1972.

Hornung, Erik. *Conceptions of God in Ancient Egypt.* Ithaca, N.Y., 1982.

Junker, Hermann. *Die Götterlehre von Memphis (Schabaka-Inschrift).* Berlin, 1940.

Kees, Hermann. *Das Priestertum in ägyptischen Staat vom Neuen Reich bis zur Spätzeit.* Leiden, 1953.

Kees, Hermann. *Der Götterglaube im alten Ägypten.* 2d ed. Berlin, 1956.

Kees, Hermann. *Totenglauben und Jenseitsvorstellungen der alten Ägypter.* 2d ed. Berlin, 1956.

Lesko, Leonard H. "Some Observations on the Composition of the Book of Two Ways." *Journal of the American Oriental Society* 91 (1971): 30–43.

Lesko, Leonard H. "The Field of Hetep in Egyptian Coffin Texts." *Journal of the American Research Center in Egypt* 9 (1971–1972): 89–101.

Morenz, Siegfried. *Egyptian Religion.* Ithaca, N.Y., 1973.

Morenz, Siegfried. *Religion und Geschichte des alten Ägypten: Gesammelte Aufsätze.* Weimar, 1975.

Morenz, Siegfried, and Dieter Müller. *Untersuchungen zur Rolle des Schicksals in der ägyptischen Religion.* Berlin, 1960.

Moret, Alexandre. *Le rituel du culte divin journalier en Égypte d'après les papyrus de Berlin et les textes du temple de Séti Premier à Abydos.* Paris, 1902.

Mueller, Dieter. "An Early Egyptian Guide to the Hereafter." *Journal of Egyptian Archaeology* 58 (1972): 99–125.

Otto, Eberhard. *Das Ägyptische Mundoffnungsritual.* Wiesbaden, 1960.

Piankoff, Alexandre. *Shrines of Tut-Ankh-Amon.* Princeton, N.J., 1955.

Piankoff, Alexandre. *The Wandering of the Soul.* Princeton, N.J., 1974.

Posener, Georges. *De la divinité du Pharaon.* Paris, 1960.

Sauneron, Serge. *Les prêtres de l'ancienne Égypte.* Paris, 1957.

Sauneron, Serge. *Les fêtes religieuses d'Esna.* Cairo, 1962.

Schweitzer, Ursula. *Das Wesen des Ka im Diesseits und Jenseits der alten Ägypter.* Glückstadt, 1956.

Sethe, Kurt H. *Dramatische Texte zu den altägyptischen Mysterienspielen.* Leipzig, 1928.

Sethe, Kurt H. *Amun und die acht Urgötter von Hermopolis.* Berlin, 1929.

Sethe, Kurt H. *Urgeschichte und älteste Religion der Ägypter.* Leipzig, 1930.

Spiegel, Joachim. "Das Auferstehungsritual der Unaspyramide." *Annales du Service des Antiquités de l'Égypte* 53 (1956): 339–439.

Vandier, Jacques. *La religion égyptienne.* Paris, 1944.

Vandier, Jacques. *Le Papyrus Jumilhac.* Paris, 1961.

Westendorf, Wolfhart, ed. *Aspekte der spätägyptischen Religion.* Wiesbaden, 1979.

Wilson, John A. *The Burden of Egypt.* Chicago, 1951.

Wolf, Walther. *Das schöne Fest von Opet.* Leipzig, 1931.

Zabkar, Louis V. *A Study of the Ba Concept in Ancient Egyptian Texts.* Chicago, 1968.

Zandee, Jan. *Death as an Enemy.* Leiden, 1960.

LEONARD H. LESKO (1987)

EGYPTIAN RELIGION: THE LITERATURE

From the dawn of Egyptian history, and throughout the three and a half millennia of their currency, religious beliefs and practices were for practical purposes committed to written form. The singular phenomenon of the nation-state the pharaohs had created put far greater stock in the hieroglyphic script, the novel creation of a bureaucracy of wise men, than it did in any memory, individual or collective, that might serve as a repository for the important knowledge of the community. The scribal tradition, therefore, at an early date took precedence over the oral in Egypt, and the scribe became recorder and transmitter of all that was deemed important among the intellectual creations of pharaonic society. Egyptian religion was practiced according to beliefs and directives "as they were [found] in writing," and scorn was poured on anything that remained in an oral stage of transmission. The latter was "the narrative discourse of the people," and was considered to be unsophisticated, hyperbolic, and unreliable.

In the light of this it should come as no surprise to learn that the scribe in ancient Egypt was the kingpin in the running of the government, and the most respected member of the community (Williams, 1972). The "scribe of the god's book," later to become the sacred scribe, and the "lector-priest" (lit., "he who carries the book role") are found already in the Early Dynastic period (c. 3000–2650 BCE). Precisely what kind of sacred literature such worthies wrote, copied, and guarded at this early time is difficult to ascertain. As the vast majority of texts, both originals and copies, were written on papyrus, it is scarcely to be wondered at that none has survived from the Old Kingdom (c. 3000–2200 BCE), and very few from the Middle Kingdom (c. 2134–1660 BCE). Something of the early history of the sacred library can, however, be reconstructed from hieroglyphic records and from the known exigencies of the cult. Thus, the overriding importance of sacred monarchy demanded that rites concerned with coronation and jubilee be regulated by written directories, and the remarkable uniformity of relief-scenes and texts commemorating these ceremonies over three millennia argues the presence, already in the Old Kingdom, of written prescriptions.

Of equal, if not greater, importance to the ancient Egyptian community were two rites intimately connected with the funerary cult—the offering to the ancestors and the mortuary liturgy. The former called forth at the very dawn of Egyptian history the offering-list, a formal and comprehensive listing of foodstuffs and other requirements of the dead, together with name and titles of the ancestor and occasionally a formulaic text to be used orally (Barta, 1963). The mortuary liturgy became the starting point for that ever-burgeoning body of texts known to the Egyptians as *sakhu* ("[funerary] beatifications"), pronounced by the lector-priest on the day of the obsequies to assist the deceased in securing a glorified existence in the beyond. Any person for whom offering-list and beatifications had been provided could *ipso facto* be termed "a competent and equipped spirit."

MORTUARY LITERATURE. Although one must await the twenty-fourth century BCE for the first extensive texts of funerary purport, from that point the genre rapidly becomes one of the most frequent in the repertoire of Egyptian writings.

The Pyramid Texts. The corpus of religious literature called the Pyramid Texts comprises approximately 760 individual paragraphs, or "spells," inscribed on the walls of the tomb chambers and entrance corridors of Egyptian kings (and occasionally queens) from Wenis (c. 2410–2380 BCE) to Aba (fl. c. 2185 BCE). As such it represents the earliest, and in some respects the most interesting, body of sacred literature in the ancient world (Faulkner, 1969; Barta, 1981). In later times the material was sporadically revived and recopied; but the original exemplars reflect its heyday. (Even when first seen, however, the corpus was undergoing a rapid evolution: Much of the content of the Wenis texts is missing and has been replaced with additional material of like sort in the pyramid of Pepi II [c. 2290–2200 BCE].) The texts follow no special sequence, other than a general "order of service" from the arrival of the funeral cortege at the pyramid to the king's acceptance by the sun god in heaven. Broadly speaking, the intent is that of an apologia on behalf of the deceased in order to secure the gods' acquiescence to his eternal stay among them. The Pyramid Texts incorporate hymns to the gods, magical incantations, prayers for the dead, liturgical pieces, and ritual texts, and as such envisage rites of embalmment and purification, the "opening of the mouth" ceremony (to revivify the mummy and the mortuary statues), coronation, rites of passage, and the offering liturgy.

While this was not their primary intent, the Pyramid Texts provide an introduction to the cult and pantheon of the gods current in Egypt during the Old Kingdom. The texts were undoubtedly produced by the theologians and scribes of the great center of sun worship, Heliopolis, where lay the "great mansion" of the sun god, Re-Atum. Reflecting the amazing political unity the Egyptian state had achieved under pharaonic administration by the middle of the third millennium BCE, these Heliopolitan priests had synthesized the religion of the Nile Valley and Delta into a unified whole, and enlisted its aid in effecting the king's journey to the solar beyond (Anthes, 1959). The Pyramid Texts can, therefore, be used—with appropriate caution—as a source for Egyptian religion during the Old Kingdom.

The Coffin Texts. This body of literature, comprising more than 1,150 "spells" and called in Egyptian the *Book of Justifying a Man in the Realm of the Dead,* is known in numerous copies from the ninth dynasty through the thirteenth (c. 2150–1650 BCE). Although a few extant fragments make it plain that the original was written up in papyrus copies, the vast majority of examples are found written in ink in vertical columns (in apparent imitation of the Pyramid Texts), on the insides of the large, rectangular wooden coffins that were characteristic of the period (Faulkner, 1973–1978). Unlike the Pyramid Texts, of which they could be considered a later development, the Coffin Texts often precede a spell with a rubric docket giving the purpose of the piece, and follow it with another supplying directions for use. The latter might suggest use by cult initiates during life, and indeed the *Book of Two Ways* has been taken to be a manual of initiation. On the other hand, the rubric headings of spells most frequently point to their construing by the ancients as magical incantations designed to circumvent obstacles, combat dangers, and ensure the well-being of the deceased in the next life. Over half of the spells are concerned with mystical transformations of the deceased into animals, gods, objects, or desirable elements in nature (the Nile, grain, air, and so on), and in a large proportion of them magical effectiveness is ensured by the knowledge of esoteric mythology to which the deceased lays claim.

Much of the Coffin Texts derives from the Pyramid Texts, and belongs under the general rubric of "beatifications," but the content and atmosphere of the Coffin Texts sometimes differ markedly from the aristocratic or royal aura of the Pyramid Texts. Often a spell from the latter is distorted and misinterpreted, either to suit the new requirements of life in a different age or, more often, through ignorance of what it originally meant. Like the Pyramid Texts, the Coffin Texts come from the context of the sun cult, but yield more information on other cult centers, such as Abydos, Mendes, and Buto. For the first time in Egyptian religious literature, prominence is given to the concept of the judgment of the dead in the afterlife; and Osiris and his cycle, on the ascendant in the later versions of the Pyramid Texts, are very much to the fore in the Coffin Texts.

Book of Going Forth by Day. By the beginning of the eighteenth dynasty (c. 1569 BCE), the vast corpus of "beatifications" represented by the Coffin Texts was being pressed into service as a source for a new document of funerary use, the *Book of Going Forth by Day,* erroneously termed the *Book of the Dead* by moderns (Allen, 1974). Written most commonly on a papyrus roll that was placed in the coffin beside the mummy (of both royalty and commoners), the *Book of Going Forth by Day* derives nearly 60 percent of its material from the known Coffin Texts; but the spells were evolving under constant pressure of reinterpretation, and new incantations were being added. Their magical intent is clearer than ever: Each spell has a title, and most a prescription for use. All were, as is to be expected, intended for the well-being of the deceased in the next life, although, as is the case with the Coffin Texts, use by the living is not entirely excluded. The *Book of Going Forth by Day* continues and expands a practice begun on a small scale by the Coffin Texts, that of glossing selected spells with colored vignettes showing the deceased before various gods or engaged in cultic acts. Whereas for the New Kingdom spells are treated as individual units having little connection with other material and no fixed position in a canonical order, the "archaizing" revival of the Kushite-Saite period (712–525 BCE) produced a standard sequence of spells that survived into Roman times.

The *Book of Going Forth by Day* shows the concept of the Egyptian afterlife at a stage from which it developed little. The concept of the judgment, or psychostasia, is virtually full-blown, the trust in the efficacy of magic at its height. It now becomes standard procedure to place certain spells on "shawabtis" (servant figurines) to activate them, or on "heart scarabs" (beetle pectorals) to prevent the heart from testifying against its owner. Proper use of chapter 125 will ensure that the deceased emerges from the divine tribunal unscathed, whether he be "guilty" or not; the pious intoning of hymns to the sun at dawn and sunset will elicit divine indulgence for eternity.

Underworld literature. From the earliest period one can sense an antithesis between Re, the supernal sun god, *fons et origo* of the universe of light, and Osiris, the passive infernal hypostasis of the mystery of fertility, death, and the earth. Every night the sun passed through the perils of the infernal regions where Osiris dwelt, and it was only by magic and the prayers of the devout that it emerged whole in the morning. The "well-equipped" soul showed an ambivalence in its postmortem desires, now striving to accompany the sun boat in its eternal round through sky and the underworld for ever, now craving identity with Osiris, embedded forever in the life-giving soil. Preoccupation with these aims, ostensibly irreconcilable, conjured up in the New Kingdom (c. 1569–1085 BCE) an ever-increasing literature on the underworld and the mystery of the eventual union of Re with Osiris (Hornung, 1980). The very names of the books comprising this esoteric library reveal the nature of the realm described: the *Book of What Is in the Underworld,* the *Book of Gates,* the *Book of Caverns,* the *Litany of Re,* the *Book of Traversing Eternity.* Though they were genuine papyrus books whose origins in some cases possibly date before the New Kingdom, most of these pieces are known from hieroglyphic copies inscribed on the walls of the tombs of the kings at Thebes. They describe an underworld divided into twelve regions (corresponding to the hours of the night), peopled by fierce demons and fraught with dangers for gods and mortals alike. It is a place of punishment from which all people fervently pray to be saved. Concern for such salvation, as well as for well-being in life, led in the first millennium BCE to the practice of placing "decrees" in the mouths of the gods on behalf of other gods and individual human beings, and inscribing them on prophylactery strips of papyrus or on tablets.

The cosmic balance between Re and Osiris and the natural principles for which they stood were of great concern in the Late period (second half of the first millennium BCE). Underworld literature envisages a union of the two at a crucial point in Re's nightly passage through the underworld. In a curious ritual called the Rite of the House of Life, designed to preserve life in the universe and prevent the sun crashing to the earth, Osiris was united with Re in the form of a mummy.

Communications between living and dead. Central to Egyptian mortuary practices was the offering to the ancestors. The entire tomb in its layout and decoration focused upon the offering station with its stone table, libation stone, and sculpted or painted representation of the deceased. Here the dead met the living, as it were, and lively "conversation" was the result. At a very early date, certainly by the close of the third dynasty (c. 2650 BCE), tomb owners had begun to use the wall space in the tomb chapel to convey messages to posterity: personal identification (name and titles), legal contracts with mortuary priests, scenes from the life of the deceased, and formal addresses to the living. The last, introduced by the heading "He [the tomb owner] says . . ." and followed by direct speech, constituted a biographical statement, and throughout Egyptian history this statement became a major source not only for history but also for personal ethics and conduct in society. Very frequently the tomb owner used it as a vehicle to cajole or harangue the passerby into either making a formal offering or (more often) pronouncing the offering formula whereby the foodstuffs named were actualized for the deceased in the next life. The tomb owner sensed that his visitor might be reluctant to comply with his request, and so he presented arguments of convenience and self-interest; at times he all but threatened. The same type of text could be used as a means of warding off would-be violators of the tomb, usually by threatening them with a lawsuit at the court of the Great God in the Beyond.

Conversation of the living with the ancestors was also possible. This took the form of "letters to the dead," written on bowls, shards, or papyrus and placed in the offering chamber of the tomb, to be seen by the spirit when it emerged to partake of the food offerings. Frequently the letters incorporated complaints that the dead relative was interfering in the writer's life.

MYTHOLOGY. No myths have come down from ancient Egypt composed solely for the sake of the narrative itself (Schott, 1945). No practical need was felt to produce an *editio princeps.* But mythology was constantly used, so powerful were its archetypal protagonists and events felt to be as a basis for cult procedure, and mythology was drawn on as an inexhaustible source of prototypes and identifications in the realm of magic. Further, the cultic and magical act enjoyed a reciprocal influence on the myth, and the latter is found evolving and reproducing under the influence of a changing cult. This evolution, however, was not in the hands of the scribe. In the cult, indeed in everyday life, the spoken word predominated; and variant forms of myth are often found developing from like-sounding words or phrases. One senses a creative impulse here that derives from the common Egyptian belief that sound structure constitutes a powerful force throughout the elements of the created world.

Cosmogonies. There is no single text from the pharaonic period whose sole purpose is to set forth a creation myth; but allusions to creation motifs are legion in all types of religious literature. Four basic patterns manifest themselves, in all of which the act of creation is construed as the elimination of chaos and the ordering of preexistent elements: (1) the primeval ocean and the creator-god or creative element that appears within it; (2) the separation of earth from sky, both personified in a sexual union; (3) creation by means of a skilled craft (e.g., the ceramic expertise of Khnum, the plastic modeling of Ptah, or the weaving of Neith); (4) the conflict between hero-god and monster, out of whose carcass the world is created. Of the four the last is the least known, the motif in Egypt having been early carried over into a cosmic explanation of the continued integrity of creation. Thanks to its espousal by the dominant solar theology of Heliopolis, the first is by far the most common, but perhaps the most crass (expectoration, masturbation, and weeping being mechanisms involved).

A rather more sophisticated approach to the problem of creation was essayed at Hermopolis and Memphis. At the former site, the abstract qualities of the Primeval Ocean (Nun) are personified as four gods (with their consorts): Nothingness, Inertness, Limitlessness, and Darkness. At Memphis, Thought and Fiat are singled out as the essence of the divine, in this case the god Ptah, and are made the sole elements in the creation process. Wherever rationality and the capability of enunciating thought exist in the created world, there exists Ptah, sustaining and informing his creation. This doctrine is most clearly set forth in the *Memphite Theology,* a commentary on a dramatic text, appearing under Shabaka (712–697 BCE) as an inscription on stone but purporting to have been copied from a much older document (Sethe, 1928). Although the alleged antiquity of the text has been doubted, the same concepts it sets forth are clearly alluded to in New Kingdom religious literature. The claim, often made, that it does in fact date from the late third millennium BCE may yet prove correct.

Myths of kingship and fertility. These center upon two great cycles of myths, the Horus-Seth conflict and the death of Osiris. The former describes the struggle of Order with Chaos, variously cast as an act of revenge, a fight over the right to rule, or simply a natural struggle. When linked with the Osiris myth, the fight is sharpened and humanized: It is not only a son's act of revenge upon his father's murderer, but also the son's assertion of his legal and political rights. When the king adopts the role of Horus and performs the obsequies for his deceased father, "Osiris," the whole myth takes on heightened significance as the mythological underpinning of the monarchy (Anthes, 1959).

From an early period the whole is inextricably intertwined with the myth of fertility, and Osiris and those gods with whom he is associated become hypostases of the principle of fertility. While it may well be a skewing of the evidence through the haphazard of preservation, texts pointing to Osiris and his congeners as associated with the Nile, the fertile soil, and the crops tend to become more numerous as the Late Period approaches.

Like cosmogonies, fertility myths are not in ancient Egypt accorded any special archetypal publication. There was no need for one. No canonical version existed, and constant use in the cult and in everyday life continued to produce changes in detail. Seldom is the myth of Osiris epitomized in the literature of the pharaonic period from beginning to end (cf. as exceptions the eighteenth-dynasty hymn to Osiris in Louvre stele c. 286 and the Plutarch version, the latter in Griffiths, 1970). But allusions of widely varying length to fertility myths are legion in all types of religious literature.

Myths about the destruction of humankind. Another well-defined group of myths centers upon a feline deity dispatched by the gods to punish humankind for disobedience. Identified as the sun's "eye" (i.e., the fierce heat of the sun disk, personified) or the goddess of plague, she ranges far over the earth effecting the gods' will; but soon she exhibits a mind of her own and refuses to follow the directives of the head of the pantheon. The plot turns on the means used by the gods to subdue her and bring her back into the divine fold (Hornung, 1981).

Mythological stories. Several pieces of writing exist that can be broadly characterized as elaborations on a mythological theme. Most date from the New Kingdom and are written in the Late Egyptian dialect (current as a literary medium from c. 1320 BCE to nearly 1000 BCE), but sporadic references suggest the presence of the genre already in the Middle Kingdom. These works center upon a known incident in a myth and rework it into a coherent narrative, often with dramatic overtones, lending a charming, human cast to the divine protagonists. Favorite foci around which interest gravitates are the topos of Isis and baby Horus hiding in the marshes of the Nile Delta, and the conflict/trial of Horus and Seth. Some, like the stories of Papyrus d'Orbiney, Papyrus Chester Beatty I, or the Amherst Papyrus, constitute independent works; others are found only in secondary contexts, where they are used as magic spells. Occasionally in the New Kingdom, themes of Canaanite mythology appear in Egyptian translation (Simpson, 1973; Lichtheim, 1973–1980).

SPECULATIVE LITERATURE. The complete collapse of society and government in the obscure "revolution" that brought an end to the Old Kingdom (c. 2200 BCE) shook the Egyptians' confidence in traditional beliefs and procedures. In the literature of the First Intermediate period that followed (c. 2200–2050 BCE) a questioning tone may be sensed; Egypt, or at least a part of it, was engaged in a fundamental reappraisal of the nation's institutions and identity. While the continuum in the mortuary cult attested by the Coffin Texts shows the presence of a traditional "mainstream" in Egyptian thought, a surprisingly large number of pieces written during the period display a questing spirit prepared to break with the past and espouse heterodox views.

Dialogues and harpers' songs. An untraditional, indeed agnostic, view of humankind's prospects beyond the tomb was the contribution of a very special group of texts that must have had their birth in the First Intermediate period. In the genre of the dialogue, two proponents of differing (if not opposing) points of view engage each other in conversation, and the views expressed are startlingly heterodox. In one example, Osiris, typifying the soul on the point of entering the afterlife, gives vent to his fear of the unknown, in spite of centuries of confident mortuary practices; and Atum is obliged to offer him the assurance of eternal survival and union with the creator himself. Even more peculiar is the *Dialogue of a Man with His Soul* (a modern title—the ancient has not survived). In the sole surviving manuscript of this work, which lacks the first few pages, an unnamed man contemplates the prospect of death and declares his determination to pursue the traditional course of preparing a tomb, the funeral service, and an endowment. His soul, however, whose acquiescence in all this is crucial to the man's hope of future existence, expresses profound doubts on the efficacy of the customary procedure, on the alleged happiness of life in the beyond, and even on man's ability to attain an afterlife (Williams, 1962).

The note of doubt sounded in these works gives over into the advocacy of a hedonistic approach to life in a well-represented genre known as "harpers' songs" (Williams, 1981, pp. 4f.). Derived from the innocuous banquet song whose sole purpose is entertainment at a social event, the harpers' songs originated in the troubled times of the twenty-second century BCE as a vehicle for the expression of a profound disillusionment with traditional views of the afterlife. Recurring themes include the desuetude of tombs and mortuary installations, the impossibility of knowing what is beyond the grave, and the need to live life to the full here and now. Although most examples of the genre are today found on tomb walls in association with a scene of the harper before the deceased, there is good reason to believe that such songs enjoyed a primary *Sitz im Leben* among the living. The content of individual pieces tends to become cliché-ridden as time goes on, but the tone is always lively, with a tendency toward impiety. Harpers' songs remained popular for centuries, and their irreverent nature occasionally evoked a counterblast from the pious.

The pessimistic view of humanity's ability to forecast what will be met beyond the grave leads naturally, though illogically, to the proposition that the afterlife, in pointed contrast to what is expected by all, is in fact a realm of gloom and misery. A story of thirteenth-century date in which a pious priest encounters the spirit of one long departed who enlightens him on this score, sets forth this view, and a few mortuary stelae of later times elaborate on the same theme.

Discourse. The Egyptians, like many ancient peoples, identified one sort of wisdom with the ability to foretell the future under divine inspiration. The verb meaning "to foretell, to announce in advance" did not, however, give rise to a genre term. More often than not it is the wise man himself whose name is the identifying element, and the text goes under the label of "The discourse (lit., *the word)* of so-and-so." Broadly speaking, such declamations are grouped by the ancients under the general rubric of "teachings."

The turbulent years of the First Intermediate period were the heyday of the prophetic discourse, although as a "literary" phenomenon it had a longer life. In the main it constituted a lament over the sorry condition of the land, gone to ruin politically and socially, and could be cast either as a backdated prediction or a contemporary description (Junge, 1977). With the coming to power of the twelfth dynasty (c. 1991–1778 BCE) the prophecy was used as a powerful tool of propaganda to bolster the regime's claim to legitimacy; it might even be placed in the mouth of a god to support the pretensions of an individual ruler.

The discourses of the First Intermediate period frequently reveal themselves as vehicles of heterodox messages. Ipuwer, an otherwise unknown wise man of the past, rails in a lengthy tirade against none other than the creator god himself, and lays at his feet the blame for having allowed the land to go to ruin under unjust administrators. A peasant, wrongfully deprived of his possessions, goes to lodge an official complaint before the appropriate magistrate, and the result is a series of paeons adulating justice and decrying civil corruption. The theme of the petitioner in a lawsuit robbed of a just hearing turns up in several works of the period.

MAGICAL TEXTS. The Egyptians conceived of magic (*heka*) as a powerful element in the universe that, if controlled, could be employed to any end, even to the constraint of the gods themselves and the dislocation of the cosmos. So dominant was the preoccupation with this possibility that literature with magical intent constitutes the most common genre in the corpus of ancient Egyptian writings. Broadly speaking, magical texts can be divided into two subgroups on the basis of purpose, those concerned with the official cult and those for private use; but the Egyptians themselves never made this distinction. Incantations are introduced under several headings: "The protection against . . ." (*sau nu . . .*), "The spell of . . ." (*ra n . . .*), "The repelling of . . ." (*sehry*), "The book of . . ." (*medjat*), "The protection of . . ." (*meket*), "The protection book . . ." (*nehet*) (Redford, 1985, p. 104, n. 60). As in the case of mortuary literature, rubrics specifying use are sometimes included, but stories in which magicians appear as protagonists often reflect the procedures involved.

The purpose of magic spells varied. Most often they were designed to ward off external forces of evil, whether ethereal or concrete. Temple ritual invoked magic to ensure the integrity of the rites, the cult personnel, the paraphernalia, and the installation. So closely intertwined in the ritual was the magical incantation that frequently it is difficult to distinguish cultic prescriptions, prayers, and hymns from texts with purely magical intent. A perusal of the famous Edfu library catalogue, for example, will reveal the startling fact that much of what would pass as ritual is subsumed under magic! Private use was concerned with protection from disease, bodily harm, or demons who effect harm, and thus was closely associated with medicine. Very common were spells to ward off snakes, scorpions, crocodiles, and other noisome animals, or to neutralize the evil intent of people (often foreign), of the dead, or of the evil eye. Formal execration of foreign enemies, employing the ritual smashing of pots and figurines, was well known in the sphere of pharaonic statecraft. Productive, as opposed to prophylactic, magic is not well attested.

By his thorough training in magical lore, the magician—the Egyptians used such a word (*hekay*), but magic could be learned by anyone intelligent enough—could confront the most powerful hostile force and triumph. Most often the speaker identified himself in a spell with a god, or invoked a mythological incident as precedent. Numerous myths are in fact known only because they were considered efficacious enough to be used as spells! Identification of celebrant or victim with a divine figure, or the extensive use of homophonous words ("pious puns"), was considered useful in ensuring the effectiveness of the spell (Borghouts, 1978).

Great compilations of magical texts were copied on papyrus and kept in temple libraries, but few of these have survived, and one is often thrown back on "unofficial" copies. Private scribal libraries have occasionally yielded magical papyri, but casual copies on ostraca are more numerous. Of special interest are the prophylactic statues of mortals or gods in various poses, covered with magical spells and provided with the means of collecting water poured over them. These usually were installed in sanatoriums attached to the temples (especially in the second half of the first millennium BCE), where sufferers from various diseases came for healing. The magical stelae and *cippi* were intended for private protection, and often show representations of the child Horus and the creatures against whom protection is sought.

WISDOM LITERATURE. The word that in Egyptian approaches closest to the concept conveyed by the Hebrew *hokhmah* ("wisdom") is *sebayt* ("teaching"), but this word is so loosely used that it can scarcely point to a formal genre. Any text with broad didactic purpose could be grouped under this heading. Thus it is found used of collections of maxims (most frequently), but also of texts of occupational guidance, model letters for students, political pamphlets, word lists, and so on. Anything, in fact, within the purview of the teacher-scribe that could be used for instruction fell broadly under this rubric.

It is, however, to aphoristic literature that the term is most often applied. A piece will begin with some such introduction as "Here begins the life-teaching, the attestations to well-being, all instructions of executive deportment and the regular procedure of courtiers" or "Here begins the instruction that educates the heart and witnesses to the ignorant." The inclusion of "testimonies" and "sayings of the way of life" generally denotes the incorporation of a collection of proverbs. The usual context of wisdom literature is the father-to-son chat, in which fatherly advice is given to the young on how to win friends and influence people and, generally, how to lead a successful life. Much of the worldly wisdom set forth suggests an origin in everyday life and a primary oral transmission. Nevertheless, from the earliest period canonical versions of many books of wisdom existed, in which wording and sequence of pericopes were of paramount importance; and the motif of a wise man's words being taken down in writing at the moment of delivery is a commonplace in Egyptian literature.

Collections of wise sayings originate in all periods of Egyptian history. Purporting to be the work of a vizier of the fifth dynasty (c. twenty-fifth century BCE), the *Wisdom of Ptahhotep* is known in a complete text, while the wisdom writings under the names of Prince Hor-djedef and Vizier Kagemni, also known Old Kingdom figures, have survived in less satisfactory condition. From the First Intermediate period comes the *Instruction for Merikare* (c. 2075 BCE), a fascinating treatise on statecraft written by a king of the tenth dynasty for his son and successor on the throne. The twelfth dynasty has bequeathed a wealth of wisdom literature, including the posthumous *Instruction of Amenemhet,* a political tract "written" from the grave and placed in the mouth of the assassinated founder of the house; a "loyalist" treatise supporting adherence to the pharaonic government; a "satire" of the trades, an early schoolboy text advocating the scribal calling; and several minor collections of maxims. The teachings of Ani and the thirty wise sayings of Amenemope come from the later New Kingdom; and the first millennium BCE has preserved the *Wisdom of Onkhsheshongy* and Papyrus Insinger, both of which show traces of foreign influence.

Although very much akin in form and content to its biblical or Akkadian counterparts, Egyptian wisdom literature had only limited influence abroad. The *Wisdom of Amenemope* had long been considered (rightly) the basis of *Proverbs* 30, and Psalm 104 seems to be more than an echo of Akhenaton's "teaching," as represented in his hymn to the sun disk (fourteenth century BCE). But biblical, Mesopotamian, and Greek folklore with a "wisdom" element owe more to local themes and sources than to Egypt (Williams, 1972, 1981).

TEMPLE LIBRARIES. While the "House of the God's Book" was originally, in the Old Kingdom, a secular registry office for royal rescripts, by the Middle Kingdom the term *god* was being construed as a reference not to the king but to a member of the pantheon, and the expression was coming to mean "temple library" (Schott, 1972, 1977). Occasionally alternating with such terms as *chamber, office,* or *hall of writings* (the last a repository of more secular documents), this department of temple administration was overseen by librarians ("keepers of the writings"), and was open to lector-priests, scribes of the god's book, and temple scribes in general. Scrolls were copied out in an adjacent scriptorium and then deposited in the library in wooden chests, less frequently in jars. Associated with the sacred library but outside the temple proper was the "House of Life," an institution open only to the highest grade of skilled scribes and to the king. Here were copied and composed the most holy rituals, hymns, commentaries, and magical texts, and here also the most esoteric rites were performed in secret.

As an archive constantly referred to in all aspects of temple life and procedure, the temple library was treated by the Egyptians as their most precious textual resource. Thoth, the inventor and master of the hieroglyphs, was the library's patron, and Seshat, the goddess of books, presided over its contents. The scribes were proud of their ability to compose, copy, and edit texts, and were strictly enjoined not to let their "fingers tamper with the god's words." One senses a continuum in the life of temple archives over many centuries in the three and a half millennia of Egyptian history. Users could ferret out scrolls of high antiquity and marvel at the difficult syntax and archaic vocabulary. The most skilled scribes boasted of their ability to restore what was lost in lacunae in moth-eaten originals. Although many such references are cliché-ridden, there is every reason to believe that a priestly scribe such as Manetho, living in the third century BCE, had access to written sources ranging back through three millennia. In the present time, although no temple library has survived intact, the contents of a typical collection are easy to reconstruct from the copious references in inscriptions and from a few papyrus caches (Reymond, 1977; Redford, 1985).

Ritual texts. Several terms designate this broad genre. The oldest, which is attested already at the dawn of Egyptian history, is *hebet* ("ritual book"), the special preserve of the *chery-hebet* (lector-priest; lit., "he who carries the ritual book"). This was a sort of breviary or missal, giving the order of service and the texts that were to be read. Occasionally the book was identified with a particular cult, as "the *hebet* of the temple of Ptah." Slightly later terms, used of documents as well as in the abstract, were *net-ʿ* ("customary procedure, ritual"; also pressed into service to render the Akkadian word for "treaty") and *iru* ("cultic forms/acts"). Sometimes "book of " is substituted for *net-ʿ*. During the Middle Kingdom a compendious order of service was referred to as "the complete [guide]," and the requirements of the ritual and, curiously, the spells to be recited were contained in the "god's offeringbook." Among the few ritual papyri that have survived, one may cite a funerary ritual and a rite of succession from the Middle Kingdom, a daily offering liturgy from the New Kingdom, and rituals for various gods' festivals from the Late period. It is important to note that, whatever mnemonic devices a priest may have employed, a ritual was always performed "in accordance with that which is in writing."

Beatifications. The category of "beatifications" (*sakhu,* from a causative root meaning "to turn someone into a glorified spirit") encompasses texts intended to "actualize" the future glorified state of the deceased in the beyond. The term is often used in captions to a scene depicting the lector-priest reading from a scroll on the day of burial. Oblique references make plain the esoteric nature of the material in their allusion to "that secret writing of the lector-priest's craft," by which beatifications are undoubtedly meant. In all probability this is the rubric under which the ancients classified such collections of mortuary spells as the Pyramid Texts and the Coffin Texts, and there can be little doubt that they were intended to be read aloud.

Hymns. In Egyptian the hymn goes under several designations. Most common is *duau* ("adoration"); less frequent, *senemehu* or *sensu* ("supplication"). Often inscribed on stelae, this adoration of the deity is sometimes explicit in its purpose, "propitiating the spirit" of the gods or goddesses addressed. Hymns are often characterized by the recurrent refrain "Hail to thee!" followed by a direct invocation of the deity, replete with epithets. Less often the key words are "Praise to thee!" The genre includes such formal hymns as cultic supplications to individual gods, litanies, and even royal apologias; but it also encompasses the popular, private hymns to the sun god at dawn and sunset, and even the inscribed "testimonies" of the semiliterate class of workers, witnessing to healing and forgiveness. By extension *duau* may also be applied to the "adorations" of Hathor, goddess of love (i.e. to love poetry). The term can refer as well to the outburst of praise, spontaneous or formal, of the king by the people.

Several longer hymns, intended for temple service, were nonetheless didactic in nature. Such were the hymns to Re-Harakhty, Amun-Re, the sun disk, and Ptah, which are known from New Kingdom exemplars. These display a sophisticated universalism, and preach (in the case of the hymn to Ptah) the same syncretistic deism as is found in the *Memphite Theology.* The monotheism of the hymn to the sun disk is well known.

Most examples imply or state directly that the hymns are to be intoned, either by private individuals as pious acts of devotion, or in a temple context by a priest or a choir. In temple ritual the papyrus containing the order of service will often give only the *incipit* of a hymn; the choristers and the celebrant undoubtedly knew it by heart.

Mythological compendiums. The Egyptians loved to compile catalogs of the salient features of the cult(s) and of the gods and their mythology for a particular nome or group of nomes. Known especially from the first millennium BCE, the genre undoubtedly has an earlier history, which is today, unfortunately, not directly attested. Late hieroglyphic texts refer to the scroll of the *Directory of Mounds of the Early Primaeval Ones* and the *Reckoning of Every Cult Seat and the Knowing of What Is in Them.* Elsewhere one hears of the *Great Plan of the Two Lands,* which contained information on Egypt and its arable land.

Chronicles and narratives. Chronicles cannot be identified as a native Egyptian genre, the form being derived from Babylonia some time in the first millennium BCE. From the early Ptolemaic period (third century BCE) comes the so-called Demotic Chronicle, in actuality a tendentious interpretation of selected events in the recent past that in form and inspiration shows strong influence from Asia. Narratives are more common. The papyrus fragments from the library of the temple of Sobek in the Fayum (the lakeland immediately west of the Nile, about fifty miles south of present-day Cairo) contained a number of quasi-legendary romances, including stories of the magician Setna, the *Romance of King Petubastis,* the story of King Djoser and his Assyrian campaign, the Amazon romance, and the *Prophecy of the Lamb.* Similar material has been unearthed in temple libraries at Saqqara, the necropolis of Memphis (Redford, 1985, chap. 8).

King-lists and offering-lists. It is most probable that temple libraries possessed historical source material in the form of king-lists and offering-lists. The offering cult of the royal ancestors had been maintained in the chief temples in the land from the earliest dynasties, and had involved an "offering invocation" in which the spirits of the deceased kings and queens were called by name to the offering table. From the twelfth dynasty at latest there had existed a formal king-list, tracing the occupancy of the pharaonic seat from the creator Ptah through an unbroken line of divine and human incumbents. Such a king-list was known to and used by Manetho, the priest-scribe who wrote a history of Egypt in Greek (third century BCE), and the relative accuracy of his *Aegyptiaca* attests to its uninterrupted and sober transmission (Waddell, 1940; Redford, 1985).

Annals of the gods. Closely allied to the compendiums mentioned above is a type of document purporting to give an account of divine acts. Derived from an old word for "annals" used originally of the yearly records of the king, the "annals of the gods" first appeared in texts of the New Kingdom and, although examples are lacking, they probably contained cosmogonic and mythological material. These "mighty acts of the gods," which of course reflect the historicization of the world of the gods, were the special preserve of the House of Life. Examples are rare in the New Kingdom. The *Book of the Cow of Heaven,* though used as a set of magic spells in the extant versions, contains an etiological account of the reign of Re (Hornung, 1981). Both Ramses II (c. 1304–1237 BCE) and Ramses IV (c. 1167–1161 BCE) refer to certain books in the House of Life that contain cosmogonic material from the reigns of the gods. Late versions of well-known myths that might qualify for inclusion in this genre are the reigns of Shu and Geb from the *Wady el-Arish naos,* the myth of Horus of Edfu, and the *Expulsion of Seth.* In using these well-known pieces, however, it is well to remember that they were recast in a period of history (fourth century BCE) when xenophobia and paranoia because of foreign conquest lent a tendentious tone to theme and content.

Directories and prescriptions. Prescriptive manuals abounded, especially in the late period. One of the earliest was the *Great Inventory,* the standard compilation of directions for the manufacture of cult images and paraphernalia, the decoration of shrines, and so on. Manuals on the construction and decoration of temples were often ascribed to Imhotep, the almost-legendary savant of the reign of Djoser (twenty-seventh century BCE). Under the same heading are directories of purification, manuals of offering, and festival calendars.

Omen texts and related genres. *Omina* are not common in the Egyptian religious corpus because they are confined to the Late period, when contact with Mesopotamia was more frequent. Hemerologies and oneiromancies, on the other hand, enjoyed native popularity and development at an early stage of Egyptian history. The former were apparently called "That Which Is in the Year," though known exemplars assign a variety of specific titles. What is important is that the explanation of why a particular day was considered propitious or inimical was always assigned a mythological context (Brunner-Traut, 1981), and in the process a myth was often adumbrated. Egyptians, like most ancient peoples, took dreams seriously, and this is reflected in the literature.

Oracle texts. The belief that a god made his will known through oracular utterances can be traced back to a relatively early period in Egypt's history, but the practice of employing oracles as an administrative and juridical mechanism dates from the nineteenth dynasty (thirteenth century BCE). Whether in the seclusion of the shrine or at the public procession of the god in his sacred bark, eliciting the god's response to solve a problem became so common that a special scribal office was called into being, that of "the scribe of oracles," to keep the records. Examples of the questions put to the god (demanding affirmative or negative responses) are extant, as are the beautiful papyrus records of the petitioner's appeal and the results. Often, especially from the twentieth to the twenty-second dynasties (c. 1200–730 BCE), a hieroglyphic record of the oracle, including a vignette showing the petitioner(s) and the divine bark, might be set up in a prominent place in the temple to serve as a legal record.

Medical texts. The writing of medical prescriptions and procedures and of the pharmacopoeia was one of the earliest acts of scribal activity in ancient Egypt. Later traditions are unanimous in ascribing certain medical books to the kings and wise men of the Old Kingdom, and in some cases the archaic syntax and vocabulary of surviving papyri bear this out. Written and edited by the sacred scribes associated with the House of Life, the papyri that have survived are collections of cases and recipes more or less united in common areas of interest or practice. Thus there are papyri on gynecology (P. Kahun), obstetrics and pediatrics (P. Ramesseum and P. Carlsberg), surgery (P. Edwin Smith), and veterinary medicine (P. Kahun); in some of the longest papyri (P. Ebers and the Berlin and London papyri) there is a miscellany of prescriptions and recipes. References to works now lost show specialization in diseases of the heart, eye, and abdomen, in anatomy and hygiene. While many magical incantations are found throughout these papyri in greater or smaller concentrations, there is everywhere in evidence an insight into pathology and pharmacology that is based on objective diagnosis and scientific deduction.

Administrative texts. In ancient Egypt the temple was not only the "god's mansion" where he resided and was ministered to by his servants, the priests, but also the hub of a large landowning institution comprising a number of disparate organs of production. Tenant farmers, herdsmen, artisans, and merchants all worked for their master, the god, and the revenue they raised provided a sizable income for the temple estate. The business documents that recorded this commercial aspect of temple life formed a major segment of any temple's archives. One of the oldest caches of papyri extant today, the Abusir Papyri, reflects the contents of such an archive from the pyramid-temple of Neferirkare I of the fifth dynasty, spanning a period of approximately fifty years several generations after the death of the king (c. 2370–2320 BCE). Here are found inventories of temple furniture, daily records of income, monthly accounts of food distribution and expenditures, and duty tables. In the Middle Kingdom, temple daybooks put in an appearance. These record income and disbursements, letters received in the temple office, celestial observations, work assignments, lists of personnel, records of cultic celebrations, and so on, all organized simply by calendrical notation. Throughout most periods, temple libraries contained inventories of land, personnel, and goods receivable; priestly correspondence; and account texts. Taxation documents, specifying quotas levied on sharecroppers and herdsmen on the temple estates or placed under obligation by the crown, were also to be found in the library. Moreover, during imperial times lists of booty from foreign wars were delivered to the temples and deposited in papyrus form in the archives there. Any records of special importance to the temple community, such as royal decrees, inductions and promotions of priests, and lists of royal and private bequests, were often culled from their primary locus in daybooks and the like, and inscribed in more permanent form on stelae, walls, and architraves for ease of reference (Redford, 1985; Reymond, 1977).

In addition to the above textual classifications, many of the genres already discussed, such as wisdom literature and magical texts, were also represented in temple libraries. There is every reason to believe that information on such subjects as geography, mineralogy, and biology was to be found there as well, but it is difficult to say whether any ancient categories corresponded to these modern terms of disciplinary research.

TEMPLE INSCRIPTIONS. The wall space provided by temple construction in ancient Egypt was used as a medium for didactic, reference, and propaganda purposes. Because the source for almost all of this textual and iconographic decoration was the temple library, temples that have survived provide a most precious record of genres whose originals have perished.

For the Old Kingdom the material is limited to a handful of royal mortuary establishments (pyramid-temples). Here the range of inscriptions is wider and more varied than was later to be the case. Decorated walls display scenes and texts recounting battles, the gathering of booty, the transportation of captives, construction, and famine, as well as singing, dancing, and royal processions. The celebration of festivals (especially the jubilee) is also present in the subject matter, but purely cultic commemoration is not as common as might be thought. The listing of townships and estates as part of the record of endowment of the temple takes the form of servant personifications, arranged in rows along the bases of walls.

While little remains from the Middle Kingdom—the eleventh-dynasty temples show *mutatis mutandis* a continuation of Old Kingdom themes, while the twelfth has left virtually nothing—the New Kingdom and later periods have bequeathed a wealth of inscriptional and iconographic evidence. As a rule, a New Kingdom "processional" (axial) temple will display on its wall surfaces texts appropriate to the status of those allowed to view them. Thus, those parts of the temple on view to the laity—external walls, pylon, and first court—are often decorated with vaguely "propagandistic" intent, and the repertoire tends toward stereotype. Here are scenes and texts of foreign wars, standard head-smiting scenes, lists of conquered places, and the welcoming of the king by the god (which continues as a major motif throughout the temple).

Most often, walls of inner courts and hypostyle hall are adorned with sequences of vignettes and accompanying texts showing the daily liturgy of waking, adorning, and offering to the god, with the king as celebrant, taken from the ritual books of the temple. Specific festivals, such as those of the jubilee, coronation, the gods Sokar and Min, the Opet feast, the foundation of the temple, and so on, are often elaborately depicted with large excerpts of accompanying texts. Processions of princes and princesses, personifications of townships, towns, and the Nile are used as decorative dadoes, or as scenes in their own right. Rooms for storage and the preparation of cult requirements are decorated with offering scenes of a "neutral" nature, which makes it difficult to ascertain the precise use of some rooms. Certain temples have preserved the records of rituals or beliefs peculiar to their localities. One may mention in this regard the Osirian rites recorded in the Sety I temple at Abydos, the Horian myths at Edfu, the ritual adapted for royal use in the Theban mortuary temples, and the jubilee rites at Soleb, Karnak, and Bubastis.

The temple courts and the immediate surroundings of the structure were deemed suitable for the display of texts set up for a variety of purposes. Prominence of place was given to royal inscriptions, either on freestanding stelae or on temple walls. These are records of royal acts or regulatory decrees affecting the temple (frequently the product of a king's speech delivered at a "royal sitting"), and often involve building inscriptions and offering endowments. The contents of such inscriptions, though rhetorically embellished for popular consumption, are usually derived from such official records as the "daybook of the king's house."

Another type of stele, set up before or just inside the temple, was inscribed with a royal encomium. Clearly associated with occasions of oral delivery, such adulations took the form either of stereotyped praise of the king in prose for his "mighty acts" or deeds, or, more often (especially in the later New Kingdom), a formal "song" to be sung to harp accompaniment, each strophe ending with the names of the king. Private individuals of high rank were allowed to set up, in an ambulatory within the temple, statues of themselves with lengthy inscriptions. Such statue inscriptions, while most often cast in the form of an address to the passerby, inevitably incorporate biographical and genealogical information of the highest importance. Citizens of low rank might, certainly in smaller temples, hope to be able to set up hymns, prayers, and testimonials to the gods on stelae where the god might see them and honor their requests.

The best-preserved temples in Egypt date from the fourth century BCE to the first century CE, and ultimately reflect the *risorgimento* of the cult during the Saite Period (664–525 BCE). In the main they follow the New Kingdom tradition, but with some modifications:

(1) Offering vignettes showing king or god before the divine owner of the temple or his guests, and derived from the daily offering liturgy, are now repeated on the walls, both interior and exterior, *ad nauseam.*

(2) The mystic birth of the god-child, offspring of the goddess of the temple, is given great prominence in text and iconography.

(3) The stone *naos* wherein the cult image resides has become a major focus of the rites, and its sides are covered with a representative list of all the divine denizens of the temple.

(4) One senses a tendency to inscribe large excerpts from ritual books, mythological compendiums, and hymns on the walls, wherever space is available, conveying a false sense of *horor vacui.*

These later temples contain a wealth of (local) mythological material, but the degree to which they reflect genuinely ancient beliefs and practices is unclear.

BIBLIOGRAPHY

Allen, Thomas George, ed. *The Book of the Dead.* Chicago, 1974. The most authoritative translation of the *Book of Going Forth by Day* in English, by a scholar who devoted his life to its study.

Anthes, Rudolf. "Egyptian Theology in the Third Millennium B.C." *Journal of Near Eastern Studies* 18 (July 1959): 169–212. The most detailed and incisive treatment of basic mythological concepts in ancient Egypt, using mainly the evidence of the Pyramid Texts.

Barta, Winfried. *Die altägyptische Opferliste von der Frühzeit bis zur griechisch-römischer Epoche.* Berlin, 1963. The standard treatment of the most common type of funerary text in ancient Egyptian tombs.

Barta, Winfried. *Die Bedeutung der Pyramidentexte für den verstorbenen König.* Munich, 1981. An excellent summary, with useful indexes and tables, of the major theories on the origins and purpose of the Pyramid Texts.

Borghouts, J. F., trans. *Ancient Egyptian Magical Texts.* Leiden, 1978. A well-written and well-translated compendium of representative incantations, with a brief but useful commentary.

Brunner-Traut, Emma. *Gelebte Mythen.* Darmstadt, 1981. A collection of five articles on specific aspects of Egyptian mythology, with a pithy introduction, useful for the student.

Faulkner, Raymond, trans. and ed. *The Ancient Egyptian Pyramid Texts.* Oxford, 1969. The most up-to-date translation into English of this early corpus of texts.

Faulkner, Raymond, trans. and ed. *The Ancient Egyptian Coffin Texts.* 3 vols. Warminster, 1973–1978. The best—and the only—comprehensive translation of the Coffin Texts available.

Griffiths, J. Gwyn, trans. *Plutarch's De Iside et Osiride.* Cardiff, 1970. There is no more authoritative treatment of the Osirian cycle of deities and their mythology in any language than this work. It is the best translation and commentary on Plutarch's *De Iside* available today.

Hornung, Erik. "Jenseitsführer." In *Lexikon der Ägyptologie,* compiled by Hans Wolfgang Helck and Eberhard Otto, vol. 3. Wiesbaden, 1980. The most recent introduction to New Kingdom literature relating to the underworld.

Hornung, Erik. *Das Buch des Himmelskuh.* Göttingen, 1981. A new publication and commentary of a long-known "underworld" book, containing the story of the destruction of humankind.

Junge, Friedrich. "Die Welt der Klagen." In *Fragen an die altägyptische Literatur,* edited by Jan Assmann et al., pp. 275–285. Wiesbaden, 1977. A study of those Middle Kingdom compositions that describe the anarchy ensuing upon the collapse of society.

Lichtheim, Miriam. *Ancient Egyptian Literature: A Book of Readings.* 3 vols. Berkeley, Calif., 1973–1980. A selection of representative texts from various genres. The translations are first-rate, and the commentary brief but very useful for the novice.

Redford, Donald B. *King-lists, Annals and Daybooks.* Toronto, 1985. A contribution to the historiography of ancient Egypt. Manetho is treated in some detail.

Reymond, Eve A. E., trans. *From Ancient Egyptian Hermetic Writings.* Vienna, 1977. Fragmentary ritual and prescriptive texts on temple buildings and cult procedure from a temple library of the Roman period. The translation is not always as reliable as one would like.

Schott, E. "Bücher und Bibliotheken im alten Ägypten." *Göttinger Miszellen* 1 (1972): 24–27 and 25 (1977): 73–75. A brief statement of work done on the study of ancient Egyptian books and libraries, an area of research in which the author's late husband excelled.

Schott, Siegfried. *Mythe und Mythenbildung im alten Ägypten.* Leipzig, 1945. A fundamental investigation of the myth-making process in ancient Egypt.

Sethe, Kurt H., ed. and trans. *Dramatische Texte zu altägyptischen Mysterienspielen.* Leipzig, 1928. A fundamental work on Egyptian religion, incorporating two studies: (1) a translation and interpretation of the *Memphite Theology;* (2) the text of a ritual papyrus of Middle Kingdom date in the British Museum.

Simpson, William K., ed. *The Literature of Ancient Egypt.* New Haven, Conn., 1973. A set of translations, by leading Egyptologists, of selected stories, wisdom texts, and poetry.

Waddell, W. G. *Manetho.* London, 1940. The only accessible translation of the history of Egypt by Manetho (third century BCE). The commentary is slim and occasionally inaccurate.

Williams, R. J. "Reflections on the Lebensmüde." *Journal of Egyptian Archaeology* 48 (1962): 49–56. Possibly the most judicious assessment of the enigmatic dialogue that goes under the title *The Man Who Was Tired of Life.*

Williams, R. J. "Scribal Training in Ancient Egypt." *Journal of the American Oriental Society* 92 (April–June 1972): 214–221.

Williams, R. J. "The Sages of Ancient Egypt in the Light of Recent Scholarship." *Journal of the American Oriental Society* 101 (January–March 1981): 1–19. An excellent summing-up of present work in the sphere of Egyptian wisdom literature, with complete bibliography.

DONALD B. REDFORD (1987)

EGYPTIAN RELIGION: HISTORY OF STUDY

The study of ancient Egyptian religion shows an enormous breadth and depth, varying over time with academic fashion and the interests of individual authors. It could be maintained that the history of the study of religion should begin in the Pharaonic period. During the long period of Egyptian history, the ancient Egyptian priesthood time and again studied and reinterpreted aspects of their ancient religious traditions. However, although evidence can be gleaned from this, there are not many actual accounts or treatises. Therefore, this survey starts with explicit evidence by several classical authors, followed by the accounts of early travelers, and concentrating on the results of modern scholarship. A distinction is made between research efforts that concentrate on the recording and publication of religious architecture and textual material on the one hand, and the analysis and interpretation of evidence for religious traditions, belief systems, and practices on the other hand. The second part is divided into several subsections, although many scholars have bridged a number of these.

RECORDING AND PUBLICATION. The accounts of sixteenth- and seventeenth-century travelers to Egypt are of great importance. Even though the authors could not decipher the hieroglyphs before the groundbreaking work of savants such as Thomas Young, and especially Jean Francois Champollion, around 1824, they have published detailed descriptions and drawings of monuments, reliefs, and inscriptions, many of which have since been damaged or completely destroyed. One of the earliest accounts is that of the English traveler, Laurence Aldersey (fl. c. 1581–1586), who visited Alexandria and Cairo in 1586. Aldersey's descriptions have been preserved by the collector of travel narratives, Richard Hakluyt (1552–1616, listed by Quinn, p. 410). Most travelers concentrated on the Giza pyramids and the sphinx, such as Pietro Della Valle (1586–1652), who also acquired Coptic manuscripts and grammars; George Sandys (1578–1644) published an account on the pyramids of Giza in 1615 (*The Relation of a Journey begun an. Dom. 1610,* in four books), which could not compete with the precise survey of John Greaves, published in 1646 (*Pyramidographia, or a Discourse of the Pyramids in Aegypt*).

The eighteenth century saw a marked growth in interest in ancient Egypt, and the increase in visitors is reflected in the number of very important collections of drawings and copies of reliefs and inscriptions. From 1743 to 1745, Richard Pococke, an English traveler, published an account of Upper and Lower Egypt, including the Valley of the Kings, in two volumes: *A Description of the East, and Some Other Countries.* Around the same time, N. Granger (d. 1733), a French physician, published the story of his travels in *Relation d'un voyage fait en Egypte en l'année 1730.* Richard Dalton (1715–1791), an English draughtsman published 131 plates in *Views and Engravings in Greece and Egypt* in 1790 and 1791. One of the great feats of Napoleon Bonaparte's expedition to Egypt from 1799 to 1801 was his involvement of a large number of scholars and artists, whose combined work was published in the *Description de l'Égypte* between 1808 and 1822.

The early nineteenth century witnessed a surge in travelers who, in many cases, went to Egypt with the explicit purpose of documenting the antiquities. Henry Salt (1780–1827) was the secretary and draughtsman to the Viscount Valentia, employed to illustrate *Voyages and Travels,* which appeared in 1809. Although Giovanni Belzoni (1778–1823) is mostly notorious for his rough approach to archaeology, he copied his discoveries diligently. His full-scale reproduction of the tomb of Seti I was exhibited in London in 1818, and he published many of his drawings in the *Narrative of Operations and Recent Discoveries* (1820). Sir Charles Barry (1795–1860) made plans and drawings of temples and tombs that are now in the Griffith Institute in Oxford. The British Museum has the collections of Robert Hay (1799–1863), comprising forty-nine volumes of drawings, plans, and copies of inscriptions and reliefs (Add. MSS. 29812-60) and no less than sixty-three volumes of drawings and plans of James Burton (1788–1862, Add. MSS. 25613-75). Baltzar Cronstrand (1794–1876) was a Swedish army officer and traveler, whose excellent drawings of Karnak temple, Medinet Habu, the Ramesseum, and the tombs of Beni Hasan are now in the National Museum of Stockholm and form an important source of information on temple architecture. Jean François Champollion organized an expedition to Egypt in 1828–1829. John Gardner Wilkinson (1797–1875) produced very precise plans and copies of hieroglyphic texts. His many publications and notes on contemporary and ancient Egypt comprise fifty-six bound volumes, which the Griffith Institute in Oxford has on loan. A brilliant draftsman and artist was Louis Maurice Adolphe Linant de Bellefonds, a French geographer and explorer (1799–1883). Copies of his notes can be found in the Louvre and the Griffith Institute in Oxford. In 1842, a well-equipped Prussian expedition set out to Egypt, directed by Karl Richard Lepsius (1810–1884). In three years' time, this expedition excavated and recorded an enormous number of individual monuments, concentrating on a precise copy of the hieroglyphic texts.

Systematic epigraphical work started in the mid-nineteenth century. The most famous and longest lasting endeavor is that of the epigraphic survey of the Oriental Institute of the University of Chicago. The publication of the temple of Medinet Habu in eight volumes (1930–1970), of the temple of Karnak in four volumes (1936–1954), of the Khonsu temple in two volumes (1979–1981) and of the temple of Luxor in two volumes (1994–1998) all mark important milestones in the epigraphy of the Theban monuments. Other major and minor temple complexes have been published by the Institut Français d'Archéologie Orientale (IFAO) in Cairo. The small but fascinating temples of Deir el-Shelwit, between Luxor and Armant, were described in four volumes by Christiane Zivie (between 1982 and 1992) and the description of the temple of el-Qa'la (north of Luxor in the village of Quft) was published by Laure Pantalaci and Claude Traunecker in 1990 and 1998. To date, seventeen volumes have been published on the temple of Dendara. Between 1870 and 1890, Auguste Mariette published six volumes, while the IFAO has published a series of eleven volumes by Émile Chassinat, François Daumas, and Sylvie Cauville. The IFAO also brought out eight volumes on the temple of Esna (between 1959 and 1982 by Serge Sauneron), and a 1995 publication on the temple of Kom Ombo (by Adolphe Gutbub). The temple of Edfu has been published in fourteen volumes, between 1897 and 1934 by Émile Chassinat and Maxence Chavet Marquis de Rochemonteix. A fifteenth volume and a second edition of the first two volumes have been published by Sylvie Cauville and Didier Devauchelle (1984–1990). The Egypt exploration society and the University of Chicago jointly published the temple of Sety I in Abydos in five volumes (in 1933 by Sir Alan Gardiner and Amice Calverley). From 1927 to 1951, Bertha Porter and Rosalind Moss published the seven volumes of their *Topographical Bibliography of Ancient Egyptian Hieroglyphic Texts, Reliefs, and Paintings,* revised and augmented from 1960 to 1972. Further revisions and the addition of an eighth volume on objects without provenance were published between 1978 and 2003 and were edited by Jaromir Malek.

Apart from texts on temple walls, funerary text collections are of great importance in the study of religion. Gaston Maspero collected the Pyramid Texts and published these between 1882 and 1893 in *Recueil des Travaux.* A publication that offered a comparison of different versions of the textual corpus was prepared by Kurt Sethe between 1908 and 1922. The fact that he transferred the columns into lines of hieroglyphs expresses that he saw the inner decoration of the pyramids mainly as textual evidence and not as an integrated composition with its own rules, orientation, word, and sign play. Sethe's rendering of the texts is very precise, but by now no longer represents all the textual variations that are known, due to the discovery of other inscribed pyramids. In 2001, the Institut Français d'Archéologie Orientale published the texts from the pyramid of Pepi I. The two volumes include a reproduction of the text by Isabelle Pierre-Croisiau, and a translation and explanation by Catherine Berger El-Naggar. In the previous edition of this encyclopedia, criticism was given to the order in which Sethe published the texts. One could say, however, that Sethe's numbering foreshadowed the later interpretation of Jürgen Osing's *Zur Disposition der Pyramidentexte des Unas* (1986): the text starts in the burial chamber, is read through the ante-chamber, and culminates towards the exit of the pyramid at the north side. The pyramid "entrance" now is interpreted as an exit toward the circumpolar stars. Thomas Allen's *Occurrences of Pyramid Texts* gives a good overview of the text publications prior to 1950, but is now outdated.

Translations of the Pyramid Texts have been published in French by Gaston Maspero and in German by Kurt Sethe (from 1935 to 1962). The first English translation was made by Samual Mercer in 1952. Alexandre Piankoff concentrated on the text from the pyramid of Unas and published an integral translation in French in 1968, while Raymond Faulkner's English translation from 1969 was based on Sethe's publication of the original hieroglyphic text.

The Middle Kingdom was heir to the religious tradition as reflected in the Pyramid Texts, which were written on the walls of the (mostly wooden) coffins. The variety of Coffin Texts is much larger than that of the Pyramid Texts: Faulkner's publication has 759 Pyramid Texts compared to the 1,200 Coffin Texts published by Adriaan de Buck. The work of the latter has provided an enormous service for the study of religious notions connected to the afterlife. As with the publication of the Pyramid Texts, the Coffin Texts are often considered without reference to their material context. The selection, order, and position of the texts on the wall of the coffins are rarely taken into consideration. An exception to this is Harco Willems's *Chests of Life*, which presents an excellent multi-disciplinary study of Middle Kingdom coffins.

Translations of the Coffin Texts have been published by Louis Speleers in *Textes des cercueils du Moyen Empire égyptien* (1947), which includes only the first two volumes of De Buck's collection of spells. Between 1973 and 1978, Raymond Faulkner published the translation in English of the entire corpus of De Buck in three volumes. A very useful publication is Leonard Lesko's *Index of the Spells on Egyptian Middle Kingdom Coffins and Related Documents* (1979), which shows the variety of texts incorporated and the order in which these texts occurred. Recently, a Web-based Coffin Text index has become available, which can be accessed through the Web page of the University of Göttingen at http://www.aegyptologie.uni-goettingen.de/. In 2000, Rami van der Molen published a dictionary to the Coffin Texts.

Collections and publications of texts of the *Book of Going Forth by Day*, also known as the *Book of the Dead* have been composed by several authors, the earliest of whom were Karl Richard Lepsius in 1842 (based on a Ptolemaic papyrus in the Turin collection) and Édouard Naville, who published many New Kingdom parallels in two volumes in 1886, following the order of Lepsius's publication. E. A. Wallis Budge published several manuscripts of the *Book of Going Forth by Day* from the collection of the British Museum. English language grammars and dictionaries generally refer to the publication of Budge by page and line number. Since his works have known several editions and reprints, this reference only works with the first edition of his *The Chapters of Coming Forth by Day* from 1898, a three-volume set of text, vocabulary, and translation.

Translations of the *Book of Going Forth by Day* have been published by Thomas George Allen in *The Egyptian Book of the Dead: Documents in the Oriental Institute Museum* (1960) and *Book of the Dead or Going Forth by Day* (1974). These publications have translations of all the spells, but do not give the illustrations known as vignettes. Paul Barguet, on the other hand, incorporated the vignettes with his translation in French published as *Le livre des morts des anciens Égyptiens* (1967) and made use of parallels in the Coffin Texts to clarify difficult or garbled passages. Raymond Faulkner published a literal translation in 1972 in *The Book of the Dead*, which was reissued by Carol Andrews in 1985 as the lavishly illustrated *The Ancient Egyptian Book of the Dead*. The standard translation in German was published as *Das Totenbuch* by Erik Hornung in 1979.

In 1915, Günther Roeder published a survey of Egyptian religious documents in *Urkunden zur Religion des alten Ägypten*. Alexandre Piankoff's *The Tomb of Ramesses VI* (1954) and *The Shrines of Tut-Ankh-Amon* (1955) provide a partial publication of several of the guidebooks to the Underworld found in the New Kingdom Royal Tombs, such as the *Amduat*, the *Book of Gates*, the *Enigmatic Book of the Netherworld*, the *Book of Caverns*, the *Book of the Earth*, the *Book of the Day*, the *Book of the Night*, and the *Book of the Heavenly Cow*. Erik Hornung published *Das Amduat* (three volumes from 1963 to 1967), *Das Buch von den Pforten des Jenseits* (1979), and a translation and commentary in his *Ägyptische Unterweltsbücher* (1972). The *Litany of Re*, published by Piankoff in 1964, is incorporated in Marshall Clagett's *Ancient Egyptian Science: A Source Book* (1989–1999), which also includes the *Book of Nut*.

Analysis and Interpretation. Herodotos traveled through Egypt in the fourth century BCE, Diodorus Siculus in the first century BCE, and Plutarch visited Alexandria in the first century CE. Their accounts reflect information provided by priests of a late, but living phase of Egyptian religion.

Before the first half of the nineteenth century, any theory on the religion of ancient Egypt was based on an interpretation of architecture and the depictions of the gods in the reliefs and tomb paintings. These early interpretations of ancient Egyptian religion focused on the most visible monuments and were intrinsically connected to biblical and koranic interpretations. In the mid-eighth century CE, Bishop Cosmas of Jerusalem maintained that he had identified the pyramids as the granaries of Joseph. The ninth century Patriarch of Antioch, who had entered a pyramid and stated that they were undoubtedly the tombs of kings, rejected this theory. In the early thirteenth century, Al-Idrisi described his visit to the pyramids with an envoy of King Friedrich II of Hohenstaufen. In his *Book of the Lights of the Pyramids*, he claimed that Latin inscriptions had been discovered in the pyramids, which he had translated into Arabic. Other Islamic scholars such as al-Maqrīzī, who lived 1364–1442, wondered whether the pyramids had been built before, or after, the Great Flood.

The German scientist and draftsman, Athanasius Kircher, wrote several works on aspects of Egyptian civilization, including its religion. His *Oedipus aegyptiacus*, published between 1652 and 1655, consisted of three volumes. His work is often ridiculed for the purely symbolic interpretation of the imagery of hieroglyphs, but his work is often misrepresented and, in hindsight, he had touched upon a relevant notion: associative sign play is an important part of the use of the Egyptian language in its religious context. Between 1750 and 1752, the German theologian and orientalist, Paul Ernst Jablonski, published three volumes on Egyptian religion, and the French priest and scholar, Antoine Banier, wrote a three-volume work on mythology and fables (expanded to eight volumes by the second edition), which was translated and published in four English volumes in 1739. Neither this work, nor the work on religion and history of Egypt by Jean François Champollion, published in 1814, was based on any translations of textual material.

Belief systems and general overviews. In most of the interpretations of ancient Egyptian religion, the implicit conviction that ancient Egypt was a high-standing culture can be discerned. The existence and form of polytheism has been explained and ordered in a wide variety of belief systems. In many cases, these seem to reflect the unconscious convictions of the modern writers and the problems they had with a multitude of gods, often in the form of animals or animal-headed human forms, rather than the core of Egyptian religion. Classical accounts and interpretations of ancient Egyptian religion led to theories of a high-brow mystery cult. The name of the god Amun, the hidden one, and the important position of his cult through much of Egyptian history, provoked theories of an inherent, but hidden, monotheism in contrast with the polytheistic, animistic, magic-ridden religion for the people. On the other hand, the worship of the Aten, in combination with biblical references to Egypt, led to theories that the cradle of Christianity stood in Egypt, while afrocentric literature emphasized the African roots of Western culture, via ancient Egypt.

Some of these theories were built on thorough scholarship, whereas others were not. Although the books of Wallis Budge are still for sale in cheap reprints, these volumes, such as *The Gods of the Egyptians* and his *Book of the Dead*, mostly serve as an example of imprecise transliterations, translations, and interpretations of the textual material. Other works that date to the same general period have withstood the test of time, and later scholarship are much better, mostly because they were written with a deeper knowledge and interpreted with a more careful approach. The oldest general overview of Egyptian religion that is still worth reading today is Adolf Erman's *Die Ägyptische Religion* (1905), later published as *Die Religion der Ägypter* (1934). In Erman's opinion, the drive behind Egyptian religion was mostly a practical, deeply felt fear of natural phenomena and an attempt to contain or control these. He disagreed strongly with the work of Alexandre Moret, who explained the multiplicity of gods from a totemic origin in which the Nome gods were united into one religious system with the political unification of Egypt (*From Tribe to Empire; Social Organization among Primitives and in the Ancient East,* translated by V. Gordon Childe from the 1923 French original, and published in 1926). In 1912, James Breasted published *Development of Religion and Thought in Ancient Egypt,* in which he presented a wealth of detail and drew broad lines on how the Egyptian religion developed from the prehistoric period to the New Kingdom. He suggested the gradual democratization of the afterlife from the Pyramid Texts to the Book of the Dead. Although not all of his ideas still stand today, the information presented in the book, and in the revised edition of 1959, is still very useful.

A great name in the study of Egyptian religion, and representative of the accepted school of thought, is Hermann Kees, whose *Götterglaube im alten Ägypten* was published in 1941. Jacques Vandier's *Religion Égyptienne* (1944) gave an excellent broad overview and is one of the classic texts, because it drew together the work of many of his contemporaries and predecessors and had an extensive bibliography.

A more anthropological approach was presented by Henri Frankfort in *Intellectual Adventure of Ancient Man* (1946) and *Ancient Egyptian Religion* (1948). He suggested replacing Breasted's interpretation that Egyptian religion is, by definition, syncretistic with the notion of "multiplicity of approaches," the existence of parallel truths. Such an interpretation could only be given by an author who did not (un)consciously try to understand Egyptian religion from within the mental boundaries of the Judeo-Christian tradition. This notion did not truly reverberate until postmodern approaches to Egyptian religion began to take some hold in the 1990s. Siegfried Morenz, for instance, published a book in which the phenomenological approach shows a bias for "religions of the word" over "cult religions" (*Ägyptische Religion,* 1960, translated as *Egyptian Religion,* 1973).

Kurt Sethe stirred up considerable controversy with his discussion of the gods and their cults in prehistoric Egypt in his *Urgeschichte und älteste Religion der Ägypter* (1930). Recent work on the predynastic period put emphasis on the context, and clearly stressed the realization that an interpretation of the earliest phases of Egyptian religion cannot be based solely on the knowledge of religious thought and practice often centuries or millennia later. Barry Kemp touched upon this theme when he discussed the colossi of Koptos and ancient temple architecture in his *Ancient Egypt: Anatomy of a Civilization* (1989).

Sydney Aufrère has written some thought-provoking publications on the relation between religion and economics, as well as religion and landscape, well-rooted in the study of material culture. Perhaps the most encompassing are *L'Univers minéral dans la pensée égyptienne* (1991) and the *Encyclopédie religieuse de l'univers végétal* (1999–2001).

The accepted approach of Egyptian religion in the late twentieth and early twenty-first centuries is one that stresses multivocality and development and change over time. Within this approach, several authors have highlighted specific aspects of Egyptian religion. The two names that dominate the field are those of Erik Hornung and Jan Assmann, the first in a much more concise fashion than the latter. In a relatively brief and yet stunningly complete overview published in 1973 (translated into English in 1983 as *Conceptions of God in Ancient Egypt: The One and the Many*), Erik Hornung provided an outline of the academic consensus regarding the Egyptian belief system. With his impressive list of publications, Jan Assmann has determined much of the discussion. His incredible mastery of the source material enables him to set up original, at times almost esoteric, theories on the religion of ancient Egypt, which are always thoroughly rooted in the textual and iconographical evidence. Perhaps the best example is *Ägypten; Theologie und Frömmigkeit einer frühen Hochkultur* (1984), published in English as *The Search for God in Ancient Egypt* (2001).

For the Greco-Roman era, there is Harold Idris Bell's *Cults and Creeds of Graeco-Roman Egypt*, published in 1953, and the contributions in *Aufstieg und Niedergang der römischen Welt* (especially II 18.5, 1995). Other important publications are *Religion in Roman Egypt: Assimilation and Resistance* by David Frankfurter (1998) and the contributions in *Ancient Egyptian Religion, the Last Thousand Years*, published in 1998 in memory of Jan Quaegebeur whose important work was brought to an end by his untimely death.

The influence of women's studies on the study of Egyptian religion is limited and plays out mostly in literature on specific goddesses or the role of women in society. Publications that stress the African origins of Egyptian culture, including the religion, are mostly considered unscholarly by mainstream Egyptology. The fact that Egypt is located in Africa and that, especially in its earliest phases, the Egyptian religion was based on oral tradition and cattle culture is only taken into account in some publications. One of the few publications to address this issue explicitly is an essay by Ann Macy Roth titled "Building Bridges to Afrocentrism: A Letter to My Egyptological Colleagues" (Web publication 1995).

Afterlife and funerary rites. Apart from his general introduction into Egyptian religion, Hermann Kees also wrote an important treatise on the early mortuary literature and the guidebooks to the netherworld. *Totenglauben und Jenseitsvorstellungen der alten Ägypter* was published in 1926 and a revised edition, in which some important corrections were made, came out in 1956. Matthieu Heerma van Voss published detailed analyses of several chapters of the Book of the Dead (cf. 1963). The great scholar of underworld books is Erik Hornung who gave an excellent overview in *Altägyptische Jenseitsbücher ein einführender Überblick*, which was translated and published in English in 1999 as *The Ancient Egyptian Books of the Afterlife*. The question whether the chthonic or the celestial and solar aspects of the mortuary cult are the most ancient, has found several discussants. Jan Assmann explicated his viewpoints in *Tod und Jenseits im Alten Ägypten* (2001). Leonard Lesko purported in his publications on the *Book of Two Ways* (1969 and 1972) that the democratization of the netherworld should be explained in terms of solarization of the Osirian cult, rather than a gradual spread of chthonic aspects. This discussion was taken up by Edmund Hermsen in *Die zwei Wege des Jenseits: das altägyptische Zweiwegebuch und seine Topgraphie*. An important shift was the change from considering funerary texts foremost as theological treatises to interpreting them primarily as ritual texts. An example was James P. Allen's "Reading a Pyramid" (1994), in which he followed up on Osing's article from 1986 and used the orientation and place of the texts to interpret their function within the ritual context. The publication of the full texts of the Pepi I Pyramid Texts will enable future testing of his interpretation.

Temple ritual. The often-underestimated connection of text and context, the placement of texts and depictions on temple walls in relation to the words spoken and actions performed inside the spaces thus decorated, has been the subject of a number of important contributions to the understanding of Egyptian religion. Already in 1962, Dieter Arnold published his *Wandrelief und Raumfunktion in ägyptischen Tempeln des Neuen Reiches*. Other work focusing on the relation between space, wall reliefs, and ritual are Rosalie David's *A Guide to Religious Ritual at Abydos* (1981) and Françoise Labrique's *Stylistique et Théologie à Edfou* (1992). An interesting approach was taken by Dimitri Meeks and Christine Favard-Meeks in *Daily Life of the Egyptian Gods* (1996 translation of 1993 French text).

Günter Dreyer's report on the Satet temple on Elephantine (1986) illustrated how archaeology can show immaterial aspects of religion such as the physical expression (in the form of a shaft) of the strong continuation in belief and ritual that connected the earliest shrine to each subsequent newly built temple phase.

Gods and goddesses. Treatises on the aspects of individual gods are found in a number of monographs, for instance in the Dutch tradition of Claas Jouco Bleeker (*Hathor and Thoth*, 1973) and Herman te Velde's *Seth, God of Confusion*, first published in 1967. Kurt Sethe discussed the Hermopolitan ogdoad in *Amun und die acht Urgötter von Hermopolis* (1929), while Karol Myśliwiec published two volumes on the god Atum (1978 and 1979). In the work on some of the goddesses, there is sometimes a more woman-centered approach to Egyptian religion, often written by female Egyptologists. Elise J. Baumgartel put an emphasis on the cow as the mother-goddess in her *The Cultures of Prehistoric Egypt* (1947). Barbara Lesko concentrated on the female perspective in *The Great Goddesses of Egypt* (1999) and Alison Roberts specifically wrote about *Hathor Rising*, with two increasingly popularizing subtitles (1995, 1997). Thorough and concentrating on the Greco-Roman and Late Antique periods were R. E. Witt's books on Isis (1971, 1979).

An important source is Christian Leitz's *Lexikon der ägyptischen Götter und Götterbezeichnungen* published in 2002, which presents an excellent overview in no less than seven volumes of the names, epithets, and cult centers of Egyptian gods and goddesses. It shows a painstakingly precise approach that undoubtedly will prove to be of considerable use for a large group of scholars.

Priesthood. Gustave Lefebvre emphasized the political and economic power of the Egyptian priesthood in *Histoire des grands prêtres d'Amon de Karnak* (1929). Serge Sauneron wrote a concise, but excellent book on priesthood in ancient Egypt in 1957, which was revised and republished in 1998, and translated for the second time into English in 2000 under the title *The Priests of Ancient Egypt*. He drew greatly on written sources from the Late Period and the Greco-Roman era. The Greco-Roman era had been discussed as early as 1905 by Walter Otto in *Priester und Tempel im hellenistischen Ägypten*, an extremely thorough work, that was reprinted in 1975 because it still had much to offer. There has been little attention to the role of women in ancient Egyptian religion. Gay Robins wrote a very useful chapter on women and the temple ritual in her book on *Women in Ancient Egypt* (1993), from which it is clear that female cult specialists exclusively occur in the realm of female goddesses. An exception is the highly politicized function of the "hand of Amun," or the Divine Adoratress / God's Wife of Amun, on which several works have been published.

Personal religion. Relatively scant attention is paid to this aspect, but *Religion in Ancient Egypt: Gods, Myths, and Personal Practice* (published in 1991, edited by Byron Shafer) did take it explicitly into account. Personal religion had a place outside the temples, in house shrines, during festivals, and especially in the realm of magic. On the latter subject, Joris Borghouts's *Ancient Egyptian magical texts* (1978) and Robert Ritner's *The Mechanics of Ancient Egyptian Magical Practice* (1993) should be highlighted. In her attempt to include social theory in an approach of Egyptian village life, Lynn Meskell put more emphasis on the agency of individuals in Deir el-Medina (1999 and 2002). Taking into account the personal choices and the mechanisms of coping of ordinary Egyptians was an important addition to the study of the religion and an aspect that had long been disregarded.

General reference works. Hans Bonnet composed the *Reallexikon der ägyptischen Religionsgeschichte* in 1952, which covered almost all aspects of Egyptian religion in brief articles and included a thorough bibliography. Many of the entries of the seven volumes of the *Lexikon der Ägyptologie*, edited by Eberhard Otto, Wolfgang Helck, and Wolfhart Westendorf (1975), catalog an even more extensive collection of brief introductions into many aspects of ancient Egyptian religion by the most important specialists of the 1970s and 1980s. The brief bibliographies per subject provide a good entry for further study. The articles dealing with religion from the *Oxford Encyclopedia of Ancient Egypt* (edited by Donald Redford, 2001) have been published in identical form under the title *The Ancient Gods Speak: a Guide to Egyptian Religion* (2002). The guide does not give an extensive update on the literature, the more recent articles do not necessarily supersede their "predecessors" in the *Lexikon der Ägyptologie*, but the fact that they are in English makes them more accessible to an English-speaking audience.

BIBLIOGRAPHY

Allen, James P. "Reading a Pyramid." *Hommage à Jean Leclant*,edited by Catherine Berger, Gisèle Clerc, and Nicolas Grimal, pp. 5–28. Vol. 1. Cairo, 1994.

Allen, Thomas George. *Occurrences of Pyramid Texts, with Cross Indexes of These and Other Egyptian Mortuary Texts.* The Oriental Institute of the University of Chicago. Studies in Ancient Oriental Civilization, No. 27. Chicago, 1950.

Allen, Thomas George. *The Egyptian Book of the Dead: Documents in the Oriental Institute Museum at the University of Chicago.* The University of Chicago: Oriental Institute Publications; Volume 82. Chicago, 1960. The facsimiles of the original texts with description, translations, and notes.

Allen, Thomas George. *The Book of the Dead: Or, Going Forth by Day: Ideas of the Ancient Egyptians Concerning the Hereafter as Expressed in Their Own Terms.* Chicago, 1974.

Arnold, Dieter. *Wandrelief und Raumfunktion in ägyptischen Tempeln des neuen Reiches.* Münchner Ägyptologische Studien 2. Berlin, 1962.

Arnold, Dieter. *Temples of the Last Pharaohs.* New York, 1999.

Assmann, Jan. *Zeit und Ewigkeit im alten ägypten: Ein Beitrag zur Geschichte der Ewigkeit.* Heidelberg, Germany, 1975.

Assmann, Jan. *Re und Amun: Die Krise des polytheistischen Weltbilds im ägypten der 18.-20. Dynastie.* Göttingen, Germany, 1983.

Assmann, Jan. *Ägypten: Theologie und Frömmigkeit einer frühen Hochkultur.* Stuttgart, Germany, 1984. Translated as *The Search for God in Ancient Egypt.*

Assmann, Jan. *Ma'at: Gerechtigkeit und Unsterblichkeit im alten Ägypten.* Munich, 1990.

Assmann, Jan. *Agypten; Eine Sinngeschichte.* Munich and Vienna, 1996.

Assmann, Jan. *Moses the Egyptian: The Memory of Egypt in Western Monotheism.* Cambridge, Mass., 1997.

Assmann, Jan. *Tod Und Jenseits Im Alten Ägypten.* Munich, 2001.

Assmann, Jan. *The Search for God in Ancient Egypt.* Translated by David Lorton. Ithaca, N.Y., 2001.

Assmann, Jan. *The Mind of Egypt: History and Meaning in the Time of the Pharaohs.* Translated by Andrew Jenkins. New York, 2002.

Aufrère, Sydney. *L'univers minéral dans la pensée égyptienne.* 2 vols. Cairo, 1991. Volume 1 is titled *L'Influence du désert et des minéraux sur la mentalité des anciens Égyptiens.* Volume 2 focuses on *L'Intégration des minéraux, des métaux et des "trésors" dans la marche de l'univers et dans la vie divine.* The two volumes focus on the relation between minerals, metals, "treasures," and the desert, where all of these originate, with the Egyptian way of thinking, the Egyptian mentality, the course of the universe, and the life of the gods.

Aufrère, Sydney. *Encyclopédie religieuse de l'univers végétal. Croyance phytoreligieuse de l'Égypte ancienne.* 2 vols. Montpellier, France, 1999–2001.

Banier, Antoine. *The Mythology and Fables of the Ancients, Explain'd from History.* 4 vols. London, 1739. Translated from the original French.

Barguet, Paul. *Le Livre des morts des anciens Égyptiens. Littératures anciennes du proche-orient.* Paris, 1967. Includes an introduction, a translation, and a commentary.

Baumgartel, Elise J. *The Cultures of Prehistoric Egypt.* Oxford and London, 1947.

Bell, Harold Idris. *Cults and Creeds in Graeco-Roman Egypt.* New York, 1953.

Belzoni, Giovanni Battista. *Narrative of the Operations and Recent Discoveries within the Pyramids, Temples, Tombs, and Excavations in Egypt and Nubia; and of a Journey to the Coast of the Red Sea in Search of the Ancient Berenice, and of Another to the Oasis of Jupiter Ammon.* London, 1820. Belzoni's drawings and an account of his work in Egypt, including a section on the women of Egypt, Nubia, and Syria by his wife, Sarah (pp. 441–483).

Belzoni, Giovanni Battista, and Alberto Siliotti. *Belzoni's Travels: Narrative of the Operations and Recent Discoveries in Egypt and Nubia.* Translated by Richard Pierce. London, 2001. A re-publication of Belzoni's most important publication, edited by Alberto Siliotti.

Bleeker, Claas Jouco. *Die Geburt eines Gottes: Eine Studie über den Ägyptischen Gott min und Sein Fest.* Leiden, 1956.

Bleeker, Claas Jouco. *Egyptian Festivals. Enactments of Religious Renewal.* Leiden, 1968.

Bleeker, Claas Jouco. *Hathor and Thoth: Two Key Figures of the Ancient Egyptian Religion.* Leiden, the Netherlands, 1973.

Bonnet, Hans. *Reallexikon der ägyptischen Religionsgeschichte.* Berlin, 1952.

Borghouts, Joris F. *The Magical Texts of Papyrus Leiden 1348.* Leiden, 1971.

Borghouts, Joris F. *Ancient Egyptian Magical Texts.* Leiden, 1978.

Breasted, James Henry. *Development of Religion and Thought in Ancient Egypt.* London, 1912. Lectures delivered on the Morse Foundation at Union Theological Seminary. Republished in 1959 and 1999.

Buck, Adriaan de. *The Egyptian Coffin Texts.* Edited by Alan H. Gardiner. Seven vols. Chicago, 1935–1963. Volume 1 (1935) *Texts of Spells 1–75.* Volume 2 (1938) *Texts of Spells 76–163.* Volume 3 (1947) *Texts of Spells 164–267.* Volume 4 (1951) *Texts of Spells 268–354.* Volume 5 (1956) *Texts of Spells 472–786.* Volume 6 (1961) *Texts of Spells 472–786.* Volume 7 (1963) *Texts of Spells 787–1185.*

Budge, E. A. Wallis. *The Chapters of Coming Forth by Day: The Egyptian Text According to the Theban Recension in Hieroglyphic.* Three vols. London, 1898. Volume 1: The Egyptian text in hieroglyphic. Volume 2: An English translation with introduction, notes, etc. Volume 3: A vocabulary in hieroglyphic to the Theban recension of the Book of the Dead. This edition has been used as a standard text edition, with later authors referring to page and line numbers.

Budge, E. A. Wallis. *The Gods of the Egyptians, or, Studies in Egyptian Mythology.* Two vols. Chicago, 1904. Reprinted in 1969 by Dover Publications, this work of Budge is still found in many bookstores, while the quality would merit it to be quietly forgotten.

Cauville, Sylvie. *Dendara Traduction. Orientalia Lovaniensia Analecta*; 81, 88, 95, 101. Leuven, Belgium, 1998–2001. Four volumes with translations of the texts from the Temple of Dendara. Volume 1 (OLA 81, 1998) concentrates on the theological texts (from the sanctuary and surrounding chapels, reproduced in Chassinat, Daumas, Cauville Le Temple de Dendara volumes 1 through 4). Volume 2 (OLA 88, 1999) is a translation of the theological and cultic texts from the crypts (Le Temple de Dendara volumes 5 and 6). The third volume (OLA 95, 2000) concentrates on the wabet, the stairs, and the kiosk (Le Temple de Dendara volumes 7 and 8), while the fourth volume (OLA 101, 2001) contains the translations of the texts from the walls of the cultic spaces such as the hypostyle hall and bordering storerooms (Le Temple de Dendara volumes 7, 9, and 11).

Champollion, Jean-François. *L'Égypte sous les Pharaohs, ou, Recherches sur la géographie, la religion, la langue, les écritures et l'histoire de l'Égypte avant l'invasion de Cambyse.* Two vols. Paris, 1814.

Champollion, Jean-François. *Monuments de L'Égypte et de la Nubie, d'apres les dessins executés sur les lieux sous la direction de Champollion-Le-Jeune.* 3 vols. Paris, 1835–1845.

Chassinat, Émile. *Le Mammisi d'edfou. Mémoires de l'institut Français d'archéologie orientale de Caire.* 2 vols. Cairo, 1910.

Chassinat, Émile, Maxence de Chalvet Marquis de Rochemonteix, Sylvie Cauville, and Didier Devauchelle. *Le temple d'Edfou. Mémoires publies par les membres de la mission archéologique française au Caire* 10–11 and 20–31. Cairo, 1897–1934. Maxence de Chalvet Marquis de Rochemonteix started with systematic recording of the reliefs of the walls of the temple of Edfu. He died in 1892, and the first volume was published by his assistant Émile Chassinat in 1897. The second and third volumes came out under both their names in 1918 and 1928. Volumes 4–14 were published with an astonishing speed by Chassinat from 1929 to 1934. A fifteenth volume, with texts and reliefs that Rochemonteix had skipped and with new photographs, was published by Sylvie Cauville and Didier Devauchelle in 1985. New editions of the two first volumes have been prepared by Cauville and Devauchelle (Volume I, parts 1 and 2 in 1984, parts 3 and 4 in 1987, Volume II, part 1 in 1987, part 2 in 1990).

Chassinat, Émile, François Daumas, and Sylvie Cauville. *Le Temple de Dendara.* 11 vols. Cairo, 1934–2000. Le Temple de Dendara 1–4 record the sanctuary and the six cult chapels (1934–1935 by Chassinat). Volumes 4, 7, and 8 record the wabet, stairs, and kiosk (1935, 1972, and 1978 by Chassinat and the latter two by Daumas). Volumes 5 (1943 by Chassinat) and 6 (1965 by Chassinat and Daumas) are a record of the crypts. The hypostyle hall and the cult chapels are subjects of volumes 9 (1987) and 11 (2000) by Daumas and Cauville, respectively. Volume 10 records the Osirien chapels (1997 by Cauville).

Clagett, Marshall. *Ancient Egyptian Science: A Source Book.* Memoirs of the American Philosophical Society; V. 184, V.214, 232. 3 vols. Philadelphia, 1989–1999. Volume 1 (1989). Knowledge and order (tomes 1–2). Volume 2 (1995). Calendars, clocks, and astronomy. Volume 3 (1999). Ancient Egyptian mathematics. Not an Egyptologist, but a historian specializing in science in the ancient world, Clagett cites considerable portions of the books of the underworld.

Clarysse, Willy, A. Schoors, and Harco Willems. *Egyptian Religion: The Last Thousand Years: Studies Dedicated to the Memory of Jan Quaegebeur.* Louvain, 1998.

Dalton, Richard. *Views and Engravings in Greece and Egypt.* London, 1790–1791. The work of Dalton, librarian to the British king, is specifically of interest because the engravings enable a comparison between the present and eighteenth-century condition of many of the Egyptian monuments.

David, A. Rosalie. *A Guide to Religious Ritual at Abydos.* Warminster, U.K., 1981.

Dawson, Warren R., and Eric P. Uphill. *Who Was Who in Egyptology.* London, 1972. A very useful encyclopedic overview of early Egyptology from the sixteenth until the mid-twentieth century.

Denon, Dominique Vivant. *Égypte, documents d'art égyptien d'apres la description de l'Égypte, expédition de l'armee française sous Napoleon Ier, l'expédition d'Égypte, dessins du Baron Denon, et le musée égyptien.* Paris, 1808–1822. The results of the scholarly team accompanying Napoleon Bonaparte from 1798–1799 on his Egyptian campaign are collected in several large volumes of descriptions and plates describing everything from contemporary crafts, flora and fauna to antiquities.

Diodorus. *The Antiquities of Egypt: A Translation with Notes of Book I of the Library of History, of Diodorus Siculus.* Translated by Edwin Murphy. New Brunswick, N.J., 1990.

Dreyer, Günter. *Der Tempel der Satet: Die Funde der Frühzeit und des alten Reiches.* Mainz am Rhein, Germany, 1986.

Erman, Adolf. *Die Ägyptische Religion.* Berlin, 1905. Reprinted in 1909 and published in an augmented and edited version under the title *Die Religion der Ägypter* in 1934.

Erman, Adolf. *Die Religion der Ägypter, Ihr Werden und Vergehen in Vier Jahrtausenden.* Berlin, 1934. Augmented version of Erman's 1905 publication.

Faulkner, Raymond Oliver. *The Ancient Egyptian Pyramid Texts.* Special edition, Oxford and New York, 1998. Reprint of the original text that was published in 1969.

Faulkner, Raymond Oliver. *The Ancient Egyptian Pyramid Texts, Translated into English.* Oxford, 1969.

Faulkner, Raymond Oliver. *The Book of the Dead: A Collection of Spells. Edited and Translated from Papyri in the British Museum.* New York, 1972.

Faulkner, Raymond Oliver. *The Book of the Dead: A Collection of Spells. Edited and Translated from Papyri in the British Museum.* London and New York, 1985. Colorful edition by C. Andrews with lavish illustrations from the British Museum papyri.

Frankfort, Henri. *Ancient Egyptian Religion, an Interpretation.* New York, 1948. Republished in 1961.

Frankfort, Henri, ed. *The Intellectual Adventure of Ancient Man: An Essay on Speculative Thought in the Ancient Near East.* Chicago, 1946. Based on lectures given at the University of Chicago by different authors. Introduction: Myth and reality, by H. and H. A. Frankfort—Egypt: The nature of the universe. The function of the state. The values of life. By J. A. Wilson—Mesopotamia: The cosmos of the state. The function of the state. The good life. By T. Jacobsen. —Conclusion: The emancipation of thought from myth, by H. and H. A. Frankfort.

Frankfort, Henri, ed. *Before Philosophy: The Intellectual Adventure of Ancient Man: An Essay on Speculative Thought in the Ancient Near East.* Harmondsworth, U.K., and Baltimore, 1949. A reworked edition of the intellectual adventure of ancient man.

Frankfurter, David. *Religion in Roman Egypt: Assimilation and Resistance.* Princeton, N.J., 1998.

Gardiner, Alan Henderson, Sir, and Amice Mary Calverley. *The Temple of King Sethos I at Abydos.* London and Chicago, 1933. A joint publication of the Egypt Exploration Society (Archaeological Survey) and of the Oriental Institute of the University of Chicago.

Granger, N. *Relation d'un voyage fait En Égypte en l'année 1730.* Paris, 1744. A description of visits of this French physician to, among other sites in Egypt, the Fayum, Beni Hassan, Abydos, Thebes, and Edfu, translated into German in 1751 and English in 1773.

Greaves, John. *Pyramidographia, or, a Description of the Pyramids in Aegypt.* London, 1646. English mathematician who set out to Cairo to measure the pyramids with the proper instruments. His thorough survey of the Giza plateau is of great interest today.

Gutbub, Adolphe. *Kom Ombo I; Les inscriptions du Naos (Sanctuaires, salle de l'ennde, salle des offrandes, coloir mystérieux).* Cairo, 1995. Text edited by Danielle Inconnu-Bocquillon.

Gutbub, Adolphe. *Textes fondamentaux de la théologie de Kom Ombo.* Bibliothèque D'étude; T. 47. 2 vols. Cairo, 1973. Translation of and commentary on inscriptions from the temple of Kom Ombo. Indexes in Volume 2.

Heerma van Voss, Matthieu S. H. G. *De Oudste Versie Van Dodenboek 17a: Coffin Texts Spreuk 335a.* Leiden, 1963.

Hermsen, Edmund. *Die zwei Wege des Jenseits: Das Altägyptische Zweiwegebuch und seine Topographie.* Obo 112. Freiburg, Gottingen, Germany, 1991.

Herodotus. *Herodotus, Book II.* Translated by W. G. Waddell. Letchworth, U.K., 1979.

Hornung, Erik. *Das Amduat: Die Schrift des verborgenen Raumes.* Agyptologische Abhandlungen. 2 vols. Wiesbaden, Germany, 1963–1967.

Hornung, Erik. *Ägyptische Unterweltsbücher: Eingeleitet, Ubersetzt und Erlautert.* 3d ed. Munich, 1972. Contains selections from various chthonic books.

Hornung, Erik. *Der Eine und die Vielen; Ägyptische Gottesvorstellungen.* Darmstadt, 1973. Translated as *Conceptions of God in Ancient Egypt: The One and the Many.* Translated by John Baines. London, 1983. A very concise, but magnificently thorough and useful introduction into ancient Egyptian religion. Has determined the development of thinking about Egyptian religion in much of the late twentieth and early twenty-first centuries.

Hornung, Erik. *Das Totenbuch der Ägypter: Eingeleitet, Übersetzt und Erläutert.* 2d ed. Zurich, 1990.

Hornung, Erik. *Das Buch von den Pforten des Jenseits: Nach den Versionen des neuen Reiches.* 2 vols. Geneva, 1979–1980. The two volumes contain the text, the translation into German, and the commentary on the Book of Gates.

Hornung, Erik. *Texte Zum Amduat.* 2 vols. Geneva, 1987–1992.

Hornung, Erik. *Altägyptische Jenseitsbücher; ein einführender Überblick.* 1997. Translated as *The Ancient Egyptian Books of the Afterlife.* Translated by David Lorton. Ithaca, N.Y., 1999. Introduction into a wide range of books dealing with the afterlife. The book contains scenes and excerpts from the Pyramid Texts, the Coffin Texts, the Book of the Dead, the Books of Breathing, the Amduat, the Spell of the Twelve Caves, the Book of Gates, the Enigmatic Book of the Netherworld, the Book of Caverns, the Book of the Earth, the Books of the Sky, the Book of Nut, the Book of the Day, the Book of the Night, the Litany of Re, the Book of the Heavenly Cow, and the Book of Traversing Eternity.

Jablonski, Paul Ernst. "Commentatio de diebus Aegyptiacis, in vetusto kalendario komano commemoratis." *Miscellanea Berolinensia Ad Incrementum Scientiarum*, vol. 7. Edited by Michaelis Berolini. Rome, 1743.

Kees, Hermann. *Totenglauben und Jenseitsvorstellungen der alten Ägypter, Grundlagen und Entwicklung bis zum Ende des mittleren Reiches.* Leipzig, 1926. Revised and republished in 1956.

Kees, Hermann. *Der Götterglaube im alten Aegypten.* Leipzig, 1941. Still a very worthwhile read. A second edition was published in 1956, reprinted in 1977.

Kemp, Barry J. *Ancient Egypt: Anatomy of a Civilization.* London and New York, 1989. Innovative thinking about aspects of Egyptian society, including some important remarks about religion, from an archaeological viewpoint.

Kircher, Athanasius. *Oedipvs aegyptiacvs hoc est vniuersalis hieroglyphicae veterum doctrinae temporum iniuria abolitae instavratio, opus ex omni orientalium doctrina & sapientia conditum, nec non viginti diuersarium linguarum authoritate stabilitum.* Published as three volumes, bound in four volumes. Rome, 1652–1655.

Kurth, Dieter. *Die Inschriften des Tempels von Edfu. Abteilung I: Übersetzungen, Bd. 1, Edfou VIII.* Wiesbaden, Germany, 1998. With contributions by A. Behrmann, D. Budde, A. Effland, H. Felber, E. Pardey, S. Ruter, W. Waitkus, S. Wiebach, and S. Woodhouse.

Labrique, Françoise. *Stylistique et théologie à Edfou: Le rituel de l'offrande de la campagne: Étude de la composition.* Louvain, 1992.

Leclant, Jean. *Les textes de la pyramide de Pepi Ier (Saqqara) reconstitution de la paroi est de L'antichambre.* Paris, 1977.

Leclant, Jean, Cathérine Berger-el Naggar, Bernard Mathieu, and Isabelle Pierre-Croisiau. *Les textes de la pyramide de Pepy Ier.* 2 vols. Cairo, 2001.

Lefebvre, Gustave. *Histoire des grands prêtres d'Amon de Karnak jusqu'a la XXIe dynastie.* Paris, 1929.

Leitz, Christian. *Lexikon der Ägyptischen Götter und Götterbezeichnungen. Orientalia Lovaniensia Analecta.* Vol. 110–116. 7 vols. Louvain, 2002. An excellent overview of the names, epithets, and cult centers of Egyptian gods and goddesses.

Lepsius, Richard Karl. *Das Todtenbuch der Ägypter: Nach dem hieroglyphischen Papyrus im Turin.* Leipzig, 1842. A translation of a Ptolemaic papyrus in the collection of the Egyptological Museum in Turin, Italy. In 1969, a reprint was published of Lepsius's text.

Lepsius, Richard Karl. *Denkmäler aus Ägypten und Äthiopien: Nach den Zeichnungen der von Seiner Majestät dem Könige von Preussen Friedrich Wilhelm IV nach Diesen Landern Gesendeten und in den Jahren 1842–1845 ausgeführten wissenschaftlichen Expedition.* 12 vols. Berlin, 1849. Published in English in 1853, with notes by Kenneth McKenzie. A reprint of 1972 provides a slightly reduced replica of the text and plates and is published by the Biblio Verlag in Osnabruck, Germany.

Lesko, Barbara S. *The Great Goddesses of Egypt.* Norman, Okla., 1999. The book presents histories of the cults of seven major goddesses and many excerpts from their literature—hymns, prayers, and magical spells as well as descriptions of ritual, temples, and clergy.

Lesko, Leonard H. *The Composition of the Book of Two Ways.* Chicago, 1969.

Lesko, Leonard H. *The Ancient Egyptian Book of Two Ways.* Berkeley, Calif., 1972.

Lesko, Leonard H. *Index of the Spells on Egyptian Middle Kingdom Coffins and Related Documents.* Berkeley, Calif., 1979.

Linant de Bellefonds, Louis Maurice Adolphe. *Linant de Bellefonds: Journal d'un voyage à Meroe dans les années 1821 et 1822.* Khartoum, 1958. Notes of Linant de Bellefonds, edited by Margaret Shinnie.

Mariette, Auguste. *Denderah: Description générale du grand temple de cette ville.* 6 vols. Paris, 1870–1890. Volume 1, *Interieur du temple.* Volume 2, *Interieur du temple.* Volume 3, *Cryptes.* Volume 4, *Terrasses.* Volume 5, *Supplement aux planches.* Volume 6, *Texte.* These six parts have been reproduced in two volumes in 1981 by G. Olms (Hildesheim and New York).

Maspero, Gaston. *Recueil des travaux relatifs a la philologie et l'archéologie égyptiennes et assyriennes.* Paris, 1882–1883.

Medelhavsmuseet (Stockholm), Baltzar Cronstrand, Beate George, and Bengt Peterson. *Die Karnak-Zeichnungen Von Baltzar Cronstrand 1836–1837.* Stockholm, 1979.

Meeks, Dimitri, and Christine Favard-Meeks. *La vie quotidienne des dieux égyptiens.* Paris, 1993. Translated as *Daily Life of the Egyptian Gods.* Translated by G. M. Goshgarian. Ithaca, N.Y. and London, 1996. This book represents an original and thorough approach to Egyptian religion.

Mercer, Samuel A. B. *The Pyramid Texts.* New York, 1952.

Meskell, Lynn. *Archaeologies of Social Life: Age, Sex, Class et Cetera in Ancient Egypt.* Social Archaeology. Oxford, U.K. and Malden, Mass., 1999.

Meskell, Lynn. *Private Life in New Kingdom Egypt.* Princeton, N.J., 2002.

Molen, Rami van der. *A Hieroglyphic Dictionary of Egyptian Coffin Texts.* Probleme Der Ägyptologie 15. Leiden and Boston, 2000.

Morenz, Siegfried. *Ägyptische Religion.* Stuttgart, Germany, 1960. Translated as *Egyptian Religion.* Translated by Ann E. Keep. London, 1973.

Moret, Alexandre, and Georges Davy. *Des clans aux empires; L'organisation sociale chez les primitifs et dans l'orient ancien.* Paris, 1923. Translated as *From Tribe to Empire; Social Organization among Primitives and in the Ancient East.* Translated by V. Gordon Childe. New York, 1926.

Myśliwiec, Karol. *Studien Zum Gott Atum.* 2 vols. Hildesheim, 1978–1979.

Naville, Édouard. *Das Aegyptische Totenbuch der XVII. bis XX. Dynastie: Aus verschiedenen urkunden Zusammengestellt und Herausgegeben.* 2 vols. Berlin, 1886. A reproduction of Naville's book appeared in 1971.

Osing, Jürgen. "Zur Disposition der Pyramidentexte des Unas." *Mitteilungen des Deutschen Archäologischen Instituts,* Abteilung Kairo (Cairo) 42 (1986): 131–144.

Otto, Eberhard, Wolfgang Helck, and Wolfhart Westendorf, eds. *Lexikon der Ägyptologie.* 7 vols. Wiesbaden, 1972–1986. A very important source of information with concise articles and references for an incredible number of entries, written by the top specialists in the field. The Lexikon was published gradually in small issues. The bibliographies are now out of date, especially for the earliest issues (Volume 1 was completely published in 1975, Volume 2 in 1977, Volume 3 in 1980, Volume 4 in 1982, Volume 5 in 1984, and Volume 6 in 1986; Volume 7 is an index volume).

Otto, Walter Gustav Albrecht. *Priester und Tempel im hellenistischen Ägypten: Ein Beitrag zur Kulturgeschichte des Hellenismus.* 2 vols. Leipzig, 1905.

Pantalacci, Laure, and Claude Traunecker. *Le Temple d'el-Qal'a.* 2 vols. Cairo, 1990–1998.

Piankoff, Alexandre. *The Tomb of Ramesses VI.* New York, 1954.

Piankoff, Alexandre. *The Shrines of Tut-Ankh-Amon.* Bollingen Series, 40:2. New York, 1955–1962.

Piankoff, Alexandre. *The Litany of Re.* Bollingen Series, 40. New York, 1964.

Piankoff, Alexandre. *The Pyramid of Unas. Texts Translated with Commentary by Alexandre Piankoff.* Bollingen Series, 40: 5. Egyptian Religious Texts and Representations. Princeton, N.J., 1968.

Plutarch. *Plutarch's De Iside et Osiride.* Translated by John Gwyn Griffiths. Cardiff, 1970.

Pococke, Richard. *A Description of the East, and Some Other Countries.* 2 vols. London, 1743. An English bishop describes his travels to many regions of the world, including Egypt.

Porter, Bertha, Rosalind Louisa Beaufort Moss, and Jaromir Malek. *Topographical Bibliography of Ancient Egyptian Hieroglyphic Texts, Reliefs, and Paintings.* 8 vols. 2d ed. Oxford, 1927–2003. Porter and Moss gave brief descriptions and plans of the temples and tombs, organized by geographical region. Between 1927 and 1951, they wrote a total of seven volumes and in 1960 started revising them. The first two volumes were revised and augmented with assistance from Ethel W. Burney. Jaromir Malek revised and augmented the third volume and added an eighth volume. Volume 1. The Theban necropolis, part 1 (1927–1960) private tombs, part 2 (1928–1964) royal tombs and smaller cemeteries. Volume 2 (1929–1972) Theban temples. Volume 3 (1931–1974) Abu Rawash to Dahshur, including the Memphis area, Volume 4 (1934) Lower and Middle Egypt (Delta and Cairo to Asyut). Volume 5 (1937) the sites of Upper Egypt (Deir Rifa to Aswan, excluding Thebes and the major temples). Volume 6 (1939) describes the best-preserved temples of Upper Egypt (excluding Thebes): Abydos, Dendera, Esna, Edfu, Kom Ombo, and Philae. Volume 7 (1951) describes the temples of Nubia, the deserts, and outside Egypt. Volume 8 was published from 1999 onwards and consists of three parts, listing objects of unknown provenance (by Jaromir Malek, assisted by Diana Magee and Elizabeth Miles).

Quinn, David Beers, ed. *The Hakluyt Handbook.* Vol. 2. London, 1974. Scholarly edition of the works of Richard Hakluyt (1552–1616), a voyager who not only recorded his own travels, but also collected the accounts of others.

Redford, Donald B., ed. *The Oxford Encyclopedia of Ancient Egypt.* New York, 2001.

Redford, Donald B., ed. *The Ancient Gods Speak: A Guide to Egyptian Religion.* Oxford and New York, 2002. A bundle of the articles from the *Oxford Encyclopedia of Ancient Egypt* that focus on religion.

Ritner, Robert Kriech. *The Mechanics of Ancient Egyptian Magical Practice.* Chicago, 1993.

Roberts, Alison. *Hathor Rising: The Serpent Power of Ancient Egypt.* Translated, Rochester, Vt., 1995.

Roberts, Alison. *Hathor Rising: The Power of the Goddess in Ancient Egypt.* Rochester, Vt., 1997.

Robins, Gay. *Women in Ancient Egypt.* London, 1993.

Roeder, Günther. *Die ägyptische Religion im Texten und Bildern.* Die Bibliothek Der Alten Welt. Reihe Der Alte Orient. 4 vols. Zurich, 1959–1961.

Roeder, Günther. *Urkunden zur Religion des alten Ägypten.* Jena, Germany, 1915.

Roth, Ann Macy. *Building Bridges to Afrocentrism: A Letter to My Egyptological Colleagues.* 1995. Available: http://www.sas.upenn.edu / African_Studies / Articles_Gen / afrocent_roth.html.

Sandys, George. *A Relation of a Journey begun An: Dom: 1610: Fovre Bookes. Containing a Description of the Turkish Empire, of Aegypt of the Holy Land, of the Remote Parts of Italy, and Ilands Adioyning.* London, 1615. Travel description that has known several editions (third edition, 1632). Sandys corrected several faulty interpretations of the pyramids, such as the one claiming that the pyramids were the granaries of Joseph and were built by the Hebrews.

Sauneron, Serge. *Les Prêtres de l'ancienne Égypte, 1957.* Translated as *The Priests of Ancient Egypt.*, 1998. Translated by David Lorton. Ithaca, N.Y., 2000. A readable and accessible account of priesthood through Egyptian history and the cults of different temples in Egypt.

Sethe, Kurt. *Die altäegyptischen Pyramidentexte nach den Papierabdrücken und Photographien des Berliner Museums.* 4 vols. in 3 vols. Leipzig, 1908–1922.

Sethe, Kurt. *Amun und die Acht Urgötter von Hermopolis: Eine Untersuchung über Ursprung und Wesen des ägyptischen Götterkönigs.* Berlin, 1929.

Sethe, Kurt. *Urgeschichte und älteste Religion der Ägypter.* Leipzig, 1930. Republished in 1960 in Liechtenstein.

Sethe, Kurt. *Übersetzung und Kommentar zu den altägyptischen Pyramidentexten.* 4 vols. Gluckstadt, Germany, 1935–1962.

Shafer, Byron E., John Baines, Leonard H. Lesko, and David P. Silverman. *Religion in Ancient Egypt: Gods, Myths, and Personal Practice.* Ithaca, N.Y., 1991.

Speleers, Louis. *Les Textes des Pyramides égyptiennes.* 2 vols. Brussels, 1923–1924.

Speleers, Louis. *Textes Des Cercueils Du Moyen Empire Égyptien.* Brussels, 1947.

Starkey, Paul, and Janet Starkey, eds. *Travellers in Egypt.* London, 1998. Edited volume with in-depth contributions on early travelers to Egypt, focusing on specific persons (such as Belzoni or Linant de Bellefonds) or on specific categories such as women, literary travelers, and Egyptian travelers to Europe.

Starkey, Paul, and Janet Starkey, eds. *Interpreting the Orient: Travellers in Egypt and the Near East.* Reading, U.K., 2001. Articles exploring the activities of nineteenth-century travelers from the West, and the influence of their accounts on the image of the Orient and the rise of orientalism.

University of Chicago. Oriental Institute. Epigraphic Survey. *Medinet Habu.* 8 vols. Chicago, 1930–1970.

University of Chicago. *Reliefs and Inscriptions at Karnak.* 4 vols. Chicago, 1936–1954.

University of Chicago. *The Temple of Khonsu.* 2 vols. Chicago, 1979–1981.

University of Chicago. *Reliefs and Inscriptions at Luxor Temple.* 2 vols. Chicago, 1994–1998.

Valentia, George, Viscount. *Voyages and Travels to India, Ceylon, the Red Sea, Abyssinia, and Egypt: In the Years 1802, 1803, 1804, 1805, and 1806.* 3 vols. London, 1809. An English benefactor, employed Henry Salt in 1802 as secretary and illustrator of this book. In 1816, Salt became British Consul-General in Egypt and carried out excavations to collect Egyptian antiquities for the British Museum.

Vandier, Jacques. *La religion égyptienne.* Paris, 1944. Second augmented edition of a publication from 1904. Part of a series on world religions, subseries on ancient oriental religions. The bibliography was made by Henri-Charles Puech. A third edition was published in 1949.

Velde, H. te. *Seth, God of Confusion: A Study of His Role in Egyptian Mythology and Religion.* Translated by G. E. van Baaren-Pape. Probleme Der Agyptologie 6. Leiden, 1967.

Wilkinson, John Gardner. *Materia Hieroglyphica. Containing the Egyptian Pantheon and the Succession of the Pharaohs, from the Earliest Times, to the Conquest of Alexander, and Other Hieroglyphical Subjects. With Plates, and Notes Explanatory of the Same.* Malta, 1828.

Wilkinson, John Gardner. *Topography of Thebes, and General View of Egypt: Being a Short Account of the Principal Objects Worth of Notice in the Valley of the Nile.* London, 1835.

Wilkinson, John Gardner. *Manners and Customs of the Ancient Egyptians, Including Their Private Life, Government, Laws, Art, Manufactures, Religions, and Early History; Derived from a Comparison of the Paintings, Sculptures, and Monuments Still Existing, with the Accounts of Ancient Authors. Illustrated by Drawings of Those Subjects.* Three vols. London, 1837. In 1841 a second series of "Manners and Customs of the Ancient Egyptians" was published, while an abridged version appeared in 1854. The 1883 edition joins the information of the two series. In 1857, Wilkinson also published an account for the Crystal Palace Egyptian collection at the World Exhibition in London.

Wilkinson, John Gardner. *A Popular Account of the Ancient Egyptians.* 2 vols. New York, 1854. A revised and abridged work of the "Manners and Customs" series. Accessible electronically at http://uclibs.org/PID/28301.

Willems, Harco. *Chests of Life: A Study of the Typology and Conceptual Development of Middle Kingdom Standard Class Coffins.* Leiden, 1988.

Zivie, Christiane M. *Le temple de Deir Chelouit.* 5 vols. Cairo, Egypt, 1982–1992.

WILLEKE WENDRICH (2005)

EIDETIC VISION SEE PHENOMENOLOGY OF RELIGION

EIGHTFOLD PATH. The noble eightfold path (Pali, *ariyo aṭṭhaṅgiko maggo)* is among the earliest formulations of the Buddhist path of practice. The *Dhammacakkhappavattana Sutta* (Setting the wheel of *dhamma* in motion), traditionally regarded as the Buddha's first discourse, introduces the eightfold path as a middle way between two extremes: indulgence in sensual pleasure and self-mortification. Sensual indulgence is condemned as "gross, domestic, common, ignoble, and not conducive to the goal." Self-mortification is condemned as "painful, ignoble, and not conducive to the goal." The eightfold path, however, is praised as productive of vision, productive of knowledge, and conducive to calm, direct knowing, self-awakening, and *nirvāṇa.* These statements are best evaluated in light of the story of the Buddha's quest for awakening, which provides the path with both narrative and theoretical context.

Having enjoyed lavish sensual pleasures in his youth, the young *bodhisattva* (Buddha-to-be) realized that these pleasures—subject to aging, illness, and death—could provide no lasting happiness. So he left home and took up the life of a wilderness mendicant to see if a deathless happiness could be attained through human effort. After six years of exploring various dead-end paths, including extreme self-mortification, he happened upon a path whose central factor consisted of a focused mental absorption called *jhāna* (Skt., *dhyāna*). Developing this absorption to a level of pure mindfulness and equanimity, he applied his mind to developing three knowledges: knowledge of previous lifetimes, knowledge of the passing away and re-arising of living beings, and knowledge of the ending of *āsavas* ("effluents" or "fermentations" that defile the mind). Through this third knowledge, the *bodhisattva* gained release from the *āsavas* of sensuality, ignorance, and "becoming"—the process whereby craving and clinging lead to rebirth. With this release, he realized the deathless and was now a Buddha: an awakened one.

The Pali discourses state that the first two of the three knowledges contained elements in common with other religious teachings of the time, but that the second knowledge also contained an element distinctive to the Buddha: his insight that the level of an individual's rebirth was due to the quality of his or her intentional actions, or *kamma* (Skt., *karman*). Actions performed under the influence of right views led to a happy rebirth on the higher levels of becoming; those performed under the influence of wrong views, led to a painful rebirth on the lower levels. Thus, action leading to rebirth was of three types: skillful, unskillful, and mixed. However, the impermanence characterizing all levels of becoming meant that they caused suffering for anyone searching for lasting happiness. Seeing this, the *bodhisattva* then applied his insight to the role of views in shaping action to see what kind of views would condition a fourth type of action, leading to the end of action and thus to the end of becoming.

This question was answered in the third knowledge: A path of action based on viewing experience in terms of four categories—suffering, its cause, its cessation, and the path of action leading to its cessation—led to a realization of the deathless. Because this path could be perfected, he realized that it was a matter of skill, rather than of grace, fate, or coincidence. Thus, to teach that skill to others, he formulated the four view-categories underlying it as the four noble truths; and the fourth truth—the path of action leading to the deathless—he formulated as the eightfold path.

The Pali discourses repeatedly cite the Buddha's insights into the nature and scope of action as the primary teachings distinguishing Buddhism from other contemporary religions. The eightfold path, as the expression of these insights, is thus the quintessential Buddhist teaching. According to the *Mahāparinibbāna Sutta,* the Buddha on the night of his passing away taught the eightfold path to his last convert in response to the question of whether teachers of other religions were also awakened. Only in a teaching that promoted the eightfold path, he maintained, could awakened people be found.

The first discourse lists the path factors without explanation: right view, right resolve, right speech, right action, right livelihood, right effort, right mindfulness, and right concentration. Other Pali discourses classify these eight factors under three headings: the first two under *discernment,* the next three under *virtue,* and the last three under *concentration.* Still others define the factors in detail. Because the path to the deathless overlaps somewhat with the actions leading to happy results in present and future lifetimes, the path can be taken as a guide, not only to transcendent happiness, but also to mundane happiness. Thus each factor of the path has a mundane and a transcendent level.

Right view on the mundane level encapsulates the *bodhisattva's* second knowledge: that there is value in the act of giving; that skillful and unskillful actions bear, respectively, pleasant and unpleasant fruit; that there are other levels of being; and that there are people who, practicing rightly, have directly known these principles for themselves. Transcendent right view encapsulates the third knowledge: knowing in terms of the four noble truths.

Mundane right resolve aims at renouncing sensual passion, at freedom from ill will, and at freedom from harmfulness. Transcendent right resolve entails directed thought and evaluation as factors of right concentration.

Right speech abstains from lies, harsh speech, divisive speech, and idle chatter. This and the remaining factors are mundane or transcendent depending on whether they are informed by mundane or transcendent right view and right resolve.

Right action abstains from killing, from stealing, and from sexual misconduct (or from sexual intercourse, according to one of the discourses).

Right livelihood, for lay people, means not selling meat, poison, weapons, slaves, or intoxicants. For monastics it means not trying to attract material support by means of scheming, persuading, hinting, belittling, or offering material incentives.

Right effort tries to prevent unskillful mental states from arising, to abandon unskillful mental states that have already arisen, to give rise to skillful mental states, and to bring already-existing skillful mental states to the culmination of their development.

Right mindfulness entails four activities. The first is keeping track of the body in and of itself—ardent, alert, and mindful—putting aside grief and distress with regard to the world. The remaining three activities follow the same formula, replacing "body" with feelings, mind states, and mental qualities.

Right concentration consists of four levels of *jhāna.* The first is composed of directed thought and evaluation focused on a single object—a classic object being the breath—accompanied by pleasure and rapture born of seclusion. The second *jhāna* consists of mental unification, devoid of directed thought and evaluation, accompanied by pleasure and rapture born of concentration. The third *jhāna* is a pleasant equanimous state, devoid of rapture. The fourth *jhāna* consists of purity of mindfulness and equanimity, free from pleasure or pain. One discourse, in defining noble right concentration, adds a fifth factor to these four *jhānas*: the ability to step back from any level of *jhāna* to observe it. Another discourse states that one may use *jhāna* as a basis for awakening by observing its factors in terms of the four noble truths, so as to develop dispassion for those factors, and then inclining the mind to the deathless.

According to the *Bhūmija Sutta,* the rightness of these factors is an objective quality, determined by their ability to issue in the deathless when put into practice, regardless of whether one expresses a wish for that aim. This principle is illustrated with similes: trying to attain the deathless by means of wrong view, wrong resolve, and so on, is like trying to squeeze sesame oil from gravel. Following the path of right view, and so on, is like obtaining sesame oil by squeezing sesame seeds.

The Pali discourses depict the relationships among these eight factors in a variety of ways, in keeping with the complexity of early Buddhist teachings on causality. Individuals at different points in the causal patterns leading to suffering will need differing explanations of how to dismantle those patterns to meet their specific needs. Some discourses depict a linear relationship among the factors, but in two different patterns: one, following the order in which the eight factors are listed; and another beginning with the virtue factors, followed by the concentration and then the discernment factors. Other discourses suggest that specific factors—such as right effort or right mindfulness—when pursued in all their ramifications, incorporate all the other path factors as well.

The most complex treatment of the relationships among the factors is found in the *Mahācattārīsaka Sutta* (The great forty), which places right concentration at the heart of the path, with the other seven factors its "requisites." This discourse adds, however, that right view, right effort, and right mindfulness underlie the development of all eight factors. This same discourse also maintains that the eightfold path leads only to a preliminary level of awakening. Full awakening requires two further factors—right knowledge and right release—although these factors are nowhere defined in the Pali discourses.

The eightfold path was central to the teachings of all the early schools of Buddhism, but succeeding generations developed it in new directions. Before the early canons were closed, the question arose as to how a Buddha's path of practice might differ from that of his *arahant* (Skt., *arhat*) disciples. The various schools mined their *jātaka* stories (accounts of the Buddha's previous lives) to produce lists of perfections (Pali, *pāramī*; Skt., *pāramitā*) that constituted the Buddha's path. The Sarvāstivādins, whose list later formed the framework for the Mahāyāna *bodhisattva* path, found six perfections embodied in their *jātakas*: giving, virtue, energy, endurance, *dhyāna*, and discernment. Five of these perfections correspond directly to factors of the eightfold path: virtue to right speech, action, and livelihood; energy and endurance to right effort; *dhyāna* to right concentration; and discernment to right view and resolve. As for giving, it derives from mundane right view.

Over time, however, Mahāyāna discourses redefined the individual perfections. The *bodhisattva's* perfection of discernment, for instance, consisted of insight into the lack of essential nature in all phenomena. His perfection of virtue allowed him to kill, for example, if his larger motivation was compassionate. In this way, the *bodhisattva* path, while retaining some of the structure of the eightfold path, filled that structure with new elements. The Theravādin school, in its commentaries, made its own *de facto* changes in the eightfold path, redefining the practice of *jhāna* and treating it as an optional factor.

In modern times, two developments—the rise of Pali studies in Japan and the rise of lay meditation movements, based on Theravāda techniques, in Asia and the West—have prompted interest in using the structure of the eightfold path to provide a guide for lay daily life.

In these ways, succeeding generations of Buddhists, lay and monastic, have continued to mine the eightfold path for guidance in their quest for happiness.

SEE ALSO Four Noble Truths.

BIBLIOGRAPHY

A modern Western introduction to the eightfold path is Bhikkhu Bodhi, *The Noble Eightfold Path* (Seattle, 1994). A modern Asian treatment is Ajaan Lee Dhammadharo, *The Path to Peace and Freedom for the Mind*, available at: www.accesstoinsight.org. The *Dhammacakkappavatana Sutta* is translated in Bhikkhu Bodhi, trans., *The Connected Discourses of the Buddha: A New Translation of the Saṁyutta Nikāya* (Boston, 2000), pp. 1843–1847. A translation of the *Maggavibhaṅga Sutta*, which analyzes the individual factors of the path, is included in the same work, pp. 1528–1529. A translation of the *Mahāparinibbāna Sutta* is included in Maurice Walsh, trans., *The Long Discourses of the Buddha: A Translation of the Dīgha Nikāya* (Boston, 1995), pp. 231–277. Bhikkhu Ñāṇamoli and Bhikkhu Bodhi, trans., *The Middle Length Discourses of the Buddha: A New Translation of the Majjhima Nikāya* (Boston, 1995), contains translations of the *Mahācattārīsaka Sutta* (pp. 934–940) and the *Bhūmija Sutta* (pp. 997–1001). Alternative translations for all of these discourses are available from Access to Insight at: www.accesstoinsight.org.

THANISSARO BHIKKHU (2005)

EINSTEIN, ALBERT (1879–1955), was the originator of the theory of relativity and widely regarded as the greatest scientist of modern times. He was born at Ulm, Germany, of particularly loving parents who were said by friends to be "always on a honeymoon." Although Jewish by descent, the family was freethinking and cared little for religious tradition. Einstein was slow in learning to speak and was far from fluent even at age nine; his parents actually feared that he might be subnormal. Furthermore, the boy intensely disliked school and did well only in mathematics and science. He learned to play the violin in childhood and maintained a lifelong interest in music; at one point he seriously considered becoming a professional violinist.

In 1895, Einstein's plan to enroll at the Swiss Federal Polytechnic School in Zurich was frustrated when he failed the entrance examination. He managed, however, to pass the exam the following year and was graduated from the school in 1900. But formal study was so disagreeable to him that he did practically nothing for a year after graduation. He stayed in Zurich and supported himself by teaching part time, for he was unable to secure a regular academic post. In 1901 he became a Swiss citizen and also published his first scientific paper. The next year, he secured a probationary position at the Swiss patent office in Bern. There, he developed several important friendships that lasted throughout his life. Also during this period, he married a fellow student from his Zurich days.

The year 1905 was Einstein's *annus mirabilis;* while still working at the patent office, he published five papers in the *Annalen der Physik* that proved to be revolutionary. Three of the papers—among the greatest in the history of science—were, in the words of J. Robert Oppenheimer, "paralyzingly beautiful." One of them outlined Einstein's special theory of relativity, on the basis of which he derived later in the same year the well-known formula $E = mc^2$, expressing the precise quantitative relationship between a particle's energy and mass. Another of these publications was an important paper on Brownian motion, and yet another dealt with the photoelectric effect. In this work, Einstein introduced a fundamental concept of quantum physics—namely, that of quanta of light energy, which were later called photons. It was actually for his work on the photoelectric effect—not for the relativity theory—that he received the Nobel Prize for physics in 1922.

Ironically, it was on the basis of Einstein's work on relativity that the University of Bern had earlier rejected him when he applied for a place on the faculty. Only in 1908, after such great physicists as Max Planck and H. A. Lorentz had recognized his genius, was he given the position at Bern. After that, academic appointments came in quick succession: In 1909, Einstein was appointed to a professorship at the university at Zurich; in 1911, to a senior professorship at the German university in Prague; and in 1912, again a position at Zurich. It was there, in 1913, that he published his first paper on the theory of general relativity. This work was brought to completion in 1916, when Einstein was a professor at the Prussian Academy and director of the Kaiser Wilhelm Institute of Physics in Berlin. Another great physicist, J. J. Thompson, called Einstein's work on the theory of general relativity "perhaps the greatest achievement in the history of human thought."

Immediately after publishing his theory of general relativity, Einstein started working out its cosmological implications, including the idea that the cosmos is, on the whole, dynamic and expanding. Back from the many travels that ensued from worldwide fame, Einstein began his last great project, the search for a unified field theory. He worked on this until the last day of his life, but the project remained unfinished. Also, by the late 1920s, the main focus of interest in physics had shifted to quantum mechanics, which proved extremely fertile in application but which lacked, as far as Einstein was concerned, philosophical rigor and aesthetic beauty. He could never accept as complete and final the probabilistic interpretation of cosmic processes offered by quantum physics, and thus he was gradually estranged from the mainstream in his field.

Einstein was always a loner, often pursuing unfashionable paths. As he, in his well-known essay "Science and Religion," wrote, "It is strange to be known so universally and yet to be so lonely." He could not accept the probabilistic interpretation of nature because of his "deep conviction of the rationality of the universe." He called this conviction a "cosmic religious feeling" and regarded it as the "strongest and noblest motive for scientific research." His intuitive feeling for this rational order was offended by quantum mechanics. He wrote to the American physicist James Franck, "I can, if the worse comes to the worst, still realize that God may have created a world in which there are no natural laws. In short, a chaos. But that there should be statistical laws with definite solutions, i.e., laws which compel God to throw the dice in each individual case, I find highly disagreeable" (*Einstein: A Centenary Volume,* p. 6).

Throughout his life, and particularly after becoming a public figure, Einstein championed the causes of social justice, freedom of conscience, and peace. When in 1933 the political situation in Germany worsened and, as a pacifist and a Jew, Einstein became a double target for the Nazis, he decided to accept a position at the Institute for Advanced Study at Princeton, New Jersey. He retired from the institute in 1945 but stayed on in Princeton, often working at the institute. In 1952 he was offered the presidency of Israel, which he declined. Einstein was active and mentally vigorous until the end. He said, a few days before his death on April 18, 1955, "Here on earth I have done my job."

Einstein described his religious feeling as one of "rapturous amazement at the harmony of natural law." Many people who knew him personally insisted that he was the most religious person they had ever met. But Einstein was not religious in any churchly or denominational manner. As he said many times and in many ways, "My religion consists of a humble admiration of the illimitable superior spirit who reveals himself in the slight details we are able to perceive with our frail and feeble minds. That deeply emotional conviction of the presence of a superior reasoning power that is revealed in the incomprehensible universe forms my idea of God."

BIBLIOGRAPHY

There is no standard biography of Einstein; perhaps the best one available is Ronald W. Clark's *Einstein: The Life and Times* (Cambridge, U.K., 2000). Leopold Infeld's *Albert Einstein: His Work and Its Influence on Our World* (New York, 1950) gives a good introduction to Einstein's scientific work by one of his collaborators. Carl Seelig's *Albert Einstein: A Documentary Biography* (London, 1956) gives the best account of Einstein's life in Switzerland, whereas Philipp Frank's *Einstein: His Life and Times* (New York, 1963) is the best report on Einstein's life in Prague. The biography by Banesh Hoffmann, with the collaboration of Helen Dukas, *Albert Einstein: Creator and Rebel* (New York, 1972), places much greater emphasis on Einstein's involvement in world affairs. The International Commission on Physics Education brought out *Einstein: A Centenary Volume,* edited by A. P. French (Cambridge, U.K., 1979); it is rich in reminiscences and contains some fine general-interest essays. *Albert Einstein: Philosopher-Scientist,* 2 vols., edited by Paul Arthur Schilpp (New York, 1951), contains Einstein's autobiography, descriptive and critical essays on his work, and Einstein's reply to these. Einstein's nonscientific writings are to be found at many places, particularly in his *Essays in Science* (1934; reprint, New York, 1955), *Out of My Later Years* (New York, 1950), and *Ideas and Opinions* (New York, 1954). The last two of these books contain his superb essay "Science and Religion."

New Sources

Aczel, Amir D. *God's Equation: Einstein, Relativity, and the Expanding Universe.* New York, 1999.

Bodanis, David. *E=mc²: A Biography of the World's Most Famous Equation.* New York, 2000.

Brian, Denis. *Einstein: A Life.* New York, 1996.

Coles, Peter. *Einstein and the Birth of Big Science.* Cambridge, U.K., 2000.

RAVI RAVINDRA (1987)
Revised Bibliography

EISAI (1141–1215) was the founder of the Rinzai (Chin., Linji) school of Zen (Chin., Chan) in Japan. A scholarly monk and religious reformer, Eisai was also the popularizer of the practice of tea drinking in Japan. Although he began life in modest circumstances, he eventually gained the patronage of the shogun heading the warrior government, the *bakufu,* in Kamakura. With the shogun's backing he built monasteries in which Zen was fostered; he was also active in the rebuilding of monasteries of the older Buddhist schools. Eisai has been eclipsed in historical reputation by such later Rinzai monks as Daitō, Musō Sōseki, Ikkyū Sōjun, and Hakuin, and by the Sōtō monk Dōgen Kigen. In his day, however, Eisai was an important figure and played a major role in securing at least partial acceptance for Zen in the Japanese religious world. Together with his near contemporaries Honen (1133–1212) and Shinran (1173–1263), the founders of popular Japanese Pure Land Buddhism, Eisai can be counted among the figures contributing to the Buddhist reformation of the thirteenth century.

Eisai's full religious name is Myōan Eisai. (The characters are sometimes read Myōan Yōsai.) He was born into the family of priests at the Kibitsu shrine in Bizen, modern Okayama prefecture. Probably through his father's influence, he began to study Buddhist texts while still a child and took the vows of a novice in the Kyoto monastery of Enryakuji at the age of fourteen. Enryakuji was a center not only for the study of the scholastic Tendai (Chin., Tiantai) Buddhism introduced to Japan by the monk Saichō (767–822), but also for Esoteric (Taimitsu, in this case) Buddhist practices. The monastery, however, had lost the spiritual vitality evident in Saichō's day. While some Tendai monks still devoted themselves to prayer and study, others made light of their vows, engaged in political intrigue, and saw little amiss in the use of military force to promote monastic interests. In this degenerating spiritual environment some earnest young monks conceived the desire to restore Enryakuji and Tendai Buddhism to their earlier glory; Eisai too became convinced of the urgent need to revitalize Buddhism in Japan. Like many monks in the ancient period, he believed that the sources of this regeneration would be found in China.

In 1168, at the age of twenty-eight, Eisai made the first of two pilgrimages to China. In his travels he became aware of the influence of Chan, but as he was in China for only six months, he did not have time to delve very deeply into its teachings. On his return to Japan Eisai brought with him some sixty volumes of Tendai-related texts, gathered on Mount Tiantai and elsewhere, which he presented to the chief abbot of Enrya kuji. For the next twenty years Eisai divided his time between Kyoto and Bizen. He led an active life, writing commentaries on the *sūtras*, lecturing on the *Lotus Sūtra (Hōkekyō),* conducting Esoteric rituals for rain or relief from sickness, and establishing small communities of disciples. Most of this activity seems to have been devoted not to the propagation of Zen but to the reform of Tendai Buddhism.

In 1187 Eisai again set out for China. His hope was to journey on to India in pilgrimage to the sacred sites associated with the life of the Buddha, but because of disturbances on the borders, his request for a travel permit was rejected by the Chinese authorities. Frustrated, Eisai made his way to Mount Tiantai. There he met the Chan master Xuan Huaichang, under whose guidance he deepened his knowledge of the tradition. Just before returning to Japan in 1191, Eisai committed himself to the *bodhisattva* precepts and was granted a monk's robe and certificate of enlightenment by Xuan.

After his second visit to China, Eisai began to actively promote Zen. He established small temples on Kyushu and along the coast of the Inland Sea, where he combined the study of Zen with devotion to the *Lotus Sūtra.* This activity did not go unnoticed in Tendai Buddhist circles. In 1194 monks from Enryakuji, arguing that Eisai was heretically engaged in an attempt to establish a new branch of Buddhism in Japan, persuaded the court to issue an edict proscribing Zen. In an attempt to defend himself and justify his espousal of Zen, Eisai wrote *Kōzen gokokuron* (Arguments in favor of the promulgation of Zen as a defense of the country). In this long work Eisai offered four major arguments in favor of Zen: that it was the very essence of Buddhism; that it was not a new teaching but had been accepted by Saichō and other patriarchs of Tendai Buddhism; that it was based on the disciplined observance of the Buddhist precepts; and that its sponsorship would certainly lead to the rejuvenation of Buddhism in Japan and to the prosperity and security of the nation.

The defense of Zen offered by Eisai did little to assuage the hostility of the Buddhist establishment in Kyoto. In 1199 Eisai set out for eastern Japan, where he found powerful patrons in the Kamakura warrior regime. Here Eisai was presented with an opportunity to spread Zen in the heartland of warrior power, well away from the interference of Enryakuji. But while he presumably talked privately to his patrons about Zen, the record of his public functions reveals only the conduct of Esoteric rituals and prayer ceremonies in Kamakura.

In 1202 Eisai returned to Kyoto. There, with the shogun Yoriie's backing, he established the monastery of Kenninji, in which Zen was to be practiced in concert with Tendai and Esoteric Buddhism. The writings and activities of the last twenty years of Eisai's life all reflect his conviction of the importance of renewing a broadly based Buddhism deriving its strength from the strict observance of the rules of lay and monastic life. This is the message of his *Nippon buppō chūkō ganbun* (An appeal for the restoration of Japanese Buddhism), written in 1204. Before his death in 1215, Eisai made one last visit to Kamakura, where he presented to the shogun Minamoto Sanetomo a treatise on the efficacy of tea drinking, the *Kissa yōjōki.*

Had Japanese knowledge of Chan come to an end with Eisai, it is unlikely that it would ever have taken deep root in Japan. Although Eisai provided a vigorous intellectual defense of Zen, he did not seek to put it on an independent footing. This was to be the task of his successors, monks such as Dōgen, Enni of Tōfukuji, and the Chinese masters who came to Japan beginning in the mid-thirteenth century. Eisai, however, framed the terms of the debate that would continue over the acceptance of Zen, and whetted the curiosity of a small band of followers, some of whom would themselves go to China in search of a deeper understanding of Zen practice.

See Also Zen.

Bibliography

Collcut, Martin. *Five Mountains: The Rinzai Zen Monastic Institution in Medieval Japan.* Cambridge, Mass., 1981.

Dumoulin, Heinrich. *A History of Zen Buddhism.* Translated by Paul Peachey. New York, 1963.

Furuta Shōkin. *Eisai, Nihon no Zen goruku.* Tokyo, 1977.

Martin Collcutt (1987)

EL. Originally an appellative that simply means "god" in common Semitic, El *(ʾil)* is the proper name of the grey-bearded patriarch of the Syro-Palestinian, or "Canaanite," pantheon. Although references to El are found in texts throughout the ancient Near East, this West Semitic deity plays an active mythological and cultic role only in the Late Bronze Age texts from the Syrian city of Ugarit (modern Ras Shamra). Here he is portrayed as a wise patriarch and the eldest of the gods, the grey-haired "father of years" (*ab šnm*). El is "the father of the gods" (*ab ilm*) and "the creator of creatures" (*bny bnwt*), while his consort, Athirat, is "the progenitress of the gods" (*qnyt ilm*). El is also credited with creating the earth in later Phoenician and Punic inscriptions, but Ugaritic texts do not include this tradition. Iconographic sources from Ugarit appear to present "beneficent El, the kindly one" *(ḷtpn ʾl dpid)* as an enthroned, bearded figure with his right hand raised in a benedictory gesture. As the "father of humanity" (*ab adm*), El is invoked to cure diseases and grant the blessing of children in Ugaritic epics.

Some scholars have argued that the Ugaritic texts portray El as an otiose deity who is replaced by the virile young Baal as the leader of the gods. Most scholars, however, now agree that El retains his authoritative position as the head of the pantheon even as the storm-god Baal exercises power over the earth on behalf of the gods. As "king" (*mlk*) and "judge" (*tpt*), El presides over the divine council, which meets at his own mountain home "at the sources of the rivers, amid the confluence of the deeps." It is El's perquisite to appoint and legitimize (*yknn*) the god who will serve as "king" (*mlk*), and so Baal rules only with the consent of the divine patriarch. El receives homage and obeisance from the gods, and apart from Anat's impetuous threats to her indulgent father, no deity openly challenges the authority of El without fear of losing his or her own position. Even Mot (Death), the "beloved of El," is subdued when the sun goddess Shapsh threatens him with El's displeasure: "Surely he will remove the support of your throne; surely he will overturn the seat of your kingship; surely he will break the scepter of your rule." The decree of El carries ultimate authority among the gods.

El's most common Ugaritic epithet is "bull" (*ṯr*), a symbol of his power and strength. One Ugaritic myth, "The Birth of the Gracious Gods," portrays El as a virile and lusty god who seduces two goddesses on the beach. Using "hand" *(yd)* as a euphemism for penis, the text states that "El's 'hand' grows as long as the sea" (*tirkm yd il kym*). He impregnates the two goddesses, who give birth to the gods Dawn and Dusk (*šḥr wšlm*). Similarly in the Baal Cycle, El welcomes the entrance of his consort to his throne room by playfully asking, "Does the 'hand' of El the King excite you, the love of the Bull arouse you?" Indeed, El can be a less-than-dignified character in Ugaritic myth. In one text, El drinks to inebriation at a divine feast (*mrzḥ*) and is berated by a god "with two horns and a tail" as he staggers home. El then collapses and apparently becomes incontinent, wallowing in his own feces and urine. (This text appropriately concludes with the recipe for a hangover remedy.) Some scholars also identify El with the "king of eternity" (*mlk ʿlm*), the divine leader of the underworld shades of deceased kings (*rpum*) in the Ugaritic corpus, but there is no consensus on this identification.

The Hebrew Bible frequently uses the word *ʾēl* as a reference to the Israelite god, both by itself and in combination with other epithets, such as El Olam, El Elyon, and El Shadday (e.g., *Gen.* 21:33; *Exod.* 6:2–3). Yahweh and El share many common features. Ugaritic El is "beneficent El, the kindly one" *(ḷtpn il dpid)*, while Yahweh is "a compassionate and gracious god" (*ʾēl raḥûm wĕḥannûn*) (*Exod.* 34:6). A Phoenician inscription from Karatepe invokes "El, the creator of the earth" (*ʾl qn arṣ*), similar to the biblical blessing of "God Most High, creator of the heavens and the earth" (*ʾē ʿelyôn qōnê šāmayim wāʾāreṣ*) (*Gen.* 14:19). Historically, El is probably identified with Yahweh in ancient Israel, as suggested by the phrase "El, the god of Israel" *(ʾēl ʾĕlōhê yiśrāʾēl)* in *Genesis* 33:20, and by the use of *ʾēl* as a common theophoric element in Hebrew names. Finally, El appears occasionally in Phoenician and Punic sources from the first millennium BCE, including the Phoenician history allegedly written by Sanchuniathon, which is partially preserved via Philo Byblius in Eusebius's *Praeparatio evangelica.*

Bibliography

Day, John. *Yahweh and the Gods and Goddesses of Canaan.* Sheffield, U.K., 2000.

Hermann, W. "El." In *Dictionary of Deities and Demons in the Bible,* edited by Karel van der Toorn, Bob Becking, and Pieter W. van der Horst, 2d ed., pp. 274–280. Leiden, 1999.

Parker, Simon B., ed. *Ugaritic Narrative Poetry.* Atlanta, 1997. Excellent and accessible English translations of the Ugaritic mythological texts.

Pope, Marvin H. *El in the Ugaritic Texts.* Leiden, 1955. A classic and still-useful study.

Smith, Mark S. *The Origins of Biblical Monotheism: Israel's Polytheistic Background and the Ugaritic Texts.* Oxford, 2001.

Smith, Mark S. *The Early History of God: Yahweh and the Other Deities in Ancient Israel.* 2d ed. Grand Rapids, Mich., 2002. An excellent introduction with comprehensive bibliographic references to recent work.

NEAL H. WALLS (2005)

ELʿAZAR BEN ʿAZARYAH (late first and early second centuries CE), Palestinian tanna, was a rabbinic sage of the Mishnaic period. Elʿazar, whose traditions are recorded in the Mishnah and related texts, is described as a wealthy priest who was a direct descendant of Ezra. It is as a result of this status that Elʿazar was appointed to be the head of the academy in Yavneh during the brief period that Gamliʾel of Yavneh was removed from that position (J.T., *Ber.* 4.1, 7d and parallels). This event is already echoed in the Mishnah (e.g., *Yad.* chap. 4), but its full import is unclear. The Babylonian tradition claims that "on that very day [when Elʿazar was appointed] *ʿeduyyot* was taught . . ." (B.T., *Ber.* 28a). Some modern scholars have understood this tradition to mean that the Mishnaic tractate *ʿEduyyot,* which they take to be the earliest tractate, was composed on that day under the direction of Elʿazar. Internal evidence, however, does not support this assertion. Whatever the nature of the event, it is clear that it had significant contemporary impact.

The position of honor accorded Elʿazar is illustrated by his frequent appearance in the company of the most respected sages of his generation. Also central to Elʿazar's image is his moderation. This is the ideal that he advocates in the Mishnah (*Avot* 3.17), where in a list of similar statements he suggests that "if there is no flour there can be no Torah, if no Torah, there can be no flour." Such moderate tendencies are particularly meaningful against the background of his prestige and legendary wealth; he is described as being especially sensitive to the difficulty of supporting oneself in this world (B.T., *Pes.* 118a). Moderation may have also been one of the lessons in his replacement of Gamliʾel; Gam-liʾel was insensitive to the difficulty of making a living, and while Gamliʾel restricted entrance into the academy, Elʿazar opened the doors to all.

Elʿazar contributed to both the legal and exegetical traditions. His legal record reflects no overall agenda or philosophy, although in certain notable cases moderation is evident. In exegesis he is considered to have been willing to accept the simple meaning of scripture.

SEE ALSO Tannaim.

BIBLIOGRAPHY

The Traditions of Eleazar ben Azariah, by Tzvee Zahavy (Missoula, Mont., 1977), is the most comprehensive work available on Elʿazar. The traditions relating the ascension of Elʿazar to the leadership of the Yavneh academy are analyzed by Robert Goldenberg in "The Deposition of Rabban Gamaliel II: An Examination of the Sources," *Journal of Jewish Studies* 23 (Autumn 1972): 167–190. Essential contributions to understanding these traditions are also made by Louis Ginzberg in *Perushim ve-ḥiddushim bi-Yerushalmi,* vol. 4 (New York, 1961), pp. 174–220.

New Sources

Boyarin, Daniel. "A Tale of Two Synods: Nicaea, Yavneh, and Rabbinic Ecclesiology." *Exemplaria* 12 (2000): 21–62.

DAVID KRAEMER (1987)
Revised Bibliography

ELʿAZAR BEN PEDAT was an amoraic authority of the third century. Of Babylonian origin (J.T., *Ber.* 2.1, 4b), Elʿazar made his career in the rabbinic academies of the Land of Israel, chiefly in Tiberias. Because both Elʿazar ben Pedat and the rather earlier Elʿazar ben Shammuʿa are frequently cited without their patronymics, some uncertainty about ascription is attached to traditions bearing their names. Nevertheless, it is clear that Elʿazar ben Pedat left Babylonia after having studied with Rav and Shemuʾel. In the Jerusalem Talmud he is once called the disciple of Hiyyaʾ bar Abbaʾ (J.T., *Qid.* 1.4, 60b), but he eventually came to be associated with Yoḥanan bar Nappahaʾ in Tiberias (J.T., *San.* 1.1, 18b). He ended his career as Yoḥanan's disciple-colleague (B.T., *B. M.* 84a) and spokesman in the academy (J.T., *Meg.* 1.11, 72b).

Possibly because of his Babylonian origins, Elʿazar was of great interest to the *naḥottei,* traveling scholars who went back and forth between Babylonia and the Land of Israel carrying reports of recent teachings of leading rabbis from one center to the other. (The work of these correspondents during the early generations of rabbinical activity in Babylonia was of great importance in preserving the unity and coordination of a movement that could have broken down into a number of relatively isolated national or regional branches.) Elʿazar's academy at Tiberias was a leading center for such exchanges of information. In the Babylonian Talmud, Elʿazar is called "the master of [or from] the Land of Israel" and the standard Babylonian formula "They sent from there" (i.e., from the Land of Israel) was understood by some as a reference to his teaching (B.T., *San.* 17b).

As a legal authority, Elʿazar was noted for his efforts to identify the masters whose teachings were incorporated without attribution in the Mishnah; he frequently sought to separate consecutive clauses of single Mishnaic pericope, saying, "Break it up; the one who taught this [part of the text] did not teach that" (B.T., *Shab.* 92b, *Ker.* 24b; see also *Bava Metsiʿaʾ* 51a). He was the author of many *aggadot* (nonlegal rabbinic teachings) but was remembered for his aversion to the esoteric lore of *merkavah* mysticism (B.T., *Ḥag.* 13a). According to the medieval *Epistle of Rabbi Sherira' Gaon* (c. 992), El'azar died in the year 279, the same year as his master Yoḥanan.

See Also Amoraim.

Bibliography

Aaron Hyman's *Toledot tanna'im ve-amora'im* (1910; reprint, Jerusalem, 1964) is an altogether uncritical compendium of traditional lore concerning El'azar. It is almost useless as a tool for modern, critical biography, but it remains valuable as an encyclopedic gathering of information. The articles titled "Eleazar ben Pedat" in the *Jewish Encyclopedia* (New York, 1906) and in the *Encyclopaedia Judaica* (Jerusalem, 1971) are also useful.

New Sources

Arbel, Vita Daphna. *Beholders of Divine Secrets: Mysticism and Myth in Hekhalot and Merkavah Literature.* Albany, N.Y., 2003.

Robert Goldenberg (1987)
Revised Bibliography

ELECTION.

The concept of divine election appears in a number of religious traditions that espouse belief in an omnipotent and personal God. Although not unknown among certain religious groups in ancient Greece and India, it has had particular significance in Judaism, Christianity, and Islam. In each of these faiths, one finds the claim that God, although universal, has freely elected or chosen a particular group of people for a particular destiny or relationship with him. While belief in the conditions and beneficiaries of election vary even within the traditions themselves, a common set of difficult, and in some cases, unanswered questions underlie this article. First, how can belief in the election of a particular group of people be reconciled with belief in a universal God? Second, does the concept of election necessarily imply belief in the superiority of the chosen? Third, what is the relationship between election, predestination, and free will? And finally, how, in the face of competing claims to election, can one know if one's own claim is true?

Judaism. Belief in God's having chosen Israel to be his *'am segullah* ("chosen people") has remained a central element of Jewish thought. Rooted in the biblical concept of covenant, it is developed further in the Talmud, in medieval philosophical and mystical writings, and in modern literary and theological texts. Although the concept of election is most closely associated with the Hebrew verb *baḥar* ("chose"), reference to election is often implied in other words. Indeed, belief in the election of Israel predates the introduction of the technical term *baḥar* in *Deuteronomy* (7:6, 14:2), a biblical text not written until the seventh century BCE. Underlying God's promises to Abraham and his descendants in *Genesis* 12, and those to Moses and the people of Israel in *Exodus* 19 as well, is the conviction that Yahveh has freely chosen a particular group of people to be "his people," thus making himself known as "their God." In the covenant that he establishes with Abraham, he promises to make of Abraham and his descendants a great nation, bringing them to a land that would be their own. The covenant that he establishes at Mount Sinai becomes a renewal and extension of the earlier, Abrahamic covenant. Establishing a special relationship with the Israelites as a whole, he here identifies himself not only as the "God of Abraham, Isaac, and Jacob" but also, more generally, as the "God of Israel."

The election of Israel, it seems, stems solely from God's love, not from any evidence of superiority or merit on Israel's behalf. Similarly, their election is one not of privilege but of obligation. "Let my people go," God repeatedly demands of Pharaoh, "that they may serve me" (*Ex.* 8:1ff.). In order to serve him, the Israelites are enjoined to refrain from worshiping or entering into a covenant with other gods (*Ex.* 20:3, 22:20, 23:32), and they are commanded to follow a clearly delineated code of moral and cultic behavior. Thus, by the eighth century BCE, the prophet Isaiah admonishes those who outwardly follow cultic prescriptions but fail to recognize either the proper intent with which sacrifices are to be offered or the kind of moral life that divine election entails. As a kingdom of priests and a holy nation, they, as the prophet Micah maintains, are to "do justice, and to love kindness, and to walk humbly with [their] God" (*Mi.* 6:8). They alone, the prophet Amos reminds them, have been known by God (*Am.* 3:2). Consequently, they bear a greater responsibility for their actions than do other people and will be punished by God for their transgressions. Nevertheless, as the eighth-century prophet Hosea insists, punishment does not negate their election. Comparing Israel to Gomer, the "wife of harlotry" whom the Lord commanded him to marry, he tells his listeners that while they have been "adulterous" in worshiping other gods and, like Gomer, will be punished for their actions, God will later renew his vow of betrothal, promising them, as Hosea promised Gomer, that if they return to him, he will "heal their faithfulness," turn aside his anger, and "love them freely" forever (*Hos.* 14:4).

According to the biblical view, certain Israelites are further elected for a specific role or office. Included are priests (*Dt.* 18:5, *1 Sm.* 2:28) as well as kings (*2 Sm.* 6:21, *Kgs.* 8:16). Emphasis is placed on the responsibilities that they are given. Here, as elsewhere, divine election clearly implies a setting apart for service.

In the sixth century BCE, following the capture of Jerusalem by Nebuchadrezzar, the destruction of the Temple, and the exile into Babylonia, the concept of election took on new and greater importance. Bereft of their holy sanctuary, with many exiled from their Holy Land, Israel, the people of God's promise, now known as Jews, came to identify suffering as a mark of their election. Although belief in the universality of their God, as expressed in the writings of the sixth-century "Second Isaiah," might have led them to conclude that their God, as God of the universe, had chosen another group of his creations to be his treasured people, their continued insistence that it was they alone whom God had chosen helped to create and nourish the hope that they would be redeemed in the future. In order to reconcile the particularity of Israel's election with the universality of God, prophets like "Second Isaiah" maintained that Israel had been chosen as a "light to the nations" (*Is.* 42:6). God had entered into a covenant with the people of Israel so that they might bear testimony to his reality, bringing others to recognize his greatness and to acknowledge that "besides [him] there is no god" (*Is.* 44:6).

The theme of Israel's election is reiterated throughout Jewish Hellenistic literature. In the Apocrypha, for example, *Ben Sira* describes the Lord as distinguishing between his creations, blessing and exalting some (i.e., Israel), cursing others (*Sir.* 33:12), while the author of *2 Esdras* specifically mentions Israel as the one people loved by God (*2 Esd.* 5:27). Philo Judaeus and Josephus similarly refer to the spiritual uniqueness of the Jews. As Philo writes in his *Life of Moses,* although "their bodies have been moulded from human seeds . . . their souls are sprung from Divine seeds, and therefore their stock is akin to God" (1.278–279).

A more exclusivist view of election appears in the writings of the Jewish schismatics living near the Dead Sea during the first centuries before and after the beginning of the common era. They alone, they claimed, were the true Israel. Pointing to the revelation of truth given by God to their Teacher of Righteousness, they saw themselves as the faithful remnant of Israel, the last in line of those whom God had chosen. They had been chosen, they believed, to receive both divine grace and eternal knowledge (*Rule of Community* 11). In return for these gifts and for the new covenant established with them, they were strictly to obey the teachings of Moses and the prophets and consciously to live their lives under the guidance of the spirit of truth. Members of the community identified themselves as sons of light, set apart and prepared for battle against the wicked sons of darkness. It was their contention that this battle would soon occur, in which they, as sons of light, would emerge victorious.

As Géza Vermès implies in his introduction to *The Dead Sea Scrolls in English* (1962), a predestinarian element seems to underlie the community's assertion that it was loved by God before creation, its members destined to become sons of light. Yet as Vermès further maintains, the Qumran community, like other Jewish groups, continually insisted that election was not an inherited privilege. Only through a freely taken oath of allegiance to God and to the teachings by which the community lived could one claim to be a member of the new covenant of grace that God had established. Only then could one claim to be a member of the elect, chosen by God "for an everlasting covenant" and for everlasting glory.

With the fall of the Second Temple in 70 CE and a Diaspora existence that forced Jews to live as a minority among people who often sought to oppress them, the concept of election continued to serve as a source of pride, strength, and hope for a better future. As rabbinic Judaism developed concepts that were to become normative for Jewish life, election remained, as Solomon Schechter (1909) notes, an "unformulated dogma" running throughout rabbinic literature. Beginning in the late first century CE with the teachings of Yohanan ben Zakk'ai, emphasis was placed not only on the close relationship that continued to exist between God and Israel but also on the life of Torah, by which Jews, chosen for holiness by God, were to live. Holiness, as ben Zakk'ai maintained, depended on neither state nor sanctuary (*Avot* 2.8) but on the fulfillment of the Torah that alone constituted what ʿAqivaʾ ben Yosef identified as the essence of Jewish existence (*Sifrei Dt.* 11.22).

According to Benjamin Helfgott (1954), rabbinic emphasis on the election of Israel needs to be seen as part of a Jewish response to the Christian claim that Jews were no longer God's chosen people. While Helfgott admits that emphasis on Israel's election as a response to an anti-Jewish polemic predates the rise of Christianity and can be found as early as 300 BCE, one can justifiably argue that the Christian challenge to the Jewish concept of election was more severe than those that predated it because Christianity's identification of the church as the true Israel posed a direct challenge to the theological foundations of Judaism itself.

The rabbis of the Talmud met this challenge not by direct debate but by reasserting their own doctrine of election with renewed emphasis and vigor. They insisted that the bond between God and Israel was indissoluble (*B.T., Yev.* 102b, *Qid.* 36a). Moreover, they maintained that even the destruction of the Second Temple needed to be seen within the larger context of a universal divine plan that included the future fulfillment of those prophetic promises made to the people of Israel. Thus, even in the face of calamity, the rabbis retained an unqualified faith in God's continuing love for Israel and Israel's love for God. To underscore their contention that God's love for Israel was not arbitrary, the rabbis offered a number of explanations as to why Israel had been chosen. According to *Numbers Rabbah* 14.10, for example, Israel was chosen because no other nation, though offered God's Torah, was willing to accept its precepts, while according to *Genesis Rabbah* 1.4, Israel's election was predestined even before the world was created. Some rabbis pointed to the humility and meekness of the Israelites as making them worthy of election, while most remained silent as to the merits or attributes that might have led to Israel's becoming the treasured people of God. None, however, believed that merit alone was sufficient cause for election. Quoting scripture to support their claim, they attributed Israel's election to God's freely given act of love.

Faith in God's special love for Israel came to be expressed most clearly in daily prayer. Biblically based concepts of election were incorporated into the liturgy as expressions of gratitude to the God who had chosen Israel from all people, loved and exalted them above others, sanctified them by his commandments, and brought them "unto [his] service." One finds these ideas articulated further in the works of such medieval thinkers as Saʿadyah Gaon, Avraham ibn Daud, Ḥasdai Crescas, and Isaac Abravanel. They receive greatest attention, however, in the twelfth-century *Sefer ha-Kuzari* by Yehudah ha-Levi, a work in which the concept of chosenness plays a central role. Written as a defense of Judaism, it identifies religious truth with that that was revealed at Sinai. Consequently, it declares that the Jews, chosen to bear that truth, are alone able to grasp what transcends the limits of reason. As Henry Slonimsky writes in his introduction to *Judah Halevi: The Kuzari* (1964), the concept of Israel's election leads ha-Levi to claim, for the Jewish people and their history, a unique and supernatural character. Yet, according to Slonimsky, it is because ha-Levi wishes to eliminate from his concept of chosenness either hatred or intolerance that he assigns other historical functions to Christianity and Islam, maintaining that in the future they will be converted to religious truth.

The assigning of supernatural uniqueness to the Jewish people finds further expression in Jewish mystical works of the Middle Ages. One finds in qabbalistic literature, for example, the claim that only the souls of Israel are from God while the souls of others are base material, or *qellipot* ("shells"). Given the precarious position of the Jew in medieval Europe, such claims, it seems, became a means of making bearable, if not intelligible, the continued oppression of the Jewish people.

Yet by the eighteenth century, with the growing acceptance of Jews into European society, the question of how one could become part of the modern world while retaining belief in a concept that clearly differentiated Jews from their non-Jewish neighbors, needed new answers. Even if one could demonstrate that the traditional concept of election was intended to imply a consecration for service rather than a claim to superiority, did not the claim serve to separate the Jews from the very people of whom they wanted to be part? Although some, like the eighteenth-century philosopher Moses Mendelssohn in his *Jerusalem,* assured his non-Jewish readers that the election of Israel did not entail privilege but obligations that could not be dismissed, nineteenth-century religious reformers in Germany, America, and later in England, emphasized the universal nature of Israel's election, reiterating that the spiritual mission with which they had been entrusted would benefit humanity as a whole.

While, as Arnold M. Eisen (1983) convincingly demonstrates, the concept of election remained a preoccupation among twentieth-century American Jewish thinkers, some, most notably Mordecai Kaplan, founder of Reconstructionism, sought to eliminate the concept altogether. In his *Judaism as a Civilization* (1934), Kaplan suggested replacing the concept of election with that of vocation. Reflecting Kaplan's own rejection of belief in a supernatural God as well as his conviction that Jews could not hope to gain acceptance in American society as long as they maintained what, protestations notwithstanding, did seem to be a claim to superiority, his concept of vocation as the communal purpose that a specific group of people choose for themselves suggests that Jews are no more unique than others.

A number of theologians recently have sought to refute, either directly or indirectly, Kaplan's notion of Jewish "normalcy." Among them has been Michael Wyschogrod, who, in *The Body of Faith: Judaism as Corporeal Election* (New York, 1983), advances the provocative claim that in choosing Israel God chose a biological rather than an ideological people. Thus, he maintains, both religious and secular Jews are exclusively loved by God and have been chosen to enter into a covenantal relationship with him. No matter what the Jew does or believes, the fact remains that he or she has been chosen to serve as the vehicle through which God acts in history.

CHRISTIANITY. The Christian concept of election is rooted in the self-identification of the early church as the true Israel. While acknowledging that the Jewish people had originally been the chosen of God, early Christian theologians insisted that those Jews refusing to acknowledge Jesus as their Messiah could no longer claim the status of divine privilege. Viewing Israel as a community of the faithful rather than as the biological descendants of Abraham, Paul declares that "not all who are descended from Israel belong to Israel" (*Rom.* 9:6). His contention here, as elsewhere, is that the concept of election, though once referring solely to the Jewish people, the Israel of the flesh, had been superseded by a new concept referring to those Jews and Gentiles who, by accepting the church's teachings, can justifiably claim to be the true Israel of the spirit. Identifying the spiritual Israel with Isaiah's faithful remnant, Paul maintains that they alone are the heirs to God's promise of redemption.

Reinterpreting the biblical concept of covenant, Paul proclaims a new covenant of salvation, available to all who profess faith in the risen Christ. Given apart from the covenant with Abraham and his spiritual seed, it actually precedes the Mosaic covenant (obedience to the Torah), which, according to Paul, is a covenant of slavery (*Gal.* 4:2–31). Although Paul does not argue that Jews should no longer keep the Law, he does insist that the Law in and of itself cannot lead to salvation. Given to Israel as a means of curbing sin, the Law, Paul says, can only bring condemnation, while the new covenant of faith brings rebirth and freedom. Paul does not deny that the Jews remain chosen by God. Indeed, in *Romans* 11:29 he states that the "gifts and the call of God are irrevocable." Yet Paul equates the Mosaic covenant simply with Law, as opposed to spirit, and with privilege, as opposed to service. Given this understanding, he then distinguishes between the Law, which is irrevocable though ultimately ineffectual, and the privileged relationship between God and Israel, which, as John Gager argues in his *The Origins of Anti-Semitism* (New York, 1983), Paul believes to have been "momentarily suspended."

Paul's extension of the concept of election to include Jews and Gentiles served as both a stimulus to greater missionary effort and as a didactic vehicle through which the responsibilities and privileges of the Christian life were made clear. By the second half of the first century, however, as the rift between Judaism and Christianity deepened, giving way to a predominantly Gentile church, Christians focused their claim to election on the church (Gr., *ekklēsia,* "the chosen") alone, with some, like Stephen, insisting that the Israelites, in his view stiff-necked and resistant to the Holy Spirit, had actually never been God's chosen people (*Acts* 7:51). According to this view, the Mosaic covenant existed only to predict the true covenant of the future. In the Gospels and other New Testament texts, emphasis is placed not only on the elect, whose righteousness and faith reveal the workings of the Holy Spirit, but also on Christ as the elect one, the model of repentance and faith necessary to enter God's kingdom (*Lk.* 9:35, 23:35). Although election ultimately rests on an act of divine grace, proof of one's election lies in obedience to the call that Christ has issued. Indeed, as John maintains, using the image of Jesus as a shepherd gathering the elect of all nations, it is only through Christ, the "door of the sheepfold," that one gains access to the Father (*Jn.* 10:1ff.).

In the epistles of the first- and early second-century bishop Ignatius, emphasis is placed on the spiritual gifts, or privileges, that divine election entails. Although all people, he writes, enjoy such temporal blessings as food and drink, only baptism leads to the bestowal of both spiritual nourishment (i.e., the Eucharist) and eternal life. From the second through the sixth century, a number of works were written proclaiming the election of the church as a substitute for the election of Israel. Thus, for example, in his *Three Books of Testimonies against the Jews,* the third-century bishop Cyprian maintains that with the cessation of all tokens of the "old dispensation," a new law, leadership, prophecy, and election would occur, with Gentiles replacing Jews as God's chosen people. Rosemary Ruether, in her *Faith and Fratricide* (New York, 1974), views this literary tradition as part of an ongoing polemic against a Judaism that by its continued and active existence seemed to challenge many of the church's teachings. Moreover, she maintains, by establishing a number of contrasting images between the synagogue and the church—carnality versus spirituality, blindness versus sight, rejection versus election—the church was better able to affirm who it was and what it hoped to be. Although the church's anti-Judaism did not always lead to a position of anti-Semitism, the use of such biblical narratives as that of the older brother Esau's forfeiting his birthright to his younger twin brother, Jacob, to convey the relationship between Judaism and Christianity powerfully underscored the church's theological claim that it alone was the true "seed of Abraham," elected by God to enter the kingdom of heaven.

The schismatic Donatist church of North Africa, originating in the early fourth century and formally denounced as heretical in the year 405, advanced its own concept of election. Formed in opposition to those bishops who, in response to the Diocletian edict of May 303, surrendered their sacred books to the civil authorities, it began to consecrate its own bishops, beginning with Majorinus as bishop of Carthage in the year 312. Claiming that the *traditores* (surrenderers) and their successors did not possess the Holy Spirit and therefore could not validly administer the rite of baptism, it maintained that it alone represented the catholic (or universal) church of Peter. Those who developed Donatist teachings, and in particular Majorinus's successor Donatus, from whom the church took its name, viewed the world as the dominion of Satan represented by the wicked "sons of *traditores.*" Forced to separate from a church that had polluted itself through its alliance with worldly powers, they insisted that only they were pure, "without spot or wrinkle." As such, they believed, they alone were the elect of God. While the opposition of Augustine and others eventually curbed its influence and growth, Donatism persisted in North Africa through the sixth century and quite probably into the seventh century and the arrival of Islam.

Between the tenth and fourteenth centuries, a number of neo-Manichaean Christian sects similarly laid claim to election. Identified by orthodox Christianity as "Manichaean" because of their dualist worldview, their identification of the God of the Hebrew Bible with Satan, and their strict asceticism—all characteristics of the Manichaean religion founded in the third century by the Persian Mani—such groups as the Armenian Paulicians, the Byzantine Bogomils, and the Latin Cathari denied that they were either heretics or Manichaeans; rather, they insisted, they alone represented true Christianity. While the label neo-Manichaean reflects the recognition by contemporary historians that Manichaean elements were present in each of these groups, scholars disagree as to whether or not a direct connection can be established between the Manichaeism of Mani and its later Christian manifestations. In either case, however, like the early Manichaeans, these medieval Christian sects divided their members into different grades or classes, including the two primary classes of the "elect" and the "hearers." Like the early gnostic pneumatics (also identified as the elect), those who were initiated into the class of the elect claimed to possess true knowledge of the self, the world, and God. Among the Cathari, the neo-Manichaean group about whom there exists greatest knowledge and whose influence seemed to be most widespread, members of the elect dressed in black, carried a copy of the New Testament in a leather bag, and embraced a rigorous asceticism that was intended to free them from contact with the material world. Bound to chastity, poverty, and abstention from meat, milk, eggs, cheese, and presumably wine, they ate only one meal (of vegetables) a day, fasted several days a week and at particular seasons, regularly engaged in prayer, and yearly accepted one new piece of clothing. Prohibited from owning property, accumulating wealth, and working in any occupation, they were cared for by the hearers, whose confessions they heard and in whose religious instruction they were engaged.

For the Cathari, as for other neo-Manichaean groups, election implied purity, perfection, and knowledge. The elect saw themselves as superior to others in having nearly achieved a state of pure spirit during their lifetime; they claimed that they alone had the privilege of entering the Paradise of Light immediately after death. According to Malcolm Lambert (1977), both religious and social considerations led many to Catharism and to preparation for their future initiation as one of the elect. While some became Cathari solely out of religious conviction, many, especially among the rural aristocracy and the lower classes, turned to Catharism as a result of their rejection of what they perceived to be the growing luxury and corruption of orthodox Christianity and as a positive affirmation of self-sacrifice and poverty. In addition, Lambert maintains, the initial equality of men and women within the class of the elect attracted a significant number of women to Catharism and to the high ritual status that it alone afforded.

Within the reformed tradition, and especially within Calvinism, the concept of election came to play a particularly prominent role. Identifying the elect as those individuals predestined for salvation, John Calvin asserted that election was rooted in a divine purpose that predated the creation of the world. According to Calvin, humanity existed in a state of total depravation. Although God had sent his son to atone for human sinfulness, the efficacy of this atonement extended only to those whom God already had chosen. Rooted solely in God's love and mercy, election, in Calvin's view, was completely gratuitous, bearing no relationship to human merit. While the few who were elected into the "covenant of life" would be redeemed, the majority of humanity, rejected by God, would be condemned to eternal damnation. In his *Institutes of the Christian Religion* (1536), Calvin describes the election of Israel as a first degree of election, superseded by a second degree in which God retains some of Israel as his children and freely adopts others. Through the preaching of the gospel and an accompanying "illumination of the spirit," the elect are called to membership in Christ, bound through their election to one another. Faith, Calvin maintains, is a seal of one's election that, together with the attaining of righteousness, becomes a confirmation to the individual that he or she indeed has been chosen.

English Puritans and their American descendants similarly placed the concept of election at the heart of their theology. Sharing Calvin's belief in a double predestination consisting of the election of the few and the condemnation of the many, they described in great detail the covenant of grace into which the elect had entered. Made possible through Christ's perfect obedience, this covenant held out both the assurance of forgiveness and the promise of salvation. According to the Puritans, this covenant needed to be appropriated in faith, with salvation subsequently mediated through established laws and institutions. Great emphasis was placed on the experience of regenerating grace as a sign of one's election. By the end of the seventeenth century, this experience became a necessary requirement for membership in both American and English Puritan churches. While the later institution of the halfway covenant enabled those who had been raised as Puritans but had not undergone the personal experience of conversion to retain their membership, Puritan churches in America continued to identify themselves as congregations of visible saints, called by God to a glorious future for which they had made elaborate preparation.

Greater awareness and appreciation of the religious beliefs of others has led a number of contemporary Catholic and Protestant theologians to reassess the traditional Christian concept of election. Ruether, for example, concludes her *Faith and Fratricide* by offering ways in which the Christian understanding of the new covenant as superseding the old might be relativized so as to acknowledge the legitimacy of ongoing Jewish claims. Similarly, Paul Van Buren, in his *Discerning the Way* (New York, 1980), suggests that Jewish and Christian concepts of election be seen as parallel claims that point toward a common hope for redemption. Sharing the concerns of both Ruether and Van Buren, Walter Bühlmann, in *God's Chosen Peoples* (Maryknoll, N.Y., 1982), suggests that chosenness be seen not as an exclusive privilege but as an inclusive model of human closeness to God. Distinguishing between a theology and an ideology of election, he warns against using religious convictions to generate and perpetuate a mentality of intolerance and supremacy.

ISLAM. Although the concept of election is not as fully articulated in Islam as it is in Judaism and Christianity, the Qurʾān frequently uses the word *ʿahd* ("injunction, command") to convey the agreement or covenantal relationship existing between Allāh and his prophets and believers. Occasionally used as a synonym for *ʿaqd* ("contract"), *ʿahd* implies the dynamic, religious engagement of the believer with Allāh, manifest through the obligations that the believer agrees to assume.

The Qurʾān affirms the election of both particular individuals, including Noah, Abraham, Moses, the Hebrew prophets, and Jesus, and their communities. It further affirms the election of God's last and greatest prophet, Muḥammad, and his community of believers. This community (the *ummah*) is identified in the Qurʾān with the biblical saving remnant. For the Muslims, other nations have sought after God, but it is the Islamic community alone that has drawn close to him. This community is not to be identified with any ethnic or social group but consists of all believers. While, according to John Wansbrough (1977), specific doctrines identifying Muslims as superior did not develop until later, the Qurʾān distinguishes Allāh's servants from others by identifying Muslims as the "purified ones" (*sūrah* 37:40) or, more simply, as "the elect" (38:47).

It is in Sufism, however, that the concept of election receives greatest attention. Developed during the ninth and tenth centuries CE, Sufism proclaimed that nothing exists but Allāh. The Ṣūfīs arrived at this claim not through intellectual knowledge but through mystical insight, or gnosis. The Ṣūfīs identified this insight as the inward essence of *islam,* or submission to God, an essence that, they maintained, could be penetrated only by the elect. According to the Ṣūfīs, the elect were those who not only experienced the divine directly but also, as Martin Lings (1961) notes, could pass with no transition from thought to action, from the "next world" and its mysteries to this world and all that it contained.

Believing that gnosis led one to attain the highest rank of human perfection, second only to the prophets, Ṣūfīs laid claim to sainthood. They based this claim not on personal merit but on Allāh's love or grace. To be chosen, then, was to receive the gift of sainthood, a gift that enabled one to penetrate into mysteries that could not be grasped through rational comprehension. Quoting a Ṣūfī poet, Lings describes the mystical intelligence of the Ṣūfī as a flawless jewel, an exquisitely beautiful gift that enables the elect to lift the veil from the "light of Allāh" and recognize that there is nothing but God.

The concept of election as a gift given to special souls even before their creation has led a number of scholars to associate the Ṣūfī claim to election with that of predestination. While these concepts are not identical with one another, the sense of being not merely called by God but overwhelmed by him, led early Ṣūfīs in particular to view their decision to leave the world and devote themselves to Allāh as a decision dictated or suggested to them. As Annemarie Schimmel writes in her *Mystical Dimensions of Islam* (Chapel Hill, N.C., 1975), the mystic has been chosen (*iṣṭafā*) by God for himself, not only to become a vessel of his love but also to participate in the primordial covenant established even before the creation of Adam and to remain pure through the meticulous observance of both Islamic law and Islamic tradition.

SEE ALSO Free Will and Determinism; Free Will and Predestination.

BIBLIOGRAPHY

While most works on election have been narrowly focused, Steven T. Katz's *Jewish Ideas and Concepts* (New York, 1977) and the essay on "Chosen People" by Nelson Glueck and others in *The Universal Jewish Encyclopedia* (New York, 1941) provide good overviews of the appearance of this concept throughout Jewish history. Harold H. Rowley's *The Biblical Doctrine of Election* (London, 1950), although written from an explicitly Christian perspective, is useful in illuminating most of the major references to this concept in the Hebrew Bible, while Solomon Schechter's *Aspects of Rabbinic Theology* (1909; New York, 1961) and Benjamin Helfgott's *The Doctrine of Election in Tannaitic Literature* (New York, 1954) remain important sources of information in discovering the development of this concept in early rabbinic literature. For a detailed description of the appearance of this concept in qabbalistic literature, see Gershom Scholem's *Major Trends in Jewish Mysticism* (1941; New York, 1961). Eugene B. Borowitz's *Choices in Modern Jewish Thought* (New York, 1983) offers a clear, though brief, summary of the development or rejection of the concept of election in the works of such twentieth-century Jewish thinkers as Leo Baeck, Mordecai Kaplan, and Richard Rubenstein. Particularly noteworthy is Arnold M. Eisen's *The Chosen People in America: A Study in Jewish Religious Ideology* (Bloomington, Ind., 1983), which offers a penetrating analysis of what Israel's election has mean to American rabbis and theologians from 1930 to the present.

J. C. V. Durell, in his *The Historic Church* (1906; New York, 1969), gives an excellent summary of the concept of election in early Christianity. The Donatist claim to election is clearly detailed in W. H. C. Frend's *The Donatist Church* (1952; Oxford, 1971). Perhaps the most extensive study of neo-Manichaeanism to date is Steven Runciman's *The Medieval Manichee: A Study of the Christian Dualist Heresy* (Cambridge, 1947). Also of interest, especially in its examination of the social conditions leading to neo-Manichaean claims to election, is Malcolm D. Lambert's *Medieval Heresy* (New York, 1977). The concept of election in Calvinism and in Reformed theology as a whole is well summarized in Heinrich Heppe's *Reformed Dogmatics* (London, 1950). For a more detailed and exhaustive examination of this concept, especially in American Puritanism, see Edmund S. Morgan's *Visible Saints: The History of a Puritan Idea* (New York, 1963).

John Wansbrough's *Quranic Studies* (Oxford, 1977) provides a fine overview of the Qur'anic concept of election, showing its relationship to themes of retribution, covenant, and exile. The development of this concept in Sufism is clearly traced by Robert C. Zaehner in his *Hindu and Muslim Mysticism* (London, 1960) and receives special attention in Martin Lings's *A Moslem Saint of the Twentieth Century: Shaikh Ahmad al-Alawi* (London, 1961).

New Sources

Abrahamov, Binyamin. *Divine Love in Islamic Mysticism: The Teachings of al-Ghazâlî and al-Dabbâgh.* Routledge Curzon Sufi Series. London and New York, 2003.

Bader-Saye, Scott. *Church and Israel after Christendom: The Politics of Election.* Boulder, Colo., 1999.

Cosgrove, Charles H. *Elusive Israel: The Puzzle of Election in Romans.* Louisville, Ky., 1997.

Jacobs, Louis. *God, Torah, Israel: Traditionalism without Fundamentalism.* Cincinnati, 1990.

Neusner, Jacob, Bruce Chilton, and William Graham. *Three Faiths, One God: The Formative Faith and Practice of Judaism, Christianity, and Islam.* Boston, 2002.

Novak, David. *The Election of Israel: The Idea of the Chosen People.* Cambridge and New York, 1995.

Peters, Francis E. *The Monotheists: Jews, Christians, and Muslims in Conflict and Competition.* Princeton, N.J., 2003.

Wells, Jo Bailey. *God's Holy People: A Theme in Bibical Theology.* Journal for the Study of the Old Testament. Supplement Series, no. 305. Sheffield, U.K., 2000.

ELLEN M. UMANSKY (1987)
Revised Bibliography

ELEPHANTS. Indigenous to both Africa and India, the elephant is the largest of all living land animals. A peaceful herbivore, the adult of the species has no fear of any other animal, with the exceptions of the human hunter and small rodents that might crawl up its trunk. Because of its awesome strength and great size, the elephant—whether wild or tamed as a beast of burden—is commonly a symbol of power: both the brute force that supports the cosmos and its life forms and the majesty of royal power. At the same time, the wild elephant demonstrates numerous characteristics shared by human beings—such as longevity, social customs, and varied personality traits—which give rise to tales in which the elephant may be a companion to humans or may exhibit humanlike qualities such as fearfulness, rage, and stubbornness.

In India, the elephant-headed god Gaṇeśa has been widely revered as a remover of obstacles, hence as a bringer of success, among both Hindus and Buddhists. His enormous popularity is also attested outside India. As Indian culture spread, the cult of Gaṇeśa was enthusiastically accepted in Southwest Asia, and in China and Japan, Gaṇeśa became well known through the introduction of Tantric Buddhism to these lands.

Since ancient times, especially in India and North Africa, the elephant has been domesticated and trained as a beast of burden. The Carthaginians, for example, rode on elephants in their war against the Romans. In Hindu mythology, elephants hold up the four quarters of the universe: the earth rests on the back of elephants, which rest, in turn, on the back of a huge tortoise. According to the *Mahābhārata,* the divine elephant Airāvata was born out of the primeval milky ocean as it was being churned by the gods and demons. This elephant was destined to be the mount of Indra, the god of thunder and battle, protector of the cosmos.

The intimate connection in Hindu mythology between Airāvata and Indra indicates that the elephant is not simply a symbol for brute force but is also most broadly associated with the powers that support and protect life. Probably because of its round shape and gray color, the elephant is regarded as a "rain cloud" that walks the earth, endowed with the magico-religious ability to produce rain clouds at will. In present-day India, the elephant plays a significant part in an annual ceremony celebrated in New Delhi for the purposes of inducing rainfall, good harvest, and the fertility of human beings and their livestock. An elephant, painted white with sandal paste, is led in solemn procession through the city. The men attending the elephant wear women's clothes and utter obscene words, as if to stimulate the dormant powers of fertility.

Although in the period of the *Ṛgveda* elephants were tamed but little used in war, by the middle of the first millennium BCE, the owning of elephants had become a prerogative of kings and chieftains, who used them in warfare and on ceremonial occasions. Elephants, particularly albino ones, became the mounts of kings and, hence, symbolic of royal power. In the mythology of kingship, the white elephant appears as one of the seven treasures of the universal monarch (*cakravartin*), who rides upon it as he sets out on his world-inspection tours.

As the embodiment of perfect wisdom and royal dignity, the Buddha himself is often referred to as an elephant. According to the older, verse version of the *Lalitavistara,* the Buddha was conceived when his mother, Maya, dreamed of his descent from heaven in the form of a white elephant. This motif is depicted in a medallion on a balustrade of the Bharhut Stupa dating from the second or first century BCE, and from that time onward, it appears repeatedly in Buddhist iconography throughout India. The later, prose version of the *Lalitavistara,* followed by the *Mahāvastu,* states more emphatically that the Buddha descended into his mother's womb in elephantine form. In subsequent centuries, the Buddhist community has generally accepted the idea that a Buddha, either of the past or of the future, must enter his mother's womb in the form of an elephant.

Many of the myths from Africa about the elephant emphasize the ways in which elephants and human beings share certain characteristics. Perhaps it is because the African elephant remained wild in comparison to its Indian cousin that its natural habits had more effect on the form of its symbolism. For instance, wild elephants are very social, living in groups with definite customs. The life expectancy of the elephant is somewhere between sixty and seventy years. It is an intelligent creature and capable of complex emotions, even neurosis and insanity. These attributes indicate ways in which human beings and elephants are similar, and therefore it is no surprise that the elephant is often regarded as a special companion of the mythical ancestors. For example, the Nandi in East Africa recount the story of how one day, when Asista, the creator, arrived on earth in order to arrange the creation, or to prepare the present condition of things, he found three beings already there, living together: the thunder, a Dorobo (a member of a hunting tribe believed by the Nandi to be their mythical ancestors), and an elephant. A similar tale is told by the Maasai. According to the Yao, the first human being emerged from the primeval wilderness carrying an elephant on his shoulders. The elephant made him a great hunter by teaching him about the natures of all the animals, granting him wild honey for food, and training him in the art of killing. Moreover, the hunter found his wife in the land of the elephants, and together they became the primordial ancestors of the Yao. In southern Africa, it is widely believed that elephants can transform themselves into human beings and vice versa.

Apparently the elephant shares with human beings the capacity for antagonizing the gods: According to the Tim in central Togo, West Africa, at the time of the beginning, the god Esso and all the animals lived together in harmony. They even shared water from the same spring. But the elephant picked a quarrel with the god, who thereupon left the earth and its inhabitants and withdrew to his heaven so that he might enjoy peace and quiet.

SEE ALSO Gaṇeśa.

BIBLIOGRAPHY

The classic analysis of elephant symbolism in India remains Heinrich Zimmer's *Myths and Symbols in Indian Art and Civilization,* edited by Joseph Campbell (1946; reprint, Princeton, N.J., 1972), pp. 102ff. A more comprehensive discussion is presented by Jan Gonda in his *Change and Continuity in Indian Religion* (The Hague, 1965), pp. 90ff. On the symbolism of the elephant in Buddhism, see Alfred Foucher's *La vie du Bouddha* (Paris, 1948), translated by Simone B. Boas as *The Life of Buddha according to the Ancient Texts and Monuments of India* (Middletown, Conn., 1963), pp. 22ff. On Gaṇeśa, there is a study by Alice Getty, *Gaṇeśa: A Monograph on the Elephant-Faced God,* 2d ed. (New Delhi, 1971).

MANABU WAIDA (1987)

ELEUSINIAN MYSTERIES.

The most important mystery cult of the ancient world was that connected with the sanctuary of Demeter Eleusinia on a hillside outside Eleusis, about fourteen miles northwest of Athens.

ORIGINS AND HISTORY. The ritual of initiation into the Eleusinian mysteries preserves memories of an earlier phase during which the mysteries were the initiation ritual of a political and, at an earlier stage, clan community, especially in the initiation of the *pais aph'hestias,* the "boy from the hearth," the religious center of house and state: he was an Athenian boy chosen by lot who underwent initiation at the cost and on behalf of the *polis* of Athens. Other traces are preserved in the cult of Demeter Eleusinia, which was widespread throughout Greece. On the island of Thasos, it was still a clan cult in the fourth century BCE; in Laconia, it concerned especially the initiation of women. These local variations show that cults of Demeter Eleusinia existed in Greece before the local ritual of Eleusis developed into the mysteries. Contrary to previous belief, however, the cult at Eleusis has no demonstrable Bronze Age roots; Mycenaean walls that have been discovered under the later sanctuary belong to secular structures. The first archaeologically recoverable sanctuary shows traces of an apsidal or oval cult house enclosed by a wall, both from the eighth century BCE. It is debatable when Athens took control of the cult—either in or before the time of Solon (c. 600 BCE) or, at the latest, in the time of Peisistratus (mid-sixth century BCE), when the sanctuary underwent a fundamental restructuring that gave it the plan it was to have for the rest of its existence.

At this time, a monumental new gateway was constructed, looking not toward Eleusis but toward Athens, and a square initiation hall (*telestērion*) was erected, incorporating the innermost sanctum (*anaktoron*) of a Solonian temple. In the second half of the fifth century BCE, the sanctuary was expanded by Ictinus and other architects to its final form. A new *telestērion* was built, large enough to accommodate several thousand initiands (*mustai*), who during the initiation rites stood on steps along the four inner walls. In the center of the *telestērion* stood the *anaktoron* in its traditional location.

By the second half of the fifth century, in the Classical period of Greek culture, participation in the rites at Eleusis, previously restricted to Athenians, was open to all Greeks. In Hellenistic and imperial times, the mysteries gained even more prestige; they were now open to *mustai* from all over the Roman Empire. The eschatological hopes offered by the rites attracted philosophers and emperors alike. Marcus Aurelius, who was both, rebuilt the sanctuary after a barbarian invasion in 170 CE. The Christian emperor Theodosius (r. 379–395) interdicted participation in the mysteries, as in all pagan cults, and shortly afterward, in 395 CE, the invading Goths destroyed the sanctuary.

ORGANIZATION. Besides the priestess of Demeter, who lived in the sanctuary, the temple of Eleusis was attended by a host of officials, both religious and secular. The main religious official was the hierophant (Gr., *hierophantes;* lit., "he who shows the sacred things"), chosen from the Eleusinian family of the Eumolpides to serve for life. From the family of the Kerukes came the *daidouchos* ("torchbearer") and the *hierokerux* ("sacred herald"), the two officials next in rank.

IDEOLOGY. The Homeric *Hymn to Demeter,* composed before Athenian control (between 650 and 550 BCE), narrates how Demeter's daughter, Kore ("maiden"), also called Persephone, was carried off by Hades. After an unsuccessful search for Kore, Demeter in human disguise came to Eleusis and was engaged as a nurse to the baby prince Demophon, whom she tried to make immortal by immersion in fire. Found out, she revealed her divinity, ordered a temple to be built, and, by stopping the growth of crops, blackmailed Zeus into restoring her daughter, at least for half a year; the other half Kore had to spend in the underworld with her husband Hades. Demeter then restored life to the crops and revealed the mysteries to the Eleusinian princes.

This narrative uses a traditional theme—the rape and restoration of a maiden are elements of a fertility theme that appears in various Near Eastern mythologies—to account for the origins of the Eleusinian cult. It is the central text for the mysteries. To those "who have seen these things," it promises a better fate after death (Homeric *Hymn to Demeter* 480ff.). In Peisistratean times, Athenian mythmakers introduced an important change: Demeter was said to have given the cereal crops to the Eleusinians, who had not known them before, and Triptolemos, one of the Eleusinian heroes, was credited with teaching the art of agriculture to humankind. Vase paintings attest to the popularity of this myth from the late sixth century onward. Not much later, another change was introduced that gave more concrete forms to the vague eschatological hopes raised by the mysteries: the *mustai* could now look forward to a blessed paradise, the uninitiated to punishments after death. From the fifth century onward, both these changes are reflected in poems ascribed to Musaios (a hero related to Eumolpos, the ancestor of the Eumolpidai) and to Orpheus.

THE RITUAL. The initiation rites were secret. Current knowledge is restricted to scraps of information provided by those who dared to divulge them (especially converted pagans) and to those rituals that were public.

The initiation formed part of the state festival of the Musteria, or Greater Mysteries, in the Athenian month of Boedromion (September–October). Initiation at Eleusis was preceded by a preliminary ritual, at Agrai, just outside Athens, that took place in the month of Anthesterion (February–March). Pictorial sources show that this ritual, called the Lesser Mysteries, had a predominantly purificatory character: it contained the sacrifice of a piglet and purifications through fire (a burning torch) and air (by means of a fan). The Greater Mysteries themselves began with preparations in Athens: assembly of the *mustai* and formal exclusion of "murderers and barbarians" (on 15 Boedromion), a ritual bath in the sea (on 16 Boedromion), and three days of fast. On 19 Boedromion, the *mustai* marched in procession from Athens to Eleusis, guided by the statue of Iacchos, the god who impersonated the ecstatic shouts (*iacchazein,* "to shout") of the crowd and was later identified with the ecstatic Dionysos.

Toward dusk, the *mustai* entered the sanctuary at Eleusis. A secret password, known through a Christian source, provides information about the preliminary rites (Clement of Alexandria, *Protrepticus* 21.8): "I fasted; I drank the *kukeōn;* I took from the chest; having done my task, I placed in the basket, and from the basket into the chest." The *kukeōn* is known to have been a mixture of water, barley, and spice, taken to break the fast (*Hymn to Demeter* 206ff.), but details of the rest of the ritual are obscure. Perhaps the *mustai* took a mortar from the sacred chest and ground some grains of wheat. They also enacted the search for Kore by torchlight (ibid., 47ff.).

The central rite is clear only in its outline. Crowded in the *telestērion* for the whole night, the *mustai* underwent terrifying darkness; then came a climax full of illumination, "when the *anaktoron* was opened" (Plutarch, *Moralia* 81d–e) and a huge fire burst forth. (Note the parallel to the motif of immersion in fire to gain immortality in *Hymn to Demeter* 239f.) Details of what followed are conjectural, based largely on the account of Hippolytus (c. 170–236). "Under a huge fire," he reports, "the hierophant shouts, 'The Mistress has given birth to a sacred child, Brimo to Brimos'" (*Refutation of All Heresies* 5.8). Perhaps "the mistress" is Demeter and the "sacred child" Ploutos (Plutus), or Wealth, symbolized by an ear of wheat, for Hippolytus describes another ritual thus: "The hierophant showed the initiates the great . . . mystery, an ear cut in silence" (ibid.).

The central rite must have evoked eschatological hopes by ritual means, not by teaching. (Teaching is expressly excluded by Aristotle, *Fragment* 15.) The symbolism of the grain lends itself to such an explanation, as does the symbolism of a new birth. A year after his initiation (*muēsis*), the *mustēs* could attain the degree of *epopteia.* The rituals of this degree are unknown; many scholars maintain that the showing of the ear belongs to this degree, on the strength of Hippolytus's terminology.

Initiation into the Eleusinian mysteries was, in historical times, an affair of individuals, as in the imperial mystery cults, but unlike them, it always remained bound to one place, Eleusis, and had presumably grown out of gentilitial cults of the Eleusinian families.

SEE ALSO Demeter and Persephone; Mystery Religions.

BIBLIOGRAPHY

The most competent archaeological account of the Eleusinian mysteries (with a much less convincing part on the ritual) is George E. Mylonas's *Eleusis and the Eleusinian Mysteries* (Princeton, 1961). Corrections regarding the Mycenaean origin are presented by Pascal Darcque in "Les vestiges mycéniens découverts sous le Telestérion d'Eleusis," *Bulletin de correspondance hellénique* 105 (1981): 593–605. The Homeric hymn has been edited, with ample commentary, by N. J. Richardson in *The Homeric Hymn to Demeter* (Oxford, 1974); the later poems are reconstructed in my *Eleusis und die orphische Dichtung Athens in vorhellenistischer Zeit* (Berlin, 1974). The iconographical sources are collected by Ugo Bianchi in *The Greek Mysteries* (Leiden, 1976). Interesting insights, despite many debatable arguments, are given in Karóly Kerényi's *Eleusis: Archetypal Image of Mother and Daughter,* translated by Ralph Manheim (New York, 1967). Walter Burkert's *Homo Necans: The Anthropology of Ancient Greek Sacrificial Ritual and Myth,* edited and translated by Peter Bing (Berkeley, Calif., 1983), approaches the mysteries through the phenomenology of sacrificial ritual; see also his short but masterly account in *Greek Religion, Archaic and Classical* (Cambridge, Mass., 1985), pp. 285–290. Bruce M. Metzger's "Bibliography of Mystery Religions: IV, The Eleusinian Mysteries," in *Aufstieg und Niedergang der römischen Welt,* vol. 2.17.3 (Berlin and New York, 1984), pp. 1317–1329, 1407–1409, covers the years 1927–1977 and is a very thorough listing, albeit without annotation.

New Sources

Alderink, Larry. "The Eleusinian Mysteries in Roman Imperial Times." In *Aufstieg und Niedergang der Römischen Welt* 2.18.2, pp. 1499–1539. Berlin and New York, 1989.

Bianchi, Ugo. "Saggezza olimpica e mistica eleusina nell'Inno Omerico a Demetra." *Studi e Materiali di Storia delle Religioni* 35 (1964): 161–193.

Burkert, Walter. *Ancient Mystery Cults.* Cambridge, Mass., 1987.

Clinton, Kevin. *Myth and Cult: The Iconography of the Eleusinian Mysteries. The M.P. Nilsson Lectures on Greek Religion, Delivered 19–21 Nov. 1990 at the Swedish Institute at Athens.* Göteborg, 1992.

Clinton, Kevin. "Stages of Initiation in the Eleusinian and Samothracian Mysteries." In *Greek Mysteries,* edited by Michael B. Cosmopoulos, pp. 50–78. London and New York, 2003.

Cosmopoulos, Michael B. "Micenean Religion at Eleusis: The Architecture and Stratigraphy of Megaron B." In *Greek Mysteries,* edited by Michael B. Cosmopoulos, pp. 1–24. London and New York, 2003.

Dietrich, Bernard C. "The Religious Prehistory of Demeter's Eleusinian Mysteries." In *La soteriologia dei culti orientali nell'impero romano. Atti del Colloquio internazionale, Roma, 24–28 settembre 1979,* edited by Ugo Bianchi and Maarten J. Vermaseren, pp. 445–471. Leiden, 1982.

Dowden, Ken. "Grades in the Eleusinian Mysteries." *Revue d'Histoire des Religions* 197 (1980): 409–427.

Foucart, Paul. *Les mystères d'éleusis.* Puiseaux, 1941, reprint 1999.

Gallant, Christine. "A Jungian Interpretation of the Eleusinian Myth and Mysteries." In *Aufstieg und Niedergang der Römischen Welt* 2.18.2, pp. 1540–1563. Berlin and New York, 1989.

Janda, Michael. *Eleusis.* Innsbruck, 2000.

Lauenstein, Diether. *Die Mysterien von Eleusis.* Stuttgart, 1987.

Motte, André. "Silence et sécret dans les mystères d'éleusis." In *Les rites d'initiation. Actes du Colloque de Liège et Louvain la Neuve, 20–21 novembre 1984,* edited by Julien Ries and Henri Limet, pp. 317–334. Louvain la Neuve, 1986.

Robertson, Noel. *Festivals and Legends: The Formation of Greek Cities in the Light of Public Ritual.* Toronto, 1992.

Robertson, Noel. "The Two Processions to Eleusis and the Program of the Mysteries." *American Journal of Philology* 119 (1998): 547–575.

Sfameni Gasparro, Giulia. *Misteri e culti mistici di Demetra.* Rome, 1986.

Sourvinou Inwood, Christine. "Festival and Mysteries: Aspect of Eleusinian Cult." In *Greek Mysteries,* edited by Michael B. Cosmopoulos, pp. 25–49. London and New York, 2003.

Speyer, Wolfgang. "Einblicke in die Mysterien von Eleusis." In *Religio Graeco-Romana. Festschrift für Walter Pötscher,* edited by Joachim Dalfen, Gerhard Petersmann, and Franz Ferdinand Schwarz, pp. 15–33. Horn, 1993.

Wasson, R. Gordon, Albert Hofmann, and Carl A. P. Ruck. *The Road to Eleusis,* preface by Huston Smith; afterword by Albert Hofmann. Los Angeles, 1998.

FRITZ GRAF (1987)
Revised Bibliography

ELIADE, MIRCEA [FIRST EDITION] (1907–1986),

Romanian-born historian of religions, humanist, orientalist, philosopher, and creative writer. The career of Mircea Eliade, who served as editor in chief of this encyclopedia, was long and multifaceted. Since this article can give only a brief, general introduction, those who wish to know more of his life and work are referred to the works cited in the following bibliography.

STUDENT YEARS. Born in Bucharest, the son of an army officer, Eliade witnessed the German occupation of his homeland when he was only nine years old. His lifelong fascination with literature, philosophy, oriental studies, alchemy, and the history of religions began when he was still at the *lycée.* An early article entitled "The Enemy of the Silkworm" reflects the boy's intense interest in plants, animals, and insects. In fact he had already published his one hundredth article by the time he entered the University of Bucharest in 1925. At the university, he became a devoted disciple of the philosopher Nae Ionescu, who taught him the importance of life experience, commitment, intuition, and the spiritual or psychological reality of mental worlds. At the university Eliade became particularly interested in the philosophy of the Italian Renaissance, especially in Marsilio Ficino's rediscovery of Greek philosophy.

Eliade was blessed with the happy combination of an unusually keen mind, strong intuition, a fertile imagination, and the determination to work hard. Much of the structure of his later thought, and some of the paradoxes of his life, were foreshadowed during his student years. Simultaneously he was both a Romanian patriot and a world citizen. He was proud of Western civilization, although he lamented its provincial character, particularly its will to "universalize" Western ideas and values into the norm for all of humankind. Looking back, he could see that in his country previous generations had had no cause to question their historic mission to consolidate Romania's national identity. His own generation, though, had experienced World War I and seemed to have no ready-made model or mission for themselves. Eliade's plea was that his compatriots should exploit this period of "creative freedom" from tradition and should try to learn from other parts of the world what possibilities for life and thought there were. His ultimate concern was the revitalization of all branches of learning and the arts, and his great hope was to decipher the message of the cosmos, which to him was a great repository of hidden meanings. Judging from his diaries and other writings, it seems that Eliade always had a strong sense of destiny, from his youth until his last day in Chicago, calling him from one phase of life to the next, though he felt he was not always conscious of what lay in store for him along the way.

Concerning his preoccupation with the Italian Renaissance in his college days, Eliade later stated, "Perhaps, without knowing it, I was in search of a new, wider humanism, bolder than the humanism of the Renaissance, which was too dependent on the models of Mediterranean classicism. . . . Ultimately, I dreamed of rediscovering the model of a 'universal man'" (*No Souvenirs: Journal, 1957–1969,* London, 1978, p. 17). As though to fulfill Eliade's preordained destiny, the maharaja of Kassimbazar offered him a grant to study Indian philosophy with Surendranath Dasgupta at the University of Calcutta (1928–1932). He also spent six months in the ashram of Rishikesh in the Himalayas. To him, India was more than a place for scholarly research. He felt that a mystery was hidden somewhere in India, and deciphering it would disclose the mystery of his own existence. India indeed revealed to him the profound meaning of the freedom that can be achieved by abolishing the routine conditions of human existence, a meaning indicated in the subtitle of his book on Yoga: *Immortality and Freedom.*

The stay in India also opened his eyes to the existence of common elements in all peasant cultures—for example, in China, Southeast Asia, pre-Aryan aboriginal India, the Mediterranean world, and the Iberian Peninsula—the elements from which he would later derive the notion of "cosmic religion." In fact, the discovery of pre-Aryan aboriginal Indian spirituality (which has remained an important thread in the fabric of Hinduism to the present) led Eliade to speculate on a comparable synthesis in southeastern Europe, where the ancient culture of the Dacians formed the "autochthonous base" of present-day Romanian culture. (Dacian culture had been reconstructed by a Romanian philosopher-folklorist, B. P. Hasdeu.) Moreover, Eliade came to believe that the substratum of peasant cultures of southeastern Europe has been preserved to this day, underneath the cultural influences of the Greeks, the Romans, the Byzantines, and Christianity, and he went so far as to suggest that the peasant roots of Romanian culture could become the basis of a genuine universalism, transcending nationalism and cultural provincialism. He believed that the oppressed peoples of Asia and elsewhere might take their rightful place in world history through such universalism. "We, the people of Eastern Europe, would be able to serve as a bridge between the West and Asia." As he remarked in his autobiography, "A good part of my activity in [Romania] between 1932 and 1940 found its point of departure in these intuitions and observations" (*Autobiography: Journey East, Journey West*, vol. 1, 1981, p. 204).

EARLY LITERARY AND INTELLECTUAL ACTIVITY. In 1932 Eliade returned to Romania and was appointed to assist Nae Ionescu at the University of Bucharest in the following year. His publication of *Yoga: Essai sur les origines de la mystique indienne* (1936), in which he attempted a new interpretation of the myths and symbolism of archaic and oriental religions, attracted the attention of such eminent European scholars as Jean Przyluski, Louis de La Vallée Poussin, Heinrich Zimmer, and Giuseppe Tucci. He also plunged feverishly into literary activities. Many people were under the impression then that Eliade thought of himself primarily as a novelist, although he was strongly motivated to engage in scholarly activities as well. Eliade had made his literary debut in 1930 with *Isabel si Apele Diavolului* (Isabel and the Devil's Water), which was obviously colored by his Indian experience. According to Matei Calinescu, in his essay "'The Function of the Unreal': Reflections on Mircea Eliade's Short Fiction" (in Girardot and Ricketts, 1982), most of Eliade's fiction inspired by India was written between 1930 and 1935, and his earlier novels with Indian themes (e.g., *Maitreyi*, 1933) were strongly autobiographical. He also points out that Eliade's later novellas on these themes, such as *Secretul Doctorului Honigberger* (The Secret of Doctor Honigberger) and *Nopţi la Serampore* (Night in Serampore), both published in a single volume entitled *Secretul Doctoru-lui Honigberger* (1940), "deal with the major problem of the fully mature Eliade, that of the ambiguities of the sacred and the profane in their characteristical relationship"; Calimescu concludes that "Eliade had discovered the 'ontological' signification of narration" by 1940 (Girardot and Ricketts, p. 142).

Eliade once stated that young Romanians had a very short period of creative freedom, and fear that this observation might apply to himself compelled him to work against the clock. Accordingly, he published not only literary works but also a series of important scholarly studies on alchemy, mythology, oriental studies, philosophy, symbology, metallurgy, and the history of religions. In 1938 he founded the journal *Zalmoxis: Revue des études religieuses.* (Unfortunately, circulation ceased after 1942.) Eliade was also active in the so-called Criterion group, consisting of male and female intellectuals. This group was a significant collective manifestation of the "young generation" of Romanians, which sponsored public lectures, symposia, and discussion about important contemporary intellectual issues as a new type of Socratic dialogue. "The goal we were pursuing," Eliade said, "was not only to inform people; above all, we were seeking to 'awaken' the audience, to confront them with ideas, and ultimately to modify their mode of being in the world" (*Autobiography*, vol. 1, p. 237).

Meanwhile, Romania could not help but be touched by the political whirlwind that was rising in Europe, manifested in the conflicts and tensions between communism and democracy, fascism and Nazism. Following the assassination of Romanian Prime Minister Duca in December 1933, Eliade's mentor Nae Ionescu was arrested on suspicion that he was an antiroyalist rightist. Also arrested were the leaders of the pro-Nazi Legion of the Archangel Michael, commonly known as the Legionnaires or the Iron Guard, and some of Eliade's friends in the Criterion group. Of course the Criterion experiment ceased to function because it was impossible for Legionnaires, democrats, and communists to share the same platform. Thus, Romania entered a "broken-off era," as Eliade called it with fear and trembling. The tense political atmosphere, the cruelties and excesses of all sorts, find their echoes in Eliade's *Huliganii*, 2 vols. (The Hooligans; 1935), although he explicitly said that the hooligans in the novel were very different from the actual Romanian hooligans of the 1930s—those "groups of young antisemites, ready to break windows or heads, to attack or loot synagogues" (*Autobiography*, vol. 1, p. 301). What concerned Eliade was not only the sad political reality of his homeland. He wrote, "I had had the premonition long before . . . that we would *not have* time. I sensed now not only that time was limited, but that there would come a terrifying time (the time of the 'terror of history')" (*Autobiography*, p. 292). In 1938 the royal dictatorship in Romania was proclaimed; then came World War II.

EMIGRATION AND DEVELOPMENT. In 1940 Eliade was appointed cultural attaché at the Royal Romanian Legation in war-torn London. In the following year he became a cultural counselor in Lisbon, in neutral Portugal. When the war was over in 1945, Eliade went directly to Paris, thus starting the life of self-imposed exile. Although he could write and lecture in French, starting a new life in a foreign country at the age of thirty-eight required considerable adjustment. On the other hand, by that time he was already a highly respected, mature scholar. "It took me ten years to understand," he said, "that the Indian experience alone could not reveal to me the universal man I had been looking for" (*No Souvenirs*, p. 17). For this task he acknowledged the necessity of combining the history of religions, orientalism, ethnology, and other disciplines. He wrote:

> The correct analyses of myths and of mythical thought, of symbols and primordial images, especially the religious creations that emerge from Oriental and "primitive" cultures, are . . . the only way to open the Western mind and to introduce a new, planetary humanism. . . . Thus, the proper procedure for grasping their meaning is not the naturalist's "objectivity," but the intelligent sympathy of the hermeneut. *It was the procedure itself that had to be changed.* . . . This conviction guided my research on the meaning and function of myths, the structure of religious symbols, and in general, of the dialectics of the sacred and the profane. (*No Souvenirs,* p. xii)

In 1946 Eliade was invited to serve as a visiting professor at the École des Hautes Études of the Sorbonne. He then proceeded to publish such famous works as *Techniques du Yoga* (1948), *Traité d'histoire des religions* (1949; revised translation, *Patterns in Comparative Religion,* 1958), *Le mythe de l'eternel retour* (1949; revised translation, *The Myth of the Eternal Return,* 1954), *Le chamanisme et les techniques archaiques de l'extase* (1951; revised and enlarged translation, *Shamanism: Archaic Techniques of Ecstasy,* 1964), and so on. He was also invited by many leading universities in Europe to deliver lectures, and he appeared in a number of seminars and conferences, for example, the annual meetings at Ascona, Switzerland.

In retrospect, it becomes clear that during his stay in Paris (1945–1955) Eliade solidified most of his important concepts and categories, including those of *homo religiosus, homo symbolicus,* archetypes, *coincidentia oppositorum,* hierophany, *axis mundi,* the cosmic rope, the nostalgia for Paradise, androgyny, the initiatory scenario, and so on, all of which became integral parts of a coherent outlook or system that aimed at what Eliade later called a total hermeneutics. This may account for the impossibility of isolating, or even criticizing, any part of his system without disturbing the entire framework. Side by side with this development, one notices the shift in his personal orientation. Before World War II, his scholarly and literary activities had focused very much on Romania. In those years, he affirmed that "the orthodox heritage could constitute a total conception of the world and existence, and that this synthesis, if it could be realized, would be a new phenomenon in the history of modern Romanian culture" (*Autobiography,* vol. 1, p. 132). After the war, he continued to regard himself as a Romanian writer, but something new was added. The sense that his experience suggested the paradigm of the homeless exile as a symbol of religious reality for modern, secularized humankind. In this situation, his literary works, too, took on the "coloring of a *redeeming force* (*forta recuperatoare*)," to quote Eugen Simion (in Girardot and Ricketts, 1982, p. 136).

METHODOLOGY AND IMAGINATION. Like many other historians of religions—for example, Raffaele Pettazzoni (1883–1959) and Joachim Wach (1898–1955)—Eliade held that the discipline of the history of religions (*Allgemeine Religionswissenschaft*) consisted of two dimensions, historical and systematic. Characteristically, he worked first on the systematic dimension (using the "morphological" method, inspired by Goethe), as exemplified by his *Traité* (*Patterns in Comparative Religion*), which presents an astonishing variety of religious data and their basic "patterns." The book starts with certain "cosmic" hierophanies (i.e., manifestations of the sacred), such as the sky, waters, earth, and stones. Analyses of these manifestations are based on Eliade's notion of the dialectic of the sacred, in order to show how far those hierophanies constitute autonomous forms. He goes on to discuss the "biological" hierophanies (from the rhythm of the moon to sexuality), "local" hierophanies such as consecrated places, and "myths and symbols." Throughout the book, Eliade examines both the "lower" and "higher" religious forms side by side instead of moving from lower to higher forms, as is done in evolutionary schemes. He takes pain to explain that "religious wholes are not seen in bits and pieces, for each class of hierophanies . . . forms, in its own way, a whole, both morphologically . . . and historically" (*Patterns in Comparative Religion,* New York, 1958, p. xvi).

It is not surprising that Eliade's morphology of religion, which is his version of the systematic aspect of the history of religions, has much in common with the phenomenology of religion of Gerardus van der Leeuw (1890–1950), a Dutch historian of religions, theologian, ethnologist, and phenomenologist. Eliade wrote a very positive review of van der Leeuw's *Religion in Essence and Manifestation* in *Revue d'histoire des religions* 138 (1950): 108–111. Although Eliade is uneasy with van der Leeuw's starting point, he praises the book because it shows that human beings can and do find religious meaning even in the most banal physiological activities such as eating and sexuality, and the book portrays the entire cosmos with its most humble parts serving as grounds for the manifestation of the sacred. It should be noted that religion has two dimensions in van der Leeuw's scheme, namely, "religion as experience," which can be studied phenomenologically, and "religion as revelation," which is basically incomprehensible and thus can be studied only theologically. Furthermore, van der Leeuw never claimed that his phenomenological study is empirical, because to him empirical research is needed only to control what has been understood phenomenologically. Similarly, Eliade never claimed that the history of religions, including its systematic task, is empirical in a narrow scientific sense, even though it certainly has empirical dimensions.

Eliade always felt a need for the alternating modes of the creative spirit—the "diurnal," rational mode of scholarship, which he expressed in his French writings, and the "nocturnal," mythological mode of imagination and fantasy, which he continued to express in Romanian. In 1955, the French translation of his major novel, *Forêt interdite,* appeared. According to Mac Linscott Ricketts, who with M. P. Stevenson translated this novel into English (*The Forbidden Forest,*

1978), Eliade felt it would be more for this work and other fiction that he would be remembered by later generations than for his erudite scholarly works. *The Forbidden Forest* is in a sense a historical novel, dealing with the events and activities of the protagonist and his lovers, friends, and foes during the turbulent twelve years from 1936 to 1948, in Romania, London, Lisbon, Russia, and Paris. In another sense it is an original novel. Eliade skillfully creates characters, all of whom are caught by "destiny," as people often are in his other stories. All of them try to escape from the network of historical events and from destructive "time," which is the central theme of this novel. The tangled story begins on the summer solstice in a forest near Bucharest. After twelve years, again on the summer solstice but in a French forest near the Swiss border, the protagonist encounters his long-lost girlfriend, and he finds salvation, which is "a kind of transcendental love for a girl—and death" (Ricketts, in *Imagination and Meaning*, p. 105). To be sure, the novels were not meant to be literary illustrations of Eliade's theories, but he admits there are some structural analogies between the scientific and literary imaginations, such as the structure of sacred and mythical space, and more especially "a considerable number of strange, unfamiliar, and enigmatic worlds of meaning" (*No Souvenirs*, p. ix).

Years in the United States. In 1956 Eliade was invited by the University of Chicago to deliver the Haskell Lectures, which were published under the title *Birth and Rebirth* (1958). In 1957 he joined the University of Chicago faculty and continued to live in that city after his retirement. At the time of his death in 1986, he was the Sewell L. Avery Distinguished Service Professor Emeritus.

Eliade's move to the United States at the age of forty-nine meant a second emigration for him, but he made an excellent adjustment to the new environment. The University of Chicago had traditionally been an important center for the study of the history of religions, and graduates trained by Eliade's predecessor, Joachim Wach, were scattered in many parts of North America and on other continents. Eliade's appointment at Chicago coincided with the sudden mushrooming of departments of religion or religious studies as part of the liberal arts programs of various colleges and universities in North America. Fortunately, his books and articles—mostly the scholarly ones and not his literary works—were beginning to be translated into English, and the reading public devoured them. Eliade made a deep impression on young readers with such works as *Cosmos and History* (1959), *The Sacred and the Profane* (1959), *Myths, Dreams and Mysteries* (1960), *Images and Symbols* (1969), *Myths and Reality* (1963), *Mephistopheles and the Androgyne* (1965), *Zalmoxis* (1972), *The Forge and the Crucible* (1962), *The Quest* (1969), and others. He also exerted a tremendous influence on more advanced students with *Yoga* (1958), *Shamanism* (1964), and *Australian Religions* (1973). The fact that Eliade was willing to use nonphilosophical and nontheological terms in an elegant literary style to discuss religious subjects attracted many secularized youths.

There were three new factors that helped Eliade's cause enormously. The first was the founding in the summer of 1961 of a new international journal for comparative historical studies called *History of Religion.* Wisely, Eliade suggested making it an English-language journal instead of a multi-language one. For the opening issue, Eliade wrote the famous article entitled "History of Religions and a New Humanism" (*History of Religions* 1, Summer 1961, pp. 1–8). In it, he expressed his sympathy with young scholars who would have become historians of religions but who, in a world that exalts specialists, had resorted to becoming specialists in one religion or even in a particular period or a single aspect of that religion. Historians of religions, he said, are called to be learned generalists. He recognized the danger of "reductionism" in the history of religions as much as in the interpretation of art and literary works. He insisted that a work of art, for example, reveals its meaning only when it is seen as an autonomous artistic creation and nothing else. In the case of the history of religions he realized that the situation is complex because there is no such thing as a "pure" religious datum, and that a human datum is also a historical datum. But this does not imply that, for historians of religions, a historical datum is in any way reducible to a nonreligious, economic, social, cultural, psychological, or political meaning. And, quoting the words of Raffaele Pettazzoni, he exhorted readers to engage in the twin (systematic and historical) tasks of the history of religions. But to him, ultimately, the history of religions was more than merely an academic pursuit. He wrote:

> The History of Religions is destined to play an important role in contemporary cultural life. This is not only because an understanding of exotic and archaic religions will significantly assist in a cultural dialogue with the representatives of such religions. It is more especially because . . . the history of religions will inevitably attain to a deeper knowledge of man. It is on the basis of such knowledge that a new humanism, on a world-wide scale, could develop. ("History of Religions," pp. 2–3)

Second, Eliade took an active part as a member (and president for a term) of a small group of North American scholars called the American Society for the Study of Religion (ASSR), established in Chicago in 1958. It was through this group that much of Eliade's personal contacts with fellow historians of religions and scholars in related fields in North America were made.

Third, Eliade, who had previously worked either on "systematic" endeavors or on studies of "particular" religious forms (e.g., yoga, shamanism, Romanian folk religion, or Australian religion) always from the perspective of the history of religions, embarked during his Chicago days on a new genre, namely, a "historical" study of the history of religions. Initially he worked on a "thematic source book" entitled *From Primitive to Zen* (1968) dealing with religious data from nonliterate, ancient, medieval, and modern religions. Then he envisaged the publication of four volumes (though his health prevented his working on the fourth volume himself) entitled *A History of Religious Ideas* (1978–1986). Although the scheme of the series follows manifestations of the sacred and the creative moments of the different traditions more or less in chronological order, readers will recognize that these books reflect faithfully his lifelong conviction about the fundamental unity of all religious phenomena. Thus, in his historical studies as much as in his systematic endeavors, he was true to his hypothesis that "every rite, every myth, every belief or divine figure reflects the experience of the sacred and hence implies the notions of *being*, of *meaning*, and of *truth*" (*A History of Religious Ideas*, vol. 1, Chicago, 1978, p. xiii).

During the latter part of his stay in Chicago, fame and honor came his way from various parts of the world. By that time, many of his books, including his literary works, had been translated into several languages. He had his share of critics. Some people thought that he was not religious enough, while others accused him of being too philosophical and not humanistic enough, historical enough, scientific enough, or empirical enough. But, as hinted earlier, he held a consistent viewpoint that penetrated all aspects of his scholarly and literary works, so that it is difficult to be for or against any part of his writings without having to judge the whole framework.

Eliade's last major undertaking in his life was the present *Encyclopedia of Religion.* As he stated himself, what he had in mind was not a dictionary but an encyclopedia—a selection of all the important ideas and beliefs, rituals and myths, symbols and persons, all that played a role in the universal history of the religious experience of humankind from the Paleolithic age to our time. It is to his credit that various scholars from every continent cooperated on the encyclopedia to produce concise, clear descriptions of a number of religious forms within the limits of our present knowledge. As soon as he had completed the major portion of his work as editor in chief of the encyclopedia, he was already thinking of several new projects, among them ones that would develop the themes of cosmos, humankind, and time. Throughout his life, Eliade never claimed that he had the answer to the riddle of life, but he was willing to advance daring hypotheses.

Once Eliade paid a high tribute to his friend and colleague, Paul Tillich, at the latter's memorial service in Chicago, and if the name of Tillich is replaced with that of Eliade, it portrays the latter admirably: "Faithful to his vocation and his destiny [Eliade] did not die at the end of his career, when he had supposedly said everything important that he could say. . . . Thus, his death is even more tragic. But it is also symbolic" (*Criterion* 5, no. 1, 1968, p. 15).

Bibliography

Both as a scholar and as a writer, Eliade was prolific throughout his life, and his works have been translated into many languages. Thus, it is virtually impossible to list all his books and articles, even the major ones, although efforts were made to include the major titles in the foregoing text. Fortunately, there are some Eliade bibliographies in English that are readily available to readers, such as the one included in *Myths and Symbols: Studies in Honor of Mircea Eliade*, edited by Joseph M. Kitagawa and Charles H. Long (Chicago, 1969), and a more up-to-date one, edited by Douglas Allen and Dennis Doeing, *Mircea Eliade: An Annotated Bibliography*, (New York, 1980). One of the best introductions to Eliade's thought is his *Ordeal by Labyrinth: Conversations with Claude-Henri Rocquet* either in its French original (Paris, 1978) or in its English translation (Chicago, 1982). This book has the virtues of unfolding Eliade's own mature views about himself, and it includes "A Chronology of Mircea Eliade's Life," which calls attention to his major writings. There are also many articles and books in various languages on Eliade's scholarly and literary works, some critical, some sympathetic, and some favorable. The third section of the abovementioned *Myths and Symbols*, as well as *Imagination and Meaning: The Scholarly and Literary Worlds of Mircea Eliade*, edited by N. J. Girardot and Mac Linscott Ricketts (New York, 1982), and *Waiting for the Dawn: Mircea Eliade in Perspective*, edited by Davíd Carrasco and J. M. Swanberg (Boulder, 1985), make helpful references to his creative writing, although his scholarly side inevitably comes into the picture too.

There are many other works (mentioning only monographs) that readers should find useful. See Douglas Allen's *Structure and Creativity in Religion: Mircea Eliade's Phenomenology and New Directions* (The Hague, 1978); Thomas J. J. Altizer's *Mircea Eliade and the Dialectic of the Sacred* (Philadelphia, 1963); Guilford Dudley's *Religion on Trial: Mircea Eliade and His Critics* (Philadelphia, 1977); Jonathan Z. Smith's *Map Is Not Territory: Studies in the History of Religions* (Leiden, 1978); Ioan Petro Culianu's *Mircea Eliade* (Assisi, 1978); and Antonio B. de Silva's *The Phenomenology of Religion as a Philosophical Problem: An Analysis of the Theoretical Background of the Phenomenology of Religion, in General, and of M. Eliade's Phenomenological Approach, in Particular* (Uppsala, 1982).

Joseph M. Kitagawa (1987)

ELIADE, MIRCEA [FURTHER CONSIDERATIONS]. Since his death in 1986 Eliade's status has been problematic and the value of his contribution to the academic study of religion has been widely debated. His presence in the English-speaking academic world has diminished since the 1980s. Use of his work in graduate courses has declined, and there has been no repetition of the large-scale conferences on his views such as those held in connection with Carrasco and Swanberg's *Waiting for the Dawn* or Ricketts and Girardot's *Imagination and Meaning.* In the 1990s considerations of his contributions were rare at American Academy of Religion Conferences, and more interest in Eliade's literature was shown by the Modern Language Association, perhaps confirming Eliade's feeling that it would be mainly for his fiction that he would be remembered. However, most of his books remain in print and continue to sell strongly to the popular reader and to academic readers elsewhere in the world.

Despite the defense of his work mounted by some writers, criticism of his thought has been consistent and influential. Beyond the scholarly debate over the academic value of his analytic categories and theoretical approach, a wealth of historical material has become available, the implications of which have also been debated. Romanian and other archives have been investigated in detail, and several biographies have appeared, raising new considerations. Much of this work remains in other European languages and is only slowly becoming available to an English readership. It is worthy of note that despite strident condemnations of Eliade's political past, this material has so far revealed no incontrovertible evidence of egregious wrongdoing. Nevertheless, the case has important implications for scholars' reflexive understanding in the study of religions, emphasizing as it does the need for meticulous self-awareness of possible complicity with institutional power structures.

It might be suggested that since Eliade's death there has been a period in which the significance of the study of Eliade has superseded the significance of his studies of religions. Whether this period will eventually result in the rejection or the rehabilitation of his work remains to be seen, but it is clear that Eliade's legacy requires further investigation. Because of his position as an internationally successful synthesizer of studies of religion, his case has become emblematic of several key issues: the role played by the "great man" figure in the establishment of the academic discipline of the study and teaching of religions; the "insider/outsider" question in the study of religion; historiography and the interpretation of historical evidence in relation to ideology; and the interpenetration of lived experience, political activity, and theoretical categories. As was the case with Martin Heidegger and Paul de Man, later scholars need to understand clearly how scholars' specifically academic production is affected by other activities.

Political Problems. The attempt to unravel Eliade's political position is an exemplar of the task confronting the historian of religions. Unearthing as much data as possible does not complete our undertaking—beyond that, there is always the call to interpret the data and to reach some conclusion while remaining scrupulously conscious of what we ourselves introduce. Eliade's political involvement in interwar Romania was largely unacknowledged in the United States until the late 1980s. However, the works of Ivan Strenski, Adriana Berger, and Leon Volovici raised specific questions: had Eliade been a supporter of the Legion of the Archangel Michael, a militant Romanian, Orthodox/nationalist organization also known as the Iron Guard? Since this organization was openly anti-Semitic, had Eliade been, and did he remain, anti-Semitic himself? The work in French of Daniel Dubuisson and Alexandra Laignel-Lavastine is particularly critical in this respect.

Saul Bellow's 2000 novel, *Ravelstein,* added to these concerns. Bellow was a close friend from Eliade's Chicago years, and the book features a Romanian historian of religions apparently concealing an anti-Semitic past. The same year saw the publication in English of the journal of Eliade's friend of the 1930s, Mihail Sebastian. Sebastian was a Jewish writer who attributed the deterioration of his friendship with Eliade to the latter's politics. Some saw his testimony as conclusive proof that Eliade was, indeed, anti-Semitic. Public reaction is suggested by a letter to the *New Yorker* from Harvey Cox, professor at the Harvard Divinity School ("A Study in Fascism," October 30, 2000), who concluded that Sebastian's *Journal* put Eliade's "virulently anti-Semitic views . . . on the record for all to see."

Even given newly available information, a clear and unambiguous judgment remains difficult to attain. There remains significant doubt that Eliade ever was "virulently anti-Semitic." While Bellow's novel may be inspired by reality, it remains fiction, although Eliade did undeniably champion the Legion of the Archangel Michael. Between January 1937 and February 1938, when he was thirty, Eliade wrote more than a dozen articles in the Legion's support, and there is some evidence that he participated in electioneering for the Legion in December 1937. However, a distinction has to be made between an involvement with the politics of the right and anti-Semitism, and a brief period of political activity does not necessarily indicate a lifelong commitment.

Through the early 1930s Eliade took a deliberately "apolitical" stance in the specific sense of withholding allegiance from the increasingly radical popular parties of both left and right. He saw these parties as rootless, foreign, brutal, and uncultured, and he championed tradition, culture, and the intellect in opposition. However, he was increasingly drawn into a nationalist position whose dangers are now all too well known. After his return from India in 1931, Eliade participated in an intellectual group called Criterion, which brought informed debate of significant issues to the Bucharest public. There were suspicions that this group was crypto-communist, and it had at least two Jewish members, but it also had members whose sympathies were to the right, and in 1932 some of these founded a review called *Axa* (*The Axis*), which gave open support to the Legion. Eliade never contributed to that journal. In fact, in 1933, along with some thirty other intellectuals and artists, he signed a protest against the return to barbarism portended by anti-Semitic persecutions in Hitler's Germany. The same year his article "Racism in the Cinema" protested against "Aryan" racist apologetics, and he explicitly rejected the confusion of nationalism and anti-Semitism in an article objecting to the expulsion from Romania of the Jewish scholars Moses Gaster and Lazăr Şăineanu in 1885 and 1901 respectively. In 1934 he wrote (under the pseudonym "Ion Plăeşu") an article, "Against Left and Right," arguing against the totalitarianism of both political extremes. However, he remained reluctant to become directly involved with political allegiances, even as he sought to clarify their foundations.

In 1934 Sebastian's autobiographical novel on the contemporary position of Romanian Jewish intellectuals appeared. *De două mii de ani* (For Two Thousand Years) bore a preface by the actively right-wing Bucharest philosopher, Nae Ionescu. Ionescu had been the professor and mentor of both Eliade and Sebastian, and editor of the widely circulated review, *Cuvântul,* to which both men had regularly contributed before its prohibition in 1934. His preface was openly anti-Semitic, in theological rather than racial terms, but Sebastian retained it out of loyalty. Eliade responded in print, attempting to mediate between his friend and their professor and to reject the latter's anti-Semitism, again on theological grounds. However, it is obvious that Eliade opposed only the most obvious manifestations of anti-Semitism and failed to appreciate the dangers of other anti-Semitic rhetoric.

At the beginning of 1935 Eliade's journalism openly continued to denounce both Nazism and Communism as forms of modern idolatry that dissolve moral distinctions in favor of biological or social criteria. He maintained his "apolitical" stance, arguing that the greatest weapon of any writer is independence vis-à-vis every political group. Yet it is in this period that the beginnings of his slide into political involvement can be seen. Eliade's "apolitical" stance was criticized from both the left and the right and attracted scant appreciation. His appeal for cultural sophistication rather than the popularist barbarism of political mass movements was largely ignored. The somewhat inept and corrupt incumbent "liberal" government failed to increase financial support for cultural activity but rather increased taxation of authors, provoking censure from Eliade. Even though he was not engaged in Ionescu's political activities, Eliade's friendship with the philosopher and his former affiliation with *Cuvântul* sufficed to establish an initial connection to the right. One of Eliade's perennial themes of the period was the unhappy financial situation of writers in Romania. When the state introduced a duty on writers' royalties in 1935, Eliade was convinced that the money would not be used for cultural advancement and reacted badly. He accused not only the state but also the bourgeois-capitalist public of indifference. Shortly after, he was threatened with the seizure of his furniture in lieu of the duty on his royalties. The refusal of the incumbent government to found an institute of Middle Eastern and Oriental Studies made Eliade sharply aware of the contrast between, for example, fascist Italy, which had such an institute, and Romania, which did not.

Eliade's scorn for the political left at that time was based mainly upon his belief that the principal superstition of the modern period concerns single, universal explanations that effectively remove human freedom. Among these he counted Hegelian historicism, Freudianism, and Marxism. Unable to sympathize with either the left or the incumbent government, Eliade in earlier articles indicated no leanings to the right either. However, in December 1935 he noted that one "youth leader" described his mission as "the reconciliation of Romania with God." Here Eliade saw a religious appeal that called upon neither class struggle, nor political interests, nor economic instincts, nor biological distinctions. The leader was Corneliu Zelea Codreanu, the founder of the Legion of the Archangel Michael, a group formed in a split from the League for National Christian Defense. This was the earliest expression of Eliade's admiration for Codreanu, and it did not, at that time, extend to the movement itself. Eliade seems to have seen Codreanu's "religious" appeal as a means of popularizing the type of cultural creation that he had previously attributed to the intellectual and writer by appealing to deep traditional roots. In another article of the same year, Eliade made it clear that he considered creators of culture to be a country's most potent force—the most effective nationalists, thanks to whom a nation "conquers eternity. . . . No matter what happens in Italy now" he wrote in October 1935, "no historical power can remove Italy from her place in eternity. No revolution, no massacre, no catastrophe can wipe out Dante, Michelangelo, Leonardo" ("România în eternitate," *Vremea,* October 13, 1935). Eliade's disposition to see the Legion as a religious cultural movement was increased by his visit in June 1936 to England as Romanian delegate to the Oxford Group, a Christian revivalist movement. It was this "religious" and "traditional" aspect of the Legion that attracted his open support. (See Nagy-Talavera's work, cited in the bibliography, for a detailed history of the Legion.)

There is disagreement as to whether Eliade actually enrolled in the Legionary movement. No Legionary records remain and possibly none were ever kept. Government archives of the period indicate that the police suspected him of joining sometime in 1935 and belonging to a Legionary cell or "nest" led by Radu Demetrescu Gyr. However, most commentators think it very unlikely that he joined before 1937, and some insist that he belonged to a different nest associated with the journal *Axa.* Thus, police suspicions remain unproven, and no certain evidence of membership has ever been brought forward. What is certain is that he contributed his written support to the Legion and thereby supported an openly anti-Semitic movement whose leader proclaimed a Jewish conspiracy, and whose second-in-command, Ion Moţa, had translated the anti-Semitic propaganda, *The Protocols of the Elders of Zion,* into Romanian.

Eliade's writings themselves express no anti-Semitism of this order. Only three of these "Legionary" articles mention Jews, and it is clear that his was, first and foremost, a rhetoric proceeding from a sentiment of general xenophobia commonly associated with nationalism. He continued to denounce elsewhere the intolerant, vulgar anti-Semitism he perceived around him. In June 1936 he had written an article in homage to Moses Gaster, who had made a large donation of old books and manuscripts to the Romanian Academy. Eliade opposed anti-Semitism that might reduce Romania's culture, as had Gaster's expulsion, but he seemed ready to accept anti-Semitism that would deny Jews equal status with ethnic Romanians. That he was also prepared to deny such status to ethnic Bulgarians and Hungarians hardly excuses this position, but it does put it into perspective: relations between ethnic and non-ethnic Romanians had been problematic since the founding of the nation in 1881.

The Legion was officially proscribed early in 1938, and Eliade's last supportive article appeared in February of that year. Codreanu was arrested in April and clandestinely executed in November. Eliade spent almost four months in a camp for Legionary sympathizers, from July to November, during which time he never acknowledged membership but refused to sign a declaration of separation from the Legion. After his release he ceased to express any sympathies for the Iron Guard but concentrated on his cultural productivity. He was appointed to the press services section of the Romanian Cultural Legation to London in April 1940. This appointment came from the royalist dictatorship that had ordered the execution of Codreanu and the massacre of some 250 Legionaries in 1939. Was Eliade's appointment a sign of his detachment from the remaining Legionaries or, on the contrary, was it a sign of the government's deliberate attempt at a rapprochement with them? That they still had considerable political influence became obvious in September 1940 when a "National Legionary State" was declared in Romania. In the legation in London, Eliade apparently boasted of his support for, and suffering on behalf of, the Legion, but the National Legionary State lasted only four months and Eliade did not benefit from it. In February 1941, when England broke diplomatic relations with Romania, he was posted to neutral Portugal. There he remained until the end of the war, after which he stayed in Paris until his employment by the University of Chicago in 1957. During his tenure as a functionary of the Office of Press and Propaganda of a country allied to Nazi Germany and a state enforcing openly anti-Semitic policies, Eliade produced neither anti-Semitic nor pro-Nazi rhetoric. Several commentators have also mentioned the fact that many colleagues and friends of Eliade's American years were Jewish and not one of them ever detected any sign of anti-Semitism in his deportment. Despite recent determined attempts to disclose anti-Semitism in Eliade's academic work, nothing indubitable has been established.

Biographical Considerations. One factor that has exacerbated suspicions about Eliade's past is his occasional tendency to "mythologize" or "fictionalize" his autobiography. This has been most clearly established in relation to Eliade's period in India but appears to be true of other portions of his life. The sometimes confused relationship between his fiction and his biography perhaps became most pointed in 1994 with the publication in English of both his 1933 novel, *Maitreyi,* and the response to it, also in novel form, from Maitreyi Devi, *It Does not Die.* Maitreyi was the daughter of Eliade's Indian host, Surendranath Dasgupta, and provided the inspiration for the eponymous character in a novel that presented itself as being uncompromisingly realistic. The protagonist of the novel, a Romanian engineer, falls in love with a Bengali woman but loses his love after their clandestine sexual liaison is discovered. Eliade was, in fact, expelled from the Dasgupta household after some kind of romantic relationship between him and Maitreyi became known. The particulars of the accounts in each novel differ considerably, although both conform to that historical basis. The true details of this affair may never be known, and it is fruitless to speculate on them here. However, it is clear that the dividing line between Eliade's biography and his fiction is not always easy to draw.

The Romanian scholar Liviu Bordaş has convincingly demonstrated that Eliade's autobiographical accounts of his stay in India suffer from some confusion of fact and fiction in other respects. Particularly "mythologized" are the accounts of his stay at the ashram at Rishīkesh, implications of esoteric initiation, the account of his forced departure from India after three years in order to satisfy his military service, and the account of his intention to eventually return to a "cave in Himalaya." While the misrepresentation of fact is not radical—six months instead of the actual three at the ashram, the exaggerated "initiation" into Tantric mysteries, his determination to perform his military duty as opposed to his inability to avoid it, and so on—this is enough to cast unfortunate doubt on the veracity of autobiographical details in other instances. Such misrepresentation can only confuse history rather than clarifying anything.

Theoretical Influences. Related to all of the above has been the question of Eliade's formative influences. As already mentioned, he championed tradition against the novelties of modernism. In March 1938 a meeting took place in Bucharest between Corneliu Codreanu and Julius Evola, an ideologue of the Italian fascists and a champion of the idea of a single unified tradition supposedly at the base of all ancient civilizations. Eliade's role in that meeting is unclear. Evola claims that Eliade arranged the meeting; Eliade denied this—but he was involved somehow, and he did have some correspondence with champions of "traditionalist" metaphysics such as Evola and Ananda Coomaraswamy. Some commentators, notably Daniel Dubuisson and Steven Wasserstrom, have argued that this is the most significant single influence on Eliade's understanding of religions. Others (Liviu Bordaş, Natale Spineto, Mac Linscott Ricketts) have made the more convincing case against this, although all recognize that Eliade was certainly not ignorant of traditionalism. A closely allied concern is the role of Eliade's experience of India in the formation of his theoretical position. Once again scholars are divided in their conclusions. Sergiu Al-George, Douglas Allen, and Bordaş emphasize the transformative effect of Eliade's visit to the subcontinent. Ricketts, Wilhelm Danca, Ansgar Paus, and A. F. C. Webster have, on the other hand, emphasized the earlier formative influences of Eastern Orthodoxy on Eliade's thought.

Academic Considerations. All of the above issues have their impact on the scholarly evaluation of Eliade's work, which has left a series of questions with contending answers.

(The annotated bibliography can be consulted for specific scholars who consider the various questions and attempt their own answers.) The clarification of Eliade's political and biographical history, and of his theoretical and cultural influences, would have significant implications for the determination of the utility of his categories and methodology. What is of importance is not so much the putative source of Eliade's terms in Indian, Eastern Orthodox, or traditionalist thought but the degree to which authoritatively identifying such a source could clarify the meaning of his terms. The implication of this must be immediately recognized—these terms are not made entirely clear by Eliade's writings. It is a particularly trenchant criticism that the "literary" prose style that made his work appealing to so many readers, especially to nonspecialists, might make his categories so indeterminate as to be obscurantist rather than helpful. The question then remains and has attracted widely divergent answers—is his analysis of religion finally accurate and coherent, and does it bring any greater clarity?

Equally unclear in the Eliadean corpus is his personal theological position. Although early articles make clear his perhaps surprisingly credulous stance in respect of claims regarding supernatural phenomena and his later theoretical work makes plain his understanding of the sacred as the real par excellence, he has also expressed a modern skepticism concerning a historically incredible God (Ricketts, 1988, p. 123; Norman Girardot in Rennie, 2001). In a body of writing as extensive as Eliade's, it may be unrealistic to expect consistency, but the debate over Eliade's theological position has been perpetuated by such apparent inconsistencies. Some have seen a latent theological agenda in his work, while others have read a strictly phenomenological description of human behaviors. So the question remains: what did Eliade himself believe, and does his personal belief add to or detract from his value as a scholar of religion?

Closely related to the question of Eliade's personal belief are questions concerning the nature of the sacred in Eliade's thought and his normativity. What did Eliade take the sacred to be? An actual and autonomous power? Or does he, rather, describe the apprehension of such power by religious believers? In so doing does he transgress appropriate limitations by assuming the rectitude of his own observations and instructing his readers in what they ought to believe and how they ought to proceed?

Other closely connected questions arising from Eliade's work concern historicism and the ubiquity of religion. It has been one of the most repeated criticisms of Eliade that he is "ahistorical" or perhaps "ahistoricist." That is, his "morphology" ignores the historical context of religious realities, grouping and analyzing by superficial similarities, and also he grants effective agency to "sacred" categories that lack historical autonomy. Eliade's position, most clearly stated in *Cosmos and History: The Myth of the Eternal Return* (1954), is that the modern evaluation of historical realities as the only source of significance, meaning, truth, and power is itself an ascription of a religious nature, brought about by developments in the history of religions. Thus, even modern historicists who limit all effective causality to historical realities can be classed as religious in this way. This gives rise to another of Eliade's widely critiqued claims: the ubiquity of religion. All human beings are religious according to the preface to *The Quest* (1969), and that the sacred is a ubiquitous category of human consciousness is his frequently repeated claim. Scholarly consensus is lacking with respect to these questions, too. Is it appropriate to describe all of humanity as religious? Is it at all helpful to redefine religion in such a way as to remove the possibility of entirely "nonreligious" people? Is it at all meaningful to recognize the active agency of "ahistorical entities"? Here the central question of reductionism appears. Eliade takes religion and religiousness to be irreducible realities. That is, they cannot be explained or defined without remainder in entirely nonreligious terms. Religion is thus a reality sui generis—of its own unique natural sort. These, too, are undecided issues in the study of religion.

The initial approach and institutional training of scholars of religion will never be disconnected from their answers to any of these questions. Those who prefer to conceive of the study of religion as an enterprise more closely allied to the social sciences than to the humanities will tend to avoid dependence upon empirically unavailable and thus "nonhistorical" concepts and categories and will be more ready to recognize a religious/nonreligious dichotomy determined along lines of dependence upon or independence from such concepts and categories. Those who prefer to conceive of the study of religion as a humanistic discipline more closely allied to a philosophical and cultural anthropology will be more open to the consideration of religious concepts and categories as the effective products of human culture whose "historical reality" may thus be constrained but is nonetheless factual. In this context the English-language distinction between the humanities and the sciences is less helpful than the Germanic distinction between *Geisteswissenschaft* and *Naturswissenschaft*. Eliade's history of religions clearly belongs to the former—on that one point at least consensus can be reached. Whatever is finally deemed to be the value of the Eliadean oeuvre, the clarification of the questions raised in its consideration can only serve to further clarify our understanding of religion and the processes involved in its study.

BIBLIOGRAPHY

The bibliography for Eliade studies is extensive. For Eliade's own works those books mentioned in the main entry on Eliade are helpful, and there is a compact but quite extensive bibliography in Rennie (1996). The most exhaustive bibliography to date is the three-volume *Biobibliografie* by Mircea Handoca, which, despite being written in Romanian, is useful to all readers since it lists Eliade's works in the languages of publication. The following works include the most significant arguments raised since his death.

Al-George, Sergiu. "India in the Cultural Destiny of Mircea Eliade." *The Mankind Quarterly* 25 (1984): 115–135. This is a consideration of Eliade's debt to Indian thought.

Allen, Douglas. *Myth and Religion in Mircea Eliade.* New York and London, 1998. Broadly favorable to Eliade as a useful guide in the study of religions, Allen's major concentration is on Eliade's normative claims.

Bellow, Saul. *Ravelstein.* New York, 2000. Despite being a fictional novel, some have seen the fact that this work was written by a close friend who spoke at Eliade's funeral as a guarantee of its historical accuracy. Closely based on Bellow's friend, Allan Bloom, the eponymous protagonist of the novel constantly warns the Jewish author that one Radu Grielecu, a Romanian professor at the University of Chicago, was once a member of the Iron Guard.

Berger, A. "Fascism and Religion in Romania." *The Annals of Scholarship* 6 no. 4 (1989): 455–465.

Berger, A. "Anti-Judaism and Anti-Historicism in Eliade's Writings." In *Tainted Greatness: Antisemitism and Cultural Heroes,* edited by Nancy A. Harrowitz, pp. 51–74. Philadelphia, 1994. Berger's earlier articles are appreciative of Eliade's theoretical position. However, in her two later articles Berger details her increasing conviction that Eliade was tainted with an anti-Semitism that pervaded his history of religions.

Cave, John David. *Mircea Eliade's Vision for a New Humanism.* New York, 1992. In a generally appreciative consideration of Eliade, Cave focuses on his new humanism as the key to understanding the scholar's thought.

Culianu, Ioan P., ed. *Geschichte der religiösen Ideen.* Vol. 4: *Vom Zeitalter der Entdeckungen bis zur Gegenwart.* Freiburg im Breisgau, Germany, 1991. Planned as a four-volume work, Eliade's *History of Religious Ideas* was not finished before his death. This entirely German anthology seeks to complete the project.

Devi, Maitreyi. *It Does Not Die: A Romance.* Calcutta, 1976. Reprinted Chicago, 1994. The response in novel form to Eliade's novel *Maitreyi* (*Bengal Nights*) by the eponymous heroine.

Dubuisson, Daniel. *Mythologies du XXe Siècle (Dumézil, Lévi-Strauss, Eliade).* Lille, France, 1993. A consideration of the three thinkers that concludes that Eliade's anti-Semitism pervades the whole of his ontological understanding of the history of religions.

Duerr, Hans Peter. *Die Mitte der Welt: Aufsätze zu Mircea Eliade.* Frankfurt am Main, Germany, 1984. A collection of articles about Eliade by authors including Paul Ricoeur, Kurt Rudolf, Ninian Smart, Ugo Bianchi, Douglas Allen, Zwi Werblowski, T. J. J. Altizer, Emile Cioran, Ioan Culianu, Mac Linscott Ricketts, Joseph Kitagawa, Adrian Marino, Eugen Simion, and Matei Calinescu.

Eliade, Mircea. *Bengal Nights.* Chicago, 1994. The English translation of Eliade's 1933 *Maitreyi.* This is the fictionalized account of Eliade's amorous relationship with the daughter of his Indian host, Surendranath Dasgupta.

Girardot, Norman. "Whispers and Smiles: Nostalgic Reflections on Mircea Eliade's Significance for the Study of Religion." In *Changing Religious Worlds: The Meaning and End of Mircea Eliade,* edited by Bryan Rennie, pp. 143–163. Albany, N.Y., 2001. Based on the author's reflections on his acquaintance with Eliade, this touches on the questions of personal belief and integrity.

Handoca, Mircea. *Mircea Eliade: Biobibliografie.* 3 vols. Bucharest, 1997, 1998, 1999. The most complete bibliography of Eliade's prodigious output yet compiled.

Idinopulos, Thomas A., and Edward Yonan. *Religion and Reductionism: Essays on Eliade, Segal, and the Challenge of the Social Sciences for the Study of Religion.* Leiden, Netherlands, 1994. Critical considerations by various authors of the question of reductionism and the interrelations of Eliade, Robert Segal, and the social scientific approach to the study of religion.

Laignel-Lavastine, Alexandra. *Cioran, Eliade, Ionesco: L'Oubli di Fascisme.* Paris, 2002. One of the most detailed attempts to assert Eliade's long-standing commitment to the Iron Guard. Despite its apparent thoroughness, this work shows signs of prejudgment and selective use of sources and has been called "excessively polemical" even by Eliade's critics.

McCutcheon, Russell T. "The Myth of the Apolitical Scholar." *Queen's Quarterly* 100 (1993): 642–646. A consideration of Eliade's case and his claims to "apolitical" status. What are the implications of an acceptance of Eliade's "apolitical" claims?

McCutcheon, Russell T. *Manufacturing Religion: The Discourse on* Sui Generis *Religion and the Politics of Nostalgia.* New York, 1997. An example of the post-Eliadean critique, particularly concerning the sui generis nature of religion.

Nagy-Talavera, Nicholas. *The Green Shirts and the Others: A History of Fascism in Hungary and Romania.* Iaşi, Oxford, and Portland, Ore., 2001. A general history of Hungarian and Romanian militant nationalism, especially of the "Green Shirts," that is, Codreanu's Iron Guard.

Olsen, Carl. *The Theology and Philosophy of Eliade.* New York, 1992. An attempt to evaluate Eliade's analysis of religion as revealing his own theology and philosophy. Olsen concentrates on the symbolism of the search for the center and Eliade's search for his own center.

Paden, William. "Before the Sacred became Theological: Rereading the Durkheimian Legacy." In *Religion and Reductionism: Essays on Eliade, Segal, and the Challenge of the Social Sciences for the Study of Religion,* edited by Thomas A. Idinopulos and Edward Yonan, pp. 198–209. Leiden, Netherlands, 1994. Paden argues that Eliade's concept of the sacred owes more to the Durkheimian understanding of the sacred as a human attribution than to Rudolf Otto's numinous sacred.

Paus, Ansgar. "The Secret Nostalgia of Mircea Eliade for Paradise: Observations on Method in the Study of Religion." *Religion* 19 (1989): 137–150. In a perception of Eliade as a "secularized mystic," Paus considers his Eastern Orthodox influences.

Rennie, Bryan. *Reconstructing Eliade: Making Sense of Religion.* Albany, N.Y., 1996. An attempt to clarify the categories of Eliade's thought and account for their prevalent misunderstanding. This addresses the questions of anti-Semitism, latent theology, and attitudes to history.

Rennie, Bryan. *Changing Religious Worlds: The Meaning and End of Mircea Eliade.* Albany, N.Y., 2001. An anthology of Anglophone scholars both critical and appreciative of Eliade, including a previously unpublished short story by Eliade and extracts from his Indian journals.

Rennie, Bryan. Review of *Journal, 1935–1944: The Fascist Years,* by Mihail Sebastian. *Religion* 32, no. 2 (2002): 172–175.

Rennie, Bryan. "Religion after Religion, History after History: Postmodern Historiography and the Study of Religions." *Method and Theory in the Study of Religion* 15, no. 3 (2003): 68–99. A consideration of contemporary understandings of the problems of historiography, including a response to Steven Wasserstrom's critique of Eliade.

Rennie, Bryan. *The International Eliade.* Albany, N.Y., 2005. An anthology of essays from non-Anglophone scholars, including considerations of many of the open questions of Eliade scholarship and an Eliade play from 1944.

Ricketts, Mac Linscott. *Mircea Eliade: The Romanian Roots, 1907–1945.* Vols. 1 and 2. New York, 1988. This meticulously researched biography of Eliade's early life reveals most of the historical details later debated.

Ricketts, Mac Linscott. *Former Friends and Forgotten Facts.* Norcross, Ga., 2003. A compilation of papers revealing in detail the inaccuracies of some criticisms of Eliade.

Ries, Julien, and Natale Spineto, eds. *Esploratori del pensiero umano. Georges Dumézil e Mircea Eliade.* Milan, 2000, pp. 201–248. Also published in French: *Deux explorateurs de la pensée humaine: Georges Dumézil et Mircea Eliade.* Turnhout, Belgium, 2003. A collection of articles on Dumézil and/or Eliade. Douglas Allen and Mac Linscott Ricketts contribute in English, while others write in Italian or French. Noteworthy are contributions by Natale Spineto, Roberto Scagno, Julien Ries, Natale Terrin, and Mircea Handoca.

Sebastian, Mihail. *Journal: 1935–1944.* Chicago, 2000. An important insight into the dynamics of anti-Semitism in 1930s Romania, Sebastian's *Journal* gives an alternative insight into Eliade's development.

Simion, Eugen. *Mircea Eliade: A Spirit of Amplitude.* New York, 2001. A detailed analysis of Eliade's literary work by the president of the Romanian Academy, who is also a professor of Romanian literature at the Sorbonne, Paris.

Smith, J. Z. *Imagining Religion: From Babylon to Jonestown.* Chicago, 1982.

Smith, J. Z. *To Take Place: Toward Theory in Ritual.* Chicago, 1987.

Smith, J. Z. *Map Is Not Territory: Studies in the History of Religions.* Chicago, 1993.

Smith, J. Z. *Relating Religion: Essays in the Study of Religion.* Chicago, 2004. Although almost all general works on the history of religions and the study of religion mention Eliade, those of J. Z. Smith are particularly thoughtful and critical, although they are not specialist studies of the complexity of the Eliadean oeuvre.

Spineto, Natale, ed. *Mircea Eliade, Raffaele Pettazzoni, L'Histoire des religions a-t-elle un sens? Correspondance 1926–1959.* Paris, 1994. This volume is an important insight into Eliade's thought by way of his lengthy correspondence with the Italian historian of religions.

Strenski, I. "Mircea Eliade: Some Theoretical Problems." In *The Theory of Myth: Six Studies,* edited by Adrian Cunningham, pp. 40–78. London, 1973.

Strenski, I. "Love and Anarchy in Romania." *Religion* 12 no. 4 (1982): 391–404.

Timuş, Mihaela, and Eugen Ciurtin. "The Unpublished Correspondence between Mircea Eliade and Stig Wikander (1948–1977)." Four Parts: *Archævs: Études D'Histoire des Religions* 4, no. 3 (2000): 157–185; 4, no. 4 (2000): 179–208; 5, nos. 3–4 (2001): 75–119; 6, nos. 3–4 (2002): 325–394. Although published in a Romanian journal of limited circulation, this is a valuable complement to the study of Eliade's life and thought.

Turcanu, Florin. *Mircea Eliade: Le Prisonnier de l'Histoire.* Paris, 2003. A detailed and well-researched biography that covers Eliade's entire life and avoids most of the polemical prejudgments of the Laignel-Lavastine volume.

Volovici, Leon. *Nationalist Ideology and Antisemitism: The Case of Romanian Intellectuals in the 30s.* New York, 1991. Although Volovici is not a specialist on Eliade, this clearly indicates the sources of the suspicions directed against him.

Wasserstrom, Steven. *Religion after Religion: Gershom Scholem, Mircea Eliade, and Henri Corbin at Eranos.* Princeton, N.J., 1999. A very well-written and compelling account of the implications of those historians of religions who attended C. G. Jung's Eranos conferences. This work is perhaps one of those showing evidence of somewhat forced argument concerning Eliade's anti-Semitism.

Webster, A. F. C. "Orthodox Mystical Tradition and the Comparative Study of Religion: An Experimental Synthesis." *Journal of Ecumenical Studies* 23 (1986): 621–649. Webster raised the question of the role of Eastern Orthodoxy in Eliade's understanding of religion. It is to be hoped that this topic will attract further study.

BRYAN S. RENNIE (2005)

ELIʿEZER BEN HYRCANUS, also known as Eliʿezer the Great, but usually simply as Rabbi Eliʿezer, was a Jewish sage of the late first and early second centuries CE, the first generation of the tannaitic period. The legends surrounding Eliʿezer's beginnings, although contradictory, are united in seeking to create an aura of greatness. According to the dominant tradition, Eliʿezer, like ʿAqivaʾ ben Yosef, was an adult before he began his studies. Despite this, he was soon found to be "explicating matters that no ear had ever before heard." Elsewhere, Eliʿezer is described as a child prodigy, and those who saw him as a child predicted that he would one day be a great sage. The legends about Eliʿezer convey a close association between him and Yoḥanan ben Zakkʾai, whom Eliʿezer and his colleague Yehoshuʿa ben Hananyah were entrusted to smuggle in a coffin from the embattled Jerusalem. The same association is emphasized in *Avot* (2.8), where Yoḥanan declares that Eliʿezer's great wisdom outweighs that of all the sages of Israel.

Eliʿezer's statements regarding himself reflect what might be termed an intense, even obsessive work ethic. He describes his extraordinary perseverance in Torah study (B.T., *Suk.* 28a), and in the same tradition he claims never to have uttered a profane word. Elsewhere Eliʿezer voices suspicion of sexuality. Most crucial, perhaps, is the claim of extreme conservatism in matters of tradition ascribed to Eliʿezer; he declares that he "never uttered a word that he did not hear from his teacher" (ibid.). Although not literally true, this accurately portrays the conservatism of Eliʿezer's legal opinions. Eliʿezer's legal concerns closely parallel those of his Pharisaic predecessors, to the extent that they can be reconstructed. His exegetical method is also often conservative, a tendency that sometimes leads him to conclusions that are harshly literal.

A picture of Eliʿezer's persona is derived to a great extent from reports of an event that led to his ban (*ḥerem*) from rabbinical circles. The traditions that describe the precipitating event (B.T., *B.M.* 59b; J.T. *Moʿed Q.* 3.1, 81c–d), composed long after it occurred, are not unified in their description, but they agree that the immediate dispute concerned the ritual purity of a certain oven ("the oven of ʿAkhnʾai"), and they appear to agree that Eliʿezer's refusal to submit to the will of the majority was the cause for his ban. This is a compelling explanation because contemporary conditions demanded cooperation with the new rabbinic center of power, the authority of which Eliʿezer was challenging. Still, other explanations for Eliʿezer's exclusion developed. One suggests that Eliʿezer's offense was his ascription to *beit Shammai* (the school of Shammai). Although widely repeated, there is no support for this conclusion in earlier sources. Another possible explanation is suggested by an enigmatic tradition that speaks of Eliʿezer's arrest for dealings with *minim* ("sectarians"; Christians?). Whatever the reason, the effect of the ban is felt in a wide variety of sources. This is particularly true in the traditions that describe Eliʿezer's death (where Yehoshuʿa arose and declared "the vow is annulled"), but it extends even to the Mishnah itself, where a few of Eliʿezer's views are explicitly suppressed.

Despite this, Eliʿezer's immense contribution to the rabbinic corpus is indicative of the respect that his genius commanded. Eliʿezer is mentioned by name in the Mishnah more often than any of his contemporaries. His opinions are often debated in the Talmuds, and despite his ban, they form the basis of halakhic (legal) decisions. Legend reflects the same conclusion. Even the text that describes the ban demonstrates heavenly support for Eliʿezer's view, support that is repeated elsewhere. Much later, respect for Eliʿezer led to the pseudonymous attribution of the Midrashic work *Pirqei de-Rabbi Eliʿezer* (ninth century) to him.

Eliʿezer's contributions are particularly prevalent in the areas of purity and sacrifice, perhaps a reflection of his belief that the Temple would soon be rebuilt. He was a zealot for the circumcision ritual, preparation for which he permitted even on the Sabbath. In matters of commandment and transgression he was concerned for the act, and not the intention.

SEE ALSO Tannaim.

BIBLIOGRAPHY

By far the best work on Eliʿezer is *Eliezer ben Hyrcanus: The Tradition and the Man,* 2 vols. (Leiden, 1973), by Jacob Neusner. Though one might dispute individual interpretations or conclusions, Neusner's work is comprehensive and his method superior to any employed previously. A useful synthetic analysis of Eliʿezer's legal traditions is Itzchak Gilath's *Rabbi Eliezer ben Hyrcanus: A Scholar Outcast* (Ramat Gan, Israel, 1984). A full review of the literature on Eliʿezer is given in volume 2 of Neusner's book, pages 249–286.

New Sources

Goldin, Judah. "On the Account of the Banning of R. Eliezer ben Hyrqanus: An Analysis and Proposal." *JANES* 16–17 (1987): 85–97.

Gutoff, Joshua. "The Necessary Outlaw: The Catastrophic Excommunication & Paradoxical Rehabilitation of Rabbi Eliezer ben Hyrcanus." *Journal of Law and Religion* 11 (1994–1995): 733–748.

Jaffé, Dan. "Les relations entre les Sages et les judéo-chrétiens durant l'époque de la Mishna; R. Eliézer ben Hyrcanus et Jacob le 'min' disciple de Jésus de Nazareth." *Pardès* 35 (2003): 57–77.

DAVID KRAEMER (1987)
Revised Bibliography

ELIJAH (mid-ninth century BCE), or, in Hebrew, Eliyyahu, was a prophet of the northern kingdom of Israel during the reigns of Ahab and Ahaziah and a leader in the opposition to the worship of Baal in Israel.

HISTORICITY OF ELIJAH. While few scholars doubt the existence of Elijah as a religious figure of great personal dynamism and conservative zeal and as the leader of resistance to the rise of Baal worship in Israel in the ninth century BCE, the biblical presentation of the prophet cannot be taken as historical documentation of his activity. His career is presented through the eyes of popular legend and subsequent theological reflection, which consider him a personality of heroic proportions. In this process his actions and relations to the people and the king became stereotyped, and the presentation of his behavior, paradigmatic. The politics of the reign of Ahab (c. 869–850 BCE) provided an appropriate occasion for cultural and religious conflict between conservative elements in Israel and the foreign Phoenician influence at the court in Samaria. But how closely the portrayal of that controversy in the biblical story of Elijah corresponds to the actual situation is an issue that cannot be easily resolved.

LITERARY SOURCES. The reason for the difficulty in assessing the biblical figure of Elijah lies in the nature of the literary sources that are contained in *1 Kings* 17–19 and 21 and *2 Kings* 1–2. (An additional story in *2 Chronicles* 21:12–15 about a letter from Elijah to Jehoram, king of Judah, is the Chronicler's invention and cannot be taken seriously as part of the Elijah tradition.) The stories about Elijah in *Kings* do not represent a unified tradition or the work of one author. Episodes narrated in *1 Kings* 20 and 22, involving two other prophets, interrupt the account of Elijah's career and give a somewhat different view of Ahab and the court. But even when these are bracketed, the resulting presentation can hardly be derived from one literary source or author. In fact, at least three separate sources may be identified: (1) *1 Kings* 17–19, usually regarded as the oldest story and the nucleus of the Elijah tradition; (2) *1 Kings* 21 and *2 Kings* 1, stories composed by the historian of *Kings* or extensively edited by him; and (3) *2 Kings* 2, an account of the transition of the prophetic office to Elisha, which is regarded as belonging to the collection of Elisha stories.

Biblical Tradition. The historian's view of Elijah in *1 Kings* 21 and *2 Kings* 1 is stereotyped. It represents the prophet as a spokesperson for the deity in issuing a reprimand and a word of judgment upon the king; Elijah's role here is similar to the role of other prophets in this source. The remarks in *2 Kings* 1:9–16 about Elijah calling down fire from heaven upon the king's soldiers present the prophet in a somewhat different role, that is, as a wonder-worker. But these verses seem superfluous; because nothing is altered by this activity, the unit has often been viewed as a later addition. Only the description of Elijah as an ascetic who wore haircloth and a leather girdle (*2 Kgs.* 1:8) suggests a distinctive tradition about an unusual personality. What is noteworthy, however, is that the historian's treatment of Elijah in *1 Kings* 21 and *2 Kings* 1 does not reflect any knowledge of the stories contained in *1 Kings* 17–19 or any suggestion of Elijah's miraculous powers.

The impression of Elijah as a major personality in Israelite history is based upon the stories in *1 Kings* 17–19. Here Elijah is a recluse and a solitary figure fed by ravens in a remote region, as well as a wonder-worker who can withhold or bring rain "by my word," who can feed a starving widow's family, and who can raise the widow's son from the dead. These stories are based upon the prophetic legend, some of them paralleling similar legends about Elisha. But all the scenes and episodes in *1 Kings* 17–19, whatever their origin, have been subordinated to the purpose of portraying the theological theme "Yahveh is God," which is also the meaning of Elijah's name.

The affirmation that Yahveh is God is demonstrated first of all by the announcement of the drought and the final coming of the rain, the events that frame and provide the background for all the scenes within chapters 17 and 18. Each episode represents a contest between Yahveh, the God of Israel, and Baal, god of the Phoenicians, whose worshipers regard him as god of the storm and the giver of rain and fertility. The contest comes to a head on Mount Carmel when the 450 prophets of Baal are unable to produce fire from heaven for their altar, while Elijah, the single prophet of Yahveh, produces fire for his altar and wins the people over. The prophets of Baal are slain, and then comes the rain. This struggle between Yahveh and Baal is not just for territory but is meant to convince Israel that Yahveh alone is God. The issue in the story is monotheism.

The flight of the prophet to Mount Horeb (*1 Kgs.* 19) takes up the theme of the faithful remnant who remains true to Yahveh as the only God in the face of great adversity. For this purpose the fear-inspiring prophet now becomes the fearful fugitive who must learn that God is not present to his people primarily in the theophany of a storm (as with Baal) but in the quiet voice of inner conviction. The faithful remnant are ultimately vindicated by the subsequent events of history.

Many scholars regard the stories in *1 Kings* 17–19 as early, even of the ninth century, and as an independent composition prior to its incorporation into the history of *Kings*. This, however, seems unlikely, because these chapters reflect nothing of the historian's editing and seem to be unknown to him. It is more plausible to suggest that *1 Kings* 17–19 is a later addition to the history of *Kings*. In it the author has portrayed the life of the prophet in such a way as to make him the medium for a theological message, one that expresses the major concerns of the exilic period. Whatever traditions lie behind these stories, they are now so thoroughly reshaped by the writer's theological interests that they cannot be recovered by a tradition history.

The story of Elijah's ascent to heaven in a chariot of fire while Elisha looks on and receives a portion of his spirit (*2 Kgs.* 2) presupposes both the reputation of Elijah as an exceptional "man of God" and the subsequent career of Elisha as wonder-worker. It was probably composed to bridge the two bodies of tradition but belongs more closely to the Elisha stories.

The manner of Elijah's ascension is so remarkable within the biblical tradition that it calls for some comment. Scholars have been quick to note that the chariot and horses of fire are strongly reminiscent of the fiery chariot of the sun so widely attested in antiquity and even in the Hebrew scriptures (*2 Kgs.* 23:11). Does this account suggest that Elijah was transported by the deity himself to a realm beyond death? Or is this an attempt to assimilate a foreign religious symbol by association with a great figure in Israel's own tradition? Whatever the explanation, the story is so exceptional in the Bible that it sets Elijah, along with Moses and Enoch, quite apart from all other mortals as one who did not die.

Finally, in *Malachi* 3:23–24 (Eng. version 4:5–6) Elijah is viewed as returning to Israel to bring the Israelites to repentance before the day of judgment. Perhaps this return is based upon the notion that Elijah never actually experienced death.

Elijah in the New Testament. The New Testament places special emphasis upon Elijah as the forerunner of the messianic age. It seems to have regarded John the Baptist and his ministry of repentance as performing in the "spirit and power of Elijah" (*Lk.* 1:17; cf. *Mt.* 11:14, 17:10–13) and as an appropriate preparation for the ministry of Jesus as the Messiah. Yet the writer of John's gospel has John the Baptist reject his identification with Elijah (*Jn.* 1:21) so as not to detract from the importance of Jesus' ministry.

Elijah also appears in a vision together with Moses at the scene of Jesus' transfiguration to speak about Jesus' own "departure" (*Mt.* 17:3–4, *Mk.* 9:4–5, *Lk.* 9:30–31). The fact that the scene is associated with prayer and a trancelike experience suggests a connection with a mystical tradition.

Elijah in Postbiblical Judaism. The biblical tradition of Elijah received a great deal of attention in Judaism: in the apocalyptic tradition, in rabbinic *aggadah,* in Jewish mysticism, and in folklore (see Ginzberg, 1909–1938). It is remarkable how the figure of Elijah could become all things to all people.

As in Christianity, Elijah was the forerunner of the messianic age, the herald of Israel's redemption (Ginzberg, 1909–1938, pp. 233–235). He would cooperate with the Messiah as a conqueror of the world powers, he would solve all the halakhic problems that still remained to be dealt with (B.T., *Meg.* 15b; *Sheq.* 2.5; *B.M.* 3.4–5), and as the one to blow the last trumpet, he would be responsible for the resurrection of the dead. He would also restore the lost furnishings of the Temple and provide for the anointing of the Messiah (*Mekhilta' de-Rabbi Shim'on bar Yoḥ'ai* 51b).

Not only is Elijah thought of in connection with the future, but he also continues to play an active role in this present age by virtue of the fact that he never actually died. Because he ascended to heaven in a miraculous way and was translated into a realm of existence akin to that of a divine being or angel, he seems to have been regarded as a special heavenly emissary who could appear in human form to righteous persons either to instruct them or to aid them in time of trouble (see Ginzberg, 1909–1938, pp. 201–203). The mystical tradition went so far as to suggest that Elijah was not human but an angel who appeared on earth for a time in human form. Perhaps as a counter to excessive veneration of the prophet, some rabbis argued that Elijah had died (B. T., *Suk.* 5a) in spite of the biblical tradition about his ascension. They were also critical of some aspects of his ministry (B.T., *B.M.* 85b; *Sg. Rab.* 1.6.1). But any efforts to downplay the prophet's reputation seem to have had little effect.

Elijah's mediation between the heavenly realm and the mundane world expressed itself in a variety of ways. To those engrossed in the study of the law Elijah might appear in a vision or dream as their counselor or teacher because he was known for his zeal for the law and the covenant (Ginzberg, 1909–1938, pp. 217–223). He was often compared with Moses, especially as one who had also received a revelation of God at Mount Horeb. A number of sayings in the Talmud are attributed to a "school of Elijah," perhaps a school founded in his honor. But in later times this notion developed into a large collection of *midrashim, Tanna de-vei Eliyyahu* (also known as *Seder Eliyyahu Rabbah* and *Zuṭa'*), which was believed to stem in some way from Elijah himself.

To the mystics of the Qabbalah Elijah was also a mystagogue who had access to the heavenly realm and could reveal its secrets (Ginzberg, 1909–1938, pp. 229–233). To others Elijah was a psychopomp who transported the souls of the righteous to paradise and the wicked to perdition (*Pirqei de-Rabbi Eli'ezer* 15). In Jewish folklore Elijah was regarded as one who still roamed the earth in the guise of a beggar or a peasant performing wondrous deeds to help the poor and the needy (Ginzberg, 1909–1938, pp. 202–211). On this level too Elijah became associated with the veneration of a number of places, either because they were identified with events in the biblical tradition or because they were places where Elijah had appeared to later generations and performed his miracles.

A number of customs are also connected with the figure of Elijah. At the ceremony of circumcision a chair is set for him in order to invoke his presence as "angel of the covenant" of Abraham to oversee and, by proxy, to carry out the requirements of the law. Elijah was also regarded as healer and guardian of the newborn because of his care for the widow's son. In this respect amulets containing the name of the prophet were good luck charms. At the Passover Seder a cup of wine is placed on the table as the cup of Elijah and is not drunk. This was interpreted eschatologically as an anticipation of the final deliverance from bondage.

Bibliography

There are few detailed monographs in English on the Elijah tradition. In German the standard treatments are Georg Fohrer's *Elia,* 2d ed. (Zurich, 1968); and Odil H. Steck's *Überlieferung und Zeitgeschichte in den Elia-Erzählungen* (Neukirchen, 1968). Two shorter essays worthy of mention are Harold H. Rowley's "Elijah on Mount Carmel," *Bulletin of the John Rylands Library* (Manchester) 43 (1960): 190–219, reprinted in his *Men of God* (New York, 1963); and Ernst Würthwein's "Elijah at Horeb: Reflections on *1 Kings* 19.9–18," in *Proclamation and Presence: Old Testament Essays in Honour of Gwynne Henton Davies,* edited by John I. Durham and J. Roy Porter (London, 1970), pp. 152–166.

For a sociological approach to the tradition, see Robert R. Wilson's *Prophecy and Society in Ancient Israel* (Philadelphia, 1980), pp. 192–200. For a psychological perspective, see Aaron Wiener's *The Prophet Elijah in the Development of Judaism: A Depth-Psychological Study* (East Brunswick, N.J., 1978).

An older but very useful commentary is the one by James A. Montgomery, *A Critical and Exegetical Commentary on the Books of Kings,* edited by Henry S. Gehman (New York, 1951). Materials on the biblical tradition of Elijah are collected in Louis Ginzberg's *The Legends of the Jews,* vol. 4 (Philadelphia, 1913), pp. 189–235, with notes in vol. 6, pp. 316–342. Especially helpful for materials on the later Jewish and Christian traditions are the articles under "Elijah" in *Encyclopaedia Judaica* (Jerusalem, 1971) and those under "Elia" in *Theologische Realenzyklopädie* (New York, 1982). This last work has a very full and up-to-date bibliography.

New Sources

Coote, Robert B., ed. *Elijah and Elisha in Socioliterary Perspective.* Atlanta, 1992.

Keinänen, Jyrki. *Traditions in Collision: A Literary and Redaction-Critical Study on the Elijah Narratives 1 Kings 17–19.* Publications of the Finnish Exegetical Society, no. 80. Helsinki, 2001.

Merchant, William Moelwyn. *Fire from the Heights.* Princeton Theological Monograph Series, no. 27. Allison Park, Penn., 1991.

Otto, Susanne. "The Composition of the Elijah-Elisha Stories and the Deuteronomistic History." *JSOT* 27 (2003): 487–508.

Speyr, Adrienne von. *Elijah.* Translated by Brian McNeil. San Francisco, 1990.

JOHN VAN SETERS (1987)
Revised Bibliography

ELIJAH BEN SOLOMUN ZALMAN SEE ELIYYAHU BEN SHELOMOH ZALMAN

ELIJAH MUHAMMAD (1897–1975), major leader of the American Black Muslim movement, the Nation of Islam, for forty-one years. Born Robert Elijah Poole on October 10, 1897, near Sandersville, Georgia, he was one of thirteen children of an itinerant Baptist preacher. He attended rural schools but dropped out at the fourth grade to become a sharecropper in order to help his family. In 1919 Poole married Clara Evans and in 1923 his family joined the black migration from the South, moving to Detroit. For six years, until the beginning of the Great Depression, he worked at various jobs in industrial plants. From 1929 to 1931 Poole and his family survived on charity and relief, an experience that was reflected in his later hostility toward any form of public assistance and in his strong emphasis on a program of economic self-help for the Nation of Islam. "Do for self" became his rallying cry.

In 1931 Poole met Wallace D. Fard (1877?–1934?, also known, among other aliases, as Walli Farrad and Prophet Fard), who had established the first Temple of Islam in Detroit. He became a totally devoted follower of Prophet Fard and was consequently chosen by Fard as a chief aide and lieutenant. Fard named him "minister of Islam," made him drop his "slave name," Poole, and restored his "true Muslim name," Muhammad. Fard mysteriously disappeared in 1934, and, after some internal conflict among Fard's followers, Elijah Muhammad led a major faction to Chicago, where he established Temple No. 2, which became the main headquarters for the Nation of Islam. He also instituted the worship of Prophet Fard as Allah and of himself as the Messenger of Allah. As head of the Nation of Islam, Elijah Muhammad was always addressed as "the Honorable." He built on the teachings of Fard and combined aspects of Islam and Christianity with the black nationalism of Marcus Garvey (1887–1940) into an unorthodox Islam with a strong racial slant. His message of racial separation focused on the recognition of true black identity and stressed economic independence.

Elijah Muhammad spent four years of a five-year sentence in federal prison for encouraging draft refusal during World War II. After his release in 1946 the movement spread rapidly, especially with the aid of his chief protégé, Malcolm X (1925–1965). During its peak years the Nation of Islam numbered more than half a million devoted followers, influenced millions more, and accumulated an economic empire worth an estimated eighty million dollars. Elijah Muhammad died on February 25, 1975, in Chicago and was succeeded by one of his six sons, Wallace Deen Muhammad.

SEE ALSO Malcolm X.

BIBLIOGRAPHY

Clegge, Claude III. *An Original Man: The Life and Times of Elijah Muhammad.* New York, 1997. A biography of Elijah Muhammad.

Elijah Muhammad. *The Supreme Wisdom: Solution to the So-Called Negroe's Problem.* Chicago, 1957.

Elijah Muhammad. *Message to the Blackman in America.* Chicago, 1965.

Essien-Udom, E. U. *Black Nationalism: A Search for an Identity in America.* Chicago, 1962. A sociological study of the Nation of Islam in Chicago.

Lincoln, C. Eric. *The Black Muslims in America.* Boston, 1961. Lincoln was officially given access to the Nation of Islam by Elijah Muhammad, and his study remains the best historical overview of the development of the movement.

Mamiya, Lawrence H. "Minister Louis Farrakhan and the Final Call: Schism in the Muslim Movement." In *The Muslim Community in North America,* edited by Earle H. Waugh, Baha Abu-Laban, and Regula B. Qureshi. Edmonton, Alberta, 1983. A study of Louis Farrakhan, who as successor to Malcolm X as "national representative," has sustained the black nationalist emphases and other teachings of Elijah Muhammad.

LAWRENCE H. MAMIYA (1987 AND 2005)

ELIMELEKH OF LIZHENSK (1717?–1787), Hasidic teacher and leading theoretician of the *tsaddiq* concept. Elimelekh and his brother, Zusya of Hanipol, who lived for some time as wandering ascetics, were both attracted to the teachings of Dov Ber of Mezhirich (Międzyrzecz, Poland) and became his disciples. After his master's death, Elimelekh settled in Lizhensk (Lesajsk, Poland) and became the major disseminator of Hasidic teachings in Galicia. Most of the later schools of Polish and Galician Hasidism, including Prsyzucha, Kotsk (Kock), Ger (Góra), Sandz (Halberstadt), and Belz (Beltsy, Moldova), are ultimately derived from Elimelekh's influence, especially through his disciple and successor Yaʿaqov Yitsḥaq, the "Seer" of Lublin (1744/45–1815). The collection of Elimelekh's homilies, published as *Noʿam Elimelekh* (1787), was one of the most popular and widely reprinted volumes of Hasidic teaching.

These homilies are primarily concerned with the promulgation of a single concept, that of the *tsaddiq.* No matter what the weekly scripture reading, Elimelekh ingeniously leads his discussion back to this theme. The *tsaddiq,* or holy man, is the necessary link between heaven and earth; the community around him is dependent upon his blessing for both spiritual and material well-being. Using strands of tradition that had a venerable history in Judaism, Elimelekh wove a picture of a universe wholly sustained by the special divine grace called forth by these few charismatic individuals. Even prayer was to be directed heavenward by means of the *tsaddiq,* because only to him were the "pathways of heaven" familiar.

An important part of the *tsaddiq* idea was the notion of his descent, usually depicted as a voluntary movement, from the heights of contemplation and absorption in God in order to raise up those more ordinary mortals who awaited his aid. Sometimes, however, this descent was also viewed as a "fall," in which the sins of the world were of such overbearing power that they caused even the *tsaddiq* to fall from his rung. In either case, this was a "descent for the sake of ascent": As he returned to his elevated state, the *tsaddiq* would carry with him those souls and sparks of holiness that had turned to him in search of redemption.

This notion of repeated descents and ascents in the life of the *tsaddiq* was adapted by Hasidism from the earlier Shabbatean movement (seventeenth century), where the "fall" or "descent" of the *tsaddiq*/messiah was used to explain Shabbetai Tsevi's bouts with depression and ultimately also to justify his seemingly treasonous act of conversion to Islam. In Hasidism the notion has been "purified" of its element of intentional sin, which was particularly prominent in the Frankist version of Shabbateanism, also current in eastern Europe. The BeSHT (Yisra'el ben Eli'ezer, c. 1700–1760) had spoken chiefly of the "uplifting of wayward *thoughts,*" portraying even the entry of a stray thought during prayer as sufficient taste of sin for the *tsaddiq.* In Elimelekh's work the rhythm of ascent and descent is also frequently used to assert the supremacy of the "revealed" *tsaddiq,* serving as communal leader, over the hidden one, who cultivates only his own mystical life. It is the *tsaddiq* serving as a public figure who "descends" in order to meet the people and can thus ascend to greater heights.

Elimelekh was known as a saintly and humble man who did not use his extreme views of the *tsaddiq*'s powers for personal gain. Abuses of this notion by later generations have often been unfairly attributed to him. During the last years of his life he withdrew from public leadership, and his disciple Ya'aqov Yitsḥaq began conducting himself as a Hasidic master, causing some conflict between them. Others of his disciples include Yisra'el of Kozienice, Mendel of Rymanów, and Naftali of Ropczyce.

Bibliography

No'am Elimelekh has been published in an annotated edition by Gedalyah Nigal (Jerusalem, 1978). The introduction to that work deals at length with major themes in Elimelekh's writings. The most complete legendary biography is the *Ohel Elimelekh* by A. H. Michelson (1910; reprint, Jerusalem, 1967).

New Sources

Elimelekh of Lizhensk. *Sidur tefilah 'Avodat Elimelekh: seder ha-tefilot le-khol yeme ha-shanah u-me'u·tar be-likutim.* Jerusalem, 1988 or 1989.

Elimelekh of Lizhensk. *Ha-Shabat no'am ha-neshamot: 'imrot ve-'uvdot be-'inyene Shabat kodesh.* Jerusalem, 2001.

Elimelekh of Lizhensk. *Shivhe ha-Rabi Elimelekh: Likut nifla mi-toldot hayav ufe'alav shel Elimelekh mi-Lizensk.* Edited by Menasheh Yitshak Me'ir Shif. Ashdod, Israel, 2002.

Arthur Green (1987)
Revised Bibliography

ELISHA (last half of the ninth century BCE) was a prophet of the northern kingdom of Israel. The prophet Elisha (Heb., Elisha') is presented in the Hebrew scriptures not primarily as a spokesperson for God to king and people, as the other prophets were, but as a holy man and a wonder-worker. In a series of hagiographic tales (*2 Kgs.* 2–8), his unusual powers are portrayed by his control over nature, his multiplication of food and oil, his healing the sick or raising the dead, and his powers of extrasensory perception. Such stories are similar to the legends of Christian saints and Jewish rabbis.

Elisha is associated with prophetic guilds known as the sons of the prophets; he served as their leader, or "father." The social status and religious purpose of such communities are quite unclear from the texts, so they shed little light on the nature of Elisha's prophetic office. In some stories Elisha is an itinerant prophet, traveling from place to place with his assistant; in others, he is a city dweller and property owner. The tradition says nothing about his teaching or his social and religious concerns. Nor does it reflect any protest against political and religious authorities, such as in the case of Elijah and the eighth-century prophets.

While some scholars accept the biblical chronology and order of events, it seems more likely that the period of Elisha's activity should be placed entirely within the reigns of Jehu, Jehoahaz, and Jehoash (c. 842–786 BCE). This was a period of Syrian domination of Israel, a fact that is reflected in several of the stories. The historian of *Kings,* however, mistakenly placed the Elisha cycle in the time before the revolt of Jehu. In this way he extended Elisha's ministry back to the time of Ahab and made him a successor of Elijah (*1 Kgs.* 19:19–21, *2 Kgs.* 2), suggesting a tradition of regular prophetic succession. Thus two quite distinct prophetic traditions influenced each other in the final formation of the text.

Bibliography

There are no extensive treatments of the Elisha cycle in English. For the present, therefore, see the brief discussion by Joseph Blenkinsopp, *A History of Prophecy in Israel* (Philadelphia, 1983), pp. 68–77. Two studies of special importance are J. Maxwell Miller's "The Elisha Cycle and the Accounts of the Omride Wars," *Journal of Biblical Literature* 85 (December 1966): 441–454, and Alexander Rofé's "The Classification of the Prophetical Stories," *Journal of Biblical Literature* 89 (December 1970): 427–440.

New Sources

Bergen, Wesley J. *Elisha and the End of Prophetism.* Sheffield, 1999.

JOHN VAN SETERS (1987)
Revised Bibliography

ELISHAʿ BEN AVUYAH (first half of the second century CE), also known as Aher (the "other"), a Palestinian *tanna* (sage), is unique among the Jewish sages of the first centuries of the common era. Even though he was thoroughly versed in rabbinic Judaism and had been the teacher of Meʾir (one of the leading sages of the latter half of the second century), Elishaʿ eventually rejected his heritage.

There are numerous accounts of the life of Elishaʿ as a rabbi and of his eventual rejection of the rabbinic teachings (B.T., *Ḥag* 14b–15b; J.T., *Ḥag* 2.1, 77b-c; *Ru. Rab.* 6.4; *Eccl. Rab.* 7.8). The Tosefta names Elishaʿ, along with Ben ʿAzzʾai, Ben Zomaʾ and ʿAqivaʾ ben Yosef, as one who entered the "orchard" *(pardes)* where he "mutilated the shoots" (Tosefta *Ḥag* 2.3), a phrase explained in several different ways in Talmudic literature (B.T., *Ḥag* 15a; J.T., *Ḥag* 77b; *Sg. Rab.* 1.4; *Dt. Rab.* 1.4).

Many have attempted to explain the apostasy of Elishaʿ in terms of the philosophical schools of his time—Gnosticism, Epicureanism, and the like—while some have seen the story of his life as presenting an opposition between Jewish and non-Jewish thought. Talmudic sources give several reasons why Elishaʿ left Judaism. One source claims that when Elishaʿ saw that the righteous suffer while the wicked were rewarded, he decided that following the laws of the Torah was of no avail. Elsewhere, the Talmud explains that while Elishaʿ was in his mother's womb, she passed by a pagan temple and the odor of the incense being burned for the idol within affected the embryo in her womb.

Elishaʿ is accused of committing a variety of sins. He is charged with killing rabbis, discouraging their disciples from continuing their studies, exacting forced labor from the Jews on the Sabbath during the persecutions of Hadrian, riding a horse on the Sabbath, and interrupting a Torah lesson on another Sabbath. The results of his actions are described in dramatic fashion. Elishaʿ claims to have heard a voice from heaven that proclaimed that all would be forgiven except for Elishaʿ. After Elishaʿ was buried, fire came forth from heaven and burned his grave.

Although the sources are unanimous in their picture of Elishaʿ as an apostate, they do not place him completely outside the rabbinical circle. Meʾir never lost respect for his teacher and continued to discuss the law with him even after his apostasy. When the daughter of Elishaʿ sought charity after her father's death, the sages stated, "Do not look at his deeds, look at his Torah," and allowed her to be supported by the community (J.T., *Hag.* 2.1, 77c). In addition, *Avot de-Rabbi Natan* contains a collection of sayings attributed to Elishaʿ that emphasize the value of good deeds.

Elishaʿ, along with Ben ʿAzzʾai, Ben Zomaʾ, and ʿAkivaʾ, is said to have entered the "orchard," or *pardes* (Tosefta *Ḥag* 2:3). The ancient sages and scholars have interpreted this episode along three major lines: (1) it hints at the mystical practices in which these four sages were engaged; (2) it is a parable about these sages' investigations into a variety mystical practices; and (3) it points to various aspects of Torah study. The passage states that Elishaʿ "gazed and cut the shoots" and then cites *Qoh* 5:5. Generations of ancient sages and modern scholars have labored fruitlessly over this passage. The most commonly held scholarly opinion is that Elishaʿ became a Gnostic dualist. This is based on Elishaʿ's confrontation with Metatron, presumably in Heaven, in which he seems to have referred to two ruling powers (B.T. *Ḥag* 15a–b). The ancient mystical traditions combine a good deal of imagery, so that Elishaʿ plays a minor role in both the Hekhalot traditions and the Merkabah traditions, based on his experience in *pardes* and his conversations with Metatron.

The story of Elishaʿ's life, his grounding in Judaism during his youth, and his rejection of it during his adulthood resonated in the souls of a number of writers who confronted the impact of modernity following the Jewish Enlightenment. Meir Halevi Letteris (c. 1800–1871), Elisha Rodin (1888–1946), and Benjamin Silkiner (1882–1933) all utilize the image of Elishaʿ in their works. In addition, Milton Steinberg used the life of Elishaʿ as the basis for his novel *As a Driven Leaf,* in which the American rabbi raises the problem of Jewish identity in a non-Jewish environment and the importance of Jewish values in comparison with those of the secular culture.

SEE ALSO Tannaim.

BIBLIOGRAPHY

For traditional views of Elishaʿ, see the *Encyclopedia of Talmudic and Geonic Literature,* edited by Mordechai Margalioth (Tel Aviv, 1945), vol. 1, pp. 105–109; Aaron Hyman's *Toledot tannaʾim ve-amoraʾim* (1910; reprint, Jerusalem, 1964), vol. 1, pp. 155–157; and Samuel Safrai's "Elisha ben Avuyah," in *Encyclopaedia Judaica* (Jerusalem, 1971), vol. 6, cols. 668–690. Milton Steinberg's *As a Driven Leaf* (New York, 1939) is a superb novel based on the life and times of Elishaʿ. For a modern critical evaluation of the Elishaʿ material, see William S. Green's "Otherness Within: Towards a Theory of Difference in Rabbinic Judaism," in *To See Ourselves as Others See Us,* edited by Jacob Neusner and E. Frerichs (Chico, Calif., 1985); Jeffrey L. Rubenstein, *Talmudic Stories: Narrative Art, Composition, and Culture* (Baltimore and London, 1999), pp. 64–104; Alan F. Segal, *Two Powers in Heaven: Early Rabbinic Reports about Christianity and Gnosticism* (Leiden, 1977); and David J. Halperin, *The Faces of the Chariot: Early Jewish Responses to Ezekiel's Vision* (Tübingen, 1988). For a recent reconsideration of the Elishaʿ tradition, see Alon Goshen-Gottstein, *The Sinner and the Amnesiac: The Rabbinic Invention of Elisha ben Abuya and Eleazar ben Arach* (Stanford, Calif., 2000).

GARY G. PORTON (1987 AND 2005)

ELIXIR, a Latinized form of the Arabic word *al-iksīr,* is related to the Greek word *xerion,* denoting a dry powder used for medicine and alchemical transmutation. Elixirs are potions believed to have restorative and curative powers. The term was first used by alchemists to describe the substance (also known as the philosophers' stone) that was believed to transmute base metal into gold, cure disease, and promise immortality. The term is also used in medical pharmacy to mean "a sweetened hydroalcoholic solution containing flavoring materials and usually medicinal substances" (*Encyclopædia Britannica,* 1964, vol. 8, p. 288). Ambrosia and nectar are related terms, especially in classical Western religion and mythology, where all three are sometimes used interchangeably for the divine drink and food of the gods. In some senses they relate to the concept of a substance that confers immortality. There is the possibility, too, that the idea of an ingestible substance of divine origin or potency may have grown out of the early sense of wonder induced by the seemingly miraculous ability of the bee to produce honey. Honey is symbolically linked to divine power in *Deuteronomy* 32:13, "he [God] made him to suck honey out of the rock and oil out of the flinty rock."

CHARACTERISTICS AND SIGNIFICANCE. In religions, myths, and fairy tales, the hope has prevailed that there exists, somewhere, a plant, fountain, stone, or intoxicating beverage that rejuvenates the old, cures the sick, and confers wealth and eternal life on those wise, lucky, or cunning enough to snatch a bite, a sip, or a sniff. In the *Epic of Gilgamesh,* the mighty king of Uruk, Gilgamesh, sets out to discover the secret of eternal life and is fortunate enough to find the miraculous plant of immortality growing at the bottom of the sea. He plucks it, but carelessly leaves it unguarded, and it is stolen by a water snake.

The belief that humanity was once immortal, and should be still, is enshrined in the many myths that tell the disastrous tale of how death entered the world. Stories such as the one from the *Epic of Gilgamesh* mentioned above appear throughout the world; all are variations on a basic myth in which a serpent or sea monster guards the source of immortality, which can be represented as a sacred spring, a tree of life, a fountain of youth, golden apples, and so on. Behind these stories lies the fear that the gods themselves are jealous and wish to keep the elixir of immortality beyond the reach of mortal hands (see *Gen.* 3:22).

THE WATER OF LIFE. In Egyptian, Hindu, Greek, Babylonian, and Hebrew creation myths, life emerges from the waters, the primal substance containing the seeds of all things. In deluge myths, life returns to the waters (undifferentiated form), from which it can reemerge in new forms. As such, water becomes the supreme magical and medicinal substance. It purifies, restores youth, and ensures eternal life in this world or the next. This magical "water of life" has taken many different forms—*soma, haoma,* ambrosia, wine—each one a sacred beverage.

ANCIENT AND TRIBAL RELIGIONS. In ancient and tribal religions characterized by shamanism, elixirs are available to the community in the form of drugs. The use of hallucinogens, intoxicants, and narcotics is important for inducing the ecstatic visions that are regarded as being able to bring shamans and their followers into contact with a spiritual world more perfect and real than that in which they live. The *soma* ritual described in the *Ṛgveda* is the oldest recorded religious ritual involving the preparation and use of an elixir. Opinion varies as to what *soma* actually was. From the research of R. Gordon Wasson (1968), however, it now seems likely that *soma* was originally extracted from the mushroom *Amanita muscaria,* the juices of which are lethal at full strength but hallucinogenic when diluted. In the case of *soma,* the visions of immortality inspired by the drink became identified with the drink itself. *Soma* was deified and the men who drank it became immortal gods.

The use of *soma* disappeared by the end of the Vedic period. Some scholars attribute this development to the migration of the Indo-Aryans away from sites where the mushrooms grew.

***KAVA* ELIXIR.** Nevertheless, a remarkable use of a nonpsychedelic, mildly narcotic, soporific muscle-relaxant drug is notable throughout many Pacific islands up until today. In its imbibable form, this drug is referred to generically as *kava,* and is derived from a shrub, *Piper methysticum,* cultivated specifically for the preparation of the drink or "elixir." "Its active principles, a series of kavalactones, are concentrated in the rootstock and roots. Islanders ingest these psychoactive chemicals by drinking cold-water infusions of chewed, ground, pounded, or otherwise macerated kava stumps and roots" (Lebot et al., 1997, p. 1). In all the different regions of its use, local mythologies commonly link *kava* to female sexuality and death. Although the drinking of *kava* is generally—but now not exclusively—limited to sexually mature males in traditional societies, it is believed to give its drinkers access to the other world and to enable them to communicate with the dead. In fact, the location of traditional *kava* drinking areas in the community is sometimes associated with burial grounds to facilitate such communication with departed ancestors (Lebot et al., 1997).

WORLD RELIGIONS. As shamanism gave way to more organized religious worship, the ritual use of elixirs in the form of mind-altering drugs was gradually discontinued or replaced by symbolic rituals that were the province of the priestly hierarchy or other religious specialists. The ritual consumption of the sacred drink *kukeon* in the Eleusinian mysteries provides an example of the way organized religion created a communal event mediated by an ordained priest. Reference to this mediation does not completely explain the experience of the initiates at Eleusis, however, since the central secret of the Mystery is still unknown and may have been of a paranormal nature.

CLASSICAL HINDUISM. From the classical period onward (after c. 600 BCE), Hinduism, perhaps under the influence of Jainism, Buddhism, and other movements originated by ascetics such as Mahāvīra or Gautama Buddha, focused more on the mystical and psychological possibilities of human consciousness in its pursuit of elevated spiritual states. The complexity of this development defies a simple elucidation, but two examples are suggestive. In the first case, the practice of yoga in its different forms, but primarily *rāja* yoga, complemented by *haṭha* yoga, required a strict ascetic discipline so that the practitioner could realize in an internal state the identity of *ātman* or *puruṣa* with the highest transcendent state beyond all physical forms. To attain this identification, the male practitioner, according to the further example of Tantra yoga, might have to learn to transform the *semen virile* into the elixir of immortality by retaining it during coitus and forcing its power or *śakti* to ascend to the highest *cakra* of the mystical physiology. The various techniques of physical yoga, whether through sexual practices or otherwise, led to internal states of bliss and spiritual intoxication that were of a nearly ineffable nature, although the nineteenth century Bengali mystic Sri Ramakrishna attempted to describe them.

The second example, among many possibilities in what is called the *bhakti* yoga tradition, is drawn from the cult of the deities Rādhā and Kṛṣṇa in medieval north-Indian Vaiṣṇavism. Their relationship is set forth in a story meant to evoke the ultimate beauty of paradise, which becomes accessible to the devotee through contemplation of the story's poetic descriptions and subsequently through rebirth in the company of the deities. Both on earth and in heaven, the goal of the devotees is to drink with their eyes the *rasa,* or elixir, as a spiritual intoxicant that fills them with unspeakable bliss in the contemplation of the divine union (White, 1977).

CHRISTIANITY. In the Christian sacrament of the Eucharist the promise of immortality implicit in the concept of an elixir is at the very heart of the ritual. According to the *Gospel of John* (6:51ff.) and other sections of the New Testament, the bread and wine—the matter of the sacrament—become the body and blood of Christ through the power of the ordained priesthood pronouncing the words of Christ recorded at the last supper. The communicant receiving the consecrated bread and wine under the right conditions is ensured eternal life. Ignatius of Antioch (c. 35–c. 107) described the Eucharist as the medicine of immortality and the antidote against death. Even though by a miracle the outward forms of the Eucharist—that is, bread and wine—remain sensible, the "substance," according to St. Thomas Aquinas and others, changes completely into the true Body and Blood of Christ. This is sometimes referred to as the Real Presence. The rite of the Eucharist may also be thought of as a reenactment of Christ's sacrifice upon the cross. Protestant Christians often interpret the Eucharist as being a memorial of the last supper, but much of the symbolism of the Eucharistic elixir is, notwithstanding, understood.

CHINESE RELIGIONS AND ALCHEMY. Eastern and Western alchemists alike claimed to have produced elixirs that rendered men immortal. But Chinese alchemists were more single-minded in their quest for physical immortality than Indian, Greek, or Western alchemists. Hence, Chinese religion is the *sine qua non* among religions with an alchemical dimension. The Chinese never made the invidious distinction between this world and the next so characteristic of Western thought, nor did they seek eventual liberation from the cosmos like Greek and Indian alchemists. For the Chinese, matter and spirit were part of an organic continuum, and the function of elixirs was to act as a kind of permanent glue, keeping body and soul eternally united, and thus preserving "spirit" *(shen).*

The Chinese were always interested in prolonging life, but the idea of an elixir of immortality appears to have first emerged in the fourth century BCE as a result of a literal interpretation of early Daoist philosophy. The term *dao* originally stood for the life force that makes material bodies develop and function. Over time, Daoist alchemists transformed this abstract principle into an edible elixir. The only difficulty lay in determining the material constituents of the *dao* and putting them in a digestible form.

The claim that the ore known as cinnabar was the ideal substance for the elixir rested on its color and chemical composition. Cinnabar is red, the color of blood, and, since cinnabar is mercuric sulfide, it can be transformed into mercury (quicksilver), the most "alive" of all the metals. The problem, of course, was that cinnabar is poisonous; but immortality was a powerful vision, and alchemists, like many others, accepted suffering as the necessary price. Between 820 and 859 CE, no fewer than six emperors were poisoned by the elixirs they took in the confident expectation that they would live forever. Joseph Needham (1947/1983) suggests that elixir poisoning was an important factor in the decline of Chinese alchemy after the ninth century. Mircea Eliade (1984), however, points out that the Chinese alchemical theories relating to the transformation of base metal into gold provide a three-part sequence: (1) the transmutation into gold; (2) the transmutation of gold into the elixir of immortality; (3) the materialization of the "immortals" who have attained the final transmutation. Access to the "immortals" on the mystical level remained a possibility throughout Daoist religious history.

MONGOLIAN RELIGION. In the related cultural area of Mongolia, the mysterious power of the world conqueror Chinggis Khan (1162?–1227) was attributed to the divine elixir that miraculously descended from the "Powerful God Khormusda" into Chinggis Khan's hands, as he sat alone in his tent-palace. The Mongolian chronicle states that he had earned the right to the elixir because of his intrepid pursuit of victory against his enemies (Bawden, 2000, p. 37).

ISLAM AND THE EUROPEAN MIDDLE AGES. In the Holy Qur'ān, the state of the blessed in heaven is linked to an elixir: "In the Gardens of delight. / On couches, facing one another; / A cup from a gushing spring is brought round for them. / White, delicious to the drinkers. / Wherein there is no headache nor are they made mad thereby." (XXXVII, 43–47; see Pickthall, 1977).

The idea of an alchemical elixir came to the West via Islam in the early Middle Ages. The story of its permutations is linked to the medieval literature of Europe. One of the most beautiful expressions of the idea of the elixir is the story of the Grail or *Gral,* most strikingly rendered in the German version of Wolfram von Eschenbach. In Eschenbach's early-thirteenth-century epic poem *Parzifal,* the Grail or *Gral* is not the chalice of the Last Supper but a magical stone:

> It is called "Lapsit exillis." By virtue of the Stone the Phoenix is burned to ashes, in which he is reborn.—Thus does the Phoenix moult its feathers! Which done, it shines dazzling bright and lovely as before! Further: however ill a mortal may be, from the day on which he sees the Stone he cannot die for that week, nor does he lose his colour . . . if anyone, maid or man, were to look at the Gral for two hundred years, you would have to admit that his colour was as fresh as in his early prime . . .—Such powers does the Stone confer on mortal men that their flesh and bones are soon made young again. This Stone is called "The Gral." (White et al., 1990, p. 463)

THE COMTE DE SAINT-GERMAIN. The story of the Comte de Saint-Germain, also called Master Rakoczi, allegedly commences in the early eighteenth century, when Saint-Germain began to be noticed in different royal courts and countries of Europe; from that time onwards, the tales of his longevity and paranormal powers proliferated. In Isabel Cooper-Oakley's biography, *The Count of Saint-Germain,* which is based on eighteenth-century sources, a couple of incidents are mentioned: In the Court of France a friend of Madame de Pompadour claimed that "during her first stay in Venice, she received from him [Saint-Germain] an Elixir which for fully a quarter of a century preserved unaltered the youthful charms she possessed at 25" (p. 31). Another person reported, "Among a number of his accomplishments, he made, under my own eyes some experiments, of which the most important were the transmutation of iron into a metal as beautiful as gold, and at least as good for all goldsmith's work" (p. 43).

In time, the roles of the "masters," who included Saint-Germain in their ranks, were extensively developed in the literature of the Theosophical Society. Other "New Age" movements were influenced by Theosophy or independently acknowledged Saint-Germain as their principal "Guide." One of the groups of this type, perhaps the most significant, bears as one of its titles the name "The Saint Germain Foundation." It is also referred to as the "'I AM' Activity,"and informally as the "'I Am' movement." The founders of this religious organization, Mr. and Mrs. Guy W. Ballard, began their work in the early 1930s under the direction of Ascended Master Saint-Germain. During their lifetimes the Ballards received numerous communications from various masters, but the originating documents of the movement, *Unveiled Mysteries* and *The Magic Presence,* discuss in detail the plan of Saint-Germain for the new age, presented to Mr. Ballard in encounters in the western mountains of the United States. These writings further report that Saint-Germain gave an elixir and a kind of energy-charged food to Mr. Ballard—who was at times in an out-of-body state—as part of Mr. Ballard's initiation into the leadership.

At the beginning of the twenty-first century, the idea of the Elixir of Immortality is very much alive. There are thousands of links on the internet to consult, including links to individuals claiming either to have drunk the elixir themselves and to be hundreds of years old or to know someone else in that condition. Along with these are listed various scientific approaches to the indefinite prolongation of human life.

SEE ALSO Alchemy, overview article; Psychedelic Drugs; Soma; and Water.

BIBLIOGRAPHY

For an excellent discussion of rebirth and regeneration and the part played in both by sun, moon, and water symbolism, see Mircea Eliade's *Patterns in Comparative Religion,* translated by Rosemary Sheed (New York, 1958). On shamanism, see Eliade's *Shamanism: Archaic Techniques of Ecstasy,* translated by Willard R. Trask, rev. and enl. ed. (New York, 1964); Weston La Barre's *The Peyote Cult,* enl. ed. (New York, 1969); and *Hallucinogens and Shamanism,* edited by Michael J. Harner (Oxford, 1973). R. Gordon Wasson identifies soma and describes its effects in *Soma: Divine Mushroom of Immortality* (New York, 1968), and Joseph Needham gives a full account of Daoist elixir addicts in *Science and Civilisation in China,* vol. 5 (1947; reprint, Cambridge, U.K., 1983). Elixirs in Eastern and Western alchemy are disussed in Allison Coudert's *Alchemy: The Philosopher's Stone* (Boulder, Colo., 1980). The amazing complexity of bee life and honey production is discussed in Thomas D. Seeley's *The Wisdom of the Hive: The Social Physiology of Honey Bee Colonies* (Cambridge, Mass., 1995). For the full story on kava, including ample scientific documentation, see Vincent Lebot, Mark Merlin, and Lamont Lindstrom's *Kava—The Pacific Elixir: The Definitive Guide to Its Ethnobotany, History, and Chemistry* (New Haven, Conn., 1997). Two classic authors discuss various aspects of yoga, including the conversion of *semen virile* into elixir: Mircea Eliade in his *Yoga: Immortality and Freedom,* translated by Willard R. Trask (New York, 1958), and Swami Agehananda Bharati (a European convert to Hinduism) in *The Ochre Robe: An Autobiography* (London, 1961; reprint, Santa Barbara, Calif., 1980) and *The Tantric Tradition* (London, 1965); also, see Benjamin Walker's *The Hindu World* (London, 1968). On Sri Ramakrishna's experiences (from 1836 to 1886), see *The Gospel of Sri Ramakrishna,* translated by Swami Nikhilananda (New York, 1942). For the *bhakti* experience of *rasa* as the elixir of divine contemplation, see Charles S. J. White's *The Caurasi Pad of Sri Hit Harivams* (Honolulu, 1977) and his "The Remaining Hindi Works of Śrī Hit Harivaṃś," *Journal of Vaiṣṇava Studies* 4, no.4 (1996): 87–104. Discussions of Chinese alchemy are contained in Mircea Eliade's *A History of Religious Ideas,* vol. 2, *From Gautama Buddha to the Triumph of Christianity,* translated by Willard R. Trask (Chicago, 1984). Discussion of Chinggis Khan's receiving the divine elixir is found in Charles R. Bawden's *Mongolian Traditional Literature: An Anthology* (London, 2000). An excerpt from Wolfram von Eschenbach's *Parzifal* is found in *Transformations of Myth through Time: An Anthology of Readings* (San Diego, Calif., 1990), prepared by Charles S. J. White et al. to accompany a PBS television course on Joseph Campbell. Muhammad Marmaduke Pickthall, a convert to Islam, produced *The Glorious Qurʾān: Text and Explanatory Translation* (Mecca al-Mukarramah, Saudi Arabia, 1977). This translation is much admired by English-speaking Muslims. Isabel Cooper-Oakley produced a biography of *The Count of Saint-Germain* (Milan, 1912; reprint, New York, 1970). The basic teaching of the "I AM" Activity is found in two books by Godfré Ray King [Guy W. Ballard], *Unveiled Mysteries,* 3d ed. (Santa Fe, N.Mex., 1939), and *The Magic Presence,* 4th ed. (Santa Fe, N.Mex., 1974). An official history by the Saint Germain Foundation is found in *The History of the "I AM" Activity and Saint Germain Foundation* (Schaumburg, Ill., 2003).

ALLISON COUDERT (1987)
CHARLES S. J. WHITE (2005)

ELIYYAHU BEN SHELOMOH ZALMAN

(1720–1797), known as the Vilna Gaon, was a scholar and theologian. Born in Selets, Lithuania, to a family renowned for its Talmudic erudition, Eliyyahu became one of the major intellectual and spiritual figures in Judaism, the preeminent representative of rabbinism in the eighteenth century. At an early age he displayed both a prodigious memory and a striking aptitude for analysis, which he applied to all branches of Jewish learning—the Torah, Mishnah, Talmud, Midrash, rabbinic codes, and Qabbalah. As a youth, his authoritative knowledge was acknowledged throughout Ashkenazic Jewry, and he soon became known simply as "the Gaon," the genius (an honorific title not to be confused with the title of the heads of the Babylonian *yeshivot* a thousand years earlier). After his marriage and a tour of the Jewish communities of Poland and Germany, Eliyyahu settled in Vilnius (Vilna), where he lived for the rest of this life except for a brief, and unsuccessful, pilgrimage to Jerusalem. In Vilnius, Eliyyahu was supported by the community although he eschewed public office and formal rabbinical positions for the life of the solitary scholar. After the age of forty, he began to lecture to a small group of disciples, who subsequently broadcast his scholarly and religious teachings through a network of Talmudic academies that was established in Lithuania and continues to this day in Israel and the United States.

At the heart of the Gaon's approach was his extreme intellectuality, his determination to reach truth through a rigorous, untrammeled study of the classics of the Jewish tradition. This belief in the supreme religious worth of study was expressed in the rabbi's quasi-ascetic regimen—he was reported to sleep only two hours a night and to forbid talk not devoted to the Torah—and, perhaps more fundamentally, in his dedication to acquiring all the skills and information essential to an elucidation of the sacred texts. Thus, following the example of a small minority of Ashkenazic sages through the centuries, Eliyyahu taught himself mathematics, astronomy, geography, and anatomy through the medium of medieval Hebrew science, and, in at least one case, approved the further transmission of scientific knowledge to traditional Jews by encouraging a student to translate Euclid into Hebrew.

Equally at variance with contemporary practice, although buttressed by precedent and authority, the Gaon opposed the practice of explaining textual problems in the Talmud through an overreliance on the hermeneutic techniques of *ḥilluq* or *pilpul* (dialectic reasoning). Instead, he insisted on a thorough study of all the cognate sources and especially the Jerusalem Talmud, which had been long neglected in favor of the Babylonian Talmud. On the basis of his mastery of classic rabbinics, but without access to manuscript variants, he was able and willing to suggest a large number of emendations and corrections in the Talmudic text, many of which resulted in contradicting the interpretations of post-Talmudic masters. This approach may be dubbed critical, and indeed Eliyyahu has been called "the father of Talmud criticism." But the Gaon's source criticism, as well as his investigations into scientific teachings, were grounded in and defined by an assumption of the infallibility of tradition. Textual emendations or astronomical charts were permissible as ancillary tools in exegesis, not as competing sources of authority. The Talmud and subsequent Jewish law could only be explicated by these devices, never overruled; indeed, the point of the endeavor was to demonstrate the eternal veracity of the biblical canon and rabbinic tradition as a whole, the possibility of understanding God's purpose through a life of uninterrupted study of his words.

This basic theological stance led the Vilna Gaon to spearhead the opposition to the new form of Jewish religiosity that emerged in his time, the Hasidic movement. Regarding the anti-intellectualism and spiritualism of Hasidism as a perversion of Judaism, Eliyyahu signed a writ of excommunication against the Ḥasidim in 1772 and refused to meet with a delegation of Hasidic masters including Shneʾur Zalman of Lyady. Under the Gaon's aegis, Vilnius became the center of anti-Hasidic propaganda and activity. The venom of the opposition was heightened in response to the publication in 1781 of one of the basic tracts of Hasidic doctrine, Yaʿaqov Yosef of Polonnoye's *Toledot Yaʿaqov Yosef,* which severely criticized the rabbinical leadership of the age and laid out the radical new doctrine of the *tsaddiq,* or "righteous man," a term referring to the Hasidic master. The Gaon again ordered the excommunication of the new sect and called for the burning of its literature. It was only after his death in 1797 that the breach between the two camps of traditional Jewry in eastern Europe could begin to be healed.

The Vilna Gaon's denunciation of Hasidism was in no way a rejection of mysticism on the part of a rigid rationalist—as it has often been portrayed in popular literature. On the contrary, the Gaon was a consistent student of Jewish mysticism, and he had an exceptionally vivid visionary life, although he consciously constrained his mystical graces and revelations from interfering in his legal and scholarly functions. He believed that true charisma inhered only in the Torah, not in its teachers. His students reveled in his personality and produced a bountiful hagiographic literature about him, and for over a century he was revered as a saint by masses of Jews in eastern Europe.

The Gaon never published his views. His writings, including notes and jottings not intended for the public eye, were published by his disciples after his death. These include commentaries on most of the Bible, the Mishnah, the Jerusalem and Babylonian Talmuds, the *Mekhilta'*, *Sifrei,* and *Sifra'* (three halakhic *midrashim*); glosses on the *Zohar, Sefer yetsirah,* and other qabbalistic classics; treatises on mathematics, astronomy, and Hebrew grammar; and perhaps his most important work, his commentary on the *Shulhan 'arukh.*

Bibliography

There is no full-fledged scholarly biography of the Vilna Gaon, although the literature on him is enormous. The most accessible treatments of his teachings and personality are two charming essays in works by major modern Jewish scholars: Louis Ginzberg's *Students, Scholars, and Saints* (Philadelphia, 1928), pp. 125–144, and Solomon Schechter's *Studies in Judaism,* vol. 1 (1896; Cleveland, 1958), pp. 298–320. More recent scholarship has revealed a good deal about Eliyyahu's personality and influence; particularly interesting are H. H. Ben-Sasson's "The Personality of Elijah, Gaon of Vilna, and His Historical Influence" (in Hebrew), *Zion* 31 (1966): 39–86, 197–216, and Immanuel Etkes's "The Gaon of Vilna and the Haskalah: Image and Reality" (in Hebrew), in *Studies in the History of the Jewish Community in the Middle Ages and Modern Times Dedicated to Professor Jacob Katz,* edited by Yosef Salmon (Jerusalem, 1982), pp. 192–217. A brief but fascinating glimpse into the Gaon's mystical life can be found in R. J. Zwi Werblowsky's *Joseph Karo: Lawyer and Mystic* (London, 1962), pp. 311–316. A succinct, useful outline of his life and teachings is the Hebrew pamphlet by Israel Klausner, *The Gaon Eliyyahu of Vilna* (Tel Aviv, 1969).

New Sources

Etkes, Immanuel. *The Gaon of Vilna: The Man and His Image.* Translated by Jeff Green. Berkeley, 2002.

Halamish, Moshe, Yosef Rivlin, and Refa'el Shuhat, eds. *Vilna Gaon and His Disciples* (in Hebrew). Ramat-Gan, Israel, 2003.

Leiman, Sid (Shnayer) Z. "When a Rabbi Is Accused of Heresy: The Stance of the Gaon of Vilna in the Emden-Eibeschuetz Controversy." *Me'ah She'arim* (2001): 251–263.

Lempertas, Izraelis, comp. *The Gaon of Vilnius and the Annals of Jewish Culture: Materials of the International Scientific Conference, 1997.* Vilnius, 1998.

Schochet, Elijah Judah. *The Hasidic Movement and the Gaon of Vilna.* Northvale, N.J., 1994.

MICHAEL STANISLAWSKI (1987)
Revised Bibliography

EMERSON, RALPH WALDO (1803–1882),

American essayist, poet, and lecturer, was a leading figure among the New England Transcendentalists. Born in Boston, Emerson was descended from a long line of Christian ministers. The son of a distinguished Unitarian minister and a deeply religious mother, he was heir to the dual legacy of Boston Unitarianism: liberalism in matters of theology and Puritan piety in matters of personal devotion, morals, and manners.

Emerson himself became a Unitarian minister, and by 1829 he had secured a desirable position as pastor of the Second Church of Boston. This followed an undistinguished four years at Harvard College, from which he graduated in 1817, and a period of study at Harvard Divinity School, during which he also worked, with little satisfaction, as a schoolmaster. With the pastorate of the Second Church, Emerson for the first time felt secure both professionally and financially. During this period he married Ellen Louisa Tucker, a younger woman of a sensitive nature and delicate health. Her death from tuberculosis, less than two years after their marriage, seems to have wrought important changes in Emerson's attitudes and thought. A rebellious strain in his character was perhaps strengthened; incipient attitudes were more strongly voiced. In his solitariness he found his faith in the primacy of the individual's relation to God strengthened, so too an impatience with the theological inheritance of received religion. He wrote in his journal in June 1831:

> I suppose it is not wise, not being natural, to belong to any religious party. In the bible you are not directed to be a Unitarian or a Calvinist or an Episcopalian. . . . I am God's child, a disciple of Christ. . . . As fast as any man becomes great, that is, thinks, he becomes a new party.

Emerson eventually gave up the pastorate of the Second Church, taking issue with the congregation's customary administration of the Lord's Supper; by 1838 he stopped preaching altogether.

Though Emerson would certainly always have considered himself a "disciple of Christ," his mature thought, as expressed in his essays and poetry, was not beholden to historical Christianity. He passionately sought for the essential spirit of religion a local habitation—temporally, geographically, and in the life of the individual. In the introduction to *Nature* (1833), which came to be his most widely read essay, he wrote: "The foregoing generations beheld God and nature face to face; we, through their eyes. Why should we not also enjoy an original relation to the universe? Why should we not have . . . a religion of revelation to us and not the history of theirs?"

Emerson was not a systematic thinker, and his ideas resist any ready summation. The essays are homiletic and aphoristic and have a cumulative power not dependent on force of logic. Certain strains can be identified, however, that undermine basic Christian conceptions. Emerson's worldview is essentially nonteleological. In his radical assertion that each individual soul must remake anew an original relation to the world, he puts the perceiving self at the center of that world. To borrow the terms of German idealist philosophy, to which he was deeply indebted, Emerson took the transcendental ego, posited as a merely formal, logical entity by Kant and subsumed under the collective will by Hegel, and made it an object of experience. In this he anticipated figures as distant as the philosophers Husserl and Sartre and the poet Wallace Stevens. That the experience of this transcendental ego is akin to mysticism as it had been known even within Christianity is apparent from this famous passage from *Nature:*

> Crossing a bare common, in snow puddles, at twilight, under a clouded sky, without having in my thoughts any occurence of special good fortune, I have enjoyed a perfect exhiliration. I am glad to the brink of fear. . . . Standing on the bare ground,—my head bathed by the blithe air, and uplifted into infinite space,—all mean egotism vanishes. I become a transparent eye-ball; I am nothing; I see all; the currents of the Universal Being circulate through me; I am part or parcel of God.

Though there is an aspect of passivity in this experience that is reminiscent of an experience of divine grace, the experience proceeds upward and outward, clearly centered in the perceiver. This spatialization is telling. Often called a pantheist, Emerson repeatedly asserted the unity of all individual souls with one another and with God. With God deposed from the pinnacle of this relationship, the world becomes not hierarchical but a plurality of parts in any of which the whole might be read: "A subtle chain of countless rings / The next unto the farthest brings."

The distance between his mature views and his Christian background seems not to have troubled Emerson, perhaps because he did not see the two as incompatible. As prophet to an age "destitute of faith, but terrified of skepticism," as his friend Thomas Carlyle characterized it, Emerson advanced his unorthodox views forthrightly and unapologetically, secure in his advocacy of "truer" religion. (We need only turn to Nietzsche, who admired the "cheerfulness" of Emerson, to be reminded of how free of anxiety the latter's writings are.) There is a consistent strain of optimism in his work that helped win him a wide audience and also has brought him some criticism, namely that he avoided any note of tragedy in his writings, even while his journal reveals that he was well acquainted with tragedy in life. Indeed his doctrine of "compensation" for evil and suffering is so philosophically ungrounded as to seem merely sentimental. But in the confidence with which Emerson forwarded his original and radical message, and in the audience he found, may be seen not merely evidence of an uncommonly balanced spirit and not merely the popular appeal of optimism; one sees the flowering of that America observed by Hegel, where "the most unbounded license of imagination in religious matters prevails."

BIBLIOGRAPHY

The primary resources for the study of Emerson are *The Complete Works of Ralph Waldo Emerson,* 12 vols., edited by Edward W. Emerson, and *The Journals and Miscellaneous Notebooks of Ralph Waldo Emerson,* 14 vols. (Cambridge, Mass, 1960–1978). The best recent biography is Gay Wilson Allen's *Waldo Emerson* (New York, 1981). Stephen E. Whicher's *Freedom and Fate: An Inner Life of Ralph Waldo Emerson,* 2d ed. (Philadelphia, 1971), is a watershed study, a point of departure for much later criticism. Jonathan Bishop's *Emerson on the Soul* (Cambridge, Mass., 1964) is another good account of Emerson's intellectual and religious development, as is Joel Porte's *Representative Man: Ralph Waldo Emerson in His Time* (New York, 1979). Two useful collections of criticism are *The Recognition of Ralph Waldo Emerson: Selected Criticism since 1837,* edited by Milton R. Konvitz (Ann Arbor, Mich.,1972), and *Critical Essays on Ralph Waldo Emerson,* edited by Robert E. Burkholder and Joel Myerson (Boston, 1983).

DAVID SASSIAN (1987)

EMPEDOCLES of Acragas (Sicily), a Greek philosopher and sage who lived in the first half of the fifth century BCE (c. 495–435 BCE) and who ended his life, according to a widespread but apocryphal tradition, by jumping into the crater of the volcano Etna. The ancient biographical tradition made him a pupil both of Pythagoras and of Parmenides of Elea and ascribed to him several texts, among others a prose treatise titled "Medical Discourses" (*Iatrikoi logoi*), the hexametrical "On Nature" (*Peri physeos*), and "Purifications" (*Katharmoi*) (which has been preserved in fragments). Both sets of information reflect what the ancient tradition, from Aristotle onwards, already regarded as the somewhat disconcerting double character of Empedocles' work—the extant hexametrical fragments combine "modern" ontology and physics inspired by Parmenides with an anthropology and eschatology that derived in large part from Pythagoras's doctrine of reincarnation (groups of Pythagoreans were active in many places in Southern Italy and Sicily during Empedocles' lifetime).

Modern interpreters usually attributed Empedocles' physical and ontological fragments to the "modern" "On Nature," and the religious teachings to "Purifications" (see the standard edition of the pre-Socratic philosphers by Herman Diels of 1903 that has been many times since reedited). Such a reading was helped by the simplistic evolutionary model "from *mythos* to *logos*" that Wilhelm Nestle's 1940 book, *Vom Mythos zum Logos,* popularized. The discovery, in 1994, of new fragments in a Strasbourg Papyrus, however, makes it more likely that all extant fragments belong to one hexametrical poem only, whose two titles are later alternatives. Neither title is likely to go back to Empedocles' epoch. It goes without saying that this discovery challenges the traditional, Aristotelian way of understanding the development of Greek thought that has survived despite growing criticism.

The consequences for Empedocles' poem have yet to be determined.

EMPEDOCLES' PHYSICS. In his physics, Empedocles reacts to Parmenides' radical separation between being and nonbeing and its concomitant rejection of the reliance on sense perception; Empedocles reasserts the validity of sense perception as a guide to humankind's understanding of nature. In a revolutionary move, he posits four "roots" of being, which he alternately calls Zeus, Here, Aidoneus, and Nestis (Diels and Kranz, 1934, 31 B 6), or, as later interpreters clarify (with disagreement in detail) fire, air, earth, and water. The divine names underline the fundamental nature of these elements. The existence of cosmos is dominated by the forces of "Friendship" (*Philotes*) and "Strife" (*Neikos*)—under their influence, the elements either congregate into bodies or disintegrate again in an eternal cycle, "and these things never cease their interchange" (Diels and Kranz, 1934, 31 B 17).

Due to its impact on later philosophers, especially on Plato and Aristotle, the theory of the four elements became fundamental in ancient, medieval, and early modern physics well beyond the revival of atomism among German doctors of the seventeenth century. Leucippus and Democritus, in turn, developed their atomism partly in reaction to Empedocles.

EMPEDOCLES' ANTHROPOLOGY. In his anthropology, Empedocles posits the divine nature of the soul; however, it does not seem to imply immortality (this would contradict his cosmology) but only a long duration of the soul's existence (Diels and Kranz, 1934, 31 B 115.5). In its original state, the soul was a *theios* or *daimōn,* "a divine being." Incarnation into a human body is an exile of the soul, due to some crime committed among the gods (Empedocles seems to draw a grim picture of human existence; Diels and Kranz, 1934, 31 B 120, 121). The aim of incarnation is punishment and purification in order to be able to return to its former divine abode. According to each life, the soul is reincarnated in a new terrestrian body that might be either a human, a plant, or an animal—the most noble plant is Apollo's laurel and the most noble animal is the lion (Diels and Kranz, 1934, 31 B 127).

A virtuous life is rewarded by a better reincarnation, the final one being that of a "seer or singer or doctor or prince among humans" (Diels and Kranz, 1934, 31 B 146). Given the range of possible incarnations, vegetarism is an inevitable consequence, as it was with the Pythagoreans, on whose doctrine Empedocles depends—he even bans the eating of some plants such as beans (again a Pythagorean prohibition) or laurel leaves (Diels and Kranz, 1934, 31 B 140). This anthropology led him to construct an evolutionary history of humanity that began in total harmony, under the reign of Aphrodite, in which humans refrained from bloodshed and from animal sacrifice (Diels and Kranz, 1934, 31 B 128). In Olympia, as is written in one anecdote, Empedocles is said to have offered an ox made of different spices.

CONCLUSION. The autobiographical statements preserved in his fragments confirm Empedocles' status as a charismatic. In a famous address to the inhabitants of Acragas, he understands himself as nearly being released from the cycle of reincarnations, as an "immortal god, no more mortal" (Diels and Kranz, 1934, 31 B 112.4). He describes how, on his arrival in the city, the people flock together and ask him for oracles and healing. He claims not only to know drugs that help fight disease—and even old age—but he also claims that he can command the weather—the wind, and the rain—and that he has an ability to call back the dead from Hades (Diels and Kranz, 1934, 31 B 111). The later biographical tradition agrees with these statements, although its reliability has always been a problem. Empedocles' pupil Gorgias claimed, however, to have seen him perform magic (*goēteuein,* Diogenes Laertius 8.59). Gorgias himself was the first highly influential teacher of rhetoric that Empedocles was said to have invented, and which some believe he may even have invented (Aristotle, in Diels and Kranz, 1934, 31 A 1.57). This ties in with other scholarship and materials that make Empedocles, against all odds, a staunch democrat, and once again underlines the complexity of his life and thought, defying easy assumptions about the development of Greek philosophy and religion.

SEE ALSO Afterlife, article on Greek and Roman Concepts; Demons, overview article; Dualism; Orpheus; Parmenides; Pythagoras; Reincarnation; Transmigration.

BIBLIOGRAPHY

Burkert, Walter. *Lore and Science in Ancient Pythagoreanism.* Translated by Edwin L. Minar, Jr. Cambridge, Mass., 1972. Diels, Hermann, ed. *Die Fragmente der Vorsokratiker,* 5th ed., chp. 31 (DK 31). Revised by Walter Kranz. Berlin, 1934. Inwood, Brad. *The Poem of Empedocles: A Text and Translation with an Introduction.* Toronto, 1992. Kingsley, Peter. *Ancient Philosophy, Mystery, and Magic: Empedocles and Pythagorean Tradition.* Oxford, 1995. Martin, Alain, and Oliver Primavesi. *L'Empédocle de Strasbourg (P. Strasb. Gr. Inv. 1665–1666). Introduction, Édition et Commentaire.* Strasbourg and Berlin, 1999. Zuntz, Günther. *Persephone: Three Essays in Religion and Thought in Magna Graecia,* pt. 3. Oxford, 1971.

FRITZ GRAF (2005)

EMPEROR'S CULT. Ruler worship was a characteristic statement of Greco-Roman paganism, reflecting its definition of godhead as a power capable of rendering benefits to the community of worshipers, and its ability to create an endless supply of cults in honor of new and specifically entitled manifestations of such beneficent divine power. The granting of cult honors to a ruler, living or deceased, was an act of homage made in return for his bestowal of specific benefits upon the community. It recognized him as the possessor of supernormal power and sought to regularize his beneficent relationship with the community by establishing the formal elements of cult, including feast days, festivals, priesthoods, and shrines.

Actual cult worship of the ruler was uncommon in pharaonic Egypt and extremely rare in ancient Mesopotamia. The Roman practice owed nothing to such Near Eastern antecedents. Rather, it was formed entirely under the impress of developments in the political and cult life of Greece. At first the Greeks offered posthumous cult honors to particular individuals distinguished for bravery or other personal prowess. Then, in the late fourth and third century BCE, it became common for individual cities to establish cults in honor of living rulers. Already in 218 BCE Roman state religion adopted the Greek practice of personifying and worshiping the collective personality of the citizen body in the cult of the Genius Populi Romani ("genius of the Roman people"). From the early second century BCE on, Rome's emergence as the dominant political force in the Greek world led individual Greek cities to establish cults in honor of Roman generals and provincial administrators who had rendered specific benefits to the community concerned. In the first century BCE, the last century of republican government at Rome, this practice of establishing municipal cults to Roman statesmen was intensified under the impact of such charismatic leaders as Pompey (d. 48 BCE) and Julius Caesar (d. 44 BCE).

After his assassination, Julius Caesar was deified. Within the context of the Roman religious mentality, this means that he was officially recognized by decree as a divine entity who had bestowed supernatural benefits upon the Roman people and in consequence had been granted immortality by the gods. Caesar was thus worthy to receive continuing cult worship from the Roman people and accordingly was adopted into the pantheon of the state religion with his own temple and feast day. With this development the imperial cult became an official part of Roman religion. The guidance and regularization of such cult expressions was a key feature in the monarchical system established during the long reign of Augustus (31 BCE–14 CE), and the forms that he established were determinative for later developments. During the first and second centuries CE, many cities throughout the empire founded cults in honor of successive emperors. The intensity of such worship began to diminish in the third century. In the fourth century, with the adoption of Christianity as the official religion and subsequent imperial prohibition of all pagan cult activity, the worship of emperors came to an end.

Under the Roman Empire there was no single imperial cult. Instead, there was a wide variety of cults of the emperors, which took three main forms: the official state cult of Rome, municipal cults of cities in the empire, and private cults.

In the Roman state cult, worship of the living emperor took the indirect form of the cult of the emperor's *genius,* the divine element and creative force that resided in the emperor and guided him like a guardian angel. Following the precedent established in the case of Julius Caesar, numerous emperors, such as Augustus, Vespasian (d. 79 CE), and Trajan (d. 117 CE), were recognized as divinities (*divi*) upon their decease; a formal ceremony and a senatorial decree attested to their apotheosis and new status as immortal. Following the tenets of Stoic philosophy and popular belief, such deification was regarded as an attestation of the "virtues" of the emperor; that is, the emperor had been the vehicle for the operation of divine and beneficent qualities like Peace, Abundance, Victory, Liberty, and Security, which through his person and activities had operated for the benefit of his fellow citizens. Under such names as Pax Augusta, Abundantia Augusti, Victoria Augusti, Libertas Augusti, and Securitas Augusti, these imperial virtues were themselves the object of widespread cult activity at both the official and the private level.

Quite apart from the official pantheon of the Roman people, cities throughout the empire established cults in honor of emperors both living and deceased. Moreover, cults of particular emperors were established by private individuals and especially by corporations. The emperor himself was the main object of cult worship; but in Roman cult, municipal cults, and private worship, deification of members of the imperial family was increasingly common from the time of Augustus on.

In founding cults, building shrines, and maintaining regular worship, the imperial cult was one of the most vital features of Greco-Roman paganism in the first two centuries of the Christian era. To be sure, there were those who criticized the worship of an emperor or of any mortal as an act of impiety; moreover, there is no real evidence that men and women turned to the divine emperor as they might to Apollo or Asklepios in time of sickness or personal crisis. But it would be wrong to dismiss the imperial cult as the empty product of political sycophancy or religious decay. The function of the emperor as divinity was not to alleviate illness or to intervene in personal crisis. His divine power functioned in the sphere of material benefits, the delivery of free grain to a famine-stricken region, gifts of money to victims of earthquakes, and the general securing of peace and prosperity throughout a vast empire. In these terms he was called and genuinely regarded as "savior and benefactor of the human race." He was regarded as a divine entity who had been chosen by the supreme god Zeus/Jupiter to rule humankind with beneficence as the earthly vicegerent of the gods. His reward for fulfilling this task was immortality. From this perspective, the imperial cult was a forceful and creative response to that need for a unity of shared belief that is essential to the integration and successful functioning of a pluralistic society. Fostered by a well-orchestrated and all-pervasive system of imperial propaganda, the image of the emperor as a divine savior sent by the supreme god and triumphant over fate and death played a seminal role in the development of the terminology and content of Christian soteriology.

SEE ALSO Apotheosis; Deification.

BIBLIOGRAPHY

For an extensive bibliography, see Peter Herz's "Bibliographie zum römischen Kaiserkult," in *Aufstieg und Niedergang der römischen Welt,* vol. 2.16.2 (Berlin and New York, 1978), pp. 833–910. Useful collections of evidence can be found in *Charisma,* 2 vols., by Fritz Taeger (Stuttgart, 1957–1960), and *The Imperial Cult in the Latin West* by Duncan Fishwick (Leiden, 1985). For interpretive studies that treat the imperial cult as a religious as well as historical phenomenon, see my *Princeps a Diis Electus: The Divine Election of the Emperor as a Political Concept at Rome* (Rome, 1977); "The Cult of Jupiter and Roman Imperial Ideology" and "The Cult of Virtues and Roman Ideology," in *Aufstieg und Niedergang der römischen Welt,* vol. 2.17.2 (Berlin and New York, 1981), pp. 3–141, 827–948; and "Gottesgnadentum," in *Reallexikon für Antike und Christentum,* vol. 11, (Stuttgart, 1950).

New Sources

Brent, Allen. *The Imperial Cult and the Development of Church Order.* Leiden, 1999.

Campanile, Maria Domitilla. "Il culto imperiale in Frigia." In *Frigi e frigio. Atti del primo Simposio Internazionale, Roma, 16–17 ottobre 1995,* edited by Roberto Gusmani, Mirjo Salvini, and Pietro Vannicelli, pp. 219–227. Rome, 1997.

Campanile, Maria Domitilla. "Ancora sul culto imperiale in Asia." *Mediterraneo Antico* 4.2 (2001): 473–488.

Campanile, Maria Domitilla. "Asiarchi e archiereis d'Asia: titolatura, condizione giuridica e posizione sociale dei supremi dignitari del culto imperiale." In *Les cultes locaux dans le monde grec et romain. Actes du colloque de Lyon 7–8 juin 2001,* edited by Guy Labarre, et al., pp. 69–79. Paris, 2004.

Cerfaux, Lucien, and Julien Tondriau. *Un concurrent du christianisme: le culte des souverains dans la civilisation gréco-romain.* Tournai, 1957.

Clauss, Manfred. *Kaiser und Gott. Herrscherkult im römischen Reiches.* Stuttgart, 1999.

de Jonge, Henk J. "The Apocalypse of John and the Imperial Cult." In *Kykeon. Studies in Honor of Hendrik S. Versnel,* edited by H. F. J. Horstmannshoff, H. W. Singor, F. T. van Straten, and J. H. M. Strubbe, pp. 127–141. Leiden, 2002.

Fischler, Susan. "Imperial Cult: Engendering the Cosmos." In *When Men were Men. Masculinity, Power and Identity in Classical Antiquity,* pp. 165–183. London, 1998.

Friesen, Steven J. *Twice Neokoros.* Leiden, 1993.

Friesen, Steven J. *Imperial Cults and the Apocalypse of John: Reading Revelation in the Ruins.* Oxford, 2001.

Gradel, Ittai. *Emperor Worship and Roman Religion.* Oxford, 2002.

Liertz, Uta-Maria. *Kult und Kaiser: Studien zu Kaiserkult und Kaiserverehrung in den germanischen Provinzen und in Gallia Belgica zur römischen Kaiserzeit.* Rome, 1998.

Price, Simon R. F. *Rituals of Power: The Roman Imperial Cult in Asia Minor.* Cambridge, U.K., 1984.

Reynolds, Joyce M. "The Origins and Beginning of Imperial Cult at Aphrodisias." *Proceedings of the Cambridge Philological Society* 26 (1980): 70–84.

Reynolds, Joyce M. "New Evidence for the Imperial Cult in Julio-Claudian Aphrodisias." *Zeitschrift für Papyrologie une Epigraphik* 43 (1981): 317–327.

Schmid, Stephan G. "Worshipping the Emperor(s)." *Journal of Roman Archaeology* 14 (2001): 113–142.

Small, Alastair M., ed. *Subject and Rulers: The Cult of the Ruling Power in Classical Antiquity. Papers presented at a Conference held in The University of Alberta on April 13–15, 1994, to celebrate the 65th anniversary of Duncan Fishwick.* Ann Arbor, Mich., 1996.

J. Rufus Fears (1987)
Revised Bibliography

EMPIRICISM is best understood not as a single doctrine but as a cluster of theses, each of which affirms the primacy of human experience in the general area of epistemology. As used here, the term *experience* refers primarily to sense experience, but it must also be extended to cover introspective experience. Insofar as other types of awarenesses, such as feeling states, pains, pangs, and so forth, are not already included in one of these categories, they too should be separately included in the general class of experiences. Following are discussions of three theses usually associated with empiricism. The first two have had considerable impact on the history of Christian theology; the third has not.

The first thesis is that ideas are derived entirely from experience. For example, the idea of red is derived entirely from experiences of red things—in this case visual sense perceptions or impressions of red objects. A complex idea such as the idea of a desk or of a unicorn may be derived directly from complex sense impressions (e.g., perceptions of desks), or may be constructed out of other ideas that are, in turn, derived entirely from sense impressions. Assuming, for instance, that no one has ever seen (i.e., had a complex sense impression of) a unicorn, still there are no elements of this idea that are not themselves derived from sense impressions.

That ideas have their origin in perception is a view worked out in some detail by Epicurus (341–270 BCE) in his work *On Nature.* It is also a thesis held by Thomas Aquinas (*Summa theologiae* 1.84.3, 6, 7) who in turn claimed to find it in Aristotle. As a doctrine of importance in modern philosophy, however, it is identified primarily with the classical British empirical tradition of the seventeenth and eighteenth centuries, as represented in the epistemological writings of Locke, Berkeley, and Hume. In contrast to the doctrine of innate ideas held by Descartes and other so-called rationalists, such as Leibniz, Locke insisted that all ideas are derived from experience. In its original state, Locke said, the mind is a blank tablet (tabula rasa) and, as such, does not possess ideas. Ideas are acquired either as a result of the operation of the sense faculties (the idea of red); or as a result of the mind's operation on the data supplied by the sense faculties (the idea of a unicorn); or as a result of introspection (what Locke called "inner sense"), observing the mind as it operates on materials supplied by the sense faculties (for instance, the idea of mind).

In Hume, the claim that all ideas are derived entirely from impressions served as the cornerstone of his empirical theory of meaning. Hume held that a word has meaning only when it is (to use his phrase) "annexed" to an idea. A term's specific meaning can be decided only by consulting the content of the idea annexed to it. But because, as Hume claimed, the content of any given idea is completely determined by the impressions from which it is derived, the meaning of a given word can be exhaustively analyzed by itemizing the impressions from which the idea annexed to that word is derived. Hume relied on this theory of meaning when he dismissed as meaningless a host of traditional metaphysical items such as the Aristotelian doctrine of substratum. With respect to the latter, Hume argued that because one has no impression of substratum, one has no such idea; thus the operative term used by metaphysicians when formulating this doctrine is without meaning. An argument of this sort was used to establish virtually all the doctrines usually associated with Hume's "skeptical" philosophy—for instance, his well-known analysis of "causation" and his highly controversial analysis of "mind."

In *Alciphron,* one of his last major works, Berkeley reviewed with approval a theory concerning the origin of the idea of God. According to the theory in question, the idea of God is a complex having as ingredients ideas generated from one's experience of creatures. Thus, for example, the idea of a being who has knowledge is derived from one's experience of finite beings like one's self. Though one does not have any direct experience of the perfect case, one can construct the idea of perfect knowledge by imagining away the imperfections (e.g., limited scope) that invariably attach to knowledge in imperfect cases. This provides the idea of omniscience, the exemplary version of knowledge. Ideas of the other so-called perfections standardly attributed to God (omnipotence, eternity, etc.) are derived by a similar process from the ideas one has of attributes possessed by finite beings. Berkeley said that this account of the idea of God is precisely the one given by Thomas Aquinas and developed by the Schoolmen under the title "analogy by proportionality." This interpretation of Thomas's doctrine of analogy is supported by a number of contemporary commentators as well (e.g., Copleston, *History of Philosophy,* vol. 2, chap. 38). It is an account that fits well both with Berkeley's and with Thomas's general empiricist stance concerning the origin of ideas.

Perhaps the most provocative empiricist account of the ideas operative in the area of religion is the one advanced by Friedrich Schleiermacher in *The Christian Faith* (1830) and subsequently expanded by his student Rudolf Otto in *The Idea of the Holy* (1917), which no doubt is the most influential study in the phenomenology of religion published in the twentieth century. According to Otto, the idea of God is derived from a complex "nonrational" (i.e., preconceptual) awareness that he referred to as "the experience of the Numen." Otto undertook to show how this primitive awareness is (as he said) "schematized" (i.e., conceptualized) in standard theological doctrines that give expression to its various ingredient feelings. Following Schleiermacher, Otto insisted that the content of the concept of God is determined by the preconceptual religious phenomena of which that concept is the schematization. Although this theory differs from the one given by Berkeley, it clearly reflects the influence of classical empiricist thought. Framed in the language of Locke or Hume, the claim is made that the idea of God comes directly from religious experiences. Berkeley (and Thomas) would disagree only with respect to the claim that the experiences in question are of a specifically religious nature.

The second thesis associated with empiricism is that human knowledge concerning matters of fact is grounded ultimately in experience. Because there is a distinction between an idea (e.g., the idea of red) and a statement (e.g., "Apples are red"), and because knowledge is formulated in statements, one must distinguish a theory concerning the origin of ideas from a theory concerning the source of knowledge. Unlike the former, the latter specifies conditions under which it can be legitimately claimed that a statement is true. These are conditions under which a knowledge claim is warranted. According to this second thesis, whatever may be the origin of one's ideas, one's knowledge of facts about the world is formulated in statements supported entirely by empirical evidence. This claim stands opposed to one made by Kant (and a number of other modern and medieval thinkers such as Descartes and Thomas Aquinas), namely, that some statements that describe facts about the world (e.g., "Every event has a cause") are known to be true a priori, that is, prior to or independent of experience. Such statements are sometimes described as self-evident. The empiricist's claim is that all factual knowledge is, by contrast, a posteriori, that is, posterior to and consequent upon experience. No factual statement is self-evident, if this means that the statement in question can be known to be true without consulting observational evidence.

It is important to note that the thesis just reviewed is explicitly restricted to knowledge about the world, that is, to knowledge of what Hume called "matters of fact." It is thus not extended to knowledge formulated in what Kant labeled "analytic" statements, that is, to statements whose truth values depend entirely on word meanings. As regards these latter statements, empiricists acknowledge that they are a priori. They add, however, that such statements are empty of factual content. This is to say that, while a priori statements may reveal something about the way one uses words or about what Hume referred to as "relations between ideas," they reveal nothing about the objects or circumstances to which these words presumably refer or to which one's ideas presumably correspond. This dichotomy between the factual a posteriori and the analytic a priori remains to this day a point of embarrassment for empiricists. The problem is not that the distinction is unintelligible or inapplicable, but rather that some knowledge statements do not fit comfortably into either class. As mentioned above, Kant thought that the statement "Every event has a cause" is of the kind last mentioned. He also thought that mathematical knowledge such as that formulated in the statement "2 + 3 = 5" defies classification in either of these categories.

The idea that knowledge about the world is grounded in experience is the hallmark of what is usually thought of as the "scientific" mentality. As such, it is antithetical to the traditional Christian insistence that revelation is the ultimate source of the factual knowledge codified in theological doctrine. Still, in the three centuries that have elapsed since the publication of Newton's *Principles,* Christian theology has exhibited some affection for the scientific style of theory construction. Largely inspired by the theological writings of Newton, eighteenth-century England was crowded with advocates of what Hume called "experimental theism," that is, theism entertained as a hypothesis and supported by reference to evidence provided by the appearance of design in nature. This trend stood in contrast to medieval methods for proving the existence of God by purely a priori considerations, as in Anselm's ontological argument, or by arguments making use of a priori (self-evident) factual premises such as the first three of Thomas's five proofs for the existence of God. Theism cast as a scientific theory and supported by the abductive logical procedures characteristic of the natural sciences reached its climax in the nineteenth century in William Paley's monumental work *Natural Theology* (1825). Although this approach to Christian apologetics is still practiced (witness Robert Clark's *The Universe: Plan or Accident,* Oxford, 1961), it is not widely held to be effective. A great many contemporary philosophers of religion think that Hume's *Dialogues Concerning Natural Religion* (1779) constitutes the definitive critique of theism as an explanatory hypothesis.

The third thesis associated with empiricism is that factual statements are meaningful only insofar as they are verifiable. If one assumes that all knowledge concerning matters of fact is ultimately grounded in experience, it follows that, except for statements whose truth values can be determined by reference to the meanings of the terms they employ, any statement known to be true is so only because it has been verified by experience. Given the same exclusion, it follows that, insofar as a statement affirms something knowable, to that extent it affirms something verifiable. Anything that cannot be verified cannot be known. Let a second assumption now be made, namely, that a statement is meaningful insofar, but only insofar, as it has a discoverable truth value. Restricting attention to statements whose truth values cannot be determined by reference to the meanings of their constituent words, this second assumption reveals that all meaningful statements affirm something that is knowable. This is so because, for any meaningful statement that is not contradictory (in which case its truth value can indeed be determined by reference to the meanings of its constituent words), there is some possible world in which it is true and in which it has been discovered (i.e., is known) to be true. It is, then, in principle knowable. But if a given statement is in principle knowable, then, by one's first assumption, it is also in principle verifiable. By this sequence of reasonings, the second empiricist thesis discussed above yields the following theory: The meaning of any statement whose truth value cannot be determined by reference to the meanings of its constituent words consists entirely of its empirically verifiable content. Of course, given this theory, any statement about the world for which no verifying observations could in principle be specified would not count as a genuine statement: it would be devoid of meaning. This is because according to the principle before us, any purported statement about the world is meaningful only to the extent that it is empirically verifiable.

This last principle, usually referred to as the verifiability principle, became the centerpiece of empiricism—called logical empiricism or more often logical positivism—during the second quarter of the twentieth century. It is important to see that it connects not only with the second of the empiricist theses treated above (as indicated in the last paragraph), but with the first as well. Here, for the second time, one is confronted with a theory of meaning. Of course the verifiability principle is not the same as the theory used by Hume. In fact, it differs on two counts: (1) it takes statements rather than individual words as the meaningful units; and (2) it requires empirical consequences rather than antecedently acquired empirical ideas as the conditions of meaning. Still, the verifiability principle is a recognizable cousin of Hume's empirical theory of meaning. It was also utilized by positivists such as A. J. Ayer, in a characteristically Humean program, to dismiss as meaningless a whole range of traditional metaphysical doctrines. At its height, positivism dominated the philosophical community, influencing as well trends in psychology (behaviorism) and in the physical sciences (operationalism). Burdened, however, by its own inability to provide a version of the verifiability principle acceptable to philosophers of science, at the end of the 1950s this theory vanished quite abruptly from the philosophical scene. It is now dead—or at least as dead as any philosophical theory can be.

As for the impact of logical positivism on theology or on religious studies more generally, there is little to say. That there exists a transcendent being who created the universe is one of the metaphysical doctrines that positivists typically dismissed as meaningless. Of course this was not atheism, if one understands atheism to be the view that God does not exist, that is, that the statement "God exists" is false. To have a truth value—that is, to be either true or false—a statement must have meaning. For positivists, the words "God exists"—being, as A. J. Ayer used to say "nonsensical"—simply did not have credentials enough to be false. As yet few (if any) religious thinkers have found this position worthy of serious attention.

See Also Logical Positivism.

Bibliography

Ayer, A. J. *Language, Truth and Logic.* 2d ed. London, 1946. See also *Logical Positivism* (Glencoe, Ill., 1959), edited by Ayer, which contains essays by most leading positivists such as Carnap, Neurath, Schlick, and Ayer himself. It also contains essays by other important twentieth-century empiricists such as Russell and Stevenson. The bibliography is amazingly complete.

Epicurus. *On Nature.* In *Epicurus: The Extant Remains,* translated by Cyril Bailey. Oxford, 1926.

Paley, William. *Natural Theology* (1802). Edited by Frederick Ferré. Indianapolis, 1963.

Schleiermacher, Friedrich. *The Christian Faith.* Translated from the second German edition. New York, 1963. Schleiermacher's best-known student and disciple was Rudolf Otto, whose study of the nature of religious experience in *Das Heilige* (Breslau, 1917), translated by John W. Harvey as *The Idea of the Holy,* 2d ed. (1950; New York, 1970), is a modern classic in religious studies.

Taylor, Richard, ed. *The Empiricists.* Garden City, N.Y., 1974. Contains a handy collection of the writings of Locke, Berkeley, and Hume. Unfortunately, Taylor's text does not include Hume's *Treatise,* which is available in *Enquiries Concerning Human Understanding and Concerning the Principles of Morals,* 3d ed., edited by L. A. Selby-Bigge (Oxford, 1975).

Thomas Aquinas. "Treatise on Man," *Summa theologiae* 1.75–89. In *Basic Writings of Saint Thomas Aquinas,* vol. 1, edited by Anton C. Pegis. New York, 1945. Helpful studies of Thomas's theory of knowledge and philosophy of mind can be found in Frederick C. Copleston's *History of Philosophy,* vol. 2 (Westminster, Md., 1952), chapter 38; and in chapter 4 of Copleston's *Aquinas* (Baltimore, 1967).

New Sources

Carruthers, Peter. *Human Knowledge and Human Nature: A New Introduction to an Ancient Debate.* New York, 1992.

Dupre, John, ed. *Human Nature and the Limits of Science.* New York, 2002.

Kitcher, Philip. *Science, Truth, and Democracy.* Oxford Studies in the Philosophy of Science. New York, 2001.

Roth, Robert. *British Empiricism and American Pragmatism: New Directions and Neglected Arguments.* New York, 1993.

Searle, Jonathan. *The Construction of Social Reality.* 1995; reprint New York, 1997.

Solomon, Miriam. *Social Empiricism.* Cambridge, Mass., 2001.

Van Fraasen, Bas C. *The Empirical Stance.* New Haven, 2002.

NELSON PIKE (1987)
Revised Bibliography

EMPTINESS SEE ŚŪNYAM AND ŚŪNYATĀ

EMRE, YUNUS SEE YUNUS EMRE

ENCHIN (814/5–891/2), posthumously known as Chishō Daishi, was the sixth patriarch (*zasu*) of the Tendai school of Japanese Buddhism and one of the so-called *nittō-hakke,* or "eight (Esoteric) masters who studied in China." Enchin, a distant cousin of Kūkai (Kōbō Daishi, 774–835), founder of the Shingon sect, was born on the island of Shikoku. From the age of fifteen he studied under Gishin, a direct disciple of Saichō (Dengyō Daishi, 767–822), founder of the Tendai sect, at the Enryakuji on Mount Hiei, the center of the Tendai monastic establishment.

Enchin was sent by the government to China, where he studied from 853 to 859, first on Mount Tiantai (center of the Tiantai sect), and then at the Qinglong Monastery in the capital, Chang'an, thus absorbing the teachings and practices of both Tendai and Esoteric Buddhism. Upon his return to Japan he was sponsored by the court (he established an initiation hall within the precincts of the imperial palace) and by the leaders of the Fujiwara clan, and took up residence in the Onjōji in Shiga prefecture, at the foot of Mount Hiei. In 868 he became *zasu* of the Tendai sect, a position he held until his death. Together with Ennin (Jikaku Daishi, 794–864), he was a central figure in the development of classical Japanese Tendai Buddhism.

Enchin's contributions gave rise to a movement that resulted in the complete esotericization of Tendai thought and practice, leading to the creation of "Tendai Esotericism" (Taimitsu, as opposed to "Shingon Esotericism," or Tomitsu). Enchin believed that the teachings of Tendai and Shingon were of equal value (in contradistinction to various hierarchical gradings fashionable at the time), but he also believed that the praxis of Shingon was superior (*ridō-jishō*). He also stated that the transcendental Buddha appearing in Tendai's major scripture, the *Lotus Sūtra,* was the same as Mahāvairocana, the main figure of the pantheon of Shingon Buddhism. Enchin was also the first proponent of the *hongaku* ("original enlightenment") theory, according to which all sentient and nonsentient beings are from the outset fully endowed with complete awakening. This theory played a central function in the evolution of Tendai doctrine and Buddhism at large, and was also instrumental in the theoretical interpretations of the associations between Shintō and Buddhist divinities (*shinbutsu-shūgō*). Finally, Enchin was also, according to the tradition, a key figure in the development of the Tendai branch of mountain asceticism (Shugendō), especially in the Kumano region.

In the generation after Enchin, the Onjōji came to be known as the Jimon branch of the Tendai sect, in opposition to the Sanmon branch located in Enryakuji. The Jimon branch was run by the disciples of Enchin, the Sanmon branch by Ennin's disciples. The patriarchs of the Tendai sect were to be chosen from either Ennin's or Enchin's lineage. This and other questions ultimately led to friction between the two institutions, and then to armed attacks, provoked largely by political considerations. During the late Heian period the so-called warrior monks (*sōhei*) of these great monasteries battled the government and each other mercilessly in a quest for privileges, land, domains, and power. This situation resulted in the demise of the Tendai institutions at the end of the medieval period, and in the total destruction of the monasteries by Oda Nobunaga in 1571.

Enchin had many disciples and composed a large number of doctrinal treatises, among which the *Dainichikyō-shiiki* (The final truth of the Mahāvairocana Sūtra) and the *Kōen-hokke-gi* (Lectures on the rites of the lotus blossom) are noteworthy. After his death, Enchin became the object of a cult centered around a sculptured representation holding his ashes.

SEE ALSO Shingonshū; Shugendō; Tendaishū.

BIBLIOGRAPHY

Chishō Daishi. Ōtsu, 1937. Published under the auspices of the Onjōji (Miidera).

Murayama Shūichi. *Hieizan to Tendai bukkyō no kenkyū.* Tokyo, 1975.

Tsuji Zennosuke. *Nihon bukkyōshi; jōsei-hen,* vol. 1. Tokyo, 1944.

ALLAN G. GRAPARD (1987)

ENCYCLOPEDIAS.

Most generally, there are two ways of understanding *encyclopedia* (from Greek *kúklos,* "circle," and *paideía,* "education"), namely: (1) after Hippias of Elis, a Sophist of the fifth century BCE, as a term denoting a universal education, subsequently the everyday education that prepares for the universal education (Isocrates, 436–338 BCE). Since Marcus Terentius Varro (116–17 BCE) the encyclopedia is organized within the system of the *artes liberales* as a preparation and introduction to philosophy, in the Middle Ages also to theology (already in Jerome's *Chronicon* (380 CE). Rabelais, in *Pantagruel* (1532), still referred to encyclopedia as a formal education and complete system of learning. From the seventeenth century onward—mainly through the influence of the French encyclopedists—it was used to denote the entirety of human knowledge. (2) *Encyclopedia* is also common to indicate a presentation of the contents of knowledge, either in certain fields of interest or in a general way, along with a detailed description of respective subjects. While in earlier times the *systematic encyclopedia* was more prominent—that is, an encyclopedia structured according to themes and issues—since the eighteenth century the *alphabetical encyclopedia* gained the upper hand. The latter is often referred to as a "General" or "Universal Encyclopedia"; in German as *Realenzyklopädie, Reallexikon, Sachwörterbuch,* or *Konversationslexikon.* Although there are many overlaps and although the differentiation is debated among scholars, it is often argued that encyclopedias explicate subjects while dictionaries explicate words. In the end, however, subjects are also words, a fact that makes the differentiation difficult.

The aim to present principally everything that is known about a great variety of subjects and fields in one publication is an ambitious project (Cappelletti, 1983). It needs the collaboration of many people over a long period of time. And it "can hardly be done without some overarching goal, some hope of making a point, or at least without reflecting on the relationship of knowledge to truth and the impact of such truth on individual and social life and the direction of history" (Sullivan, 1990, p. 317). Indeed, since presenting the complete knowledge of humankind is a futile task, it is important to note that behind encyclopedic treatment of knowledge there stands a certain ideology that structures the pieces of knowledge in a way that fits a preconceived program or discourse. Given this subtext of the encyclopedic genre, it is astonishing that encyclopedias as discursive sources, *organizing* knowledge in a meaningful way, have only rarely been the object of scholarly scrutiny (but see Kircher, 2003).

It is noteworthy that the understanding of encyclopedias as representing the ultimate knowledge of humankind is a product of an ideology that viewed the cosmos as utterly decipherable. Vincent of Beauvais, for instance, entitled his seminal medieval encyclopedia *Speculum maius* (*The Greater Mirror,* 1244) because his book was thought to represent the perfect integrity and harmony of the universe. The same is true for the twelfth-century encyclopedia *Speculum universale* (*Universal Mirror*) by the French preacher Raoul Ardent. The world itself is a text, and its hidden truth—its texture—is made accessible to humankind by means of textual representation. The claim to present the entirety of human knowledge is also a claim to master the universe, a totalizing attitude that had its impact on discourses and power relations. With the early-modern growth of scientific knowledge and the encounter with formerly unknown regions and cultures, the encyclopedia as an instrument of power gained new momentum. Examples of this are Paul Scalich's *Encyclopaedia: seu, orbis disciplinarum, tam sacrarum quam prophanum epistemon* (*Encyclopedia; or [knowledge of] the world of disciplines, both sacred and profane,* Basel, 1559), a decisively Protestant publication that for the first time used the term "encyclopedia" to designate a book; and Francis Bacon's famous encyclopedia *Instauratio magna* (*The Great Renewal,* London, 1620), with a frontispiece showing a vessel that sails through the pillars of civilization into the wide open of unknown seas to be explored.

EARLY ENCYCLOPEDIAS. The beginnings of systematic encyclopedias are usually related to Plato's nephew Speusippus (c. 408–339 BCE), but of his encyclopedia only fragments remain. Varro compiled an encyclopedic reference work for stately affairs, including information about the people and geography of the Roman Empire, government, state, law, and religion (*Antiquitates rerum humanarum et divinarum* [*History of Human and Divine Matters*]). In this tradition stood Pliny the Elder (23–79 CE) with his famous *Historia naturalis* (*Natural History,* 77 CE), in which he tackled geography, astronomy, meteorology, ethnography, anthropology, zoology, botany, medicine, dietetics, magic, mineralogy, and the arts. Along with the *Origines* or *Etymologiae* (*Etymologies,* in fact an encyclopedia with little use of etymologies in the modern sense of the word) of Isidore of Seville (560–636) and Jerome's *Chronicon*, the *Historia naturalis* remained the most influential encyclopedia for the Middle Ages.

Among the medieval encyclopedias reference must be made of the *Hortus deliciarum* (*Garden of Joy*) of Herad of Landsberg (c. 1125–1195), as this is the first encyclopedia compiled by a woman. Vincent of Beauvais's *Speculum maius* had a tremendous impact on the high Middle Ages and the Renaissance; compiled from some two thousand sources, it deals with the issues of God and creation, or the human and the divine (physics, geography, agriculture, alchemy, botany, astronomy, language, grammar, logic, rhetoric, ethics, family, economy, politics, law, handicraft, architecture, war, sports, seafaring, medicine, mathematics, metaphysics, theology, history, culture). The *Compendium philosophiae*, compiled before 1320, is usually seen as the first modern encyclopedia because it mirrors the thirteenth-century merging of Aristotelianism with the Scholastic doctrine in the genre of encyclopedia; it strives for objectivity and wants to inform about the newest scientific developments. Most encyclopedias of that time were written in Latin. There are exceptions, however. The German *Buch der Natur* (*Book of Nature*, 1350) by Konrad of Megenberg and P. Königsschlacher's untitled encyclopedia (1472) were simplified works written for a lay public; they were based on Thomas of Cantimprés's *Liber de naturis rerum* (*Book of Things in Nature*).

Particularly in the Middle Ages, the Arabic and Chinese encyclopedic literature was blossoming. In "Sources of History," Ibn Qutayba (828–889) devoted a single volume of his ten-volume encyclopedia to the issues of sovereignty, war, nobility, character, education and rhetoric, asceticism, friendship, prayer, food, and women, respectively. The encyclopedia *T'ung-tien* by Tu Yu (eighth century) informed about the sciences, educational systems, government, customs, music, army, jurisprudence, political geography, and defense. As a matter of fact, the encyclopedia as a genre of its own has a tradition in China that exceeds the Western development. From the no longer extant *Huang-lan* (*Emperor's Mirror*, compiled in 220 CE) to the revised four-hundred-volume edition of the *Qing chao xu wen xian tong kao*, edited by Liujin Zao in Beijing in 1921, Chinese encyclopedias—as their Muslim fellow publications—followed an agenda of educating the civil servants (see Giles, 1911).

Early alphabetic encyclopedias. While alphabetic encyclopedias are dominant in modernity, there are only a few forerunners in antiquity. The most important is *De verborum significatu* (*The Meaning of Words*, early first century CE) of M. Verrius Flaccus, a dictionary of rare terms with grammatical and historical explanation that transmitted the findings of late Republican scholarship (Varro) to later generations.

In the seventeenth century, three encyclopedias were influential: L. Moréri's *Grand dictionnaire historique . . .* (1674), A. Furetièr's *Dictionnaire universel des arts et sciences* (1690), and P. Bayle's *Dictionnaire historique et critique* (1696–1697). The latter is seen as a modern encyclopedia already because it puts forward a new conception with clear, brief, critical ("enlightened") articles instead of uncritical compilations of quotations. Its influence is reflected in a number of translations, among them the German version of J. C. Gottsched (*Historisches und Critisches Wörterbuch* [1741–1744]). These works set the tone for the enormous encyclopedic projects that followed the European Enlightenment.

ENCYCLOPEDIAS AND ENLIGHTENMENT. In the eighteenth century the Enlightenment led to a new phase in encyclopedic publishing (Kafker, 1981). In all cultural centers in Europe projects were launched that by far surpassed the encyclopedias known from early modern times. The underlying rationale of the eighteenth- and nineteenth-century encyclopedias was an ideology of enlightenment—sometimes in clear opposition to clerical truth claims—and of education of the masses or, rather, the middle class. Of paramount importance was the effort of the so-called encyclopedists in France.

The *Encyclopédie*. "Encyclopedists" is the name for the group of scholars that—under the direction of Denis Diderot and, in its mathematical part (until 1759), Jean le Rond d'Alembert—collaborated in the publication of the *Encyclopédie ou Dictionnaire raisonné des Sciences, des Arts et des Métiers par une société des gens de Lettres* (35 vols., 1751–1780; about 72,000 entries in seventeen volumes of letterpress, eleven volumes of engraved plates, five supplement volumes, and two index volumes). Taking up an idea of Leibniz, and building on the older English (e.g., Ephraim Chambers' *Cyclopaedia*, 1727) and French encyclopedias (e.g., Pierre Bayle's *Dictionnaire historique et critique*), the encyclopedists intended to present the complete knowledge of the time (Lough, 1971). With its discussion of all relevant problems, from general philosophical to religious, scientific, historiographical, ethical, political, and social issues, along with Voltaire's writings the *Encyclopédie* is regarded as the climax of the French Enlightenment. Of the important authors who considerably contributed to the ideological framework of the encyclopedia, alongside the editors (see particularly d'Alembert's *Discours préliminaire*, which is still read in French schools today), special mention must be made of Voltaire, who collaborated until the letter *M* before he began his own *Dictionnaire philosophique*; Holbach with his articles about chemistry; Mallet, Bergier, and others for theology and history; Yvon for ethics and metaphysics; and Montesquieu and von Grimm. The political, philosophical, and religious positions of the authors vary, although they are united in a confrontation against radicalism and control of thought that were seen in the intolerant despotism of the ancien régime and the church. With regard to religion and theology, differences can be noticed between Diderot and d'Alembert on the one hand, and Mallet and his party on the other. While Diderot in his comparative articles on religion gives long excerpts from the works of English Deism (see his articles on *Christianisme, Foi, Raison, Révélation, Religion naturelle, Thé-*

isme, Théologie, etc.), Mallet shows a determined anti-Deistic polemic (see his *Bible, Dogme, Inspiration, Prophétie,* etc.).

Censorship (or the fear of it), however, had its influence on many of the articles, a problem that increasingly troubled the whole project (see Darnton, 1979). Even d'Alembert agreed to include the *petites orthodoxies* in the encyclopedia—albeit not without trying to undermine their content with *renvois,* that is, "allusions/suggestions." On July 21, 1757, he replied to Voltaire, who had grumbled about the meekness in matters theological: "We published bad articles about religion and metaphysics; but with theological censors and such a restrictive permission of publication, I beg you to write better ones!"

Other seminal contributions. The French *Encyclopédie,* although paradigmatic in its intentions, was not the only important encyclopedia of the eighteenth century. In England, the *Encyclopaedia Britannica* (3 vols., 1768–1771) gained international fame. In 1976, the entries were divided in so-called Macropaedia (that is, the major articles in nineteen volumes) and Micropaedia (that is, the smaller articles in ten volumes). The *Encyclopaedia Britannica* became a vital reference point for the Scottish Enlightenment. How important these publications were in religious-political discourse can be seen from the fact that historian of religion William Robertson Smith (1846–1894), who was involved in the ninth edition of the encyclopedia, lost his professorship and good reputation in the Free Church of Scotland because of his article "Bible."

In the nineteenth century other seminal encyclopedias followed. For philosophical discourse, of outstanding importance was G. W. F. Hegel's *Enzyklopädie der philosophischen Wissenschaften* (1817), in which he presented his system of philosophy in three parts: Logic, Nature, and Mind. The most extensive European project to date, the *Allgemeine Encyclopädie der Wissenschaften und Künste* by J. S. Ersch and J. G. Gruber (167 vols., 1818–1889) remained unfinished. The *Conversationslexikon* of K. G. Löbel was bought in 1808 by F. A. Brockhaus, who republished it one year later and (with additional material) in 1810–1811; to the fifth edition (1819–1820), with a new academic systematization, a number of important scholars contributed. *Der Große Brockhaus* became one of the leading encyclopedias in the German language, with more than 200,000 articles in its 1928–1935 edition. As a response to Brockhaus's Protestant dictionaries, Herder's *Konversations-Lexikon* (1853–1857) was published with a Catholic agenda.

J. Meyer published *Das Große Conversations-Lexicon für die gebildeten Stände* (46 vols., 1840–1855) with the clear political intention to educate the lower and middle classes and to enable them an intellectual emancipation. This agenda can still be found in encyclopedias of the early twentieth century. In addition, accompanying the emergence of the modern nation-state, encyclopedic projects were more and more absorbed by nationalistic interests, representing the "national culture" under the auspices of the academies of arts and sciences.

ENCYCLOPEDIC WORK IN RELIGIOUS STUDIES. Encyclopedias played a crucial role in the development and emancipation of various scientific disciplines, both in the humanities and the natural sciences (chemistry, medicine, technology, geography, linguistics, musicology, etc.). With the academic study of religion emerging as a separate area of scholarship, it comes as no surprise that there was a growing interest in encyclopedias that covered either the whole of religion or specific fields of study. This does not mean, of course, that religion was an issue of less importance in earlier encyclopedic discourse—quite the contrary. Not only did religious rationales influence the structure of almost all early encyclopedias (including the "enlightened" ones), but also the customs, religious traditions, and myths of people played a significant role in all these publications. In addition, from early on there existed published encyclopedias that gave special attention to customs and mythologies. As for mythologies, one may think of Antoine Banier's *La Mythologie et les fables expliquées par l'histoire* (3 vols., Paris, 1738–1740); Benjamin Hederich's *Lexicon Mythologicum* (Leipzig, 1724); John Bell's *New Pantheon; or, Historical Dictionary of the Gods, Demi-gods, Heroes, and Fabulous Personages of Antiquity* (2 vols., London, 1790); William Sheldon's *History of the Heathen Gods, and Heroes of Antiquity* (Boston, 1810); and Henry Christmas's *Universal Mythology: An Account of the Most Important Systems* (London, 1838).

When it comes to encyclopedias that specifically focus on religion, one of the earliest major contributions is the *Real-Encyklopädie für protestantische Theologie und Kirche* (26 vols., Basel 1854–1868) by the Swiss theologian J. J. Herzog. This publication of German-speaking Protestantism was countered by French Protestants with the *Encyclopédie des sciences religieuses* (5 vols., Strasbourg 1877–1882). The editor, F. Lichtenberger, openly referred to Herzog's encyclopedia as an inspiration and provocation, and it is clear that the Strasbourg publication was meant as a nationalistic answer to the Basel project. From the Christian perspective, a number of important encyclopedic contributions came from James Hastings, a Scottish cleric. His *A Dictionary of the Bible* (London, 1898–1904), *A Dictionary of Christ and the Gospels* (London, 1906–1908), *A Dictionary of the Apostolic Church* (London, 1915–1918), and—most influential—the *Encyclopaedia of Religion and Ethics* (reprint Edinburgh, 1955) were milestones in the formation phase of (theologically informed) religious studies.

Along with the emancipation of more specialized disciplines within the academic study of religions, other encyclopedias entered the stage, among them *The Encyclopedia of Islam* (Leiden, 1913–1936, new ed., 1960) and the *Encyclopaedia Judaica* (Jerusalem, 1971–1972). German classical philology and historiography culminated in the *Real-Encyclopädie der classischen Altertumswissenschaften,* launched by August von Pauly in 1837 and revised by Georg Wissowa in 1893. In fact, the *Pauly-Wissowa* gained such fame that this encyclopedia was a main reason for earlier generations of scholars to learn German. Today, *Der Neue Pauly* and *Der Kleine Pauly* cling to this long-gone tradition of scholarship without really matching it.

Sometimes, a comparison between different editions of the same encyclopedia "offers a unique chance to have a look behind the scenes and to disclose elements of construction of an 'innocent' dictionary" (Kippenberg, 2003, p. 464), as Hans G. Kippenberg showed with regard to the celebrated *Religion in Geschichte und Gegenwart: Handwörterbuch für Theologie und Religionswissenschaft*, of which the first edition was published 1909–1913 and the fourth edition is in the process of being published (since 1998; an English translation is in preparation). A similar case can be made of the seminal *Encyclopedia of Religion* that started in 1979 as a project that strongly reflected the particular phenomenological method of its editor, Mircea Eliade, but that subsequently grew into a landmark of scholarly discussion, mirroring a variety of different approaches to the study of religion (see Sullivan, 1990, pp. 333–339).

SEE ALSO Festschriften; Reference Works.

BIBLIOGRAPHY

Brewer, Annie M., ed. *Dictionaries, Encyclopedias, and Other Word-Related Books,* 3d ed., suppl. Detroit, Mich., 1983. Along with the *World Dictionaries in Print,* a standard reference work that renders encyclopedias in hundreds of languages.

Cappelletti, Vincenzo. "Il problema dell'enciclopedia." *Veltro* 27, no. 506 (1983): 765–781. Good analysis of the problems of encyclopedic publication.

Collison, Robert L. *Encyclopedias: Their History throughout the Ages.* 2d ed. New York, 1966. Global account.

Darnton, Robert. *The Business of Enlightenment: A Publishing History of the Encyclopédie, 1775–1800.* Cambridge, Mass., 1979.

Giles, Lionel. *An Alphabetical Index to the Chinese Encyclopedia.* London, 1911.

Kafker, Frank A., ed. *Studies on Voltaire and the Eighteenth Century: Notable Encyclopedias of the Seventeenth and Eighteenth Centuries: Nine Predecessors of the Encyclopédie.* Oxford, 1981.

Kippenberg, Hans G. "A Wealth of Small Articles, but Theoretical Reflections in Tiny Doses: An Evaluation of the New RGG[4]." *Numen* 50 (2003): 464–474.

Kircher, Andreas B. *Mathesis und poiesis: Enzyklopädik der Literatur 1600 bis 2000.* Munich, 2003.

Lough, John. *The Encyclopédie.* New York, 1971.

Steinberg, Sigfrid H. "Encyclopedias." *Signature,* n.s., no. 12 (1951): 3–22. Brief, yet clear overview.

Sullivan, Lawrence E. "Circumscribing Knowledge: Encyclopedias in Historical Perspective." *Journal of Religion* 70 (1990): 315–339.

World Dictionaries in Print: A Guide to General and Subject Dictionaries in World Languages. New York, 1983. See comment for Brewer.

KOCKU VON STUCKRAD (2005)

ENDOWMENTS, MUSLIM SEE WAQF

END TIME SEE ESCHATOLOGY

ENGAGED BUDDHISM.

ENGAGED BUDDHISM. Engaged Buddhism, or "socially engaged Buddhism," denotes the rise of political activism and social service by Buddhist communities and organizations in Asia and the West since the 1950s. Paralleling a global increase of political involvement by religious groups within the Christian, Muslim, Jewish, and Hindu traditions, engaged Buddhists have supported campaigns for conflict resolution, human rights, economic development, national self-determination, and environmental protection. They have undertaken medical and pastoral care, educational programs, and community building among economically marginalized and low-caste communities, women and children, persons with HIV/AIDS, and prison inmates. They have insisted that Buddhist mindfulness, morality, and social action be integrated into all facets of daily life in both ordained and lay communities. Engaged Buddhists share the belief that mindful social action is consistent with traditional notions of Buddhist practice and its goal, the universal relief of suffering, and the awakening of human potential.

The term *engaged Buddhism* was coined by the Vietnamese Thiền (Zen) monk and teacher Thich Nhat Hanh (b. 1926), who founded peace-oriented educational and religious institutions during the Vietnam War, led antiwar protests, rebuilt villages, resettled refugees, lobbied internationally for peace talks, and published articles and books on the crisis facing his country and the Buddhist tradition. The governments of Saigon, Hanoi, and Washington opposed these actions, and thousands of Nhat Hanh's followers were killed or jailed. In 1963 photographs of a burning monk on a Saigon street appeared in the international media, illustrating the determination of the newly engaged Buddhists. After the war, Thich Nhat Hanh, exiled from his country, spread the practice and teachings of engaged Buddhism in more than eighty-five books of commentary, poetry, and meditation, through mindfulness retreats at Plum Village in southern France, and in public gatherings throughout the world (King, 1996; Hunt-Perry and Fine, 2000).

Since the 1960s Buddhist movements for nonviolent social change and human rights have proliferated in Asia and the West. In addition to the Vietnam peace movement, these include the Buddhist conversion and anticaste movement launched in 1956 by B. R. Ambedkar (1891–1956) among the *dalit* ("oppressed" or ex-untouchable) peoples of India; the Sarvodaya Shramadana (Universal Awakening through Cooperative Work) village development and peace movement of Sri Lanka, founded in 1958 by A. T. Ariyaratne; the struggle of the Tibetan people, both inside Tibet and in exile, led by the fourteenth Dalai Lama, Tenzin Gyatso, to reclaim the lands and culture devastated since the Chinese takeover of the country in 1959; the Pan-Asian movement to restore the Buddhist order of ordained women, or *bhikkhunī saṃgha*, in countries in which such ordination is opposed by male hierarchies; the three Nichiren-inspired "new religions" that took root in Japan after World War II and that have gained international followers for their peace and cultural renewal campaigns—Sōka Gakkai International (12 million members in 187 countries and territories), Risshō Kōseikai (6 million members worldwide), and Nipponzan Myōhōji (1,500 ordained and lay members worldwide); the Tzu-Chi Foundation (Fuojiao Tzu-chi Gongde Hui or Buddhist Compassionate-Relief Merit Society) founded in Taiwan in the 1960s by the nun Cheng-yen to defray medical expenses of the poor by collecting the equivalent of 25 cents per month from lay followers, which now claims 5 million members in 28 countries, runs 2 modern 900-bed hospitals, a university, a high school, and a TV channel in Taiwan, and directs $600 million in donations to medical relief projects in more than 30 countries around the world; in South Korea, the Buddhist Coalition for Economic Justice, the Jung To Society (environmental activism), Buddhist Solidarity for Reform (representing 40 civil organizations), and the Indra Net Life Community (representing 23 temples and Buddhist nongovernmental organizations); and the Thailand-based International Network of Engaged Buddhists, founded in 1989 by the Thai Buddhist writer and reformer Sulak Sivaraksa to provide a forum for the bourgeoning organizations and movements that share a socially engaged Buddhist perspective. (For surveys of engaged Buddhist movements in Asia, see Queen and King, 1996; and Queen, Prebish, and Keown, 2003.)

In North America, Europe, Australia, and South Africa, Buddhist organizations dedicated to social activism and service have also appeared with growing frequency. The California-based Buddhist Peace Fellowship, founded in 1977 by the Zen teacher Robert Aitken, coordinates programs for community development, prison reform, and international relief through chapters in the United States and its quarterly *Turning Wheel: The Journal of Socially Engaged Buddhism.* Peacemaker Circle International, headquartered in Massachusetts and founded in 1996 by Bernie Glassman, a former aeronautical engineer and lineage holder in the Japanese Sōtō Zen tradition, sponsors "bearing witness retreats" in centers of suffering and violence, such as the streets of lower Manhattan, the death-camp sites at Auschwitz-Birkenau in Poland, and Jewish and Palestinian communities in the Middle East. The International Campaign for Tibet, based in New York and Washington, D.C., coordinates public support for the refugee and exile communities of the Tibetan diaspora and organizes international pressure on the Chinese government to respect the human rights and cultural traditions of the Tibetan people, whom it has subjugated since 1959. Two engaged Buddhists have been awarded the Nobel Prize for Peace, Tenzin Gyatso, the fourteenth Dalai Lama of Tibet (1989), and Aung San Suu Kyi, the opposition leader in Myanmar (1991), and three others, Thich Nhat Hanh of Vietnam, Maha Ghosananda of Cambodia, and Sulak Sivaraksa of Thailand, have been nominated for the prize.

ORIGINS OF ENGAGED BUDDHISM. The canonical and extracanonical writings of Buddhist Asia, while focusing on monastic order, personal morality, spiritual practice, and philosophical analysis, also include teachings on service to others and social policies that promote general welfare. The Pali *Jātaka* and Sanskrit *Jātakamālā*, for example, illustrate the virtues of generosity and compassion through fables in which the future Buddha, born as a deer, a monkey, a parrot, or an elephant, risks or sacrifices his life to save others from harm. Didactic texts setting forth social ethics for laypersons include the *Cakkavattisihanada-sutta* and the *Kutadanta-sutta* of the *Dīgha-nikāya*, which argue that crimes of property and violence are often related to poverty, and that government (i.e., the righteous king) should intervene to provide farmers with grain, merchants with investment capital, and workers with fair wages in order to promote harmonious society. Indeed, instructions to the ideal monarch (Pali, *cakkavatti* or *dhammarāja*), such as the *Dhammapadāṭṭhakathā* (Buddha's advice to rulers), the "Ten Duties of the King" (*dasa-rājadhamma*, contained in the *Jātaka*), and later Mahāyāna texts such as the Indian philosopher Nāgārjuna's *Jewel Garland of Royal Counsels* (second century CE) and Japanese Prince Shōtuku's *Fourteen Article Constitution* (sixth to seventh century CE), find early expression in the rock-hewn edicts of the Buddhist king, Aśoka Maurya (reigned in northern India c. 270 to 230 BCE), promoting universal tolerance and social welfare and suggesting the pervasiveness of Buddhist ideal conceptions of a just and humane society (Harvey, 2000). The *saṃgha* (monastic order) founded by Siddhārtha Gautama, the historical Buddha, in the sixth to fifth century BCE, would appear to embody certain progressive values and social options associated with modernity in the West: equality of access to men and women of all classes and castes, a meritocracy based on personal attainment rather than birth or wealth, and a program of self-cultivation and community development based on rational analysis and practical training rather than esoteric knowledge and ritual. Furthermore, the career of the *bodhisattva* or Buddhist savior that marked the rise of Mahāyāna Buddhism in the centuries following Aśoka is based on a vow to save all sentient beings from suffering and calamity.

Yet it would be wrong to conclude that the social goals of engaged Buddhists in the early twenty-first century evolved directly from Buddhist teachings in the past. As the historian Bardwell Smith has observed,

> The primary goal of [traditional] Buddhism is not a stable order or a just society but the discovery of genuine

> freedom (or awakening) by each person. It has never been asserted that the conditions of society are unimportant or unrelated to this more important goal, but it is critical to stress the distinction between what is primary and what is not. . . . Even the vocation of the *bodhisattva* is not as social reformer but as the catalyst to personal transformation within society. (Smith, 1972, p. 106)

Since the time of the Buddha and Aśoka, many of the social and political ideals inscribed in the early literature and monuments of Buddhism have faded. Buddhist kings, such as the second-century BCE Sinhalese Duṭṭhagāmiṇī, have been as prone to wage holy war against the infidel, as were their non-Buddhist neighbors, while "Chinese and Japanese military forces have used Buddhist symbols, banners, *mudrās,* and *mantras* to empower their actions and intimidate opponents" (Harvey, 2000, p. 263). In medieval Japan, the largest monasteries supported standing armies as fearsome as those of the emperor, and as late as the twentieth century "imperial-way Buddhism" (*kōdō Bukkyō*), embraced by all schools, supported the nation's major wars: from those against China (1894–1895) and Russia (1904–1905) to World War II, when Zen temples sponsored meditation training camps for the armed forces, raised money to purchase new aircraft, and recruited and trained school boys for kamikaze missions for "love of Emperor and in service to Buddha" (Victoria, 1997, pp. 128–129).

The nineteenth and twentieth centuries saw a general decline of Buddhist institutions throughout Asia. As Ian Harris has observed: "It is difficult to point to any part of the contemporary Buddhist world that has not been massively transformed by at least one aspect of modernity, be it colonialism, industrialization, telecommunications, consumerism, ultra-individualism, or totalitarianism of the left or right. In this radically new situation Buddhists have been forced to adapt or risk the possibility of substantial decline" (Harris, 2001, p. 19). In country after country—notably China, Vietnam, Cambodia, Tibet, and Myanmar (Burma)—Buddhist leaders and institutions have been marginalized or assaulted by hostile regimes or changing social conditions. Even in nations in which the tradition was interrupted by colonialism, revolution, civil war, and invasion—such as Thailand, Sri Lanka, Japan, and Korea—the Buddhist *saṃgha* has not often been aligned with progressive politics, human rights, or social services.

Against this backdrop, progressive, nonviolent Buddhist activism has nevertheless appeared with growing frequency. "There is plenty of evidence of significant Buddhist involvement in anticolonial movements, particularly since the Second World War. Similarly, new or revamped Buddhist organizations with strongly nationalist, reformist, social-activist, therapeutic or reactionary-fundamentalist character are much in evidence throughout the 20th century," according to Harris (2001, p. 19). These spontaneous, often charismatic movements represent a marked departure from state-supported Buddhist establishments of the past. Engaged Buddhist movements of the twentieth century "direct their energies toward social conditions over which the state has legal authority, if not control; but their objective is to influence the exercise of temporal power, not to wield it" (Queen, 1996, p. 19). As Sulak Sivaraksa, Thailand's leading Buddhist intellectual and founder of the International Network of Engaged Buddhists, has written: "Buddhism, as practiced in most Asian countries today, serves mainly to legitimize dictatorial regimes and multinational corporations. If we Buddhists want to redirect our energies towards enlightenment and universal love, we should begin by spelling Buddhism with a small 'b'"—in contrast to the "capital-B Buddhism" that shares influence and favors with the power elite (Sivaraksa, 1993, p. 68).

Engaged Buddhism in Asia is thus an emerging grassroots movement that may be traced across national and sectarian boundaries—not a series of reforms instituted by local governments or religious hierarchies. Even when Buddhist movements and leaders have ties to temporal power, such as the Dalai Lama's dual role as spiritual and temporal head of Tibet, the Sōka Gakkai's affiliation with the Kōmeitō political party in Japan, and the "friendly relations" *(jie-yuan)* between the Taiwanese government and the Tzu Chi Compassionate Relief Foundation and the Foguang Shan sect of Pure Land Buddhism, each of these movements is both independent of state power (it is worth recalling that the Dalai Lama is the exiled leader of Tibet) and increasingly globalized in its relations with Tibetan, Japanese, and Taiwanese ethnic diasporas and with their nonnative members and supporters around the world. The transnational, transsectarian or nonsectarian character of engaged Buddhism often derives from the life experience of its leaders, charismatic personalities whose education and careers linked or blended Asian and Western influences. Ambedkar chose Columbia University in New York and the University of London for his graduate training; Thich Nhat Hanh studied and lectured at Princeton and Columbia, traveled to nineteen countries in Europe and North America in his quest for peace in Vietnam, and associated closely with the American religious leaders Thomas Merton and Martin Luther King Jr.; and the young Taiwanese Venerable Cheng-yen, founder of the Tzu Chi Foundation, rejected conversion to Christianity by convincing three Catholic missionary nuns of the universal compassion of the Buddha while at the same time acknowledging that Buddhists must emulate Christians in serving the poor by building hospitals and schools.

The cultural hybridity of the new Buddhism—as well as its activism and social service—may be traced to the interaction of Buddhists and Christians in the late Victorian era. Representative figures include the founders of the Theosophical Society, Henry Steel Olcott and Helena Petrovna Blavatsky, who publicly converted to Buddhism in Colombo in 1880, and their associate, the Sinhalese Buddhist activist Anagārika Dharmapāla (Don David Hewavitarne), who, with the Japanese Zen master Shaku Sōen and the Hindu swami Vivekananda, electrified crowds at the World's Parliament of Religions in Chicago in 1893 with their evangelical fervor for the wisdom of the East. By this time, Sir Edwin Arnold's romantic verse narrative of the life of the Buddha, *The Light of Asia*, had become a best-seller in the English-speaking world. Thomas Tweed remarked on the growing consensus among Buddhists and their admirers in the West regarding the social impact of religious faith: "With few exceptions, Buddhist apologists stood united with American critics, travelers, and scholars in implicitly or explicitly affirming the role of religion in stimulating effective economic, political, and social activity. Almost all participants in Victorian culture and contributors to the public discourse about Buddhism agreed: whatever else true religion was, it was optimistic and activistic" (Tweed, 1992, p. 155).

TEACHINGS OF ENGAGED BUDDHISM. Traditional teachings of the Buddhist *dharma* often find new meaning and application in the practice of engaged Buddhism. Familiar doctrines such as nonviolence, interdependence, selflessness, mindfulness, and compassion are interpreted in ways that address social and institutional dimensions of suffering in the world. Likewise, ethical guidelines such as right speech, right livelihood, and skillful means are understood in ways that acknowledge structural shifts in the economic life, geopolitics, and information technology of the early twenty-first century.

Sulak Sivaraksa interprets the traditional five precepts *(pancha shila)* to encompass institutional and transnational realities as well as interpersonal morality, for example. Nonharming is conceived in a global context:

> Hunger is caused only by unequal economic and power structures that do not allow food to end up where it is needed, even when those in need are the food producers. And we must look at the sales of arms and challenge these structures, which are responsible for murder. Killing permeates our modern way of life—wars, racial conflicts, breeding animals to serve human markets, and using harmful insecticides. (Sivaraksa, 1993, p. 74)

Likewise, non-stealing is treated in terms of economic justice ("right livelihood") and voluntary simplicity. Sexual misconduct concerns the global exploitation of women by male hierarchies, as well as the global traffic in pornography and prostitution. Avoiding false speech entails the responsible use of the mass media, education, and political discourse in order to rescue truth from propaganda and trivialization and to confront power elites with the effects of their policies. The fifth precept, against intoxicants, offers Sivaraksa the occasion to consider the economic addiction of Third World farmers to the production of heroin, coco, coffee, and tobacco as well as the use of related products that cloud the mind, for "in Buddhism, a clear mind is a precious gem" (Sivaraksa, 1993, pp. 75–79).

The twin virtues of wisdom and compassion are understood in similar ways by the Vietnamese Thich Nhat Hanh and the American Bernie Glassman, two influential voices of engaged Buddhism. In his "Tiep Hien Order Precepts," Nhat Hanh warns: "Do not think that the knowledge you presently possess is changeless, absolute truth. Avoid being narrow-minded and bound to present views. . . . Find ways to be with those who are suffering by all means, including personal contact and visits, images, sound. By such means awaken yourself and others to the reality of suffering in the world" (Nhat Hanh, 1987, pp. 90–91). Glassman Roshi invites his followers to follow the "Zen Peacemaker Order Tenets" (1998): "I commit myself to not-knowing, the source of all manifestations. . . . I commit myself to bearing witness fully by allowing myself to be touched by the joy and pain of the universe. I invite all hungry spirits into the mandala of my being and commit my energy and love to my own healing, the healing of the earth, humanity and all creations" (Glassman, 1998, pp. 68–89). In these teachings, wisdom is associated with a radical agnosticism in a world of violently competing ideologies in the hope that a mindful openness to the experience of others will result in a deeper identification and commitment to help. Likewise, both teachings illustrate a special concern for suffering beings (echoing the "preferential option for the poor" of the liberation theology of Latin American Catholicism), whereby the Buddhist vow of universal compassion is enacted in concrete programs of service and activism (Queen, 2002).

Buddhist environmentalism is a striking example of the adaptation of the traditional Buddhist worldview to contemporary modes of thought, specifically the findings of modern science. While the Buddhist teachings of the "wheel of life" and "dependent co-origination" were not based on modern theories of evolutionary biology, for example, their metaphorical expression in the ancient literature has resonated strongly for ecological activists in the early twenty-first century. Illustrating how the language of awakening and liberation may be projected from individual to ecosystem, Joanna Macy invokes the general systems theory of Ludwig von Bertalanffy and Ervin Laszlo to make the connection:

> Far from the nihilism and escapism that is often imputed to the Buddhist path, this liberation, this awakening puts one into the world with a livelier, more caring sense of social engagement. The sense of interconnectedness that can then arise, is imaged—in one of the most beautiful images of the Mahayana—as the jeweled net of Indra. It is a vision of reality structured very much like the holographic view of the universe, so that each being is at each node of the net, each jewel reflects all the others, reflecting back and catching the reflection, just as systems theory sees that the part contains the whole. (Macy, 1990, p. 61)

In practical terms, engaged Buddhist monks in Thailand have faced arrest for "ordaining" trees in the rainforests to protect them from clear-cutting by international timber cartels (Darlington, 2003), while members of the Buddhist Peace Fellowship have participated in nonviolent civil disobedience to prevent nuclear testing at the U.S. government test site in Nevada (Kaza, 2000).

Perhaps the most significant shift, or enlargement, of meaning in the practice of engaged Buddhism involves the central doctrine of suffering (Pali, *dukkha*). The Buddha is credited with saying, "In the past, *bhikkhus*, as well as now, I teach only *dukkha* and the utter quenching of *dukkha*" (*Alagaddupama-sutta, Majjhima-nikāya* [M.i.140], cited in Santikaro Bhikkhu, 1996, p. 156). As elaborated in the four noble truths, suffering is universal, it is rooted in psychological craving born of ignorance, it is "quenchable" in the peace of *nirvāṇa* (freedom from craving and other mental defilements), and it is subject to the benefits of the eightfold path: efficacious view, aspiration, action, speech, livelihood, exertion, mindfulness, and concentration. Yet the logic underlying this and other early teachings is that *dukkha* is both the experience and the responsibility of the sufferer. There can be no victims; every sufferer is held accountable for his or her own misery. Here the cure depends on the effort of the sufferer to tread the eightfold path or, in the case of the Pure Land tradition popular in central and East Asia, to entreat Amitābha Buddha to intervene on one's behalf. In the case of the Mahāyāna *bodhisattva* who vows to save all sentient beings, the mechanism remains a change of heart and behavior on the part of each being, never a group dispensation for all who are fortunate enough to hear the *dharma* and enact its injunctions or to receive the mercy of a buddha or *bodhisattva.*

The hallmark of engaged Buddhism, on the other hand, is its collectivist application of the teaching of interdependence (Pali, *paṭiccasamuppāda*) to the experience of suffering in the world. For if it is possible to suffer as a result of social conditions or natural circumstances that transcend one's psychological (or karmic) states of being—such as poverty, injustice, tyranny, or natural disaster—then *dukkha* must be addressed in a collective way to remove these conditions for all members of the affected group. Thus in Sivaraksa's interpretation of the five precepts is an abiding concern with all who are hungry and injured by wars, racial conflicts, environmental pollution, and economic conditions that favor the farming, manufacture, and marketing of deadly drugs. For Ambedkar and the 380,000 *dalits* who embraced Buddhism on October 14, 1956, the ceremony offered hope to millions oppressed by the Hindu caste system, while the college students, monks, and villagers who dig wells and build schools in more than 11,000 villages in Sri Lanka believe they embody the name of their sponsoring organization, Sarvodaya Shramadana (Universal Awakening through Cooperative Work).

This evolution of Buddhist ethics from one of individual discipline, virtue, and altruism to one of collective suffering, struggle, and liberation illustrates the cultural interaction and mutual sharing with religious and political ideas of the West, such as the notions of covenant community, social justice, and prophetic witness of the biblical Hebrews and Christians, and the secular conceptions of human rights, judicial due process, and democracy associated with Greek humanism, Roman and Anglo-Saxon law, the scientific and social Enlightenment of seventeenth- and eighteenth-century Europe, and the pragmatism and progressivism of nineteenth- and twentieth-century America. In this regard, Ambedkar stands as an exemplar of the synthesis of the ancient and modern, intellectual and activist, and personal and institutional dimensions of engaged Buddhism. As one of the first untouchables to attend college in India, Ambedkar emulated the ecumenical tolerance of the Muslim-Hindu poet-saint Kabīr (c. 1440–1580), the anticaste activism of the Maharashtrian educator Mahatma Phule (1827–1890), and the social and spiritual reformism he found in the life and teachings of the Buddha. As a graduate student at Columbia University in New York from 1913 to 1916, Ambedkar absorbed the pragmatic philosophy of his mentor John Dewey (1859–1952) as well as the Social Gospel of Protestant theologians like Walter Rauschenbusch (1861–1918), who wrote that religion is "not a matter of saving human atoms, but of saving the social organism. It is not a matter of getting individuals to heaven, but of transforming life on earth into the harmony of heaven" (Rauschenbusch, 1964/1909, p. 65). And, as an activist for untouchable rights in the decades leading up to Indian independence and as law minister and chairman of the constitution drafting committee in Jawaharlal Nehru's first government, Ambedkar added to his emerging worldview the slogans of Western progressivism, "Liberty, Equality, Fraternity" and "Educate, Agitate, Organize," and the theories of law and government he encountered at the University of London and Gray's Inn. All of these influences were woven seamlessly into the traditional rendering of the Buddha's life and teachings in Ambedkar's final work, *The Buddha and His Dhamma* (1957)—a manifesto of engaged Buddhism that remains the bible for tens of millions of Ambedkar's Buddhists followers in the early twenty-first century.

CONCLUSION. When Ambedkar was asked by reporters what kind of Buddhism he would embrace at the mass Buddhist conversion in 1956, he replied: "Our Buddhism will follow the tenets of the faith preached by Lord Buddha himself, without stirring up the old divisions of Hīnayāna and Mahāyāna. Our Buddhism will be a Neo-Buddhism—a *Navayana*" (paraphrased from Keer, 1971, p. 498). Many teachings and practices of engaged Buddhism transcend the ancient *yanas* or sectarian "vehicles"—the Hīnayāna or "elite vehicle," the Mahāyāna or "universal vehicle," and the Vajrayāna or "diamond vehicle"—by drawing teachings and practices from them all and by adapting these in keeping with modern notions of suffering, human rights, social reform, and environmental sustainability. Accordingly, some observers have proposed that Ambedkar's *Navayana* ("new vehicle"), prefiguring the beliefs and practices of engaged Buddhism as a global movement today, represents the emergence of a "fourth *yana*" in the history of Buddhism; others argue that the patterns of thought and action of the "engaged" Buddhists fall comfortably within the purview of traditional Buddhism (Queen, 2000, pp. 22–26). Whichever interpretation meets the tests of history, the sharp rise of Buddhist social engagement and activism in the twentieth century and the pervasiveness of its influence on Buddhist institutions and ideology is not in dispute.

BIBLIOGRAPHY

Aitken, Robert. *The Mind of Clover: Essays in Zen Buddhist Ethics.* San Francisco, 1984. Essays by a founder of the Buddhist Peace Fellowship.

Ambedkar, B. R. *The Buddha and His Dhamma.* 3d ed. Bombay, 2001. Has achieved canonical status for ex-untouchable Buddhist converts in India.

Chappell, David, ed. *Buddhist Peacework: Creating Cultures of Peace.* Boston, 2000. Brief essays by engaged Buddhist thinkers and movement leaders in Asia and the West.

Dalai Lama. *Policy of Kindness: An Anthology of Writings by and about the Dalai Lama.* Ithaca, N.Y., 1990. The Nobel Peace laureate reflects with others on Buddhism and history.

Darlington, Susan M. "Buddhism and Development: The Ecology Monks of Thailand." In *Action Dharma: New Studies in Engaged Buddhism,* edited by Christopher S. Queen, Charles Prebish, and Damien Keown, pp. 96–109. London, 2003.

Eppsteiner, Fred, ed. *The Path of Compassion: Writings on Socially Engaged Buddhism.* 2d ed. Berkeley, Calif., 1988. A widely influential collection featuring the most prominent actors and commentators in the late 1980s.

Glassman, Bernard. *Bearing Witness: A Zen Master's Lessons in Making Peace.* New York, 1998. Sequel to *Instructions to the Cook* (1996), detailing a Zen Roshi's innovative experiments in social engagement.

Gross, Rita. *Buddhism after Patriarchy: A Feminist History, Analysis, and Reconstruction of Buddhism.* Albany, N.Y., 1993. Historical analysis and manifesto by an activist-scholar; a touchstone of Buddhist feminism.

Harris, Ian, ed. *Buddhism and Politics in Twentieth-Century Asia.* London, 2001.

Harvey, Peter. *An Introduction to Buddhist Ethics: Foundations, Values, and Issues.* London, 2000. A useful survey of the classical foundations of engaged Buddhism.

Hunt-Perry, Patricia, and Lyn Fine. "All Buddhism Is Engaged: Thich Nhat Hanh and the Order of Interbeing." In *Engaged Buddhism in the West,* edited by Christopher S. Queen, pp. 35–65. Boston, 2000.

Kaza, Stephanie. "To Save All Beings: Buddhist Environmental Activism." In *Engaged Buddhism in the West,* edited by Christopher Queen, pp. 159–217. Boston, 2000.

Keer, Dhananjay. *Dr. Ambedkar: Life and Mission.* 3d ed. Bombay, 1971.

King, Sallie B. "Thich Nhat Hanh and the Unified Buddhist Church: Nondualism in Action." In *Engaged Buddhism: Buddhist Liberation Movements in Asia,* edited by Christopher S. Queen and Sallie B. King, pp. 321–363. Albany, N.Y., 1996.

Kraft, Kenneth, ed. *Inner Peace, World Peace: Essays on Buddhism and Nonviolence.* Albany, N.Y., 1992. Critical essays by scholars and practitioners of engaged Buddhism.

Leyland, Winston, ed. *Queer Dharma: Voices of Gay Buddhists.* 2 vols. San Francisco, 1998. Pathbreaking essays on Buddhism, gender, and sexual preference.

Ling, Trevor. *Buddhism, Imperialism, and War: Burma and Thailand in Modern History.* London, 1979.

Macy, Joanna. "The Greening of the Self." In *Dharma Gaia: A Harvest of Essays in Buddhism and Ecology,* edited by Allan Hunt Badiner. Berkeley, Calif., 1990.

Macy, Joanna. *Mutual Causality in Buddhism and General Systems Theory: The Dharma of Natural Systems.* Albany, N.Y., 1991. Offers a full exposition of a systems theory of Buddhist ethics.

Nhat Hanh, Thich. *Being Peace.* Berkeley, Calif., 1987. See pages 90–91. The most influential collection of teachings by the Vietnamese Zen teacher and activist.

Queen, Christopher S. "Introduction: The Shapes and Sources of Engaged Buddhism." In *Engaged Buddhism: Buddhist Liberation Movements in Asia,* edited by Christopher S. Queen and Sallie B. King, p. 19. Albany, 1996.

Queen, Christopher S. "The Peace Wheel: Nonviolent Activism in the Buddhist Tradition." In *Subverting Hatred: The Challenge of Nonviolence in Religious Traditions,* edited by Daniel L. Smith-Christopher, pp. 25–48. Cambridge, Mass., 1998.

Queen, Christopher S. "Engaged Buddhism: Agnosticism, Interdependence, Globalization." In *Westward Dharma: Buddhism beyond Asia,* edited by Charles S. Prebish and Martin Baumann, pp. 324–347. Berkeley, Calif., 2002.

Queen, Christopher S., ed. *Engaged Buddhism in the West.* Boston, 2000. Comprehensive treatment of eighteen movements in North America, Europe, Australia, and South Africa.

Queen, Christopher S., and Sallie B. King, eds. *Engaged Buddhism: Buddhist Liberation Movements in Asia.* Albany, N.Y., 1996. The first scholarly treatment of engaged Buddhism, surveying nine movements.

Queen, Christopher S., Charles Prebish, and Damien Keown, eds. *Action Dharma: New Studies in Engaged Buddhism.* London, 2003. Historical, ethnographic, and methodological essays from the *Journal of Buddhist Ethics* online conference.

Rauschenbusch, Walter. *Christianity and the Social Crisis* (1909). New York, 1964.

Rothberg, Donald. "Resources on Socially Engaged Buddhism." *Turning Wheel: The Journal of Socially Engaged Buddhism* (Spring 2004): 30–37. A comprehensive bibliography of books, articles, and online references.

Santikaro Bikkhu. "Buddhadasa Bhikkhu: Life and Society through the Natural Eyes of Voidness." In *Engaged Buddhism: Buddhist Liberation Movements in Asia,* edited by Christopher S. Queen and Sallie B. King. Albany, N.Y., 1996.

Sivaraksa, Sulak. *Seeds of Peace: A Buddhist Vision for Renewing Society.* Berkeley, Calif., 1993. Selected essays by the Thai Budhhist activist.

Smith, Bardwell L. "Sinhalese Buddhism and the Dilemmas of Reinterpretation." In *The Two Wheels of Dhamma: Essays on the Theravada Tradition in India and Ceylon,* edited by Bardwell L. Smith, Frank Reynolds, and Gananath Obeyesekere. Chambersberg, Pa., 1972.

Tucker, Mary Evelyn, and Duncan Williams, eds. *Buddhism and Ecology: The Interconnection of Dharma and Deeds.* Cambridge, Mass., 1998. Scholarly papers on Buddhist environmentalism presented at a Harvard University conference.

Tweed, Thomas A. *The American Encounter with Buddhism: 1844–1912, Victorian Culture and the Limits of Dissent.* Bloomington, Ind., 1992.

Victoria, Brian. *Zen at War.* New York, 1997. Pathbreaking work on Budhhism and violence.

Yarnell, Thomas Freeman. "Engaged Buddhism: New and Improved? Made in the USA of Asian Materials." In *Action Dharma: New Studies in Engaged Buddhism,* edited by Christopher S. Queen, Charles Prebish, and Damien Keown, eds., pp. 286–344. London, 2003.

CHRISTOPHER S. QUEEN (2005)

ENKI. Despite the name "lord of the earth," Enki is the god of the Abyss and is known as the "king of the Abyss." He is the poliad god of Eridu and the guardian god of Eengurra, which is built in the Abyss. Along with An and Enlil, he is part of the most powerful triad in the Sumerian pantheon and a permanent member of the assembly of the gods. He is third, after An and Enlil, and creates and organizes the world. Well-liked by Enlil, and An's favorite, he is the son of the king of heaven and earth and is Enlil's younger brother as well as the lord of plenty of the Anunna, their elder brother, and their leader. In the myth of Enki and Ninhursaga, Ninsikil is his wife, while later it is Ninhursaga or Nintu. In the myth *The Assault of the Demons on the Moon* Enki's close connection with magic and his incantations against the demons are emphasized.

SUMERIAN MYTH MAKING. The prologue of the *Debate between Bird and Fish* provides a different cosmogony from that given in many other texts. Although the three most powerful gods of the Sumerian pantheon are present, their respective roles are clearly defined. An and Enlil are the creators of the universe, but Enki, the god of wisdom, is its real organizing power.

Enki begins by creating the Tigris and the Euphrates, filling them with water, and providing irrigation channels. He then establishes the raising of livestock and a sedentary way of life with the foundation of cities, providing a king as ruler of the black-headed people. Finally, he organizes the marshy area, creating flora and fauna, which will be a blessing to humanity and the gods themselves. The text ends with the allocation of different tasks to the new creatures.

The myth *Enki and the World Order* describes the systematic organization of earthly life as the work of Enki. A thorough reading of the text makes it clear that Enki's actions have been requested by the god Enlil and that the god of wisdom has done everything to satisfy Enlil and his city Nippur. The text opens with the scribe's description of the god, in which the god is praised in terms of his relations with the other gods, with the earth, and with the human race, and as the provider of prosperity. A description immediately follows, set forth by Enki himself, praising the god's knowledge, which is fully appreciated in the divine world, and a second eulogy describes in a nutshell the role of the god in civilization and the surrounding environment. Enki decides to cross the sea in his boat and visit every country, but he especially wants to go to Sumer. After he has performed the rituals of purification, the god sails. In Sumer, Ur, Meluææa, Dilmun, and Martu, the land of nomads, he bestows his blessing and praises the progress already made. Enki addresses the natural environment and reforms human activities by putting a particular divinity in charge of each activity to oversee it and guarantee its future well-being. There follows a list of the spheres of activity and the divinities appointed.

Merely listing the activities mentioned in the myth is enough to understand and appreciate the work of the god of wisdom. But any change, by its very nature, produces some discontent, especially among those convinced that things were better as they were. This is the case with Inanna, who is displaced from her established functions. She is immediately critical of Enki's work and tries to ensure greater importance for the female goddesses of childbirth. Except for Nanshe, these goddesses were completely forgotten by Enki, and in a way Inanna completes Enki's task. Inanna continues her speech, however, stressing that her name has been totally ignored in the list given by Enki, and she asks him for a specific role. Enki answers her, listing all her spheres of activity and thus denying her a specific role in the new world order he has devised.

The events preceding the Flood are described next, starting from the observation that the human race in primordial times was not doing well. This explains the need to create the Sumerians and allow them to raise livestock and then to bestow the gifts of kingship and agriculture. When the text resumes after a lacuna, some of the gods seem perplexed by the decision. Enki broods over it and definitely does not agree. Devising a plan, he gives King Ziusudra advance warning of the Flood. The passage concerning the construction of the ship has been lost. When the text resumes, there is a description of the storm, which lasts for seven days and seven nights. At the end of the Flood, Ziusudra disembarks from the ship and offers a sacrifice to the gods. The final part of the story describes the decision of the gods to grant immortality to Ziusudra and his wife because they were the means by which the human race was saved.

AKKADIAN DEVELOPMENTS. An Akkadian incantation text is directly linked to the ritual of water purification and is directed at the river, whose waters must carry away every ill that afflicts humankind. The river bears the epithet "creator of everything" but is itself the work of the gods. In fact it is the work of the "major gods," who set all good things on its banks when they dug it out. Ea and Marduk bestowed its purifying qualities, together with "fire and rage, horror and terror" (Kramer, 1989, pp. 516–517). Because of its sacred nature, and because it runs through the innermost parts of sanctuaries, the river alone has the power of judgment over people, a privilege most often exercised in the form of trial by ordeal. After a request for quiet, it is exhorted to free humankind from sins and evil.

In another text the act of creation is attributed to two gods, Anu and Ea, with Enlil apparently not present, although he must appear in the second part of the document, which is now lost. Anu is only mentioned as the creator of the heavens and has no involvement in subsequent creative acts, leaving this to Ea alone. The title preferred by scholars, therefore, is "Ea the Creator." Ea, the main player, after creating Apsu, his home, uses a handful of clay to create Kulla (the architect god), building materials (reeds and wood), and divinities connected with the construction of sacred buildings. After making arrangements for the construction and adornment of these buildings, Ea takes care to ensure that the gods will be provided for through the production and collection of regular offerings. He thus assigns cult functions to a priestly class and entrusts the king with the provision of supplies. After establishing the divine organizational structure (building of temples, supplies for the gods, allocation of ritual and administrative responsibilities) the god finally proceeds with the creation of humankind, whose task is to carry out the work of the gods. The stress of the entire creative work is quite unique, even understanding that the theme of the passage concerning the gods and their temples, with all that it implies, was of primary importance in Babylonian religion. Hence the god of wisdom Enki carries out his creative work in an unusual order.

Various myths illustrate Enki/Ea in the role of benefactor, including the Flood narratives mentioned above and those concerning the journeys to the underworld by Inanna/Ishtar and Nergal. One text, however, seems at odds with the familiar theme of the kindness of Enki/Ea, and it tells how the god gave deceitful advice to his servant Adapa. The manuscripts that reconstruct the story of wise Adapa and how he opposed the South Wind belong to two periods of Mesopotamian civilization, the El Armana period (fifteenth century BCE and the neo-Assyrian period (seventh century BCE).

The story of Adapa is told in a Sumerian manuscript found at an Iraqi excavation at Meturan (Tell Haddad) in 1993. The text describes Adapa's normal everyday occupation as a pious, devout fisherman, his conflict with the South Wind, the summons by Anu to account for what he has done, and the advice of Ea not to accept any gifts from Anu but to curry favor with the two doorkeepers, Dumuzi and Ningizzida, at the gates of the pantheon. Finally, the ending leaves a sour taste when Anu does not intend to punish Adapa but rather to give him divine status. Adapa's refusal (as suggested by Ea) to accept the offer of divinity robs the wise man of a brighter future. At the end of the story Ea bestows a new destiny upon his favorite. Some scholars, brought out the supposition that the nature of Enki was ambiguous and supposed the figure of Enki as a trickster (Kristensen, 1947). Scholars have examined the problem of this myth and the difficulty of its interpretation, but the majority of them, despite extensive analysis from numerous angles, have not reached a satisfactory solution.

The direct link between the god Enki and water is clear in several myths. His emblem, as befits a god of water, is a fish, the mullet. But the so-called myth of Dilmun should not be ignored.

See Also Mesopotamian Religions, overview article; Ninhursaga; Tricksters, overview article; Water.

Bibliography

Albright, William F. "Ea-Mummu and Anu-Adapa in the Panegyric of Cyrus." *Journal of the Royal Asiatic Society* 26 (1926): 285–295.

Buccellati, Giorgio. "Adapa, Genesis, and the Notion of Faith." *Ugarit-Forschungen* 5 (1973): 61–66.

Cavigneaux, Antoine, and Farouk Al-Rawi. "New Sumerian Literary Texts from Tell Haddad (Ancient Meturan): A First Survey." *Iraq* 55 (1993): 91–105.

Civil, Miguel. "The Sumerian Flood Story." In *Atra-Hasīs: The Babylonian Story of the Flood*, edited by W. G. Lambert and A. R. Millard, with the Sumerian Flood story by Miguel Civil. Oxford, U.K., 1969.

Dhorme, Édouard. *Les Religions de Babylonie et d'Assyrie.* Paris, 1949.

Edzard, D. O. "Mesopotamien: Die Mythologie der Sumerer und der Akkader." In *Wörterbuch der Mythologie.* Vol. 1: *Götter und Mythen im Vorderen Orient*, edited by Hans Wilhelm Haussig, pp. 56–57. Stuttgart, Germany, 1965.

Galter, Hannes D. *Der Gott Ea/Enki in der Akkadischen Überlieferung.* Graz, Austria, 1983.

Heidel, Alexander. *The Babylonian Genesis: The Story of Creation.* Chicago. 1963.

Komoróczy, Geza. "Zur Deutung der altbabylonischen Epen Adapa und Etana." In *Neue Beiträge zur Geschichte der alten Welt*, vol. 1, edited by Hans Joachim Diesner and Elisabeth Charlotte Welskopf. Berlin, 1964.

Kramer, Samuel Noah, and John Maier, eds. *Myths of Enki, the Crafty God.* New York, 1989.

Kristensen, W.B. "De goddelijke bedrieger" (1928). In *Verzamelde bijdragen tot kennis der antieke godsdiensten,* pp. 105-124. Amsterdam, 1947.

Pettinato, Giovanni, ed. *Mitologia Sumerica.* Turin, 2001.

Picchioni, Sergio A. *Il poemetto di Adapa.* Budapest, 1981.

Giovanni Pettinato (2005)
Translated from Italian by Paul Ellis

ENLIGHTENMENT. In the context of Asian religious traditions, especially of Buddhism, what is often translated as *enlightenment* typically refers to that existentially transformative experience in which one reaches complete and thorough understanding of the nature of reality and gains control over those psychic proclivities that determine the apparent structures and dynamics of the world. As is consistent with a general South and East Asian notion that final truth is apprehended through extraordinary "sight" (hence, religious "insight" or "vision"), enlightenment is often depicted as an experience in which one is said to "see" things as they really are, rather than as they merely appear to be. To have gained enlightenment is to have seen through the misleading textures of illusion and ignorance, through the dark veils of habitual comprehension, to the light and clarity of truth itself.

The English word *enlightenment* usually translates the Sanskrit, Pali, and Prakrit term *bodhi*, meaning in a general sense "wise, intelligent, fully aware." Thus, *bodhi* signifies a certain "brightness" (again, a visual theme) to one's consciousness. The term *bodhi is* built on the same verbal root—Sanskrit *budh* ("awaken, become conscious")—as that from which derives the adjective *buddha* ("awakened one"). Thus, an enlightened being, a buddha, is one who has dispelled all of the personal and cosmic effects of ignorance and has become fully awake to reality as it truly is. From the word *bodhi* come also the terms *sambodhi* and *sambodha*, the "highest" or "most complete enlightenment."

The word *enlightenment* also, yet less often, translates other Sanskrit and Sanskrit-related terms from a variety of religious traditions other than Buddhism. The Jain notion of *kevalajñāna* (omniscience, knowledge unhindered by the karmic residues of former modes of understanding the world) describes in part the quality of an *arhat*, a person worthy of highest respect. The paradigmatic *arhats* in the Jain context are the twenty-four *tīrthaṅkaras*, those "ford-crossers" (the most recent being Vardhamāna Mahāvīra in the sixth century BCE) whose experiences of such enlightenment stand at the center of Jain religious history. Similarly, yogic Hindu traditions teach of the experience of *samādhi* ("absolute equanimity") and of *kaivalya* ("the supreme autonomous state of being free of ignorance"), both of which lead the yogin to the experience of *mokṣa*, the release from the hitherto ceaseless and painful cycle of transmigration.

But it is to Buddhist traditions that the experience of enlightenment is most pertinent. Although Buddhist lessons regarding enlightenment (*bodhi* and its correlatives, Chinese *pudi*, *wu*, or *jue*, Tibetan *byaṅ chub*, and Japanese *satori*) vary somewhat, Buddhism in general has stressed the key significance of that experience in which one fully and compassionately understands the world without discoloring or disfiguring it according to one's desires, expectations, or habits. The Buddhist insight into the nature of pain and suffering, of fear and doubt, of the feelings of insecurity and hopelessness, is that these states arise in one's ignorant mind as one selfishly tries to have reality the way one wants it rather than to know it as it is. The Buddhist way to freedom from the suffering these states cause, therefore, is to remove—usually through the practice of meditation or through the development of compassion—the conditions one places on the world, on other people, and on oneself. Thus, Buddhist enlightenment constitutes an experiential transforming and normative "deconditioning" of the self and of the world.

And what, from a Buddhist perspective, would people "see" when they have so deconditioned their response to, and analysis of, the world? Sanskrit and Pali accounts of Siddhārtha Gautama's enlightenment at the age of thirty-five as he sat under a tree near what is now the north Indian town of Bodh Gayā through the night of the full moon in the spring of *ca.* 538 BCE might well serve to summarize the elements early South Asian Buddhist understanding of the process and nature of enlightenment.

First, people would have to confront and defeat, as Gautama is reported to have done, all of the various temptations, selfish desires, and fears (sexual lust, faint-heartedness, physical weakness, passion, laziness, cowardice, doubt, hypocrisy, pride, and self-aggrandizement) that usually define and delimit their sense of identity, an exceedingly difficult task represented in Buddhist myth and iconography as Gautama's struggle in the late afternoon with the demonic and tempting Māra, the evil one.

Second—still following hagiographical accounts and traditional teachings as the paradigm—they would enter into four levels of meditative absorption (Sanskrit, *dhyāna*; Pali, *jhāna*. Technical terms will hereafter be given first in the Sanskrit, with Pali and other terms following when appropriate.) At the first level they would detach their attention from the objects of the senses and look inward into their own minds. Their thoughts would be discursive in nature, and they would feel relaxed but energetic. Entering the second level, their thoughts would no longer be discursive, but they would still feel great energy, comfort, and trust. At the third level the feeling of zest would give way to a sense of dispassionate bliss, and at the fourth level they would feel free of all opposites such as pleasure and pain, euphoria and anxiety. This fourth level of meditation would be characterized by pure and absolute awareness and complete calmness.

Gautama is said to have mastered all four of these stages of meditative concentration and could move from one to the other with ease. This was to be of central importance to his subsequent series of insights gained through the night, for through them he perceived what are known as the six types of extraordinary knowledge (*abhijñā*; *abhiññā*): magical physical powers, the ability to hear voices and sounds from all parts of the universe, the ability to know other people's thoughts, memory of his former lives, the ability to see all creatures in the world, and the extinction of all harmful psychological states. One would have to use these skills in order to understand the nature of suffering in the world, for not to do so would mean that one were merely a wizard or magician rather than a healer.

Third, having gained control over their entrapping emotions, and having mastered the four levels of contemplation, aspirants would endeavor through meditative analysis of their lives to comprehend how the present is determined by the sum total of their past actions. They would see that each person is responsible for his or her own personality and that others cannot be blamed for one's psychological predicament. This third stage of enlightenment finds narrative representation in traditional accounts of Gautama's ability to remember, in order, all of his former lives (*pūrvanivāsānusmṛti-jñāna*; *pubbenevāsānusatti-ñāṇa*) and to understand how all of those lives led to the present one. Gautama is said to have gained this insight during the first watch of the night.

Fourth, they would develop their ability to understand other people's idiosyncratic psychological and existential predicaments in the same manner as they have understood their's own. That is to say, they would be able to see how people have become who they are how they have created their own problems, even though they may not know it. Aspirants for enlightenment would then be able to respond fully and compassionately to any given situation with other people. Buddhist hagiographies say that Gautama gained such a skill during the second watch of the night, a time in which he attained the "divine vision" (*divyacakṣu*; *dibbacakkhu*) to see all of the former lives of all beings in the universe.

Finally, they would comprehend and destroy the source of all psychological "poison" (*āśrava*; *āsava:* "projection, befuddling outflow") and come to realize what are known as the four noble truths: (1) that conditioned existence is permeated by suffering (*duḥkha*; *dukkha*); (2) that this suffering has an origin (*samudāya*); (3) that, because it has its cause, this suffering, therefore, can come to an end (*nirodha*); and (4) that the way one brings an end to all suffering is to follow the Buddhist way of life, known as the Noble Eightfold Path. To tread this path, one practices: (1) the right view (*dṛṣṭi*; *ditthi*) of the true nature of things, (2) right thought, (3) right speech, (4) right action, (5) right livelihood, (6) right effort, (7) right mindfulness, and (8) right concentration.

Gautama is said to have realized the four noble truths during the third watch of the night, in the dark hours before dawn. Gaining these insights, he saw that one's ignorance of the fact that it is the thirst (*tṛṣṇā*; *taṅhā*) for sensual, emotional, or personal gratification that leads one to think and act in certain ways, and that those thoughts and actions then determine how one understands and lives one's life. In other words, it is people's desire to have the world the way they want it to be rather than to know it as it is, free of their preconceptions and demands, that leads to suffering. The cure for this disease, according to Buddhist tradition, is to relinquish one's attachment to the world as one thinks it is, or should be, so that one can be free to see it as it really is. One has to blow out the flames of one's unquenchable desires in order to know the cool waters of truth, of *dharma*.

This "blowing out" of conditioned existence, this *nirvāṇa* (*nibbāna*), is enlightenment. Gautama is said to have attained *nirvāṇa* as the sun came up, an appropriate time to be "awakened" to the nature of reality. Standing up from his place under the tree, Gautama then walked forth as the Buddha.

Theravāda Buddhism recognizes three different types of people who have gained enlightenment. The term *sāvakabodhi* ("enlightenment gained by one who has heard [the Buddha's lessons]") applies to the disciples of the Buddha; *paccekabodhi* ("enlightenment in solitude") refers to the enlightenment experienced by a person who has never actually heard the Buddha's teachings but, nevertheless, has understood in full the nature of reality. (Theravāda tradition does not recognize the teachings of a *paccekabuddha* but does not dispute the validity of his or her experience); *sammāsambodhi is* the complete and absolute enlightenment known by Gotama (Gautama) and other Buddhas in other world cycles.

Recognizing the important link between ignorance (*avidyā*; *avijjā*) of the way things are and the craving (*tṛṣṇā*; *taṅhā*) to have them otherwise, Theravāda Buddhist commentarial tradition has tended to equate the experience of enlightenment with that of the extinction of desire (*tṛṣṇākṣaya*; *taṅhākhaya*), and thus not only to *nirvāṇa* but also to the third of the four noble truths, namely, *nirodha* ("cessation"). Other near-synonyms for *nibbāna* appear throughout the earliest Pali texts: the abolition of passion (*rāgakṣaya*; *rāgakkhaya*), the cessation of hatred (*dośakṣaya*; *dosakkhaya*), the extinction of illusion (*mohakṣaya*; *mohakkhaya*), and uncompounded or unconditioned existence (*asaṃskṛta*; *asamkhata*) all restate the general connotations of the enlightenment experience.

The Mahāyāna tradition, too, has understood enlightenment to include the direct perception of things-as-they-are. According to the Mahāyāna, the enlightened being sees all beings in their "suchness" (Skt., *tathatā*, *yathābhūta*; Tib., *yaṅ dag pa ji lta ba bźin du*) or their "thatness" (*tattva*; Tib., *de kho na [ñid]*), this is to say, in their uncategorical integrity. Mādhyamika Buddhist tracts hold that to perceive all things in their suchness is to see that they are empty (*śūnya*) of any independent, substantial, essential, or eternal being. The Prajñāpāramitā (Perfection of Wisdom) school of the Mahāyāna holds that a person who is to understand the similar "emptiness" (*śūnyatā*) of the world—that nothing exists in its own nature independent of a multitude or even infinite number of interdependent causes and forces—must cultivate wisdom (*prajñā*), a wisdom that is identical with awareness of all things (*sarvajñātā*) and perfect enlightenment (*sambodhi*).

Virtually all schools of Buddhist thought recognize the key relationship between enlightenment and the practice of meditation, for it is through meditation that the mind is understood to become clear and focused enough to allow one's illuminating awareness to shine clearly. Indeed, for Dōgen, a thirteenth-century Zen master from Japan, the practice of meditation and the entry into enlightenment are one and the same thing, for meditation is a spiritual discipline that reveals one's already enlightened mind.

Buddhist though varies regarding how long it may take to gain enlightenment and whether if, once gained, it can be blurred or lost. Possible answers to these question may into some ways be represented by two attitudes toward enlightenment in the Zen tradition. In one, represented by the Chinese ideogram *kan jing* (Japanese *kanjō*), "paying attention to purity," the mind is understood to be continually fogged and distorted by various forces, so must be cleansed gradually over long periods of sitting meditation. In another, described as *jianxing* (Japanese *kenshō*),"seeing into one's true nature," there is the possibility of a sudden recognition of the awakened state that is one's inherent nature that may take place at any moment, no matter how long one has been sitting in formal meditation. In either case, enlightenment is directly associated the ability to see the "is-as-it-isness" (Japanese *kono-mama*) of the moment, free of the mind's categories, projections, habitual tendencies, desires, expectations, and demands. Indeed, according to Buddhist thought in general across its many schools, the unencumbered, direct perception into the true nature of things beyond all categorical modes of understanding, including the mind, constitutes awakened enlightenment itself.

Despite the many and long discourses on the subject, Buddhist sensibilities, particularly those associated with the various schools of the Mahāyāna, holds that the experience of enlightenment is an ineffable one, for what lies beyond all categories cannot itself be expressed in words. That it cannot be expressed, however, is part of its experience. The *Mumonkan*, a Zen Buddhist chronicle, recounts a story purported to appear in an as yet undiscovered sūtra that would exemplify this point: When asked about the nature of truth, the Buddha silently held up a flower in front of his followers. Nobody understood his point except for the venerable Kaśyapa, who said nothing but smiled softly. Seeing his smile, the Buddha knew that his disciple had understood, and declared Kaśyapa to be enlightened.

SEE ALSO Buddha; Four Noble Truths; Mokṣa; Samādhi; Śūnyam and Śūnyatā; and Truth.

BIBLIOGRAPHY

The most accessible Sanskrit account of Gautama Buddha's enlightenment is the *Buddhacarita*, Aśvaghosa's poem written in the first century CE. English translations of the sections on the temptation by Māra and the enlightenment appear in *The Buddhacarita, or Acts of the Buddha*, translated and edited by Edward H. Johnston (1935–1936; reprint, Delhi, 1972), pp. 188–217, and in *Buddhist Scriptures*, translated and edited by Edward Conze (Harmondsworth, 1959), pp. 48–53. Translations from selected Pali literatures pertinent to the enlightenment appear in Henry Clark Warren's *Buddhism in Translations* (1896; reprint, New York, 1976), pp. 129–159. Historical and analytical discussions of the Buddha's enlightenment appear in Edward J. Thomas's *The Life of Buddha as Legend and History*, 3d ed. (1949; reprint, London, 1969), pp. 61–80: Bhikkhu Ñāṇamoli's *The Life of the Buddha* (Kandy, 1972); Richard H. Robinson and Willard L. Johnson's *The Buddhist Religion*, 3d ed. (Belmont, Calif., 1982), pp. 5–20; Hajime Nakamura's *Gautama Buddha* (Los Angeles and Tokyo, 1972), pp. 57–65; and Winston L. King's *Theravāda Meditation* (University Park, Pa., 1980), pp. 1–17. On Zen definitions of and attitudes toward enlightenment, see Heinrich Dumoulin, *Zen Enlightenment: Origins and Meaning* (New York and Tokyo, 1979).

WILLIAM K. MAHONY (1987 AND 2005)

ENLIGHTENMENT, THE. The eighteenth-century European intellectual movement known as the Enlightenment was affiliated with the rise of the bourgeoisie and the influence of modern science; it promoted the values of intellectual and material progress, toleration, and critical reason as opposed to authority and tradition in matters of politics and religion. The eighteenth century itself is sometimes referred to as "the Enlightenment," but this appellation is highly misleading. For despite the patronage of a few powerful individuals (Frederick the Great of Prussia, Catherine the Great of Russia, Josef II of Austria, and Pope Boniface XIV), the Enlightenment was always a critical and often a subversive movement in relation to the established political and religious order. Its values may have dominated certain intellectual circles in the eighteenth century, especially in France, but they did not dominate the political structures or the religious life of eighteenth-century people generally; and though many political goals of the Enlightenment were largely achieved in the nineteenth century, few of them were achieved in the eighteenth. In the eighteenth century, moreover, there were other powerful movements, particularly religious ones, that diverged from and were sometimes decidedly hostile to the Enlightenment (among them, Pietism, Jansenism, and Methodism). It is also a mistake to suggest that the ideas and values of the Enlightenment were limited to eighteenth-century thinkers, for these values have had a prominent place in European thought down to the present day.

The Enlightenment has always been regarded as predominantly a French movement, but its influence was certainly felt elsewhere, chiefly in Germany, England, and the American colonies. The terms *éclaircissement* and *Aufklärung* were generally used by its proponents, but the English term *enlightenment* does not appear to have been widely used until the nineteenth century, when it had largely derogatory connotations associated with the continent. In Germany too, the movement's opponents frequently played on anti-French sentiments.

The way was paved for the French Enlightenment by the wide influence of Cartesian philosophy and science in the latter half of the seventeenth century. But it also took stimulus from philosophical and scientific advances elsewhere, particularly in England. Within France, the principal forerunner of the Enlightenment was Pierre Bayle (1647–1706), whose *Historical and Critical Dictionary* (1697) combined sharp wit, copious historical learning, and dialectical skill with a skeptical temper and a deep commitment to the values of intellectual openness and toleration, especially in religious matters. In the sciences, the Enlightenment owed much to the publicist Bernard Le Bovier de Fontenelle (1657–1757), whose long and active career brought the ideas of scientific philosophers, especially Descartes, Leibniz, and Newton, into currency in France. But the chief philosophical inspiration for the French Enlightenment was provided by John Locke (1632–1704), whose epistemology, political theory, and conception of the relation of reason to religion became models for French Enlightenment thinkers.

We may distinguish two generations of French Enlightenment thinkers, with the transition occurring around 1750. The principal representatives of the first generation were Voltaire (François-Marie Arouet, 1694–1778) and the Baron de Montesquieu (Charles-Louis de Secondat, 1689–1755). Montesquieu's chief writings were in social theory, political theory, and history. His *Persian Letters* (1721) and *The Spirit of the Laws* (1748) give the lie to the common charge that the Enlightenment perspective on society and history was shallow, naive, reductionistic, and ethnocentric. Voltaire's massive oeuvre includes poetry, plays, and novels, as well as philosophical treatises and innumerable essays on the most varied subjects. His interests were exceptionally broad, but perhaps his chief concern was with religion. Voltaire's famous motto *Écrasez l'infâme!* ("Crush the infamous thing!") accurately portrays his hostility toward the Roman Catholic Church and toward clericalism in all forms. His writings contain many eloquent pleas for religious toleration and numberless irreverent satires on the narrowness, irrationality, and superstition of traditional Christianity. Voltaire was characteristic of Enlightenment thinkers in that he was uncompromisingly anticlerical, but it would be wholly incorrect to describe him as an atheist and inaccurate to call him an irreligious man. His writings bear witness to a lifelong struggle to achieve a rational piety that might sustain a person of moral disposition in a world full of monstrous human crimes and terrible human sufferings.

The younger generation of French Enlightenment thinkers (or *philosophes*) represents a considerable variety of viewpoints, some of them far more radical politically and more antireligious than those of Voltaire and Montesquieu. The leading French philosopher of this generation was Denis Diderot (1713–1784), a versatile and gifted writer, and the principal editor of the massive *Encyclopedia*, unquestionably the greatest scholarly and literary achievement of the French Enlightenment. Diderot left no finished philosophical system, but rather a variety of writings that expressed an ever-changing point of view and covered many subjects—metaphysics, natural science, psychology, aesthetics, criticism, society, politics, morality, and religion. In religion, Diderot began as a Deist, but later abandoned this position as an unworthy compromise with religious superstition. Yet even as an atheist, he retained great sympathy for many aspects of religion, especially for the religious predicament of the conscientious individual moral agent. His atheism has sometimes been accurately (if anachronistically) described as existentialist in character. In his later years, he occasionally flirted with some form of theism, especially with a sort of naturalistic pantheism. Like Voltaire, he was adamantly opposed to the simpler and more direct atheism of materialists such as d'Holbach.

The first volume of Diderot's *Encyclopedia* was published in 1751, prefaced by the famous "Preliminary Discourse" by the scientist Jean Le Rond d'Alembert (1717–1783). Seven volumes were published by 1759, when the work was suppressed by royal decree as causing "irreparable damage to morality and religion." In the same year, Pope Clement XIII threatened those who read it or possessed copies of it with excommunication. Six years later, with tacit permission of the government, Diderot managed to publish the remaining ten volumes. The *Encyclopedia* contained articles by many distinguished French intellectuals: Voltaire and Montesquieu, Rousseau and Condorcet, Quesnay and Turgot. Some of the articles are anonymous, perhaps written by Diderot himself, or taken by him from other sources. (The article "Reason," for instance, is a close paraphrase of Coste's translation of Locke's *Essay concerning Human Understanding* [4.18.10–11], an eloquent part of Locke's treatment of the relation of reason to faith.) The *Encyclopedia* by no means disseminated a single "party line" on moral, political, or religious questions. Many of the articles on theological subjects, for instance, were by Abbé Claude Yvon (1714–1791), who, in his article "Atheists," attacks Bayle's view that atheism should be tolerated and that the morals of atheists are as high as those of believers. The real ideology behind the encyclopedia is its confidence that moral, political, and religious progress can be achieved in society by the simple means of "raising the level of debate" on these matters. It was precisely this, and not immoralist or antireligious propaganda, that aroused the fear of Louis XV and Pope Clement XIII.

The most important epistemologist and psychologist of the second-generation *philosophes* was Étienne Bonnot, abbé de Condillac (1715–1780), whose *Treatise on Systems* (1749) and *Treatise on Sensations* (1754) developed a theory of human knowledge grounded wholly on sense experience. It is probably in Condillac, in fact, together with David Hume (1711–1776), that we find the true beginnings of modern empiricism.

The *philosophes* also included some infamous philosophical radicals, particularly Julien Offroy de La Mettrie (1709–1751), Claude-Adrien Helvétius (1715–1771), and Paul-Henri Thiry, baron d'Holbach (1723–1789). La Mettrie expounded an openly materialist theory of the soul in *Man a Machine* (1748) and a blatantly hedonist ethics in *Discourse on Happiness* (1750). Helvétius's *On the Mind* (published posthumously, 1772) presents a thoroughgoing determinist and environmentalist psychology, together with a utilitarian ethical theory. D'Holbach's attack on religion was begun in his *Christianisme dévoilé* (1761; the title is cleverly ambiguous: "revealed Christianity" or "Christianity exposed"); it was continued in his materialistic, deterministic, and atheistic *System of Nature* (1770).

Elsewhere in Europe, the Enlightenment took more moderate forms. In Germany, the alleged religious unorthodoxy of the *Aufklärung*'s representatives often made them objects of controversy, sometimes victims of persecution. But in fact there was nothing more radical among them than a rather conservative form of Deism. The founder of the German Enlightenment was Christian Wolff (1679–1754). He was possessed of an unoriginal but encyclopedic mind suited to the task of exercising a dominant influence on German academic philosophy. And this he did during the whole of the eighteenth century, at least until its last two decades. Although Wolff's theology was orthodox to the point of scholasticism, his rationalistic approach to theology brought upon him the wrath of the German Pietists, who had him dismissed from his professorship at Halle in 1723. (He was reinstated by Frederick the Great, however, on the latter's accession in 1740.) Among the influential exponents of Wolffianism in the *Aufklärung* were the metaphysician and aesthetician Alexander Gottlieb Baumgarten (1714–1762), the first to describe philosophy of art as "aesthetics"; the "neologist" theologian Johann Salomo Semler (1725–1791); and the controversial early biblical critic Hermann Samuel Reimarus (1694–1768).

The *Aufklärung* flourished during the reign of Frederick the Great (r. 1740–1786). Himself a Deist and an admirer of the *philosophes*, Frederick refounded the Berlin Academy in 1744 and brought the distinguished French scientist Pierre-Louis Moreau de Maupertuis (1698–1759) to Berlin as its head, along with Voltaire, La Mettrie, and d'Alembert. The academy's nonresident members included Wolff, Baumgarten, Fontenelle, Helvétius, and d'Holbach. Beyond (or beneath) the patronage of Frederick, there were also the so-called popular Enlightenment thinkers, such as Christoph Friedrich Nicolai (1733–1811) and Christian Garve (1742–1798). By far their most distinguished representative, however, was the Jewish Deist Moses Mendelssohn (1729–1786), a gifted German prose stylist, an early advocate of the disestablishment of religion, and the grandfather of composer Felix Mendelssohn.

One of the most independent and influential voices of the German Enlightenment was that of Mendelssohn's close friend Gotthold Ephraim Lessing (1729–1781), a dramatist, critic, theologian, and admirer of Spinoza and Leibniz. Lessing's theological writings are powerful but enigmatic in content, perhaps because his aim was simultaneously to criticize the arid rationalism of Wolffian theology and to reject the irrationalism and bibliolatry of Pietism. (The term bibliolatry as an epithet of opprobrium was coined by him.)

In the second half of the eighteenth century, there arose several empiricist critics of Wolffianism in Germany, notably Johann Heinrich Lambert (1728–1777) and Johannes Nikolaus Tetens (1736–1807). But towering over them, and indeed over all other philosophers of the German Enlightenment, is the foremost critic of Wolffian philosophy, Immanuel Kant (1724–1804). It is often said that Kant's ethics displays signs of his Pietist upbringing. In fact, however, Kant's specific references to Pietist forms of religiosity (emphasis on devotional reading of the Bible and on prayer as means of raising oneself to an actual experience of grace and justification) harshly criticize them as fanaticism (*Schwärmerei*) subversive of moral autonomy. Kant's theology was always a form of Wolffian rationalism, his moral religion a form of Enlightenment Deism. Kant's famous avowal that he "limits knowledge in order to make room for faith" makes reference not to a voluntarist or irrationalist "leap," still less to a biblical faith. Kantian moral faith is a form of rational belief, justified by a subtle (and usually underrated) philosophical argument. Throughout his maturity, and even during his term as rector of the University of Königsberg, Kant refused on principle to participate in religious services (which he condemned as "superstitious pseudo-service" [*Afterdienst*] of God). His uncompromising anticlericalism and deep suspicion of popular religion ("vulgar superstition") are characteristic French Enlightenment attitudes. Kant's 1784 essay "What Is Enlightenment?" expressed wholehearted support for the movement and for the policies of academic openness, religious toleration, and anticlericalism pursued by Frederick the Great.

The Enlightenment in Britain is represented in theology by the tradition of British Deism (the position of such men as John Toland and Matthew Tindal) and in politics by Whig liberalism. Representative of both trends was the philosopher, scientist, and Presbyterian (and Unitarian) cleric Joseph Priestley (1733–1804). Other Britons displaying the impact of the Enlightenment included the utilitarian Jeremy Bentham (1748–1832), the economist and moral theorist Adam Smith (1723–1790), the historian Edward Gibbon (1737–1794), and the radical political thinker William Godwin (1756–1836). Hume is often regarded as an opponent, even a great subverter, of the Enlightenment, partly because of his political conservatism, but chiefly because of his skeptical attack on the pretensions of human reason. Hume was, however, personally on good terms with many of the *philosophes* and at one with their views on religious matters. To see Hume's attack on reason as anti-Enlightenment is to ignore the fact that it is carried on in the name of the other important Enlightenment ideal, nature. Along with Condillac and the *philosophes*, Hume views our cognitive powers as part of our natural equipment as living organisms and urges us to view our use of them as bound up with our practical needs. His skeptical attack on reason is an attack not on the faculty praised by the Enlightenment, but rather on that appealed to by vain scholastic metaphysicians and crafty sophists hoping to provide "shelter to popular superstitions" by "raising entangling brambles to cover their weakness." Far from being a critic of the Enlightenment, Hume is one of its most characteristic and articulate voices.

The founding fathers of the United States included prominent Enlightenment figures: Thomas Paine, Benjamin Franklin, and Thomas Jefferson. The Federalist suspicion of centralized state power and the hostility to clericalism motivating the complete separation of church and state in the new republic both reflect the influence of Enlightenment ideas.

Even today we still tend to view the Enlightenment through the distorting lens of nineteenth-century romanticism and its reactionary preconceptions. Enlightenment thought is still accused of being ahistorical and ethnocentric, when (as Ernst Cassirer has shown) the conceptual tools used by post-Enlightenment historians and anthropologists were all forged by the Enlightenment itself. Enlightenment thought is charged with naive optimism, despite the fact that some of the most characteristic Enlightenment thinkers (Voltaire, Mendelssohn) were historical pessimists. It is said that the Enlightenment had too much confidence in human reason, despite its preoccupation with the limits of human cognitive powers. Moreover, many of the Enlightenment thinkers who were most hopeful of salutary social change because of the progress of reason also expressed profound doubts about this (witness Diderot's posthumously published masterpiece *Rameau's Nephew*).

On the subject of religion, the common twentieth-century view—inherited from nineteenth-century romanticism—was that Enlightenment thinkers were shallow and arrogant, showing an irreverence and contempt for tradition and authority. Of course, any movement that (like the Enlightenment) sets out to deflate the pretensions of pseudo-profundity will naturally be accused of shallowness by those it makes its targets. It is equally natural that people who are outraged by crimes and hypocrisy carried on under the protection of an attitude of reverence for tradition and authority should choose irreverent wit and satire as appropriate vehicles for their criticism. In fact, the Enlightenment attack on religious authority and tradition was motivated by a profound concern for what it conceived to be the most essential values of the human spirit, the foundations of any true religion.

Kant defines "enlightenment" as "the human being's release from self-imposed tutelage"; by "tutelage," he means the inability to use one's understanding without guidance from another, the state of a child whose spiritual life is still held in benevolent bondage by his parents. Tutelage is self-imposed when it results not from immaturity or inability to think for oneself, but rather from a lack of courage to do so. Thus enlightenment is the process by which human individuals receive the courage to think for themselves about morality, religion, and politics, instead of having their opinions dictated to them by political, ecclesiastical, or scriptural authorities.

The battle cry of the Enlightenment in religious matters was toleration. The cry now sounds faint and irrelevant to us, partly because we flatter ourselves that we long ago achieved what it demands, and partly because toleration itself appears to be a value that is bloodless and without specific content. But on both counts we seriously misconceive the meaning the Enlightenment attached to toleration. Toleration is the beginning of enlightenment as Europe in the eighteenth century conceived it because it is the necessary social condition for people to use their own intellects to decide what they will believe. The Enlightenment's demand for toleration is thus the demand that people be given the opportunity to fulfill their deepest spiritual vocation: that of using their intellects to determine the faith they will live by. People miss this vocation whenever "faith" for them ceases to be a belief founded on their own evaluation of the evidence before them and becomes the submission of their intellect to some unquestioned authority. The Enlightenment's judgment on such a spiritually crippling, unenlightened "faith" was pronounced most eloquently by the father of Enlightenment thought, John Locke.

> There is a use of the word *Reason*, wherein it is opposed to *Faith*. . . . Only . . . *Faith* is nothing but a firm Assent of the Mind: which if it be regulated as is our Duty, cannot be afforded to any thing, but upon good Reason. . . . He that believes, without having any reason for believing . . . neither seeks Truth as he ought, nor pays the Obedience due to his Maker, who would have him use those discerning Faculties he has given him. (*Essay concerning Human Understanding* 4.17.24)

Enlightenment is release from tutelage. It is not surprising that a person who subjects himself to the authority of church or scripture or to his own fancies should be intolerant of others' beliefs and should attempt to impose his own upon them. "For," asks Locke, "how almost can it be otherwise, but that he should be ready to impose on others Belief, who has already imposed on his own?"

Kant, writing in 1784, did not claim to be living in an enlightened age, an age in which people had come to intellectual maturity and governed their own beliefs through reason; but he did claim to be living in an age of enlightenment, an age in which people were gaining the courage to free themselves from the spiritual oppression of tradition and authority. Before we dismiss Enlightenment thought as shallow or as irrelevant to our time, we should ask ourselves whether we can say even as much for our age as Kant was willing to say for his.

SEE ALSO Atheism; Cassirer, Ernst; Deism; Descartes, René; Doubt and Belief; Empiricism; Faith; Hume, David; Kant, Immanuel; Leibniz, Gottfried Wilhelm; Lessing, G. E.; Locke, John; Mendelssohn, Moses; Methodist Churches; Pietism; Reimarus, Hermann Samuel; Rousseau, Jean-Jacques; Spinoza, Barukh; Theism; Truth; Wolff, Christian.

BIBLIOGRAPHY

The best general study of Enlightenment thought is Ernst Cassirer's *The Philosophy of Enlightenment* (Boston, 1951). Also valuable are Paul Hazard's *European Thought in the Eighteenth Century* (New Haven, 1954) and Frederick C. Copleston's *A History of Philosophy*, vol. 6, *Wolff to Kant* (Westminster, Md., 1963), parts 1 and 2. Carl Becker's *The Heavenly City of the Eighteenth-Century Philosophers* (New Haven, 1932) is a famous and paradoxical defense of the continuity between Enlightenment thinkers and the Christian tradition they criticized. The best known of many replies to it is Peter Gay's *The Enlightenment*, 2 vols. (New York, 1966), especially volume 1, *The Rise of Modern Paganism*.

On the French Enlightenment, see Frank E. Manuel's *The Prophets of Paris* (Cambridge, Mass., 1962); on England, see John Plamenatz's *The English Utilitarians*, 2d ed. (Oxford, 1958). An excellent treatment of the German Enlightenment can be found in chapters 10–17 of Lewis White Beck's *Early German Philosophy: Kant and His Predecessors* (Cambridge, Mass., 1969). Studies emphasizing the religious thought of the four most important Enlightenment thinkers are Norman L. Torrey's *Voltaire and the English Deists* (1930; reprint, Hamden, Conn., 1967); Aram Vartanian's *Diderot and Descartes* (Princeton, 1953); *Hume on Religion* (New York, 1963), edited by Richard Wollheim; and my book *Kant's Moral Religion* (Ithaca, N. Y., 1970).

New Sources

Barnett, S. J. *The Enlightenment and Religion: The Myths of Modernity.* New York, 2003.

Darnton, Robert. *George Washington's False Teeth: An Unconventional Guide to the Eighteenth Century.* New York, 2003.

Gordon, Daniel. *Citizens without Sovereignty: Equality and Sociability in French Thought.* Princeton, 1994.

Mah, Harold. *Enlightenment Phantasies: Cultural Identity in France and Germany.* Ithaca, N.Y., 2003.

Melton, James Von Horn. *The Rise of the Public in Enlightenment Europe.* New York, 2001.

Muthu, Sankar. *Enlightenment against Empire.* Princeton, 2003.

Porter, Roy. *Flesh in the Age of Reason.* New York, 2003.

Zakai, Avihu. *Jonathan Edwards's Philosophy of History: The Reenchantment with the World in the Age of Enlightenment.* Princeton, 2003.

ALLEN W. WOOD (1987)
Revised Bibliography

ENLIL, the "wind god," was the principal god of the Sumerian pantheon and poliad god of Nippur, the religious center of the country. Enlil was also guardian god of the temple Ekur ("mountain house") and the husband of Ninlil, or Sud. Together with An and Enki, Enlil was the third member of the great triad of the Sumerian pantheon and a permanent member of the assembly of the gods. When the cosmos was divided, Enlil took the earth for himself, while An ruled the sky and Ereshkigal was given the underworld. Enlil is the elder brother of Enki, whom he entrusted with the task of putting the world in order. After the great Flood, Enlil and An gave Ziusudra (the hero of the flood) "life, like (that of) a god." The Moon god (Nanna-Sin, Ashimbabbar), Nergal, Ninazu, and Enbilulu were born from Enlil's union with Ninlil. In the myth *The Assault of the Demons on the Moon*, when the demons besiege heaven and black out the moon, Enlil deals with the situation by having Enki, the god of magic, intervene.

Piotr Steinkeller (1999) and Piotr Michalowski (1998) have cast doubt upon the Sumerian nature of the god Enlil. They discuss the actual meaning of the name, equating the Eblaite I-li-lu with Enlil. Just how at variance this is with other Sumerian myths has been shown by Manfred Krebernik and M. P. Streck, and the epithet of Enlil in Sumerian literature is *kur-gal* (great mountain), suggesting origins in eastern Mesopotamia.

The myth of *Enlil and Ninlil*, who in Mesopotamian religious tradition were seen as the principal gods of Nippur, is both a sacred marriage text (or hierogamy), as well as a theogony, since it narrates not only the marriage but also the birth of four heavenly gods, one of them the Moon god. The story begins with an introduction praising Nippur, setting the scene where the action unfolds, and a description of the two main characters, Enlil and Ninlil. Well aware of the hot-blooded nature of the youth of the city, Ninlil's wise mother, Nunbarshegunu, advises her daughter not to bathe in the river because she could tempt one of the young men. When Ninlil disobeys her mother and bathes in the river, Enlil spots her and immediately makes advances to her, which Ninlil rejects. Enlil then sails on the river with the help of his herald Nusku, and renews his advances. This time the young woman is unable to resist, so the god has intercourse with her and impregnates her with Sin-Ashimbabbar. Enlil's scandalous behavior causes the gods to banish him from the city. When he leaves the city, Ninlil follows him and finds where he is hiding, having intercourse with him three more times and producing three more gods: Nergal, Ninazu, and Enbilulu. The text concludes with a doxology praising both divinities, after a hymn in honor of Enlil.

In contrast to the preceding myth, where the circumstances in which Enlil and Ninlil marry are somewhat perplexing, another version of the myth faithfully reflects the custom and practice of Sumerian society. The story begins by introducing the characters and establishing that Enlil is not yet married. On a journey through the land of Sumer, Enlil reaches Eresh, where he meets the young Sud. He engages in conversation with her, making clear his intentions, but the god has scarcely begun to approach her when Sud proudly slams the door in his face. Enlil, already enamored, turns to Nusku and entrusts him with the task of going to Eresh to ask Sud's mother Nidaba for the hand of her daughter. Nidaba consents, but on the condition of a journey by Aruru, Enlil's sister, to Eresh, followed by her journey to Nippur. When the messenger returns to Nippur and brings back the message, Enlil prepares lavish gifts, which are taken by caravan to Eresh. The gifts are received graciously, and preparations begin for the marriage and the actual ceremony. Enlil then blesses his wife and gives her the name Ninlil.

A series of documents tell of the *Journeys of the Gods* to obtain blessings and prosperity for the cities under their protection. The first of these journeys is undertaken by the Moon god Nanna, the poliad god of Ur and son of Enlil and Ninlil, who goes to the city of his birth, Nippur. After a eulogy of his city, in which he praises its antiquity, the god Nanna sends messengers throughout the country and also to other distant countries to collect the required materials so that he can build a boat. When he has constructed the boat, there is an inventory of the goods loaded upon it, and then begins the long journey to carry the god to the city of Nippur. The boat makes several stops en route, first at Ennegi, where the goddess Ningirida, hoping to receive Nanna's precious cargo, welcomes him, but he refuses her. The same thing happens at Larsa, the home of the goddess Sherida; at Uruk, home of the goddess Inanna; at Shuruppak, home of the goddess Ninunu; and at Tummal, home of Ninlil.

The boat finally reaches Nippur, where Nanna asks for and is granted permission to enter, and he sets down the gifts he has brought. His father Enlil joyfully welcomes his son and serves a sumptuous feast for him, which ends with a request for a general blessing for the city under his protection. A special request is then put to the sovereign, but his response is ambiguous. Two other journeys concern the guardian divinities of the city of Isin, the god Pabilsag and the goddess Nininsina; both of them travel to Nippur to beg for a blessing for themselves and their adopted city.

Enlil's active involvement with humankind is shown in various documents. In *The Song of the Hoe,* Enlil, after separating heaven and earth so that humans can cultivate the earth, makes an opening in the floor of the earth. He then creates a hoe, establishes the various kinds of labor, describes the qualities of the hoe in detail, and sets it in the place where the first human being will appear. When the human race springs from mold that had been placed in the hole, and when grass grows, Enlil gives the humans the hoe, while the gods express their wholehearted approval. It is interesting to note the writer's belief, already clear from these lines, that the first human being was Sumerian.

Another document, which dates to after 1100 BCE, is the only one in which blood is necessary for the creation of humans, an element completely absent in the Sumerian creation myths and probably derived from a Semitic tradition. The story links the creation of the human race to the very beginnings of the world, when the gods had come into being, heaven and earth had been separated, and the basis for life on earth had been established by digging rivers and channels so water could flow. At a meeting involving the three main gods and the Anunna (all the great gods), Enlil poses the question as to whether or not they want him to carry on with the act of creation. Their unanimous response is to let humankind emerge in the temple of Enlil by mixing clay with the blood of the god Alla. The new creatures, called Ullegarra and Annegarra, are given the task of manual labor, and they are to make the land rich in plenty, holding sumptuous feasts for the world of the gods. This is the law laid down by Aruru, the sister of Enlil, and the goddess Nisaba ensured that it was duly observed.

The prologue of the *Debate between Sheep and Grain* contains a cosmogonic allusion to the birth of two gods that were essential for human life, Ashnan (grain) and Uttu (the spinning of wool). The god An had not created them in the beginning, so the earth did not have grain, sheep, or goats, and human beings did not have bread or clothes and were living like animals. The gods put right the forgetfulness of An by making grain and sheep appear in their house on the sacred hill, and they ate and drank plentifully, but were not sated. At this point the gods decide to bestow their new creation on humankind, and Enki advises Enlil to give sheep and grain to humans as a gift. Thus, via the intervention of these two supreme gods, sheep and grain are brought from the sacred hill to the earth for the use of human beings.

Enlil, though, is not always beneficent to humans, and the negative aspects of divine behavior towards the human race are described in the myth of Atrahasis, as well as the myth of the Sumerian flood and the *Epic of Gilgamesh.* In the *Epic of Atrahasis,* Enlil is portrayed as one who, alarmed by the rapid growth of the human race (whose noise disturbs his sleep), attempts to reduce and eventually destroy humankind by plague, by drought, and finally by flood. In the *Lament for Ur,* the destruction of the city Ur is attributed to Enlil's storm "that annihilated the land." One petitioner bemoans in a prayer the fact that Enlil is "the storm destroying the cattle pen, uprooting the sheepfold; my roots are torn up, my forests denuded."

Commencing with the Old Babylonian period, Enlil occupied a less exalted position in the pantheon. Many of his attributes were assumed by Marduk in Babylonia and by Ashur in Assyria. Indeed, it is likely that Marduk's and Ashur's prominent roles in the great Mesopotamian national epic, *Enuma elish* (in the extant Babylonian and Assyrian recensions, respectively), originally belonged to Enlil.

SEE ALSO Ashur; Marduk; Mesopotamian Religion, overview article.

BIBLIOGRAPHY

Behrens, Hermann. *Enlil und Ninlil: Ein sumerischer Mythos aus Nippur.* Rome, 1978.

Civil, Miguel. "Enlil and Ninlil: The Marriage of Sud." *Journal of American Oriental Society* 103 (1983): 43–66.

Kramer, Samuel Noah. "BM 23631: Bread for Enlil, Sex for Inanna" *Orientalia* 54 (1985): 117–132.

Krebernik, Manfred. "Ninlil (Mulliltu, Mullisu), Göttin, Gemahlin Enlils." *Reallexikon der Assyriologie* 9 (1998–2001): 453–461.

Michalowski, Piotr. "The Unbearable Lightness of Enlil." *Comptes rendues de la Rencontre Assyriologique Internationale* 43 (1998): 237–247.

Pettinato, Giovanni. *Mitologia sumerica.* Turin, 2001.

Pettinato, Giovanni. "Enlil: La parola immutabile." In *Parole, parola: Alle origini della comunicazione,* pp. 7–32. Milan, 2001.

Steinkeller, Piotr. "On Rulers and Officials in the Ancient Near East." In *Priests and Officials in the Ancient Near East,* edited by Kazuko Watanabe, pp. 103–137. Heidelberg, Germany, 1999.

Streck, Michael P. "Ninurta/Ningirsu. A. I. In Mesopotamien" *Reallexikon der Assyriologie* 9 (1998–2001): 512–522.

Such-Gutierrez, Marcos. *Beiträge zum Pantheon von Nippur im 3. Jahtausend,* Teil I and II (Materiali per i Vocabolario Sumerico) 9, nos. 1–2 (2003): 31–108.

David Marcus (1987)
Giovanni Pettinato (2005)
Translated from Italian by Paul Ellis

ENNIN (794–864), posthumous title, Jikaku Daishi; was a Japanese Buddhist monk of the Tendai school. Ennin was born in north-central Japan. At fifteen he entered the monastic center on Mount Hiei, the headquarters of the Tendai school, where he soon became a favorite disciple of Saichō (767–822), the Japanese monk who transmitted the Tendai (Chin., Tiantai) teachings to Japan from China. In 814 Ennin became a full-fledged monk, after which he studied the Buddhist precepts at Tōdaiji in Nara for seven years. Eventually, a physical ailment forced him to retire to a hut at Yokawa in the northern part of Mount Hiei, where he waited quietly for death. According to legend, Ennin devoted himself to copying the *Lotus Sūtra* (Jpn. *Hōkekyō;* Skt., *Saddharmapuṇḍarika Sūtra*) for three years, and miraculously regained his health after experiencing a vision of the Buddha in a dream. The next year (835) Ennin petitioned the court for permission to visit China. He left Japan in 838 with the last official Japanese embassy to the Tang court. Unable to gain permission to visit Mount Tiantai, eponymous headquarters of the Chinese Tiantai school, he studied Sanskrit and received initiation into the Vajradhātu Maṇḍala and the Garbhakośadhātu Maṇḍala and other Esoteric (Mikkyō) doctrines and practices.

The following year he made a pilgrimage to Mount Wutai in northern China, a center of Pure Land practices. Here, Ennin studied Tiantai texts and Mikkyō, and participated in Pure Land practices. In 840 he went to the capital, Chang'an, where for six years he deepened his knowledge and added expertise in the *susiddhi,* an Esoteric tradition as yet unknown in Japan. Ennin survived the persecution of Buddhism under Emperor Wuzong and finally returned to Japan in 847 with hundreds of Buddhist scriptures from the Tiantai, Esoteric, Chan, and Pure Land traditions, as well as treatises on Sanskrit, Buddhist images, assorted ceremonial objects, and even rocks from Mount Wutai. These are listed in the *Nittō shingu shōgyō mokuroku,* a catalogue Ennin submitted to the court. Ennin also returned with a diary, the *Nittō guhō junrei kōki,* a scrupulously accurate account of his travels and of the China of Tang times, and with new knowledge and experience to lead the Japanese Tendai school to social and doctrinal preeminence in Japan.

His busy career after returning to Japan was a combination of hectic activity and prestigious official recognition. On Mount Hiei he founded centers for Pure Land and *Lotus Sūtra* practices. He presided over an initiation for a thousand people in 849, an initiation for Emperor Montoku and the crown prince in 855, and bestowed the Mahayana precepts on Emperor Seiwa in 859. Incumbency of the office of *zasu,* or abbot, of the Tendai school was granted him by the court in 853. Ennin died in 864 (some sources have 866). In 866 he was granted the exalted title Jikaku Daishi ("master of compassionate awakening"); Saichō was (posthumously) given the title Dengyō Daishi ("master of the transmission of the teachings") at the same time. This was the first use of the title Daishi in Japan.

The contributions of Ennin to Japanese Buddhism are as follows:

(1) The transmission of Pure Land practices from Mount Wutai. Although Saichō had already introduced a type of Pure Land practice, the verbal Nembutsu introduced by Ennin provided the foundation for the later independent Pure Land schools of the Kamakura period (1185–1333).

(2) Compilation of his diary of his journey to China, an extremely valuable and unique record of Tang China.

(3) Consolidation of Tendai Mikkyō. Ennin completed Saichō's limited transmission of Mikkyō so that the Tendai Mikkyō tradition, known as Taimitsu, could successfully compete with the Tōmitsu Mikkyō of the Shingon school transmitted and founded by Kūkai (774–835).

(4) Introduction of *shōmyō,* a melodious method of chanting the scriptures, and transmission of new Pure Land, Mikkyō, confessional, and memorial ceremonies; construction of many important buildings on Mount Hiei; and development of the Yokawa area of Mount Hiei.

(5) Strengthening of the position of the Mahāyāna precepts platform on Mount Hiei through his contacts with the imperial court. Ennin's *Kenyō daikai ron,* an important treatise on the subject, further contributed to the power and influence of the ordination center on Mount Hiei.

(6) Cultivation of many important disciples. Ennin's lineage, called the Sanmon-ha, although in competition with the Jimon-ha of Enchin (814–891), dominated the Tendai hierarchy for centuries.

Ennin's legacy thus includes the development of the doctrine, practices, and social prestige of the Japanese Tendai school to the point where it dominated the Japanese Buddhist world of the later Heian period (866–1185) and provided the basis for the Pure Land, Zen, and Nichiren schools. Ennin's meticulous diary is also the best source of information on the daily life and times of Tang China.

See Also Tendaishū.

Bibliography

The only English-language work on Ennin is Edwin O. Reischauer's pioneering study, *Ennin's Travels in Tang China,* and his translation of Ennin's diary, *Ennin's Diary: The Record of a Pilgrimage to China in Search of the Law* (New York, 1955). This work is widely recognized as authoritative, but its approach is historical rather than religious and does not cover Ennin's life and contributions after his return to Japan. The most detailed study and translation of Ennin's diary in Japanese is Ono Katsutoshi's four-volume *Nittō guhō junrei kōki no kenkyū* (Tokyo, 1964–1969). There are two volumes of collected essays concerning Ennin, *Jikaku Daishi sangōshū*, edited by Yamada Etai (Kyoto, 1963), and the more scholarly *Jikaku Daishi kenkyū*, edited by Fukui Kōjun (1964; reprint, Tokyo 1980), first published on the eleven hundredth anniversary of Ennin's death. There is no single collection of Ennin's works, which are instead scattered throughout various collections of Buddhist texts.

PAUL L. SWANSON (1987)

EN NO GYŌJA (634?–701), literally, "En the ascetic (*ācārya*)"; famous Japanese mountain ascetic and *hijiri*. Details of his life have been recorded, *inter alia*, in the *Nihon ryōiki* (820) and in his biography, *En no Gyōja hongi* (724). He is also known as En no Ozunu, En no Shōzunu, Shōkaku, or simply as the Master En.

En no Gyōja was born to a family of Shintō priests in the village of Kuwahara in Yamato province (Nara prefecture). Although he converted to Buddhism as a youth, he decided to forgo ordination as a monk and to remain a layman. As a result, he is often referred to as En no Ubasoku, "the layman En," after the Japanese transcription of the Sanskrit *upāsaka* ("layman"). At the age of thirty-two he retreated to Mount Katsuragi (Nara prefecture) and adopted the severe life of a mountain ascetic, clothing himself in grasses and living on the bark of trees. In a cave on the mountainside he installed a copper statue of his patron the *bodhisattva* Kujaku Myō-ō (Skt., Mayūrīrāja), who is believed to assume the shape of a bird in order to dispense his mercies. For more than thirty years En no Gyōja practiced austerities and meditation in front of this statue. During this period he also forayed to other famous peaks, including the Omine range and Mount Kimbusen, which later became important centers of *yamabushi* activity. His experience of enlightenment, the culmination of years of ascetic practice, he recorded in this way:

> Long ago I listened to Shaka (i.e., Śākyamuni Buddha) himself as he was preaching on the Eagle mountain [Gṛdhrakūṭa]. Later I became an emperor of Japan and ruled the empire. Here I am now on this mountain in a different body, to engage in the work of saving sentient being. (Coates and Ishizuka, 1949, p. 18)

Tradition relates that with the attainment of enlightenment En no Gyōja became endowed with miraculous powers, including command of the winds and clouds and even of the indigenous *kami;* his use of a Buddhist spell (*dhāraṇī*) to exorcise the god Hitokotonushi offered vivid proof of the superior magical power available to the practitioner of Buddhism and went far to establish his reputation. Such episodes, however, brought him the disfavor of the public officials, who were chary of the potential for political and social disruption presented by such episodes, and so in the year 700 he was exiled to the island of Izu. The account in the *Nihon ryōiki* reports that during his exile he walked nightly from Izu to the mainland in order to ascend Mount Fuji. In 701 he was allowed to return to Kyoto, after which he traveled to Kyushu to continue his ascetic practices until his death later that year.

En no Gyōja's reputation as the prototypical mountain wizard, who commands the powers of nature and engages in prolific displays of magical prowess gained through his ascetic activities, led him to be canonized as the founder of the Shugendō sect of mountain ascetics. In his doctrines, En no Gyōja is recorded to have attempted to harmonize the Japanese respect for nature and belief in the sacrality of mountain precincts with the teachings of Buddhism. His followers in later generations came to recognize in certain mountain peaks and caves the indigenous equivalents of the Kongōkai (Diamond Realm) and Taizōkai (Womb Realm) *maṇḍalas* of the Tendai and Shingon esoteric traditions in Japan. En no Gyōja's legacy continued to inform the mind of Heian Japan (794–1185): instances of his legend may be found in the *Makurazōshi* (Pillow sketches) of Sei Shōnagon and in the *Konjaku monogatari* (Narratives of past and present). As late as 1799 he was awarded the honorary title Daibosatsu Shimben, "Great Bodhisattva of Divine Change."

SEE ALSO Shugendō.

BIBLIOGRAPHY

Coates, H. H., and Ryūgaku Ishizuka. *Honen the Buddhist Saint.* 5 vols. Kyoto, 1949.

Hori Ichirō. *Folk Religion in Japan.* Edited and translated by Joseph M. Kitagawa and Alan L. Miller. Chicago, 1968.

New Sources

Ishikawa, Tomohiko, and Hiromu Ozawa. *Zusetsu En no Gyōja: Shugendō to En no Gyōja emaki.* Tokyo, 2000.

Miyake, Hitoshi. *En no Gyōja to Shugendō no rekishi.* Tokyo, 2000.

Zenitani, Buhei. *En no Gyōja denki shūsei.* Osaka, 1994.

J. H. KAMSTRA (1987)
Revised Bibliography

ENOCH, or, in Hebrew, Ḥanokh (from a Hebrew root meaning "consecrate, initiate") was the son of Jared, according to biblical tradition; righteous antediluvian; and the subject of substantial hagiography in the Jewish and Christian traditions.

IN THE HEBREW BIBLE. *Genesis,* in listing the descendants of Adam until Noah and his sons, mentions Enoch, the seventh, in ways distinct from the others: Enoch "walked with God"; he lived only 365 years, a considerably shorter time than the others; and at the end of his life he "was no more, for God took him" (*Gn.* 5:21–24). Modern scholars agree that a fuller tradition about Enoch lies behind the preserved fragment. They disagree, however, on whether that tradition can be recovered from depictions of Enoch in postbiblical Jewish literature of Hellenistic times and from parallel depictions of antediluvian kings, sages, and flood heroes in ancient Mesopotamian literature.

IN JEWISH LITERATURE OF SECOND TEMPLE TIMES. The Septuagint (the Greek translation of the Bible, c. 250 BCE), *Ben Sira* (c. 190 BCE), and the *Jewish Antiquities* by Josephus Flavius (37/8–c. 100 CE) all state that Enoch was taken by or returned to the deity. The *Wisdom of Solomon* (first century BCE) explains that God prematurely terminated Enoch's life on earth so that wickedness would not infect his perfect saintliness. Philo Judaeus (d. 45–50 CE) allegorizes Enoch so as to represent the person who is ecstatically transported (echoing the Septuagint) from perishable (physical) to imperishable (spiritual and intellectual) aspects of existence, and from mortality to (spiritual) immortality. Like the Greek version of *Ben Sira,* Philo describes Enoch as a sign of repentance for having changed from the "worse life to the better." Enoch is not found among the sinful multitude but in solitude. Philo contrasts Enoch's piety with that of Abraham, which is exercised within society rather than in isolation.

The portrayals of Enoch in contemporary writings displaying apocalyptic interests are considerably more laudatory of him and expansive of the underlying biblical text. Here Enoch is depicted as a medium for the revelation of heavenly secrets to humanity: secrets of cosmology, sacred history, and eschatology. The principal sources for these traditions are *1* and *2 Enoch, Jubilees, Pseudo-Eupolemus,* and previously unknown writings among the Dead Sea Scrolls. They span a period from the third century BCE to the first century CE.

Enoch's "life" and the secrets revealed to him are summarized in *Jubilees* 4:16–26 and detailed in the *Books of Enoch.* Enoch receives these revelations first in nocturnal visions, and then in a heavenly journey lasting three hundred years, during which he dwells with angels and is instructed by them in hidden cosmological and historical knowledge. After a brief return to earth to transmit a record of his witness to his descendants, he is removed to the Garden of Eden, where he continues to testify to humanity's sins and to record God's judgments of these sins until the final judgment. Enoch is also said to officiate in paradise at the sanctuary before God. Elsewhere, certain religious laws are said to have originated with Enoch and his books. In some later parts of this literature, Enoch himself becomes a divine figure who dwells in heaven and executes justice. In most traditions, however, he is an intermediary between the divine and human, even after his transfer to paradise. Thus, Enoch combines the functions of prophet, priest, scribe, lawgiver, sage, and judge.

ANCIENT NEAR EASTERN PARALLELS. For more than a century, scholars have argued that the biblical Enoch has his roots in Mesopotamian lore about similar antediluvian figures, and that the likenesses between Enoch and such figures reemerge in the depictions of Enoch in Jewish literature of Hellenistic times. Such parallels have most frequently been drawn with the seventh (or sixth or eighth) member of the Sumerian antediluvian king-list, Enmeduranna. According to some versions of this tradition, the king, associated with the city of the sun god Shamash, is received into fellowship with the gods and is initiated into the secrets of heaven and earth, including the art of divination, knowledge of which he passes on to his son. Other scholars, noting that no mention is made of Enmeduranna's transcendence of death, find Enoch's antecedents in the wise flood heroes Ziusudra and Utnapishtim, who are said to have been rewarded with eternal life in paradise. Most recently, scholars have argued that Enoch is modeled after the *apkallu* sages, who reveal wisdom and the civilized arts to antediluvian humanity, the seventh (*utuabzu*) of whom is said to have ascended to heaven.

IN CHRISTIANITY. The church fathers exhibit considerable interest in Enoch's transcendence of death as a paradigm for Jesus and the Christian elect. However, some stress that it was only with Jesus' resurrection that Enoch's ascension was consummated. In the second and third centuries, Christian writers (among them, Tertullian and Irenaeus) place particular emphasis on Enoch's bodily assumption in support of belief in physical resurrection. Some (Tertullian, Hippolytus, and Jerome) identify him as one of the two witnesses of *Revelations* 11:3–13 who battle and are killed by the Antichrist, are resurrected a few days later, and are taken to heaven. Ephraem of Syria (fourth century) stresses that Enoch, like Jesus, in conquering sin and death and in regaining paradise in spirit as well as body, is the antipode of Adam. Because Enoch precedes the covenant of law (he is said to be uncircumcised and unobservant of the Sabbath), his faith and reward are of particular importance to Christianity in its polemic against Judaism and in its mission to the Gentiles.

IN RABBINIC JUDAISM. Rabbinic exegesis is concerned less with Enoch's righteousness during life, questioned by some early rabbis, than with the nature of his end. The main issue of dispute is whether he died like other righteous people, his soul returning to God, or whether he was transported, body and soul (like Elijah), to heaven or paradise.

Some rabbinical circles, initially those responsible for the mystical, theosophical literature of Merkavah (divine chariot) speculation (our earliest texts are from the fifth to sixth centuries), adapted prerabbinic traditions of Enoch's transformation into an angel. This angel (now identified with the archangel Metatron) is said to rule the heavenly "palace," to have a role in the revelation of Torah and its teaching on high, and to guide the righteous in their tours of heaven. The tension between the mystical exaltation of Enoch and the more qualified praise of him and denial of his assumption continues through medieval Jewish literature.

IN ISLAM. In the Qur'ān (19:57–58, 21:85), Idrīs is said to have been an "upright man and a prophet," who was "raised to a high place." While Idrīs's identity within the Qur'ān is uncertain, Muslim writers, drawing upon Jewish sources that venerate him, have regularly identified him with Enoch (Arab., Akhnūkh). He is said to have introduced several sciences and arts, practiced ascetic piety, received revelation, and entered paradise while still alive.

See Also Apocalypse, article on Jewish Apocalypticism to the Rabbinic Period.

Bibliography

There is no comprehensive work on the figure of Enoch in biblical and postbiblical religious traditions. For a thorough treatment of the biblical, Mesopotamian, and apocalyptic sources, see James C. Vanderkam's *Enoch and the Growth of an Apocalyptic Tradition,* "Catholic Biblical Quarterly Monograph Series," no. 18 (Washington, D.C., 1984). For a pastiche of some of the Jewish traditions with notes referring to most of the others, see Louis Ginzberg's *Legends of the Jews,* 7 vols., translated by Henrietta Szold et al. (1909–1938; reprint, Philadelphia, 1946–1955), vol. 1, pp. 125–140, and vol. 5, pp. 156–164. His notes, while comprehensive, are not always sufficiently critical. A collection of short treatments of Enoch in Jewish and Christian primary sources can be found in *Society of Biblical Literature 1978 Seminar Papers,* edited by Paul J. Achtemeier (Missoula, Mont., 1978), vol. 1, pp. 229–276.

On the biblical tradition of Enoch, see, in addition to Vanderkam's book, the following representative commentaries: John Skinner's *A Critical and Exegetical Commentary on Genesis,* 2d ed. (Edinburgh, 1930), pp. 131–132; Umberto Cassuto's *A Commentary on the Book of Genesis,* vol. 1, *From Adam to Noah,* translated by Israel Abrahams (Jerusalem, 1961), pp. 263, 281–286; and Claus Westermann's *Genesis (1–11)* (Minneapolis, 1984).

For a comprehensive bibliographical review of recent scholarship on the *Books of Enoch,* see George W. E. Nickelsburg's "The Books of Enoch in Recent Research," *Religious Studies Review* 7 (1981): 210–217. Important additions to that bibliography are Devorah Dimant's "The Biography of Enoch and the Books of Enoch," *Vetus Testamentum* 33 (January 1983): 14–29, and Moshe Gil's "Ḥanokh be-erets ḥe-hayyim" (Enoch in the Land of Eternal Life), *Tarbiz* 38 (June 1969): 322–327 (with an English summary, pp. I–III). On the significance of the Enochic literature for the history of Judaism, see, besides Vanderkam's work, Michael Edward Stone's essay "The Book of Enoch and Judaism in the Third Century B.C.E.," *Catholic Biblical Quarterly* 40 (October 1978): 479–492.

On the ancient Near Eastern background to the biblical Enoch and his postbiblical depictions, see Pierre Grelot's "La légende d'Hénoch dans les apocryphes et dans la Bible: Origine et signification," *Recherches de science religieuse* 46 (1958): 5–26, and Rykle Borger's "Die Beschwörungsserie Bit Meseri und die Himmelfahrt Henochs," *Journal of Near Eastern Studies* 33 (April 1974): 183–196. Both refer extensively to earlier scholarship.

On Enoch in Merkavah and related traditions, see Jonas C. Greenfield's prolegomenon to *3 Enoch, or The Hebrew Book of Enoch,* edited by Hugo Odeberg (New York, 1973), pp. xi–xlvii. For a Christian treatment of Enoch, see Jean Daniélou's *Holy Pagans in the Old Testament,* translated by Felix Faber (Baltimore, 1957), pp. 42–56. For Idrīs in post-Qur'anic Islamic literature, see Georges Vajda's "Idrīs," in *The Encyclopaedia of Islam,* new ed. (Leiden, 1960–).

New Sources

Dacy, Marianne. "Paradise Lost: The Fallen Angels in the Book of Enoch." *Australian Journal of Jewish Studies* 17 (2003): 51–65.

Hannah, Darrell D. "The Throne of His Glory: The Divine Throne and Heavenly Mediators in Revelation and the Similitudes of Enoch." *Zeitschrift für die Neutestamentliche Wissenschaft* 94 (2003): 68–96.

Nickelsburg, George W. E. *1 Enoch: A Commentary on the Book of 1 Enoch.* Hermeneia: A Critical and Historical Commentary on the Bible. Minneapolis, 2001.

Suter, David Winston. "Why Galilee? Galilean Regionalism in the Interpretation of 1 'Enoch' 6–16." *Henoch* 25 (2003): 167–212.

VanderKam, James C. "Biblical Interpretation in 1 Enoch and Jubilees." In *The Pseudepigrapha and Early Biblical Interpretation,* edited by James H. Charlesworth and Craig A. Evans, pp. 96–125. Sheffield, 1993.

Steven D. Fraade (1987)
Revised Bibliography

ENTHUSIASM. The history of enthusiasm is as much the history of the word as of the phenomenon it signifies. In the English-speaking world, the word came to prominence as a technical religious term in the seventeenth century, used always in reference to religious experience, and, for the most part, as a term of denigration. For about two hundred years, the usual usage was to denote ill-regulated religious emotion or, more specifically, fancied inspiration, the false or deluded claim to have received divine communications or private revelations. In the course of the last hundred years the technical religious meaning has been almost completely superseded by the more positive meaning now current (ardent zeal for a person, principle, or cause), though unfavorable overtones still cling to the derivative term, *enthusiast,* as connoting an impractical visionary or self-deluded person. It is, however, the technical religious term with which we are here concerned.

A discussion of enthusiasm is also a discussion of the word, in the important sense that disputes over its applicability were also disputes over the propriety and validity of any claims to divine inspiration and revelation. For those hostile to religion as such—or to any save a strictly rational religion—enthusiasm was no different from superstition, a charge which could be brought against the Jewish prophets of old, the apostle Paul, or Muḥammad with as much justice as against John Wesley (1703–1791). For members of the established church who were fearful of schism, enthusiasm was another name for sectarianism, and as such could be used of Francis of Assisi or Dominic, or "papists" in general, as well as the followers of George Fox (1624–1691) or Madame Guyon (1648–1717). For those suspicious of any display of emotion, particularly in religion, *enthusiasm* was synonymous with fanaticism. Only in the nineteenth century, under the influence of the Romantic revival, did a more positive sense of enthusiasm—as emotion deeply felt or the heightened perception of poetic inspiration—begin to free the word from the negative overtones of religious disapproval.

In a strict sense, then, the study of enthusiasm is the study of seventeenth- and eighteenth-century Christianity, understood as the study of movements within Christianity that were regarded by their critics as peripheral and as threatening to the integrity of Christianity, although perhaps it could more properly be understood as the study of the attitudes of those who condemned such movements as "enthusiastic." In addition, it should be borne in mind that *enthusiast* was used as a translation of the German *Schwärmer*, a term used by Martin Luther to describe such radical reformers as Andreas Karlstadt, Thomas Müntzer, and the Anabaptists. Like the English "enthusiasts," the German Schwärmer pretended to divine inspirations and revelations and could be classed as fanatics and sectarians. As a technical religious term, therefore, *enthusiasm* denotes the diverse expressions of radical, spiritualist, or sectarian Christianity, particularly in Europe, during the three hundred years from the beginning of the Reformation to the nineteenth century.

RONALD KNOX'S ENTHUSIASM. It is this narrowly defined enthusiasm which Ronald Knox describes in his classic study *Enthusiasm.* "Enthusiasm did not really begin to take shape until the moment when Luther shook up the whole pattern of European theology" (Knox, 1950, p. 4). "Enthusiasm in the religious sense belongs to the seventeenth and eighteenth centuries; it hardly reappears without inverted commas after 1823" (p. 6). To be sure, Knox notes that the pattern of enthusiasm is one which recurs spontaneously throughout church history, and he presents brief studies of the Corinthian church, the Montanists, the Donatists, and some medieval sects, particularly the Waldensians and the Cathari. But Donatists are hardly a good example of enthusiasm, despite their zeal for martyrdom. Knox dismisses Montanism as "naked fanaticism" (p. 49) and the medieval movements as fed by an inspiration "alien to the genius of Europe" or as "sporadic and unimportant, freaks of religious history" (p. 4). All these are brought into the picture less as examples of enthusiasm requiring analysis in their own right than as foils to the subsequent descriptions of enthusiasm proper. Even the Anabaptists, the Schwärmer themselves, are given scant treatment and serve largely as a vehicle for Knox's Roman Catholic disapproval of Luther and the Reformation. In all this, it is clear that Knox's chief objection to enthusiastic movements is their tendency to schismatic sectarianism. "The enthusiast always begins by trying to form a church within the Church, always ends by finding himself committed to sectarian opposition" (p. 109).

Knox's somewhat more sympathetic depiction of enthusiasm begins with his treatment of Fox, the founder of the Society of Friends (Quakers). His attention naturally focuses on Fox's belief in "the inner light," as illustrated by Fox's interruption of a preacher at Nottingham: "It is not the Scripture, it is the Holy Spirit by which holy men of old gave forth the Scripture, by which religions . . . are to be tried" (p. 152, note 3). In the twofold implication of this assertion, the marks of the enthusiast are clearly evident: the claim to an immediacy of inspiration (comparable to that elsewhere readily acknowledged in, but otherwise confined to, the biblical writers) not to be confused with reason or conscience; and the claim that this inner illumination is the true source of authority above the letter of scripture, the creeds, and the ordinances of church and state. The violent tremblings which often accompanied and were thought to attest to the movement of the Holy Spirit, and from which the nickname "Quakers" was derived, apparently occurred only in the very early days.

The central section of Knox's monograph is given over to a treatment of Jansenism (mid-seventeenth to mid-eighteenth centuries) and quietism (latter half of the seventeenth century). Significant certainly for their challenge to the mainstream of Roman Catholic tradition, these movements should probably not be classified as examples of enthusiasm, at least in the technical sense of the word as used by Knox. Jansenism stressed the corruption of human nature by original sin and the power of divine grace. Rigorist in character—a kind of Roman Catholic Puritanism—it came closest to enthusiasm in the degree to which it understood grace in terms of experiences of "sensible devotion" (pp. 224–225). Quietism was a doctrine of Christian spirituality which sought to suppress all human effort, so that divine action might have full sway over the passive soul. It emphasized the immediacy of contact between the soul and God, but since it also denied that such contact need be a matter of conscious experience, quietism is better studied in connection with Christian mysticism than (Christian) enthusiasm.

The real targets of Knox's critique at this point are Madame Guyon and the convulsionaries at Saint Médard. Guyon, who did much to promote quietism, evidently epitomizes a good deal of what Knox regarded as detestable in enthusiasm: particularly her spiritual "smugness" and, not least, the prominent role of influential women in supporting enthusiastic movements. The convulsions at the Paris cemetery of Saint Médard in the early 1730s (including ecstatic dancing, many alleged cures, and speaking in unknown languages) were regarded by participants as the outpouring of the Holy Spirit expected in the last days. But for Knox they are a fitting expression of popular Jansenism and a terrible warning of what can happen to a movement which sits too loose to ecclesiastical authority. Similar to the Jansenist Catholic convulsionaries were the Huguenot Camisards in southern France (late seventeenth to early eighteenth centuries), among whom a form of ecstatic prophecy, involving prostrations, trancelike states, and glossolalia, was prominent, and who in exile in Britain (where they were known as "the French Prophets") converted Ann Lee, the subsequent founder of the North American Shakers.

The other main object of Knox's analysis is Wesley. Here Knox's critique focuses on the religion of experience.

An initial chapter examines the Moravian piety inculcated in Germany by Count Nikolaus Zinzendorf (1700–1760). Like the quietists, the Moravians practiced a piety of stillness. But unlike the quietists, Zinzendorf preached religion as felt experience and salvation "as an immediate and joyful apprehension of a loving Father" (Knox, 1950, p. 410), assurance not merely as a doctrine believed but as something felt, the sense of God's protective love. It was the importance of such experience which Wesley learned from the Moravians and emphasized in his own doctrine of assurance—assurance of present pardon, the inner witness of the Spirit of God. Wesley never abandoned this belief in the importance of feelings, of "heart-religion," though he did subsequently concede that the consciousness of God's acceptance was not an invariable or essential concomitant of that acceptance (p. 539).

These examples might seem to have represented relatively mild forms of enthusiasm. But it is the consequences of such emphases, when freed from the constraints of traditional discipline and ecclesiastical authority, which concern Knox. It was the place given to the nonrational in Wesley's scheme of things which incited the famous remark of Bishop Butler to Wesley: "Sir, the pretending to extraordinary revelations and gifts of the Holy Ghost is a horrid thing, a very horrid thing" (p. 450). So, too, under the heading "Wesley and the religion of experience," Knox describes the convulsions, weeping, and crying out which often accompanied Wesley's preaching. Wesley's willingness to recognize the work of God in such paroxysms and to defend their occurrence makes the charge of enthusiast harder for him to escape, though Wesley himself resisted the charge, was never carried away with such enthusiasm, and clearly perceived its dangers. The other aspect of his teaching which might seem to merit the accusation was his view of Christian perfection, since a belief in the possibility of achieving sinless perfection results inevitably in spiritual elitism and claims of special revelation. However, "sinless perfection" was never Wesley's own phrase: what he encouraged his followers to seek was renewal in love or entire sanctification; nor did he indulge in or encourage the more extreme ideas which his teaching sometimes precipitated.

Knox's survey concludes with a brief foray into the nineteenth century and a reference to the Irvingites, the Shakers, and Perfectionism. Under the ministry of Edward Irving in London in the 1830s, prophecy and speaking in tongues became prominent, understood as utterances in the vernacular and in unknown languages prompted by the Holy Spirit, comparable to the first Christian Pentecost. For Irving, these manifestations confirmed his belief that the second coming of Christ was imminent. The Shakers emerged in the second half of the eighteenth century from a branch of English Quakers who adopted the Camisards' ritual practice of devotional dance to induce states of inspiration (the "shaking Quakers"). Under Lee, who was convinced by revelation that the millennium had already dawned, the movement was transplanted to North America in 1774. "Perfectionism" is identified by Knox with three roughly contemporaneous movements in the first half of the nineteenth century—one in Prussia, one in England, and one in North America (the only other example of North American enthusiasm that Knox really considers). All three shared the belief that the experience of conversion made sin an impossibility.

From all this it is possible to derive a thumbnail sketch of the typical enthusiast in classical terms. The fundamental belief of the enthusiast is in the immediacy and directness of his experience of God. For the enthusiast, as distinct from the quietist, this experience is self-evident and self-authenticating: self-evident, because it will be marked by distinct inward impressions (a clear sense of God's presence or acceptance, and inspiration or particular revelations, including visions) or by outward bodily manifestations (trembling or prostration, inspired utterance, or miraculous healings); self-authenticating, because it bears greater authority than scripture (as usually interpreted), ecclesiastical creed, rite, or office—greater, even, than reason itself. The enthusiast knows God's will and acts as his agent, accountable only and directly to him. Such experiences will regularly lead the enthusiast to conclude (1) that he is more spiritual than other believers, or that he has reached a higher stage in the Christian life; (2) that a less restrained form of worship should be permitted or encouraged, one in which the outward manifestations of the Holy Spirit have proper place; and (3) that any forms and structures of traditional Christianity which stifle the Holy Spirit should be dispensed with. Not untypically, such convictions can have a strong eschatological tinge—a belief that the millennium has dawned or that Christ's second coming is imminent—which invests the enthusiastic individual or sect with universal significance and can thus justify strongly antisocial or revolutionary action.

TOWARD A BROADER EVALUATION OF ENTHUSIASM. Obviously, then, the classic view of enthusiasm has to a considerable extent been determined by the negative connotations attached to the word. Within Christianity, because of fear of superstition, fanaticism, and sectarianism, claims to inspiration and fresh revelation have repeatedly been labeled as "enthusiastic" without more ado. Even Knox, in this love-hate fascination with the subject, regularly allows his account of enthusiastic eccentricities to color the total picture. However, the very evolution in the meaning of the word itself, from censure to approbation, invites a broader evaluation of the subject matter, regarding both the range of phenomena covered (outside as well as inside historical Christianity) and the possibility of a less negative appraisal. In particular, a less value-laden approach to enthusiasm must view more objectively the fact that claims to inspiration and fresh revelation are a fundamental feature of most religions, not least of all Christianity itself. Such an approach should therefore include a fuller analysis of why some such claims are acceptable and others are not.

Outside Christianity. A history of religions approach, which looks beyond the traditional intra-Christian critique of enthusiasm, broadens the range of the phenomena studied and of the tools used in evaluation.

An obvious starting point is the context of Greek thought and religion, from which the word *enthusiasm* comes, and in which one could regard enthusiasm as something positive without being uncritical. According to Plato's Socrates, "our greatest blessings come to us by way of madness, provided the madness is given us by divine gift" (*Phaedrus* 244a). Socrates proceeded to distinguish four types of this "divine madness"—as E. R. Dodds has shown in his concise summary (1951): (1) prophetic madness, whose patron god is Apollo; (2) telestic or ritual madness, whose patron is Dionysos; (3) poetic madness, inspired by the Muses; and (4) erotic madness, inspired by Aphrodite and Eros. Madness (*mania*) is not synonymous with enthusiasm (*entheos*, "full of or inspired by the god"; *enthousiasmos*, "inspiration, frenzy"), but there is considerable overlap in meaning, since *enthusiasm* also designated the classic examples of the first two kinds of madness: the Pythia of the Delphic oracle, who prophesied in a state of possession, speaking in the first person as Apollo's voice, and the frenzied dancing of the Dionysian cult, through which the devotees sought the release of ecstasy. This early recognition of a dimension of experience beyond control of the human mind—of an inspiration experienced as coming from without, to which one must yield in order to experience its full benefit—is of lasting relevance in any critique of enthusiasm, as is the recognition of a continuity or similarity between poetic inspiration and sexual ecstasy on the one hand and enthusiasm on the other. And, while Christianity looks more to the Hebrew idea of prophecy than to the ecstatic prophecy of the Hellenistic world, the phenomenology of Hebrew inspiration is not so very different, as the visions and first-person oracles of the major prophets of the Hebrew scriptures clearly testify.

The association of enthusiasm with the ancient Bacchanalia was well known by those who first used the term in the seventeenth century, which explains their heavy note of disapproval. In the past hundred years, however, documentation of similar phenomena from other cultures has grown apace. Most striking of these is shamanism, defined by Mircea Eliade as a "technique of ecstasy."

By examining the religious interpretations and intentions of shamans who communicate directly with the supernatural world, Eliade argues for a more precise distinction between ecstasy and enthusiasm. In ecstasy, the soul is believed to leave the body during a trance in order to ascend to the sky or descend to the underworld, where it may retrieve the soul of sick persons and restore them to health. Enthusiasm, on the other hand, is a term more suitably applied to cases in which a supernatural being (divinity, ancestor, or demon) inhabits or possesses an individual's body or personality. As in the many instances already mentioned, the indwelling spirit is recognized by some unusual behavior, sentiments, or especially sounds. For a parallel to the group ecstasy of the Camisards or the Shakers, we need look no further than the Muslim fraternity known as the dervishes, who since the twelfth century have sought clearer apprehension of God and greater spiritual illumination through hypnotic-like trance culminating often in a whirling dance.

A further advantage enjoyed by present-day students of enthusiasm over their predecessors is the availability of developed analyses of the social functions and psychological mechanisms of enthusiasm: for example, the shaman's role in enabling a community to cope with the unknown or with sickness and death; the techniques by which ecstasy can be induced; or the way in which ecstasy can be manipulated to strengthen and legitimize a leader's authority or to voice the protest of a deprived section of society. It would be unfortunate, however, if such analyses were confined to the field of abnormal psychology or subordinated to theories of social and economic deprivation, as has often been the case. Enthusiasm in itself deserves neither praise nor blame; it can be as integrative for some individuals and communities as it is disintegrative for others. The extreme forms of enthusiasm are just that, extreme forms, and may be as much due to the hostility of those who feel threatened by any expression of enthusiasm as to the enthusiast's own lack of control. We can speak of the cathartic benefit of phenomena such as a Dionysian ritual (and not only for the less articulate) and compare it to the temporarily inhibition-loosening benefits of a festival like the Mardi Gras. Enthusiasm can bring to expression nonrational and unconscious aspects of the personality and thus provide both release and stimulus for the individual and the community if sympathetically handled. In a fully rounded assessment of enthusiasm, psychological and sociological categories should not be permitted to squeeze out the more theological categories of symbol and sacrament.

Christian enthusiasm. A broader evaluation of enthusiasm must also take full account of the extent of enthusiasm within the Christian tradition itself. Not least in importance is the fact that Christianity in its beginnings can properly be described as an enthusiastic sect within first-century Judaism. Jesus himself can hardly be called an ecstatic, but the immediacy of his experience of God as Father and of the power of the Holy Spirit, not to mention his healings and claims to eschatological finality, are clearly attested in Christian sources and have left their mark on subsequent spirituality as well as doctrine. However, so far as enthusiasm is concerned, much more influential has been the record, given in the *Acts of the Apostles*, of the Christian movement itself, from the first Christian Pentecost onward. According to this account, ecstatic visions (described on two occasions precisely in those terms) played a significant part in directing the course of the earliest Christian expansion. Regular reports are given of miracles, including healings effected by Peter's shadow or handkerchiefs touched by Paul. The Holy Spirit was understood to come upon, enter, and fill the individual Christian with a clear physical impact which included glossolalia. Experiences of inspired utterances were evidently prized, not least as evidence that the long withdrawn spirit of prophecy had been poured out in eschatological fullness. All this is the stuff of enthusiasm throughout the history of Christianity, so it is hardly surprising that the desire to recover or experience again the Pentecostal spirit of the primitive church is one of the most recurrent features of enthusiasm from the radical Reformation onward. Similarly, it should occasion little surprise that the canonical *Revelation to John* has provided a ready source of inspiration for apocalyptic and millenarian movements within Christianity down through the centuries.

Paul was no stranger to enthusiastic phenomena, including the ascent to heaven and speaking in tongues. But his approach to excessive enthusiasm, particularly in the church at Corinth, is marked by a rare balance of sympathy and firmness. In Paul, the older Jewish recognition of the need to "test the spirits" in cases of claimed inspiration achieves a degree of sophistication seldom matched before or since. To be accepted as a manifestation of the Holy Spirit, inspiration (1) must be in accord with the gospel, whose power constituted them as Christians, (2) must be consistent with and expressive of love for fellow Christians, and (3) should aim to provide beneficial service to the community. In short, Paul viewed enthusiasm as an aberrant phenomenon only when it offended the love of neighbor which Jesus so completely embodied.

A broader critique of enthusiasm, less dominated by Western rationalist perspectives, would also take fuller account of the whole phenomenon of Eastern Christian spirituality, including such early writings as the *Odes of Solomon* and the homilies of Makarios of Egypt, and such early movements as that of the Desert Fathers and Messalianism, the latter the only Christian sect to be explicitly called "enthusiast" by the church fathers. In the medieval period, mysticism as well as millenarianism provide overlapping phenomena, and with the fuller documentation now available, it is possible to achieve a more balanced view than that attained by Knox of both the prophetic impact of Joachim of Fiore (1145–1202) and the character of the radical Reformation.

Most striking of all, for an author writing in the mid-twentieth century, was Knox's neglect of enthusiastic features of North American Christianity during the nineteenth century, particularly camp meetings, revivalism, and the holiness movement, as well as his neglect of the emergence in Britain of primitive Methodism and "higher life" teaching. Nor should the role of claimed revelations and prophecies in the beginnings of the Church of Latter-day Saints (Mormons) and of the Seventh-day Adventists be ignored.

A prime example of enthusiastic Christianity is the twentieth-century Pentecostal movement, with its special emphasis on a second experience of the Holy Spirit distinct from and subsequent to conversion, on continued bestowal of spiritual gifts, and particularly on speaking in tongues. Within the history of Christian enthusiasm, the importance of Pentecostalism can hardly be overestimated. It is the form of Western Christianity which has been least influenced by the traditions of Western rationalism and most conducive to the emergence of indigenous forms of Christianity in Africa and South America, as illustrated especially by the profusion of independent African churches which are Pentecostal (i.e., enthusiastic) in character. This suggests, once again, that European antipathy to enthusiasm reflects as much the culture patterns particularly of northern Europe as it does the emphasis of enthusiasm on experience and emotion. Furthermore, since the 1950s, Pentecostalism has been increasingly recognized as a valid and vital expression of Christianity—the first formal recognition from within mainstream Western Christianity that the enthusiastic dimension should have a place within a fully rounded Christianity. Finally, while classical Pentecostalism was largely vulnerable to reductive psychological and sociological analyses, the spread of Pentecostal emphases into the older Christian denominations with the charismatic renewal which began in the 1960s has embraced a much broader range of society and undermined many analytic stereotypes.

CONCLUDING REFLECTIONS. Enthusiasm should not be dismissed as a primitive throwback or marginal movement, whether in religion in general or in Christianity in particular. It expresses a fundamental aspect, an experiential dimension, of religion. Within the Judeo-Christian tradition, especially, it forms a strand as important as scripture, creed, or priesthood—an experience of the Spirit of God not restricted to mediation by holy book or holy ritual. The history of enthusiasm within Christianity strongly suggests that, unless given adequate expression within Christian worship and spirituality, it will burst forth sooner or later outside organized structures, often in exotic forms. This further suggests that, without checks such as those counseled by Paul, enthusiasm all too soon becomes the *reductio ad absurdum* of the religion of the Spirit. Here, too, the words of Jonathan Edwards on the similar theme of "religious affections" have continued application. "As there is no true religion where there is nothing else but affection, so there is no true religion where there is no religious affection" ([1746] 1959, p. 120).

SEE ALSO Ecstasy; Frenzy; Glossolalia; Inspiration; Moravians; Oracles; Pentecostal and Charismatic Christianity; Prophecy; Quakers; Quietism; Shakers; Spirit Possession; Wesley Brothers.

BIBLIOGRAPHY

Given the ambiguity of the word *enthusiasm*, the reader should consult Susie I. Tucker's *Enthusiasm: A Study in Semantic Change* (Cambridge, U.K., 1972), which traces the evolution of the meaning of the word.

For the background in Greek thought, see E. R. Dodds's *The Greeks and the Irrational* (Berkeley, 1951), especially chapter 3, and Walter F. Otto's *Dionysus: Myth and Cult* (Bloomington, Ind., 1973). Alfred Guillaume's 1938 Bampton Lectures, *Prophecy and Divination among the Hebrews and Other Semites* (London, 1938), treats enthusiasm in Jewish and Muslim tradition. Mircea Eliade's classic history of religions study, *Shamanism: Archaic Techniques of Ecstasy* (1951; rev.

& enl. ed., London, 1964), examines shamanism in Siberia and elsewhere. Eliade's study is complemented by I. M. Lewis's *Ecstatic Religion: An Anthropological Study of Spirit Possession and Shamanism* (Harmondsworth, 1971). Still valuable are the psychological observations of William James's *The Varieties of Religious Experience: A Study in Human Nature* (New York, 1902).

For enthusiasm within Christianity, the period of Christian beginnings is covered in P. G. S. Hopwood's *The Religious Experience of the Primitive Church* (New York, 1937) and in my *Jesus and the Spirit: A Study of the Religious and Charismatic Experience of Jesus and the First Christians as Reflected in the New Testament* (Philadelphia, 1975). Simon Tugwell provides a light introduction to the enthusiasm of Eastern Christian spirituality in his *Did You Receive the Spirit?* (London, 1972). For the medieval period, see the fascinating account of the revolutionary millenarian sects in Norman R. C. Cohn's *The Pursuit of the Millennium*, 3d ed. (New York, 1970). For one of several specialist studies of Joachim of Fiore and his influence, see Marjorie E. Reeves's *The Influence of Prophecy in the Later Middle Ages: A Study of Joachimism* (Oxford, 1969). Equally fascinating is Herbert Thurston's *The Physical Phenomena of Mysticism* (London, 1952). George H. Williams's *The Radical Reformation* (Philadelphia, 1962) corrects the traditional "bad press" given to the most enthusiastic strand of the Reformation.

Any enquiry into the Christian phenomena must begin with Ronald Knox's *Enthusiasm: A Chapter in the History of Religion with Special Reference to the Seventeenth and Eighteenth Centuries* (Oxford, 1950), which, despite the deficiencies noted above, remains a magnificent and magisterial study. From the period treated by Knox, two contributions from men of stature who knew enthusiastic movements from the inside are still worth considering: John Wesley's sermon *The Nature of Enthusiasm* (1750), usually printed as sermon 32 in standard collections of Wesley's forty-four sermons; and Jonathan Edwards's *A Treatise concerning Religious Affections* (Boston, 1746), which is reproduced in volume 2 of *The Works of Jonathan Edwards*, edited by John E. Smith (New Haven, 1959).

For the modern period, Timothy L. Smith provides a balanced view in his *Revivalism and Social Reform in Mid-Nineteenth-Century America* (New York, 1957). The compendious study by Walter J. Hollenweger, *The Pentecostals* (London, 1972), is the standard work on the subject. Kilian McDonnell provides a countercritique of the wide range of psychological and sociological analyses of Pentecostal phenomena in *Charismatic Renewal and the Churches* (New York, 1976).

James D. G. Dunn (1987)

ENUMA ELISH, the name given to the myth that contains the theological thoughts of Babylon in the first millennium, is so called from its opening words, "When above." The style and content of the poem indicate that it is indeed the authentic product of the new religious thinking that placed the god Marduk at the head of the pantheon. Manuscripts of this myth have been found at many different sites in Assyria and Babylon, covering a period from approximately 1000 to 300 BCE, so the date of composition is established with some certainty in the final period of Mesopotamian civilization.

In contrast to Sumerian mythology, which attributes the beginnings of the creation of the cosmos to two essential elements, heaven and earth, from which the gods and the human race both sprang, the *Enuma elish* myth places the origins of the cosmos before heaven and earth in a far-off time. Only primeval waters existed: salt water, called Tiamat, and sweet water, called Apsu, the first living things in the cosmos. Given the prominent part played by salt water (Tiamat) in the *Enuma elish* story, some have concluded that this myth must be non-Mesopotamian in origin, maybe Syrian or at least Semitic (Jacobsen, 1976, pp. 165–187; Durand, 1993, pp. 41–61). This theory is somewhat puzzling because the main god of the myth, Marduk, does not have the qualities of Adad, the main god of the Semitic-Occidental tale, who also appears in a different story in Assyro-Babylonian mythology.

The myth is taken from seven tablets and closes with the words of the "Hymn of Marduk" (VI.161). The hymn was certainly recited if not actually sung, as recorded in the ritual for the festival of the New Year at the temple Akitu. The festival record also notes the day on which the priest carried out the rite, the fourth day of the eleven set aside for the entire festival, which was celebrated in the month of Nisan.

The Plot. The document opens with a description of the situation in the beginning, when Apsu and Tiamat exist and mix their waters, from which emerges the first pair of primeval divinities, Lahmu and Lahama. In turn, Lahmu and Lahama produce Anshar and Kishar, from whom comes Anu, who produces Nudimmud, otherwise known as Ea, the god of wisdom (I.1–20). The new generation of gods make too much noise and disturb Apsu's sleep. Apsu becomes angry and wants to punish the young gods, but their mother Tiamat disagrees. The young gods, however, give no indication of being sorry, so Apsu, urged on by his herald Mummu, plans to destroy the troublemakers.

The young gods hear of these plans, and Ea decides to protect the new generation from Apsu's attack. Ea uses his magic to send Apsu to sleep and kills him (I.21–70). In this way Ea takes over the home of Apsu and settles in there with his consort, producing the hero of the myth, Marduk. Even at birth Marduk already demonstrates a physical strength that makes him superior to all the other gods (I.71–109).

In the meantime, Tiamat, even more upset by the noise of the young gods, seeks the help of the other primeval gods to put an end to the continuing disturbance. With the help of Æubur, who produces enormous dragons, she creates eleven giant, frightening monsters, and she engages in battle against her sons. Tiamat makes Kingu leader of her forces for the purpose, and she also marries him and entrusts him with the tablets of destiny. This news reaches of Ea, who informs the assembly of the gods (I.101–II.70).

Anshar, to whom Ea has turned, first rebukes him for killing Apsu and then sends the god of wisdom to Tiamat to calm her and thus forestall the catastrophe. Ea goes to Tiamat, who is enraged and refuses to accept his apologies, so the divine messenger returns empty-handed. Anshar tries again, sending his son Anu, who returns with the same result as Ea. A mood of dejection sets in throughout the divine world. As ever, Ea proposes the perfect solution—to call for Marduk's help. Marduk is warned in advance by his father and goes to Anshar to volunteer his services on condition that the gods grant him supreme power among the gods if he is victorious (II.71–162).

The gods hold an assembly and agree to grant Marduk the power he has requested so he can confront the hostile army straightaway (III.1–IV.34). Marduk dons his fighting gear and creates new weapons, including a spell to counteract Tiamat's poison. There is a titanic struggle, but Marduk's arrow strikes Tiamat's heart. She collapses to the ground while her army is captured (IV.35–128).

Marduk now begins his work of creation. He cuts Tiamat's body in two. With the upper part of her body he forms the heavens with all the established points, the year and the month, the sun and the moon. With the lower part he creates the earth with its mountains and rivers. Marduk receives praise and honor from all the gods. He then decides to create a suitable sanctuary for himself, which is called Babylon (IV.129–V.156). Marduk continues his work of creation, making the human race from the blood of Kingu, giving it the task of labor, and he reorganizes the pantheon into greater and lesser gods, who all sing a hymn to his glory in Babylon (VI.1–120). The poem ends with a litany of fifty names of Marduk and a doxology (VI.121–VII.162).

Directly linked to this, at least in terms of ideas, is an incantation that contains in its opening passage the story of the creation or an account of the way the earth was arranged. The god responsible for this creative process is Marduk, who has replaced the cosmic trio of Anu, Enlil, and Ea, upon whom this high honor and task is normally bestowed. This text is a forerunner of the great religious revolution by which the Babylonian priests placed their god at the head of the pantheon, a task completed by the creation of the poem *Enuma elish.*

The story may be divided into three quite distinct parts. In the first, it is clear that the earth was still untouched and all the lands still seas, so there were no cities or materials to build them, and thus no temples either (obv. ll.1–11). In the second part, Marduk intervenes and begins to separate the waters of the sea and to carry out the work that produces the present world order. He creates humanity and the animals of Sumukan, along with the entire environment, the flora and fauna, to make the world a pleasant place to visit. He of course pays a good deal of attention to Babylon and the Esagila, which the Anunna call "a pure city, home of the heart's desire" (ll.12–34). In the third part, once the earth has been made habitable, Marduk creates bricks and begins to build the Sumerian cities that had not existed previously along with their temples (ll. 35–39ff.). The cities concerned are Nippur with the temple Ekur, Uruk with the temple Eanna, Eridu with the temple Apsu, and the sacred cities of Enlil, Inanna, and Enki, the cities of the Sumerian principal gods. The symbiotic relationship between Eridu and Babylon, connected by the Esagila temple, forms the basis for the accession of Marduk to the head of the pantheon, which had once been Sumerian but has become Babylonian.

INTERPRETATION. The scribes had grasped that there were two possible ways to elevate their poliad god to a central position in the pantheon: either to link Marduk to the god of Nippur (Enlil) or, certainly more subtle, to relate him to the god Enki. It may be surprising that they chose to establish a father-son relationship between Enki and Marduk, because the former had never historically guaranteed the kingship. Yet the choice of the scribes shows a quite remarkable intelligence: they wanted to overturn historical reality and turn it to something of cosmic significance.

All the Sumerian traditions assigned the position of principal god in their pantheon to Enlil. But at the same time they emphasized that the first seat of the kingship before the Flood was the city of Eridu, the home of the god Enki, who was thus regarded as the first holder of royal power on earth. Hence the scribes decided to make Marduk the son of Enki. Their syllogistic reasoning thus becomes quite clear: if Enki the king is Marduk's father, then Marduk becomes the king. In addition, if Eridu is the home of Enki and the place of his kingship, then Babylon, the home of Marduk, is automatically the one true location of the kingship. So the words of Berossus (third century BCE) that the first royal capital on earth was Babylon explains how convincing the syllogism devised by the scribes of Babylon became for later generations.

One important indication of the process begun by Marduk's priests is the fact that among the various names of Babylon is Nun(ki), or Eridu(ki), the city sacred to the god Enki, the father of Marduk, and the first city established on earth according to Sumerian tradition. This tradition allows the Babylonian scholars to compare the two cities of Eridu and Babylon in the first instance, and then to replace the former with the latter. This is without doubt the first step in the slow development through which Babylon categorizes itself as an ancient city, dating from the earliest times and rising to the definitive status of the first city founded by the gods. The idea in the biblical story of the Tower of Babel that Babel was the first city the human race had tried to build has a perfect counterpart in a Babylonian mythological text. The Babylonian scholar responsible had subtly adapted the new reality to the earlier mythological situation. Here too, Eridu is the first city founded, but with subtle shrewdness a substitution takes place. No longer does Eridu—ancient Eridu, that is—hold the leading position, but Babylon and its main temple Esagila have become in this document the key to understanding the situation. Eridu is quite clearly an epithet of Babylon, it is Babylon where the gods decide to live, and it is Marduk, under the name Lugaldukuga, who creates the city and builds the temple dedicated to him, the Esagila.

With this delicate substitution the Babylonians manage to establish their city as the first human urban settlement, as one may deduce from the biblical narrative and, subsequently, from later literature. It is not by chance or by mistake that Berossus, when he deals in his *Babiloniaka* with the cities founded by the gods before the Flood, lists Babylon in first place, proving that the substitution effected by the Babylonians had by then become part of the accepted cultural heritage of the ancient world. The god central to *Enuma elish* is clearly Marduk, the principal god of Babylon, who was credited not only with the mythical foundation of the city but also with the creation of the other principal cities of Sumer.

FURTHER DEVELOPMENTS. The origin of the universe, as told in *Enuma elish*, has counterparts in the works of other Hellenistic and Syrian writers. A few of the surviving passages are mentioned below.

The first and the closest to the Babylonian account seems to be that in Eudemus (third century BCE), quoted by the later philosopher Damascius (fifth–sixth century CE), who put the matter as follows:

> Amongst the barbarians, it does not seem that the Babylonians talked of a single universal principle. They held the theory that there were two: Thaute and Apason, making the latter the husband of the former, whom they call the "mother of the gods." In the first instance they gave birth to a single baby, Moümis, who I suppose represented the intelligible world (derived from the two principles). Another generation followed, offspring of the same parents: Dachê and Dachos. Then a third, Kissarê and Assôros, who produced the trio Anos, Illinos, and Aos. Aos and Dauche brought into the world a son called Bel, and they say that he was the Creator. (Bottéro-Kramer, 1989, pp. 721–722)

Berossus, whose work has survived in fragments thanks to later writers, offers a vision of the origin of the world only partly similar to the Babylonian one. The principle appears to be water, more precisely salt water, called Thalatta, which had produced animals and monsters together with primitive people who lived like wild animals. Those people needed to be taught by a sage named Oan, who was half man and half fish. While these beings were living in a chaotic magma, Belos attacked and destroyed them. Belos rose up and cut Thalatta in two. With one half he made earth, with the other half, heaven. After he cut off her head, he mixed the blood that gushed out with earth and created human beings with their divine qualities, and then all the animals of the present world. These writers generally regard water as the primordial element.

The theological commentaries edited at Uruk in the final period of the cuneiform culture include accounts that would make even the most detached reader of Mesopotamian religious texts shudder. Almost nothing is known of the history of Babylon in this final time; that is, the Achemenid and Greek periods. Reading the fragments of Berossus, one is able to form the idea that the Babylonian religion centered around Marduk and that his son Nabu continued it. On the other hand little is known of the fate of the cosmic triad Anu, Enlil, and Ea, who are in a backroom position to say the least.

These commentaries, however, relate the violent end of these gods at the hands of Bel, the title assumed by Marduk when he became head of the pantheon, the greatest and most exalted of the Sumerian pantheon, to whom was attributed the creation and organization of the cosmos. The end is bloody, as subsequent texts reveal, for Marduk's father Ea, who is sent away to Apsu; for Enlil, banished to the underworld; and for Anu and his father Anshar. Ishtaran is also killed to hurt the goddess Ishtar, for reasons that remain unclear. Nabu is responsible for killing the eagle Anzu. The texts of course refer to these killings symbolically during the various ceremonies at the different festivals, especially at the most important one for the New Year. The same theological commentaries that mention the killing of the principal gods of the Sumerian pantheon, especially Anu, Enlil, and Ea, also mention the enemies of Marduk, the god of Babylon, who meet their end in the poem *Enuma elish.* The texts mention Tiamat and Kingu by name, along with their seven children and forty children respectively. Another recurring figure is Anzu. As emphasized above, the most powerful gods of the Sumerian pantheon, Anu and Enlil, along with their children, are victims of the same violent acts.

***ENUMA ELISH* AND THE BIBLE.** Ever since the first publication of the work's text, comparisons have been drawn between *Enuma elish* and the Bible, particularly the first chapter of *Genesis.* Attention has been drawn to the parallels between the seven tablets of *Enuma elish* and the biblical seven days of creation. Both stories begin with primeval water, which in the Bible is called *tehom,* the Hebrew cognate of Tiamat; the biblical spirit (or wind) of God that hovered over the waters bears some similarity to the winds of Anu that roiled Tiamat. Both stories contain the notion of creative work: the biblical sky divides the waters above from the waters below, as the upper half of Tiamat's body is divided from her lower half by the sky, and both stories depict in the same way the origin and function of the sun and the moon. However, the differences between *Genesis* 1 and *Enuma elish* are so vast that there is no reason to talk of mythological similarity or literary dependence. The similarities are evidence only of a shared cosmology, a shared "science" that saw the world as beginning in water and surrounded by it, a concept also found in early Greece. The importance of *Enuma elish* to the study of *Genesis* 1 is to demonstrate that these concepts were in fact (and were almost certainly perceived to be) common Near Eastern lore rather than data of Israel's revelation, and that Israel used this lore to convey its own independent message.

The most striking parallels between *Enuma elish* and the Bible are not to *Genesis* but to the scattered poetic passages that allude to the Lord's defeat of the sea in primordial times. This defeat of the sea is often accompanied by mention of the kingship of God, the creation of the world, and sometimes the creation of the Temple. These themes present a fundamental biblical cluster of ideas, one that has striking similarities with ideas in *Enuma elish.* This does not mean that the motifs have a Babylonian origin. The defeat of the sea, the kingship of the god, and the building of the god's palace (but not the theme of creation) are also found together in the Ugaritic Baal epic, written circa 1500 BCE and therefore (it is believed) earlier than *Enuma elish.* This cluster is not found in earlier Mesopotamian sources; most probably it was an ancient West Semitic collection of ideas that found expression in Ugaritic literary works and the Bible and that at some point was brought into Mesopotamia.

SEE ALSO Akitu; Cosmogony; Marduk; Mesopotamian Religions, overview article; Polytheism.

BIBLIOGRAPHY

Al Rawi, F. N. H., and A. R. George. "Tablets from the Sippar Library. II. Tablet II of the Babylonian Creation Epic." *Iraq* 52 (1990): 149–157.

Bottéro, Jean. *Mythes et rites de Babylone.* Paris, 1985.

Bottéro, Jean, and Samuel Noah Kramer. *Lorsque les dieux faisaient l'homme. Mythologie mésopotamienne.* Paris, 1989.

Clifford, Richard J. *Creation Accounts in the Ancient Near East and in the Bible.* Washington, D.C., 1994.

Durand, Jean-Marie."Le mithologème du combat entre le dieu de l'orage et la mer en Mésopotamie." *MARI* 7 (1993): 41–61.

Heidel, Alexander. *The Babylonian Genesis.* Chicago, 1942.

Jacobsen, Thorkild. "The Battle between Marduk and Tiamat." *Journal of the American Oriental Society* 88 (January–March 1968): 104–108.

Jacobsen, Thorkild. *The Treasures of Darkness.* New Haven, Conn., 1987.

Labat, René. *Le poème babylonien de la création.* Paris, 1935.

Lambert, W. G. "Akkadische Mythen und Epen: Enuma Elisch." In *Texte aus der Umwelt des Alten Testaments III/II,* pp. 565–601. Gütersloh, Germany, 1994.

Lambert, W. G., and Simon B. Parker. *Enuma Elish: The Babylonian Epic of Creation: The Cuneiform Text.* Oxford, 1966.

Pettinato, Giovanni. *Babilonia: Centro dell'Universo.* Milan, 1988.

Schnabel, Paul. *Berossos und die babylonisch-hellenistische Literatur.* Leipzig, 1915.

TIKVA FRYMER-KENSKY (1987)
GIOVANNI PETTINATO (2005)
Translated from Italian by Paul Ellis

EOHESUS, COUNCIL OF SEE COUNCILS, *ARTICLE ON* CHRISTIAN COUNCILS

EPHRAEM OF SYRIA (c. 306–373) was a theologian, biblical interpreter, teacher, poet, and hymnographer whose teaching activity and prolific writings have had lasting influence on the Christian tradition. Renowned for his hymns and poetic homilies, he is regarded as the preeminent Syrian father, a doctor of the universal church, and, according to Robert Murray, "the greatest poet of the patristic age . . . perhaps, the only theologian-poet to rank beside Dante" ("Ephrem Syrus, St.," in *Catholic Dictionary of Theology,* vol. 2, London, 1967, p. 222).

Born in Edessa (present-day Urfa, Turkey) in a Christian family (not a pagan household as some sources would have it), Ephraem lived for many years in Nisibis and taught at the catechetical school there. A town on the eastern Roman frontier, Nisibis was frequently pressed by the Persians. It was finally ceded to them in 363, at which time Ephraem, with the larger part of the Christian population, fled westward to Edessa, a partially Hellenized cultural center still in Roman hands. Ephraem's hymns on Nisibis reflect the vicissitudes of the Christian community there.

Edessa was a hotbed of heresies, where Arians, Manichaeans, Marcionites, and the followers of the famous Bardaisan (Bardesanes)—many of whom successfully spread their teachings through poems and songs—had confused and divided the Christians. It was here that Ephraem, perhaps ordained a deacon by this time, flourished as an orthodox teacher, effective apologist, and unifying leader.

Ephraem was called "the harp of the Spirit" by his contemporaries. His fame spread after his death, and he came to be venerated as a saint. His ancient biographers embellished his life with many accounts emphasizing his apologetic work against the Arians and highlighting the traditional view of Ephraem as father of Syrian monasticism. He is said to have visited the great monastic centers in Egypt; it is also told that upon his return he met with Basil of Caesarea, in whose presence he miraculously spoke Greek. Although Ephraem no doubt led a celibate life of evangelical fervor and simplicity and greatly admired contemporary ascetics, the traditional image of him as a monk does not fit his actual intense activity as a Christian teacher, public defender of the faith, and inspired poet who led people in song.

An immense legacy of writings in Syriac, Armenian, Greek, and Latin has been preserved under Ephraem's name, but much of it is spurious, especially the materials in Greek and Latin. Nevertheless, scholarship after World War II has uncovered an impressive body of authentic works in the original Syriac and also in Armenian versions.

Ephraem's writings consist of prose works, poetic homilies, and hymns. Of his prose works the most numerous are biblical commentaries (on *Genesis, Exodus,* the letters of Paul, and Tatian's *Diatessaron*). He also wrote prose refutations against Mani, Marcion, and Bardaisan, as well as a number of prose sermons and ascetical works the authenticity of which is disputed. Ephraem's poetical homilies are metrical sermons intended for recitation rather than singing. Among them are the six *Sermons on Faith* deriving from the Nisibine period and containing references to the Persian danger. Many other similar metrical sermons on various topics attributed to him are of doubtful authenticity.

Ephraem's fame justly rests on hundreds of exquisite poetic hymns that interpret, defend, and celebrate the basic mysteries of the Christian faith: creation, incarnation, redemption, Christ, the Holy Spirit, Mary, the church, sacraments, and the kingdom of God. They are preserved in individual collections under such titles as *Hymns on Faith, Hymns against Heresies, Hymns on the Crucifixion, Hymns on Paradise,* and *Hymns on the Church.* Acknowledged as jewels of Semitic poetry, these hymns reflect Ephraem's superb talents in their diverse symmetrical forms, cascades of imagery, breathtaking parallelisms, and artistic wordplays, all extremely difficult to render in English. Although many are composed of multiple stanzas accompanied by refrains, others are cast in the form of dramatic disputations, for example, between Death and Christ or Death and Satan, a style with Mesopotamian precedents.

Although Ephraem used traditional Christian themes and known Semitic literary forms, his originality and freshness are striking. Some examples may indicate why he is hailed as one of the world's greatest religious poets. In one hymn to Christ, translated by Robert Murray in *Eastern Churches Review* 3 (1970), Ephraem vividly associates images of the Holy Spirit's descent on Mary, Jesus' baptism, Christian baptism, and the Eucharist:

> See, Fire and Spirit in the womb that bore You!
> See, Fire and Spirit in the river where you were baptized!
> Fire and Spirit in our Baptism;
> in the Bread and the Cup, Fire and Holy Spirit!

In another incarnational hymn, Ephraem fashions extended imagery of Christ as the pearl. This hymn plays on the words *amoda* ("diver") and *amida* ("baptized"). The pearl is found by plunging into the water, but it must be pierced (a reference to Christ's suffering) before it can be set in its place of honor.

The form of the dramatic disputation is exemplified by several hymns on Christ's descent into hell that celebrate his cosmic victory over Death. In one such hymn, Death addresses Christ on the cross, challenging and taunting him in his apparent weakness. Then Jesus signals his own death with a loud cry ("Our Lord's voice rang out thunderously in Sheol"), and angels of light illumine the darkness of hell. Seized by terrible fear, Death repents of its prideful words, confesses Jesus as king, and submissively hands over Adam as the first fruits of death with the words: "As first hostage I give you Adam's body. Ascend now and reign over all, and when I hear your trumpet call, with my own hands I will bring forth the dead at your coming" (Brock, 1983, p. 44). The hymn ends in a crescendo of praise to Christ that is typical of Ephraem's poetry.

Bibliography

The following sources and studies can be recommended for further reading. A systematic study of Ephraem's theology is yet to be written.

Beck, Edmund, ed. *Corpus Scriptorum Christianorum Orientalium, Scriptores Syri.* Louvain, 1955–1975. The standard editions of the hymns and homilies of Ephraem, with German translations, are available in different volumes in this series.

Brock, Sebastian, trans. *The Harp of the Spirit.* Studies Supplementary to Sobornost, no. 4. San Bernardino, Calif., 1983. The best collection of English translations of seventeen of Ephraem's hymns and the *Homily on the Nativity.*

Gwynn, John, ed. *Selections from the Hymns and Homilies of Ephraim the Syrian.* Select Library of Nicene and Post-Nicene Fathers, second series, vol. 8, pt. 2. Grand Rapids, Mich., 1969. English translations of the hymns on nativity, Epiphany, faith, and Nisibis, as well as of the homilies on the Lord, repentance, and the Sinful Woman.

Murray, Robert. *Symbols of Church and Kingdom: A Study in Early Syriac Tradition.* London, 1975. A pioneering exploration of sources and themes of early Syrian writers, especially Aphraates and Ephraem, dealing with Christ and the church.

Vööbus, Arthur. *Literary, Critical and Historical Studies in Ephrem the Syrian.* Uppsala, 1958. An analysis of the sources, life, thought, and role of Ephraem in the tradition of Syrian monasticism.

THEODORE STYLIANOPOULOS (1987)

EPICS are extended narrative poems that establish for their hearers and/or readers a particular universe of the imagination by means of cosmogonic and sacrificial mythologies, chronicles of kings and nobles, religious and philosophical teachings, and, above all, the heroic exploits of a past age. Where a living oral tradition persists, this bygone age of gods, goddesses, and heroes may be reactualized and experienced anew each time an epic is recited or sung and performed in ritual, festival, or secular contexts. The capacity of an oral epic to change is definitive, for it is continually re-created by singers, actors, audiences, and environments, and the sequence and length of its episodes remain fluid. By contrast, epics that have passed from oral to written poetry or heightened prose with no surviving performance traditions, and epics such as Vergil's *Aeneid* that were first composed in writing, have become records of particular worldviews, histories, and religious attitudes that now are modified only by various interpretations of them.

Because they are indeed "epic" in scope, there is scarcely a dimension of human experience that may be excluded from these versified repositories. The Sanskrit *Mahābhārata,* longest of oral-literary epics with its 100,000 verses in eighteen books, serves as a vast library of mythology, folklore, religion, and philosophy, compiled from oral traditions during a period of eight centuries in the formative age of classical Hinduism. Major narrative portions are still recited in Sanskrit all over India, and various regions have vernacular versions, as is the case also with the other great Sanskrit epic, the *Rāmāyana.* In the nearly sixty thousand verses of the Persian *Shāh-nāmah,* the poet Firdawsi, working from older sources, undertook nothing less than the history of Iran from creation to the Arab conquest in the seventh century. The effort required thirty-five years, but one poet produced the Persian national epic. Even the shortest of epics, folk or classical, oral or literary, suspends in its episodes the details of a worldview. A worldview may be articulated directly or obliquely, within the context of individual heroic quests or in the intricate relations of a diverse range of characters and subcultures, in a close-knit set of episodes and locales or on a heterogeneous scale that spans generations of time and worlds of space. Some epics speak directly from living religious traditions, although the faith of contemporary singers and audiences may vary markedly from that of distant epic origins. Other epics are cryptic memorials or vague signposts to religious traditions only dimly apprehended in their narratives, as is the case with suspected Anatolian expressions fossilized, but still undeciphered, in the linguistic, folkloric, and symbolic strata of Homer's *Iliad.*

Oral epics emergent to literary forms have almost everywhere been influenced and more or less reshaped by new religions, as well as by new literary tastes and conventions. Certain themes in ancient India persisted in oral form side by side with, but unrepresented in, the thousand-year textual production of Vedic religion, then surfaced in classical Sanskrit and Tamil epics, where they were given structure and redefinition by sectarian Hinduism. Similarly, mythic themes of Iran's ancient heritage, disguised by the monotheistic reforms of Zoroaster, found new expression in the epic of Firdawsi and other Persian narrative poetry, although this time within an Islamic ethos. And as Christian tradition rides lightly on the surface of the ancient heroic mythology preserved in *Beowulf,* so too does Muslim tradition appear only marginally in the Mandingo (Malinke) epic *Sundiata* of the Mali Empire.

Some epics, such as the vast Kirghiz cycle known as *Manas,* declare mythicized history, while others, such as the *Aeneid,* display cores that are historicized myths. But almost every epic immerses its hearers and readers in the largest of human questions: human nature and its destiny; the structure of society with its hierarchies and tensions; the character of supernatural beings and powers, of gods, goddesses, demons, and of the proper human response to each of them in ritual, devotion, propitiation, or defiance; the problems of evil and good, insurrection and authority, guilt and innocence, cowardice and valor, suffering and reward. Because epics are frequently dramas of great migrations and violent conflicts in the divine and human worlds, questions of theology and history, eschatology and fate, death, regeneration, and salvation are often posed in the context of cosmic warfare (the Akkadian epic *Enuma elish*), or cultural confrontations (the *Iliad*), or dynastic strife (the Japanese *Heike monogatari*), or a melding of all of these, as in the *Mahābhārata,* where the complex destinies of the heroes are assumed into the sacrifice and regeneration of the cosmos itself.

The great majority of known epics, whether oral in composition, oral-literary, or solely literary, have been heroic ones. They are dominated by heroes (rarely heroines) whose actions and fates not only dramatize particular human emotions, predicaments, and responses, but whose destinies reinforce essential religious statements and paradigms. Among these paradigms are certain roles of the hero as shaman, sorcerer, or warrior (or combinations of these); certain concepts of space, order, time, and deity; as well as all-important expressions of the meaning of death and salvation.

SHAMANS AND JOURNEYS OF THE SOUL. The hero as shaman-sorcerer and the religious significance of the journey of the soul are well known in the oral epics of northern and central Asia and appear in such diverse characters as Grandfather Qorqut in the oldest epic of the Oghuz Turks, the *Kitabi Dedem Qorqut;* Volkh or Vseslav in the epic song form known to Russian singers as *starina (bylina);* and Gesar in the Tibetan epic that bears his name. The sage Väinämöinen journeys as a serpent to Tuonela, the netherworld, and this magical transformation in a northern Eurasian shamanic episode survives into the late compilation of the Finnish national epic, the *Kalevala.*

Several scholars have noted that sources of epic poetry may in part be sought in the narratives of shamanic visions, ecstatic journeys, and initiatory ordeals. As Mircea Eliade has shown in *The History of Religious Ideas* (vol. 1, Chicago, 1978, p. 80), Gilgamesh undergoes several ordeals of an initiatory type, and the *Epic of Gilgamesh,* "the first masterpiece of universal literature," may be understood from one perspective as the dramatization of a failed initiation. His journey to the bottom of the sea to find the plant that restores youth, a plant he then loses to a serpent in the discovery of his mortal destiny, has numerous parallels in other epics in which heroes learn of their fates in descents to the underworld and combats with chthonic powers, or in magical flights to celestial realms. The popularity of such motifs in the epic genre has carried them far from the traditional loci of Asian shamanism.

Despite reworking in the direction of medieval romance conventions, the Germanic epic *Nibelungenlied* retains such a quest in narratives of Siegfried, better known as a warrior-hero, and one with older analogues in the Scandinavian Eddas and sagas. Siegfried journeys to the land of the Nibelungen and there discovers the sword and treasure that, like Gilgamesh's plant, hold not immortality but his fate. He also gains a magic cape, as well as invulnerability, from bathing in the blood of the dragon he has dispatched in combat. And in one of South India's great store of living folk epics, the Telugu *Epic of Palnāḍu,* a performance tradition eight centuries old, continues to dramatize with a mélange of shamanic motifs the heroes' prescient skills, their ascents by magical beasts, cosmic trees, or turbans; initiatory dismemberment and reconstitution by healing; descent to the underworld; combat with monsters; trance states; nurturance by and guises as animals. These motifs in the *Palnāḍu* and certain other South Asian and Southeast Asian oral epics and songs are all the more arresting in the context of contemporary performances in which individuals emulating the heroes undergo spirit possession and séances of self-immolation and regeneration. In a word, their ancient heroes, in roles as either shaman-redeemers or warriors, are alive today in ritualized epic time.

WARRIORS AND DECISIVE BATTLES. More common in epic narrative than the high calling of the shaman who journeys to the other world and establishes defenses against demons, diseases, and death is the role of warrior in this world, often a hero of "outsiderhood" who must overcome great odds to gain or regain a heritage or position denied him or stolen from him. Strength, courage, and personal honor are his major assets. While the resourceful shamanic hero engages in fabulous struggles with death, the warrior hero stands up to its blood-red realities. At times the warrior seems to be locked in combat with himself as well as designated demons and enemies. This-worldly aspirations, the ambiguities of his morals and actions, limitations placed upon him by nature, fate, divine or human treachery, all balance out his superhuman traits and heroic pedigree (semidivine or miraculous birth, surrogate parenting by animals, discovery by shepherds or fisherfolk, precocious skills and strengths), and render him more accessible to the epic audience. There is a recognizable trajectory to his career after his astonishing youth, including confrontation with established authority, exile, return and conquest, heroic status, frequently an early death, and apotheosis. The popularity of the cult that succeeds this life cycle proves the value of his tragic death and the repeated singing of it.

It is sometimes stated that violent cultural changes and social upheavals attendant upon warfare and great migrations were productive of epic themes in a "heroic age." The history of China, however, as turbulent and war-scarred as that of any long, cumulative civilization, produced no surviving epic tradition, and only a few lines of the classic *Shi jing* (Book of poetry) recall the exploits of heroic ancestors. By contrast, a brief period of epics in the thirteenth century emerged directly from the brutal succession of wars that devastated early medieval Japan. These poetic-prose war tales (*gunki monogatari*), a genre with no counterpart in Chinese literature, were composed in the same period as the *chansons de geste* of medieval Europe and various regional battle epics of South Asia. More important than the common factor of war may have been a particular cultural glorification of the warrior. While China gave him little recognition in a social hierarchy that established the scholar-bureaucrat above peasants, artisans, and merchants, it was the epic age of medieval Japan that produced a warrior aristocracy, the samurai, and an elaborate warrior code eventually known as Bushido.

The best known of warrior cults, and prolonged epics in which their traditions are displayed, remain the Indo-European ones, and these derive from a deep and complex mythological base. Comparative studies, in particular those of Georges Dumézil and Stig Wikander, have revealed the religious significance of a Proto-Indo-European warrior tradition. Reconstruction from mythic and epic details dispersed from Iceland to India permits a vision of the parent culture as it may have existed six or seven thousand years ago, a culture in which the warrior occupied a key median position in a three-class hierarchy between the dominant priestly-sovereign class and that great bulk of society in the third estate, the producers.

Continuities between a divine tripartite trifunctional hierarchy and this human social hierarchy allowed for homologies between gods and heroes and, later, between mythic and epic themes. The fact that both the mythic human heroes and the epic warrior heroes are narrative continuations of the mythic warrior god is significant and enables us to understand certain configurations of the Proto-Indo-European warrior cult and mythology. The warrior enters, for example, a state of intoxication or heated fury, becoming invincible like fire, or he terrorizes enemies by assuming the form of a wolf or a bear, subsequent to initiatory ordeals undergone for acceptance into the warrior society. Combat with a three-headed monster, first sacrifice, and ritualized cattle raids are a part of this myth-ritual complex, as Bruce Lincoln has demonstrated for the Proto-Indo-Iranian tradition that is the backdrop to many themes of the later epics in India and Iran.

Many important themes have moved with the currents from Indo-European mythic to epic genres and surfaced in diverse regional literatures and languages (including some non-Indo-European ones), from the twelfth-century Danish historian Saxo Grammaticus's *Gesta Danorum* to Russian, Rajasthani, or Tamil oral poetry. One of Dumézil's special contributions to an ongoing profile of the warrior's "destiny" has been his study of the hero's programmatically untoward behavior that leads to self-destruction. The warrior may commit three successive sins against the three functional classes: betrayal of sovereign trust, strikingly uncharacteristic acts of cowardice within his own echelon, and crimes of avarice or rape. As a consequence he suffers successive losses of his spirituality, force of arms, and beauty or form, and dies the warrior's typical early, tragic death. Another recurrent theme is a tension between two types of warrior figures, one superhuman and aristocratic, a warrior who fights with proper weapons and, ideally, a code of chivalry (Arjuna, Sigurd, Aeneas), the other a subhuman, animalistic or monstrous hero who fights brutal, solitary battles without standard weapons or code (Bhīma, Starkad, Turnus). Still another characteristic Indo-European theme is the special relationship that may develop between the warrior and a goddess or heroine-goddess. Herakles and Hera or Athena, Camillus and Matuta, Arjuna and Draupadi (Śrī) have all provided complex illustrations of this liaison.

Divine warrior heroes such as Marduk in the Akkadian epic *Enuma elish,* the Canaanite Baal, the Hittite Taru, Zeus of the *Theogony,* or Indra of the *Ṛgveda* are all, in their respective single combats with Tiamat, Yamm, Illuyanka, Typhon, and Vṛtra, involved variously in cosmogonic acts or paradigmatic contests for celestial sovereignty. Human warrior heroes, by contrast, are most often revealed in epic action *in medias res,* preparing to defend a tribe or a nation in jeopardy. Such epics program their episodes toward decisive battles in which warrior heroes are driven to fulfill their destinies. Necessity becomes a standard impulse, as in Diomedes' terse proclamation in the *Iliad* when he and the Achaeans are backed up to the sea, their best warriors and leader Agamemnon disabled: "Let us return to the battle, wounded as we are. We must." This necessity bears the stamp of the mythic heritage: The hero, semidivine or blessed by divine guidance and the powers of order and justice, opposes an enemy, semidemonic or impelled by a hand from the powers of evil and chaos, and the tribe or nation defended represents the created world.

SPACES, TIMES, AND AUTHORITY. The notion of founding the world anew, reestablishing world space, time, and order through the holocaust of battle, is a widespread epic theme. Numerous cycles have been labeled "national epics," for they are the songs of peoples establishing identities, legitimizing traditions of particular places and events, and carrying an authority, certified by the blood of heroes, from past to present. In the singing of the epic, episode by episode, all of the true points of the world are connected once again. As Gene Roghair has said of the people who preserve the Palnāḍu epic, it "is the history of their land" and "seems largely sufficient to satisfy the local need for knowledge of the past" (Roghair, 1982, p. 70). All the features of the local villages, temples, crop fields, rivers, and roads have epic associations, and a rock inscription, for example, may be ascribed to a particular Palnadu hero, or to something done, quite simply, in "that time."

The recognition of the local region or kingdom as ordered space, and local history as ultimate time, leads also to the designation of outside space and time as disordered, wild, threatening. W. T. H. Jackson has considered the inside-outside dichotomy in European epics from Homer to *The Cid* as a theme of paradigmatic conflict between the intruder hero as mobile, active, unpredictable outsider and challenger, and the older, established king as settled, passive, predictable insider. Achilles and Agamemnon, Beowulf and Hrothgar, Siegfried and Gunther are among his examples, to which could be added for an enriched set of subthemes Arjuna and Yudhiṣṭhira, Rostam and Shāh Kāvus, the legendary Cyrus and Astyages, and others, as well as discussion of that seminal tension in Proto-Indo-European mythology between the sovereign and warrior ethos. Much of this conflict, according to Jackson, turns on the movement from an ageing king who upholds the social order to a challenger hero whose aims are personal honor and glory. What seems equally important in the structure of Indo-European epic tradition is the alliance of both ruler and heroes over against the agriculturalist-producers, and the resultant hierarchy of three ranked estates in interdependence under an ideal hero-king and divine mandate.

One of the richest themes concerning the values of space and time is that of the epic hero or heroine in exile. Banished to the wilderness or the seas, deprived of lands, family, status, and pride, the hero in exile is literally outside, in nature apart from culture. Gilgamesh as questing hero journeys outside purposefully, but the hero in exile is a wanderer. Rāma and Sītā, the Pāṇḍavas in their forest exile, and Odysseus during his nineteen years on the seas are such wanderers. The Bible, too, has been discussed in themes of exile (slavery in Egypt, the Babylonian captivity, Jesus in the wilderness or the tomb) and restoration (delivery, return, resurrection), occurring in what some have seen as a grand epic cycle of narratives moving from creation to apocalypse, and including the quest of the hero (Messiah-Christ), his early death, and apotheosis.

The importance of remembering exemplary events of the past was no doubt of central importance in the creation and preservation of epics. The compilation of the *Mahābhārata* was to some extent furthered by the demand for great cycles of songs in which local kings, performing Vedic royal sacrifices such as the Aśvamedha or the Rājasūya, were equated with victorious heroes and kings of past ages. Albert Lord's hypothesis that "the special, peculiar purpose of oral epic song at its origin . . . was magical and ritual before it became heroic" (Lord, 1960, p. 66) may not be provable, but nevertheless is cogent. In many regions of Africa and Asia today, particular epics are linked to seasonal festivals such as sowing or harvesting. Others involve not cosmic but personal time, such as those performed at life-cycle rites, in which births, puberty ceremonies or initiations, marriages, and deaths become the foci for narratives culled from mirror episodes in the life cycles of epic heroes and heroines.

DEATHS AND REGENERATIONS. It is India once again that provides the strongest drama of epic warfare as sacrifice, even cosmic destruction and renewal, although several sacred texts from Scandinavia and Iran also reveal the theme of final cataclysm. Behind them, as Wikander has shown, is a Proto-Indo-European eschatological myth in which the forces of evil and good confront one another in the decisive time. The Battle of Brávellir, an episode in Icelandic sagas and in Saxo's narratives, is the Scandinavian heroic parallel to the *Mahābhārata* eschaton.

And it is Kṛṣṇa in the *Mahābhārata,* sometimes the detached, transcendent deity Viṣṇu, beyond the tensions of battle and reconciliation, sometimes imminent counselor, involved in human time and space, who are reminders of the broad range of roles taken by deities in epics, from distant observers to randomly intrusive actors, and to immediate saviors and redeemers. Apollo moves once to restore the fallen Hektor, but cannot deter the moment of his fate. The Kirghiz Manas is in the act of prayer when his destiny traces him and, armorless, he is dispatched. Once served by fate, however, heroes may, like the world itself, be regenerated, and this is the special talent of Hindu gods and goddesses in both classical and regional epics. In the best known of Tamil literary epics, the *Cilappatikāram,* the heroine-become-goddess Kaṇṇaki restores her wrongfully executed husband, the hero Kōvalaṉ, by destroying the city (world) of injustice.

This sacrificial regeneration is perhaps the strongest of many links between classical and folk epics of South Asia and is reinforced by numerous active cults of heroes and heroines from the Sanskrit epics and uncounted regional ones. These include the enshrinement and ritual use of heroes' weapons and the sacrality of spirit residences such as caves and are reminiscent of ancient cults of heroes in Greece in which relic bones, weapons, and ships were preserved in sanctuaries, as the bones and weapons of medieval heroes and saints were kept in the churches of Europe. Unlike immortal gods, the heroes have died significant deaths and then have conquered time; their weapons are still a vivid point of contact for the religious experience of their return and, in the case of several oral epics of South India, spontaneous possession of members of the audience, whose dramatic "deaths" and revivifications while the epic is under way are undeniable proof of the living presence of the heroes.

The nearly universal appeal of the epic must reside in the charisma of an old and much-loved tale well told and the glimpse it provides into definitions of human existence. During its performance, the channels are open to a time and space that remain powerful, accessible, and paradigmatic. Heroes and heroines challenge, and thereby define, limitations placed by gods, fate, or self-absorption, as well as those social, political, economic, religious, and sexual roles by which humans divide themselves. To the audience the resolution may be clear at the outset, but the telling of the drama of transformation, sung now as it was in "that time," is itself a powerful form of renewal.

See Also Enuma Elish; Flight; Gilgamesh; Heroes; Mahābhārata; Quests; Rāmāyaṇa; Shamanism; War and Warriors.

Bibliography

Brief surveys by fifteen specialists and bibliographies for major epic traditions, including texts, translations, and studies, may be found in *Heroic Epic and Saga,* edited by Felix J. Oinas (Bloomington, Ind., 1978). Discussions of background traditions by twelve other specialists in epics are in *Traditions of Heroic and Epic Poetry,* vol. 1, *The Traditions,* presented by Robert Auty and others under the editorship of A. T. Hatto (London, 1980). Jan de Vries's *Heroic Song and Heroic Legend* (London, 1963) is a short, readable overview. *The Growth of Literature,* 3 vols. (Cambridge, 1932–1940), by H. Munro Chadwick and Nora Kershaw Chadwick remains a valuable resource despite sections now dated; particularly useful are chapters on Turkic, Russian, and Yugoslav epics.

Where comparative studies of epics are concerned it is largely the Indo-Europeanists who have been productive for the history of religions. All of the many works of Georges Dumézil have relevance for epic research. Parts of *Mythe et épopée,* 3 vols. (Paris, 1968–1973), have appeared in English translation as *The Destiny of a King* (Chicago, 1973); *Camillus: A Study of Indo-European Religion as Roman History,* edited by Udo Strutynski (Berkeley, Calif., 1980); and *The Stakes of the Warrior,* edited by Jaan Puhvel (Berkeley, Calif., 1983). See also the untranslated first volume of *Mythe et épopée* and *The Destiny of the Warrior* (Chicago, 1970). Bruce Lincoln has summarized the Indo-Iranian warrior and priestly traditions that provide much of the background to the Sanskrit and Persian epics in *Priests, Warriors, and Cattle* (Berkeley, Calif., 1981). Alf Hiltebeitel, in *The Ritual of Battle: Krishna in the Mahābhārata* (Ithaca, N. Y., 1976), has continued the pioneering efforts of Dumézil, Stig Wikander, and Madeleine Biardeau in relating the *Mahābhārata* to other Indo-European mythic and epic narratives.

An older effort accomplished in the myth-ritual context is Gertrude R. Levy's *The Sword from the Rock* (London, 1953), a broad comparative discussion of the Mesopotamian, Sanskrit, and Homeric epics. Although lacking attention to mythic themes or Indo-European studies on kingship and warrior traditions, W. T. H. Jackson provides a suggestive analysis of the confrontation between intruder-hero (individual) and establishment-king (society) in the works of Homer and Vergil and in the medieval European epics in his *The Hero and the King: An Epic Theme* (New York, 1982).

A basic discussion of epic poetry in oral composition is the work of Milman Parry and Albert B. Lord, summarized in Lord's *The Singer of Tales* (Cambridge, Mass., 1960). Theories generated by their studies of epic singers in Yugoslavia are applied to the *Iliad* and the *Odyssey.* Among recent studies of South Asian oral epics, the most complete is that of Gene H. Roghair, *The Epic of Palnāḍu* (Oxford, 1982), a translation and study of a recitation of a Telugu epic in Andhra. Farther south in India, Brenda E. F. Beck has investigated a Tamil epic in *The Three Twins: The Telling of a South Indian Folk Epic* (Bloomington, Ind., 1982). The image of the hero in a dozen sub-Saharan oral epics, and the usefulness of the Parry-Lord hypothesis, are the subjects of Isidore Okpewho in *The Epic in Africa: Toward a Poetics of the Oral Performance* (New York, 1979).

Jeffrey H. Tigay's *The Evolution of the Gilgamesh Epic* (Philadelphia, 1982) is a study of the Old Babylonian epic as it emerged from older Sumerian tales, myths, and folklore. On folkloric motifs in the *Iliad* and the *Odyssey,* see Rhys Carpenter's *Folk Tale, Fiction and Saga in the Homeric Epics* (Berkeley, 1946). Despite a Frazerian style of compilation, Martti Haavio provides important shamanic-folkloric backgrounds to themes in the *Kalevala* in *Väinämöinen, Eternal Sage* (Helsinki, 1952).

New Sources

Alles, Gregory D. *The Iliad, the Ramayana, and the Work of Religion: Failed Persuasion and Religious Mystification.* University Park, 1994.

Belcher, Stephen Paterson. *Epic Traditions of Africa.* Bloomington, 1999.

Hiltebeitel, Alf. *Rethinking India's Oral and Classical Epics: Draupadi among Rajputs, Muslims, and Dalits.* Chicago, 1999.

Hodder, Alan D., and Robert E. Meagher. *The Epic Voice.* Westport, Conn., 2002.

Honko, Lauri. *Religion, Myth, and Folklore in the World's Epics: The Kalevala and its Predecessors.* Berlin, 1990.

Jackson-Laufer, Guida M. *Encyclopedia of Traditional Epics.* Santa Barbara, 1994.

Johnson, John William, Thomas A. Hale, and Stephen Paterson Belcher, eds. *Oral Epics from Africa: Vibrant Voices from a Vast Continent.* Bloomington,1997.

Patton, Laurie L., and Wendy Doniger, eds. *Myth and Method.* Charlottesville, Va., 1996.

Schein, Seth L., ed. *Reading the Odyssey: Selected Interpretative Essays.* Princeton, N. J., 1996.

DAVID M. KNIPE (1987)
Revised Bibliography

EPIPHANY is the Christian feast of the manifestation of Jesus Christ. Traditionally celebrated on January 6; it is also celebrated by the Roman rite in some places on the Sunday following the octave of Christmas. The feast is called Epiphania ("manifestation") among Western Christians and Theophaneia ("manifestation of God") among Eastern Christians. That the feast is of Eastern origin is indicated by the Greek origin of both names. Epiphany is one of the twelve major feasts of the Orthodox church year.

The origins of Epiphany are obscure and much debated. It was originally either a feast of Christ's baptism in the Jordan or of his birth at Bethlehem. The theory that the date of January 6 corresponded to an old date for the Egyptian winter solstice has been largely discredited. The date may have at first been observed as a feast of the baptism of Christ among the second-century Basilidian gnostics. In the fourth century it was certainly a feast of the nativity of Christ, celebrated with an octave, or eight days of celebration, at Bethlehem and all the holy places of Jerusalem.

At the end of the fourth century, when the Western feast of the nativity of Christ came to be observed in the East on December 25, January 6 came to be widely celebrated as the feast of Christ's baptism, although among the Armenians Epiphany is the only nativity feast celebrated to this day. As the feast of Christ's baptism, Epiphany became for Eastern Christians a major baptismal day, and hence it was given the Greek name Ta Phota ("the lights"); baptism itself was called *photismos* ("enlightenment").

At the same time as the East was accepting the Western Christmas, the Feast of Epiphany was being adopted in the West. Outside of Rome it was celebrated as the Feast of the Three Miracles, comprising the visit of the Magi, the baptism of Christ, and the miracle of changing water into wine at the wedding feast of Cana. In Rome, however, the feast concentrated solely on the visit of the Magi, connoting Christ's manifestation to the Gentiles. With their adoption of the Roman liturgy all other Western Christians eventually came to observe Epiphany as the Feast of the Magi.

Among Eastern Christians the celebration of Epiphany is notable for several reasons. At Alexandria the patriarch would solemnly announce the date of Easter for the current year on January 6. Throughout the East, Epiphany, together with Easter, was a special day for performing baptisms. The most enduring custom, however, has been the blessing of the waters on Epiphany. There are two blessings. The first takes place during the vigil of Epiphany in the evening and is followed by the priest's sprinkling of the town or village with the blessed water. The second blessing takes place on the day of Epiphany itself, when the local waters of stream, lake, or sea are blessed by having a cross thrown into them, after which young men dive into the waters to retrieve it.

The Western observance of Epiphany has centered on the figures of the Magi, popularly called the Three Kings. Their cult was especially strong at Cologne in the Middle Ages, for their supposed relics had been brought there in the twelfth century. The idea that the Magi were kings was derived from several verses of scripture (*Ps.* 71:10, *Is.* 60:3–6). The tradition that there were three of them was probably derived from the number of gifts mentioned in the biblical account of their visit (*Mt.* 2:1–12). The account of the visit of the Magi and of the miraculous star that guided them inspired several mystery plays during the Middle Ages. The story of their visit also gave rise to the custom of gift giving on Epiphany: In Italy gifts are given on that day by an old woman named Befana, and the feast is also an occasion for gift giving in Spanish cultures.

SEE ALSO Baptism; Gift Giving.

BIBLIOGRAPHY

For a survey of the development of Epiphany and associated customs, see Francis X. Weiser's *Handbook of Christian Feasts and Customs* (New York, 1958). For a view of Epiphany from the perspective of the history of religions, see E. O. James's *Seasonal Feasts and Festivals* (New York, 1961). For Greek customs associated with Epiphany, see George A. Megas's *Greek Calendar Customs,* 2d ed. (Athens, 1963).

JOHN F. BALDOVIN (1987)

EPISCOPALIANISM SEE ANGLICANISM

EPISTEMOLOGY. This branch of philosophy studies the nature, origin, and validity of knowledge; it is sometimes called "theory of knowledge." Epistemology has been central to modern philosophy since the sixteenth century, although it originally developed in Greek philosophy in close relation to ontology (theory of being) and metaphysics. (It is an open question whether epistemology can be completely disentangled from metaphysics.)

In Greek philosophy, and especially in Plato and Aristotle, the two words used to mean "knowledge" are *epistēmē* and *gnōsis,* the former having the narrower, more scientific connotation in opposition to *doxa* ("belief"), the latter the wider one, covering also perception, memory, and experience. Plato and Aristotle relate these two conceptions to the terms *noēsis* ("thinking, intuition") and *sophia* ("wisdom"). The Western Christian tradition, however, has paid more attention to epistemology than to gnoseology; the latter plays a greater role in Eastern Christian philosophy and theology, and, it goes without saying, among the gnostics.

Among the various epistemological positions (that is, theories of knowledge in the narrower sense), realism, which is the claim—deriving from Plato and Aristotle—that forms and universals are objectively real (whether *ante rem,* "before things," as in Plato or *in re,* "in things," as in Aristotle) has had by far the longest tenure. In modern times, at least since William of Ockham in the fourteenth century, nominalism, or the view that forms and universals are only in language and in the mind, has held the field. The issue, however, is by no means dead and, oddly enough, returns in connection with modern philosophies of mathematics and even in the understanding of information theory.

A second, equally important epistemological question has been whether universal ideas are innate or only obtained through the senses. The two positions on this question were staked out by Plato and Aristotle respectively, the controversy continuing through the Middle Ages, with Augustine on the Platonic side and Thomas Aquinas on the Aristotelian. Modern philosophy begins with Descartes's emphatic support for the Platonic-Augustinian position. His contention that clear and distinct ideas are innate (a view often called epistemological idealism, to distinguish it from Plato's joint ontological and epistemological idealism) was challenged in turn by the British empiricists (Locke, Berkeley, and Hume), who sought to show that all ideas derive from the senses. Kant defined a new position by arguing the so-called presuppositional character of the "forms of perception" and "categories of understanding."

These epistemological controversies (which find remarkable—although still insufficiently studied—parallels in the histories of both Hindu and Buddhist philosophies) have had a close relation to religious practices and doctrines, not only among Christians, but also among Jews and Muslims. Thus, for example, realism appears to support the theological doctrine concerning the real presence of the body and blood of Christ in the Mass, while nominalism is more congruent with the Protestant idea of the last supper, or "meal of remembrance." Similarly, realism is helpful in harmonizing revealed and natural theology, while voluntarism and fideism are more naturally related to nominalism.

Christianity, like the other monotheistic religions, cannot submit knowledge about God to ordinary epistemic criteria. Nor can it, without abjuring the biblical conception of faith, accept the pretensions of unrestrained gnosis or esoteric accretions. The resultant difficulties have given rise to such theological maneuvers as the Averroistic "double truth" (one for the natural, the other for the revealed) and the Thomistic "analogy of being" (in which the possibility of a single univocal meaning for the word *being* is renounced). In attempting to escape the Scylla of fideism, in which knowledge ultimately has no place at all in religion, Western religions have always been in danger of running afoul of the Charybdis of gnosticism, in which there is no need or room for faith. And behind these doctrines lurk the still greater dangers of atheism and pantheism, as well as gnostic dualism.

Epistemological issues in modern times have tended to revolve around the question of the existence of God and whether it is possible to know this or to establish it by some kind of "proof." Thus Anselm's purely a priori "ontological proof" vies with Thomas Aquinas's "five ways," which allegedly derive from empirical experience. All such "proofs" were rejected by Kant in favor of a moral argument that finds God a necessary presupposition of the moral, or practical reason. Here epistemology once again is closely related to ethics, as it had been in a different way in Greek and medieval philosophy. If the medieval world culminated in Dante's visionary belief that knowledge is love, the modern world has been working out the quite different formula of Francis Bacon that knowledge is power. The limits of this power, now coming into view, suggest the limits of the conception of knowledge and perhaps the limits of the epistemological enterprise as a whole.

A word must be said also about mysticism as a way of knowing in religion, apart from both reason and ordinary experience. When, for example, the poet Henry Vaughan says, "I saw eternity the other night," or an otherwise normal and ordinary person reports, "In one moment I was liberated and knew the purpose of life," we do not have criteria for judging the validity of the "knowledge" involved. Epistemology tends to look at such matters in terms of psychology and ethics, rather than ontology and metaphysics.

Since the twentieth century there have been signs that the three-hundred-year-old predominance of epistemology in philosophy is giving way to a concern with semantics, semiology, and meaning. If epistemology cannot find its way out of either subjectivism (Cartesianism, psychologism, psychoanalysis) or objectivism (materialism, positivism, Marxism), it is perhaps because these are simply two faces of the epistemological attitude itself, which, because it begins with the separation of knower and known (and, as it were, makes this central), cannot get them back together except in these unsatisfactory ways. Seen in this light, epistemology may lose its central role in philosophy. Other ways of conceiving human involvement in the world may turn out to be more sensible and useful.

If religion has been on the defensive against science in the modern era, the difficulty may turn out to lie not so much in the differences between religious and scientific ways of knowing as in the epistemological stance itself. Important modern philosophers, particularly Martin Heidegger and Ludwig Wittgenstein, abandoned the epistemological or "representational" point of view itself in their later philosophies. And this is very likely to be the direction to which philosophy itself will go in the future.

SEE ALSO Metaphysics.

BIBLIOGRAPHY

No outstanding survey history of epistemology exists. The most important works on the subject are the classic sources themselves.

Aristotle. *Posterior Analytics.* In *The Basic Works of Aristotle,* edited by Richard McKeon. New York, 1941.

Augustine. *Concerning the Teacher.* Translated by G. C. Leckie. In *Basic Writings of Saint Augustine,* edited by Whitney J. Oates, vol. 1, pp. 361–389. New York, 1948.

Berkeley, George. *A Treatise concerning the Principles of Human Knowledge.* Edited by A. C. Frazer. London, 1901.

Descartes, René. *Meditations.* In *Philosophical Works of Descartes,* edited by Elizabeth S. Haldane and G. R. T. Ross. Cambridge, U.K., 1911.

Hegel, G. W. F. *The Phenomenology of Mind.* Translated by J. B. Baillie. New York, 1910.

Kant, Immanuel. *Critique of Human Reason.* Translated by Norman Kemp Smith. London, 1950.

Leibniz, G. W. *New Essays on Human Understanding.* Edited by A. G. Langley. La Salle, Ill., 1949.

Locke, John. *An Essay concerning Human Understanding.* 2 vols. Edited by A. C. Frazer. Oxford, 1894.

Plato. *Theaetetus.* In *Plato's Theory of Knowledge: The Theaetetus and the Sophist of Plato,* edited by Francis M. Cornford. London, 1935.

Russell, Bertrand. *Human Knowledge, Its Scope and Limits.* New York, 1948.

Thomas Aquinas. *Truth.* 3 vols. Translated by R. W. Mulligan, J. V. McGlynn, and R. W. Schmidt. Chicago, 1952–1954.

New Sources

Alcoff, Linda, ed. *Epistemology: The Big Question.* Oxford, U.K., 1998.

Anderson, Pamela Sue. *A Feminist Philosophy of Religion: The Rationality and Myths of Religious Belief.* London, 1997.

Bonjour, Laurence. *Epistemology: Classical Problems and Contemporary Responses.* Lanham, Md., 2002.

Plantinga, Alvin. *Warrant and Proper Function.* New York, 1993.

Sosa, Ernest. *Knowledge in Perspective: Selected Essays in Epistemology.* 1991; reprint Cambridge, U.K., 2003.

HENRY LE ROY FINCH (1987)
Revised Bibliography

EPOCHĒ SEE PHENOMENOLOGY OF RELIGION

EPONA

EPONA is a Celtic goddess associated with horses. Her name is attested in Gaul and throughout the Roman empire of the first three centuries CE by about 250 figurative monuments and more than 60 votive inscriptions. In fact, she is the Celtic divinity whose name, if not whose cult, appears beyond the Gaulish borders. It is also exceptional that her name has been retained by several Latin writers.

Her Celtic name is related to the general designation for the horse, *epos* (Irish, *ech;* Welsh, *ebol;* Breton, *ebeul,* "foal," from **epalo-s*), and a suffix of theonymic derivation, *-ona,* suggests that Epona was the goddess of horses, if not of stables. Actually, the Gallo-Roman iconography of Epona is divided into two main types of depictions: Epona on horseback and Epona between two facing horses. It is very likely that Epona represents a Celtic transposition and interpretation of the Hellenistic theme of the "lady of horses." The images are foreign, but the name is Celtic and has been applied to the great sovereign feminine divinity (often called Augusta and Regina in the Celtic-Roman inscriptions). There is no correspondence in the insular Celtic cultures.

Care must be taken not to see Epona as a hippomorphic divinity, that is, as one possessing equine attributes. Henri Hubert and Jean Gricourt have made comparisons—all fallacious—to insular deities, the Welsh Rhiannon ("great queen") and the Irish Macha ("plain"), eponym for Emhain Mhacha, residence of King Conchobhar in the tales from the Ulster Cycle, but neither of these mythic figures is any more hippomorphic than Epona herself. In the *Mabinogion* Rhiannon is the wife of Pwyll, and after being falsely accused of slaying her newborn son she is condemned to carry on her back the visitors to her husband's court for seven years. Macha is a war goddess of Irish tradition; after some imprudent bragging on the part of her husband, Crunnchu, Macha is forced, despite her advanced pregnancy, to run a race on a solemn feast day against the king's horses. She wins the race and then dies giving birth to twins, a boy and a girl. But before dying she hurls a cry to punish Ulates, and all the men of Ulster who hear her (and all their descendants for nine generations) are condemned not to have more strength during military encounters than a woman in childbed.

It is difficult to view Rhiannon as anything other than a queen or sovereign deity. As to Macha, she is a trifunctional divinity who also goes by the names of Bodb and Morrígan, warrior goddess of Ireland. The problem posed by Epona's plurality must be reexamined in light of these facts about Rhiannon and Macha.

SEE ALSO Horses.

BIBLIOGRAPHY

Benoit, Fernand. *Les mythes de l'Outre-Tombe, le cavalier à l'anguipède et l'écuyère Epona.* Brussels, 1950.

Le Roux, Françoise. "Epona." Ph.D. diss., École Pratique des Hautes Études, Paris, 1955.

Le Roux, Françoise, and Christian-J. Guyonvarc'h. "Morrigan-Bodb-Macha: La souveraineté guerrière de l'Irlande." *Celticum* (Rennes), no. 25 (1984).

Magnen, René, and Émile Thevenot. *Epona, déesse gauloise des chevaux, protectrice des cavaliers.* Bordeaux, 1953.

FRANÇOISE LE ROUX (1987)
CHRISTIAN-J. GUYONVARC'H (1987)
Translated from French by Erica Meltzer

EQBAL, MUḤAMMAD SEE IQBĀL, MUḤAMMAD

ERASMUS, DESIDERIUS (1469?–1536), Dutch scholar, is called the "prince of humanists." Neither the date nor the place of Erasmus's birth is known with certainty; he was probably born in 1469 in Rotterdam (he styled himself Roterodamus).

LIFE AND WORKS. Erasmus's life was wholly dedicated to scholarship. After his early education, mainly in the school of the Brethren of the Common Life at Deventer (1475–1483), his guardians sent him to the monastery of the Augustinian canons at Steyn. Ordained to the priesthood in 1492, he entered the service of Henry of Bergen, bishop of Cambrai, who gave him leave to study theology at the University of Paris (1495–1498). A visit to Oxford (1499–1500) brought him into the company of such kindred spirits as John Colet (1466?–1519) and Thomas More (1478–1535). Later he visited the cradle of the Renaissance, Italy (1506–1509), and made further journeys to England, including Cambridge, before settling in the Netherlands, at Louvain (1517–1521). There, at the height of his fame, he intended to devote himself quietly to the cause of classical and sacred literature.

But from 1518, Erasmus's labors were increasingly overshadowed by the Lutheran Reformation. He could not but welcome the addition of Martin Luther's voice to his own outspoken criticisms of ecclesiastical abuses, yet he distrusted Luther's aggressive manner, which he feared could only harm the cause of learning and piety. His friends and patrons finally induced him to challenge Luther in print. The ostensible theme of his *De libero arbitrio* (On free choice; 1524) was the freedom denied by Luther's necessitarianism, but more fundamentally the book was a warning against theological contentiousness.

In 1521, driven from Louvain by the hostility of the Dominicans to the new learning, Erasmus moved to Basel, home of publisher Johann Froben (c. 1460–1527). When Basel turned Protestant, he moved to Freiburg im Breisgau (1529–1535), but it was in Protestant Basel that he died without the ministrations of the old church, which later placed his books on the Index.

In response to the requests of his friends, Erasmus himself drew up a "catalog" of his numerous writings in nine divisions. The items vary widely in literary form, from letters to treatises, and in readership intended, from schoolboys to princes. But many of them can be distinguished by certain dominant themes. Some embody Erasmus's research on the language, literature, and wisdom of classical antiquity. Others apply the tools of classical scholarship to the original sources of Christianity, this being what is generally meant by "Christian humanism." In 1516, Erasmus brought out the first published edition of the Greek New Testament, which he furnished with a new Latin translation, notes, and prefaces, including the famous *Paraclesis* (a prefatory "exhortation" to study the philosophy of Christ). In the succeeding two decades, his series of editions of Greek and Latin fathers appeared, beginning with Jerome (1516) and ending with Origen (1536), his two favorites.

In a third group of writings, Erasmus exposed to mockery the moral failures and religious abuses of the day, notably, in his *Moriae encomium* (Praise of folly; 1511), some of the *Colloquia familiaria* (Familiar colloquies; 1st ed., 1518) and, if he did indeed write it, the anonymous pamphlet *Julius exclusus e coelis* (Julius [the warrior pope] shut out of heaven; 1517). Finally, to a fourth group of writings, which present Erasmus's own Christian vision, may be assigned the *Enchiridion militis Christiani* (Handbook [or weapon] for the Christian soldier; 1503), a powerful plea for an inward, spiritual, and moral piety that does not lean on outward religious observances. The strongly pacifist vein in Erasmus's piety is reflected in his *Institutio principis Christiani* (Instruction for a Christian prince; 1516) and especially in *Querela pacis* (The complaint of peace; 1517).

THE ERASMIAN PROGRAM. A consistent humanistic program, in which learning assumes a moral and religious character, lends unity to Erasmus's many writings. The study of ancient languages and literature is propaedeutic to following the philosophy of Christ, which can be recovered in its purity only if the theologians will leave, or at least moderate, their endless squabbles and turn back to the sources of the faith equipped with the tools of the new learning. The program is not antitheological, but it is antischolastic: Moral utility, rather than dialectical subtlety and metaphysical speculation, becomes the test of genuine theology. Erasmus proposed a new ideal of the theologian as more a scholar than a schoolman, an ideal that made a profound impact on many who did not share the Erasmian view of the gospel, including the Protestants.

What Erasmus discovered in the New Testament was, above all, the precepts and example of Christ. To be a Christian is to enlist under Christ's banner. The philosophy of Christ is not speculation or disputation, but the good life—a philosophy not essentially different from the teaching of the best classical moralists, only conveyed with unique authority and made accessible to all. It would be a mistake, however, to reduce the Erasmian imitation of Christ to mere copying of an external model; in the scriptures, as Erasmus reads them, the Savior comes alive, and Christ's philosophy is nothing less than a dying and living in him.

The work of Erasmus marked an important stage in the course of biblical and patristic scholarship. It is true that his New Testament text rested on inferior manuscripts and had no lasting usefulness, but his biblical studies, even when vitiated by overeagerness to extract an edifying lesson from the text by means of spiritual exegesis, established a new emphasis on the human and historical character of the sacred text. No less historically important is the fact that he arrived, through his study of the Gospels, at a distinctive interpretation of Christianity and of religion generally.

Stormier religious personalities, such as Luther, have found the Erasmian outlook bland. They have judged Christian existence to be neither as simple nor as placid as Erasmus supposed, because God makes a Christian not by gently strengthening a feeble will but by putting to death a vigorous, arrogant will. But the recall of Christians to a simpler, more practical ideal of discipleship has continued to win friends for Erasmus among those who doubt the usefulness of the constant refinement of dogma.

Some have hailed the Erasmian dislike of dogmatism as one source of modern undogmatic Christianity, or even of religious skepticism. Historically, that is a correct estimate of his actual influence, or at least of one strand of it. No doubt, it must be qualified by Erasmus's own professed submission to the decrees of the church. But nothing he says has quite laid to rest the suspicion that, for him, the institutional church was not so much directly salvific as a condition of that outward order and peace without which scholarship and the gospel cannot flourish.

Bibliography

Erasmus published about one hundred writings, some of which were very popular and went through several editions. Many have been translated into English. An English translation of his voluminous correspondence and all the major writings is being published as *Collected Works of Erasmus,* 40–45 vols. projected (Toronto, 1974–). Erasmus samplers are *The Essential Erasmus,* translated and edited by John P. Dolan (New York, 1964), and *Christian Humanism and the Reformation: Selected Writings of Erasmus with the Life of Erasmus by Beatus Rhenanus,* rev. ed., edited by John C. Olin (New York, 1975). Dolan has the *Enchiridion, Moriae encomium,* and *Querela pacis;* Olin includes the *Paraclesis,* perhaps the best statement of the Erasmian program. Other translations are *Ten Colloquies of Erasmus* (New York, 1957) and *The Colloquies of Erasmus* (Chicago, 1965), both translated and edited by Craig R. Thompson; *The Education of a Christian Prince,* translated and edited by Lester K. Born (New York, 1936); *The Julius Exclusus of Erasmus,* translated by Paul Pascal, edited by J. Kelley Sowards (Bloomington, Ind., 1968); and *Erasmus-Luther: Discourse on Free Will,* translated and edited by Ernst F. Winter (New York, 1961). An excellent biographical study is Roland H. Bainton's *Erasmus of Christendom* (New York, 1969), and a useful companion to Erasmus's writings is *Essays on the Works of Erasmus,* edited by Richard L. DeMolen (New Haven, Conn., 1978).

B. A. Gerrish (1987)

EREMITISM is a form of monastic life characterized by solitariness. (The term derives from the Greek *erēmos,* "wilderness, uninhabited regions," whence comes the English *eremite,* "solitary.") In this type of life, the social dimension of human existence is totally or largely sacrificed to the primacy of religious experience. It is thus understandable that Christianity has traditionally regarded eremitism as the purest and most perfect form of a life consecrated to God. While other forms of monasticism or of the religious life have striven to bring religious experience to bear on human relationships (Western Christianity especially emphasizes external service), eremitism has always been purely contemplative in thrust. Hermits live only in order to cultivate their spiritual life in prayer, meditation, reading, silence, asceticism, manual work, and, perhaps, in intellectual pursuits. In eremitism, the celibacy characteristically practiced in monachism extends to the suppression of all social relationships. While Christian monks have always stressed charity in relationships within the monastic group and, in the Middle Ages especially, written treatises on Christian friendship, Buddhist monks have emphasized the necessity for freedom from every affective relationship that might hinder the achievement of enlightenment.

While isolation for a limited period of time is common in many religions, especially as part of a process of initiation or as a special time dedicated to prayer and reflection, eremitism as a permanent vocation or prolonged phase of asceticism is found only in those religions that grant monasticism an established and determinative role. The religions in question are salvation religions, whether in the sense of self-liberation or of redemption. In Buddhism, Jainism, and Christianity religiosity has a personal character as opposed to a merely societal character (religion as a series of beliefs and rites of a tribe, *polis,* or state). Buddhism, Jainism, and Manichaeism are essentially monastic religions, owing to the importance they attach to the pursuit of the self-liberation of the human being. Christian hermits, too, often went into the wilderness in hopes of finding there the answer to the all-absorbing question: "How can I attain salvation?"

However, the theme of personal salvation does not seem to be the deepest and most constant motive behind the eremitical vocation. The Ṣūfī mystics, as well as many Christian monks and nuns, have gone primarily in pursuit of union with God. Some of them, such as Teresa of Ávila or Thérèse of Lisieux, have consecrated their lives to interceding for the world. Monks who, like Thomas Merton, distance themselves even from their own monastery, do so not to assure their own salvation but rather to devote themselves to constant prayer. In the early Christian world it was commonly said that solitaries pursued an angelic life, because they wished to be, like the angels, always in the presence of God. It can be legitimately affirmed, then, that what really permits the birth of monasticism in general and of eremitism in particular is the desire to consecrate one's whole life to religious experience.

Historically, there have been two forms of eremitism. The more common form is that of the anchorite, a term derived from the Greek verb *anachōrein,* originally used to designate the act of draft dodging or tax evasion by fleeing to out-of-the-way places. In Hellenistic times, the word came to refer generally to those who moved far away from towns and particularly to sages who withdrew in order to devote themselves to contemplation. The less common type of eremitism is that of the recluse, who often remained in town but enclosed himself in a cell, communicating with the outside world only through a small window. In the Middle East during the early Christian period there were anchorites (male and female) who not only went into the wilderness but also became recluses, in a spirit of penitence. In their different ways both anchorites and recluses profess a life of solitude as a privileged situation for personal growth.

EREMITISM IN THE ANCIENT WORLD. Eremitism first appeared as a lifelong vocation in India among the numerous ascetics on the margin of Aryan society. The ascetics stood out from the general population by their long hair and distinctive dress, or by their wearing no clothes at all. Some lived in tombs, while others, the "ascetics of the forest," lived in the woods. From them is derived the most archaic strata of the Upaniṣads and the Āraṇyakas, dating from the eighth century BCE. The Aryan ascetics withdrew from society in order to pursue individual religious experiences that were fostered by a series of extraordinary renunciations. Their ascetical discipline was aimed to induce a state characterized by illumination and by the attainment of supernatural powers. The withdrawal of these ascetics seems to have involved a rejection of priestly mediation and can be interpreted as reflecting a crisis in a ritual system that had become somewhat fossilized.

The life of Siddhārtha Gautama, called the Buddha (the Enlightened One), established the paradigm for eremitism in Indian culture. After his conversion experience, Gautama determined to become a truth-seeker and placed himself under the direction of some famous sages. After this period of discipleship, Gautama withdrew to a lovely woodland grove, where he gave himself over to the practice of extreme asceticism and came to be surrounded by a small group of disciples. One day, Gautama observed to a certain adept that physical asceticism had not led him where he wished to go and that he had therefore given it up. Upon hearing this, his disciples, bound to the ascetical tradition, abandoned him. So Gautama remained alone, and alone he ultimately reached enlightenment. After attaining this fulfillment, the Buddha went forth to preach his message. His spiritual itinerary is an exemplary instance of the four stages (*āśramas*) into which Hindu tradition divides the journey of a *brahman*: student, father of a family, forest dweller or solitary (*vānaprasthin*), and, finally, renouncer (*saṃnyāsin*), follower of an itinerant and often mendicant life. The withdrawal into solitude for a certain time is, thus, an integral part not only of Buddhist spirituality but of various forms of Hindu spirituality as well.

Withdrawal into solitude is likewise observable in other types of monastic movements that appeared in India from the sixth century BCE onward. It may also be observed in Jainism, begun by Pārśvanātha in the eighth century BCE and reformed by Mahāvīra in the sixth century BCE. Jainism aims at a life of communion with nature in places removed from the social mainstream. Both of the original great heroes of Jainism lived largely eremitical lives. Gośāla, the founder of the Ājīvikas in the sixth century BCE, began his ascetical life by withdrawing naked into the forest.

In the fourth century BCE, the conquests of Alexander the Great in the Middle East and his expeditions into India brought the Greek world into contact with Hindu philosophy and religion. Pyrrho of Elis, who took part in the Indian expedition, displayed afterward a strong inclination toward tranquil solitude, so much so, in fact, that he rarely presented himself even to the members of his household. It is said that he did so because he had heard a Hindu admonish Anaxarchos that the latter could hardly pretend to be good, let alone instruct others, because he frequented the court. Philostratus and Hippolytus later praised the asceticism of the Hindu philosophers. From about the first century BCE to the second century CE there arose in Hellenism the ideal of the sage as one who had achieved a personal contemplative relationship with the divine through the practice of solitude and certain ascetical techniques. Seneca recommended that Lucilius live a quiet and retiring life *("consistere et secum morari")*. Thus the way was paved for the emergence of the figure of the hermit. Plutarch in the first century CE speaks of a famous solitary who lived on the shore of the Eritrean Sea and communicated with others only once a year. Lucian tells of a recluse who had remained for twenty-three years in a subterranean temple, where he was instructed by Isis. Around the second century CE the verb *anachōrein* and the noun *anachōrēsis* underwent an evolution of meaning and came to indicate a withdrawal from social commitments in order to pursue inner wisdom.

The influence of these tendencies is observable also in Hellenistic Judaism. In Palestine, the Essenes withdrew from the sway of normative Judaism and created their own community of salvation with a strict, ritualized life. In Egypt, the Therapeutae mentioned by Philo Judaeus followed a predominantly eremitical form of life. They confined themselves to individual cells, where they devoted themselves to asceticism and meditation, coming together only on the Sabbath for community worship.

Ascetical renunciation became central to Manichaeism, the religion founded in Babylonia by Mani in the third century CE. Asceticism became so important because Mani attributed the material world to the workings of the principle of evil. Because the material world was thus to be shunned, this doctrine implied almost necessarily a monastic conception of life. There seems to have been some Hindu influence on the group, for its members were divided into the elect (monks) and the "hearers" (laity); the latter received the same name as was given to the laity in Jainism. The elect professed a radical poverty and sexual continence, which some carried to the point of castration. Among the elect, many were itinerant ascetics, although some of them withdrew into solitude.

Primitive Christian Eremitism. Tertullian, the celebrated African writer, stated in the second century CE that among Christians there were no naked philosophers, *brahmans*, or forest dwellers, but that all lived in moderation among the rest of those devoted to family and public life (*Apologeticum* 42.1). A century later eremitism launched a veritable invasion of Christian churches. What, one may ask, had happened to bring about this apparent reversal?

The radical commitment that Jesus asked of his disciples, involving faith, conversion, and suffering, was lived by his first followers within the context of a prophetic mission organized around the announcement of the imminence of the kingdom of God. This mission necessarily led them to involve themselves with society, and especially with those on its margins. In contrast to John the Baptist and his followers, Jesus neither practiced asceticism as a preparation for the judgment of God nor had recourse to solitude, except in decisive moments requiring prayer and reflection. It is significant, then, that the first Christian ascetics frequently invoked, not the example of Jesus, but rather that of Elijah or of John the Baptist. Early on, a group of wandering prophets who preached the imminent return of the Son of humankind seem to have taken quite literally the recommendations of Jesus on the need to abandon all things (*Didachē* 11.8). Their asceticism developed in the context of a prophetic mission, sustained by their hope in the end of the present world.

Only at a later date did this radical discipleship transform into an asceticism aimed at personal perfection or salvation. This step from commitment as a prophet to pursuit of individual asceticism—both expressions of Christian radicalism—came about simultaneously with the step from the eschatological dualism of Jesus (the "already" and the "not yet" of the kingdom of God) to the static dualism of the Hellenistic world (the world above versus the world below, spirit and body). The number of ascetics seems to have increased considerably throughout the third century. While some practiced asceticism in the cities, numerous others built cells near towns or villages and committed themselves to prayer in an early attempt at the solitary life. There were a few cases of ascetics seeking a more total isolation in the desert. Eusebius relates that Narcissus, bishop of Jerusalem, weary of slanders against him and eager to embrace a philosophical life, retired to the wilderness around 212. The ecclesiastical writer Socrates mentions a certain Eutychianus, a hermit living in Asia Minor around 310.

But it was only toward the end of the third century in Egypt that Christian eremitism appeared in a definitive and exemplary manner. Once martyrdom, as an extreme test of fidelity to the gospel, ceased to occur and once the church with its bishops became recognized as part of the urban establishment, numerous men and some women fled to the solitude of the desert in search of God. There they defiantly faced the demons whom popular belief assigned to such solitary places. Thus arose a type of Christian life characterized by solitude, constant prayer, radical poverty, manual labor, and practices of mortification.

It should be noted that, since the time of Tertullian and Origen, the two great Christian writers of the third century, the idea of retreat to the desert had become emblematic of a new religious attitude. The gospel accounts of the time Jesus spent in the desert lent a profound significance to the biblical traditions of Israel's wanderings through the wilderness and the withdrawal of some of the Israelite prophets into solitude. Tertullian wrote to the Christian martyrs that their isolation from the rest of the world during their imprisonment might well engender the spiritual benefits that the desert or solitude had given the prophets and the apostles: a lively experience of the glory of God. Origen used the desert as a symbol of spiritual progress and also transformed it into an emblem of the solitude and peace that are necessary to encounter the word and wisdom of God. It is significant that the first translators of the Greek Bible into Latin coined the noun *eremus* ("desert"), which did not exist in profane Latin. Thus the desert, the *eremus,* had been converted into a symbol of a spiritual attitude, a reliving of certain incidents in the Christ event foreshadowed by the passage of Israel through the wilderness.

These precedents must be considered in any account of the origins of Christian eremitism. The first influential Christian eremite is Anthony, a Coptic Christian born around 250. Anthony was early converted to asceticism and then retired to the desert at about age thirty-five; he enclosed himself for the next twenty years in a small, ruined fortress. Athanasius describes this period of reclusion as the phase of Anthony's mystical initiation. At the end of this period, Anthony accepted a few disciples. Toward the end of his life, he withdrew alone to a place near the Gulf of Suez, although he continued to make periodic visits to some of his anchorite followers who dwelt nearby. He died in 356, his fame widespread. His biography, written a few years after his death by Athanasius and twice translated into Latin, enjoyed a remarkable success and inaugurated a new Christian literary genre. Jerome later used Athanasius's work as a model for his lives of Paul, Malchus, and Hilarion.

Very early on, even during the lifetime of Anthony, Egypt had a large number of anchorites. Paul of Thebes, the hero whose novelistic life was written by Jerome, lived as a solitary on Mount Colzim, near the Gulf of Suez. Amun of Nitria, who like Paul was a disciple of Anthony, began a colony of hermits in the Nitrian desert (today's Wadi el Natrun) to the east of the Nile Delta. There were also the two great hermits named Makarios: Makarios of Egypt and Makarios of Alexandria, both of whom died around 390. In the desert of Scete, forty miles beyond the Wadi el Natrun, lived the celebrated Arsenius (354–449), his contemporary Agathon (a disciple of the first abbot, Daniel), and later Isaias. The sayings of the principal solitaries were gathered into popular collections called *Apophthegmata Patrum* (lit., "sayings of the fathers," but referring specifically to the Desert Fathers). The collections were first set in alphabetical order according to author by compilers writing in Greek around 450. Not long after this an excellent collection was drawn up arranged according to subject matter.

There were as well three famous women who were desert solitaries, Theodora, Sarah, and Syncletica. From the beginning of Christian monasticism, there were anchoresses, although it is impossible to accurately assess their number. That the *Apophthegmata Patrum* include the sayings of some women, and that the lives of certain spiritual women were written, suggests that any apparent silence on women is most likely due to the fact that a relatively small number settled in the wilderness. One obvious reason for a relative dearth of anchoritic women would be the frequency with which bands of robbers and highwaymen attacked isolates in the desert; women were presumably in greater danger than men. It must be acknowledged, however, that the spirituality of the first Christian anchorites had a very masculine slant, for athletic and military terminology abounds in their biographies and writings. It is not surprising, then, that this quality influenced the anchoresses, who affirmed their spiritual masculinity. Sarah stated a number of times that although she was a woman as to her sex, she was not so in spirit and resolve. Syncletica also used terminology drawn from military life and athletic contests. The practice of some anchoresses of disguising themselves as men probably arose from their concern for personal security in a time and place that was extremely hazardous for all travelers.

The most celebrated anchoress was undoubtedly Mary of Egypt (344–421), who underwent a conversion while on pilgrimage to the Holy Land and went to live in solitude on the other side of the Jordan River, where she spent the next forty-seven years. Her life, first alluded to by Cyril of Scythopolis in his sixth-century *Life of Cyriacus,* became a legend. Alexandra, a serving girl who enclosed herself in a funeral grotto, receives mention in Palladius's *Historia Lausiaca.* Another legendary figure is Theodora, a married woman who abandoned her husband and, fearing that she might be recognized by him if she entered a nunnery, decided to disguise herself as a man and managed to enter instead a monastery outside Alexandria. In time the monks accused her of being the father of a baby boy whom an unhappy young woman had left at her doorstep and expelled her from the community. She was obliged to live with the boy in the wilderness for seven years. After that time she was readmitted to the monastery, where she became a recluse in a cell apart from the rest. Syncletica (sixth century), too, withdrew to a tomb not far from Alexandria; she has the distinction of being the first Christian heroine to be the subject of a biography. Sarah lived a solitary life for some seventy years on the eastern branch of the Nile. The sayings of Theodora, Syncletica, and Sarah may be found in the *Apophthegmata Patrum.*

These anchorites and anchoresses were not the only Christians to practice the eremitical life. Alongside them, from the beginning, existed another group of solitaries: the recluses. The latter separated themselves from the world not by going to some far-off place but by enclosing or immuring themselves in cells. The great Anthony spent his first twenty years of solitude as a recluse. The famous John of Nicopolis (fourth century) lived in the same manner. Likewise, the solitaries of the Desert of Cells, east of the Nile near Cairo, preferred to live a life of withdrawal in their caves, which were "like hyenas' dens."

Anchorites and recluses held one basic attitude in common: a radical lack of interest in the world, that is, in human society and history. They called this attitude *xenoteia* (from Gr. *xenos*), the condition of being a stranger, an alien, a passerby. Their disinterest was motivated by a desire for total self-commitment to God in contemplative quiet. The Christian anchorite was at the same time in pursuit of interior peace, which could be attained only through *apatheia,* or detachment from the passions. The experience of God in his mystical fullness was for the anchorite a return to the primordial condition of the human being. One could not return to this lost paradise except by way of a continual struggle with the demons that populate society, allusions to which appear in many personal accounts. The hermits often acquired a great analytical acuteness, yet numerous allusions to dreams and visions show some of the negative effects of a life of pure interiority. Although the dialectical orientation of human nature was safeguarded by the constant dialogue with God, the fact that this dialogue was almost completely interior may well have overintensified psychic activity.

It should be remembered that at the outset hermits could not count on the help of the Christian community. They were laypersons, who had separated themselves even from ecclesiastical society and were unable to participate in the common liturgy or the sacraments. The life of Anthony makes no allusion to the Eucharist. Soon the solitaries discovered the need to consult those who were more experienced and began to make visits to them, which began with a customary greeting, "Give me a word." They also felt the need of listening to the exhortations of the most famous holy men and of celebrating the liturgy together. This gave rise to colonies of hermits who gathered together on certain days of the week for the liturgy and conferences. Anchorites who periodically went to churches for worship (this became common at an early date) were allowed to bring the Eucharist with them to their retreats, so that they could receive daily Communion alone. From the beginning, however, it was the Bible that occupied the central position in the spiritual life of the Christian hermit. Even those who did not know how to read customarily memorized psalms and New Testament passages for recitation and meditation. They turned to the Bible whenever they needed a standard for conduct. Nevertheless, the anti-intellectualism of the majority led them to oppose all theological reflection on the sacred book.

Basil of Caesarea (329?–379) is the only father of the church who ruled out the possibility of a solitary life, basing his reasoning on both anthropological (the social dimension of the human being) and religious (the Christian vocation to communion) insights. Augustine also expressed reservations regarding the eremitical life, believing that Christian charity can never prescind from the neighbor. In general, however, the church continued to regard eremitism as the highest, though most difficult, vocation, one meant only for the strongest and best-formed personalities. The vast majority of the early anchorites were simple folk with little education. Many of those of Coptic origin were ignorant of Greek; indeed, many were illiterate. Early on, it became requisite that candidates for eremitism place themselves under the direction of an experienced anchorite before undertaking the solitary life. Later, once cenobitical monasticism (monks and nuns living in community) spread, a consensus arose that subjection to the discipline of a community was the best preparation for the eremitical life. The Palestinian laura, made up of a central monastery surrounded by a scattering of eremitical cells, is based on this idea. The Trullan Synod (692) decreed that future recluses should submit to at least three years of community discipline before going into reclusion. The canonists eventually extended this norm to all solitaries.

Although the first solitaries in Egypt and Syria were for the most part unlettered countryfolk, they developed a rich spiritual doctrine. Drawing on their own experience, their prayers and their temptations, they developed and orally transmitted the first art of spiritual direction, as well as the first analyses in Christianity of interior states. Toward the end of the fourth century, a number of scholars educated in Greek culture went to listen and learn from the solitaries. Rufinus of Aquileia, a famous sage at first admired but later attacked by Jerome, arrived in Egypt in 371. Evagrios of Pontus began his apprenticeship around 383. Palladius, the future historian of the desert, arrived there around 389. John Cassian spent ten years in Egypt toward the end of the fourth century. Later, he founded two monasteries, one for men and the other for women, in Marseilles. His *Monastic Institutions* (twelve books) and his *Conferences* exercised a lasting influence on Western spirituality.

Historical Development and Spread of Eremitism. Eremitism spread rapidly throughout the Middle East. It was also developing, contemporaneously and independently, in Syro-Mesopotamian Christianity, where it assumed some quite original forms. Some eremites, the Dendrites, lived in trees or in hollow tree trunks; others lived always in the open air, either on a rocky height or in groves, while still others lived in huts. The celebrated Simeon (390?–459) mounted a pillar in order to escape the importunities of people who sought his prayers, inspiring numerous imitators (the Stylites). There were a great number of recluses who, like James and Sisinnius, dwelt in tombs or, like Thalalaeus, in hovels with roofs built so low that it was impossible to stand inside. Marana and Cyriaca loaded themselves with heavy chains. All the hermits practiced great mortifications. Some of their actions and words seem inspired by a Manichaean worldview, while others resemble the feats attributed to the Indian fakirs. Toward the middle of the fourth century, many hermits lived in the mountains near Nisibus, on Mount Gaugal in Mesopotamia, and in the mountainous region around Antioch. The origins of eremitism in Palestine are unknown; it is known only that around 330 Hilarion began a form of eremitism similar to that of the Egyptian anchorites. Throughout the fourth and fifth centuries, hermits were very common in Palestine. Around 390, the well-publicized pilgrim Egeria found them nearly everywhere.

In the West, the Latin translation of the life of Anthony seems to have given rise not only to numerous admirers but also to some imitators. Already in the second half of the fourth century, numerous hermitages appeared on the islands and islets surrounding Italy (Gallinaria, Noli, Montecristo), and a colony of Syrian hermits settled near Spoleto. By his own example Eusebius of Vercelli gave rise to a group in the mountains of Oropa. Somewhat later, there were hermitages on the hills about Rome. Ascetics had lived in France since the second half of the second century. One of the early martyrs of Lyon and Vienne had sustained himself on bread and water. But it was Martin of Tours (316?–397) who truly propagated eremitism in Gaul. His life, written by Sulpicius Severus, contributed effectively to the movement. Converted to the monastic life in Milan, Martin underwent his first anchoritic experience on the island of Gallinaria and later settled at Ligugé. There a number of disciples established their cells near his. Made bishop of Tours in 371 by popular acclamation, he alternated the exercise of his pastoral office with the life of a hermit, and in these solitary periods he was again joined by numerous disciples.

Between the fifth and eighth centuries, hermits abounded in Ireland, Scotland, and Wales. In Spain, however, solitaries were not established until the sixth century. The bishops of the Iberian Peninsula took a dim view of asceticism as a result of their struggle with the ascetic rigorism of the monk Priscillian (340?–385) and his followers, who are said to have felt the greatest scorn for those Christians who would not embrace their austerities.

In the Eastern churches, eremitism has always enjoyed great prestige, although the spread of monachism in community (cenobitism) considerably reduced the number. Periodic reactions against cenobitism, in part inspired by Basil of Caesarea, have promoted a type of monastic life focused on contemplative quiet and personal prayer, rather than on liturgical worship. Among the proponents of hesychasm (cultivators of inner peace, or *hēsuchia*) were the Sinaitic school of the seventh century and Symeon the New Theologian (949?–1022). The laura of Mount Athos was founded in 963 by Athanasius, although solitaries had already been living on the mountain. Another famous laura is the Monastery of Saint John, founded in 1068 on the island of Patmos. Both still exist today. At almost the same time, monachism was introduced into Russia by Anthony of Kiev, who had formerly been a monk at Mount Athos. When he returned to Russia, he chose as his dwelling a cave on the side of a hill that faced the city of Kiev. Numerous disciples joined him there, thus giving rise to the Pecherskaia Laura, the Monastery of the Caves. Sergii of Radonezh (1314–1392), saint-protector of Moscow and all Russia, spent several years in complete solitude. Nil Sorskii (1433?–1508) spent a great part of his life in complete solitude, developing his version of the hesychasm he had learned during a stay at Mount Athos. Cornelius of Komel shared his love of poverty and solitude. In the nineteenth century the eremitic ideal held a strong attraction for a significant group of Russian personages who spent the last stages of their lives in solitude. From this time date Feofan the Recluse (1815–1894), translator of the *Philokalia,* who remained in strict enclosure from 1872 until his death, and Serafim of Sarov (1759–1833).

The Maronite church, founded by the Syrian monk Maron (fourth century), has always professed a particular devotion to monachism. Among the Maronites, too, has arisen the practice of solitaries situating themselves in the neighborhood of its monasteries. Two Maronite hermits, the brothers Michael and Sergius ar-Rizzi, became patriarchs toward the end of the sixteenth century. The last illustrious example of this tradition is Charbel Maklouf, a popular thaumaturge of the nineteenth century.

In the West, eremites were always less numerous than in the Middle East. The teaching of Augustine on the central value of fraternal communion in the service of Christ, the preference of John Cassian for cenobitism, and, above all, the gradual conquest of the West by the *Rule of Saint Benedict* all converged to impose community monasticism as the common form. Nevertheless, even in the European West there have always been hermits. The fact that the councils of Vannes (463), Agde (506), and Toledo VI (638) all gave rules for recluses indicates that they were not a rare phenomenon. In the days of the French queen and saint Radegunda (518–587), a liturgical ceremony celebrated the entry of recluses into their cells. Grimlac, a tenth-century hermit of Lorraine, wrote the first *regula solitariorum* known in the West. Further such rules were written in the twelfth century by Ethelred of York and, for the recluses of Cluny, by Peter the Venerable. Even in a community as well organized as that of Cluny, some monks were permitted to go into reclusion and separate themselves from community life after a certain number of years. The same practice was in effect in the Cistercian monasteries, despite the communitarian spirituality that had developed at Cîteaux.

These developments were varied manifestations of a tendency toward solitude that had been growing since the tenth century. The early eleventh century saw the founding in Italy of the monastic congregations of Fuente Avellana by Peter Damian and of Camaldoli by Romuald. These monastic congregations were made up of groups of mutually independent hermitages or monasteries, or of a monastery and a colony of hermitages united under the prior of the colony. Silence and individual solitude predominated. (These congregations were joined in 1569.) In 1084, Bruno of Cologne settled in Chartreuse, France, and established there a monastery where monks lived separately in small hermitages situated around a cloister and met only for liturgical prayer in the church. Around 1090, Stephen of Muret founded the Order of Hermits of Grandmont at Haute-Vienne, France. In a short time the order had spread widely. Small groups of solitaries began to multiply in Italy and became more common in the west of France during the twelfth century. Others appeared in Italy in the thirteenth century. Francis of Assisi, for example, was strongly attracted to the eremitical life and wrote a rule for it and for his disciples.

But there were also instances of an opposite phenomenon—groups of hermits who gave rise to orders characterized by a more communal way of life. The Carmelite order, for example, was started by hermits from the West who settled at Mount Carmel in Palestine during the twelfth century; as the order spread in the West it evolved into a conventual order. Something similar happened to the Servites, founded near Florence, and to the Hermits of Saint Augustine, an order formed by the coming together of various eremitic and semi-eremitic Italian groups.

Alongside the eremitic life organized within an institutional framework, the individual eremitic life has persisted sporadically. Instances from twelfth-century England include the solitaries Henry, Caradoc, Wilfrid, and Godric. Richard Rolle de Hampole, a hermit and director of recluses, was a spiritual master and esteemed writer of the fourteenth century. The most celebrated English anchoress was Julian of Norwich, whose *Revelations of Divine Love* remains a spiritual classic. In fourteenth-century Spain, John de la Pena was the founder of a colony of hermitages. In Switzerland, there is the celebrated case of Nicholas of Flüe (1417–1487), a layman who at the age of fifty left his wife and children to go into solitude, where he spent the last twenty years of his life. "Bruder Klaus," as he is affectionately known in Switzerland, was canonized in 1947 and is venerated there by both Catholics and Protestants because of the ecumenical guidance he gave from his hermitage.

In sixteenth-century Spain, the noblewoman Catalina of Cardona escaped from the ducal palace to take refuge as a hermitess on the banks of the river Júcar. Later she founded a convent of Carmelite nuns and then spent the rest of her life in a nearby cave. In the fifteenth century an unnamed woman supposedly lived disguised as a friar in the Franciscan hermitage of the Carceri near Assisi. Another woman, who died around 1225, lived in the same manner in Burgundy. Perhaps these women were imitating the legend of the desert eremite Theodora. Some scholars have suspected that the stories of these women are fictional legends that arose in the exclusively masculine environment of the monastery, where the presence of a woman disguised as a monk could easily have been felt as a threat to the monastic vocation. Another type of mitigated feminine eremitism was initiated by Teresa of Ávila (1515–1582) under the influence of the primitive ideal of the monastery of Mount Carmel and the example of her confessor and spiritual adviser, Peter of Alcántara (1499–1562), who built a separate hut for himself in the monastery garden. Something similar happened in a number of Poor Clare convents in Spain, again under the influence of Peter of Alcántara.

In the seventeenth century, there was a new flowering of eremitical spirituality. New editions of various writings of the Desert Fathers, as well as numerous paintings of the saints Anthony and Jerome and the penitent Mary Magdalene, reflect this interest. Notable among other eremitical foundations in Spain at the time was the hillside colony at Cordova, which continued to exist until the mid-twentieth century. In the eighteenth century there were still some hermits living in the vicinity of Rome, and some new groupings of hermits arose in Germany. In the history of Christian eremitism in the West, the nineteenth century was one of the most desolate periods. Significantly, in the 1917 Code of Canon Law for the Roman Catholic church, pure eremitism disappeared as an officially recognized form of monastic life because of the code's insistence on community life as an essential element of all monastic life.

In contrast, the twentieth century witnessed a reflourishing of the eremitical life, beginning with the withdrawal of Charles-Eugène Foucauld (1858–1916), a French cavalry officer, to the Sahara. He spent the last fifteen years of his life as a hermit. John C. Hawes (d. 1956), an Anglican missionary who later joined the Roman Catholic church, spent the last years of his life as a hermit on Cat Island in the Bahamas. Foundations of eremitical groups have been established in Germany, France, and Canada. The phenomenon seems to have been particularly intense in the United States. A strong current of mystical spirituality, together with a certain disenchantment with the life of many apostolic communities, has led a certain number of religious, especially women, to seek the solitary life. The Trappist monk Thomas Merton (1915–1968) influenced this movement to a great extent. After spending twenty years at the Abbey of Gethsemani in Kentucky in an atmosphere combining total silence and intense group life, Merton arrived at a paradoxical state: He had a keen and very open awareness of a pressing need for dialogue with the contemporary world, yet he withdrew for some time into profound solitude. In 1963, he obtained permission to withdraw periodically to a small hut on a hillside near the abbey. In October 1964, thanks to his efforts, a meeting of Trappist abbots modified the order's official attitude toward eremitism. The order now regards eremitism as a possible option for monks who have spent a certain number of years in community. As he grew older, Merton's recourse to solitude became increasingly continuous. At present, a certain number of Trappists follow the eremitical life.

The Church of England has also witnessed a revival of one of its ancient traditions, in a number of women solitaries. Prayer and silence predominate in the first purely contemplative Anglican community, the Sisters of the Love of God, founded by Father Hollings in 1906. In response to this strong trend the Roman Catholic church revised its official attitude toward eremitism, as stated in the 1917 Code of Canon Law. The new code (canon 603) officially recognizes the eremitical state, even among those who do not belong to any monastic institute.

EREMITISM IN ISLAM. In Islam, eremitism is regarded as an exceptional type of life. In general, the religious life is lived either in the bosom of the family or in a community made up of a master and a number of disciples. However, a radical form of Sufism is found among itinerant monks, who express their estrangement from the world in a manner somewhat reminiscent of Hindu or Syrian practitioners of pilgrimage. Many Ṣūfīs, even if they do not fully profess this type of life, spend a certain number of years traveling throughout the Muslim world in search of a spiritual master. The ideal of the Muslim spiritual masters is "solitude in the midst of the multitude" (*kalwat dar anjuman*), that is, a state of remaining habitually in the presence of God without being touched by the tumult of one's surroundings. As means for achieving this state spiritual masters recommend detachment, silence, and interior peace. Some Ṣūfī orders insist on both material and spiritual withdrawal or retreat.

Nevertheless, a commitment to serving God while remaining in his presence has led more than a few Muslim spiritual adepts to seek material solitude. In contradistinction to the *khalwah* ("retreat," i.e., the house of a man or woman of God), *rābiṭah* designates an isolated dwelling for a person committed to the cultivation of his or her spiritual life, that is, a hermitage. Ibn al-ʿArabī tells of an Andalusian mystic, Abū Yaḥyā al-Sunhājī, who often traveled along the coast looking for solitary places in which he could live. He also tells of a holy woman of Seville who lived in a hut built so low to the ground that she could hardly stand up straight within it. Although Muslims have always professed a lively devotion toward these servants of God, there has always been also a certain opposition to what is regarded as an extreme way of life. This ambivalence is expressed in the following story. One day, a Ṣūfī who lived in a city received a visit from a pilgrim who brought him greetings from a man who had fled to the mountains. The Ṣūfī replied, "A person should live with God in the bazaar, not in the mountains" (Javad Nurbakhash, *Masters of the Path,* New York, 1980, p. 80).

EREMITISM AND COMMUNION. Eremitism in its pure form is beset with a few serious difficulties, because the solitary life projects an image of spirituality exclusively in terms of interiority, an image involving individual prayer or meditation, intense inner struggles, and so on. What role does the believing community play in this conception of spirituality? Not surprisingly, the Buddha provided certain community horizons for the individual search for salvation in order to mitigate the extremes of ascetic traditions of his day. Nor is it surprising that many Muslim teachers note that materially suppressing outward "noise" is far less important than remaining open to inner silence, even amid the bustle of the marketplace. Pure eremitism encounters insuperable objections in relation to the Christian concept of community as the vehicle of salvation. What role do the sacraments play in such a scheme?

Are rites of all sorts only for "beginners," with the more developed not in need of such props? It is easy to discern in these questions a potential for Gnostic aberrations, such as were possible in the context of the total isolation of the primitive Christian anchorites. Understandably, total and sustained isolation soon disappeared in Christianity, and the eremitical life became limited to colonies or lauras, where adherents listened to the word and participated in the sacraments. Today Christian churches would not accept any form of total isolation.

In reality, the difficulties come not only from the communitarian vocation of the believer but also from the basic social orientation of human beings. People need others, with both their experience and their limitations, in order to grow. After nine years of austere solitude, Pachomius (290?–346) reacted angrily to a slight disagreement. Seven years of fasts and vigils had not taught him patience. Here, for the first time in the history of Christian monasticism, interpersonal relationship appears as a form of mutual purification. Dorotheus of Gaza (sixth century) affirmed: "The cell exalts us, the neighbor puts us to the test." The praxis of charity shows whether personal progress has been real or illusory, but interpersonal relationships are also a source of enrichment. Dorotheus repeats a traditional saying when he states, "To stay in one's cell is one half, and to go and see the elders is the other half."

Eremitism and Human Solidarity. The quest for personal salvation, carried out in a type of life withdrawn from society and history, does not seem to leave room for solidarity with the rest of humanity. Today, when human communion and interdependence are so strongly felt, eremitism might seem like little more than a form of solitary egoism, giving rise to serious doubts as to its basic morality. The Buddhist vision of history as pure illusion presents a different perspective. From the Buddhist point of view, no good results from immersing oneself in this illusion, in this flux of sorrows and joys. On the contrary, one would do better to put oneself beyond the contingent and illusory, thus giving others the testimony of one's victory and wisdom. It is significant that in the life of the Buddha, as well as in the Hindu tradition generally, a phase of itinerant monasticism follows the period of eremitism.

Christian anchorites, too, often consider themselves alien travelers who cannot afford to be concerned with earthly affairs. But Christian eremitism constantly encounters a serious difficulty. If the transcendent God of the Bible reveals himself in the often tortuous and painful history of the human race, can any Christian turn away from history in order to encounter God? Would this God really be the God of the Bible, or would he not be some remote god encountered only in a flight from the world? Many Christian anchorites reveal the tensive pull of this implicit dualism. Nevertheless, their deep sense of being pilgrims and exiles has not prevented many of them from feeling and identifying with the problems of their contemporaries. Athanasius left his solitude and went to Alexandria in order to defend the orthodox cause against the Arians. The church meant more to him than a quest for pure interiority. Other solitaries sold their produce at market, bought what they needed for survival, and distributed among the poor any surplus before returning to their hermitages. Anthony worked not only for his maintenance but also for the needy. Poemen recommended that the brethren work as much as possible so that they could give alms.

A famous saying of Evagrios of Pontus is often quoted: "The monk lives separate from all and united to all." Significantly, he places this saying in the context of a group of sayings that stress the solitary's communion with other human beings, rejoicing in their joys, seeing God and himself in them. This meant not simply that the solitary, in finding God, finds all good things, rather that through solitude he learns to see God in his neighbor. Peter Damian explains that hermits, although they celebrate the Eucharist alone, should always use the greeting "The Lord be with you," because the solitude of the hermit is a *solitudo pluralis,* a corporate solitude, and his cell is a miniature church. The whole church is present in the solitary, and the solitary is most present to the whole church. Teresa of Ávila would invite her daughters to pray for the divided church and to respond to the division among Christians (of the Reformation and the Counter-Reformation) by intensifying their own fidelity to the gospel.

In the present era Thomas Merton has exemplified the possible ambiguity latent in the relationship between the hermit and the exterior world. Merton, who desired to devote his life to prayer in solitude, regarded the Trappist Abbey of Gethsemani as "the only real city in America" (*Secular Journal,* New York, 1959, p. 183). For years, his life involved total silence (the monks communicated their needs only by signs), common and individual prayer, and agricultural work. His first writings reflect an elitist view of contemplative monachism and a negative view of the secular milieu. In *Seeds of Contemplation* (1949) he said that whoever wanted to develop the interior life had no recourse other than to withdraw, to shun theaters, television, and the news media, and to retreat periodically from the city. In *New Seeds of Contemplation* (1979), however, he wrote that "solitude is not separation" and revealed total openness to the world. More paradoxically, during these years of growing openness he increasingly distanced himself from his community, becoming a virtual hermit.

See Also Deserts; Exile; Monasticism; Retreat; Saṃnyāsa.

Bibliography

General information on eremitism can be found in most encyclopedia articles on monasticism; see, for example, "Mönchtum," in *Die Religion in Geschichte und Gegenwart,* 3d ed., vol. 4 (Tübingen, 1960); "Monachismo," in *Enciclopedia delle religioni,* vol. 4 (Florence, 1972); and "Monasticism," in *Encyclopaedia Britannica,* vol. 12 (Chicago, 1982). On eremitism in Buddhism and Hinduism, see A. S. Geden's

"Monasticism, Buddhist" and "Monasticism, Hindu" in the *Encyclopaedia of Religion and Ethics,* edited by James Hastings, vol. 8 (Edinburgh, 1915). For the Hellenic tradition, see A. J. Festugière's *Personal Religion among the Greeks* (Berkeley, 1954). On Christian eremitism, see Clément Lialine and Pierre Doyère's "Eremitisme," in the *Dictionnaire de spiritualité,* vol. 4 (Paris, 1960); Jean Leclercq's "Eremus et eremita," *Collectanae Ordinis Cisterciensium Reformatorum* (Rome) 25 (1963): 8–30; and Louis Bouyer and others' *A History of Christian Spirituality,* 3 vols. (New York, 1963–1969). On Muslim practices, see A. J. Wensink's "Rahbaniya" and "Rahib" in the *Shorter Encyclopaedia of Islam* (Leiden, 1974) and Hermann Landolt's "Khalwa" in *The Encyclopaedia of Islam,* new ed., vol. 4 (Leiden, 1978); see also René Brunel's *Le monachisme errant dans l'Islam* (Paris, 1955) and J. Spencer Trimingham's *The Sufi Orders in Islam* (New York, 1971).

New Sources

Chevillat, Alain. *Moines du désert Egypte.* Lyon, France, 1990.

Colegate, Isabel. *A Pelican in the Wilderness: Hermits, Solitaires and Recluses.* Washington, D.C., 2002.

Coon, Linda. "Historical Fact and Exegetical Fiction in the Carolingian Vita S. Sualonis." *Church History* 72 (March 2003): 1–25.

Driot, Marcel. *Les Pères du désert: vie et spiritualite.* Montreal, 1991.

France, Peter. *Hermits: The Insights of Solitude.* London, 1996.

Jantzen, Grace. *Julian of Norwich: Mystic and Theologian.* 1987; reprint, New York, 2000.

Jotischky, Andrew. *The Perfection of Solitude: Hermits and Monks in the Crusader States.* University Park, Pa., 1995.

Jourdan, Michel. *La vie d'ermite.* Paris, 1992.

Paper, Jordan. "Eremitism in China." *Journal of Asian and African Studies* 34 (February 1999): 46–56.

Vauchez, Andri. *Sainthood in the Later Middle Ages,* translated by Jean Birrell. Cambridge, U.K., 1997.

JUAN MANUEL LOZANO (1987)
Revised Bibliography

ERIUGENA, JOHN SCOTTUS (fl. 847–877), was a Christian theologian and philosopher. Eriugena was born in Ireland in the first quarter of the ninth century, and there he received his early education (which probably included some Greek). He appeared around 847 in France at the itinerant court of Charles the Bald. Later, in Laon, he found himself in the company of a number of Irish scholars who were distinguished for their knowledge of Greek, the most important of whom was Martin Scottus. Although a teacher, Eriugena may not have been a cleric. He was invited by Archbishop Hincmar of Reims and Pardulus of Laon to refute the predestinarian errors of the theologian Gottschalk of Orbais. In so doing, he produced his first work, *On Predestination,* which did not meet with the approval of Hincmar and Pardulus and which was condemned by the councils of Valence (855) and Langres (859). Nevertheless, he was invited sometime before 859 by Charles the Bald to attempt a new translation of the writings of Dionysius the Areopagite. This work, *Translation of the Works of Saint Dionysius the Areopagite,* he completed in the years 860 to 862. Subsequently, he translated into Latin *Matters of Question* and *Questions to Thalassios* of Maximos the Confessor (862–864), *On the Making of Man* of Gregory of Nyssa, and possibly some other Greek theological texts. The effect on him of such an immersion in Greek theology was profound and abiding. From then on his compositions, despite his dependence on and reverence for Augustine of Hippo, show a strong Neoplatonic influence. Apart from his writings little more is known of Eriugena, and one loses track of him altogether around 877. There remain, however, a number of well-known legends about him.

From 859 to 860 Eriugena composed a commentary on Martianus Capella's *On the Marriage of Philology and Mercury.* This was followed by the translations mentioned above. From 864 to 866 Eriugena wrote his great original work, *Periphyseon,* also known as *De divisione naturae* (The division of nature). This was followed between 865 and 870 by *Expositiones,* or *Commentary on the Celestial Hierarchy of Dionysius the Areopagite,* and by a homily and a commentary on the *Gospel of John.* Finally, he composed some verses of only moderate poetical quality. Other works are also attributed to him. The body of his works is to be found in the edition of H. J. Floss in J.-P. Migne's *Patrologia Latina* (vol. 122).

The theology of Eriugena may be seen most clearly in his *Periphyseon,* a work of some quarter of a million words divided into five books. Nature, or all existing things, is divided or distinguished into four parts: that which creates but is not created (God as source, book 1); that which is created and creates (the Word and the primordial causes, book 2); that which is created but does not create (the created universe, book 3); and that which does not create and is not created (God as end, books 4 and 5). The work therefore takes the Neoplatonic approach of the progression from and regression of all things to the Father. The primary division of nature, however, is into being and nonbeing, both of which can be considered in five different modes: according to the perceptibility of the object; according to its order or place on the descending and ascending scale between the creator and the creature; according to its actualization (as against mere possibility); according to its perceptibility by intellect or sense; and according to its realization as the image of God.

God does not come within any of the categories of nature. He cannot be seen, although the divine nature does appear to angels and has appeared and will appear to human beings in theophanies, or appearances. One cannot know what God is, only that he is. More is known about him through negative rather than affirmative theology: One can more truly say what God is not than what he is. The primordial causes, also called divine ideas or volitions, remain invisible in the Word. In these are established the unchangeable "reasons" of all things to be made. The biblical *Book of Genesis* gives the account of how creatures, and especially human beings, were made. One can say that all things always were, are, and always will be because they always had being in God's wisdom through the primordial causes: "We should not understand God and the creature as two things removed from one another, but as one and the same thing. For the creature subsists in God, and God is created in the creature in a wonderful and ineffable way, making Himself manifest, invisible making Himself visible."

The divine nature, however, is above being and is different from what it creates within itself: In this way pantheism is avoided. The return of all things to God is best seen in the human creature, who, being body, living, sensible, rational, and intellectual, is a harmony of all things. Originally, humankind was simple, spiritual, celestial, and individual. The division into male and female was caused by sin; it was something added to true human nature. Humanity will return by stages to become intellect (here Eriugena follows Gregory of Nyssa); the body will resolve into its physical elements; the human person in the resurrection shall recover the body from these elements; the body will be changed into spirit; that spirit will return to the primordial causes. Finally, all nature and its causes will be moved toward God; there will be nothing but God alone.

The influence of Eriugena has been important and continuous in philosophy and theology. Remigius and Heiric of Auxerre and Pope Sylvester II were his early followers. Those of a mystical disposition made great use of him: the school of Saint Victor, Meister Eckhart, Johannes Tauler, Jan van Ruusbroec, Nicholas of Cusa, and Giordano Bruno. His reputation, however, suffered from the enthusiasm of Berengar of Tours, Gilbert of Poitiers, Almaric of Bena, and David of Dinant, all of whose espousal of his doctrine led to its condemnation by the councils of Vercelli (1050) and Rome (1059) and in a bull of Honorius III (1225). His ideas, nevertheless, have persisted, especially among German philosophers, and a reawakening of interest in him and his thought has begun.

BIBLIOGRAPHY

Brennan, Mary. *A Bibliography of Publications in the Field of Eriugenian Studies, 1800–1975.* Estratto degli Studi Medievali, third series, vol. 18, no. 1. Spoleto, 1977.

Cappuyns, Maieul. *Jean Scot Érigène* (1933). Reprint, Brussels, 1969. By far the best book on Eriugena's life, works, and thought.

Contreni, John J. *The Cathedral School of Laon from 850 to 930: Its Manuscripts and Masters.* Munich, 1978. Gives the context of Eriugena's life.

O'Meara, John J. *Eriugena.* Cork, 1969. A brief introduction.

O'Meara, John J., and Ludwig Bieler, eds. *The Mind of Eriugena.* Dublin, 1973. Papers of a colloquium held in Dublin (1970) by the Society for the Promotion of Eriugenian Studies. Subsequent papers from Laon (1975) and Freiburg im Breisgau (1979) were published, respectively, in *Jean Scot Érigène et l'histoire de la philosophie,* edited by René Roques (Paris, 1977), and *Eriugena: Studien zu seinen Quellen,* edited by Werner Beierwaltes (Heidelberg, 1980).

Sheldon-Williams, I. P., ed. *Iohannis Scotti Eriugenae Periphyseon.* 3 vols. to date. Dublin, 1968–1981. Two more volumes of this modern edition of the *Periphyseon,* which includes an English translation, are projected.

JOHN J. O'MEARA (1987)

ERLIK, or Erlik Khan ("King Erlik"), is a deity of the Turkic peoples of Siberia (Yakuts, Altai-Sayan Turkic tribes, Tuvin) and of the Mongolian tribes (Mongols, Buriats, Oirats/Kalmucks). Generally, Erlik is considered to be lord of the lower world and judge of the dead.

It seems, however, that Erlik (possibly meaning "the mighty one," from the Old Turkic term *erklig*) originally was a celestial god. This role can be surmised from Erlik's character as Lord Spirit of the Blue Boundlessness in the religion of the Yakuts of northeastern Siberia, who separated from their Turkic and Mongolian kinsmen in early times. Erlik's heavenly origin is also attested by Altai-Sayan Turkic tradition. Here, however, he has already been degraded to a position second to Ülgen (Kudai), their supreme deity. He is the first man, Ülgen's brother or created by him, assisting him in the creation of the earth. Erlik wants to become equal to Ülgen, however; he wants to create land himself. He also tries to seize all human beings created by Ülgen, seducing them to take forbidden food from the first tree. As a result, Erlik is banished from the celestial realm.

Thus Erlik becomes the ruler of the lower world, the king of the realm of darkness, which is opposed to the upper world, the realm of light. Erlik, his sons and daughters, and a host of other mischievous spirits created by him cause all kinds of misfortune, sickness, and death. Animals must be sacrificed to pacify the evil forces, sometimes with the help of shamans who risk the dangerous descent into Erlik's world. Specific sites in this place of horror, such as the lake of tears and the bridge of one hair that must be crossed, as well as details of Erlik's sanguinary appearance, are vividly described in various myths.

Heavenly origin is also attributed to Erlik in Buriat, Tuvin, and Mongol traditions. In Buriat shamanism, Erlen (i.e., Erlik) Khan leads the cruel black or eastern spirits against the friendly white or western spirits. At the same time he is the king of the lower world.

Erlik's role, however, has not become completely negative, as can be seen from the special relationship between him and the souls of humans. In Altai-Sayan tradition Ülgen makes the body from soil and stone, and Erlik blows in the soul. When Erlik became the devil, he remained as subject to Ülgen as he had been when he assisted him in creation. Of course, he tries to force the souls of the deceased into his realm in order to make them his servants. Soon he becomes an agent of divine justice, however, the judge of the dead who administers his office by order of Ülgen. His judgment is not arbitrary, but just.

Erlik remained a figure in the religious thought of the Christianized Turkic peoples, and he became identified with the Mongolian Buddhist judge of the dead, the Tibetan Gsinrje, and the Indian Hindu-Buddhist Yama. Erlik, the bull-headed, dreadful "protector of the [Buddhist] religion" (*nom-un sakighulsun)* and "king of Dharma" (*nom-un khan*), judges the dead using his mirror and the count of white and black pebbles representing good and evil deeds. Those condemned to hellish punishments are tortured by Erlik's executioners. There can be no doubt that Erlik also preserves traits of the Indian Yama's Iranian counterpart Yima, who is regarded as primordial man and primordial king.

See Also Ülgen.

Bibliography

Erlik's character in the religion of the Altai-Sayan Turkic peoples has been discussed by Wilhelm Schmidt in volume 9 of his *Der Ursprung der Gottesidee* (Münster, 1949). Erlik's fall is impressively related in an Altai Turkic myth translated by V. V. Radlov in his *Proben der Volkslitteratur der türkischen Stämme,* vol. 1 (Saint Petersburg, 1866), pp. 175–184. Erlen Khan of the Buriats is described in Garma Sandschejew's "Weltanschauung und Schamanismus der Alaren-Burjaten," *Anthropos* 23 (1928): 538–560, 967–986. Notes about Erlik Khan and his cult among the Mongols can be found in Aleksei M. Pozdneyev's *Religion and Ritual in Society: Lamaist Buddhism in Late Nineteenth-Century Mongolia,* edited by John R. Krueger, translated from the Russian by Alo Raun and Linda Raun (Bloomington, Ind., 1978), pp. 122–123. Important additional information about Erlik can be found in recent Russian publications, for example, see T. M. Mikhailov's *Iz istorii buriatskogo shamanizma* (Novosibirsk, 1980), pp. 168–169, which also examines divergent opinions about the etymology and character of Erlik/Erlen.

New Sources

Rinchen. *Les matériaux pour l'etude du chamanisme mongol.* Wiesbaden, 1959.

Roux, Jean P. "Les religions dans les societes turco-mongoles." *Revue de l'Histoire des Religions* 201 (1984): 393–420.

Urbanaeva, I. S., and Institut mongolovedeniia buddologii i tibetologii. *Shamanskaia filosofiia buriat-mongolov: tsentral'noaziatskoe tengrianstvo v svete dukhovnykh uchenii: v 2-kh chastiakh.* Ulan-Ude, 2000.

Klaus Sagaster (1987)
Revised Bibliography

EROS. Eros was the ancient Greek god of sexual (either homosexual or heterosexual) love or desire. The word *erōs* is the ordinary noun denoting that emotion; it could be personified and treated as an external being because of its unfathomable and irresistible power over humans (and animals and gods). This was, however, a sophisticated, largely literary phenomenon without roots in popular religion. At Thespiae (Boeotia) a sacred stone, perhaps a menhir, was venerated as Eros, but it is doubtful how old the identification was. Otherwise cults of Eros do not seem to have been established before the Classical period. He was often honored in the gymnasia (sports centers), where adolescent males were constant objects of attraction for older men. The Spartans and Cretans are said to have sacrificed to Eros before battles because the soldiers' personal devotion to one another was recognized as an important military factor.

Eros is represented in Greek literature as a beautiful youth, or later as a young boy, and as the son or attendant of Aphrodite, the goddess who presided over sexual union. He is sportive and mischievous; he plays roughly with men; he shoots arrows into them (this first in the dramas of Euripides, c. 480–406 BCE). Poetic conceit may predicate of him whatever is appropriate to the effects he produced. He can be called blind, for instance, because he chooses his victims so indiscriminately. Sometimes, in and after the fifth century BCE, poets speak of the plural *erōtes,* corresponding to the many separate loves that are always flaring up.

Eros appears in art from the sixth century BCE but becomes much more common in that of the fifth. He is usually shown as winged and carrying a lyre and a garland, both appropriate to the symposium, at which he was always active. Often he hovers above scenes of amorous import. In the fourth century the sculptors Praxiteles and Scopas portrayed him in celebrated statues. Praxiteles's mistress donated one of these to the sanctuary at Thespiae.

Eros had a special significance in cosmogonic myth. Hesiod (c. 730–700 BCE) places him among the first gods to come into being, and several later poets echo this. As they saw cosmic evolution in terms of sexual reproduction of divine entities, Eros was needed from the start to provide the impulse. In a cosmogony composed under the name of Orpheus about 500 BCE, Eros (also called Protogonos, "first-born," and Phanes, "manifest") came out of a shining egg created by Time; he fertilized the cosmic darkness, and Heaven and Earth were born. This account has connections with Semitic, Iranian, and Indian cosmogonies.

Although partially comparable with some figures (especially winged demons) belonging to the cults of the Middle East, Eros appears to be a peculiar creation of the Greeks. He is worshiped in an atypical way, with few sanctuaries (the most important of which was in the Boeotian town of Thespiae) and a scarce inventory of myths and ritual epithets. Unknown to the *Iliad,* the *Odyssey,* and the *Homeric Hymns,* Eros first appears in two passages of Hesiod's *Theogony.* In the first passage (vv. 120–122) he is presented as the most ancient god after Chaos and Gaia. He has the power to subjugate the mind and the will of both gods and men, and he has neither parents nor other deities for companions.

On the other hand, in *Theogony* (201) Eros (along with Himeros) is included in Aphrodite's retinue and accompanies her in the same way that the *paredros* of the Asian religions escorts Ishtar/Astarte. Such a subordinate figure appears different from the representation offered by Hesiod in the preceding verses (v. 120ff.), where Eros is described as a primeval, lonely, and very powerful deity.

This incongruity is only an example of the numerous contradictions in Greek literature, philosophy, and mythography dealing with Eros's character and genealogy. Pausanias (IX 27,3 = Sappho fr. 198, Voigt) claims that Sappho dedicated to Eros "a lot of poems not matching with each other." Evidence for this statement can be obtained by comparing Sappho from 159, where Eros is only a "servant" of the goddess, and Theocritus 13,1–2c (Wendel, p. 258; Sappho fr. 198b), which reports that Sappho described Eros as Aphrodites's son and attributed to him a father of such nobility as Uranus (the Sky); nevertheless it seems that, in a third poem (mentioned by Apollonius Rhodius III 26 = Sapph. fr. 198a), Sappho represented Eros as generated not by Uranus and Aphrodite but by Uranus and Mother Earth.

Different genealogies are suggested by later authors. According to Simonides (fr. 575 P.), Eros is the son of "the deceptive Aphrodite, who bore him to Ares, the contriver of frauds." In an inspired stasimon of the *Hippolytus,* Euripides says that Eros is a "son of Zeus" (v. 533). Before them, Alcaeus had suggested an original version of the matter by defining Eros as "the most terrible god, whom Iris with fine sandals bore to golden-haired Zephyr" (fr. 327 V). It is not easy to establish whether the poet drew inspiration from certain Lesbian cults or from his own imagination. If one considers the scarceness of concrete cultural evidence, it seems plausible that ancient Greek poets felt free to give personal interpretations of Eros's birth and nature.

Discordant points of view can also be found among historians and philosophers. Whereas Pherekydes (7 B 3 Diels-Kranz), Acusilaus (9 B 1 Diels-Kranz), and Parmenides (28 B 13 Diels-Kranz) seem to follow Hesiod's tradition in placing Eros in the first stage of the theocosmogonic process, Plato's reflection can be considered as a decisive turning point. In Plato's representation (*Symposium,* 203b–204a), Eros is the son of two figures suspended between myth and allegory, Poros (expedient) and Penia (poverty), and he partakes of the nature of both; he is neither a god nor a mortal, neither a sage nor a fool, but a paradoxical set of contrasting elements.

Plato's influence can be perceived in the Middle Comedy. For instance, a fragment of Alexis's *Phaedrus* (fr. 247 Kassel–Austin) describes Eros as a strange being, "neither female nor male, neither god nor man, neither foolish nor wise . . . but with a lot of aspects in one shape." It is worth noting that the iconographic type of Eros as a winged androgyne frequently appears in fourth-century South Italian pottery. A different representation is offered by Praxiteles, whose celebrated Eros looked like a young man with charming eyes.

In the same period the debate on Eros appears to attract the attention of the most important philosophical schools, giving rise to a great number of treatises on this subject. Academics, Peripatetics, Stoics, and Epicureans wrote works (mostly dialogues) with such titles as *On Love, Dialogue on Love,* and *The Art of Loving.* Although these works are almost completely lost (except for a few fragments), presumably they dwelt upon the ambiguous and contradictory nature of Eros, especially the god's habit of bringing, under different circumstances, either joy and happiness or grief and downfall (also in Cercidas's second *Meliamb,* probably influenced by Stoicism).

During the Hellenistic age, Eros was mostly represented as the little, naughty son of Aphrodite and became a stereotyped figure (see Apollonius Rhodius 3.91–99; Theocritus 19). However, he also became the hero of an inspired fable concerning his love story with a beautiful girl named Psyche. The tale probably originated within Platonic circles and owes most of its fame to a work written in the second century CE, that is, Apuleius's *Metamorphoses,* or The golden ass.

BIBLIOGRAPHY

Blanc, Nicole, and Françoise Gury. "Eros." *Lexicon iconographicum mythologiae classicae (LIMC)* 3, no. 1 (1981), 850–1049.

Calame, Claude. *The Poetics of Eros in Ancient Greece.* Translated by Janet Lloyd. Princeton, N.J., 1999.

Cavallini, Eleonora. *Il fiore del desiderio: Afrodite e il suo corteggio fra mito e letteratura.* Lecce, Italy, 2000.

Fasce, Silvana. *Eros: La figura e il culto.* Genoa, Italy, 1977.

Lasserre, François. *La figure d'Éros dans la poésie grecque.* Lausanne, Switzerland, 1946.

Page, Denys. *Sappho and Alcaeus: An Introduction to the Study of Ancient Lesbian Poetry.* Oxford, U.K., 1955.

Rudhardt, Jean. *Le rôle d'Eros et d'Aphrodite dans les cosmogonies grecques.* Paris, 1986.

M. L. WEST (1987)
ELEONORA CAVALLINI (2005)

ESCHATOLOGY

This entry consists of the following articles:

ESCHATOLOGY: AN OVERVIEW

The term *eschatology* means "the science or teachings concerning the last things." Derived from the Greek *eschatos* ("last") and *eschata* ("the last things"), the term does not seem to have been in use in English before the nineteenth century, but since then it has become a major concept, especially in Christian theology.

Most religions entertain ideas, teachings, or mythologies concerning the beginnings of things: the gods, the world, the human race. Parallel to these are accounts of the end of things, which do not necessarily deal with the absolute and final end or with the consummation of all things. The end may be conceived positively, as the kingdom of God, a "new heaven and a new earth," and the like, or negatively, for instance as the "twilight of the gods." Sometimes these accounts refer to events expected to take place in a more or less distant future. There is considerable overlap with messianism, which may, therefore, be considered as one form of eschatology.

An important distinction has to be drawn between individual and general, or cosmic, eschatology. Individual eschatology deals with the fate of the individual person, that is, the fate of the soul after death. This may be seen in terms of the judgment of the dead, the transmigration of the soul to other existences, or an afterlife in some spiritual realm. Cosmic eschatology envisages more general transformations or the end of the present world. The eschatological consummation can be conceived as restorative in character, for example as the *Endzeit* that restores the lost perfection of a primordial *Urzeit,* or as more utopian, that is, the transformation and inauguration of a state of perfection the like of which never existed before.

ASIAN RELIGIONS. Cultures that view time as an endless succession of repetitive cycles (as in the Indian notions of *yuga* and *kalpa*) develop only "relative eschatologies," because the concept of an ultimate consummation of history is alien to them. Individual eschatology means liberation from the endless, weary wheel of death and rebirth by escaping into an eternal, or rather timeless, transmundane reality that is referred to as *mokṣa* in Hinduism and *nirvāṇa* in Buddhism. Within the cosmic cycles there are periods of rise and decline. According to Indian perceptions of time, the present age is the *kaliyuga,* the last of the four great *yugas,* or world epochs. In various traditions these periods often end in a universal catastrophe, conflagration, or cataclysmic annihilation, to be followed by a new beginning inaugurated by the appearance of a savior figure, such as the *avātara* (incarnation) of a deity or the manifestation of a new Buddha.

Chinese Buddhism developed the idea of periods of successive, inexorable decline (Chin., *mofa;* Jpn., *mappō),* at the end of which the future Buddha Maitreya (Chin., Miluofo; Jpn., Miroku), who is currently biding his time in the Tuṣita Heaven, will appear and establish a kind of millennial kingdom and inaugurate a new era of bliss and salvation for all. "Messianic" and "millennial" movements in China and Southeast Asia, some of which became social revolts and peasant rebellions, have often been associated with expectations of the coming of Maitreya. Occasionally political agitation and ideologies of rebellion developed without Buddhist influences on the basis of purely Daoist or even Confucian ideas. But in these cases the ideology was "restorative" rather than eschatological in character; it announced the restoration of the lost original "great peace" (Taiping)—as, for example, at the end of the Han dynasty or in the fourth-century Maoshan sect—or propagated the message that the mandate of Heaven had been withdrawn from the reigning dynasty.

Daoism, like Buddhism, entertained notions concerning a postmortem judgment. According to Daoist belief, the judgment took place before a tribunal of judges of the dead who decided the subsequent fate of the soul and assigned it to one of the many hells or heavens that figured in the popular mythologies. Confucianism, however, has no eschatology in the narrow sense of the term; it has no doctrines concerning a day of judgment, a catastrophic end of this world, or a messianic millennium. Other Chinese ideas of individual eschatology were in part drawn from ancient lore and were later amalgamated with Buddhist and Daoist elements. Japanese Shintō has no cosmic eschatology and only vague ideas concerning the state of the dead. It is precisely this vacuum that was filled by Buddhism in the history of Japanese religion.

ZOROASTRIANISM. Individual and universal, or cosmic, eschatology merge when the ultimate fate of the individual is related to that of the world. In such a case the individual is believed to remain in a kind of "provisional state" (which may be heaven or hell, a state of bliss or one of suffering) pending the final denouement of the historical cosmic process. One religion of this eschatological type is Zoroastrianism, a religion in which world history is seen as a cosmic struggle between the forces of light led by Ahura Mazdā (Pahl., Ōhrmazd) and the forces of darkness led by Angra Mainyu (Pahl., Ahriman). This struggle will end with the victory of light, the resurrection of the dead, a general judgment in the form of an ordeal of molten metal (similar to the individual postmortem ordeal when the soul has to cross the Chinvat Bridge), and the final destruction of evil. Some of these Iranian beliefs, especially those concerning the resurrection of the dead, seem to have influenced Jewish and, subsequently, Christian eschatology.

BIBLICAL RELIGIONS. In the Hebrew Bible the terms *aḥarit* ("end") and *aḥarit yamim* ("end of days") originally referred to a more or less distant future and not to the cosmic and final end of days, that is, of history. Nevertheless, in due course eschatological ideas and beliefs developed, especially as a result of disappointment with the moral failings of the Jewish kings, who theoretically were "the Lord's anointed" of the House of David. In addition, a series of misfortunes led to the further development of these ideas: the incursions and devastations by enemy armies; the fall of Jerusalem and the destruction of the Temple in 587/6 BCE; the Babylonian exile; the failure of the "return to Zion" to usher in the expected golden age so rhapsodically prophesied by the "Second Isaiah"; the persecutions (e.g., under the Seleucid rulers and reflected in the Book of Daniel); the disappointments suffered under the Hasmonean kings; Roman rule and oppression; and finally the second destruction of Jerusalem by the Romans in 70 CE, which, after the failure of subsequent revolts, initiated a long period of exile, tribulation, and "waiting for redemption."

The predictions of the Old Testament prophets regarding the restoration of a golden age, which could be perceived as the renewal of an idealized past or the inauguration of a utopian future, subsequently merged with Persian and Hellenistic influences and ideas. Prophecy gave way to apocalypse, and eschatological and messianic ideas of diverse kinds developed. As a result, alternative and even mutually exclusive ideas and beliefs existed side by side; only at a much later stage did theologians try to harmonize these in a consistent system. Thus there were hopes and expectations concerning a worldly, glorious, national restoration under a Davidic king or victorious military leader, or through miraculous intervention from above. The ideal redeemer would be either a scion of the House of David or a supernatural celestial being referred to as the "Son of man." Significantly, Jesus, who seems to have avoided the term *messiah,* possibly because of its political overtones, and preferred the appellation *Son of man,* nevertheless was subsequently identified by the early church as the Messiah ("the Lord's anointed"; in Greek, *christos,* hence Christ) and was provided with a genealogy (see *Mt.* 1) that legitimated this claim through his descent from David.

Redemption could thus mean a better and more peaceful world (the wolf lying down with the lamb) or the utter end and annihilation of this age, the ushering in, amid catastrophe and judgment, of a "new heaven and a new earth," as in the later Christian beliefs concerning a last judgment, Armageddon, and so on. The doctrine of the resurrection of the dead played a major role in the eschatological beliefs held by the Pharisees and was also shared by Jesus. The chaotic welter of these ideas is visible not only in the so-called apocryphal books of the Old Testament, many of which are apocalypses (i.e., compositions recounting the revelations concerning the final events allegedly granted to certain visionaries), but also in the New Testament.

CHRISTIANITY. The message and teachings of the "historical Jesus" (as distinct from those of the Christ of the early church) are considered by most historians as beyond recovery. There has been, however, a wide scholarly consensus, especially at the beginning of the twentieth century, that Jesus can be interpreted correctly only in terms of the eschatological beliefs and expectations current in the Judaism of his time. The Qumran sect (also known as the Dead Sea sect) was perhaps one of the most eschatologically radical groups at the time. In other words, he preached and expected the end of this world and age, and its replacement in the immediate future, after judgment, by the "kingdom of God." Early Christianity was thus presented as an eschatological message of judgment and salvation that, after the crucifixion and resurrection, emphasized the expectation of the imminent second coming. The subsequent history of the church was explained by these scholars as a result of the crisis of eschatology caused by the continued delay of the second coming. Some modern theologians have taken up the idea of eschatology as the essence of the Christian message, though interpreting it in a less literal-historical and more spiritual or existential manner. Karl Barth, for example, has portrayed the life of the individual Christian, as well as that of the church, as a series of decisions to be apprehended in an eschatological perspective. C. H. Dodd, in his conception of "realized eschatology," has stressed the present significance of future eschatology. Christian history has been punctuated throughout by movements of a millenarian, chiliastic, and eschatological character. Certain modern movements (e.g., Marxism) are interpreted by some thinkers as secularized versions of traditional utopian eschatologies.

ISLAM. The tradition of Islam absorbed so many Jewish and Christian influences in its formative period that it is usually counted among the biblical (or "biblical type") religions. While the eschatological aspects of these traditions were deemphasized in later Islamic doctrines, they undoubtedly played a major role in the original religious experience of the prophet Muḥammad, for whom the end of the historical process and God's final judgment were a central concern. The notion of "the hour," that is, the day of judgment and the final catastrophe, the exact time of which was known to God alone, looms large in his message and is vividly portrayed in the Qurʾān (see *sūrahs* 7:187, 18:50, 36:81, and 78:17ff.). As in the Jewish and Christian traditions on which Muḥammad drew, God will judge the living and the dead on a day of judgment that will be preceded by a general resurrection (*sūrah* 75). The agents of the final hour will be Gog and Magog (*sūrahs* 18:95ff. and 21:96), led, according to some sources, by the antichrist.

There is also a messianic figure, the Mahdi (the "rightly guided one"), and Mahdist, or messianic, movements have not been infrequent in Muslim history. The eschatological Mahdi is more prominent in Shīʿah than in Sunnī Islam. In the latter, belief in the Mahdi is a matter of popular religion rather than official dogma. As regards individual eschatology, Muslim belief in Paradise and Hell, in spite of much variation in detail, is essentially analogous to that of Judaism and Christianity.

PRIMAL RELIGIONS. In most primal religions eschatology plays no major role, because they are generally based on the notion of cyclical renewal rather than on a movement toward a final consummation or end. While it is hazardous to generalize on the subject, in such traditions eschatological or messianic beliefs and expectations are often due to direct or indirect Christian or Western influences, whether relayed through missionaries or through more general cultural contact. These influences can precipitate crises that result in so-called crisis cults (many of which are of a markedly messianic character); they can also introduce eschatological notions concerning conceptions of time and history.

For example, according to the ancient Germanic myths recounted in the Eddas and the *Vǫluspá,* in the fullness of time all things are doomed to final destruction in a universal cataclysm called Ragnarǫk, the "doom of the gods." During this cataclysm there will be a succession of terrible winters accompanied by moral disintegration, at the end of which the Fenrisúlfr (Fenriswolf) will swallow the sun and then run wild; the heavens will split, the cosmic tree Yggdrasill will shake, the gods will go forth to their last battle, and finally a fire will consume all things. There are some vague but inconclusive indications that this total doom may be followed by a new beginning. Scholars are at variance on the question of possible Christian influences on Germanic mythology. Of greater methodological relevance to the present considerations is the question as to what extent this mythology was a response to a crisis. In other words, Christianity may have to be considered not as a hypothetical source of "influences" but as the cause of crises within the non-Christian cultures it confronted. Thus the "doom of the gods" mythology may have developed as an expression of the sense of doom that engulfed the original Nordic culture as a result of its disintegration under the impact of triumphant Christianity.

The contemporary sense of crisis and fear aroused by expectations of imminent nuclear catastrophe and cosmic destruction has reawakened an apocalyptic-eschatological mood in many circles. Some Christian groups, especially those in the United States, calling upon their particular interpretations of biblical prophecies, are "waiting for the end"—it being understood that the believing elect will somehow be saved from the universal holocaust, possibly by being "rapt up" and transferred to other spheres. This phenomenon is not, however, confined to the Christian West. Some of the so-called new religions in Japan and elsewhere similarly exhibit millenarian and even eschatological characteristics, often related to the figure of Maitreya, the Buddha of the future.

See Also Afterlife; Cosmogony; Cosmology; Death; Heaven and Hell; Judgment of the Dead; Messianism; Millenarianism; Paradise; Resurrection.

Bibliography

Because Judaism and Christianity possess the most highly developed eschatological doctrines, most of the relevant literature has been produced by theologians and students of these religions. In addition to the works of Albert Schweitzer, Johannes Weiss, and, in the first half of the twentieth century, the Protestant theologians Karl Barth and Emil Brunner, the following should be noted: R. H. Charles's *Eschatology,* 2d ed. (London, 1913); Hermann Gunkel's *Schöpfung und Chaos in Urzeit und Endzeit* (Göttingen, 1895); F. Holstrom's *Das eschatologische Denken der Gegenwart* (1936); Rudolf Bultmann's *History and Eschatology* (Edinburgh, 1957); C. H. Dodds's "Eschatology and History," in his *The Apostolic Preaching and Its Developments,* 2d ed. (New York, 1951); W. O. E. Oesterley's *The Doctrine of the Last Things: Jewish and Christian* (London, 1908); Paul Volz's *Die Eschatologie der jüdischen Gemeinde im neutestamentlichen Zeitalter* (Tübingen, 1934); Roman Guardini's *Die letzten Dinge,* 2d ed. (Würzburg, 1949); Norman Perrin's *The Kingdom of God in the Teaching of Jesus* (Philadelphia, 1963); and Reinhold Niebuhr's *The Nature and Destiny of Man,* vol. 2, *Human Destiny* (New York, 1943), pp. 287ff. For a review of the current interest in apocalyptic prophecy, see William Martin's journalistic but instructive report, "Waiting for the End," *Atlantic Monthly* (June 1982), pp. 31–37.

New Sources

Cohn, Norman Rufus Colin. *Cosmos, Chaos, and the World to Come: The Ancient Roots of Apocalyptic Faith.* New Haven, Conn., 1993.

Evans, Craig A., and Peter W. Flint. *Eschatology, Messianism, and the Dead Sea Scrolls.* Grand Rapids, Mich., 1997.

Polkinghorne, J. C. *The God of Hope and the End of the World.* New Haven, Conn., 2002.

R. J. Zwi Werblowsky (1987)
Revised Bibliography

ESCHATOLOGY: ISLAMIC ESCHATOLOGY

In every area of religious life, the scriptural religions have developed along courses charted between the constraints and potentialities of their sacred texts and the expectations of the popular imagination. Nowhere has this process been more evident than in the development of Islamic eschatology, which has never been completely systematized. Many intertwining factors account for this situation. Like all scriptures, the Muslim sacred book is elliptical. The Qurʾān may hammer away at the inevitability of resurrection and the rewards and punishments of the afterlife, but of the period between death and resurrection, the topography of heaven and hell, the possibility of intercession, or the nature of redemption it says little indeed.

Furthermore, the otherworldly, radical dualism of the monotheistic scriptures has rarely existed in pure form; it has usually been blurred through interaction with popular ideas and practices. Special tensions arise in the handling of death, where this world meets the next; thus eschatology becomes particularly complex. Of the monotheistic faiths, Islam had perhaps the richest backdrop and the widest cross-cultural stage. Preceded by a rich pagan heritage, the pioneers of Islam also worked within a larger monotheistic environment: some actually entered Islam from Judaism, Christianity, or Zoroastrianism; others came into contact with the practitioners of those religions. The impact of Islamic eschatology on this and other types of exposure was particularly pronounced, as was the Islamic cast given even to the most closely shared elements. Finally, the natural temporal, geographical, and ideological variations of the first thirteen centuries of an expanding Islam have been joined in its fourteenth and fifteenth centuries by modernist rethinkings.

The Qurʾanic Foundation. Not even a casual reader could miss the Qurʾān's emphasis on the final reckoning and dispensation, or its parallel concentration on the homiletic and hortatory dimensions of the prophetic role itself; almost every *sūrah* refers to eschatology, particularly to the physical rewards and punishments of heaven and hell. However, one must always keep in view the larger ethical and monotheistic context that surrounds the Qurʾān's insistence on physical resurrection and consignment; taking this insistence out of context has led many modern Western scholars to confuse the sensuous with the sensual while they ignore the equally sensuous treatments of a Dante or a Bosch.

The Qurʾān's pervasive appeal to the senses—the concrete, graphic presentation of the two dispensations and most other matters as well—is consistent not only with its oral nature but also with its need for reiterated proof of the most persuasive kind. As a didactic as well as apocalyptic work, it must argue against an archaic Arabian cosmos in which fateful time determined the course of life and assured the finality of death, neither of which depended on the creator's intentions:

> And when they see a sign [from God], they would scoff. And they say, "This is nothing but manifest sorcery. What! when we are dead and become dust and bones, shall we indeed be raised up?" (37:14–16)

In contrast, the Qurʾān's caring creator, Allāh, is also the annihilating judge who will end the human world at his chosen time (Yawm al-Qiyāmah, the Day of Resurrection; al-Sāʿah, the Hour); resurrect humans, body and soul; judge them according to their acceptance or rejection of his clear signs as elucidated by the many messengers he has sent; and consign them to their eternal reward—the fiery suffering of Jahannam (Hell, Gehenna) or the easeful pleasure of Jannah (Garden, Paradise):

> And they [the unbelievers] say, "Woe, alas for us! This is the Day of Doom. This is the Day of Decision, even that you cried lies to." (37:20–21)

The distinction between these two is stark and unequivocal, much like the distinction between desert and oasis. Fire and the Garden are a pair of polar opposites, each being everything the other is not (dead/living, shady/hot, shadowy/light), just as the inhabitants of one are everything the inhabitants of the other are not (bestial/human, deaf/hearing, ignorant/understanding, blind/ sighted, living/dead, dumb/speaking, ungrateful/grateful, neglectful/mindful, uncharitable/charitable, indecent/chaste, faithful/idolatrous, prideful/humble):

> The unbelievers . . . shall be in the fire of Gehenna, therein dwelling forever; those are the worst of creatures. But those who believe, and do righteous deeds, those are the best of creatures. (98:6–7)

Jahannam is, like the desert, hot and dry, its inhabitants always thirsty; Jannah is cool and moist, its inhabitants never wanting. Irony informs the contrast. The denizens of Hell are given "drinks," but of molten metal or oozing pus that melts the contents of their stomachs; they are "cooled" by boiling water poured over their heads, new skins replacing the burned ones; and they are "sheltered" by columns of fire over their heads. They are "clothed," but in garments of pitch or fire; they eat, but like cattle:

> As for the unbelievers, for them garments of fire shall be cut, and there shall be poured over their heads boiling water whereby whatsoever is in their bellies and their skins shall be melted. . . . (22:19–20)

The Garden has rivers flowing underneath and fountains; its inhabitants recline on cushioned couches, clothed in brocade garments, peaceful, never fatigued, sheltered, eating fruits in a refined way, drinking a musk-perfumed wine that produces no sickness or intoxication, and enjoying the presence of the *ḥūr*, "wives" made pure and untouched. (Although the Qurʾān says that women gain entrance to the Garden, too, it describes no pleasure for women equivalent to the *ḥūr*.)

> See, the inhabitants of Paradise today are busy in their rejoicing, they and their spouses, reclining upon couches in the shade; therein they have fruits, and they have all that they call for. (36:55–57)

This marvelously wrought dichotomy underscores the need for humans to choose. Fire and Garden appear not for their own sake but as signs of God's mercy or wrath. Belief in the last day is only a small part of the total challenge (see, for example, *sūrah* 2:172–173). Although Adam's expulsion from the original Garden is acknowledged, it produced no original sin that must be redeemed, even if Iblis, the fallen angel, does constantly tempt humans to wrongdoing. One earns one's fate by choosing to adhere or not adhere to clearly specified spiritual and behavioral norms. Judgment is as fair as a business transaction: one's deeds are weighed in the balance, neither wealth nor kin availing. If one has been faithful and grateful, accepted his signs and messengers as true, prayed, and given charity, one is rewarded. If one has been faithless and ungrateful, given the lie to the signs and messengers, given God partners, prayed insincerely or not at all, and been selfish with and prideful of one's material goods, one is punished. In this instance of the radical transvaluation common to the monotheistic religions, what one valued is taken away, and what one did not value becomes an eternal reward.

The signs of the advent of the Day are equally frequent and graphic: people scattered like moths, mountains plucked like wool tufts and turned to sand, earth shaken and ground to powder, heavens split and rolled back, stars scattered, seas boiling over, and sun darkened. However, not every question is anticipated, and little attention is paid to the period between revelation and eschaton, even less to the time between death and resurrection, except to say that it will seem like nothing. As later Muslims took the Qurʾanic eschatological drama to heart, they interpreted it where is was specific and elaborated it where is was not.

POST-QURʾANIC VARIATIONS. This process of elaboration produced considerable variation, in scholarly discourse as well as in the popular imagination, where the rich folklore of millennia was enriched by the new religion and transmitted in elaborate detail.

Sunnī variations. The Sunnī majority turned to the elaboration of the Qurʾanic eschatological schema as soon as the *ḥadīth* (reports about the exemplary deeds, utterances, and unspoken approval of the Prophet) began to form; significant developments continued for centuries, especially in three topic areas: (1) the period between death and resurrection; (2) the role of eschatological figures; and (3) judgment, afterlife, and the mitigation of punishment.

1. In classical thought, the word *barzakh* came to stand for both the time and place of waiting between death and resurrection, even though the Qurʾān uses the word rarely and only in the sense of a barrier. By the time of the famous theologian al-Ghazālī (d. 1111), who wrote in detail about the *barzakh*, a clearer picture had emerged. At the moment of death, ʿIzrāʾīl, the angel of death, appears; then the soul slips easily from the body, borne upward by other angels. Subsequently, the angelic pair Munkar and Nakīr question the dead in their graves about their deeds. The interrogation is followed by pressure on all grave-dwellers and punishment of some. Whether this punishment prefigures or mitigates later punishment is unclear. According to some, the dead may interact with the living during the *barzakh*, particularly in their dreams.

2. The period between revelation of the Qurʾān and the Day of Judgment, as well as the eschatological figures who function therein, also received further attention. Key figures include al-Dajjāl, the false savior or "Antichrist," and the Mahdi, the divinely guided one. Al-Dajjāl, who appears in the *ḥadīth* but not in the Qurʾān, will emerge toward the end of time after a long period of social and natural disintegration, and he will conquer the earth until killed either by the returned Jesus or the Mahdi, another non-Qurʾanic figure. The latter, in this sense, is an unnamed reforming member of the family of the Prophet who will be sent to restore peace and justice on earth for a period of time before the end and to fulfill the mission of Muḥammad as his last temporal successor (caliph), as interpreter of his revelation, and as enforcer of Islamic law (*sharīʿah*).

However, not all Sunnī Muslims expect such a figure and the term has often been used more like the related *mujaddid*, that is, a divinely guided renewer who at any point may bring the Muslim community from deviation back onto God's straight path through intellectual, spiritual, or temporal leadership. Unlike *mahdī*, *mujaddid* has cyclical connotations; it has been applied to figures at the turn of each Muslim century, from the first to the most recent. Since the eschaton failed to arrive, and since Muḥammad was believed to have purified and sealed off revelation for all time, not to reappear until the Day of Judgment, other figures could frequently rise to importance.

3. According to many post-Qurʾanic commentaries, the Day of Judgment will be announced by two blasts from the trumpet of the archangel Isrāfīl, whereupon souls will be reunited with bodies in the graves, resurrected, and assembled, perhaps to wait for an extended period of time. Their deeds will be read out of the heavenly books and weighed in the balance. When they cross the bridge over the Fire, the reckoning will be verified: sinning believers will fall into the Fire temporarily; sinning nonbelievers, permanently. Saved believers will cross safely into the Garden, where some kind of "vision" of God may await them. According to many writers, each prophet will lead his own community, with the whole procession led in turn by Muḥammad and the Muslim community. At the pool or pond *(ḥawḍ)*, the Prophet may intercede for some of the Muslim faithful in the Fire. However, some authors even argued that the Fire was a kind of purgatory for not only some but all its inhabitants.

The structure of Fire and Garden was delineated, too, with architectural models preferred, as in the Qurʾān. The Fire has seven concentric circles or layers, representing hierarchically arranged levels of punishment; the Garden has seven or eight layers, perhaps pyramidal, with the throne of God at the top. This kind of elaboration was promoted by the concomitant development of several genres of literature that detailed the Prophet's famous night journey to Jerusalem and ascension from there through the seven heavens.

Shīʿī variations. The informal structure of Sunnī eschatological figures has a formal analog in the Shīʿī imamate. Among the Twelver Shīʿah, the cosmic order and the eschaton's arrival depend absolutely on a line of descendants of the Prophet through his daughter Fāṭimah and cousin ʿAlī. These imams, as they are called, are understood to have been conceived in God's mind from one beginning as the principle of good, to have been transmitted for centuries as light in the loins of the prophets and the wombs of holy women, and to have emerged in human form as the twelve vicegerents of Muḥammad (like the twelve assistants of all previous prophets).

They suffered, as had all the prophets, and their suffering and that of all previous and subsequent humanity culminated in the martyrdom of the third of their line, Ḥusayn, at the hands of the sixth caliph, Yazīd (680–683). Ḥusayn's suffering was the central redemptive act in the cosmic drama, shared in and made visible to all previous prophets and identified with by later followers. Its final avenging on the Day of Judgment will symbolize the triumph of good over evil, justice over injustice. The followers of the imams will be redeemed not only through Ḥusayn's actions but also by the identification with his suffering they demonstrate when they weep and when they visit Karbala, the site of his martyrdom, reenacting its drama (*taʿziyah*), and reciting poetic laments.

Before the Day, the twelfth and absent imam, al-Qāʾim, will have returned as Mahdi to prepare the way. The Mahdi will arrive at the end of a long period of disintegration culminating in the appearance of al-Dajjāl, whom he will kill, just as he will kill all the enemies of the family of the Prophet. By then Jesus will have returned and will rule for a time, after which the Mahdi (and perhaps Ḥusayn himself) will reign in peace and justice, fulfilling the mission of all the prophets. The family of the Prophet will participate not only in intercession but in judgment as well, in the persons of ʿAlī or Fāṭimah or Ḥusayn.

ṢŪFĪ VARIATIONS. Muslims who adopted a Ṣūfī orientation were led to special eschatological views as a result of their asceticism, their search for union with God in this life, and their extreme love of God. Early ascetics such as Ḥasan al-Baṣrī (d. 728) stressed their fear of Hell and their desire for Paradise because they were ultrasensitive to their human sinfulness; they tended to seek the otherworld because they so strongly rejected this one. In Ḥasan's words, "Be with this world as if you had never been there, and with the otherworld as if you would never leave it." However, when love of God became a key element in Sufism, new views of the otherworld began to appear. For the earliest Muslim love mystic, the Arab poetess Rābiʿah al-ʿAdawīyah (d. 801), selfless love of God required the Ṣūfī to be veiled from both this world and the other by her vision of God, whom the Ṣūfī must love so much that Paradise and Hell are both forgotten. Ṣūfīs such as Yaḥyā ibn Muʿādh al-Rāzī (d. 871) replaced fear of punishment and hope of reward with complete trust in God's mercy and found death beautiful because it joined friend with friend. Others went much further. The Turkish poet Yunus Emre (d. 1321?) argued that the Ṣūfī must reject not only this world but also the next; some of his poems ridiculed a literal interpretation of the Qurʾān's eschatological details.

Among those Ṣūfīs who sought union with God and a vision of him in this life, that experience transformed conventional notions of Paradise and Hell. For them, the perfect Ṣūfī was not subject to changing states, including death, or concerned about created states, such as the otherworld. Some came to believe that having been touched by the primordial fire and light of God's love made them impervious to the fires of Hell, and that Paradise would provide pure experience of God, not the sensuous delights described in the Qurʾān. In the words of Shiblī (d. 945), "the fire of Hell will not touch me; I can extinguish it." Ṣūfī enlargements of Muslim eschatological thinking was not without its ironies: while popular Ṣūfī practice encouraged rituals that might increase the joys of Paradise, cultivated Ṣūfī thought discouraged hoping for Paradise even for the vision of God it might provide.

MODERN RESPONSES. Many modern Sunnī thinkers do not discuss the eschaton at all, apparently finding it too difficult to rationalize. The concerns of those who do treat the eschaton are unusually continuous with those of their premodern counterparts, but modern thinkers have also developed new emphases and rediscovered old ones.

Along the traditionalist end of the spectrum, thinkers such as Aḥmad Fāʾiz (d. 1918), Muḥammad ʿAwwād (d. 1980), Shaykh al-Islām Ibrāhīm al-Bayjūrī, Muḥammad Khalīfah, Muṣṭafā al-Ṭayr, and Ahmad Galwash tend toward various kinds of literalism, reiterating in modern language such concerns as the agony of death, questioning and punishment/reward in the grave, the awareness of the dead, and the physicality of resurrection and afterlife. At the other end of the spectrum are those, such as M. Sadeddin Evrin, who attempt to verify the Qurʾān with scientific research (the description of the signs of the eschaton, for example). Some, such as Ṭanṭāwī Jawharī (d. 1940) Muḥammad Farīd Wajdī (d. 1954), lean toward a kind of European-inspired spiritualism that posits a world from which the spirits of the dead think about and help the living. In between the two poles are various modernists who tend to downplay the traditional eschatological specifics in favor of a stress on the continuity between this life and the next, the naturalness of death and the likeness of the *barzakh* to sleep or semiconsciousness, and the nature of human responsibility and accountability. Many practice allegorical interpretations of the Qurʾān. For example, Syed Ameer Ali (d. 1928) sees a spiritual meaning in the Qurʾān's sensuous descriptions of Paradise and Gehenna. Abū al-Aʿlā al-Mawdūdī (d. 1979) stresses the practical value of Islamic eschatology in helping human beings deal with death and mortality. Muḥammad Iqbal (d. 1938), in *The Reconstruction of Religious Thought in Islam*, describes Paradise and Gehenna as states rather than localities.

Modernist thought has also taken forms much less consistent with received eschatological thinking. The founder of the Aḥmadīyah sect, Mīrzā Ghulām Aḥmad of Punjab (d. 1908), made eschatological claims of his own, asserting in 1880 that he was the Mahdi, at once the incarnation of Jesus, Muḥammad, and Kṛṣṇa. Aḥmadī Qurʾān commentaries, such as that of Maulana Muḥammad Ali (d. 1951), have continued to develop unusual eschatological views. For example, the opening of the graves is said to be prefigured by the opening of the earth to the mining of precious metals; the afterlife is seen as an example of the unceasing progress that also takes place on earth; the resurrection is presented as a new manifestation of hidden realities; and a heaven on earth is anticipated as well as a heaven after death.

The use of allegorical interpretation in the service of modernist rationalization has not been universal. Important modernists such as Muḥammad al-Mubārak, Sayyid Quṭb, Muṣṭafā Maḥmūd, and Muḥammad ʿAbduh have remained loyal to Qurʾān and *ḥadīth* in their rejection of allegorical interpretation but have also argued against literalism, finding both of them inadequate means of expressing the realities of the next world. Others have established a relationship between the eschaton and the widely perceived need for social reconstruction. For them, death and resurrection are most meaningful in the context of living an ethical life. They emphasize human accountability and focus on the ways in which considerations of the next world can promote morality in this one. These approaches have their parallel among those Shīʿī Muslims who, embarrassed by the supernaturalism of traditional eschatology, deny the return of the last imam and yet find meaning and a redemptive quality in Ḥusayn's death when it is understood as a protest against injustice and oppression. Such thinkers seem to have rediscovered ancient Qurʾānic priorities in their pursuit of modernization.

SEE ALSO Imamate; Messianism, article on Messianism in the Muslim Tradition; Miʿrāj; Nubūwah.

BIBLIOGRAPHY

The only comprehensive study of Islamic eschatology is Jane I. Smith's and Yvonne Y. Haddad's *The Islamic Understanding of Death and Resurrection* (Albany, N. Y., 1981), an unprecedented survey, largely of Sunnī thought, clearly and simply organized and concisely presented, with unusual attention given to modern thinkers of several kinds. Fritz Meier's "The Ultimate Origin and the Hereafter in Islam," in *Islam and Its Cultural Divergence: Studies in Honor of Gustave E. von Grunebaum*, edited by Girdhari L. Tikku, (Urbana, Ill., 1971), pp. 96–112, is an awkwardly translated general survey with a useful comparison of Sunnī and Shīʿī concepts of revelation, their relationship to other forms of divinely inspired knowledge and leadership, and their place in eschatology. Annemarie Schimmel's *Mystical Dimensions of Islam* (Chapel Hill, N.C., 1975) contains fascinating material on Ṣūfī eschatology throughout.

Works that address the issue of eschatology in the Shīʿī tradition in particular include S. Husain M. Jafri's *Origins and Early Development of Shīʿa Islam* (London, 1979), a straightforward, narrative, chronological account that stresses the ways in which pre-Islamic views of leadership informed various Shīʿī constituencies, concentrating on the centrist, legitimist Twelver Shīʿāh and the contributions of Jaʿfar al-Ṣādiq to their institutionalization. Mahmoud Ayoub's *Redemptive Suffering in Islam: A Study of the Devotional Aspects of ʿĀshūrāʾ in Twelver Shīʿism* (The Hague, 1978) is a moving and deeply felt rendering of eschatologically relevant piety, with suggestive comparative comments. A. A. Sachedina's *Islamic Messianism: The Idea of the Mahdi in Twelver Shīʿism* (Albany, N.Y., 1981) is a clear interpretive account of an important topic, with a particularly important analysis of the relationship between imam and prophet.

An important case study is Ignácz Goldziher's "Zur Charakteristik Gelâl ud-dîn us-Sujûtʿî's und seiner literarischen Thätigkeit," *Sitzungsberichte der kaiserlichen Akademie der Wissenschaften in Wien* 69 (1871): 7–28, a rare history and analysis of the concept of *mujaddid*, with an emphasis on one important thinker's identification with the role. John B. Taylor's "Some Aspects of Islamic Eschatology," *Religious Studies* 4 (October, 1968): 57–76, is a selective comparison of Qurʾanic and Mongol-period views, with eschatological thought divided into three categories: didactic, apocalyptic, and mystical. Taylor's references to modern Muslim responses to the topic are unfortunately seriously outdated.

Useful information can be found also in the *Shorter Encyclopaedia of Islam* (Leiden, 1974), in the following articles in particular: "Barzakh," "al-Dadjdjāl," "Djahannam," "Djanna," "Firdaws," "Ḥawḍ," "Iblīs," "ʿIsā," "Isrāfīl," "ʿIzrāʾīl," "ak-Ḳiyāma," "al-Mahdī," "Malāʾika," "Munkar wa-Nakīr," "Shafāʿa," and "Yādjūj wa-Mādjūj." However, the articles are sometimes unclearly or elliptically presented or marred by the open display or subtle influence of many of the ethnocentric biases of earlier generations of scholars, especially as regards the allegedly derivative, irrational nature of Islam.

New Sources

Cook, David B. *Studies in Muslim Apocalyptic.* Princeton, N.J., 2002.

Kelsay, John, and James Turner Johnson, ed. *Just War and Jihad: Historical and Theoretical Perspectives on War and Peace in Western and Islamic Traditions.* New York, 1991.

Robbins, Thomas, and Susan J. Palmer, eds. *Millennium, Messiahs, and Mayhem: Contemporary Apocalyptic Movements.* New York, 1997.

Schafer, Peter, and Mark R. Cohen, eds. *Toward the Millenium: Messianic Expectations from the Bible to Waco Studies in the History of Religions 77.* Boston, 1998.

Umar, Muhammad S. "Muslims' Eschatological Discourses on Colonialism in Northern Nigeria." *Journal of the American Academy of Religion* 67 (March 1999), 59–85.

MARILYN ROBINSON WALDMAN (1987)
Revised Bibliography

ESHMUN

ESHMUN was a Phoenician healer god, later identified with Asklepios, the patron of medicine, by the Greeks and the Romans. He seems to be attested since the third millennium BCE in Syria, though his physiognomy becomes clear only in the first millennium BCE. The etymology of Eshmun clearly connects him with "oil," which had therapeutic and ritual functions (in relationship with the kingship ritual) in the ancient Near East. In the Ebla archives (middle of the third millennium BCE), the theophoric element sí-mi-nu/a is found in some personal names, written dì-giš in Sumerian, meaning "oil." In the ritual texts of Ugarit and Ras Ibn Hani, in the late Bronze Age (eighteenth century BCE), the god Šmn is also mentioned as a beneficiary of offerings (*Keilalphabetischen Texte aus Ugarit* 1.164:9, 1.41:[45], 1.87:50). Unfortunately nothing is known about the functions or the role of this god in the Syrian pantheons, but his connection with oil must indicate that he was "the one who oils," and thus "the one who heals." This is surely the main reason why Eshmun was later assimilated to Asklepios/Aesculapius. His occasional *interpretatio* as Apollo (for example, in Carthage) is also based on the same background, because Apollo was also a salvific god. According to Philo of Byblos (Eus., *Praeparation Evangelica* I, 10, 38), Eshmun was Sydyk's son (Sydyk was the personification of Justice), while Damascius (*Vita Is.* ß 302) knows his father as Sadykos, who had first seven sons, the Dioscouri or Kabeiri, then an eighth son, Eshmun (Esmounos; the number 8 was a sign of election, of a special destiny). According to Pausanias (VII, 23,7–8), who refers a Sidonian testimony, Eshmun's father was Apollo, while the god himself was the Air, which brings health. According to Cicero (*Nat. deor.* III, 22, 57) and Lydus (*De mens.* IV, 142), Arsippos was the name of the third Aesculapius, that is, Rashap (Reshef), the semitic Apollo.

ESHMUN AND THE BAAL TRADITION. From a typological and historical point of view, Eshmun, though he is not a storm god, seems to be near to the Syrian Baal tradition, which emphasizes the salvific functions of the god, documented in Ugarit through Baal's connection with the Rapiu/Refaim ("the healers"=the dead). Eshmun's cult is documented not only in the sphere of public religion, but also on the level of private or popular beliefs, where the questions of health, wealth, and salvation were essential.

The earliest attestation of Eshmun seems to be the London Medical Papyrus, where we find, transcribed into Egyptian hieratic syllabic script, some short West Semitic magical texts, dated from the fourteenth to the seventeenth centuries BCE (Steiner, J. C., *Journal of Near Eastern Studies* 51, 1992, pp. 191–200). One of them (no. 28) contains the name of Eshmun and probably also of Astarte, while the text of number 33 alludes to an anonymous "healer" *(rpy)*, who is probably Eshmun.

ESHMUN IN PHOENICIA. The first epigraphical evidence related to Eshmun is the treaty (754 BCE) between Mati'el, the king of Arpad (North Syria) and Assurnirari V, king of Assyria, where Eshmun is mentioned in the group of the Syrian gods who warrant the treaty, together with Melqart (the Baal of Tyre; cf. State Archives of Assyria II, 1988, no. 2, VI, 22, p. 13). Both appear again in the treaty between Asarhaddon of Assyria and Baal of Tyre (675–670 BCE). The consequences are stated, should the Tyrian king not respect the oath: "May Melqart and Eshmun deliver your land to destruction and your people to deportation; may they [uproot] you from your land and take away the food from your mouth, the clothes from your body, and the oil for your anointing" (State Archives of Assyria II, 1988, no. 5, IV, 14–17, p. 27). The mention of the oil probably alludes to Eshmun's specific functions. The association of Melqart, Baal of Tyre, and Eshmun, Baal of Sidon, is not rare. For example, in Batsalos, near Kition (Cyprus), the double divine name, Eshmun-Melqart, indicates a strong cultural association between the two gods, who protected and defended the people.

Eshmun is also present in the onomastics of the Phoenicians who were deported to Assyria (Nimrud) in the seventh century BCE. In the fifth to fourth century BCE, Eshmun's cult is documented in Amrith, probably in connection with the salvific waters of the sanctuary (the so-called Maabed), where Melqart seems to be the major god, and in Sarepta, under the name of Asklepios (bilingual dedication made by a Cypriot in Greek and syllabic Cypriot writings, fourth century BCE). But the main center of Eshmun's cult is clearly Sidon: he is called Baal of Sidon in the famous funerary inscription of Eshmunazor II ("Eshmun has saved"), circa 475 BCE (*Kanaansische und aramsische Inschriften* [KAI] 14). He is also mentioned in the two series of Bodashtart's inscriptions (KAI 15–16), which record the restoration of the god's sanctuary, and in the inscription of the young prince Baalshillem (*Textbook of Syrian Semitic Inscriptions,* T III, no. 29). Eshmun was the most important god of Sidon, the dynastic god, the "holy prince" (*šr qdš*) of the city. He was associated, like Melqart in Tyre, with the goddess Astarte, who bore the title of *šm b'l*, "Name of Baal" (already mentioned in Ugarit). In Sidon, Eshmun had at least two sanctuaries: one in the city ("Sidon-on-the-sea") and one outside the city ("Sidon-in-the-countryside"), in Bostan esh-Sheikh, along the Nahr el-Awali (Bostrenus), near the Yidal source, where the god was associated with Astarte. Initially, in the neo-Babylonian period (sixth century BCE), a ziggurat was built, already associated with a sacral pool, probably for therapeutic rituals. The sanctuary was rebuilt in Persian times (fifth century BCE) in the Greek style. It was a very large sacral complex, with different shrines and cultural buildings. On a monumental and richly decorated podium (decorated with hunting scenes), built against the mountain, there was a sanctuary constructed of Greek marble that remained in use until the fourth century BCE. In the northwest part of the sanctuary the Eshmun's tribune (a big socle, or base, for a colossal statue or an altar) was built, seven meters high and decorated with dances and other "Apollonian" images. Another shrine, further down and located to the east, was associated with a cultic pool, and a stone throne decorated with sphinx and lions was dedicated to Astarte, the *paredros* of Eshmun. This temple complex was excavated beginning in the 1963–1964 period, and among the finds from the temple's *favissa* were votive statues dedicated to Eshmun, on behalf of children (1–2 years old) who may have been sick or were subjected to an initiation ritual (the so-called temple-boys).

Eshmun was also venerated in Berytos (Beirut), and as late as the rule of the Roman emperor Elagabalus (218–222 CE) coins of Berytos depict Eshmun on the back, usually with a caduceus or a border of snakes (symbol of healing). In the same region, according to Damascius, *Vita Is.* ß 302 (sixth century BCE), a young hunter named Asklepios was obliged to practice self-castration because of Astronoe's passion for him. The goddess, "mother of the gods," brought him to life again after the castration, using the "vital heat." This story presents several analogies with Attis's myth, but probably contains an authentically Phoenician mythical tradition. Like Melqart, a god dies and then returns to life through the actions of a goddess who gives him immortality and divine powers. It is worth noting that the Lebanese toponym Qabr Smun (Eshmun's Tomb) lies near Beirut. In this case, just like in Melqart's case, the Frazerian typology of the "dying and rising god," with its seasonal pattern, seems to be a reductive interpretation, though not completely wrong. (In *The Golden Bough* [1914], J. G. Frazer devised the category of "dying and rising gods," which included Adonis, Osiris, Attis, and others.) Besides, the fertility aspect is not the primary characteristic of Eshmun, who is first of all a healer, the Baal of the town. He is more obviously the heir of the Syrian Bronze Age traditions incarnate in Baal and the dead kings who are immortalized.

ESHMUN OUTSIDE PHOENICIA, IN THE NEAR EAST. Elsewhere in the Near Eastern world, Eshmun is attested through dedications or onomastics in Syria, Palestine, and Egypt. The Nebi Yunis inscription (third to second century BCE), which mentions a *molk* (sacrifice) in honor of Eshmun, is probably false, while the presence of Eshmun's name on an ostrakon from Shiqmona (end of the eighth century BCE) is also questionable. In Cyprus, Eshmun's cult is well documented, especially in Kition, sometimes together with Melqart (at Batsalos), probably because these two Baals had salvific functions. In Kition a god named Baal Marpe, the healing Lord, is mentioned, who could be identical with Eshmun or with Eshmun-Melqart.

ESHMUN IN WESTERN CONTEXTS. In Western contexts, Eshmun is also an important god, especially in Carthage, where he was, according to Apuleius (*Florida* 18), the city's numen. Eshmun's temple in Carthage, on the Byrsa acropolis, was indeed very famous and very rich. The Senate's meetings took placed in this sanctuary. In 146 BCE, at the end of the Third Punic War, the last defenders of the city found refuge in this temple, which was destroyed by fire. Eshmun's temple and Eshmuns priests are often mentioned in the Carthaginian inscriptions. The god was probably venerated together with Astarte, as the divine name Eshmun-Astarte is mentioned in at least one inscription. In the Roman period, Eshmun, who was named Aesculapius, continued to play an important role in the religious life of Carthage. His *paredra* (divine feminine partner) was Caelestis, with whom Aesculapius is frequently associated in Roman Africa. The Carthaginians also venerated a golden statue of Apollo, which was taken away by the Romans and placed in front of the Circus Maximus in Rome. This god could be another *interpretatio* of Eshmun.

Eshmun, under the name Aesculapius or Apollo, is also documented in Bulla Regia, Maktar, Lambesa, Oea, and elsewhere, but it is not easy to distinguish between the possible Punic roots and the Roman manifestations. The toponym Rusucmona (Cape of Eshmun) is located near Utica, where there was an important and archaic temple to Apollo.

In Sardinia, the most important evidence of Eshmun is the trilingual dedication to Eshmun/Asklepios/Aesculapius, which appears in Punic, Greek, and Latin on a bronze altar at S. Nicolò Gerrei (second century BCE). Near Cagliari, a votive hand (ex-voto) was dedicated to "Eshmun who listens," the one who fulfills prayers and heals the ill. In Spain, there probably was an Eshmun's temple in Carthagena (on the Acropolis; Polybius X, 10, 8).

Eshmun is also very frequently found in onomastics in Phoenicia and in all the "colonies" (more than seven hundred just at Carthage). The verbs linked to Eshmun in the personal names stress the healing functions of the god, who "protects," "gives (life/health)," "saves," "delivers," and so on. In the Latin transcriptions, Eshmun's name can be written as Sum/n-, San/m-, and A/Ismun-.

On the basis of such documentation, it is obviously impossible to present Eshmun as a simple "vegetation god," as suggested in the works of W. Baudissin and R. Dussaud. Like the different Bronze Age Baals, who are related to the Syrian tradition on kingship, Eshmun or Melqart, the Phoenician Iron Age Baals, are complex personalities to whom people asked a large protection: for food, for health, for stability, for fertility, for peace.

See Also Asklepios; Phoenician Religion.

Bibliography

Baudissin, W. *Adonis und Esmun.* Leipzig, 1911.

Lipinski, E. *Dieux et déesses de l'univers phénicienn et punique.* Leuven, 1985. See pages 154–169.

Mettinger, N. *The Riddle of Resurrection. Dying and Rising Gods in the Ancient Near East.* Stockholm, 2001. See pages 155–165.

Ribinichi, S. "Eshmun." In *Dictionary of Deities and Demons in the Bible,* edited by Karel van der Toorn, Bob Becking, and Pieter W. van der Horst, pp. 583-587. Leiden, 1995.

Stucky, R. A. *Tribune d'Echmoun.* Basel, 1984.

Stucky, R. A. "Das Heiligtum des Eschmun bei Sidon in vorhellenistischer Zeit." *Zeitschrift des Deutschen Palästina-Vereins* 118 (2002): 66–86.

Xella, P. "Eschmun von Sidon." In *Mesopotamica-Ugaritica-Biblica,* edited by M. Dietrich and O. Loretz, pp. 481–498. Neukirchen-Vluyn, Germany, 1993.

Xella, P. "Les plus anciens témoignages sur le dieu Eshmoun: une mise au point." In *The World of the Aramaeans,* II, *Studies in Honour of P.-E. Dion,* edited by P. M. Michèle Daviau et al., pp. 230–241. Sheffield, U.K., 2001.

Corinne Bonnet (2005)

ESKIMO RELIGION

See ARCTIC RELIGIONS; INUIT RELIGIOUS TRADITIONS

ESOTERIC BUDDHISM

See BUDDHISM, SCHOOLS OF, *ARTICLE ON* TANTRIC RITUAL SCHOOLS OF BUDDHISM

ESOTERICISM.

Esotericism has several meanings. After presenting a list of them, this article deals with the use of the term in scholarly parlance and with the various approaches toward this academic speciality in religious studies.

A Variety of Meanings. The substantive esotericism seems to have first appeared in French (*l'ésotérisme*) in Jacques Matter's *Histoire critique du Gnosticisme et de son influence* (A Critical History of Gnosticism and Its Influence), published in 1828. Along with its adjective form *esoteric,* esotericism until the early twenty-first century has carried different meanings that overlap only in part:

1. Booksellers and publishers tend to group under this heading (or under that of the occult or even metaphysics) a plethora of domains concerned with the paranormal, exotic and particularly Eastern wisdom traditions, New Age literature, and magical literature.
2. *Esoteric* is used to designate teachings or doctrines that are purposely kept secret, generally with a view to distinguish between initiates and noninitiates (the former are supposed to respect the so-called discipline of the arcane).
3. *Esoteric* refers to the hidden meanings of apparent reality (i.e., of nature, history, and mythical narratives) and to the deeper, inner mysteries of religion as opposed to its

merely external or exoteric dimensions. In this understanding, esotericism tends to designate the ways likely to provide an access to these deeper meanings. Here *gnōsis* is often used as a synonym of esotericism.

4. Within the so-called perennialist discourses, notably those of the traditionalist school of religious studies (e.g., in René Guénon's and Frtijof Schon's works), "esoterism" (used rather than *esotericism)* is the doctrine according to which there is a transcendental unity of religions—sometimes called the primordial tradition—and the ways to try to recover it.
5. The term is often used in a rather broad sense as a near synonym of (again) *gnōsis,* understood as a mode of knowing that emphasizes the experiential, the mythical, and the symbolic rather than the dogmatic and discursive forms of expression.
6. Mainly since the beginning of the 1990s, esotericism, or rather Western esotericism, has been used in academic parlance to designate (from a strictly historical perspective) a speciality covering a number of currents and traditions that present some obvious similarities. *Western* here refers to the medieval and modern Greco-Latin world in which the religious traditions of Judaism and Christianity have coexisted for centuries, visited by those of Islam. In an even stricter sense, this speciality has developed into modern Western esotericism. This expression was chosen by scholars among other available ones (e.g., hermeticism or hermetic philosophy, which some other scholars conveniently use, but they do so in the same sense). It was a matter of choosing a term to designate a historical field. This latter corresponds to a specific phenomenon that appeared at the beginning of the early modern period (i.e., of the Renaissance) and is represented by a number of specific spiritual currents.

It is in this latter, stricter sense that esotericism is intended in the present article. It is to be understood as a historical construct, not as a type of religion but as a general label for some currents in Western culture that display certain similarities and are historically related. Although there is still some debate about the definition and the demarcation of this domain, notably of its historical scope, a widespread consensus has been reached about the main currents that form its core. They are mainly of the following ones (the list is not exhaustive):

1. the Renaissance revival of hermetism (i.e., the literature bearing witness to an intense, renewed interest in the Greek *hermetica* of late antiquity, in particular in the *Corpus Hermeticum* attributed to the legendary Hermes Trismegistus);
2. Christian Qabbalah of the Renaissance and post-Christian Qabbalah;
3. the so-called occult philosophy of the Renaissance (see, for example, Cornelius Agrippa's *De Occulta Philosophia,* 1533) and its later developments;
4. alchemy of the fifteenth to the twentieth centuries, understood as a spiritual form of meditation and practice;
5. astrology (in its speculative more than its divinatory form);
6. Paracelsism (the philosophy of Paracelsus in the first half of the sixteenth century) and that of his followers bent upon giving a chemical or alchemical interpretation of nature;
7. Rosicrucianism, which began to flourish at the beginning of the seventeenth century, and its numerous varieties until the early twenty-first century;
8. theosophy (the current that began to flourish with Jacob Böhme) in the seventeenth century but also the history of the Theosophical Society since the end of the nineteenth century;
9. the so-called illuminist current (c. 1750 to 1820);
10. the occultist current (mid–nineteenth century to the first half of the twentieth century) and its related developments.

ACADEMIC APPROACHES: 1964–1990. *Giordano Bruno and the Hermetic Tradition* (1964) by Frances A. Yates has been instrumental in calling attention to the importance and significance of hermetism in the history of the Renaissance and consequently to that of the esoteric currents that flourished at that time and later. Yates's book caused a flurry of debates over what Wouter J. Hanegraaff has felicitously called "the Yates paradigm" (Hanegraaff, 2001, p. 5). Indeed Yates has created a grand narrative, as it were, based on two main assumptions. First is the existence of what she called "the Hermetic Tradition," in which she saw a more or less covert reaction against both Christianity and the rise of scientific worldviews. Second, however paradoxical it may seem, is the claim that the essential tradition of magic—which Yates considered essentially nonprogressive—was an important factor in the development of the scientific revolution. Neither of these two tenets has proved resistant to close scrutiny, but this work paved the way for an ongoing academic recognition and institutionalization of modern Western esoteric currents as a specialty in their own right.

Even within the pale of academic scholarship, the Yates paradigm was used by a number of authors with a more or less religionist-esoteric persuasion within the intellectual climate of the counterculture of the 1960s and 1970s. Indeed they were prone to consider esoteric currrents in general as a form of counterculture, just as Yates's narrative portrayed the Renaissance magus as a rebel against the dogmas of the established churches and later against the claims of mechanistic science. Such an interpretation is illustrated, for example, by many scholars associated with the Eranos group, like Carl Gustav Jung, Mircea Eliade, Henry Corbin, Ernst Benz, or Joseph Campbell (see Wasserstrom, 1999; Hakl, 2001). Therefore, on the one hand, the Eranosian production was viewed with suspicion by scholars of a a strictly historical persuasion; on the other hand and more importantly, the study of Western esotericism found in Eranos a place in which precedence was given to a "phenomenological" even apologetical approach.

What seems to be the first methodological attempt proper was proposed in 1990 by Pierre Riffard. Starting from the idea that there is a universal esotericism, this scholar attempted to find what its invariables might be. He found seven: author's impersonality, distinction between the profane and the initiated, correspondences, the subtle, arithmology (the esoteric science of numbers), occult arts, and initiation. Given its universalizing aspect in terms of areas and eras, that is, its lack of precise anchoring in history, such a position evinces a tendency toward essentialism and religionism. Nevertheless it is not devoid of interest insofar as it is likely to be appropriable by anthropology and psychology.

ACADEMIC APPROACHES: 1991–EARLY TWENTY-FIRST CENTURY. Not until as late as the beginning of the 1990s did the study of modern Western esotericism begin to be seriously recognized as an academic field of study in its own right. In these years the Yates paradigm as well as its religionist interpretation from a countercultural perspective were challenged by a different paradigm introduced by Antoine Faivre that can be seen as encompassing the entire period from the Renaissance to the early twenty-first century while still clearly demarcating the field from nonesoteric currents. As a result during the 1990s Faivre's approach was adopted by many other scholars and tended to replace Yates's grand narrative as the major paradigm in the field.

In a number of publications in the 1990s, Faivre submitted an academic construct based on empirical observations (i.e., not on an essentialist or religionist position claiming to deal with the essence of esotericism, which he considered problematic). He proposed calling esotericism in the modern West a form of thought identifiable by the presence of six characteristics distributed in varying proportions. Four are intrinsic in that their simultaneous presence is supposed to be a necessary and sufficient condition for a discourse to be identified as esoteric (although of course no discourse turns out to be that only). With them are joined two others, which he calls secondary, that is, not intrinsic, but whose presence is frequent next to the four others. That said, it is clear that none of the six characteristics belongs to esotericism alone.

The four intrinsic characteristics are:

1. The idea of correspondences. There exist invisible and noncausal correspondences between all visible and invisible dimensions of the cosmos. This is illustrated, for example, by the old notion of macrocosm and microcosm and the principle of universal relationships between all things within the universe. The latter is a theater of mirrors, a mosaic of hieroglyphs to be decoded. Everything in nature is a sign, and the least object is hiding a secret. Occult relationships govern the metals, the planets, and the parts of the human body. There are also correspondences between nature and history on the one hand and the revealed texts (the myths of foundation or origin) on the other hand.
2. Living nature. The cosmos is not merely complex or plural, nor can it be reduced to a network of correspondences. It is also alive. Viewed as a seat of sympathies and antipathies, it is palpitating in all its parts, permeated and animated by a spiritual presence, a life force, or a light—a hidden fire that circulates through it.
3. Imagination and mediations. These two notions are complementary. Rituals, *maṇḍalas*, symbols charged with polysemia, and intermediate beings (like angels) are mediators that allow the various levels of reality to be (re)connected to one another. And imagination is understood here as a specific faculty (a magical one, as it were) of the human mind to use these intermediaries, symbols, and images for acquiring a higher knowledge. Imagination (often compared here with magnet, *mageia*, imago) is the tool of knowledge of the self, of the world, of myth—it is the "eyes of fire" that makes visible the invisible.
4. The experience of transmutation. This fourth element comes in to complete the first three. It adds to them the dimension of a living experience. It may be the transmutation of oneself through an illuminated knowledge that favors a second birth but also of a part of nature itself (such is the case of course in alchemy).

The two secondary characteristics include, first, the idea of concordance, which posits the existence of common denominators (a fundamental concordance) between several or all spiritual traditions, then studies these by comparing them, in the hopes of bringing out the forgotten hidden trunk of which each particular one would be only one visible branch. Second is transmission, which has become rather common since the eighteenth century. Transmission emphasizes the importance of channels; for example, transmission from master to disciple or initiatory societies (one cannot initiate oneself). Some insist on the authenticity of the regularity of the channels of filiation supposed to transmit what could not be obtained without them.

Some aspects and implications of Faivre's construct have been challenged. Hanegraaff (1996, 2004) has cogently argued that it applies mostly to the Renaissance occult philosophy and to the late-eighteeth-century and early-ninteenth-century illuminist and Romantic contexts but fails to fully account for developments within the spiritualist-pietist context since the seventeenth century and the secularization of esotericism over the long period of the nineteenth and twentieth centuries. Kocku von Stuckrad (2004) has suggested that the limitations of Faivre's concept of a form of thought could be overcome by a discursive approach. Furthermore the relation of Western esotericism to Christianity and to the other religions of the book lends itself to ongoing debates (Hanegraaff, 1995, 2004; Neugebauer-Wölk, 2003; Stuckrad, 2004). It seems likely that such discussions, which are already operating in several directions, will contribute to further developments in the study of Western esotericism.

The Academic Institutionalization of Esotericism: A Short Overview. This long-neglected domain has been increasingly recognized in the early twenty-first century as an area of academic research and has gained a foothold in academia. It has been instrumental in bringing about a reappraisal of the understanding of Western culture in general and of its religious history in particular. Indeed even before methodological questions were seriously raised, the École Pratique des Hautes Études, Section des Sciences Religieuses (Paris, Sorbonne), created in 1964 the chair History of Christian Esotericism, which became in 1979 the History of the Esoteric and Mystical Currents in Contemporary Europe (in 2001 the adjective mystical was deleted). The University of Amsterdam in 1999 created a chair of the History of Hermetic Philosophy and Related Currents from the Renaissance to the Present, which encompasses a full academic curriculum, from the undergraduate to the doctorate levels. In Lampeter, United Kingdom, in 2001 another was established, History of the Western Esoteric Tradition. Within the American Academy of Religion, a program unit functioned from 1986 to 2000 under several titles, the latest one being Western Esotericism since the Early Modern Period. The International Association for the History of Religions held a conference in Mexico City in 2000, "Western Esotericism and the Science of Religion" (see Faivre and Hanegraaff, 1998), and another one in Durban in 2000, "Western Esotericism and Jewish Mysticism." Other similar examples could be adduced.

See Also Alchemy; Astrology; Hermetism; Nature; Theosophical Society.

Bibliography

Broek, Roelof van den, and Wouter J. Hanegraaff, eds. *Gnosis and Hermeticism from Antiquity to Modern Times.* Albany, N.Y., 1998.

Caron, Richard, Joscelyn Godwin, Wouter. J. Hanegraaff, and Jean-Louis Vieillard-Baron, eds. *Esotérisme, Gnoses, et Imaginaire symbolique: Mélanges offerts à Antoine Faivre.* Louvain, 2001.

Faivre, Antoine. *Access to Western Esotericism.* Albany, N.Y., 1994. Includes a detailed bibliography of scholarly studies devoted to specific modern Western esoteric currents, pp. 297–348.

Faivre, Antoine. *Theosophy, Imagination, Tradition: Studies in Western Esotericism.* Albany, N.Y., 2000. Includes a detailed bibliography of scholarly studies devoted to specific modern Western esoteric currents, pp. 248–259.

Faivre, Antoine. *L'ésotérisme.* Rev. and enlarged ed. Paris, 2002.

Faivre, Antoine, and Wouter J. Hanegraaff, eds. *Western Esotericism and the Science of Religion.* Louvain, 1998.

Hakl, Hans Thomas. *Der verborgene Geist von Eranos: Unbekannte Begegnungen von Wissenschaft und Esoterik; Eine alternative Geistesgeschichte des 20. Jahrhunderts.* Bretten, Germany, 2001.

Hammer, Olav. *Claiming Knowledge: Strategies of Epistemology from Theosophy to the New Age.* Leiden, 2001.

Hammer, Olav. "Esotericism in New Religious Movements." In *The Oxford Handbook of New Religious Movements,* edited by James R. Lewis, pp. 445–465. Oxford, 2004.

Hanegraaff, Wouter J. "Empirical Method in the Study of Esotericism." *Method and Theory in the Study of Religion* 7, no. 2 (1995): 99–129.

Hanegraaff, Wouter J. *New Age Religion and Western Culture: Esotericism in the Mirror of Secular Thought.* Leiden, 1996; reprint, Albany, N.Y., 1998.

Hanegraaff, Wouter J. "On the Construction of 'Esoteric Traditions.'" In *Western Esotericism and the Science of Religion,* edited by Antoine Faivre and Wouter J. Hanegraaff, pp. 11–61. Louvain, 1998.

Hanegraaff, Wouter J. "Beyond the Yates Paradigm: The Study of Western Esotericism between Counterculture and New Complexity." *Aries* 1, no. 1 (2001): 5–37.

Hanegraaff, Wouter J. "The Study of Western Esotericism: New Approaches to Christian and Secular Culture." In *New Approaches to the Study of Religion,* edited by Peter Antes, Armin W. Geertz, and Randi Warne. Berlin and New York, 2004.

Introvigne, Massimo. *Il cappello del mago.* Milan, 1990.

Laurant, Jean-Pierre. *L'ésotérisme chrétien en France au XIXè siècle.* Lausanne, 1992.

Laurant, Jean-Pierre. *L'ésotérisme.* Paris, 1993.

Matter, Jacques. *Histoire critique du Gnosticisme et de son influence.* Paris, 1828.

Neugebauer-Wölk, Monika. "Esoterik und Christentum vor 1800: Prolegomena zu einer Bestimmung ihrer Differenz." *Aries* 3, no. 2 (2003): 127–165.

Neugebauer-Wölk, Monika, ed. *Aufklärung und Esoterik.* Hamburg, 1999.

Riffard, Pierre A. *L'ésotérisme: Qu'est-ce que l'ésotérisme? Anthologie de l'ésotérisme occidental.* Paris, 1990.

Servier, Jean, ed. *Dictionnaire critique de l'ésotérisme.* Paris, 1998.

Stuckrad, Kocku von. *Was ist Esoterik? Kleine Geschichte des geheimen Wissens.* Munich, 2004.

Wasserstrom, Steven M. *Religion after Religion: Gershom Scholem, Mircea Eliade, and Henry Corbin at Eranos.* Princeton, N.J., 1999.

Yates, Frances Amelia. *Giordano Bruno and the Hermetic Tradition.* London, 1964.

Antoine Faivre (1987 and 2005)

ESSENES. The Essenes were a sect of Jews during the Hasmonean and Roman periods of Jewish history (c. 150 BCE–74 CE). This group was noted for its piety and distinctive theology. The Essenes were known in Greek as Essenoi or Essaioi. Numerous suggestions have been made regarding the etymology of the name, among which are derivation from Syriac *ḥase'* ("pious"), Aramaic *asayya'* ("healers"), Greek *hosios* ("holy"), and Hebrew *ḥasha'im* ("silent ones"). The very fact that so many suggestions as to etymology have been made and that none has carried a scholarly consensus shows that the derivation of the term cannot be established with certainty. No Hebrew cognate appears either in the Dead Sea Scrolls, taken by many scholars to be the writings of this sect, or in rabbinic literature (the Talmuds and *midrashim*). Only with the Jewish rediscovery of Philo Judaeus (d. 45–50 CE) and Josephus Flavius (d. 100 CE?) in the Renaissance was the Hebrew word *issiyyim* (Essenes) coined.

HISTORICAL SOURCES. Until the twentieth century, the Essenes were known only from Greek sources. They are described twice by Philo, in *Hypothetica* (11.1–18) and *Every Good Man Is Free* (12.75–13.91). Both of these accounts were written by 50 CE and, in turn, drew on a common, earlier source. (Philo also described a similar sect, the Therapeutae, in *On the Contemplative Life.*)

Josephus describes the Essenes in passages of several of his books. In *The Jewish War,* written around 75–79 CE, there is a detailed account (2.119–161). *Jewish Antiquities* contains a shorter account (18.18–22). In his autobiography, written about 100 CE, Josephus relates that he investigated the Essenes, among other Jewish sects, in his youth (*The Life* 2.9–11). Scattered references to the Essenes occur elsewhere in the works of Josephus.

Pliny the Elder wrote about the Essenes in his *Natural History* (5.73), completed in 77 CE. *Philosophumena* (9.18–30), considered to have been written by Hippolytus, a third-century bishop, contains a description of the Essenes that, in part, is drawn from a no longer extant source that was also used by Josephus.

Since the discovery of the Dead Sea Scrolls at Qumran in 1947, a consensus has developed that identifies the sect of the scrolls with the Essenes described by Philo and Josephus. This view has led many scholars to interpret the Greek texts describing the Essenes in light of the scrolls from Qumran, and the scrolls in light of the Greek texts, although the term *Essene* is absent from the Qumran scrolls. To avoid this methodological pitfall, evidence for the Essenes will first be presented and then compared with the corpus of the Dead Sea Scrolls.

HISTORY. No solution to the question of the origins of Essenism is likely to emerge from the available sources. Suggestions of Iranian and Hellenistic influence are possible but cannot be documented.

Josephus (*Antiquities* 13.171–173) first mentions the Essenes in his account of the reign of Jonathan the Hasmonean (r. 161–143/2 BCE). There he briefly describes the Pharisees, Sadducees, and Essenes. He himself claims to have known of the three sects through "personal experience" (*Life* 2.10–11) in the mid-first century CE. He then mentions Judas, an Essene prophet, who was instructing his disciples in fortune-telling during the reign of Judah Aristobulus I in 104 and 103 BCE (*Antiquities* 13.311–313). Herod excused the Essenes from swearing a loyalty oath because, in the view of Josephus (or his source), Menahem the Essene had foretold a lengthy reign for Herod (*Antiquities* 15.371–378). A certain Simeon the Essene predicted dire circumstances for Archelaus, the son of Herod and ethnarch of Judah (4 BCE–c. 6 CE; *Antiquities* 17.345–348); clearly, the Essenes were known for their prediction of the future.

John the Essene was one of the Jewish generals in the great revolt against Rome in 66–74 CE (*War* 2.567). Josephus relates that the Essenes were tortured by the Romans during the great revolt (*War* 2.152–153); this may indicate further their participation in the war against the Romans. An entrance through the south wall of Jerusalem was called the "gate of the Essenes" (*War* 5.145). With the destruction of the province of Judaea following in the wake of the unsuccessful uprising against Rome in 66–74 CE, the Essenes disappear from the stage of history.

THE ESSENE WAY OF LIFE. There were about four thousand Essenes, according to the testimony of Philo and Josephus. They apparently were scattered in communities throughout Palestine, although some evidence exists that they avoided the larger cities. According to Pliny, there was an Essene settlement between Jericho and ʿEin Gedi on the western shore of the Dead Sea. This description has been taken by many scholars as indicating that the Qumran sect whose library was found at the shore of the Dead Sea is to be identified with the Essenes of Philo and Josephus.

Membership and initiation. Only adult males could enter the Essene sect. Sources tell of both married and celibate Essenes. It may be assumed that in the case of married Essenes, full membership was not extended to women. Rather, their status was determined by their being wives or daughters of members. Children were educated in the ways of the community.

The Essenes were organized under officials to whom obedience was required. Members who transgressed could be expelled from the community by the Essene court of one hundred. Aspiring members received three items—a hatchet, an apron, and a white garment—and had to undergo a detailed initiation process that included a year of probation. An initiate was then eligible for the ritual ablutions. Subsequently, he had to undergo a further two years of probation, after which time he was to swear an oath, the only oath the Essenes permitted. In this oath the candidate bound himself to piety toward God, justice to men, honesty with his fellow Essenes, the proper transmission of the teachings of the sect, and the preservation of the secrecy by which the sect's doctrines were guarded from outsiders. Among the teachings to be kept secret were the Essenes' traditions concerning the names of the angels. The candidate was now able to participate in the communal meals of the sect and was a full-fledged member.

Social system. The Essenes practiced community of property. Upon admission, new members turned their property over to the group, whose elected officials administered it for the benefit of all. Hence, all members shared wealth equally, with no distinctions between rich and poor. Members earned income for the group through various occupations, including agriculture and trades. (The Essenes avoided commerce and the manufacture of weapons.) All earnings were turned over to the officials, who distributed funds for purchasing necessities and for taking care of older or ill members of the community. In addition, the Essenes dispensed charity throughout the country, much of it to those outside their group. Traveling members were taken care of by special officers in each town.

Characteristic of the Essenes was their moderation and avoidance of luxury, as evidenced in their eating and drinking habits, their clothing, and the fact that they did not anoint themselves with oil, a practice common among the Jews of the Greco-Roman period. For them, wealth was only a means to provide the necessities of life. This asceticism also manifested itself among those Essenes who were celibate. On the other hand, it appears that in many cases this celibacy was embarked on later in life, after having had children, so that it was not absolute.

Religious life. The Essenes had an ambivalent relationship with the Jerusalem Temple. While they sent voluntary offerings to the Temple, they themselves did not participate in the sacrificial worship there.

The members of the sect began their day with prayer. After prayer, they worked at their occupations. Later, they assembled for purification rituals and a communal meal that was prepared by priests and eaten while wearing special garments. After the members took their places at the table in silence, the baker and cook distributed the food to each in order of his status. A priest recited a short prayer before and after the meal. The community then returned to work and came together once again in the evening for another meal. At the setting of the sun they recited prayers to God. (These prayers cannot have been directed to the sun, as some scholars suggest, in view of the Essenes' close adherence to basic Jewish theology, that is, to a biblical conception of God.)

Ritual purity was greatly emphasized. Not only were ablutions required before the communal meals, but they were also performed after relieving oneself, or after coming in contact with a nonmember or novice. Members were extremely careful in attending to natural functions, and in bathing and expectorating. The Essenes were accustomed to wearing white garments, and rules of modesty were very important.

THEOLOGY. The Essenes are said to have believed in absolute predestination. Probably related to this doctrine was their gift of prophecy. Josephus asserts that the Essenes seldom erred in their predictions. The name of Moses was held in high esteem, and the Essenes saw blasphemy of it as a capital crime. They studied the Torah and its ethics, and interpreted the scriptures allegorically. They were extremely strict in observing the Sabbath. Their teachings were recorded in books that the members were required to pass on with great care. The Essenes were experts in medicinal roots and the properties of stones, the healing powers of which they claimed to have derived from ancient writings.

Most notable among the doctrines of the Essenes was their belief in the immortality of the soul. According to Josephus, they believed that only the soul survived after death, a concept of Hellenistic origin. However, according to the *Philosophumena* (c. 225; generally ascribed to Hippolytus of Rome), the Essenes believed that the body survived as well and would eventually be revived.

THE DEAD SEA SCROLLS. Since the discovery of the Dead Sea Scrolls, the majority of scholars have taken the view that these documents were the library of the Essenes who, accordingly, were settled at Qumran. Indeed, many parallels do exist between the sect described by the Greek sources and the seat of the scrolls from Qumran. Similar initiation ceremonies exist for both groups, although the procedure described in the classical sources diverges in some respects from that of the Qumran texts. The Essenes seem to have eaten communal meals regularly. The Qumran texts, however, envisage only occasional communal meals. For the Essenes all property was held in common, whereas at Qumran private ownership prevailed, and only the use of property was common. The Essenes' observances of ritual purity, although paralleled at Qumran, were not uncommon among the sects of this period.

The main weakness of the identification of these two groups is the fact that the word *Essene* or its equivalent is not present in the Qumran scrolls. In addition, the texts have many small discrepancies. There is no evidence that the Essenes had the apocalyptic dreams of the Dead Sea sect. Nor is it known whether they adhered to a calendar of solar months such as that which the Qumran sect followed. Scholars usually account for these minor differences by saying that the classical sources, especially Josephus, were written with a Greek-speaking audience in mind and, therefore, described the sect in terms that would be understandable to such readers.

If, indeed, the Essenes are to be identified with the sect of the Dead Sea Scrolls, then the Qumran evidence may be used to fill in the picture derived from the classical sources. If not, scholars would have to reckon with two sects having similar teachings and similar ways of life. As a matter of fact, Palestine in the Second Commonwealth period was replete with various sects and movements, each contributing to the religious ferment of the times.

JUDAISM AND CHRISTIANITY. Although the Essenes are nowhere mentioned in the New Testament, certain parallels may indicate an indirect influence of this sect on nascent Christianity. It may be generally stated that the various sects of Second Temple Judaism provide important background material for understanding the rise of the new faith.

The end product of the ferment mentioned above, combined with the great revolt of the Jews against Rome and the resulting destruction of the land, was rabbinic Judaism. Some scholars have claimed that Talmudic sources refer to the Essenes; however, the term *Essene* is not mentioned. While definite evidence is lacking, one can speculate that Essene teachings must have contributed, at least indirectly, to the subsequent development of Jewish tradition regarding such topics as purity, cult, angelology, and the division of body and soul.

See Also Dead Sea Scrolls; Judaism, overview article.

Bibliography

An excellent introduction is found in volume 2 of Emil Schürer's *The History of the Jewish People in the Age of Jesus Christ, 175 B.C.–A.D. 135,* revised and edited by Géza Vermès, Fergus Millar, and Matthew Black and translated by T. A. Burkill et al. (Edinburgh, 1979), pp. 555–597. Extremely important is Morton Smith's "The Description of the Essenes in Josephus and the Philosophumena," *Hebrew Union College Annual* 29 (1958): 273–313. Frank Moore Cross's *The Ancient Library of Qumrân and Modern Biblical Studies,* rev. ed. (Garden City, N.Y., 1961), pp. 70–106, argues for the identification of the Essenes with the Dead Sea sect. The treatment in Martin Hengel's *Judaism and Hellenism,* vol. 1, translated by John Bowden (Philadelphia, 1974), pp. 218–247, accepts this identification yet discusses at length the problem of Hellenistic influence. For the phenomenon of Jewish sectarianism in the Greco-Roman period, see my "Jewish Sectarianism in Second Temple Times," in *Great Schisms in Jewish History,* edited by Raphael Jospe and Stanley M. Wagner (New York, 1981), pp. 1–46.

New Sources

Boccaccini, Gabriele. *Beyond the Essene Hypothesis: The Parting of the Ways between Qumran and Enochic Judaism.* Grand Rapids, Mich., 1998.

Cansdale, Lena. *Qumran and the Essenes: A Re-evaluation of the Evidence.* Tübingen, 1997.

García Martínez, Florentino, and Julio Trebolle Barrera. *The People of the Dead Sea Scrolls.* Translated by Wilfred G. E. Watson. Leiden, 1995.

Hutchesson, Ian. "The Essene Hypothesis after Fifty Years: An Assessment." *Qumran Chronicle* 9 (2000): 17–34.

Stegemann, Hartmut. *The Library of Qumran, on the Essenes, Qumran, John the Baptist, and Jesus.* Grand Rapids, Mich., and Leiden, 1998.

Lawrence H. Schiffman (1987)
Revised Bibliography

ESTHER, or, in Hebrew, Ester; the daughter of Abihail, also called Hadassah; heroine of the biblical book that bears her name. Adopted and raised by her cousin Mordecai, Esther, whose name is derived from the Persian *stara,* "star," plays a crucial role in the event of persecution and deliverance of the Jews in the ancient Persian empire that the late biblical *Book* (or *Scroll) of Esther* purports to record. The story of this deliverance, which draws on ancient Near Eastern courtier motifs, wisdom themes, and, quite possibly, topoi from Mesopotamian and Persian New Year festivals, serves as a festal legend for the Jewish holiday of Purim.

The main outline of the *Book of Esther* is as follows. At the outset, the Persian ruler Ahasuerus has a grand feast that is spoiled when his wife, Vashti, refuses his demand that she perform before the assembled males. Vashti is banished, a decree is issued that all wives must honor their husbands, and the stage is set for a search to replace the defiant queen. The choice is Esther, a Jewess, who follows Mordecai's counsel not to reveal her ethnic-religious origins (*Est.* 2:1–18). While Esther keeps her secret at the court, Mordecai uncovers a plot to kill the king. Meanwhile, one of the viziers, Haman, is elevated to a position of high power. Piqued by the refusal of Mordecai to bow down in homage to him, Haman slanders the Jews to the king and, with the use of lots (Heb., *purim*), sets a date for their annihilation (*Est.* 3). Mordecai now enlists the help of Esther on behalf of her people (*Est.* 4:1–17). An initial soiree between the king and queen passes successfully. Several minor scenes follow dealing with Haman's plot to hang Mordecai (*Est.* 5:9–14) and Ahasuerus's insomnia, during which he learns of Mordecai's role in saving his life and determines to reward him, an event that provokes Haman's shame (*Est.* 6:1–14). A second soiree leads to the disgrace of Haman, the elevation of Mordecai, the disclosure of the plot against the Jews, and, finally, royal permission for the Jews to protect themselves on the day of the planned uprising (*Est.* 7:1–8:17), so that a day of national fasting and sorrow is turned into a time of joy and gladness (*Est.* 9–10).

Mordecai is presented as descended from Saul, the Benjaminite, and Haman, from Agag, the Amalekite; in this way, the novella dramatizes a typological repetition of the episode reported in *1 Samuel* 15 and recalls the divine exhortation never to forget the destructive deeds of Amalek (*Dt.* 24:17–19).

Various additions to *Esther* have been incorporated into the Apocrypha and Septuagint, and there are numerous expansions in the Aramaic *Targum sheni.* In the Middle Ages, the role of Esther took on powerful symbolic dimensions among Jews for at least three reasons. First, Esther came to symbolize the court Jew who risked everything to defend the nation so often slandered, despised, and threatened. Second, Esther, as a "hidden" Jew (together with the frequently noted absence of an explicit reference to God in the scroll), symbolized in mystical circles the hiddenness of the Shekhinah (divine feminine presence) in the world and in the Jewish exile. And finally, Esther (and the festival of Purim) was a great favorite of the Marranos in Spain and in their far-flung dispersion; they saw in her disguised condition the factual and psychological prototype of their own disguised condition.

See Also Purim.

Bibliography

Bickerman, Elias J. *Four Strange Books of the Bible: Jonah, Daniel, Koheleth, Esther.* New York, 1967. See pages 171–240.

Gaster, Theodor H. *Purim and Hanukkah in Custom and Tradition.* New York, 1950.

Ginzberg, Louis. *The Legends of the Jews* (1909–1938). 7 vols. Translated by Henrietta Szold et al. Reprint, Philadelphia, 1937–1966. See the index, s.v. *Esther.*

Moore, Carey A. "Esther." *Anchor Bible,* vol. 7B. Garden City, N.Y., 1971.

Réau, Louis. *Iconographie de l'art chrétien,* vol. 2. Paris, 1956. See pages 335–342.

Michael Fishbane (1987)

ISBN 0-02-865737-3
90000
9 780028 657370